D0119437

BRITISH
COMPANY CASES
1995

CCH EDITIONS LIMITED
TAX, BUSINESS AND LAW PUBLISHERS
TELFORD ROAD, BICESTER
OXFORDSHIRE OX6 0XD

Telephone: Bicester (01869) 253300
Facsimile: Bicester (01869) 874700
DX: 83750 Bicester 2

ABOUT THE PUBLISHER

CCH Editions Limited is part of a world-wide group of companies which specialise in tax and law publishing. The group produces a wide range of books and reporting services for the accounting, business and legal professions. The Oxfordshire premises are the centre for all UK and European operations.

All CCH publications are designed to provide practical, authoritative references and useful guides, and are written by CCH's highly qualified and experienced editorial team and specialist outside authors.

CCH Editions Limited publishes bound books and loose-leaf reporting services specific to the UK and Europe, as well as distributing the publications of the overseas affiliate companies.

Disclaimer

This publication is intended to provide accurate information in regard to the subject matter covered. Readers entering into transactions on the basis of such information should seek the services of a competent professional adviser as this publication is sold on the understanding that the publisher is not engaged in rendering legal or accounting advice or other professional services. The publisher, its editors and any authors, consultants or general editors expressly disclaim all and any liability and responsibility to any person, whether a purchaser or reader of this publication or not, in respect of anything and of the consequences of anything, done or omitted to be done by any such person in reliance, whether wholly or partially, upon the whole or any part of the contents of this publication.

Ownership of Trade Mark

The trade mark is the property of

Commerce Clearing House Incorporated, Riverwoods, Illinois, USA.
(CCH INCORPORATED)

ISBN 0 86325 420 9

ISSN 0269–0535

FOREWORD

British Company Cases 1995 reproduces the full text of British company law cases heard in the High Court, Court of Appeal, House of Lords, Judicial Committee of the Privy Council, Scottish Court of Session, Northern Ireland High Court, and reported during the year. Each case has a headnote outlining the facts, the decision and the reasons for the decision.

The decisions reproduced are listed alphabetically by name in the Cases Reported list. Cases and legislation referred to in the judgments are included in the Cases Cited list and the Legislation Finding List. The decisions are indexed by subject matter in the Topical Index.

Cases in this volume of *British Company Cases* should be cited as follows: [1995] BCC page. Thus the case of Re Sherborne Associates Ltd which appears at page 40 would be cited –

Re Sherborne Associates Ltd [1995] BCC 40.

The cases in this volume were reported by DSP Barbour, Barrister and E O'Grady, Barrister.

bcp96 prelims Mp   3

TABLE OF CONTENTS

CASES REPORTED IN 1995

This table lists all cases reported in British Company Cases 1995.
References are to pages.

Cases Reported

bcp96 prelims Mp 8

Cases Reported

Cases Reported

Cases Reported

COURTS

The following is a list of members of the judiciary in order of seniority
as at 31 December 1995

Appellate Courts

House of Lords

The Lord High Chancellor: Lord Mackay of Clashfern

Lords of Appeal in Ordinary

Lord Keith of Kinkel
Lord Goff of Chieveley
Lord Jauncey of Tullichettle
Lord Browne-Wilkinson
Lord Mustill
Lord Slynn of Hadley

Lord Woolf
Lord Lloyd of Berwick
Lord Nolan
Lord Nicholls of Birkenhead
Lord Steyn
Lord Hoffmann

Court of Appeal

The Lord High Chancellor: Lord Mackay of Clashfern
The Lord Chief Justice of England: Lord Taylor of Gosforth
The Master of the Rolls: Sir Thomas Henry Bingham
The President of the Family Division: Sir Stephen Brown
The Vice-Chancellor: Sir Richard Rashleigh Folliott Scott

Lords Justices of Appeal

Sir Brian Thomas Neill
Sir Martin Charles Nourse
Sir Thomas Patrick Russell
Dame Ann Elizabeth Oldfield
   Butler-Sloss
Sir Murray Stuart-Smith
Sir Christopher Stephen Thomas
   Jonathan Thayer Staughton
Sir Anthony James Denys McCowan
Sir Alexander Roy Asplan Beldam
Sir Andrew Peter Leggatt
Sir Paul Joseph Morrow Kennedy
Sir David Cozens-Hardy Hirst
Sir Simon Denis Brown
Sir Anthony Howell Meurig Evans
Sir Christopher Dudley Roger Rose
Sir John Douglas Waite
Sir John Ormond Roch

Sir Peter Leslie Gibson
Sir John Stewart Hobhouse
Sir Denis Robert Maurice Henry
Sir Mark Oliver Saville
Sir Peter Julian Millett
Sir Swinton Barclay Thomas
Sir Robert Andrew Morritt
Sir Philip Howard Otton
Sir Robin Ernest Auld
Sir Malcolm Thomas Pill
Sir William Aldous
Sir Alan Hylton Ward
Sir Michael Hutchison
Sir Konrad Hermann Theodor
   Schiemann
Sir Nicholas Addison Phillips
Sir Mathew Alexander Thorpe

High Court of Justice
Chancery Division
The Vice-Chancellor: Sir Richard Rashleigh Folliott Scott

Sir Jeremiah LeRoy Harman
Sir John Leonard Knox
Sir Donald Keith Rattee
Sir John Frank Mummery
Sir Francis Mursell Ferris
Sir John Murray Chadwick
Sir Jonathan Frederic Parker
Sir John Edmund Fredric Lindsay
Dame Mary Howarth Arden

Sir Edward Christopher
  Evans-Lombe
Sir Robert Raphael Hayim Jacob
Sir William Anthony Blackburne
Sir Gavin Anthony Lightman
Sir Robert Walker
Sir Robert John Anderson Carnwath
Sir Colin Percy Farquharson Rimer
Sir Hugh Ian Lang Laddie

Queen's Bench Division
The Lord Chief Justice of England: Lord Taylor of Gosforth

Sir Ronald Gough Waterhouse
Sir Christopher James Saunders French
Sir Iain Charles Robert McCullough
Sir Oliver Bury Popplewell
Sir William Alan Macpherson of Cluny
Sir Richard Howard Tucker
Sir Patrick Neville Garland
Sir Michael John Turner
Sir John Downes Alliott
Sir Harry Henry Ognall
Sir John Arthur Dalziel Owen
Sir Francis Humphrey Potts
Sir Richard George Rougier
Sir Ian Alexander Kennedy
Sir Stuart Neil McKinnon
Sir Mark Howard Potter
Sir Henry Brooke
Sir Thomas Scott Gillespie Baker
Sir Igor Judge
Sir Edwin Frank Jowitt
Sir Michael Morland
Sir George Mark Waller
Sir Roger John Buckley
Sir Anthony Brian Hidden
Sir John Michael Wright
Sir Charles Barrie Knight Mantell
Sir John Christopher Calthorpe Blofeld
Sir Peter John Cresswell
Sir Anthony Tristram Kenneth May
Sir John Grant McKenzie Laws
Dame Ann Marian Ebsworth
Sir Simon Lane Tuckey

Sir David Nicholas Ramsay Latham
Sir Christopher John Holland
Sir John William Kay
Sir Richard Herbert Curtis
Sir Stephen John Sedley
Dame Janet Hilary Smith
Sir Anthony David Colman
Sir Anthony Peter Clarke
Sir John Anthony Dyson
Sir Thayne John Forbes
Sir Michael Alexander Geddes Sachs
Sir Stephen George Mitchell
Sir Rodger Bell
Sir Michael Guy Vicat Harrison
Sir Bernard Anthony Rix
Dame Anne Heather Steel
Sir William Marcus Gage
Sir Jonathan Hugh Mance
Sir Andrew Centlivres Longmore
Sir Thomas Richard Atkin Morison
Sir Richard Joseph Buxton
Sir David Wolfe Keene
Sir Andrew David Collins
Sir Maurice Ralph Kay
Sir Frank Brian Smedley
Sir Anthony Hooper
Sir Alexander Neil Logie Butterfield
Sir George Michael Newman
Sir David Anthony Poole
Sir Martin James Moore-Bick
Sir Julian Hugh Gordon Langley

Court of Session

The Court of Session, which is the highest civil tribunal in Scotland, consists of twenty-six judges four of whom, the Lord President and three judges, sit in the First Division, and the Lord Justice-Clerk and three other judges sit in the Second Division, the two Divisions together comprising the Inner House; the remaining judges officiate in the Outer House as Lords Ordinary.

Inner House Judges

First Division

Lord Hope (The Rt Hon the Lord Hope of Craighead PC), Lord President
Lord Sutherland (R I Sutherland)
Lord Clyde (J J Clyde)
Lord Cullen (W D Cullen)

Second Division

Lord Ross (The Rt Hon D M Ross), Lord Justice-Clerk
Lord Davidson (C K Davidson)
   (*seconded to the Scottish Law Commission*)
Lord McCluskey (The Rt Hon the Lord McCluskey)
Lord Morison (A M Morison)
Lord Weir (D B Weir)

Outer House Judges

Lord Prosser (W D Prosser)
Lord Kirkwood (I C Kirkwood)
Lord Coulsfield (J T Cameron)
Lord Milligan (J G Milligan)
Lord Caplan (P I Caplan)
Lord Cameron of Lochbroom (The Rt Hon the Lord Cameron of Lochbroom)
Lord Marnoch (M S R Bruce)
Lord MacLean (R N M MacLean)
Lord Penrose (G W Penrose)
Lord Osborne (K H Osborne)
Lord Abernethy (J A Cameron)
Lord Johnston (A C M Johnston)
Lord Gill (B Gill)
Lord Hamilton (A C Hamilton)
Lord Dawson (T C Dawson)
Lord Macfadyen (D J D Macfadyen)
Lord Rodger of Earlsferry

ABBREVIATIONS

AC	Law Reports, Appeal Cases, 1891–current
ACLC	Australian Company Law Cases, 1982–current (CCH)
ACT	Advance corporation tax
A & E	Admiralty and Ecclesiastical Cases, 1865–1875
Ad & E	Adolphus & Ellis's Reports, King's Bench, 1834–1840
A-G	Attorney-General
ALJR	Australian Law Journal Reports, 1958–current
ALR	Argus Law Reports, then Australian Law Reports
All ER	All England Law Reports, 1936–current
App Cas	Law Reports, Appeal Cases, 1875–1890
Atk	Atkyn's Reports, Chancery, 1736–1755
B & CR	Bankruptcy and Companies Winding up Cases, 1915–1942
BCC	British Company Cases, 1983–current (CCH)
BCLC	Butterworths Company Law Cases
Beav	Beavan's Reports, Rolls Court, 1838–1866
Bligh	Bligh's Reports, House of Lords, 1818–1821
BR	Bankruptcy Reports (US)
B & S	Best & Smith's Reports, Queen's Bench, 1861–1870
BTC	British Tax Cases, 1982–current (CCH)
CA 1948	Companies Act 1948 (repealed)
CA 1985	Companies Act 1985
CA 1989	Companies Act 1989
CA	Court of Appeal
CB	Common Bench Reports, 1845–1856
CCC	cwmni cyfyngedig cyhoeddus (public limited company); Cox's Criminal Cases, 1843–1941
CC(CP)A 1985	Companies Consolidation (Consequential Provisions) Act 1985
CCH	CCH Editions Limited
CEC	European Community Cases, 1989–current (CCH)
cf.	(*confer*) compare
ch. (Ch.)	chapter, Chapter (of Act)
Ch	Law Reports, Chancery Division, 1891–current
Ch App	Law Reports, Chancery Appeals, 1865–1875
ChD	Law Reports, Chancery Division, 1875–1890
CJ	Chief Justice
Cl & Fin	Clark and Finnelly's Reports, House of Lords, 1831–1846
CLC	Company Law Cases (Australia), 1971–1981 (CCH) CCH Commercial Law Cases, 1994–current
CLR	Commonwealth Law Reports, 1903–current (Australia)
Cmd, Cmnd, Cm	Command Paper
CMLR	Common Market Law Reports, 1962–current
Cr App R	Criminal Appeal Reports, 1908–current
Cr App R (S)	Criminal Appeal Reports (Sentencing), 1979–current
Crim LR	Criminal Law Review, 1954–current

CS(ID)A 1985	Company Securities (Insider Dealing) Act 1985
Ct Sess	Court of Session (Scotland)
cyf	cyfyngedig (limited)
D	Dunlop (Session Cases, 2nd Series) (Scotland), 1838–1862
De G M & G	De Gex, Macnaghten & Gordon's Reports, Chancery, 1851–1857
DLR; (2d); (3d); (4th)	Dominion Law Reports (Canada), 1912–1922; (Second Series), 1923–1968; (Third Series), 1969–1984; (Fourth Series), 1984–current
DTI	Department of Trade and Industry
E & B	Ellis & Blackburn's Reports, Queen's Bench, 1851–1858
ECR	European Court Reports, 1954–current
EEC	European Economic Community
EG	Estates Gazette, 1858–current
Eq	Equity Reports, 1853–1855; Equity Cases, 1866–1875
ER	English Reports, 1220–1865
ExD	Law Reports, Exchequer Division, 1875–1880
F	Federal Reporter (US); Fraser (Session Cases, 5th Series) (Scotland), 1898–1906
Fam	Law Reports, Family Division, 1972–current
F & S	Fox & Smith's Reports
FCR	Federal Court Reports
F2d	Federal Reporter (Second Series) (US)
ff.	following
FLR	Family Law Reports, 1980–current; Federal Law Reports (Australia), 1956–current
FSR	Fleet Street Reports, 1963–current
F Supp	Federal Reporter Supplement (US)
FTLR	Financial Times Law Reports, 1986–1988
H & M	Hemming and Miller's Reports, 1862–1865
Hare	Hare's Reports, 1841–1853
HC	High Court
HL	House of Lords
HLCas	House of Lords Cases, 1846–1866
HLR	Housing Law Reports
HMIT	Her Majesty's Inspector of Taxes
ICR	Industrial Cases Reports, 1972–current
IH	Inner House (Court of Session, Scotland)
IR	Irish Reports, 1894–current
IR 1986	Insolvency Rules 1986
J	Mr Justice
JBL	Journal of Business Law
JC	Justiciary Cases (Scotland)

xvi

Abbreviations

KB	Law Reports, King's Bench Division, 1900–1952
LC	Lord Chancellor
LCJ	Lord Chief Justice
LJ	Lord Justice of Appeal;
	Law Journal Reports, New Series, 1831–1949
LJNCCR	Law Journal Newspaper County Court Reports, 1934–1947
LJ (OS)	Law Journal Reports, Old Series, 1822–1831
Ll Rep	Lloyd's Reports, 1951–current
LR	Law Reports, from 1865
LT	Law Times Reports, 1859–1947
LTJo	Law Times Newspaper, 1843–1964
Law Soc Gazette	Law Society's Gazette
Ltd	Limited
M	Macpherson (Session Cases, 3rd Series) (Scotland), 1862–1873
Macq	Macqueen's Reports (Scotland), House of Lords, 1851–1865
Meg	Megone's Company Cases, 1888–1890
Mer	Merivale's Reports, Chancery, 1815–1817
Moore Ind App	Moore's Indian Appeals, Privy Council, 1836–1872
Mor	Morison's Decisions, 1540–1808
MR	Master of the Rolls
M & S	Maule and Selwyn's Reports, King's Bench, 1813–1817
M & W	Meeson & Welsby's Reports, Exchequer, 1836–1847
My & Cr	Mylne & Craig's Reports, Chancery, 1835–1841
Myl & K	Mylne & Keen's Reports, Chancery, 1832–1835
n.b.	(nota bene) note well
ND	North Dakota
NI	Northern Ireland
	Northern Ireland Law Reports, 1925–current
NLJ	New Law Journal, 1965–current
NSWLR	New South Wales Law Reports, 1880–1900; 1971–current
NSWR	New South Wales Reports, 1960–1970
NW	North Western Reporter (US)
NZBLC	New Zealand Business Law Cases (CCH) 1984–current
NZCLC	New Zealand Company Law Cases (CCH) 1981–current
NZLR	New Zealand Law Reports, 1883–current
O.	Order
P	Law Reports, Probate, Divorce and Admiralty Division, 1891–1971
PC	Privy Council
P & CR	Property and Compensation Reports, 1950–current
PD	Law Reports, Probate Division, 1875–1890
plc	public limited company

PLR	Pension Law Reports, 1989–current
Price	Price's Reports, Exchequer, 1814–1824
Pt.	Part
Pty	Proprietary
P Wms	Peere Williams' Reports, Chancery and King's Bench, 1695–1735
QB	Law Reports, Queen's Bench Division, 1891–1900; 1952–current
QBD	Law Reports, Queen's Bench Division, 1875–1890
QC	Queen's Counsel
R	(regina) queen; (rex) king;
	Rettie (Session Cases, 4th Series) (Scotland), 1873–1898
RSC	Rules of the Supreme Court
S	Shaw (Session Cases, 1st Series) (Scotland), 1821–1838
SA	South African Law Reports, 1948–current
SALR	South Australian Law Reports, 1866–1892, 1899–1920
SASR	South Australian State Reports, 1921–current
Sav	Savile's Reports, Common Pleas, 1580–1594
SC	Court of Session Cases (Scotland), 1906–current
Sch.	Schedule
ScLR	Scottish Law Reporter, 1865–1925
Sel Cas t King	Selected Chancery Cases, 1724–1733
SI	Statutory Instrument
SIB	Securities and Investments Board
Sim	Simons' Reports, Chancery, 1826–1852
SJ	Solicitors' Journal, 1857–current
SLT	Scots Law Times, 1893–current
SRO	Self-regulating Organisation
SR & O	Statutory Rules and Orders
SSAP	Statement of Standard Accounting Practice
Stra	Strange's King's Bench Reports, 1716–1749
Swan	Swanston's Chancery Reports, 1818–1819
TC	Tax Cases, 1875–current
TLR	The Times Law Reports, 1884–1952
TMA	Taxes Management Act (1970)
TPD	Transvaal Provincial Division Reports, 1902–1946
UK	United Kingdom
US	United States of America;
	United States Reports
USM	Unlisted Securities Market
v	versus
VAT	value added tax
V-C	Vice-Chancellor
Vern	Vernon's Reports, Chancery, 1680–1719
Ves Jun	Vesey junior's Chancery Reports, 1789–1817

VLR	Victorian Law Reports, 1875–1956
VR	Victorian Reports, 1870–1872; 1957–current
WLR	Weekly Law Reports, 1953–current
WN	Law Reports, Weekly Notes, 1866–1952
WN (NSW)	Weekly Notes, New South Wales, 1884–1970
WR	Weekly Reporter, 1853–1906
Y & CC	Younge & Collyer's Company Cases, 1841–1843
¶	Paragraph

FOREIGN WORDS AND PHRASES

The following is a list of Latin and other words and phrases frequently found in decisions of the courts.

ab initio	from the beginning
ad hoc	arranged for this purpose
ad infinitum	to infinity
ad litem	for the law-suit
ad valorem	according to value
a fortiori	with stronger reason
alio intuitu	with a motive other than the ostensible and proper one
aliter	otherwise
a priori	deductively
bona fide	in good faith
caveat	warning, proviso
cadit quaestio	admitting of no further argument
certiorari	a writ, replaced by judicial review
cestui que trust	a person for whom another is trustee
contra	against
coram	before, in the presence of
corpus	the capital of a fund, as contrasted with the income
ejusdem generis	of the same kind
et al.	and others
et seq. (et sequens)	and the following
ex abundanti cautela	from excess of caution
ex debito justitiae	a remedy applicable as of right
ex gratia	as a favour
ex parte	an application in a judicial hearing made by one party in the absence of the other
hic	this, here
ibidem (ibid.)	in the same place
infra	below
in limine	at the outset
in loco parentis	in the position of parent
in re	in the matter of
in situ	in place
in specie	in its actual state, in kind
inter alia	among other things
inter partes	between or among the parties
inter se	among themselves
inter vivos	during lifetime
in toto	entirely
intra vires	within the powers of, e.g. a company
lis	legal action
locum tenens	a substitute
mandamus	a writ
modus operandi	a plan of working

Foreign Words and Phrases

mutatis mutandis	in the same manner with appropriate changes for the context
nisi	unless
nisi prius	unless before
obiter dictum	a judicial expression of opinion on a matter, not essential to the decision, and therefore not a binding authority
pari passu	rateable
passim	in various places
per alium	by means of another
per curiam	by the court
per diem	daily
per se	by itself, taken alone
prima facie	at first sight
pro rata	in proportion
quantum	a concrete quantity
quantum meruit	as much as he deserved
quid pro quo	consideration
re	in the matter of
res judicata	an issue already decided judicially
semble	it appears
sc. (scilicet)	namely, understand
sic	thus
simpliciter	without addition or qualification
sine qua non	an indispensable condition
stricto sensu	in its strict meaning
sub judice	in course of trial
sub nom	under the name of
sub voce	under a specified word
supra	above
ultra vires	beyond the powers, e.g. of (the directors of) a company
vide	see
viz. (videlicet)	in other words, namely

bcp96 prelims Mp 21

1995

BRITISH COMPANY CASES

Cited [1995] BCC

Re Gibson Davies Ltd.

Chancery Division (Companies Court).
Sir Mervyn Davies.
Judgment delivered 14 July 1994.

> *Director disqualification – Application by disqualified director for leave to act – Basis on which court would exercise discretion – Company Directors Disqualification Act 1986, s. 17.*

This was an appeal against the dismissal of an application for leave to be a director under s. 17 of the Company Directors Disqualification Act 1986.

Held, allowing the appeal and giving the appellant leave to act as a director by an order incorporating various safeguards:

1. On an application under s. 17 the court had to be satisfied that there was a need to make the order and that if the order was made the public would remain adequately protected.

2. The desire of the appellant to be a director of the company which he had devised and which was it seemed successful, was not a need for purposes of the application. On the other hand, the evidence showed that the company was in need of the services of the appellant. The judge below had concluded that the needs were overstated, but that conclusion could not be justified by consideration of the uncontradicted evidence as to the part played by the appellant in the genesis, present state and future prospects of the company.

3. Since the court was of the view that there was a need for the making of an order, the question was whether if an order was made there would be adequate protection for the public. The appellant offered ten safeguards designed to meet that point.

The following cases were referred to in the judgment:

Cargo Agency Ltd, Re [1992] BCC 388.
Lo-Line Electric Motors Ltd & Ors, Re (1988) 4 BCC 415; [1988] Ch 477.

McQuillan, Re (1989) 5 BCC 137.

Ian Croxford QC and David Lock (instructed by Edge & Ellison, Birmingham) for the appellant.

James Corbett (instructed by Wragge & Co, Brimingham) for the Secretary of State for Trade and Industry.

JUDGMENT

Sir Mervyn Davies: This is an appeal against an order made by his Honour Judge Gosling on 23 February 1994. The judge dismissed an application by Mr Alan Robert Davies, the appellant. The application was for an order that the appellant be granted leave pursuant to s. 17 of the *Company Directors Disqualification Act* 1986 to be a director of a company called Congratulations Franchising Ltd upon such terms and such

conditions as the court should think fit. In the notice of appeal dated 8 March 1994 the   A
grounds of appeal are set out under nine heads. I will mention such points later so far as
necessary.

On 1 February 1993 an order was made under the Act disqualifying the appellant for
a period of five years from 22 March 1993. That order was made on a summons by the
Secretary of State for Trade and Industry dated 7 March 1991. The order was made in
the absence of the appellant. For reasons that are not clear there were difficulties in   B
serving the appellant with a summons and other documents.

The appellant went to live in Ireland in April 1989 and, as I understand, he remained
there until May 1993. He spoke to a solicitor acting for the Secretary of State on 5 March
1992. The order dated 1 February 1993 was obtained after an order for substituted
service was made. I need not explain further the circumstances in which the original
disqualification order was obtained.

Mr Croxford appeared for the appellant and stated that no point was taken on the   C
service. Also, he said he would be in no way seeking to go behind the reasons which led
to the making of the original disqualification order. That order was made by District
Judge Hargreaves. It was made having regard to the appellant's conduct as a director of
a company called Gibson Davies & Co ('GDC'). The foundation of the order was
affidavit evidence by Mr Geoffrey Harrison, a chartered accountant who was, on
9 March 1989, appointed liquidator of GDC following a resolution for a voluntary   D
winding up.

GDC was a company incorporated in 1984. Its capital was £100 in 100 shares. The
appellant was a director at all material times. The company was at first engaged in the
business of office supplies and stationery but after a year or so supplied linen services to
the hotel trade. The company fared well up to 1989. As I have mentioned, a resolution to
wind up was then passed, Mr Harrison estimating the deficiency at £125,530. There were   E
no Crown debts and the preferential creditors were paid in full. Audited accounts had
been prepared for the years ending 31 March 1986 and 1987. Draft accounts had been
prepared for the periods ending 30 September 1987 and 31 March 1988.

Mr Harrison's first affidavit summarises the matters said to show that the appellant
and Mr Bryn Jones, who had acted as a director, were unfit to be concerned in the
management of a company. It was said: (1) that the appellant and Jones caused GDC to
enter into a transaction affording a preference to themselves, contrary to s. 239 of the   F
Insolvency Act 1986; (2) that by continuing to trade after distraint had been levied by the
Inland Revenue the appellant and Jones allowed the position of creditors to be eroded;
(3) that they raised misleading invoices; (4) that they paid undue remuneration when
trading losses were increasing; (5) that they failed to file audited accounts.

Those complaints appear to have been upheld before District Judge Hargreaves, but I
was not referred to any note of the District Judge's judgment. From the evidence adduced   G
by the appellant in the course of seeking to set aside the disqualification order and seeking
to obtain a s. 17 order it is plain that much argument might have ensued as to (1)–(5)
above had the matter been contested before the District Judge. However that may be, Mr
Croxford, as I have said, disclaimed any attempt to go behind the original disqualification
order. Although the disqualification order was made on 1 February 1993 it was not
served on the appellant until 17 September 1993. That was due to the difficulty of locating
the appellant that I have already mentioned.   H

Having been inactive in the matter for so long, the appellant, on 29 September 1993,
changed his stance. His notice of application drafted by solicitors is dated 4 October
1993. The application seeks leave to file an acknowledgement out of time and leave to file
evidence out of time, that the disqualification order be set aside and, in the alternative,
that pursuant to s. 17 he be allowed to act as a director of Congratulations Franchising.

A   Furthermore, there was an application that he be allowed to remain a director of Franchising pending the outcome of his application. In fact in a series of orders made since that time the appellant has been allowed to act as a director of Franchising, the order of 1 February 1993 notwithstanding. So it was that up to the hearing before me the appellant has at all material times continued to act as a director of Franchising. The application to set aside the disqualification order was abandoned but the application for a s. 17 order has been vigorously prosecuted.

B   Before Judge Gosling the appellant put forward seven affidavits. Three of them were by the appellant himself, two were by the appellant's present business associate, Mr S H Devine, and one was by Mr S Heer, a chartered accountant in the firm of Robson Rhodes. The seventh affidavit is of no present concern. In his affidavit sworn on 1 October the appellant speaks at length of his experience with GDC. He goes on to say that he was much affected by the failure of GDC and as well had matrimonial difficulties, now happily resolved. He went to live in Ireland. He says that at that time (i.e. 1990–

C   1992) he was in no frame of mind to defend legal proceedings of any kind. In para. 28 he says that in mid-1992 he began to regain his confidence. He says he:

> 'began to think of ideas for a new business. I began to work on a way of providing invitees to a wedding with an easy way of choosing gifts for the bride and bridegroom.'

D   A catalogue itemising articles regarded as suitable wedding gifts was published. A copy is sent to the bridal couple. The couple then indicate which articles in the catalogue are acceptable gifts. The idea is then that a list of the acceptable gifts is sent with the wedding invitations. I was shown the current 152 page catalogue in use by Franchising.

The appellant put this idea into practice in Ireland in late 1992. The appellant was assisted in this venture by Mr Devine. There was formed in Ireland a company called

E   Congratulations Ltd. The appellant owns 50 per cent of the shares, Mr Devine owns 45 per cent, with the other five per cent owned by Mr Spollane. The appellant, Mr Devine and Mr Spollane are directors of the Irish company.

Since the business in Ireland was successful it was decided to carry on the same business in England. This has been done by using Franchising for the purposes of English business. Franchising was a company which was incorporated on 5 November 1992, but its change of name to Congratulations Franchising Ltd was effected on 4 January 1993.

F   The Irish company Congratulations owns all the shares in Franchising. The directors of Franchising are the appellant, Mr Devine, and also in 1994 Mrs Jackie Richards, a chartered accountant, was appointed a director. Exhibits indicating the way in which Franchising carries on business were before me. It appears that the appellant is a key figure in the successful operation of the business.

As the word 'franchising' indicates, the business is conducted by conferring a franchise

G   on local people, who solicit orders for Franchising by sending the Franchising catalogue to persons about to wed in their local district in the hope that wedding guest lists will be sent to the Franchising headquarters at Redditch. The lists are then sent out, as I have said, with wedding invitations and the invitees may then place an order in Redditch for the dispatch of a present. It is said that Franchising has 31 franchises with customer enquiries at the date of the affidavits standing at 4,139. Business is said to be in a satisfactory state. The Bank of Ireland has, from its office in the Midlands, afforded the

H   company a £70,000 overdraft without requiring personal guarantees from the directors.

Mr Devine's first affidavit says that after setting up a successful company called Irish Fencing & Products Ltd he sold out and acquired 50,000 sq. ft. in Dublin, which is used as a central warehouse. He is, as I have said, associated with the appellant in the business of Franchising. He regards the appellant as crucial to the future of Franchising. In his second affidavit he says he made an initial investment with Congratulations of £36,000,

that sum now being part of the share capital of the company. He then worked four days   A
a week for Franchising.

The evidence of Mr Heer is that he has reviewed the internal controls and accounting
systems of Franchising, the managing accounts for 11 months ended 31 December 1993
and the trading position of the company in January 1994. The company appears to be
trading profitably and growing at a fast pace. He regards the appellant as a key man in
the company.   B

The affidavit evidence already referred to was before Judge Gosling. Before me there
was, by consent, some further evidence. This consisted of an affidavit by Mrs Jackie
Richards, a further affidavit by the appellant and a further affidavit by Mr Devine. Mrs
Richards, a chartered accountant, has been with Franchising since November 1993 and
she was appointed financial director in March with the sole responsibility for the finance
department. Mr Devine explained some difficulties which have arisen with Mr Spollane,   C
who, as I have said, has a five per cent shareholding in the Irish company. I need not
refer further to those difficulties. Mr Devine goes on to say that he now works full-time
in England in the business of Franchising. It appears that Mr Devine was, at an early
stage of his association with the appellant, made aware of the failure of the appellant's
company GDC, but whether or not Mr Devine was informed early on of the
disqualification proceedings does not expressly appear. On the other hand, it seems that
Mr Devine was told of the disqualification order in September 1993 (i.e. the month when   D
the order was served on the appellant). I need not refer to the appellant's last affidavit
sworn on 16 June 1994.

On an application under s. 17 of the Company Directors Disqualification Act the court
must be satisfied that there is a need to make the order and, more importantly, that if the
order is made the public will remain adequately protected. The concepts of need and
protection have been referred to in the context of the Act. In *Re Lo-Line Electric Motors*   E
Ltd (1988) 4 BCC 415, Sir Nicolas Browne-Wilkinson V-C at p. 419, in reference to
s. 300 of the *Companies Act* 1985 (the forerunner of s. 6 of the 1986 Act), says:

> 'The primary purpose of the section is not to punish the individual but to protect
> the public against the future conduct of companies by persons whose past records
> as directors of insolvent companies have shown them to be a danger to creditors
> and others. Therefore, the power is not fundamentally penal. But if the power to   F
> disqualify is exercised, disqualification does involve substantial interference with
> the freedom of the individual. It follows that the rights of the individual must be
> fully protected.'

So there is to be protection of the public with a measure of protection for the rights of
the individual. At p. 424 the Vice-Chancellor takes account of the 'need' of the applicant
in that case to take a managerial role.   G

In *Re McQuillan* (1989) 5 BCC 137 Murray J in the Northern Ireland High Court was
concerned with an application akin to an application under s. 11 of the 1986 Act, s. 11
being the section which debars a bankrupt from acting as a director without leave of the
court. The judge said at p. 140H:

> 'There appears to be no authority in the UK courts on the exercise of the discretion   H
> conferred on the court by art. 310 or the corresponding provision in force in
> Britain, viz. s. 11 of the *Company Directors Disqualification Act* 1986 but Mr Orr,
> for the company, helpfully referred me to a case in the Supreme Court of New
> South Wales, which has precisely the same discretion under its statute law: *Re
> Altim Pty Ltd* [1968] 2 NSWR 762, a decision of Street J given on 6 August 1968.
> The judge deals with the statutory discretion in these words (at p. 764):

A

"The section under which this application is made proceeds upon the basis that a person who is an undischarged bankrupt is prima facie not to be permitted to act as a director or to take part in the management of a company. The court is given jurisdiction to grant leave for such activities to be carried on, but an applicant who comes to the court seeking leave must bear the onus of establishing that the general policy of the legislature laid down in this section ought to be made the subject of an exception in his case. It should be borne in

B

mind that the section is not in any sense a punishment of the bankrupt. Nor should a refusal to grant leave under that section be regarded as punitive. The prohibition is entirely protective, and the power of the court to grant leave is to be exercised with this consideration in the forefront." '

So Street J emphasises the protective element of the jurisdiction.

Lastly, there is *Re Cargo Agency Ltd* [1992] BCC 388, where Harman J says (at

C

p. 393C):

'It seems to me that Mr Newey must be right that applications for leave pursuant to s. 1 should only be granted where there is a need for them to be granted, and should only be granted upon evidence of adequate protection from danger.'

The reference there to s. 1 will embrace s. 17 of the Act.

So I proceed to consider whether there is need for an order in the appellant's favour

D

and then whether or not, if an order is made, there will be adequate protection for the public. In the *Cargo* case there was plainly no need for an order, whether one considers the need of the applicant or the company of which he wished to be allowed to become a director. On the other hand, in the case of *Lo-Line* the Vice-Chancellor appeared to give weight to the need of the applicant (see p. 424).

In the case before me I recognise the desire of the appellant to be a director of the company that he devised and is now, it seems, so successful. But such desire is, to my

E

mind, not a need for present purposes. On the other hand, the evidence of the appellant, Mr Devine and Mr Heer shows that Franchising as a company is much in need of the services of the appellant as the guiding light of the company. Publicity material that is exhibited to the affidavits of Mr Davies is to the same effect, albeit that it is publicity material. In my view, I may take into account the uncontradicted evidence that Franchising has need of the appellant's services as a director. Judge Gosling does not

F

expressly address himself to the needs of the company, but he said this:

'I bear in mind what is said about the favourable prospects of the company. It is also said that if the second respondent cannot act as a director of the company, the company will fail and jobs will be lost. That would certainly be a misfortune, but I feel that these dangers are overstated and I do not see why the company should not prosper with the second respondent employed as a chief salesman.'

G

So he had in mind the needs of the company. He concluded that the needs or dangers were overstated. That conclusion cannot, in my view, be justified by consideration of the uncontradicted evidence of the appellant, Mr Heer and Mr Devine, read with the exhibited publicity material as to the part played by the appellant in the genesis, present state and future prospects of the company. Also, having regard to the size of the company, I accept the sentiment expressed in the first ground of the notice of appeal that if, as the judge suggested, the appellant were to be a chief salesman, then the appellant

H

would almost inevitably be concerned in the management of the company.

Since I am of the view that there is need for the making of an order, one goes on to consider whether, if an order is made, there will be adequate protection for the public. The appellant offered the following safeguards:

(1)   no cheque or financial agreement on behalf of the company be signed or executed by the appellant alone;

(2)   any director's loan owed by the company to the appellant shall not be repaid unless   A
all creditors of the company are paid first;

(3)   the appellant shall not be granted or accept any security over the company assets;

(4)   the appellant's total emoluments from the company shall not exceed £380 per week
or such greater sum as shall hereafter be agreed in writing by the Secretary of State,
such consent not to be unreasonably refused;

(5)   the appellant shall procure the company to file annual returns and accounts at   B
Companies House within the time limits set out in the *Companies Act* 1985;

(6)   the appellant will procure the company to complete the implementation of the
accounting controls as set out by Mr Heer of Robson Rhodes in his affidavit sworn
on 3 February 1994;

(7)   the appellant will procure the company to prepare monthly management accounts   C
and submit the said accounts to Robson Rhodes or to the company's auditors for
the time being;

(8)   Robson Rhodes, or the company's auditors for the time being, shall be instructed
to report to the board of directors in writing any matters of concern relating to the
management or financial control of the company and in default of prompt and
appropriate action by the directors of the company will bring these matters to the
attention of the Secretary of State's solicitors;   D

(9)   in the event that the company seeks to change the identity of its auditors the
appellant will procure the company only to instruct auditors who are willing to
accept and act upon the obligations set out above;

(10)   the appellant will take no step as a shareholder or director of Congratulations Ltd
(i.e. the Irish company) which would in any way impede, direct or control the
activities of the company.   E

The first nine of those safeguards were offered before Judge Gosling in written form.
The tenth safeguard was discussed but never precisely formulated. The accounting
controls referred to in item (6) are: (a) all cheques over £2,500 to be signed by more than
one director; (b) all cheques below £2,500 to be signed by both Mr Davies and the
company's financial controller, Mrs Richards; (c) monthly management accounts to be
reviewed by Robson Rhodes; (d) the company to complete the implementation of the   F
internal accounting control recommended by Robson Rhodes; (e) Robson Rhodes to
accept an obligation to bring to the attention of the directors in writing any matters of
concern relating to the management or financial control of the company and in default
of prompt and appropriate action by the directors to bring these matters to the attention
of the applicant's solicitors.

I am of the opinion that the appellant ought to be allowed to act as a director of   G
Franchising by an order which incorporates the safeguards set out above. Accordingly, I
allow the appeal and make such an order as I have mentioned.

I add that Mr Corbett for the Secretary of State drew attention here and before Judge
Gosling to difficulties that he said might arise from the fact that control over Franchising
is in the hands of the Irish company and that the appellant has a 50 per cent shareholding
in the Irish company. It was said: (1) there was a risk that conflict might arise as to the   H
appellant's dual position as director of both Franchising and the Irish company; and (2)
that the Irish company might, through its shareholding, seek to thwart any conditions
imposed on the appellant by this court. Judge Gosling briefly referred to this point in his
judgment, but the judge was not given safeguard number (10), at any rate in any written
form. To my mind, now that safeguard (10) has been offered, together with the other
safeguards, there is no occasion for withholding a s. 17 order by reason of the fact that

A   the Franchising shares are owned by the Irish company or that the shareholding of the Irish company is 50 per cent in the appellant, 45 per cent in Mr Devine and five per cent in Mr Spollane, or that the appellant and Mr Devine are directors of the Irish company.

(An amended order, reproduced below, was drawn up in this action)

ORDER

B   It is ordered that:

(i)   the appellant's appeal against the decision of His Honour Judge Gosling on 23 July 1994 be allowed save that the order for costs made by His Honour Judge Gosling and all earlier costs orders made in this action shall remain in force;

(ii)   the appellant be granted leave to be and remain a director of Congratulations Franchising Ltd for the duration of the operation of the disqualification order
C   made herein by District Judge Hargreaves of 1 February 1993 upon condition that the appellant do abide by the conditions set out in the schedule hereto;

(iii)   for the avoidance of doubt, the stay on the operation of the order herein of District Judge Hargreaves ordered by His Honour Judge Alan Taylor on 6 October 1993 and continued thereafter be forthwith lifted;

(iv)   the appellant do pay the respondent's costs of this appeal on a standard basis to
D   be taxed if not agreed, such order not to be enforced against the appellant without a further order from this court in respect of all costs incurred after 15 June 1994;

(v)   legal aid taxation of the appellant's costs.

SCHEDULE

1.   No cheque or financial agreement on behalf of Congratulations Franchising Ltd
E   ('the company') shall be signed or executed by the appellant alone.

2.   Any director's loan owed by the company to the appellant shall not be repaid unless all creditors of the company are paid first.

3.   The appellant shall not be granted or accept any security over the company's assets.

4.   The appellant's total emoluments from the company shall not exceed £380 per
F   week or such greater sum as shall hereafter be reasonably and unanimously agreed by the board of directors.

5.   The appellant shall procure the company to file annual returns and accounts to Companies House within the time limits set out in the *Companies Act* 1985.

6.   The appellant will procure the company to complete the implementation of the
G   accounting controls as set out by Mr Sukhbinder Heer of Robson Rhodes in his affidavit sworn herein of 3 February 1994, namely:

(i)   all company cheques which are required to be signed by the appellant shall also require the signature of one other director;

(ii)   the appellant will procure the prompt implementation of all internal accounting controls reasonably required by Robson Rhodes;

H   (iii)   the appellant will procure the company to prepare monthly management accounts;

(iv)   the said management accounts shall be promptly submitted to Robson Rhodes or to the company's auditors for the time being.

7.   Robson Rhodes or the company's auditors for the time being shall be instructed to report to the board of directors in writing any matters of concern related to the

management or financial control of the company, and the appellant will procure   A
the prompt implementation of any corrective action as unanimously agreed by the
board of directors to be necessary to meet those concerns.

8.   In the event that the company seeks to change the identity of its auditors, the
appellant will procure the company only to instruct auditors who are willing to
accept and act upon the obligations set out above.

9.   The appellant will take no step as a shareholder or director of Congratulations Ltd   B
(the Irish company) which will in any way impede, direct or control the activities
of the directors of the company.

———————————

C

D

E

F

G

H

A
Barclays Bank plc & Ors v British & Commonwealth Holdings plc.

Chancery Division.

Harman J.

Judgment delivered 26 July and 16 November 1994.

B
Maintenance of capital – Purchase of own shares – Redemption of preference shares – Scheme of arrangement – Reduction of capital – Shareholder wishing to sell stake issued with redeemable preference shares – Redemption underwritten by banks – Scheme sanctioned by court and reduction of capital confirmed – Company became insolvent – Banks obliged to purchase worthless shares – Banks claimed as creditors – Whether agreement which substituted claim as creditor for claim as shareholder on insolvency was objectionable – Whether claim 'in respect

C
of' failure to redeem shares – Whether there was 'financial assistance by way of indemnity' – Materiality of court order sanctioning scheme – Companies Act 1985, s. 151–153, 178, 425.

This was the determination of issues before trial under RSC, O. 33, r. 3 in an action in which seven plaintiffs, six banks and a company called Tindalk, sued British & Commonwealth Holdings plc ('B & C'). The issues were decided on a special case agreed by all parties.

D
Tindalk was the vehicle for the redemption of certain redeemable shares in B & C issued in connection with the liquidation by its owner, 'Caledonia', of a substantial stake in B & C. The scheme by which Caledonia was to cease to be a shareholder involved the cancellation of stock units in B & C held by Caledonia partly by purchase by B & C and partly by cancellation in exchange for the issue to Caledonia of new redeemable preference shares in B & C. The new redeemable preference shares would be redeemed in four equal tranches at a price of approximately £81.1m for each tranche at the wish of either the holder or B & C

E
on 31 December in each of the years 1988 to 1991. If B & C failed to redeem the relevant tranche of the shares, Caledonia was to be granted the right to sell those tranches of its redeemable preference shares at the redemption prices to Tindalk, a company formed for the purpose and to be financed by the plaintiff banks in return for B & C's covenant.

The scheme involved a reduction of the capital of B & C and in October 1987 the court made an order sanctioning the scheme under s. 425 of the Companies Act 1985 and

F
confirming the reduction of capital.

The first two tranches of shares were redeemed by B & C, but it became insolvent and administrators were appointed in 1990 and the last two tranches were not redeemed. Caledonia exercised its right to require Tindalk to purchase those shares and the banks, having financed Tindalk's purchase of the shares, claimed damages for breach of covenant by B & C in the amount paid to finance the two purchases. The economic effect was that instead of the sum required to redeem the shares being paid out of shareholders' funds, and

G
therefore ranking behind creditors, the sum claimed by the six banks as damages would rank as a creditor's claim equally with other creditors.

Held, answering the questions posed by the special case:

1. An agreement which was only likely to be called upon if a company had no distributable profits and which would, if called upon when the company became insolvent, have the effect of increasing the liabilities of the company by substituting, for rights held by

H
shareholders ranking behind creditors, rights held by a creditor ranking equally with other creditors, was objectionable by reason of the rule in Trevor v Whitworth (1887) 12 App Cas 409. (Re Walters' Deed of Guarantee [1933] Ch 321 followed.)

2. On the footings stated in the special case, the effect of the exercise by Caledonia of its put options against Tindalk, the obligation of the plaintiff banks to fund Tindalk's liabilities to pay Caledonia, and the breach of the covenants given by B & C to the plaintiff banks, led in combination to the rights of Caledonia as a preference shareholder to have its preference

shares redeemed, which rights are an obligation of B & C to one of its members and as such   A
ranked behind its obligations to unsecured creditors, being substituted, in effect, by the
rights of the plaintiff banks ranking as unsecured creditors equally with other such creditors
against B & C. The continuing existence unaltered of the preference shares did not point to
the agreement being other than an attempt to return capital unlawfully.

3. The agreement was also unenforceable as an agreement expressed to impose a liability
to make a gratuitous payment, i.e. is one not for the advancement of the company's business   B
nor made out of distributable profits, at a future date when in the event the company had no
distributable profits.

4. Allowing the banks to claim in misrepresentation rather than for breach of the
contractual warranty itself would be to allow form to prevail over substance. There could be
no misrepresentation claim based on the terms of the agreement if they were incapable of
enforcement.

5. However, the scheme had been sanctioned by the order of the court which stood until   C
set aside or rescinded. (Nicholl v Eberhardt Co Ltd (1889) 59 LT 860; (1889) 1 Meg 402
(CA) and Isaacs v Robertson [1985] AC 97 applied.)

6. The damages sought in the action were not damages 'in respect of' any failure to
redeem any shares within the meaning of s. 178(2) of the Companies Act 1985, even though
the failure was the measure of the damages claimed for breach of contract.

7. There was no 'indemnity' associated with any of the transactions (the subscription by   D
Caledonia for the issue of the preference shares and the purchase by Tindalk of the two
tranches of shares) and accordingly no 'financial assistance' within the meaning of
s. 152(1)(a)(ii) of the 1985 Act was provided by B & C in connection with those transactions.

The following cases were referred to in the judgment:

Ackbar v C F Green & Co Ltd [1975] QB 582.
ANZ Executors & Trustee Co Ltd v Qintex Australia Ltd (1990) 8 ACLC 980.   E
Australasian Oil Exploration Ltd v Lachbery (1958) 101 CLR 119.
Aveling Barford Ltd v Perion Ltd & Ors (1989) 5 BCC 677.
Bank of New South Wales v The Commonwealth (1948) 76 CLR 1.
Brady & Anor v Brady & Anor (1987) 3 BCC 535.
Charterhouse Investment Trust Ltd & Ors v Tempest Diesels Ltd (1985) 1 BCC 99,544.
Davis Investments Pty Ltd v Commissioner of Stamp Duties (NSW) (1957-58) 100 CLR   F
392.
Flynn v Graham 1964 SLT 89.
Guinness v Land Corp of Ireland (1882) 22 ChD 349.
Hadkinson v Hadkinson [1952] P 285.
Halt Garage (1964) Ltd, Re [1982] 3 All ER 1016.
Hill & Ors v Permanent Trustee Co of New South Wales Ltd & Ors [1930] AC 720.
Hutton v West Cork Railway Co (1883) 23 ChD 654.   G
Imperial Bank of China, India and Japan, Re (1866) LR 1 Ch App 339.
Isaacs v Robertson [1985] AC 97.
Jenkins v Harbour View Courts Ltd [1966] NZLR 1.
MacDougall v Jersey Imperial Hotel Co Ltd (1864) 2 H & M 568.
McGahie v Union of Shop Distributive & Allied Workers 1966 SLT 74.
Newman (George) & Co, Re [1895] 1 Ch 674.
Nicholl v Eberhardt Co Ltd (1889) 59 LT 860; (1889) 1 Meg 402 (CA).   H
Paterson v Chadwick [1974] 1 WLR 890.
Plain Ltd v Kinley & Royal Trust Co (1931) 1 DLR 468.
R v Londonderry Justices [1971] NI 91.
Redweaver Investments Ltd v Lawrence Field Ltd (1991) 9 ACLC 1032.
Ridge Securities Ltd v IR Commrs [1964] 1 WLR 479.

A
Trevor v Whitworth (1887) 12 App Cas 409.
Trustees, Executors and Agency Co Ltd v Reilly [1941] VLR 110.
Verner v General and Commercial Investment Trust [1894] 2 Ch 239.
Walters' Deed of Guarantee, Re [1933] Ch 321.
Yeoman Credit Ltd v Latter [1961] 1 WLR 828.

Robin Potts QC and Christopher Butcher (instructed by Clifford Chance) for the plaintiffs.

B
William Stubbs QC and Sir Thomas Stockdale (instructed by Wilde Sapte) for the defendants.

JUDGMENT

Harman J: One of the most dramatic of recent corporate collapses occurred on 3 June 1990 when this court made an administration order in respect of British & Commonwealth Holdings plc (hereafter 'B & C'). Such an order is only made if the court is satisfied that a company is or is likely to become unable to pay its debts: *Insolvency Act 1986*, s. 8(1)(a). B & C had a long history. It had been the owner of substantial shipping interests and a very large shareholding in it had been held by the Cayzer family. By 1987 the shipping interests had been disposed of and a man called John Gunn was the moving spirit in B & C. The Cayzer family interest in B & C's shares was largely held by Caledonia Investments plc (hereafter 'Caledonia') which wished to cease to be a large shareholder and to pursue its own interests.

D
In order that Caledonia could avoid placing very large numbers of B & C's shares on the Stock Exchange, which might have led to a substantial fall in the share price to the detriment of Caledonia and the dissatisfaction of the board of B & C, an elaborate and ingenious scheme was formulated by some of the best-known solicitors practising in the City of London with the advice of well-known specialist counsel. The scheme involved the cancellation of 90m stock units in B & C held by Caledonia partly by purchase by B & C of some stock units for £100m and partly by cancellation of the remaining stock units in exchange for the issue to Caledonia of new redeemable preference shares in B & C. The new redeemable preference shares would be redeemed in four equal tranches at a price of approximately £81.1m for each tranche at the wish of either the holder or B & C on 31 December in each of the years 1988–1991. There were provisions as to dividends which are immaterial for present purposes.

F
In order for Caledonia to be sure that it would receive its £81.1m-odd in each of the years 1988–1991 even if B & C failed to redeem the relevant tranche of the shares, Caledonia was to be granted the right to sell those tranches of its redeemable preference shares at the redemption prices to a company called Tindalk Ltd (hereafter 'Tindalk') formed for the purpose which would be financed by six banks. Further B & C was to covenant with the six banks that it would conduct its affairs so as to maintain certain asset rates. Any breach of covenant would give rise to a claim in damages by the banks against B & C.

G
The scheme involved a reduction of the capital of B & C and therefore required the sanction of the court. On 12 October 1987 this court made an order sanctioning the scheme and confirming the reduction of capital. On 16 October 1987 B & C purchased 21m-odd stock units from Caledonia for £100m and issued the new redeemable preference shares to Caledonia. Thereafter the first tranche of 'A' class redeemable preference shares was redeemed at its proper price on 31 December 1988 and the second tranche of 'B' class of such shares was so redeemed on 31 December 1989. As I have said, in the summer of 1990 B & C was held to be or to be likely to become insolvent and was placed in administration. The administrators are still running B & C and endeavouring to sort out the various claims. Naturally B & C did not redeem either the 'C' class redeemable preference shares on 31 December 1990 or the 'D' class redeemable preference shares on 31 December 1991. Further B & C was in breach of its covenants to the six banks.

Caledonia exercised its right to require Tindalk to purchase the third tranche of C class   A
preference shares, which was effected on 27 June 1991, and the fourth tranche of D class
preference shares which was effected on 23 July 1992 – a date after issue of the writ
herein. Tindalk was provided with finance to make its purchases from Caledonia by loans
from the six banks. Those loans are likely to be irrecoverable from Tindalk since the
preference shares held by it are unlikely to be of any value. Thus Caledonia has received
the same sum of money as it would have received as a shareholder if all its preference
shares in B & C had been redeemed although two tranches were not so redeemed. The   B
six banks have financed Tindalk's purchase of two tranches of preference shares and the
six banks claim damages for breach of covenant by B & C in the amount paid to finance
the two purchases. The economic effect is that instead of the sum required to redeem the
class C and class D preference shares being paid out of shareholders' funds, and therefore
ranking behind creditors, the sum claimed by the six banks as damages (which is the
same amount and has been paid to the former shareholder Caledonia) will rank as a   C
creditor's claim equally with other creditors. Plainly creditors of B & C will be much
disadvantaged by the result which is said to have been arranged.

On 16 July 1991 the seven plaintiffs, who are the six banks and Tindalk, issued a writ
against B & C. Extensive pleadings have been delivered and it emerged that there arose
points of law which might result in the action not having to go to trial. Accordingly, on
18 December 1992 Master Bagge directed pursuant to O. 33, r. 3 that issues be determined   D
before trial in the form of a document entitled 'Special case for the opinion of the court'
which was agreed by all parties. I am required to answer certain questions formulated in
para. 48, 49 and 50 of the document on the footing of the facts set out in the document.
It is of great importance to stress that I am not making any findings of fact. I have not
seen any of the original documents nor have I heard any oral evidence nor read any
affidavits. The special case is very carefully drawn and agreed by the parties. I shall not
attempt to further set out any of the facts on the footing of which I have to consider these   E
questions nor shall I make any further definitions. I adopt and hereafter use where
material the definitions set out in the special case which run for two and a half pages of
type, and I proceed upon the footing of the facts agreed by the parties for the purpose of
the trial of these issues.

The first set of questions set out in para. 48 concerns the rule of company law usually
called 'the rule in *Trevor v Whitworth*'. In my judgment there are two fundamental   F
principles of company law which can be seen in the cases cited. The first of those
principles goes back to the earliest days of English limited liability companies. The
principle is that a company cannot return capital to its members save by a reduction of
capital sanctioned by the court. This principle applies even if the company's
memorandum of association expressly provides for such a return. The principle is based
upon 'grounds of public policy' – per Page-Wood V-C (later Lord Hatherly) in
MacDougall v Jersey Imperial Hotel Co Ltd (1864) 2 H & M 568 at p. 571, the sixth   G
paragraph. The principle was thereafter before the courts many times but in my judgment
I do not need to refer to those decisions because the principle was established beyond
question in *Trevor v Whitworth* (1887) 12 App Cas 409.

There are three short passages in the speeches in the House in *Trevor v Whitworth*
which seem to me worth repeating. Lord Herschell at p. 419, citing Cotton LJ in *Guinness
v Land Corp of Ireland* (1882) 22 ChD 349 at p. 375, adopts the test then propounded: H

> '. . . whatever has been paid by a member cannot be returned to him. In my opinion
> . . . the capital cannot be diverted from the objects of the society. It is, of course,
> liable to be spent or lost in carrying on the business of the company, but no part
> of it can be returned to a member . . .'

Lord Watson at p. 423 says:

A   '. . . the effect of these statutory restrictions is to prohibit every transaction between a company and a shareholder, by means of which the money already paid to the company in respect of his shares is returned to him, unless the Court has sanctioned the transaction.'

Finally Lord Macnaghten, whose speech is most often cited and who is, of course, one of the great Victorian lawyers whose judgments so clearly lay out principles, at p. 432, five lines from the foot, said that the question involved:

B   '. . . the broader question whether it is competent for a limited company under any circumstances to invest any portion of its capital in the purchase of a share of its own capital stock, or to return any portion of its capital to any shareholder . . .'

He held that the answer to the question he had posed was 'no'.

It will be noticed that in each of those three quotations the Law Lords use the word 'return' in characterising the payment and, consistently with that word, each of them refers to transactions with shareholders. Plainly one cannot 'return' to someone that with which he has not parted. Equally plainly every shareholder must have subscribed to the company for his shares, or after a transfer of shares the new shareholder stands in the shoes of some person who subscribed for the issue of those shares. There are, and I have had cited to me, literally dozens of cases where the courts in this country, and in Australia, Canada and New Zealand (the order is alphabetical not qualitative), have considered payments to or transfers of property to shareholders and held that the payment or transfer constituted a return of capital to a member without the sanction of the court which resulted in the payment or transfer being held ultra vires, incapable of ratification and void.

The proposition that all the authorities concern payments directly or indirectly to or for the benefit of shareholders can be exemplified as follows. In *Davis Investments Pty Ltd v Commissioner of Stamp Duties (NSW)* (1957-58) 100 CLR 392 Kitto J dissented in the result so far as stamp duty was concerned but much of his reasoning was accepted by the majority. At p. 413 (line 7) that judge referred to:

'the fundamental principle of company law that the whole of the subscribed capital of a company . . . unless diminished by expenditure upon the company's object (or . . . by means sanctioned by statute) shall remain available for the discharge of its liabilities . . . *Trevor v Whitworth*; *In re Walters' Deed of Guarantee*. One aspect of this principle is that every transaction between a company (while it is a going concern) and any of its *members* by means of which any of the money paid to the company in respect of the member's shares is returned to him is prohibited unless the Court has sanctioned the transaction.' (emphasis added)

This passage was cited with approval in a judgment of the High Court of Australia, consisting of that great Australian judge Dixon CJ sitting with McTiernan and Taylor JJ, in *Australasian Oil Exploration Ltd v Lachbery* (1958) 101 CLR 119 at p. 132. The decision in that case was that the transaction before the court was an infringement of the principle although, as the judgment comments (on p. 132 before the second break):

'under the scheme envisaged by the agreement the benefits given to the shareholders would be received indirectly, through an intermediary.'

Thus indirect payment for the benefit of members is as much subject to the prohibition as any direct payment.

H   A further indication of the breadth of the principle can be seen from *Jenkins v Harbour View Courts Ltd* [1966] NZLR 1 where the point that the transaction before the court involved an unlawful reduction of capital was taken by the Court of Appeal of New Zealand themselves. The leading judgment delivered by Turner J deals with this point at p. 21, line 35 onwards. At p. 23, line 5 he says:

'This transaction, in a word, is a part of a process by which the company is to

transfer away for no return all its beneficial estate in its undertaking ... to its   A
shareholders ... I have no hesitation at all in concluding that this is in factual
essence as much a *return* of capital to shareholders as if from a fund of money a
substantial part were to be handed out ... [to] them.' (emphasis added)

He goes on at p. 23, line 37 to hold that:

'the question which the court must ask itself is – is this transaction in essence one
in which the company divests itself of part of its undertaking in favour of a   B
shareholder otherwise than in the course of a bona fide transaction entered into as
a matter of contract and not as a company/shareholder transaction.'

McCarthy J at p. 27, line 22 is to like effect:

'All parties accept this general proposition: that a limited company not in
liquidation can make no repayment by way of *return* of capital to its shareholders
except as a step in an authorised reduction of capital.' (emphasis added)   C

The judge continues, citing *Hill v Permanent Trustee Co of New South Wales* [1930]
AC 720, and goes on at line 36:

'The prohibition against a *return* of capital blocks any return whatever the form
whether it be by a payment of money, by a transfer of assets in specie or in any
other way unless the procedure stipulated by the relevant statute ... (has) been
observed' (emphasis added)   D

–and then cited Lindley LJ in *Verner v General and Commercial Investment Trust* [1894] 2
Ch 239 at p. 264. The President agreed with McCarthy J on this point, so the court are
all of the same view. All use words pointing to the relevant question being 'Does the
transaction involve a return of capital to members?'.

Mr Stubbs further cited *Re Halt Garage (1964) Ltd* [1982] 3 All ER 1016 as an example
of the court striking down an unlawful reduction of share capital. I find the actual   E
decision of Oliver J in that case difficult to accept as entirely correct. The facts in *Re Halt
Garage* were that a man and his wife were the only two directors of the company; the
company had an express power to pay directors' remuneration by resolution in general
meeting; the company resolved in general meeting to pay both husband and wife
directors' fees; the wife was ill and unable to perform any active services for the company;
the company at the end of its trading life had no distributable reserves; and the company
went into creditors' voluntary liquidation insolvent. Oliver J held that although, as he   F
said at p. 1044a–b:

'I was troubled ... by the question whether ... a payment made in these
circumstances could be apportioned. Accepting ... that directors' remuneration
under an article in this form is a gratuitous payment can part be, as it were, more
gratuitous than the rest?'

–yet he could reach the conclusion that part of the remuneration resolved to be paid to   G
the wife was a valid payment but part of the remuneration voted by that same resolution
was excessive and so void. The judge went on to hold that such an article does not
authorise what he described as 'a pure gift'. In that part of his judgment Oliver J was
echoing what that great master of the law Lindley LJ said in *Re George Newman & Co*
[1895] 1 Ch 674 at pp. 685–686.

Oliver J ended by holding at p. 1044 in *Re Halt Garage* that the payments to the wife   H
as a director who did no active work at all in excess of a limited amount less that she had
actually received, must be regarded as disguised payments out of capital and so the
liquidator's claim for repayment succeeded in part. I respectfully agree with the judge
that to call a payment 'directors' remuneration' when it was not has no effect on the
court. There is a general principle of law that *falsa demonstratio non nocet* which can be
very loosely translated as 'labels do not alter facts'. So in *Ridge Securities Ltd v IR*

A *Commrs* [1964] 1 WLR 479, to which I return later, Pennycuick J had held that the label 'interest' attached to certain payments on bogus debentures did not make the payments in law interest. Whatever the parties call a transaction its true nature will be decided by the court on the facts proved.

Further in *Re Halt Garage* it appears that the lady director was a shareholder in the company (see at p. 1020b) – so that a payment to her when there were no available
B distributable profits can properly be called 'a *return* of capital to a member'. My difficulty is that I cannot see how a single resolution passed in general meeting can be part valid and part void as ultra vires the company. As I understand the law a resolution which is part void must be invalid as a whole – see *Re Imperial Bank of China* (1866) 1 Ch App 339 at p. 347. Once the resolution passed in general meeting, expressed to resolve that £X be paid to the lady director as remuneration, is found, despite its form and the label attached, to be in fact a resolution both to pay her some remuneration and to return to
C her some capital I would have thought that the resolution as a whole was ultra vires the company, incapable of division, and so void in toto. That point does not, however, bear upon the question before me. As it seems to me the only relevant conclusion which I should draw from *Re Halt Garage* is that a payment to a corporator when a company has no distributable reserves available and the corporator has no valid claim under some right other than as a member against the company, must be an unlawful reduction of
D capital. That I entirely accept.

Out of this far too long line of authority I should finally note *Redweaver Investments Ltd v Lawrence Field Ltd* (1991) 9 ACLC 1032 from which two points emerge. First, that the judge considered the law to be that 'any agreement which in substance provides for a company to return share capital to a member is illegal and cannot be enforced' (see at p. 1036), and secondly (at p. 1037):

> 'the principle and the illegality are not limited to payments which on their face and
E according to the characterisation given to them by the parties to them are returns of capital, but the facts are examined in order to ascertain what in fact took place according to the substance of the matter.'

As I have observed elsewhere in this judgment I entirely agree that labels determine nothing, and what the quotations set out is in my judgment sound law.

All these cases therefore apply the same principle that a transaction which upon
F examination can be seen to involve a return of capital, in whatever form, under whatever label, and whether directly or indirectly, to a member, is void. In none of them was the payment made (using those words deliberately loosely) other than to or for the benefit of a shareholder, and the constant use of the word 'return' is a clear indication of the constant existence of the member/company relationship underlying the transactions. The recent decision of Hoffmann J in *Aveling Barford Ltd v Perion Ltd* (1989) 5 BCC 677, with which I agree, is, in my view, based upon the principle as I have set it out at the start
G of this paragraph. The relevant facts were that the company had no distributable profits available to pay the shareholders. The company conveyed a property which its directors and the directors of the purchaser company knew was valued at £650,000 to the purchasing company for £350,000. Not very surprisingly Hoffmann J held that the purchasing company was a constructive trustee for the vendor.

As a second ground for his decision Hoffmann J stated the proposition of law (at
H p. 682B) that:

> 'a company cannot, without the leave of the court . . . return its capital to its shareholders. It follows that a transaction which amounts to an *unauthorised return* of capital is ultra vires and cannot be validated . . .' (emphasis added)

The judge also held that the description of the transaction given to it by the parties did not bind the court. He cited a passage from Pennycuick J in *Ridge Securities Ltd v IR*

Commrs, and he referred to *Re Halt Garage*. At p. 683F Hoffmann J stated his conclusion   A
on this alternative ground:

> 'The rule that capital may not be returned to shareholders is a rule for the
> protection of creditors and the evasion of that rule falls within what I think Slade
> LJ had in mind when he spoke of a fraud upon creditors.'

He therefore held that the transfer of the property to the defendant company was an
unlawful distribution.   B

Hoffmann J reached that conclusion under the expression of the rule as 'capital may
not be returned to shareholders' although the defendant company was not itself a
shareholder of the vendor plaintiff. He did so, in my judgment, because he had defined
the defendant company as controlled by the actual shareholder in the plaintiff company,
Dr Lee. He thus regarded the transfer as a distribution to a vehicle of the shareholder
and thus indirectly to him or for his benefit. I respectfully agree with the judge's view but   C
upon that basis the case falls into precisely the same line as all the others I have mentioned
and, as I say above, the decision is based upon the principle I have set out.

Mr Potts, for the plaintiffs in the action, stressed time and time again that at the time
of the relevant agreements and indeed at all relevant times down to 3 June 1990 none of
the plaintiffs held or controlled any shares in or had any members' interest, direct or
indirect, in B & C. At the present time none of the six plaintiff banks has any such
interest. On 27 June 1991 Tindalk was registered as the holder of all the class C preference   D
shares and on 22 July 1992 Tindalk was registered as the holder of all the class D
preference shares, so that since those dates and today Tindalk is a member of B & C. The
plaintiff banks are loan creditors of Tindalk and thus their commercial interests are
greatly affected by Tindalk's rights against B & C, but on the footings stated in the issue
before me and for present purposes the plaintiff banks have no membership interest in B
& C.   E

Mr Potts therefore submitted that the principle that a company cannot make any
return of capital to its members except as authorised by statute can have no application
to the claims of the plaintiff banks which have not themselves subscribed capital to B &
C, nor have purchased shares so as to stand in the shoes of one who subscribed to B &
C, so that capital cannot be properly said to be 'returned' to them. The plaintiff banks
are not members of B & C. He added that Tindalk, although now a member of B & C
had no membership interest at all at the time the various agreements were made.   F
Accordingly, he submitted, Tindalk also is not affected by the principle commonly
referred to as 'the rule in *Trevor v Whitworth* ' which is in my judgment a fundamental
rule of company law, since the agreement at the time at which it was made did not
envisage any payment to a then member of B & C. On the basis of the authorities I have
so far cited that submission has great force.

There is however, one authority, which has so far only been mentioned in passing,   G
which affects Mr Potts' submissions above set out. That is *Re Walters' Deed of Guarantee*
[1933] Ch 321 (hereafter called the *Palm Toffee* case) which was referred to as
demonstrating the principle by Kitto J in the *Davis Investments* case at p. 413. The
decision in the *Palm Toffee* case by Maugham J, who was very experienced in company
law matters, was given extempore without citation in the judgment of any authority save
Trevor v Whitworth and, so far as the report shows, without any citation of authority by   H
the well-known specialist company law counsel for the plaintiff company. The extremely
short but clear headnote states a proposition which I am not sure the judge had uttered.
The facts as stated briefly in the report were that the defendant Mr Walters had by a deed
made between the company of the first part, himself of the second part and a trustee for
preference shareholders of the third part, guaranteed payment to the preference
shareholders for three years of dividends on the preference shares of the company. The

A   report does not indicate whether the defendant had made any payment under the guarantee, nor whether the company was solvent or had distributable reserves or not. The deed provided that the company would repay to Mr Walters on demand any amount paid by him under his guarantee to the trustee for preference shareholders.

The very short judgment of Maugham J at the top of p. 322 states that if Mr Walters, the defendant, paid any money under his guarantee he would be able to sue the company:

B   'as if he were a creditor entitled to rank in the same position as any other creditor. The capital of the company might thereby be reduced otherwise than by expenditure on the objects defined by the memorandum.'

The judge then cites *Trevor v Whitworth*. It will be noticed at once that there is no statement that Mr Walters was a member of the company, although it seems likely from other indications that he was, but plainly he was unlikely to have been a preference shareholder since he would have been guaranteeing dividends to himself. Thus there is no indication why the payment would be a return of capital to members. Maugham J states, as I respectfully think accurately, that the clause:

'purports to place the defendant in the position of a creditor who is entitled to rights against the company quite different from the right which a preference shareholder has to payment of dividends out of profits . . .'

D   I find it difficult to see on the limited facts in the report why that fact by itself brought the deed within the rule in *Trevor v Whitworth* as it has been so frequently stated. Apart from Mr Walters' right to demand payment from the company I entirely accept that the rights which he would obtain by subrogation as the guarantor who had paid to the trustee under his guarantee a sum equal to a preference dividend would simply be rights as a member of the company. But to obtain the right of subrogation the guarantor needed no agreement with the company. The right of subrogation results simply from the agreement between himself and the preference shareholder to whom the guarantee was given and payment thereunder. The right Mr Walters would obtain by subrogation is, of course, to stand in the shoes of those preference shareholders to whom he had given his guarantee and such right ranks behind the claims of creditors.

On the facts stated in the report of the *Palm Toffee* case it is not clear to me why the agreement of the company to repay Mr Walters was a breach of the rule in *Trevor v Whitworth* unless the rule extends to cover agreements with shareholders which will only fall to be performed when the company in which shares are held has no distributable reserves and is therefore unable to make some payment – whether of dividend or of a capital nature – otherwise due to the shareholders. The only rationale I can see is that if in such circumstances the agreement enables a shareholder to obtain from the third party a payment in an equivalent amount to the payment due from the company and upon so doing the third party is entitled not only to subrogation to the rights of the shareholder but also to repayment from the company, then the contract is to be held within the rule in *Trevor v Whitworth* even though at the time it is made the company has distributable reserves and there is no present difficulty in the company's making the required payments to shareholders. I do not believe that the decision in the *Palm Toffee* case has been stated to have the result I have tried to express but unless that is the ratio of the decision I find it difficult to accept.

H   The decision has stood unchallenged for sixty years and has been referred to by judges such as Kitto J (loc. cit.) without any hint of disapproval. It can be seen that the result of a guarantee to a shareholder such as that given by Mr Walters to the preference shareholders in the *Palm Toffee* case, linked with an obligation on the company to repay the guarantor, has the potential effect, if the company is insolvent or otherwise unable to pay money to shareholders, of changing claims by shareholders against a company, which rank behind claims by creditors, into a claim by a creditor ranking equally with

other creditors. That is the point stated by Maugham J although he expresses it as a   A
present and not a potential effect. It is that effect which the judge relies upon for his
conclusion that 'clause 7 is wholly ultra vires and void'.

I think it worth noting that Maugham J was careful in the last paragraph of his
judgment to preserve to the defendant his above-mentioned right arising from his
guarantee to be subrogated to the rights of preference shareholders both in respect of
dividends and 'in respect of any rights of preference shareholders in a winding-up' – see   B
the last line at p. 322. The facts reported at the start of the *Palm Toffee* case make no
reference to Mr Walters having guaranteed any rights of preference shareholders in a
winding-up. It seems likely, therefore, that the guarantee was in wider terms than stated
in the report and in fact covered all rights of preference shareholders during a three year
period. If that is correct that would lead naturally to consideration by the court of a right
to repayment of capital on a winding up which plainly is a right to a return of capital to
members and leads inevitably to consideration of the rule in *Trevor v Whitworth*.   C

As it seems to me that authority, which Mr Potts criticised but did not submit was
wrong, and which I consider I must follow and apply leaving it to a higher court to
overrule if thought fit, leads to the conclusion that any agreement which is only likely to
be called upon if the company has no distributable profits and which will, if called upon
when the company becomes insolvent, have the effect of increasing the liabilities of a
company, by substituting, for rights which are rights held by shareholders ranking behind   D
creditors, rights held by a creditor ranking equally with other creditors, is objectionable
by reason of the rule in *Trevor v Whitworth*. It is clear that, upon the footings stated in
the special case, the effect of the three stages: (a) the exercise by Caledonia of its put
options against Tindalk, (b) the obligation of the plaintiff banks to fund Tindalk's
liabilities to pay Caledonia, and (c) the breach of the covenants given by B & C to the
plaintiff banks, leads in combination to the rights of Caledonia as a preference
shareholder to have its preference shares redeemed, which rights are an obligation of   E
B & C to one of its members and as such ranking behind its obligations to unsecured
creditors, being substituted, in effect, by the rights of the plaintiff banks ranking as
unsecured creditors equally with other such creditors against B & C.

It may be said that in strict law the rights of the preference shareholder – at present
Tindalk – are not altered or, strictly speaking, replaced by substitution, if B & C pays or
is liable to pay the plaintiff banks damages under its covenants. The preference shares   F
remain in issue with their rights attached. In my judgment that is too narrow a view and
falls to take account of the inevitable realities. The plaintiff banks will never have any
claim for damages for breach of covenant unless B & C is insolvent. If it is insolvent the
rights of the preference shareholders are by definition worthless because if B & C cannot
pay its creditors in full then shareholders can get nothing. Thus B & C will never have
the double liability of first paying the plaintiff banks damages for breach of covenant,
being the amount which the plaintiff banks have to pay to enable Tindalk to meet   G
Caledonia's put option, and secondly repaying Tindalk the amount due for redemption
of the preference shares. In truth the payment to the plaintiff banks as damages of a sum
equal to the amount they have lent to Tindalk, which sum it has paid to Caledonia on
the purchase of the preference shares, will be the same as paying the redemption value of
the preference shares which will never be redeemed.

Further the objection that the payment of money or transfer of assets which was held   H
to be an unlawful reduction of capital left in force and did not alter or affect the rights of
the shareholders would have applied to many of the authorities. In the *Palm Toffee* case
itself the declaration seems to have been sought and made when no actual liability to pay
had arisen and the rights of the preference shareholders against the company remained
wholly unaffected. In *Re Halt Garage* the unlawful return of capital had no effect
whatever on the shareholding of the lady director which remained unaltered. In *Jenkins*

A   *v Harbour View Courts Ltd* the grant of a lease to a member in no way altered or affected the rights attached to the shares held by that member although the grant was an unlawful return of capital to that member. In *Redweaver Investments Ltd v Lawrence Field Ltd* the shareholding of the plaintiff remained entirely unaltered by the purported obligation to pay damages in a sum equivalent to the subscription for the shares. As a final example, in *Aveling Barford Ltd v Perion Ltd* the shareholding of Dr Lee was not affected at all by the sale of property at a gross undervalue to his controlled company, Perion Ltd. It thus

B   appears that the fact that the shareholding remains completely unaltered and the relevant company's obligations in respect of the shareholding remain in force does not affect the proposition that the transaction amounts to an unlawful return, or an agreement which may lead to an unlawful return, of capital to a member. All these cases seem to support the conclusion I have reached that the continuing existence unaltered of the preference shares on the facts stated on this issue does not point to the agreement being other than

C   an attempt to return capital unlawfully.

    I should add that the guarantee offered to shareholders in the *Palm Toffee* case against which the company was liable to indemnify the guarantor is obviously more directly linked to a member's holding of shares than is the liability in damages to the plaintiff banks for loss caused to them by making irrecoverable loans to Tindalk which loans enabled it to pay Caledonia. The indirect nature of the link between B & C's liability to

D   redeem the preference shares and the damage caused to the banks is obviously an argument for saying that the connection is too tenuous and remote. In my judgment the complexities which exist, and the varied nature of the legal rights involved, are not more than grounds for pausing to consider whether, on the footings for this issue, I should conclude that the principle that 'the whole of the capital of a company with limited liability, unless diminished by expenditure upon the company's objects (or of course by means sanctioned by statute) shall remain available for the discharge of its liabilities' as stated by Kitto J in the *Davis Investments Pty* case and adopted by Dixon CJ in the

E   *Australasian Oil Exploration* case is infringed. I have not found this an easy point to decide and other minds may well come to a different conclusion. Nonetheless if the principle is to be maintained elaborate structures put in place by highly skilled advisers cannot be allowed to divert decisions from the straight and narrow path of strict adherence to principle. I therefore conclude that the agreements do infringe the stated principle and are therefore void and unenforceable, subject to consideration of one

F   further point with which I will deal hereafter.

    The second fundamental principle of company law established by the cases is that no company may make truly gratuitous dispositions of its assets. The point is vividly expressed in the language of that great judge, Bowen LJ, in *Hutton v West Cork Railway Co* (1883) 23 ChD 654 at p. 673:

G   'The law does not say that there are to be no cakes and ale, but that there are to be no cakes and ale except such as are required for the benefit of the company . . .

        It is not charity sitting at the board of directors, because as it seems to me charity has no business to sit at boards of directors *qua* charity. There is, however, a kind of charitable dealing which is for the interest of those who practice it, and to that extent and in that garb (I admit not a very philanthropic garb) charity may sit at the board, but for no other purpose.'

H   That line of thought is echoed by Lindley LJ in *Re George Newman & Co* [1895] 1 Ch 674 at p. 686 where he says:

        'The shareholders, at a meeting duly convened . . . can, if they think proper, remunerate directors for their trouble or make presents to them for their services out of assets properly divisible amongst the shareholders themselves . . . But to make presents out of profits is one thing and to make them out of capital or out of

money borrowed by the company is a very different matter. Such money cannot   A
be lawfully divided amongst the shareholders themselves, nor can it be given away
by them for nothing to their directors so as to bind the company in its corporate
capacity.'

In *Ridge Securities Ltd v IR Commrs* Pennycuick J at p. 495 (in a passage cited by
Hoffmann J in *Aveling Barford Ltd v Perion Ltd*) expressed it thus:

'A company can only lawfully deal with its assets in furtherance of its objects. The   B
corporators may take assets out of the company by way of dividend, or with leave
of the court, by way of reduction of capital or in a winding-up. They may, of
course, acquire them for full consideration. They cannot take assets out of the
company by way of voluntary disposition, however described, and if they attempt
to do so the disposition is ultra vires the company.'

That passage seems to me to express shortly, clearly and correctly the general law. It
is, however, to be noticed that that judge, who had great experience of company law,   C
clearly speaks of what 'corporators', in other words shareholders, are permitted to do,
and ends: 'They cannot take assets out of the company, by way of voluntary disposition,
however described'. In my judgment he is plainly referring to 'voluntary dispositions' to
any person, and not only to shareholders returning capital to themselves. It is to be
noticed that neither *Trevor v Whitworth* itself nor any of the other cases on unlawful
reduction of share capital were cited to Pennycuick J or mentioned by him nor were the   D
cases on gratuitous dispositions otherwise than out of profits since they were not
necessary for the decision. The observation by Pennycuick J is one based on mere
assertion of principle, although none the worse or weaker for that.

The principle was recently summarised by Nourse LJ in *Brady v Brady* (1987) 3 BCC
535 at p. 550:

'In its broadest terms the principle is that a company cannot give away its assets.   E
So stated, it is subject to the qualification that in the realm of theory a
memorandum of association may authorise a company to give away all its assets
to whomsoever it pleases, including its shareholders. But in the real world of
trading companies – charitable or political donations, pensions to widows of ex-
employees and the like apart – it is obvious that such a power would never be
taken. The principle is only a facet of the wider rule, the corollary of limited
liability, that the integrity of a company's assets, except to the extent allowed by   F
its constitution, must be preserved for the benefit of all those who are interested in
them, most pertinently its creditors.'

Although the decision of the Court of Appeal in *Brady v Brady* was reversed in the
House of Lords this passage was not criticised. The observations of Nourse LJ were
made in a context which makes it plain that the Lord Justice is accepting the earlier
statements whereby the law imposes a limit on even an express power such as he   G
envisaged to give away all a company's assets so that such a power could only be exercised
by a company with available distributable profits. In the Canadian case of *Plain Ltd v
Kinley & Royal Trust Co* (1931) 1 DLR 468, Orde JA said at p. 479:

'a limited liability . . . company cannot do what it likes with its property . . . It
cannot lawfully give its property either to shareholders or to others. I am speaking
broadly because there are cases where in the interest of its own business a company
may [make gifts] but transactions of that character either depend upon the fact   H
that they are prudent and proper business expenditures or are made out of
accumulated profits and with the consent of the shareholders.'

These statements have been approved in Australia – see *ANZ Executors & Trustee Co
Ltd v Qintex Australia Ltd* (1990) 8 ACLC 980 at p. 988. In my judgment they are a
correct statement of English law also.

A   Mr Stubbs argued that the principle that a company cannot make a gratuitous disposition of its assets save either for the benefit of its business or out of distributable profit with the approval of its shareholders applied very widely. He submitted that a gratuitous payment by a company to the wife, mistress, niece or other friend of a shareholder when there were no distributable profits was ultra vires the company under the rule that a company cannot give away its capital. The rule operates by analogy with the rule prohibiting the unlawful return of capital to a member called the rule in *Trevor v*
B   *Whitworth*. Both types of payment have the effect of reducing capital to the detriment of creditors. That seems to me to be correct. As Mr Stubbs observed, if in the case of *Re Halt Garage* the lady director who received money described rightly or wrongly as directors' remuneration had been merely the wife of the principal shareholder and not herself also a shareholder (as she in fact was), could it be doubted that Oliver J would have held that the lady must return the money as a gratuitous payment in reduction of
C   capital, although not a *return* of capital. In my judgment that submission is correct.

     In this case at the time the option agreement and the other agreements were made B & C had available distributable profits. But as it seems to me it must equally be unlawful to make an agreement expressed to impose a liability to make a gratuitous payment, that is one not for the advancement of a company's business nor made out of distributable profits, at a future date when in the event the company has no distributable
D   profits. That brings one back to the question of the character of the payments to be made by B & C to the plaintiff banks. The claims are said to be for damages for breach of covenants as such and not claims to payments under the covenants.

     The claims made by the plaintiffs are defined in para. 44(a), (b) and (c) in the special case as the 'primary creditor claims', the 'further creditor claims' and the 'misrepresentation claims'. The primary creditor claims are for damages for B & C's breach of contract by failing to perform the covenants in the option agreement set out in
E   cl. 34(b) of the special case. These included a covenant which can loosely be summarised as that B & C would procure that its redemption reserve was sufficient to redeem such preference shares as were outstanding from time to time. That seems to me to have precisely the same commercial effect as a covenant by B & C with the plaintiff banks that it would duly redeem the preference shares as they were required to be redeemed. A breach of such a covenant would occur if B & C did not have any or sufficient distributable profits. But if B & C did not have sufficient distributable profits it could
F   only redeem the preference shares out of capital, which would inevitably be, on the authorities previously cited, an unlawful reduction of capital unless sanctioned by the court. Without such sanction the payment of the redemption moneys would be ultra vires.

     The primary creditor claims are also based on additional covenants which it is alleged B & C also broke. Some of these covenants could be broken without B & C being or
G   being about to be insolvent. For example the covenants at cl. 6.01(4) and (8) as set out on p. 27 of the special case could easily be broken without B & C being threatened with insolvency. But in fact the breaches of covenant, which are assumed for present purposes to have occurred, are the direct result, it is alleged, of B & C going into administration which, as I have set out, depends upon actual or imminent insolvency. In the circumstances, it seems to me that the operative breach upon the footing of which I am
H   to proceed is that which I have characterised as having the same commercial effect as a covenant by B & C with the six banks that it will redeem its preference shares for breach of which it will be liable to the six banks in damages to the same amount as it was liable to repay to its preference shareholders. That has the precise effect spoken of by Maugham J in the *Palm Toffee* case which he held was ultra vires and void. In my view the careful formulation adopted in the scheme constructed for Caledonia and B & C cannot be allowed to obscure the underlying reality. The truth of Mr Potts' submission that the six

banks are not members of B & C and therefore any obligation to pay damages to them   A
cannot be a *return* of capital is clear but the obligation to pay damages is a gratuitous
payment by B & C at a time when it has no distributable profits. For that reason the
obligation cannot be enforced.

The further creditor claims are made by the plaintiff banks alone and claim an
indemnity under the stand-by agreement. The stand-by agreement itself contained a
covenant by B & C that it would comply with the option agreement and an indemnity by   B
B & C to BZW (which is not a party to this action) and the original banks against loss by
reason of any default by B & C in performing the stand-by agreement. As it seems to me,
the covenant by B & C that it would comply with a term in the option agreement which
term was itself unenforceable at law cannot be the foundation for a claim at law. If it was
unlawful to perform the stand-by agreement in the circumstances which have occurred
then no loss is recoverable for that failure to perform.

The misrepresentation claims stand on a different footing to the claims to which I have   C
so far referred. As set out in para. 4(c) of the special case these claims are by the third
plaintiff bank, 'HSBC', and the sixth plaintiff bank, 'CB'. These two plaintiffs allege that
on or about 19 July 1989 they saw a draft variation of the option agreement which
variation contained a representation by B & C that it was not in breach of any term of
cl. 6.01 of the option agreement (see para. 35 of the special case) and that that
representation was untrue, material and relied upon HSBC and CB (see para. 43 of the   D
special case). On those footings the claim by HSBC and CB is said to be a straightforward
claim in tort under the *Misrepresentation Act* 1967. Mr Potts submits that the rule in
Trevor v Whitworth as applied in the *Palm Toffee* case and the rule against gratuitous
payments out of capital have nothing to do with a straightforward claim in tort and at
first sight that proposition is appealing.

However, the simple approach may obscure the true complication of the transaction.   E
Mr Stubbs submitted that if Y agrees to buy from X his holding of redeemable shares in
a company and as a term of that contract the company joins to warrant that it has, at the
date of sale, £2m of distributable profits, amply sufficient to cover the amount required
to cover the redemptions, that warranty by the company would be unenforceable by Y.
He makes that submission on the footing that if the warranty was broken because the
company has no distributable profits at the date of contract, and therefore failed to
redeem the preference shares, Y could not claim payment under the warranty as a creditor   F
and so obtain for himself a payment which as a shareholder he could not obtain. The
warranty would only be sued upon if the company failed to redeem the preference shares,
so causing loss, because it was unable for want of distributable profits to perform its
obligation. If the court were to enforce a claim for payment under the contractual
warranty it would be causing a payment which should only be made out of capital to be
made at a time when no capital was available to make that payment. It followed that the
court would refuse to enforce the claim. If that was correct, said Mr Stubbs, it would   G
make no difference if instead of the company giving a contractual warranty it made a
formal representation to Y of the same facts, knowing that Y would rely upon the
representation. If the representation was untrue, that would prima facie give rise to a
straightforward liability in tort. In Mr Stubbs' submission a conclusion that a claim in
tort would succeed where a claim in contract would fail would be to allow form to prevail
over substance.

As in other issues raised by this special case I have found my mind vacillating between   H
the two contentions so vigorously advanced in opposition to each other. In my judgment
I should prefer Mr Stubbs' submissions but plainly other minds could come to the
opposite conclusion. I am assisted to my conclusion by the consideration that if the
underlying terms of the option agreement, the continuing truth of which was represented,
on the basis upon which I have to approach this matter, were themselves incapable of an

A   enforcement (because the occasion for their enforcement by an action for damages for their breach can only be likely to arise when B & C is unable because of want of distributable profits to redeem some tranche of the preference shares) it would be odd if HSBC and CB could recover damages for misrepresentation as to those terms but the other four plaintiff banks could not recover for breach of the terms themselves.

B   I therefore reach the conclusion that none of the three types of claim identified by para. 48, 49 and 50 of the special case can be enforced because such an enforcement would be equivalent to allowing a payment out of capital when B & C at the times when the liability arose had no such capital available. On that basis the company would succeed on this question. However that is not the end of the argument on the special case.

C   As I mentioned earlier on in this judgment the scheme as defined in para. 10 of the special case was submitted to the shareholders of B & C who approved it by special resolution and the scheme was thereafter sanctioned pursuant to s. 425 of the *Companies Act* 1985 by the court on 12 October 1987. The order of the court shows that Peter Gibson J had before him counsel for B & C as the petitioner together with counsel for Caledonia and another interested party who gave undertakings to be bound by the scheme of arrangement. The order itself was in what is in my experience the most usual form. It provided that the court sanctioned the scheme 'as set forth in the first schedule hereto'. The order also provided for the reduction of capital, delivery to the registrar of companies of an office copy of the order and for advertisement in the Financial Times, all of which are usual terms of such orders.

D   The first schedule to the order contains definitions. In particular it defines the 'Caledonia preference shares', which are the class A, B, C and D redeemable preference shares in B & C, and the 'option agreement' which contains the terms giving Caledonia its options for each class of preference shares in turn entitling it to require Tindalk to purchase the relevant class of shares and the obligations upon the banks to finance Tindalk. The scheme as set out in the first schedule requires B & C and Caledonia to 'enter into and execute the option agreement'. In my judgment those provisions have the effect of incorporating by reference into the order the option agreement as if all its terms were set out.

E

F   Mr Stubbs pointed out, correctly, that the evidence in support of the scheme of arrangement made no reference to the possible effect of the option agreement in enabling the six banks to claim damages against B & C for breaches of the terms of the option agreement. It is clear that although the explanatory memorandum that accompanied the scheme documents referred to B & C paying fees to the banks for their work on the scheme, which payment might well be held to result in B & C giving financial assistance in connection with the acquisition by Caledonia of the redeemable preference shares in breach of the prohibition on such assistance, no other liability on B & C or assumption of obligation by B & C was mentioned at all. Further, section 2 of appendix III of the explanatory statement refers to B & C's contingent liabilities at its last balance sheet date in a manner which gives no hint of the large contingent liability created by the possible claims for breach of the option agreement. Mr Stubbs drew attention to further points and in general submitted that if the claims of the six banks were well founded then the explanatory memorandum was seriously misleading.

G

H   That contention may or may not be justified but in my judgment it is not a matter with which this or any court is concerned. The only question raised is as to the effect of the order made on 12 October 1987. An order of a court of unlimited jurisdiction, such as the Companies Court in which Peter Gibson J was sitting on 12 October 1987, once made stands until set aside or rescinded by some valid judicial process. See *Isaacs v Robertson* [1985] AC 97. That decision is by the board of the Privy Council and was delivered by Lord Diplock. He adopts the judgment of Romer LJ in *Hadkinson v Hadkinson* [1952] P 285 at p. 288 which itself cited a decision of Cottenham LC in 1846 to the same effect, so

that the point is covered by binding authority of the highest order. It is therefore no   A
business of this or any court to enquire into the basis for making the order of 12 October
1987 unless and until some proper application is made to set that order aside. No such
application is before me. The order therefore stands and its terms are binding and
effective.

I therefore turn to consider the effect of the order made on 12 October 1987
incorporating the terms of the option agreement. Mr Potts cited and relied upon the   B
decision at first instance and of the Court of Appeal in *Nicholl v Eberhardt Co Ltd* (1889)
59 LT 860 at first instance and (1889) 1 Meg 402 in the Court of Appeal. The decision
was widely reported in a varied series of reports, though not in the official law reports.
Counsel on the whole agreed that the report I have cited above is the best report. The
plaintiffs were suing for a declaration that agreements made in 1885 and 1886 were ultra
vires and void. The defence was that the agreements had been sanctioned by the court
under the Companies Acts 1862 and 1870. At first instance Kekewich J dismissed the   C
action saying, as reported in (1889) 59 LT at p. 863 (about three-quarters of the way
down the second column):

'the order having been made in the required form is, according to the Act of 1870,
binding not only on the creditors, not only on the liquidators but on all the
members of the company. As long as that order stands I cannot hear the plaintiffs
say they are not bound by the scheme sanctioned by that order.'   D

The Court of Appeal affirmed that decision without calling on counsel for the respondent
defendants. Lord Esher MR in (1889) 1 Meg at p. 408 says (at the foot of the page):

'the sanction of the court makes that arrangement binding also on the liquidator
and the contributories of the company. Words more plain I cannot conceive.'

Cotton LJ at p. 410 (in the middle of the page) says:

'This agreement was sanctioned by an order of the court and that being so this   E
part of the clause takes effect so long as that order stands I do not see how it is
possible to set aside the agreement.'

Fry LJ agreed.

The words of the Act of 1870 are re-enacted in s. 425(2) of the *Companies Act* 1985
which provides that:

'the . . . arrangement, if sanctioned by the court, is binding on all the creditors . . .   F
on the members . . . and also on the company . . .'

In my judgment Mr Potts' submission is correct and the terms of the option agreement
are now binding upon B & C by force of statute and therefore cannot now be impugned
by B & C. The attack upon the validity of the provisions under the rules of company law
that I have endeavoured to express above cannot be made because, by virtue of the
statute and the order made under it on 12 October 1987, the option agreement is binding
on B & C. The administrators who control B & C's affairs were not suggested to be, and   G
in my judgment are not, in any different position. It follows that the whole attack on the
option agreement based on the principle of the maintenance of capital must fail.

The special case also raises the contention that 'liability on the part of the company is
precluded by s. 178(2)' of the *Companies Act* 1985 (see para. 48(d)(ii) and 49(d)(ii)).
Section 178(2) provides that:

'The company is not liable in damages in respect of any failure on its part to   H
redeem or purchase any . . . shares.'

The question raised is whether the claims by the six banks for damages for breaches of
the terms of the option agreement or the stand-by agreement are claims for 'damages in
respect of any failure . . . to redeem . . . any shares'. Mr Stubbs submits that in reality the
claims by the six banks are raised because B & C failed to redeem the class C and class D

A tranches of preference shares. Mr Potts submits that although the failure to redeem is the occasion for the exercise by Caledonia of its put option against Tindalk and the arising of the obligation upon the six banks to provide funds to Tindalk yet it is not 'in respect of' those events that the claims in damages are made. The claims are made 'in respect of' breaches of covenant, although Mr Potts accepts that in broad, though not precise, terms the measure of loss occasioned by the breaches of covenants is the amount of the payment by Tindalk to Caledonia.

B Mr Potts submitted that the whole structure of Pt. V, Ch. VII of the *Companies Act* 1985 showed that the provisions enacted as to both the redemption of shares and the purchase by a company of its own shares were all concerned with dealings between a company and a relevant shareholder. Sections 162–169 deal with purchases by a company of its own shares and s. 171–177 provide for the redemption or purchase of shares out of capital. Section 178 itself provides in subs. (3) that subs. (2) (which I have set out above):

C   'is without prejudice to any right *of the holder* of the shares other than his right to sue the company for damages . . .' (emphasis added)

From those provisions, it is suggested, one can see that s. 178 of the Act of 1985 is concerned only with the rights of shareholders and that subs. (2) is not intended to be a general provision affecting third parties who are not shareholders. Mr Potts submitted that only a shareholder was likely to be harmed by a failure to complete a contract to buy shares or to redeem them. I am not convinced that other parties may not be so injured. Mr Stubbs cited market-makers on the Stock Exchange who were not likely to be registered as holders of shares since they would hold claims through SEPON as the agent for the Stock Exchange and who would deal not in particular shares to which they might or might not be entitled at the time of dealing, but in numbers of shares to be delivered. Market-makers might very well be affected by a failure of a company to complete a bargain made by its broker pursuant to an announced programme to buy back say ten per cent of the issued shares. If market-makers were not affected by s. 178(2) then they might well be able to formulate claims for damages against such a company. In my judgment Mr Potts' argument is not convincing on this point although I do not decide that he is wrong. I put this argument aside and turn to the second submission on the question.

Mr Potts' second submission on s. 178(2) was on the construction of the words 'damages in respect of' in the subsection. He submitted that in this context the natural and ordinary meaning of the phrase 'in respect of' could be expressed as 'for' and showed a direct causal link between the 'damages', payment of which are prohibited, and the act of 'failure to redeem' which caused the damages. In his submission the words read naturally as preventing the counterparty to the transaction with the company, that is the shareholder whose shares are not redeemed (or are not purchased), from recovering damages from the company, and do not naturally have a meaning as prohibiting all payments by the company of damages to whomsoever suffers the loss even though that party has no direct link with the company but is, for example, a banker who lent money to a shareholder on the security of redeemable preference shares which loan the banker cannot recover because of the failure to redeem the preference shares. The fact that the failure to redeem the preference shares is the occasion for the loss does not lead to the conclusion that the failure is the cause of the loss.

H In support of his submission that the natural and ordinary meaning of the phrase 'damages in respect of' is damages directly flowing from the act complained of, Mr Potts cited the decision of Croom-Johnson J in *Ackbar v C F Green & Co Ltd* [1975] QB 582. That decision turned on the true construction of the phrase 'damages in respect of' in s. 2(1) of the *Limitation Act* 1939 which is an identical phrase to that now under consideration. Croom-Johnson J's reasoning is set out at p. 588D–E of the report where he says:

'In the end if one asks the question here, "what is this action all about?", one gets A
the answer that it is about an alleged breach of contract by the defendants, as a
result of which the plaintiff lost the chance or right to recover his loss either from
the driver or from his own insurers. I do not think that the damages sought in this
action consist of or include damages in respect of personal injuries. Those damages,
which might have been recovered heretofore, are only the measure of the damages
now claimed.'

In just the same way, says Mr Potts, the damages sought in the present action do not B
consist of or include damages in respect of any failure to redeem any shares although
that failure may well be the measure of the damages claimed which are for breaches of
contract.

Mr Potts also cited *McGahie v Union of Shop Distributive & Allied Workers* 1966 SLT
74, a Scottish decision relied upon by Croom-Johnson J as supporting his conclusion,
and *Flynn v Graham* 1964 SLT 89. He submitted that *Paterson v Chadwick* [1974] 1 WLR C
890, which was a decision of Boreham J relied upon by Mr Stubbs in this case but
specifically distinguished by Croom-Johnson J in *Ackbar v C F Green & Co Ltd*, was
distinguishable in this present case also upon the ground that the statutory phrase
construed by Boreham J was 'claims in respect of' and was in the context of a provision
enabling discovery of records to be had. Boreham J had observed that the words 'in
respect of' should be given a wide meaning; in my opinion where discovery is facilitated D
by some statutory provision it is natural to read words as widely as possible. Where a
judge has to consider the quite different context of a restriction upon rights to sue for or
obtain damages the context requires a rather more careful and restrictive interpretation
of the words used. I therefore agree with and follow the distinction held by Croom-
Johnson J to apply.

Mr Stubbs submitted that the words 'in respect of' read naturally as conveying the
widest spread of meaning. He submitted that the claims for damages in the present case E
were directly related to the failure of B & C to redeem class C and class D of the preference
shares and that, adopting the test formulated by Croom-Johnson J in *Ackbar v C F Green
& Co Ltd*, if the question was asked 'what is this action all about?' the answer is that it is
about B & C's failure to redeem. Mr Stubbs cited *Paterson v Chadwick* to which I have
already referred and *Trustees, Executors & Agency Co Ltd v Reilly* [1941] VLR 110, cited
by Boreham J, where the Chief Justice of Victoria said at p. 111: F

'The words "In respect of" are difficult of definition but they have the widest
possible meaning of any expression intended to convey some connection or relation
between the two subject matters to which the order refers.'

Mr Stubbs went on to cite *Bank of New South Wales v The Commonwealth* (1948) 76
CLR 1 which was a case on the constitution of Australia. The relevant part of s. 51 of
the constitution was 'laws for . . . the good government of the Commonwealth . . . with
respect to . . .' Of that phrase Latham CJ said at p. 186: G

'A power to make laws "with respect to" a specific subject is as wide a legislative
power as can be created.'

Despite that statement the Chief Justice goes on to say:

'It is not enough that a law should refer to the subject matter or apply to the
subject matter: for example income tax laws apply to clergymen and to
hotelkeepers as members of the public; but none would describe an income tax law H
as being, for that reason, a law with respect to clergymen or hotelkeepers.'

The judgment thus demonstrates that wide words are still confined by context.

Mr Stubbs further cited *R v Londonderry Justices* [1972] NI 91 where a divisional court
of the Queen's Bench for Northern Ireland had to consider a similar power to make laws
in respect of the defence of the realm. The Lord Chief Justice considered the construction

A   of the words 'in respect of' at p. 100, line 12 to p. 102, line 35. I forbear from setting out the reasoning which is, as one would expect, impressively careful. Nonetheless I do not find the constitutional decisions of great help. Words, however wide, take their colour and meaning from their context. In my judgment in construing the phrase 'damages in respect of' in the context in which they appear in s. 178(2) of the Act of 1985, the meaning given to identical words in s. 2(1) of the *Limitation Act* 1939 by Croom-Johnson J is the true and correct meaning and I so hold. In my judgment that conclusion does not involve

B   or require the interpolation of words into the section and is mere construction and not a usurpation of the legislative function.

     I now turn to the questions raised by para. 48(d)(iii), 49(d)(iii) and 50(d)(iii) of the special case. These all turn on the terms of s. 151(1), 152(2) and 153(2) of the *Companies Act* 1985. This group of sections is in Pt. V, Ch. VI of the Act of 1985 and starts with a general prohibition against a company (including its subsidiaries) giving financial assistance directly or indirectly for the purpose of the acquisition of shares in that

C   company. The definitions for Ch. VI are set out in s. 152 and are of considerable complexity. I shall not paraphrase or set them out here but reference should be made to the statute. The important consideration for present purposes is the statutory meaning given to 'financial assistance'. The first issue is to identify what transaction is alleged to have been financially assisted. It was, in the end, I think, common ground that only three transactions were relevant: the subscription by Caledonia for the issue of all the preference shares, the purchase by Tindalk of the class C preference shares, and the

D   purchase by Tindalk of the class D preference shares. It was also, in the end, common ground that the only form of assistance allegedly given by B & C directly or indirectly for the purpose of any of those three acquisitions was that defined by s. 152(1)(a)(ii).

     The subclause is drawn in very precise terms. I have read the judgment of Hoffmann J in *Charterhouse Investment Trust Ltd v Tempest Diesels Ltd* (1985) 1 BCC 99,544 with care and admiration. I note that the judge was considering the meaning of the phrase 'financial assistance' in s. 54 of the *Companies Act* 1948, and that he observed at

E   p. 99,552:

> 'There is no definition of financial assistance in the section . . . The words have no technical meaning and their frame of reference is in my judgment the language of ordinary commerce.'

I wholly agree with those observations but I am concerned with s. 152 of the Act of 1985, which provides precisely what was not present in s. 54 of the Act of 1948, which is a

F   definition of 'financial assistance' for the purposes of Ch. VI. However, the judge added that one must bear in mind,

> 'that the section is a penal one and should not be strained to cover transactions which are not fairly within it.'

That observation I also accept and in construing the whole group of sections now governing this subject I am of opinion that the court should still bear in mind when construing documents and considering transactions the fact that the provision of s. 151(3)

G   of the Act of 1985 is penal, so as not to bring within the prohibition a transaction which can fairly be thought to be without it.

     The relevant terms of the subclause are:

> '(a) "financial assistance" means–
>
>   . . .
>
>   (ii) financial assistance given by way of guarantee, security or indemnity, other

H   than an indemnity in respect of the indemnifier's own neglect or default, or by way of release or waiver . . .'

     Mr Potts submitted that each of the acts referred to was an act known to the law and properly described as a term of art. He submitted that 'guarantee' had a precise legal meaning, so did 'security' and so did 'indemnity'. He added that 'release' and 'waiver' are also legal terms of art. The particular term relied upon as the financial assistance given by B & C in these three transactions was 'indemnity'. The meaning of 'indemnity' is established by the decision of the Court of Appeal in *Yeoman Credit Ltd v Latter* [1961] 1 WLR 828. The leading judgment was delivered by Pearce LJ and at p. 831, line 13 he holds:

> 'An indemnity is a contract by one party to keep the other harmless against loss.'

Harman LJ at p. 836, line 10 also clearly considers that an indemnity is a particular thing known to the law and having special characteristics, although at p. 835, middle paragraph, that Lord Justice deprecated the nature of the issue. Mr Potts therefore contended that since no provision of the option agreement contained any promise to pay money so as to hold the other party 'harmless against loss' it could not be said to contain any 'indemnity' and none of the three classes of claim, the primary creditor, the further creditor and a fortiori the misrepresentation claims, could involve any breach of s. 152(1)(a)(ii).

Mr Stubbs conceded towards the end of his reply, as I understood him, that if the word 'indemnity' was a term of art so that it would bear the meaning already set out then B & C could not succeed upon this point. I am of opinion that s. 152(1)(a)(ii) is composed of terms of art and that 'indemnity' is so used. Upon that basis it is clear in my judgment that there is no indemnity connected with any of the three relevant transactions and accordingly under that definition no financial assistance was provided by B & C in connection with any of those transactions.

Finally there is raised in the special case a point which, in the light of my decision that no financial assistance as defined was given in connection with the three transactions, is, I believe, academic. By para. 48(d)(iv) of the special case there is raised the issue whether the order of 12 October 1987, to which I have already referred, can render lawful what would otherwise be unlawful. For the reasons which I gave in the interlocutory judgment which I delivered on 18 January 1994 this question should be answered in the affirmative.

I therefore conclude that I should answer the questions posed by the special case as follows: question 48(d)(i), no; question 48(d)(ii), no; question 48(d)(iii), no; question 48(d)(iv), yes; questions 49(d)(i), (ii) and (iii), no; question 50(d)(i), (ii) and (iii), no; for the reasons given above. I should not part with this case without expressing my indebtedness to counsel for their labours and assistance. I have not cited many authorities that were shown to me but the industry displayed at the Bar was indomitable. The decisions have been far from easy but my task has been greatly assisted by the arguments presented.

FURTHER JUDGMENT
(Delivered 16 November 1994)

Harman J: This is a further hearing of the special case directed by an order of Deputy Master Bragge. The matter was argued on 10 or 15 (it does not matter precisely how many) days before me last spring, and I handed down a too lengthy judgment in July 1994.

The order has not yet been perfected and so the order is open for reconsideration before its perfection either by the court of its own motion or by the court on the representations of either side.

The representations made to me today by counsel for the defendant to the action are that the judgment as handed down, at p. 38E above where specific answers are given to the questions posed by the special case, is inapt in its substance because the answers given do not logically flow from the reasoning set out earlier. Further it is submitted that the argument before me, in particular submissions by Mr Potts for the plaintiffs in the action, the respondents on the special case, on days 7, 8 and 9 at various places in the transcript, showed that the whole matter was conducted on the footing that the various classes of claims might fall into different categories, whereas I have dealt with them in the judgment on the one footing.

A   The claims run in three ways: there are what are called, and are defined in the special case as, the primary creditor claims, the further creditor claims and the misrepresentation claims. The decision I reached was that in essence the primary creditor claims based on an option agreement would have been objectionable under the rule of company law, commonly called the rule in *Trevor v Whitworth* (1887) 12 App Cas 409, but were saved and made effective and binding by virtue of the statute and the decision of the Court of Appeal in *Nicholl v Eberhardt* (1889) 1 Meg 402 which I cite in the judgment.

B   The essence of the point put to me is that the reasoning in *Nicholl v Eberhardt* which I, of course, accepted and adopted is that any agreement sanctioned by the court on a scheme or other order becomes binding whether or not without such a sanction it would be binding. That therefore, as it was put, validates, or white-washes, the option agreement and, as Mr Potts expressed it, must mean that all the terms of the option agreement are thereby made effective and remedies for them must be available in the ordinary way.

C   Mr Stubbs has urged me that the claims defined as the 'further creditor claims' are based upon a different and antecedent agreement to the option agreement, an agreement referred to as 'the standby agreement', made on 8 October 1987, and not specifically mentioned or referred to in any precise way at all in the order made four days later on 12 October 1987.

     There is a reference to the purpose of the standby agreement in the scheme document put before the court leading to the making of the order sanctioning the scheme. At page
D   15 of the scheme document there is a reference to the standby facility, but no specific reference to the standby agreement itself. Therefore, says Mr Stubbs, the standby agreement is not validated by the order on the principle in *Nicholl v Eberhardt*. Further, the claims under the Misrepresentation Act, which are in respect of representations said to have been made in, I think, July or August 1989 cannot conceivably have had anything to do with the order of the court made on 12 October 1987. The mere stating of the dates shows that the one has no reference to the other. Therefore, says Mr Stubbs, it follows
E   that the *Nicholl v Eberhardt* decision, and the line of authority which it provides, have nothing to do with the misrepresentation claims or the further creditor claims.

     The answer by Mr Potts is that that is not an adequate way of approaching it. The essence of the attack upon the standby agreement and upon the misrepresentation claims is that they are affected by the decision in *Trevor v Whitworth*. That point I held was good of itself but rendered ineffective by reason of the validation of the scheme by the order. It follows that since the original attack is made ineffective the attack on the standby
F   agreement and the alleged misrepresentation cannot themselves be invalidated, although not mentioned in the order of the court and not therefore directly within the *Nicholl v Eberhardt* principle.

     As it seems to me the whole essence of the standby agreement depends upon the validity of the option agreement. If that is valid the terms of the standby agreement do not, in my own view, require further validation by any express reference.

G   The misrepresentation claims are misrepresentation about the status of the option agreement. If the option agreement is of itself validated and enforceable by reason of *Nicholl v Eberhardt* then the misrepresentation claims will be equally capable of pursuit.

     Mr Potts' submission is that the decision I set out on pp. 34–35 logically follows from the argument which I had endeavoured to set out in the reasoning in the judgment and that there should be no alteration to it.

H   I am persuaded by Mr Potts that that is correct, and I should refuse to alter the terms of the judgment at p. 38E, although I am at this point, in my judgment, entirely free to do so . . . I have also directed some alterations to the terms of the judgment which are agreed by both sides to correct an oversight.

     I conclude in substance that I should leave the judgment unaltered in that respect.

(Order accordingly)

Re Sherborne Associates Ltd.

Bristol District Registry (Mercantile List).
His Honour Judge Jack QC (sitting as a High Court judge).
Judgment delivered 5 May 1994.

> *Wrongful trading – Company went into insolvent liquidation – Whether directors should have realised company was insolvent and could not properly continue trading – Whether directors should be ordered to contribute to company's assets – Whether liquidator could continue action against director after death – Insolvency Act 1986, s. 214.*

This was an application by the liquidator of an insolvent company for a declaration under s. 214 of the Insolvency Act 1986 that three of its non-executive directors should contribute to the company's assets.

The company was incorporated in January 1987 and commenced trading as an advertising agency. Its paid-up share capital was then £36,000. Its accounts to 31 December 1986 showed a trading loss of £78,904 and there was a deficit of assets over liabilities amounting to £42,901. In 1988 further shares were issued increasing the paid-up share capital by £32,000 to £68,000. In December 1988 the three respondent directors resigned. The company was put into liquidation by its remaining directors in February 1989 with debts amounting to £178,788 and there was a deficiency of assets over liabilities of £109,237.

The liquidator alleged that by specified dates in January 1988 the three directors ought to have concluded that there was no reasonable prospect that the company would avoid going into insolvent liquidation under s. 214. One of the directors died before the application was heard and his personal representatives were respondents to the action. They argued that when the director died the liquidator lost any right to seek relief against him under s. 214.

Held, dismissing the application:

1. The liquidator was not entitled, if his case was not made out as to the dates pleaded, to argue subsequently that the directors should have concluded on subsequent dates that there was no reasonable prospect of the company avoiding liquidation. It would not be fair to the respondents to permit the liquidator to raise such a case which would have required the examination of each date for that purpose.

2. The general intention of s. 214 was to provide that a director should re-establish a company's assets where he had permitted it to trade on when insolvent liquidation was the only reasonable prospect. That was a commercial purpose and there was no reason to suppose that Parliament intended that it should be defeated by the death of a director where his estate remained sufficient to effect the purpose.

3. It was only in situations arising from the breakdown of marriage where one spouse died that it had been held that rights were lost on death. A claim under s. 214 was quite different and in other situations which had been before the courts it had been held that the statutory right or obligation survived. Therefore whether or not a liquidator's rights under s. 214 amounted to a cause of action within s. 1(1) of the Law Reform (Miscellaneous Provisions) Act 1934, they were not to be treated as ceasing upon the death of the director in question.

4. Furthermore a liquidator might have a cause of action under s. 214 within the meaning of s. 1(1) of the 1934 Act. Section 214 provided in effect that if a liquidator could establish a factual situation he might request the court to declare that the director should make a contribution to the company's assets, the amount of which was in the court's discretion: that plainly amounted to a cause of action.

5. The onus was on the liquidator to persuade the court to conclude that his case was made out by inviting the court to look at the history of the company as recorded in the

A   financial documents and in its detailed board minutes. The court must always have in mind the possibility of explanations for what had occurred from a deceased director had he lived which would rebut or tend to rebut the liquidator's case. The court should not reject that possibility unless it was fully satisfied, after rigorous examination, that it was right to do so.

     6. The court had to keep in mind: (a) that there was always a danger with hindsight of assuming that what in fact happened was always bound to happen and was apparent; B   (b) that the three non-executive directors were responsible men with considerable achievements who were applying themselves to the company's problems; and (c) the evidence heard and not heard. On the facts of the present case, it was not satisfied that any of the directors ought to have concluded that there was no reasonable prospect that the company would avoid insolvent liquidation. (Re Produce Marketing Consortium Ltd (1989) 5 BCC 520; Re Purpoint Ltd [1991] BCC 121; and Re DKG Contractors Ltd [1990] BCC 903 distinguished.)

C

     The following cases were referred to in the judgment:

Attorney-General v Canter [1939] 1 KB 318.
Barder v Caluori [1988] AC 20.
D'Este v D'Este [1973] Fam 55.
Dipple v Dipple [1942] P 65.
DKG Contractors Ltd, Re [1990] BCC 903.
D   *Garnett, Re* (1886) 31 ChD 1.
Produce Marketing Consortium Ltd, Re (1989) 5 BCC 569.
Purpoint Ltd, Re [1991] BCC 121.
Read v Brown (1888) 22 QBD 128.
Ronex Properties Ltd v John Laing Construction Ltd & Ors [1983] QB 398.
Sugden v Sugden [1957] P 120.
E   *Thomas v Times Book Co Ltd* [1966] 1 WLR 911.
United Collieries Ltd v Simpson [1909] AC 383.
Whytte v Ticehurst [1986] Fam 64.

John Briggs (instructed by Harrison Clark, Worcester) for the liquidator.

Declan O'Mahony (instructed by Richard Welsh & Co) for the first respondent.

F   David Mason, solicitor (instructed by Christopher Davidson & Co, Cheltenham) for the second respondent.

Michael Gadd (instructed by Townsends, Swindon) for the third, fourth and fifth respondents.

JUDGMENT

G   **His Honour Judge Jack QC:** This is an application made by Mr Nigel Halls as the liquidator of Sherborne Associates Ltd for a declaration under s. 214 of the *Insolvency Act* 1986 that three of Sherborne's directors should contribute to the company's assets. The action was commenced in the Bristol Chancery list and was transferred with the consent of the parties to the new Mercantile list in order to obtain an early hearing date for an action where the events are now some six or seven years distant.

H   Sherborne was incorporated on 16 January 1987 and commenced trading in the following month as an advertising agency. Its paid-up share capital was then £36,000. Its accounts to 31 December 1986 showed a trading loss of £78,904, and there was a deficit of assets over liabilities amounting to £42,901. In April and September 1988 further shares were issued, increasing the paid-up share capital by £32,000 to £68,000. In early December 1988 the three directors who are respondents to this application resigned. The company was put into liquidation by its remaining directors on 10 February 1989. As is

shown by the statement of affairs its debts amounted to £178,788 and there was a   A
deficiency of assets over liabilities of £109,237.

The discretionary jurisdiction under s. 214 comes into effect in respect of a director
where, as provided by s. 214(2)(b):

> 'At some time before the commencement of the winding up of the company, that
> person knew or ought to have concluded that there was no reasonable prospect
> that the company would avoid going into insolvent liquidation . . .'   B

The liquidator alleges that this was the case in respect of each relevant director at the
latest on 22 or 30 January 1988 when board meetings were held. The liquidator does not
allege that the directors had actually concluded as the subsection sets out, but that they
ought to have so concluded.

Figures have been agreed which show that the overall worsening in the position of the
creditors between 31 December 1987 (the nearest date to 22 or 30 January 1988 for which   C
figures were available) and 9 December 1988 was £19,615 and to 10 February 1989 was
£27,799. These figures take the benefit of the share capital put in during 1988 (£32,000),
which it was argued for the liquidator should not be done for the purpose of assessing
liability under s. 214. The hearing lasted 12 days despite the considerable use of written
submissions.

The liquidator also sought to argue that, if his case was not made out as to the dates   D
in January 1988, the directors should have concluded on subsequent dates that there was
no reasonable prospect of Sherborne avoiding going into liquidation. This alternative
case was not pleaded. It was only made clear that the liquidator was seeking to advance
such a case after the evidence had been heard. It would not be fair to the respondents to
permit the liquidator to pick a series of subsequent dates, or to invite the court to pick a
subsequent date, saying in respect of such a date or dates that at least then the conclusion
that there was no reasonable prospect that Sherborne would avoid insolvent liquidation   E
should have been reached. Such a case would have required the examination of each date
for this purpose.

The three directors in question are Mr Warwick Squire, Sir Charles Irving and Mr
David Ellwood. Mr Squire died on 5 February 1992 and his personal representatives are
respondents to the application.

In closing submissions on behalf of Mr Squire's personal representatives the point was   F
taken that when Mr Squire died the liquidator lost any right to seek relief against him
under s. 214. The decision on this point involves the consideration of a number of
authorities which, while in my view they may all point in the same direction, some at
least take different routes.

It was submitted for the liquidator that the liquidator's rights under s. 214 amounted
to a cause of action and so survived Mr Squire's death by reason of s. 1(1) of the *Law*   G
Reform (Miscellaneous Provisions) Act 1934. That section provides:

> '. . . on the death of any person after the commencement of this Act all causes of
> action subsisting against or vested in him shall survive against, or, as the case may
> be, for the benefit of his estate.'

This section was passed to reverse with specific exceptions the common law rule that
causes of action in tort abated on the death of either the person injured or the wrongdoer: H
actio personalis moritur cum persona. The general rule prior to the Act was that an action
in tort had to be begun in the joint lifetimes of the person injured and the wrongdoer.

Where a statute creates a cause of action within the meaning of s. 1(1) of the 1934 Act,
the effect of the section is that the cause of action survives the death of the person injured
or of the wrongdoer. So, in *Attorney-General v Canter* [1939] 1 KB 318 it was held by the

A
Court of Appeal that a liability to penalties under an Income Tax Act, being a cause of action, attached to a taxpayer's estate following his death. This must of course be subject to the provisions of the statute creating the cause of action: for a statute might provide that a cause of action created by it abated on death.

The *actio personalis* rule was, and so far as it may survive is, however of limited ambit. In *United Collieries Ltd v Simpson* [1909] AC 383 the House of Lords had to consider whether the right of a workman to compensation under the *Workmen's Compensation Act* 1906 passed to his widow. This was, of course, prior to the 1934 Act. Lord Macnaghten stated at p. 391:

B

C
'... I put aside the semblance of argument founded on the maxim "Actio personalis moritur cum persona." The application of that maxim is limited to actions in which remedy is sought for a tort, or for something which involves, at any rate, the notion of wrong-doing. Liability under the Workmen's Compensation Act has no connection with any wrong-doing on the part of the employer. It does not result from any neglect or any default on his part. Indeed, in the case of death, or "serious and permanent disablement," the event may be the consequence of "serious and wilful misconduct" on the part of the workman while the employer is wholly free from blame, and yet compensation may be recoverable all the same.'

D
He went on to consider the construction of the Act and concluded, as did the majority of their Lordships, that the widow could claim.

It follows that where s. 1(1) of the 1934 Act cannot be relied on because a right or obligation created by statute does not give rise to a cause of action within the meaning of the section, the *actio personalis* rule is very unlikely to be applicable. I say 'is very unlikely' rather than 'will not' because of a passage in the judgment of Donaldson LJ in *Ronex Properties Ltd v John Laing Construction Ltd & Ors* [1983] QB 398 at p. 406H as follows:

E

'The rule applied to causes of action based upon a breach of a tortious obligation owed by the plaintiff to the defendant. If in 1935 Parliament had created a new tortious obligation by statute in a form to which the Act of 1934 would not have applied, and if it had failed to make special provision for the benefit and burden of that obligation to pass to the estate of those who died before judgment, no doubt the rule would have applied.'

F
The Court of Appeal there had to consider whether a right to contribution under s. 6 of the *Law Reform (Married Women and Tortfeasors) Act* 1935 was lost on death. Donaldson LJ continued at p. 407:

'But the statutory right of contribution created by the Act of 1935 is not based upon a breach of any obligation, whether tortious or otherwise, owed to the claimant in the contribution suit by the respondent in that suit. It is based upon breaches of tortious duties owed by both parties to the contribution suit, whether jointly or severally, to a third party and, stranger to that suit, the plaintiff in the main action ... Accordingly, in my judgment, the rule has no application to Mr Stephenson's right to claim contribution under the Act of 1935 and that right has passed to his personal representatives for the benefit of his estate under the law of succession.'

G

H
Donaldson LJ there referred simply to the right passing under the law of succession. It may be that in that respect the case before him was straightforward. However, in my view, it is more correct to say that whether or not it passes is a question of construction of the Act creating the right. This was the approach of the House of Lords in the *United Collieries* case.

This brings me to a number of cases in the Family Division or its predecessor   A
concerning questions arising in a divorce or family situation and effect of the death of a
husband or wife upon them. These were strongly relied on on behalf of the personal
representatives. They have a particular background because of the effect of death on the
relationships concerned. The earlier cases were reviewed by the House of Lords in *Barder
v Caluori* [1988] AC 20. Giving the leading speech in the House of Lords, Lord Brandon
stated at p. 37D:
                                                                                  B
> 'I would state the conclusions to which I think that these authorities lead in this
> way. First, there is no general rule that, where one of the parties to a divorce suit
> has died, the suit abates, so that no further proceedings can be taken in it ...
> Secondly, it is unhelpful, in cases of the kind under discussion, to refer to
> abatement at all. The real question in such cases is whether, where one of the
> parties to a divorce who has died, further proceedings in the suit can or cannot be
> taken. Thirdly, the answer to that question, when it arises, depends in all cases on   C
> two matters and in some cases also on a third. The first matter is the nature of the
> further proceedings sought to be taken. The second matter is the true construction
> of the relevant statutory provision or provisions, or of a particular order made
> under them, or both. The third matter is the applicability of s. 1(1) of the Act of
> 1934.'

Lord Brandon then went on to examine the question before the House, namely, whether   D
on the true construction of certain rules the jurisdiction to entertain an appeal out of
time only lasted so long as the other party to the suit was alive. His examination of the
nature of the rules led him to the conclusion that they should not be construed to
terminate the jurisdiction on the death of a party to the suit.

Three of the earlier cases in this line require mention. In *Dipple v Dipple* [1942] P 65 it
was held that the right of a wife to apply for secured maintenance was not a cause of
action within s. 1(1) of the 1934 Act and did not survive the husband's death. In *Sugden   E
v Sugden* [1957] P 120 it was held that an order for maintenance for children could not be
enforced against a husband's estate in respect of the period after his death. As Lord
Brandon stated in respect of the case in *Barder* [1988] AC 20 at p. 35F:

> '... on the true construction of s. 26(1) of the Matrimonial Causes Act 1950 ...
> and of the order of the court made under that provision, the husband's obligation
> to pay lasted only so long as he lived.'   F

The judge at first instance had accepted that there was a cause of action within s. 1(1) of
the 1934 Act. Dealing with this argument Denning LJ stated at p. 134:

> ' "Causes of action" are not, however, confined to rights enforceable *by action*,
> strictly so called – that is, by action at law or in equity. They also extend to rights
> enforceable by proceedings in the Divorce Court, provided that they really are
> rights and not mere hopes or contingencies. They include, for instance, a sum   G
> payable for costs under an order of the Divorce Court, or a right to a secured
> provision under an order already made against a man before his death. . .'

The third case, *Whytte v Ticehurst* [1986] Fam 64 was cited to the House of Lords in
Barder but is not referred to in the speeches. The issue there was whether the right of a
wife to apply to the court for provision under the *Inheritance (Provision for Family and
Dependants) Act* 1975 passed on her death to her personal representatives. Booth J cited   H
the passage from *Sugden*, which I have quoted and went on to consider the terms of the
1975 Act. She concluded at p. 69–70:

> 'The claim is, as it always has been, a claim for financial provision and the purpose
> of the reformed legislation was to extend the nature of the relief which the court
> can grant. In my judgment it follows that the principles stated by Denning LJ in

A   *Sugden v Sugden* [1957] P 120 continue to apply and that it must still be the case that no enforceable right exists until the order is actually made.

Further, in my judgment, both the Matrimonial Causes Act 1973 and the Inheritance (Provision for Family and Dependants) Act 1975 by their explicit terms and by the very purposes for which they were enacted restrict the claim for financial relief to a spouse or surviving spouse.'

B   I would not want to leave these cases without quoting a passage from the judgment of Ormrod J in *D'Este v D'Este* [1973] Fam 55 at p. 59B which to my mind provides helpful insight as to the ratio of this line of cases:

'In my judgment, the real answer to this application is this, that the whole of the matrimonial causes legislation, right back to 1857, is essentially a personal jurisdiction arising between parties to the marriage or the children of the marriage.

C   The death of one or other of the parties to the litigation has nothing whatever to do with the old common law rule which was abrogated by the Act of 1934. The fact that these applications abate by death derives, in my judgment, from the legislation which created the rights, if they are rightly called "rights", and from no other source. If that is correct, then it is not necessary to examine very closely whether or not the administratrix in this case has something which could be called, by any stretch of imagination, a cause of action.'

D   Section 1(1) of the 1934 Act was enacted so that causes of action survived, which would otherwise have been lost on death by reason of the common law rule. It should not be read as providing that other rights should be lost on death because they are not causes of action. In my judgment the passages which I have cited from *Sugden* and from *Whytte v Ticehurst* should not be taken as establishing that a statutory right which does not give rise to a 'cause of action' cannot survive the death of one of the parties. That would be to give a section intended to have a constructive effect a destructive effect which is not stated

E   in the section. It would also, for example, be contrary to the actual decision in *Barder*, namely that a right to apply for leave to appeal out of time and a substantive right of appeal was not lost by the death of the proposed respondent to the appeal. The passages which I have cited should in my view be taken, first as indicating why in the context of the particular legislation the rights in question did not survive death, and second as a possible approach to like questions in other legislation. It must however, ultimately,

F   always be a question of construing the particular legislation, whether a right given by it survives death.

In the cases which I have cited the courts examined two questions, sometimes one and sometimes the other. One is whether on the construction of the Act providing the right or obligation, the right or obligation survives the relevant death. The other is whether the Act gives rise to a cause of action within s. 1(1) of the 1934 Act, and so by operation of

G   that section the cause of action survives. As I have stated, an Act could create a cause of action within that section but nonetheless provide that it should not survive death. So, in my view the better approach is to consider the question of the construction of the Act, at least first.

I find no assistance in the actual terms of the *Insolvency Act* 1986 as to whether a liquidator's right under s. 214 survives the death of a director. It is true that s. 214 refers

H   to 'a person' who is or has been a director of the company. It does not anywhere refer to his estate or personal representatives. But this is usual. It is not usual that Acts of Parliament indicate whether a right of obligation will pass on death by reference to a person's estate or personal representatives. I am therefore thrown back on the nature of this legislation to infer the intention in this respect of s. 214. The general intention of the section is to provide that a director should re-establish a company's assets where he has permitted it to trade on when insolvent liquidation was the only reasonable prospect.

This is a commercial purpose and there is no reason to suppose that Parliament intended   A
that it should be defeated by the death of a director where his estate remains sufficient to
effect the purpose. It is a situation quite different to those arising from the breakdown of
a marriage where a husband or wife dies. I remark that it is only in the latter situations
that it has been held that rights are lost on death. In other situations which have been
before the courts it has been held that the statutory right or obligation survives. I
therefore conclude that whether or not a liquidator's rights under s. 214 amount to a
cause of action within s. 1(1) of the 1934 Act, they are not to be treated as ceasing upon   B
the death of the director in question.

The conclusion which I have just reached is sufficient to determine this question. I will
however for completeness consider whether a liquidator may have a cause of action
under s. 214 within the meaning of s. 1(1) of the 1934 Act. A cause of action is
traditionally defined as a set of facts which give rise to a right of action: thus 'every fact
that it would be necessary for the plaintiff to prove, if traversed, in order to support his   C
right to the judgment of the court' – per Lord Esher in *Read v Brown* (1888) 22 QBD 128.
This definition was provided in the course of considering where a cause of action arose.
In *Sugden v Sugden* Denning LJ distinguished rights which can be enforced and mere
hopes or contingencies. He accepted that a party may have a cause of action even though
the remedy is discretionary.

Section 214 provides in effect that if a liquidator can establish a factual situation he   D
may request the court to declare that the director should make a contribution to the
company's assets, the amount of which is in the court's discretion. Here the factual
situation which the liquidator seeks to establish in respect of each respondent director is
that he should have concluded that there was no reasonable prospect that Sherborne
would avoid going into insolvent liquidation. I accept that the line may be difficult to
define but in my view this right plainly amounts to a cause of action. The position is that
the liquidator has to establish a factual situation defined by the Act and he may then ask   E
the court to exercise its discretion in his favour. That discretion will be exercised in
accordance with the principles which are being established by the decided cases in so far
as they are peculiar to this new section. The position is not very far removed from that
where a plaintiff asked the court to grant him an equitable remedy. The family law cases
lie on the other side of the line in that there are no facts to be proved, no factual situation
to be established, defined by the law beyond the status of husband, wife or child, before   F
the applicant can ask for relief.

I therefore conclude that the liquidator is entitled to proceed under s. 214 against the
personal representatives of Mr Squire. Although Sherborne went into liquidation in
January 1989 and things initially progressed quickly with draft points of claim being
provided to the three directors in September of that year, the proceedings were not
commenced until July 1992, after the death of Mr Squire. There were various reasons for   G
different periods of delay, which taken individually may be justifiable. But where the
fates combine to provide a series of difficulties a strong hand is required to ensure that
the combination does not have unacceptable consequences. The period which I have in
particular to examine, January 1988, is now over six years ago. Memories, particularly
elderly memories, become at best uncertain at that distance and may be actually
misleading.

H

The death of Mr Squire has of course meant that I have not heard his evidence. He is
the central figure in the history of the company. I have not heard his explanations, nor
have I heard them tested in cross-examination. What I do have from him is a series of
points made in two letters to his solicitor dated 25 October 1989 and 3 November 1989
which have been adduced in evidence under the Civil Evidence Act. In *Thomas v Times
Book Co Ltd* [1966] 1 WLR 911, Plowman J had to consider a case that shortly before

A   his death Dylan Thomas had made a gift of the manuscript of *Under Milk Wood*. He cited at p. 916 the dictum of Brett MR from *Re Garnett* (1886) 31 ChD 1 at p. 9:

> 'The law is that when an attempt is made to charge a dead person in a matter, in which if he were alive he might have answered the charge, the evidence ought to be looked at with great care; the evidence ought to be thoroughly sifted, and the mind of any Judge who hears it ought to be, first of all, in a state of suspicion; but if in the end the truthfulness of the witnesses is made perfectly clear and apparent, and the tribunal which has to act on their evidence believes them, the suggested doctrine becomes absurd. And what is ridiculous and absurd never is, to my mind, to be adopted either in Law or in Equity.'

The suggested doctrine had been that corroboration was required of a witness who was giving evidence against, as it were, a person who had died. Plowman J continued:

> 'Therefore, not only in this case is the onus of proof on the defendants, but I am enjoined by authority to approach their story with suspicion having regard to the fact that the other actor's story, the late Dylan Thomas, is dead and cannot therefore give his own version of what took place.'

Here the onus is on the liquidator. It is inappropriate in the circumstances to say that I should approach the case with suspicion in the sense that the word was used by Plowman J. For it is not a question of truthfulness on the liquidator's part: he is inviting me to look at the history of this company as recorded in the financial documents and in its very detailed board minutes and to conclude that his case is made out. I direct myself here that I must always have in mind the possibility of explanations for what had occurred from Mr Squire had he lived, which would rebut or tend to rebut the liquidator's case: I should not reject that possibility unless I am fully satisfied after rigorous examination that it is right to do so.

Mr Squire was effectively the founder of the company and he invited Sir Charles Irving and Mr Ellwood to invest in it and to be non-executive directors. Mr Squire became chairman and, as I will relate, came to adopt more of an executive function than was initially intended. Sir Charles Irving and Mr Ellwood were non-executive directors and never fulfilled any executive functions. Sir Charles Irving was vice-chairman but he never exercised the position. Mr Squire and Sir Charles Irving invested £13,000 each, and Mr Ellwood £1,000 making up £27,000 of the £36,000 initial capital, the remaining £9,000 coming by way of £3,000 from each of the three executive directors who were recruited.

In order to understand the role played by each of the three non-executive directors it is necessary to say a little about each of them.

It was Mr Squire who had the idea of setting up the company to carry on business as an advertising agency in Cheltenham. Mr Squire was a cost accountant by training and spent 44 years in the Dowty Group. He became a main board director and the managing director of its aerospace and defence division, which in 1984 had a turnover of £170m. He retired from Dowty in that year due to ill health. He then looked for other involvements and invested £25,000 in Mr Ellwood's company, D Ellwood Ltd, which designed and built for exhibitions. Mr Squire became chairman and was responsible for bringing financial discipline and drive to a company which under Mr Ellwood had previously had uncertain fortunes. In 1984 it had sales of £196,000 which by 1989 had increased to £958,000. At about the same time Mr Squire invested in a small engineering company, Holdcourt Ltd, which had premises adjacent to Ellwood Ltd. The idea of Sherborne must have come to Mr Squire in 1986. Advertising agencies were then doing well and Mr Squire must have seen an opportunity in the Cheltenham advertising scene. It is apparent that he thought that Sherborne's business could be to the advantage of Ellwood Ltd and vice versa. The evidence I heard concerning Mr Squire showed him as a man of strong personality and imposing physical presence; a tough but fair

businessman. It is clear that he had considerable business experience of the working of a   A
large business and by 1987 some experience of smaller ones. He had an ability with
figures. He had at the most limited experience of advertising.

Sir Charles Irving was member of Parliament for Cheltenham from 1974 to his
retirement in 1991. He was knighted in 1989. He is now 71. He was a founder of the
National Council for Care and Resettlement of Offenders, and has been a central figure
in a number of charities directed to the socially disadvantaged. His business experience   B
began as a hotelier. In 1964, when he had been a member of the Cheltenham Borough
Council and of the Gloucester County Council for 16 years, he became Director of Public
Relations, Dowty Group Services, a post which he held until 1986 when he became a
consultant. As Director of Public Relations he was involved in overseeing on a part time
basis the provision of public relations services to the Dowty group. Here he was dealing
with an aspect of the advertising and public relations world, but in a special capacity: he
had captive clients as it were, the companies within the group, and had no need to look   C
for business. He told me that he was not a man who enjoyed figures. He knew Mr Squire,
both within the Dowty group and as a friend and frequently visited Mr Squire and his
wife at their home. I deduce that Mr Squire invited him to invest in Sherborne and to
become a director because he had such money as was needed to invest, was a substantial
figure in Cheltenham, and because of his experience in the field.

Mr David Ellwood began his working life in 1940 as an apprentice fitter with Shorts.   D
By about 1955 he had worked his way up to becoming designer at Dowty with
responsibility for special purpose machinery. He started Ellwood Ltd in 1965 as a £100
company. The company survived but from time to time faced great difficulties and badly
needed the management and costing techniques which Mr Squire brought to it in 1984.
Mr Ellwood had a very high regard for Mr Squire whom he saw as his mentor. When he
said that he had but a small voice in the financial affairs of Sherborne he continued, 'at
the head of the table sat the maestro who had tutored me in accounting.'   E

The setting up of an advertising agency by persons who are outside the advertising
business presents certain problems. It requires in particular the recruitment of individuals
who will either bring business with them or be able to attract new business, or more likely
a combination of the two. The success of the company must depend upon the success
with which this recruitment is accomplished. Mr Squire found three men for this purpose
and they became the executive directors of Sherborne. They were Mr Doughty who   F
became managing director, Mr Eastwood and Mr Locke. Mr Eastwood and Mr Locke
brought business with them: Mr Doughty did not. They each contributed £3,000 to the
initial share capital of £36,000. Mr Eastwood was to leave effectively at the end of
January 1988 and Mr Doughty in mid-March. Mr Locke stayed to the end.

I will next relate in such detail as is necessary the history of the company from the
commencement of business until its liquidation. I will then return to examine in greater   G
detail the situation in January 1988. The history is largely to be extracted from the board
minutes which are unusually detailed and were accepted by all parties as being accurate.

The first meeting was held on 20 February 1987, and the six directors were elected. An
overdraft facility of £50,000 had been agreed with the Midland Bank. This was secured
by a guarantee from Mr Squire for £25,000, and guarantees from each of the five other
directors for £5,000 and also by a fixed charge on book debts and a floating charge. The
first review of the facility was scheduled for February 1988. Premises had been found.   H
They appear to have been reasonably substantial and impressive, and were probably
larger than the company needed in its early days. The lease was guaranteed by Mr Squire
and Mr Ellwood. A business plan was produced by Mr Doughty. A forecast of business
to the end of the year (i.e. 31 December 1987, the company's year end) provided for a
turnover of £450,000 as follows:

A

	£
Eastwood	151,000
Locke	105,650
New business	193,350
	450,000

B Projected costs amounted to £474,250, giving a projected loss of £24,000.

At the meeting a month later, 20 March 1987, Mr Squire stated that a turnover of at least £500,000 would be required to break even and he felt the agency could not expand as quickly as foreseen. He raised the question of taking on another accounts director. At the next meeting on 24 April there is the first reference to delaying payments to creditors. Mr Doughty recommended recruiting a further accounts director who would bring with him at least £200,000 of business. Thus both Mr Squire and Mr Doughty appear to have

C realised that the existing team might not be able to generate sufficient business, and also the difficulty of attracting new business. This search for a further accounts director is mentioned in the board minutes for 22 May, 31 July, 18 September and 27 November 1987.

At the meeting on 31 July 1987 the board were able to consider the figures for the first five months' trading. A loss of £27,638 had been incurred on sales of £136,152 mainly

D due to overheads exceeding the forecast. In his report commenting on the figures Mr Squire stated: 'While trading losses cannot be allowed to continue at this level I think that in the circumstances it was a creditable performance.' Mr Squire stated sales of £565,000 would be required to break even on the year. A forecast showing a loss in the year of £52,000 was rejected as unacceptable. July showed continuing losses. At the meeting on 1 September Mr Squire raised important questions as to the executive directors not working as a team and as to their discipline.

E A further meeting was held on 18 September 1987, which was one of the few Sir Charles Irving was unable to attend. The August figures showed a loss of £4,988 (July £2,593). The minutes state: 'Mr Squire advised that he had been disappointed at the results and that the company had until Christmas to put things right.' He asked for a revised forecast for the last three months of the year. Debtors were about £25,000, with creditors at £45,000. The bank overdraft was being kept down. So the company was

F drawing finance from a third source, namely its creditors, in addition to its shareholders, and the bank. It could be seen that, given the nature of the company's overheads, the only way into profit was by a substantial increase in sales. September was a bad month with a loss of £7,809 on sales of £43,028, the company's biggest monthly loss. By its end Sherborne's liabilities exceeded its assets and it was insolvent. At the board meeting on 23 October 1987 Mr Doughty recognised the company's position by suggesting that he investigate the possibility of re-financing it. At the meeting a revised forecast of sales for

G the last three months was tabled. I will set this out against the figures actually achieved.

Sales

1987	Forecast (23.10.87)	Actual	(Loss)
	£	£	£
October	28,750	36,214	(7,000)
November	41,000	33,580	(7,611)
December	53,500	22,882	(16,633)
	123,250	92,676	(31,244)

It should be recorded that at the meeting on 23 October 1987 Mr Squire had pointed out that the December forecast was 'perhaps a little optimistic'. Taken together the sales

for October and November just beat the forecast. But the performance for the quarter as   A
a whole involved the loss of a sum nearly equal to the company's paid up share capital.
It had already lost £43,028 on the period to the end of September giving on this basis the
loss to the year end of £74,272. However due to unidentified increases in the losses the
management figures for the year end gave a total loss of £89,108. The trading loss shown
by the audited accounts was reduced to £78,904. The sales for the year shown by the
management accounts were £350,373 which may be compared with the £450,000 shown
by Mr Doughty's business plan considered by the board on 20 February 1987. These   B
sales were later attributed at the board meeting on 22 January 1988 as £200,000 to Mr
Eastwood and £150,000 to Mr Locke; that is, none to Mr Doughty.

It was apparent following the year end that Sherborne could not continue for long
going the way it was, and it was clear also that a considerable increase in turnover leading
to profitability was required. The two board meetings held in January 1988 show this to
have been appreciated by the directors. The first was on 22 January. Only Sir Charles   C
Irving was absent. The first matter important to these proceedings was the grilling by Mr
Squire of each of the three executive directors as to their new business prospects for 1989.
Each gave optimistic figures for their total sales as follows:

	£
Mr Locke	530,000
Mr Eastwood	450,000
Mr Doughty	400,000
Total	1,380,000

Mr Squire then made a prepared statement. In it he proposed that the company cease
trading at the end of February. He had reached this conclusion, he said, because he was
no longer prepared to continue his guarantees because of the lack of business discipline
shown by the executive directors. I am satisfied in particular by the evidence of Mr   E
Ellwood and an earlier not dissimilar event concerning Ellwood Ltd that in making this
statement Mr Squire's intention was not necessarily that Sherborne should cease to trade
but to put the maximum pressure on the executive directors. Apart from the central
problem of insufficient sales, there were three problems in particular with the executive
directors: they were not working as a team; they were producing forecasts of future
business which were far too optimistic; and in respect of Mr Eastwood it was strongly   F
suspected by the three non-executive directors that not all his work was being properly
put through the company. The minutes show however that Mr Squire must have had at
least the possibility in mind that the company would cease to trade. It would follow that
he was to an extent awaiting events. The meeting ended with a row between Mr Eastwood
and Mr Squire and the outcome was that Mr Eastwood left Sherborne. Rather
surprisingly it appears he did not leave formally until 4 March. He did not attend the
board meeting on Saturday 30 January. Sir Charles Irving did. Mr Squire stated that the   G
reason for the meeting was to decide whether the company should continue to trade. He
stated the company's net indebtedness as having risen to £78,000 from £67,000 at the
year end. Revised sales forecasts were considered as follows:

	£
Mr Doughty	400,000
Mr Eastwood	61,000
Mr Locke	530,000
(with Mr Wells)	
A N Other	150,000
Total	1,141,000

A   This was taken as £1m and was approved by the board. The profit forecast based upon it was for a profit of £55,600. Mr Squire offered to become acting chief executive until 30 June 1988 on 13 conditions which he tabled. One was that there would be weekly management meetings. This offer was accepted and Sherborne continued to trade. The main issue concerning this decision, to which I will return, is whether the directors were justified in concluding there was a realistic prospect of sufficiently increased business in 1988. The liquidator's case is that the sales forecast was transparently unrealistic and

B   should have been rejected. Although there was no recorded discussion of the need to bring in a new account director (the 'A N Other' in the forecast), with the impending departure of Mr Eastwood it must have been clear to all involved that this was a priority.

Losses continued. On 14 March 1988 Mr Doughty wrote tendering his resignation. His letter refers to disagreement over matters of policy. It is likely that a major reason for his leaving was the difference between his forecasts of business and his actual business:

C   very little had materialised.

At the board meeting on 25 March 1988 Mr Squire proposed that Mr Agincourt become a director. Mr Agincourt was a man of several interests who was described in evidence as a flamboyant character. Sir Charles Irving told me that he took against him; but evidently he impressed Mr Squire. Mr Agincourt told the board of the substantial prospects which he had. It was at this meeting that it was agreed to employ Mr

D   McDonald. He had been recruited by Mr Agincourt from another agency. At a meeting on 31 March, Mr Agincourt was appointed managing director. At a meeting on 29 April Mr Squire stated that Mr Doughty had been paid £7,000 for loss of office and that he had bought his shares. It was then proposed to take on Mr Broomfield, who had also been recruited by Mr Agincourt. The figures for the first three months of the year were considered. They showed a loss of £24,859 against a forecast loss of £7,045. Mr Agincourt informed the board that a great step forward had been made in April and he was

E   confident for the future.

It was probably in the latter part of May 1988 Mr Squire had a heart attack. He was in hospital for a period, but was well enough to preside over the annual general meeting on 1 July, and the weekly management meetings thereafter. The next board meeting was on 22 July. Meanwhile on 16 June 1988 Mr Agincourt had written resigning as 'acting' managing director on the ground that 'his commitments [were] such that getting into the

F   office on a regular basis is simply out of the question'. He also wrote a letter dated 23 May 1988 stating that he was unable to continue working with Sherborne because an investigation of the company by his accountant had shown that the picture was far worse than he had been led to believe. It appears that Mr Agincourt subsequently left England and went to America. The two letters were found among Mr Squire's papers. They were not seen by Sir Charles Irving or Mr Ellwood. I have come to the conclusion that I should not put any reliance on the earlier of the two letters. The indications are all that

G   Mr Agincourt must have known the position of the company as shown by its management accounts and that these were sufficiently accurate. It is possible that he wrote as he did in the earlier letter to attempt to justify his dropping an important commitment which he should not have taken on.

The figures before the board on 22 July were those for the six months to the end of June. They showed:

H

	Sales	Profit (Loss)	
	Forecast : *Actual*	*Forecast* : *Actual*	A
	£ £	£ £	
April	107,000 : 35,737	12,451 : 2,123	
4 months to April	267,000 : 169,398	5,406 : (22,736)	
May	106,000 : 21,159	10,389 : (9,381)	B
June	107,000 : 35,469	10,383 : (2,736)	
6 months to June	480,000 : 226,026	26,178 : (34,853)	

In short, the downhill path continued. There was a discussion of future billings. Neither Mr Broomfield nor Mr McDonald had brought work with them to Sherborne. The next event was that the Midland Bank effectively declined to continue to support Sherborne. This was because of concern 'at the company's trading position and balance sheet': their letter of 9 August 1988. It should be recorded however that Sherborne had never exceeded the limit on its overdraft. Approaches were then made to other banks in Cheltenham, including Lloyds Bank and the National Westminster Bank. The proposition put to Lloyds by Mr Squire was that there would be a cash injection of £40,000 by way of an increased shareholding, coming from Mr Squire (£4,000), Mr Locke (£10,000), Mr McDonald and Mr Broomfield (£13,000 each). This was turned down by the bank in its letter of 22 August 1988 because of the results for 1987 and for the first six months of 1988: the bank felt that the debt burden incurred was already too great. The subsequent proposal to the National Westminster Bank for an overdraft at the increased figure of £75,000 was accepted. This proposal provided in addition for a further £13,000 from a new investor who was yet to be found. Guarantees were provided as follows: Mr Squire £25,000 – unchanged, Mr Locke £10,000 – previously £5,000, Mr McDonald, Mr Broomfield and the investor to be found, £10,000 each. Mr Squire's conduct at this time was criticised on behalf of the liquidator in relation to his procuring of the facility from the bank and his obtaining the undertakings to invest and guarantee from Mr McDonald and Mr Broomfield. They told me in evidence and I accept that they did so very much at Mr Squire's request. Mr McDonald and Mr Broomfield had no experience in the running of companies or finance. Mr McDonald had to borrow money to raise his investment. In the event Mr Broomfield declined to invest because he was going through a divorce. It was suggested on behalf of the liquidator that I should form an unfavourable view of Mr Squire's behaviour at this time, which in turn would assist me in forming an unfavourable review in respect of the previous January. I bear in mind the direction which I set out earlier in respect of the case against Mr Squire. I need only say that I do not feel that a sufficiently clear and strong case is made out, particularly as it is only its reflection on the earlier events of January which concerns me.

At the board meeting on 1 September 1988 Mr McDonald and Mr Broomfield were appointed directors. Approaches were being made to a parliamentary lobbyist who might come to Sherborne. There was discussion of the need to appoint perhaps two further account directors. Mr Locke pointed out that they were in very short supply and Mr Broomfield that no-one would want to join them with the company as it was. Sir Charles Irving stated that, if he had been in control of the company it would have been closed, and it was up to the three executive directors to turn the company round in the next few months. The results over the next four months of the year were as follows:

		Sales	[1987]	Profit (Loss)	[1987]
		£	£	£	£
1988	Sept	36,544	[33,286]	(5,101)	[(7,809)]
	Oct	23,890	[36,214]	(3,873)	[(7,000)]
	Nov	30,188	[33,580]	(1,026)	[(7,611)]
	Dec	22,614	[22,882]	(1,029)	[(16,633)]
	Total	93,236	[125,962]	(8,971)	[(39,053)]

The comparison with 1987 shows the improvement in the profitability in the company. If the December figure is correct, which the liquidator questioned, and if the burden of its debt is put on one side, it can be suggested that Sherborne was turning the corner.

The finale came at the board meeting on 2 December 1988. Sir Charles Irving had determined on his resignation prior to the meeting unless two accounts were confirmed, which they were not. He reached this conclusion because sales were still falling well short of forecasts. Mr Squire stated that, unless he was convinced that Sherborne would make a profit of £150,000 in 1989 he would resign. After prolonged discussion he determined on resignation. It must have been in his mind as a possibility or even a probability that he would resign at the meeting: but he does not appear to have gone into it with the fixed intention of doing so; he still had some hope for the company. The three executive directors were still at this point optimistic for the company's future and resisted its ceasing to trade. Mr Ellwood did not immediately conclude that the company could not continue. He resigned subsequently because, in further discussions with the executive directors, they were none of them prepared to act as managing director. Meetings with the bank followed. Sherborne was trading within its overdraft limit as it had throughout its life. The National Westminster saw no advantage in immediate liquidation. It was not until February 1989, following advice from insolvency experts, that Sherborne was put into liquidation.

Having completed the story, I return to the situation of Sherborne in January 1988. A strong case can be made that Sherborne was then in, and could be seen to be in, a situation which could only end in insolvent liquidation. The company had traded for some ten months and had losses in the region of £80,000 of which some £30,000 had occurred in the last three months. Against this its issued share capital was only £36,000. The way forward to profitability could only be through a substantial increase of business. How could this be achieved? The executive directors said that they could do it. Yet by the end of January it was known that Mr Eastwood, the largest producer of business, was leaving and would take his clientele with him. In addition there were doubts, perhaps grave doubts, about the ability of Mr Doughty to produce new business on the scale promised by his forecast, or anything like it. The company had been looking for a new accounts director for some time, but none had been found.

In considering the case against the respondents s. 214(4) of the Act must be applied. It provides:

'For the purposes of subsections (2) and (3), the facts which a director of a company ought to know or ascertain, the conclusions which he ought to reach and the steps which he ought to take are those which would be known or ascertained, or reached or taken, by a reasonably diligent person having both–

(a) the general knowledge, skill and experience that may reasonably be expected of a person carrying out the same functions as are carried out by that director in relation to the company, and

(b) the general knowledge, skill and experience that that director has.'

The first point to be disposed of is one arising on the pleadings. The points of claim do A
not positively assert that the forecast before the board on 30 January 1988 was unrealistic:
para. 27 begins 'If, which is not admitted, the sales forecast was unrealistic . . .' In closing
speeches it was submitted on behalf of Mr Squire's personal representatives that it was
not open to the liquidator to assert that it was unrealistic. The case was opened to me on
behalf of the liquidator that the forecast should not have been relied upon and cross-
examination was conducted on that basis. It was the essence of the liquidator's case as
presented before me. If this point was going to be taken, it should have been taken at the B
start and would no doubt have been met by an amendment.

I should keep in mind, as it seems to me on the facts of this case, the following. First,
there is always the danger of hindsight, the danger of assuming that what has in fact
happened was always bound to happen and was apparent. Secondly, the three non-
executive directors were responsible men, two of them at least with considerable
achievements, who were applying themselves to the problem: whatever else it did not go C
by default. Third, the evidence that I have heard, and the evidence which I have not
heard. I heard Sir Charles Irving and Mr Ellwood, and also Mr McDonald and Mr
Broomfield. I could not hear the evidence of Mr Squire and perhaps unsurprisingly I did
not hear from Mr Doughty, Mr Eastwood and Mr Locke. I have already set out the
approach which in my view it is appropriate for me to adopt to the case in respect of Mr
Squire as a result of his death. D

I will take first the case in respect of Mr Squire. It is plain from the minutes of the
meetings on 22 and 30 January 1988 that he recognised that the company was in a very
serious position: he expressly stated on 30 January that the issue was whether it should
continue to trade. He knew that the key question was whether the business of the
company could be expanded sufficiently to bring it into profit.

His answer to the body blow apparently dealt by the departure of Mr Eastwood is E
probably to be found in the minutes of the meeting on 26 February 1988 where he stated
the profitability on Mr Eastwood's work was only 15.7 per cent, about half of that
achieved by Mr Doughty and Mr Locke. In his letter of 25 October 1989 he stated that
this meant Mr Eastwood was therefore not covering his salary, car and all associated
expenses. Looking at the figures it seems to me unlikely that Mr Eastwood's departure
did not result in some drop in net income: but I accept it was much less harmful than it
at first would seem. There is also to be borne in mind that Mr Eastwood was seen as a F
divisive influence in the company and was suspected of doing work on the side.

So I come to the issue of the reality of the forecast of billings or sales considered on 30
January. In his letter of 25 October 1989 Mr Squire wrote:

> 'During the period between the board meeting on 23 January and that on 30
> January, 1988, numerous discussions were held with the executive directors who G
> were putting me under considerable pressure to allow the company to continue.
> The executive directors compiled new forecasts, of which I have a copy, which
> showed a figure of £1,141,000 and after intensive questioning they agreed that we
> should create a contingency of £141,000 by making the year's forecast the
> £1,000,000 I have already spoken of.'–

and, subsequently: H

> 'At that time with the information we gathered from the executive directors, we
> were satisfied that the company could be pulled round.'

It can be said that in a sense this takes the matter little further because it does not explain
how Mr Squire was persuaded to accept what the liquidator says was incredible. It is
clear however that Mr Squire was a hard-headed man. In the absence of contrary

A   evidence and in the light of the direction I have set out concerning the case against him, I should be slow to reject what he has stated.

I should also refer here to the evidence of Sir Charles Irving and Mr Ellwood concerning the forecasts. For it can be said that what was apparent to them should also have been apparent to Mr Squire. Sir Charles Irving's evidence was to the effect that by January 1988 he had no confidence in the executive directors' forecasting ability. There were some passages in the evidence of Mr Ellwood to the same effect. The evidence of Sir

B   Charles on this crucial issue appears to place great difficulty in the way of the respondents. But listening to his evidence I formed the view that time had not treated his memory kindly. There were three aspects to this. First, he now saw everything very much in black and white, Mr Doughty and Mr Eastwood being black throughout. Secondly, he had difficulty, perhaps greater than to be expected, in distinguishing in his mind the different stages of the company's progress. Third, there were also instances where Mr

C   Ellwood remembered matters concerning Sir Charles' involvement, which Sir Charles had forgotten. Through February and March 1988 it became plain beyond doubt that Mr Doughty's forecasts were of the 'jam tomorrow' variety and that he was unlikely ever to bring in substantial business. I do not consider that the position can have been so plain to Sir Charles Irving in January. He would otherwise have acted differently. I think that Mr Ellwood also had difficulty in distinguishing between what had become plain beyond doubt in mid-March and the situation in January overall. Mr Ellwood's evidence came

D   to this, that Mr Doughty was a persuasive and convincing man and that in January 1988 he had his doubts about him but still found him plausible. I accept that. Mr Doughty had emigrated from South Africa and had not found establishing himself in England easy: he was fighting for his job.

It is easy to say now that the chances of finding a replacement for Mr Eastwood who would bring substantial work with him were slight. But I do not think that the possibility

E   should be dismissed. Mr Agincourt was found and made an investment, even though he did not stay. Mr McDonald and Mr Broomfield were found. Had they been found earlier, had there not been the unforeseen setback to the company of Mr Squire's heart attack, the company would have been in a stronger position.

The outcome is that I am not satisfied that in January 1988 Mr Squire ought to have concluded that there was no reasonable prospect that Sherborne would avoid going into insolvent liquidation. I am not satisfied that he was not entitled to conclude that there

F   was a prospect for the company achieving the turnaround into profit, which was a reasonable rather than a fanciful prospect. It did not need to make the forecast profit of £55,600 to survive, something better than even would probably have done.

The liquidator's case against Sir Charles Irving and Mr Ellwood must also fail. They were in no better position than Mr Squire to conclude whether the company had reasonable prospects of success and indeed were in a rather worse position. The case

G   having failed against him, the central figure, it must fail also against them. Had I concluded that the case against Mr Squire succeeded, I would have had to consider the difficult question of the extent to which, in such circumstances, they were entitled to say that they looked to and relied on Mr Squire. I do accept that these two non-executive directors were entitled to place reliance on the highly experienced chairman who had far the greater involvement with the company and the figures. In particular it was he who

H   had the discussions with the executive directors between the two January board meetings. In my view, where in circumstances such as here, one director seeks to rely on another, the other director's view or conclusion is a matter to be taken into account with the other matters which the director should be taking into account as required by s. 214(4). I would here have had to conduct a balancing exercise between the facts which I am presuming for this purpose pointed one way and the conclusion by Mr Squire of the opposite. This is an exercise which can only be done on the basis of actual findings.

A

I was referred to three decisions on s. 214 which I have not so far mentioned. They are: *Re Produce Marketing Consortium Ltd* (1989) 5 BCC 569, *Re Purpoint Ltd* [1991] BCC 121 and *Re DKG Contractors Ltd* [1990] BCC 903. In each the liquidator was successful. I will not prolong this judgment by summarising the facts in those cases. It is enough to say that there were in each features which made the conduct of the directors plainly irresponsible as well as other matters which can be used to distinguish them from the present case.

B

(Order accordingly)

C

D

E

F

G

H

A
Sharp & Anor v (Joint receivers of Albyn Construction Ltd) v Thomson & Ors.

Court of Session (Outer House).
Lord Penrose.
Judgment delivered 11 May 1994.

B
Receivership – Crystallisation of floating charge – Property of company – Company had executed and delivered disposition of property – Disposition had not been registered – Whether property remained property of company to which floating charge attached – Companies Act 1985, s. 463.

The receivers of Albyn Construction Ltd sought declarator that a property which the company had agreed to sell to the first defenders remained the property of the company at
C
the date of the receivers' appointment and was caught by the floating charge under which they were appointed. The receivers were appointed on 10 August 1990. The company agreed to sell the property in 1989, and a disposition was delivered to the defenders on 9 August 1990 and registered on 21 August 1990.

The issue between the parties, briefly stated, was as to the effect of the crystallisation of the charge in circumstances in which Albyn had executed and delivered the disposition of the subjects to the first defenders but in which the disposition had not been recorded at the
D
date of crystallisation in the general register of sasines. For the defenders it was contended that delivery of the disposition was effective to remove the subjects from the property of Albyn and from the scope of the floating charge accordingly. Alternatively, it was argued that if ownership was not transferred by delivery of the disposition, there was to be implied a constructive trust of the subjects for the disponees.

Held, giving judgment for the receivers:
E
1. In a question with third parties the grantor of an unrecorded disposition remained fully vested with feudal right and title notwithstanding delivery of the deed, until it was recorded in the register of sasines.

2. The contractual rights of a purchaser under missives were 'property' whether or not he had received delivery of a disposition of the subjects. The incorporeal moveable jus crediti had that character. Similarly, the debtor on concluding missives subjected himself to
F
obligations one of which was to deliver a disposition conferring in the ordinary case a marketable title on the disponee. On delivery of a disposition in terms of the contract, that obligation of the seller was satisfied. The question was whether by that act the disponer transferred in whole or in part his property rights in the subjects.

3. Until recording a disposition was not effective to divest the grantor and the subjects remained comprised in his property. Thus the subjects remained in substance the property
G
of Albyn until registration by which time they were subject to the security in favour of the floating charge holder. (Young v Leith (1847) 9 D 932 applied.)

4. The argument that on delivery of the disposition there arose a constructive trust in favour of the disponee pending registration, appeared to contradict the well-settled principle that a contractual obligation with regard to property, which had not effectually and actually brought about either a security upon it or a conveyance of it, was not per se the foundation
H
of a trust or a declarator of trust. (Bank of Scotland v Liquidators of Hutchison Main & Co Ltd 1914 SC 1 applied.)

The following cases were referred to in the opinion:

Bank of Scotland v Liquidators of Hutchison Main & Co 1914 SC (HL) 1.
Bowman v Wright (1877) 4 R 322.
Caledonian Fish Selling Marine Stores Ltd v Allard Hewson & Co Ltd 1970 SLT 195.

Cameron's Trustees v Cameron 1907 SC 407.　　　　　　　　　　　　　　A
Carse v Coppen 1951 SC 233.
Clark Taylor & Co Ltd v Quality Site Development (Edinburgh) Ltd 1981 SC 111.
Cormack v Anderson (1829) 7 S 868.
Dempsey v Celtic Football & Athletic Co Ltd 1993 SLT 382; [1993] BCC 514.
Edmond v Gordon (1858) 3 McQ 116.
Embassy Picture House (Troon) Ltd v Cammo Developments Ltd 1971 SC 25.
Forth & Clyde Construction Co Ltd v Trinity Timber & Plywood Co Ltd 1984 SC 1.　　B
Fraser v Fraser & Hibbert (1870) 8 M 400.
Gibson v Hunter Home Designs Ltd 1976 SC 23.
Grant (James) & Co Ltd v Moran 1948 SLT (Sh Ct) 8.
Hawking v Hafton House Ltd 1990 SLT 496.
Heritable Reversionary Co Ltd v Millar (1892) 19 R (HL) 43.
Inland Revenue v Clark's Trustees 1939 SC 11.　　　　　　　　　　　C
Kerr's Trustees v Lord Advocate 1974 SC 115.
Life Association of Scotland Ltd v Black's Leisure Group plc 1988 SCLR 172;
1989 SLT 674.
Lombardi's Trustee v Lombardi 1982 SLT 81.
Lyle & Scott Ltd v Scott's Trustees 1959 SC (HL) 64.
Margrie Holdings Ltd v C & E Commrs 1991 SLT 38.
Melville (Viscount) v Paterson (1842) 4 D 1311.　　　　　　　　　D
Mitchell v Ferguson (1781) Mor 10296.
Musselwhite & Anor v C H Musselwhite & Son Ltd & Ors [1962] Ch 964.
Pettigrew v Harton 1956 SLT 25.
Piccadilly Radio plc, Re (1989) 5 BCC 683.
Rodger (Builders) Ltd v Fawdry 1950 SC 483.
Stevenson v Wilson 1907 SC 445.　　　　　　　　　　　　　E
Thomas v Lord Advocate 1953 SC 151.
Young v Leith (1847) 9 D 932.

P S Hodge (instructed by Paull & Williamsons) for the pursuers.

N F Davidson QC (instructed by Drummond Miller, WS) for the first defenders.

C M Campbell QC and J N Young (instructed by Dundas & Wilson, CS) for the
second defenders.　　　　　　　　　　　　　　　　　　　F

OPINION

Lord Penrose: The pursuers are joint receivers of Albyn Construction Ltd ('Albyn').
They were appointed on 10 August 1990 by instrument of appointment executed by the
Bank of Scotland as holders of a floating charge granted by Albyn, dated 2 July and
registered 16 July 1984. The floating charge was created by Albyn,　　　G

> 'over the whole of the property (including uncalled capital) which is or may be
> from time to time, while this instrument is in force, comprised in our property and
> undertaking . . .'

Albyn carried on a construction business. By missives dated 14, 21 and 29 March and
23 May 1989, they agreed to sell to the first defenders, Mr and Mrs Thomson, a basement
flat at 10 Whinhill Road, Aberdeen for a price of £40,000. The date of entry agreed in the　H
missives was 14 April 1989. On 9 August 1990 Albyn executed and the company's
solicitor delivered to Mr and Mrs Thomson's solicitor a feu disposition of the subjects of
sale. The disposition was recorded in the register of sasines for the county of Aberdeen
on 21 August 1990. The date of entry in the disposition was 14 April 1989. Mr and Mrs
Thomson granted a standard security in favour of Woolwich Building Society on 31 July
1990 and that deed was also recorded on 21 August 1990.

A   The pursuers contend that in the circumstances the subjects remained the property of Albyn at 10 August 1990 and were attached by the floating charge which crystallised on that date. The pursuers seek declarator in the first place that the floating charge did so attach. Secondly, declarator is sought that the floating charge has operated since 10 August 1990 and continues to operate as if it were a fixed security with priority over the standard security in favour of Woolwich. Thirdly, declarator is sought that the pursuers are entitled to exercise the powers conferred on them by the charge and by Sch. 2 to the

B *Insolvency Act* 1986 and in particular that they are entitled to take possession of the subjects and sell or otherwise dispose of them.

     The case was debated on procedure roll on the pleas of all three parties. Thereafter the case was put out by order and there was further discussion of additional authorities on 29 April 1994. For the pursuers counsel sought decree *de plano* on the basis that the whole averments of the defenders were irrelevant. For each of the first defenders and

C second defenders counsel sought dismissal. The issue between the parties, briefly stated, was as to the effect of the crystallisation of the charge in circumstances in which Albyn had executed and delivered the feu disposition of the subjects to the first defenders but in which the disposition had not been recorded at the date of crystallisation in the general register of sasines.

     For the second defenders it was contended that delivery of the disposition was effective

D to remove the subjects from the property of Albyn and from the scope of the floating charge accordingly. It was said that on delivery Mr and Mrs Thomson acquired the property, as a matter of general law and in the sense of the statute. The nature of the property was variously described, by junior counsel as a personal right of ownership of the subjects and by senior counsel as a *jus ad rem* or personal right in the subjects which they were entitled to vindicate. It was accepted that the right was capable of being

E defeated by a competing prior recorded disposition or security writ or completed diligence. The right acquired by Mr and Mrs Thomson was not a real right. That however was not essential. The critical question to determine was what was 'the property' of the company that was attached by the floating charge. Reference was made to observations in *Heritable Reversionary Co Ltd v Millar* (1892) 19 R (HL) 43 by Lord Watson at p. 49 and by Lord Macnaghten at p. 53. counsel submitted that the equiparation of 'property'

F and 'belonging to' and the explanation that these were not technical words in the law of Scotland but fell to be understood in their ordinary significance were observations which were equally applicable in the present context. The word 'property' was not a term of art. Infeftment was not essential to a beneficial interest in heritable subjects. An illustration of this approach was found in *Hawking v Hafton House Ltd* 1990 SLT 496. Property was, essentially, a right in an asset. Title did not characterise that right. One required a right of beneficial enjoyment. In support of this general proposition counsel referred to the observations of Lord Patrick in *Thomas v Lord Advocate* 1953 SC 151 at p. 161 and of

G Lord Justice-Clerk Thomson at p. 158. Further reference was made to *Embassy Picture House (Troon) Ltd v Cammo Developments Ltd* 1971 SC 25 and in particular to the dicta of Lord Justice-Clerk Grant at p. 28; *Gibson v Hunter Home Designs* 1976 SC 23 and the opinion of the Lord President at p. 26 and of Lord Cameron at p. 30–31; *Margrie Holdings Ltd v C & E Commrs* 1991 SLT 38 in the opinion of Lord President Hope at p. 42; *Lombardi's Trustee v Lombardi* 1982 SLT 81; *James Grant & Co Ltd v Moran* 1948

H SLT (Sh Ct) 8; and *Life Association of Scotland v Black's Leisure Group plc* 1988 SCLR 172; 1989 SLT 674. From these authorities counsel submitted that a number of propositions followed. Once a disposition had been delivered the disponee obtained property in the subjects. He could then:

(1)   grant a disposition of the subjects;

(2)   serve notices on tenants;

(3)   be subjected to the jurisdiction of the local or national courts of the country where   A
        the property was situated; and

(4)   he then had in effect the full rights and obligations associated with ownership such
        as obligations for payment of rates and rights to enjoy rents, the fruits of the
        property and generally the rights of beneficial ownership.

Once the disposition had been delivered, no other party had a right to enjoy or use the
property. On the facts of the particular case on 9 August 1990 the disposition was   B
delivered. Immediately before the appointment of the receivers the first defenders
therefore had a personal right, equivalent to a full right of ownership, albeit that their
right might be defeated in certain circumstances. The company was infeft but it had no
rights of ownership. It had effectively divested itself of those. It could not assert any of
the normal rights associated with ownership against the first defender. Although
remaining infeft, there was nothing which the company could lawfully do in respect of
the property. There was no right in the company in virtue of its infeftment to grant a   C
disposition in favour of a third party. No competing party had any right to the property.
A company which had no vestige of residual beneficial interest in an asset could not be
said to have that asset comprised in its property. The situation fell to be distinguished
from the 'race to the register' cases. Those cases depended upon the requirement, as a
matter of public policy, to make the register effective as a measurement of parties' rights.
The *Real Rights Act* 1693 provided that, assuming good faith, whoever first recorded title   D
fell to be recognised as the proprietor of the property. However, that was not the issue in
this case. If, on a sound view of the situation, the subjects remained comprised in the
property of the company then it was accepted by the second defenders that the floating
charge attached to it. If it were not comprised in the property of the company there was
no race because the receivers had no rights over the subjects in such circumstances. The
1693 Act did not create any right of property. In summary, junior counsel submitted that
there was a personal right of ownership on delivery; that the transfer exhausted the whole   E
beneficial rights of Albyn in the subjects; that following delivery the company was
divested of property, notwithstanding that it remained infeft, in respect that it could do
nothing with the subjects; and finally, that the seller required to do no more and could
do no more effectively to transfer the asset to the purchaser. In these circumstances the
heritage was no longer the property of the company on 10 August 1990 and the floating
charge did not attach.   F

Senior counsel for the second defenders adopted junior counsel's submissions but
approached the issue differently. As an overview he focussed the only question which
arose in the case as being whether or not the subjects fell within s. 462(1) of the *Companies
Act* 1985 and s. 53(7) of the *Insolvency Act* 1986. That is, the question was whether as at
the date of crystallisation the subjects formed part of the 'property' of the company and
were at that date subject to the charge. It was necessary in these circumstances to form a
clear view as to what constituted property in the law of Scotland. He adopted Erskine's   G
definition of property for this purpose, namely that it was a right recognised by law to
use and dispose of a thing as one's own. There were at least two important aspects of
this. First, property related to rights in things as opposed to rights arising as a matter of
obligation and the nature of the right was the right to use the thing as one's own. This
had an echo in the observations of Lord Macnaghten in the *Heritable Reversionary Co*
case where he spoke of ownership as relating to what 'belonged' to a person. Counsel   H
was critical of the pursuers' position which, he submitted, fell into the error of equating
property with a completed or perfected feudal title in heritable subjects. The two were
not synonymous. His submission was that in the context of general Scots law property
was not properly so defined. Alternatively he submitted that on a sound construction of
the statutory provisions in question in this case the equiparation was not sound. The
expression 'real right' had been relied on heavily and was commonly taken to be a

A   synonym for a completed feudal right or title. A more accurate usage however would be to treat a completed or perfected real right as being the equivalent of a recorded title. Reference was made to the observations of Lord Fullerton in *Young v Leith* (1847) 9 D 932. The fact that a perfected or completed feudal title or real right had to await the act of registration did not lead naturally to the view that no property right was transferred by the delivery of a conveyance prior to that event. *Young v Leith* was typical of cases involving questions of title. But that was or could be a very different question from the

B   question of property. What was in issue in *Young* was whether there had been a completed feudalised title immune from challenge. Reference was made to pp. 937–939 in this context. In the circumstances of that case the court did not require to contemplate any intermediate position. It was accepted that recording was necessary to render the disponee's right wholly immune from future successful challenge. It was however an error to assume that it followed that in the absence of a perfected or feudalised real right no

C   right of property was transferred. It was accepted that adjudication by a third party creditor was possible. However, on delivery the disponee was vested with ownership of or property in the subjects which would persist unless and until that right was defeated by a preferable title. The position of the floating charge holder fell to be distinguished from that of the holder of a decree of adjudication. The decree was the equivalent of a conveyance granted by an infeft debtor. Reference was made to Lord Cameron's observations in *Gibson v Hunter Home Designs* and Graham Stewart on *Diligence* at

D   p. 618. In applying the principle to the present case a decree of adjudication as at 10 August would have operated as if Albyn had fraudulently granted a disposition to a third party. If one had been in that position the delivery to the third party, assumed to be acting in good faith, and for value, operated as the starting gun in the race to the register. But in the situation in the present case there had been no such initiation of the race. The pursuers' rights were wholly dependent on the short question of the definition of the property rights of Albyn who had already granted a disposition. The floating charge

E   attached. Its attachment created no new or separate rights. It was not the equivalent of a fresh grant. The question here, as in *Heritable Reversionary Co*, was not as to the effect of vesting or transfer, but as to what was in the property of the company. There was no 'race to register'. There was no competition between two persons deriving separate grants from a common author. The floating charge holder did not have the benefit of a separate grant of the particular subjects. The proper focus was not on what was granted to the

F   first defenders in this case. It was on what was left with Albyn. Applying Erskine's definition of property all that could be so described was exhausted by delivery of the disposition. It followed that the floating charge did not attach to the subjects notwithstanding that the company remained feudally infeft. After delivery there was no right to use the land, no right to make grants of or connected with the land, and no right in law to do anything in relation to the subjects. Nor could any such rights ever be

G   resumed by Albyn without the consent of the purchaser. The purchaser could interdict any other disposition or deed on the basis that it would be in derogation of the grant originally made to him. On granting a disposition including absolute warrandice there was nothing left with the disponer. It was erroneous to rely upon the possibility of a valid and effective competing disposition or grant in favour of a third party for value in good faith. The pursuers' contention that '*nemo dat quod non habet*' meant that there could have been no effective divestiture of the disponer was erroneous. The source of the

H   effective disposition's validity in such circumstances was statute and not any assumed property right in the disponer. That was the policy of the 1693 Act. There was of necessity an innocent party injured in the circumstances covered by the Act. Its purpose was to prefer the party first on the register. Reference was made to the *Heritable Reversionary Co* (1892) 19 R 43 and to the observations of Lord Watson at pp. 49–50 and of Lord Herschell at p. 44. A person who held an unrecorded disposition had title to vindicate his

property rights against any third party who did not have a competing title. That was   **A**
demonstration also of ownership. The only effect of registration was to prevent the
vulnerability of the disponee's rights to defeat at the hands of third parties with
competing property rights. The policy behind the vulnerability was that in the absence of
registration creditors and purchasers could not rely upon or have the benefit intended to
be derived from the record. Reference was made to *Erskine*, vol. 1, III, ii, para. 48. In the
present case nothing had happened which defeated the rights of the defenders. There had
been no subsequent grant, express or equivalent, by the disponer the recording of which   **B**
could attract the benefit of the statute. Had it been that the disponee's right had been
defeated by a subsequent deed recorded in priority, the result would have been that
property would have passed from the disponee to the winner of the race. The property
could never return to the seller. What could have happened was that it might pass from
the disponee to the floating charge holder in certain circumstances because the floating
charge holder derived right from the debtor company but was never truly in competition   **C**
with the disponee. The floating charge holder was never vested in the subjects which were
comprised in the disposition. It would be a startling situation if on 10 August Albyn,
which had no lawful right to do anything with or in relation to the property, nevertheless
had it comprised within its property and undertaking. A property right must have
substance and content. That content could not be obtained simply by asserting a right to
make a fraudulent disposition. What 'belonged' to a person was his property. No one
would describe Albyn's rights in such terms after 9 August 1990. Whether one called the   **D**
right taken by the disponees a *jus ad rem* or a personal right was immaterial. Senior
counsel rejected the use of the expression 'personal right of property'. Until defeated the
disponee had a right in the property which he could vindicate against the world and
continued to enjoy a right of that character unless and until defeated by the recording of
a competing writ. This was *dominium*, ownership, a real right, a right in a thing. It gave
the right to use, sell, destroy, subject to standard securities, to bequeath, and to intromit   **E**
with the property in every way. Fundamentally the law of Scotland recognised only one
distinction of relevance in this context and that was between property and obligation. To
say that it was necessary to transfer a real right in order to transfer property was
erroneous. The authorities relied on by the pursuers in this context did not support the
argument advanced.

    For Mr and Mrs Thomson counsel adopted the second defenders' submissions but in   **F**
the alternative contended that *esto* ownership was not transferred by delivery of the
disposition, there was to be implied a constructive trust of the subjects for the disponees.
As a result, it was said, at the creation of the constructive trust the seller ceased to have
beneficial ownership in the subjects. The first defenders were therefore secured against
the attachment of the floating charge. It was not disputed that if there were an effective
trust the first defenders would be preferred over the pursuers' claims. Reference was made
to Wilson & Duncan on *Trusts* at p. 77 for an indication of the circumstances in which a   **G**
constructive trust might arise. Counsel relied particularly on *Stevenson v Wilson* 1907 SC
445 in this context. Further reference was made to *Lyle & Scott v Scott's Trustees* 1959
SC (HL) 64 and to the observations of Lord Sumner at pp. 72 and 73. Counsel relied
also on *Re Piccadilly Radio plc* (1989) 5 BCC 692 at p. 703H. These cases, involving the
transfer of shares in limited companies, provided an apt analogy. The primary content of
the property rights was transferred and recognised to be so, notwithstanding that title   **H**
remained in each case with the transferor. Payment of the price and delivery of the
transfer deed in Scotland and in England were treated as creating a trust. The title holder
was treated as holding for behoof of the transferee from the delivery of the relevant
transfer deed. In the present case the price had been paid and the disposition delivered.
Registration did not alter the position. The position was conceived as a matter of trust in
Gibson v Hunter Home Designs by the Lord President at p. 27. Lord Cameron's analysis

A   of the situation was in error in that case when he expressly excluded the possibility of trust. One could not properly exclude or reject the notion of a constructive trust by noting the absence of the requirements of an express trust. The approach was unsound. A series of cases supported the notion that delivery did involve the passing of property. Reference was made to *Bowman v Wright* (1877) 4 R 322 at pp. 324 and 326 and to *Heritable Reversionary Co v Millar* at p. 49-50, 43 and 46. Once the price had been paid and received and the disposition had been delivered the vendor clearly had no beneficial

B   interest in the subjects. The delivery of the disposition completed the process and it was upon that event that property passed. In the context of the creation of a formal trust reference was made to *Kerr's Trustees v Lord Advocate* 1974 SC 115 and to the observations of Lord Fraser at p. 129. Those requirements related to express trust. However, a constructive trust arose by operation of law and the identification of a point of transfer of assets to trustees was not essential in that context. The law implied a

C   constructive trust in relation to property where the circumstances existed for application of the principle. The trustee was precluded from transacting with the property as his own because he stood in a trust relationship to the beneficiary. Accordingly it was submitted that to the extent that real right was held to remain with the vendor, he held that right as a constructive trustee for the beneficiary and the property was not within the scope of the floating charge. In addition to the references to *Stevenson v Wilson*, Mr Davidson relied

D   upon *Dempsey v Celtic Football & Athletic Co Ltd* 1993 SLT 382; [1993] BCC 514 as an additional authority showing the application of the same principles and in particular relying upon *Piccadilly Radio plc* in a Scottish context.

   For the pursuers, counsel submitted that the subjects were attached by the floating charge. Reference was made to the *Insolvency Act* 1986, s. 53, 55 and 70 and for their effect to *Forth & Clyde Construction Co Ltd v Trinity Timber & Plywood Co Ltd* 1984 SC

E   1. The floating charge took effect as if it were a standard security recorded at 10 August 1990. In these circumstances the issue was whether delivery of the disposition on 9 August divested Albyn of property in the subjects so that they were not and could not have been attached by the floating charge on 10 August. In order to divest a disponer of property in Scots law it was necessary that the disposition granted be recorded in the register of sasines or that the interest of the disponee be registered in the Land Register as was

F   appropriate. Scots law initially required sasine. Thereafter registration came to be a formal requirement. Nothing in the statutory reforms of conveyancing law from the beginning of the 19th century had removed the requirement for symbolic delivery of the subjects to divest the disponer.

   Counsel made his submissions in six chapters. In the first place he submitted that there was a fundamental distinction between real and personal rights. It was necessary in order

G   to transfer property to effect a transfer of real rights. Expressions such as 'a personal right of property' had no validity. There could not be a personal right of property in any material sense. When one was dealing with competitions between creditors and disponees one was dealing with property and the distinction between real and personal right was of fundamental importance. Reference was made to T B Smith's *Short Commentary on the Law of Scotland* at p. 278 and p. 459. In the absence of trust a decision as to who had

H   property was a decision as to where lay the real right in the subjects in question. A disponer retained the real right in property until his disposition was recorded and it was only by paction that he was constrained in his conduct relative to it. Reference was made to *Erskine's Institutes*, III, i, 2 and II, iii, 48. Further reference was made to *Edmond v Gordon* (1857) 3 McQ 116 and to the speeches of Lord Cranwell at p. 122 and Lord Wensleydale at p. 129, and to Gloag and Irvine, *Rights in Security*, pp. 29 and 33–34. A *jus ad rem* fell within the category of personal right. It followed from these authorities:

(1) that there was a clear distinction between real and personal rights; A

(2) that ownership and a real right in an asset were interchangeable expressions;

(3) that both *jus crediti* and *jus ad rem* were personal rights: the only distinction between them was that in the latter case the disponee in possession of a delivered disposition had it within his power to obtain a real right without further act of or intervention by the disponer;

(4) however, even where a disponee had taken delivery of a disposition he was exposed B
to the risk that the disponer might grant a subsequent disposition which, if made real first, could defeat his rights; and

(5) it followed that even after disponer A had delivered a disposition to disponee B he retained a right of property in heritage; he could dispone the same property to C through mistake, inadvertence, fraud, and the disponee C obtained a good title if he first recorded his disposition; if disponer A did not retain a right of property he C
could not effectively have disponed to C: *nemo dat quod non habet.*

Counsel's second chapter of submissions was that, having regard to history, sasine and registration were essential to achieve transfer of heritable property. The 19th century reforms allowing registration of conveyances merely made such registration the equivalent of sasine by symbolical delivery plus the recording of an instrument of sasine without those steps being taken. Without registration of the disposition there was no D
sasine and no transfer of the land. In summary, originally three steps were required to transfer heritage. There was a requirement for a charter containing a *de praesenti* dispositive act of the disponer. That required to be delivered. And there had to be sasine, delivery of the land. In the 15th century an added solemnity was the requirement of an instrument of sasine. After 1617 there was a requirement that the instrument of sasine be registered in the register of sasines. The process in that respect had been one of increasing the requirements to achieve the transfer of property. During the 19th century the E
Infeftment Act 1845 and the *Titles to Land Act* 1858 created shortcuts. They did not otherwise change the law. Sasine and the registration of an instrument of sasine might be omitted. The other essential requirements remained. There had been no fundamental change since 1617. Counsel referred to *Stair's Institutions*, II, iii, 12, 14 and 16 to vouch the first four steps outlined in his summary. Reference was made to *Stair's* comments on the use of and effect of a disposition in the context of personal rights. Counsel referred F
to *Hume's Lectures on Conveyancing*, vol. 4, pp. 127, 151, 169, 170, 176, 178, 182, 183. On the basis of these references he submitted that prior to the middle of the 19th century the law was clear. In the absence of sasine the disponee was vulnerable to the acts of the disponer where those acts gave rise to real right in third parties. When one looked at the 19th century reforms all that they did was to provide the shortcut already mentioned. If one did not complete the process then the position was that the disponee did not have the benefit of sasine, did not have an instrument of sasine and no right of property had been G
transferred. The position had been dealt with at length in *Young v Leith* (1847) 9 D 932. Counsel referred extensively to the opinion of the majority of the court between pp. 932 and 944. In summary his submissions were that sasine remained necessary to divest the grantor of both title and beneficial interest in land; that sasine was null and void if it were not registered and the grantor was left with no more than a personal obligation to the grantee; that without registration the grantor retained the heritable right and full title to H
the property and he could divest by sale or by granting security or be divested by the act of an adjudger and lastly, that there was no intermediate stage at which or in which the grantor retained title but the grantee had taken a real right in the subjects. It amounted to this, that registration was a necessary solemnity in the transfer of property. Before 1845 and before 1858 there was no basis in law or principle to support the proposition that delivery of a deed without registration transferred ownership. The 1845 and 1858

A Acts did not alter the substance of the position. The 1845 Act provided that the recording of an instrument of sasine would have the same effect as sasine followed by the recording of such an instrument. The effect was that the recording of the deed had the same significance as both steps had previously had. The 1858 Act cut out the necessity for an instrument of sasine. That did not alter the essential structure of the requirements and permitted the omission of sasine and a recorded instrument if and only if one proceeded to record the disposition. Section 15 of the *Titles to Land (Consolidation) (Scotland) Act*
B 1868 left matters in substantially the same position. Section 163 of the 1868 Act provided that the old forms might still be used underlining the proposition that the legal principles remained the same. Consistent with this were the provisions of the *Conveyancing (Scotland) Act* 1874 that infeftment implied entry with the superior. Counsel referred additionally to *Bell's Lectures* at p. 666 and to *Cameron's Trustee v Cameron* 1907 SC 407 in support of his general proposition that in order to deliver land one must in the
C absence of sasine take the step of registration which under the legislation amounted to constructive sasine. Particular reference was made in *Cameron's Trustees* to Lord President Dunedin at p. 413, Lord Kinnear at p. 421 and Lord Low at p. 425. Counsel submitted thirdly that on analysis of *Mitchell v Ferguson* (1781) Mor 10296 there was authority for the view that an adjudger, taking *tantum et tale*, if infeft before a disponee who had prior to adjudication received a disposition, obtained a prior right. The 'race to the register' was won by him. Lord Cameron's analysis of the situation in *Gibson v Hunter*
D *Home Designs* was consistent with this principle and was correct. Counsel referred to the report of *Mitchell* at p. 10296–7. The contentions advanced by the uninfeft disponee were not dissimilar to those which had been advanced by counsel for the second defenders in the present case. Reliance was placed on the argument that a disponer could not dispone again without fraud. The arguments were rejected. That could be only because property remained with the disponer subject to purely contractual restrictions on his right to
E intromit with the asset. Considering Lord Cameron's observations in *Gibson* in the light of *Mitchell* and having regard to Graham Stewart on *Diligence* at p. 620 it was clear that Lord Cameron was applying these principles correctly. There were several cases relating to the 'race to the register' in the context of bankruptcy which were in point. Counsel referred to *Cormack v Anderson* (1829) 7 S 868 at pp. 870–871 and to the opinion of Lord Glenlee; to *Viscount Melville v Paterson* (1842) 4 D 1311 and in particular to Lord Ivory at p. 1315. Relying on these cases counsel submitted that if the position were that a
F disponee in possession of a delivered disposition had an interest which was a property interest, there would be no basis for a race to register. The existence of the race conditions was consistent only with the view that registration alone divested the grantor and invested the grantee with rights of property. Further reference was made to *Craigie's Lectures* at p. 514, and to *Goudie* at pp. 256–257 which were to the same effect. The race to the register excluded the argument of both defenders in this case.

G Counsel's fourth chapter dealt with his responses to the submissions of junior counsel for the second defenders. In relation to *Gibson v Hunter Home Designs* 1976 SC 23 he submitted in the first place that the argument between the parties was confined to analysis of the rights arising at the stage of missives. The pursuer asserted that there then arose real rights, which failing, a trust. The case did not deal with the holder of a delivered disposition on the one hand in competition with a person who had a real right on the
H other. Secondly it was clear from the summary of argument that very limited authority with a bearing on the issues involved had been cited and in particular that there had been none relating to the observations of the Lord President at p. 27. Only the *Embassy Picture House* case was referred to. It was a jurisdiction case and specialities arose in that context. Thirdly, the Lord President's observations on p. 27 relating to a 'personal right to the subjects' were made without assessment of the nature of the right and in particular without relating it to competitive rights where there was a recorded deed. In any event a

personal right of the kind identified was of no assistance to the defenders because it   A
amounted to a right personal against the disponer and was not a right available against
third parties. It was not a right of property at all. The floating charge holder was a third
party and fell to be distinguished from an heir or successor of the disponer himself.
Unless the defenders succeeded in their submission that the subjects were not property of
the company they could not succeed in this action. The correct analysis in *Gibson* was
found in the opinion of Lord Cameron at pp. 29–30 where in substance he cited the views
of Graham Stewart on *Diligence*. Turning to the jurisdiction cases on which junior   B
counsel for the second defenders had relied, counsel submitted that these were not
concerned in any way with the competition between two people deriving rights from the
same source. In such a competition title was all important. However, in the jurisdiction
cases one was not concerned with title but, as observed by the Lord Justice-Clerk in
Bowman v Wright, the 'reality and substance' of the position. That appeared also in the
Embassy Picture case, in *Caledonian Fish Selling Marine Stores Ltd v Allard Hewson &*   C
Co Ltd 1970 SLT 195 and *Fraser v Fraser & Hibbert* (1870) 8 M 400. One was not dealing
with ownership in the sense which necessarily arose in the present case in those situations.
In relation to *Thomas v Lord Advocate* 1953 SC 151 counsel observed that in that case at
p. 152 it was noted that the defenders had conceded that a transfer of property had been
completed on the delivery of a disposition. That was an important concession
fundamental to the observations of Lord Patrick. It was also wrong. The case was also   D
special in respect that the topic was as to the application of s. 11(1) of the *Customs &*
Inland Revenue Act 1889. The taxpayer's assertion had been that the gift was of a *jus ad*
rem. The considerations were wholly different from those that arose in the present
situation. Lord Patrick's views on a more relevant topic could be seen in *Pettigrew v*
Harton 1956 SLT 25. Reference was also made to Lord Mackintosh's observations on
p. 30 of that case. It was submitted that the second defenders' attempt to separate title
and beneficial interest was misconceived. 'Property' was what a company owned, and in   E
the case of heritable property that was necessarily a reference to real rights. The property
which was attached by s. 53(7) was that which would be property and would have vested
in a trustee in bankruptcy under the 1913 Act. But generally there was no separation in
Scots law of beneficial interest from title in the absence of trust. Apart from trust, in
which respect Scots law differed from other civilian systems, Scots law followed the
general civilian approach and denied separation between title and beneficial interest. It   F
was because of that that one had cases dealing with the race to the register for example.
In *Heritable Reversionary Co* at pp. 49–50 Lord Watson was making observations which
had to be understood in the context of an express trust. Otherwise his observations were
not to be relied upon. The purported analysis of interest as between legal interest and
beneficial interest was impracticable in Scots law and also was inconsistent with
authority. The reason that an adjudger took in competition with an unrecorded
disposition was simple. The disponer had both title and beneficial interest for all   G
purposes. Further, the disponer who remained on the register had the exclusive right to
sub-feu, to lease, to grant or discharge servitudes. On a proper analysis he retained all
property rights and the only restrictions on his exercise of them were derived from
contract. There was an implied term that he would not derogate from his grant in favour
of the disponee. But that was a matter of contract not affecting ownership or beneficial
interest in the property. There was no material difference in legal effect between the   H
position of the holder of a delivered disposition and the position of a purchaser under
missives. Prior to the delivery of the disposition the vendor might be in breach of contract
whereas after delivery of the disposition he would dispone again in derogation of his
prior grant. These however were not substantial differences in the present context. If it
were correct that the disponer retained title and beneficial interest and was restricted
merely by contract prior to the recording of the disposition then it was wrong and out of

A   context to talk of a 'bare' title. That was a trust concept and had no application in the context of sale. To hold otherwise would be to make a major innovation in Scots law. The factors relied on by the second defenders were all related to contract or statutory provisions. The disponee was given possession but that related to contract. The right to use an unrecorded disposition of property as a link in title was statutory: s. 3 of the *Conveyancing (Scotland) Act* 1924. The right to grant heritable security was statutory:

B   s. 12 of the *Conveyancing and Feudal Reform (Scotland) Act* 1970. The right to remove a tenant was only a partial relaxation, because the person initiating the action had to be infeft before decree could pass. However, the issue was not what rights the disponee had but whether one could separate beneficial interest and title in the absence of trust. There was no authority in Scots law that one could effect such a separation.

      Counsel's fifth chapter of submissions was in response to the contentions for the first defenders. There was no basis for constructive trust in relation to the sale of heritage.

C   Constructive trusts had been admitted in limited circumstances. None of them related to the present case. In addition to the reference to *Wilson & Duncan on Trusts*, counsel referred to vol. 24 of the *Stair Memorial Encyclopaedia* at para. 30. *Stevenson v Wilson* was recognised as an example of a constructive trust at that passage. However, it did not apply to heritable property and provided no assistance in the present case. The creation of a constructive trust on delivery of a disposition was contrary to the assumptions relied

D   upon in ordinary conveyancing practice. During the civil service strike when the registers were not available, practice had been to take an express declaration of trust. No one had relied on any implied or constructive trust in the circumstances. One of the benefits obtained from trust was that the beneficiary was protected against the insolvency of the trustee. However, the authorities indicated that the holder of an unrecorded disposition obtained no such protection and accordingly militated against the notion of constructive trust. The terms of the disposition and the right of the disponee to record and divest the

E   disponer again militated against the notion that the disponer held the property on a trust constituted by the disposition. The two stages were mutually incompatible. There already existed in Scots law a mechanism to protect the buyer from a third party purchaser. Reference was made to *Rodger (Builders) v Fawdry* 1950 SC 483. Scots law generally did not imply trust in the context of sale. One required to treat English authorities with considerable caution in the circumstances. Further, recent authorities tended to construe restrictively the requirements for the creation of a trust. Reference was made to *Kerr's*

F   *Trustees* and to *Clark Taylor & Co Ltd v Quality Site Development (Edinburgh) Ltd* 1981 SC 111. In those cases, in which the disposition created a new estate differently defined from any that had existed before, there was a difficulty in holding that a trust had been created in respect that the estate had not come to exist in any relevant sense prior to recording of the disposition. For all of these reasons there was not and could not be a constructive trust in the context of the transfer of heritage and without that no beneficial

G   interest in the land vested in the disponee. Lastly, counsel submitted that current conveyancing practice supported the pursuers. Reference was made to Professor Halliday's work at vol. 2, p. 369. In response to senior counsel for the second defenders, pursuers' counsel referred to the passages in *Erskine* and emphasised a need to see them in their context and to compare them with Erskine's other observations on the distinction between real and personal rights. Properly read Erskine supported the pursuers. In response to counsel for the first defenders, counsel extended the references relating to

H   constructive trust in England to include the case of *Musselwhite v C H Musselwhite & Son Ltd* [1962] Ch 964.

      In my opinion it is helpful to have regard to the wider statutory context in approaching the particular issue in this case. Section 462(1) of the *Companies Act* 1985 provides that it is competent under the law of Scotland for an incorporated company to create a floating charge:

'over all or any part of the property (including uncalled capital) which may from   A
time to time be comprised in its property and undertaking'.

The same language is found in s. 51(1) of the *Insolvency Act* 1986. Similar expressions
appeared in the antecedents of the current statutes. Section 1(1) of the *Companies
(Floating Charges) (Scotland) Act* 1961, in introducing the concept of the floating charge
into Scotland, provided for the creation of a floating charge by an incorporated company
'over all or any of the property, heritable and moveable, which may from time to time be   B
comprised in its property and undertaking'. In the *Companies (Floating Charges and
Receivers) (Scotland) Act* 1972, on the introduction of receivership, the specific
references to heritable and moveable property were removed, the expression was left
general and there was introduced the uncalled capital of the company, because of doubts
derived from authorities relating to equivalent English provisions. But generally the
purpose of the provisions remained the same throughout and was essentially to enable
the development of a new form of security in the case of limited companies to be created   C
in favour of creditors to provide flexible security of a kind already familiar in England.
The background, in Scots law, as is well known, was set out in Lord President Cooper's
opinion in *Carse v Coppen* 1951 SC 233 at p. 239:

> '. . . it is clear in principle and amply supported by authority that a floating charge
> is utterly repugnant to the principles of Scots law and is not recognised by us as
> creating a security at all. In Scotland, the term "equitable security" is meaningless.   D
> Putting aside the rare and exceptional cases of hypothec, we require for the
> constitution of a security which will confer upon the holder rights over and above
> those which he enjoys in common with the general body of unsecured creditors of
> a debtor, (a) the transfer to the creditor of a real right in specific subjects by the
> method appropriate for the constitution of such rights in the particular classes of
> property in question, or (b) the creation of a nexus over specific property by the
> due use of the appropriate form of diligence. A floating charge, even after   E
> appointment of a receiver, satisfies none of these requirements.'

The obstacles to recognition of the floating charge lay in Scots property law. For
present purposes, the requirement for transfer of a real right in specific subjects is
particularly important. It was obstacles of the kind identified by the Lord President which
were addressed in the 1961 Act and its successors, to enable the creation of floating
charges (CA 1985, s. 462(1)):   F

> 'for the purpose of securing any debt or other obligation (including a cautionary
> obligation) incurred or to be incurred by, or binding upon, the company or any
> other person . . . in favour of the creditor in the debt or obligation . . .'

The approach adopted did not innovate upon the general requirements of Scots
property law for the creation of any of the forms of security otherwise recognised. What
was provided was a facility, restricted to incorporated companies, intended to operate   G
within the framework of a more or less precisely defined set of rules. Of necessity, those
prescribed relationships between floating charges and rights recognised in property law
generally. In particular, priorities among secured creditors had to be regulated, and
provision had to be made to regulate competition with creditors who had done diligence.
In relation to heritable property, s. 462(5) provides that a floating charge has effect
notwithstanding that the instrument creating it is not recorded in the register of sasines,
or, as appropriate, registered in accordance with the *Land Registration (Scotland) Act*   H
1979. Section 463 provides for the effect of the floating charge on a winding up. The
charge attaches to the property comprised in the company's property and undertaking
on the commencement of the winding up. Provision is made for the competition between
the holder of the floating charge and any person who has effectually executed diligence
on the property or holds a fixed security over the property ranking in priority to the

A   floating charge or holds over the property or any part of it another floating charge ranking in priority to the charge in question. Significantly, s. 185 of the Insolvency Act is excluded, strengthening the position of the holder of the floating charge by avoiding the statutory adjudication in favour of the liquidator. The mechanism adopted in bankruptcy, and reflected in liquidation, has not been used. In s. 486 the expression 'fixed security' is defined as meaning any security other than a floating charge which on the winding up of the company in Scotland would be treated as an effective security over

B   that property and is expressly defined to include a security over heritage within the meaning of s. 9(8) of the *Conveyancing and Feudal Reform (Scotland) Act* 1970. Turning to the provisions of the *Insolvency Act* 1986 one again finds language appropriate to a context which requires consideration of rights and obligations arising as a matter of property law. Section 53(7) provides that on the appointment of a receiver under that section, that is, by the holder of the charge, the floating charge attaches to the property

C   then subject to the charge and such attachment has effect as if the charge were a fixed security over the property to which it has attached. Given the structure of these provisions, there is, at least superficially, an attraction towards a solution to the present question which acknowledges the property law context.

     In my opinion two requirements fall to be met if the contentions of the receivers are to succeed in this case: (1) the subjects must fall within the expression 'the property . . .

D   comprised in the property and undertaking' of the company on 10 August 1990; and (2) the interest of the company in the subjects on that date must have been such that as between the company and the floating charge creditor there could then attach to the subjects a standard security assumed to have been duly recorded without any act of the company being required. The operation of s. 13(7) of the 1972 Act, the predecessor of s. 53(7) of the *Insolvency Act* 1986, was considered in relation to moveable property in *Forth & Clyde Construction Co Ltd v Trinity Timber & Plywood Co Ltd* 1984 SC 1. The

E   property in question in that case consisted of a debt due to the company in receivership. At pp. 10–11, the Lord President, with whom Lord Stott and Lord Brand agreed, said:

     'The attachment of the debt due and payable by the Regional Council is, by virtue of section 13(7), to have effect *as if* the charge were a fixed security over it. The intention appears to me to be that the holder of the floating charge shall, on the appointment of a receiver, enjoy all the protection in relation to any item of

F   attached property that the holder of a fixed security over that item thereof would enjoy under the general law. A fixed security is defined by reference to those securities which would be treated by the law of Scotland as "effective securities" on the winding up of the company (section 31(1)). In the context of this Act the expression "effective securities" in section 31(1) must, I think, mean securities other than those constituted by means of diligences, for throughout the Act a sharp distinction is drawn between a fixed security and a diligence. This distinction is to

G   be found, for example, in section 1(2)(a) and (b), section 15(2)(a) and (b) and section 20(1)(a) and (b). By the language of section 13(7) one is, in my opinion, driven to ask, in attempting to define the effect of the attachment of particular property, what kind of security over that property, other than by way of diligence, would be treated by the law of Scotland on the winding up of the company in this jurisdiction as an "effective security". If, as one must, one ignores diligences, it is

H   clear that in the case of a book debt the only relevant "effective security" within the meaning of section 31(1) is an assignation in security, duly intimated to the debtor. It follows, accordingly, that in the case of an attached book debt one can only reasonably discover the effect of the attachment by treating it *as if* there had been granted in relation to it the only relevant "effective security" known to the law, namely an assignation in security, duly intimated. To adopt any other approach would in my opinion deprive the holder of the charge of the advantages

which he was intended to enjoy, namely the advantages which would be enjoyed   A
by the holder of an "effective security", recognised by the law, over each and every
form of property attached by the charge.'

In my opinion these observations are clearly general in their effect and are equally
instructive in the context of heritable as of moveable property. The words 'as if' indicate
that one must proceed on an assumption of fact, appropriate to the class of property in
question, that the property is subject to an effective fixed security in favour of the holder   B
of the floating charge on the relevant date. It follows from the same passage that the
proper analysis of the provision does not to any extent depend on forms of diligence as
direct analogues. And there is nothing in the language to suggest that one is concerned
with analogous transactions entered into by the company. The company is not assumed
to have executed any form of security deed as a voluntary act within its competence.
Substantially the same mechanisms apply on crystallisation on winding up: *Companies
Act* 1985, s. 463(1) and (2). In each case, a fixed security is assumed to attach without   C
reference to any means by which the company itself could have created such a security
by its own act, in the circumstances then obtaining. This appears to me to reflect the
general structure of the provisions. The company completes the voluntary element in the
transaction necessary on its part by executing and delivering the floating charge
instrument, always provided that timeous registration then follows. Thereafter,
attachment is a function of the registered charge, triggered by one or other of the events   D
identified in the legislation and provided for in the particular instrument.

On the other hand the essential characteristic of the charge prior to attachment is that
it does not affect the acquisition or disposal by the company of property rights, so that
assets held by the company from time to time, while 'property' of the company, remain
unaffected by any hypothetical fixed security. It appears to me to follow that a floating
charge can only attach to property, however defined, which was so held by or for the
company at the date of attachment as to be affected by a fixed security deemed at the   E
material date to have all of the characteristics of a completed and effective security over
the class of subjects in question. The company must stand in such a relationship to
heritable property that a standard security deemed to have the benefit of due recording
and identifying the property would attach to the property in a question between the
company, the floating charge creditor and competing creditors. Provided that the
property is so held, it is immaterial whether there are limitations or restrictions on the   F
capacity of the company itself to enter into any voluntary transaction which would have
that effect. There is a danger, however, in the argument that anything which could be the
subject to a fixed security would necessarily be within the meaning of 'property' on a
sound construction of the Act. In *Heritable Reversionary Co v Millar* (1892) 19 R 43 the
reasoning of the judges of the Court of Session was criticised on the ground that they had
dwelt on the effect of vesting of a bankrupt's estate in his trustee to the exclusion of the
prior question of what comprised the property sequestrated: see, for example, Lord   G
Herschell at p. 44. That case was concerned with property acquired and held by an agent
with fiduciary obligations to his principals. Mr McKay had been manager of *Heritable
Reversionary Co.* He purchased heritage for the company, using the company's money
and credit, but, it appears for convenience, took title in his own name. When he left the
company's employment he executed a declaration of trust reflecting the realities of the
situation and undertook to transfer on the company's instructions. The declaration was   H
never registered, and no transfers took place before his sequestration. So far as the public
records were concerned, McKay was owner. McKay's status as agent was amenable to
proof by his writ, and there was no question as to the facts of the case. The speeches in
the House of Lords generally use the language of trust, and at the original hearing on
procedure roll the case was dealt with in that context. *Bank of Scotland v Liquidators of
Hutchison Main & Co* 1914 SC (HL) 1 was not referred to. At the resumed hearing, Mr

A   Hodge recognised that the later case forced a shift in his position, but he contended that the decision effectively equiparated agency and trust for present purposes. That was not challenged. It was held in the House of Lords that the subjects were not 'property' of McKay for the purposes of the Bankruptcy Act then in force. In Wilson & Duncan on *Trusts*, the decision, along with that in *Bank of Scotland v Liquidators of Hutchison Main & Co*, is treated, perhaps tentatively, as referring to 'property' in the sense of the Bankruptcy Acts, partly at least because of the difficulties of reconciling dicta in those

B   cases with other decisions dealing with the property law aspects of trust. It is, in my opinion, clear that the fields of bankruptcy and the Companies Act provisions in question are closely related and one would be obliged to treat as having very high authority any general comments in those cases on the construction of expressions appearing in both. It is necessary therefore to consider whether the observations of the House of Lords go further than the immediate context and indicate a meaning for the word 'property' which

C   is particular to the context of provisions in statutes of this class. The case related to s. 102 of the *Bankruptcy (Scotland) Act* 1856. That section provided for the vesting of the bankrupt's estates in his trustee and the effect of that vesting. At p. 49 Lord Watson identified the critical parts of the provision as follows:

> 'The act and warrant of confirmation in favour of the trustees shall, *ipso jure*, transfer to and vest in him, or any succeeding trustee, for behoof of the creditors, absolutely and irredeemably, as at the date of the sequestration, with all right, title,

D   and interest, the whole property of the debtor, to the effect following.'

At p. 46, he had said:

> 'Before adverting to the language of the statute I think it may be useful to consider the nature of the relations existing between a solvent trustee who is feudally vested in the heritable estate of the trust by a title *ex facie* absolute, and his *cestui que*

E   *trust*, whose right rests upon a latent back-bond. As between them there can, in my opinion, be no doubt that according to the law of Scotland the one, though possessed of the legal title, and being the apparent owner, is in reality a bare trustee; and that the other, to whom the whole beneficial interest belongs, is the true owner . . . But in that state of the title the trustee, though his action may be in breach of duty, or even grossly fraudulent, can communicate a valid right to a purchaser or a lender on the security of the trust-estate, who transacts with him for

F   value and without notice of the interest of the beneficiary . . . it must, however, be kept in view that the validity of a right acquired in such circumstances by a *bona fide* disponee for value does not rest upon the recognition of any power in the trustee which he can lawfully exercise, because breach of trust duty and wilful fraud can never be in themselves lawful, but upon the well-known principle that a true owner who chooses to conceal his right from the public, and to clothe his

G   trustee with all the *indicia* of ownership, is thereby barred from challenging rights acquired by innocent third parties for onerous considerations under contracts with his fraudulent trustee.'

At p. 49 having quoted the provision and the terms already mentioned, his Lordship proceeds:

> 'Were the subjects in dispute the property of McKay, within the meaning of that

H   enactment at the date of his sequestration? Upon the language of the statute, that appears to me to be a very simple question, admitting only of a negative answer. An apparent title to land or personal estate, carrying no real right of property with it, does not, in the ordinary or in any true legal sense, make such land or personal estate the property of the person who holds the title. That which, in legal as well as in conventional language, is described as a man's property is estate, whether heritable or moveable, in which he has a beneficial interest which the law allows him to dispose of. It does not include estate in which he has no beneficial interest, and which he cannot dispose of without committing a fraud. It is true that the law will sustain a right created by his fraudulent alienation in the person of a *bona fide* alienee for value, but not, as has already been pointed out, upon the ground that the thing alienated was the property of his author. The respondent, as representing creditors who had no dealing with the bankrupt in relation to the estate of which the appellants had the beneficial fee, and who have given no value for the interest which he claims on their behalf, does not stand in the position of an onerous and *bona fide* alienee, and cannot take benefit from the principle which validates the right of the latter.'

Having considered the terms of superseded legislation his Lordship proceeded at the foot of p. 50 to say:

'I venture to think that the property described in these four Acts as falling within the sequestration includes no heritable or other estate of which the bankrupt was not the true owner. That construction gives effect to the literal meaning of their language; and it is to my mind hardly conceivable that the Legislature should have intended to confiscate the property of persons other than the bankrupt for the behoof of his creditors, by requiring him to execute a disposition in favour of their trustee, which but for the statute he could not have granted without being guilty of the crime of breach of trust and embezzlement . . .'

At p. 43 Lord Herschell said:

'It seems beyond dispute that as between McKay and the appellants he was a bare trustee, and they were the true and beneficial owners of the property. I do not understand it to be questioned that the law of Scotland recognises such a relationship, or that, if it appeared *ex facie* of the dispositions, the beneficiary would be regarded as the true owner as against all persons and for all purposes. Although as regards third persons the case may be very different when the trust is latent, I do not see how this can affect the relation of the trustee and the beneficiary *inter se*. If McKay had disposed of the property and converted the proceeds to his own use, he would, I apprehend, have been guilty of a breach of trust, and rendered himself amenable to the criminal law.

It is true that an onerous purchaser from him would have obtained an unimpeachable title, but this would not be because the property was his, but because the true owners had permitted him to appear on the Register of Sasines as the owner, and thus entitled anyone dealing with him for value to regard him as such. A register, whether of heritable or any other subjects, would obviously fail of its purpose unless this were the law.'

In relation to the statutory provision he said at p. 44:

'Wherever, therefore, it has to be determined whether heritable or any other estate vested in the trustee, the first question which arises is, was it the "property of the debtor"? The expression is not a technical one, but is obviously intended to comprehend all that would ordinarily be understood as covered by it. It cannot be doubted that it includes all beneficial interests possessed by the bankrupt, even though the property be vested in other persons as trustees for him. On the other hand, I cannot think, unless compelled by authority to take that view, that it includes, or was ever intended to include, estates of which the bankrupt was a bare trustee, and in which he had no beneficial interest . . . The words "belonging to" are not technical, and I do not think that a heritable estate of which the bankrupt is a bare trustee, and in which he had no beneficial interest, can with any propriety be said to "belong" to him.'

A   At p. 53 Lord Macnaghten said:

'But what is the thing which is vested? It is "the property" of the bankrupt. As regards his real estate in Scotland it is "the heritable estate belonging to him". The words "property" and "belonging to" are not technical words in the law of Scotland. They are to be understood, I think, in their ordinary signification. They are, in fact, convertible terms – you can hardly explain the one except by using the other. A man's property is that which is his own – that which belongs to him. What belongs to him is his property. No one in ordinary parlance would speak of land or funds held only in trust for another as the property of the trustee. Land or funds so held are not the trustee's property in any real sense any more than a bankrupt's sequestrated estate is the property of the trustee in bankruptcy. It is true that in the present case the complete feudal title was in the bankrupt. It is true that in a strict legal view the right of the beneficiaries was only a personal claim against their trustee. But for all that the bankrupt could not have applied the property to his own purposes, or used it for his own benefit, without committing a fraud for which he might have been made criminally responsible. The beneficiaries were the true owners all along . . .'

The circumstances in *Bank of Scotland v Liquidators of Hutchison Main & Co* 1914 SC (HL) 1 were that Hutchison Main & Co had entered into an agreement with the bank for the release of assets held by the bank as security on the basis that in substitution the company would obtain and assign to the bank a debenture from another company, Frank A Johnston Ltd, which was indebted to Hutchison Main. The debenture was granted by Johnston in March 1910. Hutchison Main's Scottish solicitors had written to the bank in February stating that as soon as the debenture reached their hands they would 'make it available' to the bank. The bank relied on the solicitors to complete the assignation. Arrangements for making the assignation were in progress when Hutchison Main went into liquidation. The bank contended that the liquidators took *tantum et tale* and that the debenture was held by Hutchison Main subject to a fiduciary obligation to make it available to the bank. The liquidators prevailed. Lord Kinnear said at p. 3:

'I do not understand it to be disputed that . . . the liquidation is exactly in the same position as an individual debtor under the Bankruptcy Acts. Rights in security which have been effectually completed before the liquidation must still receive effect which the law gives to them. Both the company and its liquidators are just as completely disabled by the winding up from granting new or completing imperfect rights in security as the individual bankrupt is by his bankruptcy . . . Every creditor is to have an equal share, unless anyone has already a part of the estate in his hands by virtue of an effectual legal right . . .'

At p. 4, he said that to make a security over debt effective, it was necessary for the assignee to have a right which he could enforce against the debtor in his own name 'because it is indispensable for the efficacy of a security that the secured creditor should have *jus in re*'. The claim that there was a trust was based on *Heritable Reversionary Co.* At pp. 5–7 Lord Kinnear explained that decision. He said at pp. 6–7 that the decision of the House of Lords proceeded on the basis that:

'. . . as between the bankrupt and his employers, the former was a bare trustee, and the latter were the true and beneficial owners of the property, which, therefore, did not belong to the bankrupt in the sense of the Act, and was not vested in the trustee. It was not disputed that third persons dealing with the bankrupt with specific reference to the property were entitled to rely on the title as it stood on the Register of Sasines, and, thus, that an onerous purchaser from him would have obtained an unimpeachable title. But it was held that this would not be because the property was his, but because the true owners had permitted him to appear on

the Register of Sasines as the owner, and thus entitled anyone dealing with him for A
value to regard him as such. The noble and learned Lords held that the rule of
personal bar which thus protects transactions of the trustee from challenge only
applies to such as have specific reference to the trust estate, and is not pleadable by
personal creditors who do not stipulate for, or obtain, any conveyance to that
estate. This appears to me to be the full force of the decision; and I am unable to
see that it has any bearing on the matter in hand. Of course it assumes, what,
indeed, was never disputed, that property admittedly held under a bare trust, B
without any beneficial interest in the trustee, would not pass to his creditors on his
bankruptcy. But the bankrupt's title of property was qualified only by a latent
trust. The question was whether this latent declaration of trust could be looked at;
and when that was once settled by the decision of this House, the rest followed as
a matter of course.

It is further to be observed that the trust so established was declared in express C
terms, and directly affected the constitution of the real right. It is a very different
thing to say that a personal obligation to give the benefit of a specific fund to a
particular creditor creates a trust which attaches to the fund and excludes it from
the estate for distribution. That the judgment in the case of *Millar* was not intended
to cover such a case as this is obvious, because Lord Herschell states the distinction
between the duty imposed by a trust and the liability created by a personal contract
in perfectly clear terms.' D

Lord Halsbury concurred in Lord Kinnear's judgment. Lord Atkinson's view was that
nothing short of the passing of the absolute and entire beneficial interest in the relevant
subjects would suffice. That could not be achieved by contract. Lord Shaw of
Dunfermline was clearly anxious that nothing should be thought to diminish the
authority of *Millar*: p. 16. His views on the scope of the decision appear at pp. 15 and 16.
The bank's contentions were characterised by him as 'mis-applying the well-known E
doctrine of apparent and real ownership'. He explained that in the context of agency,
where the agent's acquisitions of assets on behalf of his principal are correctly treated as
never having been *in bonis* of the agent, but at all times of the principal. *Heritable
Reversionary Co* was, in his view, an outstanding instance of the application of this
principle.

It is clear that assets held in trust are not 'property' of the trustee, for present purposes, F
whether the trust be expressed or latent, subject to requirements of proof. If the
observations in *Millar* are read in that context, their value may be limited. The trust
concept depends on the division of ownership from beneficial enjoyment. In *Clark Taylor
& Co* 1981 SC 111 Lord President Emslie set out the requirements for the constitution of
a trust at p. 118. In particular, he said:

'. . . there must be a beneficiary or beneficiaries with defined rights in the trust
estate; and there must also be delivery of the trust deed or subject of the trust or a G
sufficient and satisfactory equivalent to delivery, so as to achieve irrevocable
divestiture of the truster and investiture of the trustee in the trust estate.'

The requirement of investiture of the trustee reflects the first principle underlying the
doctrine of trust stated by *Bell's Principles*, s. 1991:

'That a full legal estate is created in the person of the trustee, to be held by him
against all adverse parties and interests for the accomplishment of certain ends and H
purposes.'

The trustee, whether appointed under a deed or holding that office by operation of law,
has a right of property in the assets comprised in the trust, for the purposes of the trust.
The law could not recognise the trust concept without recognising that the trust estate
vested in the trustee was, notwithstanding irrevocable investiture, so qualified by his

A   obligations as trustee relative to that estate that the assets comprised in it could not be
    treated as his property or as belonging to him in the context of his personal insolvency.
    Millar, as explained in *Hutchison Main & Co*, indicates that for certain purposes an agent
    acquiring property on behalf of a principal is in the parallel position. To recognise that
    would provide little insight into the means by which assets held by a company, as its
    undoubted and unqualified property, could cease to be its property, and in particular in
    determining the stage at which an asset sold by the company passed from its property in
B   implement of the sale. In *Millar* Lord Watson carefully distinguished cases involving a
    personal obligation to convey heritable property from the situation to which his
    comments were directed: p. 51. If one accepted Mr Hodge's submission that apart from
    the special characteristics of trust the only relevant distinction recognised in Scots law
    was the distinction between real and personal rights, the effect of *Millar* would properly
    be restricted to the context of trust and agency.

C   I consider that it is not possible to treat *Millar* in such a narrow way. The question of
    statutory construction could not, as a matter of logical analysis, be confined or
    constrained by the proper treatment of the particular case on a sound interpretation of
    the provision. The general observations are authoritative indications of the proper
    approach to the construction of the expression 'property' in the Bankruptcy Acts and in
    related contexts. The things which vest in a trustee in sequestration, and those which are
D   taken by a liquidator for the purposes of a winding up, are the things which belong to
    the debtor, which are in substance and reality his property. In my opinion the same
    approach has to be adopted in dealing with the present provisions. The terminology of
    the bankruptcy legislation remained substantially the same in the 1913 Act as it was at
    the time of *Millar*, and remained so when the *Companies (Floating Charges) (Scotland)
    Act* 1961 came into force. The contexts are sufficiently close to make it necessary to adopt
    the interpretation indicated in *Millar* for present purposes. In adopting that view it is
E   necessary to acknowledge that there are differences in the mechanisms adopted in the
    statutes. In relation to moveable property s. 97(1) of the 1913 Act provided that the
    bankrupt's moveable property vested in the trustee 'so far as attachable for debt, or
    capable of voluntary alienation'. In relation to heritage, the whole heritable estate
    belonging to the bankrupt in Scotland vested, to the same effect as if a decree of
    adjudication and implement of sale, as well as a decree of adjudication for payment and
    security of debt, subject to no legal reversion, had been pronounced in favour of the
F   trustee and recorded at the date of the sequestration, and as if a poinding of the ground
    had then been executed, subject always to such preferable security as existed at the date
    of the sequestration. These specific provisions were concerned to identify property subject
    to sequestration in terms of diligence and the claims of creditors. As observed by Lord
    President Emslie, the mechanisms adopted for the purposes of the floating charges
    legislation are materially different. However, on the approach to construction adopted in
G   *Heritable Reversionary Co* the mechanics are a subordinate factor in interpreting
    provisions such as this. In my opinion it is appropriate in these circumstances to take the
    view that the expression 'the property comprised in property and undertaking' of a
    company comprises those assets which in a true and substantial sense belong to the
    company and are held as the company's property in that sense. But it is not clear that
    that takes one any further as a matter of general interpretation. It does not provide an
    answer to the question whether it is an essential characteristic of property that it be
H   amenable to the claims of the company's creditors. Nor does it prescribe any degree of
    use or exploitation of the asset which must be available to the company before it can be
    comprised within the company's property. It is relatively easy to identify examples of
    property which the owner cannot use at all, but which remain within the limits of what is
    in reality and substance his. Use may be restricted or excluded by contract, or by other
    obligation. Disposal of an asset may be restricted similarly. A licence may exhaust for its

term the potential for enjoyment of an asset, yet fall short of the civil possession implicit   A
in the lease of the asset. The search for comprehensive interpretation of the expression
presents at least considerable difficulties and may be impossible.

The question whether delivery of a disposition eliminates the subjects from the class of
assets comprised within the property and undertaking of the disponer in the sense derived
from the authorities involves discussion of a considerable body of authority. Mr
Campbell did not seriously challenge Mr Hodge's analysis of the law relating to the   B
divestiture of an infeft proprietor of heritage, either historically or in its modern form.
From and after the 1858 Act, at least where the older forms were not used, the recording
of a dispositive deed in the register of sasines or the land register has been an essential
solemnity for the transfer of real right, failing which the granter is not divested, and the
disponee is liable to be defeated in a competition with another disponee who reaches the
register first, or to take subject to the security rights of the holder of a fixed security who
records first. The issue between the pursuers and the second defenders was whether this   C
was an essential step in transferring property for the purposes of the provisions.

In *Young v Leith* (1847) 9 D 932 the issue related to competing claims to heritable
property entailed in 1745 on a destination in favour of younger sons of Charles Gordon
of Buthlaw and the heirs male of the body of each of them respectively. The pursuers
claimed the subjects as nearest lawful heirs portioners of John Gordon and Charles
Gordon, the second and fourth sons respectively, and the defenders, the *mortis causa*   D
trustees of General Gordon who was a son of Charles Gordon, advanced their claim on
the basis of a progress of writs including a fee simple disposition by General Gordon in
favour of himself and certain heirs. General Gordon had served as heir of provision of
his father under the destination, and taken out a precept from Chancery on which he was
infeft. But his infeftment was never recorded. Charles Gordon had served as heir of
provision of his uncle, John. He also was infeft, but the sasine was not recorded
timeously. The pursuers' propinquity was not in dispute, and the issue turned on the   E
effectiveness of the unrecorded steps to alter the original destination under which the
pursuers claimed. The First Division held that General Gordon was not entitled to grant
the deeds on which the defenders relied, and granted decree of reduction, thereby
removing the obstacles in the way of the pursuers themselves serving. At p. 376, Lord
Fullerton characterised the defenders' case in this way:

> 'The defenders must maintain either that (General Gordon) was well infeft, or that   F
> he had some personal right which gave him power to execute the deeds. But it is
> impossible to say that his infeftment was good. It was not recorded at all . . . and
> there was no personal right carried by the General's service which could enable
> him to convey. There was no personal right in the parties to whom he served . . .'

The case went to the House of Lords. It was remitted back for argument viva voce before
the whole court as to the validity of the title set up by the defenders. The report in 1847   G
reflects the views taken after that hearing. Lord Medwyn, Lord Ivory and Lord
Cuninghame differed from the majority whose opinion was delivered by Lord Fullerton.
At the risk of doing injustice to the research and learning reflected in the opinions, it may
be sufficient for present purposes to identify the issue as being the effect of the
requirements of the Act of 1617 (C 16), relating to registration of the then obligatory
instrument of sasine. At p. 934, Lord Fullerton explained the purpose of the Act as
obliging parties to register and putting that obligation,   H

> 'on its true ground, viz. the security of persons dealing with the apparent
> proprietors, against the effect of latent deeds qualifying or limiting their ostensible
> rights.'

Registration was required within 60 days and the penalty for failure was that unregistered
writings:

A

'shall make no faith in judgment, by way of action or exception, in prejudice of a third party, who hath acquired an perfete and lauchful right to the said lands and heritages; but prejudice to use the said writtes against the party-maker thereof, his heirs and successors.'

The exception available to the grantor, his heirs and successors, was treated by Lord Fullerton as personal, operating in bar, see p. 935, or operating only as personal

B obligations, p. 937. Dealing with the primary effect of the provision, his view was that the effect was to annul the instruments as constituting real rights. He proceeded at p. 937:

'Besides, it will be found, on considering the true import of the terms employed, that they do amount in substance to an extinction of any real right which a valid seisin would confer. The proper object and effect of every valid seisin is to divest the granter of the heritable right, and to invest the grantee. When that legal act is

C once completed, it absolutely excludes the acquisition of any subsequent real right from the granter, preferable to that of the party seised, or, indeed, the acquisition of any real right, through any other medium than the right of the party so seised. An instrument of seisin, which has not in law that effect, is practically null as a seisin, i.e. as an act completing a real right; for it does not produce the effect which it is the sole and peculiar object of a valid seisin to secure. When it is said that the statute annuls the instrument, only *qualificate*, that is, in prejudice of a third party

D who has acquired a perfect right to the lands, it is overlooked that the very qualification excludes the notion of a real right. It is of the very essence of a real right, not only to found a preference against a less perfect right, but to prevent any third party from acquiring a perfect right to the lands, which most certainly an unregistered seisin does not.

In the case of an original conveyance, the seisin of the disponee, if unregistered, does not divest the granter; for it leaves in him the heritable right, which may be

E validly acquired from him by a second disponee completing his title by a registered seisin . . .'

The only question left was as to the extent of the exception. The minority judges differed fundamentally with the majority. At p. 969, for example, Lord Medwyn said:

'For it must always be recollected that, prior to the Act, the infeftment, with its

F extended instrument, conferred the full fee, took the lands out of the disponer, and conveyed them to the disponee. I am of opinion that it still does so, even although the further requisite of recording has not been attended to; for this is not declared a solemnity, nor has been held such, invalidating the act of delivery, when not observed; it is something superadded to the ceremony which conferred the right, and where its omission is not only not said to invalidate or nullify what previously conveyed the fee, but only the effect of what is conferred is limited and restricted

G to what does not militate against the fee being, as before, in the person infeft.'

In my opinion it is clear from this that the substantial issue of what was required to divest the grantor and invest the acquirer of heritage with a real right of property was dealt with in the case, and that registration was held to be an essential solemnity in the absence of which property was not transferred, though the rights might instruct personal obligations in any question with parties within the scope of the exception. It did not

H occur to any of the judges that a charter might transfer property. But that does not alter the point that the issue was as to the stage at which property passed.

In view of the authority of this decision, it is perhaps unnecessary to consider at length the discussions of the institutional and other writers which were cited, other than for illustration. To repeat the effect of Mr Hodge's historical analysis, the position was as follows. Prior to the *Infeftment Act* 1845, the steps necessary to transfer heritage were:

(1)   a charter containing the *de praesenti* dispositive act of the disponer;   A

(2)   delivery of that charter to the disponee;

(3)   sasine: symbolical delivery of the land;

(4)   a duly executed instrument of sasine; and

(5)   registration of the instrument of sasine in the register of sasines.

Baron Hume's Lectures 1786–1822, vol. 4 of the Stair Society Edition, at p. 182 dealing   B
with sasines says:

> 'Let us now return one step farther back on the investiture, and suppose, that
> charter only has been given, or disposition executed, but that no seisin has
> followed. You will here anticipate the consequence, which is, that there is no real
> investiture, but the constitution only of an ordinary personal right or *jus ad rem* to
> the lands – such a right as is good, indeed, against the granter and his heirs or
> others who come into his place, and are liable to the like personal objection as he,   C
> – but which shall not stand the test of trial with any perfect investiture acquired by
> a third party, who has no concern with and is not reached by that objection. The
> deed of conveyance, not followed with seisin, which is the feudal delivery of the
> lands, (and as necessary as the real delivery is in the case of moveable corpora) is a
> mere expression of consent; neither divests the disponer nor really qualifies, nor
> intrinsically limits his previous feudal right to the lands. Being still vested with that   D
> feudal right he can, therefore, effectually make it over to another, who can defend
> himself therein, and maintain his right. As to his author's personal engagements or
> contracts with respect to it, he, the singular successor, is no party to them, nor
> supposed to know of them, nor obliged to enquire about them . . . Or if John sell
> and dispone to James, and then borrows money from George, upon heritable
> bond; and if this bond is followed with seisin, while James is uninfeft, James, the
> purchaser, shall indeed have the property of the lands; but still he has it under   E
> burden only of this feudal interest and security duly vested in the person of George
> (because that has been conveyed to him only). Or again put the case, that while
> James is still uninfeft, John, the disponer's creditors, shall adjudge the lands for
> payment of their debts, and be infeft upon their diligence. These adjudications are
> effectual incumberances on the purchaser's title. As was indeed decided in the case
> of *Mitchell v Ferguson* of 13 Febry. 1781.'   F

Dealing with the Act of 1617, Baron Hume says at p. 176:

> 'We have now followed the feudal investiture through the several steps of its
> progress down to the last of all – the registration of the seisin. We have, however,
> hitherto been occupied chiefly with the detail of the forms . . . and it may therefore,
> now, be worthwhile to look back upon the space we have travelled over, and to
> consider, briefly . . . the state of the vassal's title in its several, chief, steps of
> advancement, and the influence which those steps, respectively, have on the   G
> condition of his right. I begin with the matter, which was last described – the
> Registration of the Seisin. The Statute of 1617 itself declares the consequence, if,
> in any case, this shall be entirely omitted, vizt. 'That the Seisin shall make no faith
> in Judgement, by way of Action or exception, in prejudice of any third party who
> hath acquired a perfect and lawful Right to the Lands –' that is to say, the
> unrecorded seisin shall be postponed, in competition with any perfect feudal right,   H
> which has been compleated both by due entry on Record, and in all other respects.
> Thus put the case that John gives charter of his lands to James, who is infeft, but
> neglects to put his seisin on Record; and that John shall next give charter of those
> same lands to George, who takes seisin, and records the instrument; George shall
> carry the lands. The prior seisin is nothing to him, who has no information of it, in
> the way which law has enjoyed.'

A   In my opinion Mr Hodge correctly analysed the effect of the 19th century reforms. The alternatives provided then preserved the characteristics of the old forms. Recording of a disposition was an essential solemnity of divestiture of the grantor. The *Infeftment Act* 1845 and the *Titles to Land (Scotland) Act* 1858 provided for the effective transfer of heritage without sasine, and without delivery of a duly executed instrument of sasine, where there was delivered and recorded on a warrant of registration a disposition or other conveyance of the land. These provisions were re-enacted in s. 15 of the *Titles to Land Consolidation (Scotland) Act* 1868, which again preserved the older forms: s. 163.

B   So far as it goes, Lord President Dunedin's dictum in *Cameron's Trustee v Cameron* 1907 SC 407 at p. 413 supports the equiparation of the older and more modern forms. But the decision is rather far removed from the present context to provide more than incidental support for Mr Hodge's submissions.

C   The result of these authorities, in my opinion, is that in a question with third parties the grantor of an unrecorded disposition remains fully vested with feudal right and title notwithstanding delivery of the deed, until it is recorded in the register of sasines. Baron Hume deals with the uncompleted act, in the forms of the time, as constituting in the grantee no more than a personal right or *jus ad rem* good against the grantor and his heirs but ineffective in a question with any third party who acquired a prior effective right. The specific example of a heritable bond, followed by sasine, in a question with a holder of an unregistered conveyance, is dealt with. The characterisation of the right as a *jus ad rem* requires consideration. But it appears clearly that Baron Hume considers that to be synonymous with personal right available against the grantor and his heirs only.

D

    If this is not to be determinative of the question in the present case, it must be because in applying the statutory test infeftment involves a step beyond the requirements for the transfer of property. The personal right conferred by the delivery of the disposition would require to be treated as completing the property transfer not only as between the parties but as between the disponer and his creditors. That was the position of the second defenders. Mr Campbell relied on Erskine's definition as an aid to understanding the concept of 'property' in Scots law. That definition was (Book II, i, i):

E

> 'The sovereign or primary real right is that of property; which is the right of using and disposing of a subject as our own, except in so far as we are restrained by law or paction.'

F   I have not found that helpful as a starting point. On one view it is a description of the legal incidents of property rather than an analysis of the source of those incidents. The holder of an unrecorded disposition may or may not have a right of using the subjects. That will depend inter alia on the date of entry, and may be long postponed: *Thomas v Lord Advocate* 1953 SC 151. On any view the right of use enjoyed by the holder of an unrecorded disposition is defeasible at the instance of a party holding a prior recorded writ. Typically when such a person does have the use of the property the date from which his enjoyment commences will be determined by paction. As Mr Campbell recognised, it is necessary to distinguish rights in re from rights dependent on obligation in these circumstances. In the present case, it appears for example that entry and actual occupation to the subjects were taken under the missives and could have had no source other than obligation from April 1989 at least until the delivery of the disposition. Further, I consider that Mr Hodge was correct in drawing attention to the passages in *Erskine* which show a clear recognition of the need to distinguish between real and personal rights. I refer in particular to Book III, i, 2:

G

H

> 'The essential difference may be perceived between rights that effect a subject itself, which are called real, and those which are founded in obligation, or, as they are generally styled, personal. A real right, or *jus in re*, whether of property or of an inferior kind – as servitude – entitles the person vested with it to possess the subject

as his own; or, if it be possessed by another, to demand it from the possessor, in
consequence of the right which he hath in the subject itself: whereas the creditor in
a personal right or obligation has only a *jus ad rem*, or a right of action against his
debtor or his representatives, by which they may be compelled to fulfil that
obligation, but without any right in the subject which the debtor is obliged to
transfer to him.'

It will be necessary to return to the expression '*jus ad rem*'. That apart, it appears that the
fundamental distinction lies between rights that arise directly from the relationship in
which a person stands to a subject, and rights which depend on relationships between
two or more persons affecting the subject. Even such a generalisation is open to question.
The totality of heritable rights in given subjects is not indivisible. There can clearly co-
exist rights of property in the same subjects amounting in the aggregate to *dominium
plenum* but shared in accordance with deeds, which, albeit feudalised, reflect the
agreement of parties. However, as a matter of general law, such rights become real only
when recorded. To return to the question of when heritage ceases to 'belong' to a person,
the question remains whether delivery of the disposition brings about that state. The bald
statement of the question in that way, which was the approach adopted by the second
defenders, tends to conceal a range of possible problems. As *Thomas v Lord Advocate*
demonstrated, a disposition may not carry a right of immediate entry to the subjects and
enjoyment of them. One can, on the reasoning in that case, regulate ownership
chronologically, as one may by a disposition in fee, reserving the disponer's liferent. A
pro indiviso disposition can create interests in a number of persons which in aggregate
exhaust the property rights in undivided subjects. A sub-feu would raise different issues.
The particular case is where a disposition is intended to convey the *dominium utile*, as
separate property, whether to the total exhaustion of the heritable rights of the disponer
or not, but so as to substitute the disponee for the disponer as owner of the subjects
defined in the disposition to the extent of the grant.

In my opinion the jurisdiction cases relied on by the second defenders do not assist in
resolving the issue in the present case. From the opinions of the Lord President and of
Lord Ardmillan in *Fraser v Fraser & Hibbert* (1870) 8 M 400 at pp. 404 and 405
respectively, it appears that the basis on which jurisdiction depends is beneficial
possession, whether natural or civil, of heritable estate in Scotland. The Lord President
draws attention particularly to the risks associated with the use of the term 'property' in
this context. In *Bowman v Wright* (1877) R 322 different language is used by the Lord
Justice-Clerk at p. 325, where he says that:

'the jurisdiction founded on the title to heritable property within the Kingdom
rests not on a fiction, but on a reality.'

At p. 328 Lord Gifford says:

'It appears to me that the principle on which jurisdiction is founded in respect of
heritable property rests not on merely nominal property, but on real and beneficial
interest in some heritable subject.'

Lord Hunter considered these authorities in *Caledonian Fish Selling Marine Stores Co
Ltd v Allard Hewson & Co Ltd* 1970 SLT 195. At p. 197 he said:

'The theory, which has been so accepted, appears to be that the defender should
have a beneficial right or interest in heritable property situated in Scotland, which
admits of being made available to a pursuer through the means of judgment in the
Scottish courts. The theory is, accordingly, that of effectiveness, but, as the
authorities demonstrate, it is upon technical rather than practical effectiveness that
the ground of jurisdiction depends . . .'

In my opinion nothing in *Embassy Picture House v Cammo Developments Ltd* 1971 SC
25 affects this issue. The position which emerges is that the developed law in the field of

A   jurisdiction has identified a particular character of interest in heritable property as fundamental to its use to found jurisdiction against a defender. It is impossible, logically, to develop a more general proposition on the basis of these authorities. While one might find support in them for parallel reasoning in another context, to use the observations as the basis of decision as to the requirements in such a context would involve *petitio principii*.

B   Much more substantial questions arise from the decision in *Gibson v Hunter Home Designs* 1976 SC 23 and related authorities in the series founded on by Mr Campbell for the second defenders. *Gibson* dealt with the problem which arises where a purchaser enjoys possession of subjects under missives but does not have the benefit of a delivered disposition. At p. 27 the Lord President said:

C   'Although I have every sympathy with the purchaser in the events which happened, I have not the slightest doubt that his first argument is without substance. In the law of Scotland no right of property vests in a purchaser until there has been delivered to him the relevant disposition. On delivery of the disposition the purchaser becomes vested in a personal right to the subjects in question and his acquisition of a real right to the subjects is dependent upon recording the disposition in the appropriate Register of Sasines. Putting the matter in another way the seller of subjects under missives is not, in a question with the purchaser, D   divested of any part of his right of property in the subjects of sale until, in implement of his contractual obligation to do so, he delivers to the purchaser the appropriate disposition. Until the moment of delivery the purchaser, even if he has paid the price and obtained occupation of the subjects, has no more than a right under the contract of sale, the missives, to demand performance by the seller of his contractual obligation to convey. Such right as the purchaser has, accordingly, is E   no more than a *jus crediti* until delivery of the disposition for which he contracted has been made to him . . .'

It is clearly implicit in that observation, albeit obiter, that on delivery of a disposition the grantor is divested of and the grantee is invested with a personal right to the subjects which is of the nature of a right of property. Lord Cameron's opinion was to a different effect, see pp. 29–30. Lord Johnston concurred with the Lord President. The Lord F   President's views reflect the approach adopted in *Thomas v Lord Advocate* by Lord Patrick. The context was special, and to some extent the decision may have been influenced by the concession made by the Inland Revenue as to the effect of delivery of a disposition. But none of the judges present would have expressed views on a matter of principle which were not their own. The Lord Justice-Clerk, at p. 158, spoke of the disposition as operating on delivery to confer the personal right to the lands, with postponed entry. It was 'property' which could be disposed of or used as a fund of credit. G   His opinion does not assist in this case, however, since his analysis would be consistent with 'property' in the sense he considered relevant also being held by the disponer. Lord Mackintosh dissented on the view that the disponer's continued enjoyment of the subjects over the material period excluded the disponee from beneficial possession. But he clearly considered that delivery of the disposition involved irrevocable parting with the disponer's whole rights in the lands. Lord Patrick at p. 161 made much more general H   comments. He said:

'It does not seem possible to contend that on delivery of such a disposition no property passes to the disponee. All the property the disponer had passes at once. Recording of the disposition in the Register of Sasines will only make real a right which was previously personal. As between disponer and disponee the transfer of all the former's interests is at once complete upon delivery of the disposition . . .'

Similar views were stated by Sheriff-substitute A G Walker in *James Grant & Co* 1948   A
SLT 8 at p. 9. In *Embassy Picture House* 1971 SC 25, Lord Justice-Clerk Grant said that
the right of the holder of a delivered but unrecorded disposition of heritage was 'clearly
a right of ownership'. It is clear that Lord President Emslie's dictum reflected an
established view of the effect of delivery of a disposition of heritage. It is also clear that
the context was Scots property law, in the formal sense. The case dealt with competing
claims defined in terms of real and personal rights.
                                                                                          B
Turning to the later cases, Lord Jauncey in *Lombardi's Trustee v Lombardi* 1982 SLT
81 treated the Lord President's observations in *Gibson* as trite:

> 'It is trite law that a disponer of subjects does not divest himself of any right of
> property in those subjects until he delivers actually or constructively to the
> disponee a disposition thereof.'

The citation of *Gibson* in *Life Association of Scotland* 1988 SCLR 172 does not add   C
weight to the discussion. However, in *Margrie* 1991 SLT 38 the Lord President adopted
and applied his predecessor's observations. His comment that: 'there was no divestiture
by Muirfield . . . until they delivered the disposition . . .', while in the context of VAT,
clearly reflected the application of general principle. It would be relatively easy to
distinguish these cases, or, by analysis of the precise circumstances to describe the wider
comments as obiter. In *Margrie*, the critical issue was whether Margrie has ever had a
major interest in land. The company never had anything but a right under contract.   D
There never was a disposition in its favour. In *Lombardi* the selection of the date of
delivery of the disposition was the most favourable position to adopt from the point of
view of the defender since it fixed the earliest point at which her husband's solvency could
be tested, and therefore improved her prospects of success. But the diversity of contexts
militates against any approach which is limited to piecemeal analysis and distinction.
There is a consistency of view which must be correct or in error notwithstanding the   E
authority of those expressing it.

It is necessary to define with some precision the issue which has to be resolved. There
is, in my opinion, no doubt that what the disponee has is 'property'. The contractual
rights of a purchaser under missives is 'property' whether or not he has received delivery
of a disposition of the subjects. The incorporeal moveable *jus crediti* has that character.
If such a person cannot obtain a disposition in implement of his rights under the contract,
he will normally have a right to damages in compensation for his loss, if any. If his debtor   F
is insolvent the damages realised may leave a balance which cannot be recovered. That,
however, is a function of the insolvency rather than a qualification of the right. Similarly,
the debtor on concluding missives subjects himself to obligations to the purchaser which
impose limitations on his conduct which the law will recognise and, in appropriate cases,
enforce. One of those obligations is to deliver a disposition conferring in the ordinary
case a marketable title on the disponee. On delivery of a disposition in terms of the   G
contract, that obligation of the seller is satisfied. The question is whether by that act the
disponer transfers in whole or in part his property rights in the subjects. The notion of a
partial transfer of property in the subjects appears to be fraught with difficulty. At best it
must consist in a combination of incidents which asserts the transfer of beneficial
ownership derived from, and wholly dependent on, the disposition, and divorced from
obligation founded on the contract, with retention of formal title pending recording of
the disposition. On Mr Campbell's primary argument it must be a real right in the   H
subjects. In some of the comments quoted it is characterised as a *jus ad rem*.

In *Edmond v Gordon* (1858) 3 McQ 116, Lord Cranworth, at p. 122, cast doubt on the
existence of any distinction between *jus ad rem* and *jus crediti*, and said:

> 'There may be this practical distinction, that the *jus ad rem* is a right which the
> person possessing it may make a complete right by his own act, or by some act

A   which he may compel another, without a suit, to perform; whereas a *jus crediti* may be defined to be a right which the holder of it cannot make available, if it is resisted, without a suit, to compel persons to do something else in order to make the right perfect.'

Lord Wensleydale at p. 130 characterised the right in question as 'nothing but a personal right' whatever its proper designation. In my opinion these observations suggest that the

B   *jus ad rem* and the *jus crediti* are personal rights. They do not support the view that a *jus ad rem* is a property right in the subjects to which it relates, or a real right. Attempts to analyse the rights of beneficiaries under trusts as some sort of intermediate right of property have been made but have given rise to serious criticism. McLaren on *Wills and Succession*, vol. 2, p. 832 at para. 1527 said:

C   'The distinction between the specific property or interest which forms the subject of conveyance in a deed of trust, and the beneficiary's right to that property or interest, is a very obvious one; and yet, from inattention to this distinction, the true nature of the beneficiary's right to the trust-estate has been either misunderstood, or imperfectly stated, by authorities in the jurisprudence of Scotland professing to deal with the question. The beneficiary interest has been defined as a *jus crediti* affecting the trustee; a definition which, if accurate at all, is only accurate when applied to the case of a beneficiary interest arising under an *ex facie* absolute

D   disposition, qualified by a separate declaration. The beneficiary interest under deeds of settlement, conveying the estate ostensibly for uses and purposes, may be more correctly defined as a personal right of property in the estate which is the subject of disposition. It is a right of property in the same sense that a ground-annual, real burden, or other right by reservation, or an estate standing upon a decree or minute of sale, is a right of property. For although the title to the estate stands in the person of the trustee, the interest of the beneficiary is by the terms of

E   the trust-deed protected, in so far as the nature of the property in each particular case admits of protection, against the acts of the trustee and the claims of his creditors.'

At para. 1531 he said:

F   'The beneficiary's right to estate conveyed under an *ex facie* absolute disposition is also a right of property, with this difference, that as his interest has not been made a burden upon the trustee's title, it is not a *jus in re* enforceable against onerous assignees of the trustee. It is, however, a personal right of property – *jus ad rem* – giving the beneficiary a preference in bankruptcy, and in questions with a judgers from the trustee.'

These views were not altered in *Dykes' Supplement* in 1934. However, they came under

G   critical review in *Inland Revenue v Clark's Trustees* 1939 SC 11: Lord President Normand at p. 22 and Lord Moncrieff at p. 26. *Clark's Trustees* militates against any notion of an intermediate class of property of this kind. Influenced by these authorities, *Wilson & Duncan* at p. 16 show a disinclination to use the term '*jus ad rem*' as supported by McLaren because of the confusion of thought which it involves. It is clear that in a number of situations beneficiaries under trusts do have a right to vindicate trust assets.

H   However, these situations arise generally where it is necessary in the light of some factor or circumstance external to the relationship between trustee and beneficiary to take steps for the protection or vindication of the beneficiaries' rights. Typically one has in mind circumstances in which the inmixing of trust property by a trustee in breach of trust entitles the beneficiary to trace the trust assets in the hands of third parties. The right depends, however, not on the assertion of a direct property interest but on the assertion that assets which ought properly to have been held separate and in trust have been diverted to some purpose incompatible with the trust. While the right of vindication is similar to that of an owner, the source of the right differs.

    In relation to heritable property Mr Campbell contended that one should follow *Gibson*, and that nothing in *Young v Leith* bore upon the question. He argued that that case was concerned only with the question whether General Gordon had a perfected feudal title. That, in his submission, was a different question from whether the grantor of a disposition was divested of property in the relevant sense. However, as already noted, the opinion of Lord Medwyn and Lord Ivory did seek to support an intermediate position in which the infeft disponee had a real right notwithstanding failure of due registration. Their opinion, at p. 958, identified the purpose to be served by the Act of 1617 as strictly limited, viz:

> 'That it shall not be pleadable against a third party having an onerous perfect right, acquired on the face of the records.'

At p. 959 it was said:

> 'Thus, then, according to the object and terms of the Act, while an unregistered seisin is not effectual against an onerous competing right, it is not declared null, but must be operative to all other effects, and is especially so against the superior and the granter of the right . . .'

On an analysis of the older authorities Lord Medwyn said:

> 'It has been said such decisions would not be repeated now. True, if we hold that an unregistered sasine is null; but if it be not null, and conveys a real right, these judgments are sound; and our predecessors knew as well as we, and they had more practice in such cases, what title is required to support such actions.'

It was clear that in view of the minority an intermediate position did exist in which a right of property was carried short of registration, but that the lack of registration militated against the effectiveness of that right in a question with a limited class of potential competitors. Lord Cuninghame, who returned an independent opinion, was broadly to the same effect as the other minority judges. The context of these observations was of course different from the present. However it is clear that a notion of a right of property in heritage, short of a registered or recorded right, was before the court and was the substance of the issue among the judges in Scotland. In these circumstances, in my opinion, there can be no doubt as to the force on the majority decision as expressed by Lord Fullerton as to the effect of registration, and, more particularly, as to the situation existing in the absence of registration as a necessary solemnity for divesting the grantor of a disposition in modern practice. In my opinion it follows that until recording, a disposition is not effective to divest the grantor and the subjects remain comprised in his property in circumstances such as the present. The alternative view necessarily implies a right of property in heritable subjects not only without infeftment, but while the grantor of the disposition remains infeft. In other words, it implies that the feudal fee in the undivided subjects has come to be shared between disponer and disponee on the delivery of the disposition. The disponer, having, ex hypothesi, entered with the superior, remains the feudal vassal, while already divested of the property. Any analysis of 'property' in heritable subjects in such terms appears to be inconsistent with principle and to be impossible to reconcile with the majority opinion in *Young v Leith*.

    It is with considerable hesitation that one differs from Lord President Emslie, and with the other eminent judges whose dicta on or relating to this topic have been referred to. None of them had the benefit of the citation of authority put before me, however. The case of *Young v Leith* was neither referred to nor discussed. In my view that decision, of a majority of the whole court, is binding as to the effect of the general law of property in Scotland, and leads to the view that, until recorded, a disposition is not effective to divest

A the grantor of the subjects. I take some comfort from the views of Lord Cameron in *Gibson* at pp. 24–30.

In my opinion, therefore, the subjects remained comprised in the property of Albyn, on ordinary principles of property law. I consider that this view is consistent with the 'race to the register' cases and in particular with *Mitchell v Ferguson*. That case illustrates the position in a competition between an uninfeft disponee and the creditors of the

B disponer who had adjudicated and completed their diligence by infeftment at the critical time. The disability of the disponer preventing him from alienating by voluntary act in fraud of the unrecorded disposition was relied upon. The adjudger's argument in the case prevailed. Critically it was:

> 'Such is the nature of feudal rights, that they cannot be affected, qualified, or burdened by any personal deed. Notwithstanding even a conveyance, if only
C > personal, the feudal rights still remain in the disponer.'

The other authorities in this series appear to me simply to add illustrations of the same principle. Together they imply, as Mr Hodge contended, in my opinion, that the race to register is consistent only with the view that registration alone divests the prior infeft owner and is effective to transfer property as a matter of general law. Many of the cases in this group involved competitions between the holders of grants from a common

D author. They were not all of that kind. The position of an adjudicating creditor who obtains priority over a disponee cannot be explained away on any such ground. Even in a case of competing dispositions, however, the cases appear to me to have importance. In such cases each of the dispositions is the grant of the common author, and the deduction of title on which the grant depends in setting up a valid title is, of necessity, the same. The writs which the grantor delivers are the same writs. It is the grantor's title which the disposition bears to transfer. It is impossible to accept Mr Campbell's

E submission that property is derived from the competitor who fails in the race. Mr Campbell was driven to that analysis by his contention that property passed with delivery of the disposition. Having so passed, the unrecorded disposition had to be a step in the acquisition of property by the winner of the race. I did not find that approach attractive. It appeared to give an effect to the unrecorded disposition, as a property writ derived from the disponer contributing to the rights of the winner of the race, which would be entirely at odds with its purport as a disposition in favour of the unsuccessful disponee

F who, in the circumstances, could have had no part in it, and in the typical case no knowledge of, the competing transaction. I prefer Mr Hodge's submission on this matter. The statutory preference in favour of the writ first recorded proceeds on the assumption that each writ in the race could instruct a feudal title to the subjects. It is, of course, tempting to see the race solely in terms of two competing dispositions of identical subjects, and to characterise the later disposition as fraudulent. But error may play at least as large

G a part in conveyancing conflicts as does fraud. At the resumed hearing, Mr Hodge founded on the observations of Lord President Cooper in *Carse v Coppen* as supporting his submissions on the 'race to the register' cases. In my view there is force in that submission. The Lord President emphasised the requirement for the transfer of real right to create an effective security. Lord Kinnear did the same in *Hutchison Main & Co.* It would be an unusual feature of our jurisprudence if the creation of an effective security right, a right subordinate to ownership, required the transfer of real right, whereas

H property in the subjects could be transferred by mere delivery of a disposition to the disponee which need never be made real by registration.

It remains to consider on this branch of the case whether the construction of the word 'property' derived from *Millar* alters the position. There is nothing remarkable in the adoption of definitions for particular purposes which involve the use of words or expressions in ways which differ from typical usage in a context such as property law. Mr

Hodge was critical of the concession made in *Thomas v Lord Advocate*, at p. 155, that a　　A
right of fee was passed on delivery of the disposition in question. But even if there were
such a concession, it would have been made in the context of the *Finance Act* 1894 which
defined property passing on a death primarily in terms of property of which the deceased
was competent to dispose. 'Property' was specially defined, and one might reasonably
take the view that discussion of its meaning in context would have little general
application. For the reasons already given, I consider that it is appropriate to rely on the
discussion in *Millar* so far as it is helpful. However, I am less than confident that there is　　B
much assistance to be obtained from the case in the present context. The elaboration of
the definition appears to add little or nothing of significance to one's understanding.
Rather it acknowledges synonyms for 'property' without finding in those synonyms, on
a proper analysis of their meaning, any features instructive of the characteristics of
'property' other than derive from the word itself. In *Millar* it was possible to say that the
subjects never 'belonged' to McKay in any sense. The context, as explained in *Hutchison*　　C
Main, was particular and facilitated that view. However, in the present context it is no
easier to answer the question 'when did the subject cease to belong to Albyn?' than the
question 'when did the subjects cease to be comprised in Albyn's property?'.

The case of *Thomas* undermines the equiparation of 'property' and beneficial
occupation, so far as it has general application outwith the context of the *Finance Act*
1894. Lord Patrick's comments at pp. 160–161 illustrate the position. The situation he　　D
envisaged involved a disposition in liferent and fee, duly recorded on behalf of A, the
liferenter, and B, the fiar. B's wish to dispose of his interest could be effected only by
delivery of a disposition with entry postponed until the death of A. That act, in Lord
Patrick's opinion, was sufficient to pass to the disponee B's whole interest in the lands.
But it was a right conceived in terms which excluded beneficial occupation during the
lifetime of A. Both A and B would have had to complete title by investiture in former
practice, and in current practice the same would be achieved by recording: *Stair*　　E
Encyclopaedia, vol. 18, para. 74. If B were a limited company, as might well be the case
in modern practice where institutions frequently purchase 'reversions', it could hardly be
contended that the right was not the company's property, despite the fact that there was
no present enjoyment of the subjects. Again one can readily envisage situations in which
an infeft proprietor of heritable subjects yields up possession in contemplation of a sale
subject to some suspensive condition. Enjoyment of the subjects under the contract would
not divest the proprietor. To define 'property' exclusively in terms of beneficial　　F
occupation and enjoyment would be inaccurate. Similarly, in my opinion, it would be
inaccurate to make beneficial occupation and enjoyment an essential element of the
definition of the word in the present context. It is not disputed that Albyn were the
owners of the subjects. The question is what was required to divest the company of
ownership in the relevant sense. They surrendered possession to Mr and Mrs Thomson
in terms of the missives. The disposition superseded the missives as the source of that　　G
possession, but did not alter the fact of enjoyment or its extent in any way. Delivery was
a stage in the transfer of property. In my opinion, following the analysis in *Young v Leith*,
the subjects remained, in substance, the property of Albyn until registration. By then
they were subject to the fixed security in favour of the floating charge holder.

If, notwithstanding the observations in *Heritable Reversionary Co v Millar*, it were
appropriate to have regard to the whole structure of the statutory provisions and to the　　H
mechanical provisions in particular, it appears to me that the view is strengthened that
there remains within the property of a limited company that which is liable to be affected
by securities in favour of third parties. It was not disputed between counsel that a
standard security granted by a company, and duly recorded, prior to the recording of the
disposition, would have been valid against the first defenders, even if granted after
delivery of the disposition and in derogation of the grant it contained, subject always to

A good faith on the part of the security holder. Accordingly, if vulnerability to a security writ were the test, the pursuers must succeed. And this would appear to fit the structure of the Act. Given the ranking provisions now found in the *Companies Act* 1985, one can readily envisage a situation in which a floating charge is granted, and subsequently a standard security is granted by the company over heritable subjects and that standard security is duly recorded. The ranking provisions in force might well postpone the standard security to the floating charge. Were the second defenders correct in their

B contentions, the standard security would have effect but the delivery of a disposition in favour of a purchaser in circumstances such as the present would render the floating charge ineffective as a security over the property. The result would be a conflict between the ranking of the respective security writs in terms of the statute and the writs themselves and the claim of the purchaser to take free of any obligation to the floating charge holder. The wider analysis of the statutory provisions tends further to support the view that

C subjects will be affected by the floating charge at crystallisation if they then could be affected by a standard security over them.

I turn now to Mr Davidson's argument that on delivery of the disposition there arose a constructive trust in favour of the disponee pending registration. It appears to me that the general position in Scots law is well expressed by Lord Shaw of Dunfermline in *Bank of Scotland v Liquidators of Hutchison Main & Co Ltd* 1914 SC (HL) 1 at p. 17, namely

D that there is a well-settled principle that a contractual obligation with regard to property, which has not effectually and actually brought about either a security upon it or a conveyance of it, is not per se the foundation of a trust or a declarator of trust. The hypothesis on which Mr Davidson proceeded, namely, that property had not been transferred to the first defenders but that the right remaining in Albyn had become impressed with a trust in favour of them appears to me directly to contradict this basic proposition. The authorities relating to transfer of shares appear to me to be readily

E distinguishable from the situation which arises for consideration in the present case. The matter can be illustrated by reference to *Stevenson v Wilson*. The vendor of the shares had, in common form, executed and delivered a transfer of the shares in question. He had received payment of the price. These steps had required litigation but had been effectively completed. The transfer was presented to the company. The company refused to register the transfer in favour of the transferee or to acknowledge him as a member or to pay him dividends accruing on the shares. The transferor, whose name remained on

F the register and who did not propose to annul the sale and return the price, declined to receive from the company the dividends accruing on the shares. It was held that there was a constructive trust in favour of the transferee in these circumstances. The overriding power of the company to refuse registration coupled with the transferor's insistence on maintaining the bargain readily distinguishes *Stevenson* and similar cases from the transfer of heritable property. There is no power in any third party to prevent registration

G of the disposition. In the opinion of the Lord President the importance of the company's articles is emphasised. The ratio of the decision was that where the transferor insisted on the bargain, and refused to annul it, standing the unwillingness of the company to register the transfer, the transferor was a 'quasi trustee' for the transferee. The combination of factors peculiar to the situation was clearly fundamental to the decision arrived at. In *Lyle & Scott v Scott's Trustees* 1959 SC 64 Viscount Simonds, at p. 73, expressed the

H matter more widely. He said that where the vendors having entered into an agreement for the sale of the shares had received and retained the price it followed that, whether or not they had yet done all that they ought as vendors to do, they held the shares as trustees for the purchaser. Neither Lord Keith of Avonholm nor Lord Reid found it necessary to express such a view and, in supporting the decision in *Stevenson v Wilson* avoided any more general expression that would support the notion of trust arising as an incident of an uncompleted transaction of sale. There is an obvious difficulty in applying uncritically

any rule of English law in this context. It appears to me that the discussion in Russell J's   **A**
opinion in *Musselwhite* [1962] Ch 964 at pp. 984–987 particularly, discloses the general
basis of the rule in England in a way which makes English authority an inappropriate
foundation for views in a Scottish context. In my view *Stevenson v Wilson* applies only in
the context to which it related, namely the transfer of shares in limited companies where
directors possess and exercise powers to refuse registration of transfers. There are, in any
event, in my opinion, a number of difficulties associated with the view that a trust of
heritable property arises on delivery of the disposition. The purpose of the disposition is   **B**
directly contradictory of the fundamental basis of trust namely that the infeft proprietor
should hold for a third party. The delivery of the disposition is designed to put the
disponee in a position to effect, by recording or registration, the total divestiture of the
disponer and not in any way to qualify his infeftment with any right in favour of a third
party. At the resumed hearing, Mr Davidson acknowledged that the decision in
Hutchison Main & Co affected the expression of his argument. He contended, however,   **C**
that it left the substance of the argument unaffected, and, in particular, made no impact
of his submission that the delivery of a disposition gave rise to a new situation in which
it was appropriate to imply a constructive trust for the disponee. For the reasons already
set out, I cannot accept that submission. Mr Davidson attempted to support his argument
by reference to the observations of the Lord President in *Gibson v Hunter Home Designs
Ltd* 1976 SC 23. However in my opinion those observations are destructive of the notion
that a trust arises in the context of the sale of heritage and provided no support for him   **D**
whatsoever. In my opinion the observations of Lord Cameron at p. 31 reflect the correct
position in Scots law. Mr Davidson, in my opinion, was correct to this extent, that it
cannot be the sole measure of the existence of a constructive trust to consider whether
the requirements of an express trust had been satisfied. His difficulty, however, was that
he was unable to find any content for his proposition that a constructive trust arose. In
my opinion Lord Cameron's observations are wider than the construction put on them   **E**
by Mr Davidson in any event. His Lordship was concerned with the question whether a
trust had arisen. His exclusion of that notion appears to me to be equally applicable in
the present context. In my opinion the alternative argument fails.

In the whole circumstances I shall repel the pleas-in-law for the defenders respectively,
sustain the pursuers' fourth plea-in-law and grant decree *de plano* in terms of the first
three conclusions of the summons.

  F

(Order accordingly)

  G

  H

A
Re a Company No. 0032314 of 1992.
Duckwari plc v Offerventure Ltd.
Chancery Division and Court of Appeal.
Robert Reid QC (sitting as a deputy judge); Neill, Beldam and Millett L JJ.
Judgment delivered 8 February 1993 and 7 July 1994.

B
Substantial property transactions involving directors – Company took over benefit
of contract for sale of property to connected person – Whether transaction
involved acquisition of asset by company – Whether asset was non-cash asset
exceeding requisite value – Companies Act 1985, s. 320, 322.

This was an appeal with the leave of the judge from an order of Mr Robert Reid QC
sitting as a deputy judge of the Chancery Division dismissing an appeal from an order of the
C
registrar which declared that a transaction between two associated companies was voidable
under s. 322 of the Companies Act 1985.

The appellants were 'C' and a company, 'Offerventure', of which C was a director and
shareholder. In 1989 Offerventure agreed to buy a freehold property for £495,000 and paid
a deposit of £49,500 to stakeholders. On completion the property was conveyed to another
company, 'Duckwari', of which C was a director. Duckwari paid the balance of the purchase
D
price and reimbursed Offerventure for the deposit.

Duckwari wished to avoid the transaction because the property had subsequently fallen in
value. The transaction which was said to contravene s. 320 of the 1985 Act was the
acquisition by Duckwari from Offerventure of the benefit of the contract to purchase the
property. It was accepted that Offerventure was connected with C for the purposes of
s. 320(1)(b).

E
The judge found that there was a transfer to Duckwari of the benefit of Offerventure's
interest under the purchase contract, and that the value of the asset acquired was at least
£49,500, the value of the deposit subsequently reimbursed. On the basis that the requisite
value for the purpose of s. 320 was £44,399 (ten per cent of the company's asset value shown
in the last accounts), the arrangement was one whereby the company acquired non-cash
assets of the requisite value and the registrar's decision was upheld.

F
On appeal, Offerventure and C argued that the transaction did not involve the acquisition
of an asset by Duckwari from Offerventure, but a novation of the purchase contract; and
that the judge was wrong to find that the asset was a non-cash asset and that its value was
£49,500.

Held, dismissing the appeal:

G
1. It would be arguable that Duckwari had acquired an asset from Offerventure even if
the transaction was carried out by novation. The court would assume, however, without
deciding, that the appellants would be entitled to succeed if the arrangements were carried
out by means of a novation.

2. The judge's decision that there was no novation was correct. It was in the highest
degree implausible that any novation took place and there was abundant evidence of a
H
bilateral agreement between Offerventure and Duckwari to let Duckwari take over
Offerventure's rights and liabilities.

3. The asset which Duckwari acquired was a single asset which could be described with
equal accuracy either as the benefit of the purchase contract or (what came to the same
thing) Offerventure's beneficial interest in the property. They were both non-cash assets,
within the meaning of s. 739 of the 1985 Act, worth at least £49,500.

The following cases were referred to in the judgments: A

Niltan Carson Ltd v Hawthorne (1987) 3 BCC 454.

Rasbora Ltd v JCL Marine Ltd [1977] 1 Ll Rep 645.

Edward Bannister QC (in the High Court) and Philip Hoser (instructed by Vizards) for the appellants.

David Neuberger QC (in the Court of Appeal) and Kenneth Craig and Peter Kirby (instructed by Robin Myddleton & Co, Hertford) for Duckwari.   B

HIGH COURT JUDGMENT
(Delivered 8 February 1993)

Robert Reid QC: This is an appeal from an order of Mr Registrar Scott made on 22 July 1992 by which it was declared that the acquisition by the applicant, Duckwari, from Offerventure Ltd of a contract dated 6 April 1989, between J A Bennett and another of the one part, and Offerventure Ltd of the other part, 'for the purchase of freehold   C
property known as 12 Corporation Street, High Wycombe, Bucks, is voidable under s. 322 of the *Companies Act* 1985 unless one or more of the conditions specified in s. 322(2) is satisfied'. That was a quotation for the form of the order. The order went on to make various directions for enquiries as to damages.

The facts so far as they are revealed by the evidence are simple. Mr Cooper, the second respondent, was a director of Duckwari from 4 August 1988 until sometime in 1990. He   D
was also a director of Offerventure. The shares in Offerventure were all owned by Mr Cooper and his wife and it is accepted as a result that Mr Cooper is connected with Offerventure for the purposes of s. 320 of the 1985 Act.

By a contract dated 6 April 1989 Offerventure contracted to buy 12 Corporation Street for £495,000. The contract provided for a deposit of £49,500 which Offerventure duly paid to stakeholders. Completion was fixed for 31 October 1989.
                                                                         E
On 24 August 1989, Mr Cooper on behalf of Offerventure wrote to Mr O'Neil, then a director of Duckwari, a letter the material parts of which read as follows:

'Following our recent conversation I confirm that the company has recently exchanged contracts to purchase the freehold interest in respect of the above property for £495,000. Completion is set for 31 October. I am happy to pass the property on to Duckwari at cost and have a profit sharing arrangement which I   F
will be prepared to take in shares. I shall let you have some figures very shortly. In the meantime perhaps you would like to take a look at the location and if you are happy to proceed we can get something moving between the lawyers as quickly as possible.'

Duckwari accepted that suggestion. So far as appears from the evidence before me, the acceptance was not recorded in any writing, nor was the arrangement formalised by any further documentation.   G

On or before about 30 October 1989, the board of Duckwari, at a meeting attended by Mr Cooper, resolved to borrow £350,000 from Commercial Bank Cheshire Ltd, now known as Commercial Bank Trust plc ('CBT'), to enable it to complete the contract. Duckwari completed the contract on 9 November 1989 and in accordance with the arrangement Duckwari then reimbursed Offerventure with the deposit which Offerventure had paid.   H

Subsequently, CBT became dissatisfied with Duckwari's performance and procured that its nominees took control of the board.

Duckwari's accounts for the year ended 31 December 1987, were laid before the company in general meeting on 26 September 1988. They showed net assets of £443,999. The accounts for year ended 31 December 1988, which showed net assets of £364,981, were laid before the company in general meeting on 29 September 1989.

A   The one point of issue on the evidence is the value of the property at the time of the contract. Mr Middleton, who is now a director of Duckwari, has deposed that Duckwari has been advised that the property was never worth the amount paid for it. Mr Cooper deposed to his view that the property was worth £500,000–525,000 in the autumn of 1989 and produces a valuation of £500,000 dated 19 September 1989 which was produced initially for Offerventure and subsequently supplied to, and accepted by, both Duckwari and also CBT. Mr Cooper further produced a valuation made in March 1992, valuing

B the property at £525,000 in October 1989.

In my view, there is no evidence to suggest that £495,000 was an excessive price at the date of either contract or completion.

Section 320(1) and 320(2), before amendments to financial limits which were made by SI 1990/1393 which came into effect on 31 July 1990, provided as follows:

C   '(1) With the exceptions provided by the section next following, a company shall not enter into an arrangement–

        (a) whereby a director of the company or its holding company, or a person connected with such a director, acquires or is to acquire one or more non-cash assets of the requisite value from the company; or

        (b) whereby the company acquires or is to acquire one or more non-cash assets

D   of the requisite value from such a director or the person so connected,

      unless the arrangement is first approved by a resolution of the company in general meeting and, if the director or connected person is a director of its holding company or a person connected with such a director, by a resolution in general meeting of the holding company.

      (2) For this purpose a non-cash asset is of the requisite value if at the time the

E   arrangement in question is entered into its value is not less than £1,000 [now £2,000] but (subject to that) exceeds £50,000 [now £100,000] or ten per cent of the company's asset value, that is–

        (a) except in a case falling within paragraph (b) below, the value of the company's net assets determined by reference to the accounts prepared and laid under Part VII in respect of the last preceding financial year in respect of which such accounts were so laid; and

F   (b) where no accounts have been so prepared and laid before that time, the amount of the company's called-up share capital.'

Section 322(1) is in these terms:

      'An arrangement entered into by a company in contravention of section 320, and any transaction entered into in pursuance of the arrangement (whether by the

G   company or any other person) is voidable at the instance of the company unless one or more of the conditions specified in the next subsection is satisfied.'

It is common ground that the onus is on the applicant to show that the transaction in question exceeded the financial limits of s. 320. In support of that proposition I was referred to *Niltan Carson Ltd v Hawthorne* (1987) 3 BCC 454 at p. 472. It is also common ground that the effect of s. 320 is that subject to the threshold figure of £1,000, a transaction was within s. 320 if the value exceeded £50,000 or ten per cent of the

H company's net asset value, whichever was the less. Since the arrangement in this case was made in August 1989, it would, in my judgment, fall within the section only if the value of the non-cash asset required exceeded ten per cent of the figure shown in the 1987 accounts which were then the most recent laid before the company in general meeting.

I should say that I did not hear argument on this point, because although Mr Craig did not accept that this view was correct, and would have sought to rely on the 1988 accounts, he took the view it did not matter, in the circumstances of this case, which of those accounts one looked at.

Duckwari's originating summons appeared to put its case on the basis that Duckwari's purchase of the property is voidable, but throughout the case has been argued on the basis that the relevant transaction was the acquisition of the benefit of the contract for purchase of the property by Duckwari from Offerventure.

Before me it was contended on behalf of Offerventure and Mr Cooper, first, that Duckwari did not acquire any non-cash assets from Offerventure and, second, if it did, the non-cash assets acquired did not have the requisite value.

The first argument was based upon the proposition that there was no transfer of the benefit of Offerventure's interest under its contract to Duckwari, but a novation whereby the original contract between the vendors and Offerventure was determined and the vendors and Duckwari then entered into a new contract. Thus it was argued that there was no acquisition of anything by Duckwari from a director or a person connected with a director. In support of this argument, it was pointed out that there was no evidence of any assignment in writing and in the absence of an assignment there was no explanation for the willingness of the vendors to convey into the name of Duckwari. Reliance was further placed on a letter written to Mr Cooper dated 9 November 1989, i.e. the date of completion, by the solicitors acting for Duckwari on the conveyance. It is submitted that the letter makes it clear that Offerventure had completely dropped out at some date before completion and the letter was informing Offerventure that the replacement contract, to which Offerventure was not a party, had been completed. In my judgment the letter does no such thing. It is in these terms:

'Brian Cooper Esq. Brian Cooper & Company.'

–then the address is given–

'Dear Mr Cooper,

Warnerdeal Ltd, 12 Corporation Street, High Wycombe

I refer to my telephone conversation with your secretary today and confirm the transfer of the above premises to Duckwari plc has been completed as at today's date together with the mortgage in favour of Commercial Bank Cheshire Ltd. I understand that the keys to the premises may be collected from No. 21 High Street, High Wycombe, if you do not already have these. As agreed the sum of £49,500 in respect of the deposit paid on exchange of contracts is due back to Offerventure Ltd and I have arranged for this sum to be telegraphically transferred to the account of Offerventure Ltd, Barclays Bank, 6 Monk Street, London W1.

Finally you may recall that it was a term of the contract that interest on the deposit from 30 September 1989 until completion was to accrue to the purchaser and I understand from the vendor's solicitors that the sum due is £673.84p calculated as follows . . .'

The calculation follows.

'I presume this sum when received should be paid to Offerventure Ltd but would you please confirm. In the meantime I confirm I shall now deal with the stamping and registration formalities.

Yours sincerely . . .'

–then a signature, and underneath that:

'C S O'Neil Esq, Duckwari plc.'

It will be noted it is addressed to Mr Cooper, a director of both Offerventure and Duckwari, at his business address. It has the unexplained heading 'Warnerdeal Ltd'. It

A asks for confirmation that interest due on the deposit be paid to Offerventure. It also makes reference to the collection of the keys. These matters, and the last sentence, are consistent only with the letter being sent to Mr Cooper in his capacity of director of Duckwari. The fact that a copy was also sent to S O'Neil Esq, Duckwari plc, is no indication to the contrary.

B There is, in my judgment, simply no evidence of any tripartite agreement releasing Offerventure and creating a new contract with Duckwari. Significantly, Mr Cooper gave evidence on affidavit and made no suggestion that anything of the sort had happened. In my judgment, this was simply a case where the vendors were prepared to convey into the name of the person other than the contractual purchaser, namely Duckwari, whether or not they were contractually bound to do so. As to this there might be some argument in view of the terms of cl. 7 of the contract which is in these terms:

C 'The vendor shall not be required to transfer the property to any person other than the purchaser provided the purchaser may require the vendors to transfer the property to a company associated with the purchaser at the same price payable hereunder.'

I should add that in these circumstances, I gain no assistance from *Rasbora Ltd v JCL Marine Ltd* [1977] 1 Ll Rep 645, which was cited to me.

D The second submission, that the value of the non-cash assets acquired from Offerventure was not of the requisite amount, is based upon the premise that the value of the property did not exceed £525,000 at the date of the arrangement. It is said that in those circumstances, the value of the contract, which was the non-cash asset acquired, did not exceed £30,000, so it was less than the necessary figure of £44,399.

E The taking over and later reimbursement of the deposit is characterised as being merely a matter of convenience, a banking transaction to save a series of cheques being written. It is further said that the taking of the benefit of the deposit and the reimbursement of it, could not be regarded as a separate transaction and that even if it could the taking of the benefit of the deposit could not be regarded as the acquisition of a non-cash asset. Reference was made to the definition of non-cash asset at s. 739(1). That definition is:

'In this Act "non-cash asset" means any property or interest in property other than cash; and for this purpose "cash" includes foreign currency.'

F In response to these arguments the first suggestion on behalf of Duckwari was that the value of the assets transferred was £495,000. It was submitted that what was acquired was Offerventure's equitable interest in the land which had arisen on the making of the contract and which was worth £495,000. The difficulty with this submission is that on contract an unpaid vendor's lien arose, so the equitable interest was charged with payment of the purchase price. I reject the submission that in some way which was never made clear the equitable interest was acquired by Duckwari free of the unpaid vendor's G lien.

The second submission was that under the arrangement Duckwari acquired the benefit of the contract and what had been done under it, namely, the payment of the deposit to the stakeholder. Thus, it was submitted, the value of the asset acquired was at least £49,500, being the value of the deposit which subsequently reimbursed. The fact that the deposit paid by Offerventure was released to the vendors on completion as part of H the purchase price, and that an equivalent sum was then reimbursed to Offerventure, was an indication of that value.

In my judgment this submission is correct. It does not matter that there was no assignment in writing or that the arrangement might not have been enforceable at law, nor is the contrary contended on behalf of the appellants. The reimbursement of the £49,500 deposit was an integral part of the transaction. It would not be correct to regard

the arrangement about the deposit as being a separate transaction, nor can it be regarded   A
as being an administrative matter outside the arrangement. The deposit stood as part of
the purchase price and as a result of the arrangement, Duckwari gained the benefit of it
on completion. It is true that if Duckwari had failed to complete the deposit might have
been forfeit, but that does not diminish its value. Offerventure's money remained as a
deposit and was used as part of the purchase price paid on completion. Thereafter
Offerventure was reimbursed.

      In my judgment, the acquisition of the benefit of the deposit was part of a single   B
transaction by which Duckwari acquired the benefit of the contract in its then state, i.e.
with a deposit having been paid to stakeholders and the value of the non-cash assets
acquired under that arrangement can best be judged by the amount of the reimbursement.
It follows that the arrangement made was one whereby the company acquired non-cash
assets of the requisite value and the registrar's decision was correct.

      I therefore dismiss the appeal.   C

(Appeal dismissed)

COURT OF APPEAL JUDGMENT
(Delivered 7 July 1994)

Millett LJ: This is an appeal with the leave of the judge from an order of Mr Robert   D
Reid QC sitting as a deputy judge of the Chancery Division made on 8 February 1993
dismissing an appeal from an order of Mr Registrar Scott dated 22 July 1992 by which it
was declared that a transaction between two associated companies was voidable under
s. 322(1) of the *Companies Act* 1985 (acquisition of non-cash assets from connected
persons) unless one or more of the conditions specified in s. 322(2) was satisfied.

      The facts can be shortly stated. On 6 April 1989 the appellant company,   E
Offerventure Ltd, entered into a contract to purchase a freehold property, No. 12
Corporation Street, High Wycombe, Buckinghamshire, for £495,000 and paid a ten per
cent deposit amounting to £49,500 to stakeholders. Completion was fixed for 31 October
1989. The shares in Offerventure were all owned by Mr Cooper, the individual appellant,
and his wife, and it is accepted that Offerventure was a person connected with Mr Cooper
for the purpose of the relevant statutory provision.

      Mr Cooper was also a director of the respondent company, Duckwari. On 24 August   F
1989 Mr Cooper wrote to Mr O'Neil, a fellow director of Duckwari, and offered to pass
the property on to Duckwari at cost. Duckwari decided to take up Offerventure's offer,
though its acceptance was not recorded in writing, and it is clear that the arrangement
was never approved by Duckwari in general meeting. By the end of October 1989,
Duckwari had made the necessary arrangements to finance the purchase with money
borrowed from a bank, and a board meeting was held on 13 October 1989 at which the
borrowing of the money and the granting of the necessary security to the bank were   G
formally agreed.

      The solicitors handling the purchase of the property were Nabarro Nathanson, who
took their instructions from Mr Cooper throughout. The purchase of the property was
completed on 9 November 1989, when the property was conveyed into the name of
Duckwari which paid £495,000 to Nabarro Nathanson. Nabarro Nathanson in turn paid
the balance due under the contract (£445,500) to the vendor and reimbursed the sum of   H
£49,500 to Offerventure.

      The transaction is described by Mr Cooper in para. 3 of his affidavit sworn in these
proceedings in which he says:

      'It is also true that in late August I offered to let Duckwari take over from
      Offerventure the contract for the purchase of the property and that Duckwari

A   decided to accept that offer, it paying the £495,000 purchase price rather than
     Offerventure (by paying £445,500 to the vendors and reimbursing Offerventure the
     amount of the deposit it had already paid).'

     Duckwari alleges that the value of the property is now substantially less than £495,000.
     The bank has caused directors of its own choice to be appointed to the board of Duckwari
     and has procured all the other directors to resign. Duckwari then commenced the present

B   proceedings for relief under the *Companies Act* 1985 consequential upon the
     arrangements I have described not having been approved by the members of Duckwari
     in general meeting.

     Section 320 of the *Companies Act* 1985, which is headed 'Substantial property
     transactions involving directors etc.' provides, so far as material:

         '(1) With the exceptions provided by the section next following, a company shall
C   not enter into an arrangement–

             . . .

             (b) whereby the company acquires or is to acquire one or more non-cash assets
                  of the requisite value from such a director or the person so connected,

             unless the arrangement is first approved by a resolution of the company in general
             meeting . . .'

D   Subsection (2) defines 'the requisite value' of the non-cash asset; I need not read it because
     the figure has been agreed for the purpose of this litigation.

     Section 322 sets out the liabilities which may arise from contravention of s. 320. Section
     322(1) provides that:

         'An arrangement entered into by a company in contravention of section 320, and
         any transaction entered into in pursuance of the arrangement (whether by the
E   company or any other person) is voidable at the instance of the company unless
         one or more of the conditions specified in the next subsection is satisfied.'

     Subsection (2) sets out a number of conditions. Subsection (3) provides:

         'If an arrangement is entered into with a company by a director of the company
         . . . or a person connected with him in contravention of section 320, that director
         and the person so connected, and any other director of the company who
F   authorised the arrangement or any transaction entered into in pursuance of such
         an arrangement, is liable–

             (a) to account to the company for any gain which he has made directly or
                  indirectly by the arrangement or transaction, and

             (b) (jointly and severally with any other person liable under this subsection) to
                  indemnify the company for any loss or damage resulting from the
G   arrangement or transaction.'

     The deputy judge found that there was no evidence that the price paid for the property
     (£495,000) was an excessive price. On the evidence before him, it may have been worth
     rather more; it was certainly not worth less. He also found that 'the requisite value' for
     the purpose of s. 320(1) was a minimum value of £44,399. There is no appeal from either
     of those findings.

H   Three issues have been argued before us on this appeal:

     (1)   Was the deputy judge right in characterising the transaction as the acquisition of
           an asset by Duckwari from Offerventure?

     (2)   If so, was he right in characterising it as a non-cash asset?

     (3)   If so, was he right in finding that its value was £49,500?

Characterising the transaction   A

The contract for the purchase of the property was entered into by Offerventure. It was completed by Duckwari. In layman's terms, Duckwari 'took over' the contract. The question is: how was this achieved? The appellants submit that it can only have been achieved in one of two ways:

(1)   there might have been a novation of the contract in favour of Duckwari, by which the vendor agreed to the substitution of Duckwari for Offerventure as the   B contracting purchaser;

(2)   there might have been an assignment of the benefit of the contract by Offerventure to Duckwari, with Offerventure remaining contractually liable to the vendors.

If it is equally possible that what took place was a novation or an assignment then, the appellants submit, Duckwari's claim must fail; the onus is on Duckwari to establish on a balance of probabilities that there was an arrangement under which a non-cash asset of   C a requisite value was acquired from a connected person. If it was a case of novation, it is submitted, no asset at all was acquired from Offerventure. The asset was acquired from the vendor, who was not a connected party. Novation operates to discharge the old contract and substitute the new, and not as an assignment of rights and obligations under the old contract. That undoubtedly is the case. But whether or not a novation would involve the acquisition of an asset by Duckwari from Offerventure depends upon the true construction of the relevant provisions of the *Companies Act* 1985, and in particular,   D upon the effect of s. 739(2) which provides:

'A reference to the transfer or acquisition of a non-cash asset includes the creation or extinction of an estate or interest in, or a right over, any property, and also the discharge of any person's liability, other than a liability for a liquidated sum.'

Since Offerventure's consent to a novation would be required, it is arguable that   E Duckwari acquired an asset from Offerventure even if the transaction was carried out by novation. I will assume, however, for the purpose of these proceedings, without deciding, that the appellants would be entitled to succeed if the arrangements were carried out by means of a novation.

The deputy judge found that there was no novation. There was no evidence of any tripartite arrangement involving Duckwari, Offerventure and the vendor. There was no evidence of any new contract for sale by the vendor to Duckwari. He concluded that the   F only agreement was that between Offerventure and Duckwari by which Offerventure agreed to let Duckwari take over the benefit of the contract. In the absence of any evidence that a formal assignment by the vendor had ever been executed, he inferred that the agreement between the two companies had been carried into effect by Offerventure simply directing the vendor to convey the property to the name of Duckwari, a direction with which the vendor was evidently willing to comply, whether strictly obliged to do so   G or not.

This finding of the deputy judge has been criticised by the appellants who argue that novation is the more likely characterisation of what happened. They rely on a number of features of the case. They say that the absence of any writing such as is usual in the case of an assignment points in favour of a novation.

There is no evidence that there was any formal assignment of Offerventure's rights to   H Duckwari, and the judge did not find that there was. But it is clear that Offerventure agreed to allow Duckwari to take over its right to complete the purchase *and did so*. Offerventure could have performed its part of that agreement by procuring a novation, by formal assignment, or merely by directing the vendor to convey directly to Duckwari. The judge inferred that the last was the method employed. If that is what happened, then Duckwari acquired from Offerventure, without a formal assignment, the very same right

A to complete the purchase that it would have acquired by a formal assignment. In short, the presence or absence of a formal written assignment is neither here nor there; it is sufficient that there was no novation.

Next, it is submitted that the apparent lack of any further involvement by Offerventure once it had been agreed that Duckwari should take over the deal points to novation rather than assignment, but in my judgment this merely reflects the commercial reality of
B the situation that Duckwari had taken over the deal.

Then reliance is placed upon the fact that interest earned on the deposit appears to have been repaid to Offerventure. It is said that this clearly shows that Duckwari was not acquiring the benefit of the deposit which Offerventure had paid, for had it done so Duckwari rather than Offerventure would have been entitled to the interest.

C Reliance for this purpose is placed upon a letter from Nabarro Nathanson written on the day of completion to Mr Cooper, as the judge found, in his capacity as a director of Duckwari, in which Nabarro Nathanson confirmed the transfer of the property to Duckwari and that the matter had been completed, and stated that a sum of £600 odd had been repaid by the vendor as interest on the deposit, and stated:

> 'I presume this sum when received should be paid to Offerventure Ltd but would you please confirm . . .'

D In my judgment this is at best neutral, and at worst tells against the appellants. Duckwari had as it were enjoyed the benefit of the deposit which Offerventure had paid since the date (which is unknown) when it agreed to take over the purchase, but did not account to Offerventure for the amount of the deposit until completion. It was, of course, a matter for agreement between the two companies whether and if so for what period Duckwari should pay interest to Offerventure for the notional use it had made of the
E deposit, and it is entirely possible that they overlooked the need to agree this. But if Offerventure had approached the vendor with a request for novation of the contract, it seems to me that it would almost certainly have done so through Nabarro Nathanson. Any novation agreement would have had to provide for what was to happen to the deposit already paid and interest thereon. The fact that Nabarro Nathanson had to ask Mr Cooper which of the two companies was entitled to interest, instead of advising him of the position, points against the existence of any formal novation.

F The appellants also sought to rely upon the phraseology used in the letter of 24 August 1989 and of Duckwari's board minutes, which, in my view, are neutral, and on the affidavit evidence, which being sworn by laymen is not necessarily accurate in the use of language, and is of little or no assistance.

The appellants referred to the decision of Lawton J in *Rasbora v JCL Marine* [1977] 1 Ll Rep 645 which Lawton J described as 'the clearest possible case of a true novation'. In
G that case, Mr Atkinson had commissioned the defendants to build him a boat. Shortly after the contract had been entered into, and to avoid VAT, he told the defendants that he would form a Jersey company which would be substituted as the buyer. The defendants agreed. Mr Atkinson subsequently acquired the plaintiff company, and the defendants accepted it as the buyer, and prepared the necessary documentation for presentation to Customs and Excise showing the plaintiff company to be the buyer and claiming exemption from VAT. Lawton J, as I have said, held that this was the clearest
H possible case of a true novation. I respectfully agree. Nothing could be further from the facts of the present case, where there is not a shred of evidence that the vendor ever accepted Duckwari as the contracting purchaser in place of Offerventure. All the vendor can be shown to have done is to have complied with a request to convey the property to Duckwari. Since he would not have done this unless requested to do so by Offerventure, it may readily be inferred that such a request was made and acceded to. But that is not

novation. Novation requires a substitution of the obligor, not of the party who takes the   A
benefit of the contract.

The appellants' main submission was that the judge should not have attempted to
decide whether assignment or novation was the more likely; he should have concluded
that the precise manner in which Duckwari had acquired the property was in doubt; and
that accordingly Duckwari had not discharged the burden of proof of establishing that it
had acquired a non-cash asset from Offerventure as distinct from acquiring such an asset   B
by novation from the vendor.

I disagree. It is in my view in the highest degree implausible that any novation at all
took place. In the first place, as I have already pointed out, any approach to the vendor
to agree to be party to a novation would almost certainly have been made through
Nabarro Nathanson, and would have resulted in some relevant documentation coming
into existence. In the second place, it would have been known to Offerventure, which   C
would have been a necessary party in order to obtain its release from the obligation to
pay the purchase price due on completion, so that the absence of any evidence of novation
from that source is striking. Thirdly, novation would have been pointless. There was no
useful purpose to be served by it. There was no reason for Offerventure to request it,
seeing that it must have been aware through Mr Cooper that Duckwari, an associated
company, would be in a position to complete the transaction; and there was no good
reason at all for the vendor to agree to the substitution of one associated company for   D
another.

In my judgment, what is known about the transaction is that the vendor contracted to
sell and convey to Offerventure; that in fact he conveyed to Duckwari; that he did so at
Nabarro Nathanson's request, acting on Mr Cooper's instructions; and that Mr Cooper
gave those instructions because he had agreed on behalf of Offerventure to allow
Duckwari to complete the purchase instead of Offerventure.   E

There is, therefore, abundant evidence of a *bilateral* agreement between Offerventure
and Duckwari to let Duckwari take over Offerventure's rights and liabilities; it is self-
evident that the vendor agreed to allow Duckwari to take the conveyance, that is to say,
to take the benefit of the contract; and there is not a shred of evidence of any tripartite
arrangement whereby the vendor agreed to substitute Duckwari for Offerventure as the
obligor under the contract.

In my judgment, the deputy judge was plainly right to reject the suggestion that there   F
was a novation which was entirely speculative and unfounded by any evidence of any
kind.

The identification of the asset which was acquired

The second and third questions can be taken together because they both depend on the   G
identification of the asset which Duckwari acquired from Offerventure by virtue of its
agreement to take over the contract of purchase. In my judgment, the asset which
Duckwari acquired was a single asset which can be described in either of two ways with
equal accuracy. It can be described as the benefit of the purchase contract or (what comes
to the same thing) Offerventure's beneficial interest in the property. They are both non-
cash assets – this term being defined by s. 739(1) of the *Companies Act* 1985 as 'any
property or interest in property other than cash'.   H

The benefit of the purchase contract was Offerventure's right to call for a conveyance
of the legal estate in the property free from incumbrances on payment of the balance of
the purchase price of £445,500. On the footing that the property was worth at least
£495,000, that right was worth at least £49,500. Offerventure's beneficial interest in the
property was worth the same since, until payment of the balance of the purchase price,

A its beneficial interest was subject to the unpaid vendor's lien for the balance. This is what the deputy judge found, and in my judgment he was plainly correct in doing so.

The appellants submit that what Duckwari acquired from Offerventure was the benefit of the purchase contract subject to the obligation of paying £495,000 on completion. Duckwari, it is submitted, should have paid the vendor £495,000 and Offerventure should have recovered the amount of the deposit which it had paid from the stakeholder. If (as

B appears to have happened) Offerventure paid only £445,500 to the vendor, the deposit being released to him, and paid a further £49,500 to Offerventure, that was only machinery and cannot affect the correct analysis of the transaction. If this analysis is correct, then Duckwari acquired a non-cash asset from Offerventure, but its value was nil.

I agree that the precise machinery employed on completion does not affect the correct
C analysis of the asset which was acquired from Offerventure, but I cannot accept any of the rest of that submission. In my judgment, the position is entirely straightforward and can be analysed by considering the rights and obligations which Offerventure had at the date when it offered to let Duckwari take over the contract. Offerventure had the right, on the date fixed for completion, to call for a conveyance of the property on payment of £495,000, but with the right to take credit for the value of the deposit which it had paid.
I put it that way rather than to say 'take credit for the sum of £49,500' because counsel
D for the appellants pointed to the possibility that a deposit might be paid in kind, foreign currency or by a bankers' draft of a bank which became insolvent and was therefore worth nothing at the time of completion. In the present case, where the deposit was paid in sterling and in cash, there is, of course, no difference between the two formulations.

Similarly, Offerventure had the beneficial interest in the property, subject to the unpaid vendor's lien for the purchase price of £495,000 but after receiving credit for the amount
E of the deposit already paid. That right or interest was the right or interest which Duckwari acquired from Offerventure. As against the vendor it acquired the opportunity to call for a conveyance of the property on payment of £495,000, thereby discharging Offerventure's obligation to pay that sum, but with the right to take credit for the value of the deposit held by the stakeholders.

The appellants argue that this is not a correct analysis of the position and submit that
F the true position is that Duckwari acquired an obligation to pay £495,000 in order to acquire the property, together with a separate right to use the deposit for that purpose. In my judgment, the fallacy in that argument is that the deposit was not a separate item of property, and certainly not one which was acquired from Offerventure. Offerventure had no right to the return of the deposit as against the vendor. The contract itself provided in clear terms what was to happen to the deposit on completion. Paragraph 6 of the contract between Offerventure and the vendor provided:

G
'The purchaser shall on the date of this agreement pay a deposit of ten per cent of the purchase price to the vendors' solicitors as stakeholders for the vendors as security for due performance. The purchaser hereby irrevocably authorises any stakeholder to whom any deposit has been paid to account for the same with accrued interest from the date hereof to 29 September next to the vendors . . .'

H The clause then becomes somewhat inelegant, but it provides for the payment thereafter of interest on the deposit to the purchaser:

'. . . except where completion is delayed through the default of the purchaser . . .'

–before resuming with a description of what is to happen to the deposit itself:

'. . . and in the event of the deposit becoming repayable to the purchaser it shall be repaid together with the interest accrued thereon.'

In my judgment, it is plain that on completion the deposit was payable by the   A
stakeholders to the vendors and was not repayable to the purchaser. Accordingly,
Offerventure's only right on completion, and the right which it passed on to Duckwari,
was to have the amount of the deposit taken into account in computing the balance of
the money due to the vendor.

The appellants have argued strenuously that Duckwari have the right to insist upon
paying £495,000 and making use of the deposit. I do not agree as a matter of legal   B
analysis, but in any case in my judgment nothing turns on this. There was only one asset
which was acquired from Offerventure, and that was Offerventure's rights under the
contract. If it is a question of valuing those rights, then one begins with the simple
proposition that the primary right which Duckwari acquired from Offerventure was the
right to call on completion for a conveyance of a property worth £495,000. But it was
not an unqualified right. It was subject to an obligation to pay a sum of money. In order
to value the right which Duckwari acquired from Offerventure, it is necessary to take   C
into account the obligation which Duckwari would have to discharge in order to obtain
the property. But in order to put a money value on the liability, it is necessary to have
regard to the maximum possible amount which Duckwari could be compelled to pay the
vendor in order to discharge Offerventure's obligations; and the maximum amount which
Duckwari could be compelled to pay was £445,500.

This in my judgment disposes of both arguments advanced by the appellants: first, that   D
the value of the non-cash asset was nil; and secondly, that if there was an asset acquired
which was worth £49,500 it was a cash asset, namely the amount of the deposit.

It remains necessary only to consider an argument which was advanced and rejected
by the judge below and which has been repeated before us on behalf of Duckwari,
namely, that the value of the non-cash asset acquired by Duckwari from Offerventure
was £495,000. It was submitted that the reality of the matter was that it was acquiring   E
the property or the right to buy the property and that the purchase price of £495,000 was
payable in its entirety to or to the direction of Offerventure, so that even the £445,500
which was paid to the vendor was only paid to the vendor because Offerventure so
directed. That is true, but we are concerned with the identification and valuation of the
asset which moved in the other direction; and the problem is that, although it is true that
the property itself passed from the vendor to Duckwari only because Offerventure
directed the vendor to transfer the property to Duckwari and therefore moved from the   F
vendor through Offerventure to the purchaser, the fact remains that the vendor had his
own independent valuable proprietary right in the property, namely the unpaid vendor's
lien. That had to be discharged by Duckwari by payment direct to the vendor (that was
worth £445,500) and that figure must be deducted from the value of the property acquired
from Offerventure. In my judgment, there were two assets being acquired by Duckwari.
One was the asset acquired from Offerventure, viz. the right to call on completion for the
conveyance on discharging Offerventure's obligations to the vendor and paying   G
Offerventure £49,500; and the other was the extinction of the vendors' unpaid lien by
discharging Offerventure's obligation to pay the balance of the purchase money due to
the vendor.

Duckwari has pointed to the capricious results which appear to follow from this
analysis because it makes the question whether a transaction needs to be approved by the
company in general meeting depend upon the amount, if any, of the deposit rather than   H
the value of the property being acquired by the company.

If this is an anomaly it results from a combination of the facts (1) that cash assets and
liabilities are excluded from the computation and (2) that Parliament has seen fit, for
obvious reasons, to exclude the operation of the section where the transaction is not of
substantial value. I do not think that it is possible in isolation to consider whether this

A   analysis does lead to capricious results without considering the consequences of an infringement of the section.

These proceedings have been brought by Duckwari in order to enforce the indemnity provided for by s. 322(3). Duckwari's object is to seek to recover from the appellants the amount of the loss which has resulted from the fall in market values since the date of the transaction. Whether Duckwari would succeed in that endeavour will depend upon the

B   question whether the loss or damage resulting from the arrangement or transaction referred to in s. 322(3)(b) is to be measured by the difference between the value of the property at the date of the transaction and the purchase price (which in this case was nil) or is to be measured by the purchase price and the value of the property at some other and later date. That is a question which still remains for decision, and I express no opinion at all upon it. But it must not be assumed from anything that I have said in the course of this judgment that I take any view on that one way or the other.

C   I would, however, after some discussion with counsel, substitute for the declaration made by the registrar a somewhat different declaration to the effect that the arrangement between Duckwari and Offerventure contravened s. 320(1) and delete any reference to s. 322.

Subject to that substitution, I would dismiss this appeal.

Beldam LJ: In spite of the excellent argument from Mr Hoser, I too agree that there

D   is sufficient evidence to justify the deputy judge's finding that there was an arrangement between the company and Offerventure that the company should acquire a non-cash asset from Offerventure. I also agree that the evidence upon which he made that finding was contained in Mr Cooper's affidavit where he said that in late August he had offered to let Duckwari take over from Offerventure the contract for the purchase of the property and that Duckwari had decided to accept that offer – it paying the purchase price rather

E   than Offerventure – by paying £445,500 to the vendor and reimbursing Offerventure the amount of the deposit it had already paid.

The second question was whether the cash asset was of the requisite value at the time of the arrangement as required by s. 320(2) of the Companies Act. I consider that it was at least of the value of £49,500, the amount of the credit to which the company would be entitled against the purchase price on taking over the contract. The fact that the company had agreed to pay Offerventure an equivalent sum does not in my view affect the value

F   of the asset acquired.

Accordingly, I agree with Millett LJ that this appeal fails. I also agree with the form of the declaration which he has proposed.

Neill LJ: I too agree that this appeal should be dismissed for the reasons given by Millett and Beldam L JJ. In saying that, I too would wish to pay tribute to the quality of

G   Mr Hoser's arguments. There will therefore be a declaration that the arrangement between Offerventure Ltd and Duckwari plc contravened s. 320(1) of the *Companies Act* 1985.

(*Appeal dismissed with costs. Leave to appeal to the House of Lords refused*)

———————————

H

Re Rae.

Chancery Division.
Warner J.
Judgment delivered 15 July 1994.

Bankruptcy – 'Property' of bankrupt – Whether bankrupt could retain benefit of 'entitlement' to fishing licences – Whether entitlement was property – Insolvency Act 1986, s. 363, 436.

These were appeals by a bankrupt, 'R', against county court orders relating to fishing licences held by him. At the time of the bankruptcy order against him R traded as the owner of four UK registered fishing vessels. He held licences for them under the Sea Fish (Conservation) Act 1967. The vessels themselves vested in his trustee in bankruptcy. It was common ground that the licences did not. The effect of the bankruptcy order was to invalidate them. However, the Ministry of Agriculture, Fisheries and Food, by whom the licences were granted, recognised an 'entitlement' in R, or in any person in whose favour he might waive that entitlement, to be considered for the grant of fresh licences. That entitlement had a value. The question for the court was whether that entitlement should enure for the benefit of R's creditors or for the benefit of R. The district judge decided in favour of R's creditors. R appealed.

Held, dismissing the appeals:

1. To construe the Insolvency Act and in particular s. 436 as excluding R's recognised entitlement from his property would be contrary to the purposes of the Act. Once it was conceded (as it was) that R's recognised entitlement was not excepted by s. 283(2)(a) of the Act, use of it by him would be inconsistent with the scheme of the Act.

2. The court could not conclude, merely from a consideration of the purposes of the Insolvency Act and the non-exhaustive nature of the definition of 'property' in s. 436, that any asset of the bankrupt which could be realised or turned to account was 'property' within the meaning of the Act.

3. The recognised entitlement of R as a previous owner of fishing vessels was an interest of a kind falling within the definition of property in s. 436. It was a present interest 'incidental to' property, i.e. the vessels.

The following cases were referred to in the judgment:

Ayerst v C & K (Construction) Ltd [1976] AC 167.
Bristol Airport plc & Anor v Powdrill & Ors. Re Paramount Airways Ltd [1990] BCC 130; [1990] Ch 744.
City of London Corporation v Bown (1989) 22 HLR 32.
International Bulk Commodities Ltd, Re [1992] BCC 463; [1993] Ch 77.
Kirby v Thorn EMI plc [1988] 2 All ER 947.
Nokes v Doncaster Amalgamated Collieries Ltd [1940] AC 1014.
Vine, Ex parte. Re Wilson (1878) 8 ChD 364.
Zim Properties Ltd v Procter [1985] BTC 42.

Robert Bourne (instructed by Gill Akaster, Plymouth) for the bankrupt.

Stephen Davies (instructed by Bond Pearce, Plymouth) for the trustee in bankruptcy.

JUDGMENT

Warner J: On 27 May 1993 a bankruptcy order was made against Mr Quentin Scott Rae in the Torquay County Court. This is an appeal by Mr Rae against two orders that were made subsequently by that court. The first of those orders was made on 7 September 1993 by District Judge Meredith and is the substantive order against which Mr Rae appeals. The second order, which was made on 14 October 1993 by deputy District Judge

A   Arnold, merely varied ancillary provisions of the first order as to what the parties should be permitted to do pending the outcome of the appeal. My references hereafter to 'the district judge' will be references to District Judge Meredith.

Both orders were made on the application of Mr S J Hobson, who is Mr Rae's trustee in bankruptcy. He is the respondent to the appeal.

B   At the time of the bankruptcy order against him Mr Rae traded as the owner of four UK registered fishing vessels. He held licences for them under s. 4 of the *Sea Fish (Conservation) Act* 1967. The vessels themselves vested in his trustee in bankruptcy. It is common ground that the licences did not. The effect of the bankruptcy order was to invalidate them. However, the Ministry of Agriculture, Fisheries and Food, by whom the licences were granted, recognises an 'entitlement' (I put that word in inverted commas) in Mr Rae, or in any person in whose favour he may waive that entitlement, to be considered for the grant of fresh licences. That entitlement has a value and the question in this case is, shortly stated, whether that entitlement should enure for the benefit of Mr Rae's creditors or for the benefit of Mr Rae himself. The district judge decided in favour of Mr Rae's creditors.

Section 4 of the *Sea Fish (Conservation) Act* 1967 as amended provides by subs. (1) that 'The Ministers' – an expression that is, so far as material, defined by s. 22(2) of the Act as meaning 'the Minister of Agriculture, Fisheries and Food, and the Secretaries of State respectively concerned with the sea fishing industry in Scotland, Wales and Northern Ireland' – may by order impose prohibitions on fishing 'unless authorised by a licence granted by one of the Ministers'.

Such a prohibition was imposed by the *Sea Fish Licensing Order* 1992, which replaced earlier orders. By para. 3 of that order fishing anywhere by fishing boats which are registered in the UK or are British-owned is (with certain exceptions) prohibited unless authorised by a licence granted (a) in the case of certain fishing boats registered in the Isle of Man by the Isle of Man Department of Agriculture, Fisheries and Forestry and (b) in any other case, by one of the Ministers. Mr Rae's vessels were not registered in the Isle of Man. His licences were, as I have indicated, granted by the Minister of Agriculture, Fisheries and Food.

Subsection (3) of s. 4 of the Act of 1967 provides that, where any fishing boat is used in contravention of any prohibition imposed by an order under that section, the master, the owner and the charterer (if any) are each guilty of an offence. Subsection (4) enables an order under the section to authorise the making of a charge for a licence, but the order of 1992 does not authorise the making of any such charge. Subsection (5) is important in that it provides:

'A licence under this section shall be granted to the owner or charterer in respect of a named vessel . . .'

G   The subsection goes on to provide that the licence may authorise fishing generally or may confer limited authority to fish by reference to such matters as the area within which fishing is authorised, the periods or times during which fishing is authorised and the descriptions of fish which may be taken. Mr Rae had licences in respect of each of his vessels. The authority which they conferred was limited in various ways. Subsection (8) of s. 4 provides:

'The licensing powers conferred by this section may be exercised so as to limit the number of fishing boats, or of any class of fishing boats, engaged in fishing in any area, or in fishing in any area for any description of fish, to such extent as appears to the Ministers necessary or expedient for the regulation of sea fishing.'

Subsection (9) provides:

'A licence under this section—

        (a) may be varied from time to time; and   A

        (b) may be revoked or suspended, if this appears to the Minister who granted the licence to be necessary or expedient for the regulation of sea fishing.'

It is the policy of the ministers, in the context, as I understand it, of the common fisheries policy of the European Community, to exercise their powers under s. 4 so as to prevent any increase in the capacity of the fishing fleet. The way in which effect is given to that policy is summarised in a letter dated 29 April 1994 from the legal department of   B the Ministry of Agriculture, Fisheries and Food. That letter was written for the assistance of the parties to this appeal and of the court. It explains not only the position which the ministry adopts regarding entitlements to licences under s. 4 in general but also the ministry's views on the law relevant to the present case and, to some extent, its resultant attitude to the case.

The letter explains the nature of the 'entitlement', to which I referred earlier, that the   C ministry recognises that a person may have to be considered for the grant of a licence. As to that I will read two paragraphs of the letter:

    'Licences are granted under section 4(5), Sea Fish (Conservation) Act 1967 (as amended) to the owner or charterer of a fishing vessel and . . . UK registered fishing vessels may only fish for profit if licensed by the Ministry. The Ministry takes the view that licences are not property because they only exist in relation to a named owner of a particular vessel: licences may be suspended, revoked or varied   D at any time at the discretion of the Minister. A licence is merely a personal permission given to a particular person to use a particular vessel for fishing. A licence remains in existence only so long as the vessel is owned or chartered by the licence holder. If, for any reason, ownership of the vessel changes hands, the licence becomes invalid and a fresh licence must be applied for before the vessel can be used for commercial fishing.   E

    Because of the need to conserve fish stocks, the Ministry restricts the number of licences which are granted each year by virtue of not creating any new opportunities to fish, i.e. the fishing capacity of the fleet is capped. However, in exercising its discretion to grant licences, it does recognise, in general, an "entitlement" to apply for a sea fish licence as resting with the previous licence holder who can either apply for a licence in his own name or waive his "entitlement" so that another person can apply for a licence. The Ministry will not   F grant a licence unless an existing "entitlement" has been surrendered and, if the previous licence was held by someone other than the applicant, the previous owner has waived his "entitlement" to be considered for the grant of a licence by signing the previous owner's declaration on the application form. In this way, the number of UK licences does not increase. The Ministry does not at present charge a fee for issuing licences and considers that the issue of licences, even to a previous holder,   G is ultimately based on the discretion of the Minister.'

A specimen of an application form (Form AFL2) for a licence, containing at the end of it a 'previous owner's declaration' of the kind referred to in the ministry's letter, is in evidence. By that declaration the former owner or charterer of the vessel to which the application relates confirms that the applicant is now the owner or charterer of that vessel and that he (the former owner or charterer) does not intend to apply for any licence for a   H vessel to replace it. He also confirms that he has surrendered all licences in respect of the vessel to the fisheries office from which they were issued and that he understands that, having made that declaration, any application he makes in the future for a licence may be rejected. That form of declaration is preceded in the application form by a 'transfer declaration' which the form states is 'To be completed by new owner(s)/charterer(s) when applying for a licence to be transferred from previous owner'. It is clear that the form is

A   there using loose language because licences are not transferable. On a change of ownership of a vessel, or in its charterer, the former owner or charterer's licence or licences lapse and the new owner or charterer has to apply for a fresh licence.

I return to the ministry's letter. After the paragraph that I have read, it refers to a press release by which the ministry announced its policy of recognising an 'entitlement' to be considered for a licence as subsisting for two years. The letter continues:

B   'The time would, usually, start to run from the day the licence became invalid; which, in cases of bankruptcy would, ordinarily, be the date of appointment of the trustee in bankruptcy.

Under normal circumstances trustees in bankruptcy are not treated differently from anyone else. Licences are issued to trustees in bankruptcy only if the bankrupt signs the previous owner's declaration. We understand that it was Mr Rae's refusal

C   to sign the waiver which led to the current proceedings. We have indicated to you and to the trustee's solicitors that, exceptionally, in this case, because there would be no prejudice to Mr Rae's position, the Ministry is prepared to grant licences to the trustee until the final determination of the case, even though the application submitted by the trustee does not contain Mr Rae's signature.'

As to that passage in the letter I must mention four things. First, I understand that the ministry have indicated that in the present case they would treat Mr Rae's 'entitlement'

D   to be considered for licences as subsisting for two years after the final determination of the appeal. Secondly, the ministry have in fact granted Mr Hobson a licence in respect of one of Mr Rae's four vessels for the period until the final determination of the appeal, but I understand that Mr Hobson has not made use of that licence. The four vessels are laid up in the River Dart. Thirdly, it was not on the appointment of Mr Hobson as Mr Rae's trustee in bankruptcy that Mr Rae's licences became invalid. It was, as I stated earlier, on the making of the bankruptcy order. That was because each licence contained

E   a provision the effect of which was to invalidate it if Mr Rae ceased to be a member of the South Western Fish Producers Organisation Ltd, which on the making of the bankruptcy order he did. It was on that ground that the ministry called for the surrender of the licences. Fourthly, at the request of Mr Hobson's solicitors, the legal department of the ministry set out in a letter dated 6 May 1994 the ministry's policy when a licence holder which is a company goes into liquidation and when a licence holder who is an

F   individual dies. That letter is, so far as material, in these terms:

'Where a company which holds licences goes into liquidation there is no transfer of ownership of the vessels to which the licences relate. The liquidator is appointed to act on behalf of the company and can sign documents in the company's name. Consequently the company can either request new licences or waive its entitlement to licences in favour of another and the liquidator can sign the appropriate forms

G   in the name of the company.

There are few instances when the Ministry has been asked to deal with the licence entitlement of an individual who has died. In the cases when this has happened the Minister has exercised her discretion and chosen to accept the signature of either the beneficiary of the deceased's estate or the signature of the personal representatives of the deceased, provided that the Ministry has been satisfied that there are no conflicting claims on the estate.'

H   I propose from now on to refer for convenience to the 'entitlement' that the ministry recognises a person to have to be considered for the grant of a licence as a 'recognised entitlement'. I do not of course intend to suggest, by the use of that phrase, that the entitlement is a legal right, any more than I take the ministry to have so intended by the use of the word 'entitlement' in its letters of 29 April and of 6 May. It is clear and, I think, common ground between counsel that the grant or refusal by the minister of a

licence is a matter entirely within her discretion, subject to the possibility in an
appropriate case of an exercise of her discretion being the subject of proceedings for
judicial review.

I said earlier that Mr Rae's recognised entitlement had a value. Mr Hobson in his
affidavit says:

> 'The licences have a separate value from the vessels and, although transfer of
> licences is subject to control by MAFF, licences are in practice traded for value.'

Mr Rae, in his affidavit, says:

> 'I accept that a practice has grown up whereby licence holders receive a
> consideration for the surrender of a licence thereby enabling some other person,
> being the payer of such moneys, to receive a licence at the discretion of MAFF.'

In January 1993 Mr Rae made a proposal for an individual voluntary arrangement
with his creditors. In the event that proposal came to nothing. However, in an estimated
statement of affairs as at 14 January 1993 annexed to the proposal, Mr Rae showed his
vessels as estimated to realise, without licences, £565,000 under the arrangement and
£489,000 in a bankruptcy, and the licences as estimated to realise £376,000 under the
arrangement and £326,000 in a bankruptcy. (Mr Rae now says that he believes that the
statement of affairs was incorrect in ascribing a value to the licences in the event of his
bankruptcy.) There is also in evidence a letter dated 16 February 1993 from a firm of ship
brokers and marine valuers in which they value the licences at £252,283.20 'as between a
willing seller and a willing buyer'. There is no more recent valuation of Mr Rae's
recognised entitlement and no evidence of the current value of the four vessels without
the benefit of that entitlement. Clearly, however, they would fetch substantially less
without it than with it. It is of some significance that Mr Rae's licences included one
which he 'purchased' (I put that word in inverted commas) in 1991 for £75,000.

Mr Hobson's investigations have revealed very little in the way of assets available for
Mr Rae's creditors other than his vessels and (if it is available) his recognised entitlement.
His vessels are charged to Barclays Bank plc. His licences were not. Barclays Bank's debt,
which is over £1.8m, greatly exceeds on any view the value of the vessels. If Mr Rae's
recognised entitlement is not available for his creditors, there will be very little for his
unsecured creditors, which include trade creditors for about £212,000.

Mr Hobson, following his appointment as Mr Rae's trustee in bankruptcy, wished to
sell his vessels with the benefit of his recognised entitlement. However, Mr Hobson was
informed by the Ministry of Agriculture, Fisheries and Food of its practice and told that
he could not sell the vessels with that benefit unless Mr Rae signed the previous owner's
declaration in the relevant application form. That Mr Rae declined to do. Mr Hobson
therefore made, under s. 363 of the *Insolvency Act* 1986, the application which resulted in
the district judge's order of 7 September 1993. The important paragraphs of that order
are para. 1, 2 and 3.

By para. 1 the district judge declared that 'all the right title or interest of the
respondent' – that is Mr Rae – 'in the fishing licences in respect of the fishing vessels' –
the four vessels are then named – 'and/or any entitlement to call for new fishing licences
is vested in the applicant' – that is Mr Hobson – 'by virtue of s. 283 and 306 of the
Insolvency Act 1986.'

By para. 2 the district judge made:

> 'a declaration under s. 311(3) of the *Insolvency Act* 1986 that the applicant may
> exercise such rights and do such things as may be necessary or expedient to procure
> the transfer of the licences or the grant of new fishing licences as the respondent
> might have exercised had he not become bankrupt.'

A   By para. 3 the district judge ordered that:

'In the event that the Ministry of Agriculture, Fisheries and Food does not accept the exercise by the applicant of the rights conferred by para. 1 and 2 of this order then the respondent shall pursuant to s. 363(2) of the *Insolvency Act* 1986 do all such things as may be necessary or expedient to procure the transfer of the licences or the granting of new fishing licences to the applicant or to such person or persons as the applicant may nominate and the respondent shall sign the previous owner's declaration in form AFL2 in respect of each such licence.'

I go back once more to the ministry's letter of 29 April 1994. Following the passage in that letter that I last read, the author of it continues:

'I turn now to the wording of any order which the court might be prepared to make. Clearly, given that the Ministry is not a party to the proceedings it is not bound by the court's order. Whilst the Ministry will do everything in its power to give effect to an order of the court, it must not be subsequently placed in the position where it may have to grant two licences where, previously, only one existed.

Whilst it is clearly a matter for the court to decide whether it can and should make an order under s. 363(2) of the *Insolvency Act* 1986 (with or without an order under s. 39(1) of the *Supreme Court Act* 1981), the Ministry would only entertain an application by the trustee for a licence (other than in the circumstances referred to above) if the court were to direct that Mr Rae, or someone acting on his behalf, were to sign the previous owner's declaration – and this was effected. It is our view that it is for the court and not the Ministry to assess the competing insolvency interests and to adjudicate accordingly; this is not a function which the Ministry is equipped to carry out. In the absence of an order we would continue to recognise an "entitlement" to apply for a licence as resting with Mr Rae subject to the overriding consideration that it would lapse at the end of two years. We would add that in the Ministry's view as the licences are not property the court is not entitled to make any declarations of the sort contained in para. 1 and 2 of the order of 7 September 1993.'

Mr Davies, who appears for Mr Hobson on the appeal but did not appear before the district judge, does not seek to uphold para. 2 of the district judge's order. Moreover, he accepts that para. 1 of that order is inappropriate in so far as it refers to the licences vesting in Mr Hobson, since they came to an end on Mr Rae's bankruptcy. Mr Davies put before me a draft of a declaration alternative to that made by the district judge in para. 1 of her order. That draft, among other things, omits the reference to the licences vesting in Mr Hobson and substitutes for the reference to 'any entitlement to call for new fishing licences' a reference to '(a) any entitlement to apply for new licences and/or (b) any power to waive or surrender such entitlement'.

I had the benefit of very able and detailed arguments and of an extensive citation of authority by both Mr Bourne on behalf of Mr Rae and Mr Davies on behalf of Mr Hobson. It will not be necessary for me in this judgment to go into all the details of those arguments or to refer to all the authorities that were cited to me.

Essentially Mr Bourne's contentions on behalf of Mr Rae were:

(1)   that Mr Rae's recognised entitlement was not 'property' within the meaning of that term in the *Insolvency Act* 1986 and therefore did not vest in his trustee in bankruptcy, and

(2)   that because that entitlement was not property forming part of Mr Rae's estate in bankruptcy, it was not open to the court to make under s. 363 of the Act an order

of the kind contained in para. 3 of the district judge's order directing Mr Rae in   A
effect to give the benefit of it to his creditors.

Mr Davies argued that, on the contrary:

(1)   the recognised entitlement was 'property' within the meaning of that term as
      defined by s. 436 of the Insolvency Act or at all events was a power exercisable by
      Mr Rae to which s. 283(4) of that Act applied, so that it did vest in his trustee in
      bankruptcy, and   B

(2)   alternatively, if the recognised entitlement remained vested in Mr Rae it was
      reasonable for his trustee in bankruptcy to require him, under s. 333(1)(c) of the
      Act, to take such steps as were necessary, such as signing the previous owner's
      declaration in form AFL2, to give the benefit of it to his creditors, and therefore
      proper for the court, if he refused to do so, to order him to do so under s. 363(2)
      of the Act.   C

I must now set out the main provisions of the Insolvency Act that are relevant to the
questions that thus arise.

Section 283 defines a bankrupt's estate. Subsection (1) reads:

> 'Subject as follows, a bankrupt's estate for the purposes of any of this Group of
> Parts comprises–
>   D
> (a) all property belonging to or vested in the bankrupt at the commencement of
>   the bankruptcy, and
>
> (b) any property which by virtue of any of the following provisions of this Part
>   is comprised in that estate or is treated as falling within the preceding
>   paragraph.'

Subsections (2), (3) and (3A) except certain types of property from subs. (1). Subsection   E
(2) excepts:

> '(a) such tools, books, vehicles and other items of equipment as are necessary to
> the bankrupt for use personally by him in his employment, business or vocation;
>
> (b) such clothing, bedding, furniture, household equipment and provisions as are
> necessary for satisfying the basic domestic needs of the bankrupt and his family.'

Subsection (2) is subject to s. 308 which enables the trustee in bankruptcy in certain   F
circumstances to claim property so excepted. The notice of appeal in this case
foreshadowed an argument that Mr Rae's recognised entitlement was excepted by subs.
(2), but Mr Bourne did not rely on that argument.

Subsection (3) excepts:

> '(a) property held by the bankrupt on trust for any other person, and
>   G
> (b) the right of nomination to a vacant ecclesiastical benefice.'

Subsection (3A), which was inserted by s. 117 of the *Housing Act* 1988, excepts certain
kinds of statutory tenancies, such as a protected tenancy within the meaning of the *Rent
Act* 1977 and a non-assignable secure tenancy under Pt. IV of the *Housing Act* 1985. Its
effect is, however, qualified by s. 308A, which was also inserted by s. 117 of the *Housing
Act* 1988. Under s. 308A the trustee in bankruptcy may claim any such tenancy for the   H
estate, but he may not then disclaim it without the leave of the court – see s. 315(4) as
amended by s. 117 of the *Housing Act* 1988.

Subsection (4) of s. 283, omitting immaterial words, reads:

> 'References in any of this Group of Parts to property, in relation to a bankrupt,
> include references to any power exercisable by him over or in respect of property

A　except in so far as the power is exercisable over or in respect of property not for the time being comprised in the bankrupt's estate and–

　　. . .

　　(b)　cannot be so exercised for the benefit of the bankrupt;
　　. . .'

B　Section 305(2) provides that the function of the trustee in bankruptcy is to get in, realise and distribute the bankrupt's estate in accordance with the relevant provisions of the Act. Section 306 provides that:

　'(1) The bankrupt's estate shall vest in the trustee immediately on his appointment taking effect . . .

　(2) Where any property which is, or is to be, comprised in the bankrupt's estate
C　vests in the trustee . . . it shall so vest without any conveyance, assignment or transfer.'

Section 307 contains provisions enabling the trustee, by notice in writing, to claim for the bankrupt's estate any property which has been acquired by, or has devolved upon, the bankrupt since the commencement of the bankruptcy and before his discharge.

Section 310 empowers the court to make an 'income payments order' claiming for the
D　bankrupt's estate so much of his income as does not appear to the court to be necessary for meeting the reasonable domestic needs of the bankrupt and his family. Section 333(1) provides:

　'The bankrupt shall–

　　(a)　give to the trustee such information as to his affairs,

　　(b)　attend on the trustee at such times, and

E　　(c)　do all such other things,

　as the trustee may for the purposes of carrying out his functions under any of this Group of Parts reasonably require.'

Section 333(2) requires the bankrupt to give notice to the trustee of any property which is acquired by or devolves upon him, or of any increase in his income, after the
F　commencement of the bankruptcy.

Subsections (1) and (2) of s. 363 are in these terms:

　'(1) Every bankruptcy is under the general control of the court and, subject to the provisions in this Group of Parts, the court has full power to decide all questions of priorities and all other questions, whether of law or fact, arising in any bankruptcy.

G　(2) Without prejudice to any other provision in this Group of Parts, an undischarged bankrupt or a discharged bankrupt whose estate is still being administered under Chapter IV of this Part shall do all such things as he may be directed to do by the court for the purposes of his bankruptcy or, as the case may be, the administration of that estate.'

Lastly, s. 436 provides, so far as material:

H　'In this Act, except in so far as the context otherwise requires . . .

　　"property" includes money, goods, things in action, land and every description of property wherever situated and also obligations and every description of interest, whether present or future or vested or contingent, arising out of, or incidental to, property;

　　. . .'

It is clear therefore that Mr Rae's recognised entitlement does not form part of his A estate in bankruptcy and is not vested in his trustee in bankruptcy unless it is 'property' within the meaning of the Act. Leaving aside for the moment the provisions of s. 283(4) relating to powers exercisable 'over or in respect of property', the question whether that recognised entitlement is property within the meaning of the Act turns on the definition of property in s. 436.

The first thing to be observed about that definition is that it is not exhaustive. It does B not say what 'property' means, but what it 'includes'. It may therefore be taken to imply that 'property' includes other things than those that are expressly mentioned.

Secondly, the definition to some extent defines 'property' by reference to that word itself. The first limb of the definition states that property includes 'money, goods, things in action, land and every description of property wherever situated'. What does 'property' mean in that collocation of words? As has often been said, 'property' is not a term of art, C but takes its meaning from its context – see for instance per Nicholls LJ in *Kirby v Thorn EMI plc* [1988] 2 All ER 947 at p. 953, citing Lord Porter in *Nokes v Doncaster Amalgamated Collieries Ltd* [1940] AC 1014 at p. 1051. It seems to me that in the phrase 'every description of property wherever situated' the word 'property' must connote anything which is capable of being owned and of which the ownership can be asserted or defended in legal proceedings. If so, the second limb of the definition, beginning with the words 'and also', must go wider. D

Thirdly, in construing the definition it is proper to have regard to the purposes of the Act. In *Bristol Airport plc v Powdrill* [1990] BCC 130 the Court of Appeal were concerned with the construction of the provisions of the Act relating to a company in respect of which an administration order had been made. One of the issues was whether aircraft of which the company was only a lessee were 'property' of the company. Sir Nicolas Browne-Wilkinson V-C, after summarising the issues in the case, said (at pp. 147–148): E

> 'Before dealing with the issues summarised above, it may be helpful to state what, in my opinion, is the correct approach to the construction of the provisions dealing with administrators contained in Pt. II of the Act. The judge was very much influenced in his construction by the manifest statutory purpose of Pt. II of the Act. I agree with this approach. The provisions of Pt. II themselves, coupled with the mischief identified in the Cork Report, show that the statutory purpose is to F install an administrator, as an officer of the court, to carry on the business of the company as a going concern with a view to achieving one or other of the statutory objectives mentioned in s. 8(3). It is of the essence of administration under Pt. II of the Act that the business will continue to be carried on by the administrator. Such continuation of the business by the administrator requires that there should be available to him the right to use the property of the company, free from interference by creditors and others during the, usually short, period during which such G administration continues. Hence the restrictions on the rights of creditors and others introduced by s. 10 and 11 of the Act. In my judgment in construing Pt. II of the Act it is legitimate and necessary to bear in mind the statutory objective with a view to ensuring, if the words permit, that the administrator has the powers necessary to carry out the statutory objectives, including the power to use the company's property.
>
> H
>
> On the other hand, however desirable it may be to construe the Act in a way calculated to carry out the parliamentary purpose, it is not legitimate to distort the meaning of the words Parliament has chosen to use in order to achieve that result. Only if the words used by Parliament are fairly capable of bearing more than one meaning is it legitimate to adopt the meaning which gives effect to, rather than frustrates, the statutory purpose.'

A   Sir Nicolas Browne-Wilkinson went on to consider the question whether the aircraft were 'property' of the company. He referred to the definition of 'property' in s. 436, observed at p. 148D that, 'It is hard to think of a wider definition of property', and held that the interest of the company under the lease of an aircraft was property within that definition. The grounds on which he did so were that, although the lease was only a contract, it was a specifically enforceable contract, so that the company had an equitable right in the aircraft which fell within the statutory definition as being some 'description

B of interest . . . arising out of, or incidental to' that aircraft. With his reasoning Woolf and Staughton L JJ agreed. The Court of Appeal was not in that case concerned with the question whether something not enforceable in a court of law or equity (save possibly by proceedings for judicial review), such as Mr Rae's recognised entitlement, was capable of falling within the definition of 'property' in s. 436.

C   On the propriety of having regard to the purposes of the Act in construing it, I was referred also to the decision of Mummery J in *Re International Bulk Commodities Ltd* [1992] BCC 463 where (at p. 468B) he said:

> 'In my judgment, the court should construe the relevant provisions, where the wording so permits, to promote and not to frustrate the evident legislative purpose . . .'

D   The relevant legislative purpose here is to my mind perfectly clear. Bankruptcy, putting it in the simplest terms, is a process whereby on the one hand all a debtor's property, with certain specific exceptions, is vested in his trustee in bankruptcy for realisation and distribution of the proceeds among his creditors and, on the other hand, he is forever relieved of personal liability to those creditors. The specific exceptions exist either because the property is not appropriate for distribution among the bankrupt's creditors, such as property of which he is only a trustee, or because, unlike an insolvent company, the

E bankrupt is a human being whose life must continue during and after insolvency. For this reason s. 283(2) excepts from the bankrupt's estate the tools and other items of equipment necessary for his personal use in his employment, business or vocation and also the clothing, bedding, furniture, household equipment and provisions necessary for the basic domestic needs of the bankrupt and his family. For the same reason the court may not make under s. 310 an income payments order reducing his income below what appears to the court to be necessary for meeting his reasonable domestic needs and those

F of his family. For the same reason again the bankrupt is, within limits, allowed to keep damages awarded to him for injury to his person, such as damages for slander – see *Ex parte Vine. Re Wilson* (1878) 8 ChD 364. There is no example, however, either in the Act or in the many authorities that were cited to me, of the bankrupt being entitled to retain for his own benefit a purely financial or commercial asset capable of realisation for the benefit of his creditors and not necessary for his personal use in his employment, business

G or vocation.

    As Mr Davies pointed out, the practice of the Ministry of Agriculture, Fisheries and Food, as described in its letters of 29 April and 6 May, 1994, creates an anomaly as between the position where an insolvent individual becomes bankrupt and the position where an insolvent company goes into liquidation. If Mr Rae had traded through a company which was his alter ego, the company would have owned the vessels and held the licences for them, and the vessels could have been sold by the liquidator with the

H benefit of its recognised entitlement. The difference in treatment is due only to the difference in the machinery applicable under the Insolvency Act in the case of an insolvent company and in the case of an insolvent individual. In the case of an insolvent company, the legal title to its property remains vested in it, under the control of the liquidator. In the case of an insolvent individual the legal title to his property passes to his trustee in bankruptcy. However, in both cases the property is impressed with a trust for the benefit

of creditors and the functions of a liquidator and of a trustee in bankruptcy are similar – A
see *Ayerst v C & K (Construction) Ltd* [1976] AC 167, per Lord Diplock at pp. 176–180.
(That case was decided under earlier legislation, but the *Insolvency Act* 1986 has not
materially altered the position.) In the case of a company, any surplus after satisfying the
rights of its creditors and the costs of the liquidation is distributable among the
shareholders according to their rights. In the case of the bankruptcy of an individual any
surplus after satisfying the rights of his creditors and the costs of the bankruptcy is
returnable to the bankrupt. The difference in machinery is due to the different nature of   B
a company and an individual. As I said earlier, an individual is a human being whose life
continues independently of his insolvency. But there is no reason why that should make
any difference of substance to the rights of creditors, apart from such differences as I
referred to earlier which are attributable to the fact that the bankrupt is a human being.

The conclusion I reach is that to construe the Insolvency Act and in particular s. 436
as excluding Mr Rae's recognised entitlement from his property would be contrary to the   C
purposes of the Act. Whilst being relieved of his liabilities to his creditors he would be
permitted to retain realisable assets without that retention being explicable by reference
to his needs as a human being. In saying that I do not overlook that Mr Rae could
exercise his recognised entitlement to obtain fresh licences for use in a business carried on
by him. But once it is conceded (as it is) that Mr Rae's recognised entitlement is not
excepted by s. 283(2)(a) of the Act, such use of it by him would be inconsistent with the
scheme of the Act.   D

Mr Bourne argued that the exclusion of Mr Rae's recognised entitlement from the
property vesting in his trustee in bankruptcy would not be inconsistent with the scheme
of the Act because, if Mr Rae were himself to realise its value, his trustee in bankruptcy
could claim the proceeds as after-acquired property under s. 307. Mr Davies pointed to
various difficulties that could confront the trustee in those circumstances. However, Mr
Rae need not realise his recognised entitlement for cash. He could, as I mentioned a   E
moment ago, use it to obtain fresh licences for, for instance, vessels chartered by him, in
which case the purposes of the Act, as I see them, would be frustrated.

Mr Davies put in the forefront of his argument on behalf of Mr Hobson a submission
that, in view of the non-exhaustive nature of the wide definition of 'property' in s. 436,
the fact that the exclusion of Mr Rae's recognised entitlement from the property vesting
in his trustee in bankruptcy would be contrary to the purposes of the Act was enough to   F
lead to the conclusion that that entitlement was property within the meaning of the Act.
Mr Davies submitted that the word 'property' in the Act included any asset of the
bankrupt capable of realisation for the benefit of his creditors.

Among the authorities cited to me by Mr Davies in support of that submission was
City of London Corporation v Bown (1989) 22 HLR 32. That was a case about a non-
assignable secure tenancy under Pt. IV of the *Housing Act* 1985. The Court of Appeal   G
held that such a tenancy did not vest in the tenant's trustee in bankruptcy. The case was
decided on the law as it stood before the *Insolvency Act* 1986 was amended by s. 117 of
the *Housing Act* 1988 in the ways that I mentioned earlier. The ratio of the decision was
expressed by Dillon LJ as follows (at pp. 38–39):

> '. . . I take the view that the non-assignable secure periodic tenancy of Mr Bown is
> a mere personal right dependent on the terms of the statute.' – That is a reference
> to the *Housing Act* 1985 – 'It is not an asset which the trustee in bankruptcy could   H
> realise for the benefit of the creditors and I see no reason therefore why it should
> be included in the property of the bankrupt which has vested, albeit without
> assignment, under section 306 of the Insolvency Act in the trustee in bankruptcy.'

It seems to me, however, difficult to treat that passage in Dillon LJ's judgment as
authority for the converse proposition that any asset which the trustee in bankruptcy

A   could realise for the benefit of the creditors is included in the property of the bankrupt vesting in the trustee.

Mr Davies also relied on my own judgment in *Zim Properties Ltd v Procter* [1985] BTC 42. In that case I held that a right to bring an action to seek to enforce a claim that was not frivolous or vexatious, which right could be turned to account by negotiating a compromise yielding a substantial capital sum, was an 'asset' within the meaning of that term in the capital gains tax legislation. In point was, among other provisions of that

B   legislation, s. 22(1) of the *Finance Act* 1965, which provided:

'All forms of property shall be assets for the purposes of this Part of this Act . . .'.

My decision turned on a consideration of the reasoning of the House of Lords in an earlier case in which, so it appeared to me, the House had treated as virtually irrelevant the use by s. 22(1) of the word 'property' and had held to be dominant in the legislation the word 'asset'. That word is not used in the Insolvency Act.

C   Other authorities cited by Mr Davies in support of this submission were, if I may say so, even more remote from the point.

I am not persuaded that one can, merely from a consideration of the purposes of the Insolvency Act and the non-exhaustive nature of the definition of 'property' in s. 436, reach the conclusion that any asset of the bankrupt which can be realised or turned to

D   account is 'property' within the meaning of the Act.

I have, however, after considerable hesitation, come to the conclusion that Mr Davies is entitled to succeed on one of his alternative submissions, which was that Mr Rae's recognised entitlement came within the words in s. 436 'and every description of interest, whether present or future or vested or contingent, arising out of, or incidental to property', namely his vessels. I think that the recognised entitlement is a present interest incidental to the vessels. The word 'interest' is notoriously one of wide import, the

E   meaning of which varies according to the context in which it is used. Here it is not limited to an interest in property. It extends to an interest 'arising out of, or incidental to, property'. The difficult question is whether the phrase 'every description of interest' includes an interest which is not enforceable in a court of law but which is nonetheless marketable and so capable of being turned into money. The passage that I read earlier from the judgment of Sir Nicolas Browne-Wilkinson in *Bristol Airport plc v Powdrill*

F   provides to my mind authoritative guidance in answering that question. The words 'every description of interest' are fairly capable of bearing more than one meaning. They could be construed as meaning only interests capable of being asserted or defended in legal proceedings (other than proceedings for judicial review). But there is nothing in the words themselves to confine them to that meaning. Nor do the words that follow, 'whether present or future or vested or contingent', have any obvious limiting effect. That being so it is right to adopt the meaning that gives effect to, rather than frustrates, the statutory

G   purpose.

Mr Bourne argued that Mr Rae's recognised entitlement did not arise out of, and was not incidental to, the four vessels vested in Mr Hobson. It arose, he said, from, and was incidental to, the exercise of the minister's discretion. It was an ability to apply for licences for other vessels which Mr Rae might acquire as owner or charterer; and in so far as Mr Rae was able to waive it in favour of another person, the licences applied for

H   by that other person need not be for any of the four vessels vested in Mr Hobson. I cannot accept that argument. It is not necessary, in order for an interest to come within the words of s. 436, for it both to arise out of and to be incidental to property. It is enough that it is incidental to property. It seems to me clear that Mr Rae's recognised entitlement is incidental to the four vessels. The licences were granted in respect of the four vessels and it was from his ownership of those vessels that Mr Rae derived the recognised entitlement. It is, I think, immaterial that the recognised entitlement can be

regarded as incidental also to other things, such as the exercise of the minister's discretion,   A
or indeed the licences.

The most powerful argument put forward by Mr Bourne was based on the nature itself
of the recognised entitlement. That entitlement, he pointed out, was the creature of the
minister. It existed because of an intimation by her as to the way in which she would
generally exercise her discretion to grant licences. It was defined and limited by her
practice. It existed in such person as she recognised. It could not exist in anyone else. For   B
that reason it existed in Mr Rae and existed in a company acting by its liquidator, but
did not exist in a trustee in bankruptcy.

I would have found that argument compelling and conclusive were it not for the terms
of the ministry's letter of 29 April 1994. In that letter the ministry states that in its view,

> 'it is for the court and not the ministry to assess the competing insolvency interests
> and to adjudicate accordingly; this is not a function which the ministry is equipped   C
> to carry out.'

True the ministry makes those statements in a paragraph in which it envisages the court
only making an order under s. 363(2) and in which it says that in its view the court is not
entitled to make any declaration of the sort contained in para. 1 and 2 of the district
judge's order. However, it is clear that the reason why the ministry was of the latter view
was that, 'the licences are not property'. The analysis of the legal position made by   D
counsel on this appeal has shown that whether or not the licences were property is not
really relevant, because they have ceased to exist. What is relevant is that, if I am right in
the view that I have expressed, the recognised entitlement of a previous owner of fishing
vessels is an interest of a kind falling within the definition of property in s. 436. In those
circumstances it does not seem to me that that view is invalidated by the fact that hitherto
the minister has not regarded the recognised entitlement of such an owner who has
become bankrupt as vesting in his trustee in bankruptcy. The chief concern of the   E
ministry seems to be that it should not be placed in the position where it might have to
grant two licences where previously only one existed.

In the result it is not necessary for me to express any view on Mr Davies' other
alternative submissions, that Mr Rae's recognised entitlement formed part of the
goodwill of his business, which vested in his trustee in bankruptcy, or that it was a power
to which s. 283(4) of the Insolvency Act applied. Nor need I express any view on the   F
question whether, if that entitlement was not property within the meaning of the Act, it
would have been proper to direct Mr Rae under s. 363(2) to take steps such as signing
the previous owner's declaration in form AFL2.

I turn to the form of the order that I should make. As I said earlier, Mr Davies accepts
that para. 1 and 2 of the district judge's order are inapposite. I think that para. 3 of that
order is also in some respects inappropriately worded. Nor am I entirely content with Mr   G
Davies's redraft of the declaration in para. 1 of the district judge's order. What I propose
to do, subject to any further submissions of counsel, is this.

First, I will discharge para. 1, 2 and 3 of the district judge's order.

Second, I will make a declaration (which of course will not bind the minister) that any
entitlement of Mr Rae to be considered by the Minister of Agriculture, Fisheries and   H
Food for the grant of new fishing licences consequent upon the invalidation of the licences
issued to Mr Rae in respect of the four vessels now vested in Mr Hobson as Mr Rae's
trustee in bankruptcy (those vessels being named in a schedule to the order) and any
power to waive or surrender such entitlement are property within the meaning of the
Insolvency Act 1986 and are accordingly vested in Mr Hobson as Mr Rae's trustee in
bankruptcy.

A   Third, I will make an order under s. 363(2) of the Act directing Mr Rae to do at the request of Mr Hobson all such things as may be necessary or expedient to procure that the benefit of such entitlement shall enure to Mr Hobson or to such person or persons as he may nominate and in particular (without prejudice to the generality of that direction) to sign at the request of Mr Hobson the previous owner's declaration in any form of application for such a licence.

B   I will hear counsel as to anything else that my order should say.

Stay of execution

I have come to the conclusion that in the circumstances I should not order a stay of execution in view of the cost of £1,000 a week of keeping these vessels laid up and the evidence to which Mr Davies has drawn my attention about the deterioration of the vessels while they are laid up, the likely time that it will take for the matter to be heard by the Court of Appeal and Mr Davies' undertaking on the part of the trustee in bankruptcy not to distribute any proceeds of any sale of the vessels with the benefit of the entitlement without a further order of the court.

There will be, as Mr Bourne has pointed out, if the trustee does sell the vessels with the benefit of the entitlement a problem of deciding how much of the proceeds are attributable to the vessels and how much to the benefit of the entitlement. Resolving that problem will be a question of fact which will have, if necessary, to be done on evidence. But there is no evidence, as Mr Davies has pointed out, that Mr Rae in fact has plans to use the entitlement to obtain further licences. In those circumstances it seems to me that the scales fall down on the side of letting the vessels be sold as soon as possible with the benefit of the entitlement so that the greatest possible sum can be secured for the creditors, or, if the Court of Appeal so decides, in part for Mr Rae.

E   There will be no stay of execution.

(Appeals dismissed with costs to be taxed if not agreed. Leave to appeal granted)

Re a Company No. 004539 of 1993.

Chancery Division (Companies Court).
Blackburne J.
Judgment delivered 18 July 1994.

> *Winding up – Admission and rejection of proof (creditors' meeting) – Creditor's proof marked as objected to and creditor allowed to vote – Appeal against validity of creditor's vote – Without creditor's vote different liquidator would have been appointed at meeting – Consequences of invalidity of vote – Insolvency Rules 1986 (SI 1986/1925), r. 4.70.*

This was an application by creditors for an order reversing the official receiver's decision at a creditors' meeting in a compulsory winding up to allow a creditor to vote under r. 4.70(3) of the Insolvency Rules, having marked that creditor's proof as objected to. The respondents to the application were the official receiver, the creditor and the liquidator appointed at the meeting. Without that vote, the majority in value of creditors at the meeting would have been in favour of a different liquidator.

The creditor's claim was for £6.85m representing damages for repudiation of a contract to purchase property. The applicants argued that any claim arising out of the admitted repudiation of that contract was compromised as part of an overall settlement embodied in Tomlin orders and that as a result nothing was owing.

The liquidator wished to argue that the applicants were not creditors and therefore had no standing to challenge the official receiver's decision at the meeting to admit the creditor's proof for voting purposes.

Held, declaring the vote invalid and making an order for the liquidator to be succeeded by a new liquidator:

1. Unless and until the applicants' proofs were rejected they were creditors entitled under r. 4.70(2) to appeal to the court against the official receiver's decision to admit another creditor's proof for voting purposes and the liquidator had no standing to challenge their standing to do so.

2. The task of the court on an appeal under 4.70(4) was simply to examine the evidence placed before it on the matter and come to a conclusion whether, on balance, the claim against the company was established and, if so, in what amount. In considering the matter, the court was not confined to the evidence which was before the chairman at the time that he made his decision but was entitled to consider whatever admissible evidence on the issue the parties to the appeal chose to place before the court.

3. The court was satisfied that the claim to damages was compromised, that the creditor was not entitled to vote at the meeting of creditors and that the official receiver's decision to admit the proof should be reversed.

The following cases were referred to in the judgment:

Potts, Re [1934] Ch 356.
Tilcon Ltd v Land and Real Estate Investments Ltd [1987] 1 WLR 46.

Alan Steinfeld QC and Richard Ritchie (instructed by Jacobsens) for the applicants.

Michael Todd (instructed by the Treasury Solicitor) for the official receiver.

Robin Knowles (instructed by Travers Smith Braithwaite) for the liquidator.

JUDGMENT

Blackburne J: On 30 June 1993 CFAC Ltd (formerly the Chelsea Football and Athletic Co Ltd – 'CFAC') was ordered to be wound up. On the making of that order the official receiver, by virtue of his office, became the liquidator of CFAC.

© 1995 CCH Editions Limited

bcp95 bcp 167 Mp 116 —bcp167 65

A   Six months later the official receiver decided that, having regard to information which he had received, the actions taken by the directors of CFAC and others at or about the time of the making of the winding-up order against CFAC required detailed investigation and that the creditors of CFAC should be given an opportunity to appoint a liquidator of their choice to undertake that investigation and to provide a liquidator so appointed with the required funding for that purpose. He therefore decided that meetings of the creditors and contributories of CFAC should be held to enable them to make this appointment.

B

Briefly stated, that information was as follows. In or about June 1992 CFAC's football undertaking – that of the well known Chelsea Football Club – had been transferred, for no monetary consideration, to a company called Chelsea Football Club Ltd ('the club company'). The club company was a subsidiary of Chelsea Village Ltd ('CV'). CV held a debenture, dated 28 November 1992, over CFAC's assets and undertaking. On 14 May 1993, CV had appointed an administrative receiver, Mr Papi, over CFAC's assets and undertaking, pursuant to powers contained in the debenture. On 13 June 1993, the very day upon which CFAC was ordered to be wound up, the administrative receiver had transferred to CV assets of CFAC said to be worth £519,000, leaving CFAC bereft of assets but with substantial liabilities.

C

D   The meeting of creditors took place on 5 May 1994. No separate meeting of contributories took place because none turned up in response to the notice convening it. The official receiver, in the person of Mr Pugh, presided at the meeting of creditors. Present at the meeting were proxy holders for nine creditors who had lodged proofs of debt. Those creditors were: Maybank Press (88) Ltd (in liquidation), in the sum of £62,240.62; the Commissioners of Inland Revenue and the Commissioners of Customs and Excise, in sums totalling £92,983.43; SB Property Co Ltd ('SB Property'), in the sum of £6,850,000; Reems Ltd, in the sum of £25,500; Hargreaves, Brown and Benson, a firm of accountants, in the sum of £27,500; the club company, in the sum of £1,250,862; CV, in the sum £1,039,942; and Stamford Bridge Properties Ltd ('Stamford Bridge'), in the sum of £266,455. Stamford Bridge, which had under another name previously been a subsidiary of CFAC, was, like the club company, a subsidiary of CV. For convenience, I shall refer to CV and its subsidiaries, the club company and Stamford Bridge as 'the associated companies'. Three other creditors had submitted proofs totalling £2,537,000-odd but those creditors were not represented. Of those that were, the proxy holders for the Commissioners of Inland Revenue and Customs and Excise, Reems Ltd and SB Property held special proxies for the appointment of Christopher Morris of Touche Ross as liquidator, the proxy holder for Maybank Press (88) Ltd held a general proxy and the four others, i.e. the associated companies and the accountants, were represented by Mr Doffman who held special proxies in favour of the appointment of Mr G F Hilton of Kidsons Impey, as liquidator.

E

F

G

At the start of the creditors' meeting Mr Doffman challenged the validity of the meeting. The official receiver expressed the view that it had been properly constituted and continued the meeting. At a later point in the meeting Mr Doffman challenged SB Property's claim to be a creditor. After Mr Doffman had shown a document to him, the official receiver decided to mark SB Property's proof as 'objected to' but to allow it to vote.

H

Rule 4.70 of the *Insolvency Rules* 1986, which is the relevant rule, provides, so far as material, as follows:

> '(1) At any creditors' meeting the chairman has power to admit or reject a creditor's proof for the purpose of his entitlement to vote; and the power is exercisable with respect to the whole or any part of the proof.

(2) The chairman's decision under this Rule . . . is subject to appeal to the court   A
by any creditor or contributory.

(3) If the chairman is in doubt whether a proof should be admitted or rejected, he
shall mark it as objected to and allow the creditor to vote, subject to his vote being
subsequently declared invalid if the objection to the proof is sustained.

(4) If on an appeal the chairman's decision is reversed or varied, or a creditor's
vote is declared invalid, the court may order that another meeting be summoned,   B
or make such other order as it thinks just.'

In marking SB Property's proof as objected to and allowing it to vote the official receiver
as chairman of the meeting was acting under that rule.

I take up the story from the official receiver's minutes of the meeting:

'At this point in time representatives of the Customs and Excise and the Inland
Revenue requested that the proofs for the associated companies also be marked   C
"objected to" if I was marking the proof of SB Property Co Ltd as "objected to"
as there must be considerable doubt on the validity of the transactions that had
taken place between the associated companies and the purported debenture under
which Chelsea Village Ltd had already appointed an administrative receiver who
had apparently transferred all the assets in situ to Chelsea Village Ltd. As the
evidence in support of these proofs of debt, which had only been received that   D
morning was not in any way conclusive I informed the meeting that I was prepared
to mark the proofs of Stamford Bridge Properties Ltd and Chelsea Village Ltd as
"objected to", but to allow them to vote at the meeting.'

I should add that the official receiver had earlier rejected the club company's proof for
voting purposes.

An attempt by the official receiver to persuade the meeting to appoint Mr Morris and   E
Mr Hilton as joint liquidators having failed, a vote was taken. With Maybank Press's
general proxy holder voting in favour of Mr Morris, creditors having admitted claims of
£7,032,734.05 were in favour of Mr Morris's appointment, whilst creditors having
admitted claims in the sum of £692,093.49 were in favour of Mr Hilton. The result was
that Mr Morris was appointed.

The associated companies now apply to the court for declarations that the notice
convening the meeting of creditors held on 5 May 1994 and the meeting as so convened   F
were invalid; alternatively that any resolutions passed, or purportedly passed, at that
meeting were invalid; alternatively that any resolution passed, or purportedly passed, at
the meeting purporting to remove the official receiver as liquidator and appointing
Christopher Morris in his place was invalid. The associated companies also seek a
declaration that SB Property was not entitled to be admitted to proof at the meeting and
an order reversing the official receiver's decision to admit that company to vote at the   G
meeting. Consequential relief is also claimed. The respondents to that application are the
official receiver, SB Property and Mr Morris.

Also before me is an application by the Commissioners of Inland Revenue and the
Commissioners of Customs and Excise for a declaration under the Insolvency Rules,
r. 4.70(4) that the votes of CV and Stamford Bridge at the meeting of creditors were
invalid; alternatively, an order reversing the official receiver's decision as chairman to
admit their proofs for voting purposes at that meeting; alternatively, an order under   H
r. 4.85(1)(b) expunging their proofs; alternatively an order under r. 7.50 reversing the official
receiver's decision not to reject those proofs for voting purposes and consequential relief.

I need not take up time on the associated companies' application, so far as it challenges
the validity of the creditors' meeting, or on the application of the Commissioners of
Inland Revenue and Customs and Excise challenging the validity of CV's and Stamford

A   Bridge's votes at the meeting. During the course of the hearing before me both challenges were dropped on certain agreed terms as to costs. Broadly speaking between them the associated companies have either already paid or have provided for all of CFAC's known creditors, including the two Crown departments, and, in the case of any claims which those two departments may have over and above the claims for which they have so far submitted proofs, have provided undertakings satisfactory to the two departments to discharge any further amounts which may be shown to be due. The only exception, if it

B   is an exception, is SB Property, which as mentioned earlier was admitted to proof in the sum of £6,850,000 but with its proof marked as 'objected to'.

    There is a dispute between the associated companies on the one hand and Mr Morris and the official receiver on the other as to when the associated companies first made known their willingness to discharge CFAC's known creditors and the terms of that willingness, but in view of the settlement that has been reached it would not be profitable

C   for me to dwell in any way on that dispute.

    In the result, subject to one matter, I am only concerned with the associated companies' challenge to SB Property's entitlement to vote at the meeting and the consequences of that challenge if it is successful. Although a respondent to the associated companies' application, the official receiver ceased, following the settlement, to take any further part in the hearing, leaving as an active participant only Mr Morris (for whom Mr Knowles

D   appeared). SB Property, likewise a respondent to the associated companies' application, was not represented before me and has therefore not addressed any argument in response to the associated companies' challenge to its entitlement to vote at the meeting.

    That one matter is this. Mr Knowles wished to advance argument as to whether the associated companies were indeed creditors of CFAC and whether, therefore, they had locus to challenge the official receiver's decision at the meeting to admit SB Property's

E   proof for voting purposes. This derives from the fact that under r. 4.70(2), under which the associated companies mount their challenge, it is only creditors or contributories who can appeal. Mr Steinfeld, for the associated companies, objected to this line of attack on his clients' status as creditors or at any rate on the status of CV and Stamford Bridge, the club company's proof having been rejected and against which rejection there has been no appeal. He argued that since under r. 4.70(2) it is only a creditor or a contributory who can appeal and since Mr Morris is neither and since, in the event, the two Crown

F   departments which are creditors no longer pursue their challenge, then, unless and until the proofs of CV and Stamford Bridge are rejected (and there is no evidence that either has been), those two creditors are entitled under r. 4.70(2) to appeal to this court against the official receiver's decision to admit SB Property's proof for voting purposes and Mr Morris, as liquidator, has no locus to challenge their locus to do so. In my judgment, Mr Steinfeld is correct.

G   Mr Knowles, on behalf of Mr Morris, invited me to hear from him what as liquidator Mr Morris had to say on the status of CV and Stamford Bridge as creditors, even though, as I understood it, it was not suggested that their proofs of debt had been or should be rejected. I declined the invitation. Whilst I do not doubt that I am entitled to hear what the liquidator – who in a compulsory winding up is an officer of the court – has to say on any matter affecting the winding up of the company of which he is liquidator, I do not

H   consider that where as here what is in issue is whether Mr Morris ought to have been appointed liquidator at all, I should permit him to call into question the prima facie right of CV and Stamford Bridge under r. 4.70(2) to challenge the official receiver's decision to admit SB Property to proof. Mr Morris's appointment as liquidator is in issue because if CV and Stamford Bridge are successful in their challenge, the consequence would have been that, discounting SB Property's vote, the majority in value of creditors at the meeting would have been in favour of Mr Hilton, who was the associated companies'

nominee for the office. I should add that nothing has been said to question Mr Hilton's   A
fitness for that office.

SB Property was admitted to proof for voting purposes in the sum of £6.85m.
According to the evidence submitted in support of its proof, that sum represented
damages for repudiation of a contract by CFAC to purchase Stamford Bridge football
ground from SB Property for £22.85m. The nub of the associated companies' challenge
to that claim is that any claim arising out of CFAC's admitted repudiation of that   B
contract was compromised in December 1992 as part of an overall settlement of a number
of claims between SB Property and CFAC and that, in consequence of that settlement,
nothing is owing.

Before considering the evidence bearing on that issue I should mention briefly one
preliminary question which arose and was debated before me, which was what test I
should apply in deciding that issue. Was it sufficient to show that SB Property was   C
arguably a creditor or, as it was put at one stage in the argument before me, that there
was 'a good prima facie case' that SB Property was a creditor, or ought something more
to be shown? Counsel's researches did not reveal any decision directly in point either
under r. 4.70(4) or under its statutory predecessors or in the equivalent rule in the field of
personal insolvency. It is, I think, established, on the equivalent rule applicable in
bankruptcy, that the onus of demonstrating that the chairman's decision was wrong and
should be reversed or varied lies on the creditor mounting the appeal and that the decision   D
whether any creditor should be admitted to proof for voting purposes under appeal is a
provisional one, in the sense that it is open to the chairman (whoever he might be) at
some future meeting of creditors to come to a different conclusion on the evidence then
available to him from that arrived at by the chairman at an earlier meeting in respect of
the same creditor (see *Re Potts* [1934] Ch 356).

I would also observe that, since an appeal can lie against both a decision to admit and   E
a decision to reject a proof for voting purposes, I do not consider that the burden of
proof on the objector should depend upon whether he is concerned to secure the reversal
of a decision to reject a proof or, as in the instant case, the reversal of a decision to admit
a proof. I say this in the light of a submission by Mr Knowles that the court should err
in favour of admitting a creditor to proof for voting purposes rather than reject it. For
my part, I cannot see why that should be so.   F

In my view, the task of the court on an appeal under 4.70(4) is simply to examine the
evidence placed before it on the matter and come to a conclusion whether, on balance,
the claim against the company is established and, if so, in what amount. I would only
add that, in considering the matter, the court is not confined to the evidence that was
before the chairman at the time that he made his decision but is entitled to consider
whatever admissible evidence on the issue the parties to the appeal choose to place before   G
the court.

I come then to the evidence relating to SB Property's claim. It has its origins in the
exercise by CFAC of an option to purchase Stamford Bridge Football Club (in Fulham
Road, London), together with some adjoining premises. The option was contained in a
lease of the football ground granted by SB Property to CFAC as part of a sale and
leaseback arrangement entered into in August 1982. The option was exercised in August   H
1988. There was a question whether the option had been validly exercised and three days
after exercising the option CFAC started an action designed to establish the effectiveness
of its exercise of the option. This action effectively replaced an earlier action by CFAC
against SB Property, which in general terms sought to restrain SB Property from entering
into a long lease with a third party company, the effect of which – if valid – would have
been to prevent CFAC from exercising its option.

A   SB Property and the third party company, between whom a long lease had indeed been entered into, were defendants to the new proceedings. Initially they defended CFAC's action. By 1991, for reasons which I need not explain, they abandoned their defence and in June 1991 an order was made in the proceedings declaring that the option had been validly exercised in August 1988.

B   In late November 1991 the open market value as at August 1988 of the property, subject to the exercise of the option, was determined at £22.85m. That was the price payable for it under the contract constituted by the exercise of the option. By then, with the collapse in the property market, the property was worth substantially less. This prompted CFAC to start a fresh action, 'the option damages claim', against SB Property claiming damages for the delay in the ascertainment of the price for the property as a result of SB Property's insistence – subsequently abandoned – that the option had not been validly exercised.

C   In January 1992 SB Property started its own action, 'the specific performance action', against CFAC claiming specific performance of the contract for the sale of the property resulting from the exercise of the option. It issued a summons for summary judgment under O. 86 for specific performance of the contract. At about the same time SB Property applied to strike out the option damages claim. Both applications came on for hearing before Millett J in February 1992. He decreed specific performance of the contract,

D   allowed the option damages claim to proceed and declined to delay completion of the contract until CFAC's claim for damages under its option damages claim had been ascertained. He also consolidated both actions.

     CFAC appealed the judge's refusal to delay completion of the contract pending determination of its option damages claim, and SB Property appealed the judge's refusal to strike out the option damages claim.

E   On 2 April 1992 the Court of Appeal dismissed CFAC's appeal against the decree of immediate specific performance and allowed SB Property's appeal by striking out CFAC's option damages claim.

     By December 1992 the position reached in the consolidated proceedings was that CFAC had still not completed its purchase, despite the decree of specific performance which the Court of Appeal had affirmed, but had petitioned the House of Lords for leave

F   to appeal, the Court of Appeal having refused leave.

     As if that was not litigation enough, there were by December 1992 several other sets of proceedings on foot between or involving CFAC and SB Property or persons or companies associated with them. They comprised: two petitions under s. 459 of the *Companies Act* 1985; an action by CFAC against SB Property and others in which CFAC sought the repayment of certain rent; two so-called landlord and tenant actions by CFAC

G   against among others SB Property; a so-called guarantor's action by CFAC; and a claim arising out of a planning dispute (I take these descriptions from certain heads of agreement to which I now come).

     By late 1992 the two principal actors in this welter of litigation were insolvent. CFAC had already transferred its football undertaking to the club company and was left with liabilities which exceeded its assets. In November 1992 the Royal Bank of Scotland in its capacity as chargee of the football ground had appointed receivers over that asset. This

H   led to the Royal Bank of Scotland brokering a settlement of all these various claims. The result was the preparation on 8 December 1992 of draft heads of agreement involving the Royal Bank of Scotland, SB Property (then in receivership), Apus Properties (the owner of premises adjoining the football ground), Kenneth Bates (the moving spirit behind CV – the parent company of the club company which by then was running Chelsea Football Club) and CV.

In essence the heads of agreement provided for the simultaneous sale and transfer by   A
SB Property of the football ground and by Apus of the adjoining premises to a subsidiary
of the Royal Bank of Scotland for £16.5m, with Mr Bates procuring CFAC (which by
then he controlled) to surrender its lease and any other interest in the football ground
immediately beforehand, and with the Royal Bank of Scotland releasing its mortgages
over the two properties in question, conditional on the payment to it by SB Property and
Apus of the £16.5m proceeds of sale of their two properties. The heads of agreement
further provided for two new 20-year leases of the football ground and of the adjoining   B
premises to CV, immediately following completion, at a rent equal to interest at one and
five-eighths per cent over three months LIBOR on the sum of £16.5m. Also provided
were put and call options, designed to enable a subsidiary or associated company of CV
to acquire the freehold in the football ground and the adjoining property.

Paragraph 5.1 of the heads of agreement provided as follows:

> '(a) *Litigation between the parties hereto or their associates.* On completion all   C
> parties will, and will procure that all their associates will, discontinue all legal
> proceedings to which they are a party against any other parties to these heads of
> agreement and/or their associates, on terms that there be no order as to costs, but
> without disturbing any orders for costs already made, and that all judgments, save
> as to costs, be discharged. All parties hereby agree that on and from the date of
> completion of the transactions contemplated in these heads of agreement no   D
> further or substitute actions or claims will be brought by any such party or any of
> their associates in relation to these heads of agreement, or in relation to any rights,
> claims or causes of action, in respect of which any of the parties hereto, or any of
> their associates, have commenced proceedings against any of the other parties
> hereto, or their associates. All references to proceedings, actions and claims
> include, without limitation, the proceedings referred to in subpara. 5.2 below.'

Paragraph 5.1(b) is concerned with one of the two s. 459 petitions. Paragraph 5.2 sets out   E
the various proceedings referred to in para. 5.1. These were all of the proceedings to
which I have referred including, in particular, the specific performance action.

It was thus a term of the heads of agreement that, on completion of the transactions
contemplated by the heads, SB Property would discontinue its specific performance
action against CFAC – which although not expressed to be a party to the heads of
agreement was an associate of Mr Bates who was – and that it would not bring any   F
further or substituted action or claim against CFAC in relation to any rights, claims or
causes of action arising out of the matters with which the specific performance action was
concerned. Finally, so far as material, completion of the various transactions
contemplated by the heads of agreement was fixed to take place by 15 December 1992.

Although only in draft and, in any event, expressed to be 'non-binding', it is evident
that the provisions of the heads of agreement were substantially carried into effect. My   G
attention was drawn to one or two respects in which the terms differed from those
contemplated by the heads of agreement – for example existing costs orders were
abandoned – but with the possible exception of the matters which form the basis of SB
Property's proof against CFAC, I am satisfied that the transactions contemplated by the
heads of agreement were carried into effect.

In particular various consent orders in the Tomlin form were made (although none   H
was made in the specific performance and option damages claims). The Tomlin orders
provided as follows (I read from the Tomlin order made in one of the so-called landlord
and tenant actions):

> 'In consideration of the stay of the abovementioned action, the plaintiff [CFAC]
> and the first defendant [SB Property] agree that such stay is accepted by the
> plaintiff and the first defendant in full and final settlement of all and any claims,

A   including – but not limited to – the claims and previous orders for costs in favour of and between the said parties made in these proceedings which the plaintiff and the first defendant have, or may have, against the other in respect of and/or arising out of the premises [the premises are described] . . . whether based in contract, tort, statute or howsoever arising.'

The premises include the football ground and the adjoining premises.

B   So far as concerns the specific performance action, a letter addressed to CFAC and dated 15 December 1992, was drawn up and signed. It reads as follows:

'Dear Sirs

Stamford Bridge ground

C   We refer to a lease dated 19 August 1982 made between SB Property Co Ltd, the Chelsea Football & Athletic Co Ltd (now known as CFAC Ltd) and others ("the lease") and to an option to purchase contained in para. 6 of the fourth schedule to the lease ("the option"). We also refer to an order for specific performance of the option that was made by Mr Justice Millett on 26 February 1992 in action number CH1992-S-145 ("the order").

The order, at least in so far as it will require the option to be completed, was, as you will be aware, subsequently confirmed by the Court of Appeal on 24 March

D   1992 and the time for complying with the order was extended to seven days after judgment of the Court of Appeal.'

(I am not certain that 24 March 1992 is the correct date, but it matters not).

'As the order has not yet been complied with you are in breach of the contract formed on the exercise of the option. We hereby treat this as a repudiatory breach of that contract, which repudiation is now accepted by us.

E   In the alternative, please treat this letter as a notice to complete that contract immediately by payment of the sums due under the order. If you are unable to comply with this notice then we shall treat this, similarly, as a repudiatory breach of the contract.

Yours faithfully . . .'

Then it is signed by Mr Hughes, under whose signature the following appears:

F   'C J Hughes and T R Harris, joint fixed charge receivers of the Stamford Bridge ground, as agents for SB Property Co Ltd and without personal liability.'

Also appearing is the following:

'We confirm that we accept that the contract is hereby repudiated for the reasons set out in this letter.

G   H S Todd

For and on behalf of CFAC Ltd, Director.'

At completion, on 15 December 1992, the following words were added at the end of the second paragraph of that letter, so that the sentence in question read as follows:

'We hereby treat this as a repudiatory breach of that contract, which repudiation is now accepted by us, without prejudice to our rights under the contract.'

H   Mr Richard Taylor, a partner in the firm of solicitors acting for the associated companies, says this about the addition of those words (I read from para. 16 and 17 of his second affidavit, omitting immaterial parts):

'I was present when the letter at p. 11 in Mr Morris's bundle [the letter of 15 December 1992 which I have just read] was signed by Mr Todd on behalf of the company. The purpose of the letter was to permit the overall settlement of the SB

A

dispute. Messrs Hughes and Harris had been appointed as Law of Property Act receivers in respect of the property at Stamford Bridge and not receivers to the whole company as Mr Morris appears to assume. Until the contract created by the option had been determined the LPA receivers could not sell the property to any third party. The letter determined the contract.

B

At the last moment and during the completion meeting Messrs Hughes and Harris were advised that the written amendment should be added to the letter so that there could be no question that they had compromised that which they were not entitled so to do. The company did not object to such amendment as it appreciated that only the company [it is agreed that that should be a reference to SB Property] could compromise the damages claim. Following the signing of the Tomlin orders the company withdrew its petition to the House of Lords.'

C

Had the matter rested there it would have been plain, I think, that any claim SB Property had against CFAC for damages for repudiation of contract had been abandoned as part of the December settlement.

There are, however, three letters in evidence which suggest that the inclusion of the additional words in the second paragraph of the letter of 15 December 1992 was to preserve SB Property's claim to £6.85m against CFAC. I say £6.85m because, given the price of £16m at which SB Property's receivers were disposing of the football ground to the subsidiary of the Royal Bank of Scotland, prima facie, damages in that amount were thereby crystallised. Those three letters are:

D

(1) a letter dated 25 March 1994 from Mr Harris, one of the receivers appointed by the Royal Bank of Scotland over the property to Mr Cotter, a director of SB Property in December 1992 and subsequently, in which Mr Harris states his belief that SB Property has a claim for damages against CFAC for £6m;

E

(2) a letter from Mr Cotter to the official receiver dated 8 June 1994 in which Mr Cotter appears to assume that SB Property has a claim; and

(3) a letter dated 21 June 1994 from Mr Walker, a partner in Cameron Markby Hewitt, to a partner in the solicitors acting for Mr Morris, in which Mr Walker states that:

> 'We believe that the amendment to the letter [i.e. the letter of 15 December 1992] reflected the intention of the same parties [i.e. CFAC, SB Property and, I think, the receivers appointed by the Royal Bank of Scotland] to leave outstanding claims arising from the said breach of contract [that is a reference to CFAC's failure to complete the contract].'

F

Although SB Property was not represented before me to resist the challenge to the official receiver's decision to admit it to voting at the creditor's meeting, I am satisfied by Mr Knowles that it was proper for him, on behalf of Mr Morris, to advance argument as to why I could properly come to the view that the official receiver's decision was correct.

G

In essence, Mr Knowles made three points:

(1) the evidence suggested that there was indeed an intention that SB Property's claim to damages against CFAC should be preserved, notwithstanding the settlement;

(2) it is difficult to see what the point was in adding the words to the second paragraph of the letter of 15 December 1992, if not to preserve the damages claim;

H

(3) the damages claim was something new, springing out of the acceptance on 15 December 1992 of CFAC's repudiation of the contract and being personal in nature (as distinct from being a claim to an interest in the property) was unaffected by the terms of the heads of agreement and was not caught by the terms of the

A   Tomlin orders, which related only to claims in respect of or arising out of the property.

Although the contrary is certainly arguable – as Mr Knowles' skilful submissions demonstrated – I take the view on the evidence before me that SB Property abandoned any claim to damages against CFAC arising out of CFAC's failure to complete its contract to purchase the football ground. I say that for the following reasons.

B   (1)   Although never signed, I am satisfied that the heads of agreement set out the substance of the terms of settlement, brokered by the Royal Bank of Scotland and carried into effect, to dispose of all claims between SB Property and CFAC and others relating to the property. Those claims included SB Property's claim against CFAC, arising out of CFAC's failure to complete its contract to purchase the property. That claim was not restricted to the outstanding decree of specific

C   performance but included the right to treat the contract as repudiated and to sue for damages consequent upon CFAC's continued failure to complete in accordance with the decree. I reject the submission that the claim to damages was something independent of and different in origin from the cause of action which had led to the making of the decree of specific performance. See *Tilcon Ltd v Land and Real Estate Investments Ltd* [1987] 1 WLR 46 at p. 53C, to which, after argument was concluded, my attention was drawn by Mr Knowles.

D   (2)   If it had been intended that that claim should be preserved I would have expected to see a reference to such a reservation in the heads of agreement. There is none. If, on the other hand, the terms agreed were varied at the time of completion to provide for the reservation of a right by SB Property to pursue CFAC in damages, I would have expected rather more than simply the addition of eight words at the end of the second paragraph of the letter of 15 December 1992 to herald this

E   radical departure from the terms agreed only seven days earlier. Even so, the additional words do not in terms refer to a damages claim. There is no other contemporary document suggesting that such a reservation was made.

    (3)   It is impossible to reconcile an intention to reserve a damages claim for repudiation of the contract with the wide terms of the Tomlin orders and difficult to reconcile it with the remainder of the transactions adumbrated by the heads of agreement

F   (all of which involved a stay or an abandonment of claims) and with CFAC's action in subsequently withdrawing its petition for leave to appeal to the House of Lords from the Court of Appeal's decision of 2 April 1992.

    (4)   There is no affidavit evidence from any of the others involved in the transactions at the time they were entered into to contradict what Mr Taylor says in para. 16 and 17 of his second affidavit, either from SB Property's directors or from the

G   receivers who signed the letter of 15 December 1992 or from the solicitors (apart from Mr Taylor) who were involved in the transaction and who attended on completion. It is noteworthy that, although a respondent to the associated companies' application, SB Property has not chosen to defend its claim. It is said that it is too impoverished to do so. If, in truth, it had a claim for £6.85m I am surprised that it has felt unable to mount any resistance to the associated companies' challenge.

H   (5)   The letter from Mr Walker of Cameron Markby of 21 June 1994, stating as his belief that the words were added to the letter of 15 December 1992 to reflect the parties' intention to leave outstanding any claims arising from the repudiation of the contract, is not supported by any evidence from those who were involved at the time and is contradicted by a letter from Julie Cole also of Cameron Markby dated 4 January 1993 in which she says:

'As you know, as part of the sale of Stamford Bridge it was agreed that all A
litigation relating to the site would either be discontinued or stayed.'

(6)   I can place no reliance on the letter dated 8 June 1994 to the official receiver from
Mr Cotter. It is plain from that letter that Mr Cotter, who claims to have had no
involvement in the events of December 1992, has no recollection of those events. If
SB Property had intended to reserve a claim to damages – which would not have
been swept up by the Royal Bank of Scotland charge – I would have expected SB
Property's director to have had some knowledge of the matter. Apparently he has
none.

(7)   I can, likewise, place no reliance on Mr Harris's letter to Mr Cotter of 25 March
1994. Although Mr Harris does have a recollection of events his recollection is
plainly faulty. Even then he does no more than state his 'belief' that SB Property
has a claim to damages. He does not suggest that such a reservation was ever the
subject of any negotiations to which he was a party.

In these circumstances, I propose to declare that SB Property was not entitled to be
admitted to vote at the meeting of creditors of CFAC held on 5 May 1994 and to order
that the official receiver's decision to admit SB Property to vote at that meeting be
reversed. In coming to this conclusion I intend no criticism of the official receiver. Indeed,
on the information then available to him he dealt perfectly correctly in admitting SB
Property's proof and, following Mr Doffman's intervention, marking it as 'objected to'.

I will hear counsel on whether in these circumstances I should order another meeting
of creditors to take place or whether I should make some other order instead.

Costs

What I propose to do on costs is this.

First of all, so far as the first applicant is concerned, its proof was rejected for voting
purposes and on no basis, as it seems to me, can that applicant be entitled to any costs.
That leaves simply the second and third applicants.

They had to come to court in order to establish the main relief which they were seeking,
which was a declaration that SB Property ought not to have been admitted to proof for
voting purposes at the meeting on 5 May 1994. To that extent they would have incurred
costs, in any event.

So far as Mr Morris, the third respondent to the applicants' application, is concerned
it is the submission of Mr Steinfeld, on behalf of the applicants, that their costs of this
application should be borne by him and borne by him personally, on the grounds that it
was, in substance, he who was resisting the relief which they were seeking. In my
judgment, Mr Morris acted entirely properly in laying before me matters pertinent to the
question of whether or not SB Property was or was not rightly admitted to proof for
voting purposes, more particularly as SB Property itself was not represented before me.

In all the circumstances, the order that I propose to make is this, that the costs of the
second and third applicants of their application – notwithstanding the fact that the length
of the application was, to some extent, extended by a procedural objection to the validity
of the meeting on 5 May, which objection was subsequently abandoned – should be costs
in the winding up of the company. So far as the costs of Mr Morris are concerned they
too should be treated as costs in the winding-up of the company.

That leaves only the official receiver. So far as he is concerned provision has already
been agreed between him on the one hand and the applicants on the other for his costs
and I need say nothing more about that.

Finally I should say that, in coming to the decision that I have, I attach no importance
either to the submission made to me by Mr Steinfeld, that Mr Morris or his firm solicited

A   – if, indeed, they did – the support of creditors for his appointment of 5 May, nor do I take into account (as, equally, it seems to me to be irrelevant) the fact that it was as a result of these proceedings that the applicants have been induced to pay some or all of the outstanding creditors of this company.

(*Order accordingly*)

B

C

D

E

F

G

H

Royal Trust Bank v National Westminster Bank plc & Anor.   A

Chancery Division.
Jonathan Parker J.
Judgment delivered 19 July 1994.

Charge – Company gave charge to lender over hiring agreements – Income from agreements paid into account at bank – Whether charge was specific equitable charge over hiring agreements and proceeds – Whether income received was subject to charge – Whether charge was fixed or floating – Whether bank had notice of security – Whether bank was constructive trustee of income from agreements.   B

This was an action by a bank ('RTB') claiming that another bank ('Natwest') was liable to account to RTB as constructive trustee of certain moneys received by Natwest representing payments made to a company pursuant to hire-purchase agreements and other agreements of a similar kind entered into by the company with its customers over which RTB claimed to have a specific equitable charge.   C

The company's business was providing equipment for its customers by means of hire-purchase agreements, lease-purchase agreements, and equipment leases. RTB provided loan finance to the company under a facility which provided for RTB to take a 'first legal charge' over hiring agreements deposited with RTB. Pursuant to successive facility letters the company executed successive deeds of assignment and charge under which the company assigned to RTB the benefit of the agreements deposited by the company with RTB. Income from the deposited agreements was paid into an account with Natwest, and periodic payments were made to RTB out of that account, until 26 June 1992 when Natwest refused to make further payments out of the account and demanded payment of £159,803 owing by the company to Natwest. The next day RTB wrote to Natwest claiming that payments into the account under agreements deposited with RTB were subject to a specific equitable charge in favour of RTB. Subsequently a substantial credit balance accumulated on the account deriving from payments under deposited agreements.   D   E

RTB contended that under the deed of assignment and charge there was a specific equitable charge over the hiring agreements deposited with RTB and over the income from such agreements. RTB further contended that on receipt of the letter dated 26 June 1992 Natwest became a constructive trustee for RTB of all moneys thereafter coming into its hands representing income derived from agreements subject to the charge. Natwest contended that under the charge the company retained the right to use income from the deposited agreements in the ordinary course of its business, subject only to such right being determined by RTB in accordance with the terms of the charge and that such right had not been so determined. Alternatively, Natwest contended that the company was in fact allowed to use the income in the ordinary course of business as a matter of licence by RTB, and that such licence had not been determined. Natwest further contended that any charge over income from deposited agreements was a floating charge and no crystallisation of such a floating charge had occurred. Finally Natwest contended that even if there was a specific charge over income from deposited agreements paid into the account, nevertheless the terms of RTB's letter were not such as to give Natwest actual notice of RTB's rights in respect of such income, with the result that Natwest was not accountable to RTB as constructive trustee as claimed.   F   G   H

Held, giving judgment for RTB:

1. The charge did not confer upon or reserve to the company the right to use income of deposited agreements in its hands from time to time in the ordinary course of its business (pending some act of enforcement by RTB under the terms of the charge or the occurrence

A   of an event of default). The charge covered not merely the right to income receivable in the future but also income in the hands of the company from time to time.

2. The fact that the charge fastened on agreements deposited with RTB from time to time did not render the charge ambulatory. It was a specific charge on each agreement, which arose as and when the agreement was deposited with RTB and continued unless and until the agreement expired or ceased to form part of the security pursuant to the provisions

B   for substitution.

3. Prior to the letter of 26 June 1992, RTB did consent to the company withdrawing funds from the account for use in the ordinary course of its business. The evidence failed to support Natwest's argument that such consent could only be withdrawn on adequate notice because of some equity arising by way of promissory estoppel.

4. Given the state of knowledge of Natwest prior to receipt of the letter of 26 June 1992

C   as to the security taken by RTB, the terms of that letter were adequate to constitute Natwest constructive trustee of income from agreements deposited with RTB thereafter received by Natwest.

The following cases were referred to in the judgment:

Armagh Shoes Ltd, Re [1982] NI 59; [1984] BCLC 405.
Atlantic Computer Systems plc, Re [1990] BCC 859; [1992] Ch 505.

D   *Atlantic Medical Ltd, Re* [1992] BCC 653.
Brightlife Ltd, Re (1986) 2 BCC 99,359; [1987] Ch 200.
Evans v Rival Granite Quarries Ltd [1910] 2 KB 979.
Henry v Hammond [1913] 2 KB 515.
Illingworth v Houldsworth [1904] AC 355.
New Bullas Trading Ltd, Re [1993] BCC 251; [1994] BCC 36 (CA).
Yorkshire Woolcombers Association Ltd, Re [1903] 2 Ch 284 (CA); [1904] AC 355 (HL).

E   Gregory Mitchell (instructed by Crossman Block) for the plaintiff.

David Oliver QC and Michael Fordham (instructed by Dibb Lupton Broomhead) for the defendant.

JUDGMENT

F   **Jonathan Parker J:** In this action Royal Trust Bank ('RTB') claims that National Westminster Bank plc ('National Westminster') is liable to account to RTB as constructive trustee of certain moneys received by National Westminster representing payments made to a company called Brookes Associates Finance Ltd ('the company'), pursuant to hire-purchase agreements and other agreements of a similar kind entered into by the company with its customers, over which RTB claims to have a specific equitable charge. The moneys in respect of which relief is claimed were credited by

G   National Westminster to the company's No. 2 account at National Westminster's Crawley Branch.

The defendants to the action are National Westminster and the company, but the company has not been represented and has taken no part in the proceedings.

RTB appears by Mr Mitchell of counsel, and National Westminster by Mr Oliver QC and Mr Fordham of counsel.

H   At all material times the company carried on the business of providing equipment for its customers by means of hire-purchase agreements, lease-purchase agreements, and equipment leases. Nothing turns for present purposes on the differences between these three types of hiring agreement.

RTB provided loan finance to the company for the purposes of this business under a facility the terms of which were contained in three successive facility letters. The first of

these facility letters was dated 8 September 1987, and offered a facility of up to £500,000   A
until 30 September 1988. The second facility letter was dated 21 November 1988 and
offered a facility of up to £1,250,000 until 30 November 1989. The third facility letter was
dated 10 April 1990 and offered a facility of up to £2,500,000 until 30 November 1990.
Each of the facility letters provided that the facility was to be used to finance hire-
purchase and leasing agreements (plus, in the case of the latter two facility letters, marine
mortgage agreements).

B

As to security for the facility, it was a term of each of the first two facility letters that
RTB should take a 'first legal charge' over hiring agreements deposited with RTB from
time to time, being agreements on terms and conditions acceptable to RTB and with
hirers acceptable to RTB, and that the total sums receivable under such agreements
should at all times be equal to at least 140 per cent of the principal amount currently
outstanding under the facility. The third facility letter provided that the facility was to be
secured by a deed of charge already held by RTB, together with personal guarantees by   C
two of the directors of the company, Mr Gary Brookes and Mr Jennings.

Pursuant to the facility letters, the company executed three successive deeds of
assignment and charge, under each of which the company assigned to RTB the benefit of
hiring agreements deposited from time to time by the company with RTB, subject to a
proviso for reassignment to the company on discharge by the company of its indebtedness
to RTB under the facility. The first of these three deeds was dated 31 March 1988, the   D
second 6 December 1988 and the third 10 February 1992.

In this action, RTB contends that the deed of assignment and charge dated 10
February 1992 (which I will call 'the 1992 charge') created a specific equitable charge
over hiring agreements deposited with RTB from time to time, together with the income
stream deriving from such agreements. RTB further contends that by letter dated 26 June
1992 it gave National Westminster express notice of its rights under the 1992 charge, with
the consequence that on receipt of that letter National Westminster became a constructive   E
trustee for RTB of all moneys thereafter coming into its hands representing income
derived from agreements subject to the 1992 charge (i.e. agreements deposited for the
time being with RTB). RTB claims a declaration to that effect, coupled with an order for
an account, and consequential relief.

So far as RTB's alleged rights under the 1992 charge are concerned, National
Westminster contends primarily that, whatever may be the position in relation to income   F
receivable *in futuro* under deposited agreements, on the true construction of the 1992
charge the company retains the right to use income from such agreements in its hands
from time to time in the ordinary course of its business, subject only to such right being
determined by RTB in accordance with the terms of the 1992 charge; that such right has
not as yet been so determined; and that accordingly as matters stand income of deposited
agreements coming into the hands of the company and credited to the company's No. 2   G
account at National Westminster is not subject to the 1992 charge.

Alternatively to that primary contention, National Westminster contends that even if
on its true construction the 1992 charge did not leave the company free to use income
from deposited agreements coming into its hands from time to time in the ordinary
course of its business (subject to termination of such right under the terms of the 1992
charge), nevertheless the company was in fact allowed to do so as a matter of licence by
RTB, and that such licence has not as yet been effectively determined.   H

On either basis, submits Mr Oliver, it matters not for present purposes whether the
1992 charge creates a charge over the agreements themselves or over income receivable
in futuro under such agreements, since the company has at all material times been, and it
remains, fully at liberty to deal with income from deposited agreements (as and when
received into its hands) for its own purposes, free from any charge.

A   As a second line of defence, National Westminster contends that if the 1992 charge creates any charge over income from deposited agreements coming into the hands of the company from time to time (as opposed to income receivable *in futuro*), the company's freedom to use such income in the ordinary course of its business is consistent only with such charge being a floating charge; and that in the event no crystallisation of such a floating charge has as yet occurred.

B   Thirdly, turning to the question of notice, National Westminster contends that even if (contrary to its earlier contentions) the 1992 charge created a specific charge over income from deposited agreements coming into the hands of the company and paid into the company's No. 2 account at National Westminster, nevertheless the terms of RTB's letter dated 26 June 1992 were not such as to give National Westminster actual notice of RTB's rights in respect of such income, with the result that National Westminster is not accountable to RTB as constructive trustee as claimed.

C   The factual history is not in dispute.

The first drawdown under the facility was made by the company on 2 March 1988, at which time hiring agreements (that is to say the original agreements) were deposited by the company with RTB. The total sum receivable under the agreements so deposited exceeded the amount of the drawdown by the required 40 per cent margin.

D   On 31 March 1988 the company executed the first of the three deeds of assignment and charge in favour of RTB. Nothing turns for present purposes on the terms or effect of this deed, and it is accordingly unnecessary for me to rehearse its terms.

Income from deposited agreements was, as I have said, paid by the company into its No. 2 account at the Crawley branch of National Westminster. The company also maintained a No. 1 account at the same branch. The company made periodic payments out of its No. 2 account in respect of accrued interest on its principal indebtedness under E   the facility, but prior to early 1992 no repayments of principal were made. In addition, the company made withdrawals from the No. 2 account for its own business purposes, without prior consultation with RTB. From time to time, the company's accounts went into overdraft, pursuant to an overdraft facility granted to the company by National Westminster. The No. 2 account was not designated in the books of National Westminster as a trust account, nor does the name of RTB appear on the statements F   relating to it. Moreover, it appears that although by far the greater part of the moneys credited to the No. 2 account represented income from agreements deposited for the time being with RTB, some credits to the account may have come from other sources. No income from deposited agreements was paid into the company's No. 1 account.

From May 1988 onwards the company made further periodic drawdowns under the RTB facility, on each occasion depositing further agreements so as to maintain the G   requisite margin of security. In addition, since as time passed and further payments were made to the company pursuant to deposited agreements the total sum receivable under such agreements inevitably reduced, further agreements were periodically deposited in order to maintain that margin.

By the second facility letter, dated 21 November 1988, RTB increased the facility to £1,250,000.

H   On 6 December 1988 the company executed the second of the three deeds of assignment and charge (which I will call 'the December 1988 charge').

Since the 1992 charge incorporates by reference many of the provisions of the December 1988 charge, it is necessary to refer at this stage to a number of such provisions. In the first place, a number of the definitions contained in cl. 1 of the December 1988 charge are incorporated in the 1992 charge, including the following.

The expression 'the agreements' is defined as meaning: A

'All hire lease or hire purchase agreements from time to time entered into between the company and its customer in connection with the equipment hire business carried on by the company and deposited with and assigned to the bank' – that is a reference to RTB – 'under or pursuant to this deed and any and every continuation thereof or substitution therefor.'

The expression 'the equipment' is defined as meaning: B

'the motor vehicles or any other equipment which are now or may hereafter be the subject matter of the agreements together with all replacements and renewals of such motor vehicles, the component parts thereof and all accessories and additions thereto.'

The 'charged property' is defined as meaning: 'the agreements and the equipment'.

Clause 2 of the December 1988 charge contained the company's covenant to repay   C
moneys lent under the facility in accordance with the terms of the second facility letter. Clause 3 contained the charging provisions, but since the 1992 charge contains its own charging provisions it is not necessary for me to refer to the charging provisions in the December 1988 charge.

Clauses 4–8 of the December 1988 charge were incorporated by reference into the 1992 charge. Clause 4 contained provisions for the maintenance of cover at the required level   D
of 140 per cent of current indebtedness, defined as 'the minimum level of cover'. Clause 4(3) was in the following terms:

'The bank shall be entitled in its absolute discretion to refuse to accept any agreements offered by the company for deposit hereunder, and any such agreements so refused shall be disregarded in determining the minimum level of cover default, and the company shall deposit with and assign to the bank further   E
agreements in substitution therefor.'

Clause 5 of the December 1988 charge provided that the charge thereby created should take effect as a continuing security. Clause 6 of the December 1988 charge contained a covenant by the company at the request of RTB to perfect the security thereby created in such manner as RTB might require.

Clause 7 of the December 1988 charge contained a number of covenants by the company. I must refer to three of them.   F

By cl. 7(5) the company covenanted that it would:

'strictly enforce the covenants given to it by its customers in the agreements and not without the prior consent of the bank terminate any of the agreements prior to the expiry date specified therein or otherwise vary any of the terms of the agreements, grant any time indulgence to any other party to the agreements or any guarantor or indemnifier thereof, release, set off or vary the liability of any such   G
party, guarantor or indemnifier or waive any breach of the agreements.'

By cl. 7(11) the company covenanted that it would:

'not without the prior written consent of the bank sell, transfer, assign, part with or in any other respect whatsoever deal with the charged property or any of its rights thereunder or interest therein or agree to the transfer or assignment by any of the customers of all or any of its rights, interests or obligations under any of the   H
agreements.'

Finally for present purposes, by cl. 7(12) the company covenanted that it would:

'not without the prior written consent of the bank create or permit to subsist any security interest over all or part of the charged property other than the security interest constituted by this deed.'

A   Clause 8 of the December 1988 charge contained a number of representations and warranties by the company, the terms of which are not material for present purposes.

Clause 9 of the December 1988 charge (which was incorporated into the 1992 charge with an addition, the terms of which are not material) provided, under the heading 'events of default', for the termination of the facility on presentation of an administration petition in respect of the company, on the making of any proposal for a voluntary B   arrangement under Part I of the *Insolvency Act* 1986, or on default by the company.

Clause 10 of the December 1988 charge conferred power on RTB to appoint a receiver of the whole or any part of 'the charged property' under the *Law of Property Act* 1925.

Clause 11 of the December 1988 charge was in the following terms:

C   'The statutory power of sale conferred on the bank by section 101 of the Act' – the Act in this context is the *Law of Property Act* 1925, that being a defined expression in cl. 1 of the December 1988 charge – 'shall arise on the execution hereof and may be exercised by the bank at any time in relation to any part of the charged property after the bank shall have demanded in a manner and at a time or times provided for in the facility letter the payment or discharge by the company of all or any of the secured obligations and the provisions of the Act relating to and regulating the exercise of the said power of sale shall so far as they relate to the security D   constituted by this deed be varied or extended accordingly.'

Finally, for present purposes, cl. 15 of the December 1988 charge, which was incorporated into the 1992 charge and is headed, 'collection of sums due under agreements, reads as follows:

'(1) The company shall until otherwise directed by the bank collect as agents for the bank all sums due under the agreements.

E   (2) The company shall if so required by the bank at any time open an account with the bank which shall be designated as a "rental income collection account" and pay to the credit of such account from time to time and forthwith upon the company receiving from its customers any moneys pursuant to the agreements all of such moneys so received by the company.

(3) The company shall on demand by the bank cease to collect the sums due under the agreements and shall without prejudice to the bank's right to do so at any time F   give notice to its customers in such form as may be approved by the bank from time to time to remit payments due under the agreements direct to the bank and the bank shall credit such payments to the rental income collection account referred to in subcl. (2) above or, if no such account shall have been opened by the bank, the bank shall open such an account for this purpose. Any sums collected by the company in breach of this provision shall be held on trust for the bank.

G   (4) Moneys standing to the credit of the rental income collection account shall accrue interest from day to day at the rate of . . . such interest to be computed on the basis of the number of days elapsed and a 365 day year.

(5) The company shall only be allowed to make any withdrawals or direct any payments from the rental income collection account with the prior written consent of the bank.'

H   During 1989 and 1990 the company made further drawdowns under the second facility letter and (as from 10 April 1990) under the third facility letter, which further increased the facility to £2,500,000.

By mid-1991 RTB had decided as a matter of policy to withdraw the facility, and from about October 1991 discussions took place between RTB (acting by Mr Bayes) and the company (acting by Mr Brookes) for the repayment of the company's indebtedness under

the facility. By that stage the full amount of the facility, £2,500,000, had been drawn   A
down.

In about December 1991 the company negotiated a discounting facility with Yorkshire
Bank Finance Ltd in the sum of £500,000, such facility taking the form of an offer by
Yorkshire Bank Finance Ltd to purchase from the company hiring agreements at a
discounted value, up to a limit of £500,000.

In or about early 1992 agreement was reached between Mr Bayes and Mr Brookes for   B
repayment of principal to be made by monthly payments of £85,000, and a total sum of
£170,000 was duly paid to RTB out of the company's No. 2 account, representing the
monthly instalments for January and February 1992.

On 10 February 1992 the company executed the 1992 charge.

Mr Bayes gave evidence on affidavit and orally. His evidence was not challenged, and
I accept it in its entirety.   C

He told me that he decided to take a further charge out of an abundance of caution, as
the December 1988 charge referred to the second facility letter, which had subsequently
been superseded by the third facility letter.

As I explained earlier, the 1992 charge incorporates many of the provisions of the
December 1988 charge. Thus, cl. 1 of the 1992 charge incorporates the definitions in the
December 1988 charge, save that the expression 'facility letter' is defined as meaning the
third facility letter. Clause 2 of the 1992 charge contains the company's covenant, in   D
substantially the same form as the covenant contained in cl. 2 of the December 1988
charge. Clause 3 of the 1992 charge is headed 'assignment and charge', and I must read
it in full.

'(1) As security for the payment or discharge of all the secured obligations and all
its obligations under this deed the company as beneficial owner hereby assigns to   E
the bank free and clear of all security interests all the rights benefits and interests
of the company present and future in the agreements including but without
prejudice to the generality of the foregoing:

   (i)   the right to receive all rentals and other payments whatsoever due or to
         become due under or by virtue of the agreements;

   (ii) the benefit of all guarantees indemnities charges negotiable instruments and   F
         other rights and remedies now or hereafter belonging to the company in
         connection with the agreements;

   (iii) so far as is applicable the benefits of all insurances effected by the company
         in connection with the agreements or the equipment;

   (iv) the benefit of each and every warranty or guarantee given by any person to
         the company upon the purchase by the company of the equipment or any   G
         component parts thereof;

to the extent that the same are not already effectively vested in the bank pursuant
to the deed of assignment and charge granted by the company in favour of the
bank dated 6 December 1988, to hold the same unto the bank absolutely provided
always that if the company shall make irrevocable payment of or discharge in
respect of all the secured obligations and all its obligations under this deed the   H
bank will at the request and cost of the company reassign to the company the
agreements and other rights assigned hereunder.

(2) As further security for the payment or discharge of all the secured obligations
and all its obligations under this deed the company as beneficial owner hereby
charges to the bank by way of first fixed charge the equipment to the extent that

A   the same is not already effectively vested in the bank pursuant to the said deed of assignment and charge.'

Clause 4 of the 1992 charge incorporates cl. 4–8 inclusive of the December 1988 charge. Clause 5 of the 1992 charge incorporates cl. 9 of the December 1988 charge ('events of default'), with an immaterial addition. Clause 6 of the 1992 charge effectively incorporates the provisions in the December 1988 charge relating to RTB's power to

B   appoint a receiver, and to its power of sale under the *Law of Property Act* 1925. Clause 7 of the 1992 charge incorporates cl. 12–27 of the December 1988 charge.

Returning to the factual history, Mr Bayes told me that in the course of his discussions with Mr Brookes about the repayment by the company of its indebtedness to RTB under the facility, Mr Brookes assured him that the company's No. 2 account at National Westminster was being used exclusively for the collection of income from agreements

C   from time to time deposited with RTB, and that no other moneys were credited to that account. Mr Bayes accepted this assurance. He was not aware of any credits being made to that account from other sources. On the other hand he accepted in evidence that when checking the bank statements of the account he came across standing order credits from five agreements the originals of which he could not find. It is therefore possible that such agreements had not been deposited with RTB; alternatively, they may have been deposited with RTB and subsequently lost or mislaid by RTB. In addition, Mr Bayes

D   accepted that he was unable to attribute to particular agreements payments made into the account by means of 'counter credits'.

It was arranged between Mr Bayes and Mr Brookes that periodic payments should be made to RTB out of the company's No. 2 account pursuant to direct debit instructions given to National Westminster by the company. However, on 25 June 1992 (at which point the No. 2 account was overdrawn to the tune of more than £50,000) National

E   Westminster refused to make further payments to RTB out of the account. On the same day National Westminster withdrew the company's overdraft facility and demanded payment of the total sum owing by the company to National Westminster on its accounts with National Westminster. The sum so demanded was £159,803.18.

On the following day, 26 June 1992, RTB wrote the letter to National Westminster which is relied on by RTB in support of its allegation that as from receipt of that letter,

F   if not earlier, National Westminster had actual notice that payments into the No. 2 account representing payments under agreements for the time being deposited with RTB were subject to a specific equitable charge in favour of RTB. The letter is in the following terms:

'Dear Sirs,

G   *Re Brookes Associates Finance Ltd*

You will be aware that we afford facilities to the above-named company as security for which we have a fixed charge over all payments due under the company's HP/ lease agreements which have been assigned to us pursuant to a deed of assignment and charge. This deed of assignment and charge is of course registered at Companies House.

H   As a matter of practice we understand that those sums which are charged to us are paid into the company's No. 2 account with you from which payment is made to us by way of direct debit on a monthly basis. However, two payments in the account on 25 June 1992 in the sum of £152,650 and £15,431.05 have not been honoured. Those sums are, as we have said, charged to us and in the circumstances we require an immediate banker's payment in the total sum.

Furthermore, we hereby give you formal notice that all future moneys paid to any   A
of the company's accounts with you in respect of those agreements assigned and
charged to us are to be held for our sole benefit.

Yours faithfully . . .'

In this action, RTB does not pursue the claim made in the second paragraph of the
letter (relating to payment of the two sums of £152,650 and £15,431.05). Moreover, it
makes no claim against National Westminster in relation to moneys withdrawn from the   B
No. 2 account prior to receipt by National Westminster of RTB's letter of 26 June 1992.

Mr Bayes told me that he did not send a copy of the letter of 26 June 1992 to the
company, and that it did not occur to him to do so. He was, however, in fairly regular
contact with Mr Brookes at this time.

In September 1992 (by which time a substantial credit balance had accumulated on the
No. 2 account, derived mainly, if not entirely, from payments under deposited   C
agreements) National Westminster gave notice to the company of its intention to exercise
its right of set-off, and on 11 November 1992 it combined the balances on the company's
accounts by transferring a sum of £106,328.74 from the No. 2 account to the company's
No. 1 account in order to extinguish the overdraft on the No. 1 account. This transfer
effectively reduced the credit balance on the No. 2 account to nil.

I am told that the company is now in receivership.   D

I can now return to the issues and to the arguments.

I turn first to the issue as to the rights of RTB as against the company in respect of
income from deposited agreements received into the hands of the company from time to
time.

Mr Mitchell, for RTB, submits that the 1992 charge created a specific equitable charge
over the deposited agreements themselves and over income derived from them, both   E
received and receivable. He submits that the 1992 charge possesses none of the three
characteristics of a floating charge listed by Romer LJ in *Re Yorkshire Woolcombers
Association* [1903] 2 Ch 284 in the well-known passage from his judgment (at p. 295 of
the report) where he says:

'I certainly do not intend to attempt to give an exact definition of the term "floating
charge", nor am I prepared to say that there will not be a floating charge within   F
the meaning of the Act, which does not contain all the three characteristics that I
am about to mention, but I certainly think that if a charge has the three
characteristics that I am about to mention it is a floating charge. (1) If it is a charge
on a class of assets of a company present and future; (2) if that class is one which,
in the ordinary course of the business of the company, would be changing from
time to time; and (3) if you find that by the charge it is contemplated that, until
some future step is taken by or on behalf of those interested in the charge, the   G
company may carry on its business in the ordinary way as far as concerns the
particular class of assets I am dealing with.'

Mr Mitchell further relies on the decision of the Court of Appeal in *Re Atlantic
Computer Systems plc* [1990] BCC 859. In that case the question arose whether charges
over subleases of equipment to end-users were to be characterised as fixed charges or
floating charges for the purposes of certain provisions of the *Insolvency Act* 1986. Giving   H
the judgment of the Court of Appeal, Nicholls LJ referred to the dictum of Romer LJ in
the *Yorkshire Woolcombers* case and continued (at p. 873B):

'In the House of Lords (*Illingworth v Houldsworth* [1904] AC 355 at p. 357) Lord
Halsbury LC referred to the charge in that case and stated what he considered to
be the essential characteristic of a floating security:

A
"In the first place you have that which in a sense I suppose must be an element in the definition of a floating security, that it is something which is to float, not to be put into immediate operation, but such that the company is to be allowed to carry on its business. It contemplates not only that it should carry with it the book debts which were then existing, but it contemplates also the possibility of those book debts being extinguished by payment to the company, and that other book debts should come in and take the place of those that had

B
disappeared. That . . . seems to me to be an essential characteristic of what is properly called a floating security."

Lord Macnaghten (at p. 358) also emphasised the ambulatory nature of a floating charge:

"I should have thought there was not much difficulty in defining what a floating charge is in contrast to what is called a specific charge. A specific charge, I

C
think, is one that without more fastens on ascertained and definite property or property capable of being ascertained and defined; a floating charge, on the other hand, is ambulatory and shifting in its nature, hovering over and so to speak floating with the property which it is intended to affect until some event occurs or some act is done which causes it to settle and fasten on the subject of the charge within its reach and grasp."

D
In the light of these observations we cannot accept Mr Heslop's submissions. The notable feature of the present case is that the charges were not ambulatory. The property assigned by the company was confined to rights to which the company was entitled under specific, existing contracts. The assignments consisted of the company's rights "under or by virtue of" subleases each of which was already in existence at the time of the assignments and each of which was specifically identified in the relevant deeds of assignment. In each case the payments due to the company

E
under a specific sublease were charged as security for the payments due by the company under the head lease relating to the same equipment. The company's right to receive future instalments from end users in due course pursuant to the terms of these subleases was as much a present asset of the company, within Romer LJ's reference to "present and future" assets of a company, as a right to receive payment of a sum which was immediately due. Romer LJ's reference to future

F
assets was a reference to assets of which, when the charge was created, the company was not the owner. That was the position in that case. That is not the position in this case.'

Mr Mitchell accepts that given the manner of operation of the company's No. 2 account prior to 26 June 1992, and in particular the fact that during that period withdrawals were made from the account for the general purposes of the company's

G
business, it is not open to RTB to claim a proprietary interest in income from deposited agreements credited to the No. 2 account prior to that date. He submits, however, that RTB's implied consent to such income being available to the company for the purposes of its business was withdrawn when RTB wrote the letter of 26 June 1992, and on that basis he submits that RTB has a proprietary claim to all income from deposited agreements thereafter credited to the No. 2 account.

In this connection he relies on a further passage from the judgment of the Court of

H
Appeal in the *Atlantic Computer* case where Nicholls LJ said (at p. 873H):

'We have in mind that in practice sums payable by the end users under these subleases were paid to the company and utilised by it in the ordinary course of business. In so far as this is relevant, it may well be that this was what the parties intended should happen. The company was to be at liberty to receive and use the instalments until AIB chose to intervene. We are unpersuaded that this results in

these charges, on existing and defined property, becoming floating charges. A   A
mortgage of land does not become a floating charge by reason of the mortgagor
being permitted to remain in possession and enjoy the fruits of the property
charged for the time being. This is so even if the land is leasehold and the term is
very short, and as such the asset charged is of a wasting character. So here: the
mere fact that for the time being the company could continue to receive and use
the instalments does not suffice to negative the fixed character of the charge. This
apart, we have seen nothing to lend any support to the administrators' contention.   B
In particular, we have seen nothing to suggest that after the assignment the
company was to be at liberty to deal with its rights under the subleases without the
consent of AIB.'

Mr Mitchell also relies on the decision of Vinelott J in *Re Atlantic Medical Ltd* [1992]
BCC 653 for the proposition that the distinction between a fixed charge on the deposited
agreements and a floating charge on the income from such agreements collected by the   C
company is an unreal one (see particularly p. 659H).

As I indicated earlier, Mr Oliver's primary submission is that, as a matter of contract
between the company and RTB, the company at all material times retained full freedom
to deal with income from deposited agreements from time to time in its hands, with the
result that such income is not subject to any charge created by the 1992 charge, whether
fixed or floating. He submits that such freedom is conferred by the 1992 charge itself on   D
its true construction, alternatively it must have been conferred by way of express or
implied licence dehors the 1992 charge. If it was conferred by the 1992 charge, it could
(so Mr Oliver submits) only be determined pursuant to the provisions of the 1992 charge
– e.g. by RTB invoking the provisions of cl. 15(2) or (3) of the December 1988 charge,
which RTB has not done, or by the appointment of a receiver or the occurrence of an
event of default. On the other hand, if it was conferred by licence dehors the 1992 charge,
the licence could (he submits) only be revoked by RTB on adequate notice being given to   E
the company, and there is no evidence of any such notice being given to the company. In
particular, Mr Oliver relies on the fact that a copy of the letter of 26 June 1992 was not
sent to the company.

As to cl. 15(1) of the December 1988 charge (which was incorporated into the 1992
charge), Mr Oliver submits (relying on *Henry v Hammond* [1913] 2 KB 515) that this
provision did not impose any fiduciary obligation on the company, and in particular did   F
not oblige it to place income from deposited agreements in a separate account or prevent
it from using such moneys for the purposes of its business.

Mr Oliver expressed himself as content to accept (although he did not formally
concede) that the 1992 charge created a specific equitable charge over the agreements
themselves, and very possibly also over the right to future receivables under those
agreements, but he submitted that the company's subsisting (as he would have it)   G
contractual freedom to deal with income actually received (as opposed to income
receivable *in futuro*) precludes the existence of any charge over or proprietary claim to
such income for so long as such freedom subsists.

Alternatively, Mr Oliver submits that if the 1992 charge created any charge on income
in the hands of the company, such charge must on authority be a floating, as opposed to
a specific, charge. In this connection he relies strongly, once again, on the company's
supposed contractual freedom to use income coming into its hands from time to time in   H
the ordinary course of its business.

Mr Oliver cites *Re Brightlife Ltd* (1986) 2 BCC 99,359 (a decision of Hoffmann J and
Re New Bullas Trading Ltd ([1993] BCC 251 (Knox J); [1994] BCC 36 (CA)) as examples
of cases in which freedom to deal with the charged property is recognised as an important
factor in determining the proprietary character of the security, and in support of a general

A   submission to the effect that the fact that the parties may have described a charge as being a fixed charge is not conclusive as to its nature, since the nature of the security which they have created depends upon the terms of their contract rather than on the label which they have attached to it. He also relies in this connection on the Northern Irish case of *Re Armagh Shoes Ltd* [1982] NI 59.

B   As to the passage in the judgment of the Court of Appeal in the *Atlantic Computer* case at p. 873H, cited above, Mr Oliver pointed out that the report does not set out all the relevant provisions of the charge, with the result that one cannot tell whether the company's freedom to deal with income from charged subleases in the ordinary course of its business derived from the charge itself or from some consensual arrangement outside the terms of the charge. He submits that it should be assumed that the latter was the case, since otherwise the decision would represent an erosion of the concept of a floating charge to an extent which is not justified on the earlier authorities.

C   In support of the submission that, assuming there to be a floating charge over income of deposited agreements in the hands of the company from time to time, such charge has not yet crystallised, Mr Oliver relies on *Evans v Rival Granite Quarries Ltd* [1910] 2 KB 979 as authority for the proposition that it is essentially for the parties to specify, as a matter of contract, the circumstances or events which will cause a floating charge to crystallise.

D   I turn first to the 1992 charge itself, in order to determine whether, on its true construction, it confers upon, or reserves to, the company freedom to use income of deposited agreements in its hands from to time in the ordinary course of its business, pending the occurrence of an event of default or the invoking by RTB of its specific remedies or powers under the terms of the 1992 charge.

E   In my judgment the 1992 charge does not on its true construction confer upon or reserve to the company the right to use income of deposited agreements in its hands from time to time in the ordinary course of its business, pending some act of enforcement by RTB under the terms of the 1992 charge or the occurrence of an event of default. In the first place, the charging provisions in cl. 3 of the 1992 charge are expressed to include the agreements themselves, and 'all the rights, benefits and interests of the company, present and future, in the agreements'. Looking no further for the moment, those words are in my judgment apt to include not merely the right to income receivable in the future, but also income in the hands of the company from time to time. In the second place, in my judgment cl. 15(1) of the December 1988 charge – when read in the context of the 1992 charge as a whole, and in particular in the context of the remainder of cl. 15 – clearly indicates that in collecting income as agent for RTB the company is a fiduciary. Were that not to be so, I can see no purpose at all in the inclusion of cl. 15(1). In the third place, it seems to me that, given the terms of the charging provision, clear words would be required to, in effect, exclude from the scope of the charge income of the charged property actually received, while leaving income receivable subject to the charge. The decision of the Court of Appeal in the *New Bullas* case indicates that it may be open to contracting parties to achieve such a (to my mind) odd result, but in that case there were clear words to the effect that the fixed charge was not to apply to book debts when realised: here there is no comparable provision.

H   I appreciate that the requirement that cover be maintained at 140 per cent of the company's current principal indebtedness (a requirement contained in cl. 4 of the 1988 charge and incorporated in the 1992 charge) recognises the possibility that the company may use income from deposited agreements in the ordinary course of its business, but in my judgment it does not confer upon or reserve to the company a right to do so. All it does, in my judgment, is recognise that RTB may allow the company to do so (as in the event it did).

As Nicholls LJ said in the passage from the judgment of the Court of Appeal in the   A
Atlantic Computer case quoted earlier:

'In so far as this is relevant, it may well be that this was what the parties intended
should happen.'

Nor do I see any reason to interpret Nicholls LJ's words in the restricted sense suggested
by Mr Oliver.

B

I conclude, therefore, that on the true construction of the 1992 charge income of
deposited agreements coming into the hands of the company from time to time is subject
to the charge thereby created, and that no right is thereby conferred upon or reserved to
the company to use such income in the ordinary course of its business.

I turn next to the question whether the charge created by the 1992 charge over such
income is a specific charge or a floating charge.

C

I accept Mr Mitchell's submissions that none of the three characteristics of a floating
charge described by Romer LJ in the *Yorkshire Woolcombers* case are present in the
instant case. Nor is the charge 'ambulatory', in the sense in which Lord Macnaghten used
that word in *Illingworth v Houldsworth* (see also the passage in the judgment of the Court
of Appeal in the *Atlantic Computer* case at p. 873B of the report, cited earlier in this
judgment). The fact that the charge in the instant case fastens on agreements deposited
with RTB from time to time does not render the charge ambulatory. It is a specific charge   D
on each agreement, which arises as and when the agreement is deposited with RTB and
which continues unless and until the agreement expires or ceases to form part of the
security pursuant to the provisions for substitution contained in cl. 4 of the December
1988 charge and incorporated in the 1992 charge. In that sense, the charge created by the
1992 charge is not ambulatory but stationary.

I therefore conclude that on its true construction the 1992 charge creates a specific   E
equitable charge on income from agreements deposited with RTB coming into the hands
of the company from time to time.

I turn next to Mr Oliver's alternative submission that the company's freedom to use
such income in the ordinary course of its business derives from an implied licence by
RTB outside the terms of the 1992 charge, which licence has not as yet been revoked,
there being no evidence of any notice (let alone adequate notice) of revocation having   F
been given by RTB to the company.

Plainly, prior to writing the letter of 26 June 1992, RTB did consent (it matters not
whether expressly or impliedly) to the company withdrawing funds from its No. 2
account for use in the ordinary course of its business. Moreover, on the basis of the
conclusions which I have already reached, in so consenting RTB was indeed acting
outside the terms of the 1992 charge.

G

There is, however, no evidence before me of any consideration for such consent moving
from the company. It follows that Mr Oliver's assertion that such consent can only be
withdrawn on adequate notice being given by RTB to the company must be based on the
premise that the circumstances in which the consent was given raise some equity to that
effect in favour of the company against RTB (e.g. an equity arising by way of promissory
estoppel). On the evidence before me, however, I am unable to conclude that such an
equity exists. As I said earlier, the company has taken no part in the proceedings.   H
Moreover, National Westminster elected to call no evidence.

As the matter stands before me, the position as between RTB and the company is that
at no material time did the company have any right to use the income from deposited
agreements from time to time standing to the credit of the company's No. 2 account in
the ordinary course of the company's business; that the use of such moneys for that

A   purpose required the consent of RTB; that until 26 June 1992 RTB did so consent; but that as from 26 June 1992 it did not.

In any event, even if on an investigation of all the relevant facts and circumstances it should appear that the company might have been in a position to assert some equity against RTB in relation to the withdrawal of RTB's consent – which in the event it has not sought to do – I am not persuaded, as the matter stands before me, that the existence of such an equity would affect the position as between RTB and National Westminster, B   assuming National Westminster to be fixed with notice of RTB's rights under the 1992 charge.

I accordingly reject Mr Oliver's alternative contention based on the existence of a consensual arrangement outside the terms of the 1992 charge.

I turn finally, therefore, to the question of notice.

C   It is accepted on behalf of National Westminster that on receipt of the letter of 26 June 1992, if not earlier, National Westminster had actual notice that RTB was a loan creditor of the company pursuant to a facility which it had provided to the company, and that RTB had taken security for that lending in the form of charges of some kind over hiring agreements entered into by the company. Mr Oliver submits, however, that the letter of 26 June 1992 was inadequate in that it did not identify the particular agreements which were subject to the 1992 charge as at that date. He submits that it was incumbent on D   RTB at the very least to identify each and every such agreement, and that in the absence of such identification National Westminster was not fixed with notice of RTB's rights under the 1992 charge so as to render it liable as constructive trustee as claimed.

For his part, Mr Mitchell accepts that it would have been preferable (as plainly it would) had there had been annexed to the letter of 26 June 1992 a schedule identifying all agreements deposited with RTB as at that date, but he submits that in all the E   circumstances the letter of 26 June 1992 was sufficient to render National Westminster liable as claimed. In particular, he relies on a number of internal documents of National Westminster disclosed on discovery which indicate that the National Westminster received copies of the first two facility letters from the company (containing detailed terms as to the security to be provided for the facility), and that Mr Brookes kept National Westminster regularly informed in relation to the company's dealings with RTB. Thus, an internal memorandum of National Westminster dated 7 November 1989 F   notes 'receivables £1,533,754 against loan from Royal Trust Bank £1.1m plus current borrowing taken on the No. 2 account', and further notes that the facility was to increase to £2.5m. Similarly, an internal document of National Westminster dated 13 March 1990 contains the following:

> 'Income at present £140,000/£150,000 per month on the deals they finance and Royal Trust are looking to put up the line from £1.25m to £2.5m. At present they G   pay interest only to Royal Trust, replacing expired agreements with new ones from time to time. Every time they do a drawdown with Royal Trust . . . they need to provide full details of all agreements charged to Royal Trust . . . A list was produced as at 23 February indicating balance outstanding on agreements they have financed was £1.68m with no arrears.'

An internal memorandum of National Westminster dated 8 May 1990 contains the H   following:

> '*Securities*: Is it feasible for us to have a charge over the agreements which have not been discounted with Royal Trust as security for our facility?'

–and later in the same memorandum:

> 'In respect of the agreements deposited with the Royal Trust Bank the system will need to be set up whereby we get regular information as to the agreements written,

amount receivable therefrom, those deposited with Royal Trust, balance   A
outstanding with Royal Trust and amount receivable on contracts still held by the
company.'

An internal memorandum of National Westminster dated 5 June 1990 states:

'Numerous discussions over previous two months in respect of security for present
facilities. Mortgage debenture was totally rejected and we have been exploring the
possibility of taking a charge over those lease agreements not discounted with   B
Royal Trust.'

An internal memorandum of National Westminster dated 29 November 1990 states:

'Gary [that is a reference to Mr Brookes] told me that the current block facility
through Royal Trust is fully drawn down at £2.5m against which there are
receivables of £4m. 200 borrowing lines, of which only two are in arrears . . .'

Finally, an internal memorandum of National Westminster dated 26 June 1992 (but   C
plainly written before receipt of RTB's letter of that date) comments that:

'It will obviously not be long before Royal Trust seek to obtain a secure hold on
the moneys and there is clearly a threat that we may be challenged by Royal Trust
on preference. I feel that we should take whatever we can at this stage and worry
about preference later.'

In my judgment, given the state of knowledge of National Westminster prior to receipt   D
of the letter of 26 June 1992 as to the security taken by RTB (as evidenced by National
Westminster's internal memoranda, examples of which I have given above) the terms of
that letter were adequate to constitute National Westminster constructive trustee of
income from agreements deposited with RTB thereafter received by National
Westminster. The letter of 26 June 1992 was just the attempt by RTB to 'obtain a secure
hold on the moneys' which National Westminster had been expecting. In my judgment   E
the fact that the letter did not go on to identify the particular agreements constituting
RTB's security as at that date does not, in all the circumstances of this case, suffice to
prevent National Westminster becoming liable as constructive trustee, as claimed.

Accordingly, I conclude that National Westminster is accountable to RTB as
constructive trustee in respect of all moneys credited to the company's No. 2 account
after receipt by National Westminster of RTB's letter dated 26 June 1992, being moneys
representing income from agreements for the time being deposited with RTB pursuant to   F
the 1992 charge.

(Order accordingly)

   G

   H

A

Re Moorgate Metals Ltd.
Official receiver v Huhtala & Anor.

Chancery Division.
Warner J.
Judgment delivered 23 March 1994.

B

Disqualifying unfit directors of insolvent companies – Whether respondent was de facto or shadow director – Whether respondents were unfit – Company Directors Disqualification Act 1986, s. 6.

This was an application by the official receiver for a disqualification order under s. 6 of the Company Directors Disqualification Act 1986 against two respondents, one of whom ('H') contested the application. In the case of H there were two questions for the court: (1) whether his conduct as a director of Moorgate Metals Ltd made him unfit to be concerned

C

in the management of a company, and (2) if so, for what period he should be disqualified. In the case of the other director, 'R', there were three questions, the first being whether R was a de facto or a shadow director of the company. If that question was answered in the affirmative the same two questions of unfitness and length of disqualification arose.

Moorgate had a short life. It was incorporated on 14 November 1988 and was ordered to be compulsorily wound up on 15 November 1989. It was then insolvent to the tune of over

D

half a million pounds. R was in sole charge of the company's trading as a metal merchant. It resold container loads of scrap metal at prices lower than those at which it bought them and it therefore traded at a loss. R concealed this from H by issuing invoices which went unpaid. R was at all material times an undischarged bankrupt.

Held, disqualifying the respondents for four and ten years respectively:

1. H was clearly unfit. He made an inappropriate investment of the company's money

E

without adequate documentation. He should have realised sooner that R was not to be trusted and that the company could not be saved. His remuneration and benefits at the expense of the company were excessive. He had acted irresponsibly in taking £10,000 from the company for the purchase of a property in France.

2. R was a de facto director of Moorgate. A number of facts led to that conclusion: the fact that Moorgate came into existence as a result of R inviting H to join him in a business

F

that he was minded to set up; the fact that R and H shared the responsibilities of managing the company and that R was in sole charge of the company's trading with no limit on the extent of the commitments that he could enter into on behalf of the company; and the fact that R and H received equal remuneration. Other facts supported the conclusion. The evidence pointed to H and R running the company between them as equals, and not to R being H's subordinate in any way. R was a director in all but name.

G

3. R was a thoroughly dishonest, irresponsible and unscrupulous person. The seriousness of his misconduct as a de facto director of Moorgate put his case at least at the top end of the middle (five to ten year) bracket. R's involvement in the management of Moorgate while an undischarged bankrupt spoke for itself. So did the manner in which he conducted the company's trade and the way in which he concealed what he was doing from H by means of the deception of the invoices. R was primarily the author of the company's insolvency. In the matter of the excessive remuneration R's conduct was even more irresponsible than H's

H

because R knew that profits were not being and could not be earned out of which to pay that remuneration. He was also at fault in the matter of the French property.

The following cases were referred to in the judgment:

Cargo Agency Ltd, Re [1992] BCC 388.
Godwin Warren Control Systems plc, Re [1992] BCC 557.
Hydrodan (Corby) Ltd [1994] BCC 161.

Lo-Line Electric Motors Ltd & Ors, Re (1988) 4 BCC 415; [1988] Ch 477.   A

Sevenoaks Stationers (Retail) Ltd, Re [1990] BCC 765; [1991] Ch 164.

Tasbian Ltd, Re (No. 3) [1991] BCC 435; [1992] BCC 358 (CA).

Malcolm Davis-White (instructed by the Treasury Solicitor) for the official receiver.

Charles Salter (instructed by Moss & Co) for the first respondent.

JUDGMENT   B

Warner J: This is an application by the official receiver for a disqualification order under s. 6 of the *Company Directors Disqualification Act* 1986 against each of two respondents, namely, Mr Christopher William Huhtala and Mr Lionel Rawlinson.

The application was contested by Mr Huhtala who was represented before me by Mr Salter. The application was not contested by Mr Rawlinson. On 21 February 1994, two days before the hearing began, Mr Rawlinson wrote a letter to the court to which he C attached a plea in mitigation saying that he did not wish to contest the proceedings in view of his age, 70, and of the state of his health. Mr Rawlinson is a diabetic and he suffers from a heart condition. He enclosed with his letter a doctor's certificate to the effect that because of his heart complaint he should avoid undue stress if at all possible. Mr Rawlinson had on 7 April 1992 sworn an affidavit which was read to me by Mr Davis-White on behalf of the official receiver notwithstanding an order that the evidence D of any deponent not attending for cross-examination be not read. There is also before me as an exhibit to the assistant official receiver's first report in support of the application a statement made by Mr Rawlinson on 22 November 1989 to a senior examiner in the office of the official receiver.

Subsection (1) of s. 6 provides that the court shall make a disqualification order against a person where it is satisfied (a) that he is or has been a director of a company which has at any time become insolvent and (b) that his conduct as a director of that company E makes him unfit to be concerned in the management of a company.

The company in respect of which the official receiver contends that those conditions are satisfied in the case of each of the respondents is Moorgate Metals Ltd, which I will call 'Moorgate' or 'the company'.

Moorgate had a short life. It was incorporated on 14 November 1988 and was ordered to be compulsorily wound up on 15 November 1989. It was then insolvent to the tune of F over half am pounds; its creditors included a number of small creditors. The cause of its insolvency was both simple and astonishing. Its trade was that of a metal merchant. It bought and sold large quantities of scrap metals, in particular brass, aluminium, lead and steel. For the most part it resold container loads of such metals at prices lower than those at which it bought them. Only in a few cases did it resell at a profit. So inevitably it traded at a loss and the losses mounted up. Mr Rawlinson, who was in sole charge of the G company's trading, says that this was done to secure a foothold in the market. For a long time he was able to conceal from Mr Huhtala the fact that the company was trading in that way.

Moorgate was a joint venture between Mr Rawlinson and Mr Huhtala. However, Mr Rawlinson was at all material times an undischarged bankrupt. For that reason his wife, Mrs Betty Millicent Rawlinson, acted as his nominee both as a shareholder in and as a H director of the company. The issued share capital of the company consisted of two shares of £1 each, one of which was held by Mr Huhtala and the other by Mrs Rawlinson. The formally appointed (or 'de jure') directors of the company were from the time of its incorporation Mr Huhtala and Mrs Rawlinson. The secretary of the company was Mr Rawlinson. Mrs Rawlinson took no part in the affairs of the company save that she attended the only formal board meeting ever held which was on 4 July 1989. The others

A   present at that meeting were Mr Huhtala and Mr Rawlinson. The official receiver contends that Mr Rawlinson was a de facto director or a shadow director of the company.

Thus in the case of Mr Huhtala there are two questions for my determination: (1) whether his conduct as a director of Moorgate makes him unfit to be concerned in the management of a company and (2) if so, for what period he should be disqualified.

In the case of Mr Rawlinson there are three questions, of which the first is whether he was a de facto or a shadow director of the company. If that question is answered in the affirmative the same two questions arise as in the case of Mr Huhtala.

Mr Huhtala

Mr Huhtala was born in 1946 so that at the time of the incorporation of the company he was 42. Since leaving school he had had a succession of jobs with a variety of employers including foundries in South Wales, a cigarette paper manufacturer, a multinational cosmetics company (Revlon), a small provincial wine merchant, two firms of chartered surveyors and three publishers of magazines. Some of those jobs had been fairly lowly. Thus by the South Wales foundries he had been employed as a clerk, and with the wine merchant his duties included driving a van. Others of his jobs were managerial, mostly concerned with marketing rather than financial administration. With Revlon he had, in 1978, risen to the position of European marketing and advertising manager. While at Revlon he had obtained a diploma in advertising and marketing at the City of London Polytechnic. He had also, while at Revlon, started in partnership with other employees of Revlon a business of manufacturing and selling toiletries for children. That business was eventually incorporated as Pewter Toiletries Ltd. Mr Huhtala told me that that business had been carried on with the knowledge and consent of Revlon because Revlon were not interested in children's toiletries. Be that as it may, Pewter Toiletries appears to have been financially a failure.

Mr Huhtala was an adjudicated bankrupt in 1981 and obtained his discharge in 1987. On obtaining his discharge he became a director of the third of the publishers that I have mentioned, a company called Metals and Minerals Publications Ltd (which I will call 'MMP') and also of an associated company of MMP, namely Tin Publications Ltd (which I will call 'Tin Publications').

MMP and Tin Publications published periodicals relating to the metals industry and to trade in metals. As a director of MMP and of Tin Publications Mr Huhtala had the day-to-day management of those companies. The other two directors, who were the owners of the shares in the companies, were comparatively inactive. One was resident in Australia and the other had other interests which occupied most of his time. However, Mr Huhtala was not concerned with the editorial side of the management of MMP and Tin Publications. He was not responsible for the contents of those companies' publications. In cross-examination before me Mr Huhtala acknowledged that, contrary to what he had said in a statement made to the official receiver's senior examiner on 22 November 1989, he had not 'gained quite an extensive knowledge of the metals industry during [his] career in publishing'.

I have to say that I formed the view that Mr Huhtala, who was cross-examined at length, was a very unreliable witness. Making full allowance for the fact that he was speaking of events that took place mostly five or six years ago, his answers to questions were too often obscure, confused, inconsistent with each other or otherwise unsatisfactory; and more than once his version of events changed materially as he was confronted with documentary evidence.

Mr Rawlinson

Mr Rawlinson was born in 1923. He is an experienced metals trader. He was adjudicated bankrupt three times: in 1962, in 1966 and in 1978. In 1984 an application

by him for discharge from his third bankruptcy was opposed by the official receiver on   A
the grounds of dishonest conduct on his part in a number of respects. It was refused.

The genesis of Moorgate

MMP and Tin Publications had offices at 60 Worship Street, London EC2. They had
more space there than they needed. In the autumn of 1988 Mr Rawlinson became a
tenant of some of that space, the arrangements being made on behalf of MMP by Mr   B
Huhtala. Mr Rawlinson and Mr Huhtala had known each other socially for some time.
Mr Rawlinson, who had worked as a metals trader for various employers, was minded
to set up business on his own account as a metals trader. He invited Mr Huhtala to join
him in that business and Mr Huhtala accepted the invitation. Moorgate was formed to
carry on that business. At the time of its formation the owners of the shares in MMP and
Tin Publications had decided to sell those companies and Mr Huhtala envisaged
acquiring them by way of a management buy-out. I infer that Mr Huhtala did not at that   C
time intend to work full time for Moorgate. However, soon afterwards – Mr Huhtala
told me that it must have been before the end of November 1988 – the owners of MMP
and Tin Publications sold those companies to someone else and Mr Huhtala's proposed
management buy-out fell through. Thereafter, whilst Mr Rawlinson remained in sole
charge of Moorgate's buying and selling of metals, Mr Huhtala became responsible for
all other aspects of its affairs, in particular finance and administration.   D

Moorgate's trading

From November 1988 to February 1989 Moorgate traded from 60 Worship Street. In
February 1989 it moved to premises at 42 Westbourne Grove, London W2 of which the
lease had been acquired in Mr Huhtala's name for a premium of £15,000. Mr Huhtala
told me that during the period while Moorgate was at 60 Worship Street he only visited
the office about twice a week, partly because of the presence there of the new owners and   E
directors of MMP and Tin Publications and partly because he had to spend much time
at the company's bankers, then Barclays Bank, Southampton Row.

During the whole of its life the company had only two employees apart from Mr
Huhtala and Mr Rawlinson. One was Alison Power, a secretary. She was employed by
MMP and worked part-time for the company while it was at 60 Worship Street. When
the company moved to Westbourne Grove she moved with it and became, so I   F
understood, a full-time employee. The other employee was part-time, a person who came
to the office once a week to deal with VAT, PAYE, National Insurance and the like.

When the company moved to Westbourne Grove Mr Huhtala began to keep, on the
basis of records made by Alison Power, a 'transaction journal' of all the company's
purchases and sales of metals.

The company's earliest transaction took place on 7 December 1988. It was a purchase   G
from Lion Metals Inc, an American company, which I will call 'Lion', and resale to Bhatt
International Inc, another American company, which I will call 'Bhatt', of scrap brass
for shipment to India. Thereafter Lion became Moorgate's almost exclusive supplier and
Bhatt by far its largest customer. All resales to Bhatt were made at a loss. In all Moorgate
purchased scrap metals costing US$3,882,880 from Lion of which $2,116,542 worth were
sold to Bhatt at a gross loss of $454,474. In January 1989 Mr Rawlinson visited Lion and   H
there negotiated an agreement with its directors under which Lion granted Moorgate a
credit facility of $400,000 at any one time in exchange for the right to be Moorgate's
exclusive supplier of metals in North America. The proprietor of Bhatt, Mr Nitin Bhatt,
was himself an Indian and Bhatt exported scrap brass to India. The way in which trade
with Bhatt and Lion Metals was carried out was described by Mr Rawlinson in his
statement of 22 November 1989 in these terms:

A 'Bhatt would indicate to me what his requirements were and we would agree a price. I would then go to Lion Metals and as soon as they had the brass scrap available they would agree to sell the company the amount required by Bhatt. The price was always fixed by Lion Metals. Bhatt would then make arrangements for the goods to be shipped to India and would supply the company with details of the ships and ports to which the goods were to be delivered together with a remittance to cover the cost of the goods. Usually this would be a round sum payment of
B $25,000 per container. I then contacted Lion Metals who would arrange for the goods to be taken to the ships concerned. Lion Metals bore the cost of transporting the goods to the ships and Bhatt was responsible for the cost of shipping them to India. The sale prices I agreed with Bhatt were always less than the prices at which the company could purchase them from Lion Metals because I wanted to get the company's name and reputation established in the market. I hoped that eventually
C the company would be able to increase its prices to Bhatt and so recover its previous losses or to sell directly to Bhatt customers in India.'

The company acquired a number of customers other than Bhatt with each of which it did a comparatively small amount of business, namely Walter Trapp GmbH of Frankfurt, Hoogevens Handel Metals BV of Utrecht, Trade Vent of Dubai, Anfield Ltd of Manchester and J H Rayner Ltd of the London Metal Exchange. With all of these except Anfield Ltd and J H Rayner Ltd the company traded at a loss.
D
In or about February 1989, in circumstances which were never made clear to me, Mr Rawlinson told Mr Huhtala that supplementary invoices would be sent to customers to cover the difference between the prices shown in the original invoices to them and the full price they should have paid. (At this time there had been no sale yet to Anfield Ltd or to J H Rayner Ltd.) That full price would in the case of each transaction cover Moorgate's apparent loss on the transaction and produce a gross profit of, Mr Huhtala thought,
E about six per cent on average. According to Mr Huhtala Mr Rawlinson gave him two reasons for this procedure of first undercharging the customer and then sending him a supplementary invoice. One was that in some cases the supplementary invoice was to cover additional charges for such things as insurance and special freight costs. The other was that the procedure was customary in the trade and was adopted because the customer requested it. There was no truth in either explanation but Mr Huhtala believed Mr Rawlinson. Mr Huhtala did however insist, so he told me, that supplementary invoices
F should be sent out as soon as possible. It took some time for the supplementary invoices to be prepared. It appears that some addressed to Walter Trapp were dated 30 March 1989 and a large batch addressed to Bhatt, amounting in total to $218,592, were dated 14 April 1989. The supplementary invoices became known as 'A' invoices. This was because each of them bore the same number as the original invoice in respect of the sale to which it was supposed to relate with the addition of the letter 'A'. Unbeknownst to
G Mr Huhtala or, for that matter, so it seems, to Alison Power, the 'A' invoices were not sent to the customers to whom they were addressed. Mr Rawlinson intercepted the company's outgoing mail to ensure that they were not. After March/April 1989 'A' invoices were prepared for each transaction a few days after the original invoice, but again Mr Rawlinson ensured, by the same method, that they were not dispatched.

By June 1989 the company was suffering serious cash-flow problems. In the middle of
H that month its debit balance on its running account with Lion reached a peak of over $1.3m. In July 1989 Mr Huhtala arranged for a statement of account to be sent to Bhatt which included the 'A' invoices. In the preparation of that statement Mr Rawlinson co-operated. It showed a balance due by Bhatt to Moorgate of over $400,000. The statement was of course disputed by Bhatt. Precisely what then happened is unclear, but certainly by August or early September 1989 Mr Huhtala had learned from Mr Rawlinson that the 'A' invoices had never been sent out and that the company had been trading at a loss.

By this time it was too late to save the company. In August supplies from Lion ceased   A
and on 21 September 1989 Lion served on the company a statutory demand for $897,567.
Solicitors, Messrs Holman Fenwick & Willan, were instructed on behalf of the company
and an attempt was made to raise a counterclaim against Lion. The hopeless nature of
that counterclaim is apparent from a letter written by Holman Fenwick & Willan to
Lion's solicitors on 27 September 1989. On 6 October 1989 (without waiting three weeks)
Lion presented a winding-up petition and on 9 October 1989 provisional liquidators of
the company, Mr A R Bloom and Mr S J L Adamson of Ernst & Young, were appointed   B
on Lion's application. On 15 November 1989 the winding-up order was made.
Subsequently Mr Bloom was appointed liquidator.

The case against Mr Huhtala

Many points were made by Mr Davis-White both in his opening and in his cross-
examination of Mr Huhtala to the discredit of Mr Huhtala. No-one who heard that   C
cross-examination would wish to invest in or give credit to a company managed by Mr
Huhtala. Nonetheless, in determining whether Mr Huhtala is unfit to be concerned in the
management of a company I can have regard only to his conduct as a director of
Moorgate and then only to those aspects of that conduct that are (pursuant to r. 3(3) of
the *Insolvent Companies (Disqualification of Unfit Directors) Proceedings Rules* 1987)
stated in the assistant official receiver's report to be matters by reference to which Mr
Huhtala is alleged to be unfit to be so concerned, subject to my discretion to allow the   D
official receiver to add to those matters.

I will consider the specific allegations against Mr Huhtala in the order in which Mr
Davis-White dealt with them in his final submissions.

(1) *Mr Rawlinson's involvement in the management of the company*

Under s. 11 of the *Company Directors Disqualification Act* 1986 it is an offence for a   E
person who is an undischarged bankrupt to take part or be concerned in the management
of a company. Mr Huhtala, as he acknowledged in cross-examination, knew in substance
that that was so and he knew from the beginning that Mr Rawlinson was an undischarged
bankrupt. Yet he was a party to Mr Rawlinson acting as he did.

So far as the case against Mr Huhtala is concerned, it is, I think, immaterial whether
or not Mr Rawlinson was a de facto director or a shadow director of the company. I   F
observe that the provisions of s. 6(3) and 22(4) of the Act, extending the meaning of the
expression 'director' to include a shadow director, do not apply to s. 11, no doubt because
it is unnecessary for them to do so since that section makes it as much an offence for an
undischarged bankrupt to be concerned in the management of a company as for him to
act as director of one.

Mr Huhtala knew that Mr Rawlinson was an undischarged bankrupt, but he did not   G
know that Mr Rawlinson had been bankrupt three times or that he had been refused his
discharge. Much less did he know the reasons for that refusal. Mr Huhtala, with his own
experience of applying for his discharge from bankruptcy, twice urged Mr Rawlinson to
apply for his discharge so as, as Mr Huhtala expressed it, to 'regularise his position'. He
did so at the time of the formation of Moorgate and again when in May 1989 he received
a letter from Mr D H V Robertson FCA, the company's accountant, saying that Mr
Rawlinson was clearly acting as a director or shadow director and should be invited to   H
the board. Mr Robertson of course did not know that Mr Rawlinson was an
undischarged bankrupt.

Although he knew that Mr Rawlinson was an undischarged bankrupt Mr Huhtala left
the conduct of the company's metal trading, which was its only business, and the extent
of the commitments that the company undertook in that business, wholly to him. That

A   was not only unlawful, it was manifestly unwise, though it is only with hindsight that one can see how unwise it was. It seems indeed that, at the time of the formation of Moorgate, Mr Huhtala envisaged that he himself would be managing the businesses of MMP and Tin Publications, which he told me was a very demanding task. That would necessarily have meant his having to leave the management of Moorgate almost entirely to Mr Rawlinson.

B   *(2) Investment in Communique in Print Ltd*

This is one of the matters concerning which Mr Huhtala's version of the facts changed when he was confronted with documents. Communique in Print Ltd, which I will call 'CIP', was incorporated on 30 December 1988 to carry on the business of a printer. It was originally conceived as a joint venture between Mr Stuart Payne, who was a printer, and Mr Huhtala. CIP was to print one of MMP's magazines and another magazine. Mr

C   Payne's and Mr Huhtala's consents to act as directors of CIP were dated 15 November 1988, as was Mr Huhtala's wife's consent to act as secretary. When Mr Huhtala's proposed management buy-out of MMP fell through Mr Payne set about finding other business for CIP. Mr Payne and Mr Huhtala agreed that each of them should contribute £5,000 to the capital of CIP by way of subscription for shares. Mr Huhtala's £5,000 came to CIP in January 1989 (the precise date is uncertain) in the form of a cheque from Moorgate. Thereafter Mr Huhtala maintained that it was an investment by Moorgate.

D   The shares were never issued, a neglect for which Mr Payne and Mr Huhtala blamed each other.

The official receiver's primary contention is that the £5,000 was a loan by Moorgate to Mr Huhtala in breach of s. 330 of the *Companies Act* 1985. There is, I think, no doubt that, as Mr Salter realistically conceded, Mr Huhtala used Moorgate's money because it was available. But that does not necessarily mean that it was a loan by Moorgate to Mr

E   Huhtala. There is in evidence some correspondence between Mr Huhtala and Mr Payne in September 1989 when they fell out and some later correspondence between the official receiver and a firm of solicitors acting for CIP. That correspondence appears to me inconclusive. However, a reference to CIP in the minutes of the board meeting of Moorgate on 4 July 1989 is, I think, inexplicable unless Moorgate was regarded as having an investment in CIP. On balance, therefore, I think it probable that the £5,000 was an

F   investment by Moorgate in CIP rather than a loan to Mr Huhtala.

On that footing Mr Huhtala is open to criticism on two grounds. First, the investment was inappropriate. In January 1989 Moorgate had just started to trade on an issued share capital of £2. Mr Huhtala had no reason to think that it had money to spare for investment, particularly in a speculative venture unconnected with its own business such as CIP. Secondly, it was negligent of Mr Huhtala to pay Moorgate's £5,000 to CIP without ensuring that the shares in CIP were issued to it. The lack of the appropriate

G   documentation has caused much uncertainty and waste of time, as the correspondence to which I have referred shows.

It appears that despite Mr Huhtala's hopes for CIP in January 1989 it has not been successful. Of course I accept that £5,000 is not a large sum compared to Moorgate's trading losses.

H   *(3) Accounting records*

Mr Huhtala accepted that it was his responsibility to keep Moorgate's accounting records. The official receiver alleged that the records that were kept were inadequate. In the assistant official receiver's report that allegation was made only in general terms, save that reference was made to a letter dated 11 December 1989 from Mr Robertson to the official receiver. To that letter I shall come.

Well before the hearing of this application efforts were made by Mr Huhtala's legal   A
advisers to obtain from the official receiver further and better particulars of the allegation
that Moorgate's accounting records were inadequate. None were forthcoming until the
second day of the hearing when Mr Davis-White volunteered oral particulars of the
allegation. These were, in a nutshell, to the effect that there were no or no adequate sales
and purchase ledgers showing how much was owed to or by the company at any
particular time. It seemed to me that it would be unfair to Mr Huhtala to allow such
particulars to be relied upon, at least without an adjournment. The official receiver then   B
elected not to pursue the matter.

That left the allegations in Mr Robertson's letter of 11 December 1989 of which there
were two. Of those, one was later abandoned by Mr Davis-White in view of its obscurity.
The other concerned Barclays Bank. Mr Robertson said that at the time when his firm
ceased working on the company's accounts to 30 June 1989 (because of the appointment
of the provisional liquidators) they had been 'unable to reconcile various transfers to the   C
extent that . . . there may or may not have been over £100,000 unexplained'. It seems
probable that Mr Robertson meant dollars and not pounds, and that he was referring to
some transfers from Bhatt and from Walter Trapp GmbH in December 1988 and January
1989 and to a transfer to Lion in January 1989. In answer to the allegation Mr Huhtala
produced some correspondence between himself and Barclays Bank in June and July
1989 and a letter that he wrote to Mr Bhatt in consequence. Barclays Bank's explanations   D
are obscure in the extreme and Mr Bhatt's reply, if any, is not in evidence. From the
documents and from what Mr Huhtala told me I infer that the inadequacy lay not so
much in the company's own records but in the documentation from Barclays Bank to
support them in the form of statements of account and advices. If so I think that Mr
Huhtala was at fault in not checking the statements from Barclays Bank sooner. The
total amount involved was some $141,000.

E

(4) *Moorgate's trading and the 'A' invoices*

In the assistant official receiver's report Mr Huhtala is criticised for allowing Moorgate
to trade extensively with one supplier and one customer. Rightly, in my view, Mr Davis-
White conceded that it is not improper for a director to cause his company to trade
largely or solely with one supplier or with one customer, but he pointed out that it renders
the company vulnerable and calls in particular for watchfulness by the director over the
state of the company's account with the supplier or customer.   F

It is clear that until Moorgate moved to Westbourne Grove Mr Huhtala exercised very
little control over its finances. He visited the office at Worship Street only about twice a
week and he told me himself that he had during this period been very relaxed about the
company's affairs. He also told me that he had expected Moorgate to provide him with
an agreeable way of earning a living after the pressures of running MMP and Tin
Publications.   G

With hindsight it would be easy to criticise Mr Huhtala for having believed Mr
Rawlinson when he told him of the need for the 'A' invoices and the reasons for them –
easy to say that he was excessively gullible. However, Mr Huhtala knew nothing of the
trade in metals. Mr Rawlinson was the expert.

To my mind the real criticism of Mr Huhtala is that once he knew of the 'A' invoices
he was slow to do anything to ensure that the company received payment on them. He   H
knew that without payment of those invoices the company was inevitably trading at a
loss. He did nothing about seeking payment from Bhatt until July 1989 although his
understanding was, so he told me, that the company was entitled to prompt payment of
the 'A' invoices. Nor is there any evidence that he did anything to secure payment of the
'A' invoices from any other customer, such as Walter Trapp or Hoogevens. Had he done
so he would surely have discovered that the 'A' invoices had not been sent out.

A   Mr Huhtala is, I think, also to be criticised for not having realised when Mr Rawlinson
revealed to him that the 'A' invoices had not been sent out that Mr Rawlinson was not
to be trusted and that the company could not be saved. It appears that, instead, Mr
Huhtala believed Mr Rawlinson when he said that he was in negotiation with Mr Bhatt
for payment of the $400,000-odd shown as due from Bhatt in the statement of accounts
sent to him in July and for payment by Bhatt of an additional $500,000 on account of
future trade. Mr Huhtala did not even get into touch himself with Bhatt to enquire about
B   the position. Mr Huhtala also believed Mr Rawlinson when he said that he was expecting
£250,000 from his brother for investment in the company. I do not think that such
gullibility is acceptable in a director of a company. I do not overlook, in saying that, that
Mr Rawlinson had deposited with the London branch of the Commerzbank (which had
in February 1989 replaced Barclays Bank as the company's main bankers) a cheque for
£250,000 drawn on his own building society account with instructions not to present it
C   until he notified them that funds to meet it were available.

(5) *Excessive remuneration*

From December 1988 to September 1989, both inclusive, Mr Huhtala and Mr
Rawlinson each drew £4,166.66 a month by way of remuneration from the company.
That is remuneration at the rate of £50,000 a year. In addition each received from the
D   company a contribution to his pension plan of £6,000. Mrs Rawlinson and Mr Huhtala
each benefited from private medical insurance at a cost to the company of about £400.
From February to September 1989 the company made lease payments of £260 a month
for Mr Huhtala's car. Finally, in August 1989 the company took delivery of an Alfa
Romeo car for Mr Huhtala's use which had been ordered in June and for which the
company paid £22,000.

E   The official receiver contends that that remuneration and those benefits were excessive
given Moorgate's trading and financial circumstances and were at the expense of its
creditors. In the assistant official receiver's report that allegation was made only against
Mr Rawlinson as against whom, bearing in mind what he knew, it was obviously justified.
Mr Salter did not oppose my allowing it to be extended to Mr Huhtala, but asked me to
bear in mind that Mr Huhtala had not come to court prepared to deal with it. In the
sense that he had not dealt with it in his affidavit, that is true, but there was no suggestion
F   that there was any evidence that he could have given which would have been pertinent to
it. In cross-examination Mr Huhtala accepted that, knowing the financial state of the
company, he should have forgone his salary, certainly for September 1989 and perhaps
for earlier periods.

In my judgment this matter must be looked at over the whole life of the company. In
the early stages there was no certainty about the profits that the company would make
G   and no justification for assuming that they would support a salary of as much as £50,000
a year for each of Mr Huhtala and Mr Rawlinson, plus other benefits, in addition to the
company's other overheads. From March 1989 at the latest Mr Huhtala knew that the
profitability of the company depended on the 'A' invoices being paid and thereafter he
knew that they were not being paid. By June 1989 he knew that the company was having
cash-flow problems yet he caused the company to order a car for him costing £22,000.
H   Then matters went from bad to worse – albeit that the debt to Lion was reduced from its
peak of over $1.3m to just under $900,000. Yet Mr Huhtala continued to draw his salary
and to concur in Mr Rawlinson drawing his.

To my mind Mr Huhtala and Mr Rawlinson helped themselves to remuneration and
to benefits at the expense of the company and of its creditors to an extent that was in all
the circumstances irresponsible.

(6) Purchase of a property in France   A

On 13 November 1989 Mr Huhtala and Mr Rawlinson swore a statement of affairs of the company as at 9 October 1989, the date of the appointment of the provisional liquidators. The same statement of affairs was sworn by Mrs Rawlinson on 21 November 1989. In that statement of affairs there was shown as an asset of the company 'Loan to director, not yet repaid – £10,000'. In his preliminary examination on 15 November 1989 by the official receiver's senior examiner, the record of which Mr Huhtala signed after having been informed of the provisions of s. 5 of the *Perjury Act* 1911, Mr Huhtala said:

> 'The company has made a loan to me of £10,000 in September 1989. There is no loan agreement but it was intended that the loan would carry interest at two per cent over base rate.'

Mr Huhtala expanded on that in the statement which he made to the same senior examiner on 22 November 1989, after having again been told of the provisions of s. 5 of the Perjury Act, and the record of which he signed on 7 December 1989. He said:

> 'For some time my wife and I had been looking for a holiday property in France and in September had decided to purchase a property in the Pyrenees. A deposit of £10,000 was required and it was agreed that the company could lend this money to me to enable me to complete the purchase. The company duly agreed but as there were insufficient funds in the company's bank account to enable the loan to be made Rawlinson agreed to make a loan of £25,000 to the company to enable it to make the loan to me. This was duly carried out on 29 September on which day Rawlinson paid in two cheques for £10,000 and £15,000 respectively drawn on his building society account. I then drew a banker's order' – that should read 'banker's draft' – 'for £10,000 which was debited to the company's bank account and left for France to complete the property transactions. Three days later on Monday, 2 October I telephoned Rawlinson from France to seek his confirmation that his building society cheques would be paid. He assured me that they would be. I therefore went ahead an hour later to sign the necessary papers and deposit the £10,000 banker's draft as part payment for the property I was acquiring. I returned to London on the Tuesday, the following day, and on Wednesday I was told by the bank that the building society cheques had been returned by the bank marked "Orders not to pay".'

I will come back in due course to the matter of the stopping by Mr Rawlinson of his cheques for £10,000 and £15,000 which is relied upon by the official receiver as against Mr Rawlinson as yet another manifestation of his dishonesty. I should say that the bank in question was not the Commerzbank but the National Westminster Bank's Westbourne Grove branch at which also Moorgate had an account. The important thing, however, about the passage that I have read from Mr Huhtala's statement to the senior examiner is that it confirmed what he had sworn to in the statement of affairs and had told the senior examiner at his preliminary examination, namely that he had borrowed £10,000 from the company and explained that he had done so to acquire a holiday home in France.

In those circumstances it is hardly surprising that the official receiver should have alleged against Mr Huhtala, as he did, that he borrowed £10,000 from the company in breach of s. 330 of the *Companies Act* 1985.

What is surprising is the defence raised by Mr Huhtala to that allegation in his affidavit and subsequently at the hearing before me. That defence was, shortly stated, that the property in France, which was not in the Pyrenees but on the outskirts of Albi, was being bought not as a holiday home for Mr and Mrs Huhtala but as an office for the company, the intention being that the company should eventually move there from Westbourne Grove. In cross-examination Mr Huhtala said that the purchase price of the property

A   was about £50,000 and that it was too large for a holiday home for himself and his wife. He also said that the reason why he had described the £10,000 as a loan in the statement of affairs, at his preliminary examination and in his narrative statement was that, when he was preparing the statement of affairs, he had had a conversation with someone from Ernst & Young in the provisional liquidators' team which had resulted in an understanding that that would be the best way of dealing with the matter. In support of that version of events Mr Huhtala referred to the minutes of the board meeting on 4 July

B   1989 which contained an item reading 'CH was empowered to research the siting of the overseas office and report back to the board'. He told me that he had subsequently agreed with Mr and Mrs Rawlinson that the company would acquire the property at Albi. He also told me that the purchase of the property had later been cancelled and his understanding with Ernst & Young reversed, so that the liquidator received the balance of the £10,000 after deduction of a penalty payable under French law and of the French

C   notaire's charges. That statement prompted an enquiry by the official receiver from Ernst & Young during the hearing which produced two letters to Ernst & Young from Mr Huhtala. One was a letter dated 3 November 1989 which clearly confirmed that the £10,000 was borrowed by Mr Huhtala from the company. The other was a letter dated 21 May 1990 which evinced that, on the cancellation of the purchase of the property, Mr Huhtala obtained from the French notaire a cheque for 32,000 French francs (then about £3,200) made out in favour of Ernst & Young and sent it to them. The statement

D   Mr Huhtala's evidence on this whole matter was unsatisfactory. It was not always consistent and at times it was very vague, particularly as to his conversations with Ernst & Young and as to the circumstances in which he came to obtain the cheque in their favour from the French notaire.

     It is not necessary for me to decide whether the £10,000 was a loan to Mr Huhtala or was a deposit on the purchase of the property for the company. If it was the former there

E   was a breach of s. 330 and Mr Huhtala lied to me. If it was the latter Mr Huhtala lied in the statement of affairs and lied twice to the official receiver's examiner, thereby committing breaches not only of the Perjury Act but also of s. 131 and 235 of the *Insolvency Act* 1986. In either case, taking £10,000 from the company for the purchase of the French property at the beginning of October 1989 was highly irresponsible. The company was then in severe financial difficulties. The statutory demand had been served and was being resisted only by means of a fanciful counterclaim. Mr Huhtala's case was

F   that, at the time, he believed that the company had a future because of what Mr Rawlinson had told him about his negotiations with Bhatt and because of the expectation of £250,000 from Mr Rawlinson's brother. It was not, Mr Huhtala said, until after he returned to London from France that he learned that Mr Rawlinson had withdrawn his cheque for £250,000 from the Commerzbank and that Mr Rawlinson finally told him that the 'A' invoices had not only not been sent but had been bogus. I have already

G   expressed my view of Mr Huhtala's gullibility at that time.

(7) *Conduct as a witness*

     Mr Davis-White drew my attention to *Re Godwin Warren Control Systems plc* [1992] BCC 557, where Chadwick J held that, by virtue of s. 6(2) of the *Company Directors Disqualification Act* 1986, the court could take into account, in considering a person's fitness to be concerned in the management of a company, that person's conduct in the

H   proceedings against him under s. 6 themselves, and in particular the truthfulness of the evidence given by him in those proceedings. Mr Davis-White invited me, if and in so far as I found that Mr Huhtala's evidence had been untruthful, to take that into account.

     I have already said that I found Mr Huhtala a very unreliable witness. It was demonstrated more than once that what he had said was untrue. For instance, he said in his affidavit and in cross-examination, until confronted with documents, that he had become a director of CIP because of the investment by Moorgate, and he said in cross-examination, again until confronted with a document, that he did not know of the statutory demand when he made the payment of £10,000 for the French property. And, as I have said, he must have lied to someone about that £10,000.

In the *Godwin Warren* case Chadwick J took into account the untruthfulness of the respondent concerned because it showed that he still did not appreciate what the duties of a director of a public company were and therefore showed that he was unfit to be concerned in the management of a company. In Mr Huhtala's case I am satisfied that the matters alleged and proved against him, quite apart from his conduct as a witness, clearly show him to be unfit to be concerned in the management of a company. The unreliability of his evidence adds little to that.

Conclusion as regards Mr Huhtala

Having concluded that Mr Huhtala's conduct as a director of the company makes him unfit to be concerned in the management of a company I have to decide for what period he should be disqualified. Logically perhaps, since the purpose of a disqualification order is not to punish the director concerned but to protect the public from him, he should be disqualified for ever. But Parliament has been merciful. Under subs. (4) of s. 6 the minimum period of disqualification is two years and the maximum 15. I have in the matter the guidance of the Court of Appeal in *Re Sevenoaks Stationers (Retail) Ltd* [1990] BCC 765 at pp. 771–772 and my knowledge, so far as it goes, of the disqualification periods imposed in other cases.

In all the circumstances I will order that Mr Huhtala shall not, without the leave of the court, be a director of, or in any way, whether directly or indirectly, be concerned or take part in the promotion, formation or management of a company for a period of four years from today.

The case against Mr Rawlinson

As regards Mr Rawlinson the first question is whether he was a director of Moorgate within the meaning of that expression in s. 6(1) of the Act. In his affidavit Mr Rawlinson contended that he was not. He pointed to the absence from the Act of any express mention of a de facto director and he referred to the definition of a shadow director in s. 22(5) of the Act. He said that his position was that of metal trader of the company; that every trading company on the Metal Exchange employed a metal trading expert like himself; and that the majority of such employees were not directors. He accepted that he 'controlled the company's entire trading operation', but said that that was because of his professional expertise.

Mr Davis-White referred me to a number of authorities on the matter, namely *Re Lo-Line Electric Motors Ltd* (1988) 4 BCC 415, *Re Tasbian Ltd (No. 3)* [1991] BCC 435 and [1992] BCC 358, *Re Cargo Agency Ltd* [1992] BCC 388, and *Re Hydrodan (Corby) Ltd* [1994] BCC 161. It appears to me clear from those authorities:

(1)   that the word 'director' in s. 6(1) includes a 'de facto director'; and

(2)   that for this purpose a de facto director is a person who in fact acts as a director, though not appointed as such.

Some of the expressions used by Millett J in the *Hydrodan* case could be construed as meaning that, for a person to be held to have been a de facto director, the label 'director' must have been attached to him. But I am sure that Millett J did not mean that. He was concerned to distinguish between a de facto director and a shadow director, the latter being a person in accordance with whose directions or instructions the directors of a company (whether de jure or de facto) are accustomed to act.

A   I have come to the conclusion that Mr Rawlinson was a de facto director of Moorgate. I have already mentioned many of the facts that have led me to that conclusion: the fact that Moorgate came into existence as a result of Mr Rawlinson inviting Mr Huhtala to join him in a business that he was minded to set up; the fact that Mr Rawlinson and Mr Huhtala shared the responsibilities of managing the company and that Mr Rawlinson was in sole charge of the company's trading with no limit on the extent of the commitments that he could enter into on behalf of the company; and the fact that Mr
B   Rawlinson and Mr Huhtala received equal remuneration. (Mr Huhtala had the additional benefit of motor cars but the purchase of company cars for both Mr Huhtala and Mr Rawlinson was authorised at the board meeting on 4 July 1989. I was not told why none was in fact purchased for Mr Rawlinson.) Other facts support the conclusion. Mr Huhtala told me that he consulted Mr Rawlinson on all important decisions, including the appointment of bankers, the appointment of solicitors, the appointment of
C   Mr Robertson's firm as accountants and the investment in CIP. Indeed it is clear (as I have mentioned) that Mr Robertson thought Mr Rawlinson was acting as if he were a director of the company and in his letter to the official receiver of 11 December 1989 Mr Robertson said 'We were instructed by both Mr Huhtala and Mr Rawlinson . . .' When the company's main bank account was moved from Barclays Bank to the Commerzbank, although Mr Huhtala was named in the mandate as the sole signatory on the account, Commerzbank were informed that both Mr Rawlinson (who was described as 'chief
D   executive') and Mr Huhtala (who was named second and described as 'managing director') had authority to give instructions over the telephone to effect payment orders. Lastly, there is in evidence a promotional brochure published by Moorgate which repeatedly refers to Mr Rawlinson (there described as 'senior trader') and Mr Huhtala (described as 'managing director') as 'partners'. Again Mr Rawlinson is named first. The overall picture conveyed by the evidence is of Mr Huhtala and Mr Rawlinson as equals, running the company between them, and not of Mr Rawlinson being Mr Huhtala's
E   subordinate in any way. In my view Mr Rawlinson was a director in all but name.

   Having reached that conclusion I need not advert to the question whether Mr Rawlinson could be regarded as having been a shadow director of Moorgate.

Mr Rawlinson's fitness to be concerned in the management of a company

F   In the case of Mr Rawlinson the matters by reference to which he is alleged by the official receiver to be unfit to be concerned in the management of a company to a large extent correspond to those alleged in the case of Mr Huhtala, but of course in some respects they are of greater gravity.

   His involvement in the management of Moorgate while an undischarged bankrupt speaks for itself. So does the manner in which he conducted the company's trade and the way in which he concealed what he was doing from Mr Huhtala by means of the
G   deception of the 'A' invoices. Mr Rawlinson was primarily the author of the company's insolvency. In his statement of 22 November 1989 to the senior examiner and in his recent plea in mitigation addressed to the court he made various excuses for his conduct in those respects but these do not, in my judgment, bear examination.

   In the matter of the excessive remuneration drawn by Mr Huhtala and Mr Rawlinson, Mr Rawlinson's conduct was, I think, even more irresponsible than Mr Huhtala's
H   because Mr Rawlinson knew that profits were not being and could not be earned out of which to pay that remuneration.

   In the matter of the purchase of the French property Mr Rawlinson at no time suggested that the £10,000 was other than a loan to Mr Huhtala. In his statement to the senior examiner he said that in September 1989 he was approached by Mr Huhtala 'who wished to borrow £10,000 from the company in order to finance the purchase of the

property he was in the process of acquiring in France' and that he, Mr Rawlinson, 'duly   A
agreed'. So Mr Rawlinson either concurred in the company making a loan to a director
in breach of s. 330 of the Companies Act and did so at a time when he knew that the
company was insolvent or, if Mr Huhtala's version of events is true, concurred in the
company embarking on a purchase that it was then irresponsible to make and co-
operated with Mr Huhtala in swearing a false statement of affairs and by lying to the
senior examiner.

   B

However, in the case of Mr Rawlinson, the matter goes further. As I mentioned earlier,
the stopping by Mr Rawlinson of his cheques for £10,000 and £15,000 in favour of the
National Westminster Bank is relied upon by the official receiver, rightly in my view, as
another manifestation of his dishonesty. The evidence about this consists of the passage
that I read earlier from Mr Huhtala's narrative statement to the senior examiner, a
passage in Mr Rawlinson's own statement to the senior examiner, and a letter from the
National Westminster Bank to the official receiver which is exhibited to the assistant   C
official receiver's report.

From that evidence it is clear, and undisputed, that the National Westminster Bank
agreed to issue the draft for £10,000 that Mr Huhtala took to France only because it had
received the cheques for £10,000 and £15,000 drawn by Mr Rawlinson on his building
society account. The subsequent stopping of those cheques by Mr Rawlinson meant that
the National Westminster Bank had been induced into issuing its draft for £10,000 by a   D
deception.

Another matter which forms part of the case against Mr Rawlinson, though not of the
case against Mr Huhtala, is a fax that he sent to Mr Bhatt on 6 October 1989, the day
the winding-up petition was presented, in an endeavour to mount a spurious
counterclaim against Lion. In that fax, after referring to Moorgate's dispute with Lion,
Mr Rawlinson said:

   E

'. . . It would greatly help and assist my case if I could have a fax from you referring
to your previous faxes, where you complained about the late and non-delivery of
containers, of the upsetting of your trade and financial schedule and also late
delivery of the pending 25/30 containers. It would be helpful if you could make the
fax really strong in your complaint referring also, if you can, to loss of profit
through late or non-deliveries, loss of reputation and goodwill etc. If you can put
a final figure to that of about 400/500K it would be of enormous help. Please realise   F
that this fax would be strictly confidential, only for us and would not involve or
bind you in any way, and will mean no involvement on your part. It will just be a
great help to us. If you do this fax for us, please do not refer to any request from
me for such a fax, but simply send it as if it was totally spontaneous. I hope you
can do this for me.'

Mr Rawlinson followed that fax up with another on the same day asking Mr Bhatt to: G

'Please let us have for our opening Monday, 9th, your fax stating your losses etc.
for non-delivery etc.'

–and adding:

'Please indicate the final figure at about 400K.'

Monday, 9 October was the date on which Lion's application for the appointment of
provisional liquidators was due to be heard. Fortunately Mr Bhatt did not comply with   H
Mr Rawlinson's request but showed Mr Rawlinson's faxes to Lion.

There are two comparatively minor matters in respect of which I think that Mr
Rawlinson is less to blame than Mr Huhtala. One is the investment in CIP which,
although Mr Rawlinson was consulted about it, was primarily Mr Huhtala's doing. The
other was the failure to check the Barclays Bank statements. According to the established

A   division of responsibilities between Mr Rawlinson and Mr Huhtala it was Mr Huhtala's responsibility to check the bank statements.

Conclusion as regards Mr Rawlinson

It is clear that Mr Rawlinson is a thoroughly dishonest, irresponsible and unscrupulous person. The seriousness of his misconduct as a de facto director of Moorgate puts his case, in my view, at least at the top end of the middle bracket mentioned by Dillon LJ in the *Sevenoaks* case at p. 772.

I will therefore in his case make a disqualification order in the same terms as in the case of Mr Huhtala but for a period of ten years. I realise of course that so long as Mr Rawlinson remains an undischarged bankrupt that order will have no greater effect than s. 11 of the *Company Directors Disqualification Act* 1986 save that if he contravenes it he will be punishable for contempt of court as well as liable to prosecution under s. 13 of the Act. I realise also that when the period of disqualification ends Mr Rawlinson will be 80. That does not, however, seem to me to be a reason for reducing the period.

(Order accordingly)

Secretary of State for Trade and Industry v Normand.

A

Court of Session (Outer House).
Lord Sutherland.
Judgment delivered 22 June 1994.

Disqualifying unfit directors of insolvent companies – Whether disqualification application was out of time – Company Directors Disqualification Act 1986, s. 7(2).

B

The date of an application for a disqualification order under s. 7(2) of the Company Directors Disqualification Act 1986 was the date upon which the petition was lodged in court. (Secretary of State for Trade and Industry v Josolyne 1990 SLT (Sh Ct) 48 followed.)

The following cases were referred to in the opinion:

Alston v Macdougall (1887) 15 R 78.

C

Boyle v Glasgow Corporation 1975 SC 238.
Corstorphine v Kasten (1898) 1 F 287.
Miller v National Coal Board 1960 SC 376.
North v Stewart (1889) 17 R (HL) 60.
Secretary of State for Trade and Industry v Houston (unreported, 25 June 1993).
Secretary of State for Trade and Industry v Josolyne 1990 SLT (Sh Ct) 48.

Alan Dewar (instructed by R Brodie, solicitor in Scotland to the Secretary of State for Trade and Industry) for the Secretary of State.

D

Paul Arthurson (instructed by Drummond Miller) for the respondent.

OPINION

Lord Sutherland: This is an application by the Secretary of State under s. 7(1) of the *Company Directors Disqualification Act* 1986 seeking the making of a disqualification order against the respondent under s. 6. The respondent has stated a preliminary plea to the competency on the ground that the making of the application is time-barred and the case came on procedure roll on that plea. Section 7(2) of the Act provides:

E

> 'Except with the leave of the court, an application for the making under that section of a disqualification order against any person shall not be made after the end of the period of 2 years beginning with the day on which the company of which that person is or has been a director became insolvent.'

F

No leave of the court has been sought in this case. It is a matter of agreement that the relevant company of which the respondent was a director became insolvent on 27 March 1991. It is further a matter of agreement that the present petition was presented to the court on 26 March 1993 but the interlocutor granting a first order for service on the respondent was not pronounced until 30 March 1993.

G

Counsel for the respondent argued that under the terms of s. 7(2) the date of an application for the making of an order was the date when the first order was pronounced and not the date when the petition was lodged in court. Counsel pointed out that in ordinary procedure in the Court of Session the date of commencement of any cause was the date of citation. As authority for this proposition he referred to *Erskine's Institutes* III.6.3, McLaren, *Court of Session Practice*, p. 317, *Alston v Macdougall* (1887) 15 R 78, *North v Stewart* (1889) 17 R (HL) 60 and *Corstorphine v Kasten* (1898) 1 F 287. He also referred to *Miller v National Coal Board* 1960 SC 376 and *Boyle v Glasgow Corporation* 1975 SC 238 as authority for the proposition that when time-bar is being considered the date of commencement of an action is the date of citation. Counsel deduced from these cases a principle that until a defender or respondent was convened into the process by way of citation there could be no commencement of an action against him. Apart from

H

A two cases to which I am about to refer, counsel was unable to produce any authority relating to the date of commencement of petition proceedings as opposed to proceedings commenced by way of summons. The two cases to which he did refer, which were both cases under the Company Directors Disqualification Act, were both against his proposition. The first of these is *Secretary of State for Trade and Industry v Josolyne* 1990 SLT (Sh Ct) 48 where precisely the same point as has been taken in the present case was taken. The argument for the respondent in that case was based on the principle that the commencement of an ordinary action is the service of the initial writ on the defender. In the Sheriff Court an application for an order under the Act is directed to be made by summary application and a summary application being a civil proceeding competent in the Sheriff Court is an action. That being so it should, so far as possible, be governed by the same rules as an ordinary action including the rule relating to commencement. Sheriff Principal Ireland, however, held that the difficulty about that argument was that it tended to divert attention from the statutory provision which the court is required to construe. In his view, looking at the clear meaning of the words in s. 7(2), what required to be done was that an applicant must make an application to the court and when the solicitor presented the initial writ to the Sheriff Clerk then, according to the ordinary meaning of the words he made an application to the court. Events such as making an order for service or the actual service of the writ on the respondent were events which were consequential on an application which had already been made. For these reasons the sheriff principal held that the relevant date was the date when the initial writ was presented to the court rather than the date of service. The other case to which counsel referred was *Secretary of State for Trade and Industry v James Houston* (unreported, 25 June 1993). In that case, however, the point at issue was what was the correct date of the appointment of the administrative receiver, as parties were agreed that the petition seeking the disqualification order was presented on 10 September 1991 and that that was the relevant date for the purposes of s. 7(2). The point at issue in the present case therefore was a matter of concession in *Houston*. Counsel contended that the decision in *Josolyne* was unsound in principle and should not be followed.

Counsel for the petitioner contended that the reasoning in *Josolyne* was flawless and that decision should be followed. What was important was not what the position might have been at common law in relation to ordinary actions but what is the procedure laid down under the statute with which we are concerned. Under s. 7(2) the relevant date is the date of an application for the making of an order and the date of application must be the date on which the petition was lodged in court. As Sheriff Principal Ireland pointed out, the subsequent procedures were simply consequential upon the original application which has already been lodged in court. Section 7(2) is not concerned with the date of commencement of an action which might involve the convening of a competing party but is only concerned with the date of an application to the court. For these reasons the relevant date was the date on which the petition was lodged in court, namely 26 March 1993, and accordingly the application was made within the period of two years.

There is no doubt that in an ordinary action the date of commencement of the action is the date of citation of the defender. In an ordinary action, however, the court is not involved until such time as the summons is lodged for calling. That being so, the action cannot be commenced by some unilateral action on the part of the pursuer where no formal intimation has been made to the defender and where the court has not been involved. The position, however, is different in petition procedure. Under that procedure the petition is lodged in court and then in terms of r. 195 of the Rules of Court the case will automatically be put before a Lord Ordinary in order that a first order may be pronounced. From the moment the petition is lodged the rest of the procedure follows automatically. I therefore find myself in complete agreement with Sheriff Principal Ireland when he says that the order for service and the service on the respondent are

merely events which are consequential on an application which has already been made.   A
Section 7(2) is concerned not with the convening of a respondent into the process nor
with the commencement of an action as that is understood in ordinary procedure. What
s. 7(2) is concerned with is an application to the court and it is the date of that application
that is relevant. In my opinion, there can be no doubt whatever that under the ordinary
meaning of words 'an application to the court' must be the date upon which the petition
is lodged in court. For these reasons I am satisfied that the respondent's plea to the
competency is unfounded and I shall repel that plea and, of consent, allow proof before   B
answer.

(*Order accordingly*)

C

D

E

F

G

H

A
Re Hitco 2000 Ltd.
Official Receiver v Cowan.
Chancery Division.
Jules Sher QC (sitting as a deputy High Court judge).
Judgment delivered 29 July 1994.

B
> *Disqualifying unfit directors of insolvent companies – Official receiver appealed against district judge's finding that director not unfit – Whether director traded without reasonable prospect of paying creditors – Whether official receiver could rely on new complaint on appeal – Company Directors Disqualification Act 1986, s. 6.*

C
This was an appeal by the official receiver from the district judge's dismissal of an application in the county court for a disqualification order against the respondent under s. 6 of the Company Directors Disqualification Act 1986.

Four 'charges' were found proved by the district judge: (1) misuse of the company's bank account by the respondent 'by bouncing cheques'; (2) a failure to file accounts; (3) failure to file two sets of accounts of another company; and (4) the failure to file one annual return of the company. The judge rejected an allegation of trading without reasonable prospect of paying creditors. The official receiver appealed against that finding.

D
The dispute on the appeal was about the seriousness of the proven failures and whether they justified the making of a disqualification order. The judge held that misuse of the bank account was of a 'fairly serious nature' but that the other three were less serious and that overall the four proven charges did not add up to conduct which rendered the respondent unfit to be a company director.

E
There was a further issue concerning the allegation of misuse of the bank account. At trial this was based solely on the issuing of cheques which were dishonoured; on appeal the official receiver sought to rely on the respondent's practice of leaving whole books of blank cheques signed by him with his bookkeeper as part of the case asserting unfitness.

Held, allowing the appeal and disqualifying the respondent for two years:

F
1. Signing the blank cheques was a misuse, but it was not the misuse with which the respondent was charged. The court had a discretion to allow the official receiver to rely on additional charges if this could be done without injustice, but in order to be able to rely on a new complaint as an additional charge the official receiver had to make it clear that he intended to do so. That was not done. The complaint of signing cheques in blank could not be tagged on to the substantive head of complaint alleging misuse 'by bouncing cheques' nor could it be relied on as conduct which of itself justified a finding of unfitness.

G
2. However, in so far as the evidence was relevant to any subsisting ground of complaint, whether specifically or by way of general background, it was something the court was entitled to take into account. As the allegation was consistent with what seemed from the evidence generally to have been an abdication of responsibility in the realm of financial control and failure to keep himself informed as to the financial state of the company, it was relevant to the charge of continuing to trade at the creditors' expense.

H
3. The judge was satisfied that the respondent did not have a reasonable and justifiable belief in the company's ability to trade through its difficulties from mid-February 1990 until it ceased trading in April 1990 but he rejected this period of over two months as insignificant in the life of the company. However, fresh credit continued to be incurred in this period. The respondent did not assert a conscious process of evaluation and belief at any time that it was appropriate for him to go on trading. Had he done that and had the judge believed him it would be inappropriate for an appellate court to interfere. That was not this case.

4. On the issue whether the respondent had a sufficient flow of management information   A
to enable him to take intelligent decisions as to whether to carry on trading, it was clear
that as sole director of the company he failed to fulfil his responsibilities to monitor the
company's financial position or to ensure that he had the requisite professional guidance.
The judge was wrong to reject the charge that the respondent continued to trade without any
reasonable prospect of paying his creditors. That charge was adequately proved in respect
of the period from early January 1990 onwards.
                                                                                          B
5. That conduct made the respondent unfit to be concerned in the management of a
company. His abdication of control of the financial side of the business of the company in
relation to the charge of trading at the risk of creditors was echoed by his abdication of
control in relation to the charge of misuse of the bank account by the issuance of cheques
that were dishonoured. The cumulative effect of those two proven charges confirmed the
assessment of the respondent as unfit.

6. Had the dishonoured cheques stood alone as the only charge proved, the court would   C
have hesitated to disagree with the judge. Standing alone the filing defaults would not have
added up to unfitness.

The following cases were referred to in the judgment:

Sevenoaks Stationers (Retail) Ltd, Re [1990] BCC 765; [1991] Ch 164.
Swift 736 Ltd, Re. Secretary of State for Trade and Industry v Ettinger & Anor [1993]
BCC 312.   D

Stephen Davies (instructed by the Treasury Solicitor) for the official receiver.

Philip Gillyon (instructed by Blandy & Blandy, Reading) for the respondent.

JUDGMENT

Jules Sher QC: This is an appeal from the dismissal on 16 September 1993 by District   E
Judge Sonnex in the Slough County Court of an application by the official receiver dated
12 February 1992 for a disqualification order against the respondent, John Cowan, under
s. 6 of the *Company Directors Disqualification Act* 1986 ('CDDA 1986'). I am told that,
so far as the Disqualification Unit is aware, this is the first appeal from a dismissal of an
application under the Act. The appeal is made under r. 7.47 of the *Insolvency Rules* 1986
and the procedure is governed by r. 7.49 which, in turn, applies the procedure and practice
of the Supreme Court relating to appeals to the Court of Appeal. Accordingly, I am   F
exercising a true appellate jurisdiction.

There was some debate before me as to the proper approach of an appellate court in
the context of s. 6 of the CDDA 1986. Under that section the court is obliged to make a
disqualification order in respect of the director if:

'it is satisfied–

    (a) that he is or has been a director of a company which has at any time become   G
           insolvent (whether while he was a director or subsequently), and

    (b) that his conduct as a director of that company (either taken alone or taken
           together with his conduct as a director of any other company or companies)
           makes him unfit to be concerned in the management of a company.'

Under r. 3(3) of the *Insolvent Companies (Disqualification of Unfit Directors)
Proceedings Rules* 1987 (SI 1987/2023) the evidence filed in support of the application for   H
a disqualification order must include:

'a statement of the matters by reference to which the respondent is alleged to be
unfit to be concerned in the management of a company.'

Typically in these cases there are a number of such matters or 'charges' (as they have
from time to time been described) which are included in the official receiver's reports filed

A   as evidence in support of his application. In this case such charges included, inter alia,
     'phoenix' trading, misuse of a bank account, trading at creditors' risk and breach of the
     Companies Act 1985 in connection with filing of accounts and annual returns.

     In the first instance the task of the trial judge is to determine whether these 'charges'
     are established or not. That process involves the determination of issues of primary fact.
     So far as such issues are concerned the appellate process is well known. Where the
     determination has depended upon a conflict of oral evidence, the appellate court will
B   generally defer to the judgment of the trial judge unless satisfied that he has misdirected
     himself, or, in other words, that the finding was perverse. The determination of some
     'charges' however depends, at least in part, upon an evaluation of the primary facts
     found. For example, a charge of trading without having a reasonable prospect of paying
     creditors involves a considerable degree of primary fact, in particular as to the moving
     financial picture of the company throughout the period under review. But whether the
C   director has traded without such reasonable prospect involves the additional process of
     evaluation of the facts so found in order to decide, for example, whether a reasonable
     director would have known that he should not trade beyond a particular point in time.
     Whether that further conclusion is properly described as based on inference from primary
     fact or (as I would prefer) based on evaluation (rather than proof) of primary fact, the
     fact is that the appellate court is in as good a position to make that evaluation as is the
D   trial judge, and should not shrink from differing from the trial judge if satisfied that his
     evaluation was wrong.

     There is, however, a further stage in the trial process under s. 6 of the CDDA 1986.
     The ultimate determination for the trial judge is whether the proven 'charges' render the
     director unfit to manage a company. That determination is not one of primary fact. It is
     a determination which involves the evaluation of the seriousness of the 'charges' which
     have been proved and a judgment of the trial judge as to whether, taking all the
E   circumstances into account, including all matters of mitigation and extenuation, the
     director is or is not unfit. The subjective evaluation of all this material by the trial judge
     is emphasised by the opening words of the section: 'The court shall make a
     disqualification order against a person in any case where . . . *it is satisfied* . . . that his
     conduct . . . makes him unfit' (emphasis added). Nonetheless, the ultimate conclusion as
     to fitness or otherwise is itself a conclusion of fact. In the words of Dillon LJ in *Re*
F   *Sevenoaks Stationers (Retail) Ltd* [1990] BCC 765 at p. 773G:

          '. . . the true question to be tried is a question of fact – what used to be pejoratively
          described in the Chancery Division as "a jury question".'

     Plainly, the appellate court would be very slow indeed to disturb such conclusion as to
     fitness or unfitness. In many, perhaps most, cases the conclusion will have been so very
     much assisted and influenced by the oral evidence and demeanour of the director and
     other witnesses that the appellate court would be in nowhere near as good a position to
G   form a judgment as to fitness or unfitness than was the trial judge. But there may be cases
     where there is little or no dispute as to the primary facts and the appellate court is in as
     good a position as the trial judge to form a judgment as to fitness. In such cases the
     appellate court should not shrink from its responsibility to do so, and, if satisfied that the
     trial judge was wrong, to say so.

H   **The facts**

     I start with a broad sketch of the background taken from the trial judge's judgment,
     with which sketch neither counsel has quarrelled.

          'The conduct in question relates to a company, Hitco 2000 Ltd, which became
          insolvent and was liquidated. Also relied upon is one allegation of conduct in
          relation to Jaysea Agencies Ltd, a company incorporated on 5 April 1990, which

ceased trading in December 1992 and of which the respondent has since ceased to   A
be a director.

The original allegations, ten in number, are contained in para. 158 of the official
receiver's report dated 5 January 1992. A second report of 10 November 1992
amended one and added one, namely failure to co-operate, and at a very late stage
(by a letter dated 26 August 1993) the official receiver's solicitors gave notice that
late filing and failure to file accounts in Jaysea Agencies would also be relied upon.   B
Four allegations have been withdrawn, so the net total before the court today is
eight.

I propose very briefly to review the background, to deal with each of the allegations
in turn and then to consider whether those matters that are proved suffice to satisfy
the s. 6 requirement.
   C

The respondent has followed a business career entirely devoted to sales. He was a
director of various companies over a number of years and for about five years
prior to 1988 was the director/proprietor of Hitco (UK), which was engaged in
importing fancy goods from Hong Kong to supply to mail order companies. It
had a substantial turnover but was not overall profitable. By early 1988, (UK) was
in a critical financial state and was unable to continue trading without the goodwill   D
of the supplier. The respondent's evidence, which I have no reason to doubt, is
that (UK)'s problems were attributable to unfavourable currency exchange rates.
Arrangements were made with the co-operation of Hitco (Hong Kong) for the
residual stock to be taken over by a new company, Hitco 2000, which was
incorporated on 22 March, 1988. Initially, in the light of the chronology and the
absence of certain vital documentation, the official receiver had legitimate
suspicions that this was 'phoenix trading'. It is now clear that was not the case;   E
(UK) was paid for the stock, and its creditors were paid in turn. No reliance is
placed on the respondent's conduct in (UK).

Hitco 2000 did not continue the same business; its primary line was the sale of gift-
packaged lingerie to garage forecourts and other retail outlets. The respondent was
sole director. He employed bookkeepers throughout the life of the company and
there is no allegation that his books of account were deficient, although there is an   F
admitted allegation that no annual account was filed. The company started trading
on or about 1 July 1988. Apart from stock, it had no initial working capital. The
respondent did put in a sum, he says about £6,000–£7,000, which was spent on
development costs for moulds and so forth. Later, in April 1989, the respondent
made a loan of £8,000-odd. He said that his wife also put in £3,500, but there is no
firm evidence of that.   G

From the outset debts were factored; first to Chancery factors and later to Westpac.
Notwithstanding, there were severe cash flow problems from at least March 1989
onwards, evidenced by a considerable number of bouncing cheques and aged
creditors. Draft accounts showed the first six months of trading to be good; there
was a profit before tax of £43,000. Thereafter, there are no formal accounts and
the official receiver alleges that the company was insolvent by March 1989. I shall   H
examine that proposition presently. At any rate, the company continued trading
until 29 March 1990, when a bailiff instructed by Customs and Excise took walking
possession and effectively forced a cessation. Thereafter, a winding-up petition was
presented on 6 June 1990 and an order made on 21 August. This application was
issued on 12 February 1992.'

A   **The charges**

In the event, in this appeal, there were only five charges left in the arena. Four of them were found to be proved by the trial judge and there is no appeal against those findings. Those four charges may conveniently be summarised at the outset. They are:

(1)   the misuse of the bank account of Hitco 2000 Ltd ('the company');

B   (2)   the failure to file the company's accounts for its first period of trading by 30 April 1990;

(3)   the failure to file two sets of accounts of Jaysea Agencies Ltd ('Jaysea') by 31 March 1992 and 31 March 1993; and

(4)   the failure to file one annual return of the company by 2 November 1989.

As I have said there is no dispute in this appeal that these charges were rightly found proved. The only dispute is as to the seriousness of these failures and whether they
C   justified the making of a disqualification order. The trial judge held that misuse of the bank account was of a 'fairly serious nature' but that the other three were less serious and that, overall, the four proven charges did not add up to conduct which rendered the respondent unfit to be a company director.

I would have had no hesitation in upholding the trial judge in relation to the filing defaults outlined in (2), (3) and (4) above had they stood alone. He considered all the
D   circumstances surrounding such failures and came to the conclusion that they did not exhibit unfitness as a director. I would have had considerably more hesitation however in relation to the misuse of the bank account. There was presented for payment on no less than 84 occasions (over 80 of them in the last year or so of the company's life) cheques which were dishonoured. The evidence presents a clear picture of lack of financial control. The respondent made it quite clear in evidence that his expertise lay in the buying and selling of the goods the company dealt in and that he relied on the expertise of his
E   bookkeeping staff to compile the accounting records. He told the judge that he was on the road about 85 per cent of the time and that he was a sales-orientated person and relied heavily on others to advise him. He made it quite clear that he did not understand the finer points of accounting. He was asked, 'Did you or did you not yourself go into the books to try to satisfy yourself that it was right to continue trading?' His answer was, 'No, because I would not have understood the finer points'.

F   He employed bookkeepers who had no formal qualifications, Mr Noble from August to November 1988, Mr Shepherd from November 1988 to February 1989, Mrs James from February 1989 to October 1989 and Mr Hay from then until the cessation of trading in late April 1990.

The cheques were issued by one or other of these bookkeepers, often post-dated and, as the respondent said in evidence, 'if the moneys didn't hit on that exact date problems
G   arose'. He signed whole cheque books in blank which he gave to Mr Hay and another employee, Mr Rimmell, with instructions to 'pay as many of the debts as they possibly could given the funds they had, to all the major outstanding persons concerned'. He accepted that he was aware that the employees to whom he gave the books paid the most pressing creditors or paid those whom it was considered politic to pay.

The respondent's main explanation for the bouncing cheques is that it was the fault of
H   Chancery Factors Ltd ('Chancery') to whom he factored his book debts. It was said that they did not pay on time as they were obliged to do. The judge accepted that the company had cause to complain of Chancery's conduct. That is an example of a determination of what was plainly a primary fact. I mention it because it is the only one which was challenged on this appeal. Mr Stephen Davies, counsel for the official receiver, submitted that it was not open to the judge to come to that conclusion on the evidence. Mr Philip Gillyon, counsel for the respondent, submitted otherwise. I, for my part, am by no means

convinced that significant fault lay at the door of Chancery; but there was some evidence   A
upon the basis of which the trial judge could have so found. Accordingly I do not think
it appropriate to disturb that finding. However, the trial judge went on to say that the
fault was not entirely one-sided. It is quite clear that the company got its invoicing wrong
and that this was a major cause of the cash-flow difficulties with Chancery.

At all events, as to the bounced cheques, the evidence was that one way or another,
whether out of company funds or the respondent's own personal funds, the great majority   B
of the cheques were ultimately satisfied. It is accepted by Mr Davies that the precise
number which remained unsatisfied may have been as few as four. Accordingly, it is said
that the evidence of continually bouncing cheques was not evidence of insolvency but
was the consequence of timing difficulties in matching cash receipts with cash outflow.

However true that may be there is no excuse, as the judge held, for sending out cheques
without concrete grounds for expecting them to be met. It would not be a misuse of the   C
bank account to suffer the misfortune of a cheque being referred to drawer where reliance
on a reliable customer's assurance of payment turned out to be misplaced. But, as the
judge held, it is inconceivable that such a misfortune could occur 84 times. Nor, I think,
was the respondent so bold as to suggest that such misfortune was the cause. His sole
explanation was that it was the fault of Chancery. But that explanation, thin as it was in
the period before September 1989, was unavailable in the period post 7 September 1989
when the company's factors were changed from Chancery to Westpac General Finance   D
('Westpac').

In the period after Westpac took over the factoring approximately 28 further cheques
were dishonoured. The respondent said in evidence that Westpac increased the amount
by which the face value of the invoices was discounted in the factoring process and that
was why the cash-flow problems did not resolve themselves. The judge treated that
explanation 'with a degree of caution' because, as he said, it was not contained in the   E
respondent's affidavit.

Whatever the reasons for the poor cash flow, regularly drawing cheques in the hope
that the account will be within limits when they are presented is a misuse of a bank
account and is conduct which is certainly capable of evidencing unfitness. Whether it
does so in any particular case or not is a matter to be evaluated in the light of all the
evidence in the case. The judge here held that in all the circumstances it did not indicate   F
unfitness. I shall come back to this assessment after I have dealt with the most serious
charge made by the official receiver, namely trading without reasonable prospect of
paying creditors.

Before I do that I must clear away one issue that was hotly debated before me. The
original allegation of misuse of the account was based solely on the issuing of cheques
which were dishonoured. The criticism of the respondent in leaving with his bookkeeper   G
blank cheques signed by him was raised as part of the case asserting unfitness for the first
time in this appeal. It was not put forward as a separate ground of unfitness below,
whether by way of amendment to the 'charges' or in argument. Had it been, says Mr
Gillyon, other evidence as to the way in which control was nonetheless maintained over
the use of such blank cheques could have been investigated. In particular, evidence might
have been forthcoming from Mr Noble whom it might have been possible to locate or
from Mrs Cowan who was a signatory on the account. Mr Gillyon attempted   H
(unsuccessfully) to persuade me in any event that on the evidence that was led sufficient
control was in fact maintained by the respondent in relation to the use of the blank
cheques.

In submissions before me, the use of blank cheques in this way was put by Mr Davies
as part of the charge of misuse of a bank account. In my judgment it was indeed a misuse

A   of a bank account but it is true to say that it was not the misuse with which the respondent was charged.

The issue is whether, in the circumstances, the complaint can be relied upon by the official receiver at all. In my judgment some formality must attend the raising of further charges or grounds upon the basis of which misconduct and unfitness is to be asserted. The court has a discretion to allow the official receiver to rely on additional charges if this can be done without injustice: see *Re Sevenoaks Stationers* at p. 774. But, in order to

B   be able to rely on a new complaint as an additional charge, the official receiver must make it clear that he intends to do so. That was not done here and, in my judgment, the official receiver is not entitled to rely upon the respondent's practice of leaving signed blank cheques with his bookkeeper as conduct which of itself justifies a finding of unfitness.

C   However if as here evidence comes to light – especially where it comes from the respondent's own affidavit – it would be absurd if the law required the court to ignore it altogether. In so far as the evidence is relevant to any subsisting ground of complaint, whether specifically or by way of general background, it is something the court is entitled to, indeed should, take into account.

As the allegation of misuse of the bank account was, specifically, an alleged misuse 'by bouncing cheques' the signing of cheques in blank cannot in my judgment be tagged on

D   to that substantive head of complaint. But this evidence is consistent with what seems to me from the evidence generally to have been an abdication of responsibility in the realm of financial control. As such, it is relevant to the most serious charge made against the respondent which also involves an abdication of the responsibility of a director in the realm of financial control, in the case of this charge, in monitoring continued trading and keeping himself informed as to the financial state of the company.

E   That brings me to what I see as the heart of this case and that is the allegation of continuing to trade without reasonable prospect of all creditors being paid. The company traded for a period of a year and ten months, from 1 July 1988 to late April 1990. In all that time there is no evidence that a single set of accounts comprising a balance sheet together with supporting trading and profit and loss accounts was prepared or that management accounts were produced in any form which would have enabled the

F   respondent (or anyone else for that matter) to make an intelligent appraisal of the financial health of the company. In all that period of time the business of the company was conducted without the respondent stopping once to make such an appraisal and to ask himself the question: should I stop incurring credit and cease trading? I should say immediately that there is no allegation or question of want of probity on the respondent's part. Furthermore, this is not a case where the respondent has been lining his own pocket at the expense of creditors and it is not a case where, to any significant extent, it is alleged

G   that he was financing his business by means of the involuntary credit extended by the Crown in the form of HM Customs and Excise in respect of VAT or the Inland Revenue in respect of PAYE. But it does seem to me to be a case where trade was carried on by a sole director for the most part blind as to the true financial state of his company and thus quite unable to make an intelligent projection from time to time as to whether it was right to go on or not. In my judgment the respondent's greatest failing is that he did not ensure that he was provided with regular financial management information so as to

H   enable him to answer that most difficult question which every director who trades with the privilege of limited liability is obliged to confront, especially in straitened financial circumstances, 'should I cease trading?'

That the company was in straitened financial circumstances for the most part of its existence is clear. It went into liquidation in June 1990 with a deficiency as regards creditors of over £150,000. Apart from the bouncing cheques there is a picture of writs

issued by a number of creditors for undisputed claims. In many cases the respondent said   A
he would telephone to the creditors concerned and apologise. Throughout the life of the
company creditors built up and the respondent failed to assess the extent and age of the
debts owed to creditors. The aged trade creditor list prepared by the official receiver
shows debts incurred as early as 1988 which remained unpaid at the time of the
liquidation. Debts amounting to nearly £5,000 incurred before April 1989 remained
unpaid at the end. There were constant threats of enforcement action by HM Customs
and Excise. In the handover notes to Mrs James who took over from Mr Noble in   B
February 1989 it is noted: 'check court summonses for customers not paid'.

Against this background it was all the more important that the respondent should have
before him an accurate picture from time to time of the assets and liabilities of the
company, of the profitability of the company and of the cash-flow projection for the
immediate future. How else could any reasonable decision be made as to whether
continued trading from that point of time onwards would be at the risk and expense of   C
creditors or not? I have looked in vain through the evidence to find any clear indication
that at any relevant time there was before the respondent any intelligible financial picture
upon the basis of which such a reasoned decision could be made.

It is true that there was a draft profit and loss account prepared by the bookkeeper Mr
Shepherd for the period of the first six months of trading (down to December 1988) and
headed 'for discussion purposes only'. I mention this because it was relied upon again   D
and again in the course of the hearing below as an example of the availability of relevant
accounting information. I leave aside the fact that it was a draft document for discussion
purposes only. The important point is not its existence but the absence of a similar
document for the next six months, or the six months after that. So far as it went, of
course, the draft profit and loss account showed a profit of £43,000 on a turnover of
£340,765 and it would have given comfort to the respondent. But business goes on as   E
does the continued need for financial information, and in the ensuing months turnover
was patchy and the severe cash-flow problems and their consequences manifested
themselves.

The event that plainly weighed heavily with the judge in leading to his rejection of the
allegation of trading without reasonable prospect of paying the creditors was the calling
in of Mr Matthews, an unqualified accountant, to assist in August 1989. Mr Matthews,
although unqualified, had had many years of experience. It is reasonably plain that Mr   F
Matthews was called in because of the problem the company was having with its cash
flow. As Mr Matthews said, he was 'not down at 2000 on an auditing mission; I was
down to try and assist in implementing better procedural methods'. What Mr Matthews
did while he was at the company appears most clearly from the report he prepared which
is dated 21 August 1989. The judge said that, 'he attached considerable significance to
this report'. The report concentrated on the difficulties created with Chancery in   G
connection with inaccurate invoicing by the company and offered practical advice to
avoid these problems and the cash-flow consequences they caused. Mr Matthews also
gave some advice on staffing and recommended the employment of Mr Hay as
bookkeeper in place of Mrs James. In his report to the respondent Mr Matthews said, 'I
am sure that between us we can resolve your current problems ...' and he made
suggestions in this regard in order to 'put the business on a sound footing ...' A great
deal of reliance was placed by Mr Gillyon on these positive remarks in this report.   H

Mr Matthews spent four days at the company and the judge was satisfied that he
would have become aware if the company was then trading without a reasonable
prospect. Mr Gillyon relies on Mr Matthews' report as consistent with the continuation
of trading. Certainly there was no suggestion that the company should cease to trade.
But it is tolerably clear that Mr Matthews was not sent in to advise on the question of

A   continued trading. However the judge concluded, and I would not for my part disturb this conclusion, that some comfort could have been gleaned from his report in this respect.

As to Mr Matthews' advice, the respondent carried out his recommendations with regard to the inaccurate invoicing. He also carried out Mr Matthews' advice by changing his bookkeeper. However, the most important recommendation of Mr Matthews was not followed. That was that the respondent should employ Mr Matthews initially to

B   come down for three days to assist in getting a system together to overcome the existing problems, and then to come down at monthly intervals during the first year and to carry out the 1989 audit, prepare accounts and deal with the registrar of companies and taxation.

In the ensuing three months the monthly turnover improved, reaching approximately £80,000 in the month of October 1989. There were, however, a few set-backs. First, there

C   was a burglary in November 1989 when a considerable amount of stock was taken. More importantly, what began as a potentially lucrative contract with Burton Group plc trading as Top Man for the Christmas sales turned into a disaster when Burton Group plc insisted on a sale or return arrangement after the company was already committed on its supply side; and then the Christmas sales turned out to be very poor and the returned goods ware returned damaged beyond repair. The risk of such damage fell,

D   under the contract, on the company. Turnover had fallen to some £32,000 in November and although it had risen to £52,000 in December it fell to about £13,700 in January, £20,000 in February and from then on became pretty negligible.

Despite the lack of accounting information upon the basis of which an intelligent assessment could be made, I would not differ from the judge's conclusion, in relation to the period from August to December 1989, that the respondent should not be criticised for trading at the risk of creditors. The mere presence of Mr Matthews for four days in

E   August without adverse comment from him on the question of continued trading (even though he was not put there for that purpose) coupled with the buoyant turnover in August, September and October would be enough, even without the critical accounting information I regard as so sorely lacking, to enable the respondent to escape a charge of trading at the risk of creditors. But against the straitened financial background I have mentioned, the set-backs in the period leading up to Christmas, the disappointing

F   Christmas trading period and the disastrous Top Man contract, I think January 1990 should have seen a careful consideration as to whether it was right to continue trading.

With hindsight, of course, it is plain that trading should have stopped then, if not before. Nobody is of course gifted with hindsight but I can see very little in the evidence that could, with foresight, have justified continued trading in January 1990. It is interesting to note that in a statement made by the respondent under s. 235 of the *Insolvency Act* 1986 and signed on 30 August 1990, he said:

G
        'I first became aware that debts of the company could not be paid as and when due after Christmas 1989.'

The judge, in relation to this period, relies on a further visit by Mr Matthews at this time. 'It was not the sort of detailed investigation made earlier', the judge recorded, 'but even at that stage his evidence is that he did not see anything to cause him to advise the company to stop trading'. 'Of course', the judge went on:

H
        'that decision lies with the director and not the auditor, but if the accountant who had carried out an extensive review in August saw no reason to give different advice in January, it is difficult for the court to be satisfied that the director was culpable.'

I have read Mr Matthews' evidence. I think the judge overstates the extent and content of the review in August but, more importantly, the judge's summation of Mr Matthews'

evidence in relation to January 1990 carries the implication that Mr Matthews made   A
some conscious evaluation in January 1990 as to whether the company should carry on
trading.

There is no substitute for reading the whole of the evidence of Mr Matthews and I
hesitate to quote any of it. But the following extracts from his cross-examination by Mr
Davies and his re-examination by Mr Gillyon will go some way to illustrate my point.

Cross examination   B

'Q. Did anyone ever ask your professional advice as to whether the company
should cease trading, for instance, go in and work out whether or not it should
cease trading?

A. Not to the best of my recollection, no.

Q. And indeed if they had presumably, you would have to go in and do a proper   C
and thorough job.

A. Oh, yes, you could not do that on the telephone.

Q. No, quite. And did anyone ever really concern you with the extent or the age
of the creditors after your report, the sort of global situation, if I can put it that
way?

A. No to the best of my recollection, no, because it would not be something that I   D
was dealing with.

Q. Quite. And did you concern yourself as to who was dealing with that effectively,
was that something of your concern either way?

A. Well, presumably Mr Ken Hay and Mr Cowan were dealing with that side of
it because it is a day-to-day thing rather than a systems problem.'

Re-examination   E

'Q. When you returned to 2000 in late 1989, I think you said – do you have any
idea of the date of that return visit?

A. From the invoice I would suggest it was probably about mid-January; it was
somewhere between mid-December 1989 and mid-January 1990.

Q. And did you see anything there that caused you to conclude that the company   F
should cease to trade?

A. I don't recall, but evidently not by inference in as much as if I had, I would
have mentioned it.'

It is clear from the evidence as a whole that Mr Matthews did not in the course of his
January visit review the financial state of the company and it seems plain to me from the
above extracts that Mr Matthews did not even begin to assess whether the company
should or should not continue trading; the judge was not justified, in my judgment, in   G
relying on Mr Matthews' visit in January 1990 as giving the respondent the necessary
comfort and encouragement to go on trading.

In fact, apart from the reference to expected sales on St Valentine's Day 1990 which
was mentioned for the first time in the witness-box, there was no justification put forward
by the respondent in his evidence for the continuation of trading after the Christmas
1989 period.   H

Even if on this late and flimsy evidence it was possible to conclude that there was
justification in continuing trading until 14 February 1990, there is absolutely no evidence
justifying such continuation beyond that date. The judge was satisfied that the respondent
did not have a reasonable and justifiable belief in the company's ability to trade through
its difficulties from mid-February onwards but he rejected this period (of over two

A   months) as an insignificant 'fag end' in the life of the company. Yet fresh credit continued to be incurred in this period and the only reason it seems why trading eventually stopped is because HM Customs and Excise, having taken walking possession of the assets of the company at the end of March 1990, eventually seized all its assets on or about 23 April.

So far as the respondent himself is concerned he does not assert a conscious process of evaluation and belief at any time that it was appropriate for him to go on trading. Had he done that and had the judge believed him it would be inappropriate for an appellate

B   court to interfere. That is not this case although his evidence needs to be read in full to see that this is not the case he was putting forward.

Furthermore, on the issue whether he had a sufficient flow of management information to enable him to take intelligent decisions as to whether to carry on trading, his evidence again needs to be read in the round: isolated passages can give a misleading picture.

C   Taking all the evidence as a whole, I am left wholly unconvinced that the respondent, as sole director of this company, fulfilled his responsibilities as a director to ensure that he was provided with the flow of financial information vital to enable him to monitor the company's financial position. Moreover, it is plain on his own admission, and a reading of his evidence only goes to underline the point, that he would not have understood all this financial information in any event. In the circumstances it was incumbent upon him, if he wished to run the company as sole director to ensure (at whatever cost) that he had

D   the requisite, constant, professional guidance. Far from that being the case, he rejected Mr Matthews' offer of regular assistance.

In my judgment the judge was wrong in rejecting the charge that the respondent continued to trade without any reasonable prospect of paying all the creditors. I would hold that that charge was adequately proved in respect of the period from early January 1990 onwards.

E   I am satisfied that this conduct makes the respondent unfit to be concerned in the management of a company. If the respondent were again to manage a company as sole director without ensuring an adequate flow of financial information which he could understand and act upon, the public would be likely to be hurt. He can, of course, deploy his skills on the sales side of a business but he has shown himself unfit to undertake the responsibility of a director on the financial side. His abdication of control of the financial side of the business of the company in relation to the charge of trading at the risk of

F   creditors is echoed by his abdication of control in relation to the charge of misuse of the bank account by the issuance of cheques that were dishonoured. The cumulative effect of these two proven charges confirms me in my assessment of the respondent as unfit. Had the dishonoured cheques stood alone as the only charge proved, I would have hesitated to disagree with the judge. Coupled however with the charge of trading at creditors' risk and founded, as both these charges are, on a serious lack of financial awareness and

G   control, I am satisfied that the judge was wrong and I would allow the appeal.

I have not overlooked the breaches of the *Companies Act* 1985 in relation to the failure to file the company's accounts and annual return and the failure to file one set of Jaysea's accounts on time and the failure to file the ensuing set of accounts of Jaysea at all. (Since the hearing below a compulsory winding-up order has been made in respect of Jaysea.) As I have indicated above I would not have differed from the judge's conclusion looking at these failures in isolation. Looking at them in the light of my conclusions on the more

H   serious charges, it seems to me they only add further weight to my assessment. The two defaults in relation to the filing of Jaysea's accounts in particular occurred after the issue, on 12 February 1992, of these disqualification proceedings, and at a time when the respondent was aware that failure to prepare and file accounts was a ground upon which disqualification was sought. These failures are not as serious as the failures in *Secretary of State for Trade and Industry v Ettinger & Anor. Re Swift 736 Ltd* [1993] BCC 312. But

they exhibit the same symptom of lack of financial control as do the charges which have   A
been proved. I bear in mind the words of Sir Donald Nicholls V-C in the abovementioned
case at p. 315F:

> 'Isolated lapses in filing documents are one thing and may be excusable, but not so
> persistent lapses which show overall a blatant disregard for this important aspect
> of accountability. Such lapses are serious and cannot be condoned even though,
> and it is right to have this firmly in mind, they need not involve any dishonest   B
> intent.
>
> . . .
>
> It may be that, despite the disqualification provisions having been in operation for
> some years, there is still a lingering feeling in some quarters that a failure to file
> annual accounts and so forth is a venial sin. If this is still so, the sooner the attitude
> is corrected the better it will be. Judicial observations to this effect have been made   C
> before, but they bear repetition.'

Standing alone, the filing defaults would not have added up to unfitness. Coming on
top of the other charges they certainly confirm my determination of unfitness.

As I have said, this is not a case involving want of probity. I bear in mind also that the
collapse of the company was in part due to misfortune and that the respondent hazarded
and lost a not inconsiderable sum of his own money. I regard the respondent's unfitness   D
as meriting disqualification for no more than the minimum period prescribed by s. 6(4)
of the CDDA 1986, namely two years. But I do not think that the disqualification needs
to be absolute. Taking a managerial role on the sales side of a business provided there
was firmly in place a finance director duly qualified to exercise responsible financial
control seems to me to be an acceptable way forward. I shall hear counsel on the form of
the order and any application for leave under subs. 1(1) of the Act.

E

(*Order accordingly*)

F

G

H

A
Re CSTC Ltd.
Secretary of State for Trade and Industry v Van Hengel & Anor.
Chancery Division (Companies Court).
Robert Reid QC (sitting as a deputy High Court judge).
B   Judgment delivered 29 July 1994.

Disqualifying unfit directors of insolvent companies – Whether directors were unfit – Company Directors Disqualification Act 1986, s. 6.

This was an application under s. 6 of the Company Directors Disqualification Act 1986 against two directors, 'V' and 'J'.

They were directors of a company which operated commodities and financial futures
C   syndicates until it went into liquidation in 1989. The Securities and Investments Board presented a winding-up petition which was withdrawn when the company went into creditors' voluntary liquidation.

The Secretary of State relied on six grounds for the disqualification of the two directors: (1) alleged misapplication of clients' funds; (2) failure by the company properly to maintain client trust accounts; (3) permitting the company to trade while insolvent; (4) permitting the
D   company to pay excessive remuneration to the directors; (5) convictions of the company and another director under the Prevention of Fraud (Investments) Act 1958, s. 14 (restriction on distribution of circulars relating to investments); and (6) failure to file accounts and returns on time.

Held, disqualifying V and J for six and two years respectively:

1. In relation to the misapplication of funds, V took no steps at all to see that the
E   functions for which he was responsible in the company were properly carried out. J was concerned and took certain steps to deal with the concern. His attitude did not indicate that he was unfit. With hindsight it was possible to see that the steps which he took were inadequate.

2. In relation to the client accounts, V's lack of care for his clients and his lack of any responsible undertaking of the management role for which he was responsible was such that
F   it could properly be said that he was grossly negligent in the discharge of his duties and totally incompetent in carrying them out. J had failed to bring what was obvious accounting chaos under control.

3. It could not properly be said that the attitude which the directors adopted in continuing to trade in the first part of 1988 indicated a lack of moral probity. There was in early 1988 a genuine prospect that fresh capital would be introduced, and the directors could not be blamed for allowing the company to continue to trade in circumstances where it appeared
G   that the introduction of fresh capital and changing trading circumstances would enable the company to survive properly.

4. The remuneration paid to the directors for at least the last two years of the company's existence was excessive in that it was plainly substantially more than the company could afford.

5. No culpability rested with V in relation to the conviction. J acted properly and no
H   blame attached to him either for the prosecution having been incurred or for the manner in which he dealt with it.

6. V's cavalier attitude to filing revealed he did not appreciate the nature of the duties which he had undertaken as a director. There was only one default while J was a director, but he had been financial controller for a year before his appointment to the board and knowing the history of the company's defaults in the past he should have been particularly

vigilant to ensure that when he became financial director no further lapses of the same sort occurred.   A

The following cases were referred to in the judgment:

Cladrose Ltd, Re [1990] BCC 11.
CU Fittings Ltd & Anor, Re (1989) 5 BCC 210.
Keypak Homecare Ltd, Re (No. 2) [1990] BCC 117.
Swift 736 Ltd, Re. Secretary of State for Trade and Industry v Ettinger & Anor [1993]   B
BCC 312.
Synthetic Technology Ltd, Re [1993] BCC 549.

Michael Briggs QC (instructed by the Treasury Solicitor) for the Secretary of State for Trade and Industry.

Andrew Thompson (instructed by McKenna & Co) for the fourth respondent.

The third respondent appeared in person.   C

JUDGMENT

Robert Reid QC: This is an application under s. 6 of the *Company Directors Disqualification Act* 1986. There were originally five respondents to the application, but proceedings against the first respondent, Peter Bark, have been adjourned generally as a result of his illness, and proceedings against the second respondent, Nicholas Bark (Peter   D
Bark's father) and Gavin Wetton, the fifth respondent, have been discontinued on the grounds of the age and ill health of those two respondents. It follows that this judgment is concerned only with the applications made against Peter van Hengel, the third respondent, and Alan Jones, the fourth respondent.

CSTC was incorporated on 2 March 1984. It commenced trading in January 1985. Its principal business was that of an operator of commodities and financial futures   E
syndicates. It ceased trading on 14 July 1988 when a winding-up petition was presented.

The company, in fact, went into creditors' voluntary liquidation on 15 February 1989 after which the winding-up petition was dismissed. The liquidator is Mr Christopher Morris. He had previously been appointed as special manager on the presentation of the winding-up petition at the instance of the official receiver, who had been appointed provisional liquidator.

The company's last principal trading address was 5–9 Hatton Wall, London. Its last   F
audited accounts were up to 31 December 1986. The principal shareholder in the company at the time of its liquidation was Peter Bark. Mr Jong, who had been a director until his retirement in December 1985, also held some shares. The other shareholder was the third respondent Mr van Hengel. Mr Jones, the fourth respondent, did not hold any shares. Mr van Hengel had been formally appointed a director in July 1985. Mr Jones became a director on 30 June 1987, having joined the company as financial controller a   G
year previously.

The roles of Peter Bark, Mr van Hengel and Mr Jones respectively in the running of the company can be summarised as follows. Mr Peter Bark was the managing director holding 45,500 of the 56,000 issued shares. Mr van Hengel had joined CSTC in June 1985 as trading director. According to his affidavit, his responsibility was to trade current accounts and look after syndicated accounts in the futures market. He says he was also   H
responsible for the appointment and control of commodity trading advisers and that his function included placing funds with future commission merchants and ensuring the margin requirements were met. He describes himself as being responsible for the management of individual clients and their accounts. Mr Jones, who qualified as a costs and works accountant in 1962, was recruited by the company in 1986. Mr Nicholas Bark, the father of Peter Bark, told him the company urgently needed to engage a consultant.

A   Mr Jones had previously known Mr Peter Bark and he was interested in the post. He says he expressly made it clear to Mr Peter Bark that he had no previous experience of the financial futures industry or its regulations and would be unable to bring expert knowledge to bear in this respect. He says he was assured that both Mr Peter Bark and Mr van Hengel, as well as their senior staff, were well qualified in that regard and that he could rely upon their advice and expertise. As a result, he accepted employment with the company as financial controller with effect from 30 June 1986. He describes his duties at

B   CSTC as being solely of an accounting nature. He says that originally it had been intended that he would supervise the running of the back room, the individual client information, ensuring that information on computer was accurate for all clients. However, due to the quantity of work required to clear the backlog on his appointment, this work was instead supervised by the company secretary, Mr James Wetton, the son of the fifth respondent.

C   From the very beginning the company was in default of its obligations to make annual returns and file its accounts. Its first annual return was due on 14 October 1985 but was not filed until 9 May 1986. The March 1985 accounts were due for filing on 1 January 1986 but work on their preparation did not begin until 4 March 1986, and those accounts were signed by Mr Peter Bark and Mr van Hengel on 24 April 1986. The auditors certified those accounts on 30 April and they showed a retained loss of £2,373. On 31

D   October 1986 the accounts to December 1985 were due for filing. On 22 December 1986 those accounts were signed by the company secretary by order of the board. On 13 January 1987 the second annual return was due. On 2 February 1987 the March 1985 accounts were filed, 13 months late. On 2 March 1987 accounts to December 1985 were certified by the auditors showing a retained loss of £47,821. On 25 March the second annual return was filed, two months late. On 26 March the accounts to December 1985 were filed, five months late. On 31 October the accounts to December 1986 became due

E   for filing. However, those accounts were not certified by the auditors until February 1988. They were then signed by the company secretary by order of the board. They showed a retained loss of £181,368. On 26 May 1988 the December 1986 accounts were filed, seven months late.

   On 1 June 1988 the company and Mr Peter Bark were prosecuted under the *Prevention of Fraud (Investments) Act* 1958. They were convicted and each fined. An application

F   was made that Mr Bark should be disqualified from holding directorships, but that application was refused.

   As I have already mentioned, the company's primary business was that of investing on behalf of syndicates of investors in the American futures market. It did, however, also acquire the whole issued share capital of a company called London & Sussex Investments Ltd. That company was involved in an issue under the Business Expansion Scheme on

G   behalf of a company called Wessex. I shall return briefly to that venture later.

   The way in which the syndicate business was operated was that comparatively small investors, investing sums in many cases of £2,500, paid their money to CSTC. Those moneys were then aggregated in syndicates and placed with future commission merchants. At the end of its time the company was, in fact, using only one future commission merchant, namely Thompson McKinnon of New York. The basis upon

H   which each investor invested with the company was a standard form of client agreement. This provided for the company to take certain remuneration and provided also for the client's money, apart from that remuneration, to be kept in segregated client accounts. In July 1987 the company embarked on an ambitious expansion programme which involved Mr van Hengel, although not resigning as a director, leaving England and going to Florida to set up an American subsidiary there. For this he was paid by the subsidiary $10,000 per month. He managed to obtain office premises for the American subsidiary,

but the subsidiary was never able to start trading because it was unable to obtain from
its parent company the necessary money to obtain the requisite licences from the
American authorities. The $10,000 a month paid to Mr van Hengel was paid to the
subsidiary by the parent for onward transmission to him.

The result of the American venture was that Mr van Hengel remained a director but
was never in the UK and was not available for board meetings, nor was he able to take
any active part in the management of the company. Furthermore, although he received a
substantial sum of money from the company and for a two-month period had an
assistant, at no time was he able to start up the business of the new subsidiary and such
work as he did during that period was in relation to his own particular clients and in
assisting the business of another person who was not involved with the company.

The company submitted an application for membership to the Association of Futures
Brokers and Dealers ('AFBD') and between November 1987 and June 1988 various
meetings and discussions took place between Mr Bark and representatives of AFBD.
The company was aware that it might well have difficulty in meeting the proposed capital
adequacy requirements of AFBD. With this in view, in January 1988 discussions began
with a Mr Putsfield for him to purchase a substantial holding in the company. As a result
of this it was hoped that £1m of fresh capital would become available. However, on
7 July 1988 at the request of AFBD the Securities and Investments Board instructed
Touche Ross to investigate the affairs of CSTC under s. 105 and s. 106 of the *Financial
Services Act* 1986 following concern over the company's financial position and the
management of client funds. On that same day AFBD turned down the company's
application for membership.

On 14 July 1988 the SIB presented a petition to wind-up the company on the grounds
it was insolvent and it was just and equitable a winding-up order should be made. On the
same day the official receiver was, as I have said, appointed provisional liquidator and
Mr Morris was appointed as the special manager. On 23 January 1989 the directors of
CSTC sought the court's consent to place CSTC in creditors' voluntary liquidation. That
consent was granted subject to the proviso that Mr Morris should be appointed the
liquidator. The order also provided that the appointment of the provisional liquidator
and special manager would be terminated on Mr Morris's appointment as liquidator.
Thereafter the winding-up petition presented by the SIB was withdrawn.

The winding up has indeed demonstrated that the company was insolvent. A dividend
of something over 33p in the pound has been paid to the unsecured creditors. Those
unsecured creditors included the persons who had invested through the syndicates which
were run by CSTC. They were owed some £246,000. This excludes a further sum of
£361,000-odd to which I shall return in due course.

Against that background, I turn now to the grounds alleged by the Secretary of State
for the disqualification of Mr van Hengel and Mr Jones. Those grounds are six in
number. The first and most important of them relates to the alleged misapplication of
clients' funds. The relationship between the company and its clients was governed by a
standard form of discretionary syndicate agreement. Clause 4 of the agreement required
investors' funds to be kept both by the company and by any investment manager
appointed by the company in segregated trust accounts. It provided that all interest
accruing to such accounts should be to the account of the syndicate members and that all
interest and other payments received by the company in respect of pooled funds would
be credited to the trust account. Thompson McKinnon were, as I have said, the principal
and latterly the only future commission merchant employed by the company. Before July
1987 Thompson McKinnon invested syndicate funds which were from time to time
surplus to futures and margin requirements in short-dated US dollar Treasury Bills which
were purchased at a discount to their face value. Those bills therefore produced a yield

A   on maturity. That yield accrued to the credit of the clients. From July 1987 about three-quarters of such surplus funds were held by Thompson McKinnon in sterling. This was as a result of an anticipated adverse dollar/sterling trend. No complaint is made about the decision to hold funds in sterling rather than in dollars. It is said on behalf of Mr van Hengel and Mr Jones that they believed that each of the clients was telephoned and informed this was going to be done. The complaint that arises is in relation to the interest accruing on the outstanding balances. By a telex dated 28 July 1987 the company, acting

B   through Mr Peter Bark, the first respondent, directed Thompson McKinnon to pay all interest so far earned on such sterling funds direct to the company, and to continue to do so for the future. The terms of the telex by which this request was made were as follows:

'Further to discussions held recently between James Wetton and Tony Campanali, we would like interest earned on non-utilised funds paid directly to CSTC Ltd. This should also continue on future interest earned. The reasons for this are

C   because I have been advised that UK residents paid interest on balances would be subject to a withholding tax that CSTC would have to make. We have studied the logistics and believe that it is not a worthwhile exercise bearing in mind the manpower needed to accomplish this task.

Thank you for your help in dealing with this matter and also for Edgar Barley's latest disclosure document. When will you be able to look at the new conversion?'

D   The funds in fact received by the company as a result of that telex amounted to some £361,000. None of that money was paid into any trust account; it was retained and used by the company for its own purposes. There can be no justification, under the terms of the client agreement, for that misuse of those funds, and at the hearing neither Mr van Hengel nor Mr Jones sought to justify what had happened. Mr van Hengel in his affidavit had sought to justify the retention of those funds by the company by reference to custom

E   of the trade. However, in his oral evidence he did not seek to maintain that justification. He made it plain that change in attitude was at least in part the result of Mr Peter Bark not being at the trial with him. His new approach was this was something done by Mr Peter Bark at a time when he, Mr van Hengel, had already departed to Florida, and that it not a matter with which he was concerned. In my judgment this approach reveals a complete absence of appreciation of the obligations which he had as a director of the company and, more importantly, in the duties that he had as a director primarily

F   concerned with the welfare of the clients. Even if I took at face value his assertion that Mr Peter Bark was solely responsible for the transmission of the money to the company without Mr van Hengel's knowledge and the misuse of that money by the company, which I am not able to do, Mr van Hengel is revealed as a director who left the country and thereafter took no steps at all to see that the functions for which he was responsible in the company were properly carried out. In his favour it can be said that when the issue

G   of the £361,000 was raised, he indicated to Touche Ross that he was prepared to put up a bond for $361,000 pending determination of the propriety of the company touching the money. This offer was rejected.

Mr Jones's position is rather different. Although his affidavit evidence appeared to indicate he had not looked at the standard client agreement and had simply relied on advice received by Mr Peter Bark and from Mr van Hengel, his oral evidence, which on this point I accept, placed a rather different complexion on the matter. He said in his

H   evidence that he had read the client agreement and that he was unhappy about the use of the money for the company's own purposes, that he had raised the matter with Mr Peter Bark but had been assured by Mr Peter Bark that the use of the money by the company was proper as a matter of trade custom. He also gave evidence that he then queried the appropriateness of the form of the customer agreement as it seemed to him it was misleading. His view was that he was a layman in these matters and the agreement would be misunderstood by other lay persons in the same way as he had misunderstood it. He did not seek to raise the matter at a full board meeting; indeed full meetings appear to have been a rarity in this company. He placed his reliance on the word of the managing director who was also the major shareholder of the company, and who was the man who had specific expertise in that particular field.

In my judgment Mr Jones can be criticised for taking that stance and paying too much attention to the man who, despite his protestations to the contrary while giving evidence, he regarded as his boss. But taken alone, his attitude does not necessarily indicate that he is someone who is unfit to be a director of a company. He was concerned and he took certain steps to deal with the concern. With the benefit of hindsight it is possible to see that the steps which he took were inadequate.

The second head of complaint is that the company failed properly to maintain client trust accounts. The evidence makes it clear that the trust accounts were in serious disarray by the time the company ceased to trade. The amount of claims by clients, excluding claims in relation to the £361,000 mentioned above, were admitted in the liquidation in the sum of £264,999. In his statement of affairs the first respondent had there would be a surplus on current account of somewhere in the region of £15,000.

The third respondent, Mr van Hengel, had amongst his responsibilities the management of the individual clients and their accounts. He had not relinquished this responsibility when he left the UK to go to Florida. Thereafter, according to his affidavit, he received adequate information either from Mr Bark or Mr Jones. However, according to oral evidence, he was unable to obtain proper information from Mr Bark and spoke only occasionally to Mr Jones. He says he was reduced to corresponding through Mr Cooper, a solicitor with Lovell White Durrant, who had been solicitors on the formation of the company. In my judgment he did not obtain adequate information from Mr Bark but he made little effort to do so.

Mr Bark, it seems, was less than open with his fellow directors on matters concerning the management of the company. The result of Mr van Hengel's stay in Florida and of his cavalier attitude to his responsibilities for the management of current funds was that he had no idea at the time the company came into liquidation there was anything amiss with the client account. This was not that he had made proper enquiries and been misled but because he had been fobbed off when he sought information about the state of the company and had not seen fit to do anything about it. He was well aware the company was in financial trouble. He had, for example, been unable to obtain the $25,000 necessary for the company to obtain licences for its subsidiary so the subsidiary could start trading in the USA. He may well be a very expert dealer himself and he may well be able to give proper advice to clients. There is no suggestion that he was in any way dishonest. It is clear that he spent his own money on acquiring shares in the company. It is also clear he could have earned as much, if not more, if he had remained employed with some other organisation. However, it seems to me that his lack of care for his clients and his lack of any responsible undertaking of the management role for which he was responsible was such that it can properly be said that he was grossly negligent in the discharge of his duties and totally incompetent in carrying them out.

In the case of Mr Jones, it had originally been intended he would supervise the running of the back room, that is to say the individual client information and ensuring the information on computer was accurate for all the clients. Had he been able to undertake this work, I have no doubt he would have discovered the deficiencies in the client accounts and their true extent at an early stage, and he might then have been able to take some steps to ensure the deficiencies were made good.

I reject the suggestion that it was because he had too servile an attitude to Mr Bark that this happened and that the cause of his failure to perceive the exact extent of the

A   client account deficiency at an early stage was the same. He had at the time of the liquidation of the company, however, been employed by the company or engaged as a director for a period of two years. The much more telling criticism, therefore, that can be made of him is that during that time he had failed to bring what was obvious accounting chaos under control.

B   It is always a difficult task for a director, or indeed a senior manager, to pick the point at which he should abandon his attempts to rectify matters and should instead start making demands for liquidation of the company. As Hoffmann J said in *Re CU Fittings Ltd & Anor* (1989) 5 BCC 210 at p. 213E:

> 'It may be that in January, or even earlier, a dispassionate mind would have reached the conclusion that the company was doomed. But directors immersed in the day-to-day task of trying to keep their business afloat cannot be expected to have wholly dispassionate minds. They tend to cling to hope. Obviously there comes a point at which an honest businessman recognises that he is only gambling at the expense of his creditors on the possibility that something may turn up. But this is not such a case.'

C

D   I bear this comment fully in mind when considering Mr Jones's position as a director of the company. He was a director who had earlier experience of a company as financial manager. From at any rate November 1987 on his own evidence he was aware of the difficulties in relation to client account moneys, and was aware of a deficiency in February 1988. He had signed the financial information document supplied to AFBD. That document had disclosed a client account deficiency of £17,862. In his view there was a substantially greater deficiency on the earlier of the two management accounts which he caused to be prepared. He was, however, persuaded those management accounts overstated the position. It was as a result of this that he was persuaded at the time when he made the statement of affairs to show the client account deficiency at £89,964. It seems to me that, in fact, his earlier estimate of the June management accounts of a deficiency of some £225,000 was far more accurate; indeed when one adds to this the sum of £37,000-odd in respect of cheques made payable to investors which were outstanding at the date of the commencement of liquidation and which were, therefore, not honoured, the total comes reasonably close to the total eventually proved in the liquidation.

E

F   The reason the cheques drawn on the company's account were outstanding in favour of clients was that the trust accounts held by the company were not cheque accounts, so that whenever money was to be paid to an investor what happened was that money was transferred from a trust account into the company account and the cheques drawn on the company account. This system plainly had weaknesses; for example the investor was at the mercy of the company's bank in the event the bank chose not to honour a cheque drawn on the company's account because it was overdrawn. Counsel on behalf of the Secretary of State very properly did not seek to rely on this weakness as indicating a ground of unfitness.

G

The next basis upon which the Secretary of State contends that the respondents are unfit is they permitted the company to continue trading whilst it was hopelessly insolvent in the first part of 1988. This essentially depends upon whether or not they entertained a genuine belief as to the company's entitlement to retain interest which it had accrued on the clients' surplus funds. As I have already said, neither Mr van Hengel nor Mr Jones now contends the company had any such entitlement. As I have also said, in Mr Jones case, at the time he accepted Mr Bark's word that the company was entitled to retain this money. In Mr van Hengel's case, he appears to have been ready to accept that the company could retain money without making any investigation of his own. In any event, the company was insolvent in early 1988 and had very large retained losses. The figures which it gave AFBD in February showed it had very substantial capital requirements.

H

However, I accept that in the spring of 1988 the company was beginning to trade **A**
profitably, albeit the extent of that profit was small. In part, this was as a result of its
alliance with London & Sussex. More importantly, at that time negotiations were
continuing for the introduction of £1m of fresh capital.

In my judgment, though in the event fresh capital was not introduced, there was in
early 1988 a genuine prospect that it would be introduced, and the directors cannot be
blamed for allowing the company to continue to trade in circumstances where it appeared **B**
that the introduction of fresh capital and changing trading circumstances would enable
the company to survive properly.

The question whether a risk taken when a company is in deficiency is an unwarrantable
risk of the clients' and creditors' money is inevitably a matter of judgment. I have already
cited a passage from Hoffmann J's judgment in *CU Fittings*. In my judgment it cannot
properly be said that the attitude which the directors adopted in continuing to trade in
the first part of 1988 was an attitude which can be regarded as indicating a lack of moral **C**
probity.

The fourth charge is the respondents permitted the company to pay excessive
remuneration to the directors. The figures in respect of directors' remuneration were as
follows. For the period 2 March 1984 to 31 March 1985, of which in practice only a
couple of months was a period during which the company was trading, the directors'
remuneration amounted to £2,450. The company's retained loss for that period was **D**
£2,373. The company's turnover for the period was £15,168. The directors' remuneration
amounted to a little over 16 per cent of turnover. For the period of nine months to 31
December 1985 there was a loss of £45,448 on a turnover of £218,770. The directors'
remuneration was £56,214, something over 25 per cent of turnover. For the year to 31
December 1986 the turnover was £851,689 and the company made a loss of £133,547.
The directors' remuneration was £192,550. This amounted to over 22.5 per cent of **E**
turnover.

The evidence discloses the following further information in relation to the directors'
remuneration for the 12-month period from April 1987, and I deal only with the two
respondents presently before the court, Mr van Hengel and Mr Jones. Mr van Hengel
received £18,750 for the period to 31 June 1987. He went to Florida and thereafter he
received $10,000 a month for a further eight months to 31 March 1988 totalling $80,000.
At an exchange rate of, say, $1.87 to the pound, says the deponent Mr Morris, that total **F**
is £42,780. That $10,000 a month was nominally paid by the subsidiary which never
started to trade, but the money for it to pay him was transmitted by the parent company.

The fourth respondent, Mr Jones, received £38,245 in the tax year 1987–88. Part of
that period was, of course, a period when he was still an employee and not a director.
For the period 5 April 1988 to 15 July 1988 he received remuneration amounting to
£16,083. Mr Jones's evidence, which was unchallenged on this aspect, was that he took **G**
an abatement of salary for three months during 1988 at a rate equivalent to an abatement
of £26,000 a year. Also during the previous year he deferred taking a bonus whilst
financial controller. That bonus, he deposed, would have amounted to £20,000. He told
me in the course of his oral evidence, and I accept, that he did this in an attempt to
introduce some measure of economy within the company and, by way of example, Mr
Bark and Mr Wetton also agreed to take an abatement of their entitlements, but the
abatement which they took lasted only for two months. Mr Jones's evidence was that **H**
during his time as a director of the company there was not directors' approval of salaries
and he accepts there should have been. He placed the abatement of salary which he took
at a total of about £40,000.

In my judgment the extent of the salary paid to the third respondent, Mr van Hengel,
for the period when he was in the USA, on any view, excessive. If the directors of the

A company had put their minds properly to the question of directors' remuneration, they would have appreciated that they could not justify paying such a salary to one of their number who was achieving nothing whatsoever on behalf of the subsidiary which had never begun to trade. Furthermore, in my judgment the failure of the board to grapple with the financial constraints of the company and their failure to appreciate that the company could not afford the directors' salaries which were being charged was culpable.

B Mr Jones took a very proper attitude in accepting an abatement of his own salary and a deferment of the bonus which I am told was never in the event paid. However, in my judgment he should have gone further because he was aware there were no board meetings at which directors' salaries were approved, yet on his evidence it appears he did nothing about it. Mr van Hengel was a rather different case. His position was he could have earned as much or more elsewhere and saw no reason why he should be paid less as a director of the company of which he was also a shareholder than he could command as

C an employee elsewhere. In my judgment this indicates a failure to appreciate his duties as a director. A director must bear in mind what a company can afford as well as what is the going rate for the job performed by the director if he were an employee elsewhere. Mr van Hengel never appreciated this. In my judgment remuneration paid to the directors for at least the last two years of the company's existence was excessive in that it was plainly substantially more than the company could afford.

D The next complaint is the company and the first respondent each pleaded guilty to contravention of the *Prevention of Fraud (Investments) Act* 1958. The convictions were under s. 14 and s. 19 of that Act. It related to the distribution of circulars pertaining to arrangements in property other than securities, in that brochures relating to a collective investment scheme were sent to the general public. The company had been warned at an early stage of the dangers of s. 14. A letter on 2 July 1985 from Lovell White Durrant specifically makes the point.

E The position of the two respondents presently before the court in relation to this matter was as follows. The period over which the offence was committed was 20 August 1987 to 7 January 1988. During that period Mr van Hengel was in Florida. He was not aware of the events at the time and it was not seriously suggested on behalf of the Secretary of State that any culpability rested with him in relation to this conviction. So far as Mr Jones is concerned, he became aware of the prosecution shortly before the summons was due to be heard and made enquiries of Mr Bark about the background.

F Counsel on behalf of the Secretary of State accepts that in doing so Mr Jones acted entirely properly and no blame can be attached to him either for the prosecution having been incurred or for the manner in which he dealt with it when he heard it was going to occur.

The remaining complaints relate to the failure to file audited accounts and annual returns on time. I have already given details of the dates when these documents should have been filed and the dates on which they were, in fact, filed. The position of the two

G respondents presently before the court differs in relation to these matters. Mr van Hengel took a firm view it was no part of his job to see any documents were filed in accordance with the requirements of the Companies Act. He said the only document he signed was one set of accounts and he signed that simply because he was one of only two directors who were around at the time. This cavalier attitude in my judgment reveals he did not appreciate the nature of the duties which he as a director had undertaken.

H This is not a case, such as *Re Cladrose Ltd* [1990] BCC 11, in which a director has relied on a fellow director with special expertise. In that case Harman J said at p. 13H:

'Mr Pollard told me that he relied on Mr Platt in those respects. There were management accounts, he saw regular documents, and the books of the company were properly kept up; and he assumed, because Mr Platt was a chartered accountant and responsible in Mr Pollard's mind for that side of the business, that

all was in order. As it seems to me, the directors are all responsible for the   A
preparation of formal documents in any company. They cannot excuse the failure
to produce documents by simply saying, "Oh, I relied on somebody else", but they
may be very much less blameworthy in some instances than in others if it can be
said they relied on somebody whom they had good and sufficient cause to believe
was a proper person to rely on, and who was equally with themselves responsible.'

The reason I say this is not such a case as that is that Mr van Hengel simply did not   B
bother to consider the question of responsibility for preparation of formal documents or
for those formal documents to be filed. He appeared, from his evidence, to have no
comprehension of his responsibility as a director for the preparation and filing of formal
documents. Mr Jones is in a different position because he only became a director on 30
June 1987 and there was only one default after that date.

The December accounts, which were certified by the auditors in February 1988, were
signed by the company secretary on behalf of the board in that month but were not filed   C
until 26 May, seven months late. Part of this delay was attributed by Mr Jones to the
illness of the audit partner at Binder Hamlyn, the company's auditors. He accepts,
however, that he was remiss in that he only chased up the late accounts by about three
telephone calls to the auditors. He accepts this was an inadequate response. He also fails
to explain the delay between the auditors certifying the accounts and their being filed. He
does not explain why it took from February 1988 until May 1988, some three months   D
after the accounts had been certified by the auditors and signed on behalf of the board,
before they were filed.

As Sir Donald Nicholls V-C said in Re Swift 736 Ltd [1993] BCC 312 at p. 315F:

'Isolated lapses in filing documents are one thing and may be excusable, but not so
persistent lapses which show overall a blatant disregard for this important aspect
of accountability. Such lapses are serious and cannot be condoned even though,   E
and it is right to have this firmly in mind, they need not involve any dishonest
intent.'

In Mr Jones's case he had been a financial controller for a year before his appointment
to the board and, in my judgment, knowing the history of the company's defaults in the
past, he should have been particularly vigilant to ensure that when he became financial
director no further lapses of the same sort occurred. He accepts he failed to do this. In
my judgment, therefore, although there was only one lapse during the time he was a   F
director, he simply cannot say: 'Ah, but there is only one isolated lapse in my time as a
director.'

In summary, therefore, my view in respect of Mr van Hengel is as follows. First, he
cannot escape responsibility for misapplication of clients' funds in respect of the sum of
£361,000-odd which was transferred to the company instead of being attributed to clients'
account for the benefit of clients. In my judgment he failed to take any or any proper   G
steps to see that money was properly attributed. I was not able to accept his evidence this
was done simply by Mr Bark when he, Mr van Hengel, was a long way away and knew
nothing about it. In my judgment, having seen him in the witness-box and having
considered his oral testimony and his affidavit evidence which are not consistent, I take
the view that he must bear a measure of responsibility, though not perhaps as great as
that of Mr Peter Bark, for the failure to deal properly with these client funds. So far as   H
the allegation that he was responsible in part for the company's failure properly to
maintain client trust accounts, in my judgment again here he must bear a measure of
responsibility, though not the director principally culpable. He appears to have taken no
proper interest in the way in which the company's accounts were dealt with or in the way
in which the clients' moneys were protected. As a director, he had a responsibility which
he failed to discharge. It is not a case of a man properly relying on the expertise of some

A   fellow director who was responsible for a particular part of the company's activities. He
     simply chose to leave matters in the hands of others without a thought. As to the third
     complaint that he permitted the company to trade whilst insolvent, it is true that Mr van
     Hengel was very well aware of the company's financial shortcomings. He had been, as I
     have said, unable to obtain from the company the $25,000 necessary for the company to
     start its business in the US. He had seen that after only a couple of months the company
     could no longer afford a second employee in the US. His own evidence made it clear that
B   he knew of the company's financial difficulties. However, he believed, and with some
     justification, that fresh moneys were going to be put into the company from an outside
     source. In my judgment he cannot be described as taking unwarranted risks with its
     creditors' money. I take the phrase 'unwarranted risks with its creditors' money' from
     the judgment of Evans-Lombe J in *Re Synthetic Technology Ltd* [1993] BCC 549 at
     p. 562E.

C   So far as the fourth charge is concerned, in my judgment it is clear Mr van Hengel
     took excessive remuneration. It is not a case such as *Re Keypak Homecare Ltd (No. 2)*
     [1990] BCC 117 in which one can say that the remuneration package, although fairly
     high, is not in itself something which would cause the court to think the directors have
     shown themselves to have such a lack of regard for proper standards as to be unfit to be
     directors of a company (see at p. 120F). In my judgment, given the turnover of the
D   company and the losses it was making, the remuneration which the directors were
     receiving would have caused, to use Harman J's phrase in that case, 'very serious eyebrow
     raising'. Mr van Hengel could no doubt have obtained that sort of remuneration if he
     had been employed elsewhere, but he was not employed elsewhere.

         In *Re Synthetic Technology Ltd* Evans-Lombe J said (at p. 560F):

             'In those two judgments Harman J concluded that it was not enough for a director,
             who had an equity stake in the company concerned, to say that he was being paid
E   no more than the job that he was doing was worth, where nonetheless it was
             apparent that the total remuneration package of the director, including any
             benefits of kind, was out of proportion to the company's then trading success and
             financial health.'

         In my judgment the remuneration Mr van Hengel received was of such a kind.
     Furthermore, he failed to take any steps to consider or persuade the board as a whole of
F   the overall package of directors' remuneration and the company's ability to afford it.

         So far as the conviction under the *Prevention of Fraud (Investments) Act* 1958 is
     concerned, in my judgment no blame attaches to Mr van Hengel, but in regard to the
     failure to file audited accounts on time, in my judgment Mr van Hengel has shown
     himself unfit to be a director by reason of his disregard for the obligations imposed on
     directors to procure the filing of appropriate accounts and returns. Mr van Hengel simply
G   showed he had no conception of the obligations imposed on directors.

         In my judgment, taking the test laid down by s. 6 of the Act as a whole, his conduct as
     demonstrated in the evidence before me is such as makes him unfit to be concerned in the
     management of a company. The words are ordinary English words and they are simple.
     In my judgment, they can be simply applied to this case. The appropriate safeguard for
     the public in my judgment on the facts of this case is that Mr van Hengel should be
     disqualified from being a director of a company for a period of six years. I pick that
H   period to indicate this is a case which might be described as being in 'the medium band
     of gravity' but at the bottom end of that band.

         I turn, then, to the position of Mr Jones. The first allegation against him is he is unfit
     to be a director by reason of the company's misapplication of funds. This has to be
     viewed in the context of the other allegations against him. Were that allegation a single
     allegation standing alone, I would take the view that it stood as a matter on which Mr

Jones would be criticised but which did not by itself indicate him to be a person unfit to   A
be a director of a company. He erred in the steps that he took. Undoubtedly he steps he
took were inadequate, and he should have required a meeting of the board as a whole to
express his disquiet. Further, he should have made more forcibly his point that the
language of the standard client agreement did not justify the company's retention of the
£361,000.

The difficulty that Mr Jones faces is this lapse does not stand alone. He was the   B
financial director of the company and before that he had been in charge of the accounting
procedures and he had introduced those accounting procedures to the company in order
to deal with accounting difficulties which the company had faced. Over two years, first as
a manager and then as a director, he failed to deal adequately with the difficulties. The
result was the company was in a position in which it was unable to identify the shortfall
of clients' moneys. It was also in a position where there was an acknowledged shortfall
of clients' moneys at all times while Mr Jones was the director. Mr Jones appears to have   C
taken few, if any, steps to rectify this accepted shortfall, which was certainly over £17,000.

It is to be noted that at the time the company supplied through Mr Jones financial
information to AFBD, there was an acknowledged substantial shortfall. Nothing appears
to have been done to rectify that shortfall in the period between February 1988 and the
presentation of the winding-up petition in July 1988. For this, in my judgment, Mr Jones
must bear a share of the blame. The company was a company dealing with moneys held   D
on behalf of investment clients. Mr Jones ought to have taken strenuous and immediate
steps to ensure those sums were safeguarded. In my judgment his failure to do so, though
no doubt in part influenced by his regard for Mr Bark, the managing director, was not
something which can be wholly excused.

So far as the charge that he permitted the company to pay excessive remuneration is
concerned, whilst he must be given every credit for the steps he personally took to ensure   E
economies by the reduction of his own salary, that alone was not, in my judgment,
sufficient to free him from blame. He was aware that the company was in a very poor
financial state. The steps which he took to ensure that all his fellow directors were aware
of the need to cut remuneration seem to have been inadequate. He took no steps to
procure any board meeting at any time while he was a director of the company to consider
the question of directors' remuneration. In my judgment, this was a failure in his   F
performance of his duties as a director.

The remaining matter urged against him is in relation to his failure to procure the
proper filing of the annual accounts for the year to 31 September 1986. Mr Jones properly
acknowledged his failure in this regard in the course of his evidence. On his behalf counsel
urged that, taken by itself, this was not a serious matter. I entirely accept that, had this
stood alone, this would not have been a reason for finding Mr Jones to be unfit to be a   G
company director. However, not only do I have to take that default in conjunction with
the history of the previous defaults before Mr Jones became a director, which should
have made him all the more anxious to ensure that accounts were filed on time, but also
I have to take it in the context of the other failings to which I have referred.

My judgment is that, taking these matters altogether, Mr Jones found himself in a
position where he was out of his depth. In my judgment, he failed to act properly as a   H
director, and his conduct has shown him to be unfit to be concerned in the management
of such a company. In my view, his was a far lesser failure than that of Mr van Hengel,
and in my view the appropriate disqualification in his case is therefore the minimum
provided for by the Act (which I should say in passing makes disqualification
compulsory). I therefore propose to make an order that he be disqualified for a period of
two years. In my judgment, part of his problem arose from his becoming involved in a

A   company operating in an industry with which he was wholly unfamiliar, even though he did have some accountancy qualifications.

There is at present no application before the court under s. 17 for leave for him to be concerned in the management of any company but I can well conceive that, if such an application was made in respect of some smaller company which was engaged in a less technical and difficult area of business, it would be appropriate, subject to proper

B   safeguards, to make an order under s. 17 to enable him to be concerned in the management of that company. But for the present, what I propose to do is to make orders as I have indicated disqualifying Mr van Hengel for a period of six years and Mr Jones for a period of two years.

Costs

C   I have now to deal with the costs of this application. The position in which Mr Jones finds himself is that he is the only one of the respondents who is within the jurisdiction and he is the person against whom it is likely to be easiest to enforce an order for costs. He is, however, certainly far less culpable than Mr van Hengel and the present indications would suggest – though, of course, one must not prejudge anything against Mr Bark – that he is very much less culpable than Mr Bark. In these circumstances Mr Thompson on behalf of Mr Jones has raised the issue as to how any order for costs made against his

D   client should be limited.

I start from the proposition that the Secretary of State should have his costs on a standard basis, but so far as Mr van Hengel is concerned, I think even there there must be some limitation, because a good deal of the preparation of this case was necessitated by the now abandoned proceedings against the second and fifth respondents, Mr Bark senior and Mr Wetton and, of course, the as yet unheard proceedings against Mr Peter

E   Bark.

I take the view that the appropriate order is that Mr van Hengel should pay the costs of these proceedings on a standard basis but limited to two-thirds of the costs down to the date of commencement of the hearing and not so limited thereafter.

So far as Mr Jones is concerned, he should pay the costs on a standard basis limited to one-third of those costs down to the commencement of the hearing, and one-third of those costs thereafter as well. The reason I say one-third is because, although both he

F   and Mr van Hengel fully contested the matter, a good deal of the time was devoted to points raised by Mr van Hengel and in particular the special expense of expert evidence was caused entirely by a point taken by Mr van Hengel in his affidavit evidence but abandoned when it came to his giving his oral evidence.

In those circumstances, it seems to me that it would be an injustice to Mr Jones if I put the proportion of the costs of the hearing as high as one-half, and it is for that reason

G   that I take the view that, whereas the Secretary of State should seek to enforce the whole lot of the costs of the hearing against Mr van Hengel, so far as Mr Jones is concerned, he should be able to enforce only to the extent of one-third.

(*Order accordingly*)

H

Re Dexmaster Ltd.
Secretary of State for Trade and Industry v Joyce & Anor.

Birmingham County Court and Chancery Division.
His Honour Judge Gosling; Robert Walker J.
Judgment delivered 8 February 1994 and 6 October 1994.

> *Disqualifying unfit directors of insolvent companies – Liquidator lost company*
> *documents – Whether respondent likely to be prejudiced – Whether*
> *disqualification application should be struck out or stayed – Company Directors*
> *Disqualification Act 1986, s. 6.*

This was an appeal from a county court decision refusing to strike out director
disqualification proceedings by the Secretary of State under s. 6 of the Company Directors
Disqualification Act 1986 on the grounds that documents taken from the company and from
the appellant were admittedly lost by the liquidator. It was not contended that the
proceedings commenced by the Secretary of State should be struck out because his
application had become hopeless as a result of the loss of the documents. The submission
was that the loss of the documents before they had been made available for inspection by the
appellant would be likely unfairly to prejudice his chances of getting a fair hearing. It was
oppressive for him to have to fight the application without having inspected and studied the
documents.

Held, dismissing the appeal:

There were two complaints against the appellant – non-cooperation with the liquidator
and the removing of tangible assets from the company premises – on which it was accepted
that the lost documents could have no bearing at all. The three other most serious matters
of complaint were failing to maintain accounting records, issuing cheques which the directors
knew or ought to have known could not be met and causing the company to trade when
insolvent. The lost documents might be of some, and perhaps considerable, relevance on
these issues. But any possible prejudice to the appellant, although real, was not anywhere
near sufficiently grave or certain to justify the drastic remedy of striking out.

Andrew De La Rosa (instructed by J R Hatton, Daventry) for the appellant.

Paul Girolami (instructed by the Treasury Solicitor) for the Secretary of State.

COUNTY COURT JUDGMENT
(Delivered 8 February 1994)

His Honour Judge Gosling: This is an application by Mr Seeley, the second defendant,
in an action by the Secretary of State, in which the Secretary of State is seeking to have
him and Mr Joyce disqualified from standing as directors. The application is to strike out
the Secretary of State's application or to stay this action because there are documents
which were taken from the defendant company, and indeed from Mr Seeley, by the
liquidator which it is admitted are lost.

Two points really are made on Mr Seeley's behalf. The first is that if those documents
were here it would be possible for the defendant, Mr Seeley, to show that the allegations
made against him are unfounded or certainly that the true picture which the documents
might show would move a court to the conclusion that he is not unfit to be a director,
because it gives a fuller picture of the way he dealt with things.

There is another issue and it is one, I think, that was not initially raised. What the
liquidator is saying is that he was hampered from conducting the necessary investigations
and doing the necessary negotiations that he had to do because there were no sales
invoices, no purchase invoices, no delivery notes that ever came into his possession. The
issue here is a stark issue between Mr Seeley and the liquidator, because Mr Seeley says

A   those documents were in existence and what is more, he will say – and there is some evidence to this effect – in October they were seen by Mr Gallagher, who is an accountant, and that is what he says in his affidavit. So there are the two issues.

I am going to deal with them in the reverse order. If one deals with that second issue it is simply an issue of fact that the court will have to decide. At the moment I do not know the answer to it. If it is the case that there were no invoices, no delivery notes in the

B   possession of the company at the time the liquidator took over, then it seems to me that that issue, which can be decided on evidence, is an issue decided in that way that would go against the defendant. If the issue is decided the other way it will go against the plaintiff, and it will go against the plaintiff very strongly as an issue of credibility and it is on the liquidator that the plaintiffs are depending. But the existence or non-existence of those documents could decide the case because it could settle, if I may put it that way, the credibility of the main witnesses, and it is an issue that can be decided. Therefore, it

C   seems to me that nobody is prejudiced by leaving that issue to be decided by the judge at trial and that there can be no grounds for staying these proceedings on the grounds that documents according to one witness never came into his possession and documents according to another witness did come into his possession.

The other point made is this, that the documents admittedly in the possession of the

D   liquidator have been lost and that the loss of those documents is prejudicial to the defendants and for that reason it would be wrong and an abuse of process really to allow the Secretary of State to go on with this case. Counsel for the Secretary of State has taken me through the allegations that he relies upon in order to establish that these two directors are unfit to be directors. He set them out in his skeleton argument under para. 7. First, that cheques were issued when the directors knew or ought to have known that they would not be met.

E   Now, I have been referred to various accounts and balance sheets produced by the accountants, I have been shown that there were existing, sometimes increasing, perhaps at some times decreasing, lifts in balances in the company's accounts. So far as I can see, there is nothing in the documents that are said to have been missing that relate with any directness upon the issue as to whether cheques were issued by these two men when they knew or ought to have known that they would not be met. Among the documents that

F   are missing there are bank statements and correspondence, but bank statements and correspondence are only copies of other documents, the bank statements can be got from the bank and it is certainly of no prejudice to anybody that particular copies of bank statements and correspondence have been lost, they can be recovered. It does not seem to me there is any other document that is said to have been lost that could have any bearing – obvious bearing – upon the first issue.

G   The second allegation made is that the directors failed to maintain accounting records as required. It is said, well, you cannot really judge that issue because the documents are lost. But it is not upon the nature of the lost documents that the Secretary of State is relying, he is relying on the absence of documents that ought to have been there and which do not appear upon the list of lost documents. The issue there is this: did those documents, namely invoices and so on, exist or did they not? This is the issue I have already described, and that issue can certainly be decided and it is of no prejudice in fact

H   to either side that the documents on the list have been lost, it is the same point. If the liquidator had more documents than he admits, he is going to lose credibility and his statement that the directors failed to maintain accounting records is not going to convince the court. If he did not have the documents then it is Mr Seeley who may lose credibility or Mr Gallagher. But that is an issue for the court, and the existence or non-existence of the documents listed does not affect the way in which that issue can be tried. As I say, the

Secretary of State is not relying upon documents in the list in order to establish that part   A
of the claim.

The third issue is causing the company to trade whilst insolvent. Again, I think the
same point arises that there is really little or no significance in the existence or non-
existence of the documents listed when that issue comes to be tried, it depends upon other
matters.

The fourth issue relates to Mr Seeley and I think it is conceded that the existence or   B
non-existence of these documents has no bearing on it at all. What is alleged is that he
removed assets from one part of the building into another building, I think, at the time
that the liquidator came to get hold of them. It is admitted that it happened, the question
is why did it happen, and the documents are not relevant to that.

The fifth ground is an allegation that Mr Seeley obtained goods from his supplier
against a cheque which was countermanded. The second part of para. 5 is obtaining   C
other goods against a cheque which was postdated. Again, that seems to me to be an
issue which does not turn on allegedly lost documents, but turns on the intention of Mr
Seeley when he signed the cheques and has acknowledged that he did sign, because there
is no issue as far as I can see that he did sign those cheques and that goods were obtained.

Failing to cooperate – this is a matter that cannot depend upon these documents, it is
a matter outside the scope of the objection.   D

Where Mr Joyce is concerned, the first allegation against him is that he really, as it
were, was the accomplice of Mr Seeley in removing the assets referred to in the earlier
allegation against Mr Seeley. The documents do not help on that issue.

Secondly, he is alleged to have participated in the transfer of Dexmaster assets to
himself in discharge of a personal debt to him from Mr Seeley. That, so far as I can see,
does not depend upon a scrutiny of the documents that had been lost.   E

Consequently, it seems to me that there is no ground for striking out or staying these
applications. If there is prejudice from the loss of the documents and of course the loss of
the documents means that the picture is not as full as it would be if the documents were
there, the prejudice is prejudice to both sides and indeed if one has to strike a balance it
seems to me that it is more prejudicial that the liquidator has lost the documents than
that the person in whose possession they must have been for a much longer time has lost
them. Each side will give secondary evidence, if that is necessary, about the contents of   F
the documents and one has to bear in mind throughout that the burden of making out
the case will remain throughout upon the Secretary of State and if his witness has lost the
documents he may find it difficult to discharge that burden if those documents are
pertinent to the issue.

Consequently, I reject this application.

(*Application dismissed. Costs to be paid by second defendant; not to be enforced*   G
without leave)

HIGH COURT JUDGMENT
(Delivered 6 October 1994)

Robert Walker J: Dexmaster Ltd had a short, initially promising but eventually
disastrous, history manufacturing desks, bedroom cabinets and other furniture. The   H
directors at all times have been Mr Joyce, who is not involved on this appeal, and Mr
Seeley, the appellant on this appeal who appears by Mr De La Rosa.

The appeal is from an order of His Honour Judge Gosling made at Birmingham
County Court on 8 February 1994 refusing to strike out proceedings by the Secretary of
State under s. 6 of the *Company Directors Disqualification Act* 1986. Mr Girolami appears

A   on this appeal, as he did below, for the Secretary of State. I will summarise as shortly as I can the facts leading up to the Secretary of State's application, using a chronology helpfully provided by Mr De La Rosa. The company was incorporated and commenced trading in September 1988. At the beginning of 1989 it obtained a large contract to manufacture desks. Seeing its business expanding, it moved to new premises at the Royal Ordnance Depot at Weedon in Northamptonshire using an overdraft facility obtained from the National Westminster Bank. About two months later, that is in March 1989,

B   the company obtained a further and, in relation to the company's resources, very large contract from a company named PSM to manufacture bathroom cabinets. On the strength of this contract the company, through its directors, obtained new factory equipment in place of the second-hand equipment they had previously had.

     After that it seems, although of course I make no final finding on any of these points, to have been a case of over-rapid expansion with insufficient capital and also

C   perhaps insufficient investigation of the financial standing of those with whom the company was dealing, exacerbated, it appears, by poor accounting procedures and records. (I emphasise again that I am making no final findings on this, but simply describing the general nature of the case as it appears today.)

     The company had as its auditors Fletchers of Daventry, who in June 1989 produced accounts down to the end of May of that year indicating an overall trading loss of nearly

D   £14,000. Subsequently the directors increased directors' loans to in excess of £12,000 so that there was a small difference by which the forecast loss exceeded the directors' loans. In August 1989 the bank, National Westminster, was corresponding with the directors about difficulties over security for their personal guarantees, and it seems that at that stage a separate wages account was opened by the company.

     In October 1989, Mr Gallagher, who has sworn an affidavit in the proceedings, visited

E   both the company and the bank and was involved in inspecting them on behalf of a possible purchaser. In the same month Fletchers, the company's auditors, wrote saying that they could not act further unless their own outstanding bill was paid. Later on in the same month, October 1989, Mr Gallagher visited PSM, the company with which Dexmaster had the largest contract, to negotiate payment of an outstanding debt of some £75,000 for goods supplied which it appears PSM was in no position to pay and there were negotiations about payment by instalments. There were at the same time

F   negotiations for the sale of the company to various possible purchasers, including one who was a major creditor, but that fell through, and on 7 December 1989 the company entered into voluntary liquidation.

     Mr Menzies of Robson Rhodes was appointed as liquidator. His assistant, a manager called Wendy Sharpe, removed from the company's premises some accounting and similar documents of the company. There is an issue of fact, which I cannot and make

G   no attempt to resolve, as to precisely what documents were removed and how voluminous they were. The exhibit AMM4 to an affidavit of Mr Menzies gives a not very detailed account of what the liquidator recorded as having been removed from the company's premises, and I note particularly that there were no invoices mentioned on that list, although the county court judge seems to have assumed, as Mr Girolami says, apparently in the directors' favour that this was an issue of fact which would have to be resolved in due course.

H   In November 1991 the Insolvency Service served notice of an intention to apply for disqualification orders against the two directors, and that application was made by an originating application issued in the Birmingham County Court on 28 November 1991. I should say that at that time, and for some considerable period after that, including the whole of 1991, Mr Seeley was acting in person without the assistance of a solicitor. However, he swore and filed affidavits both of himself and other deponents on his behalf.

There were various adjournments, the reasons for which have not been gone into before   A
me and which I regard as largely, if not wholly, irrelevant, though it is worth recording
that the substantive hearing of the disqualification proceedings had originally been set
for 24 and 25 May 1993 and would, it seems, have taken place then, that is some 18
months ago, had it not been that Mr Seeley then obtained legal aid and his solicitor, Mr
Hatton, wrote to the Treasury Solicitor enquiring for various documents which were
affidavits and exhibits in the case. It is not clear whether Mr Seeley himself had lost them
or failed to hand them to his solicitor or had never had them. Mr Hatton also sought   B
inspection of the documents (those listed on exhibit AMM4) which were in the possession
of Robson Rhodes. The Treasury solicitor wrote on 23 April 1993 saying without much
further comment that those documents could not be found and confirmed this, again
without as I understand it much further comment, in a letter of 21 May 1993 which I
have not seen.

No explanation of the circumstances or reasons, so far as known, for the disappearance   C
of the documents has been given. Mr Girolami has in the interests of his clients stressed
that the insolvency practitioner is by no means to be identified with the Secretary of
State, although possibly he was going a little far in describing it simply as a case where
documents had been lost by a witness. Although proceedings under the Company
Directors Disqualification Act are, as the Court of Appeal has recently reminded us,
essentially civil proceedings, they are nevertheless civil proceedings of a very special
nature in the public interest and the Secretary of State plainly has particular duties in   D
regard to taking them.

Mr Girolami for the Secretary of State submits (and Mr De La Rosa for Mr Seeley
accepts, and in my judgment rightly in each case) that this is a true appeal in which it is
open to me to vary the order of the judge below only if he exercised what is plainly a
discretionary jurisdiction on a wrong view of the law, or taking into account matters that
he should not have taken into account, or in a way that is plainly unreasonable. I   E
approach the case on that footing.

It was not contended, either before the judge below or before me, that the proceedings
commenced by the Secretary of State should be struck out because his application had
become hopeless as a result of the loss of the documents. On the contrary, the submission
went the other way: that the loss of the documents before they had been voluntarily made
available for inspection by Mr Seeley and his legal advisers would be likely unfairly to   F
prejudice Mr Seeley in such a way as to prejudice his chances of getting a fair hearing at
the substantive hearing, and so as to make it oppressive for him to have to fight the
application without having inspected and studied the documents.

There is no suggestion at all in this case that the loss of the documents, whatever the
true explanation is, was something that occurred deliberately in order to make Mr
Seeley's task more difficult. If there were any significant evidence to back a submission of   G
that sort, then plainly we would be in an area very close to abuse of process, but neither
side suggests that this is a case where anything contumacious has occurred, and it is
accepted that the sanctions such as can be applied under, for instance, O. 24, r. 16 in the
case of contumacious refusal to comply with directions for discovery have nothing to do
with this situation here.

It seems to me that the question that the judge had to ask himself was whether Mr   H
Seeley's inability to inspect and study documents as a consequence of what I assume to
have been a careless loss by some person or persons in the office of the insolvency
practitioners produce for Mr Seeley a prejudice so severe that it cannot be compensated
for at the substantive hearing of the application (which, if this matter proceeds, ought
not I hope to be greatly delayed) but should result in the immediate and drastic sanction
of being struck out.

A The court has very often stressed that striking out is a drastic remedy to be used only in clear cases, and Mr De La Rosa, whose submissions have been very clear and moderate, accepts that he cannot place before me any reasonably comparable precedent of striking out in a situation of this sort.

I have referred so far only to striking out. Mr De La Rosa asks in the alternative for a stay, but plainly a stay in order to assist him would have to be a permanent one, and I perceive no real difference between the two possible remedies.

B The judge below, in delivering what I assume to be, like this judgment, an ex tempore judgment, did not put the issue to himself, at least expressly, in precisely those terms, possibly because he thought it obvious that that was the issue. But it is, I think, implicit in the judgment below, and it is in my view the right approach, that it is not a question, where the summary remedy of striking out is concerned, of asking 'Is a fair trial more difficult?' It is a question of whether a fair trial is so likely to be prejudiced that striking out is the appropriate remedy, bearing in mind that, although Mr Seeley through his counsel complains of possible prejudice if one course is taken, equally there is possible prejudice of a serious nature to the public interest if the other drastic course were taken at this stage. It is right to reiterate again that, subject to certain qualifications because of the public interest, disqualification applications are basically like other civil proceedings, a contest between parties on which the burden of proof is on the applicant. Nothing I say today will prevent Mr Seeley, through his counsel on the hearing of the application, from submitting as fully and as forcibly as he can that the loss of the documents is, in various ways that he has urged on me today, a matter to be taken into account by the court in reaching its conclusions on the substantive application.

Mr De La Rosa politely but firmly criticised the judge below for what he describes in his skeleton argument as an item-by-item weighing up of the balance of advantage to one party or the other from the loss of the documents. As to that, I think it is right to say first (and Mr Girolami puts this in the forefront of his argument) that this is a case where, before ever the question of the loss of the documents was raised at all, the affidavit evidence on behalf of the Secretary of State was completed. The Secretary of State had taken advice and decided what documents he intended to place before the court in order to discharge the burden of proof on him, and Mr Seeley, admittedly then acting in person (and I take that into account), had himself put in quite a volume of affidavit evidence dealing with the case against him without any apparent sense of difficulty or grievance as a result of not having inspected the documents.

Secondly, on this point I think that, although the question 'Is a fair trial so seriously prejudiced as to merit striking out?' must be a question of overall judgment, it is an overall judgment that can really only be reached by looking at each individual issue, forming a view on that and then moving to an overall judgment. There are two complaints (and it may be two quite serious complaints), that is non-cooperation with the liquidator and the removing of tangible assets from the company premises, on which it seems to be accepted that really the lost documents can have no bearing at all.

The three other most serious matters of complaint (and I say parenthetically that everyone in this case seems to have taken them all in a different order and this is probably a different order again) are: failing to maintain accounting records as required by s. 221 of the *Companies Act* 1985; issuing cheques which the directors knew, or ought to have known, could not be met; and causing the company to trade when insolvent.

I certainly would not accept a submission, if it were made, that the lost documents may not be of some, and perhaps considerable, relevance on these issues. Certainly Mr Seeley, having in general terms admitted that the accounting records of the company were not satisfactory and having then sought to place the blame elsewhere, might well wish with his advisers to look again at the ledgers and daybooks that seem to have been included

in the documents listed in exhibit AMM4 and see what might be made of them. But any   A
possible prejudice, although real, is not in my judgment anywhere near sufficiently grave
or certain to justify the drastic remedy of striking out.

Mr De La Rosa relied also, although rather faintly, on delay. There has been delay.
The reasons have not been explored, except that it is apparent that the most recent lost
date was as a result of Mr Seeley very properly obtaining legal aid, and of course I do
not in the slightest criticise his obtaining legal aid; it is simply a fact that that was the   B
immediate cause, so far as I can see from the file, of the last date having to be vacated. It
seems to me that the judge's approach was basically right, as will be apparent from my
judgment. I take a slightly different view or emphasis in approaching the matter, but I
have no hesitation in reaching the same conclusion and I dismiss this appeal.

(Appeal dismissed with costs. Legal aid taxation)

                                                        C

                                                        D

                                                        E

                                                        F

                                                        G

                                                        H

A
Secretary of State for Trade and Industry v Palfreman.

Court of Session (Outer House).
Lord Johnston.
Judgment delivered 11 October 1994.

B
Disqualifying unfit directors of insolvent companies – Whether director was unfit and should be disqualified and for how long – Whether director should have leave to act as director of other companies – Company Directors Disqualification Act 1986, s. 1, 6.

This was an application for a director disqualification order. The parties were agreed that the respondent had been concerned with a company which had become insolvent, having traded for a considerable period of time without remitting income tax, NICs and VAT to the authorities. The parties were agreed that a disqualification order was appropriate and
C
suggested a period of three years. The respondent sought leave in terms of s. 1 of the Act to continue as a director of two associated companies which continued to trade after the collapse of the first company.

Held, making a disqualification order for three years with leave to the respondent to remain a director of the other companies on terms:

D
1. The company had been trading for some period using Crown debts as capital. The sums involved were substantial, although it did not appear that there was much in the way of further debt. The respondent had been a director throughout the relevant period, albeit mostly non-executive, and was aware or should have been aware of what was going on. Undoubtedly the conduct in question indicated unfitness to be a company director. On the other hand, the quality of the conduct was at the lower end of the scale of seriousness and the three years suggested was accordingly appropriate.

E
2. The other two companies had traded successfully for some time with no hint of impropriety. There did not seem to be any problem with the accounts and there were clear consequences to the company and its customers if the respondent did not continue to be involved in management. The court would grant leave to the respondent to remain a director of the two other companies on condition that the company's solicitor who was willing to serve was appointed to the board and remained on the board throughout the three-year period.

F
The following cases were referred to in the opinion:

Cargo Agency Ltd, Re [1992] BCC 388.
Chartmore Ltd, Re [1990] BCLC 673.
Lo-Line Electric Motors Ltd & Ors, Re (1988) 4 BCC 415; [1988] Ch 477.
Majestic Recording Studios Ltd & Ors, Re (1988) 4 BCC 519.
Sevenoaks Stationers (Retail) Ltd, Re [1990] BCC 765; [1991] Ch 164.

G
Alan Dewar (instructed by the Solicitor to the Secretary of State for Trade and Industry) for the Secretary of State.

Alan Hamilton (instructed by Aitken Nairn) for the respondent.

OPINION

H
Lord Johnston: This is an application at the instance of the Secretary of State for Trade and Industry seeking a disqualification order against the respondent from serving as a director or being concerned in the management of a company under and in terms of the *Company Directors Disqualification Act* 1986. After sundry procedure a proof was allowed on a record in respect of the petition and answers.

When the case was called before me counsel lodged at the bar a joint minute agreeing all material matters of fact, thus dispensing with the need for a proof. Thereafter I heard

argument as to whether or not the court should grant leave to the respondent to serve as   A
a director in respect of two specific companies.

The powers conferred on the court in this context, in terms of the *Company Directors Disqualification Act* 1986 are to be found initially in s. 1 thereof which provides:

'In the circumstances specified below in this Act a court may, and under section 6 shall, make against a person a disqualification order, that is to say an order that he shall not, without leave of the court–   B

(a) be a director of a company, or

(b) be a liquidator or administrator of a company, or

(c) be a receiver or manager of a company's property, or

(d) in any way, whether directly or indirectly, be concerned or take part in the promotion, formation or management of a company,   C

for a specified period beginning with the date of the order.'

In terms of s. 6 of the Act the court is required to impose a disqualification order on an application being made if the person in question is or has been director of a company which has at any time become insolvent, and on the basis that his conduct as a director of that company makes him unfit to be concerned in the management of a company. The court is given jurisdiction to deal with these matters under s. 17 of the Act provided the   D
company in question falls within its jurisdiction.

Without rehearsing the entire joint minute for its terms, suffice it to say that the parties were agreed that the respondent had been concerned in the management of and as a director of a company which had become insolvent, the liquidation having been initiated by the Inland Revenue as one of the main creditors. Essentially, the company had traded without remitting to the Inland Revenue and the Customs & Excise authorities, income   E
tax and National Insurance contributions and VAT respectively for a considerable period of time. The parties were agreed that a disqualification order was appropriate suggesting in the minute a period of three years, although it was accepted that it was a matter for the court on its own discretion to impose the actual order and select a length of time.

There is little authority in this context in Scotland but the matter has been considered in a number of cases in England. I was referred to *Re Lo-Line Electric Motors Ltd* (1988) 4 BCC 415 and *Re Sevenoaks Stationers (Retail) Ltd* [1990] BCC 765. Both those cases   F
indicate that the general context of the legislation is to protect members of the public from persons whose track records as directors of companies have shown them in the past to be a danger to the public and the test of whether or not a person is, or has demonstrated himself to be, unfit to be such a director implied the ordinary use of words and a practical test. I refer particularly to the judgment of Dillon LJ at p. 773 in *Sevenoaks*. In the same case the same judge at pp. 771–772 categorises the maximum   G
term that can be imposed of 15 years into three groups of five years respectively, the first five years being the least serious in terms of the conduct complained of and the need to protect the public and the last five years being equally the most serious of the three categories. I was also referred to *Re Chartmore Ltd* [1990] BCLC 673 and *Re Majestic Recording Studios Ltd* (1988) 4 BCC 519.

As indicated, the relevant company was rendered insolvent at the instance of the Inland   H
Revenue owing it and the other Crown authorities considerable sums of money. In effect, for some period, the company had been trading using those debts as capital. It did not appear that there was much in the way of further debt but the sums involved as narrated in the joint minute were substantial. The respondent had been a director throughout the relevant period albeit mostly non-executive and was obviously aware, or should have been aware, of what was going on. Undoubtedly the conduct in question contravenes the

A   test, effectively of common sense, that a person so trading, even if the Crown rather than the public is the victim, by using debts as capital is endangering the victims thereof by his conduct which can therefore be categorised as indicating unfitness to be a company director. On the other hand, the quality of the conduct is obviously at the lower end of the scale of seriousness and following the approach of Dillon LJ it seems to me that the period to be imposed should be in the lowest category and that the three years suggested is accordingly appropriate.

B

Thus far, parties were not greatly in dispute but thereafter I heard submissions as to whether or not in terms of s. 1 of the Act leave should be granted notwithstanding the disqualification now being imposed on the respondent to continue as a director of two associated companies which continued to trade and still do trade after the collapse of the first company. It was urged upon me that collectively the two companies had a substantial number of employees, in excess of 350 full-time, had traded profitably for a number of

C   years and had a substantial turnover in terms of millions of pounds. The causes of the insolvency of the first company had not repeated themselves and evidence by way of letter was produced to suggest that there were no real problems with either the Inland Revenue or the Customs & Excise authorities at the present time. It was stated that the respondent held a position of considerable responsibility in the companies which relied upon his goodwill for their successful trading and to remove him from the management

D   of the companies could have serious effects for a number of people, not least the employees. For the record, the two companies provide security services of various kinds for clients of a widely varying nature.

Counsel for the Secretary of State took a neutral position albeit setting the matter before the court in a useful exposition of the whole matter. In particular he referred me to *Re Cargo Agency Ltd* [1992] BCC 388 where this whole question was considered by

E   Harman J, the basis of his position being that applications for leave should only be granted where there was a need for them to be granted and upon evidence of adequate protection from danger. It seems that the English courts have interpreted the phrase 'with leave of the court' as empowering the court to grant leave on conditions and that is usually what tended to happen (see *Chartmore*). It is worth noting that the question of competency with regard to this interpretation has been considered in England and the view taken that 'with leave' means, or can mean, 'on such terms and conditions as the

F   court thinks fit . . .' I confess to be slightly hesitant about whether this is a proper approach but on grounds of comity would consider it inappropriate not to follow this in Scotland since the legislation is common to the UK. I therefore approach the matter upon the basis that it is competent for the court to impose conditions noting that in the cases such conditions have been the appointment of independent directors or requirements as to accounts or both. Again, it is not immediately clear to me that much protection is obtained by appointment of an independent director but it was urged upon

G   me that the responsibilities in law that such a person would be undertaking by consenting to be a director should be sufficient to enable him to exercise the sort of control and provide the sort of protection that the Act envisages for the public and for creditors.

At the end of the day therefore, it seems that the court has a discretion, first whether to grant leave at all and secondly, if so, upon what terms and conditions as it thinks fit. Obviously each case must depend upon its own facts.

H

In the present case the two companies have traded successfully for some time with no hint of impropriety. An explanation was provided for the problems with the first company, namely clashes of personality and inadequate management by one of the other directors. None of these problems have repeated themselves. There does not seem to be any problem with the accounts and the obvious consequences to the company and its customers if the respondent is not continuing to be involved in the management of them

are clear. Accordingly, I am not satisfied that there will be a real danger to the public if   A
the present situation is allowed to continue. Nevertheless, I think it appropriate for there
to be a further appointment to the board of a person independent of the family members
which comprise the management of these companies during the currency of the period of
disqualification. I was informed that the company's solicitor was willing to be so
appointed. As I have indicated previously the degree of protection that may be provided
on one view could be limited but on the other view should be sufficient to monitor
matters given the general professional responsibilities of a solicitor and the legal   B
responsibilities he would be undertaking by consenting to be appointed a director.

On the whole matter therefore, I am satisfied that a term of disqualification should be
imposed and that period will be three years. I am also satisfied, however, that it is
appropriate to grant leave to the respondent to remain a director of the two other
companies upon the condition that the nominated solicitor is immediately appointed to
the board and remains on the board of the two companies throughout the three-year   C
period.

(Order accordingly)

D

E

F

G

H

A # Re Working Project Ltd.
Re Fosterdown Ltd.
Re Davies Flooring Ltd.

Chancery Division.
Carnwath J.
B Judgment delivered 21 October 1994.

Disqualifying unfit directors of insolvent companies – Whether director disqualification proceedings should be transferred from county court to High Court – Whether county court lost jurisdiction when company ceased to be 'being wound up' – When did company cease to be 'being wound up' – Company Directors Disqualification Act 1986, s. 6(3).

C These were three cases in which it was sought to transfer director disqualification proceedings from the county court to the High Court on the ground that the companies concerned were no longer 'being wound up' as required by s. 6(3)(a) or (b) of the Company Directors Disqualification Act 1986 and that accordingly the county court no longer had jurisdiction under that section.

D The court was asked to decide whether, if proceedings under s. 6 had been validly commenced in a county court in relation to a company then being wound up by that court or which (in the case of a voluntary liquidation) that court had jurisdiction to wind up, the county court lost jurisdiction to continue the case when the winding up was concluded, and at what point the winding was up to be regarded as concluded for that purpose.

Held, refusing to transfer the cases to the High Court:

E 1. The words 'for the purpose of the commencement of proceedings' should be implied into subs. 6(3). Provided the county court had jurisdiction at the time of the commencement of proceedings, it was empowered to carry them to conclusion.

2. The words 'is being wound up' in s. 6(3) could not be read as 'is being or has been wound up'. The right to commence disqualification proceedings in the county court could not continue when the winding up had been concluded.

F 3. The winding up was complete when the company was finally dissolved, and not before. The expression 'winding up' naturally referred to the whole statutory process designed to secure the completion of the company's affairs, the distribution of its assets, and its final quietus. That process did not end until dissolution.

The following cases were referred to in the judgment:

G *Cornish Manures Ltd, Re* [1967] 1 WLR 807.
Morris v Harris [1927] AC 252.
Pinto Silver Mining Co, Re (1878) 8 ChD 273.
Stanhope Pension Trust Ltd & Anor v Registrar of Companies & Anor. Re Forte's (Manufacturing) Ltd [1994] BCC 84.

William Charles and Philip Jones (instructed by the Treasury Solicitor) for the
H Secretary of State for Trade and Industry and the official receiver.

Terence Etherton QC and Thomas Seymour (instructed by Godsiffe & Lawson, Trowbridge, Myerson Callaghan & Law, Leicester and Howes Percival, Northampton) for the directors against whom proceedings were continuing.

Robin Hollington (instructed by Hewitson Becke & Shaw, Northampton) for the disqualified director in Davies Flooring.

JUDGMENT A

Carnwath J: I have before me three matters. They have been listed together because
they raise important questions relating to the duration of the county court's jurisdiction
under the *Company Directors Disqualification Act* 1986, in cases where the company in
question has gone into compulsory or voluntary liquidation.

Statute
B
Section 6 provides:

'(1) The court shall make a disqualification order against a person in any case
where, on an application under this section, it is satisfied–

(a) that he is or has been a director of a company which has at any time become
insolvent (whether while he was a director or subsequently), and

(b) that his conduct as a director of that company (either taken alone or taken C
together with his conduct as a director of any other company or companies)
makes him unfit to be concerned in the management of a company.
. . .

(3) In this section and the next "the court" means–

(a) in the case of a person who is or has been a director of a company which *is
being wound up* by the court, the court by which the company is being wound D
up,

(b) in the case of a person who is or has been the director of a company which
is being wound up voluntarily, any court having jurisdiction to wind up the
company,
. . .

(d) in any other case, the High Court . . .' (emphasis added) E

Section 7 provides that the application may be made by the Secretary of State, or on his
direction the official receiver.

The issue in essence is the force to be given, in the definition of 'the court', to the words
underlined above. This depends on the relationship of the CDDA provisions with those
relating to winding up of companies, principally now in Pt. IV of the *Insolvency Act* 1986.
The main provisions relevant to the conclusion of the winding-up process, in the two F
types of liquidation relevant to the present case, are:

Winding up by the court

Section 146(1): If it 'appears to' the liquidator that 'the winding up of the company is
for practical purposes complete', the liquidator must summon a final meeting of creditors.

Section 172(8): After the final meeting, the liquidator 'shall vacate office' as soon as
he has given notice to the registrar of companies and to the court of the result of the G
meeting.

Section 205(2): On receipt of the notice the registrar must register it, and three months
after the date of registration (subject to any direction by the Secretary of State under
s. 205(3)) the company 'shall be dissolved'.

Section 205(3): On the application of the official receiver or any other interested
person, the Secretary of State may give a direction deferring the date of dissolution for H
such period as he thinks fit.

Creditors' voluntary winding up

Section 106(1): 'As soon as the company's affairs are fully wound up', the liquidator
must make up an account of the winding up, and call a general meeting of the company
and a meeting of the creditors.

A   Section 106(3): Within one week after the meeting, the liquidator must send his account and a return of the meetings to the registrar of companies.

Section 171(6): The liquidator must vacate office as soon as he has made his return to the registrar.

Section 201(2): On receipt of the account and return, the registrar must register them. Three months thereafter the company 'is deemed to be dissolved'.

B   Section 201(3): On application of the liquidator or an interested person, the court may make an order deferring the date of dissolution for such time as the court thinks fit.

It will be seen that the respective processes for compulsory and voluntary liquidations follow a similar pattern – a meeting called by the liquidator when he has completed his work, registration of the return of the meeting, vacation of office by the liquidator, and final dissolution following a three-month 'cooling-off' period (as it was described in

C   argument). On dissolution the company's remaining assets, if any, are disposed of as bona vacantia (*Companies Act* 1985, s. 654). At that point it ceases to exist as a legal entity, subject only to the limited possibility of reincarnation for certain purposes (CA 1985, s. 651, 653; see *Stanhope Pension Trust Ltd v Registrar of Companies* [1994] BCC 84).

It should also be noted that the liquidator acts 'as an officer of the court subject to its

D   control' in carrying out the duties imposed on the court (*Insolvency Rules* 1986, r. 4.179); and that, during any vacancy in the office of liquidator, the official receiver fills the gap (IA 1986, s. 136).

The fact that the final demise of the company is described as 'dissolution' in one case, and 'deemed dissolution' in the other, does not appear to have any practical significance. Nor does the fact that in one case the meeting is called when 'the company's affairs are

E   fully wound up' (objective wording), and in the other when 'it appears to the liquidator ... that the winding up of the company is for a practical purposes complete' (subjective wording). On the authorities, even the former wording:

> '... cannot be construed as meaning that the affairs of the company must in fact have been fully wound up. It is at least sufficient that they should have been fully wound up so far as the liquidator is aware.'

F   (*Re Cornish Manures Ltd* [1967] 1 WLR 807 at p. 812 per Pennycuick J, citing *Re Pinto Silver Mining Co* (1878) 8 ChD 273.)

Facts

The material facts in the three cases can be briefly stated.

Fosterdown

G   The company went into voluntary liquidation in or about August 1990. The final meeting of creditors was held in May 1992 (IA 1986, s. 106(1)). The liquidator's account and return to the registrar (s. 106(3)) were made on 22 June 1992. They were registered on 24 June 1992, with the consequence that the company was 'deemed to be dissolved' three months later on 24 September 1992 (s. 201(2)).

H   On 13 July 1992 (that is, after registration of the final account, but before dissolution), disqualification proceedings were begun by the Secretary of State in the Coventry County Court against one director, and are continuing.

Davies Flooring

This company went into compulsory liquidation on 9 July 1990. The final meeting of creditors (IA 1986, s. 146) was held on 29 March 1993; the return to the registrar

(s. 172(8)) was made the following day, and registered (s. 205) on 6 April 1993. The A
company was accordingly dissolved three months later on 6 July 1993 (s. 205(2)).

On 25 June 1992 disqualification proceedings were commenced by the official receiver
in the Northampton County Court against three directors. On 2 July 1993 a
disqualification order (for two years) was made against one director (represented before
me by Mr Hollington); the case against the others is continuing.

Working Project

B

The company went into voluntary liquidation on 29 April 1992. The final meeting of
creditors was held on 29 July 1994 (s. 106), and the final return was submitted to the
registrar on 10 August 1994. I assume it was registered immediately afterwards, and that
the three-month period to dissolution (s. 201) will expire some time in November.

On 12 April 1994 disqualification proceedings were commenced by the Secretary of
State in the Bristol County Court against four directors, and are continuing.

C

Issues

In each case the summons seeks to have the case transferred to this division of the
High Court for the determination of various questions relating to the jurisdiction of the
county court, and consequential matters. Two main issues arise:

(1)   If proceedings under CDDA, s. 6 have been validly commenced in a county court D
in relation to a company which 'is being wound up' by that court, or which (in the
case of a voluntary liquidation) that court has jurisdiction to wind up, does that
court lose jurisdiction to continue the case when the winding up is concluded?

(2)   If so, at what point is the winding up to be regarded as concluded for this purpose?

Issue (1)

E

On the first point, Mr Charles (on behalf of the Secretary of State and the official
receiver) says the answer must be no. He is supported by Mr Etherton, for a number of
respondents against whom proceedings are still continuing, and who could suffer
additional costs if the proceedings now had to be transferred. Only Mr Hollington makes
a contrary submission. The costs in his client's proceedings have already been incurred.
If he is correct on this point, the order already made against his client would have been
made without jurisdiction; and, because the period of the disqualification is substantially F
complete, the Secretary of State would not (as I understand it) seek to initiate new
proceedings.

On this point I agree with Mr Charles and Mr Etherton. It would be patently absurd
if disqualification proceedings, validly commenced in the county court, were at risk of
being aborted at any time (even in the middle of the hearing, or after judgment has been
reserved), simply because the liquidator has completed his work. No one has suggested G
any sensible legislative purpose for such a rule. There is no reason why the continuing
jurisdiction of the county court in the disqualification proceedings should depend on the
speed with which the liquidator is able to progress the winding up. The disadvantages of
such a rule (in terms of cost, uncertainty and delay) are obvious.

The only substantial argument in favour of that approach is that it accords with a
literal reading of s. 6. Under subsection (1) it is 'the court' which must make the
disqualification order. On a strict reading of subs. (3)(a) and (b), the county court remains H
'the court' as defined only so long as the company 'is being wound up'. Accordingly, it is
said, once the winding up has been completed, the county court ceases to have jurisdiction
to make the disqualification order – whatever stage the proceedings have then reached.

It is, however, permissible to modify a literal reading, where it produces absurdity, and
a reasonable alternative is available (see Cross, *Statutory Interpretation* (7th edn, 1990),

A   p. 47). This is such a case. Where, as here, a section defines a particular court for the purposes of proceedings under that section, the correct inference, in my view, will normally be that the definition is directed to the *commencement* of proceedings. In the absence of express provision, Parliament can be assumed to have intended proceedings properly commenced in a particular tribunal to be carried to a conclusion in that tribunal. In subs. 6(3), therefore, the words 'for the purpose of the commencement of proceedings' should be regarded as implicit. On this view, provided the respective county courts had jurisdiction at the time of the commencement of proceedings, they were, and are, empowered to carry them to conclusion; and I so hold. It follows that the order made against Mr Hollington's client was validly made.

     This is sufficient to answer the first main question in Mr Charles' favour. In an alternative submission, however, he asks me to go further. He submits that, in s. 6(3), I should read 'is being wound up' as 'is being *or has been* wound up'. The effect would be that the right to commence disqualification proceedings in the county court would continue even when the winding up had been concluded.

     I cannot accept this submission. It well illustrates the difference between what is permissible by way of statutory interpretation, and what is not. I accept that the reasons, which make the county court a suitable forum for certain disqualification proceedings, do not necessarily change merely because the winding up has been completed. The issues relevant to disqualification relate to past conduct, and will generally be the same before and after completion of the winding up. However, the language of the statute does clearly introduce a limitation related to the course of the winding up. That limitation may not be easy to explain in policy terms, but it does not produce absurdity or unworkability (provided, as I have found, it is related to the commencement of proceedings). In cases where the county court does not have jurisdiction, there is no practical difficulty in commencing proceedings in the High Court under para. (d).

Issue (2)

     The other main question only arises in the case of *Fosterdown*, where the disqualification proceedings were commenced after the registration of the liquidator's final return, but before dissolution. At which point was the 'winding up' complete – or, more precisely, at which point did the company cease to be a company 'being wound up'?

     It seems to me that winding up is complete when the company is finally dissolved, and not before. The expression 'winding up' naturally refers to the whole statutory process designed to secure the completion of the company's affairs, the distribution of its assets, and its final quietus. That process does not end until dissolution.

     Mr Etherton asks me to prefer the date when the liquidator's final return is registered. That, he rightly says, is a public record of the completion of the liquidator's work. Indeed, s. 106 expressly refers to it as occurring when 'the company's affairs are fully wound up'. Thereafter, he says, it is difficult to regard the company as 'being wound up' in any active sense. The three-month period, at least in the normal case, is one 'during which the company, stripped of its property and discharged from its debts, would have simply awaited dissolution' (*Morris v Harris* [1927] AC 252 at p. 258, per Lord Sumner).

     In my view, however, there is a distinction between the winding up of the company's affairs, and the winding up of the company itself. It is true that, if the liquidator has done his job properly, all that will be left after the final meeting is a shell. However, the three-month period recognises the possibility of other assets being found, or of a disagreement between the creditors and the liquidator as to whether his work is complete (resulting in a request to defer dissolution). There may be remaining assets, unknown to the liquidator; if there are, the company will remain their owner. During that period it remains a legal

entity. The registration of the liquidator's return may in practice mark the end of the A
company's active life, but it makes no change to its legal status; it is an administrative
act. It is not until dissolution that the company's existence ceases, and any remaining
assets are disposed of. It is not until then that the company is finally 'wound up'.

I accordingly hold that, in *Fosterdown*, as well as in the other cases, the disqualification
proceedings were properly commenced and continued in the county court. In these
circumstances, it is unnecessary to consider the other main issue which has been argued, B
namely whether a transfer to the High Court can or should be ordered.

I will hear counsel on the form of order which should be made in the light of my
conclusions.

(Order accordingly)

C

D

E

F

G

H

A **Re Westmid Packaging Services Ltd.**
Secretary of State for Trade and Industry v Griffiths & Ors.
Chancery Division (Birmingham).
His Honour Judge Micklem (sitting as a High Court judge).
Judgment delivered 31 October 1994.

B *Disqualifying unfit directors of insolvent companies – Secretary of State sought to add respondent to disqualification proceedings out of time – Whether procedure proper – Company Directors Disqualification Act 1986, s. 7(2).*

This was an application to strike out a summons of the Secretary of State seeking leave to add a respondent out of time to director disqualification proceedings.

Disqualification proceedings were launched against three directors of a failed company.
C The evidence in those proceedings led the Secretary of State to believe that a claim could be sustained that 'M' was a de facto director of the company liable to disqualification. By then the two-year period under s. 7(2) of the Company Directors Disqualification Act 1986 had expired and the Secretary of State needed leave for proceedings against M. The Secretary of State issued a summons in the existing proceedings for leave to join M as a respondent out of time. M challenged that procedure.

D *Held*, striking out the Secretary of State's summons:

The proper procedure was to start by an originating summons seeking leave to issue proceedings out of time as an entirely separate originating procedure which, when completed, would be finished and if leave was given, then a new originating summons could be issued under the Disqualification Act. The case was not to be distinguished on the ground that there were existing proceedings on foot against other directors. (Re Crestjoy Products Ltd [1990] BCC 23 followed.)

E The following cases were referred to in the judgment:

Crestjoy Products Ltd, Re [1990] BCC 23.
Probe Data Systems Ltd, Re (No. 2) [1990] BCC 21.

Martha Maher (instructed by the Treasury Solicitor) for the Secretary of State for Trade and Industry.

F John Randall (instructed by Lee Crowder, Birmingham) and Abbas Mithani for the proposed respondent.

JUDGMENT

His Honour Judge Micklem: Westmid Packaging Services Ltd went into administrative receivership on 12 December 1991. The Secretary of State took the view that three
G directors of Westmid ought to be brought before the court under the *Company Directors Disqualification Act* 1986, and shortly before the expiration of the statutory limitation period an originating summons was issued no. 30496 of 1993 in the Birmingham District Registry in the matter of Westmid Packaging Services Ltd between the Secretary of State for Trade and Industry and Sidney Griffiths, Roy Elliot Conway and John Thomas Wassell. Those three respondents had been directors of the company.

H In the course of producing evidence in support of their case one or more of those respondents called upon Mr John Richard Morrall to swear an affidavit, and he did so. When the Secretary of State saw the affidavit of John Richard Morrall in those proceedings, he took the view that there was sufficient material disclosed to suggest that a claim that Mr John Richard Morrall was a de facto director could be sustained and that it would be proper that the question should be considered by the court whether Mr Morrall also ought not to be disqualified under the Act.

But by the time this thought occurred to the Secretary of State, time had run out, that   A
is to say, the bar to be found in s. 7(2) of the *Company Directors Disqualification Act* 1986
applied. That subsection reads:

> 'Except with the leave of the court, an application for the making under that
> section of a disqualification order against any person shall not be made after the
> end of the period of 2 years beginning with the day on which the company of which
> that person is or has been a director became insolvent.'   B

So the Secretary of State needs leave.

The problem which I have to deal with today is a procedural problem as to whether
the Secretary of State for Trade and Industry has, as counsel on his behalf suggests, taken
a proper course for obtaining leave or whether, as counsel for Mr Morrall suggests, an
improper course has been taken. Procedurally the matter goes forward in two stages.
First, on 19 September 1994 the Secretary of State issued an ordinary summons in the   C
matter of Westmid Packaging Services in the matter of the Company Directors
Disqualification Act, naming the Secretary of State as applicant, and the three
respondents to summons no. 30496/93 as respondents and adding in the heading 'John
Richard Morrall, proposed fourth respondent'.

The summons says: 'Let John Richard Morrall' – and his address is given – 'attend
before the district judge on 19 October on the hearing of an application by the applicant'
– address given, for: D

> '(1) an order under s. 7(2) of the *Company Directors Disqualification Act* 1986 that
> the applicant have leave to join the respondent out of time in the existing
> proceedings between the applicant and Sidney Griffiths, Roy Elliot Conway and
> John Thomas Wassell on the grounds set out in the affidavits of Alistair Francis
> Jones and Anthony Hannan.'

There is no dispute that in the affidavits of Mr Jones and Mr Hannan the case to be   E
made if leave is given is set out against Mr Morrall and some explanation is given of the
reasons for the application being made late. Paragraph 2 of that summons invites the
court to make such other orders as the court thinks fit.

That summons was adjourned by the district judge to be heard some time in the future
before this court. In that circumstance, on 26 October 1994 Mr Morrall made an ordinary
application to the court, which is the application I now have to deal with. In that   F
application Mr Morrall describes himself as 'the intervener', and as 'a person served with'
the summons dated 19 September 1994 issued by the Secretary of the State, which I have
mentioned, and he seeks this relief:

> '1. That pursuant to the provisions of O. 15, r. 6 and/or to the inherent jurisdiction
> of the court the intervener be at liberty to intervene in these proceedings and to be
> heard in respect of the relief sought by the applicant in the summons and by the   G
> intervener in this application.'

That has not been opposed, so that I have heard the intervener.

In para. 2 Mr Morrall seeks this relief:

> 'that the court do determine as a preliminary matter in relation to the summons' –
> that is the Secretary of State's summons – 'whether the relief set forth in the   H
> summons can properly be granted by this court having regard to the following
> matters: (a) that no originating summons for leave to bring proceedings against
> the intervener out of time has been brought by the applicant under the provisions
> of s. 7(2) of the *Company Directors Disqualification Act* 1986 and/or (b) that no
> order has been made granting leave to the applicant under s. 7(2) of the Act to
> bring proceedings for the disqualification of the intervener out of time.'

A –and by para. 3:

> 'If it be so determined, that the Secretary of State's summons of 19 September be accordingly struck out and/or dismissed and/or stayed.'

It is common ground that the *Insolvent Companies (Disqualification of Unfit Directors) Proceedings Rules* 1987 (SI 1987/2023) do not identify the procedure for making an application under s. 7(2). By r. 1(3) of those 1987 rules it is stated:

B
> 'These Rules apply with respect to an application for a disqualification order against any person ("the respondent"), where made–
>
> (a) by the Secretary of State or the official receiver under s. 7(1) of the . . . Act (on the grounds of the person's unfitness to be concerned in the management of a company), or
>
> (b) . . .

C
> on or after the date on which these Rules come into force.'

Then by r. 2:

> '*Form of application*
>
> An application to which these Rules apply shall be made–
>
> (a) in the High Court, by originating summons (. . . with such adaptation as may be appropriate), and
>
D
> (b) . . .
>
> and the Rules of the Supreme Court 1965 or (as the case may be) the County Court Rules 1981 apply accordingly, except where these Rules make provision to inconsistent effect.'

The uncertainty arising from that formulation of the rule has been resolved, at least to some extent, in two cases to which I have been referred. The first is *Re Probe Data Systems Ltd (No. 2)* [1990] BCC 21. That is a decision of Millett J which he gave on 19 January 1989, and in which he went in some detail into the question of what the proper procedure should be.

He said at p. 21:

> 'This is in form an ex parte application by the Secretary of State for leave to bring an application for a disqualification order against Mr Desai . . . All that has been debated, however, is the proper procedure in such cases.'

The judge sets out s. 7(2) and records:

> 'The *Insolvent Companies (Disqualification of Unfit Directors) Proceedings Rules* 1987 contain no provisions as to the procedure to be adopted on an application for leave. Furthermore no practice direction has been issued in relation to the matter.'

G
There is still no practice direction.

Millett J continues: 'Three possible procedures have been discussed' and he rejects two of them. He says at p. 21G:

> 'One suggestion is that the proper procedure is to apply to the registrar ex parte in the first instance for leave and unless the registrar is minded to dismiss the application he should grant it. The application should then be made and it should be left to the respondent to apply inter partes to set aside the order granting leave. The pattern for that procedure is, of course, O. 11, r. 1. In my judgment that is not an appropriate precedent because where leave is granted to issue a writ out of the jurisdiction under O. 11, r. 1 the application to set aside service of the writ is made under O. 12, r. 8 and no equivalent foundation for the registrar's jurisdiction to set

aside the leave which he has, under the suggested procedure, previously granted   **A** appears to exist. Furthermore,' – and this is the important point for present purposes – '. . . it is said I think with some justification that if that procedure were adopted then an unfair onus would be put upon the respondent to show cause why leave should not have been granted.

The second and alternative pattern for emulation is that which is adopted under the *Family Provision Act* 1966, where the statute provides that no application may   **B** be made more than six months after the date of probate or letters of administration. Practice directions have been made to the effect that where any plaintiff wishes to seek such leave the application for leave should be made as a separate head of relief in the originating summons and that the matter should be adjourned by the master to the judge as soon as the evidence is complete on that question. There is, of course, some logical difficulty about seeing how a process for which leave is needed can be issued at all until the leave is given, but be that as it   **C** may a practice direction has been made and authorises that procedure. No such practice direction exists in the present context and in my judgment there are some objections to that course being followed in the context of application for the disqualification of a director. Although I recognise that the object of the Secretary of State or other applicant in seeking a disqualification order is to protect the public, the consequences of the order are penal in their consequences and it seems   **D** to me that no one should be put in peril of being described as being the subject of an application for disqualification until leave is given where that is necessary.'

That sentence is also important for present purposes.

'Accordingly I adhere to the view which I indicated at an early stage that the proper procedure in these cases, where leave is needed, is for the applicant to apply in the first instance ex parte to the registrar for leave, putting before the registrar the whole of his evidence both for leave and on the merits. If the registrar considers   **E** that there is a prima facie case for granting leave he should then give directions to the applicant to serve the respondent with the summons or other application for leave and the evidence in support. The respondent will be entitled if he so wishes to argue that leave should not be granted. The burden will still be on the applicant to show cause why leave should be granted.'

That being the first decision in 1989, a similar application came before Harman J in *Re*   **F** *Crestjoy Products Ltd* in October 1989, and that is reported at [1990] BCC 23. As to the procedure, Harman J (who had had *Re Probe Data Systems Ltd (No. 2)* cited to him) said at p. 24E:

'Three possible procedures were set out by Millett J: the first, an analogy with O. 11, r. 1, which Millett J said was unsuitable, an observation with which I, respectfully, entirely agree. The second was that under the *Family Provision Act*   **G** 1966, where, again, there was a statutory bar on applications more than six months after (in that case) the date of probate or letters of administration. In those cases practice directions have been made producing, as Millett J observed at p. 22, a logical difficulty in seeing how a process for which leave is needed can be issued at all until leave is given. But the practice direction has been made and it authorises that procedure. I agree with Millett J that that precedent is not a very happy one and should not be followed.   **H**

He does not seem to have had mentioned to him the precedent which occurs to me (and which appears to me to be the appropriate analogy for this case) which is the application for leave under the *Leasehold Property (Repairs) Act* 1938 (as amended by the *Landlord and Tenant Act* 1954) in the case of a long tenancy. In such cases a landlord issues an originating summons for leave to issue proceedings,

A   as the case may be, for forfeiture, or for damages for breach of covenant, or both, against a tenant in respect of the premises which he holds under a lease. That originating summons seeking leave to issue proceedings is an entirely separate originating procedure that is completed and brought to an end by the grant or refusal of leave to issue the further originating process.

In my view that analogy is an apt one for this sort of case and ought to be used, and has in fact been used, here.'

B   Then the judge goes on to say that in his judgment the preliminary ex parte application to the registrar suggested by Millett J is really an unnecessary extra stage.

So there is a judge-made law practice, and I have the authority of Harman J, having considered the matter carefully and having gone to the extent of slightly disagreeing with Millett J, to the effect that the proper procedure is to start by an originating summons seeking leave to issue proceedings as an entirely separate originating procedure which, C   when completed, would be finished and if leave is given, then a new originating summons can be issued under the Disqualification Act. Counsel for the Secretary of State emphasises the fact that both the case before Millett J and the case before Harman J were cases in which there were no existing proceedings on foot and suggests that this case is to be distinguished because here, she says, there is an originating process on foot, as she put it in her skeleton argument, 'in respect of the company concerned'.

D   But it seems to me that this is not a sufficient ground of distinction because with regard to applications for disqualification, the application is in each case an application against an individual director. There are no proceedings against Mr Morrall in existence. The fact that there is on foot an application against director A, director B and director C who were all directors of the company is neither here nor there when it comes to the question of seeking leave to bring proceedings against D who is or is alleged to be a director of the E   same company. The considerations affecting the fairness or appropriateness of the form of proceeding against D remain the same as those identified in the two cases I have mentioned. It seems to me, therefore, that no sufficient reason for distinguishing the procedure suggested (and I have no doubt, followed) since *Crestjoy Products Ltd* is made out.

Moreover, it seems to me that there are difficulties about the route chosen by the Secretary of State here, namely O. 15, r. 6(1):

F   'No cause or matter shall be defeated by reason of the misjoinder or nonjoinder of any party; and the Court may in any cause or matter determine the issues or questions in dispute so far as they affect the rights and interests of the persons who are parties to the cause or matter.'

The joinder or nonjoinder of Mr Morrall does not affect in any way the rights or interests of the other directors or the success or failure of the Secretary of State's claim against the G   other directors.

Then by subr. 2:

'Subject to the provisions of this rule, at any stage of the proceedings in any cause or matter the Court may on such terms as it thinks just and either of its own motion or on application–

H   (a) . . .

(b) order any of the following persons to be added as a party, namely–

(i) . . .

(ii) any person between whom and any party to the cause or matter there may exist a question or issue arising out of or relating to or connected with any relief or remedy claimed in the cause or matter which in the

opinion of the Court it would be just and convenient to determine as   A
between him and that party as well as between the parties to the cause
or matter.'

Then by subr. (3):

'An application by any person for an order under paragraph (2) adding him as a
party must, except with the leave of the Court, be supported by an affidavit
showing his interest in the matters in dispute in the cause or matter or, as the case   B
may be, the question or issue to be determined as between him and any party to
the cause or matter.'

It seems to me what has to be determined between the Secretary of State and Mr
Morrall, if leave is given, is something quite different from what has to be decided
between the Secretary of State and each of the directors against whom proceedings have
been launched. It is a jury question as to whether on the evidence Mr Morrall is unfit to   C
be concerned in the management of the company (if on the evidence he can be shown to
have been a director at all) and it is a quite separate question from the jury question
which will arise in relation to Mr Griffiths, Mr Conway and Mr Wassell. Again it is a
jury question whether those individuals are or are not in the judgment of the court unfit
to be concerned in the management of a company.

There are I think other difficulties. On the normal application under O. 15, r. 6 the
summons would be served on the three existing respondents. In this case they are not   D
parties to this summons. In answer to that the Secretary of State says, 'all that I am
asking for is leave, and on the question of leave they would have nothing to say'. But the
next step which seems to be contemplated by the Secretary of State, if his application is
successful, is an amendment to the originating summons and joinder, so that the
proposed procedure is one in which, as far as I can see, the other respondents are to have
no say and it does not seem to me on its face to be an appropriate procedure.   E

But the main ground for my acceding to the application of the intervener today is that
no sufficient reason is given for departing from the procedure which has been devised to
protect directors where there are no proceedings in existence and there is no valid
distinction made between this case and those. Therefore, I accede to the application of
Mr Morrall. I determine as a preliminary matter that this is not an appropriate procedure
and strike out the summons of the Secretary of State dated 19 September 1994.   F

(*Order accordingly*)

G

H

A Re Mordant.
Mordant v Halls (Trustee in Bankruptcy).

Chancery Division (in bankruptcy).
Sir Donald Nicholls V-C.
Judgment delivered 20 July 1993 and 9 May 1994.

B

Bankruptcy – Whether sum held to order of court was part of bankrupt's estate – Who should pay costs of application to dispose of property after bankruptcy order made – Insolvency Act 1986, s. 284.

This was an appeal from a district court decision to dismiss an application under s. 284 of the Insolvency Act 1986.

C
A husband and wife were divorced in January 1991, and a lump sum payment order was made against the husband in ancillary relief proceedings. In the course of the proceedings, the husband produced a deed of transfer of the matrimonial home in his favour. The wife claimed her signature on the document had been procured by her husband's fraud. In March 1989 the husband had borrowed £86,000 from the building society secured by a mortgage granted by him over the house as sole owner. Of this, £35,000 was used to repay an existing mortgage. The building society was given leave to intervene. The parties signed an agreement
D
in the proceedings which provided for the husband to transfer the house to the wife, and that she would charge the property in favour of the building society to secure repayment of £35,000. In the agreement the husband admitted that he owed £68,133 to the building society. Also in the course of the hearing, it came to light that the husband had around £275,000 in an Irish bank account, and the judge ordered that this sum be paid by the husband to his solicitors.

E
The building society then presented an expedited bankruptcy petition against the husband, and the bankruptcy court appointed an interim receiver to get in and protect the husband's assets. By then a further sum of £109,000 was held by the husband's solicitors. The building society contended that these funds should be made available to unsecured creditors generally and not just the wife. The bankruptcy court made an order that the money held by the husband's solicitors should be paid to the interim receiver. A bankruptcy order was made by the district judge, who rejected the contention that the petition by the building society was
F
an abuse of the process of court, and an application by the wife that, alternatively, the court should approve the disposal of £385,000 to the wife under s. 284 of the Insolvency Act.

Held, allowing the wife's appeal and ordering the building society to pay the wife's costs of the application:

G
1. When the judge directed the husband's funds to be paid to his solicitors, he intended that these should be held 'to the order of the court'. The effect of this was to afford the wife protection in respect of her claim because the money was beyond the reach of the husband and he was unable to dispose of it himself. Accordingly when the £275,000 reached the solicitors, it ceased to be part of the husband's estate and therefore the interim receiver had no right to claim it.

2. In relation to the further sum of £109,000, the same principle applied.

H
3. The direct cause of the application was the conduct of the building society which overreached itself in its desire to protect its own interests and achieve what it regarded as a fairer distribution of the husband's assets, notwithstanding its knowledge of what the court intended should be the position over the money as between, on the one hand, the building society and its unsecured claims against the husband and, on the other hand, the wife and her claims to payment of a lump sum.

The following cases were referred to in the judgment:

A

Burton v Burton [1986] 2 FLR 419.

Cretanor Maritime Co Ltd v Irish Marine Management Ltd [1978] 1 WLR 966.

Flint, Re [1993] Ch 319.

Ford, Re; ex parte the trustee [1900] 2 QB 211.

Gordon, Re; ex parte Navalchand [1897] 2 QB 516.

Sherratt (W A) Ltd v John Bromley (Church Stretton) Ltd [1985] 1 All ER 216.

B

Woodley v Woodley (No. 2) [1993] 1 WLR 1167.

Benedict Sefi (instructed by Sanders Brickwood, Cirencester) for Mrs Mordant.

John Briggs and Martha Maher (instructed by Osborne Clarke, Bristol) and Stephen Davies (instructed by Bretherton Price & Elgoods, Cheltenham) at the hearing on costs for the trustee.

Peter Griffiths at the hearing on costs (instructed by Burroughs Day, Bristol) for the Cheltenham & Gloucester Building Society.

C

JUDGMENT
(Delivered 20 July 1993)

Nicholls V-C: Mr Lionel Alfred Mordant and his wife Mee Leng were divorced in January 1991. For convenience I shall refer to them, although divorced, simply as the husband and the wife. This case concerns the interaction between a lump sum payment order made against the husband in ancillary relief proceedings and the husband's bankruptcy. It highlights the point, perhaps not widely appreciated, that under the *Insolvency Rules* 1986 an order for the payment of a lump sum in family proceedings is not provable in bankruptcy.

D

The proceedings for ancillary relief were bitterly contested. The Cheltenham & Gloucester Building Society intervened. In the course of the proceedings, the husband produced a deed of transfer of the matrimonial home at Cirencester, Gloucester, in his favour. The wife claimed that her signature, if indeed she had signed the deed at all, had been procured by the husband's fraud. The husband denied these allegations. The deed was dated December 1987. In March 1989 the husband had borrowed £86,000 from the building society secured by a mortgage granted by him over the house as sole owner. Of this, £35,000 was used to repay an existing mortgage. So the building society was given leave to intervene. The validity of its mortgage on the former matrimonial home was material to the net value of the assets available to the husband and the wife.

E

F

The hearing on 22 October 1992

The hearing took place before Rattee J as a judge of the Family Division over six days from 15 October 1992. On 22 October three events happened. First, the husband and the wife and the building society compromised their various claims about the house. Counsel for all three parties signed an agreement which provided for the husband to transfer the house to the wife, and that she would charge the property in favour of the building society to secure repayment of £35,000. In the agreement the husband admitted that the sum owing from him to the building society, after deducting the £35,000, was £68,133 (in this judgment I shall ignore pence). Further, the agreement expressly reserved the building society's right to enforce its claim to this sum against the husband.

G

In the course of the hearing before Rattee J one matter which came to light was that £275,000 was standing to the credit of the husband in a bank account in Dublin with the Allied Irish Bank. The second event which happened on 22 October was that the judge ordered this sum to be paid by the husband to his solicitors. I shall have to return to this order. The third event was that the judge reserved his judgment on the wife's application for financial relief.

H

A   **The enforcement steps taken by the building society**

The building society now found itself in the position that it was owed £68,133 by the husband, but it had no security for the debt. The society was aware of the Allied Irish Bank account money. The documents about this had been disclosed to the building society's counsel in the course of the proceedings. The building society also knew that, inevitably, the judge would be making an order for payment of a substantial lump sum by the husband to the wife; the husband had suggested £250,000, whereas the wife was asking for £450,000.

B

The building society and its lawyers decided there was no time to lose. The judge had ordered that the £275,000 was to be brought into this country and paid to the husband's solicitors. Here was a pot of gold, at risk of passing out of reach to the wife. If this happened, the building society might have difficulty in obtaining repayment of its debt. The building society moved quickly. On the following day it obtained a Mareva injunction against the husband in anticipation of proceedings in the Queen's Bench Division. Those proceedings were begun on 26 October, claiming payment of £68,133. On 9 November the building society obtained judgment. The husband had no defence and did not oppose.

C

The building society kept up the momentum. On the next day, 10 November, it served a statutory demand on the husband. That was followed at once, on 11 November, with an expedited bankruptcy petition. In the usual way a bankruptcy petition based on non-compliance with a statutory demand cannot be presented until three weeks have elapsed after service of the demand. An expedited petition may be presented if there is a serious possibility that the debtor's property will be significantly diminished within this three week period.

D

Finally, on 12 November the bankruptcy court appointed an interim receiver. His functions included getting in and protecting all the assets of the husband, including the money directed by Rattee J to be paid to the husband's solicitors.

E

In support of this application the building society's solicitor made an affidavit in which she put forward the contention that unsecured creditors of the husband, including the building society, ought to share equally with the wife in the husband's assets. The Family Court was due to give judgment on the wife's financial provision application on 13 November. Any disposition then made by the Family Court, in favour of the wife, of the sum of £275,000 held by the husband's solicitors would defeat this equal treatment.

F

Indeed, by now a further sum of £109,000 was held by the husband's solicitors. The wife had made an application to the Family Court to commit the husband to prison for breach of an undertaking given by him to the court in May 1989. The husband spent much time abroad in Singapore on business. He owned a flat there. In December 1991, in breach of his undertaking, he sold the flat for the equivalent of £109,000. After Rattee J had reserved judgment the husband, according to his evidence, borrowed a like amount from his mother. She paid it to his solicitors, to meet any order the court might make in the matrimonial proceedings. This, coupled with an apology, was intended to purge his contempt. The building society contended that both these amounts, which comprised the only funds available to the husband in the UK, should be made available to unsecured creditors generally and not just the wife.

G

H

I pause in the narrative to observe that I wholly acquit the building society's solicitor of any intention to mislead the court. I have already noted that an obligation arising under an order made in family proceedings is not provable as a debt, even though it falls within the statutory definition of a 'bankruptcy debt': see s. 382 of the *Insolvency Act* 1986 and r. 12.3(2)(a) of the *Insolvency Rules* 1986. The application and the affidavit were made in good faith. The solicitor was not, at the time, aware of this provision in the Insolvency Rules.

The hearing on 13 November 1992

A

These enforcement steps were taken by the building society without the knowledge of the wife or her lawyers. Rattee J also knew nothing, until after all had been done. On 12 November he was told of these happenings. On Friday 13 November he gave judgment in the ancillary relief proceedings. He ordered the husband to pay the wife £350,000, and a further £35,000 to discharge the amount owing to the building society on the security of the former matrimonial home.

B

Not surprisingly, the judge was unhappy about the building society situation. The society had intervened in the financial provision proceedings between the husband and the wife. After the hearing had concluded and while the judge was preparing his judgment, the society had taken steps designed to frustrate any order the court might make for a lump sum payment by the husband to the wife out of the money held by his solicitors. The judge had not foreseen the society would act in this way.

C

The judge formed an adverse view of the husband. The judge found him a thoroughly unsatisfactory witness, often devious and sometimes lying. His dishonest lack of candour about his financial position made it virtually impossible to form any reliable picture of his financial dealings. The judge concluded that, at any rate once the proceedings were determined, the husband would have ready access to large sums of money from his mother on account of his £1.5m or so share of his father's estate. The judge observed that the bankruptcy proceedings were within the husband's own control, because he had the means to pay off the building society if he chose. The husband, in other words, was using continuing non-payment of his debt to the building society as a means to delay, or defeat, payment to the wife.

D

The matter was complicated by the intervention of the interim receiver. He was not before the court in the family proceedings. In the result the judge made an order that the lump sum of £385,000 should be paid to the wife from the funds, totalling a similar amount, held by the husband's solicitors to the order of the court, subject to the effect (if any) of the bankruptcy proceedings and the orders made in those proceedings including the appointment of the interim receiver.

E

Subsequent events

I need not trace all the toings and froings that took place after this. On 17 November the bankruptcy court, on an application to which the wife was not a party, made an order that the money held by the husband's solicitors should be paid to the interim receiver. That was duly done. On 8 December a bankruptcy order was made by District Judge Bird. He rejected a contention by the wife that the petition by the building society was an abuse of the process of the court. He also dismissed an application by the wife that, in the alternative, the court should give its approval to the disposal of the £385,000 to the wife under s. 284 of the Insolvency Act.

F

G

In February 1993 a proposed appeal by the wife against the bankruptcy order was abandoned. Instead the wife launched an application to review the district judge's dismissal of her s. 284 application. That is the application now before me. I am not hearing an appeal against the bankruptcy order. The wife made an application for leave to appeal out of time against the bankruptcy order, but on 5 May Judge Weeks QC, sitting as a judge of the Chancery Division of the High Court, refused that application.

H

No right to prove

Before continuing I should note the end result for which the building society contends. Since the wife is unable to prove in the husband's bankruptcy, the position (if the building society's contentions are well founded) is that the husband's trustee must use the £385,000 in paying the trustee's expenses and remuneration and, subject to that, he must distribute

A   the money between the husband's creditors *but excluding the wife*. This would mean there would be a substantial surplus available to be returned to the husband. No doubt the wife could take steps to intercept the surplus. Even so, the result would be that the unsecured creditors would be paid in full, save for the wife. She would not receive the whole of the lump sum ordered by the judge. Indeed, far from even sharing equally with the husband's other creditors, she would rank behind them all. She would receive the crumbs from the husband's table left unconsumed by his other creditors. This is the

B   consequence of r. 12.3(2)(a) of the Insolvency Rules. An attack on the validity of this rule was rejected recently by the Court of Appeal in *Woodley v Woodley (No. 2)* [1993] 1 WLR 1167.

I feel bound to say that the exclusion of an obligation to pay a lump sum arising under an order in family proceedings from proof as a debt in bankruptcy is a matter which would bear re-examination as a matter of urgency. I echo the observations of Balcombe

C   LJ in the *Woodley* case. For the spouse to have a right to prove would not necessarily mean that the obligation would be released when the bankrupt was discharged. There are other obligations provable as debts but which survive discharge. For instance, a liability to pay damages for negligence for personal injuries is provable, but on discharge the bankrupt is released only to such extent as the court may direct: see s. 281(5)(a). As matters now stand, the remedies available to a wife or a husband under a lump sum

D   payment order are less than satisfactory. The remedy of a judgment summons is available, since it is not barred by s. 285(3). But, depending on the facts, the adequacy of that as a remedy must be questionable once bankruptcy has intervened.

The effect of the order of 22 October 1992

Section 284(1) provides:

E   'Where a person is adjudged bankrupt, any disposition of property made by that person in the period to which this section applies is void except to the extent that it is or was made with the consent of the court, or is or was subsequently ratified by the court.'

The section applies to the period beginning with the day on which a bankruptcy petition is presented and ends, in short, when the bankrupt's estate vests in a trustee after a

F   bankruptcy order has been made. The first question I have to answer is whether the money held by the husband's solicitors when the bankruptcy petition was presented on 11 November was still the husband's 'property' for the purposes of this section.

Before turning to consider more closely the purpose and effect of Rattee J's order, I mention three background matters. First, not every order which seeks to preserve a fund to meet a future judgment debt has the effect of giving the judgment creditor a proprietary interest in the fund and, to that extent, putting the fund beyond the reach of the debtor's

G   general body of creditors. A Mareva injunction is the leading example of an order which has this aim but does not have this effect. A Mareva injunction is concerned to prevent the dissipation of assets in advance of a judgment, but it is now well established that a Mareva injunction does not confer on the plaintiff claimant any proprietary interest in the defendant's assets or any charge over them. This is so even if the injunction relates only to a particularised asset. The injunction operates only in personam: see *Cretanor*

H   *Maritime Co Ltd v Irish Marine Management Ltd* [1978] 1 WLR 966.

Second, it is equally well established that where a sum is paid into court by a defendant, either voluntarily under O. 22 in satisfaction of the plaintiff's cause of action, or involuntarily, for instance under O. 14 as a condition of leave to defend, the plaintiff is treated as a secured creditor in the defendant's bankruptcy to the extent of the money paid in: see *W A Sherratt Ltd v John Bromley (Church Stretton) Ltd* [1985] 1 All ER 216.

In *Re Gordon, ex parte Navalchand* [1897] 2 QB 516 at p. 519–520, Vaughan Williams J   A
expressed the underlying rationale in the case of a voluntary payment into court:

> '. . . I am clearly of opinion that if the proof is admitted, or to the extent to which
> it is admitted, the plaintiff is a secured creditor by reason of the payment into
> court. The money paid into court, even with a plea denying liability, has become
> subject to the plaintiff's claim by the act of the defendant, who there agrees that
> the sum paid in shall remain in court subject to the conditions of Order XXII.,   B
> r. 6.'

In *Re Ford, ex parte the trustee* [1900] 2 QB 211 at p. 213, Wright J dealt with the case of
an involuntary payment by a defendant under O. 14, in these terms:

> '. . . it is settled that where money is ordered to be paid into court to abide the
> event it must be treated as a security that the plaintiff shall not lose the benefit of
> the decision of the Court in his favour . . . The very object of such an order is that   C
> the plaintiff shall be in as good a position, so far as the money paid in extends,
> against contingencies such as bankruptcy as if he had got an immediate judgment
> . . .'

The third background matter concerns the jurisdiction being exercised by the judge
when he made his order of 22 October. Section 37(2) of the *Matrimonial Causes Act* 1973
provides:

> '(2) Where proceedings for financial relief are brought by one person against   D
> another, the court may, on the application of the first-mentioned person–
>
> (a) if it is satisfied that the other party to the proceedings is, with the intention
>   of defeating the claim for financial relief, about to make any disposition or
>   to transfer out of the jurisdiction or otherwise deal with any property, make
>   such order as it thinks fit for restraining the other party from so doing or
>   otherwise for protecting the claim; . . .'   E

The words 'or otherwise for protecting the claim' are wide. I can see no justification for
cutting them down so as to exclude power to make an order which, when carried out,
will have the effect of making property security for the claim in the same way as a sum
paid into court under O. 14 or O. 22. For instance, the judge may direct that a sum shall
be paid into court to await the outcome of a claim for financial provision.

I recognise that, when ordering payment of a lump sum, the statute only gives express   F
power to direct that the payment shall be secured when payment is to be made in
instalments: see s. 23(3)(c) of the Act of 1973. Security may also be ordered in respect of
periodical payments: s. 23(1)(b). In my view this is not a good reason for cutting down
the width of the protection the court may order under s. 37(2)(a). Section 37(2)(a) applies
to all forms of financial relief, including property adjustment orders. That points to the
provision being given a wider, rather than a narrower, meaning.

Against that background, I turn to Rattee J's order. As drawn up, it provided simply   G
that the existing Mareva injunction should be discharged and that:

> 'the [husband] by the 3rd day of November 1992 cause funds presently standing to
> his credit at the Allied Irish Bank be held by his Solicitor'.

The transcript of the exchanges which took place in court when the order was made
are more revealing. From these it is clear that the judge intended, and indeed he directed,
that the Allied Irish Bank money should be paid to the solicitors to be held by them 'to   H
the order of the court'. Without some such restriction, as the judge appreciated, the
husband's solicitors would be bound to give the money back to their client if he asked
for it. When this point was raised, counsel for the husband said he had no specific
instructions, but he did not see how he could object: 'it seems a perfectly sensible way of
securing that money pending your Lordship's judgment'.

In my view, when making this order the purpose of the judge was to afford the wife protection in respect of her claim similar to the protection she would have enjoyed had he ordered payment of the money into court. I consider, further, that the judge's order was apt to achieve the purpose. Indeed, payment to the husband's solicitors was put forward by the wife's counsel as an alternative to payment into court. I do not think that, when he ordered payment to the solicitors rather than into court, the judge was intending to affect the nature of the wife's protection. Payment to the solicitors, as officers of the court, would in practice be as secure as a payment into court. Had the judge ordered that the money was to be paid into court, in my view the case would be indistinguishable in principle from the authorities I have mentioned. The money would be earmarked as the source for any lump-sum payment just as much as a payment made into court in satisfaction of an order giving leave to defend conditional upon the provision of security.

I appreciate there was no absolute certainty the judge would direct that the lump sum payment should be made from the Allied Irish Bank money held by the solicitors to the order of the court. This does not point to a different conclusion. There never is finality about the destination of a payment in court. For instance, a payment made into court under O. 22 may, exceptionally, be withdrawn with the leave of the court for good reason: see O. 22, r. 1(3). This does not detract from the conclusion that, in the solicitors' hands as much as if it had been paid into court, the money was beyond the reach of the husband. It was subject to whatever directions the court might give in the pending family proceedings. Neither in practice nor in law was the husband able to dispose of the sum in question.

Accordingly, in my view when the £275,000 odd (the precise amount was £276,601) reached the husband's solicitors, it ceased to be part of the husband's own estate. Thus the interim receiver had no right to claim this when he was appointed. He was no more entitled to claim this money than he would have been if this had been a sum of money in court.

The further sum of £109,000

In my view the £109,000 paid to the solicitors by the husband's mother stands on the same footing. The committal application was one of the matters before Rattee J. He was told of the admitted breach of the husband's undertaking. At the request of the husband and the wife, he adjourned this application to the date on which he gave his judgment on the financial provision application. He was also told by the husband through counsel that meanwhile the husband would seek to borrow a sum equal to the sale proceeds of the Singapore flat, so that this could be available to meet the wife's claim. The money was duly provided by the mother to the husband's solicitor on 29 October. The solicitor placed this money, together with the £276,601 from the Allied Irish Bank account, in a designated deposit account 'to be held to the order of the court so far as I and [the husband] were concerned'. The solicitor treated both tranches of money similarly. This was before the bankruptcy petition was issued.

In the light of these arrangements I do not think it would have been open to the husband, once the money had been received by the solicitors, to require that it should be paid to him. The money was accepted by the solicitors on the footing that it was to be held to the order of the court as part and parcel of the husband's efforts to remedy his breach of his undertaking to the court. The payment was not the subject of a court order, or of an undertaking to the court or to the wife. In that respect the position is not so clear-cut as with the money received from the Allied Irish Bank account. But the intention of the husband was that this further sum also should be produced by him and set aside by the solicitor, an officer of the court, and earmarked as available to meet the lump sum payment order.

Court orders and s. 284   A

This conclusion is sufficient to dispose of this case. Many further arguments were addressed to me, but in the circumstances it is not necessary for me to pursue them. However, there is one point to which I should draw attention. There was much discussion before me concerning the decision in *Re Flint* [1993] Ch 319. There, after a bankruptcy petition had been presented against a husband, the court made an order under s. 24 of the Act of 1973 that the husband transfer to the wife all his estate and interest in the   B former matrimonial home. The deputy judge held that this order was a disposition of property made by the husband within the meaning of s. 284 and that, accordingly, once the husband was adjudicated bankrupt, the order became void unless subsequently ratified by the court. Central to the judge's conclusion was his view (at p. 326E) that the order had the effect that the husband's equitable interest in the house passed to the wife immediately. He regarded this as a relatively straightforward example of equity treating as done that which ought to be done. The order in that case was a consent order, but the   C judge stated his decision would have been the same if the order had been made without the consent of the husband.

In *Burton v Burton* [1986] 2 FLR 419 Butler-Sloss J expressed a different view. She observed (at p. 425) that an order made under s. 23(1)(c) of the Act of 1973 for payment of a lump sum could not transfer any beneficial interest to the party in whose favour the order was made. She continued with regard to property transfer orders made under   D s. 24(1)(a):

> 'If it is an order under s. 24(1)(a), exactly the same considerations apply, because the order is that a "party to the marriage shall transfer to the other party" such property etc. as may be so specified. In my judgment, again the beneficial interest in that transfer of property does not past until the consequential documentation has taken effect, and the Act obviously allows for that; and one reason it allows   E for that, I have no doubt, is the comprehensive code which is formulated by the Law of Property Act 1925 . . . Section 53(1)(a) of the 1925 Act provides "that no interest in land can be created or disposed of except by writing, signed by the person creating or conveying the same, or by his agents thereunto lawfully authorised in writing or by will or by operation of law". In this case, of course, it would not be a voluntary disposition in writing by the husband but either he would obey the order of the court or a registrar could exercise a procedure on his behalf   F if he chose not to do so. But it is the moment of transfer, in my judgment, pursuant to the comprehensive code of the Law of Property Act, and in accordance with the order properly made under s. 24 of the *Matrimonial Causes Act* 1973 that the beneficial interest in that property or part of that property, whether it be in money or in land, will pass to the wife petitioner and not before.'

If that is correct, a property transfer order under s. 24(1)(a) is not itself a disposition   G of property. The disposition occurs only at the later stage when the order is carried out and the requisite instrument of transfer is signed.

The decision in *Burton v Burton* seems not to have been drawn to the attention of the court in *Re Flint*. In the present case it is not necessary for me to state any conclusion of my own on the divergent views expressed in those two cases, and I shall therefore refrain from doing so.   H

Conclusion

I shall make a declaration to the effect that the money held by the husband's solicitors on 13 November 1992 did not form part of the husband's estate, and accordingly the trustee in bankruptcy is not entitled thereto. I shall make no order on the trustee's

A summons seeking directions regarding the distribution of the bankrupt's estate. The conclusion I have reached on the main application makes it unnecessary for me to give any such directions.

(*Order accordingly*)

JUDGMENT ON COSTS
B (Delivered 9 May 1994)

Nicholls V-C: I must now deal with the costs of the s. 284 application on which I gave judgment last July. The respondent to the application, so far as it was before me, was Mr Mordant's trustee in bankruptcy. According to information supplied by the trustee, no assets have been realised in the husband's estate and none is expected to be realised.

On the application the applicant wife was successful and the trustee was unsuccessful.
C Against that background my attention is directed to r. 7.39 of the *Insolvency Rules* 1986 which, so far as material, provides:

'. . . where the official receiver or a responsible insolvency practitioner is made a party to any proceedings on the application of another party to the proceedings, he shall not be personally liable for costs unless the court otherwise directs.'

In seeking an order for costs against the trustee with a direction that he is to be
D personally liable, Mr Sefi submitted that r. 7.39 is not applicable in the present case. The rule is not applicable, because the trustee was not made a party to the proceedings on the application of the wife. Initially the proceedings were brought against the official receiver, and after the bankruptcy order had been made the trustee in bankruptcy became a party, but it was not on the wife's application. Mr Sefi accepted that once the bankruptcy order had been made and a trustee appointed, the trustee had to be made a respondent to the existing application launched on 4 December. Indeed, that stands to reason. Once the
E bankruptcy order had been made, the wife would not continue with her application in the absence of the trustee. He was a necessary party. His joinder, therefore, was inevitable.

In that circumstance, whether the joinder formally was made on an application by the wife or not seems to me really to be irrelevant. Given that the joinder was inevitable, the distinction sought to be drawn is one without a difference. Here, for the purposes of this
F rule, by continuing the application to which the trustee had to be joined, the wife herself was responsible for the trustee becoming a party in as much as if she herself had formally made an application in that regard.

Mr Sefi accepted that if the rule applies in this case, he cannot point to any feature which would make this a special case in which it would be right to order that the trustee should be personally liable for costs.
G
Appearing for the building society, Mr Griffiths was more guarded. He pointed out it was up to the trustee to decide whether or not to defend the proceedings. The trustee chose to do so, although he knew the position regarding the estate and its assets.

I do not think these factors lead to the conclusion that it would be right to depart from what r. 7.39 indicated is to be the starting point regarding costs orders against respondent trustees in bankruptcy, namely, there is no personal liability unless, in effect, there is
H good reason to direct otherwise. In my view this is not a case for me to direct otherwise. I shall make an order that the trustee pay the wife's costs of the application, but I will not make any contrary direction within r. 7.39.

On that footing, pausing there for a moment, without more the wife effectively will have to bear her own costs. It is in that circumstance that the wife advanced a claim against the building society. The building society was not a party to her application. So

what is invoked is the court's jurisdiction, exercisable only in exceptional circumstances,   A
to order a third party to pay the costs of one or both of the parties in the litigation.

For the wife, Mr Sefi made several points. The most important one, placed by him at
the heart of his client's case, is that the root cause of the whole of the bankruptcy
proceedings and of the s. 284 application was the building society's action. The building
society set in motion the bankruptcy proceedings with a view to thwarting any lump sum
order made by Rattee J in the proceedings pending before him. The building society did   B
so, taking care not to tell the wife what it was doing so as thereby to preclude the wife
from having an opportunity of stepping in and restoring the matter to the judge. The
steps initiated by the building society were taken with a view to the society, as the main
creditor, receiving the main share of the two sums of money in dispute. Predictably and
inevitably, those steps taken by the building society resulted in expensive litigation. The
trustee's claim that the two sums formed part of the husband's estate must have been a
claim the building society wished him to pursue.   C

For the building society, Mr Griffiths pointed out that the wife was a party to the
compromise agreement. The agreement expressly provided that nothing in the order was
to prevent the building society from taking steps to pursue and enforce its claim as an
unsecured creditor in an agreed sum against the husband. There was no term in the
agreement that the building society could not present a bankruptcy petition. There was
no term that the wife had to be given notice of any such petition. There was no term that   D
she was to be given notice of any other steps taken by the building society to seek to
recover from the husband the money he owed to the society. It was submitted that the
building society acted lawfully and properly in diligently protecting its own interests.

Further, at a previous stage in the protracted history of this matter, there was a claim
that the building society was guilty of an abuse of the process in presentation of the
bankruptcy petition. That issue was adjudicated upon. On that issue the wife lost and the
building society succeeded, and that issue is now res judicata. Thus the building society's   E
behaviour has been upheld and countenanced by the bankruptcy court.

Once the bankruptcy order was made, it was further submitted, the building society
was no longer involved in this matter. Thereafter the conduct of any disputes with the
wife was in the hands of the trustee. As a matter of public policy, once a petition has been
presented a creditor should not be at risk regarding the costs of applications made in the
bankruptcy; that should be so whether the creditor is a main creditor or not. Here the   F
building society could not control, and in fact did not seek to control, the conduct of the
trustee in the wife's application.

Further, the building society had no opportunity to appeal against the whole or part
of my decision. In the course of the proceedings the building society had no opportunity
to seek to reach a compromise with the wife, nor was the building society given any
warning until after the event, when it was of course no longer of any use, that the wife   G
might or would make an application against the society for costs.

The points made by the building society are not without force. In the end, however, I
have concluded that in the exceptional circumstances of this case it is right and proper
that the building society should pay the wife's costs of the application. The factor which
has weighed with me is that this is not a case simply of a diligent creditor. Here the
building society was a party to proceedings before Rattee J. The matter which affected   H
the society was compromised on terms which left the society with an unsecured claim
against the husband. Indeed, the society was left at liberty to pursue its remedies in
respect of that claim. However, and this is the special feature of this case, the judge had
already taken steps intended to protect the wife's lump sum claim so far as the Allied
Irish money was concerned. That sum was to be paid to the husband's solicitors to be
held by them to the order of the court and not to the order of their client, the husband.

A   Thus it was abundantly clear that the judge intended that unsecured creditors of the husband were not to be able to touch this money ahead of the wife. The money was to be out of reach of the husband, and the building society knew this. The society nevertheless proceeded as it did without telling the wife so as to prevent the wife from going back to the judge and asking for an immediate lump sum order there and then. The building society or its legal advisers knew what would have been likely to happen if such an application had been made. In other words, the society or its advisers knew, I have to

B   say, they were attempting to steal a march on the court. In colloquial terms, they were pulling a fast one, although no doubt the building society and its advisers believed they were doing no more than they were entitled to do.

     Hence, in a very powerful sense, the direct cause of the s. 284 application was conduct of the building society of which I have to say I cannot approve. The building society overreached itself in its desire to protect its own interests and achieve what it regarded as

C   a fairer distribution of the husband's assets, notwithstanding its knowledge of what the court intended should be the position over the Allied Irish money as between, on the one hand, the building society and its unsecured claims against the husband and, on the other hand, the wife and her claims to payment of a lump sum. Accordingly, since there is no money in the husband's estate to pay the wife's costs, I consider the building society has brought upon its own head an order that it should pay the wife's costs. Had the different

D   sets of proceedings all been in the one court, the building society would have got nowhere. As it is, the society took advantage of the existence of different sets of proceedings in different courts enabling it to proceed without telling the wife of what was taking place.

     In the circumstances I think it is right to make the order even though the building society had no control over the conduct of the application, no opportunity of appealing and even though it was given no prior warning. These latter factors do not tip the balance the other way. I see no reason to doubt that in fact the building society and its advisers

E   knew of what was happening, and of the course of the application, because the solicitors and counsel who acted for the trustee in the proceedings were the same solicitors and counsel who had acted for the building society throughout.

     In those circumstances I shall make an order that the building society is to pay the wife's costs of the relevant application.

(Order accordingly)

F

G

H

Re Cedar Developments Ltd.

A

Chancery Division.
J R Cherryman QC (sitting as a deputy High Court judge).
Judgment delivered 12 May 1994.

Disqualifying unfit directors of insolvent companies – Application for leave to apply out of time – Appeal against registrar's grant of leave – Whether good reason had been shown why leave should be granted – Whether delay explained – Company Directors Disqualification Act 1986, s. 7(2).

B

This was an appeal by a former company director against a registrar's order granting the official receiver leave under s. 7(2) of the Company Directors Disqualification Act 1986 to apply out of time for a disqualification order under that Act.

Held, **allowing the appeal and dismissing the official receiver's originating summons asking for leave:**

C

1. The registrar had erred in principle in not applying the correct test when considering an application for leave under s. 7(2). The correct test was whether a good reason had been shown for an extension of time. (Re Crestjoy Products Ltd [1990] BCC 23 considered.)

2. The registrar was also wrong not to take into account delay in the two-year period, for which no good reason was given, and to assume that good reason was 'semi-automatically' shown if the time limit was exceeded by a very few days due to some administrative error.

D

3. The burden on the official receiver to show good reason was not a formality but a very real onus which could not be discharged perfunctorily. Although failure to apply in time might have been due to a last-minute administrative muddle, no sufficient explanation was given of why it took the official receiver two years to organise an application and why no margin of time was allowed for unforeseen problems such as those which did occur.

E

The following cases were referred to in the judgment:

Al Tabith, The [1993] 2 Ll Rep 214.
Benson, Re (unreported, 8 March 1971, CA).
Cedac Ltd, Re [1990] BCC 555.
Copecrest Ltd, Re [1993] BCC 844.
Crestjoy Products Ltd, Re [1990] BCC 23.
Kleinwort Benson Ltd v Barbrak Ltd [1987] AC 597.
Probe Data Systems Ltd, Re (No. 3) [1992] BCC 110.
Van Stillevoldt (C M) BV v E L Carriers Inc [1983] 1 WLR 207.

F

Peter Kirby (instructed by Rich & Baily) for the appellant.

Philip Jones (instructed by the Treasury Solicitor) for the official receiver.

G

JUDGMENT

J R Cherryman QC: This is an appeal by Mr Derek Joseph Kelly, a former director of Cedar Developments Ltd, from an order of Mr Registrar Buckley dated 14 March 1994 granting the official receiver leave under s. 7(2) of the *Company Directors Disqualification Act* 1986 to apply out of time for a disqualification order under that Act.

H

The winding-up order in respect of the company in question was made on 3 September 1991 and the evidence shows that the intended proceedings under the Act were virtually ready to be issued by 25 August 1993; in other words, just within the two-year limit provided by the section. However, they were not issued within that period of two years due to what the registrar described as 'a procedural nonsense' in the official receiver's office. It appears that that mistake or nonsense and the consequences of it were not

A   discovered until too late. Hence this present application for leave was issued on 6
     September 1993.

         As well as having been a director of Cedar Developments Ltd, Mr Kelly was formerly
     a director of a number of other companies, some of which went into insolvent liquidation
     at later dates than the date of the compulsory winding-up order in respect of Cedar
     Developments. In the case of all of the companies the official receiver questioned whether
B   Mr Kelly's conduct as a director is such as made him unfit to be concerned in the
     management of a company, and the matters intended to be relied upon relate to wholesale
     failures to prepare and file accounts and returns and so on. Indeed Mr Kirby, who
     appeared for Mr Kelly, has frankly accepted that there had been a strong case against his
     client which needed to be answered, but he submitted that, if the matter was going to be
     investigated in proceedings under the Company Directors Disqualification Act, those
     proceedings must be regularly initiated in accordance with the provisions of the Act.
C
         The original intention of the official receiver had been to make the lead application
     under the Act in the matter of Cedar Developments Ltd and to refer to Mr Kelly's
     conduct as director of the other companies in support of that application (see s. 6(1)(b)
     of the Act). When the failure to issue the proceedings in the intended lead action in time
     was discovered, this application was launched and everyone appears to have overlooked
     the fact that, as the time for an application for a disqualification order had not expired
D   in respect of three of the other companies of which Mr Kelly had been a director, it would
     have been perfectly feasible without much additional paperwork being required for the
     leading disqualification application to have been made in the matter of, for instance,
     Avamelle Ltd at any time before 3 February 1994 without any application at all for leave
     being necessary.

         Section 7(2) of the Act provides:

E   'Except with the leave of the court, an application for the making under that
         section of a disqualification order against any person shall not be made after the
         end of the period of 2 years beginning with the day on which the company of which
         that person is or has been a director became insolvent.'

         The registrar has exercised his discretion to grant leave to bring disqualification
     proceedings out of time. As this is an appeal under r. 7.47 of the *Insolvency Rules* 1986,
F   the procedure and practice of the Supreme Court relating to appeals to the Court of
     Appeal apply. I can only intervene if it can be shown that the registrar in exercising his
     discretion has made some error of law or principle. I was told that the hearing before the
     registrar, who had read the papers in advance, took little more than one hour, apparently
     including judgment. The note of his judgment which counsel have agreed reads as follows:

         'I take the view that the only ground on which the respondent is relying is not one
G   that is open to him. If the reason for the application was that the official receiver
         had not got his tackle in order during the two-year period, then any delay within
         the two years would be relevant to a minor extent along with any delay after the
         expiry of the two-year period. There was no delay after the expiry of the two-year
         period. The delay within the two-year period is not responsible for the failure to
         bring proceedings within two years. The reason why the proceedings were not
         brought was a procedural nonsense – no doubt steps have now been taken by the
H   official receiver to rectify that. The official receiver is entitled to leave to pursue the
         proceedings, particularly in view of the fact that the two-year period was not the
         latest that could be selected.'

         As I say, this was a note which counsel, both of whom were also present before the
     registrar, agreed between them. It does not appear to be a note approved by the registrar,
     and for my part I think it would be desirable in appeals under the rule that I have

mentioned that any note of judgment of the registrar or district judge should be one that   A
he has had an opportunity to approve and has approved.

It is not evident from this somewhat cryptic judgment what test the registrar applied in
deciding whether leave should be granted. He appears to have regarded it as self-evident
that there should be leave in a case where the official receiver had all his tackle in order
but missed the two-year deadline by only a few days due to some administrative muddle.
In the first half of his judgment the registrar was at pains to point out why in his view Mr   B
Kelly could not successfully oppose the application by relying on delay within the two
years. In the last sentence the point the registrar appears to make (or this is what I read
into it) is that the granting of leave could not prejudice Mr Kelly because, at the expiry
of the two-year period in relation to Cedar Developments Ltd, he still remained
vulnerable to disqualification proceedings in which his conduct as director of Cedar
Developments Ltd would be gone into in relation to any of the other three companies
which I have mentioned.   C

It appears now to be well established (see per Hoffmann LJ in *Re Copecrest Ltd* [1993]
BCC 844 at p. 852) that the correct test for the court to apply when considering an
application for leave under s. 7(2) is that stated and applied by Harman J in *Re Crestjoy
Products Ltd* [1990] BCC 23 at p. 29F:

> '. . . all I can do is try and assess the whole position here and consider whether I
> am satisfied that a good reason has been shown . . . for an extension of time . . .'   D

Harman J's formulation of the test adopted by analogy the words 'good reason' from
the test propounded by Lord Brandon in *Kleinwort Benson Ltd v Barbrak Ltd* [1987] AC
597, which was a case about the extension of the validity of a writ under O. 6, r. 8. It is
important that I should pay heed to the words which Lord Brandon added at p. 622H:

> 'The question then arises as to what kind of matters can properly be regarded as
> amounting to "good reason". The answer is, I think, that it is not possible to define   E
> or circumscribe the scope of that expression. Whether there is or is not good reason
> in any particular case must depend on all the circumstances of that case, and must
> therefore be left to the judgment of the judge . . .'

I have, very properly and usefully, been referred to the way in which the court has
exercised its discretion under s. 7(2) in a number of cases, namely, including:

(1)   *Re Crestjoy* Ltd (above) (two-year time limit expired; no proceedings for two   F
      months; leave refused).

(2)   *Re Cedac Ltd* [1990] BCC 555 (proceedings issued within time but invalid on the
      view taken by the judge at first instance because the s. 16 notice was one day short;
      leave granted; appeal allowed on the ground that the proceedings were valid when
      originally issued and leave was not required).

(3)   *Re Probe Data Systems Ltd (No. 3)* [1992] BCC 110 (proceedings commenced
      within two years by the official receiver instead of the Secretary of State; leave   G
      granted for the Secretary of State to take fresh proceedings).

(4)   *Re Copecrest Ltd* [1993] BCC 844 (a director obstructed investigation by the
      Secretary of State; good reason shown; leave granted by the Court of Appeal).

These cases are, as I have said, useful illustrations, but the way in which the court
exercises its discretion in any particular case is not a precedent as to how the discretion
should be exercised in future cases, in each of which the judge or registrar exercising the   H
discretion must come to his own conclusion whether leave should be granted and must
apply the test of whether a good reason has been shown for leave.

As to the factors to be taken into account by the court when considering an application
for leave under s. 7(2), the following passage (at p. 118G) from the judgment of Scott LJ
in *Re Probe Data Systems (No. 3)* must be borne in mind:

A

'In considering an application under section 7(2) for leave to commence disqualification proceedings out of time – the court should, in my opinion, take into account the following matters: (1) the length of the delay; (2) the reasons for the delay; (3) the strength of the case against the director; and (4) the degree of prejudice caused to the director by the delay (see *C M Van Stillevoldt BV v E L Carriers Inc* [1983] 1 WLR 207 and *Re Benson* (8 March 1971 (CA), unreported but noted at p. 461 of *Williams & Muir Hunter on Bankruptcy* (19th ed.)).'

B

I have looked at the authorities referred to by Scott LJ and observe:

(1)   that they are concerned with applications for extension of time for appealing or for setting down appeals; and

(2)   that it is plain from the *Stillevoldt* case that the four matters listed by Scott LJ are not the only matters to be taken into account. All relevant factors must be taken into account.

C

In the present case in my judgment the registrar has fallen into error in the following respects, each of which, in my view, is sufficient to vitiate his decision:

(1)   It is not clear that he has applied the correct test of asking himself whether a good reason has been shown why leave should be granted. I have the distinct impression that he was asking himself whether Mr Kelly had shown cause why leave should not be granted. In my view, failing to state or make otherwise clear the test being applied is itself an error of principle.

D

(2)   It was an error, in my view, not to take delay during the two-year period, for which no good explanation was apparently given, into account (see *Re Probe Data Systems (No. 3)* at p. 118). The point about this is that, if the official receiver had not left everything till the last moment during the two-year period, the administrative muddle which in fact occurred would not have caused the time limit to be missed.

E

(3)   It was wrong to assume that good reason is, I might say, semi-automatically shown if the time limit is only exceeded by a very few days due to some administrative error or mistake having occurred.

(4)   The registrar refers obliquely to the continued availability of Avamelle Ltd beyond the two-year period relating to Cedar Developments Ltd as a vehicle for disqualification proceedings, but wholly failed to take into account the fact that a substantive application in the matter of Avamelle Ltd would have rendered an application for leave in respect of Cedar Developments Ltd completely unnecessary.

F

As in my judgment the registrar has erred in principle in this case, I must exercise the discretion afresh myself. In support of his contention that leave to issue disqualification proceedings out of time should be granted. Mr Philip Jones for the official receiver urged me to take into account, as I do:

G

(1)   that the failure to issue in time was due only to a last-minute administrative error or hitch and that the originating application for leave was made a matter of days outside the two-year period;

(2)   that the case against Mr Kelly of failing to prepare and file accounts and returns is a strong and serious one which in the public interest should be brought before the court (I pause here to point out that, as far as I am able to glean from the documents, this is not a case involving explicit allegations of fraud as such);

H

(3)   that Mr Kelly was given a s. 16 notice of intention to proceed on 16 August 1993;

(4)   that Mr Kelly will suffer no prejudice by leave being granted because, instead of applying for leave, the official receiver had plenty of time within which to make a

substantive application in the matter of one of the other companies of which Mr   A
Kelly was director, such as Avamelle Ltd.

On behalf of Mr Kelly, Mr Kirby's first submission was that, if the reason why the
substantive application is not made in time is that some administrative muddle has
occurred, that shows that there cannot be any good reason at all why leave should be
granted, so that it becomes strictly unnecessary to carry out any detailed balancing
exercise.
                                                                                    B
I do not agree that the court should, in a case such as this, disregard all the other
matters. In my judgment, all factors which could possibly be relevant must be taken into
account, and that is what I have endeavoured to do.

To my mind, as pointed out by Mr Kirby, there are a number of other potentially
potent factors pointing against the discretion being exercised so as to allow
disqualification proceedings to be brought out of time. I may mention the following:
                                                                                    C
(1)   that disqualification proceedings are quasi-penal in nature and effect and it is thus
       a serious matter when leave to issue out of time has to be sought;

(2)   that, although failure to issue in time may have ultimately been due to a last minute
       muddle, no or no sufficient explanation has been given of why it took the official
       receiver two years to get his tackle in order and why no margin of time was allowed
       for unforeseen problems or mistakes such as in fact occurred;
                                                                                    D
(3)   that on an application for leave the burden on the official receiver to show a good
       reason is not a formality but a very real onus which cannot be discharged
       perfunctorily or semi-automatically by showing that the time limit has been missed
       by a few days simply due to some administrative mistake (in my judgment there
       can hardly be a good reason for leave without a good reason being shown why the
       time limit was missed);
                                                                                    E
(4)   that it is rather extraordinary that the official receiver, having missed the time limit
       in relation to Cedar Developments Ltd, overlooked that he could have made a
       valid substantive application in respect of Avamelle Ltd instead of pursuing this
       present application for leave.

Doing the best I can to take all the factors put to me by both sides into account and
taking full account of the four matters specified in Scott LJ's formulation and applying
the good reason test, I am not satisfied in this case that the official receiver has shown   F
any good reason why leave should be granted. In case it might be suggested that (4)
above ought to be irrelevant to my consideration of this case, I should say that I would
have reached the same conclusion without that fourth point.

If I had to encapsulate my view in very few words, I would say that the official receiver
has shown a bad reason – not a good reason – why leave should be granted. I respectfully
echo what Sheen J had to say in *The Al Tabith* [1993] 2 Ll Rep 214 concerning an   G
application to extend the limitation period under s. 8 of the *Maritime Conventions Act*
1911. The passage is at p. 219:

'Mr Charlton pointed out that the words of the statute which empower the court
to extend time are entirely general. It seems to me that plaintiffs who seek to
establish that there is good reason to extend the normal period of limitation must
show that their failure was not merely due to their own mistake. It cannot be a   H
good reason for extending the time limit that the defendants are unable to show
that there would be any specific prejudice to them in conducting their defence. At
the end of the two years, or as in this case two and a half years, it would be virtually
impossible to show such prejudice. Mr Charlton invited me to consider the balance
of hardship. If balance of hardship could constitute good reason for extending the
time limit, that time limit would always be extended. A person who decides not to

issue a writ until shortly before a period of limitation will expire takes the risk that for some unexpected reason he will fail to issue the writ in time. Mr Dawson took a deliberate decision not to instruct solicitors to issue the writ until nearly at the end of the two years, and then, when that period was extended by six months, he took the deliberate decision not to instruct solicitors to issue a writ until shortly before he thought those six months expired. By reason of his own mistake he failed to give instructions in time. I can see no good reason to extend that time limit.'

For the above reasons I exercise my discretion against granting the official receiver leave to issue proceedings out of time. I therefore allow the appeal, refuse leave and conclude by dismissing the official receiver's originating summons asking for leave.

(*Appeal allowed*)

Re Bridgend Goldsmiths Ltd & Ors.

A

Chancery Division.
Blackburne J.
Judgment delivered 29 July 1994.

Individual voluntary arrangement – Court's power to fill vacancy in office of supervisor – Whether High Court had jurisdiction to fill vacancy – Insolvency Act 1986, s. 263(5).

B

This was an application by the Secretary of State for Trade and Industry under s. 263(5) of the Insolvency Act 1986 to replace the supervisor of a number of individual voluntary arrangements.

The Secretary of State had withdrawn the authority of 'E' to act as an insolvency practitioner. As a consequence E ceased to be qualified to continue acting as supervisor of 20 individual voluntary arrangements then being implemented. Each arrangement was described in the evidence by reference to a county court in South Wales, principally Swansea County Court. The Secretary of State applied under s. 265(3) for an order removing E from his offices as supervisor and appointing another practitioner in his stead.

C

Held, refusing to make the order sought:

By virtue of s. 385(1) of the Act and r. 5.5A and 6.40(3A) of the Insolvency Rules any application to the court under s. 263(5) had to be made to the relevant county court in respect of the particular voluntary arrangement. Since none was in the High Court, the High Court had no jurisdiction under s. 263(5) to make an order replacing E as supervisor of any of the 20 voluntary arrangements. (Re Parkdawn Ltd (unreported, 15 June 1993, Harman J) not followed.)

D

The following cases were referred to in the judgment:

Adams (A J) (Builders) Ltd, Re [1991] BCC 62.
Parkdawn Ltd, Re (unreported, 15 June 1993, Harman J).

E

R B Ritchie (instructed by the Treasury Solicitor) for the Secretary of State.

JUDGMENT

Blackburne J: This matter raises a question of jurisdiction under s. 263(5) of the *Insolvency Act* 1986 ('the Act').

F

With effect from 16 April 1994 Elgar Evans ceased to be qualified to act as an insolvency practitioner within the meaning of s. 388 of the Act, his authorisation so to act having been withdrawn by the Secretary of State for Trade and Industry, as the competent authority, pursuant to s. 393(4) of the Act. Mr Evans did not challenge that withdrawal.

G

One consequence of the withdrawal of authorisation was that Mr Evans automatically vacated office as liquidator of the four companies which, at the time, were in the course of being wound up voluntarily by him: see s. 171(4) of the Act and *Re A J Adams (Builders) Ltd* [1991] BCC 62. Another consequence was that he ceased to be qualified to continue acting as supervisor of 20 individual voluntary arrangements approved under Pt. VIII of the Act and then in course of implementation: see s. 388(2)(c) and s. 390(2) of the Act.

H

The Secretary of State now applies to me for an order, so far as necessary, that Mr Evans be removed from his offices as liquidator of the four companies and as supervisor of the 20 individual voluntary arrangements and for an order that Gary Stones or some other fit and proper person be appointed liquidator or supervisor, as the case may be, in his stead. The companies and individual voluntary arrangements are listed in the schedule

A   to the originating application. Mr Stones is authorised to act as an insolvency practitioner under the Act and has consented to be appointed in place of Mr Evans in each of the latter's former appointments as liquidator or supervisor, as the case may be, of the voluntary liquidations and individual voluntary arrangements.

    I am satisfied that s. 108(1) of the Act empowers me to make these appointments in relation to the four companies in creditors' voluntary liquidation since, in the case of each of the companies, there is, by reason of the withdrawal of Mr Evans's authorisation,

B   no liquidator acting. I am also satisfied that the Secretary of State is a proper person to make the application. In the circumstances I propose to make the order which the Secretary of State seeks appointing Mr Stones as liquidator in relation to each of the four companies.

    Mr Ritchie, for the Secretary of State, urges me to follow the same course in relation to the 20 individual voluntary arrangements. I am not persuaded that I have any

C   jurisdiction to do so.

    The court's power, which Mr Ritchie invites me to exercise, is contained in s. 263(5) of the Act. I am not aware that there is any other relevant power. So far as material s. 263 provides as follows:

D
      '(1) This section applies where a voluntary arrangement approved by a creditors' meeting summoned under section 257 has taken effect.'

    I pause to say that my understanding is that this is the case in respect of each of the 20 individual voluntary arrangements.

      '(5) The court may, whenever–

        (a) it is expedient to appoint a person to carry out the functions of the supervisor, and

E
        (b) it is inexpedient, difficult or impracticable for an appointment to be made without the assistance of the court,

      make an order appointing a person who is qualified to act as an insolvency practitioner in relation to the debtor, either in substitution for the existing supervisor or to fill a vacancy.'

F   I need not read the remainder of that subsection.

    The question is what, for the purposes of that subsection, is meant by 'the court'.

    Section 385(1) of the Act, which is the relevant definition provision, defines 'the court' as meaning:

      'in relation to any matter, the court to which, in accordance with section 373 in Part X and the rules, proceedings with respect to that matter are allocated or

G   transferred . . .'

    The reference to the 'rules' is to the *Insolvency Rules* 1986.

    Section 373 provides as follows:

      '(1) The High Court and the county courts have jurisdiction throughout England and Wales for the purposes of the Parts in this Group.

H
      (2) For the purposes of those Parts, a county court has, in addition to its ordinary jurisdiction, all the powers and jurisdiction of the High Court; and the orders of the court may be enforced accordingly in the prescribed manner.

      (3) Jurisdiction for the purposes of those Parts is exercised–

        (a) by the High Court in relation to the proceedings which, in accordance with the rules, are allocated to the London insolvency district, and

(b) by each county court in relation to the proceedings which are so allocated to   A
the insolvency district of that court.

(4) Subsection (3) is without prejudice to the transfer of proceedings from one court to another in the manner prescribed by the rules; and nothing in that subsection invalidates any proceedings on the grounds that they were initiated or continued in the wrong court.'

The Parts referred to in that section include Pt. VIII in which s. 263 is to be found. Part   B
VIII is concerned with individual voluntary arrangements.

In my view it is clear from s. 373(3) that the court which has jurisdiction for the purposes of Pt. VIII, and therefore which has jurisdiction under s. 263, is the court to which jurisdiction has been allocated in accordance with the Insolvency Rules.

Rule 5.5A of the *Insolvency Rules* 1986 is the relevant rule for the purposes of jurisdiction under Pt. VIII of the Act. So far as material that rule provides as follows: C

'(1) Except in the case of a bankrupt, an application to the court under Part VIII shall be made to a court in which the debtor would be entitled to present his own petition in bankruptcy under Rule 6.40.

. . .

(3) In the case of a bankrupt such an application shall be made to the court having the conduct of his bankruptcy and shall be filed with those bankruptcy   D
proceedings.'

Rule 6.40 of the Insolvency Rules, to which r. 5.5A(1) refers, is as follows:

'(1) In the following cases, the petition shall be presented to the High Court–

(a) if the debtor has resided or carried on business in the London insolvency district for the greater part of the 6 months immediately preceding the   E
presentation of the petition, or for a longer period in those 6 months than in any other insolvency district, or

(b) if the debtor is not resident in England and Wales.

(2) In any other case, the petition shall (subject to paragraph (3) below), be presented to the debtor's own county court, which is–

(a) the county court for the insolvency district in which he has resided or carried   F
on business for the longest period in those 6 months, or

(b) if he has for the greater part of those 6 months carried on business in one insolvency district and resided in another, the county court for that in which he has carried on business, or

(c) if he has during those 6 months carried on business in more than one insolvency district, the county court for that in which is, or has been for the   G
longest period in those 6 months, his principal place of business.

(3) If, in a case not falling within paragraph (1), it is more expedient for the debtor with a view to expediting his petition–

(a) it may in any case be presented to whichever court is specified by Schedule 2 to the Rules as being, in relation to the debtor's own court, the nearest full-time court, and   H

(b) it may alternatively, in a case falling within paragraph (2)(b), be presented to the court for the insolvency district in which he has resided for the greater part of the 6 months there referred to.

(3A) Notwithstanding any other provision of this Rule, where there is in force to the debtor a voluntary arrangement under Part VIII of the Act, the petition shall

A   be presented to the court to which the nominee's report under section 256 was submitted.'

I have no information about any of the 20 voluntary arrangements referred to in the schedule to the originating application except, as appears from that schedule, that each is described by reference to a county court in South Wales, principally Swansea County Court. Although this is not made clear by the evidence, reference to those courts is

B   presumably a reference to the court to which application was made, under s. 253 of the Act, for an interim order under s. 252 and to which therefore the nominee's report on the debtor's proposals would have been made under s. 256. There is nothing to suggest that that is not the position. It is also to be presumed, in the absence of any evidence to the contrary, that applications were made to those courts because, having regard to r. 5.5A, those were the appropriate courts to which to apply.

C   That being so r. 5.5A requires any application to the court under Pt. VIII of the Act, and therefore any application under s. 263(5), to be made to the particular county court referred to in the schedule in respect of the particular individual voluntary arrangement to which it relates. Since none is in the High Court I do not see that I have jurisdiction under s. 263(5) to make an order substituting Mr Stones for Mr Evans as supervisor of any of the 20 voluntary arrangements.

D   Mr Ritchie, while accepting that jurisdiction for the purposes of Pt. VIII of the Act, and therefore for the purposes of any application under s. 263(5), was indeed that of the relevant county court referred to in respect of each of the voluntary arrangements set out in the schedule to the originating application and not that of the High Court, submitted that, if nevertheless I made the order which he seeks, the order would not be without effect but, on the contrary, would be fully effective since, the proceedings in question which the Secretary of State has launched having been initiated in the wrong court,

E   s. 373(4) would apply to validate what would otherwise, having regard to s. 373(3), be an order made without jurisdiction.

I am not persuaded that s. 373(4) has any application to the circumstances of this case. If it has the effect for which Mr Ritchie contends, it would mean that subs. (3), and the division of jurisdiction between the High Court and the county court in accordance with the Insolvency Rules, could be altogether disregarded. In my view the subsection is concerned, as the first part of it makes clear, with transfers of proceedings and, in

F   particular, with the validity of proceedings in the court from which the proceedings have since been transferred. That is not this case. No question of any transfer of proceedings arises. I therefore see no basis for the application of that subsection.

I was also referred to r. 7.55 of the Insolvency Rules. That rule is concerned with formal defects and irregularities. I am unable to see that that rule has any application any more than s. 373(4) does. The plain fact of the matter is that I am being asked to

G   exercise a jurisdiction which, sitting in the High Court, I do not consider that I have.

I was also referred to the unreported decision in *Re Parkdawn Ltd*, decided on 15 June 1993. In that case Harman J made an order under s. 263(5) appointing a new supervisor of four individual voluntary arrangements to replace somebody who had fallen ill. It appeared from a letter in evidence before me from the solicitors involved in that case that the four individual voluntary arrangements in question related to arrangements in respect of which orders, presumably under s. 256, had been made in two different county courts,

H   in other words, in courts other than the High Court. The relevant passage from the judgment reads as follows:

'There are then four cases where Mr Warren is the supervisor of individual voluntary arrangements. Under s. 263(5) of the Act of 1986 the court may, whenever it is expedient, appoint a person to carry out the function of supervisor. This seems to me, plainly, a case where, in the four cases that are listed, it is

A   expedient to appoint the new office-holder in place of Mr Warren and I shall so order.'

Paying every respect to that expression of view, I do not, however, feel able to follow it. It is not clear that Harman J was taken to the various provisions of the Act and of the rules to which my attention has been drawn or what the reasoning was, apart from expedience, which persuaded him that he had jurisdiction to make the order in question.

B   With some regret therefore, particularly in view of the obvious expediency to which Harman J refers in the *Parkdawn* case, I do not feel able to make the order which the Secretary of State seeks in relation to the 20 individual voluntary arrangements. To that I would only add that if I had taken the view that I had the necessary jurisdiction, I would not have hesitated to make the order sought.

(Order accordingly)

C

D

E

F

G

H

A
Eagle Trust plc v SBC Securities Ltd & Anor.

Chancery Division.
Arden J.
Judgment delivered 28 July 1994.

> *Takeover – Rights issue – Constructive trust – Knowing receipt of trust property*
> *– Director used company money to meet sub-underwriting commitments –*
> *Whether underwriter received money as constructive trustee – Whether*
> *underwriter had actual knowledge of source of funds – Whether 'constructive*
> *knowledge' sufficient – Whether underwriter owed duties to company as financial*
> *adviser – Duties of skill and care owed by financial adviser.*

B

These were consolidated actions in which the plaintiff company sought to make the
defendants liable after the plaintiff's chief executive had sub-underwritten a rights issue by
the company and used company money to take up those shares. The defendants were
members of the same group of companies and respectively advised the company on the rights
issue and underwrote it.

C

The rights issue was part of a takeover bid by the company which included a cash
alternative offer. The underwriting agreement between the company and the defendants
imposed an obligation on the defendants to make the cash alternative offer and to purchase
the company's shares if they could not find other purchasers for them. Similarly the
defendants agreed to take up the shares offered by way of rights to existing shareholders
but not taken up by them, to the extent that they could not find other subscribers for them.
The company agreed to find sub-underwriters for roughly 25 per cent of the shares. In fact
the company struggled to find sub-underwriters. The 1987 stock market crash known as
'Black Monday' resulted in a severe reduction in the company's share price and meant that
most of the new shares would be taken up by the underwriters.

D

E

The company's chief executive, 'F', agreed to underwrite the balance of shares not taken
up by institutions, and since he had substantial business interests there was no reason to
doubt his ability to do so. F undertook to sub-underwrite 25.5m shares after Black Monday
at a loss of some £2.8m. At no stage was the company's board told formally of F's interest
as a sub-underwriter.

F

F used company money to discharge his underwriting obligations. He was subsequently
convicted of theft. The company argued that when the defendants received the company's
money from F they had actual or constructive knowledge that it was the company's money
and they accordingly held it as constructive trustees. Alternatively the company contended
that the defendants as financial advisers were in breach of various duties owed to the
company, such as to be satisfied that sub-underwriters could meet their commitments; to
ensure that the full board was informed of certain matters; to ensure full compliance with
legal and regulatory requirements for disclosure in listing particulars; and to exercise
caution when accepting sub-underwriting commitments from directors.

G

Held, dismissing the action:

1. In respect of the state of mind required to make the receiver of trust money a
constructive trustee, the defendants did not know or suspect that F had taken money from
the company to pay his sub-underwriting commitments. The defendants regarded him as an
honest and trustworthy man. So far as they were aware, there was no reason why he should

H

not have been able to raise the requisite funds from his business associates or on the security
of his other assets. The loss that he was to suffer was a large one in absolute terms but not
in the context of a businessman with major business assets. There was no motive shown for
the defendants to become knowingly involved in F's fraud: quite the reverse. It was not
shown that they either knew that the money was the company's money, or even that it was
probably the company's money, or that they wilfully shut their eyes to the obvious or

knowingly and recklessly failed to make the enquiries that a reasonable and honest man   A
would make.

2. In a 'knowing receipt' case, where receipt occurred in the discharge of a lawful debt
(at least one arising out of a transaction which did not itself constitute a breach of trust)
actual knowledge (including wilful blindness and failing to enquire) was required and the
company's claim based on 'constructive knowledge' failed.

3. The defendant owed no duty of care as financial adviser in respect of its decision as   B
underwriter to accept F and others as sub-underwriters. There was no 'industry standard'
applicable to define the circumstances in which disclosure to the board by a financial adviser
was necessary: it was within the apparent authority of executive directors to make an
agreement on behalf of the company to defer payment of the rights issue proceeds. The
financial adviser exercised reasonable care and skill in considering whether to disclose F's
interest as sub-underwriter. Unless specifically agreed the defendant's duty as a financial
adviser would not prevent it from accepting a director as a sub-underwriter even if his   C
commitment gave him a conflict of interest with the company or affected his abilities to
perform his duties as a director in some way.

The following cases were referred to in the judgment:

Agip (Africa) Ltd v Jackson & Ors [1991] Ch 547.
Baden & Ors v Société Générale pour Favoriser le Développement du Commerce et   D
de l'Industrie en France SA [1993] 1 WLR 509.
Belmont Finance Corp Ltd v Williams Furniture Ltd & Ors (No. 2) [1980] 1 All ER 393.
Blundell, Re (1888) 40 Ch 370.
Carl Zeiss Stiftung v Herbert Smith & Co & Anor (No. 2) [1969] 2 Ch 276.
Cowan de Groot Properties Ltd v Eagle Trust plc [1992] 4 All ER 700.
El Ajou v Dollar Land Holdings plc & Anor [1993] BCC 698.
Manchester Trust v Furness [1895] 2 QB 539.   E
Montagu's Settlement Trusts, Re [1987] Ch 264.
Polly Peck International plc v Nadir (No. 2) [1992] 4 All ER 769.
Sanders Bros v Maclean & Co (1883) 11 QBD 327.
Thomson & Ors (Trustees) v Clydesdale Bank Ltd [1893] AC 282.
Williams v Williams (1881) 17 ChD 437.

Richard McCombe QC and Craig Orr (instructed by Berwin Leighton) for the plaintiff.   F

Jonathan Sumption QC and Mark Hapgood QC (instructed by Linklaters & Paines)
for the defendants.

JUDGMENT

Arden J: Introduction

The claims in these consolidated actions arise out of the role played by the first   G
defendant (then called SBCI Savory Milln Ltd and hereafter referred to as 'Savory Milln')
in connection with the offer by the plaintiff (hereafter 'Eagle') in October 1987 to the
shareholders of Samuelson Group plc (hereafter 'Samuelson') to acquire their shares in
exchange for Eagle shares. Eagle was a small but acquisitive industrial conglomerate
listed on the Stock Exchange. Its chief executive was Mr John Ferriday. At the same time
as Eagle made its offer to Samuelson shareholders, Savory Milln on behalf of the second   H
defendant (hereafter 'SBCI') made an offer, which I shall call 'the cash alternative offer',
to accepting Samuelson shareholders to purchase for cash the Eagle shares to which they
became entitled. (Savory Milln and SBCI are members of the same group of companies.)
In addition Savory Milln advised the Eagle board in relation to the Samuelson offer.
Eagle's offer was recommended by the board of Samuelson. Simultaneously with the
Samuelson offer Eagle made a rights issue to its shareholders and this was underwritten

A   by SBCI. Savory Milln acting on behalf of SBCI arranged for SBCI's obligations to take Eagle shares under the cash alternative offer and rights issue to be sub-underwritten. In the event, the sub-underwriters were called on to take up shares. The plaintiff's claim is that certain payments in discharge of sub-underwriting obligations came from Eagle and were a misuse of its funds. The plaintiff contends that the defendants are liable to compensate it accordingly.

B   The principal individuals who participate in these events are the directors of Eagle, and representatives of Savory Milln. Apart from Mr Ferriday, the directors of Eagle were Mr Leslie John Thomas (chairman), Mr M C Baker (finance director), Mr Richard E Smith (managing director), Mr Robert Laurie Black (operations director), Mr Clive P Whiley (corporate development director), and three non-executive directors: Mr Hamish Timothy Warren Janson, Dr D Hardwick and Mr D M Saunders. The secretary of Eagle was Mr Alan Storey Beaumont. Mr Charles Alfred Richard Gillams, associate director

C   in Savory Milln's corporate finance department, was in day to day charge of these matters on behalf of Savory Milln until early December 1987. He was a chartered accountant by training with three years' experience in company investigations and three years' experience in corporate finance. During his time as a trainee accountant he had been involved in auditing. In charge of the corporate finance department was David George Tree who had been appointed director of Savory Milln's corporate finance department in mid-1987, having been engaged in other aspects of Savory Milln's business since 1971.

D   He and Mr Gillams shared an office, but it was not Mr Tree's function to supervise Mr Gillams. He took over from Mr Gillams when the time came to recover money from the sub-underwriters. At all material times, the solicitors to Eagle were Lovell White & King (now Lovell White Durrant). Mr John Cooper, a partner, was principally concerned on their behalf. All these individuals, save Mr Ferriday, Mr Whiley, Mr Baker, Dr Hardwick and Mr Saunders, gave evidence, the defendants calling Mr Gillams and Mr Tree.

E   Further witnesses were called as follows. The plaintiff called Mr Mark Singleton Evans as an expert on the duties of Savory Milln as a financial adviser. It also called Mr Ian Charles Lowe and Mr Andrew John Rose, partners in Berwin Leighton, its solicitors, to prove prior statements made by Mr Gillams. In addition, the statement of Robert Tennant-Ralphs, an employee of Jefferies & Co (who as later appears were sub-underwriters to the issue), adduced by the plaintiff, was accepted by all parties as evidence without need for the witness to be called. The defendants also called Mr Danny Thomas

F   Claridge, a senior cashier at Savory Milln. It will be evident that events have been retold in court in the absence of a number of material witnesses.

     The most important witness for Savory Milln was Mr Gillams. His experience in financial services, when compared with that of Mr Tree, was relatively brief. Given his relatively brief experience, that he was responsible for getting the offer and rights issue launched is impressive. It was one of the largest underwritings Savory Milln had done.

G   On the other hand, Mr Gillams did not reap the benefit of his apparent success. He was in due course declared redundant by Savory Milln and he is now working for Howmac, Mr Saunders' company. On a number of points, when challenged, he modified his story. I attribute this to a difficulty in recalling with the requisite precision events long past which were not recorded contemporaneously in file notes or memoranda. I have however had to exercise caution before finding any facts based solely on his evidence. The plaintiff invited me to take the same course with Mr Tree. I do not propose to do so. In my

H   judgment Mr Tree was a helpful and reliable witness in so far as he had any recollection of events.

Events surrounding Mr Ferriday's sub-underwriting

     I now set out the facts as I find them to be. Savory Milln were Eagle's stockbrokers. Their first involvement in the Samuelson acquisition was on Friday, 9 October 1987,

when Mr Gillams had a meeting with Mr Whiley. Savory Milln were instructed to act as   A
financial advisers in connection with the Samuelson acquisition. They agreed, and
advised on the structure of the offer. They also advised that Eagle should make an
underwritten rights issue to raise money whose purpose would be, and was in due course
stated in the documentation sent to shareholders to be, to reduce Samuelson's
indebtedness. Savory Milln, as agents for SBCI, agreed to act as underwriter to the rights
issue and to make the cash alternative offer. The fee structure for the underwriting (to
which I refer below) was agreed. SBCI's and Savory Milln's intention was to take steps   B
to allocate the underwriting to sub-underwriters and thus to take no risk themselves on
the underwriting. Savory Milln did not advise on the commercial merits of the
acquisition. The Samuelson acquisition had been introduced to Eagle by Guardian
Investments Ltd, an offshore company in which Mr Martin Boston, a solicitor and senior
partner in the firm of Martin Boston & Co, solicitors, was believed to be beneficially
interested. Eagle agreed to pay a fee for this introduction of £1m, or, if less, three per   C
cent of the price paid by Eagle for any Samuelson shares acquired subject to a maximum
of £1.25m.

Eagle had already made a number of acquisitions with Mr Ferriday at the helm. He
had become chief executive in April 1987. He was responsible for Eagle's acquisition
strategy: he played no real part in managing the group's existing businesses. He was
popularly regarded as skilled in acquisitions and it was understood that sufficient   D
shareholders would follow any recommendation of his to enable a resolution to be passed
by the company in general meetings. Within Eagle, he was autocratic in his management
style. He had a highly persuasive and self-assured manner.

After a considerable amount of activity over the weekend, involving the directors of
Eagle and principally Mr Gillams on behalf of Savory Milln, the underwriting agreement
between Eagle, Savory Milln and SBCI was signed in the early hours of Monday, 12   E
October 1987. The signatories on behalf of SBCI on the counterpart to be given to Eagle
were Mr Anthony Northrop, a director of SBCI, and Mr John Raubenheimer, in-house
legal counsel to SBCI. Mr Tree signed the underwriting agreement on behalf of Savory
Milln. The executed parts were not delivered until early afternoon on the following day
and one of the issues is the reason for this delay.

The underwriting agreement imposed an obligation on the defendants to make the
cash alternative offer to the Samuelson shareholders and to purchase the Eagle shares   F
involved if they could not find other purchasers for them. Similarly the defendants agreed
to take up the Eagle shares offered by way of rights to existing Eagle shareholders but
not taken up by them, to the extent that they could not find other subscribers for them.
There were a number of warranties, but no force majeure clause. Commission was
payable to the defendants (variable according to the period of their commitment), with a
reduction where Eagle itself introduced persons as sub-underwriters. Savory Milln and   G
Eagle had made similar arrangements in relation to previous acquisitions. Over the
weekend of 10/11 October, Mr Ferriday told Savory Milln that Mr Martin Boston,
Earnshaw Haes & Sons (hereafter 'Earnshaw Haes') and Jefferies & Co would, on Eagle's
introduction, each sub-underwrite 16.7m new Eagle shares approximately. In other
words, Eagle agreed to find sub-underwriters for 50m shares, roughly 25 per cent of the
shares that could be issued under the offer and rights issue.

At 9.23 am on 12 October 1987, there was a press announcement of the terms of   H
Eagle's offer for the shares of Samuelson. This offer was conditional inter alia upon
approval by Eagle shareholders at an extraordinary general meeting (EGM). Eagle had
agreed the terms of the offer with the board of Samuelson, and it held irrevocable
acceptances from holders of some 26 per cent of Samuelson's issued share capital. (By 14
October 1987 Eagle had purchased shares or held irrevocable acceptances in respect of

A   shares representing 50.01 per cent of Samuelson's issued share capital.) The press release
referred to the cash alternative offer to be made by SBCI and to the rights issue to be
underwritten by SBCI. (There was also a purchase invitation to existing Eagle
shareholders entitling them to apply for shares acquired by SBCI under the cash
alternative offer.) In the aftermath of the Samuelson offer, when Savory Milln was
conducting internal enquiries as to its group's underwriting arrangements with Eagle, Mr
Northrop contended, with the concurrence of Mr Raubenheimer, in a note to their senior

B   colleagues at Savory Milln (for which a Civil Evidence Act notice was given) endorsed
on Mr Gillams' memorandum dated 8 December 1987, referred to below, that Mr
Northrop had told Mr Gillams that SBCI was only happy with the underwriting going
ahead 'if the 20 per cent underwriting "taken" by Eagle was confirmed in writing *prior* to
launch on Monday morning', i.e. if the underwriters whom Eagle had said it would
introduce confirmed their commitments in writing prior to the launch on 12 October

C   1987. This did not happen (nor indeed did it happen before Mr Gillams handed over the
executed underwriting agreement). If such instructions were given, there would then be
some explanation why Mr Gillams retained the underwriting agreement signed by the
defendants after execution. However, unless Mr Gillams was deliberately disobeying
instructions, of which instructions neither he nor Mr Tree had any recollection, it would
not explain why Mr Gillams, having initially retained the signed copies of the
underwriting agreement, distributed them before he had those confirmations. Neither Mr

D   Northrop nor Mr Raubenheimer was called to give evidence. As appears above, I find
Mr Gillams' recollection of some events to be imperfect. Notwithstanding this, on this
particular issue I accept Mr Gillams' evidence that he did not have instructions that the
defendants were not to be bound to the underwriting agreement unless confirmations
from the sub-underwriters introduced by Eagle were received prior to the press release.
There is no evidence which bears out the contention made by Mr Northrop and Mr
Raubenheimer. Mr Northrop may have advised Mr Gillams that this should be done.

E   But, given that SBCI had apparently accepted the principle that it would commit itself to
the underwriting agreement before sub-underwriters had been approached, Mr Gillams
had in my judgment sufficient authority to decide for himself what evidence of the
commitment of Eagle-introduced underwriters he would accept.

I find that in the course of the morning – after the press launch – Mr Gillams made
some basic enquiries as to the status of the Eagle-introduced underwriters, and, then,

F   seeing that the sub-underwriting appeared to be going reasonably well in the course of
the morning he released the underwriting agreement. Mr Gillams' actions in holding on
to the underwriting agreement were misguided. Once the press announcement was made
it was effectively too late for the defendants to say that they were not bound by the
underwriting agreement. Mr Gillams clearly did not appreciate this at the time of the
transaction. I further find that he took no step to obtain written confirmations from the

G   Eagle-introduced sub-underwriters until after the release of the underwriting agreements.
In my judgment he was swayed into accepting the names of the Eagle-introduced sub-
underwriters without evidence of their commitment from them by the powerful
personality of Mr Ferriday. Mr Gillams' evidence was that he did not receive the names
of the Eagle-introduced underwriters until the Monday morning. The plaintiff called no
direct evidence to support their allegation that Mr Ferriday had given him the names
over the weekend. So far as I can see very little turns on this point, and I am content to

H   accept Mr Gillams' evidence on it.

The marketing operation for the shares to be sub-underwritten went well on the
morning of 12 October 1987 but in the afternoon there was increasing resistance. At the
end of the afternoon, Savory Milln had failed to find sub-underwriters for 35m Eagle
shares. Mr Gillams telephoned Mr Ferriday to enquire if he had reserve sub-underwriting
capacity, and Mr Ferriday said that he would find sub-underwriters for a further 20m

shares. In the event, he found sub-underwriters who confirmed their commitments for a   A
further 15m shares as follows: Coast Securities, 3m; Standard Chartered Bank, 2m; Bank
of Bermuda, 10m.

In addition Mr Saunders arranged for his company Howmac plc to participate for a
further 1m shares and Earnshaw Haes further increased their commitment by 5m shares
as appears below.

Letters of confirmation were sent to sub-underwriters for them to sign confirming the   B
number of shares they were willing to take. Confirmations were received from the original
three Eagle-introduced sub-underwriters for 33m shares only, not 50m as indicated by
Mr Ferriday. On 12 October 1987, Mr Boston returned his form confirming a
commitment for only 11m shares. On 14 October 1987, Jefferies & Co returned their
letter of confirmation in which they drastically reduced the number of shares they were
willing to take to 1m. On 12 October 1987, however, a commitment signed in the name   C
of Earnshaw Haes had been received for 21m shares. Subsequently, on 19 October 1987,
further confirmation signed in the name of Earnshaw Haes was received for 5m shares.
Mr Ferriday had therefore indicated that he could introduce sub-underwriters for 16m
shares more than he had been able to do.

On 19 October 1987 the Stock Exchange crash known as 'Black Monday' occurred.
This resulted in a severe and, in the period in which the events material to this action
occurred, permanent reduction in share values on the Stock Exchange. The Eagle share   D
price fell from 37.5p (the price shown in the *Financial Times* at the close of the last dealing
day prior to announcement of the Samuelson offer) to 23.5p, which was below the offer
price of 39p per share under the rights issue and also the value (in the same sum) placed
on an Eagle share for the purposes of the cash alternative offer. It was thereafter likely
that, unless the share price recovered, most of the new Eagle shares would have to be
taken up by underwriters.   E

The share price did not recover, and Mr Tree and Mr Gillams formed the view that for
Eagle to continue with the Samuelson offer on the existing terms would jeopardise its
ability to make further acquisitions for shares in the immediate future. Sub-underwriters
would have to take up substantial numbers of shares which they would want to sell and
this would depress the Eagle share price. In Savory Milln's view, there was a serious
question-mark over the transaction and, in order that no one should be misled, members   F
of the corporate finance department were forbidden to discuss the question of its
proceeding with outside bodies. On 29 October 1987, the board of Eagle met and gave
further consideration to the Samuelson acquisition in the light of Black Monday. Mr
Saunders declared his interest in the sub-underwriting. Mr Ferriday addressed the
meeting on the commercial merits of the acquisition. At a later point, Mr Gillams and
Mr Tree joined the meeting to explain their views. Mr Tree addressed the meeting and
expressed the views of Savory Milln and indeed went so far as to try to persuade the   G
board not to proceed. Having heard Mr Gillams and Mr Tree in the witness box, I am
satisfied that their views were reasonably and genuinely held. I do not find proved the
plaintiff's allegation that Savory Milln's advice on 29 October 1987 was 'not genuine or
proper' but motivated by its desire to minimise its liability as underwriter. After Mr Tree
had addressed the board, Mr Tree and Mr Gillams left the board meeting. The Eagle
board, however, decided to proceed with the Samuelson acquisition and rights issue on   H
the terms announced. The necessary documentation was approved by the board on 4
November 1987. The Eagle board recommended shareholders to vote in favour of the
Samuelson acquisition. Savory Milln were named as the board's advisers. This does not,
as the plaintiff alleges, support the allegation that the advice given to the board on 29
October was not genuine or proper. Mr Tree had expressed Savory Milln's view but the
board concluded that the commercial merits of the acquisition outweighed the

A disadvantages in Savory Milln's eyes. Savory Milln had not been involved in the commercial merits of the acquisition and it could therefore properly defer to the board's view on the matters overall. The board were reminded by Mr Cooper that on the question whether the transaction should proceed there was a conflict of interest between Savory Milln's position as financial adviser and its position as underwriter.

B Under the rules of the City Code on Takeovers and Mergers the document containing Eagle's offer had to be posted to Samuelson's shareholders on or before Monday, 9 November 1987. Savory Milln was still working to obtain outstanding confirmations of sub-underwriting commitments on the preceding Friday, 6 November 1987. An internal memorandum dated 6 November 1987 and prepared by Mr Edward Seager, who was employed by Savory Milln in its corporate finance department, shows that Savory Milln had not then received written confirmations of sub-underwriting commitments from, among others, Bank of Bermuda and Mr Ferriday. The material parts of the memorandum are as follows:

C

'To: Corporate Finance Department
From: Edward Seager
6 November 1987

SUBJECT	STATUS	RESPONSIBILITY
BANK OF BERMUDA Written confirmation of underwriting commitment	to be received by 5pm	CARG to organise via JF.
JF Written confirmation of underwriting commitment	to be received by 5pm	CARG
OTHER SUBUNDERWRITERS Written confirmation of underwriting commitment	By fax today and in writing subsequently	RC

. . .

NOTES:

. . .

G The transaction will not proceed unless Eagle Trust plc ensure the underwriting organised under their auspices has been completed, and evidence of this is offered in writing.

E.S.'

(The initials CARG are Mr Gillams' initials.)

H Mr Seager did not give evidence and there was no evidence as to the source of the information in his notes. Mr Gillams was not asked in cross-examination if he told Mr Ferriday that the transaction would not proceed if the Eagle-introduced underwriters did not produce written confirmation of their underwriting commitments. (Indeed in his witness statement Mr Gillams denies that he made any threat to withdraw from the underwriting unless Mr Ferriday personally underwrote the shortfall.) Mr Tree was asked whether the threat was communicated to Mr Ferriday but he was unable to answer from

his own knowledge. There is no evidence on which I find that the substance of Mr
Seager's note was communicated to Mr Ferriday.

It is apparent that Savory Milln had been let down by Eagle. Eagle had confidently
assured Savory Milln over the weekend of 10/11 October 1987 that they could introduce
underwriters for first 50m, and then subsequently 70m shares. There was now a shortfall
of 16m shares. If Mr Ferriday had been under the impression that Savory Milln and
SBCI would block the issue of the offer documentation and had given a sub-underwriting
commitment simply to appease them, the question might arise whether Savory Milln
were not on notice that Mr Ferriday had acted without regard to his own financial
position. This is not, however, what is alleged against Savory Milln. It is said that Mr
Gillams asked Mr Ferriday to take up the shortfall (which was stated to be 14.5m shares)
and that Savory Milln were keen that Mr Ferriday should do this for two reasons:

(1) to reduce their uncovered exposure, and

(2) to give him an incentive to vote against the Samuelson acquisition at the Eagle
     EGM.

The plaintiff also alleges that Mr Ferriday agreed to underwrite the 14.5m shares as a
favour to Mr Gillams, in the belief that he would prevent Mr Gillams from losing his job
because he had accepted Jefferies & Co without checking whether they were prevented
by US securities law from sub-underwriting. This is the case the defendants must meet.

Mr Gillams says that in a telephone conversation in the course of 6 November 1987,
Mr Ferriday asked Mr Gillams if the sub-underwriting was complete. Mr Gillams replied
that there was a shortfall of 14.5m shares and Mr Ferriday offered to sub-underwrite
these shares and thereafter signed a confirmation to that effect, which was faxed to
Savory Milln late that afternoon. (Given the wording of the memorandum, the first page
of which Mr Gillams accepts he saw, I consider this conversation must have taken place
before the memorandum was prepared.) Mr Ferriday's confirmation increased the
number of shares in respect of which Eagle had introduced sub-underwriters to 69.5m
which was beyond the 50m shares originally agreed. Mr Ferriday agreed to give this
confirmation personally because despite many requests from Savory Milln he had been
unable to come up with details of other sub-underwriters ('shapes and sizes' as Mr
Gillams put it). The parties contemplated that he might subsequently find sub-
underwriters who would then be substituted for him.

I do not find proved the plaintiff's assertion that Savory Milln had a scheme to put Mr
Ferriday in a position whereby he would vote against the Samuelson acquisition. The
suggestion is that this would enable Savory Milln to be discharged from their obligations
under the underwriting agreement and thus avoid the risk that other sub-underwriters
might renege. There was no evidence from within Savory Milln that Mr Gillams would
have lost his job because he accepted Jefferies & Co. (Indeed although Mr Gillams said
at Mr Ferriday's trial that Jefferies & Co had withdrawn because of problems in the US
he later admitted that was speculation, and Mr Tennant-Ralphs' statement shows that
Jefferies & Co had European clients to whom they sought to allocate the sub-
underwriting). I find that in the course of a conversation in which Mr Gillams pressed
for the 'shapes and sizes', Mr Ferriday volunteered to be a sub-underwriter for the
balance. He did this because he could not fulfil his promises to Savory Milln.

The table set out below shows that on share values at 6 November 1987 Mr Ferriday
stood to make a loss of £1.45m. Mr Gillams knew that but it did not occur to him to
question Mr Ferriday's ability to be a sub-underwriter. Mr Ferriday had other apparently
substantial business interests (including shareholdings in Paramount Airways and in
Wolverhampton Wanderers Football Club), a shareholding in Eagle worth
approximately £4m and an expensive lifestyle. Mr Gillams understandably took him to
be a wealthy man. I accept this evidence even though Mr Gillams appears to have told

A   Berwin Leighton in 1989 that Savory Milln did not know about Mr Ferriday's non-Eagle assets in 1987; I consider it is more likely than not that these would have come to Mr Gillams' knowledge by November 1987. Mr Tree likewise regarded Mr Ferriday as a wealthy man. Moreover, Mr Whiley later assured Mr Tree that Mr Ferriday would not take on a commitment which he could not meet. Mr Gillams, at least, was aware that Mr Ferriday shared his commitments 50:50 with his partner Mr Robert Smith, who Mr Gillams also believed to have substantial wealth outside Eagle. Mr Gillams did not know

B   what Mr Ferriday's assets were worth, but that is not surprising.

      Mr Gillams must, however, have been concerned about the shortfall of 14.5m shares until Mr Ferriday took it up. It was always the intention of SBCI or Savory Milln that the underwriting should be fully sub-underwritten. Mr Gillams sought to allay any suggestion of concern about this period by saying that he was confident that the ultimate holding company, Swiss Bank Corporation, 'could, in a worst case scenario, take a

C   "knock" on its balance sheet to the extent of this shortfall'. I am not satisfied that Mr Gillams was in an appropriate position to be unconcerned about the shortfall for that reason. In my judgment, he must have been worried that he would not find sub-underwriters for the shortfall.

      The sub-underwriting confirmation signed by Mr Ferriday does not contain any figures for the number of shares for which he was underwriting. This is consistent with his

D   underwriting the 'swing' as Mr Gillams called it, or the balance not taken up by the institutions.

      Late in the afternoon of 6 November 1987, Mr Boston faxed a letter to Mr Ferriday and one of his partners wrote to Savory Milln on his behalf. The material parts of Mr Boston's letter to Mr Ferriday are as follows:

E   'I am writing in regard to the sub-underwriting participation which I have taken on. This as you know was taken on on the basis of your agreement with me to indemnify me and to take any shares which I acquire pursuant to the sub-underwriting if I should call upon you to do so at any time within six months of 12 October 1987 at 30p per share. At the time you of course told me that the offer and rights issue would not go ahead unless I took sub-underwriting participation and further you told me that you personally would be sub-underwriting a total of 20m shares. Further you told me that all directors and major shareholders would

F   take up their rights and would participate in the purchase invitation. It was of course only on the basis of your agreement with me and on the basis of representations regarding the taking up of rights etc to which I refer above that I agreed to participate in the sub-underwriting and of course Savory Milln were fully aware that it was only upon the basis of your agreements with me and of the representations made by you (and indeed by them) that I took up the sub-underwriting.

G   I am obviously conscious of the movement in the share price of the company shares and also the general dramatic change in the financial and economic climate. I feel it is only right and proper to write to you at this stage, bearing in mind your agreement to indemnify me and to take shares if I call on you to do so. I have given some thought to the position of the underwriter and the sub-underwriters, and it seems to me that the underwriter must give serious consideration to invoking

H   any force majeure clause which, I assume in the usual way, is included in the underwriting agreements. Further I consider that the underwriter should exercise his duties as the agent of the sub-underwriters with all due care and in the interests of sub-underwriters.

      I have not of course seen the draft offer and rights issue documentation but I take it that they include the directors' undertakings in regard to taking up their rights

and also in regard to participating in the purchase invitation. I also assume that
full disclosure is given in the documentation about your agreement to indemnify
me and to take such shares as I shall call upon you to take at any time within six
months of 12 October, and further that disclosure is given of your sub-
underwriting 20m shares.'

As foreshadowed in Mr Boston's letter, the letter from Martin Boston & Co to Savory
Milln invited them to consider invoking the force majeure clause and asserted that they
owed a duty to sub-underwriters to do so. The letter was faxed to Mr Ferriday also on 6
November 1987.

Mr Ferriday immediately took advice on this letter from Mr Cooper. He confirmed to
Mr Cooper that he had indeed agreed to sub-underwrite 20m shares. Mr Cooper was
concerned that Mr Ferriday had made an arrangement with Mr Boston which ought to
have been disclosed in the listing particulars. He was also concerned that in making those
arrangements, Mr Ferriday had been acting on behalf of Eagle. Mr Ferriday denied that
he had made any such arrangements as Mr Boston alleged either personally or on behalf
of Eagle. Mr Cooper and Mr Gillams discussed the matter and Mr Gillams saw the letter
from Martin Boston & Co. Mr Gillams and Mr Cooper accepted Mr Ferriday's
assurance that no indemnity had been given. Subsequently at Mr Cooper's request Mr
Ferriday confirmed in writing to Mr Cooper and Mr Gillams that he had not given Mr
Boston any indemnity or undertaking, whether privately or on behalf of Eagle. The
posting of the offer document accordingly went ahead as planned on 9 November 1987.
Eagle shareholders were simultaneously sent a document explaining (inter alia) the
reasons for the offer and convening an EGM. The circular accompanying the notice of
meeting stated that the Eagle board 'which had been advised in relation to the offer by
Savory Milln' considered the acquisition of Samuelson to be in the best interests of Eagle
and recommended Eagle shareholders to vote in favour of the resolutions to be proposed
at the extraordinary general meeting. No reference was made in the documentation sent
to Samuelson shareholders or that sent to Eagle shareholders or in the listing particulars
to Mr Ferriday's sub-underwriting commitments. However, full particulars of the
underwriting agreement, including the rebate on commission for Eagle-introduced
underwriters appeared in the listing particulars sent to both sets of shareholders.

The letter from Martin Boston & Co to Savory Milln was delivered by hand to Savory
Milln on 9 November 1987. Mr Gillams made a report by letter to (among others) Mr
Howard Hughes, managing director of Savory Milln. He stated that in his opinion the
letter was an attempt to evade underwriting obligations. He stated that full consideration
had been given 'to the desirability of proceeding with the issue as requested by Mr
Boston'. What Martin Boston & Co had demanded was consideration of the sub-
underwriters' position, not that of Eagle. I am satisfied that Savory Milln would have
considered whether, in the light of the changed situation following Black Monday, it
could withdraw from its sub-underwriting position but, as already noted, there was no
force majeure clause (or indeed any other relevant right of withdrawal) in the sub-
underwriting agreement.

As a result of this incident, Mr Cooper became aware that Mr Ferriday was
'personally' sub-underwriting 20m shares. Mr Cooper says that he took this to be a
reference to Mr Ferriday introducing sub-underwriters for this number of shares, and
that his own personal commitment was a token one. Mr Gillams did not at any stage ask
Mr Cooper to advise on this question and in my judgment he did not do so because he
understood from a previous transaction that a director's interest as sub-underwriter did
not have to be disclosed. (He accepted, however, in his evidence at Mr Ferriday's trial
that the scale of Mr Ferriday's underwriting rendered it a material transaction which
should have been disclosed.) However, Mr Cooper did not need instructions from Mr

A Gillams to consider this question. Once he was told the facts he would naturally have considered the question of disclosure. Shortly after this incident Mr Cooper became aware that Mr Ferriday was proposing to take on a sub-underwriting commitment for 11m shares. He decided that his commitment was not disclosable because the market price per share was below the offer price. His reasoning was that no one would be influenced in their investment decision by what a director did if that position obtained. In my judgment, this was the view which he reached on 6 November 1987 in respect of

B Mr Ferriday's sub-underwriting commitment for 20m. In my judgment he must be mistaken in his recollection of the size of the commitment at the time. Mr Cooper's view when he gave evidence was that if he had been told that Mr Ferriday had agreed to sub-underwrite 50m shares before the listing particulars were issued, he would have caused a reference to the sub-underwriting commitment to be included, thus abandoning his earlier argument based on the market price. Mr Sumption QC for the defendants argued that

C Mr Cooper was simply expressing this view out of an abundance of caution. In my judgment he was clearly referring to the obligation to include matters in listing particulars as opposed to the obligation to issue supplementary listing particulars (with which he did not deal). In conclusion at this stage, I find that Mr Cooper concluded for legal reasons that Mr Ferriday's underwriting commitment was not disclosable on 6 November 1987. If his advice was wrong, that is not a matter for which Savory Milln can be held responsible.

D Mr Ferriday agreed to sub-underwrite a further 11m shares in the following circumstances. Not long after the incident involving Mr Boston, Mr Ferriday agreed to assume liability as sub-underwriter for a further 11m shares in place of Mr Boston and Savory Milln concurred in the arrangement, in which Mr Cooper was involved, which resulted in Mr Boston's release from such liability. Accordingly, to Savory Milln's certain knowledge, Mr Ferriday had undertaken to sub-underwrite 25.5m Eagle shares after

E Black Monday and at a certain loss of some £2.8m. In return for Mr Ferriday assuming his sub-underwriting obligations, Mr Boston procured Guardian Investments Ltd to accept an unconditional payment of £250,000 in lieu of the fee to which it had previously been entitled for introducing Samuelson to Eagle. The revised commission arrangements were approved by the Eagle board on 25 November 1987 but no reference was then made to Mr Ferriday taking over Mr Boston's sub-underwriting obligations. Mr Gillams,

F however, was aware of what he called 'the counter-trade'.

The arrangement was clearly disadvantageous on its face to Mr Ferriday. The defendants however rely on this transaction as showing that they can have had no doubt about Mr Ferriday's ability to meet his sub-underwriting obligations since they were accepting him as underwriter for a further 11m shares. In my judgment, they did not specifically address this issue. Their major concern was to remove the possibility of

G default by a significant sub-underwriter. On the other hand Mr Gillams did not in fact think that Mr Ferriday would take all the 25.5m shares beneficially since he and Mr Smith shared stakes of this nature and Mr Ferriday had told Mr Gillams between 6 and 30 November 1987 that the shares resulting from his sub-underwriting would be shared between him and Mr Smith. Moreover he believed as I have already said that Mr Ferriday was a man of substance. Mr Gillams had no reason to doubt Mr Ferriday's honesty at this stage.

H At about this time Mr Cooper prepared a paper showing how the Samuelson offer might be restructured so as not to involve the issue of shares. However, as Mr Cooper accepted when he gave evidence, it was not realistic to restructure the offer. However a meeting was held at the office of Lovell White & King on 19 November 1987 attended by Mr Cooper, two colleagues from Lovell, White & King, Mr Thomas, Mr Whiley and Mr Ferriday. The object of the meeting was to consider ways in which the damage to Eagle

forecast by Savory Milln could be minimised. Lovell White & King prepared a conference   **A**
note. Paragraph 1 of the note reads:

> '1. The current major shareholders list of Eagle was compared with the sub-underwriting list (so far as we knew it) and it was found to overlap in only a limited number of cases, notably Kuwait Investment Office, M & O Group, Banko Nominees, Pearl Assurance and Henderson Management. It was agreed that the principal shareholders should be approached and asked to take action to support   **B** the board at the EGM.'

The question which arises is whether the meeting had a list of sub-underwriters showing Mr Ferriday's name. Mr Cooper's evidence is that he believed Mr Ferriday to be a sub-underwriter only for the 11m shares taken over from Mr Boston. In fact Mr Ferriday had also personally agreed to sub-underwrite a further 14.5m shares. The difference is important because Mr Cooper's evidence is (as I read his witness statement) that if he   **C** had known that Mr Ferriday was sub-underwriting 25.5m shares he would have ensured that that fact was disclosed in the listing particulars and brought to the attention of the board. Mr Cooper's evidence on the sub-underwriting list however is that the meeting on 19 November 1987 did not have a physical list, that for the major shareholders the meeting looked at the names of the substantial shareholders disclosed in the listing particulars (which disclosed only Bank of Kuwait Nominees Ltd with 9.1 per cent and Barclays Nominees (M & G Group) Ltd with 5.2 per cent) and that the names of sub-   **D** underwriters were simply provided orally by Mr Whiley, who was working closely with Savory Milln. Mr Thomas could not recollect the meeting at all. None of the other attendees gave evidence. Each of the persons named in para. 1 of the conference note appears in the sub-underwriting list maintained by Savory Milln. Given the way that para. 1 is couched, I conclude that Mr Cooper's recollection is mistaken and that a list of sub-underwriters was available at the meeting and was inspected at it. Given the nature   **E** of the discussion (which was as to how shareholders would vote and whom Eagle could approach) I consider it is more likely than not that Mr Whiley or Mr Thomas would have gone through it. I am not however satisfied that Mr Cooper actually went through the list at this meeting. Furthermore, the conference note indicates that the list was not complete. There is no reference to Mr Ferriday's name. In the circumstances I am not satisfied that the list which the meeting had contained Mr Ferriday's name.

The Samuelson offer was conditional on certain ordinary resolutions being passed at   **F** an EGM of Eagle held on 25 November 1987. These resolutions were duly passed. The Samuelson offer was accordingly declared unconditional as to acceptances. The closing date for the rights issue was 30 November 1987.

When in 1989 Mr Gillams was interviewed by Berwin Leighton, Eagle's solicitors, he said (according to Berwin Leighton's attendance note) that when Mr Ferriday voted at the EGM it seemed to Savory Milln that he was voting for his own bankruptcy having   **G** regard to the number of shares which he had undertaken to underwrite. The attendance note prepared by Berwin Leighton next states that in Mr Gillams' view Mr Ferriday must have thought he could warehouse the shares and then sell them when the market went up. As soon as he received a copy of the attendance note Mr Gillams made the point that the comment on bankruptcy would only be made with hindsight. I accept that that is either what he said or what he should more accurately have said. It was not Savory   **H** Milln's view at the time that Mr Ferriday was voting for his own bankruptcy at the Eagle EGM on 25 November 1987. The fact that Mr Ferriday did not take steps to cause the resolutions to be defeated did not in my judgment give rise to a concern about whether Mr Ferriday would be able to meet his financial commitment but rather enhanced the impression already given to Savory Milln that he could carry out the acquisition, including meeting his own sub-underwriting commitments.

On 3 December 1987, the Eagle board met and all the directors were present, except Mr Saunders. At this meeting there was clearly some discussion of Mr Boston's claim as Mr Whiley is recorded in the minutes as having tabled a letter dated 6 November 1987 which he on behalf of Eagle had written in that connection and also Mr Ferriday's letter dated 6 November 1987 denying that he had given the alleged indemnity.

At no stage was the board told formally of Mr Ferriday's interest as a sub-underwriter. In his witness statement, Mr Gillams suggests that he had a conversation with Mr Thomas after the board meeting of 29 October 1987 in which he alluded to it. Mr Thomas denied the conversation and in any event at 29 October 1987 Mr Ferriday had no interest as a sub-underwriter. Mr Gillams sought to put a different interpretation on what he said but it is a strained explanation which I do not accept. On 3 December 1987, after the Samuelson offer became unconditional, a film about Samuelson was shown to a small audience including Mr Ferriday. Mr Thomas heard Mr Ferriday remark that he was one of the sub-underwriters. However this was simply a casual remark. It did not occur to Mr Thomas to pursue it. It is not the kind of remark which could put the board on notice as to the actual position as it turned out to be. However I am satisfied that Mr Baker, Mr Whiley and Mr Smith were aware that Mr Ferriday had undertaken to sub-underwrite a significant number of shares. Subject to this, at all material times prior to 10 March 1988 the Eagle board must be taken to have been unaware of the scale of Mr Ferriday's sub-underwriting commitments.

Savory Milln as underwriters were called on to take the vast majority of the shares issued under the rights issue and Samuelson offer. As a result of the cash alternative offer, Savory Milln was left with 117,514,260 new Eagle shares out of a total of 123,215,870 new Eagle shares allotted. The rights issue was taken up only as to 0.36 per cent so some 68m shares fell to be taken up by Savory Milln under the underwriting agreement.

The consideration in respect of the shares acquired under the cash alternative offer was due to be paid to the accepting shareholders on 21 December 1987. In respect of the rights issue, however, Savory Milln became obliged to make payments to Eagle. Under the terms of the underwriting agreement, these payments were due on 7 December 1987.

In late November 1987, however, Mr Gillams and Mr Whiley agreed that in principle Eagle would be flexible about the date for payment of the right issue proceeds. On 1 December 1987, Mr Gillams and Mr Baker agreed on the telephone that payment of the rights issue proceeds would not be made to Eagle until Savory Milln had itself received the corresponding proceeds from sub-underwriters. By a letter dated 1 December 1987 Mr Baker accordingly extended the time for payment by Savory Milln of the rights issue proceeds from 7 December 1987 until 16 December 1987.

In the aftermath of Black Monday it was not unknown for some indulgence to be extended to sub-underwriters who had cash flow difficulties. However none of Eagle's sub-underwriters were complaining of lack of liquidity; there was only one other underwriter who in the event contested his liability or who, like Mr Ferriday and Earnshaw Haes, made late payment. The impetus for the agreement to defer came from Savory Milln. Mr Gillams must have foreseen when he made the agreement that Mr Ferriday was one of those who would have liquidity problems. Having made the agreement to defer with Eagle, he passed the matter to Mr Tree. Mr Gillams was not immediately concerned thereafter but he must inevitably, in my view, have heard or overheard that Mr Ferriday was late in his payments to Savory Milln. The amounts which Mr Ferriday had committed himself to pay made that more than likely. Mr Gillams said in his evidence, and I accept, that nonetheless he did not conclude that Mr Ferriday was taking money from Eagle to meet his commitments until very much later. Eagle complains that Savory Milln did not disclose the deferment agreement to the board.

In my judgment, Mr Gillams was entitled to deal with Mr Whiley and Mr Baker without   A
obtaining the board's approval to the arrangement or informing the board. The
agreement was within the ostensible authority of those directors and the contrary has not
been suggested.

It then fell to Savory Milln to make demands on sub-underwriters. Mr Tree sent out
letters to sub-underwriters requesting payment by Friday, 11 December 1987.
Immediately prior to that date Mr Ferriday told Mr Tree that he would be arranging to   B
pay not only the money due from himself but also that due from Earnshaw Haes and
that it would arrive in stages. He requested that the moneys should be applied first
against the moneys due from Earnshaw Haes. Mr Tree thought that Mr Ferriday might
also have said that the money would be coming from a Jersey account. The amount due
from Mr Ferriday was £7,439,514.60 and from Earnshaw Haes the sum of £7,563,856.20.

On 8 December 1987, at the request of Mr Hughes, Mr Gillams prepared a long   C
memorandum of his recollection 'some time after the events of the chronology of the
Eagle Trust deal'. It concludes with the following statement:

> 'Problems on confirmation did not arise with the SM underwriting, however the
> c. 20% taken by Eagle did not include professional underwriters and problems did
> occur, all of which were satisfactorily handled.'

Specific mention is made of difficulties which had arisen on 12 October 1987. No   D
specific mention is made of any subsequent difficulty. Nor is there any reference to any
commitment undertaken by Mr Ferriday personally. In my judgment, the memorandum
is an attempt by Mr Gillams to minimise the difficulties that had arisen in order to avoid
criticism from his superiors. It did not fairly set out the matters which Mr Gillams would
have recollected. Even so, for the reasons already given, I am not satisfied that the note
which Mr Northrop added, on the basis of which the plaintiff contends Mr Gillams was
instructed to obtain written confirmations from Eagle-introduced sub-underwriters prior   E
to the launch, is accurate, if indeed that is how the note should be interpreted.

On 15 December 1987, Mr Tree wrote a weekly report to his management committee
on the outstanding position under the underwriting agreement. He referred to an
agreement with 'the company-nominated underwriters' to put Savory Milln in funds
before it paid the company. The only company-nominated sub-underwriter who had not
paid was in fact Mr Ferriday. The agreement was with Eagle, that it should not demand   F
payment until Savory Milln had been put in funds. Mr Tree's formulation did not make
it clear that there was no longer any scheduled date for payment to Eagle by Savory
Milln.

Each sub-underwriter was requested when making payment to quote a particular
account number. On 14, 16 and 18 December, Savory Milln received sums totalling
£13.5m at its account at the Lothbury branch of National Westminster Bank plc
(hereafter 'the bank'). The first two payments (for £2m and £3.5m respectively) were   G
made electronically. The bank advised Mr Claridge of the amounts received and quoted
a reference. The third payment was for £8m and was made via CHAPS. Mr Claridge was
informed of the receipt of this sum on 18 December 1987 but it was not until the next day
that he received a bank statement showing that the sum had come from Anser General
Investments SA (hereafter 'Anser'), a company owned by Mr Ferriday. However, Mr
Claridge knew that the moneys were for the account of Mr Ferriday whose reference had   H
been quoted.

On 16, 17 and 22 December 1987, Savory Milln made payments of £8m, £3.5m and
£8m respectively to Eagle in respect of proceeds of the rights issue.

I now turn to the circumstances of the receipt of the moneys due in respect of the sub-
underwriting obligations of Mr Ferriday and Earnshaw Haes. Payments in and out of

A   Savory Milln amounting to £50m to £100m per week were handled by the cashiers department. The sums of £2m and £3.5m were received by Savory Milln on 14 and 16 December 1987 by CHAPS (clearance house automated payment system). The amounts were credited to Savory Milln's account at the Lothbury branch of National Westminster Bank plc ('the bank'). The bank then telephoned Mr Claridge and gave him the reference accompanying payment which showed him that the payments were to discharge Earnshaw Haes' underwriting commitments. The bank statements show that these sums had come from Hambros Bank in Jersey.

B

   The further sum of £8m was received on 18 December 1987 by direct bank transfer to Savory Milln's account at the Lothbury branch of the bank. The bank telephoned Mr Claridge to inform him of the credit and on the next day Mr Claridge received an advice note from the bank showing that the moneys had come from Hambros Bank (Jersey) Ltd and that Hambros' customer was Anser. Mr Claridge made no connection between this

C   sum and the sum of £8m paid by Savory Milln to Eagle on 16 December 1987. The bank statements for the account into which the sums of £2m, £3.5m and £8m were paid show that the balance, when those sums are credited, was overdrawn although by the end of the day in which the credits were so paid respectively the account was in credit.

   There remained due from Mr Ferriday the sum of £1.25m. On 17 March 1988, Ferriday and Smith Holdings Ltd, a private holding company belonging to Mr Ferriday and Mr

D   Richard Smith, paid the sum of £1.25m in satisfaction of Mr Ferriday's outstanding sub-underwriting commitments. Savory Milln then made a final payment of £1.1m to Eagle in respect of the rights issue proceeds. This suggests that there must have been some understanding or arrangement between Savory Milln and Eagle that payment of the balance of the rights issue proceeds would not be made until this sum was discharged. There is no evidence that such an arrangement was made by Mr Gillams.

E   At its meeting on 10 March 1988, the board of Eagle was informed that Mr Ferriday and Mr Smith had each acquired 12,399,191 shares as a result of the sub-underwriting. None of the board members present at this meeting reacted to this disclosure with surprise or complained that the information should have been made available earlier.

   The following table demonstrates the very considerable loss which Mr Ferriday incurred at various dates as a result of sub-underwriting:

F

G

H

TABLE SHOWING MR FERRIDAY'S SUB-UNDERWRITING LOSS

Date/Event	Eagle share price X	Difference between share price and 30p XX	Amount called on Mr Ferriday (11.12.87)	Loss on sub-underwriting taken in Mr Ferriday's name	Amount called on Earnshaw Haes (11.12.87)	Loss on sub-underwriting taken in Earnshaw Haes' name XXX	Aggregate of loss of Mr Ferriday and Earnshaw Haes	Half share aggregate loss XXXX
9 October 1987 (last dealing day before Eagle announced its offer for Samuelson)	37.5p	–	–	–	–	–	–	–
20 October 1987 (day after 'Black Monday')	23.50p	6.5p	–	–	–	£1.69m	–	–
6 November 1987 (day on which Mr Ferriday personally undertook to sub-underwrite 14.5m shares)	20.00p	10p	–	£1.45m	–	£2.6m	£4.05m	£2.025m
9 November 1987 (date of offer document and listing particulars in which Mr Ferriday's sub-underwriting commitment was not disclosed)	16.50p	13.5p	–	£1,957,500	–	£2.6m	£5,467,500	£2,733,750
13 November 1987 (day Mr Ferriday took over Mr Boston's commitment to sub-underwrite 11m shares making Mr Ferriday's total commitment in his own name 25.5m shares)	19.00p	11p	–	£2,805,000	–	£2.86m	£5.665m	£2,832,500
25 November 1987 (Date of Eagle EGM)	17.25p	12.75p	–	£3,251,250	–	£3,315,000	£6,566,250	£3,283,125
1 December 1987 (Date of Mr Baker's letter to Mr Gillams)	17.00p	13p	£7,439,514.60p	£3,315,000	£7,563,856.20p	£3.38m	£6,695,000	£3,347,500
10 March 1988 (Day before Stock Exchange announcement of Mr Ferriday's and Mr Smith's acquisition of 12,399,191 shares each under the sub-underwriting arrangements)	19.00p	11p	–	£2,805,000	–	£2.86m	£5.665m	£2,832,500

Notes:

X   On the Stock Exchange. Figures supplied by the plaintiff.

XX   30p was the price per share (excluding commission) which underwriters and sub-underwriters undertook to pay.

XXX   In early December 1987 Mr Ferriday informed Mr Tree that he would be providing the sums necessary to meet this commitment also. Earnshaw Haes undertook to sub-underwrite 21m shares on 12 October 1987 and 5m shares on 19 October 1987. Mr Ferriday was accordingly indicating to Mr Tree that he would produce £15,003,370 in cash.

XXXX   Mr Ferriday and Mr Smith shared the loss equally. None of the figures for loss take account of commission earned.

A **Events after March 1988**

In April 1988, as a result of queries raised by Eagle's auditors, the board learned that payments amounting to £19.3m had been paid between 27 November and 18 December 1987 to Connect Parcel Distribution plc (hereafter 'Connect'). Connect became a subsidiary of Eagle in April 1988 and the board ratified payments made to it on the footing that they had been loans for the purpose of Connect's business. Prior to its
B acquisition, Eagle had been closely involved in the management of its affairs.

Subsequent to this meeting, Eagle's auditors discovered that part of the money paid to Connect appeared to have been diverted elsewhere. Mr Thomas spoke to Mr Ferriday by telephone who explained that part of the money had been diverted to Rayton-Fissore, a car manufacturer in Italy, which Mr Ferriday was proposing to acquire for Eagle. It occurred to Mr Thomas that these moneys might have been used to assist sub-underwriters other than Mr Ferriday to take up their shares. Mr Thomas asked Mr
C Ferriday to return at once from Los Angeles, where he then was, to England. On 26 April 1988, Mr Thomas confronted Mr Ferriday and asked him whether he had used the moneys lent to Connect to support the underwriting. Mr Ferriday denied this and Mr Thomas believed him. Thereafter an investigation was carried out into the Rayton-Fissore venture. A satisfactory report was received and accordingly the debt currently owed by Rayton-Fissore was treated as an asset in Eagle's accounts.

D In the course of the audit of the next year's accounts, Eagle's auditors discovered that there was some question over whether money apparently paid to Rayton-Fissore had ever reached them. This led in due course to the discovery that moneys had indeed not been paid to Rayton-Fissore but had been extracted and paid to Savory Milln in discharge of Mr Ferriday's underwriting obligations.

Subsequently Mr Ferriday was tried and convicted of the theft of £3.5m and £8m from
E Eagle on 15 and 17 December 1987.

Payments in December 1987

Payments of £3.5m and £8m were made from Eagle to Connect on 15 and 17 December 1987 and thence on 16 and 18 December to Savory Milln via the account of Anser with Hambros Bank Jersey. It is agreed that these payments to Savory Milln were made out
F of moneys belonging to Eagle. There is also no dispute as to the provenance of the sum of £2m paid by Anser to Savory Milln on 14 December 1987. It represented part of the sum of £2.5m paid by Connect to Anser which in turn represented part of a sum of £3m paid by Eagle to Connect on 10 December 1987. There is however an issue as to whether this was out of moneys belonging to Eagle or moneys belonging to Connect.

Between 27 November 1987 and 14 December 1987, Eagle Trust made payments
G totalling £6.8m to Connect as follows:

	£m
27 November 1987	0.30
2 December 1987	0.25
7 December 1987	3.25
10 December 1987	3.00
H | | 6.80 |

On 11 December 1987 the sum of £3m was paid by Connect to R Young & Co, client account, at Hambros Bank in Jersey. Of this £2.5m was immediately credited to the account of Anser with Hambros. On 14 December 1987 Anser made a payment of £2m to Savory Milln in respect of Earnshaw Haes' and Mr Ferriday's sub-underwriting commitments.

The plaintiff's case is that Mr Ferriday only formed his fraudulent intention on or   A
after 7 December 1987. It follows that the £2m paid to Savory Milln on 14 December
would only have been stolen from Eagle if the payment of £3m from Eagle to Connect
on 10 December 1987 represented moneys misappropriated from Eagle rather than
moneys lent to Connect. Connect is now insolvent. It is not a plaintiff in these
proceedings. Accordingly if the £2m represented moneys lent by Eagle to Connect, the
claim for compensation for loss of that sum made by Eagle in these proceedings must
fail.   B

There is little direct evidence as to the nature of the payment of £3m made by Eagle to
Connect on 10 December 1987. The amount is slightly different from that paid by
Connect to Anser, being the sum of £2.5m paid on the following day. It was not until 14
December 1987 that Mr Ferriday instructed Anser that it would be receiving this sum of
£2.5m, £2m of which was to be transmitted to Savory Milln. Thus the interval of time
between the payment from Eagle to Connect and the instruction to Anser is greater than   C
in the case of the other payments (12/13 December was a weekend) and the amounts of
such payments do not exactly match.

Despite the facts that Eagle had made other payments to Connect about this time and
that Connect needed money for the purposes of its business, it seems to me more likely
than not that in all the circumstances of the case the sum of £3m paid from Eagle to
Connect on 10 December 1987 was never intended to belong to Connect and was always   D
destined to be used to discharge the sub-underwriting commitments of Mr Ferriday and
Earnshaw Haes. The sum left Connect on 11 December 1987. Mr Ferriday had assumed
day to day control of Connect in early December 1987. The signatures authorising the
payment were those of Mr Black and Mr Baker. Mr Black confirmed that it was
appropriate for him to sign with Mr Baker. It is probable that Mr Baker was giving effect
to instructions from Mr Ferriday. Accordingly in my judgment Eagle is the proper
plaintiff in respect of the sum of £2.5m and not Connect.   E

Evidence of Mr Evans

From 1981 to 1993 Mr Evans was the head of the corporate finance department of
Laing & Cruikshank, stockbrokers. In that capacity he was personally involved in
advising on acquisitions and disposals, and the raising of capital. He was called to give
expert evidence as to the manner in which a financial adviser would act in a situation like   F
that of Savory Milln on the Eagle/Samuelson acquisition. Mr Evans' evidence in some
respects also extended beyond the proper scope of expert evidence. This I have had to
take into account.

The duties identified by Mr Evans can be described as follows:

(1)   a duty to be satisfied that sub-underwriters can meet their commitments if called
upon to meet them;   G

(2)   a duty to ensure that the full board is informed of certain matters;

(3)   a duty to ensure full compliance with legal and regulatory requirements for
disclosure in the listing particulars; and

(4)   a duty to exercise caution when accepting sub-underwriting commitments for
directors.   H

With respect to (1), Mr Evans' report says:

'16. It is, in my view, generally accepted that, when arranging sub-underwriting
for a share issue, a financial adviser has a responsibility to ensure that the sub-
underwriting is properly, and tidily, put in place, with sub-underwriters who
genuinely wish to become shareholders in the company. The arrangement of the

A   sub-underwriting is not a matter which is solely of concern to the financial adviser/ underwriter, for the reasons that:

> (1) the failure of any sub-underwriters, while only a matter of financial concern to the underwriter, nevertheless may create a pool of loose shares which could deflate the market price and possibly provide a threshold for a hostile bid; and

B   (2) the knowledge that sub-underwriters have failed to meet their commitments will inevitably cause concern among other sub-underwriters and might weaken their willingness to remain as investors in the company.'

Mr Evans was extensively cross-examined on this point, and it was evident that his views were inconsistent and confused. I do not accept Mr Evans' opinion on the arrangement of sub-underwriting. In allocating sub-underwriting, Savory Milln was protecting itself and SBCI against the risk of having to take up shares under the

C   underwriting agreement. Mr Evans accepted that if Savory Milln had not sought to pass this risk to sub-underwriters it could sell any shares taken up under the underwriting agreement when it liked or at least after a reasonable time after the issue had been made had passed. In my judgment sub-underwriters could not logically be bound by greater restrictions than the primary underwriters. Furthermore in underwriting, or allocating sub-underwriting, Savory Milln was not in my judgment carrying out the functions of a

D   financial adviser. It was acting as primary underwriter on its own account. No obligations to retain or ensure retention of the shares for any period or to choose any particular type of sub-underwriter for the benefit of Eagle can be implied into the underwriting agreement. An underwriter may in practice take steps to prevent a disorderly sale of shares taken up under an underwriting agreement, but this in my judgment is to enhance its own commercial reputation and not because it owes any duty to the company for

E   whom it is an underwriter.

Mr Evans concludes on the basis of para. 16 of his report, quoted above, that the financial adviser (who is also an underwriter),

> 'has a fundamental responsibility to satisfy himself that the sub-underwriters are good for their commitments if called upon to meet them.'

An underwriter is likely to allocate the sub-underwriting only to sub-underwriters whom he believes will perform their obligations if called upon. But he will do this because it is

F   in his interests as underwriter. If he fails to find satisfactory underwriters, the company may suffer damage but this is difficult to assess and a by-product of his failure to protect his own interests. An underwriter does not in my judgment take on underwriting obligations in the course of carrying out his duties as financial adviser and accordingly he cannot be treated as having some hybrid character of a 'financial adviser/underwriter' when selecting sub-underwriters.

G   Accordingly in my judgment Savory Milln owed no duty of care as financial adviser in respect of its decision as underwriter to accept Mr Ferriday, Earnshaw Haes, Boston & Co/Mr Boston and Jefferies & Co as sub-underwriters.

As to (2), there are a several matters which Mr Evans mentions in his report as matters which should be disclosed to the board or discussed with it. He says that it is the responsibility of the financial adviser to discuss with the board any potentially damaging

H   matter which involves a director and which directly impacts on the market price of its shares, or any significant development such as the incident with Mr Boston. He says that the financial adviser should disclose to the full board:

(a)   details of a director's sub-underwriting;

(b)   details of any proposed action by the financial adviser in a situation where its action may conflict with the interests of the company; and

(c)   details of any proposed arrangement between the financial adviser and a director   A
in his personal capacity.

In this context Mr Evans placed reliance on a statement of the Panel on Takeovers and
Mergers dated 30 July 1987. That statement refers to the need in appropriate situations
to place the opinion of the company's professional advisers before the whole board. The
context of the statement however is that of the responsibility of committees of a board to
keep the board informed. It does not seek to place such a duty on the professional   B
advisers themselves.

There is therefore no 'industry standard' applicable to define the circumstances in
which disclosure to the board by a financial adviser is necessary. The relevant passages
in Mr Evans' report are couched in terms of what he would expect or what Savory Milln
should do rather than in terms of an accepted market practice.

In all the circumstances I consider that, in the absence of clear evidence of an accepted,   C
relevant market practice, I should not accept Mr Evans' opinion on this matter.
Disclosure to the full board is inflexible and often impractical. The need for the full board
to be involved will prima facie depend on all the circumstances. Accordingly I find that a
financial adviser may properly (in the absence of circumstances indicating to the
contrary) rely upon a director performing any duty which he may have to disclose matters
to the board, and that, where a director is personally interested in any agreement he
proposed to make with the company, the financial adviser may properly, in appropriate   D
cases, decide to rely on the consent to the agreement given by an executive director who
is not similarly interested and who is acting in the course of his apparent authority. Thus,
in my judgment, it was sufficient in this case that Mr Ferriday's sub-underwriting, and
the agreement to defer payment of the rights issue proceeds, were known to Mr Baker
and Mr Whiley. The agreement to defer payment of the rights issue proceeds involved a
loss of interest to Eagle but the sums involved were comparatively small. I accordingly   E
infer that it was within the apparent authority of Mr Whiley and/or Mr Baker to make
that agreement on behalf of Eagle.

I should add that Mr Evans said that it was unknown for an underwriter to delay
paying amounts due under an underwriting agreement. In the light of the other evidence
I have heard, I do not consider that this observation can apply to an agreement made
with the client company to defer the date for payment in the period immediately following
Black Monday.   F

With respect to (3) Mr Evans' report says:

> '19. One of the primary roles of a financial adviser, in the context of a takeover,
> or share and rights issues, is to take full responsibility for the accurate and timely
> production and posting of the offer documentation and listing particulars required
> by the City Code and the Stock Exchange Listing Rules ("the Yellow Book"). It is
> the responsibility of the financial adviser to ensure that full and proper disclosure   G
> of all relevant and material information is made, as required by the City Code and
> the Listing Rules as well as the *Financial Services Act* 1986 (including, in particular,
> s. 146 of the Act).'

On the basis of this passage it is said that Savory Milln should have advised Eagle that
the listing particulars should disclose Mr Ferriday's interest as sub-underwriter. Indeed
Mr Evans says in his report that he personally would have given this advice to the board.   H
In cross-examination, he expressed the opinion that this information would be material
to other investors in the company and stated that it was his own firm's practice to
disclose.

The duty of the financial adviser in this regard can be no higher than one to exercise
reasonable care and skill. I have been shown no regulatory rule or enactment which in

A   terms requires disclosure of this interest. Its disclosure would depend upon the true construction of s. 146 of the *Financial Services Act* 1986 ('the 1986 Act') and the question whether a duty to disclose this information exists at common law. Section 146 of the 1986 Act requires listing particulars to contain:

> '... all such information as investors and their professional advisers would reasonably require, and reasonably expect to find there, for the purpose of making
B   an informed assessment of–
>
> > (a) the assets and liabilities, financial position, profits and losses, and prospects of the issuer of the securities; ...'

In my judgment, there can only be a legal duty of care on a financial adviser to advise upon the disclosure of any matter if that matter is required to be disclosed by law. In Mr Evans' opinion, it is rare for a director to have a sub-underwriting commitment. There
C   could not therefore in my judgment be any consensus in the market place as to the disclosure requirements in this context of which it could be said Mr Gillams should have been aware. Mr Gillams did consider the question of disclosure; he did not refer it to Mr Cooper as it might be said he should have done. But as I have already recounted Mr Cooper did in fact know of Mr Ferriday's underwriting commitment and he concluded it did not require to be disclosed. I do not consider that Mr Gillams as a layman could be expected to reach the correct conclusion as a matter of law on the meaning of s. 146 of
D   the 1986 Act or the scope of any duty at common law.

With respect to (4) Mr Evans' report says:

> '18. In this regard, a financial adviser should exercise caution when contemplating the possibility of a director of the company acting as a sub-underwriter, particularly if the contemplated commitments of the director are substantial. It would, of course, prove highly embarrassing, and potentially damaging, to the
E   company, and embarrassing to the adviser, if a director were to run into difficulties in meeting any sub-underwriting commitments which he had assumed. It is, in fact, unusual, in my experience, for directors of companies to assume sub-underwriting commitments of any magnitude in relation to issues of the company's own shares.'

In my judgment, this paragraph also confuses the position of Savory Milln as financial adviser with its position as underwriter. I have discussed this point above. The capacities do not in my judgment overlap so that the matters mentioned in the paragraph quoted
F   cannot (unless specifically agreed) form part of Savory Milln's duty as financial adviser. Accordingly that duty would not prevent Savory Milln from accepting a director as a sub-underwriter even if his commitment gave him a conflict of interest with the company or affected his abilities to perform his duties as a director in some way.

The plaintiff's allegations
G

    Eagle put its case in three ways which I will set out in turn: (1) constructive trust, (2) breach of duty, and (3) failure to discharge the amounts due.

(1) *Constructive trust*

    The material parts of the statement of claim in its present form are as follows:

> '14. The said £13.5m was received by Savory Milln (as aforesaid) and dealt with
H   (as set out in para. 10 and 12 above) in circumstances where Savory Milln deliberately or recklessly shut their eyes to the fact and/or ought to have known and/or were on enquiry that the said sums were or represented Eagle's own money.
>
> 15. Savory Milln deliberately or recklessly shut their eyes to and/or ought to have been aware of the matters aforesaid and/or were on enquiry as to the same by virtue of the following facts and matters:

(i) they knew that some £23m in sub-underwriting (some 69m shares) was being   A
arranged by or through Ferriday, the chief executive of Eagle;

(ii) they took no or no adequate steps to check that they [the Eagle-introduced
sub-underwriters] were genuinely sub-underwriting the share issues or that
they were good for their obligations. They should have been particularly
suspicious about this in the light of (a) the fact that most of these sub-
underwriters were not institutions nor persons who would normally sub- B
underwrite share issues such as this and (b) of the significant changes in the
sub-underwriting list . . . ;

(iii) Ferriday only became a sub-underwriter at all because of the difficulties
encountered by Savory Milln . . . Savory Milln accepted, and indeed pressed
for Ferriday's personal commitment in respect of 14.4m shares (some £4.3m)
without taking any steps to consider whether he was personally good for the
money. Savory Milln made no such inquiry because Gillams was concerned   C
about Savory Milln's own position as underwriters and was desperate to
cover their exposure. He knew that Ferriday, as chief executive of Eagle,
could not be seen, once committed, to default on his sub-underwriting
commitment and they preferred not to inquire as to the source from which
he would (if necessary) discharge such a commitment. The fact that he was
prepared to agree to undertake the commitment after the Stock Exchange   D
crash must have seemed remarkable to Savory Milln, if he was intending to
pay out of his own pocket, since by that time it was clear that the sub-
underwriters stood to lose substantially if the Samuelson acquisition went
ahead;

(iv) the circumstances surrounding Martin Boston & Co . . . put them on notice
that (a) Ferriday might be indemnifying some or all of the said sub- E
underwriters in respect of their liabilities and (b) that he might be doing so
on behalf of Eagle. Savory Milln and their solicitors, S J Berwin & Co, were
very concerned as to Martin Boston's allegations and considered the possible
implications of s. 151 of the *Companies Act* 1985 in this connection;

(v) after Ferriday had taken over the sub-underwriting of Martin Boston and
Co/Martin Boston his commitment was for 25.5m shares, i.e. an exposure of
more than £7.5m. All of this had been assumed only because of his inability   F
to find or maintain the sub-underwriters whom he had promised to Savory
Milln. This was a wholly unusual situation, as Savory Milln well knew.
Nonetheless and despite Martin Boston's allegations, Savory Milln chose to
take no steps to satisfy themselves as to Ferriday's ability to meet his
commitments nor to require him to provide security for the same, but
preferred not to ask any or any searching questions;   G

(vi) in fact [they knew that] although Ferriday personally was liable for at least
£7.5m in respect of his own sub-underwriting obligations, but they did not
believe that he had the funds to discharge such obligations. Mr Gillams
believed in October 1987 that Ferriday's wealth (such as it was) was tied up
in Eagle. After the stock market crash of 19 October 1987, Savory Milln
thought that Ferriday would use his vote at the extraordinary general   H
meeting of Eagle (held on 25 November 1987 to approve the offer and the
rights issue) in such a way that he did not expose himself to these liabilities.
When he voted in favour of the transaction proceeding Savory Milln thought
that he was in effect voting to bankrupt himself, but chose to take no steps
to find out how, if not from Eagle's funds Ferriday could possibly discharge
his obligations;

A (vii) Gillams did not even raise either with his superiors or with the board of directors of Eagle any concerns as to the ability of Ferriday to meet his commitment or as to how he had come to assume such extensive and unsecured liabilities. Gillams felt gratitude towards Ferriday for covering what would otherwise have been an embarrassing shortfall in the sub-underwriting for which Gillams had responsibility and preferred to ask as few questions as possible in the hope that everything worked out all right;

B (viii) when the time came for Savory Milln to decide how to deal with the £13.5m received from Anser in Jersey, Savory Milln made no inquiry as to the source from which the payments of £13.5m came. They made no or no adequate inquiry either of Hambros Bank Ltd, Hambros Bank (Jersey) Ltd or of Anser as to which payments from Jersey related to which sub-underwriter's liabilities. They made no enquiries as to who Anser was, nor its relation with

C Eagle or Ferriday or the other sub-underwriters, despite their concerns referred to in (ii)–(vii) above and despite the fact that they had to decide whether to apply the said £13.5m towards the debts of the sub-underwriters and, if so, which;

  (ix) Savory Milln made no or no adequate inquiry as to how Ferriday had managed to raise money from which to offer to pay his sub-underwriting

D obligations, if not from Eagle's own funds;

  (x) Savory Milln did not contact Earnshaw Haes to check that the said £13.5m should be applied towards the discharge of Earnshaw Haes' obligations before attributing the said payment to those obligations. Had it done so, it would have discovered that Earnshaw Haes denied that it had any liability . . . but rather that the liability had been undertaken by Michael Barnard on behalf of Ferriday. In truth the apparent Earnshaw Haes underwriting was

E really a further commitment by Ferriday, which could only be discharged by access to Eagle's own funds. Since Savory Milln did not believe that Ferriday could pay £7.5m they knew he could not possibly pay £15m, i.e. his own commitments plus those made in the name of Earnshaw Haes;

  (xi) the request by Ferriday to apply the £13.5m first towards the Earnshaw Haes' commitment and then towards his own must have or ought to have

F struck Savory Milln as very strange if Earnshaw Haes was a genuine arm's length underwriter, especially when coupled with the fact that Earnshaw Haes sub-underwriting commission (to which they were, if genuine, obviously entitled) was deducted from the final payment by Ferriday of his sub-underwriting commitment in March 1988;

  (xii) nonetheless, Savory Milln proceeded to apply the £13.5m as directed by

G Ferriday and chose to make no further inquiries of Ferriday, Earnshaw Haes or the board of Eagle before applying the said funds towards discharge of Earnshaw Haes' and then Ferriday's liabilities. Indeed Gillams did not even consult his superiors;

  (xiii) Savory Milln must have been suspicious, or ought to have been suspicious, that Ferriday was asking for more time in which to meet his sub-underwriting commitments and those of Earnshaw Haes, and that those

H sub-underwriters were unable . . . to pay their obligations on the due date, viz. 11 December 1987. The agreement reached by Tree . . . with Ferriday and Baker of Eagle that Eagle would not require Savory Milln to pay their own obligations until they had been able to collect from the sub-underwriters was a most unusual arrangement, which further indicated to Savory Milln (1) that there may have been some connection between Eagle itself and the

sub-underwriting obligations; (2) that there was a connection between   A
Ferriday and Earnshaw Haes, with a possibility that the commitments in the
name of Earnshaw Haes were in truth Ferriday's; and (3) that Ferriday did
not have, or was unable to find, the requisite funds with which to meet his
sub-underwriting commitments. Nonetheless, Savory Milln again preferred
not to ask questions about any of these matters, but simply waited for the
money to arrive.
                                                                         B
15A. If (which is denied) it is incumbent upon Eagle to prove what would have
happened if due inquiry had been made at any stage in the history set out in
para. 15 above, Eagle will contend that what would have occurred is what is set
out in para. 19 below.'

The fundamental issue here is the required state of mind of a constructive trustee who
has received trust money. (Liability in these circumstances is to be distinguished from
liability arising when a person knowingly assists in the fraudulent and dishonest design   C
of the trustee.) There is a helpful and oft-cited categorisation of the various types of
knowledge that a person may have in Peter Gibson J in *Baden v Société Générale pour
Favoriser le Développement du Commerce et de l'Industrie en France SA* [1993] 1 WLR
509n at p. 575H:

> '. . . knowledge can comprise any one of five different mental states which [counsel
> for the plaintiffs] described as follows: (i) actual knowledge; (ii) wilfully shutting   D
> one's eyes to the obvious; (iii) wilfully and recklessly failing to make such inquiries
> as an honest and reasonable man would make; (iv) knowledge of circumstances
> which would indicate the facts to an honest and reasonable man; (v) knowledge of
> circumstances which would put an honest and reasonable man on inquiry.'

The allegation in para. 14 of the statement of claim is that Savory Milln deliberately
shut their eyes to the fact that the sums totalling £13.5m were Eagle's own money. This
allegation is made only against Mr Gillams, and not against Mr Tree. I should say at   E
once that, on the facts as found by me, I am satisfied that Savory Milln did not know of,
or suspect it to be the case, that Mr Ferriday had taken money from Eagle to pay his
sub-underwriting commitments and those of Earnshaw Haes. Mr Ferriday disguised the
trail. Savory Milln regarded him as an honest and trustworthy man. So far as Savory
Milln was aware, there is no reason why he should not have been able to raise the
requisite funds from his business associates or on the security of his other assets. The loss
that he and Mr Smith were to suffer was a large one in absolute terms but not in the   F
context of businessmen with major business assets. There is, moreover, no motive shown
for Savory Milln to become knowingly involved in Mr Ferriday's fraud: quite the reverse.
My conclusion on this aspect of the case essentially follows from the issues of fact which
I have resolved in favour of Savory Milln and which appear earlier in this judgment. In
my judgment it is not shown that Savory Milln either knew that the £13.5m was Eagle's
money, or even that it was probably Eagle's money, or that it wilfully shut its eyes to the   G
obvious or that it knowingly and recklessly failed to make the enquiries that a reasonable
and honest man would make. Accordingly it did not have knowledge of types (i)–(iii) in
the passage which I have cited from Peter Gibson J in the *Baden* case. The facts as found
by me do not justify that finding or inference of such knowledge.

I now turn to constructive knowledge on which Eagle relies in the alternative. At this
stage, I should point out that the question of whether Eagle has a cause of action at all   H
on this basis was considered in depth by Vinelott J on an application to strike out the
statement of claim. The decision of Vinelott J ([1993] 1 WLR 484) was that Eagle's claim
should be struck out. In a long and closely-reasoned judgment he cited *Re Blundell* (1888)
40 ChD 370 and continued (at p. 506D):

> 'The ground of the decision [in *Re Blundell*] seems to me to be that if, in the
> ordinary course of business, a payment is made in discharge of a liability to the

A   defendant, the defendant cannot be made liable as a constructive trustee merely
upon the ground that he knew or had reason to suspect that there had been a
breach of trust disentitling the trustee to make the payment. It must be shown that
the circumstances are such that knowledge that the payment was improper can be
imputed to him.

In my judgment, therefore, in a case of this kind, in order to make a defendant
B   liable as a constructive trustee, it must be shown that he knew, in one of the senses
set out in (i), (ii) or (iii) of Peter Gibson J's analysis in the *Baden* case, post, p. 509,
that the moneys were trust moneys misapplied; or the circumstances must be such
that, in the absence of any evidence or explanation by the defendant, that
knowledge can be inferred. And it may be inferred if the circumstances are such
that an honest and reasonable man would have inferred that the moneys were
probably trust moneys and were being misapplied, and would either not have
C   accepted them or would have kept them separate until he had satisfied himself that
the payer was entitled to use them in discharge of the liability.'

Eagle appealed to the Court of Appeal against the order of Vinelott J and before the
appeal began, it amended the statement of claim. Savory Milln and SBCI accepted it as
disclosing a reasonable cause of action. The Court of Appeal accordingly set aside the
order of Vinelott J by consent and gave the plaintiff leave to amend.

D
The arguments before Vinelott J have been substantially addressed to me again. Mr
McCombe QC for the plaintiff, submits that where a person has received trust property
he incurs liability as a constructive trustee if he has knowledge of any of the five kinds
identified in the *Baden* case. Mr Sumption QC submits that in a commercial transaction,
or at least in a case such as the present involving the discharge of a lawful debt, knowledge
of types (iv) or (v) is insufficient. As there is a substantial overlap between the argument
E   presented to Vinelott J and that presented at this hearing, I will, where my reasoning is
the same as that of Vinelott J, gratefully adopt passages from his judgment.

Mr McCombe relies on a number of authorities but particularly *Belmont Finance Corp
Ltd v Williams Furniture Ltd & Ors (No. 2)* [1980] 1 All ER 393. I agree with what
Vinelott J said about this case in his judgment at [1993] 1 WLR 496F–497F. At p. 405d
Buckley LJ refers to the liability of a person who receives trust property 'with knowledge
F   (actual or constructive)'. However he does not state what kind of constructive knowledge
he means. Goff LJ speaking of the constructive trustee receiving trust property 'in
circumstances in which it knew, or ought to have known' of the breaches of trust but it is
clear from his judgment at p. 412e that he considered that the constructive trustee had
actual knowledge because the director responsible for the transaction was common to
both the company which was the victim of the breach of trust and the company which
received its property. The *Belmont* case is in any event distinguishable factually from the
G   present case because the property was received in that case under the very transaction
which constituted the breach of trust. In the present case the sub-underwriting
transaction, which gave rise to the obligation which Mr Ferriday discharged by using
Eagle's moneys, was a proper transaction in itself having no other connection with Mr
Ferriday's breach of trust.

Mr McCombe relies on the further authority of the Court of Appeal in *Agip (Africa)
H   Ltd v Jackson & Ors* [1991] Ch 547 at p. 567C–F per Fox LJ (with whom Butler-Sloss
and Beldam L JJ agreed). In this passage Fox LJ sets out the knowledge required in a
'knowing assistance' case and then sets out the passage I have cited from the *Baden* case.
Fox LJ continues:

'I accept that formulation. It is however only an explanation of the general
principle and it is not necessarily comprehensive.'

Thus the Court of Appeal accepted all five kinds of knowledge as applicable in a   A
knowing assistance case. Mr McCombe submits that Millett J in *El Ajou v Dollar Land
Holdings plc* [1993] BCC 698 at p. 717H regarded the observations as applicable to a
knowing receipt case but it seems to me that the report may have confused 'former' with
'latter' so that Mr McCombe's point may not be a good one.

Mr McCombe also referred me to *Polly Peck International plc v Nadir (No. 2) & Ors*
[1992] 4 All ER 769. At pp. 776J–777F Scott LJ said: B

'In the statement of claim actual knowledge on the part of the Central Bank is
alleged. Alternatively constructive knowledge is relied on. The mental states that
will suffice to fix a defendant with liability as a constructive trustee are not always
easy to identify. A number of learned judgments have illuminated the problem (see
e.g. *Agip (Africa) Ltd v Jackson* [1992] All ER 385, [1990] Ch 265; *affd* [1992] 4 All
ER 451, [1991] Ch 547, *Baden v Société Générale pour Favoriser le Développement
du Commerce et de l'Industrie en France SA* (1982) [1992] 4 All ER 161, *Eagle Trust*   C
plc v SBC Securities Ltd [1992] 4 All ER 488 and *Cowan de Groot Properties Ltd v
Eagle Trust plc* [1992] 4 All ER 700 . . .

Liability as constructive trustee in a "knowing receipt" case does not require that
the misapplication of the trust funds should be fraudulent. It does require that the
defendant should have knowledge that the funds were trust funds and that they
were being misapplied. Actual knowledge obviously will suffice. Mr Potts has   D
submitted that it will suffice if the defendant can be shown to have had knowledge
of facts which would have put an honest and reasonable man on inquiry, or, at
least, if the defendant can be shown to have wilfully and recklessly failed to make
such inquiries as an honest and reasonable man would have made (see categories
(iii) and (v) of the categories of mental state identified by Peter Gibson J in *Baden's*
case [1992] 4 All ER 161 at 235). I do not think there is any doubt that, if the latter
of the two criteria can be established against the Central Bank, that will suffice. I   E
have some doubts about the sufficiency of the former criterion but do not think
that the present appeal is the right occasion for settling the issue. The various
categories of mental state identified in *Baden's* case are not rigid categories with
clear and precise boundaries. One category may merge imperceptibly into another.'

Mr McCombe cited many other authorities. I hope counsel will not think it
discourteous if I do not go through all the authorities they have cited. The high water   F
mark in the authorities which support Mr McCombe's submission is I believe in the
authorities that I have cited. So I will now turn to the submissions of Mr Sumption.

Mr Sumption derives some conceptual support for his argument in the very many
authorities which hold that constructive notice is not to be extended to commercial
transactions: see for example *Thomson & Ors v Clydesdale Bank Ltd* [1893] AC 282 and
Manchester Trust v Furness [1895] 2 QBD 539. As Bower LJ said in *Sanders Bros v*   G
MacLean & Co (1883) 11 QBD 327 at p. 343: 'Credit, not distrust, is the basis of
commercial dealings'. In the field of constructive trusts, the principal authorities in favour
of Mr Sumption's approach are *Re Montagu's Settlement Trusts* [1987] Ch 264, *Carl
Zeiss Stiftung v Herbert Smith & Co & Anor (No. 2)* [1969] 2 Ch 276, *Williams v Williams*
(1881) 17 ChD 437 and *Re Blundell* (1888) 40 ChD 370. All these cases are referred to in
the judgment of Vinelott J and I gratefully adopt his analysis. In addition to those
authorities, and the decision of Vinelott J, there is the following observation of Millett J   H
in *El Ajou v Dollar Land Holdings plc* [1993] BCC 698 at p. 717H:

'In *Eagle Trust plc v SBC Securities Ltd* [1993] 1 WLR 484 at pp. 506–507, Vinelott
J based liability firmly on inferred knowledge and not on constructive notice. For
my own part, I agree that even where the plaintiff's claim is a proprietary one, and
the defendant raises the defence of bona fide purchaser for value without notice,

A   there is no room for the doctrine of constructive notice in the strict conveyancing sense in a factual situation where it is not the custom and practice to make inquiry. But it does not follow that there is no room for an analogous doctrine in a situation in which any honest and reasonable man would have made inquiry.'

Mr Sumption's argument also receives support from the decision of Knox J in *Cowan de Groot Properties Ltd v Eagle Trust plc* [1992] 4 All ER 700. His Lordship sets out the

B   authorities for and against the requirement for constructive notice in a 'knowing receipt' case. The kernel of his own decision is in the following passage at pp. 759g–760d:

'In my judgment the position of a person dealing as purchaser with a vendor company's directors on a sale is as regards potential breaches of fiduciary duty by the directors of the vendor company in many ways similar to that of a person to whom a payment is made in discharge of an obligation that they are typical

C   commercial transactions. As Vinelott J observed in *Eagle Trust plc v SBC Securities Ltd* [1992] 4 All ER 488 at 507:

'The doctrine of constructive notice was developed in the field of property transactions and at a time when full and careful investigation of title was called for before a purchaser could be satisfied that the vendor had legal title to the property sold and that there were no legal or equitable encumbrances on it.

D   Judges have frequently warned of the danger of extending the doctrine beyond these bounds."

Vinelott J quoted Lindley LJ in *Manchester Trust v Furness* [1895] 2 QB 539 at 545 and *Thomson v Clydesdale Bank Ltd* [1893] AC 282 . . . in support. Neither the fraudulent scheme that is relied upon by Eagle in the present case nor the claimed sale at a gross undervalue in my judgment constitutes the sort of encumbrance with which conveyancing investigations of title are concerned. In relation to such

E   dealings it would be inappropriate to introduce the doctrine of constructive notice. I prefer in this context as the proper test to be applied the question whether knowledge that the directors of Eagle were deliberately selling at a gross undervalue can reasonably be imputed to Mr Samuelson; it follows from this view that I do not accept the submission made to me that in the case of a knowing receipt of trust property it is not necessary to establish at least in the case of a bona fide purchaser for value of trust property that the recipient had actual knowledge

F   in categories (i), (ii) or (iii) in the *Baden* case of the breach of trust. I suspect that the inclusion of the words "bona fide" in that submission was not intended because their presence would seem to negate any possibility even of constructive knowledge, but apart from that I consider that the relegation of a purchaser for value to a category more, rather than less, exposed to claims of constructive trusteeship to be misconceived. The volunteer, such as the tenth Duke of

G   Manchester in the *Montagu* case, is not a person who is entering into an arm's length contractual bargaining transaction and the courts applying equitable doctrines would be more, rather than less, likely to impute knowledge to a volunteer than to a contracting purchaser, more especially when the subject of inquiry on the latter's part, such as the question whether the sale to him is at a deliberate undervalue, is a matter in which his commercial interest is diametrically opposed to that of the vendor.'

H   I propose in the instant case to follow the reasoning of Millett J, Vinelott J and Knox J and to hold that in a 'knowing receipt' case, where the receipt occurs in the discharge of a lawful debt (at least one arising out of a transaction which does not itself constitute a breach of trust), actual knowledge within categories (i), (ii), and (iii) in the *Baden* case is required. This seems to me the preferable position in law. Accordingly Eagle's claim in constructive trust in the case fails.

I will, however, deal with the case on the basis of Mr McCombe's submissions in case   A
I am wrong. I am satisfied on the facts that even the hypothetical honest and reasonable
man in the position of Savory Milln when it received the sums totalling £13.5m would
not in all the circumstances have realised that the moneys were probably Eagle's moneys
or been put on enquiry. To reach that conclusion, as I see it, on the matters pleaded (so
far as established in evidence) Savory Milln would have had to doubt Mr Ferriday's
honesty. Such doubt might be evidenced by some internal speculation as to how Mr
Ferriday was going to meet his commitments but there is no evidence of any discussion   B
or concern within Savory Milln of that kind. The only matter which could have given
them that concern was the incident with Mr Boston. Mr Ferriday however had denied
Mr Boston's allegations, and Mr Cooper, Eagle's solicitor, had been satisfied that Eagle
and Savory Milln could properly accept his version of events in preference to those of
Mr Boston. Mr Ferriday was the chief executive of an established client of Savory Milln.
In due course, Savory Milln received moneys at the direction of Mr Ferriday not from   C
Mr Ferriday personally but from the Jersey account of an offshore investment company.
I do not see why the facts should indicate the theft of Eagle's funds to an honest and
reasonable man. The use of nominees or investment managers is an accepted business
practice and does not connote that some dishonesty has occurred.

The only other way in which the plaintiff could in my view succeed in the circumstances
of this case on the footing of constructive knowledge would be to say that, although there
was nothing to indicate dishonesty, yet the history of the matter would have led an honest   D
and reasonable man to make enquiries to check that the funds came from a legitimate
source. No particular form of enquiries have been suggested by counsel nor has it been
submitted when or how such enquiry would be made. (The opportunity for making
enquiry must be limited: and this is a situation in which enquiries are not routinely made.)
In my judgment a person is not put on enquiry into the source of payments made by his
debtor merely because the sums were large. Given the circumstances of the case, the   E
amounts were not in my judgment so large that a creditor would be bound to hold the
payment and not use it to discharge the amount owed to it while he made further
enquiries about the source of the funds received from the debtor.

(2) *Breach of duty*

The second way in which Eagle puts its case is on the basis that Savory Milln as Eagle's
financial adviser owed a duty of skill and care in advising Eagle on the offer for   F
Samuelson (and the contemporaneous rights issue) and in acting in connection with those
matters.

Eagle further contends that as financial adviser Savory Milln owed a number of other
duties, in particular:

(1)   a duty to act bona fide in the interests of Eagle;

(2)   a duty not to permit a conflict of interest to arise without the consent of Eagle;   G

(3)   a duty to report to the Eagle board matters which might suggest that a director
        was acting in breach of his duty;

(4)   a duty not to enter into arrangements with directors which were not disclosed to
        the board;

(5)   a duty to exercise reasonable skill to ensure that the listing particulars complied
        with s. 146 of the *Financial Services Act* 1986, the Stock Exchange Listing Rules   H
        and the City Code on Takeovers and Mergers;

(6)   a duty to ensure that through the allocation of sub-underwriting 'the best quality
        of shareholders was found for Eagle';

(7)   a duty 'not to accept as sub-underwriters persons whom they did not know and
        whose financial soundness and substantiality they had not investigated';

A   (8)   a duty not to accept a director as sub-underwriter without ensuring that the situation was fully disclosed to the board and without being satisfied as to the propriety and implications of the director being a sub-underwriter.

Numerous breaches of duty are alleged. In particular Eagle contends that the following constitute breaches of duty.

(1)   Acceptance of Jefferies & Co, Martin Boston & Co/Martin Boston, Earnshaw
B   Haes and Mr Ferriday as sub-underwriters without investigation of their means.

(2)   Acceptance of Jefferies & Co as sub-underwriters without considering whether their involvement would be likely to breach US securities law.

(3)   Failure to disclose Mr Ferriday's sub-underwriting commitments to the Eagle board.

(4)   Agreeing with Eagle to defer payment under the underwriting agreement so long
C   as Savory Milln had not themselves received payment from the sub-underwriters.

(5)   Failure to report to the board Mr Ferriday's difficulty in meeting his sub-underwriting commitments.

(6)   Acceptance of the £13.5m without disclosure of the circumstances to the Eagle board.

(7)   Pressuring Mr Ferriday to take on an underwriting commitment in respect of
D   14.5m shares on 6 November 1987.

(8)   Failure to advise that the sub-underwriting commitments should be disclosed in the listing particulars.

Eagle alleges that these breaches led to the following consequences:

'19. Had Savory Milln adequately discharged their said duties, then either:

E   (i) Ferriday would never have undertaken the said sub-underwriting or the extent of it; or

        (ii) it would have been impossible for Ferriday to have access to Eagle's funds in order to discharge his liabilities; or

        (iii) the board of Eagle would have been alerted to ensure either (i) or (ii) above; or

F   (iv) when the £13.5m came in from Jersey, investigations would have been carried out by Savory Milln and/or Eagle itself, prior to the application of the said funds towards any particular sub-underwriting obligation, to discover the source thereof, which would have revealed that it had come from Eagle.

20. By reason of Savory Milln's said breaches of duty Eagle suffered loss and
G   damage, viz. loss of the said £13.5m, which would otherwise have been avoided.'

It follows from what I have already said in relation to Mr Evans' evidence that the duties alleged to be owed by a financial adviser have not been established. Accordingly this alternative claim must fail and issues of contributory negligence and causation do not arise.

(3) *Failure to discharge the amount due*

H   Eagle's pleaded case on this is as follows:

'21. Further or in the alternative, in the premises the payments [made pursuant to the underwriting agreement] did not discharge Savory Milln's obligations to Eagle pursuant to the underwriting agreement. Accordingly Savory Milln have, to the extent of £13.5m, wrongfully failed to pay their obligations to Eagle pursuant to that agreement and remain liable to pay the said sum to Eagle.'

A

This alternative claim is designed to enable Eagle to succeed if it establishes that Savory Milln had constructive knowledge that the £13.5m belonged to Eagle even if constructive knowledge is insufficient for a claim in constructive trust based on knowing receipt. In view of my decision on the constructive knowledge point this claim must fail. Savory Milln did not have constructive knowledge of theft. Hence the £13.5m cannot be traced (even if it could otherwise be traced) into Savory Milln's moneys. This makes it unnecessary for me to deal further with this claim.

B

For all these reasons I dismiss the action.

(Action dismissed)

C

D

E

F

G

H

A # Re Gordon & Breach Science Publishers Ltd.

Chancery Division (Companies Court).
Robert Walker J.
Judgment delivered 21 October 1994.

Winding up – Petition – Whether compulsory winding up should supersede
B *voluntary.*

This was a petition for the compulsory winding up of a company which was already in creditors' voluntary liquidation.

The petitioner was the company's landlord and complained that those controlling the company, which was part of a group, had extracted the assets, arranged for the satisfaction of those creditors on whom the goodwill of the business depended, and achieved the 'selective
C dumping' of what was onerous and had no effect on goodwill. The company's income stream was cut off as a direct result of a decision by other group companies; the lease of the company's business premises was assigned to an associated company, 'STBS'; and the company's accounts showed cash at bank and in hand of over £5m in June 1991 compared with £6,000 when it went into liquidation in September 1993.

The original voluntary liquidator, appointed at a creditors' meeting which the petitioner
D did not attend, was removed and replaced at a further meeting requested by the petitioner. At that meeting a new liquidator was appointed by the votes of the associated companies claiming to be creditors for about £6m in all, including a new claim by STBS for £5.5m. The petitioner argued that the new claim was a sham.

Held, making a compulsory winding-up order:

1. Fairness and commercial morality might require that a substantial independent
E creditor, which felt itself to have been prejudiced by what it regarded as sharp practice, should be able to insist on the company's affairs being scrutinised by the process which followed a compulsory order. Such a creditor was entitled to an independent investigation. That might be so even where the voluntary liquidation was already well advanced and a compulsory order might cause further expense and delay. (Re Palmer Marine Surveys Ltd (1985) 1 BCC 99,557, Re Lowestoft Traffic Services Co Ltd (1986) 2 BCC 98,945 and Re
F Falcon R J Developments Ltd (1987) 3 BCC 146 considered.)

2. Where there were inter-group trading activities, there were many opportunities for manipulating profit and loss. Given the last-minute claim for £5.5m by STBS, the inter-group trading activities required the investigation which would ensue on the making of a compulsory order.

3. The fact that the associated creditors went to such lengths to maintain the voluntary
G liquidator in office was itself enough to disqualify him in the eyes of the petitioner, and this was not an irrational view to take. In such circumstances, an impartial investigation on behalf of the general body of creditors was needed.

The following cases were referred to in the judgment:

Falcon R J Developments, Re (1987) 3 BCC 146.
Hide, Re; ex parte Llynvi Coal and Iron Co (1871) LR 7 Ch App 28.
H *Lowestoft Traffic Services Co Ltd, Re* (1986) 2 BCC 98,945.
Palmer Marine Surveys Ltd, Re (1985) 1 BCC 99,557.
Swain (J D) Ltd, Re [1965] 1 WLR 909.

John Davies (instructed by Masons) for Rainbow Office Investments Ltd.

Michael Roberts (instructed by Clintons) for STBS Ltd, G & B Science Publishers SA and General Financial Holdings AG.

Annie Hockaday (instructed by Hobson Audley) for the liquidator.   A

Rupert D'Cruz (instructed by Shepherd Harris & Co, Enfield) for Brenner Cash.

JUDGMENT

Robert Walker J: This is a petition for the compulsory winding up of a company, Gordon & Breach Science Publishers Ltd ('the company') which is already in creditors' voluntary liquidation. The company went into creditors' voluntary liquidation on 24 September 1993 and Mr Keith Goodman was appointed as liquidator at a creditors'   B meeting held on the same day. The petition was presented on 3 February 1994 and a good deal of affidavit evidence has been put in, some of it very late, on the petition. In the meantime there has been another creditors' meeting on 26 July 1994 at which Mr Goodman was removed as liquidator (the decisive vote for his removal being that of the petitioning creditor). Mr Goodman was however replaced, not by the insolvency practitioner whom the petitioning creditor proposed (Mr Peter Yeldon of Smith and   C Williamson) but by Mr Maurice Moses of Levy Gee, whose appointment was achieved by the vote of STBS Ltd ('STBS'), an associated company in the group to which the company belongs. I shall have to return to that meeting later in this judgment.

The company was incorporated in 1962 and has a paid up capital of £90,001. It carried on part of a business as scientific publishers; I will return to the nature of its operations in more detail later. Although incorporated in England, it is apparently managed from   D Switzerland. It is a member of a large group with associated companies in the US, Switzerland, the Netherlands and according to a diagram which is in evidence – but which the deponent Mrs Gloria Korenberg describes as of dubious authenticity – more exotic jurisdictions also. For present purposes the most important associated companies are STBS, an English company; G & B Science Publishers SA ('G & B Switzerland'), a Swiss company; and General Financial Holdings AG ('General Financial') a company incorporated in Liechtenstein.   E

The circumstances of the company going into creditors' voluntary liquidation and the appointment of Mr Goodman as liquidator now lie some way in the past, and counsel for opposing creditors (the three associated companies named above and Brenner Cash, a firm of chartered accountants) urge that I should regard them as irrelevant to the present situation, now that Mr Goodman is no longer liquidator. But while recognising that the situation has changed, I think they must still have an important bearing on my assessment of the motives of the parties and the solidity of their grievances, and generally   F on the justice of the case.

The petitioning creditor, Rainbow Office Investments Ltd ('Rainbow') was the landlord of the offices (on the third and fourth floors of 1 Bedford Street, London WC2) which were occupied by the company as original tenant under a lease made in 1984, the reversion to which was acquired – in two stages – by Rainbow. In its petition Rainbow claimed a debt of just over £155,000 made up mainly of a contribution to past repairs,   G rent and service charge, and a liability for dilapidations. The petition also refers to a liability, then unquantified, in respect of the residue of the term. I should add that before the presentation of the petition (in fact, on 17 November 1993) Mr Goodman had disclaimed the lease.

The statement of affairs sworn to by Mr Roger Greene on 24 September 1993 disclosed assets valued at about £38,000 and listed the companies' creditors as follows (to the nearest £1,000 and ignoring one small debt of uncertain classification): Rainbow,   H £41,000; HM Customs and Excise, £46,000; other trade and expense creditors, £43,000; STBS, £85,000; G & B Switzerland, £200,000; General Financial, £16,000.

Mr Greene also attended and chaired the first creditors' meeting. There is a detailed note prepared by Mr Goodman for oral presentation to the meeting and it included a report of the history of the company prepared by Mr Greene but read out by Mr

A   Goodman. Mr Greene was not a director of the company for the whole of the relevant period but it is clear that he did have considerable involvement in its affairs. I will read part of this report.

'Mr Greene tells me that the company became the first affiliate of Gordon & Breach Science Publishers Inc which had been founded in the USA in 1961. Subsequently, affiliates were also set up in France, the Netherlands and
B   Switzerland. In the late 1980s, the Gordon & Breach Science Publishing group . . . ceased publishing in the UK and the USA and subsequently, this operation was performed by two Swiss members of the group, Gordon and Breach Science Publishers SA and Harwood Academic Publishers GmbH.

Gordon and Breach Science Publishers Ltd continued its involvement with the group scholarly journals, not as a publisher but as a subscription agent for a territory that comprised a number of countries in various parts of the world. At
C   this time the company operated from leasehold premises at William IV Street, London WC2 and 1 Bedford Street, London WC2. The company was granted a 20 year lease from November 1984 for which £82,750 per annum was payable as rent. The William IV Street lease ended by its term in December 1991.

In 1990 the company leased premises at Reading Bridge Approach, Reading, Berkshire where a lease was taken covenanting a peppercorn for the period 25
D   March 1990–2 August 1990 and thereafter, an annual rent of £196,250 inclusive. Staff were reassigned from Bedford Street to Reading and William IV Street and the Bedford Street premises were vacated. When the William IV lease ended in December 1991, some staff were reassigned to Bedford Street and the rest to Reading. In July 1993, Bedford Street was vacated.

As a subscription agent the company was allowed a 45 per cent discount and
E   organised the collection of subscription revenue and fulfilment of subscriptions on behalf of the Swiss publishers within the company's territory. Mr Greene tells me that the company was not assisted by any loans or overdraft facilities and that the company has always been self funding. Revenue was received in the following way.

   (a) The company received a commission based upon the sales of the group's journals in a specified territory.

F   (b) The company recharged Gordon and Breach Science Publishers SA for editorial and production staff salaries together with the proportion of overheads related thereto.

   (c) The company also recharged STBS Ltd an accommodation charge for use of part of their office and facility, another group company.

Apart from acting as a subscription agent the company also performed editorial and certain other publishing services for the two Swiss publishing entities.
G
I have been advised by Mr Greene that in June of this year, the two Swiss publishers terminated their arrangements with the company. Mr Greene remonstrated with the group chairman to reconsider their actions but the plea to reconsider was to no avail. Being deprived of its mainstream source of income, Mr Greene decided to discuss the company's position with the auditors and was advised that in all of the circumstances an insolvent liquidation of the company
H   seemed inevitable and as such steps should be taken for the company to be placed into creditors' voluntary liquidation. In that regard, my firm were instructed to assist with the statutory formalities and on 9 September, the notices convening this meeting were issued.'

This passage touches on a number of matters which have been the subject of controversy before me: in particular the financial and business arrangements between

different members of the group; the Reading premises, the lease of which was assigned   A
by the company to STBS on 17 September 1993, after the Bedford Street premises had
been vacated in July 1993 and seven days before the company went into liquidation; and
the cutting-off of what Mr Greene calls the company's 'mainstream source of income' as
the direct result of a decision by other group companies.

The last sentence of the passage which I have read mentions Mr Goodman's
involvement in events before 24 September 1993. Mr Goodman had an assistant, Mr   B
Nigel Gomez-Lee, and there is documentary evidence (which neither counsel for the
opposing creditors sought to challenge) of his being privy to plans to orchestrate the
payment or non-payment of the company's debts so that certain apparently friendly
creditors (notably Summers Morgan, the company's auditors, and Brenner Cash) should
(as it is put in a note headed 'Nigel: adjustments from 8 September 1993') 'remain unpaid
until after creditors' meeting'. Other debts totalling at least £66,000 appear to have been
paid by STBS, and other debts by other group companies. Another note in the same   C
handwriting records 'unpaid – lease agreement' and 'unpaid – Bedford Street rates'. It
also states,

> 'NB there are a number of lease agreements that will – as far as I know – be 'taken
> over' by STBS/OPA.'

There is also a fax dated 9 September 1993 sent to Mr Gomez-Lee by Mr Greene. It
reads,   D

> 'Dear Nigel,
>
> Herewith is the invoice for our share of the "repairs" to Bedford Street. I have no
> problem contesting the invoice to avoid the landlord's attendance at the meeting.
> It is *not* an invoice we would pay in ten days or without documentation. Please let
> me know what you and Keith suggest. Roger.'

'Keith' seems to refer to Mr Goodman. These documents provide strong prima facie   E
evidence of improper manoeuvring in which the insolvency practitioner's assistant (and
perhaps also the insolvency practitioner himself) were engaged. No evidence in answer
on these matters has been put in by the opposing creditors, except that Mr Brenner in an
affidavit sworn on 11 October 1994 says that he was not aware of any plan. In the same
affidavit Mr Brenner is still deposing to his belief in Mr Goodman's 'obvious
impartiality'. But in my judgment the petitioning creditor, Rainbow, had ample reason   F
to feel deeply concerned and sceptical about Mr Goodman's claims to impartiality and
his assertion (in his two affidavits) that he was and would remain completely neutral and
impartial.

At the original creditors' meeting on 24 September 1993 Mr Goodman was appointed
as liquidator not (as is incorrectly stated in the petition) by the votes of the associated
companies but by the votes of three relatively small creditors in respect of professional   G
services, that is Summers Morgan, Brenner Cash and Clintons, the company's solicitors.
It will be observed that two of these creditors were identified in the note to Mr Gomez-
Lee as earmarked for that role. Rainbow did not attend or vote at the creditors' meeting
because it had not received notice of the meeting. Mr Gomez-Lee has sworn in an
affidavit that notice of the meeting was sent to Rainbow's agents Ashville Properties Ltd.
I cannot resolve that matter, but the fax from Mr Greene to Mr Gomez-Lee (referring to
avoiding the landlord's attendance at the meeting) gives obvious cause for some   H
suspicion.

Rainbow also had ample reason to feel deeply concerned and sceptical about the way
in which the creditors' voluntary liquidation fitted in with the activities of the group as a
whole: the vacation of the Bedford Street premises, the assignment of the Reading lease
to STBS, the payment-off by associated companies of selected liabilities, and the

A   switching-off (as it were) by two Swiss associated companies of the company's life-support system.

I should also mention a fax dated 15 September 1993 sent by Mr Greene to Mr Goodman and Mr Gomez-Lee (then, it will be remembered, liquidator-designate and liquidator's assistant-designate). It begins on first-name terms,

B

'Dear Keith and Nigel,

Herewith is my first draft company history which I have run past Alan Brenner and Ken Morgan. Please let me have your comments. Also herewith is the press release we intend to circulate. The G & B group has no formal legal status and merely is the way we collectively refer to all the G & B affiliated companies.'

The history which follows is plainly the genesis of Mr Goodman's report read at the first creditors' meeting. The draft press release is aptly described by Mr Davies (for the petitioning creditor, Rainbow) as 'bullish'; it gives no hint to the reader that the improved 'structural and marketing efficiency' of which it speaks involved the serious insolvency of a subsidiary which had previously been an important part of the group.

C

I see great force in Mr Davies' submission that it would not be the first time that those controlling a company have extracted assets, arranged for the satisfaction of those creditors on whom the goodwill of the business depended, and achieved what Mr Davies called 'selective dumping' of that which is onerous and has no effect on goodwill. The 'Dear Nigel' manuscript strikes me as unusually candid evidence of selective dumping.

D

I have already said something about Mr Brenner's evidence and I should add something more, especially since Brenner Cash was, until the morning of the hearing, the only opposing creditor. In his first affidavit Mr Brenner claims to have personal knowledge of some of the affairs of the company as a result of advising from 1985 until the present time. The rest of his first affidavit consists of a strenuous refutation of points made by the petitioning creditor, most of which could not be within his own knowledge unless he did indeed have a good deal of inside information as to the company's activities. Certainly he had enough inside information to put in an invoice for professional services (unusually, for work in progress) on 14 September 1993. He was a signatory to the company's bank account (although he actually signed cheques only rarely). Mr Brenner's own affidavits show his deep involvement and it is absurd for him to suggest (as he does in his third affidavit) that if his firm does not count as an independent creditor, no one can count as an independent creditor. It is also absurd for him to suggest (in the same affidavit) that inspection of the company's papers by Mr James Walker (who is a Scottish accountant, and Rainbow's managing director) did not uncover a single matter raising doubt as to the liquidator's performance or his duties. On the contrary, it seems to me that Mr Walker struck gold.

E

F

G

I have already referred to two of the three matters of complaint originally specified in Rainbow's petition: the circumstances in which the company's income stream was cut off, and the assignment of the Reading lease. The third, and the most fully canvassed before me, was the fact that the company's accounts to 30 June 1991, as certified by Summers Morgan on 30 April 1992, show the company as having cash at bank and in hand as £5,316,720 (in addition to debtors of £1,671,050) although matched by current liabilities of £7,111,956 (including an item 'subscriptions in advance' of £4,520,283) and trade creditors of £1,938,015. By the time of the liquidation the company's cash, as shown by the statement of affairs, was down to £6,337. No audited accounts had been produced in the meantime, though they should have been filed by the end of April 1993.

H

Rainbow's solicitors took this matter up with Mr Goodman in correspondence. In a letter dated 23 December (which seems to have been mainly the work of Mr Gomez-Lee) the liquidator replied that,

'The dramatic difference between cash at the bank and in hand as at 30 June 1991   A
and as at 24 September 1993 was an area which caused me some concern at the
outset. It transpires that the accounting treatment of cash at bank as at 30 June
1991 was effectively incorrect and the enclosed copy of the Board Minute of the
company passed on 18 May 1992 clearly explains the position. I have, in actual
fact, investigated this particular matter and am satisfied with the explanation as
given to me. The cash at bank as at 30 June 1991 did not actually belong to the
company.'   B

The board minute recorded a board meeting of the company held in Switzerland and
attended by Mr Martin B Gordon, Mrs Korenberg and Madeleine Villard. It records
that Mr Gordon stated that the current accounting treatment,

'was inappropriate in that, in fact, the company was an agent of the journal
publishers being paid a commission of 45 per cent of subscription price; the
company was not a principal buying journals from the publishers at a 45 per cent   C
discount . . . It was resolved that (1) commencing with the company's fiscal year
ending 30 June 1992, the company's revenue from journal subscriptions shall be
recorded in the company's books of account as commission revenue and not as
sale proceeds and that the company's accountants be so instructed.'

No other documentary evidence of these important inter-group arrangements was put in
evidence. The minute raises almost as many questions as it answers. It certainly   D
contributes to the impression that those running the group's affairs felt able to make
whatever arrangements suited themselves, without any great regard for documentation
or commercial realities. That impression is further reinforced by the computer services
episode, to which I shall come shortly.

I must, however, complete the history of the exchanges over the cash position.
Rainbow's solicitors expressed dissatisfaction at the explanation in the liquidator's letter   E
of 23 December 1993. The liquidator wrote again (and again the letter seems to have
been mainly the work of Mr Gomez-Lee) on 24 January 1994 that he was quite satisfied
with the explanation:

'You may find the explanation quite extraordinary, but it is an inescapable fact. I
do however agree that it is somewhat unusual . . . the trading activities of the group
were somewhat complex . . . It is not unusual for publishing groups to trade in this
way although the accounting treatment of such transactions can vary from group   F
to group. I am quite happy that the Board Meeting passed by the directors on 18
May 1992 does not reflect the true position and has not effectively removed any
assets from the reach of the company's creditors.'

Rainbow remained dissatisfied and its petition for a compulsory order soon followed.
The liquidator's acceptance of the explanation may ultimately prove to have been correct,
but Rainbow was in my judgment entitled to remain sceptical. There is an obvious lack   G
of evidence of any coherent documentation of the group's financial and business
arrangements, and Mr Davies rightly points out that Mr Goodman's relatively modest
fee for his services (£2,700 plus VAT) cannot have covered very many hours' investigation
of the complex trading activities of a group of which he previously knew nothing.

On 27 June 1994 Rainbow's solicitors wrote to Mr Goodman requesting a creditors'
meeting for Mr Goodman's removal as liquidator, and the meeting was called for the 26   H
July. On 19 July Rainbow wrote to the liquidator enclosing a proxy and a proof for a
sum of nearly £800,000, made up as follows:

(1)   prior to disclaimer about £75,000;

(2)   claim in consequence of disclaimer about £222,000;

(3)   claim under *Re Hide* about £500,000.

A   This claim is disputed. There was not much argument before me as to how great a discount I should apply, and I do not feel disadvantaged by the absence of any prolonged argument. On any view Rainbow is a substantial, wholly independent creditor. The real issue is whether I should, in the circumstances of this case, attach any weight to the enormous (but for the most part disputed) claims of the associated companies.

B   It will be recalled that STBS, G & B Switzerland and General Financial were originally shown in the statement of affairs as creditors for a total of about £300,000 – part but not all of which seems to have resulted from their paying the debts of selected outside creditors of the company. None of them was initially an opposing creditor.

    It appears from Mr Goodman's notes (prepared for the meeting on 26 July) that until two days before the meeting the associated companies had submitted proxies (all naming Mr Bienias of Clintons) and proofs totalling about £315,000. However on 25 July STBS put in an additional proof for £5.5m. It was signed by Mrs Korenberg and accompanied by a faxed and a couriered letter also signed by her. Mr Goodman's speaking note records his reaction:

C

> 'On 21 July I received a further letter from Messrs Clintons asking for a copy of the proof of debt lodged by the creditor who requisitioned this meeting. Pursuant to their right of inspection under r. 4.79 of the *Insolvency Rules* 1986 I duly allowed Messrs Clintons to see a copy of the proof.

D

> I have no doubt that when this meeting was requisitioned all of the 'connected' creditors of Gordon and Breach Science Publishers Ltd expected their combined claims to outweigh the claim of the requisitioning creditor, namely the company's landlords, Rainbow Office Investment Ltd. Based on the amount of the claim set out in the requisition notice that indeed was the position.

E

> However, when the revised claim of the landlords, taking account of the damages etc, was inspected by Messrs Clintons it was realised that the combined claims of the associated companies were exceeded by the revised claim of the landlord and in my view one of the connected creditors, namely STBS Ltd, sought to redress that position by submitting a late massive claim which, in my view, is manifestly tendentious and extremely questionable.

F

> There has been much correspondence between myself and Messrs Clintons regarding this claim in the last few days. However I am advised by my solicitor that at this stage I am unable to satisfactorily adjudicate on, or agree 'estimated minimum values' on unliquidated claims under r. 4.67(3) of the *Insolvency Rules* 1986.

> I am therefore further advised that I should apply r. 4.70(3) of the *Insolvency Rules* 1986 and if I am in any doubt as to the validity of any claim, admit the claim for voting purposes and mark it as *"objected to"*.

G

> Putting my own opinion aside, I firmly believe that I must act in an even handed manner and be seen to do so. I, and I am sure the landlords and their advisors, remain doubtful as to the validity of all the connected company claims. Similarly however the connected companies and their advisors express doubts over the landlords' claim. I therefore propose to admit all claims submitted for voting

H

> purposes and mark them all as *"objected to"*.'

STBS's £5.5m claim is said to be based on an agreement dated 1 April 1992 in the form of a letter, typed on STBS writing paper, signed by Mrs Korenberg for STBS and by Mr Gordon for the company. It is for a term continuing until 30 June 2007. It requires STBS to lease computing services to the company in consideration of £400,000 p.a. (plus VAT) payable quarterly (with an upwards-only index-linking every five years) for the rental of

the equipment and a further amount, ascertained by a complex formula which also   A
involves index-linking, for computing services.

Rainbow strongly objects to STBS's £5.5m claim. In an affidavit sworn on 15 August
1994 (para. 36) Mr Walker summarises his reasons for doing so:

(1)   There is no mention of the liability in the statement of affairs sworn to by Mr
      Greene, despite the fact that Mr Greene was (the deponent believes) in the position
      of a group chief executive reporting directly to Mr Gordon.   B

(2)   As late as 22 July 1994 STBS's proof was for a mere £69,615; the enormous claim
      for £5.5m was submitted only after STBS became aware of the size of Rainbow's
      claim.

(3)   The alleged contract was evidently quite new to Mr Goodman.

(4)   In a fax dated 21 September 1993 to Mr Gomez-Lee from Mr Morgan of Summers
      Morgan, it is stated that STBS overcharged the company for computer services in   C
      1992 and 1993.

(5)   The latest accounts of STBS (to 31 December 1992, filed in March 1994) show:

      (a) STBS ceased trading in December 1993,

      (b) no record of the alleged debt of £5.5m, and

      (c) a statement that STBS expected to be paid all debts due to it in December   D
           1993 (see the directors' report – signed by Mrs Korenberg – and note 1).

Mr Walker's affidavit goes on to set out his belief that STBS's additional proof is a
'complete sham', and to question the existence of a contract on which that proof is based.
However Mr Goodman felt bound to admit STBS's proof, marked 'objected to';
Rainbow's proof, similarly marked, was also admitted; and after Mr Goodman had been
removed from office by Rainbow's votes, Mr Moses was appointed as his successor by   E
the votes of STBS and the other associated companies, claiming to be creditors for about
£6m in all.

I have already referred to some affidavit evidence which has been put in very late.
Apart from an affidavit of Mr Moses (which sets out his qualifications and experience,
and asserts his independence) there are four affidavits. First, an affidavit of Mr Anthony
Millner sworn on 4 October 1994: he was the company's financial controller until he was
summarily dismissed on 22 February 1993. He deposes that he had not (until recently   F
shown copies) seen or heard of the alleged agreement of 1 April 1992 or the board minute
of 18 May 1992. As to the agreement he says that had he been aware of it, he would have
been responsible for raising quarterly charges for computer leasing and services; he is
'absolutely certain' that he never raised any invoices for these matters.

Secondly, there is an affidavit sworn by Mrs Korenberg on 7 October 1944. She gives
an address in New York, though the affidavit was sworn in London WC2. Her affidavit   G
states that, 'STBS is in principle content for the company to be compulsorily wound up',
but goes on to add various qualifications and to refer to various matters of peripheral
relevance (including proceedings by Rainbow against another associated company which
was a guarantor, and proceedings by other associated companies against another ex-
employee, Mr Michael Dougan). The most remarkable thing about this affidavit is what
it does not say. It omits reference to the alleged agreement of 1 April 1992 (to which Mrs
Korenberg was a signatory) or to the board minute of 18 May 1992 (a board meeting   H
attended by Mrs Korenberg).

Thirdly, there is an affidavit sworn on 10 October 1994 by Mr Kenneth Morgan. This
strongly disputes Mr Millner's affidavit and exhibits copies of invoices and VAT returns
– the latter apparently signed by Mr Millner which (if they are genuine) cast doubt on
the whole of Mr Millner's affidavit. Fourthly there is Mr Brewer's third affidavit, sworn

A   on 11 October 1994. I have already said all that I need to say about that affidavit. There are sharp conflicts between some of these deponents which may have to be resolved by cross-examination in due course when particular claims are investigated. I cannot resolve them, and I think I must decide what order to make on the petition without attaching any weight, at this stage, to Mr Millner's affidavit. That is not to say that I accept the opposing creditors' general submission that every 'whistle blower' is actuated by malice and is for that reason to be disregarded.

B   When the petition came on for hearing before me Mr Roberts (for STBS, G & B Switzerland and General Financial) applied to join the list of opposing creditors. His application was not opposed by Mr Davies and was allowed. I record without comment that Mr Roberts, in making his application, told me that STBS's claim was for about £85,000; I enquired whether it was not for £5.5m, and Mr Roberts demurred; later that day, however, he told me that the claim was indeed for £5.5m.

C   In exercising my discretion whether to order the compulsory winding-up of a company which is already in creditors' voluntary liquidation, I have to take account of both the quantity and the quality of the claims of the petitioning creditor (who in this case stands alone) on the one hand, and the opposing creditors on the other hand. It is not simply a question of arithmetic. Fairness and commercial morality may require that a substantial independent creditor, which feels itself to have been prejudiced by what it regards as sharp practice, should be able to insist on the company's affairs being scrutinised by the

D process which follows a compulsory order. Such a creditor is entitled to an investigation which is not only independent, but can be seen to be independent. This may be so even where the voluntary liquidation is already well advanced and a compulsory order may cause further expense and delay (and in this case STBS's enormous new claim, unless quickly proved false, must set back the progress that has been made). These principles are very clearly stated in the authorities to which I was referred – notably *Re Lowestoft*

E *Traffic Services Co Ltd* (1986) 2 BCC 98,945 and *Re Palmer Marine Surveys Ltd* (1985) 1 BCC 99,557 (two decisions of Hoffmann J made within a fortnight of each other in October 1985) and *Re Falcon R J Developments Ltd* (1987) 3 BCC 146 (decided by Vinelott J).

  These decisions are helpful in setting out the principles or guidelines on which the court's discretion is to be exercised, and it is not helpful to go into any detailed examination of the facts of other cases (Diplock LJ made the same point in *Re J D Swain*

F *Ltd* [1965] 1 WLR 909 at p. 913). It is not therefore appropriate to embark (as counsel for the opposing creditors seemed to be inviting me to do) on a detailed comparison of the facts of this case and those of the reported cases. But Mr Roberts was wrong if he submitted (as my note indicates) that *Falcon Developments* was a clear case of a majority of creditors (by value) favouring a compulsory order: in fact the figures were disputed and closely balanced, and Vinelott J made a compulsory order because he thought it

G right to disregard the views of the principal group shareholders and the associated companies (see (1987) 3 BCC 146 at pp. 155–156).

  Counsel told me that they were not aware of any reported case concerned with whether a compulsory order should be made for the winding up of a company, already in voluntary liquidation, where that company was a member of a closely integrated trading group. (The *Falcon Developments* case concerned a small group of companies, but it

H appears that they had no trading relationship.) Where there are inter-group trading activities (and especially where, as in this case, there seems to have been no other trading activity engaged in by the company) there is a good deal of room for manipulation of profit and loss. 'Transfer pricing' and similar activities may attract the notice of revenue authorities if they artificially reduce taxable profits. Equally they must attract the notice of insolvency law if they operate to the prejudice of independent creditors. In this case,

since the last-minute appearance of STBS's huge claim, the inter-group trading activities   A
seem to cry out for investigation. That is a further matter to be taken into account in the
exercise of my discretion.

In these circumstances I have no hesitation in coming to the conclusion that I should
make a compulsory order. This involves no criticism of Mr Moses, but (to paraphrase
Hoffmann J in *Palmer Marine Surveys* (1985) 1 BCC 99,557 at p. 99,563) the fact that
the associated creditors have gone to such lengths to install and maintain Mr Moses in   B
office is itself enough to disqualify him in the eyes of Rainbow; and in view of all that has
happened in this matter Rainbow's attitude cannot be dismissed as irrational. Nor can it
be characterised as a 'witch hunt'; the matters that call for investigation will be
investigated impartially, on behalf of the general body of creditors, during the process of
compulsory liquidation. I shall therefore make the usual compulsory order.

(Order accordingly)   C

A # Re Highway Foods International Ltd.
Mills & Anor v C Harris (Wholesale Meat) Ltd.

Chancery Division (Companies Court).
E G Nugee QC (sitting as a deputy High Court judge).
Judgment delivered 17 October 1994.

B *Receivership – Retention of title – Application for directions – Meat sold to buyer on retention of title terms and subsold on retention of title terms – Receivers appointed to buyer – Neither buyer nor subpurchaser had paid for meat – Seller and receivers sought payment from subpurchaser – Whether title had passed to buyer under agreement to sell – Whether reservation of title clause created security interest – Factors Act 1889, s. 2(1), s. 9.*

C This was an application by the receivers of Highway Foods International Ltd under s. 35 of the Insolvency Act 1986 for directions whether they or the respondent were entitled to the proceeds of sale of meat sold by the respondent to Highway on retention of title terms and subsold by Highway on retention of title terms.

The respondent, 'Harris', supplied meat to Highway on Harris's standard terms and conditions which included a retention of title clause. The meat was subsold on Highway's standard terms and conditions to 'Kingfry'. Again the standard terms included a retention
D of title clause. Before Highway had paid Harris or Kingfry had paid Highway for the meat (although some ten per cent of it had already been processed), Kingfry complained direct to Harris that a metal tag had been found in the meat. Harris, not having been paid, agreed to 'repossess' the 90 per cent of the meat which had not been processed, purporting to act under the retention of title clause in its contract with Highway. Harris would investigate the meat (at Kingfry's premises) and resupply it direct to Kingfry.

E Receivers were then appointed to Highway who disputed Harris's claim to be entitled to possession of the meat or to the proceeds of the subsale to Kingfry. The receivers applied to the court for directions whether Harris had a proprietary or security interest in the sum of £30,897.04 (the price Highway agreed to pay Harris for the whole consignment of meat) which had been placed on deposit by Kingfry pending resolution of the dispute.

F The receivers argued that Highway, having agreed to buy the meat and obtained possession of it with the consent of Harris, had delivered it under an agreement of sale to Kingfry; and that agreement was a sale or other disposition of goods within s. 2(1) of the Factors Act 1889; the disposition was therefore as valid as if it had been expressly authorised by Harris and title passed to Kingfry. By virtue of s. 9 of the Factors Act the fact that the contract between Highway and Kingfry was only an agreement for sale and was subject to a retention of title clause did not prevent the title passing to Kingfry.

G *Held,* determining that Harris was entitled to the purchase price of the meat it repossessed (£27,703.60) and that the receivers were entitled to the purchase price of the processed meat (£3,193.44):

1. Assuming, as required by s. 2(1) and 9 of the 1889 Act, that Highway's agreement for sale was as valid as if it had been expressly authorised by Harris, title would not have passed to Kingfry until Highway had been paid, and there would be nothing to divest Harris of the
H title it retained under its contract with Highway. The effect of s. 2(1) was only to render the buyer's agreement for sale as valid as if it had been expressly authorised by the seller; the conditions for the passing of title under the buyer's agreement for sale to the subpurchaser had still to be satisfied. Accordingly the meat was still the property of Harris when it retook possession of it and agreed to sell it to Kingfry. (*W Hanson (Harrow) Ltd v Rapid Civil Engineering Ltd* (1987) 38 BLR 106 considered.)

2. To hold that a reservation of title clause gave the seller no more than a security   **A**
interest, on the ground that his title to the goods could be defeated by the buyer's paying the
purchase price in full, would render reservation of title clauses useless in all cases unless
registered. Harris retained title to the unprocessed meat at the date it repossessed it. (Clough
Mill Ltd v Martin [1985] 1 WLR 111 applied.)

3. The fact that the time allowed for payment had not expired did not affect the fact that
Harris retained the title to the meat.
  B

4. Kingfry acquired title to the processed meat. Highway delivered possession of the meat
to Kingfry under an agreement for sale within the meaning of s. 9 of the 1889 Act. Under
s. 2(1) that disposition was as valid as if it had been expressly authorised by Harris. When
title to the meat which had been processed passed to Kingfry, the price paid for it was
subject to the retention of title clause in the contract between Harris and Highway which
gave Harris only a security interest in the proceeds of the sale by Highway to Kingfry. That
  C
security interest, being unregistered, was void against the receivers.

The following cases were referred to in the judgment:

Clough Mill Ltd v Martin [1985] 1 WLR 111.
Compaq Computer Ltd v Abercorn Group Ltd & Ors [1991] BCC 484.
Hanson (W) (Harrow) Ltd v Rapid Civil Engineering Ltd (1987) 38 BLR 106.
Modelboard Ltd v Outer Box Ltd [1992] BCC 945.
  D
Tatung (UK) Ltd v Galex Telesure Ltd & Ors (1989) 5 BCC 325.

Nigel Burroughs (instructed by Hammond Suddards) for the applicants.

Jeremy Callman (instructed by Cornish & Co) for the respondent.

JUDGMENT

  E
E G Nugee QC: This is an application for directions pursuant to s. 35 of the *Insolvency
Act* 1986. The applicants are the joint administrative receivers of Highway Foods
International Ltd ('Highway'), appointed on 2 February 1993 under the terms of a
debenture dated 31 May 1988 by which Highway charged its assets, including book
debts, to Lloyds Bank plc. I will refer to them as 'the receivers'. The respondent, C Harris
(Wholesale Meat) Ltd ('Harris'), supplied a large quantity of meat, consisting of
43,440lbs of boneless lamb breasts and other lamb and 14,278lbs of bacon trims, to
  F
Highway between 7 and 30 December 1992 at a total price of £30,897.04 on Harris's
standard terms and conditions, which were set out on the face of its invoices. Payment
was to be made within 28 days, and the conditions of sale included the following retention
of title clause:

> '5. The ownership of the goods in the original or any altered form will only be
> transferred to the buyer when he has paid all that is owing to the seller. On resale   **G**
> the buyer shall remain accountable to the seller for the whole of the proceeds of
> the sale(s) so long as any indebtedness whatever remains outstanding from the
> buyer to the seller. The seller reserves the right to enter and collect from any
> premises goods in their original or altered form where moneys are overdue, or
> where bankruptcy/liquidation proceedings are pending/effective, or a receiver has
> been appointed.'

  H
Highway sub-sold the meat (together with other meat) to Kingfry Meat Products Ltd
('Kingfry') for £33,202.16 and delivered it to Kingfry's premises between 8 December
1992 and 7 January 1993. The meat was sub-sold on Highway's standard terms and
conditions, which were printed on the back of the invoice and referred to on the face of
it. Payment was to be made within 21 days of delivery of the meat, and the conditions of
sale included a retention of title clause of which the following are the material subclauses:

A

'3. *Title to goods*

(a) In no circumstances shall legal title in the goods on any sale pass from the seller to the buyer until the buyer shall have paid the seller in full for such goods.

. . .

(c) Until title in the goods has passed to the buyer, the buyer shall hold the goods as bailee for the seller and, so long as they have not been resold by the buyer or
B incorporated with other goods not the property of the seller to the extent that they have lost their identity and cannot be extracted, shall deliver up the goods to the seller or to his order on demand.

(d) The buyer shall, if so requested by the seller at any time, at no cost to the seller keep all such goods in a separate part of the buyer's premises and shall cause them to be clearly marked with the fact of the seller's ownership on them. The seller shall
C be entitled at any reasonable time to enter any premises of the buyer, or premises where the goods or any of them are stored for the buyer, to inspect its goods or repossess them or any of them if and to the extent that they have not been lawfully resold in the ordinary course of business or incorporated with other goods not the property of the seller whereby they have lost their identity and cannot be extracted.

(e) During any such bailment of the goods, notwithstanding that the title shall not
D have passed to the buyer, the buyer shall in the ordinary course of business be entitled to resell the goods or use the goods for mixing, processing or manufacture; provided that none of the events set out above in condition 2(d) have occurred (if any such event has occurred no goods of the seller may be sold or charged, or used in mixing, processing or manufacture, or otherwise dealt with, or moved, without the seller's prior written agreement).'

On 13 January 1993 Kingfry complained to Harris that a metal tag had been found in
E the meat. Mr Alvin Harris, Harris's managing director, went to Kingfry's factory to discuss the problem, accompanied by Mr Kourouklaris, a certified meat technologist and inspector. Mr Sergiou of Kingfry told Mr Harris that Kingfry had not paid Highway for the meat, most of which was still in Kingfry's cold store, though some ten per cent of it had already been processed. Highway had also not yet paid Harris for the meat; and after further discussion it was agreed that Harris would repossess the remainder of the meat,
F purporting to act under condition 5 of its contract with Highway, would carry out a thorough investigation, and would then re-supply Kingfry with the meat once it was confident that it was safe for use. It was further agreed that the price Kingfry would pay Harris would be no more than the price Highway would have paid Harris. In fact Harris never physically repossessed the meat, which at all times remained in Kingfry's premises, where it was examined by Harris. On 29 January Harris wrote to Highway saying:

G
'Following the non-payment of these goods supplied by our company we have exercised our rights under our conditions of sale, para. 5.'

On 1 February Harris wrote to Kingfry saying:

'Under our terms and conditions of sale ownership of the goods does not vest in Highway Foods International Ltd until payment. As we have not received payment for the goods, we have exercised our rights under para. 5 of the terms and conditions of sale. . . . As you are willing to purchase the goods directly from us,
H we are arranging for a credit note to be issued to Highway Foods International Ltd and enclose our invoices for £ . . . in respect of the agreed sale of these goods.'

No invoices were in fact enclosed, but subsequently, though not until 17 December 1993 after the meat had been paid for in full, Harris invoiced Kingfry for £27,703.60, being the price for the meat remaining unprocessed (38,880lbs of lamb and 12,850lbs of bacon trims), calculated at the same rate per pound as Highway had agreed to pay. On

the same day, 17 December, Harris issued a credit note to Highway. However, despite   A
the delay in sending the invoice, I am satisfied that Mr Harris and Mr Sergiou agreed at
Kingfry's factory on 13 January that Kingfry would purchase the balance of the meat
remaining unprocessed directly from Harris.

On 15 February the solicitors for the receivers notified Kingfry that they denied
Harris's claim to be entitled to possession of the meat or to the proceeds of the sub-sale
to Kingfry. The receivers' evidence as to what happened next is as follows: B

> 'After a lengthy dispute between the joint administrative receivers, Kingfry and
> [Harris] over payment by Kingfry for the meat, £36,335.46 was paid by Kingfry to
> the joint administrative receivers and £32,368.14 was placed on deposit, of which
> the sum of £30,897.04 is claimed by [Harris].'

The directions sought by the receivers are in the following terms:

> 'Whether in the events which have happened [Harris] has a proprietary or security   C
> or any interest in the sum of £30,897.04 currently held in a deposit account at
> Midland Bank plc in the joint names of the solicitors acting for the [receivers],
> Hammond Suddards, and the solicitors acting for [Harris], Cornish & Co . . .'

The evidence did not show the reason for the difference between the £30,897.04 claimed
by Harris and the £32,368.14 placed on deposit in the joint account, and, subject to one
point on interest which I shall mention, the case has been argued on the footing that the   D
dispute relates solely to the £30,897.04 which represents the price Highway agreed to pay
Harris for the whole consignment of meat.

Harris's case, as summarised in Mr Harris's affidavit, is that:

(a)   Section 9 of the *Factors Act* 1889 did not serve to pass the title in the meat to
     Kingfry on the sale by Highway, and therefore Harris was able to repossess the
     meat and sell it directly to Kingfry. Consequently £27,703.60 of the funds held in   E
     the joint account are the proceeds of sale due to Harris directly under the
     agreement to sell entered into with Kingfry, and do not fall into the administrative
     receivership of Highway.

(b)   Alternatively, if s. 9 of the *Factors Act* 1889 does apply, then the interaction of
     s. 2(1) of the same Act with s. 9 is such that:
       (i)   either, on the facts, title did not pass to Kingfry; or   F
       (ii)   if title did pass, then the proceeds of the sale by Highway are held on trust
          for Harris.

(c)   In the further alternative, of the moneys held in the joint account either:
       (i)   £3,193.44 (being the difference between £30,897.04 and £27,703.60), if the
          court accepts Harris's arguments on s. 9 and/or s. 2(1); or   G
       (ii)   £30,897.04 if the court rules against Harris on s. 9;
     is held on trust for Harris.

Accordingly Harris claims that it has a proprietary interest in the sum held in the joint
account, either as the proceeds of a direct sale by Harris to Kingfry, or as the proceeds of
the original sale from Harris to Highway which are held on trust for Harris.   H

On behalf of Highway, the receivers' case is that:

(a)   Title to the meat passed to Kingfry on delivery to Kingfry by virtue of s. 9 of the
     Factors Act 1889, and accordingly Harris was not entitled to repossess the meat,
     and has only an action in debt or conversion against Highway, which gives it no
     proprietary interest in the proceeds of the sub-sale of the meat.

A (b) Alternatively Harris has at most not a proprietary interest in the proceeds of sale but only a security interest, and that interest is void against the receivers for want of registration under s. 395 of the *Companies Act* 1985.

(c) In the further alternative, if title to the meat remained vested in Harris after delivery to Kingfry, so that Harris was able to repossess the meat which had not been processed and resell it to Kingfry, Harris had only a security interest in the ten per cent which had been processed by Kingfry, and this interest was void against the receivers for want of registration under s. 395.

B

I turn then to the *Factors Act* 1889. Section 9 provides as follows:

'Where a person, having bought or agreed to buy goods, obtains with the consent of the seller possession of the goods or the documents of title to the goods, the delivery or transfer, by that person or by a mercantile agent acting for him, of the goods or documents of title, under any sale, pledge, or other disposition thereof, [or under any agreement for sale, pledge, or other disposition thereof], to any person receiving the same in good faith and without notice of any lien or other right of the original seller in respect of the goods, shall have the same effect as if the person making the delivery or transfer were a mercantile agent in possession of the goods or documents of title with the consent of the owner.'

C

D The section is identical with s. 25 of the *Sale of Goods Act* 1979, with the significant exception that the latter section omits the words which I have enclosed in square brackets. Section 9 of the Factors Act has not, however, been repealed, and if the words in square brackets give it a wider operation than s. 25 of the *Sale of Goods Act* 1979 advantage can be taken of them.

It has been said that the last four lines of s. 9 'give rise to considerable difficulty' (*Benjamin's Sale of Goods*, 4th edn, para. 7-081), and that 'this is a somewhat obscure provision to say the least' (McCormack's *Reservation of Title*, p. 165). They do not seem to me to present a great problem in the present case. To understand them one has to refer to s. 2(1) of the *Factors Act* 1889, which, so far as is material, provides as follows:

E

'Where a mercantile agent is, with the consent of the owner, in possession of goods . . . any sale, pledge, or other disposition of the goods, made by him when acting in the ordinary course of business of a mercantile agent, shall . . . be as valid as if he were expressly authorised by the owner of the goods to make the same; provided that the person taking under the disposition acts in good faith, and has not at the time of the disposition notice that the person making the disposition has not authority to make the same.'

F

The receivers say that Highway, having agreed to buy the meat and obtained possession of it with the consent of Harris, delivered it under an agreement for sale to Kingfry; that this agreement was a sale or other disposition of the goods within s. 2(1); that this disposition was as valid as if it had been expressly authorised by Harris; and that the title to the meat therefore passed to Kingfry.

G

There is an obvious weakness in this line of reasoning. Had Highway actually sold the meat to Kingfry, I do not think Harris could have disputed that title would have passed. But the contract between Highway and Kingfry was not a sale but an agreement for sale, under which the title was not to pass until, at the earliest, Highway had been paid in full for the meat (for the distinction between a sale and an agreement for sale see the *Sale of Goods Act* 1979, s. 2(4) and (5)). On 13 January 1993 Highway had not been paid any part of the purchase price. Assuming, as is required by the combined effect of s. 2(1) and 9, that Highway's agreement for sale was as valid as if it had been expressly authorised by Harris, title would not have passed to Kingfry by that date, and there would be nothing to divest Harris of the title which it had retained by cl. 3 of its contract with Highway. Accordingly the meat was still the property of Harris when it retook possession

H

on that date and agreed to sell it to Kingfry. This is the conclusion reached in Benjamin   A
at para. 5-128:

> 'The title of sub-purchasers from the buyer of goods supplied subject to a
> reservation of title provision in a Romalpa clause will ordinarily not be affected by
> the fact that the buyer is not the owner of the goods. They will acquire a good title
> under s. 25(1) of the *Sale of Goods Act* 1979 or under s. 2(1) of the *Factors Act*
> 1889, or because the buyer has the express or implied authority of the seller to sell   B
> the goods in the ordinary course of business and confer a good title on sub-
> purchasers. More difficulty, however, arises where the buyer in turn agrees to sell
> the goods to a sub-purchaser subject to a retention of title provision, and delivers
> the goods to the sub-purchaser. In such a case it would seem that, unless and until
> the sub-purchaser has paid the price of the goods or satisfied such other conditions
> as may have been stipulated by the buyer for the passing of property to the sub-
> purchaser, the seller would be entitled to claim the goods as his property in the   C
> hands of the sub-purchaser.'

Benjamin adds a footnote:

> '*Hanson (W) (Harrow) Ltd v Rapid Civil Engineering Ltd* (1987) 38 Build LR 106.
> But the sub-purchaser may be able to rely on the words "or under any agreement
> for sale . . . or other disposition" in s. 9 of the *Factors Act* 1889.'

Mr Burroughs, counsel for the receivers, took up the suggestion in the footnote, and   D
argued that the fact that the contract between Highway and Kingfry was only an
agreement for sale and was subject to a Romalpa clause did not prevent the title passing
to Kingfry. In my judgment the suggestion is not well-founded. It is quite true that, under
s. 9, unlike s. 25 of the *Sale of Goods Act* 1979, s. 2(1) applies where the buyer in
possession has entered into an agreement for sale to a sub-purchaser as well as where he
has actually sold; but the effect of s. 2(1) is only to render the buyer's agreement for sale   E
as valid as if it had been expressly authorised by the seller; and this is not enough to get
the sub-purchaser home if the conditions for the passing of title under the buyer's
agreement for sale to the sub-purchaser have not been satisfied.

The facts in *Hanson* were indistinguishable from those of the present case. Hanson
agreed to sell timber to Rapid subject to a retention of title clause. Rapid delivered the
timber to Usborne under a contract which provided that no property in the goods should
pass until payment of the relevant instalment under the contract. No payments were   F
made by Rapid or Usborne. Judge Davies QC had no hesitation in holding that, because
no payment was made, there was no sale within the meaning of s. 25, and accordingly
Usborne did not obtain any title to the timber. It appears that the argument on behalf of
Usborne was based solely on s. 25 of the *Sale of Goods Act* 1979 and s. 2 of the *Factors
Act* 1889, and no reliance was placed on s. 9 of the latter Act; and it is no doubt this
omission that led to the suggestion in the footnote in Benjamin. In my judgment,   G
however, Usborne would clearly have fared no better had an argument been presented
based on s. 9, since it would have been unable to point to any agreement under which
title would have passed to it had the timber belonged to Rapid at the date of the
agreement.

Mr Burroughs submitted that it was wrong to call the second agreement in the present
case an agreement to sell, because the title was still in Harris and Highway did not have
it. I do not agree. Highway had it in its power to obtain the title at any time by paying   H
the purchase price to Harris. In any event I do not see how this submission improves the
position of Highway or Kingfry.

Mr Burroughs further submitted that, because Harris's title was defeasible on payment
by Highway of the purchase price, it amounted to no more than a security interest, which
was void against the receivers for want of registration. There is much discussion in the

A cases and in the leading textbooks on the question whether a provision under which the buyer is required to pay the whole proceeds of any sale by him into a separate account, which is to remain the property of the seller, gives the seller a proprietary interest in the money in the account or merely a charge on it, on the footing that when the buyer has paid the seller the whole of the price due to him the seller must release the balance in the account to the buyer; and I shall have to refer to this when I come to consider Harris's claim to so much of the sum paid by Kingfry as relates to the ten per cent of the meat

B which had been processed. But to hold that a simple reservation of title clause gave the seller no more than a security interest, on the ground that his title to the goods could be defeated by the buyer's paying the purchase price in full, would render reservation of title clauses useless in all cases unless registered. The effectiveness of a simple provision for reservation of title, notwithstanding additional provisions in the same clause of more doubtful validity, and notwithstanding that the underlying purpose of the clause is clearly

C to provide a form of security for the payment of the purchase price, has, however, been well established from the time of the decision of the Court of Appeal in *Clough Mill Ltd v Martin* [1985] 1 WLR 111, if not earlier. So far as the unprocessed meat is concerned, therefore, I have no doubt that Harris retained the title at the date it repossessed it.

Mr Burroughs submitted further that Harris had no right, on 13 January 1993, to repossess from Kingfry the two consignments of meat which had been delivered to

D Kingfry on 30 December 1992 and 7 January 1993 (which amounted to about 17 per cent of the whole), because, under the contract between Highway and Kingfry, Kingfry had 21 days in which to pay for the meat and this period had not expired. The fact that the time allowed for payment had not expired does not in my judgment affect the fact that Harris retained the title to the meat throughout. Whether the position might have been different had Highway tendered the full price of the meat within the 28 days allowed under its contract with Harris is a question which does not arise. No such tender was

E made at any time. It may be that Harris's repossession of the meat within the 21 days or the 28 days and before the receivers were appointed amounted to a breach of its contract with Highway; but that is not a question which is before me, and it is difficult in any event to see what damage Highway suffered as a result of Harris's repossession even if it was to some extent premature.

F I hold therefore that Harris is entitled to the purchase price of the meat which it repossessed and in respect of which it sent Kingfry an invoice for £27,703.60.

Its claim to be entitled to the purchase price of the meat which had already been processed and which accordingly it did not repossess depends on rather different considerations. If Highway had been paid for this meat, Harris would have had to rely on the provision in condition 3 of its conditions of sale, that:

G 'On resale the buyer shall remain accountable to the seller for the whole of the proceeds of the sale(s) so long as any indebtedness whatever remains outstanding from the buyer to the seller.'

'The whole of the proceeds of sale' would, of course, have included Highway's profit. If the effect of this provision was to constitute Highway a trustee for Harris of the whole of the proceeds of sale, as Harris would have had to contend in order to establish a proprietary interest in such proceeds, Highway would have had a right to discharge its

H indebtedness to Harris and take the balance of the proceeds of sale for itself, thereby defeating Harris's beneficial interest in such balance. The legal consequence would be that Harris's interest in the proceeds of sale would be a security interest, which would be void against the receivers for want of registration: see *Tatung (UK) Ltd v Galex Telesure Ltd & Ors* (1989) 5 BCC 325; *Compaq Computer Ltd v Abercorn Group Ltd & Ors* [1991] BCC 484; *Modelboard Ltd v Outer Box Ltd* [1992] BCC 945.

In fact, however, Kingfry did not pay the purchase price to Highway. It paid a rather   A
larger sum into the joint account to which I have referred, to await the outcome of these
proceedings. As I have mentioned, the dispute concerns the title to part only of that sum,
namely the precise amount claimed by Harris. In these circumstances I do not think the
receivers can contend simply that the money in the joint account constitutes a larger fund
over which Harris has a charge for the smaller amount claimed by it, as would have been
the case had Kingfry paid to Highway the whole amount for which it had agreed to buy
the meat. Harris has not asserted any interest in the money in the joint account so far as   B
it exceeds the price at which it agreed to sell the meat first to Highway and then to
Kingfry, except in so far as it is entitled to interest on the purchase price; and it has not
been suggested that the rather larger sum which was paid into the joint account should
be regarded as security for the payment of a smaller sum to Harris, or that there was any
similar agreement between the parties when the payment into the joint account was made.
To the extent that Harris is entitled to be paid by Kingfry, the payment into the joint   C
account is in my view to be treated in the same way as if it were a payment to Harris. To
the extent that Highway is entitled, it should be treated as if it were a payment to
Highway.

As between Harris and Highway, Highway never acquired title to the meat which was
processed by Kingfry; but by the time it had been processed by Kingfry it had lost its
identity, and Harris did not assert a claim to ownership of it in January 1993 or at any   D
subsequent time. Kingfry clearly acquired title to the resulting product, at the latest when
it paid for the meat which it contained. As between Highway and Kingfry, in my
judgment, condition 3(c) and (d) of Highway's standard terms and conditions envisaged
that, if Highway initially had title to the meat, the title would pass to Kingfry when the
meat had been incorporated with other goods not the property of Highway whereby it
had lost its identity and could not be extracted.

At this point it is in my judgment necessary to return to s. 2(1) and 9 of the *Factors Act*   E
1889. Highway delivered possession of the meat to Kingfry under an agreement for sale
within the meaning of s. 9. Under s. 2(1) this disposition was as valid as if it had been
expressly authorised by Harris. In my judgment the terms of the disposition are therefore
binding on Harris. When title to the meat which had been processed passed to Kingfry,
the price paid for it to the receivers must in my judgment be treated as paid to Highway.

Once in Highway's hands, it became subject to the retention of title clause in the   F
contract between Harris and Highway; but, for the reasons which I have given, that
clause gave Harris only a security interest in the proceeds of the sale by Highway to
Kingfry. That security interest, being unregistered, was void against the receivers. It
cannot, I think, make any difference that the amount in issue between the parties is the
precise amount of the purchase price due to Harris: for whether the retention of title
clause creates a charge on the purchase price when paid to Highway must in my judgment   G
turn on the true construction of the clause, not on the amount paid, or treated as paid,
to Highway.

Accordingly, in my judgment, the receivers, and not Harris, are entitled to the purchase
price of the processed meat, namely £3,193.44.

Harris claimed interest on the amount due to it during part or all of the period before   H
the money was paid into the joint account. The basis of the claim was that the money
was subject to a trust in favour of Harris. In my judgment Harris's right to the £27,703.60
was the ordinary seller's right to the proceeds of the sale by Harris of the meat which it
had repossessed, and this carries no right to interest. If Harris had had to rely on asserting
a trust of the proceeds of a sale by Highway, it would have failed because of the want of
registration, and no question of interest would have arisen.

A   Any interest earned on the money in the joint account during the period since it was paid in will, of course, be divisible between Harris and the receivers in the proportions in which they are entitled to the principal.

(*Order accordingly*)

Re PFTZM Ltd (in liquidation)　　　　　　　　　　　　　　　A
Jourdain & Ors v Paul.

Chancery Division (Companies Court).
His Honour Judge Paul Baker QC (sitting as a High Court judge).
Judgment delivered 18 November 1994.

> *Liquidation – Private examination – Questionnaire – Scope of questionnaire was*　　B
> *to see whether respondents were shadow directors – Respondents refused to answer*
> *questionnaire as oppressive – Liquidator obtained ex parte order for private*
> *examination – Application to set aside ex parte order – Whether questions were*
> *oppressive – Whether prima facie case that respondents were shadow directors –*
> *Insolvency Act 1986, s. 214, 236, 251.*

This was an application to set aside an ex parte order obtained by the liquidators of　　C
PFTZM Ltd under s. 236 of the Insolvency Act 1986.

The business of the company was running a hotel/country club. It owned the freehold of
the hotel and the surrounding sites. In 1988 'S' purchased shares in the company for £4.5m
and became its managing director. He also obtained planning permission to make
improvements to the hotel at a cost of £2.25m. In March 1989 the borrowing of the company
was refinanced by 'Humberclyde', a group of bankers and financiers, to the tune of £6.75m.
The security was a 125-year lease of the company's premises which were then leased back　　D
to the company for a 25-year term. The rent under that sublease was the interest on the loan
for five years and then increased to take account of capital repayments of the loan.

In April 1990 the improved club opened for business but did not produce profits to meet
the outgoings. In January 1991 S stated the forecast profits would not be enough to service
the rent under the lease and informed Humberclyde of this. It was agreed that S would
remain as managing director but he would draw no salary until the project showed a profit.　　E
It was further agreed that weekly management meetings would be held concerning the
trading of the business, which would be attended by the applicants who were officers of
Humberclyde. This arrangement lasted for almost two years, until the company went into
liquidation.

In February 1994 the liquidators wrote to the applicants, enclosing a questionnaire
relating to their involvement with the company. These questions were answered but then
another questionnaire was sent, asking for more information. These questions were regarded　　F
as oppressive by the applicants and were not answered. The liquidator responded telling the
applicants that he intended to make an inter partes application under s. 236 of the Insolvency
Act requiring the applicants to furnish the liquidator with information relating to the
company. However the liquidator then obtained the order ex parte, and the applicants
applied to have that order set aside.

Held, setting aside the registrar's order:　　　　　　　　　　　　　　　G

1. There was no good ground for the application having been made ex parte.

2. The court would not examine whether there had been material non-disclosure of facts
to the registrar. There was no proper analogy to be drawn from other ex parte orders which
could be set aside on that ground. The court had to examine the merits of the order obtained.

3. The first questionnaire was directed to discovering whether the applicants were shadow　　H
directors. The main purpose of the supplementary questionnaire was not to elicit further
information or documents but to obtain admissions or explanations regarding the
information already obtained, to extract admissions which showed that the officers of
Humberclyde had become shadow directors. Those questions were oppressive and
misdirected being designed to furnish evidence which could be relied upon in trying to
establish liability in people who were third parties, not directors.

A   4. There was no prima facie case made out that the applicants were shadow directors, and it was unlikely that further information would come to light to show that they were. They were not acting as directors of the company; they were acting in defence of their own interests. This was not a case where the directors were accustomed to act in accordance with the directions of the applicants. It was a case where the creditor made terms for the continuation of credit in the light of threatened default. The directors of the company were quite free to take the offer or leave it.

B

The following cases were referred to in the judgment:

Bletchley Boat Co Ltd, Re [1974] 1 WLR 630.
British & Commonwealth Holdings plc, Re (No. 2). British & Commonwealth Holdings plc v Spicer & Oppenheim [1992] BCC 172 (CA); [1992] BCC 977, [1993] AC 426 (HL).
Cloverbay, Re (No. 2) [1990] BCC 414; [1991] Ch 90.
Maxwell Communications Corp plc, Re [1994] BCC 741.

C
North Australian Territory Co, Re (1890) 45 ChD 87.

David Chivers (instructed by Cameron Markby Hewitt) for the applicants.

Ashley Underwood (instructed by Hill Taylor Dickinson) for the liquidator.

JUDGMENT

D   **His Honour Judge Paul Baker QC:** This is an application to set aside an ex parte order of Mr Registrar Simmonds which he made on 3 June 1994. The order was obtained on the application of Mr Nigel Trevor Paul, one of the joint liquidators of the company, PFTZM Ltd. It was directed to Mr Michael Jourdain, Mr David Powell and Mr M J Dix, those being officers of Humberclyde Finance Group Ltd. It required them to attend before the registrar, and I quote from the order:

E   '. . . to be examined on oath in the above matters and to have and produce all books papers and other documents in their possession or under their control relating to the company.'

The order was sought under s.236 of the *Insolvency Act* 1986. Subsection (1) of s. 236 states that this section applies as does s. 234. Going back to subs. (1) of s. 234, that section applies (inter alia) in the case where the company goes into liquidation. Then the subsection finishes off:

F   '. . . and the "office-holder" means the administrator, the administrative receiver, the liquidator or the provisional liquidator, as the case may be.'

Returning to s. 236(2):

'The court may, on the application of the office-holder, summon to appear before it–

G   (a)   any officer of the company,

(b)   any person known or suspected to have in his possession any property of the company or supposed to be indebted to the company, or

(c)   any person whom the court thinks capable of giving information concerning the promotion, formation, business, dealings, affairs, or property of the company.'

H   Going on to subs. (3):

'The court may require any such person as is mentioned in subsection 2(a) to (c) to submit an affidavit to the court containing an account of his dealings with the company or to produce any books, papers or other records in his possession or under his control relating to the company or the matters mentioned in paragraph (c) of the subsection.'

That is as far as I think I need read from s. 236. One sees the essence of it is the obtaining   A
of the information concerning the business, dealings, affairs or property of the company,
and the production of books or documents relating to those matters.

Section 236 is an old provision. It first appeared in the *Companies Act* 1862, but has
recently been considered in the higher courts in this country in connection with the
Maxwell débâcle. Its purpose is to enable liquidators, who normally come in as strangers
to the affairs of a company, to obtain information to assist them in carrying out their   B
functions. There had been two views as to its scope. The narrower view was that its object
was confined to reconstituting the knowledge of the company, and thus was limited to
the obtaining of facts and documents known to the company before liquidation. The
broader view was that the scope was not so limited but extended to all facts which could
assist the liquidator in carrying out his functions, whether to get in assets or make reports
on the conduct of officers of the company. It might include the obtaining of information
which the company did not possess or could not have possessed before liquidation.   C

This division of opinion was exposed in the Court of Appeal in the case of *Re British
& Commonwealth Holdings plc (No. 2)* [1992] BCC 172, the majority, that is to say Ralph
Gibson and Woolf L JJ, favouring the broader view. That view was affirmed by the
House of Lords on appeal [1993] BCC 977; [1993] AC 426.

The broader the scope of the enquiry, the more necessary it is to guard against the
possibility of oppressive use of the power, especially when directed against third parties   D
as opposed to the officers of the company. Lord Slynn of Hadley, who delivered the only
reasoned speech, recognised that in the following passage at p. 984D. His Lordship had
been considering the previous authorities, including the one under appeal, and then he
comes to this conclusion:

> 'I am therefore of the opinion that the power of the court to make an order under
> s. 236 is not limited to documents which can be said to be needed "to reconstitute   E
> the state of the company's knowledge" even if that may be one of the purposes
> most clearly justifying the making of an order.

At the same time it is plain that this is an extraordinary power and that the
discretion must be exercised after a careful balancing of the factors involved – on
the one hand the reasonable requirements of the administrator to carry out his
task, on the other the need to avoid making an order which is wholly unreasonable,   F
unnecessary or "oppressive" to the person concerned. The latter was stressed by
Bowen LJ in *Re North Australian Territory Co* (1890) 45 ChD 87 at p. 93:

> "That is an inquisitorial power, which may work with great severity against
> third persons, and it seems to me to be obvious that such a section ought to be
> used with the greatest care, so as not unnecessarily to put in motion the
> machinery of justice when it is not wanted, or to put it in motion at a stage
> when it is not clear that it is wanted, and certainly not to put it in motion if   G
> unnecessary mischief is going to be done or hardship inflicted upon the third
> person who is called upon to appear and give information."

Such an approach was stressed more recently by Brightman J in respect of oral
examination in *Re Bletchley Boat Co Ltd* [1974] 1 WLR 630.

The protection for the person called upon to produce documents lies, thus, not in   H
a limitation by category of documents ("reconstituting the company's state of
knowledge") but in the fact that the applicant must satisfy the court that, after
balancing all the relevant factors, there is a proper case for such an order to be
made. The proper case is one where the administrator reasonably requires to see
the documents to carry out his functions and the production does not impose an
unnecessary and unreasonable burden on the person required to produce them in

A   the light of the administrator's requirements. An application is not necessarily unreasonable because it is inconvenient for the addressee of the application or causes him a lot of work or may make him vulnerable to future claims, or is addressed to a person who is not an officer or employee of or a contractor with the company in administration, but all these will be relevant factors, together no doubt with many others.'

B   The balancing exercise referred to was examined in greater detail in the judgment of Ralph Gibson LJ in the Court of Appeal. I have given the reference already and I am now referring to p. 184–185. The Lord Justice was stating certain principles which are not in dispute. His seventh principle reads as follows:

    'The matters which are relevant to the balancing of the requirements of the office holder against the risk of oppression to the person against whom the order is sought include the following.

C

    (a) The case for making an order against an officer or former officer of the company will usually be stronger than it would be against a third party because officers owe a fiduciary duty to the company and are under a statutory duty (s. 235 of the 1986 Act) to assist the office-holder.

    (b) If, by giving the information sought, a third party risks exposing himself to liability, that involves an element of oppression . . .

D

    (c) An order for an oral examination is more likely to be oppressive than an order for the production of documents: per the Vice-Chancellor in *Re Cloverbay (No. 2)* [1990] BCC 414 at p. 420.

    (d) If someone is suspected of wrongdoing, and in particular fraud, it is oppressive to require him to prove the case against himself on oath before any proceedings are brought: per the Vice-Chancellor in *Cloverbay* at p. 421A.'

E   With that examination of the law, and what I conceive to be the relevant principles, I come to the facts of the matter. The business of the company was running a hotel or country club. The company, then known as Kirtons Farm Country Club and Hotel Ltd, were the freehold owners of the hotel and the surrounding sites. In 1988 the shares in that company were bought by Mr John Steven. He thereupon became the managing director of the company. The shares were bought for the sum of £4.5m. Mr Steven

F obtained planning permission to enlarge the hotel from 30 bedrooms to 55 bedrooms and to do other improvements. The cost of that was something of the order of £2.25m.

    In March 1989 the borrowing of the company was refinanced with Humberclyde, a group of bankers and financiers, of which the main company is the one I have mentioned, Humberclyde Finance Group Ltd. It was refinanced by Humberclyde to the tune of

G £6.75m. That, of course, is the sum of the two figures that I mentioned. The security Humberclyde took was a lease for 125 years of the company's hotel and premises, and then there was a sub-lease for 25 years back to the company. The rent under that sub-lease was the interest on the loan for five years, and then increasing with capital to take account of capital repayments of the loan. I do not have to go into the full details of it, but that was the rough outline of the method of financing.

H   In April 1990 the new and improved club opened for business but it soon became evident that, despite the improvements, the club was not going to produce profits which would meet the outgoings. In January 1991 the managing director, Mr Steven, stated that the forecast profits would not be enough to service the rent under the lease, and Humberclyde were told that. Perhaps for this part of the case I should refer to the affidavit in support of the application of Mr Paul, the liquidator. I should perhaps mention that of course the liquidator did not know anything about the business before

appointment, and the information in his affidavit is gleaned from Mr Steven at an   A
interview between Mr Paul and Mr Steven. It is right, I should say, that Mr Paul adds
this:

> 'I would like to stress that none of Mr Steven's comments have been verified by
> any other party.'

Then he sets out the information which he had received from Mr Steven (at para. 7):

> 'The development was undertaken and the country club opened the new facilities   B
> in April 1990. Mr Steven stated that by January 1991, based on future bookings
> and general interest in the site, the forecast profits from the development would
> not be enough to service the rent. Mr Steven duly advised Humberclyde of this fact
> and after discussions it was agreed that Mr Steven would remain as managing
> director and 80 per cent shareholder of PFTZM Limited, although he would draw
> no salary until the project started to show a profit.   C
>
> 8. In addition it was agreed that weekly management meetings would be held
> concerning the trading of the business, which would be attended by either David
> Powell, a director of Humberclyde, or Michael Jourdain, a Manager employed by
> Humberclyde. In the event, Michael Jourdain duly attended these meetings and
> David Powell attended approximately 50 per cent of the time.
>
> 9. Mr Steven has advised me that all the revenues were to be paid into an account   D
> in the name of Humberclyde. On a four weekly basis the financial controller of
> PFTZM Ltd, Martin Johnston, would process a list of required payments (trade
> creditors, salaries, etc.) which would be discussed in detail at the meetings and
> approval would be obtained from either Mr Jourdain or Mr Powell for the specific
> payment. Mr Jourdain and/or Mr Powell had an ultimate power of veto over those
> persons being paid. Humberclyde would then transfer money from their account
> to the company's trading account at National Westminster Bank plc, Havant,   E
> sufficient to cover the approved payments. The company also had a rolling
> 3-month capital expenditure programme which again required approval by
> Humberclyde. Staff changes also had to be approved by Humberclyde.'

That was the arrangement set in train according to Mr Steven during the following
January 1991. It went on for I suppose the best part of two years because then we pick
up the story again in December 1992. Turning to para. 11 of Mr Paul's affidavit: F

> '11. At the end of December 1992, David Powell asked Mr Steven for his long-
> term views on the project.
>
> 12. On 11 January 1993, Mr Steven received a notice from the local magistrates
> asking him to surrender his liquor licence for the premises. Mr Steven spoke to Mr
> Powell concerning this and Mr Powell advised Mr Steven that Humberclyde had
> decided to foreclose on the loan and intended to grant a 15-year management   G
> contract to Resort Hotel Group, at a rent in excess of the operating profits being
> made by the company. Mr Steven was advised that the employees' jobs would be
> protected, future bookings would be honoured and certain small creditors would
> be paid, to ensure the continued trading of the business.'

That was in January 1993. Thereafter the liquidation of the company followed, I was
told, in March 1993. On 12 November 1993 Mr Paul was appointed one of the joint   H
liquidators of the company.

That is a general history of the matter as it appeared to Mr Paul, the liquidator,
following his interview with Mr Steven.

I come to the involvement of the applicants, the officers of Humberclyde, in this matter.
I now turn to the correspondence mostly between the parties and their respective

A   solicitors. I think the first letter comes from Mr Paul. It opens with a letter of 9 February 1994 which I think is one of several identical letters that were sent to each of the respondents from Mr Paul. This is from the letter to Mr Jourdain:

'I write to advise you that I was appointed liquidator of PFTZM Ltd on 12 November 1993, by the Secretary of State for Trade and Industry, at the request of the official receiver.

B   The principal purpose of this appointment is to investigate the actions of the directors of the company [and those concerned with its management].

In order to commence the investigations, I have prepared the enclosed questionnaire which I would ask you to complete and return to me within 28 days. Where you consider it appropriate, additional information may be given if this will allow me to obtain a better understanding of the transactions entered into by the company, and the ultimate responsibility for the direction of the company.'

C   This I think is important:

'The purpose of this questionnaire is to establish [your] involvement in the trading of a business which was apparently insolvent following the completion of additional extensions in early 1990.

For your information, individual questionnaires have been sent to [the board of Humberclyde and David Powell] to establish to what extent they were involved with the business . . .

D   As I am sure you are aware, I am required to report to the DTI on the actions of both directors and shadow directors and the responses to these questions will enable me to reach a view on whether Humberclyde, [yourself] or Michael Jourdain acted in the capacity of shadow directors for the purpose of the *Insolvency Act* 1986 and the Company Directors' Disqualification Act 1986 and, as such, whether they should be considered in the preparation of my report to the DTI.'

E   One sees the threat there of making investigations to see whether these officers of Humberclyde can be involved as directors and the consequence that they may be liable as such, and to be disqualified under the Act of 1986. That would seem to be then the main purpose of the questioning. The questionnaires were answered by each of the addressees and were returned on 18 March.

F   The next step of importance is that on 25 March Mr Paul submitted a further questionnaire. This is his letter on that occasion, p. 15:

'The answers you have provided are most helpful, but there are certain areas in which I require further explanation, where the reply gives rise to further questions, or where the reply does not agree with the information provided by the directors of PFTZM.

G   Accordingly, I have attached a schedule of further questions which ask for clarification of matters of concern. I have referred to the relevant questions in the original questionnaire rather than repeat the questions, and the further questions should be read in conjunction with your responses to the questionnaire.'

I will return to the nature of those questions later.

H   I turn to the response to that questionnaire which this time comes from the solicitors who act for the applicants in this case, Cameron Markby Hewitt. On 31 March, after referring to *British & Commonwealth Holdings plc v Spicer & Oppenheim* that I have already alluded to, they say:

'We therefore consider the request for answers to further wider-ranging questions to be oppressive for the reasons set out below. Our clients will not therefore be answering the further questions.'

Then I omit other passages in the letter and come to the penultimate paragraph:

A

'Nevertheless, if you consider it necessary to apply for an order requesting answers to your new set of questions, counsel can argue the issue before a registrar or judge. Please ensure such application is made inter partes. The nature of the questions posed by you is not such as to justify going ex parte for an order. It should also be clear to you that our clients will resist the making of any such order(s).'

B

The reply to that came on 14 April from Mr Paul and argued with them the applicability or otherwise of the *British & Commonwealth* case. He then said in the last paragraph:

'Notwithstanding the above, I note your comments in the penultimate paragraph of your letter and I am instructing solicitors to issue an application pursuant to s. 236 of the *Insolvency Act* 1986. I will, of course, ensure that the application is made inter partes.'

C

Such an application was made on 26 April and was directed to all those from whom answers to the questionnaires were sought, and gave notice of the hearing of the application on the part of the liquidators of the company, and then this is the relief sought:

'The parties named herein or any other officer of Humberclyde Finance Group Ltd provide assistance in the form of answers and documentation requested in the letter and enclosures of the liquidator to the parties of 25 March 1994.'

D

That was returnable initially on 16 May, but that I understand was vacated and, ultimately, 9 June was the date set for the hearing of that application.

I next look at a letter from the applicant's solicitors of 10 May in which they say:

'We are informed by our clients that [the company's] liquidation is asset-less. Therefore we do not intend to incur costs by taking this matter further unless the liquidator or your firm is able to provide evidence of the liquidator's ability to meet any costs order made against him in relation to his application. If another creditor is funding the action, please will you provide us with details of the basis and extent of this funding. Given that our clients are not only the subject of this application but are also the largest creditors of [the company], we feel we are entitled to have this information. If you and your client are unwilling to provide the information then we reserve the right to take the matter up with the court as a preliminary issue on 9 June.'

E

F

The liquidator's solicitors have now come on the scene. They write as follows on 12 May:

'You will recall that in your letter to the liquidator dated 31 March 1994 you requested an inter partes hearing in relation to the liquidator's request for further information from your clients. You are no doubt aware that the normal procedure in relation to requests for private examination is that the liquidator attends ex parte and the examinee is given an opportunity to appeal against the order. Notwithstanding the usual procedure, the liquidator has consented to your request and is therefore concerned by your clients' attempts to frustrate the hearing on 9 June by reference to the financial position of the company in liquidation.

G

Unlike the *Insolvency Rules* in relation to the convening of public examinations there is no requirement for applications pursuant to s. 236 of the *Insolvency Act* 1986 to be supported by a deposit by way of security for costs for the examination . . .

H

We anticipate that you will suggest to the court on 9 June that the application seeks an order which would be wholly unreasonable, unnecessary or oppressive to your clients. The liquidator's questions are not unreasonable. They are necessary

A to reconstitute the state of the company's knowledge. Any oppression in terms of legal costs that your clients may have had to bear in relation to the application are entirely the result of your request to the liquidator that an inter partes hearing be convened.

If you are now content to consent to the normal procedure whereby the liquidator will attempt at first instance (ex parte) to convince the court that there are bona

B fide reasons why an order should be made in terms of delivery of documentation and/or public examination of your clients then we would appreciate your setting this out in writing. This would appear to overcome your concerns regarding your clients' exposure to irrecoverable legal costs as a result of your attendance at the hearing on 9 June.'

I have to say that I regard that letter as containing a number of misconceptions. In the

C first case there is no sufficient ground shown for reneging on the consent that they had given that there should be an inter partes hearing. This was a request made through reputable solicitors on behalf of clients that had a substantial interest in the matter. The reasons given do not begin to justify going back on that agreement. I accept that the writer of the letter was not aware of the recent decision of Vinelott J which deals with this aspect of the case. It is a decision of *Re Maxwell Communications Corporation plc* [1994] BCC 741 and his Lordship had given judgment on 21 April 1994, about two or three

D weeks before in other words. It was an application for documents against a firm of solicitors, Titmuss Sainer & Webb, in the ongoing Maxwell litigation. Vinelott J says at the top of p. 747:

'However, although [the solicitors acting for the administrators] were I think justified in seeking an order under s. 236, I am not satisfied that they were justified in making the application ex parte and, when it became apparent that there would be considerable delay before an application could be heard, in failing to give TSW

E notice so that they could attend the hearing. In many if not in most cases where application is made under s. 236, the circumstances do justify the making of an application ex parte and without notice to the person against whom the order is sought. It is not infrequently the case that it is apparent when the application is made that documents which fall clearly within s. 236 will not be produced voluntarily and there may be good reasons for insisting on the confidentiality of

F the statement by the office-holder in support of the application.'

Just pausing at that point, that reason cannot possibly apply to this case. The office holder had made his statement to the court and there was no reason to preserve its confidentiality. Then going on:

'It is not infrequently the case that the production of documents is urgently required and that the delay in obtaining an inter partes hearing or in giving notice

G to the person affected would unduly hamper the office-holder's task.'

That again is not a reason which can be applicable in this case. There are cases where notice in advance of the service of the order might lead to the disappearance of the documents which the office-holder wishes to inspect. There is no suggestion here that the applicants and their solicitors would be parties to conduct leading to the disappearance of the documents.

H Those are the sort of reasons which justify an ex parte order in the view of Vinelott J. Then he goes on:

'However, an application under s. 236 must not be seen as an all embracing exception from the general rule that a person is entitled to be heard before an order of the court is made against him, more particularly if it is a mandatory order requiring the production of documents. Some good reason must be shown justifying an application ex parte. In the instant case there was no good ground for proceeding ex parte and without notice, at least when it became apparent that the application could not be heard before 14 March. The administrators' statement has in fact been made available and confidentiality has not been claimed. In these circumstances I think the inference is that if TSW had been given notice they could have satisfied themselves that the order sought fell within the scope of s. 236(2)(c) and have raised objection to the unduly wide and vague terms which para. 1 was framed. I have no doubt that if this course had been taken the extent of the documents to be produced would have been clarified and the arrangements later made for inspection and taking of copies would then have been made. The order would either not have been necessary or, if necessary, would not have provided for copies of all the documents to be made and supplied by TSW. The costs of the application to set aside the order would therefore have been saved.'

We have seen that the order that was made was for the production here of all documents.

The reasons given to me for going ex parte, which partly one collects from the letter, that it is alleged that the clients were attempting to frustrate the hearing of 9 June by reference to the financial position of the company in liquidation. It is not for the liquidator to rule on the points that are made, to judge the soundness of points that are going to be raised and go ex parte as a result of them. The judicial officer hearing the case, if he so considers, is quite capable of dealing with some point that is raised which may be frivolous or an abuse of the process of the court, or time wasting or something like that. The raising of such points is not a ground for going ex parte. It is a ground for costs following submission to the registrar in due course.

It was submitted to me by Mr Underwood that because of additional points that are going to be taken, the appointment of 9 June would have been insufficient and it would have meant prolonged hearing and it would have had to have gone over to another appointment. Accepting that to be true, that does not seem to me good ground for going to ex parte application, absent any evidence of urgency. The course adopted has taken just as long to resolve as it would have done if there had been an inter partes application in the first place.

Returning to the letter:

'The liquidator's questions are not unreasonable. They are necessary to reconstitute the state of the company's knowledge.'

That is stating too narrowly what the purpose of applications under s. 236 is. Nevertheless the scope of the questions, as stated in the earlier correspondence, was to see whether the parties involved could be shown to be shadow directors with the consequences that ensued. The ex parte application came on and, on 3 June, an ex parte order was made which I have mentioned already. It required them to attend and produce all books, papers and other documents in their possession or under their control relating to the company. So that is a much broader order than was being sought in the inter partes application. The order did give leave to apply to discharge it, and that in fact is the application that is before me. Mr Chivers in his submissions to me said that I ought to set it aside on the ground, among others, that there was a material non-disclosure of facts to the registrar.

I do not propose to do it on that ground, or spend time examining whether that was so. I just comment that I would not be guided by any analogy drawn from similar cases of ex parte orders concerned with Mareva injunctions or Anton Piller orders. The reason is that those orders have an immediate and detrimental effect to the defendant, by freezing his bank accounts, and matters of that sort. The granting of such an order can be very damaging to his commercial reputation which is very difficult later for him to recover if it is shown to be unjustified. Therefore there is a very high duty on parties

A applying for Mareva and similar injunctions to make full disclosure to the judge before whom the application comes. That has nothing like the same weight in the case of an order which merely requires a person to attend in chambers before a registrar at some date in the future to be examined, and which contains within it an order that he can apply to discharge it before any immediate detrimental public effect has been experienced. So I propose to examine the merits of the order obtained rather than dispose of it on that ground.

B

We recall from the letter of 10 March, which sent the questionnaires, that it is indicated that they were directed to discovering whether the addressees were shadow directors, whether the company has been trading while insolvent, and whether their conduct was such as to require a report to be made to the Secretary of State in connection with the *Company Directors Disqualification Act* 1986. It was argued before me by Mr Underwood that there was a strong prima facie case that they were shadow directors, and as such

C would be liable under s. 214 of the Insolvency Act in addition to any liability to be disqualified. Section 214(1):

'Subject to subsection (3) below, if in the course of the winding up of a company it appears that subsection (2) of this section applies in relation to a person who is or has been a director of the company, the court, on the application of the liquidator,

D may declare that that person is to be liable to make such contribution (if any) to the company's assets as the court thinks proper.'

The section applies to a person if:

'(a) the company has gone into insolvent liquidation,'

–that is the case here:

'(b) at some time before the commencement of the winding up of the company,

E that person knew or ought to have concluded that there was no reasonable prospect that the company would avoid going into insolvent liquidation, and

(c) that person was a director of the company at that time;

but the court shall not make a declaration under this section in any case where the time mentioned in paragraph (b) above was before 28 April 1986.'

F Then under subs. (7), directors include a shadow director.

At that point I come to look at the questions and answers which were asked. There was a point taken right at the outset on behalf of the applicants here, that the further questions were oppressive. I do not propose to read them all through, but I will pick up the questionnaire to Michael Jourdain and look for example at question number 9:

G 'Did you recommend taking steps to recover the investment of Humberclyde as soon as you became aware that profitable trading was unlikely?'

Answer:

'This option was considered but not recommended.'

In the further questionnaire, to which objection is taken, there is this under question 9:

H 'Would you please provide details of the reasons for not recommending the recovery of your investment when it was apparent that profitable trading was unlikely. Did you advise the directors that they would be continuing to trade the company whilst insolvent? Did you provide comfort to the directors by way of confirmation that all future creditors of the company would be paid in full? Were you aware of the likely consequences of your recommendations to continue trading an insolvent company which was not profitable? Did you consider the option of

recovery on more than one occasion? Please advise me of the dates on which this   A
option was considered.'

Then I can look at 12. The original question was:

'At what point in time did you become aware that the trading performance of the
company was such that Humberclyde no longer wished to support the company
under the existing financial arrangements?'

Answer: B

'As regards the March 1990 funding, in January 1991. As regards that and the
May 1991 funding, on or about 8 December 1992, but trading performance was
only one factor. JFS's [that is Mr Steven] and other hotel management personnel's
involvement in Compton Holdings, the lack of direction of the management and
the ongoing problems with internal controls including failing to account properly
for VAT were other important factors in Humberclyde's decision that they no   C
longer wished to support the company. These issues all crystallised when the
company's funding from Humberclyde ran out.'

The supplementary question in relation to that which is sought:

'The reasons which you have given for no longer supporting the company, when
considered in the light of your involvement over a considerable period, would
appear to be such that you would have been fully aware of these reasons for a   D
period prior to the expiry of formal facilities. Why was action not taken by
Humberclyde to recover their investment earlier? Why did you continue to support
the company when you considered that the management lacked direction and the
internal controls were weak? Were you not in a position to raise these matters with
the management at a much earlier stage if you were unhappy with their actions?'

I might just notice the final supplementary question which is said to be applicable to all   E
the questions:

'In view of the responses to the questionnaire, the apparent control of the
company's bank account and other matters relating to the affairs of the business,
would you please reconsider your answers to these questions, and provide me with
a full explanation of your answers.'

I am bound to say that I regard those questions as extremely oppressive and misdirected.   F
One must not forget that Humberclyde was a major creditor of this company and, what
is more, it was the owner of a 125-year lease of the property on which the company was
carrying on business. It was subject to a 25-year lease on which the company could not
pay the rent. In those circumstances why should the major creditor have to take steps to
recover its investment as soon as the company appears insolvent? Why should a creditor
not give time to a debtor company? Why should not a bank or financier agree to honour
one cheque rather than another without running the risk of being regarded as running   G
the company itself?

Just looking for a moment at what a shadow director is, I turn to s. 251 of the
Insolvency Act:

' "Shadow director", in relation to a company, means a person in accordance with
whose directions or instructions the directors of the company are accustomed to
act (but so that a person is not deemed a shadow director by reason only that the   H
directors act on advice given by him in a professional capacity) . . .'

This definition is directed to the case where the nominees are put up but in fact behind
them strings are being pulled by some other persons who do not put themselves forward
as appointed directors. In this case the involvement of the applicants here was thrust
upon them by the insolvency of the company. They were not accustomed to give

A   directions. The actions they took, as I see it, were simply directed to trying to rescue what they could out of the company using their undoubted rights as secured creditors. It was submitted to me that it was a prima facie case of shadow directors, but I am bound to say that is far from obvious. It does seem to me that the main purpose of the supplementary questionnaire is to extract admissions which show that the officers of Humberclyde have gone over the limit and become shadow directors. It is not to elicit further information or documents but to obtain admissions or explanations regarding the information already obtained.

B   I have already referred to the tests and the authorities but I will just return to the judgment again of Vinelott J in the *Maxwell* case [1994] BCC 741. I come to this passage at p. 749. He is commenting in relation to the facts before him on the principles mentioned by Ralph Gibson LJ in para. (b); the passage I read out from the Lord Justice's judgment at (b) was:

C   'If, by giving the information sought, a third party risks exposing himself to liability, that involves an element of oppression . . .'

That was the point that Ralph Gibson LJ had made. Then Vinelott J has this to say about the applicability of that to the facts before him which is some guidance to me here:

D   'As regards (b) I do not think that any significant weight should be attached to the risk that answers given in the interviews may lead to and be relied on in civil litigation brought by the administrators against TSW. The transactions in question are complex and unusual and resulted in very serious losses to MCC. The administrators must clearly make a full investigation into all the surrounding circumstances and if their enquiries reveal any shortcoming on the part of any of the professional advisers concerned with the transactions giving rise to recoverable compensation, they must take appropriate action. But the investigation is not designed to furnish evidence which can be relied upon to support a claim against TSW, though a claim may be the consequence of investigations designed to uncover the full circumstances surrounding them.'

E   In my judgment the supplementary questionnaire here is manifestly designed to furnish evidence which can be relied upon in bringing home liability to people who are third parties, not directors. Then Vinelott J goes on as to oral examinations:

F   'The factor mentioned by Ralph Gibson LJ in (d) has no relevance in this case [if someone is suspected of wrongdoing] . . .'

That does have relevance here. It is oppressive to require a person to prove the case against himself on oath. Going back to Vinelott J's judgment:

G   'In addition to these specific factors I must, of course, bear in mind that an oral examination is not only intrusive and to that extent oppressive, but will also entrench upon the no doubt valuable time of professional men and women. As against that I must bear in mind also that the collapse of the Maxwell group is a matter of wide public concern and that it has resulted in grave hardship to a large number of innocent employees and pensioners; the interests of pensioners are indirectly affected in that pension funds administrated by Bishopsgate Investment Management Ltd . . . has very large claims against MCC. In these circumstances the administrators must make and be seen to have made the fullest possible investigations.'

H   Certainly that does not apply in the present case, that there is any need of that type of investigation.

In summary I have to set the order aside. It is admitted that the applicants are not directors. The examination is directed to show that they are shadow directors. I find that there is no prima facie case made out, and it is unlikely that further information will

come to light to show that they are shadow directors. The central point, as I see it, is that **A**
they were not acting as directors of the company; they were acting in defence of their own
interests. This is not a case where the directors of the company, Steven and his colleagues
were accustomed to act in accordance with the directions of others i.e. the applicants
here. It is a case here where the creditor made terms for the continuation of credit in the
light of threatened default. The directors of the company were quite free to take the offer
or leave it.

    B

Had the original supplementary questionnaire come before the court, it is possible that
some parts of it might be salvaged. For example, question 4:

> 'In view of your answers to the above, were you under the impression that all trade
> and other creditors, other than Humberclyde, would be paid in full by funds
> provided by Humberclyde? Would you please provide me with copies of your
> regular management reports?'

    C

I am not saying it would, but I can see a case for their production.

> 'Did you advise the board of directors at the regular meetings that you attended
> that they could or could not rely on Humberclyde providing funds . . .'

That is question 5. That might be justified. Then there is one question where they had not
answered the question as to what evidence they received. That is number 8, question 6.

Be that as it may the order that was made was not justified at all. I set the order of Mr **D**
Registrar Simmonds dated 3 June 1994 aside.

    (Order set aside. Liquidator to pay applicants' costs on standard basis)

    E

    F

    G

    H

A **Official Receiver v Moore & Anor.**
Re Gower Enterprises Ltd.
Chancery Division (Companies Court).
Evans-Lombe J; Blackburne J.
Judgment delivered 24 May and 29 November 1994.

B *Disqualifying unfit directors of insolvent companies – Whether company had become insolvent – Meaning of 'expenses of winding up' – Whether liquidator's remuneration reasonable – Company Directors Disqualification Act 1986, s. 6(1)(a), 6(2)(a).*

This was the hearing of a preliminary issue and an inquiry in director disqualification proceedings as to whether the company concerned had 'become insolvent' within the meaning C of s. 6(2)(a) of the Company Directors Disqualification Act 1986.

It was not in dispute at the inquiry that the company's debts and other liabilities at the time of the winding-up order totalled not less than £528,461 (ignoring some £11,200 of further claims not referred to in the statement of affairs and subsequently admitted to proof by the liquidator). The relevant figure for assets was no greater than £636,643.11 (representing the totality of the book debts set out in the statement of affairs at their full book value and certain interest accruing before the winding-up order was made). Deducting D the figure of £528,461 for debts and liabilities from the figure of £636,643.11 for assets, there was a surplus of £108,182. Section 6(2)(a) of the Disqualification Act required 'the expenses of the winding up' to be deducted from that balance in order to establish whether, for the purposes of s. 6(1) of the Act, the company had become insolvent.

The judge's decision on the preliminary issue was to declare (1) that s. 6(2)(a) was to be construed as if the word 'reasonable' were included immediately before 'expenses of the E winding up'; (2) that in ascertaining the assets of the company for the purposes of s. 6(2)(a) of the Act, interest attributable to any period prior to liquidation was to be counted but interest accruing on debts after liquidation was to be ignored; and (3) that in ascertaining the liabilities of the company for the purposes of s. 6(2)(a) of the Act, interest payable under s. 189 of the Insolvency Act 1986 was to be ignored.

Payments made by the liquidator (other than by way of distributions to creditors) totalled F £184,410.80. The second respondent accepted that, of that sum, £82,056.16 were expenses of the winding up for the purposes of s. 6(2)(a) of the Act (including £71,990.45 paid to the DTI pursuant to the Insolvency Fees Order 1986); the balance of £102,354.62 was liquidator's remuneration which the second respondent submitted was unreasonable. The remuneration had been fixed by the creditors at ten per cent of realisations and five per cent of distributions. If the remuneration had been fixed by reference to reg. 19 of the Insolvency Regulations 1986 it would have been around £61,000, and if fixed on the time basis, it would G not have exceeded £20,000.

Held, declaring that when the company went into liquidation its assets were insufficient to pay its debts and other liabilities and the expenses of the winding up within the meaning of s. 6(2)(a):

1. 'Reasonable expenses' would include fees recoverable under the Insolvency Regulations 1986 as well as those payable pursuant to the Insolvency Fees Order 1986 as H well as legal fees, tax and disbursements of one kind or another.

2. The liquidator's remuneration as an element of those expenses meant remuneration properly payable in accordance with the Insolvency Rules and, where applicable, the Insolvency Regulations. If fixed in accordance with those rules and regulations and subject to any challenge under the Insolvency Rules 1986, r. 4.131, the liquidator's remuneration as so fixed was properly an item of the expenses of the winding up for the purposes of s. 6(2)(a)

294   Official Receiver v Moore. Re Gower Enterprises Ltd   **[1995] BCC**

(*Evans-Lombe J*)

of the Act, whether that figure was higher than, the same as or lower than the figure that   A
would have been arrived at by applying the scale laid down for the official receiver by the
Insolvency Regulations. Accordingly the figure of £102,354.64 was properly to be included
in the computation under s. 6(2)(a).

3. If the figure of £102,354 was not held to be reasonable remuneration, remuneration
fixed by reference to the scale laid down for the official receiver by the Insolvency
Regulations 1986, reg. 19 would, in the circumstances of the case, have been reasonable in   B
amount. Whether therefore £61,000 or the lesser figure of £53,241 was taken as the product
of applying that scale, the result was the same as if the actual figure of £102,354 was taken,
which was that, taken together with the other items, the expenses of the winding up exceeded
the surplus of £108,182.

Philip Jones (instructed by the Treasury Solicitor) for the official receiver.

Kate Lampard (instructed by Wedlake Bell) for the respondent.   C

JUDGMENT ON PRELIMINARY ISSUE
(Delivered 24 May 1994)

Evans-Lombe J: The matter before me is a preliminary issue in an application for the
disqualification of a director under the *Company Directors Disqualification Act* 1986. The
originating summons was issued on 28 January 1993. It seeks orders against the   D
respondent directors for their disqualification under the provisions of that Act, making a
series of allegations as to their conduct as such directors. The application relates to a
company called Gower Enterprises Ltd. The relevant provisions of the Act are contained
in s. 6 and they read as follows.

'(1) The court shall make a disqualification order against a person in any case
where, on an application under this section, it is satisfied–   E

    (a) that he is or has been a director of a company which has at any time become
        insolvent (whether while he was a director or subsequently), and

    (b) that his conduct as a director of that company (either taken alone or taken
        together with his-conduct as a director of any other company or companies)
        makes him unfit to be concerned in the management of a company.

(2) For the purposes of this section and the next, a company becomes insolvent if–   F

    (a) the company goes into liquidation at a time when its assets are insufficient
        for the payment of its debts and other liabilities and the expenses of the
        winding up,

    (b) an administration order is made in relation to the company, or

    (c) an administrative receiver of the company is appointed . . .'   G

I do not need to read the remainder of that section.

The issue arises in this way. The statement of affairs of the company sworn on 8 March
1991 as at the date of the winding up, which was 31 January 1991, shows assets of the
company with a book value of £628,939 estimated to realise a precisely similar sum. That
is because the assets of this company represented book debts which were good. The
statement of affairs shows liabilities of £528,451, and accordingly produces a surplus of   H
assets over liabilities of rather more than £100,000. The total actual realisations by the
liquidator as at 4 December 1992 and as shown by a summary of liquidator's receipts
and payments drawn to that date was £754,901. The increase over the estimated value of
the debts was not caused by contractual interest since it is common ground that no such
contractual interest had become due. It was increased first by judgment interest on the
amounts of the book debts which the liquidator was compelled to sue for, they not being

A   immediately paid by the debtors, and, secondly, gains resulting from investment of the receipts by the liquidator after the winding-up order.

The expenses of the liquidation have turned out to be £184,410.80. Those consist substantially of Department of Trade and Industry fees and the liquidator's remuneration as fixed by the creditors. There is a relatively small sum of £4,275 in respect of legal fees, presumably incurred in obtaining payment, through proceedings, of the debts which comprise the assets of the company.

B

Thus if the assets of the company are taken to be their book and estimated value at the date of the winding up, there is a deficit of approximately £80,000 on the statement of affairs position, if one adds to the liabilities the amount of the expenses which have actually been incurred in the winding up. On the other hand, if one takes into account the amount which the debts ultimately realised, and does not take into account interest becoming due under s. 189 of the Insolvency Act, there is a surplus of £38,000 approximately. If s. 189 interest is taken into account, there is sufficient only to pay 6p in the pound in respect of the resulting charge to interest under that section.

C

Whether or not the applications to disqualify the respondents as directors fall within the provisions of the Act turns on whether the condition that they must have been directors of a company which at any time became insolvent as set out in s. 6(2)(a) of the Act are met. That section therefore is the section which is fundamental to the issue which it falls to me to decide. Section 6(2) is intended to define what is meant by the words "become insolvent" in subs. (1)(a). The requirements of subs. 2(b) and 2(c) are met virtually exclusively only when a company is not able to pay its debts when due.

D

However, the question of whether a company has become insolvent within s. 6(1)(a) must be in the final analysis a question of fact. It is not in issue between the parties that that factual issue falls to be determined at the date of the liquidation. The two questions between the parties are whether the assets at that time must be treated as being worth what they ultimately realised. That is the first issue, and on that issue the official receiver contends that they do not fall to be valued in accordance with what they ultimately realised, but rather in accordance with what their value was precisely at the date of liquidation.

E

The second issue on an alternative formulation of the test is whether s. 189 interest payable to creditors proving in the liquidation, in the event that their proofs are admitted, must be taken into account in answering the question, 'Was the company at the relevant time insolvent?'

F

I will deal straightaway with the latter issue. It seems to me that s. 189 interest must not be taken into account. In no sense, in my judgment, can the words 'debts or other liabilities' of the company in subs. (2)(a) existing at the date of the liquidation be taken to include a liability to pay interest on debts admitted to proof under s. 189 becoming payable after the liquidation has commenced.

G

By parity of reasoning, it seems to me that interest and other gains accruing due after the liquidation cannot comprise an asset existing at that date within the subsection. Such interest is entirely contingent at the date of the winding up. It seems to me the contrary is the case where such interest is in respect of a period preceding the winding up which is subsequently ordered to be paid, because that is interest with which the asset, namely the debt, at the date of judgment was pregnant, in the event that, as transpired to be the case, the liquidator had to sue for it.

H

The principal difficulty in the case appears to me to arise from the words 'expenses of the winding up'. In the context in which those words are used in subs. (2)(a) their ostensible meaning is the expenses that subsequently were incurred in the course of the winding up. The amount of such expenses cannot be determined at the date of the winding up.

296   **Official Receiver v Moore. Re Gower Enterprises Ltd**   **[1995] BCC**

(Evans-Lombe J)

This result is pregnant with injustice. It must be borne in mind that whether or not a   A
company fulfils the terms of s. 6(1) and (2) of the 1986 Act may decide the question
whether the directors of the company are subject to the disqualification provisions of the
company directors Disqualification Act. It seems to me to be a basic injustice that
whether they fall within the provisions of that Act could turn on what expenses the
liquidator either advisedly or ill-advisedly incurs in the course of the winding up; for
instance a liquidator in a case such as this, where the assets and liabilities are fairly evenly
balanced, might wholly unjustifiably embark on a process of suing a particular debtor   B
whom he should well have known had insufficient assets to pay the claim and accordingly
the proceedings against him were purposeless. He might incur substantial costs in
undertaking those proceedings and the amount of those costs might push the asset
balance over the edge so that the company could be shown to be insolvent within the
meaning of s. 6.

I cannot believe that the legislature intended when it used the words, 'if the company   C
goes into liquidation at a time when its assets are insufficient for the payment of its debts
and other liabilities and the expenses of the winding up', it meant such an indeterminative
and moving test to be the test of whether the provisions of the Act applied. Accordingly
it seems to me that I would be justified in construing those words so as to include the
word 'reasonable' in the definition of expenses so that the words read, 'and the reasonable
expenses of the winding up'. What would constitute 'reasonable expenses' must be a   D
question of fact.

I would suggest that as a rule of thumb what constitutes 'reasonable expenses' should
be those fees and expenses properly chargeable by applying the official receiver's scale
fees under the *Insolvency Fees Order* 1986 to the realisable assets in the winding up. In
this case that would work out at £120,000 approximately.

I would also suggest that as a rule of thumb, if the expenses can be shown to have been   E
less than the official receiver's scale fees, the actual expenses should then be substituted
for those scale fees in arriving at a conclusion whether the company had become insolvent
within s. 6(1). If a system of calculation such as I have suggested is applied in cases such
as this, which must be rare, the potential for injustice which I have described is removed.

It follows, however, that I do not accept the submission of the second respondent that
prima facie interest accruing after the date of the winding up in respect of periods   F
commencing with the date of the winding up should be taken into account in deciding
whether the company has become insolvent within s. 6(1). Interest, it must be borne in
mind, is an award designed to compensate a creditor for not having his money available
to dispose of at the relevant time, and accordingly prima facie is self-cancelling in respect
of the period when it is accruing. If it were legitimate to take account of interest in the
assessment of solvency at the date of the winding up, it would be necessary
simultaneously to discount the debt at that date by a percentage which would represent   G
the inability of the creditor to obtain payment of his debt forthwith.

For these reasons it seems to me that I do not have sufficient information from which
to conclude the question of whether this company had or had not become insolvent
within s. 6(1) for the purposes of this application. The deficit, taking into account the
official receiver's scale fees figure of approximately £120,000, can only be some £20,000.
It is possible that the interest recovered on the debts referable to a period prior to the   H
winding up may exceed that amount.

I leave to counsel what my order should be consequent on that finding.

(Order accordingly)

A   JUDGMENT ON INQUIRY
                              (Delivered 29 November 1994)

Blackburne J: I have before me an inquiry arising in the course of an application by
the official receiver for the disqualification of two directors under s. 6 of the *Company
Directors Disqualification Act* 1986.

The two respondent directors were directors of Gower Enterprises Ltd, which was
B   placed in compulsory liquidation on 30 January 1991.

Before the court can make a disqualification order under s. 6, it must be satisfied, inter
alia, that a person against whom the order is sought 'is or has been a director of a
company which has at any time become insolvent': see s. 6(1)(a)).

Section 6(2)(a) provides that for the purposes of the section 'a company becomes
insolvent if':
C
         '(a) the company goes into liquidation at a time when its assets are insufficient for
         the payment of its debts and other liabilities and the expenses of the winding up
         . . .'

One of the issues which has arisen on this application is whether, when Gower went
into liquidation on 30 January 1991, it had become insolvent within the meaning of that
provision. This in turn has given rise to the question as to what is meant by the expression
D   'assets', 'liabilities' and 'expenses of the winding up' as used in that subsection.

That question was determined by Evans-Lombe J alone on 24 May 1994 when he
declared:

(1)   that s. 6(2)(a) must be construed as if the word 'reasonable' were included
         immediately before 'expenses of the winding up';

E   (2)   that in ascertaining the assets of the company for the purposes of s. 6(2)(a) of the
         Act, there is to be ignored in respect of any debts owing to the company any
         interest accruing on the debts after liquidation but not any interest attributable to
         any period prior to liquidation; and

(3)   that in ascertaining the liabilities of the company for the purposes of s. 6(2)(a) of
         the Act, there is to be ignored any statutory interest payable under s. 189 of the
F   *Insolvency Act* 1986.

He also directed an inquiry as to whether Gower went into liquidation at a time when
its assets were insufficient for the payment of its debts and other liabilities and the
expenses of the winding up, and gave directions for the taking of that inquiry. The
inquiry is now before me.

The two respondents were formerly in partnership as chartered accountants under the
G   name Moore Sloane & Co. Gower, of which the two respondents were its only directors,
acted as a service company to that partnership. The two respondents also owned and
controlled a company called Alandene Enterprises Ltd.

Gower's statement of affairs as at 30 January 1991, deposed to by the second
respondent on 8 March 1991, disclosed assets consisting simply of five book debts
estimated to realise £620,939, that figure also being the book value of those debts. Of
those five book debts, one was owed by the partnership, i.e. the two respondents in the
H   sum of £594,697; another was owed by Alandene in the sum of £30,192. Liabilities were
expressed to consist merely of four creditors with claims totalling £528,461, comprising
the Inland Revenue in the sum of £373,022, Her Majesty's Customs and Excise in the
sum of £155,323 and two other creditors in the aggregate sum of just £106. On the face
of the statement of affairs and ignoring the expenses of the winding up, there was a
surplus as regards creditors of £100,478.

Neither the partnership nor Alandene paid the sums admittedly due from them when   **A** they were called upon to do so and the liquidator, Mr Auger of Stoy Hayward, who was appointed on 24 April 1991, issued proceedings to recover the sums owed. On 25 June 1991, he issued proceedings against the partnership for £594,697 and interest under s. 35A of the *Supreme Court Act* 1981, calculated from 1 January 1991. On 19 July 1991, judgment was entered in default for £637,711.40 plus interest in the sum of £5,865.60 since the issue of the writ. The judgment debt was not paid. This led to the service of a statutory demand on 22 October 1991. That demand was not complied with and in due   **B** course winding-up proceedings were launched against the partnership. That resulted in the payment of £668,885.10 on 19 February 1992, the very day the petition was due to be heard. That was not enough to discharge the petition debt and costs. The petition was adjourned for seven days when a further sum of £6,349.44 was paid and the petition was dismissed. In the meantime, further interest totalling £25,416.03 had accrued due on the judgment debt. A further statutory demand was served which was not complied with and   **C** further winding-up proceedings were launched. This resulted in a final payment, in discharge of the accrued interest, on 15 September 1992, and the second petition was dismissed. It had taken the liquidator nearly 18 months to recover in full the debt of £594,697 owed to Gower by the partnership. The sum ultimately paid included interest under s. 35A in respect of the period from 1 January 1991 onwards.

Recovery of the sum of £30,192 owed to Gower by Alandene was scarcely less difficult.   **D** On 25 June 1991, a writ was issued for recovery of that sum. Default judgment was entered on 12 July 1991 and, following non-payment of the judgment debt, winding-up proceedings were launched against that company. Eventually, on or shortly before 29 January 1992, Alandene discharged the debt with a payment of £32,769-odd, in full settlement of the debt including interest.

There was a question as to whether the moneys used to discharge the partnership's indebtedness to Gower came from moneys belonging to the partnership. That is not an   **E** issue which I have needed to investigate. It is sufficient to say that on 13 April 1994 both respondents were made bankrupt and on 27 April 1994 a winding-up order was made in respect of the partnership.

Against that background, I now have to determine whether, as at 30 January 1991, Gower was insolvent within the meaning of s. 6(2)(a) of the Act.

It is not in dispute that Gower's debts and other liabilities at the time of the winding-   **F** up order totalled not less than £528,461. That figure ignores some £11,200 of further claims not referred to in the statement of affairs and subsequently admitted to proof by the liquidator.

Although there was at one stage a dispute as to what Gower's assets were at that time, including what the figure should be in respect of interest attributable to any period prior to Gower's liquidation, it is now common ground between counsel that the relevant   **G** figure was no greater than £636,643.11. That sum represents the totality of the book debts set out in the statement of affairs at their full book value and interest on the debts of the partnership in Alandene from 1 January 1991 to 30 January 1991 in the sum of £7,704.11. In fact, the liquidator recovered rather more by way of interest but interest over and above £7,704.11 represents interest which accrued after Gower's liquidation and is therefore something which, by the order of 24 May 1994, I am to ignore in determining what Gower's assets were at the date that it went into liquidation.   **H**

I say that the value of Gower's assets on the day it went into liquidation was *no greater* than £636,643.11 because, in view of the very considerable difficulties which the liquidator experienced in recovering the debts due from the partnership and Alandene, to say nothing of the doubt that exists as to the provenance of the moneys used to discharge the partnership's debt, there must be a considerable doubt whether, at the time

A   Gower went into liquidation, its book debts were then worth their full face value amount. However, I am content to proceed on the footing that they were since, in the view that I take of this matter, it makes no difference to the outcome of the inquiry if in truth they were worth less.

Deducting the figure of £528,461 for debts and liabilities from the figure of £636,643.11 for assets, there is a surplus of £108,182. From that balance must be deducted the

B   expenses of Gower's winding up in order to establish whether, for the purposes of s. 6(1) of the Act, Gower became insolvent.

By his order of 24 May 1994, Evans-Lombe J alone considered that the expression 'expenses of the winding up' should be construed as if qualified by the word 'reasonable'. In his judgment, after observing that what constitutes reasonable expenses is a question of fact, he said this:

C   'I would suggest that, as a rule of thumb, what constitutes 'reasonable expenses' should be those fees and expenses properly chargeable by applying the official receiver's scale fees under the *Insolvency Fees Order* 1986 to the realisable assets in the winding up. In this case that would work out at £120,000 approximately.'

I pause to say that there is an obvious omission in that passage in that the figure of £120,000 would only be achieved if the fees in question are those recoverable under the *Insolvency Regulations* 1986 as well as those payable pursuant to the *Insolvency Fees*

D   *Order* 1986 to which the judge refers. The calculation which produces that figure – it also includes VAT – is to be found at p. 658 of trial bundle B. The passage also omits reference to expenses, such, for example, as legal fees, tax and disbursements of one kind or another. By omitting to mention these, I do not think that the judge was intending to suggest that they should be ignored. The judge continued:

E   'I would also suggest that, as a rule of thumb, if the expenses can be shown to have been less than the official receiver's scale fees, the actual expenses should then be substituted for those scale fees in arriving at a conclusion whether the company had become insolvent within s. 6(1). If a system of calculation such as I have suggested is applied in cases such as this, which must be rare, the potential for injustice which I have described is removed.'

The injustice which the judge described was the possibility that a liquidator might

F   incur expenses ill-advisedly such, for example, as unjustifiably suing a particular debtor whom he should well have known had insufficient assets to pay the claim with the result that the proceedings against him were purposeless.

In this case payments made by the liquidator, other than by way of distributions to creditors, as at 4 December 1992 totalled £184,410.80. Miss Lampard for the second respondent – the first respondent has not so far taken any part in these proceedings – accepts that, of that sum, £82,056.16 are expenses of the winding up for the purposes of

G   s. 6(2)(a) of the Act. That sum includes £71,990.45 paid to the DTI pursuant to art. 3 of the *Insolvency Fees Order* 1986 and calculated in accordance with fee 10 in Pt. I of the Schedule to that order.

Where Miss Lampard takes issue with the list of payments which comprise the figure of £184,410.80 is over the sum of £102,354.62 paid out to the liquidator by way of remuneration. She accepts correctly that the expenses of the winding up must include

H   some remuneration for the liquidator. The *Insolvency Rules* 1986, r. 4.127(1) provides that the liquidator is:

            'entitled to receive remuneration for his services as such'.

She submits, however, that the sum paid of £102,315.62 is an unreasonable amount and that a much lesser figure, between £10,000 and £20,000, should be substituted. This figure was based on the evidence of Mr Allen, an insolvency practitioner, who gave evidence

300   **Official Receiver v Moore. Re Gower Enterprises Ltd**   **[1995] BCC**

(*Blackburne J*)

before me and who estimated, but without having had sight of the liquidator's files, that   A
remuneration calculated on a time basis would have been in the region of £10,000–
£20,000. For the purposes of the argument before me, Mr Philip Jones for the official
receiver was prepared to accept that £20,000 would have been the liquidator's
remuneration if calculated on a time basis.

By the statutory scheme provided by Parliament for the administration of insolvent
companies, the liquidator's remuneration is fixed by the *Insolvency Rules* 1986, r. 4.127.   B
Where the liquidator is not the official receiver, his remuneration, subject to a default
provision, is fixed either by the liquidation committee, if there is one, or, if there is not,
by resolution of a meeting of creditors. It is fixed either (1) as a percentage of the value
of the assets which are realised or distributed or the value of both in combination or (2)
by reference to the time properly given by the liquidator and his staff in attending to
matters arising in the winding up.

In arriving at a determination based upon time, the liquidation committee or, in   C
default, the creditors are to have regard to various matters – see the *Insolvency Rules*
1986, r. 4.127(2)–(5). Mr Allen's estimate of £10,000–£20,000 is, as I understand it, on
the footing of a determination under r. 4.127(2)(b).

The *Insolvency Rules* 1986, r. 4.127(6) contains a default provision whereby, if not
fixed as set out earlier in the rule, the liquidator's remuneration is to be fixed in   D
accordance with the scale laid down for the official receiver by general regulations. The
relevant regulation is reg. 19 of the *Insolvency Regulations* 1986. It is not I think in doubt
that if remuneration were fixed by that regulation it would have amounted, on actual
realisations, to £61,000-odd. In fact, on 28 September 1992, the liquidator's remuneration
was resolved under the *Insolvency Rules* 1986, r. 4.127(2)(a) by creditors whose debts
amounted to approximately 72 per cent of the value of Gower's creditors at ten per cent
on realisations and five per cent on distributions, yielding the figure of £102,354.64 which   E
I have mentioned.

Remuneration of £102,000-odd for what essentially was a very straightforward
liquidation seemed to me, when my attention was first drawn to it and to some extent
still seems to me, to be surprisingly high. However, as Mr Jones pointed out, this was a
liquidation where, having regard to the financial position of the principal debtor, to the
fact that apart from Gower's claims against that debtor and Alandene there were, to all   F
intents and purposes, no assets and to the fact that for many months, while expenses in
the liquidation were being incurred there was no certainty – indeed, considerable doubt –
whether he would recover anything at all, the liquidator could reasonably expect to be
treated generously by the creditors and be remunerated by reference to percentages on
recoveries and distributions rather than on a time basis.

The *Insolvency Rules* 1986, r. 4.131 enables a creditor, with the concurrence of at least   G
25 per cent in value of the creditors including himself, to apply to the court for an order
that the liquidator's remuneration be reduced on the ground that it is, in all the
circumstances, excessive. The court has power on such an application to fix the
remuneration at a reduced amount or rate. In this case, no such application has been
made. It could only be made, in the circumstances, by Her Majesty's Customs and Excise
and it is now over two years since the liquidator's remuneration was fixed.

The position therefore is that, first, the liquidator's remuneration has in fact been fixed   H
at £102,354.64 and no creditor has sought to challenge that sum. Secondly, if the
remuneration had been fixed by reference to reg. 19, it would have been around £61,000,
and thirdly, if fixed on the time basis, it would not have exceeded £20,000. I have also
been shown a calculation – I think it was the same calculation that was before Evans-
Lombe J alone – which shows that, if the debts owed to Gower had been paid immediately

A   upon the making of the winding-up order, the official receiver's remuneration for acting
as liquidator would have amounted to £53,241, ignoring VAT.

The question is whether I should include the liquidator's actual remuneration of
£102,354.64 or some lesser, and if so what, figure in the computation of 'expenses of the
winding up' for the purposes of s. 6(2)(a) of the Act.

The expression 'expenses of the winding up' is one which occurs in the *Insolvency Act*
B   1986 – see, for example, s. 175(2) and s. 214(6). In s. 156 of the Act the expression
'expenses incurred in the winding up' appears and in s. 115 the expression is 'all expenses
properly incurred in the winding up'.

In all of these cases the liquidator's remuneration as an element of those expenses
must, in my view, mean remuneration properly payable in accordance with the
Insolvency Rules and, where applicable, the Insolvency Regulations. If fixed in
C   accordance with those rules and regulations and subject to any challenge under the
Insolvency Rules 1986, r. 4.131, the liquidator's remuneration as so fixed is properly an
item of the expenses of the winding up as that expression is used in those provisions. For
my part, I see no reason why that expression, where it occurs in s. 6(2)(a) of the Act,
should be understood any differently. If, as an element of those expenses, the liquidator's
remuneration has been fixed in accordance with the Insolvency Rules and Regulations
and has not been challenged by the only persons who, under the rules, are given a right
D   of challenge, then, in my view, the remuneration as so fixed is properly part of the
expenses of the winding up for the purposes of s. 6(2)(a) of the Act, whether that figure is
higher than, the same as or lower than the figure that would have been arrived at by
applying the scale laid down for the official receiver by the Insolvency Regulations.

A question which arises is whether it is open to me to adopt that approach having
regard to the views expressed in his judgment by Evans-Lombe J alone. In my view, it is,
E   in that I do not consider that, in construing the expression 'expenses of the winding up'
as qualified by 'reasonable', the judge was doing other than referring to remuneration
properly charged in accordance with the scheme which Parliament has laid down in the
1986 Rules and Regulations. The reference in the judgment of Evans-Lombe J alone to
the unjustified incurring of expenses by a liquidator and to the need therefore to ensure
that they do not enter into the computation of the expenses of the winding up to the
disadvantage of directors facing disqualification proceedings is, of course, concerned
F   with disbursements rather than with the liquidator's remuneration which, if fixed on a
scale basis, would not be increased by the wrongful pursuit of a pointless claim. But such
expenses do not in any event constitute expenses of the winding up except to the extent
that they are properly chargeable or incurred – see the Insolvency Rules, r. 4.218(1)(a).

In these circumstances, I consider the figure of £102,354.64, admittedly large in
amount, as properly to be regarded as an expense of the winding up for the purposes of
G   s. 6(2)(a) of the Act. I am happy to reach that conclusion because it avoids the court
having to embark on what, in other cases, might be the difficult, time consuming and
therefore expensive exercise of reviewing the conduct of the liquidation. I cannot think
that that was a process which Parliament intended should be undertaken in the context
of applications for disqualification under the Act. It also avoids the possibility of coming
to a figure for remuneration different from what the creditors have resolved upon or been
content to accept and different therefore from the figure for expenses of the winding up
H   for the purposes of other provisions of the scheme.

In case I am wrong about that, and the order of Evans-Lombe J alone does require me
to take a narrower view of the matter, I consider that remuneration fixed by reference to
the scale laid down for the official receiver by the *Insolvency Regulations* 1986, reg. 19
would, in the circumstances of this case, have been reasonable in amount. When cross-
examined by Mr Jones, Mr Allen, who had been called by Miss Lampard to give evidence

on what remuneration would have been reasonable in this case, accepted that it would   A
not have been unreasonable for the liquidator to have charged on that scale.

Whether therefore one takes £61,000 or the lesser figure of £53,241 as the product of
applying that scale, the result is the same as if the actual figure of £102,354-odd is taken,
which is that, taken together with the other items, the expenses of the winding up exceed
the surplus of £108,182 referred to earlier.

The result of this conclusion is that, when Gower went into liquidation on 30 January   B
1991, its assets were insufficient to pay its debts and other liabilities and the expenses of
the winding up and I so declare in answer to the inquiry directed by the order of 24 May
1994.

(*Order accordingly*)

C

D

E

F

G

H

A **Re Dominion International Group plc.**

Chancery Division (Companies Court).

Rattee J.

Judgment delivered 16 December 1994.

Disqualifying unfit directors of insolvent companies – Order for all deponents in
B *disqualification proceedings to be cross-examined – Whether registrar had*
jurisdiction to make such order – Whether registrar had erred in principle –
Company Directors Disqualification Act 1986, s. 6, 7(1) – Rules of the Supreme
Court 1965, O. 38, r. 2(3) – Insolvent Companies (Disqualification of Unfit
Directors) Proceedings Rules 1987, r. 2, 3, 4, 6.

This was an appeal against an order made by the registrar in proceedings brought by the
C Secretary of State for Trade and Industry for the disqualification of the appellant under the
Company Directors Disqualification Act 1986.

The originating summons was issued in January 1992, and much affidavit evidence had
been filed subsequently. In October 1994 the registrar ordered under the Rules of the
Supreme Court, O. 38, r. 2(3) that all deponents of such affidavits should attend the hearing
of the originating summons for cross-examination on their affidavits, and if they did not do
so the affidavits could not be read or used in evidence without leave of the court.

D The appellant contended that the registrar had no jurisdiction to make such an order:
RSC, O. 38, r. 2(3) did not apply because the Insolvent Companies (Disqualification of
Unfit Directors) Proceedings Rules 1987 made provision to inconsistent effect. Furthermore
if the registrar did have jurisdiction, he had erred in principle in the way in which he had
exercised his jurisdiction because it was wrong to make an order for cross-examination of
the respondent in disqualification proceedings because they were in the nature of penal
E proceedings. Alternatively it was wrong in principle to make an order for cross-examination
of deponents living abroad if the effect of such an order was to deprive the respondent to the
disqualification proceedings of a right to introduce that deponent's evidence.

Held, dismissing the appeal:

1. There was nothing in the 1987 rules inconsistent with the power in O. 38, r. 2(3) to
order cross-examination on affidavits in disqualification proceedings. The registrar had
F jurisdiction to make the order.

2. The registrar did not err in principle in exercising the jurisdiction. Disqualification
proceedings were penal and the court would not compel a respondent to give evidence but if
a respondent chose to swear an affidavit and file it under r. 6 there was no reason why he
should not be subject to an order for cross-examination on that affidavit. (*Comet Products
UK Ltd v Hawkex Plastics Ltd* [1971] 2 QB 67 distinguished.)

G 3. The effect of the registrar's order was that the court retained a discretion to permit
the appellant to use in evidence any of the affidavits filed under r. 6, even if the deponents
did not attend for cross-examination. The registrar properly took the view that it was
desirable in the interests of the just determination of the issues that would have to be
determined at the trial that the court should, to the extent possible, hear cross-examination
of all deponents, leaving it to the court at a later stage to consider any application by the
H appellant to use in evidence, without cross-examination, the affidavit of any deponent as to
whom the appellant could satisfy the court that cross-examination was impracticable.

The following cases were referred to in the judgment:

City Investment Centres Ltd, Re [1992] BCLC 956.
Comet Products UK Ltd v Hawkex Plastics Ltd & Anor [1971] 2 QB 67.
Moonbeam Cards Ltd, Re [1993] BCLC 1099.

Rover International Ltd & Ors v Cannon Film Sales Ltd [1987] 1 WLR 1597.   A
Williams (Rex) Leisure plc, Re [1994] BCC 551; [1994] Ch 350.

Elizabeth Gloster QC and Richard Snowden (instructed by North & Co) for the
applicant.

A G Bompas QC (instructed by the Treasury Solicitor) for the Secretary of State for
Trade and Industry.

                                                                                 B
                              JUDGMENT

Rattee J: This is an appeal against an order made by the Companies Court registrar
on 17 October 1994 in proceedings whereby the Secretary of State for Trade and Industry
applies under s. 7 of the *Company Directors Disqualification Act* 1986 for a
disqualification order in respect of the appellant under s. 6 of the Act.

The originating summons initiating the proceedings was issued as long ago as 21   C
January 1992. Over the last two and a half years a great deal of affidavit evidence has
been filed in support of the originating summons, in answer and in reply.

On 17 October 1994 the registrar ordered that all deponents of such affidavits should
attend the hearing of the originating summons for cross-examination on their affidavits
and if they did not do so the affidavits could not be read or used in evidence without
leave of the court. This was a common form order made (or purportedly made) under   D
O. 38, r. 2(3) of the Rules of the Supreme Court. The appellant contends:

(1)   that the registrar had no jurisdiction to make such an order; and

(2)   that if he had jurisdiction, he erred in principle in the way in which he exercised his
        discretion.

It was agreed between the parties that if indeed the registrar did have jurisdiction to
make the order, I cannot properly interfere with the exercise of his discretion under that   E
jurisdiction, unless I am satisfied that he erred in principle in that exercise.

The reason why, according to the appellant's submission, the registrar had no
jurisdiction to make the order is because O. 38, r. 2(3) does not apply to proceedings
under the *Company Directors Disqualification Act* 1986 ('disqualification proceedings').

I should at this stage read O. 38, r. 2(3). It is in these terms:

> 'In any cause or matter begun by originating summons, originating motion or   F
> petition, and on any application made by summons or motion, evidence may be
> given by affidavit unless in the case of any such cause, matter or application any
> provision of these rules otherwise provides or the Court otherwise directs, but the
> Court may, on the application of any party, order the attendance for cross-
> examination of the person making any such affidavit, and where, after such an
> order has been made, the person in question does not attend, his affidavit shall not   G
> be used as evidence without the leave of the Court.'

These proceedings were begun by originating summons. So in terms O. 38, r. 2(3)
applies to them. However, the appellant argues that it does not in fact apply because of
the effect of the *Insolvent Companies (Disqualification of Unfit Directors) Proceedings
Rules* 1987 ('the 1987 rules'). Those rules apply to an application for a disqualification
order made by the Secretary of State or the official receiver under s. 7(1) of the 1986 Act
and, therefore, to these present proceedings. I should refer then to r. 2, 3, 4 and 6 of the   H
1987 rules. Those rules provide as follows:

> '2 An application to which these Rules apply shall be made—
>
> (a)   in the High Court, by originating summons (Form 10 in Appendix A to the
>   Rules of the Supreme Court, with such adaptation as may be appropriate),
>   and

(b) in a county court, by originating application, such an application being nevertheless referred to in these Rules as a summons;

and the Rules of the Supreme Court 1965 or (as the case may be) the County Court Rules 1981 apply accordingly, except where these Rules make provision to inconsistent effect.'

Rule 3, headed 'The case against the respondent', is as follows:

'(1) There shall, at the time when the summons is issued, be filed in court evidence in support of the application for a disqualification order; and copies of the evidence shall be served with the summons on the respondent.

(2) The evidence shall be by one or more affidavits, except where the applicant is the official receiver, in which case it may be in the form of a written report (with or without affidavits by other persons) which shall be treated as if it had been verified by affidavit by him and shall be prima facie evidence of any matter contained in it.

(3) There shall in the affidavit or affidavits or (as the case may be) the official receiver's report be included a statement of the matters by reference to which the respondent is alleged to be unfit to be concerned in the management of a company.'

Rule 4 is headed 'Endorsement on summons' and is as follows:

'There shall on the summons be endorsed information to the respondent as follows–

    (a) that the application is made in accordance with these Rules;

    (b) that, in accordance with the relevant enactments, the court has power to impose disqualifications as follows–

        (i) where the application is under section 7 of the Company Directors Disqualification Act, for a period of not less than 2, and up to 15, years; and

        (ii) where the application is under section 8 of that Act, for a period of up to 15 years;

    (c) that the application for a disqualification order may, in accordance with these Rules, be heard and determined summarily, without further or other notice to the respondent, and that, if it is so heard and determined, the court may impose disqualification for a period of up to 5 years;

    (d) that if at the hearing of the application the court, on the evidence then before it, is minded to impose, in the respondent's case, disqualification for any period longer than 5 years, it will not make a disqualification order on that occasion but will adjourn the application to be heard (with further evidence, if any) at a later date to be notified; and

    (e) that any evidence which the respondent wishes to be taken into consideration by the court must be filed in court in accordance with the time limits imposed under Rule 6 (the provisions of which shall be set out on the summons).'

Rule 6, headed 'Evidence', is in the following terms:

'(1) The respondent shall, within 28 days from the date of service of the summons, file in court any affidavit evidence in opposition to the application he wishes the court to take into consideration and shall forthwith serve upon the applicant a copy of such evidence.

(2) The applicant shall, within 14 days from receiving the copy of the respondent's evidence, file in court any further evidence in reply he wishes the court to take into consideration and shall forthwith serve a copy of that evidence upon the respondent.'

In *Re Rex Williams Leisure plc* [1994] BCC 551, the Court of Appeal held that the   A
effect of r. 6 is that any evidence a respondent to disqualification proceedings wishes to
be taken into consideration must be in the form of affidavits filed under r. 6, and that
additional oral evidence in-chief at the trial would be allowed only at the discretion of
the court. As Hoffmann LJ said at p. 555E, the words of r. 6(1),

> 'only make sense if they mean that the evidence [the respondent] wishes the court
> to take into consideration must be filed on affidavit.'   B

It is in my judgment clear from the words of r. 2, which I have read, that like all other
potentially relevant Rules of the Supreme Court, O. 38, r. 2(3) applies to disqualification
proceedings unless the 1987 rules 'make provision to inconsistent effect'. Miss Gloster
submitted that they do for the following reasons.

(1)   The mandatory effect of r. 6 of the 1987 rules that the respondent must file his
      evidence in the form of affidavits (unlike the effect of its predecessor, r. 6 of the   C
      Insolvent Companies (Disqualification of Unfit Directors) Proceedings Rules 1986,
      which provided that the respondent to disqualification proceedings 'may' file
      affidavit evidence) is inconsistent with O. 38, r. 2(3) of the Rules of the Supreme
      Court, which deals with procedures begun by originating summons where evidence
      'may be given by affidavit' (see the words of O. 38, r. 2(3) itself).

(2)   It would be unfair if the court could, by an order for cross-examination under   D
      O. 38, r. 2(3) prevent the respondent to disqualification proceedings adducing
      affidavit evidence of a deponent he cannot produce for cross-examination when at
      the same time, by virtue of r. 3(2) of the 1987 rules, at least in a case where the
      application is made by the official receiver, the applicant can adduce hearsay
      evidence without its being subject to being tested by cross-examination: see *Re City
      Investment Centres Ltd* [1992] BCLC 956 and *Re Moonbeam Cards Ltd* [1993]
      BCLC 1099.   E

(3)   It is to be implied into the 1987 rules and, in particular, r. 6(1), that the court will
      take into consideration any affidavit filed by a respondent pursuant to r. 6(1)
      without cross-examination of the deponent. This implication is strengthened by
      the absence from the information to be endorsed on the originating summons
      under r. 4 of any warning to the respondent that the effect of filing an affidavit
      may be to make the deponent liable to cross-examination as a pre-condition of the   F
      affidavit being considered by the court.

Despite the ingenuity of these submissions of Miss Gloster on behalf of the appellant,
I do not consider that any of them justifies a conclusion that any of the 1987 rules contain
anything inconsistent with the application of the power in O. 38, r. 2(3) of the Rules of
the Supreme Court to make an order for cross-examination on affidavits in
disqualification proceedings. In my view the answers to the three submissions of Miss
Gloster to the contrary are as follows.   G

(1)   There is nothing inconsistent between the power in O. 38, r. 2(3) to order cross-
      examination on affidavits and the fact that under the 1987 rules all evidence has to
      be by affidavit in the first instance.

(2)   The alleged unfairness (if it exists, which I do not accept) results from r. 3(2) of the
      1987 rules. There is nothing inconsistent with the provisions of that rule and the
      court having power to order cross-examination of deponents.   H

(3)   I do not consider that there is any ground for implying into r. 6 some provision
      that all affidavits will be taken into consideration without cross-examination,
      especially bearing in mind that r. 2 makes, inter alia, the power to order cross-
      examination applicable in the absence of some inconsistent provision in the 1987
      rules.

A   Accordingly in my judgment the registrar was right in his view that he had jurisdiction under O. 38, r. 2(3) of the Rules of the Supreme Court to make the order for cross-examination that he made.

Did the registrar err in principle in exercising the jurisdiction?

B   Miss Gloster, on behalf of the appellant, put two wholly separate arguments under this head:

(1)   It is wrong in principle to make an order for cross-examination of the respondent in disqualification proceedings because they are in the nature of penal proceedings.

(2)   It is wrong in principle to make an order for cross-examination of deponents living abroad if the effect of such an order is to deprive the respondent to the disqualification proceedings of a right to introduce that deponent's evidence under C   s. 2 of the *Civil Evidence Act* 1968.

I fail to see any reality in the first argument in the present case, because Miss Gloster made it quite clear, no doubt on instructions, that the appellant intends in any event to submit himself for cross-examination at the trial on his own affidavits, because he appreciates that his evidence will carry less weight if untested by cross-examination. However, the argument was pressed by Miss Gloster and I should deal with it.

D   The submission, as I understand it, was to the following effect. The order for cross-examination of the appellant on his affidavits has the effect of compelling him to give evidence by submitting himself to cross-examination at the trial, even if he should decide that he does not wish to rely on his affidavit. This would be wrong in principle, particularly in penal proceedings such as disqualification proceedings. Miss Gloster relied on the decision in *Comet Products UK Ltd v Hawkex Plastics Ltd & Anor* [1971] 2 QB 67 E   on what she described as an analogous principle in proceedings for contempt of court.

In that case the Court of Appeal did decide that a respondent to a committal motion would not be compelled to give evidence. However, the court also took the view that if the respondent chose to put an affidavit sworn by him before the court, there was no reason in principle why he should not be ordered to be cross-examined on it. As Cross LJ said at p. 77F:

F   'It is, I think, only in a very exceptional case that a judge ought to refuse an application to cross-examine a deponent on his affidavit.'

In fact the court held that circumstances of that case were exceptional in the sense that counsel for the applicant had made it plain that he wished to cross-examine the respondent on matters far outside the limited question of breach of an injunction relevant on the committal motion, and to extend his cross-examination to matters which the court G   considered were germane to a pending passing-off action, rather than to the committal motion. For that reason the court refused to make an order for cross-examination. Megaw LJ at pp. 76–77 considered that the fact that the proceedings concerned – namely the committal proceedings – were penal proceedings was a proper factor to be taken into account in exercising the court's discretion to order cross-examination, but the court did not regard that factor as any bar to such an order had it otherwise been appropriate.

H   I accept that disqualification proceedings are of a penal nature and that the court will not in such proceedings compel a respondent to give evidence. This is reflected in the 1987 rules which impose no obligation on a respondent to adduce any evidence. If, as the appellant has done, he chooses to swear an affidavit and file it under r. 6 as evidence which he wishes the court to take into consideration, I see nothing in the decision in *Comet Products UK Ltd v Hawkex Plastics Ltd* or in principle to suggest that he should not be subject to an order for cross-examination on that affidavit.

Miss Gloster argued that such an order deprived the appellant of his right to make the   A
Secretary of State prove his case by his own evidence without recourse to cross-
examination of the appellant. I do not accept this. Of course the appellant had the
opportunity before filing his evidence to consider whether to rely on defects in the
Secretary of State's own evidence as enabling the appellant to submit that the Secretary
of State had not made out a case of disqualification and to file no evidence of his own.
That is, no doubt, one purpose of the requirement of r. 3 of the 1987 rules that the
Secretary of State's evidence must be served with the originating summons, so that the   B
respondent has 28 days under r. 6 in which to consider whether to file evidence himself
or to rely on submitting that he has no case to answer.

I reject the argument that an order for cross-examination of a respondent to
disqualification proceedings is wrong in principle.

Miss Gloster's second ground for her argument that the registrar erred in principle was
based on the premise that (contrary to Miss Gloster's primary submission) the effect of   C
the order for cross-examination is that if a particular deponent does not attend for cross-
examination pursuant to the order, the appellant will be debarred from adducing the
affidavit of that deponent as a statement under s. 2 of the *Civil Evidence Act* 1968. Thus
the first question to determine in relation to this submission is whether, indeed, the
appellant will be so debarred. This question is of wide import. It applies not only to
disqualification proceedings but to all proceedings in which an order for cross-   D
examination is made under O. 38, r. 2(3).

Mr Bompas QC, counsel for the Secretary of State, argued that indeed the appellant
will be debarred from adducing (without the leave of the court) as evidence under the
Civil Evidence Act any affidavit whose deponent does not attend for cross-examination,
for the effect of a deponent's not attending the trial for cross-examination pursuant to
the registrar's order is, according to O. 38, r. 2(3) of the Rules of the Supreme Court, that
'his affidavit shall not be used as evidence without the leave of the court'.   E

Miss Gloster's response to this argument was that O. 38, r. 2(3) must take effect subject
to s. 2(1) of the *Civil Evidence Act* 1968. This response is not, on the face of it, very
promising in the light of the actual terms of s. 2(1). That subsection provides that:

> 'In any civil proceedings a statement made, whether orally or in a document or
> otherwise, by any person, whether called as a witness in those proceedings or not,
> shall, *subject to this section and to rules of court*, be admissible as evidence of any   F
> facts stated therein of which direct oral evidence by him would be admissible.'
> (emphasis added)

However, Miss Gloster submitted that the 'rules of court' to which s. 2(1) is expressly
made subject are limited to rules of court made pursuant to the power in s. 8 of the *Civil
Evidence Act* 1968 itself, which do not include O. 38, r. 2(3).

I do not accept that the apparently general reference to rules of court in s. 2(1) should   G
be construed as limited in this way. In my judgment s. 2(1) takes effect subject to the
Rules of the Supreme Court as a whole, and to O. 38, r. 2(3) in particular: see to similar
effect *Rover International Ltd v Cannon Film Sales Ltd* [1987] 1 WLR 1597 at p. 1600H.

Thus, in my judgment, if an order for cross-examination is made under O. 38, r. 2(3)
and the deponent fails to attend for such cross-examination, his affidavit cannot (without
the leave of the court) be used in evidence whether pursuant to s. 2(1) of the *Civil Evidence*   H
Act 1968 or otherwise.

It was next submitted by Miss Gloster, in reliance on a course approved by Harman J
in *Rover International Ltd v Cannon Film Sales Ltd* [1987] 1 WLR 1597, that even if the
effect of the order for cross-examination is, if the deponent does not attend for cross-
examination, that the appellant cannot adduce that deponent's affidavit in evidence as a

A   statement under s. 2(1) of the *Civil Evidence Act* 1968, there is nothing to stop the appellant adducing it as a statement with the omission of the jurat. I do not accept this. The statement would in my judgment remain the affidavit made by the deponent and as such excluded from evidence by the terms of O. 38, r. 2(3) on the assumption that the deponent has failed to attend for cross-examination.

B   As a third alternative Miss Gloster argued that even if the affidavit could not be introduced under the Civil Evidence Act, there would be nothing to stop the appellant obtaining the same evidence from the deponent as was included in the inadmissible affidavit in the form of, for example, a letter and then adducing the letter under s. 2 of the *Civil Evidence Act* 1968.

This last submission is, in my judgment, unreal in the present context for the effect of r. 6 of the 1987 rules is, as I have said, that the appellant cannot, without the leave of the court, adduce any evidence in the disqualification proceedings other than evidence in the form of affidavits filed in accordance with that rule. It follows in my judgment that the appellant cannot adduce any evidence not in the form of an affidavit under the Civil Evidence Act or otherwise without the leave of the court. In the case of a deponent who does not attend for cross-examination pursuant to an order under O. 38, r. 2(3), it would be pointless for the court to consider the grant of leave to adduce under the Civil Evidence Act, for example, a letter from the same deponent containing the same statement as his affidavit, rather than considering the grant of leave to rely on the affidavit itself, under the power to grant such leave expressly reserved by O. 38, r. 2(3).

The reality of the situation is that the effect of the registrar's order is that the court retains a discretion to permit the appellant to use in evidence any of the affidavits he has filed under r. 6 of the 1987 rules, even if the deponents do not attend for cross-examination. If, as the appellant fears, he is unable to produce one or more of his foreign resident deponents for cross-examination, no doubt he will seek leave of the court to use the affidavits nonetheless and the court will consider all the circumstances in deciding whether or not to grant such leave. At present the appellant admits that he does not know which of his deponents, if any, will not attend the trial for cross-examination. As appears from the note of his decision the registrar took this into account and also took into account the fact that the court will be able to consider at a later stage whether to allow an affidavit to be used without cross-examination. Had the appellant submitted to the registrar that in respect of any one or more foreign resident deponents they would not, in fact, attend for cross-examination, no doubt the registrar would have considered whether, in those circumstances, it was right to order cross-examination of that, or those deponents, bearing in mind the appellant's right to seek leave to adduce those deponents' evidence under the *Civil Evidence Act* 1968.

As the matter was presented to him the registrar clearly took the view that it was desirable in the interests of the just determination of the issues that will have to be determined at the trial that the court should, to the extent possible, hear cross-examination of all deponents, leaving it to the court at a later stage to consider any application by the appellant to use in evidence, without cross-examination, the affidavit of any deponent as to whom the appellant could satisfy the court that cross-examination was impracticable. Far from being satisfied that the registrar erred in principle in exercising his discretion in this manner, in my judgment he exercised it entirely correctly and I shall dismiss this appeal.

(Appeal dismissed with costs. Leave to appeal refused)

George Fischer (Great Britain) Ltd v Multi-Construction Ltd. Dexion Ltd (third party).

Court of Appeal (Civil Division).
Glidewell and McCowan L JJ and Sir Michael Kerr.
Judgment delivered 21 December 1994.

Breach of contract – Damages – Plaintiff holding company sued for breach of contract – Holding company alleged loss by its operating subsidiaries – Whether subsidiaries' loss was holding company's loss – Whether losses too remote – Whether amount of losses proved.

This was an appeal by the third party against the decision of an official referee giving judgment for the plaintiff against the defendant for £567,839 damages (£702,102 with interest), and for the defendant against the third party in the same sum. The third party and the defendant had admitted liability and the defendant had ceased to take part in the action, which continued against the third party as defendant.

The plaintiff was a holding company, owning 100 per cent of the shares in a number of operating subsidiaries. The plaintiff and the defendant entered into a contract for the design and construction by the defendant of a warehouse and distribution centre. Three cranes were designed and installed by the third party as subcontractors. The design of the cranes was defective, and the third party admitted liability for faults in the cranes.

The plaintiff claimed damages under three heads: (1) the cost of the repairs to the cranes (£76,839); (2) increased costs of operation (£262,000); and (3) loss of sales (£229,000). The third party did not accept liability for (2) and (3) which were losses suffered by the operating subsidiaries. The official referee accepted that although the loss of £491,000 had been suffered directly by its subsidiaries, the plaintiff had itself suffered indirect loss in the same sum because the decrease in the subsidiaries' profits had resulted in an equal loss to the value of its shares in the subsidiaries and/or to the plaintiff's own profits.

The issue on the appeal was whether as a matter of law, a shareholder in a company was entitled to recover damages for a diminution in the value of its shareholding in the company or in the distribution by way of dividends or otherwise of profits of the company, where such diminution resulted from loss inflicted on the company by the defendant's breach of its contract with the plaintiff. The plaintiff also had to prove that: (1) it had suffered a loss; (2) it could quantify the loss by evidence; and (3) the loss was not too remote. The plaintiff submitted that as a matter of general principle, if these three items were proved, it should be awarded damages for its loss, even though that loss was indirect and not the direct result of the defendant's breach. The defendant argued there was authority to the contrary in Prudential Assurance Co Ltd v Newman Industries Ltd & Ors (No. 2) [1982] Ch 204.

Held, dismissing the appeal:

1. The issue was not whether the shareholder had a right of action at all, but rather under what heads damages were recoverable by a party who had a right of action for breach of contract. (Dicta in Prudential Assurance Co Ltd v Newman Industries Ltd & Ors (No. 2) [1982] Ch 204 distinguished.)

2. The plaintiff's evidence to the effect that a £1 loss to the subsidiary company as a result of a breach of contract would result in a £1 loss to the balance sheet or profits of the holding company, was effectively not challenged.

3. The loss claimed by the plaintiff was not too remote. (Lee v Sheard [1956] 1 QB 192 considered.)

The following cases were referred to in the judgments:
Foss v Harbottle (1843) 2 Hare 461; 67 ER 189.
Hadley v Baxendale (1854) 9 Exch 341.

A   *Lee v Sheard* [1956] 1 QB 192.
Prudential Assurance Co Ltd v Newman Industries Ltd & Ors (No. 2) [1982] Ch 204.
Roberts v Douglas Smith Stimson (1988) 46 BLR 50.
Victoria Laundry (Windsor) Ltd v Newman Industries Ltd [1949] 2 KB 528.

Christopher Purchas QC and Simon Brown (instructed by Wyeth & Co, Dartford) for Dexion.

B   William Crowther QC and Howard Palmer (instructed by Masons) for George Fischer (Great Britain) Ltd.

JUDGMENT

Glidewell LJ: This is an appeal by the third party, Dexion, against a decision of His Honour Judge Hicks QC, sitting as an official referee on 3 December 1992 when he gave
C   judgment for the plaintiff against the defendant for £567,839 damages and £134,263 interest, a total of £702,102, and also gave judgment for the defendant against the third party in the same sum, together with judgment for the defendant against the plaintiff on a counterclaim for a total (including interest) of £67,658.38 with consequent orders for costs. On the third and fourth days of the trial, counsel for Dexion and for the defendant made admissions that their clients were liable respectively to the defendant and in turn to
D   the plaintiff for breach of contract. The defendant therefore ceased to take part in the action, which continued against Dexion as if it were the defendant. This appeal has been similarly conducted.

After the admissions, the issues at the trial related solely to the damages recoverable by the plaintiff. The issues on the appeal are similarly limited, but only some of those argued at the trial have been argued before us. In particular, by reason of RSC, O. 58, r. 4 no appeal lies against a decision of an official referee on any question of fact without
E   the leave of the official referee or of this court. On 18 July 1993 Steyn LJ refused an application for such leave. The issues argued on the appeal have therefore been limited to questions of law.

The facts

F   The plaintiff, George Fischer (Great Britain) Ltd is a holding company, owning 100 per cent of the shares in a number of operating subsidiaries, in particular George Fischer Sales Ltd (GF Sales), George Fischer Castings Ltd (GF Castings), and George Fischer Plastics Ltd (GF Plastics). GF Castings manufactures metal pipework together with parts and fittings. GF Plastics manufactures plastic pipes, fittings and valves. GF Sales sells both products. It is the principal (though not the sole) customer of both GF Castings and GF Plastics and they are its principal, although not sole, suppliers.

G   The plaintiff and the defendant entered into a contract for the design and construction by the defendant of a warehouse and distribution centre at Coventry. There were to be installed in the warehouse three cranes, each of which would move up and down one of the three aisles in the warehouse. The purpose of the cranes was to store the products which came into the warehouse on appropriate racks, and thereafter to retrieve or 'pick' those products when they were required in order to fulfil an order. The defendant
H   subcontracted to Dexion the design, supply, installation and commissioning of the cranes. Unfortunately the design of the cranes was defective in a number of respects. The two most important faults were in the vertical brake control system and in the gearbox of the cranes. The first fault was eventually diagnosed by Dexion, traced and rectified. At the time of the trial the fault in the gearbox remained, and would remain until the gearboxes were replaced by heavier rating gearboxes. It is for these and other faults in the cranes that Dexion admitted liability.

The warehouse was intended to be and was occupied by GF Sales as a storage and   A
distribution depot for the metal and plastic pipes and fittings. The judgment does not
indicate the nature of the agreement between the plaintiff and GF Sales under which GF
Sales occupied the warehouse, although we have been told that it paid a rent to the
plaintiff.

Damages were claimed by the plaintiff against the defendant (and thus after the
admission effectively against Dexion) under three heads: B

(1)   the cost of repairs to the cranes, both past and prospective;

(2)   increased costs of operation; and

(3)   loss of sales.

The cost of repairs had been borne, and the cost of the future repairs was to be borne,
by the plaintiff. These costs were agreed in the sum of £76,839. Thus Dexion admits that
it is liable in damages to the plaintiff at least in that sum. It does not accept however that   C
it was liable for damages under either heads (2) or (3), and the amount of damages to be
awarded if they could properly be claimed under those heads was not agreed.

The plaintiff's case as to its claim for damages representing the increased costs of
operation and the loss of sales was that, as a result of Dexion's breach of contract, the
work at the distribution centre was much disrupted. GF Sales therefore suffered an
increase in its operating costs and a loss of sales. GF Castings and GF Plastics
manufactured their products elsewhere, and as I have already said both sold the greater   D
part of their output to GF Sales. As a result of the disruption to the distribution of
products in and from the warehouse, those sales also decreased, and GF Castings and
GF Plastics therefore also suffered losses.

The judge quantified the loss of the three subsidiary companies as follows:

		£
Increased operating costs – GF Sales		262,000
Loss of sales – GF Sales		134,000
Loss of sales – GF Castings		42,000
Loss of sales – GF Plastics		53,000
TOTAL		491,000

E

The addition of the repair cost of £76,839 brings the total of these figures to £567,839,   F
the amount of the damages awarded by the judge. The quantification of the loss and
damage is of course a question of fact, against which there is thus no appeal.

The plaintiff sought to prove that, although the total of £491,000 loss was suffered
directly by its subsidiary companies, it had itself suffered indirect loss in the same sum
because the decrease in the profits of the subsidiaries had resulted in an equal loss to the
value of the shares in the subsidiaries and/or to the plaintiff's own profits.   G

Mr Purchas for Dexion submitted to the official referee that the plaintiff was not
entitled to recover any damages for such loss for the following reasons:

(1)   A shareholder suffers no recoverable loss by diminution in the value of his
shareholding or reduction in distributions to him as a member of the company.

(2)   Objection (1) cannot be circumvented by recourse either to ignoring the separate
corporate entities of the companies and treating them as parts of a single   H
commercial unit or to treating the plaintiff as agent for its subsidiaries.

(3)   On the evidence no loss by the plaintiff was proved; in particular there was no
ground for inferring that the value of its shareholding in its subsidiaries decreased,
£ for £, by the amount of their losses and expenses, and no alternative basis for
damages was advanced.

A   (4)   Any such loss was too remote as not being within either limb of *Hadley v Baxendale*, and in particular was not within the contemplation of the defendant when entering into the contract.

The judge ruled in the plaintiff's favour on the first issue. The first question in this appeal is whether he was right to do so. Having decided that issue in favour of the plaintiff, the judge did not decide the second issue. As to the third issue, he decided this also in the plaintiff's favour, and this is the second question which arises on this appeal.

B   On the fourth issue he found on the facts that three of the defendant's employees:

'acquired a good knowledge of the way in which (the plaintiff) is structured and the intercompany trading relationship which exists between each of the relevant subsidiary companies.'

He therefore concluded:

C   'On that evidence, which I accept, I find that at the time when the defendant entered into its contract with the plaintiff it may reasonably be supposed to have been within its contemplation that breaches of contract of the kind now admitted would be liable to result in a diminution in the value of the plaintiff's shareholdings in GF Sales, GF Castings and GF Plastics by reason of losses and expense suffered by them.'

This again is a finding of fact against which there is no right of appeal.

D

The plaintiff's case

The plaintiff contends that it was and is entitled to damages resulting from Dexion's breach of contract in two capacities:

(1)   as the owner of the newly constructed warehouse, for the cost of repairs to the equipment in the warehouse, i.e. the cranes; and

E   (2)   as 100 per cent shareholder in each of its subsidiary companies, for loss occasioned to the value of its shareholding in each of those companies, or for the loss of its profits resulting from the diminution in the subsidiaries' profits.

By a respondent's notice, the plaintiff seeks to keep open the two questions which the judge did not decide, i.e. whether it is right to ignore the separate corporate entities of the companies and treat them as part of a single commercial unit, or whether the plaintiff could properly be regarded as acting as agent for its subsidiaries. We have so far only heard argument on Dexion's appeal, not on the issues raised in the respondent's notice. For the purposes of this judgment I therefore disregard those issues.

The issues in the appeal

The first and major issue can be expressed as follows. As a matter of law, is a shareholder in a company entitled to recover damages for a diminution in the value of its shareholding in the company or in the distribution by way of dividends or otherwise of profits of the company, where such diminution results from loss inflicted on the company by the defendant's breach of its contract with the plaintiff?

It is common ground between the parties that, assuming the answer to this question is 'Yes', in order to succeed, the shareholder must go on to prove that:

(1)   it did suffer such a loss;

H   (2)   it can quantify the loss by evidence; and

(3)   the loss is not too remote, i.e. because on the facts known to the defendant at the time of the contract it was reasonably foreseeable that if the defendant was in breach of contract, the plaintiff would suffer such a loss. See as to this the classic statement in the judgment of the court delivered by Asquith LJ in *Victoria Laundry (Windsor) Ltd v Newman Industries Ltd* [1949] 2 KB 528 at pp. 539–540.

I have already said that the official referee found facts which established that, if the   A
plaintiff did suffer recoverable loss, that loss was not too remote. Dexion's contention
that the plaintiff failed to prove or to quantify its loss is the subject of the second issue in
this appeal.

In effect Mr Crowther for the plaintiff submits that as a matter of general principle, if
a plaintiff proves these three matters to the satisfaction of a judge, there is no reason in
law why it should not be awarded damages for its loss, albeit that loss is indirect not the   B
direct result of the defendant's breach. Mr Purchas, however, submits that there is
authority to the contrary, namely, the decision of this court in *Prudential Assurance Co
Ltd v Newman Industries Ltd & Ors (No. 2)* [1982] Ch 204. Prudential held three per cent
of the shares in Newman. Prudential alleged that B, the chief executive, and L, a director
of Newman, had conspired to bring about the purchase by Newman of the assets of
another company in which B and L had a major interest and which was in serious
financial difficulties. That purchase benefited that other company and was alleged to be   C
detrimental to Newman and thus to its shareholders, including Prudential. An
extraordinary general meeting of Newman approved the purchase of the assets of the
other company. On the appeal, it was held:

(1)   that where fraud was practised on a company, it was the company that prima facie
should bring the action and it was only in circumstances where the board of the
company was wider the control of the fraudsters that a derivative action should be   D
brought;

(2)   that the plaintiff's personal action was an action to recover damages on the basis
that the company in which the plaintiff held shares had suffered damage; that,
since the plaintiff's right as holder of the shares was merely a right of participation
in the company on the terms of the Articles of Association, any damage done to
the company had not affected that right and, accordingly, the action was
misconceived.   E

It is the second proposition on which Mr Purchas relies. In support of it he quotes a
passage from the judgment of the court at p. 222G:

'In our judgment the personal claim is misconceived. It is of course correct, and
the judge found and Mr Bartlett did not dispute, that he and Mr Laughton, in
advising the shareholders to support the resolution approving the agreement, owed
the shareholders a duty to give such advice in good faith and not fraudulently. It   F
is also correct that if directors convene a meeting on the basis of a fraudulent
circular, a shareholder will have a right of action to recover any loss which he has
been personally caused in consequence of the fraudulent circular; this might
include the expense of attending the meeting. But what he cannot do is to recover
damages merely because the company in which he is interested has suffered
damage. He cannot recover a sum equal to the diminution in the market value of   G
his shares, or equal to the likely diminution in dividend, because such a "loss" is
merely a reflection of the loss suffered by the company. The shareholder does not
suffer any personal loss. His only "loss" is through the company, in the diminution
in the value of the net assets of the company, in which he has (say) a three per cent
shareholding. The plaintiff's shares are merely a right of participation in the
company on the terms of the articles of association. The shares themselves, his
right of participation, are not directly affected by the wrongdoing.'   H

Later in the judgment there is a further relevant passage to the following effect at
p. 223G:

'A personal action could have the most unexpected consequences. If a company
with assets of £500m and an issued share capital of £50m were defrauded of
£500,000 the effect on dividends and share prices would not be discernible. If a

A company with assets of £10m were defrauded, there would be no effect on share prices when the fraud was discovered; if it were first reported that the company had been defrauded of £500,000 and subsequently reported that the company had discovered oil in property acquired by the company as part of the fraud and later still reported that the initial loss to the company could not have exceeded £50,000, the effect on share prices would be bewildering and the effect on dividends would either be negligible or beneficial.

B The plaintiffs in this action were never concerned to recover in the personal action. The plaintiffs were only interested in the personal action as a means of circumventing the rule in *Foss v Harbottle*. The plaintiffs succeeded. A personal action would subvert the rule in *Foss v Harbottle* and that rule is not merely a tiresome procedural obstacle placed in the path of a shareholder by a legalistic judiciary. The rule is the consequence of the fact that a corporation is a separate
C legal entity. Other consequences are limited liability and limited rights. The company is liable for its contracts and torts; the shareholder has no such liability. The company acquires causes of action for breaches of contract and for torts which damage the company. No cause of action vests in the shareholder. When the shareholder acquires a share he accepts the fact that the value of his investment follows the fortunes of the company and that he can only exercise his influence over the fortunes of the company by the exercise of his voting rights in general
D meeting.'

The rule in *Foss v Harbottle* (1843) 2 Hare 461 is that in general if a wrong (whether a breach of contract or a tort) is done to a company, only the company may sue for the damage caused to it; a shareholder has no right to bring an action on behalf of the company in order to protect the value of his shares. The rule preserves the rights of majority shareholders against an attempt by a minority shareholder to bring an action
E where the majority do not wish such an action to be brought. There is for this reason an exception to the general rule where it is alleged that those in control of a company have defrauded it.

The part of the passage in *Prudential v Newman* on which Mr Purchas particularly relies, which I have quoted first above, if read in isolation might appear to support Mr Purchas's submission. But, like any other dictum in a judgment, it must be read in its context and not in isolation. The context of the passage is that the issue then under
F consideration in *Prudential v Newman* was whether the shareholder (Prudential) had a right of action at all, in a case in which the company had and was willing to exercise its right of action if a conspiracy were proved to exist. *Prudential v Newman* is not an authority on the question, under what heads are damages recoverable by a party who has a right of action for breach of contract? For this reason in my view, the dicta in the judgment *Prudential v Newman* were not directed to, and thus have no application to,
G that issue, which is the issue in the present case.

Lee v Sheard [1956] 1 QB 192, was also a decision of this court. Mr Lee was one of two directors of, and held 45 per cent of the shares in, a small private company which carried on business as textile merchants. Mr Lee did both the buying and the selling for the company. He was injured in a car accident caused by the defendant's negligence. As a result of his injuries, the company's business suffered, and thus there was a reduction in the profits available for distribution both to him and his co-director. It was held that the
H loss which Mr Lee thus suffered was a head of damages for which he was entitled to claim, and was not too remote. Giving a judgment with which Hodson LJ and Morris LJ agreed, Denning LJ said at p. 195:

'I am of the opinion that Mr Lee succeeds. The loss which he suffered is a real loss of £1,500. He is entitled to recover that sum from the wrongdoer unless it is too remote, or there is some other good reason why he should not get it.'

In the present case the official referee took the view (as had the late Judge Newey in an   A
earlier decision of his, *Roberts v Douglas Smith Stimson* (1988) 46 BLR 50) that the
decisions of this court in *Prudential v Newman* and *Lee v Sheard* were irreconcilable, the
one with the other. Judge Newey in his decision had followed *Prudential v Newman*.

In his judgment Judge Hicks said:

> 'In this case the plaintiff has an undoubted right of action and its subsidiaries do
> not. I therefore consider that I am bound by *Lee v Sheard* and that *Prudential v*   B
> *Newman* is to be distinguished. That also seems to me to accord with principle.
> Loss which is actually caused to a plaintiff by the defendant's actionable wrong
> should be recoverable, if within the general limits set by concepts such as
> remoteness and mitigation. Restrictions arising from the need to protect a specific
> rule primarily concerned with entitlement to sue rather than measure of damages,
> such as the rule in *Foss v Harbottle*, should not be applied more widely than their
> reason for existence requires.'   C

As I have explained, in my judgment the principle to be derived from *Prudential v*
Newman does not apply to the issue in the present case. However, except that *Lee v*
Sheard was an action in tort, that decision was based on the principle for which Mr
Crowther for the plaintiff contends. Like the judge, I think that that principle applies just
as much in relation to damages for breach of contract as it does in tort. Save that, for the
reasons I have explained, it is not necessary to distinguish *Prudential v Newman*, but   D
rather to say that it simply does not apply, I agree with Judge Hicks on this issue. I
therefore reject Mr Purchas's argument on this first and major issue.

The second issue is expressed as follows in the notice of appeal:

> 'The learned judge erred in law in accepting the contention made by an expert
> witness and chartered accountant that:
>
> > "the plaintiff as the holder of 100 per cent of the shares in GF Sales, GF Plastics   E
> > and GF Castings suffered a loss equal to that suffered by each of them in the
> > internal quote when there was no evidence to support that contention." '

Mr Philip Kabraji FCA gave evidence for the plaintiff. In his report which was put in
evidence, he said:

> 'Every £1 loss in a subsidiary company represents £1 lost in GF (Great Britain),
> since each of these companies is 100 per cent owned by GF (Great Britain). GF   F
> (Great Britain) is therefore entitled to the whole of the profit earned by a
> subsidiary. Thus, if the profits of a subsidiary are reduced by £1, the value of GF
> (Great Britain)'s investment in the subsidiary is also reduced by £1. This remains
> true whether the profits of the subsidiaries are distributed to GF (Great Britain)
> by way of dividend or whether they are retained within the individual subsidiaries
> own working capital. It is by virtue of this relationship within the Group   G
> companies that I have included the subsidiaries' losses in my quantification of the
> claim for damages.'

When he was cross-examined he said that if he was valuing the shares in a subsidiary
company for the purposes of a sale by the parent company, a common way of valuation
would be to look at the profits of the subsidiary company for the past two or three years,
estimate from that the estimated profits for the future and apply to that figure a number
of years' purchase. He agreed that a loss in profits in one particular year would not   H
necessarily result in the sale price of the shares being reduced by precisely the amount of
that loss. He said however:

> 'In a situation where there is no sale contemplated, it is a reduction in the
> investment of the parent company in the subsidiary, because it has lost those
> moneys. Its balance sheet is now smaller than it would otherwise have been.'

A He added:

'There is of course the point that of course if these profits had been made, they would have been paid out as dividends to the parent company and therefore formed part of the parent company's assets.'

He said that dividends were paid between the subsidiaries and the parent company. He concluded on this subject:

B 'It is necessarily a £ lost, as I said, for a number of reasons. First, it affects the balance sheet of the subsidiary company and therefore it could affect the valuation of the investment in the parent company. Secondly, dividends can be paid up by the subsidiary to the parent company. Thirdly, there could be a shortfall in capital in the subsidiary and therefore the parent company might have to make up the working capital. Fourthly, the money could be invested in assets in that company C which would generate future profits or increase the future profits of that particular company and increase its valuation to any prospective purchaser.'

Mr Purchas submits that Mr Kabraji was doing no more than giving theoretical evidence about the effect on the value of the shares in subsidiary companies generally, not about the actual effect of loss caused to the subsidiaries in this case by Dexion's breach. Such evidence, he submits, was strictly inadmissible, or at least as a matter of law D did not prove the plaintiff's loss. In order to prove that loss, it was necessary for the plaintiff to call detailed evidence about the actual effect of the loss to the subsidiaries on the balance sheet and profits of the plaintiff company, and there was no such evidence.

For the defendant and Dexion, Mr Aldous, chartered accountant, was called. In his report he said:

'GT (Grant Thornton, Mr Kabraji's firm, the accountants for the plaintiff) assert their view that £1 lost in the subsidiary is a £1 loss to the holding company. This E action is brought by the non-trading holding company for the UK, GF (Great Britain) Ltd. GT's contention may or may not be the case. Each corporate entity is a separate entity. The overall decision-making of their management and their overall trading may improve, or damage, the value of the investment which the holding company has in each subsidiary.'

In his evidence in-chief he was not asked to add to or expand on this comment, and F thus naturally he was not cross- examined about it.

In my view, considering Mr Kabraji's evidence as a whole, it was to the effect that a £1 loss to the subsidiary company as a result of a breach of contract would result in a £1 loss to the balance sheet or profits of the holding company, unless some other extraneous factor produced a different result. In effect, that is what Mr Aldous said. Certainly he did not disagree with the proposition. Dexion and Mr Aldous had access to the plaintiff's G books and accounts, but no attempt was made on behalf of Dexion to prove that there was some other extraneous factor which would displace the effect to which Mr Kabraji referred in his evidence. It follows that Mr Kabraji's evidence on this matter was effectively not challenged.

In my view Mr Kabraji's evidence was admissible, and the judge was entitled to accept it as he did as proving the plaintiff's loss. I view this as a matter of fact, on which as I have said Dexion is not entitled to appeal, rather than a matter of law.

H Mr Purchas, however, advanced an alternative argument based upon this part of the evidence and a passage in the judgment, which I suspect had not been advanced in the court below. He put it in these terms:

'On the facts of this case, there being no evidence of a reduction in dividends, the judge had to ask whether there was evidence on which he could assess whether there had been a diminution in the value of the shares, and if so to what extent.'

Mr Purchas then pointed to the judge's finding on foreseeability, which I have already   A
quoted. He points out that Judge Hicks in that passage said that it might reasonably be
supposed to have been within the plaintiff's contemplation that:

> 'Breaches of contract of the kind now admitted would be liable to result in a
> diminution in the value of the plaintiff's shareholdings in its subsidiary companies.'

Mr Purchas submits that the judge did not there find that the plaintiff should
reasonably have contemplated that the plaintiff would suffer loss in one of the other ways   B
advanced by Mr Kabraji in the last answer which I have quoted from his cross-
examination.

I do not find this a convincing argument. I have no doubt that Judge Hicks expressed
himself as he did in this paragraph because at that point nobody had suggested that if it
was reasonably foreseeable that the breach of contract would result in a diminution of
the value of the shareholding in the subsidiaries, it might not also or alternatively result   C
in a diminution of dividends paid to the plaintiff or in loss in one of the other ways
referred to by Mr Kabraji. It must follow that if the one form of loss could reasonably
have been contemplated so could the others. If the matter had been brought to his
attention, I have no doubt that the judge would so have worded the passage in his
judgment. Thus in my view this point does not avail the appellant. It is clear to me that
the judge's finding on this issue was intended to be and was indeed a finding that the
damages claimed by the plaintiff were not too remote. I would thus reject the argument   D
on this issue also.

It is for these reasons that I would dismiss the appeal.

It is therefore unnecessary for us to hear argument about, or to reach any conclusions
about, the issues raised in the respondent's notice.

McCowan LJ: I agree.

Sir Michael Kerr: I also agree. The so-called rule in *Foss v Harbottle*, and its discussion   E
in *Prudential v Newman*, were both concerned with situations in which the company in
question had a right of action, or would have had such a right if the alleged wrong done
to it – whether it be tort or breach of contract or both – were established. The effect of
the rule is accordingly that, save in exceptional circumstances, it must be left to the
company, i.e. effectively to the majority of its shareholders, to exercise the company's
right of action.   F

In the present case, however, the position is the opposite. The plaintiff, the 100 per
cent shareholder in its three subsidiaries, has an unquestionable – and indeed admitted –
right of action for damages (at least nominal) for breach of contract. The companies, on
the other hand, have no right of action. The only issues which arise are therefore
concerned with the determination of the loss, if any, which the shareholder plaintiff has
suffered as the result of the breach of contract, and whether damages may be recovered   G
for it. That determination involves questions of evidence, foreseeability and remoteness
which were decided by the judge in favour of the plaintiff on the facts and on which there
can be no appeal in this case. It follows that the present case is quite unaffected both by
Foss v Harbottle and *Prudential v Newman*. I would accordingly dismiss this appeal for
the same reasons as Glidewell LJ.

(Appeal dismissed)   H

A **Powdrill & Anor v Watson & Anor (Paramount Airways Ltd).**
Talbot & Anor v Cadge & Anor (Leyland DAF Ltd).
Talbot & Anor v Grundy & Anor (Ferranti International plc).
House of Lords.
Lord Keith of Kinkel, Lord Browne-Wilkinson, Lord Mustill, Lord Woolf,
B Lord Lloyd of Berwick.
Judgment delivered 16 March 1995.

> *Administration orders – Whether administrators had 'adopted' contracts of*
> *employment – Administrators dismissed employees – Whether claims of employees*
> *under employment contracts were secured on company's assets in priority to*
> *administrators' remuneration – – Whether administrators could contract out of*
> C *'adoption' – Insolvency Act 1986, s. 19(5).*

> *Administrative receivership – Whether administrative receivers had 'adopted'*
> *contracts of employment – Whether receivers were personally liable on contracts*
> *– Whether receivers could contract out of 'adoption' – Insolvency Act 1986,*
> *s. 44(1)(b).*

These were appeals by the joint administrators of Paramount Airways Ltd ('Paramount')
D and the administrative receivers of two companies ('Leyland DAF' and 'Ferranti') from
judgments of the Court of Appeal [1994] BCC 172 and Lightman J [1994] BCC 658
respectively that the contracts of employment of former employees of the companies had
been adopted by the administrators within the meaning of s. 19(5) of the Insolvency Act
1986 and by the receivers under s. 44 of the 1986 Act.

Paramount
E
The administrators were appointed to Paramount on 7 August 1989. They caused
Paramount to continue trading with a view to seeking a buyer for its business as a going
concern. On 14 August, the administrators wrote to the employees stating that they did not
and would 'not at any future time adopt or assume personal liability in respect of your
contracts of employment'. Attempts to find a buyer failed and the employees were dismissed
at the end of November.
F
Two employees petitioned under s. 27 of the 1986 Act claiming that various sums including
pay in lieu of notice, unpaid holiday pay, so-called loyalty bonuses agreed with the
administrators and pension contributions, were payable under s. 19(5). Evans-Lombe J
[1993] BCC 662 held that an administrator could contract out of the adoption of contracts
of employment, but that the administrators' letter of 14 August was ineffective to exclude
adoption of the contracts which the administrators had procured Paramount to continue to
G perform. Accordingly liabilities incurred under those contracts of employment while the
joint administrators were in office were charged on the assets of the company under s. 19(5)
in priority to the administrators' remuneration and expenses. Such liabilities included
payments in lieu of notice, holiday pay and pension contributions. The agreement to pay
bonuses was a separate agreement and claims under it and claims for compensation for
unfair dismissal did not attract the protection of s. 19(5) because they did not arise under
the relevant contract of employment. The administrators appealed. The respondents cross-
H appealed in relation to the bonus payments.

The Court of Appeal held that by continuing to employ staff and pay them in accordance
with their previous contracts, after the 14-day period mentioned in s. 19(5), the
administrators had adopted those contracts of employment. The word 'adopted' in s. 19(5)
connoted, in relation to contracts of employment, 'the continuance of which is expressly or
impliedly accepted'. The assertion by an administrator that he was not adopting the

contract, such as the letter, was mere wind with no legal effect. The employees were entitled   A
to two months' pay in lieu of notice out of the property of the company in the custody or
under the control of the administrators. The same applied in relation to pension contributions
and holiday pay. The bonus agreement was a separate contract and not covered by s. 19(5)
as a contract of employment adopted by the administrators.

Leyland DAF and Ferranti
                                                                                                    B
In the case of both companies the receivers wrote to the employees stating that they 'ha[d]
not adopted, do not adopt, and will not at any future date adopt' contracts of employment
with the companies. The Leyland DAF receivers paid employees' wages post-receivership as
and when the liability to pay arose. Some 957 Leyland DAF employees made redundant
after the 14-day period in s. 44(2) had claims relating to pay in lieu of notice, pension
contributions, redundancy payments, benefits under company car and medical and accident
insurance policies, and holiday pay. The Ferranti receivers caused Ferranti to pay the   C
employees' wages for the periods in which they continued to work. Some 106 employees
were made redundant after the 14-day period. Their claims related to payments in lieu of
notice, severance payments, holiday pay, pension contributions, and company car benefits.

Lightman J held that the receivers had adopted the contracts of employment; had not
contracted out of their personal liability; and were personally liable (coextensively with the
companies) in respect of all contractual (but no other) liabilities under the contracts of   D
employment of the employees irrespective of the dates on which they accrued or the periods
in respect of which the liability arose.

The administrators and receivers appealed.

Held, dismissing the appeals but varying the order of the Court of Appeal in Paramount
so as to declare that sums in respect of holiday pay were only payable by the administrators
in respect of months of employment after the administrators' appointment, and varying the   E
orders of Lightman J by setting aside his directions in relation to entitlement to private
medical insurance, accident insurance and holiday pay in Leyland DAF and in relation to
health care schemes, the provision of motor cars, holiday pay and sums due under the terms
of a severance payment and redevelopment agreement in Ferranti and referring those
matters back to the Chancery Division:

1. For the purposes of both s. 19 (administration) and s. 44 (receivership) an employee's   F
contract of employment was 'adopted' if he was continued in employment for more than 14
days after the appointment of the administrator or receiver.

2. It was not possible for an administrator or receiver to avoid this result or alter its
consequences unilaterally by informing employees that he was not adopting their contracts
or was only doing so on terms.

3. In the case of both administration and receivership the consequence of adoption was to   G
give priority only to liabilities incurred by the administrator or receiver during his tenure of
office.

The following cases were referred to in the speech of Lord Browne-Wilkinson:

Anchor Line (Henderson Bros) Ltd, Re [1937] Ch 1.
Botibol, Re [1947] 1 All ER 26.
Davis (S) & Co Ltd, Re [1945] Ch 402.
Joel's Will Trusts, Re [1967] Ch 14.   H
Levi & Co Ltd, Re [1919] 1 Ch 416.
Mack Trucks (Britain) Ltd, Re [1967] 1 WLR 780.
Nicoll v Cutts (1985) 1 BCC 99,427.
Oak Pits Colliery Co, Re (1882) 21 ChD 322.
Rochester (Bishop of) v Le Fanu [1906] 2 Ch 513.

A *Specialised Mouldings Ltd, Re* (unreported, 13 February 1987, Harman J).
United Club and Hotel Co Ltd, Re (1889) 60 LT(NS) 665.

Jonathan Sumption QC, Patrick Elias QC and Mark Phillips (instructed by Wilde Sapte) for the administrators and Leyland DAF receivers and (instructed by Allen & Overy) for the Ferranti receivers.

B Robin Potts QC, Richard Snowden and Brian Napier (instructed by Burrough & Co) for the Paramount employees.

Charles Purle QC, David Bean and Ross Crail (instructed by Rowley Ashworth) for the employees in Leyland DAF and Ferranti.

SPEECHES

Lord Keith of Kinkel: For the reasons given in the speech to be delivered by Lord
C Browne-Wilkinson, which I have read in draft and with which I agree, I would vary the order of the Court of Appeal in the *Paramount* case and that of Lightman J in the *Leyland DAF* and *Ferranti* cases in the manner he proposes and otherwise dismiss the appeals.

Lord Browne-Wilkinson: When a company is in severe financial difficulties its bankers or other holders of a floating charge normally enforce their security by appointing a
D receiver. In many cases it is in the interests of the secured creditor that the whole or part of the company's business should continue, notwithstanding the receivership, so that it can be sold as a going concern rather than on a break-up basis. For this purpose it is necessary for the company, acting by the receiver, to continue to employ some or all of the workforce. Where no receiver has been appointed out of court, the court instead of making an immediate winding-up order can now appoint an administrator for the purpose of continuing the business of the company with a view to procuring its survival
E for the more advantageous realisation of its assets on a going concern basis. For that purpose the continued employment of part of the workforce will again normally be essential. These three appeals raise questions as to the rights of employees whose employments have been continued by a receiver or administrator. Those rights have been clarified for the future by the *Insolvency Act* 1994. However, in relation to employments continued by an administrator or receiver between 1986 and 1994 these questions remain
F live.

In outline the question is whether on the true construction of the *Insolvency Act* 1986, s. 19 (which relates to administrators) and s. 44 (which relates to administrative receivers) gave such employees the right to be paid in full, and in priority to all other creditors, not only for services actually rendered during the administration or receivership but also other payments not referable to such services to which the employees were entitled under their contracts of employment with the company, e.g. holiday pay referable to a period
G before the receiver or administrator was appointed and payments in lieu of notice.

Section 19 of the 1986 Act deals with the vacation of office by an administrator; subs. (4) and (5) provide as follows:

'(4) His remuneration and any expenses properly incurred by him shall be charged on and paid out of any property of the company which is in his custody or under his control at that time in priority to any security to which section 15(1) then
H applies.

(5) Any sums payable in respect of debts or liabilities incurred, while he was administrator, under contracts entered into or contracts of employment adopted by him or a predecessor of his in the carrying out of his or the predecessor's functions shall be charged on and paid out of any such property as is mentioned in subsection (4) in priority to any charge arising under that subsection.

A

For this purpose, the administrator is not to be taken to have adopted a contract of employment by reason of anything done or omitted to be done within 14 days after his appointment.'

The question in administration therefore is whether in the case of any given employee the administrator has 'adopted' the employee's contract of employment and, if so, whether the sum claimed under the adopted contract is a sum 'payable in respect of debts or liabilities incurred while he was administrator'.

B

Sections 44 and 45 deal with employees in an administrative receivership as follows:

'44(1) The administrative receiver of a company–

(a) is deemed to be the company's agent, unless and until the company goes into liquidation;

(b) is personally liable on any contract entered into by him in the carrying out of his functions (except in so far as the contract otherwise provides) and on any contract of employment adopted by him in the carrying out of those functions; and

C

(c) is entitled in respect of that liability to an indemnity out of the assets of the company.

44(2) For the purposes of subsection (1)(b) the administrative receiver is not to be taken to have adopted a contract of employment by reason of anything done or omitted to be done within 14 days after his appointment.

D

45(3) Where at any time an administrative receiver vacates office–

(a) his remuneration and any expenses properly incurred by him, and

(b) any indemnity to which he is entitled out of the assets of the company,

shall be charged on and paid out of any property of the company which is in his custody or under his control at that time in priority to any security held by the person by or on whose behalf he was appointed.'

E

The question therefore in administrative receivership is whether the receiver has 'adopted' the contract of employment and, if so, whether the sum claimed is a liability 'on' the adopted contract.

F

The facts

There are three appeals before your Lordships. One (*Paramount Airways Ltd*) is concerned with administration; the other two (*Leyland DAF Ltd* and *Ferranti International*) are concerned with receivership.

G

Paramount

Paramount carried on business as a charter airline for which purpose it employed the respondents two pilots. Under their contracts of employment they were entitled, in addition to their wages, to the payment by the company of contributions into a retirement pension plan. Under cl. 8 of their contracts of employment the pilots were also entitled to take 28 days paid holidays in each year beginning 1 April. Clause 8(f) provided as follows:

H

'(f) On termination of employment, other than for misconduct, your holiday entitlement will be paid on the basis of 1/12th of the annual entitlement for each full calendar month's service from the previous 1 April or, if you commenced employment after such date, then your date of commencement, less any leave taken.'

A   The appellants were appointed joint administrators by an order of Warner J made on 7 August 1989. On 14 August 1989 the administrators wrote to all employees as follows:

> 'I write to advise you that [we] were appointed joint administrators of the above company by an order of the High Court dated 7 August 1989. Under the provisions of the *Insolvency Act* 1986 the joint administrators act as agents of the company.

B
> We are currently investigating the company's position but as yet we are uncertain as to the true contractual position between yourself and the company.

> Nothing in this letter is to be taken to affect the true identity of your employer. However, we should like to take this opportunity of reassuring you that the company will continue to pay your monthly salary during the interim period, including that payable on 31 August 1989 together with any other sums which you are contractually entitled to pursuant to the terms and conditions of your contract
C
> of employment. We hope that we may have your co-operation during this period.

> We wish to make it clear that the joint administrators act at all times as agents for the company and without personal liability. The administrators are not [sic] and will not at any future time adopt or assume personal liability in respect of your contracts of employment.'

D   Thereafter the administrators sought to find a buyer for the business as a going concern and caused Paramount to continue trading, paying the salaries and pension contributions of all the employees. The administrators made it clear throughout that the employees were continuing to be employed under their existing contracts of employment with Paramount and it was obvious to the pilots that the payment of their salaries was an expediency measure in order to keep Paramount trading.

E   Attempts to find a buyer having failed, on 30 November 1989 the administrators informed a meeting of employees that the majority were to be made redundant with immediate effect. On 5 December 1989 the administrators sent letters to the pilots and other employees which letters terminated their employment with effect from 30 November 1989. The pilots and others claimed, inter alia, that they were entitled under s. 19 of the 1986 Act to be paid two months' salary (including pension contributions) in lieu of notice and sums in respect of holiday pay. These claims were upheld by Evans-
F Lombe J ([1993] BCC 662). The employees also advanced claims to additional sums under a bonus agreement and awards for unfair dismissal: these latter claims were dismissed by the judge and nothing turns on them in this appeal. The decision of Evans-Lombe J was, in substance, affirmed by the Court of Appeal (Dillon, Leggatt and Henry L JJ): see [1994] BCC 172.

G   **Leyland DAF**

    The Leyland DAF receivers were appointed on 3 February 1993. At the date of the appointment Leyland DAF owed approximately £570m to secured and unsecured creditors. It employed 5,371 employees, the monthly wage bill being in the region of £7m. The Leyland DAF receivers had no immediate access to cash to fund post-appointment trading but were able to secure some limited funding by borrowing.

H   On the day of their appointment, the Leyland DAF receivers, following the then accepted practice of receivers, wrote to all employees a letter which included the following passages:

> 'The receivers currently contemplate causing the company, for such period as the receivers think fit, to continue to pay remuneration to you in accordance with your contract of employment . . .

... Section 44(1)(b) of the *Insolvency Act* 1986 provides that an administrative   A
receiver of company is "personally liable on any contract of employment adopted
by him in the carrying out of his functions".

The receivers have not adopted, do not adopt and will not at any future date adopt,
your contract of employment with the company ...

... Section 44(1)(b) also provides that "an administrative receiver of a company is
personally liable on any contract entered into by him in the carrying out of his   B
functions (except in so far as the contract otherwise provides)". The receivers
themselves have not intended to enter nor do they intend to enter into any contract
of employment with you. Nevertheless, to avoid any doubt, it is stressed that in
any event the receivers have not assumed and will not at any future date assume
any personal liability in relation to your present or future employment.'

The Leyland DAF receivers caused Leyland DAF to pay the employees' wages for the   C
periods post-receivership during which they continued to work. Some employees were
made redundant within the 14-day period after the appointment of the receiver. Between
26 March 1993 and 10 September 1993, 957 employees were made redundant.
Contractual notice was not given to these employees. The receivers continued to trade
and completed a series of sales of the business of Leyland DAF. Approximately 2,700
employees were retained in the transferred businesses by the purchasers and their
immediate continued employment thereby secured. The receivers assumed that the claims   D
of any employees not transferred to the purchasers would fall to be dealt with in a
subsequent liquidation.

The contractual position of the Leyland DAF employees is as follows. There are two
classes of employee, namely, workshop employees of whom the respondent Mr Sumner
is one, and staff employees of whom the respondent Mr Cadge is one. Under their
contracts of employment they are entitled to benefits under four heads: E

(1) *Notice*

(a)   Workshop employees are generally entitled to one week's notice for each year of
        service up to a maximum of 12 weeks. Mr Sumner was entitled to 12 weeks' notice
        and (subject to mitigation) claims £2,915.28.

(b)   Staff employees have different periods of notice. Mr Cadge was entitled to three   F
        months' notice and claims £6,671.08.

The estimated total value of potential claims against the receivers for payments in lieu of
notice is £3,421,615 odd.

(2) *Pensions*

(a)   Mr Sumner's claim for pension contributions falling due during the period for
        which he should have received notice is £116.61.   G

(b)   Mr Cadge's claim for pension contributions during the same period is £266.84.

(3) *Medical and accident insurance*

Some employees, including Mr Cadge, were entitled to participate in Leyland DAF's
BUPA scheme.

The estimated total value of the claims for pensions and medical and accident insurance   H
during the notice period is £148,463-odd.

(4) *Holiday pay*

(a)   Mr Sumner was entitled to 25 days' holiday in accordance with cl. 7.1 of the
        collective agreement. His claim to holiday pay is £291.53.

A   (b)   Mr Cadge's claim to holiday pay arises under cl. 1.5 and 1.6 of the staff employment terms and conditions. He claims £307.90 under this head.

The estimated total value of potential claims to holiday pay is £143,573.41.

Ferranti

The Ferranti receivers were appointed on 1 December 1993. At that date Ferranti
B   owed approximately £114m to secured creditors, £5m to preferential creditors and £44.7m to unsecured creditors. It had approximately 3,200 employees and the monthly wage bill was about £4.7m. The businesses of the Ferranti group were sophisticated and highly complex. The receivers' ability to sell the businesses as going concerns depended upon the continued performance of hundreds of contracts and on Ferranti's ability to secure future contracts. To ensure that Ferranti had the funds to continue trading whilst the Ferranti receivers carried out their investigations, they borrowed £5m on the basis of
C   their personal liability.

On 2 December 1993 the Ferranti receivers wrote to all employees a letter which stated inter alia:

'1. The receivers themselves are not and will not become your employer.

2. On the contrary, the companies have remained and, for so long as your employment continues, will remain your employer.

D   3. The receivers have not assumed, and will not at any future date assume, any personal liability in relation to your employment.

4. Section 44(1)(b) of the *Insolvency Act* 1986 provides that an administrative receiver of a company is "personally liable on any contract of employment adopted by him in the carrying out of his functions". The receivers have not adopted, do not adopt and will not at any future date adopt, your contract of employment with
E   the companies.

5. Section 44(1)(b) also provides that "an administrative receiver of a company is personally liable on any contract entered into by him in the carrying out of his functions (except in so far as the contract otherwise provides)". The receivers themselves have not intended to enter nor do they intend to enter into any contract of employment with you. Nevertheless, to avoid any doubt, it is stressed that in any event the receivers have not assumed and will not at any future date assume
F   any personal liability in relation to your present or any future employment.'

The Ferranti receivers caused Ferranti to pay the employees' wages for the periods post-receivership during which they continued to work.

Some employees were made redundant during the period of 14 days after the appointment of the receivers. Between 16 December 1993 and 1 October 1994, 229
G   employees were made redundant of whom some were employed on Ferranti's executive contract and others on the non-executive contract. As at 1 October 1994, 706 employees were still employed by Ferranti. Some of Ferranti's business units had been sold and 1,484 employees transferred to employment with the purchasers, their immediate continued employment being thereby secured.

Ferranti had two classes of employees employed under two standard forms of contract. The executive staff contract applies only to senior managers, of whom the respondent
H   Mr Parry is one. Mr Parry was made redundant on 14 January 1994 without notice having been given. The non-executive staff contract applies to all other grades of staff, including the respondent Mrs Grundy. Mrs Grundy was made redundant on 4 February 1994 without notice being given.

Under their contracts, the respondent employees are entitled to benefits under six heads:

Notice   A

(a) Under cl. 12 of the executive contract, Mr Parry was entitled to six months' notice of termination and claims £17,336.52. The estimated total of potential claims under this head by executive staff amounts to £1,397,012.

(b) Non-executive staff are entitled to four weeks' notice plus an additional week for every year after five years' service up to a maximum of 12 weeks. Mrs Grundy was entitled to 12 weeks' notice and claims £1,845.72. The estimated total of potential claims by non-executive staff for payments in lieu of notice amounts to £356,054.

Severance payment

(a) Under a severance payment and redeployment agreement dated 14 February 1991, Mr Parry was entitled to a severance payment of one month's pay plus 514 weeks' pay totalling £6,376.63. The estimated total of potential claims by executive staff under this head is £108,037.

(b) Under the severance agreement, Mrs Grundy was entitled to a payment of one month's salary plus the maximum additional severance payment of 12 weeks' pay. Her claim is for £2,514.80. The estimated total of potential claims by non-executive staff under this head is £385,029.

Holiday pay   D

(a) Under the executive contract, Mr Parry was entitled to 33 days of paid holiday. Under cl. 6(d) of his contract holiday pay on termination was calculated based on the number of completed weeks of service from 1 January until the date of termination less holiday taken. Mr Parry claims £132.85.

(b) Under the non-executive contract, Mrs Grundy was entitled to 37 days of paid holiday. Holiday pay was calculated on the same basis as under the executive contract. Mrs Grundy claims to be entitled to 21/2 days of holiday pay totalling £132.85.

The estimated total of potential claims for holiday pay is £50,280.

Pensions

Both Mr Parry and Mrs Grundy were members of Ferranti's pension scheme under which the company was bound to pay contributions. The estimated total of potential claims for damages for non-payment of pension contributions in respect of the notice period is under the non-executive contract, £39,086 and under the executive contract, £361,296.

Mr Parry's company car

Under cl. 2.4 of his contract Mr Parry was provided with a car. The estimated total of potential claims for non-provision of motor cars is £8,157 under the non-executive contract and £22,986 under the executive contract.

Health care scheme

Under cl. 5 of the executive contract, Mr Parry was entitled to membership of the company's health care scheme. The estimated total of potential claims in respect of this benefit is £2,922 under the non-executive contract and £4,265 under the executive contract.

The estimated total personal liability of the Ferranti receivers to employees made redundant since 15 December 1993 is about £3.9m if the decisions appealed from are upheld. In the circumstances of this case, the assets of Ferranti are sufficient to provide an indemnity to the receivers in respect of those claims. The Ferranti receivers' best

A   estimate is that, if the judgment is overturned, the prospects of a return to the Ferranti pension scheme, a secured creditor ranking behind the first secured creditors, would be improved.

Lightman J held ([1994] BCC 658) that the employees of both Leyland DAF and Ferranti were entitled to be paid in priority, under s. 45, all the sums claimed by them whether or not the liabilities were incurred during the receivership. The respondents, with

B   leave, appeal directly to your Lordships' House.

The history of the legislation

At common law a receiver appointed by the court was not the agent of the company and was therefore personally liable for any contracts entered into by him. In the case of receivers appointed out of court by debenture holders the position was different. The

C   debenture normally provided that the receiver was to be the agent of the company, from which it followed that contracts made by the receiver after his appointment were made on behalf of the company as principal and did not expose him to personal liability. This position was altered by the *Companies Act* 1947 (re-enacted in s. 369(2) of the *Companies Act* 1948) which provided that a receiver appointed out of court should be personally liable on any contract entered into by him in the performance of his functions and entitled in respect of that liability to indemnity out of the assets. The result of the

D   statutory indemnity given to the receiver against his personal liability was to give a right, by subrogation, to the other party to the contract to be indemnified out of the receivership assets in priority to the debenture holders. However, it is to be noted that the section did not deal with the liability of a receiver on contracts entered into by the company before his appointment.

The appointment of a receiver by a debenture holder does not, in itself, terminate the

E   contracts of employment of the employees. If the receiver continues their services they remain the employees of the company, see *Re Mack Trucks (Britain) Ltd* [1967] 1 WLR 780. In practice, receivers wishing to carry on the business of the company retain the work force paying wages as they fall due. The wages so paid by the receiver are costs and expenses of the receivership: accordingly they are payable in priority to the secured creditors. Until 1985 it had not arisen for decision whether an employee whose employment the receiver had caused the company to continue but whose wages had not

F   been paid in full was entitled to the same priority in respect of the unpaid wages.

That question arose for determination in *Nicoll v Cutts* (1985) 1 BCC 99,427. Mr Nicoll had a five-year service contract with a company. A receiver was appointed by debenture holders, a bank, on terms which made the receiver the agent of the company. The receiver did not immediately take steps to terminate Mr Nicoll's contract. The receiver used his services to a limited extent without paying his salary. Five weeks after

G   his appointment, the receiver gave Mr Nicoll one month's notice to terminate his contract: the report does not disclose how this was possible given that he had a five-year service contract. Mr Nicoll claimed against the receiver that he was entitled to his salary from the date of the receiver's appointment to the date of the expiry of the notice. The claim was based on s. 369(2) of the *Companies Act* 1948 (i.e. on the grounds that the receiver was personally liable); alternatively, on the ground that the salary was a cost and expense of the receivership and accordingly payable out of the assets in priority to any

H   payment to the bank. The Court of Appeal rejected the claim on both grounds. It was held, correctly, that Mr Nicoll's employment by the company was not terminated by the appointment of the receiver and that s. 369(2) did not apply to a pre-existing contract the performance of which was continued by the receiver as opposed to a new contract made by the receiver after his appointment. The alternative claim based on the unpaid salary being a cost and expense of the receivership was, with regret, rejected on the grounds

that, although employees' salary actually paid by the receiver would rank in priority as   A
part of the costs and expenses of the receivership, unpaid salary could not.

Immediate steps were taken to correct the law as stated in *Nicoll v Cutts*. At the time
of that decision, an Insolvency Bill had already been introduced into Parliament. In that
Bill the statutory predecessor of what is now s. 44 of the Act of 1986 contained no
reference to contracts of employment being 'adopted'. Amendments to the Bill were
made to include liability under contracts of employment 'adopted' by administrators   B
(s. 19(5)), administrative receivers (s. 44(1)(b)), other receivers appointed out of court
(s. 37(1)(a)) and receivers under Scottish law (s. 57). There is no doubt, indeed it is agreed,
that these amendments were introduced to correct the mischief disclosed by *Nicoll v
Cutts*, viz. the inability of an employee who has rendered services during the receivership
to recover his wages for such services if they remain unpaid.

The Insolvency Acts 1985 and 1986 introduced for the first time the machinery of the   C
court-appointed administrator. This was done on the recommendations contained in the
report of the Cork Committee on insolvency law and practice (1982, Cmnd 8558).
Chapter 9 of the report draws attention to an advantage which attaches to cases where
an out of court receiver is appointed, viz. the ability of the receiver to carry on the
profitable parts of the business of the company with a view either to procuring its
recovery or to its disposal as a going concern. It said that such 'preservation of the
profitable parts of the enterprise has been of advantage to the employees, the commercial   D
community and the general public'. The report states that where a receiver had not been
appointed by a debenture holder, in a significant number of cases companies had been
forced into liquidation and potentially viable businesses capable of being rescued had
been closed down. To meet this need the committee recommended the creation of a court-
appointed administrator who should have similar powers to those customarily conferred
on a receiver appointed out of court. Part II of the Act of 1986 implements that
recommendation.   E

This 'rescue culture' which seeks to preserve viable businesses was and is fundamental
to much of the Act of 1986. Its significance in the present case is that, given the
importance attached to receivers and administrators being able to continue to run a
business, it is unlikely that Parliament would have intended to produce a regime as to
employees' rights which renders any attempt at such rescue either extremely hazardous
or impossible.   F

Following the passing of the Act of 1986, it became the practice for receivers and
administrators to send to employees whose services the company still required letters
such as those sent in the present cases, i.e. emphasising that the receiver or administrator
was neither 'adopting' the contract of employment nor accepting personal liability but
was not terminating the employees' contract with the company and would cause the
company to continue to pay the employees' salary so long as they were at work. This   G
practice was widespread and was said to be based, perhaps unwisely, on an unreported
decision in 1987 in *Re Specialised Mouldings Ltd* for which the judge had given no
reasons.

When the decision of the Court of Appeal in the *Paramount* case was announced, it
caused a furore in the insolvency world. The Court of Appeal held that, if employees
continued to work and be paid after the appointment of an administrator, letters of the
kind sent in these cases were ineffective. By continuing the employment the administrator   H
had 'adopted' the contracts of employment within the meaning of s. 19(5) of the Act of
1986 and accordingly liabilities incurred to such employees while he was administrator
(including payments in lieu of notice and holiday pay payable on dismissal) were payable
in priority to all other debts. The Court of Appeal described the letters which sought to
avoid this result as mere 'ritual incantation'.

A   The furore was understandable. The result of the decision was to make it extremely hazardous for administrators to keep on the employees necessary to enable the company's business to continue. If, instead of an administration order, the company had been wound up employees would be creditors entitled to prove in the liquidation in relation, for example, to their claims for payment in lieu of notice but (save to a limited extent) enjoying no priority. Whereas, if an administration order was made and employees kept on for more than 14 days, the contracts would have been 'adopted' and

B   the retained employees would immediately become entitled to super-priority, ahead not only of secured, preferential and ordinary creditors but even of the costs of administration: see s. 19(4) and (5). In relation to receiverships, under the Court of Appeal decision in *Paramount* the position was even worse. If receivers are to be taken to have 'adopted' contracts of employments, they become personally liable for *all* liabilities 'on' contracts. The fear (subsequently confirmed by the decision of Lightman J) was that

C   the receivers' liability on adopted contracts might extend to all liabilities under the contracts of employment whether incurred before, during or after the receivership. In the ordinary case, a period of 14 days during which no adoption can take place is quite inadequate to enable the receiver or the administrator to access the relative merits of, on the one hand, an immediate closure of the business involving the dismissal of the employees and a sale on a breakup basis and, on the other, the continuance of the business and its employees for the purpose of seeking to sell on a going concern basis.

D   The outcry following the *Paramount* decision caused Parliament to act with almost unprecedented speed. Little over a month after the Court of Appeal decision in *Paramount* the *Insolvency Act* 1994 received Royal Assent. Under that Act the liability of administrators under s. 19, administrative receivers under s. 44, Scottish receivers under s. 57 and Northern Ireland receivers under the *Insolvency (Northern Ireland) Order* 1989 (but not that of non-administrative receivers under s. 37) on contracts of employment

E   'adopted' by them on or after 15 March 1994 is restricted to payment of wages, salary and contributions to a pension scheme in respect of services rendered after the adoption of the contract. The Act of 1994 had no impact on contracts adopted before 15 March 1994: hence these appeals.

    Although the position is thus resolved for the future, if the decisions appealed from are correct the large number of receiverships and administrations which have taken place between 1986 and 1994 will have been conducted on the wrong basis and very large sums

F   are at stake. In administration, employees should have received payments in lieu of notice or holiday pay for the notice period. So far as completed administrations are concerned these employees rights may be barred by the release given by s. 20 of the Act of 1986. But continuing administrations will be affected. In the case of receiverships the position is more acute. Under the judgment of Lightman J the receivers are personally liable for past, present and future liabilities under contracts of employment which they continued.

G   If the receivership has been completed and the assets distributed, the receiver is left with no assets out of which to satisfy his indemnity. In continuing receiverships the rights of secured and unsecured creditors alike will be prejudiced by the large sums payable in priority to employees whose employment was continued.

    These background facts disclose a number of points of central importance in construing s. 19 and 44 of the Act of 1986. First, the mischief sought to be remedied by

H   the introduction of the concept of 'adopting' contracts of employment was the decision in *Nicoll v Cutts*. Second, that decision related only to liability to pay the employees wages falling due, but not paid, during the receivership: it was not concerned with other liabilities arising before or after the receivership. Third, the amendments made to the Insolvency Bill to meet that mischief related to administrators appointed by the court as well as to receivers: it would be strange if Parliament intended to produce different results in the two cases. Fourth, the rescue culture designed to promote the ability to continue

the company's business was a basic feature of the Act of 1986. Fifth, any provision which   A
loads the company administration or receivership with imponderable liabilities to
employees who are continued renders it extremely hazardous for administrators or
receivers to continue the company's business, i.e. if the judgments appealed from are
correct they militate against the rescue culture. Sixth, although the Act of 1994 is not a
legitimate aid to the construction of the Act of 1986, the fact that Parliament moved so
fast to correct the decision in *Paramount* shows that the construction put on the Act of
1986 by the Court of Appeal operates in a manner contrary to the public interest.   B

The decisions in the courts below

In the *Paramount* case the argument was taken in two stages: first, had there been an
adoption of the contracts of employment; second, what was the consequence of such an
adoption? As to the first question, the Court of Appeal thought it almost self evident that
by procuring the company to continue to pay wages as they fell due the administrators   C
had adopted the contracts. The Court of Appeal said 'One wonders how, if [the
administrators] had not adopted the contracts, these employees . . . came to be in their
employment at all'. Adoption was considered to be all or nothing: if the employment
continued and wages were paid the whole contract of employment had been adopted and
nothing that the administrators said in their letters to the employees could alter that fact.
Once it was decided that the administrators had adopted the contracts, s. 19(5)
automatically produced the result that debts or liabilities incurred while they were   D
administrators were payable in full. The liabilities incurred during this administration
included the obligation to pay wages (including pension contribution) for the period for
which notice of termination of employment should have been given and the sums due for
holiday pay, which liabilities were incurred when the administrators summarily dismissed
the employees. It is a striking fact, that, in construing s. 19, the Court of Appeal made no
reference to the statutory history to which I have referred, possibly because it was not   E
drawn to their attention. According to the report, not even *Nicoll v Cutts* was cited to
them.

In *Leyland DAF* and *Ferranti* Lightman J adopted the same two- stage approach. He
first held that the contracts had been adopted because the pre-existing contracts of
employment had been continued after the appointment of the receivers. He relied on two
decisions relating to the adoption by liquidators of pre-existing contracts (*Re Anchor*   F
Line (Henderson Brothers) Ltd [1937] Ch 1 and *Re S Davis & Co Ltd* [1945] Ch 402) and
on the Court of Appeal decision in *Paramount*. He held that the receivers could only have
limited their liability under contracts of employment by terminating the existing contracts
and entering into new contracts of employment with them. On the second issue, Lightman
J fully took into account the background facts which I have referred to and expressed the
view that Parliament may well not have intended the 'windfall for employees' involved in
holding that the employees were entitled to be paid all liabilities whenever incurred and   G
of whatever kind under the adopted contracts. But he held that the statutory words were
too clear to lead to any other result.

The approach to construction

I cannot accept that this two-stage approach to the construction of s. 19 and 44 of the
Act of 1986 is correct. The words used by Parliament must be construed as a whole and   H
in their context including, if it can be discovered, the mischief aimed at. In the present
case the mischief aimed at (the inability of the employees to obtain unpaid wages payable
in respect of services actually rendered to a receiver) is clearly identified. Parliament may
intend to go further than remedying an identified mischief, but it is difficult to attribute
to Parliament an intention not only to remedy an identified mischief but to create a new
and greater one.

A   In my judgment, in order to determine Parliament's intention it is necessary to look at the joint effect of adoption followed by the statutory consequences said to flow from it. If the words used by Parliament have a meaning which is consonant with its presumed intention not to frustrate the rescue culture and not to produce unworkable consequences, then in my judgment that construction should be adopted. If, having had regard to those factors, it is impossible to detect a more limited parliamentary intention then the literal words of the sections must be given effect to. Only if the consequences of not

B departing from the literal meaning of the words produces an absurd result is it legitimate for the court to reject those words and seek to determine what Parliament in fact meant. I will therefore first consider the consequences of the decisions appealed from in somewhat greater detail, before turning to the proper construction of the statutory words.

The practical consequences of the decisions appealed from: receivership
C

     If the decision in *Leyland DAF* and *Ferranti* relating to receivership is correct the fate of employees of an insolvent company which subsequently goes into liquidation depends entirely upon whether or not they are employed in a sector of the company's business which the receiver decides to keep going. If their employment is not terminated by the receiver within 14 days, they will have the following entitlement in priority to all other creditors whether secured or unsecured. First, they keep their jobs and are paid for their

D services during the receivership. Second, all liabilities of the company to them under their contracts of employment accruing before the receivership, e.g. arrears of salary, any right of action for breach of contract, arrears of contributions to occupational pension schemes (which, depending on the terms of the contract, may include not only current payments but also lump sum top up payments) and bonus payments relating to earlier years. Third, payments in lieu of notice. Fourth, all sums falling due under the contract of employment after the termination of the receivership, i.e. if the receiver sells or transfers the company

E or its business to a third party in circumstances where the contract of employment is not terminated, the receiver will remain liable for breaches of contract committed after such transfer or sale. Compare that position with that of the employee whose employment is not continued by the receiver. Not only does he lose his job immediately but his only right will be to prove in the liquidation for arrears of wages and notice payments falling due before the winding up. By s. 386 and Sch. 6 of the Act of 1986, he is given a limited

F priority for salary and holiday pay due in respect of the services rendered in the period of four months prior to the appointment of the receiver: but such preferences are not only 'capped' at a limited amount but rank after the rights of continued employees to be paid in full all the claims I have mentioned. Even if it would be right (as Lightman J considered) to attribute to Parliament a special tenderness towards employees, it is most improbable that Parliament intended to produce such an unfair disparity between some

G employees and others, such disparity depending entirely on whether or not they are dismissed within 14 days of the receiver's appointment.

     Again the construction adopted by Lightman J renders the position of a receiver considering whether or not to continue the business almost impossible for the reasons I have already given, viz. he has only 14 days to try to assess whether or not the increased price to be realised on a going concern basis will be greater than the increase in imponderable liabilities consequent on the adoption of contracts of employment which

H will take priority over the secured rights of the debenture holder whose interest he was appointed to protect. Moreover, the fact that the receiver's personal liability extends to future liabilities incurred to the employee after the receiver ceases to be in control of the management of the company presents very great practical difficulties in the completion of any receivership. Say that the receiver has otherwise completed his task and wishes to hand over the fruits of his realisation to the debenture holder. He cannot safely do so

(save on the receipt of an indemnity from the debenture holder) because he will be left   A
without any assets out of which to satisfy his indemnity against future personal liability.

For these reasons, I am forced to the conclusion that it would be absurd to attribute
to Parliament an intention to produce these unjust and haphazard results so inimical to
the rescue culture. It follows in my judgment that, in relation to receiverships, the
construction adopted by Lightman J cannot be correct. Either it is wrong to treat
'adoption' as the automatic consequence of a receiver continuing the employment of   B
employees or some special meaning has to be attached to the concept of the receiver
being liable 'on' an adopted contract of employment.

The practical consequences of the decisions appealed from: administration

Although the concept of 'adopting' contracts of employment is common to both s. 19
and 44, in the case of administrators s. 19 expresses the consequences of such adoption   C
much more narrowly than does s. 44. Under an adopted contract of employment
employees in an administration have the right to 'any sums payable in respect of debts
and liabilities incurred *while he was administrator*'. Mr Potts, for the employees in
Paramount, accepts that this form of words cannot give rise to any right to payment of
liabilities incurred before the appointment or after the discharge of the administrator. He
submits that a liability is incurred within the meaning of the section when the liability
first becomes due, even though it does not then become immediately payable. Thus, on   D
his argument, s. 19 does not confer any rights in respect of unpaid wages or other debts
(e.g. bonus payments, contributions to pensions) which fell due before the appointment
of the administrator. Moreover, he submits that the *Apportionment Act* 1870 applies to
such arrears. Thus, for example, if wages are payable monthly in arrears and the
administrator is appointed halfway through the month, under the Apportionment Act
the wages are to be treated as having accrued due on a daily basis even though not
immediately payable. Liability for wages in respect of the period before the appointment   E
of the administrator was therefore incurred before the appointment and the administrator
is only liable for the wages accruing in respect of the period after the appointment.
However, so Mr Potts submits, the liability to pay wages in lieu of notice does not accrue
until the employment is terminated.

I accept Mr Potts's submissions on this part of the case. Mr Sumption, for the
administrators, submitted that the *Apportionment Act* 1870 did not operate to apportion   F
the liabilities to pay a sum in the nature of income but only to apportion the right to
receive such income. He relied on *Re United Club and Hotel Co Ltd* (1889) 60 LT(NS)
665 in which it was held that a winding-up petition presented halfway through a quarter
could not be based on an apportioned part of the current quarter's rent due under a lease
since it was not immediately payable at the date of the presentation of the petition. In my
judgment that case is explicable on the basis that, until the *Companies (Consolidation)*   G
Act 1908, a winding-up petition could not be based on a contingent or prospective debt.
It is quite inconsistent with a series of decisions which, in my judgment correctly, hold
that the Apportionment Act does operate to apportion liabilities between obligors:
Bishop of Rochester v Le Fanu [1906] 2 Ch 513; *Re Joel's Will Trusts* [1967] Ch 14 and the
cases there cited.

Therefore, the temporal limitation in s. 19(5) ('liabilities incurred while he was   H
administrator') operates to exclude most of the absurd consequences which flow from a
literal construction of s. 44. Even so, s. 19 as construed by the Court of Appeal gives rise
to many anomalies. First it goes beyond the mischief disclosed by *Nicoll v Cutts*. Second
it is incompatible with the rescue culture since as I have already discussed it is very
difficult for an administrator to assess within 14 days of his appointment the respective
merits of continuing or closing down parts of the company's business. Third, in addition

A to the unfair distinction between employees to which I have referred above, the right to payments in lieu of notice is dependent upon whether the administrator himself terminates the employment (in which case the liability is incurred by him and obtains priority) or first applies for his discharge without terminating the employment in which case it is the winding-up order which produces the termination and there is no priority. Fourth, there is the strange feature that under s. 19(5) the rights of employees under adopted contracts are given super-priority over other expenses of the administration and

B the administrators' own remuneration. Although such priority is understandable in relation to payment for services actually rendered in the administration under continued contracts of employment, it is difficult to accept that Parliament intended to give such super-priority to payments in lieu of notice which, by definition, cannot produce any benefit to the administration.

C These factors persuade me that it is improbable that, in relation to administrations, Parliament intended to produce these anomalous results. However, in the context of administration the temporal limitation on liability contained in s. 19(5) prevents the result being, in my view, so absurd as to entitle the court to construe s. 19 in a way which the words used by Parliament do not themselves sustain. In the light of these circumstances, I turn to consider the actual construction of the sections.

D **The meaning of 'adopt'**

At the conclusion of the argument I was persuaded that it was possible to construe the word 'adopt' in such a way as to avoid all the anomalies which I have mentioned above. The word 'adopt' is not a term of art but takes its colour from the context in which it is used. In referring to the adoption of children or the adoption by a principal of an agent's unauthorised contract, the word has quite different connotations. In s. 323(4) of the

E *Companies Act* 1948, the word 'adopt' was used to describe the consequence of a liquidator failing to disclaim an unprofitable contract. In that context 'adopt' plainly means failure to disclaim, i.e. leaving in being an existing contractual relationship between the company and the creditor so as to permit the creditor to prove in the liquidation for subsequent breaches. Under the salvage principle, a liquidator who uses leasehold property or goods for the better conduct of a liquidation becomes liable for the rent or contract price: such use by the liquidator has been judicially referred to as

F 'adoption' of the contract by the liquidator: see *Re Anchor Line* (above) at pp. 8, 9 and 15; *Re S Davis & Co Ltd* (above) at p. 406. In those cases adoption does not connote accepting personal liability. Yet in *Re Botibol* [1947] 1 All ER 26 the word 'adoption' was used to describe the acceptance of personal liability by a receiver.

The meaning of the word 'adopt' in s. 19 and 44 of the 1986 Act therefore has to be gathered from the context in which it is used. It is important to bear in mind that the

G appointment of an administrator or receiver does not terminate the employee's contract of employment with the company. Only if the company (acting by the receiver or administrator) gives notice terminating the employment or, by failing to pay wages as they accrue due, repudiates the contract of employment will the contract with the company terminate. Therefore, so long as wages are paid by the company the employee remains the employee of the company. The Court of Appeal lost sight of this factor when, in the passage I have quoted, they wondered how the employee continued to be

H employed if there had been no adoption by the receiver. Therefore, the mere continuation of the employment by the company does not lead inexorably to the conclusion that the contract has been adopted by the administrator or receiver.

It is common ground that adoption does not mean an assumption of personal liability by the administrator or receiver since there is no question of an administrator accepting personal liability under s. 19. Nor in my judgment can it mean 'fail to disclaim' as in

s. 323 of the *Companies Act* 1948 since, as I have said, the issue is not whether the   A
company is liable on the continued contract but whether the liability on the contract is to
have a higher priority. Nor can adoption connote doing such acts as would be sufficient
to make the payments due an expense of the administration since s. 19(4) gives such
expenses a different and lower level of priority and in *Nicoll v Cutts* it was held that such
liability was not an expense of the receivership. In my judgment, as Mr Sumption
submitted, adoption in s. 19 and 44 can only connote some conduct by the administrator
or receiver which amounts to an election to treat the continued contract of employment   B
with the company as giving rise to a separate liability in the administration or
receivership.

If that is the right meaning of 'adoption' in s. 19 and 44, the question arises whether
adoption of the contract is an all or nothing matter involving the acceptance or rejection
of the contract as a whole or whether it is open to an administrator or receiver so to
conduct itself as to show that he is only prepared to treat certain liabilities under the   C
contract as liabilities in the administration or receivership. To my mind this is the most
difficult question in the case. On the one side it is said that Parliament cannot have
intended the administrator or receiver to be able to 'cherry pick', taking the benefits of
the contract but rejecting the burdens. On the other, it is said that adoption of a contract
is a unilateral act and there is nothing to prevent the adopter from attaching conditions
to its adoption.

In favour of the view that the administrator or receiver can attach conditions to his
adoption, Mr Sumption submits that there is no a priori reason why the adopter should
not state which liabilities he is accepting and which he is not. The contract of employment
with the company continues in any event and the company is fully liable for any breaches.
Conditional adoption by the administrator or receiver does not in any way alter the
underlying contract as between the parties to it. Second, the sections equate liability
under adopted contracts with liability under contracts entered into by the administrator   E
or receiver. In the case of new contracts made by the administrator or receiver he can
stipulate which obligations he is accepting as liabilities or for which he will be personally
liable. Why, asked Mr Sumption should this not be possible when a contract of
employment is adopted? Third, such a conclusion gives effect to the underlying rescue
culture of the 1986 Act. Unless the administrator or receiver can limit the extent to which
he is accepting responsibility, for the reasons which I have given it will frequently be   F
impossible for him to assess the desirability of continuing the workforce.

My views on this argument have varied. But eventually I am, with regret, forced to the
conclusion that there is no halfway house such as Mr Sumption proposes. The mischief
aimed at by the Act (i.e. the decision in *Nicoll v Cutts*) must mean that the concept of
adoption of the contract covers at least accepting liability for payment for services
rendered to the administrator under contracts which he has continued. If it were to be
open to the administrator or receiver to exclude such liability, the Act fails to remedy the   G
mischief. Therefore the concept of adoption of the contract is inconsistent with an ability
to pick and choose between different liabilities under the contract. The contract as a
whole is either adopted or not: the consequences of adoption are then spelt out by the
Act. If the employment is continued for more than 14 days after the appointment of the
administrator or receiver, there seems to be no escape from the conclusion that the whole
contract has been adopted. If the result of this view would be to produce an absurdity it   H
would be permissible to reject the plain meaning of the words. But in relation to
administration, the consequences of giving the word 'adoption' its all or nothing
meaning, although unfortunate, are not absurd. There is nothing absurd in the view that
an administrator can only use the services of employees on the basis that they are entitled
to be treated in accordance with their contract of employment and, for example, to be
given contractual notice of termination or paid in lieu of notice.

A   For these reasons I am most reluctantly forced to the view that in the 1986 Act the contract of employment is inevitably adopted if the administrator or receiver causes the company to continue the employment for more than 14 days after his appointment. Since adoption must have the same meaning in both s. 19 and 44, it follows that in these cases the contracts of employment were adopted by the administrators and receivers.

B   **The consequences of adoption: administration**

    So far as administration is concerned, s. 19 only applies to liabilities incurred during the administration. On the literal meaning of these words, such liabilities include liability for wages accruing during the contractual period of notice or the damages payable for the failure to give such notice. Mr Sumption submitted that the words should be read as being limited to those liabilities incurred in return for services actually rendered for the benefit of the administration. He relied by analogy on the salvage cases which render

C assets in liquidation liable for expenses incurred by the liquidator for the purpose of the more beneficial realisation of the company's assets: see *Re Oak Pits Colliery Co* (1882) 21 ChD 322. However, I do not think these principles assist Mr Sumption. Although the authorities show that debts incurred before the liquidation do not obtain priority, they indicate that even on the salvage principle all liabilities under a contract incurred after the time of adoption of the contract by a liquidator are entitled to priority. Thus in *Re &*

D *Davis & Co Ltd* (above) damages for failure to deliver up goods bailed to a company under a bailment contract 'adopted' by a liquidator were held entitled to priority even though the obligation to deliver up only arose after the liquidator had ceased to manage the company's business. Again in *Re Levi & Co Ltd* [1919] 1 Ch 416 sums due under a covenant to deliver up in good repair at the termination of a lease of premises which had been used by a liquidator were held entitled to priority on the salvage principle even though some of the disrepair occurred during a period before the liquidator took

E possession. The salvage principle in liquidation indicates that if a liquidator adopts a contract for the purpose of the more beneficial conduct of a liquidation all such liabilities under such contract after the date of adoption are entitled to priority. This principle is therefore of no assistance in seeking to limit the administrator's liability in this case.

    I therefore reach the view that in the *Paramount* case the employees are entitled under s. 19 to payment in lieu of notice, including pension contributions in respect of the notice

F period.

    As to holiday pay, the question is whether the sum payable to dismissed employees under cl. 8(f) on termination of their employment in respect of paid holiday not yet taken at that date is a liability incurred during the administration. One view is that since such sum is not payable until termination of the employment by the administrator the whole liability is incurred at that time. The alternative view is that under cl. 8(f) the employer

G incurs at the end of each month a liability to pay a sum equal to 1/12th of the holiday entitlement of the employee for the year such liability being contingent upon the employee ceasing to be employed during the holiday year. On this latter view, liability for holiday pay referable to the months before the appointment of the administrator will not have been incurred during the administration and the employee will only be entitled under s. 19(5) to the proportion of the sum payable on termination which is referable to the months of employment since the appointment of the administrator.

H   In my view the latter is the correct construction. As was common ground between the parties, a liability can be incurred before it becomes payable. Under cl. 8(f) a liability arises at the end of each month to pay 1/12th of the holiday entitlement. That liability is contingent upon the termination of the employment in the holiday year and may also be reduced in amount by the employee subsequently taking holidays. But the basic liability arises from the employee having been employed throughout that calendar month. In my

judgment the liability under cl. 8(f) was therefore incurred at the end of each calendar   A
month although only payable on a contingency at a later date. Holiday pay referable to
complete months of service expiring before the date of the administrator's appointment
are therefore not liabilities incurred while he was administrator and do not fall within
s. 19(5).

The consequences of adoption: receivership
B
I have already expressed the view that the consequences of the literal construction of
s. 44 adopted by Lightman J produces an absurd result which cannot reflect the intention
of Parliament. On the view I have expressed, the receivers have undoubtedly adopted the
contracts of employment in the present case. Therefore to avoid the absurdity which
Parliament cannot have intended the words in s. 44(1) which make a receiver personally
liable 'on any contract' must be given a forced construction.

C
In my judgment the liability of a receiver 'on' any adopted contract must be read as
subject to the same restriction as applies to contracts adopted by an administrator under
s. 19, i.e. as being restricted to liabilities incurred under the contract while he was receiver.
I reach this view for two reasons. First, the liabilities have to arise under a contract
adopted in the carrying out of the receiver's functions as a receiver. Parliament must have
been addressing the ordinary case where a receiver in pursuance of his functions could
not normally adopt a contract of employment with propriety so as to give the employee   D
priority for liabilities other than those incurred during the receivership. Although there
may be special cases in which the employee stipulates for greater protection, I do not
think that this was within the contemplation of Parliament. Second, and more important,
there is no conceivable logic in giving employees of a company in receivership any
different rights from those enjoyed by employees of a company in administration. So far
as the employees are concerned there is no distinction between the two regimes. The
wording of s. 44 differs from that of s. 19 only because receivers are personally liable   E
whereas administrators are not. It is impossible to believe that Parliament intended this
factor to confer greater rights on employees in a receivership.

Summary
I therefore reach the following conclusions:
F
(1)   For the purposes of both s. 19 and s. 44 an employee's contract of employment is
       'adopted' if he is continued in employment for more than 14 days after the
       appointment of the administrator or receiver;

(2)   it is not possible for an administrator or receiver to avoid this result or alter its
       consequences unilaterally by informing the employees that he is not adopting their
       contracts or only doing so on terms;

(3)   in the case of both administration and receivership the consequence of adoption of   G
       contracts of employment is to give priority only to liabilities incurred by the
       administrator or receiver during his tenure of office.

I would therefore vary the order of the Court of Appeal in the *Paramount* case so as to
declare that the sums in respect of holiday pay payable under cl. 8(f) of the respondents'
contracts of employment are only payable by the administrators in respect of months of
employment after the appointment of the administrator. I would otherwise dismiss the   H
appeal. The costs of the respondents before your Lordships' House should be paid by the
administrators as administration expenses, such costs to be taxed on an indemnity basis
if not agreed.

As to the *Leyland DAF* and *Ferranti* appeals, your Lordships were not addressed by
counsel as to which of the benefits claimed by the employees would be payable if your

A   Lordships determined the appeals in the sense I have suggested. I would therefore vary
     the order of Lightman J in the *Leyland DAF* case by setting aside his directions in relation
     to entitlement to private medical insurance, accident insurance and holiday pay and refer
     those matters back to the Chancery Division for determination in accordance with your
     Lordships' views. Similarly, in the *Ferranti* case I would vary the order of Lightman J by
     setting aside his determination in relation to health care schemes, the provision of motor
     cars, holiday pay and sums due under the terms of the severance payment and
B   redevelopment agreement and refer those matters back to the Chancery Division for
     determination. I would otherwise dismiss the appeals. The costs of the respondents before
     your Lordships' House in both appeals should be paid by the receivers, such costs to be
     taxed on an indemnity basis if not agreed.

        Lord Mustill: I have had the advantage of reading in draft the speech prepared by
     Lord Browne-Wilkinson. I agree with it and for the reasons he gives I too would dismiss
C   these appeals.

        Lord Woolf: For the reasons given in the speech to be delivered by Lord Browne-
     Wilkinson, which I have read in draft and with which I agree, I too would dismiss these
     appeals in the manner which he proposes.

        Lord Lloyd of Berwick: I have had the advantage of reading in draft the speech
     prepared by Lord Browne-Wilkinson. For the reasons he gives I too would dispose of
D   these appeals in the manner which he proposes.

                                   (*Appeals dismissed*)

E

F

G

H

Re Estate Acquisition & Development Ltd.

Chancery Division.
Ferris J and Warner J.
Judgment delivered 6 March 1992 and 2 March 1993.

Unfair prejudice petition – Whether right under articles or Companies Act infringed – Whether petitioner established legitimate expectations extending beyond those rights – Whether order for costs should be enforced against petitioner's shares – Companies Act 1985, s. 459.

These were an unfair prejudice petition pursuant to s. 459 of the Companies Act 1985 and a hearing on costs.

The company was a private property company in which the petitioner held 11.59 per cent of the shares. In 1988 one of the petitioner's co-directors and shareholders offered to buy the petitioner's shares and later asked the petitioner to resign as a director. The petition complained, first, of proposals to remove the petitioner as a director and appoint other directors, secondly, of an attempt to alter the memorandum and articles and, thirdly, of failure to provide information to the petitioner to enable her to carry out her duties as a director, to know whether the company's affairs were being properly managed, and to value her shares.

At a subsequent hearing, the respondents applied for leave to enforce the order for costs made against the petitioner, and for a charging order on the petitioner's shares in the company.

Held, dismissing the petition with costs and giving the respondents leave to enforce the order for costs against the petitioner's shares in the company:

1. The petition failed because the petitioner could not establish any infringement of a right under the articles or the Companies Act and could not establish that she had any expectations over and above those rights deserving of the court's protection.

2. The court gave the respondents leave to enforce the order for costs against the petitioner but only against her shares in the company, made a charging order on the petitioner's shares, and directed that in subsequent proceedings for the sale of the shares under an order of the court, the majority shareholders were to offer to buy them at their fair value.

The following cases were referred to in the judgments:

Abbey Leisure Ltd, Re [1990] BCC 60.
Cade (J E) & Son Ltd, Re [1991] BCC 360.
Company, Re a [1983] Ch 178.
Company No. 007623 of 1984, Re a (1986) 2 BCC 99,191.
Company No. 008699 of 1985, Re a (1986) 2 BCC 99,024.
Company No. 00477 of 1986, Re a (1986) 2 BCC 99,171.
Company No. 00314 of 1989, Re a [1990] BCC 221.
Crystall v Crystall [1963] 1 WLR 574.
Ebrahimi v Westbourne Galleries Ltd & Ors [1973] AC 360.
Elgindata Ltd, Re [1991] BCLC 959.
Kenyon Swansea Ltd, Re (1987) 3 BCC 259.
Posgate & Denby (Agencies) Ltd, Re (1986) 2 BCC 99,352.

Stephen Davies (instructed by Wallace & Partners) for the petitioner.

Robin Hollington (instructed by Harkavys) for the respondents.

JUDGMENT ON PETITION
(Delivered 6 March 1992)

Ferris J: I have before me a petition under s. 459 of the *Companies Act* 1985 in relation to the affairs of a company named Estate Acquisition & Development Ltd ('the company'). The petitioner is Mrs Audrey Pamela Felton, who holds just under 12 per cent of the shares in the company. The respondents, other than the company itself, which is merely a nominal respondent, are some, but not all, of the other shareholders in the company and also certain individuals who are directors of but not shareholders in the company. The primary relief which is sought by Mrs Felton is an order requiring the respondents to purchase her shares in the company. The petition also seeks an order requiring the respondents to provide or procure the provision to Mrs Felton of certain information concerning the affairs of the company, but Mrs Felton has shown no enthusiasm for this relief during the course of the hearing. The other relief claimed by the petition has either been struck out by order of the court, which I shall mention later, or was purely interlocutory in nature.

The company was incorporated on 13 August 1963. At the outset the principal individuals behind the company appear to have been Mr Michael Felton, who was a solicitor and formerly the husband of Mrs Felton, and Mr Maurice Scott, an estate agent who, through a company controlled by him and known as Jalside Ltd, carries on an estate agency business in South Ruislip, Middlesex, under the name of Laurance & Co. From its incorporation the company has carried on business as a property company, primarily it seems holding and investing in property rather than dealing in it. It appears to have built up a portfolio consisting of a large number of residential properties and ground rents the gross value of which is said to be of the order of £1m.

In the first 25 years of its existence, or thereabouts, the company seems to have been managed by Mr Felton and Mr Scott, both of whom were directors of it. I did not hear any evidence which would enable me to form a view as to whether one of them was more active than the other, and this probably does not matter for present purposes. Mrs Felton became a director in 1979, at which time she was not a shareholder in the company. Mrs Felton does not, however, appear to have played any active part in the management of the company at any time. Unless one meeting at her house at which her husband, Mr Scott and she were present is to be regarded as a board meeting, she does not claim ever to have attended a meeting of directors of the company. She first became a shareholder in the company in February 1982, when she purchased 5,160 shares which were transferred to her by nine different transfers all dated 15 February 1982. A further 277 shares were transferred to her on 7 May 1984 and another 275 shares were transferred to her on 18 April 1985. All these transfers were made to give effect to purchases, not gifts or voluntary dispositions. I was told nothing about the individual transactions under which Mrs Felton acquired shares, but the average price paid by her was stated to be about £2.50 a share, giving a cost of £15,000 or a little less for her total holding of 5,712 shares.

The authorised capital of the company is £100,000 divided into 96,000 ordinary shares of £1 each and 4,000 8.5 per cent cumulative preference shares of £1 each. No cumulative preference shares appear ever to have been issued. At all material times since 1986, if not before then, 47,774 ordinary shares of the company have been in issue. According to the annual return of the company as at 18 July 1988 these shares were held as follows: by Mrs Felton 5,712 shares, which is 11.59 per cent of the total; by Michael Felton 7,669 shares or 16.05 per cent of the total; by Mr Scott 100 shares, which is a minute 0.2 per cent of the total; by a Miss Inge O'Donnell 34,154 shares, which is 71.49 per cent of the total, by Mrs Braithwaite, who will be mentioned later in this judgment, one share, and by nine other shareholders who are not parties to this action, a total of 108 shares, the

proportion held by Mrs Braithwaite and these other nine shareholders being thus a mere   A
0.22 per cent of the total.

A number of observations need to be made in relation to these shareholdings. First, at the time of the annual return in question, Mr Michael Felton had been imprisoned for an offence of dishonesty. He had sold his practice as a solicitor late in 1984 or early in 1985. He had become bankrupt in 1985. Part of his shareholding had been charged to Lloyds Bank and another part had been charged to Barclays Bank. Accordingly, subject   B
to these charges, the 7,669 shares registered in his name were in fact vested in his trustee in bankruptcy. Mr Michael Felton's marriage to Mrs Felton had broken down and they had been divorced in February 1988. Turning to Miss O'Donnell, who was the largest shareholder at 18 July 1988, she had received all, or all but 100 of her shares as a gift from Mr Scott made between September 1986 and January 1987. Miss Inge O'Donnell has since become the wife of Mr Scott.

Three provisions of the articles of association of the company adopted on its   C
incorporation call for mention. First, art. 65 provided in relation to general meetings that, except in respect of the choice of a chairman, the declaration of a dividend and the adjournment of the meetings, 'the quorum shall be five members personally present'. Secondly, in relation to board meetings, art. 110 provided as follows:

> 'The directors or any committee of directors may meet together for the despatch of business, adjourn and otherwise regulate their meetings as they think fit and   D
> determine the quorum necessary for the transaction of business. Until otherwise determined, five shall be a quorum.'

The article contains two other sentences which do not matter for present purposes.

There is no evidence that the directors ever did expressly determine that the requisite quorum should be less than five. A requirement for a quorum of five at directors' meetings was, however, likely to give rise to difficulty in this company. According to the annual   E
return as at 18 July 1988 there were only five directors in office, namely Mrs Felton, Mr Scott, Miss O'Donnell, Mrs Braithwaite and a Mr David Simms-Davies. Accordingly it would be necessary for all these directors to attend board meetings if a quorum was to be present.

Thirdly, art. 127 of the company's articles provided as follows:

> 'The directors shall from time to time determine whether and to what extent and   F
> at what times and places and under what conditions or regulations the accounts and books of the company or any of them, shall be open to the inspection of members and no member not being a director shall have any right of inspecting any account or book or document of the company except as confirmed by the statutes or authorised by the directors or by a resolution of the company in general meeting.'
  G

The matter with which this petition is concerned began in about June 1988. At that time Mrs Felton was recently divorced from her husband, who had become bankrupt and had recently begun a term of imprisonment of three or three-and-a-half years for an offence or offences involving dishonesty. I find no difficulty in accepting that she was at that time depressed. Her financial position was, as she put it, 'quite dreadful'. Her evidence that Mr Scott had been quite a close friend until shortly before that time and that he knew of her financial circumstances was not challenged.   H

The first event on which Mrs Felton relies is a telephone conversation which took place between her and Mr Scott in June 1988. Mrs Felton said that Mr Scott telephoned her out of the blue and offered to purchase her shares in the company at £2.50 each. There had never been any previous suggestion that she should sell her shares to Mr Scott or to anyone else. Mrs Felton said that she was astounded by the offer and very angry and the

A   conversation was very short. The reason why she was angry was because she was certain that £2.50 was much too low a price. It was about the price that she had paid for the shares when she acquired them and she was aware that, in the intervening period, there had been considerable inflation and a boom in property values. Mrs Felton said that she was not in a position to make an informed decision and she probably mentioned to Mr Scott that she would have to get legal and financial advice. It is clear that she rejected Mr Scott's proposal either immediately or very soon after it was made. Her evidence was

B   that the matter was not raised again by Mr Scott. None of this evidence was challenged and I accept it as being correct.

Some time after the offer was made in June, probably in July or early in August 1988, Mr Scott telephoned Mrs Felton and asked her to resign as a director of the company. Mrs Felton said that he was direct and made his meaning quite clear. In answer to a question by her he said that he did not claim that she had done anything wrong but he

C   just did not want her name on the paper. She replied to the effect that she was certainly not prepared to resign. Mrs Felton's evidence about this was not challenged and I accept it.

On 18 August 1988 solicitors instructed by the company sent to Mrs Felton a copy of a notice signed by Mr Scott and addressed to the directors of the company proposing that Mrs Felton be removed from office as a director. Mrs Felton then instructed her

D   present solicitors who, on 15 September, wrote a long letter to the directors of the company setting out various information which Mrs Felton required. This information was divided into two categories. First, as shareholder, Mrs Felton sought information under seven heads, all but one of which was cross-referenced to a section of the *Companies Act* 1985 giving her the right to the information sought. I will refer to the first category of information as 'the shareholder information'. Secondly, in her capacity as director, Mrs Felton sought information under nine further heads. I will refer to this

E   second category as 'the management information', although I am not thereby meaning to indicate any view whether or not Mrs Felton was entitled to all this information in her capacity as director or otherwise.

On 20 September 1988 the company's auditors replied to the letter of 15 September on behalf of the company offering inspection of the statutory books of the company by appointment. As to the request for management information, the auditors stated that

F   this would have to await Mr Scott's return from holiday.

Some time between 20 September and 7 October 1988 a representative of Mrs Felton's solicitors visited the company's office to inspect its statutory books. It seems that all the shareholder information was provided during that visit or at about this time, because the request for it does not feature again in the correspondence. It was discovered during that visit that the company purported to have adopted a new memorandum and new articles

G   of association at an extraordinary general meeting said to have been held on 5 July 1988. Mrs Felton said that she had received no notice of any directors' meeting at which a decision to call such an extraordinary general meeting was to be discussed. Indeed she said that she had never received notice of any directors' meeting up to this time. She also said that she had not in her capacity as a member been given any notice of the extraordinary general meeting.

H   In the petition Mrs Felton complains of this purported alteration of the company's memorandum and articles as being ineffective on the ground that no meeting was in fact held on 5 July 1988 and that if any meeting was held it was irregularly convened in that she received no notice of it. It is convenient to deal with this allegation immediately. I accept Mrs Felton's evidence that she received no notice of any directors' meeting before the notices which I shall mention later on; and I also accept her evidence that she received no notice of any general meeting to be held on 5 July 1988. I very much doubt whether

any such meeting took place. No minutes of any such meeting have been produced. There   A
are minutes of a purported directors' meeting said to have been held on 5 July and also
of a purported annual general meeting on the same date. The minutes of the annual
general meeting do not mention who is said to have been present save that Mr Scott is
said to have been in the chair. In respect of the supposed extraordinary general meeting,
the only record which exists is a document purporting to be a copy of a special resolution
expressed to adopt the new memorandum and articles which has been certified as correct   B
by Mr Scott and which was in due course registered at the Companies Registry. The
respondents called the secretary of the company, Mrs Braithwaite, to give evidence at the
trial, apparently with a view to proving that notices of certain later meetings had duly
been sent out. Mrs Braithwaite was not specifically asked to give evidence about the
notices of the meetings purportedly held on 5 July 1988, although if her evidence about
the procedure in relation to notices generally was true, she must have had the same
participation in respect of the notices of the July meeting as she had in respect of the   C
notices of the later meetings. No other evidence was called by the respondents. In the
light of this and having regard to the action taken later in relation to the memorandum
and articles, I find that the new memorandum and articles were not validly adopted in
July 1988. The probability is that there was no meeting held and no special resolution
was passed. At the very least, if there was a meeting, I find that Mrs Felton was not given
notice of it and the failure to give her notice cannot be excused as being merely accidental.
Accordingly the meeting, if held, was invalid.   D

The discovery in relation to the new memorandum and articles was the subject of a
letter from Mrs Felton's solicitors to the company dated 7 October 1988.

It appears that the company at this time claimed also to have convened an
extraordinary general meeting for 13 October at which the resolution to remove Mrs
Felton as a director was to be proposed. In a letter dated 11 October 1988, Mishcon de   E
Reya, expressing themselves to be solicitors for Mr Scott, informed Mrs Felton's
solicitors that in order to avoid a costly dispute as to whether this meeting, that is to say
the meeting on 13 October, had been properly convened, the resolution for the removal
of Mrs Felton would not be put. I do not know whether a meeting was in fact held on 13
October. If a meeting was held Mrs Felton was not present at it and it is clear that no
business was transacted at it.

F
Under cover of a letter from Mishcon de Reya dated 2 November 1988 there was sent
to Mrs Felton's solicitors a notice convening a meeting of the directors of the company
on 9 November 1988 to consider a requisition from Mr Scott, Miss O'Donnell, Mr
Simms-Davies and Mrs Braithwaite, seeking the calling of an extraordinary general
meeting of the company to consider resolutions adopting a new memorandum and
articles (which were, in fact, the same as those purportedly adopted at the suggested
meeting held on 5 July), appointing four new directors of the company and removing   G
Mrs Felton as a director. The notice convening the board meeting contained a note to
the effect that if the board did not convene the meeting within 21 days the requisitionists
would be entitled to do so in accordance with the Companies Act. It is said that Mrs
Felton also received notice of this board meeting direct from the company and this is one
of the matters on which Mrs Braithwaite was called to give evidence. I will deal with this
point later, but it is not of significance by itself because Mrs Felton undoubtedly received   H
notice of the meeting through her solicitors and she made it clear, through them, that she
did not intend to be present at the meeting. There exists a document which purports to
be a minute of a directors' meeting held on 9 November at which only Mr Scott, Miss
O'Donnell, Mr Simms-Davies and Mrs Braithwaite were present. These minutes state
that as there was no quorum the meeting was closed without transacting any substantive
business.

A   Thereafter, by a notice which is dated 18 November 1988, the requisitionists convened an extraordinary general meeting of the company for 13 December 1988 to transact the business which they had specified in their requisition, save that the proposal to remove Mrs Felton as a director was omitted. There is an issue whether this notice was sent to or received by Mrs Felton herself and I shall return to this point. There is no doubt, however, that a copy of the notice was sent to Mrs Felton's solicitors under cover of a letter dated 30 November 1988 from Mishcon de Reya. It is said that an extraordinary

B general meeting was duly held on 13 December, although Mrs Felton made no attempt to attend it, and that the resolutions specified in the notice were duly passed. There exists a document which appears to constitute minutes of such a meeting together with a note of the persons said to have been present at the meeting, namely, Mr Scott, Miss O'Donnell, Mr David Davies, Mrs Braithwaite and Mr James Green, all of whom were shareholders in the company. Mrs Felton does not accept that the meeting was ever held

C and this is a matter to which I shall return.

     With regard to the provision of information, the visit to the company's offices which I have already mentioned seems to have been regarded as satisfying Mrs Felton's request for the shareholder information. As regards the management information, nothing was forthcoming even though Mr Scott must have returned from holiday some time in October 1988. Through her solicitors Mrs Felton stated that she did not propose to attend board meetings until the information was provided and various reminders about

D the outstanding request for information were given by Mrs Felton's solicitors on a number of occasions. A more vigorous protest was made by a letter dated 1 December 1988. In response to this Mishcon de Reya, who appear by now to have begun to act on behalf of the company, rather than simply on behalf of Mr Scott, provided the audited accounts for the years ended 29 September 1986 and 1987 under cover of a letter dated 9 December 1988. Mishcon de Reya also stated in that letter that the rest of the

E management information, with the exception of the directors' minute book, might be examined by Mrs Felton at the company's registered office on giving reasonable notice. It was made clear in that letter that Mrs Felton would only be allowed to inspect the relevant documents, not to take copies. Mrs Felton's solicitors described this, in a letter of 12 December 1988, as a cynical disregard of Mrs Felton's rights. The offer to inspect documents was not taken up prior to the presentation of the petition. In the same letter

F of 12 December 1988, Mrs Felton's solicitors made it clear that Mrs Felton would not be attending the extraordinary general meeting convened for 13 December, stating that in view of the denial of information to her 'it would not be meaningful for her to attend meetings where she can take no active part in a reasoned discussion'.

     In connection with her evidence Mrs Felton waived privilege in certain communications between herself and her solicitors from which it appears that by 18 December 1988 she had resolved to present a petition under s. 459, if possible before

G Christmas that year, and that a draft petition had been prepared by that date. In the event, however, the petition was not presented until 18 January 1989. In the meantime, on 6 January, the company gave notice of an extraordinary general meeting to be held on 8 February 1989 to consider a resolution removing Mrs Felton as a director. This meeting was not, however, proceeded with.

     In the petition, apart from formal and uncontroversial allegations, Mrs Felton refers

H to the requirement of a quorum of five at board meetings; to Mr Scott's offer for her shares in June 1988; to his subsequent request for her to resign as a director, which is said to have been made 'a few weeks after the said suggestion [i.e. the share purchase offer] had been made and rejected'; to the suggested adoption of a new memorandum and articles at an extraordinary general meeting purportedly held on 5 July 1988, of which Mrs Felton was given no notice; to the events in October and November concerning meetings, which I have already narrated; and to the position, as at the date of the petition,

in respect of Mrs Felton's requests for the management information. There was also an   A
allegation in relation to a share transfer purportedly signed by Mrs Felton, but this has
not been pursued. It is relevant to read two more general paragraphs of the petition.
First, in para. 24 it is alleged that:

> 'Without the relevant information the petitioner is not in a position (i) adequately
> to carry out her duties as a director of the company and/or (ii) to know whether
> the affairs of the company are being managed in the best or alternatively a proper   B
> manner in the interests of its members including and in particular herself, (iii) to
> have any idea of the true value of her shareholding in the company.'

The 'relevant information' referred to in this paragraph means the information which I
have described as the management information. Secondly, in para. 28 of the petition it is
alleged as follows:

> 'In the premises the actions and omissions of the respondents and each of them   C
> have not been prompted by any business considerations or any solicitude for the
> welfare of the company but are designed to exclude the petitioner from any or any
> effective part in the company and further to prevent the petitioner from knowing
> whether the suggested sales price for her shares is fair or reasonable.'

The respondents to the petition are, in addition to the company, Mr Scott, Miss
O'Donnell, Mrs Braithwaite, who are directors and members of the company, and Mr
Tullett, Mr Coburn and Mr and Mrs Thevitt who are not members of the company but   D
are said to have been elected as directors of it at the meeting held on 13 December 1988.
I observe at once that it is difficult to see how the last four persons can be held in any
way responsible for any acts or omissions which occurred before the time of their election
as directors, which was only a few weeks before the presentation of the petition and no
more than a few days before the time when, it appears, Mrs Felton resolved to present
the petition.   E

I have indicated the relief sought by the petition at the beginning of this judgment. I
add only that Mrs Felton seeks not only an order that the respondents and each of them
are to purchase her shares, but an order that they must do so at a price which takes no
account of the fact that Mrs Felton's holding is a minority holding.

On 7 February 1989 the registrar made an order for service of points of claim, points
of defence and points of reply. Points of claim were served on 5 May 1989. The   F
respondents then applied by notice of motion dated 3 July 1989 to strike out the points
of claim. This application came before Mummery J in December 1989 (see [1990] BCC
221). In his judgment, given on 14 December 1989, Mummery J struck out the claim for
winding up on just and equitable grounds because there was no allegation that the
company had been formed on a basis that involved a special relationship of mutual
confidence or that there was a special relationship which entitled Mrs Felton to continue
to participate in the management of the company. Accordingly, he held that the claim   G
for winding up was bound to fail. Mummery J refused, however, to strike out the claim
for relief under s. 459–461 of the *Companies Act* 1985.

After the decision of Mummery J, points of defence and points of reply were served,
but nothing in these pleadings calls for mention. Nor, I think, do I need to refer to
anything in the affidavit of Mrs Felton sworn in support of the petition on 16 January
1989. There was no other affidavit evidence sworn in support of or in opposition to the
petition. There was affidavit evidence in relation to the motion to strike out the points of   H
claim in so far as that motion was founded upon the inherent jurisdiction of the court. I
do not think that I need to refer to any of this, except to mention that in an affidavit
sworn on 8 December 1989 Mr Jeffrey Hodson, an accountant engaged on behalf of Mrs
Felton to examine the affairs of the company, mentioned certain dealings between the
company and Mr Scott which may be said to have given rise to loans of £10,000 and

A   £6,000 by the company to Mr Scott. Of these possible loans only £5,000 out of the £10,000 transaction remained outstanding for any substantial period. The only significance of this evidence for present purposes seems to be that, if the right analysis of the transactions is that there were loans, a statement made to Mrs Felton's solicitors that there were no loans to directors of the company was incorrect.

B   Mrs Felton gave oral evidence at the trial. I have incorporated in the foregoing summary the essence of what she said about Mr Scott's proposal to purchase her shares, his request for her resignation and the non-receipt by her of notices of directors' and general meetings prior to October 1988. Clearly Mrs Felton is an intelligent and articulate witness and her evidence seemed to be wholly credible. I confess, however, that doubts about her credibility were raised in my mind when in cross-examination she emphatically denied that her former husband Michael Felton had assisted her in the preparation of her petition, but then had to accept that she had visited him in prison on 18 December

C   1988 and had discussed the petition with him. I accept her evidence that the visit was occasioned by a personal family matter, but it is apparent from a letter which Mrs Felton wrote to her solicitor the same day as the visit to her husband (privilege in which letter was waived) that Mrs Felton discussed the petition with her former husband and that he wrote some notes which Mrs Felton sent to her solicitor. These notes were subsequently embodied in Mrs Felton's affidavit almost word for word and in that affidavit Mrs Felton deposed to the matters stated in the notes as being her knowledge when in fact

D   they appear to have been the knowledge of her former husband. In the result I would have considerable reservations about accepting Mrs Felton's evidence on disputed matters where her evidence is not corroborated. Nevertheless I am prepared to accept her evidence to the extent to which I have already mentioned.

   The only other witness to be called at the trial was Mrs Braithwaite whose evidence I shall consider when I deal with the issue concerning the meeting said to have been held

E   on 13 December 1988.

   So far as the law is concerned, s. 459 applies in this case without the amendment made by para. 11 of Sch. 19 to the *Companies Act* 1989, an amendment which would, I think, have no practical import even if it were applicable to this case. Accordingly what Mrs Felton has to establish is that:

F   'the company's affairs are being or have been conducted in a manner which is unfairly prejudicial to the interests of some part of [its] members (including at least [herself]) or that [some] actual or proposed act or omission of the company . . . is or would be so prejudicial.'

In setting out the relevant terms of the section in this way I have made certain minor linguistic adjustments to meet the present context, but these do not affect the sense of the section.

G   I accept with gratitude the following summary of the guidance which may be extracted from the decided cases which was given by Mummery J in his judgment on the application to strike out the points of claim in this case. I cite from *Re a Company No. 00314 of 1989* [1990] BCC 221 at p. 225-226:

   '(1) The provisions confer on the court a very wide jurisdiction and discretion, so wide that it has to be carefully controlled in order to prevent it from being used as

H   a means of oppression by a dissident shareholder (*Re a Company No. 007623 of 1984* (1986) 2 BCC 99,191 at p. 99,196). In that case Hoffmann J, on the hearing of the petition, dismissed the claims of a minority shareholder who was seeking to use the petition under s. 75 of the 1980 Act to compel the majority shareholders to buy his shares in circumstances where the company's articles provided a means for determining the fair value of those shares and that provision had not been invoked by him. In those circumstances he held that there were no grounds for

characterising the conduct of the majority as unfair and it was neither necessary   A
nor appropriate to present such a petition. I note in passing that the articles of this
company do not provide any special machinery for the purchase or valuation of
members' shares.

(2) The statutory provisions were enacted for the "protection of the company's
members against unfair prejudice". They were not enacted so as to enable a
"locked-in" minority shareholder to require the company to buy him out at a price   B
which he considers adequately reflects the value of the underlying assets referable
to his shareholding (*Re a Company* [1983] Ch 178 at p. 191C).'

Then I omit a sentence from the summary.

'(3) The provisions apply to conduct which is unfairly prejudicial to the interests
of the member *qua* member. They do not extend to conduct which is prejudicial to
other interests of persons who happen to be members of the company (*Re a*   C
Company [1983] Ch 178 at p. 189E and *Re a Company No. 00477 of 1986* (1986) 2
BCC 99,171 at p. 99,174). The interests of the member(s) referred to in the section
are not, however, necessarily limited to his strict legal rights under the constitution
of the company. The concept of "unfair prejudice" to "interests" clearly embraces
a wider range of complaints than infringement of a member's legal rights under
the articles and under the Companies Acts.

(4) A resolution of a company is capable of being regarded as unfairly prejudicial   D
within the meaning of s. 459 if it has been proposed and would be prejudicial if
carried through, even though there is no immediate threat that the offending
resolution would be passed (*Re Kenyon Swansea Ltd* (1987) BCC 259 at pp. 264–
265). There cannot be any valid objection to the present petition on the ground
that the resolutions which have been proposed from time to time have not been
validly passed or have not been passed at all.   E

(5) The past acts of the company are also capable of being regarded as unfairly
prejudicial within the meaning of s. 459 even though at the date of the petition, or,
I would add, at the date of the hearing, the unfairness has been remedied (*Re
Kenyon Swansea Ltd* at p. 265). Thus, if the withholding of the information
requested by the petitioner in this case is capable of being unfairly prejudicial to
her within the meaning of this section the petition does not cease to be maintainable   F
on the ground that the information has been supplied subsequent to the
presentation of the petition.'

In reading this summary I have omitted certain comments made by Mummery J under
proposition (2) which do not seem to me to be relevant for present purposes. In relation
to his comments on proposition (1) the authority referred to has in effect been overruled
by the Court of Appeal's decision in *Re Abbey Leisure Ltd* [1990] BCC 60, which I shall
mention later, although I do not think that the general proposition that the jurisdiction   G
needs to be controlled in order to prevent it from being used as a means of oppression by
a dissident shareholder has in any way been qualified. I shall have to make comments of
my own at a later stage in relation to the matters dealt with in Mummery J's propositions
(4) and (5).

As regards proposition (3) in Mummery J's summary, he does not appear to have been
referred to some observations of Hoffmann J in *Re Posgate and Denby (Agencies) Ltd*   H
(1986) 2 BCC 99,352 at p. 99,357. These observations are not in any way inconsistent
with Mummery J's summary but in my view they add to it in an illuminating way. What
Hoffmann J said was as follows:

'In the absence of a breach of fiduciary duty . . . the equity shareholders plainly
have no right under the articles to prevent the directors from exercising the

A   company's power to sell its assets. But the concept of unfair prejudice which forms
the basis of the jurisdiction under s. 459 enables the court to take into account not
only the rights of members under the company's constitution but also their
legitimate expectations arising from the agreements or understandings of the
members inter se. There is an analogy in Lord Wilberforce's analysis of the concept
of what is "just and equitable" in *Re Westbourne Galleries*. . . The common case of
such expectations being superimposed on a member's rights under the articles is
B   the corporate quasi-partnership, in which members frequently have expectations
of participating in the management and profits of the company, which arise from
the understandings on which the company was formed and which it may be unfair
for the other members to ignore. The question is therefore whether (the petitioner)
can be said to have had a legitimate expectation that in the circumstances which
exist in this case, the board would not dispose of the syndicates without the
C   approval of the holders of a majority of the equity shares.

Although the answer to this question must in each case depend on the particular
facts, it is well to recall that in *Re.Westbourne Galleries Ltd* Lord Wilberforce said
that in most cases the basis of the association would be "adequately and
exhaustively" laid down in the articles. The "superimposition of equitable
considerations" requires, he said, something more. This was said in the context of
D   the "just and equitable" ground for winding up, but in my judgment it is equally
necessary for a shareholder who claims that it is "unfair" within the meaning of
s. 459 for the board to exercise powers conferred by the articles to demonstrate
some special circumstances which create a legitimate expectation that the board
would not do so. Section 459 enables the court to give full effect to the terms and
understandings on which the members of the company became associated but not
to rewrite them.'

E   In *Re Elgindata Ltd* [1991] BCLC 959 Warner J referred to *Re Posgate and Denby
(Agencies) Ltd* and another authority and went on to say (at p. 985C) that:

'In general members of a company have no legitimate expectations going beyond
the legal rights conferred on them by the constitution of the company, that is to
say its memorandum and articles of association.'

F   On behalf of Mrs Felton, Mr Davies pressed me to adopt a rather wider approach. He
relied heavily on another decision of Hoffmann J in *Re a Company No. 008699 of 1985*
(1986) 2 BCC 99,024. It is convenient to refer to this case as 'the 1986 case' in order to
distinguish it from the many other cases reported simply as 'Re a Company'. In that case
Hoffmann J was asked to strike out a petition under s. 459 which complained of a circular
issued by the chairman of a company urging shareholders to accept the lower of two rival
take over bids and suggesting that the higher bid would not succeed on various grounds.
G   The chairman and other directors of the company were financially interested in the lower
bid and wanted it to succeed. Hoffmann J held that the interest of a shareholder in being
able to sell his shares at the best price was an interest unfair prejudice to which was
capable of founding a petition under s. 459. He went on to say this at p. 99,029:

'The next point taken by (counsel for the respondents) was that the petitioners'
interest as shareholders comprised a "bundle of rights and obligations" (see
Farwell J in *Borland's Trustee v Steel Brothers*. . .) and that unless they could show
H   some infringement of rights other than those conferred by s. 459 itself, their
interests as shareholders could not be said to have been prejudiced within the
meaning of s. 459. In this case, he said, failure to take steps which would result in
the petitioners being able to accept the better offer did not infringe any of the rights
attached to their shares. I think that this is too restrictive an interpretation of the
section. The concept of unfairness which was chosen by Parliament as the basis of

the jurisdiction under s. 459 in my judgment cuts across the distinction between   A
acts which do or do not infringe the rights attached to the shares by the constitution
of the company. (Counsel for the respondents) referred me to *Re Carrington
Viyella plc...* in which Vinelott J said that:

> "... to bring a petition under s. (459) the petitioner must show not simply that
> his rights as a shareholder have been infringed but that the affairs of the
> company have been conducted in a way unfairly prejudicial to some part of the   B
> members."

He invited me to infer that it is a necessary but not sufficient condition for relief
under s. 459 that the petitioner's rights as a shareholder must have been infringed.
I do not think that Vinelott J was addressing himself to the question of whether
such infringement was a necessary condition and in my judgment it is neither
necessary nor sufficient. Unfairness is a familiar concept employed in ordinary
speech, often by way of contrast to infringement of legal right. It was intended to   C
confer a very wide jurisdiction upon the court and I think it would be wrong to
restrict that jurisdiction by adding any gloss to the ordinary meaning of the words.'

Mr Davies contended that this passage showed that the rights of a shareholder include
a right not to be unfairly prejudiced and that if there is an infringement of this right the
case will be within s. 459. The inquiry to be made is, therefore, an inquiry whether,
looking at the matter objectively, the way in which the petitioner has been treated can be   D
said to be unfair. Mr Davies said that this approach was supported by a passage in the
judgment of Mummery J on the strike-out application in this case, as reported in [1990]
BCC 221 at p. 227D. The passage relied on by Mr Davies is as follows:

> 'In my judgment, when regard is had to the totality of the allegations in this
> petition and in the points of claim, the petitioner has an arguable case that the
> combination of proposals to remove her as a director, to appoint other directors,   E
> to alter the memorandum and articles and to offer to purchase her shares without
> providing her with information relevant to ascertaining their value or to the
> running of the company in the interests of the members, amounts to conduct of
> the affairs of the company which is unfairly prejudicial to her interests as a member
> of the company. Such conduct may affect the real value of her shares which
> represent her interests in the company'.   F

However, the passage continues immediately as follows:

> 'Looking at the facts which are alleged in the petition and in the points of claim in
> the context of the wording of s. 459–461 and the breadth of the court's discretion
> under those provisions, I feel unable to say summarily at this stage that the
> petitioner's complaint of unfair prejudice to her interests is so clearly unarguable
> that it should be struck out. At the hearing of the petition the respondents may   G
> well succeed in satisfying the court that the petition should be dismissed because
> the petitioner cannot establish any infringement of a legal right under the articles
> or under the Companies Acts and cannot establish that she has any expectations
> over and above those legal rights deserving of the court's protection. I regard all
> those matters as suitable for decision on the hearing of the petition, but not now.'

In my judgment it is clear that Mummery J was not attempting to lay down a general
rule, still less to prejudge this case. He was merely stating the basis on which he was not   H
sufficiently satisfied at the stage before him that the present petition was doomed to
failure.

Reverting to the 1986 case, I cannot accept that Hoffmann J is to be taken to state a
general proposition to the effect contended for by Mr Davies. Such a general proposition
would have been quite unnecessary to the decision which he actually made in that case.

A The 1986 case was decided by Hoffmann J on 13 February 1986. His decision in *Re Posgate and Denby* was given on 20 June 1986. In his judgment in the later case, Hoffmann J said nothing to indicate that the scope of s. 459 as he then described it was narrower than he had considered it to be some four months earlier. This is not surprising in my view because in fact the scope described in the later case was not narrower than that described in the earlier one. Nothing which was said in the 1986 case justifies the wider approach contended for by Mr Davies.

B This conclusion is, I think, consistent with the way in which Warner J treated a similar argument in *Re J E Cade & Son Ltd* [1991] BCC 360 at pp. 370-372. In particular Warner J rejected an argument based on *Re Abbey Leisure Ltd* [1990] BCC 60 which was, in effect, repeated by Mr Davies before me. I reject that argument on the same grounds as Warner J.

C I now turn to the particular matters relied upon in this case. Although Mrs Felton relies primarily upon the matters alleged in her petition taken in conjunction, it is necessary, in my view, to start by considering separately the various elements in her complaint.

The first of these elements is Mr Scott's offer to purchase her shares in June 1988. This does not appear to me to be capable of being treated as part of the conduct of the company's affairs. It was a proposal made by Mr Scott on his own behalf. Mr Scott did

D not give evidence and it is not possible to know what were his reasons for making the offer. In an affidavit sworn on 23 January 1992 on behalf of the respondents by their solicitor in connection with an application for discovery, it is said that the sum offered by Mr Scott was 'substantially less than what the shares were worth', that Mr Scott knew that Mrs Felton was in financial difficulties and 'as it were tried it on'. On behalf of Mrs Felton there was complaint that this view of the matter was put forward only at a very

E late stage and through the mouth of Mr Scott's solicitor. But in essence it amounts to an admission of Mrs Felton's own case that the offer was a derisory one. Moreover, as I have noted, Mrs Felton makes it clear that the offer was rejected some weeks before Mr Scott asked for Mrs Felton's resignation as a director. All that the allegation about the incident of June 1988 amounts to is that Mr Scott, on his own behalf and not on behalf of the company, made a derisory offer for Mrs Felton's shares which she rejected either immediately or very soon after it was made.

F The next matter is the proposal to remove Mrs Felton as a director. Such a proposal was clearly put forward on a number of occasions in 1988 and early in 1989. The first occasion was Mr Scott's request for Mrs Felton to resign made in or shortly before August 1988. Next was the notice of 17 August 1988 from Mr Scott to the directors of the company of his intention to move a resolution for Mrs Felton's removal at an extraordinary general meeting of the company. This resolution was to have been

G considered at a general meeting purportedly called for 13 October 1988, although it was not proceeded with then. Next a resolution to the same effect was included in the requisition for a general meeting, although it was omitted from the notice which subsequently convened a general meeting on 13 December. The matter was revived at a board meeting held on 5 January 1989, which led to a formal proposal to be considered at a general meeting on 8 February 1989. The resolution was not proceeded with at that meeting and it seems that no further resolution of this kind has been proposed while the

H petition has been pending. There must, however, be a substantial prospect that the proposal will be put forward again once the petition has been disposed of.

The first and most important point to be noted in relation to this matter is that every director of a company is subject to the possibility of being removed as a director by ordinary resolution under s. 303 of the *Companies Act* 1985. Accordingly it cannot be said that, in the absence of special circumstances, a member who happens also to be a

director of a company has any right to remain in office and to participate in the   A
management of a company's business. There may, of course, be special circumstances
which have the result that, if removal takes place under the statutory provisions, there
will be grounds for complaint under s. 459. Circumstances of the kind which existed in
Ebrahimi v Westbourne Galleries [1973] AC 360 constitute a typical example. But in the
present case no such circumstances are pleaded and I was wholly unpersuaded that any
could be said to exist.

  B

That is enough to dispose of the threat to remove Mrs Felton as a director as a ground,
by itself, for relief under s. 459. But it would be unrealistic not to recognise that in the
present case ample grounds seem to exist to justify such removal. Although Mrs Felton
is undoubtedly an intelligent woman, there is nothing to suggest that she has any qualities
which make her particularly suited to being a director of this company. She has been a
director since 1979 without, it seems, ever attending a directors' meeting except possibly
an informal meeting at her home. Her protestation that her absence has been attributable   C
to the fact that she has not received notice of meetings (which I accept in respect of the
period down to October 1988) is greatly diminished in force by the fact that she showed
no interest in the affairs of the company before about September 1988 and that she has
declined to attend meetings of directors held since then, despite the fact that she has had
notice of them.

The third element in Mrs Felton's complaint is the adoption of a new memorandum   D
and articles of association. There are two main aspects of this to be considered, namely
the procedural position and the substantive effect of the change.

As to the procedural position, I have already held that the new memorandum and
articles were not effectively adopted in July 1988. The fact that a special resolution was
registered at the Companies Registry in respect of a meeting which was probably not held
and which, if held, was not the subject of proper notice, is no doubt a serious criticism of   E
Mr Scott and the others who were in de facto control of the company's affairs at that
time. The next question is whether the new memorandum and articles were effectively
adopted at the meeting said to have been held on 13 December 1988. This was the main
matter in respect of which Mrs Braithwaite was called to give evidence.

I have to say that if Mrs Braithwaite had not given evidence I would have had little
difficulty in concluding that the meeting of 13 December 1988 was validly convened and   F
duly held. Having heard Mrs Braithwaite, however, I have had my doubts about this. I
found Mrs Braithwaite a most unsatisfactory witness. She has worked for very many
years for Mr Scott's estate agency business and is a director of Mr Scott's company
Jalside Ltd. She is and has been since before 1988 the secretary of the company. Her
evidence in chief was to the effect that the requisition for a general meeting, the notice of
a directors' meeting for 9 November 1988 to consider that requisition, and the notice of
the meeting to be held on 13 December were all sent out by her, or under her personal   G
supervision, and that the minutes of the directors' meeting on 9 November 1988 and of
the meeting of 13 December were prepared by her from notes taken at the time. Her
evidence was, in effect, that all notices of meetings and minutes were dealt with in a
similar way. After cross-examination, however, I entertained the gravest doubts whether
this was so. Some notices which Mrs Braithwaite originally claimed to have sent out
herself seem almost certainly to have been sent out by the company's auditors, Pinnick   H
Lewis. These included, as I think Mrs Braithwaite herself eventually accepted, all those
on which her name was typed rather than signed and on which the address of the
company's registered office which is the office of Pinnick Lewis, is stated as being Mrs
Braithwaite's address. I found it difficult to accept that the minutes which Mrs
Braithwaite claimed to have been prepared by her were in fact so prepared, as distinct
from being prepared by the auditors or someone else. At the end of Mrs Braithwaite's

A   evidence I felt doubtful about almost everything which she had said except some matters which were uncontroversial and some other matters where I was sure that she was wrong.

This has caused me to have considerable doubt about the meeting of 13 December. In the end, however, I have come to the conclusion that this meeting was properly convened and duly held. It is clear from a letter from Mishcon de Reya to Mr Lewis, which is expressed to be dated 10 August 1988 but which must have been written on 10 November
B   1988 that, in relation to this meeting, the company was acting under careful legal advice designed to secure that Mrs Felton could not object to what was done. A proper notice concerning the meeting was undoubtedly prepared and a copy of it was sent to Mrs Felton's solicitors under cover of a letter from Mishcon de Reya dated 30 November 1988. I think the probability is that a copy of this notice was sent to Mrs Felton herself on or about 18 November 1988. Undoubtedly Mrs Felton knew that a meeting was to be held on 13 December, and although she did not attend such a meeting, her intention not
C   to attend was only communicated to Mishcon de Reya in Mrs Felton's solicitor's letter of 12 December 1988 which was, presumably, received by Mishcon de Reya on the very day of the meeting. As a quorum of five was required and the persons said to be present at the meeting included Mr James Green, a shareholder who apparently had not previously taken any part in meetings, it seems that the organisation of a quorum had required a certain amount of effort. It would have been the height of folly for Mr Scott
D   and the others concerned to have refrained from holding a proper meeting, when they were on notice that Mrs Felton was complaining about irregularly convened meetings; when the main business was to regularise something which, on good grounds, was said to have been done irregularly in July; and when Mrs Felton might, notwithstanding what had been said in her solicitor's letter, have put in an appearance. It seems to me improbable that Mr Scott and those advising or supporting him were guilty of such folly. In all the circumstances I find myself able to accept Mrs Braithwaite's evidence that she
E   distinctly remembers a meeting being held on 13 December, notwithstanding my scepticism or disbelief concerning most of the rest of her evidence. I also accept that the persons present at such meeting were those whose names are listed in the note attached to the minutes of that meeting and that at the meeting the new memorandum and articles were adopted and the four persons proposed for election as directors were duly elected.

Turning to the substance of the new memorandum and articles, two complaints are
F   made, namely, first the adoption of new objects and, secondly, the adoption of new provisions as to the quorum for general meetings and board meetings. As to the objects, it is asserted in the petition that the changes involve a considerable expansion of the objects for which the company is established. When I asked for particular extensions to be pointed out, Mr Davies mentioned only certain rather general provisions of the kind all too often found in memoranda of association. I think there is nothing in this complaint.

G   As to the provisions relating to quorum, it will be recalled that the previous articles of association of the company provided for a quorum of five at both general meetings and board meetings. The new articles incorporate, subject to minor variations and some omissions, the regulations contained in Table A in the *Companies (Tables A–F) Regulations* 1985 (SI 1985/805). The new quorum at general meetings is that prescribed by reg. 40, namely two persons. The new quorum at directors' meetings is that prescribed
H   by reg. 89, which is likewise two persons unless some other number is fixed by the directors.

It is, I think, a surprising notion that the adoption of the provisions of Table A is, or is part of, conduct which is unfairly prejudicial to a member's interests for the purposes of s. 459, although I should hesitate to hold that it can never be so. Mrs Felton's complaint in relation to general meetings was not expanded in argument and is, in my

judgment, without any foundation whatsoever. The substance of her complaint as   A
regards board meetings is that, before the new articles were adopted, she was one of five
directors who could only hold an effective board meeting if all five were present. She
could thus prevent the board from transacting business by the simple expedient of staying
away from the meetings. Even though the directors had, under the previous articles,
power to fix a quorum other than five Mrs Felton could prevent this being done by
preventing a quorum being present at any meeting called to fix a lower quorum. This is
scarcely an attractive proposition and I find it difficult to see how a director can ever   B
have a legitimate interest in preserving a position of this kind where the inevitable result
is to stultify the conduct of the company's affairs. Apart from this, however, it cannot, in
my view, be suggested that this complaint brings Mrs Felton's case within s. 459. In her
capacity as a member, which is the only relevant capacity for the purposes of s. 459, she
has no legitimate expectation to remain as a director of the company whatever the
quorum for board meetings, for reasons which I have explained. In any event she could   C
not have legitimately objected to a proposal under the old articles to increase the number
of directors to such a total as would be likely to secure a quorum at any meeting, whether
or not Mrs Felton herself was present. Quite apart from all this, the rights of any member
of a company under its articles are liable to be changed by special resolution and this is
all that has happened here. In the absence of special circumstances involving abuse of the
rights of the majority, a change in the articles, particularly a change of the kind made in
this case, is one of the ordinary incidents to which a member of a company cannot validly   D
object. Mr Davies sought to persuade me that Mrs Felton had a right to be consulted
before any change in the memorandum and articles was proposed, but I see no basis for
this. The right of a member in relation to such matters is the right to have the matter
considered by a duly convened meeting of the company at which he or she is free to vote.
Mrs Felton was afforded this right.

Apart from his points concerning of the adoption of the new memorandum and   E
articles, Mr Davies also sought to develop an objection to the appointment of four new
directors at the meeting held on 13 December 1988. His contention was that Mrs Felton
was entitled to be consulted before resolutions for such appointment were put forward
for consideration at a meeting. I see no basis at all for this complaint.

The final element in Mrs Felton's complaint is that the management information had
not been provided. Mr Davies relied upon the position as at the date of service of the
points of claim in May 1989. He cited *Re Kenyon Swansea Ltd* (1987) 3 BCC 259 in   F
support of the proposition that past conduct can constitute unfair prejudice for the
purposes of s. 459. As a general proposition that may be so, but I do not think it can be
said that information provided subsequent to the date of petition is irrelevant. I do not
think that Mummery J intended to say it was irrelevant in his comments on proposition
(5) in the passage from his judgment on the strike-out application in this case which I
have already read. Mummery J was concerned with a different aspect of the point, namely   G
whether the subsequent provision of information made the petition unmaintainable. In
my judgment the subsequent provision of information must be a material consideration,
if only because the natural remedy for a failure to provide information is an order that
the information be provided and there can be no purpose in making such an order when
the information has in fact been provided before the order is made.

As I have said, the information said not to have been provided is that specified in para.   H
23 of the petition and it is the same as the management information sought by the letter
of 15 September. It is thus information which at the outset was information which Mrs
Felton sought in her capacity as a director, not in her capacity as a member. I have heard
no argument which satisfies me that Mrs Felton had any right to this information in her
capacity as member. Indeed, art. 127 of the articles of association of the company which
applied prior to 13 December 1988 specifically excludes any such right. It seems to me,

A therefore, that refusal of this information, if there has been refusal, cannot be conduct which is unfairly prejudicial to Mrs Felton's interests as a member and thus within s. 459.

Mrs Felton's case that there has been a failure to supply the requisite information is set out in particulars given under para. 14 of the points of claim on 30 March 1990, which deal with the matter as at the time of service of the points of claim on 5 May 1989. In my judgment many of the complaints summarised in these particulars are, even looked

B at as at May 1989 without regard to what has happened subsequently, ill-founded or insubstantial. Thus in relation to item (1), which is documentation disclosing the nature and value of the company's assets, Mrs Felton's case appears to be that this information was purportedly made available in documents enclosed with the respondents' solicitors' letter of 21 February 1989, but Mrs Felton does not admit that all the relevant information under this head was made available by that letter. As it is for Mrs Felton to make good her complaint a non-admission of this kind gets her nowhere.

C Item (2), relating to documents concerning liabilities, is dealt with in a similarly ineffective manner. Item (3) relates to documents concerning negotiations between the company and Mr Michael Felton's trustee in bankruptcy which appear now to be accepted never to have taken place. Item (4) relates to the transfer of shares from Mr Scott to Miss O'Donnell which seems to me to have little relevance to anything that Mrs Felton is properly concerned with and which has since been provided anyway. Item (5)

D relates to the directors' minute book, which had been made available by 5 May 1989. Item (7) relates to current valuations of the company's properties, which Mrs Felton appeared at one time to require to be made at the company's expense but which she now accepts that she cannot require to be brought into existence simply for her benefit. The remaining items, namely (6), (8) and (9), relate to draft accounts and detailed matters concerning directors' remuneration and dealings with the company. The precise significance of these items was not developed in argument before me, except that Mr

E Davies pointed out the arguably incorrect answer which had been given to the effect that there were no directors' loans. I find it difficult to evaluate what the effect of a complete refusal of information of these kinds may have been.

It is not necessary, however, to dwell on this matter. I have already mentioned that the offer made by Mishcon de Reya in their letter of 9 December 1988 to give inspection of the documents containing the management information was not taken up at that time.

F In a long letter dated 21 February 1989 Harkavys, who had become the solicitors to the respondents in succession to Mishcon de Reya at about the time the petition was presented, dealt with most of Mrs Felton's complaints in what seems to me to be a reasonable way and offered to make arrangements for the inspection of the company's documents relating to the management information and for the copying of documents required by Mrs Felton at her expense. This offer was not taken up on behalf of Mrs Felton until September 1989, apparently because Mrs Felton wanted an accountant to

G do the inspection on her behalf and authority had to be obtained from the Legal Aid Board to incur the necessary expense. Mr Hodson, the accountant instructed by Mrs Felton, inspected documents on 25 September 1989 and raised numerous points with Pinnick Lewis, who offered further inspection of documents and also discussions about them. The process seems to have continued through the winter of 1989/90, culminating in a visit to inspect further documents specified by Mrs Felton's solicitors on 18 April 1990. In a letter of 10 May 1990 Harkavys asked Mrs Felton's solicitors for confirmation

H that they were not awaiting further information. No such confirmation was given and in letters of 15 June 1990 and 19 March 1991 Mrs Felton's solicitors required further documents and information. The first of these letters was dealt with by the production of further documents and the second by a suggestion that Pinnick Lewis be approached again. Some at least of the points raised in the second letter seem to me almost to indicate a desire on the part of Mrs Felton to supervise the activities of the directors of the

company without attending board meetings and raising genuine matters of concern in   A
the usual way. For example, the letter includes requests for information whether the
auditors have made a physical check of the title deeds for the company's properties and
for confirmation that all the properties have sufficient fire cover and that premiums had
been paid up to date. The impression that I have is that in the course of the proceedings
Mrs Felton's demands for information have become insatiable and oppressive.

Even taking up a stance at the date when the points of claim were served, as Mr Davies   B
invites me to do, and overlooking the important point that any entitlement of Mrs Felton
to the management information was an entitlement as director and not as member, I find
it impossible to say that the non-provision of the management information, in so far as
it had not been provided at that date, amounts to conduct of the kind mentioned in
s. 459. Even if it was, the only remedy which would be appropriate to this complaint
standing by itself, would be an order for the provision of the missing information. As I
have mentioned, the petition seeks such an order, but as the matter was presented to me   C
Mrs Felton seems now to be interested only in an order that her shares be purchased by
one or more of the respondents. In any event, having regard to the very free access to
information which has been made available to Mrs Felton, and her advisers in the course
of the proceedings, I would not think it necessary or desirable to make such an order. I
believe that if such an order were made it would itself be used by Mrs Felton as an
instrument of oppression.   D

Having dealt at some length, perhaps at undue length, with the individual component
parts of Mrs Felton's case I must now turn to the case which she seeks to make on the
basis of these component parts taken in conjunction with each other. However, I find this
a troublesome task because, although Mr Davies made it clear throughout that he relied
upon the matters pleaded as a whole rather than individually, I found it difficult to
understand precisely what the whole is said to be beyond the sum of its component parts.
At one time I thought that Mrs Felton was trying to make good a case that the various   E
acts or omissions which she alleges subsequent to June 1988 were part of a plan to bring
pressure to bear upon her to accept Mr Scott's derisory offer for her shares. But such a
case is not open on the pleadings and if pursued, which it was not, would face the
difficulty that no offer, derisory or otherwise, was on the table for acceptance after the
initial offer was made and rejected in June 1988. Mr Davies confined himself, as he must,
to what is said in the pleadings which, so far as a general case going beyond the specific   F
matters is concerned, seems to be limited to para. 24 and 28 of the petition, which I have
already read. When I pressed Mr Davies to formulate the proposition which he advanced
as defining the interests of Mrs Felton which had been unfairly prejudiced, he put it in
this way:

> 'In a company of this sort, in which the rights and liabilities of members inter se
> are not absolutely governed by the memorandum and articles of association of the   G
> company, a member to whom an offer is made for the purchase of that member's
> minority shareholding, certainly if made by the person who is in control of the
> company, has a right to the provision of all information necessary to enable her to
> decide whether she is willing to be a vendor or prospective vendor of her shares.
> Her position as a prospective vendor is part of her position as a member of the
> company.'

H

I have endeavoured to set out the proposition exactly as it was put by Mr Davies and
I make no criticism of any linguistic inelegance which might have been avoided if it had
been formulated otherwise than in the course of Mr Davies' oral submissions. The last
sentence of the proposition, relating to the minority shareholder's position as a
prospective vendor being part of her position as a member, is supported by the decision
in the 1986 case of Hoffmann J. Mr Davies submitted that the rest of the proposition was

A   also supported by the 1986 case, but this would only be so if that case established that a member has the right not to be unfairly prejudiced without the need to identify the prejudice with any separate interest of the member. As I have indicated, I reject the view that the 1986 case is authority for such a proposition.

Apart from this the submission runs into a number of other difficulties. Mr Davies did not put it forward as a proposition applicable to all companies but limited it to 'a company of this sort in which the rights and liabilities of members inter se are not absolutely governed by the memorandum and articles'. But, as Lord Wilberforce said in *Ebrahimi v Westbourne Galleries* [1973] AC 360 at p. 379E, in most cases the basis of the association between members will be 'adequately and exhaustively' laid down in the articles and the superimposition of equitable considerations will require something more. There is nothing in the pleadings in this case, and there was nothing in the evidence, to indicate what is distinctive about this company or what it is that has the effect that the rights and liabilities of its members are not governed by the memorandum and articles of association of the company.

Beyond this, the proposition makes no allowance for the fact that, as I find, Mr Scott's offer was made in his personal capacity and not as part of the conduct of the company's affairs and was a once and for all offer which ceased to operate once it had been refused, as it was immediately after it was made. I cannot see how a single offer of this kind can trigger a right to have information which did not previously exist and which goes well beyond the usual rights that a member has to information about the company's affairs.

In any event, as I have held, the company has in the event provided Mrs Felton with a great deal of information, probably going well beyond what she would be entitled to even if Mr Davies's proposition were correct. While it is true that the management information has been provided during the course of the proceedings rather than before the presentation of the petition and it is also time that the provision of information at that stage is not by itself a bar to an otherwise well-founded petition based on the failure to provide information, I cannot accept that the failure to give effect to the right asserted in Mr Davies's proposition could lead to the remedy sought by Mrs Felton, namely the purchase of her shares. In other words, even if I were to accept Mr Davies's proposition, which I do not, and were also to accept that the failure to provide management information at an earlier stage constitutes unfair prejudice to Mrs Felton's interests as a member of the company, I do not see how this could, in the circumstances of the present case, lead to anything more than an order for the provision of the missing information which, for the reasons I have indicated, I regard as being unnecessary and inappropriate.

In the result I conclude that this petition must be dismissed. I add only this. The evidence indicates that prior to October 1988 the affairs of the company had been conducted with a degree of informality and a disregard for the provisions of the company's constitution which is unacceptable. Although the irregularities which have occurred do not, in my judgment, entitle Mrs Felton to the relief which she has sought on this petition, it must not be thought that the dismissal of the petition entitles those who control the company's affairs to revert to the old irregular ways.

(Petition dismissed with costs)

JUDGMENT ON COSTS
(Delivered 2 March 1993)

Warner J: On 6 March 1992, Ferris J dismissed a petition under s. 459 of the Companies Act, which had been presented by Mrs Audrey Pamela Felton against eight respondents. The first respondent was the company, the conduct of whose affairs was in question in the petition, namely, Estate Acquisition & Development Ltd. The second respondent was Mr Maurice Scott, a director and shareholder in the company. The third respondent was his wife, named in the petition as Inge O'Donnell. She is a shareholder in the company. I am not sure whether she is or was also a director. The fourth to eighth respondents were other individuals who were shareholders or directors of the company.

Ferris J ordered Mrs Felton to pay the costs of the petition but, since she was legally aided, he directed that the order for costs should not be enforced without the leave of the court. The costs have since been taxed in the sum of £39,843.98. I now have before me an application by the respondents for leave to enforce that order for costs, coupled with an application for a charging order on Mrs Felton's shares in the company.

The company is a property holding company and it is common ground for the purposes of this application that its net asset value is about £1.1m. The issued share capital of the company is £47,774, divided into shares of £1 each.

The petitioner holds 5,712 shares, which is about 12 per cent of the issued share capital. If one divides £1.1m by 47,774, one gets about £23 per share. On that basis, a basis which is of course quite unrealistic, the value of Mrs Felton's shares is about £131,000.

Mr Scott holds 914 shares and his wife (whom I will call 'Mrs Scott') holds 34,150. Mrs Scott's holding represents about 71 per cent of the issued share capital of the company and, of course, it is more realistic to value her holding on an assets basis. On that basis, at £23 per share, her holding is worth £785,542 or thereabouts. On the same basis, Mr Scott's holding is worth about £21,000.

Mrs Felton's former husband, Mr Felton, is the registered holder of 7,669 shares, representing about 16 per cent of the share capital of the company; but the beneficial interest in those shares is vested in Mr Felton's trustee in bankruptcy.

The petition had been presented on 18 January 1989 and the dispute that led to it had originated in June 1988.

I must now read the relevant parts of s. 17 of the *Legal Aid Act* 1988. Subsection (1) provides:

> 'The liability of a legally assisted party under an order for costs made against him with respect to any proceedings shall not exceed the amount (if any) which is a reasonable one for him to pay having regard to all the circumstances, including the financial resources of all the parties and their conduct in connection with the dispute.'

Subsection (2) provides for regulations to be made as to the court, tribunal or person by whom that amount is to be determined and the extent to which any determination of that amount is to be final.

Subsection (3) provides:

> 'None of the following, namely, a legally assisted person's dwelling house, clothes, household furniture and the tools and implements of his trade shall–
>
> (a) be taken into account in assessing his financial resources for the purposes of this section, or
>
> (b) be subject to execution or any corresponding process in any part of the United Kingdom to enforce the order,
>
> except so far as regulations may prescribe.'

It is common ground that the regulations do not prescribe anything that is material for present purposes.

As to the financial resources of the respondents, other than the company, I have before me an affidavit of Mr Scott. As I have already said, it is common ground that the net asset value of the company is of the order of £1.1m, but of course the company played in the proceedings on the petition the limited role which is usual in s. 459 proceedings.

A   In his affidavit, Mr Scott says that he and his wife have agreed to indemnify all of the other individual respondents in these proceedings in respect of any costs involved and that, for that reason, they are not giving evidence on this application as to their means. I can, therefore, take it that those other individual respondents will be unaffected by the decision on this application one way or the other. The liability of the respondents for costs simply does not affect them.

B   Mr Scott then exhibits what he calls a brief statement of his and his wife's affairs as at April 1992 and he says that, as can be seen from that, he and his wife are able to afford the costs involved in this affair, should Mrs Felton not be ordered to pay them. Indeed, Mr Hollington, on behalf of the respondents, has told me that it is accepted that Mr and Mrs Scott could bear those costs without hardship.

   The statement of affairs exhibited to Mr Scott's affidavit shows his net assets to be worth about £212,000 and his wife's net assets to be worth about £170,777. Mr Davies has criticised that statement of affairs, quite properly, for not mentioning any income of Mr Scott or Mrs Scott. Mr Scott carries on, through a company called Jalside Ltd, the business of an estate agent and one imagines that he derives an income from that. Mrs Scott, according to an affidavit sworn by Mrs Felton, derives an income of £19,200 a year from the company.

D   Mr Davies also invites me to treat with caution Mr Scott's valuation of his shares in Jalside Ltd at £25,000. He does so because, in his statement of affairs, Mr Scott has taken his and his wife's shares in the company Estate Acquisition & Development Ltd at £5 each which, particularly bearing in mind that they have between them control of the company, is a patent undervalue. The only asset of Mrs Scott put into the statement of affairs is her 34,154 shares in the company which, as I mentioned earlier, on a purely arithmetical assets basis are worth £785,000 odd.

E   Mrs Felton has put in an affidavit in which she states her financial resources. She is the freehold owner of her home at 90 Maida Vale, London W9. That has been on the market for something between 18 months and two years and the current asking price is £315,000. It is charged to Barclays Bank plc for sums totalling about £270,000 and it is indeed at Barclays Bank's instance that it is being sold, Barclays Bank having obtained judgment and an order for possession against Mrs Felton. However, Mrs Felton is still occupying the property, by agreement with Barclays Bank, pending its sale, on payment by her of a monthly sum in respect of interest on her debt.

   Mrs Felton's father has a second charge on the property for £25,000, which he lent to her in March 1984. Mrs Felton's other assets are of negligible value. She has been unemployed for approximately five years and is in receipt of income support. She says that she has incurred debts to family and friends of £30,000, which she has borrowed in order to maintain her monthly interest payments to Barclays Bank, and that she owes a further sum of £2,000 to Thames Water.

   She, of course, has her 5,712 shares in the company and about those she says this, in para. 22 of her affidavit:

> 'In practical terms I am unable to deal with those shares or to dispose of them to anyone other than an existing member of Estate Acquisition and Development Ltd and the only buyers are likely to be those in control, namely Mr and Mrs Scott who between them own approximately 73.44 per cent. Even if I were to find a purchaser for those shares and transfer the shares to that purchaser the directors of the first respondent have an absolute discretion to refuse to register that transfer. The purpose of my petition initially was to achieve an order that my shares be purchased for a proper value and that my association with the company be terminated. As I have stated previously regrettably my petition did not succeed

and accordingly I remain locked into a company over which I can exercise no   A
control.'

Then in para. 23 she says that, if the application to enforce the order for costs against
her should succeed and a charging order be made over her shares, it is not credible that
any purchaser other than an existing member of the company would come forward.

Indeed, it is common ground that Mrs Felton's only prospect of selling her shares is to
one or more of the respondents and that the shares are valueless to her at the moment.   B
They do not yield any income.

I turn to the conduct of the parties in connection with the dispute.

Mr Hollington, on behalf of the respondents, has pointed to three aspects of Mrs
Felton's conduct which, he submits, are open to criticism. The first, and least important,
is that the petition originally sought not only relief under s. 459 but also the winding up
of the company on the just and equitable ground. A few months after the presentation of   C
the petition, an application by the respondents for an order striking out the petition came
before Mummery J. He struck out the claim for winding up on the ground that there was
no reasonable cause of action for it. He did not strike out the claim for relief under s. 459
and he reserved the costs of the application.

The second aspect of Mrs Felton's conduct that Mr Hollington criticises is summed up
in a passage in the judgment of Ferris J, at p. 354A, where he said:

> 'The impression that I have is that in the course of the proceedings Mrs Felton's   D
> demands for information have become insatiable and oppressive.'

Ferris J, having stated his reasons for thinking that Mrs Felton was not entitled to an
order for the provision of information, went on:

> 'I believe that if such an order were made it would itself be used by Mrs Felton as
> an instrument of oppression.'

Having read Ferris J's judgment and having also been taken through the   E
correspondence between the solicitors for Mrs Felton and the respondents' solicitors for
the period 1 February 1989–21 February 1992, just before the petition was heard by
Ferris J, I can well understand why Ferris J made those comments and why Mr
Hollington criticises that aspect of Mrs Felton's conduct.

Mr Davies sought to belittle it and to persuade me that it had no important impact on
costs. I cannot, of course, assess what impact it had on costs but it must have had some   F
impact and it is quite certainly something to which the court must have regard under
s. 17(1).

The third aspect of Mrs Felton's conduct which is criticised by Mr Hollington is
something which, of course, Ferris J did not have before him. It is the conduct of Mrs
Felton in response to overtures by Mr Scott beginning in November 1989 with a view to
endeavouring to compromise the proceedings initiated by the petition. I have been taken   G
through the 'without prejudice' correspondence between the solicitors and there again I
can well understand the basis of Mr Hollington's criticism. Of course, one does not know
what would have happened if Mrs Felton had responded to those overtures by making
some sort of counter-offer at an early stage. She did make a counter-offer in the week
before the petition was due to come on for hearing but that came to nothing. There again,
Mr Davies sought to belittle the consequences of her inactivity and sought to persuade
me that her conduct had not been as unwise as it seemed to me at first sight. However,   H
the fact is that Mr Scott repeatedly, through his solicitors, made very clear his keenness
to try to settle the matter without the proceedings having to go to trial and that there was
no or virtually no helpful response from Mrs Felton's side.

As regards the conduct of the respondents in connection with the dispute, Mr Davies
referred me to passages in the judgment of Ferris J in which he set out the way in which

A the dispute had originated and developed up to the time of the presentation of the petition. Mr Davies submitted that it was apparent from that that Mr Scott and the other directors had brought the petition on themselves by their actions against Mrs Felton and by irregularities for which they were responsible in the conduct of the company's affairs from June 1988 onwards. Their conduct, said Mr Davies, was the cause of the petition being brought. He pointed out that Mummery J had declined to strike out the claim under s. 459 and that Ferris J, at the end of his judgment, had said this:

B 'In the result I conclude that this petition must be dismissed. I add only this. The evidence indicates that prior to October 1988 the affairs of the company had been conducted with a degree of informality and a disregard for the provisions of the company's constitution which is unacceptable. Although the irregularities which have occurred do not, in my judgment, entitle Mrs Felton to the relief which she has sought on this petition, it must not be thought that the dismissal of the petition entitles those who control the company's affairs to revert to the old irregular ways.'

C That I take into consideration.

Mr Hollington submits that, in the circumstances, it would be reasonable and just for me to make an order which resulted in the payment of the taxed costs of the petition by Mrs Felton, provided that only her shares in the company were resorted to for that purpose and that steps were taken to ensure that she received a fair price for her shares.

D I have come to the conclusion that, in principle, Mr Hollington is right. What Mr Hollington envisages, in effect, is that I should make an order giving the respondents leave to enforce Ferris J's order for costs but only against Mrs Felton's shares in the company; that I should couple with that leave a charging order on Mrs Felton's shares; and that, in any subsequent proceedings by originating summons for the sale of the shares under an order of the court, Mr and Mrs Scott should offer to buy them at their fair value. Mr Hollington has produced a minute of the proposed order on those lines.

E There has been some discussion of the terms of that minute and further discussion of those terms is undoubtedly needed.

Mr Hollington suggested that, these being proceedings inter partes, I could make a charging order absolute. However, as I indicated during the argument, I think that, if there is to be a charging order, Mrs Felton's other creditors ought to have an opportunity of being heard before it is made absolute. In her affidavit, Mrs Felton names two of her creditors, Barclays Bank plc and Thames Water, but she does not name her father or her other creditors and it will be necessary for her to do so.

F Mr Davies argued that I had no power to make such an order. He pointed out that in *Crystall v Crystall* [1963] 1 WLR 574 the Court of Appeal held that the financial resources of the assisted party were a most compelling circumstance to be taken into account by the court when exercising its discretion under the predecessor of s. 17(1). That meant, said Mr Davies, that the court must make an assessment of the assisted party's resources in terms of cash. Mr Davies conceded that the court could take into account the value of shares held by the assisted party where that value was easily realisable, for instance, in the case of shares in a quoted company; but he submitted, as I understood his argument, that the court could not take into account the value of assets which were realisable only on the satisfaction of conditions, and here a string of conditions was envisaged: that I should make a charging order nisi; that that order should be made absolute; that there should then be an application for an order for the sale of the shares; that on that order being made, Mr and Mrs Scott should make an offer to buy them at their fair value; and that that offer should in fact result in their purchase from Mrs Felton at their fair value. Nor, said Mr Davies, did I know what that fair value might turn out to be.

G

H

I have felt the force of that argument and that is one of the reasons why I am so concerned that my order should be in such a form as to ensure that Mrs Felton is

protected against things going wrong. But I cannot accept the premise of the argument. A
Section 17(1) does not require the court to make an assessment of the financial resources
of the assisted party in cash terms. It requires only that the liability of the assisted party
under an order for costs made against him should not exceed the amount, if any, which
is a reasonable one for him to pay having regard to all the circumstances, including of
course the most important circumstance, his financial resources. If, as here, those
resources include an asset that is only realisable on the satisfaction of conditions, there is
no reason why that asset should be ignored if means can be found of satisfying those B
conditions. Nor do I think that, if the means of satisfying those conditions require the
exercise by the court of other powers that it has, the court is precluded by s. 17(1) from
exercising those powers so as to achieve justice between the parties.

Another argument put forward by Mr Davies rested on the terms of s. 17(3), which
require that in assessing the financial resources of the assisted person there should be left
out of account, inter alia, his dwelling house. Mr Davies pointed out that the subsection C
said nothing about liabilities. It followed, he said, that in assessing the financial resources
of the assisted person, one should leave out of account his dwelling house but not his
liabilities even if secured on his dwelling house. In other words, one should regard those
liabilities as deductible from his resources other than his dwelling house.

I cannot accept that argument, which I felt was put forward by Mr Davies with his
tongue in his cheek. No doubt the court is precluded by s. 17(3) from regarding the D
assisted person's dwelling house as an asset forming part of his financial resources; but
the court must take the facts as it finds them to be. The facts here are essentially that Mrs
Felton's house is charged to Barclays Bank and then to her father and that, because it is
charged to Barclays Bank, it is to be sold. For me to refuse to make the order sought by
the respondents would not preserve it for her.

Then Mr Davies argued that, in deciding under s. 17(1) how much it is reasonable for E
the assisted person to pay, the court must have regard to the relative wealth of the assisted
party and the persons in whose favour the order for costs has been made. He pointed to
the evidence about the net asset value of the company, the wealth of Mr and Mrs Scott
and the lack of evidence about the financial resources of the other individual respondents.

However, I do not think that s. 17(1) is to be construed as meaning that an order for
costs against an assisted party should never be enforced in favour of a wealthy party or
against a party who will suffer no substantial financial hardship if it is not enforced. The F
fact that a successful unassisted party will suffer no financial hardship if the order is not
enforced does not necessarily mean that it is reasonable and just that he should bear all
his own costs. My attention was drawn to the contrast between s. 17 and s. 18, which
relates to the payment of the costs of a successful unassisted party by the legal aid board.
An order under s. 18 can only be made in respect of costs incurred in a court of first
instance if the court is satisfied that the unassisted party will suffer severe financial G
hardship unless the order is made.

Next, Mr Davies submitted that there was a sinister motive for this application, its real
purpose being to enable the respondents to get rid of Mrs Felton as a shareholder in the
company. In support of that submission, Mr Davies pointed to two matters. One was a
comment made by Mr Hollington at the end of his submissions to the effect that a
charging order over Mrs Felton's shares would protect the respondents against a new H
petition under s. 459 by Mrs Felton. The other was the way in which Mr and Mrs Felton
had, since the judgment of Ferris J, taken proceedings against, among others, the
company and Mr Scott in respect of irregularities in the conduct of the company's affairs.
Mr Scott and the company have been convicted of a number of offences under the
Companies Act in the Harrow Magistrates' Court as a result of prosecutions brought,
some of them by Mr Felton and some of them by Mrs Felton. There have also been

A   proceedings by Mr Felton in this court for a declaration that the annual general meeting of the company purportedly held on 17 June 1992 was invalid and for consequential relief. Those proceedings were compromised on the basis that a new meeting would be held and that Mr Felton's costs would be paid by the defendants.

Mr Hollington, in his reply, explained to me what he had meant by his remark at the end of his submissions. So explained, I do not think that there was anything sinister at all about it. I do not doubt that the respondents would be glad to be rid of Mrs Felton as
B   a shareholder, but that is not a reason for depriving them of the order they seek if it is otherwise an order which it is proper to make.

Lastly, Mr Davies took two points in support of his contention that I should not make a charging order. First, he pointed out that there was no affidavit from the respondents complying with O. 50, r. 1(3). That is true, but substantially all the information that is required to be given by such an affidavit is before the court. The defect is, therefore, a
C   technical one and Mr Hollington has offered an undertaking to remedy it by putting in a formal affidavit complying with r. 1(3). I think I can dispense with that formality.

Secondly, Mr Davies pointed out that the value of Mrs Felton's shares was not at present known, so that it was impossible for me to tell how many of her shares needed to be charged in order to cover the sum of £39,843.98. He did tell me that to raise £40,000 the shares would have to be worth about £7 each.

D   Be that as it may, the answer to this point was I think, as Mr Hollington pointed out, that the problem can be dealt with in the proceedings for the sale of the shares. Their value should be ascertained in those proceedings and, when it has been ascertained, the number of shares that needs to be sold can be determined and the charging order can be discharged as to any balance.

I conclude that, in all the circumstances, it would be reasonable and just that I should
E   make the order sought by Mr Hollington. I do not think that there is any ground on which I should give the respondents leave to enforce the order for costs in their favour in respect of part only of the £39,843.98, as was tentatively suggested by Mr Davies.

(*Order accordingly*)

F

G

H

Barrett v Duckett & Ors.

A

Court of Appeal (Civil Division).
Russell, Beldam and Peter Gibson L JJ.
Judgment delivered 27 July 1994.

*Minority shareholder's action – Derivative action – Striking-out motions –
Winding-up petition – Plaintiff 50 per cent shareholder alleged wrongdoing by
other shareholder – Other shareholder presented winding-up petition – Whether
plaintiff was suing for ulterior motive – Whether winding up was alternative
remedy – Whether derivative action should be struck out.*

B

These were appeals from a judgment of Sir Mervyn Davies refusing motions to strike out
a derivative action by a 50 per cent shareholder in a company (see [1993] BCC 778).

The plaintiff sued four defendants: (1) "D", the other 50 per cent shareholder in the
company; (2) D's wife; (3) the company; and (4) another company owned and controlled by
D and his wife. The plaintiff complained that the fourth defendant company was acquired
by D and his wife for the purpose of acquiring assets rightly belonging to the company and
diverting business from the company and that business had been diverted; that D had
extracted cash from the company; and that D and his wife had paid themselves excessive
remuneration. The plaintiff's case was that it was impossible for her to set the company in
motion to bring the action because she had only an equal shareholding with D and D was
the sole director.

C

D

The defendants argued that the action was not a permissible derivative action because the
plaintiff had an alternative remedy. D had presented a winding-up petition on grounds of
insolvency and deadlock before the action was commenced. If a winding-up order was made
the question of proceedings against D could be considered by the liquidator. The defendants
also argued that the plaintiff was unlikely to be able to exercise independent and unbiased
judgment when conducting an action on the company's behalf and was therefore not a proper
person to bring the action. In particular it was said that while she had made claims against
D and his wife she had made no claim against her daughter although she was a director of
the company at the time and had allegedly benefited from the misappropriation of money.

E

Sir Mervyn Davies refused to strike out the action and directed it to be heard with the
winding-up petition. He held that (1) the company was prima facie entitled to the relief
claimed, (2) the plaintiff, although a 50 per cent shareholder, was able to bring a derivative
action, (3) winding up could not properly be described as an alternative remedy, and (4) the
plaintiff's personal attitude did not debar her from pursuing the action. The defendants
appealed.

F

The main debate in the Court of Appeal revolved around the applicability of the
proposition that a derivative action would not be allowed to proceed if brought for an
ulterior purpose or if another adequate remedy was available.

G

Held, allowing the appeal and striking out the action:

1. The plaintiff lacked the means to pursue the action further. As the company did have
some money which might be used in litigating the claims, it was better that the decision
whether or not to use the money should be taken by an independent liquidator rather than
the plaintiff. In the unusual circumstances of the case, the opportunity to put the company
into liquidation could be said to provide an alternative remedy which made the derivative
action inappropriate.

H

2. Personal rather than financial considerations appeared to be impelling the plaintiff to
pursue the action, in the outcome of which she would have no financial interest if the
company were insolvent, and in preventing a winding up when that would provide the only
practical means of obtaining some benefit from her shares if the company were in fact

A solvent. She was not pursuing the action bona fide on behalf of the company. If she had been, she would have sued her daughter no less than the petitioner in respect of the diverted moneys, whereas she was pursuing the other defendants as far as she could, regardless of whether there was any real likelihood of recovery. That was not a satisfactory basis for an action on behalf of the company.

The following cases were referred to in the judgments:

B *Ebrahimi v Westbourne Galleries Ltd & Ors* [1973] AC 360.
Fargro Ltd v Godfroy (1986) 2 BCC 99,167; [1986] 1 WLR 1134.
Ferguson v Wallbridge [1935] 3 DLR 66.
Nurcombe v Nurcombe & Anor (1984) 1 BCC 99,269; [1985] 1 WLR 370.
Wallersteiner v Moir (No. 2) [1975] QB 373.

Philip Cayford (instructed by Harris Rosenblatt & Kramer) for the first defendant.

C Anthony Mann QC (instructed by Ines de Vecchi) for the second and fourth defendants.

David Guy (instructed by Nathan Silman) for the plaintiff.

JUDGMENT

Peter Gibson LJ: This is a most unhappy case. On its face it is an action brought by a
D shareholder to right grievous wrongs done to the company of which she is a shareholder. But unfortunately the circumstances in which the action is brought and pursued include a bitter matrimonial dispute between the plaintiff's daughter and the primary defendant. That bitterness appears to have infected decisions taken in relation to these proceedings, added to which there has been a notable lack of realism on the part of the plaintiff and her advisers. The litigation, even though it has not progressed beyond certain interlocutory steps, appears to have exhausted the finances of the plaintiff and, while the
E amounts claimed for the company are large, to an objective observer the likelihood of significant recoveries seems very small indeed. The two individual defendants who have been served with the proceedings are on legal aid. The result so far is that this litigation has been ruinous to the plaintiff and has caused heavy costs to be incurred by the public purse.

The appeal is brought by the first defendant, Christopher Duckett ('Christopher'), the
F second defendant, Janet Duckett ('Janet') and the fourth defendant, Nightingale Coaches Ltd ('Coaches'), from the order of Sir Mervyn Davies, sitting as a judge of the High Court, on 28 July 1993 (see [1993] BCC 778). Those defendants had applied by motion to strike out or stay the action brought against them by the plaintiff, Elizabeth Barrett ('Mrs Barrett'), suing on behalf of the third defendant, Nightingale Travel Ltd ('Travel'), as well as herself. The judge by his order made no order on the motions and ordered that the action should be set down for hearing with a petition presented by Christopher for
G the winding up of Travel. The judge refused leave to appeal but such leave was granted by Hoffmann LJ.

Mrs Barrett is the widow of Mr A E Barrett and the mother of Carol Duckett ('Carol'). Carol was married to Christopher until their divorce on 11 February 1991. She was joined as a third party by Christopher and we have also been shown an order by the judge on 28 July 1993 by which she was made the fifth defendant and Christopher's
H father was made the sixth defendant in the action. This order has not been served on Carol or Christopher's father and the pleadings have not been amended to include claims against them.

Mr Barrett had carried on a coach hire business in his own name until Travel was incorporated in 1979 and took over that business. Christopher had worked for Mr Barrett and on Travel's incorporation he and Mr Barrett each took 50 of the 100 £1

shares in Travel and each became a director. On 19 February 1983 Mr Barrett died. Mrs A
Barrett inherited his shares and for 10 months was a director, but she resigned at the end
of 1983 when Carol became a director in her place. Christopher was the managing
director and the business expanded. Travel acquired and operated several bus routes,
Christopher holding the necessary certificate of competence. Travel earned profits
sufficient to provide Christopher and Carol with what Mrs Barrett called 'a good living'
and Mrs Barrett said that whilst their marriage subsisted she had no cause for concern
about the way in which Travel's business was being conducted. She has never received B
any dividends from her shares nor worked for Travel.

But in February 1989 Christopher's and Carol's marriage broke down. He started to
cohabit with Janet, then a certified accountant working for Travel's accountants. Later
that year he offered her a job with Travel as its accountant at an annual salary of £28,000
and she commenced work at the end of October 1989. She married Christopher in August
1991. That month she was appointed company secretary, a position which she still holds. C

Coaches was incorporated on 13 July 1990. It was acquired by Janet and Christopher,
each of whom took one £1 share, and was given the name Portledge Coaches Ltd, which
they changed to its present name on 8 January 1991. Janet was the sole director of
Coaches until December 1991, when she resigned as director and became the company
secretary of Coaches. Christopher then became the sole director until August 1992 when
he resigned and Janet and Christopher's father became the directors of Coaches. D
Christopher at that time also sold his one share to his father for £2,000.

In the divorce there are still unresolved ancillary relief proceedings, and it was in those
proceedings that Christopher revealed serious misfeasances which had been occurring.
He acknowledged that since October 1986 he had diverted cash receipts of Travel into
two Post Office Giro accounts, one in the joint names of himself and Carol and the other
in his sole name. Sums amounting to £89,000 were placed in the joint account and E
£128,000 in the sole account. Moreover those receipts were not recorded in the books or
accounts or tax returns of Travel. Part of those moneys was used in the refurbishment of
a second home for Christopher and Carol, 'The Noakes' in Herefordshire. Once the
diversions of Travel's moneys were revealed, draft accounts for Travel were prepared,
showing those moneys as directors' loans, and the Revenue were informed. Not only was
tax payable on those undeclared receipts but also such loans had adverse tax F
consequences, attracting as they did advance corporation tax in a substantial sum on
which interest ran until the loans were repaid, when there would be a right to recover the
tax and interest would cease to accrue. The commonsense solution was to extinguish the
loans as quickly as possible.

On the breakdown of the marriage, Carol had remained with Christopher's and her
two children in the jointly owned but heavily mortgaged matrimonial home in Gerrards G
Cross, while Christopher and Janet lived in another even more heavily mortgaged
property of which Janet is the beneficial owner. The one disposable asset available to
Christopher and Carol to reduce the debt to Travel was The Noakes. But Carol refused
to sell The Noakes. On 27 September 1990, however, Christopher and Carol met with
the Revenue and it was agreed that The Noakes should be transferred to Travel as soon
as possible. But Carol refused to cooperate with Christopher on this and other matters
relating to Travel; for example she refused to sign the accounts of Travel which could H
therefore not be filed, in breach of the directors' statutory duties. To break the impasse
Christopher attempted to have another director appointed in 1990, but Mrs Barrett
opposed this. However on 3 June 1991 in the matrimonial proceedings, Carol gave an
undertaking to the court to resign as director and secretary of Travel forthwith and to
transfer The Noakes to Travel. Despite the undertaking Carol refused to resign and it

A   was only after an application for her committal that she finally resigned on 17 August 1991, leaving Christopher as the sole director of Travel.

A further difficulty arose between Christopher and Carol over the operation of Travel's bank account on which Carol was a signatory. The defendants say that she continued throughout 1989 and 1990 to draw cheques on that account for her own purposes and the evidence from Janet before us is that over £20,000 of what was agreed with the Revenue to be treated as the directors' loan account is represented by such drawings.

B   Janet says that to enable Travel to have banking facilities, cheques payable to Travel from December 1990 were paid through Coaches' bank account, Coaches in turn paying cheques on behalf of Travel and supplying cash for wages; £308,000 was paid into Coaches' bank account in this way and, it is said by Janet, paid out by Coaches on Travel's behalf.

C   In the meantime there had been an offer by Travel to purchase Mrs Barrett's 50 shares for £40,000 in September 1989. Those negotiations failed, but on 24 April 1991 Mrs Barrett offered to sell her shares to Christopher for £70,000 plus a tax indemnity. Christopher offered £70,000 without the indemnity, but she gave as her price, if she had to pay capital gains tax, the sum of £85,000, which was increased to £90,000 on 17 July 1991. Intertwined with the sale of shares in these negotiations was the transfer of The Noakes to Travel, consent to which was sought from Mrs Barrett, who said she would

D   agree to it if the sale of her shares was agreed. But Christopher was unable to raise the purchase moneys demanded, and Mrs Barrett withheld her consent to the transfer and Carol hers to a sale of The Noakes. Christopher applied in the matrimonial proceedings for an order to compel Carol to sign a contract for the sale of The Noakes and on 24 February 1992 by a consent order Carol undertook to sign a sale contract and to allow the sale proceeds to go to Travel subject to a capital gains tax retention. Three months

E   later, alarmed by the risk of repossession of the matrimonial home because no mortgage payments had been made for some months, she successfully applied to the court to be released from her undertaking to allow the sale proceeds of The Noakes to go to Travel on the ground that it represented the only available capital with which she and her children could be rehoused if they lost their home. In December 1992 The Noakes was sold and the net proceeds of just under £100,000 are held on deposit in the joint names of the solicitors of Christopher and Janet pursuant to an order of the court. Thus although

F   Christopher had declared himself on 20 December 1990 a trustee for Travel of his interest in The Noakes, no part of the proceeds has gone to reduce the debt to Travel and interest on the tax on the directors' loans continues to accrue. On 29 May 1992 Travel's auditors advised it that the Revenue were owed £180,000, excluding penalties for the incorrect returns which have yet to be quantified.

G   In July 1992 the auditors advised Christopher that Travel might be insolvent and on their advice he consulted an insolvency practitioner in Pannell Kerr Forster ('PKF'). PKF advised on 10 August 1992 on the options for the company. They pointed out that to continue trading Travel needed continued support from the bank to which it owed £25,000 and that support was not forthcoming, the bank having requested repayment by the end of September 1992. They concluded that it would be difficult to continue trading in the long term and suggested asking the bank to appoint a receiver, which they accepted

H   it might well not be willing to do. They continued:

> 'this presents a problem to the director as on past performance Mrs E Barrett would not pass a resolution to wind up the company. The way round this would be for the director to petition the court to wind up the company due to a break down between the shareholders, the company being insolvent and no longer able to continue trading.'

That advice (in draft) had been received a little earlier and on 8 August 1992 Travel
ceased to trade. It sold to Coaches its tangible assets (including its vehicles subject to
hire-purchase liabilities taken over by Coaches) for £36,895, that being the value put on
the assets by an independent valuer. The purchase price was largely borrowed from a
bank on security provided by Christopher's father. Christopher called an extraordinary
general meeting of Travel at which he proposed that it enter a creditors' voluntary
winding up and that a partner in PKF be appointed liquidator. But as PKF correctly
forecast, that resolution was defeated by Mrs Barrett's opposition on 29 October 1992.
Accordingly on 13 November 1992 Christopher petitioned in the Leicester County Court
for the compulsory winding up of Travel. He did so on two grounds: one was that the
company was insolvent and unable to pay its debts as they fell due; the other was on the
just and equitable ground because of the deadlock position in which the company found
itself. The petition has been advertised, but no creditor has appeared to support it. Mrs
Barrett opposes the petition. The petition has been transferred to the High Court on the
order of Vinelott J.

An estimated statement of affairs at 29 October 1992 shows that Travel's assets at their
book value exceed its liabilities by £46,743. But that assumes that the directors will repay
their loan account of £239,000. Even if the proceeds of The Noakes were paid to the
company in part payment of the loans with a consequent reduction in the sum owed to
the Revenue, the liabilities would substantially exceed the assets in the absence of further
repayment of the loans.

On 11 March 1993 this action was commenced by the issue of a specially indorsed writ.
By the statement of claim Mrs Barrett states that she 'brings this action in a representative
capacity on behalf of Travel and/or on behalf of herself' and 'is an oppressed minority
shareholder and is entitled to bring this action to recover on behalf of Travel and/or on
behalf of herself'. Relief is sought under the following heads:

(A)   against Christopher, damages of at least £217,000, the moneys diverted into the
Post Office Giro accounts;

(B)   against Christopher and/or Janet, who is alleged to be a de facto director of Travel,
damages of at least £268,000, being as to £27,000 one year's pay to Janet and as to
the remainder remuneration paid to Christopher between 1986–87 and 1990–91,
no resolution having been passed by Travel for directors' remuneration;

(C)   against Christopher, Janet and Coaches, who are alleged to have entered into a
conspiracy together,

     (1)   damages of at least £308,000 (I have already referred to what Janet has said
of this sum);

     (2)   accounts and enquiries in respect of the transfer of assets (including
confidential information) from Travel to Coaches;

     (3)   declarations that the shares in Coaches are held for Travel and that the
assets of Coaches are held for Travel; and

     (4)   a declaration that Travel is entitled to an indemnity against any liability to
the Revenue arising out of the matters the subject of complaint.

On the same day Mrs Barrett moved ex parte for and obtained from Mummery J
injunctive relief in Mareva form and what may be called a modified Anton Piller form,
that is to say requiring the immediate disclosure of the whereabouts of documents
comprising all the financial records of Travel and Coaches for the period 1 November
1989 to 31 October 1992. The applications were supported by an affidavit in which Mrs
Barrett swore to her belief that Christopher, Janet and Coaches would seek to hide or
destroy documents. One curious feature in respect of this order is the fact that on 19
January 1993 a draft affidavit to be sworn by Mrs Barrett in the winding-up proceedings

A and exhibiting a draft statement of claim for the intended Chancery proceedings (the draft being in almost identical form to that actually issued) was served on Christopher. I find it difficult to believe that Mummery J could have had his attention drawn to the fact that for more than seven weeks Christopher had been alerted to the allegations against him.

B The order made by Mummery J was executed and Mrs Barrett obtained access to the records of Travel and Coaches which she sought. An affidavit was sworn by Christopher verifying his and Travel's assets. He has an equal interest with Carol in the former matrimonial home in Gerrards Cross, but because of the increasing mortgage arrears as well as 'heave' problems, it is doubtful what that interest is worth, if anything. He has an interest under Travel's pension scheme, but it is inherently improbable that he could presently obtain any moneys therefrom. He has already declared himself a trustee for Travel of his interest in The Noakes and so has no interest in its proceeds. Apart from C that he has 50 shares in Travel. Janet has sworn an affidavit verifying her and Coaches' assets. She owns the equity of the house where Christopher and she live but the equity in it is only said to be worth some £20,000–£30,000. She has no other assets apart from her one share in Coaches. Coaches has vehicles worth £80,000 (subject to hire-purchase liabilities) and its cash at its bank less its debt to the bank is £7,000. Christopher, Janet and Coaches promptly applied to discharge Mummery J's order, but that application has D not yet been heard.

On 9 June 1993 Christopher, Janet and Coaches issued their notices of motion to strike out the action or to stay it until after the hearing of the winding-up petition presented by Christopher. They did so on the basis that an alternative remedy to the derivative action existed and that Mrs Barrett is an inappropriate person to conduct such litigation on behalf of the company. Janet also applied under O. 18, r. 19 to strike out the claims made against her as a de facto director. The judge rejected those claims, holding that the E practical course was to list the action for hearing with the petition.

The general principles governing actions in respect of wrongs done to a company or irregularities in the conduct of its affairs are not in dispute:

(1)   The proper plaintiff is prima facie the company.

(2)   Where the wrong or irregularity might be made binding on the company by a
F   simple majority of its members, no individual shareholder is allowed to maintain an action in respect of that matter.

(3)   There are however recognised exceptions, one of which is where the wrongdoer has control which is or would be exercised to prevent a proper action being brought against the wrongdoer: in such a case the shareholder may bring a derivative action (his rights being derived from the company) on behalf of the company.

G (4)   When a challenge is made to the right claimed by a shareholder to bring a derivative action on behalf of the company, it is the duty of the court to decide as a preliminary issue the question whether or not the plaintiff should be allowed to sue in that capacity.

(5)   In taking that decision it is not enough for the court to say that there is no plain and obvious case for striking out; it is for the shareholder to establish to the
H   satisfaction of the court that he should be allowed to sue on behalf of the company.

(6)   The shareholder will be allowed to sue on behalf of the company if he is bringing the action bona fide for the benefit of the company for wrongs to the company for which no other remedy is available. Conversely if the action is brought for an ulterior purpose or if another adequate remedy is available, the court will not allow the derivative action to proceed.

Although Mrs Barrett is not a minority shareholder but a person holding the same   A
number of shares as the other shareholder, Christopher, in the circumstances of this case
she can be treated as being under the same disability as a minority shareholder in that as
a practical matter it would not have been possible for her to set the company in motion
to bring the action.

The debate before the judge and before us has largely turned on the applicability of the
propositions in para. 6 to the facts of the case, and because of their importance I will   B
illustrate those propositions by reference to three authorities.

First on the necessity for the absence of an ulterior purpose, the words of Lawton LJ
in *Nurcombe v Nurcombe* (1984) 1 BCC 99,269 at p. 99,273 are apposite:

> 'It is pertinent to remember, however, that a minority shareholder's action in form
> is nothing more than a procedural device for enabling the court to do justice to a
> company controlled by miscreant directors or shareholders. Since the procedural
> device has evolved so that justice can be done for the benefit of the company,   C
> whoever comes forward to start the proceedings must be doing so for the benefit
> of the company and not for some other purpose. It follows that the court has to
> satisfy itself that the person coming forward is a proper person to do so.'

Second on the availability of alternative remedies, there are two authorities on the
effect of liquidation in relation to a derivative action. In *Ferguson v Wallbridge* [1935] 3
DLR 66 Lord Blanesburgh delivering the judgment of the Privy Council said at p. 83:   D

> 'in their Lordships' judgment, [the present action] could have been so maintained
> if the company were not in liquidation. *Cook v Deeks* (1916) 27 D.L.R. 1 is clear
> authority for this. But could it be so maintained now that the company is assumed
> to be in liquidation? And the answer must again, as their Lordships think, be in
> the negative.

> The permissibility of the form of proceedings thus assumed, where the company   E
> concerned is a going concern, is an excellent illustration of the golden principle
> that procedure with its rules is the handmaid and not the mistress of justice. The
> form of action so authorised is necessitated by the fact that in the case of such a
> claim as was successfully made by the plaintiff in *Cook v Deeks* – and there is at
> least a family likeness between that case and this – justice would be denied to him
> if the mere possession of the company's seal in the hands of his opponents were to   F
> prevent the assertion at his instance of the corporate rights of the company as
> against them. But even in the case of a going company a minority shareholder is
> not entitled to proceed in a representative action if he is unable to show when
> challenged that he has exhausted every effort to secure the joinder of the company
> as plaintiff and has failed. But *cessante ratione legis, cessat lex ipsa*. So soon as the
> company goes into liquidation the necessity for any such expedient in procedure
> disappears. Passing over the superficial difficulty that a company in compulsory   G
> liquidation cannot be proceeded against without the leave of the court, the real
> complainants, the minority shareholders, are no longer at the mercy of the
> majority, wrongly retaining the property of the company by the strength of their
> votes. If the liquidator, acting at the behest of the majority, refuses when requested
> to take action in the name of the company against them, it is open to any
> contributory to apply to the court.' – and then he refers to the Canadian statute –   H
> 'And under section 234 of the Provincial Companies Act, which corresponds to
> section 252 of the Companies Act 1929' – now s. 112 of the *Insolvency Act* 1986 –
> 'it is open to the court, on cause shown, either to direct the liquidator to proceed
> in the company's name or on proper terms as to indemnity, and otherwise give to
> the applicant leave to use the company's name as plaintiff in any action necessary
> to be brought for the vindication of the company's rights.'

A   That reasoning was applied by Walton J in *Fargro Ltd v Godfroy* (1986) 2 BCC 99,167. In that case a minority shareholder in a company which was deadlocked wished to bring a derivative action, alleging that the other shareholder and directors had diverted assets and opportunities belonging to the company to their own use. Before the writ was issued the company went into liquidation. When the plaintiff issued the writ, the defendants applied to strike out. The application succeeded. Walton J said at p. 99,169:

B   'But once the company goes into liquidation the situation is completely changed, because one no longer has a board, or indeed a shareholders' meeting, which is in any sense in control of the activities of the company of any description, let alone its litigation. Here, what has happened is that the liquidator is now the person in whom that right is vested.

Now, that being the case, the plaintiff can take a variety of courses. The plaintiff can ask the liquidator to bring the action in the name of the company. Doubtless, as in virtually all cases, the liquidator will require an indemnity from the persons who wish to set the company in motion against all the costs, including, of course, the costs of the defendant, which he may have to incur in bringing that action. The liquidator may ask for unreasonable terms or, on the other hand, the liquidator may be unwilling to bring the action, and under those circumstances it is always possible for the shareholders who wish the action to be brought to go to the court asking for an order either that the liquidator bring the action in the name of the company or, more usually, that they are given the right to bring the action in the name of the company, of course, against the usual type of indemnity, which will, if there is any difficulty about the matter, be settled by the court. And I think that this has been the practice and procedure for a very long time indeed.'

He then cited *Ferguson v Wallbridge* and commented:

E   'So there is clear authority in the Privy Council as to the vast distinction that there is between the position where the company is a going concern and the minority shareholders' action can be brought, and a case where, when it goes into liquidation, there is no longer any necessity for bringing a minority shareholders' action. Because, subject if necessary to obtaining the directions of the court, which is in itself an excellent thing as acting as a filter against any totally wrong-headed action, the action can be brought directly in the name of the company as it should be so brought.'

In the *Fargro* case the liquidator had in fact agreed to bring the action, but it is clear from the reasoning of both Lord Blanesburgh and Walton J that even if the liquidator's views were unknown the derivative action would not be allowed to proceed. The obvious factual difference between *Fargro* and the present case is that Travel, unlike the company in *Fargro*, was not in liquidation at the time the derivative action was commenced. I shall return later to the question whether this difference is of crucial importance in the present case.

At this point it is convenient to rehearse what seem to me to be the salient features of this case.

1. Mrs Barrett was until the breakdown of her daughter's marriage a merely passive shareholder, taking no part after 1983 in the running of Travel. She received no dividends from her holding in the company. Her only prospect of obtaining a benefit from her shares has been and is if there were to be a winding up or a sale of her shares to Christopher or the company. It is inconceivable that an outside purchaser could be found for her shares alone. At an extraordinary general meeting of Travel on 16 June 1992, her accountant and proxy, Mr Wellstood, when asked whether she was aware that her refusal to consent to the transfer of The Noakes into Travel effectively reduced her shareholding

in the company to a negligible value whilst also putting the company at risk, replied that   A
she did understand this and had written off her interest in Travel.

2. For a considerable time after being aware of the conduct of Travel's affairs of which complaint is now made by her and which plainly could be said to have been conduct in a manner which was unfairly prejudicial to her interest as a shareholder, she took no legal action, but participated in active negotiations for the sale of her shares which she offered to sell. That was a realistic attitude as she is a lady of 73 and no one has been put forward   B
as available to run the company other than Christopher. But when those negotiations broke down on price, despite having professional advisers she did not avail herself of what one would have thought was the plain and obvious legal remedy available to her, namely a petition under s. 459 of the *Companies Act* 1985, asking for relief under s. 461(2)(d), viz. the purchase of her shares, with the alternative, if she thought the company should be recovering what had wrongly been taken from it, of seeking relief   C
under s. 461(2)(c), viz. authority for civil proceedings to be brought in the name and on behalf of the company by such person or persons and on such terms as the court may direct.

3. Travel is deadlocked, has not traded since August 1992 and is probably insolvent. On the evidence before this court Christopher and Carol are unable to repay the directors' loans in full.

4. When Christopher attempted to put Travel into a creditors' voluntary liquidation,   D
Mrs Barrett prevented it.

5. Christopher's attempt to put Travel into compulsory liquidation is opposed by Mrs Barrett because she says that she believes Travel has a future. But that future depends on her succeeding in her claim that the shares in and assets of Coaches are held in trust for Travel and also that Mr Wellstood is right in his advice to Mrs Barrett in an unsworn report made by him on 27 May 1993 after the action commenced and after examination   E
of the documents produced by the order of 11 March 1993. In it he said that had Travel's business been offered for sale on the open market:

> 'I suspect that a price of six times pre-tax profits (that is the adjusted profit after adding back excess remuneration, etc.) would have been established, giving a value of approximately £400,000.'

I have to say that I regard that suspicion which is based on a large number of assumptions, as unrealistically optimistic given that it is through Christopher holding a   F
certificate of competence that bus routes have been and are operated and that Christopher appears to have no service agreement with Travel (or Coaches for that matter).

6. It was only after Christopher's attempts to put Travel into liquidation that Mrs Barrett belatedly commenced this action. Thereby she has demonstrated that she is not content that it should be left to a liquidator to bring proceedings but that she wants   G
control of such proceedings.

7. Travel has arguable claims against Christopher, Janet and Coaches, and some against Christopher are undisputed. There is however dispute as to whether some particular claims are arguable. For example, on the evidence before this court it may be doubted whether Mrs Barrett's advisers, in causing her to claim damages of £308,000, have understood what occurred in relation to the £308,000, and Janet hotly denies ever acting as de facto director. But it is unnecessary to decide these disputes, given that it is   H
conceded that there are claims which in a properly constituted action should be allowed to go to trial.

8. Travel has arguable claims against Carol. In Mrs Barrett's own words (in her affidavit of 1 March 1993 in support of her application for Mareva and Anton Piller injunctions):

A   'It would seem that . . . . [Christopher] and, to a lesser extent Carol, have diverted funds or stolen moneys belonging to Travel and have thereby caused Travel to incur a very large liability for advance corporation tax, interest and, probably, associated fines and/or penalties.'

9. Mrs Barrett has no moneys of her own to continue this action. She says that she incurred legal costs prior to 28 July 1993 of £52,000 which used up her life savings. Surprisingly in view of *Wallersteiner v Moir (No. 2)* [1975] QB 373 at pp. 392 and 400, she was granted legal aid until the certificate was discharged on 8 April 1994. She has applied to this court (but we have not yet heard the application) for an order that Travel should indemnify her for the costs which she has expended and will have to expend in this action, this appeal and that application. The only moneys presently available to Travel are the £36,895 proceeds of the sale to Coaches.

10. Mrs Barrett remains close to Carol and as she frankly acknowledged in her affidavit of 1 June 1993:

'I would be less than truthful if I were to deny that I was reluctant to sue my own daughter.'

The joinder of Carol as a defendant to the action remains, in the absence of amendment of the statement of claim to include claims against her and in the absence of service of proceedings on Carol, a token gesture.

Mr Anthony Mann QC for Janet and Coaches and Mr Cayford for Christopher point out that the circumstances of the present case are unprecedented. In all the reported cases on derivative actions the wrongdoer has by his exercise of control over the company prevented proceedings being brought against him, whereas in the present case the alleged wrongdoer, by trying to put the company into liquidation, has attempted before the action commenced and is attempting to create a situation where the allegedly oppressed minority shareholder is no longer at the mercy of the controlling shareholder and director. In my judgment the court is entitled to view with suspicion and caution the actions of the alleged wrongdoer lest on their true interpretation they are no more than attempts to defeat or at least to defer judgment being obtained against him. But in the present case it is significant that Christopher's attempts to put the company into liquidation (1) came after a long period of deadlock during which he was frustrated in his attempt to put The Noakes or its proceeds into Travel to reduce the directors' loan account and the tax debt, (2) followed advice from an insolvency practitioner in a well-known firm of accountants, and (3) preceded not only the commencement of the action but also any intimation that the action would be commenced.

Mr Guy for Mrs Barrett submitted that the judge was right to reject the contention that she had another available remedy through proceedings in the liquidation of Travel.

G   First he said that it was not certain that Travel would be wound up on Christopher's petition. But that ignores the fact that Mrs Barrett was given, but rejected, the opportunity to have Travel put into a creditors' voluntary liquidation, and whilst I accept that it is possible that the court in the exercise of its discretion would not on an opposed petition compulsorily wind up the company when the petitioner is the alleged wrongdoer, that possibility is only a live one because of her opposition. Even if she continued to oppose the petition, the court may be driven to accept that there is no alternative to a winding up, given the apparent insolvency and worsening financial position of Travel while further interest accrues to the Revenue and given the deadlock in the company.

Second, Mr Guy supported the judge's comment that there was no certainty that the liquidator would sue and that Mrs Barrett had no means of compelling him to sue. Mr Guy said that the liquidator needed to incur the cost of applying to the court to sue. It is of course correct that the liquidator has a discretion. A liquidator in a compulsory liquidation can bring an action with the approval of either the liquidation committee or the court (s. 167(1) of the *Insolvency Act* 1986). If Mrs Barrett is aggrieved by the decision of such a liquidator, she can apply to the court under s. 168(5). In the case of a voluntary winding up, the liquidator is not obliged to obtain the sanction of the court or liquidation committee to bring any proceedings (para. 4 of Sch. 4 to the 1986 Act) and an aggrieved contributory has power to apply to the court under s. 112(1). But in any event it is apparent from the reasoning of Lord Blanesburgh in the *Ferguson* case and of Walton J in the *Fargro* case that the fact that a liquidator has a discretion in relation to the bringing of an action is no answer to the objection based on the availability of an alternative remedy. No doubt the liquidator may be inhibited from pursuing claims by the shortage of available funds and may seek an indemnity from Mrs Barrett if she wants him to pursue claims which the assets available to him would not justify. But I see no injustice in that. On her own evidence she lacks the means to pursue this action further. As the company does have some money which might be used in litigating the claims, it is in my opinion manifest that it is better that the decision whether or not to use the money should be taken by an independent liquidator rather than by Mrs Barrett.

I therefore conclude that in the unusual circumstances of this case, the opportunity that Travel be put into liquidation which was offered and continues to be offered by Christopher can be said to provide an alternative remedy such as makes the derivative action inappropriate.

But the matter does not stop there. I turn to the second ground on which Mr Mann and Mr Cayford submit that this action should not be allowed to proceed, namely that Mrs Barrett has an ulterior motive which makes her an inappropriate person to bring these proceedings. On this the judge commented:

> 'No doubt there is ill feeling between Mrs Barrett and Mr Duckett but that in itself cannot debar Mrs Barrett – were it to do so, most derivative actions would be frustrated.'

I see the force of that, but I am not persuaded that it is a sufficient answer to the point put against her in the light of the particular circumstances. Here I repeat what I have referred to as the salient features of this case. Personal rather than financial considerations would appear to be impelling her to pursue an action, in the outcome of which she would have no financial interest if the company were insolvent, and in preventing a winding up when that would provide the only practical means of obtaining some benefit from her shares if the company were in fact solvent.

I can well understand that Mrs Barrett is upset at what has occurred between Christopher and Carol and that she is indignant at the supplanting of Carol by Janet. But her partiality shows through all her evidence, and it is by her behaviour in relation to the claims against Carol, in contrast to the claims against Christopher and Janet, that I have become convinced that she is not pursuing this action bona fide on behalf of the company. If she had been, she would have had to sue Carol no less than Christopher in respect of diverted moneys. She claims that she did not sue Carol because Carol does not have any assets. But when Mr Guy was asked what assets Christopher had to make him worth suing, the first two items listed by Mr Guy were the jointly owned former matrimonial home in Gerrards Cross and the proceeds of The Noakes in each of which Carol retains her interest. Mr Guy sought to assure us that now that the decision had been made to sue Carol, the action would proceed against her. I am afraid that I simply do not believe that Mrs Barrett would pursue any claim against her daughter to the point of enforcing judgment: to my mind it is improbable in the extreme that she would force her daughter and grandchildren out of their home and I quite understand why she would not. Her failure to take the order making Carol a defendant any further speaks volumes. On the other hand I do not doubt that she would pursue the other defendants as far as

A   she could, regardless of whether there is any real likelihood of recovery. This is not a satisfactory basis for an action on behalf of the company.

I am left in no doubt that this is an action which should not be allowed to proceed. Hoffmann LJ in giving leave to appeal said:

B
> 'As a matter of common sense, it seems arguable that the parties should not be subjected to lengthy and costly proceedings exacerbated by family hostilities when an independent liquidator might decide that the action could be settled on reasonable terms.'

I entirely agree with such argument. I hope that even now Mrs Barrett will agree to a voluntary winding up to save costs and that she will promptly give the liquidator the benefit of all the work that has been done in this case on her behalf to facilitate any proceedings which he may wish to pursue.

C
For these reasons I respectfully differ from the judge in his conclusions. I would allow the appeal and strike out this action.

Beldam LJ: In this unprofitable litigation a once successful family venture has been brought to ruin by false accounting and tax evasion for which Christopher Duckett must bear the main responsibility. The company's resulting insolvency could perhaps have been retrieved had not Carol Duckett been supplanted as wife and director by Janet
D   Duckett. The impasse in the company's affairs is a predictable result, as is Mrs Barrett's desire, so far as she could, to ensure that Christopher and Janet Duckett should not deprive her daughter and grandchildren of a share in the profits of the business of the company her husband had built up and in which she held 50 per cent of the shares. Mrs Barrett may not have been well advised on the choice of the steps available to her; her daughter may have gone back on an undertaking to assist in the transfer to the company of 'The Noakes', though the court undoubtedly considered she had grounds which
E   justified releasing her from the undertaking. For all this, I am unimpressed by the criticisms voiced by counsel for Christopher and Janet Duckett. It does not lie well in the mouth of those who have effectively ousted Mrs Barrett's family from sharing in the profits of the company to be critical of her, or to question her motives. Nevertheless with reluctance, rather than by persuasion by the argument, I too have reached the conclusion that the action brought by Mrs Barrett should not proceed. I have sympathy for the
F   dilemma which faced the judge and as I am differing from his solution I shall state my reasons.

Between 1986 and 1990 a sum of £212,500 was diverted from the company's trading receipts into private accounts of the directors, Christopher and Carol Duckett. These substantial depredations seem to have escaped the notice of the company's accountants and auditors and only came to light when, in divorce proceedings between Christopher
G   and Carol Duckett, her claim to ancillary relief for herself and the children was vigorously contested. It appears that Christopher Duckett was then advised by the company's accountants to disclose this dishonesty to the Inland Revenue and to seek the advice of insolvency practitioners. The result was an insolvency practitioner's report of 10 August 1992 with attached estimate of the state of affairs of the company showing the debt due from the directors under the cosmetic sobriquet 'Directors' loan account, £240,000'. To
H   this arrangement it is said the Inland Revenue agreed. I find it difficult to see how this sum could legitimately be regarded as a loan made by the company to the directors when by s. 330 of the *Companies Act* 1985 the company would have been prohibited from making it. As appears from the affidavits put before the court, there is no reasonable prospect of either of the directors making any significant reduction in this debt. The company is insolvent and has ceased to trade. The principal creditor appears to have decided to let matters drift.

Peter Gibson LJ has fully described the events leading up to Mrs Barrett's resistance   A
to a creditor's voluntary winding up and to the presentation of the winding-up petition
by Christopher Duckett. Those events do not persuade me that the absence of merit on
her part exceeds that of the other parties in this dispute.

If, as the judge decided, both the derivative action and the winding-up petition were to
continue, the result would be even more wasteful of the company's meagre resources than
the proceedings to date. Neither the action nor the petition would inevitably resolve the   B
stalemate. Ultimately, I think, the court would be required to choose between allowing
the plaintiff to pursue the company's remedies when she has not and could not
realistically be expected to pursue them with the impartiality necessary for such an action
or having to accede to a petition to wind up the company by a director whose criminal
conduct has instigated its insolvency, a question which clearly troubled Vinelott J when
he heard the application to transfer the petition to London. The public interest lies in
adopting the course which is most likely to recover the revenue of which it has been   C
defrauded.

Whilst it will be for the court hearing the winding-up petition to decide if the order can
be justified on either of the grounds put forward by Christopher Duckett, I find difficulty
in understanding how it could be said to be just and equitable for the court to wind up
the company in these circumstances. In *Re Westbourne Galleries Ltd* [1973] AC 360 Lord
Wilberforce, after reviewing the authorities which led to the adoption of the words 'just   D
and equitable' in company and partnership law, said at p. 379B:

> 'The words are a recognition of the fact that a limited company is more than a
> legal entity, with a personality in law of its own: that there is room in company law
> for recognition of the fact that behind it, or amongst it, there are individuals, with
> rights, expectations and obligations inter se which are not necessarily submerged
> in the company structure. That structure is defined by the Companies Act and by   E
> the articles of association by which shareholders agree to be bound. In most
> companies and in most contexts, this definition is sufficient and exhaustive, equally
> so where the company is large or small. The "just and equitable" provision does
> not, as the respondents suggest, entitle one party to disregard the obligation he
> assumes by entering a company, nor the court to dispense him from it. It does, as
> equity always does, enable the court to subject the exercise of legal rights to
> equitable considerations; considerations, that is, of a personal character arising   F
> between one individual and another, which may make it unjust, or inequitable, to
> insist on legal rights, or to exercise them in a particular way.'

In the circumstances of this case the court could hardly decide that it is just and
equitable for a defaulting director to exercise his right to petition to wind up this company
if it is opposed by another and equal shareholder. As Lord Cross said in the same case at
p. 387G: G

> 'A petitioner who relies on the "just and equitable" clause must come to court with
> clean hands, and if the breakdown in confidence between him and the other parties
> to the dispute appears to have been due to his misconduct he cannot insist on the
> company being wound up if they wish it to continue.'

Nor do I think it relevant in the circumstances of this case that Mrs Barrett was a   H
'passive' shareholder, content to receive no dividend from her holding, until her daughter
was ousted from the company by the arrival of Janet Duckett. It is not suggested that
Mrs Barrett was aware that the company's receipts were being diverted for the purpose
of evading tax. She was no doubt content that her daughter and grandchildren should
receive any benefits which might otherwise have accrued to her in the form of a dividend
on her shares.

A   As to the other ground on which the petition is based, the company is undoubtedly insolvent. Both Christopher and Carol Duckett are liable to the company for the majority of the deficiency. The company has ceased trading as its assets and goodwill have been transferred to Nightingale Coaches Ltd. The company's only additional 'asset' is its undeniable cause of action against its former directors and the possibility of a claim against Janet Duckett. If a liquidator were appointed, he would be bound to proceed against the former directors and would no doubt obtain summary judgment. Any claim
B   against Janet Duckett and Nightingale Coaches Ltd is more problematical and its pursuit would require resources which neither the company nor Mrs Barrett have. A decision whether to pursue the claim in the interests of the company having regard to the limited resources available is, in my judgment, better left to a liquidator. But there still remains the difficult question whether it is an insuperable bar to the making of a winding-up order on the ground that the company is insolvent that its insolvency was caused by the conduct
C   of the petitioning director in taking the company's moneys and by his inability to pay them back.

    I am not convinced that in all circumstances a director's past wrongdoing should be regarded as a bar to his presenting a winding-up petition. It is not in the public interest to deter those who have defrauded the Revenue from coming forward to admit their wrongdoing. Although the disclosure in the present case was prompted rather by
D   necessity than conscience, if a winding-up order is made a liquidator would be in a position to ensure so far as he could that Christopher and Carol Duckett fulfilled their obligation to reimburse the company. No doubt some of the earnings which accrue to Christopher Duckett from the use of the assets acquired from the company could be used for this purpose.

    In their original application before the judge all the appellants applied for an order that Mrs Barrett's action either be struck out or stayed. At one time I was attracted to
E   the latter course but, on reflection, I consider that the public interest in recovering the misappropriated assets would be better served by dismissing her action and allowing the winding-up petition to continue.

    Russell LJ: I agree that this appeal should be allowed and Mrs Barrett's action struck out for all the reasons appearing in the judgment of Peter Gibson LJ.

F   (*Appeal allowed. Plaintiff to pay costs in Court of Appeal and below (save in relation to the period 29 July 1993–8 April 1994). No order as to indemnity*)

G

H

Adams v R.

Privy Council.
Lord Templeman, Lord Jauncey of Tullichettle, Lord Browne-Wilkinson, Lord Woolf, Lord Lloyd of Berwick.
Judgment delivered 31 October 1994.

Appeal against conviction for conspiracy to defraud – Elements of offence – Directors' duties – Whether directors were under a duty to disclose information to company – Effect of dishonest concealment of information.

This was an appeal against a New Zealand Court of Appeal decision upholding the appellant's conviction for conspiring to defraud the company of which he was a director.

The appellant was the deputy chairman of 'EHL', the holding company of a group which was placed in statutory receivership. The appellant was charged with a number of offences. The appeal was concerned with a charge of conspiring to defraud any one or more of EHL, its subsidiary companies and others by using dishonestly a system of disguising the source and utilisation of moneys from legitimate inquiry by the use of off-shore companies and bank accounts. That system was referred to as the Yeoman Loop and there were five transactions which made use of it. The Court of Appeal was satisfied that there was ample evidence enabling the inference to be drawn beyond reasonable doubt that the appellant had agreed to the Loop being set up and used for the purpose of concealing the origin and use of money received and that such concealment was fraudulent. The court went on to hold that the Loop was fraudulent because it made it difficult for the company's other directors and its auditors to conduct legitimate inquiries into the source of the moneys concerned to ascertain whether the group had any interest in them. The appellant argued that this went too far and that a conspiracy to defraud required a fraudulent act or omission adversely affecting an interest of the person to be defrauded. The appellant further argued that since he was not found to have acted dishonestly in relation to the funds which formed the subject of any of the five transactions, one of the ingredients necessary to a conviction for conspiracy to defraud was missing; it was not enough that the use of the Yeoman Loop had been found by the judge to be dishonest.

The Court of Appeal had quashed the appellant's conviction on another count relating to dishonestly obtaining shares in one of the company's subsidiaries. In doing so the court referred to a practice whereby sales of shares to directors were not formally notified to the board nor recorded, as supporting an honest belief that no disclosure to the board was called for. The appellant argued that the Court of Appeal had failed to take into account the effect which the acquittal on that charge had upon the appellant's conviction on the charge in question.

Held, dismissing the appeal:

1. A person was not prejudiced if he was hindered in inquiring into the source of moneys in which he had no interest. Where possible economic loss was concerned there had to be some right or interest in the victim which was capable of being prejudiced whether by actual loss or by being put at risk.

2. The existence of a practice of non-disclosure involving breach of fiduciary duty did not per se absolve those operating the practice from dishonesty. If non-disclosure would have been dishonest, but for the practice, they could not rely on that practice which they had instituted to negative dishonesty. The Court of Appeal was in error in concluding that there was no obligation to disclose the dealings with the subsidiary's shares. Hence the quashing of the appellant's conviction on that count did not affect his conviction on the conspiracy to defraud count.

3. The appellant as a director of EHL and some of its subsidiaries was under a duty, when entering into a transaction with those companies or when using the resources of the

A   companies for his own benefit, to act with perfect good faith and to make full disclosure to
     the company in question of all material circumstances. Since a company was entitled to
     recover from directors secret profits made by them at the company's expense, it would follow
     that any dishonest agreement by directors to impede a company in the exercise of its right
     of recovery would constitute a conspiracy to defraud. A person could be guilty of fraud when
     he dishonestly concealed information from another which he was under a duty to disclose to
     that other or which that other was entitled to require him to disclose. (R v Governor of
B   Pentonville Prison, ex parte Tarling (1978) 70 Cr App R 77 distinguished.)

     4. It followed that the appellant, having been party to the use of the Yeoman Loop in the
     case of four out of the five transactions for the purpose of dishonest concealment of
     information which, as a director, he was under a duty to disclose to the company, was
     properly convicted.

C   The following cases were referred to in the judgment:

     Aberdeen Railway Co v Blaikie Bros (1854) 1 Macq HL 461.
     R v Governor of Pentonville Prison, ex parte Tarling (1978) 70 Cr App R 77.
     R v Scott [1975] AC 819.
     R v Terry [1984] AC 374.
     Wai Yu-tsang v R [1992] 1 AC 269.
     Welham v DPP [1961] AC 103.

D   John McLinden and Suzanne Clark (both New Zealand Bar) (instructed by
     Cruickshanks) for the appellant.

     WGGA Young QC and M A Woolford (both New Zealand Bar) (instructed by
     Allen & Overy) for the Crown.

                                      JUDGMENT
E   (Delivered by Lord Jauncey of Tullichettle)

     This appeal from the New Zealand Court of Appeal relates to the dramatic rise and
     fall of the fortunes of the Equiticorp group of companies. Equiticorp Holdings Ltd
     ('EHL'), which was the holding company of the group, was formed in March 1984 and
     went public in June of that year. Its accounts, as at 31 March 1987, showed total assets
     of $2.167 billion and a group net profit after tax of $104.9m. On 22 January 1989 the
     whole group was placed into statutory receivership and the shares in EHL became
F   worthless. Throughout the period Allan Robert Hawkins was the chairman of directors
     and managing director of EHL and from the outset he or companies associated with him
     controlled 40 per cent of the shares in EHL. During the same period Grant Adams, the
     appellant, was deputy chairman of EHL and either chairman or director of other
     companies in the group. Maxwell Colin Taylor was initially company secretary of EHL
     and became a director in 1985. Russell John Curtayne joined EHL in September 1985
G   and became, on 1 April 1986, general manager of the investment group of companies
     within the Equiticorp group. Kevin James Gillespie and Ian Lindsay Gunthorp were also
     executive directors, the former until July 1987, the latter until the group was placed into
     statutory receivership. These six men formed what was known as the investment team
     which dealt inter alia with all major investment projects for the group. There were in
     addition three other executive directors and three non-executive directors whom it is
     convenient to describe collectively as the independent directors. The solicitor to EHL was
H   Robert Paul Darvell who was a senior partner in Rudd Watts and Stone ('RWS'), one of
     the largest legal firms in New Zealand.

     Consequent upon the collapse of EHL the Crown preferred an indictment containing
     thirteen counts against the six members of the investment team and Mr Darvell. Not
     every individual was concerned in each count and it is sufficient for the purposes of this
     appeal to refer only to those in which the appellant was concerned. Nevertheless having

referred by name to all the persons who were charged it is right to point out that Taylor,   **A**
Gillespie and Darvell were ultimately acquitted of all the counts relating to them. The
counts relating to the appellant were in the following terms:

'*Count 1*

The Solicitor-General charges that Allan Robert Hawkins, Grant Adams, Maxwell
Colin Taylor, Russell John Curtayne and Robert Paul Darvell between 1
December 1986 and 28 February 1988, at Auckland and elsewhere, did conspire   **B**
with one or more of the others by deceit, falsehood and other fraudulent means to
defraud any one or more of Equiticorp Holdings Ltd, its subsidiary companies
and others in that they did agree to use dishonestly a system of disguising the
source and utilisation of moneys from legitimate inquiry by the use of off-shore
companies and bank accounts and Rudd Watts and Stone.

Count 2   **C**

The Solicitor-General further charges that Allan Robert Hawkins, Grant Adams,
Maxwell Colin Taylor, Kevin James Gillespie, Ian Lindsay Gunthorp, Russell
John Curtayne and Robert Paul Darvell between 1 November 1986 and 31 October
1987, at Auckland and elsewhere, did conspire with one or more of the others by
deceit, falsehood and other fraudulent means to defraud any one or more of
Equiticorp Holdings Ltd, Equiticorp Finance Group Ltd, Beid Pty Ltd, Equiticorp   **D**
Tasman Ltd and Feltex International Ltd in that they did agree to obtain
dishonestly for themselves, other than Robert Paul Darvell or for associated
interests, the benefit of funds derived from the Equiticorp group of companies,
being management fees paid by Equiticorp Tasman Ltd and Feltex International
Ltd.

Count 4   **E**

The Solicitor-General further charges that Allan Robert Hawkins, Grant Adams,
Maxwell Colin Taylor, Kevin James Gillespie, Ian Lindsay Gunthorp, Russell
John Curtayne and Robert Paul Darvell between 1 October 1986 and 30 November
1987, at Auckland and elsewhere, did conspire with one or more of the others by
deceit, falsehood and other fraudulent means to defraud any one or more of
Equiticorp Holdings Ltd, Equiticorp Industries Group Ltd and Equiticorp
Investments (Hong Kong) Ltd in that they did agree to obtain dishonestly for   **F**
themselves, other than Robert Paul Darvell or for associated interests, shares and
warrants in Keady Ltd and the benefits of their realisation.'

After a six-month trial before Tompkins J sitting in the High Court without a jury the
verdicts on these counts were as follows: count 1; Hawkins, the appellant and Curtayne
guilty, Taylor and Darvell not guilty; count 2: Hawkins, Gunthorp and Curtayne guilty,
the appellant and Taylor and Gillespie not guilty; count 4: Hawkins, the appellant and   **G**
Taylor guilty, the remaining accused not guilty.

The Court of Appeal quashed the convictions of Hawkins, the appellant and Taylor
on count 4 but upheld their convictions on count 1. The appellant now seeks to have his
conviction on that count quashed by this board.

The facts giving rise to the counts are complex. Those relevant to count 1 centre   **H**
around what became known as the Yeoman Loop and five transactions which made use
of it. Count 2 arose from an abortive attempt by an EHL subsidiary to take over an
Australian company, and count 4 from dealings in shares of a Hong Kong company in
which another EHL subsidiary had acquired some 97 per cent of the shareholding. Their
Lordships are much indebted to counsel on both sides for the assistance which they gave
in dealing with these complex matters. Mr McLinden, who had the difficult task of

A   opening the appeal, guided their Lordships through the complexities of the various transactions and presented his arguments with considerable clarity and skill.

The Yeoman Loop

Some time prior to March 1987 Hawkins asked the appellant to set up an overseas structure to receive moneys which he, Hawkins, was expecting from overseas. Three companies were acquired and the shares therein were registered in the names of Darvell and another partner in RWS. They held as nominees for Hawkins and not as beneficial owners. Bank accounts were opened for each of the companies by RWS and their names, countries of registration and bank accounts were as follows: Barley Grange Ltd, Cook Islands, Bank of Canton in Singapore ('BGL'); Mercantile Finance Corporation Ltd, Turks and Caicos Islands, Hong Kong and Shanghai Bank Corporation in Hong Kong ('MFC'); Yeoman Ltd, Vanuatu, Bank of Canton Ltd in Hong Kong. On 9 August 1987 Yeoman Ltd changed its name to First Pacific Finance Ltd and was referred to by Tompkins J in his judgment as Yeoman-First Pacific ('YFP').

The appellant in evidence stated that the purpose of setting up the Yeoman Loop was to receive two sums of money known as the 'H' fee and the 'retreat' fee and subsequent payments from other transactions to which reference will be made later. He acknowledged that it was deliberately set up with the intention that ownership of the structure should be anonymous and incapable of being detected. The judge, after reviewing all the relevant evidence, concluded that the purpose of setting up and using the Yeoman Loop was for concealment. The use of the Yeoman Loop was described by him as follows:

'The structure was used on five occasions, referred to at the time and during the trial as transaction 1, transaction 2 etc. But for transactions 1 and 5, the method used was the same. The money to pass through the Yeoman Loop was converted into Singapore dollars, paid into the Barley Grange account in the Bank of Canton, Singapore, converted into Hong Kong dollars, paid into the account of Mercantile Finance at the Hong Kong and Shanghai Bank Corporation in Hong Kong, still in Hong Kong dollars, paid to Yeoman's account at the Bank of Canton in Hong Kong, converted into NZ dollars and paid on every transaction except transaction 2 to Rudd Watts and Stone's trust account, from where it was paid out. In the case of transaction 1, Barley Grange and Mercantile Finance were omitted. In the case of transaction 5, all three companies were used, but through various accounts in Australia.'

The 'H' fee

Before turning to the details of the five transactions which made use of the Yeoman Loop something must be said about the 'H' fee which the judge found to refer to a sum of approximately A$70m to be paid from Australia. It was originally expected to arrive early in 1987 probably in time for some of it to be used by Hawkins and the other members of the investment team to take up their rights under a one for four cash issue by EHL, for which payment was due on 31 March 1987. In the event it was paid in two parts, the first on 12 January 1988 and the second on 7 September 1988, each by the same method.

Mr Fitzgerald, the managing director of Equiticorp Australia ('EAL') in Sydney was instructed by Hawkins to set up foreign exchange transactions to deal with moneys owing to Hawkins' companies from Elders IXL. The *first* operation took place in December 1987 and January 1988 and was deliberately contrived so that Elders IXL appeared to have lost A$39.5m and BGL to have gained A$39.1m, the difference of A$400,000 being the profit to the Bank of New Zealand ('BNZ') for constructing the transaction.

Confirmation advice of this transaction was sent by BNZ to BGL marked for the   A
attention of Fitzgerald. Thereafter the A$39.1m were passed in Australian dollars
through MFC to YFP where it was divided as follows:

(1)   A$37.2m were paid into BNZ in Singapore, converted into NZ$39.9m and paid as
      to NZ$29.5m to Richardson Camway Ltd ('RCL') (one of Hawkins' companies)
      thence to Equiticorp Finance Group Ltd ('EFGL') and then back in two sums on
      different dates to RCL.   B

(2)   A$1.2m was converted into New Zealand dollars by the National Bank of New
      Zealand and then passed through RWS to another of Hawkins' companies for
      equal division between Gunthorp and the appellant, the latter's share being paid
      into his Australian trust which never paid any tax. This operation constituted
      transaction five.

(3)   A$0.8m was paid as to A$200,000 each to Curtayne and Taylor and as to   C
      A$400,000 to EAL.

The *second* operation took place in September 1988 and involved a similar contrived
transaction involving NZ whereby Elders IXL appeared to have lost A$27m and
Sharpers Mart, a Hong Kong company owned by EHL, to have gained A$26.6m, a
difference of A$400,000 being once again the profit to BNZ. It is not necessary to follow
the travels of the money from Sharpers Mart, suffice it to say that it did not pass through
the Yeoman Loop.   D

The judge held that the Crown had been unable to establish what the 'H' fee was, from
whom it came, why it was paid or to whom it was payable. Although the appellant
received the sum of A$200,000 from the 'H' fee he professed ignorance as to what the fee
was, a profession which the judge found to be incredible in view of the appellant's direct
involvement in the complicated financing transaction. However, after analysing the
evidence relating to it and remarking upon the A$800,000 cost of the contrived foreign   E
exchange dealings, the judge concluded that despite the suspicions that surrounded it he
could not make an affirmative finding that the 'H' fee itself was fraudulent.

The five transactions

Transaction 1. On 23 April 1987 a sum of just over $6m was converted into Hong
Kong dollars by Equiticorp Tasman ('ET') and paid into YFP's account with the Bank   F
of Canton in Hong Kong. On 24 April 1987 it was paid out in two amounts, namely (i) a
sum which was converted back into New Zealand dollars and paid into the trust account
of RWS on 28 April 1987 in the name of the members of the investment team other than
the appellant, and (ii) a lesser sum which was converted into Australian dollars and paid
to EAL for the credit of the appellant's trust, after which it was divided between him and
Hawkins and Taylor. The appellant was unable to explain why the $6m had been paid
through YFP rather than directly to RWS and EAL. The $6m was derived from   G
transactions by the investment beam in shares in a Hong Kong company which will be
considered in more detail when dealing with count 4.

Transaction 2. On 20 May 1987 a bank draft for A$1.5m was received in the mail from
the Netherlands by the Bank of Canton in Singapore for BGL's account. It was paid
through MFC and YFP and thence to Equiticorp Investment Group Ltd ('EIGL'). It
was ultimately applied in part payment of existing YFP loans owing to a company,   H
Avant Garde Ltd, forming part of a chain of companies known as the Ewoch chain used
by the Equiticorp group for reasons relating to withholding tax. There was no suggestion
by the Crown that the use of this chain of companies was dishonest. The sum of A$1.5m
was known as the 'retreat' fee but it remains shrouded in as much mystery as did the 'H'
fee. The appellant was unable or unwilling to explain why the sum had been paid from
the Netherlands or why it was paid through the Yeoman Loop to EIGL. The judge

A   concluded that the only feasible reason for paying it through the Yeoman Loop was to
     make it more difficult for an inquirer to find out what it was and whence it came.
         Transaction 3. Between 20 and 28 May 1987 a sum of $869,272, which was the balance
     of an account in the name of Beid with Equiticorp Financial Group Ltd ('EFGL') was
     moved round the Yeoman Loop into the trust account of RWS arriving there as
     $861,794. Between 2 and 16 June 1987 this sum was divided by the investment team in
     the proportion of 7/12 to Hawkins and 1/12 to each of the other five members. This sum
B   represented part of management fees totalling $3,296,800 charged by EHL to ET and a
     company called Feltex International Ltd, 49.9 per cent of whose shares were owned by
     EHL, in connection with an unsuccessful but profitable attempt by ET to take over an
     Australian company. The remainder of the management fees had been used to purchase
     shares in EHL which were then divided among the investment team in the same
     proportions of 7/12 and 1/12. Thus the entire management fees charged by EHL to these
C   two companies found their way into the hands of the investment team or their trusts or
     associated companies. The appellant was unable to explain why his share of what started
     as the sum of $869,272 was paid through the Yeoman Loop but the judge found that by
     having his share paid offshore through YFP he was evading tax. This transaction was
     the subject of count 2.
         Transaction 4. On 7 August 1987 a sum of $1,325,600 was dispatched from RWS trust
D   account round the Yeoman Loop, arriving back six days later less some $37,000 in the
     trust account, whence it was passed along the Ewoch chain of companies to reduce the
     debt owed by YFP to Avant Garde Ltd. This money derived from further dealings in the
     shares and warrants of the Hong Kong company referred to in transaction 1 which will
     be described in more detail in relation to count 4. Although the appellant gave the
     instructions to RWS to send money round the Yeoman Loop he was unable to explain
     the reasons therefor. The judge again concluded that for reasons which are not apparent
E   those involved, principally Hawkins and the appellant, wished to conceal the
     transactions.
         Transaction 5. This has already been described in the context of the 'H' fee.
         It is now time to turn to the judge's conclusions in relation to counts 1, 2 and 4.
         Count 1. The judge found in relation to each of the five transactions that concealment
     was their purpose. He concluded that the purpose of setting up and using the Yeoman
F   Loop was apparent beyond reasonable doubt and that it was:

         '. . . set up and used in order to conceal the payments that were intended to be, and
         were, made, and to make it difficult for any person who had cause to enquire, to
         find out what they were, and their source. The cumulative effect of all the evidence
         to which I have referred leads to the clear conclusion that the only reasonable
         inference that can be drawn is that that concealment was dishonest – that is, with
G   intent to defraud. Concealment for innocent reasons is not a reasonably possible
         inference.'

     He went on to pose the question 'was anyone defrauded?' and answered it in this way:

         'If the purpose of the structure were dishonest concealment, the question answers
         itself. The persons the conspirators intended to defraud were those from whom it
         was intended to conceal. It is not necessary that these be specifically identified. But
H   it is easy to see that they would embrace the directors of EHL (other than the
         conspirators), other employees of Equiticorp who may talk about these exceptional
         transactions, the auditors, who would be intensely interested in any of those
         transactions that did or may have involved an Equiticorp company, the Revenue,
         and enforcement agencies on both sides of the Tasman.'

     He might also have added creditors of Equiticorp.

Count 2. This count related to the appropriation by the investment team of the   A
management fees charged by EHL to ET and Feltex International, already referred to in
the context of transaction 3. The defendants, other than Hawkins, maintained that they
honestly believed that the shares and cash given to them were bonuses for which Hawkins
had obtained proper authorisation from the independent directors in accordance with
the normal practice. The judge concluded that Hawkins stole the shares and the cash and
that this was known to Gunthorp and Curtayne. In acquitting the appellant, Taylor and
Gillespie he found it impossible to exclude as a reasonable possibility that they were told   B
that the shares and cash were a bonus for which they were entitled to assume that
Hawkins had obtained the authority of the independent directors. The appellant's
acquittal on this count does not of course affect the judge's conclusions as to the reason
why he made use of the Yeoman Loop for his cash share.

Count 4. In late 1986 EHL decided to expand into Hong Kong and the appellant and
Taylor were placed in charge of the operation. A Hong Kong company was acquired by   C
EHL, was renamed Equiticorp Investments (Hong Kong) Ltd ('EIHK') and after certain
further dealings became the owner of 1,945m ten cent shares (in all 97.25 per cent of the
capital) in a company called Keady Ltd ('Keady'). In December 1986 the appellant and
Hawkins decided that 60m Hong Kong one dollar shares in Keady should be offered to
the investment team at HK$1.50. After a rights issue the number of shares to be allocated
was reduced to 45m and the price increased to HK$2, this being 50 per cent over net
tangible asset value. However between 6 and 12 February 1987 and before the 2,000m   D
ten cent issued shares were consolidated into 200m shares of HK$1, 20,440,000 shares
and 111,000 warrants, being options to purchase shares, were sold for HK$37,456,876
and the proceeds paid to EIHK which deducted therefrom the cost price of 20 cents.
From these net proceeds NZ$6m reached ET which sum was later passed to YFP as
transaction 1 and ultimately into the hands of the investment team or their interests. The
balance of the net proceeds was used to purchase and later sell shares in ET for the   E
benefit of the investment team. As a result of the sale of the above ten cent shares and
warrants and the transactions consequent thereupon the investment team made a very
substantial profit of which the appellant's share was $1,427,587.

On 20 February 1987 the 2,000m ten cent shares in issue were consolidated into 200m
shares of HK$1 each and on the same day a rights issue of HK$1 share for every two
HK$1 shares issued was announced. In April 1987 Hawkins and the appellant decided
that the bulk of the shares still held by the investment team should be sold back to EHL   F
at HK$2.50, being 50 cents more than the team had agreed to pay for them but about
HK$1.50 below market price. The profit on the shares sold was to be used to pay for the
remaining shares which the members held. Finally in July 1987 the balance of the shares
held by the investment team was exchanged for warrants. Five members of the investment
team other than Gillespie sold their warrants to ET for a consideration consisting of
some $8.525m in cash and 1.5m shares in EHL valued at $6.75m. Most of the cash was   G
used to buy further shares in EHL with the result that the foregoing five members all
ended up as owners of substantial numbers of shares in EHL, in the case of the appellant
some 1,116,923 with a market value of $4.50m. The balance of the $8.525m amounting
to some $1,325,600 was passed round the Yeoman Loop to Ewoch, constituting
transaction 4.

The judge found that in the papers prepared for submission to the EHL board and in   H
the minutes of board meetings between February and May 1987 there was no indication
of any sale of Keady shares by EIHK to the investment team or their trusts. Indeed the
board papers showing the percentage of Keady shares held by or on behalf of EHL did
not reflect the sale of any shares to or for the benefit of the investment team. At a board
meeting of EHL on 23 February 1987 there was a discussion about the trading in the
market of 44m Keady shares at extraordinary prices but although all members of the

A   investment team were present none of them mentioned the fact that they personally had sold half of that number. On 21 May 1987 EHL's auditors asked Hawkins to provide confirmation that the independent directors had approved the sale by EIHK of Keady shares to the investment team. The appellant at the request of Hawkins thereupon drafted a minute of a meeting of 28 January 1987 showing that two of the independent directors were present thereat and had approved the allocation of shares. In fact no such meeting took place and the two independent directors were at no time aware of the investment

B   team's acquisition of and subsequent dealings in the shares, there having been no disclosure, formal or informal, to them as directors. The minute was accordingly a deliberate piece of deception.

The judge concluded that the Crown had failed to prove that members of the investment team had not entered into binding agreements to purchase the shares or at least did not honestly believe that they had by 6 February 1987. It followed that it was

C   not dishonest for them to sell some of their shares between 6 and 12 February.

The judge then went on to deal with the contention of the Crown that the defendants had dishonestly concealed from the EHL board their acquisition of and dealings in Keady shares. He referred to the fact that Hawkins was wont to decide whether shares in the EHL group should be allocated to executive directors and that it was not the practice for such transactions formally to be notified to the board nor for the transactions to be

D   recorded with a disclosure of interest, albeit the practice contravened both s. 199 of the *Companies Act* 1955 and EHL's articles of association. However the judge concluded that the allocation of Keady shares to the investment team was no ordinary share allocation to which past established practice could properly be applied since a glaringly obvious conflict of interest existed. After referring to the instances of concealment above referred to, as well as a number of similar instances, the judge said:

E   'What was required was not some figures from which an astute director might be able to deduce that some of his fellow directors were selling Keady shares. What was required was a full, frank and open disclosure to the other directors of what the investment team had done and was proposing to do. Given the pronounced conflict of interest, honesty demanded nothing less.

Was there an agreement dishonestly to conceal?

F   The conflict of interest, and the obligation that that imposed on honest directors to make disclosure to their fellow directors, were so clearly apparent that the only reasonable inference was that those intimately involved in the transaction agreed amongst themselves to keep it secret. And they did so dishonestly, with intent to deceive their fellow directors, and thereby defraud EHL.'

Their Lordships entirely agree with the view that a full and frank disclosure was required of the investment team. The judge then went on to consider the effect of concealment

G   from the independent directors and said that the board of EHL:

'. . . could legitimately have considered that if profits were being made on the sale of Keady shares, that were still in the name of Equiticorp Investments (HK), some if not all of those profits should belong to EHL. Had they been aware of the later proposals for the investment team to sell some of their Keady shares back to EHL they would, having regard to the obvious conflict of interest, want to be informed

H   about, and be satisfied as to, the terms. The same applies to the later shares for warrants swap. But the concealment of all of these transactions from the board deprived them of that opportunity.'

The judge convicted Hawkins, Taylor and the appellant because they dishonestly concealed from the EHL board their involvement in the Keady transaction and EHL was, or may have been, prejudiced as a result. In relation to count 1 the Court of Appeal

were satisfied that there was ample evidence enabling the inference to be drawn beyond   A
reasonable doubt that Hawkins and the appellant had agreed, prior to March 1987, to
set up and use the Yeoman Loop for the purpose of concealing the origin and use of
money received and that such concealment was fraudulent. They concluded:

> 'Whoever took part in the agreement to use the Loop for them must be seen as
> intending to practise a fraud on at least the other directors of Equiticorp and its
> auditors, by making it difficult for them to conduct legitimate inquiries into the   B
> source of the moneys concerned *to ascertain whether the Equiticorp group had any
> interest in them*. The conviction of Hawkins and Adams on count 1 was inevitable.'
> (emphasis added)

In quashing the convictions of Hawkins, Taylor and the appellant on count 4 the
Court of Appeal concluded that since it was implicit in the judge's conclusions that the
investment team honestly believed that they held the shares pursuant to an allocation
properly made and taken up there was no occasion for them to disclose to other directors   C
and executives what was their personal business. The judgment referred to the practice
whereby sales of shares to directors were not formally notified to the board nor recorded
with a disclosure of interest as supporting an honest belief that no disclosure to the board
was called for. The judgment criticised the judge for equating secrecy in respect of share
dealings and breach of fiduciary duty with dishonesty and intent to deceive and thereby
defraud EHL. The judgment referred to the following passage in the speech of Lord   D
Wilberforce in *R v Governor of Pentonville Prison, ex parte Tarling* (1978) 70 Cr App R
77 at p. 110:

> 'Breach of fiduciary duty, exorbitant profit making, secrecy, failure to comply with
> the law as to company accounts (I state these as assumptions) are one thing: theft
> and fraud are others.'

–and ultimately concluded that the investment team were entitled to the benefits of their   E
realisation and under no obligation to disclose them to anyone.

Although it does not affect the position in relation to count 4 their Lordships take
issue with these conclusions, on two grounds. *First* Lord Wilberforce's observations in
Tarling were made in the context of charges of conspiracy to defraud. The Divisional
Court had already held that the evidence on these charges fell far short of setting up a
prima facie case of dishonesty (p. 96). Lord Wilberforce at p. 111 said: F

> 'The highest, in my opinion, that the evidence can be put is that the participants
> made a secret profit at the expense probably of HPBHK (but Mr Tarling was not
> a director of HPBHK), possibly and indirectly of HPBIL and, that they kept it
> secret: it would not otherwise be a secret profit. This by itself is no criminal offence
> whatever other epithet may be appropriate.'

Lord Keith of Kinkel at pp. 137–138, after stating that the alleged conspirators were in   G
breach of their fiduciary duty to disclose the share dealings in question, continued:

> 'But that does not in itself constitute a crime under the law of England. The
> evidence, while clearly showing that Mr Tarling and those of his co-directors who
> were party to the dealings missed a number of suitable opportunities for disclosing
> these dealings, does not indicate that positive steps were taken to conceal them.'

Neither Lord Wilberforce nor Lord Keith of Kinkel went further than to say that non-   H
disclosure per se amounting to breach of fiduciary duty did not amount to a crime. They
were not dealing with a situation where there was a positive finding of dishonest
concealment on the part of the defendants. In this case not only had the defendants sold
both shares and warrants back to EHL and ET respectively without disclosing that they
were the vendors but the Yeoman Loop, whose purpose the judge had found to be
dishonest concealment, had been used on two occasions in connection with the

A   transactions in Keady shares. Furthermore the appellant and Hawkins had prepared a minute of a meeting of the board of EHL which had never taken place, with the clear intention as the judge found of 'fraudulently misleading by indicating to the auditors that two independent directors at the time were aware of and had approved the sale to the Keady consortium'. In these circumstances their Lordships consider that the situation obtaining in this case is significantly different from that which obtained in *Tarling* and that the dictum of Lord Wilberforce upon which the Court of Appeal relied does not

B   apply. In the *second* place the existence of a practice of non-disclosure involving breach of fiduciary duty does not per se absolve those operating the practice from dishonesty. Actions which are basically dishonest are not rendered honest by repetition. Hawkins was chairman and managing director of EHL and the appellant deputy chairman throughout its life. They were both therefore substantially responsible for the practice of non-disclosure to the board of share allocations to directors. If non-disclosure would

C   have been dishonest, but for the practice, they cannot rely on that practice which they had instituted to negative dishonesty. It must in any event be remembered that the practice as found by the judge was related only to allocation of shares to directors and not to resale by directors at a profit to EHL or its subsidiaries. Their Lordships cannot accept the proposition that a director of a company who acquires assets from that company, whether openly or clandestinely, is then entitled to trade those assets with the company without disclosing that he is so doing.

D   It is now time to turn to the arguments in relation to count 1. Mr McLinden advanced four main arguments, namely (1) that the Court of Appeal had extended the ambit of a conspiracy to defraud beyond any limit which had previously been set; (2) that a conspiracy to defraud could only take place where there existed (i) an interest of the person to be defrauded, (ii) a fraudulent act or omission adversely affecting that interest, and (iii) dishonest concealment of the fraudulent act, in short double dishonesty; (3) that

E   the Crown was required to prove that the appellant knew and agreed that the Yeoman Loop would be used to launder money stolen from Equiticorp; and (4) that the Court of Appeal had failed to take into account the effect which their acquittal of the appellant on count 4 had upon his conviction by the judge on count 1.

   (1) Mr McLinden criticised the passage in the judgment of the Court of Appeal relating to count 1 which has already been referred to and in particular the words emphasised therein. This statement was, he submitted, in far too broad terms and would

F   allow A to be convicted of defrauding B of moneys in which B had no interest whatsoever merely because A's actions made it more difficult for B to ascertain whether or not he had any interest therein. Their Lordships consider that there is force in that submission. In *Welham v DPP* [1961] AC 103 Lord Radcliffe at p. 124 said that:

> 'What [the law] has looked for in considering the effect of cheating upon another person and so in defining the criminal intent is the prejudice of that person . . .'

G   A person is not prejudiced if he is hindered in inquiring into the source of moneys in which he has no interest. He can only suffer prejudice in relation to some right or interest which he possesses. This was made clear in *Wai Yu-tsang v R* [1992] 1 AC 269, where Lord Goff of Chieveley, delivering the judgment of the board, referred at p. 276E to the expression 'intent to defraud' and continued:

> 'In broad terms, it means simply an intention to practise a fraud on another, or an

H   intention to act to the prejudice of another man's right.'

Lord Goff further stated at pp. 279–280:

> 'The question whether particular facts reveal a conspiracy to defraud depends upon what the conspirators have dishonestly agreed to do, and in particular whether they have agreed to practise a fraud on somebody. For this purpose it is enough for example that, as in *R v Allsop* and in the present case, the conspirators

have dishonestly agreed to bring about a state of affairs which they realise will or   A
may deceive the victim into so acting, or failing to act, that he will suffer economic
loss or his economic interests will be put at risk.'

This passage must, of course, be read together with the earlier observations in the
judgment made with reference to *Welham v DPP* [1961] AC 103 which was followed in *R
v Terry* [1984] AC 374 that conspiracies to defraud are not restricted to cases of intention
to cause the victim economic loss. However where possible economic loss is concerned   B
there can be no doubt that there must exist some right or interest in the victim which is
capable of being prejudiced whether by actual loss or by being put at risk. It follows that
the Court of Appeal have gone too far in overlooking the need for the existence of such
a right or interest in the victim which must be prejudiced.

(2) Mr McLinden submitted that, since the appellant was not found to have acted
dishonestly in relation to the funds which formed the subject of any of the five
transactions, one of the ingredients necessary to a conviction for conspiracy to defraud   C
was missing. It was not enough that the use of the Yeoman Loop had been found by the
judge to be dishonest. This submission, however, ignores the fact that the appellant as a
director of EHL and some of its subsidiaries was throughout his tenure of these offices
under a duty, when entering into a transaction with these companies or when using the
resources of these companies for his own benefit, to act with perfect good faith and to
make full disclosure to the company in question of all material circumstances. A director   D
is in the same position as an agent (*Aberdeen Railway Co v Blaikie Bros* (1854) 1 Macq
HL 461 at p. 471) and it is trite law that 'no agent may enter into any transaction in
which his personal interest might conflict with his duty to his principal, unless the
principal, with full knowledge of all the material circumstances and of the exact nature
and extent of the agent's interest, consents' (*Bowstead on Agency* (15th edn) p. 164). This
proposition is further expanded in the above work at p. 167:

> 'Where an agent enters into any contract or transaction with his principal, or with   E
> his principal's representative in interest, he must act with perfect good faith, and
> make full disclosure of all the material circumstances, and of everything known to
> him respecting the subject matter of the contract or transaction which would be
> likely to influence the conduct of the principal or his representative.'

Furthermore an agent has a duty to obtain his principal's informed consent before he
uses the latter's property for his own personal benefit (*Bowstead*, p. 175). In applying   F
these principles to conspiracy to defraud, regard must be had to the following dictum of
Viscount Dilhorne in *R v Scott* [1975] AC 819 at p. 840:

> '. . . it is clearly the law that an agreement by two or more by dishonesty to deprive
> a person of something which is his or to which he is or would be or might be
> entitled and an agreement by two or more by dishonesty to injure some proprietary
> right of his, suffices to constitute the offence of conspiracy to defraud.'   G

Since a company is entitled to recover from directors secret profits made by them at the
company's expense, it would follow that any dishonest agreement by directors to impede
a company in the exercise of its right of recovery would constitute a conspiracy to
defraud. In their Lordships' view a person can be guilty of fraud when he dishonestly
conceals information from another which he was under a duty to disclose to that other
or which that other was entitled to require him to disclose. It was the element of dishonest
concealment which was absent in *Tarling*.   H

Taking transactions 1 and 4 together certain things clearly emerge. The appellant and
the other defendants acquired Keady shares and warrants from EIHK without disclosure
to the board of EHL. They sold all these shares and warrants at a large profit, a
substantial number of them being sold back to EHL or ET, once again without disclosure
to the board of EHL. Until the resales the shares appeared to be registered in the name

A   of EIHK. Thereafter Hawkins and the appellant concocted a minute of a fictitious
    meeting in order to deceive EHL's auditors into thinking that the board of EHL had
    sanctioned the allocation to the investment team of Keady shares. $6m from the February
    1987 sale of some 20,440,000 ten cent Keady shares which had been received by EIHK
    was paid to ET in Australia and then for unexplained reasons by way of YFP's account
    in Hong Kong to RWS or EAL whence it found its way into the hands of the investment
    team or their various interests. After five members of the investment team sold their
B   Keady warrants to ET at a very large profit they passed a substantial sum of money
    round the Yeoman Loop' for unexplained reasons at a cost of $37,000. The appellant
    and his co-defendants were accordingly not merely failing to disclose their activities to
    the board of EHL but they were taking positive steps whose only object was to make it
    more difficult for persons such as other directors, the shareholders and the auditors of
    EHL, who had a legitimate interest in the transactions, to discover what they were doing.
C   The board could, as the judge said:

       '. . . legitimately have considered that if profits were being made on the sale of
       Keady shares, that were still in the name of Equiticorp Investments (HK), some if
       not all of those profits should belong to EHL. Had they been aware of the later
       proposals for the investment team to sell some of their Keady shares back to EHL
       they would, having regard to the obvious conflict of interest, want to be informed
D   about, and be satisfied as to, the terms. The same applies to the later shares for
       warrants swap. But the concealment of all of these transactions from the board
       deprived them of that opportunity.

       There is a further aspect. The secrecy that surrounded the activities of Adams and
       Taylor on behalf of the investment team, and the lack of any documentary evidence
       in the hands of anyone other than Adams and Taylor, meant that they had
E   effectively hedged their bets. If, contrary to all the indications, the February sales
       had not yielded a worthwhile profit, they could have decided that the shares sold
       were not theirs, but Equiticorp Investment (HK)'s. They were still in the name of
       Equiticorp Investments (HK). As no one else knew whose were the shares being
       sold, that could and would not be challenged. Leaving that option in their hands
       was also to EHL's detriment.'

F   Although these observations were made in relation to count 4 they are equally applicable
    to consideration of transactions 1 and 4 in the context of count 1.

    In the case of transaction 2 the Crown was unable to prove that the investment team
    derived any benefit from the 'retreat' fee. The appellant would not or could not explain
    its origin nor why it was passed round the Yeoman Loop instead of being paid direct
    from BGL's account in Singapore to EIGL. The interposition of the Yeoman Loop
G   between BGL and EIGL necessarily rendered more difficult legitimate inquiries into the
    origin of the money and the reason for its payment to EIGL. However, notwithstanding
    the unusual nature of the transaction their Lordships do not feel able to affirm that on
    the facts as found by the judge the investment team were under a duty of disclosure in
    relation to the 'retreat' fee.

    Transaction 3 was used to transfer moneys payable against invoices issued by EHL for
H   services performed by EHL from an account with EFGL around the Yeoman Loop and
    through RWS into the hands of the investment team or their trusts or companies at a
    cost of some $7,500. Even although the appellant may have thought that his share of the
    money was a bonus authorised by the independent directors, that did not absolve him
    from his duty of disclosure at least to the shareholders. Once again the interposition of
    the Yeoman Loop between EFGL and RWS's trust account impeded inquiries into
    money in which EHL had an undoubted interest.

The position in relation to transaction 5 is somewhat different from that obtaining in   A
relation to the other four transactions in as much as it was not established that EHL or
any of its subsidiaries had any interest in the 'H' fee, nor was it proved that it was per se
dishonest. However the resources of EHL in the form of EAL were used to set up a
contrived foreign exchange transaction and the Yeoman Loop was then used to conceal
what had gone before, as well as the origin of the benefits to the investment team. To
whomsoever the 'H' fee may have belonged in law, Hawkins and the appellant at least
were aware that the Yeoman Loop was being used to conceal the obviously dishonest   B
foreign exchange transaction in Australia, a transaction which because of its use of EHL's
resources they were under a duty to disclose. Thus transaction 5 was itself dishonest.

It follows that the appellant, having been party to the use of the Yeoman Loop in the
case of four out of the five transactions for the purpose of dishonest concealment of
information which, as a director, he was under a duty to disclose to EHL, was properly
convicted on count 1. This conclusion also disposes of Mr McLinden's third point. It   C
only remains to say a word about Mr McLinden's fourth submission to the effect that
the Court of Appeal, in upholding the appellant's conviction on count 1, had failed to
take into account their quashing of his conviction on count 4. Their Lordships have
already indicated why they consider that the Court of Appeal were in error in concluding
that the investment team were under no obligation to disclose their dealings with the
Keady shares. Thus although the Court of Appeal order on count 4 must stand all the   D
circumstances surrounding the dealings in the Keady shares can properly be looked at in
the context of count 1 to which they are as already explained highly relevant.

For the foregoing reasons their Lordships will humbly advise Her Majesty that the
appeal should be dismissed.

(Appeal dismissed)

E

F

G

H

A
Re Edennote Ltd.
Tottenham Hotspur plc & Ors v Ryman & Ors.

Chancery Division.
Sir John Vinelott.
Judgment delivered 9 November 1994.

B
Application to set aside assignment by liquidator – Removal of liquidator – Whether creditor was 'person aggrieved' – Whether liquidator acted reasonably in granting assignment of company's action – Whether court should remove liquidator – Insolvency Act 1986, s. 168, 172.

This was an application by creditors under s. 168(5) of the Insolvency Act 1986 to set aside a deed of assignment between the liquidator of Edennote Ltd and 'V', and to remove the liquidator under s. 172 of the 1986 Act.

C
V was the chief executive of 'Tottenham plc' under a service agreement and was the manager of 'Tottenham Ltd' (the football club subsidiary of Tottenham plc) under a management agreement made with V's company, Edennote. Edennote held shares in Tottenham plc and when the service agreement and the management agreement were terminated, Edennote presented a petition under s. 459 of the Companies Act 1985. V and Edennote also commenced proceedings against Tottenham plc and Tottenham Ltd,

D
claiming, in the case of Edennote, damages for breach of the management agreement, and, in V's case, damages for breach of the service agreement. The petition was dismissed when Edennote failed to provide security for costs. The applicants (respondents to the petition) having obtained an order for costs against Edennote had it wound up as insolvent. The defendants in the action then sought security for costs.

Edennote's liquidator agreed to assign its interest in the action to V for £7,000 plus ten

E
per cent of the net proceeds recovered. The defendants applied to have the assignment set aside and to have the liquidator replaced.

Held, setting aside the deed of assignment and removing the liquidator:

1. A creditor could be a person aggrieved under s. 168(5).

2. An exercise by a liquidator of powers conferred on him by statute could be called into question not only if it could be shown that the exercise of the power was utterly unreasonable

F
– that it went beyond what any reasonable person properly instructed could have considered proper – but also if it was shown that the person exercising the power, though acting in good faith, took into account considerations which he ought not to have taken into account or failed to take into account considerations which he ought to have taken into account.

3. The assignment could not stand. It should have been obvious to the liquidator as soon as he was approached by V that the sale of Edennote's right of action to V would put into

G
V's hands a very powerful weapon which he could use in negotiations for the settlement of both claims. The claim in the hands of V had a very considerable nuisance value. In the event Tottenham plc or perhaps Tottenham Ltd was prepared to pay £75,000 to avoid that risk. At the very least the liquidator should have inquired whether Tottenham were willing to enter into negotiations. Whatever may have been his motives for not doing so, he in fact failed to consider one of the two possible ways of realising the company's claim in an advantageous way.

H
4. The task confronting the liquidator was to consider whether to accept the offer of £75,000 made in settlement of the claim against Tottenham Ltd, whether to invite V to make a further offer of an increased share of the proceeds of the litigation, and if V did, how to evaluate the likely prospects of recovery in costly and protracted proceedings. The applicants or other creditors could not fairly be asked to accept the liquidator's decision after it had been shown that he was willing to enter into an assignment to V without giving

any consideration to the possibility of negotiating a satisfactory compromise with   A
Tottenham plc and Tottenham Ltd.

The following cases were referred to in the judgment:

Associated Provincial Picture Houses Ltd v Wednesbury Corporation [1948] 1 KB 223.

Bang and Olufsen v Ton Systeme Ltd (unreported, 16 July 1993, CA).

Burn, Re; ex parte Dawson & Ors [1932] 1 Ch 247.

Debtor, Re a; ex parte the Debtor v Dodwell [1949] Ch 236.

   B

Freightex Ltd v International Express Company Ltd & Ors (unreported, 27 July 1981, CA).

Keypak Homecare Ltd, Re (1987) 3 BCC 558.

Leon v York-O-Matic Ltd & Ors [1966] 1 WLR 1450.

Peters, Re. Ex parte Lloyd (1882) 47 LT 64.

Pitman (Harold M) & Co v Top Business Systems (Nottingham) Ltd (1985) 1 BCC 99,345.

   C

Ramsey v Hartley [1977] 1 WLR 686.

Sidebotham, Re; ex parte Sidebotham (1880) 14 ChD 458.

Richard McCombe QC and Jonathan Crow (instructed by Herbert Smith) for the applicants.

David Neuberger QC and Susan Prevezer (instructed by Nabarro Nathanson) for the first respondent.

   D

Jonathan Rayner James QC and Michael Jefferis (instructed by John Bowden Trainer & Co) for the second respondent.

JUDGMENT

Sir John Vinelott: This is an application to set aside a deed of assignment dated 28 July 1994 and made between the first respondent, Mr Stephen Blandford Ryman as liquidator of Edennote Ltd and Mr Terence Frederick Venables. The application arises   E out of a long running and widely publicised dispute between the third applicant, Mr Alan Michael Sugar, and Mr Venables over the management of the first applicant, Tottenham Hotspur plc (which I will abbreviate to 'Tottenham plc') and its wholly owned subsidiary Tottenham Hotspur Football Athletic Co Ltd (which I will abbreviate to 'Tottenham Ltd'), which I must briefly describe. The second applicant, Amshold Ltd, is a private company, all or substantially all of the shares of which are owned by Mr Sugar. At all   F material times it has had a substantial shareholding in Tottenham plc sufficient to give Amshold de facto control of Tottenham plc. Those shares were acquired in 1991 when Mr Sugar and Mr Venables joined in acquiring shares of Tottenham plc owned by others who held a controlling interest. Later, a rights issue was taken up by Mr Sugar and Mr Venables. The shares acquired by Mr Sugar and Mr Venables were acquired in the names of Amshold and Edennote, a company the shares of which have at all material times been held by Mr Venables, respectively.   G

On 9 June 1991 Mr Venables entered into a service agreement with Tottenham plc under which he agreed to serve as chief executive of Tottenham plc for a term of five years at a basic salary of £225,000 per annum with an annual bonus and other benefits. That agreement was in effect superseded by two agreements, both executed on 7 September 1992. The first of them, 'the management agreement', was made between Tottenham Ltd and Edennote Ltd. By the management agreement Edennote agreed to   H provide the services of Mr Venables as manager of the football club operated by Tottenham Ltd for a term expiring on the same day as the expiry of the service agreement. The consideration was an annual sum of £150,000. The second was a supplemental agreement varying the terms of the service agreement but providing in effect that Mr Venables' duties to Tottenham plc were to be subject to the prior claims of Tottenham Ltd and reducing his salary under the service agreement to £75,000. In summary, after

A 7 September 1992 Mr Venables was the chief executive of Tottenham plc, the terms of his appointment being governed by the original service agreement as amended and, through Edennote, the manager of Tottenham Ltd, his original basic remuneration being split between them.

Not long after the execution of these two agreements there were disputes between Mr Sugar and Mr Venables, and on 14 May 1993 the service agreement and the management

B agreement were terminated. That led, first, to a petition presented by Edennote under s. 459 of the *Companies Act* 1985. Edennote joined Tottenham plc and Amshold and Mr Sugar as respondents. The relief sought included a claim for the reinstatement of Mr Venables as chief executive of Tottenham plc and as manager of Tottenham Ltd and an order that Amshold's shares of Tottenham plc be sold to Mr Venables and Edennote at a price to be ascertained by the court. Shortly before the presentation of the petition Edennote obtained an injunction ex parte from Arden J designed to preserve the position

C of Mr Venables until the hearing of an application for an injunction covering the period until the s. 459 petition could be heard. The application for an injunction came before Sir Donald Nicholls V-C between 7 and 14 June 1993 and was dismissed. Tottenham plc, Amshold and Mr Sugar as respondents to the s. 459 petition were concerned with the financial position of Edennote and its ability to meet any order for costs and applied for an order that Edennote provide security. On 29 July 1993 Edennote was ordered to

D provide security in the sum of £300,000 within 21 days. Edennote was in no position to provide security, and on 13 September 1993 Chadwick J dismissed the s. 459 petition and ordered Edennote to pay the taxed costs of the respondents to the petition. Shortly afterwards Edennote sold its shares in Tottenham plc.

In the meantime on 17 July 1993 Mr Venables and Edennote had commenced proceedings against Tottenham plc and Tottenham Ltd, claiming, in the case of Edennote, damages for breach of the management agreement, and, in the case of Mr

E Venables, damages for breach of the service agreement. There followed a minor diversion in that litigation. The defendants were a few days late in serving their defence, and on 15 October Edennote and Mr Venables obtained a judgment in default of defence. That was set aside by consent on 21 January 1994 when a defence and counterclaim was served. During that interlude the applicants (the respondents to the s. 459 petition) had delivered a bill of costs amounting to £460,000. It was delivered on 27 October 1993. In January

F 1994 Herbert Smith, the solicitors acting for the applicants (Tottenham plc, Mr Sugar and Amshold) discovered that on 24 August 1993 Edennote had executed charges over the shares it then held in Tottenham plc in favour of Mr Venables and his solicitors, Kanter Jules Grangewoods ('Grangewoods'), to secure sums of £1.211m and £450,000 respectively and in favour of a Mr Igal Yawetz who had lent moneys to Edennote towards the rights issue. The shares were sold shortly thereafter and substantial sums were paid to Mr Venables, Grangewoods and Mr Yawetz. Herbert Smith were concerned that any

G delay might prejudice the ability of the liquidator, if appointed, to have the charges and payments set aside under s. 240 of the *Insolvency Act* 1986, and on 12 January 1994 Tottenham plc presented a petition for the compulsory winding up of Edennote. The costs had not then been taxed. They were taxed in the sum of £335,000 on 26 January and the taxing master issued an interim certificate for £183,750 on 21 February 1994. Objections to the taxation were later raised but have since been abandoned. The costs have been agreed between the official receiver and Tottenham plc in the sum of £350,000.

H The winding-up petition came before Rattee J on 12 May 1994 and he made the usual compulsory winding-up order (see [1994] BCC 681). The petition had been opposed by Edennote on the grounds, first, that the applicant had no locus standi to present the petition, there having been no taxation when the petition was presented, and, secondly, that the court should exercise its discretion against the petitioners because the winding up of Edennote would stifle its claim against Tottenham Ltd.

Those objections were rejected by Rattee J. I should refer to one passage in his   **A**
judgment where in giving a number of reasons for rejecting the second ground he said (at
p. 686H):

> '. . . a winding-up order will take the prosecution of the order by the company
> against the subsidiary of Tottenham plc out of the hands of the company but will
> enable a liquidator appointed in a winding up to pursue it if he thinks fit, taking
> account of the strength of the claim and of the wishes of Mr Venables as the largest   **B**
> creditor of the company with the benefit of an indemnity if proferred by Mr
> Venables as to costs, in circumstances where, if there were no winding up, Mr
> Venables anyway would appear to be the only person in a position to finance the
> further prosecution of the claim for the time being.'

The usual compulsory order included, of course, an order that the costs of the applicants,
the petitioning creditor and the company be paid out of the assets of the company, but
the applicants were given leave to apply for an order that they be paid by Mr Venables   **C**
personally. Those costs have yet to be taxed. No doubt in view of the opposition to the
petition the costs will be substantial.

At this point I must advert briefly to the action brought in the Queen's Bench Division
('the Queen's Bench action'). On 11 January 1994 Tottenham Ltd and Tottenham plc
applied for an order for security for their costs. On 3 May that application was adjourned
pending the outcome of the winding-up petition. Following the making of the winding-   **D**
up order the official receiver became the liquidator. Herbert Smith wrote to him on 31
May drawing his attention to the outstanding application for security for costs and
expressing anxiety that the application should be heard speedily before any further costs
were incurred in the Queen's Bench action. The official receiver replied on 6 June to say
that he proposed to convene a meeting of creditors on 29 July to appoint a liquidator in
his place and asked if Herbert Smith would be willing to adjourn the application for
security until 10 August so that the liquidator when appointed could give consideration   **E**
to the issues in the Queen's Bench action before the application for security was heard.
He said that unless Herbert Smith would agree an adjournment he would have to invite
the Secretary of State to exercise his powers to appoint a liquidator forthwith. Herbert
Smith were not prepared to agree an adjournment until after the creditors' meeting
because they feared that there would be disputes about the appointment of a liquidator
and that the application for security might not be heard until later in the year. Mr Ryman   **F**
was appointed liquidator by the Secretary of State on 15 June. On 23 June the application
for security was restored for 29 July. Then, on 27 July Mr Ryman notified all known
creditors that he did not intend to call a meeting of creditors unless required by creditors
holding one-tenth of the company's aggregate debt to do so. He instructed Nabarro
Nathanson to act as his solicitor. On his appointment Mr Ryman had received from the
official receiver his report to creditors; it gave as the only asset of Edennote a refund due
from the Inland Revenue of £35,000 in respect of franked investment income. It gave   **G**
Edennote's total liabilities as £2,918,486. They included the £460,130 claimed by the
applicants, £930,000 due on a loan account of Mr Venables and a claim for VAT of
£221,399. The assets, of course, would also include any sum recovered in the Queen's
Bench action if it succeeded. Further, only 25 per cent had been paid on the ordinary
shares of Edennote, 5,000 in number, and a call on Mr Venables, the sole shareholder,
would produce a further £37,500. In addition, Edennote had a prima facie claim to set   **H**
aside the charges in favour of Mr Venables, Grangewoods and Mr Yawetz and the
payments to them. However, it was clear to Mr Ryman that urgent consideration would
have to be given to the claim in the Queen's Bench action before the application for
security for costs was heard. On 28 July the assignment to Mr Venables was completed.
I shall have to return to deal in some detail with the events between the appointment of
Mr Ryman and the execution of the assignment in a moment.

A   I should first say something about the terms and the effect of the assignment and the court's jurisdiction to set it aside.

The assignment

The assignment starts with a number of definitions. They include definitions of: 'the action' as 'the proceedings issued by the assignor jointly with the assignee against B Tottenham (which is not defined) and Tottenham Hotspur' (defined to mean Tottenham plc), and the definition gives the action number; of the expression 'the assigned rights' as 'such property right title and interest as the assignor may have in the action'; and of 'the proceedings' as 'the action or any subsequent proceedings issued by the assignee in relation to the assigned rights or in relation to any breach of the management agreement.'

By cl. 1 Edennote is expressed to assign to Mr Venables the assigned rights. By cl. 2 C the consideration is expressed to be £7,000 and ten per cent of the proceeds of the action after deducting the costs and expenses incurred by Mr Venables in pursuing the proceedings. Literally construed this would include any costs incurred by Mr Venables in pursuing his own claim against Tottenham plc, but Mr Rayner James QC, who appeared for Mr Venables, made it clear his client accepted that he was only entitled to deduct the costs incurred in relation to the claim by Edennote against Tottenham Ltd.

D   It was provided by cl. 4.4 that neither Mr Ryman nor Edennote was to have any liability for costs and expenses incurred by Mr Venables in pursuing the proceedings or in issuing further proceedings based on the assigned rights.

The assignment is not very artistically drawn. I have already referred to the absence of any definition of 'Tottenham'. Mr McCombe QC, who appeared for the applicants, submitted that on a literal construction the assignment purports to be an assignment of E the action, which, of course, is something strictly incapable of assignment. I think that may be too narrow a view. The assignment extends to Edennote's rights against Tottenham Ltd, and it was clearly contemplated that the assignee might commence a fresh action on the assigned cause of action. However, I do not need to express any concluded opinion on this point. Mr McCombe agreed that, as that issue was one which it would be open to Tottenham Ltd to pursue in the Queen's Bench action, the present appeal should proceed on the footing that the assignment was or included an assignment F of Edennote's right of action.

It is well-settled that a trustee's statutory power of sale creates a statutory exception from the rules as to maintenance and champerty: see *Ramsey v Hartley* [1977] 1 WLR 686, a case concerning the estate of a bankrupt where the earlier authorities are reviewed and where it was held that a trustee in bankruptcy could validly assign a cause of action in return for an indemnity as to costs and 35 per cent of any recovery. In the unreported G decision of the Court of Appeal in *Bang and Olufsen v Ton Systeme Ltd* in which judgment was given on 16 July 1993 the Court of Appeal affirmed that the principles applied in *Ramsey v Hartley* apply equally in the liquidation of a company.

I initially felt some doubt whether, once an action had been commenced, the cause of action could be severed and assigned, thereby removing the foundation of the action. I was later referred to another recent unreported decision of the Court of Appeal in *Freightex Ltd v International Express Company Ltd & Ors*, in which this precise situation H arose. The benefit of an action was assigned after an action had been commenced and, indeed, after the liquidator had agreed in principle to give security for the costs of the action. The Court of Appeal reversed the decision of May J who had refused to make an order substituting the assignee for the insolvent company as plaintiffs. The question I have to decide is whether the assignment should be set aside as an improper exercise of Mr Ryman's power of sale.

Setting aside: jurisdiction   A

Section 167 of the *Insolvency Act* 1986 confers wide discretion on a liquidator to exercise the powers conferred by Sch. 4. Those in Pt. I and II can only be exercised with the sanction of the court or the liquidation committee. Those in Pt. III, which include a power of sale over the company's assets, can be exercised without that consent. Under subs. (2) a liquidator (not being the official receiver) before disposing of an asset of a company to a connected person must give notice to the liquidation committee if there is   B one. However, it is common ground that in the absence of a liquidation committee the liquidator is not bound to give notice to the Secretary of State or the official receiver.

Subsection (3) reads as follows:

'The exercise by the liquidator in a winding up by the court of the powers conferred by this section is subject to the control of the court, and any creditor or contributory may apply to the court with respect to any exercise or proposed   C exercise of any of those powers.'

Under s. 168(3) the liquidator is given power to apply to the court for directions as to the exercise of any of his powers. Section 168(4) and (5) I must again read in full.

'(4) Subject to the provisions of this Act, the liquidator shall use his own discretion in the management of the assets and their distribution among the creditors.

(5) If any person is aggrieved by an act or decision of the liquidator, that person   D may apply to the court; and the court may confirm, reverse or modify the act or decision complained of, and make such order in the case as it thinks just.'

Mr Rayner James submitted that s. 167(3) is what he described as a directions section. Section 168(5) confers a separate and distinct power which can only be invoked by a person aggrieved. A creditor as such, he submitted, cannot claim to be a person aggrieved within s. 168(5). I think that is too narrow an approach. Section 167(3) confers on a   E creditor a right to apply to the court with respect to any exercise as well as any proposed exercise of the liquidator's powers. The right to seek the directions of the court as to a proposed exercise of his power is to be found in s. 168(3). Subsection (5), like subs. (3), is ancillary to s. 167(3) and gives to, amongst others, a creditor or contributory the right to apply to set aside a decision or act of a liquidator. That that is the proper construction of s. 168(5) is supported by its legislative history. The ancestor of both s. 167(3) and of s. 168(5) is s. 20 of the *Bankruptcy Act* 1869. The penultimate paragraph of that section   F read as follows:

'A bankrupt or any creditor, debtor or other person aggrieved by any act of a trustee may apply to the court and the court may confirm, reverse or modify the act complained of and make such order in the premises as it thinks just. The court may from time to time during continuation of a bankruptcy summon general meetings of the creditors for the purpose of ascertaining their wishes and may if   G the court thinks fit direct the registrar to preside at such meetings.'

In my judgment the words 'persons aggrieved' in section 168(5) are no more than shorthand for the longer description, 'any creditor, debtor or other person aggrieved'.

Mr Rayner James relied upon a decision of the Court of Appeal in *Re Burn, ex parte Dawson & Ors* [1932] 1 Ch 247 as authority for the proposition that a creditor as such cannot claim to be a person aggrieved within s. 168(5). On a proper analysis I do not   H think that *Re Burn* is authority for that proposition. The trustee had applied unsuccessfully in the county court for an order for the payment of moneys out of the bankrupt's earnings, and Mr Dawson, a creditor who had been made a respondent to that application in respect of another matter raised in the application, sought to appeal against the refusal by the county court to make the order sought. He had no locus standi to appeal. A right of appeal was conferred by s. 108 at the instance of any person

A   aggrieved. The divisional court, followed the decision in *Re Sidebotham; ex parte Sidebotham* (1880) 14 ChD 458, where James LJ explained the meaning of a 'person aggrieved' in this context. In that case Bramwell B, agreeing with James LJ, said at p. 466:

B   'Supposing that the Comptroller has a right to appeal from the refusal of the judge to act upon his report, and he does not think fit to do so, is there to be an appeal by the bankrupt or by any of the creditors? Is the Comptroller to be satisfied, and yet is the bankrupt or any creditor to be entitled to appeal? I do not say that such a state of things is impossible, but certainly the general rule is that an appeal must be by the party who has endeavoured to maintain the contrary of that which has taken place. It is not so much that there is a disability on the part of the bankrupt to appeal, as that no one but the Comptroller is entitled to appeal.'

C   So, in that case, the creditor, who was not a party to the relevant application, had no right of appeal.

It has been stressed in many cases that the power to set aside an act of a trustee or liquidator is to be sparingly exercised. In *Re Peters* (1882) 47 LT 64 where a trustee in bankruptcy with the support of a majority of the creditors had refused to sell reversionary interests expectant on the death of an elderly man, Sir George Jessel MR said:

D   'Independently of the resolution of the creditors against the sale, there is no locus standi for any one creditor to interfere and ask the court to order a sale, except on the ground that the trustee has not exercised his discretion bona fide. Here the appellant says that the refusal to sell is an absurd exercise of the discretion of the trustee. But the court will not interfere unless the trustee is doing that which is so utterly unreasonable and absurd that no reasonable man would so act. He is certainly not doing anything of the kind in the present case, and, in my opinion, the appeal ought to fail.'

E

He clearly did not mean that the applicant, a creditor, had no right to apply to the court (the application was made under s. 20 of the 1869 Act) but that the application would not be entertained unless it was shown that the trustee's refusal to sell was an absurd exercise of his discretion.

F   *Re Peters* was applied by Plowman J in *Leon v York-O-Matic Ltd* [1966] 1 WLR 1450, a case where the plaintiff, a creditor of the company being wound up who had made an offer to the liquidator for assets of the company, applied to restrain completion of a sale to another at what he claimed to be an undervalue. The claim that it was at an undervalue was rejected. Plowman J, having held that the principles in *Re Peters* applied in the winding up of a company, cited with approval a passage in the judgment of Harman J in *Re a Debtor; ex parte the Debtor v Dodwell* [1949] Ch 236 at p. 241, another bankruptcy

G   case, where he said:

'It seems to me clear that there must be circumstances in which the court can interfere at the instance of a bankrupt to control the actions of the trustee: this is apparent from the terms of s. 80 itself, and is confirmed by the all-embracing language of s. 105.

H   I need not, I think, attempt to define what these circumstances are. They cannot, I think (in the absence of fraud) justify interference in the day-to-day administration of the estate, nor entitle the bankrupt to question the exercise by the trustee in good faith of his discretion, nor to hold him accountable for an error of judgment. administration in bankruptcy would be impossible if the trustee must answer at every step to the bankrupt for the exercise of his powers and discretions in the management and realisation of the property.'

Nourse J in *Harold M Pitman & Co v Top Business Systems (Nottingham) Ltd* (1985)   A
1 BCC 99,345 accepted counsel's submission at p. 99,348 that:

> '. . . before the court could have made any order restraining a sale proposed, to
> which I have referred, it would have been necessary to show either that the
> liquidator was acting fraudulently or that he had in some way not exercised his
> discretion bona fide or that he was proposing to do something which was so utterly
> unreasonable and absurd that no reasonable man would do it.'   B

A little later he added:

> 'It does seem to me that it would run very contrary to the view which the
> Companies Court has always taken of the desirability of a liquidator, whether in a
> winding up by the court or in a voluntary winding up, being able to exercise his
> powers without undue fetters if I were to say that there should be some lower
> standard to be established in order to enable the court to intervene.'   C

I must not be taken as in any way differing from these authoritative statements of the
law if I add that in the light of the modern development of the law of judicial review an
exercise by a liquidator of powers conferred on him by statute had to be judged by
reference to what is commonly referred to as the *Wednesbury* test, that is that an exercise
of a statutory power or discretion may be called in question, not only if it can be shown
that the exercise of the power is utterly unreasonable – that it went beyond what any
reasonable person properly instructed could have considered proper – but also if it is   D
shown that the person exercising the power, though acting in good faith, took into
account considerations which he ought not to have taken into account or failed to take
into account considerations which he ought to have taken into account.

Setting aside: the facts

I must now return to a detailed examination of the events between the appointment of   E
Mr Ryman as liquidator and the execution of the assignment by Mr O'Reilly as his
attorney.

Very shortly after his appointment Mr Ryman was telephoned by Mr Eddie Ashby,
Mr Venables' assistant manager who wished to discuss the future of the Queen's Bench
action and the pending application for security for costs. On 22 June a meeting took
place between Mr Ryman, Mr Ashby and Mr Trainer of John Bowden Trainer & Co,
who had recently been appointed as Mr Venables' solicitors. It was attended also by Mr   F
Chapman of Edennote's auditors. The possibility of Mr Venables purchasing Edennote's
claim in the Queen's Bench action was raised. Mr Ryman says that at that time he had in
mind the observation of Rattee J, which I have read, and an observation of counsel for
Tottenham plc and Tottenham Ltd, mentioned by Rattee J in his judgment, that it was
always incumbent upon any liquidator of Edennote in deciding what action to take with
regard to prosecuting the action to consider the wishes of Mr Venables as the largest   G
creditor of Edennote. Two days later Mr Ryman received a letter from Mr Trainer
confirming Mr Venables' wish to acquire Edennote's claim. On 27 June Mr Ryman
instructed Nabarro Nathanson to consider the legal requirements for such an assignment.

On 5 July there was a further meeting with Mr Ashby to discuss the impending
application for security for costs. It was attended by Mr Ashby, Mr Salber, a solicitor
with Grangewoods, who were still the solicitors on the record for the plaintiffs in the
Queen's Bench action, Mr Trainer, and Miss Alison Cutler, a solicitor employed by   H
Nabarro Nathanson. Mr Ryman had apparently been advised by Miss Cutler that it was
highly probable that an order for security would be made on 29 July, and that if it were
made Edennote would incur considerable costs which would be payable as an expense of
the litigation. It was agreed that Nabarro Nathanson would consider with counsel the
'mechanics of a possible assignment and whether this would be possible'. Mr Ashby

A confirmed that Mr Venables would indemnify Edennote and Mr Ryman up to £2,000 to meet the costs of obtaining legal advice. Miss Cutler instructed Miss Prevezer of counsel on the following day. Miss Prevezer advised in conference on 13 July. Miss Prevezer confirmed Miss Cutler's advice that if the liquidator adopted the Queen's Bench action, in particular by defending the application for security for costs, he would make Edennote liable for costs which would rank ahead of all other expenses in the liquidation. She was pessimistic about the possibility of defending or of obtaining an adjournment of the

B application for security and advised that Mr Ryman should make up his mind what course of action he wished to pursue before the application, then some two weeks ahead, was heard. She pointed out that if the Queen's Bench action were to be continued with the support of Mr Venables the liquidator would have to be satisfied that he had a satisfactory indemnity in the form of cash equal to Edennote's costs and the costs that might be awarded against him, a potential total liability of over £400,000. She advised

C that an assignment was the preferable course 'as it does not have the same costs implications within the liquidation so long as it is effected prior to the security for costs application and the liquidator has not adopted the proceedings', and that an assignment for a suitable consideration plus a share of any damages recovered would not be void as champertous. Her conclusion was that:

> 'The plaintiffs must make a decision very swiftly as to what they intend to do with Edennote's part of the proceedings. The liquidator cannot continue them unless he
> D receives a substantial indemnity which, given the costs implications within the liquidation, should be backed by a substantial deposit of funds. Alternatively, the liquidator can assign the proceedings to Mr Venables for a fixed sum plus a share of the proceeds. Further examination of the merits of the claim is necessary to establish what a suitable figure for the assignment should be.'

There was a further meeting on 18 July attended by Mr Ryman, Mr O'Reilly, Mr
E Saville, a managing clerk with Mr Ryman's firm, Mr Trainer, Mr Ashby and Miss Cutler. Miss Prevezer's opinion was discussed. Mr Ryman said that:

> 'He could not risk continuing the litigation without funds as he would be responsible for the costs which would rank as an expense in the liquidation.'

He confirmed that an indemnity from Mr Venables would not be sufficient and added:

> 'If Mr Venables wished him to continue the litigation he must put up cash up front
> F to cover the estimated costs. The other option is to assign.'

Mr Ryman is there reported as having asked Mr Ashby whether he had a figure in mind. Mr Ashby said that Mr Venables would be back in the country very shortly and he would then discuss the matter with him and an offer would be made.

Between 5 and 21 July there were a number of discussions between Mr Ryman and those representing Mr Venables to discuss the merits of Edennote's claim in the Queen's
G Bench action. An oral offer was made by Mr Ashby on 21 July. It was confirmed in a letter of 22 July. On the same day Mr Ryman telephoned Miss Cutler to say that he had agreed to assign Edennote's interest in the claim in the Queen's Bench action for £7,000 plus ten per cent of the net proceeds recovered. She was asked to draft an assignment. Mr Ryman also wrote to the official receiver with an application for sanction 'to compromise a potential debtor of the company by assigning the rights to a third party'. I

H am bound to say that I find that sentence unintelligible. The order which the official receiver was actually asked to make was included; it was an order allowing Mr Ryman to assign Edennote's rights in the Queen's Bench action to Mr Venables. The official receiver replied on 26 July to say that it was not clear that the proposed assignment fell within the category of a compromise, but that he was content that it should proceed without his sanction. Mr Ryman started his holiday on the same day as the letter came from Mr Ashby, that is 22 July (which was a Friday), leaving matters in the hands of Mr

O'Reilly. Miss Cutler had already drafted an appropriate power of attorney under which   A
Mr O'Reilly would execute the assignment. She prepared a draft assignment and sent it
to counsel for approval on 26 July and, later on the same day, to Mr Trainer. She also
drafted a letter to Herbert Smith. It was not sent until 9.54 on the following day, 27 July.
Miss Cutler left for three weeks' holiday, having handed over responsibility for the
completion of the transaction to Miss Picton-Howell. On 27 July Herbert Smith received
the fax letter dated 26 July from Nabarro Nathanson. Mr O'Reilly also received a copy
of the proposed assignment from Nabarro Nathanson and forwarded it to Mr Venables   B
on the same day. Later, he sent the engrossment for execution; it was returned duly
executed with a cheque for £7,000 on 28 July.

The precise time when Mr O'Reilly received and executed and dispatched the engrossed
assignment is not clear from the correspondence. No evidence from Mr O'Reilly has been
adduced. However, it is possible to ascertain the sequence of events from a careful reading
of the correspondence. Nabarro Nathanson's letter of 26 July was faxed to Herbert Smith   C
at 9.54 on 27 July. Mr Watts, the solicitor with Herbert Smith responsible for the conduct
of the Queen's Bench action and the application for security, in replying to that letter by
fax on 27 July refers to a conversation between himself and Mr Saville in the course of
that morning. I was told by Mr McCombe that that conversation in fact took place at
11.30am. The points raised by Mr Watts were repeated in the letter to which I shall turn
in a moment. That letter was sent to Nabarro Nathanson by fax at 4.30 in the afternoon,   D
and it is I think probable that a copy was faxed to Rothman Pantall, Mr Ryman's firm,
with a covering letter headed 'for the attention of Mr Saville' at about the same time.
Miss Picton-Howell in her affidavit evidence says that she sent the assignment to Mr
O'Reilly, the engrossment that is, after she had received Herbert Smith's faxed letter. As
I have said, on 28 July Mr O'Reilly faxed a further letter to Herbert Smith informing him
that the assignment had been completed. In the light of these developments Herbert
Smith had no alternative but to agree an adjournment of the application for security.   E
The letter, dated 26 July but faxed to Herbert Smith at 9.54am on 27 July, was the first
that Herbert Smith had heard of any proposal to assign Edennote's claim in the Queen's
Bench action to Mr Venables or at all. It is clear from that letter that it was sent to
Herbert Smith, not as solicitors for the applicants in their capacity as creditors of
Edennote, but as solicitors to Tottenham plc and Tottenham Ltd in their capacity as
defendants to the Queen's Bench action. Herbert Smith were told that the liquidator was
in the process of assigning Edennote's claim and that notice was being given to Herbert   F
Smith to avoid unnecessary costs being incurred in relation to the application for security.
However, in their reply Herbert Smith made it clear that they were concerned that any
assignment of the claim might prejudice their client's position as creditors and at the fact
that no one except Mr Venables had been approached to see what he was prepared to
pay. Clearly the objection was that neither Tottenham Ltd or Tottenham plc had been
approached. There was no other potential purchaser. They posed a number of questions   G
which the writer, Mr Watts, said had been put to Mr Saville on the morning. One was:

> 'Were any other persons approached as to the possible assignment of the cause of
> action?'

Mr Watts said that he had been informed by Mr Saville that he would need to consult
with Mr O'Reilly. There is no evidence from Mr Saville or Mr O'Reilly as to what, if
anything, passed between them. Herbert Smith asked for an assurance that no further   H
step would be taken without a full explanation being given as to the circumstances
surrounding the assignment. As I have said, the assignment was in fact executed after
that conversation and after that letter had been sent to Nabarro Nathanson and a copy
also sent to Rothman Pantall. Mr O'Reilly replied on the following day to say that the
assignment had been executed and that in consideration of the assignment Mr Venables
had paid £7,000 and had given an undertaking to pay the liquidator ten per cent of any

A   net proceeds recovered by him. He confirmed that no one else had been approached and
he added:

> 'I am sure that you will agree that it would be highly inappropriate to have
> contacted either yourself or your clients as your clients are the defendants to the
> said proceedings. Faced with your clients' application for security of costs at the
> date of our appointment it was clear that it would be necessary for us to carry out
B   an investigation as to the merits of the case and to take appropriate action. Counsel
> was instructed who advised that the most appropriate course of action for the
> liquidator to follow would be to seek an assignment of the action to the other
> plaintiff.'

Nabarro Nathanson on the same day, referring to that letter, sent Herbert Smith a
copy of the assignment. That letter crossed with a letter from Herbert Smith enclosing a
copy of Rothman Pantall's letter in which, referring to the paragraph of the letter from
C   which I have cited a passage, they claimed that:

> 'We would have thought that it was an obvious course of action to approach the
> defendants in the litigation to see whether or not they would in effect be interested
> in settling the litigation. Without making such an approach how can the liquidator
> be assured that he is acting in the best interests of the creditors as a whole?'

D   The correspondence continued with two faxed letters on 29 July. In the first Nabarro
Nathanson, replying to Herbert Smith's letter of 28 July, complained that an assignment
to any person other than Mr Venables would have offended the rules against champerty.
In fact, as I have said, a liquidator exercising a power of sale can sell a cause of action.
The rules against champerty do not apply to such a sale; they would apply to a sale of
the proceeds of an action leaving the cause of action vested in the liquidator but that was
not a course that had been contemplated. Miss Prevezer erred in thinking that an
E   assignment to Mr Venables was permissible only because Mr Venables had a legitimate
interest in the action. That error is understandable and I think irrelevant. The true
position did not become apparent until the hearing of this application. However, it was
clear that Herbert Smith were concerned that Tottenham plc and Tottenham Ltd had
not been approached and there was no possible question that a settlement of the action
as between Tottenham Ltd and Edennote could have been champertous. Herbert Smith
in their letter of 29 July pointed out that:
F

> 'To act in the best interests of the creditors as a whole, your clients should have
> secured the best consideration possible for the claim before disposing of one of
> Edennote's two assets. It may well have been that our clients, if approached, would
> have offered a sum which would have exceeded the nominal payment made by Mr
> Venables and the possible future payment.'

That led to a somewhat strange reply from Nabarro Nathanson on 3 August where it
G   was said:

> 'We note your comments on the assignment to Mr Venables. Mindful of the fact
> that there are two plaintiffs in this action and our client is liquidator of one of
> them, he did not want to do anything to weaken the other plaintiff's position. The
> decision to assign to Mr Venables was taken following careful consideration by
> our client and after advice from both counsel and ourselves.'

H   Herbert Smith in reply to that reiterated that:

> 'The interests your clients should have been paying attention to were not those of
> Mr Venables but those of the creditors as a whole. Any reasonable liquidator
> would have sought to have secured the best possible price before relinquishing the
> claim. In that regard the obvious parties to have approached would have been the
> defendants to see what proposal they had to make. In order to dispose of the

matter, our clients would have been prepared to make an offer in excess of the   A
price received from Mr Venables.'

In her affidavit evidence Miss Howell explains that Miss Cutler before she left
explained the position to her and asked her to 'manage' the transaction. She, Miss Cutler,
had already drafted the assignment and the letter which was faxed to Herbert Smith on
27 July. After receiving Herbert Smith's faxed letter of 27 July she spoke to counsel but
there was insufficient time to ask counsel to consider her reply. As to her observation in   B
her reply of 3 August that Mr Ryman did not want to do anything to weaken Mr
Venables' position she explains that she 'now understands that this was not a point on
which any weight was placed in advising Mr Ryman with regard to the assignment'. No
evidence has been filed by Mr O'Reilly explaining what he meant by saying that it would
have been 'inappropriate' for the liquidator to have contacted Herbert Smith or their
clients.

Matters did not rest there. On 10 August Herbert Smith wrote to Nabarro Nathanson   C
to say that their clients intended to apply to the court to have the assignment set aside.
They referred to Nabarro Nathanson's letter of 3 August as demonstrating the liquidator
had had regard only to the interests of Mr Venables and not to the interests of the
creditors as a whole. Later, Mr Watts received a telephone call from Mr Ryman who
suggested that they should meet to discuss the position, an invitation which Mr Watts
declined. Mr Watts' evidence is that Mr Ryman went on to discuss the assignment. Mr   D
Watts expressed the view that it was inappropriate for him not to have approached
Tottenham Ltd or the applicants. He, Mr Watts, says that Mr Ryman replied that he
had considered such an approach but that Mr Venables had made it clear that he would
not agree to any such course of action. Mr Watts' account of this conversation is disputed
by Mr Ryman. His account is that Mr Watts said that if his clients had been approached
they might have been willing to offer as much as £50,000. Mr Ryman replied that he
thought he had taken care to ensure that the transaction was properly handled and had   E
acted in accordance with the advice of solicitors and counsel. He went on to say:

> 'I had been concerned at the time of the assignment that I was not laying Edennote
> open to a claim by Venables that it had somehow prejudiced his position in relation
> to the proceedings. Whilst this was not something which I had discussed with
> Nabarro Nathanson or counsel, it was at the back of my mind, given the
> contentious nature of the proceedings.'   F

He explains that he has since been advised by Nabarro Nathanson that his concern about
a possible claim by Venables against Edennote with respect to any action by Edennote in
relation to the proceedings was 'misfounded'.

Before turning to the submissions by counsel there is one other aspect of this case
which I should mention. In his affidavit in support of this application Mr Watts exhibited
a letter to Grangewoods dated 12 April in which Herbert Smith expressed willingness to   G
consider a commercial settlement of the Queen's Bench action. He went on to set out a
possible basis for settlement and ended by saying that the offer would remain open for
seven days and no longer. He also referred to a letter from Grangewoods dated 18 April
in which Grangewoods said that they were taking their client's instructions. He then adds
that he had heard nothing further. He refers to a subsequent conversation with Mr Salber
of Grangewoods in which he confirmed that his clients would be willing to consider a   H
commercial settlement and again says that he heard nothing further. The conversation
with Mr Salber is said in a later affidavit to have taken place on 10 June, that is after the
winding-up order had been made but while Grangewoods were still on the record as
solicitors for the plaintiffs in the Queen's Bench action. That evidence is criticised by Mr
Venables and Mr Ryman as incomplete. In fact there was a further letter from
Grangewoods, not referred to by Mr Watts, which is dated 23 April in which

A   Grangewoods explained that their clients were willing to consider a commercial settlement and suggested a meeting and, following the conversation with Mr Salber, a letter from Mr Trainer dated 5 May in which, after referring to a without prejudice meeting which had been arranged for the following Monday to discuss the settlement of the action, he made it clear that he wanted prior confirmation that Herbert Smith would consent to the winding-up petition being taken out of the floating list. Herbert Smith replied on the same day to say that they did not accept that any without prejudice meeting should involve discussions as to the future of the winding-up petition. I think Mr Watts, if he was to exhibit without prejudice correspondence concerning proposals for settlement, should have exhibited all the correspondence, though I accept that he did not intend to mislead the court. The purpose of referring to the letter of 12 April was to show that an offer of settlement had been made. Reference to the subsequent correspondence would have shown only that the possibility of a settlement was abandoned, not because terms could not be agreed, but because Mr Venables' solicitors sought to attach a condition which would have resulted in the adjournment of the winding-up petition. Herbert Smith were, I think, clearly justified in their refusal to adjourn the winding-up petition while negotiations for a settlement were continuing.

    The case for the liquidator can be shortly stated. It is said that on his appointment the liquidator was faced with the prospect that an order for security for costs would be made on 29 July and that unless some means could be found of financing the litigation Edennote would lose the benefit of a claim, which, apart from the prospect of recovering sums paid out to Mr Venables, Grangewoods and Mr Yawetz, was the only substantial asset. When he was first approached on behalf of Mr Venables he explored the possibility of continuing the action if funded by Mr Venables, not only for his own costs but as to any costs that might be awarded against Edennote. When it became apparent that Mr Venables could not afford to do so he took the only course that seemed to him available, to dispose of the right of action for a cash sum which would give him the financial assistance he needed in the liquidation and a share of the proceeds recovered. In doing so he had to evaluate the prospect that the claim would succeed. It did not occur to him to approach Tottenham Ltd or Tottenham plc, who at the time were vigorously pursuing their application for security and had already refused an adjournment. He did not enter into the assignment in order to prefer or assist Mr Venables, nor did he deliberately conceal his intention to enter into the assignment until it was too late for the applicants to object. If he did err in not approaching Tottenham Ltd and the applicants to explore the possibility of a compromise it was an error of judgment, but no more. It cannot be said that it was so gross an oversight as to justify setting aside the assignment. He was advised by solicitors and counsel and neither warned him that he should not proceed with the assignment without first exploring the possibility of a compromise. The fault, it is said, lies as much with the applicants and their advisers as with him. They should have renewed their offer as soon as they learned of his appointment.

    The objectionable term introduced by Mr Venables' solicitors (the postponement of the winding-up petition) had disappeared when the winding-up order was made. Mr Neuberger, who appeared for the liquidator, went so far as to say that the applicants when they failed to raise with the liquidator the possibility of a compromise did so because they preferred to gamble on the prospect that the liquidator would do nothing and that the action would come to an end without further expense to them. Having gambled and lost, they cannot now complain.

    I have after careful consideration come to the conclusion that I cannot accept these submissions. I accept that it is only in very exceptional circumstances that the court will interfere with the exercise by a liquidator of his discretion to sell the assets of an insolvent company. However, in my judgment it should have been obvious to Mr Ryman as soon as he was approached by Mr Venables that the possibility of a sale of Edennote's right of

action to Mr Venables put into his, Mr Venables', hands a very powerful weapon which   A
he could use in negotiations for the settlement of both claims. In everyday language, the
claim in the hands of Mr Venables, whose personal claim against Tottenham plc was
confronted with the contention that he had fully mitigated his loss, had a very
considerable nuisance value. In the event Tottenham plc or perhaps Tottenham Ltd was
prepared to pay £75,000 to avoid that risk. At the very least Mr Ryman should have
inquired from Herbert Smith whether they were willing to enter into negotiations and, if
they proved protracted, to have asked them either to adjourn the application for security   B
or not to apply for judgment in default of compliance while the negotiations were
pursued. Whatever may have been Mr Ryman's motives for not doing so, he in fact failed
to consider one of the two possible ways of realising the company's claim in an
advantageous way. Mr Ryman says that he was concerned that if he approached
Tottenham plc or Tottenham Ltd he might lay himself open to a claim by Mr Venables.
However, he sought no advice on this point during the period between Mr Ashby's first   C
approach and the date that Mr Ryman sought advice from Nabarro Nathanson. Even
then the propriety of approaching Tottenham plc and Tottenham Ltd was not
considered. It is clear from Mr Ryman's evidence that Nabarro Nathanson were
consulted as to the most appropriate method of transferring the claim to Mr Venables
and as to the mechanics for doing so. By the time that Mr Venables consulted Nabarro
Nathanson they were the only matters which had to be considered.

Great stress was placed by Mr Rayner James and Mr Neuberger on the fact that   D
neither Miss Cutler nor Miss Prevezer drew attention to the possibility that a more
favourable deal could be struck with Tottenham plc and Tottenham Ltd. There are two
answers to that submission. First, the question is whether the transaction was one which
a reasonable liquidator, who took into account all relevant and no extraneous
considerations, could have entered into. It is no answer to say that the liquidator acted
in accordance with professional advice if that advice was in fact wrong. That could only   E
be material if the claim were a claim for damages for negligence. The second is that, as I
have already observed, Nabarro Nathanson were consulted after Mr Ryman had agreed
in principle to assign the cause of action to Mr Venables. They were not asked to advise
whether he should endeavour to negotiate better terms with Tottenham plc and
Tottenham Ltd, the only persons who would be interested in the outcome of the claim,
before proceeding to assign to Mr Venables. Very senior and experienced solicitor and
counsel might have raised the point and warned Mr Ryman of the risk he would run if   F
he failed to pursue the possibility of a compromise. But he cannot complain if Miss
Cutler and Miss Prevezer did not step outside the matter on which their assistance was
sought. Then it is said that Mr Ryman should not be criticised for an honest mistake
made under conditions of great urgency. In fact it is clear from *Freightex* that the urgency
was not as great as he and his advisers thought. If negotiations had been opened and had
been protracted until after 29 July and if Tottenham plc and Tottenham Ltd had
withdrawn from negotiations after an order for security had been made it would still   G
have been open to Mr Ryman to have assigned the cause of action to Mr Venables at
any time before the action was actually dismissed. I cannot criticise Miss Cutler and Miss
Prevezer for ignorance of a recent and unreported decision of the Court of Appeal.
However, the urgency was self-created. The question is not whether Mr Ryman should
have told Herbert Smith of the intended assignment in the brief interval between the time
when instructions were given to Miss Cutler to prepare it and the time when it was   H
executed. The questions are whether Mr Ryman should not have opened negotiations
with Tottenham plc and Tottenham Ltd as soon as an approach had been made by Mr
Venables seeking an assignment, and whether Mr O'Reilly as Mr Ryman's delegate was
justified in executing the assignment after Herbert Smith had objected that more could
be obtained for a settlement of Edennote's claim, albeit that that objection was made
(through no fault on the part of Herbert Smith and their clients) at the eleventh hour.

A   For the reasons I have given I do not think that this assignment can stand.

The removal of Mr Ryman as liquidator

Under s. 172 of the 1986 Act a liquidator of a company which is being wound up by the court can be removed by the court or at a general meeting of creditors summoned for that purpose. The possibility of summoning a general meeting was considered by Herbert Smith and rejected, rightly I think, because Mr Venables claims to be a creditor with a

B   claim much in excess of the applicant's debt and would inevitably vote against the resolution. A creditors' meeting therefore would inevitably be followed by a dispute and litigation as to whether he should be allowed to vote. Herbert Smith invited the official receiver to ask the Secretary of State to exercise his power to remove Mr Ryman. The Secretary of State expressed the view that, as the validity of the assignment would not be resolved by the removal of Mr Ryman as liquidator, it would be more appropriate if the

C   matter were referred to the court at the same time. No objection has been raised by Mr Ryman's advisers to this application on the ground that the application should first have been canvassed at a meeting of creditors.

The power of a court to remove a liquidator was considered by Millett J in *Re Keypak Homecare Ltd* (1987) 3 BCC 558. There the liquidation was a creditors' voluntary liquidation and the application was made under s. 108(2). Under that subsection the

D   court can remove a liquidator on cause shown. Those words do not appear in s. 172(1). The explanation I think is that a liquidator in a compulsory winding up is an officer of the court. The liquidator in a voluntary winding up is not, and the court cannot act unless on some cause shown. However, the difference in the language of the two sections is immaterial for the purposes of this case.

In *Keypak* Mr Edgar had been appointed liquidator at a creditors' meeting by a

E   majority in number but not in value of the creditors. A number of smaller creditors had given a proxy to the managing director who exercised the proxy votes in favour of the appointment of Mr Edgar. The principal complaint was that a company previously dormant had come to life and was trading from the same premises with the same staff and equipment and was selling the company's stock and that it was a Phoenix company, created or revived to continue the insolvent company's trade without paying for its goodwill or more for its stock than a forced sale valuation. It was said that Mr Edgar

F   had accepted a fait accompli and had not taken proper steps to investigate the transaction or to recover stock of the company which appeared to be missing. Millett J observed (at p. 561) that if Mr Edgar believed that exacting,

> 'a forced-sale price for the stock that he could trace, then that was all the creditors could reasonably expect. If that was the view that Mr Edgar took it was a view, unfortunately, which has been all too prevalent amongst liquidators and has been the cause of very considerable disquiet among creditors, and it is a view which I

G
> hope will not be held again. It is an attitude which it is one of the purposes of the Insolvency Act 1986 to change.'

He decided that Mr Edgar should be removed, and said at pp. 563–564:

> 'It was submitted to me that the rule laid down in that last case (a reference to *Re Adam Eyton Ltd* (1887) 36 ChD 299), that in order to effect the removal of the liquidator the court needs only to be satisfied that it is for the general advantage of

H
> those interested in the assets of the company that the liquidator be removed, must be read in the context of the facts of the case and that very special circumstances must exist before the power can be exercised in a case in which no personal misconduct or unfitness can be shown on the part of the liquidator.

> There were special circumstances in that case, but I do not read the general principle laid down by the Court of Appeal as being limited to cases in which

special circumstances can be shown. On the contrary, the words of the statute are   A
very wide and it would be dangerous and wrong for a court to seek to limit or
define the kind of cause which is required. Circumstances vary widely, and it may
be appropriate to remove a liquidator even though nothing can be said against
him, either personally or in his conduct of the particular liquidation.

In the present case I approach the matter in this way. There is nothing that can be
said against Mr Edgar so far as his personal propriety is concerned. There is no   B
evidence of any misconduct or wrongdoing on his part, or of his intimacy or
friendship with the directors of the company at all. He is a professional,
independent, and experienced liquidator. But I am not impressed by his
performance in the conduct of this liquidation. I take the view that his experience,
gained in times when liquidators were accustomed to directors simply removing
the stock before liquidation and then paying for them afterwards at forced-sale
values, has stood him in ill stead. As a result, he has adopted a relaxed and   C
complacent attitude to such conduct, and in my judgment the creditors, who were
outraged by what they believed had happened, were perfectly reasonable in the
view that Mr Edgar was not likely to pursue the directors with anything like
sufficient vigour. If that was the view they adopted at the meeting, then it has been
amply confirmed by all that has taken place since. I, too, take the view that Mr
Edgar is unlikely to pursue the directors with anything like sufficient vigour.   D

Mr Edgar may well have a justified feeling that he is being treated a little like
Admiral Byng, and that he is being removed from office "in order to encourage
the others". I do not shrink from that. In an insolvency the stock is not there to be
taken by the outgoing directors and traded with for weeks before the
commencement of the liquidation and then simply paid for at an artificially low
forced-sale valuation; and the sooner that liquidators recognise that the better.

In circumstances such as the present, the creditors are entitled to expect either the   E
suspicious matters to be cleared up very shortly after the creditors' meeting, or
proceedings to be commenced against the former directors with speed and pursued
with vigour. A liquidator who can see from the statement of affairs that there are
likely to be insufficient assets to enable him to discharge his duties ought to make
the position clear at the meeting of creditors and insist upon being authorised by
those present at the meeting to take such steps as may be necessary. But simply to   F
stand back and do nothing and then claim that that is justified by the lack of
finance is not, in my judgment, good enough.'

Mr Neuberger and Mr Rayner James pointed out that in that case Millett J was
influenced by general considerations of policy, the need not to be seen to countenance
the continuation of practices which the 1986 Act was designed to prevent. However, his
decision is founded on and usefully illustrates the general principle that liquidators must
act in the interests of the general body of creditors and should not continue in office if in   G
the circumstances the creditors no longer have confidence in his ability to realise the
assets of the company to their best advantage and to pursue claims with due diligence.

A number of criticisms of the liquidator's conduct have been made. They are as
follows:

(1)   Mr Venables' shares of Edennote were partly paid. They were purportedly   H
transferred to another company controlled by Mr Venables, which it is said is
unlikely to be able to meet a call, but that was after the winding-up petition had
been presented and is void under s. 127 of the 1986 Act. A request for payment of
the sums due was met with a claim that Mr Venables proposed to meet the call by
way of adjustment to his loan account. Nabarro Nathanson then pointed out that
a call on a contributory could not be set off against a claim against the company

A and said that on the expiry of 21 days from the request the official receiver would be asked for leave to make a call. I understand that an application to the court under r. 4.204 has now been made and is due to be heard in a week or so's time. Mr Venables now accepts that he is not entitled to set off the call against a debt claimed against the company. The liquidator might, I think, have acted more diligently, bearing in mind that he had no other cash resources and that one reason for executing the assignment is said to have been to obtain money with which to

B carry out his duties, £7,000 of which £2,000 was absorbed in the liquidator's costs of the assignment. The matter was first raised in mid-September. However, the dispute concerning the assignment must clearly have taken precedence in the liquidator's mind, and I do not think that any serious criticism can be made of his failure to demand that Mr Venables pay the sum claimed, £37,500, coupled with a threat that an application to the court to enforce a call would be made unless it

C was promptly paid.

(2) Mr Venables claims to be a creditor in the sum of £972,000. The liquidator has been criticised for his failure to investigate this claim. The circumstances in which this debt arose are shortly as follows. A loan of approximately £1m was made by a company called Landhurst Leasing to enable Edennote to take up the rights issue by Tottenham plc. Mr Venables says that the loan was made to him and by him to

D Edennote. It was credited to his loan account and from time to time Edennote made repayments to Landhurst which were debited to his loan account. Landhurst is in administrative receivership, and I understand that it is also the subject of an enquiry by the Department of Trade and Industry. The receiver supplied Herbert Smith with a copy of what purports to be a lease-back agreement between Landhurst and Edennote under which Edennote was paid £1m for assets which were then leased back to Edennote. This document came into the hands of Herbert

E Smith subject to an undertaking of confidentiality pending the showing of a television programme, 'Panorama', originally fixed for the penultimate Monday in October, though it was later postponed until Monday of last week. Mr Venables claims that what purports to be his signature on the document was either a forgery or that the document was altered after he had signed it. He also relies on an agreement dated 10 September 1993 between himself, Landhurst and the receiver, the result of which, he says, is that some payments were made to Landhurst by

F Edennote but liability for substantial sums are recoverable by him but not by the receivers of Landhurst from Edennote. I find it unnecessary to explore this dispute, and it would be wrong to do so on this occasion. The dispute has already been the subject of considerable publicity. All that can be said is that these matters will have to be investigated by the liquidator before the claim is admitted in full. I should add that it seems probable from the documents I have seen that Mr Venables will

G be a substantial creditor of Edennote even if the transaction with Landhurst is left out of account.

(3) Mr Venables was paid £435,966, ostensibly in part repayment of his loan account on 15 September 1993. Payments were also made to Grangewoods and to Mr Yawetz, in whose favour charges had been created, also within the six months preceding the presentation of the winding-up petition. These charges and payments are prima facie unlawful preferences within s. 240. What is said is that, although

H there might be difficulty in recovering from Mr Venables, there is no reason why a claim should not have been made against Grangewoods and if necessary pursued by an application to the court as a matter of extreme urgency.

I do not think that any of these criticisms would by themselves justify removing Mr Ryman. They, or at least the first and third of them, are at the most matters to be weighed in the balance, and I do not think that great weight should be given to them. However, I

406
           Re Edennote Ltd   **[1995] BCC**
           (Sir *John Vinelott*)

have come to the conclusion after some hesitation that the right course is to remove Mr   A
Ryman. I reach this conclusion primarily on the ground that the first task that will
confront the liquidator will be to consider whether to accept the offer of £75,000 now
made in settlement of the claim against Tottenham Ltd, whether to invite Mr Venables
to make a further offer of an increased share of the proceeds of the liquidation, and, if he
does, how to evaluate the likely prospects of recovery in proceedings which are bound to
be costly and protracted and the expense of which is unlikely to be fully reflected in any
order for costs. I do not think that the applicants or the other creditors can fairly be   B
asked to accept the decision of Mr Ryman now that it has been shown that he was willing
to enter into an assignment to Mr Venables without giving any consideration to the
possibility of negotiating a satisfactory compromise with Tottenham plc and Tottenham
Ltd and in proceeding with the assignment (by his attorney Mr O'Reilly) after objection
had been made by Mr Watts. That, I think, is sufficient in itself.

I should add that it seems to me also better in the interests of Edennote and its creditors   C
that the winding up should be in the hands of a liquidator with the resources to investigate
claims which are likely to be resisted. An insolvency practitioner of the highest repute,
Mr Neil Cooper, a partner in Robson Rhodes, has been approached by the applicants
and is willing to act if given an indemnity by the applicants for his costs and remuneration
which are not recovered in the liquidation. At present the liquidator has no funds to
which he can have resort except the £37,500 due from Mr Venables, which will soon be   D
absorbed in costs if it has not been absorbed already.

There is a claim for repayment of tax on franked investment income but that will not
be paid unless a claim for VAT on the purported lease-back transaction which the Crown
will be entitled to set off is shown to have been unfounded. Mr Ryman, if he remains the
liquidator, will be wholly dependent on a rapid resolution of the claims against
Grangewoods and Mr Yawetz. There is no real prospect that other creditors will be
willing to support the costs of a liquidation by him.   E

In these circumstances I think the right course is to remove Mr Ryman as liquidator. I
understand that no objection is raised to the appointment of Mr Neil Cooper and that
Mr Venables is willing to accept his appointment without a reference to chambers. As I
am removing Mr Ryman as liquidator I think I should stress that no attack has been
made on his integrity and good faith. It would be wrong to conclude on the evidence that
I have seen that his intention to assign the benefit of the claim to Mr Venables was   F
deliberately concealed from the applicants. But in my judgment fairness to the other
creditors, in particular the applicants, requires that the disposal of the claim against
Tottenham Ltd, whether by assignment or compromise, be confided to a new liquidator
who can bring a fresh mind to bear on this question.

I will reserve argument on the question of costs until the parties have had an
opportunity of considering this judgment.   G

(*Order accordingly*)

   H

A
New Zealand Guardian Trust Co Ltd v Brooks & Ors.

Privy Council.
Lord Keith of Kinkel, Lord Oliver of Aylmerton, Lord Mustill, Lord Lloyd of Berwick, Lord Nicholls of Birkenhead.
Judgment delivered 17 November 1994.

B
Negligence – Whether directors acting within scope of agency – Whether company vicariously liable.

This was an appeal from a decision of the Court of Appeal of New Zealand. The question at issue was whether or not the directors of a company which under the terms of a debenture trust deed was obliged to furnish to the trustee of the deed regular certificates as to certain aspects of the company's affairs, signed by two of the directors on behalf of all of them, were or were not joint tortfeasors with the company in respect of alleged negligence in the preparation of the certificates.

C

When the company fell into financial difficulties and was unable to repay the advances made by the debenture holders, they sued the appellants, the trustee under the debenture, to recover the shortfall alleging breaches of the duties owed to them under the trust deed. The appellants joined as third parties the directors of the company at the material time, claiming indemnity or contribution in respect of the claims against them by the debenture holders.

D
The appellants had released the company from liability and the directors argued that that released them. The appellants argued that the duty under the trust deed to furnish directors' quarterly reporting certificates to the trustee imposed on the directors a personal duty to exercise reasonable care and skill in the preparation of the requisite certificates, quite independent of any duty which might be incumbent on the company. Therefore the directors were not joint tortfeasors with the company. The High Court as a preliminary issue decided in favour of the appellants. The Court of Appeal allowed the directors' appeal.

E
Held, dismissing the appeal:

1. The directors were the company's agents and were acting within the scope of their agency when they prepared the certificates. They could not have prepared them if they had not been authorised by the company to do so, and their doing so was for the benefit of the company because the rendering of the certificates was necessary to the maintenance of the loans to it.

F
2. The fact that the directors assumed a personal responsibility to see that the certificates complied with the requirements of the trust deed and to exercise reasonable care in their preparation and that the company might not itself have owed any duty of care to the appellants in relation to the preparation of the certificates did not necessarily mean that the company could not be liable for the negligence of its directors acting within the scope of their authority.

G
3. There was nothing in the trust deed which showed an intention that any liability for the negligent preparation of certificates was to rest on the directors alone, to the exclusion of the company.

4. The company was vicariously liable for the negligence of its directors in the preparation of the certificates and was accordingly a joint tortfeasor with them. The release of the company therefore had the effect of releasing also the directors.

H
The following cases were referred to in the judgment:

Cassidy v Ministry of Health [1951] 2 KB 343.
Kuwait Asia Bank EC v National Mutual Life Nominees Ltd [1990] BCC 567; [1991] 1 AC 187.
Lloyd v Grace, Smith & Co [1912] AC 716.
McGowan & Co v Dyer (1873) LR 8 QB 141.

J G Miles QC and G W Hall (both New Zealand Bar) (instructed by Dibb Lupton   A
Broomhead) for the trustee company.

Rhys Harrison QC and Gerard Kilpatrick (both New Zealand Bar) (instructed by
Wray Smith & Co) for the directors.

JUDGMENT
(Delivered by Lord Keith of Kinkel)   B

This is an appeal from the Court of Appeal of New Zealand. The question at issue is
whether or not the directors of a company which under the terms of a debenture trust
deed was obliged to furnish to the trustee of the deed regular certificates as to certain
aspects of the company's affairs, signed by two of the directors on behalf of all of them,
are or are not joint tortfeasors with the company in respect of alleged negligence in the
preparation of the certificates.

The company, Budget Rent A Car Ltd ('Budget'), borrowed money from a consortium   C
of financiers and bankers. The advance was secured by a debenture trust deed dated
5 May 1987 entered into between Budget, Budget Lease Management (Car Sales) Ltd
and the present appellants ('NZGT'), the holders of the debentures being the lenders
mentioned above. The total moneys advanced amounted to $17.25m. Budget fell into
financial difficulties and was unable to repay the advances made by the debenture holders.
Two of these, Westpac Securities Ltd ('Westpac') and DFC Financial Services Ltd   D
('DFC') entered into a deed of compromise with Budget dated 30 July 1990 by which
they agreed to accept $10.537m in full and final settlement of their claims. This sum was
in fact advanced to Budget under new financing arrangements. There was a shortfall of
$2.712m in respect of the claims in question, and Westpac and DFC are suing NZGT to
recover this sum alleging breaches of the duties owed to them under the trust deed.
NZGT have joined as third parties the directors of Budget at the material time, claiming
indemnity or contribution in respect of the claims against it by Westpac and DFC. By   E
deed dated 7 August 1990 NZGT released Budget from all liabilities towards it. The
release did not cover the directors of Budget.

The directors of Budget, in answer to the claim against them, pleaded the release of
7 August 1990. The effect of this was tried, as a preliminary issue under r. 418 of the High
Court rules, before Barker J. By judgment delivered on 2 August 1993 he decided the
issue in favour of NZGT. The directors appealed, and on 17 December 1993 the Court   F
of Appeal (Sir Robin Cooke P, Richardson and Casey JJ) reversed the judgment of
Barker J and dismissed NZGT's claim against the directors.

Under cl. 6.01 of the trust deed Budget covenanted with NZGT that it would from
time to time during the currency of the deed do various things, including:

'Furnish directors' quarterly reporting certificates
(h) on or before the last day of the month (or such later date as the trustee shall in   G
writing agree) after the end of each financial quarterly period of the company in
each year and at any other dates the company may elect and if so required by the
trustee, on or before the last day of the month following any month during which
the trustee shall request the same (which request shall only be made if the trustee
considers that special circumstances warrant such request and so certifies in writing
to the company specifying such special circumstances), furnish to the trustee a
certificate signed by not less than two directors on behalf of the directors, in such   H
form and with such qualifications (if any) as the trustee in its discretion may
approve:
(A) stating to the best of the directors' knowledge and belief after having made
all due enquiry, whether or not since the date as at which the last such
certificate was given, or in the case of the first such certificate, since the date

A   of this deed (each such date being referred to in this para. (h) as a 'certification date'):

> (i) any matters have in their opinion occurred to affect adversely the interests of the stockholders, and if so giving particulars thereof; . . .'

There followed a great many other matters which it is unnecessary to set out.

B   Counsel for the appellants before the board did not dispute the existence and continued validity in New Zealand of the rule that the release of one joint tortfeasor from liability operates to release also all the others. The argument was that the effect of cl. 6.01(h) of the trust deed was to impose upon the directors of Budget a personal duty owed to NZGT, quite independent of any duty which might be incumbent on Budget, to exercise reasonable care and skill in the preparation of the requisite certificates. Therefore the directors were not joint tortfeasors with Budget.

C   The respondents' case is that Budget is vicariously liable for the negligence of the directors in the preparation of the certificates and is accordingly a joint tortfeasor with them on that basis.

In *Lloyd v Grace, Smith & Co* [1912] AC 716 at p. 737 Lord Macnaghten quoted with approval the following passage from the judgment of Blackburn J in *McGowan & Co v Dyer* (1873) LR 8 QB 141 at p. 145:

D
> 'In *Story on Agency*, the learned author states, in section 452, the general rule that the principal is liable to third persons in a civil suit "for the frauds, deceits, concealments, misrepresentations, torts, negligences, and other malfeasances or misfeasances, and omissions of duty of his agent in the course of his employment, although the principal did not authorise, or justify, or participate in, or indeed know of such misconduct, or even if he forbade the acts, or disapproved of them."
>
E
> He then proceeds, in section 456: "But although the principal is thus liable for the torts and negligences of his agent, yet we are to understand the doctrine with its just limitations, that the tort or negligence occurs in the course of the agency. For the principal is not liable for the torts or negligences of his agent in any matters beyond the scope of the agency, unless he has expressly authorised them to be done, or he has subsequently adopted them for his own use and benefit." '

F   The directors of Budget were its agents, and the question is whether or not they were acting in the course of their agency when they prepared the certificates. There can be no doubt that they were acting in their capacity as directors when they did so, and indeed this was conceded by counsel for the appellants. Further, they were acting within the scope of their agency. They could not have prepared the certificates if they had not been authorised by Budget to do so, and their doing so was for the benefit of Budget because the rendering of the certificates was necessary to the maintenance of the loans to it. It is

G to be accepted that the directors assumed a personal responsibility towards NZGT to see that the certificates complied with the requirements of the trust deed and to exercise reasonable care in their preparation, but in most if not all cases where the acts of an employee or agent render the employer or principal vicariously liable it is because the employee or agent was in breach of a duty which he personally owed to the injured party.

There are, of course, cases where the principal or employer himself owes a duty of care

H to the person who has been injured by the act of the agent or employee. That was the basis of the decision in *Cassidy v Ministry of Health* [1951] 2 KB 343 where it was held that a hospital authority which had undertaken the treatment of a patient owed the patient a duty of care in relation to the treatment, and could not escape liability on the ground that the injury had resulted from negligence on the part of the medical staff who had actually administered the treatment. But vicarious liability can and very frequently does arise in the absence of any duty directly owed by the principal or employer. A

familiar instance is that of negligence on the part of the driver of a vehicle. The employer   A
of the driver does not himself owe any duty to users of the highway in relation to the
manner of driving of the vehicle, yet is liable for the negligence of his employee. So in the
present case the fact that Budget may not itself have owed any duty of care to NZGT in
relation to the preparation of the certificates does not necessarily mean that it cannot be
liable for the negligence of its directors acting within the scope of their authority. It is no
doubt possible that the terms of a contract such as that which is here involved may be
such as to make it plain that any liability for the negligent preparation of certificates is to   B
rest on the directors alone, to the exclusion of the company. But their Lordships can find
nothing in the general structure of this trust deed or the particular language of cl. 6.01
capable of evincing an intention that such should be the position in the present case.
Their Lordships were not referred to any authority or statement of principle indicating a
possible basis of distinction between cases where the negligence of directors acting within
the scope of their authority might engage the liability of the company and cases where it   C
does not. In the circumstances they cannot perceive any valid grounds upon which
vicarious liability of the company might be negatived in the instant case.

Counsel for the appellants sought to derive support for their argument from certain
dicta of Lord Lowry in *Kuwait Asia Bank EC v National Mutual Life Nominees Ltd* [1990]
BCC 567. That case was similar to the present in that it involved a claim arising out of
alleged negligence on the part of directors of a company ('AICS') in preparing certificates
to be furnished by the company to the trustee for deposit holders. Two of the directors in   D
question (House and August) were employees of the Kuwait bank, which had nominated
these employees as directors. The trustee sought to make the Kuwait Bank liable for their
negligence, but although succeeding before the Court of Appeal of New Zealand failed
before the judicial committee.

Lord Lowry, delivering the advice of the board, said at p. 586D–F:

> 'House and August owed three separate duties. They owed in the first place to   E
> AICS the duty to perform their duties as directors without gross negligence; the
> liability of a director to his company is set forth in the judgment of Romer J in *Re
> City Equitable Fire Insurance Co Ltd* [1925] Ch 407. They owed a duty to [the
> plaintiff] to use reasonable care to see that the certificates complied with the
> requirements of the trust deed. Finally, they owed a duty to their employer, the
> bank, to exercise reasonable diligence and skill in the performance of their duties   F
> as directors of AICS.
>
> If House and August did not exercise reasonable care to see that the quarterly
> certificates were accurate, they committed a breach of the duty they owed to [the
> plaintiff] and may have committed a breach of the duty they owed to AICS and a
> breach of the duty they owed to the bank to exercise reasonable diligence and skill.
> But these duties were separate and distinct and different in scope and nature. The   G
> bank was not responsible for a breach of the duties owed by House and August to
> AICS or to [the plaintiff] any more than AICS or [the plaintiff] were responsible
> for a breach of duty by House and August.'

Later at p. 588A, he said:

> 'The only rights and remedies of [the plaintiff] were against AICS for breach of
> contract and against the directors of AICS who owed a duty to [the plaintiff]. By
> the trust deed, the quarterly certificates were rendered on behalf of the directors   H
> and nobody else.'

The issue before the board was whether the Kuwait bank was liable to the plaintiff trustee
for breaches of the duty owed to it by House and August. That issue was answered in the
negative. No question arose as to whether AICS was liable for these breaches of duty.
There was no argument about that. It was clearly not in the forefront of Lord Lowry's

A   mind. It is difficult to understand what may have been in his mind when he referred, in the last two lines of the passage first quoted above, to the possibility of the plaintiff being liable for a breach of duty by House and August. In the result the passages in question, which are purely obiter, cannot be regarded as expressing a considered view upon the sort of question which arises in the present appeal. In their Lordships' opinion Budget was vicariously liable for the negligence of its directors in the preparation of the certificates and was accordingly a joint tortfeasor with them. The release of Budget
B   therefore had the effect of releasing also the directors.

     For these reasons their Lordships will humbly advise Her Majesty that the appeal should be dismissed. The appellants must pay the respondents' costs before their Lordships' board.

(Appeal dismissed)

C

D

E

F

G

H

Re McKeen (a Debtor).

Chancery Division (Manchester District Registry).
Morritt J.
Judgment delivered 1 April 1992.

Bankruptcy – Voluntary arrangement – Post arrangement creditor obtained bankruptcy order – Debtor sought to annul bankruptcy order – Whether voluntary arrangement terminated on making of bankruptcy order – Whether debts in voluntary arrangement were bankruptcy debts – Insolvency Act 1986, s. 282(1)(b), 283(5), 382(1).

This was an appeal by the debtor against the district judge's refusal to annul a bankruptcy order under s. 282(1)(b) of the Insolvency Act 1986.

After a voluntary arrangement had been approved in relation to the debtor, rent became due on the debtor's business premises and the landlord served a statutory demand and obtained a bankruptcy order. The debtor applied to the court for the annulment of the bankruptcy order under s. 282(1)(b), the debt and costs due to the landlord and the official receiver's costs having been paid. The district judge concluded that the debts due to the creditors bound by the voluntary arrangement were bankruptcy debts within s. 382(1) of the 1986 Act and that they had not been paid in full or secured to the satisfaction of the court.

On appeal the debtor submitted that the making of the bankruptcy order did not terminate the voluntary arrangement, and that the effect of the voluntary arrangement was to novate the pre-existing liabilities to the creditors bound thereby to a right to share pari passu in the property subject to it so that at the date of the bankruptcy order the debtor was no longer subject to those liabilities. In the alternative he submitted that the debts of the creditors bound by the voluntary arrangement had not been proved in the bankruptcy, and that there was no point in giving them the opportunity to prove therein because they had indicated no wish to do so.

Held, allowing the appeal and annulling the bankruptcy order:

1. The debtor did not contend that the voluntary arrangement imposed a trust in favour of the creditors bound thereby on the property subject to it. Nor was it contended that the voluntary arrangement gave rise to any security in their favour. Thus the bankruptcy order had the consequence of vesting in the trustee the assets comprised in the voluntary arrangement.

2. The trustee took the property comprised in the voluntary arrangement subject to the rights of the creditors to have it applied for their benefit in accordance with the provisions of the voluntary arrangement. Therefore the voluntary arrangement did not terminate on the making of the bankruptcy order.

3. The voluntary arrangement continued notwithstanding the bankruptcy order, and the debts thereunder were not bankruptcy debts within s. 382(1). The debtor was not subject to any debt or liability in respect of those debts at the date of the bankruptcy order. The creditors having agreed to the voluntary arrangement had precluded themselves from proof in the bankruptcy so long as the voluntary arrangement continued.

Anthony Elleray (instructed by R C Moorhouse, Leeds) for the debtor.

Mr McCarthy appeared as the representative of the official receiver.

JUDGMENT

Morritt J: This appeal raises questions concerning the effect on a voluntary arrangement entered into by a debtor with his creditors pursuant to Pt. VIII of the *Insolvency Act* 1986, of a subsequent bankruptcy order against the debtor made on the petition of a creditor who is not bound by the voluntary arrangement.

A   The debtor and Mr Fineberg carried on business in partnership as a recruitment
agency. Due to the insolvency of various substantial debtors to the partnership, by
2 April 1990 the partnership itself was insolvent. The partners consulted an authorised
insolvency practitioner who drew up a statement of affairs as at 23 May 1990. On the
same date, the Leeds County Court made an interim order under the *Insolvency Act* 1986,
s. 252.

B   The partners were lessees of the premises from which the business was conducted. The
lease was granted in 1987 for a ten-year term with power to terminate at three-yearly
intervals. In the statement of affairs, the landlord was shown as a creditor whose debt for
rent had been paid by 23 May 1990 so that nothing was owed at that date. But on 24
June 1990, further rent became due. The lease was terminated by notice expiring on 29
September 1990.

C   On 4 June 1990, the nominee referred to in the debtor's proposals reported to the court
that in his opinion a meeting of the debtor's creditors should be summoned to consider
the debtor's proposals. Such a meeting was convened for and duly held on 26 June 1990
when the proposals with one amendment were approved unanimously by all creditors
present in person or by proxy. Notice of the meeting had not been given to the landlord
because when given to the other creditors the landlord was not then a creditor to whom
a debt was presently due.

D   In the proposals approved by the creditors the debtor stated:

> 'I, Stephen Alexander McKeen of Larkhill, Linton Common, Linton, Wetherby,
> make the following proposal to my creditors for a voluntary arrangement in
> satisfaction of my debts. I am insolvent and wish to make an equitable distribution
> of my property between my creditors. I consider that the implementation of a
> voluntary arrangement will be quicker and cheaper than bankruptcy proceedings
E   > to the corresponding benefit of my creditors.'

He then described the partnership and its insolvency, and dealt with the requirements of
the *Insolvency Rules* 1986, r. 5.3(2). The assets to be subject to the arrangement were to
be the partnership assets and his personal assets excluding the employment agency licence
and his personal chattels respectively. Preferential creditors were to be paid in full by the
supervisor. Secured creditors were to be dealt with by agreement or refinancing.

F   The material provisions of the proposal are as follows:

> 'The duration of the proposed voluntary arrangement is two years or such longer
> time as shall be to the sole discretion of the supervisor, absolutely necessary for the
> supervisor to realise the assets, agree the claims of creditors and deal with all
> matters arising during the voluntary arrangement.

G   > For the purpose of a distribution, the liabilities shall be as at the date of the
> meeting of creditors under s. 257.

> I propose that proofs submitted to rank for payment of a dividend in the voluntary
> arrangement shall not bear interest from the date of the implementation of the
> arrangement.

> I propose that all my creditors, including those whose claims are contingent or as
H   > yet unquantified, should be invited to submit particulars of their proof as at the
> date of implementation of the voluntary arrangement to the supervisor. I further
> propose that in admitting proofs of debt under this arrangement, the supervisor
> shall apply those provisions of the rules relating to admission for payment of
> proofs of debt by a trustee in bankruptcy. In the event of any proof being rejected,
> the creditor shall have right of application to the court for directions on the
> admissibility or otherwise of such proof.

It is proposed to deal with all other liabilities by payment of an interim dividend   A
as quickly as possible and a second and final distribution will be paid as close as
practicable to the first anniversary of the commencement of the arrangement.

In the event of the termination of the arrangement, any funds held by the
supervisor for the purpose of payment to creditors but not so paid, are to be held
on deposit or invested in recognised securities until payment to any trustee in
bankruptcy subsequently appointed. If no such bankruptcy proceedings are   B
commenced, the balance is to be paid to such person as the court may direct on the
application of an interested party.

The proposed functions of the supervisor are to agree the creditors' claims and to
realise, bank and distribute the funds to be included in the arrangement. I propose
to give the supervisor specific powers to dispose of property belonging to the
partnership, to sign any transfer or conveyance necessary to effect this, and to give   C
a valid receipt for moneys. The supervisor is to keep such records of his receipts
and payments and of his acts and dealings as are required by law.'

Corresponding proposals were made by Mr Fineberg and approved by his creditors.

In April or May 1991, the landlord served a statutory demand on the debtor in respect
of rent due on or after 24 June 1990. The debtor did nothing then, or when the
bankruptcy petition was served on him on 7 October 1991 because the supervisor's   D
assistant informed him that the landlord was bound by the terms of the voluntary
arrangement.

A bankruptcy order was made on 22 November 1991, and on 2 December 1991 the
debtor applied to the court for the annulment of the bankruptcy under s. 282(1)(b) of the
Insolvency Act 1986. That section provides, so far as material:

'The court may annul a bankruptcy order . . . if it at any time appears to the court–   E

    . . .

    (b) that, to the extent required by the rules, the bankruptcy debts and the
         expenses of the bankruptcy have all, since the making of the order, been
         either paid or secured for to the satisfaction of the court.'

By the time the application was made, the debt and costs due to the landlord, and the   F
costs of the official receiver had been paid in full by the debtor's employer; but those
creditors who were bound by the voluntary arrangement had not been.

The district judge found himself in some difficulty, with which I sympathise, because
the circumstances of the case were novel, and the application to annul was supported by
the official receiver and there was no opposition. The district judge concluded that the
debts due to the creditors bound by the voluntary arrangement were bankruptcy debts as   G
defined in the *Insolvency Act* 1986, s. 382(1) and as they had not been paid in full or
secured to the satisfaction of the court he dismissed the application.

His reasons are clearly set out on pp. 4 and 5 of his judgment in the following terms:

' "(a) . . . any debt or liability to which he is subject at the commencement of the
bankruptcy."

The question therefore to be decided is whether or not all the debts or liabilities to   H
which the debtor was subject on 22 November 1991 have been paid or secured to
the satisfaction of the court, and more particularly are the debts of the voluntary
arrangement debts to which the bankrupt is subject.

Section 260 of the Act is the only section that gives an explanation of the effect of
the approval of the arrangement by all creditors. It says:

A

"The approved arrangement takes effect as if made by the debtor at the meeting and binds every person who in accordance with the rules had notice of, and was entitled to vote at, the meeting (whether or not he was present or represented at it) as if he were a party to the arrangement."

It becomes a quasi contractual arrangement bound by the arrangement, and cannot take any further proceedings against the debtor personally.

B

They relied on the supervisor to pay the dividend. The arrangement could not be any more powerful than s. 252(2) which prevents proceedings, or execution, or legal process by those creditors against a debtor; but it cannot mean the debtor is not still subject to those liabilities.

If the supervisor were under appropriate circumstances to petition the court to make a bankruptcy order, the arrangement would fall down and the creditors

C

would be entitled to petition in the bankruptcy for all their debts. Similarly, if a creditor who was not bound by the voluntary arrangement were to seek a bankruptcy order against a debtor, and the power was annulled, the creditor should try to get an annulment, and the creditors subject to the voluntary arrangement would have no call with the other creditors to claim against the assets of the debtor surely; but an individual could argue that the creditors subject to the

D

voluntary arrangement have to do the best they can with what was available for them, and that the other creditors may divide up later assets. It cannot be that the potential creditor – the landlord in this case – should be paid in full when none of the other creditors have received any payment at all.

I accept wholeheartedly that the creditors under a voluntary arrangement cannot press the debtor for earlier payment so long as the voluntary arrangement continues. They have to wait for action from the supervisor to have the bankrupt

E

made bankrupt whether by default, as in this case, or even by a petition. It seems to me that the debts which are then owed by the debtor are debts to which he is subject, being the date of the bankruptcy order. The crucial date is the date of the bankruptcy order. It is on that date the debts of the bankruptcy order are crystallised.'

The district judge also made certain criticisms of the debtor's disclosures to the official

F

receiver. I admitted a further affidavit from the debtor which explains to my satisfaction what appeared to the district judge to be discrepancies.

The debtor appeals on the ground that the district judge was wrong in law in his construction of 'bankruptcy debts' in the *Insolvency Act* 1986, s. 382(1). Before me, there was no one interested in opposing the appeal, but counsel for the debtor has helpfully taken me through the relevant provisions of the Act and the rules. He submitted that the

G

making of the bankruptcy order did not terminate the voluntary arrangement, and that the effect of the voluntary arrangement was to novate the pre-existing liabilities to the creditors bound thereby to a right to share pari passu in the property subject to it so that at the date of the bankruptcy order the debtor was no longer subject to those liabilities. In the alternative he submitted that the debts of the creditors bound by the voluntary arrangement had not been proved in the bankruptcy, and that there was no point in giving them the opportunity to prove therein because they had indicated no wish to do

H

so.

Individual voluntary arrangements are dealt with in Pt. VIII of the Insolvency Act. There is no restriction on the proposals which a debtor may put forward to his creditors. It is up to the creditors to decide whether or not to accept them. Thus a voluntary arrangement may take many different forms. As the district judge noted only s. 260 indicates the effect of a voluntary arrangement. Subsection (2) provides that:

'The approved arrangement–

(a) takes effect as if made by the debtor at the meeting, and

(b) binds every person who in accordance with the rules had notice of, and was entitled to vote at, the meeting (whether or not he was present or represented at it) as if he were a party to the arrangement.'

Thus, the debtor and the creditors referred to in para. (b) are to be treated as parties to the arrangement; that is bound by a contract imposed by statute. Such contract may provide expressly or by necessary implication for its termination in the event of the subsequent bankruptcy of the debtor. But if, as in this case, it does not, the question arises whether it necessarily terminates in consequence of the bankruptcy.

The only provision of the *Insolvency Act* 1986 which deals expressly with the termination of a voluntary arrangement is s. 262 which enables the court to revoke a voluntary arrangement within a limited time in the event of unfair prejudice or material irregularity.

By s. 264(1)(c), and s. 276, the court may make a bankruptcy order against the debtor on the petition of the supervisor or a creditor bound by a voluntary arrangement if the debtor has failed to comply with his obligations or has misled his creditors. But the Act is silent as to the consequences for the voluntary arrangement of such an order. In this case there are no circumstances which could bring any of these provisions into operation. By s. 306 on the making of a bankruptcy order the bankrupt's estate, as defined by s. 283 vests in the trustee. The only exclusion material in the circumstances of a voluntary arrangement is s. 283(3)(a) which excludes property held by a bankrupt on trust for any other person.

The debtor did not contend that the voluntary arrangement imposed a trust in favour of the creditors bound thereby on the property subject to it. Nor was it contended that the voluntary arrangement gave rise to any security in their favour. Thus in my judgment the bankruptcy order in this case had the consequence of vesting in the trustee the assets comprised in the voluntary arrangement. But I do not think it follows that the voluntary arrangement was terminated by the making of the bankruptcy order. The debtor was bound to ensure that his property comprised in the voluntary arrangement was applied in accordance with its terms. That obligation confirmed correlative rights on the creditors bound by the voluntary arrangement. By s. 283(5) it is provided that:

'For the purposes of any such provision in this Group of Parts, property comprised in a bankrupt's estate is so comprised subject to the rights of any person other than the bankrupt (whether as a secured creditor of the bankrupt or otherwise) in relation thereto, but disregarding–

(a) any rights in relation to which a statement such as is required by section 269(1)(a) was made in the petition on which the bankrupt was adjudged bankrupt, and

(b) any rights which have been otherwise given up in accordance with the rules.'

Thus the trustee took the property comprised in the voluntary arrangement subject to the rights of the creditors to have it applied for their benefit in accordance with the provisions of the voluntary arrangement.

Therefore, I agree with the debtor's first submission that the voluntary arrangement did not terminate on the making of the bankruptcy order. It may well be (but it is not necessary for me to decide) that a voluntary arrangement might be liable to be discharged after a bankruptcy order pursuant to s. 345.

Given that the voluntary arrangement continued notwithstanding the bankruptcy order, were there any bankruptcy debts within s. 382(1) arising thereunder? In my

A   judgment there were not. It is plain from para. 1 of the proposal that the rights conferred on creditors bound thereby were in satisfaction of the pre-existing debts. Those rights were to receive an interim dividend and final distribution from the proceeds of sale of the property comprised in the voluntary arrangement. There was no right to receive anything from the debtor personally. In those circumstances, the debtor was not, in my judgment, subject to any debt or liability on the date of the bankruptcy order in respect of those debts.

B

The district judge was impressed by the consequence of the supervisor obtaining a bankruptcy order under s. 276, and the position of a creditor who was not bound by the voluntary arrangement obtaining payment in full from after-acquired property. But with regard to the first point, the effect of such an order would be to enable the court in the bankruptcy to remedy the default which justified the order in the first place. It would not necessarily require the termination of the voluntary arrangement. In the case of the

C   second point, if the form of the agreement is to exclude the creditors bound by it from sharing in after-acquired property that is what they have agreed to. And in either case it is possible to provide in the voluntary arrangement for its termination on the making of a bankruptcy order or for a right to share in after-acquired property if that is what is wanted.

It follows from my decision so far that I also agree with the debtor's second point. The

D   creditors having agreed to the voluntary arrangement have precluded themselves frown proof in the bankruptcy so long as the voluntary arrangement continues. Thus in the words of s. 282(1)(b): 'to the extent required by the rules' there are no bankruptcy debts.

In my judgment the terms of s. 282(1)(b) permit the annulment in this case of the bankruptcy order and there are no reasons to refuse the order the debtor seeks. Accordingly, I allow this appeal.

E

(*Order accordingly*)

F

G

H

Re Bradley-Hole (a Bankrupt), ex parte Knight.

Chancery Division.
Rimer J.
Judgment delivered 18 November 1994.

Individual voluntary arrangement – Bankruptcy order made on post arrangement debt – Whether arrangement terminated by subsequent bankruptcy order – Whether assets remained distributable in arrangement or passed to trustee – Position of creditor entitled to vote in respect of one debt but not in respect of another – Insolvency Act 1986, s. 257, 260(2)(b), 263(4), Pt. VIII; Insolvency Rules 1986 (SI 1986/1925), r. 5.17(3).

This was an application for directions by the supervisor of an individual voluntary arrangement, approved on 11 May 1990, resulting from the making of a bankruptcy order against the debtor on a petition based on a debt which arose after that date.

A bankruptcy order was made against the debtor on his own petition on 6 April 1990. A proposal for a voluntary arrangement was then sent to 15 creditors, including his former wife ('Mrs B-H'), and was approved with certain modifications at a meeting at which only three creditors were present or represented. There were at least two creditors to whom notice of the meeting was not given.

At the date of the subsequent bankruptcy order (in September 1992) the supervisor had realised £65,231.55 net after costs and disbursements. There were claims totalling approximately £98,000 in the voluntary arrangement and Mrs B-H also claimed to be a creditor in the arrangement in respect of various orders for financial relief made in divorce proceedings ('the matrimonial debts'). The supervisor disputed her entitlement in its entirety. The district judge who made the 1992 bankruptcy order assumed that its consequence was to bring the voluntary arrangement to an end.

The supervisor's application under s. 263(4) of the Insolvency Act 1986 asked whether the bankruptcy order had brought the voluntary arrangement to an end or whether the assets remained distributable in accordance with the terms of the arrangement. If the voluntary arrangement survived the bankruptcy order there were issues as to how much Mrs B-H was entitled to under the voluntary arrangement. She claimed mortgage arrears which the debtor had been ordered to pay; a sum secured by a second charge over the matrimonial home which the debtor was ordered to transfer to her free of encumbrances; arrears of maintenance; and costs of the matrimonial proceedings. The supervisor argued that her claims were not within the voluntary arrangement and he disputed the quantum of two of her claims.

Held, declaring that the voluntary arrangement was not at an end, that the assets were held on trust for the creditors in the voluntary arrangement and that Mrs B-H was entitled to participate in the arrangement:

1. There was nothing in the provisions of the Insolvency Act 1986 sufficient to warrant the inference that a bankruptcy order (or, at any rate, one made on a petition presented by someone other than a s. 264(1)(c) petitioner) was intended to have the effect of automatically terminating a prior voluntary arrangement.

2. The assets held by the supervisor on the terms of the arrangement were held by him on trust for the creditors who were parties to the arrangement. As a consequence the bankrupt retained no beneficial interest in those assets (save only an interest in any surplus after the payment of the creditors in full) and none of the assets vested in the bankrupt's trustee.

3. Further, any 'unrealised' assets of the bankrupt held or owned by him at the date of the arrangement were similarly impressed with a trust for the benefit of the creditors who were party to the voluntary arrangement.

A   4. Although notice of the s. 257 meeting was sent by the nominee to Mrs B-H not as a creditor in respect of the matrimonial debts, but in case she had any other non-matrimonial claims as a creditor (which she did not), she was validly given notice of the meeting for the purpose of s. 260(2)(b). It was irrelevant that the nominee did not know that her claims in respect of the matrimonial debts entitled her to be given notice of the meeting.

5. Mrs B-H was a person who 'had notice of, and was entitled to vote at, the meeting' for the purposes of s. 260(2)(b) and was bound by the arrangement as if she were a party to it in respect of the entirety of her proved indebtedness, even though she may not have been entitled to vote at the meeting in respect of her claim for costs because that debt was either 'for an unliquidated amount' or was one 'whose value is not ascertained' within r. 5.17(3) of the Insolvency Rules.

6. As at 6 April 1990 Mrs B-H had an enforceable claim against the debtor to discharge the then amount of the second charge on the matrimonial home or to indemnify her against it. She could only claim for the amount of the indebtedness secured by the second charge as at that date. She was not entitled to claim in the arrangement for a greater sum.

7. In respect of the periodical payments order made in the divorce proceedings, Mrs B-H was entitled to claim in respect of the arrears which had accrued due down to 6 April 1990, but not in respect of any payments which were to fall due after that date.

The following cases were referred to in the judgment:

Ayerst v C & K (Construction) Ltd [1976] AC 167.
Campbell v Campbell [1922] P 187.
Cranley Mansions Ltd, Re [1994] BCC 576.
Debtor (No. 64 of 1992), Re a [1994] BCC 55; [1994] 1 WLR 264.
Hawkins, Re; ex parte Hawkins [1894] 1 QB 25.
James v James [1964] P 303.
Kerr v Kerr [1897] 2 QB 439.
Leisure Study Group Ltd, Re [1994] 2 BCLC 65.
Linton v Linton (1885) 15 QBD 239.
McKeen, Re [1995] BCC 412.
Watkins v Watkins [1896] P 222.
Woodley v Woodley (No. 2) [1994] 1 WLR 1167.

Philip Hoser (instructed by Max Barford & Co, Tunbridge Wells) for Mrs C Bradley-Hole.

C M Curtis (instructed by Dakers Seymour & Co, Brighton) for the bankrupt.

G Crawford (instructed by Burstows, Brighton) for the supervisor of the voluntary arrangement.

Richard Ritchie (instructed by the Treasury Solicitor) for the official receiver.

JUDGMENT

Rimer J: Introduction

This is an application for directions made pursuant to s. 263(4) of the *Insolvency Act* 1986 ('the Act') by the supervisor of an individual voluntary arrangement made under Pt. VIII of the Act. The supervisor is Mr William Jeremy Jonathan Knight, a chartered accountant and licensed insolvency practitioner ('the supervisor'). The debtor is Mr Anthony John Wyndham Bradley-Hole. The voluntary arrangement was approved on 11 May 1990. The need for the present application has arisen because on 28 September 1992 a bankruptcy order was made against the debtor (whom I shall call 'the bankrupt') on a petition based on a debt which arose after 11 May 1990.

I have been asked to determine four questions of which the first two concern the effect, if any, of the bankruptcy order on the voluntary arrangement. In short, they ask whether

the bankruptcy order has brought the voluntary arrangement to an end, with the
consequence that assets which would otherwise be distributable in accordance with its
terms now form part of the estate in bankruptcy of the bankrupt; or whether those assets
remain distributable in accordance with the terms of the arrangement. The other two
questions arise only if I conclude that the voluntary arrangement survived the
bankruptcy.

The background facts

The bankrupt was formerly married to Mrs Carolyn Bradley-Hole. On 25 September
1987 she petitioned for a divorce and a decree absolute was granted on 9 March 1989. In
the course of the divorce proceedings Mrs Bradley-Hole obtained various orders for
financial ancillary relief against the bankrupt and she claims to be a creditor of the
bankrupt by virtue of those orders. They were made by the Tunbridge Wells County
Court on 9 January and 5 May 1989 and 15 February 1990. I shall refer to Mrs Bradley-
Hole's claims against the bankrupt arising under them as the 'matrimonial debts'.

On 6 April 1990 a bankruptcy order was made against the bankrupt based on his own
petition. He then determined instead to try to put in place an individual voluntary
arrangement under Pt. VIII of the Act. On 9 April 1990 he applied under s. 253 of the
Act for an interim order. On 20 April 1990 an interim order was made and on the same
day the supervisor, acting at that stage as the nominee, submitted a proposal for a
voluntary arrangement of the bankrupt's affairs to 15 of his creditors, including Mrs
Bradley-Hole, and gave notice, pursuant to s. 257, of a meeting of creditors to be held on
11 May 1990.

The bankrupt's proposal was approved at that meeting, although with certain
modifications. Only three creditors were present or represented, namely W J Hayes, the
Inland Revenue and HM Customs & Excise, their debts totalling £73,660.11. There were
at least two creditors to whom notice of the meeting was not given.

The effect of the approval of the arrangement at that meeting was, as provided by
s. 260(2) of the Act, that:

'(2) The approved arrangement–

(a) takes effect as if made by the debtor at the meeting, and

(b) binds every person who in accordance with the rules had notice of, and was
entitled to vote at, the meeting (whether or not he was present or represented
at it) as if he were a party to the arrangement.'

The principal provisions of the arrangement were as follows.

Paragraph (p) provided that Mr Knight 'be appointed ... supervisor in order to
administer the arrangement'.

By paragraph (a) the bankrupt provided that:

'the whole of my assets of any nature whatsoever to which I was entitled at the
date of the bankruptcy order and to which I might become entitled up to the date
of the approval by the creditors of the terms of this my proposed voluntary
arrangement, be available for the benefit of my creditors.'

Paragraph (b) recited that the bankrupt was the licensee of the Shepherd and Dog
public house in West Sussex, that its lease was due to expire on 24 June 1990, but that he
proposed to renew it, if possible. One of the agreed modifications to the arrangement
provided that he would pay to the supervisor 'all net profits for the trading at Shepherd
and Dog after provision for income tax liabilities'.

Paragraph (e), as modified, provided that the arrangement was to continue until all
creditors were paid in full.

A   Paragraph (f) provided that 'distribution to creditors will be made when funds are available'.

Paragraph (k) provided that:

'Funds received by the supervisor will be banked in a local bank account pending distribution to creditors. Any moneys surplus to immediate requirements will be placed on interest bearing deposit account for the benefit of creditors.'

B   Paragraph (l) provided that:

'Any surplus funds remaining after payment to creditors in full will be returnable [to the bankrupt] after termination of the arrangement.'

Finally, paragraph (o) provided that the bankrupt undertook that he would:

C   'give my full co-operation to the supervisor to enable him to realise my assets and to enable payments to be made to creditors in accordance with these proposals.'

I should refer also to r. 5.21(1) of the *Insolvency Rules* 1986 ('the rules'), which provides that:

'(1) Forthwith after the approval of the voluntary arrangement, the debtor in Case 2, and the official receiver or trustee in Case 1, shall do all that is required for putting the supervisor into possession of the assets included in the arrangement.'

D   The present was a Case 1 case, as the bankrupt was an undischarged bankrupt at the date of the approval of the arrangement (see r. 5.1).

On 18 May 1990 the bankruptcy order was ordered to be annulled, the annulment taking effect on 15 June 1990. On 24 June 1990 the bankrupt's lease of the Shepherd and Dog terminated and was not renewed, although a new lease was granted to Jessica Thompson. She and the bankrupt married on 6 July 1991. The non-renewal of the lease

E   brought to an end the expected flow into the hands of the supervisor of the net profits from the trade of the Shepherd and Dog.

On 28 September 1992 a further bankruptcy order was made against the bankrupt on a petition presented in the Brighton County Court by Phoenix Brewery Co Ltd. Their debt was £2,379.20 and was incurred after the approval of the voluntary arrangement. As at the date of that order, the supervisor had realised £65,231.55 net after costs and

F   disbursements. As a result of subsequent realisations and the accruing of interest he now has in his hands, in a bank account in his name, assets of approximately £76,000. He has been notified of claims totalling approximately £98,000, which he acknowledges rank for dividend in the voluntary arrangement. In addition, Mrs Bradley-Hole also claims to be a creditor in the arrangement with matrimonial debts originally put by her at £95,987.89, although she has since reduced her claim. The supervisor disputes her entitlement in its

G   entirety.

The district judge who made the bankruptcy order assumed that its consequence was to bring the voluntary arrangement to an end, an assumption which the supervisor shared. As a result of that common assumption the supervisor was appointed the bankrupt's trustee in bankruptcy. Subsequently, the supervisor was advised that the bankruptcy did not necessarily terminate the voluntary arrangement. That possibility

H   raised an obvious potential for conflict in the discharging by the supervisor of his dual roles of supervisor and trustee, and on 25 May 1993 an order was made in the Brighton County Court rescinding his appointment as trustee, whereupon the official receiver became trustee. In the meantime, on 25 October 1992, the supervisor had also applied in the bankruptcy proceedings, in his capacity as supervisor, for various directions. On 25 May 1993 the bankruptcy proceedings were transferred to the High Court pursuant to r. 7.11(2).

Questions 1 and 2   A

Paragraphs 1 and 2 of the application dated 25 October 1992 raise the following questions.

> '1. Whether the individual voluntary arrangement approved on 11 May 1990 under Pt. VIII of the *Insolvency Act* 1986 in respect of Anthony John Wyndham Bradley-Hole ("the bankrupt") is at an end by virtue of the bankruptcy order made herein on 28 September 1992 or otherwise.   B

> 2. Whether the funds held by the applicant as such supervisor and whether unrealised assets as may have been owned by the bankrupt on 11 May 1990 form part of the estate in bankruptcy of the bankrupt divisible amongst all the creditors of the bankrupt in accordance with Pt. IX of the *Insolvency Act* 1986 or are held by the applicant on trust or otherwise only for the benefit of creditors bound by the individual voluntary arrangement.'   C

On those questions I have heard argument from Mr Crawford (for the supervisor), Mr Hoser (for Mrs Bradley-Hole) and Mr Ritchie (for the official receiver). Mr Crawford and Mr Hoser made common cause and argued that the funds held by the supervisor as such and any unrealised assets of the bankrupt as at 11 May 1990 are held for the exclusive benefit of the creditors bound by the voluntary arrangement. Mr Ritchie argued that the effect of the subsequent bankruptcy was to bring the arrangement to an end,   D with the consequence that all such assets became part of the bankrupt's estate in his bankruptcy.

I should mention why it is that Mrs Bradley-Hole has a special interest in asserting the survival of the voluntary arrangement and proving her right to participate in it. That is because, as her claims against the bankrupt arise under orders made in family proceedings, it was common ground between counsel that they are expressly excluded   E from being provable in his bankruptcy by r. 12.3(2)(a), which provides that:

> '(2) The following are not provable–

>> (a) in bankruptcy, any fine imposed for an offence, and any obligation arising under an order made in family proceedings . . .

It was, however, also common ground that the matrimonial debts are in principle   F capable of ranking for a dividend in the bankrupt's voluntary arrangement. This is because at the date of the arrangement the bankrupt was an undischarged bankrupt under his earlier bankruptcy and s. 257(3) of the Act provides, in effect, that the creditors of such a debtor who are entitled to participate in his voluntary arrangement include:

> '(a) every person who is a creditor of the bankrupt in respect of a bankruptcy debt
> . . .'   G

That subparagraph is then elucidated in part by s. 382(1), which provides that:

> '(1) "Bankruptcy debt", in relation to a bankrupt, means (subject to the next subsection) any of the following–

>> (a) any debt or liability to which he is subject at the commencement of the bankruptcy,   H

>> (b) any debt or liability to which he may become subject after the commencement of the bankruptcy (including after his discharge from bankruptcy) by reason of any obligation incurred before the commencement of the bankruptcy . . .'

–and further, by s. 383(1)(a), which provides that:

A '(1) "Creditor"–

(a) in relation to a bankrupt, means a person to whom any of the bankruptcy debts is owed . . . and

(b) in relation to an individual to whom a bankruptcy petition relates, means a person who would be a creditor in the bankruptcy if a bankruptcy order were made on that petition.'

B Counsel are agreed that those provisions in principle enable claims of the nature of Mrs Bradley-Hole's matrimonial debt to rank for dividend in the voluntary arrangement, there being no provision comparable to r. 12.3(2)(a) which would exclude them from so ranking. There is, however, an issue as to whether, on the particular facts of this case, Mrs Bradley-Hole is entitled to participate in the voluntary arrangement. That issue is the subject of question 4.

C The arguments of Mr Crawford and Mr Hoser in support of the contention that the voluntary arrangement survives the bankruptcy unscathed were essentially along the same lines. Their submission is that it has not been determined by the bankruptcy and that the assets which the supervisor has in his hands as such and also any unrealised assets of the nature referred to in question 2 fall to be distributed exclusively among the creditors bound by the arrangement.

D They pointed first to s. 253(2) of the Act, which provides that:

'(2) The proposal must provide for some person ("the nominee") to act in relation to the voluntary arrangement either as trustee or otherwise for the purpose of supervising its implementation.'

They then submitted that, consistently with that provision, the supervisor holds those assets which he has in his hands upon trust exclusively for the benefit of the participating E creditors in accordance with the terms of the arrangement and that the bankrupt has no beneficial interest in such assets at all, or only an interest in any surplus after the creditors have been paid in full.

In support of this argument they relied on some observations of Harman J in *Re Leisure Study Group Ltd* [1994] 2 BCLC 65. That case concerned a company in respect of which a creditor's voluntary arrangement had been made. Mr Judd, the supervisor, had certain funds in his possession and an administrative receiver of the company applied F to restrain him from distributing them to the creditors under the arrangement. Harman J refused the application, holding that Mr Judd held the assets as trustee for the creditors and that there was no basis on which the administrative receiver could restrain distribution.

At p. 67g Harman J said:

G 'The question must at once arise: "on what basis does the supervisor, as the legal owner of the money, hold that money?" I say "the legal owner" because the funds are in, as I understand, an interest-bearing bank account in the name of the supervisor and he is therefore the owner in law of that chose in action. The first indication of the capacity in which the supervisor would hold the money comes from s 1(2) of the 1986 Act, which I quote:

H "A proposal under this Part is one which provides for some person (the nominee) to act in relation to a voluntary arrangement either as trustee or otherwise for the purpose of supervising its implementation; and the nominee must be a person who is qualified to act as an insolvency practitioner in relation to the company.'

That plainly fits Mr Judd exactly. He is a licensed insolvency practitioner and entitled to act in relation to this company. He was asked to supervise the

implementation of the voluntary arrangement and prima facie one would think he A
was asked to act in relation to the voluntary arrangement as a trustee.

As a matter of the English language that word is the most obvious word that could
be used and, to my mind, it is also the most appropriate word that could be used
in the law. A person who holds property not for his own beneficial interest but for
the benefit of others is normally and properly described as a trustee for those other
persons who are normally considered to be beneficiaries of his. The term "trustee"
is commonly used, after all, when property is purchased by an individual in the B
name of another, or indeed by a company in the name of another, wholly paid for
by the purchaser out of his or its own money. The person in whose name the
property is registered is always, and has always been, described by the law as
holding the property upon a resulting trust. He is a trustee. It is in my view the
obviously appropriate term to apply.

. . . Mr Judd is thus not holding the fund on behalf of the company, save in respect C
of the residual rights under cl 17 of the voluntary arrangement whereby at the end
of the ten-year period any moneys remaining would then result back to the
company. In my judgment it is plain beyond peradventure that until that date he
holds those funds as a trustee for the creditors on whose behalf he is appointed.

The argument by the administrative receiver seems to be that he as administrative
receiver in some way has a claim to these funds. The claim, be it noted, is not the D
claim of the bank, which is not a party to this application at all. The administrative
receiver is of course the agent of the company but, as is quite apparent, the
company cannot have any claim to these funds paid to Mr Judd pursuant to the
voluntary arrangement and held by him on trust for the creditors, and it is difficult
if not impossible to perceive upon what basis the administrative receiver thinks he
personally can assert a claim to these funds. The moneys are, in my judgment, in
law the property of Mr Judd and in equity held by him upon trust for the creditors E
who appointed him at the approval of the voluntary arrangement. It therefore
seems to me that this application in so far as it seeks to restrain Mr Judd from
dealing with his trust funds as a trustee for the benefit of his beneficiaries is wholly
and totally unwarranted and has no legal basis of any sort.'

Mr Crawford and Mr Hoser argue that similar considerations apply to the present
case and that the supervisor became a trustee of the assets held by him, the beneficiaries F
under the trust being the creditors bound by the voluntary arrangement. They say that
the bankrupt has made an outright disposal to the supervisor of the assets so held for the
benefit of the participating creditors and that such trust was not brought to an end by the
subsequent bankruptcy. They submit that, whilst it might be possible for a voluntary
arrangement to provide for its determination upon the occasion of a subsequent
bankruptcy, there is no express such provision in the present arrangement and no basis
for implying any such provision into it. They submit further that there is nothing in the G
Act which provides that the bankruptcy was to have the effect of terminating the
arrangement and that, absent any such provision, there is no basis on which I ought to
hold that it did have such effect.

On the contrary, Mr Crawford points to s. 264(1)(c) and 276(2) of the Act as providing
internal support for the inference that its scheme does not intend that a subsequent
bankruptcy will ordinarily bring a voluntary arrangement to an end. Section 264(1)(c) H
provides that the persons who may present a bankruptcy petition include:

'(c) . . . the supervisor of, or any person (other than the individual) who is for the
time being bound by, a voluntary arrangement proposed by the individual and
approved under Part VIII . . .'

–and section 276(2) provides that:

A '(2) Where a bankruptcy order is made on a petition under section 264(1)(c), any expenses properly incurred as expenses of the administration of the voluntary arrangement in question shall be a first charge on the bankrupt's estate.'

Mr Crawford argued that it is implicit in these provisions that a bankruptcy order made on a petition presented by a s. 264(1)(c) petitioner does bring the voluntary arrangement to an end and that it is for that reason that express provision is made in

B s. 276(2) enabling the costs of its administration to be recovered out of the bankrupt's estate in his bankruptcy. However, there is no provision comparable to s. 276(2) governing the case in which the debtor is made bankrupt on a petition presented by a person other than a s. 264(1)(c) petitioner. Mr Crawford submits that the reason for this is that such a bankruptcy order has no effect on the voluntary arrangement and that therefore there is no need for any such provision.

C Mr Hoser did not also embrace this last argument, since he foresees a possibility that a petition might hereafter be presented by a s. 264(1)(c) petitioner and, for reasons that I have given, he would be anxious on Mrs Bradley-Hole's part to argue that not even a bankruptcy order made on such a petition would bring the voluntary arrangement to an end. Both counsel submitted, however, that in any event the assets held by the supervisor are simply not part of the bankrupt's estate within the meaning of s. 283 of the Act and thus are not comprised in the assets which vest in the bankrupt's trustee pursuant to

D s. 306.

I was referred to a decision of Morritt J on 1 April 1992 in *Re McKeen* [1995] BCC 412, which also raised a question as to the effect on a voluntary arrangement of a subsequent bankruptcy order. In that case the debtor convened a meeting with his creditors on 26 June 1990 in order to consider his proposed voluntary arrangement. The creditors present unanimously approved it. On 24 June 1990 rent became due from the debtor to his landlord, but notice of the meeting had not been given to the landlord, as

E he was not a creditor at the date that the notices were given. It followed from s. 260(2) of the Act that the landlord was not bound by, or treated as a party to, the arrangement. In 1991 the landlord served a statutory demand on the debtor for the rent due on or after 24 June 1990 and on 22 November 1991 a bankruptcy order was made on the landlord's petition. On 2 December 1991 the debtor applied to the court for the annulment of the bankruptcy under s. 282(1)(b) of the Act. That provides that:

F '(1) The court may annul a bankruptcy order if it at any time appears to the court–

(a) . . .

(b) that, to the extent required by the rules, the bankruptcy debts and the expenses of the bankruptcy have all, since the making of the order, been either paid or secured for to the satisfaction of the court.'

G By the time the application came on the debt and costs due to the landlord and the costs of the official receiver had been paid in full by the landlord's employer, but those of the creditors who were bound by the voluntary arrangement had not. The district judge declined to annul the bankruptcy, on the ground that the debts due to the creditors bound by the voluntary arrangement were bankruptcy debts which had not been 'paid or secured for to the satisfaction of the court'.

H Morritt J allowed the debtor's appeal and annulled the bankruptcy. No argument was advanced to him by anyone interested in opposing the appeal and it appears from the judgment that, in contrast to the submissions made in this case, the debtor's counsel did not contend that the voluntary arrangement operated to impose a trust on the property subject to it in favour of the creditors bound by it. In the absence of any such contention, Morritt J held that the bankruptcy order had the consequence of vesting in the trustee the assets comprised in the voluntary arrangement. However, he held that it did not follow that the arrangement was terminated by the bankruptcy. He pointed out that the debtor was bound to ensure that the property comprised in the arrangement was applied in accordance with its terms, being an obligation which conferred correlative rights on the creditors bound by the arrangement. Morritt J then referred to s. 283(5) of the Act, which provides that:

> '(5) For the purposes of any such provision in this Group of Parts, property comprised in a bankrupt's estate is so comprised subject to the rights of any person other than the bankrupt (whether as a secured creditor of the bankrupt or otherwise) in relation thereto, but disregarding–
>
> > (a) any rights in relation to which a statement such as is required by section 269(1)(a) was made in the petition on which the bankrupt was adjudged bankrupt, and
> >
> > (b) any rights which have been otherwise given up in accordance with the rules.'

–and he held that the trustee took the property comprised in the voluntary arrangement subject to the rights of the creditors to have it applied for their benefit in accordance with its terms. Morritt J held that it followed that the voluntary arrangement did not terminate with the bankruptcy, that the rights conferred on the creditors by the arrangement were in satisfaction of their pre-existing debts and that the debtor was not subject to any debt or liability on the date of the bankruptcy order in respect of them.

Mr Crawford and Mr Hoser submitted that that case was correctly decided but on the basis of incorrect reasoning. The thrust of the criticism was that, given that the judge decided the case on the basis that the voluntary arrangement impressed the property subject to it with neither a trust nor a security in favour of the participating creditors, it was difficult to see on what ground those creditors were regarded as still having specific rights against the property within the meaning of s. 283(5). They submitted that the case should have been decided on the basis that the arrangement property was trust property which did not vest in the trustee at all.

Question 2

Question 2 raises an issue as to the effect of the bankruptcy on 'unrealised assets . . . owned by the bankrupt on 11 May 1990'. By 'unrealised' the question refers to assets which the supervisor has not taken into his possession. The evidence is that, save for a suggestion that the bankrupt may then have had a half interest in a vehicle of unknown value, no such assets are known to exist, so that this part of the application may be somewhat academic. However, Mr Crawford and Mr Hoser argue that any such assets are similarly impressed with the trust in favour of the participating creditors. They submit that a voluntary arrangement takes effect as if it were in the nature of a statutory contract between the debtor and the participating creditors (see again s. 260(2) of the Act).

In the present case the contract was one by which the bankrupt agreed to devote the entirety of his assets to his creditors, with those creditors giving full consideration by compromising their claims in respect of their pre-existing debts. Once the arrangement was approved, nothing further remained to be done by the creditors by way of performance of their own contractual obligations. The whole beneficial interest in such assets was thus vested in them and they were in the position of being entitled to compel the realisation and distribution of the assets in accordance with the scheme of the arrangement. Thus, the argument ran that the unrealised assets were and are trust assets for the benefit of the creditors, just as much as are the assets in the hands of the supervisor.

Mr Hoser submitted that the trust so arising was essentially analogous to the type of trust which is impressed upon the property of a company upon the making of a winding-up order. He referred me to the speech of Lord Diplock in *Ayerst v C & K (Construction)*

A   *Ltd* [1976] AC 167, in which there is a discussion of the sense in which a company's property becomes trust property to be applied in a particular way upon its winding up. Mr Hoser referred to the following part of Lord Diplock's judgment at p. 179E:

> 'The question of the beneficial ownership of the company's property was dealt with explicitly by both James L.J. and Mellish L.J. in *In re Oriental Inland Steam Co.* (1874) 9 Ch. App. 557:

B

> > "The English Act of Parliament has enacted that in the case of a winding up the assets of the company so wound up are to be collected and applied in discharge of its liabilities. That makes the property of the company clearly trust property. It is property affected by the Act of Parliament with an obligation to be dealt with by the proper officer in a particular way. Then it has ceased to be beneficially the property of the company; . . ." (*per* James L.J. at p. 559).

C

> > "No doubt winding up differs from bankruptcy in this respect, that in bankruptcy the whole estate, both legal and beneficial, is taken out of the bankrupt, and is vested in his trustees or assignees, whereas in a winding up the legal estate still remains in the company. But, in my opinion, the beneficial interest is clearly taken out of the company. What the statute says in section 95 is, that from the time of the winding-up order all the powers of the directors of

D

> > the company to carry on the trade or to deal with the assets of the company shall be wholly determined, and nobody shall have any power to deal with them except the official liquidator, and he is to deal with them for the purpose of collecting the assets and dividing them amongst the creditors. It appears to me that that does, in strictness, constitute a trust for the benefit of all the creditors, . . ." (*per* Mellish L.J. at p. 560).

E
> The authority of this case for the proposition that the property of the company ceases upon the winding up to belong beneficially to the company has now stood unchallenged for a hundred years. It has been repeated in successive editions of *Buckley on the Companies Acts* from 1897 to the present day. Nevertheless your Lordships are invited by the appellant company to say that it was wrong because it was founded on the false premise that the property is subject to a "trust" in the strict sense of that expression as it was used in equity before 1862.'

F   The House of Lords refused that invitation.

Those various arguments by Mr Crawford and Mr Hoser have, in my judgment, considerable force. One difficulty which they do, however, involve is the fact that the scheme of Pt. VIII of the Act appears to be such that it is perfectly possible that one or more of a debtor's creditors might, perhaps quite innocently, be excluded from participation in his voluntary arrangement. For example, the nominee might overlook

G   one of the creditors and not give him notice of the meeting to consider the proposed arrangement; or his notice of the meeting to a creditor may be lost in the post and never received. In either case, as counsel accepted, that creditor will not be a party to or bound by the voluntary arrangement and will not be entitled to participate in it. In *Re a Debtor (No. 64 of 1992)* [1994] BCC 55, a decision of mine sitting as a deputy judge of the Chancery Division, I held that such a debtor will in principle be entitled to petition for the debtor's bankruptcy. I did not, however, have to decide what, if any, consequences a

H   bankruptcy order on such petition would have on the prior voluntary arrangement. However, if the voluntary arrangement survives the bankruptcy for the exclusive benefit of its participating creditors, then the presentation of a bankruptcy petition may in practice be a worthless course for the excluded creditor to take. This consideration has raised in my mind a concern as to the correctness of the arguments of Mr Crawford and Mr Hoser.

They both accepted that the scheme of Pt. VIII is such that, either by bad luck or   A
innocent error, one or more creditors might find themselves excluded from the approved
voluntary arrangement. They recognised also that such a creditor would probably not be
entitled to apply to challenge the arrangement under s. 262 of the Act. They submitted,
however, that these consequences are simply the result of the manner in which the Act
was drafted and do not detract from the overall integrity of their arguments.

Mr Ritchie, for the Official Receiver, submitted that it is implicit in the scheme of the   B
Act that a voluntary arrangement and a bankruptcy are not intended to co-exist as
concurrent insolvency regimes and that a voluntary arrangement automatically comes to
an end upon the making of a subsequent bankruptcy order. He referred to various
provisions of the Act which he submitted provided support for his basic proposition.

He referred to s. 253, which provides for the making by the debtor who is proposing
a voluntary arrangement of an application for an interim order and, in particular, to
subs. (5), which reads: C

'(5) An application shall not be made while a bankruptcy petition presented by
the debtor is pending, if the court has, under section 273 below, appointed an
insolvency practitioner to inquire into the debtor's affairs and report.'

He further referred to s. 252(2) which provides that:

'(2) An interim order has the effect that, during the period for which it is in force–   D

(a) no bankruptcy petition relating to the debtor may be presented or proceeded
with, and

(b) no other proceedings, and no execution or other legal process, may be
commenced or continued against the debtor or his property except with the
leave of the court.'

Mr Ritchie also referred to s. 261(1), which provides that: E

'(1) Subject as follows, where the creditors' meeting summoned under section 257
approves the proposed voluntary arrangement (with or without modifications) and
the debtor is an undischarged bankrupt, the court may do one or both of the
following, namely–

(a) annul the bankruptcy order by which he was adjudged bankrupt;

(b) give such directions with respect to the conduct of the bankruptcy and the   F
administration of the bankrupt's estate as it thinks appropriate for
facilitating the implementation of the approved voluntary arrangement.'

Mr Ritchie submitted that these last provisions contemplated either the annulment of
the prior bankruptcy order or at least the making of directions of a nature friendly to the
implementation of the voluntary arrangement. He gave as an example an instance in
which the court might direct the trustee who was in the course of realising a particular   G
asset to continue to do so, but for the benefit of the voluntary arrangement and the
creditors participating in it. He submitted that, in default of any order under either
subparagraph of s. 261(1), it was a necessary inference that the voluntary arrangement
would come to an end.

Mr Ritchie referred also to s. 264(1)(c) and 276 of the Act, which I have already
mentioned, and submitted that a bankruptcy order made on a petition presented by a
person entitled under s. 264(1)(c) would terminate the voluntary arrangement. As I have   H
said, Mr Crawford submitted likewise and I have outlined how he relied on these
particular provisions as supporting his argument rather than the contrary one. I do not
find it necessary to decide whether a bankruptcy order made on a s. 264(1)(c) petition
would automatically result in the termination of the prior voluntary arrangement.
However, even if it would, I find nothing in either of s. 264 and 276 to support Mr

A   Ritchie's wider proposition that the same consequence also follows regardless of who the petitioner is.

Next, Mr Ritchie relied on s. 312(1) and (2), which provide that:

'(1) The bankrupt shall deliver up to the trustee possession of any property, books, papers or other records of which he has possession or control and of which the trustee is required to take possession.

B   This is without prejudice to the general duties of the bankrupt under section 333 in this Chapter.

(2) If any of the following is in the possession of any property, books, papers or other records of which the trustee is required to take possession, namely–

     (a) the official receiver,

C   (b) a person who has ceased to be trustee of the bankrupt's estate, or

     (c) a person who has been the supervisor of a voluntary arrangement approved in relation to the bankrupt under Part VIII,

the official receiver or, as the case may be, that person shall deliver up possession of the property, books, papers or records to the trustee.'

D   Mr Ritchie said that subs. (2) provides tacit support for his submission that a voluntary arrangement terminates on the occasion of a subsequent bankruptcy, because he says that it shows that the supervisor has to hand over to the trustee, inter alia, 'property', which is in his hands, including property which has presumably only come into his hands in his capacity as supervisor. In my view, however, these provisions do not bear the weight which Mr Ritchie seeks to put on them. Subsection (2) bites only on 'property . . . of which the trustee is required to take possession . . .' That will only include property in the hands of a supervisor and subject to a prior voluntary arrangement if the

E   consequence of the bankruptcy is that it does terminate the voluntary arrangement. That is the very question that I have to decide and, in my view, subs. (2) sheds no light on it.

Mr Ritchie also relied on the point to which I have already referred, namely the problem raised by the creditor who is, perhaps innocently, excluded from the voluntary arrangement. He submitted that the scheme of the Act is that all creditors are intended to be bound by a voluntary arrangement. He recognised the possibility of one or more

F   creditors being excluded, through no fault of their own, from participation in it and recognised also that they might have no standing to apply to challenge the arrangement under s. 262. He submitted that it could not have been Parliament's intention that such creditors should be so sidelined and deprived of a right to participate in a division of such of the debtor's assets as have been devoted to the arrangement, which might well represent the bulk of them (and, in the present case, in fact represented all of them). Mr

G   Ritchie submitted that it is implicit in the scheme of the Act that such a creditor is entitled to petition for the debtor's bankruptcy and that the consequence of a bankruptcy order will be that the voluntary arrangement is thereupon terminated. He submitted that in that event assets undistributed to the creditors who were party to the arrangement would then devolve on to the trustee, although he did not suggest that the trustee could upset distributions already made. He submitted that both Morritt J's reasoning and his decision in *Re McKeen* (above) were wrong.

H   Having considered the arguments advanced before me, I have come to the conclusion that those of Mr Crawford and Mr Hoser are to be preferred. I do not find in any of the provisions in the Act to which Mr Ritchie referred me any sufficient warrant for the inference that a bankruptcy order (or, at any rate, one made on a petition presented by someone other than a s. 264(1)(c) petitioner) is intended to have the effect of automatically terminating a prior voluntary arrangement. I accept the argument that the

assets held by the supervisor on the terms of the present arrangement are held by him on   A
trust for the creditors who are parties to the arrangement. In my judgment, the
consequence of that is that the bankrupt retains no beneficial interest in those assets (save
only an interest in any surplus after the payment of the creditors in full) and that none of
such assets vest in the bankrupt's trustee. The trust simply continues, notwithstanding
the bankruptcy. I also accept that any unrealised assets of the bankrupt held or owned
by him on 11 May 1990 are similarly impressed with a trust for the benefit of the creditors
who are party to the voluntary arrangement and that such trust continues   B
notwithstanding the bankruptcy.

I recognise that this conclusion could result in what might be regarded as an injustice
to any creditors of the bankrupt who, for one reason or another, were not given notice
of the proposed arrangement and had no opportunity to participate in it. However, any
such injustice appears to me to be a consequence of the manner in which Pt. VIII of the
Act has been drafted and enacted. I recognise also that the reasoning which has led me   C
to my decision differs somewhat from that of Morritt J in *Re McKeen*. However, my
decision itself is, I think, essentially in line with the decision in that case.

I answer question 1 by declaring that the voluntary arrangement is not at an end,
whether by the 1992 bankruptcy order or otherwise, and I answer question 2 in the sense
of the second alternative. I shall deal with question 4 next and then with question 3.

Question 4   D

Question 4 asks:

> '4. As to how much the claim by Mrs Carolyn Mary Elizabeth Bradley-Hole ranks
> for dividend under the individual voluntary arrangement.'

Mrs Bradley-Hole originally claimed to be entitled to rank as a creditor in the
arrangement in the sum of £95,987.89. Her claim was broken down under seven heads.   E
However, Mr Hoser abandoned her claim in respect of three of them. The ones in which
she has persisted are as follows.

(1)   £2,411.42 in respect of arrears of instalments for a period to 5 May 1989 and due
       under a Nationwide Anglia Building Society mortgage over the former
       matrimonial home at Woodlands, The Street, Fulking, West Sussex ('Woodlands').
       The bankrupt was ordered to pay the instalments by the order of 9 January 1989.   F
       He failed to do so and the arrears have been paid by Mrs Bradley-Hole.

(2)   A sum secured by a second charge over Woodlands in favour of National
       Westminster Bank plc. This claim derives from the order of 5 May 1989, whereby
       the bankrupt was ordered to transfer to Mrs Bradley-Hole his entire interest in
       Woodlands, subject to the Nationwide Anglia mortgage, but otherwise free from
       encumbrances. When eventually Woodlands was transferred to Mrs Bradley-Hole   G
       it was still subject to the second charge.

       On 11 May 1990, the date of the approval of the arrangement, the amount secured
       by that charge was £36,530.60. Woodlands was subsequently sold, with completion
       taking place on 29 April 1993. At that date the charge secured £47,697.74. At and
       after that date Mrs Bradley-Hole was engaged in correspondence with the bank
       disputing whether it was entitled to take the full £47,697.74 out of the proceeds of
       sale. It is unnecessary to detail the nature of the dispute between Mrs Bradley-Hole   H
       and the bank, but its outcome was that in November 1993 the bank repaid to Mrs
       Bradley-Hole the sum of £6,702.34, with the result that the net amount received by
       the bank out of Woodlands' proceeds of sale was £40,995.40.

       Mrs Bradley-Hole deposes in an affidavit that she does not intend to take any
       further action against the bank with regard to the dispute. She contends that, had

A   the bankrupt honoured the order of 5 May 1989, the proceeds of sale of Woodlands would not have been reduced by the sum of £40,995.40, and she claims to rank in the arrangement for that sum.

(3)   £17,920 in respect of arrears of maintenance which the bankrupt was ordered to pay to Mrs Bradley-Hole for the Bradley-Hole children. This was ordered on 5 May 1989 at the rate of £140 per week. Mrs Bradley-Hole claims for a period of 128 weeks from 18 September 1989 to the date of the notification of her claim to the supervisor. This period expired long after the first bankruptcy order, which was 6 April 1990, and down to that date the arrears were some £3,920.

(4)   £19,683.29 in respect of the taxed costs of the matrimonial proceedings payable by the bankrupt by virtue of an order of 15 February 1990. The costs were taxed on 19 December 1991 and were to be paid on or before 17 January 1992.

C   Mr Crawford submitted that Mrs Bradley-Hole is not entitled to participate in the voluntary arrangement in respect of any of these claims. He submitted that, although notice of the s. 257 meeting was sent by the nominee to Mrs Bradley-Hole, it was not sent to her as a creditor of the bankrupt in respect of the matrimonial debts, but was so sent in case she had any other non-matrimonial claims as a creditor. This was because, at the time that he sent out the notices convening the meeting, the nominee incorrectly assumed that Mrs Bradley-Hole would not be entitled to participate in the arrangement by virtue of her claims in respect of the matrimonial debts. Further, no such debts were referred to in the bankrupt's statement of affairs. In fact, Mrs Bradley-Hole has no non-matrimonial claims against the bankrupt. Mr Crawford argued that in all these circumstances the notice of the meeting sent to Mrs Bradley-Hole could not be regarded as a notice to her as a creditor; that she was therefore not a person who, for the purpose of s. 260(2)(b), 'had notice of' the meeting and that she was not bound by, or entitled to participate in the approved arrangement.

E   I do not accept this argument. Mrs Bradley-Hole was a creditor entitled to notice of the s. 257 meeting and the nominee gave her notice of it. It is in my view irrelevant that he did not know that her claims in respect of the matrimonial debts entitled her to be given notice of the meeting. He did the right thing by giving notice to her, albeit that he did not realise it, and the notice was not rendered ineffective by his unawareness in this respect. I hold that Mrs Bradley-Hole was validly given notice of the s. 257 meeting.

F   Mr Crawford referred next to r. 5.17, headed 'Voting rights', and to r. 5.18 headed 'Requisite majorities'. He relied on these rules to support an argument that, even if Mrs Bradley-Hole was a person who 'had notice' of the s. 257 meeting for the purposes of s. 260(2)(b), she was not 'entitled to vote at' it within the meaning of the same subparagraph and was in consequence neither a party to, nor bound by, the arrangement. To explain this argument, I must set out both r. 5.17 and 5.18, which provide as follows:

G   '5.17 *Voting rights*

(1) Subject as follows, every creditor who was given notice of the creditors' meeting is entitled to vote at the meeting or any adjournment of it.

(2) In Case 1, votes are calculated according to the amount of the creditor's debt as at the date of the bankruptcy order, and in Case 2 according to the amount of the debt as at the date of the meeting.

H   (3) A creditor shall not vote in respect of a debt for an unliquidated amount, or any debt whose value is not ascertained, except where the chairman agrees to put upon the debt an estimated minimum value for the purpose of entitlement to vote.

(4) The chairman has power to admit or reject a creditor's claim for the purpose of his entitlement to vote, and the power is exercisable with respect to the whole or any part of the claim.

(5) The chairman's decision on entitlement to vote is subject to appeal to the court by any creditor, or by the debtor.

(6) If the chairman is in doubt whether a claim should be admitted or rejected, he shall mark it as objected to and allow the creditor to vote, subject to his vote being subsequently declared invalid if the objection to the claim is sustained.

(7) If on an appeal the chairman's decision is reversed or varied, or a creditor's vote is declared invalid, the court may order another meeting to be summoned or make such other order as it thinks just.

The court's power to make an order under this paragraph is exercisable only if it considers that the matter is such as to give rise to unfair prejudice or a material irregularity.

(8) An application to the court by way of appeal under this rule against the chairman's decision shall not be made after the end of the period of 28 days beginning with the day on which the chairman's report to the court is made under section 259.

(9) The chairman is not personally liable for any costs incurred by any person in respect of an appeal under this Rule.

5.18 *Requisite majorities*

(1) Subject as follows, at the creditors' meeting for any resolution to pass approving any proposal or modification there must be a majority in excess of three-quarters in value of the creditors present in person or by proxy and voting on the resolution.

(2) The same applies in respect of any other resolution proposed at the meeting, but substituting one-half for three-quarters.

(3) In the following cases there is to be left out of account a creditor's vote in respect of any claim or part of a claim–

    (a) where written notice of the claim was not given, either at the meeting or before it, to the chairman or the nominee;

    (b) where the claim or part is secured;

    (c) where the claim is in respect of a debt wholly or partly on, or secured by, a current bill of exchange or promissory note, unless the creditor is willing–

        (i) to treat the liability to him on the bill or note of every person who is liable on it antecedently to the debtor, and against whom a bankruptcy order has not been made (or, in the case of a company, which has not gone into liquidation), as a security in his hands, and

        (ii) to estimate the value of the security and (for the purpose of entitlement to vote, but not of any distribution under the arrangement) to deduct it from his claim.

(4) Any resolution is invalid if those voting against it include more than half in value of the creditors, counting in these latter only those–

    (a) to whom notice of the meeting was sent;

    (b) whose votes are not to be left out of account under paragraph (3); and

    (c) who are not, to the best of the chairman's belief, associates of the debtor.

(5) It is for the chairman of the meeting to decide whether under this Rule–

    (a) a vote is to be left out of account in accordance with paragraph (3), or

    (b) a person is an associate of the debtor for the purposes of paragraph (4)(c);

A   and in relation to the second of these two cases the chairman is entitled to rely on the information provided by the debtor's statement of affairs or otherwise in accordance with this Part of the Rules.

(6) If the chairman uses a proxy contrary to Rule 5.16, his vote with that proxy does not count towards any majority under this Rule.

(7) Paragraphs (5) to (9) of Rule 5.17 apply as regards an appeal against the
B   decision of the chairman under this Rule.'

In reliance on these rules, Mr Crawford made two submissions. The first was that, as Mrs Bradley-Hole had not given written notice of any of her claims to the chairman or nominee prior to the meeting, the true effect of r. 5.18(3)(a) is that she was not 'entitled to vote at' the meeting in respect of any of those claims within the meaning of s. 260(2)(b). Thus he said that she was not bound by or a party to the arrangement in respect of any
C   of her claims.

I am unable to accept this argument. Rule 5.18 is, in my judgment, concerned not with entitlement to vote but, as is indicated by its contents and heading, with 'Requisite majorities'. In particular, in directing that certain votes are to be left out of account, r. 5.18(3) proceeds in my view on the premise that the person casting them has in principle an entitlement to vote, but that in the particular circumstances any votes so cast are not to be counted. A vote cannot be left out of account unless it has first been cast and I
D   consider that the better approach to the construction of r. 5.18(3) is that it presumes that there was a basic entitlement to vote in the first place. I cannot read r. 5.18(3) as having the consequence that creditors whose votes are so to be left out of account are to be equated with creditors who have no entitlement to vote at all. Were that the intention, then I consider that the matter would have been dealt with by r. 5.17, which is, in terms, concerned with 'voting rights'.

E   Secondly, and alternatively, Mr Crawford submitted that, as Mrs Bradley-Hole's costs recoverable against the bankrupt (item (4) of her claim) had not been taxed at the date of the bankruptcy order or the date of the approval of the arrangement, her debt in respect of costs was either 'for an unliquidated amount' or was one 'whose value is not ascertained' within the meaning of r. 5.17(3). There was no agreement with the chairman to put an estimated minimum value on such debt for the purpose of voting (note the words 'for the purpose of entitlement to vote' in rule 5.17(3)). Thus, submitted Mr
F   Crawford, Mrs Bradley-Hole was not 'entitled to vote' at the s. 257 meeting in respect of her costs claim within the meaning of s. 260(2)(b) and was for that reason excluded from participation in the arrangement in respect of such claim. Mr Crawford relied on the reasoning to the like effect of Ferris J in *Re Cranley Mansions Ltd* [1994] BCC 576 at pp. 593D–594F.

Mr Hoser accepted that Mrs Bradley-Hole's costs claim was one either 'for an
G   unliquidated amount' or for a 'debt whose value is not ascertained' within the meaning of r. 5.17(3). He also accepted that, if this had been her only claim, the consequence of no agreed estimated minimum value having been put on it by the chairman would be that she was not 'entitled to vote' for the purpose of s. 260(2)(b) and thus not bound by the arrangement.

However, he submitted that in the particular circumstances of this case, Mrs Bradley-
H   Hole was 'entitled to vote at, the meeting' within s. 260(2)(b) and that she is a party to and bound by the arrangement in respect of all the matrimonial debts, including the costs claim. His argument was that (1) she was entitled to vote at the meeting in respect of her claims other than her cost claim, albeit that she did not choose to attend the meeting and exercise her rights; (2) she is therefore a person who was 'entitled to vote at the meeting' within s. 260(2)(b); (3) in a case where a creditor is entitled to two or more separate debts owed by the debtor, that subparagraph does not purport to limit his participation in the

arrangement to the extent only of that debt or those debts in respect of which he has an　A
entitlement to vote; and (4) therefore an entitlement to vote in respect of one or some
only of the creditors' debts will entitle him to participate in the arrangement, not just in
respect of that or those debts, but in respect of the entirety of his claims.

The respective arguments of Mr Crawford and Mr Hoser thus pose this question. If a
creditor has two claims against the debtor, one being an unliquidated claim in respect of
which, in default of satisfying the provisions of r. 5.17(3), the creditor has no entitlement　B
to vote and the other being a liquidated claim in respect of which he is entitled to vote, is
the consequence that the creditor is (1) bound by and party to the arrangement in respect
of both debts; or (2) bound by and party to it for the purpose of the debt in respect of
which he is entitled to vote, but not in respect of the other debt?

I do not find either of these alternatives satisfactory. Each of them could in my view,
and in the varying circumstances that might arise in any particular case, result in a degree
of unfairness towards the creditor concerned. I have not been referred to any provision　C
in the Act or the rules which sheds any direct light on the point. However, with some
hesitation, I have come to the conclusion that Mr Hoser's argument is to be preferred.

To the question whether Mrs Bradley-Hole is a person who 'had notice of, and was
entitled to vote at, the meeting' for the purposes of s. 260(2)(b) the answer must in my
judgment be 'yes', albeit that her voting entitlement was based on debts other than the
costs claim. So answering this question, s. 260(2)(b) in terms provides that Mrs Bradley-　D
Hole is bound by the arrangement as if she were a party to it; and I find it difficult to
conclude otherwise than that the effect of the subsection must be that she is so bound
and is such a party in respect of the entirety of her proved indebtedness, even though she
may not have been entitled to vote at the meeting in respect of one or more heads of such
indebtedness. To conclude otherwise involves reading into s. 260 words that are not
there. I recognise that my preferred conclusion may, on the facts of any particular case,
result in what may be perceived to be an element of unfairness to any creditor so bound.　E
However, I consider that the scheme of the Act is that the remedy of any such creditor is
to apply to the court under s. 262 to challenge the decision of the s. 257 meeting.

I accordingly hold that Mrs Bradley-Hole is in principle bound by, and entitled to
participate in, the arrangement in respect of her four surviving heads of claim. However,
Mr Crawford disputed the quantum of two of these heads. I will take each of the four
heads in turn.　F

(1) The claim for £2,411.42 in respect of instalment arrears under the Nationwide
Anglia mortgage. There is no dispute on the amount of this claim.

(2) The claim in respect of the second charge over Woodlands. Mrs Bradley-Hole's
claim is for £40,995.40, the amount ultimately taken out of the sale proceeds by the bank
in 1993. Mr Crawford submits that the maximum amount of the claim is for the sum
secured by the second charge on 6 April 1990, the date of the first bankruptcy order,　G
which he says is the relevant date by reference to which the participating creditors must
prove their claims. There is no evidence as to what the amount was on this date, but it is
likely to have been approximately the same as, probably slightly less, than the
indebtedness at 11 May 1990 of £36,530.60.

Mr Hoser does not, I think, submit that 6 April 1990 is not the relevant date at which
the amounts of the creditors' respective debts are to be determined, but he says that such
determination is governed in part by the provisions of s. 382(1)(b) of the Act, which I　H
have set out earlier in this judgment. In reliance on that provision, Mr Hoser argues that,
as at 6 April 1990, the bankrupt was under an existing obligation to transfer Woodlands
to Mrs Bradley-Hole free from the second charge. However, the extent of his liability to
her by virtue of such obligation only crystallised in 1993, when the amount of the
proceeds of sale taken by the bank in satisfaction of its charge was fixed at £40,995.40.

A   He says that the liability to which the bankrupt became subject at that point is thus squarely within s. 382(1)(b) and that Mrs Bradley-Hole's claim in respect of such amount is provable in the voluntary arrangement in full.

I do not accept that argument. In my view, s. 382(1)(b) is primarily directed at the type of liability which, as at the date of the bankruptcy order, is in the nature of a future, prospective or contingent one; that is to say a liability which will or may arise at some B   future time, but which has not yet crystallised. Even assuming expressly without deciding, that the terms of the voluntary arrangement in the present case did permit creditors to claim in respect of such liabilities, I cannot, however, regard the present claim as within this class of liability. The position is that, as from 5 May 1989, Mrs Bradley-Hole had an enforceable right to compel the transfer to herself of Woodlands free from the second charge and she still had such a right as at 6 April 1990. It may be that she could not in practice have achieved the transfer free from the second charge and that she might, as C   eventually she did, have to settle for a transfer subject to it. In principle, however, she did, as at 6 April 1990, have an enforceable claim against the bankrupt to discharge the then amount of the second charge or to indemnify her against it. Her claim against the bankrupt as at 6 April 1990 cannot, in my judgment, be regarded as a future, prospective or contingent one. His liability to her was then a present one and payment to her at that date of the amount then secured by the charge would have enabled her to discharge it in D   full. I cannot see how it can be just for her to be entitled to claim in the arrangement for a greater sum. That sum has, presumably, subsequently grown primarily because of the accruing of interest due to the bank. I take it to be clear that, in the case of interest-bearing debts, creditors cannot claim in the arrangement for interest accruing after 6 April 1990. In my view, Mrs Bradley-Hole's claim for the full £40,995.40 is, in essence, a claim for interest accruing due since 6 April 1990.

E   I therefore hold that Mrs Bradley-Hole may only claim for the amount of the indebtedness secured by the second charge as at 6 April 1990. I would expect the parties to be able to agree what this figure is but in case of any difficulty over it, I will give them liberty to apply.

(3) The claim for maintenance. Mrs Bradley-Hole claims some £17,920, being arrears of maintenance ordered to be paid to her on 5 May 1989 for the benefit of the four children of the family. Her claim is (a) for arrears due by 6 April 1990, which total some F   £3,920, and (b) in respect of payments which became due subsequently down to 12 March 1992, when her claim was notified to the supervisor. Her claim in respect of (a) is based on s. 382(1)(a); and that under (b) is based on the proposition that, as at 6 April 1990, these payments were in the nature of a debt or liability within s. 382(1)(b), being a claim which became quantified at a cut-off point chosen by her in 1992, when she gave notice of her claim.

G   The claim is in respect of payments due to Mrs Bradley-Hole under a periodical payments order made in the course of the divorce proceedings. Payments of this nature have always been regarded as of a personal and inalienable nature. Further, the court has always retained a jurisdiction to vary, discharge or suspend such orders or to remit the payment of any arrears (see s. 31 and 32 of the *Matrimonial Causes Act* 1973). The special nature of such payments has resulted in their special treatment in the case of the H   bankruptcy of the party ordered to pay them, a matter to which I should refer briefly.

Thus, s. 382(1)(a) and (b) of the Act, on which Mr Hoser relies, are derived from s. 30(3) of the *Bankruptcy Act* 1914, a section headed 'Description of debts provable in bankruptcy', which was itself derived from s. 37 of the *Bankruptcy Act* 1883. It was, however, clear law under those latter Acts that no proof could be made in the bankruptcy in respect of (a) arrears of any periodical payments at the date of the receiving order or

(b) future payments due to be made after the date of the receiving order (see, for example,   A
Linton v Linton (1885) 15 QBD 239, *Re Hawkins* [1894] 1 QB 25, *Kerr v Kerr* [1897] 2 QB
439, *James v James* [1964] P 303 and *Woodley v Woodley (No. 2)* [1994] 1 WLR 1167 at
p. 1178H). The reasoning underlying these decisions was that neither the arrears nor the
future periodical payments were capable of valuation or estimation, since it was within
the discretion of the court as to how far arrears might be enforced and the court could
also vary its order as to any future payments. The inability to prove for these payments
in the bankruptcy did not, of course, mean that their beneficiary was remediless. They   B
simply remained personal liabilities from which the bankrupt was not discharged by his
bankruptcy and the intended beneficiary could continue to look to enforce payment of
them out of his personal earnings.

The new insolvency regime introduced in 1986 has preserved these principles, although
deals with the matter differently. I consider that, on a natural reading of the definition of
a 'bankruptcy debt' in s. 382, it can be said to include indebtedness under periodical   C
payments orders, a construction which appears to be supported by s. 281(5) which is
concerned with the effect of discharge from bankruptcy. That subsection reads:

'(5) Discharge does not, except to such extent and on such conditions as the court
may direct, release the bankrupt from any bankruptcy debt which–

(a) ...

(b) arises under any order made in family proceedings.'   D

However, what is in any event clear is that no proof can be made in bankruptcy for
any obligation arising under, inter alia, a periodical payments order, and I have already
referred to r. 12.3(2) which so provides.

It is against this background that Mr Hoser argues that Mrs Bradley-Hole can,
however, claim in the voluntary arrangement in respect of the periodical payments order.   E
The argument is that (1) the bankrupt's liability under such an order is a 'bankruptcy
debt', (2) s. 257(3) provides that, in a Case 1 case, the creditors entitled to be given notice
of the meeting to approve the voluntary arrangement include 'every person who is a
creditor of the bankrupt in respect of a bankruptcy debt' and (3) there is no provision
equivalent to r. 12.3(2) preventing a claim in respect of such liabilities being made in the
voluntary arrangement.   F

Taking first the claim in respect of the maintenance payments due after 6 April 1990,
in my judgment that argument is insufficient to get Mr Hoser home.

Mr Crawford's main submission in answer to it is that it is implicit in the bankrupt's
proposal for the voluntary arrangement that the only debts which were to rank for
payment under it were those for which the debtor had already become liable and that
it was no part of the proposal to extend it to debts or liabilities which would or might   G
only arise in the future. He may be right about that, but I consider that there is a
more fundamental difficulty in the way of Mrs Bradley-Hole's claim in respect of the
post-6 April 1990 payments. As well as being personal and inalienable, the benefit of a
periodical payments order is also incapable of being released. It can only be discharged by
the court. That was decided by the decision of the Court of Appeal in *Watkins v Watkins*
[1896] P 222. The principle was later succinctly expressed by the President, Sir Henry
Duke, in *Campbell v Campbell* [1922] P 187 at p. 192, as follows: H

'The order of May, 1914, assigned no property and created no debt. What is
created by the order is not a chose in action in the petitioner, but an obligation in
the respondent to pay to his wife what has been called a purely personal allowance
for her maintenance. She cannot issue execution without leave, or assign or release
her interest. This appears from cases like *Linton v. Linton* (1885) 15 QBD 239 and

A
    Watkins v. *Watkins* [1896] P 222. Since an express agreement by the wife would not discharge the husband's liability, it clearly cannot be discharged by tacit consent or mere inaction.'

    In my view, this principle prevents Mrs Bradley-Hole from claiming in the voluntary arrangement in respect of payments destined to accrue in the period after 6 April 1990. The essence of a voluntary arrangement is that under it each creditor compromises or

B
releases his rights against the debtor in respect of his pre-existing debt and receives in exchange and in full satisfaction whatever payment terms are being offered by the debtor. It appears to me that any claim by Mrs Bradley-Hole in respect of these particular payments can only be on the basis that she has compromised or released her rights under the order against the bankrupt in exchange for the payment terms offered under the arrangement. In my judgment, it was not competent for her to make such a compromise or release. I therefore conclude that she is not entitled to claim in the arrangement for

C
any maintenance payments which fell due after 6 April 1990.

    The position with regard to the arrears which had accrued due by 6 April 1990 is different. Mr Crawford expressly admitted that Mrs Bradley-Hole is entitled to claim in respect of these arrears, which total at most £3,920, and has not sought to argue the contrary. Further, it is unclear that the principle which I consider precludes Mrs Bradley-Hole from claiming in respect of future maintenance payments also prevents her from

D
releasing or assigning her rights in respect of any arrears. In particular, in *Watkins v Watkins* at p. 228, Lindley LJ stated his opinion that a divorced wife 'may release and I suppose assign her right to arrears', although I do not read that dictum as forming part of the decision in the case.

    In these circumstances I direct that Mrs Bradley-Hole is entitled to claim in respect of the arrears which had accrued due down to 6 April 1990, but not in respect of any payments which were destined to fall due after that date. Again, I hope that there will be

E
no difficulty in the parties agreeing the precise figure but, if there is, they may have liberty to apply.

    (4) The claim for costs, taxed in the sum of £19,683.29. The order for costs in Mrs Bradley-Hole's favour was made before the bankruptcy order, although the costs were only taxed afterwards. The taxation rendered certain the amount of costs due to Mrs Bradley-Hole by the bankrupt as at 6 April 1990. I did not understand Mr Crawford to

F
argue against a claim by Mrs Bradley-Hole for the full amount of the taxed costs and I take the view that she is so entitled and I so direct.

Question 3

Question 3 asks:

G
    '(3) Whether the applicant as such supervisor should convene a meeting of those creditors bound by the individual voluntary arrangement and directions as to the terms of reference of that meeting.'

    The suggested need for the calling of such a meeting was justified in the supervisor's evidence by three factors to which he referred, but Mr Crawford relied on only one of them. The supervisor's principal concern is that the consequence of my decision is that

H
Mrs Bradley-Hole is entitled to participate in the arrangement in respect of indebtedness of a substantial amount, being indebtedness of which the other creditors who are party to the arrangement may well have been ignorant at the time that it was approved. He is concerned that those creditors may feel that all the bankrupt's cards were not placed face up on the table at that time and that, for the reasons I have earlier outlined, had they been better informed about the bankrupt's affairs, they would have preferred to have rejected his proposal for a voluntary arrangement.

I propose to say no more about the position than that, in my view, it would be just   A
that the arrangement creditors should have an opportunity to consider their position. I
will direct that the supervisor is at liberty to notify them of such matters as he considers
ought to be drawn to their attention, either by way of a circular letter or by way of a
meeting.

(*The official receiver's and Mrs Bradley-Hole's costs to be paid out of the supervisor's
fund. Leave to appeal granted to the official receiver and Mrs Bradley-Hole*)   B

C

D

E

F

G

H

A # Re AMF International Ltd.

Chancery Division.
Ferris J.
Judgment delivered 24 November 1994.

B *Liquidation – Members' voluntary liquidation superseded by creditors' – Creditor applied for proof to be admitted, for creditors' meeting and liquidator's removal – Liquidator replaced at creditors' meeting – Creditor sought costs of application from liquidator – Insolvency Act 1986, s. 108; Insolvency Rules 1986 (SI 1986/ 1925), r. 4.143(4).*

This was a hearing on the costs of an application by a creditor for its proof to be admitted and paid in the liquidation of AMF International Ltd, for a meeting of creditors to be
C summoned under s. 95 of the Insolvency Act 1986, and for the liquidator to be removed from office pursuant to s. 108.

The applicant was the assignee of the reversion of AMF's business premises. AMF went into members' voluntary liquidation. The liquidator made distributions to AMF's parent ('Minstar') and took an indemnity from Minstar. Having paid rent under the lease, the liquidator realised that the lease was a liability and disclaimed it, giving rise to a claim by
D the applicant under s. 178(6) of the Act. The liquidator admitted the applicant's proof of debt in a sum greater than that which remained in his hands and made a payment on account. A creditors' meeting pursuant to s. 95 was then held and a new liquidator appointed for the resulting creditors' voluntary liquidation.

The applicant wanted the liquidator to pay the costs of the application personally: the reason why the application for substantive orders was not effective was that, as a result of
E the liquidator's own acts in paying a contributory before he had satisfied AMF's liabilities, AMF appeared to be insolvent and the liquidator, having lost the confidence of the applicant as principal creditor, had been displaced. Under r. 4.143(4) of the Insolvency Rules, the costs of an application for the removal of a liquidator were, subject to any contrary order of the court, not payable out of the company assets. Against this the liquidator argued that there was no real impropriety in his making payments to Minstar when he did, because he
F reasonably believed at that time that the assets remaining in his hands as liquidator were sufficient to satisfy the outstanding liabilities of AMF.

Held, ordering the liquidator personally to pay the applicant's costs of the proceedings on the standard basis and his own costs:

In making payments to Minstar the liquidator acted at his peril. If Minstar did not honour its undertaking, he might find himself personally liable to the new liquidator in respect of
G any deficiency of assets in the liquidation or to the applicant for breach of his statutory duty to pay the debts of the company out of its assets. Moreover he had acted with unacceptable dilatoriness in dealing with the applicant's claim. He had brought the proceedings upon himself. Further, if the result desired by the applicant had not been achieved by means of s. 95 of the Insolvency Act, the court would have made an order for his removal from office.

The following cases were referred to in the judgment:
H
Armstrong Whitworth Securities Co Ltd, Re [1947] Ch 673.
Keypak Homecare Ltd, Re (1987) 3 BCC 558.
Pulsford v Devenish [1903] 2 Ch 625.

Paul Girolami (instructed by Rabin Leacock Lipman) for the applicant.

Richard de Lacy (instructed by Nabarro Nathanson) for the respondent.

JUDGMENT   A

Ferris J: In the events which have happened, the application in this matter has been effective only in respect of the costs of the application. But, in order to decide how those costs should be borne, I shall have to set out in some detail the relevant facts. For the most part, these facts emerge from the documents which are before me and the primary facts are not in dispute.

At all material times, AMF international Ltd ('AMF') has been the wholly owned   B
subsidiary of an American corporation, incorporated in the State of Minnesota, named Minstar Inc ('Minstar'). AMF occupied, for the purposes of its businesses, premises on the Newbridge Trading Estate, Bristol, under a lease of those premises dated 13 May 1976 creating a term of 25 years from 24 June 1976 with five-yearly rent reviews. AMF was the original lessee under the lease and covenanted in the usual way to pay the rent becoming due throughout the term. At the time with which I am concerned, the passing   C
rent under the lease was £110,000 per annum. The reversioners entitled to the property subject to the lease have at all material times been the individuals who are the applicants in these proceedings. They were not the original lessors, but they took an assignment of the reversion in August 1986.

On 29 November 1991, the directors of AMF made a declaration of solvency and on 17 December 1991 AMF entered into members' voluntary liquidation, Mr W J H Elles, of the Southampton office of Ernst & Young, being appointed liquidator. In the   D
statement of assets and liabilities annexed to the declaration of solvency, the major assets of AMF were said to consist of trade debtors whose debts amounted to some £5.9m. It has subsequently emerged, however, that to the extent of about £4.5m this sum represented not trade debts but money due to AMF from its parent Minstar in respect of a loan or loans made by AMF to Minstar. After taking into account other assets and estimated liabilities, the surplus estimated to be available for contributories of AMF was   E
stated to be £5,946,913. In arriving at this estimate no allowance was made for the value of AMF's rights and obligations under the lease, either as an asset or as a liability.

Presumably this was because it was considered at the date of declaration of solvency that the residue of the term created by the lease could be disposed of without cost or gain to AMF.

After the commencement of the liquidation, AMF appears to have sub-let part of the   F
premises demised by the lease, but the particulars of the receipts got in and payments made by the liquidator indicate that the rents obtained from sub-letting were not enough to cover the rent payable to the applicants under the lease. Nevertheless, the rent under the lease was paid by the liquidator, albeit somewhat irregularly, during 1992 and the early part of 1993.

During 1992, before completing the liquidation so far as payment of liabilities was   G
concerned, the liquidator made certain distributions to Minstar, as contributory. These distributions included a cash payment of £470,000 on 12 May 1992 and another cash payment of £450,000 on 8 June 1992. These payments reduced the cash balance remaining in the liquidator's hands to about £28,000. The balance was further reduced in July 1992 but, notwithstanding the payment of certain liabilities, it had risen to about £217,000 at the end of 1992, mainly as the result of the receipt of a substantial corporation tax refund. The liquidator appears also to have treated the benefit of the loan or loans made by AMF   H
to Minstar as having been distributed in specie to Minstar. Certainly he made no attempt to get in the amount of any such loan.

In anticipation of the distributions which I have mentioned being made to Minstar, on 25 March 1992 Minstar gave the liquidator an indemnity in writing. It is addressed to the liquidator, and it reads:

A   'In consideration of you as liquidator of the above named company making a distribution of a substantial portion of the surplus assets of the company without first obtaining tax clearances and settling other liabilities, we hereby agree to pay, satisfy and discharge all the liabilities of the company, including your reasonable remuneration and disbursements of the liquidator, to the extent that the remaining assets of the company are not sufficient and to meet those in full, limited to the amount that we have received from the liquidator.'

B   That is signed on behalf of Minstar by an individual who was its vice president.

Neither the distributions to Minstar nor the existence of the Minstar indemnity were known to the applicants in these proceedings until after the proceedings had been commenced.

C   In 1993, if not before, the liquidator had come to appreciate that the lease of the premises occupied by AMF was a liability rather than an asset. There appear to have been some negotiations directed towards the surrender of the lease to the applicants but these negotiations were inconclusive. On 10 March 1993, the liquidator's solicitors stated that AMF was insolvent and that steps were being taken to convert the liquidation into a creditors' voluntary liquidation and to disclaim the lease. The statement as to insolvency was withdrawn a fortnight later, it being said that it was based on a misunderstanding within the solicitors' firm. Further negotiations took place but without positive result. Matters seem to have come to a head after the applicants, on 4 May 1993, demanded payment of the rent which had become due on 25 March 1993 and threatened proceedings if payment was not made within seven days. On 12 May the liquidator paid the rent and on 13 May he filed a formal notice of disclaimer in respect of the lease. The validity of this disclaimer has not been challenged. Accordingly, pursuant to s. 178(6) of the *Insolvency Act* 1986, the applicants are deemed to be creditors of AMF to the extent of the loss or damage suffered by them in consequence of the disclaimer.

E   On 2 July 1993 the liquidator, by his solicitors, asked the applicants' solicitors to provide particulars of the damages claimed to have been suffered by the applicants. In response, on 2 August 1993, the applicants' solicitors put the applicants' claim at more than £1.2m. This claim was acknowledged on 12 August, the liquidator's solicitors saying that they would write further in due course. No substantive reply was, however, written during the rest of 1993.

F   On 26 January 1994 the applicants' solicitors, who expressed concern at the absence of a substantive response to their letter of 2 August 1993 – although it is fair to say that they had not chased the matter in the meantime – wrote formally to set out the applicants' proof of debt. This was put at £793,349 and was said to be supported by a number of documents which were enclosed with the letter. Proceedings under s. 112 of the Insolvency Act were threatened unless a satisfactory response was received within 28 days. It now transpires that an acknowledgement of this letter was written by the liquidator's solicitors on 31 January but this acknowledgement was not received by the applicants' solicitors. So far as the applicants were concerned, all that happened in the next ten weeks was some desultory contact between the surveyors to the parties. On 19 April 1994 the applicants issued the originating application in this matter. By it they sought orders that the liquidator should admit and pay in full their proof of debt; alternatively, that he summon a meeting of creditors in compliance with s. 95 of the *Insolvency Act* 1986; and, in the further alternative, that he be removed from office pursuant to s. 108.

On 3 May 1994 the liquidator's solicitors, in formal response to the applicants' solicitors' letter of 26 January said:

'You are well aware that our clients do not admit your clients' claim in the sum alleged. It is admitted that your clients are entitled to damages following the

disclaimer but the level of such damages must be the subject of proper   A
determination with recourse to expert evidence.'

Thereafter there was some correspondence about the quantum of the applicants' claim
and there were agreed procedural directions in the originating application, as a result of
which para. 3 of that application, relating to the removal of the liquidator from office,
was adjourned into court for a substantive hearing on 22 July, subsequently postponed
to 25 July 1994.   B

On 22 July 1994, after the liquidator had received advice from his surveyors, his
solicitors wrote to the applicants' solicitors stating that the liquidator was prepared to
admit the applicants' proof of debt in the sum of £572,444. This was stated to be the
undisputed part of the debt, but in a statement enclosed with the letter it was made
apparent that, in respect of one item included in the total of £572,444, a sum of £100,000
had been admitted as a provisional figure, the liquidator reserving the right to revise this   C
figure either upwards or downwards. The liquidator proposed to satisfy the sum of
£572,444 as to £200,000 by means of a payment from the liquidation account with the
Insolvency Services Agency and as to the balance of £372,444 by calling on Minstar to
pay this sum under its indemnity by 15 August. It was proposed that the balance of the
applicants' claim be discussed between the surveyors to the parties. In the light of this
proposal, the hearing date for 25 July was very understandably vacated, the matter being
adjourned until the Michaelmas term. In the event, it was fixed to come before me on 9   D
November and it is this matter with which I am now concerned. I need, however, to state
some further events which have occurred subsequently.

On 16 August the applicants received from the liquidator the sum of £200,000, which
was accepted by them on account of the £572,444 agreed to be paid. Minstar did not,
however, make any payment to the liquidator pursuant to his demand, with the result
that the liquidator made no further payment to the applicants. Minstar indicated,   E
through the liquidator, that it wished to deal with the applicants direct, but this was not
acceptable to the applicants. On 19 August the liquidator convened a creditors' meeting,
pursuant to s. 95, to be held on 7 September. When that meeting was held, a new
liquidator was voted into office for the purposes of the resulting creditors' voluntary
liquidation.

No question of the removal of Mr Elles from office now arises because he has already
ceased to hold office as liquidator. Moreover, the applicants will now have to deal with   F
the new liquidator, not Mr Elles, as regards payment of the balance of their admitted
claim and the agreement or determination of the part of their claim which is not admitted.
It is not known whether the new liquidator will be able to enforce Minstar's undertaking
so as to put himself in funds. It is obvious, however, that no relief could now be granted
on para. 3 of the originating application and on behalf of the applicants no such relief
has been pressed for. I have only been asked to make an order as to the costs of the   G
application. For this purpose, it has been agreed between the parties that I should treat
the whole of the originating application as being before me and dispose of it accordingly.

On behalf of the applicants, it is submitted that I should order that the liquidator, Mr
Elles, should personally pay the applicants' costs and should not be allowed to recover
either his own costs or any costs paid by him to the applicants out of the assets of AMF.
Alternatively, it was argued that if I were minded to allow Mr Elles to recover any costs   H
out of the assets of AMF, his right of recoupment should be expressed to arise only after
all the creditors of AMF have been paid in full. If any right of recoupment is not excluded
or postponed by an order of the kind proposed on behalf of the applicants, then the
applicants will, in effect, bear their own costs and the costs of the liquidator unless
Minstar honours its indemnity to the extent required to satisfy all costs and pay the
applicants' debt in full.

A   The grounds upon which the applicants contend that I should make an order of the kind which they seek can, I think, be summarised as follows. Although the liquidator has said, in the narrative attached to a statement of affairs signed by him on 12 September 1994, that it appeared from the declaration of solvency that the lease had been disposed of by AMF before the liquidation, the liquidator knew, by a date soon after his appointment, that this was not the case.

B   Indeed, he made payments on account of rent in January, February, April and May 1992, all before the cash distributions to Minstar. He must have realised that the lease would or might give rise to liabilities in the liquidation, because he was or should have been aware that AMF was original lessee and thus liable on the lessee's covenants throughout the term; he was also aware that the rent received from sub-lettings did not cover the rent payable under the lease; and his own efforts to dispose of the lease or to sub-let vacant parts led to no solution. Nevertheless, in May and June 1992 he made cash

C distributions to Minstar without quantifying or providing for any liabilities under the lease. In doing so, he acted in breach of 'the cardinal principle that in a winding-up shareholders are not entitled to anything until all the debts have been paid' (see *Re Armstrong Whitworth Securities Co Ltd* [1947] Ch 673 at p. 689 per Jenkins J). He therefore acted at his peril, as, in effect, he recognised by taking the indemnity from Minstar. But he also brought about a potential conflict of interest between his personal

D position and his duties as office-holder. This conflict of interest is said to have arisen from the existence of a temptation to resist bona fide claims from creditors lest the indemnity proved to be insufficient or unenforceable and he had to satisfy those claims personally. This, it was said, conflicts with his duties as office-holder, which include a statutory duty to pay the debts of the company out of its assets (see *Pulsford v Devenish* [1903] 2 Ch 625 at pp. 632–633). This statutory duty imports a duty impartially to examine and admit all proper claims from creditors.

E   It was further pointed out that from 2 August 1993 the liquidator was on notice that the applicants had a claim to be creditors for a large sum, which they then put at £1.2m. The liquidator appears, however, to have taken no steps to evaluate this claim. So far as the applicants were aware the position did not change after 26 January 1994, when they lodged a proof of debt for £793,349. Even if they had received the letter of 31 January 1994, this would not really have changed matters because it was a mere

F acknowledgement. Although the rules do not now provide a time within which a liquidator must accept or reject a proof, it was submitted that he must do so within a reasonable time. In this case proceedings were not launched until 19 April, by which time a reasonable time had expired. It was said, therefore, that the liquidator had brought the application upon himself.

     It was further argued that even after the commencement of proceedings the liquidator

G had behaved unreasonably. He had concurred in the giving of directions and the filing of evidence to lead to a contested hearing on 22 July without having obtained expert advice which enabled him to know whether or to what extent the applicants' claim to have suffered loss could be resisted. When he did finally obtain advice on the very date which had been fixed for the contested hearing, he conceded over 70 per cent of the claim and proposed to enter into negotiations as to the balance. The only reason why the application for substantive orders is not now effective is that, as a result of the liquidator's

H own acts in paying a contributory before he had satisfied AMF's liabilities, AMF appears to be insolvent and the liquidator, having lost the confidence of the applicants as principal creditors, has been displaced.

     My attention was drawn to r. 4.143 (4) of the Insolvency Rules, under which the costs of an application for the removal of a liquidator are, subject to any contrary order of the court, not payable out of the company assets.

Against this it was argued on behalf of the liquidator that there was no real impropriety   A
in him making payments to Minstar when he did so, because he reasonably believed at
that time that the assets remaining in his hands as liquidator were sufficient to satisfy the
outstanding liabilities of AMF.

As matters now stand, it is not known whether or not the applicants will succeed on
the balance of their claim which has not been admitted. Nor is it known whether the new
liquidator will seek to enforce Minstar's indemnity or, if he does so, whether he will   B
recover sufficient to satisfy the applicants in full so far as their claim is found to be valid.
It was contended that in these circumstances it would be premature to make any such
order for costs as the applicants seek.

It was further argued that any apparent delay on the part of the liquidator in dealing
with the applicants' claim is excusable and should be excused. The evidence shows, it was
said, that on 15 February 1994 the liquidator instructed his surveyors, a firm named   C
Pringle Denny, who already were acting on his behalf, to assess the claim of the applicants
set out in the letter of 26 January. On 7 March Pringle Denny produced what they
described as an 'initial overview', as a result of which the liquidator authorised them to
instruct an expert in the Bristol property market to work with them. It was said that
Pringle Denny then spent several weeks interviewing firms in the Bristol area, and chose
Chestertons, whose appointment they confirmed on 28 April. Unfortunately, after having
received detailed instructions on 17 May, Chestertons discovered that they had a conflict   D
of interest and they notified Pringle Denny on 26 May that they could not act. A
substitute firm, Hartnell Taylor Cook, were instructed on 14 June. All this was set out in
a letter from the liquidator's solicitors dated 21 July 1994, although it was unknown to
the applicants until that time. At the time that that letter was written by his solicitors, the
liquidator did not have the report of Hartnell Taylor Cook. That report, which is dated
22 July, was sent to Pringle Denny by fax on the same date. Its contents were presumably
conveyed at once to the liquidator who, also on the same date, made the admission which   E
I have already mentioned, leading to the adjournment of the hearing then fixed for 25
July. It was submitted that the liquidator acted with great promptness on and after 22
July and that any apparent dilatoriness before that date was not his fault because he had
frequently stressed the need for urgency upon Pringle Denny.

It was submitted that in these circumstances I should order the costs of the applicants
and of the liquidator to be paid as expenses of the winding up. It was accepted that the   F
result of such an order would be that the costs would be paid in priority to the debt due
to the applicants. It was suggested that, if I were to feel anxiety lest the amount due to
the applicants might not be paid in full because of the non-recovery of money from
Minstar, I should give leave for the applicants to apply at some future date for the
payment of Mr Elles' costs to be postponed to the applicants' right to recover their debt
pursuant to s. 156 of the Insolvency Act.
                                                                                              G
I accept in substance the argument of the applicants and I reject that put forward on
behalf of Mr Elles. The one respect in which I do not wholly accept the argument for the
applicants is that part of it which depends upon a conflict of interest. As to that, I think
there was a potential conflict but I do not find that this affected Mr Elles' judgment. I do,
however, expressly find that in making payments to Minstar Mr Elles acted at his peril.
If Minstar does not honour its undertaking, Mr Elles may yet find himself personally
liable to the new liquidator in respect of any deficiency of assets in the liquidation or to   H
the applicants for breach of the statutory duty held to exist in *Pulsford v Devenish*.

Moreover it seems to me that Mr Elles has acted with unacceptable dilatoriness in
dealing with the applicants' claim. It was not safe for him to assume that the claim
originally put at £1.2m in August 1993 would be substantially reduced in January 1994,
yet he appears to have taken no effective steps to evaluate the claim between these two

A dates (a period of nearly six months in total). He did take some steps towards an evaluation from February 1994 onwards and, if he is right, he was seriously let down by the dilatoriness of his own agents. Even so he cannot, in my view, escape responsibility for this delay. Moreover he did not disclose his difficulties to the applicants until 21 July, by which time the application had been launched and, so far as para. 3 was concerned, was about to go to an effective hearing. The least he should have done, in my view, was to explain his difficulties when the proceedings were commenced and to keep the
B applicants fully and frankly informed of the progress, or lack of it, which was being made thereafter. If he had done so he might have received a measure of sympathy from the court, even if the patience of the applicants had been exhausted.

In my judgment Mr Elles has brought these proceedings upon himself. Further, if the result desired by the applicants had not been achieved by means of s. 95 of the Insolvency Act, it appears to me that, applying the test which emerges from *Re Keypak Homecare*
C *Ltd* (1987) 3 BCC 558, I would inevitably have made an order for Mr Elles' removal from office. In these circumstances it would not be right, in my view, to deal with the costs in the way proposed on behalf of Mr Elles. If such an order were made and if Minstar does not honour its indemnity to the extent necessary to pay in full both the costs and the amount admitted or found to be due to the applicants, the applicants will be left to make another application to the court under s. 156. This would not, in my view, be just.

D Moreover r. 4.143(4) suggests that an order of the kind asked for on behalf of Mr Elles is to be regarded as an exceptional order.

It was argued on behalf of Mr Elles that the rule is for the protection of the general body of creditors against action taken by a single creditor or a small group of creditors, and that it is not really applicable in a case of the present kind, where the applicants appear to be the only unpaid creditors. I do not, however, accept this argument. In my
E view, r. 4.143(4) has a general application to all cases where an application is made to remove a liquidator, including this case.

In my judgment the right order to make is that Mr Elles must himself pay the applicants' costs of these proceedings on the standard basis and must bear his own costs. I have hesitated as to whether I should attach a proviso to my order to the effect that, if and when all creditors of AMF have been paid in full, Mr Elles shall be entitled to have reimbursed to him out of the assets of AMF the amount which he has had to pay to the
F applicants and to bear in respect of his own costs. But the burden of such a proviso would fall upon Minstar, which is not before me, not upon the applicants. In view of this I have concluded that I should go no further at this stage than to give Mr Elles liberty to apply for an order to the effect which I have mentioned once all creditors have been paid in full. The justice of such an order can then be argued, if there is a dispute about it, between the parties who would be affected by it, namely Mr Elles, the new liquidator and
G Minstar. The affected parties will not include the present applicants.

(*Order accordingly*)

H

Acatos & Hutcheson plc v Watson.

Chancery Division.
Lightman J.
Judgment delivered 13 December 1994.

Plaintiff company wished to purchase company whose sole asset was shareholding in plaintiff – Whether prohibition against company acquiring own shares applied – Companies Act 1985, s. 23, 143, 162.

This was a summons by the plaintiff company, ' A & H plc', to determine whether the prohibition against a company acquiring its own shares under the rule in Trevor v Whitworth (1887) 12 App Cas 409 and s. 143 of the Companies Act 1985 precluded the plaintiff acquiring the whole issued share capital of 'A Ltd' whose sole asset was a 29.4 per cent shareholding in the plaintiff.

Shareholders in A & H plc contemplating making an offer for the company used A Ltd to build up a stake. After the intention of making such an offer was abandoned, all sides wished A Ltd's holding to be eliminated and it was agreed that A & H would buy the entire issued share capital of A Ltd in exchange for an issue to A Ltd's shareholders of new shares in A & H. The agreement required the court to determine that by acquiring A Ltd as a wholly owned subsidiary the plaintiff would not be held to be acquiring its own shares contrary to the rule in Trevor v Whitworth ('the rule') and s. 143 of the Act and without complying with s. 162.

Held, granting the declarations sought by the plaintiff:

1. Where it might be inferred from the facts (including the fact that the only asset of the intended subsidiary was shares in the holding company) that the intended subsidiary was set up as the first of two stages in a single scheme to evade the rule (the first being the acquisition by the intended subsidiary of shares in the holding company; and the second being the subsequent acquisition by the holding company of the intended subsidiary) the corporate veil might require to be lifted. But that situation was far from the present case.

2. The acquisition by the plaintiff of the shares in A Ltd was outside the rule and there was no occasion to pierce the corporate veil. If the takeover of a target company were precluded by virtue of its holding of shares in the acquiring company, the acquisition by the target company of such a holding would be an effective defence to such a takeover. It was plain that the rule had no such far reaching consequences. The application of the rule could not depend on or be affected by the size of the holding by the target, the percentage of the assets of the target represented by the holding or the motive for acquisition of the target.

3. Section 143 prohibited a company acquiring its own shares, not merely by purchase, but also 'otherwise', e.g. by an exchange. However it did not in terms prohibit (any more than did the rule) the acquisition by the plaintiff of A Ltd. That there was no such prohibition was put beyond question by s. 23 which expressly entitled A Ltd on the acquisition to retain its shareholding (and any bonus shares subsequently issued) in the plaintiff, albeit the voting rights in respect of those shares were suspended during its ownership.

The following cases were referred to in the judgment:

Adams & Ors v Cape Industries plc & Anor [1990] BCC 786; [1990] Ch 433.
August Investments Pty Ltd v Poseidon Ltd & Samin Ltd [1971] 2 SASR 71.
Bank of Tokyo Ltd v Karoon & Anor [1987] AC 45.
DHN Food Distributors Ltd v Tower Hamlets LBC [1976] 1 WLR 853.
Dyason v JC Hutton Pty Ltd (1935) ALR 419.
Littlewoods Mail Order Stores Ltd v McGregor [1969] 1 WLR 1241.
Salomon v A Salomon & Co Ltd [1897] AC 22.
Trade Practices Commission v Australian Iron & Steel Pty Ltd (1990) 22 FCR 305.
Trevor v Whitworth (1887) 12 App Cas 409.

A   Elizabeth Gloster QC (instructed by Frere Cholmeley Bischoff) for the plaintiff.

Terence Mowschenson (instructed by Frere Cholmeley Bischoff) for the defendant.

JUDGMENT

Lightman J: I have before me an originating summons in respect of which the plaintiff,
Acatos & Hutcheson plc, seeks declarations that (a) it has power to acquire the entire
B   issued share capital of Acatos Ltd ('Acatos') and (b) the prohibition against a company
acquiring or dealing in its own shares under the rule in *Trevor v Whitworth* (1887) 12 App
Cas 409 ('the rule') and s. 143 of the *Companies Act* 1985 does not apply to the acquisition
by the plaintiff of the entire issued share capital of Acatos. The defendant, Mr Watson,
who is the registered holder of shares in the plaintiff, but not in Acatos, has been joined
as a representative defendant. The originating summons raises the issue of law as yet
C   undecided in this jurisdiction whether the rule or s. 143 precludes the plaintiff acquiring
100 per cent of the issued share capital of Acatos whose sole asset is a holding of some
29.4 per cent of the voting share capital of the plaintiff.

Facts

The plaintiff, which is a company registered in Great Britain quoted on the London
D   Stock Exchange, is one of the world's largest processors of agricultural products for the
food industry. Acatos is a private UK company whose shares are held by Mr Ian
Hutcheson ('Mr Hutcheson'), members of his family, his family trusts and investment
companies established by his family and certain other individuals (shareholders whom
together I shall refer to as 'the Hutcheson associates'). In early 1990 the Hutcheson
associates contemplated making an offer to acquire all the share capital of the plaintiff
not already owned by them and consolidated their interest by exchanging their shares in
E   the plaintiff for shares in Acatos. Acatos, which was until that time a dormant private
company, was the vehicle through which it was intended that any offer for the plaintiff
would be made. Pursuant to this exchange, on 4 October 1990 Acatos acquired its
substantial share holding in the plaintiff.

In November 1990, Acatos abandoned its intention of making an offer for the plaintiff.
Since then the only function of Acatos, beyond holding the shares in the plaintiff, has
F   been to provide under a contract ('the Acatos service agreement') to the plaintiff the
services of Mr Hutcheson as chairman and chief executive of the plaintiff together with
his support staff. Acatos has no other material trading activities, assets or liabilities.

The Acatos shareholding structure has restricted the ability of the Hutcheson
associates to trade freely their indirect interest in the plaintiff, and the existence of a single
29 per cent holding of the shares in the plaintiff has an adverse effect on the level of
G   activity in trading in the plaintiff's shares. Accordingly the plaintiff and the Hutcheson
associates are anxious to eliminate the present shareholding of Acatos in the plaintiff and
to return to the Hutcheson associates their direct interests in the plaintiff, and at the same
time to reduce the costs presently incurred by the plaintiff under the Acatos service
agreement. The straightforward method of doing so by putting Acatos into liquidation
and distributing its holding to its shareholders has a substantial tax cost, and hence the
need to adopt some other course. Accordingly the Hutcheson associates and the plaintiff
H   have entered into an agreement dated 26 September 1994 ('the agreement') designed to
achieve the same goal.

The agreement provides for the sale by the Hutcheson associates of the entire issued
share capital of Acatos to the plaintiff in exchange for an issue to the Hutcheson
associates of new shares in the plaintiff. At completion, it is anticipated that the net assets
of Acatos other than its shareholding in the plaintiff will be negligible. The agreement

has been negotiated at arm's length. Both the Hutcheson associates and the independent
directors of the plaintiff have been separately advised by solicitors and accountants, and
in particular the independent directors have been advised that the transaction is in the
interests of the plaintiff and its shareholders. After completion of the agreement, the
plaintiff proposes to alter the rights attaching to the shares in the plaintiff held by Acatos
so that:

(1)   the shares will carry no right to vote or receive dividends;

(2)   the shares will be deemed on a winding up to have a nominal value of 50 pence
       irrespective of any reduction in the nominal value of the shares.

Thereafter, an application will be made to the court to sanction a reduction of capital
on the basis that:

(1)   the par value of the shares will be reduced to a nominal sum (0.01p); and

(2)   the capital reserve created on the reduction of the shares will be utilised to permit
       the investment in Acatos to be written off against it.

The plaintiff has however been quite properly concerned, in the absence of any English
authority or textbook guidance on the question, that an argument might be raised against
the validity of the agreement on the ground that by acquiring Acatos as a wholly owned
subsidiary the plaintiff will in substance be acquiring its own shares without complying
with s. 162 of the *Companies Act* 1985 and accordingly fall foul of the rule and s. 143. In
these circumstances, the agreement provides that completion shall not take place unless
and until on or before 28 February 1995 (inter alia) the necessary resolutions were (or
have been) passed at general meetings of the plaintiff and:

'(e) a declaration [is] made by the High Court of Justice in England and Wales, in
form and substance satisfactory to the parties, to the effect that the acquisition of
the shares pursuant to this agreement is intra vires the buyer and does not involve
an unauthorised reduction of the buyer's capital nor a dealing in its shares . . .'

The originating summons seeking this declaration was issued on 7 November 1994 and
affidavits have been sworn verifying the facts I have recited by Mr Hutcheson and Mr
Ian Caunt, the plaintiff's finance director.

The plaintiff was represented by Miss Elizabeth Gloster QC and Mr Watson by Mr
Terence Mowschenson who have both given me all available assistance on the issues
raised.

Law

(a) *The rule*

The rule lays down as a fundamental principle of English company law that a limited
liability company shall not reduce its capital or purchase its own shares save in
accordance with the statutory provisions which permit this course and then subject only
to strict compliance with requirements and procedures designed to provide due protection
for creditors. The rationale is stated by Lord Herschell in *Trevor v Whitworth* (1887) 12
App Cas 409 at p. 415 thus:

'What is the meaning of the distinction thus drawn between a company without
limit on the liability of its members and a company where the liability is limited,
but, in the latter case, to assure to those dealing with the company that the whole
of the subscribed capital, unless diminished by expenditure upon the objects
defined by the memorandum, shall remain available for the discharge of its
liabilities? The capital may, no doubt, be diminished by expenditure upon and
reasonably incidental to all the objects specified. A part of it may be lost in carrying
on the business operations authorized. Of this all persons trusting the company are

A   aware, and take the risk. But I think they have a right to rely, and were intended by the Legislature to have a right to rely, on the capital remaining undiminished by any expenditure outside these limits, or by the return of any part of it to the shareholders.'

The rule is confirmed and supplemented by s. 143 to which I will refer later in my judgment.

B   In accordance with this principle, it is ultra vires for a company to buy its own shares, unless statutory authorisation has been obtained, and it is irrelevant how far such purchase is in the interests of the company or its shareholders as a whole. The plaintiff could not therefore purchase the shareholding held by Acatos. The question raised is whether it is possible to sidestep the rule by the plaintiff purchasing instead the issued share capital of Acatos, a course which has the same economic consequences for the plaintiff and its creditors – the capital of the plaintiff is expended in buying (in effect) its
C own shares. Miss Gloster submits that this course is permissible because in law the plaintiff is purchasing the shares in Acatos, and not the assets of Acatos. She cites in support certain Australian decisions and in particular the judgments of Bray CJ and Hogarth J in *August Investments Pty Ltd v Poseidon Ltd and Samin Ltd* [1971] 2 SASR 71 ('the *Poseidon* case'). Mr Mowschenson submits that to prevent the rule and s. 143 being circumvented the court should lift the corporate veil, in order to ensure that
D the spirit of the principle of maintenance of capital is not infringed, the court should treat the plaintiff as acquiring its own shares. He relies on a passage in the judgment of Mitchell J at p. 90 in the *Poseidon* case and (as examples of the lifting of the veil) two English authorities where the veil was lifted, namely *DHN v Tower Hamlets* [1976] 1 WLR 852 at pp. 860A–E, 861D–862D and 867C–D and *Littlewoods Mail Order Stores Ltd v McGregor* [1969] 1 WLR 1241 at p. 1254.

E   In Australia this question has been considered in three cases. The first is *Dyason v J C Hutton Pty Ltd* (1935) ALR 419 when Martin J in a very short judgment upheld the validity of a purchase by a wholly owned subsidiary of shares in its holding company. He is reported as saying:

> 'The company, in addition to being a trading company, is also an investment company, and there is no reason in law why it should not exercise its power of investing in the shares of another company. Whatever ultimate effects may follow
F   in dealing with the shares acquired, it cannot be said that the action now proposed is a purchase by the company of its own shares, either directly or indirectly.'

In the *Poseidon* case, the Supreme Court (Zelling J) and the Supreme Court (in banc) refused an injunction to restrain Poseidon proceeding with a takeover offer to acquire the shares in Samin in exchange for shares in Poseidon, the complaint being that Samin held 200,000 shares in Poseidon. Bray CJ held that the rule did not apply because
G Poseidon was acquiring shares in Samin, not its own shares; and because in any event, even if treated as acquiring its own shares, it was not thereby reducing its capital, but was acquiring them for new shares from its unissued capital, in effect exchanging assets for assets. He refused the invitation to pierce the corporate veil and look at the commercial realities. He accepted that there were occasions when the courts have lifted the corporate veil to look at the commercial reality underneath, for example, in order to prevent the
H evasion of fiscal, social and administrative legislation (citing inter alia *Littlewoods Mail Order Stores Ltd v McGregor*) but said that such consideration had no place in this context. He found support in the decision of Martin J in *Dyason v J C Hutton* above. After stating that this result was clear on general principles, he went on to say that the matter was put beyond doubt by a legislative provision much to the effect of s. 23 of the *Companies Act* 1985 to which I will refer later. He went on to hold that the validity of the purchase of the shares in Samin was unaffected either by the size of the holding of shares

held by Samin in Poseidon, the percentage of the assets of Samin represented by the   **A**
holding, or the existence or non-existence on the part of Poseidon as the motive for the
acquisition of Samin of the desire to acquire its own shares.

Hogarth J gave a judgment much to the same effect, emphasising that the question
raised was whether in law Poseidon was purchasing its own shares, not whether this
might be the commercial result of the transaction (see p. 83). His judgment, as that of
Bray CJ, supports the contentions of Miss Gloster.   **B**

The concurring judgment of Mitchell J contains the following passage:

> 'This is not a case in which it appears that the company intended to become the
> subsidiary company has been set up in reality for the purpose of acquiring shares
> in the holding company. If that were so, then there might be ground for describing
> the intended subsidiary company, as Lord Denning described the subsidiary
> company in *Littlewoods Mail Order Stores Ltd v McGregor*, as "the creature, the   **C**
> puppet (of the holding company) in point of fact". If the sole asset of the intended
> subsidiary company were a parcel of shares in the proposed holding company it
> seems to me that the court might be entitled, in looking at the realities of the
> situation, to say that the proposal by the latter company was to purchase its own
> shares, notwithstanding the fact that nominally it was acquiring shares in the
> former company. However, this is not the position in the matter before the court.'

Mr Mowschenson quite naturally seizes on this passage as authority for the   **D**
proposition that the corporate veil should be pierced without more where, as in the
present case, the sole asset of the company whose shares are to be purchased (i.e. Acatos)
is shares in the acquirer (i.e. the plaintiff). So read, the judgment directly contradicts the
views of the majority. I cannot so read the judgment. It seems to me that Mitchell J was
postulating the situation where it might be inferred from the facts (including the fact that
the only asset of the intended subsidiary was shares in the holding company) that the
intended subsidiary was set up as the first of two stages in a single scheme to evade the   **E**
rule: the first being the acquisition by the intended subsidiary of shares in the holding
company; and the second being the subsequent acquisition by the holding company of
the intended subsidiary. In such situation, as Mitchell J says, the corporate veil may
require to be lifted, but that situation is miles away from the present case, as it was from
the facts in the case before him.

The third decision is that of Lockhart J in the Federal Courts of Australia New South   **F**
Wales District Registry General Division (1990) 22 FCR 305. He held that for the
purposes of the *Australian Trade Practices Act* 1974 the acquisition by a wholly owned
subsidiary did not constitute the acquisition directly or indirectly by the holding
company, and that an indirect acquisition was an acquisition by someone acting as agent,
trustee or nominee. It is sufficient to say that Lockhart J cited with approval the judgment
of Bray CJ in the *Poseidon* case and expressed views much to the same effect.   **G**

The three Australian authorities all support the view that the acquisition by the
plaintiff of the shares in Acatos is outside the rule and that there is no occasion to pierce
the corporate veil.

Authorities in this jurisdiction on the principles governing the piercing of the corporate
veil are to the same effect. English law insists on recognition of the distinct legal
personality of companies unless the relevant contract or legislation requires or permits a   **H**
broad interpretation to be given to references to members of a group of companies or the
legal personality is a mere façade or sham or unlawful device (see *Adams & Ors v Cape
Industries plc & Anor* [1990] BCC 786). The cases relied on by Mr Mowschenson (*DHN v
Tower Hamlets* [1976] 1 WLR 853 and *Littlewoods Mail Order Stores v McGregor* [1969]
1 WLR 1241) fall within the established exception. Outside these exceptions, the plaintiff
is entitled to organise and conduct its affairs in the expectation that the court will apply

A the principle of *Salomon v A Salomon & Co Ltd* [1897] AC 22 in the ordinary way. The language of Robert Goff LJ in *Bank of Tokyo Ltd v Karoon & Anor* [1987] AC 45 at p. 64 (approved by Slade LJ in *Adams v Cape* at p. 538) is apposite:

> '[Counsel] suggested beguilingly that it would be technical for us to distinguish between parent and subsidiary company in this context; economically, he said, they were one. But we are concerned not with economics but with law. The distinction between the two is, in law, fundamental and cannot here be bridged.'

B

If the takeover of a target company were precluded by virtue of its holding of shares in the acquiring company, the acquisition by the target company of such a holding would be an effective defence to such a takeover. It is plain that the rule has no such remarkable or far reaching consequences. Like Bray CJ, I cannot think that the application of the rule can depend upon or be affected by the size of the holding by the target, the percentage of the assets of the target represented by the holding or the motive for acquisition of the target.

C

(b) *Sections 143 and 23*

Section 143(1) provides as follows:

> 'Subject to the following provisions, a company limited by shares . . . shall not acquire its own shares, whether by purchase, subscription or otherwise.'

D

Section 23 (so far as material) reads as follows:

> '(1) Except as mentioned in this section, a body corporate cannot be a member of a company which is its holding company and any allotment or transfer of shares in a company to its subsidiary is void.
>
> . . .

E

> (4) Where a body corporate became a holder of shares in a company–
>
> (a) before 1st July 1948, or
>
> (b) on or after that date and before 1st November 1990, in circumstances in which this section as it then had effect did not apply,
>
> but at any time on or after 1st November 1990 falls within the prohibition in subsection (1) above in respect of those shares, it may continue to be a member of that company; but for so long as that prohibition would apply, apart from this subsection, it has no right to vote in respect of those shares at meetings of the company or of any class of its members.

F

> (5) Where a body corporate becomes a holder of shares in a company on or after 1st November 1990 in circumstances in which the prohibition in subsection (1) does not apply, but subsequently falls within that prohibition in respect of those shares, it may continue to be a member of that company; but for so long as that prohibition would apply, apart from this subsection, it has no right to vote in respect of those shares at meetings of the company or of any class of its members.

G

> (6) Where a body corporate is permitted to continue as a member of a company by virtue of subsection (4) or (5), an allotment to it of fully paid shares in the company may be validly made by way of capitalization of reserves of the company; but for so long as the prohibition in subsection (1) would apply, apart from subsection (4) or (5), it has no right to vote in respect of those shares at meetings of the company or of any class of its members.'

H

Section 143 both confirms and extends the rule. It prohibits a company acquiring its own shares, not merely by purchase, but also 'otherwise'. Accordingly, though the rule may not extend to an exchange of shares as held by Bray CJ in the *Poseidon* case, such an exchange is prohibited by the section. Section 143 however does not in terms prohibit

(any more than the rule) the acquisition by the plaintiff of Acatos. That there is no such   A
prohibition is put beyond question by s. 23 which expressly entitles Acatos on the
acquisition to retain its shareholding (and any bonus shares subsequently issued) in the
plaintiff, albeit the voting rights in respect of those shares are suspended during its
ownership. Like Bray CJ, I find this section a compelling consideration (if I were
otherwise in doubt) that the acquisition by the plaintiff of Acatos in no wise contravenes
the rule or s. 143.

   B

Conclusion

I accordingly hold that the plaintiff is entitled to the declarations which it seeks. I
should add that, whilst such a purchase by one company of a shareholder in it is not
absolutely prohibited, in view of the potential for abuse and for adverse consequences
for shareholders and creditors, the court will look carefully at such transactions to see
that the directors of the acquiring company have acted with an eye solely to the interests   C
of the acquiring company (and not, for example, to the interests of the directors) and
have fulfilled their fiduciary duties to safeguard the interests of shareholders and creditors
alike. These requirements have been amply satisfied in this case.

(Order accordingly)

   D

   E

   F

   G

   H

A **Re Bank of Credit and Commerce International SA (No. 4).**

Chancery Division.
Sir Richard Scott V-C.
Judgment delivered 19 December 1994.

Winding up – Liquidators sought authority to enter into agreements compromising
claims between company and majority shareholders and pooling assets of group
B *companies.*

This was an application following on from the application made in June 1992 by the
English liquidators of Bank of Credit and Commerce International SA (see [1992] BCC
715) in which Nicholls V-C authorised them to execute and carry into effect a contribution
agreement (settling the claims between BCCI companies and the majority shareholders in
return for a payment into the liquidation by the majority shareholders) and an agreement
C pooling the assets of BCCI companies.

The agreements were conditional on their being approved by the Luxembourg court and
that court's approval of the contribution agreement was overturned on appeal. However, the
pooling agreement stood.

The English liquidators sought authority to execute a revised contribution agreement and
a supplementary pooling agreement relating to companies in the ICIC group.

D *Held*, giving the liquidators authority to execute the two agreements:

Two factors had not changed since the previous contribution agreement was approved.
One was the length of time it would take to come to a resolution of, and the complexity of,
litigation between the parties. The other was the inherent uncertainty of any complex
litigation. Those two factors no amount of further discovery could cure. For the depositors
their only chance of getting a reasonably prompt return, even if, as a number of depositors
E would think, it was a less than adequate return in respect of their lost money, was for the
agreements to go ahead. That was underlined by the approval of these agreements by the
vast bulk of the creditors.

The following case was referred to in the judgment:
Bank of Credit and Commerce International SA, Re (No. 2) [1992] BCC 715.

F Michael Crystal QC and Adam Goodison (instructed by Lovell White Durrant) for
the English liquidators of BCCI SA.

Martin Pascoe (instructed by MacKenzie Mills) for the liquidators of the ICIC
companies.

Ajmalul Hossain (instructed by Hallewell Bunyard) for former employees of BCCI.

Michael Todd (instructed by Manches & Co) for former employees of BCCI.

G Peter Scott QC and Richard Hacker (instructed by Simmons & Simmons) for the
majority shareholders.

Mark Pelling (instructed by Warner Cranston) for three former directors of BCCI.

JUDGMENT

Scott V-C: The application before me today is made by the English liquidators of
H BCCI SA. They ask for authority to execute the revised agreements and the ICIC pooling
agreement, both described in the papers placed before me, and to be authorised to
implement and carry those agreements into full force and effect and to comply with and
perform their obligations thereunder in accordance with the terms of those agreements.

This application follows on from the application made in June 1992 to my predecessor,
Sir Donald Nicholls (see [1992] BCC 715). Nicholls V-C was asked to authorise the

English liquidators to execute and carry into effect two agreements: one described as a   A
contribution agreement; and the other the main pooling agreement. The contribution
agreement was an agreement which, in effect, sought to settle the claims and cross-claims
between the several BCCI companies on the one hand and the majority shareholders so-
called – i.e. the ruler of Abu Dhabi, the government of Abu Dhabi and the Abu Dhabi
investment authority – on the other hand in return (this is a very free summary of the
essence of that agreement) for a payment into the liquidation by the majority
shareholders of a sum to be calculated by reference to a formula, depending upon the   B
extent of recoveries obtained by the Liquidators, that might have varied between $1.2
billion and $2.2 billion.

A particular feature of that contribution agreement was that creditors could participate
in the financial consequences of the payments by the majority shareholders into the
liquidation only if they gave releases to the majority shareholders and others of claims
which they, the creditors, might have. If they did not give those releases those creditors   C
who declined to do so would have to be content with obtaining their dividend from the
assets and the liquidation deriving from other sources but not including that payment to
come from the majority shareholders.

Second, there was a pooling agreement, whereby the assets of all the various BCCI
companies in liquidation were to be brought into a common pool, thereby rendering it
unnecessary to decide the perhaps insoluble but, in any event, very difficult and complex   D
questions of identifying the owner of the particular assets as between the various
companies, each of which had its own creditors. Once brought into the pool, the assets in
the pool would be used to provide dividends for all the creditors of all the companies pari
passu.

Those two agreements the English liquidators were authorised to enter into. The
agreements were, however, conditional upon their being approved by all the courts
having jurisdiction in the liquidation – i.e. the courts of this country, the courts of the   E
Cayman Islands and the courts of Luxembourg. Those latter courts, of the Cayman
Islands and Luxembourg, are the courts of the countries in which the principal
companies, BCCI SA (Luxembourg) and BCCI Overseas (Cayman Islands), are
incorporated. So the agreements were conditional upon approval being obtained from
the courts of those three countries. In England the approval that was sought by the
liquidators was opposed, staunchly opposed, by a number of creditors claiming to   F
represent the bulk of the creditors in the BCCI companies' liquidation. At that stage no
formal creditors' committee or liquidation committee had been established.

Sir Donald Nicholls V-C authorised the English liquidators to enter into those
agreements and carry them into effect, notwithstanding the opposition of the creditors
(claiming, as I have said, to represent the bulk of the creditors). Some of the disappointed
creditors appealed to the Court of Appeal on an issue of law. It was contended that the   G
court did not have power to authorise the liquidators to enter into a compromise on the
terms of the contribution agreement. The particular point that was taken was that the
effect of the contribution agreement would be to produce two different classes of
creditors, those who were willing to grant releases to the majority shareholders and those
who were not, who would not rate equally among themselves in a sharing of the assets
that the liquidators had for distribution among creditors. Various other legal points as
well were taken but that I take to be the main point.   H

The Court of Appeal dismissed the appeal and held that the Vice-Chancellor had had
power under the relevant empowering legislation to give the authority sought by the
liquidators. The Court of Appeal did not enter into the question of whether the Vice-
Chancellor had correctly exercised his discretion in authorising the liquidators to enter
into those agreements. That was a matter for the court of first instance and the exercise

A   of discretion had not been challenged on appeal. The points that had particularly influenced the Vice-Chancellor in the exercise of his discretion were the impossibility of seeing an end to the litigation that would be necessary between the liquidators and the majority shareholders in order to resolve the cross-claims between themselves and the difficulties of identifying the assets of each of the companies and of identifying the creditors who could claim in each liquidation. The need for a cutting of the Gordian knot in the interests of all the creditors and with a view to their obtaining some benefit by way of dividend from the assets that were available in the liquidation, supplemented – as those assets would be – by the payment from the majority shareholders, was the most dominant consideration in the mind, I think, of the Vice-Chancellor, as appears from his judgment.

B   The appeal from his judgment was dismissed on 17 July 1992 (see [1992] BCC 715).

C   In Luxembourg the court ordered a ballot of creditors in order to seek their views on the agreements. The result of the ballot was that over 93 per cent of the creditors who responded and who had validly voted were in favour of the agreements. The Luxembourg court on 22 October 1992 – not surprisingly in view of that ballot result – made an order approving the agreements, subject to a minor amendment of the pooling agreement. The minor amendment was subsequently accepted by the courts in this country and in the Cayman Islands.

D   However, three of the creditors who had opposed the approval in Luxembourg appealed to the Luxembourg Court of Appeal on 24 December 1992. The appeal was finally determined in Luxembourg on 27 October 1993 where the appeal was allowed. The appeal was on a ground of law, as had been the appeal in this country. As I understand it, the point of law taken was – to all intents and purposes – the same as the pari passu point taken before the Court of Appeal in this country and to which I have referred. At the foot of the Luxembourg Court of Appeal decision the contribution

E   agreement had fallen. There had been an appeal in Luxembourg against the pooling agreement but that appeal had been abandoned, so the pooling agreement stood, having been approved at that stage by the courts of all three jurisdictions.

Negotiations were then resumed between the liquidators and the majority shareholders and led to a further agreement. Non-binding heads of agreement were signed by the liquidators and the majority shareholders, or the Abu Dhabi authorities, on 3 March

F   1994 and a draft of a legally binding agreement was finalised in July.

In September 1994 an English liquidation committee, which had been established in the meantime, voted unanimously in support of the new revised contribution agreement, save that an Abu Dhabi representative on the committee did not vote on the ground, obviously, of conflict of interest.

G   On 28 September a Luxembourg creditors' committee of BCCI SA and also of BCCI Holdings held a composite meeting. Six out of eight of the members voted in favour of the new revised agreement. Of the two who did not vote in favour, one was the Abu Dhabi representative, who again, very properly, refrained from voting and the other, as I understand it, did not attend the meeting. The stage was therefore set for a further application to this court and to the Luxembourg and Cayman Island courts for approval of the revised contribution agreement.

H   On 25 November 1994 the liquidators made an up to date report to this court. The report dealt not only with the manner in which the revised contribution agreement to which I have referred had come about but also with a proposed supplemental pooling agreement, whereby the companies in the ICIC group would be brought into the pool that had been established by the main pooling agreement that had already been approved. The manner in which the ICIC companies' affairs are entwined with those of the BCCI companies is dealt with in the liquidator's report in para. 29 and 30. Paragraph 30 of the

report says that the principal ICIC companies and in particular ICIC Overseas   A
(incorporated in the Cayman Islands) functioned as a bookkeeping centre for
transactions initiated and coordinated by Abedi and Naqvi, they being two of the
executives of BCCI. The report goes on:

> 'Many of these transactions were part of arrangements designed to manipulate the
> financial position of the BCCI group. The principal ICIC companies were the
> recipients of substantial funds from the principal BCCI companies and in   B
> particular BCCI Overseas. The application of those funds includes:
>
> – financing of BCCI Holdings shares and capital notes and shares in Credit
> and Commercial American Holdings ... including the use of nominees
> (controlled, under powers of attorney, by Abedi and Naqvi and persons
> acting under their direction), buy-back arrangements, non-recourse
> arrangements and guaranteed minimum returns on "investments";   C
>
> – routing of funds to disguise the true nature of transactions being undertaken
> and the financial effect on BCCI: in particular, funds from BCCI were routed
> through principal ICIC companies to service false and delinquent loans in
> the books of BCCI to pay interest on unrecorded liabilities of BCCI;
>
> – payment of expenses incurred by BCCI;
>
> – many loans in ICIC's portfolio were approved by the central credit   D
> committee of the BCCI group. Loans were either transferred to principal
> ICIC companies from principal BCCI companies or were funded by ICIC
> on the instruction of the central credit committee;
>
> – other loans appear to have been booked in ICIC to cover losses sustained
> from trading activities incurred by the BCCI group ... ;
>
> – in some instances, security for loans booked in ICIC was either taken in the   E
> name of a BCCI company or was not assigned to ICIC at the time the loan
> was transferred to ICIC from BCCI.'

That being the background, the conclusion of the liquidators (para. 29 of the report)
was that:

> 'The affairs of the principal BCCI and ICIC companies were so commingled that
> it would be impracticable without very considerable delay and enormous expense,   F
> and might well be impossible:
>
> (a) to determine as between each group of companies and as between companies
> within those groups, what property is the property of one rather than the
> other; or
>
> (b) to determine what amounts, if any, are due from one company to another
> as a result of acts and omissions in relation to transactions which have taken   G
> place (or should have taken place) between them.'

In short, the case for the ICIC companies entering the pooling arrangements already
concluded between the BCCI companies is the same case as persuaded the Vice-
Chancellor to approve the main pooling agreement. If the ICIC companies are not
brought into the pooling arrangement the consequent delay and uncertainty in sorting
out the affairs of the two respective groups would be bound to lead to a long period
before the liquidators could undertake any payment of dividend for want of certainty as   H
to the assets from which the dividends could be paid.

It is a feature of the main pooling agreement that realisations of assets which come to
the hands of the English liquidators will, after due provision has been made for various
matters (one of which I will in a moment mention), be transferred to the Luxembourg
liquidators (Luxembourg being the principal liquidation centre, given that BCCI SA was

A incorporated in Luxembourg.) That has produced one particular problem in relation to which a point has been made before me today. The law of Luxembourg on insolvency is not identical to the law of England on insolvency. There may be creditors who can claim under the law of this country who would be unable to claim under the law of Luxembourg or whose claim in that jurisdiction might be reduced in amount, as compared with their entitlement under the law of this country. The pooling agreement enables the English liquidators to retain out of the assets in their hands sufficient funds to compensate those

B creditors for the prejudice which they might otherwise suffer if they had to claim and could claim only in Luxembourg. Rut, in addition, there are a number of claims which have been made which have a proprietary base. The extent to which proprietary claims are possible must depend upon the facts peculiar to each claim but it is undoubtedly the case that there are circumstances in which liquidators can be faced with proprietary claims which take priority over any claims of creditors and, indeed, sometimes take

C priority over any costs and expenses of the liquidation itself. As I say, whether that is so in any particular case must depend upon the facts of the particular case. Rut if such claims can be brought against the liquidators in this country they must plainly retain sufficient funds out of the assets in their hands to cover those claims. The main pooling agreement provided for the liquidators to retain such sums as they might think fit to cover themselves against claims of that proprietary sort, as well as in relation to other types of claims for which provision needed to be made.

D Before I come to deal with the merits of the agreements that are before me for approval today there is one further detail I should mention. On 10 November 1994 the main pooling agreement and a number of other subsidiary pooling agreements consequent upon it were executed and have therefore become final. The ICIC subsidiary pooling agreement will, if it is approved and entered into, bring the ICIC companies into the pool established by the execution of those agreements on 10 November.

E The revised contribution agreement is conditional. The conditions are set out in para. 21.9 of the liquidators' report. The conditions are:

'(a) the liquidators obtain requisite court approvals and authorisations [that refers to approvals and authorisations in the three jurisdictions I have mentioned];

(b) the government of Abu Dhabi obtain requisite approvals and authorisations;

F (c) the pooling agreement and the proposed ICIC pooling agreement are executed; and

(d) certain claims and debts arising in the ordinary course of banking business owed to the majority shareholders and various related entities are admitted in the relevant liquidations to a value of at least US$1,250m as ordinary unsubordinated claims . . .'

G The result of the condition that relates to the government of Abu Dhabi obtaining requisite approvals and authorisations means, in effect, that the majority shareholders will not become bound by the agreement until completion. They remain able to withdraw from it. The debts owed to the majority shareholders that have so far been admitted in the relevant liquidations fall short by some $12m of the minimum $1,250m figure mentioned in the last of those foregoing conditions. It did at one time occur to me to wonder how long the agreement might remain open-ended with uncertainty as to whether or not that condition would be fulfilled. On reflection, and with Mr Crystal's assistance,

H I do not think that is a matter that need concern me because if the majority shareholders want to execute the revised agreement, assuming that all the relevant courts authorise the liquidators to proceed with those agreements, then the majority shareholders will do so whether or not the admitted claims have reached the $1,250m figure. If there is a shortfall that may or may not be a reason why the majority shareholders will wish to withdraw from the agreement. It will, in the end, be a matter for their decision.

The financial effect of the revised contribution agreement is dealt with in para. 36 of   A
the liquidators' report. In that paragraph, subject of course to the conditions to which I
have referred, the liquidators express it to be their aim to declare an interim dividend of
about 20 per cent in the summer of 1995. That is – as the paragraph expresses it to be –
no more than an aim, but it is an aim that, if everything goes well, I understand them to
believe to be practicable. They have some optimism about its achievement.

In the next paragraph the liquidators express the opinion that the ultimate return to   B
creditors at the end of the day (that may still be some years off) may be in the region of
30–40 per cent.

It is, in my opinion, a matter of very great significance that the creditors – so far as the
proceedings before the creditors' committees and the liquidation committees are
concerned – almost unanimously have approved these agreements. Nicholls V-C had to
deal with the application before him in June 1992 on the other footing, namely, that the   C
creditors before him were opposing. It is a strong thing to go against the expressed wishes
of the creditors, whose money it is that is being talked about.

There were reasons which drove Nicholls V-C to the conclusion that he should approve
the proposed contribution agreement notwithstanding creditors' opposition. As the
matter stands today, however, the converse is the case. I would need a very strong reason,
in the face of the creditors' approval of the agreement, to decline to approve it.   D

Miss Shahidi, whose mother is a depositor and a creditor in the liquidation of one of
the BCCI companies (and it matters not which), for a sum – as I understand it – in the
region of £100,000, has addressed me on behalf of her mother. She emphasised to me the
hardship caused to her mother and to her mother's family, a hardship shared with a very
large number of individual depositors both in this country and abroad, brought about
by the fraudulent manner in which the affairs of BCCI and the management of its funds
were conducted. The strength of feelings of the depositors, in the circumstances in which   E
they find themselves, is of course entirely understandable but it cannot stand in the way
of the liquidators' attempts to rescue as much as is able to be rescued from the wreck.
The vast bulk of the creditors – as I have said – now support the proposed arrangements.
The case for approving the arrangements, in order to reduce, so far as possible, delay
before at least some substantial dividends can be paid is as great if not greater now than
it was when the matter was last before the court in June 1992.   F

Miss Shahidi made an appeal to the ruler of Abu Dhabi to come to the assistance of
the depositors to a greater extent, as one of the majority shareholders, than he has so far
done. I do not know whether what she said will be conveyed to him but it is not a matter
that I, as a judge in this court, can take any further. I must deal with the proposed
agreement on the basis that it is a result, as it plainly is, of arm's length negotiation
between the liquidators and the majority shareholders, and on the basis that the   G
alternative to the resolution by compromise of the impasse in which the parties find
themselves would be intractable, lengthy and speculative litigation.

My predecessor saw, on a confidential basis, the legal opinions that had been supplied
to the liquidators regarding the prospects of that litigation and I have been allowed, on
the same basis, a sight of the opinions. Since the date of those opinions a considerable
degree of discovery has been obtained by means of documents handed over by the Abu
Dhabi authorities to the liquidators. These documents have not yet been the subject of   H
any intensive approval but, as I understand the position, there has been a cursory
inspection of the more important of them, sufficient to enable those advising the
liquidators to have supplied a more informed opinion on the prospects of the litigation
that would be the alternative to entry into the agreements now before the court for
approval. I have seen that opinion as well.

A   It is true to say, as one would expect, that the additional discovery has had the result that in some respects the prospects of the litigation are not as speculative as they were before that discovery was available. The more information any litigant gets about the background to his cause of action or to the causes of action proposed against him, the more informed will be the view as to the likely consequence. A more informed view is now possible than was possible when Nicholls V-C dealt with the matter in June 1992.

B   But two factors have not changed. One is the length of time it would take to come to a resolution of and the complexity of any such litigation. The other is the inherent uncertainty of any complex litigation. Those two factors no amount of further discovery can cure. For the depositors their only chance of getting a reasonably prompt return, even if, as a number of depositors thinking along the lines of Miss Shahidi will surely think, it is a less than adequate return in respect of their lost money, is for the agreements now before the court to go ahead. That this is so is underlined by the approval of these

C   agreements by the vast bulk of the creditors.

Accordingly, it seems to me that I ought to approve the agreements as asked by the liquidators. There have been objections to my doing so put forward by counsel on behalf of three parties. I must deal now with their respective points.

Mr Hossain represents some 26 ex-employees of BCCI companies and members of their families who claim to be entitled to proprietary remedies against the assets of BCCI

D   arising from improper use of trust funds in respect of which they, the employees, claim to be interested. The amount of money involved in the trust claim is put, in a document which Mr Hossain handed to me, at $150m with some $80m of interest to be added. They claim also to be depositors in respect of a sum of some $33m, and they claim a sum of $64m-odd in respect of shares in what is described as the 'staff benefit fund'.

Apart from the $33m deposit claims, these claims are put as proprietary claims, and Mr Hossain asks for some direction to be given to the liquidators requiring them to

E   retain in this country, before remission of assets to the Luxembourg liquidators, sufficient to cover the amount of this proprietary claim.

Mr Todd has appeared before me for some 95 ex-employees of one or other of the BCCI companies who have very recently obtained legal aid to pursue a claim against the companies. This claim, too, as I understand it and as they would hope to put it, is for a proprietary remedy enabling them to claim assets under some constructive trust. I know, as is already perhaps apparent, very little of the way in which the claim will be put, but

F   so, I think, does Mr Todd. The details have not yet been worked out. Mr Todd supports Mr Hossain in saying that there ought to be some direction given to the liquidators to make sure that sufficient funds are kept in this country to cover the proprietary claim of his clients if it should prove to be successful.

I have no means of knowing what, if any, substance there is behind the claims of Mr

G   Hossain's clients or of Mr Todd's clients. I have no means of knowing to what extent those claims can be couched in terms of proprietary remedy so as to take priority over the claims of ordinary creditors. On the information I have it would be wrong of me to express any view at all as to whether, assuming they could establish the requisite ingredients to the requisite degree of proof for interlocutory purposes, it would be possible for them to obtain interlocutory orders of the sort mentioned. I am quite clear that the orders mentioned do not arise directly or, indeed, indirectly, out of the relief

H   sought by the liquidators, that is to say approval of the two agreements.

If Mr Hossain's clients or Mr Todd's clients can establish their locus standi, can obtain the requisite leave to sue the companies in liquidation, and believe they can persuade the appropriate judge that they ought to have interlocutory relief requiring the liquidators to hold particular funds of money in this country to answer their claims if successful, then they can make an application and seek that relief in that application. I do not believe that

this is a matter with which I should be dealing today. There is no application before the   A
court and there is insufficient evidence before the court to allow the matter to be properly
dealt with.

Finally, Mr Pelling has appeared on behalf of three ex-directors, non-executive
directors of BCCI SA, BCCI Overseas and BCCI Holdings, who are in dispute with the
majority shareholders or one or other of the Abu Dhabi authorities. One of the features
of the revised contribution agreement, as also the original contribution agreement, is that   B
there are mutual releases by the majority shareholders of the companies, and by the
companies of the majority shareholders, of claims and cross-claims which they have
against one another, with the exception of claims arising in the normal course of banking
business.

The releases to be given by the liquidators of the BCCI companies are expressed to be
releases to the majority shareholders and to a class of persons described as 'related
persons'. Related persons are identified in a schedule to the agreement. The schedule   C
includes the three non-executive directors who are Mr Pelling's clients. But the revised
agreement also contains a provision to the effect that the majority shareholders may, if
they want, remove from the list of related persons any of the individuals whose names at
the moment appear in the list, provided they do so before completion of the agreement.
So, just as it was the decision of the majority shareholders that particular individuals
should be named in the list of related persons in the first place, so they reserve to   D
themselves the right to amend the list, up to the time of completion, by removing any
names as they may think fit.

As I understand it, these three ex-directors have commenced proceedings against the
majority shareholders, or some of them, in New York under an Act designed to provide
remedies against racketeering called the RICO Act. I cannot remember what RICO
stands for, but at any rate it is concerned with the prevention of fraudulent racketeering.   E
It is a piece of legislation which provides for multiple damages, as a penal disincentive,
to be awarded against unsuccessful defendants. The fear, I have no doubt it may be a
well founded fear, on the part of the three non-executive directors is that they may be
shortly told by the majority shareholders, or by the Abu Dhabi authorities, that unless
these New York proceedings are stopped they can expect to find their names removed
from the list of related persons. In that event the releases given by the BCCI companies
will not cover them. This is given added point by the fact that the BCCI companies in   F
liquidation have already commenced proceedings against these three non-executive
directors and others in Luxembourg. If they are not covered by the related persons
releases they have no immediate way of avoiding the Luxembourg proceedings that are
being brought against them.

Mr Pelling submits that it is quite wrong for me to authorise the approval of an
agreement, some of the provisions of which place the majority shareholders in a position   G
to coerce these non-executive directors to abandon proceedings they have started in a
foreign jurisdiction, namely New York. In my opinion this is not a point with substance.
The question of who are to be named as related persons in the revised agreement is a
matter for the majority shareholders. If they remove the names of one or two or three or
more of the presently named related persons, that will be to the advantage of the BCCI
companies in liquidation, because there will be more persons against whom companies
can still bring actions for damages on such causes of action as may be available.   H

If the agreements fail to proceed because I withhold the approval that is being sought
today, there is nothing to stop the majority shareholders from immediately offering to
enter into another identical agreement but with the three names removed. The fears that
the three non-executive directors have are well understandable, but an analysis of the
position fails to persuade me that it is of any moment to this court, or that it is anything

A   that this court is in a position to prevent. Accordingly, I do not propose to accept that point as a ground for declining to give the liquidators the authority that they seek.

For these reasons I have come to the conclusion that I should accede to the application that has been made to the court today and I should give the liquidators authority to proceed to execute and carry into effect the two agreements to which I have referred.

(*Order accordingly*)

462

Huish v Ellis & Ors.

Queen's Bench Division (Bristol Mercantile Court).
His Honour Judge Raymond Jack QC.
Judgment delivered 5 January 1995.

Mortgage – Mortgagor alleged that assets were sold by mortgagee for less than they should have been – Extent of mortgagee's duty on sale – Whether mortgagee's valuers owed duty to mortgagor.

This was a claim by a mortgagor that assets which the mortgagee bank had taken possession of under the charge had been sold for less than they should have been.

The plaintiff was a farmer and the assets were a farm and buildings and a milk quota. The bank sold the farm and quota together for £425,000. The plaintiff argued that the land and quota should have been sold separately (which would have required the plaintiff's cooperation). The bank submitted that its duty as mortgagee did not require it to sell the land and quota separately and that in any event in the circumstances it was an abuse of process for the plaintiff to allege that the bank should have sold them separately.

The plaintiff also alleged that valuers who advised the bank and receiver and another finance company in connection with the realisation of assets owed a duty to the plaintiff.

Held, striking out the claims as disclosing no cause of action:

1. The quota could only be sold separately in cooperation with the plaintiff and by him; the bank had no power or right to deal separately with the quota. The bank was free to decide whether it preferred the simple course of selling the land so that it carried the quota, or whether it preferred to run the risks attached to trying to arrange a separate sale of the quota in cooperation with the plaintiff. The bank owed no duty to the plaintiff in making that decision. The limit of the bank's duty was to take reasonable care to obtain a proper price for the land when sold in circumstances where it would carry the quota with it. (*Downsview Nominees Ltd v First City Corporation Ltd* [1993] BCC 46 applied.)

2. The facts were consistent only with an intention on the part of the plaintiff that the bank should sell the farm with the quota. They were wholly inconsistent with an intention that the bank should sell the farm separately from the quota to the highest bidders. If the bank did what the plaintiff intended or if he constrained the bank to act as the bank did, the bank would have a defence to his claim. He had made an assertion which lay at the foundation of his claim against the bank while his documented actions and the documents emanating from him demonstrated the opposite. In the circumstances striking out was a proper exercise of the court's jurisdiction to prevent abuse of its process.

3. The weight of authority appeared to be in favour of a mortgagee being liable where he employed a reputable agent but the agent was negligent. That indicated that an agent employed by a mortgagee to advise him was under no duty to the mortgagor in giving that advice. A duty owed to the mortgagor might conflict with the agent's duty to the mortgagee.

The following cases were referred to in the judgment:

Arbuthnott v Fagan and Feltrim Underwriting Agencies Ltd [1994] CLC 918; [1995] 2 AC 145.
Caparo Industries plc v Dickman & Ors [1990] BCC 164; [1990] 2 AC 605.
China & South Sea Bank Ltd v Tan Soon Gin [1990] 1 AC 536.
Cuckmere Brick Co Ltd & Anor v Mutual Finance Ltd [1971] Ch 949.
Downsview Nominees Ltd v First City Corporation Ltd [1993] BCC 46; [1993] AC 295.
Faulks v Faulks [1992] 1 EGLR 9.
Harrison (Saul D) & Sons plc, Re [1994] BCC 475.
Hedley Byrne & Co Ltd v Heller & Partners Ltd [1964] AC 465.
Johnson (B) & Co (Builders) Ltd, Re [1955] Ch 634.

A   *McNaughton (James) Paper Group Ltd v Hicks Anderson & Co* [1990] BCC 891; [1991]
      2 QB 113.
      Pacific Associates Inc & Anor v Baxter & Ors [1990] 1 QB 993.
      Parker-Tweedale v Dunbar Bank plc & Ors [1991] Ch 12.
      Rich (Marc) & Co AG & Ors v Bishop Rock Marine Co Ltd & Ors [1994] CLC 133;
      [1994] 1 WLR 1071.
      Ross v Caunters [1980] Ch 297.
B   *Smith v Eric S Bush* [1990] 1 AC 831.
      Tomlin v Luce (1889) 43 ChD 191.
      Tse Kwong Lam v Wong Chit Sen & Ors [1983] 1 WLR 1349.
      White & Anor v Jones & Anor [1993] 3 WLR 730 (CA).

      Simon Edwards (instructed by Clark Willmot & Clarke, Bristol) for the plaintiff.

      The first defendant did not appear.

C   Stephen Davies (instructed by Lawrence Tucketts, Bristol) for the second defendant.

      Milwyn Jarman (instructed by Morgan Bruce, Cardiff) for the third defendant.

      Paul Darlow (instructed by John Neal, Bristol) for the fourth defendant.

JUDGMENT

His Honour Judge Raymond Jack QC: The plaintiff in this action, Mr Huish, is a
D   farmer and in 1987 he farmed Caerforiog Farm at Sovla near Haverfordwest in Dyfed.
      The farm was largely but not wholly a dairy and cattle breeding enterprise. It had a milk
      quota of a little over 1m litres, which was substantial for the size of the farm. Both herd
      and farm had a high reputation. The enterprise was financed in part from two sources.
      One was the second defendant, Barclays Bank. The bank held a legal charge over the
      farm and the buildings, and also an agricultural mortgage over the assets of the farming
      enterprise being carried on at the farm. Each gave the bank the right to appoint a receiver
E   following a demand for payment. On 12 November 1986 the bank was owed £508,119
      and on 14 November it appointed the first defendant as receiver under the agricultural
      mortgage. On 17 August 1987 the bank took possession of the farm and buildings as
      mortgagee under the charge and ultimately it sold them with the milk quota to Mr C J
      Smith on 11 April 1988 for £425,000.

      The second source of finance was the fourth defendants who had advanced money
F   under an agreement of hire purchase covering a stock of cattle. I will call them 'Francis
      Finance'. The dairy herd was sold by them in January 1987. The relationship between
      their rights and the bank's agricultural mortgage so far as cattle is concerned is unclear,
      but does not appear material to the questions considered in this judgment.

      The third defendant is a firm of surveyors, auctioneers, valuers and land agents, who
      were instructed by the receiver (and perhaps also the bank) and by Francis Finance to
      advise in connection with the realisation of assets. I will refer to them as 'John Francis'.
G   In broad terms Mr Huish's claim was that the various assets were sold for less than they
      should have been.

      On 30 September 1994 an order was made that there be heard together:

      (1)   the bank's application to strike out the claim against them as disclosing no
            reasonable cause of action and as constituting an abuse of the process of the court;

      (2)   the issue raised by John Francis, whether the facts set out in para. 20–22 of the
H   amended statement of claim disclose any cause of action against them; and

      (3)   the issue raised by Francis Finance, whether the facts set out in para. 23–27 of the
            amended statement of claim disclose any cause of action against them.

      These questions were heard on 29 and 30 November 1994. The receiver was not involved
      in the hearing, his attitude was to support his co-defendants but to await the outcome of
      their applications.

Although solicitors for Mr Huish had indicated in correspondence that no further   A
amendments of the statement of claim would be forthcoming, a few days before the
hearing the defendants were presented with important reamendments proposed by Mr
Edwards on behalf of Mr Huish. These, together with further simplification of Mr
Huish's case during the course of the hearing, substantially narrowed the court's task.

I will take first the position of Francis Finance, because this can be quickly concluded.
The amended statement of claim made two claims against them. First it was alleged that   B
they should have sold the herd in June 1987 through a specialist firm alternatively under
Holstein Friesian Society rules, and damages were claimed totalling £95,498 for their
failure to do so. This claim was abandoned by the proposed reamendment. The second
claim accepted the actual sale date in January 1987 but made the same point in respect of
a specialist firm and the rules. The damage claimed was £11,400. As it is accepted that
there is owing to Francis Finance £7,532 to be set off against that claim in any event, the
sum remaining in dispute was thus reduced to some £4,000. In these circumstances Mr   C
Darlow for Francis Finance was content that the question raised by the issue should
remain undetermined at this stage.

The starting point for the examination of the position between Mr Huish and the bank
is Mr Edward's acceptance in the course of his reply on Mr Huish's behalf that, to show
a loss to Mr Huish, Mr Huish would have to establish that the bank should have sold the
land and the milk quota attached to it separately. That claim, that the land and quota   D
should have been sold separately, thus becomes the only claim which I need consider.
The relevant paragraphs of the statement of claim in its reamended form are 14, 16(4)
and 12(1). Mr Davies submitted on behalf of the bank, first that the bank was under no
such duty in law, second that, in any event, given the indisputable facts, it was an abuse
of the court's process for Mr Huish to allege that the bank should have sold them
separately, and third, that Mr Huish could establish no loss. I will take these in turn.

Many people may consider that a milk quota is in reality a species of property which   E
can be bought and sold. Its legal nature was considered in *Faulks v Faulks* [1992] 1 EGLR
9, where Chadwick J held that a milk quota registered in the name of a partnership
farming land held under a tenancy which was not a partnership asset, was not itself a
partnership asset and in effect attached to the tenancy. It is sufficient here to have in
mind that the bank had no charge or other right over the quota; that if the land were sold
by the bank without more, the quota would effectively with it; that the quota was
registered in the name of Mr Huish and that in the situation which existed the cooperation   F
of Mr Huish would have been required to enable the quota to be sold separately from
the land.

The law relating to the duty of a mortgagee with a power of sale to the mortgagor may
be found in a trilogy of modern cases in the Privy Council, which, it is plain, state the law
of England as applicable to the appeals before the board. I will take them in order of
decision.   G

In *Tse Kwong Lam v Wong Chit Sen* [1983] 1 WLR 1349, on appeal from Hong Kong,
the mortgagee had put up for public auction the property which constituted the security
and it was sold to a company in which he had an interest. In giving the judgment of the
board Lord Templeman referred to the well-known passage in Lord Salmon's judgment
in *Cuckmere Brick Co Ltd v Mutual Finance Ltd* [1971] Ch 949 at pp. 968–969 that:

> 'a mortgagee in exercising his power of sale does owe a duty to take reasonable   H
> precautions to obtain the true market value of the mortgaged property at the date
> on which he decides to sell it.'

—and stated (at p. 1356G):

> 'In the result their Lordships consider that in the present case the company was
> not debarred from purchasing the mortgaged property but, in view of the close

A   relationship between the company and the mortgagee and in view in particular of the conflict of duty and interest to which the mortgagee was subject, the sale to the company for $1.2m can only be supported if the mortgagee proves that he took reasonable precautions to obtain the best price reasonably obtainable at the time of sale.'

B   It was held that the mortgagee should have taken expert advice as to the method of sale, as to the steps reasonably to be taken to make the sale a success and as to the amount of the reserve. He was not bound to postpone the sale in the hope of obtaining a better price, or adopt a piecemeal method of sale which could only be carried out over a period and at some risk of loss. It was held the mortgagee had not established that he had taken due precautions to obtain the best price reasonably obtainable at the time of sale. It would appear that it was because of the relationship between the mortgagee and the purchasing company that the onus was placed on the mortgagee to justify what he

C   had done rather than on the mortgagor to show that the mortgagee had failed to take reasonable precautions to obtain a proper price. The decision confirms the duty of a mortgagee when he actually comes to sell and identifies the ambit of the duty on the facts of the case.

D   In *China & South Sea Bank Ltd v Tan Soon Gin* [1990] 1 AC 536, also on appeal from Hong Kong, shares were mortgaged to secure a loan which was also supported by a guarantee. The debtor defaulted. Although the shares were then still worth more than the loan, the creditor did not realise them. Later they became worthless and the creditor proceeded against the surety. The surety alleged that the creditor should have realised the shares following the default while they retained their value, and so could not proceed against him. The judgment of the board was again delivered by Lord Templeman. It was held that the surety had no defence. Lord Templeman stated (at p. 545D):

E   'If the creditor chose to exercise his power of sale over the mortgaged security he must sell for the current market value but the creditor must decide in his own interest if and when he should sell . . .

The creditor is not obliged to do anything . . . it appears . . . that . . . the creditor did no act injurious to the surety, did no act inconsistent with the rights of the surety and the creditor did not omit any act which his duty enjoined him to do.

F   The creditor was not under a duty to exercise his power of sale over the mortgaged securities at any particular time or at all.'

The third and perhaps most comprehensive of the trilogy, is *Downsview Nominees Ltd v First City Corporation Ltd* [1993] BCC 46, an appeal from New Zealand. Here again the judgment was delivered by Lord Templeman. The facts were complicated, and I need not go into them. It had been argued, citing in particular the dictum of Salmon LJ in

G   *Cuckmere* which I have quoted, that a mortgagee was under a general duty of care towards a mortgagor. This was rejected. At pp. 53–54 Lord Templeman stated:

'From these principles flowed two rules, first, that powers conferred on a mortgagee must be exercised in good faith for the purpose of obtaining repayment and secondly that, subject to the first rule, powers conferred on a mortgagee may be exercised although the consequences may be disadvantageous to the borrower.

H   These principles and rules apply also to a receiver and manager appointed by the mortgagee.'

Then, on p. 55C–D:

'The duties owed by a receiver and manager do not compel him to adopt any particular course of action, by selling the whole or part of the mortgaged property or by carrying on the business of the company or by exercising any other powers

and discretions vested in him. But since a mortgage is only security for a debt, a   A
receiver and manager commits a breach of his duty if he abuses his powers by
exercising them otherwise than "for the special purpose of enabling the assets
comprised in the debenture holders' security to be preserved and realized" for the
benefit of the debenture holder.'

On pp. 55H–56C:

    'The general duty of care said to be owed by a mortgagee to subsequent   B
encumbrancers and the mortgagor in negligence is inconsistent with the right of
the mortgagee and the duties which the courts applying equitable principles have
imposed on the mortgagee . . . If a mortgagee exercises his power of sale in good
faith for the purpose of protecting his security, he is not liable to the mortgagor
even though he might have obtained a higher price and even though the terms
might be regarded as disadvantageous to the mortgagor. *Cuckmere Brick Co Ltd v*   C
Mutual Finance Ltd [1971] Ch 949 is Court of Appeal authority for the proposition
that, if the mortgagee decides to sell, he must take reasonable care to obtain a
proper price but is no authority for any wider proposition . . . The duties imposed
by equity on a mortgagee and on a receiver and manager would be quite
unnecessary if there existed a general duty in negligence to take reasonable care in
the exercise of powers and to take reasonable care in dealing with the assets of the
mortgagor company.'   D

Mr Edwards submitted for Mr Huish that the claim that the farm and milk quota
should have been sold separately came within the bank's obligation arising if it decided
to sell, to take reasonable care to obtain a proper price. For this purpose I accept that
there is an arguable case that, if the land and quota had been sold separately, the total
realised would have been more than if the land had been sold so as to carry the quota
with it. Mr Edwards submitted that, if the land alone was to be looked at, because the   E
bank only had a charge over the land, then, if the land was sold so that it carried the
quota with it, the value of the quota if sold separately had to be deducted from the price
to give a price for the land alone. That then, he submitted, on the basis of Mr Huish's
figures, gave a very low one.

Mr Davies for the bank submitted that it was clearly within the power of the bank to
sell the land so that it carried the quota with it; if the bank did so, the price receivable for   F
the bank's benefit was thereby enhanced; the quota could only be sold separately in
cooperation with Mr Huish and by him; the bank had no power or right to deal separately
with the quota; the limit of the bank's duty was to take reasonable care to obtain a
proper price for the land when sold in circumstances where it would carry the quota with
it.

In my view the bank's duty was limited as submitted by Mr Davies. The bank was free   G
to decide whether it preferred the simple course of selling the land so that it carried the
quota, or whether it preferred to run the risks attached to trying to arrange a separate
sale of the quota in cooperation with Mr Huish. The bank owed no duty to Mr Huish in
making that decision. In my view the cases which I have cited establish that, provided a
holder of security exercises his powers in good faith for the purpose of obtaining
repayment, he is free to exercise those powers as he chooses: to quote from the judgment
of Jenkins LJ in *Re B Johnson & Co (Builders) Ltd* [1955] Ch 634 at p. 661, approved by   H
Lord Templeman in *Downsview*, the bank had 'full discretion as to the exercise and mode
of exercising those powers'. What may be called the *Cuckmere* duty of care has a strictly
limited ambit of application, namely to the sale itself once the creditor has decided what
and when to sell. That is consistent with the facts before the Court of Appeal in *Cuckmere*
and it is established by *Tse Kwong Lam* and by *Downsview*. The limited ambit is in

A   particular made plain by Lord Templeman in *Downsview* at pp. 55–56 in a passage which I have already quoted in full.

I conclude, therefore, that Mr Huish's claim against the bank is bad in law. In case I am wrong in that, I will go on to the bank's two further submissions.

The bank submits that, regardless of the legal position as to duty, Mr Huish's allegation that the land and milk quota should have been sold separately is on the uncontrovertible facts an abuse of the process of court. Where proceedings are alleged to

B   be an abuse of the court's process, affidavit evidence may be put before the court and the court may examine the facts. That examination is usually kept within a narrow ambit, and it is not usually appropriate to enter on any wide ranging enquiry as to the facts: for, if that is necessary, the court will normally conclude that the facts should be investigated at a trial. The bank's case here is that it is plain and incontrovertible that Mr Huish

C   conducted himself to force them to make the sale which they did to Mr Smith, who was Mr Huish's friend and ally, and that Mr Huish did all he could to frustrate any other course. I was referred to the Court of Appeal's decision in *Re Saul D Harrison & Sons plc* [1994] BCC 475. There the court held that a petition under s. 459 of the *Companies Act* 1985 should be struck out on the basis that there was no evidence which the petitioner could adduce to support the case she sought to make. While an analogy can be drawn between that case and the bank's submission here, the proceedings are very different. I

D   approach the bank's submission on the basis that I must not be drawn into a consideration of factual issues which should properly be left to the trial.

I will next summarise the relevant facts which have been put in evidence and which are nearly all of them established by the documents.

(a)   The sale of the land by the bank faced the following complications:

E   (i)   Any sale of milk quota separate from the land required the cooperation of Mr Huish and the bank. The position is set out in the Milk Marketing Board's letter to the bank of 13 November 1986.

       (ii)   On 3 December 1986 Mrs Huish registered a class F land charge against the land. (Divorce proceedings were then, or were about to be, in train.)

F   (iii)   In the latter part of 1986 a neighbouring farmer, Mr Woolrich, advanced a claim that part of the milk quota attaching to the farm should be allocated to him. Details are set out in a letter to the Milk Marketing Board from Mr Woolrich's advisers dated 16 April 1987.

The bank were naturally aware of the options as to the sale of the farm and were in receipt of advice as to them. Thus the receiver's letter of 30 December 1986 enclosed a review of some possibilities including separate sales of the whole or part

G   of the quota. The bank's response of 8 January 1987 favoured a separate sale of the whole quota. This was confirmed by a letter of 17 February 1987.

(b)   On 2 February 1987 Mr Smith offered £400,000 for the farm with the milk quota. This was considered insufficient. Mr Huish alleges that a similar offer had been made by Mr Smith in November 1986. On 30 March 1987 Mr Forrister offered £450,000 for the farm and quota. On 2 June 1987 Mr Forrister made a further offer of £350,000 to include 750,000 litres of milk quota from the total of some

H   1.1m litres. In June 1987 Mr Smith made an offer to buy the land and buildings alone for £200,000. This offer was apparently made on behalf of Mr Huish, whom Mr Smith was prepared to finance. The bank however decided to sell the farm with the quota as a single unit, as is set out in letters of 1 July 1994. Paragraph 15 of Mr Huish's affidavit sworn on 25 October 1994 states that he was informed of the bank's decision on 23 June 1988.

(c)   On 26 June 1987, unknown at the time to the bank, Mr Huish purported to sell the   A
farm with the quota to Mr Smith for £345,000. An estate contract was registered.
The sale was subject to Mrs Huish's charge and Mr Woolrich's claim. On 3 July
1987 John Francis wrote asking for Mr Smith's highest offer, to state whether milk
quota was included and if so, the quantity, and saying that they were anxious to
bring matters to a head. On 7 July Mr Huish's solicitors wrote to the bank,
informing the bank of the sale to Mr Smith at £345,000, saying that this was 'an
open market valuation that has been carried out by Messrs J J Morris'.   B

(d)   On 29 July 1987 Mr Forrister increased his offer to £485,000, to include all the
quota.

(e)   On 3 August 1987 the bank paid £37,500 to secure the removal of Mrs Huish's
charge.

(f)   On 5 August 1987 Mr Huish's solicitors wrote saying that they would be very
surprised if a price higher than £345,000 subject to the two claims could be   C
obtained, and that it was considered a realistic figure by J J Morris. The bank was
urged to cooperate in the sale to Mr Smith at that price, otherwise the value of the
quota might be lost.

(g)   From August 1987 the bank sought Mr Huish's cooperation in the transfer of the
quota. He refused. On 13 August 1987 he applied to the board to transfer the
quota on a temporary basis to Mr Smith. His position is shown in two letters to   D
the Milk Marketing Board dated 18 October 1987 and 7 March 1988 (misdated
1987). In the former he stated that the bank had no rights over the quota, that Mr
Smith had taken possession of the farm with cattle following the sale to him, and
that he would not agree to any transfer of the quota to the bank. In the second
letter Mr Huish stated his case that Mr Smith was entitled to the transfer of the
whole quota and asked the board that it be effected.

(h)   On 14 August 1987 Mr Woodham offered £490,000 for the farm with the full   E
quota.

(i)   On the same day the bank took possession of the farmland and buildings using
chains and padlocks. These were removed. Mr Huish remained in the farmhouse.

(j)   At a meeting with the bank on 7 October 1987 attended by Mr Huish and Mr
Smith, Mr Smith indicated that he was willing to increase his offer above £345,000
plus the £37,500 paid by the bank to Mrs Huish, i.e. above £382,500. By letter of   F
9 October Mr Smith made an offer equivalent to that figure and to take on Mr
Woolrich's claim.

(k)   On 6 November 1987 the bank obtained a possession order against Mr Huish
suspended for 28 days. It had not made Mr Smith a party to the proceedings. The
court was informed by Mr Huish's solicitors that Mr Smith was in possession.

(l)   On 5 January 1988 (dated 1987) the National Farmers Union wrote a letter   G
effectively on behalf of Mr Huish asking the bank to resolve matters so he could
become farm manager for Mr Smith which, the letter stated, would solve the quota
problem.

(m)   On 14 March 1988 the Ministry of Agriculture, Fisheries and Food informed the
bank that as Mr Smith was in possession it was proposed to accord him the use of
the quota.

(n)   On 24 March 1988 Mr Huish swore an affidavit in the possession proceedings   H
asking for leave to appeal out of time and stating that, so far as he was aware, Mr
Smith's offer was the best received, with or without quota, and therefore the sale
to Mr Smith should go ahead and the order for possession be refused 'upon the
basis that (the bank) will be paid the full value of their security and that they could
not, by means of an order for possession, obtain more'.

A   (o)   On 31 March 1988 the bank accepted an offer from Mr Smith to purchase the farm
           with quota for £425,000 subject to Mr Woolrich's claim. The conveyance was
           effected on 11 April 1988. Mr Huish continued to live in the farm house and to
           manage the farm. The bank remained out of pocket by £223,356.

     (p)   On 9 August 1988 Mr Huish entered a voluntary arrangement with his creditors.
           The debts amounted to £365,558.

B   (q)   In March 1989 Mr Huish repurchased the farm with 235,000 litres of quota from
           Mr Smith for £200,000. Mr Smith retained 230,000 litres of quota. A half of the
           original quota was also sold by Mr Smith. The effect of these transactions was that
           Mr Smith recouped what he had paid to the bank. It appears that the value of milk
           quota had risen in the meanwhile. In June 1992 Mr Huish sold the farm for
           £460,000.

C   Mr Huish's case was advanced to me on the basis that it was only when the bank made
     it clear that the land and quota were to be sold together (and it must be his case that this
     happened on about 23 June 1987) that he decided to cease cooperating, and that if the
     bank had relented at any time into 1988 he would have cooperated. I proceed for the
     present purpose on the basis that the bank reached a definite decision towards the end of
     June 1987 that the land and the quota should be sold together. It cannot, of course, be
     said to have been irreversible.

D   In my judgment the facts which I have set out are consistent only with an intention on
     the part of Mr Huish that the bank should sell the farm with the full quota to Mr Smith.
     They are wholly inconsistent with an intention that the bank should sell the farm
     separately to the quota to the highest bidders. I refer to all the events which I have set
     out, but it is made most plain by his solicitors' letter of 5 August 1987 and by his affidavit
     in the possession proceedings which I have quoted. It is unnecessary for me to conclude
     why this was Mr Huish's intention. Nonetheless the subsequent events in which things
E   worked so well for Mr Huish indicate a reason if one is needed. Mr Edwards accepted
     that, if the bank did what Mr Huish intended, or, if he constrained the bank to act as the
     bank did, the bank would have a defence to a claim brought under what was called the
     Cuckmere principle. He was plainly right to do so. I find therefore that, even if it were
     good in law, the making of this claim would be an abuse of the court's process.

F   Before leaving this subject I should consider whether I have overstepped those bounds
     of a striking-out application to which I earlier referred. Mr Huish has made an assertion
     which lies at the foundation of his claim against the bank while his documented actions
     and the documents emanating from him demonstrate the opposite. I am satisfied that in
     the circumstances of the case it is a proper exercise of the court's inherent jurisdiction to
     prevent abuse of its process to reach the conclusion which I have.

G   I come to the third submission made by the bank, that in any event Mr Huish cannot
     establish that he has suffered any loss by reason of the bank not having sold the milk
     quota separately. Mr Huish's case is that the land and quota sold separately should have
     achieved £695,100, which betters by £270,100 that received from Mr Smith. The bank
     would have taken some £225,000, which would leave some £45,000 for Mr Huish's
     general creditors and his case is that he has been disadvantaged in that amount. The
     bank's answer is that, even accepting the figure of £695,100, no loss is shown because Mr
H   Huish must give credit for the financial advantage of the transactions with Mr Smith. It
     was submitted for Mr Huish that no such credit need be given: it is irrelevant or too
     remote. The decision on this point depends at least in part on findings as to the
     relationship between Mr Smith and Mr Huish. It is not a matter than can be concluded
     on this application.

          The case against John Francis is that they owed a duty to Mr Huish in advising the
     receiver, the bank and Francis Finance in connection with the realisation of assets. It was

submitted by Mr Jarman on behalf of John Francis that they owed a duty only to those   A
who instructed them and none to Mr Huish.

This raises the question whether one who tenders advice to a mortgagee or chargee in
connection with the realisation of the security owes any duty to the mortgagor or chargor
in the giving of that advice. It is submitted that there should be a duty because, if the
advice is acted on by the mortgagee, this may affect the proceeds of realisation and hence
the surplus, if any, to which the mortgagor is entitled. This situation is different from   B
that where the claimant has himself relied on a statement or advice emanating from the
defendant and seeks to recover the loss which he says has occurred as a result of his
reliance. It is the latter which has more often been before the courts in recent decisions.

The question of the duty of the adviser to the mortgagee towards the mortgagor must
be considered in conjunction with the duty of the mortgagee himself.

Save for a dictum by Cross LJ in *Cuckmere* there appears to be no decision on the
point, and I have to approach it as a matter of principle. It had been sought to raise in   C
the Court of Appeal in *Cuckmere* the issue whether it was open to a mortgagee to answer
a mortgagor's claim by asserting that he had acted on the advice of a competent agent in
connection with the sale. The issue had not been raised at the trial and the court refused
to allow it to be raised before them. The court nonetheless had something to say about
it, and I will have to return to that. It was in this context that, at p. 973C in *Cuckmere*,
Cross LJ stated: D

> 'Of course, in many cases the mortgagee may suffer no damage himself by reason
> of the agent's negligence because the purchase price, though less than it should
> have been, exceeds what is owing to the mortgagee. In such circumstances it may
> be that nowadays the law would allow the mortgagor to recover damages directly
> from the agent although not in contractual relations with him; but that was
> certainly not so a hundred years ago when *Wolff v. Vanderzee* (1869) 20 L.T. 353
> was decided.'   E

The point as to the mortgagor's right to sue the agent had not been raised or argued
before the Court of Appeal, and I do not think that I should take the passage as more
than an indication that the point is open to argument, particularly in view of the
important decisions in the law of negligence since 1971.

In this situation I may begin with the decision of the House of Lords in *Caparo
Industries plc v Dickman* [1990] BCC 164. This was a claim by investors in a company   F
against its auditors on the basis that the auditors had negligently prepared accounts on
which the investors relied in investing. It was held on a preliminary issue that no duty
was owed to the investors by the auditors. In his speech Lord Bridge stated at p. 169C:

> 'What emerges is that, in addition to the forseeability of damage, necessary
> ingredients in any situation giving rise to a duty of care are that there should exist
> between the party owing the duty and the party to whom it is owed a relationship   G
> characterised by the law as one of "proximity" or "neighbourhood" and that the
> situation should be one in which the court considers it fair, just and reasonable
> that the law should impose a duty of a given scope upon the one party for the
> benefit of the other . . . I think the law has now moved in the direction of attaching
> greater significance to the more traditional categorisation of distinct and
> recognisable situations as guides to the existence, the scope and the limits of the
> varied duties of care which the law imposes.'   H

The argument before me accepted this as a proper starting point for my decision. As I
understood the argument for John Francis it was also accepted that the proximity or
neighbourhood test was satisfied. The argument centred rather on whether it was fair,
just and reasonable to impose a duty in the circumstances. I was referred to a number of
decisions on each side.

A   The plaintiff in *Parker-Tweedale v Dunbar Bank* [1991] Ch 12 had a beneficial interest in mortgaged property which was sold. He asserted that the sale was at an under-value and made a claim against the mortgagee. It was held by the Court of Appeal that no duty was owed. Nourse LJ stated at page 19D:

> 'Once it is recognised that the duty owed by the mortgagee to the mortgagor arises out of the particular relationship between them, it is readily apparent that there is no warrant for extending its scope so as to include a beneficiary or beneficiaries under a trust of which the mortgagor is the trustee. The correctness of that view was fully established in the clear and compelling argument of Mr. Lloyd, who drew particular attention to the rights and duties of the trustee to protect the trust property against dissipation or depreciation in value and the impracticabilities and potential rights of double recovery inherent in giving the beneficiary an additional right to sue the mortgagee, a right which is in any event unnecessary.'

C   In *James McNaughton Paper Group Ltd v Hicks Anderson & Co* [1990] BCC 891 the Court of Appeal held that auditors who had prepared accounts and made statements concerning a company were not liable to plaintiffs who subsequently took over the company. So, like *Caparo* and unlike here, the case concerned a situation where there was reliance by the plaintiffs on material emanating from the defendants. In his judgment Neill LJ listed six headings to cover the areas to be examined to see whether it was appropriate to decide that a duty was owed. As they are intended for situations where advice is given which is relied on by a plaintiff to his detriment, they are of limited assistance here.

    In *Smith v Eric S Bush* [1990] 1 AC 831 one issue before the House of Lords was whether a professional valuer employed by a prospective mortgagee to value a house for the purpose of a mortgage by the prospective purchaser owed a duty of care to the purchaser in circumstances where it was unlikely that the purchaser would instruct his own surveyor. It was held that there was a duty: the valuer must be taken to have known that the purchaser would only buy if the valuation was satisfactory. I do not find the case of particular assistance here.

    The plaintiffs in *Pacific Associates Inc v Baxter* [1990] 1 QB 993 had contracted to do dredging work under a contract to be supervised by the defendant engineers who had certification functions under the contract. It was held that the engineers owed no duty to the plaintiffs in respect of their certifications. This was not a case involving reliance by the plaintiffs: it was the plaintiffs' employers under the contract who relied on the certificates in not paying the plaintiffs until the plaintiffs proceeded against them by arbitration. An important factor among the several featuring in the judgments of the Court of Appeal was the contractors' right to arbitrate against the employers and thereby to put in question certificates issued by the engineers.

    The plaintiffs in *Marc Rich & Co AG v Bishop Rock Marine Co Ltd* [1994] CLC 133 were cargo owners. The vessel had developed a crack in its hull and was then inspected by a surveyor on behalf of a classification society. He advised that after specified repairs it could continue on the voyage. It did so and sank, and the cargo was lost. The plaintiffs sued the shipowners and settled on the basis of what they could recover under the Hague rules. The action continued against the society. The Court of Appeal held that the society owed no duty to the cargo owners. The society's primary duty to the shipowners and the established international code applying between the society and the owners were important features in the decision.

    I am informed that *Marc Rich* is under appeal to the House of Lords. Until their decision on that appeal is given, their Lordships' last word in this area of law is to be found in *Arbuthnott v Fagan and Feltrim Underwriting Agencies Ltd* [1994] CLC 918. The issue was whether Lloyd's underwriting agents owed a tortious duty of care to their names. It was held that they did. In the leading judgment Lord Goff took the governing principle from *Hedley Byrne & Co Ltd v Heller & Partners Ltd* [1964] AC 465, which is the origin of the modern law of negligent misstatement and economic loss. Lord Goff took from that case the concept of 'assumption of responsibility', which he applied to the situation of the agents to find that they were under a duty to their Names.

I take last *White v Jones* [1993] 3 WLR 730 because it is a case where a party who had placed no reliance on anything done by the defendant was held entitled to recover. Two potential beneficiaries under an undrawn will recovered against solicitors who had negligently delayed in drawing it, when the testator died. The earlier first instance decision to the same effect of *Ross v Caunters* [1980] Ch 297 was approved. It was an important feature of the Court of Appeal's judgments that, if there was no liability to a beneficiary, there would be no remedy in respect of the negligence. Sir Donald Nicholls V-C stated at p. 740F:

> 'Then it is eminently fair, just and reasonable that the solicitor should be liable in damages to the intended beneficiary. Otherwise there is no sanction in respect of the solicitor's breach in his professional duty. Thus there is a special relationship between the solicitor and intended beneficiary which should attract a liability if the solicitor is negligent.'

These cases provide guidance as to the approach of the court and as to the particular aspects which should be examined. What are the features of the situation in which Mr Huish asserts that John Francis owed him a duty of care?

(1)   Any balance from the proceeds of realisation held by the bank after the satisfaction of secured creditors was held for Mr Huish. Therefore, if John Francis gave negligent advice to, for example, the bank, as to the realisation of its security, and the bank acted on it, that balance due to Mr Huish might be diminished.

(2)   It was the bank's reliance on the advice which might injure Mr Huish and not his own reliance. In this respect the case is different from those which are in what might be called the *Hedley Byrne* line, but has a parallel with *Pacific Associates v Baxter* and with *Marc Rich v Bishop Rock Marine*.

(3)   John Francis were employed to give advice to the security holders. They owed a duty in contract to advise them as to their best interests in the situation.

(4)   The interests of the security holders might not be the same as those of Mr Huish. It was submitted that there was an identity of interest, namely to raise as much money from the security as possible. In very broad terms that is true. But it is notorious that creditors and debtors are frequently in conflict as to what should be done with regard to security, as to what should be sold and how and when. The reason is that there are often conflicts of interest between the two. I have set out in my consideration of the case against the bank, the bank's duties arising in equity in the exercise of its powers, and it is necessary here only to emphasise the discretion which is given to a security holder.

(5)   If the duty of the security holders and Mr Huish may conflict and the duty of John Francis is to the security interests, how can they also owe a duty to Mr Huish? The only answer which can be given is that they owe a duty to him when their primary duty to the security holders permits. That can be met by limiting the ambit to what I have called the *Cuckmere* duty, namely the duty to take reasonable care to obtain a proper price. It would then be a similar duty owed to both security holder and owner. Such a concept, however, presents a problem. In my view John Francis either owed a duty of care to Mr Huish when they were advising the security holders or they did not. A duty limited in the way suggested is not consistent with the concept of duty of care as developed in English law.

A   (6)   The bank owed Mr Huish a duty to take reasonable care to obtain a proper price. It was submitted that there is no need to place John Francis under a like duty in order to provide Mr Huish with a remedy: compare *Parker-Tweedale v Dunbar Bank* and *Marc Rich v Bishops Rock Marine.* This was met with the submission that it might well be an answer for the bank to say that they had taken advice from a reputable firm and they were not responsible if the advice turned out to be negligent. So, it was submitted, a remedy against the agent might be required. I was not addressed as to whether it would indeed be an answer. In *Cuckmere* the defendants sought to raise the point in the Court of Appeal but were not permitted to do so. Nonetheless Salmon LJ pointed out at p. 969 that to allow the defendants to escape on the ground they had taken advice from a reputable firm would be contrary to the view of Cotton LJ in *Tomlin v Luce* (1889) 43 ChD 191, but expressed no concluded view. Cross LJ, however, went further at p. 975 and stated that a mortgagee was liable for the negligence of his agent. The weight of authority therefore appears to be in favour of a mortgagee being liable where he employs a reputable agent but the agent is negligent. If that is right, to place John Francis under a duty to Mr Huish would be to duplicate a remedy already available against the bank.

I conclude that it would not be fair, just and reasonable that an agent employed by a mortgagee to advise him should be under a duty of care to the mortgagor in giving that advice. The question has to be looked at in the round, but the factor which I find particularly persuasive is the combination of the last two points which I have set out.

Mr Edwards sought to introduce a new para. 20A into the statement of claim to raise an argument based on the receiver being appointed as agent for Mr Huish under the terms of the agricultural mortgage. I did not hear argument on this due to shortage of time, but put it back for written submissions. In the event Mr Huish's solicitors wrote stating that the proposed reamendment would not be pursued.

I conclude that the facts pleaded in para. 20–21 of the amended statement of claim as proposed to be reamended do not disclose a cause of action against John Francis.

It is to be hoped that counsel will be able to agree an order to give effect to this judgment. In the event that they cannot, the case should be relisted for further hearing.

(Order accordingly)

Neptune (Vehicle Washing Equipment) Ltd v Fitzgerald.

Chancery Division.
Lightman J.
Judgment delivered 10 February 1995.

Directors – Sole director – Enforcement of fair dealing – Directors to disclose interest in contracts – Sole director authorised payment to himself and resigned – Company sought repayment – Articles permitted self dealing – Whether director had complied with statutory requirement to disclose interest at directors' meeting – Whether and how to disclose interest at directors' meeting in sole directorship company – Companies Act 1948, s. 199 (repealed; see Companies Act 1985, s. 317).

This was an appeal (raising an issue under s. 317 of the Companies Act 1985) from a master's order in an action by a company against its former sole director who had authorised payment to himself of £100,000 which he said was due to him under his contract of employment.

After the defendant as sole director of the plaintiff had purported to terminate his contract of employment and procured the payment to himself, he retired as director (as he was obliged under his contract of employment to do on termination of his employment). The plaintiff under a new director required repayment of the moneys. The moneys were paid into an account in the names of the parties' solicitors pending (according to the plaintiff) the resolution of the plaintiff's claim to the moneys, but (according to the defendant) resolution of the plaintiff's claim and of the defendant's claims for damages for wrongful and unfair dismissal.

The master upheld the plaintiff's proprietary claim on the grounds that the defendant's conduct constituted unlawful self-dealing and breach of fiduciary duty, but was unable to resolve the issue as to the terms of the solicitors' agreement on the material before him.

On appeal it was common ground that the defendant's conduct constituted self-dealing. Article 13 of the company's articles permitted such self-dealing but left intact the requirement to comply with the predecessor of s. 317 of the Companies Act 1985 requiring a director to declare an interest at a meeting of directors. The question was whether and how s. 317 was to be complied with in a company with a sole director.

Held, allowing the defendant's appeal and giving leave to defend:

1. For the purpose of s. 317 there could be a directors' meeting in case of a sole directorship. When holding the meeting alone, a sole director had to make the declaration to himself and record the declaration in the minutes. The court might find it difficult to accept that the declaration had been made if it was not so recorded. If the meeting was attended by anyone else (e.g. the company secretary), the declaration had to be made out loud and in the hearing of those attending, and again had to be recorded. If it was proved that the declaration was made, the fact that the minutes did not record the making of the declaration would not preclude proof that it had been made.

2. The obligation to declare the interest at a directors' meeting imposed by s. 317(1) extended to contracts etc. whether or not considered or resolved upon by a meeting of directors. The statutory obligation was not to be construed as confined to the situations specified in s. 317(2). So to construe s. 317(1) would be to place an unjustified restriction on the generality of the words used and enable the statutory obligation to be sidestepped by avoiding consideration of and decisions on such contracts at directors' meetings. Accordingly a sole director could not evade compliance with s. 317 by considering or committing the company to a contract in which he was interested otherwise than at a directors' meeting or by delegating the decision-making to others.

A　The following cases were referred to in the judgment:

East v Bennett Brothers Ltd [1911] 1 Ch 163.
Foster v Foster [1916] 1 Ch 532.
Guinness plc v Saunders & Anor [1990] BCC 205; [1990] 2 AC 663.
Imperial Mercantile Credit Association (Liquidator of) v Coleman (1873) LR 6 HL 189.
Lee Panavision Ltd v Lee Lighting Ltd [1991] BCC 620.
B　*London Flats Ltd, Re* [1969] 1 WLR 711.
Movitex Ltd v Bulfield & Ors (1986) 2 BCC 99,403.
Runciman v Walter Runciman plc [1993] BCC 223.

Elizabeth Jones (instructed by Harbottle & Lewis) for the plaintiff.

Michael Roberts (instructed by Amery Parkes) for the defendant.

C　　　　　　　　　　　　　　JUDGMENT

Lightman J: I have before me an appeal from an order of Deputy Master Weir made on 6 October 1994 raising a novel question of law under s. 317 of the *Companies Act* 1985 which I am required to determine under RSC, O. 14A.

Facts

D　The plaintiff is a private company. The defendant was the managing director employed under a contract of employment dated 1 January 1991. Under this contract (as subsequently varied) the defendant was entitled to six months' notice of termination, save in case of termination 'pursuant to group restructuring' in which case he was entitled to twelve months' notice.

Since the retirement of the only other director in November 1993, the defendant was the sole director of the plaintiff.

E　In November 1993 the majority shareholding in the plaintiff was acquired by a company called Wesumat GmbH ('the holding company'), and the holding company appointed Mr Donald Phillips, who was a director of a fellow subsidiary of the holding company, as its representative with responsibility for the plaintiff. By a fax dated 22 December 1993 the holding company directed the defendant to take instructions from Mr Phillips. Mr Phillips refused the defendant's request for the appointment of a second F　director of the plaintiff.

According to the defendant, in November and December 1993 Mr Phillips took an increasingly active role in the plaintiff, until a time was reached when the defendant concluded, he says both honestly and reasonably, that his services were no longer required.

After taking certain advice from the plaintiff's solicitors, on 5 January 1994 the G　defendant passed resolutions as sole director of the plaintiff purporting to terminate his contract of employment and authorise payment to himself of the sum of £100,892.62 which (he says) was due to him in this event under his contract of employment. He thereafter procured such payment to be made. At or about the same time the defendant retired as director (as he was obliged under his contract of employment so to do on termination of his employment). The plaintiff under a new director immediately challenged the validity and propriety of the resolutions and required repayment of the H　moneys paid. The solicitors for both parties thereafter entered into an agreement ('the solicitors' agreement') that the moneys be paid into an account in the joint names of both firms pending (according to the plaintiff's solicitors) the resolution of the plaintiff's claim to entitlement to the moneys, but (according to the defendant's solicitors) resolution of the plaintiff's claim and resolution of the defendant's claims for damages for wrongful and unfair dismissal.

On 28 January 1994, the plaintiff commenced this action asserting the plaintiff's   A
proprietary claim seeking a declaration that the defendant had received the moneys as
trustee for the plaintiff and payment. On 16 February 1994 the plaintiff took out a
summons for summary judgment. The defendant intends to counterclaim in this action
for damages for wrongful dismissal, and has already instituted before an industrial
tribunal proceedings for unfair dismissal, which have been adjourned by the tribunal
pending determination of these proceedings. The defendant correctly concedes that he
cannot set off any claim for damages against the plaintiff's proprietary claim. But in   B
answer to the plaintiff's application, besides disputing the challenges to the propriety and
validity of the resolutions, he contends that pursuant to the solicitors' agreement the
moneys in the joint account should not be paid out to the plaintiff until after
determination of his claims for damages for wrongful dismissal and unfair dismissal.

The master in a careful judgment upheld the plaintiff's proprietary claim on the
grounds that the defendant's conduct in passing the resolutions constituted both an   C
unlawful self-dealing and a breach of fiduciary duty by the defendant. But, feeling unable
to resolve the issue as to the terms of the solicitors' agreement on the material before him,
he directed that an inquiry be held before him (with cross-examination of the solicitor
deponents on their affidavits) as to the terms of the contract. It is common ground that
likewise I cannot resolve this issue on the evidence before me, involving as it does or may
resolution of conflicts between accounts of various telephone conversations. I think that
pleadings are required for the satisfactory resolution of this issue and that the resolution   D
should be at a trial before a judge rather than by means of an inquiry before the master
and more particularly the judge at the trial of all issues in this action outstanding after
judgment on this summons. It will be apparent that until this issue is resolved, the money
in issue remains secure and available to meet any entitlement of the plaintiff.

On the hearing of this appeal I have the advantage of certain further evidence of some
importance regarding the circumstances in which the resolutions were passed not   E
available to the master. In the special circumstances of this case (and not as a matter of
course) as an indulgence to the defendant I allowed this evidence to be adduced.

There are two distinct issues which I must consider, one essentially of law and the other
of fact, on either of which, if the plaintiff succeeds in showing that there is no seriously
arguable defence, the plaintiff must be entitled to the relief sought. On the issue of law,
both parties are agreed that in order to save costs, having heard full argument, I should   F
under RSC, O. 14A decide all questions that I can and leave over for trial only such that
on the current state of the evidence I feel unable to resolve. I shall follow this course. I
shall consider the two issues in turn.

1. Self-dealing
                                                                                        G
A director of a company owes a fiduciary duty to the company to act bona fide in the
best interests of the company and to prefer its interests to his own where they conflict. If
a director on behalf of the company enters into any arrangement or transaction with
himself or with a company or firm in which he is interested, that arrangement or
transaction may be set aside without enquiry as to whether the company has suffered
thereby ('the self-dealing rule'); but it is a defence to such a claim that the shareholders
of the company have consented to the transaction, and if the articles of association of the   H
company provide that a director may vote in matters in which he is interested the self
dealing rule is excluded, see: *Movitex Ltd v Bulfield & Ors* (1986) 2 BCC 99,403: *Guinness
plc v Saunders* [1990] BCC 205 at pp. 210–213; [1990] 2 AC 663 at pp. 689–693.

The plaintiff's articles adopt the articles contained in Pt. I of Table A in the First
Schedule to the *Companies Act* 1948, as modified by the Companies Acts 1948 to 1981

A ('Table A') save in so far as they are varied by the express provisions of the articles. The relevant clauses of Table A are as follows:

'84(1) A director who is in any way, whether directly or indirectly, interested in a contract or proposed contract with the company shall declare the nature of his interest at a meeting of the directors in accordance with section 199 of the Act.

B (2) A director shall not vote in respect of any contract or arrangement in which he is interested, and if he shall do so his vote shall not be counted, nor shall he be counted in the quorum present at the meeting [subject to certain inapplicable exceptions].

(3) A director may hold any other office or place of profit under the company (other than the office of auditor) in conjunction with his office of director for such period and on such terms (as to remuneration and otherwise) as the directors may
C determine . . .

(4) A director, notwithstanding his interest, may be counted in the quorum present at any meeting whereat he or any other director is appointed to hold any such office or place of profit under the company or whereat the terms of any such appointment are arranged, and he may vote on any such appointment or arrangement other than his own appointment or the arrangement of the terms
D thereof.

86. The directors shall cause minutes to be made in books provided for the purpose–
     . . .

     (b)   of the names of the directors present at each meeting of the directors and of any committee of the directors;

E   (c)   of all resolutions and proceedings at all meetings . . . of the directors, and of committees of directors;

and every director present at any meeting of directors or committee of directors shall sign his name in a book to be kept for that purpose.

102. The directors may delegate any of their powers to committees consisting of such member or members of their body as they think fit; . . .
F
106. A resolution in writing, signed by all the directors for the time being entitled to receive notice of a meeting of the directors, shall be as valid and effectual as if it had been passed at a meeting of the directors duly convened and held.'

The relevant articles of the company provide as follows:

'1. The regulations contained in [Table A] . . . shall apply to the company save in
G so far as they are varied hereby: and in addition to the . . . clauses of Table A, as varied hereby, the following shall be the regulations of the company.

2. The company is a private company . . .

9. Unless and until the company in general meeting shall otherwise determine, there shall not be any limitation as to the number of directors. If and so long as there is a sole director, he may exercise all the powers and authorities vested in the
H directors by these articles or Table A.

13. A director may vote as a director in regard to any contract or arrangement in which he is interested or upon any matter arising thereout, and if he shall so vote his vote shall be counted and he shall be reckoned in estimating a quorum when any such contract or arrangement is under consideration; and cl. 84 of Table A shall be modified accordingly.'

It is common ground that the defendant's conduct in respect of the passing of the   A
resolutions constituted self-dealing. Subject to one qualification suggested by Miss Jones,
it is likewise common ground that the company's art. 13 (modifying Table A, reg. 84(2))
permits such self-dealing. Miss Jones submits that Table A, reg. 84(4) survives or operates
as a gloss on the company's art. 13 precluding (by implication) a director voting in respect
of his own appointment or an arrangement in respect of its terms. I reject this suggested
qualification. Table A, reg. 84(4) assumes that a director will only vote in respect of
contracts or arrangements of other directors because Table A, reg. 84(2) already expressly   B
precludes his voting on his own. Article 13 in modifying Table A, reg. 84(2) removes the
objection of self-dealing as much in one class of contract or arrangement as in another.

The modification leaves intact the requirement of Table A, reg. 84(1) for compliance
with s. 199 of the *Companies Act* 1948, now replaced by s. 317 of the *Companies Act*
1985, and it is accordingly a condition of reliance on art. 13 that reg. 84(1) and s. 317 are
complied with.   C

Section 317 (so far as is relevant) provides as follows:

'(1) It is the duty of a director of a company who is in any way, whether directly
or indirectly, interested in a contract or proposed contract with the company to
declare the nature of his interest at a meeting of the directors of the company.

(2) In the case of a proposed contract, the declaration shall be made–   D

(a) at the meeting of the directors at which the question of entering into the
contract is first taken into consideration; or

(b) if the director was not at the date of that meeting interested in the proposed
contract, at the next meeting of the directors held after he became so
interested;

and, in a case where the director becomes interested in a contract after it is made,   E
the declaration shall be made at the first meeting of the directors held after he
becomes so interested.

(3) [This subsection provides for a director giving a general notice]

(5) A reference in this section to a contract includes any transaction or
arrangement (whether or not constituting a contract) made or entered into on or
after 22 December 1980.   F

(7) A director who fails to comply with this section is liable to a fine.

(8) This section applies to a shadow director as it applies to a director, except that
a shadow director shall declare his interest, not at a meeting of the directors, but
by a notice in writing to the directors which is either–

(a) a specific notice given before the date of the meeting at which, if he had been
a director, the declaration would be required by subsection (2) to be made;   G
or

(b) [a general notice under subs. (3)].'

It is convenient at this point to set out certain provisions in s. 382 of the *Companies
Act* 1985:

'(1) Every company shall cause minutes of all proceedings . . . at meetings of its   H
directors . . . to be entered in books kept for that purpose.

(3) Where a shadow director by means of a notice required by section 317(8)
declares an interest in a contract or proposed contract, this section applies–

(a) if it is a specific notice under paragraph (a) of that subsection, as if the
declaration had been made at the meeting there referred to, and

A   (b) otherwise, as if it had been made at the meeting of the directors next
following the giving of the notice;
and the making of the declaration is in either case deemed to form part of the
proceedings at the meeting.

(5) If a company fails to comply with subsection (1), the company and every
officer of it who is in default is liable to a fine and, for continued contravention, to
B   a daily default fine.'

In this judgment, as in s. 317, the term 'contract' will be used to include a transaction
or arrangement.

It is clear that, for the defendant to invoke art. 13 as justifying the self-dealing, he must
be able to show that he has complied with Table A, reg. 84(1) and s. 317. The important
and novel question raised is whether there must or can be compliance, and if so how, in
C   the case of a company with a sole director. The question is important, for the situation
and articles in place in this case are of common occurrence, and non-compliance (if
compliance is required by s. 317) may lead, not merely to serious civil law consequences,
but the criminal sanction of a fine which (in case of a trial on indictment) may be of an
unlimited amount. The question is novel, for the researches of counsel have revealed no
authority on the question or guidance in the textbooks.

D   Miss Jones for the plaintiff submits that the word 'meeting' prima facie means 'a
coming together of more than one person' (citing as authority for this proposition *East v
Bennett Brothers Ltd* [1911] 1 Ch 163 and *Re London Flats Ltd* [1969] 1 WLR 711); and
that accordingly in case of a sole director there can be no meeting of directors at which
the sole director can declare his interest in a proposed contract. She argues that for a
director to meet with himself, let alone make a declaration to himself of what he already
knows, is somewhat fantastical and cannot be what the statute insists on. Section 317,
E   she says, is designed to create a safeguard for shareholders and for this purpose imposes
as a pre-condition before such a contract is considered or entered into that the procedure
of a declaration at a meeting is gone through. If (because of the existence of a sole
directorship) the pre-condition cannot be complied with (because there can be no meeting
and no declaration), there can be no such consideration or decision as to entry by the
director. Accordingly, she submits, in any case where there is a possibility of the company
entering into a contract in which the director is interested, the consideration and decision
F   whether the company should enter into it must be left to the shareholders. It is well
established that, where the directors for any reason, e.g. deadlock, are disabled from
exercising their powers, those powers may be exercised in default by the shareholders in
general meeting: see e.g. *Foster v Foster* [1916] 1 Ch 532. Where the sole director is also
sole shareholder, this creates no problem. But if that is not the case, it is reasonable that
the shareholders should have the opportunity to participate in the decision making.

G   If this novel contention is correct, it has the most far reaching and to date unrecognised
effect, substantially negating the plain intention of members framing the articles in the
form of the articles of the plaintiff that a sole director should have power to enter into
contracts in which he is interested without reference to the members. It seems to me quite
inconceivable that in enacting s. 317 (and its statutory predecessor) Parliament had any
such intention, and reg. 84(1) of Table A cannot carry the matter further.

H   I am satisfied that for the purpose of s. 317 there can be a directors' meeting in case of
a sole directorship. In order to determine whether the word 'meeting' in s. 317 has a
meaning different from the ordinary meaning of a 'coming together of more than one
person' I must have regard to the object of s. 317: see Warrington J in *East v Bennett
Brothers Ltd* [1911] 1 Ch 163 at p. 169.

Section 317 'shows the importance which the legislature attaches to the principle that
a company should be protected against a director who has a conflict of interest and duty'

per Lord Templeman in *Guinness v Saunders* [1990] BCC 205 at p. 214F; [1990] 2 AC 663   A
at p. 694E. The requirement is for a full and frank declaration by the director, not of 'an'
interest, but of the precise nature of the interest he holds, and, when his claim to the
validity of a contract or arrangement depends upon it, he must show that he has in letter
and spirit complied with the section and any article to like effect: see Lord Cairns in
Liquidator of Imperial Mercantile Credit Association v Coleman (1873) LR 6 HL 189 at
p. 205.
                                                                                         B
The object of s. 317 is to ensure that the interest of any director and of any shadow
director in any actual or proposed contract shall (unless the procedure has been adopted
of giving a general declaration under subs. (3)) be an item of business at a meeting of the
directors. Where a director is interested in a contract, the section secures that three things
happen at a directors meeting. First, all the directors should know or be reminded of the
interest; second, the making of the declaration should be the occasion for a statutory
pause for thought about the existence of the conflict of interest and of the duty to prefer   C
the interests of the company to their own; third, the disclosure or reminder must be a
distinct happening at the meeting which therefore must be recorded in the minutes of the
meeting under s. 382 and reg. 86 of Table A (consider in particular s. 382(3)). Failure to
record the declaration (if made) exposes the company and every officer in default to a
fine (see s. 382(5)) but does not preclude proof that the declaration was made and that
s. 317 was complied with. The existence of this record operates as a necessary caution to   D
directors and shadow directors who might otherwise think that their interest might pass
unnoticed if the contract falls to be scrutinised at some later date; and it affords valuable
information as to the existence of any interest and its disclosure and thereby protection
for shareholders and creditors alike in case they later wish to investigate a contract. A
sole director will know of his own interest, but he may not know of the interest of any
shadow director: s. 317 ensures that he should know. The reminder of his duty and the
making of the record required by s. 317 must have enhanced value and importance in   E
case of a sole director, where there are no other directors to witness or police his actions.

The statutory object is achieved by requiring the director interested in any contract of
the company to make a declaration of interest at a meeting of directors. The declaration
must be made at the meeting at which the contract or arrangement is considered if the
director is interested at the date of such meeting. If the interest is only acquired after the
meeting has considered or resolved to enter into the contract, the interested director must   F
make the required declaration at the next directors' meeting (see s. 317(2)). But the
obligation to declare the interest at a directors' meeting imposed by s. 317(1) is perfectly
general and extends to contracts whether or not considered or resolved upon by a meeting
of directors, e.g. if the subject of a resolution authorised by Table A, reg. 106 or entered
into by the managing director in exercise of his powers as such. The statutory obligation
is not to be construed as confined to the situations specified in s. 317(2). So to construe   G
s. 317(1) would be to place an unjustified restriction on the generality of the words used,
enable the statutory obligation to be sidestepped by avoiding consideration and decisions
on such contracts at directors' meetings and emasculate the statutory policy and
protection. I am comforted having reached this conclusion to know that it accords with
the view expressed in *Gower's Principles of Modern Company Law* (5th edn) p. 577. In a
situation where s. 317(2) does not apply or where the obligation under s. 317(2) could   H
not be fulfilled because, for example, the interested director by reason of illness was
unable to attend and make the required declaration at the meeting where the contract
was considered or decided on, the director is duty bound to ensure that a meeting is held,
if necessary convening it himself, so as to make the required declaration and thereby
procure that its making and his interest are recorded in the minutes. Accordingly a sole
director cannot evade compliance with s. 317 by considering or committing the company

A   to a contract in which he is interested otherwise than at a directors' meeting or by delegating the decision-making to others.

In the context of legislation which specifically authorises sole directorships and where Table A provides for a committee of one, the legislature cannot have intended by use of the word 'meeting' in s. 317 to exclude from its ambit and the achievement of the statutory object sole directors, and I so hold. This conclusion is reinforced by the consideration

B   that the concept of the holding of a directors' meeting in case of a sole directorship is familiar to company lawyers.

Two different situations may arise. The sole director may hold a meeting attended by himself alone or he may hold a meeting attended by someone else, normally the company secretary. When holding the meeting on his own, he must still make the declaration to himself and have the statutory pause for thought, though it may be that the declaration does not have to be out loud, and he must record that he made the declaration in the

C   minutes. The court may well find it difficult to accept that the declaration has been made if it is not so recorded. If the meeting is attended by anyone else, the declaration must be made out loud and in the hearing of those attending, and again should be recorded. In this case, if it is proved that the declaration was made, the fact that the minutes do not record the making of the declaration will not preclude proof of its making. In either situation the language of the section must be given full effect: there must be a declaration

D   of the interest.

In the present case, the meeting at which the resolutions were passed was attended by the defendant as sole director and by the company secretary. The minute makes no reference to any such declaration being made, but that is not conclusive. There is a substantial issue between the parties which I cannot resolve on the affidavit evidence before me whether the necessary declaration was made. I must therefore leave over this

E   issue to the trial as also the vexed question of law (which will only arise if the declaration was not made) whether this failure is fatal to any defence to the plaintiff's claim for recovery on grounds of self-dealing. The trial judge will in this event have to decide whether (in accordance with orthodox doctrine) the rule of equity gives the plaintiff an absolute right to recovery or whether today the rule is more flexible and the court has some residual discretion, at least if there is 'a mere technical non-declaration' of an interest shared by or known to all the directors: consider *Lee Panavision Ltd v Lee*

F   *Lighting Ltd* [1991] BCC 620 at p. 637 and *Runciman v Walter Runciman plc* [1993] BCC 223 at p. 233.

2. Breach of fiduciary duty

The plaintiff contends that in passing the two resolutions and procuring the plaintiff to pay him the money, the defendant was seeking to further his own interests, and not those of the company, and accordingly was in breach of fiduciary duty to the plaintiff. If

G   the plaintiff establishes this claim, the plaintiff will have a proprietary claim to the money.

The defendant has on affidavit disputed this claim. He says that he honestly and reasonably took the view that the plaintiff did not need his services any more because of the increasing involvement of Mr Phillips who wished to take over his functions; and that he voted himself no more than that to which he considered himself entitled under his contract. There is independent evidence that Mr Phillips had decided to get rid of him

H   and there were communications between the defendants and the plaintiff's solicitors regarding his entitlement as well as with the company secretary. On the other hand there are very serious questions raised about his conduct. Despite the solicitors' advice he did not inform or consult Mr Phillips about the proposed resolutions before they were passed. The apparent reason was that he knew (by reason of Mr Phillips' rejection of the defendant's proposals for the determination of his employment on like terms) that Mr

Phillips would object and prevent him from proceeding in this way. There are grave   A
difficulties justifying the quantification of the payments made, in particular in respect of
bonus and commission for the year 1994.

The court must be slow to make a finding on an application for summary judgment
under O. 14 that the defendant has acted in bad faith when the defendant denies it and
affords some justification for his conduct. If the court thinks that the defence is shadowy,
it may order payment of the moneys in issue into court. But in this case the moneys are   B
already secured. The action must in any event proceed to trial to determine the issues
relating to the solicitors' agreement and there can be no payment out to the plaintiff until
this issue is resolved. Further the defendant's counterclaim for damages for wrongful
dismissal involves a substantial overlapping of the events and issues the subject of the
plaintiff's claim.

In all the circumstances, I think that the defendant has a sufficient case to justify the
grant of leave to defend on the issue of breach of fiduciary duty and this is a proper case   C
to go to trial on this issue. I should not embarrass the trial judge by any further expression
of view on the issues raised.

Conclusion

I shall allow the appeal and give the defendant leave to defend (a) in respect of the
claim for actionable self-dealing on the issues whether (1) at the directors' meeting at   D
which the resolutions were passed the defendant made the declaration required by s. 317
and reg. 84(1) of Table A and (if not) (2) the court has a discretion whether or not to
grant to the plaintiff the relief it seeks and, if it has such a discretion, whether the court
ought to decline to exercise it; and (b) generally on the issue of breach of duty.

The plaintiff has expressed doubt whether the defendant really intends to pursue his
claim for damages. I shall give a strict timetable for pleadings, discovery and the further   E
conduct of this action. This course should resolve that doubt.

As regards costs, subject to hearing any argument on the question, having regard to
the result of the hearing and the indulgence granted to the defendant in respect of the
further evidence admitted, I think that justice would be served by an order that costs
before the master and before me shall be costs in cause.

(*Order accordingly*)   F

G

H

A **Re Pinecord Ltd.**
Bennett & Anor v Rolph.
Chancery Division (Companies Court).
Lightman J.
Judgment delivered 16 February 1995.

B *Liquidation – Application for order to vary list of contributories – Whether loan agreement effected netting off of loan to company and liability unpaid on shares – Insolvency Rules 1986 (SI 1986/1925), r. 4.199.*

This was an application by shareholders of a company in liquidation for an order under r. 4.199 of the Insolvency Rules 1986 varying the list of contributories to show the shares held by the applicants as fully paid.

C In 1990 the company was desperate for additional finance of £1m and a rights issue and an issue of convertible loan stock were agreed on. The applicants were to subscribe £245,000 for 950 shares and C, a company which they controlled, was to subscribe £105,000 for loan stock. The applicants paid £100,000 of the £245,000 due on their shares and by a shareholders' agreement the balance of £145,000 was 'payable at any time at their option'. C, as well as subscribing £105,000 for loan stock, lent £145,000 to the company. This was repayable when the applicants paid up the amounts outstanding on the shares. On a winding up or receivership that loan was to rank for payment with capital repayable to ordinary shareholders in the company 'as though the moneys outstanding had been repaid . . . and (the applicants) had paid a sum equivalent to the amount outstanding . . . to the company pursuant to their obligations to subscribe for ordinary shares in the company' (cl. 6 of the loan facility agreement).

E In 1991 the company went into administrative receivership and then liquidation. The liquidator contended that £145,000 was outstanding on the shares and placed the applicants on the list of contributories as the first step to requiring payment. The applicants argued that cl. 6 was meant on a receivership to effect a netting off of the liability for unpaid calls and the moneys due from the company to C alternatively to operate as an agreement between C and the company that the company should not sue the applicants for any sum due in respect of unpaid calls.

F *Held,* dismissing the application:

Clause 6 did not effect the discharge of C's loan or the liability for calls or any set off. It was only a somewhat complicated subordination clause intended to relegate C as lender to the level which the applicants would have held if they had paid the £145,000 due on their shares instead of procuring payment of a loan by C with the advantage in a liquidation of C ranking in respect of such payment as a creditor.

G The following cases were referred to in the judgment:
Cordova Union Gold Co, Re [1891] 2 Ch 580.
Fowler v Broad's Patent Night Light Co [1893] 1 Ch 724.
Hirachand Punamchand & Ors v Temple [1911] 2 KB 330.
Overend Gurney & Co, Re. Grissell's Case (1866) LR 1 Ch App 528.
Wragg Ltd, Re [1897] 1 Ch 796.

H Michael Todd (instructed by Hughes Watton) for the applicants.
Ceri Bryant (intructed by Field Fisher Waterhouse) for the respondent.

JUDGMENT

Lightman J: I have before me an application by Michael and Maurice Bennett ('the applicants') to which Mr Rolph, the liquidator of the company, is the respondent, for an

order pursuant to r. 4.199 of the *Insolvency Rules* 1986 varying the list of contributories   A
of Pinecord Ltd ('the company') to show the shares held by the applicants as fully paid.
This application raises a question as to the substantive rights and liabilities of the
applicants. The applicants also seek directions pursuant to s. 112 of the *Insolvency Act*
1986 whether the list of contributories has been properly settled. The application for
directions raises certain procedural questions, but it is common ground that the
irregularities in settling the list arising from certain delays on the part of the liquidator
can and should be cured by granting an extension of time, and this I will do.   B

Facts

The company was incorporated on 14 April 1976 as a company limited by shares. On
26 October 1989, the company executed a debenture in favour of Midland Bank plc
('Midland') containing a fixed and floating charge over all its assets. At the beginning of
1990 the company was experiencing financial problems. By the end of February 1990 the   C
financial position had so deteriorated that (1) the company was in breach of certain
covenants it had given Midland, (2) Midland required new equity to be injected and (3)
the board considered that there was an immediate requirement for additional finance of
£1m before the end of March. At a board meeting held on 28 February 1990 the board
agreed to ask the shareholders for a capital injection. At a further board meeting on 28
March 1990, the company's solicitors produced documentation to effect a rights issue
and an issue of convertible loan stock. There were then executed some five documents of   D
which four require consideration:

(a) *A memorandum agreement ('the shareholders' agreement')*

The shareholders' agreement executed by all the shareholders (1) recorded the
agreement of the shareholders to raise £1m, as to £700,000 by means of an issue of 2,715
new shares of £1 each in the company at the price of £257.79 per share and as to £300,000   E
by the issue of new convertible loan stock; (2) provided that the applicants should
subscribe £245,000 for 950 shares and that Camion Finance Ltd ('Camion'), a company
which they controlled, should subscribe £105,000 for loan stock; and (3) stipulated that
the loan stock should be unsecured but should carry interest. Clause 3.3 of the
shareholders' agreement is in the following terms:

> '3.3 Michael and Maurice Bennett's subscription for 950 new [shares] shall only
> be paid as to £100,000 on subscription with the outstanding balance being payable   F
> at any time at their option. In consideration of the agreement by the company to
> allow such moneys to remain outstanding Michael and Maurice have undertaken
> with the company to procure that a sum equivalent to their outstanding
> subscription moneys (£145,000) should be provided on subscription by way of an
> unsecured interest-free loan by Camion Finance Ltd. The terms and conditions of
> such loan shall be evidenced in a short loan agreement between the company and   G
> Camion Finance Ltd. In particular such loan shall not be repayable until Michael
> and Maurice Bennett pay over the balance of the subscription moneys for their
> 950 new ordinary shares.'

(b) *A subordinated loan facility letter ('the loan facility letter')*

By the loan facility letter, Camion and the company agreed that Camion should lend
to the company £145,000 interest free and unsecured. Clauses 3 and 6 of the letter provide   H
as follows:

> '3. *Repayment*
>
> All amounts borrowed and outstanding hereunder shall be repaid by the Borrower
> (save as hereinafter provided) at such time as the sum equivalent to the amount
> outstanding hereunder has been paid to the company by Michael and Maurice

A   Bennett pursuant to their outstanding obligations to pay up the ordinary shares in
     the company subscribed by them pursuant to an agreement dated 28 March 1990.

     6. *Winding up*

     On the winding up of the company or on its going into receivership or an
     administration order being made in respect of it any sums then borrowed and
     outstanding hereunder shall rank for repayment pari passu with any capital
B   repayable to ordinary shareholders in the company (including any premium) paid
     by the latter on the subscription by the latter for ordinary shares of £1 each in the
     company as though the moneys outstanding hereunder had been repaid in full
     prior to the date of liquidation, receivership or granting of the administration
     order as the case may be, and Maurice and Michael Bennett had paid a sum
     equivalent to the amount outstanding hereunder to the company pursuant to their
     obligations to subscribe for ordinary shares in the company pursuant to an
C   agreement dated 28 March 1990.'

     (c) *A board resolution ('the resolution')*

     This resolution resolved the allotment of the new shares to the applicants (spelling out
     that only £100,000 was payable on subscription) and the allotment of the stock to Camion
     and that the company sign the loan facility letter.

D   (d) *An instrument creating the loan stock ('the stock instrument')*

     This created stock to the value of £300,000 unsecured but carrying interest repayable
     at any time at the will of the company but in any event repayable in full at par on 31
     October 1990, and in default of such repayment (apparently) automatically converted
     into shares. Clauses 4 and 15 of the stock instrument provide as follows:

     '4. *Ranking of stock*

E   The original stock and all further stock as and when application has been or will
     be made to any Stock Exchange for permission to deal in or for an official or other
     quotation for the stock issued shall subject to the provisions for subordination
     hereinafter contained rank pari passu equally and rateably without discrimination
     or preference as an unsecured obligation of the company notwithstanding that any
     part or parts thereof shall have been issued on different dates.

F   15. *Subordination*

     In the event of the winding up of the company the claims of the stockholders will
     be postponed to the claims of all other creditors of the company to the extent that
     such claims are admitted in the winding up.'

     The applicants were duly allotted 950 new shares and subscribed £100,000, leaving
     unpaid £145,000. The applicants duly procured Camion to lend £145,000 to the company
G   on the terms of the loan facility letter. Camion also duly subscribed and paid £105,000
     for loan stock.

     On 24 January 1991, Midland appointed administrative receivers of the company. On
     15 April 1993 these receivers petitioned in the name of the company to have the company
     wound up by the court, and this order was duly made on 9 June 1993. The liquidator was
     appointed liquidator of the company on 20 August 1993.

H   **Legal issue**

     The applicants at the date of the liquidation of the company were members registered
     as holders of the 950 new shares subscribed for by them on or about 28 March 1990. The
     critical issue is whether these shares were only part paid for at that date. The liquidator
     contends that £145,000 was outstanding and accordingly placed them on the list of

contributories as the first step to requiring payment. The applicants contend that the   **A**
liability had been discharged under and by virtue of the provisions of the various
documents I have set out, at the latest on the date of appointment of the receivers.

Decision

By common consent, the question before me is one of construction, and I think that it
is right, as submitted by Mr Todd for the applicants, that all the documents should be   **B**
construed as all forming part of one transaction.

So far as the company was concerned, the transaction revolved around the need of the
company for £1m and the desire of all parties to facilitate this injection of funds. So far
as the applicants and Camion were concerned, the scheme was that they should provide
between them £350,000, that is to say £105,000 by way of subscription by Camion for
loan stock, £100,000 by way of part payment by the applicants for new shares and the   **C**
balance of £145,000 at the option of the applicants either by payment of the £145,000
outstanding in respect of the shares or by way of a loan from Camion of this sum. It was
clearly agreed that, if Camion made this loan, the company should not be entitled to
payment by the applicants of £245,000 due in respect of the allotment of shares unless
and until the loan of £145,000 was repaid to Camion. This scheme was no doubt effective
protection for the applicants preventing the company prior to liquidation 'having its cake
and eating it', that is to say requiring payment of the subscription moneys without   **D**
repaying the loan.

The problem facing the applicants is that, notwithstanding the agreed protection of the
applicants and constraint on the company, on liquidation the liability of the applicants
to calls for the outstanding £145,000 (unless previously discharged) became an immediate
unconditional liability enforceable by the liquidator, for:

(1)   the protective provision in cl. 3.3 of the shareholders agreement, that payment of   **E**
the outstanding balance on the shares was 'payable at any time at their option',
does not survive liquidation: see *Re Cordova Union Gold Co* [1891] 2 Ch 580 and
Fowler v Broad's Patent Night Light Co [1893] 1 Ch 724; and

(2)   the liability for calls cannot be set off against any liability of the company to the
applicants: see *Re Overend Gurney, Grissell's Case* (1866) LR 1 Ch App 528.

With that protection removed, the question arises whether the documents furnish any   **F**
basis for treating the applicants' liability as discharged or otherwise unenforceable prior
to the date of liquidation. The only sustainable argument is that the liability was
discharged on the appointment of the receivers under the provisions of cl. 6 of the loan
facility agreement. Liability for calls can be satisfied by set off, accord and satisfaction as
well as payment prior to liquidation: see *Re Wragg* [1897] 1 Ch 796.

Mr Michael Todd for the applicants submits that cl. 6 is more than a provision   **G**
subordinating Camion in respect of the loan to the company so that Camion's loan ranks
for repayment pari passu with ordinary shareholders. The parties knew how to effect in
simple and clear terms a provision for subordination when they wanted to: see cl. 15 of
the stock instrument. Clause 6 could have effected subordination if it had stopped short
at the conclusion of the first part of the clause (with the words '£1 each in the company')
and omitted the rest of the clause (beginning with the words 'as though'). Mr Todd   **H**
submits that the second part of the clause was expressed and intended on the receivership
prior to liquidation of the company to effect a payment and discharge (or 'netting off')
of the liability for unpaid calls out of and with the aid of the moneys due from the
company to Camion; or alternatively to operate as an agreement between Camion and
the company that the company should not sue the applicants for any sum due in respect
of unpaid calls, an agreement which would preclude the company (and the liquidator)

A   suing the applicants, citing for this purpose *Hirachand Punamchand & Ors v Temple* [1911] 2 KB 330.

I have been much troubled with the construction of cl. 6, but after anxious consideration I have reached the conclusion that the clause does not reasonably admit of either construction advanced. I do not think that cl. 6 contemplates (let alone is intended to effect) the discharge of the Camion loan or the liability for calls or any set off. Indeed the position is quite to the contrary, for both liabilities are recognised and intended to

B   subsist, but by virtue of the documentation to have specific incidents. As we have seen, under the shareholders' agreement the liability for calls was to be at the will of the applicants. The Camion loan, as well as repayable only on the payment of the calls, was by cl. 6 of the loan facility letter to rank as a subordinated debt.

I think that cl. 6 is indeed a somewhat complicated subordination clause intended to relegate Camion as lender to the level which the applicants would have held if they had

C   paid the £145,000 due on their shares instead of procuring payment of a loan by their creature Camion. The draftsman intended that the applicants by this device of providing moneys required by the company as a loan through their company instead of paying in full for their shares, should not achieve any advantage in case of the company's liquidation by Camion ranking in respect of such payment as a creditor. But whilst the draftsman appears to have been astute in perceiving this possibility and precluding any

D   such advantage being obtained by the applicants, he was not astute enough to appreciate or provide for cancellation of the disadvantage to the applicants of having to pay calls in full whilst Camion could only prove (and prove as subordinated creditor) in respect of the loan. If the draftsman had been so astute, he could have provided that on receivership both debts should cancel each other out. But I cannot read cl. 6 as achieving any such thing. It was not designed to do this and I cannot rewrite it to achieve this object, however reasonable this result may appear to be or however much I might think that the parties

E   would have insisted on a provision to that effect if they had occasion to consider it. No such protection was plainly considered necessary: protection was seen to lie in the words of cl. 3.3 of the shareholders' agreement 'payable at any time at their option'. The frailty of this protection was unobserved and no such additional protection was provided in cl. 6 of the loan facility letter. Accordingly despite the persuasive and able arguments of Mr Todd, I must dismiss his application.

F   *(Application dismissed)*

G

H

Deutsche Genossenschaftsbank v Burnhope & Ors.

A

Court of Appeal (Civil Division).
Staughton, Waite and Peter Gibson L JJ.
Judgment delivered 27 October 1994.

Theft by company – Insurance policy covered 'theft by persons on premises' – Whether 'persons' included corporations – Whether presence of company required presence of directing mind and will – Theft Act 1986, s. 1; Companies Act 1985, s. 375; Law of Property Act 1925, s. 61.

B

This was an appeal by a bank against a decision dismissing its action against insurers on the ground that the points of claim disclosed no cause of action.

The appellants were insured by the defendants against (inter alia) 'theft . . . committed by persons present on the premises of the assured'. The bank claimed to have suffered a loss of £9m as a result of theft by a customer, the Wallace Smith Company. In reliance on false representations made by the company to the bank, the latter had handed over securities to an employee. The bank made a claim to the insurers and when they refused to pay, started an action. The judge dismissed the action holding that the points of claim disclosed no cause of action because the policy referred only to natural persons, and not theft by a company, present on the premises; secondly, that a company could only be present in a place by its directing mind and will.

C

D

Held, allowing the appeal:

1. A company could, for some purposes, be present in a place by somebody who was not its directing mind and will, but a mere employee or agent.

2. (Per Waite and Peter Gibson L JJ) There was no context to displace the prima facie construction of 'persons present on the premises' as including both corporate and natural persons.

E

3. (Per Staughton LJ dissenting) The context did require companies to be excluded from 'persons present on the premises'. The parties were not concerned with such an artificial legal concept as the presence of a company in the bank. They were concerned with the presence or absence of actual real live people. That was what was meant in simple ordinary English by the word 'persons'. In those circumstances there was no theft by a real live person in the bank. The only relevant person there was the temporary employee who was innocent and not a thief.

F

David Donaldson QC and Rory Phillips (instructed by Herbert Smith & Co) for the appellants.

Gordon Langley QC and Guy Philipps (instructed by Berwin Leighton & Co) for the respondents.

G

JUDGMENT

Staughton LJ: The plaintiffs and appellants are a bank. They carry on business at 10 Aldersgate Street, London EC1 and, presumably, elsewhere. The defendants are Lloyd's underwriters, and insurance companies. They issued policies of insurance to the bank for the year 31 December 1990–31 December 1991. By those policies the insurers undertook to make good direct financial loss sustained by the bank as stated in the insuring clauses.

H

Insuring clause no. 2 was not the one in the original form of the policy, but one that was amended, presumably for this occasion. In the margin it is described as 'On Premises', but that means primarily that it refers to property which is on premises. It is not an insurance on buildings. The clause reads as follows:

'By reason of property being lost through:

A   A. (a) burglary, robbery or hold-up, or

(b) theft, larceny or false pretences, committed by persons present on the premises of the assured or on the premises where the property is located, or

(c) mysterious unexplainable disappearance, or

(d) being damaged, destroyed or misplaced howsoever or by whomsoever caused.'

B

And there are then words which apply to (a), (b), (c) and (d):

'whilst such property is in or upon any premises wherever situated.

B. Property being lost through any of the perils specified in A above, while in the possession of a customer or any representative of such customer, when on the premises of the assured, whether or not the assured is legally liable for such loss, subject always to general condition 8, and excluding in any event loss caused by such customer or representative.

C

Special exclusion: This insuring clause of the policy DOES NOT cover loss of or damage to property while the same is in the mail.'

The bank claim that they suffered a loss of £9m on Friday, 26 April 1991. The insurers declined to pay, so the bank started an action. They applied for summary judgment by

D   summons in the commercial court. Hobhouse J thought that the insurers had an arguable defence. He also thought that they had a complete answer to the claim because the points of claim disclosed no cause of action. So he treated the summons as an application for the determination of a question of law as a preliminary issue. He might equally have treated it as an application under O. 14A, if that is any different.

Having already heard all the argument, he then reserved judgment for a week, when

E   he dismissed the action. In other words, he held that the points of claim disclosed no cause of action. It was in a sense a preliminary issue because, if he had decided it in favour of the bank, there would have had to be a trial on the facts, or some of them.

The passages in the points of claim, which it is necessary to look at to determine if the judge was right that they disclosed no cause of action, begin at para. 4:

'4. At all material times Wallace Smith Trust Co Ltd ('Wallace Smith') was a

F   customer of the plaintiff at Aldersgate. In 1984 Wallace Smith opened a money market line of credit with the plaintiff. By April 1991 the terms of that facility were as follows:

(i) An unsecured credit line of up to DM 2m (or £700,000); and

(ii) A credit line of up to DM 28m (or £9m) secured by physical possession by the plaintiff of securities of a type acceptable to the plaintiff amounting to

G   total face value of at least £9m.

5. On 22 April 1991 Mr Wallace Duncan Smith, the chairman of Wallace Smith requested and the plaintiff agreed to a variation in the facility terms pleaded in para. 4 above whereby the plaintiff would permit Wallace Smith to take possession of the securities held by the plaintiff until close of business on any day in exchange for a letter of undertaking from Wallace Smith to the plaintiff by which Wallace Smith would undertake to the plaintiff to produce specified securities acceptable to

H   the plaintiff by the close of business on that day.

6. On 25 April 1991 the plaintiff held the following securities pursuant to the facility terms pleaded in para. 4 above ('the securities'):

(a) four treasury bills of £250,000 each;

(b) four Lloyd's Bank certificates of deposit of £1m each;

(c) two Credit Agricole certificates of deposit of £1m each;   A

(d) one National Westminster Bank certificate of deposit of £1m; and

(e) one Westpac certificate of deposit of £1m.'

I omit para. 7.

'8. On Friday, 26 April 1991, Mr Towers of Wallace Smith telephoned the plaintiff at Aldersgate and stated that Wallace Smith wished to withdraw the securities B pursuant to the agreement pleaded in para. 5 above in exchange for a letter of undertaking from Wallace Smith to the plaintiff by which Wallace Smith would undertake to deliver to the plaintiff the following securities ('the alternative securities'):

(a) Credit Lyonnais certificates of deposit of £5m.

(b) Morgan Guaranty Trust Co certificates of deposit of £4m.'   C

These alternative securities were acceptable to the plaintiff.

'9. At all material times Mr Towers acted or purported to act in relation to the plaintiff as agent for Wallace Smith.

10. Following the above telephone conversation, Mr Towers came to Aldersgate on 26 April 1991 and handed over a letter of undertaking from Wallace Smith dated 26 April 1991 ('the letter of undertaking') in the following terms: D

"Dear Sirs,

We undertake to guarantee to deliver to you today as soon as received by us the following bank bills/certificates of deposits . . ."''

and the certificates in the sum of £9m are set out.

'. . . "Yours faithfully, for Wallace Smith Trust Co Ltd."   E

11. Mr Towers handed the letter of undertaking to Miss Dar of the plaintiff's loan administration department. Miss Dar asked Mr Towers when she could expect delivery of the alternative securities. Mr Towers stated that they would be delivered to the plaintiff by the close of business that day.

12. By the letter of undertaking dated 26 April 1991 and by Mr Towers' statement to Miss Dar, Wallace Smith made the following representations to the plaintiff: F

(1) That Wallace Smith had rights over the alternative securities which would enable the alternative securities to be used by Wallace Smith as collateral for their money market credit line from the plaintiff; and/or

(2) That Wallace Smith had or would have the alternative securities available to it by close of business on 26 April 1991 so that they would be able to deliver them and would deliver them to the plaintiff as soon as they received them   G or by close of business on 26 April 1991 at the latest; and/or

(3) That Wallace Smith intended so to deliver the alternative securities in accordance with the terms of the letter of undertaking.

13. In reliance on these representations the plaintiff handed over to Mr Towers the securities.

14. In breach of the undertaking given in the letter of undertaking, Wallace Smith H did not deliver the alternative securities to the plaintiff by close of business of 26 April 1991 or at all.

15. On Monday 29 April 1991, the banking and trading activities of Wallace Smith were suspended on the orders of the bank of England and Mr Wallace Duncan Smith was arrested.

A   16. On 30 April 1991 solicitors acting on behalf of the bank of England presented
a petition for the winding-up of Wallace Smith. On that date Mr Wallace Duncan
Smith was charged with fraudulent trading under s. 458 of the *Companies Act*
1985.
        17. On 30 April 1991 the plaintiff's money market credit line loan to Wallace
Smith, which then, with accrued interest, amounted to £9,012,452.05 fell due for
B   repayment. On that date the plaintiff made written demand for repayment to
Wallace Smith. No repayment of any sum has been made.'
        It is said that the loss was either by false pretences or because the securities were stolen.
Particulars are then given in which it is said:

        'Each of the representations pleaded in para. 12 above was false and was made
        dishonestly in order to induce the plaintiff to hand over the securities to Wallace
C   Smith in that Wallace Smith and/or their agent Mr Wallace Duncan Smith knew
        that the same was false.'

        Those are the relevant passages in the points of claim. One should notice two things.
First, that there is no allegation of dishonesty by Mr Towers. He was a temporary, and
relatively junior, employee of the Wallace Smith company. Secondly, the only natural
person who entered the bank's premises from the Wallace Smith company during this
affair was Mr Towers. As the judge records, it was admitted before him that there was a
D   loss and that, on the facts pleaded in the points of claim, it was a loss by theft by the
Wallace Smith company. That is because their chairman, Mr Wallace Duncan Smith,
was acting dishonestly on the facts pleaded, and he was the directing mind and will of the
company. It followed that the company was guilty of theft, even though the hand that
took the securities was the hand of Mr Towers, the innocent temporary employee.
        Those concessions are made on the basis of the facts pleaded, which are not altogether
E   admitted and may be denied. For the purposes of determining whether the points of
claim disclose a cause of action, one must take those facts to be true.
        Mr Donaldson, who appears for the bank appellants, accepts that there has to be a
theft shown by somebody. An honest taking from the bank, even if it was unjustified,
would not amount to a theft within the policy. There must be a theft in terms of s. 1 of
the *Theft Act* 1968 which says that a person is guilty of theft if he dishonestly appropriates
F   property belonging to another with the intention of permanently depriving the other of
it.
        Although there was no theft by Mr Towers, as is common ground, there was, on the
assumed facts, a theft by the company. What is more, the appropriation took place on
the bank's premises. There is no dispute about that. The judge held that there was no
cause of action disclosed because of the words in the clause:
G   'Theft . . . committed by persons present on the premises of the assured.'
        What the judge said about that was this:

        'The defendant's argument gives effect to the natural meaning of the words used
        for: "Theft . . . committed by persons present on the premises." Mr Towers was
        the only person present on the premises. He did not commit the crime of theft. The
        plaintiffs' argument really has to omit the words "by persons present" and treat
        the relevant phrase as if it simply said "committed on the premises". Alternatively,
H   they have to say that the word "by" should be read as "through". As will be
        appreciated, such submissions involve making alterations to the actual wording of
        the clause. Their argument runs into further difficulties when one considers what
        agency would suffice for the purposes of their construction.

        A servant is, after all, no more than an agent of his employer. He, unlike an alter
ego, cannot be identified as the corporate entity. On the plaintiffs' argument the

clause would also be satisfied if it had just been a messenger who delivered the   A
letter and picked up the securities.'

It seems to me that the judge was taking two points there. First, he was saying that the
clause in the policy referred only to natural persons, and not to theft by a company,
present on the premises. Secondly, he was at any rate tending to the view that a company
can only be present in a place by its directing mind and will. A number of metaphors are
used to identify the natural person who may be equated to a company. If we are not   B
allowed Latin nowadays, my preferred choice for the alter ego is the word 'soul'.

Taking point 2 first, there is authority not cited to the judge, which in my view shows
that a company can at any rate for some purposes be present in a place by somebody
who is not its directing mind and will, but a mere employee or agent. That conclusion is
reached by looking for example at the *Companies Act* 1985, s. 375, referring to the
representation of corporations at meetings.

C

'(1) A corporation, whether or not a company within the meaning of this Act,
may–

     (a) if it is a member of another corporation, being such a company, by
       resolution of its directors or other governing body authorise such person as
       it thinks fit to act as its representative at any meeting of the company . . .'

'(2) A person so authorised is entitled to exercise the same powers on behalf of the   D
corporation which he represents as that corporation could exercise if it were an
individual shareholder . . .'

The footnote in *Halsbury's Statutes*, vol. 8, p. 447 reads:

'A representative of a corporation which is a shareholder may be counted in
ascertaining whether or not there is a quorum (*Re Kelantan Coconut Estates Ltd
and Reduced* (1920) 64 Sol Jo 700).'

E

Section 370(4) of the Companies Act provides in the relation to general meetings:

'Two members personally present are a quorum.'

The bank say that the combined effect of those sections and the *Kelantan* decision is
that, if a company is represented by its nominee, the company is to be taken to be
personally present at the meeting. There is further support for that in reg. 54 of Table A:

'Subject to any rights or restrictions attached to any shares, on a show of hands   F
every member who (being an individual) is present in person or (being a
corporation) is present by a duly authorised representative, not being himself a
member entitled to vote, shall have one vote . . .'

So one reaches the position that for some purposes of law a company is deemed to be
present at a place where an employee of any grade is present on its behalf. It can be
argued that the Wallace Smith company was present by Mr Towers in the bank on   G
Friday, 26 April 1991.

One comes to the other reason given by the judge. Does this limitation in the insurance
policy refer to both natural and artificial persons, or only to natural persons? To reach a
conclusion one must first pause to consider, what is the purpose of this limit in the policy?
I must say that no obvious purpose springs to my mind, and none has been put forward
by counsel. It may be that the insurers were anxious to limit this category of loss to
something happening on somebody's premises, because the risk would be less than in the   H
street; or because there were likely to be witnesses, and therefore the risk of fraudulent
claims was reduced. That is the merest speculation. It certainly does not produce any
plausible and convincing purpose for the limit.

There are two clauses in the policy under the heading 'General Exclusions' which use
a somewhat similar notion.

A

'9. Any loss through the surrender of property away from premises of the assured as a result of a threat

    (a) to do bodily harm to a director or employee of the assured or to any other person except loss of property in transit in the custody of any employee PROVIDED THAT, when such transit was initiated, there was no knowledge by the assured of any such threat, or

B

    (b) to do damage to the premises or to any property whatsoever including property of the assured or of any other person

unless such threat is perpetrated by or in collusion with an employee and such loss is covered by insuring clause no. 1.

10. Any loss resulting directly or indirectly from remote or off-premises manipulation of any computer system owned, operated or time shared by the assured, unless such loss is covered by insuring clause no. 1.'

C

That does not take one much further. So it was not relied on by either counsel. At the very highest, those clauses show that the insurers may have had some concern that events happening on the bank's premises, or on the premises generally, were in a different category from events happening elsewhere.

In the course of the argument, although apparently not at any earlier stage, reference was made to s. 61 of the *Law of Property Act* 1925:

D

'In all deeds, contracts, wills, orders and other instruments executed, made or coming into operation after the commencement of this Act, unless the context otherwise requires . . .

    (b) "Person" includes a corporation . . .'

So one starts from the position that the words in the policy: '. . . committed by persons present on the premises' may include a company that is present on the premises, unless the context otherwise requires.

E

In my judgment it does otherwise require. I reach that conclusion with great hesitation because I think that this is a very difficult point. But it seems to me that this clause was not drafted by a lawyer, or not by a very skilled lawyer. It was not part of the original policy but, apparently, compiled for this purpose. I do not believe that the parties to this insurance contract were concerned with such an artificial legal concept as the presence of a company in the bank. I think that the parties were concerned with the presence or absence of actual real live people. That is what is meant in simple ordinary English by the word 'persons'. In those circumstances there was no theft by a real live person in the bank. The only relevant person there was Mr Towers, who was innocent and not a thief. I would, therefore, agree with the judge's conclusion that the points of claim disclose no cause of action, and I would dismiss this appeal.

F

G

Waite LJ: On what is accepted to be a finely balanced point of construction, I find that my own mind has come down in favour of the opposite view. I can discover no context here to displace the prima facie construction of 'persons present on the premises' as including both corporate and natural personalities. It is common ground that theft was committed when the securities were handed over by the bank to Mr Towers on their premises in exchange for the letter of undertaking. Of course a corporate entity can never be present anywhere in the literal sense. You cannot set its common seal upon a chair and say: 'There it sits.' Instances abound, however, where companies can achieve the effect of presence – as, for example, where they are represented at a shareholders' meeting by an individual who can exercise on their behalf all the powers which the company would have enjoyed if it had been a natural person, even to the extent of ranking as a constituent element in a quorum.

H

There was a theft committed that day on the bank's premises. The company was the   A
thief. The appropriation was carried out by Mr Towers, innocently (although his mens
rea is not for present purposes relevant). The element of dishonest intent or permanent
deprivation was supplied by the guilty mind of Mr Smith as the directing mind and will
of the company. In my judgment, the company was 'present' through its representative,
Mr Towers, at the moment when the theft was committed every bit as effectively as, again
through Mr Towers, it carried out the act of appropriation. I would allow the appeal.

   B

Peter Gibson LJ: The short but teasingly difficult question of construction raised is
whether, on the true construction of the policy, 'theft [is] committed by persons present
on the premises' in circumstances where theft is committed by a body corporate, but the
necessary act of appropriation is committed on the premises by an innocent agent of the
body corporate (that agent carrying out the instructions of the body corporate), the
dishonest directing mind of which is that of a person not on the premises.

Two questions arise on this appeal. The first is whether a company is included within   C
the meaning of the word 'persons' in the phrase from the policy which I have mentioned.
One starts, as Staughton LJ has done, with the statutory presumption that in a contract
like this a reference to a person includes a reference to a company. That presumption can
be displaced if the context otherwise requires. Does it so require here? For my part I can
see nothing to displace the presumption.

It is true that the theft must be committed by persons 'present on the premises' and   D
that limitation must have a purpose. It is difficult to be certain what that purpose can be,
but it may be that the parties contemplated that there would be a greater degree of
security if the circumstances of the theft were so limited, 'premises' being defined as, in
effect, anywhere from which the assured, that is to say the bank, carries on business.
Such a purpose does not, to my mind, afford any reason to distinguish between natural
persons and companies in relation to the commission of the necessary offence. The
assured is a bank against which theft could be committed by a company no less than by   E
an individual. The context does not seem to require that only an individual should be the
thief on the premises.

I see no real difficulty in the concept of a company being treated as doing physical acts
or being present in a particular place. Take the case where someone like Mr Smith, the
directing mind of the company, is present in the name of and on behalf of the company
to carry out the company's policy. I can see no sufficient reason why, had Mr Smith been   F
in Mr Towers' place, it could not properly be said that the theft was being committed by
the company being present on the premises through Mr Smith. It may be, in that example,
that Mr Smith would also have been guilty of theft, but that is not the material question.
For these purposes the company is the thief. As Staughton LJ has pointed out, the
Companies Acts have long been interpreted as allowing a company shareholder to be a
person present at a meeting of shareholders through the presence of a representative,
even if that representative is not the directing mind of the company. I, therefore, conclude   G
on the first question that the reference to 'persons' does include a reference to a company.

The second question arises on a further point taken by Mr Langley. Even if the
company were present by Mr Towers, is the condition in the relevant clause of the policy
satisfied when not all the elements for the commission of theft have been found present
on the premises? He submits that it is not sufficient that the actus reus, the appropriation,
should have occurred on the premises. He submits that the mens rea must also be present   H
there in the form of Mr Smith, the directing mind of the company.

I am not persuaded that that is correct. I can see no reason why it should matter to the
parties in agreeing the policy where the guilty directing mind of the company happened
to be. For example, if Mr Smith had been in his car immediately outside the bank's
premises (to imagine a possible scenario), or in any other place, whether on or off the

A   premises, but he did not himself perform the act of appropriation, his location is surely immaterial provided that the agent doing the will of the company and carrying out the company's instructions by committing the act of appropriation was physically on the premises.

For these reasons, it seems to me that in the present case it can be said that theft was committed by a person, the company, present on the premises by its agent. I therefore

B   respectfully disagree with the conclusion reached by the judge and I too would allow the appeal.

(Appeal allowed. Costs of appeal and of preliminary issue before the judge to be the plaintiffs' costs in any event. Costs of O. 14 summons before the master to be the defendants' costs in any event. Leave to appeal refused)

C

———————————

D

E

F

G

H

Masport Ltd v Morrison Industries Ltd.

A

Privy Council.
Lord Keith of Kinkel, Lord Oliver of Aylmerton, Lord Mustill, Lord Lloyd of Berwick, Lord Nicholls of Birkenhead.
Judgment delivered 14 November 1994.

> *Accounting policies – Agreement for purchase of 'stock, including raw materials, work in progress, spares and finished goods' – Purchase price to be aggregate book value of assets – Accounts stated that general principles of historical cost accounting applied – Whether valuation on basis of latest invoiced costs complied with contract.*

B

This was an appeal and cross-appeal from a decision of the Court of Appeal of New Zealand.

C

The appellant agreed to buy all the respondent's stock, including raw materials, work in progress, spares and finished goods. The purchase price was to be 'the aggregate book value of the assets as at 31 December 1986 using as the basis therefor the book values as per (the respondent's) accounts'. Attached to the agreement were accounts which stated that the general principles of historical cost accounting applied and that trading stock was valued at the lower of cost or net realisable value. However, the basis adopted in the accounts was not that of historical cost, but latest invoiced cost, with some modifications. A dispute arose as to the value the books could properly ascribe to the raw materials. The appellant's evidence was that there was an overvaluation of between $332,000 and $562,000. The New Zealand Court of Appeal accepted the higher figure. The appellant having failed to make payments under the agreement argued that because of the incorrect stock valuation it was not in default, which would give rise to a liability to pay interest.

D

Held, varying the order of the Court of Appeal by substituting $332,000 for $560,000 as the amount of the overvaluation to be deducted from the sums to which the respondent was entitled under the agreement, with a consequential adjustment in the amount of interest payable, and otherwise dismissing the cross-appeal and the appeal:

E

1. The respondent's directors were concerned to obtain a price equal to the value at which, obsolescent stock apart, the stock appeared in the company's books. However, the attached statement of accounting policies was unequivocal in what was said concerning the manner of compilation of the accounts. Presumably the respondent's directors did not appreciate the consequences of this. Had they done so, the accounting policies statement, strictly incorrect so far as the raw materials were concerned, would not have been included in that form in the accounts. In the result the respondent would be paid, so far as could be ascertained, an amount equal to the price it paid for the raw materials; it would not be paid anything in respect of the unrealised profit element built into the stock valuation in its books.

F

2. In calculating his higher figure the appellant's expert made assumptions concerning the percentage of stock which had been subject to two revaluations. These assumptions lacked a persuasive factual base. The reasoning in support of the lower figure was cogent.

G

3. In the context of the agreement 'default' meant no more than failure to pay the amount due under the agreement at the relevant date. A determination of value, correct in every respect, was not a condition precedent to the appellant being under an obligation to make any payment on the prescribed dates. If the auditors were in error, and the figures were incorrect, this did not displace the appellant's obligation to pay. If the appellant successfully challenged the determination its obligation was to pay only the reduced amount. In that event it was not in default in respect of the excess. But as to the sum found to be due, that should have been paid on the prescribed date. If the appellant chose to pay a lesser amount, it was at risk as to interest so far as the balance was concerned.

H

A   Peter Scott QC and Richard Wallis (New Zealand Bar) (instructed by Clifford Chance) for the appellants.

Rhys Harrison QC and Sandra Grimshaw (both New Zealand Bar) (instructed by Alan Taylor & Co) for the respondents.

JUDGMENT
(Delivered by Lord Nicholls of Birkenhead)

B   This appeal and cross-appeal from a decision of the Court of Appeal of New Zealand raise questions on the proper interpretation of a written agreement between the parties and questions of fact. No point of law of general importance is involved. The judgments in the courts below set out the basic facts very fully; the judgment of Williams J in the High Court covered 125 pages of the record of the proceedings, and the judgment of the Court of Appeal 35 pages. It would be of no assistance to the parties, or anybody else,

C   for their Lordships to recapitulate the background facts yet again.

Their Lordships will therefore turn straight to the issues raised by the respondent Morrison Industries Ltd ('Morrison') in its cross-appeal, after referring to the principal terms of the parties' agreement. The agreement was dated 29 September 1986. By this agreement the appellant Masport Ltd ('Masport') agreed to buy from Morrison all its stock, including raw materials, work in progress, spares and finished goods located in New Zealand or Australia. The purchase price was to be 'the aggregate book value of the

D   assets as at 31 December 1986 using as the basis therefor the book values as per Morrison's accounts', subject to a reduction for obsolete or unusable stock (para. 6). Provision was made for arbitration on the amount of this reduction if the parties could not agree. The first $2m of the price was to be paid on the date of settlement, which was fixed for three months ahead, on 31 December 1986. The balance was payable in two instalments over the next 18 months. One-third of the balance was to be paid on 30

E   September 1987, and the remainder on 30 June 1988. Immediately upon the value of the stock being determined, Masport was to issue to Morrison bills of exchange payable on 30 September 1987 and 30 June 1988 for the amounts then payable less, in the case of the earlier bill, the amount of $0.5m. Stock was to be taken on the date of settlement by Morrison under the direction and control of Arthur Young and Co, who were Morrison's auditors, 'as though for audit purposes'. Masport was entitled to have observers present at the stocktaking, and to confer with Arthur Young 'as to the financial determination

F   resulting'. For the purpose of fixing the time when Masport should issue the bills of exchange, the value of stock so determined, without any deduction for obsolete or unusable stock, was 'deemed to be the determination of the value of stock' (para. 8).

Several documents were attached to the agreement when it was signed. Each page of these documents was initialled by the persons who signed the agreement. Among these documents, although not referred to in the text of the agreement, was one which had

G   formed part of Morrison's accounts for the financial year ending 31 March 1986. It was headed 'Statement of accounting policies'. Under the heading 'Accounting convention' appeared this statement:

> 'The general principles of historical cost accounting have been applied in the preparation of these financial statements except for . . .'

Under a further heading, 'Valuation of assets – Inventories', the document stated:

H   > 'Trading stock, raw materials and work in progress are valued at the lower of cost or net realisable value. The standard cost method has been used to determine cost . . .'

The book values as per Morrison's accounts

Morrison's financial year ended on 31 March, so in the ordinary course the usual statutory accounts would not be prepared as at 31 December 1986. For this reason there

could be no question of Arthur Young determining the value of the stock for the purposes   A
of the agreement by simply going to the books and extracting the values of the stock as
recorded therein for the purpose of the year-end accounts. Hence the agreement
envisaged that, as at the settlement day of 31 December 1986, the 'books' of Morrison
would have to be specially written up with the values of the stock, and that for this
purpose there would be a stocktaking by Morrison under the direction of Arthur Young
as though they were conducting a year-end audit.
                                                                                              B
In dispute is the value the books could properly ascribe to the raw materials, including
the raw material element in the work in progress and finished goods. Clearly, and the
contrary has not been suggested, Morrison was not at liberty at settlement to adopt
whatever inflated value it might choose, however absurd. But there are several different
ways in which the value of raw materials can be assessed. For instance, they may be
valued at actual cost, or at replacement cost, or at net realisable value. Paragraphs 6 and
8 of the agreement did not set out which basis was to be used in the books of Morrison   C
when the stock in hand in three months' time came to be valued. On this the agreement
was silent.

However, as already noted, the parties did attach and initial an extract from the March
1986 accounts, setting out the basis on which those accounts had been completed. The
general principles of historical cost accounting had been adopted. In agreement with the
Court of Appeal, their Lordships consider that from this the conclusion which inexorably   D
follows is that it was implicit in the agreement that the valuation method used for the
stock at settlement date would be the same as, or not less favourable to the buyer than,
the method currently being used by Morrison in its books as stated in the attached
statement of accounting policies, namely, historical cost. By attaching and initialling this
statement the parties must be taken to have intended that the statement should have
some legal effect for the purposes of their agreement. One obvious respect in which the
statement must have been intended to have legal effect was that the buyer could rely on   E
this as a statement of the way Morrison kept its books on which the price would be
calculated.

Before the board, as before the trial judge and the Court of Appeal, submissions were
directed at the sentence in this statement which reads 'The standard cost method has
been used to determine cost'. Their Lordships consider that, in this context, this sentence
is empty of content and that it does not detract from the unambiguous statement   F
concerning the use of historical cost accounting principles. Reference to 'the standard
cost method' tells the reader nothing about which of the several possible alternatives is
the basis used in calculating the standard cost. A standard costing system may produce
figures approximating to any of the various methods of calculating cost, such as 'first-in,
first-out', weighted average, 'last-in, first-out', and latest purchase price. Of these
methods, some approximate to historical cost, others do not: 'first-in, first-out' does so   G
approximate, latest purchase price does not.

The basis of valuation in Morrison's books

Their Lordships turn next to consider what happened when settlement day arrived.
The books were then written up in the sense that a stock valuation was prepared. Whether
that valuation, as at 31 December 1986, was prepared on the same basis as the valuation
in the March accounts is open to question. However, it is not necessary to pursue that   H
issue. Even if the value of the stock at the later date was calculated in all respects on the
same basis as the earlier date, it is clear that the basis adopted in the March 1986 accounts
was not that of historical cost. The basis adopted was that of latest invoiced cost, with
some modifications. This is established by the evidence. Further, that this was the basis
used in the stock valuation of 31 December 1986 is expressly stated in Arthur Young's

A   letter of determination dated 9 April 1987. In an inflationary economy this method aims at a different target from actual cost. Where raw materials in hand, or incorporated into work in progress or finished goods, derive from several batches of materials bought over a period of months, the latest invoiced cost may be a useful guide to replacement cost, but it is not a sound guide to actual historical cost. The latest invoice price tells one the price most recently paid for the lawnmower engines, or the bicycle parts, or the nuts or bolts, or whatever. It does not tell one the price actually paid, over a period of months,

B   for all the raw materials in question.

The extent of overvaluation

The next step is to identify the extent to which the amount as determined by Arthur Young ($7,944,339) exceeded the proper figure, that is, the value of the stock which would have been recorded in Morrison's books if they had been compiled on the basis of

C   historical cost. This is a question of fact, on which the burden of proof rested on Morrison. It was for Morrison to establish the amount properly due to it from Masport under the terms of the agreement.

On this question the Court of Appeal took a different view from the trial judge. Williams J much preferred the evidence of Morrison's witnesses, Mr France, Mr Gair and Mr Tonkin, to the evidence of Mr Leaning who was called by Masport. Mr Tonkin's

D   conclusion was that the review exercise carried out by him in conjunction with Mr Fox showed an overstatement of book value in comparison with historical cost of raw materials on a FIFO basis of only 1.3 per cent. If this figure is sound, Masport's case must fail. Valuation of stock in a manufacturing business of any size can only be an approximation. However diligently records are kept, in practice it will be impossible to identify the precise purchase order from which emanated each item of raw material being valued, either in stock or as a component of work in progress or finished goods. An

E   overstatement of 1.3 per cent would be well within the bounds of acceptable variation from one calculation to the next.

Mr Tonkin's conclusion was not challenged by cross-examination. Despite this, and despite the trial judge's acceptance of Mr Tonkin's evidence, their Lordships consider it was open to the Court of Appeal to reject Mr Tonkin's conclusions. The review exercise, as described by Mr Fox and Mr Tonkin, was open to the criticisms set out by Robertson

F   J in his judgment. In particular, the 1.3 per cent figure was not extrapolated and carried into the calculation of the value of the raw material elements in work in progress and finished goods. That emerged from Arthur Young's letter dated 4 December 1987. Even with the unused raw materials, the adequacy of the sample tested was questionable. Stocks of items whose aggregate value was less than $3,000 were not tested at all. These comprised 39 per cent in value of raw materials in stock. And the items tested included, as a major element, one item (engines) whose price history may well have been exceptional

G   and hence unrepresentative and distorting to the overall result when included in the sample.

The trial judge, while preferring the evidence of Morrison's witnesses, stated that he did not doubt Mr Leaning's integrity. But if the results of the exercise carried out by Mr Fox and Mr Tonkin are to be discounted, Mr Leaning's evidence was the only credible evidence on this point. Mr Leaning's conclusion was that the extent of the overvaluation

H   was in the range between $332,000 and $562,000. Their Lordships consider that, overall, Mr Leaning's reasoning in support of the lower of these two figures is cogent.

Mr Leaning described his lower figure as conservative. The Court of Appeal preferred the top end of Mr Leaning's range and accepted his higher figure. On this their Lordships have to part company with the Court of Appeal. In his second calculation Mr Leaning made assumptions concerning the percentage of stock which had been subject to two

revaluations. Their Lordships consider these assumptions lack a persuasive factual base.   A
Accordingly their Lordships consider that Morrison established an entitlement to the
amounts claimed less $332,000.

Before turning to Morrison's cross-appeal, their Lordships add a general observation
on this part of the case. They recognise that the directors of Morrison were concerned to
obtain a price equal to the value at which, obsolescent stock apart, the stock appeared in
Morrison's books. The only discount they were prepared to agree was that the price   B
could be paid, free of interest, over a period of 18 months. On the face of it, para. 6 of
the agreement achieved that objective. However, the attached statement of accounting
policies was unequivocal in what was said concerning the manner of compilation of
Morrison's accounts. The directors of Morrison may well not have appreciated the
consequences of this. Presumably they did not. Had they done so, the accounting policies
statement, strictly incorrect so far as the raw materials were concerned, would not have
been included in that form in the March 1986 accounts. In the result Morrison will be   C
paid, so far as can now be ascertained, an amount equal to the price it paid for the raw
materials; it will not be paid anything in respect of the unrealised profit element built into
the stock valuation in its books.

Interest
                                                                                          D
Paragraph 5 of the agreement set out the dates on which payment was due, as already
noted. Paragraph 5 continued:

> 'No interest shall be payable on any unpaid portion of the purchase price except
> that if Masport shall default in making any of the above payments on due date
> Masport shall pay interest at the rate of 20 per cent on the amount in default from
> the date of default until payment is made but without prejudice to any other rights   E
> or remedies of Morrison in relation to such default.'

Masport contended that since the stock value as determined by Arthur Young was
prepared on an incorrect basis, it was not in 'default' when it failed to make any payment
either in September 1987 or June 1988, beyond issuing two bills of exchange for a further
$2m altogether.

The Court of Appeal declined to accept this submission. Their Lordships agree. In the   F
context of this paragraph, 'default' meant no more than failure to pay the amount due
under the agreement at the relevant date. Their Lordships do not accept that a
determination of value, correct in every respect, was a condition precedent to Masport
being under an obligation to make any payment on the prescribed dates. There needed
to be a determination. That triggered an obligation to issue the bills, in accordance with
para. 8. But Masport's obligation was to pay a price calculated in accordance with para.
5 and 6. Arthur Young's determination was no more than machinery in that regard.   G
Under the agreement the price would be book value, with the books compiled on the
basis of historical cost. The figures were to be audited by Arthur Young, who were to
report the result. If their auditing exercise was erroneous, and the figures were incorrect,
this did not displace Masport's obligation to pay, on the due dates, the correct sums
calculated in accordance with the terms of the agreement. If Masport successfully
challenged Arthur Young's determination, its obligation was to pay only the reduced   H
amount. In that event Masport was not in default in respect of the excess. In respect of
the excess, Masport was never under a contractual obligation to pay. But, as to the sum
found to be due, that should have been paid on the prescribed date. If Masport chose to
pay a lesser amount, it was at risk as to interest so far as the balance was concerned. This
approach did not work hardly on Masport for it was in possession of the assets and ran
the business from settlement date onwards.

A **Conclusion**

Their Lordships will humbly advise Her Majesty that Morrison's cross-appeal should be allowed to the extent of varying the order of the Court of Appeal by substituting $332,000 for $560,000, with a consequential adjustment in the amount of interest payable. The cross-appeal is otherwise dismissed, as is Masport's appeal. There will be no order as to costs before their Lordships' board and the orders as to costs in the courts below
B will not be disturbed.

(*Order accordingly*)

C

D

E

F

G

H

Royscot Spa Leasing Ltd v Lovett & Ors.

Court of Appeal (Civil Division).
Nourse and Beldam L JJ and Sir Christopher Slade.
Judgment delivered 16 November 1994.

Transactions defrauding creditors – Discovery – Judgment creditors sought discovery in proceedings to set aside transfer of property – Whether documents protected by legal professional privilege – Whether prima facie case of defrauding creditors made out – Whether purpose to be established was substantial purpose or dominant purpose – Insolvency Act 1986, s. 423.

This was an appeal against an order for discovery made in proceedings under s. 423 of the Insolvency Act 1986 (transactions defrauding creditors).

The appellant tried to remortgage the matrimonial home after the plaintiffs had issued proceedings against him as guarantor of the debts of his business. The house was remortgaged after the appellant had transferred it to his wife and stepson. The plaintiffs then obtained judgment against him and applied for a declaration that the transfer of the property constituted a transaction defrauding creditors within the meaning of s. 423 and should be set aside. It was common ground that the transfer provided for the appellant to receive no consideration within the meaning of s. 423(1).

The judge in the s. 423 proceedings ordered discovery of documents which would otherwise have had the protection of legal professional privilege. He concluded that a prima facie case of fraud had been established: the transaction was at a substantial undervalue with £200,000 being transferred for less than half its value. Secondly, the transfer was made three days before the plaintiffs obtained summary judgment against the appellant. Against that there was evidence that the transfer was suggested by a mortgagee and that the purpose was to raise money, rather than to make it impossible for the applicants to recover their judgment debt.

On appeal the principal question for the court was whether it was satisfied that the transaction was entered into for one or other of the purposes mentioned in s. 423(3).

Held, allowing the appeal:

1. The fact that the transfer was made for no consideration could not by itself establish the requisite purpose of defrauding creditors. The requirements for the operation of the section imposed by s. 423(3) were additional to those imposed by s. 423(1) so that the actual purpose of the transferor had to be investigated. The test was not a solely objective one. For the purposes of the appeal (though without deciding the point) the court assumed in favour of the plaintiffs that the relevant purpose which had to be established in the application of s. 423 was substantial purpose, rather than the stricter test of dominant purpose.

2. The evidence was not inconsistent with the existence of an intention on the part of the appellant to place his interest in the property beyond the reach of the plaintiffs, being one substantial purpose of the transfer. That, however, was not enough. The plaintiffs had failed to show a prima facie case that a substantial purpose of executing the transfer was that of putting assets beyond the reach of the plaintiffs or otherwise prejudicing their interests.

The following cases were referred to in the judgment:

Chohan v Saggar & Anor [1992] BCC 306.
Derby & Co Ltd v Weldon (No. 7) [1990] 1 WLR 1156.
Moon & Ors v Franklin (The Independent, 22 June 1990).

Vincent Williams (instructed by Chambers Rutland & Crauford) for the appellant.
Martha Maher (instructed by Willans, Cheltenham) for the plaintiffs.

JUDGMENT

Sir Christopher Slade: This is an appeal by Mr Derek Victor Lovett, pursuant to leave granted by the judge, from an interlocutory order of His Honour Judge Moseley QC, sitting as a judge of the High Court, made on 25 February 1993. The appeal raises questions concerning the rules governing legal professional privilege. It stems from a voluntary transfer of property made on 25 January 1991 by Mr Lovett and his wife, Mrs Delia Lovett, and his stepson, Mr Heywood, which is said by the respondents to have constituted a transaction made with intent to defraud creditors within the meaning of s. 423 of the *Insolvency Act* 1986 ('the 1986 Act'). The relevant facts, so far as they appear from the evidence before the court, may be stated as follows, more or less in chronological order.

The appellant, Mr Lovett, and his wife have at all material times been the joint owners of a property known as 3 Westminster Road, Hanwell, London W7, which they purchased in their joint names in November 1984 for £63,000. For this purpose they borrowed £36,000 from the Alliance and Leicester Building Society. Mr Lovett found himself in severe financial difficulties, partly or largely because of a disastrously unsuccessful business venture in which he had been involved together with Mr Sands. They initially traded as a firm under the name of Premet UK, but subsequently traded as a company called Premet (UK) Refinery Ltd ('Premet'). He found himself liable for debts of the business, either personally or as a result of his guarantees of Premet's debts, in particular to National Westminster Bank.

At all material times there have been living in the property Mr and Mrs Lovett, her son Mr Heywood, Mrs Lovett's mother and Mr and Mrs Lovett's young son. In May 1989 National Westminster Bank took a second charge on the property to secure indebtedness of £10,000. In June 1989 the property was remortgaged to the Bank of Ireland to secure an advance of £50,000. This advance was used to discharge the existing liability to the Alliance and Leicester Building Society and to pay off certain other creditors of Mr Lovett.

On 9 January 1990 Royscot Spa Leasing Ltd and two other associated companies ('the plaintiffs') issued a writ against Mr Sands and Mr Lovett claiming a sum of £30,711.17 under a contract of indemnity by which they had agreed to indemnify the plaintiffs against loss arising out of certain hire agreements entered into by the plaintiffs with Premet. Mr Lovett served a defence to those proceedings on 20 February 1990.

On 31 July 1990, National Westminster Bank wrote to Mr Lovett stating that they intended to enforce their security held for the guarantee liability.

On 2 August 1990, Mr Lovett's wife, according to his evidence, telephoned that bank and explained his financial difficulties. The bank suggested that the only practical course of action was to enter into a further remortgage of the property to raise sufficient funds to discharge the first charge to the Bank of Ireland and to clear his debt to the National Westminster Bank. The bank, according to Mr Lovett's evidence, agreed to withhold further action provided these arrangements were completed quickly.

On 6 August 1990, the plaintiffs' solicitors notified Mr Lovett's solicitors of their intention to apply for summary judgment.

Also in August 1990, taking up the suggestion of National Westminster Bank, Mr and Mrs Lovett instructed a broker, Mr Pate, to apply for a new loan of £65,000 on mortgage from the Birmingham Midshires Building Society ('Birmingham Midshires'). Mr Tunnicliffe, its general manager, has stated in an affidavit that the information received from Mr Pate was that Mr and Mrs Lovett wished to obtain an advance of £65,000 to enable them to remortgage the property because they needed some capital and desired to complete improvements to it, but that Mr Lovett had a county court judgment registered

against him. (In fact, as Mr Lovett deposes, he had at that time several county court   A
judgments registered against him.) As a result, Mr Tunnicliffe deposed, Mr Lovett was
precluded from being considered by Birmingham Midshires as an applicant for an
advance. Accordingly, in discussion with Mr Pate, it was agreed to substitute Mr
Heywood for Mr Lovett himself as an applicant, subject to the property being transferred
into the joint names of Mrs Lovett and Mr Heywood with Mr Lovett's consent. Mr
Tunnicliffe's evidence (none of which I see reason to doubt) is that Birmingham
Midshires would not have made the advance (which it later did) until the property was   B
transferred into the names of Mrs Lovett and Mr Heywood.

With this in anticipation, on 22 August 1990, Mrs Lovett and Mr Heywood made a
written application to Birmingham Midshires seeking a loan of £65,000 to be secured on
the property. The application attributed to the property a value of £200,000.

On 10 September 1990, Birmingham Midshires produced a valuation report which
attributed to the property a value of £130,000 in its present condition, retention for   C
recommended repairs £5,000 and, when satisfactorily repaired, £5,000.

On 8 October 1990, National Westminster Bank wrote to Mr Lovett requiring
repayment proposals for the discharge of his mortgage liability within 21 days.

On 19 October 1990, Birmingham Midshires made an initial offer of an advance of
£65,000, a condition of the offer being that the Bank of Ireland charge be redeemed.
   D
On 31 October 1990, the plaintiffs' solicitors notified Mr Lovett's solicitors of a new
date for the hearing of the O. 14 application, namely 13 December 1990.

On 22 November 1990, a revised offer of a loan of £65,000, with a retention of £5,000
for repairs, was received from Birmingham Midshires. Also on that day, Mr Lovett's
solicitors submitted their report on title to Birmingham Midshires and requested the
advance cheque of £60,000 to enable completion to take place on 4 December 1990. This
cheque was in due course provided on 3 December 1990.   E

However, after they had submitted their report on title, Mr Lovett's solicitors learned
from a land registry search of the existence of the second charge in favour of National
Westminster Bank. Mr Lovett's evidence is that, while he thought he had raised this
matter with his solicitors, he 'cannot be sure'. In any event, it became necessary to enter
into further negotiations with that bank and Birmingham Midshires' cheque was
therefore returned pending resolution of this problem.   F

On 30 November 1990, the Bank of Ireland issued a redemption quotation in the sum
of £51,364.02.

On 7 December 1990, National Westminster Bank wrote to Mr Lovett's solicitors
making two alternative offers, one of which was an offer to accept £10,925 in full and
final settlement of the mortgage liability.

On 13 December 1990, Mr Lovett was given unconditional leave to defend the   G
plaintiffs' action by the district registrar.

On 18 December 1990, Mr Lovett's solicitors wrote to National Westminster Bank, in
answer to its letter of 7 December, stating that Mr and Mrs Lovett would like to avail
themselves of the offer to accept £10,925. They said that 'Mr. and Mrs Lovett are keen
to finalise matters without delay'.

On 19 December 1990, the plaintiffs' solicitors notified Mr Lovett's solicitors of their   H
intention to appeal from the district registrar's order.

On 19 January 1991, Mr Lovett's solicitors wrote to National Westminster Bank
asking for a reply to their letter of 18 December 1990 'as our clients are anxious to
complete the proposed transfer and subsequent remortgage of the property . . . without
further delay'. During the course of the following few days an arrangement was agreed

A between the bank and Mr Lovett's solicitors which included (inter alia) a new loan in favour of Mrs Lovett.

On 16 January 1991, the Bank of Ireland provided a revised redemption quotation in the sum of £52,521.79. The preparations thus having been duly made, a number of transactions were effected, more or less simultaneously, on 25 January 1991, that is to say:

B (1)   Mr and Mrs Lovett executed a transfer of the property in favour of Mrs Lovett and Mr Heywood, the transfer being expressed to be 'in consideration of the natural love and affection of [Mr] Lovett for [Mr] Heywood';

(2)   a mortgage of the property was executed by Mrs Lovett and Mr Heywood in favour of Birmingham Midshires;

C (3)   an advance of £60,000 was made by Birmingham Midshires to Mrs Lovett and Mr Heywood;

(4)   out of that advance, the Bank of Ireland and National Westminster Bank were repaid the sums demanded by them and released their charges on the property.

Three days later, on 28 January 1991, the plaintiffs' appeal from Mr District Registrar Greenslade's judgment was heard and succeeded. His Honour Judge Fallon made an
D order for summary judgment in favour of the plaintiffs for a sum of £35,544:63 (including interest).

On 23 January 1992, the plaintiffs issued an originating application joining as defendants Mr Lovett, Mr Heywood and Mrs Lovett, claiming a declaration that the transfer of the property dated 25 January 1991 constituted a transaction defrauding creditors within the meaning of s. 423 of the 1986 Act and should be set aside accordingly. They followed this by issuing two summonses respectively dated 10 February 1993 and
E 22 February 1993, joining as respondents the three last-mentioned parties and Birmingham Midshires, seeking an order for discovery of certain classes of documents which they considered would or might assist this claim. It was and is common ground that all these documents were subject to the protection of legal professional privilege unless they fell within an exception to the rules governing such privilege.

On 25 February 1993, the judge ordered that:

F (1)   Mr and Mrs Lovett should forthwith produce all correspondence between them and their solicitors and the attendance notes and statements from the conveyancing files of their solicitors concerning the transfer of the equity in and remortgage of the property;

(2)   Mr Lovett should forthwith produce all correspondence, documents, notes and memoranda, including all solicitor/own client correspondence written by or to his
G solicitors and attendance notes created by them in the defence on his behalf of the action brought by the plaintiffs and relating to the issues between the parties in the present proceedings.

Mr Lovett now appeals to this court from this order.

Section 423 of the 1986 Act is headed 'Transactions defrauding creditors' and, so far
H as material for present purposes, provides:

'(1) This section relates to transactions entered into at an undervalue; and a person enters into such a transaction with another person if–

(a) he makes a gift to the other person or he otherwise enters into a transaction with the other on terms that provide for him to receive no consideration;

. . .

(c) he enters into a transaction with the other for a consideration the value of   A
which, in money or money's worth, is significantly less than the value, in
money or money's worth, of the consideration provided by himself.

(2) Where a person has entered into such a transaction, the court may, if satisfied
under the next subsection, make such order as it thinks fit for–

    (a) restoring the position to what it would have been if the transaction had not
been entered into, and   B

    (b) protecting the interests of persons who are victims of the transaction.

(3) In the case of a person entering into such a transaction, an order shall only be
made if the court is satisfied that it was entered into by him for the purpose–

    (a) of putting assets beyond the reach of a person who is making, or may at
some time make, a claim against him, or

    (b) of otherwise prejudicing the interests of such a person in relation to the claim   C
which he is making or may make.'

It is common ground that the transfer dated 25 January 1991 constituted a transaction
providing for Mr Lovett to receive no consideration within the meaning of s. 423(1). If
and when the plaintiffs' originating application comes to be heard, the principal question
for the court will therefore be whether it is satisfied that the transaction was entered into
for one or other of the purposes mentioned in s. 423(3), so as to satisfy one or other of   D
the conditions precedent to obtaining relief under the section. If, but only if, they are able
so to satisfy the court, they will have established that the transfer was a transaction made
for the purpose of defrauding creditors.

A long line of authority recently examined in detail by Vinelott J in *Derby & Co Ltd v
Weldon (No. 7)* [1990] 1 WLR 1156 establishes that a claim for legal professional
privilege which a party to litigation might otherwise enjoy may be lost if the evidence   E
before the court reveals a prima facie case that the documents in question came into
existence either for the purpose of advising and assisting that party in preparation for
contemplated fraudulent conduct or in the course of such conduct itself. This line of
authority, however, also shows that since legal professional privilege is founded on
important considerations of public policy (namely that a citizen should be able to speak
frankly to his legal adviser) the court will be slow to displace this privilege and will require
evidence of a prima facie case of fraud before it does so. Where no prima facie case has   F
yet been established, it will not order discovery on the mere suspicion that disclosure of
the relevant documents might perhaps enable the party seeking it to prove fraud
thereafter; it will not allow him discovery simply to assist him in embarking on a fishing
expedition.

In the present case the judge gave his reasons for concluding that a prima facie case of
fraud had been established as follows: G

    'I look at all the facts of the case, including the facts put forward by the
respondents, and I must decide whether the applicants have shown a prima facie
case that the case falls within the exception indicated. I am not entitled to make a
decision on the facts. Have the applicants shown a prima facie case that this case
is within the exception? In their favour, it is said that the transaction was at a
substantial undervalue with £200,000 being transferred for less than half its value.   H
Secondly, the coincidence must be explained that the transfer was made three days
before the liability of the first respondent was decided in summary judgment
proceedings. Against this is the evidence that the transfer was suggested by a third
party and that the purpose was to raise money, rather than to make it impossible
for the applicants to recover their judgment debt. In my opinion, the applicants
have made out a prima facie case. There ought to be an order for disclosure because

A   the documents show an undervalue and bring the case within s. 423 and are not therefore privileged.'

The judge in his judgment also considered various other points which had been argued before him, in particular a submission made on behalf of Mr Lovett (which the judge rejected) that in any event a distinction fell to be drawn between documentation which came into existence for the dominant purpose of being used in pending or contemplated
B   legal proceedings and other documentation.

In this court it has been common ground that the plaintiffs, in order to obtain the discovery which they seek, have to satisfy us that on the available evidence a prima facie case has been established that the transfer of 25 January 1991 which is under attack was effected for one or other of the purposes mentioned in s. 423(3) of the 1986 Act, i.e. for the purpose:

C   '(a) of putting assets beyond the reach of a person who is making, or may at some time make, a claim against him, or

(b) of otherwise prejudicing the interests of such a person in relation to the claim which he is making or may make.'

The word 'purpose', when appearing in a statute, frequently gives rise to difficulties in its application. There was some discussion in this court as to whether the purpose which
D   has to be established under s. 423 is a 'sole' purpose or a 'substantial' purpose or a 'dominant' purpose. I would, for my part, reject without hesitation any suggestion that a sole purpose has to be established. On this point I find entirely convincing the reasoning of Mr Edward Evans-Lombe QC, then sitting as a deputy High Court judge, in *Chohan v Saggar* [1992] BCC 306 at p. 321E where he said:

E   'As Lord Oliver in the well-known case of *Brady v Brady* [1989] AC 755; (1988) 4 BCC 390 at p. 779F–G; 408 acknowledged, the word "purpose" is a word of wide content. But he went on to say that it must be construed bearing in mind the mischief against which the section in which that word appears is aimed. Here, the purpose or mischief against which the section is aimed, namely s. 423, is the removal of assets by their owner, in anticipation of claims being made or contemplated, out of the reach of such claimants if those claims ultimately prove to be successful. It would defeat that purpose if it were possible successfully to
F   contend that if the owner was able to point to another purpose, such as the benefit of his family, friends or the advantage of business associates, the section could not be applied.'

In that case the judge (at p. 323B) construed s. 423(3) as requiring a plaintiff to demonstrate 'a dominant purpose to remove assets from the reach of actual or potential claimants or creditors, but as not excluding the possibility that there might also be other
G   purposes behind the relevant transfer'. In *Moon & Ors v Franklin* decided on 20 June 1990 (*The Independent*, 22 June 1990), Mervyn Davies J similarly appears to have considered that 'predominant purpose' was the relevant test.

For the purposes of this appeal, though without deciding the point, I am content to assume in favour of the plaintiffs that the relevant purpose which has to be established in the application of s. 423 is *substantial* purpose, rather than the stricter test of dominant
H   purpose.

In the present case it is not open to the plaintiffs to argue that the very fact that the transfer was made for no consideration by itself establishes the requisite purpose of defrauding creditors. The requirements for the operation of the section imposed by s. 423(3) are additional to those imposed by s. 423(1) so that the actual purpose of the transferor has to be investigated. The test is not a solely objective one.

The suspicion with which the plaintiffs view the transfer under attack is   A
understandable, having regard to the very short interval of time (three days) by which it
preceded the order for summary judgment. This was naturally one of the main points
relied on by Miss Maher in her admirable argument for the plaintiffs. She submitted that
despite an apparently inexplicable order made by the district registrar giving
unconditional leave to defend, Mr Lovett must at all material times have been aware that
he had no defence to the plaintiffs' action and his counsel, Mr Vincent Williams, who
signed his pleading in that action and has appeared on his behalf in this court, accepted   B
that this was no more than a 'holding' defence. It was obvious, in her submission, that
the transfer was made in anticipation of the summary judgment which was about to be
given in favour of the plaintiffs as creditors for a very substantial sum and for the purpose
of putting Mr Lovett's interest in the property beyond the reach of the plaintiffs when
they came to execute this judgment.

Miss Maher did not accept the explanation for the transfer advanced on behalf of Mr   C
Lovett, which was that it was in response to pressure from National Westminster Bank.
This, she submitted, does not square with the stated purposes for which the loan was
required in the mortgage application dated 22 August 1990, namely '(1) pay off Bank of
Ireland, (2) central heating, rewiring, new bathroom'. Furthermore, the debt owed to
National Westminster Bank was only £10,925, while the plaintiffs' debt was over £40,000
and would in due course be enforceable by a charging order after summary judgment   D
was obtained. The threat from the plaintiffs, it was pointed out, had existed since January
1990 when their writ was issued and, at least as early as March 1990, Mr Lovett's
solicitors were making representations to the plaintiffs' solicitors as to his financial
difficulties owing to the activities of his former business partner. More than a month
before the transfer (on 19 December 1990), the plaintiffs' solicitors had notified Mr
Lovett's solicitors of their intention to appeal from the district registrar's order and the
letters of 18 December 1990 and 9 January 1991 indicate that by that time Mr Lovett was   E
anxious to complete the proposed transfer and subsequent remortgage of the property.
The fact that Mr Lovett had apparently not informed his solicitors of National
Westminster Bank's charge would appear to suggest that at that time this charge was not
uppermost in his mind.

I see the force of all these points, which were forcefully submitted by Miss Maher.
They are certainly not inconsistent with the existence of an intention on the part of Mr   F
Lovett to place his interest in the property beyond the reach of the plaintiffs being one
substantial purpose of the transfer of 25 January 1991. That, however, is not enough.
The plaintiffs have to show a prima facie case that this was a substantial purpose and in
my judgment they have not done so. I can state my reasons quite shortly.

The available evidence shows that:

(a)   as at the beginning of August 1990, Mr Lovett was under genuine pressure from   G
        National Westminster Bank and was fearful that they might seek to enforce their
        security and deprive him and his family of their home;

(b)   because of his weak financial position, he had no money available with which to
        pay them off and was not in a position to borrow from other sources without a
        remortgage;

(c)   the suggestion of a remortgage emanated in the first instance from National   H
        Westminster Bank in a telephone conversation with Mrs Lovett on 2 August 1990
        and was made for the purpose of providing one way in which the money could be
        raised to pay off the bank;

(d)   the subsequent suggestion of a transfer of the property into the names of Mrs
        Lovett and Mr Heywood was made by Birmingham Midshires in August 1990

A   because they were not prepared to advance money on a mortgage of the property under which Mr Lovett was one of the mortgagors;

      (e)   the pressure from National Westminster Bank was renewed when it wrote its letter of 8 October 1990 requiring repayment proposals.

Against this background, despite the existence of the proceedings instituted by the plaintiffs, I think it scarcely arguable on the available evidence that from August to
B   October 1990 the wish to keep his interest in the property outside the reach of the plaintiffs as creditors was a substantial purpose of Mr Lovett in initiating and pursuing arrangements for a remortgage of the property to Birmingham Midshires, coupled with the transfer of the property which would be necessary if that remortgage was to be effected. On the evidence, the transfer of the property had been suggested, and before November 1990 was in contemplation, because this appeared to be the best way of
C   dealing with a pressing creditor, National Westminster Bank, which, unlike the plaintiffs, had a charge on the property, and retaining the family home.

The plaintiffs' strongest point on this appeal, in my view, arises from the events following National Westminster Bank's letter of 8 October 1990. It could be said, and has been said, that in the succeeding months, while the pressure from that bank to some extent relaxed, the pressure from the plaintiffs' side to some extent increased, first with the prospect of the hearing before the district judge in December and then with that of
D   the subsequent hearing before the judge. Miss Maher relied strongly on the apparent reversal of roles of the bank and Mr Lovett in December 1990 and January 1991 when his solicitors were pressing the bank for replies (albeit themselves delaying in answering the bank's letter of 11 December for 11 days). In my judgment, however, whatever conjectures the court might make as to Mr Lovett's purpose or purposes by the time he came to execute the transfer on 25 January 1991, the evidence does not establish a prima facie case that a substantial purpose of its execution had become that of putting assets
E   beyond the reach of the plaintiffs or otherwise prejudicing their interests. The available evidence, in my judgment, is equally consistent with the conclusion that the purpose of Mr Lovett in effecting the transfer in January 1991 was the same as it had continuously been since the transaction was first suggested to him in August 1990, namely that of satisfying National Westminster Bank and keeping a home for himself and his family, as he himself has deposed.

F   No doubt the *result* of the transfer was to put assets beyond the reach of the plaintiffs and otherwise to prejudice their interests, but in applying the section, result cannot be equated with *purpose*; and as yet, in my judgment, no prima facie case showing the relevant purpose has been established. Accordingly, while I have some sympathy with the plaintiffs, they cannot, in my judgment, properly be allowed the discovery which they seek.

G   In these circumstances, it is not necessary to consider the other issues concerning privilege dealt with by the judge. I would allow this appeal and set aside para. 2 of his order of 25 February 1993.

      Beldam LJ: I agree.

      Nourse LJ: I also agree.

H   (*Appeal allowed with costs. Applicants to pay three-quarters of the respondents' costs in the court below. Paragraph 2 of the judge's order discharged. Leave to appeal to the House of Lords refused. Legal aid taxation for the appellant's costs*)

Steans Fashions Ltd v Legal and General Assurance Society Ltd.

A

Court of Appeal (Civil Division).
Nourse, Staughton and Leggatt L JJ.
Judgment delivered 9 December 1994.

Striking defunct companies off register – Objection to striking off – Company was B
plaintiff in action – Company had been struck off register – Company applied for
restoration to register – Defendant in action obtained judgment and indemnity
costs order against company's solicitors – Company was restored to register –
Company appealed against judgment and solicitors appealed against costs order –
Whether action should have been stayed pending restoration application –
Companies Act 1985, s. 652, 653(2).

This was an appeal by the plaintiff company, which had been restored to the register, C
against a judge's decision that, the plaintiff having been struck off the register and dissolved,
the defendant was entitled to judgment.

On the morning of the trial of the plaintiff's action the defendant discovered that the
plaintiff had been struck off the register pursuant to s. 652 of the Companies Act 1985. The
plaintiff made an application to the Companies Court for the restoration of its name to the
register pursuant to s. 653(2) of the 1985 Act. The defendant applied for judgment and D
sought an indemnity costs order against the plaintiff's solicitors on the ground that they had
acted without authority since the striking off. The plaintiff urged the judge to adjourn the
defendant's application pending the outcome of the proceedings in the Companies Court.
The judge declined to accede to that suggestion.

The company was restored to the register and appealed against the judge's order arguing
that the action should have been adjourned or stayed pending the restoration application. E
The solicitors appealed on the ground that restoration cured the want of authority,
alternatively that there was no basis for refusing to adjourn.

Held, allowing both appeals:

In the circumstances the judge was wrong to dismiss the action rather than to grant a stay
pending the outcome of the plaintiff's application under s. 653(2). (*Eastern Capital Holdings
Ltd v Fitter* (unreported, 19 December 1991, Evans J) approved.) F

The following cases were referred to in the judgment:

Eastern Capital Holdings Ltd v Fitter (unreported, 19 December 1991, Evans J).
Tyman's Ltd v Craven [1952] 2 QB 100.
Yonge v Toynbee [1910] 1 KB 215.

Stewart Boyd QC (instructed by Mishcon de Reya) for the appellant.
G
Cyril Kinsky (instructed by Clyde & Co) for the defendant.

JUDGMENT

Nourse LJ: When this appeal was called on yesterday I had gained two impressions of
it from a perusal of the papers beforehand: first, that the problem to which it gives rise
must be of very rare, if not unique, occurrence; secondly, that it ought to be susceptible
of a simple and straightforward resolution. Now a recognition that the first of those H
impressions was incorrect has only served to confirm my belief in the correctness of the
second.

On the morning of 22 March 1993 Mr Patrick Bennett QC, sitting as a deputy judge
of the Queen's Bench Division, was about to start the trial of an action nominally brought
by the plaintiff, Steans Fashions Ltd, against the defendant, Legal and General

A   Assurance Society Ltd, in which the plaintiff's claim was for payment under a policy of
     goods in transit insurance. Earlier that day the defendant's solicitors, on making a
     company search against the plaintiff, had discovered that on or about 14 May 1992 its
     name had been struck off the register and the plaintiff dissolved pursuant to s. 652 of the
     Companies Act 1985 for failure to deliver to the registrar of companies its annual returns
     for the years 1990–1992. The immediate result was that the trial was adjourned until the
     following day so that the position could be clarified. On the same day, 22 March, the
B   plaintiff made an application to the Companies Court for the restoration of its name to
     the register pursuant to s. 653(2) of the 1985 Act.

        On the morning of 23 March counsel for the defendant applied to the judge for
     judgment on the basis that, the plaintiff having ceased to exist, the defendant was entitled
     as of right to judgment on both claim and counterclaim. He also sought an indemnity
     costs order against the plaintiff's solicitors on the ground that they had acted without
C   authority since 14 May 1992. On the other side, counsel for the plaintiff urged the judge
     to adjourn the defendant's application pending the outcome of the proceedings in the
     Companies Court. The judge declined to accede to that suggestion.

        By his order and judgment made on 23 March the judge gave judgment for the
     defendant against the plaintiff on both claim and counterclaim, with costs up to 14 May
     1992 to be taxed on the standard basis, and against the plaintiff's solicitors for the
D   amount of the defendant's costs incurred from and after 14 May 1992 to date, to be taxed
     on an indemnity basis. He also made an order for payment out of £50,000 which had
     been paid into court as security for the defendant's costs, subject to the usual undertaking.

        Four weeks later, on 20 April 1993, Morritt J, sitting in the Companies Court, on
     certain undertakings by the plaintiff, made an order restoring its name to the register
     pursuant to s. 653(2) of the 1985 Act. On the subsequent delivery of an office copy of the
E   order to the registrar of companies pursuant to s. 653(3), the plaintiff, in the words of
     that subsection, was 'deemed to have continued in existence as if its name had not been
     struck off'.

        The plaintiff and its solicitors now appeal against the order of Mr Patrick Bennett QC.
     The essence of the plaintiff's appeal, as stated in its amended notice of appeal, is
     contained in ground 7:

F   'In all the circumstances the only reasonable decision to which the judge could
          have come was that the defendants' application should be adjourned for a short
          period alternatively that the action should be stayed pending the plaintiffs'
          application to the Companies Court for its name to be restored to the register.'

        The essence of the solicitors' appeal, as stated in their notice of appeal, is contained in
     ground 6:

G   'In all the circumstances, and the plaintiff company having been restored to the
          register, there was no basis for making the order made at the time that it was made.
          Alternatively by reason of the restoration of the company to the register, that basis
          is no longer sustainable. Alternatively there was no basis for refusing to adjourn
          the matter for hearing at a time when the solicitors would have had time to adduce
          evidence.'

H   The distinction between those two grounds was that the plaintiff was asking this court
     to look at the matter as it stood before the judge and, on that footing, to say that in not
     granting a short adjournment or a temporary stay he erred in principle or gave a decision
     that was plainly wrong; whereas the solicitors were asking the court to look at the
     position as of today and to hold that, by virtue of s. 653(3), there had been a statutory
     ratification of their acts, so that the authority that they undoubtedly lacked on 23 March
     1993 had been retrospectively supplied. However, in opening the appeals, Mr Boyd QC,

who appears for both appellants, has submitted that we should in both cases look at the   A
position as of today, the effect of s. 653(3) having been retrospectively to cure the
plaintiff's inability to maintain the action on 23 March 1993 no less than the solicitors'
lack of authority. He fully accepts that the plaintiff and the solicitors, or one of them,
should bear the defendant's costs thrown away by reason of the aborted trial. But he
submits that, subject to provision for those costs, the judge's order should be set aside in
its entirety, so that the action can proceed as it would have proceeded had it not been for
the plaintiff's temporary dissolution.   B

On the other side, Mr Kinsky, for the defendant, submits that the plaintiff's correct
course was to apply for the judgment to be set aside under the Rules of the Supreme
Court, O. 35, r. 2 and, that course not having been taken, that the judge's order should
stand and the plaintiff should be left to pursue its claim in the fresh action which has now
been started by a writ issued and served but in which no further steps have yet been
taken. Mr Kinsky complains that the new case is one which was not made in the plaintiff's   C
notice of appeal, albeit that it must have appeared tolerably clear from the solicitors'
notice of appeal that it was one which might be made. Procedurally I see no objection to
Mr Boyd's now taking a pure point of law whose outcome could not have been affected
by any further evidence which might have been adduced below.

Mr Boyd objects to the suggestion that the judge's order should stand, first, because it
might leave some question of issue estoppel in the air, particularly in regard to the   D
judgment on the counterclaim and, secondly, because some additional costs and delay
would necessarily be incurred and caused if the plaintiff was forced to pursue the second
action rather than continue with the first. These objections undoubtedly have substance
and my strong inclination is to accede to Mr Boyd's proposal that the judge's order
should simply be set aside, subject of course to appropriate provision for the costs thrown
away.   E

The position is not, however, as simple as that. It is not, as I see it, open to us to deal
with the matter without considering the validity of the plaintiff's original case on the
appeal, namely that the judge erred in principle or gave a decision that was plainly wrong.
There are, I think, two reasons for that. First, Mr Kinsky has submitted, and he may be
right, that if the judge's order were to stand, the defendant could apply for a stay of the
second action until the costs of the first action had been paid. Secondly, the point would
in any event have to be considered in relation to the costs of the plaintiff's appeal to this   F
court.

Mr Kinsky has argued that the judge had no course open to him but to dismiss the
action; alternatively, that if he did, he exercised his discretion in a manner with which
this court cannot interfere. The point is one of some general importance. It is therefore
on every ground appropriate that it should be dealt with, although I propose to do so as
briefly as I reasonably can.   G

Contrary to my expectation, it appears that the problem which faced the judge in this
case is one with which several judges of first instance, mainly in the Commercial Court,
have had to wrestle in recent years, rather laboriously as it seems to me. Mr Kinsky has
referred us to a number of authorities, culminating in the unreported decision in *Eastern
Capital Holdings v Fitter* (19 December 1991). In that case Evans J, having carefully
considered the earlier authorities, including the decision of this court in *Tyman's Ltd v
Craven* [1952] 2 QB 100, took the view, with which I entirely and respectfully agree, that   H
not only did the action not have to be dismissed but that the correct course was to stay it
pending the outcome of the plaintiff's application under the Guernsey equivalent of
s. 653(2). He said:

'In my judgment, on further analysis both logic and convenience point to the
action being stayed rather than dismissed. Whatever order is made now during the

A   period of dissolution, it will be retrospectively validated when, and if, the company is restored to the register. An order of dismissal would have to be set aside because it would be inconsistent with the action being resumed. An action which may be revived should not sensibly be dismissed now. But an action which is presently 'dead' may sensibly be stayed, assuming that any order can be made now, until such time as circumstances change and the action is revived.'

B   In my view, although the matter remains one for the discretion of the judge on the facts of the particular case, the course adopted by Evans J will generally be appropriate, subject always to proper provision for costs. I think it possible that the judges who considered the matter in the earlier cases, like the deputy judge in this case, did not fully appreciate the probability of success in the application under s. 653(2). While not suggesting that such an application is a formality, far less that success in it is a foregone conclusion, I rely on my own experience as a judge of the Companies Court for believing

C   that the practice is to make the order if a real advantage will accrue to the contributories or creditors of the company from its revival and if all defaults are remedied, the costs of the registrar of companies are provided for and the Treasury Solicitor has stated that no objection is taken on behalf of the Crown in right of bona vacantia; see also the notes to the predecessor provision to s. 652 and 653, s. 353 of the *Companies Act* 1948, in *Buckley on the Companies Acts* (14th edn) vol. 1 at p. 808, under the heading: 'Going company'.

D   I turn to Mr Kinsky's alternative submission that this was a case where the discretion could properly be exercised in the way in which the judge exercised it. He has referred us to passages in the transcript of the argument on 23 March 1993 and the judgment given by the judge. He has also relied on evidence now before the court which shows that the plaintiff's sole director, and possibly a barrister employed by its solicitors, although not the responsible partner himself, knew as early as January 1993 that the plaintiff had been struck off the register. I take full account of Mr Kinsky's submissions in this respect. But

E   I have to say that the circumstances of the present case were not in my opinion such as to make it appropriate for the judge to take the course that he did. I think that he was wrong to dismiss the action there and then rather than to grant a stay over the hearing of the application under s. 653(2). In defence of the judge I should make it clear that only one authority, *Yonge v Toynbee* [1910] 1 KB 215, was discussed before him. That case goes only to the solicitors' implied warranty of authority. The judge was not, for example,

F   referred to Evans J's judgment in *Eastern Capital Holdings v Fitter*.

     For these reasons I think that ground 7 in the plaintiff's amended notice of appeal is a good one; so also is ground 6 in the solicitors' notice of appeal. I would therefore allow both appeals, set aside the judge's order and judgment and make a joint and several order against the plaintiff and the solicitors for payment of the defendant's costs thrown away, those costs to be taxed if not agreed on the standard basis. The precise form of the order can be discussed with counsel after judgment.

G   **Staughton LJ:** I agree.

     Leggatt LJ: I agree.

     (*Both appeals allowed with 80 per cent of costs. Judge's order and judge's statement set aside. Joint and several order made against plaintiff and solicitors for the payment of the defendant's costs thrown away, to be taxed if not agreed on the standard basis*)

H

Re Lewis's of Leicester Ltd.

A

Chancery Division.
Robert Walker J.
Judgment delivered 13 January 1995.

Administration – Application for directions – Company operated department store – Department store contained 'shop within a shop' concessions – Concessions operated by licensees on various contractual bases – Before insolvency company paid takings into separate account – Whether licensee could trace into general company account – Whether company had created trust in favour of licensees – Whether trust was preference or transaction at undervalue or infringed pari passu distribution rule – Insolvency Act 1986, s. 14(3), 107, 238, 239.

B

This was an application for directions made under s. 14(3) of the Insolvency Act 1986 by the joint administrators of Lewis's of Leicester Ltd ('the company').

C

The company, which traded as a department store, went into administration in January 1994. The store had been bought from receivers in 1991 by staff and management, but trading under the staff/management buy-out was unsuccessful and the store went into 'closing down sale mode' in March 1993. A number of licensees occupied 'shop within a shop' concessions in the store and arrangements were made at the end of 1993 to segregate money received by the company from some of its licensees. The administrators' application was to determine the destination of moneys in the company's accounts which were the subject of claims by the licensees.

D

The licensees fell into several different categories: (1) those who sold their own goods but put the takings in the company's tills on standard terms which provided for them to receive from the company a payment equivalent to gross takings less returns and commission. This category was subdivided into those whose gross takings were in fact paid into a separate bank account and those whose takings were (through error) not so paid. (2) A second category of licensees had withdrawn from the proceedings. (3) The third category of licensees had non-standard forms of agreement which provided for their takings (less agreed commission and other agreed deductions) to be held on trust. This category was subdivided into the majority where no payments were made into the separate bank account and the minority which had the benefit both of an express trust stipulation and (in the event) of payment into a separate account.

E

F

The issues for the court were whether a category (3) licensee could trace into the company's general bank account in respect of sales after 8 December 1993, the last date on which the account was overdrawn; whether the company had by its actions in December 1993 in paying takings into segregated accounts created a trust in favour of claimants in the first subcategory (it being conceded that their standard-form agreements did not create a trust of the takings); and whether such a trust was a preference or transaction at an undervalue or infringed the rule of pari passu distribution.

G

Held, giving directions accordingly:

1. It was possible for the category (3) claimant to trace into the company's general bank account after it had returned to credit.

2. In relation to the category (1) claimants the mere opening of the new bank account was not without more sufficient to create a trust, but in this case there was evidence from which it could be inferred that the company did intend that moneys paid into the new account should be trust moneys. In that way the formula in the standard-form agreements was shifted from the contractual to a trust context. The trust covered the gross takings paid into the account and the company was a beneficiary under the trust to the extent of its right to commission.

H

A   3. The creation of the trust did not infringe s. 238 or 239 of the Insolvency Act 1986 or the residual principle of public policy striking down a mechanism outside charge or trust purporting to vary the rule of pari passu distribution in the event of insolvency.

The following cases were referred to in the judgment:

Barlow Clowes International Ltd v Vaughan [1992] 4 All ER 22.

Bishopsgate Investment Management Ltd v Homan & Ors [1994] BCC 868; [1995] Ch 211.

B   *British Eagle International Airlines Ltd v Compagnie Nationale Air France* [1975] 1 WLR 758.

Chelsea Cloisters Ltd, Re (1980) 41 P & CR 98.

Devaynes v Noble. Clayton's Case (1816) 1 Mer 572; 35 ER 781.

Eastern Capital Futures Ltd, Re (1989) 5 BCC 223.

Hallett's Estate, Re (1880) 13 ChD 696.

C   *Hunter v Moss* [1993] 1 WLR 934.

Kayford Ltd, Re [1975] 1 WLR 279.

M C Bacon Ltd, Re [1990] BCC 78.

Multi Guarantee Co Ltd, Re [1987] BCLC 257.

National Westminster Bank Ltd v Halesowen Presswork & Assemblies Ltd [1972] AC 785.

D   David Marks (instructed by Harvey Ingram, Leicester) for the administrators.

David Eaton Turner (instructed by Howes Percival, Northampton) for the first respondent.

Lexa Hilliard (instructed by Cole & Cole) for the third respondent.

JUDGMENT

E   **Robert Walker J:** This is an application for directions made under s. 14(3) of the *Insolvency Act* 1986 by the joint administrators of Lewis's of Leicester Ltd ('the company'). The company petitioned for an administration order on 31 December 1993 and the order was made, because of the urgency of the matter, on 5 January 1994. The only purpose of the administration order was to achieve a more advantageous realisation of the company's assets.

F   At that time the company was trading as a department store at Humberstone Gate, Leicester. It had a lease of the premises which was, since notice had been served under a break clause, known to be coming to an end on 9 February 1994. A substantial amount of rent was due under the lease. The staff (just over 100 part-time and full-time employees) had in October 1993 been given 90 days' notice that they were being made redundant. In these circumstances the administration had the very short-term purpose of enabling the store to remain open during the January sales period. It finally closed on 22 January 1994, leaving about three weeks to remove stock and vacate the premises before the lease G   ended on 9 February.

The matter on which the joint administrators seek directions arises from the unusually high degree to which the company used its department store as a base for concessions of the 'shop within a shop' variety. About 120,000 square feet, that is about half of the sales area of the store, was by the end of 1993 occupied by concessionaires who were licensees employing their own sales staff and owning their own merchandise, although the terms H   on which the merchandise was sold varied, and it is because of that and because of arrangements that were made at the end of 1993 to segregate money received by the company from some of its licensees, that this application has become necessary.

Before describing those matters in more detail I should perhaps go back a little further into the company's history as it appears from the second appendix to the financial report prepared by Pannell Kerr Forster. Before 1991 the store was owned by Lewis's Group

Ltd, which went into receivership at the beginning of 1991. After months of negotiations   A
the business was taken over by the company. The company had been formed by staff and
management who put up equity capital of £350,000. Loan capital was provided in the
form of a £400,000 overdraft from National Westminster Bank plc and a £100,000 loan
from British Coal Enterprises Ltd. Most unfortunately, trading under the staff/
management buy-out was unsuccessful, really it seems from the first, and the introduction
of more and more licensees was a means of easing the company's cash flow problems
since it was the licensees rather than the company who were tying up their capital in stock   B
held on the premises for retail sale. The company made a loss of about £547,000 in the
period from February to July 1992 (that is a period not including the all-important
Christmas and January sales season) and a loss of about £226,000 in the same period in
1993. In March 1993 the store was, in the words of appendix 2 of the report, put into a
closing down sale mode. It was decided to try to trade through Christmas 1993 but long
before then the final closure had been decided on.   C

The licensees fall, for the purpose of adjudicating on their claims, into several different
categories. This is reflected in the fact that there have in the course of this application
been five separate respondents, three in a representative capacity, but in the event only
two respondents have been represented before me. In describing the different categories
of licensees I should follow the terms used in the affidavit evidence and in counsel's
submissions, although some of the terminology is not particularly apt.   D

The first category is the concession holders who sold their own goods, although on
standard-form terms under which all the takings were paid into tills controlled by the
company which was under an obligation to pay to the concession holder, either on a
weekly or a monthly basis, a sum equal to the gross takings (including receipts from
credit sales) less (1) refunds made to customers on goods returned or exchanged during
the relevant period and (2) commission allowable to the company. Commission was at
different rates for different concession holders but 25 per cent was a typical figure. The   E
first category must in the events which happened be subdivided into those whose gross
takings were in fact paid and those whose gross takings were (through error) not paid
into the separate bank account which I shall mention shortly. (There were in fact two
separate bank accounts, but for the present I shall refer to them as a single account.) The
first subcategory number 24 and the second subcategory (inappropriately termed the
'deemed concession holders') number seven. Their claims amount in very round figures
to £65,000 and £15,000 respectively. I mention these figures only to show the relatively   F
small sums involved. I shall, as I am asked to, deal with the matter as a matter of principle
and not get involved with precise figures.

The first subcategory of concession holders are represented by the first respondent,
Kordenate Ltd, which appears by Mr Eaton Turner. The second subcategory was not
initially represented by anyone, but in the event Miss Hilliard, whose principal
constituency is the so-called hybrid category to which I shall come in a moment, has   G
without any material conflict of interest felt able to make submissions on behalf of the
second subcategory also, and Miss Hilliard has, for the assistance of the court, accepted
that further responsibility.

The second category of licensees were the so-called 'pay on sales' category. They also
had a standard-form agreement but in a crucially different form in that it provided for
their goods to become the property of the company immediately before sale to a   H
customer, so that the sale to the customer was treated as a purchase and subsale by the
company at an enhanced price, the difference corresponding to the company's
commission. The implications of this rather artificial arrangement as regards VAT were
faithfully reflected in the standard-form agreement. The pay on sale licensees, who
number 42, were not intended to participate and in no case did they participate in the
arrangement for a separate bank account. They were originally represented by the second

A respondent, the Original Trading Co Ltd, but last November, having taken counsel's opinion and found it unfavourable, the second respondent withdrew its claim and withdrew from the proceedings by consent on terms of getting its costs down to the time of its withdrawal. This seems to me to be a proper concession rightly made in order to save costs of arguing a hopeless claim, although I can well understand the strong feeling of the pay on sale licensees (whose total claims amount to about £200,000) when they found that they had in effect been unknowingly subsidising the final period of the company's trading activities. It is also thoroughly understandable that the hybrid category, who took the trouble to insist on express trust stipulations which were then ignored, should also feel aggrieved. In the circumstances any resolution of these questions is bound to seem arbitrary, but I have no jurisdiction to impose what I regard as a fair result rather than attempting an analysis of the legal consequences of the unfortunate sequence of events which in fact occurred.

B

C The third category of licensees have non-standard forms of agreement, apparently prepared by themselves rather than by the company, which expressly provided for the takings of their concessions, less the agreed commission and other agreed deductions, to be held in trust for them. The precise form of words varies, but in every case there was an express reference to a trust or trusteeship. The third category is again subdivided into the majority (numbering I think eight) where no payments were made into the separate bank account, and the fortunate minority, that is Dannimac Ltd and Antler Ltd, which had the benefit both of an express trust stipulation and (in the event) of payment into the separate account. The claims of these two companies are agreed to be irresistible and the parties have agreed a form of consent order, which I will make, for payment in full of their claims (but without interest) from the separate account. That again saves costs by dispensing with the need for separate representation of those two companies before me.

D

E The less fortunate majority of the hybrid category did not get the benefit of the separate banking arrangements, apparently because the company did not realise that their claims were as strong, indeed because of the express trust stipulation much stronger, than the first category of concession holders. It appears that the company did not check the non-standard forms of agreement or take advice at the time as to their legal effect. The company may not even have held copies of the non-standard agreements at its offices. This seems most regrettable to say the least, although I bear in mind that all this happened in circumstances of considerable stress and urgency. But on this application I am concerned only to determine the destination of moneys in the segregated accounts and the general bank accounts. That is the only subject-matter of this application.

F

As I have mentioned, Miss Hilliard appears for the representative of the hybrid category other than Dannimac and Antler, that is the third respondent, the Floridan Group Ltd. The total claims of this representative group (excluding Dannimac and Antler) are of the order of £65,000, of which about £25,000 relates to the period since 8 December 1993. The significance of that date is that it is the last date at which the company's general current account was overdrawn. Since that date, as is clearly shown in a schedule exhibited to an affidavit of Miss Elizabeth Dickin, there has always been a credit balance exceeding the amount of Miss Hilliard's hybrid clients' claims in respect of sales since that date.

G

Mr David Marks for the joint administrators has helpfully formulated the issues which I have to consider and decide. Apart from the consent order in respect of Dannimac and Antler which I have already covered, and costs which I defer, there are five issues as follows:

H

(1) Can Miss Hilliard's hybrid clients trace into the company's general bank account and assert a proprietary claim to the sum of about £25,000 in respect of their sales since 8 December 1993?

(2)   Can Mr Eaton Turner's clients in respect of whom payments were made into the   A
segregated account assert a proprietary claim as beneficial owners under the trust
in respect of the moneys equal to their gross takings after 21 December 1993 paid
into the segregated accounts? In short, and subject to the technical points in (3)
and (4) below, did the company's actions on 21 December 1993 (which I have yet
to describe in detail) coupled with payments into the new segregated account, and
the further segregated account which replaced it on the commencement of the
administration, effectively create a trust?   B

(3)   If so, was the creation of the trust a preference infringing s. 239 of the *Insolvency
Act* 1986 or a transaction at an undervalue infringing s. 238?

(4)   Was the creation of the trust an attempt to contract out of s. 107 of the *Insolvency
Act* 1986, and so ineffective on the principles stated by the House of Lords in
National Westminster Bank Ltd v Halesowen Presswork & Assemblies Ltd [1972]
AC 785 and *British Eagle International Airlines Ltd v Compagnie Nationale Air*   C
France [1975] 1 WLR 758?

(5)   If Mr Eaton-Turner succeeds on points (3) and (4) above how should the
segregated fund be distributed?

I can deal quite shortly with point (1) above and I shall then set out more fully the
facts relevant to the remaining points.   D

(1) Tracing by the hybrid concessionaires

It is clear that Miss Hilliard's clients had the benefit of express trust stipulations in
their agreements, but an express declaration of trust is no help in an insolvency unless
there is some identifiable trust property to which it relates. The Court of Appeal has
recently reaffirmed that (with a possible special exception for so-called backward tracing   E
which is not now relevant) equitable tracing cannot extend to an overdrawn bank
account. When the account becomes overdrawn the trail is lost and it can be picked up
again if the account returns to credit only in respect of later payments in of trust moneys
(*Bishopsgate Investment Management Ltd v Homan & Ors* [1994] BCC 868). But in respect
of the sum of about £25,000 of hybrid concessionaires' money paid into the company's
general account since it returned to credit on 9 December 1993 no one has argued that
tracing is not possible and appropriate, and I shall direct that tracing is both possible and   F
appropriate.

(2) Is the segregated account a trust account?

Mr Eaton Turner has not attempted to argue that the standard-form concession
holders whom he represents got the benefit of what would have amounted to an implied
trust stipulation in their agreements. I think he was right not to do so. The argument   G
would not have perhaps been completely hopeless, but I do not think I would have
accepted it, however fully and attractively it had been developed. Nevertheless Mr Eaton
Turner did point out that the commercial substance of the transaction between his clients
and the company was that the former became licensees of selling space for the latter,
almost like stall holders in a market, for a licence fee which was not fixed but varied with
the licensees' trading turnover. The express provisions for payment into tills controlled
by the company and general control over takings by the company can be seen, Mr Eaton   H
Turner suggests, as a practical means of ensuring that the company got its variable
licence fees by deduction at source.

I see considerable force in these submissions and I think they are relevant as part of
the commercial context (in the well-known phrase first used, I think, by Lord
Wilberforce) in which the first segregated account was opened shortly before Christmas

A 1993. At that time the company and its advisers, who had since 1991 included KPMG Peat Marwick (double-banked from December 1993 by Pannell Kerr Forster as the proposed administrators), knew that the company was insolvent and that the inevitable outcome was administration if ordered by the court and then, or alternatively, if there was no administration, winding up. (I add parenthetically that the company has not yet been wound up but only because it was thought best for saving costs for this application to continue to be made in the administration.)

B The various categories of licensees, by contrast, may not have been aware of the company's dire financial situation. Certainly they knew that the department store was to close, but they may have thought that that was because of the landlord's intention to redevelop the site after regaining vacant possession of the premises. The licensees had received a circular letter from the company in September 1993 but no party has put that letter in evidence. There is no point in my speculating on its contents, except to say it

C seems to me very unlikely that it gave either a clear or candid picture of the company's financial difficulties. I say that simply because if it had it seems inconceivable that at least some of the concession holders would not have taken a different course. The action taken by the company on 21 December 1993 was not therefore taken at the request of all or any of the licence holders. It was not even known to them, it seems, until 6 January 1994, the day after the administration order was made, when a meeting of licence holders was

D called and they were informed of the position.

The company's decision is recorded in minutes of a board meeting held on 29 December 1993. There is no suggestion that these minutes do not correctly record what had occurred just over a week before. I will read part of para. 4 headed 'Future of the store'.

E 'Following the correspondence noted in the minutes of the board meeting of 1 December, a meeting took place on 21 December with Messrs Brian and Bob Hamblin of Pannell Kerr Forster . . .' – they are of course the joint administrators now making this application – 'They were accompanied by Mr David Chapel of KPMG Peat Marwick and the mechanics of proceeding towards achieving an administration order were discussed in some detail.

It was agreed that concessions needed a high level of protection as the company was acting as an agent for handling their money and a new bank account was

F opened on 21/12/93 to cover this situation.'

The rest of the paragraph deals with preparations for the application for the administration order. That is, I believe, the only truly contemporaneous written indication of the company's intentions in setting up the new bank account.

It is obviously lacking in legal precision, but the same was true of the comparable

G arrangements considered by Megarry J in *Re Kayford Ltd* [1975] 1 WLR 279 and by the Court of Appeal in *Re Chelsea Cloisters Ltd* (1980) 41 P & CR 98. In the latter case there seems to have been no truly contemporaneous documentary evidence before the court at all, but the Court of Appeal had no hesitation in relying on the affidavit of Mr Iredale, who was the chartered accountant supervising the affairs of Chelsea Cloisters Ltd at the material time, as to his intentions (see especially the speech of Bridge LJ at p. 103).

H The separate bank account was opened on 21 December and the gross takings of some but not all of the licence holders was, as I have already mentioned in describing the different classes of claimants, paid into it. Another account replaced it when the administration order was made. There is a good deal of affidavit evidence about the intentions of the company's directors (especially Mr Peter Wilson who has made more than one affidavit), acting as they were on the advice of chartered accountants (including the two accountants who have since become the joint administrators). I will not set out

all of the relevant passages verbatim, but the affidavits of both Mr Brian Hamblin and   A
Mr Robert Hamblin indicate that they advised that the separate account should be set
up in order to segregate third party moneys, that is moneys that did not belong to the
company.

Paragraph 5 of the accountants' report, prepared in support of the administration
petition, refers to the money in the separate accounts being subject to a trust. Perhaps
most important, Mr Wilson in his most recent affidavit sworn on 29 November 1994   B
said:

> 'It was agreed that a fund should be set up to protect those operators who had
> "money only" clauses by which was meant those operators whose money the
> company was holding rather than their goods. So far as the directors were
> concerned these were third party moneys and as such should be protected because
> they did not belong to the company. I was of the view that those operators' moneys
> should be held in "trust" for them and a separate account was therefore opened   C
> that day. All the sales receipts taken by those operators were to be paid into that
> account and the company was thereby giving up its claim to those moneys.'

Then a little further down he said:

> 'Once the administration order was made the intention was to distribute the
> moneys to the operators that they were paid in for, subject of course to their being
> entitled to those moneys.'   D

This important evidence has in the course of the hearing attracted a good deal of
discussion and a certain amount of criticism (including I may say criticism from Mr
Marks, who took the opportunity to inform me that he did not draft that particular
affidavit).

For my part, I have found the reference to a 'money only' clause rather baffling, but
on any view the passages which I have read are indicative of Mr Wilson's belief that the   E
money of Mr Eaton Turner's clients, or at least the balance of it after payment of
commission, did not belong to the company. It is true that in the last sentence which I
have quoted Mr Wilson has added 'subject of course to their being entitled to those
moneys', but that prudent qualification is plainly justified having regard to the variety
and sophistication of the arguments which have been placed before me. It does not to my
mind affect the substance of Mr Wilson's affidavit evidence on this point.

In setting up the separate account the company, acting on professional advice, was   F
intending to achieve something sensible. There are, it seems to me, only three possible
explanations of what it was intending to do: first, to ensure that future receipts of
concession holders' takings, believed to be already subject to a trust under the standard-
form agreements, were kept separate and identifiable; second, to ensure that future
receipts of concession holders' takings, although not trust moneys under the existing
standard-form agreements, should become trust moneys and should be kept separate and   G
identifiable; third, simply to preserve the status quo pending legal advice at a later date.

Mr Marks, making submissions on behalf of the general body of unsecured creditors,
has argued moderately but persuasively for the third possibility, that is maintaining the
status quo or, as he put it, holding the ring. With hindsight, action simply to hold the
ring (and probably in respect of all the different categories of licensees) might have been
a sensible course. But it seems to me it is simply not what the affidavit evidence points to.   H
With the bare exception of the words 'subject of course to their being entitled to those
moneys' which I have already commented on, the evidence points, to my mind quite
clearly, to the first of the three possible explanations – the company thought that these
moneys simply were not the company's moneys. The company was therefore, in view of
Mr Eaton Turner's correct concession as to the construction of the standard-form
concession agreement, mistaken in its belief in a pre-existing trust.

A   Mr Marks and Miss Hilliard have submitted that this mistake is one reason, and a compelling reason, for ruling against the creation of a trust, since if a person believes that he is already a trustee he cannot logically intend to create a trust for the first time, except I suppose if he is acting simply for the avoidance of doubt. Mr Wilson and his advisers do not seem to have felt much, if any, doubt in December 1993 that the concession holders' takings were indeed third party moneys. But in the *Chelsea Cloisters* case this very point was considered by Bridge LJ, who said at p. 103:

B

'It may even be that Mr Iredale supposed that the terms of clause 1 of the tenancy agreement had in fact impressed these deposits with a trust. That would have left unresolved the question arising out of the terms of that agreement. But, if he was mistaken in that belief, it would not – as Mr Parker has satisfied me in his reply – have prevented his intention from being effective, if his intention in setting aside what he believed to be trust moneys was to ensure that they were available for what he believed to be the trust purposes.'

C

Mr Marks submits that this is dictum which I need not and should not follow, but I find it does give me useful guidance. If a person thinks that he ought to segregate property subject to an existing trust and acts accordingly, the court may infer that that existing property and, a fortiori as it seems to me, subsequent receipts which he pays into the same account, are effectively impressed with the trust.

D   The evidence from which such an intention can be inferred is in my judgment stronger in the present case than in the *Chelsea Cloisters* case. In the passage from the affidavit of Mr Wilson which I have already quoted the word 'trust' is indeed explicitly used, albeit in inverted commas. I fully accept Mr Marks' submission that the mere opening of a new bank account is not without more sufficient to create a trust, but in this case there is, it seems to me, much more to the evidence than that. I infer that the company did intend that moneys paid into the new account should be trust moneys.

E   Apart from technical points on the Insolvency Act, the other submissions made to me by Mr Marks and Miss Hilliard against an effective trust largely turned on the three certainties necessary for the creation of a trust. In this case, because of the rather rudimentary character of the trust contended for, the three tests of certainty – that is words, subject-matter and objects – tend to run into each other. In particular, some rather imprecise language in para. 4 of Mr Wilson's affidavit, from which I have already quoted and on which I have already commented, has led to a debate as to whether there was a trust of the concession holders' net entitlements (that is after commission and any adjustments for goods returned) under which the concession holders were entitled to 100 per cent of the beneficial interest, or a trust of the gross takings under which the concession holders were entitled to part only, to be computed by the application to different constituent parts of the fund, of different commission percentages and by any

F

G   necessary adjustment for returns.

It has also been submitted, especially by Mr Marks, that the need for a complex formula, not specified or even hinted at in the board resolution, is a strong reason for scepticism as to the creation of a trust. Again, Mr Marks developed this submission persuasively, but I am not convinced by it for several reasons. First, there was no need for the board resolution to state or restate the appropriate formula. It was there in the standard-form agreements (cl. 4) and the formula had simply to be shifted from a contractual context to a trust context in just the same way as it was in the *Re Kayford Ltd* and the *Chelsea Cloisters Ltd* cases. Secondly, the formula was not particularly complex. Clause 4 of the standard-form agreement is reasonably simple and straightforward, as indeed are the express trust stipulations which were in Miss Hilliard's clients' non-standard agreements from the beginning (although most regrettably, as we have seen, they were overlooked except in the cases of Dannimac and Antler). Third,

H

even if the formula had been much more complicated, the trust is a versatile medium   A
which can be and is used for a wide variety of commercial purposes, sometimes involving
very complicated arrangements. As just one instance out of many I could refer to the
clauses dealing with equalisation of income distributions commonly found in the trust
deeds of authorised unit trusts. If it is objected that those clauses are expertly drafted and
precise and that that is what saves them from uncertainty I think it may be said, as Mr
Eaton Turner did say in his reply, that even in their absence the court would not be
inclined to wash its hands of the matter and declare that the trust was too uncertain to   B
be given effect to, but would if necessary give directions as to the proper methods of trust
accountancy to be used to work out the details of the trust operation. Mr Colin Rimer
QC seems to have taken much the same view when in *Hunter v Moss* [1993] 1 WLR 934
at p. 945 he was invited to consider (or perhaps I should say inveigled into considering)
various hypothetical questions which had certainly not been raised in *Re Kayford Ltd.*

Coming back to the general issue of certainty of subject-matter and objects it is in my   C
judgment clear that the intention was to subject to a trust everything that was paid into
the new account. It was a situation of stress and urgency and the new arrangement had
to be one which was capable of being put in place quickly and operated reasonably
simply. All the gross takings were to go into the new account. But it seems to me, despite
Mr Wilson's apparent (but I think inadvertent) statement to the contrary, the company
had no intention of giving up its right to commission in respect of sums paid into the
account, and the company was therefore a beneficiary under the trust to the extent of   D
those rights in respect of commission. Apart from *Hunter v Moss*, Mr Marks also showed
me two cases on claims to boxes of wine arising in the liquidation of wine merchants. I
do not think I need refer to those cases any further as they were dealing with such a
different subject-matter, but I should perhaps refer to a passage on which Mr Marks
relied in *Re Multi Guarantee Co Ltd* [1987] BCLC 257 at p. 266H where Nourse LJ said:

> '... common sense suggests to me that it is almost inconceivable that [the director   E
> in question] could have intended that [the action taken in that case] should result
> in Multi Guarantee's being thereafter divested of all possible beneficial interest in
> the moneys.'

I would indeed echo that comment, despite what Mr Wilson has deposed to, and say that
it is inconceivable that the company in this case intended to give up a claim to commission
in respect of the money paid into the separate account. But I do not read Nourse LJ's   F
words, directed as they were to the particular and unusual facts of the *Multi Guarantee*
case, as excluding the possibility of a trust of money to be divided according to a known
or ascertainable formula with the company participating as a beneficiary under that
formula. *Re Kayford Ltd* and *Re Chelsea Cloisters Ltd* are indeed both examples of that
type of case where the company participated, to the extent of payments for filled orders
in the former case and payments in respect of proper dilapidation claims in the latter
case.   G

For these reasons I decide the second issue in favour of Mr Eaton Turner. It is no
disrespect to counsel or to their interesting submissions that I shall deal with the next
three points much more quickly.

(3) Preference and transaction at undervalue

  H

In my judgment there is nothing in this case that infringes s. 238 or 239 of the *Insolvency
Act* 1986. It seems to me reasonably clear from the evidence that the company took the
action that it did on the advice of experienced insolvency practitioners for two principal
reasons: first in the company's interests because the company was, no doubt rightly,
concerned that a sudden defection of licence holders, possibly just before Christmas,
would make the store look more like a morgue than a market during its final weeks of

A   trading; and secondly, because the company thought that the concession holders who were believed to have this right were entitled to have this action taken (and indeed some of them were, although unfortunately it was only in two cases that the company was correct about the identities of those who were undoubtedly entitled to the right).

Going back to the first of these reasons, I recognise that there is an apparent lack of logic about taking action in order to provide a reassurance to licence-holders and keep
B   them trading in the store if they are then not told of this action taken in their interests. This is a question to which I see no wholly satisfying answer, unless it be, as was suggested to me, that in this hectic pre-Christmas period there was simply not enough time to do everything which would have been done had there been more time to reflect on the position and all its implications. But at least it can be said that once the separate account was in place it could be used to reassure any concessionaire who, hearing rumours perhaps of the company's financial difficulties, went to the company's management and
C   sought reassurance.

However that may be, it seems to me on the evidence that there was no intention, still less any desire, to grant a preference in what the company did just before last Christmas. In the light of *Re M C Bacon Ltd* [1990] BCC 78 (see especially at p. 87) I find this a conclusive answer to the suggested argument for an improper preference, and I find it unnecessary to consider the further submissions that I heard, interesting though they are,
D   as to the precise meaning in this sort of context of the expression 'creditor'. I note in passing that Oliver LJ in the remarks which he made about a possible improper preference in the *Chelsea Cloisters* case specifically limited his remarks to the amount of deposits which had already been paid and were in Mr Iredale's hands at the time the account was opened. They were in a sense therefore assets of Chelsea Cloisters Ltd which were being, on one view, subjected to a trust for the first time rather than being receipts which came in to the company and from the moment of their receipt went straight into a
E   trust mechanism. But it is not, it seems to me, necessary for me to go into that point further, nor do I base my decision on it.

There was also in my judgment no transaction at an undervalue. The company's assets were not diminished by what was in substance an arrangement for accelerated payment of future – and I emphasise only future – sums due to concession holders in respect of trading which took place in the future.
F

(4) The British Eagle point

Mr Marks was right to draw this point to my attention, but having considered it I am quite unconvinced that there is a problem here under this residual principle of public policy. The principle is probably limited, it seems to me, to cases where parties have, albeit for good commercial reasons, attempted to use the law of contract to create a
G   mechanism outside the familiar fields of charge or trust which will in the event of one party's insolvency purport to vary the pari passu principle now embodied in s. 107 of the *Insolvency Act* 1986. If I am right so far, the company set up a valid trust mechanism which does not fall foul of either s. 238 or s. 239 of the Insolvency Act, and the trust mechanism cannot in my judgment be caught by this further residual principle which, at least since the coming into force of the *Insolvency Act* 1986, must now apply only in
H   special cases of the type mentioned above.

(5) The destination of the segregated fund

If I am right so far, the segregated fund is held in trust for the so-called concession holders (but not the so-called deemed concession holders or the hybrids) and, to the extent of its claim for commission, the company. The concession holders must in my view participate rateably both as between themselves and with the company according to their

net entitlements, that is (in the case of the concession-holders) net of commission, which   **A**
is as I have said at varying rates, and net of refunds on returned goods, if any. This is not
a case where the company has in any meaningful sense mixed trust money with its own –
quite the reverse – and so I see no reason to apply the rule in *Re Hallett's Estate* (1880)
13 ChD 696, nor has any counsel before me contended that I should. Nor is it appropriate
in my view to consider applying the first in, first out principle in accordance with
Clayton's Case (1816) 1 Merrivale 572. To do so would in my judgment be an expensive
and pointless exercise (see *Re Eastern Capital Futures Ltd* (1989) 5 BCC 223, a decision   **B**
of Morritt J, and the decision of the Court of Appeal in *Barlow Clowes International Ltd
v Vaughan* (1992) 4 All ER 22).

(Order accordingly)

—————————

C

D

E

F

G

H

A
Re a Debtor No. 10 of 1992.
Peck v Craighead & Ors.

Chancery Division (in bankruptcy).
Martin Mann QC (sitting as a deputy High Court judge).
Judgment delivered 18 January 1995.

B
Individual voluntary arrangements – Whether meeting approving IVAs had wrongly affected right of secured creditor – Whether execution creditor with benefit of seizure under writ of fi. fa. was secured creditor – Whether there was a material irregularity at creditors' meeting – Insolvency Act 1986, s. 258(4), 262, 383(2).

These were applications by a creditor under s. 262 of the Insolvency Act 1986 challenging
C
approval of individual voluntary arrangements.

The applicant had obtained a judgment against the debtors; execution proceeded under a writ of fi. fa. and the sheriff took walking possession of chattels. Thereafter the debtors' IVAs were approved.

The applicant contended that his interests as a creditor had been unfairly prejudiced under s. 262(1)(a) on three grounds: first, that approval of the IVAs contravened his rights as a secured creditor under s. 258(4); the second and third grounds assumed that he was not a
D
secured creditor.

Held, directing a further meeting under s. 262(4)(b):

There was no reason in principle to conclude that an execution creditor's security constituted by seizure under a fi. fa. was excluded from s. 258(4). The applicant was a secured creditor for the purposes of s. 258(4) whose security right had been wrongly affected by the approval of the IVAs. That was a material irregularity within s. 262(1)(b).

E
The following cases were referred to in the judgment:

Clarke (Charles), Re [1898] 1 Ch 336.
Slater v Pinder (1871) LR 6 Ex 228; (1872) LR 7 Ex 95.
Williams, Ex parte (1872) LR 7 Ch App 314.

Lexa Hilliard (instructed by Carter Vincent Jones Davis, Bangor) for the applicant.

F
Mark Cawson (instructed by Rosalind Hallifax & Co) for the debtors.

John Briggs (instructed by Booth & Co, Leeds) for the supervisor.

JUDGMENT

Martin Mann QC: On 6 January 1993 Raymond Craighead and Patricia Craighead ('Mr and Mrs Craighead') received the approval of a meeting of creditors summoned
G
under s. 257 of the *Insolvency Act* 1986 to individual voluntary arrangements ('IVAs') in identical terms. (In the remainder of this judgment references to statutory provisions will be to the Insolvency Act unless otherwise indicated.) The precise terms of the IVAs are largely immaterial, though I shall make reference to specific effects later in this judgment. Neither is much of the detail of the events which led to their having to enter into the IVAs, as an alternative to bankruptcy, material, although, inevitably, certain of it is and to that extent I shall recount it.

H
Applications in respect of the IVAs are now before this court by way of transfer from the Bangor County Court. They consist of two sets of identical consolidated applications for s. 262 relief and declarations. In each case the applicant is Julian Hannavelle Ackroyd Peck ('Mr Peck').

Mr Peck is a creditor of Mr and Mrs Craighead in the following circumstances (so far as material). Mr and Mrs Craighead acquired and ran as partners a country house hotel

in North Wales. Mr Peck invested £25,000 in the venture and was employed as general   A
manager but otherwise had no interest in it. The hotel turned out to be seriously affected
by dry rot. It could not open to the public as anticipated and expected revenue inflows
were inadequate to service the debt incurred to the National Westminster Bank plc ('the
bank') on the acquisition and for working capital and to pay trade creditors.

Having come under pressure from their creditors, Mr and Mrs Craighead each decided
to accept the shelter of the statutory moratorium available to applicants under s. 252 and   B
to propose individual voluntary arrangements. They applied for and obtained interim
orders on 15 October 1992. Mr Craighead's proposal (which, in effect, subsumed Mrs
Craighead's) noted negligible assets, that the bank was a secured creditor in respect of
the hotel to the extent of about £600,000 of a debt of £1.3m and unsecured creditors in
substantial amounts such that their appeared to be a deficit as regards unsecured creditors
of about £1.2m of which some were preferential but the bulk were trade creditors. It also
noted (inter alia) that creditors might expect to receive a better distribution pursuant to   C
the IVAs than they would in a bankruptcy.

Final approval under s. 257 was, as I have stated, secured on 6 January 1993. Such
approval was to modifications of original proposals. I have not been told the date of the
report to the court with respect to the creditors' meeting under s. 259 but it is axiomatic
that there was such a report and common ground that Mr Peck's challenges under s. 262
were within time, that is, within 28 days of the report, when issued on 2 February 1993.   D

As to the terms of the IVAs: these envisaged the supervisor selling the hotel as a going
concern, Mr and Mrs Craighead in the meantime to receive a small income out of trading
profits should any arise. The supervisor was to monitor the business and to call a meeting
of creditors for the purpose of reconsidering this state of affairs should the business turn
out to have traded unprofitably for any period exceeding two months. It was implicit
that the bank, though secured only as to part of its debt, would not enforce its security   E
until sale. Other than household and personal effects, no assets were to be excluded from
the IVAs.

In the meantime, Mr Peck had on 9 March 1992 commenced an action in the Bangor
District Registry of the High Court against Mr and Mrs Craighead for arrears of salary
and repayment of his investment. His total claim plus interest amounted to somewhat
over £54,040. A default judgment was entered on 10 April 1992 and on 14 April 1992   F
execution proceeded under a writ of fi. fa.

Several interlocutory applications followed the entry of the default judgment but
eventually Mr and Mrs Craighead consented to judgment in respect of part of Mr Peck's
claim, that is, for £35,000 and costs, on the basis that the balance of the claim would go
to trial. The consent judgment was made on 17 June 1992.

The sheriff acted immediately under the fi. fa. by taking walking possession over some   G
626-odd chattels comprising most, if not all, of the hotel furniture, furnishings, fittings
and motor vehicles ('the chattels').

It is obvious that the business could not have been continued had the chattels been
sold by the sheriff, since they could not realistically have been replaced. Unsurprisingly,
therefore, one of the interlocutory applications to which I have made brief reference was
for a stay of execution while yet another was an interpleader by the sheriff, who, or   H
course, needed to know how matters stood; not least because he needed to know to whom
he should look for his charges amounting, I have been told, to £4,000. The interpleader
was issued on 20 August 1992 but has not been heard.

It is convenient to note in this context s. 252(2), which provides:

'An interim order has the effect that, during the period for which it is in force –

A

      (a) no bankruptcy petition relating to the debtor may be presented or proceeded with, and

      (b) no other proceedings, and no execution or other legal process, may be commenced or continued against the debtor or his property except with the leave of the court.'

–and s. 254, which provides:

B

    '(1) At any time when an application under section 253 for an interim order is pending, the court may stay an action, execution or other legal process against the property or person of the debtor.

    (2) Any court in which proceedings are pending against an individual may, on proof that an application under that section has been made in respect of that individual, either stay the proceedings or allow them to continue on such terms as it thinks fit.'

C

The interim order has not been renewed since its automatic lapse 28 days after the report to the court under s. 259.

Accordingly, if Mr Peck is a secured creditor, there is no longer anything (absent any prior security right) to prevent the sheriff selling the chattels or to prevent Mr Peck giving him a good receipt for the proceeds of sale to the extent of his debt and the sheriff's charges. This is because secured creditors are in the special position recognised by s. 258(4). The subsection provides:

D

    'The meeting shall not approve any proposal or modification which affects the right of a secured creditor of the debtor to enforce his security, except with the concurrence of the creditor concerned.'

E

It is a fortiori that if a meeting approves a proposal or modification which in some way affects or purports non-consensually to affect security rights its business is to such extent irregular and legally ineffective. However, in my judgment, that fact can only be asserted by challenging the meeting's decision under s. 262 because subs. (8) of that section provides:

    'Except in pursuance of the preceding provisions of this section, an approval given at a creditors' meeting summoned under section 257 is not invalidated by any irregularity at or in relation to the meeting.'

F

It is noteworthy that Mr Peck challenges the IVAs on grounds that they unfairly prejudiced his interests as a creditor rather than on grounds of irregularity.

However, it is first for determination whether an execution creditor who has the benefit of a walking possession agreement entered into by a sheriff under a fi. fa. is a secured creditor for the purposes of s. 258(4).

G

Section 383(2) provides:

    'Subject to the next two subsections and any provision of the rules requiring a creditor to give up his security for the purposes of proving his debt, a debt is secured for the purposes of this Group of Parts to the extent that the person to whom the debt is owed holds *any* security for the debt (whether a mortgage, charge, lien or *other* security) over any property of the person by whom the debt is owed.'

H

(emphasis added)

Section 383(4) provides:

    'In subsection (2) the reference to a security does not include a lien on books, papers or other records, except to the extent that they consist of documents which give a title to property and are held as such.'

These subsections offer the only express statutory guidance. However, it is clear from   A
the breadth of the language and the express exclusion of specific types of lien that
subs. (2) contemplates, quite literally, *any* security afforded recognition under the law.

There is therefore no reason in principle to conclude that an execution creditor's
security constituted by seizure under a fi. fa. is excluded from s. 258(4) absent any limiting
provision; and there is none. For the proposition that a security is so constituted, see per
Lindley MR in *Re Charles Clarke* [1898] 1 Ch 336 at p. 339:   B

> 'It is very true that the property in goods seized under a fi. fa. remains in the
> execution debtor until sale: *Giles* v. *Grover* 1 Cl. & F. 72. But it is no less true that
> after seizure and before sale the execution creditor is as regards those goods in the
> position of a secured creditor: see *Ex parte Williams* L.R. 7 Ch. App. 314 and
> *Slater* v. *Pinder* L.R. 7 Ex. 95. He had a legal right as against the execution debtor
> – i.e. owner of the goods – to have the goods sold and to be paid out the proceeds
> of sale.'   C

Ex parte Williams, cited above, was not read to me in argument and I shall not cite it
here, but I have found it instructive as to the nature of the security right since it explains
that at common law the execution creditor had security from the teste of the writ of fi. fa.
but that this was changed as regards third parties by the Statute of Frauds to the date of
the delivery of the writ to the sheriff (which, in the sense that a writ binds the property in
the debtor's goods, is the position today by virtue of s. 138(1) of the *Supreme Court Act*   D
1981). The sheriff obtained a qualified property in the goods upon seizure like that of a
factor, albeit distinct from that of a legal mortgagee, but until then he merely had a right
of seizure. This right, Sir G Mellish LJ decided, could not properly be called a security
(pp. 317–318 of the judgment).

I infer that the security right which an execution creditor has under a fi. fa., which has
been acted upon by seizure, is not unlike a lien, which is a security right expressly   E
contemplated by s. 383(2). The fact that such a security right has not been enforced is
nothing to the point. It is enough that the debtor's property in the goods is bound. It is
clearly irrelevant that the property has not yet passed out of the debtor's hands as on
completion of the execution by sale.

By contrast, there is a statutory limiting provision in the bankruptcy context. For that
circumstance, s. 346(1) provides: F

> 'Subject to section 285 in Chapter II (restrictions on proceedings and remedies)
> and to the following provisions of this section, where the creditor of any person
> who has been adjudged bankrupt has, before the commencement of the
> bankruptcy–
>
> (a) issued execution against the goods or land of that person, or
>
> (b) attached a debt due to that person from another person,   G
>
> that creditor is not entitled, as against the official receiver or trustee of the
> bankrupt's estate, to retain the benefit of the execution or attachment, or any sums
> paid to avoid it, unless the execution or attachment was completed, or the sums
> were paid, before the commencement of the bankruptcy.'

And s. 346(5) (so far as material) provides:

> 'For the purposes of this section–   H
>
> (a) an execution against goods is completed by seizure *and* sale . . .' (emphasis
> added)

Hence, in bankruptcy an execution creditor is deprived of his security right under a fi. fa.
delivered to the sheriff until after the property in the debtor's goods seized has passed out
of the debtor's hands.

A   Since there is but one definition of secured creditor it might perhaps be concluded that
           Parliament intended the treatment accorded to such execution creditors in bankruptcy to
           be the same for an IVA. However, an examination of the origins of s. 346 suffices to
           dispel any doubts in this respect, for although s. 346 sits within a new insolvency code it
           is nonetheless the successor of the *Bankruptcy Act* 1914, s. 40, which reinstated the effects
           of s. 184 of the *Bankruptcy Act* 1849 (repealed by the *Bankruptcy Act* 1869), and its
           purpose must be construed accordingly. These sections were enacted to provide execution
B   creditors who had obtained security over a debtor's goods under a fi. fa. and sheriffs with
           a degree of protection from the effects of the doctrine of relation back which upon
           adjudication served automatically to divest the creditor of the security so obtained in
           favour of the debtor's assignee: see the helpful treatise in *Slater v Pinder* (1871) LR 6 Ex
           228 at p. 234. (Cf., in the company context, s. 183 – the successor of the *Companies Act*
           1948, s. 325.)

C   It is unsurprising that there is no comparable provision applicable to an IVA because
           in this situation the supervisor does not obtain the property in the debtor's goods or any
           prior right to it. The execution creditor does not find that his security has been divested
           and the sheriff does not become a wrongdoer by virtue of the IVA if he deals with the
           goods.

           In my judgment, therefore, Mr Peck is a secured creditor for the purposes of s. 258(4)
D   whose security right has been wrongly affected by the approval of the IVAs. I interpose
           that it has not been asserted that Mr Peck consented to his security right being affected,
           and that it was intended to be so affected is self-evident from the terms of the IVAs which
           I have described.

           Section 262 (so far as material) provides:

               '(1) Subject to this section, an application to the court may be made, by any person
E   specified below, on one or both of the following grounds, namely–

                   (a) that a voluntary arrangement approved by a creditors' meeting summoned
                        under s. 257 unfairly prejudices the interests of a creditor of the debtor;

                   (b) that there has been some material irregularity at or in relation to such a
                        meeting.'

           It must follow that the creditors' meeting which on 6 January 1993 approved the IVAs
F   was materially irregular in the sense of subs. (1)(b) rather than unfairly prejudicial in the
           sense of subs. (1)(a).

           However, Mr Peck also contends that his interests as a creditor have been unfairly
           prejudiced on three grounds. These, broadly stated, are, first, that the meeting
           contravened s. 258(4), as I have held it did. The other two grounds predicate that Mr
           Peck is not a secured creditor. They are, second, that because the IVAs incorporate no
G   provision for the payment of the sheriff's charges as an expense of the administration he
           will have to meet those charges himself yet will receive no corresponding benefit from the
           seizure; and, third, that the IVAs are inherently unfair to unsecured creditors in his
           position because only the bank and the hotel's suppliers will benefit if the business trades
           profitably until sale while their interests must be correspondingly harmed if it does not
           do so (which in the event turned out to be the case).

H   Mr Peck argued these unfair prejudice points against the possibility of failure under
           s. 258(4), but while he has challenged under s. 262(1)(a) he has not done so under
           s. 262(1)(b). Even so, technically he has succeeded, and the procedural irregularity is not
           such, in my judgment, as to cause any discernible prejudice to anyone. Subject to
           submissions of counsel for the parties, therefore, I am minded to allow Mr Peck to amend
           his s. 262 application to introduce the subs. (1)(b) condition as a ground. The amendment
           is necessary because, in my judgment, irregularity involving unlawfulness at a meeting of

creditors is conceptually different from unfair prejudice which predicates unfairness   A
inherent in a proposal or modification which otherwise lawfully affects a creditor's
interest.

I shall deal with the second and third unfair prejudice grounds in short order since they
do not now arise. As to the second, it is, in my judgment, clear that there is no relevant
unfairness if I am incorrect in holding that Mr Peck is entitled to a security right which
has been wrongly affected by the IVAs. This is because the unfairness complained of   B
stems from statute rather than from the IVAs for they simply omit to make provision
which Parliament, in its wisdom, did not ordain unreasonable or unfair to exclude as a
statutory requirement. The weakness of the proposition that the omission renders the
IVAs unfairly prejudicial is, moreover, exemplified by the fact that if such were held to
be the case, it is practically impossible to conceive of any case in which an IVA similarly
deficient could not be challenged successfully on precisely the same ground.

The third ground begs the question whether and in what circumstances the court   C
should interfere with the commercial judgment of men of business failing evidence of bad
faith and absent any statutory indication that the objectives of a majority of creditors by
value can be circumscribed by the judiciary. The possibility, as yet unproven and, I have
to say, barely articulated, that the majority might in this case have been interested in the
hotel continuing to trade, even at a loss for a short while, for reasons not necessarily
wholly connected with the prospect of a sale as a going concern at an enhanced price is   D
not, in my judgment, sufficient to discharge the burden of proof which rests upon a
minority to show that his or its interests as a creditor are unfairly prejudiced.

Subject to the amendment which I am minded to allow, the remedy which Mr Peck
seeks as a consequence of the infringement of s. 258(4) is a declaration (so far as material)
that the execution can proceed notwithstanding the IVAs. If necessary, I shall make
one, but it will be conditioned upon the exercise of the court's powers under s. 262.
By subs. (4):   E

'Where on an application under this section the court is satisfied as to either of the
grounds mentioned in subsection (1), it may do one or both of the following,
namely–

(a) revoke or suspend any approval given by the meeting;

(b) give a direction to any person for the summoning of a further meeting of the   F
      debtor's creditors to consider any revised proposal he may make . . .'

There is, however, power under subs. (6) and (7) to give further and supplemental
directions.

I have not heard argument concerning the exercise of my discretion. Subject, therefore,
to such further argument as the parties through their counsel wish to advance, I am
presently minded to give a direction under subs. (4)(b) rather than immediately to revoke   G
or suspend the approval given on 6 January 1993 and, if appropriate, to renew the
interim order in the meantime.

(*Order accordingly*)

H

A **Soden & Anor v British & Commonwealth Holdings plc & Anor.**
Chancery Division.
Robert Walker J.
Judgment delivered 12 April and 27 April 1995.

B
Scheme of arrangement – Liability of contributories – Parent sued insolvent subsidiary for misrepresentation – Whether any damages awarded to parent would be due to parent in its 'character of a member' – Whether parent's claim would be subordinated – Whether separate class meeting required to approve arrangement – Companies Act 1985, s. 425; Insolvency Act 1986, s. 74(2)(f).

This was an originating summons by the administrators of Atlantic Computers plc who had proposed a scheme of arrangement under s. 425 of the Companies Act 1985 which was approved by creditors and sanctioned by the court.

C
Before its collapse Atlantic had been acquired by British & Commonwealth Holdings plc ('B & C'), advised by Barclays de Zoete Wedd ('BZW'), for a total consideration in cash and shares of over £400m. The collapse of Atlantic led to the collapse of B & C which also went into administration.

After the scheme of arrangement between Atlantic and its creditors was approved, B & C commenced two actions, one against Atlantic and others (all but one of whom were directors of Atlantic) for damages for negligent misrepresentations said to have induced B & C to acquire

D Atlantic's shares, and a second against BZW for damages for breach of duty. In the second action BZW issued a third-party notice against (among others) Atlantic claiming indemnity, contribution and damages.

On the basis that success by B & C in its claim against Atlantic would turn it from a holder of worthless shares into a creditor, the administrators sought the determination of the court on the question whether damages awarded to B & C would be sums owing to B & C 'in (its) character of a member' within the meaning of s. 74(2)(f) of the Insolvency Act

E 1986 (though Atlantic was not yet in liquidation). The same question arose if BZW was found liable to B & C and succeeded in its third-party proceedings against Atlantic. (Subsidiary questions related to whether successful claims by B & C and BZW against Atlantic would give rise to 'scheme liabilities' under the scheme of arrangement.)

Held, ruling accordingly:

1. For a sum to be due to a member in his character of a member by way of dividends, profits or otherwise it had to result from a claim directly relating to the contractual nexus between

F company and members and members amongst themselves ('the corporate nexus'). This was the right approach to identifying a claim as characteristically a member's claim, rather than just a claim which happened to be made by a member.

2. The question was therefore whether a claim made by an open-market purchaser of shares in a company such as B & C (as opposed to an original subscriber or allottee), the claim being based on negligent misrepresentation by the company as to its assets, was sufficiently closely related to the corporate nexus as to be characteristically a member's claim.

G
3. The wrong of which B & C and BZW complained was separate from any transaction by which any original holder took up shares and so became a member of the company and was not sufficiently central as to lead to their claims being characterised as claims by members as such. (Webb Distributors (Aust) Pty Ltd v State of Victoria (1993) 11 ACLC 1178 followed.)

4. Atlantic's administrators were right to proceed on the footing that (apart from preferential and secured creditors) there was only one class of ordinary unsecured creditors,

H and no need for separate class meetings.

The following cases were referred to in the judgments:

Addlestone Linoleum Co, Re (1887) 37 ChD 191.
Automatic Bread Baking Co, Re (1939) 40 NSW 1.
Barclays Bank plc & Ors v British & Commonwealth Holdings plc [1995] BCC 19.
Borland's Trustee v Steel Brothers & Co Ltd [1901] 1 Ch 279.
British & Commonwealth Holdings plc, Re (No. 3) [1992] BCC 58; [1992] 1 WLR 672.

Cinnamond Park & Co Ltd, Re [1929] NI 47.   A
Dale and Plant Ltd, Re (1889) 43 ChD 255.
Dividend Fund Inc, Re [1974] VR 451.
Eutrope (W H) & Sons Pty Ltd, Re [1932] VLR 453.
Harlou Pty Ltd, Re [1950] VLR 449.
Holliday (L B) & Co Ltd, Re (1986) 2 BCC 99,031.
Houldsworth v City of Glasgow Bank (1880) 5 App Cas 317.
Howard's Will Trusts, Re [1961] Ch 507.
Leicester Club and County Racecourse Co, Re, ex parte Cannon (1885) 30 ChD 629.   B
New British Iron Co, Re, ex parte Beckwith [1898] 1 Ch 324.
New Chile Gold Mining Co, Re (1890) 45 ChD 598.
Ooregum Gold-Mining Co of India v Roper [1892] AC 125.
Prenn v Simmonds [1971] 1 WLR 1381.
Pyramid Building Society, Re (1992) 10 ACLC 1205.
Simpson (Harry) & Co Pty Ltd, Re (1963) 81 WN (Pt. 1) NSW 207, (1966) 84 WN   C
(Pt. 1) NSW 455 (CA).
Sovereign Life Assurance Co v Dodd [1892] 1 QB 405.
Webb Distributors (Aust) Pty Ltd v State of Victoria (1993) 11 ACLC 1178.

William Stubbs QC and Catherine Roberts (instructed by Stephenson Harwood) for
B & C.

Anthony Mann QC, Professor Dan Prentice and David Chivers (instructed by Cameron
Markby Hewitt) for Atlantic.   D

Leslie Kosmin QC and Robin Dicker (instructed by Lovell White Durrant) for BZW.

JUDGMENT
(Delivered 12 April 1995)

Robert Walker J: Introductory

This originating summons raises difficult questions arising out of the collapse of Atlantic   E
Computers plc ('Atlantic') and British & Commonwealth Holdings plc ('B & C'). During
the summer of 1988 B & C acquired the whole of Atlantic's share capital, initially by
purchases in the market, and then by a general offer which was recommended by Atlantic's
board of directors. In the litigation which I am about to mention it is B & C's case that at
the time of the acquisition (for a total consideration in cash and shares of over £400m)
Atlantic was worthless, or almost worthless, as a result of unsound procedures and practices
in the computer leasing businesses carried on by some of its most important subsidiaries. As
is well known, both Atlantic and B & C went into administration in 1990.   F

The collapse of these companies has led to a good deal of litigation. Two actions are
relevant for present purposes:

(1)   in an action designated as 1994 Ch B 2747 ('the main action') B & C is suing Atlantic
        and seven other defendants (all but one of whom were directors of Atlantic) for
        damages for negligent misrepresentations said to have been made at different dates
        between May and September 1988, so as to induce B & C to acquire Atlantic's shares;   G

(2)   in an action designated as 1994 Ch B 2448 ('the BZW action') B & C is suing Barclays
        de Zoete Wedd ('BZW') its adviser on the acquisition, for damages for breach of
        duty, and BZW has issued a third-party notice against (among others) Atlantic
        claiming indemnity, contribution and damages.

Both those actions are at an early stage. The damages claimed in the actions are enormous.
The costs already incurred in the actions are substantial, and if the actions go to trial – quite
apart from possible appeals – the costs also will be enormous.   H

The first action has the unusual feature that it is a claim by a holding company against its
wholly-owned subsidiary. Such a claim would be pointless if the subsidiary had a surplus of
assets over liabilities, since it would not change the economic position of the holding
company's shareholders (except by putting group funds in the lawyers' pockets). But
Atlantic has liabilities far in excess of its assets, and so B & C's administrators have an
obvious interest in translating B & C's position into that of creditor, if they can.

A   I will briefly summarise the events leading up to the originating summons that is now
before me. I will postpone, for the present, any detailed description of the scheme of
arrangement referred to in the title to the originating summons.

Atlantic was put into administration by an order made on 16 April 1990. Mr J F Soden
and Mr P S Padmore, the plaintiffs in these proceedings, were appointed as administrators.
The original purpose of the administration was the more advantageous realisation of the
company's assets, but by an order of Millett J made on 24 January 1994 the sanctioning of
B   a scheme of arrangement under s. 425 of the *Companies Act* 1985 was added as a further
purpose of the administration. In the meantime B & C had also been put into administration,
by an order made on 3 June 1990, and a scheme of arrangement between B & C and its
preferential and ordinary creditors was approved, although only after a challenge by
subordinated creditors: see *Re British & Commonwealth Holdings (No. 3)* [1992] BCC 58.

After the order of Millett J, Atlantic's administrators took steps to prepare and propose
a scheme of arrangement between Atlantic and its 'scheme creditors' as defined (I shall have
C   to return to this expression, but it certainly excluded preferential and secured creditors). On
1 February 1994 the administrators issued an originating summons for leave to call a
meeting of scheme creditors, and by an order made on the same day Mr Registrar Buckley
gave leave and gave directions for calling the meeting. The meeting was called for 16 March
and notice of it was given to known scheme creditors, including two B & C subsidiaries, one
of which was B & C Group Finance Ltd ('BCGF'), but not B & C itself. BCGF's claim
amounted, with interest, to over £88m.

D   On 9 March 1994 Stephenson Harwood, the solicitors acting for B & C's administrators,
gave the first written intimation to Cameron Markby Hewitt, the solicitors acting for
Atlantic's administrators, of the claim by B & C now put forward in this main action. No
formal details of the claim were sent to Atlantic's administrators before the meeting on 16
March, when the proposed scheme of arrangement was approved without any opposition
from any of the creditors represented at it. The scheme of arrangement was then approved,
E   without opposition, by an order of Mr Registrar Buckley made on 30 March 1994.

On or about 29 April 1994 Atlantic's administrators received formal notices of claim, on
the footing that they were scheme creditors, from B & C and BZW. B & C's claim was for
£500m with interest from 19 July 1988, the nature of its claim being described as 'for
damages for negligence and/or breaches of duty and/or negligent misstatements and/or
misrepresentations and/or breaches of warranty' on the part of Atlantic, with some added
particulars. BZW's claim was described as,

F   'Indemnity and/or contribution and/or damages from (Atlantic) in respect of BZW's
           liability (if any) to (B & C) arising out of B & C's acquisition of Atlantic in
           1988. The best particulars that BZW can presently provide as to the quantum of the
           claim are that it believes that B & C may claim a sum reflecting the amount of the
           write-off of its investment in Atlantic of about £550m plus interest.'

The writ in the BZW action was issued on 29 April 1994, and BZW's third-party notice
G   against Atlantic on 10 June 1994. In the meantime B & C's writ in the main action against
Atlantic had been issued on 18 May 1994.

The originating summons commencing these proceedings was issued on 6 September
1994. It has been amended once with the leave of the master and again, with my leave,
during the course of the hearing. As amended, it raises in relation to both B & C's and
BZW's claims a series of questions of some complexity. In very general terms, the questions
go to whether and to what extent B & C's claim against Atlantic in the main action – if
H   upheld at trial and on appeal – will succeed in turning B & C's position from that of a holder
of worthless shares into that of a creditor ranking with ordinary unsecured creditors of
Atlantic; and whether, and to what extent, BZW's claim against Atlantic in the BZW action
– if upheld at trial and on appeal, and within the limits stated in its notice of claim – must
share in any subordination to which B & C's claim is subject. (No one suggests that BZW
can possibly be in a worse position than B & C on this main issue, or that it can be
subordinated otherwise than as a result of B & C's being subordinated.)

Section 74(2)(f) of the Insolvency Act 1986   A

Counsel sensibly agreed that the most convenient way to argue the questions raised in the originating summons was by taking in their logical order pairs of questions, or pairs of groups of questions, relating to B & C on the one hand and to BZW on the other hand. Consequently I first heard argument on the issue common to para. 1 and 7 of the amended originating summons. I shall take that issue first in this judgment.

Section 74 of the *Insolvency Act* 1986 has a prominent position at the beginning of Pt. IV, Ch. 1 of that Act, which contains general provisions relating to all types of winding   B
up of registered companies. The section begins:

> '(1) When a company is wound up, every present and past member is liable to contribute to its assets to any amount sufficient for payment of its debts and liabilities, and the expenses of the winding up, and for the adjustment of the rights of the contributories among themselves.
>
> (2) This is subject as follows–'   C

(and then after a number of paragraphs which may be relevant as context, but are not directly in point):

> '(f) a sum due to any member of the company (in his character of a member) by way of dividends, profits or otherwise is not deemed to be a debt of the company, payable to that member in a case of competition between himself and any other creditor not a member of the company, but any such sum may be taken into account for the purpose   D
> of the final adjustment of the rights of the contributories among themselves.'

This provision has a long legislative history, going back – in virtually identical language, except for changing habits in punctuation – through s. 502 of the *Companies Act* 1985 and s. 212 of the *Companies Act* 1948, right back to s. 38 of the *Companies Act* 1862. It is also to be found, with some variations of language (notably 'capacity' for 'character' in the company law of Victoria, see e.g. *Webb Distributors (Aust) Pty Ltd v State of Victoria* (1993) 11 ACLC 1178 at p. 1181) in various company law statutes in force in Commonwealth   E
territories.

As Mr William Stubbs QC (who appeared with Miss Catherine Roberts for B & C) had occasion to remind me in more than one context, Atlantic is in administration but is not yet in liquidation. So questions raised in the originating summons as to the treatment in a future winding up of Atlantic of damages and costs to be awarded at the future trial of proceedings in which the pleadings are not yet closed are, it might be said, future and hypothetical questions twice over. But the court will decide such questions if satisfied that there is a   F
sufficiently good reason to do so. Counsel were unanimous in asking me to decide this question, despite my initial doubts on the point. On reflection I am satisfied that the question is one that I ought to answer, despite its future and hypothetical element, because it has a direct bearing on what Atlantic's administrators may or may not do under the scheme of arrangement – and in particular, whether the hopes of Atlantic's ordinary creditors, who had been hoping to receive a significant distribution in May 1994, must continue to be disappointed.   G

It is easy to understand and state, in the most general terms, what is the legislative purpose underlying the rule now embodied in s. 74(2)(f). It is (in the apt phrase of Mr Anthony Mann QC, who appeared with Professor Dan Prentice and Mr David Chivers for Atlantic) that 'members come last'. In other words, a general subordination of the rights of members to those of creditors is part of the price that Parliament exacts for the conferment of the privilege of incorporation, especially with limited liability. The rules or principles requiring the maintenance of a company's capital, and forbidding shares to be issued at a discount   H
(and numerous associated or subsidiary rules or principles) can be seen in the same way. The point was well expressed by Tadgell J in the Supreme Court of Victoria (Appeal Division) in *Re Pyramid Building Society* (1992) 10 ACLC 1205 (from which *Webb Distributors* was a further appeal) at p. 1217:

> 'Limited liability of a member of a company involves exemption, at a price, from what would otherwise be unlimited liability. As Lord Macnaghten put it in *Ooregum*

A   *Gold-Mining Co of India v Roper* [1892] AC 125, 145, citing *Buckley on the Companies Acts*–

"The dominant and cardinal principle of these Acts is that the investor shall purchase immunity from liability beyond a certain limit, on the terms that there shall be and remain a liability up to that limit." '

It is also easy to see that it would be absurd, in blind obedience to the very general principle that 'members come last', to discriminate against a creditor of a company simply
B   because he happens to be a member of the company, if his claim as a creditor has no close connection with his membership (it will of course often have *some* connection, since a shareholder-director of a small trading company is more likely to lend his surplus funds to his company rather than to another company in which he has no other interest). That is covered by the all-important parenthesis 'in his character of a member', echoed by the following words 'by way of dividends, profits or otherwise'. Even if membership of the company is a necessary condition of the debt arising, the debt will not be caught if the
C   condition of membership can be seen as irrelevant. Kay J gave a rather fanciful example in *Re Dale and Plant Ltd* (1889) 43 ChD 255 at p. 258-259:

'Suppose a company bought a million of bricks from a man who was a brick-maker. If he happened to be a shareholder, no one could doubt that that circumstance would not prevent him from proving in competition with the other creditors. But suppose that the articles of association contained provisions that no bricks should be bought of any person who was not a shareholder in the company. Is, then, the money paid as
D   the price of the bricks money due to the vendor of them in his character of member? Certainly not. It is not money due to him in his character of member, but money due to him in his character of brick-maker or brick-seller, and the fact that one of the articles provided that the company should not buy of any one who was not a member would not make the price of the bricks money due to him in his character of member, any more than it would be if there were no such article.'

Although the general principle is clear enough, it is not easy to discern any single reliable
E   test for the borderline cases which occur. Rights which a person has in the character of a member can undergo a transmutation (the expression used by Mervyn Davies J in *Re L B Holliday & Co Ltd* (1986) 2 BCC 99,031 at p. 99,038) into rights which the same person has in the character of a creditor. The commonest example is where a shareholder does not call for payment of dividends to which he is entitled, but instead leaves them with the company (without waiving them). His entitlement may become an unsecured loan. Whether it does so is simply a question of fact to be determined on evidence that may be ambiguous or
F   incomplete (this is illustrated by the New South Wales case of *Re Harry Simpson & Co Pty* (1963) 81 WN (Pt. 1) NSW 207, (1966) 84 WN (Pt. 1) NSW 455, where the question was finally decided by the appellate court's decision to admit fresh evidence). The authorities on this type of case are reviewed in *Re L B Holliday*, above.

Another type of case is a director's claim for unpaid remuneration. In *Re Leicester Club and County Racecourse Co, ex parte Cannon* (1885) 30 ChD 629 the claimant director was regarded by Pearson J as a sort of 'working member' and as claiming in that character (see
G   at p. 633). But that approach has not been followed either in England, Northern Ireland or Australia: see *Re Dale and Plant* (1889) 43 ChD 255 at pp. 259–260; *Re New British Iron Co, ex parte Beckwith* [1898] 1 Ch 324; *Re Cinnamond Park* [1929] NI 47 at p. 56; *Re Automatic Bread Baking Co* (1939) 40 NSW 1 at p. 7. I agree with the more recent authorities that *ex parte Cannon* can no longer be regarded as sound. It is true that in some of the later 19th century cases it was distinguished, partly it seems on the rather surprising ground that in that case no director's share qualification was requisite (as it certainly was in the *Dale and*
H   *Plant* and *Automatic Bread Baking* cases). So the weight of authority establishes that it is not sufficient, to make a person claim against a company in his character of a member, that the holding of shares is a necessary ingredient in his claim.

The strongest cases of this type are two Australian cases, *Re W H Eutrope Pty* [1932] VLR 453 and *Re Harlou Pty* [1950] VLR 449. *Re W H Eutrope Pty* shows the principle that directors' remuneration is not due to members as such being followed even in the case of a 'two-man company' where the director-shareholders' decision to distribute profits by way

of remuneration, rather than dividend, was motivated by tax considerations. As Mann J   A
said (at p. 459) it is not in the power of the court to turn a resolution fixing directors'
remuneration into a resolution declaring a dividend.

In *Re Harlou Pty* a company had, on employing a bookkeeper, required him to apply and
pay for 500 shares in its capital, subject to an obligation on the company, if his employment
was for any reason terminated within six months, to find a purchaser for the shares at not
less than par. The bookkeeper left within six months. The company failed to find a purchaser
for the shares, and soon afterwards went into liquidation. The case turned mainly on ultra   B
vires and financial assistance for purchase of shares, but there was also argument on the
Victorian equivalent of s. 74(2)(f). The contract was held to be valid and lawful, and O'Bryan
J (without reference to authority) rejected the argument for subordinating the bookkeeper's
claim:

'The £500 due to the appellant is not due to him in his character of a member at all.
It is not because he is a shareholder that he is entitled to these damages, but it is
because he has made a contract with the company of the character to which I have   C
referred, which contract the company has broken, that he is entitled to damages.'

Mention of *Re Harlou Pty* leads on to three other cases in which a claim for damages,
closely connected with the holding of shares, has been considered in the context of provisions
equivalent to s. 74(2)(f). *Re Addlestone Linoleum Co* (1887) 37 ChD 191 is a curious case
decided before the House of Lords (in the *Ooregum* case) removed any remaining doubt
about a limited company issuing shares at a discount. The company had purported to issue
£10 preference shares on payment of only £7.10s., but the shareholders received certificates   D
stating that their shares were fully paid. When the company was wound up these preference
shareholders were placed on the list of contributories and calls of £2.10s. per share were
made on them. Some applied for leave to prove in the liquidation for 'damages for breach
of contract or otherwise' in connection with the issue of the shares.

Before Kay J there was extensive argument on s. 38(7) of the *Companies Act* 1862, the
forerunner of s. 74(2)(f). Kay J said (at p. 197):
                                                                                                   E
'Now, unquestionably the applicants – retaining these shares and claiming damages
because the shares are not exactly what they were represented to be – are making such
claims in the character of members of the company, and the only question is whether
such claims are for sums "due by way of dividends, profits or otherwise". To
determine that it is necessary to consider the scope and intent of this provision in the
statute. The obvious analogy is the case of a partner attempting to prove in
bankruptcy in competition with the creditors of the firm. But whether this section is   F
intended to have entirely the same effect or not, it is quite clear from the language of
it that a debt due to a member in that character, such as for dividends, directors' fees,
or the like, could not be so proved.'

Kay J went on to say (at p. 198) that the applicants admitted their liability as
contributories to help meet the claims of creditors but were,

'. . . yet seeking to get part of it back out of the pockets of those very creditors
themselves. I confess it seems to me that the money so claimed is not only claimed in   G
the character of members but that the claim is just as unreasonable as if it were a
claim of dividends or profits, and that, accordingly, it comes within the words "or
otherwise", which I have read from section 38.'

The decision of Kay J in *Addlestone* seems not to have been cited to (or recalled by) the
same judge when he decided *Re Dale and Plant* only two years later, when he reached a
different decision about directors' remuneration, and said (43 ChD at p. 259) that 'the words
"or otherwise" must mean something analogous to dividends or profits on his shares'.   H
Addlestone went to the Court of Appeal, which upheld Kay J, mainly by reference to the
decision of the House of Lords in *Houldsworth v City of Glasgow Bank* (1880) 5 App Cas
317. But Cotton LJ said (37 ChD at p. 205) that it would have been very difficult to come to
the conclusion that the preference shareholders, if allowed to prove at all, could compete
with outside creditors. Lopes LJ said (at p. 206) that he agreed with Kay J as to the
construction of s. 38(7). Lopes LJ also said (at p. 206) that the difference between the claim

A for damages for misrepresentation in *Houldsworth*'s case, and the claim for damages for breach of contract in the case before him, was not a substantial distinction.

The decision in *Houldsworth*'s case (which Mr Stubbs described, at an earlier hearing, as being of legendary impenetrability) has recently been altered by statute (s. 111A of the *Companies Act* 1985, introduced by the *Companies Act* 1989) but it was not suggested by counsel that the statutory change has any bearing on what I have to decide. So the main point that I get from *Addlestone* is that two members of the Court of Appeal seem to have

B regarded a claim for damages for breach of contract, because shares issued to the claimants were 'not exactly what they were represented to be', as falling within what is now s. 74(2)(f).

Two years later Stirling J decided *Re New Chile Gold Mining Co* (1890) 45 ChD 598. In that case a former shareholder whose shares had been wrongly forfeited (at a time when they were worth nearly four times their par value) sought to prove for damages in the subsequent liquidation of the company. Stirling J allowed the claim. After discussing whether s. 38(7) of the *Companies Act* 1862 could in any circumstances apply to an ex-

C member the judge said (at p. 605):

> 'I do not, however, decide the case on that ground, because I have come to the conclusion that, supposing the applicant to be a past member within the meaning of that sub-section, the sum in question was not due to him in his character of a member; but, as it appears to me, it was, on the contrary, due to him in the character of non-member. What he claims is not any sum which is payable to a member, but damages
>
D > payable to him by reason of his having been deprived of the rights of a member by an irregular act on the part of the company in respect of which the contract, contained in the articles of association, entitles him to damages.'

Much more recently the High Court of Australia in *Webb Distributors (Aust) Pty v State of Victoria* (1993) 11 ACLC 1178 considered claims by holders of non-withdrawable shares in three building societies (which were to be wound up in accordance with the Victorian company law code). The claimants complained that they had been misled as to the nature

E of their shares, being told that they were redeemable and 'like a deposit'. As with *Addlestone* in the Court of Appeal, the case turned largely on *Houldsworth*'s case and its incorporation into Victorian company law. But the majority of the High Court (Mason CJ and Deane, Dawson and Toohey JJ discussed *Addlestone* at some length. They quoted (at p. 1184) the observations of Cotton LJ about the preference shareholders in that case, that 'now they come here as shareholders, and in substance retain their shares, and seek to sue the company for breach of the contract under which they took them'. The majority of the High Court took the view that s. 360(1)(k) of the Companies (Victoria) Code (which is equivalent to

F s. 74(2)(f), though it refers to 'capacity' rather than character) had the same meaning as Kay J's interpretation of s. 38(7).

The majority of the High Court then said (at p. 1185):

> 'Paragraph (k) of s. 360(1) will not prevent claims by members for damages flowing from a breach of contract separate from a contract to subscribe for the shares [at this point there is a footnote, forming part of the judgment, referring to *Re Dale and Plant*
>
G > and *Re Harlou Pty*]. But, in the present case, the members seek to prove in the liquidation damages which amount to the purchase price of their shares, which is a sum directly related to their shareholding. Moreover, they sue as members, retaining the shares to which they were entitled by virtue of entry into the agreement and they seek to recover damages because the shares are not what they were represented to be. Accordingly, the claim falls within the area which s. 360(1)(k) seeks to regulate: the protection of creditors by maintaining the capital of the company.'

H I was referred to a number of other authorities including the recent decision of Harman J in *Barclays Bank plc & Ors v British & Commonwealth Holdings plc* [1995] BCC 19. That case was mainly concerned with the principle of maintenance of a company's capital (a principle which the High Court of Australia regarded as closely connected with the subordination of claims of members as such, as has just been seen). Mr Mann relied on the *Barclays Bank* case mainly for the general proposition (on which, at p. 33, Harman J accepted the submission of Mr Stubbs, while commenting that other minds might come to

the opposite conclusion) that form should not be allowed to prevail over substance. I readily   A
accept that I must look for the substance of the matter, but – as in the *Barclays Bank* case –
it is not obvious where the substance is to be found.

Mr Stubbs submits that the search for substance (or principle) must start with the
essentials of membership of a company. He refers to the basic provisions now found in
s. 14 and 22 of the *Companies Act* 1985, and to Farwell J's well-known definition of a share
in *Borland's Trustee v Steel Brothers & Co Ltd* [1901] 1 Ch 279 at p. 288. The essence of
membership, Mr Stubbs submits, is in the bundle of rights which are inseparable from (or   B
characteristic of) membership. I accept Mr Stubbs' submission (which was not disputed by
Mr Mann or by Mr Leslie Kosmin QC who appeared with Mr Dicker for BZW) that that is
the right starting-point.

The commonest constituent elements of a member's 'bundle of rights' (so far as rights to
money are concerned, and in the case of a prosperous company) are dividends. These are
specified, together with profits, in s. 74(2)(f), and it was common ground that Kay J was
right when he said that the words 'or otherwise' must mean something analogous to   C
dividends and profits. Examples of analogous claims would be claims to sums due on a
reduction of capital approved by the court, or sums due on an authorised redemption of
redeemable shares (see *Re Dividend Fund* [1974] VR 451). On this approach, which I believe
to be the correct approach, the words 'by way of dividends, profits or otherwise' do not
either restrict or extend the natural meaning of 'in his character of a member'; their function
is to help to explain that expression. The real issue for decision, it seems to me, is how far
the analogy implicit in 'or otherwise' is to be stretched.   D

Mr Stubbs formulates and puts forward a four-part test, that is that to fall within
s. 74(2)(f) the sum due to a member must be:

(1)   contractual in nature, arising from the contract which a company's articles establish
        between the company and all its members (and between its members themselves),
        either alone or in conjunction with one or more resolutions;

(2)   for something analogous to dividends or profits;

(3)   (in the words of his skeleton argument) 'in respect of a right which is part of the   E
        bundle of rights and obligations making up the share itself'; and

(4)   a liquidated sum.

Mr Kosmin takes a similar line, emphasising the 'analogous' requirement and also the fact
that BZW is not, and never has been, a member of Atlantic.

Mr Mann emphasises (as I have already noted) the importance of substance prevailing
over form. He relies on *Addlestone* and *Webb Distributors* as persuasive authorities. He   F
submits that they should be seen as cases where a claim for the loss of value of shares was
treated as a claim made in the character of a member. He formulates a two-part test, that
the sum due should be on a claim which (1) is made in respect of shares and (2) could not be
made except by a holder of shares. He disputes the first and last of Mr Stubbs' four points.
Mr Mann does, however, concede that costs awarded against Atlantic in the two sets of
pending proceedings would not fall within s. 74(2)(f), so that the argument has been on
damages only. Mr Stubbs criticizes Mr Mann's test as relying on the vague expression 'in   G
respect of' (and it certainly is a wide and vague expression, as the court has often observed).
In making this criticism Mr Stubbs may have overlooked the appearance of the same
expression (with rather more wrapping) in the third part of his own test.

Neither Mr Stubbs' four-part test nor Mr Mann's two-part test can be fully reconciled
with all the authorities. Mr Stubbs' biggest difficulty is with the claims for damages which,
in *Addlestone* and *Webb Distributors*, were treated as within the equivalent of
s. 74(2)(f). Mr Mann's biggest difficulty is in applying *Addlestone* and *Webb Distributors* to   H
a situation in which the claimant became a member of the company by buying shares from
existing shareholders, rather than as an original subscriber or allottee; and in which the
misrepresentation complained of was as to the asset backing of the company's shares, and
not as to their legal nature. Mr Mann also has a problem with *Re Harlou Pty*.

I cannot accept the fourth element of the test that Mr Stubbs proposes. It is perfectly clear
that not merely liquidated debts, but also unliquidated claims, can be admitted to proof in

A   a winding up. That has been the case for many years, although it was only under the *Insolvency Act* 1986 that unliquidated claims in tort become provable. In my judgment the context of s. 74 as a whole strongly requires, and the language of s. 74(2)(f) permits, the expression 'sum due' to include an unliquidated claim which does in other respects fall within the paragraph. Any other construction would produce an extraordinary anomaly. The fact that an unliquidated claim falling within the paragraph would be a rarity may partly explain the choice of language (which is, as Mr Stubbs says, of venerable antiquity)

B   but ought not to be taken as a reason for restricting its meaning. Examples of unliquidated claims which might exist at the commencement of a winding up, and which would clearly (as I see it) be claims by members in their character as such, would be claims under s. 92 (breach of duty in respect of pre-emptive rights) or s. 359 (rectification of the register) of the *Companies Act* 1985.

     Mr Stubbs points to the words 'debts and liabilities' in s. 74(1), and seeks to draw a contrast. But the argument can be run both ways. As Viscount Simonds said in *Government*

C   *of India v Taylor & Anor* [1955] AC 491 at p. 509:

> '. . . though I accept the proposition that a word should be used in the same sense throughout a statute, it is by no means a universal rule and I am not pressed by it in construing a section of an Act so long and complex as the *Companies Act* 1948 . . .'

Moreover Mr Stubbs' submission on this point is contrary to the view of the law that seems to have been taken in *Addlestone* and *Webb Distributors*, though it is true that the point does not seem to have been argued.

D   Mention of s. 92 and 359 of the *Companies Act* 1985 leads on to the first element of Mr Stubbs' test, that the claim must be contractual in nature. If I understand Mr Stubbs correctly, his argument does not require that the claim must be for damages for breach of contract, but rather that it must be a claim directly relating to the contractual nexus between company and members, and members amongst themselves, which I have already referred to as the starting point of his submissions (I will call this 'the corporate nexus'). Seen in this way even a claim in tort (such as the claim in deceit in *Houldsworth*'s case) would fall within

E   this category so long as it relates sufficiently closely to the relationship established by the corporate nexus.

     Whether or not I have fully understood Mr Stubbs' submissions, I think that this is the right approach to identifying a claim as characteristically a member's claim, rather than just a claim which happens to be made by a member. Indeed, I rather think that all three elements of Mr Stubbs' test, apart from the liquidated sum point which I reject, are really three different ways of putting the same essential point. On this approach claims under

F   s. 92 and 359 of the *Companies Act* 1985 can be seen as arising out of the corporate nexus as added to by statute. This approach also fits in with the views expressed in earlier cases that it does or should make no difference whether the claim is in contract or tort (see Lopes LJ in *Addlestone* 37 ChD at p. 206; *Re Dividend Fund* [1974] VR at p. 454).

     Ultimately the point comes down to whether a claim made by an open-market purchaser of shares in a company (as opposed to an original subscriber or allottee), the claim being based on negligent misrepresentation by the company as to its assets, is sufficiently closely

G   related to the corporate nexus as to be characteristically a member's claim. *Addlestone* and *Webb Distributors* were both claims by original members. The claimants were complaining of the very transaction under which, by becoming members, they had contributed part of the company's capital. That is the point emphasised in the passage from the majority judgment in *Webb Distributors* (11 ACLC at p. 1185) that I have already quoted from; the passage points to the close connection between the Victorian equivalent of s. 74(2)(f) and the principle of maintaining capital for the protection of creditors.

H   In this case, by contrast, B & C was never an original member in respect of any shares in Atlantic (and as Mr Kosmin rightly submits, this and the following points apply still more strongly to BZW). Nether B & C nor BZW seeks to withdraw from Atlantic, directly or indirectly, any capital which either has ever contributed. In this respect their position is stronger than that of the ex-employee who was the claimant in *Re Harlou Pty*. He was allowed to prove as an ordinary creditor for the company's failure to find a buyer for the shares which he had taken up as an original allottee. Mr Mann submits that the case was

wrongly decided and that I ought not to follow it, but to my mind it is an example of a claim   **A**
made by a member, but not in his character of member. The ex-employee's near-equivalent
of a put option was distinct from his relationship with the company under the corporate
nexus.

It is also of interest to consider the case (perhaps unlikely but not impossible) of a
company which, by negligently *understating* the value of its assets, induces members to sell
their shares on the market at less than their fair value. If later the company really does fall
on hard times and goes into liquidation, the former members who had sold their shares at   **B**
what was (at the time) an undervalue might have difficulty in establishing their loss (that is,
in proving that they would have sold at the top of the market) but they could not, it seems
to me, be subordinated by s. 74(2)(f). It may be said (as Stirling J said in the *New Chile* case)
that the reason for that would be that they were claiming as non-members. But an equally
valid reason would be that their former membership, although a necessary condition of their
claims, was not sufficiently central as to lead to their claims being characterised as claims by
members as such.   **C**

For these reasons I will answer the questions in para. 1 and 7 of the reamended originating
summons in the negative sense. In doing so I follow what I understand to be the principle
stated by the majority of the High Court of Australia in the *Webb Distributors* case: the
wrong of which B & C and BZW complain is separate from any transaction by which any
original holder took up shares and so became a member of the company. A claim that the
company's wrongful representation induced a purchaser of its shares to overestimate their
asset backing is not the same as a claim that it misled persons taking up shares as to their   **D**
legal nature. I must emphasise that at the moment B & C's and BZW's claims are unproven.

The scheme of arrangement

In view of my answer to the questions in para. 1 and 7 of the reamended originating
summons the questions in para. 2, 2A and 8 do not arise. I consider that Atlantic's
administrators were right to proceed on the footing that (apart from preferential and secured
creditors) there was only one class of ordinary unsecured creditors, and no need for separate   **E**
class meetings.

Had I taken a different view on s. 74(2)(f) there should have been a separate creditors'
meeting for those subordinated under that provision, and in the absence of such a meeting
the scheme of arrangement would not have bound the subordinated creditors: *Sovereign
Life Assurance Co v Dodd* [1892] 1 QB 405. I should add, however, that had I taken a
different view I would have found it impossible to accept Mr Stubbs' argument that the
scheme of arrangement (which was prepared and considered in ignorance of the claims of B   **F**
& C and BZW, and seems to have been approved without reference to them) could have
had the totally unexpected effect of promoting subordinated claims so that they ranked with
those of ordinary unsecured creditors. The commercial context of the arrangement was to
provide for the orderly processing of ordinary creditors' claims in a way that avoided some
of the expenses which would have attended the same process if carried out in the course of a
winding up, and the references in the arrangement to 'all creditors' could not be allowed to
override or subvert that obvious purpose.   **G**

In the circumstances, however, I need not go further into the submissions addressed to
me on this point.

(*Order accordingly*)

SUPPLEMENTARY JUDGMENT
(Delivered 27 April 1995)   **H**

Robert Walker J: On 12 April I handed down a written reserved judgment most of which
was concerned with the questions (as to s. 74(2)(f) of the *Insolvency Act* 1986) raised in
para. 1 and 7 of the re-amended originating summons. I answered those questions in the
negative sense, so that the questions in para. 2, 2A, and 8 of the re-amended originating
summons (which are expressed to arise only if the questions in para. 1 and 7 are answered
in the affirmative) did not fall to be answered, although I heard argument on them.

A   At the end of my judgment I gave a brief indication of my view on the questions which had been argued before me, but which in the event did not arise. Counsel for Atlantic and B & C have asked me to amplify my judgment on these questions, for the possible assistance of the Court of Appeal in the event of an appeal, and I now do so in this supplementary judgment. It does not in any way defer or affect my order on the questions raised in para. 1 and 7 of the re-amended originating summons.

      The background facts are summarised in the first section of the main written judgment.
B   The most relevant dates for present purposes were 24 January 1995, when Millett J altered the terms of Atlantic's administration so as to add the purpose of the sanctioning of a scheme of arrangement under s. 425 of the *Companies Act* 1985; 1 February, when an originating summons was issued by the administrators for leave to call a creditors' meeting, and Mr Registrar Buckley gave leave and gave directions for the meeting; 7 February, the date of the formal proposal in relation to a scheme of arrangement which was circulated to known scheme creditors; 9 March, when solicitors acting for B & C's administrators notified
C   solicitors acting for Atlantic's administrators of B & C's claim; 16 March when the creditors' meeting was held; and 30 March, when the scheme of arrangement was approved, without opposition, by Mr Registrar Buckley.

      It will be apparent from this summary of dates that the scheme of arrangement was prepared and proposed in ignorance of, and without regard to, the enormous claims now put forward by B & C and (in third party proceedings) BZW. B & C's claim was notified to Atlantic's administrators before the creditors' meeting, but only just, and only in very
D   general terms: there is no indication that anyone (at least on Atlantic's side) had time, before the creditors' meeting, to reach any considered view as to the possible application of s. 74(2)(f) of the 1986 Act, or that the proposed scheme was altered significantly in order to take account of B & C's last-minute claim. Such negative indicators as there are (for instance, the fact that no one seems to have considered going back to Mr Registrar Buckley and asking him to direct the calling of a separate meeting of creditors who might be subordinated under s. 74(2)(f)) point the other way.

E   This group of questions in the re-amended originating summons essentially raises issues of two types: what does the scheme of arrangement mean? and whom does the scheme of arrangements bind? The latter issue was raised in relation to B & C, at Mr Stubbs' request, in para. 2A; Mr Kosmin did not ask for a similar question to be raised in relation to BZW.

      Normally the issue of what a contractual document means is quite distinct from the issue of whom it binds. But in this case the two issues tend to become entangled. The jurisdiction of the Companies Court to sanction an arrangement under s. 425 of the *Companies Act* 1985
F   is exercisable so as to bind 'all the creditors or the class of creditors' (see s. 425(2)). It seems reasonably clear that the order of Mr Registrar Buckley was intended to bind 'scheme creditors' as defined in the scheme – that is all persons with claims against Atlantic in respect of (and I quote from the definition of 'scheme liabilities'):

> 'debts and liabilities (other than the preferential or secured liabilities) that would be provable under r. 12.3 of the Insolvency Rules if the company were to be placed into compulsory liquidation on the [date when the sanctioned scheme takes effect] and in
G   > this definition the words 'debts' and 'liabilities' shall have the meanings ascribed to them in r. 13.12 of the Insolvency Rules as if the company were being wound up.'

      The crucial provisions of the scheme were that there was to be a general moratorium on the enforcement of scheme liabilities otherwise than under the scheme (para. 2) and that under the scheme established claims in respect of scheme liabilities are to be met rateably, after discharge of the preferential liabilities (para. 3). The main purpose of the scheme was (as appears from the formal proposal for the scheme) to enable Atlantic's ordinary creditors
H   to be paid in an orderly fashion, so far as funds permitted, by a process that appeared to have advantages over both a company voluntary arrangement and a winding up.

      That is the background to this group of questions, and I am entitled to take it into account as part of the commercial context in which the scheme was prepared, voted on and sanctioned by the Companies Court. All counsel invited me to apply the principles stated in the very well-known speech of Lord Wilberforce in *Prenn v Simmonds* [1971] 1 WLR 1381, although they differed as to the conclusions I should reach by the application of those

principles. Counsel agreed that I could and should look at the formal proposal as   A
explanatory of the scheme of arrangement, and I think they were right in this. On the other
hand the details of correspondence between solicitors immediately before the creditors'
meeting, discussing small textual changes, are not in my view admissible (or, if I am wrong
on that, helpful) in construing the scheme.

In addition to the general guidance that I get from *Prenn v Simmonds*, I think I must also
attach great weight to the fact that I am considering a scheme sanctioned by the Companies
Court. A construction of such a scheme – or, I would add, of an arrangement approved by   B
the court under the *Variation of Trusts Act* 1958 – which produces arbitrary or absurd results
is to be rejected if a fair and sensible reading is possible. When a testator is disposing of his
own property, eccentricity of disposition is permissible and its preservation may even be
regarded as an objective of public policy (see Wilberforce J in *Re Howard's Will Trusts*
[1961] Ch 507 at p. 523) but eccentricity is not acceptable in fiduciaries disposing of property
which is not theirs; still less in the High Court when exercising a statutory jurisdiction so as
to bind absent creditors (or minor or unborn beneficiaries).   C

I am therefore deeply sceptical of the view that the scheme could possibly have been
intended to have the effect, or did have the effect, of promoting any subordinated creditor
(if, contrary to my judgment, B & C and BZW would be subordinated creditors) to the
status of an ordinary unsecured creditor where there seems to me no possible reason for the
existing ordinary unsecured creditors, or the court, to regard such a promotion as expedient
or justified. It seems to me that the form of para. 2A of the re-amended originating summons
was a tacit recognition of this: Mr Stubbs wanted to find out first whether the meaning of   D
the scheme was favourable to his clients, and to argue that he was not bound only if the
scheme failed to give his clients an unexpected promotion.

That is not, it seems to me, a logical or practical way to approach these issues. If, contrary
to what I have decided, the claims of B & C and BZW are within s. 74(2)(f), then they
constitute a separate class of subordinated creditors, for whom (if they were to be bound) a
separate class meeting should have been called. In the absence of those steps being taken,
the scheme could not have bound them: see *Sovereign Life Assurance Co (in liq) v Dodd*   E
[1892] 1 QB 405.

The scheme was intended to bind 'scheme creditors' on the assumption – which is
abundantly clear both from the scheme itself, and from admissible surrounding
circumstances – that there was (apart from secured and preferential creditors) only one class
of creditors, whose claims ranked pari passu. I find a high degree of unreality in being asked
to construe a scheme, which was prepared, voted on and sanctioned by the court on this
clear assumption, so as to permit a class of (on this hypothesis) subordinated creditors to   F
take the benefit of a scheme which does not bind them. Mr Mann suggested that the way
out was to be found in r. 12.3(3) of the *Insolvency Rules* 1986; I cannot accept that
submission, since r. 12.3(2A)(c) seems much more apt to cover a case within s. 74(2)(f) of
the 1986 Act. I prefer to reach the obvious conclusion on the simpler and broader ground
that no one who was not bound by the scheme was intended to take the benefit of it, and
that that is necessarily implicit in para. 3 of the scheme.

Had they arisen for decision, I would therefore have answered the question in   G
para. 2A of the re-amended originating summons by declaring that B & C was not bound,
and the questions in para. 2 and 8 by declaring that the claims of B & C and BZW did not
give rise to a scheme liability – that is, they were not liabilities of the sort intended to be
dealt with by the scheme.

(Ruling accordingly)

  H

A ## Stein v Blake.

House of Lords.
Lord Keith of Kinkel, Lord Ackner, Lord Lloyd of Berwick, Lord Nicholls of
Birkenhead and Lord Hoffmann.
Judgment delivered 18 May 1995.

B *Bankruptcy – Mutual credit and set-off – Trustee in bankruptcy assigned claim
against defendant back to bankrupt – Defendant had counterclaim and argued
that there could be no assignment because of statutory rules of set-off – Whether
causes of action survived bankruptcy or merged in net balance after taking account
– Whether net balance could be assigned – Whether net balance had been assigned
– Insolvency Act 1986, s. 323.*

C This was an appeal from a decision of the Court of Appeal (see [1993] BCC 587) on the
effect of s. 323 of the Insolvency Act 1986 (mutual credit and set-off).

The plaintiff had commenced proceedings against the defendant in 1987. The defendant
had a counterclaim. In 1990 the plaintiff was adjudicated bankrupt. In 1991 the trustee
assigned the benefit of the action back to the bankrupt in return for 49 per cent of the net
proceeds.

D The defendant applied to stay the action on the ground that until an account had been
taken by the trustee under s. 323 there was nothing to assign. The defendant relied upon the
decision of Neill J in *Farley v Housing and Commercial Developments Ltd* (1984) 1 BCC
99,150. He succeeded before the deputy master and, on appeal by the plaintiff, before the
judge.

The Court of Appeal allowed the plaintiff's appeal, holding that debts due to and from a
E bankrupt did not disappear on the making of the bankruptcy order. The separate causes of
action did not cease to exist until the set-off had been completed by payment one way or the
other. *Farley's* case was wrongly decided.

Held, dismissing the defendant's appeal:

1. Section 323 operated at the time of bankruptcy without any step having to be taken
by either of the parties. The taking of the account in accordance with s. 323(2) meant no
F more than the calculation of the balance due. The set-off was mandatory and self-executing
and resulted, as of the bankruptcy date, in only a net balance being owing. The cross-claims
ceased to exist as choses in action (though they had to be considered separately for the
purpose of ascertaining the balance) and were replaced by a claim to a net balance. (*Farley
v Housing & Commercial Developments Ltd* (1984) 1 BCC 99,150 approved.)

2. The trustee could assign the right to the net balance like any other chose in action.

G 3. The deed executed by the trustee did have the effect of carrying the net balance.

The following cases were referred to in the speech of Lord Hoffmann:

Daintrey, Re, ex parte Mant [1900] 1 QB 546.
Day & Dent Constructions Pty Ltd v North Australian Properties Pty Ltd (1982) 150
CLR 85.
Dynamics Corporation of America, Re [1976] 1 WLR 757.
Farley v Housing & Commercial Developments Ltd (1984) 1 BCC 99,150.
H *Forster v Wilson* (1843) 12 M & W 191; 152 ER 1165.
Gye v McIntyre (1991) 171 CLR 609.
Mersey Steel and Iron Co v Naylor Benzon & Co (1882) 9 QBD 648.
National Westminster Bank Ltd v Halesowen Presswork & Assemblies Ltd [1972] AC
785.
New Quebrada Co Ltd v Carr (1869) LR 4 CP 651.

Ramsey v Hartley [1977] 1 WLR 686.

Sovereign Life Assurance Co v Dodd [1892] 2 QB 573.

Michael Mark (instructed by Maislish & Co) for the appellant.

Edward Bannister QC and Philip Hoser (instructed by Bray Walker) for the respondent.

SPEECHES

Lord Keith of Kinkel: For the reasons given in the speech to be delivered by Lord Hoffmann, which I have read in draft and with which I agree, I would dismiss this appeal.

Lord Ackner: I have had the advantage of reading in draft the speech prepared by Lord Hoffmann. For the reasons he gives I too would dismiss this appeal.

Lord Lloyd of Berwick: I have had the advantage of reading in draft the speech prepared by Lord Hoffmann. For the reasons he gives I too would dismiss this appeal.

Lord Nicholls of Birkenhead: I have had the advantage of reading in draft the speech prepared by Lord Hoffmann. For the reasons he gives, with which I agree, I too would dismiss this appeal.

Lord Hoffmann: 1. The issues

If A and B have mutual claims against each other and A becomes bankrupt, does A's claim against B continue to exist so that A's trustee can assign it to a third party? Or is the effect of s. 323 of the *Insolvency Act* 1986 to extinguish the claims of A and B and to substitute a claim for the net balance owing after setting off the one against the other? And if the latter is the case, can the trustee assign the net balance (if any) before it has been ascertained by the taking of an account between himself and B? If yes, is that what the trustee in this case has done? These are the issues in this appeal.

2. The facts

The plaintiff Mr Stein was adjudicated bankrupt on 16 July 1990. He was at the time a legally aided plaintiff engaged in suing the defendant Blake. It is unnecessary to go into the details save to say that Mr Stein was claiming damages for breach of contract and a declaration that he was entitled to be indemnified against certain tax liabilities. Mr Blake was counterclaiming for damages for misrepresentation and had in addition an indisputable cross-claim under various orders for costs in any event. Mr Blake perhaps hoped that Mr Stein's trustee, in whom the right of action (if any) had vested, would decide that it was not in the interests of creditors to spend money on pursuing the litigation. If so, he was right, but the trustee did not abandon the claim. Instead he executed a deed dated 4 April 1991 by which he assigned the benefit of the action back to Mr Stein in return for 49 per cent of the net proceeds. Mr Stein again obtained legal aid. Mr Blake applied to have the proceedings dismissed on the ground that a claim subject to a set-off under s. 323 of the *Insolvency Act* 1986 could not validly be assigned. The application succeeded before the judge but his decision was reversed by the Court of Appeal (see [1993] BCC 587; [1994] Ch 16). Mr Blake now appeals.

3. Bankruptcy set-off

Section 323 reads, so far as relevant, as follows:

'(1) This section applies where before the commencement of the bankruptcy there have been mutual credits, mutual debts or other mutual dealings between the bankrupt and any creditor of the bankrupt proving or claiming to prove for a bankruptcy debt.

A

(2) An account shall be taken of what is due from each party to the other in respect of the mutual dealings and the sums due from one party shall be set off against the sums due from the other.

(3) . . .

(4) Only the balance (if any) of the account taken under subsection (2) is provable as a bankruptcy debt or, as the case may be, to be paid to the trustee as part of the bankrupt's estate.'

B

4. Bankruptcy set-off compared with statutory legal set-off

Section 323 is the latest in a line of bankruptcy set-off provisions which go back to the time of Queen Anne. As it happens, legal set-off between solvent parties is also based upon statutes of Queen Anne. But the two forms of set-off are very different in their

C

purpose and effect. Legal set-off does not affect the substantive rights of the parties against each other, at any rate until both causes of action have been merged in a judgment of the court. It addresses questions of procedure and cash-flow. As a matter of procedure, it enables a defendant to require his cross-claim (even if based upon a wholly different subject-matter) be tried together with the plaintiff's claim instead of having to be the subject of a separate action. In this way it ensures that judgment will be given simultaneously on claim and cross-claim and thereby relieves the defendant from having

D

to find the cash to satisfy a judgment in favour of the plaintiff (or, in the 18th century, go to a debtor's prison) before his cross-claim has been determined.

Bankruptcy set-off, on the other hand, affects the substantive rights of the parties by enabling the bankrupt's creditor to use his indebtedness to the bankrupt as a form of security. Instead of having to prove with other creditors for the whole of his debt in the bankruptcy, he can set off pound for pound what he owes the bankrupt and prove

E

for or pay only the balance. So in *Forster v Wilson* (1843) 12 M & W 191 at p. 204 Parke B said that the purpose of insolvency set-off was 'to do substantial justice between the parties'. Although it is often said that the justice of the rule is obvious, it is worth noticing that it is by no means universal. (Wood on *English and International Set-off* (1989), para. 24-49–24-56. It has however been part of the English law of bankruptcy since at least the time of the first Queen Elizabeth (*op. cit.* para. 7-26).)

F

Legal set-off is confined to debts which at the time when the defence of set-off is filed were due and payable and either liquidated or in sums capable of ascertainment without valuation or estimation. Bankruptcy set-off has a much wider scope. It applies to any claim arising out of mutual credits or other mutual dealings before the bankruptcy for which a creditor would be entitled to prove as a 'bankruptcy debt'. This is defined by s. 382 of the *Insolvency Act* 1986 to mean:

G

'(1) . . . any of the following–

(a) any debt or liability to which he is subject at the commencement of the bankruptcy,

(b) any debt or liability to which he may become subject after the commencement of the bankruptcy (including after his discharge from bankruptcy) by reason of any obligation incurred before the commencement

H

of the bankruptcy . . .

(3) For the purposes of references in this Group of Parts to a debt or liability, it is immaterial whether the debt or liability is present or future, whether it is certain or contingent or whether its amount is fixed or liquidated, or is capable of being ascertained by fixed rules or as a matter of opinion; and references in this Group of Parts to owing a debt are to be read accordingly.'

5. Taking the account under s. 323

A

Bankruptcy set-off therefore requires an account to be taken of liabilities which, at the time of bankruptcy, may be due but not yet payable or may be unascertained in amount or subject to contingency. Nevertheless, the law says that the account shall be deemed to have been taken and the sums due from one party set off against the other as at the date of the bankruptcy. This is in accordance with the general principle of bankruptcy law, which governs payment of interest, conversion of foreign currencies etc., that the debts of the bankrupt are treated as having been ascertained and his assets simultaneously distributed among his creditors on the bankruptcy date: see *Re Dynamics Corporation of America* [1976] 1 WLR 757 at p. 762. It is clear, therefore, that when s. 323(2) speaks of taking an account of what is 'due' from each party, it does not mean that the sums in question must have been due and payable, whether at the bankruptcy date or even the date when the calculation falls to be made. The claims may have been contingent at the bankruptcy date and the creditor's claim against the bankrupt may remain contingent at the time of the calculation, but they are nevertheless included in the account. I consider next how this is done.

B

C

6. Quantifying the cross-claims

How does the law deal with the conundrum of having to set off, as of the bankruptcy date, 'sums due' which may not yet be due or which may become owing upon contingencies which have not yet occurred? It employs two techniques. The first is to take into account everything which has actually happened between the bankruptcy date and the moment when it becomes necessary to ascertain what, on that date, was the state of account between the creditor and the bankrupt. If by that time the contingency has occurred and the claim has been quantified, then that is the amount which is treated as having been due at the bankruptcy date. An example is *Sovereign Life Assurance Co v Dodd* [1892] 2 QB 573, in which the insurance company had lent Mr Dodd £1,170 on the security of his policies. The company was wound up before the policies had matured but Mr Dodd went on paying the premiums until they became payable. The Court of Appeal held that the account required by bankruptcy set-off should set off the full matured value of the policies against the loan.

D

E

But the winding up of the estate of a bankrupt or an insolvent company cannot always wait until all possible contingencies have happened and all the actual or potential liabilities which existed at the bankruptcy date have been quantified. Therefore the law adopts a second technique, which is to make an estimation of the value of the claim. Section 322(3) says:

F

> 'The trustee shall estimate the value of any bankruptcy debt which, by reason of its being subject to any contingency or contingencies or for any other reason, does not bear a certain value.'

G

This enables the trustee to quantify a creditor's contingent or unascertained claim, for the purposes of set-off or proof, in a way which will enable the trustee safely to distribute the estate, even if subsequent events show that the claim was worth more. There is no similar machinery for quantifying contingent or unascertained claims *against* the creditor, because it would be unfair upon him to have his liability to pay advanced merely because the trustee wants to wind up the bankrupt's estate.

H

7. The occasion for taking the account

In what circumstances must the account be taken? The language of s. 323(2) suggests an image of the trustee and creditor sitting down together, perhaps before a judge, and debating how the balance between them should be calculated. But the taking of the account really means no more than the calculation of the balance due in accordance with

A   the principles of insolvency law. An obvious occasion for making this calculation will be the lodging of a proof by a creditor against whom the bankrupt had a cross-claim. Indeed, it might have been thought from the words 'any creditor of the bankrupt proving or claiming to prove for a bankruptcy debt' in s. 323(1) that the operation of the section actually depended upon the lodging of a proof. But it has long been held that this is unnecessary and that the words should be construed to mean 'any creditor of the bankrupt who (apart from s. 323) would have been entitled to prove for a bankruptcy

B   debt'. Thus the account to which s. 323(2) refers may also be taken in an action by the trustee against a creditor who, because his cross-claim does not exceed that of the trustee, has not lodged a proof: see *Mersey Steel and Iron Co v Naylor Benzon & Co* (1882) 9 QBD 648 and *Re Daintrey, ex parte Mant* [1900] 1 QB 546 at p. 568.

Once one has eliminated any need for a proof in order to activate the operation of the section, it ceases to be linked to any step in the procedure of bankruptcy or litigation.

C   This is a sharp contrast with legal set-off, which can be invoked only by the filing of a defence in an action. Section 323, on the other hand, operates at the time of bankruptcy without any step having to be taken by either of the parties. The 'account' in accordance with s. 323(2) must be taken whenever it is necessary for *any* purpose to ascertain the effect which the section had. This is shown most clearly by the Australian case of *Gye v McIntyre* (1991) 171 CLR 609. In 1980 Gye, Perkes and three others bought a hotel in

D   New South Wales from a company for $1.25m. For this purpose they borrowed $200,000 from Mrs McIntyre, who was the company's tenant. The business was a failure and in June 1982 Mrs McIntyre obtained judgment by default for $224,000 in respect of her loan, interest and costs. Execution was stayed while Gye and Perkes pursued an action for damages against Mrs McIntyre for having fraudulently induced them to buy the hotel from the company by overstating its profits. In 1985 both Gye and Perkes entered into binding compositions with their creditors under which they assigned certain assets and

E   promised certain payments to a trustee for the benefit of their creditors. The assigned assets did not include the benefit of the action against Mrs McIntyre and she did not prove as a creditor in either composition. In 1988 the action against Mrs McIntyre was successful and Gye and Perkes obtained judgment in the sum of $214,600. They claimed a declaration that she was not entitled to set off the 1982 judgment, for which she could have proved in the compositions. The *Australian Bankruptcy Act* 1966 provides, if I may paraphrase in English terminology, that bankruptcy set-off shall apply in a composition

F   as if a bankruptcy order had been made on the day on which the resolution accepting the composition was passed and the trustee of the composition was the trustee in bankruptcy.

It will be observed that in this case the creditor was neither seeking to prove nor being sued by the trustee in bankruptcy. The issue was the effect which the deemed bankruptcy had had upon a claim which had never passed to the deemed trustee and which was later litigated between the bankrupt and the creditor. The High Court of Australia held that

G   bankruptcy set-off applied. The judgment of the court said, at p. 622:

> 'Section [323] is a statutory directive ("shall be set off") which operates as at the time the bankruptcy takes effect. It produces a balance upon the basis of which the bankruptcy administration can proceed. Only that balance can be claimed in the bankruptcy or recovered by the trustee. If its operation is to produce a nil balance, its effect will be that there is nothing at all which can be claimed in the bankruptcy

H   > or recovered in proceedings by the trustee. The section is self-executing in the sense that its operation is automatic and not dependent upon 'the option of either party': see, per Lord Selborne LC in *In re Deveze; Ex parte Barnett* (1874) 9 Ch. App. 293, 295.'

The court noted the majority decision of this House in *National Westminster Bank Ltd v Halesowen Presswork & Assemblies Ltd* [1972] AC 785 that the application of s. 323 is

mandatory in the sense that it cannot be excluded by prior agreement of the parties. But A
it said that whether or not it could be excluded by agreement, its operation did not
depend upon any procedural step. If, for example, the cross-claims produced a nil
balance, one would hardly expect either the creditor to prove or the trustee to sue. But
there could be no doubt that if the question subsequently needed to be decided, the two
claims would be treated as having extinguished each other. The court said:

> 'Even if one were to accept the dissenting view of Lord Cross of Chelsea in the B
> *National Westminster* case [1972] AC 785, 813-818 to the effect that the otherwise
> automatic operation of a provision such as [section 323] may be excluded by an
> antecedent agreement, it would be wrong to attribute to the legislature the illogical
> intent that a directive which was intended to be otherwise automatic in its
> operation and to apply in circumstances where set-off produced a nil balance
> should not operate at all unless and until either the bankrupt's creditor saw fit to
> exercise the option of lodging a formal proof of debt or the trustee in bankruptcy C
> instituted proceedings for recovery of a debt due to the bankrupt.'

8. Do the causes of action survive?

The principles so far discussed should provide an answer to the first of the issues in
this appeal, namely, whether if A, against whom B has a cross-claim, becomes bankrupt, D
A's claim against B continues to exist as a chose in action so that A's trustee can assign it
to a third party. In my judgment the conclusion must be that the original chose in action
ceases to exist and is replaced by a claim to a net balance. If the set-off is mandatory and
self-executing and results, as of the bankruptcy date, in only a net balance being owing, I
find it impossible to understand how the cross-claims can, as choses in action, each
continue to exist.

This was the conclusion of Neill J in *Farley v Housing & Commercial Developments Ltd* E
(1984) 1 BCC 99,150. Mr Farley was the principal shareholder in W Farley & Co
(Builders) Ltd, which in 1972 had entered into two agreements with the defendant
company to build blocks of flats. Both led to disputes, with claims by the building
company for money due under the contracts and cross-claims by the defendant for
damages. In 1975 the building company went into insolvent liquidation. In 1979 the
liquidator purported to assign to Mr Farley the benefit of the agreements and all moneys F
payable thereunder. Mr Farley then commenced arbitration proceedings under the
agreements. The arbitrator stated a special consultative case (p. 99,154) asking:

> '(1) Whether by reason of the provisions of [the then equivalent of s. 323 as applied
> to companies] upon the contractor becoming insolvent and being wound up ...
> the debts due under the [two agreements] ceased to have a separate existence as
> choses in action (and thus thereafter could not be assigned) being replaced by a G
> balance of account under [section 323].'

Neill J answered in the affirmative. I think that he was right. The cross-claims must
obviously be considered separately for the purpose of ascertaining the balance. For that
purpose they are treated as if they continued to exist. So, for example, the liquidator or
trustee will commence an action in which he pleads a claim for money due under a
contract and the defendant will counterclaim for damages under the same or a different H
contract. This may suggest that the respective claims actually do continue to exist until
the court has decided the amounts to which each party is entitled and ascertained the
balance due one way or the other in accordance with s. 323. But the litigation is merely
part of the process of retrospective calculation, from which it will appear that from the
date of bankruptcy, the only chose in action which continued to exist as an assignable
item of property was the claim to a net balance.

A   **9. The reasoning of the Court of Appeal**

The Court of Appeal took the view that Farley was wrong and that the separate causes of action survived the bankruptcy and could be assigned, subject to the 'equity' of the bankruptcy set-off. My Lords, the notion of an assignment subject to equities looks plausible when one is dealing with an assignment of the only claim which the bankrupt has against a creditor. In such a case it produces the same result as an assignment of the
B   net balance. But the fallacy is exposed if the bankrupt has more than one claim. Take, for example, the two contracts in Farley's case and assume that the liquidator at first assigns only one to Mr Farley. If each contract continues to exist as a chose in action, each can be the subject of a legal assignment. Mr Farley sues on his contract and by way of defence the defendants plead counterclaims for damages under both contracts. The court decides that the damages exceed the sums due under the contract and dismisses the action. The liquidator then assigns the other contract to Mrs Farley. She is not bound by
C   the decision in her husband's case and the defendant would have to plead and prove its counterclaims all over again. The account envisaged by s. 323 would have to be taken twice (with possibly differing results) when the section plainly contemplates a single calculation.

The argument for the plaintiff, which was recorded and accepted by Balcombe LJ in the Court of Appeal [1993] BCC 587 at p. 590F, began with the proposition that:

D   'Nothing in the wording of s. 323 changes the *nature* of set-off as it operates between solvent parties; it merely widens the categories of claim capable of being, and which must be, set off.'

I hope I have demonstrated that this submission is fundamentally wrong. It is true that bankruptcy set-off does cover a much wider range of claims than legal set-off. But for present purposes the important difference is that the latter must be pleaded and is given
E   effect only in the judgment of the court, whereas the latter is self-executing and takes effect on the bankruptcy date.

Secondly it was submitted for the plaintiff (p. 590G) that:

        'the language of the section draws a distinction between what is *due* – which is the word used in subs. (2) and (3) – and what is payable or recoverable – as under subs. (4). The separate causes of action (claim and cross-claim) remain due, and do
F   not cease to exist, until the set-off has been completed by payment one way or the other.'

This argument is derived, via *Derham on Set-off* (1987), p. 74, from a dictum of Mason J in *Day & Dent Constructions (Pty) Ltd v North Australian Properties (Pty) Ltd* (1982) 150 CLR 85. The judge said that 'due' in the Australian equivalent of s. 323(2) meant due at the date when the account had to be taken and he relied upon this construction to
G   explain why a creditor should be entitled to set off a debt which was contingent at the bankruptcy date. I would respectfully disagree because I think that 'due' merely means treated as having been owing at the bankruptcy date with the benefit of the hindsight and, if necessary, estimation prescribed by the bankruptcy law. The valuation provision in s. 322(3) shows that the contingency need not have occurred even at the time when the account has to be taken. But the point was not necessary for the decision and was in any
H   case addressing the question of what obligations should be taken into account in arriving at the net balance rather than whether those obligations survived as choses in action.

Thirdly, Balcombe LJ placed much weight upon a dictum of Brett J in *New Quebrada Co Ltd v Carr* (1869) LR 4 CP 651 at pp. 653–654. This was an action by a company in liquidation for calls against three partners, joint owners of shares in a company. The plea was a set-off of a debt alleged to be owing by the company to the shareholders. It is important to bear in mind that this was pleaded as a legal set-off under the Statutes of

Set-off, not a bankruptcy set-off arising on the liquidation of the company. Bankruptcy   A
set-off did not apply to company liquidations until the *Judicature Act* 1875. It was
therefore essential that the debt relied upon as set-off should have been legally actionable
by the defendants. The replication was that after the action had been brought and before
the plea, one of the partners had become bankrupt and his interest in the company's
alleged debt had vested in his assignee. It had therefore ceased to be actionable by him.
There was a demurrer to this replication. In support of the demurrer it was argued that
the bankrupt's share in the debt had not vested in his trustee because under s. 171 of the   B
Bankruptcy Act 1849 (the then equivalent of s. 323 of the *Insolvency Act* 1986) it was on
his bankruptcy automatically set off against the calls due to the company. Bovill CJ,
applying an earlier decision, disposed of the case on the ground that s. 171 applied only
to a sole trader and not to one partner in a firm. Byles J and Montague Smith J agreed.
Brett J also agreed, but went on to consider obiter what the effect of s. 171 would have
been if the bankrupt had been a sole trader. In his view, the debt owing to the bankrupt   C
would have vested in his trustee and therefore ceased to be actionable by the bankrupt.
Having so vested, it would then have been liable to be set off *in the bankruptcy* against
the company's claim to prove for calls. He added:

> '[Section 171] does not, I think, extinguish the mutual debts, but if it did, I should
> have thought it would have answered the plea of set-off. In either view I think it
> does not leave a right of action in the bankrupt against the plaintiffs, and that he   D
> cannot, therefore, avail himself of his claim against the plaintiffs under an ordinary
> plea of set-off, and that, on the present pleadings and argument, it seems to me, is
> all we have to decide.'

It should be noticed that s. 171 of the *Bankruptcy Law Consolidation Act* 1849 (12 &
13 Vict, c 106) said that 'one debt or demand *may* be set against another', as opposed to
the words 'the sum due from the one party *shall* be set off against any sum due from the
other party' which were used in the equivalent section [section 39] of the *Bankruptcy Act*   E
1869 (32 & 33 Vict, c 71) and all its successors. It is therefore perhaps not surprising that
the mandatory and self-executing nature of the set-off was not as fully apparent under
the Act of 1849 as it is today. At any rate, I do not think that despite the eminence of its
author, this somewhat throw-away dictum on the *Bankruptcy Act* 1849 can be regarded
as authoritative on the construction of s. 323 of the *Insolvency Act* 1986.

F

10. Can the net balance be assigned?

The next question is whether the trustee can assign the net balance. (I should mention
that the question was not put to Neill J in *Farley v Housing & Commercial Developments
Ltd* (1984) 1 BCC 99,150.) The duty of the trustee under s. 305(2) is to realise the
bankrupt's estate and the right to the net balance is part of the property of the bankrupt
vested in the trustee. One method of realisation is to transfer or assign the individual   G
assets for value. In *Ramsey v Hartley* [1977] 1 WLR 686 the Court of Appeal, following
authority which went back more than a century, held that even a bare right of action was
property which the trustee was entitled to assign. His statutory duty to realise the estate
excluded the doctrines of maintenance and champerty which would otherwise have struck
down such an assignment. Likewise, there is no rule to prevent him from assigning such
a right of action to the bankrupt himself. So why should a trustee not assign the right to
the net balance?   H

Mr Mark, for the appellant, says that the right cannot be assigned until the balance
has been quantified by the account taken under s. 323. The reason, he says, is that the
trustee must be party to the taking of that account. Bankruptcy set-off is, as Lord Simon
of Glaisdale said in *National Westminster Bank Ltd v Halesowen Presswork & Assemblies
Ltd* [1972] AC 785 at p. 809, part of a 'code of procedure whereby bankrupts' estates . . .

A   are to be administered in a proper and orderly way'. So, for example, s. 322(3) (which I have already quoted) requires the value of a contingent or otherwise unascertained debt to be estimated by the trustee.

I think that this submission of Mr Mark is wrong for the same reasons that persuaded me that his submission on the first issue was right. If bankruptcy set-off is self-executing, it does not require the trustee or anyone else to execute it. The argument gives too literal a meaning to the notion of taking an account. The case of *Gye v McIntyre* (1991) 171

B   CLR 609 shows the account being taken in proceedings to which the trustee was not a party. It is true that the situation arose because in a composition the parties are able to decide which property should vest in the trustee and could exclude the claim against Mrs McIntyre. In the case of a bankruptcy vesting is determined by the law. But for present purposes I can see no logical distinction between a case in which the trustee assigns the right to the net balance and one in which the bankrupt's claim, though subject to

C   bankruptcy set-off, did not vest in him in the first place.

It is true that the trustee will ordinarily not be party to the action between assignee and creditor. So if the creditor is asserting that there is actually a net balance in his favour for which he is entitled to prove, a successful outcome of the action will not, as a matter of res judicata, oblige the trustee to allow his proof. But there is no reason why a defendant should not, with leave, join the trustee as a defendant to his counterclaim. Even if the

D   action had been brought by the trustee, the creditor would have needed the leave of the court to make a counterclaim. In these circumstances, there seems to me little additional inconvenience in having to add the trustee as a party. I would therefore hold that a trustee may assign the right to the net balance like any other chose in action.

11. Questions of construction

E   Did the actual deed executed by the trustee have the effect of carrying the net balance? That is a question of construction. If a trustee purports to assign the bankrupt's rights in a cheque for £10,000, it would be absurd to hold that the deed has no effect because it turns out that the drawer of the cheque has some small counterclaim against the bankrupt. The intention of the parties is clear enough. If the assignment would have carried the original cause of action, it will also, as a matter of conveyance, carry the right to the balance after deduction of the cross-claim. Whether the assignee would have any

F   claim against the trustee for having purported to assign a greater interest than he actually had need not here be considered.

There is greater difficulty if the trustee has assigned *less* than the net balance, i.e. to have kept back some credit item in the calculation. This would be an assignment of a part of a debt. On ordinary principles it would not be enforceable in proceedings to which the trustee was not a party. Only if the trustee joined as a plaintiff could the single

G   account envisaged by s. 323 be taken.

In this case the deed of assignment of 4 April 1991 recited that the trustee had agreed with the bankrupt for the assignment to him of:

> 'such claims and legal rights of action as are hereinafter mentioned which the trustee as trustee in bankruptcy of the assignee may have against [the defendant]'.

The operative part said in cl. 1 that the trustee assigned to the bankrupt:

H

> 'such claim or claims against Mr Blake as the trustee may have as trustee in the bankruptcy of the assignee as presently formulated, or as amended by counsel with the trustee's approval, based only on the facts pleaded in consolidated action no. Ch 1989 S-8148 and 1988 S-4555 ('the claim') to the intent that the assignee shall be entitled (subject as hereinafter mentioned) to such moneys as Mr Blake may be to the assignee in settlement of the claim.'

By cl. 6(ii) the parties agreed, for the avoidance of doubt, that:

'nothing in this agreement shall affect the trustee's right to take action against Mr Blake if so advised in relation to matters not arising out of the facts other than those pleaded in the aforesaid consolidated action.'

My Lords, the fact that the assignment makes no express reference to the defendant's cross-claim is, for the reasons I have given, no obstacle to holding the assignment effective to carry whatever balance is due after its deduction. But if the effect of this last clause was that the trustee retained a part of his claim to the net balance against Mr Blake, then in my judgment the action would not have been properly constituted until the trustee had been added as a party. Mr Blake could not be put in a position in which he had to raise the same cross-claim in two sets of proceedings. His remedy would have been to apply to have the action stayed until the trustee had been added. Before your Lordships' House, however, Mr Bannister QC for the plaintiff said that the trustee asserted no other causes of action against Mr Blake. He is willing to make it clear that he is assigning the whole of the net balance due to the bankrupt's estate. In these circumstances it is unnecessary to discuss further the question of what might have happened if there had been an application for a stay on the grounds that the proceedings were not properly constituted. The application to which the judge actually acceded was to dismiss the action on the ground that Mr Stein had no title to sue. For the reasons which I have given, which I think were the alternative reasons of Staughton LJ, the Court of Appeal was in my judgment right to hold that the judge's order could not be supported. I would therefore dismiss this appeal.

12. The wider issues

I should add in conclusion that although the appeal may have turned on a somewhat technical question, it is a symptom of a wider problem. Although Mr Mark argued that it was inconvenient and unjust that the account under s. 323 should be taken between him and Mr Stein, rather than between him and the trustee, he frankly admitted that his main grievance was that despite the bankruptcy, he was still being pursued by Mr Stein with the benefit of legal aid. But he acknowledged that this complaint would have been the same if there had been no counterclaim and the case had not fallen within s. 323 at all.

It is a matter of common occurrence for an individual to become insolvent while attempting to pursue a claim against someone else. In some cases, the bankruptcy will itself have been caused by the failure of the other party to meet his obligations. In many more cases, this will be the view of the bankrupt. It is not unusual in such circumstances for there to be a difference of opinion between the trustee and the bankrupt over whether a claim should be pursued. The trustee may have nothing in his hands with which to fund litigation. Even if he has, he must act in the interests of creditors generally and the creditors will often prefer to receive an immediate distribution rather than see the bankrupt's assets ventured on the costs of litigation which may or may not yield a larger distribution at some future date. The bankrupt, with nothing more to lose, tends to take a more sanguine view of the prospects of success. In such a case the trustee may decide, as in this case, that the practical course in the interests of all concerned (apart from the defendant) is to assign the claim to the bankrupt and let him pursue it for himself, on terms that he accounts to the trustee for some proportion of the proceeds.

It is understandable that a defendant who does not share the bankrupt's view of the merits of the claim may be disappointed to find that notwithstanding the bankruptcy, which he thought would result in a practical commercial decision by an independent trustee to discontinue the proceedings, the action is still being pursued by the bankrupt. His disappointment is increased if he finds that the bankrupt as plaintiff in his own name

A   has the benefit of legal aid which would not have been available to the trustee. Similar considerations apply to an assignment of a right of action by the liquidator of an insolvent company to a shareholder or former director. In such a case there is the further point that the company as plaintiff can be required to give security for costs. The shareholder assignee as an individual cannot be required to give security even if (either because he does not qualify or the legal aid board considers that the claim has no merits) he is not in receipt of legal aid.

B   I mention these questions because they were alluded to by Mr Mark as a policy reason for why the courts should be restrictive of the right of bankruptcy trustees or liquidators to assign claims. But the problems can be said to arise not so much from the law of insolvency as from the insoluble difficulties of operating a system of legal aid and costs which is fair to both plaintiffs and defendants. Mr Blake is in no worse position now than he was before the bankruptcy when Mr Stein was suing him with legal aid (although

C   this would not have been the case if the plaintiff had been a company). Mr Blake's complaint is that the bankruptcy has brought him no relief. But whether it should seems to me a matter for Parliament to decide.

(Appeal dismissed)

D

E

F

G

H

Re Grayan Building Services Ltd.
Secretary of State for Trade and Industry v Gray & Anor.

Chancery Division (Companies Court) and Court of Appeal.
Arden J; Neill, Hoffmann and Henry L JJ.
Judgment delivered 5 August 1993 and 10 November 1994.

Disqualifying unfit directors of insolvent companies – Whether directors' conduct rendered them unfit – Appeal – Whether court was concerned with unfitness at time of hearing – When appellate court could interfere with decision on fitness – Whether directors' conduct had fallen below appropriate standard – Company Directors Disqualification Act 1986, s. 6, s. 9(1).

This was an application under s. 6 of the Company Directors Disqualification Act 1986.

The respondents were directors of Grayan Building Services Ltd ('Grayan') which went into voluntary liquidation on 10 February 1989.

The complaints made against the respondents were (1) making payments which were preferences; (2) trading at the risk of creditors; (3) making a prohibited loan to themselves; (4) failure to keep accounting records; and (5) late filing of accounts for 1987. In respect of the alleged preferences the respondents had repaid £25,000 to the liquidators.

The judge made no disqualification order. In respect of complaint (1) other remedies had been pursued and their conduct in relation to the preferences did not render them unfit at the date of the hearing. Complaints (4) and (5) did not render them unfit since they had taken steps to improve the company's accounting systems and the late filing of the 1987 accounts was an isolated incident. In respect of complaint (3) the sums drawn by the respondents did not strictly constitute 'loans' for the purposes of s. 330 and were, in any case, of minimal amounts. Finally, in respect of complaint (2) the respondents should have realised that certain claims against another company (of which they were subcontractors) would not be met. However that was shortly before liquidation took place. Their failure to reach the same conclusion significantly earlier, however regrettable it might have been, was not such as to render them unfit. The Secretary of State appealed, accepting the judge's findings of fact but challenging the evaluation of them and the decision that they did not amount to conduct falling below the requisite standard.

Held, allowing the appeal and disqualifying the respondents for two years:

1. The word 'makes' in s. 6(1)(b) of the Disqualification Act did not allow the court to consider the need for disqualification at the time of the hearing. The court was concerned solely with the conduct relied on as showing unfitness, in order to decide whether that conduct, viewed cumulatively and taking into account any extenuating circumstances, fell below the appropriate standards of probity and competence. Where the conduct did fall below that standard, the making of a disqualification order was mandatory whether in the individual case the court thought this was necessary in the public interest or not.

2. Since the question for the court was a narrow one, namely whether specific conduct measured up to a standard of probity and competence fixed by the court, the appellate court was in as good a position as the trial judge to form a judgment as to unfitness where there was little or no dispute as to the primary facts.

3. The judge's reasoning on the preferences was wrong in principle. There was also force in criticism of the test applied in relation to the allegation of trading while insolvent. Taking into account the preferences, which the judge disregarded for an inadmissible reason, the conduct of the directors did fall below the appropriate standard for persons fit to be directors of companies.

A   The following cases were referred to in the judgments of Arden J and Hoffmann LJ:

Bath Glass Ltd, Re (1988) 4 BCC 130.
Benmax v Austin Motor Co Ltd [1955] AC 370.
Coventry (deceased), Re [1980] Ch 461.
ECM (Europe) Electronics Ltd, Re [1991] BCC 268.
Hitco 2000 Ltd, Re [1995] BCC 161.

B   *Lo-Line Electric Motors Ltd & Ors, Re* (1988) 4 BCC 415; [1988] Ch 477.
Mitchell (George) (Chesterhall) Ltd v Finney Lock Seeds Ltd [1983] 2 AC 803.
Pamstock Ltd, Re [1994] BCC 264.
Polly Peck International plc, Re [1993] BCC 890.
Sevenoaks Stationers (Retail) Ltd, Re [1990] BCC 765; [1991] Ch 164.
Swift 736 Ltd, Re [1993] BCC 312.

C   Roger Kaye QC (in the Court of Appeal) and Malcolm Davis-White (instructed by the Treasury Solicitor) for the Secretary of State for Trade and Industry.

Edward Bannister QC (in the Court of Appeal) and Robin Hollington (instructed by Field Seymour Parkes, Reading) for the first respondent.

HIGH COURT JUDGMENT
(Delivered 5 August 1993)

D   **Arden J:** This is an application by the Secretary of State for Trade and Industry against Walter Gifford Gray (whom I shall call Mr Gray) and David Erskine Paterson (whom I shall call Mr Paterson). The Secretary of State has been represented by Mr Malcolm Davis-White, and Mr Gray has been represented by Mr Robin Hollington. Mr Paterson appeared in person.

The application is under s. 6 of the *Company Directors Disqualification Act* 1986 ('the Act') and seeks an order that the respondents should not, without the leave of the court, be directors or be concerned in, or take part in, the management of a company for a period of not less than two and not exceeding 15 years from the date of such order.

Section 6 of the Act provides in material part as follows:

'(1) The court shall make a disqualification order against a person in any case where, on an application under this section, it is satisfied–

    (a) that he is or has been a director of a company which has at any time become insolvent (whether while he was a director or subsequently) and

    (b) that his conduct as a director of that company (either taken alone or taken together with his conduct as a director of any other company or companies) makes him unfit to be concerned in the management of a company.

(2) For the purposes of this section and the next, a company becomes insolvent if–

    (a) the company goes into liquidation at a time when its assets are insufficient for the payment of its debts and other liabilities and the expenses of the winding up . . .

(3) . . .

(4) Under this section the minimum period of disqualification is 2 years, and the maximum period is 15 years.'

H   Mr Gray and Mr Paterson were directors of Grayan Building Services Ltd (which I shall call 'Grayan') from respectively 14 December 1984 and 9 January 1985 until 10 February 1989 when Grayan entered voluntary liquidation. The first condition is in my judgment satisfied: I give details as to the position in the liquidation below. So the only issue is whether the second condition is likewise satisfied. The conduct which the application requires me to consider is the conduct of the respondents as directors of Grayan.

Section 9(1) of the Act provides: A

'(1) Where it falls to a court to determine whether a person's conduct as a director or shadow director of any particular company or companies makes him unfit to be concerned in the management of a company, the court shall, as respects his conduct as a director of that company or, as the case may be, each of those companies, have regard in particular–

   (a) to the matters mentioned in Part I of Schedule 1 to this Act, and   B

   (b) where the company has become insolvent, to the matters mentioned in Part II of that Schedule;

and references in that Schedule to the director and the company are to be read accordingly.'

Schedule 1 contains two parts. The first sets out matters applicable in all cases; the second sets out matters applicable where the company has become insolvent. Mr Davis-White relied on the following paragraphs: C

'*Part I – Matters Applicable in all Cases*

1. Any misfeasance or breach of any fiduciary or other duty by the director in relation to the company.

2. Any misapplication or retention by the director of, or any conduct by the director giving rise to an obligation to account for, any money or other property of the company.   D

3. . . .

4. The extent of the director's responsibility for any failure by the company to comply with any of the following provisions of the Companies Act, namely–

   (a) section 221 (companies to keep accounting records) . . .   E

5. The extent of the director's responsibility for any failure by the directors of the company to comply with–

   (a) section 226 or 227 of the Companies Act (duty to prepare annual accounts) or,

   (b) section 233 of that Act (approval and signature of accounts).   F

Part II – Matters Applicable Where Company Has Become Insolvent

6. The extent of the director's responsibility for the causes of the company becoming insolvent.

7. The extent of the director's responsibility for any failure by the company to supply and goods or services which have been paid for (in whole or in part).

8. The extent of the director's responsibility for the company entering into any transaction or giving any preference, being a transaction or preference–   G

   (a) liable to be set aside under . . . sections 238–240 of the Insolvency Act . . .'

In *Re Sevenoaks Stationers (Retail) Ltd* [1990] BCC 765; [1991] Ch 164, Dillon LJ held that the word 'unfit' in s. 6(1)(b) was an ordinary English word and that the question whether a person was 'unfit' to be concerned in the management of a company within the meaning of s. 6(1)(b) of the Act was a question of fact. At p. 773B; 176A Dillon LJ   H
held:

'It is beyond dispute that the purpose of s. 6 is to protect the public, and in particular potential creditors of companies, from losing money through companies becoming insolvent when the directors of those companies are people unfit to be concerned in the management of a company.

A   The test laid down in s. 6 – apart from the requirement that the person concerned is or has been a director of a company which has become insolvent – is whether the person's conduct as a director of the company or companies in question 'makes him unfit to be concerned in the management of a company'. These are ordinary words of the English language and they should be simple to apply in most cases. It is important to hold to those words in each case.

B   The judges of the Chancery Division have, understandably, attempted in certain cases to give guidance as to what does or does not make a person unfit to be concerned in the management of a company. Thus in *Re Lo-Line Electric Motors Ltd* [1988] Ch 477; (1988) 4 BCC 415 the Vice-Chancellor said at p. 486; 419:

> "Ordinary commercial misjudgment is in itself not sufficient to justify disqualification. In the normal case, the conduct complained of must display a lack of commercial probity, although I have no doubt in an extreme case of
C   gross negligence or total incompetence disqualification could be appropriate."

Then, at p. 492; 424, he said that the director in question,

> "has been shown to have behaved in a commercially culpable manner in trading through limited companies when he knew them to be insolvent and in using the unpaid Crown debts to finance such trading."

D   Such statements may be helpful in identifying particular circumstances in which a person would clearly be unfit. But there seems to have been a tendency, which I deplore, on the part of the Bar, and possibly also on the part of the official receiver's department, to treat the statements as judicial paraphrases of the words of the statute which fall to be construed as a matter of law in lieu of the words of the statue. The result is to obscure that the true question to be tried is a question of fact – what used to be pejoratively described in the Chancery Division as a "jury
E   question".'

In the *Sevenoaks* case itself, the respondent was not found to be dishonest but to be incompetent or negligent 'in a very marked degree' (p. 780C; 184B). Significantly Dillon LJ did not think it necessary for incompetence to be total as suggested by Browne-Wilkinson V-C in *Re Lo-Line Electric Motors Ltd* (1988) 4 BCC 415; [1988] Ch 477 at p. 419; 486 to render a director unfit to take part in the management of a company (see
F   per Dillon LJ at p. 780C; 184C).

The background in this case is that Grayan provided a package of heating, electrical, ventilation and plumbing services (often to be performed by subcontractors of Grayan) when buildings were in the course of construction. At all material times the respondents were the only directors. Grayan had some three major contracts:

(1)   (started August 1987) in connection with the refurbishment of the Prince of Wales
G   Hotel, Kensington, London;

(2)   (started February 1987) in connection with the erection of a block of luxury flats in Avenue Road, St John's Wood, London NW8; and

(3)   (started April 1988) in connection with the erection of the Randsworth Centre.

These contracts were subcontracts with Fairclough Building Ltd (hereafter 'Fairclough'),
H   which was the main contractor on the site. The contracts provided that Fairclough would only be bound to pay Grayan if it in turn was paid by the building owner (a 'pay when paid' clause). Fairclough was not paid by the owner of the property in Avenue Road and in reliance on its rights under its contract Fairclough did not pay Grayan. It did not (until January 1989) in terms tell Grayan that it would not be paying Grayan's outstanding claims in respect of this contract. But according to Mr Vooght (one of the joint liquidators of Grayan as appears below) Fairclough had in fact decided before

Grayan went into liquidation not to pay its claims in respect of Avenue Road. Mr Vooght A
accepted that Fairclough's failure to state its position earlier was commercially dishonest
or immoral. Grayan did not have a 'pay when paid clause' in its contracts with its
subcontractors and accordingly Grayan remained liable to pay them even though it had
not been paid by Fairclough. Some subcontractors were persuaded not to take action
against Grayan while Grayan itself was waiting for payment. In the end, however,
Grayan ran out of money, and the respondents caused Grayan to enter creditors'
voluntary liquidation after receiving advice from Cork Gully. The joint liquidators are B
Nicolas John Vooght and John Martin Iredale whom I shall call Mr Vooght and Mr
Iredale respectively.

The matters on which the Secretary of State relies as demonstrating that the
respondents are unfit to be concerned in the management of a company are as follows:

'(a) That the respondents caused Grayan to enter into a transaction that afforded
a preference by repaying its bank overdraft of which they were guarantors at a C
time when they knew or should have known that Grayan was insolvent (see
para. 41–50).

(b) That the respondents caused Grayan to make a payment of £12,000 to Grayan
Construction Ltd, a company of which they sole directors at a time when they
knew, or should have known, that Grayan was insolvent (see para. 51).

(c) That the respondents caused Grayan to continue trading at a time when there D
was no reasonable prospect of making payment for creditors' claims (see para. 52–
66).

(d) That the respondents caused Grayan to make loans to themselves in
contravention of the provisions of s. 339 of the *Companies Act* 1985 (see para. 37–
40).

(e) That the respondents failed to ensure that accounting records were maintained E
in accordance with the provisions of s. 221 of the *Companies Act* 1985 (see
para. 37–40).

(f) That the respondents failed to ensure that audited accounts were filed with the
registrar of companies in accordance with the provisions of s. 242 of the *Companies
Act* 1985 (see para. 33–36).'

(Affidavit of Mr Vooght sworn on 1 February 1991, para. 67). F

Mr Vooght, Mr Elles and Mr Gray gave evidence and were cross-examined. Mr
Paterson did not himself give evidence, expressing himself content to adopt what Mr
Gray had said. Mr Davis-White gave an indication on behalf of the Secretary of State
that he would not seek to invite the court to draw inferences from the fact Mr Paterson
had not given evidence. In the circumstances, I have had to assess the conduct of Mr
Paterson and Mr Gray as directors, on the same evidence. G

I will now set out the facts as I find them to be:

1. In its first two financial years (ending 31 March 1986 and 31 March 1987
respectively) Grayan made losses and these resulted in a debit balance on profit and loss
account at 31 March 1987 of £140,336.

2. The last date for filing Grayan's accounts for the period ended 31 March 1987 was
31 January 1988. They were not in fact filed until 15 December 1988. H

3. In the year ended 31 March 1988 Grayan made a profit of £114,737. The deficit on
profit and loss account was thereby reduced to £25,599. Grayan continued to trade until
the date of the commencement of its liquidation.

4. The statement of affairs sworn by the respondents showed an estimated deficiency
as regards creditors of some £745,087. In the statement of affairs, contracts were written

A   down from their book value of £1,653,967 to £150,000. The liquidators have in fact realised only some £69,073 in respect of these contracts. In the result, only a small dividend has been paid to preferential creditors and no dividend has been paid to unsecured creditors.

    5. The respondents each held 50 per cent of the issued share capital of Grayan (£20,000). Mr Gray was chairman and chief executive with responsibility for sales. Mr Paterson was managing director and had responsibility for general administration. The respondents shared responsibility for the accountancy function.

    6. Grayan's borrowings were by overdraft from National Westminster Bank plc (hereafter 'the bank'). The overdraft facility was originally £30,000 but it was increased to £80,000 by the end of 1986. On 8 February 1989 the facility was increased to £85,000. The respondents and their wives had executed unlimited guarantees of this facility, secured by second charge on their homes. At the date of the liquidation the amount of the overdraft had been reduced to £2,604.

    7. At all material times, the auditors of Grayan were Ernst & Whinney and the partner in charge of the audit was William Jason Hugh Elles (whom I shall call Mr Elles).

The Avenue Road contract

    8. This contract was scheduled to commence in February 1987 and to be completed by December 1987. It was not in fact completed until some nine months later. Grayan submitted a loss and expense claim to Fairclough in the sum of £338,048. Fairclough did not reject this offer but declined to accept Grayan's offer in October 1988 to settle it on the basis of a discount of some seven per cent.

    In relation to this contract, and in relation to the Prince of Wales Hotel contract, Grayan had a financing arrangement with Fairclough to certify payments on a fortnightly basis in return for a financing charge.

    Grayan gave preliminary notice to Fairclough of its loss and expense claim on this contract in January 1988. By letter dated 16 September 1988, it sought payment of the balance of its measured claim (less a retention) amounting to £61,750 and a payment on account of its loss and expense claim.

    Mr Gray's evidence was that he had no reason to believe but that, once the flats were sold, Grayan's account would be paid in full. The flats were however luxury flats with sale prices in excess of £1m at a time when there was a slump in the property market. The Secretary of State's case was that it was unreasonable for Grayan to expect that its loss and expense claim would be met in full. In January 1989 Fairclough told Grayan that its claim on this contract would not be met.

Prince of Wales Hotel contract

    9. Work on this contract worth £1.9m began late and had not been completed by the date of the liquidation. The project was beset with problems from the start. Ownership of the hotel changed and this led to delays and variations. Moreover in the summer of 1988 there was a change in the project surveyor and consulting engineers which caused further problems.

    Grayan made complaints to Fairclough about the late payment of its claims on this contract from about March 1988.

    In September 1988, Grayan wrote to its principal subcontractors on the Prince of Wales site to advise them of its cashflow difficulties. I have not seen a copy of this document.

    On liquidation Grayan withdrew from this site to enable Fairclough to complete the contract using Grayan's subcontractors.

The Randsworth Centre   A

10. Work commenced on this contract, an office development, in April 1988. The design of the installation was not compatible with the building and numerous changes were required. The final account had not been agreed by the date of liquidation. The quantity surveyors had required a fully documented account of the variations to prove the ineffectiveness of the original design and the subsequent design changes by others. It had become clear in January 1989 that prompt settlement on this contract was unlikely.   B

Grayan sought payment on account of these variations from Fairclough from about November 1988. The total claim was in excess of £400,000.

On liquidation Grayan ceased work on this site and Fairclough employed its subcontractors direct so as to minimise possible claims against Grayan.

11. Grayan came under pressure from its creditors towards the end of 1988 and a number of writs were issued.   C

Meeting with the bank on 31 January 1989 and subsequent events

12(a) On 31 January 1989 Mr Gray and Mr Paterson had a meeting at their request with the manager of the bank at its Caversham branch. Grayan was clearly under pressure from its creditors. Mr Gray sought an increase in Grayan's facility from £80,000 to £200,000. The request was referred to Area Head Office and Mr Gray and Mr Paterson were advised to consult Ernst & Whinney.   D

(b) On 1 and 2 February 1989 the respondents had meetings with Jeff Knight (to whom I shall refer as Mr Knight) of Ernst & Whinney who suggested various alternative ways for raising fresh funds. They also met with Mr Elles. Mr Elles advised the directors not to make payments to creditors although payments essential for keeping the company alive were probably all right. Mr Elles says that he advised that such payments might be preferences (he could not remember if he had used that term as such) for which the directors might be personally liable. Mr   E
Elles agreed with Mr Gray that the directors were not specifically told not to make payments into the existing bank account of Grayan.

(c) On 6 February 1989 Mr Gray, Mr Paterson, Mr Knight and Mr Elles attended a further meeting with the bank at the bank's Reading Business Centre.

There is a detailed note of this meeting prepared by one of the managers of the   F
bank, Mr Fitzgerald. It appears from it that one of the reasons why the Caversham branch had not granted an increase in the facility was that the directors were unwilling to allow their houses to stand as security for any increase in the facility. It also appears that Grayan had summonses and writs issued against it totalling £65,000 and that writs and summonses claiming a further £110,000 were threatened. Various possibilities for future action were canvassed including administration and liquidation. The respondents accepted responsibility for   G
Grayan's financial position. The figures produced to the bank showed a peak borrowing requirement of some £371,000 in March or April 1989. The bank made it clear that it would be unwilling to advance further funds if the directors were not willing to provide further security over their houses. The directors indicated that they might be prepared to do this if the bank would commit itself to seeing Grayan through its current problems. The note compiled by Mr Fitzgerald then states: H

'... I, therefore, suggested that if there was a way forward then this would need to be against the close involvement of auditors, Ernst & Whinney, with Jason Elles's insolvency department undertaking a brief review of certain aspects to give the bank comfort. Providing the information was acceptable then against mortgage debenture security the bank may be prepared to provide the support that the company needs.

A   It was, therefore, left that the directors would discuss with Ernst & Whinney the bank's requirements which were namely:

1. A revised cash flow forecast from the company with an overview by Ernst & Whinney to confirm accuracy.

2. Management accounts, including balance sheet and profit & loss, to be drawn at 31.1.89 to confirm the current levels of profitability.

B   3. Ernst & Whinney to undertake a scrutiny of debtors to confirm that these are bona fide with no outstanding claims and should be readily collectible.

4. Ernst & Whinney to undertake an assessment of current contracts to confirm profitability of each.

C   5. Confirmation by Ernst & Whinney that creditors had agreed a moratorium on repayment which was reflected in the new cash flow.'

The note concludes with discussion of the need for funding in the period to 13 February 1989, as the investigation requested could not be completed until then.

The note records that in the early part of the meeting Ernst & Whinney confirmed that Grayan had traded profitably in the current year, and that 'a quick estimate was that net profit for the 10 months trading period of the existing year would be D   in the region of £20,000'. I accept Mr Elles' evidence that this confirmation came from Mr Knight and that it would have been based on information provided to Ernst & Whinney by the directors. I thus reject Mr Gray's explanation that this figure was produced by Ernst & Whinney from information in their own files. The statement was not one that Ernst & Whinney could be expected to make without information from the directors.

E   (d) After this meeting, Mr Elles told Mr Gray and Mr Paterson that Ernst & Whinney would require their outstanding fees to be reduced by £12,000 before undertaking any further work. Mr Gray and Mr Paterson therefore decided to produce a business plan themselves. There is in evidence a business plan which Mr Gray says was prepared after the meeting with the bank on 6 February 1989. However it contains information which was already then available. The business plan comprised:

F   (i) an 11 point plan for improving the administration and concluding that the cash requirement of Grayan would diminish;

(ii) a single page explaining why Grayan had been short of cash. This contains six numbered paragraphs including 5 and 6 as follows:

'5. The accounting system does not easily allow for extraction of G   necessary management information and it is planned to introduce, with immediate effect, a computerised system using software that is in regular use in the contracting industry to produce the information necessary.

6. There are currently on going claims for extensions of time payment which are shown on the schedule, some are progressing more positively than others, for this reason it would be realistic to allow for H   a 25 per cent success rate and accordingly in the fullness of time – probably the next six months – we can expect payments of about £125,000 which have *not* been included in the cash flow forecast.'

(iii) A list of debtors showing that on the basis that loss and expense claims were worth their full amount, debtors exceeded creditors by some £207,067.51. I would comment that this statement is subject to the qualifications:

    (a) that such claims may be worth less than their face amounts; and   A

    (b) that such claims may not be realised for some time.

  (iv) Schedules showing contractual payments and retention.

   (v) A cash flow statement for February 1989 to January 1990 and assumptions. This showed a peak borrowing requirement of £371,000 to March 1989, and an overdraft to January 1990 of some £246,000.

  (vi) A list of summonses and writs totalling £64,768.06.

 (vii) A list of subcontractors' claims totalling £458,197.77 and the amounts at which they could be expected to accept now namely, £287,865, leaving a balance of £170,332 payable in March 1989.

(viii) A list of the claims, totalling £110,005.88, of the creditors who had issued letters before action.

  (ix) A summary of the order book, value £2,038,011.

   (x) A list of creditors with the dates when their claims became due.

The total shown for creditors was £621,439.51, of which £504,650.70 fell due in December 1988. Most of the balance had fallen due in September, October or November 1988.

(e)   On 7 and 8 February 1989 Mr Gray and Mr Paterson pressed debtors including Fairclough for payment. This appears to have been in accordance with advice given by Ernst & Whinney. On 8 February 1989 Mr Gray had a meeting with Mr Batchelor of Fairclough. He did not make any promises as to payment but said he would see what he could do.

(f)   On 9 February 1989 Mr Batchelor telephoned Grayan's offices and left a message that a cheque for £80,500 was available for collection to be paid against the Prince of Wales site. Mr Gray says that there were no 'strings' attached to this cheque and that Grayan was not obliged to use the cheque to pay specified subcontractors. On previous occasions, starting in late 1988, Fairclough had approved a list of subcontractors who were to be paid out of the moneys it paid. In my judgment it is more probable than not that to obtain any moneys from Fairclough Mr Gray had to explain Grayan's financial situation and why it needed the money, so leading Fairclough to believe that the money would be used in a particular way.

(g)   The cheque was collected by an employee of Grayan called Richard Hunt, who had attended some of the earlier meetings with the bank, Ernst & Whinney and Mr Batchelor. He paid the cheque into Grayan's account at the branch of the bank nearest to Fairclough's offices. Mr Gray said that it was the normal practice to collect cheques and to pay them in as quickly as possible so that subcontractors could be paid. In fact Grayan had already issued cheques totalling £60,000 earlier in the week and placed a stop on them after the meeting with the bank when it was clear that there would be no immediate increase in the facility. Mr Gray executed a written confirmation of the stop at the bank's offices early on the morning of Thursday, 9 February 1989. A further cheque for £2,000 was banked on 10 February 1989. Mr Gray's explanation for not lifting the stop immediately was that the directors were going to decide which creditors to pay after the meeting with the bank fixed for 13 February 1989.

(h)   Later on the same day, in the afternoon, Mr Gray and Mr Paterson had a meeting with Ernst & Whinney. There was a discussion of the various alternatives for refinancing Grayan that had been investigated, but, as nothing had borne fruit, Ernst & Whinney advised that Cork Gully should be called in to advise. Mr Gray says that this was the first indication he had from Ernst & Whinney that Grayan

A   might go into receivership or liquidation. On this I prefer Mr Elles' evidence that liquidation would have been among the options considered at the meetings with them on 1 and 2 February.

(i)   Cork Gully attended the premises of Grayan on the morning of Friday 10 February. After some examination of Grayan's financial position they advised that the right course was for Grayan to enter liquidation. Subsequent to that, on the same day, the respondents as the only members of Grayan passed a resolution for voluntary liquidation.

(j)   At the date of liquidation, Grayan had confirmed orders of some £2m.

I now take the matters relied upon by the Secretary of State in more detail:

(A) *Payment to the bank of £80,500 and £2,000 on 8 and 10 February 1989 respectively*

It is said that these payments were preferences by virtue of s. 239 of the *Insolvency Act 1986* which provides in material part as follows:

(2) Where the company has at a relevant time (defined in the next section) given a preference to any person, the office-holder may apply to the court for an order under this section.

(3) Subject as follows, the court shall, on such an application, make such order as it thinks fit for restoring the position to what it would have been if the company had not given that preference.

(4) For the purposes of this section and section 241, a company gives a preference to a person if–

(a) that person is one of the company's creditors or a surety or guarantor for any of the company's debts or other liabilities, and

(b) the company does anything or suffers anything to be done which (in either case) has the effect of putting that person into a position which, in the event of the company going into insolvent liquidation, will be better than the position he would have been in if that thing had not been done.

(5) The court shall not make an order under this section in respect of a preference given to any person unless the company which gave the preference was influenced in deciding to give it by a desire to produce in relation to that person the effect mentioned in subsection (4)(b).

(6) A company which has given a preference to a person connected with the company (otherwise than by reason only of being its employee) at the time the preference was given is presumed, unless the contrary is shown, to have been influenced in deciding to give it by such a desire as is mentioned in subsection (5).'

The payments made on 8 and 10 February 1989 were made at a 'relevant time' for the purposes of s. 239. As Mr Gray and Mr Paterson had guaranteed the bank overdraft, s. 239(6) applies. The onus would therefore be on them to show the requisite desire to prefer did not exist.

The liquidators took out preference proceedings against the bank. In February 1992, these proceedings were settled on terms that the respondents contributed £12,000 to the costs of the bank and paid £25,000 to the liquidators.

(B) *Payment of £12,000 to Grayan Construction Ltd (hereafter 'Construction') on 8 February 1989*

I make the following additional findings in relation to this matter:

(i)   Construction was owned by the respondents. It had lent some £29,000 to Grayan.   A
It needed to recover back some of that money to meet its own liabilities.
Construction was then trading but has since ceased to trade.

(ii) On 8 February 1989 Mr Paterson drew a cheque on Grayan's account in favour of
Construction.

(iii) On 26 February 1990 the liquidators obtained judgment against Construction in
the sum of £12,000 in proceedings alleging that this payment was a preference.   B

(C) *Trading at the risk of creditors: September 1988 to 10 February 1989*

In my judgment, the Secretary of State has established that Grayan was insolvent from
September 1988 and unable to meet its liabilities as they fell due, and further that this
would have been known to the respondents. The Secretary of State relied on the following
matters which I find as facts:

(i)   Grayan's 1987 accounts were the subject of a going concern qualification by the   C
auditors in these terms in their report dated 28 November 1988:

'The accounts have been prepared on a going concern basis. This basis may not
be appropriate because the company incurred a loss of £83,508 during the year
ended 31 March 1987 and at that date its liabilities exceeded its assets by
£120,336 and its current liabilities exceeded its current assets by £155,066.

Should the company be unable to continue trading, adjustments would have to   D
be made to reduce the value of assets to their recoverable amount, to provide
for any further liabilities which might arise and to reclassify fixed assets and
long term liabilities as current assets and liabilities.'

(ii) Between September and October 1988, Grayan received some four writs for sums
between £500 and £5,000 respectively. These sums were not material but are
indicative of an ability to meet liabilities as they fell due.   E

(iii) At the date of liquidation, Grayan owed £18,246 in respect of PAYE for 1988/89.

(iv) Grayan wrote to subcontractors on the Prince of Wales site in September 1988
informing them of its difficulties.

(v)   The report given to creditors at the creditors' meeting to approve the appointment
of the liquidators admitted that Grayan had difficulties meeting its liabilities from
October/November 1988. This report was based on information provided by the   F
respondents.

(vi) In December 1988 Grayan made a number of round sum payments to creditors to
appease them.

(vii) From August 1988 onwards Grayan was receiving money from Fairclough on
condition that it would then be paid to specified creditors.

(D) *Loans in breach of s. 330 of the Companies Act 1985*   G

Section 330 prohibits a company from making a loan to a director. The prohibition is
subject to a number of exceptions, none of which is relevant. What happened in the
instant case was that the respondents drew sums from Grayan to meet expenditure or on
account of remuneration. The accounts of Grayan showed the sums as moneys lent to
the respondents because the situation was only regularised after the year end. In the case
of the last year, amounts totalling £7,679 remained outstanding at the date of liquidation   H
which have not been recovered. (After the liquidation the Revenue agreed to treat the
amounts owing as remuneration but this was only for tax purposes as after liquidation
the amounts could not be authorised as remuneration by the respondents.) However, Mr
Davis-White accepted that the indebtedness probably did not strictly constitute 'loans'
for the purposes of s. 330 and in view of the small sums involved he did not pursue this
allegation.

A　(E) *Failure to keep accounting records in accordance with s. 221 of the Companies Act 1985*

Section 221 provides:

'(1) Every company shall keep accounting records which are sufficient to show and explain the company's transactions and are such as to–

B
　(a) disclose with reasonable accuracy, at any time, the financial position of the company at that time, and

　(b) enable the directors to ensure that any balance sheet and profit and loss account prepared under this Part complies with the requirements of this Act.

(2) The accounting records shall in particular contain–

　(a) entries from day to day of all sums of money received and expended by the company, and the matters in respect of which the receipt and expenditure takes place, and

C
　(b) a record of the assets and liabilities of the company.

(3) If the company's business involves dealing in goods, the accounting records shall contain–

　(a) statements of stock held by the company at the end of each financial year of the company,

D
　(b) all statements of stocktakings from which any such statement of stock as is mentioned in paragraph (a) has been or is to be prepared, and

　(c) except in the case of goods sold by way of ordinary retail trade, statements of all goods sold and purchased, showing the goods and the buyers and sellers in sufficient detail to enable all these to be identified.'

E　The Secretary of State's case is that:

(a)　in relation to stock, that Grayan failed to maintain stock records or any stock control system; and

(b)　in relation to work in progress, Grayan failed to keep records which would enable overheads and costs to complete to be allocated to particular contracts. The Secretary of State relied inter alia upon the fact that the 1987 accounts of Grayan

F　were qualified on this basis by a further paragraph in Ernst & Whinney's audit report as follows:

'During the year the company did not, in our opinion, maintain adequate accounting records in relation to contract work in progress. As a consequence, we have been unable to satisfy ourselves as to the appropriateness of the allocation of overheads to individual contracts or of the estimated costs to

G　complete contracts in progress at the year end. Accordingly, we are unable to satisfy ourselves as to the carrying value of contract work in progress included in these accounts at £416,202 or whether the profit for the year is fairly stated.'

As to (a), I find the allegation proved but the respondents say, and the Secretary of State accepts, that the amounts involved were immaterial. In those circumstances, it is not necessary for me to make further findings in relation to these matters.

H　As to (b), Mr Gray's evidence was that the requisite information as to labour, material and overheads was in the job files handed to the liquidators. Mr Vooght denied that this was so. Mr Vooght said that this was also the opinion of Mr Sandford, the specialist quantity surveyor, who following an initial report which is in evidence, went through the job files and raised questions with the respondents for some two weeks after the liquidation. Following the 1987 audit report, the respondents were conscious of the need to improve the accounting systems of Grayan and they had engaged Mr Hunt to assist in

that. But in my judgment the situation remained that the accounting records in relation   A
to work in progress did not comply with s. 221. Even if Mr Gray is right that the
information necessary to show Grayan's financial position in respect of work in progress
was in the job files but was difficult to extract from them, the job files would still not have
complied with s. 221(1) which requires that information to be readily available and
properly organised.

I find as a fact that Grayan did not produce regular monthly management accounts.   B
Its failure to do so no doubt meant that the directors were less well-informed about the
financial position of Grayan than they might otherwise have been, but the failure was
not a breach of s. 221 and is not a matter which I have taken into account.

(F) *Late filing of the 1987 accounts*

The Secretary of State's allegation that these accounts were filed in breach of s. 242(1)
is in my view unanswerable. The question is whether the directors can rely on s. 242(4):   C

> '(4) It is a defence for a person charged with an offence under this section prove
> that he took all reasonable steps for securing that the requirements of subsection
> (1) would be complied with before the end of the period allowed for laying and
> delivering accounts and reports.'

The directors say, however, that the delay was due to delays on the part of Ernst &
Whinney. Mr Gray says he had one or two rows with Mr Knight on the telephone over   D
the accounts but was too busy to write to him to press him to finalise the audit.

Conclusions

Apart from the alleged preferences, the case for the Secretary of State is based on the
incompetence of the respondents. I approach the case on that basis.

The crucial word is not however 'dishonest' but 'unfit' (see s. 6(1) of the Act). There   E
are likely to be many personal characteristics which taken singly or together make a
person unfit to be a director. If a director is found to be unfit, the Act requires a period
of disqualification to be imposed for a minimum period of two years. Thus any finding
of unfitness is a grave and serious matter though, as Mr Davis-White pointed out, it is
always open to the person disqualified to apply to the court for leave. I bear in mind that
the consequences of disqualification are grave. As Mr Hollington said, disqualification is
not imposed for mere errors of judgment: see *Re ECM (Europe) Electronics Ltd* [1991]   F
BCC 268. However, at the same time I bear in mind that the purpose of the Act is to
protect the public.

In the present case, there were, in my judgment, serious shortcomings in the
respondents' conduct as directors for the following reasons.

1. In the course of its business, Grayan secured major contracts with Fairclough. The   G
fact that it did so may well be due to the credit of the technical skills of those who worked
for Grayan. On the other hand it seems clear that Grayan overstretched itself in financial
terms. These large contracts were extended in point of time and Grayan incurred major
liabilities to subcontractors. In turn, the directors had failed to foresee this possibility
and to ensure that Grayan had adequate financial backing in terms of share capital and
banking facilities such as would enable it to trade out of a difficult contractual situation.

By the end of 1988 Grayan had three very large claims against Fairclough which   H
remained outstanding.

The respondents, particularly Mr Gray, took the view that these claims would
eventually be met. That view was optimistic. Fairclough did not accept the claims and
made no payment on account. The property market was in difficulties and the owner of
Avenue Road was known to be in financial trouble. If the optimism was not borne out,

A subcontractors would not be paid. Moreover Grayan was continuing to trade and indeed was taking on new work potentially increasing the amount of claims affected. By the time the business plan was prepared, the respondents either had or ought to have had doubts as to whether the claims that the respondents ought to have realised that their claims would not be met in full. I accept this, but it has not been shown that they should, prior to January 1989, have expected that Grayan's claims would be reduced to such an extent that it could not discharge its liabilities, or that the failure to do so was more than an error of judgment on the respondents' part.

B

It is said that the respondents caused Grayan to trade on for the benefit of creditors and in particular so as to enable subcontractors to get the benefit of any recovery on those claims. If Grayan had gone into liquidation the likelihood was that Fairclough would have refused to pay any sum. However, the difficulty with that argument, even if it were otherwise a good one, is that it has no basis in the directors' own evidence. In the absence of such a basis, that argument cannot be pursued. It is said that creditors were not prejudiced by the continuation of trading but there is no evidence to support this. The fact Grayan continued to trade would seem to militate against this.

C

2. At the eleventh hour the respondents took advice from Ernst & Whinney. They were told not to make payments to creditors. They received a large payment of £80,500 from Fairclough which was then paid into the bank account. This was used to make a payment of £12,000 to a connected firm Grayan Construction Services Ltd. In my judgment both the respondents bear a responsibility for this payment. It was paid in the knowledge there was a risk that a liquidator would seek to claim it back and thus the directors were prepared to take their chance on this. In my judgment the payment was a serious error of judgment on the part of the respondents. As regards the repayment of overdraft by National Westminster Bank, it is said that the respondents proposed to review who should be paid out of the bank facility on the following Monday. In my judgment this particular answer does not ring true since the bank had already made it clear that it needed a report from Ernst & Whinney. If that report were not produced there seems to me to have been a real risk known to the respondents that the bank would call in its facility so that Grayan would not be able to pay creditors. Likewise, I reject as unlikely the directors' explanation that they did not appreciate that the risk of preference extended to paying off the overdraft by credits into Grayan's bank account. In all the circumstances, it seems to me that the Secretary of State has established that the respondents would be unable to rebut the presumption in s. 239(6) of the *Insolvency Act 1986* in relation either to the payment to the bank or the payment of £12,000 to Construction. These payments, particularly that to the bank, conferred substantial personal benefits on the respondents.

D

E

F

3. As I have already explained, the job files did not in my judgment comply with s. 221 of the *Companies Act* 1985 and it was not suggested that the respondents should not bear some responsibility for this.

G

4. The 1987 accounts were filed 18 months late. There were important going concern and accounting records qualifications in the audit report on these accounts. I find that the respondents did not press Ernst & Whinney to finalise their audit work and that accordingly they cannot rely on s. 242(4) of the *Companies Act* 1985.

H

I have reached the view that the matters mentioned in (2)–(4) above did not render the respondents unfit to be directors for the purposes of s. 6 of the Act for these reasons.

(a)   As to the preferences, other remedies exist and have been pursued. The consequences of a preference will have been brought home to the respondents in those proceedings, and accordingly I do not consider that their conduct in relation to the preferences renders them now unfit for the purposes of s. 6(1).

(b)   As to the failure to keep accounting records, this is not a case where the significance   A
or the consequences of the failure have been explored. Moreover the respondents
did take steps to improve the accounting systems of Grayan and, serious though a
breach of s. 221 is, I do not consider their responsibility for it, in all the
circumstances of this case, renders them unfit for the purposes of s. 6(1).

(c)   As to the late filing of the 1987 accounts, I have heard no evidence which suggests
that the respondents were deliberately preventing the issue of those accounts.
Obviously, the late filing was serious, but it was isolated. As the unchallenged   B
evidence of Mr Gray suggests that the respondents were not wholly to blame, I do
not find that this matter renders the directors unfit for the purposes of s. 6(1).

In the circumstances, I make no disqualification order.

(*Order accordingly*)

   C

COURT OF APPEAL JUDGMENT
(Delivered 10 November 1994)

Hoffmann LJ: This is an appeal by the Secretary of State from a refusal of Arden J to
disqualify two company directors. We are told that it was the first appeal to this court
from such a refusal, although there has been a successful appeal by the Secretary of State
from a county court to a judge of the Chancery Division: see *Re Hitco 2000 Ltd* [1995]   D
BCC 161 (Jules Sher QC sitting as a deputy High Court judge, 29 July 1994).

The application in this case was made by the Secretary of State under s. 7(1)(a). The
Secretary of State may make such an application if it appears to him expedient in the
public interest that a disqualification order under s. 6 should be made.

These are the other relevant provisions of the Act:

'1. *Disqualification orders: general*   E

(1) In the circumstances specified below in this Act a court may, and under section
6 shall, make against a person a disqualification order, that is to say an order that
he shall not, without the leave of the court–

(a) be a director of a company, or

(b) be a liquidator or administrator of a company, or

(c) be a receiver or manager of a company's property, or   F

(d) in any way, whether directly or indirectly, be concerned or take part in the
promotion, formation or management of a company,

for a specified period beginning with the date of the order.

(2) In each section of this Act which gives a court power or, as the case may be,
imposes on it the duty to make a disqualification order there is specified the
maximum (and, in section 6, the minimum) period of disqualification which may   G
or (as the case may be) must be imposed by means of the order.

6. *Duty of court to disqualify unfit directors of insolvent companies*

(1) The court shall make a disqualification order against a person in any case
where, on an application under this section, it is satisfied–

(a) that he is or has been a director of a company which has at any time become   H
insolvent (whether while he was a director or subsequently), and

(b) that his conduct as a director of that company (either taken alone or taken
together with his conduct as a director of any other company or companies)
makes him unfit to be concerned in the management of a company.

. . .

A   (4) Under this section the minimum period of disqualification is 2 years, and the maximum period is 15 years.

9. *Matters for determining unfitness of directors*

(1) Where it falls to a court to determine whether a person's conduct as a director or shadow director of any particular company or companies makes him unfit to be concerned in the management of a company, the court shall, as respects his conduct

B   as a director of that company or, as the case may be, each of those companies, have regard in particular–

    (a) to the matters mentioned in Part I of Schedule 1 to this Act, and

    (b) where the company has become insolvent, to the matters mentioned in Part II of that Schedule;

and references in that Schedule to the director and the company are to be read

C   accordingly.

17. *Application for leave under an order*

(1) . . .

(2) On the hearing of an application for leave made by a person against whom a disqualification order has been made on the application of . . . the official receiver . . . the . . . official receiver . . . shall appear and call the attention of the court to

D   any matters which seem to him to be relevant, and may himself give evidence or call witnesses.

Schedule 1 – Matters for Determining Unfitness of Directors

Part I – Matters Applicable in all Cases

1. Any misfeasance or breach of any fiduciary or other duty by the director in

E   relation to the company.

2. Any misapplication or retention by the director of, or any conduct by the director giving rise to an obligation to account for, any money or other property of the company.

3. . . .

4. The extent of the director's responsibility for any failure by the company to

F   comply with any of the following provisions of the Companies Act, namely–

    (a) section 221 (companies to keep accounting records) . . .

Part II – Matters Applicable Where Company Has Become Insolvent

6. The extent of the director's responsibility for the causes of the company becoming insolvent.

G   7. . . .

8. The extent of the director's responsibility for the company entering into any transaction or giving any preference, being a transaction or preference–

    · (a) liable to be set aside under section 127 or sections 238 to 240 of the Insolvency Act . . .'

    The two respondents had both been directors of Grayan Building Services Ltd

H   ('Grayan'), a company formed on 12 December 1984 which commenced trading on 1 January 1985 and went into creditors' voluntary liquidation on 10 February 1989. The company paid a dividend of 15.7 pence in the pound on its £94,000 of agreed preferential claims and nothing on its £1m or so of trade debts. The condition in s. 6(1)(a) was therefore satisfied and the question for the judge was whether condition (b) was satisfied, that is to say, whether the conduct of the respondents as directors of Grayan made them unfit to be concerned in the management of a company.

I summarise the facts as found by the judge. Grayan carried on business as a heating   **A** and ventilation contractor. It was lightly capitalised with an initial share capital of £20,000 and a bank overdraft facility of £30,000 which was increased to £80,000 in 1986. In the 15 months to 31 March 1986 it made a loss of £27,000 on a turnover of £622,000. The year to 31 March 1987 showed a loss of £84,000 on a turnover of £605,000, but the accounts (which were not filed until 15 December 1988, shortly before the liquidation) were qualified by the auditors who said that the company did not maintain adequate accounting records in relation to contract work in progress. They therefore felt unable to   **B** be satisfied that the profit/loss for the year was fairly stated. In the year to 31 March 1988 the company greatly expanded its business. The draft accounts showed a turnover of £3.89m and a profit of £128,000.

By 1988 the company had developed a close relationship with a building contractor called Fairclough Building Ltd ('Fairclough') which employed it as subcontractor on three major sites. Grayan in turn subcontracted a good deal of the work. All three were   **C** beset by delays and difficulties. The first was a block of luxury flats in St John's Wood which began in February 1987, was supposed to have been completed by December 1987 but took another nine months. Grayan notified Fairclough of a loss and expense claim of £338,000 in January 1988 which remained unpaid at the date of liquidation. The second was the refurbishment of a hotel in Kensington which began in August 1987, suffered substantial delays and was still incomplete at the date of liquidation. From   **D** March 1988 Grayan was complaining to Fairclough about late payment of its claims and in September 1988 it wrote to its own subcontractors saying that it had cash flow difficulties and asking for forbearance. Some forbore and others pressed for payment. The third was a large office development where work began in April 1988. There were numerous variations in the course of construction which may have been due to deficiencies in the original design. In November 1988 Grayan made a claim for over £400,000 in respect of variations which Fairclough did not pay.   **E**

The weakness of Grayan's position was that its contract with Fairclough had a 'pay when paid' clause which meant that when the developer ran into financial difficulties (as happened in St John's Wood) or Fairclough itself came under financial pressure or was involved in disputes, Grayan did not get paid. On the other hand, there was no such clause in Grayan's contracts with its own subcontractors. The judge found that by September 1988, when the first writs began to arrive, Grayan was insolvent in that it was   **F** unable to pay its debts as they fell due and this would naturally be known to the directors. Fairclough, which was concerned to keep Grayan's subcontractors on site, was making payments to Grayan on condition that the money was used to pay specified contractors. In December 1988 Grayan made a number of round-figure payments to pressing creditors.

In January 1989 Fairclough said in terms to Grayan that its loss and expense claim   **G** made a year earlier on the St John's Wood contract would not be paid. On 31 January Mr Gray and Mr Paterson went to see their bank (National Westminster, Caversham branch) to ask for an increase in the overdraft facility. The manager advised them to consult their auditors, Ernst & Whinney, and referred the request to his regional head office at Reading. On the following day Mr Gray and Mr Paterson went to see Ernst & Whinney. The partner in charge of their annual audit discussed with them the possibility of liquidation and advised them not to pay any creditors unless it was essential to keep   **H** the company alive. Otherwise, he said, the directors might be personally liable for the payments.

On 6 February 1989 Mr Gray and Mr Paterson went to the bank's Reading Business Centre. They produced figures which showed a peak borrowing requirement of £371,000 in March or April 1989. The bank said that it was a condition of any further advances

A   that the directors should give security in the form of charges over their houses. The directors were reluctant to do so unless the bank would commit itself to keeping Grayan afloat. The bank said that before it could undertake any such commitment it would need Ernst & Whinney's confirmation of a number of aspects of the company's financial position. The difficulty was that Ernst & Whinney were unwilling to do the work unless a substantial payment was made in respect of outstanding fees. So Mr Gray and Mr Paterson decided to produce their own business plan instead. This was obviously not going to satisfy the bank. On 8 February Mr Gray made a last-ditch attempt to persuade Fairclough to pay a substantial sum. This resulted only in a payment of £80,500 on the following day, in circumstances to which I shall return. But it was not enough to keep the company going. On 9 February Ernst & Whinney recommended that Cork Gully be called in to give specialist insolvency advice and on their advice the company resolved to wind up on the following day.

C   By r. 3(3) of the *Insolvent Companies (Disqualification of Unfit Directors) Proceedings Rules* 1987 the evidence on behalf of the Secretary of State in a disqualification application must include 'a statement of the matters by reference to which the respondent is alleged to be unfit to be concerned in the management of a company'. One or two of those listed by the Secretary of State in this case were not pressed at the hearing, but the following are those which were:

D   (1)   causing Grayan to trade and incur substantial debts between September 1988 and February 1989 when there was no reasonable prospect that creditors would be paid;

        (2)   failing to ensure that proper accounting records were kept, contrary to s. 221 of the *Companies Act* 1985 (a matter to which the court's attention is specifically directed by para. 4(a) of Sch. 1 to the Act);

E   (3)   failing to file the 1987 audited accounts by 31 January 1988 (these accounts, which contained the auditor's qualification which I have mentioned and another qualification as to whether the accounts could properly be prepared on a going concern basis, were not filed until 15 December 1988);

        (4)   two preferential payments on 8 and 9 February which I must now describe in more detail.

F   6 February 1989, when Mr Gray and Mr Paterson went to the bank at Reading, was a Monday. They had previously issued cheques totalling about £60,000, but when the meeting ended without any immediate increase in the facility and (in view of Ernst & Whinney's refusal to undertake a review of their financial position) little prospect of such an increase in the future, they decided to stop the cheques.

     Mr Gray and Mr Paterson also controlled an associated company called Grayan
G   Construction Ltd ('Construction') which was owed £29,000 by Grayan on inter-company loan account. It was also in serious financial difficulties, and on 8 February needed £12,000 to pay one of its creditors. Mr Paterson drew a cheque for £12,000 on Grayan's account which was paid into the account of Construction and used to pay its creditor.

     On Thursday, 9 February Mr Batchelor of Fairclough, whom Mr Gray had been pressing for money on the previous day, telephoned to say that a cheque for £80,500 in
H   respect of the Kensington hotel contract was ready to be collected. Fairclough had for some months been making payments under this contract on condition that the money was used to pay specified sub-contractors. Mr Gray said in evidence that on this occasion there were 'no strings attached' but the judge did not accept this and found that payment had been made upon the representation that it would be used to pay subcontractors. An employee, Mr Hunt, went to collect the cheque and, as usual, paid it into the company's bank account. As there was a stop on the cheques which had been drawn on the account

(Mr Gray had confirmed the stop in writing early on that Thursday morning) the effect   A
was virtually to pay off the company's overdraft, which had been guaranteed by the
directors. Another cheque for £2,000 was paid into the same account on 10 February,
hours before the resolution to wind up. Although the first cheque was banked by Mr
Hunt, there is no suggestion that Mr Gray and Mr Paterson were not aware that it would
be paid into the account and that there was a stop on payments out. The judge rejected
their explanation that they were intending to wait for a further meeting with the bank on
the next Monday, 13 February, before deciding which creditors to pay.   B

After the liquidation, the liquidator obtained judgment against Construction for the
£12,000 it had been paid. We do not know how much of this judgment was satisfied. The
liquidator commenced proceedings against the directors for repayment of the £82,500 as
a preference under s. 239 of the *Insolvency Act* 1986. The relevant parts of this section
are:

> '(4) . . . a company gives a preference to a person if–   C
>
> > (a) that person is . . . a surety or guarantor for any of the company's debts . . .
> > and
> >
> > (b) the company does anything . . . which . . . has the effect of putting that
> > person into a position which, in the event of the company going into
> > insolvent liquidation, will be better than the position he would have been in
> > if that thing had not been done.   D
>
> (5) The court shall not make an order under this section in respect of a preference
> given to any person unless the company which gave the preference was influenced
> in deciding to give it by a desire to produce in relation to that person the effect
> mentioned in subsection 4(b).
>
> (6) A company which has given a preference to a person connected with the
> company . . . at the time when the preference was given is presumed, unless the   E
> contrary is shown, to have been influenced in deciding to give it by such a desire as
> is mentioned in subsection (5).'

In February 1992 the preference proceedings were settle on terms that Mr Gray and
Mr Paterson paid £25,000 to the liquidator and £12,000 to the bank in respect of its
costs.

The making of preferences is something to which the court is required particularly to   F
have regard by para. 8(a) of Sch. 1. The judge found that the preference to Construction
was a 'serious error of judgment'. The directors knew that there was a risk that the
liquidator would claim it back and 'were prepared to take their chance'. She held that the
£82,500 payments were also preferences. She rejected Mr Gray's evidence that he did not
appreciate that a payment into the company's overdrawn bank account which he had
guaranteed might be a preference and held that the directors would be unable to show   G
that they were not influenced by a desire to improve their position in the event of a
liquidation.

As to the other three matters upon which the Secretary of State relied to show unfitness,
the judge's findings were as follows:

(1) *Trading while insolvent*

The judge found, as I have said, that from September 1988 the directors knew that the   H
company was insolvent in the sense of being unable to pay its debts as they fell due. She
said that in 1988 the company had overstretched itself in financial terms. It did not have
enough resources to be able to trade out of its difficulties with the three large contracts.
But she said that the directors had taken the view that their claims against Fairclough
'would eventually be met' and that the company would then be able to pay its creditors.

A This was an optimistic view, particularly when one of those claims had been outstanding since the previous January, but the judge said that the failure of the directors to realise that they would not be paid enough to meet their liabilities was 'no more than an error of judgment' and not such as to render them unfit to be directors of a company.

(2) *Failing to keep proper accounting records*

B The judge found this allegation proved. The auditor's certificate on the 1987 accounts, which were signed off on 28 November 1988 but no doubt known in substance to the directors a good deal earlier, told them that their accounting records were inadequate. Nevertheless, the judge said that the situation remained that the records did not comply with s. 221 of the *Companies Act* 1985. The company also did not produce monthly management accounts. These are not required by the Companies Act and the judge said that it was therefore a matter which she had not taken into account. On the other hand, C the absence of up-to-date figures about the company's financial position is relevant to whether it is reasonable for directors to allow a company to continue trading at a time when it is unable to pay its debts as they fall due.

(3) *Failure to file the 1987 accounts in time*

The judge found this allegation 'unanswerable'. She held that the statutory defence of having taken 'all reasonable steps' to secure compliance (s. 242(4)) was not made out.

D In the result, therefore, the judge held that the allegation of wrongful trading while insolvent was not made out but that all the other allegations were. She described the proven allegations as 'serious shortcomings in the respondents' conduct as directors'. Nevertheless she found that they had not been shown to be unfit. In regard to the preferences, she said that:

E '. . . other remedies exist and have been pursued. The consequences of a preference will have been brought home to the respondents in those proceedings and accordingly I do not consider that their conduct in relation to the preferences renders them *now* unfit for the purposes of s. 6(1).' (emphasis added)

She said that a breach of s. 221 was a serious matter but that the directors did take steps to improve the company's accounting systems and that although the late filing of accounts was 'obviously serious', the delay was partly the fault of Ernst & Whinney and F an isolated event. Neither was sufficient to render the directors unfit.

The Secretary of State says that on the judge's findings of fact, she was wrong to hold that the respondents had not been shown to be unfit. Mr Bannister for the respondents says that whether the respondents were unfit is a value judgment which an appellate court should not disturb unless it was founded upon an error of principle or was plainly wrong. In this case he says that the judge had the advantage of, at any rate, seeing Mr Gray in G the witness-box (Mr Paterson did not swear an affidavit or give evidence) and was entitled on all the evidence to form the view that they were not unfit to be directors.

Before I come to the function of a court hearing an appeal from the making or refusal of a disqualification application, it will be convenient to consider the nature of the decision which the trial judge has to make. The question is whether, in the words of s. 6(1), 'his conduct as a director . . . makes him unfit to be concerned in the management of a company'. Mr Bannister submitted that this required the court to be satisfied that H the respondent was at the time of the hearing a person who, for the future protection of the public, should not be allowed to concern himself in the management of a company. For this purpose the court could look at any evidence which showed that despite the respondent's shortcomings in the past, he was unlikely to offend again.

I do not agree. It is true that the subsection uses the present tense 'makes' but I agree with Peter Gibson J in *Re Bath Glass Ltd* (1988) 4 BCC 130 at p. 132 that this means

only that the court has to make the decision on the evidence put forward at the hearing. A
In that case the judge, rightly in my view, rejected the submission that the court could
consider conduct 'other than conduct as a director of the insolvent company or other
companies relied upon by the [official receiver] to obtain a disqualification order'. The
court is concerned solely with the conduct specified by the Secretary of State or official
receiver under r. 3(3) of the Disqualification Rules. It must decide whether that conduct,
viewed cumulatively and taking into account any extenuating circumstances, has fallen
below the standards of probity and competence appropriate for persons fit to be directors B
of companies.

   In my view the construction for which Mr Bannister contends is not consistent with
the court having a *duty* to disqualify a director whose conduct has shown him to be unfit.
If the court always had to be satisfied at the hearing that the protection of the public
required a period of disqualification, there would be no need to make disqualification
mandatory. Even if the court had a discretion, it would not, having formed the view that C
disqualification was necessary in the public interest, be acting judicially if it did not make
a disqualification order. The purpose of making disqualification mandatory was to ensure
that everyone whose conduct had fallen below the appropriate standard was disqualified
for at least two years, whether in the individual case the court thought that this was
necessary in the public interest or not. Parliament has decided that it is occasionally
necessary to disqualify a company director to encourage the others. Or as Sir Donald D
Nicholls V-C said in *Re Swift 736 Ltd* [1993] BCC 312 at p. 315:

> 'Those who make use of limited liability must do so with a proper sense of
> responsibility. The director disqualification procedure is an important sanction
> introduced by Parliament to raise standards in this regard.'

If this should be thought too harsh a view, it must be remembered that a disqualified
director can always apply for leave under s. 17 and the question of whether he has shown E
himself unlikely to offend again will obviously be highly material to whether he is granted
leave or not. It may also be relevant by way of mitigation on the length of disqualification,
although I note that the guidelines in *Re Sevenoaks Stationers (Retail) Ltd* [1990] BCC
765 are solely by reference to the seriousness of the conduct in question.

   It follows that I agree with the approach of Vinelott J in *Re Pamstock Ltd* [1994] BCC
264, when he said (at p. 282) that it was his duty to disqualify a director whose conduct F
'fell short of the standard of conduct which is today expected of a director of a company
which enjoys the privilege of limited liability' even though he did so with regret because:

> '[the] respondent seemed to me (so far as I can judge from the evidence before me)
> to be a man who today is capable of discharging his duties as a director honestly
> and diligently.'

But, as the judge said, the court is required to disqualify a director whose conduct has G
made him unfit:

> 'even though the misconduct may have occurred some years ago and even though
> the court may be satisfied that the respondent has since shown himself capable of
> behaving responsibly.'

I am not sure whether in *Re Polly Peck International plc* [1993] BCC 890 at p. 898 H
Lindsay J's discussion of the need to prove *present* unfitness was intended to express a
different view. Some of the examples given by the judge are of extenuating circumstances
which accompanied the conduct in question. These are matters which it seems to me it
would always be proper for the court to take into account. On the other hand, if the
judge meant that the court was concerned with anything other than whether that conduct,
taken in its setting, fell below the appropriate standard, I would respectfully disagree.

A   Once one is clear about the precise nature of the decision which the judge has to make, it is easier to decide how an appellate tribunal should approach an appeal against his decision. The judge is deciding a question of mixed fact and law in that he is applying the standard laid down by the courts (conduct appropriate to a person fit to be a director) to the facts of the case. It is in principle no different from the decision as to whether someone has been negligent or whether a patented invention was obvious (see *Benmax v Austin Motor Co Ltd* [1955] AC 370). On the other hand, the standards applied by the law in different contexts vary a great deal in precision and generally speaking, the vaguer the standard and the greater the number of factors which the court has to weigh up in deciding whether or not the standards have been met, the more reluctant an appellate court will be to interfere with the trial judge's decision. So in *George Mitchell (Chesterhall) Ltd v Finney Lock Seeds Ltd* [1983] 2 AC 803 at pp. 815–816, Lord Bridge of Harwich was considering the application of the test of 'fair and reasonable' in the *Unfair Contract Terms Act* 1977. He said:

> 'It would not be accurate to describe such a decision as an exercise of discretion. But [such] a decision . . . will have this in common with the exercise of a discretion, that, in having regard to the various matters to which . . . s. 11 of the Act of 1977 direct[s] attention, the court must entertain a whole range of considerations, put them in the scales on one side or the other and decide at the end of the day on which side the balance comes down. There will sometimes be room for a legitimate difference of judicial opinion as to what the answer should be, where it will be impossible to say that one view is demonstrably wrong and the other demonstrably right. It must follow, in my view, that, when asked to review such a decision on appeal, the appellate court should treat the original decision with the utmost respect and refrain from interference with it unless satisfied that it proceeded upon some erroneous principle or was plainly and obviously wrong.'

E   Similar comments were made in this court in *Re Coventry (deceased)* [1980] Ch 461 about a decision as to whether a testator had made 'reasonable financial provision' for a dependant for the purposes of the *Inheritance (Provision for Family and Dependants) Act* 1975. Buckley LJ described such a decision as a 'value judgment' which should not be disturbed unless the judge had made an error of principle.

F   These cases are at one end of a spectrum and decisions such as whether a motorist has driven with due care and attention are probably somewhere near the other end. Where lies the decision that a director's conduct fell below the appropriate standard? In my view, nearer to the negligence end than that represented by *Finney Lock* or *Coventry*. If Mr Bannister were right in saying that the judge was involved in a general inquiry about the respondent's current fitness to be a director, then I think he would probably also be right about the approach to an appeal from such a decision. But since I think that the true question is a much narrower one, namely whether specific conduct measures up to a standard of probity and competence fixed by the court, I agree with the way in which the matter was put by Mr Jules Sher QC sitting as a deputy High Court judge in *Re Hitco 2000 Ltd* [1995] BCC 161. After citing a passage of *Re Sevenoaks Stationers (Retail) Ltd* [1990] BCC 765; [1991] Ch 164 at p. 773; 176 in which Dillon LJ referred to the question of unfitness as a 'jury question', the learned deputy judge went on (at p. 163F):

H   > 'Plainly, the appellate court would be very slow indeed to disturb such conclusion as to fitness or unfitness. In many, perhaps most, cases the conclusion will have been so very much assisted and influenced by the oral evidence and demeanour of the director and other witnesses that the appellate court would be in nowhere near as good a position to form a judgment as to fitness or unfitness than was the trial judge. But there may be cases where there is little or no dispute as to the primary facts and the appellate court is in as good a position as the trial judge to form a

judgment as to fitness. In such cases the appellate court should not shrink from its   A
responsibility to do so, and, if satisfied that the trial judge was wrong, to say so.'

In this case Mr Kaye, for the Secretary of State, makes no attack upon the judge's
findings of primary fact. He is content to accept her findings on every point. It is the
evaluation of those facts, the decision as to whether they amounted to conduct falling
below the requisite standard, that he challenges.

First, there is the finding that because other remedies exist for preferences and the   B
liquidator pursued them, thereby bringing home to the respondents the consequences of
a preference, the conduct in that regard did not show that the directors were *now* unfit.
Mr Kaye says that this reasoning is erroneous in principle. The statute requires the court
to have particular regard to the extent of the director's responsibility for the company
giving a preference. But the fact that a preference has been given inevitably means that
the company will have its remedy under the Insolvency Act and if a recovery seems
possible, the liquidator is likely to pursue it. To take these matters into account by way   C
of mitigation will deprive the specific reference to preferences in Sch. 1 of any effect in
most of the worst cases, namely where the director has preferred himself. In my view
there is force in this criticism. It also seems to me that the emphasis on whether the
directors are *now* unfit and the taking into account of matters subsequent to the relevant
conduct was, for the reasons I have earlier stated, wrong in principle.

Mr Kaye next says that the judge applied too lenient a test in relation to the allegation   D
of trading while insolvent. She absolved the directors on the ground that she was not
satisfied that they should have known that Fairclough would not *eventually* pay enough
to enable the creditors to be paid. Even if Fairclough did eventually pay, the respondents
must have known (even if only from the writs they were receiving) that there was a high
risk that before that date the company would have been forced into insolvent liquidation.
Mr Kaye says that it was enough to constitute unfit conduct that they were from
September 1988 pursuing a policy of deliberately delaying payment to all creditors whose   E
goodwill as subcontractors or otherwise was not essential to the company's survival.
Only when it became apparent that this policy would not create enough involuntary
credit at the expense of trade creditors and the Inland Revenue did they approach the
bank for a larger facility and only then, at the prompting of the bank, did they seek
advice from their accountants. The judge described this as having been at the eleventh
hour. Mr Kaye says that their conduct was similar to the conduct of the director in *Re*   F
Sevenoaks Stationers (Retail) Ltd [1990] BCC 765; [1991] Ch 164, of whom Dillon LJ
said at p. 779; 183:

> 'Mr Cruddas made a deliberate decision to pay only those creditors who pressed
> for payment. The obvious result was that the two companies traded, when in fact
> insolvent and known to be in difficulties, at the expense of those creditors who,
> like the Crown, happened not to be pressing for payment. Such conduct on the   G
> part of a director can well, in my judgment, be relied on as a ground for saying
> that he is unfit to be concerned in the management of a company.'

In this case Mr Kaye says that the directors were even less justified in trading at the
risk of creditors because they knew that they had inadequate information about the true
financial position of the company. Again, I think that there is force in these criticisms.

Finally, Mr Kaye says that the judge dealt with each allegation separately and did not   H
have regard to them cumulatively. I am not sure about this point; she does not expressly
mention their cumulative effect but it is hard to believe that she did not take that into
account. But I am certainly of the view that taking into account the preferences which
the judge disregarded for, as I think, an inadmissible reason, the conduct of the directors
in the round fell below the appropriate standard for persons fit to be directors of
companies. It was therefore her duty to make a disqualification order.

A   The appeal must therefore be allowed and the question arises of the period for which the directors should be disqualified. The Secretary of State does not contend that the conduct was more serious than the lowest bracket in the *Re Sevenoaks Stationers (Retail) Ltd* guidelines. Having regard to the fact that the directors have been in jeopardy for a very considerable time, I think that the justice of the case does not require disqualification for longer than the statutory minimum of two years.

B   **Henry LJ:** I am in entire agreement with the judgment of Hoffmann LJ and wish only to add a word on the judge's duty to give reasons as to why the court, having made its primary findings of fact, does or does not conclude that the respondent was unfit.

This court will always respect the trial judge's primary findings of fact, and does so here. But here I find a mismatch between those findings of fact and the conclusion drawn, namely that the conduct of these men as directors of the failed company had not satisfied the court that they were unfit to be concerned in the management of a company. I have not been able to find in the judgment reasons which would justify that conclusion given the findings of primary facts made.

The concept of limited liability and the sophistication of our corporate law offers great privileges and great opportunities for those who wish to trade under that regime. But the corporate environment carries with it the discipline that those who avail themselves of those privileges must accept the standards laid down and abide by the regulatory rules and disciplines in place to protect creditors and shareholders. And while some significant corporate failures will occur despite the directors exercising best managerial practice, in many too many there have been serious breaches of those rules and disciplines, in situations where the observance of them would or at least might have prevented or reduced the scale of the failure and consequent loss to creditors and investors.

Reliable figures are hard to come by, but it seems that losses from corporate fraud and mismanagement have never been higher. At the same time the regulatory regime has never been more stringent – on paper even if not in practice. The Parliamentary intention to improve managerial safeguards and standards for the long term good of employees, creditors and investors is clear. Those who fail to reach those standards and whose failure contributes to others losing money will often both be plausible and capable of inspiring initial trust, often later regretted. Those attributes may make them attractive witnesses. But as s. 6 makes clear, the court's focus should be on their conduct – on the offence rather than the offender. The statutory corporate climate is stricter than it has ever been, and those enforcing it should reflect the fact that Parliament has seen the need for higher standards. Where serious breaches have been shown, tribunals when deciding the question of fitness should give clear reasons why they reached the decision they did on that question. I could not find such reasons here.

Neill LJ: I also agree. Those who trade under the regime of limited liability and who avail themselves of the privileges of that regime, must accept the standards of probity and competence to which the law requires company directors to conform.

Although an appellate court should always be cautious before interfering with a judge's conclusion as to fitness or unfitness for the purposes of s. 6(1) of the 1986 Act, I am satisfied in the respects identified by Hoffmann LJ that the judge in this case erred in principle in her approach to the primary facts. I am also further satisfied for the reasons given by Hoffmann LJ that the primary facts found by the judge clearly established conduct which made the two respondents unfit to be concerned in the management of a company within the meaning of s. 6.

(Order of 5 August 1994 set aside. Disqualification order for two years against first and second respondents to run from 10 November 1994. No order against second respondent in respect of costs in Court of Appeal. Costs order in favour of the second respondent below

A

set aside. Respondents to repay costs paid below. Legal aid taxation of first respondent's costs below on standard basis, costs incurred since 17 March 1993 not to be enforced without leave of the court. Order for costs against second respondent below. Order nisi against legal aid board for balance of first respondent's costs in Court of Appeal. Legal aid taxation. Leave to appeal to the House of Lords refused)

B

C

D

E

F

G

H

A
Re Manlon Trading Ltd.
Official Receiver v Aziz.
Chancery Division (Companies Court) and Court of Appeal.
Evans-Lombe J; Staughton, Beldam and Peter Gibson L JJ.
Judgment delivered 22 July 1994 and 12 April 1995.

B *Disqualifying unfit directors of insolvent companies – Application to strike out disqualification proceedings for want of prosecution – Whether public interest made disqualification proceedings sui generis – Whether there had been inordinate and inexcusable delay – Whether there had been serious prejudice to respondent – Company Directors Disqualification Act 1986, s. 6, 7(2); Rules of the Supreme Court, O. 25, r. 1.*

C This was an appeal by the official receiver from Evans-Lombe J's decision to strike out director disqualification proceedings brought against 'A' under s. 6 of the Company Directors Disqualification Act 1986.

The proceedings were commenced in 1990 on the day before the expiry of the two-year period prescribed by s. 7(2) of the 1986 Act and the official receiver accepted that the proceedings were not advanced between May 1991 and September 1992 as a result of inordinate and inexcusable delay.

D The judge held that disqualification proceedings were sui generis in the field of striking out for want of prosecution. The delay had not given rise to a substantial risk that it was not possible to have a fair trial of the issues in the case, but there had ceased to be an obvious public interest in obtaining a disqualification order against the respondent. If that approach was wrong, the test for ordinary private litigation was met and the proceedings should be struck out: there had been delay which had prolonged the time during which the proceedings

E had been pending by more than two years and during that period the respondent had suffered the prejudice to any businessman inherent in having disqualification proceedings, making serious allegations against him, hanging over his head. The official receiver appealed.

Held, dismissing the appeal:

1. The fact that director disqualification proceedings were not brought to enforce private rights but in the public interest was only a factor to be balanced against any prejudice caused

F to the defendant by inordinate and inexcusable delay, and did not justify discarding the conventional approach to striking out for want of prosecution.

2. Greater diligence in prosecuting proceedings was expected where the institution of proceedings under s. 6 of the 1986 Act was delayed until the end of the permissible two-year period. (Dictum of Vinelott J in Re Noble Trees Ltd [1993] BCC 318 at p. 321H approved.)

G 3. The prejudice to a director inherent in the prolongation of disqualification proceedings, which the judge relied on, and the prejudice caused to the respondent through the effect of delay on the memories of witnesses together amounted to prejudice which was sufficiently serious to outweigh the public interest in pursuing the disqualification proceedings.

The following cases were referred to in the judgments:

Allen v Sir Alfred McAlpine & Sons Ltd & Anor [1968] 2 QB 229.

H *Attorney-General's Reference (No. 1 of 1990)* [1992] QB 630.
Birkett v James [1978] AC 297.
Biss v Lambeth, Southwark and Lewisham Health Authority [1978] 1 WLR 382.
Carecraft Construction Co Ltd, Re [1993] BCC 336; [1994] 1 WLR 172.
Department of Transport v Chris Smaller (Transport) Ltd [1989] AC 1197.
Eagil Trust Co Ltd v Pigott-Brown & Anor [1985] 3 All ER 119.
Grayan Building Services Ltd, Re [1995] BCC 554; [1995] Ch 241.

Lo-Line Electric Motors Ltd & Ors, Re (1988) 4 BCC 415; [1988] Ch 477.   A
Noble Trees Ltd, Re [1993] BCC 318.
Official Receiver v B Ltd [1994] 2 BCLC 1.
Roebuck v Mungovin [1994] 2 AC 224.
Sevenoaks Stationers (Retail) Ltd [1990] BCC 765; [1991] Ch 164.

AWH Charles QC and Guy Newey (Mark Cunningham in the Court of Appeal)
(instructed by the Treasury Solicitor) for the official receiver.
                                                                                            B
Edward Bannister QC (Matthew Collings in the Court of Appeal) (instructed by
Simons Platman & Rechnic) for the respondent.

HIGH COURT JUDGMENT
(Delivered 22 July 1994)

Evans-Lombe J: This case concerns an application to strike out proceedings for want
of prosecution. It is unusual because the proceedings sought to be struck out are   C
proceedings by originating summons brought by the official receiver under the provisions
of the *Company Directors Disqualification Act* 1986 for an order under s. 6 of that Act
that the respondent, Haroon Abdul Aziz, be disqualified from acting as a director or
being directly or indirectly concerned in the promotion or management of the company
without the leave of the court.

I will now set out the background facts of the case from which the application arises.   D

Manlon Trading Ltd (to which I will hereafter refer as 'the company') was
incorporated in 1972. It seems that in or about 1976 the company was carrying on
business as steel exporters. At about that time the respondent's family acquired a
shareholding interest in the company though it is not clear whether the respondent was
at any stage a direct shareholder in it. The respondent had been deported from Malawi
where he and his family had been in business. In September 1977 the respondent was   E
appointed general manager of the company. In the evidence filed in the proceedings he
accepts that from that date he acted as a shadow director of the company and that the
nominal directors of the company had no executive function. His explanation for this
state of affairs is that the company's principal area of business was Africa and, in
particular, Malawi where the respondent retained a number of useful business contacts.
It would not, it seems, have assisted the company's business had the company's filed
records shown the respondent as a director because of his previous deportation from that   F
country. By early 1978 the company had ceased to carry on business as a steel exporter
and its business had become exclusively that of a confirming agent, that is an intermediary
between businesses primarily situated in the UK who wished to trade into Africa and in
particular into Nigeria. The company's bankers were Johnson Matthey Bankers, later
renamed Minories Finance.

An important area of the company's business was centred on Nigeria where the   G
company had clients from whom there became due substantial sums of money. In 1983
there was a military coup in Nigeria and rigid exchange control was imposed by the new
regime which prevented the company's Nigerian debtors from paying their indebtedness
to the company. Thereafter a system of payment was adopted whereby foreign creditors,
including the company and its UK customers, were paid by promissory notes issued by
the Nigerian government for payment in the future, that government taking payment
from the company's Nigerian customers in Nigeria.   H

In 1984 Johnson Matthey Bankers got into financial difficulties with the result that the
bank called in its loan portfolio. In mid-1986 the bank obtained judgment against the
company for approximately £4.5m and against the respondent for rather more than
£100,000 being part of the amount of the company's indebtedness to the bank for which
the bank held the respondent's guarantee. On 28 February 1988 the company ceased

A   trading and on 30 March 1988 the bank presented a winding-up petition against the company. On 22 April 1988 the company presented a petition for administration. As part of the evidence in support of that petition the company put forward accounts showing a balance sheet surplus as at 31 March 1988 of £770,000 approximately and that it traded profitably for the period ending on that date. Those accounts, however, showed debtors to the company of some £21,700,000 estimated as being realisable in full. However a large proportion of these debtors were subject to Nigerian exchange control.

B   The petition for administration was dismissed on 10 May 1988 and a compulsory winding-up order was made against the company on 8 June. Meanwhile bankruptcy proceedings had been commenced against the respondent based on his indebtedness under his guarantee to the bank and on 4 August 1988 a bankruptcy order was made against him.

C   The liquidator embarked upon an investigation of the company's affairs. In February and November 1989 the respondent was privately examined on oath in his bankruptcy proceedings.

The proceedings to disqualify him were commenced on 7 June 1990, the day before the expiry of the period prescribed for the commencement of such proceedings by s. 7(2) of the *Company Directors Disqualification Act* 1986 (to which I will hereafter refer as 'the Act').

D   Thereafter the proceedings appear to have adopted a normal, if not over-expeditious course until 15 April 1991 when at a directions hearing before the registrar the official receiver was ordered to file and serve evidence in reply on or before 13 May 1991 and the matter was stood over for further directions to 20 May 1991. Thereafter there commenced a period ending in October 1992 when the applicant appears to have taken virtually no steps to advance the proceedings towards a hearing. A curious feature of this period is that during it there appear to have taken place five directions hearings before the registrar on 20 May, 1 July, 22 July, 21 October and 11 November of 1991. On each occasion the official receiver accepts that the respondent did not attend because, save as to the first, he was given no notice of the hearing. On each occasion the official receiver's time for filing his evidence in reply was extended. On the first occasion the official receiver was ordered to pay the respondent's costs in any event notwithstanding that he took no part in the hearing and the respondent was given liberty to apply before 24 June. Thereafter the costs of the successive directions hearings were made costs in cause. On the last occasion provision was made for the cross-examination of witnesses and the matter was adjourned to be heard in court on a date to be fixed. I received no satisfactory explanation for how these orders came to be made in the absence of the respondent and why when made, they were never communicated to him or his solicitors save that made on 11 November 1991 in the manner which I will describe.

G   The official receiver accepts that between May 1991 and September 1992, a period of some 17 months, the proceedings were not advanced as a result of delays on his part which were inordinate and inexcusable. I was told that the reason for the delays was that the file had been assigned to a member of the staff of the Disqualification Unit at the Treasury Solicitor's office, who became ill. Very properly that reason for the delay was not advanced as any sort of excuse.

H   It seems that in October 1992 the file was taken over by another member of the staff of the Disqualification Unit and work recommenced on preparing the case for trial.

Meanwhile on 4 August 1991 the respondent was discharged from his bankruptcy and thereafter again became able to act as a director of companies.

By letter dated 11 November 1992 from the Treasury Solicitor to solicitors then acting for the respondent, the Treasury Solicitor served on the respondent notice of intention to

proceed. At the same time the respondent was provided with a copy of the order for　A
directions made on 11 November 1991. Thereafter there were two changes of solicitor for
the respondent. The final notice of change accompanied a letter of 15 January 1993 from
the respondent's present solicitors to the Treasury Solicitor.

The respondent's reply to the Treasury Solicitor's letter of 11 November 1992 was by
letter from his solicitors of 21 January 1993. That letter was divided into five paragraphs.
The first two paragraph sought copies of documents material to the case. The third　B
paragraph complained about the use to which transcripts of private examinations of the
respondent in the bankruptcy proceedings had been put. The fourth and fifth paragraph
read as follows:

> '4. We are presently awaiting our client's files from DJ Freeman. In the meantime
> our client assures us that he has rebutted every allegation made against him.
> Indeed, the proceedings brought by the liquidator have been settled out of court.　C
> In these circumstances, it is wholly unfair and inequitable to have the
> disqualification proceedings hanging over our client's head like the sword of
> Damocles. The proceedings brought by you have lain dormant for the past 18
> months. Please inform us whether it is your intention to either withdraw or
> prosecute the claim.
>
> 5. In the absence of any satisfactory response and/or action from you by 11　D
> February 1993, we reserve the right to make an application to strike out the
> proceedings for inexcusable delay.'

The reference to a settlement out of court was a reference to a settlement agreement of
various proceedings brought by the liquidator of the company against members of the
respondent's family and companies controlled by them, reached in October 1992.

On 26 January 1993 the Treasury Solicitor replied, dealing with the questions as to　E
documents and the complaint about the transcript and concluded:

> 'I confirm that I am instructed to proceed with this application and look forward
> to receiving the exhibits referred to in my letter of 21 January 1993.'

Unusually in cases of this kind an order for cross-examination of the deponents to the
evidence in support and in opposition to the application to strike out has been made. The
affidavit in answer was sworn on behalf of the official receiver by Mrs Oliver, the head of　F
the Disqualification Unit in the Treasury Solicitor's department. In the course of her
evidence she said that after service of the notice of intention to proceed and receipt of the
respondent's solicitor's letter of 21 January 1993 she anticipated that an application to
strike out the proceedings for want of prosecution would be made by the respondent. In
the event no such immediate application was made notwithstanding the respondent's
solicitor's deadline for action of 11 February 1993, in particular notwithstanding that the　G
official receiver had still not filed his evidence in reply which, by this time, was 14 months
overdue from the date it was ordered to be served by the court's order of 11 November
1991, and was 20 months overdue from the date it was ordered to be served on the last
application for directions upon which the respondent appeared.

Mrs Oliver gave evidence both in her affidavit and in cross-examination of the steps
thereafter taken by the official receiver through the Treasury Solicitors to get the case　H
ready for trial. Those steps included correspondence with the respondent's solicitors who
sent four letters to the Treasury Solicitor dated 29 January, 2 July, 31 August and 5
October 1993. The principal subject of that correspondence appears to have been the
collation of documents for an anticipated trial of the case. In none of these letters from
the respondent's solicitors was any indication given of a renewed intention to seek to
strike out the proceedings for want of prosecution.

A   The respondent's solicitors were also in communication with the liquidator writing three letters dated 21 October and 2 and 10 December 1993. These letters in addition to seeking documentation were directed to attempting to obtain from the liquidator a fresh report to the court, in the light of his administration of the winding up, which it appears the respondent hoped would exonerate him from the charges brought against him in the proceedings. The first paragraph of the letter of 21 October 1993 reads:

B   'As you aware the proceedings against me are continuing despite our previous agreements whereby it was agreed that a revised factual report would be sent by your office to the board of Trade as per new facts/evidence available to you in the course of various court actions.'

A large part of what appears to have occupied the Treasury Solicitor in the ensuing months seems to have been the reconstitution of the Treasury Solicitor's file dealing with the case, the bulk of the contents of which appear to have been mislaid. Procedurally all

C   that remained to do before the case could be brought on for trial was for the official receiver to file his long overdue evidence in reply. In the result this was not achieved until 24 January 1994 when a six-paragraph affidavit of the liquidator largely devoted to bringing up to date the most recent statement of affairs of the company and a 28-paragraph further report of the deputy official receiver which in fact contains very little new information and largely consists of argument, were filed and served rather more than

D   15 months after the serving of notice of intention to proceed.

On 14 February the Treasury Solicitor wrote to the respondent's solicitor seeking a response to the request in their letter of 24 January for the name of counsel to be instructed by the respondent so that a convenient date for the hearing could be fixed. The respondent's solicitors' immediate response was by letter dated 17 February in which they object to being subjected to pressure to fix a date when it had taken the official

E   receiver two and a half years to file his evidence in reply. Finally in response to a letter from the Treasury Solicitor dated 22 February detailing steps being taken to obtain a date for the trial the respondent's solicitors wrote on 17 March 1994 revealing their intention to apply to strike out the proceedings for want of prosecution.

In the course of his submissions Mr Charles conceded that had the case been pursued with proper diligence by the Treasury Solicitor it would have come for hearing in the first half of 1992. In the result had not the application to strike out intervened I would have

F   been dealing with the substantive hearing of the official receiver's application to disqualify the respondent.

The matters alleged in the official receiver's proceedings against the respondent as indicating unfitness, to which I will refer as 'the charges', were 17 in number. One of the charges is not proceeded with. One charge involves the allegation that a property of the company was transferred to a company controlled by the respondent's mother on 31

G   March 1988, rather more than two months before the winding up at an undervalue. Four charges involve payments of substantial sums for no apparent consideration to family or connections, one on 28 April 1988 shortly before the winding up. Five charges involve the transfer of promissory notes issued by the Nigerian government shortly before and shortly after the winding up, to banks who would otherwise have made claims on the family of the respondent and to the respondent's relatives and connections. One charge

H   involves the allegation that the money to subscribe for Manlon's shares held by a company controlled by the respondent's family was entirely provided by the company itself. The respondent is charged with taking payment of substantial sums in May 1986 for no apparent consideration. There is a charge of failing to keep proper accounting records, and a charge of failing to co-operate properly with the liquidator, in particular providing inaccurate statements of affairs and failing to disclose debts due to the company. It is alleged that the respondent contributed to the company's collapse by

failing to ensure that there was appropriate Export Credits Guarantee Department cover   A
for its exporting operations in place at all times and there is an allegation that the
company was permitted by the respondent to continue to trade while insolvent and while
there was no realistic hope that it would recover solvency. Mr Charles, who appeared for
the official receiver, described as the most serious charges those which involved
dispositions of the company's assets shortly before and shortly after the winding up. He
said that if those serious charges were made out the case would be likely to fall into the
middle bracket of seriousness as defined in the *Sevenoaks Stationers* case [1990] BCC 765   B
and so warrant a period of disqualification of between five and ten years. All the charges
are denied by the respondent who has filed extensive evidence supported by exhibits. It is
no part of my function to come to any assessment of the strength of the case against the
respondent. It is sufficient for my purpose to note that the allegations are, by common
consent, of a serious nature and would amount to a serious attack on the reputation and
competence of any businessman in the eyes of his fellows.   C

In the *Supreme Court Practice 1993* at note 25/1/6, what is required to be established
for the court to exercise its power to strike out for want of prosecution, certainly in cases
between private litigants, is defined in the following terms:

> 'The requirements are: (a) that there has been inordinate and inexcusable delay on
> the part of the plaintiff or his lawyers, and (b) that such delay will give rise to a
> substantial risk that it is not possible to have a fair trial of the issues in the action   D
> or is such as is likely to cause or to have caused serious prejudice to the defendants
> either as between themselves and the plaintiff or between each other or between
> them and a third party.'

That passage was approved by the House of Lords in *Birkett v James* [1978] AC 297
at p. 318. In the *Department of Transport v Chris Smaller (Transport) Ltd* [1989] AC
1197 the House of Lords again addressed the question. At p. 1207C of the report Lord   E
Griffiths is recorded as saying:

> 'However, Mr Connell submits that once the limitation period has expired so that
> the plaintiff cannot commence a fresh action, inordinate and inexcusable delay in
> the conduct of the litigation should be a ground for striking out even though there
> can be a fair trial of the issues and the defendant has suffered no prejudice from
> the delay. What would be the purpose of striking out in such circumstances? If   F
> there can be a fair trial and the defendant has suffered no prejudice, it clearly
> cannot be to do justice between the parties before the court; as between the plaintiff
> and defendant such an order is manifestly an injustice to the plaintiff. The only
> possible purpose of such an order would be as a disciplinary measure which by
> punishing the plaintiff will have a beneficent effect upon the administration of
> justice by deterring others from similar delays. I have no faith that the exercise of   G
> the power in these circumstances would produce any greater impact on delay in
> litigation than the present principles.'

Then at the bottom of that page he continues:

> 'The principles in *Allen v McAlpine* and *Birkett v James* are now well understood
> and I have not been persuaded that a case has been made out to abandon the need
> to show that the post writ delay will either make a fair trial impossible or prejudice   H
> the defendant. Furthermore, it should not be forgotten that long delay before issue
> of the writ will have the effect of any post writ delay being looked at critically by
> the court and more readily being regarded as inordinate and inexcusable than
> would be the case if the action had been commenced soon after the accrual of the
> cause of action. And that if the defendant has suffered prejudice as a result of such
> delay before issue of the writ he will only have to show something more than

A   minimal additional prejudice as a result of the post writ delay to justify striking out the action.

Alternatively, Mr Connell submits that at least the burden should be upon the plaintiff guilty of inordinate post writ delay to prove that the defendant will not suffer prejudice as a result of the delay. I regard this as a wholly impractical suggestion.'

B   Then at the bottom of p. 1208 he continues:

'Mr Laws, on behalf of the plaintiffs, submitted that the prejudice that entitled a defendant to strike out an action should be limited to proof of prejudice in the conduct of the litigation. This seems to me to be another way of saying that delay has prevented a fair trial of the action: but in both *Allen v McAlpine* and *Birkett v James* reference is made both to the risk that there could not be a fair trial of the action and of prejudice to the defendants, which, one would suppose, was intended to mean some prejudice other than mere inability to have a fair trial.'

Then in the middle of p. 1209 he continues having cited authority:

'These authorities clearly establish that prejudice may be of varying kinds and it is not confined to prejudice affecting the actual conduct of the trial. It would be foolish to attempt to define or categorise the type of prejudice justifying striking out an action but there can be no doubt that if the defendants had been able to establish significant damage to their business interest, flowing directly from the culpable delay of 13 months after the issue of the writ, a judge would have been entitled to regard it as prejudice justifying striking out the action.'

In *Roebuck v Mungovin* [1994] 2 AC 224 the House of Lords returned to the subject of striking out for want of prosecution and in particular the question of the effect of waiver by the defendant. In his speech at p. 236F Lord Browne-Wilkinson said:

'Where a plaintiff has been guilty of inordinate and inexcusable delay which has prejudiced the defendant, subsequent conduct by the defendant which induces the plaintiff to incur further expense in pursuing the action does not, in law, constitute an absolute bar preventing the defendant from obtaining a striking-out order. Such conduct of the defendant is, of course, a relevant factor to be taken into account by the judge in exercising his discretion whether or not to strike out the claim, the weight to be attached to such conduct depending upon all the circumstances of the particular case.'

Mr Charles submitted that the law established by the series of cases starting with *Allen v Sir Alfred McAlpine & Sons Ltd & Anor* [1968] 2 QB 229 and continuing through the three decisions of the House of Lords which I have cited and other authorities, apply in relation to applications to strike out proceedings such as the present case notwithstanding that those authorities are all decided in the context of private litigation concerning the rights of individuals. Accordingly he submitted that in order to succeed the respondent must establish that he had suffered prejudice as a result of the periods of inordinate and inexcusable delay which are admitted by the official receiver or which the court finds to have taken place. Such prejudice can be either prejudice to a fair trial of the case or other prejudice, which I will refer to as 'collateral prejudice'. Such collateral prejudice could either be specific actual prejudice suffered by the respondent or prejudice to the respondent inherent in the existence of the proceedings of the type found to exist by the Court of Appeal in *Biss v Lambeth, Southwark and Lewisham Health Authority* [1978] 1 WLR 382 and in respect of which Lord Griffiths in his speech in *Department of Transport v Smaller* [1989] AC 1197 at p. 1209 quoted a passage from his judgment in *Eagil Trust Co Ltd v Pigott-Brown & Anor* [1985] 3 All ER 119 at p. 124G where he said:

'Any action is bound to cause anxiety but it would as a general rule be an A exceptional case where that sort of anxiety alone would found a sufficient ground for striking out in the absence of evidence of any particular prejudice. *Biss's* case is an example of such an exceptional case, the action hanging over for eleven and a half years, with professional reputations at stake.'

Mr Charles submitted that the evidence did not support the existence of any such collateral prejudice in this case.

It is convenient at this stage in my judgment to deal with two issues which depend on fact and which relate to alleged prejudice.

The first issue is whether, after the delay which there has been in this case, there can now be a fair trial. Mr Charles indicated in the course of his submissions that if I were to take that view then it would be appropriate to strike out the proceedings notwithstanding that it might not be possible precisely to show that the prejudice to a fair trial arose as a result of any specific period of delay admitted or found to be inordinate and inexcusable.

This is a case where extensive affidavit evidence has been sworn on both sides, seven of the nine affidavits being sworn in 1990 or 1991. From the exhibits it is apparent that the issues are extensively documented. Mr Bannister does not contend that as a result of the delay any particular witness is not available, nor that any particular documents have been lost. In the *Eagil Trust* case Griffiths LJ said at p. 123E describing what the judge in that case was considering:

'He clearly had in mind, it appears to me, as a part of the submissions that he was being invited to draw the inference from mere delay, either that there could not be a fair trial of the action or that the defendants would be prejudiced. But, as to that, although he did not spell out his reasons in detail for rejecting such a submission, there was ample material to support his view. This was not a case where Mr Taylor and Mr Pye, on whose evidence the issue of whether or not these guarantees had been discharged would depend, were being called on for the first time to think about what had happened at the beginning of 1976; Mr Taylor had prepared a memorandum in 1979, which he had exhibited to an affidavit sworn in 1979, just three years after the event; and Mr Pye himself had sworn an affidavit dealing with the matter in 1981. Furthermore, this is not an issue which is going to turn on the minutiae of recollection of the words exchanged at the meeting between Mr Taylor, Mr Pye and a Mr Rieck in which it is alleged that this discharge of the guarantees was given on behalf of the plaintiff company. There is a very broad issue here; either it was agreed between those parties to discharge the guarantee or it was not. It would not depend on the judge trying to assess the recollection of the precise words exchanged.'

It is very difficult for a judge to assess at an interlocutory stage precisely how issues in any trial will ultimately emerge. However it seems to me that the sort of considerations which guided Griffiths LJ into dismissing the defendant's appeal in the *Eagil Trust* case are applicable to the present case and lead me to the conclusion that there is no 'substantial risk that it is not possible to have a fair trial of the issues' in these proceedings.

The second matter with which I have to deal is whether notwithstanding the finding that I have just made, the respondent has established that he has been caused serious collateral prejudice by reason of the delay in bringing the proceedings to trial.

A large part of the evidence sworn in this application by the respondent is concerned to prove that he has suffered specific collateral prejudice. It was also submitted that he must be treated as having suffered prejudice to his reputation and standing as a businessman inherent in the fact that these proceedings had been brought against him by the official receiver, which prejudice has been prolonged by the prolongation of the proceedings due to the official receiver's delays.

A   The respondent's allegations of specific prejudice can be grouped under four heads. The first head is the allegation made in respect of seven named companies that when, after his discharge from bankruptcy on 4 August 1991 the respondent again became able to assume directorships of companies he was, by reason of these proceedings being still pending, prevented from taking up directorships of those seven companies and thus lost the director's fees that had to be paid to other individuals who were appointed in his place. The seven companies concerned were either controlled by his family or by business associates of the respondent.

B

     The second head is the allegation that the respondent has had to decline appointment as a trustee of four trusts. It is not suggested that the respondent suffered any financial penalty as a result of having to do so.

     The third head is the allegation that as a result of the pendency of the proceedings and the resulting inability of the respondent to deal with the primary banks with a view to getting loans, as opposed to insurance companies and building societies, he has lost the opportunity presented by two commercial transactions: the first, the opportunity to acquire with a group of friends and associates the operations of a major manufacturer of batteries in Malawi, Zambia and Zimbabwe; the second, the opportunity to act as manager for remuneration of the operations of two companies based in South Africa and Malawi in the UK.

C

D   The fourth head of prejudice is the allegation that the respondent's claims to recover property expropriated from him in Malawi by proceedings in that country and otherwise has been prejudiced by the continued existence and pendency of the allegations against him in these proceedings which, he suggests, undermines his credibility in pursuing his claims in court and otherwise.

     It is clear from the passage in the speech of Lord Griffiths at p. 1208C of the report of the House of Lords decision in *Department of Transport v Chris Smaller (Transport) Ltd* [1989] AC 1197 which I have set out above that the burden of proof of establishing prejudice rests on the party seeking to strike out the relevant proceedings for want of prosecution.

E

     The respondent was cross-examined at some length before me on these allegations of specific prejudice. I do not propose, in this judgment, to rehearse the respondent's evidence on each separate item and his answers given to the questions put to him by Mr Charles. I will confine myself to saying that in my judgment he failed to discharge the burden of proof which rests upon him and that I am unable to find proved that the respondent has suffered prejudice flowing from the prolongation of the proceedings by the delays of the official receiver in the specific ways which he alleges and certainly not prejudice which could be categorised as 'serious', in the context of this case and the circumstances in which the respondent was living and continuing to work from the time when these proceedings were commenced and, in particular, after his discharge from bankruptcy.

F

G

     I turn to consider the second type of prejudice, which does not involve a risk to a fair trial, which a defendant or respondent can suffer and which is inherent in the pendency of the proceedings in question. This sort of prejudice of which an example is to be seen in *Biss's* case in the anxiety caused to nurses of the continuing challenge to their professional competence, is of a type which usually cannot be directly proved. It is also of a type, in so far as it concerns anxiety caused by the pendency of proceedings, in respect of which Lord Griffiths in *Department of Transport v Chris Smaller (Transport) Ltd* said at p. 1209F:

H

     'I would, however, express a note of caution against allowing the mere fact of the anxiety that accompanies any litigation being regarded as of itself a sufficient prejudice to justify striking out an action.'

–and in respect of which he quoted from his own judgment in the *Eagil Trust* case in   A
which he said that only in exceptional cases of this kind would such prejudice justify
striking out.

In my judgment, however, the prejudice suffered by businessmen against whom
proceedings are brought under the Directors Disqualification Act to disqualify them
from acting as directors of companies is of a different nature to that with which the Court
of Appeal was dealing in *Biss's* case and upon which Lord Griffiths was commenting in   B
the *Eagil Trust* and *Department of Transport* cases. Much will depend on the nature of
the allegations being made to justify disqualification. However, any case brought to
disqualify an individual from acting as a director will involve allegations which, if proved,
would undermine the status and reputation of a businessman against whom they are
made. In the present case Mr Charles accepts that the allegations are rather more than
that since he contends that, if established, they would bring the case into the medium
band of seriousness as defined in the *Sevenoaks Stationers* case.   C

It was suggested by Mr Charles that by contrast with what may be the position of the
majority of businessmen, I could be satisfied on the evidence before me that the
respondent in this case was cocooned from such prejudice by the network of family
businesses and companies in which he has worked since the proceedings were launched
against him. I cannot accept that submission. It involves my finding that the respondent
had during that period no ambitions in business outside the circle of his family and their   D
immediate business associates. There is no justification on the evidence for any such
finding. In my judgment it is inherent in the nature of proceedings brought under the
Directors Disqualification Act, launched as they are by a government department and
brought in the public interest for the protection of the public, that they will prejudice the
business interests of the respondent to those proceedings so long as they remain pending,
save in the most exceptional cases of which this is not one. Such prejudice will result from
loss of business opportunities, whether known to the respondent or not, simply brought   E
about by the existence of the proceedings and the nature of the allegations contained in
them becoming known to potential business partners. In the present case the respondent
gave evidence of how business enquiries about him were passed to the liquidator of the
company who then informed the enquirer of the existence of the proceedings. Prejudice
may also arise from the inability to order a businessman's affairs with a view to the future
because his status, in particular his ability to manage the business affairs of the company,   F
will remain in question until the proceedings are determined. In this regard it is important
to bear in mind that the prohibition resulting from disqualification set out in s. 1(1) of
the 1986 Act is extended in subs. (d) of that section to being concerned 'in any way,
whether directly or indirectly ... in the promotion, formation or management of a
company', a much broader restriction than simply from being formally appointed
director. It is the existence of this almost inevitable prejudice which, in my judgment,
requires the applicant in proceedings under the 1986 Act, once they have been   G
commenced, to take all steps to ensure that those proceedings are brought to trial at the
earliest possible moment commensurate with the court being able to do justice between
the parties. It is the existence of this sort of prejudice which makes a case such as the
present one, where the applicant has been compelled to accept that for a period of 17
months the matter was not advanced due to the inordinate and inexcusable delay of the
applicant and those advising him and in which after the expiry of such period, and   H
notwithstanding a threat to have the proceedings struck out for want of prosecution, it
took the applicant a further 15 months to prepare and serve two affidavits of modest
length and content, a matter of some anxiety to the court. I accept that the respondent
will have suffered prejudice of this type during the period of approximately four years
during which these proceedings have been pending that period itself commencing two
years after the commencement of the winding up.

A   Mr Bannister's broad submission for the respondent was that the rules established by
the long series of cases starting with *Allen v Sir Alfred McAlpine & Sons Ltd & Anor*
[1968] 2 QB 229 and of which the three House of Lords cases which I have cited are
leading examples, and which were all decided in the context of private litigation, are
inapplicable to public law cases where the applicant is a regulatory authority and the
respondent is an individual who, it is alleged, has broken relevant rules and against whom
a statutory remedy is sought to be enforced. Accordingly he submits that I should not be
B   bound by the minutiae of the rules applied to private litigation by those authorities and
should not, for example, require to have proved prejudice flowing from any period of
inordinate and inexcusable delay established before exercising the jurisdiction to strike
out if otherwise satisfied that it is an appropriate case to do so. He submitted that there
was a duty on the regulatory authority once proceedings against a respondent had been
decided upon, to press on with those proceedings. Any failure to do so should be
C   interpreted by the court as a loss of confidence by the regulatory authority that the
proceedings were indeed required to be pursued in the public interest which, if prolonged,
should be dealt with by the court by striking out the proceedings. If this involved the
court exercising the jurisdiction to strike out as a goad to the regulatory authorities then
so be it.

Mr Bannister referred me to what appear to be the only two reported cases where
D   applications to strike out proceedings under the Directors Disqualification Act have been
made.

The first is a decision of Vinelott J in *Re Noble Trees Ltd* [1993] BCC 318. The grounds
upon which the Secretary of State in that case relied for seeking the disqualification of
the respondent are summarised by the judge at p. 318G in the following terms:

E   '. . . that he caused the company to trade knowing it to be insolvent, that he had
misapplied company moneys for his own benefit, that he had issued cheques which
he knew would be dishonoured and that he had failed to co-operate with the
receivers.'

These appear to be serious charges reflecting some of the charges made in the present
case. In the result Vinelott J, dealing with a case which, like this one, was commenced
right at the end of the two-year statutory period, and which was before him some five
years after the winding up of the company concerned, dismissed the proceedings for want
F   of prosecution. In doing so he does seem to have followed the rules prescribed in the civil
litigation cases. Thus, whereas he did not find potential prejudice to a fair trial, he did
find specific prejudice to the respondent flowing from the proceedings. He did not,
expressly, balance such prejudice to the respondent against the public's interest in
continuing the proceedings to obtain the protection of a disqualification order. This case
was before the *Roebuck* case and accordingly the judge considered whether in the
G   circumstances of that case there had been a waiver by the respondent of a right to apply
to strike out consequent on delay by the applicant. At p. 322E of the report the judge
said:

'Mr Yeudell [of the Treasury Solicitors] in his affidavit evidence explains the great
pressure of work that he was under during this period. I do not underestimate his
difficulties. I think I am entitled to take notice of the fact that the Treasury Solicitor
and the legal department of the DTI are seriously understaffed. But I cannot take
H   these difficulties into account in considering whether there has been inordinate and
inexcusable delay. If legislation to provide for the disqualification of persons who
are shown to be unfit to be directors is required in the public interest, the
government must find ways of providing adequate resources. It seems to me
intolerable in the public interest that if the Secretary of State considers a person to
be unfit to be a director of a company that he should be allowed to remain free so

to act for as long as the period of five years which in this case elapsed after the   A
insolvency which gave rise to the report and enquiries which in turn led the
Secretary of State to take that view.

It is also unfair to the individual concerned that the proceedings should remain in
suspense for such a protracted period.'

The second case is *Official Receiver v B Ltd* [1994] 2 BCLC 1 in which judgment was
given by Judge Paul Baker QC, sitting as a judge of this division of the High Court, on 6   B
April 1993. Again in this case proceedings were started right at the end of the two-year
period prescribed by s. 7(2) of the Act. A number of the allegations against the two
director respondents were dropped in the course of the proceedings. Those which were
pressed are summarised in a letter from the Treasury solicitor to the respondents'
solicitors quoted (at pp. 2–3) as follows:

> '(i) the failure to file accounts as required by statute; (ii) the advances to associated   C
> companies and general intermingling of the companies' affairs to the ultimate
> detriment of creditors; (iii) trading whilst insolvent by the non-payment of Crown
> moneys; and (iv) to the extent that it is accepted by your clients that some cheques
> were issued which were not honoured, the dishonoured cheques.

> Some of these allegations relate to more than one of the companies to which your
> clients were directors.'

In this case as in the present case, a period of inordinate and inexcusable delay in the   D
prosecution of the proceedings was admitted by the Treasury Solicitor. In the result
Judge Baker, who was dealing with the case some four and a half years after the relevant
winding up, dismissed it for want of prosecution.

Judge Baker seems also to have applied the civil litigation rules and looked for proof
of prejudice before striking out the proceedings. However at pp. 10–11 the following
passage appears: E

> 'Mr Briggs, in relation to the principles I have been reviewing with the aid of these
> authorities [the civil litigation cases], submitted that these principles should be
> applied in a modified way to disqualification proceedings and he gave two reasons
> for this. The first was that this was not ordinary private litigation, but was brought
> by the Secretary of State or the official receiver in the public interest. It is in the
> public interest that unfit directors should be disqualified and the fact of delay in   F
> the proceedings is no reason for not going on in the public interest. So in balancing
> the position as between the respondent's private interest and the public interest,
> the court should tend to exercise the discretion which the court has towards
> allowing the proceedings to continue. I am unable to accept that submission. It is
> equally important to do justice to a respondent as it is to protect the public from
> unfit directors. Further, if a respondent is unfit it is all the more important that he   G
> should be disqualified promptly . . .'

In the present case Mr Charles made a similar submission to that made by Mr Briggs
in the *B Ltd* case as an alternative submission when I put to him that there will almost
always be prejudice to respondents to disqualification cases which is likely to be serious
and which results from the prolongation of the proceedings resulting from delay.

Judge Baker then goes on to quote the passage which I have cited from the judgment
of Vinelott J. Then at p. 15 Judge Baker is recorded as saying: H

> 'The evidence on the part of Mr Edwards and Mr O'Brien [as to specific collateral
> prejudice] is not very specific as regards dates, but the situation is a continuing one.
> It is a situation of uncertainty. Mr Briggs suggested it was no more than the state
> of anxiety against which Lord Griffiths warned as justifying dismissal. This
> however goes further. As I would see it the business interests of the directors are

A
affected and have been prejudiced by the delay. Had the official receiver prosecuted the case expeditiously during 1991 it would have been heard a year ago and the situation clarified. Where a businessman has proceedings of this kind hanging over him, their mere existence is prejudicial in that he cannot order his affairs with any certainty. To some degree he has to accept that. If the application is prosecuted diligently, albeit taking advantage to the full of the time limits which the law allows, he cannot complain of the effect upon the ordering of his affairs. Further if

B
he is found unfit, he cannot complain he cannot continue to have the benefit of trading with the benefit of a limited liability for the period of disqualification save with the leave of the court which may be withheld or granted subject to restrictive conditions. Nevertheless the right to be a director of a limited company is an important right: it prejudices a businessman to leave him in a state of uncertainty for an inordinate period of time in relation to a specific business opportunity or

C
interest which involves him becoming a director of a particular company.'

It is of note that in both these cases the judges placed emphasis on the duty of the regulatory authority to press on with the proceedings because of the unfairness to the respondent in leaving them hanging over him for an unnecessarily long period.

In my judgment the approach of the court in applications to strike out cases brought under the Directors Disqualification Act cannot be the same as the approach of the court

D
to ordinary private litigation. I do not think that the Court of Appeal in *Allen v McAlpine* and the House of Lords in *Birkett v James* and its successor cases had in mind the applicability of the rules they were prescribing for private litigation cases to cases of this type. Disqualification cases, and probably other proceedings brought by regulatory authorities, are sui generis and the rules established in the 'private litigation' authorities can only be applied to them with considerable modifications.

In the first place this is because the proceedings concern the status of the respondent

E
and are not to resolve disputes as to private rights where applications to strike out involve considerations of when the right to enforce such private rights in the courts falls to be extinguished as a result of delay and which may properly involve a balancing by the court of the conduct and circumstances of both parties to produce a result which does justice between them. In disqualification cases the proceedings are brought by a regulatory authority, the Secretary of State or the official receiver on his behalf, who has no direct

F
personal interest in the result.

The proceedings are brought in the public interest in order to protect the public, and in particular the business community, from the depredations of persons who, by their past conduct of the affairs of insolvent companies have demonstrated that they are unfit to conduct the business of a company with the protection of limited liability. If as a result of incompetent presentation the proceedings fail it is the public which is disadvantaged

G
by the absence of the protection which a disqualification order confers.

However, the Act places an upper limit on the period of disqualification which the court can impose. It follows, therefore, that the legislature did not regard indefinite disqualification of those who, in the past, have shown themselves to be incompetent or not to be trusted, as being in the public interest. The legislature must have envisaged that it was in the public interest that a businessman, whose past conduct had justified disqualification, should, after an appropriate period in which the public was to be

H
protected and during which it must be presumed he became aware of the consequences of his past failings, have restored to him the right to manage businesses with the protection of limited liability. The legislature must have realised that the institution of such proceedings would usually have a serious inhibiting effect on a businessman, but also that the process of education and reform would also start with the commencement of the proceedings. It follows that, by contrast with private litigation where the plaintiff's

interest in enforcing his private rights against the defendant remains constant, the interest   A
of the public in obtaining the protection of the disqualification order must diminish as
time passes from the commencement of the relevant liquidation and certainly from the
commencement of the proceedings to disqualify.

Disqualification proceedings involve a process akin to sentencing in criminal cases.
Delay in bringing the matter before the court may handicap that process from doing
justice. There is no equivalent in private litigation. It is possible to envisage a situation   B
where delay might produce a wholly artificial and unjust result. Thus in the present case
it is conceded that if the proceedings had been properly conducted they would have come
for trial in 1992. If, contrary to Mr Charles' submissions, the court had found the case to
be proved but only at the less serious end of the *Sevenoaks* test and had imposed a period
of two years' disqualification only, that period would now have expired and the
respondent would be free again to be a director. However in fact as a result of the delay
the case was only ready to be brought on after six years from the winding up and four   C
years from the commencement of the proceedings. On the assumption that the court had
made the same basic finding as to unfitness it would have been bound by s. 6 of the Act
to have imposed a minimum period of two years' disqualification which the respondent
would only now be embarking upon. Thus a two-year delay would impose on the
respondent two more years before he could put behind him the inhibitions and
disadvantages flowing from the pendency of the proceedings and the period of   D
disqualification consequent upon them. I accept, as was submitted by Mr Charles, that
where the court was considering a longer period of disqualification, because it took a
more serious view of the case, it might be able deliberately to reduce that period in the
light of the delays in bringing the case to trial. Such an approach is consistent with the
approach of Ferris J in *Re Carecraft Construction Co Ltd* [1993] BCC 336. However the
potential for injustice remains.

Finally, by contrast with private litigation, there will almost always be serious collateral   E
prejudice, inherent in the existence of the proceedings which in private litigation would
justify striking out.

Concluding as I do that disqualification proceedings must be treated as sui generis in
the field of striking out for want of prosecution I would with some diffidence suggest the
following as a practical approach to the question whether proceedings to disqualify
should be so struck out: F

(1)   The court, having determined that there has been inordinate and inexcusable delay
       in the conduct of the proceedings by the applicant, should then decide whether
       such delay has given rise to a substantial risk that it is not possible to have a fair
       trial on the issues raised in the case.

(2)   If the court concludes that there cannot be a fair trial the court will generally
       dismiss the proceedings. The applicant has control of the case and is under a duty   G
       to press on with it. Only in exceptional cases would the court treat conduct of the
       respondent in relation to the proceedings as justifying allowing the case to proceed.

(3)   Where no prejudice to a fair trial is established the court should permit the case to
       proceed unless, having regard to all the circumstances of the case including:

       (a) the nature of the allegations;   H

       (b) the likely period of disqualification which would be imposed if those
            allegations were proved;

       (c) the time which has elapsed since the relevant winding up or the
            commencement of the disqualification proceedings and the application to
            strike out these proceedings;

A
    (d) the continuing inherent prejudice to the respondent (which can usually be assumed); and

    (e) the impact and seriousness of specific prejudice to the respondent which the court finds to have resulted or which is resulting from the pendency of the proceedings,

there has ceased to be an obvious public interest in obtaining a disqualification

B
order against the particular respondent for the protection of the public which outweighs the interest of the respondent (and of the public) in the respondent being able to pursue his business affairs without fetter.

With relation to (c) I would attach no great significance to delay in launching the disqualification proceedings late in the two-year period. In any reasonably complicated insolvency it will take the office-holder an appreciable time to investigate the company's

C
affairs so as to be in a position to report on the conduct of directors.

In the present case I am only concerned with para. (3). In the result, I am not satisfied that there exists such an obvious public interest and accordingly I would strike out the proceedings.

If, contrary to my conclusions, the rules as to private litigation are applicable to this case the result, in my judgment, should be the same. Inordinate and inexcusable delay for

D
a period of 17 months is admitted. A large part of the period from the service of notice of intention to proceed until the applicant's evidence in reply was served must also, in my judgment, be treated as delay of a similar nature. Such delay has prolonged the time during which the proceedings have been pending by more than two years. During that period the respondent has suffered the prejudice to any businessman inherent in having proceedings of this kind, making serious allegations against him, hanging over his head. I am not prepared to treat such prejudice as other than serious notwithstanding that the

E
respondent has been unable to point to the consequential loss of specific business opportunities. In the result the test set out at note 25/1/6 which was approved in *Birkett v James* is met and the proceedings should be struck out.

(Order accordingly)

COURT OF APPEAL JUDGMENT

F
(Delivered 12 April 1995)

Peter Gibson LJ: This is an appeal by the official receiver from the dismissal by Evans-Lombe J of disqualification proceedings brought against Haroon Abdul Aziz. Whilst this case, like others of its kind, ultimately turns on its own particular facts, an important issue raised on this appeal is the correct approach to applications to strike out such proceedings for want of prosecution.

G
Manlon Trading Ltd ('Manlon') was incorporated in 1972 and initially traded as a steel exporter, its principal area of business being Africa and in particular Malawi. Mr Aziz and his family had been in business in Malawi, but he was deported from there. In 1976 Mr Aziz's family acquired a shareholding in Manlon and in September 1977 Mr Aziz was appointed general manager. It would not have assisted Manlon's business in Malawi if the company's filed records showed him, a deportee, as a director. However, he accepts that he acted as a shadow director of Manlon from 1977 until it was wound

H
up, the nominal directors having no executive function. By early 1978 Manlon's business had become exclusively that of a confirming agent, acting as an intermediary between businesses, primarily in the UK and businesses in Africa, and particularly Nigeria.

Manlon's bankers were Johnson Matthey Bankers Ltd ('the bank').

In 1983 there was a military coup in Nigeria. Rigid exchange control was imposed by the new regime, and this prevented Nigerian debtors from paying their substantial

indebtedness directly to Manlon. Those debtors paid the Nigerian government which   A
gave Manlon promissory notes. In 1984 the bank, being in financial difficulties, called in
its loans. In 1986 the bank obtained judgment against Manlon for some £4.5m and
against Mr Aziz for some £100,000 in respect of a guarantee by him of part of Manlon's
debt. On 28 February 1988 Manlon ceased trading and on 30 March 1988 it was
compulsorily wound up. On 4 April 1988 the bank obtained a bankruptcy order against
Mr Aziz. He was discharged from his bankruptcy on 4 August 1991.

   In the meantime on 7 June 1990 the official receiver commenced disqualification   B
proceedings against Mr Aziz as a shadow director of Manlon under s. 6 and 22(4) of the
Company Directors Disqualification Act 1986 ('the Act'). The originating summons was
supported by a report to the court of the deputy official receiver. In the report he alleged
that by reference to the following matters Mr Aziz was unfit to be concerned in the
management of a company:

(1)   Mr Aziz misapplied company assets by causing Manlon: C

     (a)   to transfer a property at an undervalue to a connected company on 31
         March 1988;

     (b)   to make substantial payments to companies and individuals not in the
         normal course of business and for which no explanation had been received,
         including a payment on 9 September 1987 to his cousin Mr Ibraimo and a
         payment on 27 May 1987 to one Latif;   D

     (c)   to make payments to relatives after the presentation of the winding up
         petition without explanation or consideration;

     (d)   to assign promissory notes both before and after commencement of the
         winding up to relatives, a friend and banks whose loans were guaranteed by
         him or by relatives of his;

     (e)   to make payments to his brother Abdul within two years of the   E
         commencement of the winding up for no consideration.

(2)   He caused Manlon in June 1981 to apply moneys in financing the subscription for
     its own shares.

(3)   He withdrew moneys from Manlon on 13 May 1986 for his own purposes for no
     consideration.
       F
(4)   He failed to ensure that adequate accounting records were kept by Manlon, the
     complaint being that whilst all transactions were entered in the records there was
     often no proper explanation of the payments and receipts (and numerous examples
     of the alleged failures dating from 1980 onwards are referred to in the report).

(5)   He failed to provide the liquidator of Manlon with information and in particular
     with adequate explanation of the circumstances leading to many of Manlon's
     transactions, some of which took place many years before the commencement of   G
     the liquidation.

(6)   He caused the failure of Manlon by failing to arrange Export Credits Guarantee
     Department cover and by failing to ensure that its transactions were of a genuine
     nature (the report refers to transactions going back to 1983).

(7)   He knowingly continued Manlon's business beyond a date when there was no
     reasonable prospect of all creditors being paid, that date being said to be in 1983.   H

   None of these allegations is accepted by Mr Aziz (and we have been told that one
allegation forming part of (1)(b) is not being pursued by the official receiver). Mr Aziz
responded to the report by an affirmation on 12 April 1991. Other evidence sworn of his
behalf came from Manlon's bookkeeper, Mr Patel, and a partner in Manlon's auditors,
Mr Ling.

A   Notwithstanding that the commencement of these proceedings was delayed until the very last day of the two-year period allowed by s. 7(2) of the Act the official receiver did not pursue the proceedings with any expedition. At a hearing on 15 April 1991 the official receiver was directed by the companies registrar to file and serve evidence in reply by 13 May 1991. At each of five subsequent hearings before the registrar, successive extensions of time were sought and obtained for the filing of that evidence in reply. Mr Aziz was given no notice of any save the first of those hearings nor were the orders made at those

B   hearings communicated to Mr Aziz save the order made at the last of those hearings on 11 November 1991.

By letter dated 11 November 1992 the Treasury Solicitor on behalf of the official receiver served on Mr Aziz notice of intention to proceed after the expiration of one month by serving and filing the evidence in reply. Mr Aziz was also sent a copy of the order for directions made one year earlier. The solicitors then acting for Mr Aziz on 21

C   January 1993 wrote to the Treasury Solicitor, saying that Mr Aziz had rebutted every allegation made against him, that proceedings brought by the liquidator of Manlon against Mr Aziz had been settled out of court, and continued:

'In these circumstances, it is wholly unfair and inequitable to have disqualification proceedings hanging over our client's head like the sword of Damocles. The proceedings brought by you have laid dormant for the past eighteen months. Please

D   inform us whether it is your intention to either withdraw or prosecute the claim.

In the absence of any satisfactory response and/or action from you by 11 February 1993, we reserve the right to make an Application to strike out the proceedings for inexcusable delay.'

The Treasury Solicitor on 26 January 1993 replied that he was instructed to proceed with the application. But despite all the extensions of time for service of the evidence in

E   reply, and although the final extension granted on 11 November 1991 was only for one week to 18 November 1991, that evidence was not filed and served until 24 January 1994. As the judge records, all that such evidence consisted of was an affidavit of six paragraphs by the liquidator, largely devoted to bringing up to date the most recent statement of affairs of Manlon, and a further report of 28 paragraphs by the deputy official receiver, containing very little new information and largely consisting of argument. On 27 March 1994 Mr Aziz applied to strike out the proceedings for want of prosecution.

F   The official receiver surprisingly applied, and even more surprisingly the registrar acceded to the application, for liberty that the deponents on each side on Mr Aziz's application be cross-examined. That order is not under appeal before us, but I feel bound to comment that in my opinion it would require highly exceptional circumstances, which do not appear to me to have been present in this case, to justify such an order. The rules and practice of the court allow interlocutory applications to be made for the purpose of

G   bringing to an end or reducing the scope of proceedings. It would destroy the utility of such applications if they became occasions for lengthy trials within trial, extended by oral evidence.

At the hearing before the judge, Mrs Oliver, the head of the Disqualification Unit in the Treasury Solicitor's department, who had sworn an affidavit in which she explains the delays that had occurred, and Mr Aziz, who in an affirmation had claimed to have

H   suffered specific prejudice caused by the delays (such as that he would have become a director of seven named companies but could not do so because of the pending disqualification proceedings), were cross-examined. The judge found that there was no substantial risk that it was impossible to have a fair trial of the issues in the proceedings and that Mr Aziz had not discharged the burden on him of satisfying the judge of the specific prejudice that had been claimed. However, the judge said that disqualification proceedings were sui generis, so that the rules for striking out for want of prosecution in

private litigation did not apply, that the interest of the public in obtaining the protection　A
of a disqualification order diminishes as time passes from the commencement of the
liquidation and that he was not satisfied that there existed such an obvious public interest
and accordingly he struck out the proceedings. He also, in the alternative, considered the
application of the rules for striking out for want of prosecution in private litigation and
on that basis held that the inherent prejudice, in having disqualification proceedings
hanging over Mr Aziz in the period of inordinate and inexcusable delay, was serious and
accordingly he held that he would strike out the proceedings on that approach, if　B
applicable to disqualification proceedings.

The official receiver now appeals. Mr Charles submits that:

(1)　the judge was wrong to treat disqualification proceedings as sui generis;

(2)　alternatively, the judge's reasoning and decision on a sui generis approach were
　　　wrong; and　　　　　　　　　　　　　　　　　　　　　　　　　　　　　　C

(3)　the judge's alternative decision misinterpreted and misapplied the tests applicable
　　　to ordinary applications to strike out for want of prosecution.

Mr Collings for Mr Aziz, whilst supporting the judge's conclusion, has concentrated
primarily on the alternative decision and has in addition by a respondent's notice
challenged the finding by the judge that there can be a fair trial; he relies in particular on
the prejudice caused by fading memories.

At this point it is convenient to set out the statutory framework against which the　D
application fell to be considered. The Act provides for the making of a disqualification
order, that is to say an order that a person shall not without the leave of the court for a
specific period, beginning with the date of the order, be a company director or liquidator
or administrator or receiver or manager of a company's property or in any way, whether
directly or indirectly, be concerned or take part in the promotion, formation or
management of a company (s. 1). Such an order may be made by the court in a variety　E
of specified circumstances, but the court is obliged to make an order under s. 6 in any
case where, on an application under the section, it is satisfied of both of two conditions
(s. 6(1)). One is that the person is or has been a director of a company which has at any
time become insolvent. The other (so far as material to the present case) is that his
conduct as a director of that company makes him unfit to be concerned in the
management of a company. The matters to which the court is to have regard in　F
determining such fitness are set out in Sch. 1 to the Act and several of those matters
require the court to consider the extent of the director's responsibility for the company's
actions or omissions. Whether an application under s. 6 should be made is left to the
Secretary of State, his power to do so being conditional on it appearing to him that it is
expedient in the public interest that a disqualification order under s. 6 should be made
against the person (s. 7(1)). Except with the leave of the court, the application is not to
be made more than two years from the company in question becoming insolvent. An　G
order made under s. 6 must be for a minimum period of two years (the maximum being
15 years). In contrast if it appears to the Secretary of State after a statutory investigation
and report that a disqualification order should be made, no time limit is prescribed for
the application to be made nor is any minimum period for the disqualification (s. 8).

I turn next to the court's power to strike out proceedings for want of prosecution.
There are express provisions of the Rules of the Supreme Court which empower the court　H
to strike out when a plaintiff omits to do what he is required by the rules to do. But in
addition the court has inherent jurisdiction to dismiss proceedings for want of
prosecution where there has been default in complying with the rules or with an order of
the court or there has been excessive delay in the prosecution of proceedings. In the
absence of contumelious default, the conventional approach to striking out for want of
prosecution in all civil proceedings has been since *Birkett v James* [1978] AC 297 to

A   inquire whether there has been inordinate and inexcusable delay on the part of the plaintiff (or his lawyers) and whether such delay will give rise to substantial risk that it is not possible to have a fair trial of the issues in the proceedings or is such as is likely to cause or to have caused serious prejudice to the defendant.

The judge's favoured approach appears to have been devised by him and it departs from the approach taken by Vinelott J in *Re Noble Trees Ltd* [1993] BCC 318 and by
B   Judge Paul Baker QC (sitting as a judge of the Chancery Division) in *Official Receiver v B Ltd* [1994] 2 BCLC 1. Both were cases of striking out disqualification proceedings for want of prosecution and in both the conventional approach was adopted. But the judge was surely right to point out that considerations additional to those referred to in the formulation of the test on the conventional approach have their place in the court's decision. As he said, the proceedings are not brought to enforce private rights but are brought in the public interest in order to protect the public. That must be a factor
C   militating against the striking out of such proceedings.

However, for my part I would not accept that this was a sufficient factor to justify discarding the conventional approach altogether, as distinct from modifying it so that in disqualification proceedings that factor must be balanced against the prejudice caused to the defendant by the inordinate and inexcusable delay.

I have other difficulties with the details of the judge's favoured approach which was in
D   three parts.

(1)   He said that the court, having determined that there has been inordinate and inexcusable delay in the conduct of the proceedings, should then decide whether such delay has given rise to a substantial risk that it is not possible to have a fair trial. On the conventional approach, the defendant complaining of inordinate and inexcusable delay can apply to strike out either on the ground that there can be no
E   fair trial or on the ground of serious prejudice. I do not understand why the judge would not allow an application to strike out on the latter ground, unless it is that he had in mind the rule in criminal proceedings that the defendant complaining of delay must establish that no fair trial can in consequence be held. It is of course true that a disqualification order has serious consequences for the disqualified person and that the contravention of an order carries criminal penalties (s. 13). But the primary purpose of disqualification proceedings is the protection of the public
F   and not the punishment of the director (*Re Lo-Line Electric Motors Ltd* (1988) 4 BCC 415; [1988] Ch 477 at p. 419; 486). Further, there is no limitation period for criminal proceedings. In contrast, an application for an order made under s. 6 must be made within two years of the commencement of the liquidation. Mr Charles did not contend that the rule in criminal proceedings applied, and I think he was right not to do so.

G   (2)   The judge said that if the court concludes that there cannot be a fair trial, the court will 'generally' dismiss the proceedings, allowing in exceptional cases the proceedings to continue because of the conduct of the director. For my part, I cannot see that there can ever be such an exception. If there cannot be a fair trial, the court will surely strike out the proceedings.

(3)   The judge said that where there can be a fair trial, the court should permit the case
H   to proceed unless, having regard to all the circumstances of the case, including

      (a)   the nature of the allegations,

      (b)   the likely period of disqualification which would be imposed if the allegations were proved,

      (c)   the time elapsed since the liquidation or the commencement of disqualification proceedings and the application to strike out,

(d) the continuing inherent prejudice to the director from the pendency of the   A
proceedings, and

(e) the impact and seriousness of specific prejudice resulting from that
pendency,

there has ceased to be an obvious public interest in obtaining a disqualification
order against the particular respondent for the protection of the public which
outweighs the interest of the respondent (and of the public) in the respondent being   B
able to pursue his business affairs without fetter.

A number of points arise on this. First, whilst it is of course right that the court should
have regard to all the circumstances, some of the circumstances identified by the judge
call for comment.

For my part, I regard the assistance derived from circumstance (b) (viz. knowing the
maximum likely period of disqualification in the event of total success by the official   C
receiver) as likely to be limited. The court will usually not be in a position to assess
whether such total success is likely. Take the present case. There are numerous allegations
made against Mr Aziz, all of which are conceded to be arguable but are nevertheless
challenged, and it is impossible for this court to say at this stage which allegations would
succeed. It is likely that the judge had in mind the point put to him by Mr Charles that if
the allegations are established, the period of disqualification that would have been
ordered had there been a trial in 1992 (as would probably have occurred but for the   D
official receiver's delays) would still be running and the delays could be taken into account
by the court when determining the period of disqualification (see *Re Grayan Building
Services Ltd* [1995] BCC 554 at p. 577A). But the possibility cannot be ignored that the
official receiver might only achieve partial success justifying a disqualification for a period
at or close to the minimum possible, in which case the delays could not be taken into
account adequately or at all.   E

As for circumstance (c), the judge commented that he would attach no great
significance to delay in launching the disqualification proceedings late in the two-year
period. But in *Re Noble Trees Ltd* at p. 321H, Vinelott J took the opposite view. He said:

'Greater diligence in prosecuting proceedings is expected of a litigant who delays
issuing proceedings until the end of a limitation period and I see no reason why a
different approach should be adopted if the Secretary of State delays the institution   F
of proceedings under the 1986 Act until the end of the permissible period.'

I respectfully agree with Vinelott J. In doing so I do not in any way overlook or seek
to minimise the very great difficulties facing the Secretary of State in bringing
disqualification proceedings quickly. The matters to be considered before a decision is
taken to seek an order are very wide-ranging and co-operation from those concerned is
not always readily available. But Parliament, by laying down a two-year period, has   G
given a clear indication of the expedition which it expects if proceedings are to be brought
and the court must take note of that.

In relation to circumstances (d) and (e), in my judgment what is of importance is
prejudice caused by delay before the proceedings are brought, as well as prejudice caused
by the delay of the Secretary of State or official receiver after the proceedings have been
commenced. Prejudice resulting from the mere pendency of proceedings, if not caused by
such delay, seems to me irrelevant.   H

Second, the judge in suggesting a test measured by the cesser of a public interest in
obtaining a disqualification order, was referring to a theory which he had earlier
advanced, that the interest of the public in obtaining the protection of the order must
diminish with the passage of time. This was apparently based on the fact that the Act
imposes a maximum period of disqualification and on the judge's belief that a 'process of

A   education and reform' would start with the commencement of disqualification proceedings. I can accept none of this. The scheme of s. 6 is to direct attention to the past conduct of a director for the purpose of ascertaining whether the director is unfit to be concerned in the management of a company. Present unfitness is judged by that past conduct (see, for example, *Re Grayan Building Services Ltd* at p. 576C). In the light of that, I cannot see that the public interest in obtaining the protection of a disqualification order diminishes as time goes by. However the passage of time may lead to consequences

B   which have greater weight than that public interest.

It follows that I cannot agree with the approach favoured by the judge or his conclusion consequent on adopting that approach.

I turn next to the conventional approach. It is not disputed by the official receiver that there was some inordinate and inexcusable delay and the period of that delay is said to

C   be between May 1991 and September 1992. The judge also found that a large part of the period from the service of the notice of intention to proceed until the evidence in reply was served must also be treated as a delay of a similar nature. I do not understand why the whole of the period from September 1992 (and not merely from the service on 11 November 1992 of the notice of intention to proceed) until service of the evidence in reply is not a period of inordinate and inexcusable delay. Nothing happened at the end of September 1992, other than administrative changes internal to the Treasury Solicitor's

D   department, and throughout the period the official receiver was in breach of the order requiring him to serve his evidence by 18 November 1991. Until that order was complied with, the proceedings could not progress. The entire period of delay from May 1991 until January 1994 can be contrasted with the two-year period allowed by s. 7(2) for the commencement of proceedings.

It is at first sight a little surprising that the judge should find against Mr Aziz on the

E   specific prejudice alleged by him and yet find for him on the basis of the prejudice inherent in the pendency of disqualification proceedings. Mr Charles referred to authorities which establish the principle that where a plaintiff has delayed commencing proceedings until just before the end of the limitation period, it is only necessary for the defendant to establish more than minimal prejudice from delay after the commencement of proceedings. He rightly pointed out that those authorities clearly indicate that the principle depends on serious prejudice having been caused by the delay before the writ

F   was issued (see, for example, *Department of Transport v Chris Smaller (Transport) Ltd* [1989] AC 1197 at p. 1208). But here the judge has found serious prejudice in the delay since the commencement of proceedings.

Mr Charles also made the submission that the judge was wrong to say that the prejudice to a director which is inherent in disqualification proceedings was of a different nature from that in issue in *Biss v Lambeth, Southwark and Lewisham Health Authority*

G   [1978] 1 WLR 382. The judge himself said of prejudice inherent in the pendency of proceedings (at p. 587H):

'This sort of prejudice of which an example is to be seen in *Biss's* case in the anxiety caused to nurses of the continuing challenge to their professional competence, is of a type which usually cannot be directly proved.'

H   The judge also referred to what Lord Griffiths said in *Department of Transport v Smaller* at pp. 1209–1210, where he expressed a note of caution against accepting anxiety caused by the pendency of proceedings as sufficient prejudice in itself to justify striking out. But to my mind it is clear that the judge was not suggesting that the inherent prejudice in the pendency of disqualification proceedings consisted of anxiety to the director through the continuing challenge to his professional competence. Instead he was relying on the practical disadvantages to the director through his status and reputation

being called into question as a result of the institution in the public interest of the   A
disqualification proceedings. He went on to say (at p. 588D) that such proceedings:

> '. . . will prejudice the business interests of the respondent to those proceedings so
> long as they remain pending, save in the most exceptional cases of which this is not
> one. Such prejudice will result from loss of business opportunities, whether known
> to the respondent or not, simply brought about by the existence of the proceedings
> and the nature of the allegations contained in them becoming known to potential   B
> business partners.'

He also referred to the possible prejudice to a businessman in being unable to order his
affairs with a view to the future, because his status will remain in question until the
proceedings are determined.

Mr Charles expressly accepted that there was an inherent prejudice to a director in the
pendency of disqualification proceedings and that this could be inferred by the court even   C
without evidence of specific prejudice. But he questioned whether that prejudice in this
case was sufficient to justify a striking out. I have considerable doubt whether the judge
was right to find the inherent prejudice, which he had identified, as alone sufficient in
view of the Judge's earlier finding that a fair trial was possible and his rejection of the
specific prejudice asserted by Mr Aziz, particularly when against that evidence must be
set the public interest in obtaining a disqualification order against a delinquent director.
The mere pendency of disqualification proceedings does not of course as a matter of law   D
prevent the director from acting or continuing to act as a director of a company. In my
opinion it would be a rare case where the judge would be justified in striking out on the
sole ground of such inherent prejudice inferred from the nature of disqualification
proceedings without other prejudice being shown to have occurred as well.

Mr Collings submitted that the judge had in fact found actual prejudice in the following
sentence which came immediately after the passage last cited from the judgment (at   E
p. 588E):

> 'In the present case the respondent gave evidence of how business enquiries about
> him were passed to the liquidator of the company who then informed the enquirer
> of the existence of the proceedings.'

But I read that as a recitation of the evidence to illustrate the point being made by the
judge of the loss of business opportunities, rather than as a finding of fact. Indeed, having
looked at the transcript of Mr Aziz's evidence, I think it doubtful whether Mr Aziz was   F
giving evidence of facts within his own knowledge rather than mere hearsay.

However, in my judgment, the judge's conclusion can be supported on the facts of the
present case by the addition of the prejudice caused to Mr Aziz through the effect of
delay on the memories of witnesses. In *Roebuck v Mungovin* [1994] 2 AC 224 at p. 234
Lord Browne-Wilkinson said that in the ordinary case the prejudice suffered by a
defendant and caused by the plaintiff's delay is the dimming of witnesses' memories and   G
that a judge can infer that any substantial delay at whatever period leads to a further loss
of recollection. I have already set out the summary of the numerous allegations made by
the official receiver against Mr Aziz. Because of the nature of the allegations it is for Mr
Aziz to explain and excuse, if he can, his conduct and the conduct of others in Manlon
for whose actions he was responsible. Some of his explanations and excuses refer to
transactions which he said occurred even earlier than the impugned actions. Some of   H
those impugned actions occurred six years before the service of the evidence in reply.
Others occurred years before that; for example, the fraudulent trading allegation goes
back to 1983. On the particular facts of this case I do not regard the vast quantities of
documents put in evidence as indicating that oral testimony by witnesses such as Mr Aziz
would have little or no importance at the trial when explanations and excuses would be
proffered and be the subject of cross-examination. I have no difficulty in inferring that

A   the substantial culpable delay by the official receiver has caused prejudice in this respect to Mr Aziz.

I would add that, as I have already pointed out, there is a risk that, by reason of the obligation on the court, if on an application under s. 6 the statutory conditions are satisfied, to make a disqualification order for a minimum of two years, the lengthy delay caused by the official receiver could not be taken into account adequately or at all in the
B   length of the disqualification ordered.

I would hold therefore that the inherent prejudice on which the judge relied and the additional prejudice to which I have referred together amount to serious prejudice. Further, in my judgment, it is sufficiently serious to outweigh the public interest in pursuing the disqualification proceedings to protect the public.

I reach this conclusion with some regret. I am conscious of the practical difficulties
C   faced by those who have to take decisions to seek such disqualification orders and by those who have the conduct of such proceedings. The public interest is not best served if a shadow director, whose conduct, in the view of the Secretary of State, renders him unfit to be a director, can escape from proceedings brought against him without any determination by the court on the merits of the application for a disqualification order. But to my mind it is plain that in this case matters were allowed to go seriously awry by the dilatory prosecution of the proceedings and that Mr Aziz cannot fairly be penalised
D   for the consequences of the official receiver's delay. For these reasons I would dismiss this appeal.

Beldam LJ: I, too, would dismiss this appeal. The facts which gave rise to the official receiver's application under s. 6 of the *Company Directors Disqualification Act* 1986, for an order that Mr Aziz be disqualified on the ground that his conduct as shadow director made him unfit to be concerned in the management of a company, have been fully set
E   out in the judgment of Peter Gibson LJ. If established, the grounds for seeking the order amount to serious misconduct by Mr Aziz in his capacity as a shadow director and would justify the court in making the order sought. If the court is satisfied that an order should be made, the minimum period of disqualification is two years and the maximum 15. Without full consideration of all the charges laid at the door of Mr Aziz, it is impossible to say what period the court would fix as appropriate in his case.

Before making an application to the court under s. 6, the Secretary of State must be
F   satisfied that it is expedient in the public interest that a disqualification order should be made, and unless the court gives leave, any application for such an order must be made within a period of two years beginning with the day on which the company became insolvent. In my view the provision of a comparatively short period within which such proceedings must be started is a clear indication that they should be commenced without delay. Equally I have no doubt that, once commenced, they should be pursued with
G   expedition.

In the present case the official receiver has been guilty of delay in the prosecution of the proceedings. If the proceedings had been between litigants in a civil dispute, unquestionably the delay would be categorised as inordinate and inexcusable. In this appeal the official receiver places great emphasis on the public interest in being protected from misconduct by a director responsible for the affairs of a company which has become insolvent. It is argued that the public interest in the proceedings is a special circumstance
H   which should lead the court to apply different criteria in judging whether to exercise its inherent jurisdiction to strike out the proceedings for want of prosecution.

In arriving at his decision the judge held that such proceedings were in a category of their own and he suggested that when asked to strike them out the court should not follow the guidelines laid down in *Allen v Sir Alfred McAlpine & Sons Ltd & Anor* [1968] 2 QB 229 and in *Birkett v James* [1978] AC 297 but should favour a practical approach

founded on the public interest in such proceedings. Like Gibson LJ, I have reservations   A
with the considerations on which the judge, albeit with diffidence, founded his approach
to the question of dismissing the proceedings for want of prosecution. I do not doubt
that the public interest expressly referred to in s. 7 of the Act is an important
consideration. But the interest of the public in being protected from further misconduct
by a director of an insolvent company is not the only public interest involved. Even if it
were, it could hardly be served by inordinate and inexcusable delay in prosecuting such
proceedings. There is a public interest in the efficient administration of justice and it is   B
widely acknowledged that justice is not only impeded by such delay but is brought into
disrepute. Any system of justice which appears to countenance a disregard of the court's
procedure and orders and inordinate delay forfeits public esteem. I can see no advantage
to the public interest in the court adopting a more lenient stance to the inefficient and
dilatory preparation of proceedings because they are said to be taken in the interest of
the public. Nor do I agree with the judge that it is material that the proceedings are taken   C
by a regulatory body which has no direct personal interest in the result. The consequences
of dismissing an individual litigant's claim for want of prosecution have been said to be
draconian and clearly may in some cases involve great hardship. Why should it be
material that the regulatory body has no direct personal interest in the result? The
director against whom the order is sought has a very great personal interest not only in
the result but that the charges against him should be decided as soon as possible. The
official receiver accepted in the course of argument that although there was no legal   D
barrier to a director against whom charges had been preferred accepting an appointment
while proceedings are pending, in practice no director would do so.

Analogies were drawn in the course of argument between proceedings under s. 6 of the
Company Directors Disqualification Act and criminal proceedings in the Crown Court
but there is a obvious distinction that in such proceedings time cannot run against the
Crown whereas a specific and comparatively short period has been decreed by Parliament   E
for disqualification proceedings. I also have serious reservations about the official
receiver's argument that any prejudice caused to the director against whom the charges
are laid could be mitigated by taking into account the delay in any period of
disqualification imposed. Such an approach assumes that the charges or some of them
have been satisfactorily proved, that those proved are sufficiently serious to warrant a
penalty great enough to accommodate the period of inordinate and inexcusable delay
and at the same time leave room for the minimum period. On these matters the court   F
would be required to form its assessment on inadequate material and without the whole
of the evidence. In short, I cannot see that prejudice caused by delay could properly be
regarded as mitigated by a hypothetical penalty which might be imposed for an unproved
allegation.

The judge thought that it would be appropriate to regard the public interest as
diminishing over the period of the delay. I do not think it does. I think the truth is that   G
the interest remains as important as ever but that if those responsible for pursuing it do
so in such a dilatory fashion that it can no longer fairly be vindicated, it must like the
interest of a private litigant yield to the interests of justice.

The judge placed no great weight on the fact that the proceedings had been initiated at
the very end of the two-year period. He said (at p. 593C):

> 'In any reasonably complicated insolvency it will take the office-holder an   H
> appreciable time to investigate the company's affairs so as to be in a position to
> report on the conduct of directors.'

That may well be so and the time taken within the period provided by Parliament to
bring the proceedings cannot of itself amount to inordinate delay but, as Lord Diplock
said in *Birkett v James* [1978] AC 297 at p. 322G:

A
> 'A late start makes it the more incumbent upon the plaintiff to proceed with all due speed and a pace which might have been excusable if the action had been started sooner may be inexcusable in the light of the time that has already passed before the writ was issued.'

In the result, the judge dismissed the proceedings because he considered that there no longer existed such an obvious public interest as would justify their continuance.

B
Approaching the case on the alternative basis that the rules as to private litigation were applicable, he reached the same conclusion stating that the proceedings had been prolonged by more than two years. He said (at p. 593D):

> 'During that period the respondent has suffered the prejudice to any businessman inherent in having proceedings of this kind, making serious allegation against him, hanging over his head. I am not prepared to treat such prejudice as other than

C
> serious notwithstanding that the respondent has been unable to point to the consequential loss of specific business opportunities.'

Accordingly he held that there was additional prejudice to Mr Aziz beyond the prejudice inherent in the late start to the proceedings.

The judge had found that a fair trial of the issues was still possible in spite of the inordinate delay. That was a conclusion to which it was open to him to come and I would

D
not disturb it. Equally I consider that this court is not in a position to disagree with his finding that Mr Aziz had not satisfied him of the specific prejudice of which he complained. The official receiver contended that the judge was wrong to take account of the prejudice to any businessman inherent in having proceedings of this kind, making serious allegations against him, hanging over his head. I do not think he was. The judge was referring not just to prejudice inherent in the bringing of the proceedings but to the fact that that prejudice had been prolonged by the official receiver's inordinate and

E
inexcusable delay. The official receiver had conceded that in practice a businessman would be prevented from obtaining directorships until the proceedings were concluded. It is accepted that in some cases charges of professional negligence which have been hanging over the head of a defendant for a prolonged period may be sufficient, though not as a rule in itself sufficient to constitute prejudice. Accordingly I consider the judge was entitled to take the prolongation of the admitted disadvantages into account.

F
There is, however, a further matter and that is the very substantial period added to the proceedings which would be likely to have an effect on the ability of Mr Aziz and any witnesses to recall the events leading up to the insolvency of the company. I agree that the judge's conclusion can be supported by an inference that such a substantial delay in the prosecution of the proceedings has added to the dimming of witnesses' memories as referred to by Lord Browne-Wilkinson in *Roebuck v Mungovin* [1994] 2 AC 224 at p. 234. For these reasons, I would support the judge's decision founded on the conventional

G
basis for the exercise of the court's jurisdiction to dismiss for want of prosecution.

Staughton LJ: In my opinion, the test for deciding whether this present action should be dismissed for want of prosecution is not in all respects the same as that which prevails in a dispute between citizens about their civil rights. There is a public interest that those who are unfit to be company directors should be disqualified. That public interest must be taken into account. The action is not a contest between two adversaries either of

H
whom is entirely at liberty to abandon his case for good or bad reason or for no reason at all.

However, I would not go so far as to apply to the present proceedings the rules laid down for criminal cases in *Attorney-General's Reference (No. 1 of 1990)* [1992] QB 630. There the topic is to be found under the description abuse of process, rather than dismissal for want of prosecution. It was said (at p. 644A):

A

'. . . no stay should be imposed unless the defendant shows on the balance of probabilities that owing to the delay he will suffer serious prejudice to the extent that no fair trial can be held.'

There is for the most part no limitation period for criminal prosecutions. By contrast there is a time limit of two years (subject to an extension by leave of the court) for proceedings under s. 6 of the *Company Directors Disqualification Act* 1986. So the public interest in the disqualification of unfit directors may, when s. 6 is invoked, have to yield to the lapse of time.

B

I would agree with the list of circumstances to be taken into account which was set out by Evans-Lombe J at (a)–(e) in para. (3) of his test, which Peter Gibson LJ has cited. They must be considered against the public interest in disqualification; and the judge must decide where the balance of justice comes down. I would not myself say that the question is whether 'there has ceased to be an obvious public interest in obtaining a disqualification order'. But I agree that it is whether that public interest is outweighed by the requirements of justice to the director in the particular circumstances of the case.

C

The judge in this case found that there could still be a fair trial. I would not interfere with his conclusion on that issue. He rejected the specific instances of prejudice put forward by Mr Aziz. There is no challenge to his decision on that issue. But he found that the general prejudice inherent in the fact that an application for disqualification is pending, and subsisting in this case for a period of four years, outweighed the public interest.

D

In my judgment, the judge was entitled to reach that conclusion. I can find nothing in the speech of Lord Griffiths in *Department of Transport v Chris Smaller (Transport) Ltd* [1989] AC 1187, which shows that collateral prejudice (i.e. prejudice which is not derived from the difficulty of having a fair trial) cannot of itself be sufficient. Serious, or significant, collateral prejudice is an alternative requirement. Furthermore, there is a mandatory period of two years as the minimum under s. 6. In a case of delay which is thought to have brought hardship on the director, the court may make a reduction in the period of disqualification that it would otherwise have imposed (as was done in *Re Grayan Building Services Ltd*). But it cannot go below two years. That of itself convinces me that long delay may justify dismissal even if a fair trial is still possible.

E

I too would dismiss this appeal. I would only add that it seems to me quite extraordinary that the registrar ordered discovery of documents, subpoenas and cross-examination on affidavits. No doubt the official receiver had little or no direct evidence to counter the affirmations of Mr Aziz. But he could have argued that nevertheless they were not to be believed; and the judge would have been able to give affect to that argument if he thought fit. The object of the application that the action be dismissed for want of prosecution was to *avoid* a trial. Surely it cannot have been right to have a trial in order to see whether the application succeeded.

F

(Appeal dismissed)

G

H

A
Re Fleet Disposal Services Ltd.
Spratt v AT & T Automotive Services Ltd & Ors.

Chancery Division (Companies Court).
Lightman J.
Judgment delivered 31 January 1995.

B
Creditors' voluntary liquidation – Application for directions – Agency – Trust – Creditor made proprietary claim to moneys in bank account of company in liquidation – Moneys were proceeds of sales by company as agent – Whether proceeds were subject to trust in favour of creditor.

This was an application for directions by the liquidator of a company for determination of the question whether the respondent, 'Nortel', had any proprietary interest in assets held C by the liquidator representing proceeds of sales of cars by the company as agent for Nortel.

The agreement between the company and Nortel provided for the company to pay sale proceeds (less commission and agreed costs) to Nortel five days after receipt by the company. An addendum provided that all repayments should be made on separate cheques. All proceeds of sale were paid into one account and all payments to Nortel were made out of that account, although there was no provision in the agreement for a separate account and the account was used for the proceeds of sale of other principals' cars. It was common D ground that if Nortel established that the company received the proceeds of sale of its cars as trustee, the proceeds were traceable to the sum of £27,417 in the company's bank account.

Held, ruling that Nortel had made out its proprietary claim to the sum of £27,417:

1. The question whether Nortel had a proprietary interest in the proceeds of sale was one of construction of the agency agreement in the light of the surrounding circumstances including the intention of the parties.

E
2. Considering the payments into and out of the account and the terms of the agency agreement, the court inferred that there was a trust relationship between the parties.

The following cases were referred to in the judgment:

Cotten, Re (1913) 108 LT 310.
Devaynes v Noble. Clayton's Case (1816) 1 Mer 572; 35 ER 781.
F
Hallett's Estate, Re (1880) 13 ChD 696.
Napier and Ettrick (Lord) & Anor v Hunter & Ors [1993] AC 713.
Neste Oy v Lloyds Bank plc [1983] 2 Ll Rep 658.

Robin Dicker (instructed by Pitmans, Reading) for the liquidator.

Lexa Hilliard (instructed by the legal department of Northern Telecom Europe Ltd) for Northern Telecom Europe Ltd.

G
JUDGMENT

Lightman J: I have before me an application by the liquidator of Fleet Disposal Services Ltd ('the company') for directions. The company carried on the business of selling cars both as principal and as agent. As agent the company sold fleets of cars for the first to thirteenth respondents, and there are sums outstanding and due to each of them. The fourteenth and fifteenth respondents provided moneys to enable the company H to give bonds securing the payment of sums due from the company to its principals in respect of certain sales. The question raised by the liquidator is whether any of the 15 respondents has any proprietary interests in assets held by the liquidator representing the proceeds of sale of their cars and in particular funds in accounts of the company with the Midland Bank plc ('the bank'). Since the issue of the application, all the respondents except the eleventh, Northern Telecom Europe Ltd ('Nortel'), have conceded that they

have no claim. Nortel however contends that it does have a proprietary interest in the   A
sum of £27,417 representing the traceable proceeds of the sale of vehicles sold by the
company as their agent.

Facts

The company was incorporated on 28 March 1989 with a share capital of £1,000
owned by Mr Ian Collins ('Mr Collins') and his wife. Its primary business was that of   B
acting as selling agent for major car leasing companies.

The company used standard sale terms and conditions incorporated in its invoices
when selling cars to members of the public. These made clear that the company was
selling as agent and required payment of the purchase price to the company; that title
should pass (in case of payment by cheque) only on clearance of the cheque; and that in
case of any breach of contract by the purchaser the company should be free to sell to a
third party.   C

Until the start of 1993 the company did not have standard written terms and conditions
of business when contracting with its fleet suppliers ('the principals'). A standard contract
('the standard contract') was drafted by the company's solicitors between December 1992
and January 1993. This included provisions that the company should 'act in accordance
with [principals'] agreed instructions and in the [principals'] best interest at all times' (a
provision which can only be expressing what would otherwise be implied); that nothing   D
in the agreement should be deemed to create an agency between the company and the
principals (a provision which, as totally inconsistent with the relationship created by the
substantive terms, must be legally without effect); and that 'repayment of the [principals']
sale proceeds will be made' less the specified sale fee (or commission) and any other
agreed costs exactly five days after the company first receives payment.

The company had six accounts with the bank, only three of which are material. There   E
was at all times a direct account used for sales of cars owned by the company. VAT was
payable in respect of such sales and it was considered administratively convenient in
respect of accounting for VAT for the company to operate a separate account for such
sales. There was also at all times a current account which was used for payment of the
company's general expenses, VAT, costs and overheads. Until May 1991 this account
was used for the receipt of the proceeds of sale of principals' cars sold by the company as
agent and for payment of the net proceeds of sale to the principals. In May 1991 however   F
it was decided at the suggestion of the bank that it would be administratively convenient
that there should be opened a separate account for receipt of such proceeds and for
payment to principals. Such account was duly opened and called the 'agency account',
though it was apparently also referred to within the company as 'the trading account'. It
is quite clear on the evidence of contemporary documentation as well as from the
company's conduct, e.g. in making substantial transfers thereout to the current account,   G
and the oral evidence of Mr Collins that it was the intention and understanding on the
part of the company and the bank that receipts of the company on the sale of principals'
cars and the moneys in the agency account should be and were the free moneys of the
company and in no wise trust or client moneys.

During 1992 the company required further capital, and the fourteenth respondent
agreed to provide some £100,000 on the terms set out in an agreement with the company
and Mr Collins dated 30 October 1992 ('the finance agreement'). Clause 7 of the finance   H
agreement reads as follows:

> '7.1 The company hereby agrees that from the date of this agreement all
> transactions where it acts as agent for its clients will be dealt with only through the
> agency bank account, and will record all such transactions in the books of account
> as agency transactions

A
       7.2 The company further agrees that the direct bank account from the date of the agreement shall only be used for the purchase, transfer and repair of 'own stock' cars for retail and direct sale

       7.3 Unless agreed in writing by the 'A' shareholders the total indebtedness to the bank for the combined sum of the agency, direct and main bank accounts shall not be allowed to exceed £50,000.'

B
       Clause 7.1 stipulated the continued use of the agency account for the specified purpose, and cl. 7.3 recognises the agency account as, not a trust account, but (like the others) a repository of the company's free funds.

       Towards the end of 1992, concern was however felt by the company's solicitors that the terms 'agent' used in reference to the relationship of the company with its principals and 'agency' in reference to the bank account might give cause for argument that receipts of proceeds might be moneys held on trust for principals and that the moneys in the
C
agency account were likewise trust moneys. It was for this reason that the standard written terms included the (nugatory) provision disclaiming any agency relationship; and that the company decided to change the name of the account to 'trading account' and indeed to close the account and transfer the net sum standing to the credit of this account to the current account. The agency account was duly closed and transfers were made of £317,000 on 6 April and of £5,012.70 on 7 April 1993.

D
       Until about November 1992, Nortel used as agent for fleet disposals a company called A G Bayliss. When this agent then went into insolvent liquidation occasioning the loss of £20,000 in respect of the outstanding net proceeds of sale of Nortel cars, Mr Farrington (the senior manager support services of Nortel) arranged to meet Mr Collins and Miss Brady of the company at Mr Farrington's office to discuss the company taking over as agent. This meeting took place at some date between 23 November and 3 December
E
1992. Mr Farrington has told me that he did not have in mind at this meeting anything other than the replacement of A G Bayliss as agent by the company; he did not have in mind any need for tighter contractual terms to avoid any repetition of the loss occasioned to Nortel by the liquidation of A G Bayliss.

       A critical conflict in the evidence of the only two witnesses who gave oral evidence, Mr Farrington and Mr Collins, arises as to what was said at the meeting. I accept that both witnesses are honest but I must weigh the testimony of one as against the other as to
F
what occurred at this meeting some time ago.

       Mr Collins in his evidence deposes that at this meeting he told Mr Farrington that the funds from the sale of Nortel cars would be paid into an account referred to as an agency account and repayment would be made less commission and other agreed charges five days after the company received payment. Mr Farrington in his evidence goes further and says that Mr Collins gave him a specific assurance in respect of the possible
G
insolvency of the company, namely that the company had set aside a specific account (the agency account) to receive the proceeds of sale of cars sold as agent and that these funds would be available for payment to Nortel in case the company became insolvent. Mr Collins challenges this evidence and in particular that he made any reference to insolvency or gave any assurance referable to possible insolvency. He says that, if Mr Farrington had raised any anxieties of this character, he would have offered a bond securing payment, a course followed in the case of other principals who had raised such
H
anxieties.

       On this issue whether insolvency was referred to, I prefer the evidence of Mr Collins. As appears from Mr Farrington's own evidence, he did not attend the meeting looking for any assurance in case of insolvency. He never made any attendance note or reference to any other person of this or any such assurance. The contractual documentation between the company and Nortel ('the agency agreement') is silent in this regard. It seems

to me improbable that any such assurance would be given or received without some   A
reference being made to it by Mr Farrington to Nortel's legal department who were
subsequently involved in agreeing the contractual documentation or some note or
memorandum or confirmatory letter to Mr Collins.

The agency agreement signed by Nortel on 16 December 1992 and the company on 9
January 1993 is not in the form of the standard contract, but as I see it in substance there
is no real distinction. The company therein is expressly referred to as Nortel's agent (as it   B
plainly was), and undertook to act in accordance with its principal's agreed instructions
and in the best interest of the principal at all times, and to pay 'sale proceeds less our
commission and any other agreed costs in . . . five days after receipt of moneys'. An
addendum dated 11 December 1992 provided that all repayments should be made on
separate cheques.

The company ceased trading on 8 April 1993 and the company went into creditors'
voluntary liquidation on 27 April 1993 with an estimated deficiency of some £726,000 of   C
which over £650,000 is due to the first to thirteenth respondents, and £45,000 is due to
Nortel. It is common ground that, if Nortel can establish that the company received the
proceeds of sale of its cars as trustee, and on the basis that no other respondent has a
competing right to trace into the same funds, under the rule in *Clayton's Case* the
proceeds are traceable to the sum of £27,417 standing to the credit of the company in the
current account with the bank and Nortel is entitled to such moneys. As I have said, the   D
other respondents have conceded that they have no competing right, and I must direct
the liquidator to proceed on this basis.

Issue to be tried

The issue of law raised is whether in the relevant surrounding circumstances upon the
true construction of the agency contract the company received the sale price of cars sold
as agents for Nortel as trustees for Nortel. Ms Lexa Hilliard, counsel for Nortel, sought   E
at the hearing to raise an alternative argument that the conversation between Mr
Farrington and Mr Collins gave rise to a collateral contract creating a trust of receipts in
respect of such proceeds of sale. No hint of a suggestion of such a collateral contract was
given prior to the hearing, and when (as I required it to be) the claim was fully pleaded in
a draft pleading, it was apparent that the claim was not merely unsupported by, but
inconsistent with, the evidence of Nortel. Accordingly I did not allow that contention to   F
be proceeded with.

Law

The question whether Nortel had a proprietary interest in the proceeds of sale of its
cars on receipt of the same by the company is one of construction of the agency agreement
in the light of the surrounding circumstances at the time when it was made, and these
circumstances include the intentions of the parties express or to be inferred: see *Neste Oy*   G
v Lloyds Bank plc [1983] 2 Ll Rep 658 at p. 663.

The intentions for this purpose are limited to intentions of the parties communicated
to, or reasonably to be inferred by, each other, and do not extend to private
uncommunicated intentions. Accordingly the established but uncommunicated
intentions on the part of the company (and its advisers and the bank) that the company
should be entitled to use the moneys in the agency account as its own free moneys is not   H
relevant for this purpose, for it was never so stated nor reasonably to be inferred.

One surrounding circumstance was that the agency account existed; that all sale
proceeds of cars sold as agent were paid into this account and all payments to principals
were made out of this account; that this arrangement was intended to continue; and that
this was communicated by the company to Nortel as (in the words of Mr Dicker, counsel

A   for the liquidator) a selling point of the company as agent. For this purpose, I attach little (if any) importance to the designation of this account as 'the agency account', for Mr Farrington did not attach importance to the name; indeed he was uncertain as to the name of the account. The importance is the existence of the separate designated account.

I turn second to the relationship between the parties. The company was Nortel's agent for sale. As it seems to me, notwithstanding 'the general disinclination of the courts to
B   see the intricacies and doctrines connected with trusts introduced into everyday commercial transactions' (see *Neste Oy v Lloyds Bank* [1983] 2 Ll Rep 658 at p. 665), that is a relationship where, in respect of moneys received by the agent representing the proceeds of sale of the principals' property, the court is particularly ready to infer a trust: it is not readily to be inferred that the agent is intended to be able to finance his business out of the proceeds of sale of his principal's property: see e.g. *Re Cotten* (1913) 108 LT 310 and *Re Hallett's Estate* (1880) 13 ChD 696.
C   I turn third to the agency agreement. It contains no express term whether the proceeds of sale should be held as trustee or retained in a separate account. But there are indications of a trust relationship, or at least language consistent with it. Provision is made for 'payment of sale proceeds five days after receipt of moneys' (a short period) and payment by separate cheques – language and provisions at least to some degree apposite to a trust and inapposite to a mere accounting relationship – certainly inapposite
D   to a running account.

Taking these factors together, it seems to me that a trust relationship is appropriate to the commercial relationship which existed between these parties and I can see no unfair or undue consequences for the company or its unsecured creditors (consider *Lord Napier and Ettrick & Anor v Hunter & Ors* [1993] AC 713 at p. 744C–H). Indeed the company had the opportunity expressly to exclude any trust obligation when it drafted its standard contract and agreed the agency contract, for it had this matter very much in mind. Far
E   from doing so, the selling point was made of the separate account and no disclaimer of any trust obligation was expressed.

Against finding such a trust relationship I must balance the factors stressed by Mr Dicker.

(a) *Absence of express term*
F   It is correct that Nortel did not insist on any express provision in the agency agreement for a separate account; but this was because Mr Collins stated the position regarding the agency account.

(b) *Interest*
    Mr Collins intended the company to retain the interest earned on the moneys in the agency account and Mr Farrington had no intentions regarding interest. I see no reason
G   why consistently with Nortel's proprietary claim it may not reasonably be inferred as the common intention of the parties that the company could retain the interest in respect of the five-day period, even as it could retain its commission and other agreed costs.

(c) *Other moneys in the account*
    The agency account was to be and was used as the receptacle for the proceeds of sale of all principals' cars, and not merely Nortel's, and all the first to thirteenth respondents
H   (other than Nortel) have conceded that the proceeds of their cars were the free money of the company. Accordingly the money claimed by Nortel was mixed, and was free to be mixed, in the account with free moneys of the company. Whether or not the concession by the other principals was necessary or correct (and the facts relating to Nortel have distinct features) the fact that the proceeds of Nortel cars could be mixed in this way with the free moneys of the company, whilst a factor to be taken into account, is not a bar to

the existence of a proprietary claim: see e.g. *Re Hallett's Estate* (1880) 13 ChD 696. In   A
the circumstances of this case, there is no reason to infer that Nortel should have
anticipated that the legal rights of other principals in respect of the proceeds paid into
the account differed from those of Nortel or that the receipts in the case of the other
respondents might be the free moneys of the company. In the circumstances, the
fortuitous circumstance that the proceeds of sales of the cars of other principals paid into
the account are, or may be, the free moneys of the company can really carry little, if any,
weight.   B

(d) *Absence of recognition of trust*

Mr Farrington did not appreciate that the agency contract and the arrangements
regarding the agency account might give rise to a trust relationship between the company
and Nortel. He saw the practical value in the arrangements for a separate banking
account, but (being a non-lawyer) he did not appreciate or have in mind the legal   C
consequences of a proprietary claim. I do not think this matters. His subjective
impression and his unexpressed analysis (or lack of analysis) of the arrangements cannot
prejudice the rights of Nortel.

I therefore conclude that Ms Hilliard in her forceful submissions on behalf of Nortel
has made out its proprietary claim to the sum of £27,417.

(Order accordingly)   D

E

F

G

H

A # Framlington Group plc & Anor v Anderson & Ors.

Chancery Division.

Blackburne J.

Judgment delivered 7 February 1995.

Directors' duties – Conflict of interest – Defendant directors ran investment
B *management business for plaintiffs – Purchaser of business issued shares as*
consideration to plaintiffs and defendants – Plaintiffs alleged that defendants were
in breach of duty and held shares as constructive trustees – Whether defendants
were in breach of duty.

This was the trial of an action arising out of the circumstances in which the second
plaintiff ('FIM') agreed to sell to the fourth defendant, 'Rathbone', part of FIM's private
client fund management business, which was then managed by the first, second and third
C defendants (who were employees and directors), and of the circumstances in which, and the
terms on which, those defendants took up employment with Rathbone on and subsequent to
completion of the sale.

The price Rathbone paid was roughly £3.48m, two per cent of the value of the funds under
management, of which one per cent was payable to 'Framlington', which owned FIM, and
one per cent was expected to be payable to the defendants in return for entering into five
D year service contracts containing post-employment restrictions via a company set up by the
defendants to supply their services to Rathbone. Framlington did not find out that the
defendants' personal services company was being sold to Rathbone in consideration of the
issue of shares in Rathbone, until the deal was made public. The management of Framlington
had told the defendants that it was not concerned with the terms of their remuneration deal
with Rathbone, and the defendants (two of whom were directors of Framlington) were
excluded from any involvement in the negotiations between Framlington and Rathbone.
E
Framlington took action to recover the consideration shares arguing that they were
consideration properly payable to Framlington and that negotiating the transfer of the
shares to themselves was a breach of their duty of good faith and of their fiduciary duty as
directors of FIM and of Framlington. In consequence, they held the consideration shares
(and any benefits derived or to be derived from those shares) on constructive trust for the
plaintiffs.

F *Held*, dismissing the action:

1. The consideration shares did not represent a payment to the three managers for an
asset which belonged to FIM nor did they acquire them by the use of some property or
confidential information of FIM which came to them as directors of FIM. The consideration
shares were the price which the three were willing to accept in return for binding themselves
under five-year service contracts to make the goodwill which attached to them as the persons
G who had over many years managed their clients' investments, available to Rathbone, and
for restricting their freedom, after the termination of their service contracts, to exploit that
client goodwill for themselves or for others. The three managers were free to negotiate
whatever price they could from Rathbone for their future services to that company.

2. The three managers did not divert to themselves any maturing business opportunity
which should have been made available to the plaintiffs. The opportunity which the plaintiffs
had of extracting a payment from Rathbone in consideration of a transfer by FIM to
H Rathbone of the private client investment management business, was one which Framlington
was free to exploit and did exploit.

3. In failing (if they did) to assist FIM to obtain the best price reasonably obtainable for
what FIM was negotiating to sell to Rathbone, the three did not act in breach of any general
duty to act bona fide in FIM's interests. There was no evidence to indicate what part, apart
from managing clients' investments, each of the three managers was expected to play within

FIM. In any event as regards the sale to Rathbone, the three were instructed not to take   A
part in the sale negotiations. (**Furs Ltd v Tomkies (1936) 54 CLR 583 distinguished.**)

4. **The negotiation by the three of the remuneration package that they could expect to
receive on joining Rathbone was not in itself, with or without disclosure to FIM, a breach of
any general duty of good faith owed by them to FIM.**

The following cases were referred to in the judgment:

Balston Ltd v Headline Filters Ltd [1990] FSR 385.   B
Bell & Anor v Lever Bros Ltd & Ors [1932] AC 161.
Bishopsgate Investment Management Ltd v Maxwell [1993] BCC 120.
Boardman & Anor v Phipps [1967] 2 AC 46.
Boulting & Anor v Association of Cinematograph, Television and Allied Technicians
[1963] 2 QB 606.
Furs Ltd v Tomkies (1936) 54 CLR 583.   C
Industrial Development Consultants Ltd v Cooley [1972] 1 WLR 443.

Christopher Pymont (instructed by Stephenson Harwood) for Framlington.

Daniel Serota QC and Andrew Clarke (instructed by Allen & Overy) for the
defendants.

JUDGMENT
       D

Blackburne J: This is the trial of an action arising out of the circumstances in which,
in late 1991, the second plaintiff ('FIM') agreed to sell to Rathbone Brothers plc
('Rathbone') that part of its private client fund management business which was then
managed by the first, second and third defendants and of the circumstances in which,
and the terms on which, those defendants took up employment with Rathbone on and
subsequent to completion of the sale in early January 1992.

FIM is the wholly owned subsidiary of the first plaintiff ('Framlington plc') and forms   E
part of the Framlington group of companies. It was the fund management arm of the
group. The first, second and third defendants ('the three managers') were employees and
directors of FIM. Mr Clarke, the second defendant, was its managing director. Mr Clarke
and Mr Lanyon, the third defendant, were also directors of Framlington plc.

The business in question was sold by an agreement entered into by the plaintiffs with
Rathbone on 1 November 1991. It consisted of the benefit of FIM's right to manage the   F
investment portfolios of the private clients managed on FIM's behalf by the three
managers pursuant to standard discretionary investment management agreements. The
benefit of the right to manage a number of personal equity plans was also included. The
sale price under the sale agreement was geared to the value of the funds of those private
clients who could be persuaded by a certain date to enter into new management
agreements with Rathbone in place of those that they had had with FIM or, in the case
of personal equity plans, could be persuaded to substitute Rathbone for FIM as plan   G
manager. The price paid by Rathbone under the agreement ultimately worked out at
£1.75m satisfied as to all but £164,037, which was paid in cash, by the issue to
Framlington plc of shares in Rathbone.

At the time of the sale agreement the three managers were free, subject to giving not
more than three months' notice to FIM and to resigning as directors of FIM (and, in
addition, in the case of Mr Clarke and Mr Lanyon to resigning as directors of   H
Framlington plc), to set up in business in competition with FIM and to solicit for
themselves (or for their new employers) all or any of FIM's clients and employees.

The sale was precipitated by the wish of the three managers to leave the Framlington
group and take up employment with Rathbone. The sale agreement was negotiated on
the basis that they would do so. The negotiation of its terms was conducted by Mr Paul

A   Loach, managing director of Framlington plc, on behalf of the plaintiffs and Mr Michael
     Ingall, chief executive of Rathbone, on behalf of Rathbone. The three managers took no
     part at all in those negotiations: indeed they were told by Mr Loach not to do so. On 3
     January 1992 the three managers' employment with FIM ceased and they resigned their
     directorships. On 6 January they took up employment with Rathbone. The terms which
     they agreed with Rathbone included the issue to them by Rathbone, pursuant to an
B   agreement entered into on 17 August 1992, of shares in Rathbone ('the consideration
     shares') valued at £1.67m in return for which each of the three entered into a five-year
     service contract. The service contract provided for an annually reviewable salary of
     £55,000 and various in-service benefits and contained restrictions against solicitation of
     clients, acting for clients, or solicitation of Rathbone's employees during differing periods
     after the termination for whatever reason of their employment with Rathbone. The sum
     of £1.67m was calculated by reference to the value of the funds under management by
C   them transferred to Rathbone. Most of that sum was attributable to funds transferred
     pursuant to the sale agreement.

         At the time of the sale agreement the plaintiffs, although they knew that the three
     managers would be transferring to Rathbone's employment (the sale agreement assumed
     that they would), were unaware that, as part of their arrangements with Rathbone, the
     three managers would receive benefits related (as the consideration shares were) to the
D   value of the managed funds transferred from FIM to Rathbone pursuant to the sale
     agreement. At the time of the sale agreement the three managers had not entered into
     any binding agreement with Rathbone to receive any such benefits or even to be employed
     by Rathbone. On the other hand they had been given to understand by Mr Ingall, and
     expected, that they would be taken into Rathbone's employment on a long-term basis,
     that they would be subject to restraints following termination of their employment and
     that, in return, they would receive benefits calculated by reference to a percentage, not
E   exceeding one per cent, of the value of managed funds transferred to Rathbone by some
     date, as then unspecified, in 1992. Those terms, with others, eventually found expression
     in the agreement of 17 August 1992.

         The plaintiffs contend that the consideration shares together with any income and
     other profits which those shares have earned since they were beneficially acquired by the
     three managers are secret profits for which the three managers are accountable to FIM
F   and they seek relief accordingly.

         Those are the bare essentials of the dispute. I now proceed to fill in some of the details.

         Before joining the Framlington group the three managers had, with others, been
     partners in Laurence Prust and Co. The discretionary fund management part of that
     business was purchased by Framlington plc in late 1986. The precise manner in which
G   the purchase was structured does not matter. The upshot was that the company into
     which that part of Laurence Prust's business had been transferred was acquired by
     Framlington plc and its name changed to FIM. As part of the purchase terms the former
     Laurence Prust partners who remained with FIM (there were eight in all) became
     directors of FIM and entered into various restrictive covenants designed to protect the
     business which Framlington plc had purchased. In 1988 or so control of Framlington plc
     passed to Throgmorton Trust. That takeover had been opposed by the former Laurence
H   Prust partners (including the three managers) who had remained with FIM.

         For reasons which it is not necessary to go into in any detail the three managers
     became increasingly disenchanted with the Framlington group. Private client fund
     management formed only a small part of the business of the group following its takeover
     by Throgmorton Trust. The former Laurence Prust partners felt that the group did not
     regard private client fund management as of much importance. They felt that their

department was drifting. Over and above that they did not always see eye-to-eye with Mr   A
Paul Loach who was the managing director of Framlington plc at the time.

The result was that four of the former partners left. The sale by Throgmorton Trust of a 25 per cent share in Framlington plc to Credit Commercial de France, a former shareholder of Framlington plc, in early 1990 did not give rise to any improvement. However that sale did lead to the release in 1990 of the restrictive covenants which the former Laurence Prust partners, including the three mangers, had entered into on the   B sale of the discretionary fund management business to Framlington plc. Some doubts apparently existed as to the extent of that release but it is common ground that the restrictions ceased to have any validity from and after May 1991. At the latest from that date, therefore, the three managers were free, once they had ceased to be CCH FIM's employees and had resigned their directorships, to set up or join a competing business and take with them or solicit clients of the Framlington group, whether or not the clients were ones   C whom the three managers had managed, and solicit employees of the Framlington group to join them. It is also common ground, as I have mentioned, that they were entitled to terminate their employment on giving not more than three months' notice.

From time to time, particularly once it had become common knowledge, as apparently it did, that they were no longer subject to any restrictive covenants, each of the three managers had been approached by outsiders to see if he would be willing to consider employment elsewhere. Eventually, in late June 1991, Mr Anderson, the first defendant,   D was approached by Mr Doulton, a near neighbour of his in Hampshire. Mr Doulton was a colleague of Mr Ingall, to whom I have already referred, who was and remains a director and chief executive of Rathbone. Mr Doulton had tried to interest Mr Anderson in joining Rathbone on two or so prior occasions but without success. Mr Doulton mentioned that Rathbone was looking to expand and enquired whether Mr Anderson would be interested in joining. Mr Anderson indicated that he was unhappy at FIM and   E was considering a move. Mr Doulton suggested that he go and see Mr Ingall to see what each had to offer. This led to a meeting between Mr Anderson and Mr Ingall on 2 July 1991. That was followed by a further meeting on 29 July attended on this occasion by Mr Lanyon as well. The upshot was that Mr Ingall was indeed interested in taking them on as investment managers in Rathbone. The terms on offer by Rathbone were a lower salary (£50,000 shortly to be increased to £55,000) than they had been receiving at FIM (£63,000) and lesser in-service benefits of one kind or another. On the other hand, as Mr   F Ingall explained to them, Rathbone had a policy of paying lower salaries than its competitors but of incentivising senior staff through the ownership of shares in Rathbone. Mr Ingall suggested that if the two were free to move to Rathbone they should do what other staff at Rathbone had done by forming a personal services company to act as a vehicle for incorporating their capacity to introduce new business to Rathbone together with their client and professional connections and goodwill, and that they should   G sell the company as a trading company to Rathbone in consideration of the issue to them of shares in Rathbone. He explained that if Rathbone were to acquire such a company the two would need to be committed to Rathbone as long-term employees for a minimum of five years subject to various restrictions after termination of their employment. By proceeding along that route it was Mr Ingall's understanding, as I have no doubt he explained to Mr Anderson and Mr Lanyon, that the acquisition of shares in Rathbone   H by way of exchange for their shares in a personal services company would not be an event which would give rise to any charge to tax. In short the use of a personal services company was understood to be a tax efficient method of enabling persons, such as Mr Anderson and Mr Lanyon, offering their services as investment managers to Rathbone, to do so without suffering an immediate charge to tax on the acquisition by them of shares in that company. I express no view whether that understanding was well founded.

A   Because Mr Anderson and Mr Lanyon had been in fund management for many years (since 1969 in Mr Anderson's case and 1973 in Mr Lanyon's) and had acted for many of their clients for considerable periods of time, they had no doubt that if they were to move elsewhere many of their clients would follow them bringing their investment management business with them. In the absence of restraint (as by mid-1991 was the case), Mr Anderson and Mr Lanyon would be free to act for any clients who chose to keep their business with them and would be free also to approach clients to persuade them to follow them to their new employer. They recognised, however, that the actual mechanics of

B   transfer were far from straightforward, not only because of the large number of clients for whom they acted (there were several hundred accounts) but also because of the logistical problem of transferring clients' stock from a single pool held by one nominee but embracing holdings owned by others. In the interests of their clients they wanted to have an orderly transfer of the managed funds and for this the co-operation of the

C   Framlington group would be needed. It occurred to them that the best way of achieving this was to see whether the group would be willing to sell to Rathbone the benefit of the private client business which they managed for FIM. They also recognised, however, as did Mr Ingall whom they next saw on 2 September 1991, that Framlington plc, when told of their wish to transfer to Rathbone, might simply send them away on three months' 'garden leave' and refuse to entertain any kind of negotiated arrangement with Rathbone.

D   It was in case that happened that, on 3 September 1991, Mr Ingall sent to each of the two a letter with a formal offer of employment from a date to be agreed and at a commencing salary of £55,000 subject to a review in January 1993 together with various other in-service benefits but expressed to be subject to three months' notice on either side. The letter also contained various restraint provisions designed to take effect on termination of their employment but made clear that, should they leave Rathbone for whatever reason before completion of an agreement by them to sell their personal services

E   company to Rathbone, they would be entitled to take with them such clients as they had introduced to Rathbone. The letter also referred to the basis upon which Rathbone would be willing to buy that company. It did so by reference to an example which showed them receiving 1.57 per cent of the value of funds under management over a certain level valued as at 30 September 1992.

     It was in a state of uncertainty as to what Framlington's attitude would be that Mr Anderson and Mr Lanyon first mentioned to FIM's managing director, Mr Clarke, that

F   they had decided to leave the group. That was on 3 September 1991. Mr Clarke had not himself at that stage been a party to any of the discussions which Mr Anderson and Mr Lanyon had had with Mr Ingall and was unaware, until he was told, of their wish to leave the Framlington group to join Rathbone. At Mr Clarke's suggestion the two set out in writing their reasons for wanting to leave, after which they saw the deputy chairman of Framlington plc and, later that same day, Mr Loach, Framlington plc's

G   managing director.

     The witnesses were not clear about precisely what was said at the various meetings of which there were several at around this time. I am satisfied, however, that either at the first meeting with Mr Loach after they had announced their intended departure, which was on 3 September 1991, or on the second meeting with him about the matter, which was on the following day, it was agreed that the best course would be an orderly transfer to Rathbone of the management of the portfolios of the various private clients which Mr

H   Anderson and Mr Lanyon managed. Mr Loach claims that it was he who made the suggestion. Messrs Anderson and Lanyon say that they had had in mind that an orderly transfer was desirable. In my view it matters not who first broached the matter since it is common ground that it was agreed that that was the best manner of proceeding.

     According to the evidence of Mr Anderson and Mr Lanyon, at the second meeting with Mr Loach Mr Anderson began to outline the nature of the remuneration that they

would be receiving at Rathbone and how, in particular, they would be receiving a smaller   A
salary. At that point, according to their evidence, Mr Loach interrupted to say that he
was not interested in their personal negotiations with Rathbone. Mr Loach's account,
when cross-examined on the matter, was slightly, but in my view not significantly,
different. He was under the impression that, at the first of the two meetings, at a time
when the two had not identified who their new employer would be, Mr Lanyon told him
that they would be paid less by the new employer than they were receiving from FIM at
which point, and without interrupting, Mr Loach said that he did not want to know   B
about their salaries. This was to some extent in conflict with his own witness statement,
which stood as his evidence in chief, where he stated that he was not interested in their
'remuneration package' but only in what price Framlington should receive on a transfer
of the management of the funds in question.

My conclusion on this issue, the relevance of which will emerge later, is that, at the
second of the two meetings and in the course of some remarks by Mr Anderson about   C
the different remuneration that he and Mr Lanyon would be receiving at Rathbone, Mr
Loach indicated that he was not interested in the remuneration that they would be
receiving from Rathbone, that there was no intention on the part of Mr Anderson or Mr
Lanyon to deceive Mr Loach as to what that remuneration was expected to consist of,
and that Mr Anderson and Mr Lanyon emerged from the meeting having been given to
understand by Mr Loach that the management of the Framlington group, represented
by Mr Loach as managing director of the parent company, was not concerned with the   D
terms of any deal over their remuneration which Mr Anderson and Mr Lanyon were able
to strike with Rathbone as their prospective new employer. A part of that remuneration
was to consist of the consideration shares which each was to receive in return for entering
into five year service contracts containing post-employment restrictions.

Not only did Mr Loach make it clear that he was not concerned about the
remuneration terms that Mr Anderson and Mr Lanyon might negotiate with Rathbone   E
but he made it clear that he did not want Mr Anderson and Mr Lanyon to take part in
his negotiations with Mr Ingall for the sale by Framlington to Rathbone of the
management of the private client funds managed by them or even to attend any of the
discussions between him and Mr Ingall. And in the event neither did so.

The imminent departure of Mr Anderson and Mr Lanyon prompted Mr Clarke to
consider his future with the Framlington group. With Mr Loach's approval Mr Clarke
and Mr Ingall met and either on 4 or 5 September (the date is unimportant) Mr Ingall   F
offered the same terms to Mr Clarke as he had discussed with Mr Anderson and Mr
Lanyon. Specifically Mr Clarke was given to understand that the number of shares in
Rathbone that he might expect to receive would be calculated by reference to the value
of the funds which he, together with Mr Anderson and Mr Lanyon, would be managing
and would be subject to restrictions on disposal and that in return he would be expected
to enter into a five-year service contract containing restrictive covenants. After some   G
hesitation and after considering various alternatives Mr Clarke decided to accept Mr
Ingall's offer of employment with Rathbone. That occurred around the middle of
September 1991. Thenceforward Mr Clarke found himself in the same position as Mr
Anderson and Mr Lanyon. Although he continued for a short while to be managing
director of FIM (he was replaced by Mr Loach before the sale agreement was signed) he
ceased thereafter to attend any board meetings of either FIM or Framlington plc (of
which, as I have mentioned, he was also a director). Like Mr Anderson and Mr Lanyon   H
Mr Clarke was excluded from any involvement in the negotiations between Mr Loach
and Mr Ingall over the terms of transfer to Rathbone of management of the private client
funds managed by those three.

Initially in his negotiations with Mr Ingall Mr Loach asked for three to four per cent
of the value of the funds transferred (this related to the funds which Mr Anderson and

A   Mr Lanyon managed because at that time the funds managed by Mr Clarke had not come into play) as FIM's price for co-operating in an orderly transfer and Mr Ingall countered with an offer of $\frac{1}{2}$ per cent. By the middle of September, however, a compromise percentage of one per cent was agreed which applied also to the funds managed by Mr Clarke when he decided to leave the Framlington group to join Rathbone. There is some evidence to indicate that at a meeting on 9 September between Mr St Giles, the chairman of Framlington plc, and Mr Anderson and Mr Lanyon (at
B   which, according to both managers, Mr St Giles adopted a hostile attitude to them) Mr Lanyon indicated that in his view it would be, in his words, 'non-amicable' if Framlington were to hold out for three per cent of the funds under management. I am satisfied that in so stating Mr Lanyon's concern was to assist in achieving an agreed transfer of the funds which he plainly recognised as being in everybody's interests, not least the clients whose funds were in question. It is also the case that at a meeting with Mr Loach on 10
C   September Mr Lanyon stated that, in his view, four per cent would be 'completely outside our ball park'. There is nothing to indicate, however, that these remarks by Mr Lanyon had the slightest impact on Mr Loach's negotiations with Mr Ingall. In his witness statement and in his oral evidence before me Mr Loach made no mention of them.

During the period that he was negotiating with Mr Loach Mr Ingall was in contact from time to time with the three managers. That contact was, until a meeting on 26 September, largely if not entirely by telephone. The three managers, whilst not denying
D   that such contact occurred, were unable to recall those contacts but Mr Ingall said that they occurred and I am satisfied that they did. It would have been surprising if there had been no contact. Because of the nature of the transaction that was under negotiation between Mr Loach and Mr Ingall involving, as it did, a transfer to Rathbone of the greater part of FIM's business managed by the three managers (the management by them of institutional and charitable funds was not included), a move by the three managers to
E   Rathbone's employment and the entering into by the three (and by Rathbone) of covenants designed to protect from solicitation the remainder of FIM's business, Mr Ingall was surprised (his expression was 'nonplussed') by Mr Loach's refusal to allow the three managers to be involved in the negotiation. He was, however, permitted by Mr Loach to contact them to let them know what was going on.

In one of his communications with one or other of the three managers (he thinks it was
F   Mr Anderson but he could not recall when it occurred) Mr Ingall indicated that the terms which he had earlier discussed with Mr Anderson and Mr Lanyon for paying them 1.57 per cent or thereabouts of the value of the funds transferred in return for their agreement to enter into restrictions following termination of their employment with Rathbone had been on the assumption that there would be no agreement with the Framlington group. He indicated that those terms no longer applied now that Rathbone might be agreeing to pay to Framlington one per cent of the value of funds transferred. In particular he
G   mentioned that the result of agreeing a payment of one per cent to Framlington would be that Rathbone would have to cut back severely on any deal he might be able to do with them.

By the end of September, by when he had agreed a figure of one per cent with Mr Loach, Mr Ingall indicated to the three managers that he was willing to pay them one per cent rather than some lesser percentage. This figure was eventually carried into the agreement of 17 August 1992 to which I have already referred. He felt able to offer this
H   amount as Rathbone's share price was going up (which enabled Rathbone to issue fewer shares in satisfaction of any given sum of money) and Mr Ingall regarded the acquisition of the management of the private client funds in question as a very significant deal and saw enormous advantages if the handover could be undertaken amicably.

There was extensive reference in the cross-examination of the three managers and Mr Ingall to a list of points in Mr Lanyon's handwriting for a meeting on Thursday 26

September. The list is of points of concern to the three managers affecting their   A
arrangements with Rathbone, some of which impacted on the terms over which Mr Ingall
was in negotiation with Mr Loach. They included, for example, whether the one per cent
of the value of funds under management to be transferred would be inclusive of various
expenses involved in the transfer of the funds, whether a sufficient period was being
allowed for completion of the sale and what staff the three would like to take with them
to Rathbone from FIM. Mr Anderson and Mr Clarke were very vague about the list and
the meeting to which it related. It seems however that later that day there was a meeting   B
with Mr Ingall although who from among the three mangers, apart from Mr Lanyon,
attended the meeting was unclear. At that meeting matters concerned with the transfer to
Rathbone were discussed. Whether any of the matters discussed at that meeting had any
impact on the terms which Mr Ingall agreed with Mr Loach seems to me, on the evidence,
to be extremely doubtful. They do not appear to have had any bearing on the price to be
paid by Rathbone to Framlington the amount of which (one per cent of the funds under   C
management transferred) had been discussed and agreed some days earlier. Mr Ingall
thought that it was at this meeting that, as he put it, he 'firmed up' on the percentage
(one per cent of the funds under management transferred) that he could offer them. A
few days later, on 30 September 1991, draft heads of agreement were agreed between
Framlington plc and Rathbone, and the matter was thereafter put into the hands of
solicitors. The agreement for sale itself was entered into on 1 November 1991.

The sale agreement of 1 November 1991 lists, by way of schedule, each of the fund   D
management agreements which was the subject of the sale. The schedule was missing in
the copies of the sale agreement in evidence before me but I understand that the list
referred to several hundred. The portfolios totalled in value, as at November 1991,
approximately £180m. The actual number of clients was rather fewer since a number of
clients had more than one portfolio. In addition a number of the clients were connected
with each other. Mr Anderson and Mr Lanyon managed their clients jointly. Those   E
clients had a value of £120m or thereabouts as at November 1991. Of those clients 80 per
cent in value were represented by approximately 100 family groupings. Those managed
by Mr Clarke which accounted for the balance in value numbered 350-odd.

The success of the sale depended upon persuading the clients in question, who were
entitled in all cases, as I understand it, to terminate forthwith on notice the discretionary
fund management agreements which they had entered into with FIM, to transfer the
management of their funds from FIM to Rathbone. It was therefore a term of the sale   F
agreement that FIM and Rathbone should cooperate fully with a view to ensuring that
the clients in question would enter into replacement contracts with Rathbone (or
Rathbone's nominated subsidiary) in place of the clients' agreements with FIM. In
practice that meant that the three managers, as the persons who knew the clients (it was
not suggested that anyone else did), had the task of persuading the clients to transfer to
Rathbone.   G

The price paid by Rathbone under the sale agreement for those clients who did transfer
to Rathbone was one per cent of the aggregate value of the portfolios of the clients in
question valued as at close of business on 5 January 1992. The more clients that could be
persuaded to transfer, therefore, the greater the amount of the consideration that
Framlington plc would receive. The contract contained a provision for valuing the
portfolios in default of agreement. The price once ascertained was satisfied by the   H
allotment to Framlington plc, or as it might direct, of that number of 5p ordinary shares
in Rathbone, credited as fully paid at a value of 357.5p per ordinary share, whose value
equalled the price. The sale agreement also provided that if at any time after 5 January
1992 but before close of business on 30 June 1992, Rathbone or any of its subsidiaries
should become fund managers of any portfolios in respect of which a replacement
contract had not by 5 January 1992 been entered into (or, in the case of personal equity

A   plans, Rathbone or any subsidiary had not by then become plan manager), then Rathbone would pay a sum equal to one per cent of the value of the portfolio in question valued as at 5 January 1992. Such further contracts were referred to before me as 'stragglers'. Payment for stragglers was to be satisfied by either shares (calculated on the same basis as before) or cash at Rathbone's option. Rathbone opted to pay for stragglers in cash. The overall price paid was £1,754,601. Of that sum £1,590,564 was satisfied by the allotment to Framlington plc of 444,930 ordinary 5p shares in Rathbone and the

B   balance of £164,037 represented cash paid for stragglers. Shortly after the sale was completed (on 13 January 1992) Framlington plc sold the shares at 430p each thus realising a substantial gain over the nominal amount of the sale consideration.

It was a term of the sale agreement that on completion Rathbone and the three managers would each enter into a deed of non-solicitation with FIM. Notwithstanding that none of the managers was a party to the sale agreement and obtained no

C   consideration from FIM or Framlington plc for doing so each executed such a deed. By the deed each manager and Rathbone undertook to Framlington plc not during a period of two years after completion to solicit orders, in connection with any business competing with the fund management business as at 1 November 1991 of Framlington plc or its subsidiaries and not sold under the terms of the sale agreement, from anyone who had been a client of such business during the 12 months prior to 7 January 1992. FIM and

D   Framlington plc for their part undertook to Rathbone that neither FIM nor any company carrying on any business in succession to FIM nor any company which was then or might thereafter become a member of the Framlington group would during a like period solicit orders, in connection with a business competing with the business sold to Rathbone under the sale agreement, from anyone who had become a customer or client of Rathbone pursuant to the sale agreement.

E   With effect from Monday 6 January 1992 each of the three mangers took up employment with Rathbone, their employment with and directorships of FIM (and, in the case of Mr Clarke and Mr Lanyon, their directorships of Framlington plc) having terminated the preceding Friday. Until 17 August 1992 their employment was regulated by the terms of a letter dated 9 December 1991 under which each was appointed an investment manager reporting to Mr Ingall in return for a commencing salary of £55,000. It was expressed to be terminable on three months' notice on either side. In addition each

F   was provided with a car and the right to join Rathbone's pension scheme and health insurance and death in service schemes. Each undertook to be bound during his employment with Rathbone and at all times thereafter not to divulge any secrets or other confidential information relating to the business or affairs of Rathbone or any of its subsidiary or associated companies and not at any time after termination of his employment for whatever reason to represent himself as connected with or interested in

G   Rathbone's business or to solicit, interfere with or endeavour to entice away any employee of Rathbone or of any of its subsidiary or associated companies. They were otherwise free of restraint on the termination of their employment with Rathbone.

I have already referred to Mr Ingall's suggestion that the three managers form a personal services company through which the three could provide their services to Rathbone, and which they could sell to Rathbone in exchange for shares in Rathbone. The corporate vehicle chosen for the purpose was acquired off-the-shelf on 30 December

H   1991 when the three were appointed directors of it. On 6 January its name was changed to Laclan Associates Ltd ('Laclan') and the two subscriber shares in it were transferred to Mr Lanyon and Mr Anderson respectively. On 7 January a further 998 shares were allotted resulting in 308 shares held by Mr Lanyon and 308 shares by Mr Anderson, 309 shares by Mr Clarke and 25 shares by each of those members of FIM's staff (of whom there were three) who transferred to Rathbone with the three managers.

Six months later, on 22 June 1992, Laclan entered into an agreement with Rathbone   A
which, according to cl. 1, was deemed to have come into effect on 6 January (the date
when the three managers took up their employment with Rathbone). Notwithstanding
that as from that date each of the three was employed full time by Rathbone as an
investment manager reporting to Mr Ingall pursuant to the letter of 9 December 1991,
the agreement of 22 June 1992, to which none of the three was a party, provided that
each would act as an investment manager to introduce clients to and act for Laclan and
that Laclan would (1) introduce new clients to Rathbone and carry on the management   B
of the investments of those clients as undisclosed agent for Rathbone (the agreement says
undisclosed agent for Laclan but that is obviously an error) (2) use its best endeavours to
procure that private clients using the fund management services of FIM should terminate
their contracts with FIM and enter into contracts for fund management services with
Rathbone (this was assumed on both sides to be a reference to securing for Rathbone the
so-called 'stragglers'), and (3) use its best endeavours to retain as clients of Rathbone   C
those private clients who were the subject of the sale agreement of 1 November 1991. The
agreement provided for Rathbone to pay quarterly to Laclan a sum equal to the
management fees derived by Rathbone from the private clients as a result of Laclan's
services, and to provide all administrative and support services needed to enable Laclan
to conduct its investment business in consideration of a quarterly fee equal to 90 per cent
of Laclan's profits before tax.

On 17 August 1992 the six shareholders in Laclan entered into the agreement which I   D
have already briefly mentioned. It was a share sale agreement with Rathbone whereby
the six shareholders sold their shares in Laclan to Rathbone in consideration of
£1,666,677 satisfied by the allotment and issue credited as fully paid of 846,029 ordinary
shares of 5p each in Rathbone. Those are the consideration shares referred to earlier. The
sale was expressed to be conditional on each of the three managers entering into
prescribed service agreements with Rathbone by 31 August 1992 failing which the   E
agreement was declared to be null and void. On the same day the prescribed service
agreements were entered into thereby fulfilling the condition in the share sale agreement
and the consideration for the purchase was paid by the issue of the consideration shares.

Under the service agreements each of the three managers undertook for a period of
five years to serve Rathbone as an investment manager in return for a basic annual salary
of £55,000 and the use of a motor car. The service agreement made provision for holidays,
sickness pay, membership of Rathbone's pension and death in service schemes, and   F
private medical insurance. More particularly the service agreements contained a number
of restraint provisions on each manager's part intended to take effect on termination of
his employment. Among those restraints were (1) an agreement not for the period of two
years after the end of his employment to solicit or endeavour to entice away from
Rathbone (or any of its subsidiary or associated companies) anyone who in the previous
year had been a customer of it (or of any such subsidiary or associated company) or who   G
had been in the habit of dealing with Rathbone (or any of is subsidiary or associated
companies), (2) an agreement not at any time after the end of his employment to solicit,
interfere with or endeavour to entice away any employee of Rathbone (or any of its
subsidiary or associated companies), and (3) an agreement for the period of one year
after the end of his employment not to act for or deal with anyone for whom he had
acted or with whom he had had any dealings during his employment by Rathbone.

Similar restrictions were also contained in the share sale agreement of the same date.   H
The share sale agreement also contained a restriction on the ability of the three managers
to dispose of the consideration shares. The restrictions prevented them from disposing of
any of those shares while in Rathbone's employment except with Rathbone's consent,
such consent not to be unreasonably withheld, and provided for the consideration shares
to be registered, as they were, in the name of the fourth defendant. Although not happily

A   worded the restriction appeared to envisage that each manager might dispose of up to 20 per cent of his consideration shares in any of the calendar years of 1992–1996.

I must now go back in time to shortly after the sale agreement was signed. On 6 November 1991 Mr Ingall faxed to Mr Loach a suggested Stock Exchange announcement of the sale agreements which had been entered into five days earlier. Two features of that announcement evoked great surprise within the Framlington group and B   led to a series of meetings between Mr Loach and the three managers at which Mr Loach expressed his anger at the discovery of the terms apparently agreed between Rathbone and the three managers. The first was the reference in the draft announcement to the expectation that Rathbone would acquire a company owned by the three managers which would provide services in the procurement and the management of the investment management business that Rathbone had agreed to acquire from Framlington. The second was the reference to an expectation that the total consideration for the C   acquisitions, dependent upon a valuation of the funds under management as at 5 January 1992, would not exceed £3.48m.

The reference to a company owned by the three managers was to the personal services company which, as I have mentioned, was later acquired and renamed Laclan. The reference to the figure of £3.48m was, it seems, to Rathbone's estimate of two per cent of the value of the funds under management which it was expected would transfer to D   Rathbone. The figure was two per cent because, broadly speaking, one per cent was payable to Framlington plc under the sale agreement and one per cent was expected to be payable to the three managers on the acquisition of Laclan.

I need not set out in any detail the course of the communications which took place between Mr Loach and the three managers and between Mr Loach and Rathbone once the press release had come to his notice. It is clear and is not in dispute that the plaintiffs E   (through Mr Loach) regarded the payment which the three managers could expect to receive as 'consideration properly payable to this company [i.e. Framlington plc] for the private client fund management business which is being sold by Framlington Investment Management Ltd to Rathbone' and its negotiation as 'a clear and gross breach of your duty of good faith to this company as your employer and, even more seriously, of your fiduciary duty as a director both of this company and Framlington Investment Management Ltd.' See Mr Loach's letter of 7 November 1991 sent to each of the three F   managers.

In a later letter to the three managers, dated 11 November 1991, Mr Loach stated the position as he understood it as follows (I read from the letter sent to Mr Anderson):

> 'Each of you, Bob Clarke and Richard Lanyon are directors of FIM and Bob Clarke and Richard Lanyon are also directors of Framlington Group plc. That G   places certain duties on you in addition to those which you have in any event as an employee of Framlington.
>
> Looking first at your position as an employee, there is a basic rule that you are bound to account to your employer for any secret profit received in connection with your employer's affairs. As directors, you are not entitled to profit from your position without complying with various requirements, namely full disclosure to H   the rest the board and approval by them or, in certain circumstances, the shareholders. Failure to comply with these requirements gives rise to an obligation to account to the company for the profits made. The way in which the profits are made is irrelevant. There does not have to arise any question that property has been mishandled – it is enough if a director has enriched himself without the required disclosure and approval. The obligation to account does not depend in any way on fraud or lack of good faith, or even whether the profit in question

would ever have gone to the company. Motive is irrelevant as is the question   A
whether any loss has actually been suffered by the company.

That is the basic law in a nutshell. To apply it to the present situation, it appears
that consideration is passing to the three of you in connection with the sale by
Framlington of its private client find management business.'

Having reserved the rights of Framlington plc and FIM to proceed against the three
managers arising out of what had been discovered of their arrangements with Rathbone,   B
Mr Loach made clear that completion of the sale agreement was without prejudice to
that right.

In their letters of reply dated 20 November (a draft of which, dated 11 November, had
been delivered to Mr Loach) the following appears (I read from the letter sent by Mr
Anderson):

> 'You have been aware for some time of my intention to leave Framlington to join   C
> Rathbones. My contract of employment with the company does not contain any
> restrictions which prevent me from competing with it or soliciting business from
> its customers following the termination of my employment. Rather than simply
> leaving and competing, however, I approached you with a suggestion that an
> orderly transfer of the private client business, which would inevitably have
> followed me to Rathbones would be in the best interests of everybody and in
> particular the clients themselves.   D

> After I had mentioned this, you entered into negotiations with Rathbones and
> agreed terms which would apply to the transfer. I had no part in these negotiations.
> I did not act for Framlington nor did I act for Rathbones.

> It was always apparent and indeed was recognised by you, that I would be
> negotiating the terms of an employment agreement which would take effect on
> joining Rathbones. As yet no agreement on this or the payment of any   E
> consideration has been finalised. However, in discussions Rathbones indicated that
> they would wish me to enter into a long fixed term agreement containing restrictive
> covenants. The aim of this was to protect the business which they were acquiring
> and for which they had paid you a consideration. In consideration for my agreeing
> to this and to ensure that I was provided with a suitable incentive, Rathbones
> offered me an equity stake in the company. . . .

> I was under no obligation to inform you that I was leaving to join Rathbones or   F
> to give you the opportunity of negotiating the sale of Framlington's private client
> fund management business. I have acted in good faith throughout. The
> arrangements proposed with Rathbones represent remuneration and not a
> commission on the sale of a business as you suggest. I did not use my fiduciary
> position as a director of Framlington Investment Management Ltd in any way in
> negotiating with Rathbones. It is disingenuous to suggest that my negotiation of a   G
> new employment agreement relates to the affairs of Framlington or can be said to
> have been done in the course of the management of its business. It does not utilise
> an opportunity coming to Framlington or my special knowledge as a director.
> Furthermore the terms, which I would reiterate have not yet been finalised, cannot,
> by any stretch of the imagination, be described as a secret payment to induce me
> to act in Rathbones' interests on the sale of the business as I was not involved in   H
> the negotiations.

> The fact that I am a director of Framlington Investment Management Ltd does
> not oblige me to disclose terms of employment with a new company which will
> apply once my directorships and my employment with Framlington has come to
> an end. Indeed, you recognised this yourself by saying that you were not interested
> in the deal that we did with Rathbones.'

A   The question is which of these rival contentions is correct. Before coming to that I make the following further observations on the evidence.

(1)   It was suggested to Mr Loach that he was aware from early September 1991 or at any rate before the sale agreement was entered into that Rathbone was in the habit of incentivising senior employees by means of an issue of shares in exchange for the acquisition of a personal services company belonging to the incoming employee. That awareness was said to derive from his reading of the published accounts of Rathbone for 1990. I do not consider that the evidence justifies that conclusion.

(2)   Although at the time of the sale agreement no binding agreement had been entered into by Rathbone with any of the three managers their expectation was as set out in the letter of 20 November from which I have quoted. In addition it was their expectation that the consideration which they would receive would be calculated by reference to one per cent of the value of funds under management by the three to be transferred to Rathbone.

(3)   I accept the evidence of Mr Ingall, supported by that of the three managers, that the reason why no commitment to the offer of long-term employment had been entered into at the time of the sale agreement on 1 November 1991 was that they wanted to ensure that before doing so they would settle in comfortably at Rathbone. They all had every expectation that they would. Until they did, as Mr Ingall made clear, Rathbone carried the risk, having paid £1.75m to Framlington, that they might not and that they would be free to solicit the clients in question to go elsewhere.

(4)   I accept that the incorporation and later sale to Rathbone of Laclan as the personal services company of the three managers was intended as a tax efficient manner of proceeding. The scheme was very much the brainchild of Mr Ian Harvey, finance director of Rathbone. The three managers who when cross-examined about its terms did not seem to have much of an understanding of it, appear simply to have accepted the terms of the scheme, doubtless in the expectation that if it was apt to avoid an immediate charge to tax they would be foolish not to follow it. I certainly see nothing sinister in the fact that none of them took separate advice on the terms of the Laclan transaction or of their service contracts.

(5)   I regard each of the witnesses who gave evidence before me as honest. In any event it was not suggested, indeed it was expressly accepted by Mr Loach, that the three managers had acted otherwise than in good faith. All of the witnesses, however, had great difficulty in recalling quite what had been said and when and tended to try and reconstruct what would or must have happened rather than what they recall having happened. There was in evidence a quantity of manuscript notes of meetings which were taken mostly by Mr Winterton, newly recruited as in-house lawyer within the Framlington group. On the very few relevant issues of fact which arise, however, the manuscript notes provide no assistance.

(6)   I was not assisted by the evidence by Mr Hickey, a tax partner in KPMG Peat Marwick. He was called by the plaintiffs with a view to expressing views on the taxation consequences of the sale by the three managers of their shares in Laclan in exchange for shares in Rathbone. In the absence of a suggestion that the agreements which the three managers and Laclan made with Rathbone were in some way shams (and no such suggestion was made) it does not seem to me to matter what precisely the taxation consequences were of the Laclan transaction.

(7)   Nor was I assisted by the evidence of Mr Sainty, an expert in executive recruitment specialising in the financial services sector with particular expertise in the fund management industry. He was called by the defendants to express views on the

range and nature of the remuneration which fund mangers could expect to receive   A
in 1991/1992 on accepting employment as a fund manager with an employer such
as Rathbone. The burden of his evidence was that increasingly these days fund
managers such as the three managers can expect to be provided with equity as a
substitute for year on year bonus performance remuneration and that the
remuneration package (including equity participation in Rathbone) provided to
them by Rathbone fell within the parameters of what could be expected from an
employer such as Rathbone.   B

The essence of the plaintiffs' case as originally pleaded was that prior to 1 November
1991 (when the sale agreement was entered into) the three managers had reached an
understanding with Rathbone (whether or not of contractual effect) which they failed to
disclose to the plaintiffs whereby each would receive a substantial capital benefit as a
result of the transfer to Rathbone of the fund management business of FIM which they
managed, that the consideration shares received by the three mangers were the fruits of   C
that understanding and that, in consequence, the three hold the consideration shares (and
any benefits derived or to be derived from those shares) on constructive trust for the
plaintiffs. See para. 22 of the statement of claim.

When Mr Pymont opened the case for the plaintiffs he put more flesh on that claim by
submitting that the three managers, although not involved in the negotiations between
the plaintiffs and Rathbone, were, as directors of FIM, under a fiduciary duty to give   D
disinterested advice and assistance to the plaintiffs (or at any rate to FIM) concerning
the person to whom and the price at which the private client business which the three of
them were managing should be sold, that by negotiating a deal with Rathbone without
disclosing to the plaintiffs the terms of what they were negotiating (other than that they
would be receiving a lower salary) they put themselves in a position where their duty to
FIM (to give such advice and assistance) conflicted with their personal interest (in the
deal that they were negotiating with Rathbone) and that accordingly they became   E
accountable to the plaintiffs for the undisclosed benefits obtained by them, namely the
consideration shares and any benefits derived or to be derived by them from those shares.

During the course of his closing submissions, and in response to a complaint by Mr
Serota QC on behalf of the defendants that the case which Mr Pymont was now
advancing was not one which had been adequately pleaded, Mr Pymont sought leave,
which I gave, to amend his statement of claim by pleading (1) the duty with which the   F
three managers' personal interest in negotiating their understanding with Rathbone
without disclosing it to the plaintiffs was said to be in conflict and (2) the conflict and its
consequences. Accordingly the statement of claim was amended by the addition of two
additional paragraphs. The first was as follows:

'3A. It was at all material times the duty of the individual defendants, as directors
of FIM, to act bona fide in the interests of FIM and, further or in particular, in the
event of negotiations with a third party at arm's length for the sale of that part of   G
the business of FIM which was entrusted to them, to assist FIM in obtaining the
best price reasonably obtainable therefor.'

Mr Pymont made clear that the duty of the three managers to assist FIM to obtain the
best price reasonably obtainable for that part of the business of FIM which was entrusted
to them was one which arose as a consequence of the fact that the three were directors of
FIM and not in consequence of any particular direction or instruction given to them or   H
to any other special circumstance (other than the fact that, as set out in that paragraph,
the business being sold was one which they had been managing).

Paragraph 22 of the statement of claim was amended to include the following plea:

'(c) Until 3 January 1992 (when they resigned as aforesaid) the individual
defendants put themselves in a position where their interests (pursuant to the

A agreement or understanding referred to in (a) above and in the negotiations therefor) [that is a reference to what I have described as the understanding] were in conflict with their duties identified in para. 3A as directors of the second plaintiff and thereby acted in breach of the obligation in equity not to put themselves in such a position and further failed to make any or any adequate disclosure to the second plaintiff as to the existence or terms of that agreement or understanding or those negotiations; in consequence the individual defendants are disabled from

B retaining for their own benefit as against the second plaintiff the benefits received by them under the Laclan agreement (save as aforesaid)' [the parenthesis is a reference to the benefits receivable by the three managers under their respective long-term service contracts].

In his closing submissions Mr Pymont amplified that plea by submitting that, as soon as the plaintiffs and Rathbone entered into negotiations for the sale of that part of the

C business that the three managers had been managing and throughout the period of those negotiations, the three were in a position where their duty to assist FIM to obtain the best possible price was in conflict with their personal interest in negotiating a deal with Rathbone. If as a result of that conflict they derived a benefit they became liable, he submitted, to account to FIM for that benefit unless they could show that they had made full disclosure of it to FIM. Since no such disclosure was made except as to the salaries that they would be receiving (implicit in which were, he submitted, the other in-service

D benefits to which they became entitled under those service contracts, being benefits of a kind which could be expected as part of a normal service contract), the three managers became obliged to account for the consideration shares which they received.

The fact that Mr Loach told Mr Anderson and Mr Lanyon that he was not interested in their remuneration package and instructed them not to become involved in the negotiations between the plaintiffs and Rathbone (an instruction which, when he said

E that he intended to leave the Framlington group and join Rathbone, extended to Mr Clarke) could, he submitted, be ignored because Mr Loach had not been told the full position: he was told of the smaller salaries that they would be receiving but was not told of the understanding of which, even then (early September) Mr Anderson and Mr Lanyon had that they would receive a payment, over and above their salaries, linked to the value of the managed funds transferred. In short Mr Loach's instruction was uninformed and

F therefore irrelevant to the extent of the duty of the three managers to assist FIM to obtain the best possible price in its negotiations with Rathbone and irrelevant to the existence of the conflict between the proper execution by them of that duty and their interest in negotiating what they were to receive from Rathbone.

What, according to Mr Pymont in his closing submissions, lies at the heart of the claim was not that the three managers, while still directors of FIM, were negotiating their remuneration with a future employer – without more, he accepted, the plaintiffs could

G have no complaint about that – but that, so soon as the plaintiffs entered upon negotiations with that future employer for the sale of a part of FIM's business to that future employer, an inevitable conflict arose if the three managers were thereafter to continue, as they did, to negotiate their future remuneration with that employer. This conflict arose, he submitted, from the fact that the amount which Mr Loach, as the person who had the conduct of the negotiations on behalf of the Framlington group, was

H negotiating to receive from Rathbone was potentially affected by the amount which, concurrently, the three managers were negotiating to receive from Rathbone. This was because, unknown to Mr Loach, Rathbone, in the person of Mr Ingall, was willing to pay a sum equivalent to two per cent or so of the value of the funds under management likely to be transferred to it as a result of his negotiations (the press release indicated that Rathbone expected that the overall amount to be paid would not exceed £3.48m) so that by negotiating with Mr Ingall that they should receive one per cent of the value of funds

transferred but without disclosing that fact to Mr Loach, the three were restricting the   A
amount that, in negotiations with Mr Loach, Mr Ingall was likely to concede to the
plaintiffs. In fact, submitted Mr Pymont, a linkage between the two amounts was
established on the evidence in that, according to Mr Ingall, having agreed with Mr Loach
that the plaintiffs should receive one per cent of the value of funds transferred, he
informed the three managers that he could no longer offer 1.57 per cent of the value of
funds transferred but would only be willing to concede between one-half to one per cent,
a figure which was firmed up in late September, at a time when no concluded deal with   B
Rathbone had been entered into, to one per cent. If, submitted Mr Pymont, the three
managers had told Mr Loach of what was on offer to them, as they should, Mr Loach
might have been able to hold out for more than the one per cent which was agreed and
was carried into the sale agreement.

Mr Pymont grounds his claim on the well known rule that a person in a fiduciary
position may not place himself in a position where his fiduciary duty and his interest   C
conflict or, as it is sometimes put, may not enter engagements in which he has, or can
have, a personal interest conflicting, or which may conflict, with the interest of those
whom he is bound to protect.

The authorities in which this rule has been recognised and discussed are numerous. I
propose to cite from four of them only.

In his speech in *Boardman v Phipps* [1967] 2 AC 46 Lord Upjohn stated the rule and   D
adverted to its limitations in the following terms at p. 123:

> 'Rules of equity have to be applied to such a great diversity of circumstances that
> they can be stated only in the most general terms and applied with particular
> attention to the exact circumstances of each case. The relevant rule for the decision
> of this case is the judgmental rule of equity that a person in a fiduciary capacity
> must not make a profit out of his trust which is part of the wider rule that a trustee   E
> must not place himself in a position where his duty and his interest may conflict. I
> believe the rule is best stated in *Bray* v. *Ford* [1896] A.C. 44, 51 by Lord Herschell,
> who plainly recognised its limitations:
>
> > "It is an inflexible rule of a Court of Equity that a person in a fiduciary position,
> > such as the respondent's, is not, unless otherwise expressly provided, entitled to
> > make a profit; he is not allowed to put himself in a position where his interest
> > and duty conflict. It does not appear to me that this rule is, as has been said,   F
> > founded upon principles of morality. I regard it rather as based on the
> > consideration that, human nature being what it is, there is a danger, in such
> > circumstances, of the person holding a fiduciary position being swayed by
> > interest rather than by duty, and thus prejudicing those whom he was bound to
> > protect. It has, therefore, been deemed expedient to lay down this positive rule.
> > But I am satisfied that it might be departed from in many cases, without any   G
> > breach of morality, without any wrong being inflicted, and without any
> > consciousness of wrong-doing. Indeed, it is obvious that it might sometimes be
> > to the advantage of the beneficiaries that their trustee should act for them
> > professionally rather than a stranger, even though the trustee were paid for his
> > services."

It is perhaps stated most highly against trustees or directors in the celebrated
speech of Lord Cranworth L.C. in *Aberdeen Railway* v. *Blaikie*, 1 Macq. 461, 471   H
where he said:

> "And it is a rule of universal application, that no one, having such duties to
> discharge, shall be allowed to enter into engagements in which he has, or can
> have, a personal interest conflicting, or which possibly may conflict, with the
> interests of those whom he is bound to protect."

A   The phrase "possibly may conflict" requires consideration. In my view it means that the reasonable man looking at the relevant facts and circumstances of the particular case would think that there was a real sensible possibility of conflict; not that you could imagine some situation arising which might, in some conceivable possibility in events not contemplated as real sensible possibilities by any reasonable person, result in a conflict.'

B   Although, in that case, Lord Upjohn dissented on the facts his statement of the rule has not, I think, been doubted. The last sentence of that citation echoes a passage in his earlier judgment in the Court of Appeal in *Boulting v ACTAT* [1963] 2 QB 606 at p. 637 where, in discussing the rule, he said:

'There was some discussion before us as to the ambit of the rule. It was submitted that it could not apply to cases where a managing director negotiates too high a salary with his company or takes too long a holiday, or stays at an unnecessarily
C   luxurious hotel when on the company's business. However, a broad rule like this must be applied with common sense and with an appreciation of the sort of circumstances in which over the last 200 years and more it has been applied and thrived. It must be applied realistically to a state of affairs which discloses a real conflict of duty and interest and not to some theoretical or rhetorical conflict.'

The obligation of a director to account to his company for profits made by him was
D   also discussed by Lord Blanesburgh in *Bell v Lever Brothers Ltd* [1932] AC 161. At p. 194 of his speech the following appears:

'. . . the liability of a director in respect of profits made by him from a contract in which his company also is concerned is one thing: his liability, if any there be, in respect of his profits from a contract in which the company has no interest at all is quite another. In the first case, unless by the company's regulations the director is permitted, subject to or without conditions, to retain his profit, he must account
E   for it to the company. In the second case, the company has no concern in his profit and cannot make him accountable for it unless it appears – this is the essential qualification – that in earning that profit he has made use either of the property of the company or of some confidential information which has come to him as a director of the company.'

I also find helpful the remarks of Falconer J in *Balston Ltd v Headline Filters Ltd* [1990]
F   FSR 385 at p. 412 where the following appears:

'In his statement of the overriding principle by Roskill J. in the *I.D.C.* case, namely "that a man must not be allowed to put himself in a position in which his fiduciary duty and his interests conflict," the conflict contemplated must be one with a specific interest of the company (or other body or person) to whom the fiduciary duty is owed, as, for example, a maturing business opportunity, as in *Canaero*, or the plaintiff's interest in the contract secured by the defendant in the *I.D.C.* case,
G   or a contract falling within the first class of contracts in Lord Blanesburgh's dichotomy in *Bell v Lever* (p. 194), or the use of some property or confidential information of the company which has come to a director as such (Lord Blanesburgh's qualification of his second class). In my judgment an intention by a director of a company to set up business in competition with the company after his directorship has ceased is not to be regarded as a conflicting interest within the context of the principle, having regard to the rules of public policy as to restraint
H   of trade, nor is the taking of any preliminary steps to investigate or forward that intention so long as there is no actual competitive activity, such as, for instance, competitive tendering or actual trading, while he remains a director.'

Wherein then lies the conflict? What is the specific interest of FIM which is in conflict with the three managers' conduct in negotiating for themselves a generous remuneration package with Rathbone at the time that Mr Loach was in negotiation with Mr Ingall?

It is not suggested, although initially in the correspondence it was, that the   A
consideration shares represented a payment to the three managers for an asset which
belonged to FIM or that they acquired them by the use of some property or confidential
information of FIM which came to them as directors of FIM. The shares were paid in
consideration of an asset of the three managers which they were willing to bring to
Rathbone – an asset which belonged to them and which, on leaving the Framlington
group's employment they were free to exploit for themselves, namely the client goodwill
which attached to them as the persons who had, over many years, managed their clients'   B
investments. The consideration shares were the price which the three were willing to
accept in return for binding themselves under five year service contracts to make that
goodwill available to Rathbone and for restricting their freedom, after the termination of
their service contracts, to exploit that client goodwill for themselves or for others.

Nor is it suggested, or can be suggested, that the three managers diverted to themselves
some kind of maturing business opportunity which should have been made available to   C
the plaintiffs of the kind which featured in *Industrial Development Consultants Ltd v
Cooley* [1972] 1 WLR 443 to which I was referred. The opportunity which the plaintiffs
had of extracting a payment from Rathbone in consideration of a transfer by FIM to
Rathbone of one of its assets, namely its client goodwill in the private client investment
management business which the three managers had been managing, was one that Mr
Loach, on behalf of the group, was free to exploit and did exploit.   D

It is not suggested, and cannot be, that the consideration shares represented some kind
of secret bribe or commission for having introduced Rathbone to the Framlington group.
The many authorities to which I was referred on that topic did not seem to me to be in
point. The consideration shares were payment for securing the long-term service of the
three managers and with it their client goodwill.

Nor can it be suggested that the three managers were not free to negotiate whatever   E
price they could from Rathbone for their future services to that company. The fact that
the consideration for so doing took one form (a regular salary, in-service benefits and
equity participation in the employer calculated by reference to the value of funds
transferred) rather than another (a salary, in-service benefits and an annual profit bonus
dependent upon profits achieved, or participation in an executive share option scheme)
was, in itself, entirely a matter for the three managers. I mention this because at times
during his submissions Mr Pymont appeared to be contending that a director   F
contemplating joining a new employee was under an obligation to disclose to the
company of which he is a director any unusually generous terms (such as a large capital
payment) that the new employer is offering to pay him to secure his services. I cannot see
why.

One of the duties with which the three managers' interest is said to have been in conflict
was their duty, as it is put in para. 3A of the statement of claim, 'to assist FIM in   G
obtaining the best price reasonably obtainable' for what FIM was negotiating to sell to
Rathbone. I do not consider that that did form any part of the three managers' duty.
Nor, to make the point clear, do I consider that in failing (if they did) to assist FIM to
obtain the best price reasonably obtainable for what FIM was negotiating to sell to
Rathbone, the three acted in breach of any general duty to act bona fide in FIM's
interests. What precisely a director's duty is within a company must depend, as Hoffmann
LJ observed in *Bishopsgate Investment Management Ltd v Maxwell* [1993] BCC 120 at   H
p. 139C (when commenting on whether a director is under a duty to participate in the
management of a company) 'upon how the particular company's business is organised
and the part which the director could reasonably have been expected to play'.

In this case there was no evidence to indicate what part, apart from managing clients'
investments, each of the three managers was expected to play within FIM and I am not

A   willing to assume, without more, that each was under the particular duty alleged. But the point is academic because it is clear that, as regards the sale to Rathbone, the three were instructed by Mr Loach speaking on behalf of Framlington plc (the sole beneficial shareholder of FIM) not to take part in the sale negotiations with Mr Ingall. I reject any suggestion that, because neither Mr Anderson nor Mr Lanyon informed Mr Loach of all of the terms which Mr Ingall was then offering to them if they were willing to join Rathbone, that instruction can be ignored. Knowing that they would be joining

B   Rathbone Mr Loach clearly realised that it would be quite impossible for those two to be involved in negotiating the price which Rathbone should pay to the Framlington group to secure the latter's co-operation to a smooth transfer to Rathbone of the private client business. Furthermore, it seems to me that the three did assist FIM to obtain the best price reasonably obtainable for its private client business because, as I have earlier related, the three, without being under the least obligation to do so, entered into deeds of

C   non-solicitation with FIM on completion of the sale agreement on 13 January 1992. That there should be such deeds in order to protect what remained of FIM's business after the sale to Rathbone was a part of the bargain struck by the plaintiffs with Rathbone embodied in the sale agreement.

     Nor do I consider that the negotiations by the three with Mr Ingall, at a time when the group was in negotiation with Rathbone, of the remuneration package that they could expect to receive on joining Rathbone was in itself, with or without disclosure to FIM, a

D   breach of any general duty of good faith owed by them to FIM. In the absence of some special circumstance (for example a prohibition in a service contract) a director commits no breach of his fiduciary duty to the company of which he is a director merely because, while a director, he takes steps so that, on ceasing to be a director (and, if he is one, an employee of that company), he can immediately set up in business in competition with that company or join a competitor of it. Nor is he obliged to disclose to that company

E   that he is taking those steps. See *Balston Ltd v Headline Filters Ltd* [1990] FSR 385 at p. 412.

     In any event Mr Loach made it clear to Mr Anderson and Mr Lanyon that he was not concerned with the remuneration terms that they might negotiate with Rathbone. Those terms included the acquisition of the consideration shares in return for entering into the five-year service contracts. It is not suggested that Mr Loach's attitude differed in this

F   respect once Mr Clarke had decided to join Rathbone and had told Mr Loach of that fact. Since I do not consider that Mr Loach's remark was in any way improperly induced I do not see how it lies in the plaintiffs' mouths to say that the three should not have taken that remark at face value which, on the facts, they plainly did.

     The fact, if fact it was, that Rathbone set a ceiling on the amount it was willing to pay to acquire the goodwill in the private client investment management business which attached partly to FIM and partly to the three managers so that whatever the three

G   managers were able to negotiate was likely to be at the expense of what Mr Loach could negotiate for the plaintiffs did not, in my judgment, involve any breach of duty or obligation in equity on the part of the three managers. Specifically I see no reason why a director cannot, without committing any breach of his duty of good faith, seek to drive as hard a bargain as he is able with his future employer over the terms on which he is to be employed and the fact, if fact it be, that the result of so doing may be that the employer

H   is deprived of assets which that employer might otherwise have devoted to trading with or acquiring an asset from the company of which the director is still then a director seems to me to be of no consequence. If Mr Loach had thought that the price which Mr Ingall was willing to pay for the transfer to Rathbone of the private client business was too little he was free to reject it. He did not, presumably because he came to the view, uninfluenced on the evidence by anything the three managers said or did, that, in ail the circumstances, it was acceptable in amount.

Were it otherwise it is difficult to see what the three managers could do. Supposing the A
three had agreed their remuneration package with Rathbone before any question of a
sale by the group to Rathbone had arisen. What are the three to do once the group
decides to negotiate a sale of its interest to Rathbone? Disclosing to the group what they
have agreed is not likely to affect the amount that Rathbone is willing to pay to the group
but even if it might, it is difficult to see on what basis, in these circumstances, the three
are accountable to FIM for the fruits of what they have negotiated. I cannot see that the
fact that, at the time the group embarks upon its negotiation with Rathbone, no deal has B
been struck between the three managers and Rathbone makes any difference. Rathbone
plainly needed to secure the services of the three managers otherwise the sum it was
willing to pay the group might turn out to be largely if not wholly wasted: unless
Rathbone secured their services, the three would be free to go elsewhere and take with
them as many of the private clients as they could. I am quite unable to see why, merely
because at the time a deal was being negotiated between the group and Rathbone the C
three were in negotiation with Rathbone over the terms of their remuneration package,
the three are accountable to FIM for the undisclosed part of what they eventually
negotiated when, if they had not embarked on their negotiations until after 1 November
1991, or had concluded a binding agreement with Rathbone before the group had decided
to offer the private client business to Rathbone, they would not.

But I question, in any event, the factual premise on which the case is based. The D
amount that Mr Ingall was willing to pay to the plaintiffs was not limited by what he was
willing to pay to the three. On the contrary Mr Ingall made clear that, once he was
embarked on negotiations for a purchase from the plaintiffs, he was no longer willing to
offer to the three as much as he had indicated at his meeting with Mr Anderson and Mr
Lanyon on 2 September (which was before he had even met Mr Loach) that he might be
willing to offer to them. It was only on 26 September 1991, after he had agreed with Mr
Loach the basis on which Rathbone should make payment to the plaintiffs, that he E
returned to a discussion with the three managers of the basis on which they should be
paid in return for their long-term commitment to Rathbone.

What is crucial, to my mind, is that the three managers were not involved in the
negotiations between the Framlington group and Rathbone. That distinguishes the case
from *Furs Ltd v Tomkies* (1936) 54 CLR 583, which bears a superficial similarity to this
case. The facts of that case are conveniently set out in the headnote. F

> 'T., while managing director of the appellant company, was authorized by the
> directors to negotiate for the sale of the tanning, dressing and dyeing part of its
> business. He eventually arranged with L., who was the promoter of a company to
> be formed, to sell it to that company for £8,500. Pursuant to this arrangement the
> plaintiff sold to the defendant F.D. Ltd. T. was an expert in the processes of
> tanning, dressing and dyeing and was familiar with the secret formulae used by the G
> appellant for these purposes. In the course of the negotiations for sale L. told him
> that the new company would want his services, and he so informed the appellant's
> chairman of directors. The chairman, after consultation with some of the other
> directors, advised him to make the best arrangements for himself that he could
> with the purchaser. Before the terms of sale were agreed upon T. arranged a
> contract between himself and the company to be formed in which it was agreed
> that he should serve that company and in that service disclose all his knowledge H
> and information about the process of the tanning, dressing and dyeing and should
> receive shares in the company and £4,000, in addition to an annual salary. This
> transaction, which if carried out would make its formulae valueless to it, was not
> disclosed to the appellant. After incorporation F.D. Ltd. adopted the contract with
> T., issued the shares to him and gave him promissory notes for the £4,000.'

A   To that statement of facts I would only add that one of the terms of the agreement
     between T (i.e. Tomkies) and L (Mr Lumb) was that Tomkies should serve the new
     company for three years as an employee and should thereafter be bound for a period of
     five years by a restrictive covenant. The court held that Tomkies was accountable to the
     plaintiff for the £4,000 payment.

          The ratio of the judgment of the majority of the court (Rich, Dixon & Evatt JJ with
B   whom McTiernan J agreed) was expressed in the following passage starting at p. 597:

          'The fact was that he occupied an exceptional situation. He was manager of the
          section of the business under offer and armed with all the knowledge used in
          conducting it, whether knowledge forming part of the stock he was entitled to
          carry away from the appellant company's employment or secret information to
          which that company alone was entitled. He was the director to whom the
C   negotiations of the sale had been largely entrusted. No doubt, too, his influence
          with his board was not negligible. When he demanded £5,000, it is not surprising
          that the purchasers thought good reason existed for paying it to him. They did not
          stop to analyse the ingredients in the situation which enabled him to ask for a lump
          sum. They expressed the payment one way in their preliminary letter, probably
          without any particular design. The solicitors expressed it in another way in the
          service agreement he drew up, probably seeking the most plausible and respectable
D   basis on which the payment could be justified. When, later on, they required a
          consideration to support an issue of shares, the purchaser described it in a third
          way. There was some ground for each of the complexions given to the payment. It
          wore more than one aspect. But the fact of paramount legal significance is that the
          payment was obtained by the respondent in course of a transaction which he was
          carrying out on behalf of the company in execution of his office of managing
E   director. It was only because it fell to his lot to negotiate the sale on behalf of his
          company that he was able to demand and obtain the sum. His fiduciary character
          was alike the occasion and the means of securing the profit for himself.

          To our minds it is quite plain that, by doing so, he greatly diminished the price
          obtainable by the company. He himself admitted on his cross-examination that his
          entering into the service agreement decidedly depreciated the formulas as an asset
F   for sale and that no value would be left to them. It is not improbable that the price
          which the company might have got was diminished to the full extent of £5,000. But
          this is just one of the inquiries that is excluded. So too, on the question of liability
          to account, is the inquiry into the advantages which the purchasers expected, or
          had a right to expect, in return. The respondent had a plain duty with which he
          brought his private interest into conflict and that is enough.'

G   The fact that his co-directors confided the negotiations to Tomkies and told him that
     he was free to make the best deal he could with the new company was found to be
     irrelevant because the action of his directors could not relieve Tomkies of the obligation
     which, as a director, he owed to the plaintiff company (i.e. its shareholders). This appears
     from the following passage (at p. 599) in the judgment of the majority:

          'No doubt his co-directors' action in confiding the negotiations to the respondent
          and advising him to look after himself exposed him to the temptation of preferring
H   his own advantage to the interests of the company. But the board could not relieve
          him of the equitable obligations which arose out of this conflict of duty and of
          private interest. His one resource, if he was resolved to adopt the unwise course of
          acting in the transaction on behalf of his company and yet seeking a profit for
          himself, was complete disclosure to and confirmation by the shareholders. But
          complete disclosure he was not prepared to make.

We are unable to agree with the view that the respondent's principal placed him in   A
a position in which his duty and interest conflicted and thus waived the right to the
performance of an undivided duty. The board of directors could not do this in the
case of a fellow director and, even if it could, no one contemplated anything but
an ordinary agreement of employment at a salary.'

The course of action which the defendant should have followed if he wanted to avoid
the conflict was explored in the judgment of Latham CJ in the following passage at   B
p. 590:

'It has been said that the position was a difficult one for the defendant. In a sense
this was the case. But there is really nothing unusual in the requirement that a
person occupying a position of trust and confidence should subordinate his own
interests to the interests of another person to whom he stands in a fiduciary
relation. The defendant might have proposed the postponement of any discussion
of the terms upon which he would accept employment until after the agreement of   C
sale had been made for the plaintiff company or he might have offered to retire
altogether from the negotiations as soon as the difficulty became apparent. It is
true that the purchaser might have refused to continue negotiations until he had
made sure that the defendant would carry on with the new owner of the business
upon satisfactory terms. In that event the proper course for the defendant to adopt,
if the negotiations went on, was to make a full disclosure to the shareholders of the
arrangements which he had made on his own behalf with the company to which   D
the plaintiff was selling its business. In fact, however, he made an agreement with
respect to his own interests first, and the negotiations then proceeded between
Lumb and the plaintiff (represented in part by the defendant and in part by
Cropely) upon the basis, known to Lumb and the defendant, but not known to
any of the other directors or to the shareholders of the company that the purchaser
had already agreed to pay Tomkies £5,000 in addition to a salary.'   E

Here, by contrast, the three managers were not involved in the negotiations between
Framlington group and Rathbone. Additionally, although I do not consider that this
was critical, the three came to no understanding with Mr Ingall until after the basis upon
which Rathbone would pay the plaintiffs had been agreed between Mr Loach and Mr
Ingall.

In the result I can find no basis upon which the three managers can be made to account   F
to the plaintiffs for the consideration shares and the action therefore falls to be dismissed.

This conclusion makes it unnecessary to decide what relief I would have granted if I
had been in Mr Pymont's favour. Whether, in that event, I would have granted relief to
the three managers under s. 727 of the *Companies Act* 1985 and if not whether I would
have ordered them to account to FIM on the basis of the highest value that the
consideration shares attained from time to time (and otherwise on the terms of the draft
form of order which Mr Pymont helpfully supplied to indicate precisely what relief he   G
was seeking) would very much have depended on the extent to which and why I was in
his favour.

Finally I should mention one further matter. At a late stage in his closing submissions
Mr Pymont sought leave to amend his statement of claim not just in the way that I have
earlier mentioned and which I allowed, but also by alleging a failure on the part of the
three managers to disclose their interest in the sale agreement to FIM's board when a   H
resolution of the board was passed (I suspect by passing around the resolution for
signature by the various board members) authorising Mr Loach to sign the sale
agreement on behalf of FIM and appointing him as managing director of FIM in Mr
Clarke's place. The resolution in question is undated and shows each of the three
managers as 'having declared an interest in the contract' (i.e. the sale agreement) and as
having 'abstained'. I refused to allow the amendment. By the time the application was

A made the evidence had long since been closed and Mr Serota had concluded his submissions on behalf of the defendants. To have allowed the amendment would have necessitated, as Mr Serota submitted and I accept, recalling witnesses and investigating the circumstances in which the resolution came to be passed. That in turn would have necessitated adjourning the trial. It did not seem right to allow that to happen at so late a stage in the action.

B *(Action dismissed with costs)*

_____

Re a Company No. 007923 of 1994.
Re a Company No. 007924 of 1994.

Court of Appeal (Civil Division).
Nourse and Waite L JJ.
Judgment delivered 18 January 1995.

Public interest winding-up petitions – Appeal against judge's refusal to restrain B
advertisement – Secretary of State presented winding-up petitions in public
interest – Companies applied to restrain advertisement – Whether test for
restraining advertisement same as test for restraining presentation – Test for
restraining advertisement of public interest petition – Insolvency Act 1986,
s. 124A; Insolvency Rules 1986 (SI 1986/1925), r. 4.11(1).

These were appeals against the judge's refusal to direct under r. 4.11(1) of the Insolvency C
Rules 1986 that winding-up petitions presented by the Secretary of State in the public
interest pursuant to s. 124A of the Insolvency Act 1986 should not be advertised.

Held, allowing the companies' appeal and directing that the petitions should not be
advertised over the hearing of the Secretary of State's application for appointment of a
provisional liquidator:

D

1. The test for restraining presentation (that the petition would constitute an abuse of
process) could not be equally applicable to a restraint on advertisement. That was primarily
and conclusively demonstrated by the discretion exercisable under r. 4.11(1), an exercise
which did not come into a decision on abuse of process.

2. Since r. 4.11(1) required advertisement unless the court directed otherwise, it was for
the company to show sufficient reason to depart from the normal practice. (Re Normandy E
Marketing Ltd (Company No. 007946 of 1993) [1993] BCC 879; [1994] Ch 198 approved.)

3. Considering the circumstances in the light of the purposes of advertisement, it appeared
that a restraint on advertisement, at all events in the short term, would not deprive creditors
of the companies of any significant advantage they would otherwise have had; that the
contributories already had effective notice of the petitions; and that those who might trade
with the companies during the period between the presentation of the petitions and their final F
determination would be protected by an order under s. 127. Those considerations would not,
however, together provide a sufficient ground for departing from the normal practice.

4. The companies had to show that advertisement might cause serious damage to the
reputation and financial stability of the companies. Although the harmful effects of
advertisement were liable to be exaggerated, the companies' evidence was sufficient to
establish that advertisement could cause serious damage to their reputation and financial G
stability. Adding that consideration to the likelihood that if there was no advertisement in
the short term no significant disadvantage would be caused to those whose interests had to
be considered and to the likely imminence of the hearing of the application for a provisional
liquidator, the court would direct that the petitions should not be advertised over that
hearing.

The following cases were referred to in the judgments: H

Bradford Navigation Co, Re (1870) LR 5 Ch App 600.
Bryanston Finance Ltd v De Vries (No. 2) [1976] Ch 63.
Coulon Sanderson & Ward Ltd v Ward (1986) 2 BCC 99,207.
Golden Chemical Products Ltd, Re [1976] Ch 300.
Morgan Roche Ltd v Registrar of Companies (1987) 3 NZCLC 100.

A *Normandy Marketing Ltd, Re (Company No. 007946 of 1993)* [1993] BCC 879; [1994]
   Ch 198.
   S N Group plc v Barclays Bank plc [1993] BCC 506.

   Leslie Kosmin QC and Fernanda Pirie (instructed by Berrymans) for the appellants.

   Roger Kaye QC (instructed by the Treasury Solicitor) for the Secretary of State.

B   JUDGMENT

   Nourse LJ: Rule 4.11(1) of the *Insolvency Rules* 1986, which applies to all petitions for
   the compulsory winding up of companies other than those presented by contributories,
   provides:

        'Unless the court otherwise directs, the petition shall be advertised once in the
C   Gazette.'

   In this case the Secretary of State for Trade and Industry, pursuant to s. 124A of the
   Insolvency Act 1986, has presented petitions against two associated insurance broking
   companies on the ground that it is expedient in the public interest that they should be
   wound up. The companies, while accepting that the petitions are not demurrable, seek to
   restrain their advertisement until after there has been a full hearing on the merits. The
   principal subject of debate has been the test to be applied in deciding whether to direct
D that a petition presented under s. 124A should not be advertised.

   The companies were incorporated in England as private companies in December 1990
   and February 1993 respectively. The first has an issued and paid up share capital of
   £10,000 and the second of £1,000. In June 1993 the business of the first company was
   largely taken over by the second, which has carried it on in the same manner as before.
   On 4 July 1994 the Secretary of State authorised one of his officers to require both
E companies, together with a third, to produce to him any documents which he might
   specify. The investigating officer's oral enquiries were concluded on 23 August. The
   petitions were presented on 13 December, alleging that from the information and
   documents obtained in the investigation it appeared to the Secretary of State that it was
   expedient in the public interest that the companies should be wound up. The essence of
   the case against both companies can be taken from para. 10 of the petition relating to the
   first of them (the corresponding paragraph in the petition relating to the second company
F is in nearly identical terms):

        'In carrying on its business the company acted for overseas insurers or reinsurers
        and exercised a great deal of delegated authority on behalf of such insurers or
        reinsurers. In doing so it aided and abetted such insurers and reinsurers to operate
        in the UK in carrying on insurance business without authority in breach of s. 2 of
        the *Insurance Companies Act* 1982 and itself committed breaches of that section.'

G The petitions, together with voluminous affidavit evidence in support (principally that
   of the investigating officer), were served on the companies on 14 December, no
   intervening communication having been received from the department after 23 August
   nor any indication that the companies were or might be trading unlawfully.

   On 19 December there was a hearing before Ferris J when both sides were present. By
   that stage a director of both companies had sworn an affidavit whose principal purpose
H was to oppose an application, first made by the Secretary of State on 16 December, for
   the appointment of a provisional liquidator. In it he said:

        'The companies do not believe that they have carried out insurance business
        contrary to s. 2 of the *Insurance Companies Act* 1982 or done anything else which
        is unlawful. In the circumstances they fully intend vigorously to defend the petition
        to wind them up.'

Later he said: A

> 'If, which is denied, there has been a breach of s. 2 of the *Insurance Companies Act*
> 1982, such breach has been committed without intent or an intention to deceive
> and in any event no policyholder has suffered any loss as a result of any such
> breach.'

The application for a provisional liquidator was stood over to come on for hearing
before the judge on the first available date after 31 January 1995, with a time estimate of   B
two days and liberty to apply to fix a date on the basis that the matter required a certain
degree of expedition. Also before Ferris J were cross-applications by the companies for
relief pursuant to s. 127 of the 1986 Act and a direction that the petitions should not be
advertised. They were supported by a further draft affidavit sworn by the same director.
Upon undertakings by the companies, in particular an undertaking not to write any new
insurance business or to renew any existing insurance policies in the UK, whether as   C
agent or otherwise, other than with insurance companies which were authorised to carry
on insurance business in the UK, the judge made an order under s. 127 whose effect, it is
agreed, was to enable the companies to carry on business except in the respects covered
by the undertaking.

Ferris J refused the companies' application for an order restraining advertisement. In
doing so, he said:
                                                                                       D
> 'I have been directed to what was said in the cases of *Coulon Sanderson & Ward
> Ltd v Ward* (1986) 2 BCC at p. 99,207 . . . That was a case where objection was
> taken to the presentation of a petition. The principle was applied to a case where a
> similar argument was raised in connection with advertisement, in *S N Group plc v
> Barclays Bank* [1993] BCC at p. 506, and it was held by Parker J that the same
> principle was applicable.
>   E
> The principle, as I apprehend it, is that a party which has presented a petition
> should not be restrained from proceeding with that petition, including the
> advertisement of the petition in accordance with the rules, unless there is prima
> facie evidence that the petition is more or less bound to fail, in which case the court
> may be prepared to conclude that the petition is an abuse of the process. It could
> not possibly be said in this case that the petition of the Secretary of State is more
> or less bound to fail, or that its presentation was an abuse of the process.'   F

The judge refused the companies leave to appeal. On 22 December they applied for the
leave of this court.

The original return date for the petitions was today, 18 January. It has now been put
back until 1 February. Last week, the Secretary of State having intimated his intention
to initiate the procedure for advertisement today, the companies asked for this   G
application to be dealt with urgently. A direction was made for it to come on for an early
inter partes hearing before the full court, with the appeal to follow if leave was granted.
Further evidence has now been filed in the shape of an affidavit sworn on 16 January by
another director of the second company to which reference will be made hereafter. The
companies' detailed evidence on the merits is not yet ready. Both sides believe that it will
be possible to have an effective two-day hearing of the application for a provisional
liquidator, possibly of the petitions as well, in early February. The companies seek a   H
direction restraining advertisement of the petitions over that hearing.

In this court the case has been argued on behalf of the companies and the Secretary of
State by Mr Kosmin QC and Mr Kaye QC respectively, neither of whom appeared before
the judge. The arguments have been fuller than they were below and additional
authorities have been cited. The basic submission of Mr Kosmin is that the judge was

A   wrong to equate the test to be adopted on an application to restrain advertisement of a petition already on the file with that adopted on an application to restrain the presentation of one which has not yet reached it.

In *Coulon Sanderson & Ward Ltd v Ward* (1986) 2 BCC 99,207 this court, building on its earlier decision in *Bryanston Finance Ltd v De Vries (No. 2)* [1976] Ch 63, propounded a general rule that the court should not on an interlocutory motion, whether made ex parte or inter partes, restrain what would otherwise be the legitimate presentation of a

B   winding-up petition by someone qualified to present it, unless the company establishes on the evidence a prima facie case for holding that the petition would constitute an abuse of process. That that test cannot be equally applicable to a restraint on advertisement is primarily and conclusively demonstrated by the discretion exercisable under r. 4.11(1), an exercise which does not come into a decision on abuse of process. Moreover, Mr Kosmin has referred us to an observation of Buckley LJ in the *Bryanston Finance* case at

C   p. 78F and to the decision of Eichelbaum J in the New Zealand High Court in *Morgan Roche Ltd v Registrar of Companies* (1987) 3 NZCLC 100, 189, both of which support the view that there is a clear distinction between the two tests.

While emphasising that he was not referred to some of the authorities most in point, I therefore respectfully think that Ferris J was wrong in equating the two tests. As for *S N Group plc v Barclays Bank plc* [1993] BCC 506, on which the judge relied, I am doubtful whether Jonathan Parker J, at p. 508G, was saying anything more than that the

D   advertisement of a petition already on the file which constitutes an abuse of process will be restrained in like manner as its presentation. If he was saying that, he was right. If he was saying more than that, his view was obiter and in my respectful view wrong.

What then is the test to be applied in the case of a public interest petition presented under s. 124A? The conduct of such a petition is governed by the rules in ch. 3 of Pt. 4 of the 1986 rules, which, as their language recognises, apply principally to creditors'

E   petitions. Although it is not uncommon for a public interest petition to contain an allegation, usually subsidiary to others, that the company is insolvent, there is no necessity for such an allegation, it being obvious that it must sometimes be in the public interest that a solvent, even a profitable, company should be wound up. But it is no less obvious that in applying a provision such as r. 4.11(1) to such a case there are relevant considerations different from those applicable where there is an allegation of insolvency,

F   the position being more akin to a contributory's petition, where, under r. 4.23(1)(c) in ch. 4, it is left to the court to direct on the return day or afterwards whether and, if so, by what means the petition is to be advertised.

The different considerations were recognised by Brightman J in *Re Golden Chemical Products Ltd* [1976] Ch 300, a case where the petition had been presented by the Secretary of State under the then equivalent of s. 124A. At p. 309G, he said:

G   'The advertisement of a winding up petition is highly damaging to the reputation of a company and is likely to lead creditors to believe that the company is no longer able to meet its liabilities, although in fact it may be fully solvent . . . I think that Mr Muir Hunter is entirely correct when he says that the power given to the Secretary of State by section 35 is of a most formidable nature, which may cause serious damage to the reputation and financial stability of the company.'

At p. 310H, the judge said:

H   '. . . having regard to the implications for a company if a winding up petition is presented under section 35, I think that the Department of Trade might consider whether it would, generally speaking, be right to defer advertising the petition (unless the court otherwise directs) until the last moment that is practical, provided that the company in question desires to continue trading and is not prima facie insolvent.'

It has been rightly pointed out that Brightman J suggested only that advertisement　A
might be deferred. He did not suggest that it might be dispensed with. That no doubt was
because until 1979 the matter was governed by r. 28 of the *Companies (Winding-up)
Rules* 1949, under which advertisement, sooner or later, was mandatory. The
observations of Brightman J are nevertheless valuable in determining the approach of the
court to the advertisement of a public interest petition under r. 4.11(1).

Mr Kaye has told us on instructions from the Treasury Solicitor that, so far as he is　B
aware, there has been no case in which the advertisement of a public interest petition has
been restrained, either permanently or temporarily. It appears that the only reported case
in which the question has arisen is *Re Normandy Marketing Ltd (Company No. 007946
of 1993)* [1993] BCC 879; [1994] Ch 198 where Morritt J, correctly in my opinion, held
that since r. 4.11(1) requires advertisement unless the court otherwise directs, it is for the
company to show sufficient reason to depart from the normal practice. On the facts of
that case and in the exercise of his discretion, the judge refused to direct that the petition　C
should not be advertised. He assumed that an early determination of the petition was
unlikely and observed that it would not be consistent with the normal practice of the
court to permit a petition to remain unadvertised for a lengthy period. Here Ferris J did
not exercise his discretion because he thought, erroneously, that he had to apply a test in
which no such exercise was involved. That means that we in this court must exercise our
own discretion in the matter and we must, I think, exercise it in the circumstances of the　D
case as they stand today.

It is helpful to start with a consideration of the purposes of advertisement. The primary
purpose must be to give notice of the petition to those who are entitled to be heard on it,
namely the creditors (whether actual, contingent or prospective) and contributories of
the company. Although it was held in the early days of limited liability that the judge has
a discretion to hear someone who has no such entitlement to be heard 'as amicus curiae,
if you have an interest, that I may know what public grounds there are' – see *Re Bradford　E
Navigation Co* (1870) LR 5 Ch App 600 at p. 603, per James LJ, it is difficult to think of
circumstances in which the court would exercise that discretion in the case of a public
interest petition, where the interests of the public generally are necessarily represented by
the Secretary of State. The secondary, but no less important, purpose of advertisement
must be to give notice to those who might trade with the company during the period
between the presentation of the petition and its final determination and who might thus　F
be adversely affected by the provisions of s. 127 of the 1986 Act.

In the light of those purposes, how ought the discretion to be exercised in the present
case? Its principal features appear to be the following. First, there is no allegation, either
in the petition or in the supporting evidence, that the company is insolvent. Second, on
the assumption that the allegations made in the petitions will be proved, there is not, on
the arguments we have heard, any substantial ground for thinking that the rights of　G
policyholders under policies unlawfully effected by the companies, whose rights will lie
primarily, if not exclusively, against the insurers, will have been prejudiced. Third, it
appears from the evidence in support of the petitions that the contributories of the
companies are either their directors or companies owned or controlled by them. Fourth,
the companies' undertakings to the court on 19 December will ensure that no further
unlawful business is undertaken. Fifth, the order then made under s. 127 will ensure that,
in regard to business lawfully undertaken thereafter, third parties will be protected.　H

It therefore appears that a restraint on advertisement, at all events in the short term,
would not deprive creditors of the companies, who may or may not include policyholders,
of any significant advantage they would otherwise have had; that the contributories
already have effective notice of the petitions; and that those who might trade with the
companies during the period between the presentation of the petitions and their final

A   determination will be protected by the order under s. 127. Those considerations would not, however, together provide a sufficient ground for departing from the normal practice. Unless the companies can show that advertisement may, in the words of Brightman J, cause serious damage to the reputation and financial stability of the companies, advertisement there must be.

     The case for the companies on this aspect of the matter has been compendiously stated

B   in the affidavit sworn on 16 January. In summary, it is said that all the directors of the companies have unblemished records; that the insurance industry operates in a closed world where the placing of business depends very much on the confidence that one individual has in the reputation of another; that knowledge of the existence of the petitions amongst others in the industry will inevitably cast a slur on the directors' reputations, which in turn will inevitably do lasting damage to their business prospects as well as putting it beyond doubt that the companies will never be able to trade again;

C   and, in short, that if the petitions are advertised the effect will, in practice, be the same as if the companies were wound up, so that there would be little point in their continuing to oppose them. The affidavit also criticises the lack of communication by the department, between the completion of the oral enquiries and the presentation of the petitions, and of any preliminary warning to the companies. While those criticisms are barely relevant to anything we have to decide today, I will, without going into detail, record my opinion that they are unjustified.

D   Although it has been well observed that the harmful effects of advertisement are liable to be exaggerated, as they may have been here, the companies' evidence is in my view sufficient to establish that it could cause serious damage to their reputation and financial stability. Adding that consideration, first, to the likelihood that if there is no advertisement in the short term no significant disadvantage will be caused to those whose interests must also be considered and, secondly, to the likely imminence of the hearing of

E   the application for a provisional liquidator, I have come to the view that we ought to direct that the petitions should not be advertised over that hearing. Thereafter the matter will rest with the decision of the judge conducting it.

     I would therefore give the companies leave to appeal and allow their appeal accordingly.

F   **Waite LJ:** I agree that an application by a company for an interlocutory order restraining presentation of a public interest petition altogether on the ground of alleged abuse of the process stands in a different category from cases where the relief sought by the company is limited to a direction under r. 4.11(1) of the Insolvency Rules prohibiting or postponing advertisement of the petition; and that the two forms of application fall to be dealt with on different principles.

     Where it is sought to restrain presentation of the petition, there must be prima facie

G   evidence that the company would succeed in establishing that the proceedings sought to be restrained would constitute an abuse of process – *Coulon Sanderson & Ward Ltd v Ward* (1986) 2 BCC 99,207 applying *Bryanston Finance Ltd v De Vries (No. 2)* [1976] Ch 63.

     Where, on the other hand, the company applies only for a direction against advertisement, the court is not so much concerned with protecting its own process from abuse as with the need to strike a fair balance between two different aspects of public

H   policy. One is the concern of the court to ensure that the proceedings are brought to the attention of all those who may be presumed to have an interest in resisting or supporting them – i.e. actual, contingent and prospective creditors, contributories, and those dealing or proposing to deal with the company in the ordinary course of its business. The other is an appreciation by the court of the serious consequences for the reputation and financial stability of the company to which advertisement of the petition may give rise

(see *Re Golden Chemical Products Ltd* [1976] Ch 300 per Brightman J at p. 309). The   A
circumstances of each particular case (given the starting point that the onus is on the
company to show sufficient reason to depart from the normal practice of advertisement
– see Morritt J in *Re Normandy Marketing* [1993] BCC 879) will determine how those
objectives are to be reconciled.

In the present case the judge incorrectly applied the abuse of process test to the issue
of advertisement. His error requires the discretion under r. 4.11 to be exercised by this   B
court. For the reasons given by Nourse LJ, with which, as with all the reasoning in his
judgment, I am in full agreement, I would exercise that discretion by ordering that the
petitions should not be advertised over the relatively short period that is anticipated to
elapse between now and the conclusion of the hearing of the application for the
appointment of a provisional liquidator.

I too would allow the appeal.
  C

*(Leave to appeal granted and appeal allowed, with costs; para. 6 of judge's order of 19
December 1994 discharged, and direction given in terms to be agreed between counsel.
Leave to appeal to the House of Lords refused)*

D

E

F

G

H

A
Re a Company No. 007923 of 1994 (No. 2).
Re a Company No. 007924 of 1994 (No. 2).
Chancery Division (Companies Court).
Knox J.
Judgment delivered 28 February 1995.

B
Public interest winding-up petitions – Whether insurance brokers were carrying on unauthorised insurance business – Whether insurance brokers were aiding and abetting carrying on of unauthorised insurance business – Whether brokers should be wound up in public interest – Insurance Companies Act 1982, s. 2; Insolvency Act 1986, s. 124A.

These were petitions presented by the Secretary of State pursuant to s. 124A of the
C Insolvency Act 1986 for the winding up of two companies in the public interest.

The companies acted as insurance brokers, dealing with offshore insurers and reinsurers. Neither the companies nor the insurers nor the reinsurers were authorised to carry on insurance business in the UK under the Insurance Companies Act 1982. Their activities amounted to the carrying on of insurance business in the UK by the offshore insurers through the companies as agents contrary to s. 2 of the Insurance Companies Act 1982. The
D companies were not agents of the reinsurers.

Held, dismissing the winding-up petitions:

1. The companies were not themselves in breach of s. 2 but they aided and abetted the insurers in committing breaches of s. 2. The companies' directors believed their activities to be lawful, although their investigations into the legality of what they proposed and did was totally inadequate. Had there been no other relevant features, those considerations would
E have led to the making of winding-up orders since it was in the public interest that unlawful activities were made to cease and were discouraged.

2. However, the business done by the companies was not intrinsically against the public interest. The risks insured against were perfectly normal; the companies' authorities from the insurers required the risks to be fully reinsured; the underwriting was done carefully as the favourable claims experience showed; and claims were met promptly in accordance with reputable loss adjusters' advice. There was no evidence of the public being misled or financial
F unsoundness or of inadequate books. The evidence fell some way short of establishing the potential insolvency that the Secretary of State suggested was shown.

3. A second mitigating factor was the degree of uncertainty about the precise ambit of carrying on insurance business and the fact that the directors believed they were acting lawfully.

G
4. It was material that the directors of the companies had taken steps to replace on renewal all insurances with authorised insurers or with Lloyd's.

The following cases were referred to in the judgment:

Bedford Insurance Co Ltd v Instituto de Resseguros do Brasil [1985] QB 966.
D R Insurance Co v Seguros America Banamex [1993] 1 Ll Rep 120.
Jacob (Walter L) & Co Ltd, Re (1989) 5 BCC 244.
Pepper v Hart [1992] BTC 591; [1993] AC 593.
H
Phoenix General Insurance Co of Greece SA v Halvanon Insurance Co Ltd [1988] QB 216.
R v Jefferson [1994] 1 All ER 270.
Sayce v Coupe [1953] 1 QB 1.
Scher & Ors v Policyholders Protection Board [1994] 2 AC 57.
United General Commercial Insurance Corp Ltd, Re [1927] 2 Ch 51.

Roger Kaye QC and Stephen Moverley Smith (instructed by the Treasury Solicitor)　A
for the petitioner.

Terence Cullen QC and Fernanda Pirie (instructed by Berrymans) for the companies.

JUDGMENT

Knox J: There are before the court petitions presented by the Secretary of State for
Trade and Industry for the winding up of two companies, No. 007923 and 007924 of　B
1994, pursuant to s. 124A of the *Insolvency Act* 1986. That reads so far as relevant:

> 'When it appears to the Secretary of State from–
>
> (a)　any report made or information obtained under Part XIV of the Companies
>   Act 1985 . . .
>
> that it is expedient in the public interest that a company should be wound up, he
> may present a petition for it to be wound up if the court thinks it just and equitable　C
> for it to be so.'

There was an investigation made under s. 447, which is within Pt. XIV of the
Companies Act 1985, by Mr Matthew Thomas Sullivan, a chartered accountant, into
company No. 007923 of 1994 and company No. 007924 of 1994 and these petitions are
based on his findings.

There were also adjourned to be heard at the same time applications for the　D
appointment of provisional liquidators of the same two companies, but those
applications have not been pursued before me since such appointments would be either
inappropriate or unnecessary according to whether or not winding-up orders are made.
The winding-up petitions have not been advertised pursuant to an order of the Court of
Appeal on 18 January 1995 (see [1995] BCC 634).

I have reached the conclusion that although company No. 007923 of 1994 and　E
company No. 007924 of 1994 have been involved in the carrying on within this country
of an illegal business, it would not, in all the circumstances of the case, be just and
equitable for me to order them to be wound up. My reasons are as follows.

The issues on these petitions were almost entirely limited to questions of law and how
discretion should be exercised by the court rather than questions of fact. Both company
No. 007923 of 1994 and company No. 007924 of 1994 are insurance brokers. They have,
at all material times, only dealt with other brokers and insurance companies from whom　F
they have held binding authorities and they have not, therefore, had any direct dealings
with the insured members of the public. The insurers, from whom binding authorities
were held, were successively Societe Centrale D'Assurances Sal (Lebanon), which I will
call 'SCA Sal' and Baltic Insurance Group (Lithuania), which I will call 'Baltic'. All risks
insured were 100 per cent reinsured. The principal reinsurers involved were Dai Ichi
Kyoto Reinsurance Co SA (Belgium) ('Dai Ichi') and Kobe Reinsurance SA (Belgium)　G
('Kobe').

The business in which company No. 007924 of 1994 and company No. 007923 of 1994
were involved and which gave rise to these petitions was insurance of commercial
premises where the risks were difficult to place either because of the insured's trade or the
locality of the insured premises.

The business was originally the product of two approaches received by Mr 'P', a　H
director of both company No. 007924 of 1994 and company No. 007923 of 1994, who
was their principal witness before me. The first was in 1992 from M Elie Chebli, who
controlled SCA Sal, a small Lebanese insurer, which Mr Chebli suggested could insure
risks if a suitable reinsurer could be found. The second approach was from Mr John
Mitchell, whom Mr P already knew as a representative of Dai Ichi and Kobe. Mr Mitchell
said that those companies were reinsurance companies only and were looking for insurers

A   to reinsure. Dai Ichi and Kobe are both registered in Belgium. They are not authorised to carry on insurance business in Belgium, but in Belgium, unlike this country, reinsurance business as opposed to insurance business carried on in Belgium does not have to be authorised. Neither company No. 007924 of 1994, company No. 007923 of 1994, SCA Sal, Dai Ichi or Kobe have ever been authorised in this country to carry on insurance business within the UK.

B   The manner in which the business was handled in this country, at first by company No. 007924 of 1994 until June 1993 when company No. 007923 of 1994 took over most of its functions, was not significantly in dispute and it was accepted before me by Mr Cullen, on behalf of company No. 007924 of 1994 and company No. 007923 of 1994, that the activities involved amounted to the carrying on of insurance business within the UK by the insurers, SCA Sal and Baltic, through their agents, company No. 007924 of 1994 and company No. 007923 of 1994. Those were not admissions which were made by C   those insurers, who are not parties to these proceedings, but they do make it unnecessary to go into minute details of how the business was conducted.

The following statements contained in the petition before me regarding company No. 007923 of 1994 were accepted as factually correct. I quote:

'(a) It is the main link in organising a consortium of insurers and reinsurers who offer in the UK a product or insurer's package known as combined commercial D   insurance.

(b) It negotiates with brokers seeking insurance on behalf of clients.

(c) It, through its directors or staff, sets the amount of premium sought in each case and sends an offer to the client's brokers to insure for such premium.

(d) It deals with the paperwork for completing the insurance contract and accepts the premiums.

E   (e) If necessary, it instructs surveyors to examine the risks sought to be insured and decides on any requirements with which the insured must comply.

(f) It collects premiums and distributes commissions following appropriate deductions from the premium moneys collected.

(g) It procures the issuing of policies and forwards them to the insured's brokers. It appears that the paperwork for such policies is done in England and a director F   of the company, Mr P, signs them on behalf of the insurers. He apparently takes them to Cyprus and signs them there, but this is a cosmetic exercise of no real significance.

(h) It receives claims forwarded by brokers for the insured.

(i) It reviews, and if appropriate settles, claims of less than £1,000.

(j) It refers claims of £1,000 or more to loss adjusters. If the loss adjusters G   recommend settlement up to £50,000, the company arranges payment without reference to the insurers or their reinsurers.

(k) If the loss adjusters recommend settlement of between £50,000 and £200,000, the company refers the matter to another English company in London (CRM) who have authority to agree payment without reference to the overseas reinsurers and insurers.'

H   Similar statements applied to the activities of company No. 007924 of 1994 before July 1993 after which company No. 007923 of 1994 took over the underwriting activities, which were based in Bolton, while company No. 007924 of 1994, based in London, dealt with the onward transmission to insurers and reinsurers of net premiums and bordereaux.

The binding authorities which company No. 007924 of 1994 and later company No. 007923 of 1994 had were on terms that the risks should be fully reinsured. This was done

by means of reinsurance treaties into which the reinsurers, Dai Ichi and Kobe, entered,   A
which bound them to reinsure the risks that the insurers SCA Sal and Baltic insured.
There was a close link between the reinsurers and company No. 007924 of 1994 and
company No. 007923 of 1994 in that both Dai Ichi and Kobe were represented in London
by CRM Insurance Services Ltd ('CRM'), a company which owns 35 per cent of the
issued share capital in company No. 007924 of 1994 and is itself owned by two directors
of company No. 007924 of 1994 other than Mr P.

In November 1993, the reinsurers, Dai Ichi and Kobe, agreed to the addition to the   B
policies issued of a cut-through clause which permitted the insured to approach the
reinsurers direct. This did not purport to confer any legal rights upon the insured against
the reinsurers, nor did it do so, but it could well have been of practical utility had it been
necessary to rely upon it, an event which, on the evidence, has not occurred.

Another aspect of the business of company No. 007924 of 1994 and company No.
007923 of 1994 not mentioned in the petitions was the creation of a £500,000 retention   C
fund out of premiums payable to the insurers and reinsurers between November 1993
and April 1994. This was held by company No. 007923 of 1994 in a separate account in
order to enable claims to be met quickly although legally the money was payable to the
reinsurers had they demanded it. In fact, it was never resorted to for either the purpose
of meeting claims or to pay the reinsurers, but it remains intact.

The evidence of the directors of company No. 007924 of 1994 and company No.   D
007923 of 1994 was that the arrangements by way of binding authority given by the
insurer within stated limits for individual risks on terms of 100 per cent reinsurance and
for reinsurers to enter into reinsurance treaties binding themselves to reinsure any risk
accepted by the insurers were in accordance with normal practice in the insurance
industry, as was the cut-through clause. There was no evidence to the contrary filed by
the Secretary of State. Indeed, the principal witness for the Secretary of State was Mr
Sullivan, the chartered accountant, who had conducted investigations under s. 447 of the   E
Companies Act 1985, but he disclaimed any familiarity with either the insurance industry
or its practices.

I therefore accept the directors' evidence on the above-mentioned matters regarding
what is normal practice. In the circumstances, I see no reason to disregard the clear legal
structure of insurer and reinsurer with the former, but not the latter, giving a broker a
binding authority. This serves to dispose of the suggestion that was put more than once   F
to witnesses for company No. 007924 of 1994 or company No. 007923 of 1994 that those
companies were agents for the reinsurers. The actions of the directors and staff of
company No. 007924 of 1994 and company No. 007923 of 1994 in underwriting risks on
behalf of the insurers had the known effect of binding the reinsurers because the
reinsurance treaties were the mirror image of the binding authorities given by the insurers,
but that did not make company No. 007924 of 1994 or company No. 007923 of 1994 the   G
agents of the reinsurers.

Reliance was placed, on behalf of the Secretary of State, upon the inadequacy of the
investigations made by the directors of company No. 007924 of 1994 and company No.
007923 of 1994 before embarking upon the business. Their investigations as to the legality
of what they were proposing to do and later on were doing were indeed totally
inadequate. This was the main obstacle to my exercising my discretion against making
winding-up orders.   H

The attitude that what is commonly done must be permissible is a very dangerous one
and not one which I would wish to encourage, but it is the main explanation rather than
justification for the belief which I accept the directors of company No. 007924 of 1994
and company No. 007923 of 1994 genuinely held that the activities of those companies
were not illegal.

A Mr P, who was the director principally concerned with the management of company No. 007924 of 1994, although a director of both companies, said he was aware that some insurance companies were authorised in this country and some were not, but that he understood a company did not need authorisation to place a risk with an offshore insurer so long as the broker revealed that it was not authorised. He denied that the scheme, as it evolved, was devised in order to avoid the need for authorisation and I accept that evidence. Mr P assumed that what his companies did was just placing risks with offshore

B insurers and that was the point where he fell into error. Although his practice of signing in Cyprus the policies issued by SCA Sal was explained by him as one which he followed because he did not think it right to sign on their behalf outside their office and they had no office in England, I do not accept that was the whole story. I find that he wished to preserve the image of an offshore insurer because he was in a rather imprecise way aware that company No. 007924 of 1994 and company No. 007923 of 1994 needed to be seen

C to be placing risks with offshore insurers.

When the switch from SCA Sal to Baltic was effected in April 1994, the practice of signing policies outside this country was continued, but they were signed on Baltic's behalf in Brussels. It was not suggested by anyone that the place where the policy was signed could, of itself, be determinative of the question whether insurance business was being carried on within the UK and that makes the note to s. 2(1) of the *Insurance*

D *Companies Act* 1982, which I will call 'the ICA 1982', at p. 165 of *Halsbury's Statutes*, vol. 22, under 'Carry on . . . insurance business', 'Insurance business is carried on where the contracts are made and the policies of insurance are issued, not where the risks are situated; see *Re United General Commercial Insurance Corp Ltd* [1927] 2 Ch. 51', well capable of misleading. It did not mislead Mr P or his fellow directors because they made no legal enquiries whatever, let alone consult *Halsbury's Statutes* or the notes therein.

E One of the other directors who gave evidence was, if anything, even more ignorant of the law governing insurance business. Mr J was the director primarily responsible for company No. 007923 of 1994 underwriting in Bolton and his evidence was that he did not even know that some companies needed to be authorised to carry on insurance business in the UK since he was unaware of the concept of authorisation.

Mr B, the director of company No. 007923 of 1994, concerned with the financial as opposed to the underwriting side of the business, said that he had heard of the ICA 1982

F and that he knew of the need for authorisation to carry on insurance business within the UK, but that as all company No. 007923 of 1994 was doing was acting under a binding authority, he did not think there was anything wrong in what was done.

There was no suggestion made that the business done by company No. 007924 of 1994 and company No. 007923 of 1994 was intrinsically against the public interest. The risks

G insured against were perfectly normal. The claims experience was exceptionally favourable to date with only some ten per cent of premium income in the way of claims, but this was attributed, in significant measure, to good luck as well as careful surveys before risks were accepted and it was not suggested that such favourable claims experience would continue in the long term.

The financial substance of the insurers and reinsurers was the subject of criticism on

H behalf of the Secretary of State. So far as SCA Sal was concerned, it was common ground that it had no substantial assets, but as it carried none of the risk that feature was submitted not to imperil the insureds' security. Baltic, on the evidence, does have more substantial assets, viz. US$40m, although some doubt was cast upon their location and the extent to which they were under the control of their auditor, Prof Dr Walter Missorten. Their initial accounts only covered the period 25 May to 30 June 1993 and stated that Baltic would start operating on 1 August 1993, but they stated share capital

at US$40m, of which $18,000 were capitalised start-up expenses, and the balance cash   A
and securities valued at fair market price.

Mr Sullivan's principal affidavit says that:

> 'These accounts purport to have been audited by Blanckaert Missorten
> Spaenhoven & Co, representatives in Brussels of the Horwath international
> network of accountants. The audit certificate purports to have been signed in
> Vilnius by Prof Dr W Missorten.'   B

The use of the word 'purport' twice over, if and in so far as it carries any implication
that the accounts were not prepared and signed by reputable and competent accountants,
was only supported by evidence of a conversation by a third party with Dr Missorten,
who is reported to have said that he, Dr Missorten, had not verified the assets, but had
relied on a director's valuation of those assets which he understood to be in Lithuania
under the director's control. In the light of the 100 per cent reinsurance of these policies,   C
the financial soundness of the reinsurers is of far greater moment than that of the insurers,
but I would observe in passing that a statement that the company's assets are within the
director's control is not in itself either surprising or alarming.

As regards the reinsurers, there was put in evidence a good deal of press speculation
about the irregularities in the conduct of Dai Ichi some three years ago and, more
seriously, doubt about the ownership of Dai Ichi which does appear to have migrated   D
from Japan to Delaware to this jurisdiction without much compliance with the
requirements of company law.

I do not find it necessary to set out the detail of these matters because what seemed to
me to be significant for my purposes is how the directors of company No. 007924 of 1994
and company No. 007923 of 1994 conducted themselves regarding Dai Ichi and Kobe as
very important reinsurers upon whose financial stability the business which they handled
very largely depended. For this purpose, I am satisfied that Dai Ichi was a company that   E
needed investigation by the directors of company No. 007924 of 1994 and company No.
007923 of 1994 before they could conscientiously embark upon the scheme which they
promoted.

The directors of company No. 007924 of 1994 and company No. 007923 of 1994 in
general, and Mr P and Mr B in particular, accepted that the financial soundness of Dai
Ichi and Kobe was very important and they claimed to have made adequate enquiries on   F
the subject. What they did, according to Mr P, was initially to obtain the balance sheets
of Dai Ichi and Kobe which showed that their accounts were audited by reputable
auditors, in the case of Kobe by a representative of Deloitte Touche Tohmatsu, with
whom Mr B checked up shortly before December 1992 and received a reply that they
were indeed the auditors and that the financial statements for the 19 months ending 31
March 1992 gave a true and fair view.   G

As regards Dai Ichi, the auditors for the year ending 31 December 1992 were a Belgian
firm with offices in Belgium, Luxembourg and Germany, about whom I heard no
evidence. Secondly – and I suspect as far as Mr P is concerned more importantly – he
obtained a list of brokers, insurance companies and Lloyd's syndicates, which was sent
by an agent of Kobe saying it was a list of persons dealing with Kobe and Dai Ichi. Mr
P checked with a small number out of a very long list and heard nothing to put him off.   H

Thirdly, Mr P passed over what information he had to his accountant, Mr Passmore,
who is acquainted with insurance business as well as being a chartered accountant, and
asked him what he thought. Mr P, in his oral evidence, did not say that Mr Passmore
gave him a positive clearance as he had said to Mr Sullivan during the latter's
investigations, but he did say that he heard nothing against the reinsurers from Mr
Passmore.

A   By the time that negative was established, company No. 007924 of 1994 had received its binding authority dated 1 November 1992 from SCA Sal and was conducting this business with Dai Ichi and Kobe as reinsurers. These were enquiries which were less than thorough given the critical importance of the soundness of the reinsurers and in this respect too I consider that the directors of company No. 007924 of 1994 are open to criticism. In fact, their optimism was reinforced by the receipt by Mr J of a Standard & Poor rating dated August 1993 for the year 1992 which rated Dai Ichi as BBisc.

B

The evidence before me was that numerous quite reputable insurers have such a rating and I accept that a small company like company No. 007924 of 1994, without a security department, was entitled to be encouraged by it, more especially in view of the fact that their business was of a short tail nature. None of its directors took time to study the text or figures of the Standard & Poor rating and I do not propose, therefore, to examine it. I heard evidence from Mr Stephen John Forrest of FMW International Insurance Brokers

C   Ltd that in the latter part of 1993, his company had investigated company No. 007923 of 1994 and its relations with Dai Ichi and Kobe and was satisfied as regards the latter.

The loss adjusters employed by company No. 007923 of 1994 were also consulted and they gave company No. 007923 of 1994 a clean bill of health. It was also verified that professional indemnity cover was held by company No. 007923 of 1994 and in general Mr Forrest's company was content to do and did do business with company No. 007923

D   of 1994 and appreciated that the cover offered was offshore, but took the view that it did not need authorisation.

Mr Sullivan's last affidavit contained evidence that Standard & Poor had given Dai Ichi a 'U' rating as at October 1994, i.e. no rating, but that is so close to the date when the petition was presented that it does not impinge significantly upon the steps taken by the directors of company No. 007924 of 1994 and company No. 007923 of 1994 to

E   monitor the performance and standing of the reinsurers they were using.

Overall, I take the view that the directors of company No. 007924 of 1994 and company No. 007923 of 1994 cut corners and relied very much on market talk to assess and monitor their reinsurers' financial standing, but they were not out of line in this respect with the attitudes adopted by numerous other brokers who did business with them while acting for clients. Such brokers were, in the great majority, aware who the

F   reinsurers were and were at liberty to, and in some cases did, make their own enquiries which did not, in general, put them off.

The first main issue of law was whether Mr Cullen, for the Secretary of State, was right in submitting that company No. 007924 of 1994 and company No. 007923 of 1994 were themselves in breach of s. 2(1) of the ICA 1982. It reads:

'Subject to the following provisions of this section, no person shall carry on any

G   insurance business in the United Kingdom unless authorised to do so under section 3 or 4 below.'

Section 14 of the 1982 Act provides that the unauthorised carrying on of insurance business is a criminal offence. Section 3 provides for the grant of authorisation by the Secretary of State. Subsection (1) reads:

'The Secretary of State may authorise a body to carry on in the United Kingdom

H   such of the classes of insurance business specified in Schedule 1 or 2 to this Act, or such parts of those classes, as may be specified in the authorisation.'

Section 4 provides for the continuation of authorisation under the previous Insurance Companies Act, in this case the 1981 Act. The rest of Pt. I of the ICA 1982 provides for the mode and conditions for the grant and withdrawal of authorisation under s. 3. For example, s. 7 provides inter alia as follows:

'(1) The Secretary of State shall not issue an authorisation under section 3 above   A
to an applicant whose head office is in the United Kingdom unless the applicant is:

    (a) a company as defined in section 735 of the Companies Act 1985 or article 3
         of the Companies (Northern Ireland) Order 1986, or

    (b) a registered society, or

    (c) a body corporate established by royal charter or Act of Parliament and
         already authorised under section 3 or 4 above to carry on insurance business   B
         (though not to the extent proposed in the application).

. . .

(3) The Secretary of State shall not issue an authorisation under section 3 above
to an applicant whose head office is in the United Kingdom if it appears to the
Secretary of State that any director, controller, manager or main agent of the
applicant is not a fit and proper person to hold the position held by him.'   C

There is a similar provision to s. 7(3) in s. 9(5), which deals with applicants from
outside the Community.

Part II of the ICA 1982 provides for the regulation of insurance companies to the
extent indicated in s. 15, subs. (1) of which provides:

    'Subject to the provisions of this section, this Part of this Act applies to all   D
    insurance companies, whether established within or outside the United Kingdom,
    which carry on insurance business within the United Kingdom.'

Later subsections. qualify that general provision. Subsequent sections of Pt. II of the
ICA 1982 provide for a variety of requirements such as annual accounts, balance sheets
and margins of solvency which, in my view, make it plain beyond argument that
companies carrying on insurance business within the UK, so that Pt. II of the ICA 1982
applies to them, are limited to the principal insurers and do not extend to agents of such   E
insurers.

Similarly, the scheme of Pt. I of the ICA 1982, in my view, makes it clear that it is
principal insurers and not their agents that are intended to be within the ambit of that
Part. The expression 'carrying on insurance business' is not defined as such in the ICA
1982 although insurance business is described by s. 95 in terms which all start with the
words, 'The effecting and carrying out of' a variety of transactions of one sort and   F
another. Similarly, Sch. 2 to the ICA 1982, which sets out the classes of business into
which insurance business is now classified for authorisation purposes, also describes each
class in terms which start, 'Effecting and carrying out contracts of insurance . . .' There
is one slight exception to this. In the second part of class 15, suretyship, such transactions
as fidelity bonds are not called contracts of insurance, but nothing turns on this.

The conclusion therefore follows that carrying on an insurance business within the UK   G
within the meaning of the ICA 1982 is an amalgam of effecting and carrying out the
relevant contracts and that equally necessarily it involves a whole range of activities
which include, but are far from limited to, making the relevant underwriting decisions,
processing premiums and dealing with and settling claims: compare *Scher v Policyholders
Protection Board* [1994] 2 AC 57 at p. 101 by Lord Goff of Chieveley.

The parties are understandably at one in agreeing before me that on the evidence the   H
business conducted by company No. 007924 of 1994 and company No. 007923 of 1994
was insurance business and that the totality of the acts done by those companies
amounted to carrying on insurance business within the UK by the relevant insurers under
whose authority company No. 007924 of 1994 and company No. 007923 of 1994 acted.
Re United General Commercial Insurance Corp Ltd [1927] 2 Ch 51 shows that a single
factor, such as the location of the risk insured against, is not determinative. As already

A   mentioned, it is not authority for the proposition that the place where the policy is signed is determinative either.

     The submission was made to Mr Adrian Hamilton QC, sitting as a deputy High Court judge, in *D R Insurance Co v Seguros America Banamex* [1993] 1 Ll Rep 120, that the test was whether the business was carried on substantially in Great Britain. He did not have to adopt that formulation any more than I do because there is no issue before me but
B   that what was done in the UK did indeed amount to carrying on insurance business here. In the *D R Insurance Co* case, the contention which Mr Adrian Hamilton QC had to deal with and rejected, rightly if I may say so, was that it was essential to the carrying on of insurance business in the UK that the final decision to effect the insurance be taken within the UK. That reinforces the conclusion that no such single act out of the multiplicity of acts that go to make up the carrying on of insurance business can be isolated and treated as determinative of a place where such business is carried on.

C   For the Secretary of State, it was argued that because company No. 007924 of 1994 and company No. 007923 of 1994 did the physical acts in question, they were carrying on insurance business here and the fact that they did not carry the insurance risk was irrelevant. Reliance was placed on the width of the prohibition in s. 2 of the ICA 1982, 'no person shall carry on any insurance business in the United Kingdom unless authorised', and on the fact that this is wider in scope than the enabling and regulatory
D   provisions in the following sections of the Act which were limited to, for example, provisions regarding authorisations for bodies, which unlike the expression 'person' does not include individual humans, to carry on insurance business.

     This is correct in that the prohibition and the original sanction are directed at a wider field of possible offenders than the field of potential authorised insurers. It is necessary to prevent enterprising, but financially insubstantial individuals from carrying on insurance
E   business within the UK, but it does not prove anything about the meaning of the phrase, 'carrying on insurance business'.

     Similarly, analogies drawn from the fields of tort and the general law of principal and agent do not seem to me to advance the argument. It was submitted, correctly, that where an agent commits an unlawful act on behalf of a principal, principal and agent are both liable, but that begs the question by postulating an unlawful act in the first place. The issue here is whether the unlawful act is carrying on an insurance business as principal or
F   whether it is carrying it on whether as principal or agent and that must turn on the provisions of the ICA 1982.

     In my view, the ICA 1982 is so framed that it is clear that when it speaks of carrying on insurance business, it is referring to the risk-bearing activity that an insurer embarks on as a whole. That conclusion is reinforced by a consideration of what the situation would be if Mr Kaye's argument, for the Secretary of State, was right on this point and
G   there was an insurer situated outside the UK which was authorised to carry on certain classes of insurance business within the UK, but it did so through a binding authority to a broker in this country, which was given authority rather on the lines of those given to company No. 007924 of 1994 and company No. 007923 of 1994 in this case, and acted upon it and effectively carried on the business singlehanded without any reference to the authorised principal.

H   If Mr Kaye's construction of the meaning of 'carrying on insurance business' is right, the broker, as well as the insurer, would be carrying on the business and would need authorisation. It would be surprising, to put it mildly in those circumstances, if the broker incurred criminal penalties for lawfully operating its principal's authorised and lawful business unless the broker also obtained an authorisation. No such difficulties arise if the ICA 1982 is construed as referring to the conduct by an insurer when it speaks of carrying on an insurance business.

On that basis, I do not consider that company No. 007924 of 1994 and company No.   **A**
007923 of 1994 committed a breach of s. 2, but that brings me to the second issue,
whether they aided and abetted the insurers in such breaches. In my view, they did. That
the insurers were in breach was accepted by Mr Cullen. He also accepted that the
common law notion of aiding and abetting an offence was of general application to all
statutory offences unless specifically excluded by statute.

R v Jefferson [1994] 1 All ER 270 was accepted by both sides as establishing that. In   **B**
Jefferson's case, the appellant was convicted of aiding and abetting the offence of violent
disorder, an offence under s. 2(1) of the *Public Order Act* 1986 which reads:

> 'Where three or more persons who are present together use or threaten unlawful
> violence and the conduct of them (taken together) is such as would cause a person
> of reasonable firmness present at the scene to fear for his personal safety, each of
> the persons using or threatening unlawful violence is guilty of violent disorder.'   **C**

It was submitted for the appellant that s. 6 of the 1986 Act required a particular *mens
rea* for that and other offences, the particular relevant provision being s. 6(2), which
reads:

> 'A person is guilty of violent disorder or affray only if he intends to use or threaten
> violence or is aware that his conduct may be violent or threaten violence.'

This was argued to have the effect of making violent disorder an offence for principals   **D**
only and, in particular, to exclude s. 8 of the *Accessories and Abettors Act* 1861, which
reads:

> 'Whosoever shall aid, abet, counsel, or procure the commission of any indictable
> offence, whether the same be an offence at common law or by virtue of any Act
> passed or to be passed, shall be liable to be tried, indicted, and punished as a
> principal offender.'   **E**

As to this argument, Auld J said, giving the judgment of the Court of Appeal, Criminal
Division (at p. 280e):

> 'In our judgment, the offences created by the 1986 Act may be committed by aiders
> and abettors as well as by principals. As counsel for the Crown pointed out, the
> question is not whether s. 6 of the 1986 Act excludes s. 8 of the 1861 Act, and it is
> only in part one of construction. An aider and abettor of an offence is a common   **F**
> law notion, not a creation of statute. It is of general application to all offences,
> whether at common law or of statutory creation, unless *expressly excluded* by
> statute. Section 8 of the 1861 Act is merely a deeming provision as to how aiders
> and abettors are to be dealt with at trial. The proper approach is to consider
> whether there is anything in the 1986 Act which excludes, in relation to the public
> order offences created by it, the general common law principles of aiding and   **G**
> abetting.
>
> In our view, s. 6 is concerned only with identifying, in statutory form, the requisite
> mens rea for each of the offences provided for in ss. 1–5. It does not exclude or cut
> down in relation to any of those offences the liability of an aider and abettor who
> is aware of and party to the requisite intent of the principal offender.'

It seems to me that by the words 'expressly excluded', which I have emphasised, Auld   **H**
J probably intended to refer to a statutory provision which necessarily excluded liability
as an aider and abettor just as much as to a statutory provision which said in terms, 'No
one shall be liable to be punished for aiding and abetting such-and-such a crime.' That
seems to me to follow from the next sentence where he states the proper approach to be
to consider whether there was anything in the 1986 Act which excluded the general
common law principles of aiding and abetting. Whether I am right or not about that, the

A   minimum requirement is that it should be a necessary implication from the statutory language; probability is not enough.

Mr Cullen submitted that there was such a necessary implication to be found in two sections of the ICA 1982. The first was s. 74, which authorises regulations to be made for requiring intermediaries, who make offers to persons to take any steps with a view to entering into insurance contracts in relation to an insurance company which is not an authorised insurer, to inform the person to whom the invitation is made that the insurer
B   is not authorised. Regulations have been made.

In my view, this falls a long way short of proving that Parliament intended to prevent intermediaries, who aided and abetted insurers in breach of s. 2 of the ICA 1982, from being prosecuted for aiding and abetting. The regulations under s. 74 seem to me to be aimed at a different field, namely, those who are only acting as intermediaries of unauthorised insurers, who are not committing breaches of s. 2. If s. 74 and the
C   regulations thereunder are thus construed, they do not carry any implication, let alone a necessary implication, that intermediaries may not commit the offence of aiding and abetting an infringement of s. 2.

The other section relied upon by Mr Cullen was s. 91. Subsection (1) provides:

> 'Where an offence under this Act committed by a body corporate is proved to have
D   been committed with the consent or connivance of, or to be attributable to any neglect on the part of, any director, chief executive, manager, secretary or other similar officer of the body corporate or any person who was purporting to act in any such capacity, he, as well as the body corporate, shall be guilty of that offence and liable to be proceeded against and punished accordingly.'

Here again, I remain quite unconvinced that there is a necessary incompatibility between the limited extent of liability in the stated events of senior officers and employees
E   of corporate offenders on the one hand and liability by agents generally for aiding and abetting an of fence under s. 2 on the other. Here again, although there might possibly be an overlap between the circumstances that fell within both offences, the offences are significantly different. Under s. 91, only individuals of particular seniority and guilty knowledge are made punishable for of fences under any part of the ICA 1982 of their corporate body. The general offence of aiding and abetting a breach of s. 2 is, in my view,
F   essentially different; in some respects wider and in others narrower, but there is no impossibility at all involved in contemplating that Parliament, at one and the same time, intended to punish senior officers in the circumstances stated in s. 91 and, at the same time, make agents or others liable for aiding and abetting offences under s. 2.

Mr Cullen advanced a floodgates argument against aiding and abetting of offences under s. 2 of the ICA 1982 being itself an offence in that very large numbers of persons, notably including insured persons, would be guilty of the offence. He cited *Sayce v Coupe*
G   [1953] 1 QB 1 for the proposition that a purchaser of goods could be guilty of the offence of aiding and abetting an unlawful sale where he knows the circumstances which made that sale unlawful.

Lord Goddard CJ there said at p. 8, in answer to an argument that since the relevant statute (the *Tobacco Act* 1842) did not make it an offence to buy but only to sell tobacco by a person who was not a licensed dealer, the court should hold that the offence of
H   aiding and abetting should not be preferred. He said:

> 'The statute does not make it an offence to buy, but obviously, on ordinary general principles of criminal law, if in such a case a person knows the circumstances and knows, therefore, that an offence is being committed and takes part in, or facilitates the commission of the of fence, he is guilty as a principal in the second degree, for it is impossible to say that a person who buys does not aid and abet a sale.'

If anything, *Sayce v Coupe* seems to me to support the Secretary of State's case on   A
aiding and abetting because it illustrates the difficulty in implied exclusions of the offence
of aiding and abetting. The appellant's submission, rejected by Lord Goddard CJ, did at
least show a strong argument by implication that Parliament, while forbidding sale in
stated circumstances, did not intend to penalise the purchaser from the simple fact that
only sales and not the correlative purchase was prohibited, but that was not enough.
Moreover, in relation to the floodgates argument, it is to be borne in mind that what the
ICA 1982, s. 2(1) prohibits is carrying on a business rather than the sale of an article and   B
I do not accept that the very simple corollary between prohibited sale and purchase of an
article necessarily applies to the prohibited conduct of a business and a single transaction
with a third party in the course of that business. The link is far looser.

Similar considerations, in my view, govern what was said in Parliament on the second
reading of the Insurance Companies Bill, to which I was referred in reliance on *Pepper v
Hart* [1992] BTC 591; [1993] AC 593. Assuming, for the moment, that there is sufficient   C
ambiguity in the ICA 1982 to render what was said in Parliament admissible in evidence
at all, it does no more than evince a decision not to regulate the activities of brokers to
any extent greater than that specifically provided for. I do not, for my part, see that that
amounts to awarding them carte blanche to aid and abet their principals' offences under
the ICA 1982.

Finally, on this aspect, I am fortified by what was said, albeit obiter, by Parker J in   D
Bedford Insurance Co Ltd v Instituto de Resseguros do Brasil [1985] QB 966. In that case,
agents, Gerald Herbert Ltd, in breach of the financial limitation on their authority and
without the knowledge or consent of Hong Kong resident insurers, who had no
authorisation to carry on insurance business of the relevant class under the provisions of
the *Insurance Companies Act* 1974, which correspond to s. 2(1) of the ICA 1982, did the
following things: (1) they wrote in London, on the plaintiffs' behalf, a large number of
risks; (2) collected premiums and settled claims thereon in London; (3) reinsured such   E
risks as to part; and (4) paid premiums and collected claims under such reinsurances.

Of that state of affairs, Parker J said this at p. 980E:

'It is clear that, through Gerald Herbert Ltd. and/or Mr. Gerald Herbert, and with
the consent and connivance of Mr. Gerald Herbert, their director, the plaintiffs
were throughout the years 1977 to 1982 carrying on insurance business in London
in contravention first of the Act of 1974 and later of the Act of 1981. The plaintiffs   F
and, by virtue of section 79 of the Act of 1974, Mr. Gerald Herbert were thus
throughout the period from 1973 guilty of offences under first one and then the
other Act. Gerald Herbert Ltd. aided and abetted those offences for it is clear from
the documents that they knew full well that what they were doing was illegal and
deliberately set out to create a false impression.'

The issue in the proceedings was whether the reinsurance contracts were void through   G
illegality, as Parker J held they were, a decision later approved and followed by the Court
of Appeal in *Phoenix General Insurance Co of Greece SA v Halvanon Insurance Co Ltd*
[1988] QB 216, but substantially reversed by s. 132 of the *Financial Services Act* 1986.

The question whether Gerald Herbert Ltd were guilty of aiding and abetting the
plaintiffs in the illegal conduct of insurance business was not something which Parker J
had to decide, but it is clear enough that Parker J had no doubt that the offence against
the prohibition against unauthorised carrying on of insurance business in this country   H
was committed by the unauthorised foreign principal insurer, aided and abetted by the
agent in this country, which performed all the acts that constituted the carrying on of the
unauthorised insurance business. His views were, in my view, not only obiter, but also
right in a case which, in the factual background to the issue of illegality of reinsurance,
bore a striking resemblance to the one now before me.

A   This brings me to the question of how I should exercise the discretion, which it was common ground exists, whether or not to order the respondent companies to be wound up. It was argued that I should be guided by what Nicholls LJ said in *Re Walter L Jacob & Co Ltd* (1989) 5 BCC 244 where the Court of Appeal, reversing the decision of Harman J, who had dismissed a public interest winding-up petition presented by the Secretary of State, said (at p. 250H):

B   '. . . the opinion of the Secretary of State that it is expedient in the public interest that a company should be wound up is the prerequisite to the presentation by him of a winding-up petition under s. 124(4)(b).'

I pause there to observe that the jurisdiction is now in s. 124A of the *Insolvency Act* 1986, but nothing turns on the amendments which are purely formal. Nicholls LJ continued at p. 251A:

C   'Forming and holding the relevant opinion gives the Secretary of State standing to present his petition. That is their only legal effect. . . .

A petition having been duly presented by the Secretary of State, the next stage is when the petition comes before the court. At this second stage, the court is concerned with the whole of the evidence before it and the submissions made thereon by the parties. The court is not concerned with what was the material D before the Secretary of State at the earlier stage when he formed his opinion. Nor, it seems to me, is the opinion as such of the Secretary of State, or an official in his department, reached at the earlier stage on whatever factual matter was before him in a report made by inspectors, or resulting from a books and papers investigation, normally of materiality to the Companies Court when it decides the petition. The court's task, in the case of so-called public interest petitions, as in the case of all other petitions invoking the court's winding-up jurisdiction under s. 122(1)(g), is E to carry out the balancing exercise described above, having regard to all the circumstances as disclosed by the totality of the evidence before the court. In respect of all such petitions, whoever may be the petitioner, the court has to weigh the factors which point to the conclusion that it would be just and equitable to wind up the company against those which point to the opposite conclusion. It is to the court that Parliament has entrusted this task, in all cases. Thus, where the F reasons put forward by the petitioner are founded on considerations of public interest, the court, if it is to discharge its obligation to carry out the balancing exercise, must itself evaluate those reasons to the extent necessary for it to form a view on whether they do afford sufficient reason for making a winding-up order in the particular case.

In the case of "public interest" petitioners, the court will, of course, carry out that G evaluation with the assistance of evidence and submissions from the Secretary of State and from other parties. When doing so the court will take note that the source of the submissions that the company should be wound up is a government department charged by Parliament with wide-ranging responsibilities in relation to the affairs of companies. The department has considerable expertise in these matters and can be expected to act with a proper sense of responsibility when seeking a winding-up order. But the cogency of the submissions made on behalf of H the Secretary of State will fall to be considered and tested in the same way as any other submissions. His submissions are not ipso facto endowed with such weight that those resisting a winding-up petition presented by him will find the scales loaded against them. At the end of the day the court must be able to identify for itself the aspect or aspects of public interest which, in the view of the court, would be promoted by making a winding-up order in the particular case. In many, perhaps most, cases that will be a simple exercise in which the answer will be self-evident. In other cases the answer may not be so obvious.'

I turn to the third matter which formed the subject-matter of argument before me, namely, the consequences pursuant to s. 132 of the *Financial Services Act* 1986 of the insurance contracts in the present case having been effected in contravention of s. 2(1) of the ICA 1982. This is an independent point from the issues whether company No. 007924 of 1994 and company No. 007923 of 1994 have been acting illegally and is one which would have arisen in any event given the admission that the insurers were in contravention of s. 2 of the ICA 1982.

Under s. 132(6) of the *Financial Services Act* 1986, contracts in contravention of s. 2 of the ICA 1982 are only partly invalidated, that is to say, to the extent provided for by the earlier parts of the section. The general principle is that the insured can recover any money paid and receive compensation for any loss sustained as a result of having paid it. There are two qualifications to this. First, anyone relying on his right to recover money paid cannot enforce the contract of insurance and, secondly, the court has a discretion to allow money paid under the contract to be retained if it is satisfied (a) that the person carrying on insurance business reasonably believed that his entering into the contract did not constitute a contravention of s. 2 of the ICA 1982 and (b) that it is just and equitable for the money paid to be retained. The section in fact refers not only to money paid, but also to property transferred, but where, as here, the contract is for insurance against a money premium, it is only money paid that has any practical significance.

There are various matters to be observed on the potential operation of s. 132 of the *Financial Services Act* 1986. First, it is against the insurers that remedies for recovering the premium are primarily conferred since it is the insurer that was the contracting party. Secondly, it does not necessarily follow that the insured would seek to recover their premiums. Those who had successful claims met would be most unlikely to do so because they would have to refund their claim, but even those who had not successfully claimed might well prefer to continue to have the benefit of their insurance policy rather than claim a refund and set about finding a fresh insurer. It is to be assumed that the primary objective of the insured was to secure insurance cover rather than secure an adventitious benefit by way of refund of premiums through the rights conferred by s. 132 of the *Financial Services Act* 1986.

Thirdly, although it is not for me to anticipate a decision of the court, charged with the task of deciding the point, I do not rate highly the chances of the insurers succeeding in satisfying the court that they reasonably believed that their entry into insurance contracts did not constitute a contravention of s. 2 of the ICA 1982. If, as seems likely, they took as few steps as the directors of company No. 007924 of 1994 and company No. 007923 of 1994 to verify the legal position, it is not easy to see how it could be said their belief was reasonable. It may even be that they had no belief at all on the subject, but had not bothered to consider the point.

Fourthly, if and to the extent to which claims were made against company No. 007924 of 1994 and company No. 007923 of 1994, the premium reserve of £500,000 is an available source of funds, but in relation to premiums paid over to the insurers it does not seem to me that company No. 007924 of 1994 and company No. 007923 of 1994 are liable at all. Overall, I have reached the conclusion that the evidence falls some way short of establishing the potential insolvency that Mr Kaye, for the Secretary of State, suggested was shown.

Finally, before I summarise the factors that have influenced me in my decision, I should mention that I have not attached significant weight to the proposal made at one time on behalf of company No. 007924 of 1994 for an indemnity bond to be entered into.

A   This never materialised into a transaction at all and did not, in my view, warrant the description of 'a scheme' as suggested on behalf of the Secretary of State.

I turn to consider the factors for and against making a winding-up order. The most important argument in favour of making winding-up orders is the fact that both company No. 007924 of 1994 and company No. 007923 of 1994 have engaged in illegal activities on a substantial scale. Allied to that is the fact that virtually no attempt was made to find out whether what was done was or was not lawful. It is, of course, the responsibility of those who conduct businesses to ensure that their activities are lawful. Had there been no other relevant features, those considerations would have led me to make winding-up orders since it is in the public interest that unlawful activities are made to cease and are discouraged.

In particular, it is entirely unsatisfactory for directors just to assume that because their colleagues in the same line of business do not raise any questions as to the propriety of their activities, those activities comply with the law. However, there are other factors which, I believe, mitigate the above consideration.

First of all, the business, questions of authorisation apart, was perfectly legitimate and above board. In this respect, there is a major distinction from *Re Walter L Jacob & Co Ltd* where the respondent company's business was found to fall below generally accepted minimum standards of commercial behaviour. In the case before me, the evidence was that it was difficult, when the business started in 1992, to obtain cover in the UK market for difficult risks such as those dealt in by company No. 007924 of 1994 and company No. 007923 of 1994. To the extent that that need was satisfied, it was beneficial to the insured. The underwriting was done carefully, as was the surveying as the favourable claims experience shows. In addition, claims were met promptly in accordance with reputable loss adjusters' advice. On the other hand, this was not, on the evidence, cut price insurance likely to lead to the sort of insurance débâcle which has caused scandal in the past. There was no evidence of the public being misled or financial unsoundness or of inadequate books. Generally, the reputability of the business, authorisation apart, goes some way to mitigate the illegality. It does not, of course, excuse it, but what I have to decide is whether I should impose the severe penalty of winding up, and not whether the two companies have been conducted in a blameless way.

A second mitigating factor is the degree of uncertainty that there is about the precise ambit of carrying on insurance business. That is perhaps best illustrated by the fact that submissions were made to me on behalf of the Secretary of State which seemed to me incorrect. There is also the note in *Halsbury's Statutes*, which I have already remarked upon, which is apt to mislead. All this would be of greater weight if there was any evidence that the directors of company No. 007924 of 1994 and company No. 007923 of 1994 took any legal advice, but they did not. Nevertheless, I do not consider that it would be right for me not to give credit for the fact which I have found that the three directors whom I heard giving evidence all honestly believed that they were acting lawfully and that others of considerable experience in the same line of business took the same view.

It is, however, high time that it was widely recognised in insurance circles that the authorisation requirements of the ICA 1982 do not automatically become inapplicable if the insurer is an offshore entity and that what is critical is where the insurance business is carried on. Although it was held in *Re Walter L Jacob & Co Ltd* that it was no sufficient answer that the respondent company had ceased its offending practices just before the petition was presented, it is of materiality that the directors of company No. 007924 of 1994 and company No. 007923 of 1994 have at once taken steps to replace on renewal all insurances with authorised insurers or with Lloyd's. I accept the submission made to me by Mr Cullen that it was not shown to be necessary to wind up the two companies in order to protect the public.

Finally, although, as I have found earlier, the enquiries made into the financial   A
standing of the reinsurers left a good deal to be desired, I do not consider that those
shortcomings should tip the scales in favour of making up winding-up orders. I have
found this very much a borderline case and I would emphasise that I am not by any
means absolving the directors of company No. 007924 of 1994 and company No. 007923
of 1994 from blame. I have reached the conclusion that the public interest does not
require me to make a winding-up order in either case and I decline to do so.

B

(Order accordingly)

C

D

E

F

G

H

A ## Re Pearl Maintenance Services Ltd.
Re Pearl Building Contracts Ltd.

Chancery Division (Companies Court).
Carnwath J.
Judgment delivered 2 March 1995.

B *Receivership – Payment of preferential debts out of assets subject to floating charge – Whether debenture created floating charge over book debts – Whether proceeds of book debts assigned under factoring agreement were floating charge assets – Whether receivers should continue in office after debenture-holder fully paid off – Insolvency Act 1986, s. 40.*

This was an application by receivers of two companies for directions under s. 35 of the Insolvency Act 1986. The companies had entered into an agreement with 'TSB' by which
C they factored their book debts to TSB. The companies had also given TSB a debenture granting a 'specific' charge over the companies book debts. TSB appointed receivers to the companies in February 1994. TSB was fully paid off on 9 March 1994. The companies went into creditors' voluntary winding up on 12 April 1994.

The issues raised were, in summary: (1) whether the charges over book debts created by the debentures were floating charges; (2) whether the proceeds of the book debts assigned to
D TSB under the factoring agreement were floating charge assets for the purpose of the receivers' duties under s. 40 of the Insolvency Act 1986; (3) whether the receivers should continue in office once TSB was fully paid off and whether an agreement between TSB and the receivers for TSB to collect the book debts after TSB was paid off and receive commission for doing so was effective. (There were also issues as to interest on the amounts held by TSB and whether certain fees were properly claimed by the receivers.)

E *Held*, giving directions accordingly:

1. The charge in the debentures was a floating charge. There were no restrictions on the freedom of the company to realise its book debts, and to use the proceeds in the ordinary course of business. (Re Brightlife Ltd (1986) 2 BCC 99,359; [1987] Ch 200 applied; Re New Bullas Trading Ltd [1994] BCC 36 considered.)

2. The proceeds of the book debts were floating charge assets for the purpose of the
F receivers' duties under s. 40. Section 40 applied in the case of a debenture 'secured by a charge which, as created, was a floating charge'. It having been established that the charge was created as a floating charge, it did not matter when or by what route the book debts found their way into the receivers' hands. Once within the receivers' hands they came within the scope of the duty under s. 40(2), and remained subject to it so long as the duty continued.

3. Although the receiver started as the appointee of the debenture-holder, statute imposed
G upon him a duty to the preferential creditors under s. 40 which was capable of having a separate life of its own. It did not cease merely because the debenture-holder was satisfied. The receiver remained under a duty to meet the claims of the preferential creditors, so far as could be done out of floating charge assets. The receivers' continuing duty under s. 40 gave them authority to make the agreement with TSB to continue collecting the book debts and receive commission.

The following cases were referred to in the judgment:
H *Brightlife Ltd, Re* (1986) 2 BCC 99,359; [1987] Ch 200.
Charge Card Services Ltd, Re (No. 2) (1986) 2 BCC 99,373; [1987] Ch 150.
Craven-Ellis v Canons Ltd [1936] 2 KB 403.
IR Commrs v Goldblatt & Anor [1972] Ch 498.
Lewis Merthyr Consolidated Collieries Ltd, Re [1929] 1 Ch 498.
New Bullas Trading Ltd, Re [1994] BCC 36.

Rottenberg & Ors v Monjack & Anor [1992] BCC 688.   A
Saunders (G L) Ltd, Re [1986] 1 WLR 215.
Welsh Development Agency v Export Finance Co Ltd [1992] BCC 270.
Westminster Corporation v Haste [1950] Ch 442.
Yorkshire Woolcombers Association Ltd, Re [1903] 2 Ch 284 (CA); [1904] AC 355 (HL).

Richard Adkins (instructed by Lawrence Graham) for the receivers.

Philip Hoser (instructed by Michael Wydra) for TSB Factors Ltd.   B

Clare Hoffmann (instructed by Judge Sykes & Harrison) for the liquidator.

JUDGMENT

Carnwath J: This is an application by the receivers for directions under s. 35 of the *Insolvency Act* 1986. They were appointed joint receivers on 25 February 1994 under two debentures created in November 1993 in favour of Chancery Factors Ltd (now TSB   C
Factors Ltd), who were also parties to a factoring agreement made at the same time. The debentures are in identical terms. The main issue is whether the receivers' duties continue for the purposes of s. 40 of the Insolvency Act, notwithstanding that the debenture-holder was fully paid off on 9 March 1994. The effective respondent is the liquidator of the two companies, whose appointment took effect on the voluntary winding up of the companies on 12 April 1994.   D

Background

The Pearl businesses were started in 1975 and operated from five regional offices in Glasgow, Manchester, Leeds, Rugby and Barnet. In November 1993 they were sold to Streetlarge Ltd, a company owned by the companies' directors. The business was mainly concerned with term maintenance contracts and special works contracts. Towards the   E
end of 1993 it became clear that the companies were faced with a cash-flow crisis, and under severe pressure from creditors. This led to the receivers being appointed by TSB on 25 February, and the companies ceasing business on 2 March. Although TSB's own interests were fully discharged by 9 March, it continued to collect book debts for the receiver; and an agreement was concluded by them on 15 April with the receiver, providing for a commission of 4.5 per cent. The company went into voluntary liquidation on 12 April 1994.   F

I am concerned principally with the terms of the factoring agreement and related debenture. The factoring agreement was signed by the companies on 9 November 1993. By it TSB agreed to 'factor book debts of your business on the terms and conditions set out below'. Material parts of the contract read as follows:

'1. *Purchase of book debts and advance payments*   G

1.1 You will sell to us and we shall purchase all debts arising from the sale of goods or the rendering of services by you on credit terms to customers of the following class or description:

All customers to which any invoice is to be rendered by you to an address in the UK or the Republic of Ireland pursuant to the relevant contract of sale (excluding those customers referred to in special terms 6.8 and 6.9) ("book debts") which are   H
in existence one day after your acceptance of this offer ("the start of factoring") and all book debts which come into existence after the start of factoring during the period of this agreement so that ownership of all book debts in existence on the start of factoring shall vest in us on the start of factoring and of all book debts coming into existence thereafter shall vest in us upon their coming to existence without further formality . . .

A 1.2 The purchase price payable by us to you for every book debt purchased by us hereunder . . . shall be the amount payable by the customer in respect of such book debt . . . less the factoring charge referred to below and less any discount or allowance allowed or allowable to the customer. We shall within seven days of our receipt of a notification relating to any book debt pay you such amount ('the advance payment') not exceeding 70 per cent of the amount specified in the notification of the book debt . . .

B 1.3 You will ensure that all invoices and other notices requiring payment of a book debt purchased by us are clearly endorsed with a notice in such form as we may for the time being approve that we have purchased the book debt concerned and the payment is to be made to us accordingly . . .

C 1.6 You will from time to time at our request and whether before or after termination of agreement arising from this offer execute and deliver to us duly stamped legal assignments in our favour in respect of all or any of the book debts purchased by us. If in relation to any book debt purchased by us hereunder such assignment shall not be effective in law or if the ownership of the book debt shall not effectively vest in us (in either such case) you will hold in trust for us and separately from your own property such book debt (or any money or other property received in payment thereof . . .).'

D Clauses 6.8 and 6.9 of the special clauses excluded certain categories of book debt, including those in respect of the Ministry of Defence and Lord Chancellor's office.

By cl. 4.1 it was provided that in the event of a customer disputing his obligation to pay a debt:

'we may at any time thereafter either require you to repurchase all or the relevant part of such book debt in which event you will immediately pay to us the repurchase price thereof or require you to reduce the purchase price to us of such book debt by an amount equivalent to that subject to rejection or in dispute . . .'

E By cl. 2 the factoring charge to be deducted in the calculation of the purchase price was fixed as a sum equal to 0.875 per cent of the amount of the book debt.

Turning to the debenture which was also executed on 9 November 1993, the relevant provisions are as follows:

F '2. The company as beneficial owner hereby charges with the payment and discharge of all moneys and liabilities hereby covenanted to be paid or discharged by the company:

. . .

(iv) by way of specific charge all book debts and other debts now and from time to time due or owing to the company;

. . .

G (vii) by way of floating security its undertaking and all its rights whatsoever and wheresoever present and/or future including those for the time being charged by way of specific charge pursuant to the foregoing paragraph if and to the extent that such charges as aforesaid shall fail as specific charges but without prejudice to any specific charges as shall continue to be effective;

But so the company is not to be at liberty to create any mortgage or charge upon and so that no lien shall in any manner arise on or affect any part of the property hereby charged either in priority to or pari passu with the charges hereby created and further that the company shall have no power to sell let part with possession or otherwise dispose of any part of the property referred to in subcl. (i)–(vi) above and shall only have power to part with or dispose of any part of the property referred to in subcl. (vii) above by way of sale in the ordinary course of its business . . .'

Statute

A

The relevant statutory provisions are contained in the *Insolvency Act* 1986. Section 35 enables a receiver of the property of a company appointed under a debenture to apply to the court for directions 'in relation to any particular matter arising in connection with the performance of the functions of the receiver'. The court may give such directions or make such order declaring the rights of persons before the court or otherwise as it thinks just. Section 40 is important and I set it out in full:

B

'*Payment of debts out of assets subject to floating charge*

(1) The following applies, in the case of a company, where a receiver is appointed on behalf of the holders of any debentures of the company secured by a charge which, as created, was a floating charge.

(2) If the company is not at the time in course of being wound up, its preferential debts (within the meaning given to that expression by section 386 in Pt. XII) shall be paid out of the assets coming to the hands of the receiver in priority to any claims for principal or interest in respect of the debentures.

C

(3) Payments made under this section shall be recouped, as far as may be, out of the assets of the company available for payment of general creditors.'

Section 175 deals with preferential debts in a winding up of the company and provides that they shall be paid in priority to all other debts.

D

Section 386 defines categories of preferential debts by reference to Sch. 6. Preferential debts include money owed to the Inland Revenue for income tax deducted at source, and other things such as VAT, car tax and social security contributions, and also employees' remuneration. Under Sch. 6 the existence and amount of preferential debts is related to 'the relevant date', which in the case of a company in receivership is the date of the appointment of the receiver by debenture-holders, and in the case of a voluntary winding up is the date of the passing of the resolution for the winding up (s. 387(3) and (4)).

E

Issues

The issues raised in this case are, in summary:

(1) Whether the charges over book and other debts created by cl. 2(iv) of the debentures were floating charges (although described in the debentures as 'specific charges').

F

(2) Whether the proceeds of the book debts assigned to TSB under the factoring agreement were floating charge assets for the purpose of the receivers' duties under s. 40.

(3) Whether the receivers should continue in office notwithstanding their having achieved sufficient realisations of the assets to enable them to discharge principal and interest due to TSB as holders of the debentures.

G

(4) Whether the agreement between TSB and the receivers entered into on 15 April, including TSB's right to the commission payments, is effective. There is also an issue as to interest on the amounts held by TSB pending the resolution of the present dispute.

(5) Certain work was done by the receivers before their formal appointment on 25 February 1994. There is a question as to whether fees are properly claimed by them.

H

Although the matter has been hotly contested before me, there was no evidence from the liquidator to explain precisely whose interest the liquidator was seeking to protect. It is true that on the figures shown to me, the amount of preferred debt is substantially greater if the 'relevant date' is that applicable to the receivership rather than that

A applicable to the liquidation. However, allowing for the expenses of the receivers and the liquidator, it seems that there is unlikely to be any money available beyond that due to preferential creditors, whichever figure is used for the preferred debts. It is not clear, therefore, who else has a substantial interest. It is said that the figures may be affected by a potential dispute about the level of the receivers' fees, but that this has not been elaborated in evidence. However, in the absence of evidence to the contrary, I must assume that the parties are conscientiously discharging their duties, and that these issues

B do matter in the real world. If not, it would be unfortunate that the diminishing assets of this company were being further dissipated by litigation between those whose job it is to realise them for the benefit of the creditors.

I should add that although the TSB have been represented before me and have generally taken a position supportive of the receivers, they are in substance neutral, apart from the issue of their commission and interest. Otherwise they have been content to

C continue to collect the book debts and hold them pending the resolution of the present dispute. The preferential creditors have not been separately represented, their interests being sufficiently covered by the receivers.

Question (1)

The first question turns on the construction of the debenture. For this purpose, it is

D correct in my view to consider it independently of the factoring agreement, which, although concluded at the same time, was designed to give rise to distinct legal rights and remedies.

On this first question, Miss Hoffmann for the liquidator submits that the charge on book debts is (as stated in the debenture) 'specific' or fixed', not 'floating'. If this is correct, then the case is outside s. 40 altogether, and the other questions arising from that

E section become academic. She does not suggest that the wording of the charge is itself conclusive. Furthermore, she concedes that, in spite of differences of wording, the essential characteristics of the present charge are not materially different from those found to constitute a 'floating charge' in *Re Brightlife* (1986) 2 BCC 99,359; [1987] Ch 200. However, she submits that the reasoning in that case has to be reconsidered in the light of the recent judgment of the Court of Appeal in *Re New Bullas Trading Ltd* [1994]

F BCC 36.

That submission faces the difficulty that the Court of Appeal in that case, far from overruling *Re Brightlife*, implicitly approved and distinguished it. Nourse LJ, who gave the leading judgment, referred without dissent to the earlier cases, starting with *Re Yorkshire Woolcombers Association* [1903] 2 Ch 284 and including *Re Brightlife*, and said (at p. 37H):

G 'In each of the previous authorities the draftsman treated book debts indivisibly, the question being to which form of charge they had, as such, been subjected. Here, for the first time in a reported case, the draftsman has deliberately and conscientiously set out to subject them to a fixed charge while they are uncollected and a floating charge on realisation. The essential question, as it has emerged in this court, is whether the law allows them to be treated in that fashion.'

H That decision has promoted considerable academic interest (see e.g. Goode, 110 LQR 592, Lightman & Moss on *Receivers* (2nd ed.), p. 35ff.). However, the court in terms treated the case as turning on the specific wording of the clause in the debenture before it. It does not give any basis for revisiting the earlier authorities in cases where the debenture does not draw the same sharp distinction between the treatment of the book debts and their proceeds. Those authorities will have been consistently acted upon by draftsmen, receivers and others. Whatever the precise limits of the *New Bullas* approach, it offers no excuse (certainly at first instance) for introducing uncertainty in relation to forms of charge whose interpretation has been treated as settled.

In the *Re Brightlife* debenture:

'. . . the significant feature (was) that Brightlife was free to collect its debts and pay the proceeds into its bank account. Once in the account, they would be outside the charge over debts and at the free disposal of the company.'

(per Hoffmann J at p. 99,363; 209). The same can be said here. There are no restrictions in the debenture on the freedom of the company to realise its book debts, and to use the proceeds in the ordinary course of business. In particular, it is not suggested that such realisation would amount to a 'sale', 'parting with possession' or 'disposal' of the book debts within the restriction in cl. 2. On the first question, in my view, the receivers are correct.

Question (2)

Question (2) has generated arguments of impressive complexity and ingenuity. In so far as I understood them, they can be summarised as follows.

Miss Hoffmann pointed to the fact that on the day following the creation of the charge over the book debts – existing and future – in favour of TSB, those same book debts (other than the excluded debts) were, by virtue of the factoring agreement, assigned to TSB. Book debts subsequently coming into existence would vest automatically. Accordingly, she says, the companies ceased to have any beneficial interest in the book debts upon which the charge could bite. If instead it were to be argued that the charge could bite on the companies' right to the purchase price under the factoring agreement, that is 'conceptually impossible', being a charge on a debt from TSB itself (see *Re Charge Services Ltd (No. 2)* (1986) 2 BCC 99,373; [1987] Ch 150 at p. 99,391; 175 per Millett J). This, she says, continued to be the position up to the appointment of the receivers. At that point the floating charge would have crystallised. Accordingly, after that date, even if the book debts were theoretically reassigned from TSB to the receivers, they would by then be fixed charge assets, and therefore outside the scope of s. 40.

Mr Adkins, for the receivers, met this problem by analysing the transactions as creating two concurrent equitable assignments of the book debts in favour of TSB in separate capacities – one as debenture-holder, the other as factor. On this basis, they remained at all times within the scope of the debenture and the floating charge, even though the factoring agreement would have priority until reassignment. He also drew attention to Court of Appeal authority to show that Millett J's 'conceptual' principle cannot be accepted without qualification or exception (*Welsh Development Agency v Export Finance Co Ltd* [1992] BCC 270). Mr Hoser, for TSB, generally supported Mr Adkins' submissions. But he also made the point – correctly in my view – that once TSB's own entitlement had been paid off, as it was on 9 March, any book debts remaining in, or coming into, TSB's hands would be held on behalf of the company, which would thus have sufficient interest on which the charge could bite.

In my view, however, refined legal analysis of this kind is not necessary. The receivers were appointed under the debenture to get in the various assets, whether subject to fixed or floating charges. The problem of categorisation for present purposes only arises under s. 40, when it becomes necessary to decide the scope of their duty to the preferential creditors. The answer must be found in the proper construction of that section. By subs. (1), it applies in the case of a debenture 'secured by a charge which, *as created*, was a floating charge'. Although not repeated in subs. (2), those words also implicitly limit the scope of the assets in respect of which the preferential creditors have priority (*Re Lewis Merthyr Consolidated Collieries Ltd* [1929] 1 Ch 498). As I see it, they require one to go back to the document which created the charge, even in relation to assets which were not

A in the company's hands, or even in existence, at the time the charge was created. As I have already found, the charge over the book debts was created as a floating charge. That having been established, it does not seem to me to matter very much when or by what route those book debts find their way into the receivers' hands. The nature of the charge *as created* remains the same. Once within the receivers' hands they would come within the scope of the duty under s. 40(2), and remain subject to it so long as the duty continued (see below).

B Question (2) must therefore be answered in the affirmative.

Question (3)

On the third question, Miss Hoffmann submits that the receivers' primary duty is to the debenture-holders; the s. 40 duties are no more than a statutory appendage. Once the primary duty has been discharged, she says, the appendage can have no separate life of

C its own. The statutory responsibility for the protection of the preferential creditors then shifts to the liquidator. She relies on dicta in two authorities. In *Re G L Saunders Ltd* [1986] 1 WLR 215, as in this case, there was a dispute between the receiver and the liquidator; the preferential creditors sided with the receiver, because the amounts having priority under a liquidation would be significantly less than under the receivership. The issue was whether the predecessor of s. 40 imposed any duty on the receiver to meet

D preferential debts out of fixed charge assets. Nourse J held that it did not (applying *Lewis Merthyr Consolidated Collieries Ltd*). In commenting (obiter) on some of the submissions of counsel for the receiver, he said (at p. 219G):

'If the debenture holder's debt has been extinguished, there is no principal or interest owing to the debenture holder and the preferential creditors can no longer look to the receiver but only to the company.'

E If these words are taken out of context, they could be read as supporting Miss Hoffmann's submission. However, it is clear that Nourse J was not addressing the situation which arises here. As he indicates earlier in the judgment (p. 218A), it was common ground that money realised from the floating charges was 'clearly payable to the preferential creditors'. There was no suggestion that their right to that payment was in any way affected by the satisfaction of the debenture-holder's entitlement.

F A similar comment may be made on the other authority – *Rottenberg v Monjack* [1992] BCC 688. In that case the judge (Judge Roger Cooke) adopted the following statement from Picarda, *Law relating to Receivers, Managers and Administrators* (2nd ed, 1990) (at p. 690H):

'Once the receiver and manager has sufficient funds to pay off the debenture-holder's debt and his own remuneration and costs, charges and outgoings incurred in the proper exercise of his powers, a receiver and manager should call a halt to

G his management of the company. His job is done and if it goes beyond this point he may be liable to account as a trespasser, as well as running the risk of getting no reward or even indemnity for his labours or expenditure.'

Again, however, the judge was not addressing s. 40, or in particular the treatment under that section of a surplus on floating charge assets. The passage from Picarda does, however, underline the importance for receivers of having a clear rule.

H In my view, the answer to this question becomes apparent if one considers the nature of the duty and rights created by s. 40. The cases show that s. 40 creates a positive duty (not merely a restriction) in favour of the preferential creditors, and that it is a duty enforceable by action in tort for damages (*Westminster Corporation v Haste* [1950] Ch 442; *IR Commrs v Goldblatt* [1972] Ch 498). Thus it is a duty which creates statutory private rights, enforceable as such by the preferential creditors. This being so, it would

be very odd if those rights disappeared, merely because the debenture-holder (who in the   A
context of these statutory rights is a third party) has been paid off. It is no answer to say
that the rights are recreated by s. 175 in the liquidation. As the figures in this case (and in
G L Saunders) show, the preferred debts under s. 175, which are determined by reference
to a different date, may be much less valuable.

Thus, although the receiver starts as the appointee of the debenture-holder, statute
imposes upon him a duty to the preferential creditors which is capable of having a   B
separate life of its own. It does not cease merely because the debenture-holder is satisfied.
The receiver remains under a duty to meet the claims of the preferential creditors, so far
as can be done out of floating charge assets.

Question (4)

In view of that answer, the fourth question, which concerns the rights of TSB to their
commission under the agreement with the receiver on 15 April, does not arise. If the   C
receivers' duty to the preferential creditors in respect of book debts continued, they had
the authority to make that agreement.

In any event, I would have held that the liquidator was bound in equity. TSB were
employed by the receivers to get in the book debts. That was a role which had to be
performed by someone, and TSB were best equipped for the task. TSB set out the terms
on which they were willing to act on 28 March, and proposed that any arrangement   D
should start from that date. By then both parties were treating the factoring agreement
as effectively dead. The new agreement was not in fact concluded until 15 April, three
days after the liquidator's appointment took effect. But, as one would expect, the receiver
and the liquidator were in communication, and the liquidator did nothing to question
the arrangement with TSB. On the contrary, at a meeting on 9 May, the liquidator (Mr
Langley) is recorded as having been 'favourably disposed' to TSB continuing to collect
debts for a fee. He even suggested that the fee should be increased 'as time goes on'.   E
According to Mr Jerrard (of TSB), that was a reference to an increase from the 4.5 per
cent agreed with the receivers. Nor is there anything from the liquidator to counter Mr
Jerrard's evidence that 4.5 per cent is a normal rate of commission for this type of work.

The circumstances fall well within the principles established by such cases as *Craven-
Ellis v Canons Ltd* [1936] 2 KB 403 (see Goff & Jones, *Restitution* (4th ed.), pp. 478ff.).

A point was also raised as to the interest to be paid by TSB on the money held by it   F
pending this dispute. Mr Hoser floated an argument, based on para. (xv) of the agreement
of 15 April, that interest should be limited to 2.5 per cent. That provides:

> '(TSB) will agree to make a rebate equivalent to $2^1/_2$ per cent per annum for
> clearance purposes from the effective date . . . on all surplus sums retained over the
> outstanding obligations of the companies of £1 each, so that we can rebut any
> challenge by any appointed liquidator.'   G

As Mr Hoser frankly admitted, this does not appear to have anything to do with the
present issue. TSB must of course account for the interest earned by it on the money
collected by it under the April agreement. On the material before me, I see no reason why
its obligation in respect of interest should be less or more than that.

Question (5)

Finally, a point was raised about the fees incurred by the receiver before his   H
appointment. The background to this is explained in the first affidavit of Mr Dobson
(solicitor for the receiver). These fees were claimed by the present applicants, not as
expenses of the receivership as such, but as costs incurred by them on instruction from
TSB under cl. 4.8 of the factoring agreement. This entitled TSB to recover from the
companies:

A
> 'any legal and other costs, charges and expenses reasonably and properly incurred by (TSB) in obtaining the release of book debts from charges or other liens or encumbrances or in enforcement of (TSB) in relation to such book debts.'

There seems no reason to question this explanation. In the end, as I understood her, Miss Hoffmann did not press the point.

B
Conclusion

In the light of the above reasoning, the receivers are entitled in substance to the relief which they seek under their originating summons of 18 July 1994. I will hear any submissions on the form of order or ancillary matters.

(Order accordingly)

C

D

E

F

G

H

Re Lineas Navieras Bolivianas SAM.

A

Chancery Division.
Arden J.
Judgment delivered 20 December 1994.

*Winding up – Stay of proceedings – Creditor arrested ship – Creditors issued writs
in rem – Whether in rem claimants needed leave to proceed – Whether claimants
should have leave – Insolvency Act 1986, s. 126–130.*

B

These were applications in the winding up of Lineas Navieras Bolivianas SA ('Linabol')
for leave to continue actions in the Admiralty Court so as to receive a share of the proceeds
of sale of Linabol's ship, 'Bolivia'.

On 7 December 1993 a creditor, 'Tramp Oil', arrested the Bolivia in Liverpool. On 29
December 1993 'Doraship' issued a writ in rem, and between 29 December 1993 and 14
February 1994 other creditors issued writs in rem. On 14 February 1994, however, Doraship
presented a petition for the winding up of Linabol as an unregistered company, since Linabol
was incorporated outside the jurisdiction. In the period from 24 February 1994 through to
12 April 1994 the five applicants issued their writs in rem. On 18 March 1994 Tramp Oil
obtained judgment in default and an order for the appraisement and sale of the ship, subject
to leave of the Companies Court. Leave was granted on 12 May 1994 provided no
distribution of the proceeds took place without further leave. On 13 April 1994 Linabol had
been ordered to be wound up. By the date of the winding-up order only one of the applicants'
writs had been served.

C

D

The question was whether the in rem claimants who issued proceedings in the Admiralty
Court between the date of the presentation of the winding-up petition and the date of the
winding-up order should be given leave to proceed in the Admiralty Court so as to receive a
share of the proceeds of sale of the ship the subject of those proceedings.

(There was a subsidiary question, whether the claimants did in fact have in rem claims. It
was common ground that their claims were arguably in rem. In those circumstances, the
question whether they were in rem claims or not was to be determined in the Admiralty
Court.)

E

Held, granting the applicants leave to proceed:

1. By arresting the ship prior to the presentation of the petition, Tramp Oil had security
and thus there could be no objection to its enforcing its security by obtaining an order for
sale. (Re Aro Co Ltd [1980] Ch 196 applied.)

F

2. The effect of the order for sale made by the Admiralty Court on the assets of the
company was to convert the company's interest in the ship into a right to receive the balance
of the proceeds of sale remaining after satisfaction of the prior claimants. As a result it
appeared that the applicants did not in fact require leave under s. 130(2) because they were
not proceeding against either the company or the company's property.

G

3. If it was necessary so to hold to avoid the effect of s. 129(2), such conversion must, in
the event of an order for sale, be deemed in law to have taken effect from the execution of
the warrant for arrest, when the ship entered the custody of the Admiralty Marshal on
behalf of the Admiralty Court.

4. Alternatively if leave were needed, leave should be given because it would be inequitable
not to grant it for the following reasons. (1) The order for sale showed that the Admiralty
Court contemplated that the proceeds of sale would be distributed by it in the usual way;
that was, prima facie, to all claimants who made their claims in time. (2) The writs were
validly issued so far as the Insolvency Act 1986 was concerned. There was nothing in any of
the provisions of the Insolvency Act to divest the applicants of their security. (3) The refusal
of leave would amount to preventing the applicants from enforcing security and would enable

H

A   some only of the claimants on the proceeds of sale to scoop the pool. (4) The ship was kept in the jurisdiction by use of the powers of the Admiralty Court and a better price was obtained because the sale was by the Admiralty Marshal as opposed to being a sale by the liquidator.

The following cases were referred to in the judgment:

Albert Life Assurance Co, Re. The Delhi Bank's Case (1871) 15 SJ 923.

B   *Aro Co Ltd, Re* [1980] Ch 196.

Australian Direct Steam Navigation Co, Re (1875) LR 20 Eq 325.

Ayerst (Inspector of Taxes) v C & K (Construction) Ltd [1976] AC 167.

Constellation, The [1966] 1 WLR 272.

Monica S, The [1968] P 741.

Roberts Petroleum Ltd v Bernard Kenny Ltd [1983] 2 AC 192.

C   *Roundwood Colliery Co, Re* [1897] 1 Ch 373.

Rudow v Great Britain Mutual Life Assurance Society (1881) 17 ChD 600.

Zafiro, The [1960] P 1.

Lionel Persey (instructed by Constant & Constant) for the applicant.

Peter Havey (instructed by Hill Dickinson Davis Campbell, Liverpool) for the respondent.

D

JUDGMENT

Arden J: These are applications in the winding up of Lineas Navieras Bolivianas SA (hereafter 'Linabol') for leave to continue actions in rem now pending in the Admiralty Court against the ship 'Bolivia'. Details of the names of the applicants appear from Exhibit ME/1 to the affidavit of Mr Nigel Emerson sworn on 22 November 1994. They are claimants nos. 8, 9, 10, 12 and 15 in that list. They are represented by Mr Lionel

E   Persey. The application is opposed by the joint liquidators of Linabol who are Mr C J Barlow and Mr N Palios. The applications were served on other creditors, but none of them appears. The liquidators are represented by Mr Peter Havey.

The question is whether the in rem claimants who issued proceedings in the Admiralty Court between the date of the presentation of a petition for winding up and the date of the winding-up order should be given leave to proceed in the Admiralty Court so as to

F   receive a share of the proceeds of sale of the ship the subject of those proceedings.

There is a subsidiary question whether the claimants do in fact have in rem claims. It is common ground that their claims are arguably in rem. In those circumstances, the question whether they are in rem claims or not should, in my judgment, be determined in the Admiralty Court and not here, but that point only arises if the application succeeds.

G   The facts can be shortly stated. On 19 November 1993 a creditor issued a writ in rem against the Bolivia. On 22 November 1993 another creditor, Doraship SA (hereafter 'Doraship') obtained a Mareva injunction against Linabol. On 7 December 1993 a third creditor, Tramp Oil Schiffahrts und Kandeligesellschaft mbH & Co KG (hereafter 'Tramp Oil'), arrested the Bolivia in Liverpool. On 29 December 1993 Doraship issued a writ in rem, and between 29 December 1993 and 14 February 1994 there were five creditors who issued writs in rem.

H

On 14 February 1994, however, Doraship presented a petition for the winding up of Linabol as an unregistered company. Linabol is a company incorporated outside this jurisdiction. In the period from 24 February 1994 through to 12 April 1994 the five applicants issued their writs in rem. On 18 March 1994 Tramp Oil obtained judgment in default and an order for the appraisement and sale of the ship, subject to leave of the Companies Court. This order was expressed in these terms:

'1. That judgment be given for the plaintiff in the sum of US \$120,357.06;   A

2. That subject to the proviso in para. 3 of this order the Bolivia be appraised and sold by the Admiralty Marshal, and that the proceeds of sale thereof be paid into court with all questions of priority being observed;

3. That the order for appraisement and sale in para. 2 of this order shall not take effect unless and until the plaintiff has obtained the leave of the Companies Court.'

Then the order dealt with costs.   B

On 12 May 1994 the registrar of the Companies Court indeed granted leave, and his order was in these terms:

'It is ordered that the applicants have leave to proceed with the appraisement and sale of the vessel Bolivia as directed by Clarke J on 18 April 1994 provided no distribution of the proceeds of sale shall take place without further leave of this court.'   C

On 13 April 1994 Linabol was wound up by the court on the petition of Doraship. The petition was not opposed. By the date of the winding-up order one only of the applicants' writs had been served. On 12 May, as I have recounted, the registrar made his order giving leave to proceed with the sale.

I now turn to the relevant provisions of the *Insolvency Act* 1986. I start with s. 126. This provides in material part as follows: D

'(1) At any time after the presentation of a winding-up petition, and before a winding-up order has been made, the company, or any creditor or contributory, may–

    (a) where any action or proceeding against the company is pending in the High Court or Court of Appeal in England and Wales or Northern Ireland, apply to the court in which the action or proceeding is pending for a stay of proceedings therein . . .'   E

I need not read further from that subsection.

Section 127 provides:

'In a winding up by the court, any disposition of the company's property, and any transfer of shares, or alteration in the status of the company's members, made after the commencement of the winding up is, unless the court otherwise orders, void.'   F

By virtue of s. 129(2) the winding up of Linabol began at the time of the presentation of the petition for winding up.

I next turn to s. 128. Subsection (1) provides:

'Where a company registered in England and Wales is being wound up by the court, any attachment, sequestration, distress or execution put in force against the estate or effects of the company after the commencement of the winding up is void.'   G

I then turn to s. 130. Subsection (2) provides:

'When a winding-up order has been made or a provisional liquidator has been appointed, no action or proceeding shall be proceeded with or commenced against the company or its property, except by leave of the court and subject to such terms as the court may impose.'   H

Therefore by virtue of s. 130 the stay took effect in this case on the making of the winding-up order. The presentation of the petition did not stop the issue or service of proceedings, although s. 126 contains a power to apply for a stay where the proceedings are against a company.

A   I now turn to s. 183 of the Act. This provides in subs. (1) that:

> 'Where a creditor has issued execution against the goods or land of a company or has attached any debt due to it, and the company is subsequently wound up, he is not entitled to retain the benefit of the execution or attachment against the liquidator unless he has completed the execution or attachment before the commencement of the winding up.'

B   All those provisions which I have read are in Pt. IV of the *Insolvency Act* 1986. Linabol was in fact wound up under s. 221 in Pt. V of that Act. I will go first to s. 220 because that defines 'unregistered company'. It says:

> 'For the purposes of this Part, the expression "unregistered company" includes any association and any company, with the following exceptions–
>
>   (a) (repealed)
>
> C   (b) a company registered in any part of the United Kingdom under the Joint Stock Companies Acts or under the legislation (past or present) relating to companies in Great Britain.'

Section 221(1) provides that:

> 'Subject to the provisions of this Part, any unregistered company may be wound up under this Act; and all the provisions of this Act and the Companies Act about D   winding up apply to an unregistered company with the exceptions and additions mentioned in the following subsections.'

I then turn to s. 229 of the *Insolvency Act* 1986. This provides that:

> 'The provisions of this Part with respect to unregistered companies are in addition to and not in restriction of any provisions in Part IV with respect to winding up companies by the court; and the court or liquidator may exercise any powers or do E   any act in the case of unregistered companies which might be exercised or done by it or him in winding up companies formed and registered under the Companies Act.'

Mr Persey submits that the provisions of Pt. V of the Act dealing with unregistered companies do not incorporate s. 128 which avoids sequestrations after the winding up, but I reject that submission because s. 221, as I have read, makes it clear that all the F   provisions of the Act about winding up apply to an unregistered company, and s. 128 is, in my judgment, such a provision. In my judgment, the effect of Pt. V of the Act is to make the whole of Pt. IV applicable in the case of an unregistered company, and in that regard see *Rudow v Great Britain Mutual Life Assurance Society* (1881) 17 ChD 600.

I now turn to the aspects of Admiralty procedure to which my attention has been drawn and which are material for this case. There are two types of claimant in Admiralty which should be distinguished. First there is the claim of a maritime lienor. In his case G   the lien attaches to the ship as soon as the circumstances occur which gave rise to the lien. In contradistinction a statutory lien granted by s. 20 of the *Supreme Court Act* 1981 does not affect the ship until the writ is issued. Section 21 of that Act deals with the manner in which Admiralty jurisdiction is to be exercised, and I draw attention to s. 21(6) which provides:

> 'Where, in the exercise of its Admiralty jurisdiction, the High Court orders any H   ship, aircraft or other property to be sold, the court shall have jurisdiction to hear and determine any question arising as to the title to the proceeds of sale.'

The effect of arrest and priorities on sale are also relevant in this case. I have been referred to a book entitled *Admiralty Jurisdiction and Practice* by Nigel Meeson from which I should like to quote. I start at p. 124 under the heading 'Property under arrest'. Mr Meeson's book states that:

'Once the warrant for arrest has been executed, the property is arrested and in the custody of the Admiralty Marshal on behalf of the court. Interference by any party with the arrest process such as removing the property to be arrested with knowledge that an arrest has been issued is a contempt of court punishable by committal, as is any interference with the custody of the property after arrest such as moving the property within the jurisdiction without authority, or removing it from the jurisdiction.'

In relation to the effect of a sale ordered by the Admiralty Court, Mr Meeson says this (at p. 142–143):

'The sale of a ship or other property by the court gives the purchaser title free of all maritime liens and other encumbrances, and after the sale all claims or demands against the ship can only be enforced against the proceeds of sale. Thus in *The Tremont* Dr. Lushington said: "The jurisdiction of the court in these matters is confirmed by the municipal law of this country and by the general principles of the maritime law; and the title conferred by the court in the exercise of this authority is a valid title against the whole world, and is recognised by the courts of this country and by the courts of all other countries." And in *The Acrux* Mr Justice Hewson said: "The title given by such process [a sale by the Admiralty Marshal] is a valid title and must not be disturbed by those who have knowledge or may receive knowledge of the proceedings in this court. So far as all the claimants against this ship before her arrest are concerned, their claims are now against the fund in this court and not against the ship properly sold to an innocent purchaser free of encumbrances . . ." '

At p. 160 Mr Meeson deals with the prima facie order of priorities in relation to proceeds of sale. He says this – and I am only going to read the material parts:

'The overall framework of priorities is straightforward and is as follows.

(i) A claim with a maritime lien ranks first and has priority over all other types of claim. However, the maritime lien attaches to the ship in connection with which the claim arose and so where the claim is enforced by means of the sister ship provision, the claim will not be to enforce a maritime lien, but will be only a statutory right of action in rem and will have the lesser priority accorded to such claims.

(ii) The claim of a mortgagee is postponed to a claim with a maritime lien whether arising before or after the mortgage and will also be subject to any claim secured by the issue of an Admiralty writ in rem issued prior to the date of the mortgage even if such claim does not carry a maritime lien . . .

(iii) The claims of others entitled to proceed by Admiralty action in rem will be subject to all maritime liens and mortgages, but will have priority over general creditors of the shipowner, except those who have perfected their execution prior to the issue of the writ in rem.

(iv) The claims of in personam creditors of the owner of the res will be last, having no priority. However, an execution creditor who has caused the ship to be seized by the sheriff pursuant to a writ of fieri facias will stand in the position of a secured creditor as from the time of such seizure. Accordingly, he will have priority over an Admiralty writ in rem issued after the execution in respect of a claim not giving rise to a maritime lien, but the execution will be subject to prior maritime lien, statutory rights of action in rem where the writ was issued prior to execution and to mortgages or other charges granted prior to execution.

(v) The owner of the res is entitled to the balance remaining, if any.'

A   I then turn to p. 166 for an explanation of why it is stated that the order is only a prima facie order of priorities, and it is there stated that the usual order of priorities is only a prima facie order and may be departed from by the court upon equitable grounds.

Subject to the effect of the presentation of the winding-up petition, the applicants here would (if their claims were to be in rem claims) be within para. (iii). It was established in *Re Aro Co Ltd* [1980] Ch 196 at p. 209B–D that a statutory in rem creditor acquires the

B   status of a secured creditor when he issues his writ. It does not matter if he does not serve it, or if he does not arrest the ship. In that case the applicant had issued his writ in rem before the presentation of the petition. He applied for leave under the predecessors of s. 130(2). The applicants were given leave to proceed with their action under what is now s. 130(2), first, because they had already acquired the status of secured creditor; second, on the basis that the court had a discretion to permit the applicants to proceed, even if by so doing they acquired priority over other creditors.

C   I would like to read some passages from the judgment. Starting at p. 209B, Brightman LJ said the following:

> 'In our judgment there is no particular reason for equating the date of the creation of the status of a secured creditor with the date of when the Admiralty jurisdiction can be said to be 'invoked' for the purposes of section 3 of the *Administration of Justice Act* 1956. It seems more logical to test the position of the plaintiffs by

D

> asking whether, immediately before the presentation of the winding-up petition, they could properly assert as against all the world that the vessel *Aro* was security for their claim, not whether they could assert that they had invoked the jurisdiction of the Admiralty Court within the meaning of section 3 of the Act of 1956. If it is correct to say, as was not challenged in the court below and is not challenged in this court, that after the issue of the writ in rem the plaintiffs could serve the writ

E

> on the *Aro*, and arrest the *Aro*, in the hands of a transferee from the liquidator and all subsequent transferees, it seems to us difficult to argue that the *Aro* was not effectively encumbered with the plaintiffs' claim. In our judgment the plaintiffs ought to be considered as secured creditors for the purpose of deciding whether or not the discretion of the court should be exercised in their favour under section 231.'

Brightman LJ then deals with the alternative ground and says as follows:

F

> 'There is an alternative approach. The dispensing power in section 231 is not in terms dependent upon the plaintiffs' establishing the status of secured creditors, but on the exercise of the court's discretion. The discretion is conferred by the words "except by leave of the court and subject to such terms as the court may impose". In section 325(1)(c) the discretion exercisable by the court in favour of the execution creditor is conferred by the words "the rights conferred by this

G

> subsection on the liquidator may be set aside by the court in favour of the creditor to such extent and subject to such terms as the court may think fit". The nature of this latter discretion has been considered in three recent cases. In *In re Grosvenor Metal Co. Ltd.* [1950] Ch. 63, 65, Vaisey J. said: 'The section seems to give the court a free hand to do what is right and fair according to the circumstances of each case.' In *In re Suidair International Airways Ltd.* [1951] Ch. 165, Wynn-Parry J. adopted the same construction of the subsection, as also did Pennycuick J. in *In*

H

> *re Redman (Builders) Ltd* [1964] 1 W.L.R. 541. We consider that those cases were correctly decided. The only appreciable difference between the wording of the two sections is that section 325 includes the words "to such extent" as well as the words "subject to such terms". This appears to us a trivial distinction on which to found a decision that the discretion under section 231 is somehow narrower than the discretion under section 325. We adopt the definition of the discretion under

section 325 as applied in the three cases mentioned and we consider that the   A
discretion of the court under section 231 gives the court an equal freedom to do
what is right and fair in the circumstances.

If the liquidator's contention were correct, it would follow that every plaintiff in
rem suing a ship already under arrest would have to cause a further arrest to be
made unless he knew for a certainty that there would be no liquidation. Quite
apart from causing additional and unproductive expense, this would be contrary   B
to the normal practice well established in Admiralty matters over the years.'

Then I can take it up at p. 210G:

'Lastly, if the court's discretion under section 231 is to be exercised only in favour
of a plaintiff who arrests, a problem will arise in every case where the second or
subsequent claimant is proceeding in the county court. The county court has no
jurisdiction to issue a warrant for arrest unless it be shown to the satisfaction of   C
the judge that it is probable that the vessel will be removed out of the jurisdiction
before the plaintiff's claim is satisfied: section 83 of the *County Courts Act* 1959.
That could hardly be proved of a vessel which is already in the custody of the
Admiralty Marshal. In these circumstances there seems to us a powerful argument
for leaving undisturbed a long established practice whereby second and subsequent
claimants protect their position by caveat against release rather than by multiple   D
arrests.

We see no virtue in confining relief under section 231 in this type of case to a
claimant who has served his writ on the ship as distinct from the claimant who has
issued his writ but not served. The service of the writ adds nothing to the status of
the claimant vis-à-vis the vessel sued. This is established by the issue of the writ. As
between plaintiff and defendant, service merely causes time to commence running
within which the defendant must enter an appearance in order to avoid being a   E
respondent to a motion for judgment by default.

We therefore reach the conclusion that leave ought to be granted to the plaintiffs
under section 231 even if it is incorrect to regard them as having been secured
creditors at the commencement of the winding up.

On these two grounds we allow the appeal.'
   F
The other member of the court was Stephenson LJ, and he asked Brightman LJ to
read the judgment of the court.

In this case, of course, writs were not issued until after the presentation of the winding-
up petition, contrary to the position in the *Aro*. Mr Havey reserved the right to challenge
the correctness of the decision in the *Aro* in the higher court. I understand that the point
which arises in this case is of importance to those practising in this field. If the applicants
do not have leave it will always be open to a creditor who is an ordinary unsecured   G
creditor to prevent the statutory in rem claimants from proceeding against the ship or its
proceeds in accordance with Admiralty jurisdiction by presenting a winding-up petition.

Mr Persey for the applicants made in essence two submissions. His first submission
was that the statutory lien attached on issue and that, he said, is established by the *Aro*.
He says that there is no distinction between those who issued before the presentation of
the petition and those who issued after.   H

His second and alternative submission was that it was right and fair that the applicants
should have leave to proceed, and he urged me to apply the test which the Court of
Appeal in the *Aro* had themselves applied in the passage which I have quoted. As regards
the reasons why he says it is fair and right that the applicants should have leave to appeal,
he submitted as follows:

A   (1)   that the only asset of Linabol within the jurisdiction was the Bolivia;

      (2)   that the ship was in the jurisdiction because it was arrested by maritime claimants invoking the Admiralty jurisdiction. Had the Admiralty jurisdiction not been invoked, there would have been no basis upon which Doraship would have been able to commence winding-up proceedings;

B   (3)   that by the time the winding up was commenced, several writs had been issued against the ship, and accordingly the Admiralty Court was seized with jurisdiction in respect of claims against and over the ship and, but for the winding up, would have administered those claims and any subsequent claims in accordance with its usual procedures;

      (4)   that the applicants have an unarguable statutory right to proceed in rem and they have exercised that right against the ship in accordance with Admiralty jurisdiction;

C

      (5)   that the Admiralty jurisdiction is derived from international convention, and in Mr Persey's submission it is desirable that maritime claims should, so far as just and possible, be dealt with by the Admiralty Court;

      (6)   that it was not right and fair that a party that does not itself have a valid action in rem should be able by the commencement of the winding-up proceedings to pre-empt and prejudice the rights of those who do have arguable statutory rights in rem simply because the latter have not yet issued proceedings, although they would have done so in the ordinary course of Admiralty procedure.

D

I should explain, as regards the last point, that, as can be seen from the order of Clarke J, the question of priorities is dealt with after sale and those who want to make a claim to the proceeds of sale have a period of time set by the Admiralty Court in which to make those claims.

E

I should also explain that Doraship had a claim which was in part an in rem claim and in part an unsecured claim.

Mr Havey for the liquidators submitted as follows. He submitted first that the arrest and sale of the ship was in the form of a sequestration. On this point he referred me to *The Constellation* [1966] 1 WLR 272. It can be seen from p. 272H that the crucial facts were as follows. A petition was presented for the winding up of the defendant company on 8 July 1965. The defendant company owned a number of vessels, and after the date of presentation of the petition various writs were issued against those vessels, which were arrested, and on 26 July an order for the winding up of the defendant company was made. Thereafter there were various applications that the vessels be appraised and sold pendente lite. The court adjourned those motions to enable the liquidator of the defendant company to apply to the Companies Court for directions, and the registrar gave leave to the liquidator to cause appearances to be entered on behalf of the defendant company in various of the Admiralty actions. He also gave leave to the plaintiffs in the case which is reported at the point at which I am reading, and to interveners to proceed with their actions, notwithstanding the terms of the winding-up order.

F

G

The terms of the order made by the registrar was that no monetary judgment was to be enforced in any such action without the leave of the Companies Court against any assets of the company other than the ship or ships to which such action related or the proceeds of sale thereon. The matter thus came before the Admiralty Court, and it is the hearing before the Admiralty Court which is reported, and the position is that the judge, Hewson J, held that although arrest and sale of a ship were equivalent to sequestration and execution for the purpose of what is now s. 128 of the *Insolvency Act* 1986, s. 128 had to be read subject to what is now s. 130(2) of the *Insolvency Act* 1986, and, in view of the leave given by the Companies Court, the Admiralty Court could and would order the

H

appraisement and sale of the three remaining vessels and declare that the order for   A
appraisement and sale previously made should be effective.

Mr Havey submits that the issue of a writ in rem and/or the service of the writ in rem
should be regarded as analogous to the taking of first steps towards sequestration. In my
judgment, whether or not this is not correct, the issue and service of the writ in rem were
not part of the process of sequestration. If the applicants had issued a warrant for arrest
of the ship and the ship had been arrested, sequestration would have occurred and s. 128   B
would apply to it, but there is nothing in the *Insolvency Act* 1986 to prevent them from
issuing or serving their writs in rem unless the court was able to stay the proceedings
under s. 126. However, I would accept that, subject to the effect of the order for sale
obtained by Tramp Oil, the applicants would need leave if they now sought to arrest the
ship or to proceed with their actions.

Mr Havey submitted as follows. First, he submitted that the applicants do not come
within the principles laid down by the Court of Appeal in the *Aro* because they had not   C
invoked the in rem jurisdiction prior to commencement of winding up and therefore did
not encumber the Bolivia with their claim prior to that date, and he refers me to the *Aro*
at an earlier passage than I have read. At p. 207B–E the argument on behalf of the
applicants in that case is set out, and in that case counsel submitted the following
propositions:

> '(i) The discretion of the court under section 231 is unfettered. The court should   D
> do what is fair and just in all the circumstances of the particular case. (ii) In
> general, in exercise of that discretion the court should allow a maritime claimant
> to commence and to continue an action in rem notwithstanding the fact that a
> winding up has commenced, in order to ensure the priority of maritime claimants
> whether the priority is that of the holder of a maritime lien, or a mortgagee, or the
> holder of a statutory lien, that is to say the holder of a statutory right of action in
> rem. A claimant who has issued a writ in rem before the commencement of the   E
> winding up should in general be allowed to continue his action, notwithstanding
> the winding up, because he has an accrued right of arrest.'

In my judgment it is apparent, as Mr Havey submits, that when the Court of Appeal
deals with these submissions in the passage that I have already read at p. 209B–D, it is
accepting the narrower proposition of counsel in the sentence which begins 'A claimant
who has issued a writ in rem', and terminating with the words 'an accrued right of arrest',   F
rather than the earlier more general proposition in the sentence beginning: 'In general, in
exercise of that discretion the court should allow a maritime claimant . . .'

Mr Havey further submits that the commencement of the winding up is the critical
time to consider the status of a creditor and whether he should be allowed to enforce his
claim or prove in the liquidation. If the creditor has 'put in force' his proceeding prior to
the commencement of the winding up, he will be permitted to continue; otherwise he will   G
not, save where there are special circumstances which would render this inequitable, and
he cites an earlier decision of the Court of Appeal, *Re Roundwood Colliery Co* [1897] 1
Ch 373 which is in fact approved in the *Aro* [1980] Ch 196 at p. 204F–H.

Mr Havey further submits that the rationale for this is that the overriding principle
behind corporate liquidation is that, once the liquidation has commenced, inroads into
the assets of the company at the expense of unsecured creditors in the liquidation ought
to be precluded and the court should exercise its discretion under s. 130(2) so that the   H
assets fall within the statutory scheme of the insolvency, i.e. so that the property should
be distributed pari passu. Mr Havey referred me to *Roberts Petroleum v Bernard Kenny
Ltd* [1983] 2 AC 192 at p. 208D.

Mr Havey also submits that there is no reason in principle, nor is there any authority,
which requires that the present applicants be allowed to escape from the statutory

A   scheme. Furthermore he submits that unless the applicants can demonstrate that they are to be treated as secured creditors, or virtually secured creditors, by reason of having put their proceedings in force before the commencement of the winding up, leave to proceed should not be given in the absence of exceptional circumstances, and he refers me to a number of textbooks which support the submission that he has already made based on *Re Roundwood Colliery*, namely *Halsbury's Laws*, vol. 7(2), para. 1884, n. 16, 17, *Palmer's Company Law*, para. 15.443 and *Corporate Insolvency Law & Practice* by Milman (2nd edn), p. 132.

B

   Finally, Mr Havey submitted that there was no exceptional circumstance in the present case, and he submitted that it was appropriate that the in rem proceedings should be dealt with in the winding up and that that would be consistent with the course taken in *Re Australian Direct Steam Navigation Co* (1875) LR 20 Eq 325.

C   Mr Havey amplified his submission on the statutory scheme resulting from a winding-up order as follows. Upon commencement of the winding up the assets passed into the statutory scheme for dealing with the assets for the benefit of all creditors. Therefore there was not the necessary unity of ownership of the vessel between the time the claim arose and the time the claim was asserted by issue of the writ in rem (see *The Monica S* [1968] P 741). If the liquidator as opposed to the Admiralty Marshal sold the vessel, it would be encumbered by the claims of those who issued their writs in rem prior to the

D   commencement of winding up when the vessel was still owned by Linabol, but it would not be encumbered by the claims of these applicants. On Mr Havey's submission there was no reason in principle why the applicants should have any claim to the proceeds of sale of the vessel superior to the other unsecured creditors, and therefore there was no basis on which leave should be given to them to enable them to convert themselves into secured creditors by continuing their actions to judgment.

E   The statutory scheme which arises on liquidation was described thus in *Roberts Petroleum Ltd v Bernard Kenny* in the passage which Mr Havey has cited.

> 'An order for the compulsory winding up of a company, or a resolution of the company in general meeting for voluntary winding up, in each case brings into operation a statutory scheme for dealing with the assets of the company: see *Ayerst v. C & K (Construction) Ltd* [1976] A.C. 167. Save for some procedural details, there is no difference in this respect between a compulsory and a voluntary winding up. The statutory duty of the liquidator in each case is to collect the assets of the
F   company and to apply them in discharge of its liabilities. For this purpose unsecured creditors, unless preferred or deferred, rank equally and share pari passu (section 317 of the *Companies Act* 1948). The assets which the liquidator is able to collect and distribute are however necessarily those which are free from a charge.'

   The nature of a company's interests in its assets once it has entered liquidation was
G   considered in more detail in a case referred to in that passage, namely, *Ayerst v C & K (Construction) Ltd* [1976] AC 167. That was also a decision of the House of Lords and Lord Diplock, giving the principal judgment in that case, said at p. 179C:

> 'The nature of a company's interest in its assets after a winding-up order had been made first fell to be considered by the Court of Chancery under the *Companies Act* 1862. It was, perhaps, inevitable that the court should find the closest analogy in
H   the law of trusts.'

He then quotes *Re Albert Life Assurance Co, The Delhi Bank's case* (1871) 15 SJ 923, and continues:

> 'The question of the beneficial ownership of the company's property was dealt with explicitly by both James L.J. and Mellish L.J. in *In re Oriental Inland Steam Co.* (1874) 9 Ch. App. 557:

"The English Act of Parliament has enacted that in the case of a winding up the   A
assets of the company so wound up are to be collected and applied in discharge
of its liabilities. That makes the property of the company clearly trust property.
It is property affected by the Act of Parliament with an obligation to be dealt
with by the proper officer in a particular way. Then it has ceased to be
beneficially the property of the company . . ." *(per* James L.J. at p. 559)

"No doubt winding up differs from bankruptcy in this respect, that in   B
bankruptcy the whole estate, both legal and beneficial, is taken out of the
bankrupt, and is vested in his trustees or assignees, whereas in a winding up the
legal estate still remains in the company. But, in my opinion, the beneficial
interest is clearly taken out of the company. What the statute says in section 95
is, that from the time of the winding-up order all the powers of the directors of
the company to carry on the trade or to deal with the assets of the company
shall be wholly determined, and nobody shall have any power to deal with them   C
except the official liquidator, and he is to deal with them for the purpose of
collecting assets and dividing them amongst the creditors. It appears to me that
that does, in strictness, constitute a trust for the benefit of all the creditors . . ."
(per Mellish L.J. at p. 560).

The authority of this case for the proposition that the property of the company
ceases upon the winding up to belong beneficially to the company has now stood   D
unchallenged for a hundred years. It has been repeated in successive editions of
Buckley on the Companies Acts from 1897 to the present day.'

In my judgment, a critical feature of this case was that on 18 March 1994 Tramp Oil
obtained an order for the sale of the ship. Once that happened, the proceeds of sale were
held by the Admiralty Court to be applied in accordance with its procedures. Tramp Oil
had arrested the ship prior to the presentation of a petition. It therefore had security (see
the *Aro* case) and thus there could be no possible objection to its enforcing its security by   E
obtaining an order for sale. Indeed following the order for sale and subsequent winding-
up order the Companies Court gave leave for the sale to proceed, albeit on terms
precluding any distribution of the proceeds of sale without leave. The effect of the order
for sale made by the Admiralty Court on the assets of the company must, it seems to me,
have been to convert the company's interest in the ship into a right to receive the balance
of the proceeds of sale remaining after satisfaction of the prior claimants. As a result of   F
conversion it would appear that the present applicants do not in fact require leave under
s. 130(2) because they are not proceeding against either the company or the company's
property. Furthermore, if it is necessary so to hold to avoid the effect of s. 129(2), I hold
that such conversion must, in the event of an order for sale, be deemed in law to have
taken effect from the execution of the warrant for arrest, when the ship entered the
custody of the Admiralty Marshal on behalf of the Admiralty Court.

If that is wrong and leave is needed, then in my judgment leave should be given. I   G
consider that both the test propounded by Mr Persey, and that propounded by Mr
Havey, are met, and in my judgment it would be inequitable not to grant leave for the
following reasons.

First, neither the ship nor the proceeds of its sale has ever been in the custody of this
court. They have at all material times been in the custody of the Admiralty Court. The
order for sale shows that the Admiralty Court contemplated that the proceeds of sale   H
would be distributed by it in the usual way; that is, prima facie, to all claimants who
make their claims in time.

Second, the writs were validly issued so far as the *Insolvency Act* 1986 is concerned.
They are not, in my judgment, affected by either s. 127 or s. 128 of that Act. There is no
reason therefore why the applicants should not be treated as secured creditors in the same

A   way as the applicants in the *Aro* were. There is nothing, as I see it, in any of the provisions of the Insolvency Act cited to me to divest the applicants of their security.

Third, the refusal of leave would amount to preventing the applicants from enforcing security and would enable some only of the claimants on the proceeds of sale to scoop the pool.

B   Fourth, the ship was kept in the jurisdiction by use of the powers of the Admiralty Court, and I am told that a better price was obtained because the sale was by the Admiralty Marshal as opposed to being a sale by the liquidator. I see that the course which I propose to take is consistent with that which was taken by the registrar in *The Constellation*. As it will be recalled, the registrar there gave leave for the claimants to proceed to money judgment in the Admiralty Court and to enforce their claims against the ship against which they had issued writs. Moreover, in that case, the arrests occurred after the presentation of the winding-up petition.

C   The conclusion which I have reached is not, in my judgment, inconsistent with that which was reached in the case to which I was referred by Mr Havey, namely, *Re Australian Direct Mutual Steam Navigation* (1875) LR 20 Eq 325. The circumstances in that case were that on 17 April 1875 the company had been ordered to be wound up and a liquidator had been appointed. After that date the master of the ship proceeded to commence proceedings in the Admiralty Court with a view to establishing a lien on a ship owned by the company for the amount due to him, and he obtained an order that the ship be arrested, and in due course the liquidator brought proceedings in the Companies Court to prevent the master from further prosecuting his Admiralty proceedings. In this case therefore the winding-up order had preceded any step which was taken in the Admiralty Court.

D   The judgment of the court was given by Sir George Jessel MR. He said as follows:

E   'In my opinion the arrest of a ship is a sequestration within the 163rd section of the Companies Act, 1862. The term 'sequestration' has no particular meaning; it simply means the detention of property by a Court of Justice for the purpose of answering a demand which is made. That is exactly what the arrest of a ship is; consequently, as I read the 163rd section, it is void in the case of a creditor who can prove under the winding-up, if the sequestration takes place after the winding-up order has been made, as is the case here. Then the only other point is whether the creditor has a maritime lien independently of the proceedings in the Admiralty Court. Whether those proceedings were necessary to complete the creditor's title, I do not mean to say; but if they were, then his title was inchoate and not complete at the time of the winding-up order, of which he had full notice. If, on the other hand, he had a complete lien before the winding-up order, the proper way of enforcing that lien was by taking out a summons in the matter of the winding-up, and asking that the property subject to the lien might be realized and the proceeds applied in satisfaction of the lien, or else that sufficient security might be given, so that the amount due to the creditor should be forthcoming. There is no hardship in this upon the creditor. Instead of going to the Admiralty Court he could have applied to this court by a process at least as cheap and at least as speedy as that in the Admiralty Court. I think the proper order will be that a sum be carried to a separate account in the winding-up to answer the claim, and thereupon all proceedings in the Admiralty Court must be stayed . . .'

As regards that decision, it seems to me that it was more convenient from the point of view of administering the winding up in that case that the master should proceed in the manner explained in the Companies Court, and that it was not unjust to require him to do so, because a sum could be set aside to meet his claim so that he would not be prejudiced. As a separate point, I note that the time which the Master of the Rolls

considered to be the appropriate time for assessing whether the master had a valid claim   A
to a lien was not the date of the presentation of the petition but immediately prior to the
making of the winding-up order. Thus the retroactive effect of the order was not taken
into account for this purpose.

Another decision was cited to me, namely *The Zafiro* [1960] P 1. This was a decision of
Hewson J in the Admiralty Court. What had happened in this case was that a company
had given notice of its intention to convene a meeting for voluntary winding up, but   B
before that meeting was held the plaintiffs had issued a writ in rem against the Zafiro and
arrested the vessel. At a later date the creditors passed a resolution that the company
should be wound up and appointed a liquidator. Subsequently the Admiralty Court
ordered that the vessel be appraised and sold, and she was in fact sold and the proceeds
of sale were paid into court. Therefore the motions before the court were on the one hand
a motion for judgment in default of defence by the arresting party against the company
in liquidation, and a motion also by the company that the action be stayed on the   C
grounds that, since the writ had been issued, the company had gone into liquidation, and
that before the plaintiffs had issued their writ in rem and arrested the ship, they had
received notice that a meeting was to be held for the purposes of voluntary liquidation.
The company also sought an order that the proceeds of sale be paid out to it after
satisfaction of the claims of the owner of another vessel who had, however, previously
obtained judgment against the Zafiro in a collision action.

Hewson J held that the arrest of the vessel was not an execution within the meaning of   D
what is now s. 183 of the *Insolvency Act* 1986, and accordingly that the plaintiffs were
entitled to keep the benefit of the arrest of the Zafiro against the liquidator in spite of the
prior notice of meeting at which the resolution for voluntary winding up was to be
proposed. He also held that, by arresting the Zafiro, the plaintiffs had become secured
creditors; and thirdly, that the general practice of the court was to stay actions against a
company after commencement of voluntary winding up, save in special circumstances. It   E
being an action for necessary disbursements (i.e. to enforce a statutory lien), Hewson J
held that, since the writ was issued and the vessel was arrested before the passing of the
resolution for voluntary liquidation (which was the time when in law the voluntary
liquidation commenced), the arrest constituted a special circumstance.

The decision in *The Zafiro* has to be read bearing in mind the subsequent decision of
the Court of Appeal in *Aro* that the issue of the writ constituted the security for an in rem   F
claimant. The point which arises in the present case did not arise in *The Zafiro*, and in
the circumstances I derived little assistance from it.

Finally, in my judgment, the situation in this case is not wholly dissimilar from that in
the *Aro*. In that case the in rem claimants obtained security on issue of their writ, because
at any time thereafter they could have arrested the ship. In this case the applicants could
likewise have arrested the ship immediately following at least the issue of their writs in   G
rem. There was no application under s. 126 of the *Insolvency Act* 1986 to prevent them
from doing so, and there must be some doubt whether an order could indeed have been
made under that section since it requires proceedings to be 'against the company'. Here
the proceedings were in rem against the ship. Section 126 does not use the words 'against
the company or its property': compare the different wording in s. 128 and s. 130(2). I
need not consider the position after the winding-up order because by that time Tramp
Oil had obtained the order for sale.   H

In those circumstances I propose to give the applicants leave to proceed.

(Order accordingly)

A
Secretary of State for Trade and Industry v Carmichael.

Edinburgh Sheriff Court.

John Horsburgh.

Judgment delivered 29 December 1994.

B
Disqualifying unfit directors of insolvent companies – Whether leave should be given for disqualification proceedings out of time – Proceedings issued one day late – Delay increased to three months by court process – Whether good cause for delay shown – Company Directors Disqualification Act 1986, s. 7(2).

This was a preliminary application to commence proceedings for a disqualification order outwith the period of two years from the date of liquidation set by s. 7(2) of the Company Directors Disqualification Act 1986.

C
Held, granting leave to proceed:

1. At each stage of the investigative and preparatory processes appropriate steps were taken, having regard to other priorities, to secure a timely and proper consideration of the case. The deadline was missed due to an unfortunate oversight and that was an acceptable explanation for the delay.

D
2. There was no prejudice to the defender which would merit the refusal of leave. The fact that the defender might be disqualified for a minimum period of two years did not constitute prejudice. That would be a consequence of the mismanagement of the company's business.

The following cases were referred to in the judgment:

Cedac Ltd, Re. Secretary for Trade v Langridge [1991] BCC 148; [1991] Ch 402.
E
Copecrest Ltd, Re [1993] BCC 844.

Crestjoy Products Ltd, Re [1990] BCC 23.

Probe Data Systems Ltd, Re (No. 3) [1992] BCC 110.

Tasbian Ltd, Re (No. 3) [1992] BCC 358.

C J Tyre (instructed by the solicitor to the Secretary of State) for the pursuer.

C S Wilson (Brodies WS) for the defender.
F

NOTE OF JUDGMENT

John Horsburgh: This is a preliminary application to commence proceedings for a disqualification order outwith the period of two years from the date of liquidation set by s. 7(2) of the *Company Directors Disqualification Act* 1986.

G
Counsel for the pursuer explained that the last day for lodging the application had been Friday, 19 August 1994, and that the defender had received timeously the ten days' notice of the pursuer's intention to apply in terms of s. 16(1) of the Act. The application had been lodged on Monday, 22 August. On 22 September it had been withdrawn with leave of the court, and a fresh one received. A hearing on competency was eventually fixed for 21 November. The original delay of one day had been increased to about three months by the court process. He made reference to r. 2 and 3 in the *Insolvent Companies*
H
(Reports on Conduct of Directors) (No. 2) (Scotland) Rules 1986 (SI 1986/1916 (S 140)) which obliged the liquidator to make a return to the pursuer within six months of the liquidation, which then gave the pursuer a further 18 months to decide whether or not an application should be made. He also referred to *Re Probe Data Systems Ltd (No. 3)* [1992] BCC 110, *Re Tasbian Ltd (No. 3)* [1992] BCC 358, and *Re Copecrest Ltd* [1993] BCC 844.

From the cases he derived these propositions: A

In considering an application for leave the court should take into account the length of the delay, including that occurring within the two-year period, and the reasons for it; the strength of the case against the director; and the degree of prejudice caused to the director by the delay.

Leave should not be granted if the application was bound to fail, but it should if there was a fairly arguable case, unless factors such as prejudice to the director were present.   B

The two-year period gave the pursuer a contingency allowance for unexpected delays for which he was not responsible. Thus any lapse of time up to its expiry fell to be taken into account, since it is in the public interest that the fitness or otherwise of a person to be a director should be decided as early as possible.

Counsel divided the lapse of time into three periods.

Between the date of the liquidation on 21 August 1992 and the lodging of his return   C
on 6 July 1993 the liquidator had to investigate a substantial unfair preference. He had subsequently raised an action in Glasgow Sheriff Court which had been settled by the return of certain assets to him.

Between 6 July 1993 and 28 June 1994 officers in the pursuer's insolvency unit had prioritised the more urgent of the 200 reports they considered annually. This case was scheduled appropriately. Thereafter its investigation proceeded. After meetings with the   D
liquidator and the assembly of documents it was decided to send the papers to the solicitor's office. This process, locally and in London, took the normal period of four months. The papers were received by the solicitor's office on 23 June. It was decided to proceed with the application, and the appropriate diary entries were made. Matters more urgent were processed first. The s. 16(1) notice was timeously sent on 8 August. Unfortunately the lodging of the application on 19 August was overlooked.
                                                                                    E
It could not be said that there was no case to answer, since the company had traded at creditors' expense, its indebtedness increasing by £26,000 between March and August 1992. The real delay had been one day only. The delay which had occurred since the case had come into court was not material. The only prejudice to the defender was that, should the application be granted, he could be prevented from being a director of a company till a later date, but it would be open to him to seek recall.

The solicitor for the defender submitted that it was not clear from r. 3(1) of the *Act of*   F
Sederunt (Company Directors Disqualification) 1986 (SI 1986/2296) (S 168) whether an application for leave required to be made separately from an application for an order. That had not been done in this case, and there may be a question of competency arising. However, the defender was in no difficulty in responding to the present application.

He accepted the propositions derived by counsel from the cases cited as setting out the appropriate test. He added references to *Re Crestjoy Products Ltd* [1990] BCC 23 at p. 29   G
and the opinion of Mervyn Davies J in *Copecrest* at p. 849, emphasising the need for those responsible for its preparation to pay attention to the case when the time limit was approaching. He also made reference to the obiter dictum of Nourse LJ in *Re Cedac Ltd* [1991] BCC 148 at p. 163; [1991] Ch 402 at p. 424.

He contended that in considering the preliminary application for leave the period of delay to be considered ran from 21 August 1992 to the date of lodging of the present   H
application, namely 22 September 1994. The explanation for delay in the period to 6 July 1993 was undermined by the fact that the liquidator's return had been lodged before the action was raised on 26 August 1993. The contemplated proceedings did not excuse the six weeks' delay after the return was lodged. In any event, such delay had to be taken into account, and the pursuer still had over 13 months to decide to proceed. It had been with the Insolvency Unit almost one year before being passed to the solicitor's office. It

A   should have been obvious that the time limits were fast approaching, and steps to prioritise the matter should have been taken. While the solicitor's office doubtless had other pressing matters, the s. 16 notice had been sent timeously, and the application should have been made timeously.

It was conceded that there was a case to answer, but since that almost always must be so, that made the issue of delay of greater importance. Since the minimum period of disqualification was two years, and the discretionary maximum 15 years, the

B   consequences for the defender could be serious. While the legislation was designed to give protection to the public, a balance had to be struck with the interests of the defender, who also had to be protected. Accordingly good cause had to be shown to justify a late application. Even though the deadline had been missed by one day only, it should not be granted.

C   I am of the opinion that this application should be granted. I consider the propositions derived from the cases cited, and assented to on the defender's behalf, correctly state the tests to be applied in determining a preliminary application such as this.

On the issue of competency I formed the view that the terms of r. 3(1) of the *Act of Sederunt (Company Directors Disqualification)* 1986 (SI 1986/2296) do not require separate applications to be made by the pursuer for leave to apply late and for seeking a disqualification order itself. The former is a mere preliminary, if circumstances require it,

D   to the latter, which is one of the substantive rights created by the Act. I take the reference to 'leave of the court' to relate to the provisions in the Act which afford a variety of disqualified persons corresponding rights of dispensation, on their application to the court. In any event, it was very fairly indicated that the issue of competence was not being pressed, and it was stated on the defender's behalf that this application had placed him in no difficulty so far as making a response was concerned.

E   On its merits I was satisfied that at each stage of the investigative and preparatory processes appropriate steps were taken, having regard to other priorities, to secure a timely and proper consideration of the case. During the first year the liquidator had to concentrate on the issue of an unfair preference, and it was only when a decision had been taken to raise an action that any assessment of the likely assets of the company could be made. During the period to 23 June 1994 most of the time available had been devoted to dealing with more urgent reports. This case had been slotted in to the schedule in reasonable time, and the time required to process it had been within the normal span.

F   It is plain that when the case was in the hands of the solicitor's office it was scheduled appropriately, having regard to more urgent matters which required to be dealt with, and when it was taken up, it was proceeded with at an appropriate speed, as timeous dispatch of the s. 16 notice would indicate. It was due to an unfortunate oversight that the deadline was missed. I regarded that as an acceptable explanation for the delay.

G   It was accepted that there was a case to answer. I did not consider that any prejudice had been occasioned to the defender which would merit the refusal of leave even upon the view that 22 September should be taken as the terminal date. The fact that the defender might be disqualified for a minimum period of two years does not constitute prejudice. That would be a consequence of his mismanagement of the company's business, if proved. It does not stem from the failure to lodge the application in time. In this case prejudice could only arise from the fact that any period of disqualification would

H   commence from a date some weeks later than might otherwise have been the case, and end correspondingly later. I do not consider this is a matter of materiality.

For the foregoing reasons I consider the application for leave should be granted.

(*Order accordingly*)

————————————

Re Full Cup International Trading Ltd.

A

Chancery Division (Companies Court).
Ferris J.
Judgment delivered 3 February 1995.

*Unfair prejudice petition – Unfair prejudice proved – Petitioner sought order under
s. 461 for respondents to purchase his shares – Court's discretion under s. 461 –
Whether winding up was appropriate remedy – Companies Act 1985, s. 459, 461.*

B

**Under s. 461 of the Companies Act 1985 the court had a discretion as to the relief it
would grant if it found that a petition under s. 459 was well founded. That discretion
extended to the refusal of specific relief under s. 461 in a case where the court was unable to
devise relief which would constitute an appropriate remedy or where some other course of
action seemed preferable. No relief which would meet the justice of the case and which would
be more advantageous than a winding up was capable of being devised. The court was not
prepared to grant relief under s. 461, but would allow the petition to be amended so as to
seek winding up on just and equitable grounds, with a view to a winding up order being
obtained when the formalities had been complied with.**

C

The following case was referred to in the judgment:

XYZ Ltd, Re (Company No. 004377 of 1986) (1986) 2 BCC 99,520; [1987] 1 WLR 102.

D

Ian Lamacraft (instructed by the Luper Partnership) for the petitioner.

JUDGMENT

Ferris J: I have before me a petition by Mr Linos Antoniades ('the petitioner') seeking
relief under s. 459 and 461 of the *Companies Act* 1985 in relation to the affairs of Full
Cup International Trading Ltd ('the company'). The petitioner is one of only three
shareholders in the company. The other shareholders are Miss Landy Wong Chet Kin
and Mr Jackson Yuen Man, who are the first and second respondents to the petition. I
will refer to them jointly as 'the respondents' although they are not the only respondents.
The company itself is named as third respondent, although in the usual way it has taken
no part in these proceedings. After the petition was presented a company named Full
Cup Ltd was added as fourth respondent. Its part in the events with which I am concerned
will appear hereafter, but it too has taken no part in the proceedings.

E

F

It is appropriate to note at the outset that, as a result of orders made in May and July
1994, the respondents have been debarred from defending the petition. They were present
in person throughout the hearing and I thought it right to inquire whether they claimed
to be entitled to address me on any point, notwithstanding the debarring order. They
evidently have very little command of English and at their request I thought it proper to
hear Mr Gerry Wood and an interpreter on their behalf. In the event, however, I heard
little or nothing of any relevance from their side and there was no need for me to consider
to what extent, if at all, the debarring order left it open to them to make submissions.

G

As a result of the debarring order I have heard no oral evidence and no witness has
been cross-examined. The consequence has been greatly to increase the difficulty of the
task of adjudicating on the petition. There has been a mass of affidavit evidence filed
during the course of numerous interlocutory applications but the case of neither side has
been at all clearly deployed in that evidence. On behalf of the petitioner Mr Lamacraft
sought to present the case to me by taking me to certain parts of the evidence of the
petitioner and the other witnesses on his side and to some parts of the evidence of the
respondents and their witnesses which, he claimed, constituted admissions. I did not find
this approach to be satisfactory, despite Mr Lamacraft's efforts to assist me by a written
summary of his main points cross-referenced to the parts of the evidence relied upon.

H

A   After reserving judgment I have thought it right to read the whole of the affidavit evidence, although not all the exhibits, in the order in which the affidavits were sworn, in order to try to ascertain the history of the matter. That reading will inevitably colour the summary of the relevant facts which I am about to give, but I have endeavoured to keep in mind the making of the debarring order and its effect and to exclude from my consideration matters which are not properly before me.

B   At the end of 1992 the petitioner was, and had been for some time, carrying on the business of the wholesale and retail sale of clothing through a company named Hardline Ltd ('Hardline') in which he held 99 of the 100 issued shares, his wife holding the other share. Hardline traded from premises at No. 177 Seven Sisters Road, Finsbury Park, London.

The respondents are Hong Kong Chinese who, at the end of 1992, were trading in clothing in or from Hong Kong under the name Full Cup International Company C   ('FCIC'). FCIC appears to have been a Hong Kong partnership in which the respondents were the only partners. According to Miss Landy Wong the respondents came to England in December 1992 with a view to establishing contacts with one or more English traders through whom FCIC could sell in England the garments in which it dealt, which appear to have been obtained for the most part from manufacturers based in China. The respondents made contact with the petitioner and certain associates of his and agreed to D   establish some kind of joint venture through a new company which was to be incorporated. The company was incorporated as the intended joint venture company on 3 February 1992. The parties did not, however, wish to wait for the incorporation of the company and its registration for VAT before beginning to trade. It appears to have been agreed that in the first instance, pending the establishment of the company, Hardline would trade as agent for the intended joint venture. There is in evidence a copy of an invoice from FCIC to Hardline for goods sent by air from Hong Kong on 8 January E   1993, and there are other invoices for subsequent shipments of garments, all before the incorporation of the company.

The company seems to have been activated after a board meeting of its directors held on 23 February 1993. By this time the associates of the petitioner who had originally been interested in the venture had dropped out. The petitioner and the respondents became the only directors of the company and 91 shares in the company were allotted, F   33 to Miss Landy Wong, 33 to Mr Jackson Yuen and 25 to the petitioner. Presumably these 91 shares were intended to include the original subscribers' shares. The 91 shares are the only shares in the company which have been issued and they remain held by the petitioner and the respondents in the numbers agreed on 23 February 1993.

Even after the activation of the company in this way on 23 February the actual trading of the joint venture continued to be carried on through Hardline. The reason for this G   appears to have been connected with accountability for VAT. On the importation of goods from Hong Kong VAT had to be paid and it was important that this should be done by a trader registered for VAT and that the subsequent sale of the goods should be by the same trader. Hardline was a VAT registered trader and it was able to use its registration for VAT by trading as agent for the company pursuant to s. 32 of the VAT Act. The company was not registered for VAT until 17 March 1993. It was intended that it should take over trading from Hardline on 1 April 1993, the take-over extending not H   only to the trade in goods imported from the respondents in Hong Kong but to all the trade previously carried on by Hardline.

Before 1 April, however, disputes appear to have arisen between the petitioner on the one hand and the respondents on the other. The evidence does not disclose with any degree of clarity what was the nature of these disputes, but they involved complaints by the respondents that the petitioner was failing to account properly for trading done by

Hardline on behalf of the company and complaints by the petitioner that the respondents   A
were requiring the whole of the proceeds of sales to be remitted to FCIC in Hong Kong
without allowing proper deductions for the costs of selling. The precise terms on which
FCIC was supplying goods to Hardline on behalf of the joint venture were not established
by the evidence, but it was the case of both parties that there was some kind of sale or
return arrangement and that goods were supplied subject to a retention of title provision.

On 16 March 1993 the respondents approached Mr Stephen Wong, a certified   B
accountant and partner in the firm of Heneghan Joseph & Co practising as accountants
from an office in Wembley, for advice concerning their complaints against the petitioner.
From then on the respondents appear to have had assistance from Mr Wong at every
important stage of their dealings with the petitioner, who had his own accountants.

Towards the end of March 1993 the respondents became interested in a company
named Boldflag Ltd. This company had been incorporated on 19 January 1993 but there
is no evidence to connect the respondents with it until 24 March, when they became its   C
directors. A company search shows that on the same date Miss Landy Wong held 99 of
the 100 issued shares in Boldflag Ltd and Mr Jackson Yuen held 1 share. On 6 April 1993
Boldflag Ltd changed its name to Full Cup Ltd. I shall refer to it as 'FCL'.

At about the beginning of April the respondents caused the stock of garments held for
sale on behalf of the joint venture to be removed from Hardline's premises at 177 Seven
Sisters Road and placed in storage with a company named Total Storage Ltd which was   D
unconnected with any of the parties. At some time during the same month new shop
premises at No. 132A Seven Sisters Road were acquired on lease, apparently at the
instance of the respondents. The petitioner has said in his evidence that he understood
that No. 132A Seven Sisters Road was to be a retail shop for the company and there is
evidence to suggest that the company paid the initial rent for these premises. It seems
reasonably clear, however, that No. 132A was intended by the respondents to be the
trading premises for FCL. In para. 26 of her first affidavit, sworn on 16 July 1993, Miss   E
Landy Wong referred to the acquisition of No. 132A and said:

> 'The shop I proposed to use as a showroom to retail some of the stock purchased
> from FCITL' [i.e. the company] and the rear for storage of the stock on behalf of
> FCITL.'

She did not explain what she meant by 'the stock purchased from FCITL'. Earlier she
had simply referred to the removal of the stock from the premises of the company. She   F
claimed to have organised this in order to protect the company from what she regarded
as the misconduct of the petitioner. In her second affidavit she said that her concern was
that the goods supplied to the company by FCIC had been purchased on credit from
suppliers on the Chinese mainland. These suppliers were looking to FCIC for payment
which, by implication from Landy Wong's evidence, FCIC was unable to make because
it had not been paid by the company. Landy Wong sought to explain that: G

> 'The intention was for [FCL] to take delivery of the goods supplied from Hong
> Kong which would be transferred to [the company] as and when necessary.'

The position is a confused and unsatisfactory one. It is, however, clear that the
respondents took unilateral action to remove unsold goods from the company, where
they were effectively under the control of the petitioner, and, after a period in which the
goods were in the custody of Total Storage Ltd which acted on the directions of the
respondents, put them in the custody of FCL, which they controlled. If they had not been   H
debarred from defending they would apparently have sought to contend that this was a
justified measure to prevent the petitioner from dealing with these goods in a way which
they considered to be for his own benefit and to the detriment of the company. As this
affirmative case is not open to the respondents as a result of the debarring order I cannot
proceed on the basis that it is shown to be justified, but equally I cannot, I think, wholly

A ignore the fact that this was the justification that the respondents sought to advance as soon as these proceedings were commenced in July 1993.

There is a certain amount of evidence which indicates that FCL did not function merely as an intermediary between FCIC and the company but traded on its own account with goods belonging to the company. The most direct evidence consists of copies of two documents exhibited to the affidavit of Polycarpos Spyrou sworn on 29 July 1993. One

B document appears to be a summary of goods sold by FCL on 15 May 1994. The other is an invoice in respect of the very same goods from the company to FCL at wholesale price. This invoice is dated 14 May, but the inference that it was brought into existence only after the goods had been sold on a retail basis by FCL is irresistible. It seems that on this occasion the whole of the money received by FCL was in fact paid into the company's bank account, but this was only because FCL did not have its own bank account at that time. A bank account for FCL was opened shortly afterwards. In his first

C affidavit the petitioner stated that a short time after the stock was transferred to No. 132A Seven Sisters Road,

> 'it developed that the proceeds of all sales were banked in the account of FCL rather than that of [the company], despite the fact that invoices were raised by [the company].'

The want of particularity in this assertion is unsatisfactory, but the statement is consistent

D with what is shown by or to be inferred from the documents which I have just mentioned and with other evidence which I accept concerning the activities of FCL and, in the absence of admissible evidence to the contrary, I accept it.

Later in May there was an incident concerning a cheque for £17,000 drawn on the company's bank account. The terms of the company's bank mandate were such that cheques had to be signed by both the petitioner and Miss Landy Wong. The petitioner's

E evidence was that on about 22 May 1993 Landy Wong asked him to sign a cheque in order to pay the sign-writer who had painted the shop sign at 132A Seven Sisters Road. As the amount to be paid to the sign-writer was not known the petitioner signed the cheque with the amount left blank. He said that he subsequently found that the sum of £17,000 had been paid to Landy Wong on this cheque. I find it impossible to evaluate this evidence without taking into account the explanation given by Landy Wong, although to do so is in conflict with the debarring order. She does not comment on what

F the petitioner said about the cheque being for a payment to the sign-writer but she accepts that the cheque was made out for £17,000 and that this sum was received by her. The explanation which she gave was that the company owed her £17,300 and that the £17,000 was part payment of this sum. The particulars which she gives to support the indebtedness of £17,300 are complicated and impossible to understand properly on the material which is before me. But I think it would be unsound to accept the petitioner's evidence on this

G point when it is untested by cross-examination and I know that the respondents would have wished to contradict it.

In April 1993 a company named Full Cup Industrial Co Ltd had been incorporated in Hong Kong, with the respondents as its directors and shareholders. This company, which I shall refer to as 'FCICL', appears to have traded from the same premises as FCIC. It may have been intended to take over the business of FCIC but there is no evidence of

H this and in July 1993 both FCIC and FCICL appear to have been active. It seems probable that in April and May 1993 some at least of the goods supplied to the company from Hong Kong were supplied by FCICL rather than by FCIC. But it is doubtful whether any new goods at all were supplied to the company after about the first week of June. It appears from what is said in the second affidavit of Stephen Wong that the company ceased to trade on 18 June 1993. The petitioner has not expressly accepted this but he has not denied it either and I accept it. It seems that the relationship between the

petitioner and the respondents had broken down completely by the first or second week   A
of June. Moreover by the latter part of June, and perhaps from an earlier time, the
respondents were causing FCIC and FCICL to press the company for payments alleged
to be due from it and to threaten to take back unsold goods pursuant to its retention of
title.

At a meeting between the petitioner and the respondents which took place on 25 June
1993 the petitioner was handed an already written letter of resignation as a director of
the company which the respondents asked him to sign. When he declined to do so the   B
respondents handed him a notice signed by Landy Wong purporting to be a notice of an
extraordinary general meeting of the company to be held on 8 July at which,

> 'An ordinary resolution is proposed to remove and re-appoint the existing board
> of directors and secretary.'

The petitioner interpreted this as manifesting an intention to remove him without re-
appointing him. Although this interpretation was contrary to the linguistic sense of the   C
notice I think it was probably correct.

On 7 July 1993 the petitioner, in advance of presenting the petition in this matter,
applied ex parte to Arden J for injunctive relief restraining the respondents from taking
steps to remove him as a director of the company and Arden J granted such relief until
after 19 July. In the petition, which was presented within a day or so thereafter, the
petitioner alleged that an agreement had been made between himself and the company   D
on or about 23 February 1993 under which the petitioner was to receive a salary and a
share of profits (neither of which were quantified in the petition) and to make a
contribution of capital to the company. It was alleged that he had made a capital
contribution of at least £5,180 but had received no payments of salary or profits. Matters
relating to the extraordinary general meeting proposed to be held on 8 July were then
pleaded. These and the non-payment of salary and profits were relied upon as conduct   E
unfairly prejudicial to the petitioner.

The petitioner's first affidavit in support of the petition and his claim for interlocutory
relief was sworn on 8 July. Not surprisingly it went into somewhat greater detail than the
petition and it particularised the agreed salary as being £400 per week. Somewhat
strangely, having regard to the fact that the agreement for a salary was said to have been
made at the time when the petitioner agreed to become a director, that is to say about 23
February, it was alleged, apparently by way of complaint, that the petitioner had last   F
been paid a salary on 29 January 1993. Any such payment must have been made by
Hardline, not the company, and cannot be relevant to the existence or non-existence of
the agreement alleged.

An affidavit in answer to the petitioner's first affidavit was sworn by Landy Wong on
16 July 1993 and an affidavit of Stephen Wong in support of the respondents' case was
sworn on 19 July. On the latter date the petitioner swore a further affidavit dealing with   G
some of the points made by Landy Wong and indicating his intention to apply for leave
to amend the petition so as to raise further complaints of unfairly prejudicial conduct.
When the motion for interlocutory relief came before the court again on 23 July it was
stood over to be heard as a motion by order, the injunctions granted by Arden J being
continued until after the hearing.

On 22 July, on the application of the petitioner, Mr Registrar Buckley gave leave for   H
the petition to be amended and the amendments were duly made shortly afterwards. The
amendments substituted new paragraphs for all the paragraphs of the petition except
those making purely formal allegations. The new paragraphs include, in addition to
reformulated claims regarding non-payment of salary and the intention to remove the
petitioner from office, allegations concerning the incorporation of FCL, the removal of
the company's stock from its premises and the placing of them under the control of the

A   respondents, the sale of goods belonging to the company by or for the benefit of FCL, the incident of the cheque for £17,000 and the refusal of information concerning the accounting records of the company.

A good deal of further affidavit evidence on both sides was sworn, mainly during the last week or so of July 1993. On 30 July 1993 the respondents applied to Harman J, ex parte but on notice, for certain relief relating to the payment of some alleged liabilities of

B   the company, but Harman J declined to make an order. Thereafter there appears to have been a good deal of procedural activity by way of service of a defence on 15 September 1993, points of reply on 29 September 1993, a request for further and better particulars of the defence on 8 October 1993, the administration of interrogatories on behalf of the petitioner on the same date and the service of some answers to these interrogatories on 10 November 1993.

C   In the course of this activity it became apparent that FCIC or FCITL, or perhaps both of them, had during July 1993 claimed to assert title under the retention of title provision subject to which goods had been supplied to the company and, pursuant to that provision, to direct that the unsold goods be transferred to FCL. However documents which purport to show that stock had been sold by the company to FCL were also brought into existence. These documents include an invoice which is dated 2 July 1993 and which purports to record a sale of goods by the company to FCL at the price of

D   £273,831.80 plus VAT of £47,920.57, making a total of £321,752.37. No such sum was, however, paid by FCL to the company, either at that time or subsequently. This document must have been in existence by 29 July 1993 when a copy of it was exhibited to an affidavit sworn by Mr de Silva, the respondents' solicitor. In a later affidavit, sworn on 12 November 1993, Mr de Silva referred to a meeting between representatives of HM Customs and Excise, Mr Stephen Wong and the petitioner at which the company's liability for VAT as at 31 August 1993 was discussed. Mr de Silva said that this liability

E   was some £67,000 by reason of the transfer of goods from the company to FCL. According to Mr de Silva, Mr Stephen Wong claimed that VAT was not payable on such transfer, but I think that Mr de Silva must have meant to say that this contention was advanced by the petitioner, for Mr Stephen Wong was acting for the respondents whose interest it was, in the circumstances which I shall come to, to cause the company to pay VAT. The point is of relatively minor importance, however, because the representatives

F   of Customs & Excise maintained that VAT was payable. The respondents appear then to have drawn a cheque for £67,000 on the company's account in favour of Customs & Excise in respect of the VAT liability. They presented this cheque to the petitioner for him to countersign, but he declined to do so.

The petitioner's motion which had been directed to be heard as a motion by order appears to have come before Sir Mervyn Davies on 11 November 1993. The injunction

G   originally granted by Arden J was continued until the substantive hearing of the petition. In addition Sir Mervyn Davies restrained the respondents from altering the company's bank mandate, with the result that the company's VAT liability remained unpaid.

The reason why it was in the interest of the respondents that the company should be liable to VAT in respect of the goods transferred to FCL was that FCL, through Mr Stephen Wong, intended to claim repayment of this VAT as input tax suffered by it, against which it had no output tax for which to account. In October 1993 Mr Stephen

H   Wong submitted on behalf of FCL a claim for repayment of VAT amounting to £65,464.60. In support of this claim there was submitted to Customs & Excise an invoice purporting to be dated 2 July 1993 which is expressed to be in respect of the sale by the company to FCL of the goods which were the subject of the earlier invoice dated 2 July 1993 which I have mentioned and some other goods. The price was expressed to be £374,083.44 plus VAT of £65,464.60 making a total of £439,548.05. Presumably this

invoice was intended to supersede the earlier invoice of 2 July because of the overlap in   A
the goods covered by the two invoices. From the printed serial number on the invoice it
appears to have been the next invoice in the book after the first invoice of 2 July. I infer,
however, that it was brought into existence at a much later date, after the meeting with
representatives of Customs & Excise held to discuss the company's VAT liability as at 31
August 1993. This meeting must have taken place in September 1993. If the invoice had
been in existence at 29 July 1993 I think Mr Stephen Wong would have told Mr de Silva
about it and Mr de Silva would have exhibited a copy of it to his affidavit sworn on that   B
date. If it had been in existence at the time of the September meeting with Customs and
Excise, I would expect it to have been produced then, but there is nothing to suggest that
this was done. The petitioner, in an affidavit sworn on 7 January 1994, deposes to some
information obtained by him from Customs & Excise from which it seems that the invoice
was produced to Customs & Excise at a VAT inspection of FCL which took place on
1 October 1993. I infer that it was brought into existence some time during September   C
1993.

Going hand in hand with the new invoice of 2 July and no doubt brought into existence
at the same time as that invoice are two documents described as 'official receipts' each
dated 2 July 1993, typed on the printed letterhead of the company and addressed to FCL.
One such receipt is expressed to be for the sum of £360,814.38 made up as to £306,652.91
by the 'cost value' of goods and as to £54,161.47 VAT thereon. This sum is expressed to
have been received, 'in the form of consideration stated below for stock supplied on   D
2.7.93'. There then follows a note:

> *'Form of consideration*
>
> A letter of release from Full Cup Industrial Co Ltd (registered in Hong Kong)
> formally releasing our debt to the value of £360,814.38.'

The other receipt is in identical form save that it is expressed to be for the sum of   E
£78,733.66 made up as to £67,430.53 the 'cost value' of goods and as to £11,303.13 VAT
thereon. The sums mentioned in the two receipts amount in the aggregate to the amount
stated in the new invoice of 2 July as being the price of the goods which are the purported
subject matter of that invoice, together with the VAT thereon and that invoice is referred
to by its number in the two receipts.

The release referred to in the two 'official receipts' appears to be a message dated   F
6 August 1993 signed on behalf of FCICL (but not FCIC) and addressed to the company
stating:

> 'We confirm that as the unsold goods shipped to you have now been confiscated
> by Full Cup Ltd on our behalf as a consequence of your non-payment, that you
> are released from payment of those [sic] goods.
>
> As for the goods already sold by you we expect payment within 24 hours.'   G

This material was received by the petitioner shortly before 15 December 1993, although
it is not clear from what source he received it. At the same time he became aware that
Customs & Excise had acceded to the repayment claim of FCL and had repaid the VAT
as claimed. On 16 December 1993 he applied ex parte to Warner J for Mareva injunctions
freezing the assets of the respondents and FCL, which was added as a respondent to the
petition. An order was made as asked until after 12 January 1994 and, by an order of
Knox J made on 12 January this relief was continued until after the hearing of the   H
application as a motion by order.

In a disclosure affidavit sworn in accordance with the order of Warner J on 17 January
1994, Miss Landy Wong exhibited a copy of the bank statement of FCL from which it
could be seen that £65,935.19, which is clearly the VAT repayment, was received by FCL
on 17 November and that on 26 November £65,000 was transferred out of FCL's current

A   account. Miss Landy Wong said in her affidavit that this sum was transferred to a high
interest rate account from which it was withdrawn and paid in cash to a representative of
China Huran Wall Shine Imports ('Huran') on or about 23 December 1993. In the
subsequent applications to the court there was a good deal of evidence directed to the
question whether the payment to Huran was made after the respondents had notice of
the injunction granted by Warner J, but as there are no proceedings for contempt on foot
I shall not attempt to make findings about this.

B
What is more significant for the purposes of this narrative is that, after this disclosure
that the money had been paid away by FCL, the petitioner sought an order that the
respondents be cross-examined on their disclosure affidavits and restrained from leaving
the jurisdiction until after such cross-examination. On 18 January Knox J made an order
restraining the respondents from leaving the jurisdiction until after the hearing of the
motion for an order that they be cross-examined. This motion came before Millett J on

C   24 January, when an elaborate order was made. It is not necessary for me to go into the
detailed terms of this order, for these were to cease to have effect if £65,000 was paid into
court and that sum was in fact paid in by or on behalf of the respondents on 31 January
1994.

The other steps in the s. 459 petition which are relevant call for only a brief mention.
They are the making of the unless order by Mr Registrar Buckley on 11 May 1994, his

D   subsequent declaration on 27 June that the respondents are debarred from defending the
petition and the refusal of Mr Registrar Simmonds on 18 July to allow further time for
compliance with the unless order. Finally, on 27 July 1994, on an ex parte application by
the petitioner, Blackburne J appointed the petitioner to be the receiver of the assets and
business of the company until the final determination of the petition. The evidence in
support of the application shows that the main purpose of the receivership was to enable
certain liabilities of the company to be paid out of its bank account, which was in credit

E   to an amount of about £85,000 at the time of the application. In particular the amount
of the VAT in dispute as a result of the purported transfer of goods to FCL, that is to
say approximately £65,000, had to be paid in order to enable the company to pursue its
appeal against the VAT liability. I understand that this payment has now been made.

I now turn to the allegations of unfairly prejudicial conduct. I propose to consider all
the complaints which are raised in the re-amended petition, even though some of these

F   were, at best, only faintly relied upon before me.

The most important of these complaints relate to the transfer of the stock and business
of the company to FCL. It is convenient to consider the allegations in two parts. The first
part includes complaints concerning the removal of the company's stock to the
warehouse of Total Storage; and the sale of goods belonging to the company by the
respondents and the crediting of the proceeds of sale of these goods to FCL. There is no

G   doubt that the company's stock was removed to the warehouse of Total Storage at the
instance of the respondents and that from then on it was under the de facto control of
the respondents to the exclusion of the petitioner. At some stage the stock seems to have
been taken to No. 132A Seven Sisters Road, and at that stage it seems to have come
under the control of FCL, but in practical terms this was a continuation of control by
the respondents. I also accept that in substance the allegation that sales have been made
for the benefit of FCL is made good. I have already mentioned the sales which are the

H   subject of the invoices dated 15 and 16 May 1993. Although the proceeds of these
particular sales came into the company's bank account this was a matter of convenience
resulting from the fact that at that time FCL had no bank account of its own. So far as
the respondents were concerned the retail sales were made for the benefit of FCL and the
company was entitled only to the wholesale price. As I have stated already, I accept the
evidence of the petitioner that 'after a while', which seems to mean from about the middle

of May onwards, the proceeds of sale of the company's goods found their way into FCL's A
bank account. This was clearly the result of action taken by the respondents and
constituted a breach of the fiduciary duties owed by them to the company, as was the
very establishment of FCL to compete with, or even supersede, the company as the seller
of goods supplied by FCIC or FCICL. In my judgment these breaches of fiduciary duty
constituted not only wrongs done to the company but the conduct of the company's
affairs by the respondents in a manner which was unfairly prejudicial to the interests of
the petitioner as the only other member of the company.   B

The second part of the complaint relates to the transactions concerning the company's
stock which took place during July 1993. These are not the subject-matter of detailed
allegations in the petition, but they fall within the general scope of the complaints made
in para. 14 and 22 and I think I must deal with them. Unfortunately no particulars are
given in para. 14 and 22 and the relevant evidence is piecemeal and confusing.
Nevertheless the end result of these transactions is clear, namely that the company ceased C
to hold any of the stock supplied from Hong Kong and ceased to trade while FCL took
over all the stock and all the trade. It is also clear that this happened at the instance of
the respondents. But it is necessary to analyse with some care precisely what it is that the
respondents did and in what capacity they did it.

One analysis is that, as partners in FCIC or directors of FCICL, the respondents
caused those entities to assert their title as suppliers of the goods under the retention of D
title provision and to cause the goods to be sold to a new customer, namely FCL. Such
conduct would not, in my judgment, be something done in the course of the company's
affairs and could not be the basis for an application under s. 459. It was action taken by
the partners of FCIC or the directors of FCICL in the management of the affairs of those
undertakings. On this analysis even the taking over of the trade by FCL might be
excusable because, the company having been forced to cease trading as a result of the E
legitimate action of its suppliers, it is not easy to see what was wrong in FCL seizing the
resulting commercial opportunity.

There is, however, an alternative analysis of what was done, which is that,
notwithstanding any retention of title provision, the company was recognised as the legal
owner of the goods supplied by FCIC and FCICL and was caused by the respondents to
sell those goods to FCL on the terms of the invoices and official receipts subsequently F
brought into existence and dated 2 July 1993. If this were the true nature of the
transaction then the company has disposed of its entire stocks in return for nothing more
than a release of the amounts owed to FCIC or FCICL. (I assume that the release is to
be regarded as given on behalf of both, notwithstanding that it is expressed to be given
only by FCICL. If FCIC is not bound by the release then the transaction was even more
unfavourable to the company and the failure to obtain an effective release from FCIC
was itself a serious dereliction of duty.) These amounts do not seem to have been greater G
than the prices, net of VAT, mentioned in the invoices of 2 July. No account seems to
have been taken of the fact that, on the footing that there was a sale to FCL, the company
rendered itself liable to account for more than £65,000 in VAT even though it received
no part of the price in cash. Even if the VAT liability were disregarded the transaction
would still be objectionable, because the respondents clearly failed to consider whether
some course other than a sale at cost price to FCL might be more beneficial to the
company. On this analysis the conduct of the respondents would, in my judgment, H
amount to a serious breach of their fiduciary duties to the company. It would tend to
deplete the assets of the company and thus affect adversely all its shareholders. But two
of those shareholders, namely the respondents, obtained benefits in their capacity as
shareholders in FCL which were not available to the petitioner, who had no interest in
FCL. If, therefore, there was a sale to FCL, the bringing about of that sale at the instance

A   of the respondents amounted, in my view, to the conduct of the affairs of the company in a manner unfairly prejudicial to the petitioner.

It is necessary, therefore, for me to choose between the alternative analyses. Neither party has, to my mind, behaved entirely consistently. The respondents have been inconsistent in first asserting the title of FCIC and FCICL and then, by recording a sale by the company, proceeding on the basis that the company had a title to sell. As for the

B   petitioner, he complains of the respondents' dealings with the goods as unfairly prejudicial conduct but also, as I understand it, claims against Customs & Excise that the company cannot have made a taxable supply to FCL because the goods had already been 'confiscated' by FCIC and FCICL. My conclusion is that the respondents cannot escape the consequences of the documents they have brought into existence for the purpose of evidencing a transaction under which the company would be liable to pay VAT and FCL would be entitled to recover it. This transaction must have been intended

C   by them to be an effective one, otherwise it could not have the tax consequences from which they have sought to benefit their own company, FCL. Accordingly I find that their dealings with the company's stock did constitute unfairly prejudicial conduct towards the petitioner.

What I have said so far deals, so far as I find myself able to do so, with the allegations made in para. 12–14 and 22 of the petition, as elaborated in the evidence. The remaining

D   allegations made in the petition can be dealt with more briefly.

In para. 15 there is an allegation that the respondents have on diverse occasions since May 1993 passed off the goods of FCL as the goods of the company. There was no evidence whatever to support this complaint.

In para. 16 there is a complaint that, since May 1993, the respondents have caused FCL to make sales to customers of the company and of Hardline, in breach of their duties to the company. There was little detailed evidence in support of this allegation, but

E   I am prepared to infer that it is correct because the actions of the respondents have ensured that the company ceased to carry on any effective business after the end of June 1993 or thereabouts, while FCL has continued in business in the same field, initially trading with the same stock, since that time. It must surely be the case that in doing this FCL has traded with parties who were previously customers of the company or Hardline. This was unfairly prejudicial conduct, although I think it adds little of substance to what

F   I have already found as regards dealings with the company's stock.

In para. 17 the allegation regarding the cheque for £17,000 is made. I have already indicated the rival accounts of this cheque given by the petitioner and Landy Wong respectively. I could only accept the petitioner's account of the matter and find unfairly prejudicial conduct if I were to ignore or reject the explanation given by Landy Wong. I do not think that the fact that she is debarred from defending the petition obliges me to

G   take this course. In the result I am simply unable to form a conclusion as to the primary facts concerning this cheque. The petitioner's allegations concerning the cheque are not proved to my satisfaction.

Paragraph 18 makes allegations that FCICL supplied goods to the company at prices above their market value, some of which goods were defective, and that the respondents refused the petitioner's requests that goods be supplied at lower prices or from suppliers other than FCICL. There was no evidence beyond mere assertion to support these

H   complaints. Moreover, even if they were well founded I would not be satisfied that they would demonstrate unfairly prejudicial conduct of the company's affairs on the part of the respondents.

Paragraphs 19–21 deal with the failure of the company to pay to the petitioner what he claims to have been an agreed salary or to repay to him money said to have been lent by him to the company. As to these matters, I am not satisfied that there was such an

agreement for the payment of salary as the petitioner claims or that the money referred   A
to was a loan to the company. Further, on the petitioner's own case the amounts in
question were not to be paid or repaid until the company was 'sufficiently profitable'. I
am not satisfied that this requirement was ever satisfied.

Paragraph 23 complains of the respondents' intention to cause the company to remove
the petitioner from office. Having regard to the request for the petitioner's resignation
and the notice of the intended extraordinary meeting I am satisfied that the respondents   B
did have this intention. But such an intention is not necessarily unfairly prejudicial
conduct (see *Re XYZ Ltd* (1986) 2 BCC 99,520). In order to conclude that removal of the
petitioner was unfairly prejudicial I would need to conduct a much fuller investigation of
the facts concerning the intentions of the parties as to their entitlement to participate in
the management of the company than has been possible on the evidential material
actually deployed.

Much the same goes for the complaint in para. 24 as to refusal of access to the   C
company's accounting records. This is an area in which the parties have been making
allegations and counter-allegations almost since the commencement of their joint venture.
I do not find myself able to reach a reliable conclusion on the largely unparticularised
claims of the petitioner and his disorganised evidence.

In the result I find unfairly prejudicial conduct in one area only, namely that involving   D
dealings with the company's stock and the transfer of the company's business to FCL.
This conduct is, however, relatively serious, in that the respondents have, in effect, stifled
the company's business, deprived the company of its stock and taken over both business
and stock for the benefit of a company in which they, but not the petitioner, are
interested. On behalf of the petitioner it is submitted that, in these circumstances, I ought
to grant relief under s. 461 of the *Companies Act* 1985 and, in particular, that I ought to
order the respondents to purchase the petitioner's shares in the company. At first sight it   E
may be thought that this would represent a comparatively simple remedy, but this
appearance is rapidly dispelled when it is seen how the petitioner asks for it to be applied.
The minutes of order submitted on his behalf provide for two inquiries to be made,
namely:

(1)   an inquiry as to the value of the business of the respondent as a going concern at
the date of the petition 'on the basis . . . that the matters complained of in the said   F
petition had not occurred'; and

(2)   an inquiry as to the greatest gross profit from sales that might have been achieved
by the company from 1 April 1993 until the date of the order, the company's
turnover being taken to be such turnover as the company would have achieved
were it not for the matters complained of in the petition.

The value of the petitioner's shares is then proposed to be ascertained on the basis that: G

(1)   a sum representing the value of the company's business was paid to the company
at the date of the petition;

(2)   the amount of the gross profit ascertained on inquiry (2) has been paid to the
company;

(3)   the sum of £17,000 has been repaid to the company;   H

(4)   the company has no other assets or liabilities other than for corporation tax on the
gross profit; and

(5)   there is no discount in the value of the petitioner's shares by reason of the fact that
they constitute a minority holding.

A   I see many objections to such an order, of which the following are the more important:

(a)   To order inquiries as to value or turnover 'on the basis . . . that the matters complained of in the petition had not occurred' throws onto the person conducting the inquiry many of the difficulties concerning what happened, whether it was objectionable and, if so, who was to blame which I have experienced in hearing the petition. There would be some simplification as a result of my refusal to accept the

B   petitioner's case concerning a number of matters, which would thus have to be removed from the category of those things which are to be disregarded. But I can see no satisfactory way in which one could define, for the purposes of the inquiry, how the conduct in relation to the transfer of the stock and business of the company to FCL and the trading of FCL with the company's stock before its transfer is to be disregarded.

C   (b)   I see no justification for ordering an inquiry as to the *gross* profit which the company would have earned on a particular hypothesis, still less as to the *greatest* such gross profit. Taken with the assumption that, for the purpose of ascertaining the value of the petitioner's shares, the company is to be treated as having received this gross profit and the absence of any allowance for the cost of goods which, on any view, has not been paid or for selling costs the formula is calculated to produce a price which is thoroughly distorted in favour of the petitioner. Mr Lamacraft

D   appeared to be wholly unashamed about this. He said that if it became necessary to ascertain what was due to the Hong Kong suppliers of the goods in which the company traded and is to be assumed to have continued to trade, there would be no end to the inquiry. That may well be so, but it cannot possibly justify the adoption of a formula which, in my view, is bound not to yield a fair price.

(c)   It cannot be right, in my view, to assume that the company has no other assets or
E   liabilities than certain stated assets, when all the evidence points to the fact that the affairs of the company were never satisfactorily managed and that there are many matters which remain to be accounted for both as between the company and outside parties and as between the petitioner, the respondents and the company.

I would not, therefore, be prepared to make an order of the kind proposed on behalf of the petitioner, even with such modifications as might be thought to be appropriate to reflect the findings of fact which I have felt able to make. If there were to be an order for

F   the purchase of the petitioner's shares by the respondents it would have to be, in my view, an order for the purchase of those shares at a price which represents a due proportion of the net assets of the company (I would have no difficulty in disregarding the minority position) ascertained after taking full accounts in order to ascertain all the assets and liabilities of the company and appropriate steps to redress or compensate for all wrongs done to the company by any of its directors, including the petitioner.

G   Such an order would not, however, constitute a practicable proposition. It would encounter the difficulties concerning the ascertainment of the sums due to suppliers which led Mr Lamacraft to propose his own, in my view impermissible, short cut. It would also require the resolution of a multitude of matters which I have not been able to resolve in dealing with the petition, including the taking of a proper account of the trading undertaken by Hardline on behalf of the company. Although both sides in the petition

H   have maintained that the company is solvent, I am by no means satisfied that this will be found to be the case if proper accounts are taken. Such an order will also involve the court, whether by the judge or a registrar, embarking upon an extremely laborious and expensive process which it will be unable to achieve without a degree of co-operation by the parties which seems hitherto to have been lacking. I am not sure that even the petitioner would want such an order to be made, for it would lead to many of the

difficulties which he has sought to avoid by asking for a different order which I am not   A
prepared to make.

There is also a further consideration. The company is completely dormant so far as
trading is concerned. Neither side has any use for the company as a going concern. Under
the only form of order for the purchase of his shares which I would think it right to make
the petitioner would receive no more than he would on the liquidation of the company,
assuming that the liquidator takes appropriate action to redress the wrongs done to the   B
company, whether by the respondents or the petitioner. I do not suggest that a liquidation
would be straightforward, but a liquidator would, in my view, be in a better position to
carry out investigations into the facts and to arrive at the proper return (if any) which is
due to the petitioner than the court would be in as the result of an order under s. 461
directing the necessary accounts and inquiries. If it were objected that a liquidator will
not find it commercially sensible to follow up all the avenues of inquiry which are open,
then this would merely support my own view that the court will be unable to do better   C
under s. 461.

As I read the opening words of s. 461 the court has a discretion as to the relief it will
grant if it finds that a s. 459 petition is well founded. This discretion must, in my view,
extend to the refusal of specific relief under the section in a case where the court is unable
to devise relief which would constitute an appropriate remedy or where some other course
of action seems to be preferable. I take the view that no relief which would meet the   D
justice of the case and which would be more advantageous than a winding up is capable
of being devised. It seems to me that there can be no real argument against a winding-up
order, but as such an order has not been asked for in the petition I cannot make one
immediately. I merely say that I am not prepared to grant relief under s. 461 in this case,
but that if I were asked to do so by either side I would allow the petition to be amended
so as to seek winding up on just and equitable grounds, with a view to a winding up
order being obtained when the formalities as to advertising have been complied with.   E

There are a number of ancillary matters which I must deal with. First the order of
Blackburne J appointing the petitioner to be receiver of the company made that
appointment only until the final determination of the s. 459 petition. Having regard to
what I have just said concerning the possible amendment of the petition it may be that
my decision today does not amount to the final determination of the petition and that
the receivership continues. But it is clearly desirable that the matter shall be put beyond   F
doubt. If I am asked to do so I will continue the receivership expressly for a limited
period, not longer than a month or six weeks, in order to allow time for consideration
whether to apply for a winding-up order and, if such application is made, for the
necessary advertisement to take place. I must make it clear, however, that I would not be
willing to continue the receivership indefinitely as an alternative to winding up.

Secondly there is an application of the petitioner by summons dated 26 May 1994 for   G
an order that the £65,000 in court be paid out. The summons asked that this sum be paid
out to HM Customs & Excise for the purpose of discharging the company's liability for
VAT for the period to 31 July 1993, but that liability has since been satisfied by payment
made out of the company's own money. Mr Lamacraft asked that the money in court be
paid to the company. But I consider that such an order would be right only if I were
satisfied that the respondents are bound to recompense the company for the VAT liability
resulting from the purported sale of stock to FCL. I am, however, not satisfied about this   H
at present. Not only does the company have on foot an appeal against the VAT liability
but, even if the appeal fails, it seems to me that it will be necessary to consider the whole
of the company's VAT position, including the amount of input tax it has paid on
importation of the goods purportedly sold, before there will be any degree of clarity.
These are matters which a liquidator of the company will have to consider if there is a

A   winding-up order. At this stage I shall do no more than give all parties, including the company, liberty to apply for an order for payment out of the money in court.

Thirdly there are certain reserved costs which will have to be dealt with. I shall leave these for consideration after I have heard the parties when this judgment is handed down.

Fourthly there are the costs of a separate winding-up petition which I have not yet mentioned. On 13 January 1994 a petition for the winding up of the company was

B   presented in the Leeds District Registry by a petitioner identified in the petition as 'Full Cup Industrial Company of 1713A Park-Inn Commercial Centre, 56 Dundas Street, Kowloon, Hong Kong'. On the face of it this appears to be FCIC, or in other words the respondents, but the solicitors purporting to act for the petitioner, a firm named Brooke North and Goodwin of Leeds, have not acted for the respondents in the s. 459 petition. The petition was expressed to be based upon the non-payment of a debt of £58,708.77 said to be due from the company to the petitioner.

C   After the winding-up petition came to the notice of the petitioner and his advisers, Brooke North & Goodwin were asked questions about the identity of the petitioner in that petition, but nothing of any utility was revealed. On the application of the company, on whose behalf the petitioner claimed to give instructions, the winding-up petition was transferred to London to be heard together with the s. 459 petition. An application was then made to have the winding-up petition dismissed as an abuse of the process and this

D   application came before Rattee J on 10 March 1994. I was told that on that occasion the respondents denied that they had given instructions for the winding-up petition to be issued. Rattee J dismissed the petition but he reserved the question of costs for consideration at the hearing of the s. 459 petition. This question is accordingly now before me. The company, through the petitioner, asks that the costs of the winding-up petition shall be ordered to be paid by the respondents or, if the respondents did not give

E   instructions for the petition to be presented, by Brooke North & Goodwin.

It is accepted that I cannot deal with the application against Brooke North & Goodwin at this stage, since they have not had notice of the application. In the circumstances it would not be convenient to deal with the possible liability of the respondents for the costs, for that is likely to depend upon the same issue as that which will govern the possible liability of Brooke North & Goodwin. As I see the matter at present, if the respondents gave instructions for the winding-up petition to be issued on behalf of FCIC

F   they will have no answer to the application that they pay the costs of the petition and Brooke North & Goodwin will not be liable unless the circumstance would justify a wasted costs order against them. If, however, Brooke North & Goodwin were not authorised by the respondents to present the petition on behalf of FCIC it is difficult to see from what other source they could have obtained the necessary authority and they will almost certainly be liable to an order for costs on the ground that they have

G   commenced proceedings without the authority of the client they claim to represent. These matters will have to be gone into on a future occasion.

(Order accordingly)

H

Re Atlantic Computers plc (in administration). National Australia Bank Ltd v Soden & Anor.

Chancery Division (Companies Court).

Chadwick J.

Judgment delivered 16 February 1995.

Scheme of arrangement – Bank's claim to be a creditor – Whether letter of comfort imposed contractual promise as to future conduct.

This was an application by a bank ('NAB') seeking to reverse the decision of administrators of a scheme of arrangement relating to Atiantic Computers plc ('Atlantic') rejecting NAB's claim to be a creditor. NAB's claim arose under two letters of comfort given by Atlantic in connection with facilities granted by NAB to Atlantic Medical Ltd ('AML'), a former subsidiary of Atlantic Computers. The letters provided, by para. (c), that if Atlantic Medical Ltd was unable to meet its commitment, the parent company would take steps to make arrangements for Atlantic Medical Ltd's present, future or contingent obligations to the bank both for capital and interest to be met. The final paragraph of the letters stated that para. (c) was 'an expression of present intention by way of comfort only'.

Held, dismissing the application and confirming the decision of the scheme administrators:

Paragraph (c), read independently of the final paragraph in the letter, was phrased in terms which were sufficiently certain to give rise to an enforceable obligation. However para. (c) was qualified by the final paragraph in the letter. The court's task was to ascertain what common intention should be ascribed to the parties from the terms of the document and the surrounding circumstances. The common intention to be ascribed to the parties appeared plainly from the terms of the letter. It was an intention that Atlantic Computers should give no more than a warranty as to present intention by way of comfort only. A document in the terms of the two letters of comfort did not impose a contractual promise as to future conduct.

The following cases were referred to in the judgment:

Banque Brussels Lambert SA v Australian National Industries Ltd (1989) 21 NSWLR 502.

Chemco Leasing SpA v Rediffusion (19 July 1985, Staughton J); [1987] 1 FTLR 201 (CA).

Kleinwort Benson Ltd v Malaysia Mining Corporation Bhd (1988) 4 BCC 217, [1988] 1 WLR 799; (1989) 5 BCC 337; [1989] 1 WLR 379 (CA).

Rose & Frank Co v J R Crompton & Bros Ltd & Ors [1925] AC 445.

Hugh Mercer (instructed by Laytons) for the applicant.

Jonathan Nash (instructed by Cameron Markby Hewitt) for the respondents.

JUDGMENT

Chadwick J: On 30 March 1994, the court sanctioned a scheme of arrangement between Atlantic Computers plc and its creditors. That scheme provided for creditors to lodge claims with the scheme administrators. In particular, para. 7.6 enabled a creditor whose claim was rejected by the scheme administrators to apply to the court for an order that that decision be reversed.

The applicant, National Australia Bank Ltd ('NAB'), claims to be a creditor of Atlantic Computers. On 26 April 1994, NAB lodged a claim for a sum of £922,195.72. That claim was rejected by the scheme administrators on 9 August 1994. The application now before me is for that decision to be reversed. The scheme administrators are the respondents to the application.

A   NAB's claim arises under two letters of comfort, dated respectively 30 December 1986 and 31 March 1987. Those letters were given in connection with leasing or hire-purchase facilities granted by NAB to Atlantic Medical Ltd, a former subsidiary of Atlantic Computers. Atlantic Medical Ltd ('AML'), is now in liquidation and is thought to be insolvent. The two letters of comfort are in identical terms, save as to the description of the facilities to which they respectively relate. It is not suggested that there is any material difference arising from the circumstances in which each was given.

B   I will read the letter of 30 December 1986. It is addressed to NAB by Atlantic Computers:

> 'Dear Sirs,
>
> *Letter of Comfort*
>
C   We hereby confirm that Atlantic Medical Ltd is wholly owned by Atlantic Computers plc. We confirm that we are aware of the facility detailed below and which your bank has granted to Atlantic Medical Ltd.'

The facility is then described as a hire-purchase facility expiring on 30 December 1993. The letter continues:

> 'In consideration of the bank granting such credit, we undertake that without the prior consent of the bank:
>
D   > (a)   that the beneficial ownership of Atlantic Medical Ltd will be maintained by this company during the currency of the facility now to be made available by the bank;
>
> (b)   that the moneys owing by Atlantic Medical Ltd to the parent company will not be repaid in priority to any moneys owing or contingently owing by Atlantic Medical Ltd to the bank;
>
E   > (c)   that if Atlantic Medical Ltd is unable to meet its commitment, the parent company will take steps to make arrangements for Atlantic Medical Ltd's present, future or contingent obligations to the bank both for capital and interest to be met.
>
> This document is not intended to be a guarantee and, in the case of para. (c) above, it is an expression of present intention by way of comfort only.'

F   NAB's claim is made under para. (c) of that letter. It is said, and it is not in dispute, that AML is unable to meet its commitment to NAB under the hire-purchase facility described in the letter and that accordingly the parent company, Atlantic Computers, has come under a liability to make arrangements for AML's indebtedness to be met in full. The amount of the claim has been calculated after taking into account the dividend expected to be received in the liquidation of AML. The amount itself is in dispute, but it is agreed that questions of computation and quantum should not be argued before me. I

G   am concerned only to decide liability.

        If it were not for the final paragraph in the letter of comfort, I should have no real doubt that Atlantic Computers had accepted an obligation to ensure that AML's present, future and contingent obligations in relation to the hire-purchase facilities described were met. Although not strictly a guarantee, in that the obligation could be fulfilled without direct payment by Atlantic Computers to NAB – for example by the parent company

H   putting its subsidiary in funds sufficient to enable AML to meet its commitments – the obligation which Atlantic Computers had assumed would, I think, have been that of a surety.

        I do not accept the submissions, made on behalf of the scheme administrators, that para. (c), read independently of the final paragraph in the letter, is phrased in terms which are insufficiently certain to give rise to an enforceable obligation. I am satisfied

that, if para. (c) had remained unqualified by the final paragraph in the letter, Atlantic   A
Computers would have been well aware of what it had to do to perform the obligation
which it had undertaken; and that the court would have had no difficulty in deciding
whether that obligation had been performed.

But para. (c) does not stand alone. It is qualified by the final paragraph in the letter. In
particular, it is made clear in that final paragraph that para. (c) is intended to take effect
as 'an expression of present intention by way of comfort only'.
                                                                                            B

If para. (c) is to take effect only as an expression of present intention, it can contain no
contractual promise as to the future policy or intentions of Atlantic Computers. It must
be treated as nothing more than a warranty that, at the relevant date, 30 December 1986
or 31 March 1987 as the case may be, Atlantic Computers did intend that, if in future
AML was unable to meet its commitment to NAB, then the parent would stand behind
its subsidiary. That warranty may or may not have given comfort to NAB; but as is made   C
clear by the final paragraph, it was not intended to do more than give such comfort as
NAB might derive from an expression of present intention.

It is not suggested – and on the evidence before me it could not be suggested – that
Atlantic Computers did not have a present intention on 30 December 1986 (or 31 March
1987) in the terms which I have described. Nor is it suggested that that present intention
did not continue up until 14 December 1989, when AML wrote to NAB to confirm that
the 1986 comfort letter remained in place.   D

In those circumstances, there can be no claim for breach of warranty; and, there being
no contractual promise as to future conduct, there can be no claim for breach of such a
promise.

It was contended on behalf of NAB that to treat the final paragraph of the letter as
qualifying para. (c) in the way that I have described is to destroy an obligation which had
already arisen under para. (c). It was said that, as a matter of construction, the final   E
paragraph cannot be allowed to have that effect and that it must be struck down on the
grounds of repugnancy. NAB sought to rely on the principle that a later clause in a deed
which is repugnant to an earlier clause cannot be allowed to take effect. In my view, the
answer to that contention is to be found in the judgment of Lord Phillimore in *Rose &
Frank Co v J R Crompton and Brothers Ltd* [1925] AC 445, in particular at p. 454.

The letter must be read as a whole. Reading the document as a whole, it cannot make   F
any difference that the qualification 'in the case of para. (c) above, it is an expression of
present intention by way of comfort only' appears where it does. The qualification might
equally well have appeared immediately before para. (c), in the form 'para. (c) below is
intended as an expression of present intention by way of comfort only.' Those who enter
into letters of this kind cannot be taken to have had a different intention because they
choose to introduce the qualification immediately after rather than immediately before
the relevant paragraph.   G

I was, quite properly, referred to other decisions on letters of comfort – in particular,
to the decisions of Staughton J and of the Court of Appeal in *Chemco Leasing SpA v
Rediffusion* [1987] 1 FTLR 201 and to the decisions of Hirst J and of the Court of Appeal
in *Kleinwort Benson Ltd v Malaysia Mining Corporation Bhd* (1989) 5 BCC 337; [1989] 1
WLR 379. As the Court of Appeal has made clear in *Kleinwort Benson* the question for
the court in each case is whether as a matter of construction, in the light of whatever   H
surrounding circumstances may be relevant and admissible, the parties intended to make
a contractual promise for the future or to give only a warranty as to present intention.

Although for reasons explained by Staughton J in *Chemco Leasing SpA v Rediffusion
Ltd* (unreported, 19 July 1985) in a passage cited by Hirst J in *Kleinwort Benson* ((1988) 4
BCC 217 at p. 223; [1988] 1 WLR 799 at p. 806G), it may be artificial to assume that

A   parties to a letter of comfort had any common intention at all as to the effect of that letter which they have signed, nevertheless the court's task in these cases is to ascertain what common intention should be ascribed to them from the terms of the document and the surrounding circumstances. In my view, the common intention to be ascribed to these parties appears plainly from the terms of the letter. It was an intention that Atlantic Computers should give no more than a warranty as to present intention by way of comfort only.

B

   I was referred also, understandably, to the decision of Rogers CJ in the Supreme Court of New South Wales in the case of *Banque Brussels Lambert SA v Australian National Industries Ltd* (1989) 21 NSWLR 502. It is clear from remarks on p. 523 that the Chief Justice found the approach of the Court of Appeal in *Kleinwort Benson* somewhat unreal. He took the view that the construction reached by the Court of Appeal rendered the document in that case nothing but a scrap of paper.

C

   It would not be open to me to follow the Chief Justice's decision, even if I were to accept his criticism of the Court of Appeal's approach; but I draw attention to the fact that, as he acknowledged, the test prescribed by the law of Australia to determine whether a statement is promissory or only representational is different from that in England (see p. 524A). In my view, the law of England is clear. A document in the terms of these two letters of comfort does not impose a contractual promise as to future conduct.

D   Accordingly, I dismiss the application and confirm the decision of the scheme administrators.

(Application for leave to appeal refused)

E

F

G

H

Preston Borough Council v Riley & Anor.   A

Court of Appeal (Civil Division).
Russell and Hobhouse L JJ and Sir Roger Parker.
Judgment delivered 23 March 1995.

*Insolvency – County court administration order – Whether liability for unpaid
community charge was debt within county court administration order – County
Courts Act 1984, Pt. VI.*   B

**County court administration orders under Pt. VI of the County Courts Act 1984 in favour
of the respondents properly included their liability for unpaid community charges under the
Local Government Finance Act 1988 and the Community Charge (Administration and
Enforcement) Regulations 1989. Against the background of the law of bankruptcy the
words 'debt' and 'indebtedness' in Pt. VI on their ordinary meaning included the respondents'
liability for unpaid community charge. There was nothing in the 1984 Act to show that a   C
narrower meaning was intended, and nothing in the 1988 Act and 1989 regulations sufficient
to take the debt arising from the making of a liability order out of Pt. VI of the 1984 Act.**

The following cases were referred to in the judgment of Hobhouse LJ:

Liverpool Corporation v Hope [1938] 1 KB 751.
McGreavy, Re [1950] Ch 269.
Pascoe, Re [1944] Ch 310.   D
St Aubyn v A-G [1952] AC 15.
Savundra, Re [1973] 1 WLR 1147.
Seaman v Burley [1896] 2 QB 344.

W Braithwaite QC and M Mulrooney (instructed by the solicitor to Preston Borough
Council) for the appellants.

A Rumbelow QC and W Hunter (instructed by Sutcliffe Reed, Preston) for the   E
respondents.

JUDGMENT

Hobhouse LJ: The *County Courts Act* 1984 consolidated various statutes dealing with
the constitution, jurisdiction and procedure of the county courts. Part VI contains the
provisions covering the making of administration orders in the county court: F

'112(1) Where a debtor–

(a) is unable to pay forthwith the amount of a judgment obtained against him;
and

(b) alleges that his whole indebtedness amounts to a sum not exceeding the
county court limit, inclusive of the debt for which the judgment was
obtained,   G

a county court may make an order providing for the administration of his estate.'

Before it makes the order, the court has to give notice to each of the creditors whose
name the debtor has given (subs. (3)). Creditors representing debts of over £1,500 may
petition for the debtor's bankruptcy, provided he or they do so within 28 days (subs. (4)).
By subs. (6):

'An administration order may provide for the payment of the debts of the debtor   H
by instalments or otherwise, and either in full or to such extent as appears
practicable to the court under the circumstances of the case, and subject to any
conditions as to his future earnings or income which the court may think just.'

Section 113 provides for the marshalling of the debts and gives creditors the right to
object to the order or its terms. It is implicit, with an immaterial exception, (d), that all

A   creditors rank equally. (See also O. 18, r. 18.) Section 114 provides that, subject to preserving a landlord's right to distrain for rent,

> '. . . when an administration order is made, no creditor shall have any remedy against the person or property of the debtor in respect of any debt–
>
>   (a) of which the debtor notified the appropriate court before the administration order was made; or
>
B
>
>   (b) which has been scheduled to the order,
>
> except with the leave of the appropriate court, and on such terms as that court may impose.'

The court has the power to allow execution in certain circumstances (s. 115). When a debtor has fully complied with the order he is discharged from his debts to the scheduled creditors (s. 117).

C   Part VI therefore contains a simplified scheme for dealing with insolvent debtors in the county court. It has some of the features of the provisions of the *Bankruptcy Act* 1914, now superseded by the *Insolvency Act* 1986, and in a simplified way deals with the same problems as those Acts. In my judgment it is the bankruptcy legislation which provides the context in which the provisions of Pt. VI have to be construed.

D   The point raised by this appeal is whether a liability for unpaid community charge under the *Local Government Finance Act* 1988 is a 'debt' for the purpose of Pt. VI of the 1984 Act. Is it part of the debtor's 'whole indebtedness' for the purpose of s. 112(1)(b)? Is it a 'debt' for the purpose of s. 114? We understand that different county courts have given differing answers to these questions and that an authoritative resolution of these differences is required. The community charge has now been replaced by the council tax and Pt. VI of the 1984 Act will shortly have been amended by the *Courts and Legal Services Act* 1990. But we are told that the decision of this court upon the meaning of Pt. VI will still have value.

E   The rival arguments can be shortly stated. The judgment debtors, Mr and Mrs Riley, adopt the language of Somervell LJ in giving the judgment of the Court of Appeal in *Re McGreavy* [1950] Ch 269 at p. 275, when considering whether a liability for rates came within the term 'debt' as used in the *Bankruptcy Act* 1914:

> 'In the first place, we think that the word "debt", apart from any indication from
F
> the context to the contrary, would in its natural meaning cover a liability for rates. It is undoubtedly a sum due. If a man were asked to make a list of his debts he would clearly include it.'

On this basis, they say the words in Pt. VI should be given their ordinary meaning. A man who is asked to list his whole indebtedness would certainly include the unpaid community charge which he owed to the local authority.

G   The council refer to other dicta. In *Seaman v Burley* [1896] 2 QB 344 at p. 347 Lord Esher MR said:

> 'But I do not think it is true to say that the obligation to pay the rate is a debt. It is certainly not a debt in the ordinary sense of the term. No one can bring an action for it. It is a payment to be made in pursuance of a public duty, which cannot be enforced by action or in any other way than by proceedings before magistrates.'

H   In *Liverpool Corporation v Hope* [1938] 1 KB 751 at p. 754, Slesser LJ said, in relation to an attempt to bring a civil action to recover unpaid rates:

> 'As to the first ground, which appears on the face of it to be an ordinary common law claim for debt, it is clear to my mind that the only remedy which is afforded to a local authority entitled to rates is the remedy of distress. A rate is not a common law liability, it is the creature of statute.'

Thus, the council argue, debt does not as such include a liability for a tax. The community   A
charge was a tax. It falls to be collected within the scheme laid down in Sch. 4 of the 1988
Act as elaborated by the *Community Charge (Administration and Enforcement)
Regulations* 1989. In law it gives rise to a liability not a debt. The relevant judicial
proceedings for the collection of the tax are in the magistrates' court not by action in the
county court as would be the case if there were a debt.

Whereas the statement relied upon by Mr and Mrs Riley was made in the context of   B
considering the *Bankruptcy Act* 1914, those relied upon by the council were made in
rather different contexts – whether the recovery proceedings were criminal or civil –
whether a council was confined to proceedings in the magistrates' court. But the council
submit that they should guide our decision and support the decision of Judge Holt that
unpaid community charge was not a 'debt'.

These quotations suffice to show that the word 'debt' has been understood in different
senses. It can be wide enough to include a liability such as that with which we are   C
concerned; it can be more restricted and not include statutory liabilities for which
remedies are provided in the magistrates' courts. The word is capable of being used to
express wider and narrower meanings. In any given statute the sense in which it is used is
to be derived from its context in the statute itself and the context of the statutory scheme
into which the statute in question has to fit. It is necessary to make this choice in deciding
in what sense the words 'whole indebtedness' and 'debts' have been used. In *McGreavy*   D
the court did not treat as decisive their view of the ordinary meaning of the word; they
went on to consider in detail the structure and provisions of the 1914 Act.

In 1991, judgments were given against Mr and Mrs Riley in the Preston County Court
for sums which they owed to the Electricity Board. They asked the court to make
administration orders. They listed sums which they said they owed to other creditors.
Mrs Riley listed four creditors and Mr Riley three. He included the rent which he owed   E
to the council. Each included as well a sum of £449 which he/she said he/she owed to the
council for unpaid community charge for an earlier year. The council had taken
proceedings against each of them in the magistrates' court and on 22 February 1991 had
obtained 'liability orders' against them under Pt. 4 of the 1989 regulations. This had not
however led to the recovery of the tax. The county court made administration orders in
favour of Mr and Mrs Riley and directed that they could pay off their debts at the rate
of £10 per month; it seems that they have no money and are living on social security   F
payments.

When they heard about the administration orders, the council objected to them; they
said that the orders should not have included the sums of uncollected community charge.
The district judge rejected their application. They appealed to the judge. Judge Holt
allowed the appeal and amended the administration orders so as to exclude the unpaid
community charges. Mr and Mrs Riley have appealed to this court.   G

Judge Holt gave a careful judgment setting out the arguments in full and referred to
the decision of another county court judge. She recognised the force of the debtors'
argument and accepted what Somervell LJ had said in *McGreavy*. She was persuaded to
take a different view by a consideration of the 1989 regulations. She held that 'total
indebtedness in s. 112 must relate to debts which are recoverable by action'. Her
reasoning can be criticised since she appears to use later regulations made under a later
and distinct Act of Parliament as an aid to the construction of the Act of 1984; but this   H
of course does not necessarily mean that her conclusion was wrong.

The question raised by this appeal has two aspects: first what is the meaning of Pt. VI
of the 1984 Act; secondly, whether unpaid community charge comes within it. The answer
to the first question is largely determinative of the answer to the second. There has been
little dispute about the character of the liability for community charge; it is accepted, by

A   analogy from *Liverpool Corporation v Hope*, that it does not give rise to a civil cause of action. There is no statutory provision making the unpaid tax recoverable by a civil action even after a liability order has been made. The relevance of the 1988 Act and the 1989 regulations is primarily to identify the character of the liability which has given rise to this dispute but the council have advanced an argument based upon the Act and regulations.

B   The law recognises that monetary liabilities can arise in different ways and give rise to different legal consequences. For instance, a contract can give rise to a debt. A tort or a breach of contract or a breach of statutory duty can give rise to a liability in damages which may be liquidated or unliquidated. A statutory provision may give rise to a monetary liability. That liability may be recoverable as a civil debt but it need not be. It is a matter of implication from the terms of the statute. If the statute makes special

C   provision for the recovery of the relevant sum in a particular way, it can carry the implication that the remedy of a civil action is not open to the claimant. This was the basis of the decision in *Liverpool Corporation v Hope*. An Act, whilst laying down a special enforcement procedure, may provide that the relevant sums shall also be recoverable as a civil debt.

  Historically the remedy of an action in debt was available for a wide range of liquidated monetary liabilities. It was not restricted to liabilities in contract. It served 'for the

D   recovery of statutory penalties, of forfeitures under bye-laws, of amercements, and of moneys adjudged by a court to be due': Maitland: *The Forms of Action at Common Law*, Lecture 5. Debts of record were recoverable in this way. In *Re Pascoe* [1944] Ch 310, it was held that a fine imposed after the conviction of the bankrupt at the Newcastle Assizes was a debt of record due to the Crown provable in his bankruptcy. The court held that the fine came within the term 'debt' in the *Bankruptcy Act* 1914 (per Morton J at pp. 313 and 317):

E

> '. . . I feel no doubt that the fine was a debt if the word "debt" is to bear its ordinary meaning. It is a debt of record due to the Crown.'

> '. . . the fact that a fine is also a punishment does not make it any the less a debt . . .'

(See also *Re Savundra* [1973] 1 WLR 1147.)

F   The magistrates' court which made the liability orders against Mr and Mrs Riley is not a court of record. But there is a close analogy with debts of record and judgment debts. The liability of Mr and Mrs Riley is of a character which would historically have been recognised as a debt: it properly comes within the term 'debt'. The two cases which are concerned with the law of bankruptcy, *McGreavy* and *Pascoe* both give a wide interpretation to the word 'debt'.

G   It is against this background of the existing law of bankruptcy that the 1984 Act re-enacted the provisions for administration orders in the county court. The words 'debt' and 'indebtedness' are unqualified. On their ordinary meaning they include the liability for the unpaid community charge. In my judgment there is nothing in the 1984 Act to show that a narrower meaning is intended. The scheme is clearly intended to be comprehensive. If some classes of debts are to be excluded from the scope of s. 114, it is difficult to see how the orders will work in practice. That the scheme is intended to be

H   comprehensive is supported by the safeguards built into it. The court has an overriding discretion under s. 112 when the order is applied for; after an order has been made, the court has under s. 114 the power to permit other remedies and under s. 115 the duty to permit execution if assets above a certain limit exist. The creditor also has the opportunity to present a petition provided he complies with s. 112(4). As has been held in the cases cited, the existence of procedures in the magistrates' court does not imply that the relevant

A

debt should be excluded from the scope of provisions such as these; see, for example, the similar argument rejected by the Court of Appeal in *McGreavy* at p. 278.

The arguments of the council upon the construction of Pt. VI of the 1984 Act do not succeed. There remains the argument which persuaded the judge. Is it implicit in the 1988 Act and the regulations of 1989 that the liability for unpaid community charge shall not be treated as a debt for the purposes of legislative provisions such as those contained in Pt. VI? By the time that the 1988 Act was passed, the law of insolvency had been extensively recast by Acts which were then consolidated into the *Insolvency Act* 1986.

B

The community charge was introduced by Pt. I of the *Local Government Finance Act* 1988 in substitution for the domestic rate. It imposed a statutory liability upon defined classes of individuals to pay the charge. Under s. 9(6), the individual is required to discharge the liability by making payments in accordance with the administrative provisions in the second schedule to the Act and regulations made under it. Under s. 22(3) the fourth schedule is to take effect in relation to the recovery of sums due. Sch. 4 empowers the minister to make regulations. It covers a range of remedies: the making of liability orders by magistrates' courts, attachment of earnings, deductions from income support, distress, commitment to prison, bankruptcy, winding up, and charging orders. Paragraphs 9 and 10 are those which relate to bankruptcy and winding up. Each cross-refers to the *Insolvency Act* 1986 and states that regulations may be made which provide that, following a liability order, the amount due shall be deemed to be a debt for the purposes of a creditor's petition for a bankruptcy order (s. 267) or a winding-up order (s. 122 and s. 221). A regulation in the terms of these paragraph was made in 1989: it is reg. 44. The schedule and the regulations refer to a person against whom a liability order has been made as the 'debtor'.

C

D

The council submits that para. 9 and 10 and reg. 44 show that without such a provision the liability would not be a debt. This argument has to be taken to the length of saying that the 1988 Act and the 1989 regulations implicitly provide that the liability shall *not* be a debt save for the limited purposes stated, that is, that it shall not be a debt for the purpose of Pt. VI of the 1984 Act. The use of the word 'deemed' is capable of carrying this implication but does not necessarily do so (*St Aubyn v A-G* [1952] AC 15 at p. 53, per Lord Radcliffe). It is the case that the paragraphs and regulation are confined to the right of the creditor to petition; they do not refer to the right of the debtor to do so nor do they deal with rights of proof. I consider that the correct understanding of these provisions is that they are, for the avoidance of doubt, concerned with the legal proceedings which may be taken by the creditor. In the absence of such a provision it might be inferred that a creditor was not to be permitted to bring such a petition. The provisions do not touch upon the status of the liability in general, nor do they address the position of the debtor and his right to petition for his own bankruptcy (or, in the case of a company, for its own winding up or the making of some other order). The schedule and the regulations are dealing with the remedies open to the creditor; they do not suffice to support the implication which the council need; they do not suffice to take the debt that has arisen from the making of a liability order out of Pt. VI of the 1984 Act.

E

F

G

It follows that in my judgment this appeal should be allowed and the order of the district judge should stand.

Sir Roger Parker: I agree.

Russell LJ: I also agree.

H

(*Appeal allowed*)

Re a Company No. 007936 of 1994.

Chancery Division (Companies Court).
Roger Kaye QC (sitting as a deputy judge of the Chancery Division).
Judgment delivered 23 March 1995.

Winding-up petition – Just and equitable ground – Striking-out application – Petition alleged exclusion from management in quasi-partnership – Petition alleged fear that company might be insolvent – Whether petition demurrable as containing no averment that petitioners had tangible interest in winding up – Whether petition showed how expectation of participation in management arose – Insolvency Act 1986, s. 122(1)(g); Rules of the Supreme Court, O. 18, r. 19.

This was an application by the company to strike out a contributories' winding-up petition under s. 122(1)(g) of the Insolvency Act 1986 on the ground that it disclosed no reasonable cause of action under RSC, O. 18, r. 19.

The company argued that the petition was demurrable because it alleged that the company was insolvent which was inconsistent with the need to aver that the petitioners had some tangible interest in the winding up. Secondly, the company argued that the petition disclosed no cause of action because it merely alleged that the company was a quasi-partnership and that the relationship between the quasi-partners had broken down, but did not describe how the quasi-partnership and legitimate expectation of taking part in management arose.

Held, striking out the petition:

1. The petitioners did show a sufficient locus standi to petition. They were, in substance and by implication, if not expressly, alleging that they were unable to state whether there would be some tangible interest available to them on a winding up owing to the lack of information. There was no need for the petition to go further and show or aver that the petitioners would be entitled to or were likely to be entitled to some such tangible interest, where they alleged instead the company's own default in providing proper access to financial information. Further, the plea as to a 'fear' that the company might be trading while insolvent was not necessarily an averment that the company was in fact insolvent.

2. It was not sufficient for the petitioner simply to aver there was a legitimate expectation of taking part in the management. That did not of itself 'specify the grounds' of the petition. It must at least be stated how that expectation arose and what agreement or understanding there was as the basis for subjecting the exercise of legal rights to equitable considerations. Without 'something more' over and above the rights and expectations shareholders expected from the company's constitution and the fact of their association in the company, the petition failed to disclose any basis on which the court could order the winding up of the company.

The following cases were referred to in the judgment:

Chesterfield Catering Co Ltd, Re [1977] Ch 373.
City and County Bank, Re (1875) LR 10 Ch App 470.
Ebrahimi v Westbourne Galleries Ltd [1973] AC 360.
Harrison (Saul D) & Sons plc, Re [1994] BCC 475.
Newman and Howard Ltd, Re [1962] Ch 257.
Othery Construction Ltd, Re [1966] 1 WLR 69.
Practice Director No. 1 of 1990 [1990] BCC 292.
Rica Gold Washing Co, Re (1879) 11 ChD 36.
Ringtower Holdings plc, Re (1989) 5 BCC 82.
Rolled Steel Products (Holdings) Ltd v British Steel Corporation (1984) 1 BCC 99,158; [1986] Ch 246 (CA).
Unisoft Group Ltd, Re (No. 2) [1994] BCC 766.

Robert Miles (instructed by Ince & Co) for the applicant.

Ashley Underwood (instructed by Hill Taylor Dickinson) for the respondents.

JUDGMENT A

Roger Kaye QC: On 14 December 1994 a petition dated 12 December 1994 was presented to the court for the winding up of the applicant company under the provisions of the *Insolvency Act* 1986 by certain of the contributories of that company. The particular ground relied on for the winding up of the company is s. 122(1)(g) of that Act, namely that it is just and equitable to do so. Before me is an application dated 20 December 1994 by the applicant company seeking to strike out the petition under RSC, O. 18, r. 19. In the alternative, should that application fail, the applicant seeks joinder of certain additional parties to the petition and also security for costs. It was agreed that I should deal first with the strike-out application and, subject to that, then proceed to hear submissions on the remainder of the company's application. The grounds on which the strike-out application are based are that the petition discloses no reasonable cause of action, that it is scandalous, frivolous or vexatious or is otherwise an abuse of the process of the court. C

Since the petition has not been advertised I propose to refer to the applicant simply as 'the company' and to certain material individuals and others, namely 'Mr I', 'Mr E', 'Mr L' and the 'L' family, by those letters rather than their full names.

The petition is supported by an affidavit of verification sworn on the same date by an associate solicitor of the petitioner's solicitors. This supporting affidavit exhibited three exhibits: first, the petition; secondly, the memorandum and articles of association of the company; and, thirdly, a bundle of documents said to have been provided by Mr I, a director of the company. D

The petition is presented by two named trustees of a family settlement dated 28 September 1989, one is a company, which I shall call 'MSL', and the other is an individual, Mr M. Both give addresses in Limassol, Cyprus. Paragraph 5 of the petition contains what may be described as its 'guts' and alleges: E

'The company has been operating as a quasi-partnership. The relationship of mutual trust and confidence between the quasi-partners has broken down and [Mr E] is not being allowed to take part in the management, which he has a legitimate expectation of doing. In the circumstances it is just and equitable that the company be wound up.'

Below this paragraph is a subheading, 'Particulars', followed by a series of F subparagraphs to which I shall have to return. Paragraph 6 of the petition avers that:

'The petitioner will consent to an order pursuant to s. 127 of the *Insolvency Act* 1986 in the standard form.'

The purpose of that averment was that, notwithstanding the presentation of the petition, dispositions of property otherwise rendered void after the presentation of the winding-up petition should be validated at the earliest opportunity under that section: G see para. (5) of *Practice Direction No. 1 of 1990: Companies Court Contributory's Petitions* [1990] BCC 292. Despite that averment, subpara. 5(i) of the particulars given under para. 5 contains this:

'[Mr I] fears that, although the company has been trading profitably, it may now be trading whilst insolvent, as:

  (i) he has not received explanations for many concerns he has raised as to H profitability;

  (ii) it has been conceded that [Mr L] has received payments of over £100,000 wrongly described as dividends and which are recoverable, and the company asserts that he will be paid a bonus so as to extinguish his indebtedness, but has implied that the company cannot afford to pay it.'

A   On the face of it the petitioners seemed, at first blush, to have been implying, by para. 6, that the company was solvent, but by para. 5(i) that it (or rather they fear that it) may be insolvent. Faced with this ambiguity the company applied, ex parte, to Lindsay J on 16 December 1994 for an order under s. 127. The judge granted a temporary order validating dispositions of the company until the matter could be heard inter partes on 20 December 1994. On that occasion, on the company expressly assuring Arden J that the company was able to meet its liabilities as they fell due, the judge made a s. 127 order

B   over until judgment on the petition or further order in the meantime. On the same day, 20 December, the company made the application which is now before me to strike out the petition and for the additional relief I have already mentioned.

     The petition came before Mr Registrar Buckley on 12 January 1995 for its first directions hearing. The registrar ordered the petition to stand as points of claim and directed it be not advertised. Mr Registrar Buckley further gave directions for the filing

C   of evidence on the present application and adjourned the petition to the judge. The purpose of ordering the petition to stand as points of claim seems to me to have been, amongst other things, to avoid the necessity for the lengthy affidavits of evidence that was a familiar feature of cases of this sort.

     The petition in the present case therefore stands both as a petition and as points of claim. It is not disputed by Mr Underwood, counsel for the petitioners, that a petition is

D   susceptible of being struck out under O. 18, r. 19(1), for the provisions of that rule, which on its face embraces 'any pleading', also expressly extends to a petition by virtue of O. 18, r. 19(3). This is even though the requirements as to form and contents of pleadings (in, for example, O. 18, r. 12) do not otherwise so extend since O. 1, r. 4(1) defines 'pleading' as not including a 'petition'. That O. 18, r. 19(1) also extends to a document entitled or ordered to stand as 'points of claim' cannot, I think, be in any doubt. As a 'petition' it is expressly within O. 18, r. 19(3). As points of claim it is also, in my judgment,

E   caught by that rule. It is plain that the registrar, in ordering the petition to stand as points of claim, intended it to be read and treated as a pleading in 'insolvency proceedings' (which these undoubtedly are: see r. 13.7 of the *Insolvency Rules* 1986) and to which the Rules of the Supreme Court and the practice of the High Court are to apply 'except so far as inconsistent with the Insolvency Rules': see r. 7.51 of those rules. I see nothing in a petition being ordered to stand as points of claim as being 'inconsistent' with the

F   Insolvency Rules. I am fortified in this conclusion having noted that Harman J reached a similar view in *Re Unisoft Group Ltd (No. 2)* [1994] BCC 766 at pp. 768–769.

     It is, of course, common ground that I must approach the strike-out application so far as it is based on the ground of no reasonable cause of action on the footing that the averments in the petition are true, irrespective of what might or might not be proved on the effective hearing of the petition. Moreover the court must scrutinise the averments,

G   and, if necessary where it is legitimate to do so, the evidence in support of the petition, with care in order to see if the petitioners really do have an arguable case and an entitlement, at trial, to the relief sought on that case. Only if the court comes to the clear view that the petitioner's case is plainly and obviously unsustainable should it be struck out: see, for example, *Re Saul D Harrison & Sons plc* [1994] BCC 475 at p. 492 per Hoffmann LJ.

H   Each case depends, of course, on its own facts. Mr Underwood acknowledged that the petition is not as detailed as might customarily be the case with a contributory's petition but sought, in the circumstances of this case, to persuade me to apply a gloss to this test and to adopt a more lenient or flexible and less rigorous approach to the petition. In elaboration of this he deployed two arguments. First, he argued that, where, as here, it is contemplated that the court might order points of claim, the petition ought, therefore, to be regarded as akin to a generally endorsed writ. On this basis he argued that just as the

courts are slow to strike out defects of particularity in a generally endorsed writ, since   A
they can be cured either by amendment or by service of a statement of claim, so I ought
to be slow to strike out the petition in this case. He drew my attention to a supporting
passage for this proposition in relation to generally endorsed writs on p. 36 of vol. 1 of
the *Supreme Court Practice 1995* under the heading 'Indorsement of Claim. 1. Statement
of claim not indorsed' where it is stated:

> 'Where an indorsement of claim lacks particularity, the defect does not render the   B
> writ a nullity (*Pontin v Wood* [1962] 1 QB 594; and see *Auster v London Motor
> Coach Works* (1914) 31 TLR 26). The defect may be cured by amendment or by
> the service of a statement of claim (*Hill v Borough of Luton* [1951] 2 KB 387).'

Secondly, he argued that by consenting to the registrar's order that the petition should
stand as points of claim, the company became estopped from taking any pleading point
against the petition as points of claim over and above any criticism they could legitimately
make of the petition viewed, as it were, as a generally endorsed writ.   C

I do not accept these submissions. There is, in my judgment, no reason for departing
from the usual test, which I have referred to above, to be applied to an application based
on non-disclosure in the petition of a reasonable cause of action, namely is it plain and
obvious that the petition will not succeed. It is this test which is to be applied to this
petition. My reasons are as follows:

(1)   A petition is a formal document which initiates the winding-up process against a   D
company. This much is clear from s. 124(1) of the *Insolvency Act* 1986 providing
(so far as relevant) that 'an application to the court for the winding up of a
company shall be by petition'.

(2)   Rule 4.22(1) of the *Insolvency Rules* 1986 requires a contributory's winding-up
petition to 'specify the grounds on which it is presented'. Whilst I was not referred
to the authorities cited in support of the passage quoted above from the *Supreme*   E
Court Practice, I am prepared to accept that the general practice of the court in
relation to lack of particularity in generally indorsed writs is as Mr Underwood
describes it and as the passage quoted states it to be, but the petition in this case is
not such a writ. Despite being ordered to stand as points of claim the petition is,
and started life as, a petition and, as such, is susceptible to a different regime. That
regime is governed not by the rules of pleadings as set out in the Rules of the   F
Supreme Court (with the exception in O. 18, r. 19 I have mentioned) but by the
Insolvency Rules 1986 (as amended). Rule 4.22(1) of these rules, applicable to
contributories' petitions (see r. 4.2(4)), provides, as I have said, that:

> 'The petition shall specify the grounds on which it is presented . . .'

That is complementary to s. 122(1) of the *Insolvency Act* 1986 which prescribes the
grounds on which a company may be wound up.   G

(3)   The fact that the registrar ordered the petition to stand as points of claim does not
make it any the less a petition. That the registrar had jurisdiction to make that
order is clear from r. 4.23(1) of the *Insolvency Rules* 1986 conferring on the registrar
power to make such orders as he thinks fit for the procedure to be followed on the
petition: see r. 4.23(1)(b) and (e). Viewed, of course, from the standpoint of the
date of presentation of the petition (and therefore prior to his order), it was by no   H
means absolutely guaranteed that the registrar would make the order he did. The
registrar had a discretion at large, to be exercised judicially as he thought fit in the
circumstances. On the other hand, unless the court gives leave to the contrary, a
generally indorsed writ must be followed by a statement of claim (see O. 18, r. 1)
which must, in turn, comply with the pleading requirements contained in O. 18
(see, for example, O. 18, r. 12). Otherwise, the statement of claim must be itself

A   endorsed on the writ and, where appropriate, comply with the same requirements. I do not, therefore, find Mr Underwood's analogy either helpful or relevant.

(4)   As a document initiating the process against the company, the grounds relied on must disclose valid grounds upon which the court can validly order the winding up of the company under s. 122 and those grounds must be specified with clarity and sufficient precision to enable the company to know the case it has to meet at trial.

B   Hence, even if I were to accept that the registrar's order was a consent order (although it does not so appear on its face), the effect of r. 4.22(1) and the registrar's order under r. 4.23(1) seems to me merely to emphasise and underline the importance of the petition as a formal document initiating the present litigation. The effect of the order was to dispense with the need for an affidavit in answer. Instead, the company (subject to the present application) could, no doubt, answer the petition by points of defence. The winding up of an active company is a serious

C   step with serious consequences for all concerned, creditors as well as contributories. It therefore behoves petitioners to set out their case in the petition with clarity, substance and precision so that the respondent company knows, and the court knows, what case the company has to meet. The petition must, either in its original form or as amended, therefore contain all the material averments or, to use the words specified in r. 4.22(1), 'the grounds' upon which it is based. It is these

D   grounds which the company here has to meet and it is these grounds which the petitioners must prove at trial, on the ordinary civil burden of proof, if it is to have any hope of succeeding in obtaining the winding-up order it seeks. The analogy from the realm of pleadings which I do find helpful, and which is, in my judgment, useful to bear in mind can be taken from the words of Lawton LJ in *Rolled Steel Products (Holdings) Ltd v British Steel Corporation* [1986] Ch 246 CA at p. 309; (1984) 1 BCC 99,158 at p. 99,203, words which appear to me to be wholly apposite

E   to petitions:

       'I wish, however, to add a comment about the pleading points which have had to be considered in this appeal. From the way they were raised by counsel and dealt with by the trial judge I was left with the impression that neither the judge nor defending counsel appreciated as fully as they should have done the need for precision and expedition when dealing with pleading points. My recent experience in this court shows that some counsel and judges are not giving

F   pleadings the attention which they should. Pleadings are formal documents which have to be prepared at the beginning of litigation. They are essential for the fair trial of an action and the saving of time at trial. The saving of time keeps down the costs of litigation. A plaintiff is entitled to know what defences he has to meet and a defendant what claims are being made against him. If the parties do not know, unnecessary evidence may be got together and led or, even

G   worse, necessary evidence may not be led. Pleadings regulate what questions may be asked of witnesses in cross-examination.'

(5)   If, therefore, the pleadings do not show the ground on which a court could validly make a winding-up order or if, on the grounds that are pleaded, it is plain and obvious that, even if proved at trial, the petitioners must fail, the court will and must exercise the exceptional jurisdiction to strike out the petition. To do otherwise would be to prolong for more than is necessary the state of uncertainty that a

H   petition inevitably brings to an operating company's activities and plans. All these points merely serve, in my judgment, to emphasise once again the duty on petitioners to ensure that their petition contains the material facts on which the petition is based.

(6)   Even if, as to which I say nothing, an estoppel could operate in this field, by the time the registrar made his order the company had already issued its application

to strike out the petition. For my part, therefore, I cannot see how any estoppel   A
can be said to have arisen against the company.

(7)   There has been no application to amend the petition in this case at any stage of the
present proceedings hitherto nor before me. The petitioners therefore stand or fall
by the petition in its present form.

With these observations in mind I must, therefore, now turn to the petition itself as it
stands.   B

The petition alleges, in para. 1 and 4, that the company was incorporated on 29 April
1971 under the Companies Acts 1948–1967 to carry on business as a travel agency and
tour operator. Paragraph 2 gives the registered office of the company. In para. 3 it is
alleged that the nominal capital of the company is 38,889 'A' ordinary shares and 11,111
'B' ordinary shares all fully paid up or credited as paid up. I have already set out para. 5
above. I must now refer to the particulars given under that paragraph. By para. 5(a) it is   C
alleged that the company was founded by the L family who own or control the A shares.
Paragraph 5(b) alleges that in September 1977 Mr E joined the company as an employee
but in April 1978 he bought the 'B' shareholding and became the financial director.
Paragraph 5(c) pleads that the articles were revised to give rights to the 'B' shareholders,
and in particular art. 17 gives power to appoint a 'B' director; art. 3 provides a veto over
allotment and disposal of shares; art. 7, 8 and 9 provide a pre-emption procedure; art. 22
provides a veto over five categories of activity; and art. 24 provides a veto over the   D
appointment of a managing director. Beyond that the articles are not set out (though
they are exhibited to the supporting affidavit). Paragraph 5(d) alleges that in 1980 Mr E
was appointed joint managing director, and in 1987 became the sole managing director.
It goes on:

'He was the main point of contact with joint venture partners who provided the
substance of the company's business. By that stage the company was run on a basis   E
of mutual trust and co-operation and it was understood that [Mr E] was entitled
to take a part in the management.'

Paragraph 5(e) alleges that in 1989 the L family and Mr E constituted trusts to hold the
shareholdings and Mr E transferred all the 'B' shares to 'the petitioner'. 'The transfers',
it goes on, 'made no difference to the running of the company.' Paragraph 5(f) says that
on 3 September 1993 Mr E 'was summarily dismissed as managing director for alleged   F
financial irregularities'. 'The allegations', it is averred, 'are false, and [Mr E] has issued
proceedings for wrongful dismissal. The company has counterclaimed in respect of the
alleged irregularities. It is the petitioner's case that this court cannot resolve those
disputes'. Pausing there I was told that these proceedings are currently pending in the
Queen's Bench Division, are hotly disputed, and have already reached the stage of a
rejoinder. Paragraph 5(g) alleges that Mr I was appointed as 'B' director by the petitioner   G
(sic) in place of Mr E but 'has been refused proper access to financial information and
has not been allowed to participate properly in management'. This subparagraph then
concludes after that averment: 'The petitioners will rely on the substantial
correspondence exhibited to the affidavit verifying this petition, as the particulars are too
numerous to be conveniently set out here'. Paragraph 5(h) says that there is no managing
director. I have already referred to para. 5(i). Paragraph 5(j) (the last of the
subparagraphs under the heading 'Particulars') states the following: H

'The petitioners believe that the pre-emption rights in the articles would operate to
their disadvantage and to the advantage of the [L] family because:

(i) the valuation is to be undertaken, so as to be binding, by the auditors. They
have compiled the case against [Mr E] which comprises the counterclaim
referred to in (f) above and which [Mr E] asserts to be false;

A
    (ii) there is no mechanism set out for the valuation;

    (iii) there is no protection for the fact that the 'B' shareholding is a minority interest;

    (iv) the petitioners believe that the company may have been mismanaged since the dismissal of [Mr E] so as to reduce the value of the shares.'

B
I have already set out para. 6 above and para. 7 concludes the material averments of the petition by repeating the last sentence of para. 5. There then follows the usual plea for a winding-up order. That is the petition.

Mr Miles, on behalf of the company, submits, first, that the petitioners have no locus standi to present their petition because, whilst the petition does contain an averment that all the shares are fully paid, it contains no averment that the petitioners have some tangible interest in the winding up. That, he submits, renders the petition demurrable on
C
its face. He points out, correctly, that whilst the petition contains no actual averment that the petitioners have some tangible interest in the winding up, it must at least contain some averment that there will be a substantial surplus for distribution among the shareholders, or at least that the petitioners will be entitled, on a winding up, to some interest qua member or shareholder and not merely to some private, or personal, right. That, he says, the petition does not do, but, instead, implies rather by para. 5(i) that the
D
company is insolvent, and that is therefore fatal to the survival of the petition.

Mr Underwood relies on the allegations in para. 5(g) and 5(i) as constituting sufficient averments for these purposes. He submits that it is sufficient for the petitioners to allege, as they in effect do, that because Mr I, their appointed director, has been refused proper access to financial information, they are unable to say whether there will be such a surplus and, accordingly, by para. 5(i), fear that the company may be insolvent or, by para. 5(j),
E
that the shares in the company may have been reduced in value by reason of mismanagement.

There are, of course, a number of authorities on this topic. I can begin, I think, as did Mr Miles, with the classic statement of Sir George Jessel MR in *Re Rica Gold Washing Co* (1879) 11 ChD 36 at p. 42 where he said:

F
'Now I will say a word or two on the law as regards the position of a Petitioner holding fully paid-up shares. He is not liable to contribute anything towards the assets of the company, and if he has any interest at all, it must be that after full payment of all the debts and liabilities of the company there will remain a surplus divisible among the shareholders of sufficient value to authorize him to present a petition. That being his position, and the rule being that the Petitioner must succeed upon allegations which are proved, of course the Petitioner must shew the court by sufficient allegation that he has a sufficient interest to entitle him to ask
G
for the winding-up of the company. I say "a sufficient interest," for the mere allegation of a surplus or of a probable surplus will not be sufficient. He must shew what I may call a tangible interest. I am not going to lay down any rule as to what that must be, but if he shewed only that there was such a surplus as, on being fairly divided, irrespective of the costs of the winding-up, would give him £5, I should say that would not be sufficient to induce the court to interfere in his behalf.'

H
In *Re Newman and Howard Ltd* [1962] Ch 257 a contributory who had failed, after many requests, to obtain information or accounts from the company presented a petition on ground that it was, in those circumstances, just and equitable to wind up the company. On presentation of the petition the accounts were forthcoming and the petition withdrawn. The sole question was whether the company should pay the petitioner's costs. The company contended that it should not since the petition was demurrable as it had failed to allege that assets would be available for the petitioner in the winding up.

Pennycuick J held that the petition was not demurrable and that the company should   A
pay the petitioner's costs. It is quite apparent from the judgment that the judge did not
in any shape or form resile from what he described as the general rule as stated by the
Court of Appeal in *Re Rica Gold Washing Co* (above). Instead, he said (at p. 262):

> 'In the case where a petition is based on a failure to supply accounts and
> information, with the consequence that the petitioner is unable to tell whether or
> not there will be a surplus available for the contributories, it cannot really be the   B
> law that the petitioner is bound to allege and to verify on oath the statement that
> the company has surplus assets when, by reason of the company's own default, he
> is not in a position to tell whether or not that statement is true. Nor, I think, can it
> really be the law that the petitioner is bound in such a case to make some vague
> statement such as "the accounts may show that there will be surplus assets
> available for the contributories".'

Mr Underwood, not unnaturally, relied on that passage. This case was referred to in   C
Re Othery Construction Ltd [1966] 1 WLR 69. There a fully paid up shareholder
petitioned to wind up the company on the grounds that it was insolvent. Buckley J
dismissed the petition and a submission, based on *Re Newman and Howard Ltd* (above),
that it was no longer necessary for a contributory to show that there is likely to be a
surplus of assets available for distribution in the winding up. Buckley J pointed out that
Pennycuick J had recognised the 'general rule' as laid down in *Re Rica Gold Washing Co*   D
(above) and only qualified it by reference to the particular facts of the case that made it
difficult for the petitioner to allege whether there would or would not be a surplus
available for distribution. He summarised the position thus (at p. 75):

> 'Nevertheless it remains the rule that, before a contributory can petition
> successfully for the winding up of the company, he must show either that there will
> be a surplus of assets available for distribution amongst the shareholders or that
> the affairs of the company require investigation in respects which are likely to   E
> produce such a surplus.'

Mr Miles relies on that for his contention that, far from averring that an investigation
is likely to produce such a surplus, the petitioner in this case seems to be alleging the
contrary, namely that the company may be insolvent.

These cases were considered in *Re Chesterfield Catering Co Ltd* [1977] Ch 373. There
the executors of a shareholder who was a lessee of premises owned by the company   F
wished, in order to facilitate the sale of the lease, to deal with an independent liquidator
of the company since there were no directors or secretary of the company. They
accordingly petitioned for the winding up of the company on the grounds of insolvency
but no creditor appeared to oppose or support the petition. The question arose whether
the executors had locus standi to petition and Oliver J held that they did not but, in the
circumstances, nevertheless stood the petition over for a short time to see if any creditor   G
would appear to support it. After referring to the passage I have quoted from *Re Rica
Gold Washing Co* (above) Oliver J said this at p. 379D:

> 'It should, I think, be noted that Jessel M.R. was there purporting to lay down a
> rule. Mr. Heath says, however, that the rule is not one which does not admit of
> exceptions and he points to Jessel M.R.'s own statement, at p. 43, "There will be,
> no doubt, some exceptions," and to *In Re Newman and Howard Ltd.* [1962] Ch.
> 257, which is referred to by Buckley J. in *In Re Othery Construction Ltd.* [1966] 1   H
> W.L.R. 69 and in which Pennycuick J. declined to treat as demurrable a petition
> presented by a shareholder whose complaint was that no accounts had been
> furnished which would enable an allegation of solvency to be made.
> I think that what Mr. Heath says is right, but I do not think that as the law now
> stands the exception goes beyond this: that a petition will not be regarded as

A   demurrable on the ground of the petitioner's lack of locus standi if his inability to prove his locus standi is due to the company's own default in providing him with information to which, as a member, he is entitled.'

At p. 380G Oliver J added this:

B   '. . . it seems to be contrary to the principle of all the cases to suggest that, even allowing that there may be exceptions to the general rule, a petitioner can demonstrate his locus standi by pointing to some private advantage which he may derive from the winding up and which is unconnected with his membership of the company.'

C   Now I entirely accept Mr Miles' point that para. 5(g) of the petition does not allege, in terms, that *the petitioners* have been refused proper access to financial information. What it does allege, however, is that the petitioner (in the singular, but nothing, I think, turns on that; nobody can be in any doubt as to whom that referred to) appointed Mr I as 'B' director in place of Mr E. That the petitioners were entitled to do so is apparent from para. 5(c) of the petition referring to this power having been given to the 'B' shareholders under art. 17 of the articles of association of the company. It was, however, Mr I, not the petitioners, who was refused proper access. Given that Mr I was a director and not a shareholder it could be said that the refusal to provide him with information was a refusal qua director, not qua member, but I do not think that, for these purposes, such a D distinction matters. It is reasonably plain from the petition that Mr E before him, and Mr I on his appointment, was regarded by the petitioners as the conduit for such information. Thus it seems to me that the petitioners are, in substance and by implication, if not expressly, alleging that they are indeed unable to state whether there would be some tangible interest available to them on a winding up owing to the lack of information. In as much as Mr Miles submits that the petition must go further and show E or aver that the petitioners will be entitled to or are likely to be entitled to some such tangible interest, then I do not think that, on the authorities I have cited, they need do so where, instead, they allege, as here, the company's own default in providing proper access to financial information.

Nor do I think that para. 5(i) goes as far as Mr Miles contends. He submitted that this must be taken to be a positive averment of insolvency. I do not so read it. In its context, particularly following on from the averment in para. 5(g) about lack of financial F information, it is perhaps hardly surprising that Mr I 'fears that, although the company had been trading profitably, it may now be trading while insolvent'. That is a plea as to a 'fear' that is held, not necessarily an averment that the company is in fact insolvent. Whilst I consider there is much more force in Mr Miles' point that this pleading, so viewed, may be irrelevant, it does not follow that it is enough, on this point, to drive the petitioners from the judgment seat. Accordingly, in my judgment, on this aspect of the G case Mr Underwood succeeds and the petitioners do show a sufficient locus standi to petition.

I should perhaps add, lest there be any remaining doubt about the matter, that at one point, in response to a query of my own, since the petition does not also contain any averment that the petitioners have held their shares registered in their name for at least six months during the 18 months before the presentation of the petition, Mr Miles contended that this too was a ground on which the petition was demurrable: see s. 124 of H the *Insolvency Act* 1986. However, the further researches of counsel, for which I am indebted, revealed that in *Re City and County Bank* (1875) LR 10 Ch App 470 (where just this point was taken) James LJ at p. 474 declared that the petition was not demurrable but the point could be set up by way of answer for it is something within the knowledge of the company. In the light of that Mr Miles, rightly, in my view, abandoned the point. No doubt, as the editors of *Buckley on the Companies Acts* (14th ed., vol. 1)

note at p. 540 it is desirable to contain in the petition a plea showing that s. 124 is   A
complied with, but its absence is not, per se, fatal to it.

I must therefore now deal with Mr Miles' second ground of attack, that the petition
discloses no cause of action. The basis of the petition is, as I have said, contained in
para. 5. At its core is a complaint that Mr E has been excluded from the management of
the company.

Mr Miles submitted, however, that it is not sufficient for the petition merely to allege,   B
as it does, in para. 5, that 'the company has been operating as a quasi-partnership' nor
that:

> 'the relationship of mutual trust and confidence between the quasi-partners has
> broken down and [Mr E] is not being allowed to take part in the management,
> which he has a legitimate expectation of doing.'

These expressions, 'quasi-partnership', 'trust and confidence' and 'legitimate expectation'   C
are, he says, mere legal descriptions, not allegations of the material facts giving rise to
those descriptions. He argues that the particulars given under para. 5 take these assertions
no further. They do not describe how the 'quasi-partnership' or 'mutual trust and
confidence' arose beyond reliance on the articles which he submits is not enough.
Likewise the petition does not describe how the 'legitimate expectation' of Mr E's taking
part in management arose beyond reliance on three things: first, on the articles giving Mr   D
E (as the 'B' shareholder) the right to nominate himself as director; secondly, the assertion
in para. 5(d) that by 1987 the company was run on the basis of mutual trust and co-
operation; thirdly, it was by that stage understood that Mr E was entitled to take part in
the management. Each of these three factors, he says, merely brings one back to the
articles, the foundation of Mr E's right to take part in management. What these
averments do not show, he submits, is how Mr E's 'legitimate expectations' could
continue after he transferred the shares to the petitioners in 1989, still less do they show   E
how the petitioners had such expectation beyond the rights conferred by the articles. In
short, he says, it is quite apparent from the petition that the petitioners' case (and Mr E's
case) is based, and based solely, by reference to the articles and his position, derived from
those articles, of managing director. True it is averred in para. 5(e) that the 'transfers [of
the shares to the petitioners in 1989] made no difference to the running of the company'
but that, he argues, is self-evident since the articles continued in being governing the
relationship of the parties. Since therefore, for whatever reason, Mr E ceased to be a   F
director in 1993, after he had transferred his shares to the petitioners, his right to continue
in office also ceased and neither he, nor the petitioners, had nor have any continuing
right to remain in office, certainly not qua shareholder (for he had ceased to be one).
Instead they had a right to appoint another 'B' shareholders nominee director, which
they did in Mr I. On the contrary, it is contended (in para. 5(g)) that on the appointment
of Mr I in place of Mr E, Mr I was deprived of financial information and not allowed to   G
take part in management. That latter right too, Mr Miles points out, is derived from the
articles, not from something more. It is 'the something more' that is missing from this
petition. Mr E, he argues, is fully protected because if he conceives he has been improperly
dismissed he can litigate the matter, as he has done, by action in the Queen's Bench
Division. That does not entitle him or the petitioners to petition for the winding up of
the company.

In my judgment Mr Miles is right and I accept these submissions. The relevant   H
principles applicable to petitions of this kind have been oft stated and are well known. I
do not think I need set out all the relevant quotations. It is clear from the speech of Lord
Wilberforce in *Re Westbourne Galleries Ltd* [1973] AC 360 at pp. 379B–380B, from the
judgment of Peter Gibson J in *Re Ringtower Holdings plc* (1989) 5 BCC 82 at p. 93 and
from the judgments of Hoffmann LJ and Neill LJ in the Court of Appeal in *Re Saul D*

A   *Harrison & Sons plc* [1994] BCC 475 at pp. 489–490 and 500 respectively, that the following principles may be said to be applicable to the consideration of whether a court can and should make a winding-up order on the just and equitable ground in a case such as this:

(1)   In general shareholders have no legitimate expectations beyond the legal rights conferred on them by the memorandum and articles of association.

B   (2)   Part of those general expectations, even in a small company, is that those responsible for the management of the company can be expected to have trust and confidence placed in them by the shareholders. In the absence of proof of some additional agreement or understanding these factors do not make the association of the shareholders formed on the basis of the company's constitution a partnership or quasi-partnership with partner-like obligations owed by each to the others.

C

(3)   Additional rights, obligations and expectations may, however, be conferred or superimposed on those normal constitutional rights and expectations by virtue of some agreement or understanding between the shareholders and the management.

(4)   To justify the court imposing equitable considerations by the making of a winding-up order, there must be 'something more' over and above those general rights and expectations that the shareholders may be expected to have from the company's constitution or from the mere fact of their association in the company. In the absence of 'something more', in the absence, in other words, of some such agreement or understanding there is no basis for subjecting the exercise of legal rights to equitable considerations by the making of a winding-up order on the just and equitable basis. As Lord Wilberforce expressed it in *Re Westbourne Galleries Ltd* [1973] AC 360 at p. 379E–F:

E   'It would be impossible, and wholly undesirable, to define the circumstances in which these [equitable] considerations may arise. Certainly the fact that a company is a small one, or a private company, is not enough. There are very many of these where the association is a purely commercial one, of which it can safely be said that the basis of association is adequately and exhaustively laid down in the articles. The superimposition of equitable considerations requires something more . . .'

F   I have searched long and hard in the petition and the evidence for the 'something more' in this case. Mr Underwood urged me to ignore the transfer by Mr E to the petitioners of his shareholding in 1989, suggesting that whilst the petitioners are not his nominees, the transfer was, nevertheless, for some fiscal or other advantage. On no basis, so far as I can see, is it legitimate so to do. It would ignore the plain facts as pleaded in the petition, that by the time Mr E was dismissed, he was no longer a shareholder. Nor do I think that even if I were to ignore it and if, for one moment, I was able to say it was Mr E who was the petitioner, not the trustees, would I still be able to discern the 'something more' required. it is not Mr E who is the petitioner, but Mr M and MSL. The relevant question then is have they disclosed a ground on which the company could be wound up? If only for the reasons given earlier in this judgment, I do not think that it is sufficient for the petitioner simply to aver there was a legitimate expectation that Mr E could take part in the management. That does not, of itself, 'specify the grounds' of the petition. it must at least be stated how that expectation arose and what the 'something more' was or is that might justify a winding-up order at the end of the day. Whichever way one turns on this petition one comes back to the proposition that the petitioners' case is at best simply based on the articles. That does not, however, assist them with this petition. As I said, the central thrust of the petition is the dismissal of Mr E. But, he having been dismissed at a time when he was no longer a shareholder, had not even that expectation of

continuing in office. I can see no basis on which it can be alleged that the petitioners have　A
a legitimate expectation of his continuing in office (and it is, of course, not so alleged,
para. 5 of the petition alleging instead that 'he', Mr E, not the petitioners, had the
expectation). The petitioners had a right under the articles to appoint Mr I in his place
and did so. Mr I, as the petitioners' nominee, had and has the right to be a director under
the articles. He is a director. The company is still running under the protection of the
s. 127 order I referred to earlier. If Mr I or the petitioners are not obtaining the
information to which they are entitled, then no doubt other legitimate remedies and　B
means are available to them to correct that deficiency but that absence of information is
not the basis or ground on which the petition is presented. Mr E, as Mr Miles observed,
is fully protected for if he is right and the reasons for his dismissal were and are ill-
founded then, no doubt, that will be reflected in the Queen's Bench action.

My judgment is therefore quite simply that, on this petition as drafted, and for the
reasons given, it manifestly fails to disclose any basis on which the court could order the　C
winding up of the company.

Mr Miles also made a number of submissions, somewhat in the alternative, that the
petition was embarrassing in that it failed to particularise the grounds with any clarity or
precision. There was much force in this. On this ground, too, I would have been prepared
to strike out the petition even though the application did not specifically refer to this
ground (Mr Underwood very properly took no point on that). in a petition of this nature　D
it must be regarded as thoroughly unsatisfactory for the company to be met with wholly
vague but potentially important allegations of a 'quasi-partnership' and 'quasi-partners'
without saying between whom the partnership was constituted or who are or were the
quasi-partners. I have also already stated that I accept Mr Miles' criticisms of the failure
to specify how the legitimate expectation arose, and how or between whom it was
understood Mr E was entitled to take part in management. I have also already
commented on the irrelevance of the pleading as to Mr I's 'fears' in para. 5(i). In truth,　E
of course, many of these points under this additional ground of attack overlapped to
some extent with the attack based on lack of reasonable cause of action. I must, however,
also mention one other aspect that is, in my view, to be regarded as completely
unacceptable. I have already referred to para. 5(g) of the petition and its reference to
reliance on 'the substantial correspondence exhibited to the affidavit verifying this
petition.' Any averment in a petition that expects the respondent and its advisers to trawl　F
through a mass of indigestible correspondence, minutes and other documents in order to
find out what the case is against them in a material respect is to be regarded, in my view,
as bad. It is completely impossible to answer and defeats the whole object of pleadings or
petitions being essential for the fair trial of the action as indicated by Lawton LJ in the
passage I quoted earlier in this judgment, and of saving time and costs.

Modern litigation is expensive enough without needlessly adding to it. I accordingly
propose to order that the petition be struck out.　　　G

(Order accordingly)

H

A
Re Butlers Wharf Ltd.

Chancery Division (Companies Court).
Richard Sykes QC (sitting as a deputy High Court judge).
Judgment delivered 30 March 1995.

Suretyship – Whether sureties for part of debt entitled to share in security for whole debt with principal creditor.

B

This was an application by receivers and a bank raising the question whether a surety for a part of a larger debt who had discharged the full amount for which he was surety was entitled to share rateably with the principal creditor in security which had been given for the whole debt.

The bank had made available to the company a facility of £40m in connection with a property development. This was secured by fixed and floating charges and a performance guarantee provided by 'Clydesdale'. There was also a further facility of £10m for the redemption of redeemable shares in the company ('the redemption advance'). The security package for the redemption advance included the deposit of listed securities by a shareholder, 'Conran', and a guarantee from Clydesdale of £800,000 plus interest, capped at £1m in aggregate. The company defaulted and receivers were appointed.

C

D

The deposited shares were sold and Clydesdale paid £1m under its guarantee. The amounts so recovered, totalling £10,889,882.11, were credited to suspense accounts in the bank's name. The full amount of the redemption advance with interest was £10,790,504.52.

Held, ruling accordingly:

1. The redemption advance must be regarded either as having been discharged when the amount held on suspense account was no less than the amount owed in respect of the redemption advance or as due to be discharged immediately by the application of the amounts held in suspense accounts.

E

2. The security given by the company for the whole debt had to be shared between the bank and Clydesdale and Conran who had discharged their obligations as sureties for part of the debt. The circumstances in which the redemption advance was made and the security was provided were not sufficient to displace the prima facie rule in favour of permitting them to share in the security. (*Goodwin v Gray* (1874) 22 WR 312 applied.)

F

3. The bank argued that the Conran memorandum of deposit was expressed not to 'affect' any other security and that the security which the bank took from the company was affected if it was prevented from appropriating realisations of the company's security to that part of the debt which did not comprise the redemption advance. However the memorandum of deposit did not affect the security given by the company, but rather affected the bank's enjoyment of that security.

G

The following cases were referred to in the judgment:

Aldrich v Cooper (1803) 8 Ves Jun 382; 32 ER 402.
Barclays Bank Ltd & Ors v TOSG Trust Fund Ltd & Ors (1984) 1 BCC 99,017; [1984] AC 626.
Farebrother v Woodhouse (1856) 23 Beav 18; 53 ER 7.
Forbes v Jackson (1882) 19 ChD 615.
Goodwin v Gray (1874) 22 WR 312.
Gray v Seckham (1872) LR 7 Ch App 680.
Hobson v Bass (1871) LR 6 Ch App 792.
Kirkwood's Estate, Re (1878) 1 LR Ir 108.
Midland Banking Co v Chambers (1869) LR 4 Ch App 398.
Nicholas v Ridley [1904] 1 Ch 192.
Paul v Spierway Ltd (in liquidation) [1976] Ch 220.

H

Rouse v Bradford Banking Co Ltd [1894] AC 586.   A
Sass, Re [1896] 2 QB 12.
TH Knitwear (Wholesale) Ltd, Re (1988) 4 BCC 102; [1988] Ch 275.
Thornton v McKewan (1862) 1 H & M 525; 71 ER 230.
Wade v Coope (1827) 2 Sim 155; 57 ER 747.
White v Bristol Aeroplane Co Ltd [1953] Ch 65.
Williams v Owen (1843) 13 Sim 597; 60 ER 232.
Yonge v Reynell (1852) 9 Hare 809; 68 ER 744.   B

Simon Mortimore QC and J McCaughran (instructed by Clifford Chance) for the
applicants.

Peter Goldsmith QC and Mark Phillips (instructed by Freshfields) for the respondents.

JUDGMENT

Richard Sykes QC: The respondents are Sir Terence Conran, Five Arrows Ltd and   C
Clydesdale Bank plc. The questions I have to consider are concerned with whether Sir
Terence and Clydesdale have rights of subrogation: in order to explain how the questions
arise I must first outline the relevant facts.

The facts

The company was acquired by Sir Terence Conran in order to buy and develop Butler's   D
Wharf, a property on the south bank of the Thames near Tower Bridge, London.

On 30 May 1984 the share capital of the company was increased to some £4.2m and
additional shareholders were brought in, comprising LET Investments Ltd, a subsidiary
of Five Arrows, Sir Robert McAlpine & Sons (Trade Investments) Ltd, Conran Roche
Ltd and Mr Roger Seelig. The share capital was divided into redeemable shares and
ordinary shares.

On 31 May 1984 the company purchased the Butler's Wharf property for   E
approximately £3.65m and entered into a building contract with Sir Robert McAlpine &
Sons Ltd under which the contract price of £27.4m was paid in advance. The company
borrowed the requisite funds from Morgan Grenfell & Co Ltd, which took as security a
performance guarantee provided by Clydesdale, bankers to the McAlpine group.

On 5 November 1984 Midland first came on the scene: by a facility letter of that date
it made available to the company a £32m facility (terminating in November 1989) to   F
provide working capital and to replace the Morgan Grenfell loan. Midland took full
security in the form of fixed and floating charges over all the assets and undertaking of
the company as security for 'all moneys and liabilities which now are or shall at any time
hereafter be due owing or incurred to the bank by the company'. Midland also took an
assignment of the Clydesdale performance guarantee as part of its security package.

At the same time Midland granted facilities of £6.4m to Sir Terence and £800,000 to   G
LET for the purpose of enabling them to subscribe for redeemable shares in the company.
The security for these advances comprised a deposit of all the issued shares in the
company: additionally Sir Terence and LET deposited marketable securities to a value
of 50 per cent of the loans made to them respectively as security therefor and Five Arrows
gave a guarantee for LET's loan. The redeemable shares were subscribed in February
1985.

In 1988 a further rearrangement of the company's financing was effected. After   H
protracted negotiations and changes of plan Midland agreed, by its facility letter dated
20 December 1988, to make available to the company a facility of £40m and a further
facility of £10m specifically to permit the redemption of the redeemable shares. This latter
advance was in the facility letter and elsewhere described as the long-term facility and in
other places as the redemption advance: I shall refer to it by the latter term.

A The security for the £40m facility was the same security as had been given for the original advance.

Paragraph 2.2 of the facility letter required as security for the redemption advance memoranda of deposit and charge by Sir Terence, Five Arrows, McAlpine and Conran Roche in the form set out in an appendix 'or such other security that is satisfactory to' Midland.

B The intention was that the security to be provided should be worth 125 per cent of the amount to be advanced. The redemption advance was to be repaid by quarterly instalments of £500,000 commencing on 31 March 1992.

Ultimately the security provided for the redemption advance was as follows:

(1) Sir Terence provided a memorandum of deposit and charge under which he was to deposit securities listed on the Stock Exchange having a value equal to 100.14 per
C cent of the redemption advance.

(2) Five Arrows provided a similar memorandum of deposit and charge: the requisite value of the securities to be deposited was 9.37 per cent of the redemption advance.

(3) McAlpine provided a guarantee of Clydesdale for £800,000 plus interest (capped at £1m in aggregate) in fulfilment of McAlpine's obligation to provide satisfactory
D security.

(4) Conran Roche provided an unsecured guarantee in the standard Midland Bank form.

The downturn in the property market in 1989 had the effect that the company went into default under the second facility. Further discussions with the bank ensued and the third facility was entered into on 12 September 1990. The general facility was increased
E to £58m over and above the £10m redemption advance. All the facilities became repayable on demand and a mistake in the memoranda of deposit given by Sir Terence and Five Arrows (which would have rendered them useless) was corrected. I shall in this judgment refer to these memoranda in their corrected form: nothing turns on the correction.

The third facility only succeeded in delaying disaster for a short time. On 13 December
F 1990 Midland appointed the receivers as administrative receivers under the fixed and floating charges in the company debenture. The receivers have effected some realisations, made some payments to Midland and continue in office.

As respects the security provided by shareholders for the redemption advance:

(1) The listed shares held under Sir Terence's memorandum of deposit were sold and the net amount realised amounted to £8,380,565.67.

G (2) Clydesdale paid the amount of £1m under its guarantee.

(3) Five Arrows paid the sum of £1,359,213.59 to Midland and obtained a release of the shares deposited by it: it was agreed that these acts were in full and final settlement of all claims which Midland and Five Arrows might otherwise have against each other. Five Arrows has played no part in these proceedings.

(4) Nothing has been recovered from Conran Roche. Indeed the evidence before me
H discloses no demand on them.

The amounts so recovered, totalling £10,889,882.11, were credited to suspense accounts in the name of Midland. The full amount of the redemption advance with interest accrued to 4 July 1991 (when the last of the above realisations was effected) was £10,790,504.52. Midland did offer to return the surplus of just over £99,000 to the shareholders but later withdrew that offer.

The issues: repayment of the redemption advance.   A

Logically, the first question I should decide is whether the redemption advance has
been or must now be repaid.

As appears from my recital of the facts, Midland has received from the guarantors of
the redemption advance an amount which is greater than the amount of that advance
plus interest. There are two separate elements to the question:

(1)   Must all the amounts recovered be applied in discharge of the redemption advance   B
       or can, in particular, recoveries from Clydesdale be applied towards discharge of
       the remainder of the company's indebtedness to Midland?

(2)   Is Midland entitled to hold recoveries on suspense account? If so, for how long
       may it do so?

(1) Recoveries under the Clydesdale guarantee   C

The following are the substantive provisions of the Clydesdale guarantee:

'In consideration of your extending facilities to Butlers Wharf Ltd of the Butlers
Wharf Building, 36 Shad Thames, London SE1 2YE on a long term construction
loan as defined in a facility letter dated 20 December 1988, we hereby establish our
irrevocable guarantee in your favour in the sum of £800,000 (eight hundred
thousand pounds sterling) plus interest at a rate of 0.75% over London Interbank   D
Offer Rate as published from time to time, subject to our maximum liability not
exceeding £1,000,000 (one million pounds sterling) inclusive of interest to 31 March
1992. After 31 March 1992, the amount of this guarantee will be as specified in the
attached schedule.

The guarantee will be payable upon first demand following demand for repayment
by Midland Bank under the terms of the said facility letter dated 20 December
1988.   E

The guarantee will cease to be effective after 31 December 1996. This guarantee is
not assignable and is for your exclusive benefit. This guarantee shall be construed
in accordance with English law.'

The schedule attached shows the amount guaranteed reducing by £50,000 per quarter
from 31 March 1992, in line with the scheduled repayments under the redemption
advance.   F

The expression 'long term construction loan' deserves an explanation. It is not in fact
defined in the facility letter to which it refers but there are definitions of 'long term
advance', 'long term facility' and 'long term loan', all of which refer to the redemption
advance and I do not doubt that the Clydesdale guarantee must be treated as being given
in consideration of Midland granting the facility of the redemption advance.

Mr Simon Mortimore QC, who appeared for the applicants, argued that under the   G
terms of the Clydesdale guarantee, Midland was entitled to apply recoveries from
Clydesdale in whatever way it wished: it was not obliged to apply such recoveries towards
discharge of the redemption advance. Clydesdale was not in the position of a surety but
rather in the same position as one who gives a performance bond in support of a
construction contract, for example.

These submissions were particularly based on the second paragraph of the Clydesdale   H
guarantee and the use of the words 'first demand'. Mr. Mortimore accepted that, taking
the first paragraph on its own, the Clydesdale guarantee would be a conventional
guarantee in respect of the redemption advance. Mr Peter Goldsmith QC, appearing for
Sir Terence and Clydesdale, submitted that the right to be treated as a surety and to be
subrogated did not depend on whether the obligation was conditional or collateral as
between the obligor and the principal creditor. What was necessary, he said, was that the

A   obligation should be collateral as between the principal debtor and the obligor and that that fact should be communicated to the principal creditor.

In my judgment the first paragraph of the Clydesdale guarantee is, as a matter of construction and especially seen against the factual matrix in which it was given (particularly cl. 2.2 of the facility letter dated 20 December 1988), a guarantee of the redemption advance in the proper sense of that term.

B   Is the position changed by the second paragraph? In my opinion it is not. The important thing about that paragraph is that the obligation of Clydesdale is conditional: it is conditional on demand being made under the facility letter and hence on the company being liable to pay (inter alia) the redemption advance.

A considerable amount of authority was cited on this point. In view of my conclusion as to construction, I do not need to go into it in detail.

C   As mentioned above, Mr Goldsmith submitted that I did not need to go so far as to say that the Clydesdale guarantee was in law a guarantee. I agree with this submission and, if wrong about construction, would rely on the principle to which Mr Goldsmith referred me: see *Rouse v Bradford Banking Co Ltd* [1894] AC 586. It is clear from all the circumstances that Midland knew Clydesdale's guarantee was provided by way of security for the obligation of the company as principal to repay the redemption advance:

D   in this respect I need only refer to para. 2.2 of the facility letter.

(2) Recoveries under the memoranda of deposit and charge provided by Sir Terence and Five Arrows

It is not disputed that Sir Terence and Five Arrows, who gave collateral security without personal covenants, are in the position of guarantors. Nor is it disputed that the guarantees given by them were limited in amount to the amount of the security provided

E   and were guarantees in respect of the redemption advance.

(3) Can Midland hold recoveries in suspense account and claim that the redemption advance has not been paid off?

There is no doubt that as between itself and the company Midland may hold amounts recovered by it under its security in suspense account. A typical clause, in Midland's legal

F   charge dated 5 November 1984, is as follows:

> '13. All monies received recovered or realised by the bank under this charge (including the proceeds of any conversion pursuant to cl. 12 above) may in the discretion of the bank be credited to any suspense or impersonal account and shall bear interest at such rate, if any, as may be agreed in writing between the bank and the mortgagor and may be held in such account for so long as the bank may think
G   fit pending the application from time to time (as the bank shall be entitled to do as it may think fit) of such moneys and accrued interest thereon if any in or towards the discharge of any of the moneys and liabilities.'

That clause is confined to moneys realised under the company's charge as opposed to moneys recovered from third parties, however, and in any event cannot possibly bind any of the guarantors since none was a party to the company's security documentation.

H   It is relevant that, whilst the Midland standard form guarantee given by Conran Roche contained provisions which enabled Midland to credit to suspense account 'any moneys received recovered or realised hereunder', the Clydesdale guarantee is silent as to suspense account.

As to the memoranda of deposit Mr Mortimore submitted that the right to carry proceeds of realisation to suspense account was to be found in the words:

'. . . and so also that you [Midland] shall be entitled to apply the proceeds of sale   A
and disposal in or towards the discharge of the amounts and liabilities referred to
in para. 2 of this memorandum *in such manner as you may think fit. . .*' (emphasis
added)

Can the words emphasised be read as permitting Midland not to apply proceeds of
realisation towards discharging the amounts or liabilities referred to but to hold them in
suspense account?   B

In my judgment it is plain that those words cannot be so read. What they clearly do
give to Midland is the right to decide in which order the various amounts and liabilities
referred to in cl. 2 (principal, interest, costs, commissions and charges) shall be
discharged. In my view they do not give more than this.

I reach the conclusion that the redemption advance must be regarded either as having
been discharged when the amount held on suspense account was no less than the amount   C
owed in respect of the redemption advance or as due to be discharged immediately by the
application of the amounts held in suspense accounts. I have not heard argument on
which of these is correct and will hear counsel further on this point if either side regards
it as having significance.

Is subrogation available?

Having reached this conclusion I now turn to the question mainly debated before me,   D
which is this: is a surety for a part of a larger debt who has discharged the full amount
for which he is surety entitled to share rateably with the principal creditor in any security
which has been given for the whole debt? Three principles have been established beyond
question:

(1)   The surety, in the situation described above, is entitled both to an indemnity claim
against the principal debtor and to all securities which the principal debtor gave to   E
the principal creditor in respect of and limited to the guaranteed part of the debt:
Aldrich v Cooper (1803) 8 Ves Jun 382, *Yonge v Reynell* (1852) 9 Hare 809 at
p. 818.

(2)   The surety is neither entitled to amounts paid voluntarily by the debtor in respect
of the part of the debt not guaranteed by the surety nor to security given only for
the part of the debt not so guaranteed: *Wade v Coope* (1827) 2 Sim 155.   F

(3)   The surety is entitled, upon the insolvency of the principal debtor, to share rateably
with the principal creditor in amounts paid by way of dividend in respect of the
whole debt: *Thornton v McKewan* (1862) 1 H & M 525, *Gray v Seckham* (1872) LR
7 Ch App 680.

Each of these principles is of course subject to express terms of the guarantee to the
contrary effect.   G

All the textbooks which deal with the subject regard a fourth principle as established,
namely that any security given by the principal debtor for the whole debt must be shared
between the principal creditor (the remainder of whose debt remains outstanding of
course) and the surety: *Goodwin v Gray* (1874) 22 WR 312 is the authority most often
cited for this principle. It is this principle on which the respondents in this case seek to
rely and which the applicants seek to undermine.

Mr Mortimore's points are these: H

(1)   he criticises the decision in *Goodwin v Gray* (above);

(2)   he invites the court to prefer *Farebrother v Woodhouse* (1856) 23 Beav 18;

(3)   he relies on the law in the USA.

I shall deal with these points in order.

A   As to *Goodwin v Gray* Mr Mortimore says that Sir George Jessel MR was wrong to rely on *Thornton v McKewan* as authority supporting his decision, because it was a dividend case and not a security case. I am entirely unpersuaded and can see no distinction of any significance between the case of dividends from an insolvent and proceeds of realisation of security. In both cases the amount concerned is not and cannot be appropriated to one part of the whole debt; the amount is received on account of the debt as a whole. Since, whatever else may be the position, the surety has become, on

B   payment off of the part of the debt guaranteed by him, in the position of the principal creditor in respect of that part, at least as respects the monetary claim, he is entitled to share in amounts received in respect of that part, whether received as dividends or proceeds of realisation of security.

     I recognise that it is possible for a principal creditor, by contract with the surety, to require that dividends and realisations shall be appropriated to the second debt until it is

C   paid off but in my opinion equity would not permit such appropriation, either in the case of dividends or in the case of realisations, in the absence of contract with the surety.

     It is also suggested by Mr Mortimore that the relevant point in *Goodwin v Gray* was conceded by counsel for the defendant. I do not think this is strictly correct, although I do not regard the question as one of great significance: the Master of the Rolls certainly made his decision on the basis of his view that it was governed by *Thornton v McKewan*.

D   Mr Mortimore's sheet anchor, *Farebrother v Woodhouse*, is a case where the right to tack securities came into conflict with the principles of subrogation and the former was held to prevail over the latter. I say this with some confidence for it seems plain to me that there were two separate debts with separate security and that, in the absence of the right to tack, the sureties for part of the advance would have been entitled, on payment of the part of the debt guaranteed by them, to the benefit of the security for that part of the advance in accordance with the first established principle referred to above. Indeed

E   Sir John Romilly MR put the question thus (at p. 25):

> 'In other words, does the mortgagee, by obtaining a third person to become surety for one debt, relinquish the right he would otherwise have to tack.'

Basing himself upon *Williams v Owen* (1843) 13 Sim 597, Sir John answered his question 'no', although with some hesitation.

F   Mr Goldsmith, after submitting that *Farebrother* was a tacking case, also pointed out that the subsequent history of *Farebrother* has not been one of universal acclaim. In particular:

(1)   *Williams v Owen* was considered in *Forbes v Jackson* (1882) 19 ChD 615 no longer to be good law and the *Farebrother* decision was criticised in that case.

(2)   The decision was criticised in *Re Kirkwood's Estate* (1878) 1 LR Ir 108 in which

G   case Flanagan J said (at p. 113):

> 'The case seems not to have been approved by the profession, and was eventually compromised.'

(3)   When followed in *Nicholas v Ridley* [1904] 1 Ch 192 by Byrne J it was followed with considerable reluctance. The successful appeal in that case went off on a different point.

H   In my judgment *Farebrother v Woodhouse* is of no assistance in this case simply because it was a decision based on the right to tack: additionally, it is doubtful whether it was ever good law.

     I can take the US law very shortly: I invited Mr Goldsmith not to address me on it.

     It certainly appears to be the case that the law in the US is different, but according to my reading of the materials put before me by Mr Mortimore that is largely because of

statutory provisions. I do not propose to lengthen this judgment by discussing it: I regard   A
it as irrelevant to my decision.

I conclude this section of my judgment by saying that in my judgment *Goodwin v Gray* remains good law and as upholding what I have above described as the fourth principle. I do not consider *Farebrother v Woodhouse* as throwing any doubt on that principle.

Even if I entertained doubts about the question, which I do not, I should be very reluctant to make a decision which ran counter to the settled practice and the law as it   B has been perceived to be for well over 100 years not only in England and Wales but also in Ireland, Canada, Australia and New Zealand and probably other commonwealth countries. As to this, see *Halsbury's Laws of England*, vol. 26, para. 581 and cases there cited.

This is not the end of subrogation. It is submitted by Mr Mortimore that the circumstances in which the redemption advance was made and the security was provided   C by the shareholders were such as to displace any prima facie rule in favour of permitting the respondents to share in the security.

The starting point for this argument is some general statements about the law of subrogation in *Paul v Spierway Ltd (in liquidation)* [1976] Ch 220 at p. 232 and in *Re T H Knitwear (Wholesale) Ltd* (1988) 4 BCC 102; [1988] Ch 275 at p. 106; 283.

I have not quoted the passages relied on because I do not think they advance the   D question. Both those cases were concerned with the question whether a particular set of circumstances should provide a party with a right of subrogation: not surprisingly, notions of equity and unjust enrichment were relevant.

Subrogation in the case of guarantees is and has for over 150 years been part of English law and to such an extent that it has been given statutory clothing in s. 5 of the *Mercantile Law Amendment Act* 1856, though both counsel agree that that section is not applicable here. It is far too late to be considering whether it is just that subrogation should be   E permitted in the factual circumstances which exist in the present case: subrogation has become part of the armoury available to a surety when he has discharged the whole of the debt guaranteed.

Mr Mortimore submitted that the providers of the shareholders' security had 'no legitimate expectation' of being able to participate in the security given to Midland. Alternatively, he said, it is to be assumed that there was no common intention that there   F should be such participation.

I do not intend to discuss the background circumstances advanced by Mr Mortimore. Suffice it to say that if the providers of security had neither a legitimate expectation nor even an intention of participation that is in my judgment no bar to their participation, except in a case where they have contracted not to participate.

This conveniently brings me to the last major point.   G

Clauses 3 and 8 of the Conran memorandum of deposit

Clause 3 provides that the security provided shall be 'a continuing security'.

Clause 8 provides as follows:

> 'This security is in addition to and shall not affect or be merged in any bills, notes,   H
> guarantees, indemnities, undertakings, mortgages, charges, pledges, liens or other
> security whatsoever which you may hold now or hereafter in connection with the
> original facility letter [the facility letter dated 20 December 1988 above referred
> to].'

Mr Mortimore argues that these clauses have the effect of preventing Sir Terence from participating in the security provided by the company until Midland has been paid in

A   full. His argument is that if Midland is, because of the Conran memorandum of deposit, prevented from appropriating realisations of the company's security to that part of the debt which does not comprise the redemption advance then the security which Midland took from the company is 'affected'. He supports his case by reference to authority.

In *Re Sass* [1896] 2 QB 12 the question before the court was as to the amount for which a creditor bank might prove in the bankruptcy of a principal debtor, the guarantor having already paid £300, the maximum amount recoverable under his guarantee.

B

Vaughan Williams J held that the bank was entitled to prove for the whole amount of its debt, without giving credit for the amount received from the guarantor. The judge reached this conclusion on the ground that the guarantor was surety for the whole of the debt, with a limit on his liability, rather than surety for part of the debt: the result of that was that no right of proof would pass to the guarantor until the bank had been paid in full.

C

In order to explain the importance which Mr Mortimore attaches to this case I must quote the guarantee in full:

> 'I hereby guarantee to you the payment of any sum or sums of money which may be now or may hereafter from time to time become due or owing to your bank anywhere from or by E. Sass his executors or administrators (who are all hereinafter referred to as "the said debtor") either solely or jointly with any other person or persons in partnership or otherwise upon banking account or upon any discount or other account or for any other matter or thing whatsoever including the usual banking charges. This guarantie is to be a security for the whole amount now due or owing to you or which may hereafter from time to time until the expiration of the notice hereinafter mentioned become due or owing to you by the said debtor but nevertheless the total amount recoverable hereon shall not exceed £300 in addition to such further sum for interest and other banking charges and for costs as shall accrue after the date of demand by you upon me for payment. This guarantie is to be in addition and without prejudice to any other securities which you may now or hereafter hold from or on account of the said debtor and is to be binding on me my estate and effects as a continuing security notwithstanding any settlement of account or my being under any disability or my death until the expiration of one calendar month from the time when you shall receive notice in writing to the contrary from me my executors administrators or legal representatives.

D

E

F

> . . .

> You are to be at liberty without thereby affecting your rights hereunder at any time to determine or vary any credit of the said debtor to vary exchange or release any securities held or to be held by you from or on account of the said debtor to renew bills or promissory notes in any manner and to compound with give time for payment to accept compositions from and make any other arrangements with the said debtor or any obligants on bills, notes or securities held or to be held by you from or on behalf of the said debtor. And in case of bankruptcy liquidation by arrangement or composition with creditors any dividends you may receive from the estates of the said debtor or others shall not prejudice your right to recover from me my executors or administrators to the full extent of this guarantie any sum which after the receipt of such dividends may remain owing to you by the said debtor.'

G

H

–and the following passage from the judgment of Vaughan Williams J (at p. 15):

> 'Now for the purpose of this guarantie all I have to determine here is, whether, as between the bank and the surety, the surety became a surety for the whole of the

debt or for a part. In my judgment the surety here became a surety for the whole   A
of the debt. It is true that his liability was to be limited; but still, notwithstanding
that, his suretyship was in respect of the whole debt, and he, having paid only a
part of that debt, has in my judgment no right of proof in preference or priority to
the bank to whom he became guarantor. I should have said that myself upon the
first paragraph in this guarantie; but if there was any doubt about it, it seems to
me that the last clause is also amply sufficient, either by itself or in conjunction
with the earlier parts of the guarantie, to shew that, as between the bank and the   B
surety, the bargain was that the bank should have the benefit of all sums paid by
the debtor whether by way of dividend or otherwise, and of all securities held by
the bank against the debtor's liability, until the whole amount of the debt due from
the debtor to the bank was discharged; and that it would have been manifestly
wrong on the words of this guarantie to hold that the surety could, as against the
bank, get any right to dividend or security or anything else by reason of the   C
payment of this part of what was to be treated, as between him and the bank, as
the whole debt, unless and until the bank had received every sixpence of the full
debt.'

A matter debated before me was as to the words of the guarantee referred to by the
judge when he referred to 'the first paragraph of this guarantie' and 'the last clause'.

Mr Mortimore argued that the last clause was the sentence immediately before the   D
asterisks, while Mr Goldsmith suggested that the reference was to the concluding words
quoted above. Oliver LJ in an obiter dictum in *Barclays Bank Ltd & Ors v TOSG Trust
Fund Ltd & Ors* (1984) 1 BCC 99,017; [1984] AC 626 at p. 99,028; 644, may have been
persuaded to read *Re Sass* in the same sense as Mr Mortimore is urging me to read it. He
said:

'Where the guarantee is of the whole of a fluctuating balance (e.g. as in the case of
a guarantee of the debtor's current account with a bank) with a limit on the liability   E
of the surety, such a guarantee is to be construed as a guarantee of part only of the
debt and the surety paying up to the limit of his liability will be entitled to that
extent to stand in the creditor's shoes and prove in priority to him (see *Ex parte
Rushforth* (1804) 10 Ves 409 and *Gray v Seckham* (1872) LR 7 Ch App 680). The
right of the surety in these circumstances to prove in priority to the principal
creditor can, however, (as it normally is in bank guarantees) be excluded by the
express terms of the contract of guarantee. A provision that the guarantee is to be   F
in addition and without prejudice to any other securities held from or on account
of the debtor and that it is to be a continuing security notwithstanding any
settlement of account is probably sufficient for this purpose (see *Re Sass* [1896] 2
QB 12) but at least there must be some express clause in the contract which can
fairly be construed as a waiver by the surety of his rights in favour of the principal
creditor (contrast *Hobson v Bass* (1871) LR 6 Ch App 792 with *Midland Banking*   G
Co v Chambers (1869) LR 4 Ch App 398). Such a provision will not readily be
inferred merely from the form which the transaction takes (see *Gray v Seckham*
LR 7 Ch App 680.'

Of the two cases referred to by Oliver LJ, in *Hobson v Bass* there was no provision
preventing the surety from exercising his right of proof after payment in full and in
Midland Banking Co v Chambers the relevant provision was to the effect that all dividends   H
and other payments received from the principal debtor should be taken and applied as
payments in gross and that the guarantee should apply to and secure any ultimate balance
remaining due to the principal creditor.

Taking the point in stages:

(1)   I am not convinced that Vaughan Williams J in *Re Sass* placed any reliance on the
      words relied on by Mr Mortimore. It seems clear to me that he came to his

A   conclusion that the suretyship was in respect of the whole debt by reference to the
           wording of the first and second sentences of the guarantee and that when he
           referred to the last clause he was intending to refer to the last sentence quoted
           above, which is paraphrased in his judgment.

(2)   I, accordingly, do not feel it necessary to attribute the weight I otherwise would to
           the dictum of Oliver LJ in *Barclays Bank Ltd & Ors v TOSG Trust Fund Ltd &
B   Ors.*

(3)   My own conclusion, untrammelled by authority, is that cl. 3 and 8 of the Conran
           memorandum of deposit do not constitute wording 'which can fairly be construed
           as a waiver by the surety of his rights in favour of the principal creditor' as Oliver
           LJ put it.

(4)   The only verb in cl. 8 which might be relevant is 'affect'. I do not regard the
           memorandum of deposit as having 'affected' the security given by the company
C   which remained precisely the same security as previously but rather as affecting
           Midland's enjoyment of that security, which is something different. The distinction
           between affecting rights and affecting the enjoyment of rights is clearly recognised,
           in a rather different field, in *White v Bristol Aeroplane Co Ltd* [1953] Ch 65.

(5)   By way of background it is of significance:

           (a)   that Midland's standard form of guarantee, as given by Conran Roche Ltd,
D   contained a clause in terms similar to cl. 8 but also contained a clause which
                 unequivocally postponed the surety's right of proof and subrogation until
                 payment of the whole amount of the debt;

           (b)   that cl. 8 had a place in the memorandum of deposit given by Sir Terence
                 for his own borrowing in 1985 and cannot in that case have been inserted in
                 order to cover a subrogation question.

E   In all the circumstances I reject the contentions of the applicants on this point. I,
           accordingly, reach the conclusion that the respondents are entitled to be subrogated and
           to participate in the security provided to Midland by the company. This brings me to the
           last point argued before me.

To whom should the receivers account?

           The extreme positions adopted by the parties were:

F   (1)   in the case of the applicants, that the respondents should receive their entitlement
                 simply as passive beneficiaries, the obligation to account to them arising as money
                 had and received, constructive trust or because of a lien;

           (2)   in the case of the respondents, that the receivers are obliged to account direct to
                 the respondents.

           In the course of argument, it became clear and was, I believe, accepted by both counsel
G   that neither extreme position was wholly tenable.

           It is inescapable that Midland is the legal owner of the security provided by the
           company. In my judgment, Midland and the respondents are the beneficial owners of
           that security which is held for them as tenants in common by Midland as trustee. The
           proportion of the security attributable to the respondents and hence their proportionate
           beneficial interest falls to be determined following further argument. The rights of the
H   respondents vis-à-vis the security and the receivers appointed under it are those of
           equitable tenants in common. If there is any difficulty in relation to these rights no doubt
           further application to the court can be made, though I see no reason why there should be
           any difficulty.

                                        (*Order accordingly*)

                                        _____

Doorbar v Alltime Securities Ltd (No. 2).

Chancery Division.
Knox J.
Judgment delivered 16 June 1995.

Individual voluntary arrangement – Whether approval of arrangement should be revoked – Landlord had rights under lease exercisable against debtor's wife on bankruptcy – Whether inability to invoke clause was unfairly prejudicial – Whether rights under lease were interests of landlord as a creditor – Chairman at creditors' meeting allowed landlord to vote for one year's future rent – Whether chairman erred in valuing landlord's claim – Whether material irregularity – Insolvency Act 1986, s. 262(1)(a), (b).

This was an appeal from a district judge's decision revoking a debtor's voluntary arrangement which was challenged by the debtor's landlord on grounds of unfair prejudice and material irregularity under s. 262(1)(a) and (b) of the Insolvency Act 1986.

The landlord argued that approval of the voluntary arrangement was unfairly prejudicial to its interests, because the lease contained a clause which provided that the debtor and his wife would take a new lease on the debtor's bankruptcy. The landlord attached value to its rights against the wife under the clause. The district judge held that inability to activate the clause, which would be available in a bankruptcy, constituted unfair prejudice.

The material irregularity alleged was the chairman's refusal to value the future rent under the lease for voting purposes as the annual rent multiplied by the number of years left to run. The chairman offered to put one year's rent as the minimum value. The district judge decided that there had been a material irregularity at the meeting in that the chairman 'did not make a reasonable valuation of future rent but concerned himself with the duty to mitigate which was wrong'.

Held, allowing the appeal:

1. The unfairness in view under s. 262 was unfairness brought about by the terms of the voluntary arrangement. (Re a Debtor (No. 259 of 1990) [1992] 1 WLR 226 followed.)

2. The landlord's right of re-entry in the lease was a security and was unaffected by the voluntary arrangement by virtue of s. 258(4). There was no relevant prejudice in relation to that right because it was unaffected. (Exchange Travel Agency Ltd v Triton Property Trust plc & Anor [1991] BCC 341, and Re Olympia & York Canary Wharf [1993] BCC 154 followed.)

3. The question was whether the landlord's rights under the clause were within the ambit of interests as a creditor of the debtor under s. 262. In light of the characteristics of the prejudice relied on, and more especially the fact that the right in question was exercisable against a person other than the debtor and was a right which arose on the determination through disclaimer of the debtor's liability and was therefore a substitute for rather than a constituent part of the debtor's indebtedness, it was outside the ambit of s. 262(1)(a).

4. If the question of unfairness had arisen, the balance had to be struck between the prejudice to the landlord in having its right against the debtor's ex-wife restricted on the one hand, and the prejudice to the general body of creditors in being prevented from having the benefit of any voluntary arrangement which included future payments of rent under the lease on the other. In the circumstances the prejudice to the landlord would not be unfair, primarily because it had its security against the debtor in the shape of a right of re-entry unaffected by the voluntary arrangement.

5. On the question of material irregularity in the process of valuation by the chairman of the meeting, the chairman was justified in making allowance for the probability of re-entry and effectively treating the landlord as not standing to lose the rent for the whole of the rest

A   of the term. The latter was not a realistic assumption. Although it was a misdescription to describe the allowance as a duty to mitigate, the chairman was not so far in error as to make his conduct a material irregularity.

The following cases were referred to in the judgment:

Company (No. 00314 of 1989), Re a [1990] BCC 221.
Debtor (No. 222 of 1990), Re a, ex parte Bank of Ireland & Ors [1992] BCLC 137.

B   *Debtor (No. 259 of 1990), Re a* [1992] 1 WLR 226.
Doorbar v Alltime Securities Ltd [1994] BCC 994.
Exchange Travel Agency Ltd v Triton Property Trust plc & Anor [1991] BCC 341.
Naeem (a Bankrupt), Re [1990] 1 WLR 48.
Olympia & York Canary Wharf Ltd, Re [1993] BCC 154.
Weller (Sam) & Sons Ltd, Re (1989) 5 BCC 810; [1990] Ch 682.

C   Antony Zacaroli (instructed by Isadore Goldman) for the debtor.

Amanda Tipples (instructed by Tinklin Springall) for the landlord.

JUDGMENT

Knox J: This is an appeal from District Judge Gamba's decision on 17 February 1995 in the Eastbourne County Court revoking a voluntary arrangement approved by a meeting of creditors of the debtor on 4 October 1993. This is the second stage in an

D   application originally made on 18 October 1993 by Alltime Securities Ltd ('Alltime'). That application by amendment contains an application for a declaration that the debtor's voluntary arrangement does not include future rent under a lease with the applicant Alltime dated 3 April 1981 and does not affect the first respondent's liability for the same, the first respondent being the debtor.

That was dealt with by District Judge Hollis in the Eastbourne County Court on 5

E   July 1994, who granted that declaration as well as permitting the amendment raising that issue. On 3 November 1994 I reversed that decision and held (1) that future payments of rent were included by a modification in the voluntary arrangement, and (2) that the chairman of the meeting on 4 October 1993, Mr Bradshaw, had agreed to put a minimum value on Alltime's right to future rent. This is, in fact, a reported decision in [1994] BCC 994, and I understand it is under appeal. Accrued rent was also due to Alltime, but that was accepted as being included within the voluntary arrangement and no problem

F   regarding that arises.

The lease mentioned in that application was dated 3 April 1981, made between Alltime of the first part, which was the landlord, Menage Graphic Production of the second part, and the debtor and his wife (as she then was) of the third part, and the latter were described as 'hereinafter called "the surety".' The expression Menage Graphic Production appears, although there may be some doubt about this at the end of the day,

G   not to represent a legal person but to be a trade name used by the debtor, and on that basis it was the debtor who was the tenant under the lease, and that is certainly the basis upon which the matter proceeded in the county court.

The term reserved was one of 20 years from 4 April 1981. The initial rent was £7,500 per annum. There were provisions for upward rent reviews which were activated on 29 September 1990 so as to increase the rent to £13,830, which is the present rent reserved. There is a right of re-entry in common form, which I need not, I think, read. It is

H   exercisable inter alia on non-payment of rent for 21 days after becoming payable, but the clause that principally matters is cl. 5, which I should read. It is as follows:

'If the tenant' –and this is the debtor– 'shall go into liquidation and the liquidator shall disclaim this lease, or if the tenant shall be wound up or cease to exist (or if the tenant for the time being shall be an individual and shall become bankrupt and the trustee in bankruptcy shall disclaim this lease) and if the landlord shall within

three months after such disclaimer or other event putting an end to the effect of   A
this lease as aforesaid so far as concerns the tenant by notice in writing require the
surety to accept a lease of the premises for a term commensurate with the residue
which if there had been no disclaimer or if this lease had continued to have had
effect as aforesaid would have remained of the term hereby granted at the same
rent and subject to the like covenants and conditions as are reserved by and
contained in this lease (with the exception of this clause) the said new lease and the
rights and liabilities thereunder to take effect as from the date of the said disclaimer   B
or of this lease ceasing to have effect as aforesaid then and in such case the surety
shall pay the costs of and accept such new lease accordingly and will execute and
deliver to the landlord a counterpart thereof.'

It will be recalled that the debtor and his wife at the outset of the lease were described as
'the surety'. No one suggests that the difference between the singular and the plural
makes any difference. There is no suretyship clause in any ordinary sense of a guarantee   C
of a tenant's obligations, and the only justification for the use of the expression 'sureties'
is to be found in cl. 5, which I have read.

The acceptance of a new lease by the debtor himself pursuant to cl. 5 would fairly
clearly be a nugatory operation if he was bankrupt and his trustee in bankruptcy had just
disclaimed. His wife has filed evidence directed to show that she did not intend to enter
into any suretyship obligations, and how far that may be a defence to an action against   D
her for specific performance has not been explored before me. Alltime considers her to be
worth suing and attaches value to its rights under cl. 5. They, of course, arise only on
bankruptcy, not on entering into a composition with creditors.

The other paragraphs in the application that was originally made, para. 1 of which
was dealt with by itself, were restored for a further hearing in the Eastbourne County
Court, and the ones that matter read as follows: E

'2. Further or alternatively, the approval to the debtor's proposed voluntary
arrangement given by the meeting of creditors held on 4 October 1993 be revoked
on the ground that the voluntary arrangement as approved unfairly prejudices the
interests of the applicant as a creditor of the debtor.

3. Further or alternatively the approval to the debtor's proposed voluntary
arrangement given by the meeting of creditors held on 4 October 1993 be revoked   F
or suspended on the ground that there was a material irregularity at the meeting.'

Two issues arise, one on each of those two paragraphs in the application, and they
reflect two paragraphs in the relevant section which is s. 262 of the *Insolvency Act* 1986.
Subsection (1) of that section reads:

'Subject to this section, an application to the court may be made, by any of the
persons specified below, on one or both of the following grounds, namely–   G

     (a) that a voluntary arrangement approved by a creditors' meeting summoned
         under section 257 unfairly prejudices the interests of a creditor of the debtor;

     (b) that there has been some material irregularity at or in relation to such a
         meeting.'

There is no doubt but that Alltime was one of the persons who might apply under this
section. They are listed in subs. (2) but I need not read that subsection.   H

The unfairness in view is, under the section, unfairness brought about by the terms of
the voluntary arrangement. This appears from inter alia the decision *Re a Debtor (No.
259 of 1990)* [1992] 1 WLR 226. The facts appear from the headnote as follows:

'At a meeting summoned under section 257 of the Insolvency Act 1986 only four
creditors were present in person or by proxy. The applicant, also a creditor, had

A   instructed his solicitor to attend the meeting, but no proxy entitling her to vote on his behalf had been filed. The debtor's ex-wife, who had a claim to arrears of maintenance, had not been notified of the meeting. At the meeting, a scheme of arrangement was approved whereby all creditors would receive 10p in the pound. The applicant applied under section 262(1) of Act of 1986 for the scheme to be revoked on the ground that false or misleading information had been presented at the meeting, in that the debts owed to the creditors who voted for the scheme were

B   suspect, and that such conduct constituted unfair prejudice within section 262(1)(a).'

With regard to that, Hoffmann J said (at p. 228C):

'At the first hearing of the application under section 262 the only ground relied upon was unfair prejudice, but on the application to review that decision it was also alleged that there had been a material irregularity. The allegations of unfair

C   prejudice were based upon evidence at first deposed to on information and belief by Mr. Kee's solicitor but subsequently by the source of that information, namely a Mr. Webster.'

Passing over what Mr Webster says, the judge says this about it:

'The substance of Mr. Webster's allegations is that in his view all the debts owed to the creditors who voted for the arrangement are suspect.'

D   The judge expressed his conclusions on those objections as follows at the foot of p. 228:

'It seems to me that as a matter of construction section 262 is talking about unfairness brought about by the terms of the voluntary arrangement. This conclusion, as Miss Agnello for the debtor pointed out, is supported by the scheme of the Act, and in particular by the provisions of sections 264(1)(c) and 276. A

E   creditor who is bound by a voluntary arrangement can nevertheless present a petition for bankruptcy under section 262(1)(c). However, section 276 provides that in such a case the court shall not make a bankruptcy order unless it is satisfied of one or other of various matters, of which one is:

(b) that information which was false or misleading in any material particular or which contained material omissions – (i) was contained in any statement of affairs or other document supplied by the debtor under Part VIII to any person,

F   or (ii) was otherwise made available by the debtor to his creditors at or in connection with a meeting summoned under that Part . . .'

That shows that if Mr. Kee is right in his claim that the statement of creditors in the debtor's statement of affairs is a fabrication, he is not without remedy. It is a ground upon which he can, notwithstanding the voluntary arrangement, present a petition for bankruptcy.'

G   That ground of there being a separate remedy is not available here and is not an issue before me.

Unfair prejudice, therefore, is a reference to a degree of prejudice to one creditor or class of creditors as compared with other creditors or class of creditors. It involves an assessment of any imbalance between possible prejudices to one or the other. The statutory scheme envisages differences of opinion on whether an arrangement should be

H   approved and provides for a minority in certain circumstances to be overridden. The actual rule on the subject is to be found in r. 5.18(1) of the *Insolvency Rules* 1986 which provides as follows:

'Subject as follows, at the creditors' meeting for any resolution to pass approving any proposal or modification there must be a majority in excess of three-quarters in value of the creditors present in person or by proxy and voting on the resolution.'

A

The concept of unfair prejudice is aimed at disproportionate prejudice on one side or the other. The prejudice to Alltime relied on is a restriction on its ability to use cl. 5 of the lease because there will foreseeably not be a bankruptcy if the voluntary arrangement stands and it is complied with. The result of that, so far as Alltime is concerned, is that it will probably be deprived of the exercise of such rights as it has against the debtor's ex-wife. This is the product not so much of a particular term of the arrangement as of s. 260(1) and (2) of the Insolvency Act. They define the effect of approval of a voluntary arrangement as follows:

B

'(1) This section has effect where the meeting summoned under section 257 approves the proposed voluntary arrangement (with or without modifications).

(2) The approved arrangement –

(a) takes effect as if made by the debtor at the meeting, and

(b) binds every person who in accordance with the rules had notice of, and was entitled to vote at, the meeting (whether or not he was present or represented at it) as if he were a party to the arrangement.'

C

There are restrictions, as appears from the last authority to which I have referred, on rights to petition for the bankruptcy of a debtor who has entered into a voluntary arrangement. They are contained in s. 264 of the Insolvency Act:

'A petition for a bankruptcy order to be made against an individual may be presented to the court in accordance with the following provisions of this Part–

D

(a) by one of the . . . creditors . . .

. . .

(c) by the supervisor of, or any person (other than the individual) who is for the time being bound by, a voluntary arrangement proposed by the individual and approved under Part VIII . . .'

E

Section 276, which is referred to in Hoffmann J's judgment, in subs. (1) has the qualification in relation to the making of bankruptcy orders where there has been a voluntary arrangement. It appears from Hoffmann J's judgment and I need not repeat it.

It is also to be noted that s. 258(4) forbids interference with any right of a secured creditor of a debtor to enforce his security except with the creditor's concurrence or an order of the court. The right of re-entry in the lease was submitted by Mr Zacaroli on behalf of the debtor to be a security of Alltime for relevant purposes. I was referred to *Re Naeem (a Bankrupt)* [1990] 1 WLR 48 where the headnote reads as follows:

F

'A bankrupt sought approval for a voluntary arrangement with his creditors under section 260 of the Insolvency Act 1986. The arrangement as approved, which was to be implemented through a nominee appointed pursuant to section 253(2) of the Act, provided, inter alia, that the bankrupt's leasehold interest in a shop under a lease which contained a forfeiture provision should be marketed immediately and sold as soon as possible. The landlord, a creditor for arrears of rent under the lease, obtained an order revoking the creditors' approval of the arrangement on the ground that it was unfairly prejudicial to his interests. The respondents to the application, the bankrupt and his nominee and two creditors, were ordered to pay the costs of the landlord's application.

G

On appeal by the bankrupt and his nominee:

H

Held, allowing the appeal, that the voluntary arrangement was intended to bind the bankrupt's creditors only as creditors and did not affect any proprietary rights such as that of the landlord to forfeit the lease (subject to the court's discretion to grant relief); that since the effect of the arrangement was to modify the claims of all the creditors there would be no unfairness to the landlord, as a creditor, in the

A   modification of his claim for rent arrears; and that, accordingly, the registrar would
be wrong to revoke the creditors' approval of the arrangement.'

At p. 50D Hoffmann J said:

'Of course the effect of the interim order was to hold up the landlord's right to
forfeit, but under section 260(4) of the Act of 1986 the interim order ceases to have
effect 28 days after the date on which the report of the outcome of the creditors'
B   meeting has been given to the court under section 259. Accordingly the interim
order no longer applies and the landlord is free to commence such proceedings for
forfeiture as it may be advised. What the arrangement does do is to bind the
landlord as a creditor for the unpaid rent. To that extent it has indirectly an effect
on the landlord's right to forfeit for non-payment of rent. Apart from the
arrangement, the bankrupt would only have been relieved against forfeiture for
non-payment of rent on condition that all the arrears were paid. Equally the
C   landlord could have proceeded on the same grounds against an assignee of the
tenant, and the assignee too could have obtained relief only on the same terms.

While the terms of relief are a matter for the discretion of the judge to whom the
application is made, it is unlikely that, after the landlord's right to arrears of rent
has been extinguished and replaced by its rights in the arrangement, any condition
of full repayment would be imposed before the bankrupt or an assignee could
D   obtain leave. Mr. Lewison submits that this would be unfair prejudice to the
landlord. I do not agree. The right to forfeit for non-payment of rent is in order to
provide the landlord with security for payment of that rent, whatever it may be.
The effect of the arrangement is to modify the landlord's claim for arrears of rent
in the same way as the claims of other creditors. It does not appear to me to be
unfair prejudice that after such modification the right to forfeit should only stand
as security for recovery of the modified debt rather than the original one.'

E   Similarly in *Exchange Travel Agency Ltd v Triton Property Trust plc & Anor* [1991]
BCC 341; [1991] BCLC 396, the headnote is quite brief and reads:

'The phrase "other security" in s. 248(b) of the Insolvency Act 1986 is wide enough
to cover a right of re-entry conferred on a landlord by the terms of a lease and
therefore once an administration order is made a landlord is precluded by s.11(3)(c)
F   of the 1986 Act from exercising his right of re-entry without the consent of the
administrator or the court.'

In that case there was argued on one side as follows:

'In this case Mr Snowden argues that the rights created by a proviso for re-entry
in a lease are and have for some centuries been described as giving security to the
landlord for the observance by the tenant of his obligations under the lease.'

G   Then various authorities were cited in support of that argument. That is at pp. 343–
344. On the other side, counsel argued in terms that are recorded as follows at p. 344D:

'Mr Marks did not doubt that the word "security" has been applied to the proviso
for re-entry in a lease for generations by distinguished property lawyers and is
undoubtedly so regarded. He said, however, that it was not a security within the
definition in s. 248 of the 1986 Act. That provides in s. 248(b),

H   " 'security' means–

         (i) in relation to England and Wales, any mortgage, charge, lien or other
            security . . .' "

Sir Nicolas Browne-Wilkinson V-C has said that the word "security" should be
construed in its ordinary and natural sense. Mr Marks asserted that a proviso for
re-entry was not a security in the ordinary sense of that word. The taking of

possession was not similar to enforcing a security over the property of the debtor,   A
since it was merely the retaking by the landlord of his own property. Mr Marks
also argued that enforcing a proviso for re-entry was not analogous to the
enforcement of a mortgage, a charge or a lien, because the landlord was asserting
a paramount right. He asserted that a lease was not a relationship of the same
nature as a relationship created by a mortgage, or charge, or lien and that on the
ejusdem generis principle of construction introduced by the word "other" before
"security", one could see a genus in the phrase "mortgage, charge, lien", and any   B
other form of security must be within that genus to be within the section.'

On that, Harman J said at p. 345D:

'The right to re-enter has always been regarded as a security, and that word has
always been used to describe that right. It is a way of securing the observance of
the tenant's obligations. So, also, when a mortgagor charges his premises to a
mortgagee, the mortgagee is entitled to sue for his money under the covenant in   C
the mortgage and is also entitled under the right given by the mortgage to enter
upon the premises for the better security of his debt. The analogies are, of course,
not perfect, but they seem to me sufficiently close to allow the reading of the words
"other security" in s. 248 to extend to cover the right to re-enter peaceably
conferred by a proviso for re-entry in a normal lease.'

That decision, that a right of re-entry is a security within s. 248 of the Insolvency Act,   D
was followed by Millett J in *Re Olympia & York Canary Wharf* [1993] BCC 154 where at
p. 156E, having quoted a passage from Harman J's judgment, Millett J said:

'I respectfully agree. In my judgment the peaceable re-entry is a step in the
enforcement of a landlord's security over the property of a tenant, and if the tenant
is a company in administration the taking of that step requires the prior consent of
the administrator or the leave of the court.'

   E

Consistently with those authorities, I consider that Alltime's right of re-entry under the
lease should be regarded as a security which it holds over the debtor's property. I do not
accept the argument advanced by Miss Tipples that the right of re-entry is one over the
property of Alltime and not over the property of the debtor. That seems to me to be
indistinguishable from the argument that was rejected by Harman J in the *Exchange
Travel* case. The consequences are, first, the right of re-entry is unaffected by the
voluntary arrangement. Section 258(4) forbids that. Secondly, there is no relevant   F
prejudice in relation to that right because it is unaffected.

The prejudice which is relied upon has the following features. First, it is a restriction of
a right prospectively exercisable against a person other than the debtor. Second, it is the
product of the statutory consequences of the approval of the voluntary arrangement,
which includes the right to future rent, rather than the result of any particular term of the
arrangement. Third, the right which is prejudicially affected is one which arises under the   G
lease and therefore pre-exists the voluntary arrangement and has no connection with the
voluntary arrangement save that its value increases if and to the extent that the debtor is
insolvent. Fourth, the right which is prejudicially affected is not a right over the debtor's
property but a contingent personal right against the third party, the debtor's ex-wife.
Five, the right prejudicially affected is one to substitute in place of rights against the
debtor corresponding rights against the debtor and another. It is therefore in practice a
right to release the debtor and substitute another. The new covenant by the debtor ex   H
hypothesi after his bankruptcy is practically worthless and would involve a merger of the
debtor's existing covenant. Finally, there is no question of Alltime's rights of re-entry
having been prejudiced by the voluntary arrangement.

Mr Zacaroli submitted that the alleged prejudice arose not from the terms of the
voluntary arrangement but from the terms of the lease and that it would not be right to

A   allow Alltime effectively to veto any voluntary arrangement which included the right to future rent because of what in his submission was a defect in the drafting of cl. 5 of the lease. He also submitted that it was material in assessing whether the prejudice was unfair to take into account as well as Alltime's prejudice the countervailing prejudice to the general body of creditors other than Alltime, all of whom voted for the voluntary arrangement and would be prejudiced by its non-approval if Alltime's objection that it was unfairly prejudiced succeeded.

B

There are really two questions.

(1)   Is the prejudice identified one which comes within the statutory wording: 'voluntary arrangement approved by a creditors' meeting . . . unfairly prejudices the interests of a creditor of the debtor'?

(2)   If so, is this prejudice unfair?

C   As to (1), 'interests' is a very wide word and it seems to me that some limits should be set upon it. For example, if a trust existed which provided for property presently settled on the debtor for life to go over to the creditor if the tenant for life became bankrupt, the creditor would have an interest in that property contingent upon the debtor's bankruptcy. But it does not seem to me likely that Parliament intended that that fortuitous circumstance would enable a voluntary arrangement otherwise fit to be approved and, in fact, approved by all unsecured creditors, to be set aside. The natural limitation which

D   can be divined from the words of the statute is that the interests to be prejudiced must be interests which the creditor has in his capacity as a creditor of the debtor.

This was an aspect which was not fully considered during the oral argument before me; nor indeed was it addressed by the district judge in his judgment under appeal. Counsel on both sides at my invitation have submitted supplementary written submissions on this aspect from which it is apparent that it is indeed common ground (a)

E   that some limitation upon the interests in question needs to be applied and (b) that the limitation should be to interests as a creditor of the debtor. This would exclude the fortuitous interests under a trust, such as I mentioned above.

I was referred to a somewhat similar turn of phrase in s. 459 of the *Companies Act* 1985 where there is a wide jurisdiction to grant relief where the company's affairs are being or have been conducted in a manner which is unfairly prejudicial to the interests of

F   its members generally or of some part of its members (including at least himself), i.e. the petitioner. A series of decisions under that section has established that it is only to interests as a member that the court will have regard in deciding whether relevant interests have been prejudiced. Thus Mummery J in *Re a Company (No. 00314 of 1989)* [1990] BCC 221 at p. 226C said:

G   'The provisions apply to conduct which is unfairly prejudicial to the interests of the member qua member. They do not extend to conduct which is prejudicial to other interests of persons who happen to be members of the company . . . The interests of the member(s) referred to in the section are not, however, necessarily limited to his strict legal rights under the constitution of the company. The concept of "unfair prejudice" to "interests" clearly embraces a wider range of complaints than infringement of a member's legal rights under the articles and under the Companies Acts.'

H   See also *Re Sam Weller & Sons Ltd* (1989) 5 BCC 810; [1990] Ch 682 at p. 814; 690, where Peter Gibson J made the point considered in the last sentence of that extract from Mummery J's judgment somewhat more fully. It is the latter aspect that was relied upon by Miss Tipples for Alltime. She accepted that s. 262(1)(a) of the *Insolvency Act* 1986 was not concerned with any interest of a creditor which was wholly unrelated to any interest of his as a creditor of the debtor, but she submitted that the rights conferred by cl. 5 of

A

the lease against the debtor's ex-wife constituted a privilege of Alltime's and that it was inextricably linked with Alltime's right to receive future payments of rent from the debtor. As such, it was, she claims, an interest of Alltime qua creditor of the debtor.

B

I have already sought to analyse the characteristics of the prejudice relied upon, and the question which arises is whether Alltime's interest is within the ambit of interests as a creditor of the debtor. In the light of those characteristics, as I sought to set them out, and more especially of the fact that the right in question is one exercisable against another person than the debtor and is a right which arises on the determination through disclaimer of the debtor's liability and is therefore a substitute for rather than a constituent part of the debtor's indebtedness, I have come to the conclusion that it is outside the ambit of s. 262(1)(a). As I have said, this is not an aspect dealt with at all in the judgment appealed from. The conclusion of District Judge Gamba on this point is stated in the sentence:

C

> 'Having taken into account the various arguments, I am forced to the conclusion that the inability to activate cl. 5 of the lease, which is something which is regularly done in circumstances of winding up and bankruptcy, has constituted an unfair prejudice.'

D

I am not altogether clear what it is that is regularly done in bankruptcy. The terms of cl. 5 may possibly be common form, although to describe the lessee and his wife as 'the surety' in relation to a clause such as cl. 5, which is not anything which can properly be called a guarantee of the lessee's obligations, does seem to me rather more eccentric than common form. However that may be, it does not touch the question whether the interest is within s. 262(1)(a) and, for the reasons which I have given, I do not think it is.

E

That renders academic the question whether the prejudice would be unfair, but I should mention that an issue which was debated before me was whether, in striking the appropriate balance to see whether there was unfairness, regard should be had to the interests of the unsecured creditors other than Alltime in approving and securing the benefits of a voluntary arrangement which includes future payments of rents under the lease. Miss Tipples submitted that I should not put those interests into the scale but should concentrate on comparing the way the voluntary arrangement affected Alltime (adversely as regards rights against the debtor's ex-wife) and the way it affected other creditors (beneficially it must be assumed, because they presumably voted for it because they considered they would get more under a voluntary arrangement than a liquidation). Given that there are virtually no assets in the bankruptcy, that is a realistic assumption. I do not accept that that is the appropriate test, given that the relevant prejudice, which I assume, contrary to my earlier decision for present purposes, is relevant, is one which, if operative, precludes any voluntary arrangement that includes future rent payments. In those circumstances, it seems to me that any realistic assessment of what is fair or unfair prejudice has to take account of the result of holding that it is unfair, and that is that there can be no voluntary arrangement whatsoever which includes the future payments of rent under the lease.

F

G

Since I do not consider that there is a relevant prejudice, I do not propose to do more than state my conclusion on the question where the balance, which would have to be struck, lies as between the prejudice to Alltime in having its right against the debtor's ex-wife restricted on the one hand, and the prejudice to the general body of creditors in being prevented from having the benefit of any voluntary arrangement which includes future payments of rent under the lease on the other. The balance is not an easy one, but I consider that the prejudice would not in the circumstances be unfair, primarily because Alltime does have its security against the debtor in the shape of a right of re-entry unaffected by the voluntary arrangement.

H

A   Upon the question of material irregularity the issue revolves around the process of valuation by the chairman of the meeting. Mr Bradshaw, who was that chairman, said in his affidavit on this subject in para. 4:

'I would ask the court to note that at the meeting on 4 October 1993 I invited the applicant to submit a claim for the future rent liabilities in the sum of one year's rent. I would not accept a calculation of all the future rent because there was a duty to mitigate, but I would have been prepared to accept one year's future rent.
B   The applicant did not ask for such a sum to be included in the voting and as such its vote was in the sum of £32,911.61. Even if one year's rent (in the sum of £13,830) had been admitted for the purposes of voting, the proposal would still have been approved by the requisite majority.'

I should mention that the figure of £32,911 was the accrued rent and not the future
C   rent. In his report after the holding of the meeting, he included the following:

'Mr Bradshaw was asked about cl. 12 of the proposals and it was confirmed that it was intended that any liabilities arising under the lease of premises should be included in the arrangement. Mr Springall suggested that the whole of the future rent should therefore be included but Mr Bradshaw said that this could not be so because there had to be mitigation for the likelihood of the property being relet and it was therefore not possible to quantify a liquidated sum due. The only
D   liquidated sum due at today's date was the figure claimed in Alltime Securities' proof of debt in the sum of £32,911.61.'

Miss Tipples argued that Alltime was effectively being compelled to accept only a dividend on future rent payments for the whole duration of the voluntary arrangement and therefore should have been allowed to vote on the product of the current annual rent and the number of years that the lease had to run, i.e. until its expiry on 3 April 2001.
E   That certainly has the merit of mathematical simplicity. I was referred to *Re a Debtor (No. 222 of 1990), ex parte Bank of Ireland & Ors* [1992] BCLC 137 where the facts can be found sufficiently from the headnote which reads:

'On 4 January 1991 a meeting of C's creditors was held to consider whether to approve a voluntary arrangement proposed by C. At the meeting, the chairman, S, ruled that five creditors who had been given notice of and were present at the
F   meeting were not entitled to vote on the ground that their claims were for unliquidated amounts or their value was not ascertained within r. 5.17(3) of the Insolvency Rules 1986. The debts of the five creditors arose out of guarantees given to them by C in respect of the liabilities of two companies and they were disputed by C on the grounds that representations had been made in each case that the creditor would not enforce the guarantees until the primary liability of the companies had been fully enforced. The voluntary arrangement was approved at
G   the meeting. The five creditors sought orders against C and S pursuant to s. 262 of the Insolvency Act 1986 and r. 5.17(3) and (7) of the 1986 Rules that the decision of S be reversed and the approval given at the meeting to the voluntary arrangement be revoked.'

In relation to that, Harman J said at p.144:

H   'In my judgment the scheme of the meeting rules in r. 5.17 is quite plainly a simple one. As one would expect the meeting is not the place to go into lengthy debates as to the exact status of a debt, nor is it the time to consider such matters as this court, sitting as the Companies Court, frequently has to consider such as whether a debt is bona fide disputed upon substantial grounds, an issue which leads to a great deal of litigation and frequently takes a day or so to decide. None of that could possibly be a suitable process to be embarked upon at a creditors' meeting.

The scheme is quite clear. The chairman has power to admit or reject; his decision   A
is subject to appeal; and if in doubt he shall mark the vote as objected to and allow
the creditor to vote. That is easily carried out upon the basis advanced by Mr.
Moss QC, Mr. Mann and Mr. Trace. It provides a simple clear rule for the
chairman, not a lawyer, faced at a large meeting with speedy decisions necessary
to be made to enable the meeting to reach a decision. On that basis the chairman
must look at the claim; if it is plain or obvious that it is good he admits it, if it is
plain or obvious that it is bad he rejects it, if there is a question, a doubt, he shall   B
admit it but mark it as objected. This chairman does not appear to have followed
that process.'

Then he goes on to deal with what happened in that particular case.

The relevant Insolvency Rules are as follows. They are all in 5.17. I need not read
subr. (2). Subrule (3):
  C

'A creditor shall not vote in respect of a debt for an unliquidated amount, or any
debt whose value is not ascertained, except where the chairman agrees to put upon
the debt an estimated minimum value for the purpose of entitlement to vote.

(4) The chairman has power to admit or reject a creditor's claim for the purpose
of his entitlement to vote, and the power is exercisable with respect to the whole or
any part of the claim.
  D

(5) The chairman's decision on entitlement to vote is subject to appeal to the court
by any creditor, or by the debtor.

(6) If the chairman is in doubt whether a claim should be admitted or rejected, he
shall mark it as objected to and allow the creditor to vote, subject to his vote being
subsequently declared invalid if the objection to the claim is sustained.

(7) If on an appeal the chairman's decision is reversed or varied, or a creditor's   E
vote is declared invalid, the court may order another meeting to be summoned, or
make such other order as it thinks just.

The court's power to make an order under this paragraph is exercisable only if it
considers that the matter is such as to give rise to unfair prejudice or a material
irregularity.'

The future rent in this case was an unliquidated amount. I have already held (subject,   F
of course, to the Court of Appeal's decision not yet received) that the chairman did agree
to put upon the debt an estimated minimum value. That is in terms of subr. (3). While I
quite accept that it is eminently desirable that a chairman of a creditors' meeting, who is
unlikely to be even a valuer let alone an actuary, should not be expected to indulge in
actuarial niceties, it is inescapable that some sort of assessment of minimum value should
be made. Reference to minimum value contains a recognition that there will in many
cases be a bracket of values covering various shades of opinion and somewhere within   G
which no doubt will lie the best estimate of open market value and perhaps other values
on different bases. There is no guidance whatever in the rules how the process is to be
done, but I do not accept that it necessarily has to be done on a basis which is
mathematically simple if that basis does not reflect the value which the relevant creditor
has at stake. What is clear is that the rules do not contemplate perfection in the valuation
process, partly because it is only agreement to put a minimum value and not the correct   H
value, and partly because an appeal can only succeed if there is unfair prejudice or
material irregularity. What happened here is that the chairman offered to put one year's
rent as the minimum value and the representatives of Alltime contended for the aggregate
of rent for the whole of the rest of the term. I accept that if and to the extent that the
chairman relied upon a duty placed upon Alltime under the law of contract to mitigate
its loss, that was wrong. Equally, I am satisfied that Alltime's approach to the valuation,

A   while short and simple, is also wrong. It seems to me that what the chairman was basically trying to do was to estimate what was likely to happen if the voluntary arrangement was approved, and he took the view that in those circumstances the right of re-entry was likely to be exercised. He was wrong in saying, if he did, that there was a duty to exercise it. He was at least arguably right in considering that it was likely to be exercised, because there is no reason to suppose that Alltime, armed, as I believe it is, with a right of re-entry, will fail to exercise it and sit meekly by receiving only a small dividend in respect

B   of every gale of rent for the whole of the rest of the term. I therefore conclude that the chairman was justified in making allowance for the probability of re-entry and effectively treating Alltime as not standing to lose the current open market rent for the whole of the rest of the term. The latter is not in my judgment a realistic assumption.

      Mr Zacaroli rationalised this on two alternative bases. First, taking into account contingencies and, secondly, treating the security aspect of Alltime's rights, i.e. the right

C   of re-entry, as unaffected by the voluntary arrangement. Both routes reached the conclusion that the true value of what Alltime had at stake as regards future rent was the capitalised value of the difference between the rent reserved and the rent obtainable in the open market. There is absolutely no valuation evidence before the court whatsoever. In principle, I have no doubt that Mr Zacaroli's approach is a great deal more realistic as an appraisal of what Alltime had at stake than the claim which they did advance for the whole of the rent for the whole of the term with no element of discount even for

D   accelerated payment or allowance for the possibility, which I regard as a probability, of the exercise of the right of re-entry. In my judgment, the chairman was well entitled to reject such a claim as unrealistic. Placed in the difficult position he found himself in of an unrealistic claim being advanced on behalf of a creditor with a debt for an unliquidated amount, I am of opinion that there was no material irregularity involved in his willingness to put upon the claim as a minimum value for the purpose of entitlement to vote one

E   year's rent at the current rent. The judgment under appeal dealt with this issue, too, fairly briefly, the conclusion being stated as follows:

> 'I am also further forced to conclude that there has been a material irregularity at the meeting in that the chairman did not make a reasonable valuation of future rent but concerned himself with the duty to mitigate which was wrong.'

      I fear that here, too, I disagree with the view expressed about the valuation process.

F   The obligation is not, in fact, to place a reasonable value but a minimum value and, for the reasons given above, I am of opinion that it was right to take into account the possibility of re-entry although it was, I agree, a misdescription to describe the allowance as a duty to mitigate. In valuation terms, however, in my view, a rose by any other name would smell as sweet, and I consider that the chairman was not so far in error as to make his conduct a material irregularity. The appeal therefore will be allowed subject, of course, to the Court of Appeal's decision on my earlier decision.

G

(Order accordingly)

H

Re Dollar Land (Feltham) Ltd & Ors.

Chancery Division (Companies Court).
Blackburne J.
Judgment delivered 6 July 1995.

A

B

Winding-up orders – Winding-up petitions adjourned to explore possibility of voluntary arrangements – Further adjournment refused in absence of opposing creditors and winding-up orders made – Companies appealed against winding-up orders and sought rescission – Whether opposing creditors could appear on rescission application – Whether winding-up orders should be rescinded – Insolvency Rules 1986 (SI 1986/1925), r. 4.16(5), 7.47(1), (2).

These were appeals by eight companies under r. 7.47(2) of the Insolvency Rules against the making of winding-up orders and alternatively applications to rescind the winding-up orders under r. 7.47(1).

C

The petitioner was the Inland Revenue. The petitions had been adjourned for 28 days while the possibility of the companies' entering into voluntary arrangements was further explored. When a further 28-day adjournment was sought the Revenue and a supporting creditor obtained winding-up orders in the absence of opposing creditors.

Held, rescinding the winding-up orders:

1. The registrar had jurisdiction to refuse the adjournment of the petitions and, given that the commissioners' petition debts were not disputed, to make winding-up orders on each of the petitions. Nor did the registrar misdirect himself in the exercise of his jurisdiction: he was entitled on the material before him to come to the decision that he did. In the absence of any material misdirection on the registrar's part the companies' appeals failed.

D

2. The court hearing an application to rescind a winding-up order under r. 7.47(1) had a discretion under r. 4.16(5) to give leave to opposing creditors to appear and be heard. It was right to give such leave because the court was satisfied as to the reasons why they failed to give notice in time for the previous hearing and more generally because this was a matter in which it was of particular importance to the court to know what the views were of the companies' creditors.

E

3. The purpose of the rescission applications was not to secure the dismissal of the winding-up petitions so that the companies were free to resume trading, their purpose was merely to secure a further short adjournment of the petitions to see whether proposals for company voluntary arrangements could be worked up to a state which would enable the nominees to recommend that meetings should be summoned.

F

4. The court had to be and was satisfied on the evidence that there was a real prospect that proposals could be formulated which would command the necessary approvals. Also a significant body of the companies' creditors, and possibly the vast majority in value of them, were in favour of the rescission of the winding-up orders and the further short adjournments which the eight companies sought. It was also relevant that the commissioners and the supporting creditor would suffer no prejudice. A number of matters which in the official receiver's view merited further investigation did not lead the court to dismiss the applications.

G

The following cases were referred to in the judgment:

Calgary and Edmonton Land Co Ltd, Re [1975] 1 WLR 355.
Practice Note [1974] 1 WLR 4.
Telescriptor Syndicate Ltd, Re [1903] 2 Ch 174.

H

Simon Mortimore QC (instructed by Herbert Smith) for the applicant companies.

The official receiver appeared in person.

Nicholas Peacock (instructed by the Solicitor of the Inland Revenue) for the petitioning creditor.

A   Thomas Grant (instructed by Walker Morris) for Holmes Building plc.

Hilary Stonefrost (instructed by Nabarro Nathanson) for GE Capital Corp (Funding) Ltd.

Lloyd Tamlin and Sandra Bristoll (instructed by Davis Hanson) for Channel Hotels and Properties Ltd.

Lloyd Tamlin and Sandra Bristoll (instructed by Alexander Stone & Co) for Alexander
B   Stone & Co.

Andreas Gledhill (instructed by Adler & Co) for Fuchsia Establishment.

JUDGMENT

Blackburne J: On 13 April 1995 the Commissioners of Inland Revenue presented petitions for the winding up of eight companies in the Dollar Land group of companies. All eight are subsidiaries of Dollar Land Holdings plc. The petitions are based on sums
C   claimed by way of income tax in respect of periods after September 1992, payable under para. 4 of Sch. 16 to the *Income and Corporation Taxes Act* 1988, and interest under s. 87 of the *Taxes Management Act* 1970. The petitions were presented following written demands made on 6 April 1995. The petition debts total £4,153,128 and range from £1,236,607 in the case of Dollar Land (Feltham) Ltd (or Feltham for short) to £70,184-odd in the case of Dollar Land Industrial Ltd. The indebtedness is not disputed.

D   Each of the eight companies is or was once a property owning company. The business of the companies and of the other companies in the group, Dollar Land Holdings plc having 40 or more active subsidiary and sub-subsidiary companies including the eight companies with which I am concerned, is that of property investment. The commissioners also claim further sums from the eight companies relating to unpaid Sch. 16 tax and s. 87 interest in respect of periods prior to October 1992, the total of such further sums being
E   just over £7m, including £2,379,453 said to be owed by Feltham. Those further claims do not form the subject-matter of any of the petitions owing, it seems, to a doubt on the part of the commissioners as to the basis upon which they could be claimed. This was because there had been an agreement entered into in late 1992 between the Revenue and the eight companies with other companies in the Dollar Land group for a lesser sum to be paid in satisfaction of the tax and interest then outstanding, but which the companies thereafter failed to pay.

F   Following service of the demands on 6 April, the eight companies sought insolvency advice from Stoy Hayward. Owing to a conflict of interest Stoy Hayward found that they were unable to continue advising, and on or about 20 April the companies turned to other accountants, namely Buchler Phillips, for advice. Buchler Phillips are well-known and experienced insolvency practitioners. By the beginning of May, Buchler Phillips began to give consideration to the possibility of each company entering into a company voluntary arrangement. By then winding-up petitions had been presented and, with the
G   exception of Dollar Land Cumbernauld Ltd, served on each of the eight companies. Cumbernauld, as I shall call it, was served in mid-May.

On 2 May the eight companies retained the services of Herbert Smith to advise them in connection with the proposal that there should be company voluntary arrangements. They and Buchler Phillips have since continued to advise the eight companies in these matters.
H   The first hearings for the petitions were fixed for 24 May. Some days in advance of those hearings an affirmation by Mark Stern, a director of Feltham, was served with a view to the companies obtaining a 28-day adjournment of the eight petitions, while the possibility of the eight companies entering into company voluntary arrangements was further explored. According to Mr Stern's affirmation, a review of the financial position of the eight companies undertaken by their directors in conjunction with Buchler Phillips

and Herbert Smith indicated that a liquidation of the eight companies would not result   A
in any funds becoming available to unsecured creditors, inasmuch as all of the properties
owned by the eight companies were fully charged, and that the affairs of the Dollar Land
group, which extended beyond the eight companies, were complex and interrelated.

It was considered by the companies, and those advising them, that the key to any
voluntary arrangements would lie in securing the co-operation of GE Capital
Corporation (Funding) Ltd (or GE Capital for short). GE capital was and is the major   B
secured creditor of six of the eight companies. At the time, that is to say in mid-May
1995, the overall claim of GE Capital against the six was thought to amount to £37.5m
although later evidence indicates that the overall total is around the £40.8m mark. A
major debtor among the six is Feltham, to which considerable sums have been advanced
by GE Capital in connection with the acquisition and refurbishment of a substantial
retail and office development in Feltham. By May 1995 the refurbishment of the
development was nearing completion.   C

According to Mr Stern's affirmation, in the course of discussions held at the end of
April 1995, GE Capital indicated to representatives of the eight companies, including
Buchler Phillips, that it was concerned to avoid a situation which the liquidation of the
eight companies would precipitate, which would leave it with no option but to enforce its
security with the result that the properties over which it held charges would be sold on a
forced sale basis. GE Capital indicated, however, that it would consider the possibility of   D
releasing a portion of its security which could be applied for the benefit of unsecured
creditors by means of a company voluntary arrangement. It was to carry forward the
possibility of a scheme of voluntary arrangements, involving the release of part of its
security by GE Capital, that an adjournment of the eight petitions was sought at that
first hearing.

In the result the Commissioners of Inland Revenue, as petitioning creditors in respect
of the eight petitions, were persuaded to agree to the 28-day adjournment which the eight   E
companies were seeking, and on 25 May Mr Registrar Buckley, before whom the
petitions came, made orders to that effect.

On 20 June, the twenty-seventh day of the adjournment, Mr Stern made a further
affirmation with a view to securing a further 28-day adjournment of the eight petitions.
Exhibited to the affirmation was a report by Buchler Phillips. After setting out the steps
taken by them since their appointment and the appointment of Herbert Smith, Buchler   F
Phillips' report continues as follows. I take it up at para. 4:

> '4.1 It is proposed that David Julian Buchler and Lee Anthony Manning, both
> partners and licensed insolvency practitioners of Buchler Phillips, act as nominees
> in relation to the proposed company voluntary arrangements of the Dollar Land
> companies, and that they are subsequently appointed as joint supervisors in the
> event that creditors approve the terms of the company voluntary arrangements.   G
>
> 4.2 An essential feature of the proposed company voluntary arrangements
> comprises a refurbishment and sale of a substantial retail and office development,
> the freehold of which is owned by Dollar Land Feltham Ltd. This property is
> known as the Centre, Feltham, Middlesex – the Feltham Centre.
>
> 4.3 The Feltham Centre is currently in the final stages of a major refurbishment
> programme which is being funded by GE Capital. GE Capital has already
> advanced a sum of approximately £2.8m to Dollar Land Feltham Ltd for this   H
> purpose, and is prepared to make available a further advance of £724,000. These
> sums are in addition to approximately £18m which GE Capital advanced to Dollar
> Land Feltham Ltd to fund the acquisition of the Feltham Centre.
>
> 4.4 GE Capital has security over all the property and assets of Dollar Land
> Feltham Ltd, including the Feltham Centre. Its security is cross-collateralised

A throughout the group to which the Dollar Land companies belong. In total GE Capital is owed approximately £50m by the Dollar Land companies and other companies in the same group.

4.5 The directors of the Dollar Land companies have instructed professional surveyors and valuers to provide a report and valuation of the Feltham Centre. The present indications which have been given by the professional surveyors and valuers employed by the directors of the Dollar Land companies indicate that once

B the refurbishment of the Feltham Centre and its letting had been completed the value of the Feltham Centre is likely to exceed £24m. A full valuation report is expected within 14 days.

4.6 It is presently proposed that GE Capital will limit the amount of proceeds due under the terms of its security from the sale of the Feltham Centre as follows:

C 4.6.1 all proceeds up to £22m will be paid to GE Capital;

4.6.2 all proceeds between £22m and £24.5m will be made available for the purposes of the proposed company voluntary arrangements (the "available") realisations; and

4.6.3 all proceeds over £24.5m will be paid to GE Capital in reduction of the total liability due and owing to GE Capital.

D 4.7 The outline proposal referred to in sub-paragraph 4.6 above has been discussed between the directors and GE Capital at a number of meetings held in London for that purpose. GE Capital has indicated that it is prepared to consider proposals for company voluntary arrangements on the basis of the above referred to outline proposal. GE Capital has informed the directors of the Dollar Land Companies that it would require at least seven days to consider any company voluntary arrangement documentation submitted to it by them. GE Capital have

E informed the directors of the Dollar Land companies that such a period of time would be required in order to submit the documentation to its credit committee in the United States for approval, and to obtain its own legal advice from its solicitors, Nabarro Nathanson. Herbert Smith have already had a number of meetings with Nabarro Nathanson to discuss GE Capital's security position in general.

4.8 In order to finalise proposals for submission to creditors, the professional

F advisers to the Dollar Land companies require further time to complete their due diligence investigations into the positions of, inter alia, other secured and unsecured creditors of the Dollar Land companies.

4.9 The directors of the Dollar Land companies recognise that the outline proposal mentioned above is dependent on sale of the Feltham Centre in a fully let and refurbished condition. To take account of unforeseen eventualities it is

G proposed that Dollar Land Holdings plc, the parent company of the Dollar Land companies, will make a number of payments to the proposed supervisors amounting in aggregate to a sum in the region of £450,000 over a period of three years, from implementation of the proposed company voluntary arrangements. It is proposed that such moneys will be held by the proposed supervisors in an interest bearing bank account to be applied towards meeting any shortfall in the potential

H dividend payable to unsecured creditors out of the available realisations referred to in sub-paragraph 4.10 below.

4.10 Pending completion of the due diligence investigations referred to above, receipt of completed valuation advice and clarification of GE Capital's position, the directors of the Dollar Land companies are not in a position to submit a finalised proposal for company voluntary arrangements of the Dollar Land companies to creditors. However, on the basis of information received from the

directors, and our investigations to date, Buchler Phillips estimate that the likely   A
potential dividend will be in the region of 14–25p in the pound.

4.11 A number of issues need to be addressed by the directors of the Dollar Land
companies in order that this level of dividend to unsecured creditors may be
achieved through company voluntary arrangements. These issues will require a
substantial amount of management and professional time to resolve satisfactorily.
It is anticipated that these remaining issues will be resolved within the next 14 days.   B

4.12 The issues of on-going funding and liabilities of the Dollar Land companies,
including on-going tax liabilities to the Inland Revenue, are being considered by
the directors and their professional advisers. These issues will be addressed in the
proposals.

5.1 The draft estimated statements of affairs prepared by Buchler Phillips on the
basis of information provided by the directors of the Dollar Land companies show   C
that the Dollar Land companies are all insolvent on a net assets basis. They are
also insolvent on the grounds that they are unable to pay their debts as evidenced
by their inability to meet the demands of the Inland Revenue. The due diligence
procedure in relation to these statements of affairs is also continuing . . .

5.2 Buchler Phillips have considered the effects of alternative insolvency regimes
under the Act including administration, administrative receivership and
liquidation. Buchler Phillips have concluded that there is no real prospect of any   D
alternative regime to company voluntary arrangements which is capable of
producing a dividend of between 14 and 25p in the pound for the unsecured
creditors of the Dollar Land companies.

5.3 The assets of the Dollar Land companies are at present fully secured, therefore
unsecured creditors are unlikely to receive any dividend under an alternative
insolvency regime.'   E

And the report concludes:

'6.2 We are, therefore, of the view that the outlined company voluntary
arrangement for the Dollar Land companies is likely to be the most expedient
course of action available and is likely to realise the best return for unsecured
creditors.

6.3 Accordingly, we consider that a further adjournment for 28 days of the Inland   F
Revenue's petitions should enable the directors of the Dollar Land companies
together with their professional advisers to finalise proposals for company
voluntary arrangements in a form which can then be submitted to their creditors.'

I have quoted at length from that report because, notwithstanding its contents, on the
adjourned hearings of the eight petitions on 21 June the registrar refused to grant the
adjournment sought, but acceded to the request of the commissioners as petitioning   G
creditors that the eight companies should be wound up. He accordingly made orders then
and there winding up each of the eight companies. In this the commissioners were
supported by Holmes Building plc, separately represented before him, which claims to be
a creditor of Feltham in the sum of £141,000-odd.

I have a very brief note of the registrar's judgment prepared by Mr Peacock, appearing
then as now for the commissioners, and agreed by Mr Mortimore QC, appearing then as
now for the eight companies. The note, which has not been submitted to the registrar for   H
his approval, is in the following terms:

'In the absence of the opposing creditors I should make the winding-up orders
sought today. If there were creditors who wished to oppose their chance to do so
was today. It does not seem to me in any case that the winding up of these
companies will prevent the disposal to whatever best advantage can be achieved of

A   the Feltham Centre. That can be equally well done in liquidation. I make the orders sought.'

The reference to no opposing creditors is to the fact that no creditors were represented before him to oppose the making of the winding-up orders in respect of any of the eight companies. The only creditors represented before the registrar were the commissioners and Holmes Building, both of whom, as I have mentioned, were pressing for immediate winding-up orders.

B   Before me are appeals by each of the eight companies brought under r. 7.47(2) of the *Insolvency Rules* 1986 against the winding-up orders which the registrar made, and in the alternative, applications by each of them to rescind the winding-up orders brought under r. 7.47(1). Notices of appeal have not yet been issued, or had not when the hearing before me began, but against the non-objection of the commissioners, and in the case of Feltham, Holmes Building plc, who appears before me by Mr Grant, I agreed to hear the appeals on the undertakings of the companies to issue the appropriate notices of appeal.

C   It was common ground between counsel that I should first hear the appeals and, only if I were against the eight companies on those appeals, hear the applications to rescind the winding-up orders brought under r. 7.47(1). It was also common ground between counsel that on hearing the appeals I should confine myself to a consideration of the evidence that was before the registrar when he made the winding-up orders on 21 June against which the eight companies now appeal.

D   For the eight companies Mr Mortimore made the following submissions in support of their appeals. First, that because the making of the winding-up orders was opposed by the eight companies which were seeking further adjournments of 28 days for the purpose of formulating proposals for company voluntary arrangements, the registrar had no jurisdiction to make winding-up orders. Instead he should have granted the adjournment sought, or adjourned the matter to the judge in accordance with the Practice Direction in force since April 1991 governing the jurisdiction of the registrar. That Practice Direction is to be found in vol. 2 of the *Supreme Court Practice*, para. 831.

E   Secondly, that in any event the registrar failed to ask himself the question which he should have considered, which was whether the company voluntary arrangement proposals enumerated in the Buchler Phillips report were something he should take into account, and if so whether those proposals were of sufficient quality to be put to creditors (for which purpose there would necessarily have to be an adjournment of the petitions) but instead took into account as fatal to the company's adjournment applications a consideration which in the circumstances was irrelevant, namely that there were no creditors represented before him who opposed the making there and then of the winding-up orders.

F   Thirdly, that the registrar failed to give effect to what he described as the 'rescue culture' embodied in the provisions of the *Insolvency Act* 1986, by failing to give sufficient weight to the views of Buchler Phillips as responsible and experienced professional insolvency specialists, who were stating in the course of a detailed and carefully prepared report that further time was required to formulate and put forward proposals for company voluntary arrangements.

G   I have some doubt whether, given the companies' request for a further adjournment of the petitions, supported as it was by the Buchler Phillips report, and implicit within which was opposition to the making of immediate winding-up orders, it was appropriate for the registrar to deal with the matter himself, rather than to adjourn the petitions to the Companies Judge to be dealt with on the following Monday. I do not, however, doubt that the registrar had jurisdiction to refuse the adjournment of the petitions and, given that the commissioners' petition debts were not disputed, to make winding-up orders on each of the petitions. I therefore reject Mr Mortimore's first submission.

H   Nor am I persuaded that the registrar misdirected himself in the exercise of his jurisdiction. Mr Peacock told me, and I accept, that the registrar was taken through the

Buchler Phillips report, that he, Mr Peacock, criticised the draft voluntary arrangement　A
proposals set out in that report, drew the registrar's attention to the fact that despite the
initial 28 day adjournment, the draft voluntary arrangement proposals were a long way
from being finalised, and were at best tentative and conditional in nature, and pointed
out that the only creditors represented before him were creditors opposed to voluntary
arrangements and in favour of immediate winding-up orders.

I do not consider that, brief though the note is of the registrar's decision, the registrar,　B
who has vast experience in these matters, could have been unmindful of the evidence,
such as it was, of the draft voluntary arrangement proposals. After all he had just been
taken through them by counsel before him. Or that he considered that the absence of any
opposing creditors before him was in itself and without more a sufficient reason for
making winding-up orders. I therefore reject Mr Mortimore's second submission.

The other matters urged on me by Mr Mortimore for submitting that the registrar's
decision should be upset on appeal go to the exercise of his discretion. In my judgment　C
the registrar was entitled on the material before him to come to the decision that he did.
The fact that in his place I might, and probably would, have come to a different view is,
in the absence of any material misdirection on the registrar's part, beside the point. In
my judgment, therefore, the companies' appeals fail.

I come now to the applications to rescind the winding-up orders brought under
r. 7.47(1). On 27 June each of the eight companies applied to the registrar to review and　D
rescind the winding-up orders he had made six days earlier, and sought instead orders
that he adjourn the hearing of the winding-up petitions for 28 days, alternatively that he
adjourn the petitions for hearing to the judge. They also sought a stay of all further
proceedings in the winding up of the eight companies pending determination of appeals
against the winding-up orders.

The applications came before the registrar the following day when, upon various　E
undertakings by the directors of the eight companies, he adjourned the applications to
the judge (in the event myself) to be heard as soon as possible, ordering that the winding-
up orders be not drawn up until after the hearing of the applications, stayed all
proceedings in the winding up in the meantime, and gave leave for further evidence to be
filed. Before him on that occasion were counsel for the commissioners and the eight
companies, together with counsel for GE Capital and two other creditors. The official　F
receiver was also in attendance.

Starting with a lengthy further affirmation by Mark Stern made on 27 June, a
substantial body of further evidence has been filed. It is not in dispute that on an
application to rescind a winding-up order made, as these applications are, under r. 7.47,
it is open to the court to receive further evidence. Nor is it in dispute that although the
applications must be made to the court that made the orders under review, it is open to
the court (in this case the registrar) to adjourn the applications to the judge (in this case　G
myself) for hearing and determination.

Before me on the hearing of the applications to rescind the winding-up orders was
Miss Stonefrost, representing GE Capital, claiming to be creditors of six of the eight
companies in sums totalling £40.8m, Miss Bristoll, representing two further creditors,
Channel Hotels and Properties Ltd (CHAPS for short) claiming to be a creditor of each
of the eight companies in the sum of £6.5m, and Alexander Stone & Co, a firm of　H
Glasgow solicitors, claiming to be creditors of Cumbernauld in the sum of £95,000-odd,
and Mr Gledhill, on behalf of a Liechtenstein Anstalt called Fuchsia Establishment,
claiming to be a creditor of each of the eight companies, also in the sum of £6.5m,
alternatively £5.7m. Those creditors have all now served notices under r. 4.16 of the
Insolvency Rules with a view to opposing the winding-up petitions against the eight
companies, or in the case of Alexander Stone against Cumbernauld.

A   All have served evidence explaining why they were not represented before the court in opposition to the petitions on 21 June. They support the companies' applications for the winding-up orders to be rescinded and the petitions adjourned to enable properly formulated company voluntary arrangement proposals to be prepared and considered.

For the commissioners Mr Peacock submitted that because those creditors did not serve notices under r. 4.16 in time for the hearing of the petitions before the registrar on

B   21 June when he made the winding-up orders, I have no power under the Insolvency Act or under the Insolvency Rules to permit appearances by those creditors on these applications, and therefore none can properly appear and be heard before me. He submitted that the relevant rule permitting creditors to be heard in support of an opposition for petition is r. 4.16, which permits appearances only on the hearing of the petition. These applications, he submitted, are not the hearing of the petition.

C   In my judgment that is altogether too narrow a view of the scope of r. 4.16, and a misunderstanding of the nature of an application to review, made as these are, under r. 7.47(1). So far as material, r. 4.16 provides as follows:

> (1) Every person who intends to appear on the hearing of the petition shall give to the petitioner notice of his intention in accordance with this Rule.
>
> . . .

D
> (4) The notice shall be sent so as to reach the addressee not later than 16.00 hours on the business day before that which is appointed for the hearing (or, where the hearing has been adjourned, for the adjourned hearing).
>
> (5) A person failing to comply with this Rule may appear on the hearing of the petition only with the leave of the court.'

These applications are in nature applications to the court which heard the petitions to

E   review the decisions which it made on the hearing of those petitions. In essence, they are applications to rehear the petitions. In this connection my attention was drawn to para. 841 of vol. 2 of the *Supreme Court Practice* which states in connection with applications to rescind a winding-up order that:

> 'There is no need to issue a formal application as the petition is restored before the court.'

F   In my view r. 4.16 extends as much to an application under r. 7.47(1) to rehear a petition as it does to the first or any adjourned hearing of the petition. As the court hearing these applications, I have therefore a discretion under r. 4.16(5) to give leave to the four creditors to appear and be heard on these applications.

I propose to give leave to each of them to appear and be heard. In my view it is right that I should do so, both because I am satisfied as to the reasons why they failed to give

G   notice in time for the hearing on 21 June and more generally because this is a matter in which it is of particular importance to the court to know what the views are of the companies' creditors. It was, in part at any rate, because there were no opposing creditors before him that the registrar made winding-up orders on 21 June. It would in my view have been an exceedingly odd result if, on an application to him to review his orders, the Insolvency Rules did not permit him to hear from the very persons whose views, if they had been before him, as they are now before me, would, as Mr Peacock accepted, have

H   led the registrar either to grant the 28-day adjournment sought or at least to adjourn the petitions to me for hearing, and would not in either case have led to the making of the winding-up orders.

Mr Peacock, supported by Mr Grant for Holmes Building plc, submitted that before acceding to an application to rescind a winding-up order, the court must be satisfied in respect of three things: first, that the debt of the petitioning creditor has been paid, or will be paid, when each winding-up order is rescinded; second, that the company is solvent at least on the basis that it can pay its debts as and when they fall due; third, that the official receiver is satisfied from his work that there is nothing that requires investigation of the affairs of the company and that his costs can be paid.

It was submitted by Mr Peacock that the practice of the court, when rescinding winding-up orders, is akin to its jurisdiction to stay winding-up proceedings pursuant to what is now s. 147 of the Insolvency Act. In this connection my attention was drawn to *Re Telescriptor Syndicate Ltd* [1903] 2 Ch 174 and *Re Calgary and Edmonton Land Co Ltd* [1975] 1 WLR 355. It was submitted that none of these three requirements is satisfied in these cases, and accordingly that the applications should be dismissed.

My attention was also drawn by Mr Peacock to a practice note of 30 November 1970 to be found in [1974] 1 WLR 4 where the following appears:

> 'The making of the order [that is a winding-up order] however, affects all creditors of the company and gives the Official Receiver authority to act forthwith, and in the circumstances the inherent power of the court to revoke or vary an order at any time before it is perfected is one that ought to be exercised with great caution.'

Although the matter is now governed by r. 7.47(1) and (4) it was submitted that the need for great caution remains when exercising the jurisdiction to rescind a winding-up order.

In my judgment, whilst accepting that the jurisdiction is one to be exercised with caution, I do not accept that the jurisdiction is properly exercisable only where the full requirements have been satisfied to which Mr Peacock referred me. I do not accept that the jurisdiction is as narrowly confined as that. I can well see that where the purpose of the rescission application is to secure the dismissal of the winding-up petition, so that the company in question is free to resume trading, the three requirements to which Mr Peacock refers will ordinarily and possibly invariably have to be satisfied, but that is not the purpose of these applications. Their purpose is not to secure the immediate dismissal of the winding-up petitions, so that the eight companies can continue to trade, but merely to secure a further short adjournment of the petitions to see whether proposals for company voluntary arrangements can be worked up to a state which will enable David Buchler and Lee Manning, partners of Buchler Phillips, and licensed insolvency practitioners, as nominees, to submit a report to the court under s. 2 of the 1986 Act recommending that meetings of the companies' members and creditors be summoned under s. 3.

Inherent in the whole process is that the companies are not solvent, and that the commissioners, as petitioning creditors, have not been and will not be paid in full as a condition of the rescission of the winding-up orders, but will only be paid in accordance with the terms of the voluntary arrangements if approved. For my part I can see no good reason why, if the evidence justifies this course, I should not rescind the winding-up orders and adjourn the eight petitions for the short period that the companies request, and not simply leave it to the liquidators of the companies to bring forward proposals, if they consider it appropriate, at some later stage, assuming by then, contrary to the Buchler Phillips report, that the matter has not been overtaken by events which render impractical any possibility of a voluntary arrangement.

The question then is whether, on the evidence, it is appropriate for me to accede to the course which the eight companies, together with their parent company, Dollar Land Holdings plc, and supported by the four opposing creditors, invite me to follow. I must, I think, be satisfied on the evidence that there is a real prospect that proposals can be formulated which will command the necessary approvals. In my judgment the evidence does so satisfy me. It is evident from Mark Stern's fourth affirmation that the eight companies, together with their advisers, have been active in working towards the production of what is described in that affirmation as a credible draft document

A embodying draft proposals for submission to creditors, and that the proposals have been developed to provide additional benefits for creditors in the shape of enhanced payments. It is not necessary to set out in this judgment how the draft proposals now stand. The matter is set out at length in para. 3.2.2 of Mr Stern's fourth affirmation.

I am also satisfied from the evidence filed by the four opposing creditors, including in particular and critically GE Capital, and from what their respective counsel have said to B me, that a significant body of the companies' creditors, and possibly the vast majority in value of them, are in favour of the rescission of the winding-up orders and the further short adjournments which the eight companies seek.

It is also relevant to consider whether the commissioners and Holmes Building plc, who oppose these applications, will suffer any prejudice if I accede to these applications. Despite Mr Peacock's valiant efforts to persuade me otherwise, I am quite unable to see that they will. In particular, the fact that by acceding to these applications the companies C may succeed in bringing forward proposals which will be approved by the meetings summoned under s. 3 does not seem to me of itself to be prejudice of a kind which should incline me to refuse these applications.

It was submitted by Mr Peacock that I should discount the views of CHAPS and Fuchsia Establishment because of connections of one kind or another said to exist between those two creditors and the Dollar Land group of companies. It is not in doubt D that Fuchsia Establishment is a minority shareholder in two of the eight companies, Dollar Land Industrial Ltd and Dollar Land Marton House Ltd. Beyond that it is denied by those companies that there exists any connection such as to render them other than independent creditors. On the evidence as it stands, I am quite unable to come to any view on the matter. Moreover, I accept the submissions of Mr Gledhill and Miss Bristoll that the question of independence is irrelevant at this stage, where the question is essentially whether the eight companies should have the opportunity by means of a E further short adjournment to see whether voluntary arrangement proposals can be finalised for consideration by creditors. If any connection is found to exist within the meaning of s. 249 of the Act, the provisions of r. 1.19(4) of the Insolvency Rules regulating the requisite majorities needed at any meeting with creditors summoned under s. 3, will operate to ensure that the views of connected creditors do not prevail.

There remains for consideration whether I should decline to grant the relief sought on F these applications by reason of the matters brought to my attention by the official receiver. He highlighted four matters from the affidavit of Philip Grant, an inspector of taxes, filed on behalf of the commissioners which, in the official receiver's view, merited further investigation. They were: first, that from 1987 onwards companies in the Dollar Land group, including the eight companies, have deducted over £12m in income tax, but have not paid one penny piece of that to the Inland Revenue as required by Sch. 16; second, that two other companies in the Dollar Land group have gone into liquidation, G one in early 1993 and the other in late 1994, each owing £600,000 by way of unpaid PAYE tax and National Insurance contributions after the Dollar Land group withdrew its financial support; third, that another company in the Dollar Land group appears to have transferred its property assets to a subsidiary of CHAPS in what, on the available evidence, are confusing circumstances, giving rise, according to Mr Grant, to doubts as to the propriety of the transaction, coupled with the suspicion that Cumbernauld, and another of the eight companies, Dollar Land Thameway Ltd, may have done likewise; H and, fourth, that in November 1990 the eight companies executed assignments in favour of GE Capital of their rental income and effectively, as I understand it, of the totality of their income at a time when they were failing to discharge their Sch. 16 liability, and when arguably therefore they should have gone into liquidation instead.

The official receiver suggested that an investigation of these matters, in the liquidation of the eight companies might justify a report to the Secretary of State, leading to the

A

commencement of disqualification proceedings against one or more of the responsible directors, or other action.

Like the official receiver I am troubled by the matters disclosed in Mr Grant's affidavit, in particular the amount and period of default in respect of the non-payment of Sch. 16 tax liabilities. I am not persuaded, however, that these matters should lead me to dismiss these applications and leave the eight companies in liquidation. First, the fifth affirmation of Mr Stern rejects any improprieties. I do not think it would be right at this stage, and

B

on disputed evidence, to assume against the eight companies that the official receiver's concerns are well founded and deny to the eight companies the opportunity to lay company voluntary arrangement proposals before their creditors at a meeting summoned under s. 3 if the nominees report to the court that such meetings should be convened. Second, under r. 1.3(2)(c)(iii) the directors of the eight companies must in their voluntary arrangement proposals deal with whether, to their knowledge, any circumstances exist which might give rise to claims in the liquidation inter alia that transactions have been

C

entered into at an undervalue, and this is a matter which before reporting to the court under s. 2 the nominees will plainly want to give their attention to. Third, it will be a matter for creditors whether they vote to approve the company voluntary arrangements, assuming proposals can be produced to lay before them, rather than allow the companies to go into liquidation. As matters presently stand on the evidence the vast majority in value of the creditors represented before me wish to have that opportunity. I am therefore most loath to deny them that opportunity. Fourth, any improper conduct on the part of

D

directors meriting disqualification in relation to their conduct of the affairs of the two companies which went into liquidation in 1993 and 1994 can, if appropriate, be the subject of disqualification proceedings irrespective of what happens to these eight companies. Fifth, and in the last resort, it is always open to the Secretary of State to bring public interest petitions against some or all of the eight companies under s. 124A of the Act following a report made or information obtained under Pt. XIV of the *Companies Act* 1985.

E

In the result I propose to accede to these applications by rescinding the winding-up orders made against the eight companies on 21 June, and by adjourning the eight petitions to a suitable date in the last week of this term.

Costs

First of all, I will deal with the opposing creditors. They will bear their own costs, and I need say no more about that. So far as the appeal is concerned, I direct that the appeals having failed the commissioners' costs of the appeals should be paid by the unsuccessful appellant companies but out of third party sources, i.e. out of sources other than those of the eight companies. If that means that they have to come from Dollar Land Holdings plc so be it.

F

So far as the rescission applications are concerned, I direct that all of the costs of the commissioners, and of the supporting creditor, and of the companies are to be costs in the respective petitions. I think I omitted the position of the supporting creditor in relation to the appeals. Its costs likewise should be paid for by the successful appellants and should be otherwise than out of the resources of the eight companies.

G

So far as the official receiver's costs are concerned, they should paid for by the eight companies and Dollar Land Holdings plc otherwise than out of the resources of the eight companies, and they should be paid forthwith. I shall give liberty to apply in case there is any problem about that.

H

(*Order accordingly*)

A
Beverley Group plc v McClue.
Chancery Division (Companies Court).
Knox J.
Judgment delivered 19 July 1995.

B
Winding-up petition – Company voluntary arrangement – Whether petitioner was bound by voluntary arrangement – Whether petitioner had notice of meeting – Whether petitioner was entitled to vote at meeting – Insolvency Act 1986, s. 5(2)(b); Insolvency Rules 1986 (SI 1986/1925), r. 1.9, 1.17.

This was an application by a company for an order restraining the petitioner in a winding-up petition from proceeding further upon the petition whether by advertising the same or otherwise.

C
The debt was not in dispute. The issue was whether a company voluntary arrangement in relation to the company was binding on the petitioner.

The company's evidence was that notice of the proposed CVA was sent to the petitioner. The petitioner's evidence was that he did not receive notice of the CVA as a creditor but that he was aware of the proposed CVA and attended the members' meeting as a director of an investor in the company. At the creditors' meeting no value was put on the petitioner's claim. The petitioner argued that he had no notice of and was not entitled to vote at the creditors' meeting and was therefore not bound under s. 5(2)(b) of the Insolvency Act 1986.

D
Held, dismissing the petition:

1. On the evidence the notice was sent and might have gone astray, but nevertheless the creditor was aware of the meeting and the proposals to be made at it. Since the rules were complied with for sending the notice and the creditor did, albeit perhaps from a third party, have the requisite notice, no injustice was caused by regarding him as having had notice in accordance with the rules.

E
2. The petitioner was at the date of the meetings a creditor with a debt for an unliquidated amount. He was entitled to vote under r. 1.17(1) of the Insolvency Rules 1986 and was not disentitled by any failure to agree a minimum value under r. 1.17(3), because r. 1.17(3) only applied to persons present or represented at the meeting.

The following cases were referred to in the judgment:

F
Cranley Mansions Ltd, Re [1994] BCC 576; [1994] 1 WLR 1610.
Debtor No. 64 of 1992, Re a [1994] BCC 55; [1994] 1 WLR 264.
Doorbar v Alltime Securities Ltd [1994] BCC 994.

Richard Sheldon (instructed by Field Fisher Waterhouse) for the company.

D Garland (instructed by Ian Newbery & Co, Poole) for the petitioner.

G
JUDGMENT

Knox J: The application before the court is made by a company ('the company') for an order that Mr William Alan McClue, the petitioner named in a petition presented to the court on 22 June 1995, be restrained from proceeding further upon the petition whether by advertising the same or otherwise. That petition was a petition for the winding up of the company based on the following allegations in the petition:

H
'The company is indebted to the petitioner in the sum of £8,061.35' – and details of VAT are given – 'in respect of costs incurred in an action in the Queen's Bench Division' – and the reference to that action is given. 'On 16 June 1995 the petitioner's solicitor served on the company a copy order dated 13 June 1995 requiring the company to pay the said sum, which order was in the prescribed form'

–and putting it shortly, the company did not pay.

The debt as such is not in doubt. The factual background is that on 20 December 1993   A
the company started proceedings against Mr McClue. On 10 May 1994 a summons
issued under O. 14 by the company for judgment was dismissed with costs to be paid in
any event in favour of Mr McClue. The terms of the order are in fact in evidence.
Nothing turns on the precise wording of it.

The next significant event is that on 19 December 1994 the company, through its
solicitors, sent to Mr McClue a notice saying: B

> 'Take notice that the plaintiff hereby discontinues this action as against you in
> respect of the whole of the claim made within this action.'

Finally, on 13 June 1995 a certificate was issued pursuant to that notice of discontinuance
that the costs of Mr McClue, the defendant, had been taxed in the sum of £8,061.35,
which is the figure mentioned in the petition.

   C

The issue on the application is principally whether a company voluntary arrangement,
which was approved on 20 December 1994, in relation to the company is binding on Mr
McClue. If it is, it is accepted that he was not in a position to present a winding-up
petition; if it is not, he was in a position to do so.

As regards the voluntary arrangement, there is before me evidence on the company's
side by, first, Mr Colin Sidney Robinson, chairman and chief executive of the company.
He, having set out what I have already stated briefly with regard to Mr McClue's   D
entitlement in respect of that order for costs, went on to deal in his affidavit with the
proposals for the company voluntary arrangement and he says, inter alia:

> 'The CVA proposal was one document addressed to both members and all known
> creditors. From 30 November 1994 to 20 December 1994, I was involved in the
> drafting and the placing of an open offer document and dealing with various
> administration matters with regard to the CVA. On 17 November 1994 David   E
> Buchler and Lee Manning were appointed to be the joint nominees of the proposals
> and following approval of the proposal to become the supervisor of the CVA.'

He then refers to the terms of the CVA document, which was sent out in accordance with
the rules, and a little later he goes on to deal with how notice of the proposal for a
company voluntary arrangement was sent out and he says:

   F

> 'On or around 29 November 1994 and before 2 December 1994, I instructed my
> personal assistant, Mrs Felicia Boss-Walker, to ensure and confirm to me that a
> CVA document had been posted to Mr McClue at his home address. I also
> instructed Mr Bridge to verify that this had been done. I received confirmation
> from Mrs Boss-Walker and Mr Bridge that the CVA document had been posted
> to Mr McClue. At the same time, I had also given to Mrs Boss-Walker and to Mr
> Bridge a similar instruction regarding CVA documents which were to be sent to   G
> persons whom I listed to Mrs Boss-Walker and which I now see listed in an exhibit
> to her affidavit.'

He confirms that having read copies of her affidavit in particular, he believes that Mr
McClue was sent the CVA document. Mrs Boss-Walker has, as indicated, also sworn an
affidavit. She says:

   H

> 'On or before 29 November 1994, Mr Robinson instructed me either orally or by
> handwritten notes to post to each of certain names at given addresses a copy of the
> company's company voluntary arrangement proposal document.'

She then produces a list that she made of the names that Mr Robinson gave to her and
in that list, second on it, is Mr McClue's name and an address which coincides exactly
with the address that he gives in his own affidavit. Her affidavit goes on:

A 'Between Tuesday, 29 November 1994 and Friday, 2 December 1994, I personally placed in an envelope a print of the CVA document and wrote on each envelope the name and address for each of the names on the list. I then sealed each envelope. I caused each envelope referred to in para. 5 to be posted by being delivered under my control to the company's receptionist for franking on the company's franking machine at the letter first-class rate and inclusion into the company's mail bag for collection by the Post Office.'

Finally, so far as this aspect of the matter is concerned, there is an affidavit from Nicky Matthews, who was employed by the company as a receptionist at the relevant time, and she gives evidence as to the practice with regard to outgoing mail. She says:

'It was the usual practice for items of outgoing mail to be handed in at the company's reception desk by employees. A tray was provided at the reception into which the outgoing mail was placed. At approximately 3.00 p.m. each day either I or Mr Pett' – he was described as the driver for the chairman of the company – 'would then pass the mail through the franking machine at first-class letter rate and then put the mail into the Post Office mail bag for collection'

–and she states the times at which collection was made and says that it was extremely rare for any items of post to be left until the next day and says that that would only occur if the item was delivered to reception after the mail had been collected. She also says:

'In the period from 29 November to 6 December 1994 I was carrying out my duties. To my knowledge all items of post delivered to reception in that period were franked at the first-class letter rate and put in the mail bag for collection the same day. To my knowledge during my employment with the company, no item of post ever went missing or was lost before franking and putting in the mail bag for collection.'

It seems to me that on a balance of probabilities on that evidence it should be found that the letter was posted to Mr McClue. Mr McClue's account of the matter is to be found in an affidavit that he has sworn. He says, amongst other things:

'I am a creditor of the company in respect of my costs. I am further interested in the applicant' – by which he means the company that I am referring to as 'the company' – 'via a company called Sandford Investment Services Ltd, which is an investment vehicle belonging to myself and my wife equally and of which she and I are directors. Sandford was beneficial owner of 500,000 shares in the applicant company which were held by Bank of Scotland Central Nominees Ltd on its behalf. After proceedings had been brought against me by the applicant company this shareholding was reduced to 10,000.

The applicant is now subject to a company voluntary arrangement under the Insolvency Act and I accept that as a creditor if I was served with notice of the creditors' meeting and was entitled to attend and vote at that meeting then I am bound by the terms of the CVA whether or not I attended or voted. I did not personally receive notice of the CVA as a creditor and no package for me was delivered to my home address. Papers relating to the CVA were sent to Bank of Scotland Central Nominees Ltd on behalf of Sandford as a shareholder and were in due course forwarded on to Sandford, inevitably taking some little while to reach me and did not arrive until after the meetings had taken place. Nonetheless, I became aware of the proposed CVA both because of press reports and because other people told me about it. Had I been invited to attend the creditors' meeting I would certainly have done so because I had and have serious misgivings about the management of the applicant company, which in a very sort space of time has lost a considerable amount of money. If the creditors had not agreed to a CVA and the company had gone into liquidation a DTI inquiry could have followed.

Nonetheless, I was in London on 20 December and arranged to attend at the offices of Buchler Phillips where the meeting was to be held in my capacity as a director of Sandford as shareholder in the applicant, where I met up with Mrs Wise, a colleague of mine who was attending the meeting.'

His solicitor has also sworn an affidavit and so far as relevant he says:

'On 12 December, I received a facsimile message from my client who had been notified by a third party of the proposal CVA of the applicant. He had not at that stage received from the applicant any paperwork relating to the CVA. On 14 December, I received a telephone call from Mr Rose of Field Fisher Waterhouse, acting on behalf of the applicant. He told me that in view of the proposed CVA, which was due to be decided upon the following week, his client proposed settling the action on the basis that they would withdraw their claim with each side paying its own costs including the costs of the O. 14 proceedings'

–and he draws the conclusion that:

'It is plain from this that after that my client was not being treated as a creditor of the applicant at that time. This seemed a somewhat unattractive proposition and was not accepted by my client.

On 19 December, I received by fax notice of discontinuance and having discussed the matter with my client wrote to Field Fisher Waterhouse on that date.'

That letter is in evidence. It is of course dated 19 December 1994 and addressed to Field Fisher Waterhouse and sent by Mr McClue's solicitors.

'We thank you for your letter received by fax this afternoon'

–that was a covering letter with the notice of discontinuance and did not say anything other than that the notice of discontinuance was sent.

'Our client had been proposing to attend the shareholders' meeting tomorrow in order to raise various points but as all that remains outstanding between our respective clients is the amount and payment of costs, we trust that this will no longer be necessary. We attach a schedule setting out our costs in this matter and trust that you will be able to agree the same and arrange for us to be in funds prior to tomorrow's meetings.'

The first reference to a meeting is in the singular, the shareholders' meeting, the second is in the plural. There was indeed attached a bill of costs which added up in total to £7,150.26 and obviously bears a very close family connection with the taxation of costs that subsequently ensued.

There is a good deal of evidence about what happened thereafter, which I do not think is directly relevant to anything that I have to decide.

Mr McClue, it is common ground, did attend the members' meeting on 20 December 1994, which was held immediately after the creditors' meeting. As to the conduct of the creditors' meeting, Mr Robinson in his affidavit says this:

'An integral part of the preparation for the creditors' meeting was that the directors reviewed all possible creditor claims, especially those claims which may have been of a difficult nature to assess for voting purposes. Until Mr McClue's solicitors' letter of 19 December 1994 was received, whilst it was difficult for the company to put any figure on Mr McClue's claim the company was considering putting a value of about £10,000 on his claim were he to attend and vote at the creditors' meeting. On 19 December 1994, after receipt of the letter of that date from Mr McClue's solicitors the value of Mr McClue's claim for voting purposes was estimated by myself to be £10,000, which was made up of £7,150.26 plus 17.5 per cent VAT,

A giving £8,401.55, all rounded to £10,000 to allow for any interest or other costs which may eventually be claimed.

I gave this information to Buchler Phillips at the meeting for the purposes of this being allocated against Mr McClue in the event of him attending and voting at the meeting. As Mr McClue did not attend the creditors' meeting or complete a proxy form, the chairman of the meeting, in accordance with cl. 5.2.1 of appendix 4 of the CVA document, did not have formally to allocate any figure against Mr

B McClue's claim, hence in Mr Buchler's report dated 21 December 1994 submitted to the court Mr McClue is not listed in sch. 2 to that report because Mr McClue neither attended nor voted at the creditors' meeting nor did he submit a proxy form for that meeting.'

He goes on to say that the members' meeting was attended by Mr McClue and that Mr McClue voted against the CVA, although it is the fact that his right to cast a vote in

C respect of shares held by a nominee for Sandford Investment Services Ltd was at best somewhat dubious. Nothing much turns on whether he was entitled to do so or not.

That is the evidence with regard to the basic facts. This is an interlocutory application and there has been no cross-examination of the witnesses. It is therefore inappropriate to make findings of fact where they depend entirely on the veracity or reliability of the deponents and are challenged. It is clear nevertheless that Mr McClue was aware of the

D proposed creditors' meeting before 20 December 1994. Although neither he nor his solicitor says so in terms, it seems to me highly probable that he had the proposal for the CVA but when he received it is a matter which is in dispute. There are therefore three factual possibilities: one is that he was bound by the CVA, the second is that he was not bound by it and the third is that that is a question which is the subject of a genuine dispute.

The relevant legislation is as follows. I start with the Insolvency Act itself. Part I of the

E first group of parts deals with company voluntary arrangements. I need not go through all the detail of it but the relevant provisions are as follows. Section 3(1) provides:

'Where the nominee under section 1 is not the liquidator or administrator, and it has been reported to the court that such meetings as are mentioned in section 2(2) should be summoned, the person making the report shall (unless the court otherwise directs) summon those meetings for the time, date and place proposed in

F the report.'

Pausing there for a moment, that all happened. This was a case where the nominee was not the liquidator or administrator; there was not either a liquidator or an administrator. There was a report which was filed in court on 29 November 1994. Section 3(2) provides as follows:

'Where the nominee is the liquidator or the administrator, he shall summon

G meetings of the company and of its creditors to consider the proposal for such a time, date and place as he thinks fit'

–and that is the pendant to s. 3(1) which I have just read. It is not directly relevant. Subsection (3) reads:

'The persons to be summoned to a creditors' meeting under this section are every creditor of the company of whose claim and address the person summoning the

H meeting is aware.'

The other important provision in the Act is s. 5(2). That provides as follows:

'The approved voluntary arrangement–

(a) takes effect as if made by the company at the creditors' meeting, and

(b) binds every person who in accordance with the rules had notice of, and was entitled to vote at, that meeting (whether or not he was present or

represented at the meeting) as if he were a party to the voluntary   A
arrangement.'

I have not read the provisions that deal with the actual decisions of the meeting; there is
no dispute about that.

The relevant rules are in the Insolvency Rules, and they are as follows. In r. 1.9, headed
'Summoning of meetings under section 3', subr. (1) reads: B

'If in his report the nominee states that in his opinion meetings of the company
and its creditors should be summoned to consider the directors' proposal, the date
on which the meetings are to be held shall be not less than 14, nor more than 28,
days from that on which the nominee's report is filed in court under Rule 1.7.'

That did in fact happen. As I have mentioned, it was filed in court on 29 November 1994
and the date of the meeting was, as I have also mentioned, 20 December, which was
clearly within that bracket.   C

'(2) Notices calling the meetings shall be sent by the nominee, at least 14 days
before the date for them to be held–

     (a) in the case of the creditors' meeting, to all the creditors specified in the
          statement of affairs, and any other creditors of the company of whom he is
          otherwise aware; and

     (b) in the case of the meeting of members of the company, to all persons who   D
          are, to the best of the nominee's belief, members of it.'

I should mention that so far as the statement of affairs is concerned, which, as required
by the rules, was annexed to the document that was sent around, Mr McClue was not
listed as one of the creditors and he falls into the category of 'other creditors of the
company of whom he is otherwise aware'.

Rule 1.17 deals with entitlement to vote and voting. It is headed 'Voting rights   E
(creditors)' and the two relevant subrules are (1) and (3). They read as follows:

'(1) Subject as follows, every creditor who was given notice of the creditors'
meeting is entitled to vote at the meeting or any adjournment of it.

(3) A creditor shall not vote in respect of a debt for an unliquidated amount, or
any debt whose value is not ascertained, except where the chairman agrees to put
upon the debt an estimated minimum value for the purpose of entitlement to vote.'   F

It seems to me that the expression 'every creditor who was given notice of the creditors'
meeting' in r. 1.17(1) should be interpreted as the corollary of the provision in s. 5(2),
which I have read, 'the approved voluntary arrangement . . . binds every person who in
accordance with the rules had notice of . . . that meeting'. Having notice within that
subsection and being given notice in r. 1.17(1) seem to me to be two sides of the same
coin.   G

The provisions with regard to service, so far as material, are r. 12.10, which deals with
service by post.

'(1) For a document to be properly served by post, it must be contained in an
envelope addressed to the person on whom service is to be effected, and pre-paid
for either first or second class post.'

Then there are subrules which deal with the date at which a document which is thus dealt   H
with is treated to be served. With regard to first-class post it is the second business day
after the date of posting; with second-class post it is the fourth business day after the date
of posting, unless the contrary is shown. Rule 12.16 reads:

'Where in accordance with the Act or the Rules a meeting of creditors or other
persons is summoned by notice, the meeting is presumed to have been duly

A   summoned and held, notwithstanding that not all those to whom the notice is to be given have received it.'

Finally, r. 13.3 provides that:

'(1) A reference in the Rules to giving notice, or to delivering, sending or serving any document, means that the notice or document may be sent by post, unless under a particular Rule personal service is expressly required'

B   –and there is no requirement for personal service in any of the rules with which I am concerned.

There are two legal questions that arise out of the provisions of s. 5(2) of the Act. One is, did Mr McClue 'have notice' in accordance with the rules? The other is, was Mr McClue entitled to vote in accordance with the rules? It seems to me, on the true construction of s. 5(2), that the words 'in accordance with the rules' govern both 'had

C   notice of' and the words 'was entitled to vote at, that meeting'. The whole phrase, it will be recalled, reads: 'binds every person who in accordance with the rules had notice of, and was entitled to vote at, that meeting'.

For the company it was argued that notice is satisfied if notice is actually received, by whatever means, and secondly, that where notice is served in accordance with the rules it is to be treated as received. I was referred to a decision of Mr Rimer QC called *Re a*

D   *Debtor No. 64 of 1992* [1994] BCC 55. In that case, the issues concerned bankruptcy but there is an exact parallel, with irrelevant exceptions, between the provisions that deal with individual voluntary arrangements and the provisions from which I have read extracts which deal with company voluntary arrangements. It was accepted that decisions on the one are very likely to be of assistance on the other. In that particular case the notice of the individual voluntary arrangement – because it was a bankruptcy case – was sent to the wrong address so there was no service under the rules. What was relied on was

E   constructive notice, and in particular r. 12.16 formed an important plank in that argument. Mr Rimer rejected that argument, rightly in my view, and it was not relied on before me by the company. It is perfectly clear that r. 12.16 is concerned with the validity of the meeting rather than with the efficacy of notice or service on an individual creditor. Mr Rimer did, however, decide that 'notice' meant actual notice and at p. 66 he said:

F   '. . . accepting (as is admitted) that the society [the creditor] had no actual notice of the meeting, is it nevertheless open to the society to deny that it is one of the persons whom s. 260(2)(b) provides are bound by the arrangement approved at the meeting?'

I pause there to observe that s. 260(2)(b) is the bankruptcy pendant to s. 5(2)(b), which is the section that governs the company voluntary arrangement and which I have read.

G   'The district judge appears to have answered "No" to this question. However, I respectfully disagree. I draw attention to the fact that, in specifying whether or not a creditor is bound by the arrangement, s. 260(2)(b) focuses on whether or not he "had notice of" the meeting (i.e., in my view, had received notice of it). By contrast, the presumed validation of a meeting under r. 12.16 depends essentially on whether or not the notice was duly sent, whether or not actually received. Further, the only presumption that r. 12.16 in terms raises is as to the validity of the summoning and holding of the meeting: it does not purport also to raise a presumption that a

H   creditor had notice of the meeting when in fact he had none.

In my judgment, these considerations point to the conclusion that, even though a s. 257 meeting may be presumed by r. 12.16 to have been duly summoned and held, nevertheless a creditor who had no actual notice of it will not be bound by any arrangement which was approved at it. The reason why he is not so bound is that s. 260(2)(b) provides that the arrangement binds those persons (and, in my

view, only those persons) who (inter alia) had "notice" of the meeting, whereas   A
such a creditor had none.'

He also said, at p. 68, in relation to a passage which I need not read from *Muir Hunter on Bankruptcy*:

'I in any event respectfully disagree with the suggestion in it' – that is in that text book – 'that a creditor who does not receive, and remains in ignorance of, the notice of a meeting which is sent to him can (in the bare circumstances apparently   B envisaged by *Muir Hunter*) nevertheless still have "constructive notice" of such meeting. A person ordinarily only has "constructive notice" of a fact when he is put on notice of matters whose investigation would lead him to discover it, an investigation which he abstains from making; or where he anyway deliberately or carelessly fails to make inquiries which a prudent person in his position ought to have made and which, if made, would have led him to discovery of the fact. However, a creditor, such as the society, which never received a notice of a meeting   C which is said to have been sent to it, cannot in my view, and without more, be said to have "constructive notice" of the convening of the meeting. In particular, and as I have earlier pointed out, r. 12.16 does not deem the creditor to have had notice of the meeting: it merely provides (in effect) that the non-receipt by him of a notice duly sent will not by itself be sufficient to enable him to say that the meeting had not been duly summoned and held.'   D

It was submitted that having notice was enough and that in this case Mr McClue had notice, principally because of his solicitors' letter of 12 December. Mr Rimer, in the case which he decided, was only concerned to deal with an argument that constructive notice was good enough and to dispose of that it was sufficient for him to say that what was needed was actual notice. It was quite unnecessary to say how such notice had to be had because in the particular case there was no actual notice. Mr Rimer's decision is not of   E direct assistance save in rejecting the argument that r. 12.16 is of assistance, and in any event that was not relied on before me.

The words in s. 5(2) 'in accordance with the rules had notice of' require, in my judgment, the relevant notice to be in accordance with the rules and that includes the requirement that notice be sent by the nominee at least 14 days before the meeting as well as the requirements for service.   F

On the evidence before me it is possible, in my view, to say that Mr McClue was aware of the creditors' meeting before it was held and to that extent he had actual notice of it. Even making all due allowance for the impossibility of resolving conflicts of evidence on affidavit, it is in my judgment clear, even on the evidence of Mr McClue and his solicitor, that Mr McClue knew that there were to be creditors' and shareholders' meetings and what the meetings were called to approve. It is also possible to say that the notice was sent to him at least 14 days before 20 December. What it is not possible to say is whether   G that notice reached him 14 days before the meeting. In my judgment, so long as the notice is sent according to the rules and the creditor is in fact aware of the notice before the meeting the strict requirements of the rules are complied with. The great majority of cases will fall into one or other of two categories: (1) cases where notice was sent in accordance with the rules and that notice was received accordingly by the creditor, and (2) cases where notice was not sent in accordance with the rules and was not received by the creditor. The case dealt with by Mr Rimer in the judgment that I have referred to falls   H into this latter category.

The case before me is the exceptional case where, on the evidence, the notice was sent and may well, for what the evidence satisfactorily establishes, have gone astray but nevertheless the creditor was aware of the meeting and the proposals to be made at it. Since the rules were complied with for sending the notice and the creditor did, albeit

A perhaps from a third party, have the requisite notice I do not consider that any injustice is caused by regarding him as having had notice in accordance with the rules.

I turn to the question of entitlement to vote in accordance with the rules. Mr McClue was, on 20 December 1994, the date of the meetings, a creditor with a debt for an unliquidated amount. So much is common ground. Mr Robinson, in para. 23 of his affidavit, which I have read, said that he gave information to Buchler Phillips (Mr Buchler being the chairman of the meeting) regarding the expected quantum of Mr McClue's

B claim based on the solicitors' letter which I have read of 19 December 1994, 'for the purposes of this being allocated against Mr McClue in the event of his attending and voting at the meeting'. It was submitted that this was enough to satisfy the requirement in r. 1.17(3), 'agrees to place a minimum value'. That is a phrase that has already given to some divergence of judicial views. In *Re Cranley Mansions Ltd* [1994] BCC 576, Ferris J held that the word 'agree' involved a bilateral operation and that what was needed was

C agreement on the value between the chairman and the creditor in question. In *Doorbar v Alltime Securities Ltd* [1994] BCC 994, I expressed the view that all a chairman had to do was agree to put a minimum value on an unliquidated claim. An important factor in my reaching that conclusion was that it seemed to me unlikely that it was intended that a creditor with an unliquidated demand could avoid being entitled to vote by the simple expedient of refusing to agree a value for his contingent claim. However, in both *Cranley Mansions* and in *Doorbar v Alltime Securities* the creditor, with the unliquidated demand,

D was present at the creditors' meeting and neither case is of direct assistance on the problem of the absent creditor with the unliquidated demand. Here again, I have great difficulty in accepting that the draftsman intended that such a creditor with proper notice of the proposals could avoid being bound by simply staying away. Mr Sheldon submitted that all that was needed to satisfy 'agrees' was a subjective and unexpressed willingness in the chairman to agree. I do not feel able to put so robust a construction on r. 1.17(3);

E 'agrees' seems to me to require an overt expression of willingness to place a minimum value. Although it does appear to be something of an empty formality, if one supposes that a creditor with an unliquidated demand who has had notice of the proposal and of the meeting does not attend and is therefore not there to be party to any agreement of any sort, it would be possible for the chairman of such a meeting to say that he had had notice of the following persons with unliquidated or contingent claims upon which he records his willingness to place a minimum value on their several claims.

F The other possibility is that r. 1.17(3) only applies to persons present or represented at the meeting. This is the construction which I prefer. It is to be noted that r. 1.17(1) speaks of 'entitled to vote', which is in fact the phrase that is used in s. 5(2) of the Act. Rule 1.17(3) does not speak of entitlement to vote, it just contains a prohibition on voting except in a stated case. That prohibition only makes sense in relation to a creditor who is in a position physically to vote, i.e. is either present or is represented. If r. 1.17(3) is thus interpreted as being limited to those who are in a position to vote in person or by proxy,

G there does seem to be a sensible scheme for dealing with the various categories of creditors with notice of the meeting. Those who do not turn up and are not represented are liable to be bound by s. 5(2). Those who do attend in person or by proxy with unliquidated or unquantified claims are entitled to vote if the chairman agrees to put a minimum value on the claim but not if he does not. On that basis, Mr McClue was entitled to vote under the rules.

H I am therefore left with the position that Mr McClue was both entitled to vote in accordance with the rules and had notice, in my view, in accordance with the rules. It was common ground that if that conclusion was reached he was bound by the voluntary arrangement and not entitled to present a winding-up petition.

(*Petition struck out with costs. Leave to appeal granted*)

Grovewood Holdings plc v James Capel & Co Ltd.

Chancery Division.
Lightman J.
Judgment delivered 19 July 1994.

> *Maintenance and champerty – Liquidator agreed that backers of litigation should have half the recoveries in exchange for funding action – Whether agreement champertous – Whether action should be stayed – Insolvency Act 1986, Sch. 4, para. 6.*

This was a summons by the defendant ('Capel') seeking an order that proceedings be stayed on the ground that the action was being funded pursuant to a champertous arrangement.

In 1989, Capel acted as stockbroker and adviser to the plaintiff ('Grovewood') on an acquisition which proved disastrous and occasioned the collapse of Grovewood which went into liquidation. Grovewood commenced the action against Capel alleging negligence and misrepresentation whilst acting as Grovewood's financial adviser. The claim was for £38m. The liquidator of Grovewood entered into two successive 'sponsorship agreements' with backers under which, in return for the necessary funding, he agreed that the backers should receive one-half of the recoveries of the action.

Held, granting a stay:

1. A transfer of a half beneficial interest in recoveries in return for financing the action was a 'sale' for the purpose of para. 6 of Sch. 4 to the Insolvency Act 1986.

2. The statutory power of sale of a bare cause of action conferred on such a sale immunity from the (otherwise) applicable law of maintenance and that immunity had by judicial decision been recognised as extending to sales on terms providing for a division of recoveries, but there was no basis in principle or authority for extending the statutory exemption applicable in case of sales of bare causes of action to sales of the fruits of litigation which included provision for the purchaser to finance the litigation.

3. Proceedings maintained champertously were an abuse of process and should be stayed. The acknowledged impropriety of any liquidator proceeding on the basis of such an agreement was a further reason for granting a stay.

The following cases were referred to in the judgment:

Bang & Olufsen UK Ltd v Ton Systeme Ltd (unreported, 16 July 1993, CA).
Giles v Thompson [1994] 1 AC 142.
Glegg v Bromley [1912] 3 KB 474.
Goldsmith v Sperrings Ltd [1977] 1 WLR 478.
Guy v Churchill (1888) 40 ChD 481.
Martell & Ors v Consett Iron Co Ltd [1955] Ch 363.
Papaloizou, Re (unreported, 4 December 1980, Browne-Wilkinson V-C).
Park Gate Waggon Works Co, Re (1881) 17 ChD 234.
Ramsey v Hartley [1977] 1 WLR 686.
Seear v Lawson (1880) 15 ChD 426.
Weddell & Anor v J A Pearce & Major & Anor [1988] Ch 26.
Westminster Property Group plc, Re [1985] 1 WLR 676.
Wild v Simpson [1919] 2 KB 544.

Rupert Jackson QC and Simon Monty (instructed by Reynolds Porter Chamberlain) for the plaintiff.

Jonathan Sumption QC and Paul Wright (instructed by Cameron Markby Hewitt) for the defendant.

A   JUDGMENT

Lightman J: 1. Introduction

I have before me a summons issued on the application of the defendant, James Capel
& Co Ltd ('Capel'), seeking an order that the proceedings be stayed on the ground that
the action is being funded pursuant to a champertous arrangement.

B   **2. Facts**

The facts can be shortly stated. In 1989, Capel acted as stockbroker and adviser to the
plaintiffs, Grovewood Holdings ('Grovewood'), on a successful bid for, and acquisition
of, a listed property company known as Local London Group plc. The acquisition proved
disastrous and occasioned the collapse of Grovewood which in December 1991 went into
insolvent voluntary liquidation. In May 1992 (prior to liquidation) Grovewood
C   commenced this action against Capel alleging negligence and misrepresentation whilst
acting as Grovewood's financial adviser. The claim is now for £38m. The allegation is
firmly denied. Since liquidation the liquidator has manfully fought to continue the action.
He has sought support from the creditors and shareholders, but in vain. In order to keep
the action going, he has been driven to enter into two successive agreements entitled
'sponsorship agreements' with backers under which, in return for the necessary funding,
he has agreed that the backers should receive one half of the recoveries of the action.
D   Authority to enter into agreements with third parties to fund the action was conferred on
the liquidator by the duly constituted liquidation committee on 10 December 1991.

The two sponsorship agreements are respectively dated 16 December 1992 and 13 May
1994. They are in substantially the same terms. I am only concerned with the second,
which I shall call 'the 1994 agreement'. This is constituted by two documents. I shall give
a brief summary of their contents. The first is entitled 'Sponsorship agreement' and one
E   only of the two sponsors is party to it. (That sponsor is referred to in the 1994 agreement
as 'the sponsor' and the other as 'the provider', and I shall refer to them in the same
way). There are three parties, namely (1) the liquidator; (2) the sponsor and (3) the
liquidator's solicitors ('the solicitors'). After reciting the issue of the writ, the insufficiency
of assets in Grovewood to fund the litigation, and the agreement of the sponsor to fund
the litigation, it is agreed that:

F   (1)   the sponsor shall at his own cost in the name of Grovewood diligently pursue the
              litigation 'without being subject to the control or interference of the liquidator';

(2)   the liquidator shall give the sponsor, so far as the rules and practice of the court
              permit, all assistance and information requested by the sponsor;

(3)   the solicitors agree to defer charging the sponsor their reasonable profit costs until
              determination of the litigation;

G   (4)   all recoveries in the action shall be paid into the solicitors' client account and be
              held on trust to pay:

(a) all costs;

(b) the costs due to the solicitors in respect of the action for the period prior to
                    liquidation, namely £225,000; and

(c) as to the balance, 50 per cent to the liquidator and 50 per cent to the sponsor;

H   (5)   any insufficiency in the recoveries to meet costs incurred or liability for costs
              ordered to be paid to Capel is to be made good by the sponsor.

The second document is an agreement to which the sponsor and provider alone are
parties. In short it provides for the sponsor and provider to share the liabilities (and in
particular any sum ordered to be paid into court as security for costs) and the 50 per cent
share of recoveries. Beyond this, the second agreement enables the sponsor to 'unitise' or

sell off to other providers the share of the recoveries to which he is entitled in return for　A
payments of or contributions towards the half share of any security for costs which the
sponsor is liable to provide.

Capel have for some time been concerned as to the method adopted by the liquidator
to finance the action. The liquidator has not been forthcoming in this regard, and only
recently has the general character of the arrangements emerged, and indeed the
sponsorship agreements were first disclosed at the hearing. The reason for the liquidator's　B
reticence has been the concern of the sponsors for anonymity, and this has been preserved
on production of the sponsorship agreements by masking out their names. This concern
may explain why the sponsors have been willing to acquire a share in the recoveries as
opposed to acquiring the cause of action, in which case they would have to be plaintiffs
and to disclose their identities. This summons was issued on 7 June 1994. In the
circumstances I can see no substance in any complaint as to delay by Capel in making
the application for a stay.　C

3. Law

The general principles of the law of maintenance and champerty are stated in
Halsbury's Laws of England (4th edn), vol. 9, para. 400:

> 'Maintenance may be defined as the giving of assistance or encouragement to one
> of the parties to litigation by a person who has neither an interest in the litigation　D
> nor any other motive recognised by the law as justifying his interference.
> Champerty is a particular kind of maintenance, namely maintenance of an action
> in consideration of a promise to give the maintainer a share in the proceeds or
> subject matter of the action.

> Since 1967 both criminal and tortious liability for maintenance and champerty
> have been abolished; but the abolition of these forms of liability does not affect　E
> any rule of law as to the cases in which a contract involving maintenance or
> champerty is to be treated as contrary to public policy or otherwise illegal.'

There may be maintenance of a plaintiff or a defendant, but champerty is confined to
assistance to a plaintiff (or counterclaiming defendant) who is making a claim and agrees
to share recoveries in return for the assistance or encouragement. Champerty is often
referred to in the cases as an aggravated form of maintenance: see e.g. *Guy v Churchill*　F
(1888) 40 ChD 481 at p. 489.

In the case of *Giles v Thompson* [1994] 1 AC 142, the House of Lords (1) reaffirmed
that the policy underlying the prohibition on champertous agreements was to prevent
wanton and officious intermeddling with the disputes of others in which the intermeddler
has no interest and where his assistance was without justification or excuse and with a
view to division of the spoils; (2) made plain that the objection to trafficking in litigation　G
gave rise to the continuing denial of recognition to the assignment of a bare right of
action; and (3) gave guidance that in applying the law of champerty regard should be
had to its origins as a principle of public policy designed to protect the administration
and purity of justice and the interests of vulnerable litigants.

It is common ground in this case that the 1994 agreement is prima facie champertous.
It is not alleged that the sponsors have the requisite interest or motive to justify or excuse　H
their intermeddling. The issues raised on this application are twofold: (1) whether a
liquidator is in effect given exemption from the law of maintenance and champerty in so
far as necessary to conclude such an agreement as the 1994 agreement and achieve some
realisation for creditors from the cause of action sued on in these proceedings; and (2)
whether, if the liquidator has no such exemption, a stay can and should be granted on
the ground that the agreement is champertous.

A   (a) *Liquidators and champerty*

The *Bankruptcy Act* 1869 (which is the ancestor of modern bankruptcy legislation) provided that all the property (defined to include choses in action) of a bankrupt vested in his trustee in bankruptcy; and empowered the trustee in bankruptcy to sell to anyone all the property (likewise defined) of the bankrupt. The Court of Appeal in *Seear v Lawson* (1880) 15 ChD 426 held that a bare right to sue was included within the term 'property' for the purpose of both provisions and accordingly (by way of statutory exception to the rules against maintenance) the trustee could sell a bare right of action.

B   Jessel MR remarked (at p. 433):

'The proper office of the trustee is to realize the property for the sake of distributing the proceeds amongst the creditors. Why should we hold as a matter of policy that it is necessary for him to sue in his own name? He may have no funds, or he may be disinclined to run the risk of having to pay costs, or he may consider it undesirable to delay the winding-up of the bankruptcy till the end of the litigation.'

C

The following year, in the case of *Re Park Gate Waggon Works Co* (1881) 17 ChD 234, the Court of Appeal held that s. 95 of the *Companies Act* 1862 (the ancestor of modern company legislation) which authorised a liquidator to sell the property (similarly defined) of the company likewise permitted the liquidator to sell causes of action, notwithstanding the rule against maintenance.

D

In *Guy v Churchill* (1888) 40 ChD 481, Chitty J held that the statutory authorisation of a sale by a trustee in bankruptcy of a cause of action free from the rules against maintenance extended so far as to permit a sale on terms that the assignees should fight the action at his own expense and share any recoveries with the trustee. He reasoned (at pp. 488–489):

E   'The policy of the statute appears to be to give power to the trustee, with the sanction of the committee, to make arrangements in reference to *choses in action* which are considered beneficial to the creditors. It would be a strange and inconsistent result to say that although the right of action may be sold out and out it cannot be disposed of on the terms that some part of the fruit of the action if successful shall come back to the bankrupt's estate for division among his creditors . . . It would be too fine a distinction to hold that the arrangement . . . is void merely because the bankrupt's estate gets back part of any money that may be recovered in the action.'

F

In the case of *Ramsey v Hartley* [1977] 1 WLR 686, the Court of Appeal, applying *Guy v Churchill* (above), held that under the parallel section (s. 55) of the *Bankruptcy Act* 1914, a trustee could validly sell a cause of action in return for an indemnity for costs and 35 per cent of any recovery. Megaw LJ held that the presence of the statutory power of sale distinguished the case (as that of *Guy v Churchill*) from the ordinary run of cases where the assignment of a bare cause of action was held invalid. In this context, he said (at p. 694B):

G

'One may not automatically bring doctrines from other branches of the law into the statutory code of bankruptcy.'

In the recent unreported decision in *Bang & Olufsen UK Ltd v Ton Systeme Ltd* (16 July 1993) the Court of Appeal affirmed that the law is likewise in respect of a sale by a liquidator of a cause of action in return for a share of recoveries. The statutory power of sale of the cause of action precludes any taint of champerty or maintenance in respect of the transaction. Balcombe LJ in his judgment, after referring to *Ramsey v Hartley*, said:

H

'it was held [in that case] that an assignment made by a trustee in bankruptcy is valid if it is within the powers conferred by statute upon the trustee, notwithstanding that it might otherwise be held void for maintenance or champerty, because one may not automatically bring doctrines from other branches of the law into the statutory code of bankruptcy. There would appear to be no valid distinction on this point between the law of bankruptcy and the law of insolvent liquidation. They are both now governed by the *Insolvency Act* 1986, and there is no relevant difference between the two schedules; Schedule 4 which deals with powers of a liquidator, and Schedule 5 which deals with powers of a trustee in bankruptcy.'

The powers of a voluntary liquidator are conferred by s. 165 and 166 of and Sch. 4 to the *Insolvency Act* 1986 ('the Act'). Paragraph 6 of Sch. 4 reads as follows:

'Power to sell any of the company's property by public auction or private contract.'

'Property' is defined in s. 436 as including 'things in action . . . and every description of property . . . and every description of interest . . . arising out of, or incidental to, property.'

In short, the statutory language describing the power of sale, the property which may be the subject-matter of a sale and the absence of any qualification of the prospective purchaser (implicit in the provision for sale by auction) remains (at least for present purposes) the same as in the earlier legislation.

Accordingly the authorities established beyond question that both a trustee in bankruptcy and a liquidator are given statutory power to sell a cause of action on terms that the assignees by way of consideration will pay over a share of the recoveries. This statutory power necessarily precludes any challenge on grounds of maintenance or champerty to such an agreement.

Mr Jackson for the liquidator does not, and cannot, contend that there was any sale of a cause of action in this case. The sale (if any) was of a one-half beneficial interest in the net recoveries. Such a sale, he says, is likewise authorised by the Act and likewise is exempt from application of the law of maintenance and champerty and accordingly a sale of half the recoveries subject to the purchaser agreeing to pay the costs of the action is free from taint. That the Act authorises a sale of such an interest (being property of the company) cannot be disputed: what is in issue is (1) whether the 1994 agreement constitutes a sale; and (2) if so, whether such a sale enjoys exemption from the law of maintenance and champerty.

(b) *Sale*

Mr Sumption has submitted that the transaction between the liquidator and the sponsor is not a sale and accordingly is beyond the powers of the liquidator conferred by para. 6 of Sch. 4: it is merely a funding agreement. He cited *Re Westminster Property Group plc* [1985] 1 WLR 676 where the general rule is laid down that in the absence of a special context the word 'sale' in a statute denotes an exchange of property for cash. It seems to me however that a special context exists in the Insolvency Act and its statutory predecessors. For it is quite clear from all the cases I have referred to and the unreported decision of Browne-Wilkinson V-C in *Re Papaloizou* (4 December 1980) that a transaction involving a transfer of a cause of action in return for financing an action and a share of recoveries has been treated uniformly by the courts since 1880 as a sale. After reaching this conclusion, I found the decision of Scott J in *Weddell v Pearce & Major* [1988] Ch 26 at pp. 34-35 to this very effect. Since this decision is merely confirmation of the conclusion I had already reached, I have not thought it necessary to cause the parties to incur further costs in making submissions relating to this authority. If a transfer of a cause of action in return for financing an action and a share of recoveries is a 'sale' for the purpose of para. 6, so must I think a transfer of a half beneficial interest in recoveries in return for financing the action.

A   (c) *Exemption*

The insuperable difficulty, as I see it, in the way of Mr Jackson's submission of the existence of such an exemption is that in the absence of any agreement by the purchaser to finance the action, a sale of the recoveries in an action (as distinct from the cause of action) has long been regarded as valid and unobjectionable on grounds of maintenance (see *Glegg v Bromley* [1912] 3 KB 474). No special statutory exemption from the law of B   maintenance is required to enable a trustee in bankruptcy or liquidator to dispose of such property. In this respect there is a critical distinction between a sale of the recoveries (or an interest in the recoveries) and a sale of a bare cause of action. The statutory power of sale of a bare cause of action would be empty of effect if it did not at the same time confer on such a sale an immunity from the (otherwise) applicable law of maintenance and this immunity has by judicial decision been recognised as extending to sales on terms providing for a division of recoveries.

C   I can see no basis in principle or authority for extending the statutory exemption applicable in case of sales of bare causes of action to sales of the fruits of litigation which include provision for the purchaser to finance the litigation. The references in the judgments of Megaw and Balcombe L JJ to not bringing into the law of bankruptcy doctrines applicable in other fields can only be intended to apply to doctrines expressly or by implication inconsistent with the provisions or scheme of the bankruptcy code. So D   far as the Act confers powers on liquidators and trustees other than the power to sell bare causes of action, the law of maintenance has full force and effect.

I therefore reach the firm conclusion that the 1994 agreement is champertous since the consideration for the assignment of a share of the fruits is the purchaser's obligation to finance the action, the Act confers no relevant exemption from the law of champerty and accordingly the proceedings are being maintained champertously.

E   **4. Stay**

Mr Sumption submits that, when proceedings are maintained champertously, the proceedings constitute an abuse of process and should be stayed. This appears to me to be both logical and right in any ordinary case. The law of champerty is based on public policy considerations designed to protect both the administration of justice and the defendant from the prosecution of such proceedings. If the court does not intervene, it F   may be taken to be countenancing this abuse of its process.

Mr Jackson first submits that even if the proceedings are champertous, the court should not intervene to grant a stay because the liquidator is acting meritoriously in the interests of creditors, because it is the merest technicality that the right assigned is to the fruits rather than the cause of action, and because there is evidence of a wind of change in attitudes to champerty manifested in the imminent changes in the law allowing for the G   charging of contingent fees subject to certain stringent conditions. I must reject this submission. The law draws distinctions (perhaps fine) between what is and what is not champertous, and where the arrangement fails into the category of champerty and there is no statutory exemption, the court must set its face against such an arrangement however well-intentioned it may be.

Mr Jackson secondly submits that I am precluded from taking the action of imposing H   a stay by the views expressed by Danckwerts J and the Court of Appeal in the case of *Martell v Consett Iron Co Ltd* [1955] Ch 363. In that action the defendants had applied for a stay on the ground that the action was being maintained by a third party who did not have a sufficient common interest recognised by the law in the subject-matter of the action. Danckwerts J and the Court of Appeal held that the third party did have a sufficient interest, but expressed the view obiter that a stay is inappropriate in case of illegal maintenance.

A number of different grounds were given for this view.   A

(1)   First and foremost is a ground reflecting the fact that at that time, but no longer, maintenance was a criminal offence. The ground was that the course of applying for a stay on this ground involved trying the question whether or not the alleged maintainer was committing a crime in the absence of the accused maintainer (see Jenkins LJ at p. 422 and Hodson LJ at p. 429). This ground (with the abolition of the criminal offence of maintenance) can no longer have any weight.   B

(2)   A second related ground was that, if a stay was to be granted on the ground of maintenance, the criminal taint of illegality could only be purged by discontinuing and starting a fresh action. This would elevate maintenance to a defence to the action which it is not (per Jenkins LJ at pp. 421–422). This ground ceases to have any force with the abolition of the crime of maintenance, and the recognition of so many grounds for a stay which do not constitute defences, e.g. absence of authority of the plaintiff's solicitors, forum non conveniens or the fact that the action is   C brought for a collateral (improper) purpose.

(3)   A third related ground was that it would be inappropriate to stop an action before the damage to the applicant necessary to constitute a cause of action for maintenance has occurred (see Danckwerts J at pp. 388–389). Again with the abolition of the tort of maintenance, the foundation for this ground is removed.

(4)   Danckwerts J also expressed anxiety at the absence of any precedent where a stay   D had been granted on this ground (ibid). No doubt the criminal and tortious sanctions for maintenance were in the ordinary course sufficient sanctions and deterrents to maintenance with no need for recourse to an application for a stay. The criminal and tortious sanctions have gone.

(5)   A fifth ground was special to the case of maintenance, and inapplicable to a case of champerty, and may be termed 'mutuality'. It was that if a plaintiff's claim   E could be stayed for maintenance, so by parity of reasoning should a defendant's defence if he is illegally maintained. But in the latter case a stay would be inappropriate, and if an abuse of process were to demand retribution, the defence would have to be struck out and judgment entered for the plaintiff. This would be objectionable as tantamount to holding illegal maintenance of the defendant a ground for holding the plaintiff entitled to judgment (per Jenkins LJ at p. 422 and Hodson LJ at p. 429).   F

Atkin LJ in *Wild v Simpson* [1919] 2 KB 544 at p. 564 made 'a not unfavourable comment' on the availability of a stay in case of champertous proceedings: see Danckwerts J in *Martell v Consett Iron* (above at p. 388). Whether or not the expressions of opinion in *Martell* remain good law in the case of maintenance where there is no 'aggravation', I have no doubt that I am free in case of a champertous agreement such as the present to grant a stay to prevent a continuing abuse of process which the court as   G well as Capel have an interest in bringing to an end. If the court can stay proceedings because brought for a collateral (improper) purpose, as they can (see *Goldsmith v Sperring Ltd* [1977] 1 WLR 478), the court can likewise stay proceedings if champertous. I have no doubt that in this case a stay should be granted.

I should add that I asked Mr Jackson when he opposed the grant of the stay whether there could be any reality in his opposition, since it appeared inconceivable that a reputable liquidator, such as the liquidator in this case, would or could proceed with an   H action pursuant to an agreement which was held champertous. He agreed that it was inconceivable, but nonetheless he opposed the stay. In my view, if additional grounds for a stay were required (and I do not think that this is so) I would take the view that the acknowledged impropriety of any liquidator proceeding on the basis of such an agreement was a further reason for granting the stay.

A   I would wish to make it clear, since the question was discussed before me, that the 1994 agreement (even if otherwise valid) appears to be flawed in two particular respects. First, I cannot see how a liquidator can properly or at all surrender his fiduciary power to control proceedings commenced in the name of the company. Second, I consider the provision for unitisation and further trafficking in the litigation objectionable. Mr Sumption has also objected to the provision for payment of the £225,000 pre-liquidation costs to the solicitors as a preference only to be justified if sanctioned by the court or

B   liquidation committee: see s. 165(1) and Sch. 4, para. 1 of the Act. There is no evidence as to the existence of this sanction but this sum was due to the solicitors in respect of work done prior to the liquidation and secured by a lien over the solicitors' files. The existence of the lien removes any reality for the 'preference' apparently given. In any event, I do not think that this objection (which is an internal question in the liquidation) is a matter to be explored in these proceedings.

C   I should, however, make it clear that in respect of all or any of the deficiencies in the arrangements made between the liquidator and the sponsors no personal criticism can be made of the liquidator, sponsors or the solicitors, for they at all times acted on the advice of specialist insolvency and Chancery counsel – not (I should add) the counsel appearing for the liquidator on this application.

(Order accordingly)

D

E

F

G

H

Anthony & Ors v Wright & Ors.

Chancery Division.
Lightman J.
Judgment delivered 29 July 1994.

Auditors' liability – Negligence – Duty of care – Whether auditors of trustee for investors owed duty to investors.

This was an application by auditors to strike out an action as against them under RSC, O. 18, r. 19.

The plaintiff investors had placed money with the company which held it as trustee in client accounts. The company went into liquidation with a deficiency caused by theft and breaches of trust by directors. The statement of claim alleged that the auditors owed a duty to the investors co-extensive with that owed to the company and that the auditors were in breach of such duties and that the breaches had caused the investors loss. If the auditors had revealed the breaches of trust that had been perpetrated, the company would have put a halt to further breaches and perhaps remedied past breaches.

The question was whether the investors had a maintainable case that the auditors owed any duty of care to them in respect of their audits.

Held, striking out the claim against the auditors:

There was no apparent assumption on the part of the auditors of any responsibility towards the investors, no intention that the investors should rely on them and no suggestion of any actual reliance by the investors on the audit reports. There was no feature so significantly unique to the investors (as distinguished from shareholders and creditors) and so compelling as arguably could establish the necessary close relationship to found a claim by the investors. The one unique feature was the trust relationship. That was not sufficiently significant. No special case existed for a claim by the investors against the auditors.

The following cases were referred to in the judgment:

Al Saudi Banque & Ors v Clark Pixley (1989) 5 BCC 822; [1990] Ch 313.
Barclays Bank Ltd v Quistclose Investments Ltd [1970] AC 567.
Caparo Industries plc v Dickman & Ors [1990] BCC 164; [1990] 2 AC 605.
Galoo Ltd & Ors v Bright Grahame Murray [1994] BCC 319; [1994] 1 WLR 1360.
Luscombe v Roberts and Pascho (1962) 106 SJ 373.
Ministry of Housing and Local Government v Sharp & Anor [1970] 2 QB 223.
R v Deputy Governor of Parkhurst Prison, ex parte Hague [1992] 1 AC 58.
Ross v Caunters [1980] Ch 297.
Steamship Mutual Underwriting Association Ltd v Trollope & Colls (City) Ltd (1986) 33 BLR 81.
White v Jones [1995] 2 AC 207.

Edward Davidson QC and Rosalind Nicholson (Berry & Berry) for the plaintiffs.

Michael Burton QC and Jonathan Simpkiss (instructed by Squire & Co) for the defendants.

JUDGMENT

Lightman J: Nature of application

I have before me a summons dated 11 January 1994 issued by the seventh defendant, Sieff Davidson (a firm) ('the auditors'), seeking an order that the writ and amended statement of claim be struck out as against the auditors pursuant to O. 18, r. 19 of the Rules of the Supreme Court and under the inherent jurisdiction of the court on the grounds that they disclose no cause of action against the auditors and are an abuse of process.

A   The summons comes before me by way of appeal from the decision of Master Barratt given on 14 April 1994 who dismissed the application. The application proceeded without evidence before the master. Since that hearing, the auditors have served an affidavit sworn by Mr John Tattershall of the firm of Coopers & Lybrand in support of the application. The court must be slow to allow a party to have two bites at the cherry and, after failing before the master without filing evidence, to seek to reinforce the appeal with such evidence. Such a course devalues hearings before the master. The plaintiffs opposed

B   my granting leave to the auditors to adduce such evidence, and I refused leave. The contents of the affidavit are plainly contentious. Accordingly the matter has proceeded, as it proceeded below, as an application to strike out on the ground that the statement of claim as pleaded discloses no cause of action. No evidence is to be considered save that the parties have agreed that certain guidelines to auditors referred to in the pleadings may be taken into account. For the purpose of this application I must assume to be

C   correct the facts alleged in the statement of claim, and I shall refer to them for convenience in this judgment as facts, though they are only facts for the purpose of this application and may or may not be proved to be facts at trial if this action proceeds to trial.

Pleaded facts

D   There are 90 or so plaintiffs, mainly individuals, who placed about £3m with Garston Amhurst Associates Group (Holdings) Ltd ('GAA') which carried on business as insurance brokers and consultants and was the holding company of a group of other companies (which I shall call 'the group'). Some 40 of the plaintiffs (whom I shall call 'the investors') placed with GAA about £1.3m in varying amounts from £1,000 to about £200,000 between 1981 and 30 June 1986, the agreed date on which the auditors signed off their audit report for the year ending 1985. (Application may be made to include

E   investors who placed funds in the period until 11 November 1987.) The moneys were received and held by GAA as trustee for the investors. GAA maintained a designated 'client account' at the fifth defendant, Barclays Bank plc ('Barclays'), and at the sixth defendant, the Royal Bank of Scotland plc ('RBS'), to which, with one exception, all moneys invested by the plaintiffs were credited. Trust moneys were thus initially segregated from company moneys.

F   The auditors were the accountants and auditors of GAA between 1980 and 1990, and as such 'prepared, audited and published the accounts of GAA in respect of the accounting years to 31 August 1981, 1982, 1983, 1984, 1985 and prepared the accounts for 1986–1989'. I have been told since reserving judgment that the auditors also audited the accounts for the year ended 31 August 1986 signed on 11 November 1987, but (unlike the other accounts) not filed. It was however in argument common ground that the only

G   relevant role and conduct in this case of the auditors is their auditing the accounts (on the pleadings) for the years to 31 August 1985 (application may be made to amend to include the year to 31 August 1986). Each year's audit included either in the balance sheet or a note two entries: 'Amounts due to clients' and 'Less: clients' bank balances' the figures in respect of each item being the same, the two entries accordingly cancelling themselves out.

H   On 7 March 1990, an order was made for the compulsory winding up of GAA. A statement of assets made by two directors showed a deficiency of £4.5m. The investors have received nothing from GAA in the liquidation on account of their investments. The immediate cause of the deficiency was the fraud of the first four defendants, the directors of GAA ('the directors'), who during the period 1980–1990 applied the investors' (trust) moneys for their personal benefit, to repay investors whose money had been dissipated and for other improper purposes. The directors were all charged and on 15 July 1991

convicted on charges relating to the affairs of the group of conspiracy to obtain property   A
by deception, of obtaining property by deception and of conspiracy to steal.

These defalcations and breaches of trust were not uncovered or revealed by the
auditors. How and why this is so the investors say they cannot tell until they have
inspected the audit files. These, the investors say, will only become available on discovery,
though they have never yet even asked to examine them. The only evidence of any default
on the part of the auditors known and relied on by the investors at this stage is the fact   B
that (1) on over 50 occasions between 1981 and 30 June 1986 the trust account at Barclays
was overdrawn in sums between £145 and £28,000; (2) the investors can identify in respect
of the relevant period some (as they admit) small defalcations, namely 13 totalling some
£10,000. (In the period until November 1987 there were two further defalcations totalling
some £11,000.)

The statement of claim includes amongst the plaintiffs claiming against the auditors   C
not merely the investors who had placed money with GAA during the period covered by
the 1981–1985 audits, but also persons who were at that time prospective investors. Mr
Davidson, counsel for the plaintiffs, however withdrew any claim on their behalf and
limited his claim to the investors when he opened his submissions. There is no allegation
that in any way did any of the investors rely on the auditors' audit. The allegation is that,
in acting as auditors in respect of the audits over the years in question, the auditors owed
a duty to the investors co-extensive with that owed to GAA, that the auditors were in   D
breach of such duties, and that these breaches of duty:

> 'have caused the investors and each of them loss and damage in respect of which
> [the auditors] are liable in that each of the [investors] has lost his investment with
> GAA, together with interest thereon to which he would have been entitled.'

Mr Davidson explained, though this is not apparent from the statement of claim itself,
but would (he says) have become if the auditors had served a request for particulars, that   E
the causation relied on is that, if the auditors had revealed the breaches of trust that had
been perpetrated, GAA and its directors would have taken action to put a halt to further
breaches and perhaps remedied past breaches.

Duty to investors

The first and critical question is whether the investors have a maintainable case that   F
the auditors in respect of their audits owed any duty of care to them. If the answer to this
question is in the negative (as Mr Burton for the auditors submits), then the action must
fail and accordingly the application should succeed.

The law is well established that auditors do not in respect of their audits owe a duty of
care to anyone other than the company itself save in exceptional circumstances where a
special duty has been treated as assumed to a third party. Thus in principle no duty is   G
owed to shareholders or prospective shareholders in respect of investment decisions made
regarding the purchase or sale of shares in the company; nor to existing or future creditors
who may rely on the audited accounts in leaving debts outstanding or making loans to
the company: see *Al Saudi Banque v Clark Pixley* (1989) 5 BCC 822; [1990] Ch 313
approved by the House of Lords in *Caparo Industries plc v Dickman* [1990] BCC 164;
[1990] 2 AC 605. A special relationship is required and in particular intention (actual or
inferred) on the part of the auditors that the third party shall rely, and reliance by the   H
third party, on the audit, before a claim in negligence against the auditor can be
maintained: see *Galoo Ltd v Bright Grahame Murray* [1994] BCC 319.

There are two remarkable features about the investors' claim in this case. First, there
is no apparent assumption on the part of the auditors of any responsibility towards the
investors and no intention that the investors should rely on them. Second there is no

A   suggestion of any actual reliance by the investors on the audit reports: reliance is
        specifically disavowed.

        Mr Davidson in a vigorous argument for the investors submits that a sufficient special
        relationship nonetheless exists in this case by reason of the special status of the investors
        as beneficiaries under trusts of which GAA was trustee and of whose existence the
        auditors were fully aware.

B   Mr Davidson can cite no case where such a trust relationship has been held sufficient
        to force a duty of care on auditors. Mr Davidson submits that a duty to the beneficiaries
        should be recognised because (1) there is no conflict between the auditors' duties to GAA
        and to the investors; (2) the investors are a finite class and the amount involved is limited;
        (3) the prospective liability is not additional to liability to GAA; (4) from the investors'
        point of view the auditors' remedy against GAA may be inadequate, for recoveries will
        swell the fund available to creditors generally or GAA may not have the funds to proceed
C   with an action; (5) if GAA (the trustee) is in a sufficient state of proximity, so should the
        beneficiary investors; and (6) GAA's finances were such that the investors were likely to
        be prejudiced by misapplication of client moneys.

        If there is a special relationship sufficient to create a duty of care wherever a trust exists
        in favour of beneficiaries, this will have far-reaching implications. Trusts can arise in the
        course of any company's business and trading: e.g. a *Quistclose* trust under which money
D   is paid to a company for a designated purpose, generally to discharge specific debts and
        on occasion all debts; on the conclusion of a specifically enforceable contract of sale; or
        on receipt of money paid under a mistake of fact.

        Mr Davidson however fastens on the decision of the Court of Appeal in *White v Jones*
        [1995] 2 AC 207 (in respect of which the decision of the House of Lords is pending). In
        that case, it was held that a solicitor owed a duty of care to a prospective beneficiary
E   under a second proposed will of a testator and that the prospective beneficiary could
        recover in damages for the loss occasioned when the solicitors' negligence resulted in the
        second will not being duly executed. In his judgment, Nicholls V-C said at p. 221B:

            'The House of Lords' decision in *Caparo Industries plc. v. Dickman* [1990] 2 A.C.
            605 established that, for there to be a duty to take reasonable care to avoid causing
            damage of a particular type to a particular person or class of persons, three factors
            must coalesce: foreseeability of damage, a close and direct relationship
F   characterised by the law as "proximity" or "neighbourhood", and the situation
            must be one where it is fair, just and reasonable that the law should impose the
            duty of the given scope upon the one party for the benefit of the other.'

        Nicholls V-C went on to say (at p. 222A):

            '. . . their Lordships have emphasised the importance of reliance in pure economic
            loss cases. But I do not find in those speeches any indication, still less express
G   statement, that in all cases reliance is a prerequisite to the existence of liability.'

        The Court of Appeal in that case referred to one case, *Ministry of Housing and Local
        Government v Sharp* [1970] 2 QB 223 when such liability was upheld in the absence of
        reliance, and held that the solicitor was liable despite the absence of reliance.

        It would seem to me remarkable and quite unjust and unreasonable that a company
        by the method of conduct of its business, its creation of a trust or acceptance of trust
H   moneys, should be able to impose on an auditor a duty to the beneficiaries irrespective of
        the wishes or acceptance of such a duty by the auditor.

        I think it quite plain that the decision in *White v Jones*, following the earlier decision
        to like effect in *Ross v Caunters* [1980] Ch 297, holding the solicitor liable in the absence
        of reliance is 'in a category of its own' (see Farquharson LJ at p. 232E and Steyn LJ at
        pp. 238B and 239H). If the prospective beneficiary under the will cannot sue, no claim

for damages (other than nominal) is maintainable in respect of the loss occasioned by the   A
solicitors' negligence. Hence the need for a special rule. But the Court of Appeal took
pains to make it clear that they accepted the rules laid down in *Caparo* and subsequent
cases requiring the necessary close relationship and reliance for a claim against an auditor
in respect of his audit (see e.g. Nicholls V-C at p. 222E–F).

I do not find in the six considerations relied on by Mr Davidson any feature so
significantly unique to the investors (as distinguished from shareholders and creditors)   B
and so compelling as arguably can establish the necessary close relationship to found a
claim by the investors. The one unique feature is the trust relationship. I do not think
that that is sufficiently significant. A remedy in respect of defalcation lies at the instance
of the liquidator for the benefit of all creditors including the investors; and the investors
as beneficiaries under a trust have a special personal and direct claim against the directors
for procuring or participating in the breaches of trust, a claim maintained in this action
against the directors. No special case exists for a claim by the investors against the   C
auditors.

The view which I express, I am comforted to find, is supported by Jackson & Powell,
Professional Negligence (3rd edn) para. 8.50 and is in accord with all the cases there cited.
Unlike Mr Davidson and the authors of that work, I find no real indication of a contrary
view on the part of Megaw J in *Luscombe v Roberts and Pascho* (1962) 106 SJ 373. In
that case a solicitor hopefully but unsuccessfully claimed damages against his accountant   D
for negligence in preparing his account: if the accountant had acted with due care, the
solicitor's irregularities, which were not merely technical, but deliberate, would have been
revealed earlier. In the course of his judgment, Megaw J said, obiter:

> 'The partner [in the accountancy firm] had failed to appreciate to a proper extent
> that his duty as an accountant was wider than merely to protect the solicitor but
> extended to protecting clients and the public against carelessness or dishonesty on   E
> the part of the solicitor himself.'

This dictum surely only meant that the statutory requirement for accountants' audit
certificates was imposed for the purpose of protecting the clients' and public interest: not
that a private law duty was owed to either: consider *R v Deputy Governor of Parkhurst
Prison, ex parte Hague* [1992] 1 AC 58 at 170–171A per Lord Jauncey. The dictum, if
wider than this, cannot stand with the decision in *Caparo*.

   F

Other grounds

In view of my decision in respect of absence of any duty of care owed by the auditors
to the investors, it is unnecessary to consider the other grounds on which Mr Burton
seeks to strike out the action as against the auditors and I shall only consider them briefly.

The investors plead that (beyond what I would call the conventional duties of auditors)
auditors in case of companies holding funds as trustees have a specific duty to call for   G
and verify payments into and out of client accounts.

I can find no hint of any such additional duty imposed by the *Companies Act* 1985 or
its statutory predecessors in any authority or the guidelines before me. Certainly such a
duty may exist under and by virtue of the *Financial Services Act* 1986 in case of companies
holding trust funds and not exempted by that Act. But the *Financial Services Act* 1986
came into force after the last of the pleaded audits in this case and GAA was in any event   H
exempted. I do not think it arguable that such duty existed in this case.

So far as any breach of duty by the auditors is concerned, I can find in the statement
of claim no such case as justifies the prosecution of these proceedings for breach of
professional duty. The hint of wrongdoing is apparently to be found in the overdrafts
(never at year's end) in the Barclay's account. This hint, it is alleged, should have

A   occasioned the auditors to examine payments in and out of the account and this would have led to detection of the defalcation.

To establish the necessary hint of wrongdoing, the investors have two hurdles to overcome. The first must be to show that the overdrafts (which were never at year end) came or should have come to the auditors' notice. I do not think that this should be assumed. The second is that the mere existence of the overdrafts manifested wrongdoing.

B   But whether the existence of the overdrafts was wrongful depended on the terms of the agreement with the investors, the timing of their investments and the circumstances in which the overdrafts arose.

I do not think that the overdrafts put the auditors on notice of potential wrongdoing or otherwise required the auditors to proceed on the basis that there may have been a breach of trust, and accordingly required them to search for defalcations. The overdrafts appear to me to be consistent with the conduct by GAA of its business in a legitimate

C   manner. Rather this action has all the hallmarks of a fishing expedition designed to search and find a cause of action on discovery with none yet apparent and available to be pleaded. I do not think that this is an acceptable use of the court's process (see e.g. *Steamship Mutual Underwriting Association Ltd v Trollope & Colls* (1986) 33 BLR 81 at pp. 86–89) and I would accordingly strike out this claim against the auditors on this ground also.

D

(*Order accordingly*)

E

F

G

H

Re National Employers Mutual General Insurance Association.

Chancery Division (Companies Court).

Rattee J.

Judgment delivered 22 September 1994.

Winding up – Consequences of winding-up order – Whether action commenced without leave against company in compulsory liquidation was a nullity – Insolvency Act 1986, s. 130(2).

Section 130(2) of the Insolvency Act 1986 constituted an absolute bar upon the commencement of an action against a company in compulsory liquidation without first obtaining the leave of the court, the court had no jurisdiction retrospectively to authorise the commencement of an action, and an action when commenced without leave or purportedly commenced without leave was a nullity. (Wilson v Banner Scaffolding Ltd (The Times, 22 June 1982) followed.)

The following cases were referred to in the judgment:

Stevenson (D M) & Co Ltd v Radford & Bright Ltd (1902) 10 SLT 82.
Wilson v Banner Scaffolding Ltd (The Times, 22 June 1982).

Nicholas Yell (instructed by Ryall & Lee, Peterborough) for the applicant.

Sara Williams (instructed by Paris & Co, Warwick) for the liquidators.

JUDGMENT

Rattee J: This is an appeal brought against the decision of Mr Registrar Rawson made in the Companies Court on 16 September 1994. The appeal arises in this way. The action concerned was begun against a company defendant on 21 May 1992, notwithstanding that a compulsory winding-up order had been made in respect of the company on 3 October 1990. It is not disputed on behalf of the company that the plaintiff's solicitors were not told by the company's solicitors (or solicitors who entered an appearance on behalf of the company) of the fact that the company was the subject of a winding-up order until comparatively recently, indeed in July 1994. It is not plain to me (and I do not think it is relevant for present purposes) why the fact of the winding-up order was not made apparent to the plaintiff earlier.

The action having therefore been commenced against the company after the company was made the subject of a winding-up order, it became necessary for the plaintiff's advisers, once they had realised that the company was already in liquidation, to consider the effect of s. 130(2) of the *Insolvency Act* 1986, which is in these terms:

'When a winding-up order has been made or a provisional liquidator has been appointed, no action or proceeding shall be proceeded with or commenced against the company or its property, except by leave of the court and subject to such terms as the court may impose.'

The plaintiff's advisers realised that that subsection placed an obstacle in their way in pursuing the action unless the plaintiff could succeed in obtaining from the court some sort of retrospective leave authorising their commencement without leave of the action against the company in liquidation, and the plaintiffs accordingly applied to Mr Registrar Rawson for that leave.

I am told that it was conceded before the registrar that if the court had power to give the leave that was sought it was a case in which the court would probably think it appropriate to exercise its discretion to give such leave having regard to the circumstances to which I have already referred, namely, that the action was begun against the company

A   in liquidation without the plaintiff or the plaintiff's advisers appreciating the fact that a winding-up order had been made.

However, Mr Registrar Rawson decided that it was not within his power to give the leave that was sought because he was bound (he took the view) by a decision of Milmo J made in the case of *Wilson v Banner Scaffolding Ltd* (*Times*, 22 June 1982) to the effect that proceedings begun against a company in respect of which a winding-up order has

B   been made without first obtaining leave of the court under the predecessor of s.130(2) of the 1986 Act (namely, s. 231 of the *Companies Act* 1948) were a nullity and could not be validated by some retrospective leave from the court.

The plaintiff in the action appeals to me to reverse the decision of the registrar on the ground that in this court I am not bound by the first instance decision of Milmo J, even though Mr Registrar Rawson may have been.

C   It is submitted on behalf of the plaintiff that Milmo J's decision was wrong. Milmo J decided the point in the context of a question as to whether the action in that case had begun within the relevant limitation period under the provisions of the *Limitation Act* 1939. Again in that case, as in this, the action was begun after a winding-up order had been made in respect of the defendant company.

Milmo J held that s. 231 of the *Companies Act* 1948, which was for all present purposes in terms identical to the terms of s. 130(2) of the *Insolvency Act* 1986,

D   'was a statutory bar intended to protect the interests of the creditors of the company in liquidation.'

He went on to hold, according to the report, that:

'the writ as originally issued with the name of the second defendants upon it was a nullity so far as the second defendants were concerned. The prohibition against issue without leave of the court imposed by section 231 of the *Companies Act* 1948

E   was absolute and unqualified.'

Mr Yell on behalf of the plaintiff in the present case rightly points out that Milmo J in making his decision was not, as far as one can tell from the report in the Times (although of course one does not know from that what cases were referred to at the hearing before Milmo J), referred to a decision of the Outer House of the Scottish Court of Session made in 1902 and reported in 10 SLT 82: *Stevenson & Co v Radford & Bright*. In that

F   case again an action had been started against a company after, indeed nearly two years after, an order had been made by the English High Court for the compulsory winding up of that company. It was argued that, as a result the proceedings ought to be regarded as a nullity. The judge, while accepting, as he said, the logic of that argument, said (at p. 83):

'But this, after all, is a matter of expediency, and the action being in court, and it being perfectly possible, I say no more than that, that the English court may take the view that this action ought to be allowed to proceed, I think I ought to give the

G   pursuers an opportunity of applying in England for that purpose.'

The relevant section of the companies legislation in force at the time of that decision was s. 87 of the *Companies Act* 1862, which again appears from the report of the Scottish case to have been in terms indistinguishable for present purposes from the provisions of s. 231 of the *Companies Act* 1948 or s. 130(2) of the *Insolvency Act* 1986.

H   Mr Yell on behalf of the plaintiff submits that the decision of Lord Stormont Darling in that Scottish case is authority for his proposition that the mere fact that proceedings have been commenced in breach of the provision of the statute in force at the time against a company in liquidation without prior leave of the court does not mean that the proceedings are, ipso facto, void but does mean that the winding-up court has a discretion to authorise retrospectively the commencement of the proceedings in breach of the statute.

I am not sure that in fact the Scottish case can really be said to have decided the point   A
presently before me because it would seem that what the judge in that case had in mind
was that he was not going to decide the question of the future of the proceedings before
him but was going to leave it for the English court to consider, on an application under
the then applicable section of the Companies Act, whether it was a case in which the
court could and should give leave for the proceedings to carry on. However, even if, as
Mr Yell submits, the Scottish decision is authority for his proposition in the sense that
the Scottish court could be said to have decided that an action brought in breach of the   B
provision in the terms of s. 130(2) of the Insolvency Act without leave is not ipso facto a
nullity, it seems to me that, faced with the decision of Milmo J plainly to the contrary
effect in the English court, I should follow Milmo J's decision unless I am satisfied that it
was plainly wrong. I am not so satisfied. It seems to me that, with great respect to Milmo
J, his decision represented the natural construction of the words of, in his case, s. 231 of
the *Companies Act* 1948 and in the present case subs. (2) of s. 130 of the *Insolvency Act*   C
1986. Each of those provisions provide in the clearest possible terms that no action shall
be commenced against a company in liquidation without the leave of the court. That is,
in my judgment, as Milmo J held it was, a provision constituting an absolute bar upon
the commencement of an action against a company in liquidation without first obtaining
the leave of the court.

As Milmo J in the 1982 case also pointed out, that provision was intended by the   D
legislature to protect the interests of the creditors of a company in liquidation by
preventing the company being subjected to actions once it has gone into liquidation
without the court first considering whether such an action ought to be allowed.

Mr Yell submitted that the conclusion to which Milmo J came creates, as he put it,
bizarre consequences in the sense that a potential plaintiff such as the plaintiff in the
present case may find, as the present plaintiff does find, him or herself in the position that
he started an action in perfectly good faith against a company without any knowledge   E
that the company was in liquidation, only to discover that the company is in liquidation,
if at all, long after proceedings have been commenced and possibly after the limitation
period has expired. Mr Yell submitted that the court should not accept as a proper
construction of the statutory provision that it is open to a potential defendant, being a
company in liquidation, to conceal the fact of its liquidation from the plaintiff, thereby
preventing the plaintiff recovering effective judgment against it if, by the time the plaintiff   F
learns of the fact of liquidation, the limitation period has expired.

I do not accept that argument based on the inconvenience or irrationality of the
conclusion reached by Milmo J. As Mr Yell properly accepts, it is open to any potential
plaintiff in an action against a company to ascertain whether the company is in
liquidation simply by carrying out a search of the companies registry. If a winding-up
order has been made, it will appear on the register. The fact that in very many cases a   G
plaintiff intending to pursue an action against a company does not take the trouble to
search the register in advance does not alter the fact that it is not open to a potential
defendant company in liquidation to protect itself by concealment of the fact of its
liquidation because that fact is a matter of public record available to anyone who pays
the appropriate fee and searches at the registry.

Accordingly, I am not satisfied that the decision reached by Milmo J on s. 231 of the   H
Companies Act 1948 produces any such inconvenient or arbitrary consequences as to
justify its reconsideration as representing a proper construction of that statutory
provision. In my judgment, with great respect to Milmo J, he was right in the conclusion
he reached on the 1948 Act and I see no reason to reach a different conclusion in relation
to the (for present purposes) indistinguishable provisions of subs. (2) of s. 130 of the
Insolvency Act 1986. In my judgment, the registrar was right in holding that he had no

A   power retrospectively to authorise the commencement of the action in the present case and that the action when commenced without leave or purportedly commenced without leave was a nullity.

(*Appeal dismissed*)

———————————

B

C

D

E

F

G

H

Re Dynaspan (UK) Ltd.

Chancery Division.
Robert Walker J.
Judgment delivered 14 February 1995.

Security for costs – Plaintiff company incorporated and resident in Northern Ireland and in administration – Whether security for costs could and should be ordered – Rules of the Supreme Court, O. 23, r. 1(1)(a).

The court had jurisdiction to order a company incorporated and resident in Northern Ireland to give security for costs under RSC, O. 23, r. 1(1)(a) (DSQ Property Co Ltd v Lotus Cars Ltd (1986) 2 BCC 99,539 followed); exercising the discretion afresh, on appeal from the master, and influenced by the apparent strength of the claim, the vicissitudes suffered in pursuing the claim, the risk of the claim being stifled and the fact that the plaintiff had been awarded costs of an interlocutory issue, the right order was to make no order for security.

The following cases were referred to in the judgment:

Berkeley Administration Inc & Ors v McClelland & Ors [1990] BCC 272; [1990] 2 QB 407.
Crozat v Brogden [1894] 2 QB 30.
DSQ Property Co Ltd v Lotus Cars Ltd & Ors (1986) 2 BCC 99,539; [1987] 1 WLR 127.
Kohn v Rinson & Stafford (Brod) Ltd [1948] 1 KB 327.
Mund & Fester v Hatrex International Transport (Case C-398/92) [1994] ECR I-467.
Pearson & Anor v Naydler & Ors [1977] 1 WLR 899.
Porzelack KG v Porzelack (UK) Ltd [1987] 1 WLR 420.
Raeburn v Andrews (1874) LR 9 QB 118.
Thune & Anor v London Properties Ltd & Ors [1990] BCC 293; [1990] 1 WLR 562.
Trident International Freight Services Ltd v Manchester Ship Canal Co & Anor [1990] BCC 694.
Wilson Vehicle Distributions Ltd v Colt Car Co Ltd [1984] BCLC 93.

James Guthrie QC (instructed by Jeffrey Green Russell) for the plaintiff.

David Sears (instructed by Cameron Markby Hewitt) for the second defendant.

JUDGMENT

Robert Walker J: This is an appeal from an order of Deputy Master Bragge ordering security of costs in the sum of £21,788.25 to be given by Dynaspan (UK) Ltd ('Dynaspan'). That order gave effect to a reserved decision dated 11 November 1994 in which the deputy master decided not to make any provision for what he called the pt. 1 costs; he ordered full provision for what he called the pt. 2 costs, and he left open the possibility of a further application in respect of what he called the pt. 3 and pt. 4 costs – in effect the costs of a full trial.

Dynaspan is a company incorporated and resident in Northern Ireland. It is in administration. It is in the position of plaintiff within the meaning of RSC, O. 23, r. 1 in that having been made a third party in proceedings (now discontinued by the original plaintiff) it has a counterclaim against the second defendant in the original proceedings and also against Miss Marianne Katzenberger, who is the second defendant to the claim as personal representative of her late husband, Mr Helmut Katzenberger.

It will be apparent from what I have just said that these proceedings have had a rather complicated history and I think I must try to summarise it briefly, even though some of it is now merely historical background.

A

So far as the proceedings are concerned the story begins on 18 August 1989 when a Jersey company, Romara Ltd ('Romara'), issued a writ in the Queen's Bench Division against an English company, Katzenberger Products Ltd ('Products') claiming possession of and mesne profits or arrears of rent in respect of premises at Colnbrook near Slough. The statement of claim was extensively amended and an Austrian entity, H Katzenberger Baukonstruktionen Gesellschaft ('Bauko') was added as a defendant. I say 'entity' because there seems to have been some controversy about its juridical status under Austrian law.

B

It appears that Products had been owned as to 80 per cent by Bauko (under the ultimate control of Mr Katzenberger) and as to 20 per cent by Mr Munday. Bauko was sued as a guarantor of the obligations of Products as tenant. The sale of Products in 1988 (so that it ceased to be part of Mr Katzenberger's empire) lies at the heart of the third-party claim and it is the factor which has complicated the proceedings.

C

Products defended the proceedings brought by Romara and counterclaimed for breach of an oral agreement (said to have been made by Mr Forest of Romara) for the landlord to carry out work on the premises.

On 6 December 1989 the proceedings were transferred to the Mayor's and City of London court.

D

On 5 June 1990 the second defendant, Bauko, obtained leave to issue a third party notice against Dynaspan. This referred to a written agreement dated 8 July 1988 between (1) Bauko and Mr Munday (2) Dynaspan and (3) Products. Also on 5 June 1990 Bauko issued a notice under O. 12, r. 5 of the County Court Rules claiming an indemnity from Products.

On 9 June 1990 Mr Helmut Katzenberger died. On 22 June Bauko issued a third-party notice contending that by the agreement of 8 July 1988 Dynaspan agreed (for a consideration which I shall come to in a moment) to try to obtain Bauko's release as guarantor, and in the meantime to indemnify Bauko against its liabilities to Romara. On 5 July 1990 Dynaspan put in a defence and counterclaim in the third party proceedings initiated by Bauko. The counterclaim alleged that Dynaspan (which is in the business of manufacturing and selling pre-cast concrete products) had by the agreement of 8 July 1988 agreed to buy the share capital of Products from Bauko and Mr Munday, and that Dynaspan or Products was to buy a stock of concrete girders from Bauko.

E

F

The counterclaim pleaded that this agreement was induced by a misrepresentation on the part of Mr Katzenberger, on behalf of Bauko, as to Bauko's ability to grant exclusive rights for distribution in the UK and the Republic of Ireland, for an initial period of five years (and then for a further period of five years, subject to sufficient purchases) of 'Montaquick' girders. The counterclaim alleged that this representation was false, and deliberately false. Some detailed particulars are given. The counterclaim also relied on warranties given by Bauko as to Products' financial position.

G

On 21 September 1990 the proceedings were transferred from the Mayor's and City of London court to the Chancery Division. Since the proceedings were transferred to the Chancery Division there have been numerous interlocutory applications – the case seems to have been conducted with great vigour, not to say hostility – but the only events that I need mention are as follows:

H

(1)   On 18 January 1991 Bauko was deleted from the Commercial Register in Austria. Apparently this is termed dissolution although the consequences under Austrian law are not the same as under English law. Bauko's dissolution was unknown to Dynaspan and indeed to Bauko's own English solicitors.

(2)   On 7 May 1992 Dynaspan was placed in administration.

(3)   On 24 July 1992 Bauko obtained leave (by consent, given in ignorance of its dissolution) to continue proceedings against Dynaspan. It made an application for security for costs against Dynaspan.

(4)   On 6 August 1992 Dynaspan heard of the dissolution of Bauko. The application for the security of costs was adjourned.

(5)   On 1 September 1992 Bauko's solicitors ceased to act and came off the record.

(6)   On 6 October 1992 Deputy Master Rawson gave the original plaintiff leave to discontinue its action (Bauko having proved to be a man of straw).

(7)   On 16 September 1993 Master Gowers on an ex parte application joined Mrs Marianne Katzenberger (in her capacity as her late husband's personal representative) as defendant to the counterclaim and gave Dynaspan leave to serve out of the jurisdiction.

(8)   On 10 June 1994 Mrs Katzenberger's application to set aside service was dismissed by Master Gowers. There was talk of an appeal, but it was not proceeded with.

(9)   The present summons for security for costs was then issued by Mrs Katzenberger on 25 August 1994 – say ten weeks later. In the meantime, a letter seeking security had been sent but not acceded to.

As I have already noted, the summons before Deputy Master Bragge was issued under O. 23, r. 1(1)(a), not under s. 726 of the *Companies Act* 1985. A company incorporated in Northern Ireland is not a company within the meaning of the Companies Acts. In relation to plaintiffs – or at any rate individual plaintiffs – resident in Scotland or Ireland (or, since the establishment of the Irish Republic, Northern Ireland) the practice had been firmly established, since the decision of the Divisional Court in *Raeburn v Andrews* (1874) LR 9 QB 118, of not making orders for security of costs, because the *Judgments Extension Act* 1868 enabled an English judgment to be enforced in Scotland or Ireland (or, later, Northern Ireland). In that case the three members of the Divisional Court (Blackburn J, Quain J and Archibald J) gave three short, separate judgments against ordering security to be provided by an individual plaintiff resident in Scotland: all three judgments were expressly based on the principle that as a result of the 1868 Act, the reason for the court's previous practice had ceased. The judgments very clearly proceed on the footing that the court's inherent jurisdiction to order security for costs is based, not on a plaintiff's lack of means, but on his being beyond the reach of the court's power to enforce its judgments; that basis was removed, within the UK, by the 1868 Act.

The court's power to order security for costs against a company incorporated under the Companies Acts originated under s. 69 of the *Joint Stock Companies Act* 1856 (which applied throughout the UK as it then was). It is thus a statutory jurisdiction and it is based on a quite different principle, that is that the privilege of limited liability should not be used, without control by the court, to subject a defendant to the risk of incurring irrecoverable costs in the successful defence of proceedings brought by a plaintiff who enjoys that privilege (see the observation of Nourse LJ in *Trident International Freight Services Ltd v Manchester Ship Canal Co* [1990] BCC 694 at p. 699, quoting Sir Robert Megarry V-C in *Pearson v Naydler* [1977] 1 WLR 899 at p. 904).

The fact that the *Companies Act* 1929, and all subsequent Companies Acts, have applied only to companies incorporated in Great Britain (as opposed to the UK) has given rise to a curious question as regards an application for security for costs against a company incorporated in Northern Ireland. That question has been considered in two reported decisions of distinguished judges, who reached different conclusions: and I have the unenviable task of deciding which to follow.

In *Wilson Vehicle Distributions Ltd v Colt Car Co Ltd* [1984] BCLC 93, Bingham J decided that he should follow and apply the *Raeburn v Andrews* practice in relation to a

A   company incorporated in Northern Ireland. But Millett J came to a different conclusion in *DSQ Property Co Ltd v Lotus Cars Ltd* (1986) 2 BCC 99,539; [1987] 1 WLR 127.

Bingham J's decision was based fairly and squarely on *Raeburn v Andrews* and on the principle stated in that case, which Bingham J expressed in the Latin maxim: *ratione cessante, cessat ipsa lex.*

Millett J found the consequences of Bingham J's decision 'startling' and thought it B   right to consider the point afresh; he also, it seems, heard fuller argument on it. He traced the history of the inherent jurisdiction from the eighteenth century, and the history of the Companies Acts jurisdiction from its inception in 1856. Of *Wilson Vehicle Distributions Ltd v Colt Car Co Ltd* (above) he said (at p. 99,542; 130):

> 'Bingham J held that he was precluded by the decision in *Raeburn v Andrews* from exercising [the jurisdiction ostensibly conferred by RSC, O. 23, r. 1(1)(a)]. The C   result, as he put it, was that the defendant fell uncomfortably and perhaps expensively between two stools. Security could not be ordered under the relevant section of the *Companies Act* 1985 because the plaintiff was, for the purposes of that section, treated as a foreign corporation, but equally security could not be ordered under O. 23, r. 1(1)(a) or the inherent jurisdiction of the court because the plaintiff was, for those purposes, to be treated as if it were resident in England. Can this really be the law?'

D   Millett J proceeded to hold that it was not the law, and he respectfully declined to follow the earlier decision of Bingham J in the *Wilson Vehicle* case. Millett J said (at p. 99,542; 131):

> 'It does not appear whether the plaintiff in *Raeburn v Andrews* was with or without means, but then that was irrelevant; in the case of an English resident lack of means was not sufficient, and in the case of a foreign resident it was not necessary. The E   plaintiff was an individual resident within the UK and amenable to the process of our courts. The fact that he happened to be resident in Scotland was irrelevant. There was no reason to discriminate against him by treating him any differently from a plaintiff similarly placed but resident in England.
>
> That, however, is simply not the present case. The plaintiff is not an individual but an insolvent company with limited liability. If it were incorporated and resident in F   Great Britain security could be ordered against it under s. 726 of the *Companies Act* 1985. This is not a case in which the defendants seek to discriminate against a resident of Northern Ireland, but where the plaintiff seeks to be treated differently and more advantageously than a plaintiff similarly placed in England. In my judgment, that stands the decision in *Raeburn v Andrews* on its head.
>
> In my view the true ratio of *Raeburn v Andrews* proceeds upon the straightforward principle that irrelevant circumstances should be ignored, and that plaintiffs in G   similar circumstances should be similarly treated. Where the plaintiff is an individual, with or without means, his residence in Scotland or Northern Ireland is irrelevant. He is resident within the reach of our process, and security should not be ordered against him any more than it would be ordered against an individual plaintiff resident in England. In my view that is still the law. But *Raeburn v Andrews* had, and could have had, no application to a plaintiff which was an insolvent H   company with limited liability. Here, too, in 1874, its foreign status was irrelevant, though the consequences were different; wherever incorporated and resident within the UK, security for costs could be ordered against it. That remained the law until 1929, but it has not been the law since. There is, however, in my judgment, nothing in *Raeburn v Andrews* which requires an insolvent company with limited liability incorporated and resident in Northern Ireland to be treated like an impecunious individual resident in England.'

This is a trenchant passage, but I must confess to some difficulty in following Millett J's   A
description of the true ratio in *Raeburn v Andrews* as 'that irrelevant circumstances should
be ignored, and that plaintiffs in similar circumstances should be similarly treated' – my
difficulty being especially with the first limb of this proposition. If it means that the effect
of the *Judgments Extension Act* 1868 (in making judgments 'portable' within the UK)
made it irrelevant whether a plaintiff was resident in London, Cardiff, Edinburgh or
Belfast, then that proposition prima face applies whether the plaintiff is an individual or   B
a limited liability company.

So when Millett J goes on to say, '*Raeburn v Andrews* had, and could have had, no
application to a plaintiff which was an insolvent company with limited liability' he must,
I think, have had in mind that in the case of a company incorporated under the
Companies Acts its exposure to enforcement of an English judgment is irrelevant to the
question of ordering security for costs, since the Companies Acts apply a different and
more stringent test to artificial persons who have been accorded the privilege of limited   C
liability. For them limited liability and doubtful capacity to meet an order for costs
against them, rather than immunity from having judgment enforced (or easily enforced)
against them, is the test. That such immunity from enforcement is crucial to security for
costs under RSC, O. 23, r. 1(1)(a) appears from many authorities, including *Porzelack
KG v Porzelack (UK) Ltd* [1987] 1 WLR 420, where Sir Nicolas Browne-Wilkinson V-C
said (at p. 422H):   D

> 'The purpose of ordering security for costs against a plaintiff ordinarily resident
> outside the jurisdiction is to ensure that a successful defendant will have a fund
> available within the jurisdiction of this court against which it can enforce the
> judgment for costs. It is not, in the ordinary case, in any sense designed to provide
> a defendant with security for costs against a plaintiff who lacks funds. The risk of
> defending a case brought by a penurious plaintiff is as applicable to plaintiffs
> coming from outside the jurisdiction as it is to plaintiffs resident within the   E
> jurisdiction.'

The Vice-Chancellor then went on to refer, by way of contrast, to s. 726 of the *Companies
Act* 1985 and the *DSQ Property* case. He did not express any discernible view on that
case, and Bingham LJ's comment on it in *Thune v London Properties* [1990] BCC 293;
[1990] 1 WLR 562 at p. 300; 573 is unsurprisingly delphic. Counsel's researches have not
produced any other decision, reported or unreported, in which the conflicting decisions   F
of Bingham J and Millett J have been considered.

I add – but only parenthetically, because neither side took any point on the European
aspect – that the notion of portable judgments originating in the *Judgments Extension
Act* 1868 can be traced through to Pt. II of the *Administration of Justice Act* 1920, the
Foreign Judgments (Reciprocal Enforcement) Act 1933 and (a matter of great current
importance) the Brussels and Lugano Treaties as embodied in the *Civil Jurisdiction and
Judgments Act* 1982 (as amended): see *Kohn v Rinson & Stafford (Brod) Ltd* [1948] 1 KB   G
327; *Porzelack v Porzelack (UK)* (above); *Thune v London Properties* (above); and
Berkeley Administration Inc v McClelland [1990] BCC 272; [1990] 2 QB 407 – a decision
of the Court of Appeal which may possibly be affected by the recent decision of the
European Court in *Mund & Fester v Hatrex International Transport* (Case C-398/92)
[1994] ECR I-467.

Returning to the judgment of Millett J in the *DSQ Property* case, I note that at   H
p. 99,543; 132 Millett J (in commenting on a submission that any injustice resulted from
the limited scope of s. 726 of the *Companies Act* 1985) said:

> 'The injustice results, not from the limited scope of the section, which is entirely
> appropriate, nor from any deficiency in the jurisdiction conferred by O. 23,
> r. 1(1)(a), which is wide enough to deal with the situation, but from the application

A   in very different circumstances of a rule of practice, incapable when laid down of
        affecting a plaintiff like the present, to produce consequences diametrically
        opposed to those which were then in contemplation.'

Millett J went on to say that even if *Raeburn v Andrews* was not, as he thought,
distinguishable, he would not be prepared to treat it as laying down an inflexible rule of
practice which had survived the introduction in 1964 of the present Rules of the Supreme
B   Court – a change which had certainly displaced any 'inflexible rule' that a plaintiff
resident outside the jurisdiction, and having no assets within the jurisdiction, must give
security as a matter of course (for that old rule see *Crozat v Brogden* [1894] 2 QB 30).
Whatever difficulty I have in completely understanding Millett J's observations about the
true ratio in *Raeburn v Andrews*, I find the latter part of his judgment wholly convincing,
and I respectfully prefer to follow it rather than the judgment of Bingham J in the *Wilson
Vehicle* case, where the matter seems not to have been so fully investigated and argued.
C
        On the basis that there was no settled practice preventing the deputy master from
exercising his jurisdiction, I have a discretion (to be exercised afresh, since this is not a
true appeal from the deputy master) whether to order full security for costs, or limited
security, or none at all. The main matters that have been canvassed by counsel as bearing
on the exercise of my discretion are (1) Dynaspan's very limited financial means, (2) the
alleged delay on the part of Mrs Katzenberger in applying for security, (3) the history of
D   Bauko's involvement in this litigation, so far as it is relevant, (4) the strength of
Dynaspan's claim, and (5) the possible stifling of Dynaspan's claim.

        Dynaspan is in a dire financial position. If it fails in its counterclaim, Mrs Katzenberger
may not recover in full any costs which she is awarded against Dynaspan. But that
prospect arises from Dynaspan's lack of funds, not from its incorporation and residence
in Northern Ireland; and so Dynaspan's lack of funds, although a factor to be taken into
E   account (see Bingham LJ in *Thune v London Properties* [1990] BCC 293; [1990] 1 WLR
562 at pp. 299–301; 571–573) cannot in my judgment be as weighty a factor as it might
have been on an application under s. 726. In the *DSQ Property* case Millett J treated the
absence of any s. 726 jurisdiction over a Northern Ireland company as a reason for
exercising his jurisdiction under RSC, O. 23, r. 1(1)(a), but he did not see that as equating
the two jurisdictions – which, as I have said, are based on quite different principles.
Moreover in this case Dynaspan's poor financial position cuts both ways, because it
F   raises the possibility of a valid claim being stifled. I return to that aspect below.

        Mr Sears (who appeared for Mrs Katzenberger) submitted that there had been no
substantial delay on her part in seeking security for costs. She was, he says, entitled to
challenge the jurisdiction of the English court, and so long as that challenge was on foot
(as it was until his client decided not to pursue an appeal) an application for security for
costs might have waived any objection to the jurisdiction. That is so, and I do not think
G   that Mrs Katzenberger or her advisers have been guilty of substantial delay in the sense
that their acts or omissions call for censure (nor do I think that Dynaspan and its advisers
should be censured for delay in joining her as a party, so long as Bauko was believed to
be a substantial defendant). Nevertheless, the fact is that in this hotly-contested litigation
the challenge to jurisdiction has made Dynaspan's counterclaim more protracted and
more expensive. Dynaspan was awarded costs of the jurisdiction issue, but there was no
order for those costs to be taxed and paid forthwith. That is, it seems to me, something
H   that I should take into account.

        I think I should also take into account, but only to a very limited extent, the
extraordinary episode of Bauko's English solicitors having apparently continued to
conduct litigation ostensibly on its behalf (including making an application for security
for costs) at a time when Bauko, if not dissolved in the sense that an English lawyer
would understand it, was at least no longer competent to give instructions. It appears

that the English solicitors were acting innocently in the matter, and Mr James Guthrie   A
QC (who appeared for Dynaspan) fairly accepts that responsibility for Bauko's
dissolution (and any accompanying stripping-out of its assets) is not to be laid at Mrs
Katzenberger's door. For that reason, I cannot attach much weight to the episode. But I
think I can, and should, take it into account as another matter which (although through
no fault of Mrs Katzenberger) has made the course of the litigation longer and harder
for Dynaspan.
                                                                                          B
    That brings me to the strength of Dynaspan's claim and the risk of a valid claim by
Dynaspan being stifled for lack of funds. The Court of Appeal has several times deplored
time being spent, on applications for security for costs, on lengthy investigation (through
a 'mini-trial' on affidavit evidence) of the merits of a claim. Nevertheless, on this
application (the hearing of which was quite brief, because of the excellent skeleton
arguments prepared by counsel on both sides, and the sensible use that they made of
them) Mr Guthrie was able to satisfy me, without any lengthy investigation, that   C
Dynaspan's claim in this case is a strong claim. That is partly because of unchallenged
contemporaneous correspondence, and partly because of a witness statement from a
solicitor which seems unlikely to be capable of serious challenge. Against that, however,
I must take account of the fact that the counterclaim has now become a claim against the
estate of a deceased person, and that the claim is for fraud. Even if Mrs Katzenberger
herself can produce no positive evidence to dispute the claim, the standard of proof must
be very high.   D

    I cannot therefore regard the strength of Dynaspan's claim as a decisive factor, or near
to a decisive factor. But I am satisfied that it is a strong, genuine claim, and one that
ought not to be stifled by an order for security which the company would be unable to
meet.

    Dynaspan's administrators have (as Dynaspan's solicitor, Mr Price, deposes) 'no funds
available in the administration or from Dynaspan's creditors or elsewhere' with which to   E
satisfy an order for security for costs, if such an order were made. It is clear that
Dynaspan's administrators have already invested (if that is the right word) a considerable
sum in litigating Dynaspan's counterclaim, and I think I am entitled to feel a little
sceptical about the bald statement, even from responsible and respectable insolvency
practitioners, that no funds at all would be available to meet an order for security for
costs. However, I accept that an order for security might prove to be the last straw in the   F
pursuit of the counterclaim; administrators have to take a realistic view of their duties,
and there may come a point when they decide that they would be throwing good money
after bad.

    Deputy Master Bragge gave a careful written decision, and if this were a true appeal
from the exercise of his discretion I am not sure that it would be right for me to differ
from the order that he made. But exercising my discretion afresh, I am on balance
influenced by the apparent strength of Dynaspan's counterclaim, the vicissitudes which   G
it has suffered in pursuing its claim (even though those are not all to be laid at Mrs
Katzenberger's door) and the risk of its claim being stifled. I am also influenced by the
unsatisfied order for costs which Dynaspan has left over from the jurisdiction issue, so
that Dynaspan is, as it were, in credit so far as costs are concerned; I do not think the
deputy master sufficiently recognised that merely by making no order against Dynaspan
for security in respect of what he called 'the pt. 1 costs'. I see no point in ordering   H
Dynaspan to give security in a more or less nominal amount. On the whole, I think that
the right order is to make no order for security, and I will therefore allow this appeal.

                                   (*Appeal allowed*)

A # Style Financial Services Ltd v Bank of Scotland.

Court of Session (Inner House).
Lord Justice-Clerk Ross, Lord Sutherland and Lord Coulsfield.
Judgment delivered 3 March 1995.

B *Tracing – Recompense – Pursuers sought to recover money paid into overdrawn bank account – Whether bank knew that pursuers' moneys were paid into G's account by G as agent – Whether pursuers could trace moneys in account – Whether pursuers' averments sufficient to make out case based on recompense.*

This was a reclaiming motion in an action in which the pursuers, a consumer credit company, were seeking to recover from the defenders, a bank, payment of a sum in excess of £3m with interest.

C The money was in the account of 'G' which went into receivership. The pursuers' case was that the bank were or ought to have been aware that the moneys were remitted to G's account by G as agents for the pursuers and that G had no beneficial interest therein, and that they knew or ought to have known that they were not entitled to retain the said sums in permanent reduction of the indebtedness on G's overdrawn account.

Held, upholding the Lord Ordinary's interlocutor allowing a proof before answer:

D 1. The terms of the bank mandate expressly authorised the defenders to place at the credit of G's account with them cheques and postal orders drawn in favour of the pursuers. Standing the terms of the mandate, there could be no question of there being any breach of fiduciary duty on the part of G or the defenders merely because the payments were paid into G's account with the defenders.

E 2. It must have been in contemplation of the parties that any account which G held with the defenders might be overdrawn. When money was paid into an overdrawn account, the banker was not bound to enquire into how the payer came by the money being paid into the account, but was entitled to set off the money paid into the account against the debt on the overdrawn account. (Thomson v Clydesdale Bank Ltd (1893) 20 R (HL) 59; [1893] AC 282 applied.)

F 3. Once the sums had been paid into the bank account and had served to reduce pro tanto the debit balance on the account, they had ceased to exist and could not thereafter be traced. Accordingly if the present case were to be regarded as based upon the doctrine of tracing it would be irrelevant. (Hofford & Ors v Gowans (1909) 1 SLT 153 applied; Bishopsgate Investment Management Ltd v Homan [1994] BCC 868; [1995] Ch 211 and Kensington v Liggett (Re Goldcorp Exchange Ltd) [1994] CLC 591; [1995] 1 AC 74 considered.)

G 4. The pursuers had averred sufficient to support a case that there was a fiduciary relationship between G and the pursuers and there were sufficient averments to support the view that the defenders knew of the existence of this relationship and that there had been a breach of that fiduciary relationship. If the defenders were aware of the existence of this fiduciary relationship and that the funds paid into G's account were the pursuers' funds, then sufficient had been averred to entitle the pursuers to seek to make out a case based on recompense. The real issues between the parties could only be established after enquiry.

The following cases were referred to in the opinion of the court:

H *Bishopsgate Investment Management Ltd v Homan & Ors* [1994] BCC 868; [1995] Ch 211.
Bodenham v Hoskins (1852) 21 LJ(Ch) 864.
Clydesdale Banking Co v Paul (1877) 4 R 626.
Frith v Cartland (1865) 2 H & M 417; 71 ER 525.
Gibbs v British Linen Co (1875) 4 R 630.
Gillespie v City of Glasgow Bank (1879) 6 R(HL) 104.

Hallett's Estate, Re (1880) 13 ChD 696.   A
Henry v Hammond [1913] 2 KB 515.
Heritable Reversionary Co Ltd v Millar (1892) 19 R(HL) 43.
Hofford & Ors v Gowans (1909) 1 SLT 153.
Jopp v Johnston's Trustee (1904) 6 F 1028.
Kensington v Liggett (Re Goldcorp Exchange Ltd) [1994] CLC 591; [1995] 1 AC 74.
King v Hutton [1900] 2 QB 504.
Neste Oy v Lloyds Bank plc [1983] 2 Ll Rep 658.   B
New Mining and Exploring Syndicate Ltd v Chalmers & Hunter 1912 SC 126.
Roscoe (James) (Bolton) Ltd v Winder [1915] 1 Ch 62.
Smith & Ors v Liquidator of James Birrell Ltd 1968 SLT 174.
Stodart v Dalzell (1876) 4 R 236.
Thomson & Ors v Clydesdale Bank Ltd (1893) 20 R(HL) 59; [1893] AC 282.
Westpac Banking Corporation v Savin [1985] 2 NZLR 41.   C

Arthur Hamilton QC and Gordon Reid QC (instructed by Dundas & Wilson CS) for the pursuers.

James Drummond Young QC and Patrick Hodge (instructed by Dorman Jeffrey & Co) for the defenders.

OPINION OF THE COURT   D
(Delivered by Lord Justice-Clerk Ross)

In this action the pursuers are seeking to recover from the defenders payment of a sum in excess of £3m with interest. The pursuers are a company engaged in the business of consumer credit, and were originally a wholly owned subsidiary of A Goldberg and Sons plc ('Goldberg'). In January 1986 the Royal Bank of Scotland Group plc acquired a controlling interest in the pursuers and they subsequently acquired all the equity share capital of the pursuers.   E

The basis upon which the pursuers put forward their claim is fully described by the Lord Ordinary in his opinion as follows:

'Style evolved a credit card system whereby a "Style card" was issued to a customer. Consumer credit facilities were obtainable from certain specified retailers and the arrangement is described in art. 3 and 4 of the condescendence. In summary, a customer who made purchases by means of the credit card received   F from time to time an account from the pursuers. When this happened the customer was obliged to make payment to the pursuers. Under the arrangement he could settle his indebtedness either directly with the pursuers or by making payment at the premises of Goldberg or other specified retailers as the case might be. When the customer settled the account by means of a cheque at Goldberg it is averred that he could do so either by making payment in favour of the pursuers or in   G favour of Goldberg.

The defenders were Goldberg's bankers. When sums received in settlement of the Style account from customers were paid into Goldberg's account with the defenders arrangements were made between the pursuers and Goldberg whereby sums so received by Goldberg were remitted to Style from time to time. Such sums were not paid into any special or separate account with the defenders. The pursuers   H aver that in the autumn of 1989 the defenders became apprehensive about the financial stability of Goldberg. Their account with the defenders became substantially overdrawn and on 8 June 1990, a receiver was appointed. It is averred that at the time the receiver was appointed the sums paid in Goldberg's account which were accountable to the pursuers amounted to a figure in excess of £3m. These sums were paid into an account which was and remained in overdraft. It is

A averred that those sums were all paid into Goldberg's account with the defenders between February 1990 and 8 June 1990 and were specified as being payable to the pursuers in details provided by Goldberg to them. The defenders have refused to pay these amounts to the pursuers and that is the reason for this litigation.

The basis of the pursuers' case is that in collecting money from customers Goldberg were acting as agents of the pursuers and that a fiduciary duty of accounting for
B the proceeds thereby arose. The sums in question were paid into Goldberg's account with the defenders which had the effect of reducing, but by no means eliminating the overdraft. The pursuers aver that the defenders were aware of the relationship of agent and principal as between Goldberg and them. They knew that the sums paid into the overdrawn account did not belong to Goldberg but belonged to the pursuers. The point is made specifically in art. 8 of the condescendence . . .'

C The Lord Ordinary then sets forth a passage from art. 8 of the condescendence.

Both parties have pleas to the relevancy. The pursuers' plea to relevancy is to the effect that the defences are irrelevant and lacking in specification and should be repelled and decree pronounced *de plano*. The defenders' plea to relevancy seeks dismissal of the action. After hearing parties on Procedure Roll, the Lord Ordinary repelled the defenders' fifth plea-in-law based upon indemnity, and thereafter allowed a proof before
D answer with the exception of two passages in the pleadings. The first excepted passage consisted of the last sentence of answer 8 and related to the case based upon indemnity, and the second passage consisted of the penultimate sentence of answer 5. Against that interlocutor of the Lord Ordinary the defenders have reclaimed, and the pursuers have taken advantage of the reclaiming motion by cross-appealing. Accordingly, before this court, the defenders repeated their submission that the pursuers' action was irrelevant and should be dismissed; alternatively they maintained that the Lord Ordinary was
E correct to allow a proof before answer. The pursuers, on the other hand, repeated their submission that the defences were irrelevant and that decree should be pronounced *de plano*; failing which the proof should be limited to quantum; failing which there should be a proof before answer.

In the course of their submissions, both parties referred to the terms of a mandate and indemnity, a trading agreement dated 1985 and a merchant agreement dated 25 May
F 1990. The relevant parts of these documents are referred to by the Lord Ordinary in his opinion. As already observed, the Lord Ordinary repelled the defenders' fifth plea-in-law based upon the obligation to indemnify contained in the mandate and indemnity and excluded from probation inter alia the final sentence of answer 8 which founded upon these provisions. Counsel for the defenders intimated that they were not challenging that part of the Lord Ordinary's interlocutor, and accordingly nothing more need be said
G about the argument so far as based upon indemnity. The defenders, however, did maintain that the Lord Ordinary had been in error in excluding from probation the penultimate sentence of answer 5, and if an enquiry were to take place they maintained that the averments in the penultimate sentence of answer 5 should go to proof along with the other averments in the case.

The fundamental basis of claim appears in art. 8 of the condescendence where the pursuers aver:
H
'In the foregoing circumstances, the defenders were or ought to have been aware that the said sums amounting in total to £3,095,895.72 truly belonged to the pursuers and that they were remitted to Goldberg's account with the defenders by Goldberg as agents for and on behalf of the pursuers and that Goldberg had no beneficial interest therein. They knew or ought to have known that they were not entitled to retain the said sums in permanent reduction of the indebtedness on

Goldberg's overdrawn account. By so retaining the said sums the defenders have   A
acted in bad faith. In these circumstances, the defenders are under obligation to
make payment to the pursuers of the said sum of £3,095,895.72 which is the sum
sued for and which is accordingly due and resting owing by the defenders to the
pursuers.'

Counsel for the defenders maintained that the pursuers' claim was for wrongful
retention of the sum sued for, and they submitted that such a claim was plainly irrelevant   B
in view of the fact that the mandate and indemnity expressly authorised the defenders to
credit Goldberg's account with cheques expressed to be payable to the pursuers. Counsel
submitted that what the pursuers were endeavouring to do in this action was to trace and
recover the money represented by cheques in favour of the pursuers which had been paid
into Goldberg's account. However, as soon as these sums of money were placed at the
credit of the overdrawn account of Goldberg, they fell to be set off against the debit
balance in Goldberg's account which was overdrawn with the result that the funds paid   C
into the account ceased to exist with the consequence that any remedy of tracing ceased
to be available.

There is obviously great force in that submission, and at the end of the day we
understood counsel for the pursuers' submission to be that the present action should be
seen as one of recompense rather than as one where the pursuers were seeking to trace
and recover the funds paid into Goldberg's bank account with the defenders.   D

The pursuers have two pleas-in-law dealing with the substance of the action. They are
in the following terms:

'1. The said sum sued for having been remitted to Goldberg's account with the
defenders by Goldberg as agents for and on behalf of the pursuers, as
condescended upon, the pursuers are entitled to payment thereof from the
defenders.   E

2. The sum sued for being due and resting owing by the defenders to the pursuers,
as condescended upon, decree should be pronounced as concluded for.'

The pursuers' pleas-in-law ought to contain the legal propositions upon which the
pursuers claim is based. These two pleas-in-law do not specify in any detail the legal basis
of the pursuers' case. It appears to us that they are habile to cover a tracing case, but
they are also habile to cover a case based on recompense, although it is surprising that   F
there is no specific mention of recompense.

We are satisfied that if it were to be contended that this was a tracing case, the pursuers'
case would be irrelevant. The terms of the mandate and indemnity expressly authorised
the defenders to place at the credit of Goldberg's account with them cheques and postal
orders drawn in favour of the pursuers. In these circumstances, in terms of the mandate
and indemnity the defenders were authorised to place such cheques drawn in favour of   G
the pursuers into 'the accounts maintained or to be maintained' in the name of Goldberg.
It must have been in contemplation of the parties that any account which Goldberg held
with the defenders might be overdrawn, and we did not understand the pursuers to
dispute that. The effect of paying funds into a bank account is clear. There is no fiduciary
relationship between a banker and customer in respect of money paid into a bank. The
relationship between the banker and his customer is one of debtor and creditor. The   H
customer has the right to repayment of the money which he has deposited with the
banker (Wallace & McNeil's *Banking Law* (10th edn) 9). When money is paid into an
overdrawn account, the banker is not bound to enquire into how the payer came by the
money being paid into the account, but is entitled to set off the money paid into the
account against the debt on the overdrawn account (*Thomson v Clydesdale Bank Ltd*
(1893) 20 R (HL) 59). In that case at p. 60, Lord Herschell LC said:

A
'It cannot, I think, be questioned that under ordinary circumstances a person, be he banker or other, who takes money from his debtor in discharge of a debt is not bound to enquire into the manner in which the person so paying the debt acquired the money with which he pays it. However that money may have been acquired by the person making the payment, the person taking that payment is entitled to retain it in discharge of the debt which is due to him.'

B
At p. 61 Lord Watson said:

'In this case a broker employed by the appellants to sell stock and invest the proceeds, sold and received payment of the price by a cheque of the purchasing broker payable to himself. He then passed the cheque to the credit of his current account with the respondent bank, which at the time was largely overdrawn. The course thus followed was a usual one, and in strict accordance with the practice of the Edinburgh Stock Exchange. The payment to the bank was onerous in so far as

C
concerned the respondents, because, whenever made, it operated in law as a discharge by them pro tanto of the broker's liability for the debt balance on his account; and several drafts were made by him and honoured before his dishonesty became known.'

We are accordingly satisfied that when cheques drawn in favour of the pursuers were placed at the credit of Goldberg's overdrawn account with the defenders, in accordance

D
with the terms of the mandate, the result was that the debit balance on the overdrawn account was reduced pro tanto by the amount of the cheques. We recognise that the mandate is only expressed as dealing with cheques drawn in favour of the pursuers, and that some of the cheques paid into Goldberg's account were drawn in favour of Goldberg's themselves, and that other sums placed at the credit of that account by Goldberg were sums which they had received from Style customers in cash. Nevertheless, since the defenders had express authority from the pursuers to place in the credit of

E
Goldberg's account cheques drawn in favour of the pursuers, it can hardly be contended that the defenders lacked authority to place at the credit of Goldberg's account with them any cheques drawn in favour of Goldberg or sums of cash. We are therefore satisfied that all these payments into Goldberg's account with the defenders must have had the effect of reducing pro tanto the amount of Goldberg's overdraft.

Standing the terms of the mandate and indemnity, there can be no question of there

F
being any breach of fiduciary duty on the part of Goldberg or the defenders merely because these payments were paid into Goldberg's account with the defenders.

There is another consequence which flows from the fact that these payments into the bank account acted to reduce pro tanto the debit balance on Goldberg's account with the defenders. Once these sums have been paid into the bank account and have served to reduce pro tanto the debit balance on the account, they have ceased to exist, and

G
accordingly cannot thereafter be traced. *Hofford & Ors v Gowans* (1909) 1 SLT 153 was a case where the petitioners sought to trace and recover sums which had been paid into the overdrawn bank account of a firm of stockbrokers. At p. 154 Lord Skerrington after stating the facts said:

'From this statement of the facts it follows, in my opinion, that the petitioners' money disappeared once for all when their cheques were paid into the firm's overdrawn bank account. It would of course have been different if the account had

H
been at credit. In that case the petitioners' money would have been converted into a bank credit, and it might have been traced and recovered, notwithstanding that the total balance at credit was made up also of sums belonging to the firm and to other clients.'

We agree with that statement by Lord Skerrington. That the position would be different if the bank account into which the payments were made had been in credit

appears to be vouched by *Jopp v Johnston's Trustee* (1904) 6 F 1028 and *Re Hallett's* A
Estate (1880) 13 ChD 696. In the latter case Jessel MR at p. 719 quotes from the judgment
of Wood V-C in *Frith v Cartland* (1865) 2 H & M 417:

> 'The guiding principle is, that a trustee cannot assert a title of his own to trust
> property. If he destroys a trust fund by dissipating it altogether there remains
> nothing to be the subject of the trust. But so long as the trust property can be
> traced and followed into other property into which it has been converted that B
> remains subject to the trust.'

Re Hallett's Estate was distinguished in *James Roscoe (Bolton) Ltd v Winder* [1915] 1
Ch 62. In that case Sargant J at p. 68 said:

> 'You must, for the purpose of tracing, which was the process adopted in *In re
> Hallett's Estate*. . . put your finger on some definite fund which either remains in
> its original state or can be found in another shape. That is tracing, and tracing, by C
> the very facts of this case, seems to be absolutely excluded except as to the 25l.
> 18s.'

In our opinion, these dicta all support the view that once the cheques were paid into
Goldberg's overdrawn account with the defenders and operated to reduce that overdraft
pro tanto, there was nothing left which could be traced by the pursuers. That this is so
appears to derive support from a recent case in the Court of Appeal in England and a
recent Privy Council case. In *Bishopsgate Investment Management Ltd v Homan* [1995] D
Ch 211; [1994] BCC 868 at p. 216F; 870F Dillon LJ observed that the judge of first
instance whose decision was affirmed had held that the recognised principles of equitable
tracing did not permit tracing through an overdrawn bank account – whether an account
which was already overdrawn at the time the relevant moneys were paid into it or an
account which was then in credit, but subsequently became overdrawn by subsequent
drawings. He also referred to *Kensington v Liggett (Re Goldcorp Exchange Ltd)* [1994] E
CLC 591; [1995] 1 AC 74. Similar views were expressed by Leggatt LJ.

In *Re Goldcorp Exchange Ltd*, which was a Privy Council case, at p. 610C; 104H Lord
Mustill who delivered the judgment of the Judicial Committee stated:

> 'Their Lordships should, however, say that they find it difficult to understand how
> the judgment of the board in *Space Investments Ltd v Canadian Imperial Bank of
> Commerce Trust Co (Bahamas) Ltd* (1986) 2 BCC 99,302; [1986] 1 WLR 1072, on F
> which the claimants leant heavily in argument, would enable them to overcome the
> difficulty that the moneys said to be impressed with the trust were paid into an
> overdrawn account and thereupon ceased to exist: see, for example, *Re Diplock*
> [1948] Ch 465. The observations of the board in *Space Investments* were concerned
> with a mixed, not a non-existent, fund.'

It therefore appears to us to be clear from the authorities that tracing cannot take G
place once the funds have ceased to exist. Plainly the moneys in question which were paid
into the bank account of Goldberg with the defenders have ceased to exist, and we are
accordingly satisfied that if the present case were to be regarded as based upon the
doctrine of tracing it would be irrelevant.

It is not entirely clear from the Lord Ordinary's opinion whether the case before him
was argued by the pursuers as one of tracing or one of recompense. Senior counsel for H
the pursuers contended that tracing and recompense were not discrete. It appears to us
however that the pursuers' case can be regarded as one of recompense, and it is
accordingly necessary now to consider whether the pursuers have pleaded a case on that
basis which is sufficiently relevant to go to enquiry. Put shortly the pursuers' case against
the defenders appears to be that there was a fiduciary relationship between the pursuers
and Goldberg, that the defenders knew of the existence of this relationship, its terms and

A   the fact that there had been a breach of that fiduciary relationship, and that accordingly the pursuers were entitled to recover the sum sued for from the defenders. Alternatively, it was contended that even if there was no breach of that fiduciary duty, when the money was paid into Goldberg's account with the defenders, the defenders knew that the funds had been received by Goldberg for the specific purpose of remitting these funds in due course to the pursuers, that accordingly Goldberg and the defenders were only entitled to retain these funds for a limited period, and that accordingly the defenders were not entitled to use the funds in such a way that they were liable to be destroyed; in particular by knowing what they did, they were not entitled to use these funds to reduce pro tanto Goldberg's indebtedness to them. Counsel maintained that it was clear that the defenders had obtained benefit from these funds, and were *lucrati*. They accordingly maintained that they had an obligation to restore these funds to the pursuers. Counsel maintained that the pursuers' case based upon recompense was sufficiently relevant to go to enquiry, and that the case could not be decided against the pursuers at this stage.

In support of the proposition that the defenders were aware of the existence of the fiduciary relationship between the pursuers and Goldberg, and knew that there had been a breach of that fiduciary relationship and that Goldberg were only entitled to retain the funds for a limited use, the pursuers relied upon their averments in art. 6 of the condescendence regarding the meetings which had taken place between representatives of Goldberg and the defenders' staff, and in particular the defenders' minutes of various meetings which had been produced and were referred to on record.

The pursuers' case based upon the proposition that a fiduciary relationship existed between the pursuers and Goldberg depended upon a consideration of the training agreement, the merchant agreement and the mandate. The pursuers also relied upon a large number of authorities including *Thomson v Clydesdale Bank*; *Jopp v Johnston's Trustees*; *Gillespie v City of Glasgow Bank* (1879) 6 R(HL) 104; *King v Hutton* [1900] 2 QB 504; *Henry v Hammond* [1913] 2 KB 515; and *Neste Oy v Lloyds Bank plc* [1983] 2 Ll Rep 658.

In support of the proposition that a person with knowledge of a breach of fiduciary duty was not entitled to benefit from that breach, counsel for the pursuers founded upon inter alia *Clydesdale Bank v Paul* (1877) 4 R 626 and *Gibbs v British Linen Co* reported therein as a footnote; *New Mining and Exploring Syndicate Ltd v Chalmers & Hunter* 1912 SC 126; *Bodenham v Hoskins* (1852) 21 LJ(Ch) 864; *Heritable Reversionary Co Ltd v Millar* (1892) 19 R(HL) 43; *Smith & Ors v Liquidator of James Birrell Ltd* 1968 SLT 174; and *Stodart v Dalzell* (1876) 4 R 236. In addition they referred to a number of other authorities which we have already cited. As before the Lord Ordinary, they also relied upon *Westpac Banking Corporation v Savin* [1985] 2 NZLR 41.

In answer to the pursuers' alternative basis of claim, counsel for the defenders again emphasised the terms of the mandate. If it was the intention that the defenders were obliged to make future payments to the pursuers, that should have been expressed in the mandate. Likewise, if the mandate imported any obligation to keep money separate from other payments into Goldberg's account, there is no provision in the mandate to that effect. They submitted that all that the defenders had done was in accordance with the mandate from the pursuers, and that accordingly there could be no question of bad faith at the time when the sums were credited to Goldberg's account with the defenders.

They also submitted that the pursuers had failed to make relevant averments from which the court could hold that the relationship between the pursuers and Goldberg was a fiduciary one rather than one of debtor and creditor. However, counsel did concede that the averments were sufficient to demonstrate some degree of agency as between the pursuers and Goldberg, but they maintained that no fiduciary relationship resulted from that.

We have come to the conclusion that the pursuers have averred sufficient to support a   A
case that there was a fiduciary relationship between Goldberg and the pursuers. We are
also satisfied that there are sufficient averments to support the view that the defenders
knew of the existence of this relationship and that there had been a breach of that
fiduciary relationship. Although the averments regarding what was contained in the
minutes can be criticised, we have come to the conclusion that sufficient has been averred
from which the court might draw the inference that the defenders were aware of the
existence of this fiduciary relationship. If the defenders were aware of the existence of this   B
fiduciary relationship and that the funds paid into Goldberg's account were the pursuers'
funds, then we are satisfied that sufficient has been averred to entitle the pursuers to seek
to make out a case based on recompense. We recognise that there is much to be said for
the view that the relationship between the pursuers and Goldberg was essentially one of
debtor and creditor, but we are satisfied that sufficient has been averred to entitle the
court to draw the inference that there was a fiduciary relationship.   C

The real issues between the parties can only be established after enquiry. Since it will
be necessary for an enquiry to take place, it would not be appropriate for this court to
say more at this stage regarding the legal submissions made to us. Nor would it be
appropriate at this stage for the court to comment in any detail upon the various
authorities which were cited to us.

We are also satisfied that the defenders' averments will also have to go to enquiry   D
including the penultimate sentence of answer 5. It is clear that the issues in dispute
between the parties cannot be properly determined until the facts have been established.
We are accordingly of opinion that the Lord Ordinary arrived at the correct conclusion
in this case in allowing a proof before answer. We shall, however, allow the reclaiming
motion to the extent of deleting from the Lord Ordinary's interlocutor of 23 March 1994
the exclusion from probation of the penultimate sentence of answer 5. *Quoad ultra* we
shall refuse the reclaiming motion and adhere to the interlocutor of the Lord Ordinary.   E

(*Order accordingly*)

F

G

H

A **Scmlla Properties Ltd v Gesso Properties (BVI) Ltd.**

Chancery Division.
Stanley Burnton QC (sitting as a deputy judge of the Chancery Division).
Judgment delivered 17 March 1995.

B *Insolvency – Disclaimer – Freehold land – Escheat – Liquidator disclaimed freeholds – Mortgagee subsequently sold freeholds – Whether disposal of freeholds to purchaser was effective – Whether tenants' statutory right of pre-emption arose on disposal of disclaimed freeholds – Effect of disclaimer on freeholds and interests thereunder – Effect of escheat of disclaimed freeholds to the Crown on tenants' pre-emption rights – Insolvency Act 1986, s. 178; Landlord and Tenant Act 1987, Pt. I.*

C This was an action in which tenants sought to enforce the right which they claimed under Pt. I of the Landlord and Tenant Act 1987 to purchase the freehold of premises from the defendant.

The relevant freehold titles were formerly vested in 'G Ltd'. By a legal charge they were charged by G Ltd to a bank as security for the indebtedness of 'H Ltd'. When a demand for repayment of the sum secured was not complied with the bank appointed receivers of the freeholds. G Ltd went into insolvent liquidation and the official receiver, as liquidator,
D disclaimed the freeholds pursuant to s. 178 of the Insolvency Act 1986. Subsequently the bank, as mortgagee, concluded a contract for the sale of the freeholds of the premises to the defendant. The defendant took the view that Pt. I of the 1987 Act, which gave qualifying tenants a right of pre-emption, did not apply to its purchase.

Held, deciding that Pt. I of the 1987 Act applied to the disposal of the freeholds notwithstanding that the land in question was then vested in the Crown:

E 1. The consequence of the disclaimer of a freehold under s. 178 of the 1986 Act was necessarily to determine the freehold interest.

2. On an escheat brought about by disclaimer under the 1986 Act the Crown became the owner of the land in question freed from the previous freehold interest, without any action on the part of the Crown to bring about that result.

F 3. Quite apart from the provisions of s. 178(4) of the 1986 Act, the legal charge over, and the leases of the tenants created out of, the freeholds in question survived the disclaimer of those freeholds.

4. The transfer of the freeholds by the mortgagee to the defendant was effective. The defendant was the proprietor of the freeholds and became so by reason of a disposal within the meaning of s. 4(1A) of the 1987 Act.

G 5. The disposal of the freeholds by the mortgagee, which would otherwise be a relevant disposal by virtue of s. 4(1A) of the 1987 Act, should not be held to be outside the scope of the Act because the land at that moment was vested in the Crown. The freeholds were outside the provisions of s. 56 of the 1987 Act.

The following cases were referred to in the judgment:

A E Realisations (1985) Ltd, Re (1987) 3 BCC 136; [1988] 1 WLR 200.
H *Anon* (1557) 73 ER 318.
Attorney-General v Parsons & Ors [1956] AC 421.
Attorney-General of Ontario v Mercer (1883) 8 App Cas 767.
Beale v Symonds (1853) 16 Beav 406; 51 ER 835.
Bedford (Duke of) v Coke (1751) 2 Ves Sen 116; 28 ER 76.
British General Insurance Co Ltd v Attorney-General (1945) 12 LJNCCR 113.
Burgess v Wheate (1759) 1 Eden 177; 28 ER 652.

Clark v Downes (1931) 145 LT 20.   A

Department of Transport v Egoroff [1986] 1 EGLR 89.

Downe (Viscount) v Morris (1844) 3 Hare 394; 67 ER 435.

Hastings Corporation & Anor v Letton [1908] 1 KB 378.

Hindcastle Ltd v Barbara Attenborough Associates Ltd & Ors [1994] BCC 705; [1995] QB 95.

Ho Young & Anor v Bess [1995] 1 WLR 350.   B

James (David) & Co Ltd, Re [1991] 1 NZLR 219.

King v York (1919) 88 LJKB 839.

Lowe's Will Trusts, Re [1973] 1 WLR 882.

Mercer & Moore, Re (1880) 14 ChD 287.

Middle Harbour Investments Ltd, Re [1977] 2 NSWLR 652.

Nottingham General Cemetery Co, Re [1955] 1 Ch 683.

Rogers v Maule (1841) 1 Y & CCC 4; 62 ER 765.   C

Rudler v Franks [1947] KB 530.

Strathblaine Estates Ltd, Re [1948] 1 Ch 228.

Suarez, Re (No. 2) [1924] 2 Ch 19.

Tulloch Ltd, Re (1978) 3 ACLR 808.

Walton, Ex parte (1881) 17 ChD 746.

Wells, Re [1933] Ch 29.

Wirral Estates Ltd v Shaw [1932] 2 KB 247.   D

Yonge & Conwey (1580) Sav 7; 123 ER 982.

James Thom (instructed by Malkins) for the plaintiff.

Sian Thomas (instructed by Alice Shackleton) for the defendant.

David Elvin as amicus curiae.

     E

JUDGMENT

Stanley Burnton QC: Introduction

This case raises a difficult but important point as to the application of the *Landlord and Tenant Act* 1987 to premises the freehold of which has been disclaimed on the insolvency of the landlord. If the argument of the defendant is well-founded, there is a significant lacuna in the provisions of the Act, resulting from the operation of the   F medieval doctrine of escheat. I have to say that I was initially amused, but ultimately dismayed, that the rights of the parties under a modern statute reforming the law of landlord and tenant should depend on the vestiges of feudal land law. My dismay grew as it became apparent that my decision in this case involved an examination of fundamental concepts of our land law, and an examination of concepts and authorities dating back several centuries. It was with some relief that I noted that the last authority   G to be cited in this case was a textbook dating from as recent a date as 1794; but even that referred me back to medieval writs of escheat.

I should like to express my appreciation of the work carried out by all counsel in this legally difficult case. The submissions of Mr Elvin, the *amicus curiae*, were the result of a thorough study of the authorities and analysis of the issues raised by the case. Miss Thomas's presentation of the historical material and the candour and practicality of Mr   H Thorn's submissions have also been of considerable assistance to me. Information as to the practice of the Crown Estate Commissioners in relation to Crown land was also of great help. I have to say, however, that it is regrettable that a case involving the law of landlord and residential tenant, where the parties (and in particular the tenants) are unlikely to have considerable means at their disposal to spend on lawyers' fees, should require such extensive legal research, analysis and argument.

A   **The issues**

Part I of the *Landlord and Tenant Act* 1987 confers on qualifying tenants of premises
to which that Part applies a right of first refusal on the disposal by their landlord, or by
their landlord's mortgagee, of his interest in the premises. In effect, qualifying tenants are
given a right of pre-emption in respect of their landlord's interest. The legislation was
introduced as a result of the Nugee Report on the management of privately owned blocks
B   of flats. Part I of the 1987 Act does not apply to what I may broadly describe as non-
private landlords, by virtue of s. 1(4) and s. 58, which exclude from Pt. I premises of
which the landlord is a local authority, the Housing Corporation, registered and fully
mutual housing associations, and other specified bodies, and by virtue of s. 56, which
relates to Crown land, and to which I shall have to return below.

In these proceedings the plaintiff, as the person nominated, for the purposes of s. 12 of
C   the 1987 Act, by the majority of the tenants of 1–90 Southwold Mansions and 1–60
Cleveland Mansions in Maida Vale in London, seeks to enforce the right which it claims
under Pt. I of the Act to purchase the freehold of the premises (consisting of three
registered titles) from the defendant. For convenience I shall refer to the plaintiff as 'the
tenants'.

The relevant freehold titles were formerly vested in the previous landlord of the
premises, Grantborough Ltd. By a legal charge dated 31 March 1988 they were charged
D   to the Royal Trust Bank, the name of which was subsequently changed to Gentra Ltd,
as security for the indebtedness to the chargee of Hanpier Ltd. On 18 October 1991,
Royal Trust Bank made written demand on Hanpier Ltd for payment of the sum secured
by the legal charge. It is to be assumed that the demand was not complied with. On 30
April 1992, Royal Trust Bank appointed receivers of the freeholds. On a date prior to 20
April 1993 Grantborough went into insolvent liquidation. On 20 April 1993 the official
receiver, as liquidator of Grantborough Ltd, disclaimed the freeholds pursuant to s. 178
E   of the *Insolvency Act* 1986. On 29 October 1993 Gentra, selling as mortgagee, concluded
a contract for the sale of the freeholds of the premises to the defendant. The contract was
completed on the same date. The price paid was £90,000. The defendant took the view
that Pt. I of the 1987 Act did not apply to its purchase, and cl. 11 of the contract recorded
that the vendor had not served any notice pursuant to the Act and contained an
indemnity by the defendant against any costs claims or proceedings relating to that
F   omission.

The point argued by the defendant is simply stated. It argues that on the disclaimer of
the freeholds, they vested in the Crown as an escheat. Legislation does not apply to the
Crown unless it expressly so provides or such application is necessarily to be implied.
The 1987 Act, like the old Rent Acts, apply in rem rather than in personam. Except as
provided in the Act, it therefore has no application to any premises in which the Crown
has an interest. At the relevant time, when the mortgagee disposed of the freeholds to the
G   defendant, they were vested in the Crown; the Act therefore did not apply to the disposal;
and the plaintiff has no right under the Act resulting from that disposal. The Act, it is
argued, was not applicable notwithstanding that the Crown received no benefit from the
vesting of the freeholds in it and took no step to assert its ownership or to exercise any of
the rights of ownership; and notwithstanding further that the Crown ceased to have any
interest in the freeholds as a result of the very transaction which, if the Act applied, would
H   have conferred on the tenants the right to acquire them under the 1987 Act.

The tenants dispute this conclusion. Their principal argument is that the 1987 Act
applies not in rem but in personam. On this basis, since it is not sought to exercise the
rights conferred by the 1987 Act against the Crown, and indeed the Crown would be
unaffected by their exercise, the fact that the Act has limited application to the Crown is,
it is argued, irrelevant.

At the conclusion of the original hearing, in view of the issues which had arisen as to   A
the vesting of disclaimed freehold land in the Crown, and the application of the 1987 Act
to Crown land, I asked the Attorney-General whether he wished to make submissions on
behalf of the Crown. He decided not to do so; but Mr Elvin was appointed *amicus curiae*,
and the case restored for further argument. The issues now before me are important and
potentially far-reaching. They include: whether escheat to the Crown on disclaimer of a
freehold is automatic, or whether escheat to the Crown is at its option; whether a freehold
interest in land is determined on disclaimer of the freehold under s. 178 of the *Insolvency*   B
Act 1986; whether, if the freehold interest is determined, derivative interests such as
charges, mortgages and leases are similarly determined; and whether Gentra Ltd had in
the circumstances an effective power of sale of the freeholds in question.

The Landlord and Tenant Act 1987 in outline

C

Most of the argument in this case has concerned the effect of the disclaimer of the
freeholds under s. 178(4) of the *Insolvency Act* 1986. Before coming to that, however, it
is convenient to summarise the relevant provisions of the *Landlord and Tenant Act* 1987.

Part I of the 1987 Act confers on tenants of certain premises a right of first refusal
when their landlord proposes to sell the freehold reversion. If a sale of the reversion takes
place without tenants who are entitled to a right of first refusal being accorded that right,
s. 12 confers on the tenants a right to compel the sale to them of the reversion by the   D
subsequent purchaser from their landlord. By virtue of s. 4(1A), the Act applies to
disposals by a mortgagee of the landlord as it applies to disposals by a landlord himself.
Part II of the Act confers on tenants of flats the right to apply to the court for an order
appointing a manager to act in relation to the premises, for example, to execute works of
repair which are the obligation of the landlord. Part III of the Act enables qualifying
tenants of flats to make application to the court for an order providing for the   E
compulsory acquisition by a person nominated by them of their landlord's interest. Part
IV of the Act enables a party to a long lease of a flat to make application to the court for
an order varying the lease, where the lease fails to make satisfactory provision with
respect to repair, maintenance or other specified matters. Part V of the Act is concerned
with the management of the property and in particular service charges, and Pt. VI
imposes obligations on landlords to give certain information to tenants. I have
summarised these provisions because s. 56, to which I shall have to refer below, is not   F
limited to Pt. I of the Act, under which the right claimed by the tenants in this case arises.
Similarly, as I understand it, the defendant's submission that the 1987 Act applies in rem
is not limited to Pt. I of the Act.

Section 178 of the Insolvency Act 1986

G

Section 178 of the 1986 Act is, so far as is relevant, as follows:

'*Power to disclaim onerous property*

(1) This and the next two sections apply to a company that is being wound up in
England and Wales.

(2) Subject as follows, the liquidator may, by the giving of the prescribed notice,   H
disclaim any onerous property and may do so notwithstanding that he has taken
possession of it, endeavoured to sell it, or otherwise exercised rights of ownership
in relation to it.

(3) The following is onerous property for the purposes of this section–

(a) any unprofitable contract, and

(b) any other property of the company which is unsaleable or not readily saleable or is such that it may give rise to a liability to pay money or perform any other onerous act.

(4) A disclaimer under this section–

(a) operates so as to determine, as from the date of the disclaimer, the rights, interests and liabilities of the company in or in respect of the property disclaimed; but

(b) does not, except so far as is necessary for the purpose of releasing the company from any liability, affect the rights or liabilities of any other person.'

It is not disputed that the disclaimer of the freeholds in question by the liquidator of Grantborough Ltd was effective 'to determine . . . the rights, interests and liabilities of the company in or in respect of the property disclaimed'.

Mr Elvin, Miss Thomas and Mr Thom were unanimous in submitting that the effect of disclaimer of a freehold interest is to determine that interest. This is, to a non-property lawyer, a surprising result of disclaimer; but I accept their submission. The real issue between them was as to whether derivative interests, such as leases and mortgages of a freehold, survive disclaimer. Mr Elvin submitted that they do not. Miss Thomas and Mr Thom submitted that they do.

Does disclaimer determine the freehold interest?

However, before dealing with the effect of disclaimer of a freehold on interests created out of the freehold, I should set out my reasons for accepting the submission that the consequence of the disclaimer of a freehold under s. 178 of the 1986 Act is necessarily to determine the freehold interest.

It is, first, clear that a freehold may constitute 'onerous property' for the purposes of s. 178. The wording of s. 178(3)(b) is quite general in its terms. Freeholds were the subject of disclaimer in *Re Mercer & Moore* (1880) 14 ChD 287, *Ex parte Walton* (1881) 17 ChD 746 and *Re Nottingham General Cemetery Co* [1955] 1 Ch 683. There are provisions in s. 179 and 182 of the 1986 Act relating specifically to leaseholds which have no counterpart in relation to freeholds, but one cannot infer from these provisions that freeholds are outside the scope of the power to disclaim. Disclaimer of freeholds seems to have received scant, if any, attention from the legislature, notwithstanding that such disclaimers have become increasingly common: I was told that there are about 200 escheats per year.

In considering the effects of disclaimer of a freehold, the nature of a freehold interest must be borne in mind. A freehold is not absolute ownership: it is a form of tenure. The position is summarised in Megarry & Wade, the *Law of Real Property* (5th edn), at p. 36, as follows:

'*Tenure and Ownership Today*

There is only one feudal tenure left today, namely socage, now called freehold. Feudal incidents have in practice disappeared, except for land formerly held in grand sergeanty, petty sergeanty or copyhold, where some traces of the former tenure remain. Except in the case of land formerly copyhold, mesne lordships are nearly all untraceable, for it is many years since there were any enforceable rights to preserve evidence of the relationship of lord and tenant; consequently the courts are ready to act on the presumption that the land is held directly of the Crown, e.g. for the purposes of escheat.

Yet despite the sweeping changes made by statute, "the fundamental principles of   A
the law of ownership of land remain the same as before the legislation of 1925.
Land is still the object of feudal tenure; the Sovereign remains the lord paramount
of all the land within the realm; every parcel of land is still held of some lord . . .
and the greatest interest which any subject can have in land is still an estate in fee
simple and no more". The title "tenant in fee simple" is still the technically correct
description of the person who is popularly regarded as the owner of land, and
every conveyance in fee simple substitutes the new tenant for the old as provided   B
by the statute *Quia Emptores* 1290. Nevertheless, as will be seen, for all practical
purposes ownership in fee simple "differs from the absolute dominion of a chattel
in nothing except the physical indestructibility of its subject". Our law has
preferred to suppress one by one the practical consequences of tenure rather than
to strike at the root of the theory of tenure itself. It remains possible, therefore,
that in rare cases not covered by the statutory reforms recourse may have to be   C
had to the feudal principles which still underlie our land law.'

It is because all land is held, ultimately, of the Crown that the definition of land in the
Law of Property Act 1925 and in the *Land Registration Act* 1925 includes 'land of any
tenure'. It is because the Crown cannot hold land of itself that the ancient lands of the
Crown are not registered as freeholds. To this extent, there is a major, but unremarked,
lacuna in the system of land registration in England and Wales.

Tenure requires a tenant. At common law, in the absence of a tenant, an interest in   D
land escheated to the lord holding the superior interest. As Megarry and Wade puts it (at
p. 34 of the *Law of Real Property*):

> 'Escheat is a principle inseparable from tenure which ensures that land can never
> be without an owner, for if there is no tenant and no mesne lord it will return to
> the Crown.'

The principle of modern land law which does not permit an estate in land to be without   E
an owner is basic to the common law, although it appears to postdate the development
of tenure and escheat as an incident of tenure (Simpson, *History of the Land Law* (2nd
edn) pp. 47–48; Megarry & Wade, pp. 12–14). In its original form, it is found in Glanvill,
Book VII, Ch. 17 (*De Ultimis Heredibus*, translated and edited by Hall (2nd edn, 1993)):

> 'The ultimate heir of any person is his lord. When, therefore, anyone dies without
> a certain heir – for example, without son or daughter or anyone who is without   F
> doubt the nearest and right heir, the lords of the fees may, as the custom is, take
> and keep those fees in their hands as their escheats, whether such lord is the king
> or someone else. If anyone later comes and says that he is the right heir, and is
> allowed by the grace of his lord or by a write of the lord king to pursue his claim,
> he shall sue and may recover such right as he may have . . . However, if no-one
> appears and claims the inheritance as heir, then it remains perpetually with the
> lord as an escheat, and so he may dispose of it, as of his own property, at his   G
> pleasure . . . Again, if anyone is convicted of or confesses a felony in court, he is
> disinherited by the law of the realm and his land escheats to his lord . . . To put it
> generally, whenever anyone does or says anything in court of which he is
> disinherited by judgment of the court, his inheritance escheats to the lord of the fee
> from whom he holds it . . .'

In *Attorney-General of Ontario v Mercer* (1883) 8 App Cas 767 at pp. 771–772, the Earl   H
of Selborne LC (giving the judgment of the Privy Council) stated:

> 'All land in England, in the hands of any subject, was holden of some lord by some
> kind of service, and it was deemed in law to have been originally derived from the
> Crown, "and therefore the King was Sovereign Lord, or Lord paramount, either
> mediate or immediate, of all and every parcel of land within the Realm" (Co. Litt.
> 65a). The King had "dominium directum", the subject "dominium utile" (Ibid.

A 1a). The word "tenure" signified this relation of tenant to lord. Free or common socage was one of the ancient modes of tenure ("A man may hold of his lord by realty only, and such tenure is tenure in socage", Litt., sect. 118), which, by the statute 12 Car. 2, c. 24, was substituted throughout England for the former tenures by knight service and by soccage in capite of the King, and relieved from various feudal burdens. Some, however, of the former incidents were expressly preserved by that statute, and others (escheat being one of them), though not expressly mentioned, were taken away.

B

" 'Escheat' is a word of art, and signifieth properly when by accident the lands fall to the lord of whom they are holden, in which case we say the fee is escheated" (Co. Litt. 13a). Elsewhere (Ibid., 92b) it is called "a casual profit", as happening to the lord by "chance and unlooked for". The writ of escheat, when the tenant died without heirs, was in this form: "The King to the Sheriff, & Co Command A., & Co., that he rendered B. 10 acres of land, with the appurtenances, in N., which C. held of him, and which ought to revert to him, the said B., as his escheat, or that he said C. died without heirs" (F.N.B., 155F). If there was a mesne lord, the escheat was to him; if not, to the King.

C

From the use of the word "revert" in the writ of escheat, is manifestly derived the language of some authorities which speak of escheat as a species of "reversion". There cannot, in the usual and proper sense of the term, be a reversion expectant upon an estate in fee simple. What is meant is that, when there is no longer any tenant, the land returns, by reason of tenure, to the lord by whom, or by whose predecessors in title, the tenure was created. Other writers speak of the lord as taking it by way of succession or inheritance, as if from the tenant, which is certainly not accurate. The tenant's estate (subject to any charges upon it which he may have created) has come to an end, and the lord is in by his own right.

D

E As stated in Megarry & Wade, in modern times, the possibility of there being a mesne lord holding an interest between the freehold and the Crown is generally so remote that it can be disregarded (see *Re Lowe's Will Trusts* [1973] 1 WLR 882); escheat will therefore generally be to the Crown. In this case it is agreed that the possibility of there being a mesne lord is so remote that it can be ignored.

F The most common causes of escheat have been abolished by statute: escheat on conviction for treason by the *Forfeiture Act* 1870 and escheat on intestacy by s. 45(1)(d) of the *Administration of Estates Act* 1925. The common law rules applicable to escheat on conviction for treason ('propter delictum tenentis') and escheat on intestacy ('propter delictum sanguinis') are not necessarily applicable to disclaimer of a freehold under the *Insolvency Act* 1986. However, the theory of both of these instances of escheat was that there was, as a result of intestacy or of conviction for treason (which was considered so to corrupt the blood of the convicted person as to render him incapable of holding land and incapable of having heirs to inherit his estate) no tenant holding the interest in land in question. This is precisely what occurs on disclaimer under s. 178: the company ceases to hold the freehold interest. The analogy between personal intestacy and corporate dissolution was relied upon by Lawrence LJ in *Re Wells* [1933] Ch 29 at p. 50 in relation to bona vacantia, and is equally good in relation to escheat of freeholds. It seems to me therefore, that I should have regard to the authorities on escheat on intestacy or conviction for treason in order to ascertain the consequences of disclaimer under the Insolvency Act.

G

H

According to the last sentence of the extract from the judgment of Lord Selborne in *Attorney-General of Ontario v Mercer* cited above, the effect of escheat was that the escheated interest came to an end. Escheat was applicable only to freehold land; and it follows that on escheat the freehold interest came to an end. Most authorities are to this

effect. In the well-known article by T Cyprian Williams, 'The Fundamental Principles of   A
the Present Law of Ownership of Land' (1931) 75 SJ 843, cited by Megarry and Wade at
p. 36 of the *Law of Real Property* he stated:

> 'The word *escheat*. . . does not of itself carry any implication of failure of heirs; it
> simply means the falling-in of the land to the lord. (Just as, in common parlance,
> leases for years are said to fall in when the terms granted come to an end. The case
> of escheat is exactly analogous.)   B

> I submit that . . . escheat may still take place whenever an estate in fee simple is
> brought to an end or extinguished from some other cause than want of heirs . . . it
> seems to me that the words of (s. 54 of the *Bankruptcy Act* 1914 providing for
> disclaimer by a trustee in bankruptcy) are quite sufficient to determine the
> bankrupt's estate in fee simple in any freehold property of his, which the trustee
> has disclaimed. And upon such determination, as I submit, the immediate lord of
> the fee must be entitled to enter upon the land, as his escheat.'   C

Similarly, *Halsbury's Laws of England*, at para. 1435 of vol. 17, describes escheat as
follows:

> 'The tenant's estate, subject to any charges upon it which he may have created, had
> come to an end, and the lord was in by his own right.'

Megarry and Wade, the *Law of Real Property* (5th edn) states, at p. 17:   D

> 'Escheat occurred on the extinction of a tenancy; the immediate lord became tenant
> in demesne and entitled to occupy the land.'

The operation of escheat is put clearly in Enever on *Bona Vacantia* (1927) at pp. 15–
16:

> 'In the case of the Crown's title by way of escheat in respect of the real estate of
> inheritance of a person dying before 1926 intestate and without an heir at law the   E
> Crown did not acquire any right or interest of the deceased, but continued to be
> the owner of the land, freed from the estate previously carved out of the Crown's
> interest in the land.'

In *Re Mercer and Moore* (1880) 14 ChD 287, Jessel MR said at p. 295:

> 'There is no person literally entitled upon the determination of the freehold to take
> except the Crown. If a freehold estate comes to an end by death without an heir,   F
> or by attainder, it goes back to the Crown on the principle that all freehold estate
> originally came from the Crown, and that where there is no one entitled to the
> freehold estate by law it reverts to the Crown.'

Reference may also be made to Challis's *Law of Real Property* (3rd edn, 1911) at p. 33,
and to Williams, *Principles of the Law of Real Property* (1865) at p. 116:

> '. . . so the lord, of whom an estate in fee simple is held, possesses, in respect of his   G
> lordship, or seignory, a similar, though more uncertain advantage, in his right of
> escheat; by which, if the estate happens to end, the land reverts to the lord, . . .'

In *Burgess v Wheate* (1759) 1 Eden 177 Lord Mansfield LCJ said at p. 227:

> 'This brings me to consider the nature of this right by escheat.

> It has been truly said in the beginning of feudal tenure, this right was a strict
> reversion. The grant determined by failure of heirs, the land returned as it did upon   H
> the expiration of any less temporary interest. It was no fruit, but the extinction of
> tenure (as Mr Justice Wright says); it was the fee returned.'

All these authorities indicate that the freehold determines on an escheat; indeed, it is
the determination of the freehold which brings about the escheat. The possibility of a
freehold determining is envisaged by s. 7(2) of the *Law of Property Act* 1925, and by

A   s. 118; but these provisions are concerned with determination of a freehold vested in a corporation on its dissolution, and were presumably drafted in the light of the statement in *Co. Litt.* 76 that a freehold property of a dissolved company reverted to the grantor, and the decision in *Hastings Corporation v Letton* [1908] 1 KB 378, which was disapproved by the Court of Appeal in *Re Wells* [1933] Ch 29 at pp. 47 and 60ff., and which Jenkins J refused to follow in *Re Strathblaine Estates Ltd* [1948] 1 Ch 228. These two cases, *Re Wells* and *Re Strathblaine Estates Ltd*, appear to be the only authorities

B   for the survival of a freehold interest after escheat. In *Re Wells* the point was not before the Court of Appeal: the case concerned leaseholds rather than freeholds, and bona vacantia rather than escheat. (See also the argument of the Solicitor General at p. 35: 'It is admitted that the case of escheat is quite different from that of bona vacantia' and the statement in the judgment of Lord Hanworth MR at p. 47 that the decision in *Hastings Corp v Letton* [1908] 1 KB 378 was not relevant. R E Megarry (as he then was) described

C   the decision in *Re Wells* as 'controversial': (1964) 62 LQR 223.) The court was concerned to reject the suggestion that on dissolution of a company its freeholds and leaseholds reverted to the grantor; and authorities on the question whether a freehold survives escheat (such as *Attorney-General of Ontario v Mercer*), were not relevant and were not cited. In *Re Strathblaine Estates Ltd* the authorities on escheat were not examined, presumably because the case concerned properties of a company which had been

D   dissolved, and were therefore deemed to be bona vacantia by virtue of s. 71 of the *Companies Act* 1928, re-enacted in s. 296 of the *Companies Act* 1929 and s. 354 of the *Companies Act* 1948.

     In *Re Strathblaine Estates Ltd*, Jenkins J was similarly concerned to reject the theory that land held by a dissolved company reverted to the grantor rejected by the Court of Appeal in *Re Wells*. Jenkins J held that the freeholds of the dissolved company had vested in the Crown as bona vacantia, and there was no submission before him that the

E   effect of such vesting was to determine the freehold; and he did not consider whether the effect of a freehold passing to the Crown might be to determine it. I accord great weight to this decision of Jenkins J, particularly since it has stood for some time and forms the basis of the practice of the court in relation to freeholds of dissolved companies; and Parliament may have had his decision in mind when subsequent Companies Acts and the Insolvency Act were passed. However, I do not think that his decision that the freeholds

F   survived dissolution of the freehold owner can stand, in relation to a freehold disclaimed under s. 178 of the *Insolvency Act* 1986, in the face of the authorities before me. Indeed, it is because of the weight of the older authorities that Mr Thom and Miss Thomas felt constrained to accept, and to submit, that the consequence of disclaimer is the termination of the freehold disclaimed.

     Lastly, the authorities on escheat were comprehensively reviewed by Judge Wethered

G   in *British General Insurance Co Ltd v Attorney-General* (1945) 12 LJNCCR 113. He concluded at p. 126:

         'that the correct manner in which the law on this subject should be stated is that escheat to the lord of the fee occurred in all cases when a freehold estate of a subject was determined from whatsoever cause . . .'

H   A number of additional points fall to be mentioned in this connection. First, Mr Elvin argued for determination of a freehold on disclaimer on the basis of authority and principle. I have already referred to the authorities. The principle is simply that the Crown cannot hold property of itself. Tenure implies that the superior lord and the tenant are different persons. On escheat, he argued, the freehold merges in the Crown's interest. Merger is a technical and unpopular doctrine, and its operation is capable of giving rise to injustice. My immediate reaction was that merger might be avoided by

reason of s. 185 of the *Law of Property Act* 1925. However, Mr Thom pointed out to me   A
that this provision cannot be applied to escheat, by virtue of s. 208(2) of that Act.

Secondly, there is an analogy between the disclaimer of a freehold and the disclaimer
of a lease. Both are forms of tenure, and a lease for 999 years is almost as great an interest
as a freehold. It was common ground before me that the effect of the decisions in *Re A E
Realisations (1985) Ltd* (1987) 3 BCC 136; [1988] 1 WLR 200, and *Hindcastle Ltd v
Barbara Attenborough Associates Ltd* [1994] BCC 705; [1995] QB 95 is that on disclaimer   B
of a lease it ceases to exist, although it may be deemed to continue to exist for certain
purposes if the lease is not vested in the original lessee when it is disclaimed. To hold that
a freehold similarly ceases to exist may be surprising, but places leases and freeholds on
the same footing on disclaimer. Any injustice which might otherwise be caused by
disclaimer of a freehold may be avoided by the making of a vesting order under s. 181 of
the 1986 Act. I bear in mind that there are no provisions in the Insolvency Act relating
to freeholds equivalent to s. 179 and 182; but I do not think that the absence of such   C
provisions a sufficient reason to lead me to doubt my conclusion on this point.

Thirdly, Mr Thom submitted that escheat had been abolished in relation to registered
land by the *Land Registration Act* 1925. His submission was based on the difference
between the wording of s. 105 of the *Land Transfer Act* 1875 and that of s. 80 of the *Land
Registration Act* 1925. Both the 1875 Act and the 1925 Act provided that registration of
a freehold interest in registered land vested or conferred on the registered proprietor an
estate in fee simple 'free from all other estates and interests whatsoever, including estates   D
and interests of Her (in the case of the 1925 Act, His) Majesty'. Section 105 of the 1875
Act provided:

> 'Nothing in this Act shall affect any right of Her Majesty to any escheat or
> forfeiture.'

Section 80 of the 1925 Act, however, is as follows: E

> 'Subject to the express provisions of this Act relating to the effect of . . . registration
> of a disposition for valuable consideration, nothing in this Act affects any right of
> His Majesty to any bona vacantia or forfeiture.'

As can be seen, the reference to escheat was omitted.

It would, of course, be undesirable to introduce any difference between the
transmission of registered and of unregistered land, particularly where it is difficult to see   F
any basis for distinguishing between them. Furthermore, the *Land Registration Act* 1925
was a consolidating Act, so that the abolition of escheat is unlikely to have been intended.
I have no doubt that the reconciliation of the words of, for example, s. 5 of the 1925 Act
'free from all . . . estates and interests of His Majesty' and those of s. 80 of that Act is
that set out in the judgment of Romer J in *Re Suarez (No. 2)* [1924] 2 Ch 19. The object
of the cited words in s. 5 is to ensure that the proprietor of a registered title is not exposed
to the risk of an argument that his land was escheated to the Crown before, possibly long   G
before, registration. Those words do not affect the seignory of the Crown, which is not
an 'estate' or an 'interest' within the meaning of s. 5 and 20(1) of the 1925 Act, and
therefore do not affect liability to escheat after the date of registration. On this basis, the
omission of the reference to escheat in the saving provisions of s. 80 is of no effect. I have
no doubt that the reference to escheat was omitted from s. 80 of the 1925 Act because the
draftsman mistakenly believed that all cases of escheat had been abolished. I conclude   H
that the 1925 Act was not intended to abolish, and did not abolish, escheat in relation to
registered land.

Does the Crown automatically acquire the land?

Mr Elvin submitted that although disclaimer necessarily involves the determination of
the freehold interest disclaimed, the land does not automatically vest in the Crown. I was

A   informed that the Crown is most concerned that it should not be bound to take disclaimed land. This is understandable, given that the power to disclaim is only exercisable in respect of land which is 'unsaleable or not readily saleable or is such that it may give rise to a liability to pay money or perform any other onerous act' (s. 178(3)(b) of the 1986 Act). A similar concern influenced the House of Lords in deciding that the statutory provision for forfeiture to the Crown in the *Mortmain and Charitable Uses Act* 1888 conferred on the Crown a right to forfeit a lease, but that the lease was not automatically forfeited to the Crown. In effect, forfeiture was at the option of the Crown: see *A-G v Parsons* [1956] AC 421.

B

C

D

A number of authorities on this issue must be considered with some care. References to the right of the lord to take possession on an escheat (for example, Williams on the *Law of Real Property* (24th edn, 1926) at pp. 43–44) are, in my view, equivocal as to whether escheat was automatic or at the instance of the lord. In practice, if the lord did not take possession of the land in question, it would presumably have been occupied by squatters or relatives of the deceased or of the traitorous freeholder. See, for example, Blackstone, *Commentaries*, Book II, Ch. 15. The position is further complicated by the fact that a series of statutes required an inquisition to he held before the Crown could enjoy land claimed as an escheat. If the Crown did not cause an inquisition to be held, it effectively waived its claim to the land. It is not obvious whether an inquisition which upheld the right of the Crown to an escheat was declaratory of the Crown's entitlement or effective to create that entitlement.

Nonetheless, the authorities suggest that escheat to the Crown was automatic. *Anon* (1557) 73 ER 318 states that 'the act of his (the Duke of Suffolk's) attainder vests the real and actual possession and seisin in the king without office found, and so does the statute 33 H 8'. In *Yonge & Conwey* (1580) Sav 7, a case of intestacy, the Barons held that 'le terr eschete a le Roy, & le Roy est seisie de le franckt sons office trove'. Staunford,

E   *Exposition of the King's Prerogative* (1607) at pp. 54–56, on 'the King's seisin, possession or title' distinguishes between the King's 'possession of the right of the thing' and his 'possession of the profit thereof'. The former passed to the King without any office or matter of record 'or else the freehold should be in suspense, which may not be . . .' I read this as authority for the proposition that the right of the King to escheated land as a matter of law was independent of any action on his part. In *Co. Litt.* 18b one finds the

F   following passage:

> 'And so it is of an escheat or the like, because the inheritance is cast upon, or a title vested in the lord by act in law, and not by his own deed or agreement, as our author here saith.'

The commentary is as follow:

> 'It should be considered, that though the lord must do some act to put himself into
G   the actual possession, yet his title to take possession commences immediately on the want of a tenant, and this title is vested in him without waiting for his own deed or agreement, and as much by mere act of law as the title of an heir is in the case of a descent; . . .'

Romer J in *Re Suarez (No. 2)* stated (at p. 24):

> '. . . when once the event has happened the Crown has an estate and interest in the
H   land even without any inquest of office.'

He approved the statement in an article by Mr Hardman in 15 LQR 318 that:

> 'Where a person seised of lands in fee dies intestate and without heirs, and no mesne lord is proved to exist, the right of escheat at once accrues to the Crown, and the title and possession are cast upon the king at common law. Notwithstanding the doubts expressed by Lord Ellenborough (12 East, 109, 110),

it is believed to be the better opinion that an inquest of office is only a proceeding   A
to ascertain the title of the Crown by escheat, and not an essential condition to the
vesting of such title, "or else the freehold should be in suspense, which may not
be" (Staunf. Prerog. 54A). But the law vests in the king nothing more than a bare
right, and no beneficial enjoyment of the property can in general be had until after
office found.'

It is to be noted that in that case counsel for the Attorney-General stated that he could: B

'not dispute that as soon as the right of the tenant in fee simple determines the
legal interest remains in the Crown . . . In face of the authorities it is not possible
to deny that the estate of the Crown, whatever form it takes, arises on the
happening of the event on which the escheat takes place.'

I note also that in *Re Nottingham General Cemetery Co* [1955] 1 Ch 683, counsel for
the Commissioner of Crown Lands intimated that he was prepared to admit that upon   C
disclaimer by the liquidator the freehold land held by the company would vest in the
Crown, but that he would contend that the Crown would only become involved in any
liability if and when it entered into possession: see at pp. 688–689. According to the
report of his argument, at pp. 685–686, he distinguished between seisin in law, which
passes to the Crown automatically, and seisin in deed, which required actual re-entry by
the Crown.

Thus the great weight of authority is in favour of automatic escheat. So is the principle   D
of the thing. If the effect of disclaimer is that there is no tenant of the freehold, and clearly
it is, then there is no one holding any interest below, or adverse to, that of the Crown.
The Crown therefore has an unfettered right to the land; to put it more accurately, the
Crown's seignory is no longer encumbered by the freehold interest.

The principle of *nulle terre sans seigneur* referred to at p. 34 of Megarry & Wade, in
the sentence cited above, compels the same conclusion. After the conclusion of oral   E
argument in this case, Mr Thom brought to my attention the recently reported decision
of the Privy Council in *Ho Young v Bess* [1995] 1 WLR 350. In that case the Privy Council
stated at p. 355E, 'the general proposition that the law abhors a vacuum and that title to
land must always be in someone, whether the Crown or a subject', and on the basis of
that proposition decided, consistently with *A-G v Parsons*, that the words 'shall be
forfeited' in the statute under consideration meant 'shall be liable to be forfeited' and did
not operate so as automatically to forfeit land to the Crown. Since disclaimer of a   F
freehold ipso facto determines the company's interest in the land, this general proposition
requires title on disclaimer to be immediately and automatically in the Crown.

Any doubt I might otherwise have is resolved by the terms of s. 8(3) of the *Crown
Estate Act* 1961, which provides as follows:

'Where land escheats to Her Majesty in right of the Crown or of the Duchy of
Lancaster, or to the Duke of Cornwall or Her Majesty in right of the Duchy of   G
Cornwall, then (without prejudice to the rights of other persons) the land shall vest
accordingly and may be dealt with, and any proceedings may be taken in relation
to it, without the title by escheat being found of record by inquisition or otherwise.'

Only a strained construction of this provision would enable me to hold that the vesting
of land in the Crown on an escheat depends on an election by the Crown to take the land.

I am fortified in my view by the fact that a number of statutory provisions assume that   H
land may vest in the Crown automatically, without any election by the Crown: see, for
example, s. 180 of the *Insolvency Act* 1986, and s. 40(4) of the *Crown Proceedings Act*
1947 which is as follows:

'Where any property vests in the Crown by virtue of any rule of law which operates
independently of the acts or the intentions of the Crown, the Crown shall not by

A   virtue of this Act be subject to any liabilities in tort by reason only of the property being so vested; but the provisions of this subsection shall be without prejudice to the liabilities of the Crown under this Act in respect of any period after the Crown or any person acting for the Crown has in fact taken possession or control of any such property, or entered into occupation thereof.'

B   These provisions distinguish between the liabilities of the Crown when it has seisin in law and those when it has seisin in deed, to use the language of counsel for the Commissioners of Crown Lands in *Re Nottingham General Cemetery*.

This provision should give some comfort to the Crown as to the consequences of automatic escheat. Furthermore, escheat differs from forfeiture under the Mortmain Acts in that it does not result in the estate in question vesting in the Crown as such. Forfeiture under the *Mortmain and Charitable Uses Act* 1888 led to the lease in question vesting in
C   the Crown, which would become liable under the tenant's covenants in the lease: see the speech of Lord Jowitt in *A-G v Parsons* at [1956] AC 435. On escheat, the freehold does not pass to the Crown, but determines. (To this extent, s. 8(3) of the *Crown Estate Act* 1961 is imprecisely drafted.) The Crown does not, by virtue of escheat alone, assume the liabilities of the freeholder to, for example, lessees of the freehold. Following escheat, there is no privity of contract between lessees and the Crown; the Crown is not a successor in title to the freeholder and does not derive title under him (cf s. 79 of the *Law of*
D   *Property Act* 1925); and the Crown's seignory is not the reversionary estate immediately expectant on the term granted by the freeholder or his predecessor in title (cf s. 142 of the *Law of Property Act* 1925). In any event, the Crown is entitled to the benefit of s. 178(4)(b) of the Insolvency Act, which provides that a disclaimer does not affect its rights or liabilities. Similarly, the Crown does not come under any personal obligation to a mortgagee in respect of the mortgage debt. This is, I think, the position at common law; but it too is made clear by s. 178(4)(b) of the Insolvency Act. I was warned of the
E   possibility that the Crown, or officers of the Crown, might come under criminal liabilities as a result of escheat, if it operates independently of the wishes and acts of the Crown; but I was not given any example of such liability arising in the case of land in respect of which the Crown took no action at all. If there is a risk of such liability, the answer must, I think, be the enactment of legislation equivalent to s. 40(4) of the Crown Proceedings Act.

F   I conclude that I am bound to hold, and I do hold, that on an escheat brought about by disclaimer under the 1986 Act the Crown becomes the owner of the land in question freed from the previous freehold interest, without any action on the part of the Crown to bring about this result.

There is a curious result of this conclusion. Section 654 of the *Companies Act* 1985 deems all property whatsoever vested in a dissolved company to be bona vacantia and
G   provides that it accordingly belongs to the Crown. Curiously, as in the case of the disclaimer provisions of the Insolvency Act, leaseholds are specifically mentioned, but not freeholds: however, as in the case of s. 178 of the Insolvency Act, the wording is quite general and clearly includes freeholds. I note that under s. 654 of the 1985 Act acquisition by the Crown is automatic. However, by s. 656, the Crown is empowered to disclaim such property, and s. 657 provides that, as regards property in England and Wales, s.
H   178(4) and s. 179–182 of the Insolvency Act apply as if the property had been disclaimed by the liquidator immediately before the liquidation of the company. The result of the disclaimer by the Crown of a freehold of a dissolved company appears to be, therefore, that the property ultimately comes back to the Crown as an escheat. It is difficult to see the object of these provisions, in so far as they concern freeholds. The boomerang effect of disclaimer by the Crown under what are now s. 651 et seq. of the Companies Act was the subject of comment at (1954) 70 LQR 25, but has not been explained. One is left with

the impression that the draftsman forgot that bona vacantia could, by reason of the   A
statutory deeming provision, include freeholds, or that no consideration was given to the
effect of disclaimer of a freehold under s. 178 of the Insolvency Act.

The effect of escheat on subordinate interests

Mr Elvin submitted that the result of the determination of the freehold is that
subordinate interests, such as a lease, are similarly determined. It is, he argued, a general   B
principle of the common law that when an interest in land is determined, all interests
created out of that interest similarly come to an end; a principle exemplified by the effect
of the forfeiture or disclaimer of a lease on subleases. On this basis, on the disclaimer of
the present freeholds, the tenants' leases, unbeknownst to them, ceased to exist, as did
the interest of the mortgagee, since its charge by way of legal mortgage took effect as a
mortgage by demise: s. 87 of the *Law of Property Act* 1925.

C

The logic of Mr Elvin's argument must be admitted. It is indeed difficult to understand
how a subordinate interest, created out of a freehold, can survive the termination of the
freehold interest, any more than a sublease can survive the determination of a head lease.
However, I feel bound to reject the argument. No case was cited to me in which an
escheat was held to have brought about the termination of a subordinate interest. On the
other hand, in a number of cases it has been assumed that mortgages by demise survive
escheat: see *Rogers v Maule* (1841) 1 Y & CCC 4 (where the Crown did not, however,   D
claim the freehold) and *Viscount Downe v Morris* (1844) 3 Hare 394, in which the Vice-
Chancellor held that the lord of a manor taking by escheat, on the death of a tenant
without heirs, the fee simple of lands subject to a demise for a term of years by way of
mortgage created by the freeholder is entitled, as against the mortgagee, to redeem the
term. It was implicit in this decision that the term of years survived the escheat. *Viscount
Downe v Morris* was adversely commented upon by Sir John Romilly MR, who had been
the unsuccessful counsel in that case, when he came to decide *Beale v Symonds* (1853) 16   E
Beav 406, in which he held that the equity of redemption of a fee did not escheat to the
Crown, but belonged to the mortgagee. However, the debate in these cases is not whether
the mortgage survives the escheat, but to whom the equity of redemption passes on
intestacy. In *Duke of Bedford v Coke* (1751) 2 Ves Sen 116, Lord Hardwicke LC had held
that on an escheat the Crown was bound by bona fide charges and encumbrances, but
was not otherwise liable for the debts of the freeholder: F

> 'the crown on a forfeiture takes the estate subject to all charges and incumbrances,
> which would have bound the party forfeiting, and must be bound too, where no
> fraud in respect of the crown.'

As has been seen, in his exposition of escheat in *A-G of Ontario v Mercer*, Lord Selborne
stated that:

> 'The tenant's estate (subject to any charges upon it which he may have created) has   G
> come to an end, and the lord is in by his own right.'

This dictum was accepted and applied in New South Wales in *Re Middle Harbour
Investments Ltd* [1977] 2 NSWLR 652.

Textbook authority is similarly in favour of the survival of derivative interests. Ing,
Bona vacantia (1971) at p. 128, states that the Crown will take an asset subject to any
liability secured on that asset, such as a mortgage (although no authority is cited). In the   H
article on 'The Law of Escheat' in (1888) 4 LQR 318 approved by Romer J in *Re Suarez
(No. 2)*, Frederic Hardman said:

> 'The position of the lord taking by escheat with regard to the escheated property is
> not in all respects the same as that of a person taking by grant, devise or descent.
> The lord comes in by title paramount: his estate is quite independent of the estate

A   of the tenant which has expired. He comes to the estate in the *post*, according to the old technical phraseology; that is to say, by a title paramount that of the person on whose death without heir the right of escheat attaches. His independences of the estate of the last tenant is attended with peculiar consequences, which may work either in his favour or to his disadvantage. Thus it is laid down that the lord by escheat shall have the rent reserved on a lease by the tenant, but he cannot re-enter for condition broken, because he has no privity with the lessor. The right of

B   distraining for the rent is in the lord, not as heir, but as incident to his reversion. Again, for the purpose of binding the lord in escheat, deeds have been held good against him that would have been void or voidable in other respects, as a feoffment of an infant with livery. The lord will also take subject to any incumbrances created by the last tenant, because the power of creating lesser estates is incident to a fee simple, and an exercise of that power is therefore binding on the lord. Thus if the

C   last tenant had granted a rent or demised the land for a term of years, by way of mortgage or otherwise, these partial alienations will bind the lord. So the incidents of dower and courtesy may attach to the land in derogation of the lord's right. The lord is sometimes prejudicially affected, not only by the act of the last tenant or by rules of law annexing incidents to the tenant's estate, but by statutory enactments impressing certain qualities upon the land itself. Thus in *Evans v Brown*, 5 Beav 114, it was held that under Romilly's Act, 3 & 4 Will. IV. c. 104, lands coming to

D   the lord by escheat were assets in his hands for the payment of the debts of the last tenant. This Act, however, would probably be held not to apply where the escheat is to the Crown, as the Crown is not expressly named in it. The reason that the lord taking by escheat is subject to incumbrances in general is that they are annexed to the possession of the land without respect to any privity; but the lord is not subject to any incumbrances annexed to the privity of estate. A trust for instance, is only a personal confidence between the trustee and the *cestui que trust*, and such

E   confidence is a privity confined to them. On the death of the trustee, therefore, intestate and heirless, an escheat took place, and after considerable conflict of views, it was the better opinion that the lord took the land freed from the trust, and from any obligation to the *cestui que trust*. The same result took place where a mortgage in fee had been made, and the mortgagee died intestate and without heirs. But it was naturally thought to be inequitable that any benefit should be

F   taken by the lord when a merely technical escheat of this kind took place, and various statutes were passed to mitigate or obviate such an inconvenient result.'

    The survival of subordinate interests on escheat is also supported by Simpson, *A History of the Land Law* (2nd edn) at p. 53, by Milsom, *Historical Foundations of the Common Law* (2nd edn) at pp. 111–114, and by Holdsworth, *A History of English Law* (3rd edn) vol. 3, p. 43:

G   'If lands escheated to the crown the tenant held these lands from the crown ut de honore. The scutages formerly payable to the mesne lord were now payable to the king.'

    Indeed, it was because the superior lord was bound by subinfeudation for a nominal service, like the traditional rose at midsummer, that the statute Quia Emptores was passed. Lastly, the survival of subordinate interests is also supported by Robertson, the

H   *Law and Practice of Civil Proceedings by and against the Crown* (1908) pp. 424–427.

    On the other hand, Professor Jenks, in *Modern Land Law* (1899), at p. 216, stated that escheat necessarily avoids all interests derived out of the freehold. However, he did not refer to the authorities to which I have referred above, and his statement receives scant, if any, support from the authority which he does cite. In these circumstances, I cannot regard his statement as authoritative.

I consider that I should follow the authorities referred to above, other than Professor   A
Jenks. I should not assume that the judges of the 18th and 19th centuries misunderstood
the legal position of subordinate interests on escheat, or that the legal writers to whom I
have referred, other than Professor Jenks, were mistaken in their accounts of the history
of English land law. It is not suggested that there is in the present connection any relevant
difference between escheat to a mesne lord and escheat to the Crown. I consider that I
should proceed on the basis, artificial though it may well be, that when Parliament   B
enacted the Insolvency Act and the Companies Acts it had in mind the authorities to
which I have referred, and assumed them to represent the law. I can see no difference
between the survival of a mortgage by demise, a charge by way of legal mortgage and a
demise otherwise than by way of security. Accordingly, I hold that, quite apart from the
provisions of s. 178(4) of the Insolvency Act, the legal charge dated 31 March 1988 over,
and the leases of the tenants created out of, the freeholds in question in this case survived
the disclaimer of those freeholds.   C

My conclusion happily makes it unnecessary for me to decide whether s. 178 of the
Insolvency Act, and in particular s. 178(4)(b), binds the Crown, and I express no view on
it.

**The effect of s. 178(4) of the Insolvency Act on the tenants' rights under Pt. I of the
Landlord and Tenant Act 1987**
   D
Mr Thom submitted that the right of the tenants to acquire the freeholds was preserved
by s. 178(4) of the Insolvency Act, which provides that:

'A disclaimer under this section–

. . .

  (b) does not, except so far as is necessary for the purpose of releasing the
      company from any liability, affect the rights or liabilities of any other   E
      person.'

However, at the date of the disclaimer, the tenants had no right to be preserved by
s. 178(4). The right which they claim to enforce in these proceedings arose, if at all, as a
result of the disposal of the freeholds by their mortgagee subsequently to the disclaimer.
The right to compel a sale by a new landlord arises on a 'relevant disposal' affecting
premises to which Pt. I of the 1987 Act applies: see s. 12(1)(a); see also s. 1(1), 5(1) and
11(1). Whether the tenants do have such a right must be determined as at the date of that   F
disposal. Incidentally, it was not argued that the disclaimer of the freeholds under s. 178
itself constituted a 'disposal' within the meaning of s. 4 of the *Landlord and Tenant Act
1987*.

Was the transfer of the freeholds by Gentra to the defendant effective?

In *Re Tulloch* (1978) 3 ACLR 808, Needham J said, with regard to the position of a   G
mortgagee of freehold property disclaimed under the provisions of s. 296 of the
Companies Act 1961 (NSW):

'There can remain no personal covenant and, as the Crown would take not as
successor to the company but by operation of law, the various provisions of the
mortgage would not apply to it. There being no obligation on the company to
comply with the contractual covenants, there could be, it would seem, no default   H
in complying with them which would permit the mortgagee to exercise its powers,
e.g. of sale. Where, however, the default already exists, it would follow, in my
opinion, that the right to sell vested in the mortgagee is one of the rights not
affected by the disclaimer by virtue of s. 296(2).'

The wording of s. 296(2) of the New South Wales Act is practically identical to that of
s. 178(4) of the Insolvency Act. *Re Tulloch* was first cited by Mr Elvin. As a result of its

A   citation, Miss Thomas sought to establish that the mortgagee in this case, Gentra Ltd, had been entitled to exercise its power of sale before the disclaimer of the freeholds. An affidavit was filed exhibiting a copy of a written demand dated 18 October 1991 from the Royal Trust Bank, as it was then called, to Hanpier Ltd, for the balance due from it to Royal Trust bank. I accept this affidavit as prima facie evidence that a demand of which the copy was exhibited was sent to Hanpier Ltd. No demand on Grantborough was exhibited, although it will be remembered that on 30 April 1992 Royal Trust Bank

B   appointed receivers of the charged property. Clause 2.3 of the legal charge provided that:

> '. . . the owner (Grantborough) agrees to pay to the bank or otherwise discharge on demand the secured amounts . . .'

'On demand' here means 'on demand on the owner'. 'The secured amounts' were sums due from Hanpier Ltd. Since Grantborough was a surety and not a principal debtor it would seem to follow that in the absence of a demand on it, the secured sum was not due

C   from it. However, cl. 6(4) of the legal charge was as follows:

> '. . . at any time after the bank shall have demanded payment or discharge of the secured amounts or if requested by the company (Hanpier) or the owner the bank may exercise all or any of the powers conferred on mortgagees by the *Law of Property Act* 1925 . . .'

But for the reference to the request of the company in this clause, I should have been

D   inclined to construe it too as requiring demand on the owner. This reference, however, suggests that the power of sale may become exercisable without any notice to, or even knowledge on the part of, the owner, and gives support to Miss Thomas's submission that notice on Hanpier sufficed. If it did, the power of sale of the mortgagee had arisen before disclaimer, and was preserved by s. 178(4), assuming it to be binding on the Crown.

E   However, I am very reluctant to allow the point that the power of sale conferred by the legal charge did not become exercisable to be taken in these proceedings. First, these proceedings assume that the defendant is the owner of the freeholds: the plaintiff seeks an order that the freeholds be transferred by the defendant to the plaintiff. It is only if there was a disposal of the freeholds to the defendant that any right under Pt. I of the 1987 Act can have arisen. If the acquisition of the freeholds by the defendant is to be contested by the tenants, that must be done in other proceedings. If this point had been

F   taken at an early stage by the tenants, those other proceedings might have been heard with the present proceedings. However, the point only arose at a very late stage. Furthermore, the defendant is the registered proprietor of the freeholds. It is entitled to be treated as the proprietor of the freeholds unless and until proceedings are brought to rectify the register.

Secondly, in my view, the personal covenant of a borrower-mortgagor or surety-

G   mortgagor to repay the sum secured is not a liability 'of the company in or in respect of the property disclaimed' within the meaning of s. 178(4)(a) of the Insolvency Act. There is a distinction between, for example, the covenants of a lessor, which are clearly such liabilities, and indebtedness secured by, and in a sense arising independently of, a mortgage. It would be odd if a partially secured mortgagee should, as a result of a disclaimer of the mortgaged property, lose the entirety of his debt, including his right to prove. The only authorities on this point to which I was referred were *Re Middle Harbour*

H   *Investments Ltd* [1977] 2 NSWLR 652 and *Re Tulloch*, which are, of course, not binding on me. In my view the liability of Grantborough to Gentra to pay or discharge the secured indebtedness was not determined by the disclaimer.

Thirdly, it is clear that if the power of sale had arisen and been exercised, the freehold was validly vested in the defendant. The sale by a mortgagee in such circumstances is effective by virtue of s. 88 and 104(1) of the *Law of Property Act* 1925, which is binding

on the Crown: see *British General Insurance Co v A-G* at p. 124. In such circumstances,   A
the freehold must be regarded as reviving.

Section 104 of the *Law of Property Act* 1925 is as follows:

'*Conveyance on sale*

(1) A mortgagee exercising the power of sale conferred by this Act shall have
power, by deed, to convey the property sold, for such estate and interest therein as
he is by this Act authorised to sell or convey or may be the subject of the mortgage,   B
freed from all estates, interest, and rights to which the mortgage has priority, but
subject to all estates, interests, and rights which have priority to the mortgage.

(2) Where a conveyance is made in exercise of the power of sale conferred by this
Act, or any enactment replaced by this Act, the title of the purchaser shall not be
impeachable on the ground–

     (a) that no case had arisen to authorise the sale; or   C

     (b) that due notice was not given; or

     (c) where the mortgage is made after the commencement of this Act, that leave
        of the court, when so required, was not obtained; or

     (d) whether the mortgage was made before or after such commencement, that
        the power was otherwise improperly or irregularly exercised;   D

and a purchaser is not, either before or on conveyance, concerned to see or inquire
whether a case has arisen to authorise the sale, or due notice has been given, or the
power is otherwise properly and regularly exercised; but any person damnified by
an unauthorised, or improper, or irregular exercise of the power shall have his
remedy in damages against the person exercising the power.

(3) A conveyance on sale by a mortgagee, made after the commencement of this
Act, shall be deemed to have been made in exercise of the power of sale conferred   E
by this Act unless a contrary intention appears.'

The object of s. 104(2) of the *Law of Property Act* 1925 is to avoid a purchaser having
to make any enquiry as to whether the mortgagee's power of sale has in fact arisen. It
would be highly unfortunate if the acquisition of a disclaimed freehold by a purchaser
from a mortgagee were to depend on whether the mortgagee's power of sale had actually
arisen before the disclaimer, thus producing an exception to the generality of s. 104(2),   F
and a trap for the unwary. The question whether a power of sale has arisen should
concern rights and liabilities as between mortgagor and mortgagee, and should not affect
third parties. (In this connection, the fact that the mortgagee in the present case appointed
receivers of the mortgaged property may be significant.) Section 104(2) is general in its
terms, and provides that the title of the purchaser 'shall not be impeachable' where a
conveyance is made in exercise of the power of sale conferred by the Act. The conveyance   G
by Gentra to the defendant was made by Gentra 'in exercise of the power of sale conferred
by the charge dated 31 March 1988 . . .' However, the only power of sale conferred by
the legal charge was the statutory power of sale: see cl. 6(4) cited above. It follows that
s. 104(2) is applicable, and that the conveyance to the defendant is 'unimpeachable'.
Section 104, of course, binds the Crown.

I conclude that the defendant is indeed the proprietor of the freeholds and became so
by reason of a disposal within the meaning of s. 4(1A) the 1987 Act. For the reasons   H
which I have indicated above, if I have to decide this issue, I hold that the freehold was
effectively vested in the defendant.

I add that after the conclusion of oral argument in this case, and after I had drafted
the preceding part of my judgment, Miss Thomas brought to my attention the decision
of the High Court of New Zealand in *Re David James & Co Ltd* [1991] 1 NZLR 219. My

A   conclusions on this part of the case are supported by the judgment of Holland J in that case.

The application of Pt. I of the Landlord and Tenant Act 1987 to the acquisition of the freeholds by the defendant

Miss Thomas's argument that the 1987 Act applied in rem rather than in personam
B   relied substantially on the authorities on the in rem application of the Rent Acts, and on similarities between the language of the Rent Acts and the 1987 Act, and in particular the use of phrases such as 'premises to which this Act (or Part) applies' in both the Rent Acts and the 1987 Act. The meaning of the application in rem of a statute is by no means obvious, since all legislation relating to property manifestly applies to a rem, while on the other hand all legislation ultimately works by affecting the rights and liabilities of legal (and in the final extreme, natural) persons. It is therefore convenient to consider the Rent
C   Act authorities first, since they show what may be meant by the in rem application of legislation.

The Rent Acts authorities

The first of the so-called Rent Acts was the *Increase of Rent and Mortgage Interest (War Restrictions) Act* 1915. In 1920 the existing legislation was repealed and replaced
D   by the *Increase of Rent and Mortgage Interest (Restrictions) Act* 1920, which provided the basis of the rent and security of tenure legislation until the *Rent Act* 1968. The Rent Acts gave rise to a plethora of case law, and it was said that Megarry J, the author of the essential handbook for all practitioners in this area, *Megarry's Rent Acts*, was the only person who fully understood the legislation and jurisprudence. The object of the Rent Acts, so far as tenancies were concerned, was to restrict the rent recoverable in respect of residential tenancies of dwelling houses below a specified rateable value to (in the 1920
E   Act) a 'standard rent', and to give to residential tenants of such premises a high degree of security of tenure.

The original Rent Act was a war-time measure, and the legislation was intended to be temporary. The 'standard rent' of a dwelling house was the rent payable in respect of it at the commencement of the First World War, i.e. 3 August 1914, but it could be increased in specified circumstances. In *King v York* (1919) 88 LJKB 839 the question
F   arose whether the restrictions on rent imposed by the Rent Acts continued to apply on a change in the tenancy of a dwelling-house. The Divisional Court held that the restrictions under the Act continued to apply notwithstanding any change in the tenancy of the premises. Lush J said at p. 840:

> 'There is no doubt that, under s. 2, subs. 5, once the Act has become applicable to a dwelling-house, it does not matter that, during the time the Act is in force, it comes to be used for other purposes. The Act, having once applied, continues to
G   > apply whether there has been a change in the character of the occupation or not.'

Sankey J said:

> 'The Act applies to objects, not to persons; it operates in rem and not in personam; and it stereotypes the rent of the particular house in question.'

The application of the Rent Acts to Crown property was considered in *Clark v Downes*
H   (1931) 145 LT 20. The 1923 Act had provided for houses to be gradually released from control by the Acts ('de-controlled') as landlords obtained possession. Sitting tenants remained controlled: see *Megarry's Rent Acts* (11th edn) p. 1. *Clark v Downes* concerned a number of huts which the government had built for munitions workers. They became vacant after 1923, but were re-let to tenants in 1924 and 1925. In 1928 the Crown sold the property in which the huts had been built to a company which in turn leased the property on to the plaintiff. The county court judge had refused to make an order for

possession against two tenants of the huts, whose tenancies had commenced in October 1924. It is not easy to see the basis of the argument for the tenants, since it was admitted, on appeal, that the Crown had had vacant possession of the huts after 31 July 1923, the effective date for the purposes of the 1923 Act, so that, if the huts had throughout been in private ownership, they would have been decontrolled by the 1923 Act. Be that as it may, the case was decided on appeal on the basis that the Rent Acts did not bind the Crown (this being conceded by tenants), and that the sale of the property by the Crown did not have the effect of making the Rent Acts applicable. Lord Hanworth MR said at p. 21:

> 'The assumption [that the Crown was not bound by the Rent Acts] is made because it is presumed that the Legislature does not intend to deprive the Crown of any right or property unless it expresses its intention to do so in explicit terms or makes the inference irresistible, and so where the language of a statute is general and in its general sense would not deprive the Crown of any right or property the ordinary rule is that the Crown is not so deprived.'

Romer LJ said, at p. 22, in a passage on which Miss Thomas placed great reliance, and which I therefore cite in full:

> 'It is agreed by both parties to this appeal that the Rent Restrictions Acts do not affect the rights of the Crown. It is also agreed that having regard to the authorities these Acts must be treated as operating *in rem* and not *in personam*. That being so, it seems to me that we must read subsect. (2) of sect. 12 of the Act of 1920, which is defining what houses are within the Acts, as though it in express terms said: This Act shall apply to a house other than a house belonging to the Crown, and so on. It has been laid down by the Court of Appeal that for the purpose of considering whether a house does or does not come within the provisions of that subsection the time to be regarded is not the time at which somebody is seeking to put in operation some rights in respect of the house or to resist some application made in respect of the house, but the time at which the house is let. That being so, it seems to follow that this house is not within the operation of the Acts, because clearly it was not within the operation of the Acts at the time of the letting. The argument for the respondent would, I think, be a good one so far as it is based upon the Act of 1920 if that Act operated not *in rem* but *in personam*, because then one need not except from the definition clause houses belonging to the Crown. Houses belonging to the Crown would be within the definition clause, but the Acts operating *in personam* and not barring the Crown, the Crown would not be subject to any of the restrictions imposed by the Acts in respect of the houses belonging to the Crown, leaving the houses to become subject to the operation of the Acts if and when some person other than the Crown is the person to be affected by the restrictive sections of the Act. But even if the respondent could get so far he would then, I think, be defeated by the provisions of sect. 2, sub-sect. (1), of the Act of 1923, because in that case the house would be a house within the operation of the Acts and the Crown would be the landlord within the meaning of that subsection, although the Crown would not be subject to the operation of the restrictive sections of the Acts. However, as I have said, it is conceded, and rightly conceded, that these Acts operate *in rem* and not *in personam*.

> I only want to add to this. The Acts not binding the Crown, it is the duty of the courts so to construe the Acts that the Crown and its property are in no way prejudicially affected by the Acts. Now, if the learned county court judge is right and these houses became subject to the operation of the Acts, the moment they passed out of the ownership of the Crown it follows that the reversion to the houses while in the possession of the Crown was worth considerably less than it would

A   have been but for the Acts. The Acts so construed, therefore, would have prejudicially affected the property of the Crown. Having regard to what I have said, the Acts should therefore not be construed in that way.'

The dictum of Romer LJ in *Clark v Downes*, to the effect that the Acts must be interpreted so that the Crown and its property are in no way prejudicially affected by them, did not meet with wholehearted approval. In *Wirral Estates Ltd v Shaw* [1932] 2
B   KB 247, it was held that the Acts did apply to a new tenancy created by a private purchaser of Crown land and granted to a tenant who had also been the tenant of the premises in question when they were owned by the Crown. Talbot J said, at p. 250– 251:

'I confess that if the point arose and if we were competent to deal with it, or if it arose before a Court which considered itself to be competent to deal with it, I think the question would be open to argument whether the learned Lord Justice was not going beyond what is necessary for the maintenance or the prerogative doctrine
C   with regard to the operation of statutes upon the Crown . . . I, personally, am not prepared, in the absence of any authority, to extend what possibly may in itself seem to be rather an extreme application of the doctrine with regard to the affect of statutes on the Crown.'

In the Court of Appeal, Lawrence LJ, who was sitting with Lord Hanworth MR and Romer LJ, declined to express any opinion as to whether *Clark v Downes* was correctly
D   decided.

The decision of the Divisional Court in *Clark v Downes* was applied in *Rudler v Franks* [1947] KB 530 so as to exclude from the application of the Acts a sub-tenancy created by a letting by a private tenant of the Crown of Crown property. Lord Goddard CJ said at p. 531:

'. . . I think it must be a surprise for anyone to learn that if the property sought to
E   be recovered is Crown property, notwithstanding that the tenancy is a sub-tenancy created by the tenant of the Crown, the Rent Restriction Acts do not apply to the cottage or house so long as the property remains Crown property. I need not consider what would happen if the Crown sold the reversion. So far as this court is concerned, it seems that the case is concluded by the decision of the Divisional Court, consisting of Lord Hanworth M.R. and Romer L.J., sitting as additional judges of the King's Bench Division, in *Clark v Downes*. That case has also been
F   considered and must be taken as approved by the Court of Appeal of which the same two judges were members, in *Wirral Estates Ltd v Shaw* [1932] 2 KB 247. As I understand the decision it is this. The Rent Restriction Acts apply in rem and not in personam. The meaning of that is that the Rent Restriction Acts attach or apply to the property itself, and therefore, as the Crown is not bound by the Rent Restriction Acts the cottage or house as long as it remains Crown property, never
G   becomes affected by them. If the tenancy of the cottage had been granted by the Crown, I think no one could have disputed the fact that the Rent Restriction Acts would not apply, because the Crown not being named in the Acts, obviously upon all the well-known rules of construction is not affected by the Acts. The reason why the Acts do not apply when the tenants of the Crown create a sub-tenancy is first because, as I have just said, the Acts operate in rem and not in personam and so are never attached to the house at all.'

H   The decision in *Rudler v Franks* was reversed by statute, by the *Crown Lessees (Protection of Sub-Tenants) Act* 1952. The *Rent Act* 1968 similarly limited the exemption of the Crown to immediate tenancies from the Crown: see s. 4, s. 70(3)(a) and s. 116; and this policy was continued in the *Rent Act* 1977: see s. 13, s. 19(5)(b) and s. 154 of the 1977 Act. Subsequently, by s. 73(1) of the *Housing Act* 1980, properties under the management of the Crown Estate Commissioners were removed from the Crown exemption: see

s. 13(2) of the *Rent Act* 1977, as amended by the 1980 Act. There is therefore little left of   A
the exemption of Crown property from the Rent Acts. As to the rule that they operate in
rem, *Megarry's Rent Acts*, in the latest (11th) edition, states at p. 31:

> 'Today it seems best to regard the Acts as primarily applying to contracts or "in
> pacta".'

The Landlord and Tenant Act 1987   B

In support of the submission that the 1987 Act applies in rem, Miss Thomas relies on
the similarity of the language used in relation to qualifying premises. Both the Rent Acts
and the 1987 Act are concerned with the law of landlord and tenant. Both the Rent Acts
and the 1987 Act conferred important rights on tenants going beyond those which they
enjoyed at common law. But that is as far as the similarity goes. There are considerable
differences between the respective legislation, and apart from authority I should be
cautious indeed before seeking to determine points of controversy as to the interpretation   C
or application of the 1987 Act by reference to the Rent Acts, particularly in regard to a
point which has been largely reversed by legislation.

Miss Thomas relied on the decision of the Court of Appeal in *Department of Transport
v Egoroff* [1986] 1 EGLR 89, in which it was held that the Crown was not bound by the
provisions of s. 32 and 33 of the *Housing Act* 1961 (since replaced by s. 11–16 of the
Landlord and Tenant Act 1985) as to implied covenants in short leases obliging the lessor   D
to repair the demised premises. The 1961 Act did not expressly bind the Crown, and it
was conceded that there was nothing in the statute to justify an implication that the
Crown was bound. Parker LJ referred to the Rent Acts in order to refute the submission
of the tenant that the Crown was bound by the sections in question because they were
intended to suppress a wrong: so were the Rent Acts, but they did not bind the Crown.
Counsel for the tenant sought to distinguish the Rent Acts on the basis that the 1961
legislation applied to the premises, whereas the Rent Acts applied in personam. That   E
submission was doomed to failure because, as Parker LJ pointed out, it is a truism to say
that the Rent Acts applied in rem. I do not read his judgment as requiring the 1961 Act
to be interpreted on the basis that it was *in pari materia* with the Rent Acts in any
technical sense. The case was decided on the basis of the well established rule as to the
application of statutes to the Crown. Parker LJ said at p. 90:

> 'There being, as I see it, no relevant distinction between the two sets of provisions   F
> [the Rent Acts and s. 32 and 33 of the 1961 Act], and in the light of what is said in
> (*Bombay Province v Bombay Municipal Corporation* [1947] AC 58), to which I have
> already referred, it appears to me that the test must be either an examination of
> the wording of the Act or in certain specific cases a demonstration that the purpose
> of the sections would be wholly frustrated unless the Crown were bound. That
> might raise a necessary implication outside the wording of the Act. But unless the   G
> matter can be taken that far, and in this case it certainly cannot, it does not seem
> to me that an Act of this sort can possibly be said to bind the Crown.'

This is the rule which is to be applied in determining, in the absence of express provision,
whether the 1987 Act applies to the Crown.

It is correct that both the Rent Acts and Pt. I of the 1987 Act use similar language. The
Rent Acts referred to 'any dwelling house to which this Act applies' (see, e.g., s. 1 of the
1920 Act), while Pt. I of the 1987 Act refers to premises to which it applies (s. 1). However,   H
I do not derive much assistance from this similarity. Any legislation relating to property,
unless it applies to all property, must define the property to which it applies. I should be
wary of drawing any significant inference from this similarity of language, which may be
coincidental. Furthermore, this wording is not to be found in every part of the 1987 Act.
It does not appear in Pt. IV or Pt. V, or in s. 18–30 of the *Landlord and Tenant Act* 1985

A amended by that Part. I mention this because s. 56 of the 1987 Act, which concerns the application of the Act to the Crown, is not restricted to Pt. I of the Act. Any criterion for the application of the Act to Crown property must, therefore, apply equally to all Parts of the Act.

There are also important differences between the wording and effect of the Rent Acts and the 1987 Act, and in particular Pt. I. As has been seen, *King v York* established that
B once the Rent Acts applied to premises, they continued to apply notwithstanding a change in the person of the tenant or even a change in the character of the occupation. The application of the Rent Acts was similarly independent of any change in the person of the (private) landlord of premises. In this sense they operated in rem. However, Pt. I of the 1987 Act is, in a real sense, temporary in its application. Section 1(1) provides:

C 'A landlord shall not make a relevant disposal affecting any premises to which *at the time of the disposal* this Part (of the Act) applies unless . . .

he serves notice in accordance with s. 5 and the disposal complies with s. 6–10 (emphasis added).

In the present case the tenants claim to exercise the right conferred on them by s. 12 to compel the sale to them of an interest acquired by a purchaser as a result of the failure of a landlord to comply with s. 1. This section similarly contains a timing requirement:

D '(1) Where–

(a) paragraphs (a) and (b) of section 11(1) apply to a relevant disposal affecting any premises to which at the time of the disposal this Part applied (other than a disposal consisting of such a surrender as is mentioned in section 15(1)(b)), and

E (b) those premises are still premises to which this Part applies,

the requisite majority of qualifying tenants of the constituent flats may, before the end of the period specified in subsection (2), serve a notice ("a purchase notice") on the new landlord requiring him (except as provided by the following provisions of this Part) to dispose of the estate or interest that was the subject-matter of the original disposal, on the terms on which it was made (including those relating to
F the consideration payable), to a person or persons nominated for the purposes of this section by any such majority of qualifying tenants of those flats.

(2) The period referred to in subsection (1) is–

(a) in a case where a notice has been served on the new landlord under section 11(1), the period of three months beginning with the date on which a notice is served by him under section 11(3); and

G (b) in any other case, the period of three months beginning with the date mentioned in section 11(2).'

It is to be noted that the application of Pt. I of the Act to the premises depends on more than 50 per cent of the flats in them being occupied by qualifying tenants: s. 1(2). Thus changes in the occupation of individual flats may take the premises out of Pt. I; and such a change, if occurring after a disposal by a landlord in contravention of the right
H created by s. 1, may cause tenants to lose their right to purchase the landlord's interest from its purchaser.

So far as the Crown is concerned, s. 56(1) expressly provides that the Act shall apply to a tenancy of Crown land if there has ceased to be a Crown interest in the land: compare *Clark v Downes*, in which it was held that a sale of property by the Crown did not bring a tenancy within the Rent Acts.

The provisions of Pt. I of the 1987 Act can in my view be sensibly characterised as A
creating personal rights exercisable by qualifying tenants against their landlord in respect
of premises to which that Part applies. This is consistent with the long title of the Act:
'An Act to confer on tenants of flats rights with respect to the acquisition by them of
their landlord's reversion . . .' It follows that but for the provisions of s. 56 of the 1987
Act I should have rejected Miss Thomas's submission that the Act applies in rem rather
than in personam.
B

However, the question I have to decide concerns the application of Pt. I to land held
by the Crown, which is expressly and specifically dealt with in s. 56. It provides as follows:

'*Crown Land*

(1) This Act shall apply to a tenancy from the Crown if there has ceased to be a
Crown interest in the land subject to it.

(2) A variation of any such tenancy effected by or in pursuance of an order under C
section 38 shall not, however, be treated as binding on the Crown, as a predecessor
in title under the tenancy, by virtue of section 39(1).

(3) Where there exists a Crown interest in any land subject to a tenancy from the
Crown and the person holding that tenancy is himself the landlord under any other
tenancy whose subject-matter comprises the whole or part of that land, this Act
shall apply to that other tenancy, and to any derivative sub-tenancy, D
notwithstanding the existence of that interest.

(4) For the purposes of this section "tenancy from the Crown" means a tenancy
of land in which there is, or has during the subsistence of the tenancy been, a
Crown interest superior to the tenancy, and "Crown interest" means–

   (a) an interest comprised in the Crown Estate; E

   (b) an interest belonging to Her Majesty in right of the Duchy of Lancaster;

   (c) an interest belonging to the Duchy of Cornwall;

   (d) any other interest belonging to a government department or held on behalf
        of Her Majesty for the purposes of a government department.'

Section 56 is to be compared with s. 1(4): F

'This Part also does not apply to any such premises at a time when the interest of
the landlord in the premises is held by an exempt landlord or a resident landlord.'

In s. 56 the applicability of the Act in relation to the Crown is dealt with on a
proprietary rather than a personal basis: as Miss Thomas and the Rent Act authorities
say, in rem rather than in personam. Section 56(1) addresses the application of the Act
to the Crown not by reference to the question whether it is sought to exercise rights G
against the Crown, but by reference to the question whether there has ceased to be a
Crown interest in the land in question. In addition, it is clear from the remainder to the
section that there is a Crown interest in land within the meaning of subs. (1) even if that
interest is not the interest of the immediate landlord of premises, but is a superior interest:
hence subs. (3). Given that legislation is, in the absence of express stipulation or necessary
implication, inapplicable to the Crown, and given the wording of s. 56(1), it follows that
the Act is inapplicable to a tenancy if and for so long as there is a Crown interest in the H
land subject to it even if it is not sought to exercise any right against the Crown
personally, unless it is made applicable to the tenancy by virtue of s. 56(3). In other
words, I read s. 56(1) as if it said:

'This Act shall apply to a tenancy from the Crown if (but, subject to subsection
(3), only if) there has ceased to be a Crown interest in the land subject to it.'

A   Such wording is in fact found in s. 94 of the *Leasehold Reform, Housing and Urban Development Act* 1993. This Act is *in pari materia* with the 1987 Act, and s. 94 is relied upon by Miss Thomas as elucidating s. 56 of the 1987 Act. Mr Thom, on the other hand, submits that the difference in wording is significant, and that a difference in meaning must have been intended. I accept Miss Thomas's submission in this respect. I see no reason why Parliament should have intended to adopt a different policy as to the application of the 1993 Act to the Crown from that to be found in the 1987 Act. The

B   wording of the 1993 Act reinforces my conclusion as to the meaning and effect of s. 56(1) of the 1987 Act.

However, 'Crown interest' and 'tenancy from the Crown' are specially defined by s. 56(4) of the 1987 Act. In the present case it is disputed whether there was a 'Crown interest' in the freeholds in question at the time of their disposal to the defendant. The tenants contend that there was not; the defendant contends that at the relevant time the

C   freeholds were comprised in the Crown Estate, and were therefore within s. 56(4)(a). Mr Elvin submitted that the freeholds were not, at any relevant time, comprised in the Crown Estate. If the freeholds were, at the date of their disposal by Gentra to the defendant, comprised in the Crown Estate, the plaintiff's claim under Pt. I of the 1987 Act must fail.

It is not suggested that the Crown entered upon the freeholds, or exercised any power of ownership in relation to them. The crucial question, therefore, is whether on being

D   vested in the Crown by virtue of s. 8(3) of the *Crown Estate Act* 1961, the freeholds ipso facto became part of the Crown Estate.

Section 8(3) of the 1961 Act itself is of little if any assistance in this connection: as has been seen, it provides only that the land vests 'accordingly', and is a miscellaneous provision amending the law of escheat rather than one dealing with the content of the Crown Estate. The meaning of 'the Crown Estate' is to be found in s. 1(1) of the 1961

E   Act. It is as follows:

'*Continuance of Crown Estate Commissioners, and general provisions as to their constitution and functions*

(1) The Crown Estate Commissioners (in this Act referred to as "the Commissioners") shall continue to be a body corporate for all purposes, charged on behalf of the Crown with the function of managing and turning to account land and other property, rights and interests, and of holding such of the property, rights

F   and interests under their management as for any reason cannot be vested in the Crown or can more conveniently be vested in the Commissioners; and the property, rights and interests under the management of the Commissioners shall continue to be known as the Crown Estate.'

Miss Thomas submitted that land vested in the Crown as an escheat becomes the

G   responsibility of the Crown Estate Commissioners, who are 'charged with the function of managing and turning to account land and other property . . .'; and that it therefore comes 'under the management of the Commissioners', and within the definition of the Crown Estate. I do not accept this submission. Section 1(1) does not purport to entrust to the commissioners the management of all land belonging to the Crown. Indeed, there is Crown land which is not under their management, in particular the Royal Parks,

H   which, by virtue of the *Crown Lands Act* 1851 and subsequent legislation are administered by the Department of the Environment rather than the Crown Estate Commissioners. In my judgment, the words 'the property, rights and interests under the management of the Commissioners' connote a factual test: they refer to the property etc. which is in fact under the management of the commissioners. Land which is vested in the Crown, but in respect of which the commissioners have not exercised any dominion or sought to do so, is not land under their management and is not part of the Crown Estate.

On this basis, s. 56 does not deal comprehensively with land vested in the Crown. That   A
this is so is confirmed by a comparison of that section with para. 11 of Sch. 1 to the
Housing Act 1988, which is as follows:

'*Crown tenancies*

(1) A tenancy under which the interest of the landlord belongs to Her Majesty in
right of the Crown or to a government department or is held in trust for Her
Majesty for the purposes of a government department.   B

(2) The reference in sub-paragraph (1) above to the case where the interest of the
landlord belongs to Her Majesty in right of the Crown does not include the case
where that interest is under the management of the Crown Estate Commissioners.'

It is implicit in para. 11(2) that there is land which belongs to Her Majesty in right of the
Crown but which is not under the management of the Crown Estate Commissioners.

Since the freeholds in question in the present case were outside the provisions of s. 56   C
of the 1987 Act, I must consider whether Pt. I of the Act should be held not to apply to
the tenants' tenancies by reason of the interest of the Crown. It is not suggested that this
case involves any in personam application of the Act to the Crown: the Crown has
already been divested of its interest, and will be unaffected by the enforcement of the
rights of the tenants under Pt. I, if it is applicable. The question is whether the criterion
for the application of the Act to this residual category of land should be in rem or in   D
personam. I have concluded that the test for the application of the Act should be in
personam: is it sought to enforce the provisions of the Act against the Crown, or to
contend that the Crown is bound by its provisions? My reasons are as follows.

First, in considering whether the 1987 Act should be held to apply to disclaimed land
in respect of which the Crown has exercised and sought to exercise no power of
ownership, I am seeking to ascertain the intention of Parliament on a question of, or akin
to, public policy. The in rem provisions of s. 56 of the Act are confined to specific   E
categories of property. I am not compelled to apply the same test in respect of property
which, possibly deliberately, was excluded from the scope of s. 56. Indeed, the
presumption must be that the normal tests should be applied, namely whether it is sought
to enforce the rights conferred by the Act against the Crown, and whether the Act binds
the Crown expressly or by necessary implication.

Secondly, in seeking to ascertain the intention of Parliament, I consider that I should   F
have regard to the fact that Parliament has itself virtually abolished the in personam test
for the application of the Rent Acts to the Crown, and that the practical effect of s. 56 of
the 1987 Act is to apply an in personam test: subtenants from the Crown are entitled to
exercise the rights conferred by the Act against their immediate landlords.

Thirdly, with the greatest of respect to Romer LJ, I find the test he set out in the last
paragraph of his judgment in *Clark v Downes* too vague and uncertain to be a satisfactory   G
test for the application of legislation to the Crown. I was not referred to any other case
in which such a test has been applied. The principle there stated by Romer LJ is not to be
found in the judgment of Lord Hanworth MR; it was not part of the ratio decidendi of
Romer LJ's judgment; and it was the subject of criticism in *Wirral Estates v Shaw*.

Fourthly, in seeking to ascertain the presumed intention of Parliament, I should
consider a purposive approach. One can discern from the provisions of the Act an   H
intention that it should apply to private tenants rather than to tenants of public
authorities. The exclusion of public authority landlords is effected by s. 56 so far as the
Crown is concerned, and by s. 1(4) and the definition of 'exempt landlord' in s. 58 with
regard to other public authorities, such as local authorities, the Housing Corporation
and most housing associations. The Act was passed as a result of the *Report of the
Committee of Inquiry on the Management of Privately Owned Blocks of Flats*, of which

A   the chairman was E G Nugee QC. Its terms of reference referred to 'the management of privately owned blocks of flats'. If I ask myself whether the tenants of the blocks of flats in the present case, the freehold of which temporarily vested in the Crown by escheat, without any action by the Crown to bring about that vesting, and in respect of which the Crown neither exercised nor sought to exercise any attribute of ownership, should sensibly be regarded as public authority tenants for the purposes of the 1987 Act, my answer is negative. The tenants in the present case did not in any meaningful sense

B   become tenants of the Crown. Furthermore, as I stated above, the Crown did not, by virtue of the escheat alone, assume the liabilities of the freeholders to the tenants. It would have been different if the Crown had exercised some dominion over the property; but in that case I apprehend that it would have been the Crown Estate Commissioners who would have exercised that dominion, and in consequence the land would have become under their management and part of the Crown Estate.

C   Furthermore, the distinction which I find to be applicable, between land which vests in the Crown by operation of law, independently of the acts and intentions of the Crown, and land in respect of which the Crown has exercised some attribute of ownership or possession, is to be found in other contexts, as has been seen.

There is considerable force in Mr Elvin's submission that the true question is whether the disposal of the freeholds by Gentra, which would otherwise be a relevant disposal by

D   virtue of s. 4(1A) of the 1987 Act, should be held to be outside the scope of the Act because the land at that moment was vested in the Crown. The relevant disposal in the present case was not by the Crown, but by Gentra.

The only consideration which might lead me to a different conclusion is that, if the 1987 Act does apply in the present case, it seems that it would not have applied if the land in question had been within Lancaster or Cornwall. Whereas s. 56(4)(a) requires, as

E   I have held, that the interest in question be managed by the Crown Estate Commissioners, s. 56(4)(b) and (c) require only that the interest be one 'belonging' to Her Majesty in right of the Duchy of Lancaster or to the Duke of Cornwall. It follows that any land within the duchies which is disclaimed will ipso facto come within these provisions.

It is undoubtedly highly undesirable to interpret and to apply the 1987 Act so as to create such an anomaly. If, however, I construe the Act as inapplicable to the present

F   freeholds, I shall create a different anomaly, by which the tenants are treated as having been tenants of the Crown, and therefore outside the Act, notwithstanding the fact that the Crown did not seek to become their landlord, did not at any time exercise, or seek to exercise, any right or power of a landlord in relation to them and did not assume the liabilities of their landlord. I have no doubt that the draftsman of the 1987 Act, or rather of the provisions of the *Housing Act* 1988 which inserted s. 4(1A) into the 1987 Act and brought a disposal by a mortgagee clearly within the scope of Pt. I of that Act, did not

G   have the present circumstances in mind. I have no doubt that if the present case had been before Parliament, it would have expected the Act to be applicable to Gentra's sale of the freeholds.

Accordingly, I hold that Pt. I of the Act applied to the disposal of the freeholds by Gentra to the defendant notwithstanding that the land in question was then vested in the Crown.

H   There is one last matter I wish to mention. It is not entirely inappropriate that this judgment comes to be given two days after the Law Commission has commented on the substantial legal costs incurred as a result of the need to construe and to apply archaic statutes. Much, if not all, of the legal costs in the present case would have been avoided if Parliament had expressly legislated on the consequences of the disclaimer of freehold land, in relation to the Crown and generally, and if the position of the Crown in regard

A

to escheated land had similarly been the subject of express provision in the *Landlord and Tenant Act* 1987. In addition, s. 179 and 182 (and s. 317 and 321) of the Insolvency Act should be amended so as to extend their provisions to freehold properties. The disclaimer of freeholds has generally escaped legislative attention. It is an omission which should be rectified.

(*Order accordingly*)

B

C

D

E

F

G

H

A

Shire Court Residents Ltd & Anor v Registrar of Companies.

Chancery Division.

Carnwath J.

Judgment delivered 12 April 1995.

B

Restoration to register – Residents' property management company struck off register as defunct – Company held head lease of flats – Head lease disclaimed by Crown – Residents applied for restoration of company – Certain mortgagees of flats accepted new leases – Whether company should be restored – Effect of restoration on new leases – Companies Act 1985, s. 653.

This was an application under s. 653 of the Companies Act 1985 for an order restoring Shire Court Residents Ltd ('the company') to the register.

C

Shire Court was a block of flats and the company was established by the developer to act as a residents' management company. The individual flats were held on long leases from the company which took a head lease from the developer. The company's affairs were not properly administered, ground rent was not passed on to the lessor and the company was struck off the register pursuant to s. 652. The freehold reversion was later acquired by the second respondent who was aware that no ground rent had been paid and also of the possibility of proceedings to restore the company to the register.

D

The second respondent offered the lessees new leases. None of the residents accepted. They applied for a vesting order in relation to the head lease which had passed bona vacantia to the Crown and been disclaimed. Three flats were not included in that application, having been repossessed by mortgagees. New leases were granted of those three flats.

The registrar stayed the vesting order application on the basis that an application would be made to restore the company.

E

Held, restoring the company to the register:

1. In principle the most satisfactory solution was the restoration of the company on terms.

2. There would be no injustice to the second respondent provided the problem of the three new leases could be resolved and provided it was reasonably protected in relation to costs.

F

3. It was wrong to disturb the arm's length arrangements which had resulted in the new leases except in so far as was shown to be necessary in order to restore a practical system of management. That could be achieved by a direction that the company's restored lease would take effect subject to the three new leases, with the result that those leases continued but with the company as intermediate landlord.

The following cases were referred to in the judgment:

A E Realisations (1985) Ltd, Re (1987) 3 BCC 136; [1988] 1 WLR 200.

G

Allied Dunbar Assurance plc v Fowle & Ors [1994] BCC 422.

Benedictus v Jalaram Ltd [1989] 1 EGLR 252.

Fuller v Judy Properties Ltd [1992] 1 EGLR 75.

Tyman's Ltd v Craven [1952] 2 QB 100.

Alistair Craig (instructed by Townsends, Swindon) for the second applicant.

Alexander Hill-Smith (instructed by Pye-Smiths, Salisbury) for the second respondent.

H

JUDGMENT

Carnwath J: This is an application under s. 653 of the *Companies Act* 1985 for an order restoring the company, Shire Court Residents Ltd, to the register.

Shire Court is a block of 18 flats in Swindon. The company was established by the developer, T C Titcombe and Sons Ltd, to act as a residents' management company. The individual flats were leased for 99-year terms under underleases from the company which took a head lease from the developer. Mr Iles, the present applicant, is the owner of no. 6 under a lease which was granted on 6 October 1982.

The company had a share capital of £18 divided into 18 shares which, under the articles, could only be held by the individual underlessees. The register of members and Mr Iles's own certificate have been lost; but copies of others are available and Mr Iles's lease recites that he owned one share. In the absence of evidence to the contrary, I accept, applying the presumption of regularity, that he became a member in due form.

The administration of the company's affairs was entrusted to a firm of solicitors, Kinneirs. Unfortunately, the arrangements did not work as planned. The position is explained by the present solicitor, Mr Birch, in his affidavit at para. 8 where he says this:

> 'After its incorporation, a firm of solicitors, (then known as Kinneirs but subsequently merged within Messrs Bevan Ashford) which had drawn up the lease documentation, were instructed to administer the company's affairs. However, it would appear, firstly, that they failed to take any such steps, secondly, the company's books appear to have been lost, thirdly, ground rent was not passed on to the lessor and fourthly, no annual returns were ever filed at Companies House.'

Payments were apparently made by the lessees to Kinneirs but were not passed on to the freeholders under the head lease.

On 4 March 1986, the registrar of companies struck off the company pursuant to s. 652. On 8 January 1993 the freehold reversion was acquired by Sarum Heritage Ltd ('Sarum') who were aware that no ground rent had been paid and also of the possibility of proceedings to reinstate the company. I say that by reference to a letter dated 8 January 1993, from the former freeholders to Sarum which refers to the position generally and mentions the fact that the solicitors for the residents were thought to be considering an application 'to reconstitute the management company'.

The involvement of Sarum brought matters to life on a number of fronts. On 19 February, 1993, they commenced proceedings in the Swindon County Court for forfeiture for non-payment of rent under the head lease. An order was made on 6 July 1993, and an application for relief was made by the underlessees but on 17 September 1993, the court declared the proceedings to be a nullity on account of failure to serve all the underlessees and mortgagees.

Meanwhile Sarum had contacted the Treasury Solicitor in right of the Crown's interest in the head lease as *bona vacantia* following dissolution of the company. He purported to disclaim the head lease under s. 656. On 28 April Sarum offered new leases to each underlessee for premiums between £1,500 and £2,300, which were explained as intended to cover arrears of rent and interest and costs. In their letter Sarum said that, in preparing their calculations, they had taken 'what we consider to be a reasonable expectation of our own and our clients' costs to come on the assumption that the matter can be dealt with relatively smoothly and amicably'. The calculation indicates that a likely settlement figure required from each sub-tenant, if all 18 cases were dealt with together, would be in the region of £1,400 to £1,500, whereas if all cases were dealt with separately it would be in the region of £2,200 or £2,300.

The new leases were offered in accordance with Sarum's standard lease. They would have been 99-year leases which would have represented an effective extension of 11 years over the original leases. None of the residents accepted, although it seems that some interest was shown. In August Townsends were instructed by the underlessees and they wrote to the former solicitors, now incorporated into Bevan Ashford, raising allegations of negligence. They were faced with the problem of trying to sort out the position against a background that the majority of lessees were of limited means with little or no equity in their flats.

A   In November, following a request from Townsends, the Treasury Solicitor issued a new disclaimer of the leases, doubts having been raised about the validity of the first. There then followed correspondence between Townsends and Sarum in which Townsends indicated their intention to apply for vesting orders and Sarum indicated an intention to oppose on the grounds that vesting orders would be 'impractical, unnecessary and unduly expensive'. Notwithstanding that, on 20 December 15 of the lessees applied for a vesting order under s. 181 of the *Insolvency Act* 1986; Sarum were joined in those proceedings and the matter was transferred to the Companies Court.

B

     The three flats, no. 4, 5 and 7, which were not included in that application, were vacant, having been repossessed by the building societies as mortgagees. At some point Sarum re-entered these flats, thereby forfeiting the sub-leases. New leases were granted by agreement. For no. 4 a new lease was granted to the Bradford and Bingley Building Society on 28 June 1994, for a premium of £4,850. For no. 5 a new lease was granted to the Halifax Building Society for the same premium; that lease on 15 March 1994, was assigned to Mr Kiamtia who transferred it to Mary Durup for £22,000. She apparently is a resident of Cyprus. For no. 7, a new lease was granted for the same premium to Abbey National in August.

C

     Sarum renewed its offers of new leases to the other residents, although the premium was increased to the same amount as had been agreed with the building societies, that is £4,850. This was explained in the correspondence as being to ensure that Sarum was:

D

> 'fully indemnified in respect of arrears of rent and interest thereon, the buildings insurance premium which had been expended with regard to the estate by our client, and its legal and administrative costs. The figure also takes into account that each of the former lessees at Shire Court could effectively be obtaining a 12-year lease extension at no additional cost.'

E   That is a letter of 23 June 1994.

     The offers were not accepted, although some of the mortgagees of the residents were amenable. Then in December 1994 the matter came before Mr Registrar Buckley. By that stage it had been decided that it would be possible to apply for restoration of the company and this seemed, to the registrar, to be a more appropriate route. He stayed the vesting order applications on the basis that an application would be made to restore the company, subject to returns and accounts being drawn up, which has now been done.

F

     According to Mr Birch, the possibility of taking this course arose because in November 1994, following their correspondence with Bevan Ashford and the allegations of negligence, the Solicitors Indemnity Fund in November 1994 indicated its willingness to indemnify the applicants against the costs of the application to restore. In that way the matter now comes before me.

G

     I should mention briefly the occupational leases, because there are some differences in detail. The lease granted to Mr Iles by the company in 1982 was for a period, as I have said, of 99 years from 1 January 1982. The rent was £30 per annum for the first 20 years, £60 for the next forty years and £100 thereafter, and there was provision for a management fund for maintenance with provision for contributions by the lessees. The new leases granted by Sarum were, as I said, in their standard form, which is different in layout and format, although for the main part the substance appears to be similar. The rent, however, is different. It was £75 from the commencement until 2000 and subject to review thereafter in accordance with a formula set out in the schedule and there is then provision for the service charges to be paid by way of further rent.

H

     As will become apparent, one of the points that needs to be dealt with is to reconcile the system of the original leases with that implicit in the three new leases.

I turn to the statutory provisions. The power to strike off the company arises, as I have   **A**
said, under s. 652; by s. 654 the property becomes *bona vacantia*, hence the Treasury
Solicitor's interest, and there is provision for the Crown to disclaim under s. 656–657
with the result that the relevant provisions of the Insolvency Act apply.

Section 653 deals with restoration and I should set it out in full:

'*Objection to striking off by person aggrieved*

(1) The following applies if a company or any member or creditor of it feels   **B**
aggrieved by the company having been struck off the register.

(2) The court, on an application by the company or the member or creditor made
before the expiration of 20 years from publication in the Gazette of notice under
section 652, may, if satisfied that the company was at the time of the striking off
carrying on business or in operation, or otherwise that it is just that the company
be restored to the register, order the company's name to be restored.   **C**

(3) On an office copy of the order being delivered to the registrar of companies for
registration the company is deemed to have continued in existence as if its name
had not been struck off; and the court may by the order give such directions and
make such provisions as seem just for placing the company and all other persons
in the same position (as nearly as may be) as if the company's name had not been
struck off.'   **D**

The court's powers have been considered in a number of cases; in particular in *Tyman's
Ltd v Craven* [1952] 2 QB 100 the Court of Appeal emphasised the wide powers of the
court to restore the 'as you were position'. I read Evershed MR at p. 111 where he says:

'In my judgment, the final words of the subsection can properly and usefully be
regarded as intended to give to the court, where justice requires and the general
words would or might not themselves suffice, the power to put both company and   **E**
third parties in the same position as they would have occupied in such cases if the
dissolution of the company had not intervened. More generally the final words of
the subsection seem to me designed, not by way of exposition, to qualify the
generality of that which precedes them, but rather as a complement to the general
words so as to enable the court (consistently with justice) to achieve to the fullest
extent the 'as-you-were position' which, according to the ordinary sense of those   **F**
general words is prima facie their consequence.'

Hodson LJ is to similar effect on p. 126.

The provisions for vesting orders are to be found in s. 181 and 182 of the *Insolvency
Act* 1986. Section 181 gives the jurisdiction to the court to make a vesting order on an
application following a disclaimer. Section 182 deals with leaseholds. Section 182(1)
provides: **G**

'The court shall not make an order under section 181 vesting property of a
leasehold nature in any person claiming under the company as underlessee or
mortgagee except on terms making that person–

(a) subject to the same liabilities and obligations as the company was subject to
under the lease at the commencement of the winding up, or

(b) if the court thinks fit, subject to the same liabilities and obligations as that   **H**
person would be subject to if the lease had been assigned to him at the
commencement of the winding up.'

(2) For the purposes of an order under section 181 relating to any part of any
property comprised in a lease, the requirements of subsection (1) apply as if the
lease comprised only the property to which the order relates.'

A   It will be seen, therefore, that there is reference to the possibility of part only of the property being the subject of the vesting order but the Act contains little guidance as to how, as a matter of mechanics, the objects of (1) are to be achieved where the property interest has to be divided in that way. I should note here that under r. 4.194(3)(c) of the *Insolvency Rules* 1986 the applicant for a vesting order is required to specify the order he seeks. In this case the application did not in fact do that and, as will be seen, there are acknowledged to be considerable problems in drafting an order which achieves the

B   purposes of the section.

Turning to the present proceedings, Mr Iles is, as I said, a member and therefore entitled to apply for restoration. As I understand it, he is supported by the other lessees, other than the three lessees under the new leases. Sarum has appeared before me by Mr Hill-Smith. Notice of the proceedings has been served on the owners of the three flats covered by the new leases but they have not appeared. Two of them are building societies

C   who can be assumed to be able to look after their own interests. Mrs Durup is apparently a private individual and she has been, I understand, supplied with copies of the papers but has not made any representations.

I should make two preliminary points on the effect of the statute. First, as to the status of the underlessees following disclaimer, this was discussed by Vinelott J in *Re A E Realisations (1985) Ltd* (1987) 3 BCC 136; [1988] 1 WLR 200, where he considered the

D   evolution of the legislation and the relevant authorities. What emerges from that is that, once the head lease has been disclaimed, the sublessees remain entitled to occupy, enjoying what Vinelott J described at p. 145; 213 as 'a bundle of rights' which included:

> 'the right to remain in possession of the house during the term created by the underlease, so long as the lease did not become liable to forfeiture and subject to the lessor's right of distraint and to apply to have the lease so far as it affected the

E   > house comprised in the underlease vested in her at an apportioned rent'.

Thus, one has the not wholly satisfactory position that the residents have something which is not a conventional lease but is a bundle of rights. They have no privity of estate or contract with the head lessor.

The other preliminary matter is the effect on the disclaimer of restoration of the company. By s. 653(3) the company is deemed to have continued in existence, although

F   never struck off. It has been held that one effect of this is that a disclaimer is treated as never having happened, so that the restoration of the company results also in the restoration of the company's lease, assuming it has not been forfeited in the interim: see *Allied Dunbar Assurance plc v Fowle* [1994] BCC 422.

I turn then to the issues in this case. The main issue is how best to remedy the position created by the past inadequate management so that the administration of the property can now be put on a proper footing with the legitimate interests of the lessors and lessees

G   protected and the bundles of rights which the flat owners currently enjoy being restored to interests of a more conventional and saleable nature.

The two principal points of complication I have already noted: first, how to deal with the three flats in respect of which new leases have been granted and, secondly, how to deal with the freeholder's claim to a substantial premium to cover what it says are its costs and other matters.

H   Mr Craig, for the applicants, suggests there are really four possible solutions, in order of preference from his point of view: first, to restore the company and order that the new leases granted by Sarum be unenforceable (to use his words); secondly, to restore the company without prejudice to the three new leases, by which I understood him to mean that the three new leases would be left unaffected by the restoration and their lessees' covenants would therefore continue to be directly with Sarum; thirdly, to reinstate the

vesting order application; fourthly, to dismiss the applications, leaving the parties free to   A
accept the Sarum offer, an offer which Sarum has undertaken to keep open.

Before considering the merits, it is convenient to deal with three technical points raised
by Mr Hill-Smith for Sarum. First, he says that the application for the vesting order is
defective due to non-compliance with r. 4.194, which I have mentioned. This is not purely
a procedural point since, as Mr Craig conceded, there would be considerable difficulty in
drafting an appropriate order so as to create individual leases containing covenants which   B
comply with the objectives of s. 182. For these and other reasons, neither party shows
enthusiasm for the third of Mr Craig's suggested solutions, and I agree with them.

The second point is estoppel. Mr Hill-Smith says that the claim for the vesting order in
respect of all but three flats depended on the premise that disclaimer of the head lease
was effective, since that is a foundation of the jurisdiction, and he says it is inconsistent
with an application to restore a company which seeks to undo the effect of the disclaimer.   C
He says that Mr Iles is approbating and reprobating and cannot be allowed to go back
on his election, at any rate once Sarum has relied on it by disposing of the three flats
which were not covered by the vesting application.

The principles are not in doubt and are fully explained in Spencer Bower, *Estoppel by
Representation*, p. 324 and 333. I was given a recent illustration in *Benedictus v Jalaram*
[1989] 1 EGLR 252.

However, I think the key to this point really can be found in the footnote to Spencer   D
Bower, p. 333, which says this in relation to the heading, 'Election in the conduct of
litigation':

> 'It is submitted that in cases where the proceedings are still pending before one
> tribunal they may be discontinued and another jurisdiction invoked upon payment
> of costs in the first proceeding without any election arising except where the   E
> opposite party has been irremediably prejudiced by the representator's action in
> invoking the first jurisdiction'.

I think the word 'irremediable' is important. There would be force in Mr Hill-Smith's
point if the court did not have power to deal with the problems created by the grant of
the three leases under its powers in s. 653. But that section gives wide powers, as I said,
to ensure that justice is done to all parties on the restoration. As will become apparent, I   F
think, that can be achieved in this case.

The third point made by Mr Hill-Smith is under the heading 'Concurrent leases'. He
says that the effect of the restoration is that the disclaimer is treated as of no effect. The
head lease is restored as though never disclaimed. Therefore, he says, the new leases of
the three flats must be treated as granted at a time when there was in existence a lease of
the whole property in favour of the company. Thus, they can only operate as concurrent
or reversionary leases subject to the company's restored lease so long as it continues. He   G
refers me to *Megarry and Wade*, p. 664.

I understand the logic of that submission but I am not sure that it can be applied with
such rigour to the artificial situation created by restoration. I refer, by way of analogy
(although I accept it is not an exact analogy), to the position where relief against forfeiture
is granted to a former tenant following the grant by the landlord of a new lease to a third
party. Although the relief is retrospective, the restored lease takes effect subject to the   H
new lease, not vice versa: see *Fuller v Judy Properties Ltd* [1992] 1 EGLR 75.

I accept that that is the exercise of a discretionary power to grant relief but I see no
reason in principle why a similar effect cannot be achieved by a direction under s. 653(3)
without needing to decide what would be the precise legal consequences of restoration
simpliciter in the absence of such direction.

A　　I turn, therefore, to the fundamental question which is: what does justice require? I have no doubt that in principle the most satisfactory solution is the restoration of the company. This will restore the position to that originally contemplated and contracted for by all parties or their predecessors with a single company responsible for managing the property under the control of the residents and responsible in turn to the freeholder.

B　　Mr Chandler refers in his affidavit to practical problems but there is nothing unusual about this particular block of flats and nothing unusual about the arrangement. Arrangements for such management companies are, of course, common and indeed encouraged by the policy of recent legislation.

C　　Mr Iles in his affidavit proposes that the first members' meeting be asked to approve the appointment of a management firm to ensure that the company's duties are complied with and accountants have already prepared annual returns. The solicitors hold funds on their client account to meet arrears of ground rent and, if further funds are required, to meet other liabilities; the company will have powers to recover them from the lessees and in turn Sarum will have its remedies as head lessor. I see no reason in principle why the restoration of the company should not work in practice.

D　　There also need be no injustice to Sarum, provided the problem of the three new leases can be resolved and provided they are reasonably protected in relation to their costs. I bear in mind that they were aware of problems when they bought and they were aware that restoration at that stage was a possible route. I do not think they are to be criticised for dealing separately with the mortgagees in possession, who had obvious reasons for wanting to secure a clear, saleable interest as soon as possible. Once the other lessees had opted for the vesting order route in respect of their individual flats, Sarum were entitled to take other measures to deal with the three not included in that application. However, they must have been aware that, granting leases in a different form, whatever their motives, would be likely to cause complications so long as the treatment of the remainder of the old leases or 'bundles of rights' remained unresolved. I do not think those complications in themselves should be a reason for rejecting the best overall solution, and I do not understand Mr Hill-Smith to suggest that they are insuperable.

E

F　　The fourth option, which is that proposed by Sarum, namely the offers of new leases, is, to my mind, a less attractive solution. It is at best uncertain whether individual lessees will be able to pay the premium. There is, therefore, a serious risk of a patchy result, with some flats having new leases and others having bundles of rights in the old form, and continuing uncertainty as to the chain of responsibilities.

G　　Furthermore, the case for a premium of the size claimed has not been fully made out. It was accepted by the building societies but they would, as I have said, have had reasons for seeking a quick solution. It is true that the lessees apparently made no counter-offers; but the Act gives them an alternative remedy and they were entitled to pursue it, rather than allowing the freeholder to dictate terms.

H　　I turn, therefore, to the terms to which restoration should be made subject. Mr Hill-Smith asks for the following, most of which are not in issue: first, the arrears of ground rent with interest. The amount, as I understand it, has now been agreed. There was a possible dispute about whether rent in respect of the three new leases should be treated as covered by the premiums. However, even if, as appears, rent was part of the calculation of the premium in Sarum's mind, the payment was not in terms made referable to arrears of rent but was a premium for the grant of a new lease, so the company's liability for the ground rent of those three flats would remain and, in the end, I did not understand Mr Craig to wish to quibble on this point.

Then the question of interest: Mr Craig suggested that it should be restricted to the ordinary limitation period, although he accepts that there is a wide discretion given under

s. 653 which would enable a longer period to be allowed if appropriate, see *Palmer's*   A
Company Law, para. 15-489.

It is, of course, impossible to know what would in fact have happened if the company
had remained in existence. There is very little evidence on either side as to what was
happening between 1986 and 1993. It does not appear that the former freeholders were
active, either before or after the striking off of the company, in seeking to regularise the
position or pursue their right to rent.   B

In these circumstances, although Mr Craig does not seek to challenge recovery of the
full arrears of rent, he submits that interest should run only from the date when Sarum
acquired, which is 8 January 1993. I think that is an appropriate approach, to reflect the
doubts as to whether any effective action would have been taken by the former owners.

Then, insurance premiums: it is accepted that the company must account for the
insurance premiums paid by Sarum.   C

Next, grant of new leases: Sarum asked for its costs in connection with the grant of
new leases to the three lessees and an indemnity against possible claims made by the
building societies and the costs involved. As I see it, however, the only substantive matter
which needs to be addressed in relation to these transactions is to bring the flats within
the jurisdiction of the company so that responsibility for repairs and other services is
unified. I shall return to this below.   D

From what I have heard, I see no reason why the costs incurred and payments made
in respect of the new leases should concern the court. Admittedly, they would not have
happened if the company had still been in existence but the parties were content to incur
those costs and payments as a result of deliberate decisions to use a particular means of
sorting out their interests. That purpose has been achieved and will not be materially
affected by my order. I do not see why their financial position should be altered   E
retrospectively merely because other lessees have decided to pursue a different solution.
Furthermore, as I have said, the building societies have been informed of these
proceedings and have chosen not to take any part in them.

However, I accept that I cannot in the present proceedings wholly rule out the
possibility of such a claim being advanced. It is fair, therefore, that Sarum should be
indemnified against a possibility of claims by those interested in the three flats. Mr Iles   F
himself is not in a position to offer such an indemnity but Mr Craig on instructions
indicates that the Solicitors Indemnity Fund would be willing to do so. A suitable
undertaking should therefore be given by them.

Then the vesting order proceedings: if an order is made restoring the company, the
vesting order proceedings are no longer needed. They face considerable problems in any
event, as I have indicated. Mr Hill-Smith submits that if the restoration is ordered it
should be on terms that the vesting order proceedings are discontinued and his client's   G
costs paid in any event. I agree.

I note in parenthesis that Mr Iles was not the only applicant in those proceedings but I
understand the others are associated with him, so that he should be in a position to secure
the discontinuance by all parties. Again, I understand that the Solicitors Indemnity Fund
will accept responsibility for those costs.

Then the new leases: this leaves only the question of how the three new leases are to be   H
dealt with. In his skeleton argument Mr Craig asked me to order that the three new leases
are unenforceable. Clearly this could not be done without specific notice to the lessees in
question that such an order is proposed. In any event, assuming, without deciding, that I
have power to do this under s. 653 it would not, in my view, be just to do so. As I have
said, the new leases are not simply mirror images of the old. They involve substantial

A extensions of the effective length of the lease and a change to the ground rent, as well as other more minor changes.

I think it is wrong to disturb these arm's length arrangements except in so far as is shown to be necessary in order to restore a practical system of management. In principle I see no reason why the new leases of the three flats should not coexist with the old leases on the remainder, so long as arrangements are made to ensure that the company becomes

B the immediate lessor rather than Sarum. As I have said, this would, in my view, be achieved by a direction that the company's restored lease would take effect subject to the three new leases, with the result that those leases continue but with the company as intermediate landlord. No doubt there will need to be some adjustment to the company's liabilities under the head lease, for example, to take account of the altered rent. It is likely, however, that the principle having been established, the mechanics of this are best worked out between the parties with due notice to the three new lessees. Failing

C agreement, the court will have to rule but I will hear the parties on how best to take the matter forward now in the light of this judgment.

That deals with the principle. I have indicated there that I think it is going to be best probably to let the parties absorb that and see if they can reach agreement on how the mechanics can best be sorted out.

D **Costs**

I think the right order is no order as to costs. On the one hand, I have certainly been very much assisted by Sarum's and Mr Hill-Smith's submissions but, on the other hand, I think they bought into a problem and the particular solution they have put forward has not been one which has gained favour with me. I think the fair order is to say there will be no order for costs in these proceedings.

E *(Order accordingly)*

F

G

H

Euro Commercial Leasing Ltd v Cartwright & Lewis.

Chancery Division.
Evans-Lombe J.
Judgment delivered 1 May 1995.

Administration order – Solicitors' lien – Solicitors held company's money on clients account – Administrators appointed to company – Solicitors paid money out of clients account to discharge outstanding fees – Solicitors repaid money to clients account and sought leave to pay money out – Whether solicitors' lien was destroyed by payment out – Insolvency Act 1986, s. 11(3)(c), 234(2).

These were two applications, the first by administrators of a company under s. 234(2) of the Insolvency Act 1986 for an order that certain moneys held by a firm of solicitors on clients account be paid over to the administrators; the second by that firm of solicitors under s. 11(3)(c) for the sanction of the court for payment of those moneys to office account under that section.

The firm held some £9,320 for the company on clients account and had delivered bills to the company in respect of work done amounting to some £16,000 when administrators were appointed to the company. The solicitors notified the administrators of their intention to discharge in part their bill by the application of the sum on clients account and that was done. On an application by the administrators to recover the amount so paid the deputy judge held that prior to payment from clients to office account, the solicitors had a general lien over the moneys in their hands, and that had they sought leave under s. 11 of the 1986 Act to enforce their lien they would have been given it. He later intimated that in his view, the solicitors being officers of the court, it would be appropriate for them to pay the money back into their clients account, and thereafter to seek the sanction of the court under s. 11(3)(c).

The administrators argued that the solicitors' lien was destroyed by the payment out and that when the money was paid back from office to clients account the money so paid back became the company's money for the purposes of s. 234(2), and accordingly was recoverable by the administrators.

Held, giving the solicitors leave under s. 11(3)(c) to pay themselves from the funds paid back into the clients account:

1. Assuming that the solicitors' lien was destroyed by the payment out and assuming that the money paid back became the company's property, the solicitors acquired a fresh general lien for their unpaid fees upon that sum being brought back into clients account.

2. There remained a technical breach of s. 11(3)(c) but no damage resulted from the breach because the act complained of in respect of which damages would be sought had the effect of destroying what had been a previously impregnable position held by the solicitors, in which they had a lien over property of their client, which s. 11 would not have had the effect of removing.

3. Section 11 did not deprive the solicitors of the security constituted by the lien over the reconstituted clients account.

The following cases were referred to in the judgment:

Bristol Airport plc & Anor v Powdrill & Ors (Re Paramount Airways Ltd) [1990] BCC 130; [1990] Ch 744.
Jones v Pearle (1736) 1 Stra 557; 93 ER 698.
Loescher v Dean [1950] Ch 491.
Sweet v Pym (1800) 1 East 4; 102 ER 2.
TEA (1983) Ltd v Uniting Church (NSW) Trust Association [1985] VR 139.

A   N Palmer (instructed by Hill Taylor Dickinson) for the administrators.

James Quirke (instructed by Cartwright & Lewis, Birmingham) for the solicitors.

JUDGMENT

Evans-Lombe J: I have to deal with two applications, the first by administrators of the
company, under s. 234(2) of the Insolvency Act, for an order that certain moneys held by
B   a firm of solicitors on clients account be paid over to the administrators; the second, by
that firm of solicitors, under s. 11(3)(c), for the sanction of the court for payment of those
moneys to office account under that section.

Section 11(3)(c) reads as follows:

'During the period for which an administration order is in force–

. . .

C
(c) no other steps [other than set out in (a) and (b) immaterial to this judgment]
may be taken to enforce any security over the company's property, or to
repossess goods in the company's possession under any hire-purchase
agreement, except with the consent of the administrator or the leave of the
court and subject (where the court gives leave) to such terms as the court
may impose . . .'

D   Section 234(2) provides:

'Where any person has in his possession or control any property, books, papers or
records to which the company appears to be entitled, the court may require that
person forthwith (or within such period as the court may direct) to pay, deliver,
convey, surrender or transfer the property, books, papers or records to the office-
holder.'

E   The background facts of the present case are as follows. In 1989, the company
employed the respondent firm of solicitors as its solicitor for a number of matters. Prior
to July 1993, those solicitors held some £9,320.12 on clients account, representing moneys
recovered on behalf of the company, acting on the company's instructions.

In July 1993, the solicitors delivered to the company bills in respect of work done by
solicitors on behalf of the company, amounting in total to some £16,000. On 30 July
F   1993, an administration order was made against the company, and administrators were
appointed. The administrators, it appears, continued to employ the respondent solicitors
in the company's affairs.

There was an exchange of correspondence on 26 and 27 August 1993, when the
solicitors indicated their intention to discharge in part their bill by the application of the
sum that they held on clients account to the credit of the company. That was done in
September 1993, and it was done, I am told, and there is no issue as to this, in pursuance
G   of advice sought from and given by the Law Society, which sanctioned the proposed
payment over.

Subsequently the administrators brought proceedings to recover the amount so paid
over. On 19 December 1994, that question, on the administrators' application, came
before Mr Mann QC, sitting as a deputy judge of this court. He gave judgment on 21
December.

H   He found that prior to payment from clients to office account, the solicitors had a
general lien over the moneys in their hands, which would not have been affected in any
way as a result of the provisions of s. 11. I quote from the final page of the transcript of
his judgment, where he said:

'It must follow, in my judgment, that in the context of s. 11(3)(c), the mere assertion
of the lien as against an administrator is a step to enforce a security which must be

taken no further without the leave of the court. In the result, therefore, Cartwright   A
& Lewis, the solicitors, fail on this issue as well, which is doubly unfortunate
because there can be little doubt that had they sought leave to enforce their lien
they would have been given it. As to that, I can do no better than to cite Browne-
Wilkinson V-C's words in *Bristol Airport v Powdrill* [1990] BCC 130 at p. 154G:

> "In my judgment, whilst the administration procedure should not be used so
> far as possible to prejudice those who are secured creditors at the time when the   B
> administration order was made in lieu of a winding-up order, nor should it be
> used so as to give the unsecured creditors at that time security which they would
> not have enjoyed had it not been for the administration.'"

It seems that the matter was brought back before the deputy judge later on the same
day in which he gave judgment. On that occasion, he intimated that in his view, the
solicitors being officers of the court, it would be appropriate for them to pay the money   C
back into their clients account, and thereafter to seek the sanction of the court under
s. 11(3)(c). That was done on 23 January 1995.

On 27 January, the administrators refused permission to transfer that sum back from
clients account to office account, and these proceedings were launched. It was argued on
behalf of the administrators that the solicitors' lien was destroyed by the payment out in
August 1993, pursuant to the indication that the solicitors were going to do so, in the
course of correspondence on 26 and 27 August.   D

For the purposes of these proceedings, I am prepared to accept that such occurred.
That question may turn on what factually happened to the money in the solicitors'
accounts: see *Loescher v Dean* [1950] Ch 491 per Harman J.

As I said, I am prepared to accept that, for the purpose of this case, the lien which it is
accepted was constituted by the holding by the solicitors of the sum of £9,320.12 in their   E
clients account, at a time while they had outstanding to the same client unpaid fees which
had been billed, was destroyed as a result of the payment over to office account.

It was further argued, on the basis that that lien was so destroyed, that when the money
was in January 1995 paid back from office to clients account, and credited to the client,
that by that process, described as a 'process of attornment', the money so paid back
became the company's money for the purposes of s. 234(2), and accordingly was   F
recoverable by the administrators pursuant to that subsection.

I am not at all sure that the money so paid back in fact became company's money, and
so company's property, for the purpose of s. 234(2). Again, I am prepared to assume that
it did. It seems to me, however, that if it did become company's property, that the
solicitors acquired a fresh general lien for their unpaid fees upon that sum being brought
back into clients account.

There were cited by counsel for the administrators two cases, *Jones v Pearle* (1736) 1   G
Stra 557, an innkeeper's lien case, and *Sweet v Pym* (1800) 1 East 4, an artificer's lien
case.

There was also cited Peyton on *Bailment in the Common Law* (1952), and a passage at
p. 350, which reads as follows:

> 'The right of lien has never been carried further than while the goods continue in   H
> the possession of the party claiming it,'

and that is a quotation from *Sweet v Pym*. Then the author continues,

> 'This seems the better view than that of Dallas CJ, who thought that even if
> possession is surrendered a lien could arise if the res lawfully came back into the
> possession of the person claiming the lien.'

A   In my judgment, those cases and that passage in Professor Peyton's book are not analogous to the present situation, and are not analogous in particular with a solicitor's general lien over the property of his client in respect of outstanding fees which have been billed.

   At para. 227 in *Halsbury's Laws of England* (4th edn), vol. 44 on solicitors, the following passage appears:

B   'The general rule is that the retaining lien [that is the general lien of which I speak] extends to any deed, paper or personal chattel which has come into the solicitor's possession in the course of his employment, and in his capacity as solicitor, with the client's sanction, and which is the client's property.

   Thus, a bill of exchange, a cheque, a policy of assurance, a share certificate, an application for shares, a debenture trust deed, letters patent, letters of administration, money, including money in a client account although only the amount due to the solicitor and maintenance received by a solicitor if not subject to an order as to its application or bound to be applied, in effect, as trust money, or documents in a drawer of which the solicitor is given the key, may be subject to the lien.

   The lien does not extend to a client's original will or to a deed in favour of the solicitor but reserving a life interest and power of revocation to the client, or to original court records or to documents which did not come into the solicitor's hands in his capacity as solicitor for the person against whom the lien is claimed or his successors, but as mortgagee, steward of a manor or trustee. Moreover, where documents are delivered to a solicitor for a particular purpose under a special agreement which does not make express provision for a lien in favour of the solicitor, as perhaps the raising of money, or money is paid to the solicitor for a particular purpose so that he becomes a trustee of the money, no lien arises over those documents or that money unless subsequently left in the solicitor's possession for general purposes. Otherwise the lien extends to the property whatever the occasion of delivery, except that where a solicitor acts for both mortgagor and mortgagee and the mortgage is redeemed the solicitor cannot set up a lien on the deeds against the mortgagor.'

F   As I have said, it seems to me that the cases and the extract from Professor Peyton's book are not analogous to a solicitor's general lien arising in the circumstances which are set out in *Halsbury*. It seems to me that there is no reason for taking the view that a fund reconstituted in the way that this fund was reconstituted, by the payment of money from office account to clients account, would not be covered by the general lien arising from the fact that the same firm of solicitors has outstanding unpaid fees which have been billed, and the money which reconstitutes the account is taken to be a payment to the company's client in question.

G   There is, in my judgment, no analogy to be drawn between the innkeeper's lien and artificer's lien cases, and circumstances where a lien over one sum of money has been given up by a lienee, but that lienee thereafter receives another sum of money over which he is entitled to enforce a lien when it comes into his possession, and subsequently seeks to enforce it.

H   There is nothing here equivalent to the reacquisition of chattels over which liens have been exercised, but in respect of which the lien has been given up by redelivery of the chattel, such as took place in the innkeeper's and artificer's lien cases, and in such cases as *TEA v Uniting Church* [1985] VR 139.

   In my judgment, if reconstitution of the clients account is taken to create a fund constituting property of the company, as to which I have in the circumstances of this case

A

some doubts, a fresh general lien attaches to that money in the account as so reconstituted. That general lien arises, in my judgment, from the original solicitor and client relationship, starting in this case in 1989. That conclusion seems to me to be consistent with the judgment of Harman J in *Loescher v Dean*.

There remains, of course, a technical breach of s. 11(3)(c). The remedy for such breach, it is common ground, is a claim in damages. Plainly in the present case, there could be no damage resulting from such breach because, as is not in issue, the act complained of in respect of which damages would be sought had the effect of destroying what had been a previously impregnable position held by the solicitor respondents, in which they had a lien over property of their client, which s. 11 would not have the effect of removing: see the *Bristol Airport* case.

B

This result, I have to say, seems to me to accord with the justice of the case.

In the circumstances, I need not consider the respondents' application at any length. Section 11, as I have said, cannot deprive the respondents of the security constituted by the lien over the reconstituted clients account.

C

Insofar as it is necessary to do so, in my judgment, the solicitors should have leave under s. 11(3)(c) to pay themselves from the funds held by them, namely the sum of £9,320.12, paid back into the clients account on 23 January 1995.

For these reasons, it seems to me that the applicant administrators' application fails, but the respondent solicitors' application succeeds.

D

(Order accordingly)

E

F

G

H

A # Re Blackspur Group plc.

Chancery Division.
Carnwath J.
Judgment delivered 2 May 1995.

B *Disqualifying unfit directors of insolvent companies – Disqualification proceedings issued in time but without full evidence – Application for extension of time or to file evidence – Proceedings stayed by agreement pending outcome of criminal proceedings – Whether good reason had been shown why leave should be granted – Company Directors Disqualification Act 1986, s. 7(2).*

This was an appeal by respondents to director disqualification proceedings against a decision of the registrar allowing an application by the Secretary of State for an extension of time under s. 7(2) of the Company Directors Disqualification Act 1986 alternatively an
C extension of time for filing evidence under the Insolvent Companies (Disqualification of Unfit Directors) Proceedings Rules 1987 (SI 1987/2023). The disqualification proceedings were issued at the end of the two-year period permitted by s. 7(2) with what was in effect outline evidence indicating the nature of the charges but not incorporating any supporting documentation because the Secretary of State's evidence was not ready to be filed with the summons. At the same time the application was made for an extension of time under s. 7(2)
D or alternatively an extension of time for evidence under the rules.

The companies concerned went into administrative receivership in July 1990. The report of the receiver was sent to the Secretary of State in August 1991, and a decision in principle was made to initiate disqualification proceedings. However, action was then delayed, mainly by attempts to secure assistance in the preparation of evidence from the Serious Fraud Office, which was involved and had possession of much of the relevant documentation. The registrar found that the length of the delay was not inordinate; the strength and seriousness
E of the case against the respondents was amply sufficient; no prejudice to the respondents was either alleged or proved; and that the disqualification proceedings could not realistically be brought to trial until criminal proceedings had been disposed of. After his decision the disqualification proceedings were by agreement stayed pending the outcome of the criminal proceedings.

On appeal there was further evidence on whether the SFO papers were available to the
F Secretary of State and it was accepted that the judge should exercise his discretion anew, although giving due weight to the views of the registrar.

Held, dismissing the appeal:

1. There was some force in the criticisms of the delay if the reasons for the delay were looked at on their own. However, other factors had to be brought into play.

2. The receiver could have reported earlier, but there was no practical advantage in an
G earlier report since the Secretary of State would not have been able to do anything without the detailed material. In relation to the Secretary of State's action, in practice the SFO held the key to progress in the matter since any criminal proceedings were always going to take precedence. The delay of some five to six months in getting the application in order had not delayed the overall resolution of the matter. That had had to await the outcome of the criminal proceedings in any event.

H 3. If, as must be accepted, there was a serious case against the defendants which the Secretary of State considered it right in the public interest to pursue, it should not be defeated merely because of some delay which had not in itself added to the overall time scale nor materially affected the defendants' ability to defend themselves.

The following cases were referred to in the judgment:

Al Tabith, The [1993] 2 Ll Rep 214.

Cedac Ltd, Re. Secretary of State for Trade and Industry v Langridge [1991] BCC 148;   A
[1991] Ch 402.
Cedar Developments Ltd, Re [1995] BCC 220.
Copecrest Ltd, Re [1993] BCC 844.
Crestjoy Products Ltd, Re [1990] BCC 23.
Kleinwort Benson Ltd v Barbrak Ltd [1987] AC 597.
Probe Data Systems Ltd, Re (No. 3) [1992] BCC 110.
Revici v Prentice Hall Inc [1969] 1 WLR 157.   B
Salmon, Re [1981] Ch 167.
Van Stillevoldt (CM) BV v EL Carriers Inc [1983] 1 WLR 207.

Richard Gillis (instructed by the Treasury Solicitor) for the Secretary of State for Trade and Industry.

Michael Briggs QC and Paul Girolami (instructed by Peters & Peters) for the first and fourth respondents.

P Hampton, solicitor of Piper Smith & Basham, for the third respondent.

The second and fifth respondents did not appear and were not represented.

JUDGMENT

Carnwath J: This is an appeal by the respondents from the decision of Mr Registrar Buckley. It concerns proceedings under the *Company Directors Disqualification Act* 1986 against five directors of companies within the group known as the Blackspur group. The five companies all went into administrative receivership in July 1990, four on 2 July and one on 10 July. The report from the receiver, Mr Brierley of Arthur Andersen, made under s. 7 of the Act, was sent to the Secretary of State on 28 August 1991, and a decision in principle was made to initiate disqualification proceedings. However, action was then delayed, mainly by attempts to secure assistance in the preparation of evidence from the Serious Fraud Office, who were also involved and had possession of much of the relevant documentation.

As a result, detailed preparation of the case was not put in hand until at the earliest March 1992 by which time the end of the limitation period under the Act, which was due to expire in July, was almost at hand. I will need to come back to the sequence of events in that period in more detail later. In the event the Secretary of State's evidence was not ready by the time required; and on 1 July proceedings were commenced by originating summons, with what was in effect outline evidence indicating the nature of the charges but not incorporating any supporting documentation. At the same time an application was made for an extension of time under s. 7(2) or alternatively an extension of time for evidence. Section 7(2) reads as follows:

'Except with the leave of the court, an application for the making under that section of a disqualification order against any person shall not be made after the end of the period of 2 years beginning with the day on which the company of which that person is or has been a director became insolvent.'

It is common ground that the relevant dates were 2 July or 10 July 1992, being two years from the date of the receiverships.

The procedure adopted in this case follows a suggestion made by Harman J in a case called *Crestjoy*, to which I will be coming, where he encouraged the making of an application within the two-year time limit, even if it was necessary at that point to seek extensions in order to be able to complete the evidence.

The application for the extensions was allowed by Mr Registrar Buckley on 27 January 1994 and there is an appeal from him to me. I should say that there is no suggestion that there should be any difference of approach to the extension of time under s. 7(2) and the

A   extension of time under the rules. The relevant rules are the *Insolvent Companies (Disqualification of Unfit Directors) Proceedings Rules* 1987 (SI 1987/2023). Rule 3 requires that evidence should be filed with the summons, but it is clear that that time limit can be extended under the general powers available under the Rules of the Supreme Court.

      Taking up the sequence again, the evidence of the Secretary of State was put in order
B   by December 1992, with the filing of further affidavits and extensive documentation which runs to some 12 lever arch files. In the meantime the criminal proceedings against the second to fifth defendants were being progressed by the SFO. In March 1994 following the decision of Mr Registrar Buckley to which I have referred, it was agreed that further proceedings in relation to the 1986 Act would be stayed pending the outcome of the criminal trial. That took place in June 1994. The fourth and fifth defendants were acquitted at trial. The second and third were convicted but their appeals were
C   subsequently allowed by the Court of Appeal in February 1995. The first defendant was not the subject of criminal proceedings. So we have now arrived at the point where there are no outstanding criminal charges against any of the defendants.

      Notwithstanding that, the Secretary of State has decided to proceed to seek disqualification orders under the 1986 Act, as he is entitled to do. The defendants have, through their representatives before me or individually, drawn attention to the hardship of having these proceedings hanging over them, having already faced a criminal trial and
D   been acquitted. While recognising that potential hardship, I must emphasise that it is not my function here to review the merits of the Secretary of State's decision. I am solely concerned with the delay between 1991 and 1992, and whether an extension of time should be allowed having regard to the reasons for that delay and its consequences.

      I turn then to the principles on which my discretion has to be exercised. I should say at once that it is accepted that, for reasons which will become apparent, I am entitled to
E   look at the matter anew and that, whatever the position may be in other cases, I am not confined simply to reviewing the approach of the registrar.

      The principles have been authoritatively stated in a number of cases, most recently by the Court of Appeal in a case called *Re Copecrest* [1993] BCC 844, where Hoffmann LJ said at p. 852B:

> 'The judge asked himself whether the Secretary of State had shown a good reason
F   > for an extension. This seems to me a correct way of putting the question. The matter was elaborated by Scott LJ in *Re Probe Data Systems Ltd (No. 3)* [1992] BCC 110 at p. 118 where he said:
>
> > "In considering an application under s. 7(2) for leave to commence disqualification proceedings out of time the court should, in my opinion, take into account the following matters: (1) the length of the delay; (2) the reasons
G   > > for the delay; (3) the strength of the case against the director; and (4) the degree of prejudice caused to the director by the delay".'

      That indication of the principles is drawn really from two sources. The *Probe Data* case to which Hoffmann LJ refers specifically was, as he says, a decision of the Court of Appeal, and the passage which he quotes comes from the judgment of Scott LJ, with whom the other members of the court agreed. The four matters which are there set out as being relevant are derived from various cases, including *Van Stillevoldt BV v EL*
H   *Carriers Inc* [1983] 1 WLR 207, which was a case concerned with the extension of time for leave to appeal to the Court of Appeal.

      The reference to 'good reason' is derived from a different pedigree. Harman J in the case of *Crestjoy* [1990] BCC 23, which I have already mentioned, referred by way of analogy to the speech of Lord Brandon in *Kleinwort Benson Ltd v Barbrak Ltd* [1987] AC 597. Harman J said at p. 29F:

'It seems to me, as I avoid at Mr Bompas' request any attempt to lay down   A
guidelines, that all I can do is try and assess the whole position here and consider
whether I am satisfied that a good reason has been shown (and I adopt the words
"good reason" from Lord Brandon's speech in the *Kleinwort Benson* case (at
p. 622G–H) by analogy) for an extension of time from 20 November to 14 March.'

The *Kleinwort Benson* case was concerned with a somewhat different context, that is
the extension of the validity of a writ. Lord Brandon, who gave the leading speech,   B
explained at p. 615H that there were three main categories of case in which questions of
limitation of action might arise in cases where a writ had been issued before the relevant
period of limitation. He said:

'Category (1) cases are where the application for extension is made at a time when
the writ is still valid and before the relevant period of limitation has expired.
Category (2) cases are where the application for extension is made at a time when
the writ is still valid but the relevant period of limitation has expired. Category (3)   C
cases are where the application for extension is made at a time when the writ has
ceased to be valid and the relevant period of limitation has expired.'

The passage to which Harman J drew particular attention comes at p. 622G where Lord
Brandon says:

'I think on the whole that it has been unhelpful to put the condition for extension
as high as "exceptional circumstances", an expression which conveys to my mind   D
at any rate a large degree of stringency. The old rule in force until 1962 referred to
"any other good reason", and I think that the new rule should be interpreted as
requiring "good reason" and no more.

The question then arises as to what kind of matters can properly be regarded as
amounting to "good reason". The answer is, I think, that it is not possible to define
or circumscribe the scope of that expression. Whether there is or is not good reason   E
in any particular case must depend on all the circumstances of that case, and must
therefore be left to the judgment of the judge who deals either with an ex parte
application by a plaintiff for the grant of an extension, or with an inter partes
application by a defendant to set aside an extension previously granted ex parte.

Good reason is necessary for an extension in both category (2) cases and category
(3) cases. But in category (3) cases the applicant for an extension has an extra   F
difficulty to overcome, in that he must also give a satisfactory explanation for his
failure to apply for extension before the validity of the writ expired.'

It should be said that the analogy between that last consideration of category (3) and
the present case is not exact because here the application for extension was made within
the limitation period, not outside it. However that may be, the question, as Hoffmann LJ
made clear, is whether there is 'good reason for an extension of time' and that is to be   G
considered having regard to the four factors outlined in the *Probe Data* case.

Before leaving the questions of principle, I should refer to two other points which have
been raised in argument. First, Mr Briggs for two of the appellants suggests in his
skeleton argument that a particularly stringent test is to be applied where, as he says,
'limitation questions arise'. He refers me to a judgment of Sir Robert Megarry V-C in *Re
Salmon* [1981] Ch 167. That was concerned with the *Family Provision Act* 1966 as
amended by the *Inheritance (Provision for Family and Dependants) Act* 1975, s. 4 of   H
which reads as follows:

'An application for an order under section 2 of this Act shall not, except with the
permission of the court, be made after the end of the period of six months from the
date on which representation with respect to the estate of the deceased is first taken
out.'

A   That is similar to s. 7 of the 1986 Act to the extent that there is a specific time limit together with a power in the court to extend it. Commenting on that at p. 175 the Vice-Chancellor said:

> 'First, the discretion is unfettered. No restrictions or requirements of any kind are laid down in the Act. The discretion is thus plainly one that is to be exercised judicially, and in accordance with what is just and proper. Second, I think that the
B   onus lies on the plaintiff to establish sufficient grounds for taking the case out of the general rule, and depriving those who are protected by it of its benefits. Further, the time limit is a substantive provision laid down in the Act itself, and is not a mere procedural time limit imposed by rules of court which will be treated with the indulgence appropriate to procedural rules. The burden on the applicant is thus, I think, no triviality: the applicant must make out a substantial case for it being just and proper for the court to exercise its statutory discretion to extend the time.'

C   Taken overall, I do not see any difference between that and what has been said by Hoffmann LJ in *Probe Data*, in relation to the need to show good reason for the extension. However, the contrast drawn there between a substantive provision laid down in the Act and 'a mere procedural time limit imposed by rules of court' might be misleading if too broadly applied. The Vice-Chancellor was not speaking against the background of the strict practice which has been applied in relation to extensions of time
D   for appeal in the Court of Appeal in more recent years, and certainly the cases in relation to that show that time limits laid down by the rules can be as strict as time limits imposed by the statute.

The second point which I should mention is by reference to cases such as *Revici v Prentice Hall Inc* [1969] 1 WLR 157, which indicate that in the absence of any explanation for the delay an application for extension will fail. On this basis, Mr Briggs advances an
E   argument that there must not only be a reason, but a *good* reason, for the delay since, as he says, a bad reason is no better than no reason at all. He finds some support for this submission in the judgment of Mr Cherryman QC, sitting as a deputy judge of the High Court, in *Re Cedar Developments Ltd* [1995] BCC 220. In that case there was a short delay caused by an 'administrative lapse', and an extension of time was refused even though it was accepted to be a serious case and there was no prejudice.

F   The deputy judge drew attention to the relevant principles at p. 223, and I do not think there is any challenge to that. At p. 224 he rejected the suggestion that the reason for the delay could be taken out and treated, as it were, as a preliminary consideration. However, he went on to say at p. 224D:

> '(3) that on an application for leave the burden on the official receiver to show a good reason is not a formality but a very real onus which cannot be discharged perfunctorily or semi-automatically by showing that the time limit has been missed
G   by a few days simply due to some administrative mistake (in my judgment there can hardly be a good reason for leave without a good reason being shown why the time limit was missed) . . .'

He went on to hold that the administrative muddle was not a good reason but in fact a 'bad' reason. He referred to a judgment of Sheen J in *The Al Tabith* [1993] 2 Ll Rep 214 and in particular to the following statement:

H
> 'A person who decides not to issue a writ until shortly before a period of limitation will expire takes the risk that for some unexpected reason he will fail to issue the writ in time.'

Although Mr Briggs' argument is attractively developed, I think it is misleading to equate what he calls a 'bad reason' with 'no explanation at all'. The court is undoubtedly entitled to an explanation for any delay, but once an explanation is proffered it then

becomes a matter to be considered in the light of all the other factors. I do not think it is   A
helpful to apply epithets such as 'good' or 'reasonable' or 'adequate' in the abstract, since
they beg the question of the standard to be applied. For example, it is hard to see how in
the abstract a mistaken view of the law can ever be a 'good reason'; but it may be an
understandable reason, and it may be an excusable reason, particularly if it causes no
prejudice. So, in another case to which I was referred in the Court of Appeal, *Secretary
of State for Trade and Industry v Langridge (Re Cedac Ltd)* [1991] BCC 148; [1991] Ch   B
402, Nourse LJ drew attention to the fact that the failure in that case had been in
ignorance of what was the true view of a particular statutory provision. At p. 163; 425 he
said that the judge had been entitled to treat 'the department's ignorance as excusable
and thus as a good reason for the omission to make the application in due time'. He took
into account the fact that no prejudice had been shown and there were other
considerations.

So it is impossible, in my view, to judge the weight to be given to a particular reason   C
without regard to the context, and in particular to the prejudice which may result. Indeed,
with respect to the deputy judge in *Cedar*, an administrative muddle might in certain
circumstances be viewed in the same way. It may not be a good reason as such; but,
human weakness being what it is, administrative muddles do happen, and if the delay
caused is minimal and no prejudice suffered it seems wrong that the public interest in
pursuing the matter should be defeated.   D

I turn then to the present case. The registrar, as I say, allowed the application. He gave
a written judgment. He referred to the facts of the case, and in particular he noted the
estimated deficiency in the group after some three years of trading of £34m, which as he
said was on any view 'a spectacular failure'. He referred to what he understood to be the
main difficulty facing the Secretary of State in formulating his case, which he described
thus: E

> 'The main difficulty which I do not think can be seriously disputed was that the
> Serious Fraud Office was not prepared to let the Secretary of State have access to
> the papers relating to the Blackspur Group of which the Office had taken
> possession in relation to its own investigation. Eventually in about May 1992, but
> too late for the purposes of the disqualification unit, those papers were made
> available and the evidence of the Secretary of State on the disqualification   F
> proceedings was in fact completed and served in December 1992.'

I shall need to return to that particular point. He rejected the respondents' argument that
the 'good reason' issue should be treated as a preliminary issue. I have already discussed
that point and I agree with the registrar. He held, rightly in my view, that it was necessary
to look at all the relevant factors. In conclusion he said:

> 'Those factors are first, the length of the delay; secondly the reasons for the delay;   G
> thirdly the strength of case against the respondents; fourthly the seriousness of the
> allegations; fifthly the degree of prejudice caused to the respondents by the delay;
> and sixthly – although this is probably only an aspect of prejudice – the extent to
> which the delay will postpone the eventual substantive hearing of the application.
> Even if I were persuaded that the question of the adequacy of the reasons for delay
> was a preliminary issue, I would and do decide it against the respondents. As to   H
> the remaining factors, it does not seem to me that the length of the delay was
> inordinate; the strength and seriousness of the case against the respondents appear
> to me to be amply sufficient; no prejudice to the respondents is either alleged or
> proved; and it is, I think, common ground that the disqualification proceedings
> cannot realistically be brought to trial until the criminal proceedings have been
> disposed of.'

That consideration of the relevant factors by the registrar is not seriously in issue apart from the one point about the reasons for delay. Mr Briggs in his skeleton says:

> 'The first and fourth respondents accept that the totality of the evidence now adduced in support of the proceedings against them raises a prima facie case which if proved (which they contend it will not be) will constitute a relatively serious case of unfitness. The first and fourth respondents also accept that they are unable to point to any specific prejudice which they have suffered as a result of the Secretary of State's delay in commencing properly constituted proceedings other than a six month delay in the time by which they received both proper notice of the allegations against them and the documentary evidence on which they were based.'

The other respondents broadly adopted Mr Briggs' approach, although I was urged not to be over-influenced by the headline figure of £34m without considering the factors which make it up. Accepting that, I do not understand there to be any major disagreement with Mr Briggs' assessment.

As to the delay, it is necessary to look at the evidence which was before the registrar and what has happened subsequently. There was an affidavit from Mr Brierley himself to whom I have referred. On the relevant point, having referred to the complexity and difficulties of the matter, he said:

> '7. Together with my staff I performed a detailed examination of the policies adopted by the companies and we examined the effect the adoption of these policies had on the reported profits of the companies. In view of the poor condition of the companies' books and records and the complicated transactions into which they had entered, this task took a long time to complete. In addition, I consulted counsel in relation to the transactions entered into by the companies and the legal position of the directors who had set up the transactions and entered into them on behalf of the companies.

> 8. During the first few months of the receivership I and my staff contacted the Serious Fraud Office . . . to advise them of our initial findings and our concerns. The fact that the SFO then commenced their own investigations, and retained documentation relating to the companies, made our investigation procedure more difficult, as did the need to obtain documentation from the companies' previous solicitors, Clifford Chance.

> 9. Therefore, although I could have reported upon the conduct of the directors at an earlier stage, it was not until I had completed the complicated and lengthy investigation of the companies' accountancy procedures and unravelled the various transactions which they had entered into that I was in a position to report meaningfully on their activities.'

The other relevant affidavit is from Mr Chillery, who is the Principal Examiner in the Disqualification Unit of the Department of Trade and Industry. He refers to the decision being taken at the end of September 1991 that disqualification proceedings were appropriate. But then, he says:

> 'On 1 October 1991, enquiries were made of the SFO, but no substantive answer was received.'

The case was allocated to Mr Holden at the beginning of December. He again contacted the SFO, and was informed that they were not going to make a final decision as to criminal proceedings until after publication of a report to the department by inspectors appointed to investigate a company named Atlantic Computers Ltd, with which some of the Blackspur directors had been associated. This report apparently was expected by the end of January 1992 and the SFO were expecting to make a decision in about February. Mr Chillery says, in the light of that:

'A decision was taken on behalf of the applicant that there was no alternative but to wait for the decision of the SFO. The SFO had taken charge of many of the companies' books and papers (the exhibits in the SFO inquiry total some 42,000 items) and it was hoped that the SFO would be able to assist the Secretary of State in preparing evidence of unfitness, since the SFO's investigation had necessarily been more comprehensive than that of the joint administrative receivers.'

Nothing then happened until 4 March when Mr Holden again contacted the SFO and was told that a final decision had not been made and the Atlantic Computers report had not yet been published. On 13 March someone within the department apparently decided that the Secretary of State should consider commencing proceedings on the basis of Mr Brierley's information; and the SFO apparently said that they were not prepared at that stage to disclose the papers in their possession to the Secretary of State. There was then some delay in contacting Mr Horn, who was Mr Brierley's assistant, who was on holiday at this time. In April there were discussions with Mr Horn about the preparation of evidence, and it emerged that Mr Brierley's knowledge of the matter of which the SFO had documentation was not complete. Then there were various exchanges of drafts. By the beginning of May, the department informed the SFO that the case would be weaker without the SFO's input. The Treasury Solicitor was instructed on behalf of the Secretary of State, and on 21 May there was a meeting with the representatives of the SFO at which it was agreed that SFO material could be released and made available to the Secretary of State. It was really after that meeting that serious work commenced on getting the case in order for the disqualification proceedings, but there was no prospect by then of it being ready by July.

On the basis of that evidence, the registrar understood, as I have said, that the SFO papers were not available to the Secretary of State until May 1992. Further light has been thrown on that matter by more recent correspondence which is appended to the affidavit of Miss Rickards, the solicitor to the first and fourth respondents. She challenged the statement that this material would not have been available, and in a letter of 14 April 1994 the Treasury Solicitor commented in these terms, having consulted Arthur Andersen and the SFO:

'a. Arthur Andersen confirm that the records of Blackspur plc and Blackspur Graphics Ltd have at all times remained in their direct custody. However, they inform me that these documents had only limited relevance to their main areas of investigation.

b. The SFO removed from the administrative receivers the bulk of the Blackspur Leasing plc "trading" files in the period September to December 1990, and from that time onwards the SFO held these papers initially at its offices in London, and from November 1992 at Maidstone Police Station.

c. The SFO has allowed Arthur Andersen to have access to the records of the companies held by the SFO for the purpose of the administrative receivership.

d. Arthur Andersen inform me that it was rarely possible to obtain immediate access to those records and that usually appointments had to be made several days in advance, since an officer of the SFO had to be present. Moreover the available photocopying facilities at the SFO were poor, and if the SFO were using any particular documents, these could not be viewed by Arthur Andersen at the same time. These factors made it difficult for the administrative receivers to progress their own investigation.

e. It was not until May 1992 that the SFO decided to make available to the administrative receivers and the Secretary of State (for the purposes of the disqualification application) certain material gathered by the SFO pursuant to s. 3(5) of the Criminal Justice Act 1987, e.g. witness statements, exhibits, interview transcripts and the findings of SFO accountants. You will appreciate that these are not historic company records and that neither the Secretary of State nor the administrative receivers had a right of access to them.

f. The SFO inform me that this additional material was withheld from the DTI and Arthur Andersen whilst it was considering whether to bring prosecutions, and that even now it has not made available all documents to the DTI and the administrative receivers. Your assertion that, throughout the receivership, Arthur Andersen have had access to all documentation is therefore incorrect. In contrast, your firm has had access to all the SFO's used and unused material, for the purpose of defending Mr Andrew in the criminal case.'

There was some further pressing by Miss Rickards and on 22 March 1995 the Treasury Solicitor said this:

'Having gone through the papers, I feel there is little I can add to Mr Crane's letter dated 14 April 1994. The administrative receiver had immediate and unlimited day-to-day access to the company records of Blackspur plc and Blackspur Graphics which were always in his possession. The records of Blackspur Leasing were, in the main, held by the SFO and so were held away from the office of the administrative receiver and, indeed, from November 1992 held at Maidstone. Consequently, whilst the administrative receiver was never refused access to the documents, there were, in fact, considerable practical difficulties in gaining immediate access to the documents as and when required.'

In the light of that new evidence, as I have said, it is accepted that I should exercise my discretion anew, although obviously giving due weight to the views of the registrar. Mr Briggs has given me an analysis of the evidence which was eventually put in by the Treasury Solicitor in December and he says that on examination it is clear that with diligence it could have been prepared in time to meet the statutory limit. In particular he refers to the major affidavit prepared by Mr Ballamy of Price Waterhouse. He was an accountant who was seconded in October 1990 to the SFO to work on this case. He now has prepared a substantial affidavit giving largely expert evidence arising from his view of the documentation which he has been able to study. It appears that it was not until May 1992, following the meeting with the SFO, that he began work on a report specifically for the Secretary of State. Mr Briggs says that there is nothing in his affidavit which could not have been provided by any competent expert if instructed in time, given that, as now appears, access was available to the relevant documentation, albeit with some practical difficulties.

As he says, the real problem is not, as the registrar thought, the unavailability of the papers, but that the department allowed the matter to drift in the Micawberish hope that something would turn up from the SFO. He says that it is particularly odd to allow delay pending the Atlantic Computers report, when the department must have been aware of the programme for that and that it was unlikely to be available for many months. He also says that Mr Brierley himself was at fault for not reporting sooner, as he was obliged to do under s. 7(3), once he was satisfied that there was a case under the Act.

Against this, Mr Gillis for the Secretary of State says that it was clearly sensible to avoid duplication of work in this complex matter. Even if access was in theory possible the practical difficulties would have added to the delay and costs involved and it was sensible therefore to wait for Mr Ballamy who had been working on the matter for some months already and was in a much better position to produce a report for the department.

It is certainly difficult to criticise the sentiment of wishing to avoid duplication of work and the desire to wait for Mr Ballamy. However, the difficulty with that is that there is no evidence that a considered judgment of that kind was made in December 1991. It is not even clear from the evidence whether the department knew of Mr Ballamy's

involvement at that time. Indeed, there is no indication that anyone in October or   A
December 1991 addressed their mind to the problem of getting the case ready by July.
On any view the case was going to take some months to prepare even with the full
cooperation of the SFO and the July date was not far off. There is no indication that
anyone tried to establish a realistic programme to enable the time limits to be met or, if
that was not going to be possible, to seek extensions. As far as one can ascertain from the
evidence it was not really until the meeting with the SFO in May 1992 following the
involvement of the Treasury Solicitor that work progressed in earnest, by which time of   B
course there was no hope of meeting the deadline. Thus, I see some force in the criticisms
made by Mr Briggs, if the reasons for delay are looked at on their own.

However, it is at this point that the other factors must be brought into play. As far as
Mr Brierley is concerned, although technically, as he says, he could have reported earlier,
there was no practical advantage in an earlier report since the Secretary of State would
not have been able to do anything without the detailed material. More generally, and in   C
particular in relation to the Secretary of State's action, in practice, as everyone knew, the
SFO held the key to progress in the matter since any criminal proceedings were always
going to take precedence. That is what has in fact happened. The delay of some five to
six months in getting the application in order has not delayed the overall resolution of
the matter. That has had to await the outcome of the criminal proceedings in any event.
The policy of waiting for the SFO has not caused any harm, and from the public point   D
of view it has no doubt saved some duplication of work by the involvement of Mr
Ballamy. If, as must be accepted, there is a serious case against the defendants which the
Secretary of State considers it right in the public interest to pursue, it does not seem to
me that it should be defeated merely because of some delay in getting his tackle in order,
where that delay has not in itself added to the overall time scale nor materially affected
the defendants' ability to defend themselves. Accordingly, when I weigh up all the
relevant factors, as I am required to do by the *Probe Data* approach, it seems to me that   E
the registrar's decision was correct and this appeal must fail.

(*Appeal dismissed*)

F

G

H

A # Eberhardt & Co Ltd v Mair.

Chancery Division.
Evans-Lombe J.
Judgment delivered 2 May 1995.

B *Bankruptcy – Issue estoppel – Petition based on statutory demand – Application to set aside statutory demand dismissed – Whether petition should be adjourned or bankruptcy order made – Whether debtor estopped from arguing that debt disputed on substantial grounds – Insolvency Rules 1986 (SI 1986/1925), r. 6.25.*

This was an appeal by the petitioning creditor from a district judge's order standing over a bankruptcy petition.

C The petitioning creditor argued that the judge had erred in refusing to make a bankruptcy order. The petition was based on a statutory demand which the debtor had applied to set aside. The debtor's application was dismissed as was a further application for review of that dismissal. The petitioning creditor argued that since the matters raised by the respondent had already been rejected by the court on two previous occasions there were no grounds for refusing to make a bankruptcy order.

Held, dismissing the appeal:

D 1. Subject to the special powers of the bankruptcy court, on the material before the district judge the debtor was bound by an issue estoppel arising from the decision on the application to set aside the statutory demand that the petitioner's claim was not disputed on substantial grounds.

2. However no issue estoppel could be finally binding on a court of bankruptcy at the point when that court came to consider whether to make a bankruptcy order.

E 3. Had both parties been anticipating a full hearing of the petition the district judge would have been wrong to adjourn the petition since he did not appear to have had any material before him which justified his going behind the conclusion on the application to set aside the statutory demand nor any indication that such evidence might be available in the future. However it did seem that the debtor and those representing him were not anticipating a full hearing of the petition, and that there was reasonable cause for their taking such a view.

F The following cases were referred to in the judgment:

Heyl, Re [1918] 1 KB 452.
Kibble, Ex parte (1875) LR 10 Ch App 373.
Platts v Western Trust & Savings Ltd (unreported, 1 April 1993, CA).
Van Laun, Re [1907] 1 KB 155; [1907] 2 KB 23 (CA).
Yeatman, Re (1880) 16 ChD 283.

G Raquel Agnello (instructed by Sherwin Oliver, Portsmouth) for the petitioning creditor.

Paul McCormick (instructed by Llewellyn & Co, Portsmouth) for the debtor.

JUDGMENT

Evans-Lombe J: This is an appeal from the order of District Judge Cawood made on
H 14 March 1995 on the adjourned hearing of a petition in bankruptcy against the respondent, Robert Mair. By that order he stood over the petition and gave directions for the purposes of a later hearing of the petition which, it was anticipated, would last a full day.

As at 14 March no notice of opposition had been filed by the debtor. Consequentially on the directions of the district judge such a notice was filed on 22 March. The grounds of opposition contained in it read as follows:

'1. I am not justly and truly indebted to the petitioner for the sum claimed in the A bankruptcy petition or any sum. If any such sum is due and owing (which is not admitted) the liability is that of a limited company, Bedhampton Glass Ltd and/or one Brian Wilson personally.

2. Failure to comply with provisions of r. 6.7 and 6.8 of the *Insolvency Rules* 1986.

3. Failure to comply with r. 6.12 of the said rules.

4. Delay in presenting the bankruptcy petition.

5. I appear able, and am able, to pay the sum referred to in the bankruptcy petition.'

The petitioning creditor appeals against the order of District Judge Cawood on the following grounds:

'1. The district judge erred in refusing to make a bankruptcy order on 14 March C 1995 in that on the evidence before the court, there were no grounds upon which the district judge should have refused to make a bankruptcy order, in particular:

(a) There were no grounds of opposition raised either in any notice of opposition which should have been filed pursuant to r. 6.21 of the *Insolvency Rules* 1986 (SI 1986/1925), or in any affidavits or by way of submissions which would have entitled the district judge to refuse in all the circumstances D to make the bankruptcy order sought.

(b) The only grounds of opposition which were raised were identical to those grounds of opposition raised by the respondent at the hearing before the court on 20 August 1993 on the respondent's application to set aside the statutory demand dated 12 March 1993 when District Judge Hurley dismissed the respondent's application after a full hearing.

(c) The only grounds of opposition raised by the respondent were identical to E those raised by the respondent on 2 December 1993 when the respondent sought a review of the order of District Judge Hurley dismissing his application to set aside the statutory demand. The said application for review was dismissed by District Judge Bailey-Cox on 2 December 1993.

2. The district judge erred in granting an adjournment to the respondent and F giving directions for the hearing of the petition in the circumstances in that the matters raised by the respondent had already been adjudicated upon by the court on two previous occasions and in those circumstances the respondent is not entitled to seek a further hearing in relation to matters which have already been adjudicated upon by the court.'

The background facts of the case are that in June 1991 the petitioner supplied signs to Ashby's Wine Bar in Southsea where a business was being conducted by the debtor, G apparently, in association with Mr Wilson. The order for the signs was placed by Mr Wilson. It seems that the premises at the time were being refurbished by a building company of which the debtor and Mr Wilson were directors and shareholders. That company has ceased to trade. The petitioners sought payment of their account from the debtor who in 1991 and 1992 made three payments on account totalling some £600 leaving a balance outstanding on the petitioners' invoices of £2,200.03. Upon further H payment not being forthcoming the petitioners served a statutory demand for that amount on the debtor on 15 March 1993. On 6 April the debtor applied under r. 6.4 of the Insolvency Rules to set aside the statutory demand. In support of that application he swore an affidavit. Two affidavits in answer were sworn on behalf of the petitioners and the debtor swore an affidavit in reply. It was the debtor's case that he was not trading in any sort of partnership with Mr Wilson, that Mr Wilson did not have his authority to

A place an order for signs with the petitioners and that that order had either been placed on behalf of the company of which he and Mr Wilson were directors and which was concerned with the refurbishment of the wine bar, or was made by Mr Wilson personally.

The debtor's application to set aside the statutory demand came to be dealt with by District Judge Hurley on 26 August 1993 when it was dismissed. On 3 September an attempt was made to lodge an appeal on behalf of the debtor at the Portsmouth County Court. Since the Portsmouth County Court had no jurisdiction to hear such an appeal it B was declined. On 6 September a similar attempt was made to lodge such an appeal at the Winchester District Registry of the High Court. This was also declined on the ground that the Winchester District Registry had no jurisdiction to accept such an appeal.

On 14 October 1993 an application was made by the debtor in the Portsmouth County Court seeking a review of District Judge Hurley's decision of 20 August under the provisions of s. 375(1) of the Insolvency Act. That application came to be dealt with on C 2 December by Deputy District Judge Bailey-Cox when it was dismissed. It seems that the district judge, in accordance with the practice and the authorities, took the view that since there had been placed before him no new material which had not been before District Judge Hurley, it was not a case for review but rather for appeal. The district judge also purported, it would seem without jurisdiction, to extend the time for lodging an appeal. Nevertheless on 14 December a document purporting to be a notice of appeal D was also sent to the petitioners' solicitors. It was also sent for lodgement to the High Court but was not, apparently, accepted on the ground that it was out of time, it being pointed out in a letter from the Deputy Chief Clerk to the debtor's solicitors that only the High Court had power to extend time within which to file notice of appeal.

Nothing then appears to have happened until on 15 December 1994 the petitioners presented a bankruptcy petition against the debtor and filed an affidavit by their solicitor E verifying the petition. The first hearing of the petition was fixed for 7 February 1995 but since the petition was only served on the debtor on 25 January it was stood over to 1 March. At the hearing on 1 March the debtor produced a further affidavit sworn on that day. That affidavit drew the court's attention to the appeal from District Judge Hurley's order of 20 August 1993 and sought an adjournment. The affidavit added nothing of substance on the merits of the debtor's case that he did not owe the petitioners the balance of £2,200.03 due under their invoices and which amount comprised the F petitioning debt. The matter was dealt with by District Judge Willis who stood the matter over for 14 days in order that the status of the appeal could be clarified. When the matter came back on 14 March before District Judge Cawood he made the order which I have summarised. It was the debtor's contention before him that the matter had been adjourned on 1 March on the basis that on 14 March there would be a short ten-minute hearing only when the debtor would report on the status of his appeal. For that purpose G the debtor's solicitor swore an affidavit.

On 22 March 1995 a notice of opposition was filed in the manner which I have described. Also, consequentially on District Judge Cawood's order the respondent has sworn a further affidavit on 10 April. That affidavit again deals with the merits of the debtor's defence to the petitioners' claim but does not appear to add any new material. I was told, however, that it may be sought to subpoena Mr Wilson to give evidence at any further hearing of the petition.

H It is the petitioners' submission that the debtor's substantive defence to the petition arises under para. 1 of the notice of opposition and that the remaining matters set out in the notice have no substance. For the debtor it was accepted that no valid complaint arose for failure to comply with the provisions of r. 6.7 of the Insolvency Rules. As to para. 1 the petitioners submit that whether or not the debtor has raised a bona fide dispute as to the petitioners' claim against him under the contract for the supply of signs

has been decided against the debtor in the course of his application to set aside the   A
statutory demand. That decision not having been reversed on review, and there being no
effective appeal from it, it could not be re-opened at the hearing of the petition. No
further evidence on the central issue of liability was before District Judge Cawood on 14
March which was not before District Judge Hurley on 20 August 1993. Even if it was
possible to obtain further material, such as evidence from Mr Wilson, that should have
been put before the court on a further application to review the order of District Judge
Hurley and not on the hearing of the petition. In effect the petitioner was contending that   B
an issue estoppel bound the debtor on the central issue of liability for the petitioning
debt. Accordingly it was contended that District Judge Cawood should not have
adjourned the petition but should have made a bankruptcy order. It does not seem that
the remaining matters in the notice of opposition were raised before the district judge on
14 March.

It was submitted on behalf of the respondents that on 14 March the district judge had   C
a discretion whether or not to make a bankruptcy order. In the event in the exercise of
that discretion he elected not to do so but to stand over the petition for a full hearing
giving the parties an opportunity to adduce further evidence. In any event it would have
been unjust to make a bankruptcy order on 14 March because the debtor was not
anticipating a final hearing of the petition on that day. If he had done so he would have
made efforts to obtain further relevant evidence including attempting to subpoena Mr   D
Wilson.

The material provisions of the *Insolvency Act* 1986 are to be found in s. 267, 268 and
271 as follows:

'267(1) A creditor's petition must be in respect of one or more debts owed by the
debtor, and the petitioning creditor or each of the petitioning creditors must be a
person to whom the debt or (as the case may be) at least one of the debts is owed.   E

(2) Subject to the next three sections, a creditor's petition may be presented to the
court in respect of a debt or debts only if, at the time the petition is presented–

(a) the amount of the debt, or the aggregate amount of the debts, is equal to or
exceeds the bankruptcy level,

(b) the debt or each of the debts, is for a liquidated sum payable to the
petitioning creditor, or one or more of the petitioning creditors, either   F
immediately or at some certain, future time, and is unsecured,

(c) the debt, or each of the debts, is a debt which the debtor appears either to be
unable to pay or to have no reasonable prospect of being able to pay, and

(d) there is no outstanding application to set aside a statutory demand served
(under section 268 below) in respect of the debt or any of the debts.   G

. . .

268(1) For the purposes of Section 267(2)(c), the debtor appears to be unable to
pay a debt if, but only if, the debt is payable immediately and either–

(a) the petitioning creditor to whom the debt is owed has served on the debtor
a demand (known as "the statutory demand") in the prescribed form
requiring him to pay the debt or to secure or compound for it to the   H
satisfaction of the creditor, at least 3 weeks have elapsed since the demand
was served and the demand has been neither complied with nor set aside in
accordance with the rules, or

(b) execution or other process issued in respect of the debt on a judgment or
order of any court in favour of the petitioning creditor, or one or more of

A   the petitioning creditors to whom the debt is owed, has been returned unsatisfied in whole or in part.

. . .

271(1) The court shall not make a bankruptcy order on a creditor's petition unless it is satisfied that the debt, or one of the debts, in respect of which the petition was presented is either–

B

     (a) a debt which, having been payable at the date of the petition or having since become payable, has been neither paid nor secured nor compounded for, or

     (b) a debt which the debtor has no reasonable prospect of being able to pay when it falls due.'

C   I have omitted the provisions dealing with debts becoming due in the future which are not material to the present case.

Chapter 1 of Pt. 6 of the Insolvency Rules deals with statutory demands. Chapter 2 deals with creditor's petitions. Rule 6.11 in ch. 2 requires a petitioning creditor as a condition of presenting the petition where non-compliance with the statutory demand is being relied on to file an affidavit proving service of such statutory demand. Rule 6.12 requires the filing of an affidavit, inter alia, by a solicitor who has been concerned in the

D   matters giving rise to the presentation of the petition, verifying its contents.

Under the heading 'Decision on the Hearing', r. 6.25 provides:

'(1) On the hearing of the petition, the court may make a bankruptcy order if satisfied that the statements in the petition are true, and that the debt on which it is founded has not been paid, or secured or compounded for.'

E   One such statement would necessarily be the allegation that the debtor was indebted to the petitioner in respect of the petitioning debt. It is the practice under r. 6.25(1) also for the petitioning creditor to file a certificate that the petitioning debt is still outstanding at the date of the hearing and has not been paid, secured or compounded for.

The procedure for setting aside statutory demands is dealt with in r. 6.5 in ch. 1. Subrule (1) empowers the court in an appropriate case to dismiss the application summarily without a hearing. That did not happen here. Subrules (2) and (3) provide as

F   follows:

'(2) If the application is not dismissed under paragraph (1), the court shall fix a venue for it to be heard, and shall give at least 7 days' notice of it to–

     (a) the debtor or, if the debtor's application was made by a solicitor acting for him, to the solicitor,

G   (b) the creditor, and

     (c) whoever is named in the statutory demand as the person with whom the debtor may enter into communication with reference to the demand . . .

(3) On the hearing of the application, the court shall consider the evidence then available to it, and may either summarily determine the application or adjourn it,

H   giving such directions as it thinks appropriate.'

It was under the provisions of subr. (3) that District Judge Hurley dismissed the debtor's application.

Subrule (4) of r. 6.5 sets out the circumstances in which the court may grant an application to set aside a statutory demand. So far as the present case is concerned the material provision is para. (b) which provides:

'The court may grant the application if—

A

(b) the debt is disputed on grounds which appear to the court to be substantial . . .'

In vol. 16 of *Halsbury's Laws of England* (4th edn) at para. 977 under the heading 'Issue estoppel' the editors say:

'A party is precluded from contending the contrary of any precise point which having once been distinctly put in issue has been solemnly and with certainty determined against him. Even if the objects of the first and second actions are different, the finding on a matter which came directly (not collaterally or incidentally) in issue in the first action, provided it is embodied in a judicial decision that is final, is conclusive in a second action between the same parties and their privies. This principle applies whether the point involved in the earlier decision, and as to which the parties are estopped, is one of fact or one of law, or one of mixed fact and law. The conditions for the application of the doctrine have been stated as being that:

(1) the same question was decided in both proceedings;

(2) the judicial decision said to create the estoppel was final; and

(3) the parties to the judicial decision or their privies were the same persons as the parties to the proceedings in which the estoppel is raised or their privies.'

B

C

D

It seems to me that, subject to the special powers of the bankruptcy court, on the material before the court on 14 March the debtor was bound by an issue estoppel arising from the decision of District Judge Hurley on 20 August 1993 that he was not satisfied that the petitioners' claim was disputed on grounds which appeared to him to be substantial. No direct authority on the point has been cited to me but it seems to me that a precisely similar issue arises when a petitioning creditor is required to establish the truth of the statement in the petition that the debtor is liable for the petitioning debt. It is clearly established in companies winding-up cases that the remedy of winding up is not available where the debt upon which the winding-up petition is based is bona fide disputed. The position should be the same where the petition is for a bankruptcy order.

E

Nonetheless as r. 6.25(1) makes plain the making of a bankruptcy order is a matter of discretion. It has long been established that the bankruptcy court has a power and indeed a duty to ensure that a bankruptcy is not instituted in circumstances which amount to injustice and has exercised a power to enquire into the consideration for the petitioning debt even to the extent of going behind judgments, see such cases as *Ex parte Kibble* (1875) LR 10 Ch App 373. In *Re Van Laun* [1907] 1 KB 155 at p. 163 Bigham J said:

F

'No judgment recovered against the bankrupt, no covenant given by or account stated with him, can deprive the trustee of this right. He is entitled to go behind such forms to get at the truth, and the estoppel to which the bankrupt may have subjected himself will not prevail against him.'

G

This passage said in the context of an appeal against a rejection of proof by a trustee in bankruptcy was approved by the Court of Appeal ([1907] 2 KB 23). Again there is no direct authority on the point but there would seem to be no reason to take the view that the power of the bankruptcy court to enquire into the consideration for the petitioning debt and in the process to go behind judgments or orders has not survived the coming into force of the *Insolvency Act* 1986.

H

It seems to me that just as the bankruptcy court would, in an appropriate case, go behind a judgment for the petitioning debt, so it would go behind any issue estoppel resulting from a judgment in the proceedings themselves. It follows, it seems to me, that no issue estoppel can be finally binding on a court of bankruptcy at the point when that

A   court comes to consider whether to make a bankruptcy order. I am confirmed in this conclusion by the striking fact that there appears to be no decided case under either the pre-1986 Act law or the law post the coming into force of the 1986 Act where this point has arisen, let alone been decided against the debtor. It must be borne in mind that under the pre-1986 Act law there existed, in the procedure for setting aside bankruptcy notices, a procedure, analogous to the statutory demand procedure, under which the enforceability of the petitioning debt could be tested before the petition itself was heard.

B   This conclusion is also, in my judgment, consistent with the decision of the Court of Appeal in *Platts v Western Trust & Savings Ltd* (unreported, 1 April 1993) see per the judgment of Sir Christopher Slade where he says:

> 'The phrase "on the evidence then available to it" in r. 6.5(3) by itself makes it clear that the court has a discretion to dismiss an application to set aside a statutory demand on the incomplete evidence before it without adjourning it for full
> C   evidence. If it saw fit in the light of the evidence before it, the court would still be free to go into the question of value on the hearing of the petition.'

On the hearing of the petition the court has a discretion whether or not to make a bankruptcy order or whether to adjourn the petition for further evidence etc. Where, however, the petitioner has complied with r. 6.25(1) by establishing the facts alleged in the petition and by proving that the petitioning debt remains outstanding, the court

D   should not adjourn the petition save for good cause such as the real anticipation of payment in the immediate future or the real prospect of either of the parties being able to adduce further relevant evidence: see such cases as *Re Yeatman* (1880) 16 ChD 283 and *Re Heyl* [1918] 1 KB 452 per Swinfen Eady LJ at p. 456.

Applying these principles to the present case, had I been satisfied that on 14 March both the parties were anticipating a full hearing of the petition I would have taken the view that the district judge, on the material before him, exercised his discretion to adjourn

E   the petition wrongly since he did not appear to have had any material before him which justified his going behind the conclusion of District Judge Hurley on 20 August 1993 nor any indication that such evidence might be available in the future. However it does seem that the debtor and those representing him were not anticipating a full hearing of the petition, and that there was reasonable cause for their taking such a view, and that they were contemplating obtaining further evidence for the hearing of the petition, in

F   particular subpoenaing Mr Wilson to give evidence. For these reasons, in any judgment, I cannot take the view, sitting as an appellate court from the exercise of discretion by the district judge, that he exercised that discretion so unreasonably as to justify my interference in it.

As an alternative counsel for the petitioner sought an order setting aside the various directions of the district judge for the hearing of the petition so as to make this a much less substantial matter. I do not feel myself justified in interfering with that aspect of the

G   district judge's order either. It may well be, at the hearing of the petition, if no further material evidence is available which was not before District Judge Hurley, that the proceedings may not last very long.

It seems to me therefore that for these reasons this appeal falls to be dismissed.

(Appeal dismissed)

H

Sharp & Anor (Joint receivers of Albyn Construction Ltd) v Thomson & Ors.

Court of Session (Inner House).
Lord President Hope, Lord Sutherland and Lord Coulsfield.
Judgment delivered 4 May 1995.

Receivership – Crystallisation of floating charge – Property of company – Company had executed and delivered disposition of property – Disposition had not been registered – Whether property remained property of company to which floating charge attached – Companies Act 1985, s. 463.

This was a reclaiming motion by the second defenders from an interlocutor of the Lord Ordinary: see [1995] BCC 57.

The receivers of Albyn Construction Ltd sought declarator that a flat which the company had agreed to sell to the first defenders remained the property of the company at the date of the receivers' appointment and was caught by the floating charge under which they were appointed. The receivers were appointed on 10 August 1990. The company agreed to sell the property in 1989, but a disposition was only executed and delivered to the first defenders on 9 August 1990. The disposition was registered on 21 August 1990; on the same date a standard security was recorded which the first defenders had granted in favour of the second defenders.

The defenders argued that the flat, once the disposition was executed and delivered, was no longer 'property' of Albyn within the meaning of the floating charge and Pt. XVIII of the Companies Act 1985; alternatively, if delivery of the disposition did not have that effect the same result should be achieved by implying a constructive trust of the subjects for the disponees.

The Lord Ordinary held that until recording a disposition was not effective to divest the grantor and the subjects remained comprised in his property. Thus the flat remained in substance the property of Albyn until registration by which time it was subject to the security in favour of the floating charge holder. The constructive trust argument was also rejected. The second defenders reclaimed.

Held, refusing the reclaiming motion:

1. There could be attached by means of a floating charge all property of the company which could be, at the critical date, the subject of a fixed security as defined in s. 70(1) of the Insolvency Act 1986. The only relevant test as to what was and what was not the property of the company was that provided by Scots property law. The second defenders' argument that the phrase 'property and undertaking' should be interpreted in a commercial sense, as meaning the assets of the company which were being used for the purposes of its business for the time being was rejected.

2. The terms of the floating charge were not inconsistent with the pursuers' argument that the charge extended to all heritable property of the company until a real right in it had been transferred.

3. Delivery of the disposition did not transfer the property in the land from the company to the purchaser. The property passed only when the disposition was recorded in the appropriate register, and only then could it be said with complete accuracy that the land had passed irrevocably from the property of the company. The second defenders' argument that on delivery of the disposition the flat ceased to form part of the company's property and undertaking, although the feudal title to it nevertheless remained in the company, was rejected.

4. A constructive trust did not arise following delivery or constructive delivery of property to a purchaser, pending the completion of the steps which were required to transfer the real

A   right. Where, as in this case, the transaction proceeded upon the ordinary course provided
for by the contract, the matter rested throughout entirely upon personal obligation and there
was no room for holding that there was, by implication, a constructive trust. (Bank of
Scotland v Liquidators of Hutchison Main & Co 1914 SC (HL) 1 applied; Stevenson v
Wilson 1907 SC 445 distinguished.)

The following cases were referred to in the opinions:

B   *Bank of Scotland v Liquidators of Hutchison Main & Co* 1914 SC (HL) 1.
Bowman v Wright (1877) 4 R 322.
Caledonian Fish Selling Marine Stores Ltd v Allard Hewson & Co Ltd 1970 SLT 195.
Carse v Coppen 1951 SC 233.
Dowie (Peter) & Co v Tennant (1891) 18 R 986.
Edmond v Gordon (1855) 18 D 47; (1858) 3 Macq 116.
C   *Embassy Picture House (Troon) Ltd v Cammo Developments Ltd* 1971 SC 25.
Forth & Clyde Construction Co Ltd v Trinity Timber & Plywood Co Ltd 1984 SC 1.
Fraser v Fraser & Hibbert (1870) 8 M 400.
Fraser v Magistrates of Aberdeen (unreported, 11 April 1977).
Gibson v Hunter Home Designs Ltd 1976 SC 23.
Glasgow (City of) v McEwan (1899) 2 F (HL) 25.
Grant (James) & Co Ltd v Moran 1948 SLT (Sh Ct) 8.
D   *Heritable Reversionary Co Ltd v Millar* (1892) 19 R (HL) 43.
Inland Revenue v Clark's Trustees 1939 SC 11.
Kibble v Stevenson (unreported, 23 September 1831).
Lee v Alexander (1882) 10 R 230.
Leeds Permanent Building Society v Aitken, Malone & Mackay 1985 SC 375.
Lombardi's Trustee v Lombardi 1982 SLT 81.
Macdonald v Scott's Executors 1981 SC 75.
E   *Margrie Holdings Ltd v C & E Commrs* 1991 SLT 38.
Mitchell v Ferguson (1781) Mor 10296.
Munro v Brodie (1844) 6 D 1249.
Musselwhite & Anor v C H Musselwhite & Son Ltd & Ors [1962] Ch 964.
National Bank of Scotland Glasgow Nominees Ltd v Adamson 1932 SLT 492.
National Commercial Bank of Scotland Ltd v Liquidators of Telford Grier Mackay &
F   *Co* 1969 SC 181.
Panama, New Zealand and Australian Royal Mail Co Ltd, Re (1870) LR 5 Ch App 318.
Parker v Lord Advocate 1960 SC (HL) 29.
Robertson v Duff (1840) 2 D 279.
Stevenson v Wilson 1907 SC 445.
Thomas v Lord Advocate 1953 SC 151.
Union Bank of Scotland Ltd v National Bank of Scotland Ltd (1886) 14 R (HL) 1.
G   *Young v Leith* (1847) 9 D 932; 2 Ross's Leading Cases 81.

Arthur Hamilton QC and Andrew Young (instructed by Dundas & Wilson, CS) for
the second defenders and reclaimers.

Ronald Mackay QC and Patrick Hodge (instructed by Paull & Williamsons) for the
respondents.

H   OPINIONS

Lord President Hope: This is a reclaiming motion by the second defenders in an action
of declarator. The pursuers are the joint receivers of Albyn Construction Ltd, who were
the heritable proprietors of a plot of ground at 10 Whinhill Road, Aberdeen. A
development of five flats was erected on this plot of ground. Albyn entered into missives
with the first defenders for sale of the basement flat to them for a price of £40,000,

14 April 1989 being the agreed date of entry. It was not until 9 August 1990 that Albyn executed and the company's solicitors delivered a disposition of the property to the first defenders' solicitor. One day later, on 10 August 1990, the pursuers were appointed as receivers of the company by instrument of appointment executed by the Bank of Scotland as holders of a floating charge granted by Albyn, dated 2 July and registered on 16 July 1984. The disposition in favour of the first defenders was recorded in the general register of sasines for the county of Aberdeen on 21 August 1990. On the same date there was recorded a standard security of the subjects which the first defenders had granted in favour of the second defenders on 31 July 1990. The action has been brought in order to resolve the competing claims to the flat of the pursuers, who maintain that as the disposition was not recorded until after the crystallisation of the floating charge it remained Albyn's property at that date and was attached by the floating charge when they were appointed on 10 August 1990, and of the defenders, who maintain that property in the flat passed from Albyn to the first defenders when the disposition was delivered to their solicitor on 9 August 1990.

The Lord Ordinary, before whom the case was debated on the procedure roll on the pleas of all three parties, decided this issue in favour of the pursuers, see [1995] BCC 57. By interlocutor dated 11 May 1994 he repelled the defenders' pleas in law, sustained the pursuers' fourth plea in law which was a plea to the relevancy, and granted decree de plano in terms of the first three conclusions of the summons. These were to the effect that the floating charge had attached to the flat on the appointment of the pursuers as joint receivers, that the floating charge operated as if it were a fixed security with priority over the standard security granted in favour of the second defenders by the first defenders, and that the pursuers as joint receivers were entitled to take possession of the flat and sell or otherwise dispose of it in the exercise of the powers conferred on them by the floating charge and by Sch. 2 to the *Insolvency Act* 1986. It is against that interlocutor that the second defenders have now reclaimed. The first defenders did not reclaim against it and they were not represented at the hearing of the reclaiming motion.

General background

Although the facts of this case are not complicated, there were a number of points of detail on which the information before us differed from that which was before the Lord Ordinary. These details do not have any material bearing on the competing arguments which we have to resolve, but it is as well that they should be placed on record in the interests of accuracy.

The first point relates to the relationship between the first defenders. They were referred to both in the missives and in the disposition as Steven Thomson and Mrs Carol Thomson, and this description of them was repeated in the instance of the summons when the action was raised. We were informed, however, that Steven Thomson and Carol Thomson are in fact brother and sister, and that the description of Carol Thomson as Mrs Thomson was a mistake.

The second point relates to the disposition. This was referred to in the pleadings and in the joint minute for the parties as the feu disposition. But it is clear upon an examination of the terms of the deed that this was not a case of subinfeudation by which the first defenders were to hold the flat in a feudal relationship with Albyn as their superiors, but that it was a straightforward disposition to the first defenders of Albyn's interest in the flat as heritable proprietors.

The third point relates to averments which the second defenders were allowed to make to their pleadings by amendment in the inner House and to averments which the pursuers were allowed to make in answer to the second defenders' averments. As a result of these amendments it is now a matter of admission between these parties that the flat was

A disponed by Albyn to the first defenders in the ordinary course of business and that the Bank of Scotland executed a deed of restriction disburdening the flat of a standard security in its favour. The second defenders aver that the deed of restriction, which was dated 27 July 1990, was delivered to the first defenders' solicitor along with the disposition, which the pursuers believe to be true. The pursuers also aver that, following the conclusion of the missives on 23 May 1989, the first defenders took entry and paid the price to Albyn on or about 12 June 1989. They also aver that on 8 June 1989 the

B Bank of Scotland executed a certificate of non-crystallisation of the floating charge by which they undertook:

'1. That at this date we have taken no steps to crystallise the said bond and floating charge;

2. We shall take no steps to deprive the said Albyn Construction Ltd of the right to validly convey the above subjects provided the disposition by them is recorded

C in 21 days of this date.'

The second defenders make no admission about the existence or otherwise of the certificate of non-crystallisation. This is not said by the pursuers to have been exhibited to the first defenders' solicitors. But a copy of it was produced in the respondents' appendix to the reclaiming motion, and it was accepted by the second defenders' counsel that it could be assumed that the bank were willing on 8 June 1989 to grant a certificate

D in these terms and that such a certificate could have been provided to the first defenders' solicitor if he had asked for it.

It should also be recorded that counsel for the second defenders made it clear in the course of their submissions that they did not take issue with what the Lord Ordinary said in his opinion about the wider statutory context and the requirements which must be met, having regard to the terms of the floating charge, if the pursuers were to succeed in

E this case. In this passage of his opinion (see [1995] BCC 57; 1994 SLT 1068 at pp. 67H–69E; 1076E–1077L), the Lord Ordinary referred first to the provisions of s. 462(1) of the *Companies Act* 1985, by which it is provided that it is competent under the law of Scotland for an incorporated company to create a floating charge 'over all or any part of the property (including uncalled capital) which may from time to time be comprised in its property and undertaking', and to s. 51(1) of the *Insolvency Act* 1986, by which it is provided that it is competent under the law of Scotland for the holder of a floating charge

F to appoint a receiver of such of the property of the company as is subject to the charge. He referred to the history of the introduction of the floating charge into Scots law, in the light of the observations of Lord President Cooper in *Carse v Coppen* 1951 SC 233 at p. 239 that a floating charge was utterly repugnant to the principles of Scots law and was not recognised by us as creating a security at all. He drew attention to the requirement identified by the Lord President for the constitution of a security, other than by diligence,

G which would confer upon the holder rights over and above those which he enjoys in common with the general body of unsecured creditors of a debtor, namely:

'the transfer to the creditor of a real right in specific subjects by the method appropriate for the constitution of such rights in the particular classes of property in question.'

It was that requirement which was particularly important for present purposes, and it

H was obstacles of that kind which were addressed in the *Companies (Floating Charges) (Scotland) Act* 1961 and its successors to enable floating charges to be created for the purpose of securing any debt or other obligation. In the course of his analysis of the provisions now to be found in s. 462(5) and 468 of the 1985 Act and s. 53(1) of the 1986 Act, he observed that the approach adopted did not innovate upon the general requirements of Scots property law for the creation of any of the forms of security otherwise recognised and that the language used in these provisions was appropriate to a

context which required consideration of rights and obligations arising as a matter of   A
property law.

The Lord Ordinary then said at p. 69D; 1077E:

> 'In my opinion two requirements fall to be met if the contentions of the receivers
> are to succeed in this case: (1) the subjects must fall within the expression "the
> property . . . comprised in the property and undertaking" of the company on 10
> August 1990; and (2) the interest of the company in the subjects on that date must   B
> have been such that as between the company and the floating charge creditor there
> could then attach to the subjects a standard security assumed to have been duly
> recorded without any act of the company being required.'

He went on to say, under reference to what Lord President Emslie said in *Forth &
Clyde Construction Co Ltd v Trinity Timber & Plywood Co Ltd* 1984 SC 1 at pp. 10–11 in
regard to property which consisted of a debt due to the company, that these observations   C
were clearly general in their effect and equally instructive in the context of heritable as of
moveable property. In his opinion the words 'as if' in s. 53(7) of the *Insolvency Act* 1986
indicated that one must proceed on an assumption of fact, appropriate to the class of
property in question, that the property is subject to an effective fixed security in favour
of the holder of the floating charge on the relevant date. I agree entirely with these
observations, which were not challenged to any extent by counsel for the second
defenders in the course of their argument. In my opinion they are crucial to a proper   D
understanding of the issues which arise in this case.

Mr Hamilton also stated, at the outset of his submission for the second defenders, that
he was unable to resist the following propositions which had formed part of the argument
advanced for the pursuers by Mr Hodge. These were (1) that if Albyn had granted a
subsequent disposition of the flat to another purchaser bona fide and for value and that
disposition had been recorded before the disposition to the first defenders was recorded   E
together with the standard security, the second purchaser would have taken the flat in
preference to the first defenders unencumbered by the standard security; (2) that if Albyn
had granted a standard security to a lender taking it bona fide and for value which was
recorded prior to the first defenders' disposition and standard security, the granter of
that security would have taken the benefit of it in preference to the first and second
defenders; (3) that if a creditor of Albyn holding a decree of adjudication had recorded
his decree prior to the recording of the disposition to the first defenders, the creditor   F
would have obtained a preference to the property which would have prevailed over the
first and second defenders; and (4) that the first defenders did not, on 10 August 1990,
have a complete real right in the flat of the kind described in *Young v Leith* (1847) 9 D
932 at p. 945.

Mr Hamilton accepted that the first two propositions could not be resisted, in view of
the importance to be attached to the security of the public records as between persons   G
transacting with each other in good faith, and that the third proposition was the effect of
the decision in *Mitchell v Ferguson* (1781) Mor 10296. In regard to the fourth proposition
he explained that it was not the purpose of his argument to undermine the position of the
law of property in Scots law. He said that it was accepted by the second defenders that
the feudal title to the flat had not been attached by the floating charge. It was not part of
their argument that the same interest in the same item of property could for the same
purpose be held by two or more people at the same time. The true question in this case,   H
so far as the second defenders were concerned, was whether upon a proper construction
of the floating charge the flat remained in Albyn's property and undertaking after the
delivery of the disposition to the solicitor for the first defenders. The possibility of a
separation of the interests of the owner of the property at that stage had to be recognised.
He proposed to contend that, as a result of this fragmentation of interests on delivery of

A   the disposition, the flat ceased to form part of Albyn's property and undertaking, although the feudal title to it nevertheless remained in Albyn.

Although the issue as focused by Mr Hamilton may seem to be a relatively narrow one, I consider that it raises questions of a fundamental kind about the relationship between property law and the law of obligations. It seems to me therefore to be an inevitable part of the examination of his argument that one should have a clear

B   understanding of that relationship and of the true nature of the real right according to Scots property law. I shall address myself first to this matter before I come to examine the second defenders' argument about the proper interpretation of the floating charge and their alternative argument based on the contention that the delivery of the disposition gave rise to a constructive trust in favour of the purchasers.

C
The property law context

Mr Hamilton submitted that the transfer of property and heritage involved two elements within a single transaction. These comprised the delivery of the disposition and the recording or registration of that disposition in the appropriate public register. It was wrong to regard these two stages as separate and distinct from each other. Each was an integral part of the whole and both steps were necessary. While it was accepted that a complete right of property, or a complete real right, did not pass until the recording or

D   registration of the disposition in the public register, delivery of the disposition had the effect of passing a beneficial interest in the form of an inchoate or incomplete right of property to the disponee. In any event it was appropriate for certain purposes to regard the heritage as being, at this stage in the transaction, the property of the disponee and not that of the disponer.

These submissions find some support in the dicta of judges in a substantial number of

E   cases, including *Gibson v Hunter Home Designs Ltd* 1976 SC 23 where Lord President Emslie set out at p. 27 his analysis of the three stages by which a right of property in heritage is transferred from the transferor to the transferee. The clarity of that exposition added weight to its authority, and it was followed without critical examination in a number of later cases. But the competition which has arisen in this case has made it necessary for us to look again at these dicta. The question is whether they are soundly based in principle, having regard to the framework and structure of the law of property

F   in Scots law.

I believe that the answer to this question lies in the distinction between the law of property and the law of obligations. This is one of the most fundamental of all the divisions which exist in our law. It is upon this division that a proper understanding of the distinction between real rights and personal rights depends. Real rights and personal rights differ both in their origin and subject-matter and in the way in which they are

G   created and transferred. A competition between the purchaser of heritage and the holder of a security over the same property which was created by the seller of it requires a careful examination of the point in time at which the ownership of the heritage passes from the seller to the purchaser.

In the typical case of a fixed security, the problem is resolved by the application of the principle that parties dealing with each other in good faith are entitled to proceed upon the information in the public register. Where there is a competition between unrecorded

H   titles or fixed securities, the preference is accorded to him who succeeds in the race to the register. In the case of a floating charge however there is no such race nor is there reliance on the public register. The floating charge has effect in relation to heritable property in Scotland notwithstanding that the instrument creating it is not recorded in the register of sasines or, as appropriate, registered in the Land Register: *Companies Act* 1985, s. 462(5). Yet its instant effect upon crystallisation is that it attaches, without the need to go first to

the public register, as if it were a fixed security over the property to which it has attached: A
Companies Act 1985, s. 465(2); *Insolvency Act* 1986, s. 53(7), 54(6). As the late Professor
W A Wilson observed, in his article on 'Floating charges', 1962 SLT (News) 53 at p. 55,
the introduction of a security in this form causes problems for the conveyancer. The
problem which he foresaw was that the purchaser of heritage would be affected by the
crystallisation of the floating charge if this were to occur before the disposition in his
favour was recorded. His observation was, I think, based on the assumption that the
right of property remained with the seller until the disposition was recorded or registered   B
in the public register.

The tripartite classification of the Roman law between persons, things and actions was
noted by Stair: I.i.23. In the previous paragraph, I.i.22, he had described the several
rights as three in number, personal liberty, dominion and obligation. He described
dominion as the power of disposal of the creatures in their substance, fruits and use.
Obligation was that which was correspondent to a personal right which, as he put it, was   C
'nothing else but a legal tie, whereby the debtor may be compelled to pay or perform
something, to which he is bound by obedience to guard, or by his own consent and
engagement'. Dominion, by contrast, was called a real right, 'because it respecteth things
directly, but persons, as they have meddled with those things'. In this brief discussion the
same distinction is made between real rights and personal rights as is to be found in later
authorities. He dealt with personal rights in his treatment of obligations from the   D
beginning of title iii to the end of Book I. In Book II he dealt with real rights in his
treatment of dominion, or the law of property. The same division of treatment was
followed by Erskine and by Bankton. Erskine dealt in Book II with the law of property
and in Book III with the law of obligations. His definitions in II.i.1 of the real right as
'the right of using and disposing of a subject as our own, except in so far as we are
restrained by law or paction', and in III.i.2 of rights found in obligation as 'a legal tie by
which one is bound to pay or perform something to another', follow the description   E
previously given by Stair. There then follows this passage in Erskine III.i.2:

> 'From the above definition, the essential difference may be perceived between
> rights that affect a subject itself, which are called *real*, and those which are founded
> in obligation, or, as they are generally styled, *personal*. A real right, or *jus in re*,
> whether of property or of an inferior kind – as servitude – entitles the person vested
> with it to possess the subject as his own; or, if it be possessed by another, to   F
> demand it from the possessor, in consequence of the right which he hath in the
> subject itself; whereas the creditor in a personal right or obligation has only a *jus
> ad rem*, or a right of action against the debtor or his representatives, by which they
> may be compelled to fulfil that obligation, but without any right in the subject
> which the debtor is obliged to transfer to him.'

The distinction between real rights and personal rights was the subject of an   G
observation by Professor T B Smith, *A Short Commentary on the Law of Scotland* (1962)
at p. 278, where he said:

> 'The Objects of Law may either be Real Rights (or Property) which may be
> vindicated generally, or Personal Rights (Obligations) which may be created with
> a view to transferring Real Rights, but in general create rights and duties only
> between the parties or their assignees.'   H

It is described also in the introduction to Professor KGC Reid's important title on
property law in 18 *Stair Memorial Encyclopaedia*, para. 1–3. In my opinion Mr Mackay
for the pursuers was well founded when he said that the distinction between the law of
obligations and of property was fundamental to the operation of our law. Where there is
interaction between a real and a personal right this is because the owner of a real right

A   may create by paction a right in others, the effect of which will be to restrain him in his
right to use or dispose of the subject as his own.

The classification noted by the institutional writers provides no support for Mr
Hamilton's argument that there is an intermediate, or incomplete, right which lies
between the personal right on the one hand and the real right on the other. According to
their classification a transaction for the transfer of ownership in a thing depends for its
B   enforceability upon paction, and it is not until the transaction is completed by delivery
that the real right is transferred. That, in regard to a transaction relating to heritage, was
clearly the view of Erskine, who stated in II.iii.48:

C
> 'A charter or disposition which is not followed by seisin, creates in the disponee a
> right barely personal. It lays the granter, and his heirs, under an obligation to
> divest themselves agreeably to the tenor of the grant. But it has not the effect of
> transferring to the acquirer the feudal right of the lands; and consequently, the
> subject may be affected and carried off from the disponee, before his taking
> infeftment, by any debt or diligence which is capable of divesting the disponer, in
> whom the feudal right of the land still continues vested. A creditor or purchaser,
> therefore, contracting with one who has a bare personal right to the subject, rests
> not on the security of the records, but contracts at his peril, and must accept of the
> right as it stands, with all its burdens, and be affected with every declaration or
D   > deed, however latent, that could affect his author. But from the moment that the
> author perfects his right by seisin, the grantee, if he purchases from the true
> proprietor, acquires a complete real right in the subject; which therefore secures
> him, as soon as his own right is perfected by seisin, against the consequence of all
> deeds, even seisins themselves, the registration of which is posterior, though the
> charters that they proceed upon should be prior in date to his.'

E   The question whether there was a distinction between a jus ad rem and a jus crediti,
the former being a right of a higher class, was considered by the House of Lords in
Edmond v Gordon (1858) 3 Macq 116. The jus ad rem was described by Lord Cranworth
at p. 122 as a right 'which the person possessing it may make a complete right by his own
act, or by some act which he may compel another, without a suit to perform'; whereas a
jus crediti was a right which the holder of it cannot make available without suit, if
resisted, in order to make the right perfect. While he saw this practical distinction between
F   the two rights, Lord Cranworth was unable to find anything which definitely explained
the distinction between them. Lord Wensleydale said at p. 130 that whether the personal
right, which the bankrupt unquestionably had to the lands in that case, was treated as a
jus ad rem or as a jus crediti was immaterial, and added:

> 'It is at all events clearly nothing but a personal right, and if, whatever may be its
> proper designation, it passed by the assignation contained in the heritable bond, it
G   > can make no difference in the case.'

The reference by Erskine to the purchasers acquiring 'a complete' real right by sasine,
and to his 'perfecting' his right by this means was founded upon by Mr Hamilton in
support of his argument that there was an intermediate right, distinct from the purely
personal right which preceded the delivery of the disposition, which, being of the same
nature as a right of ownership, was capable of being made real by the modern equivalents
H   of sasine. The same wording appears in the speech of Lord Cranworth in *Edmond v
Gordon* at p. 122 and 123, and in several other cases to which we were referred. In my
opinion this argument reads too much into the use of these words. Erskine at least is
clear as to the distinction between real and personal rights, and there is no suggestion
anywhere in his discussion that there is something which could be described as an
intermediate right of ownership in the subject matter which falls short of a real right.
What he is talking about in II.iii.48 is perfecting the personal right by the acquisition of

a real right in the subject. The personal right is incomplete because it does not have the effect of transferring the feudal right in the lands to the grantee. It is the acquisition of the real right which concludes the transaction and makes it perfect, by transferring ownership in the subject to the purchaser. This alone secures him against the consequences of all deeds the registration of which are posterior to his.

The discussion of this matter in Baron Hume's *Lectures*, in the Stair Society edition, supports this approach. In vol. II at p. 2 he states:

'We have thus, in those several situations, rights which arise upon grounds and connections that are materially different from each other, and which may therefore be expected to be attended with different qualities and effects in law. This accordingly is the case. Rights are divided in all regular systems of law into real and personal, as they arise from one of these sources or the other; and these are very different from each other in their ways of operating and applying.'

As to the distinction between the two he goes on to say this on the same page–

'The owner's right was not founded on any relation, contracted to this or t'other individual. It was founded on a connection formed with the thing itself, independently of all personal considerations, and without regard to the will, consent, or situation of anyone. This class of rights, which follow and are exerted over their ultimate objects everywhere, without respect of persons or circumstances, are therefore with propriety termed real rights.

Those rights, again, that spring from a connection which is formed with an individual, have for that reason a much more limited and uncertain operation. In these, as in all other instances of right, there is to be sure a corresponding obligation somewhere; but it lies in this case with that individual alone who has been applied to or bargained with as the means of getting at the thing. He, to be sure, in return for what he has received, or in fulfilment of the expectations he has raised, is bound to make good his word, and put me in possession of the thing in question. But with respect to all the rest of the world, who have had no sort of concern with this bargain of mine, and are probably ignorant even of any such having been made; I have no manner of claim nor bond upon them to repair my loss or consider my disappointment. If, therefore, in contempt of his word, the person with whom I have bargained for this thing shall afterwards again deal with another person for it, and actually deliver it to him in consequence, I cannot here, as in the case of a real right, apply to this possessor and insist on his surrendering of his acquisition. My remedy is only by an action of damages for the want of it, against the person, his author, whose wrong has occasioned me the disappointment.'

In my opinion this passage accurately describes the position in which the holder of the unrecorded disposition finds himself if he loses the race to the register with an adjudger or a subsequent disponee transacting with his author in good faith and for value. Hume is equally clear in vol. III, p. 245 about the requirement of delivery, real or symbolic, to transfer the real right:

'The natural way of transferring property, whether moveable or immoveable, is by an agreement to convey as in property, followed with delivery, real or symbolical, of the thing. These two circumstances (I have said) must concur in any case towards transference of the real right. The delivery of possession shall not transfer it, unless it follow on a suitable contract, on a habile title for transference of property, such as sale, gift or barter, in contra-distinction to the more limited titles of loan, pledge, deposit, or the like. On the other hand, the mere consent or agreement to convey as in property is equally ineffectual to transfer, unless this be followed with delivery and possession: so that if one sell the same subject successively to two persons, he

A shall have the property, in whose favour delivery is made, although on the posterior contract. The prior vendee has his claim of damages only against the vendor for breach of bargain. This plainly is the expedient as well as the equitable and natural rule of preference. Without delivery, the buyer does not form any real connection with the thing, to make his claim attach on it. And possession is a substantial and an ouvert circumstance, the outward evidence of right to guide and direct third parties conveniently, easily and safely in these transactions with the possessor. It is

B the only ready, practicable, and suitable and patent criterion of right.'

The position of the adjudging creditor was considered in *Mitchell v Ferguson* (1781) Mor 10296. The competition in that case was between David and Hugh Mitchell, creditors of the common author William Donald, and William Ferguson, to whom an unrecorded disposition of the house had been assigned by its purchaser. Ferguson was the prior disponee but his title was unrecorded. According to the narrative of the case he

C had a personal right only. The Mitchells were posterior adjudgers but their diligence was completed by infeftment. The court held that the adjudication and the infeftment following upon it were preferable to 'the personal disposal' founded on by Ferguson. It is clear from that decision that the court accepted the adjudger's argument that personal deeds cannot affect feudal rights. The same point was developed by Hume, vol. IV, pp. 182–183:

D 'Let us now return one step farther back on the investiture, and suppose, that charter only has been given, or disposition executed, but that no seisin has followed. You will here anticipate the consequence which is, that there is no real investiture, but the constitution only of an ordinary personal right or jus ad rem to the lands – such a right as is good, indeed, against the granter and his heir, or others who come into his place, and are liable to the like personal objection as he, – but which shall not stand the test of trial with any perfect investiture acquired by

E a third party, who has no concern with and is not reached by that objection. The deed of conveyance, not followed with seisin, which is the feudal delivery of the lands (and as necessary as the real delivery is in the case of moveable corpora) is a mere expression of consent; neither divests the disponer nor really qualifies, nor intrinsically limits his previous feudal right to the lands. Being still vested with that feudal right he can, therefore, effectually make it over to another, who can defend himself therein, and maintain his right.'

F It was submitted by Mr Young for the second defenders that it was not to be taken from that decision that all property rights remained with the seller following delivery of the disposition to the purchaser. All that was needed to explain the decision was that some property rights remained with him, in the form of a residual right sufficient to enable the adjudger to become infeft. Mr Hamilton submitted that the case depended for its decision on the principle that the adjudger was entitled to the benefit of the register,

G not upon the assumption that there was no divestiture to any extent of the common author in his right of property. In my opinion, however, it is sufficiently clear from this decision that it was based on the proposition that until the disposition was recorded the purchaser had a personal right only and was not vested with a real right in the property. That in any event is Hume's analysis of the position, which in my opinion is entirely consistent with the structure of the law. It is significant also that what the adjudger obtained on recording his decree in the public register was a real right in the property to

H the entire exclusion of the purchaser. There was no contractual or other relationship between the adjudger and the purchaser, so the decision is explicable on the basis only that the right of ownership remained throughout with the seller and that the purchaser's rights were personal only and not in any respect rights of ownership.

This view of the matter is supported further by the opinion of the majority of the consulted judges in *Young v Leith* (1844) 6 D 370; (1847) 9 D 932 which was later affirmed

by the House of Lords: see 2 Ross's Leading Cases 81. The Lord Ordinary has described   A
the issue which arose for decision in that case at p. 76D; 1081K–L, and I do not need to
repeat what he has said. It may be, helpful however, to put the case into its historical
context, to note the stage which the law of Scotland had then reached in regard to the
steps necessary to transfer property in land.

This subject is dealt with in the Lord Ordinary's opinion at pp. 59–60 and 77; 1073L–
1074G and 1082K–L, and a more detailed outline of the history is to be found in 18 *Stair*   B
Memorial Encyclopaedia para. 87–93. I think that it is sufficient for present purposes to
note that Scots law has always required a public act of some kind to transfer property in
land. This step is the equivalent of *traditio* in the case of moveables. It is an essential step
in the process of transferring ownership, according to the maxim *traditionibus non nudis
pactis transferuntur rerum dominia*. Originally there were three steps: (1) the execution of
a charter containing a *de praesenti* dispositive act of the disponer; (2) delivery of that
charter to the disponee; and (3) seisin, which was the formal public ceremony, enacted on   C
the land in question, by which the land was delivered to the disponee by handing over to
him the symbols of earth and stone. In the fifteenth century a further solemnity was
added to this list: (4) the execution of an instrument of sasine prepared by a notary who
was present to record the ceremony in a notarial instrument, as the only competent
evidence of the fact that seisin had been taken: Hume's *Lectures*, vol. IV, p. 167. Then,
by the *Registration Act* 1617 (cap 16): (5) registration of the instrument of sasine and   D
public register within 60 days was made compulsory. The penalty of non-registration
within the prescribed period was that the unregistered writings,

> 'shall make no faith in judgment, by way of action or exception, in prejudice of a
> third party, who hath acquired an perfete and lauchful right to the said lands and
> heritages; but prejudice to use the said writtes against the party-maker thereof, his
> heirs and successors.'   E

It was the effect to be given to that provision that was the principal issue for decision
in *Young v Leith*. Reforms introduced during the nineteenth century, by the *Infeftment
Act* 1845 and the *Titles to Land Act* 1858, made it possible to dispense with steps (3) and
(4). So the ceremony of sasine and the execution and registration of an instrument of
sasine might be, and in practice are now always, omitted. But it was not sufficient for the
transfer of property to carry out only steps (1) and (2). Step (5) was the statutory   F
equivalent of sasine, the fundamental importance of which is recognised in the maxim
nulla sasina nulla terra: Stair II.iii.16.

Young v Leith, of course, was concerned with the situation immediately prior to the
introduction of the first of the two reforms by which steps (3) and (4) were dispensed
with. Despite the opinion of the majority of the consulted judges in *Kibble v Stevenson* 23
September 1831 (see 2 Ross's Leading Cases at p. 109), the wording of the Act 1617, cap   G
16 continued to give rise to some uncertainty as to whether an unregistered sasine was a
nullity in regard to the transfer of the real right to the grantee. That issue was resolved
by the decision of the House of Lords in *Young v Leith* in conformity with the opinion of
the majority of the consulted judges that the unregistered sasine was an absolute nullity.
Lord Campbell observed at pp. 107–108:

> 'and I am very glad that this is the result, because it is in accordance with that most   H
> excellent principle which prevails in Scotland, that everything shall be recorded –
> that all titles are to be traced by recorded sasines – and that you are not in danger
> of being misled or deceived by anything to which there is not a plain and open
> access; and, therefore, I am very glad that the result is such as my noble and
> learned friend proposes, and that now, on the authority of this House, it will be
> clearly taken as the law of Scotland, that unrecorded sasines are a nullity.'

A   Mr Hamilton submitted that the issue which was decided in *Young v Leith* was not the question for decision in this case. He said that it was concerned only with the question as to the steps necessary to divest the granter of the heritable right and to invest that right in the grantee: see Lord Fullerton's opinion at p. 937. The comment at p. 938 that every feudal grant must necessarily remain incomplete and personal until it be perfected by sasine was a further indication to this effect. Although the discussion at pp. 944–945 was plainly obiter, the references here to the completion of a real right, in a question between

B   granter and grantee, showed that the issue was between a completed real right in one party and an incomplete real right in the other. The case was, he said, of no assistance where, as here, the issue was whether the heritage was the property of the grantee not that of the grantor once the disposition had been delivered to the grantee.

       I have already said that in my view the arguments relating to the use of the phrase 'complete real right' read too much into the use of these words. But on closer examination

C   of the opinion delivered by Lord Fullerton, it is, I think, clear beyond question that the judges in that case were intent in resolving the issue of what was required to divest the grantee of his right of property and to invest a right in the grantee. I agree with the Lord Ordinary's analysis of the case at p. 77H; 1082F–J. Lord Fullerton drew a clear distinction at p. 937 between real rights and personal rights, in a passage where he applied to instruments of sasines the spirit of the provisions of the Act in regard to reversions

D   and the other writings enumerated:

> 'Now, as to the latter, there can be no doubt that the failure to register did, by taking them out of the Act 1469, absolutely annul them as real rights, though it left them operative as personal obligations. And applying the same construction to the provision as to [instruments] of seisin, those instruments must be held to be annulled as constituting real rights, whatever personal obligation may possibly be left behind – whether positive, binding the granter and his heirs to complete the

E   right, or negative, barring those parties from objecting to its non-completion.'

       At p. 938 he went on to say:

> 'The existence of the unregistered sasine does not prevent the party who "hath not, as yet, a perfect right to the lands," from making his right perfect, by taking seisin on the conveyance in his favour; and the reason is obvious, because the grantee in the second right has the means of completing a perfect right, with which the

F   unregistered seisin cannot enter into a competition.'

       Although he refers at pp. 938 and 945, among other passages, to the completion of the real right, it is plain from the decision as a whole that what he is talking about is the constitution of the real right in the grantee – a phrase which he himself used at p. 941. Then there is the following passage at p. 945 which draws the discussion of this point to a conclusion:

G   'The operation of a personal right, founded on an unregistered seisin, whether by way of obligation against the granter of the precept to do something, or as a personal bar against the granter, pleading that something has not been done by the grantee, is quite intelligible. But a completed real right, good in a question between granter and grantee, and bad against all the rest of the world, is an absolute legal contradiction in terms. For it is of the very essence of a real right

H   that it shall be good against all claiming from the same author; who, by giving a complete real right to one, is understood to be divested of all power of giving it to another. He cannot be divested, till the grantee is fully vested. An intermediate state of things, which leaves the granter's own seisin entire, as retaining the real right in him, while at the very same time, another real right in the identical fee is completed in the person of the grantee, is an absolute incongruity, according to the principles of our law.

It would appear to us, then, that the only effect which a seisin, bad against all third   A
parties, can have against the granter or his heirs, is a merely personal effect, like
that of the other writings referred to in the statute.'

In my opinion it is plain from that decision, taken together with *Mitchell v Ferguson*,
the institutional writers and the illuminating discussion in Hume's *Lectures*, that Scots
law does not recognise a right which lies between the personal right on the one hand and
the real right on the other. A personal right, once created, is of course a species of   B
incorporeal property, which can be transmitted from one person to another by
assignation. But it remains at all times a right based solely on the law of obligations, until
it is replaced by the real right which alone invests the grantee with a right of property in
the thing which is the subject of the transaction. Various steps are necessary to complete
the transaction from start to finish, and each step is different. But there is no such thing
as a real right which is imperfect or incomplete. Until the real right is transferred the   C
matter rests entirely upon personal obligation.

The contrary dicta

Much of the argument both before the Lord Ordinary and before us was taken up with
an examination of a series of cases where views have been expressed, with varying degrees
of emphasis and clarity, which may appear to be contrary to the opinion which I have
just set out. I have found it difficult to isolate all these cases into distinct groups, although   D
there is one group of which the leading example is Lord President Emslie's dictum in
Gibson v Hunter Home Designs Ltd and another which is composed of cases about what
constitutes ownership of heritable property for the purposes of establishing that the
defender is subject to the jurisdiction of the Scottish court. I shall deal first with these two
groups in that order, and then deal with what seemed to me to be the more important of
the remaining cases to which we were referred. I shall conclude this chapter with a
reference to *Heritable Reversionary Co Ltd v Millar* (1892) 19 R (HL) 43 and *Bank of*   E
Scotland v Liquidators of Hutchison Main & Co Ltd 1914 SC (HL) 1, in order to see how
the important dicta in those cases affect the opinion which I have formed on the
fundamental issue of principle.

In *Gibson v Hunter Home Designs Ltd* Lord President Emslie described the three stages
in the transfer of land from the seller to the purchaser in these terms (at p. 27):

'In the law of Scotland no right of property vests in a purchaser until there has   F
been delivered to him the relevant disposition. On delivery of the disposition the
purchaser becomes vested in a personal right to the subjects in question and his
acquisition of a real right to the subjects is dependent upon recording the
disposition in the appropriate Register of Sasines. Putting the matter in another
way the seller of subjects under missives is not, in a question with the purchaser,
divested of any part of his right of property in the subjects of sale until, in   G
implement of his contractual obligation to do so, he delivers to the purchaser the
appropriate disposition.'

There can be no dispute about the analysis as to the first stage, which is the stage when
missives are completed, or the third stage, which is when the real right is obtained by
recording the disposition in the appropriate register. The difficulty arises at the second
stage, in defining the position of the holder of a delivered but unrecorded disposition.
The dictum appears to recognise that by delivering the disposition to the purchaser the   H
seller divests himself of some part of his right of property in the subject with which the
purchaser is thereby invested. If it is read in this way, the proposition cannot be reconciled
with the opinion of the majority of the consulted judges in *Young v Leith*, and it is in
conflict with the view that there can be no passing of the real right until registration. As
Professor KCG Reid has pointed out in 18 *Stair Memorial Encyclopaedia*, para. 603,

A Scots law, following Roman law, is unititular, which means that only one title of ownership is recognised in any one thing at any one time. Although this title can be shared, as in the case of common property, only one person can be the owner in competition with others about ownership. There is no opportunity for fragmentation of the concept of ownership, as the transfer of ownership one to the other occurs in a single moment which, in the case of heritable property, is that of recording the disposition in the appropriate register.

B

In *Lombardi's Trustee v Lombardi* 1982 SLT 81 Lord Jauncey, following Lord President Emslie's dictum, said that it was trite law that a disponer of the subject does not divest himself of any right of property in those subjects until he delivers the disposition to the disponee. The dictum was quoted with approval by Lord Grieve in *Macdonald v Scott's Executors* 1981 SC 75 and by Lord Allanbridge in *Leeds Permanent Building Society v Aitken, Malone & Mackay* 1985 SC 375, and I did the same thing in

C my opinion in *Margrie Holdings Ltd v C & E Commrs* 1991 SLT 38 at p. 41E. But in none of these cases was the dictum subject to critical analysis, and none of them was concerned with its application at the second stage. These observations were therefore plainly obiter, but so also was Lord President Emslie's description of the second stage as *Gibson* was concerned with a transaction which had not proceeded beyond the stage of completion of the missives. The feu disposition had not been delivered prior to the

D commencement of the liquidation of the company. It was not necessary in that case to analyse the position of the holder of a delivered disposition prior to the recording of it in the appropriate register. Lord Cameron said nothing in his opinion which can be taken to support Lord President Emslie's description of what happens at the second stage. His observation at p. 30, that even if the obligation to convey the subjects has been so far implemented as by delivery of a conveyance or disposition an adjudger infeft before the disponee will be preferred, suggests that he did not see any part of the seller's right of

E property in the subject as passing to the purchaser at that stage.

From the note of the argument in *Gibson* it appears that neither *Mitchell v Ferguson* nor *Young v Leith* were cited in the course of the debate in that case. It also shows that the source for the analysis of the second stage by Lord President Emslie can be traced back to the opinion of Lord Justice Clerk Grant in *Embassy Picture House (Troon) Ltd v Cammo Developments Ltd* 1971 SC 25, which was cited in *Gibson*, where he said, at

F p. 28:

> 'In my opinion, there is a fundamental distinction between the position of a person who has a personal right under a disposition and that of one whose right derives solely from missives of sale upon which no delivered disposition has followed. The former right is clearly a right of ownership, even if feudal infeftment has not followed and even although, until infeftment follows, it is a right which is to some

G extent at peril and which might indeed, in certain circumstances, be lost.'

Here again, however, the dictum was obiter and *Young v Leith* was not among the authorities to which the court was referred in the course of the argument. The case was concerned only with the question of jurisdiction in the sheriff court. Section 6(d) of the *Sheriff Courts (Scotland) Act* 1907 provides that the sheriff court has jurisdiction 'where the defender is the owner . . . of heritable property within that jurisdiction, and the action

H relates to such property and to his interest therein'. The action was for implement of missives of sale of heritable property, and it was held that the concluded bargain constituted by the missives did not make the defenders owners of the property within the meaning of s. 6(d). It was conceded in the argument for the pursuers that the concept of 'owner' for jurisdiction purposes was not confined to possessors of a full feudal right, and reference was made to the cases about the jurisdiction of the Court of Session which established that when an absolute conveyance was granted the grantor of it ceased to be

subject to the jurisdiction even although he had not been feudally divested. It is important   A
also to note that the case was not one which involved a competition between two persons
deriving right from the same author as to who was the owner of the subjects for the time
being.

In my opinion the dictum in *Gibson* as to what happens at the second stage in the
transaction when the disposition is delivered to the purchaser was not, with great respect,
entirely accurate. It proceeded upon an incomplete examination of the distinction   B
between the personal rights conferred on the purchaser by the seller at each of the first
two stages and the real right in the subjects, which can be obtained only at the third stage
by recording the disposition in the public register. At the second stage the purchaser is
no doubt in a stronger position then he was at the stage when the missives were
completed. He has secured performance by the seller of the obligation to deliver to him a
duly executed disposition of the subjects and all other deeds necessary for settlement of
the transaction. His possession of the disposition puts it in his power, without the need   C
to take any further steps to implement the contract, to go to the register and obtain the
real right. He can grant a conveyance of the property and create an effective security over
it to which the grantee, if he proceeds first to the register, may obtain a good title by
virtue of s. 5 of the *Conveyancing (Scotland) Act* 1924. But the relationship remains
essentially a personal one between the seller and the purchaser. The right of ownership
remains vested in the seller so long as he retains the real right. All that can be said is that
he is restricted in the exercise of his rights of ownership by his contract with the purchaser.   D
At the first stage the contract is to be found in the missives. At the second stage the
contract is to be found in the disposition which, according to the rule in *Lee v Alexander*
(1882) 10 R 230, has superseded the missives and become the sole measure of the rights
and liabilities between the parties.

I turn now to the jurisdiction cases, although I have little to say about them because I
agree with the Lord Ordinary's observation at p. 80E; 1084G that they do not assist in   E
resolving the issues in the present case. The difference between cases where there is a
competition about ownership and cases as to whether the defender is subject to the
jurisdiction is plain to see from Lord President Inglis' opinion in *Fraser v Fraser &
Hibbert* (1870) 8 M 400 at p. 404 where he said:

> 'It is also clearly settled by a chain of decisions that the nature of the defender's
> title is of no importance to the question of jurisdiction. It does not need to be a   F
> complete feudal title. A personal right on a disposition is as good a title as an
> infeftment. The mere title of apparency, without any possession, has been held
> sufficient. In other cases the possession of a bare superiority, of no pecuniary value,
> has been held sufficient. Lastly, a beneficial interest in lands held under trust has
> been held sufficient to found jurisdiction. It is plain, therefore, that the nature of
> the title is not important.'
>   G

Later on the same page he expressed the opinion that the beneficial possession, whether
natural or civil, of a moveable estate within the realm, whether permanently or
temporarily, upon a good title of possession, was sufficient to found jurisdiction. In
Bowman v Wright (1877) 4 R 322 it was held that a proprietor of heritage in Scotland
ceases to be subject to the jurisdiction of the Scottish courts when he grants an absolute
conveyance of the subject, although he has not been feudally divested. Some of the dicta
in that case may seem at first sight to support the second defender's argument, for the   H
reasons explained in more detail by Lord Coulsfield. Lord Justice Clerk Moncreiff said
at p. 325 that the seller had ceased to be the proprietor,

> 'for he had sold what he previously had, and the right to it was vested in the
> purchaser, so far at least as he, Wright, was concerned. I do not think that it
> matters that under the Act of 1617, cap 17, the disponee's right might have been

A   evacuated in favour of a second bona fide purchaser first infeft, or might have been
burdened by a lease granted after the date of the disposition. These are rights which
the Legislature has thought proper to confer on bona fide purchasers, taking
advantage of our system of registration, and upon tenants, but not rights remaining
in the original seller, who has done all he could to divest himself.'

Lord Ormidale also said at p. 326 that ,the seller was 'neither the owner nor possessor
B   of heritable estate in Scotland' at the time the action was raised, and at p. 327 that it was
impossible to hold that the defender was 'in any fair or correct sense', when the action
was raised, the owner or the possessor of the subject. But in my opinion these
observations cannot stand alongside the opinion of the majority in *Young v Leith*. The
observations of the Lord Justice Clerk are almost indistinguishable from those of Lord
Medwyn in that case at p. 969, and he was one of the minority. In *Dowie & Co v Tennant*
(1891) 18 R 986 missives had been entered into and conveyance of the subjects in favour
C   of the purchaser had been executed. But it was still in the post from America on the
critical date. It was held that the transfer of the subjects had not been completed and the
seller's plea of no jurisdiction was repelled. The case is important here only because of
the observations of Lord McLaren at pp. 988–989 which might seem to indicate that in
his opinion delivery of the deed to the purchaser was sufficient to transfer the property to
the grantee. But this adds nothing to what was said in *Bowman*, and in my opinion must
D   be taken to be an incorrect analysis where the question arises in a competition between
two persons as to who is the owner of the subjects which are in dispute. The more recent
cases of *Caledonian Fish Selling Marine Stores Co Ltd v Allard Hewson & Co Ltd* 1970
SLT 195 and *Embassy Picture House (Troon) Ltd v Cammo Developments Ltd* show that
it is now well established in this field that interest in heritable property based on the
theory of effectiveness as described by Lord Hunter in *Caledonian*, will be sufficient to
found jurisdiction against the defender. But it is not possible consistently with *Young v*
E   *Leith* to extend the application of these decisions or any of the dicta in them to the point
at issue in this case.

Among the other cases to which we were referred were *James Grant & Co Ltd v Moran*
1948 SLT (Sh Ct) 8 and *Thomas v Lord Advocate* 1953 SC 151. Counsel for the second
defenders relied strongly on the observations of Lord Patrick in *Thomas v Lord Advocate*
at p. 161 which, they said, supported the argument that delivery of the disposition to the
F   disponee had the effect of transferring rights of property from the disponer to the
disponee and that these rights were rights of a different kind from those conferred by the
missives because they could be made real by recording the disposition in the appropriate
register. The question in that case was whether the appellant's father had made a gift to
him of certain heritable subjects more than five years before his death which was effective
to exclude those subjects from the property which was deemed to pass on his death for
the purposes of estate duty. In order to be effective for that purpose, in terms of the
G   relevant legislation relating to estate duty, bona fide possession and enjoyment of the
property taken under the gift had to be assumed by the donee immediately upon the gift
and thereafter retained, to the entire exclusion of the donor of any benefit to him by
contract or otherwise.

Lord Justice Clerk Thomson dealt with the case at p. 158 on a basis which is, I think,
entirely in accordance with the pursuers' approach to the problem raised in the present
case. He said that it was beyond doubt that when the disposition was delivered to him
H   the donee obtained something which was of undoubted value, namely the personal right
to the lands, which was property taken under a gift, bona fide possession and enjoyment
of which he immediately assumed. This approach looks to the subject-matter of the gift,
namely the rights which were created in the donee, and to the vesting of those rights in
him on delivery of the disposition to the entire exclusion of the donor. It is not concerned
with the question whether the donor had divested himself of his rights of property in the

subjects or of any part of them. It is consistent with a gift which depended entirely upon   A
the creation of personal rights as between donor or donee which were effective to exclude
the donor, in a question with the donee, from the possession and enjoyment of the
property. Lord Patrick however set out at p. 161 his analysis of the effect of the delivery
of the disposition:

> 'Immediately on delivery of the disposition to the disponee there passed to him all
> the interests of the disponer in the lands. At once the transfer is complete, as   B
> between disponee and disponer, and the latter can no longer deal with the interests
> which he formerly possessed in the lands, except by a disposition in fraud of the
> disponee . . . It does not seem possible to contend that on delivery of such a
> disposition no property passes to the disponee. All the property the disponer had
> passes at once. Recording of the disposition in the Register of Sasines will only
> make real a right which was previously personal. As between disponer and
> disponee the transfer of all the former's interests is at once complete upon delivery   C
> of the disposition and, if the disposition is gratuitous, the gift of such interests in
> land as the disponer had to give is complete.'

Later, on the same page, Lord Patrick said that immediately upon delivery of the
disposition to the donee there passed to him all the interests the donor previously had in
the lands, and at p. 162 he said that the gift was conferred by the direct conveyance to
the donee of the property passing under the gift. These passages show that Lord Patrick   D
was thinking in terms of divestiture by the donor to the donee of his interest in the lands
and that he saw the disposition as having that effect immediately upon its delivery to the
donee. I do not think that his observations can be regarded as obiter. They were the basis
for his decision in favour of the appellant that the contention for the Crown was unsound.
But in my opinion they do not stand up to the close analysis which is required in the
present case under reference to *Mitchell v Ferguson* and *Young v Leith*, which were not
cited in that case. They cannot be regarded as a sound statement of the law to be applied   E
to a case such as the present where the question of rights of ownership of the lands is
directly in issue as between two parties who are competing with each other in regard to
those rights. The observation by Sheriff Substitute Allan G Walker in *James Grant & Co
v Moran* that a purchaser who obtains a valid disposition from a seller with immediate
entry then becomes for the first time 'the owner of the property' is consistent with the
approach taken by Lord Patrick, but for similar reasons I do not think that any weight
can be attached to it in the present context.   F

I do not find it necessary to say much in this chapter about *Heritable Reversionary Co
Ltd v Millar* and *Bank of Scotland v Liquidators of Hutchison, Main & Co Ltd* or *Union
Bank of Scotland Ltd v National Bank of Scotland Ltd* (1886) 14 R (HL) 1 to which we
were also referred. These cases were grouped together by Mr Hamilton as dealing in
various respects with the doctrine of apparent ownership. The *Union Bank* case was
concerned with a right in security constituted by a disposition which was *ex facie* absolute   G
together with a back letter which was not recorded. *Millar* was concerned with the
question whether heritable property vested in a bankrupt, which was subject to a latent
trust, passed to the trustees in his sequestration free of that trust to be held for distribution
among his personal creditors. *Hutchison Main* was concerned with a claim by the bank
in the liquidation of the company under a debenture in its favour which the company
was under a contractual obligation to assign to it but which had not yet been assigned to   H
the bank. In the *Union Bank* case there was a discussion of the nature of the transaction
by which heritable property was disponed absolutely in security, especially in regard to
the nature of the right of the disponer in a question with the disponee. Lord Watson said
at p. 4 of that, apart from considerations of feudal law, the radical right remained with
the disponer in the sense that, according to the reality of the transaction, she was the only
person who had a proprietary interest in the subjects of the security. In *Millar* the

A   relationship was that between a bare trustee, formally vested in the heritable estate of the
     trust under a title *ex facie* absolute, and the beneficiaries under the trust. It was held that
     the heritable estate did not belong to the bare trustee, as the beneficiaries were the true
     and beneficial owners of the property, so it did not pass to the trustee in his sequestration
     as his 'property' within the meaning of the Act. A distinction was drawn both by Lord
     Herschell at p. 44 and by Lord Watson at p. 51 between the case of a latent trust by
B   which the owner appearing on the register is a bare trustee, and that where the owner is
     under a contractual obligation, or mere personal contract, to convey the property to
     another. In *Hutchison Main* the personal obligation to assign the debenture to the bank
     was held to be nothing more than an unfulfilled promise which did not have the effect of
     depriving the company of its beneficial interest in the property.

         Mr Hamilton accepted that none of these cases were dealing with the situation which
     arises in this case. His argument, following a point which had been developed by Mr
C   Young in regard to *Millar* and *Hutchison Main*, was that they provided support for the
     view that it was possible, at stage two in the *Gibson* analysis, to separate out the position
     of the true owner from that of the apparent owner, in recognition of a relationship which
     was different from that which in terms of pure property law would apply. In any event,
     he said, there was nothing in any of the dicta in these cases which contradicted his
     argument. The references in *Millar* to the contractual obligation or mere personal
D   contract were dealing with stage one in the *Gibson* analysis, not with stage two. They also
     supported the view that the word 'property', where used in a statute or instrument, does
     not have a fixed or technical meaning but should be construed according to the reality of
     the situation. This was important to the background to the argument which he was to
     submit about the proper construction of the provisions of the statute in this case and
     those of the floating charge.

E   It is true that there are dicta in all three cases which may be used to support the view
     that a distinction can be drawn between the apparent title and the beneficial interest in
     the property where questions arise as to who is owner of it. But here again the analogy
     which the second defenders seek to draw from these dicta seems to me to break down on
     closer analysis. In the *Union Bank* case Lord Watson at p. 4 recognised that in form the
     right of the disponer under the back letter was a personal right, and he made it clear, in
     his description of the radical right, that he was not proceeding upon feudal principles. I
F   do not think that one can, with safety, draw any conclusion from his observations in that
     case in support of the arguments which the second defenders wish to advance about the
     effect of the delivery of the disposition to the disponee by a person who was undoubtedly
     the owner of the property on entering into the transaction which he was thereby
     implementing. In *Millar* the only question which required to be decided was whether the
     heritable property was the 'property' of the debtor, within the meaning of that expression
     as used in s. 102 of the *Bankruptcy Act* 1856. The decision that it was not his property in
G   the sense of the Act was based on dicta, endorsed in *Hutchison Main* by Lord Shaw of
     Dunfermline, which may seem to have a wider significance. But in *Inland Revenue v
     Clark's Trustees* 1939 SC 11 Lord President Normand said at p. 22 that the right of a
     beneficiary under a trust was 'nothing more than a personal right to sue the trustees and
     to compel them to administer the trust in accordance with the directions which it
     contains'. This observation was referred to with approval by Lord Keith of Avonholm in
H   *Parker v Lord Advocate* 1960 SC (HL) 29 at p. 41. Lord Moncrieff in *Clark's Trustees* at
     p. 26 said that he had difficulty in seeing how the right of a beneficiary could properly be
     defined, as McLaren had defined it in *Wills and Succession*, II, p. 832, as 'a personal right
     of property in the estate which is the subject of disposition', and then said:

              'In my view, the right of property in the estate of the trust is vested in the trustees
          to the exclusion of any competing right of property, and the right of the beneficiary

... is merely a right in personam against the trustees to enforce their performance   A
of the trust.'

In this matter I agree with the views expressed in Wilson and Duncan, *Trusts, Trustees
and Executors* (1975) at pp. 14 and 15, contrary to the dicta in the cases about apparent
ownership, that the preponderance of authority is to the effect that the property, in the
normal sense, is vested in the trustee. This is consistent with the basic structure of the law
of Scotland as already discussed, which draws a distinction between the law of property   B
and the law of obligations, and with the statement in Bell, *Commentaries*, i, 36 that the
beneficial interest gives only a *jus crediti* or personal action against the trustee. In my
opinion it is not part of the law of Scotland that there exist in the trustee and the
beneficiary concurrent rights of ownership in the property which is subject to the trust.
The argument that there can be a separation of interests of ownership according to what
was described as the reality of the situation is contrary to principle. The doctrine of
apparent ownership seems to me to have no place in a discussion about the effect of the   C
delivery of a disposition of heritable property to the disponee.

The scope of the floating charge

I turn now to what Mr Hamilton recognised was the principal issue in this case, namely
whether, upon a proper construction of the floating charge, the flat was part of the
property and undertaking of Albyn at the date of crystallisation. He said that, although   D
questions of property law arose in this case, the true question was as to the sound
construction of a commercial instrument, executed under powers given by the legislature,
which was designed to secure a practical commercial objective. He said that there was a
danger of losing sight of the essential issue if the rules of what he described as pure
property law were to be applied.

This argument was directed both to the terms of the floating charge itself and to the   E
terms of the statute. The critical phrase, which is to be found both in s. 462(1) of the
Companies Act 1985 and s. 51(1) of the *Insolvency Act* 1986, is contained in the expression
'the property (including uncalled capital) which may from time to time be comprised in
the property and undertaking' of the company. This expression was repeated, without
any significant alteration, in the floating charge which created in favour of the bank a
floating charge over 'the whole of the property (including uncalled capital) which is or
may be from time to time, while this instrument is in force, comprised in our property   F
and undertaking'.

It was submitted by Mr Young for the second defenders that the phrase 'property and
undertaking' should be interpreted in a commercial sense, as meaning the assets of the
company which were being used for the purposes of its business for the time being. He
said that it related essentially to something which was an asset of the company and of
value to it and that, as one would not normally regard heritable property as an asset of   G
the company once the disposition had been delivered to the purchaser, the phrase should
be construed as comprising such property only up to the date of settlement. Mr Hamilton,
while adopting Mr Young's argument, said that the phrase in the statute should receive
a purposive interpretation. He maintained that its proper scope was to include only those
assets which were deployed, or were capable of being deployed, for the purposes of the
business activities of the company, in accordance with the statement of its objects in the   H
company's memorandum. He submitted that the commercial objective, as indicated by
the eighth report of the Law Reform Committee for Scotland on the constitution of
security over moveable property and floating charges (June 1960, Cmnd 1017), was to
make available to Scottish companies the ability to deploy their assets which were subject
to this form of security as they thought fit for the purposes of the company's objects, not
to include within the security items which were irretrievably beyond the scope of its

A property. So in terms of the statute property over which a floating charge could competently be created did not include property which had irrevocably been taken out of what was referred to as the going concern of the company, and the floating charge itself contained within it indications that it was not intended to have any wider scope in regard to the property which was to be subject to the floating charge. Mr Hamilton pointed out that, according to the principles discussed in *Heritable Reversionary Co Ltd v Millar*, property which was subject to a latent trust was excluded from the charge. He said that,

B once this exception was recognised, the universality of the approach based on pure property law could be seen to be flawed. So a purposive approach to the meaning of the statute, and of the floating charge which had taken its language from the statute, was the appropriate one to adopt.

These submissions go to the heart of the controversy which has arisen about this case. Numerous letters and articles have appeared in the *Scots Law Times* news section and

C the *Journal of the Law Society of Scotland* on one side or the other in response to the decision by the Lord Ordinary. These illustrate very clearly the division of opinion on this issue. On the one hand there are those who support the Lord Ordinary's decision on the grounds that it is the result of a correct and inescapable application of the principles of Scots property law – of pure property law, as Mr Hamilton has described it. On the other hand there are those who regard the decision, with varying degrees of emphasis, as

D a grossly unjust result and as an affront to our legal system. They point to the hardship which it creates for the innocent purchaser and to the difficulties to which it gives rise for the conveyancer. We have been urged to correct this injustice by the application of equitable principles and to adopt the purposive approach contended for by Mr Hamilton. It should not be thought that the court is unaware of these arguments or of the importance of the issue for the future development of Scots law. Our task however is to apply the law as we find it, in a way which is consistent with our legal principles. If the

E result is unattractive, the decision will at least provide a secure platform for discussion as to whether the law should be amended so as to improve the position of the uninfeft purchaser.

In my opinion the only conclusion which properly can be drawn from a purposive approach to the phrase as used in the statutes is that these words were intended to give to a Scottish company the widest scope for the creating of a floating charge over its

F property. We were referred to passages in *Palmer's Company Law* (20th edn, 1959) pp. 399–400 to illustrate the historical development of the floating charge in England, and to the broad interpretation which was given to the word 'undertaking' in *Re Panama, New Zealand and Australian Royal Mail Co Ltd* (1870) LR 5 Ch App 318 by Giffard LJ at p. 322 where he said that this word 'had reference to all the property of the company, not only which existed at the date of the debenture, but which might afterwards become the property of the company'. I can find nothing in this history to suggest that a narrow

G approach should be adopted to the meaning of the phrase in the statutes, by the introduction of a test not used there, to confine the charge to assets of one kind or another and thus to exclude what, according to the meaning of the words in their ordinary sense, would otherwise be included in the scope of the charge. Nor is there anything in the discussion of the question over what property it should be competent to create a floating charge in para. 27–30 of the eighth report of the Law Reform Committee to encourage this approach. The recommendation of this committee shows no sign of an

H intention to limit the scope of the charge, nor indeed does the committee seem to have addressed itself to the issue as to whether, in view of the differences between English and Scots property law, this might be desirable. The last two sentences of this discussion, in para. 30, are in these terms:

> 'Moreover in the field of commercial law, unless there is good reason to the contrary, it is desirable that the law of England and Scotland should be the same.

We recommend that it should be competent to grant a floating charge over all or   A
any part of the property, heritable and moveable, of the borrower.'

Not only does the background to the legislation fail to provide support for Mr
Hamilton's argument, but the legislation itself does not support it in view of the terms in
which it has been enacted and the structure which it adopts. The word 'property' is used
without qualification or restriction. The result is that the sole question which has to be
answered, with regard to property both heritable and moveable, is whether it is the   B
property of the company, and not the property of someone else, at the critical date.
Questions as to the use to which it is being put, or as to whether it is of value to the
company or is, on a true and fair view, an asset of the company for the purposes of its
balance sheet are left out of account. The effect of the charge is to attach the property as
if it were a fixed security over it, but subject to the rights of any person who has effectually
executed diligence over it or holds a fixed security over it or a floating charge having
priority over or ranking pari passu with the floating charge. The mechanism which is   C
adopted here is that appropriate to a fixed security over the property. There seems no
reason to doubt that it was intended that there could be attached by means of a floating
charge all property of the company which could be, at the critical date, the subject of a
fixed security as defined in s. 70(1) of the 1986 Act. In this field the only relevant test as
to what is and what is not the property of the company is that provided by Scots property
law.

   D

To depart from this approach would, in my view, give rise to consequences which
would be unacceptable. Any restriction in the scope of the expression would have to be
applied to moveable as well as heritable property. Questions would arise as to what was
to be done about sold and undelivered goods which had been paid for but the property
in which had not yet passed because the time had not yet arrived when it was intended to
pass: *Sale of Goods Act* 1979, s. 17. Questions would arise about other kinds of moveable
property the title to which requires to be registered before it is held to vest in the   E
purchaser: see Goudy on the *Law of Bankruptcy* (4th edn) p. 254. The suggestion that the
floating charge should be restricted to property which was being used by the company
for the purposes of its business for the time being would give rise to problems about
assets which were held in reserve or which, although in the ownership of the company,
were for the time being, for whatever reason, not being used by it. The test would be
likely to give rise to delay and difficulty in the practical working out of the attachment in   F
the event of a receivership. The suggestion that it should be restricted so as to include
items which were irrevocably beyond the scope of the company's property raises further
difficulties about the meaning of that expression and how it is to be applied over the
whole range of assets comprised in the expression 'property'. The suggestion was that
heritable property passed irrevocably from the company on delivery of the disposition to
the purchaser, but that cannot be said to be true in all situations and for all purposes.
The fact is that delivery of the disposition does not transfer the property in the land from   G
the company to the purchaser. The property passes only when the disposition is recorded
in the appropriate register, and only then can it be said with complete accuracy that the
land has passed irrevocably from the property of the company.

As for the wording used in the floating charge, the words which describe the scope of
the charge follow that of the statute. They refer to 'the whole of the property' comprised
in the property and undertaking of the company. There is no indication here of an   H
intention to restrict the charge to a part only of the company's property. It was suggested
that the scope of the charge had been cut down by the obligations undertaken by the
company to 'at all times keep in good repair such heritable property, plant and
machinery, fixtures, fittings and other effects as shall from time to time be comprised in
our undertaking', not to dispose of or let the same without the written consent of the
bank and to ensure and keep the property insured against loss or damage by fire and

A   such other risks as the bank might from time to time require. The way in which these obligations were expressed was said to indicate that the floating charge was intended to cover only such property as was from time to time being used for the business of the company. In my opinion however the inclusion of conditions in these terms did not have the effect of limiting the scope of the security. They are additional conditions of a kind similar to those found in the standard conditions which apply to a standard security: see *Conveyancing and Feudal Reform (Scotland) Act* 1970, Sch. 3, standard conditions 1 and

B   5 in regard to maintenance and repair and insurance of the security subjects. The practical working out of these conditions will vary from case to case, depending on the terms of the missives and the agreed date of entry. Their inclusion in the floating charge is not inconsistent with the pursuers' argument that the charge extends to all heritable property of the company until a real right in it has been transferred.

      The Lord Ordinary said at p. 87A; 1088I–K that, if vulnerability to a security writ

C   were to be the test, the pursuers must succeed, that this would appear to fit the structure of the Act, and that a wider analysis of the statutory provisions tended further to support the view that subjects will be affected by the floating charge at crystallisation if they would be affected by a standard security over them. I agree with his conclusions on this point, and I am not persuaded that the wording of the floating charge itself supports the second defenders' argument. The exception in favour of property held in trust, according

D   to the principles described in *Heritable Reversionary Co Ltd v Millar*, is now well established in the Scots law of insolvency. But it is an exception which must be regarded as sui generis, not capable of being extended to other situations contrary to the established rules of Scots property law.

Constructive trust

E   This argument was present by counsel for the second defenders as an alternative to the other arguments previously discussed in this opinion. It was submitted that, if they were wrong in the other arguments, the flat was nevertheless outwith the scope of the floating charge by virtue of its being impressed with a constructive trust in favour of the first defenders. It was accepted, for the purposes of this branch of the argument, that the feudal title to the flat remained with Albyn, but the effect of the delivery of the disposition to the purchaser and the receipt of the purchase price was said to give rise to a fiduciary duty upon Albyn to hold the feudal title for behoof of the purchaser. Reference was made

F   to *Stevenson v Wilson* 1907 SC 445 in order to show that it was possible for a contract of sale to give rise to a situation where there was a constructive trust. Thus, if an asset had been sold and transferred to the purchaser but further steps were needed for the purchaser to complete title to it, the holder of the title was to be regarded as holding the property subject to a constructive trust in favour of the purchaser until the transfer of title to the purchaser had been achieved. Counsel recognised that this was a broad proposition

G   which did not depend upon circumstances which were special to this case and that, if the proposition was sound, its result would have to be that the asset was to be regarded as held by the vendor in trust for all purposes in the event of the vendor's insolvency.

      In *Gibson v Hunter Home Designs Ltd* it was held that entry to the subjects and payment of the price, referable to the terms of missives, did not instruct the existence of a trust pending delivery of the disposition to the purchaser. That decision, which no one

H   suggested was unsound in any respect, was based on the observations in *Heritable Reversionary Co Ltd v Millar* by Lord Herschell at p. 44 and Lord Watson at p. 51 that a mere personal contract, or personal obligation, to convey heritable estate did not confer on the purchaser either the character or rights of a trust beneficiary, and on observations to the same effect in *Bank of Scotland v Liquidators of Hutchison, Main & Co Ltd* by Lord Kinnear at p. 57 and Lord Shaw of Dunfermline at p. 17 that a contractual obligation with regard to property is not of itself the foundation of a trust which attaches

to that property and excludes it from distribution in the event of insolvency. Mr Hamilton   A
submitted however that the decision in *Gibson*, and all these dicta, were concerned only
with stage one of the *Gibson* analysis. He maintained that nothing was said in any of
these cases which excluded the possibility of a constructive trust arising at stage two.
There was no reason in principle, once the vendor had implemented his part of the
contract by the irrevocable act of delivery to the purchaser, why he should not be
regarded as holding his title to the property in trust in the meantime. He accepted that
this argument would not prevail in a question with an adjudger who obtain a prior   B
infeftment standing the decision in *Mitchell v Ferguson*. But he submitted that, as no
argument based on constructive trust was advanced there and the doctrine had been
developed subsequently, the decision in that case might be open to reconsideration on
this point.

A constructive trust is created, as Wilson and Duncan, *Trusts, Trustees and Executors*
point out at p. 77, by circumstances. The mere fact that a person has come under a   C
contractual obligation to convey property to another is not, of itself, sufficient to create
a trust over it. What are required are other circumstances, which are not referable to the
parties' contract, sufficient to create fiduciary duties in favour of the party to whom the
property is to be conveyed. The position is different in England where, as can be seen
from various dicta mentioned by Russell J in *Musselwhite v C H Musselwhite & Son Ltd*
[1962] Ch 964 at pp. 985–986, the vendor becomes, from the moment the contract is
entered into, a trustee of the property for the purchaser. That doctrine is not part of Scots   D
law, as is plain from the decision in *Gibson*. But a constructive trust was held to exist in
Stevenson v Wilson, where shares in a company had been sold to a purchaser and the
purchaser had paid the price and received a transfer of the shares from the vendor, but
the directors of the company had refused to register the purchaser as proprietor of the
shares or to pay him the dividends accruing on those shares. The question is whether an
analogy can be drawn from that case which applies to the situation which arises where   E
the disposition of subjects has been delivered to the purchaser but he has not yet obtained
a title to, and thus a real right in, the property.

In *National Bank of Scotland Glasgow Nominees Ltd v Adamson* 1932 SLT 492 at
p. 495 Lord Moncrieff rejected an argument based on *Stevenson v Wilson* that the debtor
by contracting to sell shares had become a trustee for the purchasers with a duty
thereafter to hold the shares for their sole interest and behoof. He acknowledged that a   F
seller of shares may, in very special circumstances, by the operation of the sale itself find
that he has incurred a duty of quasi-trust administration for behoof of the purchaser. But
he said that any such duty would necessarily arise as a consequence, and not as a medium,
of a transfer of the property rights in the shares. Here again a contrast is drawn between
the personal obligations of the seller which are referable to the contract and circumstances
which arise from the operation of the contract and have not been provided for by it. It is
the circumstances, not the personal obligations, which can be relied upon as having   G
created, by the operation of a constructive trust, fiduciary duties in favour of the
purchaser. It may not be helpful to say that a constructive trust can arise only in very
special circumstances, but the use of that phrase is a reminder of the essential point that
it is the circumstances and not the obligations under the contract which must be relied
upon to show that there is a constructive trust.

The circumstances in *Stevenson v Wilson* were undoubtedly special, in that a situation   H
arose which the parties had not provided for in their contract by reason of which, after it
had been performed on both sides, it proved to be impossible to complete the transaction
by registering the transfer with the company. It is not clear why the court was willing to
adhere to Lord Salvesen's decision to grant declarator in terms of the second conclusion
to the effect that the shares were held in trust for the purchaser's behoof as from 23
January 1900 which was the date of the offer to purchase. That detail is not discussed in

A the opinions. The sole reason for the decision seems to be, as stated by Lord President Dunedin at p. 456, the impossible position resulting from the vendor's attitude by which he was insisting on keeping the money and yet not putting himself to the trouble of giving over the dividends. The circumstances were special to that case, not circumstances which arise in transactions for the purchase and sale of shares generally. In my opinion the case cannot be regarded as authority for the view that a constructive trust arises in all cases of sale following delivery or constructive delivery of the property to the purchaser, pending

B the completion of the steps which are required to transfer the real right. Where, as in this case, the transaction has proceeded upon the ordinary course provided for by the contract, the matter rests throughout entirely upon personal obligation and there is no room for holding that there is, by implication, a constructive trust.

Conclusion

C In the result I consider that the holder of a floating charge is entitled to prevail in a competition with a disponee of heritable property, where the charge has crystallised after delivery of the disposition but before it has been recorded in the appropriate register. The established principles of our law point inevitably to that conclusion. The result is unsatisfactory, but it is the consequence of the introduction by Parliament of a concept which is alien to Scots law with a view to its commercial advantages but without sufficient

D regard to the protection which may be needed to avoid hardship to the purchaser. There are some features of the present case which suggest that it would be unwise to draw any conclusions from its particular circumstances. No explanation has been offered as to why the certificate of non-crystallisation which the bank was willing to give was not delivered to the first defenders' solicitor or for the long delay in presenting the disposition for recording in the appropriate register. But it has revealed a defect in the law which can only now be corrected by the introduction of appropriate measures by the legislature.

E In my opinion we should refuse the reclaiming motion and adhere to the Lord Ordinary's interlocutor.

Lord Sutherland: In 1961 floating charges were introduced into the law of Scotland, having previously been described by Lord President Cooper in *Carse v Coppen* 1951 SC 233 as being utterly repugnant to the principles of Scots law. The current legislation so far as relevant to this case is to be found in s. 462–464 of the *Companies Act* 1985 and

F s. 53(7) of the *Insolvency Act* 1986. The floating charge which was granted by Albyn was over,

> 'the whole of the property (including uncalled capital) which is or may be from time to time, while this instrument is in force, comprised in our property and undertaking.'

Counsel for the reclaimers argued that a purposive construction should be given to the

G terms of the floating charge. It was argued that the background to the legislation was to secure for commercial purposes a facility to raise funds and the scope of the property covered by the floating charge should be confined to assets deployed or capable of being deployed for the purposes of the business activities of the company. The purpose was to make available to the company assets over which security could be obtained, but it was not intended that a floating charge should cover items of property which had passed irrevocably beyond the control of the company. The difficulty with this approach is to

H decide precisely what is the purpose behind the legislation. While it is true that one of the main purposes was to provide additional assets over which security could be arranged, and in particular to enable moveable as well as heritable property to be used for the purposes of security while allowing the company to use its property in the meantime, equally it may be said that one of the purposes of the legislation was to provide a security holder with maximum protection. It may be, and in particular in the present case it may

be, that these purposes are difficult to reconcile. It is clear from the legislation that as far   A
as security over heritable property is concerned, a floating charge is equated to a fixed
security in the event of crystallisation and there are provisions in the legislation relating
to the ranking of floating charges with other securities. It is against that background that
the definition of 'property' and 'property and undertaking' must be considered. As far as
'property' is concerned this is a very wide word and it is given no form of definition in
the legislation. It would therefore, in my view, be reasonable in the context to say that
property constitutes anything which could be annexed for the purposes of security. It   B
would be illogical if particular subjects could be used for the purpose of creating a fixed
security but could not be used for the purpose of creating a floating charge. Accordingly,
in my opinion, when dealing with heritage it must be a matter of property law to decide
whether or not particular subjects can be so annexed. As far as the words 'property and
undertaking' are concerned, again these are words given no precise definition. It is not in
dispute in this case that the subjects of sale prior to delivery of the disposition were   C
subjects which were held by Albyn as part of their property and undertaking. That being
so, if the subjects still constitute property after delivery of the disposition within the
meaning of the legislation, these subjects must be property comprised in the property and
undertaking of Albyn. In my opinion therefore there is no escape from the proposition
that one must look at property law to decide whether or not the subjects were still
property in the hands of Albyn subsequent to the delivery of the disposition.

  D

    The pursuers and respondents contend that the real right in property remains with a
disponer until such time as a disposition in favour of a purchaser has been recorded and
that any rights created in the disponee are purely personal rights which are not effective
against a creditor of the disponer. The reclaimers contend that while a real right may
remain with the disponer that is a bare feudal title, there having been transferred to the
disponee all rights of any significance which can constitute the right of property. Certain
matters are not in dispute. The reclaimers accept that a real right to the property remains   E
with the disponer until a disposition is recorded. The pursuers and respondents accept
that the disposition was signed and delivered and possession of the subjects given to the
first defenders and that, accordingly, nothing remained to be done to complete the
defenders' right to the property other than recording. What therefore has to be considered
is the nature of the various rights held by the disponer and the disponee respectively at
various stages in the transaction.

  F

    Without going into the historical background in detail it is sufficient to say that since
1617 registration in the public registers has been an essential step to transfer heritable
property. The real right to the property is indivisible, although the holder of a real right
may grant subsidiary real rights in the same property as, for example, servitudes. This,
however, is the grant of an independent real right and not the transfer of any part of the
grantor's right to the grantee. It is quite clear that at the stage when missives have been
completed for the sale of property the purchaser obtains certain rights but these rights   G
are purely personal and based entirely on a personal contract between him and the seller.
When a disposition has been executed and delivered there is a clear difference in the
position inter se of the purchaser and seller. The seller, by delivery of the disposition, has
empowered the purchaser to record the deed and thus divest the seller of any feudal title
or right to the property. The purchaser no longer requires to enforce his rights under the
contract by way of action but is in a position at his own hand to divest the seller. The   H
alteration of the position of the seller and purchaser inter se however begs the question
as to what difference, if any, there is in the relationship between either of them and third
parties. If the position be under property law that the right of property remains with the
person who has a right which is valid against the whole world then it matters not what
difference may have taken place in the relationship of the purchaser and seller under the
law of obligations.

A   The law of Scotland has always recognised a clear distinction between property law on the one hand and the law of obligations on the other. This distinction was made clear in Erskine's *Institute* III.i.2 and the effect made clear at II.iii.48:

> 'A charter or disposition which is not followed by seisin creates in the disponee a right barely personal. It lays the grantor, and his heirs, under an obligation to divest themselves agreeably to the tenor of the grant. But it has not the effect of
B   transferring to the acquirer the feudal right of the lands; and consequently, the subject may be affected and carried off from the disponee, before his taking infeftment, by any debt or diligence which is capable of divesting the disponer, in whom the feudal right of the land still continues vested.'

The distinction is also made quite clear in the majority decision of the full court in *Young v Leith* (1847) 9 D 932 (affirmed in the House of Lords, 2 Ross's Leading Cases 81) where it was decided that in the absence of registration a sasine was a nullity. The opinion of
C   the majority makes it clear that an unregistered sasine may be left operative as a personal obligation but cannot constitute a real right. The effect of the distinction has long been recognised as, for example, in *Mitchell v Ferguson* (1781) Mor 10296 where a registered decree of adjudication took preference over an unregistered disposition. Nothing in the older authorities or the institutional writers gives any countenance to the contention that there is some form of inchoate right of property greater than a personal obligation but
D   less than a real right which is transferred by the delivery of a disposition, which is what I understand to be the ultimate contention of the reclaimers. It may be my fault but I confess that I was never clear during the course of the argument precisely what the nature of this inchoate right was supposed to be, and as junior counsel for the respondents correctly pointed out an analysis which depends upon a fundamental conceptual uncertainty is unlikely to be a valid one. While phrases may be found such as 'perfects his right by sasine' (Erskine), 'inchoate or personal right to the subjects' (*Munro v Brodie*
E   (1844) 6 D 1249), 'make the right perfect' (*Edmond v Gordon* (1858) 3 Macq 116 per Lord Cranworth at p. 122), all of these references and other similar ones are in the context of a personal right or obligation and there is no suggestion that the disponee has received or the disponer has lost any real right nor that any right transmitted to the disponee has any validity against any one other than the disponer. A right which has no validity against third parties and which can be defeated by a subsequent disponee who registers his disposition first or a heritable creditor who registers his security first or by an adjudger
F   who registers his decree first cannot, in my opinion, be described as a real right whether complete, partial, inchoate, fragmented or anything else. The right obtained by a disponee may indeed be a valuable one but so long as it is valid only as against the disponer, it cannot, in my view, be described as anything other than a personal right.

Counsel for the reclaimers founded upon a number of authorities from which it was said there could be extracted a principle that a right of property of some kind at least was
G   transferred from the disponer to the disponee on delivery of the disposition. I do not regard jurisdiction cases as being of assistance, as these cases are decided on the basis of the law relating to jurisdiction and not on questions of property law. *Thomas v Lord Advocate* 1953 SC 151 is also in my view of no assistance. In the first place there was a concession relating to the material point and, in any event, under revenue law there was no reason why even a personal right should not be regarded as property for taxation purposes. Lord Patrick at one point indicates that it is not possible to contend that on
H   delivery of a disposition no property passes to the disponee and all the property the disponer had passes at once. Immediately following that observation he says 'Recording of the disposition in the Register of Sasines will only make real a right which was previously personal'. He accordingly makes it clear that he is talking in terms of personal obligations and in any event in the context of that case the important matter was what had passed as between the disponer and disponee, and the rights of third parties were not

material. The case founded upon most strongly by the reclaimers was *Gibson v Hunter*   A
Home Designs Ltd 1976 SC 23 and in particular the dicta of Lord President Emslie who
said (at p. 27):

> 'In the law of Scotland no right of property vests in a purchaser until there has
> been delivered to him the relevant disposition. On delivery of the disposition the
> purchaser becomes vested in a personal right to the subjects in question and his
> acquisition of a real right to the subjects is dependent upon recording the   B
> disposition in the appropriate Register of Sasines. Putting the matter in another
> way the seller of subjects under missives is not, in a question with the purchaser,
> divested of any part of his right of property in the subjects of sale until, in
> implement of his contractual obligation to do so, he delivers to the purchaser the
> appropriate disposition. Until the moment of delivery the purchaser, even if he has
> paid the price and obtained occupation of the subjects, has no more than a right
> under the contract of sale, the missives, to demand performance by the seller of his   C
> contractual obligation to convey. Such right as the purchaser has, accordingly, is
> no more than a *jus crediti* until delivery of the disposition for which he contracted
> has been made to him.'

The first thing to be observed about that case is that the contention of the pursuer was
that he had acquired a right to the property on the conclusion of missives. Accordingly it
was unnecessary for the purposes of that case to decide what rights, if any, passed to a   D
disponee on delivery of a disposition. When the Lord President first talks of the delivery
of the disposition he points out that the purchaser becomes vested in a personal right to
the subjects and his acquisition of a real right is dependent upon recording. When he
mentions the seller being divested of any part of his right of property in the subjects of
sale he does so in the context of a question between the seller and the purchaser and not
a question between the seller or purchaser and third parties. In my opinion while the   E
Lord President negatives any suggestion that there is any transfer of property prior to
delivery of a disposition he does not necessarily imply that any real right of any kind is
transferred after delivery of the disposition. The question of what rights were transferred
after delivery of a disposition was not a question before the court in *Gibson* and, in any
event, the court was not favoured with the extensive citation of authority with which we
were favoured. The subsequent cases in which Lord President Emslie's dicta were quoted   F
with approval, namely *Macdonald v Scott's Executors* 1981 SC 75, *Lombardi's Trustee v
Lombardi* 1982 SLT 81, *Leeds Permanent Building Society v Aitken, Malone & Mackay*
1985 SC 375 and *Margrie Holdings Ltd v C & E Commrs* 1991 SLT 38 again were not
concerned with the question which we require to decide. From the report of the
arguments in *Gibson* it appears likely that Lord President Emslie's dicta were based on
observations of Lord Justice Clerk Grant in *Embassy Picture House (Troon) Ltd v
Cammo Developments Ltd* 1971 SC 25. That was another jurisdiction case and again was   G
concerned with the position of a purchaser under missives. The Lord Justice Clerk refers
to the position of a person who has a personal right under a disposition and says that
that right is clearly a right of ownership, even if feudal infeftment has not followed. What
is important to note, however, from the Lord Justice Clerk's observation is that while it
may be described as a right of ownership it is nevertheless in his view a personal right
under the disposition and not any form of real right. Phrases such as 'a right of
ownership' or 'a personal right to the lands' may be apt to describe the position of a   H
purchaser in relation to the seller. They are not, however, apt to describe his position in
relation to a third party. As far as a third party is concerned he is entitled to rely upon
the faith of the Register and so long as the seller remains the registered holder of the
subjects, a purchaser, even with a delivered disposition which has not been recorded,
cannot, in my opinion, have any right of property in relation to the third party.

A The cases of *Union Bank of Scotland Ltd v National Bank of Scotland Ltd* (1886) 14 R (HL) 1, *Heritable Reversionary Co Ltd v Millar* (1892) 19 R (HL) 43 and *Bank of Scotland v Hutchison Main & Co* 1914 SC (HL) 1 were founded on by the reclaimers as dealing with the matter of apparent ownership for the purpose of showing that it is possible to have apparent ownership according to the Register while beneficial ownership lies with another party. The difficulty in that approach, as was made clear in *Inland Revenue v Clark's Trustees* 1939 SC 11, is that the right of property in the estate of a trust is vested

B in the trustees to the exclusion of any competing right of property, and the right of the beneficiary is merely a right in personam against the trustees to enforce their performance of the trust. Accordingly, in my view, cases relating to trusts, or the rather anomalous situation of the *ex facie* absolute disposition, do not assist the reclaimers in their argument.

On the whole matter I am satisfied that the only right of property valid against the

C whole world is that which is in the hands of the person who, on the basis of the register, is the holder of that property. He may, under the law of obligations, be restricted in what he can do with that property as far as a purchaser is concerned. If he chooses to breach such an obligation however there is no restriction on his right of property as far as a third party is concerned. If there had passed from a purchaser to a seller some real right in the property, even of an inchoate nature, it is difficult to see in principle how the seller could grant any form of title to a third party which would be valid, but there is no doubt that

D such a title can be granted. I am therefore satisfied that even after a disposition has been delivered the only real right in the property remains with the seller and in the context of property law that must be property in his hands. If it remains property in his hands, over which he can grant a valid heritable security, it must inevitably follow that it is also property in his hands which will be attached by the crystallisation of a floating charge which is deemed by the legislation to be equivalent to the registration of a fixed security.

E The final suggestion advanced by the reclaimers was that *esto* a seller retained the right of property, nevertheless he retained it only as a trustee for the purchaser. The foundation for this proposition was *Stevenson v Wilson* 1907 SC 445. That, however, was a very special case on its facts where the actings of the seller had resulted in an impasse and the court found that the only way to resolve the problem was to hold that the shares were held in trust. It would be a major step to extend, by analogy, the result of that case to a

F situation where property law was the relevant consideration, and, in any event, the idea that trust could arise generally in cases of sale and purchase was rejected comprehensively in *Bank of Scotland v Hutchison Main*. While the idea of a constructive trust may have its attractions in equity, there is, in my view, no room for such a concept in relation to the sale of heritage.

On the whole matter, therefore, I am satisfied that when the floating charge crystallised after the delivery of the disposition, the subjects of sale were still the property of Albyn

G and accordingly the floating charge attached to that property. It is said that this is an inequitable result in that the creditors obtain the benefit both of the purchase price and of the subjects while the purchaser, having paid the purchase price, receives nothing. It is true that this may seem to be an inequitable result but unfortunately in most cases arising out of bankruptcy or insolvency some innocent party may suffer. The inequity suffered in this case is no greater in principle than that suffered by many unsecured creditors in the ordinary case. The inequity arises not through any fault in the law of property or the

H law of obligations. It may be that particular difficulties arise because of the form of the legislation which provides for the possible creation of the equivalent of a fixed security which is effective without having to appear on the register, and which gives no restrictive definition to the word 'property'. Any such problems, however, cannot alter the basic principles of the law of property and obligations. In my opinion the Lord Ordinary reached the correct conclusion in this case and the reclaiming motion must be refused.

Lord Coulsfield: The essential facts can be stated very shortly. Albyn Construction Ltd   A
('Albyn') carried on business as a construction company. On 2 July 1984, Albyn granted
a floating charge in favour of the Bank of Scotland and that charge was registered on 16
July 1984. The charge was described as:

> 'A floating charge over the whole of the property (including uncalled capital) which
> is or may be from time to time, while this instrument is in force, comprised in our
> property and undertaking.'
>
>   B

The floating charge contained a prohibition against the creation in favour of any
creditor other than the bank of any fixed security or floating charge ranking *pari passu*
with the floating charge, or having priority over it, and also provided that the grantors
should not be at liberty to dispose of their property otherwise than in the ordinary course
of business. Further clauses of the floating charge obliged Albyn to keep heritable and
other property belonging to them in good repair and to insure it. By missives dated 14,
21 and 29 March 1989 and 23 May 1989, Albyn agreed to sell a basement flat at 10   C
Whinhill Road, Aberdeen to the first defenders. It is now agreed that the sale of property
was a sale in the ordinary course of Albyn's business. The date of entry under the missives
was 14 April 1989. The price was paid and the first defenders obtained entry to the
subjects on 12 June 1989. It also appears that the bank had, on 8 June 1989, executed a
certificate that the floating charge had not crystallised and an undertaking not to deprive
Albyn of the right to validly convey the subjects, provided that a disposition was recorded   D
within 21 days, and that that, or a similar, certificate could have been provided to the
purchaser if it had been requested. No disposition was, however, executed until 9 August
1990. On that date Albyn did execute a disposition, which was delivered by Albyn's
solicitor to the first defenders' solicitor. There was also delivered, at the same time, a deed
of restriction dated 27 July 1990 executed by the Bank of Scotland disburdening the
subjects of a standard security in favour of the bank. On 10 August 1990, the pursuers
were appointed joint receivers of Albyn by an instrument of appointment executed by   E
the Bank of Scotland. The disposition in favour of the first defenders was recorded in the
register of sasines for the county of Aberdeen on 21 August 1990. The first defenders
had, on 31 July 1990, granted a standard security in favour of the second defenders and
that standard security was also recorded on 21 August 1990.

The current legislation governing floating charges in Scotland is found in Pt. XVIII of
the *Companies Act 1985* and in the *Insolvency Act* 1986. Section 462(1) of the 1985 Act   F
provides that it is competent under the law of Scotland for an incorporated company to
create a floating charge over all or any part of the property, including uncalled capital,
which may from time to time be comprised in its property and undertaking. Section 463
provides for the attachment of the floating charge on the commencement of a winding
up of a company, subject to the rights of persons who have executed diligence or hold
other securities; and subject also to the provisions governing the attachment of a floating
charge on the appointment of a receiver under the 1986 Act. The effect of an appointment   G
such as was made in the present case is governed by s. 53 of the 1986 Act and, in
particular, s. 53(7), which provides:

> 'On the appointment of a receiver under this section, the floating charge by virtue
> of which he was appointed attaches to the property then subject to the charge; and
> such attachment has effect as if the charge was a fixed security over the property
> to which it has attached.'
>
>   H

The issue in this case is whether the heritable subjects which Albyn had agreed to sell
to the first defenders continued to be part of the property of Albyn at the date of
crystallisation of the floating charge, so as to be attached by the charge and available to
the receivers. The Lord Ordinary held that the subjects were attached by the floating
charge (see [1995] BCC 57). In outline, his reasons were that, notwithstanding a number

A   of observations in the decided cases which suggest that the holder of a delivered, but unrecorded, disposition enjoys some right of property in the heritable subjects comprised in the disposition, nevertheless, on the ordinary principles of property law, the subjects remained comprised in the property of Albyn at the relevant date; that there was no divestiture of Albyn in any relevant sense; and that it could not be said that, following the delivery of the disposition, the subjects were held by Albyn in trust for the first defenders. He accordingly granted decree of declarator that the floating charge attached

B   to the subjects on 10 August 1990, that the charge operated as if it were a fixed security with priority over the standard security granted by the first defenders in favour of the second defenders, and that the receivers were entitled to exercise the powers conferred by the floating charge and the legislation and, in particular, to take possession of the subjects and sell or otherwise dispose of them.

C   The provisions of the 1985 Act concerning the attachment of floating charges are substantially the same as those which have governed the attachment of such charges since their first introduction by the *Companies (Floating Charges) (Scotland) Act* 1961. In *National Commercial Bank of Scotland v Liquidators of Telford Grier Mackay & Co* 1969 SC 181 Lord President Clyde observed that as from the crystallisation of a floating charge, which in that case took place on the commencement of a liquidation, the holder was to be treated as if he were the holder of a real security over the debtor's property

D   which gave him a *jus in re* over the specific property for the repayment of the sum due. Substantially the same view was taken in *Forth & Clyde Construction Co Ltd v Trinity Timber & Plywood Co Ltd* 1984 SC 1, a case concerned with a competition between a floating charge and an arrestment of a debt due and payable to the company in the hands of a third party. It was held that since there was only one form of effective security over such a debt due to the company, namely, an assignation in security duly intimated, the floating charge must be treated on crystallisation as having the effect of an intimated

E   assignation of the debt. By the same reasoning, the effect of the crystallisation of a floating charge in relation to heritable property must be equivalent to that of a standard security duly registered in the register of sasines at the date of crystallisation. Since the method of regulating the priority of floating charges in competition with other rights and claims adopted in the legislation has been to equate such charges, on attachment, with heritable securities in the ordinary form, it is necessary to pay attention to the effect which such securities in ordinary form do have in competition with other rights: and for

F   a proper understanding of the effect of such securities, it is necessary to have regard to the way in which the Scottish system of property law has developed and, in particular, to the way in which it has been affected by the compulsory registration of rights relating to heritable property. Apart from one issue, there was little dispute between the parties on this part of the case, but it is, I think, necessary to set out the position as briefly as possible as a background to the contentions of the parties in the present case.

G   Descriptions of the development of the Scottish system can be found in a number of sources, but one of the clearest and most authoritative is found in Hume's *Lectures* (Stair Society edition, vol. IV, Pt. IV, ch. I). Hume begins by pointing out that there are two written instruments which establish and are indispensable to the investiture of a real right in land, namely the charter or dispositive act on the part of the superior and the sasine or act of delivery and symbolical apprehension in pursuance of that deed of conveyance. He

H   proceeds to point out, under reference to Stair, *Institutions* III.ii.3, that it is essential that the charter or disposition should contain words of present conveyance, as opposed to a mere undertaking or intention to convey. As regards the feudal investiture or sasine, Hume explains that a ceremony of investiture was originally conducted on the lands, but that from a fairly early date some written record came to be considered necessary. The written record may originally have been crude and informal, but it became the practice for a formal instrument of sasine to be prepared by a public official or notary and, again

on the authority of Stair II.iii.16, such an instrument of sasine became not only a means   A
of proof that sasine had been given, but a necessary solemnity to accomplish the right.
The requirement that instruments of sasine should be recorded was introduced by the
Act 1617, cap. 16. That Act required that every sasine should be recorded within 60 days
of its date and that otherwise it should make no faith in judgment to the prejudice of any
third party who might have acquired a perfect and lawful right to the lands; but without
prejudice to the use of such writs against the party-maker thereof and his heirs and
successors. The original enactment contained certain deficiencies and obscurities, but   B
these were remedied by subsequent legislation, ending with the Act 1693, cap. 14. The
purpose and effect of the legislation is described by Hume as follows:

> 'But to make a sasine good to all effects – against all the lieges and in every
> competition of rights – it is further necessary that it be published in a certain, sure
> and solemn fashion to the world, *viz.* by insertion on a certain record where all
> concerned are presumed to enquire for and peruse it. Now here I need hardly point   C
> out to you the uses – the several high and beneficial uses – which such an institution
> is calculated to serve. It is obviously a matter of the greatest convenience and
> highly conducive to the ends of justice and fair dealing. It settles and proclaims the
> state of ownership of the whole lands of the Kingdom.'

Hume then points out that registration was not necessary to secure publicity in a
question with the grantor of the deed and that for that reason an unrecorded sasine might   D
form the ground of a good personal objection against the grantor or anyone representing
him. As regards any competition between disponees, however, Hume observes:

> 'Let us now return one step further back on the investiture and suppose that
> charter only has been given or disposition executed but that no sasine has followed.
> You will here anticipate the consequence which is that there is no real investiture
> but the constitution only of an ordinary personal right or *jus ad rem* to the lands –   E
> such a right as is good indeed against the grantor and his heirs or others who come
> into his place and are liable to the like personal objection as he – but which shall
> not stand the test of trial with any perfect investiture acquired by a third party who
> has no concern with and is not reached by that objection. The deed of conveyance
> not followed with sasine which is the feudal delivery of the lands (and as necessary
> as the real delivery is in the case of moveable *corpora*) is a mere expression of
> consent; neither divests the disponer nor really qualifies nor intrinsically limits his   F
> previous feudal right to the lands. Being still vested with that feudal right he can,
> therefore, effectually make it over to another who can defend himself therein and
> maintain his right. As to his author's personal engagements or contracts with
> respect to it, he, the singular successor, is no party to them, nor supposed to know
> of them nor obliged to enquire about them.'

The effect of an unrecorded sasine was considered by the whole court in *Young v Leith*   G
(1847) 9 D 932. The case had previously been considered in the Court of Session and the
House of Lords and remitted for consideration by the whole court, and it was
subsequently heard a second time in the House of Lords, but the fullest discussion of the
issues, and the relevant statements of principle, are found in the opinion of the majority
of the whole court drawn by Lord Fullerton, reported in 9 D (above). The case was
concerned with the validity of certain deeds granted in 1810 and thereafter, purporting   H
to alter the destination in an entail. The first of these deeds was a procuratory of
resignation executed by Thomas Gordon dated 10 April 1810. Thomas Gordon's title to
grant those deeds depended upon the efficacy of two sasines taken earlier, one by Charles
Gordon in 1776 and one by Thomas Gordon in 1797: the first was not registered within
the requisite period and the second was never registered at all. The opinion of the whole
court begins by stating:

A
'We do not understand it to be disputed that the validity of a procuratory of resignation must rest on the completed real right of the party by whom it is granted: and, consequently, the only point in dispute is whether an unregistered sasine be a nullity in regard to real right, or truly completes a real right to the lands.'

It is, therefore, clear from the outset of the opinion that the principal issue in the case was whether an unregistered sasine could be regarded as, in any sense, constituting a
B   *completed* real right. The argument was largely concerned with the question whether the exception to the Act 1617, cap. 16 could be regarded as conferring on an unregistered sasine the effect of a real right, in some sense, in a question between the holder of the sasine and a representative of the grantor. It was held that there could only be one real right, at one time, in relation to particular heritable subjects and the essential reason for that decision can be seen in two relatively short quotations. Firstly, at p. 937:

C
'The proper object and effect of every valid sasine is to divest the grantor of the heritable right and to invest the grantee. When that legal act is once completed, it absolutely excludes the acquisition of any subsequent real right from the grantor, preferable to that of the party seized, or, indeed, the acquisition of any real right, through any other medium than the right of the party so seized. An instrument of sasine, which has not in law that effect, is practically null as a sasine, i.e., as an act
D   completing a real right; for it does not produce the effect which it is the sole and peculiar object of a valid sasine to secure. When it is said that the statute annuls the instruments only *qualificate*, that is, in prejudice of a third party who has acquired a perfect right to the lands, it is overlooked that the very qualification excludes the notion of a real right. It is of the very essence of a real right not only to found a preference against a less perfect right, but to prevent any third party from acquiring a perfect right to the lands, which most certainly an unregistered
E   sasine does not.'

Secondly, at p. 945:

'The operation of a personal right, founded on an unregistered sasine, whether by way of obligation against the grantor of the precept to do something, or as a personal bar against the grantor, pleading that something has not been done by the grantee, is quite intelligible. But a completed real right, good in a question
F   between grantor and grantee, and bad against all the rest of the world, is an absolute legal contradiction in terms. For it is of the very essence of a real right that it shall be good against all claiming from the same author; who, by giving a complete real right to one, is understood to be divested of all power of giving it to another. He cannot be divested, till the grantee is fully vested. An intermediate state of things, which leaves the grantor's own sasine entire, as retaining the real
G   right in him, while at the very same time another real right in the identical fee is completed in the person of the grantee, is an absolute incongruity, according to the principles of our law.'

I shall revert to the significance of that decision in relation to the present case. Before doing so, it is helpful, I think, to complete the summary of the development of the system of registration of land rights. The *Infeftment Act 1845* made it unnecessary for the
H   ceremony of sasine to be performed and provided that sasine should be effectually given by the production of the appropriate writs to the notary public and the expeding and recording of an instrument of sasine. The *Titles to Land (Scotland) Act* 1858 made it unnecessary to expede and record an instrument of sasine and permitted the conveyance itself to be registered in the register of sasines, on being presented with a warrant for registration specifying the person or persons on whose behalf it was to be registered; and further provided that the conveyance:

'being so recorded along with such warrant shall have the same legal force and   A
effect in all respects as if the conveyance so recorded had been followed by an
instrument of sasine duly expede and recorded at the date of recording the said
conveyance according to the present law and practice.'

That provision was repeated in the *Titles to Land (Consolidation) (Scotland) Act* 1868
and although the older forms remained competent, the practice of recording the
conveyance has been normal since that date. The process was carried one stage further   B
by s. 4 of the *Conveyancing (Scotland) Act* 1874 which provided that every proprietor
duly infeft should be deemed to be entered with the nearest superior as at the date of
registration of his infeftment. Finally, by the *Conveyancing (Scotland) Act* 1924 it was
made possible for the holder of, inter alia, a disposition delivered but unrecorded to
convey the property comprised in the disposition to another person by a disposition
which includes a clause of deduction of title specifying the links by which title is derived
from the last infeft proprietor; the recording of such a disposition on behalf of the   C
disponee is sufficient to confer on the disponee a complete real right to the subjects.
Before 1924, the normal practice was for the holder of an unrecorded disposition to
transfer the property by a deed known as a disposition and assignation which contained
a clause of disposition of the lands themselves. In Menzies, *Lectures on Conveyancing*
(3rd edn, 1863), however, it is observed that disponing words are not essential (p. 652);
and, later, that the use of the word assignation indicates the personal nature of the right,
and that the effect of the deed is only to transfer to the receiver the same personal right   D
which belonged to the grantor (p. 653). It is not necessary to consider the provisions of
the *Land Registration (Scotland) Act* 1979: although that Act alters the system of
registration, it has not made any change in principle relevant for the purposes of the
present case.

To a large extent, there is no dispute between the parties as to the development of the
conveyancing system, as I have endeavoured to outline it, and the principles on which it   E
operates. There were, however, some points upon which the parties were at issue. The
reclaimers maintained that the effect of 19th century statutory reforms to the system of
conveyancing was only that the end result of the process of granting and recording a
disposition should be deemed to be the same as that of granting a disposition, and
expeding and recording an instrument of sasine, under the old procedure: and that it did
not necessarily follow that the effect of the grant and delivery of a conveyance remained
what it always had been. The reclaimers further submitted that the delivery of a   F
disposition and the recording of it were not two separate transactions or separate steps,
but parts of a single transaction, so that it was not necessarily wrong to say that property
in the subjects was, in some sense, transferred by the delivery of a disposition. These
contentions went with an argument that the decision in *Young v Leith* (above) was only
concerned with the question whether there could be two completed real rights in
particular subjects at the same time.   G

In my opinion, the first two of these points can be readily dismissed. It seems to me to
be clear that there is nothing in the statutory reforms which implies any alteration in the
status of an unrecorded disposition, whether delivered or undelivered. The purpose of
the reforms was to simplify the mechanics by which a conveyancing transaction is carried
out, not to blur the distinction between the grant and delivery of a disposition on the one
hand, and the recording of it on the other. That is, I think, the view which has been taken   H
by authorities on conveyancing: reference may, for example, be made to Bell's *Lectures*,
vol. I, p. 675. The argument in support of the second contention began with an analysis
of a passage in Stair III.ii.3ff., which, it was said, supported the view that a disposition
was a unilateral act conferring rights or interests or status on the disponee rather than
something purely contractual. It is true that in that passage Stair begins by distinguishing
three acts of the will about the disposal of rights, namely a resolution to dispone, a

A   paction or obligation to dispone and a present will or consent that that which is the disponer's be the acquirer's: and that he further says that it must be the present dispositive will of the owner which conveys the right to any other. In that particular paragraph, however, Stair is, as he has stated earlier, considering how far dominion and property is competent by the law of rational nature. In subsequent paragraph he goes on to consider rules of positive law such as the necessity of delivery for the transfer of title to moveables; and, in III.ii.8ff., he discusses the rules applicable to the transmission of real rights in

B   heritable property, including the necessity for sasine and recording. The reclaimers also referred, in support of this argument, to comments in later authorities which will be discussed later in this opinion. In my view, however, it is fairly easy to see that the starting point of this part of the argument on behalf of the reclaimers has no real foundation. As regards the significance of the decision in *Young v Leith*, it is, I think, correct to say that the point actually decided in the case was limited in the way that the reclaimers suggest,

C   and, for that as well as other reasons, the decision does not directly rule the question in the present case. Nevertheless, the principles upon which the decision proceeded, as indicated in the quotations set out above, are significant since they amount to an emphatic rejection of any qualified right of property in heritage. In that respect, the decision is fully consistent with the adoption of a generally civilian approach to the transfer of real rights in property by the institutional writers (see e.g. Erskine *Institute* II.i.1) and with the equation by Hume (above) and other writers of completion of

D   infeftment in heritage with delivery of moveables, in regard to the transfer of property. Such an approach involves, as your Lordship has explained, a clear distinction between real and personal rights, and between property and obligation.

     As I have mentioned, apart from the particular issues to which I have just referred, the parties were not in disagreement about the principles of the law. They were further agreed on certain propositions which are more closely related to the facts of this particular case.

E   They were agreed, firstly, that if Albyn had granted a disposition to another bona fide purchaser for value subsequent to the delivery of the disposition to the first defenders and this latter disposition had been first recorded, the disponee in that disposition would take the property unaffected by the earlier disposition: secondly, that if Albyn had granted a standard security to a bona fide lender for value which had been recorded before the disposition to the first defenders, that standard security would have had a preference over the first defenders' disposition: and thirdly, that if a creditor of Albyn

F   had adjudicated and had recorded the decree of adjudication before the recording of the disposition to the first defenders, that creditor would have obtained a preference. These three propositions are really a consequence of the fact, on which the parties were not at issue, that the first defenders did not, as at the date of attachment of the floating charge, have a completed or a complete real right to or in the subjects.

     Nevertheless, despite the principles of the law which I have attempted to summarise, it

G   is also clear that there has been some recognition of a difference between the position of a disponee who holds a disposition delivered but unrecorded and that of a purchaser who has not yet received a disposition, although he is entitled, by contract, to demand one. It can also be said to be clear that there are certain cases which do not fit easily, or without some explanation, with the civilian principles of property law, which assume an undivided concept of ownership. These cases are trust; *ex facie* absolute dispositions; some of the decisions dealing with the jurisdiction of the Court of Session; and some other more

H   marginal examples, such as cases involving rating issues, of which *City of Glasgow v McEwan* (1899) 2 F (HL) 25 is an example. As will be seen, a substantial part of the reclaimers' argument in the present case depended upon the law in relation to these special issues.

     The broad lines of the argument submitted on behalf of the reclaimers may be summarised as follows:

(1)   The question whether the subjects are caught by the floating charge depends on   A
the proper construction of the word 'property' in the statute and the floating
charge.

(2)   The word 'property' does not have a single and invariable meaning but can take
its meaning from its context.

(3)   The holder of a delivered but unrecorded disposition has been recognised as
enjoying a status beyond that of a mere personal creditor, such that it is not   B
inappropriate to regard him as having property in the subject of the disposition.

(4)   That view is supported by an examination of the cases, such as that of trust, which
do not fit easily with the broad principles of the law of heritable property.

(5)   An analysis of the rights actually enjoyed by the holder of a delivered but
unrecorded disposition confirms that view.

(6)   The preference obtained by a disponee who reaches the register first has its roots   C
and its justification in public policy designed to protect the faith of the records;
and the corollary is that it cannot be said that the disponer who has granted a
disposition retains a *right* to dispone the same subjects, or any other right which
can be regarded as property.

(7)   Alternatively, it was submitted that once a disposition has been granted and
delivered the disponer holds any remaining right of property which he has in trust,   D
or subject to a constructive trust, for the disponee.

The arguments of the respondents can likewise be briefly summarised as follows:

(1)   Scots Law in company with other civilian systems has adopted a clear distinction
between real and personal rights and a unitary theory of ownership, including a
rule that ownership is transferred at one moment in time only.

(2)   Consistently with that view, any references in the authorities to the position or   E
status of the holder of an unrecorded disposition can be construed as no more than
statements of a personal right, which is not appropriately described as being, or as
being included in, ownership or property.

(3)   The exceptional cases are either not real exceptions to the principle of unity of
ownership, as in the case of the jurisdiction cases and the cases of *ex facie* absolute
dispositions, or, if truly anomalous, are to be regarded as exceptions established in   F
the law, as in the case of trust.

(4)   The institution of the floating charge has been tied by statute into the law of
property in such a way that the attachment of the charge must have the effect of
giving the creditor a fixed security, equivalent to a standard security which prevails
by virtue of the deemed registration which that security enjoys under the statute.

(5)   There is no basis in the law for regarding the disponer as being a trustee, or a   G
constructive trustee, for the disponee after the delivery of the disposition.

These summaries of the competing arguments will, I hope, make it plain that the
ultimate issue in this case is an issue of construction of the statutory wording. It seems to
me, however, that the statutory words must be construed in the context of the system of
property law within which floating charges are designed to operate. It is, therefore,
necessary to enquire, in the first instance, whether it is possible to find within the existing   H
system of law governing the creation and transfer of rights in heritage, some meaning for
the expression 'property' which might appropriately be taken to be applied or adopted in
the statute. If there is no such meaning to be found, that is not an end of the reclaimers'
case, because it is still necessary to consider whether an examination of the statute itself,
and a consideration of its purposes, suggest that the word 'property' should be given
some special meaning in the provisions with which we are concerned. It does seem to me,

A   however, that, if that approach required to be adopted it would only be right to give a special meaning to the word 'property' within the statute if that meaning could clearly be derived from the statutory wording by the ordinary processes of construction.

     The appropriate course, therefore, appears to me to consider first whether any basis can be found in the existing law for a meaning of the word 'property', other than that of a completed real right, which might be said to be enjoyed by the holder of an unrecorded

B   disposition. In doing so, I think the first stage is to ask what rights and powers such a holder has which are not possessed by the purchaser under missives, who has a contractual right to a conveyance but has not yet received a disposition. The most obvious advantage enjoyed by the disponee who holds a delivered disposition is that he has the power to obtain, or complete, a real right by registering the disposition at any time. He is no longer dependent upon obtaining, voluntarily or by compulsion, a grant from the disponer. Secondly, the holder can grant a conveyance of the property or create

C   an effective security by virtue of the deduction of title provisions in the 1924 Act. Those provisions, however, amount to no more than a statutory simplification of the mechanics by which the property can be transmitted to a third party: before 1924 the normal means was to grant a disposition and assignation and it seems to me difficult to suppose that the 1924 legislation made any difference in principle to the position of the holder of an unrecorded disposition. Thirdly, the holder of the disposition has certain rights in relation

D   to possession of the subjects and tenancies of them. He is, assuming the date of entry has arrived, entitled to enter into possession and to collect rents. He is also entitled to serve a notice to quit, but only an infeft proprietor is entitled to obtain decree in an action of removing (see *James Grant & Co v Moran* 1948 SLT (Sh Ct) 8). To some extent, therefore, the holder is entitled to exercise rights and powers of a proprietor, but the exercise of these rights can also be explained as the consequences of the personal contract between the disponee and the disponer. The essential feature of the position of the disponee, upon

E   which the reclaimers placed most stress, was that first mentioned above, namely that the disponee is entitled to constitute his right as a real right of property and is not dependent upon the co-operation of the disponer.

     In the course of the argument reference was made to a considerable number of comments in the authorities and decided cases on the position of the holder of a disposition which has not been recorded or, as he is sometimes called, the uninfeft

F   proprietor. It is, I think, convenient to collect, first, a number of observations on the position of such a proprietor in the institutional writers and textbooks. Stair does not, so far as I am aware, either use the expression 'uninfeft proprietor' or comment directly on the rights or status of such a person. Erskine states (*Institute* II, iii, 48):

> 'A charter or disposition which is not yet followed by sasine creates in the disponee a right barely personal. It lays the grantor and his heirs under an obligation to

G   > divest themselves agreeably to the tenor of the grant. But it has not the effect of transferring to the acquirer the feudal right of the land; and consequently the subject may be affected and carried off from the disponee, before his taking infeftment, by any debt or diligence which is capable of divesting the disponer, in whom the feudal right of the lands still continues vested.'

     Later in the paragraph, Erskine refers to the right as a personal right, and as an

H   incomplete or personal right; and he also speaks of 'perfecting' the right by sasine. It should be observed, however, that in discussing the title of a proprietor to remove tenants, in Institute II, vi, 52, Erskine does use the expression 'a proprietor not infeft'.

     I have already referred to Hume's *Lectures* in which the author states (Stair Society Edition, vol. 4, p. 182), with reference to the position of a charter or disposition on which no sasine has followed:

'You will here anticipate the consequence, which is, that there is no real investiture,   A
but the constitution only of an ordinary personal right or *jus ad rem* to the lands –
such a right as is good, indeed, against the grantor and his heirs or others who
come into his place, and are liable to the like personal objection as he – but which
shall not stand the test of trial with any perfect investiture acquired by a third
party, who has no concern with and is not reached by that objection.'

Hume later observes that the disposition without sasine is a mere expression of consent   B
which does not divest the disponer nor qualify nor intrinsically limit his previous feudal
right. Craigie (*Heritable Rights*, p. 434ff.) discusses the transmission of 'the personal title'
to the lands and draws a distinction between the method of transmission of such a title
by a disposition and assignation or by assignation of an unrecorded conveyance and the
assignation of the *jus crediti*: in the latter case, priority is obtained by prior intimation of
the assignation while in the former case priority depends on priority of registration. That
rule seems to be consistent with Hume's opinion that there is no divestiture of the granter   C
until sasine has been taken. The position is discussed in more detail, but somewhat
inconclusively, in Gloag and Irvine, *Rights in Security*, p. 33. The authors state:

'A personal right to land may be described as the status of one who is in a position
to take infeftment, but who has not done so. It is the right of a man who has a
disposition in his favour which he has not recorded, or of an heir who has not
served. Beyond the general statement that it constitutes a *jus ad rem* and not a *jus*   D
in re, and yet is more than a mere *jus actionis*, it would be difficult to define it.'

We were referred to a number of decisions and I should first deal with three, which, in
my view, are of no real assistance, on this part of the case at least. We were referred to
observations by Lord Watson in *Union Bank of Scotland v National Bank of Scotland Ltd*
(1886) 14 R (HL) 1, but that was a case concerned with *ex facie* absolute dispositions
and, as Lord Watson observed at p. 4, did not depend on feudal principles. *Peter Dowie*   E
& Co v Tennant (1891) 18 R 986, a case concerned with an issue of jurisdiction, arose in
circumstances in which the proprietor of heritable subjects had dispatched a disposition
which had not been received until after the service of the summons: the case was dealt
with on the basis that there had not been any delivery of the disposition. *Fraser v*
Magistrates of Aberdeen (11 April 1977, unreported) was a case concerned with the
meaning of the word 'proprietor' in s. 32 of the *Conveyancing (Scotland) Act* 1874 and
Lord Keith's decision was, as I read it, based on a construction of the particular provision   F
and consideration of its purpose. The case supports the argument that the word
'proprietor' in a statute, does not necessarily have a fixed meaning, but is not otherwise
of any real assistance.

A further case which, in my view, is of no real assistance in the present issue, is *Thomas*
v Lord Advocate 1953 SC 151. The facts were that the proprietor of certain heritable
subjects had executed a disposition of them in favour of his son. The disposition was   G
delivered on 6 May 1945 but entry was postponed until Whitsunday 1945. The proprietor
died on 12 May 1950 and the question arose whether estate duty was payable. The effect
of the relevant legislation, s. 2 of the *Finance Act* 1894 taken with s. 38 of the *Customs*
and Inland Revenue Act 1881, as amended, was that estate duty was payable if the
property could be said to fall within the description 'property taken under any gift,
whenever made, of which property *bona fide* possession and enjoyment should not have   H
been assumed by the donee immediately upon the gift and thence forward retained to the
entire exclusion of the donor'; and if the gift was made within five years of the deceased's
death, subject to certain qualifications. The revenue case was that the subject of the gift
was the land itself and that accordingly no gift took place until a point of time within the
five years before the donor's death. The taxpayer's case was that the gift was made when
the disposition was delivered, that after that date nothing remained to be done by the

A donor and that there was nothing inchoate or imperfect about the gift. The court cited a number of cases concerned with the question what property should be considered to be the subject of a gift for the purposes of estate duty. The Lord Justice Clerk expressed his conclusion as follows (at p. 158):

B 'If one thinks only in terms of the lands conveyed, there can be no doubt that the donee cannot be said to have assumed possession and enjoyment of the lands themselves till 15 May 1945. But it is equally beyond doubt that when the disposition was delivered to him on 6 May 1945, the donee obtained something which was of undoubted value, *viz.*, the personal right to the lands, albeit with entry postponed. That was something which he could have disposed of or used as a fund of credit. That right was something which he took on delivery of the disposition and which was property taken under a gift, *bona fide* possession and enjoyment of which he immediately assumed. It seems to me that the revenue can

C succeed only by ignoring the existence of this right which the donee immediately acquired and from which the donor was immediately and wholly excluded. The revenue case is an undue simplification of the problem. Erskine defines property as "the right of using and disposing of a subject as our own". The revenue case confines itself to the former of these elements. I can see no ground for reading "property" as used in the enactment under consideration as excluding the right of

D disposal of what was given on 6 May. It may be that, were the revenue to approach the question of dealing with a bundle of interests on the lines on which it was ultimately dealt with in *In re Cochrane*, some sort of discrimination could be made, but nothing of that sort was mooted before us.'

It is, I think, of some interest to pay attention to the last sentence of the Lord Justice Clerk's observations. The issue before the court in that case was presented as a black and

E white issue, so that the whole property either fell within the charge to tax or fell outside it. There is, however, no reason why a personal right to lands, or indeed a *jus crediti* in respect of lands, should not be treated as property for taxation purposes, and therefore, in such a situation, there could well be room for an apportionment of the 'property' between donor and donee. That emphasises, in my view, that the question before the court in *Thomas v Lord Advocate* was a question of a very different kind from that which arises in the present case. It is true that Lord Patrick made certain observations (at

F p. 161) which, on their face, would appear to have some bearing on the position of an uninfeft proprietor. He said:

'It does not seem possible to contend that on delivery of such a disposition no property passes to the disponee. All the property the disponer had passes at once. Recording of the disposition in the Register of Sasines will only make real a right which was previously personal.'

G In the context of the case, however, I do not think that Lord Patrick was really saying any more than was said by the Lord Justice Clerk and, in the whole circumstances, it does not seem to me that the decision is of any real assistance in the present problem.

I turn therefore to cases which do have a direct bearing upon the issue. I propose to mention first *Gibson v Hunter Home Designs Ltd* 1976 SC 23 because although it is one

H of the latest of the relevant cases, the observations of Lord President Emslie focus very clearly on the issues relevant in the present case. *Gibson* was concerned with the application of s. 372(1)(b) of the *Companies Act* 1948 which provided that a winding up of a company should be equivalent to a decree of adjudication of the heritable estates of the company at the date of the winding up. Missives for sale of a heritable property had been concluded at the date of the winding up of a company and a feu disposition had been executed but not delivered. The question raised was whether property in the subjects

had passed to the purchaser at the date of commencement of the winding up. It was held   A
that no property had passed. Lord President Emslie said (at p. 27):

> 'Although I have every sympathy with the purchaser in the events which happened,
> I have not the slightest doubt that his first argument is without substance. In the
> law of Scotland no right or property vests in a purchaser until there has been
> delivered to him the relevant disposition. On delivery of the disposition the
> purchaser becomes vested in a personal right to the subjects in question and his   B
> acquisition of a real right to the subjects is dependent upon recording the
> disposition in the appropriate Register of Sasines. Putting the matter in another
> way the seller of subjects under missives is not, in a question with the purchaser,
> divested of any part of his right of property in the subjects of sale until, in
> implement of his contractual obligation to do so, he delivers to the purchaser the
> appropriate disposition. Until the moment of delivery the purchaser, even if he has
> paid the price and obtained occupation of the subjects, has no more than a right   C
> under the contract of sale, the missives, to demand performance by the seller of his
> contractual obligation to convey. Such right as the purchaser has, accordingly, is
> no more than a *jus crediti* until delivery of the disposition for which he contracted
> has been made to him. In this case the purchaser's entry before the passing of any
> right of property was expressly provided for in the missives and his occupation of
> the subjects thereafter was ascribable to the contract and nothing else.'
                                                                                       D
The case also dealt with the issue whether there was in the circumstances a trust for the
purchaser. I shall return to these observations after looking at some of the other relevant
decisions, but it is relevant to observe, at this stage, that the issue in *Gibson* was as to the
status of a purchaser under missives, not that of the holder of a delivered but unrecorded
disposition, and that while the Lord President negatived the transfer of any property
before delivery of the disposition, he did not, to any extent, analyse or comment upon   E
the position of the holder of a delivered disposition or the nature of any right of property
which such a holder might have. The observations in *Gibson* have been cited in a number
of subsequent cases, including *Margrie Holdings Ltd v C & E Commrs* 1991 SLT 38, but
it was not necessary, in any of those cases, for the court to scrutinise the observations
closely or consider how they might stand with the authorities to which we have been
referred, and I do not think that these later citations add anything to the case of *Gibson*
itself.   F

The remaining cases can conveniently be considered in chronological order. The first
is *Munro v Brodie* (1844) 6 D 1249. That, again, concerned the position of a purchaser of
land whose right depended on the contract of sale, and who had not received delivery of
a disposition. The purchaser granted a bond and disposition in security over the subjects
of sale and the creditor in that bond was infeft on it. Before the purchaser obtained a
disposition from the seller, and took infeftment on it, a creditor of the seller had obtained   G
a bond and disposition in security and become infeft upon it and another creditor had
used inhibition. The decision was that the purchaser's ultimate infeftment on the
disposition, when he received it, could not be allowed to set up by accretion the bond in
disposition in security granted by the purchaser in favour of his creditor. Once again,
therefore, the case was not concerned with the status or rights of the holder of an
unrecorded disposition. Attention was, however, drawn to the observations of the Lord
Ordinary, Lord Ivory, (at p. 1253) who said, after drawing attention, to the fact that the   H
right was only a right under missives:

> 'Such a case differs in many respects from that where the party has a personal right
> by disposition; for the infeftment afterwards passed upon that disposition forms,
> with the disposition itself, but one feudal investiture, and the ultimate and more
> perfect real right absorbs the less perfect and merely inchoate or personal right,

and (where there is no mid impediment) may be allowed, without any great violence, to draw back to its date. A mere missive on the contrary is not as regards the real subject even an inchoate title.'

It is also clear, however, that the purchaser in that case did not even have a written contract as the basis of his claim to have a *jus crediti* and therefore anything said by Lord Ivory in relation to the holder of a personal title was obiter. Further, the reference to the feudal investiture drawing back to the date of the disposition was made with reference to the effect of the ultimate investiture for the purposes of accretion, in the absence of some mid impediment, and while Lord Ivory does regard the whole process of disposition and infeftment as completing one feudal investiture, he does so when looking at the whole position after the investiture is complete and is not paying attention to the situation of the holder of the personal right prior to completion. Accordingly, although the observations go some way to support the contention that some important rights are transferred by the delivery of the disposition, they do not really assist in the analysis of the status and rights of the disponee before infeftment is completed.

Edmond v Gordon & Ors (1855) 18 D 47 concerned a bankrupt who had apparently acquired lands by transmission from a person to whom they had originally been feued. It was discovered, however, on the bankruptcy, that the original charter had been defective and consequently that no valid feudal right to the lands had ever been constituted. The trustee sued the successors of the original grantor to obtain a charter in his favour as trustee, but the action was opposed by persons to whom the bankrupt had granted a bond and disposition in security which had been registered in the register of sasines. The effect of the decision, put shortly, was that although the bankrupt had never had a valid feudal title, he had enjoyed a personal right which he was entitled to assign and that the publication of the bond and disposition in security by registration in the register of sasines was equivalent to an intimation and therefore gave the bond holders a priority over the trustee. The contention of the bond holders, which was upheld, was put by the Lord President (at p. 52) in this form:

'Then, again, the other party says that it may be that Nicol was a creditor of the Magistrates to compel them to fulfil that obligation and that his trustee now is so, in virtue of the transference clause in the *Bankrupt Act*; but they say that Nicol had given away part of his personal right, or at least an interest in it to them or their representatives, who had lent money in security to him.'

That being so, I think it is reasonably clear that the decision was not concerned with a question of rights of property, but with a competition between personal rights. However, in argument some weight was put upon the opinion of Lord Deas who said (at p. 57):

'The next question is, had the bankrupt a good personal right to the lands? It appears to me that he had. I do not mean a personal right (as it has been called in the argument) to get a charter or disposition from the burgh – such as a purchaser has under mere missives of sale or articles and minutes of roup – but a personal right to the lands such as a disponee has whose disposition has not been followed by a valid infeftment.'

It was submitted that the use of the expression 'a personal right to the lands' pointed towards some species of right which could be regarded as being, or as being equivalent to, some kind of property. But that construction appears to me to place too much weight on what is, I think, merely a passing reference to the position of the holder of an unrecorded disposition: and, as has been seen, there are certain practical differences between the position of such a holder and the position of a person entitled to a mere *jus crediti*. The decision was affirmed in the House of Lords (see (1858) 3 Macq 116), and some of the observations in speeches in the House were also referred to. In particular, Lord Cranworth said (at p. 122):

'I must confess that upon this subject I think there is a great deal of doubt and
obscurity, from the want of anything definitely explaining the distinction between
jus ad rem and *jus crediti*, because I think I find that these words have been used in
many cases interchangeably, without any clear distinction of the one from the
other; but there may be this practical distinction, that the *jus ad rem* is a right
which the person possessing it may make a complete right by his own act, or by
some act which he may compel another without a suit to perform; whereas a *jus
crediti* may be defined to be a right which the holder of it cannot make available, if
it is resisted, without a suit to compel persons to do something else in order to
make the right perfect.'

Lord Wensleydale (at p. 130) added that whether the right was treated as a *jus ad rem*
or a *jus crediti* it was, at all events, clearly nothing but a personal right. The observations
in the House of Lords, therefore, are definitely adverse to the recognition of any form of
right of property in the holder of an unrecorded conveyance.

The case which gives the greatest support to the reclaimers is, in my view, *Bowman v
Wright* (1877) 4 R 322. The point decided in the case, as summarised in the head note, is
that the jurisdiction of the Scottish courts, founded on proprietorship of heritage in
Scotland, ceases when the proprietor grants an absolute conveyance of the subjects,
although he has not been feudally divested. The grounds of decision are summed up in
the opinion of the Lord Justice Clerk (at p. 325) :

'The only question, therefore, is, was Wright proprietor at the date of citation of
any heritage within Scotland, for it is admitted that has acquired none since? I am
of opinion that he was not, for he had sold what he previously had, and the right
to it was vested in the purchaser, so far at least as he, Wright, was concerned. I do
not think that it matters that under the Act of 1617 Cap. 17, the disponee's right
might have been evacuated in favour of a second *bona fide* purchaser first infeft, or
might have been burdened by a lease granted after the date of the disposition.
These are rights which the legislature has thought proper to confer on *bona fide*
purchasers, taking advantage of our system of registration, and upon tenants, but
not rights remaining in the original seller, who has done all he could to divest
himself. It comes to this, that anything which the defender could have done to
affect the property would not have been the exercise of a right but the commission
of a fraud, and the power to affect property by the commission of a fraud cannot
be treated as a right of property. Being thus of the opinion this matter is to be
looked on according to the reality and substance of the thing, I am clear that we
have no jurisdiction over this defender and have no alternative but to dismiss the
action.'

Similar views were expressed by Lord Ormidale who said (at p. 327) that it was impossible
to regard the defender as in any fair or correct sense the owner or possessor of the
heritable subjects at the date of raising the action; and by Lord Gifford who said (at
p. 328) that the principle upon which jurisdiction is founded depended upon the
possession of some real or beneficial interest in some heritable subject, something real
and substantial, not a mere fiction.

This case was concerned with jurisdiction and it can be said, as the respondents
submitted, that the principles upon which jurisdiction rests are different from those of
the law of property in itself. In particular, underlying the rules governing jurisdiction
based on ownership of heritable property in Scotland is the principle that jurisdiction
should only be exercised where it can be made effective. Nevertheless, the observations
of the judges in *Bowman v Wright* are a forceful expression of the view that, once a
disposition has been granted and delivered, the truth and reality of the situation is that
the property has been transferred and that what remains with the disponer is a nominal

A   or fictional title; and that the reason why a second disponee obtains a good title if he records his disposition first has nothing to do with any rights of property which may remain in the grantor but everything to do with the principle that the faith of the records must be maintained, even at substantial cost in justice. It is for that reason that, in my view, this decision lends the most powerful support to the reclaimers' argument.

The remaining cases can be dealt with, in my view, much more briefly. *James Grant &*
B   *Co Ltd v Moran* (above) concerned the validity of a notice to quit given by a person who at the date of the notice was merely a purchaser under missives. Sheriff Substitute A G Walker held that such a person was not, in line with previous authority, entitled to give a notice to quit. The observation founded upon, which came in the course of contrasting the position of a purchaser with that of the holder of a disposition, was as follows:

C   'A purchaser who obtains a valid disposition from a seller with immediate entry then becomes for the first time the owner of the property. It is true that his title is still a personal title, but it is a title which he can complete and convert by infeftment into a real right at his own hand at any time. As soon as he receives the disposition he can occupy the property and collect the rents and he becomes liable for the burdens.'

The sheriff did therefore go so far as to treat the holder of an unrecorded disposition
D   as in some sense owner of the property, but he did so in the context of dealings with tenants and the decision contains no real analysis of the position in a question of competition of title, with which the case had no concern. *Embassy Picture House (Troon) Ltd v Cammo Developments Ltd* 1971 SC 25 was another case concerning jurisdiction, this time of the sheriff court. The defenders were purchasers of a property in terms of missives but they had not received a disposition. It was held that they were not owners of the property for the purposes of the relevant provisions of the Sheriff Courts (Scotland)
E   Acts. In the course of his opinion, Lord Justice Clerk Grant contrasted the possession of purchasers under missives with the holders of a delivered disposition, which latter he described as clearly a right of ownership, even if feudal infeftment had not followed and even if, in certain circumstances, it might be lost. In my view, that observation is primarily an application of the decision in *Bowman v Wright* (above): the case can be regarded as giving support to the approach taken in *Bowman v Wright* but like that case it was not a decision on a question of competing titles. It should perhaps be added that Lord Walker
F   (at p. 30) pointed out that it was not necessary to discuss what might be sufficient tradition or delivery to transfer ownership.

Looking at the position so far, it seems to me that there is no support either in the general structure of the system of property in land in Scotland or in the cases concerned with property rights and competition between such rights for the view that any right which could be described as ownership or property passes to the disponee upon mere
G   delivery of the disposition. On the contrary, these authorities seem to me to support the view that ownership or title only passes upon completion of the process of feudal investiture, and that up to that point whatever rights the disponee may have acquired upon delivery of the disposition remain merely personal rights. Further, where expressions have been used which tend to suggest that some form of property might have passed to the disponee, they seem to have been used, as was pointed out in the House of
H   Lords in *Edmond v Gordon* (above) and by Gloag and Irvine (above), without any clear definition or analysis of what was meant by the property said to have been transferred or what the nature and incidents of such property or proprietorial right might be. Further, although, as I have indicated, I recognise the force of the reasoning in *Bowman v Wright* (above) it seems to me that it goes much too far if it is taken as directly applicable in the context of the law of property. When it is, as it has been, well recognised that the solemnities of infeftment, whatever they may have been from time to time, are essential

in order to divest the grantor and invest the grantee with a right of property, I do not see   A
how it can properly be said that what remains with the grantee after the delivery of a
disposition but before completion of infeftment is only some kind of fictional or nominal
property. Further, although the policy of the statutory provisions is no doubt intended
to preserve the faith of the records, these statutory provisions nevertheless do, in my
opinion, affect the character of any rights which can be said to be held by a disponee who
has not registered his disposition. I do not doubt the force of the reasoning in *Bowman v*
Wright and other cases of that class in the context of the law governing jurisdiction, but   B
I do not think that that reasoning can simply be lifted from that context and applied to
the context of the law of property. Similarly, I do not think there is any reason to doubt
that the observations made in *Gibson v Hunter Home Designs* (above) were appropriate
in the context of that case. There is a real difference between the position of a disponee
who has received a disposition and that of a person who only has a right under missives,
as the authorities have repeatedly pointed out; and I do not think that the court in *Gibson*   C
was concerned to do more than to point out these differences. It was not concerned to
analyse the position of the holder of an unregistered disposition or the sense, if any, in
which such a holder could be said to have a right of property. In the end, the reclaimers'
submission was, as I understood it, that the effect of the delivery of a disposition before
recording was, on the basis of the authorities, to transfer in inchoate form, a right pre-
existing in the disponer, that this was a transfer of a real right, although incomplete, and
that the completion of an incomplete real right, although difficult as a concept, was not   D
so legally impossible as to be ruled out altogether. In my view, that argument has no
basis apart from the practical distinction between the position after the delivery of a
disposition and the position before such delivery and it is impossible to draw from the
authorities any ground for saying that the holder of such a disposition has any recognised
or clear status which can be equated with or properly described as ownership or property.

The next stage is to consider those cases which might be regarded as exceptions to, or   E
as posing some difficulty for, the scheme of property law in Scotland understood as a
system in which, in principle, ownership belongs to a single person at any one time and is
transferred at one single moment in its entirety. I have already referred to the cases
concerned with jurisdiction, and I do not think it is necessary to say more about them.
Reference was made, as I have indicated, also to *City of Glasgow v McEwan* (above), but
that was a case on a rating question and does not seem to me really to assist on a question   F
of property. The two situations which do require some further consideration are that of
trust and that of the *ex facie* absolute disposition. On the view which I take, however,
neither of these situations requires to be treated at very great length. Although it has been
argued, for example, by Sir Thomas Smith (*Studies Critical & Comparative*, p. 198ff.)
that the concept of trust is not necessarily inconsistent with civilian views of the nature
of property, it seems to me that it has always been evident that there is some difficulty in
reconciling the concept of a trust with the principle of unity of ownership. That difficulty   G
has manifested itself in, for example, attempts to explain a trust as a combination of the
contracts of mandate and deposit, an explanation which is manifestly inadequate, for the
reasons explained in Wilson & Duncan (*Trusts, Trustees & Executors*, p. 12ff). The same
difficulty also manifests itself, in my view, very clearly in the discussion of trust in South
African law in Frere Smith's *Manual of South African Trust Law* to which we were
referred by the respondents. It further seems to me that notwithstanding decisions such
as *Clark's Trustees v Inland Revenue* 1939 SC 11, in practice most lawyers dealing with   H
trusts in Scotland do so on the assumption that the trustee enjoys a legal estate or legal
title and the beneficiary an equitable or beneficial title, very much as those concepts are
understood in English law. The case principally relevant for the present purpose is
Heritable Reversionary Co Ltd v Millar (1892) 19 R (HL) 43 and it is interesting that the
Lord Chancellor in that case, at a very early stage in his opinion, remarked that he did

A   not understand it to be questioned that the law of Scotland recognised the relationship of trustee and beneficial owner. The question in the case was whether heritable property to which a bankrupt had an unqualified feudal title vested in his trustee in bankruptcy, and it was held that it did not, on the basis that such property was not property of the bankrupt at all. The bankrupt was the manager of the beneficiaries, had purchased certain property on their instructions and with their money, but had taken title in his own name. He had executed an express declaration of trust, although there was no reference to that declaration *ex facie* of the deeds. The essential grounds of the decision are, in my view, found in two passages from Lord Watson's speech. First, (at p. 49) Lord Watson said:

B

> 'Were the subjects in dispute the property of Mackay within the meaning of that enactment at the date of his sequestration? Upon the language of the statute, that appears to me to be a very simple question admitting only of a negative answer. An apparent title to land or personal estate, carrying no real right of property with it, does not, in the ordinary or in any true legal sense, make such land or personal estate the property of the person who holds the title. That which in legal as well as in conventional language is described as a man's property is estate, whether heritable or moveable in which he has a beneficial interest which the law allows him to dispose of. That which in legal as well as in conventional language is described as a man's property is estate, whether heritable or moveable, in which he has a beneficial interest which the law allows him to dispose of. It does not include estate in which he has no beneficial interest and which he cannot dispose of without committing a fraud. It is true that the law will sustain a right created by his fraudulent alienation in the person of a *bona fide* alienee for value, but not, as has been already pointed out, upon the ground that the thing alienated was the property of his author.'

C

D

E   Secondly, (at p. 50) Lord Watson said:

> 'I venture to think that the property described in these four Acts as falling within the sequestration includes no heritable or other estate of which the bankrupt was not the true owner. That construction gives effect to the literal meaning of their language; and it is to my mind hardly conceivable that the legislature should have intended to confiscate the property of persons other than the bankrupt for the behoof of his creditors by requiring him to execute a disposition in favour of their trustee which, but for the statute, he could not have granted without being guilty of the crime of breach of trust and embezzlement.'

F

G   Although there is some relationship between Lord Watson's reasoning, in so far as it refers to fraudulent alienations or dispositions, and the reasoning in *Bowman v Wright* (above), the position in this case is in my view very different. The case is not concerned with property which had ever belonged, or which continued to belong, up to the date of transfer, to the transferor. It is concerned with property which, according to an established rule of law, is not to be treated as being part of the transferor's property at all. The fact that property held in trust is not property of the holder of the apparent title is, in my view, really to be regarded as an established exception to the rules which govern the acquisition and transmission of rights of property in other cases. Attempts have been made to extend the application and effect of the concept of trust, but as is shown by the decision in *Bank of Scotland v Hutchison* 1914 SC (HL) 1, such attempts have so far been rejected.

H

The position in regard to *ex facie* absolute dispositions, is, in my view, similar. The leading case is *Union Bank of Scotland Ltd v National Bank of Scotland Ltd* (above). Notwithstanding Lord Watson's comment (at p. 4) on the case of *Robertson v Duff* (1840) 2 D 279, there may, in my view, be force in the argument that the recognition that for

certain purposes the holder of an *ex facie* absolute disposition is affected by the back   A
letter, and is treated as the holder of a mere security, may owe something to concepts of
trust. As finally expressed by Lord Watson, however, the basis of the recognition that the
radical right in the subjects remains with the disponer under a disposition *ex facie*
absolute but truly in security is that the truth and reality of the situation is that the
transaction was one of security and nothing else. Again, although it seems to me that it
can fairly be said that the recognition of *ex facie* absolute dispositions cannot easily be
fitted into a conception of the law of property based upon civilian principles, it is, at   B
most, an anomalous exception to those principles.

I should also mention at this point that the respondents found on *Mitchell v Ferguson*
(1781) Mor 10296 and other cases grouped together under the heading of 'race to the
register' cases. I do not, however, think that these cases require to be discussed in detail.
They confirm, in various contexts, that the general rule is that the person who first
registers his right prevails and to that extent are adverse to the recognition of any   C
intermediate right between a personal and a real right but do not, I think, advance the
argument much further.

On the whole matter, so far, with the greatest respect to those dicta of eminent judges
which suggest otherwise, it seems to me that it would be inconsistent with principle to
regard the holder of an unregistered disposition as enjoying any kind of property right in
any sense recognised by the general law of property. There is no clear definition of any   D
such right or of its incidents and consequences. It is conceptually difficult to understand
what such a right might be, particularly if there were, at any given time, more than one
personal right or personal title in existence. There is no basis for extension or
generalisation of any of the exceptions to the principles of the system of property law to
which reference has been made and it is difficult to see how some such intermediate right
could be recognised as a unique phenomenon on its own.
                                                                                              E
I therefore turn to the question of statutory construction, which is, in the end, the
decisive question in the case. I do so on the basis that the law of property, apart from the
floating charges legislation, does not afford to the reclaimers a definite sense in which the
expression 'property' could be understood and that any such sense must be derived from
the provisions of the statute itself. I also recognise that there are grounds for saying that
the result in the present case is unfair, if the respondents' property based argument
prevails, and that it is not a happy situation to be holding that the requirements of a   F
coherent system of property law defeat what appears to be a fair claim in an individual
case. Having said that, however, I think that it must also be recognised that there are
many other situations in bankruptcy and liquidation proceedings which give rise to
comparable unfairness. The supplier who has provided goods or services for which he
has not been paid suffers a loss every bit as great as that of the person who has paid for
property which he does not receive; and there may be force in the comment which has   G
been made (1994 SLT (News) 92) that the particular perception of unfairness in the
present case derives from an undue concentration upon the law governing domestic
conveyancing. However that may be, it seems to me that it is necessary, if the reclaimers
are to succeed, that they should be able to put forward a coherent meaning for the
expression 'property' which can be said to be derived from the provisions of the statute.

The reclaimers' arguments can be summarised, I think, as follows. Firstly, even in an   H
insolvency statute expressions such as 'property' and 'belonging to' are not necessarily
technical ones, and for this they cite *Heritable Reversionary Co v Millar* (above), *Fraser v
Magistrates of Aberdeen* (above) and other cases. Secondly, the attachment of a floating
charge does not necessarily occur only in an insolvency situation and therefore the
wording used must be construed in the context of the use of the charge as a commercial
instrument. Thirdly, in the end the question is whether Albyn intended, as disclosed by

A the terms of the floating charge which they granted, that heritage sold in the ordinary course of business, for which a price had been received and a disposition delivered, fell within the description of property in the instrument creating the charge. Fourthly, delivery was the final act of Albyn so far as within its power to take the subjects out of its property; and since the transfer of property in heritage involves a single transaction constituted in modern times by the delivery and the registration of a disposition it was not an affront to language to regard property as passing on the delivery of the disposition.

B Fifthly, a purposive rather than an analytical approach to the statute is appropriate, especially when the construction for which the respondents contend fails to achieve the objects of the statute, one of which was that a similar rule should operate in Scotland as in England. In support of these contentions, the respondents submitted that the phrase in the statute 'property from time to time comprised in its property and undertaking' was different from phrases such as 'any part of its property' and directed attention to something less than property in the absolute sense, namely to the assets which were deployed or capable of being deployed for the purposes of the business activities of the company. The same construction would apply, they accepted, to other cases in which an act of registration was necessary to transfer property such as transfers of shares, ships or aircraft. The construction proposed could, however, operate clearly because it was not difficult to determine whether an irrevocable act had taken place. The reference to a fixed security in the statutory provisions was, they submitted, a part of the mechanics of D constituting the security only.

The respondents submitted that the floating charge was an import into Scots law of an institution derived from a different system to which effect had been given in Scots law by connecting it to the law of property and making its attachment equivalent to a standard security. The phrase 'property and undertaking' had an established meaning comprising the whole of what belonged to the company and the legislation had been framed to catch E such property whether present or future. There was no hint in the statute or in any report which preceded it of any special meaning being devised for the expression 'property'. The commercial construction proposed by the reclaimers was unworkable and, for example, a balance sheet test on the lines proposed by the reclaimers would not work because accountants preparing such a balance sheet were not concerned with an issue of property but with a question of what was a true and fair view of the company's affairs.

F In approaching this final question, it seems to me that, although weight should be given to the arguments that the purity of Scots law, as a system based on the civil law, should be maintained and the unitary conception of ownership preserved, these arguments should not be overemphasised or treated as in themselves decisive. The ultimate question in this case is a practical and limited one, concerned with the operation of a particular form of security and, as some of the authorities referred to above show, exceptional situations have been accommodated within the system in the past. The G difficulty, however, which I find with the reclaimers' contentions is that, just as it seems to me impossible to derive from the general law concerning the ownership and transmission of heritage any clear defined or coherent meaning for the expression 'property' other than that of the full real right in the subjects, so it seems to me that there is no basis in the statutory provisions for deducing or establishing any such clear and coherent meaning capable of being consistently applied. The weakness of the reclaimers' H argument seems to me to be indicated by their attempt to establish a sufficiently clear meaning for the word 'property' in the statute by making reference, in some sense, to Albyn's intentions in granting the floating charge, and by suggesting that it could be inferred that the property covered by the charge was property deployed or capable of being deployed in the business of the company. Not only does it seem to me that there is no warrant for restricting the effect of the charge to property actually or potentially employed for business purposes, as opposed to any other property there might be, it also

seems to me that the tests suggested are uncertain to a very high degree. In the end, a
floating charge does operate on property, and affect proprietary rights, and it seems to
me that, for that reason, it is important that there should be clarity and certainty in its
operation. I do not think that the reclaimers obtain any assistance in surmounting this
fundamental difficulty either from reference to the wording of the floating charge itself,
or from the argument that the effect of the Lord Ordinary's decision is that, contrary to
the apparent intention of those who first recommended the introduction of such charges
in Scotland, there will be important differences between the effect of such charges in
Scotland and in England. In my view, the court must construe the legislation as it is, in
the context of the rules of property law as we have them. In all these circumstances, in
my opinion, the reclaimers have failed to show that the Lord Ordinary reached an
incorrect conclusion on this part of the case.

In the course of the debate, there was some discussion of steps which might be open to
a purchaser of heritage to protect himself against the risk that a floating charge granted
by the seller might crystallise, as in the present case, before a disposition could be
recorded. I do not, however, think it appropriate to consider whether and to what extent
any such steps might be effective. If it is the case that there are no effective steps which
can be taken, that may provide a strong argument in favour of some statutory reform of
the law, but it does not assist in solving the fundamental problem in the reclaimers'
contention. In any event, this question only arose as an incidental issue, and I am not
convinced that we heard sufficient argument to enable us to determine it properly.

The reclaimers also submitted, as an alternative, that in the circumstances Albyn
should be regarded as having held the property, after delivery of the disposition, subject
to some sort of trust or constructive trust in favour of the first defenders. I do not think
it is necessary to examine this contention at length. The argument that some sort of trust
could be said to arise in cases of sales and purchases generally was rejected in *Bank of
Scotland v Liquidators of Hutchison Main & Co Ltd* (above). It is very difficult to see how
a trust could be recognised in the circumstances of this case without recognising some
radical modification of the rules of Scots law in relation to sales and purchases and the
introduction of something very much akin to the English concepts of equitable interests,
which, whatever may be the position in proper trusts, have never been adopted into the
Scots common law of sale. For the reasons given by your Lordship, *Stevenson v Wilson*
1907 SC 445 was a very special case and does not assist the reclaimer. In the end, it
seemed to me that this part of the argument was not pressed with very great enthusiasm
by the reclaimers and it is sufficient to say that in my view the Lord Ordinary reached a
correct conclusion on this part of the case also.

In the whole circumstances, in my opinion, this reclaiming motion falls to be refused.

(*Order accordingly*)

_____

A
Royal Brunei Airlines Sdn Bhd v Tan Kok Ming.

Privy Council.
Lord Goff of Chieveley, Lord Ackner, Lord Nicholls of Birkenhead, Lord Steyn
and Sir John May.
Judgment delivered 24 May 1995.

B
*Trust – Breach of trust – Knowing assistance by third party – Dishonesty – Travel
agent required to account to airline for money from ticket sales – Moneys not
retained in separate account but used for general company business in breach of
trust – Whether dishonesty by third party required to be accessory to breach of
trust – Whether dishonesty by trustee necessary ingredient of liability of third
party – Whether director liable as accessory to breach of trust by company.*

C
This was an appeal from a decision of the Court of Appeal of Brunei Darussalam allowing
an appeal by 'T', the managing director and principal shareholder of a company ('Travel'),
from the decision of the Chief Justice who held that T was liable as constructive trustee for
moneys received by the company from the sale of airline tickets.

In 1986 the airline appointed Travel to act as its general travel agent for the sale of
passenger and cargo transportation. Travel was controlled by T, the managing director and
D
principal shareholder. The appointment was set out in a written agreement by which Travel
was required to account to the airline for all amounts received from the sale of tickets. The
agreement was expressly subject to the regulations of the International Air Transport
Association which provided that all moneys collected by the agent were the property of the
carrier and held in trust by the agent for the carrier until accounted for. Despite the terms
of the agreement Travel did not maintain a separate bank account for the airline's money
but paid it into Travel's ordinary current account with its bank. By a standing arrangement
E
any balance over a stated amount was transferred from the current account into a fixed
deposit account or to T's account. Travel was required to pay the airline within 30 days, but
fell into arrears at various times. In August 1992 the airline terminated the agreement and
in January 1993 brought an action against T for unpaid money. T was not a party to the
agency agreement but had signed it on behalf of Travel.

F
At the trial the judge held that T was liable as constructive trustee on the basis of knowing
assistance as accessory to Travel's breach of trust. Judgment was entered for the airline in
damages. T appealed. The Court of Appeal of Brunei Darussalam allowed T's appeal on
the ground that an essential prerequisite to accessory liability, a dishonest and fraudulent
design on the part of Travel as trustee, had not been established in relation to the sums held
in trust for the airline. The airline appealed.

Held, allowing the airline's appeal:

G
1. Liability as an accessory to a breach of trust by a trustee required dishonesty on the
part of the accessory, whether or not the trustee was also acting dishonestly. Dishonesty on
the accessory's part was sufficient to render him liable to make good the loss resulting from
his dishonest procurement of or assistance in a breach of trust or fiduciary obligation.

2. The money paid to Travel on the sale of the airline's tickets was held by Travel upon
H
trust for the airline. The trust gave Travel no authority to use the money in the conduct of
its business. By failing to hold the airline's money separately from its general business
account Travel committed a breach of trust, in which T knowingly assisted. It followed that
both T and Travel were acting dishonestly in so doing, since T's state of mind was to be
imputed to the company. Travel's inability to pay the airline was a direct consequence of the
breach of trust. Accordingly T was liable in damages to the airline as an accessory to
Travel's breach of trust.

The following cases were referred to in the judgment: A

Agip (Africa) Ltd v Jackson & Ors [1990] Ch 265.
Attorney-General v Corp of Leicester (1844) 7 Beav 176; 49 ER 1031.
Baden & Ors v Société Générale pour Favoriser le Développement du Commerce et de l'Industrie en France SA [1993] 1 WLR 509.
Barnes v Addy (1874) LR 9 Ch App 244.
Belmont Finance Corp Ltd v Williams Furniture Ltd & Ors [1979] Ch 250.   B
Carl Zeiss Stiftung v Herbert Smith & Co (No. 2) [1969] 2 Ch 276.
Consul Development Pty Ltd v DPC Estates Pty Ltd (1975) 132 CLR 373.
Cowan de Groot Properties Ltd v Eagle Trust plc [1992] 4 All ER 700.
DPC Estates Pty Ltd v Grey & Anor [1974] 1 NSWLR 443.
Eagle Trust plc v SBC Securities Ltd [1993] 1 WLR 484.
Eaves v Hickson (1861) 30 Beav 136; 54 ER 840.
Equiticorp Industries Group Ltd v Hawkins [1991] 3 NZLR 700; (1991) 5 NZCLC   C
67,201.
Fyler v Fyler (1841) 3 Beav 550; 49 ER 216.
Karak Rubber Co Ltd v Burden (No. 2) [1972] 1 WLR 602.
Marr v Arabco Traders Ltd (1987) 1 NZBLC 102,732.
Marshall Futures Ltd v Marshall [1992] 1 NZLR 316; (1991) 5 NZCLC 67,238.
Montagu's Settlement Trusts, Re [1987] Ch 264.
Nimmo v Westpac Banking Corp [1993] 3 NZLR 218; (1993) 4 NZBLC 103,134.   D
Polly Peck International plc v Nadir (No. 2) [1992] 4 All ER 769.
Powell v Thompson [1991] 1 NZLR 597.
R v Ghosh [1982] QB 1053.
Selangor United Rubber Estates Ltd v Cradock (No. 3) [1968] 1 WLR 1555.
Springfield Acres Ltd (in liquidation) v Abacus (Hong Kong) Ltd [1994] 3 NZLR 502.
Westpac Banking Corp v Savin [1985] 2 NZLR 41; (1986) 1 NZBLC 102,345.   E

Michael Beloff QC, Murray Hunt and Raymond Lam (of the Brunei Bar) (instructed by Norton Rose) for the appellant airline.

Daljit S Sandhu and Geoffrey Sim (both of the Brunei Bar) (instructed by Denton Hall) for T.

JUDGMENT   F
(Delivered by Lord Nicholls of Birkenhead)

The proper role of equity in commercial transactions is a topical question. Increasingly plaintiffs have plaintiffs have recourse to equity for an effective remedy when the person in default, typically a company, is insolvent. Plaintiffs seek to obtain relief from others who were involved in the transaction, such as directors of the company, or its bankers, or its legal or other advisers. They seek to fasten fiduciary obligations directly onto the   G company's officers or agents or advisers, or to have them held personally liable for assisting the company in breaches of trust or fiduciary obligations.

This is such a case. An insolvent travel agent company owed money to an airline. The airline seeks a remedy against the travel agent's principal director and shareholder. Its claim is based on the much-quoted dictum of Lord Selborne LC, sitting in the Court of Appeal in Chancery, in *Barnes v Addy* (1874) LR 9 Ch App 244 at pp. 251–252:

     H

> 'That responsibility [sc., the responsibility of a trustee] may no doubt be extended in equity to others who are not properly trustees, if they are found ... actually participating in any fraudulent conduct of the trustee to the injury of the *cestui que trust*. But ... strangers are not to be made constructive trustees merely because they act as the agents of trustees in transactions within their legal powers, transactions, perhaps of which a Court of Equity may disapprove, unless those

A   agents receive and become chargeable with some part of the trust property, or unless they assist with knowledge in a dishonest and fraudulent design on the part of the trustees.'

In the conventional shorthand, the first of these two circumstances in which third parties (non-trustees) may become liable to account in equity is 'knowing receipt', as distinct from the second where liability arises from 'knowing assistance'. Stated even more

B   shortly, the first limb of Lord Selborne's formulation is concerned with the liability of a person as a *recipient* of trust property or its traceable proceeds. The second limb is concerned with what, for want of a better compendious description, can be called the liability of an *accessory* to a trustee's breach of trust. Liability as an accessory is not dependent upon receipt of trust property. It arises even though no trust property has reached the hands of the accessory. It is a form of secondary liability in the sense that it

C   only arises where there has been a breach of trust. In the present case the plaintiff relies on the accessory limb. The particular point in issue arises from the expression 'a dishonest and fraudulent design on the part of the trustees'.

The proceedings

D   The essential facts are these. In 1986 Royal Brunei Airlines Sdn Bhd appointed Borneo Leisure Travel Sdn Bhd ('BLT') to act, in various places in Sabah and Sarawak, as its general travel agent for the sale of passenger and cargo transportation. The terms of the appointment were set out in a written agreement of 1 April 1986. BLT was required to account to the airline for all amounts received from sales of tickets. For its services it was to be paid a sales commission. The agreement was expressed to be subject to the regulations of the International Air Transport Association, one of which provided:

E   'All moneys collected by the agent for transportation and ancillary services sold under this Agreement, including applicable commissions which the agent is entitled to claim thereunder, shall be the property of the Carrier and shall be held by the agent in trust for the Carrier or on behalf of the Carrier until satisfactorily accounted for to the Carrier and settlement made . . . Unless otherwise instructed by the Carrier the agent shall be entitled to deduct from remittances the applicable commission to which it is entitled hereunder.'

F   It was common ground that the effect of this provision was to constitute BLT a trustee for the airline of the money it received from the sale of passenger and cargo transportation by the airline.

In practice what happened was that money received by BLT on behalf of the airline was not paid into a separate bank account. It was paid into BLT's ordinary, current account with its bank. By a standing arrangement with the bank, any balance in its current account in excess of a stated amount was transferred to a fixed deposit account

G   of BLT or, at times, of Mr Philip Tan Kok Ming. Mr Tan had founded BLT. He was managing director and principal shareholder. He was effectively in charge and control of BLT. The other director and shareholder was his wife. Nothing turns on these transfers of money to other accounts because, with one immaterial exception, all the transferred money eventually found its way back to BLT's current account.

BLT was required to pay the airline within 30 days, but at various times from 1988 onwards it was in arrears. In August 1992 the airline terminated the agreement. In

H   January 1993 the airline commenced this action against Mr Tan in respect of the unpaid money. Mr Tan was not himself a party to the agency agreement, although he had signed it on behalf of BLT.

At the trial held in October 1993 the Chief Justice, Dato Sir Denys Roberts, rejected a claim by the airline that Mr Tan had orally guaranteed payment of the money. The Chief Justice also rejected a claim that Mr Tan had diverted the money to his own use. The

Chief Justice upheld a claim that Mr Tan was liable as a constructive trustee, under the   A
accessory limb of Lord Selborne's formulation. Although not particularised, this issue
was pleaded explicitly and unequivocally. Mr Tan knew there was an express trust of the
money. The money appeared to have been used by BLT for its ordinary business
purposes, paying salaries, overheads and other expenses, and keeping down its bank
overdraft. It must be assumed that Mr Tan authorised the use of the money for these
purposes. That was sufficient to make him liable. A fraudulent and dishonest design is
not confined to personal gain. It is sufficient if the stranger knowingly assists in the use   B
of trust property in a way which is not permitted by the trust. Judgment was entered for
the airline for B$335,160.

The Court of Appeal of Brunei Darussalam allowed Mr Tan's appeal. Counsel for Mr
Tan conceded that a trust of the money had been created, and that there had been a
breach of that trust in which Mr Tan had assisted with actual knowledge. The issue was
whether a dishonest and fraudulent design on the part of BLT had been established. The   C
court held that the evidence revealed a sorry tale of mismanagement and broken
promises, but that it was not established that BLT was guilty of fraud or dishonesty in
relation to the amounts it held in trust for the airline. Delivering the judgment of the
court, Fuad P stated:

> 'As long standing and high authority shows, conduct which may amount to a
> breach of trust, however morally reprehensible, will not render a person who has   D
> knowingly assisted in the breach of trust liable as a constructive trustee, if that
> conduct falls short of dishonesty.'

This view of the state of the law has the support of the (English) Court of Appeal. In
Selangor United Rubber Estates Ltd v Cradock (No. 3) [1968] 1 WLR 1555 at p. 1591,
Ungoed-Thomas J held that the expression 'dishonest and fraudulent design' was to be
understood according to the principles of a court of equity. That approach was   E
emphatically rejected by the Court of Appeal in *Belmont Finance Corporation Ltd v
Williams Furniture Ltd & Ors* [1979] Ch 250. Buckley LJ observed at p. 267 that the rule
as formulated by Lord Selborne had stood for more than 100 years, and that to depart
from it would introduce an undesirable degree of uncertainty to the law over what degree
of unethical conduct would suffice if dishonesty was not to be the criterion. Goff LJ at
p. 274 agreed that it would be dangerous and wrong to depart from 'the safe path of the
principle as stated by Lord Selborne' to the 'uncharted sea of something not innocent   F
. . . but still short of dishonesty'.

In short, the issue on this appeal is whether the breach of trust which is a pre-requisite
to accessory liability must itself be a dishonest and fraudulent breach of trust by the
trustee.

The honest trustee and the dishonest third party   G

It must be noted at once that there is a difficulty with the approach adopted on this
point in the Belmont case. Take the simple example of an honest trustee and a dishonest
third party. Take a case where a dishonest solicitor persuades a trustee to apply trust
property in a way the trustee honestly believes is permissible but which the solicitor
knows full well is a clear breach of trust. The solicitor deliberately conceals this from the
trustee. In consequence, the beneficiaries suffer a substantial loss. It cannot be right that   H
in such a case the accessory liability principle would be inapplicable because of the
innocence of the trustee. In ordinary parlance, the beneficiaries have been defrauded by
the solicitor. If there is to be an accessory liability principle at all, whereby in appropriate
circumstances beneficiaries may have direct recourse against a third party, the principle
must surely be applicable in such a case, just as much as in a case where both the trustee
and the third party have been dishonest. Indeed, if anything, the case for liability of the

A   dishonest third party seems stronger where the trustee is innocent, because in such a case the third party alone was dishonest and that was the cause of the subsequent misapplication of the trust property.

The position would be the same if, instead of *procuring* the breach, the third party dishonestly *assisted* in the breach. Change the facts slightly. A trustee is proposing to make a payment out of the trust fund to a particular person. He honestly believes he is

B   authorised to do so by the terms of the trust deed. He asks a solicitor to carry through the transaction. The solicitor well knows that the proposed payment would be a plain breach of trust. He also well knows that the trustee mistakenly believes otherwise. Dishonestly he leaves the trustee under his misapprehension and prepares the necessary documentation. Again, if the accessory principle is not be artificially constricted, it ought to be applicable in such a case.

C   These examples suggest that what matters is the state of mind of the third party sought to be made liable, not the state of mind of the trustee. The trustee will be liable in any event for the breach of trust, even if he acted innocently, unless excused by an exemption clause in the trust instrument or relieved by court. But *his* state of mind is essentially irrelevant to question whether the *third party* should be made liable to the beneficiaries for the breach of trust. If the liability of the third party is fault-based, what matters is the nature of his fault, not that of the trustee. In this regard dishonesty on the part of the

D   third party would seem to be a sufficient basis for his liability, irrespective of the state of mind of the trustee who is in breach of trust. It is difficult to see why, if the third party dishonestly assisted in a breach, there should be a further pre-requisite to his liability, namely, that the trustee also must have been acting dishonestly. The alternative view would mean that a dishonest third party is liable if the trustee is dishonest, but if the trustee did not act dishonestly that of itself would excuse a dishonest third party from

E   liability. That would make no sense.

Earlier authority

The view that the accessory liability principle cannot be restricted to fraudulent breaches of trust is not to be approached with suspicion as a latter-day novelty. Before the accessory principle donned its *Barnes v Addy* straitjacket, judges seem not to have

F   regarded the principle as confined in this way. In *Fyler v Fyler* (1841) 3 Beav 550 at p. 568, Lord Langdale MR expressed the view that if trustees invested in an unauthorised investment, solicitors who knowingly procured that to be done for their own benefit 'ought to be considered as partakers in the breach of trust' even though the trustees intended in good faith that the investment would be beneficial to the life-tenant and not prejudicial to the beneficiaries with interests in capital. The same judge, in *Attorney-General v Corporation of Leicester* (1844) 7 Beav 176 at p. 179, stated:

G

> 'it cannot be disputed that, if the agent of a trustee, whether a corporate body or not, knowing that a breach of trust is being committed, interferes and assists in that breach of trust, he is personally answerable, although he may be employed as the agent of the person who directs him to commit that breach of trust.'

In *Eaves v Hickson* (1861) 30 Beav 136 trustees, acting in good faith, paid over the fund

H   to William Knibb's adult children on the strength of a forged marriage certificate produced to them by William Knibb. Sir John Romilly MR held that William Knibb was liable to replace the fund, to the extent that it was not recovered from his children, and to do so in priority to the liability of the trustees. Far from this being a case of fraud by the trustees, the Master of the Rolls at p. 141 described it as a very hard case on the trustees, who were deceived by a forgery which would have deceived anyone who was not looking out for forgery or fraud.

This point did not arise in *Barnes v Addy*. There the new sole trustee was engaged in a   A
dishonest and fraudulent design. He intended to misapply the trust fund as soon as it
reached his hands. The two solicitors were held not liable because there was no evidence
that either of them had any knowledge or suspicion of this.

What has gone wrong? Their Lordships venture to think that the reason is that ever
since the *Selangor* case highlighted the potential uses of equitable remedies in connection
with misapplied company funds, there has been a tendency to cite and interpret and   B
apply Lord Selborne's formulation as though it were a statute. This has particularly been
so with the accessory limb of Lord Selborne's apothegm. This approach has been inimical
to analysis of the underlying concept. Working within this constraint, the courts have
found themselves wrestling with the interpretation of the individual ingredients, especially
'knowingly' but also 'dishonest and fraudulent design on the part of the trustees', without
examining the underlying reason why a third party who has received no trust property is
being made liable at all. One notable exception is the judgment of Thomas J in *Powell v*   C
Thompson [1991] 1 NZLR 597 at pp. 610–615. On this point he observed (at p. 613):

> 'Once a breach of trust has been committed, the commission of which has involved
> a third party, the question which arises is one as between the beneficiary and that
> third party. If the third party's conduct has been unconscionable, then irrespective
> of the degree of impropriety in the trustee's conduct, the third party is liable to be
> held accountable to the beneficiary as if he or she were a trustee.'   D

To resolve this issue it is necessary to take an overall look at the accessory liability
principle. A conclusion cannot be reached on the nature of the breach of trust which may
trigger accessory liability without at the same time considering the other ingredients
including, in particular, the state of mind of the third party. It is not necessary, however,
to look even more widely and consider the essential ingredients of recipient liability. The
issue on this appeal concerns only the accessory liability principle. Different   E
considerations apply to the two heads of liability. Recipient liability is restitution-based,
accessory liability is not.

No liability

The starting point for any analysis must be to consider the extreme possibility: that a
third party who does not receive trust property ought never to be liable directly to the   F
beneficiaries merely because he assisted the trustee to commit a breach of trust or
procured him to do so. This possibility can be dismissed summarily. On this the position
which the law has long adopted is clear and makes good sense. Stated in the simplest
terms, a trust is a relationship which exists when one person holds property on behalf of
another. If, for his own purposes, a third party deliberately interferes in that relationship
by assisting the trustee in depriving the beneficiary of the property held for him by the   G
trustee, the beneficiary should be able to look for recompense to the third party as well
as the trustee. Affording the beneficiary a remedy against the third party serves the dual
purpose of making good the beneficiary's loss should the trustee lack financial means and
imposing a liability which will discourage others from behaving in a similar fashion.

The rationale is not far to seek. Beneficiaries are entitled to expect that those who
become trustees will fulfil their obligations. They are also entitled to expect, and this is   H
only a short step further, that those who become trustees will be permitted to fulfil their
obligations without deliberate intervention from third parties. They are entitled to expect
that third parties will refrain from intentionally intruding in the trustee-beneficiary
relationship and thereby hindering a beneficiary from receiving his entitlement in
accordance with the terms of the trust instrument. There is here a close analogy with
breach of contract. A person who knowingly procures a breach of contract, or knowingly

A   interferes with the due performance of a contract, is liable to the innocent party. The underlying rationale is the same.

Strict liability

The other extreme possibility can also be rejected out of hand. This is the case where a third party deals with a trustee without knowing, or having any reason to suspect, that

B   he is a trustee. Or the case where a third party is aware he is dealing with a trustee but has no reason to know or suspect that their transaction is inconsistent with the terms of the trust. The law has never gone so far as to give a beneficiary a remedy against a non-recipient third party in such circumstances. Within defined limits, proprietary rights, whether legal or equitable, endure against third parties who were unaware of their existence. But accessory liability is concerned with the liability of a person who has not received any property. His liability is not property-based. His only sin is that he interfered

C   with the due performance by the trustee of the fiduciary obligations undertaken by the trustee. These are personal obligations. They are, in this respect, analogous to the personal obligations undertaken by the parties to a contract. But ordinary, everyday business would become impossible if third parties were to be held liable for *unknowingly* interfering in the due performance of such personal obligations. Beneficiaries could not reasonably expect that third parties should deal with trustees at their peril, to the extent

D   that they should become liable to the beneficiaries even when they received no trust property and even when they were unaware and had no reason to suppose that they were dealing with trustees.

Fault-based liability

Given, then, that in some circumstances a third party may be liable directly to a beneficiary, but given also that the liability is not so strict that there would be liability

E   even when the third party was wholly unaware of the existence of the trust, the next step is to seek to identify the touchstone of liability. By common accord dishonesty fulfils this role. Whether, in addition, negligence will suffice is an issue on which there has been a well-known difference of judicial opinion. The *Selangor* decision in 1968 was the first modern decision on this point. Ungoed-Thomas J (at p. 1590) held that the touchstone was whether the third party had knowledge of circumstances which would indicate to 'an

F   honest, reasonable man' that the breach in question was being committed or would put him on enquiry. Brightman J reached the same conclusion in *Karak Rubber Co Ltd v Burden (No. 2)* [1972] 1 WLR 602. So did Peter Gibson J in 1983 in *Baden & Ors v Société Générale pour Favoriser le Développement du Commerce et de l'Industrie en France SA* [1993] 1 WLR 509. In that case the judge accepted a five-point scale of knowledge which had been formulated by counsel.

G   Meanwhile doubts had been expressed about this test by Buckley LJ and Goff LJ in the *Belmont* case (at pp. 267 and 275). Similar doubts were expressed in Australia by Jacobs P in *DPC Estates Pty Ltd v Grey* [1974] 1 NSWLR 443 at p. 459. When that decision reached the High Court of Australia, the doubts were echoed by Barwick CJ, Gibbs J and Stephen J: see *Consul Development Pty Ltd v DPC Estates Pty Ltd* (1975) 132 CLR 373 at pp. 376, 398, and 412.

H   Since then the tide in England has flowed strongly in favour of the test being one of dishonesty: see, for instance, Sir Robert Megarry V-C in *Re Montagu's Settlement Trusts* [1987] Ch 264 at p. 285, and Millett J in *Agip (Africa) Ltd v Jackson & Ors* [1990] Ch 265 at p. 293. In *Eagle Trust plc v SBC Securities Ltd* [1993] 1 WLR 484 at p. 495, Vinelott J stated that it could be taken as settled law that want of probity was a prerequisite to liability. This received the imprimatur of the Court of Appeal in *Polly Peck International plc v Nadir (No. 2)* [1992] 4 All ER 769 at p. 777, per Scott LJ.

Judicial views have diverged also in New Zealand. In *Westpac Banking Corporation v*   A
Savin [1985] 2 NZLR 41 at p. 70; (1986) 1 NZBLC 102,345 at p. 102,369 Sir Clifford
Richmond preferred the Belmont approach, as did Tompkins J in *Marr v Arabco Traders
Ltd* (1987) 1 NZBLC 102,732 at p. 102,762. In the *Powell v Thompson* case, at pp. 612,
613, 615, Thomas J considered that the suggestion that negligence is not enough to found
liability is to be resisted. The test is one of unconscionable behaviour. This, and
knowledge to match, whether actual or constructive, will suffice to herald a visit from
equity. In *Equiticorp Industries Group Ltd v Hawkins* [1991] 3 NZLR 700 at p. 728; (1991)   B
5 NZCLC 67,201 at p. 67,228 Wylie J disagreed. He adhered to the concept of want of
probity as the standard by which unconscionability was to be measured. In *Marshall
Futures Ltd v Marshall* [1992] 1 NZLR 316 at p. 325; (1991) 5 NZCLC 67,238 at p. 67,247
Tipping J was concerned about the difficulty of identifying as unconscionable conduct
which was less reprehensible than conduct which can be described as dishonest. He
would, he said, prefer the herald of equity to be wearing more distinctive clothing than   C
that suggested by Thomas J. In *Nimmo v Westpac Banking Corporation* [1993] 3 NZLR
218 at p. 228; (1993) 4 NZBLC 103,134 at p. 103,142 Blanchard J preferred a test of
dishonesty. Most recently, in *Springfield Acres Ltd (in Liquidation) v Abacus (Hong
Kong) Ltd* [1994] 3 NZLR 502 at p. 510, Henry J observed that the law in New Zealand
could not be regarded as settled.

Most, but not all, commentators prefer the test of dishonesty: see, among others, Peter   D
Birks (1989) LMCLQ 296; MJ Brindle and RJA Hooley 61 ALJ 281; Charles Harpum
102 LQR 114, 267, and *The Frontiers of Liability* (ed. P Birks) vol. 1, 9; Patricia Loughlan
9 OJLS 260; Parker and Mellows, *Modern Law of Trusts* (6th edn) 253; Pettit, *Equity and
the Law of Trusts* (7th edn) 172; Philip Sales 49 CLJ 491; *Snell's Equity* (29th edn) 194;
and Underhill and Hayton, *Law Relating to Trusts and Trustees* (14th edn) 355 and noter-
up.

   E

Dishonesty

Before considering this issue further it will be helpful to define the terms being used by
looking more closely at what dishonesty means in this context. Whatever may be the
position in some criminal or other contexts (see, for instance, *R v Ghosh* [1982] QB 1053),
in the context of the accessory liability principle acting dishonestly, or with a lack of
probity, which is synonymous, means simply not acting as an honest person would in the   F
circumstances. This is an objective standard. At first sight this may seem surprising.
Honesty has a connotation of subjectivity, as distinct from the objectivity of negligence.
Honesty, indeed, does have a strong subjective element in that it is a description of a type
of conduct assessed in the light of what a person actually knew at the time, as distinct
from what a reasonable person would have known or appreciated. Further, honesty and
its counterpart dishonesty are mostly concerned with advertent conduct, not inadvertent
conduct. Carelessness is not dishonesty. Thus for the most part dishonesty is to be   G
equated with conscious impropriety.

However, these subjective characteristics of honesty do not mean that individuals are
free to set their own standards of honesty in particular circumstances. The standard of
what constitutes honest conduct is not subjective. Honesty is not an optional scale, with
higher or lower values according to the moral standards of each individual. If a person
knowingly appropriates another's property, he will not escape a finding of dishonesty   H
simply because he sees nothing wrong in such behaviour.

In most situations there is little difficulty in identifying how an honest person would
behave. Honest people do not intentionally deceive others to their detriment. Honest
people do not knowingly take others' property. Unless there is a very good and
compelling reason, an honest person does not participate in a transaction if he knows it

A   involves a misapplication of trust assets to the detriment of the beneficiaries. Nor does an honest person in such a case deliberately close his eyes and ears, or deliberately not ask questions, lest he learn something he would rather not know, and then proceed regardless. However, in the situations now under consideration the position is not always so straightforward. This can best be illustrated by considering one particular area: the taking of risks.

B
Taking risks

All investment involves risk. Imprudence is not dishonesty, although imprudence may be carried recklessly to lengths which call into question the honesty of the person making the decision. This is especially so if the transaction serves another purpose in which that person has an interest of his own.

C   This type of risk is to be sharply distinguished from the case where a trustee, with or without the benefit of advice, is aware that a particular investment or application of trust property is outside his powers, but nevertheless he decides to proceed in the belief or hope that this will be beneficial to the beneficiaries or, at least, not prejudicial to them. He takes a risk that a clearly unauthorised transaction will not cause loss. A risk of this nature is for the account of those who take it. If the risk materialises and causes loss, those who knowingly took the risk will be accountable accordingly. This is the type of

D   risk being addressed by Peter Gibson J in the *Baden* case, at p. 574G, when he accepted that fraud includes taking 'a risk to the prejudice of another's rights, which risk is known to be one which there is no right to take'.

This situation, in turn, is to be distinguished from the case where there is genuine doubt about whether a transaction is authorised or not. This may be because the trust instrument is worded obscurely, or because there are competing claims, as in *Carl Zeiss*

E   *Stiftung v Herbert Smith & Co & Anor (No. 2)* [1969] 2 Ch 276, or for other reasons. The difficulty here is that frequently the situation is neither clearly white nor clearly black. The dividing edge between what is within the trustee's powers and what is not is often not clear cut. Instead there is a gradually darkening spectrum which can be described with labels such as clearly authorised, probably authorised, possibly authorised, wholly unclear, probably unauthorised and, finally, clearly unauthorised.

F   The difficulty here is that the differences are of degree rather than of kind. So far as the trustee himself is concerned the legal analysis is straightforward. Honesty or lack of honesty is not the test for his liability. He is obliged to comply with the terms of the trust. His liability is strict. If he departs from the trust terms he is liable unless excused by a provision in the trust instrument or relieved by the court. The analysis of the position of the accessory, such as the solicitor who carries through the transaction for him, does not lead to such a simple, clear cut answer in every case. He is required to act honestly, but

G   what is required of an honest person in these circumstances? An honest person knows there is doubt. What does honesty require him to do?

The only answer to these questions lies in keeping in mind that honesty is an objective standard. The individual is expected to attain the standard which would be observed by an honest person placed in those circumstances. It is impossible to be more specific. Knox J captured the flavour of this, in a case with a commercial setting, when he referred to a person who is 'guilty of commercially unacceptable conduct in the particular context

H   involved': see *Cowan de Groot Properties Ltd v Eagle Trust plc* [1992] 4 All ER 700 at p. 761H. Acting in reckless disregard of others' rights or possible rights can be a telltale sign of dishonesty. An honest person would have regard to the circumstances known to him, including the nature and importance of the proposed transaction, the nature and importance of his role, the ordinary course of business, the degree of doubt, the practicability of the trustee or the third party proceeding otherwise, and the seriousness

of the adverse consequences to the beneficiaries. The circumstances will dictate which one
or more of the possible courses should be taken by an honest person. He might, for
instance, flatly decline to become involved. He might ask further questions. He might
seek advice, or insist on further advice being obtained. He might advise the trustee of the
risks but then proceed with his role in the transaction. He might do many things.
Ultimately, in most cases, an honest person should have little difficulty in knowing
whether a proposed transaction, or his participation in it, would offend the normally
accepted standards of honest conduct.

Likewise, when called upon to decide whether a person was acting honestly, a court
will look at all the circumstances known to the third party at the time. The court will also
have regard to personal attributes of the third party such as his experience and
intelligence, and the reason why he acted as he did.

Before leaving cases where there is real doubt, one further point should be noted. To
enquire, in such cases, whether a person dishonestly assisted in what is later held to be a
breach of trust is to ask a meaningful question, which is capable of being given a
meaningful answer. This is not always so if the question is posed in terms of 'knowingly'
assisted. Framing the question in the latter form all too often leads one into tortuous
convolutions about the 'sort' of knowledge required, when the truth is that 'knowingly'
is inapt as a criterion when applied to the gradually darkening spectrum where the
differences are of degree and not kind.

Negligence

It is against this background that the question of negligence is to be addressed. This
question, it should be remembered, is directed at whether an honest third party who
receives no trust property should be liable if he procures or assists in a breach of trust of
which he would have become aware had he exercised reasonable diligence. Should he be
liable to the beneficiaries for the loss they suffer from the breach of trust?

The majority of persons falling into this category will be the hosts of people who act
for trustees in various ways: as advisers, consultants, bankers, and agents of many kinds.
This category also includes officers and employees of companies, in respect of the
application of company funds. All these people will be accountable to the trustees for
their conduct. For the most part they will owe to the trustees a duty to exercise reasonable
skill and care. When that is so, the rights flowing from that duty form part of the trust
property. As such they can be enforced by the beneficiaries in a suitable case if the trustees
are unable or unwilling to do so. That being so, it is difficult to identify a compelling
reason why, in addition to the duty of skill and care vis-à-vis the trustees which the third
parties have accepted, or which the law has imposed upon them, third parties should also
owe a duty of care directly to the beneficiaries. They have undertaken work for the
trustees. They must carry out that work properly. If they fail to do so, they will be liable
to make good the loss suffered by the trustees in consequence. This will include, where
appropriate, the loss suffered by the trustees being exposed to claims for breach of trust.

Outside this category of persons who owe duties of skill and care to the trustees, there
are others who will deal with trustees. If they have not accepted, and the law has not
imposed upon them, any such duties in favour of the trustees, it is difficult to discern a
good reason why they should nevertheless owe such duties to the beneficiaries.

There remains to be considered the position where third parties are acting for, or
dealing with, dishonest trustees. In such cases the trustees would have no claims against
the third party. The trustees would suffer no loss by reason of the third party's failure to
discover what was going on. The question is whether in this type of situation the third
party owes a duty of care to the beneficiaries to, in effect, check that a trustee is not
misbehaving. The third party must act honestly. The question is whether that is enough.

A   In agreement with the preponderant view, their Lordships consider that dishonesty is an essential ingredient here. There may be cases where, in the light of the particular facts, a third party will owe a duty of care to the beneficiaries. As a general proposition, however, beneficiaries cannot reasonably expect that all the world dealing with their trustees should owe them a duty to take care lest the trustees are behaving dishonestly.

Unconscionable conduct

B   Mention, finally, must be made of the suggestion that the test for liability is that of unconscionable conduct. Unconscionable is a word of immediate appeal to an equity lawyer. Equity is rooted historically in the concept of the Lord Chancellor, as the keeper of the Royal Conscience, concerning himself with conduct which was contrary to good conscience. It must be recognised, however, that unconscionable is not a word in everyday use by non-lawyers. If it is to be used in this context, and if it is to be the

C   touchstone for liability as an accessory, it is essential to be clear on what, *in this context*, unconscionable *means*. If unconscionable means no more than dishonesty, then dishonesty is the preferable label. If unconscionable means something different, it must be said that it is not clear what that something different is. Either way, therefore, the term is better avoided in this context.

The accessory liability principle

D   Drawing the threads together, their Lordships' overall conclusion is that dishonesty is a necessary ingredient of accessory liability. It is also a sufficient ingredient. A liability in equity to make good resulting loss attaches to a person who dishonestly procures or assists in a breach of trust or fiduciary obligation. It is not necessary that, in addition, the trustee or fiduciary was acting dishonestly, although this will usually be so where the third party who is assisting him is acting dishonestly. 'Knowingly' is better avoided as a

E   defining ingredient of the principle, and in the context of this principle the *Baden* scale of knowledge is best forgotten.

Conclusion

From this statement of the principle it follows that this appeal succeeds. The money paid to BLT on the sale of tickets for Royal Brunei Airlines was held by BLT upon trust for the airline. This trust, on its face, conferred no power on BLT to use the money in the

F   conduct of its business. The trust gave no authority to BLT to relieve its cash flow problems by utilising for this purpose the rolling 30-day credit afforded by the airline. Thus BLT committed a breach of trust by using the money instead of simply deducting its commission and holding the money intact until it paid the airline. Mr Tan accepted that he knowingly assisted in that breach of trust. In other words, he caused or permitted his company to apply the money in a way he knew was not authorised by the trust of

G   which the company was trustee. Set out in these bald terms, Mr Tan's conduct was dishonest. By the same token, and for good measure, BLT also acted dishonestly. Mr Tan was the company, and his state of mind is to be imputed to the company.

The Court of Appeal held that it was not established that BLT was guilty of fraud or dishonesty in relation to the amounts it held for the airline. Their Lordships understand that by this the Court of Appeal meant that it was not established that Mr Tan intended to defraud the airline. Mr Tan hoped, maybe expected, to be able to pay the airline, but

H   the money was lost in the ordinary course of a poorly-run business with heavy overhead expenses. These facts are beside the point. Mr Tan had no right to employ the money in the business at all. That was the breach of trust. The company's inability to pay the airline was the consequence of that breach of trust.

The Court of Appeal observed that it would have been unrealistic to expect BLT to keep the money in a separate bank account and not use any of the money in the conduct

A

of the business, particularly as BLT was also the ticketing agent for a number of other airlines. Their Lordships express no view on this, or on what the parties are to be taken to have intended would happen in practice when the company's current bank account was overdrawn. It is possible that in certain circumstances these points might sustain an argument that, although there was a failure to pay, there was no breach of trust. They do not arise in this case because of Mr Tan's acceptance that there was a breach of trust.

B

Their Lordships will report their advice to His Majesty The Sultan and Yang Di-Pertuan that this appeal should be allowed, the order of the Court of Appeal set aside, and the order of the Chief Justice restored. The respondent must pay the appellant's costs before their Lordships' board and before the Court of Appeal.

(*Appeal allowed*)

C

D

E

F

G

H

A # Re Oasis Merchandising Services Ltd.

Chancery Division.

Robert Walker J.

Judgment delivered 7 June 1995.

Wrongful trading – Champerty – Liquidator assigned 'fruits' of wrongful trading
B *claim in return for share of proceeds – Whether claim should be stayed as*
champertous – Insolvency Act 1986, Sch. 4, para. 6.

These were applications by directors to stay wrongful trading proceedings brought by the
liquidator under s. 214 of the Insolvency Act 1986 on the ground that the proceedings were
being funded by London Wall Litigation Claims Ltd ('London Wall') under a champertous
agreement and constituted an abuse of process.

C Under the agreement the liquidator 'in respect of his rights in respect of the fruits of the
s. 214 action' thereby sold and assigned to London Wall absolutely all the rights of himself
and the company in the action. Other clauses provided for London Wall to be in control of
the action and for the liquidator to concur and co-operate so far as he properly could, for
the financing of the litigation by London Wall and division of the fruits of successful
litigation in varying percentages for different tranches once London Wall had been
reimbursed for its expenditure on the litigation.

D *Held*, staying the s. 214 action:

1. An agreement to dispose of the fruits of a s. 214 claim was not a sale of property of
the company so as to be within the liquidator's power of sale under para. 6 of Sch. 4 to the
1986 Act. Any contribution to the company's assets was not to be deemed to have been an
asset of the company immediately before the commencement of the winding up. Not being
within the liquidator's power of sale the agreement was champertous (Re M C Bacon Ltd
E (No. 2) [1990] BCC 430 and dicta of Knox J in Re Ayala Holdings Ltd (unreported, 20
May 1993) considered.)

2. An application under s. 214 could not be regarded simply as ordinary civil litigation.
It was litigation which had, at least potentially, a public or penal element. In such litigation
the court was entitled to expect to have the assistance of the liquidator. A claim under s. 214
was simply incapable of outright legal assignment – it could only be made and pursued by a
F liquidator – and even a partial loss of control of the litigation was objectionable where the
claim had a public or penal element.

The following cases were referred to in the judgment:

Ayala Holdings Ltd, Re (unreported, 20 May 1993, Knox J).
Ayerst v C & K (Construction) Ltd [1976] AC 167.
Brownton Ltd & Ors v Edward Moore Inbucon Ltd & Ors [1985] 3 All ER 499.
G *Cyona Distributors Ltd, Re* [1967] Ch 889.
Glegg v Bromley [1912] 3 KB 474.
Grovewood Holdings plc v James Capel & Co Ltd [1995] BCC 760; [1995] Ch 80.
Guy v Churchill (1888) 40 ChD 481.
James, Ex parte (1874) LR 9 Ch App 609.
Leitch (William C) Brothers Ltd, Re [1932] 2 Ch 71.
H *Leitch (William C) Brothers Ltd, Re (No. 2)* [1933] Ch 261.
M C Bacon Ltd, Re (No. 2) [1990] BCC 430.
Papaloizou, Re (unreported, 4 December 1980, Browne-Wilkinson J).
Park Gate Waggon Works Co, Re (1881) 17 ChD 234.
Produce Marketing Consortium Ltd, Re (1989) 5 BCC 569.
Ramsey v Hartley [1977] 1 WLR 686.
Seear v Lawson (1880) 15 ChD 426.

Stein v Blake [1995] BCC 543; [1995] 2 WLR 710.   A
Trendtex Trading Corp v Credit Suisse [1982] AC 679.
Yagerphone Ltd, Re [1935] Ch 392.

Michael Crystal QC and Robin Dicker (instructed by Ashurst Morris Crisp) for the fourth and fifth respondents.

Martin Mann QC and Elspeth Talbot Rice (instructed by Jay Benning Levine & Peltz) for the first and second respondents.   B

Robert Wright QC (instructed by Ingledew Brown Bennison & Garrett) for London Wall.

Christopher Brougham QC (instructed by Whatley Weston & Fox, Worcester) for the liquidator.

JUDGMENT   C

Robert Walker J: Oasis Merchandising Services Ltd ('the company') was incorporated in 1985 and traded in video and audio cassettes and associated products. In 1986 it became a subsidiary of Beaverbrook Investments plc ('Beaverbrook') and Beaverbrook became a secured creditor under a debenture dated 12 September 1986. Beaverbrook appointed administrative receivers to the company on 9 November 1987. A compulsory winding-up order was made on 17 January 1988. Mr Barry Ward, a licensed insolvency   D
practitioner, was appointed as the company's liquidator on 6 January 1989.

The liquidator, continuing investigations started by the official receiver, came to the conclusion (in a report dated 2 October 1989 which I have not seen) that there was a prima facie case of wrongful trading. On 12 October 1992 the liquidator issued an originating application against five individuals claiming relief under s. 214 of the *Insolvency Act* 1986. (In this judgment all subsequent references to statutory provisions   E
are to those of the *Insolvency Act* 1986, except where otherwise stated.) These five individuals were at some stage directors, or are said to have been shadow directors, of the company. The sums claimed from these five individuals (whom I shall refer to for convenience, and without prejudging anything, as 'the directors') are substantial. The directors vigorously contest the claims.

I am not concerned with the substance of the claims. I have to rule on two applications   F
by the directors to stay proceedings on the originating application on the ground that the proceedings are being funded by London Wall Litigation Claims Ltd ('London Wall') under a champertous agreement and constitute an abuse of process. London Wall has been joined as a party by a recent order of Rattee J.

The agreement in question ('the 1991 agreement') was made on 18 November 1991 between the company, the liquidator and London Wall. The 1991 agreement recited that the company by the liquidator believed that there was a cause of action against some or   G
all of the directors for wrongful trading under s. 214. I will quote the next three recitals in full:

'(E) Due to the statutory basis of the s. 214 action the s. 214 action must be brought by the liquidator in his name and not by [the company] itself.

(F) The liquidator is unwilling to incur liability for the costs and expenses of   H
pursuing the s. 214 action or any other cause of action against the [directors] or others and [London Wall] has agreed to finance the s. 214 action or other actions as hereinafter provided in cl. 2 and 3 below.

(G) The liquidator considers it desirable that he himself and/or [the company] by him should sell and assign to [London Wall] all the "fruits" of the s. 214 action and (as provided in such cl. 2 and 3 below) his or [the company's] rights in respect

A   of the fruits of any other action or actions upon the terms hereof and in this agreement or the schedule hereto the said "fruits" shall mean any sum or sums of money (including any amount or amounts which shall have been received in respect of interest costs charges disbursements and expenses) received by the liquidator as plaintiff or as liquidator of [the company] or by [the company]

       (i) under and by virtue of final judgment in or compromise or settlement of the
B   proposed litigation including the s. 214 action, or

      (ii) in any way received from all or any of the [directors] (whether directly or indirectly) or from any other defendant or defendants or from any third person or persons on their behalf in settlement of any such claim or claims against all or any of them and whether before or after any proceedings shall have been issued or commenced.'

C   The 1991 agreement then went on to recite the consent of the liquidation committee. Clause 1 of the operative part made it conditional on the Companies Court giving the liquidator liberty to enter into it. By cl. 2 the company, acting by the liquidator, and also the liquidator himself made an assignment to London Wall, expressed as an equitable assignment by way of sale. The wording of the assignment is rather convoluted and I should perhaps quote the exact language:

D   '[the company] acting by the liquidator and the liquidator himself in respect of his rights in respect of the fruits of the s. 214 action hereby sells and assigns to [London Wall] absolutely all the rights of himself and [the company] respectively (i) in the s. 214 action to be brought by the liquidator on behalf of [the company] against the [directors] or any one or more of them . . .'

and then there is a reference to other possible legal proceedings that I need not go into. Clauses 4, 5, 6 and 11 relate to the conduct of the litigation; I shall have to come back to
E   these, but their general effect is for London Wall to be in control and for the liquidator to concur and cooperate so far as he properly can. Clause 7 contains detailed provisions about the financing of the litigation by London Wall. Most of the rest of the 1991 agreement (including two schedules) is concerned with division of the fruits of successful litigation. The general effect of these provisions (which, again, are rather convoluted) is in substance for London Wall to be reimbursed for its expenditure on the litigation and
F   (under the 'long term agreement' in the second schedule, which would now apply) for the excess to be divided in varying percentages for different tranches of excess, with the liquidator's percentage rising from ten per cent to a maximum of 50 per cent on any excess of £500,000. As a matter of form, however, this is expressed as additional consideration for the purchase by London Wall of all the fruits. The second schedule also contains an option for London Wall to take over the litigation in certain circumstances, subject to certain restrictions.

G   As I have mentioned, the 1991 agreement was conditional on the liquidator getting authority from the Companies Court to enter into it. Such authority was given by Mr Registrar Pimm on an ex parte application on 16 October 1991 (so that in fact the agreement never had effect conditionally; it had been approved before it was executed). So if the directors' application for a stay is well-founded, the Companies Court has inadvertently approved an agreement that is contrary to public policy. If so, the
H   liquidator could not be criticised for having acted within the authority conferred by the court, but the error should be corrected by the court of its own motion. It is right to point out that Mr Registrar Pimm had before him a joint opinion of very experienced company counsel confirming the propriety of London Wall's activities (I have not seen the opinion, and I do not know whether it addressed the terms of the 1991 agreement also). It is also right to point out that at least three of the relevant authorities have been decided since the order of 16 October 1991 was made.

The issue is, therefore, whether the 1991 agreement is, in relation to the proceedings   A
under s. 214, contrary to public policy on the ground of champerty. It has not been
argued that I ought not, in that event, to follow the recent decision of Lightman J in
Grovewood Holdings v James Capel [1995] BCC 760 in granting a stay (it is argued,
however, that I ought not to follow the first part of that decision and that I should find
that the agreement is not champertous).

In *Grovewood* at pp. 762–765 Lightman J summarised the present state of the law on   B
maintenance and champerty, and the history of the implicit exemption (established by a
long line of authority) for sales by liquidators and trustees in bankruptcy. The authorities
begin with the decision of the Court of Appeal in *Seear v Lawson* (1880) 15 ChD 426, a
bankruptcy case. Both that case and *Re Park Gate Waggon Works Co* (1881) 17 ChD
234 (another decision of the Court of Appeal relating to an assignment by a company in
liquidation) were cases of an outright legal assignment of cause of action for a monetary
consideration which did not depend on the success of the litigation. A contingency   C
element first appeared in *Guy v Churchill* (1888) 40 ChD 481. The trustee of a bankrupt
timber merchant entered into an agreement with one of the creditors for the creditor to
take an assignment of the right to continue a pending action against the bankrupt's
former agent, on terms that the creditor would continue the action in his name and at his
own risk and expense, and pay to the trustee (as the only consideration for the
assignment) one quarter of any net recovery (after payment of taxed costs not recovered   D
from the agent). It was argued that this arrangement was clearly champertous and not
sanctioned by *Seear v Lawson*, but Chitty J followed that decision, commenting (at
p. 488):

> 'It would be a strange and inconsistent result to say that although the right of
> action may be sold out and out it cannot be disposed of on the terms that some
> part of the fruit of the action if successful shall come back to the bankrupt's estate   E
> for division among his creditors.'

The agreement containing the arrangement is summarised quite fully in the report (at
pp. 482–484) and there are some signs that it has acted as a precedent in later cases.

Guy v Churchill was considered and applied by the Court of Appeal in *Ramsey v
Hartley* [1977] 1 WLR 686, where a trustee in bankruptcy assigned a cause of action (in
tort against an accountant) to the bankrupt himself, in consideration of receiving 35 per   F
cent of any net recovery. The Court of Appeal held that this amounted to an outright
legal assignment of an entire right of action, in consideration of a covenant to pay a sum
of money determined by a formula, and was not merely an equitable assignment of 65
per cent of the right; and that the fact that the bankrupt himself was the assignee was not
a reason for distinguishing *Guy v Churchill*. (Whether it is desirable for a trustee in
bankruptcy to assign a cause of action to the bankrupt has more recently been considered   G
by Browne-Wilkinson J in *Re Papaloizou* (4 December 1980, unreported) and by Lord
Hoffmann in *Stein v Blake* [1995] BCC 543; but I need not go further into that aspect.)

In *Grovewood* itself that company's liquidator entered into two 'sponsorship'
agreements under which its claim in proceedings against a firm of stockbrokers (for
allegedly negligent advice) was to be pursued in the company's name, but at the expense
of the sponsors, and with the assistance, but not subject to the control or interference, of   H
the liquidator. Net recoveries were to be divided equally between the liquidator and the
sponsors. It was common ground that the agreements did not effect any assignment (legal
or equitable) of the company's cause of action, but together amounted to an agreement
to assign (and, as Lightman J held, a sale) of half of the beneficial interest in the net
recoveries (see at p. 764F). This distinction was crucial to the outcome of the case
(p. 765A–E).

A   Because of the importance attached to the distinction in *Grovewood* it may be useful, at the risk of stating the obvious, to set out some very basic principles. There are three routes, at different levels, by which one person may dispose of, and another person may acquire, the prospect of benefiting from current or future litigation against a third party.

(1)   A transfer of property will normally carry with it as a matter of course the right to prosecute any cause of action closely related to that property. The most obvious

B   example is the absolute assignment of a debt (the very expression chose in action reflects that the debt, and the cause of action to recover it, are almost interchangeable). Examples could be multiplied: for instance a freeholder's right to sue on a tenant's covenants, or to seek rectification of the register to correct his boundaries; the field is very wide. A transfer of property with its concomitant associated causes of action can never be champertous because the transferee obtains a legitimate interest in the subject-matter of the litigation. In *Seear v*

C   *Lawson* the Court of Appeal seem to have been half inclined to the view that the case fell within this category, but then assumed against the trustee in bankruptcy that it fell within the next.

(2)   The assignment of a bare cause of action (or bare right to litigate) 'in origin ... meant no more and no less than a right to claim damages divorced from any transfer of property': Lloyd LJ in *Brownton Ltd v Edward Moore Inbucon Ltd*

D   [1985] 3 All ER 499 at p. 507. Lloyd LJ then quoted Parker J in *Glegg v Bromley* [1912] 3 KB 474 at p. 490:

> 'The question was whether the subject-matter of the assignment was ... property with an incidental remedy for its recovery, or was a bare right to bring an action either at law or in equity.'

Such assignments are in general against public policy: *Trendtex Trading Corp v*

E   *Credit Suisse* [1982] AC 679 at pp. 694–695 (Lord Wilberforce) and pp. 702–703 (Lord Roskill).

(3)   The third and most abstract level is the assignment, not of property (in the ordinary sense) or of a bare right to litigate, but simply of the damages or other monetary compensation that may be awarded in an action in which judgment has not been given. *Glegg v Bromley*, above, is of this type; Mrs Glegg assigned to her husband, by way of further security, any damages which she might obtain in her slander

F   action against Lady Bromley. The case was argued (as an interpleader issue) mainly on whether the assignment was made in good faith and for value, but the Court of Appeal clearly stated that because Mr Glegg had no right to influence the course of the proceedings there was no question of unlawful maintenance or champerty. Vaughan Williams LJ said ([1912] 3 KB 474 at p. 484), 'I know no rule of law which prevents the assignment of the fruits of an action. Such an assignment does

G   not give the assignee any right to interfere in the proceedings in the action'; see also at pp. 488–489 (Fletcher Moulton LJ) and pp. 490-491 (Parker J).

An assignment within the third category must be supported by consideration, because it is on analysis an agreement to assign future property (damages if and when awarded). It can therefore operate only in equity. A transfer or assignment in the other categories may operate either at law or in equity. If it operates only in equity one important practical consequence is that the assignor will (in normal circumstances) continue to be the proper

H   plaintiff in any litigation, and will continue to be at risk as to the costs (subject to any effective indemnity which he may have obtained).

It is common ground that the 1991 agreement is an agreement for the assignment of 'fruits' if and when they come into existence, rather than a legal or equitable assignment of a cause of action itself. The language of cl. 2 of the agreement is to my mind imprecise and confused, but I think counsel must be right in accepting that that is its effect.

I have heard submissions for a stay of the s. 214 proceedings from Mr Michael Crystal   A
QC (who appeared with Mr Robin Dicker for two of the directors), his submissions being
adopted and supported by Mr Martin Mann QC (who appeared with Miss Elspeth
Talbot Rice for another two directors). I have heard submissions against a stay from Mr
Robert Wright QC (who appeared for London Wall) adopted and supported by Mr
Christopher Brougham QC (for the liquidator). The points on which the argument
concentrated can be labelled as the 'property' point, the 'office of liquidator' point and
the 'fruits' point. The first two points are specific to proceedings under s. 214, and there   B
is a good deal of overlap between them. The third point is (apart from a subtlety in
para. 11(2) of Mr Wright's skeleton argument) more general and (in Mr Wright's primary
submission on this point) involves saying that *Grovewood* was wrongly decided.

Section 214 deals with wrongful trading and is (apart from its fleeting appearance in
the *Insolvency Act* 1985) a new statutory provision, expressed to be without prejudice to   C
s. 213 (which deals with fraudulent trading and has a much longer history, going back to
s. 275 of the *Companies Act* 1929). Proceedings under s. 214 are possible only if a
company is in insolvent liquidation, and the application can be made only by the
liquidator. In this it resembles s. 213, and under both sections the primary relief capable
of being granted is a declaration (in the case of s. 214) that a person to whom the section
applies is liable to make 'such contribution (if any) to the company's assets as the court
thinks proper' (in s. 213 it is 'persons' and 'contributions' in the plural). Section 214   D
applies to a person who was a director or shadow director of the company which has
gone into insolvent liquidation, if (subject as provided in subs. (3)–(5)) he knew or ought
to have known, at some time before the commencement of the liquidation, that there was
no reasonable prospect of insolvent liquidation being avoided.

Although s. 213 refers to 'contributions . . . to the company's assets' its statutory
predecessors did not do so. Section 275 of the *Companies Act* 1929 and s. 332 of the   E
Companies Act 1948 permitted an application by a creditor or a contributory, as well as
by the official receiver or a liquidator, and the court's primary power was to declare that
any person who was knowingly a party to fraudulent trading should 'be personally
responsible, without any limitation of liability, for all or any of the debts or other
liabilities of the company'. The nature of this jurisdiction, and in particular what degree
of discretion it conferred on the court, was considered in *Re William C Leitch Brothers
Ltd* [1932] 2 Ch 71 (Maugham J), *Re William C Leitch Brothers Ltd (No. 2)* [1933] Ch   F
261 (Eve J) and by the Court of Appeal in *Re Cyona Distributors Ltd* [1967] Ch 889
(where Russell LJ differed from Lord Denning MR and Danckwerts LJ as to the nature
of the jurisdiction, but reached the same result by a different route).

Mr Wright submits that the fruits which may be received in respect of the s. 214 claim
are within the very wide definition of 'property' in s. 436, and moreover that they are or
would be property of the company, so as to be within the liquidator's power of sale under   G
Sch. 4, para. 6. Mr Wright submits that the reference in s. 214 to making a 'contribution
. . . to the company's assets' (and the similar reference in s. 213) are a significant change
in the legislative scheme: the reference to a trust for creditors in *Re Yagerphone Ltd* [1935]
Ch 392 (a fraudulent preference case) is not therefore applicable, he says, to a s. 214 case.

Against that Mr Crystal submits that where there is a claim under s. 214 neither the   H
fruits, nor indeed the cause of action itself, can be property of the company capable of
being sold under Sch. 4, para. 6. Mr Crystal emphasises that a s. 214 claim is simply not
a possibility until a company has gone into insolvent liquidation, and when that happens
it is no longer beneficial owner of its assets, which become subject to a statutory trust for
creditors (see the well-known speech of Lord Diplock in *Ayerst v C & K (Construction)
Ltd* [1976] AC 167 at pp. 176–180).

A I can go along with Mr Wright's submission as to the width of the definition of 'property' in s. 436, but his further submission seems to me to be contrary to both principle and authority. In *Re M C Bacon Ltd (No. 2)* [1990] BCC 430 Millett J had to consider (in the context of the final incidence of an order for costs) claims unsuccessfully made by a liquidator against a bank (1) challenging a floating charge as a voidable preference or a transaction at an undervalue and (2) under s. 214, on the ground that the bank, by appointing an administrative receiver, had become a shadow director. After

B considering (at p. 434) whether an attack on a voidable preference could be regarded as a claim to realise or get in any asset of the company (and after deciding that it could not be so regarded) Millett J continued (at p. 435F):

'In my judgment, the same reasoning applies with even greater force to a claim brought under s. 214 of the Act, which can be brought only by a liquidator not an administrator and in the absence of an insolvent liquidation cannot be brought at

C all. In any case, I do not see how an application for such an order under the section can properly be described as an attempt to realise or get in an asset of the company. This must, in my view, mean an existing asset and, until the order has been made and complied with, there is no such asset.'

The context is different but the reasoning is clear and general in its application. I would follow it unless convinced that it is wrong. In fact I respectfully think that it is correct

D and I follow it.

I was also referred to the unreported decision of Knox J in *Re Ayala Holdings Ltd* (20 May 1993). In that case Knox J had to decide a number of preliminary issues related to an attempt by Mr Menzies, a creditor of the company, to pursue against the National Bank of Kuwait claims under s. 127 (of the *Insolvency Act* 1986) and s. 395 of the *Companies Act* 1985 which would normally be pursued by a liquidator. Since both Mr Menzies and the liquidator appeared in person, and seem not to have had legal advice in

E preparing the documentation which Knox J had to consider, the judgment covers a number of points, some of little general interest. But in a passage at pp. 24–31 of the transcript (in the original numbering) Knox J referred to,

'an important distinction between property of the company, on the one hand, and the rights and powers of a liquidator on the other. The property of a company includes rights of action against third parties vested in a company at the commencement of winding up and to that extent the principles in *Ramsey v Hartley*

F undoubtedly apply and such rights can, as I see it, be sold by a liquidator pursuant to para. 6 of Sch. 4. What is to be distinguished in my view are the statutory privileges and liberties conferred upon liquidators as such . . . who are officers of the court and act under the court's direction.'

Then after referring to and quoting extensively from *M C Bacon (No. 2)* Knox J

G reiterated,

'the fundamental distinction between assets of a company and rights conferred upon a liquidator in relation to the conduct of the litigation. The former are assignable by sale under para. 6 of Sch. 4, the latter are not because they are an incident of the office of liquidator.'

Knox J then referred to s. 167(3), which gives the court general supervision of a

H liquidator's conduct in a winding up by the court. Knox J found it difficult to accept that Parliament could have contemplated that a liquidator should be free to assign his powers to an assignee who was not subject to the control of the court.

Mr Wright submits, correctly, that *Ayala* was not concerned with a s. 214 claim. But Knox J's general distinction between a company's property and a liquidator's powers is equally applicable to a s. 214 claim. Arguably it is even more strongly applicable, since a

claim based on s. 217 does at least relate to some asset which belonged to the company   A
before the commencement of the winding up.

Reference to *Ayala* leads on (indeed, has already led on) to the office of liquidator
point. But before going further into that point I should say a little more about the change
in the law made when s. 332 of the *Companies Act* 1948 was replaced by s. 213 and 214. I
accept Mr Wright's submission that this was a significant change in the law. But I also
accept Mr Mann's submission that the purpose of the change, apart from the   B
introduction of the new concept of wrongful trading, was to resolve doubts (raised or
illustrated by the difference of opinion in the Court of Appeal in *Cyona*) as to the nature
of the remedy contemplated by s. 332. The new sections make clear that any clawback of
money achieved under them is to enure for the general benefit of unsecured creditors of
the company in question, and not a limited class of creditors whose claims date from the
final period of the company's trading. But that does not necessarily involve (indeed, in
line with *Yagerphone* it necessarily does not involve) deeming the money clawed back to   C
have been assets of the company immediately before the commencement of its winding
up. The point was clearly spelled out by Millett J in *M C Bacon (No. 2)* in the passage
([1990] BCC at p. 435) that I have already quoted. The particular language that
Parliament has chosen to use to describe the new remedies ('contribution[s] . . . to the
company's assets') can possibly be traced back to the language used by Eve J in *Leitch
(No. 2)* [1933] Ch at p. 266, where he drew an analogy with B contributories.

Mr Wright and Mr Brougham concede that the 1991 agreement is on the face of it   D
champertous, and that if it is to be upheld it must be by virtue of the liquidator's statutory
power, under Sch. 4, para. 6, to sell property of the company. I have reached the
conclusion that an agreement to dispose of the fruits of a successful s. 214 claim is not a
sale of property of the company, and that must by itself be decisive of this application.
But because the other points have been argued at some length, and because all the points
tend to interact on each other, I should state my views on the other submissions made to   E
me.

The jurisdiction under s. 213 and 214, when successfully invoked, has the effect of
increasing the fund available for a company's unsecured creditors, and so it can be seen
as a specialised civil remedy. But it also has a public or penal aspect. In *Leitch* [1932] 2
Ch at pp. 79–80 Maugham J inclined to the view that s. 275 of the *Companies Act* 1929
(the predecessor of s. 213) was in the nature of a punitive provision, and that the court   F
had discretion to order payment of a larger sum than the amount due to creditors who
had suffered as a result of fraudulent trading. Knox J considered this in *Re Produce
Marketing Consortium Ltd* (1989) 5 BCC 569 at pp. 596–597 and took the view that the
court's jurisdiction under s. 214 is primarily compensatory rather than penal. He said (at
p. 597G):

> 'Prima facie the appropriate amount that a director is declared to be liable to   G
> contribute is the amount by which the company's assets can be discerned to have
> been depleted by the director's conduct which caused the discretion under s. 214(1)
> to arise. But Parliament has indeed chosen very wide words of discretion and it
> would be undesirable to seek to spell out limits on that discretion.'

It is also noteworthy that a declaration under s. 213 or s. 214 may be the occasion for the
court making an order under the *Company Directors Disqualification Act* 1986, whether
or not any specific application is made for such an order: see s. 10 of that Act.   H

In these circumstances an application under s. 213 or s. 214 cannot in my judgment be
regarded simply as ordinary civil litigation. It is litigation which has, at least potentially,
a public or penal element. In such litigation the court is entitled to expect to have the
assistance of the liquidator, who as an authorised insolvency practitioner will be aware
of his statutory responsibilities. Putting the point at its lowest, Knox J's observations in

A   *Ayala* on the subject of s. 167(3) must apply with especial force to an application under
s. 213 or s. 214, which can only be made by a liquidator and cannot be regarded simply
as ordinary civil litigation.

Mr Wright pointed out to me that under the 1991 agreement the liquidator will remain
the applicant in respect of the s. 214 claim, and that his subjection to London Wall's
requirements, and his obligation to render assistance to London Wall, are qualified by
B   reference to what is lawful (that is true of cl. 4 and 11 of the 1991 agreement, and the 'QC
clause' in cl. 6 no doubt has a similar effect in relation to any decision on compromise;
but except in relation to a compromise, it does not seem to be true of cl. 5, unless it must
be read as impliedly subject to cl. 4).

Mr Wright then went on to submit that where a liquidator makes an outright legal
assignment of the entirety of a cause of action, he loses any vestige of control over the
future conduct of the litigation; whereas under an equitable assignment of fruits of
C   litigation, his loss of control is not complete. Partial loss of control must, he submitted,
be less objectionable than complete loss of control. In the present case there is, it seems
to me, a short answer to this point, that is that a claim under s. 214 is simply incapable
of outright legal assignment – it can only be made and pursued by a liquidator – and that
even a partial loss of control is objectionable where the claim has a public or penal
element. So my view on the office of liquidator point – in the context of s. 214 – strongly
D   reinforces my conclusion on the property point.

Outside the context of s. 214 (or s. 213) Mr Wright's point is not without force, but is
still open to debate. The basic principle underlying *Seear v Lawson* and all the authorities
that come after it may be seen as a recognition that there is a public interest in trustees in
bankruptcy and liquidators being able to realise assets (including causes of action)
expeditiously and economically, and that this warrants their statutory powers being
construed widely rather than restrictively. I remind myself that Chitty J said in *Guy v*
E   *Churchill* (the first case where a liquidator covenanted to assist the assignee, and agreed
to take a share of any recoveries as the only consideration) in a passage which I have
already quoted (40 ChD at p. 488),

> 'It would be a strange and inconsistent result to say that although the right of
> action may be sold out and out it cannot be disposed of on the terms that some
> part of the fruit of the action if successful shall come back to the bankrupt's estate
F   > for division among his creditors.'

It might perhaps have been argued that this would not be a strange or inconsistent result,
since under an outright assignment for a non-contingent consideration the liquidator is
relieved of any further involvement in the litigation, even as an assistant, and does receive
some money as a 'bird in the hand' for early distribution to the company's creditors; and
so a situation in which a liquidator continues to be involved may in practice be less
G   desirable than when he sells a cause of action outright, for cash, and has no further
involvement. However *Guy v Churchill* has stood for over 100 years and was approved
by the Court of Appeal in *Ramsey v Hartley*. It will be for decision in future cases how
Knox's J's observations in *Ayala* on s. 167(3) are to be reconciled with the statutory
power, which a liquidator undoubtedly has, to make an outright assignment, for cash, of
a bare cause of action in ordinary civil litigation (for instance, it may one day have to be
considered whether any duty arising under the rule in *Ex parte James* (1874) LR 9 Ch
H   App 609 is capable of surviving such an assignment).

The last point on which I should say something is what I have called the fruits point.
Mr Wright invited me not to follow the part of Lightman J's judgment in *Grovewood*
headed 'Exemption' ([1995] BCC 765A–E) which decides that the *Insolvency Act* 1986
confers no exemption from the law of champerty on a sale of fruits of litigation (as
opposed to the sale of a bare cause of action).

Since it is not necessary for disposing of the applications before me it would be wrong   A
for me to express any definite view on this point. But I have to say, with great respect to
Lightman J, that I have considerable difficulty with this part of his judgment. The
decision in *Glegg v Bromley* proceeds on the principle that a sale (or as in that case)
charge of mere fruits of litigation, *if not accompanied by any interference in the litigation*,
does not savour of maintenance or champerty: that is clear from all three judgments in
the Court of Appeal, in passages I have already referred to. Therefore (as Lightman J   B
recognised) *Glegg v Bromley* is not authority for the proposition that a sale of fruits of
litigation to a purchaser who *does* have the right to interfere in or control the litigation
does not require what the judge called 'special statutory exemption'. In practice, a
commercial purchaser such as London Wall (unlike the husband in *Glegg v Bromley*) is
likely to require some measure of control over the litigation.

It is, I think, the reference to 'special statutory exemption' which lies at the heart of my
difficulty. Although there is no doubt in one sense a special statutory exemption, it is not   C
an express exemption. Schedule 4, para. 6 says nothing about maintenance and
champerty, nor did any of its statutory antecedents or any parallel provision in the law
of personal insolvency. What has happened is that since 1880 the court has repeatedly
held, and Parliament in successive reviews of the insolvency legislation must be taken to
have accepted, that the statutory powers of sale conferred on liquidators and trustees in
bankruptcy may be validly exercised without any breach of the rules of public policy   D
concerning maintenance and champerty.

In these circumstances it seems to me that it is a question, not of extending or declining
to extend a statutory exemption, but of construing the statutory power of sale. If, as
Lightman J held in the preceding section of his judgment headed 'Sale', an agreement to
assign a share of future recoveries (or fruits of litigation) is a sale within the meaning of
Sch. 4, para. 6, then I would be inclined to conclude that it too must be authorised by
that provision, notwithstanding the rules of public policy as to maintenance and   E
champerty. But I emphasise that I express no definite view on the point, on which I heard
argument from Mr Wright, but little from Mr Crystal or Mr Mann.

For the reasons set out earlier in this judgment, I will accede to the applications made
by Mr Crystal and Mr Mann, and grant a stay of the s. 214 proceedings against their
clients. I will also withdraw the approval of the 1991 agreement granted by the registrar's
ex parte order of 16 October 1991. Mr Wright and Mr Brougham did not suggest that I   F
could not do this, and it seems to me that the court should of its own motion correct a
direction or authority given to a liquidator which subsequently appears to have been
given in error. The withdrawal of approval does not of course expose the liquidator to
any personal liability or criticism.

(Order accordingly)

   G

   H

A

Re Oakleague Ltd.

Chancery Division (Companies Court).
Robert Walker J.
Judgment delivered 12 June 1995.

B

Power of court to declare dissolution of company void – Liquidator assigned company's right of action to former director/shareholder – Action commenced by assignee – Company dissolved – Defendant in action opposed company's restoration to the register – Whether company should be restored – Companies Act 1985, s. 651.

This was an appeal from an order of the registrar declaring void the dissolution of Oakleague Ltd ('the company') and restoring it to the register under s. 651(1) of the Companies Act 1985.

C

The restoration application was made by the company's liquidator and by 'W', a director and 50 per cent shareholder. The application was opposed by an intervener, 'Afroze'. Disputes between W and Afroze had led to a Queen's Bench action commenced by Afroze suing on bills of exchange. The company had gone into liquidation and the liquidator had assigned to W the company's right of action against Afroze in respect of alleged defects in the goods which were the subject-matter of the bills of exchange. W as the company's assignee commenced a Queen's Bench action against Afroze. Afroze sought to strike out the second Queen's Bench action as an abuse of process arguing inter alia that the assignment to W was invalid because made for no consideration and because it was outside the liquidator's powers.

D

Held, dismissing the appeal:

The liquidator of the company knew that there was a possible claim against Afroze for defective goods but, at the stage that he assigned it, thought that it had no monetary value since he assigned it for no consideration other than the indemnity which he took. That situation was well within the legislative purpose of s. 651. The attitude of the Companies Court was that provided the application for restoration fell within the general legislative purpose the company would be restored, and whether the restoration did anyone any good or not was a matter to be decided by another tribunal in the future.

E

The following cases were referred to in the judgment:

Grovewood Holdings plc v James Capel & Co Ltd [1995] BCC 760; [1995] Ch 80.
Guy v Churchill (1889) 40 ChD 481.
Park Gate Waggon Works Co, Re (1881) 17 ChD 234.
Seear v Lawson (1880) 15 ChD 426.
Servers of the Blind League, Re [1960] 1 WLR 564.
Stanhope Pension Trust Ltd v Registrar of Companies [1994] BCC 84.
Weddell & Anor v J A Pearce & Major & Anor [1988] Ch 26.

F

G

N Leviseur (instructed by Pannone & Partners) for the appellant.

E Cohen (instructed by Gordons) for the respondent.

JUDGMENT

H

Robert Walker J: This is an appeal from Mr Registrar Buckley, who on 21 February 1995 made an order declaring void the dissolution of Oakleague Ltd ('the company') and restored it to the register under s. 651(1) of the *Companies Act* 1985. The application had been made by Mr Fatehali Ramji, who is an insolvency practitioner and was appointed as the company's liquidator on 23 June 1992, and as second applicant Mr Farouk Walji, who was a director and 50 per cent shareholder of the company. The application had been opposed by an intervener named Afroze Textile Industries (Private) Ltd ('Afroze').

Afroze is a company incorporated under the laws of Pakistan. As intervener it appeared   A
by counsel before the registrar but Mr Registrar Buckley did not give any reasoned
judgment in deciding to make the order that he did.

The disputes between the parties go back at least to 1989 and I will summarise them as
briefly as I can, relying gratefully for that purpose on the statement of facts in the
judgment of Judge Marr-Johnson, sitting as a judge of the Queen's Bench Division, when
he gave judgment on 22 March 1995 on an application which I will mention in a moment.   B

There have been two Queen's Bench actions in the course of the disputes between the
parties. The first, 1991/A/8900, was commenced by Afroze suing on bills of exchange and
the later one, 1993/W/1274, was commenced by Mr Walji. Judge Marr-Johnson was
hearing an appeal on a striking out application made in the second action. Judge Marr-
Johnson upheld the decision of Master Hodgson and struck out the second action but
that decision is in turn currently on appeal to the Court of Appeal pursuant to leave   C
given by a single Lord Justice, Hirst LJ. The dispute had begun over goods ordered from
Afroze by a purchaser in the name of Vogue Marketing. There is doubt whether this was
simply a trading name of the company or was a partnership in which the company was a
partner. The first action was on bills of exchange and was initially against Vogue
Marketing but Mr Walji was then brought in as a defendant. Meanwhile the company
had gone into liquidation and on 28 July 1992 Mr Ramji, as liquidator, made an
assignment to Mr Walji of the company's right of action against Afroze in respect of   D
alleged defects in the goods which were the subject-matter of the bills of exchange. That
assignment is of central importance to this appeal.

On 10 March 1993 the company was dissolved. I should add that the originating
summons seeking its restoration was issued on 21 December 1994 within the two-year
limit imposed by s. 651(4). On 7 May 1993 summary judgment was given against Mr
Walji in the first Queen's Bench action. On 23 July 1993 Mr Walji as the company's   E
assignee commenced the second Queen's Bench action, which is a claim for damages in
respect of defects in the goods delivered. Afroze, having resisted or at any rate not
suffered service of the proceedings outside the jurisdiction for some months, then sought
to strike out the second Queen's Bench action as an abuse of process. That application
relied on three main points. First, that the complaint should, it was said, have been raised
by counterclaim in the first action and it was unfair to allow it to be the subject-matter of
a second later action; second, that the assignment to Mr Walji was invalid because made   F
for no consideration; third, that it was invalid because it was outside the liquidator's
powers.

I am not concerned with the first point. The second and third points are fairly closely
connected. A liquidator has power under the *Insolvency Act* 1986, Sch. 4, para. 6 to sell
any of the company's property. Since 1880 it has been established that the statutory
antecedents of the liquidator's power of sale and the similar statutory powers of a trustee   G
in bankruptcy enable either office-holder to make an assignment for value of a cause of
action: see *Seear v Lawson* (1880) 15 ChD 426, *Re Park Gate Waggon Works Co* (1881)
17 ChD 234. A sale authorised by these statutory provisions, whether it takes effect as a
legal or equitable assignment, cannot be attacked as champertous even if the
consideration consists of a covenant to pay to the assignor a sum linked to the net
recovery in the action: see *Guy v Churchill* (1889) 40 ChD 481; see also the full survey of
the authorities by Lightman J in *Grovewood Holdings plc v James Capel & Co Ltd* [1995]   H
BCC 760. Moreover, the statutory power of sale has been liberally interpreted: see the
decision of Scott J in *Weddell & Anor v J A Pearce & Major & Anor* [1988] Ch 26,
especially at pp. 34–35. It is useful to note those general points even though on this
appeal Mr Leviseur, who appears for Afroze, does not take points on champerty which
are mentioned in affidavit evidence sworn on the strike-out application. Mr Leviseur

A   rightly accepts that the place for those points to be argued is in the Court of Appeal and not on this appeal.

The assignment of 28 July 1992 was signed by Mr Ramji as the company's liquidator. It was quite short and I will read it. After an appropriate heading, it says:

B   'This is to confirm that on behalf of Oakleague Ltd, I as liquidator hereby assign all the rights and claims against the above suppliers in respect of supplying defective bathrobes and towels to yourself as from today's date.'

That assignment should be read in conjunction with a letter written by the liquidator some eight days earlier, in which he had said:

C   'I as liquidator would be willing to assign all the rights and claims in this matter to yourself on acceptance that the liquidator would not be called upon to meet any costs for litigation or otherwise and you would indemnify the liquidator against any claims from the above parties that may result in consequence of any action or counter action taken by yourself against them.'

I read that paragraph because the indemnity mentioned there, on the basis of which the assignment was completed eight days later, is relied on as consideration supporting the transaction and enabling it to constitute, it is said, a sale within the liquidator's statutory powers.

D   I should add also that in an affidavit sworn on 23 December 1994 (again in connection with the strike-out application in the second Queen's Bench action) Mr Ramji, the liquidator, has deposed:

'Mr Walji has now agreed that he will allow Oakleague 75 per cent of any such surplus after costs which is an agreement I would have made in July 1992 had I been aware of the possibility of a surplus.'

E   Mr Cohen, who appears for the respondents to this appeal, accepts that that cannot have the effect of renegotiating or rewriting the transaction effected in July 1992 and that transaction must stand or fall on the basis of what happened at the time. However, Mr Cohen does urge on me that the possibility of the liquidator receiving funds under this undertaking, even if the later undertaking is itself unsupported by consideration, is something to be taken into account.

F   It would not be appropriate for me to express any definite view, still less to decide the validity of the assignment of 28 July 1992. That is, as I have already noted, one of the issues in the appeal to the Court of Appeal for which Hirst LJ, having read a draft notice of appeal, gave leave on 10 May 1995. Hirst LJ noted that the draft notice of appeal cited numerous authorities which Judge Marr-Johnson had not had the benefit of when he was hearing the appeal from Master Hodgson.

G   It seems to me that whichever way the appeal may go Afroze is faced with something of a dilemma in seeking at this stage and by this means to cut short the second Queen's Bench action by opposing the company's restoration to the register. If the appeal to the Court of Appeal succeeds then (depending on the reasons for its success and any views that may be expressed on the subject by the Court of Appeal), Mr Walji may be shown to have locus standi as at least an equitable assignee of the company's right of action although he would still, it seems, need the company to be joined as a party in the second Queen's Bench action before any final judgment for damages could be recovered: see

H   *Weddell v Pearce & Major* (above) at pp. 41–43. The restoration of the company to the register would enable that more or less technical requirement to be satisfied. If, on the other hand, there is a substantial defect in the assignment and as a result in Mr Walji's claim in the second Queen's Bench action, then the company's restoration to the register would very probably serve no useful purpose and any further attempt to give Mr Walji locus standi to bring yet a third action very likely would be blocked by the statute of

A

limitations. Whether that occurs or not depends on other proceedings which remain to be heard both in the Court of Appeal and, if the Court of Appeal allows the appeal from the strike-out, in the subsequent course of the second Queen's Bench action. It remains to be seen whether it will do any good to anyone or not but what I have to decide is whether it is right that Afroze should be able, by intervening in the s. 651 proceedings, to achieve a quick kill and knock out any further possibility of a successful claim either in the current Queen's Bench proceedings or in any future proceedings.

B

It comes down, it seems to me, to the principle on which the jurisdiction of the Companies Court under s. 651 is to be exercised. On that Hoffmann LJ, giving a judgment with which the other members of the Court of Appeal concurred in *Stanhope Pension Trust Ltd v Registrar of Companies* [1994] BCC 84 at p. 87D said:

> 'I think it would therefore be nowadays more accurate to say that ordinarily the purposes of s. 651 are either to enable the liquidator to distribute an overlooked asset or a creditor to make a claim which he has not previously made.'

C

Hoffmann LJ then went on to refer to the decision of Pennycuick J in *Re Servers of the Blind League* [1960] 1 WLR 564 as an example of a quite other case where the application for restoration to the register fell well outside that statutory purpose. The passage from the judgment of Hoffmann LJ which I have just read is, in my respectful view, a very useful and accurate statement of the purpose underlying s. 651 but it is not to be construed like an Act of Parliament. In particular the reference to an asset being overlooked is not, in my judgment, to be limited to a situation in which a liquidator was quite unaware of an asset belonging to a company over whose liquidation he was presiding. It is also, it seems to me, apt to cover analogous situations such as where a liquidator is aware of an asset but unaware that that asset has any realisable value. That is the type of situation that I am faced with. The liquidator of the company knew that there was a possible claim against Afroze for defective goods but at the stage that he assigned it can have thought that it had no monetary value since he assigned it for no consideration other than the indemnity which he took.

D

E

It seems to me that this situation is well within the legislative purpose of s. 651 as it is described in the *Stanhope Pension Trust* case. Mr Leviseur also relies on delay and backs up his reliance on delay by referring to the non-disclosure of the assignment for a considerable period of time while the first Queen's Bench action was reaching its conclusion and the second Queen's Bench action no doubt being considered. That was a matter of complaint considered on the strike-out application in the second Queen's Bench action. I am far from convinced that it is a matter to which I should attach any significance in exercising the discretion that I have under s. 651. What is more to the point is that once it became apparent from the decision of Master Hodgson that Mr Walji was regarded as having no locus standi in the second Queen's Bench action it was after a very short period – to be precise 14 days – that the originating summons seeking restoration to the register was issued. On those parts of the background which I regard as material I do not find any delay on the part of the applicants such as should lead me to refuse to exercise my discretion in their favour on that ground. In any case where there is a two-year statutory time limit it would be relatively unusual that any other equitable limitation period should in normal circumstances be applied.

F

G

As often occurs in cases of this sort the restoration of the company to the register may do it some good or it may not. The attitude of the Companies Court is that provided the application for restoration falls within the general legislative purpose as I have described it the company will be restored, and whether the restoration does anyone any good or not is a matter to be decided by another tribunal in the future. Mr Leviseur relies also on the effect of O. 59, r. 13, that an appeal does not operate as a stay and urges on me that the second Queen's Bench action unless and until the Court of Appeal allows the appeal

H

A   has been struck out. That is perfectly true. Equally, it is perfectly true that at present the company is back on the register unless and until this appeal is allowed.

It seems to me that in a situation of this sort I have to look at the realities. The realities are that there almost certainly is no room for any further Queen's Bench action because the claim very probably would be statute-barred. Nor is there any further scope for any application under s. 651, the two-year period having now elapsed. It seems to me that the

B   right course was that taken by Mr Registrar Buckley in restoring the company to the register on the basis that it fell within the statutory purpose and might eventually serve some useful purpose, and the matters relied on in front of me by Mr Leviseur, who has said all that possibly could be said on behalf of the appellants, are not matters that should carry any or much weight in the exercise of my discretion. I shall therefore dismiss this appeal.

C   *(Appeal dismissed)*

D

E

F

G

H

Re Farmizer (Products) Ltd.

Chancery Division (Companies Court).
Blackburne J.
Judgment delivered 13 June 1995.

A

Wrongful trading – Striking out for want of prosecution – Limitation period
appropriate for wrongful trading action – Whether there had been inordinate and
inexcusable delay in prosecuting action – Whether respondents had been
prejudiced by delay – Insolvency Act 1986, s. 214.

B

These were applications by the two respondents to a wrongful trading claim under s. 214 of the Insolvency Act 1986 for the claims against them to be dismissed for want of prosecution.

Held, striking out the liquidators' claims:

C

1. The facts which a liquidator had to prove to establish a claim for wrongful trading were those set out in s. 214(2). The statutory cause of action created by the section accrued on the occurrence of the latest of the matters to which the subsection referred, that was when the company in question went into insolvent liquidation.

2. The liquidators' claim was for the recovery of a sum and the appropriate limitation period was therefore six years under s. 9(1) of the Limitation Act 1980.

D

3. It was incumbent on the liquidators, having only launched their claim four and a half years into the applicable limitation period, to prosecute their claim with a minimum of further delay. Regrettably, however, that had not been the case and there were in particular two periods of delay which were both inordinate and inexcusable.

4. The ability of witnesses to recall the course of events during the relevant period would be of significance to the outcome of the liquidators' claims. After the passage of so many years, this was likely to prove extremely difficult. The question was whether their ability to recall events had been made more difficult as a result of the 18 months or so of culpable delay on the liquidators' part in prosecuting the claim. A total of 18 months or so out of the period of up to nine years or so since the events occurred with which the proceedings were concerned was significant. The applicants had suffered something more than minimal additional prejudice as a result of the liquidators' delay since the proceedings were launched.

E

F

5. The fact that the applicants faced a very substantial uninsured claim and that the existence of that claim had caused and continued to cause them much strain did not of itself constitute prejudice of a kind to justify making a striking-out order.

The following cases were referred to in the judgment:

Allen v Sir Alfred McAlpine & Sons Ltd & Anor [1968] 2 QB 229.
Birkett v James [1978] AC 297.
Coburn v Colledge [1897] 1 QB 702.
Collin v Duke of Westminster [1985] 1 QB 581.
Department of Transport v Chris Smaller (Transport) Ltd [1989] AC 1197.
Eagil Trust Co Ltd v Pigott-Brown [1985] 3 All ER 119.
Molyneux v Bull (unreported, 7 May 1991, CA).
Roebuck v Mungovin [1994] 2 AC 224.
Trill & Anor v Sacher & Ors [1993] 1 All ER 961.

G

H

Richard de Lacy (instructed by Dibb Lupton Broomhead) for the liquidators.

Sarah Harman (instructed by Sprecher Grier) for the first respondent.

Michael McParland (instructed by Penningtons) for the second respondent.

A
JUDGMENT

Blackburne J: I have before me separate applications by the two respondents to a wrongful trading claim under s. 214 of the *Insolvency Act* 1986. The respondents seek orders for the claims against them to be dismissed for want of prosecution. The respondents, Mr and Mrs Gadd, are husband and wife and, at the relevant time, were the sole shareholders and directors of Farmizer (Products) Ltd.

B
The background

The company carried on business as a grain trader, partly by the wholesaling and shipping of grain, partly by trading in grain futures and partly by dealing in what is described in the evidence as 'circle and difference trading'. From 1982 onwards the company also traded in potato futures.

C
It had been incorporated on 28 July 1969. In the 1970s the company traded with a measure of success. Its business expanded so that, by the early 1980s, the company's annual turnover had climbed to £20m and more. It was moderately profitable although in the year ended 30 June 1992 it recorded a loss of £219,000. According to its audited accounts, in the following year it made a net profit of £212,000-odd on a turnover of just under £25.4m and in the year ended 30 June 1984 it made a net profit of £31,000-odd on a turnover of just over £30.4m. It appears, however, that in the remaining three or so
D
years of the company's trading life it suffered a serious reversal of fortune resulting in the company becoming hopelessly insolvent.

The applicants, who are the joint liquidators of the company and who were appointed as such when the company was placed in creditors' voluntary liquidation on 12 October 1987, now seek to recover from the Gadds a contribution of at least £1.25m to the company's assets on the basis that, by 30 April 1986 (two days later than the earliest date
E
available under s. 214), the Gadds, as directors of the company at the relevant time, each knew or ought to have concluded that there was no reasonable prospect that the company would avoid going into insolvent liquidation.

The claim turns in part on events which occurred in connection with the preparation by the company's accountants and auditors, Jones Avens, of accounts for the company for the years ended 30 June 1985 and 30 June 1986. There was delay in the finalisation of
F
the June 1985 accounts owing to the absence of year end stock figures. Eventually, however, in April 1986 Jones Avens were able to complete draft accounts on the basis of a stock figure of £893,000-odd supplied to them by Mr Gadd's daughter, Mrs Vanessa Chick. Initially, in his evidence, Mr Gadd thought that it was he who had supplied the information. There is also some uncertainty in the evidence as to precisely when it was that the information was supplied to Jones Avens.

G
Based on stock in that amount the company's accounts, when completed in draft by Jones Avens, disclosed a loss of £365,000. Mr Beirne, the partner (since retired) in Jones Avens who dealt with Mr Gadd, expressed surprise at the level of loss but was reassured by Mr Gadd telling him that 'the position had recovered and the company was back in profit'.

In a letter to Mr Gadd dated 30 June 1986 Jones Avens wrote as follows:

H
'Further to our meeting last week I have now briefed myself as to the matter holding up the finalising of these accounts. When you saw Mrs Smallwood [she was employed by Jones Avens] you showed her a rough schedule of stock held on behalf of the company by third parties and it was arranged that you would ask the third parties to write in with certificates of the amount of stock they held on your behalf at 30 June 1985. I am not sure whether you actioned this but having regard to the total amount of stock being not far off £1m (i.e. £893,853), I am sure you

will agree it is essential that we have independent certificates of the stocks held by   A
the various people. I would be grateful if you would organise the supply of the
necessary certificates and let me have them . . .'

It is said by the liquidators that the amount of stock held by third parties was never
certified although it is claimed by Mr Gadd that Mrs Chick asked each of the stores
where the stock was held to provide certificates direct to Jones Avens. At all events the
accounts for the year ended 30 June 1985 were never finalised. According to Mr Gadd   B
the stock figure had been calculated by Mrs Chick (in his initial affidavit sworn on 7
December 1992 he referred to the calculations having been done by one of his staff) going
through unshipped contracts to establish what had been bought but not yet shipped. This
was a method of calculating stock which, according to him, he had employed since the
company's incorporation in 1969 and which had never been queried by the accountants.

The audit of the company's accounts for the year ended 30 June 1986 began in   C
November 1986 but, like the accounts for the previous year, was held up by the absence
of any stock figures. On 13 April 1987, however, Mr Gadd attended Mr Beirne's office
with a revised stock figure for 30 June 1985 of £354,673 (£539,186 less than the stock
figure which had been supplied to Jones Avens a year earlier) thereby throwing up a loss
of £912,784 for that earlier year. The draft accounts for the year ended 30 June 1986
disclosed a trading loss for that year of £304,121.

On 1 May 1987 Jones Avens wrote to Mr Gadd as follows: D

'. . . I gather . . . the year end positions have not altered the position shown by the
draft accounts, so that taking the two years together you have made a loss in excess
of £1m. I think you must think very seriously about your position now as to
whether you continue trading. Some months ago we had a meeting when I
suggested at that time that you should seek the advice of a lawyer experienced in
insolvency and liquidation matters and now I must reinforce that advice tenfold.'   E

I pause to say that Mr Gadd denies ever having been so advised.

'Following the passing of the *Insolvency Act* 1986 in certain circumstances directors
of companies which are insolvent can be held to be personally liable, whether they
knew they were trading whilst insolvent or not. We have recently taken the advice
of . . . a partner of Glanvilles in Portsmouth, and unless you know someone else I
would suggest you make an early appointment to see him to discuss the position. I   F
do urge you to seek advice at the earliest time. When these accounts are presented
to the bank I cannot think that they will wish to continue to support you.'

It was plain that the company was insolvent. Advice was taken and the decision made
to apply for an administration order. The upshot was that on 29 May 1987 an
administration order was made and joint administrators appointed. It appears that the
company, acting by its administrators, continued trading for a while. The administration,   G
however, was not successful and, on 12 October 1987, the company went into creditors'
voluntary liquidation and the applicants were appointed joint liquidators. An estimated
statement of affairs as at 23 July 1987 disclosed an estimated deficiency of £2.7m as
regards unsecured creditors with claims totalling £3.3m. It is said by the liquidators that
the stock figure in the accounts for the year ended 30 June 1986 was also overstated with
the result that the actual deficiency as at 30 June 1986 was £1.5m approximately. The
liquidators also say that the deficiency was increased by a further sum of at least £1.25m-   H
odd in the period 30 June 1986–29 May 1987 when the administration order was made.

The progress of the wrongful trading claim

Although the company went into liquidation as long ago as 12 October 1987 the
liquidators did not get around to launching their wrongful trading claim against the

A   Gadds until 13 April 1992. That was exactly four and a half years after the winding up had started and nearly five years after the company had gone into administration. There was no letter before action and no intimation of any kind to the Gadds, in advance of the issue of the originating application under s. 214, that such a claim was in the offing. Indeed, the Gadds' uncontroverted evidence is that they did not receive any correspondence of any kind from the liquidators between the end of 1988 and the service on Mr Gadd of the s. 214 application on 15 April 1992. The claim came as a complete
B   shock to them.

Through their solicitors, Sprecher Grier ('SG'), who acted for both of them at that stage, the Gadds protested at the delay and absence of any warning of any possible claim. They asked that the matter should proceed with formal pleadings. In their reply the liquidators' solicitors, Dibb Lupton Broomhead ('DLB') stated that 'the issues involved in the case are relatively straightforward and are in any event largely a matter of evidence which are better dealt with by way of affidavit'. They expressed the view that 56 days for
C   service of the Gadds' evidence in answer would be ample.

One of the difficulties faced by the Gadds was that they had not seen any documents concerned with the company's affairs for a number of years but were being asked to recall matters occurring between five and eight years previously. The upshot was that, on the directions hearing which took place on 7 May 1992, directions were made for
D   discovery by exchange of lists within 21 days with inspection seven days thereafter, and for the Gadds to file and serve their evidence in answer within 56 days and for the liquidators to serve their evidence in reply (if any) within 28 days of the service on them of the Gadds' evidence. The purpose of ordering discovery and inspection before service of their evidence in answer was plainly to enable the Gadds to refresh their memories by seeing the relevant documents.

E   Notwithstanding the liquidators' wish to stick to a tight timetable the liquidators were themselves three weeks late in serving their list. That list consisted of the enumeration, largely by reference to box numbers or to bundles, of all of the company's books and records in their possession, custody or control, whether or not relevant to the proceedings. It comprised 50 boxes of assorted documents held in a strong room plus a mass of books and records held by the liquidators. It is said that there were over 20,000
F   documents.

There then ensued correspondence over the mechanics of inspection. By late August, however, a quantity of copy and original documents were sent by DLB to SG. In the meantime SG were in correspondence with Jones Avens with a view to inspecting their working papers relating to the preparation of the company's accounts for the years ended June 1985 and June 1986. Until they received a letter from the liquidators' solicitors authorising them to release the documents in question, Jones Avens were not willing to
G   part with their documents to the Gadds or their advisers. The necessary authorisation was produced, enabling inspection to take place, in late October 1992. Whilst correspondence on this matter was in train SG discovered that a number of the documents which they had asked to inspect had not been sent by DLB and that a great many other documents, estimated to number some 800, had been sent which did not relate to the company at all. There was a further delay before that matter was dealt with when the originals of a large number of documents consisting of some 12 boxes were
H   couriered to SG. By now it was late November 1992, and the 56-day period for service of the Gadds' evidence in answer had long since expired. There was a disagreement over whether the 56 days ran from the date of the order, 7 May 1992, or from inspection. The liquidators called for the Gadds' evidence to be served by 7 July 1992, even though, by then, there had been no inspection at all by the Gadds or their advisers. Unless orders for the service of the Gadds' evidence were made, initially on 13 October 1992 for service

of their evidence by 10 November 1992 and, subsequently, on 5 November 1992, for   A
service of their evidence by 1 December 1992. A further extension of time to 8 December
1992 was agreed and on 7 December 1992 Mr Gadd's affidavit, together with a number
of exhibits, was served. Mrs Gadd, who by now was acting by separate solicitors,
Penningtons, had served her evidence on 13 November 1992. Her evidence consisted of a
denial of any knowledge of the company's affairs, the handling of which she had left
entirely to her husband, Mr Gadd, apart from signing the company's cheques and signing
off various company documents at her husband's request.   B

Although by early December 1992 the original timetable for the giving of discovery
and inspection and for the service of evidence had slipped by some five months the blame
for the delay lay, in my view, as much with the liquidators as with the Gadds. In the
meantime another area of discovery requested by SG, concerning the period when the
company was in administration, remained unresolved. SG wished to see documents ('the
administration documents') relating to the trading which the administrators had   C
undertaken. This matter was to remain unresolved for a number of months.

On 15 December 1992, a week after the service of Mr Gadd's affidavit, SG returned
the original documents which had been supplied to them by DLB. Certain documents
were omitted. SG returned the missing documents to DLB under cover of a letter dated
21 January 1993.

By letter dated 13 January 1993 DLB indicated that the liquidators did not propose   D
filing any evidence in reply – the 28-day period for doing so having in any event expired
– but that they would be serving interrogatories 'in due course' and that 'at this time we
propose issuing a summons for further directions for trial'. Apart from a letter dated 25
January 1993 from DLB, questioning certain copying charges and stating that they had
made a further request to the administrators for access to the administration documents,
no more was heard by the Gadds or their respective solicitors from the liquidators or   E
DLB for a further five months. In the meantime, by a letter dated 23 February, SG wrote
to DLB reminding them that leave would be necessary for the service of interrogatories
and pressing them for discovery of the administration documents.

The matter came to life again five months later when, by a letter dated 21 June 1993,
DLB sent copy interrogatories which they said they would be seeking leave to serve. The
letter also stated that the liquidators had been 'actively pursuing a number of lines of
inquiry' in relation to the administration documents which SG had asked to inspect. SG   F
replied expressing surprise and dismay at the five months' delay and complaining that it
was over eight months since they had asked for discovery of the administration
documents. A few days later, in early July, DLB issued an application for further
directions. This resulted in a consent order of 22 July 1993 giving leave to the liquidators
to serve interrogatories on Mr Gadd, for the interrogatories to be answered within 70
days of service, for the liquidators to provide discovery of the administration documents   G
within 28 days (i.e. by 19 August 1993), for the Gadds to be at liberty to serve further
evidence within 70 days of the order, for the exchange of expert evidence within 28 days
thereafter, and for the action to be set down for trial after 90 days upon the filing of a
certificate of readiness by either party. Provision was also made for the exchange of
witness statements not less than six weeks before trial.

On 2 August 1993 the interrogatories were served. Under cover of a letter of the same   H
date DLB delivered 15 boxes of documents to SG who had requested their return. On
8 September 1993 SG wrote to DLB drawing attention to their failure to give further
discovery in accordance with the 28-day direction. The liquidators eventually served their
list on 20 September 1993. It was served on SG only. It was a month out of time. There
was then a delay in providing copies of certain of the documents disclosed by that list:
they were not supplied until early November 1993, despite chasing letters from SG. In

A   the meantime, on 13 October 1993, a day or so out of time, Mr Gadd answered the
     interrogatories. It had been agreed between DLB and SG that the time for service by Mr
     Gadd of a further affidavit should be extended to 10 November 1993. On that date a
     further affidavit by Mr Gadd, together with various exhibits, was served.

         Twelve days later, on 22 November 1993, DLB requested the return of all original
     documents which had been delivered to SG stating that the documents were 'required by
B   our clients for finalising their expert evidence'. The documents in question were returned
     under cover of a letter dated 23 December 1993. At the time it was thought that all of the
     documents had been returned. On 20 January 1994 SG wrote to DLB to ask when the
     liquidators would expect to be in a position to exchange reports, stating that they were
     ready to do so themselves. Three and a half months were to pass before DLB got around
     to replying to that letter. They did so on 4 May 1994 when they sent a letter requesting
     the return of the company's trading book which they believed was still in SG's possession.
C   They stated that they needed that book for the purposes of their expert's report. The
     trading book related to the company's trading position between August 1986 and August
     1987. Chasing letters from DLB seeking the return of the trading book were sent on 16
     and 25 May. Eventually, on 7 July, the trading book together with certain other
     documents which SG discovered that they still possessed but which they had omitted to
     return the previous December were sent back to DLB. In mid-September SG returned
     two other files which they came across and which they should have returned the previous
D   December. It has not, however, been suggested before me that any of these documents or
     files, with the exception of the trading book, was of any materiality in the preparation of
     his report by the liquidators' expert.

         Apart from a brief exchange of correspondence during the course of September 1994
     in which DLB sought the return of certain day books but which it turned out SG had
     never received in the first place nothing more was heard by the Gadds or their respective
E   solicitors from DLB or the liquidators for another three months or so. On 23 December
     1994 SG wrote to DLB complaining that, despite the directions for setting down made
     on 22 July 1993 and the fact that they had been ready to exchange experts reports since
     January 1994, the liquidators had not progressed the matter. They put DLB on notice of
     Mr Gadd's intention to apply to the court in the New Year to have the liquidators' claim
     against him dismissed for want of prosecution. This evoked an immediate reply from
F   DLB complaining that any delay had been caused by Mr Gadd and that they had already
     forwarded to the court a formal notice of intention to proceed. Another fortnight was to
     pass before the notice to proceed was served on SG. No attempt was made to serve the
     notice on Mrs Gadd or her solicitors who had received no communication of any kind
     from the liquidators or DLB since 6 October 1993 and who had not even been served
     with the liquidators' further list directed by the consent order of 22 July 1993. On 16
     January 1995 SG issued Mr Gadd's application to dismiss the claim for want of
G   prosecution, followed a week later by the issue by Mrs Gadd's solicitors of her application
     for the same relief. Directions on the two applications were made on 2 March 1995.

         Notwithstanding that time for exchange of experts' reports expired in early December
     1993 it appears that it was not until 28 March 1995 that DLB indicated in correspondence
     that they were ready to exchange reports. That was some 15 months out of time.

H   **The jurisdiction to strike out**

         It is common ground between counsel that, following the principles laid down in
     Birkett v James [1978] AC 297, I have power to strike out the liquidators' claim for want
     of prosecution if I am satisfied that there has been inordinate and inexcusable delay on
     the liquidators' part in prosecuting the claim and that the delay will give rise to a
     substantial risk that it is not possible to have a fair trial of the issues or is such as is likely

to cause or to have caused serious prejudice to the Gadds. It is also common ground that   A
the power to strike out should not normally be exercised when there is no limitation
period or the relevant limitation period has not expired.

The issues

The issues that arise are (1) whether there has been any and if so what period or periods
of inordinate and inexcusable delay on the liquidators' part; (2) whether any such delay   B
has been causative of what compendiously I shall describe as prejudice to the Gadds; and
(3) whether there is any limitation period applicable to the liquidators' claim and, if there
is, whether that period has expired. I shall deal first with the issue of limitation.

Limitation

It was submitted by Miss Harman for Mr Gadd and by Mr McParland for Mrs Gadd
that the claim brought by the liquidators is for the recovery of a sum recoverable by   C
virtue of an enactment, namely s. 214 of the *Insolvency Act* 1986, and that, accordingly,
the relevant limitation period is governed by s. 9(1) of the *Limitation Act* 1980 which
provides that:

> 'An action to recover any sum recoverable by virtue of any enactment shall not be
> brought after the expiration of six years from the date on which the cause of action
> accrued.'   D

Relying on what was said in *Coburn v Colledge* [1897] 1 QB 702 at p. 706, they submitted
that the cause of action in this case arose when there existed every fact which it would be
necessary for the liquidators, as applicants, to prove, if traversed, in order to support
their claim to judgment under the section, and that those facts are the matters set out in
s. 214(2) of the Act. They submitted that, assuming those facts can be established, the
last in time to occur was when the company went into insolvent liquidation (see   E
s. 214(2)(a)) which was on 12 October 1987. They submitted that the six-year limitation
period prescribed by s. 9 of the 1980 Act expired on 11 October 1993.

Mr de Lacy for the liquidators submitted that no limitation period is applicable to
claims under s. 214, alternatively that a claim under s. 214 is an action on a specialty to
which s. 8(1) of the 1980 Act applies, which provides for a 12-year limitation period
which, on any view, has not yet expired, and, in the further alternative, that, if s. 9(1) of
the 1980 Act is the applicable provision, the six-year period prescribed by that section   F
only began to run when these very proceedings were commenced, i.e. 13 April 1992, with
the consequence that the six-year period still has just under three years to run.

The basis for Mr de Lacy's contention that no limitation period is applicable to s. 214
claims was, as I understood it, as follows. The only possible provisions of the *Limitation
Act* 1980 which could apply to the liquidators' claims are s. 8 and 9 both of which refer
to the date on which the cause of action in question accrued. The notion of a date on   G
which a cause of action accrues presupposes that it is objectively possible to determine
when the claim has accrued, i.e. when the facts occurred which it is necessary for the
plaintiff to prove in order to obtain the court's judgment. Wrongful trading claims,
however, are not of that nature. This is because of the incorporation into s. 214(1) of the
words 'if in the course of the winding up of a company it appears that subs. (2) of this
section applies . . .' That suggests, he submitted, that a necessary ingredient of a claim   H
under the section is that it must appear to the liquidator that wrongful trading has taken
place. Since this may happen at any time during the liquidation, depending on what
evidence the liquidator has been able to gather and what advice he has taken on that
evidence, a claim under s. 214 does not give rise to a cause of action which can be said to
'accrue' at any ascertainable time. Moreover the reference in subs. (1) to 'in the course of
the winding up' suggests that it is open to a liquidator to make an application under the

A   section at any time during the course of a winding up, however protracted the winding
up may be: that is a notion, he submitted, which is contrary to the idea of a cause of
action accruing at some objectively ascertainable moment.

I am quite unable to agree with Mr de Lacy's submissions on this point. In my view it
is clear that the facts which a liquidator must prove to establish a claim for wrongful
trading are those set out in subs. (2) of the section and no others. The statutory cause of
B   action created by the section accrues on the occurrence of the latest of the matters to
which the subsection refers: that is self-evidently when the company in question goes into
insolvent liquidation. The phrase 'it appears' in subs. (1) means that if it appears to the
court, i.e. if it is established on evidence before the court to which the application under
the section is made, that the ingredients of the claim are established then the court may
make a declaration that the person in question is to make a contribution to the company's
assets in such amount as the court shall think proper. The reference in the subsection to
C   'in the course of the winding up of a company' is intended, in my view, to make clear that
the jurisdiction conferred by the section is limited to companies which are in the course
of winding up. It is true, as Mr de Lacy pointed out, that that is in any event obvious
from the reference in the subsection to the application being made by the liquidator and
to the requirement in subs. (2) that the company shall have gone into insolvent
liquidation. It is to be observed, however, that the expression 'if in the course of the
D   winding up of a company it appears' also appears in s. 212 and 213 of the *Insolvency Act*
1986 and has appeared in predecessors of those two provisions to be found in the
Companies Act 1948 and in earlier enactments. In my judgment the expression does no
more than define when a claim under s. 214 (or under s. 212 or 213 as the case may be)
can be advanced, i.e. when the company in question is in the course of being wound up,
and it is wrong to seek, as Mr de Lacy invited me to do, to read some greater significance
into those words.

E   Mr de Lacy's second submission was that a wrongful trading claim is an action upon
a specialty to which s. 8(1) of the 1980 Act applies with the result that the limitation
period of 12 years prescribed by that section has not on any view expired. Having regard
to what was said in *Collin v Duke of Westminster* [1985] 1 QB 581 (especially at pp. 601–
603) it is clear, in my view, that a wrongful trading claim, which derives from s. 214 and
from that section alone, is a claim upon a specialty. Section 8(2) of the 1980 Act
F   prescribes, however, that 'subs. (1) above shall not affect any action for which a shorter
period of limitation is prescribed by any other provision of this Act'. The question,
therefore, is whether the appropriate limitation period is six years on the basis that the
claim is for the recovery of a sum and is thus within s. 9(1) of the 1980 Act. No other
provision of the Act was suggested.

In my view the liquidators' claim is for the recovery of a sum and that the appropriate
G   limitation period is therefore governed by s. 9(1) of the 1980 Act. Although s. 214
provides for the making of a declaration that the person in question shall make a
'contribution' to the company's assets, rather than for the payment of a sum of money,
and provides that the amount of such contribution shall be 'such . . . as the court thinks
proper' the substance of the claim is for the payment of a sum of money. The fact that
the amount to be paid is in the court's discretion and that, by s. 215(2), the court is
empowered to give effect to its declaration in such manner as it thinks proper including,
H   in particular, by way of a charge, does not seem to me to detract from the essential nature
of the claim under s. 214(1) which is for the recovery of a sum of money from the person
declared liable under the subsection.

That only leaves for consideration Mr de Lacy's third point which was that if s. 9(1) of
the 1980 Act is the applicable limitation provision with the result that the relevant
limitation period is six years, the cause of action only accrues when the claim under the

section is launched. That was not a submission which he advanced with any enthusiasm.   **A**
As I have already stated, the cause of action under the section accrues, in my view, when
the company in question goes into insolvent liquidation. That is when the last of the
events occurs which it is necessary for the liquidator to prove in order to establish his
claim. The fact that it may only be at some later date, when the liquidator has had a
chance to investigate matters and take advice, is in a position to come to a view whether
there is the basis for a wrongful trading claim and make the necessary arrangements to
issue the proceedings, that the claim is instituted does not seem to me to be material to a   **B**
determination of the date when the cause of action arises. It is frequently the case that a
plaintiff does not know, and cannot be expected to know, that he has a cause of action
until some time after the cause of action has accrued. Fraud, concealment and mistake
apart, the fact that the facts which are relevant to a cause of action are not known to the
plaintiff at the date of accrual of his cause of action is irrelevant. That this is so is implicit
in the special provision made by, for example, s. 14A of the 1980 Act in relation to   **C**
actions for damages for negligence with which that section is concerned.

In my view, therefore, the relevant limitation period applicable to the liquidators' claim
is six years as prescribed by s. 9(1) of the 1980 Act. That period began to run on 12
October 1987 when the company went into liquidation and accordingly expired six years
later on 11 October 1993.

  D

Inordinate and inexcusable delay

The liquidators did not launch their wrongful trading proceedings against the Gadds
until some four and a half years had elapsed of the six year period of limitation applicable
to the claim. Why it should have taken them so long to do so has not been explained. It
is clear, however, that where, as here, the originating process is issued within the relevant
limitation period the delay in so doing cannot be regarded as 'inordinate' for the purpose
of the exercise of the court's jurisdiction to strike out.   **E**

It is also well established, as Neill LJ pointed out in *Trill v Sacher* [1993] 1 All ER 961
at p. 979b, that where a plaintiff has delayed issuing proceedings until towards the end of
the limitation period he is under a duty to prosecute his claim with reasonable diligence,
with the result that a court will look strictly at any subsequent delay which is in excess of
the period allowed by the rules of court for taking the relevant step (or, I would add, in
complying with a timetable of steps laid down in accordance with the court's directions)   **F**
and may regard such subsequent delay as inordinate even though a similar lapse of time
might have been treated less strictly had the action been started earlier.

In this case, as it seems to me, it was incumbent on the liquidators, having only
launched their claim four and a half years into the applicable limitation period, to
prosecute their claim with a minimum of further delay. Regrettably, however, that has
not been the case and there are in particular two periods of delay which were, in my view,   **G**
both inordinate and inexcusable.

First there was a five month period from mid-January to mid-June 1993. I have already
set out the relevant events. Mr Gadd's affidavit in answer was served on 7 December
1992. In accordance with the court's directions made on 7 May 1992, the liquidators had
28 days within which to serve any evidence in reply. By mid-January 1993 they had
decided, on counsel's advice, not to serve any evidence in reply but to serve
interrogatories instead which, according to DLB's letter of 13 January 1993, 'counsel is   **H**
currently settling'. When the interrogatories eventually appeared, in late June 1993, they
were 18 in number, were straightforward in nature and ran to no more than a few pages
in length. I do not see why those interrogatories could not have been settled within the 28
day period allowed for the service of any evidence in reply. DLB's letter of 21 June 1993,
which was DLB's next communication to SG following the five month interval, referred

A to them having over the intervening five months 'been actively pursuing a number of
lines of enquiry not only in relation to the preparation of the interrogatories but also to
clarify the position concerning various post-administration documents'. Quite what those
lines of enquiry were was not explained. In the circumstances I am not persuaded that
anything in that letter or anything else that I have been told provides any kind of excuse
for this five-month period of delay. In my judgment it was both inordinate and
inexcusable.

B
The second period of delay was the time which elapsed between mid-December 1993
and early January 1995 when, following SG's warning letter of 23 December 1994, the
liquidators finally got around to serving a notice of intention to proceed. Even then it
took them another two and a half months to indicate that they were ready to exchange
experts' reports. In the meantime no step had been taken to set the application down for
trial.

C
What had happened during that very lengthy period is to some extent set out in
evidence filed on behalf of the liquidators. It appears that, in late February 1994, the
liquidators decided to change their expert and to instruct someone different. The person
selected, a Mr Peters of Touche Ross, was only approached two months later, in April
1994, when there was an initial meeting at which Mr Peters was informally instructed 'to
review the books and records' in the liquidators' possession 'with a view to preparing an
D expert's report.' Nothing more happened at that stage. The books and records were sent
to Mr Peters the following month. It was when Mr Peters or his staff began 'during the
latter part of May 1994' to review the books and records to ensure that they were
complete that Mr Peters discovered that 'some significant information was missing'. Of
that information, it is listed in Mr Peters' affidavit, one and only one item turned out to
have been retained in error by SG, namely the trading book, and not returned to DLB
the previous December. As I have earlier mentioned certain other files were also found
E by SG and returned but it has not been suggested that any of those other documents were
among the significant information which Mr Peters had found to be missing. The trading
book was returned by SG *to* DLB in early July 1994. Almost another month was to pass
before, on 3 August 1994, Touche Ross 'formally accepted' the liquidators' instructions
to act as experts in the case and agreed the objectives of the work to be undertaken by
them. I then take up the story in Mr Peters' own words:

F
'8. From that time onwards I (together with staff under my direction) began work
in earnest on the preparation of my expert report. Between that time and December
1994 we spent a total of some 650 hours in re-creating records and analysing the
ledgers and accounting records of the company.

9. This was found to be a difficult task. Particular points of difficulty were:

G
(a) Attempting to recreate the missing books and records for 1985–86 including
the sales and purchase day books of the company for the year ended 30 June
1986.

(b) Reconciling my analysis of the source documents to the draft accounts for
the year ended 30 June 1986.

(c) The books and records which were available (the majority of which had
been provided in May 1984) were not all in the boxes set out in the
H applicant's list of documents. A considerable amount of time and effort was
expended in examining the contents of the boxes we received and re-
referencing those to the list of documents provided.'

None of the missing books and records, which included the company's sales and
purchase day books and cash books for the year ended 30 June 1986, had been retained
by the Gadds or their advisers. That was established by the exchange of correspondence

between DLB and SO in September 1994 to which I have earlier referred. Mr Peters then   A
summarised the conclusions he had arrived at concerning the management of the
company in the years 1985–1987 and the Gadds' role in it.

It is surprising to me that it was only towards the middle of 1994 that the liquidators,
both of whom who are accountants and experienced insolvency practitioners, got around
to instructing their independent expert and that they did so without themselves having
taken steps to discover whether he had the information needed to prepare his report. Mr   B
de Lacy conceded that the delay between mid-December 1993 and May 1994 was
inordinate and inexcusable but sought to justify the delay which subsequently occurred
on the basis that it was necessary for the newly instructed independent expert to recreate
the company's records and analyse the results. I do not agree that this does provide any
justification. This is an exercise I would have expected the liquidators to have carried out
long before then; indeed I would have expected the exercise to have been completed or
largely completed during the four and a half years that elapsed between their   C
appointment as liquidators and the launch of their wrongful trading claim. In my
judgment the whole of this lengthy period constituted delay which was both inordinate
and inexcusable.

Prejudice

In *Allen v Sir Alfred McAlpine & Sons Ltd* [1968] 2 QB 229 at p. 260 Diplock LJ said: D

> 'But it must be remembered that the evils of delay are cumulative, and even where
> there is active conduct by the defendant which would debar him from obtaining
> dismissal of the action for excessive delay by the plaintiff anterior to that conduct,
> the anterior delay will not be irrelevant if the plaintiff is subsequently guilty of
> further unreasonable delay. The question will then be whether as a result of the
> whole of the unnecessary delay on the part of the plaintiff since the issue of the   E
> writ, there is a substantial risk that a fair trial of the issues in the litigation will not
> be possible.'

That passage was referred to and followed by the Court of Appeal in *Trill v Sacher*
and approved by the House of Lords in *Roebuck v Mungovin* [1994] 2 AC 224. I refer to
that passage because, subsequent to the first of the two periods of inordinate and
inexcusable delay that I have identified, the Gadds consented to the further order for   F
directions made on 22 July 1993 and Mr Gadd proceeded thereafter to serve his answers
to the liquidators' interrogatories, to serve a further affidavit, to have an expert's report
prepared and to announce to the liquidators that the report was held ready for exchange.
The Gadds had little choice but to go along with the steps taken at that stage by the
liquidators to prosecute their claim: until October 1993 the limitation period applicable
to the liquidators' claim had not expired so that they could not in any event before that
date apply to have the claim against them dismissed for want of prosecution. It does not   G
follow from the fact that the Gadds acted as they did during that period that I must leave
out of any account the fact and consequence of the five months of delay which occurred
between January and June 1993 in deciding whether I should exercise my discretion to
strike out the liquidators' claim. What weight I attach to the Gadds' action in taking
steps toward proceeding with a trial of the liquidators' claim during the second half of
1993 is a matter for my discretion. See the remarks of Lord Browne-Wilkinson in
Roebuck v Mungovin at pp. 236–237. I take the view that there is nothing in the Gadds'   H
conduct (or in that of their respective solicitors) that justifies me in disregarding that
earlier period of delay in deciding whether the Gadds have suffered prejudice as a result
of the liquidators' inordinate and inexcusable delay in prosecuting their claim.

In considering the question of prejudice I bear in mind the following remarks of Lord
Diplock in *Birkett v James* [1978] AC 297 at p. 323G:

A
> 'To justify dismissal of an action for want of prosecution some prejudice to the defendant additional to that inevitably flowing from the plaintiff's tardiness in issuing his writ must be shown to have resulted from his subsequent delay (beyond the period allowed by rules of court) in proceeding promptly with the successive steps in the action. The additional prejudice need not be great compared with that which may have been already caused by the time elapsed before the writ was issued; but it must be more than minimal . . .'

B
Those remarks were echoed by Lord Griffiths in the later case of *Department of Transport v Chris Smaller (Transport) Ltd* [1989] AC 1197 at p. 1208.

I also bear in mind what Lord Browne-Wilkinson said in *Roebuck v Mungovin* at p. 234E:

C
> 'In the ordinary case the prejudice suffered by a defendant caused by the plaintiff's delay is the dimming of witnesses' memories. Where there are two periods of delay, how can it be shown that a witness has forgotten during the later, rather than the earlier, period? We were referred to an unreported decision of the Court of Appeal, *Hornagold v Fairclough Building Ltd* (unreported) 27 May 1993; Court of Appeal (Civil Division) Transcript No. 634 of 1993, where there was a difference of opinion as to whether in such a case [i.e. a case where it was alleged the defendant had waived or was estopped from complaining about an earlier period of inordinate and inexcusable delay on the part of the plaintiff] it was necessary to adduce specific evidence that the prejudice flowed from the loss of memory in the later period. I have no doubt that such evidence is not necessary and that a judge can infer that any substantial delay at whatever period [i.e. since the issue of the proceedings] leads to a further loss of recollection. But even so the attempt to allocate prejudice to one rather than another period of delay is artificial and unsatisfactory.'

D

E
The Gadds point to essentially two kinds of prejudice suffered by them as a result of the period of culpable delay by the liquidators in prosecuting this claim: failing memories and business prejudice. I deal first with prejudice based on failing memories.

This turns essentially on the extent to which the issues will depend on the ability of Mr Gadd, and to a lesser extent the ability of Mr Beirne and Mrs Chick, to recall the events leading up to May 1987. It is accepted by Mr McParland that, as Mrs Gadd took no part in the running of the company's business, she has nothing to recall about the way in which the business was conducted. Instead she prays in aid the failing recollections by others of the material events as prejudicing her prospects of a fair trial. This is because the liquidators do not rely, as against her, on matters over and above those on which they rely as against Mr Gadd.

F

G
It is said by Mr de Lacy on behalf of the liquidators that this is a claim which turns substantially on the documentation; that no prejudice has been suffered by the Gadds from any culpable delay on the liquidators' part over and above the prejudice that they have suffered from the fact that the originating application was issued five or more years after the events with which the trial will be concerned; and that the Gadds had access to the material documents in June 1992 or thereabouts since when they have been able to interview and take proofs from any witnesses whose evidence they will wish to rely on at the trial. Specifically the liquidators' case, which is to a significant extent based on the recollections of Mr Beirne, is that in April 1986 Mr Beirne was concerned at the level of loss, then thought to be £365,000, disclosed by the draft accounts for the year ended 30 June 1985; that those accounts had been drawn up on the basis of stock figures supplied by Mr Gadd; that Mr Gadd reassured Mr Beirne that there was no cause for concern because the position had recovered and the company was back in profit (thus repeating the company's experience when it recovered to make net profits of £212,000 odd after it

H

had made a loss of £219,000 in the year ended 30 June 1982); that, although Mr Beirne   A
continued to press Mr Gadd 'over the next year' for information supporting the stock
figure, it was not until April 1987 that Mr Gadd supplied such further information; that
when he did so the stock figure for the year ended 30 June 1985 was £538,000 or so less
than the figure supplied the previous year; that, by April 1986, Mr Gadd must have been
aware that the company's position had worsened because by then according to the
company's records the company had sustained further and substantial losses; and that
Mr Gadd could not have expected to bring about a revival in the company's fortunes   B
which continued thereafter to decline.

I consider that this is to oversimplify the nature of the investigation which will be
necessary if this matter goes to trial. Areas which will require close examination will
include the circumstances in which the incorrect stock figure for the year ended 30 June
1985 came to be produced; the steps taken to verify the stock figure supplied to Jones
Avens in or about April 1986 for the year ended 30 June 1985; the manner in which   C
futures trading by the company was treated in the assessment of the company's financial
position at its year end; and the extent to which Mr Gadd was justified in believing, if he
did, that, despite knowing that the company had traded at a considerable loss in the year
ended 30 June 1985, nevertheless the company had since traded profitably and that the
company would continue to trade profitably.

A significant part of the company's trading was in futures. In his affidavit sworn on   D
7 December 1992 Mr Gadd said this of the manner in which such trading was dealt with
in the company's books:

> 'A particular problem that the company faced in assessing its correct position
> dealing with the open book. I would conduct some of the company's trade on the
> basis of committing the company to large purchases of grain for delivery at some
> considerable time in the future and that ultimately when the date approached
> regarding the purchase of that grain I would either have found or been in the   E
> process of finding a seller. In due course the buyer and seller would be matched
> and the grain would be shipped off directly from the supplier to the end user. When
> a purchaser was established I would receive a telex and possibly other
> documentation confirming that I had agreed to purchase the grain concerned and
> giving other details regarding weight and price and this document would then be
> filed in a memorandum file. It would *not* be entered into the accounting records of   F
> the company until such time as the second leg of the contract, typically a sale, had
> been executed. The company's records therefore did not recognise any losses, or
> indeed profits that might have been committed but not yet entered into the records.'

One of the questions at the trial will be the extent to which Jones Avens were aware of,
accepted and gave effect to the company's manner of recognising the profits and losses
arising from its futures trading.
                                                                                        G
In his affidavit in support of his strike-out application Mr Gadd says this:

> 'my "recollection" of the majority of events can now be little more than a
> reconstruction based on the documents which the applicants have disclosed. As I
> have stated above, the amount of documentation is vast. I have been through *many*
> of these documents in conjunction with my expert Mr Michaelson, but clearly I
> would need to go through them in further detail before the trial in effect, it will be
> necessary to reconstruct in detail all of the business which the company carried on,   H
> at least during the 1980s. I now find it extremely difficult to remember some of the
> events to which the documents relate and to put the documents into their necessary
> context.'

He then refers to an extract from the company's trading book for December 1986 as an
indication of the volume of trading in which the company was then engaged:

A   'Those contracts are relevant to the company's financial position at that time and to my knowledge of that position, but after such a long lapse of time I cannot recall the details of them. Those documents are simply an indication of the extent of the company's business; and in 1985 and 1986 the company in fact was party to hundreds of such contracts for thousands of tonnes of different commodities. Additionally, it is likely that at the trial of these proceedings the applicants (and the court) would want to enquire into the various matters to which I refer in my first and second affidavits for example:

B

  30.1 the reasons why I believed that the company would recover from its 1985 losses in a similar way to its recovery from previous losses;

  30.2 the profitability of the potato trading business and the business of shipping milling wheat to Ireland;

C

  30.3 the accounting treatment of the long term contracts;

  30.4 the manner in which the company dealt with its open book;

  30.5 my review of the company's open book in February 1986;

  30.6 my review of the company's books in the spring of 1986;

  30.7 my contact with the various shipping companies;

D

  30.8 my contact with the various brokers and the advice which they gave me;

  30.9 the circumstances of the production of the stock figures for 1985 and 1986;

  30.10 my discussions with Jones Avens; and

  30.11 the various complaints which I make about the conduct of the administration.

E

      My recollection of such matters, which forms the basis for my first and second affidavits, is only in very general terms . . .'

    I do not consider that these are matters which will turn simply on a review of the company's records. As is evident from the extent to which the liquidators themselves rely on what they had been informed by Mr Beirne, much will turn on the recollection of events by Mr Beirne. The same is true, but to a greater extent, of the ability of Mr Gadd and, to a lesser extent, his daughter, Mrs Chick, to recollect events. As is evident from

F the passage of Mr Gadd's affidavit from which I have just cited, Mr Gadd will need to be able to recall how, from month to month, he understood the company's position and prospects. He and his daughter will have to recall the steps taken by them to obtain year end stock figures. There will also be evidence of the communications passing between Mr Gadd and Mr Beirne (or his firm) concerning the preparation of the company's accounts for the year ended 30 June 1985, the manner in which stock had been calculated in past

G years, and the warnings, if any, which Mr Beirne gave to Mr Gadd about the company's solvency prior to May 1987.

    It is plain that recalling the events of the period from late April 1985 to mid-1987 will be very far from straightforward. Apart from the company's own trading records there would appear to be very few if any communications passing between the company and Mr Beirne. Some of the relevant financial records for the period no longer exist: Mr Peters' evidence indicates the extent to which he had recognised that 'significant

H information' was missing and the huge number of hours taken by him and his staff to 'recreate' the company's records and analyse the company's ledgers and accounting records.

    In my view the ability of Mr Gadd, and to a lesser extent Mr Beirne and Mrs Chick, to recall the course of events during this period will be of significance to the outcome of the liquidators' claims. After the passage of so many years, this is likely to prove

extremely difficult. The question is whether their ability to recall events has been made   A
more difficult as a result of the 18 months or so of culpable delay on the liquidators' part
in prosecuting this claim. I have come to the conclusion that it has, at any rate in the case
of Mr Gadd. Loss of recollection is a progressive matter. A total of 18 months or so out
of the period of up to nine years or so since the events occurred with which these
proceedings are concerned is significant. In my judgment the Gadds have suffered
something more than minimal additional prejudice as a result of the liquidators' delay
since these proceedings were launched.   B

That conclusion makes it unnecessary to express any view on the prejudice which it is
said the Gadds have suffered and continued to suffer from the fact that they have had so
large a claim (at least £1.25m) hanging over them throughout the period of the
liquidators' culpable delay. My attention was drawn in this connection to an unreported
judgment of the Court of Appeal in *Molyneux v Bull* delivered on 7 May 1991. In that
case the court, consisting of Lord Donaldson MR and Ralph Gibson LJ, dismissed an   C
appeal against an order upholding a registrar's decision striking out a personal injuries
claim for want of prosecution. The claim related to the injuries the plaintiff claimed that
she had suffered when the defendant kicked her during the course of what was described
as 'some form of horseplay in the office' where she and the defendant were employed.
The plaintiff claimed that the kick caused her to suffer severe damage to her coccyx as a
result of which she suffered and continued to suffer considerable discomfort. One of the
items of prejudice upon which the court relied in concluding that the appeal should be   D
dismissed was the prejudice suffered by the defendant during the eight months of culpable
delay which the court found to exist through having a large uninsured claim hanging
over him. In his judgment Lord Donaldson MR said this:

> 'Furthermore it is said in the affidavit on behalf of the defendant that the eight
> months' additional delay would cause substantial hardship to him in that he could   E
> not know what was the value of this claim in terms of organising his life. He could
> not know what capital he was going to have, what the extent of her claim might be
> and, quite clearly, her claim could be of considerable dimensions if she could make
> good causation in full and the viciousness of the attack. Those are matters on
> which anybody would be in difficulty. Mr Hay says that there is no evidence that
> he did want to sell his house or make a major capital investment or anything of
> that sort. That is right, there is not. On the other hand, assuming, as I do assume   F
> for reasons that I have already given, that he is not insured and this is not an
> insurance claim, for anybody to be faced with a potential claim of this magnitude
> must be a very considerable hardship to him, and to that extent, by having the
> time of uncertainty extended by eight months I think he suffered a good deal more
> than normal prejudice.'

The report of that case is very brief and it is not possible to say what the extent of the   G
evidence was which was before the court. Nor does it appear from the judgment what the
size of the plaintiff's claim was but it plainly cannot have amounted to more than a
fraction of the (uninsured) claim which the Gadds face in the proceedings before me.

I confess that I have some difficulty in reconciling the approach in that case with the
general view that the mere fact that a defendant faces a claim, even a substantial one,
cannot of itself constitute prejudice of a kind to justify the exercise of the strike out
jurisdiction.   H

In the *Chris Smaller* case Lord Griffiths, after rejecting a submission that the prejudice
that entitled a defendant to succeed on a strike out application should be limited to proof
of prejudice in the conduct of the litigation, drew attention to other forms relevant
prejudice including what was described as 'business prejudice'. He then went on to say
(at pp. 1209–1210):

'These authorities clearly establish that prejudice may be of varying kinds and it is not confined to prejudice affecting the actual conduct of the trial. It would be foolish to attempt to define or categorise the type of prejudice justifying striking out an action but there can be no doubt that if the defendants had been able to establish significant damage to their business interest, flowing directly from the culpable delay of 13 months after the issue of the writ, a judge would have been entitled to regard it as prejudice justifying striking out the action. I would, however, express a note of caution against allowing the mere fact of the anxiety that accompanies any litigation being regarded as of itself a sufficient prejudice to justify striking out an action. Mr Connell did not seek to argue that the anxiety occasioned by the extra 13 months in this case should be regarded as a sufficient ground of prejudice to justify making a striking out order. There are, however, passages in some of the judgments that suggest that the mere sword of Damocles, hanging for an unnecessary period, might be a sufficient reason of itself to strike out. On this aspect I repeat the note of caution I expressed in the Court of Appeal in *Eagil Trust Co Ltd v Pigott-Brown* [1985] 3 All ER 119, 124, where I said:

"Any action is bound to cause anxiety, but it would as a general rule be an exceptional case where that sort of anxiety alone would found a sufficient ground for striking out in the absence of evidence of any particular prejudice. *Biss's* case is an example of such an exceptional case, the action hanging over for 11 1/2 years, with professional reputations at stake."'

The evidence before me flied on behalf of the Gadds refers, not surprisingly, to the enormous strain that this litigation has imposed on them including the threat of bankruptcy if the claim were to succeed. It is not suggested that the liquidators' inordinate and inexcusable delay in prosecuting the claim has forced the Gadds, or either of them, to defer making business decisions of one kind or another which might otherwise have been made. In these circumstances, paying heed to the words of caution uttered by Lord Griffiths in the *Chris Smaller* and *Eagil Trust* cases, and notwithstanding the apparent approach of the Court of Appeal in *Molyneux v Bull*, I do not consider that the fact that the Gadds face a very substantial uninsured claim and that the existence of that claim has caused and continues to cause them much strain *of itself* constitutes prejudice of a kind to justify making a striking out order. If I am wrong in that conclusion then I would agree with Miss Harman and Mr McParland that the continued existence of so large a claim did cause the Gadds to suffer additional prejudice during the period of the liquidators' culpable delay.

In the result the Gadds' applications succeed and I shall make an order on each application striking out the liquidators' claims.

(*Order accordingly*)

Meridian Global Funds Management Asia Ltd v Securities Commission.

Privy Council.
Lord Keith of Kinkel, Lord Jauncey of Tullichettle, Lord Mustill, Lord Lloyd of Berwick, Lord Hoffmann.
Judgment delivered 26 June 1995.

Company's state of mind – Whether company knew that it was a 'substantial security holder' in a public issuer – Employees had used company money improperly to acquire relevant notifiable interest – Whether knowledge of employees to be attributed to company – New Zealand Securities Amendment Act 1988, s. 20(3), (4).

This was an appeal from the Court of Appeal of New Zealand raising the question whether a company, 'Meridian', was a 'substantial security holder' for the purposes of s. 20(4)(e) of the New Zealand Securities Amendment Act 1988 (a fact of which notice had to be given under s. 20(3) of the Act).

Meridian had a 'relevant interest' in five per cent or more of the voting securities in a 'public issuer' when its money was used to buy a 49 per cent holding in a publicly listed New Zealand company, 'ENC'. This was done by Meridian's chief investment officer, 'Koo', and a senior portfolio manager, 'Ng', improperly using their authority.

Heron J held that Meridian knew that it was a 'substantial security holder' in ENC for the purposes of s. 20(4)(e). He arrived at this conclusion by attributing to Meridian the knowledge of Koo and Ng, who undoubtedly knew all the relevant facts. If Koo and Ng had authority to enter into the transaction, their knowledge that they had done so should be attributed to Meridian. The New Zealand Court of Appeal affirmed the decision of Heron J on somewhat different grounds. It decided that Koo's knowledge should be attributed to Meridian because he was the 'directing mind and will' of the company. Meridian appealed arguing that its only directing mind and will was that of its board, or possibly of its managing director, but not Koo, whom the Court of Appeal correctly described as 'under' the managing director in the corporate hierarchy.

Held, dismissing the appeal:

1. It was a necessary part of corporate personality that there should be rules by which acts were attributed to a company. A company's primary rules of attribution would generally be found in its constitution, typically the articles of association, or implied by company law. Added to the primary rules of attribution were general rules of attribution which were equally available to natural persons, namely, the principles of agency. However, there were cases in which the court had as a matter of interpretation to fashion a special rule of attribution for the particular substantive rule, to decide whose act or knowledge was intended to count as the act or knowledge of the company. The 'directing mind and will' would often be the most appropriate description of the person designated by the relevant attribution rule, but not every such rule had to be forced into the same formula. (Tesco Supermarkets Ltd v Nattrass [1972] AC 153 and Re Supply of Ready Mixed Concrete (No. 2) [1995] 1 AC 456 considered. Dictum of Viscount Haldane LC in Lennard's Carrying Co Ltd v Asiatic Petroleum Co Ltd [1915] AC 705 at p. 713 explained.)

2. For the purpose of s. 20 of the New Zealand Securities Amendment Act 1988 the person whose knowledge was to count as the knowledge of the company was the person who with the authority of the company acquired the relevant interest. Otherwise the policy of the Act would be defeated. The fact that Koo did the deal for a corrupt purpose and did not give such notice because he did not want his employers to find out did not affect the attribution of knowledge and the consequent duty to notify.

A   The following cases were referred to in the judgment:

Bolton (H L) (Engineering) Co Ltd v T J Graham & Sons Ltd [1957] 1 QB 159.
Lady Gwendolen, The [1965] P 294.
Lennard's Carrying Co Ltd v Asiatic Petroleum Co Ltd [1915] AC 705.
Moore v I Bresler Ltd [1944] 2 All ER 515.
Multinational Gas and Petrochemical Co v Multinational Gas and Petrochemical
B   *Services Ltd* [1983] Ch 258.
Supply of Ready Mixed Concrete, Re (No. 2) [1995] 1 AC 456.
Tesco Supermarkets Ltd v Nattrass [1972] AC 153.
Truculent, The [1952] P 1.

Michael Beloff QC, John Stevenson (of the New Zealand Bar) and Andrew Tabachnik
(instructed by Bower Cotton & Bower) for Meridian.

C   Robert Dobson and Norman Miller (both New Zealand Bar) (instructed by Alan
Taylor & Co) for the Securities Commission.

JUDGMENT
(Delivered by Lord Hoffmann)

In 1990 a group of people in New Zealand, Malaysia and Hong Kong tried to gain
control of a cash-rich publicly listed New Zealand company, Euro-National Corporation
D   Ltd ('ENC'), and use its assets for their own purposes. The predators included a New
Zealand businessman called David Lee Sian Mun, two Hong Kong investment managers
called Norman Koo Hai Ching ('Koo') and Norman Ng Wo Sui ('Ng'), who were
employed by the appellants Meridian Global Funds Management Asia Ltd ('Meridian'),
and members of a Malaysian sharebroking firm called Hwang & Yusoff Securities Sdn
Bhd ('Hwang & Yusoff'). Their scheme required the purchase, through apparently
respectable New Zealand merchant bankers, of a 49 per cent controlling holding in ENC
E   for NZ$18.2m. The intention was to fund this purchase out of ENC's own assets, but
bridging finance was needed to fill the gap between buying the shares and gaining control
of the company's money. This was provided by Koo and Ng out of funds managed by
Meridian. Meridian is a substantial Hong Kong investment management company, a
subsidiary of National Mutual Life Association of Australasia Ltd. Koo was its chief
investment officer, Ng a senior portfolio manager. Their Lordships do not know exactly
F   how they were to receive their share of the spoils. But they funded the scheme by
improperly using their authority to buy and sell Asian shares. They contracted on behalf
of Meridian, through Hwang & Yusoff, to buy a parcel of shares in Malaysian and
Indonesian companies from ENC for $21m and at the same time to resell the same shares
to ENC for a slightly greater price. Payment for the purchase was made to Hwang &
Yusoff on 30 October and payment for the resale was to be made by ENC on 19
November. ENC did not own the shares in question and the persons who purported to
G   sell on its behalf had at that stage no authority to do so, but Meridian paid the money
and on 9 November Hwang & Yusoff used $18.2m to buy the shares in ENC. But the
scheme to pay Meridian back out of ENC's money on 19 November was frustrated by
the independent directors of ENC, who imposed conditions on the use of the company's
funds with which the predators could not comply. Unable to get their hands on the
company's money, they had to unwind the scheme as best they could. It is unnecessary
to go into the details of how the participants tried to extricate themselves except to notice
H   two matters. First, that on 10 December 1990 Koo, on behalf of Meridian, agreed to
release its rights under the original funding arrangements and accept instead a payment
and undertakings from Hwang & Yusoff. Secondly, that the net result was that the funds
under Meridian's management suffered a loss, which the Australian parent company had
to make good to the beneficial owners of the funds when the affair was discovered some
six or seven months later.

Stockmarket regulators have found that one way to help boards and investors to resist   A
such raids is to require immediate disclosure to the target company and the stock
exchange of the identity of anyone acquiring a substantial interest of any kind in the
company's shares. This enables the board and the investors to know who is behind the
respectable nominees. Part II of the *New Zealand Securities Amendment Act* 1988 was
intended, among other things, to introduce such transparency into dealings in publicly
quoted securities. The relevant duties of disclosure are contained in s. 20(3) and (4):

> '(3) Every person who, after the commencement of this section, becomes a   B
> substantial security holder in a public issuer shall give notice that the person is a
> substantial security holder in the public issuer to–
>
> (a) the public issuer; and
>
> (b) any stock exchange on which the securities of the public issuer are listed.
>
> (4) Every notice under subsection (3) of this section shall–   C
>
> (a) be in the prescribed form; and
>
> (b) contain the prescribed information; and
>
> (c) be accompanied by, or have annexed, such documents, certificates, and
> statements as may be prescribed; and
>
> (d) be given in the prescribed manner; and   D
>
> (e) be given as soon as the person knows, or ought to know, that the person is
> a substantial security holder in the public issuer.'

A 'public issuer' means a company listed on the New Zealand Stock Exchange and
'substantial security holder' means a person who has a 'relevant interest' in five per cent
or more of the voting securities in the public issuer. The definition of 'relevant interest' in
s. 5 is both complicated and comprehensive, but there is no need to examine its terms   E
because, although the matter was disputed in the courts below, the appellants have
accepted before their Lordships' board that the effect of the transaction was to give
Meridian a relevant interest in the 49 per cent holding in ENC between 9 November
1990, when its money was used to buy it, and 10 December 1990 when the scheme was
unwound. It gave no notice under s. 20(3).

Section 30 of the Act provides that where there are 'reasonable grounds to suspect'
that a substantial security holder has not complied with, among other provisions, s. 20,   F
the court may, on the application of the Securities Commission, make one or more of a
number of orders mentioned in s. 32. These range from ordering the substantial security
holder to comply with the Act to forfeiting the shares in which he has an interest. After
holding its own inquiry in March 1991, the Commission applied for orders against
various participants in the scheme. Meridian was not among the original defendants but
was joined a few days before the trial began.   G

Heron J held that Meridian knew on 9 November that it was a 'substantial security
holder' in ENC for the purposes of s. 20(4)(e). He arrived at this conclusion by attributing
to Meridian the knowledge of Koo and Ng, who undoubtedly knew all the relevant facts.
He did not go into the juridical basis for this attribution in any detail. It seemed obvious
to him that if Koo and Ng had authority to enter into the transaction, their knowledge
that they had done so should be attributed to Meridian. It had therefore been in breach   H
of its duty to give notice under s. 20(3). In view of the fact that its relevant interest had
ceased on 10 December 1990 the judge made no order against Meridian except that it
should pay $50,000 towards the Commission's costs and $15,000 towards the costs of a
minority shareholder in ENC. The finding that Meridian was in breach was incorporated
in a declaration made by the judge at the request of Meridian so that it could have an
order against which to appeal. The Court of Appeal affirmed the decision of Heron J on

A somewhat different grounds. It decided that Koo's knowledge should be attributed to Meridian because he was the 'directing mind and will' of the company. The Court of Appeal received some evidence about how Meridian functioned. The members of the board lived partly in Hong Kong and partly in Australia and met only once a year, for the formal business before the annual general meeting. Other matters which required a board resolution were circulated by post. Koo used to be managing director but was replaced by Mr Armour on 1 August 1990. Although Koo thereafter in theory reported

B to Mr Armour, in the matter of buying and selling securities he went on in the same way as before. The ENC purchases and sales were openly recorded in the books but Koo did not specifically report them to Mr Armour, who only found out about them after Koo had left. Nor did Koo report anything else and there was no evidence that Mr Armour or the other members of the board tried to supervise what he was doing. By leave of the Court of Appeal, Meridian now appeals to their Lordships' board. It says that its only

C directing mind and will was that of its board, or possibly of Mr Armour, but not Koo, whom the Court of Appeal correctly described as 'under Mr Armour' in the corporate hierarchy.

The phrase 'directing mind and will' comes of course from the celebrated speech of Viscount Haldane LC in *Lennard's Carrying Co Ltd v Asiatic Petroleum Co Ltd* [1915] AC 705 at p. 713. But their Lordships think that there has been some misunderstanding of the true principle upon which that case was decided. It may be helpful to start by

D stating the nature of the problem in a case like this and then come back to *Lennard's* case later.

Any proposition about a company necessarily involves a reference to a set of rules. A company exists because there is a rule (usually in a statute) which says that a *persona ficta* shall be deemed to exist and to have certain of the powers, rights and duties of a natural person. But there would be little sense in deeming such a *persona ficta* to exist

E unless there were also rules to tell one what acts were to count as acts of the company. It is therefore a necessary part of corporate personality that there should be rules by which acts are attributed to the company. These may be called 'the rules of attribution'.

The company's primary rules of attribution will generally be found in its constitution, typically the articles of association, and will say things such as 'for the purpose of appointing members of the board, a majority vote of the shareholders shall be a decision

F of the company' or 'the decisions of the board in managing the company's business shall be the decisions of the company'. There are also primary rules of attribution which are not expressly stated in the articles but implied by company law, such as 'the unanimous decision of all the shareholders in a solvent company about anything which the company under its memorandum of association has power to do shall be the decision of the company': see *Multinational Gas and Petrochemical Co v Multinational Gas and*

G *Petrochemical Services Ltd* [1983] Ch 258.

These primary rules of attribution are obviously not enough to enable a company to go out into the world and do business. Not every act on behalf of the company could be expected to be the subject of a resolution of the board or a unanimous decision of the shareholders. The company therefore builds upon the primary rules of attribution by using general rules of attribution which are equally available to natural persons, namely, the principles of agency. It will appoint servants and agents whose acts, by a combination

H of the general principles of agency and the company's primary rules of attribution, count as the acts of the company. And having done so, it will also make itself subject to the general rules by which liability for the acts of others can be attributed to natural persons, such as estoppel or ostensible authority in contract and vicarious liability in tort.

It is worth pausing at this stage to make what may seem an obvious point. Any statement about what a company has or has not done, or can or cannot do, is necessarily

a reference to the rules of attribution (primary and general) as they apply to that　A
company. Judges sometimes say that a company 'as such' cannot do anything; it must
act by servants or agents. This may seem an unexceptionable, even banal remark. And
of course the meaning is usually perfectly clear. But a reference to a company 'as such'
might suggest that there is something out there called the company of which one can
meaningfully say that it can or cannot do something. There is in fact no such thing as the
company as such, no *ding an sich*, only the applicable rules. To say that a company　B
cannot do something means only that there is no one whose doing of that act would,
under the applicable rules of attribution, count as an act of the company.

The company's primary rules of attribution together with the general principles of
agency, vicarious liability and so forth are usually sufficient to enable one to determine
its rights and obligations. In exceptional cases, however, they will not provide an answer.
This will be the case when a rule of law, either expressly or by implication, excludes
attribution on the basis of the general principles of agency or vicarious liability. For　C
example, a rule may be stated in language primarily applicable to a natural person and
require some act or state of mind on the part of that person 'himself', as opposed to his
servants or agents. This is generally true of rules of the criminal law, which ordinarily
impose liability only for the actus reus and mens rea of the defendant himself. How is
such a rule to be applied to a company?

One possibility is that the court may come to the conclusion that the rule was not　D
intended to apply to companies at all; for example, a law which created an offence for
which the only penalty was community service. Another possibility is that the court might
interpret the law as meaning that it could apply to a company only on the basis of its
primary rules of attribution, i.e. if the act giving rise to liability was specifically authorised
by a resolution of the board or a unanimous agreement of the shareholders. But there
will be many cases in which neither of these solutions is satisfactory; in which the court　E
considers that the law was intended to apply to companies and that, although it excludes
ordinary vicarious liability, insistence on the primary rules of attribution would in
practice defeat that intention. In such a case, the court must fashion a special rule of
attribution for the particular substantive rule. This is always a matter of interpretation:
given that it was intended to apply to a company, how was it intended to apply? Whose
act (or knowledge, or state of mind) was *for this purpose* intended to count as the act etc.
of the company? One finds the answer to this question by applying the usual canons of　F
interpretation, taking into account the language of the rule (if it is a statute) and its
content and policy.

The fact that the rule of attribution is a matter of interpretation or construction of the
relevant substantive rule is shown by the contrast between two decisions of the House of
Lords, *Tesco Supermarkets Ltd v Nattrass* [1972] AC 153 and *Re Supply of Ready Mixed
Concrete (No. 2)* [1995] 1 AC 456. In *Tesco* the question involved the construction of a　G
provision of the *Trade Descriptions Act* 1968. Tesco were prosecuted under s. 11(2) for
displaying a notice that goods were 'being offered at a price less than that at which they
were in fact being offered . . .' Its supermarket in Northwich had advertised that it was
selling certain packets of washing powder at the reduced price of 2s 11d, but a customer
who asked for one was told he would have to pay the normal price of 3s 11d. This
happened because the shop manager had negligently failed to notice that he had run out　H
of the specially marked low-price packets. Section 24(1) provided a defence for a
shopowner who could prove that the commission of the offence was caused by 'another
person' and that:

> 'he took all reasonable precautions and exercised all due diligence to avoid the
> commission of such an offence by himself or any person under his control.'

A   The company was able to show that it owned hundreds of shops and that the board had instituted systems of supervision and training which amounted, on its part, to taking reasonable precautions and exercising all due diligence to avoid the commission of such offences in its shops. The question was: whose precautions counted as those of the company? If it was the board, then the defence was made out. If they had to include those of the manager, then it failed.

B   The House of Lords held that the precautions taken by the board were sufficient for the purposes of s. 24(1) to count as precautions taken by the company and that the manager's negligence was not attributable to the company. It did so by examining the purpose of s. 24(1) in providing a defence to what would otherwise have been an absolute offence: it was intended to give effect to 'a policy of consumer protection which does have a rational and moral justification' (per Lord Diplock at pp. 194-5). This led to the conclusion that the acts and defaults of the manager were not intended to be attributed

C   to the company. As Lord Diplock said at p. 203D:

> 'It may be a reasonable step for an employer to instruct a superior servant to supervise the activities of inferior servants whose physical acts may in the absence of supervision result in that being done which it is sought to prevent. This is not to delegate the employer's duty to exercise all due diligence; it is to perform it. To treat the duty of an employer to exercise due diligence as unperformed unless due

D   diligence was also exercised by all his servants to whom he had reasonably given all proper instructions and upon whom he could reasonably rely to carry them out, would be to render the defence of due diligence nugatory and so thwart the clear intention of Parliament in providing it.'

On the other hand, in *Ready Mixed Concrete*, a restrictive arrangement in breach of an undertaking by a company to the Restrictive Practices Court was made by executives of the company acting within the scope of their employment. The board knew nothing of

E   the arrangement; it had in fact given instructions to the company's employees that they were not to make such arrangements. But the House of Lords held that for the purposes of deciding whether the company was in contempt, the act and state of mind of an employee who entered into an arrangement in the course of his employment should be attributed to the company. This attribution rule was derived from a construction of the undertaking against the background of the *Restrictive Trade Practices Act* 1976: such

F   undertakings by corporations would be worth little if the company could avoid liability for what its employees had actually done on the ground that the board did not know about it. As Lord Templeman said, at pp. 1254–1255, an uncritical transposition of the *Nattrass* construction:

> 'would allow a company to enjoy the benefit of restrictions outlawed by Parliament and the benefit of arrangements prohibited by the courts provided that the

G   restrictions were accepted and implemented and the arrangements were negotiated by one or more employees who had been forbidden to do so by some superior employee identified in argument as a member of the "higher management" of the company or by one or more directors of the company identified in argument as "the guiding will" of the company.'

Against this background of general principle, their Lordships can return to Viscount

H   Haldane. In *Lennard's* case the substantive provision for which an attribution rule had to be devised was s. 502 of the *Merchant Shipping Act* 1894, which provided a shipowner with a defence to a claim for the loss of cargo put on board his ship if he could show that the casualty happened 'without his actual fault or privity'. The cargo had been destroyed by a fire caused by the unseaworthy condition of the ship's boilers. The language of s. 502 excludes vicarious liability; it is clear that in the case of an individual owner, only his own fault or privity can defeat the statutory protection. How is this rule to be applied

to a company? Viscount Haldane rejected the possibility that it did not apply to   A
companies at all or (which would have come to the same thing) that it required fault or
privity attributable under the company's primary rules. Instead, guided by the language
and purpose of the section, he looked for the person whose functions in the company, in
relation to the cause of the casualty, were the same as those to be expected of the
individual shipowner to whom the language primarily applied. Who in the company was
responsible for monitoring the condition of the ship, receiving the reports of the master
and ship's agents, authorising repairs, etc.? This person was Mr Lennard, whom Viscount   B
Haldane described as the 'directing mind and will' of the company. It was therefore his
fault or privity which s. 502 attributed to the company.

Because Lennard's Carrying Co Ltd does not seem to have done anything except own
ships, there was no need to distinguish between the person who fulfilled the function of
running the company's business in general and the person whose functions corresponded,
in relation to the cause of the casualty, to those of an individual owner of a ship. They   C
were one and the same person. It was this coincidence which left Viscount Haldane's
speech open to the interpretation that he was expounding a general metaphysic of
companies. In *H L Bolton (Engineering) Co Ltd v T J Graham & Sons Ltd* [1957] 1 QB
159, Denning LJ certainly regarded it as a generalisation about companies 'as such'
when, in an equally well-known passage at p. 172, he likened a company to a human
body: D

'It has a brain and nerve centre which controls what it does. It also has hands
which hold the tools and act in accordance with directions from the centre.'

But this anthropomorphism, by the very power of the image, distracts attention from
the purpose for which Viscount Haldane said he was using the notion of directing mind
and will, namely to apply the attribution rule derived from s. 502 to the particular
defendant in the case (at p. 713):   E

'For if Mr Lennard was the directing mind of the company, then his action must,
unless a corporation is not to be liable at all, have been an action which was the
action of the company itself *within the meaning of s. 502.*' (emphasis supplied)

The true nature of the exercise became much clearer, however, in later cases on the
Merchant Shipping Act 1894. In the *Truculent* [1952] P 1, an action to limit liability for   F
damage caused by collision under s. 503, which also required the owner of the ship which
caused the collision to show that the casualty happened without his 'actual fault or
privity', the offending ship was a Royal Navy submarine. Her collision with a fishing
vessel had been caused by the inadequate system of navigation lights then carried by
submarines. Willmer J held that for this purpose the 'directing mind and will' of the
Crown, which owned the submarine, was the Third Sea Lord, to whom the board of
Admiralty had entrusted the function of supervising such matters as the systems of   G
navigation lights carried by warships. That function was one which an individual owner
of a ship would be expected to fulfil. In the *Lady Gwendolen* [1965] P 294 the owners of
the ship were Arthur Guinness, Son & Co (Dublin) Ltd. The collision occurred because
the master, in accordance with his custom, had taken his vessel laden with stout up the
Mersey Channel to Liverpool at full speed in dense fog without more than the odd casual
glance at his radar. Owning ships was a very subsidiary part of the company's activities.   H
It had a traffic department which managed the ships under the general supervision of a
member of the board who was a brewer and took no interest in the safety of their
navigation. The manager of the traffic department knew about railways but took equally
little interest in ships. The marine superintendent, one beneath him in the hierarchy,
failed to observe that the master of the *Lady Gwendolen* was given to dangerous
navigation although, as Willmer LJ said at p. 338:

A

'It would not have required any very detailed examination of the engine room records in order to ascertain that The Lady Gwendolen was frequently proceeding at full speed at times when the deck log was recording dense fog.'

In applying s. 503 of the *Merchant Shipping Act* 1894, Sellers LJ said of the company at p. 333:

B

'In their capacity as shipowners they must be judged by the standard of conduct of the ordinary reasonable shipowner in the management and control of a vessel or of a fleet of vessels.'

The court found that a reasonable shipowner would have realised what was happening and given the master proper instruction in the use of radar. None of the people in the company's hierarchy had done so.

C

It is difficult to see how, on any reasonable construction of s. 503, these findings would not involve the actual fault or privity of Guinness. So far as anyone in the hierarchy had functions corresponding to those to be expected of an individual owner, his failure to discharge them was attributable to the company. So far as there was no such person, the superior management was at fault in failing to ensure that there was. In either case, the fault was attributable to the company. But the Court of Appeal found it necessary to identify a 'directing mind and will' of the company and lodged it in the responsible member of the board or (in the case of Willmer LJ) the railway expert who managed the traffic department.

D

Some commentators have not been altogether comfortable with the idea of the Third Sea Lord being the directing mind and will of the Crown or the traffic manager being the directing mind and will of Guinness. Their Lordships would agree that the phrase does not fit the facts of the *Truculent* or the *Lady Gwendolen* as happily as it did those of *Lennard's* case. They think, however, that the difficulty has been caused by concentration on that particular phrase rather than the purpose for which Viscount Haldane was using it. It will often be the most appropriate description of the person designated by the relevant attribution rule, but it might be better to acknowledge that not every such rule has to be forced into the same formula.

E

Once it is appreciated that the question is one of construction rather than metaphysics, the answer in this case seems to their Lordships to be as straightforward as it did to Heron J. The policy of s. 20 of the *Securities Amendment Act* 1988 is to compel, in fast-moving markets, the immediate disclosure of the identity of persons who become substantial security holders in public issuers. Notice must be given as soon as that person knows that he has become a substantial security holder. In the case of a corporate security holder, what rule should be implied as to the person whose knowledge for this purpose is to count as the knowledge of the company? Surely the person who, with the authority of the company, acquired the relevant interest. Otherwise the policy of the Act would be defeated. Companies would be able to allow employees to acquire interests on 'their behalf which made them substantial security holders but would not have to report them until the board or someone else in senior management got to know about it. This would put a premium on the board paying as little attention as possible to what its investment managers were doing. Their Lordships would therefore hold that upon the true construction of s. 20(4)(e), the company knows that it has become a substantial security holder when that is known to the person who had authority to do the deal. It is then obliged to give notice under s. 20(3). The fact that Koo did the deal for a corrupt purpose and did not give such notice because he did not want his employers to find out cannot in their Lordships' view affect the attribution of knowledge and the consequent duty to notify.

F

G

H

It was therefore not necessary in this case to inquire into whether Koo could have been described in some more general sense as the 'directing mind and will' of the company.

But their Lordships would wish to guard themselves against being understood to mean   A
that whenever a servant of a company has authority to do an act on its behalf, knowledge
of that act will for all purposes be attributed to the company. It is a question of
construction in each case as to whether the particular rule requires that the knowledge
that an act has been done, or the state of mind with which it was done, should be
attributed to the company. Sometimes, as in *Ready Mixed Concrete* and this case, it will
be appropriate. Likewise in a case in which a company was required to make a return for   B
revenue purposes and the statute made it an offence to make a false return with intent to
deceive, the divisional court held that the mens rea of the servant authorised to discharge
the duty to make the return should be attributed to the company: see *Moore v I Bresler
Ltd* [1944] 2 All ER 515. On the other hand, the fact that a company's employee is
authorised to drive a lorry does not in itself lead to the conclusion that if he kills someone
by reckless driving, the company will be guilty of manslaughter. There is no
inconsistency. Each is an example of an attribution rule for a particular purpose, tailored   C
as it always must be to the terms and policies of the substantive rule.

The Commission in their printed case put forward an alternative argument based upon
s. 35 of the Act, which creates a presumption of knowledge:

> 'In any proceedings under this Part of this Act, it shall be presumed in the absence
> of proof to the contrary, that a person knew, at a material time, of the existence of
> a relevant interest in voting securities in a public issuer or of a fact or matter   D
> concerning the existence of a relevant interest in the securities if, at that time, an
> employee or agent of that person knew in his or her capacity as employee or agent
> of the existence of the relevant interest or of a fact or matter concerning the
> existence of it.'

Their Lordships did not find it necessary to call upon counsel for the Commission on this
or any other point and have therefore heard no oral submissions in support of the
Commission's alternative argument. But they find it difficult to see how, on the facts of   E
this case, s. 35 can advance the matter. There is no doubt that the knowledge of Koo and
Ng would have activated the presumption. But the presumption may be rebutted by
'proof to the contrary'. Proof of what? Proof, presumably, that in fact none of the persons
whose knowledge counted as the knowledge of the company did know about the relevant
interest. But the section gives no guidance as to who those persons are. That is left to the
process of construction of s. 20(4)(e) which their Lordships have undertaken. If, as they   F
think, Koo's knowledge was attributable to the company, the evidence made reliance on
the presumption unnecessary. And if only the knowledge of Mr Armour or the board
was so attributable, then the evidence showed clearly that they did not know and the
presumption was rebutted. Either way, it would have had no effect on the outcome of the
case.

Their Lordships will humbly advise Her Majesty that the appeal should be dismissed.   G
The appellants must pay the costs of the Commission before their Lordships' Board.

(*Order accordingly*)

———————————

H

A   # Mach Marketing International SA v MacColl.

Court of Session (Outer House).
T G Coutts QC (sitting as a temporary judge).
Judgment delivered 10 May 1995.

B   *Company formed for purposes of loan agreement – Company sued for return of
advance fee – Action based on false representations made by defender – Whether
representations irrelevant as made before company formed.*

**This was an action which raised the question inter alia whether the pursuing company
could maintain the action based on representations made before the company was formed.**

**Two individuals, B and W, sought financial backing for a proposed company buy-out.
The defender represented himself as legal adviser to a finance company which it was said**
C   **would only deal with a corporate entity. B and W then procured the formation of the pursuer
and were appointed directors. The pursuer sued first for £65,000, said to be for expenses
incurred as a result of the defender's actings, and second for US$100,000 being a sum which
was paid into the defender's hands as an advance fee for a loan agreement and which he
appropriated to his own use.**

Held, allowing a proof before answer:

D   **1. There were adequate averments to set out a case that it was at all times contemplated
by the defender that B and W would be influenced by his representations which were averred
to be false and that the defender knew that the pursuer, formed as a result of his insistence,
would act on those representations. (Leslie Leithhead Pty Ltd v Barbour (1965) SR (NSW)
172 considered.)**

2. The pursuer had set out just sufficient to entitle them to an enquiry on the merits by
E   **way of a proof before answer, with certain exceptions.**

The following case was referred to in the opinion:

Leslie Leithead Pty Ltd v Barber (1965) 65 SR (NSW) 172.

AJS Glennie (instructed by Fraser Brooks & Co, SSC) for the pursuers.

GC Bell QC (instructed by Balfour & Manson Nightingale & Bell, for Burnside,
F   Advocates, Aberdeen) for the defender.

OPINION

T G Coutts QC: In this action, which came before me on procedure roll, the pursuing
company sues first for £65,000, said to be for expenses incurred as a result of the
defender's actings, and second for US$100,000 being a sum which they aver that they
G   paid into the defender's hands and which, in effect, they aver in condescendence 10 he
appropriated to his own use.

The matters are averred to have arisen as a result of two individuals, Busch and
Walker, seeking financial backing for a proposed buy-out of a company called Icis-Lor
Group Ltd. These persons were introduced to the defender and to two other persons by
name of Kusel. One Kusel was said to be a banker and the other a trustee for a trust.
H   That trust was said to be a possible source of finance. They were introduced for a fee of
£3,000 by a gentleman who has now disappeared. Meetings took place at various
locations in Europe thereafter which involved the defender. He admits that he represented
himself as legal adviser to a company with the title Nikon Trust Corporation Ltd. This
company, registered in the Turks and Caicos Islands, had the pursuers averred, not only
no funds to the defender's knowledge but also no connection with any Japanese industrial
concern of a similar name.

The pursuers in their pleadings set out the various representations made to Busch and   A
Walker, including the important averment that the defender advised Busch and Walker
that he could not allow his clients (the trust) to deal with them unless they had a corporate
entity. He also advised them that the trust had been established for investors all over the
world and was well-known; and that the Kusels were highly respected and successful
businessmen. He admitted in answer 4 that he was legal adviser to Mr R Kusel. The
pursuers aver that R Kusel had been declared bankrupt. A draft agreement which was
produced at a meeting was given to Walker and Busch. That draft agreement was framed   B
in terms which can only be described as astonishing and which, inter alia, demanded an
advance fee of US$100,000.

Busch and Walker, who seem to have acted throughout with almost incredible naiveté,
then procured the pursuing company (a Panamanian company) and were appointed
directors on 30 October 1987.

The first point made by senior counsel for the defender was that all these above   C
narrated representations were not relevant and should be deleted. The company did not
come into existence, so far as Busch and Walker were concerned, until 30 October 1987.
The venture, he said, was until that date that of Busch and Walker and not the company,
and accordingly no representations were made to the company.

In reply, counsel for the pursuers referred to the only case cited to me at debate in
which the New South Wales Appeal Court had to deal with a similar factual situation.   D
That case *Leslie Leithhead Pty Co Ltd v Barbour* (1965) SR (NSW) 172 had involved a
proof. The plaintiff company sued for damages and recovered £8,520. The action was
based on false representations to Mr Hart. It was held (1) that as it was common ground
that the purchase was to be made by the company to be formed by Hart that the
representation could only have been made to him as a representative of the company; it
was at all times contemplated that the company, when formed, would act upon the false
representation; (2) that Hart, and thereby the plaintiff company, were in fact induced by   E
the false representation to buy the shares.

That litigation arose, it was said, out of a flagrant fraud carefully planned and
executed. On appeal it was suggested to the court that the false representation was not
made to the company but to an individual but the appellate court agreed 'wholeheartedly'
that it was at all times contemplated that the purchase was to be effected by a company
to be formed and controlled by Mr Hart. It was thereafter inferred that the inducement
offered to Mr Hart was intended to be communicated to and acted upon by the company   F
when formed.

I am of the opinion that there are adequate averments in the present case to set out a
case that it was at all times contemplated by the defender that Busch and Walker would
be influenced by his representations which are averred to be false and that the defender
knew that the pursuers, formed as a result of his insistence, would act on those
representations. In such circumstances I find no substance whatsoever in the first point   G
made for the defender, which in any event appears to me to be unsound in principle.

The pursuers thereafter were advised by another individual, Urban, recommended by
the defender and said to be a professor. He has also disappeared. He had been convicted
for fraud. Urban professed to be independent and expressed confidence in the
contemplated transaction proceeding. The pursuers followed that advice and entered into
a contract with the defender's clients, Nikon Trust, which the defender represented to
have connection with the Japanese conglomerate. The pursuers did not at once get a copy   H
of the contract which was held by the defender pending delivery of the US$100,000
therein demanded.

The pursuers then tried to act in terms of the contract to get bank guarantees. No
reputable bank would involve themselves in such a transaction. That situation would
come as no surprise to anyone considering the terms of the contract.

A   In February 1988 the defender next represented that he would attempt to vary the contract for a payment of a further $50,000.

The pursuers' position on the whole matter is summarised in condescendence 10. They aver a fraudulent scheme by the defender to obtain the $100,000 in which the Kusels and Urban participated. They also aver:

B
> 'The defender must, and any solicitors of ordinary skill exercising ordinary care would have known that the proposed contract executed on or about 9 December 1987 was not a proper loan agreement at all. It was ambiguous in material respects such as to be void for uncertainty. It contained provisions, in particular in cl. 9, which were, in practicable (*sic*) terms, impossible of fulfilment, but was couched in such terms as to induce the pursuer into believing that it was readily capable of fulfilment.'

C   The averments in condescendence 7 and the following articles of condescendence were attacked in matters of detail by senior counsel for the defender. He took several points of specification, e.g. that as it was Urban's advice not the defender's that was acted upon, there was no proper specification of what false or fraudulent representations were made to the company, and he also criticised the averments above quoted as being of no relevance to any fraudulent scheme.

D   Counsel for the pursuers invited me to consider the pleadings as a whole, disregarding infelicities of expression and, while conceding that the matters could have been better focused, submitted that they did provide a sufficient basis giving proper notice of the pursuers' case to entitle the pursuers to a proof before answer.

I consider having regard to the whole pleadings that the pursuers have, just, set out sufficient to entitle them to an enquiry on the merits by way of a proof before answer, with the undernoted exceptions. I accede to counsel for the defender's submissions to the extent that I exclude from probation the words 'and any solicitor of ordinary skill

E exercising ordinary care would' and, 'It was ambiguous in material respects such as to be void for uncertainty', which averments appear in condescendence 13. These, I agree, have no relevance to the issue of the defender's conduct which is under challenge.

A supplementary point was made in relation to condescendence 15, which relates to the first conclusion. Professional fees are claimed as are incidental costs and expenses. A schedule was produced and incorporated in the pleadings *brevitatis causa* which consisted

F of the professional's fee note which gives some specification of the work done and relates that to hours charged and also expenses, amounting to £50,000. There was also produced a document entitled 'Analysis of expenditure', that bears to be for certain matters between 1 October 1987 and November 1988. It produces a figure which does not correspond to either of the other figures in condescendence 15 which deal with costs and expenses and it observably contains material which has relation to the activities of Walker and Busch prior to the company's involvement with them as directors. It does not bear

G to be the pursuers' costs or expenses.

I was not convinced that the pursuers were entitled to probation on anything other than the £50,000 fee note which, after some hesitation, I think contains sufficient notice to form a basis for probation. However, I do not think that the following two sums in condescendence 15 are sufficiently specified for the purposes of a proof and I refuse to allow them to go to probation. It follows that proof of the damages sued for in condescendence 1 will be restricted to £50,000, being the sum specified in the fee note for

H professional hours and expenses.

No specific argument was addressed to me in relation to the defender's plea 5, but I was asked to uphold it. I could see no reason for so doing and repel it.

(*Order accordingly*)

Merrick Homes Ltd v Duff & Ors.

A

Court of Session (Inner House).
Lord Justice Clerk Ross, Lord Prosser and Lord MacLean.
Judgment delivered 17 May 1995.

Caution for costs – Lord Ordinary refused to order pursuing company to give additional caution for costs – Reclaiming motions – Whether additional caution should be ordered – Companies Act 1985, s. 726(2).

B

These were reclaiming motions by the first and third defenders against an interlocutor refusing their motions to have the pursuers ordained to find further caution for expenses.

The pursuers had been ordained to find caution for £14,000 in favour of each of the first and third defenders, in addition to sums already lodged, based upon an assessment by all counsel involved that the proof would be concluded in eight days or less. Refusing the defenders' motions for further caution the Lord Ordinary expressed the view that the court should be reluctant to accede to a step-by-step approach to the ordaining of caution, and that it was a sufficient reason for refusing the motions that the defenders seriously underestimated the duration of the proof.

C

Held, ordaining the pursuers to find additional caution in the sum of £10,000 in respect of each of the first and third defenders:

D

1. The Lord Ordinary had erred in two respects. He failed to attach sufficient weight to the fact that what was being sought by the motions was additional caution, and that he was not dealing with the question whether it was appropriate to order the pursuers to find caution at all. Secondly, he erred in failing to appreciate that part at least of the responsibility for the underestimate of the time the proof would take rested upon the pursuers.

2. The court was not satisfied that there was any general rule to the effect that the court should be reluctant to accede to a step-by-step approach to the ordaining of caution. In any event, the reason for the motions was simply that all parties were mistaken in their estimate of the number of days required for proof. It appeared that a further eight days might be required and if that had been known to the judge, the probability was that he would have fixed caution at a larger figure in favour of each of the first and third defenders.

E

The following cases were referred to in the opinion of the court:

F

Brownrigg Coal Co Ltd v Sneddon 1911 SC 1064.
New Mining and Exploring Syndicate Ltd v Chalmers & Hunter 1909 SC 1390.
Thomson v Corporation of Glasgow 1962 SC (HL) 36.

W Galbraith QC (instructed by Simpson & Marwick, WS) for the pursuers.

T G Coutts QC (instructed by Brodies, WS) for the first defenders.

Laurence Murphy (instructed by Dundas & Wilson, CS) for the third defenders.

G

OPINION OF THE COURT
(Delivered by Lord Justice Clerk Ross)

In this action, the pursuers are seeking implement of missives allegedly entered into between themselves and the first defender in January 1990 for the purchase by the pursuers of certain lands at Lochmaben. Failing implement, the pursuers seek certain alternative remedies. Proof in the action has been partly heard, and on 12 April 1995, the Lord Ordinary heard motions at the instance of the first and third defenders to have the pursuers ordained to find further caution for expenses. After hearing counsel he refused the motions. Subsequently he granted leave to reclaim against the interlocutor of 12 April 1995, and the first and third defenders have both reclaimed against that interlocutor.

H

A   In presenting the reclaiming motion for the first defender, Mr Coutts reminded us that orders for caution or its equivalent had been made previously in this action. This is referred to by the Lord Ordinary in his opinion. In June 1992 the first defender enrolled for an order on the pursuers to find caution, and subsequently the pursuers undertook to provide £2,000 to be placed on deposit receipt in joint names of the parties' solicitors in lieu of the caution for which the first defender had enrolled.

B   In June 1993, the first defender and the third defender each enrolled for an order on the pursuers to find caution for £7,500. The motions were subsequently dropped after the pursuers had agreed to lodge £2,500 in respect of each of the first and third defenders in lieu of caution.

By interlocutor dated 15 December 1994, another Lord Ordinary (Lord Weir) ordained the pursuers to find caution for £14,000 in respect of each of the first and third defenders. These sums were additional to the sums already lodged.

C   In moving the court to grant the reclaiming motion, Mr Coutts for the first defender maintained that the Lord Ordinary had erred in a number of respects. Mr Murphy for the third defender, in support of his reclaiming motion, also contended that the Lord Ordinary had erred in refusing to ordain the pursuers to find further caution.

Mr Galbraith for the pursuers, on the other hand, submitted that the reclaiming motions should be refused. He contended that the Lord Ordinary had applied the proper

D   tests. All counsel referred to the terms of s. 726(2) of the *Companies Act* 1985. Mr Galbraith maintained that the Lord Ordinary had a wide discretion when determining an issue of this kind, and he submitted that this court would only be entitled to interfere with such an exercise of discretion by the Lord Ordinary if it was satisfied that the Lord Ordinary had gone completely wrong. He submitted that the court could not be so satisfied in the present case, and that accordingly this court was not entitled to interfere.

E   Section 726(2) of the *Companies Act* 1985 is in the following terms:

'Where in Scotland a limited company is pursuer in an action or other legal proceeding, the court having jurisdiction in the matter may, if it appears by credible testimony that there is reason to believe that the company will be unable to pay the defender's expenses if successful in his defence, order the company to find caution and sist the proceedings until caution is found.'

F   Mr Galbraith founded strongly upon two cases relating to s. 278 of the *Companies (Consolidation) Act* 1908 which was in similar terms to s. 726(2) of the Act of 1985. In *New Mining and Exploring Syndicate Ltd v Chalmers & Hunter* 1909 SC 1390 at p. 1392 Lord President Dunedin said of s. 278 of the Act of 1908:

'One has only to read the section to see that it entrusts the judge with a discretion, and where a statute entrusts a judge with such a power and he exercises it, though

G   I do not say that his exercise of it will never be open to review, yet before the court will interfere it must be shewn that he has gone completely wrong.'

In *Brownrigg Coal Co Ltd v Sneddon* 1911 SC 1064, under reference to the same section Lord Dundas at p. 1067 said after referring to *New Mining Syndicate v Chalmers & Hunter*:

'It just comes to this, I think, that the Inner House, while it does not refuse to

H   consider such a motion as the present, will not reverse the judgment of the Lord Ordinary, in whichever way he has exercised his discretion, unless they are satisfied that he has plainly erred.'

We readily accept that that is the approach which the Inner House requires to adopt in cases of this kind. Indeed these cases are merely examples of the general rule that an appellate court will not overrule the discretion of a lower court merely because the

appellate court thinks that it might have exercised the discretion differently. The
circumstances in which an appellate court would be entitled to overrule the exercise of
discretion by a lower court have been described in *Thomson v Corporation of Glasgow*
1962 SC (HL) 36 by Lord Reid at p. 66:

> 'We might do so if some irrelevant factor had been taken into account, or some
> important relevant factor left out of account, or if the decision was unreasonable,
> and we would no doubt do so if the decision could be said to be unjudicial.'

A number of arguments were put forward in support of the submission that the Lord
Ordinary in this case had erred. We do not find it necessary to deal with all the arguments
presented to us because we are satisfied that in the present case the Lord Ordinary did err
in two important respects. In the first place we are of opinion that the Lord Ordinary
failed to attach sufficient weight to the fact that what was being sought by these motions
was additional caution, and that he was not dealing with a case where the question which
had to be determined was whether it was appropriate to order the pursuers to find caution
at all. Thus in the final paragraph of his opinion, the Lord Ordinary describes the final
consideration which weighed with him which was that this is not a simple litigation in
which the approach to expenses will be straightforward. That is no doubt so and that
was no doubt a relevant consideration at the time when Lord Weir in December 1994
ordained the pursuers to find caution of £14,000 in respect of each of the first and third
defenders. However the question at this stage is not whether it is appropriate to ordain
the pursuers to find caution, but whether it is appropriate that they should be ordained
to find additional caution.

In the second place, the Lord Ordinary in the penultimate paragraph of his opinion
expresses the view that it is a sufficient reason for refusing these motions that the first and
third defenders seriously underestimated the duration of the proof. He points out that
caution was ordered by Lord Weir upon an estimate that the proof would take eight
days, and he expresses the view that the first and third defenders share responsibility for
that serious underestimate. However, at an earlier point in his opinion the Lord Ordinary
has recorded that the sums of caution fixed by Lord Weir were based on an assessment
by all counsel involved that the proof would be concluded in eight days or less. Counsel
confirmed that the situation had been that counsel for the pursuers as well as counsel for
the first and third defenders were agreed in December 1994 that the proof should not
take more than eight days. This was also in accordance with the information contained
in Form 63 signed by counsel and lodged with the Keeper of the Rolls. We were informed
that to date seven days of evidence have been heard, and that the pursuers have not yet
closed their case. It is apparently their intention at the continued proof to call the third
defender as one of their witnesses.

In these circumstances we are satisfied that the Lord Ordinary was in error when he
held that the first and third defenders fully shared responsibility for the unreliable
estimate that the proof would take eight days. The pursuers must clearly share
responsibility for that estimate, and the pursuers indeed should have been in the best
position to estimate how long the proof was to take. The pursuers' proof has already
occupied seven of the eight days, and additional days are apparently required before the
pursuers will be in a position to close their case. In these circumstances we are clearly of
opinion that the Lord Ordinary was in error in holding that it was a sufficient reason for
refusing the motions that the first and third defenders required to accept responsibility
for underestimating the time which the proof would take. He erred in failing to appreciate
that part at least of the responsibility for the underestimate rested upon the pursuers.

Since the Lord Ordinary did err in these respects, we are satisfied that this court is
entitled to review the Lord Ordinary's exercise of his discretion, and that the issue of
whether or not the motions should be granted is now at large for this court.

A   In determining that issue, the starting off point must be that in December 1994, Lord Weir was satisfied that it was appropriate to ordain the pursuers to find caution in favour of each of the first and third defenders. It appears that the sums which Lord Weir fixed were based upon an assessment by all counsel involved that the proof would be concluded in eight days or less. If in December 1994 Lord Weir had been informed that the proof was likely to take 16 days instead of eight days, we are of opinion that the probability is that he would have fixed caution at a larger sum than £14,000 in respect of each of the first and third defenders. It appears that caution of £14,000 in respect of each of the first and third defenders was fixed upon an inaccurate estimate of the time required for the proof, and that that inaccurate estimate had been agreed by all parties. In his opinion the Lord Ordinary expresses the view that the court should be reluctant to accede to a step-by-step approach to the ordaining of caution. We are not satisfied that there is any general rule to that effect. For example, it may be appropriate for caution to be ordained to cover the situation up to a decision on procedure roll as to whether or not an inquiry is necessary, and thereafter for further caution to be ordained once it is known that an inquiry is to take place. In any event, we do not regard the present case as one where the first and third defenders have adopted a step-by-step approach. The reason for the present motion is simply that all parties were mistaken in their estimate of the number of days required for proof in this action. It now appears that a further eight days may be required in order to complete the proof. As we say, if that had been known to Lord Weir in December 1994, the probability is that he would have fixed caution at a larger figure than £14,000 in favour of each of the first and third defenders.

We are accordingly satisfied that in the very special circumstances of this case, it is appropriate to ordain the pursuers to find additional caution. Mr Galbraith submitted that if additional caution was ordered it was possible that the pursuers would be unable to find such additional caution in which case all their expenditure to date would have been rendered abortive, but it is significant that he did not maintain that the pursuers would be unable to find additional caution. He merely stated that ordaining the pursuers to find additional caution had the potential to render the previous expenditure by the pursuers abortive. Mr Coutts invited the court to ordain the pursuers to find caution in the sum of £30,000, and Mr Murphy for the third defenders moved the court to ordain the pursuers to find caution in favour of his clients in the sum of £25,000. Both counsel recognised that these sums might be regarded as on the high side, and that in the circumstances the court might be disposed to fix a lower sum for additional caution. One can only approach the matter of caution upon a broad basis, and having regard to all the circumstances we have come to the conclusion that it would be appropriate now to ordain the pursuers to find caution in the sum of an additional £10,000 in respect of each of the first and third defenders. We will accordingly grant the reclaiming motions, recall the interlocutor of the Lord Ordinary dated 12 April 1995, and we shall ordain the pursuers to lodge additional caution for expenses in respect of each of the first and third defenders in the sum of £10,000.

(*Order accordingly*)

———————————

R & H Electrical Ltd & Anor v Haden Bill Electrical Ltd & Ors.

Chancery Division (Companies Court).
Robert Walker J.
Judgment delivered 24 May 1995.

> *Unfair prejudice petition – Petition alleged that minority shareholder was to have certain rights of control so long as company controlled by him remained a loan creditor – Whether petitioner prejudiced in his capacity as a shareholder – Whether petitioner had legitimate expectation of management; whether company quasi-partnership – Companies Act 1985, s. 459, 461.*

These were an unfair prejudice petition under s. 459 of the Companies Act 1985, and a writ action seeking to establish that 'P' had not been validly removed from effective control of Haden Bill Electrical Ltd.

P held 25 per cent of the shares in Haden Bill. Another company ('R & H') of which P was a director and shareholder was a loan creditor of the company having provided the whole of the company's working capital. The proceedings in the action and the petition overlapped in that both asserted an agreement, understanding or situation of estoppel under which P was to have certain entrenched rights of control so long as R & H should remain a creditor of Haden Bill. The petition relied on the assertion that Haden Bill was formed on the basis of mutual trust and confidence between the shareholders and on the ouster of P as amounting to conduct of the company's affairs which was unfairly prejudicial to P.

Held, making an order under s. 461 for P's shares to be bought by the majority without a discount for a minority shareholding and for R & H's loans to be repaid as soon as reasonably possible (and leaving over the question of relief in the writ action for further argument, if necessary, at such time as the precise form of relief to be granted under s. 461 was determined):

1. P's primary claim in the writ action based on the assertion of a binding oral contract failed. It was doubtful whether the factual basis for an equitable estoppel was made out. In any event the breakdown in confidence between the shareholders made the granting of injunctive relief inappropriate.

2. The company was planned, formed and set up in business on the basis of mutual trust and P did have a legitimate expectation of being able to participate in the management of the company at least for so long as R & H remained a significant loan creditor (and so long as P was closely associated with R & H). (Tay Bok Choon v Tahansan Sdn Bhd (1987) 3 BCC 132 applied.)

3. The fact that P and R & H were separate legal persons did not exclude P from seeking relief under s. 459 on the basis that R & H's loans to the company were procured by P and formed an absolutely essential part of the arrangements entered into for the venture to be carried on by the company.

The following cases were referred to in the judgment:

British Murac Syndicate Ltd v Alperton Rubber Co Ltd [1915] 2 Ch 186.
Cade (J E) & Son Ltd, Re [1991] BCC 360.
Company No. 00477 of 1986, Re a (1986) 2 BCC 99,171.
Ebrahimi v Westbourne Galleries Ltd [1973] AC 360.
Ringtower Holdings plc, Re (1989) 5 BCC 82.
Tay Bok Choon v Tahansan Sdn Bhd (1987) 3 BCC 132.
Tecnion Investments Ltd, Re [1985] BCLC 434.
XYZ Ltd (Company No. 004377 of 1986), Re (1986) 2 BCC 99,520; [1987] 1 WLR 102.

A   Christopher Parker (instructed by Bevirs, Swindon) for the plaintiffs.

Kenneth Farrow (instructed by Ormerod Wilkinson Marshall, Croydon) for the defendants.

JUDGMENT

B   **Robert Walker J:** Two sets of proceedings have been heard together before me. One is an action commenced by writ on 15 March 1994. The plaintiffs are R & H Electrical Ltd ('R & H') and Mr Duncan Pitt. The defendants are Haden Bill Electrical Ltd ('Haden Bill'), Mr Gordon Hogg, his wife Mrs Sally Hogg, and Mr Adrian Watkins. Mr Pitt and the three individual defendants have at all times been shareholders in equal 25 per cent shares in Haden Bill, which was incorporated on 24 November 1989. The four shareholders were initially all directors of Haden Bill, but this has changed, as will appear.

C   R & H is a loan creditor of Haden Bill. Indeed R & H provided Haden Bill with the whole of its working capital (except for equity capital of £100) during its early years. Mr Pitt owns about 22 per cent of the shares in R & H; about 28 per cent are held by Mr Pitt and his brother as trustees of his late father's estate; and 50 per cent belong to an overseas body called Esscee Anstalt. At all relevant times the only directors of R & H have been Mr Pitt and Carol Rankin, representing the Anstalt.

D   The relief claimed in the writ action is largely by way of declaration and injunction, the general aim of the proceedings being to establish that Mr Pitt had not been validly removed from effective control of the affairs of Haden Bill. There was a great deal of interlocutory activity, including at one stage a motion to commit the three individual defendants (whom I will refer to as 'the majority shareholders'). The outcome of the interlocutory battles was that initially Mr Pitt succeeded in obtaining relief (granted by an order of Morritt J on 27 April 1994) but about six months later there was an order of

E   Judge Weeks which on terms (including the provision of a bond guaranteed by the Bank of Scotland for payment-off in specified circumstances of Haden Bill's liability to R & H) had the effect of transferring control of Haden Bill to Mr and Mrs Hogg and Mr Watkins.

Mr Pitt was then removed as a director of Haden Bill at an EGM of the company held on 24 October 1994. Attempts to remove him had by then been on foot for some 18 months and had been the cause of the writ action; until the order of Judge Weeks, Mr

F   Pitt's removal had been prevented by injunction. His actual removal on 24 October 1994 seems to have been, in turn, the cause of the petition – the other set of proceedings before me – which was presented on 19 December 1994. The petitioner is Mr Pitt and the respondents are the majority shareholders of Haden Bill.

The petition seeks an order under s. 459 of the *Companies Act* 1985 that the majority shareholders should be ordered to purchase Mr Pitt's shares for £60,000 (though if such

G   an order is to be made, it is agreed that the purchase price should not be fixed at this hearing); alternatively the petition asks that Haden Bill should be wound up on the ground that it is just and equitable for such an order to be made. The majority shareholders will if necessary contend (in reliance on s. 125(2) of the *Insolvency Act* 1986) that they should become purchasers of Mr Pitt's shares rather than a winding-up order being made.

H   The proceedings in the action and the petition overlap in that both assert an agreement, understanding or situation of estoppel under which Mr Pitt was to have certain entrenched rights of control so long as R & H should remain a creditor of Haden Bill. But the petition goes further and (as well as covering more recent events) relies on (first) the assertion that Haden Bill was formed on the basis of mutual trust and confidence between the shareholders, (second) the ouster of Mr Pitt from his entrenched rights and (third) certain payments made by Haden Bill (which are said to have been made without

Mr Pitt's approval and otherwise than in the interest of the company as a whole) as   A
amounting to conduct of the company's affairs which is unfairly prejudicial to Mr Pitt.

Those are, in brief summary, the issues to be resolved. Their resolution requires, as is
so often the case on a s. 459 petition, a fairly detailed examination of evidence which, as
Hoffmann J said in *Re XYZ Ltd* (1986) 2 BCC 99,520 at p. 99,526:

'tracks the breakdown of a business relationship commenced in hope and
expectation of profitable collaboration.'   B

But in this case personal relationships were involved as well. The facts are unusual, and I
have to try as best I can to disentangle the threads of shareholder relationships, debtor-
creditor relationships and personal relationships.

Mr Pitt is an experienced businessman who lives near Swindon. His marriage has been
dissolved. He has one grown-up daughter, Tracey, who works for him and was indeed
company secretary of Haden Bill until her removal. Mr Pitt's most important company   C
is R & H, which is a wholesaler in electrical goods, but he is a director (and indeed
chairman) of nearly 20 companies in all. He first joined R & H in 1960.

Mr Hogg is aged 34. He has known Mr Pitt, on and off, for more than half his life,
since he first joined R & H, working as a storeman, when he was 16. That was in 1977.
He says that he got on really well with Mr Pitt and looked up to him as a sort of father
figure. Mr Hogg worked for R & H for about three years and then left for other   D
employment. Mr Hogg again worked for R & H between 1981 and 1982, when he left
because he was dissatisfied with the pay. He then worked as a salesman for AC Electrical,
a direct competitor of R & H in the Swindon area, but he remained in touch with Mr
Pitt. He sometimes telephoned Mr Pitt and challenged him to a game of snooker at Mr
Pitt's house, but Mr Pitt declined to play with him until about 1988 when Mr Hogg was
promoted by AC Electrical and moved to become manager of their Trowbridge branch
so that Mr Hogg was no longer part of the direct competition in the Swindon area.   E

Meanwhile Mr Hogg had married his wife, Sally. They have three children including a
daughter, Hayley. She is married to Mr Euan Carscadden (who also plays a part in the
story).

Mr Watkins worked for R & H for nearly 19 years, from 1974 until 1993. For the last
12 years of this period he was general manager of R & H and its associated companies
(though he was never a director of R & H). Mr Pitt described Mr Watkins as his right-   F
hand man. Mr Hogg said in his oral evidence that he assumed that Mr Watkins would
always vote with Mr Pitt although in the event there was a bitter parting of the ways
between them over a personal matter. Mr Pitt said in his oral evidence that he did not
expect there to have to be any votes taken, because he assumed that all four director-
shareholders would, after any necessary discussion, reach a consensus. He said that he
wanted to be chairman not for a casting vote but simply because he wanted to take the   G
chair at meetings.

It was during a game of snooker at Mr Pitt's house, some time in the spring or early
summer of 1989, that discussions began which led to the formation of Haden Bill. These
discussions were initially between Mr Pitt and Mr Hogg. Mr Hogg spoke of his ambitions
for having his own business. Mr Pitt warned him to be careful (since Mr Hogg had a
family as well as a mortgage) but indicated that if Mr Hogg was seriously interested he
(Mr Pitt) might be willing to help. Mr Pitt made clear, however, as the discussions   H
developed, that if Mr Hogg was to have a new electrical wholesale business it must be
well away from areas in which R & H (or AC Electrical) was trading: and for that reason
Mr Hogg decided to look to Scotland, where he had roots.

At some stage (Mrs Hogg thinks it was July 1989, which she remembers because she
was heavily pregnant with her third child) there was a meeting between Mr Pitt, Mr

A   Watkins and Mr and Mrs Hogg, the prospective shareholders in the new company. Mr and Mrs Hogg did not relish having Mr Watkins as a shareholder, but Mr Pitt insisted on Mr Watkins being involved. Part of Mr Pitt's motivation was, it seems, to confer a sort of bonus on Mr Watkins, who was not investing more than a nominal sum and was not going to be a working director, but was to have one-quarter of the equity. Originally R & H was to provide loan capital of £100,000, but this figure doubled when it was decided, with Mr Pitt as the moving force, to acquire freehold premises in Scotland. Such

B   premises – at 19 Faraday Road, Glenrothes – were eventually acquired in July 1990 and trading commenced a month later. In the meantime Haden Bill had been incorporated and (after an interregnum during which Mr Broadbent, Mr Pitt's accountant, was sole director) the first board meeting (other than purely formal meetings) was held on 10 May 1990. At that date Mr Hogg had only just reached the end of his employment by AC Electrical.

C   One of the issues in this case is whether the arrangements made during 1990 for the management of Haden Bill's affairs just happened, so to speak, or whether they were the result of a binding oral agreement between the shareholders, or (as is put forward in amendments and reamendments to the statement of claim and in the petition) a non-contractual understanding capable of giving rise to estoppel. Another issue is whether those arrangements were made (in Lord Wilberforce's words in *Re Westbourne Galleries*

D   *Ltd* [1973] AC 360 at p. 379F) 'on the basis of a personal relationship, involving mutual confidence' – that being a typical if not essential ground on which it may be equitable to view a private company as a quasi-partnership. There is a conflict of oral evidence on these points. Mr Pitt says that it was orally agreed between the four shareholders that so long as R & H was providing loan capital, Mr Pitt would control Haden Bill's bank account as sole signatory with possession of the only chequebook (and with the possibility of two other directors, or one other director and the company secretary, Mr Pitt's

E   daughter, signing cheques in emergencies only) and that Mr Pitt (with the assistance of his office staff at Swindon) would keep Haden Bill's books of account and generally see to its financial affairs. Mr Pitt saw this as having a double function. On the one hand, it gave him a sort of informal security, in that he monitored expenditure, including wages; moreover in practice it led to any questionable items of proposed expenditure being discussed in advance, on the telephone, between himself and Mr Hogg. On the other hand, it provided a benefit for Haden Bill which would otherwise have had to incur extra

F   expenditure on a bookkeeper's wages. Mr Pitt says that this happened under an oral agreement made when the four shareholders first decided to form Haden Bill. Mr Hogg accepts that the bookkeeping facility was useful but does not accept the security aspect, and denies that there was any oral agreement for the bookkeeping arrangement to continue for any particular period.

G   Mrs Hogg and Mr Watkins also assent that there was no oral agreement before the board meeting of 19 May 1990, and that the decisions at the board meeting do not go any further than is recorded in the minutes.

   Such documentary evidence as there is on these disputed issues is largely negative – that is, there was no written shareholders' agreement, formal or informal. The minutes of the board meeting record the opening of an account at Midland Bank, Swindon (where Mr Pitt's other companies banked) with cheques to be signed by Mr Pitt or any two other

H   directors, but do not state that this arrangement was to continue so long as R & H remained a creditor (or for any other period).

   In the absence of documentary evidence I must consider and assess the oral evidence which I heard from Mr Pitt, Mr Hogg, Mrs Hogg and Mr Watkins. But before I do so it is convenient to summarise the rest of the story and identify the other factual issues that arise.

At the board meeting on 10 May 1990 25 ordinary shares of £1 each in Haden Bill   A
were allocated, for cash, to each of the four shareholders. The board minutes refer to R
& H advancing a maximum of £100,000 but it is clear that the plan for buying freehold
premises in Scotland was by then already well advanced, and R & H advanced to Haden
Bill £200,000 in two tranches, in July and August 1990. A mortgage in Scottish form of
the Glenrothes premises was executed on 28 July 1990 to secure £95,000 (the purchase
price) with interest at 12 per cent per annum. The balance of the loan remained, at this
stage, unsecured (except for what Mr Pitt regarded as his informal security) and interest-   B
free. The secured loan has been referred to as the building loan and the unsecured loan
as the stock loan.

Haden Bill made six monthly payments of £2,000 to reduce principal on the building
loan (as well as paying interest) but discontinued these, with Mr Pitt's concurrence, in
January 1991; and in February 1991, October 1991 and March 1992 R & H made further
advances of £20,000 (on each occasion) so as to increase the stock loan. The second of   C
these further advances was quickly repaid and repayment of instalments of principal on
the building loan (at the rate of £2,500 per month) were resumed in March 1992.

In the meantime, in January 1991, Mr Pitt on the advice of Mr Broadbent, the
accountant, arranged for payments of interest on the interest-bearing part of the loans to
be designated as management charges. This was apparently done for some reason
connected with VAT or corporation tax. Since R & H was using its staff and facilities to   D
provide Haden Bill with bookkeeping services it was, it seems to me, open to the two
companies to agree to a charge for these services, and it may have been open to R & H
to waive interest on the building loan in the meantime, but I express no view as to
whether these transactions were in fact carried out, or whether the label 'management
charges' was a sham. In the event this was a further source of confusion and dispute after
the shareholders fell out.

On 8 February 1991 the first AGM of Haden Bill was held at the Balbirnie Hotel,   E
Markwinch. Mr Broadbent was in attendance and presented the audited accounts for
1990 (the company's accounting date was 31 December, so that the audit must have been
carried out with commendable speed). It is not surprising (since the company had only
just started trading, and had a paid up capital of only £100) that the accounts showed a
loss of about £27,000 and a deficiency of assets of about the same size. It seems that Mr
Broadbent, with encouragement from Mr Pitt, emphasised the company's precarious   F
state and the directors' responsibilities; he explained the 'going concern' basis which
depended on R & H's continuing support; and there was mention of R & H taking a
fixed and floating charge over all Haden Bill's assets. There is a dispute as to what (if
anything) was said on this occasion about the chairmanship of Haden Bill.

R & H did continue to support Haden Bill, as already mentioned, and its business
began to prosper. In 1991 it made a net profit of about £24,000 (after administrative   G
charges in lieu of interest of about £13,000) but still had a small deficiency of assets. In
1992 the net profit was about £39,000, and a dividend of £30,000 was declared. This was
arrived at after discussion at an EGM and board meeting held at the Roscobie Hotel,
Leslie, Fife on 19 February 1993. Mr Broadbent recommended an increase in the
company's paid up capital and the decision finally arrived at was that after the
declaration of a dividend of £30,000, £20,000 would be capitalised and £10,000 credited
to the shareholders 'to be drawn when finances permit'. This required a special resolution,   H
which was passed, to increase the authorised capital to £50,000.

At a further board meeting of Haden Bill on the following day it was resolved that R
& H would, in relation to £90,000 of the stock loan, accept repayment of principal at the
rate of 'at least' £2,000 per month and would not call in this sum so long as such
repayments were made. This was said (in the Haden Bill board resolution) to be for the

A

protection of Haden Bill and it plainly was beneficial to it – the expediency of the transaction would seem to have been a matter for debate at a board meeting of R & H rather than Haden Bill, but if the Anstalt's representative director felt any qualms about Mr Pitt's generosity with R & H's shareholders' fund, there is no hint in the papers that she ever expressed them.

B

This decision (which was embodied in a deed dated 5 April 1993) has also given rise to some confusion, especially as regards the implications for payment of interest (or administrative charges in lieu of interest) but that is not an issue before me. There are separate proceedings about it in the Swindon County Court. In the proceedings before me the only issue connected with this episode is as part of Mr Pitt's estoppel argument.

By the beginning of 1993 the seeds of conflict between the shareholders were already germinating and sprouting. Mr and Mrs Hogg were living in Glenrothes and running the business, except for bookkeeping. As to that the practice was that invoices were shuttled

C

to Swindon, generally on a weekly basis, and cheques were signed and sent out by Mr Pitt at Swindon. Mr Pitt provided Mr Hogg with management figures on a monthly basis. Mr and Mrs Hogg were receiving £20,000 a year between them as salary, which they understandably regarded as low remuneration for the managers of a business which was starting to thrive, especially as Mrs Hogg had to use the services of a childminder to look after her youngest child while she was working. Mr Pitt, on the other hand, stressed

D

the need for economy and sacrifice until the business was really well established, and its debts to R & H repaid. Mr Pitt agreed the cost of the childminder, and the Hoggs' combined salary went up to £25,000, but an exchange of letters between Mr Pitt and Mr Hogg in September 1992 shows that all was not well between them. Mr Pitt's letter was firm but moderate in tone, and Mr Hogg's reply was for the most part conciliatory, but the exchange does not seem to have cleared the air or produced any permanent improvement in the situation. At the same time, quite independently and unknown to the

E

Hoggs until about March 1993, a personal crisis was developing as between Mr Pitt and Mr Watkins.

During 1993 there were negotiations for Mr Pitt to buy out Mr Watkins' shareholdings in various companies in which they both held shares, including Haden Bill; but no agreement was reached. During the second half of 1993 Mr Watkins was still employed by R & H, but was not in fact going to work at Swindon.

F

In November 1993 Mr Hogg discovered that his personal bank account was overdrawn. This seems to have upset him. At about the same time Mr Watkins and his wife were visiting the Hoggs in Scotland. On 14 November Mr Hogg had a long talk on the telephone with Mr Pitt. After the conversation Mr Hogg said to Mr Watkins (in Mr Hogg's own words), 'I have worked it out, the old man is greedy'. It seems clear that from that date there was an alliance between the majority shareholders against Mr Pitt.

G

It was not until the following February, however, that the majority shareholders made their move.

On 2 February 1994 notice was given for the AGM of Haden Bill to be held at Glenrothes on 4 March. There was an item on the agenda, 'to consider and approve the resignation of Mr A Watkins' (Mr Pitt seems to have thought that Mr Watkins had agreed to resign, or would in the event resign). Mr Hogg had been due to stay with Mr

H

Pitt at the latter's house on 5 February, but the arrangement was cancelled at short notice. On 10 February T D Young & Co ('Youngs'), solicitors practising at Glenrothes, sent a faxed letter to Mr Broadbent telling him of their clients' intention to remove Mr Pitt as a director of Haden Bill. Youngs' clients were named as Haden Bill and the three majority shareholders. The letter said that Mr Pitt would receive notice of a board meeting to be held in Glenrothes on Monday, 14 February approving the calling of an EGM. On Saturday, 12 February Mr Pitt received through the post draft minutes of such a board meeting, showing that it was proposed to change Haden Bill's banking arrangements (opening an account with the Bank of Scotland), to remove Mr Pitt as chairman and his daughter as company secretary (with Mr Watkins and Mr Hogg being appointed in their respective places) and to convene an EGM for 21 March 1994 to remove Mr Pitt as a director.

Youngs' letter to Mr Broadbent was promptly passed to Mr Pitt's solicitors, Bevirs, who protested in a faxed letter dated 11 February at the shortness of the notice. There ensued a vigorous correspondence which I need not trace in detail. Mr Farrow makes the point, which carries some weight but not to my mind a great deal, that it was not until some weeks later that Bevirs contended for a contractual basis for objecting to the majority shareholders' action against their client.

The board meeting was postponed by one day but was held on 15 February, Mr Pitt being absent, as was Mr Watkins. Mr and Mrs Hogg proceeded to transact the business set out in the draft minutes, which were signed by Mr Hogg.

The AGM of Haden Bill was held on 4 March. It was attended by the three majority shareholders with Mr Wilson of Youngs in attendance but no one else. The accounts were not available and for reasons that I have already touched on they were not produced until finally signed off by new auditors on 30 March 1995; they showed a net profit of about £55,000. The notes to the balance sheet showed that at 31 December 1993 there was £53,000 of principal repayable to R & H within one year (reflecting monthly instalments of £4,500) and £82,000 repayable after more than a year – so a total of £135,000 principal was due to R & H at that stage.

At the AGM Mr Watkins said that he did not intend to resign as a director, and the meeting passed a vote of confidence in him. On 15 March Mr Pitt issued his writ and a notice of motion for interlocutory injunctions. That motion was stood over on undertakings. On 24 March Haden Bill launched its own motion for delivery up of its books and records.

During April, despite the undertakings given to Warner J on 18 March 1994, Haden Bill made payments of three types on which the committal proceedings against the majority shareholders were later based:

(1)   a total sum of £3,500 paid to Mr and Mrs Hogg on 18 April in respect of dividends declared but not previously paid (no corresponding payment was offered to Mr Pitt);

(2)   a total of about £8,000 paid to Youngs in March or April 1994 in respect of legal costs (there was an error in computation of the exact amount which it is not necessary to pursue); and

(3)   a sum of £500 described as an instalment of bonus paid to Mr Carscadden (then Hayley's fiancé) on 14 April.

These payments are also relied in the petition as instances of unfairly prejudicial conduct by the majority shareholders.

On 7 November 1994 Jacob J made no order in the committal motion except that the majority shareholders should in any event pay the costs of the motion on any indemnity basis, to be taxed and paid at once. I need not go further into the interlocutory stage of the proceedings.

I heard oral evidence from Mr Pitt, Mr and Mrs Hogg, Mr Watkins and Mr Broadbent. Mr Pitt and Mr Hogg were cross-examined at some length. The other witnesses were cross-examined only briefly.

Mr Pitt is an experienced businessman who believes in hard work, economy, and keeping things simple. On several occasions he did not proceed with formal documents

A   (such as a shareholders' agreement and a debenture secured by a fixed and floating charge) which were recommended to him by professional advisers. Speaking of his relations with his fellow shareholders in Haden Bill he said that they did, in the end, rely just on trust. He knew that the chairmanship of Haden Bill gave him a casting vote but he said that if you got to a stage where you needed a casting vote, you were in trouble. He expected Mr Watkins to go along with his views but he did not expect differences with the Hoggs either – at any rate, differences that were incapable of being talked

B   through and resolved by discussion, rather than by taking a vote. He thought (justifiably, it seems to me) that the arrangement was so beneficial to the Hoggs that he did not expect trouble from them.

     Mr Pitt gave his evidence in a straightforward way which largely concealed the strong feelings that he has about the case. On most points I prefer his evidence to that of Mr Hogg, where their testimony is in conflict. But on the crucial question of the oral

C   agreement I think that Mr Pitt's strong feelings have led him into the mistaken belief that his plans and expectations – which were no doubt discussed at length with Mr Hogg during 1989 – amounted to a binding oral contract between himself (acting on behalf of R & H) and the three other shareholders. I am not satisfied, on the balance of probability, that there was any such binding oral contract. The assertion of a contract is to a considerable extent negated by Mr Pitt's own evidence as to relying on trust. Mr Pitt is

D   not only an experienced businessman but also a strong character. He was Mr Watkins' boss (though as he put it, talking of being boss was not his style) and he was (as both agree) a sort of father figure to Mr Hogg. It seems to me much more probable, and I so find, that the discussions during 1989 and early 1990 were just that – discussions – and that Mr Pitt expected his fellow shareholders to go along with his views about the management of the company's affairs (and in particular, its financial control), not because they were contractually bound to do so, but because they would have been

E   foolish – as well as ungrateful – not to do so.

     Mr Hogg is a very ambitious man with a much keener awareness of his talents (as he sees them) than his limitations. He seems quite unaware of how much he owes Mr Pitt for giving him the chance to be (in Mr Hogg's words) 'his own guvnor'. In 1989 he had twice left R & H's employment (where he had worked as a storeman and a salesman) and he was just starting to acquire some managerial experience as a branch manager of a

F   rival wholesaler. For the sum of £50 Mr Hogg and his wife acquired 50 per cent of the shares in a company which was to be loaned £100,000 interest-free (soon supplemented by a further £100,000 at a reasonable commercial rate, and by further advances); and the company was to have the benefit of Mr Pitt's experience, and R & H's office facilities, in looking after the books and supplying management information.

G   Mr Hogg's apparent lack of awareness of the value of these benefits merely underlines, to my mind, his lack of business experience. When asked why he wanted to be chairman of Haden Bill from the outset (something he pressed for, but Mr Pitt refused to agree) Mr Hogg said that it was because it was the 'top job'; he readily admitted that he knew nothing about a chairman's boardroom responsibilities. Mr Watkins in his evidence made very clear that in his view the Hoggs simply did not have the skill or experience to maintain the necessary accounting records in Scotland, and that Mr Hogg would have

H   been foolish not to accept Mr Pitt's offer.

     I accept that Mr and Mrs Hogg both worked very hard, for relatively low remuneration, during the first few years of Haden Bill's operations. I think they are quite wrong if (as appears to be the case) they feel a sense of grievance against Mr Pitt about that. Mr Pitt gave Mr Hogg the chance to be his 'own guvnor' but any young man who is building up his own business (or a business in which he and his wife have acquired a

half-share for a nominal consideration) must expect to receive less, in the way of   A
immediate income, than a less ambitious man who remains in paid employment.

I accept most of Mr Hogg's evidence on matters of primary fact, though I do not
accept his evidence that there was no discussion of the chairmanship at the Balbirnie
Hotel or his assertion that he had nothing to do with the letter from Mr Carscadden's
solicitors. More importantly, I do not accept Mr Hogg's assessment of the commercial
realities of the situation.   B

Mrs Hogg's evidence was marked by its strength of feeling against Mr Pitt, but added
little to my understanding of the facts. Mrs Hogg asserted that Mr Watkins was a 'rubber
stamp' for Mr Pitt but that the same was not true of herself and her husband. I do not
consider that either Mrs Hogg or Mr Watkins was simply a 'rubber stamp', either in 1989
or later, but I do consider that they were both fairly inactive during the discussions
leading up to the incorporation of Haden Bill.   C

I found Mr Watkins a reliable witness. He accepted that the arrangement was beneficial
to him. I think he summed up the position correctly when he said that it would have been
logical for Mr Pitt to have insisted on an agreement such as he now contends for, but
that Mr Pitt did not in fact do so.

On these findings of fact, Mr Pitt's primary claim in the writ action, based on the
assertion of a binding oral contract, must fail. Mr Christopher Parker (for Mr Pitt) then
falls back on estoppel, submitting that an estoppel can be based on less certain and clearly   D
defined representations or undertakings. That is no doubt so, up to a point, but I doubt
whether the factual basis for an equitable estoppel (as opposed to the general equitable
principles on which a winding-up order may be made on just and equitable grounds) has
been made out here. In any event I do not think it appropriate to grant any of the
injunctive relief sought in the writ action. In view of the breakdown in confidence between
the shareholders, and the hostility which the majority shareholders now feel towards Mr   E
Pitt, it would be unthinkable to attempt to compel them to work together in harmony
(compare *British Murac Syndicate Ltd v Alperton Rubber Co Ltd* [1915] 2 Ch 186). I do
not think it could possibly be right to go through the motions of restoring Mr Pitt
temporarily to the board of Haden Bill simply in order to trigger off a payment under
the Bank of Scotland bond. The wording of the bond is not appropriate to the situation
as it has developed since the order of Judge Weeks (though the developments were,
perhaps, predictable). That may be because it was redrafted at the last moment, under   F
pressure. But I cannot allow speculation as to the contractual position between the bank
and the majority shareholders to affect my judgment as to what order (if any) should be
made in the writ action. I shall come back later to whether any relief at all (such as a
declaration) should be granted in the writ action.

I come on then to the relief under s. 459 sought on the petition. Mr Kenneth Farrow
(for the respondents) relies on four main points in resisting relief on the petition. First,   G
Mr Farrow submits that Mr Pitt's only real involvement was as an agent for R & H,
which was a loan creditor, not a shareholder, of Haden Bill; therefore, he says, there was
no prejudice to Mr Pitt in his capacity as a shareholder. Second (reiterating the distinction
between Mr Pitt and R & H with the emphasis the other way round) Mr Farrow submits
that if the investor with a real complaint is R & H, it would be contrary to principle to
ignore the distinction and treat Mr Pitt (the only petitioner) as if he were identical with R
& H. Third, Mr Farrow submits (especially in connection with the disputed payments   H
made in April 1994) that relief under s. 459 must be appropriate, and that that involves
the principle of proportionality. Fourth, he submits that Haden Bill should not be
regarded as a quasi-partnership founded on mutual trust.

I can readily accept Mr Farrow's third point, but the others call for closer examination,
with some reference to authority.

A   The first point, as to the capacity in which the petitioner complains, was fully considered by Warner J in *Re J E Cade & Son Ltd* [1991] BCC 360, both in relation to s.459 and in relation to winding up on the just and equitable ground: see at pp. 373 and pp. 376–378 respectively. The facts of the *Cade* case were unusual and I think that Mr Parker is right in submitting that it was an extreme case in that it was fairly obvious that the petitioner was (in Warner J's words at p. 374C) 'pursuing his interests as a freeholder of the farm and not his interests as a member of the company'. There are other reported

B cases in which the interests of a shareholder either as an employee, or as a contingent creditor (by subrogation) of the company, or even as a creditor of other shareholders in the company, have been treated as relevant for the purposes of s. 459 or the Malaysian equivalent of what is now s. 122(1)(g) of the *Insolvency Act* 1986. In *Re a Company No. 00477 of 1986* (1986) 2 BCC 99,171 Hoffmann J referred (at p. 99,173) to the submission that s. 459:

C   'must be limited to conduct which is unfairly prejudicial to the interests of the members as members. It cannot extend to conduct which is prejudicial to other interests of persons who happen to be members.'

Hoffmann J commented at p. 99,174:

D   'In principle I accept this proposition, as did Lord Granchester QC in *Re a Company* [1983] Ch 178. But its application must take into account that the interests of a member are not necessarily limited to his strict legal rights under the constitution of the company. The use of the word "unfairly" in s. 459, like the use of the words "just and equitable" in s. 517(1)(g) enables the court to have regard to wider equitable considerations.'

Then after quoting a well-known passage in the speech of Lord Wilberforce in *Re Westbourne Galleries* [1973] AC 360 at p. 379, Hoffmann J continued,

E   'Thus in the case of the managing director of a large public company who is also the owner of a small holding in the company's shares, it is easy to see the distinction between his interests as a managing director employed under a service contract and his interests as a member. In the case of a small private company in which two or three members have invested their capital by subscribing for shares on the

F   footing that dividends are unlikely but that each will earn his living by working for the company as a director, the distinction may be more elusive. The member's interests as a member who has ventured his capital in the company's business may include a legitimate expectation that he will continue to be employed as a director and his dismissal from that office and exclusion from the management of the company may therefore be unfairly prejudicial to his interests as a member.'

G It is not suggested in the present case that Mr Pitt (or Mr Watkins) was to be a working director of Haden Bill and remunerated as such; but the passage which I have quoted supports the general proposition that the court should take a broad view of what may properly be regarded as a petitioner's interest as a member.

H Similarly in *Tay Bok Choon v Tahansan Sdn Bhd* (1987) 3 BCC 132 the Privy Council (in a judgment delivered by Lord Templeman) took into account (as relevant to the creation of relations of confidence in which it was inequitable for the petitioner to be ousted) (1) that the chairmanship had been promised to the petitioner; (2) that he had contributed further equity capital after becoming a shareholder (he had not been an original shareholder); (3) that he (and his co-directors) had guaranteed the company's liabilities to a loan creditor (which the petitioner had introduced); and (4) that the petitioner had made large loans to fellow shareholders (apparently to enable them to contribute further equity capital). After listing and commenting in these four points Lord Templeman said (at p. 135):

'Viewing the facts as a whole their Lordships are satisfied, as the trial judge was   A
satisfied, that the petitioner was led to believe, even in the absence of any express
assurance, that he would participate in the management of the company and that
he would in any event be entitled to a seat on the board so long as he held one-
quarter of the issued share capital of the company. Their Lordships have no doubt
that the other shareholders were glad in 1980 to obtain the co-operation and
support of the petitioner as a financier and businessman on terms that he would
participate and would be appointed director. Although no specific undertakings   B
may have been given an obligation is to be implied or inferred from the conduct of
the parties to allow the petitioner to participate in management and to be a director
unless by withdrawal of his support or for some other good reason a change in
management and control became necessary.'

In that case, as in the present case, the petitioner had been chairman and an important
member of the board, but had not been a remunerated working director. Again, the case   C
shows the court taking a broad view of what can be seen as the interests of a member as
such. *Tay Bok Choon* was not cited in *Cade*, but the two cases are not to my mind
inconsistent. *Cade* should, it seems to me, be seen as illustrating that even if a broad view
is to be taken, there must be a limit beyond which further extension is not permissible
(see [1991] BCC at pp. 377–378). If Mr Pitt himself had been Haden Bill's loan creditor,
under arrangements made between him and the majority shareholders when the company
was first being planned and formed, I should have had little hesitation in coming to the   D
conclusion that the arrangements were a reflection of, and sufficiently closely connected
with, Mr Pitt's membership of Haden Bill as to be within the scope of s. 459.

I have to consider, therefore, whether the fact that Mr Pitt and R & H were separate
legal persons is a crucial distinction which should lead to a different conclusion. I was
not referred to any authority clearly dealing with this point (in the context of s. 459 or
winding up on the just and equitable ground). In *Tay Bok Choon* the Privy Council did,   E
as already noted, take account of the petitioner's loans to fellow shareholders (a
transaction also at one remove, though in a different way, from a direct loan by a
shareholder to the company); but it is not clear whether there was any argument on the
point. The point is touched on in a case which was not cited to me, *Re Tecnion Investments
Ltd* [1985] BCLC 434. That was the decision of the Court of Appeal on discovery on a
s. 459 petition, where discovery was sought (but, on appeal, not allowed) of documents
said to be held by companies controlled by the alleged oppressors. But discovery is a   F
technical matter on which the court has to take a technical view, and I do not think the
case gives me any clear guidance as to the inviolability of the corporate veil on the
substantive hearing of a s. 459 petition. For that reason I have not thought it necessary
to invite further argument about *Tecnion*.

On the whole I have come to the conclusion that I should not treat the separateness of
Mr Pitt and R & H as excluding him from seeking relief under s. 459 on the basis that R   G
& H's loans to Haden Bill were procured by Mr Pitt and formed part (and an absolutely
essential part) of the arrangements entered into for the venture to be carried on by that
company. That way of looking at the matter seems to me to be in line with the broad
approach adopted in the cases already referred to. It is also (and this is to my mind very
important) the way that the parties themselves seem to have looked at the matter. They
are not lawyers or accountants and they all seem to have regarded R & H as Mr Pitt's
company (Mr Farrow told me that it was only on delivery of Mr Pitt's supplementary   H
witness statement that his clients learned who were the shareholders in R & H). It is clear
from some attendance notes that at one stage (shortly before the Glenrothes premises
were acquired) Mr Hogg thought that Mr Pitt personally was going to lend the second
£100,000, and there is no indication that it made any difference to any of the majority
shareholders whether the money came from Mr Pitt himself or from R & H.

On the last of Mr Farrow's four points, I feel no doubt but that Haden Bill was, during 1989 and 1990, planned, formed and set up in business on the basis of mutual trust. At that time there was certainly trust between Mr Pitt and Mr Watkins as a pair, between Mr and Mrs Hogg as a pair, and between Mr Pitt and Mr Hogg as a pair. Such reservations as there may have been between the Hoggs and Mr Watkins, or on the part of Mrs Hogg towards Mr Pitt, cannot in my judgment negate that conclusion. The fact is that numerous contractual documents which were discussed or drafted (including the two already mentioned, and also a service agreement for Mr Hogg) were never completed because the parties decided to proceed on the basis of trust. The situation was the antithesis of one where a petitioner has entered into 'massively detailed and professionally drawn agreements' (see Peter Gibson J in *Re Ringtower Holdings plc* (1989) 5 BCC 82 at p. 92G). Had Mr Hogg been told that because he had no written service agreement he was not entitled to remuneration as a working director, he would have indignantly, and rightly, objected that that was part of the basic understanding on which Haden Bill had been formed.

In these circumstances Mr Pitt did in my judgment have a legitimate expectation of being able to participate in the management of Haden Bill, at least for as long as R & H remained a significant loan creditor (and so long as Mr Pitt was closely associated with R & H). This expectation was in my judgment similar to that of the petitioner in *Tay Bok Choon*, as described by Lord Templeman in the passage that I have already quoted.

Lord Templeman qualified the expectation of the petitioner in that case by limiting it to the period until 'for some other good reason a change in management and control became necessary'; and that qualification is no doubt appropriate in any similar case, including the present case. The personal troubles between Mr Pitt and Mr Watkins (which were acknowledged but not investigated in the course of cross-examination of Mr Pitt) made it inevitable that there should be a change in management and control, and Mr Watkins' alliance with the Hoggs (an unlikely event, viewed from 1989) made it inevitable that Mr Pitt should be the one to go, regardless of the rights and wrongs of the personal troubles. Conversely, however unmeritorious Mr Pitt's personal conduct, it could not in my judgment justify the majority shareholders in summarily ejecting him without consultation or discussion about the future of Mr Pitt's equity capital, and R & H's loan capital, in Haden Bill. It was largely for that reason that I would have rejected any suggestion (which was only mentioned, and not pressed) that the personal troubles should be investigated by recall of witnesses and further cross-examination.

Had the position been considered and discussed between the majority shareholders and Mr Pitt in February 1994, I think the solution likely to have emerged, and a fair solution, would have been that Mr Pitt should cease to be chairman and a director of Haden Bill, that his shares should be bought by the majority shareholders without a discount for its being a minority holding, and that R & H's loans to Haden Bill should be repaid as soon as reasonably possible (either by refinancing or out of retained profits, but in any event substantially sooner than if the minimum instalments fixed by the deed of 5 April 1993 had continued).

I will make an order under s. 461 on those general lines, but I will refrain from any further definition until the parties have had the opportunity to consider this judgment and see whether they can agree on the details, or alternatively formulate what detailed points on the form of the order are in dispute. But the valuation should (as both sides have already invited me to direct) be made as at 1 February 1994 (or some other convenient date close to 1 February), taking account of the terms for the repayment of R & H's loans ultimately agreed or directed (and any consequent strain on Haden Bill's cash flow), but otherwise without the benefit of hindsight (especially as to Haden Bill's litigation costs incurred from March 1994).

A

That approach has the great advantage, as counsel recognised, of making it unnecessary for me to rule on, or consider granting separate relief in respect of, the disputed payments made in April 1994. I will say no more than that none of them appears to me to be an obvious or flagrant misuse of the board's powers, though the legal costs seem questionable. Mr Pitt will remain a creditor of Haden Bill for any unpaid dividends due to him, and their payments should be provided for in the order.

B

Earlier in my judgment I referred to the question whether I should grant any relief in the writ action. In my judgment the disputed board meeting of 14 February (then deferred to 15 February) 1994 was called on notice which was unreasonably short. The notice must have been known to be inadequate and must have been intended to put Mr Pitt and his advisers in a difficult position. However all that is now past history, except so far as it may have symbolic significance in connection with the costs of the writ action. I have in mind that there was a lot of interlocutory skirmishing in the writ action which ended with an order for costs in cause; and that because the petition was launched at a late stage but then managed to catch up with the writ action for trial, the separate costs of the petition may be – in relative terms – on a fairly low level. For all these reasons I shall leave over the question of relief in the writ action for further argument, if necessary, at the same time as I deal with the precise form of relief to be granted on the petition, and with the costs of both sets of proceedings.

C

(Order accordingly)

D

E

F

G

H

^A Inland Revenue Commissioners v a Debtor.

Chancery Division.
Robert Walker J.
Judgment delivered 20 June 1995.

^B *Bankruptcy petition – Whether Revenue's refusal of debtor's offer was unreasonable – Capacity of appeal tribunal to differ from registrar on issue of unreasonable refusal if he had not erred in law – Insolvency Act 1986, s. 271(3).*

This was an appeal by the Inland Revenue as petitioning creditor against a registrar's order dismissing a bankruptcy petition on the ground that the Revenue had unreasonably refused an offer to secure the debt under s. 271(3) of the Insolvency Act 1986.

^C The debtor did not dispute that he owed the Revenue about £36,000 but offered a third charge over his house. The debt could then be paid by the house being sold in exercise of the power of sale which the Revenue would obtain under the charge. The house was probably worth £150,000 but was not easy to sell.

Held, allowing the appeal and making a bankruptcy order:

1. The court was as well placed as the registrar to evaluate the issue of whether the Revenue's refusal of the debtor's offer was unreasonable. (Benmax v Austin Motor Co
^D [1955] AC 370 applied; Re Grayan Building Services Ltd [1995] BCC 554 considered.)

2. A charge taken by the Revenue would have to be enforced by sale, and on the facts there was reason to suppose that a sale might be very difficult. The officials of the Revenue concerned with collection ought not (and therefore were, on the face of it, unlikely) to refuse an offer which increased the likely net recovery to public funds, but the Revenue was, on the face of it, the best judge of what internal costs and diversion of resources might be involved in accepting security. There was no evidence of institutional oppression, and it was not
^E contended that the Revenue were bound to state their reasons and were bound by them.

3. The Revenue had not gone outside the 'range of reasonable positions' and acted unreasonably. Therefore, the registrar erred in deciding that the factual preconditions for the exercise of discretion under s. 271(3) were satisfied. (Re a Debtor (No. 32 of 1993) [1994] BCC 438 followed.)

^F The following cases were referred to in the judgment:

Barclays Bank plc v O'Brien & Anor [1994] 1 AC 180.
Benmax v Austin Motor Co [1955] AC 370.
Debtor (No. 32 of 1993), Re a [1994] BCC 438; [1989] 1 WLR 899.
Debtor (No. 415/SD/93), Re a [1994] 2 All ER 168.
Gilmartin, Re [1989] 1 WLR 513.
Grayan Building Services Ltd, Re [1995] BCC 554; [1995] Ch 241.
^G *Tredegar (Viscount) v Harwood & Ors* [1929] AC 71.

Christopher Tidmarsh (instructed by the Solicitors for Inland Revenue) for the Inland Revenue Commissioners.

Christopher Brougham QC and M Fay (instructed by Dallow & Dallow) for the respondent.

^H JUDGMENT

Robert Walker J: This is an appeal by the Commissioners of Inland Revenue ('the Revenue') from an order of Mr Registrar Rawson made on 31 March 1995 by which he dismissed a bankruptcy petition presented by the Revenue on 30 June 1994.

The appeal concerns s. 271(3) of the *Insolvency Act* 1986 and is a true appeal. So far as the exercise of discretion is concerned, I can reach a different conclusion only if the

registrar failed to exercise his discretion on correct principles, or at not all. This was   A
decided by Harman J in *Re Gilmartin* [1989] 1 WLR 513, itself an appeal from a decision
under s. 271(3). I shall have to come back to analyse how the outcome of the present
appeal depends on issues of law, fact and discretion.

The primary facts are that the debtor was formerly a self-employed steel erector liable
to income tax under Sch. D. In 1989 and 1990 the turnover of his business was of the
order of £90,000 a year. He is aged about 58 and for the last four years he has been in   B
poor health, and unable to work. He and his wife own a house called Sans Souci on the
edge of the Ashwood Marina near Greensforge in Staffordshire. The house has
unfortunately not lived up to its name. The debtor and his wife bought it for just under
£100,000 in 1985 and they have been trying to sell it since November 1990. The present
asking price is £160,000. It has been as high as £200,000. About ten months ago local
valuers advised that:

'a figure in the order of £150,000 would be achievable, even allowing for the   C
limitations being imposed by the design of the property etc.'

This refers, I think, to the house being of modern design, with flat roofs, and therefore
not so easily marketable as a house of more traditional construction.

Under the conveyance dated 10 December 1985, the house belongs to the debtor and
his wife as joint tenants beneficially. £64,200 was (last March) due to the Nationwide
Building Society under a first charge.   D

When the petition was presented the debtor owed the Revenue over £33,000 for
Sch. D income tax, interest and National Insurance contributions going back to 1989.
Since 1989 the debtor has paid only about £9,000 out of a principal tax liability of about
£35,000; with further accrued interest the total liability is about £36,000. The debtor does
not dispute this liability but (after earlier hearings in connection with a statutory demand
dated 14 June 1993 which I need not go into further at present) he opposed the petition,   E
when it was heard by the registrar, on the ground that he had made an offer to secure the
debt and that the Revenue had unreasonably refused his offer.

Section 271(3) of the *Insolvency Act* 1986 provides:

'The court may dismiss the petition if it is satisfied that the debtor is able to pay all
his debts or is satisfied–

(a) that the debtor has made an offer to secure or compound for a debt in   F
respect of which the petition is presented,

(b) that the acceptance of that offer would have required the dismissal of the
petition, and

(c) that the offer has been unreasonably refused;

and, in determining for the purposes of this subsection whether the debtor is able   G
to pay all his debts, the court shall take into account his contingent and prospective
liabilities.'

It will be noted that this subsection confers a statutory discretion on the court exercisable
only if the factual preconditions which it mentions have been established to the
satisfaction of the court.

In an affidavit sworn on 17 August 1994 the debtor deposed that he and his wife had   H
offered the Revenue a second charge over their house, and that there was still sufficient
equity in the property to satisfy the debt. That referred, I think, to what had happened at
an earlier hearing (on 12 August 1993) before the district judge. Until that earlier hearing
all that had been offered had been an undertaking to pay the debt out of the net proceeds
of the house, when sold. Then at the hearing before the district judge, and at his
suggestion, a charge was offered. The district judge then set aside the statutory demand,

A   but the Revenue's appeal against that decision was allowed, without opposition, because of the intervening decision of Jacob J in *Re a Debtor (No. 415/SD/93)* [1994] 2 All ER 168.

On 1 March 1995 Mr Srodzinsky (a legal executive with the debtor's solicitors) swore an affidavit on behalf of the debtor deposing to a possible exchange transaction which, if successful, would have brought the debtor and his wife a substantial sum of money, but
B   unfortunately that transaction, like some previous sales, seems to have fallen through. In the same affidavit the deponent disclosed for the first time (so far as the Revenue is concerned) a second charge on the house to National Westminster Bank plc, for £15,000. The debtor and his wife can therefore now offer only a third charge.

On 28 March 1995 (only three days before the hearing before the registrar) the debtor's wife swore an affidavit deposing that she was well aware of the bankruptcy proceedings, that she had been advised to take separate advice but did not wish to do so, and that she
C   was willing to agree to the charge. The significance of this affidavit is of course in connection with the special position of security gratuitously provided by a married woman as established by the House of Lords in *Barclays Bank plc v O'Brien & Anor* [1994] 1 AC 180.

There is a note, signed by the registrar, of the hearing before him. It records that it was common ground that the test of unreasonableness was satisfied if no reasonable
D   hypothetical creditor would have refused the offer to secure the debt in the circumstances of the particular case. The note then records five submissions made on behalf of the debtor. I will come back to these. The note then continues:

> 'I have concluded that the debtor has made an offer to secure the debt for the purposes of para. (a) of subs. (3) and that the acceptance of that offer would have required the dismissal of the petition for the purposes of para. (b). I am also
E   > satisfied that the Revenue's refusal for the reasons stated is unreasonable. I accordingly dismiss the petition.'

Mr Tidmarsh for the Revenue criticised the registrar's decision on a number of grounds. One of the most obviously cogent is that the registrar carefully recorded the five points made on behalf of the debtor but seems not to have recorded – at least in his written statement of reasons – submissions made on behalf of the Revenue. There is also
F   unfortunately a lack of total agreement as to what submissions were made by the Revenue at the hearing.

But before coming on to that in detail I should, I think, consider the legislative purpose of s. 271(3), and what ought to be the general approach of the court in deciding what is or is not an unreasonable refusal of an offer to secure or compound for a debt.

There was agreement between counsel as to three general points. First, the provision has no clear antecedents in the old bankruptcy law. There was a reference in the
G   *Bankruptcy Act* 1914 to compounding or securing a debt to the satisfaction of the court, but there is no authority on that which assists me in looking for the legislative purpose of the new provision. However it does seem to be implicit in the new provision that it is possible for a petitioning creditor to act unreasonably in refusing to accept an offer to compound – that is, to pay less than 100p in the pound in satisfaction of a debt. Mr Christopher Brougham QC (who appeared with Mr Fay for the debtor) argued from that starting-point that Harman J may not have been right, in *Re Gilmartin* (above) at p. 516,
H   to approve the registrar's observation 'that a petitioning creditor is entitled to be paid his debt in full on the hearing of a petition unless it is adjourned on the ground that there is a reasonable prospect of him being paid within a reasonable time'. I do not think I can usefully pursue that argument, except to say that the juxtaposition of securing and compounding (which are different types of transactions) makes it more difficult to discern a clear legislative purpose.

Second, both sides accepted that the test must be objective and related to matters which   A
bear objectively on the debtor/creditor relationship. Here at least I think there is a parallel
with the law of landlord and tenant, where reasonable withholding of consent to the
assignment of a lease must be directly concerned with the relationship of landlord and
tenant, with the result that unreasonableness has (in that context) gone at least halfway
to becoming a term of art. I should add, however, that Mr Tidmarsh deprecated any
close parallel with the law of landlord and tenant, and I think he must be right at least as   B
to the giving of reasons (where there is now a specific statutory duty under the *Landlord
and Tenant Act* 1988, which has no parallel in s. 271).

Third, it seems to me reasonably clear (and Mr Brougham did not argue to the
contrary) that in considering an offer a creditor is entitled to have regard to his own
interests (so long as they are his interests as a creditor, and not in some other capacity so
as to bring in collateral considerations). The creditor is not required to balance his
interests against those of the debtor, or to take a chance, or to show patience or   C
generosity, even though some creditors might do so. As Lord Phillimore put it in *Viscount
Tredegar v Harwood & Ors* [1929] AC 72 at p. 82, acting reasonably is not the same as
acting justly, fairly or kindly. That was a landlord and tenant case but this point at least
is of general application.

These general observations are, I think, much in line with the careful reserved judgment
of Mr Timothy Lloyd QC in *Re a Debtor (No. 32 of 1993)* [1994] BCC 438 (a   D
compounding case). At p. 447F the deputy judge formulated the test as,

> 'whether a reasonable creditor, in the position of this petitioning creditor, and in
> the light of the actual history as disclosed to the court, would have accepted or
> refused the offer.'

The deputy judge continued,

> 'However, I think it has to be borne in mind that there could be a range of   E
> reasonable positions on the part of hypothetical reasonable creditors. In order to
> conclude that the refusal was unreasonable, it seems to me that the court has to be
> satisfied that no reasonable hypothetical creditor would have refused the offer and
> that the refusal of the offer was therefore beyond the range of possible reasonable
> actions in the context.'

I respectfully agree with the deputy judge's statement of the principle (which was plainly   F
the source of the common ground before the registrar). Towards the end of his judgment
the deputy judge touched on another point which is relevant to this appeal. I respectfully
doubt whether there can be any strong presumption that large and impersonal creditors
(such as the insurance company in that case, or the Revenue in the present appeal) are
unlikely to act unreasonably. In a perfect world all creditors, large and small, would
always act reasonably. Large and impersonal bodies are much less likely to act
unreasonably from motives of personal vindictiveness (as the deputy judge must have   G
had in mind at p. 448F) but bureaucratic inflexibility can sometimes produce an
impersonal sort of oppression. On the other hand, large organisations constantly have to
take decisions affecting large numbers of debtors (whether they are taxpayers, borrowers
or trade debtors) and they can sensibly do so only by delegating the decisions to be made
in accordance with coherent in-house policies. I shall come back to this in connection
with what has been said about the Revenue's having a set policy.
                                                                                               H
The issue on which this appeal turns is whether the Revenue's refusal of the debtor's
offer was unreasonable. If it was, the exercise of the registrar's discretion to dismiss the
petition is not challenged. If it was not, the registrar had no discretion to exercise, and no
jurisdiction to dismiss the petition under s. 271(3). The issue of unreasonable refusal is a
question of fact, but it is not a simple question of primary fact. It is a process which
involves finding the primary facts (and here they are not really in dispute, although there

A are a few gaps in the evidence) and then (in the expression used by Viscount Simonds in the very well-known case of *Benmax v Austin Motor Co* [1955] AC 370 at p. 373) to make an evaluation of them. This process involves the making of a value judgment, but not the exercise of a discretion (in its semi-technical legal sense). In that process of evaluation an appellate tribunal is as well placed as the tribunal of first instance, especially where the evidence at the first instance was given on affidavit, without cross-examination. That is the point in the *Benmax* case. This is a true appeal but I must reject Mr Brougham's

B submission that I am for that reason unable to differ from the registrar, on the issue of reasonableness, unless he made an error of law.

I turn again to the primary facts, adopting Mr Tidmarsh's summary with some modification.

(1) The Revenue accept that an offer was made, although its content changed materially with the affidavit of 1 March 1995 (when the second charge securing

C £15,000 was disclosed for the first time). The offer was really only finally confirmed with the affidavit of the debtor's wife sworn on 28 March 1995.

(2) The debtor made clear that the only way the debt could be paid was by the house being sold in exercise of the power of sale which the Revenue would obtain under the charge. Indeed, the debtor held it out to the Revenue as an attraction that they would have control of the sale. In other words the Revenue was being offered not

D simply a security, but a security which it would in practice have to enforce (unless a prior chargee did so first).

(3) The value of the house is probably the order of £150,000 (Mr Tidmarsh suggested a bracket of £150,000–£180,000 and a mid-point of £165,000 which I suspect may be on the optimistic side). On any view the house is, for whatever reason, not easy to sell. The DSS is not meeting the whole of the payments on the Nationwide

E mortgage and the total amount secured on the house seems to be increasing.

(4) Although there is no reason to think that the debtor has been deliberately secretive or evasive the Revenue still does not have a compete picture of the debtor's financial position, especially as regards the second charge.

Mr Tidmarsh then proceeded to draw up a sort of balance sheet of advantages and disadvantages, from his clients' point of view, of accepting the offer made by the debtor

F and his wife. He stated the disadvantages first, and in brief summary they are:

(1) that the charge offered will in practice have to be enforced;

(2) that enforcement by sale would probably be difficult and protracted;

(3) that the Revenue might be forced into the problems of a mortgagee in actual possession;

G (4) that the Revenue is not in the business of lending money, on security or otherwise, and does not have the administrative resources that would be available to a big commercial lender;

(5) that it would be unable to charge and recover its internal costs of becoming an unwilling mortgagee;

(6) that the debtor should have paid his tax years ago;

H (7) that after a bankruptcy order the Revenue would have all the debtor's assets available as a possible source of payment, and a reasonable prospect of achieving full recovery; and

(8) that the debtor did not put his cards on the table until as recently as 1 March 1995.

The items that Mr Tidmarsh acknowledged as going into the other side of the balance, as advantages to the Revenue in the debtor's offer (on behalf of himself and his wife)

largely corresponded to the reasons which Mr Brougham puts forward in arguing that   A
the Revenue have been unreasonable in refusing the offer. Those reasons are essentially
the same (with a little embellishment) as the five points recorded in the written reasons of
the registrar. They are, in brief summary:

(1)   that the offer would provide adequate security even if the debt were to double (or,
as Mr Brougham now puts it, were to increase substantially) with accruing interest;

(2)   that some interest on the first charge is being paid by the DSS;   B

(3)   that if the debtor is made bankrupt, only half the equity in the house would be
available and the Revenue would suffer a shortfall;

(4)   that the proposed security would enable the Revenue to take possession and sell
the house as quickly as (and probably more quickly than) a trustee in bankruptcy;

(5)   that the associated costs would be smaller; and
         C
(6)   that the Revenue's policy (if it exists) of not accepting security cannot by itself be
a good reason for refusing the offer.

In connection with his point (4) Mr Brougham referred me to s. 336 of the *Insolvency Act*
1986 and submitted (as I accept) that in practice a trustee in bankruptcy would be more
likely to wait for a year so as to get the benefit of s. 336(5).

Mr Brougham also criticised Mr Tidmarsh's points (1)–(5) (which are to my mind the   D
only substantial points made on behalf of the Revenue, on the facts of this case) as being
points that are inherent in any taking of security, and argued that since Parliament
plainly contemplated that it might be unreasonable for a creditor to refuse security, a
creditor could not reasonably object to the very notion of taking security. At that very
high level of generality, there is force on Mr Brougham's argument. But there is also
force in Mr Tidmarsh's riposte that the Revenue is not objecting to the notion of taking
security as such, but to the proposal that it should take security in the form of a third   E
charge which (unless a prior chargee acted first) would have to be enforced by sale. Mr
Tidmarsh tells me that the Revenue has no rigid policy against accepting security. Each
case is, he says, considered on its own merits, although usually the result of case-by-case
consideration is a decision against taking security. (If that was the case two years ago the
official from the Enforcement Office must have been mistaken, or at least imprecise, in
what he said to the district judge: the note of the hearing is the official's own note.)
         F
In practice a charge taken by the Revenue would have to be enforced by sale, and on
the facts of this case – which are not necessarily the fault of the debtor and his wife, but
are facts nevertheless – there is reason to suppose that a sale may be very difficult,
presenting the vendor with serious problems about (among other things) when to take
possession (with all the responsibilities involved in that) and at what minimum price this
difficult property shall be sold (bearing in mind a mortgagee's duties in exercising his
power of sale). To say that the Revenue could appoint outside solicitors to act for it is far   G
from answering these problems: outside solicitors would have to receive instructions for
which the Revenue would be responsible.

Having looked at the rival submissions in some detail I remind myself that the crucial
question is: am I satisfied that the Revenue has acted unreasonably in rejecting the offer?
The Revenue is, as Mr Tidmarsh says, under a statutory duty to collect tax (and interest
on tax) that is due but unpaid. The officials of the Revenue concerned with collection   H
ought not (and therefore are, on the face of it, unlikely) to refuse an offer which increases
the likely net recovery to public funds. But the Revenue is, on the face of it, the best judge
of what internal costs and diversion of resources may be involved in accepting security in
a case like this. Without going back on what I have said about the possibility of
institutional oppression, I see no real evidence of it in this case. At worst some officials
have been careless and imprecise in explaining the Revenue's position. Mr Brougham

A does not contend that the Revenue were bound to state their reasons and are bound by them.

Bearing in mind the 'range of reasonable positions' mentioned in the observations of Mr Timothy Lloyd QC in *Re a Debtor (No. 32 of 1993)* (above) at p. 447 – observations with which I fully agree – I am not in the end satisfied that the Revenue have in this case gone outside that range and acted unreasonably. I conclude, therefore, that the registrar

B erred in deciding that the factual preconditions for the exercise of discretion under s. 271(3) were satisfied. I shall therefore allow this appeal and make a bankruptcy order.

Since this judgment was completed there has been a report of the decision of the Court of Appeal in *Re Grayan Building Services Ltd* [1995] BCC 554, a case on the *Company Directors Disqualification Act* 1986. The judgment of Hoffmann LJ (with which Neill LJ and Henry LJ agreed) considers (at p. 575) with fuller analysis and citation of authority,

C a point similar to that which arose on this appeal, as to an appellate tribunal's freedom to review a finding of fact which involves a value judgment.

I think it would not be right for me, without hearing counsel, to make any alteration to my judgment to take account of what was said by the Court of Appeal in *Grayan*. It is not clear where exactly a value judgment as to unreasonableness under s. 271(3) of the *Insolvency Act* 1986 ought to come in the 'spectrum' to which Hoffmann LJ refers. But in this case there was no oral evidence, and little dispute as to the primary facts, and I do

D not understand the decision of the Court of Appeal as restricting the powers of an appellate tribunal in such a case.

However I am prepared to hear brief submissions on *Grayan* if either side wishes to make them.

(Order accordingly)

E _____

F

G

H

Barclays Bank plc v Eustice.

A

Court of Appeal (Civil Division).
Butler-Sloss, Aldous and Schiemann L JJ.
Judgment delivered 6 July 1995.

*Transactions defrauding creditors – Discovery – Bank sought declarations that
transactions entered into by defendants were void – Bank obtained order for
discovery of documents between defendants and legal advisers – Appeal – Whether
strong prima facie case that transactions were at undervalue – Whether strong
prima facie case that purpose of transactions was to prejudice creditor – Scope of
discovery of documents relating to transactions defrauding creditor – Insolvency
Act 1986, s. 423.*

B

This was an appeal against an order for discovery of documents in an action in which the
plaintiff bank sought, amongst other relief, a number of declarations pursuant to the
provisions of s. 423 of the Insolvency Act 1986 to the effect that various transactions entered
into by the defendants were void because they defrauded the creditor bank.

C

The first defendant ('E') was farming in partnership with his mother. Part of the land they
farmed was held under a tenancy between himself as freeholder and his mother and himself
as tenants. Other land was held by E as freeholder. E wished to acquire more land. He
approached the bank and it was agreed that he should borrow £550,000 on a 20-year loan
with a separate overdraft facility of £100,000. The bank took charges over his freehold land.
Soon further funds were needed. The bank was prepared to increase the overdraft facility to
£150,000, but only on terms that the 20-year loan was converted to a 12-month facility and
that agricultural charges were given over all the agricultural assets. E accepted. The bank
later agreed to increase the overdraft limit to £200,000. At this time, E entered into three
agreements: an assignment of the lease of land by E and his mother to his sons; an agreement
granting a tenancy to his sons of the other land; and an agreement for the sale of listed
agricultural assets by E to his sons. The bank was not informed of these agreements until
such time as it called in its loans.

D

E

In proceedings under s. 423 the bank sought an order that the defendants should disclose
all documents containing or evidencing communications between the defendants and their
legal advisers relating to the transactions. The judge ruled in favour of the bank (excepting
documents obtained or created for the dominant purpose of being used in pending or
contemplated proceedings). The defendants appealed.

F

The questions on appeal were whether the judge was entitled to find that the evidence
disclosed a strong prima facie case in favour of making the s. 423 order sought by the bank,
and if so, whether legal professional privilege attached to documents containing or
evidencing communications between the transferor and his legal advisers relating to
transactions entered into by the transferor at an undervalue for the purpose of prejudicing
the interest of persons making a claim against him.

G

Held, dismissing the appeal:

1. The judge was right in the conclusion to which he came on undervalue. In effect what
had happened was that the partnership which borrowed from the bank on the security of
certain assets had parted with those assets in return for some covenants. The recipients of
the assets had received more than they had paid for because the price was only payable in
the future and because if the bank wished to realise its security the recipients would have a
certain ransom value. There was a strong prima facie case that the transactions were entered
into for a consideration the value of which was significantly less than the value of the
consideration provided by the recipients and therefore the undervalue test in s. 423 was
fulfilled.

H

A   2. There was a strong prima facie case that the bank's security had been transferred to
members of the family at a time when action by the creditor was clearly anticipated by the
debtor and that those transfers were at an undervalue and that what remained in the hands
of the debtor barely if at all covered the debt. E's intention was to prevent the bank enforcing
its security which would give him time and if all went well might enable him to pay off the
bank. There was a strong prima facie case that the purpose of the transactions was to
prejudice the interests of the creditor bank.

B   3. One of the factors which the court would often find relevant was the purpose for which
the advice was sought. The court would be more hesitant to lift the cloak of privilege where
advice was sought to explain the legal effect of what had already been done and was the
subject of existing or imminent litigation. The present case was essentially one about advice
sought on how to structure a transaction, advice coming into existence for the dominant
purpose of stopping the bank interfering with the defendants' use of what they regarded as
C   family assets.

      4. Prima facie E was seeking to enter into transactions at an undervalue for the purpose
of prejudicing the bank. That purpose was sufficiently iniquitous for public policy to require
communications between E and his solicitor in relation to the setting up of the transactions
to be discoverable. (*Ventouris v Mountain* [1991] 1 WLR 607 applied.)

      The following cases were referred to in the judgment of Schiemann LJ:

D   *Agricultural Mortgage Corporation plc v Woodward & Anor* [1994] BCC 688.
      Arbuthnot Leasing International Ltd v Havelet Leasing Ltd & Ors (No. 2) [1990] BCC
      636; [1992] 1 WLR 455.
      Bullivant & Ors v A-G for Victoria [1901] AC 196.
      Chohan v Saggar & Anor [1992] BCC 306.
      Crescent Farm (Sidcup) Sports Ltd v Sterling Offices Ltd & Anor [1972] Ch 553.
E   *Derby & Co Ltd & Ors v Weldon & Ors (No. 7)* [1990] 1 WLR 1156.
      Gamlen Chemical Co (UK) Ltd v Rochem Ltd (unreported, 7 December 1979, CA,
      CAT No. 777/79).
      O'Rourke v Darbishire & Ors [1920] AC 581.
      R v Cox & Railton (1884) 14 QBD 153.
      R v Haydn (1825) 2 F & S 379.
      Royscot Spa Leasing Ltd v Lovett & Ors [1995] BCC 502.
F   *Ventouris v Mountain* [1991] 1 WLR 607.

      Paul Morgan QC and Siobhan Ward (instructed by Burges Salmon, Bristol) for the
defendants.

      Anthony Mann QC and Stephen Rees Davies (instructed by Bond Pearce, Plymouth)
for the plaintiff bank.

G   JUDGMENT
      Schiemann LJ: On 21 June 1995 we dismissed an appeal against an order for discovery
made by Judge Jack QC. These are my reasons for approving that course. The action in
which that order was made was one in which the plaintiff bank sought, amongst other
relief, a number of declarations pursuant to the provisions of s. 423 of the *Insolvency Act*
1986 to the effect that various transactions entered into by the defendants were void
because they defrauded the creditor bank. In the interlocutory proceedings with which
H   this appeal is concerned the bank sought an order that the defendants should disclose all
documents containing or evidencing communications between the defendants and their
legal advisers relating to the transactions. The defendants claimed that these documents
were privileged from disclosure on the basis of legal professional privilege. The judge
ruled in favour of the bank and the defendants appeal against that order by leave of this
court.

The appeal raises two questions the first of which is of interest only to the parties but   A
the second of which is of some general significance. The first question is whether the judge
was entitled to find that the evidence disclosed a strong prima facie case in favour of
making the s. 423 order sought by the bank. The second question arises only if the answer
to the first question is in the affirmative. It is this: does legal professional privilege attach
to documents containing or evidencing communications between the transferor and his
legal advisers relating to transactions entered into by the transferor at an undervalue for
the purpose of prejudicing the interest of persons making a claim against him? This is, so   B
far as the researches of counsel go, the first time that this question has fallen for decision.

Mr Morgan QC who appeared on behalf of the appellant concentrated his submissions
on the second question which raises a point of law or policy rather than on the first which
is purely factual. However, he did not concede that the present was a case where the
evidence disclosed a strong prima facie case in favour of making an order under s. 423. It
is common ground that, absent a prima facie case, legal privilege is available for the   C
documents in question. It is therefore necessary to consider the factual position first.
There was some argument as to whether the persons seeking discovery and inspection
needed only to make out a prima facie case or whether they needed to demonstrate a
strong prima facie case. Since, for reasons which will appear, I regard the present case as
being a strong prima facie case I do not need to express an opinion on the point. The
next section of this judgment sets out my reasons for concluding that there is here a
strong prima facie case on the facts for the making of such an order. Having done so I   D
shall move to consider the point of law of general significance.

The case for the making of a s. 423 order

Section 423(1) of the *Insolvency Act* 1986 provides:

'This section relates to transactions entered into at an undervalue; and a person
enters into such a transaction with another person if–
    (a) . . .   E
    (b) . . .
    (c) he enters into a transaction with the other for a consideration the value of
        which, in money or money's worth, is significantly less than the value, in
        money or money's worth, of the consideration provided by himself.'

Section 423(3) says: F

'In the case of a person entering into such a transaction, an order shall only be
made if the court is satisfied that it was entered into by him for the purpose–
    (a) of putting assets beyond the reach of a person who is making, or may at
        some time make, a claim against him, or
    (b) of otherwise prejudicing the interests of such a person in relation to the claim
        which he is making or may make.'
Section 423(2) gives the court a discretionary power of making such order as it thinks   G
fit for restoring the position to what it would have been if the transaction had not been
entered into and protecting the interests of persons who are victims of the transaction.

'Transaction' is defined in s. 436 as including a gift, agreement, or arrangement.

It is thus apparent that before an order can be made under the section the court must
be satisfied:
(1)   that a transaction was entered into at an undervalue; and   H
(2)   that it was entered into for a prohibited purpose.

The judge summarised the background in his judgment of 10 January 1995 in words
which are not criticised and which I gratefully adopt:

'The background to the application is as follows. The Eustice family have farmed
in Cornwall for some 170 years. In 1992 Paul Eustice was farming in partnership

A

with his mother, Inez Eustice. Part of the land they farmed, Tregotha Farm, was
held under a tenancy between himself as successor to his late father as freeholder
and his mother and himself as tenants. Other land was held by Mr Eustice as
freeholder. There were some 300 acres in all. Mr Eustice wished to acquire a further
200 acres from his uncle and to develop a strawberry farm. His bank, the National
Westminster Bank, would not agree to fund the venture and he approached the
plaintiff bank, Barclays, whom I will call "the bank". In November/December

B

1992 it was agreed between the bank and Mr Eustice that he should borrow
£550,000 on a 20-year loan with a separate overdraft facility of £100,000. The bank
took charges over his freehold land. He asserts that it was agreed that the project
should be considered on a long-term basis and that the overdraft facility could be
increased if further funds were needed until the strawberry venture was established.
There would be a limit imposed by the available security.

C

By November 1993 further funds were needed. The bank was prepared to increase
the overdraft facility to £150,000, but only on terms that the 20-year loan was
converted to a 12-month facility and that agricultural charges were given over all
the agricultural assets. Mr Eustice says that he protested against the bank's breach
of its promises but had no option but to accept. He did so, he asserts, on the basis
of an assurance from the bank that the bank would exhaust every alternative
course before exercising any remedy under the agricultural charges.

D

The accounts for the year ending 31 March 1994 showed a net loss of £116,028
and during 1994 the bank watched the progress of the business with care. On 9
June 1994 the bank agreed to increase the overdraft limit from £150,000 to
£200,000. Their letter of that date sets out the terms on which this was offered. In
accordance with those terms the bank reduced the limit to £150,000 by letter of 5
August, but on 25 August agreed to reinstate the £200,000 limit. The strawberry

E

season was in progress over this period. In August Mr Eustice proposed to the
bank the sale of certain inessential assets to raise some £300,000. By 16 December
some £120,000 had been applied from this source to reduce the overdraft. On 5
October the bank sought and later obtained Mr Eustice's agreement to the
appointment of Andersons, who are farming consultants, to prepare a report on
the business. The context is found in the bank's letter of that day. This referred in

F

particular to a projected overdraft of £185,000 at the end of December as opposed
to approximately £105,000 projected for then as recently as August, and to an
overdraft of £200,000–£240,000 at the end of June 1995. It pointed out that there
were no longer reserves of assets to finance future loss.

On 10 November 1994 the Inland Revenue distrained goods on the farms to cover
amounts due for PAYE and National Insurance contributions totalling £9,982.83
and served notice to that effect on Mr Eustice.

G

In that month Mr Eustice himself sought the assistance of agricultural consultants
named Braybrook Agriculture. On 18 November three agreements were entered
into, as follows:

    (a) An assignment of the lease of Tregotha Farm by Mr Eustice and his mother
        to his sons, Charles and Giles Eustice.

    (b) An agreement granting a tenancy to his sons of the other land.

H

    (c) An agreement for the sale of listed agricultural assets by Mr Eustice to his
        sons. This included assets within the Inland Revenue's distraint.

For the time being the bank was not informed of these agreements. Other than
saying that they were 'made as a result of consulting Braybrook Agriculture', Mr
Eustice is silent as to their genesis or purpose. Although the point was not raised
before me, it is clear that, at least so far as banking was concerned, the business

continued to be run as before. I say that because the bank did not notice any A
change. If the income of the enterprises had stopped being paid into the same
partnership account of Mr Eustice and his mother the bank would have noticed.
Whether the sons now have separate banking facilities is not known to me. It was
suggested to me on behalf of the bank that there are now no facilities. This was not
contradicted.

In late November 1994 Andersons produced their report. It put forward three B
options:

(1) to continue to support and manage the business as at present, monitoring it
closely, with a review at the end of each of the primary crop seasons, and in
the event of significant shortfall and further depletion of the equity taking
immediate action;

(2) selling all the land except the 53 acres on which is the farm shop;

(3) a managed programme of realisation of all the assets.   C

The report did not recommend which should be followed, but it pointed to
disadvantages with the second.

On 8 December 1994 the position was reached that the bank wished to discuss the
report with Mr Eustice, but he did not wish himself to do so. He had instructed
solicitors, Burges Salmon, with whom he wished the bank to deal. The bank had
not been provided by Mr Eustice's accountants with cash flow figures and details D
of debtors and creditors for October because he had given no information to his
accountants. The bank took the view that Mr Eustice was taking a confrontational
approach and that it must protect its position. It did not yet know of the
transactions of 18 November. On the same day, 8 December, it called in its loans
and made demands on Mr Eustice and his mother for a total of £758,476. On 9
December the bank appointed Mr Watson and Mr Haworth as receivers under its E
charges over the land. On 12 December Burges Salmon wrote informing the bank
of the assignment and tenancy agreements. On 21 December the Eustices disclosed
to Burges Salmon the existence of the sale agreement.'

Was the transaction entered into at an undervalue?

1. *The sale agreement*
                                                           F
The judge said this of the sale agreement whereby particular assets were sold to Charles
and Giles Eustice:

'Those assets include some but not all of the assets covered by the agricultural
charges. They include some of those covered by the Inland Revenue's distraint.
Points were made on behalf of the bank as to the valuation of particular items. But
I am prepared to proceed on the basis that overall the figures represent their actual
value but no more. The price, however, is to be paid by ten annual instalments G
commencing on 17 November 1995. There is no provision for interest. It is
remarkable that, despite the bank's appointment of receivers under the agricultural
charges on 16 December 1994, this agreement was not disclosed until 21 December.
Mr Tamlin submitted I should conclude that it is a sham. I express no view on
that. I am, however, satisfied that the agreement falls within s. 423(1)(c) because
the provision for deferred payment renders the consideration received significantly H
less than the value of goods sold.'

2. *The tenancy agreement*
As to this the judge said:

'This provides for an annual rental of £93,000. There is no evidence to suggest that
this is or is not a market figure. In the first year only £45,000 is to be paid and is to

A

be paid in arrears on 17 November 1995. In the second year £93,000 is to be paid in arrears on 17 November 1996. In the third year £141,000 (that is £93,000 plus £93,000 less £45,000) is to be paid in arrears on 17 November 1997. These deferment provisions may render the transaction vulnerable. But what is, I consider, more likely to be fatal is its close similarity to that before the Court of Appeal in *Agricultural Mortgage Corporation plc v Woodward* [1994] BCC 688.

B

There a borrowing of £700,000 was secured on a farm which would have been worth over £1m with vacant possession. The farmer fell into arrear and some £850,000 was due. Just before a deadline given by the mortgagee expired he entered into a tenancy agreement at a market rent with his wife. The intent was to preserve the farm from the bank. The effect was to reduce the value of the freehold of the farm to less than £500,000. The court held that, because the wife would be placed in a "ransom position" as regards the mortgagee, viewing the transaction as a

C

whole the benefits conferred by the farmer on his wife were significantly greater in value, in money or money's worth, than the value of the consideration given by her: the transaction fell within s. 423. I can see no ground for distinguishing the tenancy in the present case from that before the Court of Appeal. The bank appears to have an unanswerable case for it to be set aside.'

3. *The assignment of the lease*

D

The judge said this of the lease of the 91 acres of Tregotha Farm to Mr Eustice and his mother made in 1990 and the assignment of that lease to the sons on 18 November 1994:

'Following the death of his father Mr Eustice became the freeholder and landlord. The rent is £2,000 per annum payable in half-yearly instalments in arrear. The term is 15 years from 1 April 1979 and so expired on 31 March 1994. I was not addressed as to that and will proceed on the basis that the lease is still on foot

E

either by holding over or in some other way. The assignment provides for the tenants to hold from year to year, which supports that approach. It simply vested the interest under the lease in the sons for a consideration of £1.

When the bank took its charge over the freehold of Tregotha Farm it was unaware of the lease: it thought that it was dealing with Mr Eustice as freeholder of a freehold in hand. How this came about is not dealt with in the evidence. The charge describes Mr Eustice as "the proprietor" and his mother as "the occupier". There

F

must however be a very real possibility that the bank is entitled to deal with Mr Eustice and his mother on the basis that Mr Eustice held an interest in hand rather than a reversion. If the bank is so entitled then either the sons have taken no interest as a result of the assignment or, if they have, the assignment must be liable to be set aside under s. 423 because of the ransom position identified by the Court of Appeal in *Agricultural Mortgage Corporation plc v Woodward*.'

G

4. *Each side invited us to look at these three legal arrangements as one transaction consisting of three parts – that seems realistic*

Mr Morgan QC who appeared for the Eustices made his submissions with elegant tenacity coupled with realism. He accepted that the comments of the judge in relation to the sale agreement could not be gainsaid. He accepted that it was unusual in agricultural tenancies to have rent payable in arrears yearly and that it was clear that during the year

H

until 17 November 1995 not a penny was due to Mr Eustice by way of rent under the tenancy agreement. He accepted that it was probable, on the material before the court, that money by way of interest would be payable to the bank before that date and that, if these transactions are to be taken at face value, there would be no assets available to Mr Eustice from which to pay that interest. He accepted that the tenancy agreement was determinable by the tenant giving 12 months' notice which renders questionable the right

of the landlord to receive in the future a rent allegedly in excess of the market rent. He A
accepted that there was no evidence before the judge or before us in support of the
submission which I understand will be made on behalf of the defendants at the trial to
the effect that £93,000 is substantially in excess of the market rent. He accepted that there
was nothing to suggest that any rent payable under the lease of Tregotha Farm was
above the market rent which might have made this a case where a negative premium for
taking over the lessees obligations might be appropriate.

Faced with the ransom point adumbrated in the *Woodward* case Mr Morgan sought B
to distinguish it by pointing out that there the value of the freehold after the transactions
was less than the amount owing to the plaintiffs whereas in the present case, so he
maintained the transactions left the bank no worse off than if they had not taken place.
He submitted that the total indebtedness to the bank as at November 1994 was £759,000
and indicated that there was material (not I think before the court) which suggested that
the value of the land encumbered by the transactions of 18 November was £800,000, C
although unencumbered that value had been £1m. So, he submitted, the fact that prior
to those transactions the unencumbered value was significantly higher than £800,000 was
nothing to the point: the bank still had enough to cover its debt and therefore the
beneficiaries of the challenged transactions had no ransom value.

There are two answers to this submission. The first is that so far as the issue of
undervalue is concerned the late payment provisions are enough to lead to a strong prima D
facie case that the sale agreement and the tenancy agreement were concluded at an
undervalue and therefore the ransom point is not needed. The second answer to the point
lies in the fact that there was no realistic possibility of the bank being able to realise the
freehold in November 1994 and that the indebtedness was increasing daily. In
consequence the probability was that at the time of any realisation by the bank of its
security it would need to sell with vacant possession in order to be able to cover the
indebtedness and the realisation charges. In those circumstances the transferees would be E
in a position to ask for a ransom from the bank before giving vacant possession. In
consequence the ransom point has force in showing that the transferees were obtaining
more than they were paying for.

I consider the judge was right in the conclusion to which he came on undervalue. In
effect what has happened here is that the partnership which borrowed from the bank on
the security of those assets has parted with those assets in return for some covenants. The F
recipients of the assets have received more than they have paid for because the price is
only payable in the future and because if the bank wishes to realise its security the
recipients will have a certain ransom value. To put it no higher, there is a strong prima
facie case that the transactions were entered into for a consideration the value of which
is significantly less than the value of the consideration provided by the recipients and that
therefore the undervalue test in s. 423 is fulfilled.

G

Was the transaction entered into for a prohibited purpose?

The next question is whether there is also a strong prima facie case that the transaction
was entered into for the purpose of prejudicing the bank's interests.

Mr Eustice claims that if only the bank had left him alone to run his business the bank
would have been paid off by November 1996 and that if he wins this action that will still
be the case. It is possible that this is right although there is nothing in the material to H
which our attention has been drawn which makes this conclusion likely. It may be that
the reasoning of Mr Eustice is that the farm will be so profitable that there will be ample
out of which to pay the bank. Even if this turns out to be the case there is nothing in the
documents which obliges the sons to give to their father the profits from the farm
enterprise (if they eventuate) save in so far as he is owed sums as landlord.

A   Mr Morgan conceded that the effect of the transactions was to make it more difficult for the bank to get its money during 1995. That is manifestly correct. I have no hesitation in going further and agreeing with the judge that there is a strong prima facie case that the transactions were entered into for that very purpose. In those circumstances there is a strong prima facie case that they were entered into for the purpose of prejudicing the interests of the bank.

B   The judge put it this way:

> 'I am satisfied that there is a strong case here that in entering these transactions the aim of the defendants, and I put it in plain language, was to prevent the bank getting its hands on the land and other assets. In para. 38 of his first affidavit, Mr Paul Eustice deposed:
>
> > "The purpose of the transactions entered into on 18 November 1994 was solely to ensure to the best of my ability that my family was able to complete the agreement with the bank of November 1992. I wanted to ensure my family would still farm and progress new business until November 1996 without interference from the bank in accordance with the agreement in the event that contrary to the agreement, the bank sought to enforce its security."
>
> I underline those last words. That, indeed, is what the bank has done.
>
> At para. 39 he deposed:
>
> > "There is no intention on my part to prejudice the bank or any other creditors. It is my belief that if my family is permitted to continue the business without interference from the bank and consequential costs then the enterprise will be a success by November 1996 ensuring the protection of the bank's investment and rewarding the hard work of my own family."
>
> The effect of that so far as the bank's position is concerned is, in short, this: that it was Mr Eustice's intention by the transactions to prevent the bank enforcing its security which would give him time and, if all went well, might enable him to pay off the bank.
>
> However, meanwhile, the bank would be unable to enforce its security interests. The rights which the bank would otherwise have to obtain possession of the land, to obtain the sale of the land, would be defeated. In my view there is a strong case that the situation falls within those sub-subsections of subs. (3) of s. 423.'

F   I gratefully adopt the reasoning of Mr Evans-Lombe QC in *Chohan v Saggar* [1992] BCC 306 at p. 321:

> 'As Lord Oliver in the well known case of *Brady v Brady* [1989] AC 755; (1988) 4 BCC 390 at p. 774F–G, 408 acknowledged, the word "purpose" is a word of wide content. But he went on to say that it must be construed bearing in mind the mischief against which the section in which that word appears is aimed. Here, the purpose or mischief against which the section is aimed, namely s. 423, is the removal of assets by their owner, in anticipation of claims being made or contemplated, out of the reach of such claimants if those claims ultimately prove to be successful. It would defeat that purpose if it were possible successfully to contend that if the owner was able to point to another purpose, such as the benefit of his family, friends or the advantage of business associates, the section could not be applied.'

H   This passage was approved by the Court of Appeal in *Royscot Spa Leasing Ltd v Lovett & Ors* [1995] BCC 502.

    Once one accepts that there is a strong prima facie case that the bank's security has been transferred to members of the family at a time when action by the creditor was clearly anticipated by the debtor and that these transfers were at an undervalue and that

A

what remains in the hands of the debtor barely if at all covers the debt, there is in my judgment a strong prima facie case that the purpose of the transactions was to prejudice the interests of the creditor. I accept that there can easily be cases where part of the security is transferred at an undervalue and thus the security is reduced in value and yet still amply covers the debt. In such cases there may well be an argument that the transactions do not prejudice the interests of the creditor. The present case does not however fall into that category. On Mr Morgan's figures, the bank was left with a margin of five per cent (£800,000–£759,000) in circumstances where even this is reducing because of accruing interest charges. This is to be left in a situation which is significantly more precarious than one which provides for a margin of 30 per cent (£1,000,000–£759,000). The fact that there will be costs of realising the security adds force to this consideration.

B

For these reasons I agree with the judge that there is a strong prima facie case that the preconditions for making an order under s. 423 are fulfilled in the present case.

C

The scope of privilege

I turn therefore to the question of general interest in relation to the law governing discovery. We start for this purpose from the position that there is a strong prima facie case that Mr Eustice ('the transferor') entered into transactions at an undervalue and that his purpose in so doing was to prejudice the interests of the bank ('the claimant'). It is also common ground that these documents are relevant to the issues between the parties and therefore disclosable. The question which falls to be resolved is whether legal professional privilege attaches to documents containing or evidencing communications between the transferor and his legal advisers relating to transactions entered into by the transferor at an undervalue for the purpose of prejudicing the interest of persons making a claim against him. If it does then the documents need not be produced for inspection.

D

In the resolution of this question there are two conflicting desiderata in the background:

E

(1) Discovery of every relevant document is desirable to help the court decide what happened and why. The right answer is more likely to be arrived at by the court if it is in possession of all relevant material.

(2) It is desirable that persons should be able to go to their legal advisers knowing that they can talk frankly and receive professional advice knowing that what each party has said to the other will not be revealed to third parties.

F

This second desideratum has recently been expressed thus by Bingham LJ in *Ventouris v Mountain* [1991] 1 WLR 607 at p. 611C and I gratefully adopt his words:

'The doctrine of legal professional privilege is rooted in the public interest, which requires that hopeless and exaggerated claims and unsound and spurious defences be so far as possible discouraged, and civil disputes so far as possible settled without resort to judicial decision. To this end it is necessary that actual and potential litigants, be they claimants or respondents, should be free to unburden themselves without reserve to their legal advisers, and their legal advisers be free to give honest and candid advice on a sound factual basis, without fear that these communications may be relied on by an opposing party if the dispute comes before the court for decision. It is the protection of confidential communications between client and legal adviser which lies at the heart of legal professional privilege ... Without the consent of the client, and in the absence of iniquity or dispute between client and solicitor, no inquiry may be made into or disclosure made of any instructions which the client gave to the solicitor or any advice the solicitor gave the client, whether in writing or orally.'

G

H

It will be noted that in the last sentence cited Bingham LJ referred to the 'absence of iniquity'. In so doing he was recognising the effect of a line of cases which have

A established that advice sought or given for the purpose of effecting iniquity is not privileged.

The present appeal is concerned essentially with the question whether the effecting of transactions at an undervalue for the purpose of prejudicing the interests of a creditor can be regarded as 'iniquity' in this context. 'Iniquity' is, I believe, without having done any research on the point, Bingham LJ's word. The case law refers to 'crime or fraud' (*R v Cox & Railton* (1884) 14 QBD 153 at p. 165), 'criminal or unlawful' (*Bullivant v A-G for Victoria* [1901] AC 196 at p. 201) and 'all forms of fraud and dishonesty such as fraudulent breach of trust, fraudulent conspiracy, trickery and sham contrivances' (*Crescent Farm (Sidcup) Sports Ltd v Sterling Offices Ltd* [1972] Ch 553 at p. 565). The case law indicates that 'fraud' is in this context used in a relatively wide sense. Thus in *Gamlen Chemical Co (UK) Ltd v Rochem Ltd* (unreported, 7 December 1979, CA) Goff LJ cited and approved a passage in the judgment of Goulding J in the court below where
C he had said in the language of an age which has passed:

> 'For servants during their employment in breach of their contractual duty of fidelity to their master, to engage in a scheme secretly using the master's time and money, to take the master's customers and employees and make profit from them in a competing business built up to receive themselves on leaving the master's service, I would have thought that commercial men and lawyers alike would say
D that is a fraud.'

On the other hand the courts have shown themselves reluctant to extend the concept indefinitely and have warned against an indiscriminate setting aside of legal privilege. Thus in the *Gamlen* case Goff LJ stated:

> 'The court must in every case, of course, be satisfied that what is prima facie proved really is dishonest and not merely disreputable or a failure to maintain good ethical standards and must bear in mind that legal professional privilege is a very necessary
E thing and is not likely to be overthrown, but on the other hand the interests of victims of fraud must not be overlooked. Each case depends on its own facts.'

In the *Crescent Farm* case the court was not willing to extend the concept to the tort of inducing a breach of contract.

One of the factors which the court will often find relevant and which may be decisive
F in a particular case is the purpose for which the advice is sought. Is it sought to explain the legal effect of what has already been done and is now the subject of existing or imminent litigation? Or is it sought in order to structure a transaction which has yet to be carried out? In the former class of case the court will be more hesitant to lift the cloak of privilege than in the latter. As Lord Wrenbury said in *O'Rourke v Darbishire & Ors* [1920] AC 581 at p. 632:

> 'Not every document relevant to the issue of fraud but documents which are not
G upon some other ground privileged, are exposed to production. For the present purpose it is sufficiently accurate to say that documents relating to the conception and carrying out of the alleged fraud are not, but documents arising in professional confidence as to defence against the alleged fraud are protected.'

Thus the court would be reluctant – it is not presently necessary to decide the point – to force a legal adviser to give evidence or produce documents as to what a client had
H said when seeking advice as to how to respond to a criminal charge which had been preferred against him. That, normally at any rate, would be unjustifiably to invade the defendant's rights to silence and would be against the public interest to which Bingham LJ referred in the passage I have cited.

I regard the present case however as being essentially one about advice sought on how to structure a transaction.

I accept that it must have been obvious to the defendants that the bank might, once it learned of the challenged transactions, start proceedings. It was faintly submitted on behalf of the defendants that therefore advice as to structuring the transactions was to be regarded as advice coming into existence for the dominant purpose of being used in contemplated proceedings. That submission I reject. The dominant purpose was to stop the bank from interfering with the defendants' use of what they regarded as family assets.

The first main submission made by Mr Morgan was based on the decision of Scott J in *Arbuthnot Leasing International Ltd v Havelet Leasing Ltd & Ors (No. 2)* [1990] BCC 636. In that case Scott J was prepared to accept that an intention to put a debtor's assets out of the reach of a creditor was not necessarily a dishonest motive but held that even so it could suffice for the purposes of s. 423. Mr Morgan relied on this and went on to submit that the case law had in effect confined the possibility of lifting the privilege to cases where there was dishonesty.

I reject this submission. Scott J was not concerned with whether legal professional privilege should be lifted. His use of the word dishonest was not in that context. In any event he was merely indicating that he was prepared to accept something which he did not need to decide and which had been submitted by the losing party. Moreover, as I have indicated, various words other than 'dishonest' have been used in the course of the cases in which privilege has been in issue. However to me the most important consideration is that we are here engaged not in some semantic exercise to see what adjective most appropriately covers the debtor's course of conduct but in deciding whether public policy requires that the documents in question are left uninspected. I do not think it does. Adopting the approach of Vinelott J in *Derby v Weldon (No. 7)* [1990] 1 WLR 1156, discovery followed by inspection would not here result in an unjustified interference with the defendants' property or right to privacy.

The second main submission made by Mr Morgan was based on the analysis of Stephen J in *R v Cox and Railton* (1884) 14 QBD 153 which is often cited in cases concerned with privilege. Stephen J said at p. 165:

'The question therefore is, whether, if a client applies to a legal adviser for advice intended to facilitate or to guide the client in the commission of a crime or fraud, the legal adviser being ignorant of the purpose for which his advice is wanted, the communication between the two is privileged?'

At pp. 166–167 he quotes Lord Brougham in an early case as saying:

'If, touching matters that come within the ordinary scope of professional employment legal advisers receive a communication in their professional capacity . . . from a client . . . or . . . commit to paper in the course of their employment on his behalf matters which they know only through their professional relation to the client, they . . . will not be compelled to disclose the information . . .'

Then Stephen J said the following on p. 167:

'The reason on which the rule is said to rest cannot include the case of communications, criminal in themselves, or intended to further any criminal purpose, for the protection of such communications cannot possibly be otherwise than injurious to the interests of justice . . . Nor do such communications fall within the terms of the rule. A communication in furtherance of a criminal purpose does not "come into the ordinary scope of professional employment".'

Mr Morgan submitted that the cloak of privilege should only be lifted if either the solicitor was a party to the 'crime' or the client uses the solicitor's advice or assistance for a criminal or fraudulent purpose not contemplated by the solicitor so that the solicitor is an unwitting accomplice to the client's fraud or crime. He submitted that no one had alleged that the solicitors in question were engaged in crime and that the defendants and the solicitors had jointly and openly engaged in a purpose which was both overt and

A   lawful, namely seeking and giving advice as to how to remove Mr Eustice's assets out of the temporary reach of the bank without rendering the transactions liable to be set aside under s. 423.

Mr Morgan relied on the observations of Bushe CJ in an Irish case *R v Haydn* (1825) 2 F & S 379 where he said at p. 381:

B   'If any man should confide to a professional person, that he had a treasonable or felonious intention, and wished to know how he might execute it so as to escape punishment, it would be too much to say that such communication which might make the man consulted guilty of misprision, was privileged; but if a man meditates an act which, exceeding certain limits, would become criminal, and confined within certain bounds would be perfectly justifiable, the person asking the advice must be considered as seeking how he may *avoid* and not how he may *commit* a crime, and it is impossible that an attorney should be obliged to disclose such communication.'

C   Mr Morgan also relied on what Lord Sumner said in *O'Rourke v Darbishire* [1920] AC 581 at p. 613:

'No one doubts that the claim for professional privilege does not appl to documents which have been brought into existence in the course of or in furtherance of a fraud to which both solicitor and client are parties. To consult a solicitor about an intended course of action, in order to be advised whether it is
D   legitimate or not, or to lay before a solicitor a fact relating to a charge of fraud, actually made or anticipated, and make a clean breast of it with the object of being advised about the best way in which to meet it, is a very different thing from consulting him in order to learn how to plan, execute, or stifle an actual fraud.'

These submissions were attractively presented but I reject them. For reasons given earlier in this judgment we start here from a position in which, on a prima facie view, the client was seeking to enter into transactions at an undervalue the purpose of which was
E   to prejudice the bank. I regard this purpose as being sufficiently iniquitous for public policy to require communications between him and his solicitor in relation to the setting up of these transactions to be discoverable.

If that view be correct, then it matters not whether either the client or the solicitor shared that view. They may well have thought that the transactions would not fall to be set aside under s. 423 either because they thought that the transactions were not at an
F   undervalue or because they thought that the court would not find that the purpose of the transactions was to prejudice the bank. But if this is what they thought then there is a strong prima facie case that they were wrong. Public policy does not require the communications of those who misapprehend the law to be privileged in circumstances where no privilege attaches to those who correctly understand the situation.

These cases can indeed throw up difficult problems of policy and one sees frequent
G   references in the case law to the desirability of deciding each case on its facts. The evidence in the present case reveals a strong prima facie case of what the sidenote to s. 423 refers to as 'transactions defrauding creditors'. The evidence which is sought to be inspected may help the plaintiffs overcome a detriment to which they ought not to have been exposed and to which they were exposed by the action of the defendants. Mr Morgan, when asked to identify the prejudice which inspection might cause to his client could do no more than indicate that material might emerge which would indicate to the plaintiffs
H   various weaknesses in the defendants' position. In those circumstances I do not consider that the public interest requires these communications to be kept secret. If the strong prima facie case turns out to be correct then the defendants have deliberately indulged in something which I would categorise as sharp practice.

I do not consider that the result of upholding the judge's order in the present case will be to discourage straightforward citizens from consulting their lawyers. Those lawyers

should tell them that what is proposed is liable to be set aside and the straightforward
citizen will then not do it and so the advice will never see the light of day. In so far as
those wishing to engage in sharp practice are concerned, the effect of the present decision
may well be to discourage them from going to their lawyers. This has the arguable public
disadvantage that the lawyers might have dissuaded them from the sharp practice.
However it has the undoubted public advantage that the absence of lawyers will make it
more difficult for them to carry out their sharp practice. In my judgment the balance of
advantage is in permitting inspection of the material as ordered by the judge. I would
dismiss the appeal.

The respondents' notice under O. 59, r. 6(1)(a)

The judge followed the decision of Vinelott J in *Derby & Co Ltd & Ors v Weldon & Ors
(No. 7)* [1990] 1 WLR 1156 at p. 1174–1175 that:

'The plaintiffs are not entitled to disclosure of any documents which fall under a
different head of privilege: legal advice obtained and documents coming into
existence for the dominant purpose of being used in pending or contemplated
proceedings.'

The order under appeal provided that discovery should:

'include all documents containing or evidencing communications between the
defendants and their legal advisers relating to the tenancy agreement and the
assignment in their respective possession, custody or power (excepting documents
to which a bona fide claim of privilege is made on the ground that the same were
obtained or created for the dominant purpose of being used in pending or
contemplated proceedings).'

It is common ground that the order should also have referred to the sale agreement. The
order of the court will reflect that.

It was submitted on behalf of the plaintiffs that the words in brackets were too wide.
The original cause for the respondents' notice which encapsulated this ground was a fear
that the defendants' solicitors might consider that all the documents referring to the
transactions might be subject to what is known as litigation privilege because the
transactions were set up at a time when litigation was contemplated. There was ground
for that fear at the time but now that this judgment has been delivered it is obvious that
such an attitude by the solicitors would be indefensible.

The plaintiffs nevertheless submitted that the order instead of referring to documents
obtained or created for the 'dominant purpose of being used in pending or contemplated
proceedings' should have referred to the 'sole purpose'. In my judgment the reference to
dominant purpose correctly reflects in the circumstances of the present case what justice
and public policy require and I would not propose altering the judge's order in this
respect.

Aldous LJ: I agree.

Butler-Sloss LJ: I also agree.

(Order accordingly)

A # Eurocross Sales Ltd & Anor v Cornhill Insurance plc.

Court of Appeal (Civil Division).
Sir Thomas Bingham MR, Auld and Ward L JJ.
Judgment delivered 13 July 1995.

B *Security for costs – Legal Aid – Company sold its business including insurance claim to individual plaintiff – Company's action stayed on failure to give £5,000 security for costs – Plaintiff joined subject to condition that he paid £5,000 into court – Appeal and cross-appeal – Whether joinder should have been ordered on terms – Whether joinder should be set aside as device to circumvent order for security against company – Whether joinder should be set aside as device to enable plaintiff to obtain Legal Aid – County Court Rules 1981, O. 13, r. 1(8).*

C This was an appeal against an order that the appellant be added as plaintiff in proceedings brought by a company against an insurer subject to his paying £5,000 into court and a cross-appeal by the insurer for the joinder of the appellant to be set aside.

A company of which 'S' and his wife were the directors and shareholders had an insurance claim against 'Cornhill' in relation to a damaged consignment of fruit. The company then sold its business, including the potential claim against Cornhill, for a nominal £1 consideration to another company of which S and his wife were the directors and D shareholders. That company issued proceedings against Cornhill and was ordered to give security for costs in the sum of £5,000. The company sold its business to S for £1 and he applied to be substituted as plaintiff in the action. The proceedings by the company were stayed because security was not given. On the assumption that the company had validly assigned its claim to S, S was given leave to be joined, by way of addition rather than substitution, on condition that he paid £5,000 into court. S obtained Legal Aid to appeal E against the imposition of terms on his joinder. Cornhill cross-appealed on the basis that the assignment was a sham designed to circumvent the court's order for security and the rule that corporations were not eligible for Legal Aid.

Held, allowing S's appeal and dismissing Cornhill's cross-appeal:

1. Since S was applying for joinder, the judge was entitled to impose appropriate conditions which might in principle have included any term which matched the justice of the F case. The condition most often imposed on the joinder of a plaintiff was that he pay the costs of and occasioned by the joinder and that he pay the costs incurred up to the date of joinder or thrown away as a result of the joinder.

2. However, the basis of the judge's order, which was that Cornhill should enjoy the same protection in relation to costs against S as it already enjoyed against the plaintiff company, could not be justified. If there had been no basis for a security order against the company, G no order against S would have been contemplated. The making of an order against the company, which had the practical effect of paralysing the company's action, did not alter the position.

3. There were no grounds for treating the sale, even if it was made with a view to avoiding an order for security to which the company would have been subject, as a colourable device which the court could or should strike down. Nor would the court set aside the joinder of S H on the ground that the sale was effected in order that S might apply for Legal Aid, a course not open to the company.

The following cases were referred to in the judgment of the court:

Advanced Technology Structures Ltd v Cray Valley Products Ltd & Anor [1993] BCLC 723.
Bowring (C T) & Co (Insurance) Ltd v Corsi & Partners Ltd [1994] BCC 713.

Kinnell (Charles P) & Co Ltd v Harding, Wace & Co [1918] 1 KB 405.   A
Tetley Tea Co Ltd v Alderson [1969] 1 WLR 102.

Dr Satvinder Juss (instructed by Dickinson, Parker Hill & Sons, Ormskirk) for the applicants.

Sarah Lee (instructed by Clyde & Co) for the respondents.

JUDGMENT OF THE COURT
(Delivered by Bingham MR)   B

The director and major shareholder of a small company bought the company's business, which included an insurance claim. The director then applied to be added as plaintiff in county court proceedings brought by the company against the insurer. It was ordered that he should be added, subject to his paying £5,000 into court, in effect as security for the insurer's costs of the action, the company already being subject to an order that it give security in that sum for the insurer's costs of the action. If added as C plaintiff the director became eligible for legal aid, which the company would not have been. Should the director have been added as plaintiff? If so, did the court have power to impose a condition on his joinder that he pay £5,000 into court? If it did, was that a proper exercise of the court's power on the facts? Should the joinder now be set aside? These are the questions which arise for our decision.

I. [Background]
D

In the autumn of 1991 a consignment of soft fruit was carried by sea from the US to this country. On arrival here it was found to be damaged. The consignment was owned by Eurocross Ltd, a small company of which Mr Sood and his wife were the directors and shareholders. The company had insured its cargo interests with Cornhill Insurance plc. The company claimed against Cornhill for the damage to the fruit but the claim was rejected.   E

On 31 March 1992 Eurocross Ltd sold its business to Eurocross Sales Ltd for the nominal consideration of £1. The business sold included 'potential claim against Cornhill Insurance for damage to plums imported in October 1991, a claim denied by the insurers, but which may have to go to court for redress'. Eurocross Sales was another company of which Mr Sood and his wife were the shareholders and directors. Mr Sood executed the sale agreement on behalf of both companies. Later that year Eurocross Ltd was wound F up on a creditor's petition.

On 14 April 1992 Eurocross Sales Ltd issued proceedings against Cornhill in the Mayor's and City of London Court claiming damages of some £27,500 and interest. Cornhill delivered a defence denying the claim.

In the summer of 1993 there were four relevant events: Eurocross Sales Ltd sold its business to Mr Sood; Cornhill applied that the particulars of claim be struck out as G disclosing no cause of action and that the action be dismissed; Cornhill also applied for an order that Eurocross Sales Ltd give security for its costs of the proceedings; and Mr Sood applied to be substituted as plaintiff in the action. The precise sequence of these events is in dispute, and it is not clear to what extent one move was prompted by or made to anticipate another.

By an agreement dated 2 July 1993 Eurocross Sales Ltd sold its business to Mr Sood for the nominal consideration of £1. The express reason for the sale was that the company H wished to diversify into publishing and to free itself of problems associated with the fruit business. The sale was to become effective on 30 July. Mrs Sood executed the agreement on behalf of Eurocross Sales Ltd, Mr Sood on his own behalf.

Cornhill's application to strike out the particulars of claim and dismiss the action was dismissed by District Judge Woodcraft on 10 November 1993, when he gave the plaintiff

A   leave to amend. There has been no appeal against this decision. The proceedings must be regarded as raising a serious triable issue as to Cornhill's liability as insurer.

Having warned Eurocross Sales Ltd of its intention to do so, Cornhill on 19 July 1993 issued an application for security for costs. The security sought was £11,900 in the form of a first class bank guarantee, and the ground relied on was s. 726(1) of the *Companies Act* 1985 (that the company would be unable to pay the defendant's costs if the defendant

B   were successful in its defence). This application also came before District Judge Woodcraft on 10 November 1993. He ordered that the company give security for costs in the sum of £5,000 within 28 days and that in default the proceedings should be stayed. There has been no appeal against this order. Nor has security been given, although the time allowed to the company has been extended. The proceedings by Eurocross Sales Ltd are accordingly stayed.

C   At the same hearing on 10 November 1993 District Judge Woodcraft refused Mr Sood's application to be substituted for Eurocross Sales Ltd as plaintiff in the action. Against this decision Mr Sood appealed.

His appeal came before His Honour Judge Byrt QC (we are told, despite the dating of the order and the transcript, on 10 February 1994). The issue was whether Mr Sood should be added, not substituted, as plaintiff, and if so on what terms. Assuming for purposes of his decision (although this has always been in issue and may have to be

D   decided) that the company had validly assigned its claim against Cornhill to Mr Sood, the judge held that Mr Sood had a strong claim upon the exercise of the court's discretion to allow him to be added or substituted as a plaintiff. The judge accepted that the company had limited resources and that Mr Sood wanted to protect it against the consequences of failure in litigation. But he found merit in Cornhill's submission that since the validity of both assignments was in issue Mr Sood should become a party by way of addition rather than substitution. He then considered whether Mr Sood's joinder

E   should be on terms and, if so, what terms. He said:

> 'The Rules of the Supreme Court, O. 15, r. 6(2), make plain that at the time of directing a party be joined, the Court has power to stipulate the terms upon which he should be so. I have come to the conclusion I must ensure the defendants are adequately and properly protected on the issue of costs, bearing in mind that they already have an order for the security of costs against the plaintiff company.

F
> I think it would be wrong for the court to collaborate with Mr Sood in such a way that would enable the plaintiff company to escape the effects of that order by allowing Mr Sood to join as a party without himself being subjected to terms. Accordingly, I shall make it a condition of Mr Sood being joined as a party that he should be subject to terms. The question then is, what terms those should be.

G
> I know nothing about Mr Sood's means and in consequence the order I make is not based upon the fact that he has or has not the money to comply with the condition. However, I think it is important that if the defendant is to be adequately protected here then Mr Sood should be placed on terms similar to those of the order for the security of costs against the plaintiff company.

> Accordingly, I propose to direct that he shall be allowed to join as a party to the action on condition that he pays into court the sum of £5,000 within 28 days. Of

H
> course, if he defaults on that, he does not join as a party to the action. That will be the order I make in respect of that part of Mr Sood's application.'

Mr Sood applied for leave to appeal against the judge's decision to impose terms on his joinder. For purposes of his appeal he applied for and was granted legal aid. When the grant of legal aid came, belatedly, to the notice of Cornhill, on the eve of a hearing in this court, it prompted a notice of cross-appeal by Cornhill seeking that the joinder of

Mr Sood should be set aside. The essential basis of this was that the assignment to Mr Sood was a sham, or a colourable device, or an abuse of the process of the court, designed to circumvent the court's order for security and the rule that corporations are not eligible for legal aid, and that the court should not give effect to such a design.

It appeared to this court on 29 March 1995 when the matter first came before it that issues of some possibly far-reaching significance were raised. It accordingly adjourned the matter for fuller argument (written and oral) and offered the Legal Aid Board an opportunity to attend and make representations if it wished. The Legal Aid Board did not see fit to do so.

II. [The rules]

Order 15, r. 1(1)(b) of the County Court Rules empowers the county court to allow any person to be added or substituted as a party to proceedings if the High Court would have power to allow joinder in a like case. The power of the High Court under O. 15, r. 6(2)(b)(ii) is at any stage of the proceedings and on such terms as the court thinks just to order the addition as a party of any person between whom and any party to the cause there may exist an issue connected with the relief claimed in the cause which the court considers it just and convenient to determine in that cause. Where the interest of one party is assigned to another, O. 5, r. 11 of the County Court Rules gives the court a further discretionary power to order the joinder of the assignee.

Order 13 of the County Court Rules governs applications made in the course of proceedings. Rule 1(1) provides:

'Except as otherwise provided, the following paragraph of this rule shall have effect in relation to any application authorised by or under any Act or rule to be made in the course of an action or matter before or after judgment.'

Rule 1(8) provides:

'The court may as a condition of granting any application, impose such terms and conditions as it thinks fit, including a term or condition requiring any party to–

    (a) give security,

    . . .

    (c) pay money into court,

    (d) pay all or any part of the costs of the proceedings . . .'

Order 13, r. 8(1) of the County Court Rules empowers the court to order security for costs against a plaintiff ordinarily resident out of England and Wales if, having regard to all the circumstances, it thinks it reasonable to do so. The county court also enjoys the power to order security under s. 726 of the Companies Act. But it lacks the little-used power to order security which the High Court has under RSC, O. 23, r. 1(1)(b), (c) and (d).

III. [The jurisdiction to order security]

The jurisdiction to order security for costs exists 'to prevent the injustice which would result if a plaintiff who was in effect immune from orders for costs were free to litigate at the defendant's expense even if unsuccessful' (*C T Bowring & Co (Insurance) Ltd v Corsi & Partners Ltd* [1994] BCC 713 at p. 724H per Millett LJ). A plaintiff may, on appropriate facts, be regarded as so immune because it is not ordinarily resident within the jurisdiction or, if a limited company, because it lacks the wherewithal to pay the defendant's costs. In the case cited, Millett LJ described RSC, O. 23 as 'a complete and exhaustive code' (p. 729D). Dillon LJ found it 'difficult to envisage the court creating a new category of case in which a plaintiff or defendant can be required to give security,

A   without leaving that to the Rules committee or Parliament' (p. 722D). It seems plain that the county court had no jurisdiction under CCR, O. 13, r. 8 to order Mr Sood as a personal plaintiff to give security, whatever his financial position, and the judge did not purport to do so. His order was that Mr Sood pay £5,000 into court as a condition of being joined. No reference appears to have been made to CCR, O. 13, r. 8. The judge's order had much the same effect as an order for security (save that the penalty for non-compliance was non-joinder and not a stay) and gave Cornhill the same protection

B   against Mr Sood as it had previously enjoyed against the company, but the order was imposed as a condition of joinder and not as an order for security.

The discretionary power of the High Court to impose terms as a condition of ordering the addition of a party under RSC, O. 15, r. 6 is expressed in wide terms and we see no reason to restrict the meaning to be given to them. We accept as accurate the statement in the *Supreme Court Practice 1995* at 15/6/15: 'On giving leave to amend as to parties,

C   the court may impose such terms as may be just having regard to all the circumstances'. This wide discretionary power must of course, like any other judicial discretionary power, be exercised in accordance with settled practice or for relevant and sustainable reasons. The condition most often imposed on the joinder of a plaintiff is that he pay the costs of and occasioned by the joinder and that he pay the costs incurred up to the date of joinder or thrown away as a result of the joinder.

D   Where the court may properly refuse an order which a party is seeking it may, if appropriate, make the order on terms that the applicant party give security for the costs of the other party: *ibid*, per Millett LJ at p. 730. So if a party seeks an adjournment of a hearing, the county court may under CCR, O. 13, r. 1(8) put him on terms to give security for costs and order him to pay the costs thrown away: *Tetley Tea Co Ltd v Alderson* [1969] 1 WLR 102.

E   We are of the opinion that Judge Byrt had no power to (and did not) order Mr Sood to give security for Cornhill's costs under CCR, O. 13, r. 8. But since Mr Sood was applying for an order, the judge was entitled to impose appropriate conditions which might in principle have included any term which matched the justice of the case including (if appropriate on the facts) an order that Mr Sood give security for Cornhill's costs. The central question is whether, in the circumstances as they were presented to him, the judge was entitled to impose the condition he did.

F

IV. [The order made]

The sum of £5,000 which Eurocross Sales Ltd was ordered to pay by way of security was less than half the sum for which Cornhill had applied, but the order was made on an application to cover Cornhill's costs up to and including the trial and there is no suggestion that the order was made on an instalment basis to cover Cornhill up to any

G   interlocutory stage. At the date of application Cornhill claimed to have incurred costs of £7,500. It was not suggested that the joinder of Mr Sood increased the costs of the action or in any way altered (save in relation to the validity of the sale to him) the issue already joined between insured and insurer. Thus the judge's order cannot be read as a condition that Mr Sood secure Cornhill against the costs caused by or thrown away as a result of his joinder (which Mr Sood was not in any event ordered to pay). It seems clear that the basis of the judge's order was his judgment that Cornhill should enjoy the same

H   protection in relation to costs against Mr Sood as it already enjoyed against the plaintiff company under the unappealed order of the district judge.

It is of course true that as a result of the joinder Cornhill exchanged an opponent which could only proceed if it provided security for Cornhill's costs for an opponent who could (unless the judge's condition were upheld) proceed without providing such security. To that extent the joinder would, in the absence of such a condition, put it in a worse

position. That would be even more obviously so if, as may be the case, the company   A
cannot provide security of £5,000, because Cornhill would (on this hypothesis) exchange
an opponent who is effectively paralysed for one who is not. On the other hand, Cornhill
is in no worse a position than if the company had sold its business to Mr Sood before
bringing proceedings, and he had been the plaintiff from the outset. It is in no worse a
position than if, instead of being joined, Mr Sood had commenced a fresh action as
plaintiff. And the potential injustice against which the security order was intended to
protect Cornhill no longer exists: the company's action is stayed unless and until it   B
provides the security ordered; but in Mr Sood it faces a personal plaintiff who is liable to
the extent of his available assets to meet any costs order made against him. Depending
on his means, he may or may not be able to meet such an order, but the law affords a
defendant no protection against costs which may not be paid by impecunious personal
plaintiffs.

Had Mr Sood been ordered to pay, and give security for, the costs occasioned by or   C
thrown away as a result of his joinder, there could in our judgment have been no
sustainable objection to the order. But we can find no justification for the order in fact
made. If there had been no basis for a security order against the company, we cannot
imagine that an order against Mr Sood would have been contemplated. We see no reason
why the making of an order against the company, which had the practical effect of
paralysing the company's action, alters the position. Instead of sheltering behind the
limited liability of his company, Mr Sood has chosen to expose himself to the liability of   D
a personal plaintiff. That is not, without more, something for which he should be
penalised.

V. [The sale as a device]

The affidavit evidence before us raises the factual possibility that the sale by Eurocross
Sales Ltd was made in order to circumvent an application for security which Mr Sood   E
knew Cornhill would make or guessed it might. Mr Sood disputes this. We cannot resolve
this factual issue. But Mr Sood is not a stranger to litigation, nor is he ignorant of the
law, nor is he fearful of conducting litigation himself. So it is necessary to ask: if it were
true that the sale by Eurocross Sales Ltd to Mr Sood was made to circumvent an
application for security by Cornhill, would that affect the conclusion expressed above?

Miss Sarah Lee, for Cornhill, does not suggest that the sale agreement was   F
champertous, and she does not challenge the sale as any breach of the company's or the
directors' obligations. She did at first submit that the sale agreement was a sham, but we
cannot for our part see that it involved any element of pretence, of saying one thing and
doing another, of disguising the true nature of the transaction. The sale may or may not
turn out to be valid, but there is no indication that the company was to retain any interest
in any recovery made by Mr Sood against Cornhill. There is inevitably some factual
artificiality in the distinction between Mr Sood and his company, but the sale agreement   G
appears to represent the deal which was, for whatever reason, done. It was not in our
view a sham.

On the present hypothesis, the sale agreement was a device in the sense that it was a
transaction effected to circumvent a procedural disadvantage to which the company but
not (as must have been supposed) Mr Sood might be subject. Is the court entitled,
assuming that hypothesis to be correct, to impose the disputed payment condition on Mr   H
Sood?

In contending that it is, Miss Lee relies strongly on *Advanced Technology Structures
Ltd v Cray Valley Products Ltd & Anor* [1993] BCLC 723. The facts of the case are
important. The plaintiff company issued a writ against the defendants claiming large
damages. An employee of the company agreed to help it in its litigation against the

A   defendants in return for a share of the damages it recovered. An order for security for costs was made against the company which it provided, but it had no further means of financing the litigation. The company thereupon assigned its claim against the defendants to the employee for a nominal consideration, on terms which gave the employee a right to prosecute the action in the name of the company and provided for a sharing of the proceeds. The employee obtained legal aid and applied under RSC, O. 15, r. 7(2) (which corresponds to CCR, O. 5, r. 11) to be added or substituted as plaintiff. The judge

B   rejected the application. The Court of Appeal upheld the judge's decision on a number of grounds: (1) that no substitution was needed, since the employee could prosecute the action in the company's name; (2) that the assignment was a sham and a mere stratagem or device to enable the company to litigate with the support of the employee's legal aid; and (3) that the assignment agreement was champertous.

     The first and third of these grounds of decision were plainly correct, in our respectful

C   view, but they have no application here. We think the court may have been treating 'sham' as equivalent to 'a mere stratagem or device', and if so we think it was wrong; but there was an element of pretence about the assignment agreement; and for the employee to obtain legal aid to prosecute a claim more for the company's benefit than his own plainly involved a colourable evasion of the rule which precludes the grant of legal aid to companies. There was, however, no reliance on the order for security made against the

D   company, and no suggestion that joinder of the employee should be subject to a similar term.

     It will be necessary to refer to this authority again below in relation to legal aid, but we do not think it provides us with any ground for treating the sale in the present case, even if made with a view to avoiding an order for security to which Eurocross Sales Ltd would have been subject, as a colourable device which the court should or properly could strike down. The rules provide a safeguard against a defined risk: it cannot in our view

E   be legally objectionable to remove the risk so as to remove the need to provide the safeguard.

VI. [Legal aid]

     When the case was before Judge Byrt, the possibility that Mr Sood might seek and obtain legal aid had not arisen and he did not address it. So far, Mr Sood's legal aid

F   extends only to this appeal, but Cornhill is apprehensive that he may hereafter obtain legal aid to prosecute the action, and if that were to occur it would be put at a disadvantage. Cornhill attacks the sale by Eurocross Sales Ltd to Mr Sood as a stratagem or device to enable Mr Sood to obtain legal aid, and on that basis submits that the joinder order should be set aside.

     On the dates disclosed to us it appears somewhat unlikely that the sale to Mr Sood was

G   effected to enable Mr Sood to obtain legal aid. But this again is an issue we cannot resolve, and for purposes of this judgment it may be assumed that the sale was effected in order that Mr Sood might apply for legal aid, a course not open to the company.

     It is undoubtedly true that the company as plaintiff was ineligible for legal aid, and it appears that Mr Sood is eligible. In contrast with the *Advanced Technology Structures* case, however, there is nothing to found an inference that Mr Sood is, to any extent, to conduct the action on behalf or for the benefit of the company. If the joinder takes effect

H   the company will for all practical purposes be out of the action and it will be his action as a personal plaintiff.

     If Mr Sood remains as plaintiff, and if he applies for legal aid, the Legal Aid Board will have to consider whether the sale to Mr Sood was effected to enable him to prosecute this claim personally with the benefit of legal aid instead of through his company without that benefit, and if so whether it would be unreasonable that he should have legal aid.

Under Pt. V of the *Civil Legal Aid (General) Regulations* 1989 (SI 1989/339) the board   A
has power to refuse a certificate if 'it appears unreasonable that the applicant should
receive legal aid in the particular circumstances of the case': reg. 34(1)(e). In our judgment
the position is clear. If the grant of legal aid in present circumstances would be
unreasonable, the board could refuse it, and presumably would. That is a judgment the
board is well fitted to make. If the grant in present circumstances is not unreasonable,
the board may not (in the absence of some other ground for refusal) refuse it. But in that
event it would not in our view be open to us to set aside the joinder of Mr Sood on the   B
ground that it would open the door to an abuse of legal aid. We readily accept that the
courts must be astute to detect and ready to stamp on abuses of legal aid, but we do not
see the present case as one of abuse and the Legal Aid Board have not attended to argue
that it is.

We would decline to set aside the joinder of Mr Sood on this ground.

   C

VII. [Company representation]

In July 1992, when Eurocross Sales Ltd was the sole plaintiff, an order was made that
in all further hearings the company should be represented by solicitors or counsel. Mr
Sood challenged that order before Judge Byrt on 10 February 1994, but he affirmed it.
Mr Sood has sought to appeal to this court against that decision of the judge.

There is in the County Court Rules no provision equivalent to the general prohibition   D
in RSC, O. 5, r. 6(2) and O. 12, r. 1(2) on the conduct of proceedings by a body corporate
otherwise than by a solicitor. In the county court a company director without legal
qualifications may, generally speaking, address the court only where the court has
granted him a right of audience in relation to those proceedings: *Courts and Legal
Services Act* 1990, s. 27(2)(c). The decision whether to grant the director a right of
audience in a particular case is one to be made by the court in the exercise of its discretion.
In *Charles P Kinnell & Co Ltd v Harding, Wace & Co* [1918] 1 KB 405 at p. 413 Swinfen   E
Eady LJ said:

> 'It is left to his discretion, but except under special circumstances he would
> doubtless only sanction some director or officer or regular employee of the
> company so appearing instead of the company, and would limit his permission to
> cases which he thought could properly be disposed of before him, without the
> assistance of either counsel or solicitor.'   F

In the present case the judge did not misdirect himself in any way, and he was abundantly
justified in holding that the case raised issues which might be very hard to resolve fairly
unless the company were professionally represented. There is no ground for impugning
his judgment on this point, which would now appear to be academic.

VIII. [Conclusion]   G

We would grant Mr Sood leave to appeal and Cornhill leave to cross-appeal.

We would allow Mr Sood's appeal to the extent of setting aside the condition that he
pay £5,000 into court. Otherwise we would affirm the judge's order.

We would dismiss Cornhill's cross-appeal.

We do not reach this decision without some unease. One need not be clairvoyant to   H
foresee the possibility of abuse if the practice were to become prevalent of impecunious
companies, unable to meet anticipated orders for security, assigning claims to penniless
directors who would then litigate the claims without giving security, perhaps with the
benefit of legal aid and taking advantage of the rights accorded even in the higher courts
to unrepresented personal litigants. These are not fanciful risks. But we think that the
safeguard must be found (a) in the fiduciary duty owed by directors to their companies,

A   which must ordinarily prohibit transfer of a company asset to a director at an undervalue; (b) in the right of the Legal Aid Board to refuse the grant of legal aid where it would be unreasonable to grant it; and (c) if need be, in amendment of the rules of court. On the facts and argument in this case, we do not think that the apprehension of future abuse would justify the court in making any order other than that which we propose. As Samuel Johnson observed, 'Sir, you must not neglect doing a thing immediately good from fear of remote evil'.

B

(*Order accordingly*)

C

D

E

F

G

H

Neptune (Vehicle Washing Equipment) Ltd v Fitzgerald (No. 2).

Chancery Division.
A G Steinfeld QC (sitting as a deputy judge of the Chancery Division).
Judgment delivered 18 July 1995.

> *Director's duties – Sole director – Enforcement of fair dealing – Directors to disclose interest in contracts – Sole director terminated own service contract and withdrew company money as compensation – Plaintiff sued for return of money; defendant counterclaimed for wrongful dismissal – Whether defendant had made sufficient declaration of interest – Whether defendant in breach of duty to act in best interests of company – Whether defendant retained authority to withdraw company money – Whether court should grant relief to defendant – Companies Act 1985, s. 317, 727.*

This was an action by a company against its former sole director who at a board meeting of the company attended by the defendant and the company's secretary, had resolved as sole director that his own service contract should be terminated and had resolved that the sum of £100,892 should be paid to him by way of compensation for the termination of his service contract.

The company sought return of the money arguing (1) that the defendant made no or an insufficient 'declaration of the nature of his interest' in the transaction as required by the company's articles of association and s. 317 of the Companies Act 1985 so as to take the transaction out of the strict equitable rule against self-dealing; (2) that the defendant in making the relevant resolutions and the payment pursuant thereto was acting in breach of his fiduciary duties owed to the company by preferring his own interest over that of the company; or (3) at the time when the sum was withdrawn from the company's bank account the defendant was no longer a director of the company and, accordingly, no longer had any authority to authorise the company's bank to make that payment.

The defendant argued that he did make a sufficient declaration, that he was acting bona fide in the best interests of the company, and that he was authorised to withdraw the money. In any event relief should be granted to the defendant pursuant to s. 727 of the Companies Act 1985 and the court ought only to direct repayment of the money on terms that the defendant be permitted to retain such part of it as the court regarded as fair and reasonable. In addition the defendant maintained a counterclaim for damages for his alleged wrongful dismissal.

Held, giving judgment for the plaintiff:

1. The company's articles excluded the strict equitable rule against self-dealing but that did not entail that the director was relieved from his other obligations to the company, including his duty to act bona fide in the company's interests. (Farrar v Farrars Ltd (1888) 40 ChD 395 and Guinness plc v Saunders & Anor [1990] BCC 205 applied.)

2. The defendant acted in breach of his fiduciary duties to the company in passing the board resolutions and procuring the payment to himself of the sum of £100,892.62 from the company's bank account by not acting bona fide in the interests of the company but preferring his own interests to those of the company.

3. The defendant failed to make a sufficient declaration of the nature of his interest to the board meeting on 5 January in compliance with the company's articles and the Companies Act.

4. The defendant ceased or was to be regarded as having ceased to be a director immediately after the board resolutions were made and thus did not have the authority of the company to make the said payment.

A 5. There was no power to grant relief to the defendant pursuant to s. 727 of the Companies Act 1985 since it did not appear that the defendant had acted reasonably.

6. There was no justification in the circumstances of the case for exercising any power which the court might have to subject the company's prima facie entitlement to repayment in full to any term that would allow the defendant to retain some part of the sum wrongly paid. Any power to award remuneration was restricted to cases where it could not have the effect of encouraging a conflict of interests. (*Guinness plc v Saunders & Anor* [1990] BCC 205 applied.)

B

7. The counterclaim for damages for wrongful dismissal was dismissed because the defendant's contract of employment was terminated by the defendant's own wrongful repudiation of it by the action which he took in passing the resolutions, which was to be regarded as accepted by the company by the actions taken on behalf of the shareholders the following day.

C

The following cases were referred to in the judgment:

Aberdeen Railway Co v Blaikie Bros (1854) 1 Macq HL 461.
Boston Deep Sea Fishing and Ice Co v Ansell (1888) 39 ChD 339.
Farrar v Farrars Ltd (1888) 40 ChD 395.
Guinness plc v Saunders & Anor [1990] BCC 205; [1990] 2 AC 663.
Hindle v John Cotton Ltd (1919) 56 ScLR 625.

D

Lee Panavision Ltd v Lee Lighting Ltd [1991] BCC 620.
Movitex Ltd v Bulfield & Ors (1986) 2 BCC 99,403.
Neptune (Vehicle Washing Equipment) Ltd v Fitzgerald [1995] BCC 474.
Phipps v Boardman [1967] 2 AC 46.
Roith (W & M) Ltd, Re [1967] 1 WLR 432.
Runciman v Walter Runciman plc [1993] BCC 223.

E

Smith (Howard) Ltd v Ampol Petroleum & Ors [1974] AC 821.
State Trading Corp of India v M Golodetz Ltd [1988] 2 Ll Rep 182.

Elizabeth Jones (instructed by Harbottle & Lewis) for the plaintiff.

Michael Roberts (instructed by Amery Parkes) for the defendant.

JUDGMENT

F

A G Steinfeld QC: Introduction

By this action the plaintiff company ('the company') seeks the repayment from the defendant, who was formerly its managing director, of the sum of £100,892.62 which the defendant withdrew by bankers' draft from the company's bank account on the afternoon of 5 January 1994. That sum represents the aggregate of sums which at a board 'meeting' of the company attended by the defendant alone as sole director of the company

G

and with the company's secretary, Mr Peter Phillips, in attendance held on the morning of 5 January 1995, the defendant had, as sole director, resolved should be paid to himself by way of compensation for the termination of his own service contract. At the same meeting the defendant had resolved that such service contract should be terminated. The sum claimed has in fact at an early stage of the proceedings been paid by agreement into an account in the joint names of the company's and the defendant's respective solicitors. There is an issue as regards the exact terms of that agreement and, in particular, as to

H

whether, even if the company were to succeed in its claim in this action, the deposited sum should be retained to meet an outstanding claim by the defendant for compensation for unfair dismissal which he is pursuing in the industrial tribunal. This being a discrete issue which only arises for possible determination depending upon the outcome of this action, I directed at the outset of this trial that the same should be heard and determined following judgment.

The company maintains its claim on essentially three alternative bases, namely: A

(1)   the defendant made no or an insufficient 'declaration of the nature of his interest' in the transaction to the 'meeting' of directors at which the transaction was resolved upon as required by the company's articles of association and s. 317 of the *Companies Act* 1985 so as to bring the transaction outside of the strict equitable rule which prohibits a director (save with the informed consent of the shareholders in general meeting) from entering into any transaction with the company in which   B
his personal interest conflicts with his duty to the company; or

(2)   the defendant in making the relevant resolutions and the payment pursuant thereto was acting in breach of his fiduciary duties owed to the company by preferring his own interest over that of the company; or

(3)   at the time when the sum was withdrawn from the company's bank account the defendant was no longer a director of the company and, accordingly, no longer   C
had any authority to authorise the company's bank to make that payment.

The various defences to the claim are, in summary:

(1)   the defendant *did* make a sufficient 'declaration of the nature of his interest' at the board meeting on 5 January 1994;

(2)   in making the resolutions and causing the payment to be made the defendant was acting in what he bona fide believed to be the best interests of the company and   D
was thus not in breach of his fiduciary duties as a director of the company;

(3)   the defendant did not resign his directorship of the company until 6 January 1994 and, accordingly, was still a director and thus authorised to withdraw the money the previous afternoon or, alternatively, even if he was not then a director, the resolutions passed that morning entitled him to withdraw the money in any event;

(4)   in any event relief should be granted to the defendant pursuant to s. 727 of the   E
Companies Act 1985 for any breach of duty or breach of trust which, by withdrawing the sum in question, he may have committed;

(5)   further and in any event the court ought only to direct repayment of the money on terms that the defendant be permitted to retain such part of it as the court regards as fair and reasonable.

In addition the defendant maintains a counterclaim for damages for his alleged wrongful   F
dismissal.

The preliminary ruling

I ought to say something as regards the first matter relied upon by the company, namely the alleged failure of the defendant to declare the nature of his interest to the board meeting on 5 January 1994. Regulation 84(1) of Table A in the first schedule to the *Companies Act* 1948 (as modified by the Companies Acts 1948 to 1981) ('Table A'),   G
which is incorporated with certain modifications into the company's articles of association, provides that a director who is in any way interested in a contract or proposed contract with the company 'shall declare the nature of his interest at a meeting of the directors in accordance with s. 199 of the [Companies] Act [1948]' (now s. 317 of the *Companies Act* 1985). It might at first blush be thought that such provision could not apply in the case of a sole director proposing to enter into such a contract. In the first   H
place it might be thought that, although a sole director might well be able to exercise all the powers of the board of directors, there cannot, so long as he remains a sole director, be as a matter of ordinary English any 'meeting' of the directors to whom such declaration can be made.

Secondly, it might be thought to be somewhat artificial and pointless for a director to declare to himself something of which he is, of course, only too aware. In those

A   circumstances it might have been thought that, even in a case where, as here, the articles permit a director to vote in respect of a contract in which he is interested (cl. 13 of the company's articles), if there is a sole director who, ex hypothesi, cannot declare the nature of his interest to a 'meeting' of the directors, a transaction of this sort is one which, being within the equitable rule forbidding self-dealing, can only be entered into by the director with the informed consent of the shareholders in general meeting. However, by a judgment delivered on 10 February 1995 ([1995] BCC 474), Lightman J, on an appeal

B   from the master upon the company's application for summary judgment, ruled that this was not the case. The judge held in substance that, for the purposes of reg. 84(1) of Table A and s. 317, the word 'meeting' must, in the case of a company having, as here, a sole director entitled to exercise all the powers of the board and to vote in respect of contracts in which he was interested, have a meaning different from its ordinary meaning of a 'coming together of more than one person' and could extend to a 'meeting' of that sole

C   director. He went on to observe that two different situations could arise (at p. 481B), namely:

> 'The sole director may hold a meeting attended by himself alone or he may hold a meeting attended by someone else, normally the company secretary. When holding the meeting on his own, he must still make the declaration to himself and have the statutory pause for thought, though it may be that the declaration does not have to be out loud, and he must record that he made the declaration in the minutes.

D   > The court may well find it difficult to accept that the declaration has been made if it is not so recorded. If the meeting is attended by anyone else, the declaration must be made out loud and in the hearing of those attending, and again should be recorded. In this case, if it is proved that the declaration was made, the fact that the minutes do not record the making of the declaration will not preclude proof of its making. In either situation the language of the section must be given full effect:

E   > there must be a declaration of the interest.'

There was no appeal against that judgment and it is accepted by both the counsel before me that the ruling made by the judge is to be regarded as the determination of a point of law pursuant to RSC, O. 14A and is thus binding on the parties as a matter of res judicata. Accordingly, it is a ruling which I am bound to follow and apply even if I had doubts as to its correctness.

F   **The company and Wesumat**

The company was incorporated on 10 November 1983, for the purpose of selling and servicing in the UK vehicle washing machines manufactured in France by its holding company, a company called Neptune SA. This company owned virtually the whole of the company's issued share capital. There was another registered shareholder, Mr Perkins, who, it seems, had sold his shareholding in the company to Neptune SA prior to

G   the events giving rise to this action, although he still remains registered as the holder of a minute shareholding. No point is taken in regard to that shareholding and for the purposes of this action it can, in my judgment, be assumed that until the events to which I now come the company was the wholly owned subsidiary of Neptune SA. In 1993, prior to these events, the sole directors of the company were the chairman of Neptune SA, a gentleman called M Miossec, who gave evidence before me, and the defendant. Neptune

H   SA was in turn a subsidiary of a company called IPIC. A co-subsidiary of IPIC was a company incorporated in Germany which I shall call Wesumat GmbH. That company also manufactured vehicle washing machines (although not truck and bus washing machines) and, like Neptune SA, had a wholly owned subsidiary in England, which I shall call Wesumat UK, for the purpose of selling and servicing its machines in the UK. At all times material to this action the chairman of Wesumat GmbH was a gentleman called Herr Decker and the managing director of Wesumat UK was a gentleman called

Mr Don Phillips. Both these gentlemen gave evidence before me. Prior to the events of   A
1993 the Wesumat companies and the Neptune companies traded (somewhat surprisingly
given that they were all subsidiaries of the same ultimate holding company) in
competition with and at arm's length from each other.

In April 1993 Neptune SA got into financial difficulties due, it seems, to a particular
loss-making plant and provisions of French law which made it difficult, if not impossible,
for that plant lawfully to be closed and its employees made redundant. Accordingly on   B
21 April 1993, it was placed by the French court into what has been described by the
parties to these proceedings as 'administration', being an insolvency procedure seemingly
not dissimilar from an English administration. During the summer of 1993 the court-
appointed administrator invited bids for the assets of Neptune SA. Wesumat GmbH
made a bid for all these assets, including, therefore, Neptune SA's shareholding in the
company, which was accepted by the administrator and approved by the French court
by order made on 29 September 1993. The price to be paid for the various assets was to   C
be determined by an expert. It appears that there has been a delay in the determination
by such expert of the price which has resulted in a delay in the formal transfer of the
various assets, including Neptune SA's shares in the company, to Wesumat GmbH.
Nevertheless, it appears clear on the evidence before me that as from 29 September 1993,
the company falls for all practical purposes to be regarded as a wholly owned subsidiary
of Wesumat GmbH, that company having full authority to exercise all voting and other   D
powers attached to Neptune's SA's shares in the company. I am told that a formal
transfer of these shares to Wesumat GmbH is expected in the next few weeks.

The defendant's service contract

The defendant was recruited to take over as managing director of the company towards
the end of 1990 by Mr Railton, who has some form of association with the ultimate   E
shareholders of IPIC. Mr Railton also gave evidence before me. The terms of the
defendant's employment with the company were at all material times regulated by a
written service contract between the defendant and the company dated 1 January 1991.
So far as material for the purposes of this action, the service contract provided as follows:

(1)   The defendant was to serve the company in the capacity of managing director until
the contract was terminated by either party giving not less than six months' notice   F
in writing (cl. 2 and cl. 3(a)).

(2)   The defendant was to devote the whole of his time, attention and abilities during
normal business hours to the business of the company and was to serve the
company 'well and faithfully' (cl. 3(b) and (c)).

(3)   The defendant was to be entitled to a fixed salary of £45,000 per annum increasing
each year in line with inflation (cl. 4(a) and (c)) and to a bonus each year of not   G
less than five per cent of the company's pre-tax annual profits (cl. 4(d)).

(4)   The defendant was to be entitled to 25 working days' holiday per annum but was
not entitled to payment in lieu of any holidays not taken nor was he entitled to
carry forward his holiday entitlement from one year to the next unless agreed
between him and the chairman of the board (cl. 6).

(5)   The company was entitled to terminate the defendant's employment without notice   H
in the event, inter alia, of any wilful default by the defendant in the discharge of
his duties thereunder or any wilful breach by him of any of the terms of his service
contract (cl. 9(a)).

(6)   The defendant was 'forthwith' to resign his directorship if at any time his
employment came to an end.

A   The service agreement was varied in two respects, namely:

(1)   By a letter from the company to the defendant signed by M Miossec dated 18 January 1991, it was agreed that, in addition to the bonus provided for under the terms of the service contract, the defendant was to be entitled to a further bonus equal to one per cent of sales (exclusive of VAT).

(2)   By a letter from the company signed by M Miossec on 5 October 1992, it was
B   agreed that the period of notice would be extended to 12 months if the company gave notice of termination 'further to group restructuring'. This letter concluded by stating 'If payment is made in lieu of notice then your full salary, benefits, commissions and bonuses shall be paid upon such notice being given'.

Events leading to the termination of the service contract

C   I now deal with events which began in the autumn of 1993 following the takeover of the company by Wesumat GmbH and which culminated in the termination in January 1994 of the defendant's employment with the company.

The period in the immediate aftermath of the takeover was one of considerable uncertainty so far as concerns the affairs of the company. Herr Decker has told me (and I accept) that he found the affairs of Neptune SA in complete disorder and was unable
D   throughout that year to make any final decisions about what was to be done. However, at an early stage, it appears to have been decided that Neptune SA would cease producing car washing equipment (but might continue to produce truck and bus washing equipment) and that the business or remaining business of the company would by some means or another be merged with the business of or taken over by Wesumat UK. This inevitably entailed close and continual contact between the defendant as managing director of the company and Mr Don Phillips as managing director of Wesumat UK.

E   There is little, if any, dispute between the parties as to what happened in the period from October 1993 until towards the end of November. There was a meeting in France at the premises of Neptune SA attended, amongst others, by Herr Decker and the defendant at which the defendant sought information, which Herr Decker was unable to give, as to Wesumat's intentions concerning the company. This was followed on 19 October 1993, by a meeting between the defendant and Mr Don Phillips at the company's
F   offices in Southampton. There were a number of matters discussed at that meeting in consequence of which Mr Phillips on 25 October 1993, sent a fax to Herr Decker which was copied to the defendant setting out his initial thoughts for an ultimate merger of the business of the company and that of Wesumat UK. It can, I think, fairly be said that at this stage and, indeed, at all times down to about the end of November or the beginning of December the relations between the defendant and Mr Phillips were cordial. The defendant was concerned – and rightly so – on a number of matters concerning the future
G   prospects for the company, including in particular its solvency and what was to happen to its staff. So far as the former was concerned, the defendant's major concern was that, although on paper the company was perfectly solvent and, indeed, had a substantial credit balance at its bank, a large part of its assets consisted of sums due to it from its parent company which had, of course, by this stage, gone into administration. Those sums were roughly cancelled out by other sums owed by the company to Neptune SA
H   but all the parties were at this stage uncertain as to whether set-off applied. Another source of worry was the transfer of staff. This would in the normal way be achieved by a simple transfer of Neptune staff into the employment of Wesumat. However, this would have to be on the same terms as they were employed by the company by reason of the Transfer of Undertakings Regulations ('the regulations'). This was something which Mr Phillips felt could not be done because in many, if not most, cases Wesumat's level of pay to its own workforce was significantly below that being paid to the company's staff. The

plan which soon emerged to deal with this was to make all the company's staff redundant   A
and then for Wesumat to make fresh offers of employment to such of the staff as
Wesumat wished to retain. The defendant stated in his evidence before me that he was
concerned that such a scheme would fall foul of the regulations and could result in
considerable liability being incurred by the company, although I have to say that such
concern does not appear to me to be reflected in any of the contemporaneous documents.

It may be convenient if at this stage I made certain observations as to certain of the   B
witnesses.

Herr Decker

He gave evidence that right up until the end of 1993 and beyond he had so little
information concerning the affairs of the Neptune group that he was unable to come to
any final decision as to what would happen with the company nor to answer the various
questions or give the various confirmations which the defendant had (entirely   C
understandably as he conceded) raised during this period.

Whilst I am prepared broadly to accept this evidence, it seems to me that (a) to some
extent Herr Decker must be exaggerating and (b) it would obviously have been more
helpful if Herr Decker had, in answer to the defendant's queries, spelt this out. Instead,
as can be seen from my findings below, he ignored the defendant's perfectly legitimate
request for information contained in his faxed letter dated 2 December, 1993, for nearly   D
three weeks. And when he did respond to that fax, he did so in an abrupt and somewhat
unhelpful way. Herr Decker explained that he was irritated by what he felt was the
defendant's constant request for information and confirmations which he, the defendant,
knew could not be given. It seems to me that the real reason was that Herr Decker
regarded the defendant as being no more than one of his employees who was expected to
do what he was told forthwith and without question. That is, of course, to ignore the
special role and responsibility of a managing director of an English limited company.   E

Mr Don Phillips

I found Mr Don Phillips to be an entirely truthful and on the whole reliable witness.
He himself was the first to admit that on matters of detail, such as whether particular
conversations took place at a meeting or on the telephone and, if at a meeting, where
exactly the meeting was held, his recollection was not necessarily entirely accurate,   F
although he insisted that he had a good recollection of exactly what was said in the course
of a given conversation. It seems to me that in certain respects his recollection of what
exactly was said in particular conversations may be less than perfect.

The defendant

As to the defendant himself, he is clearly a most intelligent and capable person with a
highly personable personality. Up to a point I found his evidence to be entirely truthful   G
and reliable. However, when it came to the crucial matters in question in this action,
namely the reasons why he took the actions which he did on 5 January and the events
leading up to it, I have to say that found his evidence less than convincing. His answers
to many, if not most, of the questions addressed to him in relation to these matters were
peppered, in my judgment, with prevarication and evasiveness. And his explanations,
when he was forced to give them, were in many, if not most, cases unconvincing. A   H
simple example suffices at this juncture. The money which was in dispute was withdrawn
by banker's draft on the afternoon of 5 January. The defendant had himself written the
letter to the company's bank authorising the drawing of that draft in his favour. Whilst
giving his evidence in chief I enquired of the defendant why he had gone to all this trouble
when he could simply have written a cheque in his favour drawn on the company's bank
account. The answer to this question was obvious, as he was ultimately forced to concede

A   in cross-examination, namely that he wanted to ensure that he was paid before the company, in the shape of Mr Don Phillips, found out about it and took steps to prevent the payment by stopping the cheque. But this was not the reply that he gave to me. He told me that he had done it this way because his solicitors, Innes & Co, had suggested that it be done this way, that they did not explain why nor did he ask, that it seemed 'like a good idea to me' and that 'we did not take the matter any further'. I am afraid that I
B   find that answer evasive in the extreme and symptomatic of the sort of answers which the defendant gave on numerous occasions in regard to the events of 5 January and the events leading up to it.

To return to the narrative, throughout the remainder of October and November there were a number of communications and discussions between the defendant and Mr Don Phillips regarding the affairs of the company into the details of which I need not go. On a number of occasions the defendant, again entirely properly, sought advice on various
C   matters, including his responsibilities as a director of the company, from both the company's solicitors, White & Bowker, and its auditors, Marshall Roche. At this stage there had been, so far as the evidence before me went, no or little discussion as to the defendant's own personal future once the merger or takeover was completed. The defendant appears to have been under the impression that he would be offered the position of managing director of Wesumat UK on the basis that Mr Phillips, who he
D   thought was nearing retirement age, might be persuaded to step down and become executive chairman. But this was not a proposition that appears to have had much appeal, if any, to Mr Phillips himself. It does appear, however, that by the middle of November the defendant was becoming concerned as to his own future since an attendance note of Mr Short of White & Bowker records that on 15 November 1993 he discussed with the defendant 'suitable alternative employment and (briefly) constructive dismissal'. Significantly in that same conversation Mr Short records that he advised the
E   defendant as to a possible conflict of interest and suggested that he seek the consent of the company if he wanted to take advice from Mr Short in his personal capacity.

On 22 November M Miossec resigned as a director of the company leaving the defendant as sole director. The defendant was unhappy with this position, primarily, it seems, because it entailed that he would have to shoulder alone the responsibility if it should transpire that the company was trading whilst insolvent. He wanted Mr Phillips to become a director, but Mr Phillips refused to do so. He gave in evidence two grounds.
F   The first was that by so doing he might be placing himself in a position in which there was a conflict between his duties as managing director of Wesumat and his duties to the company as one of its directors. Secondly, that he knew so little about the affairs of the company and was concerned that, if there should be an insolvent liquidation, he should not be left having to answer to angry unpaid trade creditors. The latter reason I find entirely convincing. It admittedly left the defendant in a difficult position. The suggestion
G   was made that he should appoint as director one of his own staff, and at one point one of them, Mr Colin Russell, was suggested and took advice from the company's solicitors as to his duties as director. But in the end he refused to accept the appointment in case it should impede his ability to find alternative employment in the future. In any event, this was not what the defendant desired. He wanted, as he told me and I entirely accept, a representative of the shareholders to be on the board.

H   As I have said, up to now relations between the defendant and Mr Don Phillips were reasonably cordial. That relation became strained, however, and commenced to break down from about the end of November 1993. It had been agreed between Mr Phillips and the defendant that, in view of the rumours which were now rife as to the impending demise of the company, there should be an address to the staff as to what was going on and what was to happen to them in the future. On 29 November 1993, Mr Phillips sent to the defendant a draft of his intended speech to the staff. The defendant thought it was

too negative in tone and faxed it back with a number of suggested amendments. Mr   A
Phillips took strong exception to this and telephoned back angrily rejecting the suggested
amendments. Whatever the rights and wrongs about this, I have no doubt that by this
time the defendant realised that he could not work amicably with Mr Don Phillips, and
it was likely, therefore, that he would have ultimately to seek employment elsewhere.

On 2 December 1993, the defendant telephoned Mr Dunn of White & Bowker, who
was their employment law expert. By his attendance note Mr Dunn records that he was   B
asked by the defendant to advise whether if the directors were not given adequate
information to perform their duties this could amount to constructive dismissal, but gave
a negative answer. The following day Mr Short of White & Bowker felt it right to write a
letter to the defendant reminding him of his duties as director. The letter stated that he
must always be able to demonstrate that the actions which he had taken as a director
were in the company's best interests (although they might also be in his own personal
interests) and that, if that put the defendant in an untenable position, he would have no   C
alternative but to offer his resignation as director. On the same day by a separate letter,
Mr Short advised the defendant that, following the resignation of M Miossec as director,
there were two courses open to him. The first was to appoint a new director. The second
was for the defendant to resign as company secretary and for a new secretary to be
appointed. In the event it was this latter course that was adopted by the subsequent
appointment of Mr Peter Phillips, the company's internal accountant, as company   D
secretary. These two letters of advice were written one day after the defendant had, as I
have already mentioned, sent to Herr Decker in Germany a fax asking for information
and instructions as regards a variety of matters, including who should be appointed a
further director of the company.

The next event of importance with which I must deal was a meeting that took place on
16 December 1993, between the defendant and Mr Don Phillips. There were quite
apparently a variety of matters concerning the affairs of the company that were discussed   E
at that meeting. One of them was a problem that had arisen because in error the factory
in France had produced parts for 30 more vehicle washing machines than had been
expected and Herr Decker was insisting that the company seek to dispose of these
machines on the UK market. The defendant regarded this as being an impossible task,
not least because in the light of the previous information given, the sales team had been
telling customers that Neptune machines were now discontinued. He politely made his   F
views on this subject known in a fax to M Miossec sent three days later and copied to Mr
Phillips. Taking on board the points made in that fax the decision was subsequently
made and communicated to the defendant by fax from Mr Phillips dated 22 December
1992, to produce from the relevant parts 12 'Euro Duo' machines instead. But the
defendant has told me in evidence, which again I entirely accept, that he did not regard
this as much comfort since those machines, being approximately double the price, were
even more difficult to sell than the original ones.   G

One of the other major matters discussed at the meeting was the defendant's own
future. Mr Phillips had previously suggested to the defendant that he might be offered
the position of general manager of Wesumat, but without a place on the board. At that
meeting Mr Phillips repeated this offer and outlined the terms. The defendant did not
find these terms appealing, not least because the remuneration package which he was
being offered was about one-half of his existing package. The defendant says that at the   H
meeting Mr Phillips agreed that he, the defendant, would be made redundant 'forthwith',
paid a year's salary in lieu of notice and then immediately re-engaged as a consultant on
the same remuneration terms as under his existing service contract. Mr Don Phillips
denies that there was even a discussion in this regard let alone an agreement. To an extent
both of these differing versions are supported by contemporaneous documents. On the
very day of the meeting Mr Phillips sent a three-page fax to Herr Decker which makes

A   reference to his having offered the defendant the position of general manager and to the fact that such did not appear to appeal to the defendant but makes no reference to the agreement alleged by the defendant. The defendant supports his version by a fax which he sent the following day to Mr Phillips in which the alleged agreement is referred to in para. 4. Mr Phillips did not formally reply to that fax denying the alleged agreement until a fax dated 31 December 1993, although he asserts that he did speak to the defendant denying the agreement prior to that time. On the defendant's fax of 17 December 1993,

B   Mr Phillips wrote, he tells me on the date when he received it, the words 'definitely *not* agreed' beside para. 4.

In my judgment the truth of this matter lies somewhere between the two versions. It is, in my judgment, highly unlikely that the defendant would have written in the terms that he did in para. 4 of his fax of 17 December if there had been no discussion whatsoever in regard to the matters there referred to. Furthermore the fact that, as appears from Mr

C   Phillips' fax to Herr Decker of 16 December, there clearly was discussion at that meeting concerning the defendant's existing service contract and the amount of notice required to terminate it, tends to suggest that it is likely that there was some discussion, at least, on this matter. In addition, it is to be noted that Mr Phillips' comment which he endorses on the defendant's fax is not 'not even discussed' but 'not agreed'. The likelihood, in my judgment, is that the sort of matters referred to in para. 4 were, indeed, raised by the

D   defendant at the meeting. At this stage, in my judgment, the defendant had clearly decided that it was extremely unlikely he was going to go over to Wesumat once the merger took place and his main aim at that stage was to maximise the money that he could obtain from the company when he left. It is, however, in my judgment inconceivable that any actual agreement could have been reached with Mr Phillips at that meeting. Mr Phillips, as the defendant well knew, had not even seen let alone obtained advice in regard to the

E   terms of the defendant's service contract. Moreover the defendant himself in evidence conceded that the proposal for him to be re-employed as a consultant was an integral part of what was proposed – and that the full terms of such consultancy had yet to be negotiated. In my judgment the defendant's fax of 17 December 1993, was the first move by the defendant in his plan to leave the company with the maximum amount of compensation.

F   As appears from a letter from Mr Dunn of White & Bowker dated 17 December 1993, on the same day as his meeting with Mr Phillips, the defendant telephoned White & Bowker seeking, so it would appear, advice in general terms as to how his entitlement under his service contract could reasonably be calculated on the basis, as appears from that letter, that the same was being done by agreement with 'the shareholders' representative'. No less than three times in that letter it was emphasised that whatever he was proposing to do should be confirmed and agreed with that representative. On the

G   same day, that is 17 December 1993, the defendant prepared a fax to be sent to Mr Phillips setting out as 'guideline figures' amounts, which totalled just under £152,000 which he claimed. There are a number of copies of that fax disclosed on discovery. Each has marked on it a notation to the effect that it had not been sent. The defendant asserts that it was faxed on 24 December with a re-fax to Mr Phillips of his other fax of 17 December (which as I have already observed was actually sent) which had not yet been answered. I cannot accept this evidence. Mr Phillips denies receipt of any such fax and it

H   is, in my judgment, extremely unlikely that the defendant would have sent it to him on 24 December. The fax stated that the figures would have to be checked with 'our accountant/lawyer'. In fact by 24 December the figures had indeed been checked, in a general sort of way, by Ms Booth of White & Bowker who had on 21 December 1993, written back querying in certain material respects the figures given. Having received that letter it seems to me unlikely to the point of being inconceivable that the defendant would have sent the fax to Mr Phillips in the same form as he had originally drafted it on 17 December.

On 20 December 1993, various meetings were held with all the staff, other than the sales staff, of the company to explain the position and the future prospects. Mr Phillips had on 18 December faxed to the defendant a revised version of the speech which he wanted the defendant to deliver. The first such meeting was with the southern engineering staff. The engineering staff of the company, numbering approximately 52, were vital for the company's business, since it was they who were servicing the machines installed by the company. This was a lucrative business for the purpose of which it was necessary to have a large quantity of spare parts. The exact date of the transfer of this business to Wesumat had not yet been decided. The following day at a meeting which was to be held between Mr Phillips and Herr Decker in Germany it was in fact decided to retain this business in the company until at least the end of March 1994. This was not known on 20 December and the defendant asserts that he was not informed of this decision until a conversation with Mr Phillips on 29 December. Mr Phillips says that he told the defendant of his decision soon after he came back from Germany on 22 December. Whilst I prefer Mr Phillips' evidence in relation to this, I do not think it matters. For at all events the defendant was aware that the servicing side of the company's business would have to be retained at least until the end of February 1994, when the various maintenance contracts were due for renewal. Thus the defendant was well aware that the engineering staff and the spare parts for servicing machines would have to be retained at least until then. In the event, it is common ground that the meeting with the engineering staff went very well. Mr Phillips addressed the staff and, to the defendant's relief, discarded the draft speech which he had prepared. There were a number of questions to which satisfactory answers appear to have been given. There was, apparently, another meeting later that day with the northern engineering staff. There is no evidence to suggest that this meeting went any less well. Later that day there was also a meeting with the administration staff, most of whom were in any event going to be made redundant by the end of the year.

The events of 22 December 1993, represent something of a watershed. In the first place there was a meeting arranged in the morning with the sales staff, the object being to persuade them to transfer to Wesumat. This meeting went disastrously badly by all accounts. Mr Phillips was not there and instead sent his sales director, Mr Ian Kemp. According to the defendant – and I entirely accept this – without consulting with him Mr Kemp announced to the staff that they were to be made redundant at the end of the year, which led the sales team, as the defendant put it, 'silently to accuse me of leading them like lambs to the slaughter'. Mr Kemp was unable to tell the sales staff anything more about their prospects of employment with Wesumat other than that the prices for the machines would be up by 20 per cent, he was not sure who was going to get any offers and when, and any offer would be bound to be on terms of remuneration less than they were presently receiving. The upshot of the meeting was that the sales team took off almost en masse to join a competitor, namely the vehicle washing machine division of a company called May Holdings Ltd trading as 'Brushwash', which was expanding at that time its operations in the UK. The sales team must have been thinking of joining Brushwash before that date. The board minutes of May Holdings of the same day record that two of their directors 'were currently in negotiation to recruit a number of Neptune's senior staff for Brushwash', and Mr Round, a director of that company who gave evidence for the defendant, stated that the negotiations would have commenced some time before that date. On the same day the defendant received the fax from Herr Decker to which I have already referred. This fax was abrupt in its terms and told the defendant that he was to regard Mr Phillips as the shareholders' representative and that he was to obey his instructions without 'discussions and handwritten comments'. He also on the

A   same day received a fax from Mr Phillips telling him that he must make every effort to sell what had now become the 12 Euro Duo machines which, as already stated, the defendant felt to be an impossible task.

On the afternoon of 22 December the defendant decided to consult his own solicitors. He telephoned Miss Hoskins of Innes & Co. Her advice is confirmed in a letter dated 30 December 1993. The first paragraph sets out Miss Hoskins' advice as to the payment to

B   which he would be entitled if what is referred to therein as a 'redundancy notice' were to be given to him. The next paragraph sets out Miss Hoskins' advice to the effect that he would not be entitled to any payment if he obtained a new job before such notice was given. The defendant was asked in cross-examination why he should be seeking such advice on 22 December, but was unable to give any explanation. He indeed questioned whether he had, indeed, sought advice on this matter on 22 December. In my judgment the letter of 30 December makes it quite clear that he had done so. The reason, in my

C   judgment, is equally clear. On any basis he had by this time twice been approached by Mr McMillan, the managing director of May Holdings, with a view to offering him a senior position with Brushwash. The first time had been in the summer of 1993, when the defendant had said he was not interested as he was happy in his present employment. The next approach came when it became apparent that the company was going to be 'wound up'. When exactly this was was never made clear in the evidence, but it appears

D   it must have been shortly before Christmas. Mr McMillan himself was not available to give evidence at this trial being on the high seas in a yacht. Mr Railton, in evidence admissible under the Civil Evidence Act, recounted a telephone conversation which he had with Mr McMillan in which Mr McMillan, according to Mr Railton, told him that he had offered a job to the defendant prior to Christmas. However, in a letter dated 11 May 1995, which Mr McMillan wrote to Mr Railton following that telephone conversation, he was somewhat less specific as to when the actual offer of employment

E   was made. The defendant asserts that no actual offer of employment was made to him until by letter dated 24 January 1994. The defendant accepts that an approach was made to him prior to Christmas, which must, in my judgment, have coincided with the approach made to the sales team. However, he is equally adamant that his response to that approach was that, since he was still a director of the company, he was not at liberty to discuss the matter with Mr McMillan. In the absence of Mr McMillan's evidence being tested by cross-examination, I would give the defendant the benefit of the doubt in this

F   regard. It does not, however, in my judgment matter very much. The fact remains that by 22 December 1993, the defendant, who had by now twice been approached on behalf of Brushwash and whose sales team had been recruited by Brushwash, must have been only too aware that the extreme probability was that, once he left the company, he was likely to be offered a position with Brushwash, as, indeed, he was. In my judgment everything that occurred on and after 22 December 1993, points to the fact that the

G   defendant was now intent on leaving the company at the earliest opportunity in order to join Brushwash but wanted to ensure that, before so doing, he was paid the maximum amount of compensation.

The following day without reference to or consultation with Mr Phillips the defendant sent out a circular to the staff. Mr Phillips says that he did not receive a copy of that circular until one was received by him from an anonymous source in the post on 4 January 1994. The defendant says that a copy was sent to Mr Phillips. This was never

H   put to Mr Phillips in cross-examination and I wholly reject it. The explanation for the sending out of that circular given by the defendant is obscure. He said that since the meetings with staff on 20 December 1993, he had been bombarded with questions from the staff which required answers and he felt that the best way to do it was to set out the various questions that had been asked with the answers in a circular to the staff. I find this explanation difficult to accept given that the only relevant staff now were the

engineering staff (the sales staff had already gone to Brushwash and the administrative   A
staff were, in any event, going to be made redundant). The meetings with the engineers
had by all accounts gone well and all the questions raised at the meetings by all accounts
were satisfactorily answered. The defendant asserts that the object of this letter was to
give accurate factual information to the staff. Yet an analysis of the letter shows that it is
riddled with inaccuracies. The defendant is, as I have said, a person who strikes me as
being highly intelligent and articulate. The letter is itself in various express and sometimes
subtle ways extremely disparaging of Wesumat. In para. 12 there is set out a list of all the   B
major firms in the UK carrying on the car washing machine business to which staff were
invited to look for alternative employment. Brushwash is given a glowing testimonial. I
have no doubt that the purpose of this letter was to dissuade staff from joining Wesumat
and persuade them instead to join Brushwash, which is the company which the defendant,
as I have already said, anticipated would shortly be employing him.

On 24 December the defendant again consulted Mr Short of White & Bowker.   C
According to Mr Short's attendance note, the advice which was given to the defendant
was that the matters of which he then complained did not justify his resigning.

M Miossec gave evidence to the effect that the defendant was constantly in this period
on the telephone to him complaining about the actions that were being taken, but had
been told that he should, in effect, knuckle down and co-operate. On 27 December 1993,
M Miossec wrote to the defendant a letter which makes it clear that he had understood   D
at that time from the defendant that he was leaving the company. On 29 December 1993,
Mr Marshall of Marshall Roche wrote, referring to a recent telephone conversation with
the defendant, reminding him of his duties as director and strongly recommending that
he obtain clear instructions from the shareholders before taking any further action which
might prejudice the future of the company. The letter went on to give advice in general
terms as to how stock might be disposed of. On the same day the defendant sent a fax to
Mr Phillips stating that he proposed to take steps to dispose of assets, in particular 'some   E
machine stocks', because the advice which he had received was that he would obtain
greater revenue from 'selling off certain items now rather than waiting for a liquidator
and that this would be the responsible path to follow'. I can see nothing in Mr Marshall's
letter which even remotely amounts to such advice. The fact of the matter is that, as the
defendant himself confirmed in his evidence, the spare parts in question would only be of
any real use to a person who was going to take over the maintenance contracts. This is   F
something that would not be known until the end of February, when the maintenance
contracts were going to be renewed. And in any event, the defendant was well aware that
it was Wesumat, the company's sole shareholders, who were intent on taking over that
business. It is difficult in the circumstances to know why the defendant sent a fax in these
terms to Mr Phillips. It may be that he was seeking to provoke Mr Phillips into dismissing
him, so that he could then obtain what he thought would be substantial compensation
(he had not yet been advised that any earnings made in the year during which notice was   G
to be given would have to be taken into account in mitigation of his damages). It may be
that this was, at the time, intended to be the first step towards disposing of the spare
parts in favour of Brushwash and thus enabling them to take over the servicing business.
The latter is lent support by the fact that the defendant on the same day prepared circulars
to be sent to, inter alia, Brushwash, offering the spare parts for sale, although these faxes
were never in fact sent. The predictable response of Mr Phillips by fax of the same day   H
was to ask the defendant to take no action concerning the disposal of the assets since, as
it was put, all were required for the company's operations. The same fax indicated that a
decision had been made (the defendant says communicated for the first time) to retain
the company as a legal entity pro tem. The fax enclosed a proposed draft letter to staff
which indicated that the service operations side of the business was to continue into 1994.
The defendant responded by fax of the same date still threatening to sell certain assets,

A   asking for the 'German guarantees' (this refers to confirmation in writing that the intercompany debt would be written-off) and refusing to send the letter to staff until this had been done. I need not comment on the various other faxes that passed that day.

On 30 December 1993, there was a lengthy conversation between the defendant and Mr Phillips. Mr Phillips thought that this conversation had taken place at a meeting but was prepared to accept that it might have been, as the defendant asserted, on the
B   telephone. The terms of that conversation were confirmed in a fax sent by Mr Phillips to Mr Fitzgerald the following day. That fax made it quite clear that he did not agree to the defendant being made immediately redundant and paid a year's salary. On the same day the defendant consulted Innes & Co and spoke to Mr Sears of that firm. He agreed to try and arrange a conference with counsel for Tuesday, 4 January 1994 (the counsel was in fact Mr Roberts who appears in this action for the defendant). Mr Sears' attendance note records that he prepared on that day a statement of the defendant and instructions to
C   counsel. The instructions to counsel are illuminating. What was sought essentially was advice in relation to constructive dismissal and, as regards alternative employment, the 'need to determine current employment by constructive dismissal with little or no notice without jeopardising claims for constructive dismissal'. The tone of these instructions is highly corroborative, in my judgment, of the fact that by this time the defendant was intent on leaving the company as soon as possible so as to join Brushwash and was concerned that he should be able to do so without jeopardising any claims that he might
D   have to compensation. That is corroborated further by his statement in which he stated: 'I fear that my position is untenable and feel that now I have been constructively dismissed. I am hopeful of obtaining other employment soon but want to assure myself of all my rights under my service contract.' The conference with Mr Roberts was duly held on 4 January 1994. The attendance note of that conference records that the gist of the advice was that, whilst the defendant had a case for constructive dismissal, the
E   damages which he could claim would be small if he were to be re-employed within a short while since he would have to bring in his earnings from his new employment in mitigation of those damages. Counsel went on to advise that 'the best effective tactical move' was for the defendant to convene a board meeting, terminate his contract of employment and pay himself out the amount due under the contract, namely '12 months' notice plus any accrued bonuses or other amounts that he is entitled to'. Counsel went on to advise that he should hold the meeting and pass a resolution as soon as possible but not resign as
F   director until the moneys had been taken from the company's bank account.

The defendant then proceeded with speed to act on that advice. By this time I should say the defendant had already decided, according to the evidence which he gave me, that his employment by the company should be, to use a neutral phrase, terminated. He gave evidence to the effect that, being left alone on New Year's Eve, he had carefully contemplated what in this regard would be in the best interests of the company, and tried
G   to put himself in the position of Mr Phillips as a reasonable director of the company. I reject that evidence completely. The defendant did not strike me as a person who would be capable of carrying out such a dispassionate consideration of matters which vitally concerned his own personal interests. Furthermore, such a dispassionate consideration of what was in the interests of the company is not consistent with the tone of the instructions to counsel which had been prepared on his instructions to Mr Sears on the same day, nor with his own statement likewise prepared. I am prepared to accept that the
H   defendant on New Year's Eve made the final decision to leave the company. But he did so, in my judgment, in his own interests and not having in any dispassionate manner considered the interests of the company.

Following the advice given by counsel events moved relatively swiftly. On the morning of 4 January 1994, the defendant had sent a somewhat truculent fax to Mr Phillips which included a suggestion that they should have a meeting on either 5, 6 or 7 January. By this

time, of course, Mr Phillips had received the staff circular of 23 December and decided   A
to sack him. He tried to contact the defendant to arrange a meeting for the following day
but was unable to do so. Accordingly he sent a fax seeking a meeting at the defendant's
office the following afternoon. The defendant faxed back to say that he was not going to
be there as he had taken a previous fax cancelling a meeting 'at face value'. What of
course the defendant did not say was where he in fact intended to be the following
afternoon, namely at the company's bank at Cheapside armed with a letter of authority
entitling him to draw over £100,000 from the company's bank account. On the morning   B
of 5 January 1994, he convened with Mr Peter Phillips a board meeting at which he
signed and got Mr Phillips to countersign as company secretary the resolutions which are
in dispute in this action. The first was a resolution that the defendant's employment with
the company be terminated with immediate effect. The second was that the defendant be
paid various sums totalling £100,892.62 'in accordance with his contract and in lieu of
notice'. Prior to the meeting he had already prepared and, so his evidence goes, signed a   C
letter instructing the company's bank to issue a draft in his favour in the sum resolved
upon. The defendant then appears to have cleared out his office and departed for the
bank to withdraw the draft. In fact the bank was not satisfied with the letter and required
him to sign a further instruction in the bank's standard form for the issue of the draft.
The draft was then promptly deposited by the defendant in his bank account. Not a word
about all this was communicated to Mr Phillips, despite the plethora of faxes which had
previously been passing between them. The defendant did not even promptly fax a copy   D
of the resolutions to Mr Phillips. Instead he merely posted it to Mr Phillips by recorded
delivery post on 6 January 1994 (a Thursday). On the same day he did send a fax to Mr
Phillips but this fax merely said that he had 'put a letter in the post to you which will be
self-explanatory and will negate the need for your proposed meeting'. That fax said
nothing whatever about the events of 5 January. I asked the defendant why he had taken
this course and his answer was that he had been advised to do so by Innes & Co. I regard
this as an unsatisfactory answer. In my judgment the reason is obvious. Whilst the   E
defendant had obviously been advised that he had to advise at some stage Mr Phillips as
the representative of the shareholders as to what had occurred, he also desired to delay
for so long as reasonably possible the time when they would find out. The letter was not
in fact received until the following Monday.

In the event Mr Phillips was unable to meet up with the defendant on 5 January 1994
and came again to the company's offices on 6 January 1994. He came accompanied by   F
Mr Dutton who on 4 January he had retained as a fill-in for the defendant once he was
dismissed. On 6 January at an EGM of the company which Mr Phillips purported to
hold, Mr Phillips on behalf of the company's shareholders terminated or purported
summarily to terminate the defendant's contract of employment, based mainly on the
defendant's having sent out the circular to staff of 23 December. He is alleged to have
told the staff after the meeting that he had been instructed to do this before Christmas.
However, this was never put to Mr Phillips and the witnesses who gave evidence on this   G
matter on behalf of the defendant were, it seems to me, prepared to accept that what Mr
Phillips may well have said was that the sacking of the defendant was something that
should have been done before Christmas. This would be an oblique reference to the staff
circular of 23 December. It is, in my judgment, plain on the evidence that it was not until
Mr Phillips received in the post on 4 January a copy of the staff circular that any decision
was made to terminate the defendant's employment.

After this, I am afraid, over-long review of the facts, I turn to consider the different   H
bases upon which the claim against the defendant is made.

Breach of fiduciary duty

The law in this regard is well established, and can for present purposes be summarised
as follows. A director owes fiduciary duties to his company. In consequence as a matter

A of the general law he is not permitted to enter into a transaction with his company in which he has a personal interest save with the informed consent of the shareholders given in general meeting. If he does so, the transaction is voidable at the suit of the company. This rule, often referred to as the 'self-dealing rule', is an application of the general principle of trust law which forbids a trustee from profiting from the trust and from placing himself in a position in which his duty to his beneficiaries conflicts with his own personal interest. It is a rule founded on the proposition that, human nature being what
B it is, it would be too much to expect any fiduciary in regard to such a transaction to be truly able to place the interests of his beneficiaries above his own personal interests. The rule is a strict and inflexible rule of equity which, if breached, automatically entitles the beneficiaries (subject to defences such as laches, acquiescence or impossibility of restitutio in integrum) to have the transaction set aside without enquiry as to whether it was in fact on proper and fair terms (see *Aberdeen Railway Company v Blaikie Bros* (1854) 1 Macq
C 461 per Lord Cranworth at p. 472: 'So inflexible is the rule that no enquiry on the subject is permitted'). However, as already observed the articles of association of most companies exclude the self-dealing rule and permit a director to contract with the company provided, generally, that certain formalities are complied with. Such a provision is reg. 84 of Table A (which is incorporated into the articles of association of the company) which permits a director to enter into a contract with a company in which he has an interest provided that he declares the nature of his interest to a meeting of the directors in accordance with
D what is now s. 317 of the *Companies Act* 1985. As already mentioned, Lightman J has in this case held that these provisions apply even in the case of a sole director who, prima facie, cannot declare his interest to a 'meeting' of the directors since in those circumstances the 'meeting' is regarded as sufficiently constituted by the sole director alone (see [1995] BCC 474). I deal below with the question of whether a sufficient such declaration was made in this case. For the purposes of considering this basis of claim I
E shall proceed on the assumption that it was.

Accordingly, although the transaction here in question was plainly within the self-dealing rule, it is a transaction which the defendant was not prohibited by the strict equitable rule from entering into. That, however, does not mean, in my judgment, that in causing the company to enter into the transaction, the defendant was absolved from discharging his duties owed as a director to the company. Indeed, the contrary was not argued. The legal position is in my judgment, well stated by Vinelott J in *Movitex Ltd v*
F *Bulfield & Ors* (1986) 2 BCC 99,403 at p. 99,432 as follows:

> 'The true principle is that if a director places himself in a position in which his duty to the company conflicts with his personal interest or his duty to another, the court will intervene to set aside the transaction without enquiring whether there was any breach of the director's duty to the company. That is an overriding principle of equity. The shareholders of the company, in formulating the articles, can exclude
G > or modify the application of this principle. In doing so they do not exempt the director from or from the consequences of a breach of a duty owed to the company.'

As to what the duty of a director to his company relevant for present purposes is, again there was no serious dispute before me. The general principles are, in my judgment, well set out in *Gower's Principles of Modern Company Law* (5th edn) at p. 553 in the following
H terms:

> 'In applying the general equitable principle to company directors four separate rules have emerged. These are: (1) that directors must act in good faith in what they believe to be the best interests of the company; (2) that they must not exercise the powers conferred upon them for purposes different from those for which they were conferred; (3) they must not fetter their discretion as to how they shall act;

and (4) that, without the informed consent of the company, they must not place   A
themselves in a position in which their personal interests or duties to other persons
are liable to conflict with their duties to the company.'

The last principle mentioned has, of course, been excluded in this case by the company's
articles. But the other three have not. For present purposes the most important of these
is the first. In that regard the passage immediately following that which I have cited is, in
my judgment, most helpful. It reads as follows: B

'1. *Acting in good faith*

In most cases compliance with the rule that directors must act honestly and in
good faith is tested on commonsense principles, the court asking itself whether it is
proved that the directors have not done what they honestly believe to be right, and
normally accepting that they have unless satisfied that they have not behaved as
honest men of business might be expected to act. Directors are required to act   C
'bona fide in what they consider – not what a court may consider – is in the
interests of the company . . .' (*Per* Lord Greene M.R. in *Re Smith & Fawcett Ltd.*
[1942] Ch. 304 at 306, C.A.). On the face of it, this duty is simply to display
subjective good faith. But, notwithstanding that it is for the directors and not the
court to consider what is in the interests of the company, they may breach that
duty notwithstanding that they have not acted with conscious dishonesty but have
failed to direct their minds to the question whether a transaction was in fact in the   D
interests of the company.'

The illustration given immediately after this passage is *Re W & M Roith Ltd* [1967] 1
WLR 432, where the court set aside a service contract between the company and its
director on being satisfied that the sole object of the contract was to make provision for
the director's widow.

In *Howard Smith Ltd v Ampol Petroleum* [1974] AC 821 the Privy Council (at p. 835)   E
cited the following passage from the speech of Viscount Finley in *Hindle v John Cotton
Ltd* (1919) 56 ScLR 625 at pp. 630–631) as the clearest statement of the law:

'Where the question is one of abuse of powers, the state of mind of those who
acted, and the motive from which they acted, are all important, and you may go
into the question of what their intention was, collecting from the surrounding
circumstances all the materials which genuinely throw light upon that question of   F
the state of mind of the directors as to show whether they were honestly acting in
discharge of their powers in the interests of the company or acting from some bye-
motive, possibly of personal advantage, or for any other reason.'

In the defence it is pleaded (para. 9(a)) that, by reason of the fact that the company's
articles permitted the defendant to enter into a contract with the company in which he
had a personal interest: G

'there was no conflict between the defendant's contract of employment and his
fiduciary duty as director of the plaintiff since the articles of association
contemplated that the defendant could, acting as a sole director, pass board
resolutions in relation to any transaction or arrangement concerning his contract
of employment, including without prejudice to the generality of the foregoing, the
termination of the contract and his financial entitlement pursuant thereto
consequent upon such a termination'.   H

If that is intended to be a contention that merely because the articles permit it the
conflict disappears, I emphatically reject such a contention which was, indeed, not argued
before me. As already illustrated, the mere fact that the strict equitable self-dealing rule
is excluded or modified, does not entail that the director is relieved from his other
obligations to the company, including his duty to act bona fide in the company's interests.

A   The conflict between a director's duty to the company and his personal interest does not disappear merely because the strict equitable rule against self-dealing has been excluded. On the contrary, if the conflict remains, there is a distinct danger that the director will be tempted, in breach of his duty to the company, to place his interests before that of the company. It is indeed, this very danger that gave rise to the strict equitable rule. When the rule has, as I see it, been excluded it becomes the duty of the court, in my judgment,

B   to scrutinise the transaction with great care so as to determine whether in carrying it out the director truly has managed to avoid the temptation of putting his personal interests before that of the company. This, in my judgment, emerges very clearly from the approach of the Court of Appeal in *Farrar v Farrars Ltd* (1888) 40 ChD 395 (dealing with a sale by a mortgagee to a company in which he was interested), the explanation of which is, in my judgment, correctly set out by Vinelott J in the *Movitex* case (above) at p. 99,434. Indeed, I venture to suggest that the greater the interest of the director and the

C   more apparent the conflict, the more 'jealously' (to use the word of Vinelott J) the court should look at the transaction. It is difficult to conceive of a matter where there is a greater conflict between the personal interest of a director and his duties to the company than the question of whether the director's own service contract should be terminated and, if so, upon what terms as to compensation. Further, the court's concern is bound to be even greater – and hence its scrutiny of the transaction even closer – where the transaction is determined by that director alone acting as sole director.

D   Applying these principles to the present case, I have no doubt that in acting as he did on 5 January the defendant was not acting in what he honestly and genuinely considered to be in the best interests of the company but rather was acting exclusively to further his own personal interests. The following, which is not intended to be an exhaustive list, points, in my judgment, inevitably to this conclusion:

(1)   It is quite apparent that the defendant knew full well that the action which he was
E   proposing to take on 5 January was action to which Mr Phillips as representing the sole shareholder of the company would be totally opposed. The defendant was not prepared in his evidence before me to admit this. The furthest he was prepared to go was to concede that he thought that his action *might* be opposed by Mr Phillips. In my judgment, this is evasive. Mr Phillips had on 31 January told him by fax that he was wholly opposed to the defendant's proposal (which had been put in the form of an agreement) to terminate his contract of employment and pay
F   himself a year's salary. Accordingly, it was quite apparent to the defendant that the shareholders, in the shape of Mr Phillips, did not regard the termination of his contract and the payment of compensation to him as being in *their* interests. By 5 January the defendant had already been advised by counsel that set-off would apply to the intercompany debts so that on that basis the company was at that time wholly solvent. If the action taken was not in those circumstances, what the shareholders considered to be in their best interests, it is impossible to see how the
G   defendant could properly have concluded that the action he was taking was in the best interests of the company.

(2)   The action was taken furtively and secretly behind the backs of the shareholders and with the object of facing them with a fait accompli which they might have some difficulty in setting aside. This is not the hallmark of a director bona fide and honestly carrying out his duties to the company but rather the reverse.
H   Significantly, the defendant in his evidence before me refused to concede what his real motivations in this regard were. I have already mentioned his lack of candour in relation to the obtaining of the bankers' draft. When asked why he did not communicate his decision to terminate his service contract to Mr Phillips, his only answer was that he had been advised that he had the authority to do so without consulting with Mr Phillips. Bearing in mind that he had been consulting with Mr

Phillips over the previous three months and, moreover, that one of his major A
complaints was the way he was being instructed by Mr Phillips in regard to the
discharge of his duties as managing director, I find this answer totally
unsatisfactory. Equally unsatisfactory, in my judgment, was his explanation, if
such it can be called, as to why he thought it right to send a copy of the resolutions
to Mr Phillips by post on 6 January instead of immediately on the previous day
informing Mr Phillips directly by fax or telephone of what he had done. His B
explanation, namely that he did this on the advice of Innes & Co but without being
able to offer any reason why that advice was given, is one which I find evasive and
entirely lacking in candour. In my judgment, a director honestly and bona fide
carrying out his duties to the company, which is what the defendant claims to have
done in the present case, does not act in the way that the defendant acted on 5
January.

(3)   The defendant on his own evidence acted in the way he did on 5 January on the C
basis of the advice which he had received from his own solicitors, Innes & Co,
following the conference with counsel. Indeed, his oral evidence was peppered with
references to 'we' decided this and 'we' decided that. The expression 'we' was
explained by the defendant as being a reference to himself on the advice of his
solicitors. But he finally accepted in evidence that what he had gone to Innes & Co
for was to seek advice as to how to get out of his service contract with little or no
notice and without jeopardising his claim for constructive dismissal, whilst D
ensuring that the company had money to meet his claim. Counsel had advised
taking the action which he did on 5 January on the basis that it was the 'best
tactical move' for the defendant. He accepted in evidence that he understood that
as meaning the best way from his point of view of getting out of his service contract
and being paid 12 months' notice, which was the end which he wished to achieve.
All this points, in my judgment, almost inevitably to the conclusion, which is E
already borne out by my findings of fact in the earlier part of this judgment as to
the defendant's motives from just before Christmas until the date of his departure,
that, in acting as he did on 5 January, the defendant was acting for the purpose of
promoting his own personal interests and not acting in any way the interests of the
company.

(4)   The defendant in evidence accepted that there was still a great deal of work to be F
done for the purpose of winding up the affairs of the company and that, if he left,
there would be a hole in the management of the company which would have
immediately to be filled. The interests of the company in those circumstances
dictate that before he left the defendant should have taken steps to ensure that that
hole was immediately filled. The natural such step to take would have been to
forewarn Mr Phillips so that he could find an immediate replacement – but this
was, of course, the last thing that the defendant wished to do because he G
appreciated that, if he did this, his plan would be discovered and stopped in its
tracks. At the very least, if he truly had the interests of the company in mind he
would have informed Mr Phillips of his departure immediately it had taken place.
This he did not do either. This again, in my judgment, points to the fact that the
last thing that the defendant truly had in mind on 5 January was the interests of
the company.

(5)   The defendant had in December sought and obtained from White & Bowker as H
solicitors for the company advice in general terms as to the payment that might
reasonably be made to him by way of compensation for termination of his
contract. However, that advice had been obtained on the basis that the termination
of his contract and the payment of compensation had been agreed between him
and the shareholders. As mentioned already, White & Bowker stressed in their

A   advice to the defendant that he should revert to the shareholders for confirmation
in regard to any amount to be paid to him. Notwithstanding that advice at no time
did the defendant go back to White & Bowker for their advice as solicitors for the
company in regard to the propriety of the action which he was proposing to take
in the altered circumstances that the same was being taken without the agreement
or, indeed, knowledge of the shareholders. The advice that would probably have
been given would have been that he should not do what he was proposing to do
B   but, if he found it intolerable any longer to continue as managing director of the
company, he should resign and seek to maintain a claim against the company for
constructive dismissal. But the defendant obviously did not wish to have advice of
this sort given to him since he had already been advised that, even assuming that
he had a claim for constructive dismissal, in monetary terms that claim would not
be worth much if, as he fully expected, he was shortly thereafter to be re-employed.
C   This is not the hallmark of a person who has at all in mind the interests of the
company as opposed to his own personal interests.

(6)   The amount which the defendant awarded to himself was plainly, in my judgment,
computed without the slightest regard to the interests of the company. The
defendant asserts that he regarded that sum as the minimum to which he was
entitled. Even assuming it was in the interests of the company to terminate the
defendant's contract of employment, I cannot see what possible interest of the
D   company could be served by the company then and there agreeing the amount of
compensation to be paid. The proper and obvious course would be to leave the
question of compensation to be negotiated subsequently as between the defendant
and his successors on the board of the company appointed by the shareholders. It
is plain, in my judgment, that the defendant awarded himself the amount in
question for his own personal benefit and having no regard whatever to the
E   interests of the company. Thus he awarded himself a whole year's salary without
(i) taking into account the possibility that as a matter of the true construction of
his service contract as amended the company's termination thereof might not in
the circumstances properly be regarded as being 'further to group restructuring' so
as to require only six months' notice; (ii) taking any legal advice from White &
Bowker in relation to that matter; and (iii) taking into account the fact that it was
highly likely that in the course of the year he would be obtaining alternative
F   employment. He awarded himself bonuses for 1993 and 1994 notwithstanding that
(i) the profit figure for 1993 had not yet been ascertained and (ii) not only ex
hypothesi had the 1994 figures not been obtained, but it was highly likely that
during that year there would be no or minimal sales/profits achieved by Neptune.
He further awarded himself holiday pay for untaken holidays in 1993 entirely
disingenuously stating in the minutes that that was 'per D Phillips fax of 08/12/93'.
G   In fact by that fax Mr Phillips stated in clear terms that he *objected* to moneys
being paid in lieu of holiday not taken by any staff, although he stated that he was
prepared to agree in certain circumstances to holiday untaken for 1993 being taken
in 1994. Further, the defendant neither made allowance for any tax that would be
payable and assessed upon the company on the sums which he awarded himself
nor took any advice from either the company's solicitors or its accountants in that
regard.

H   By his defence the defendant pleads a variety of matters which he contends justified
the actions which he took as being in the interests of the company. None of these, even if
established on the facts, which in most cases they were not, even remotely touches upon
the question of why it was in the interests of the company not merely to terminate his
service contract but also then and there to resolve on the quantum of any compensation.
I should add, in this regard, that reject the suggestion brought in by late re-amendment

that, by the last sentence of M Miossec's letter of 6 October 1992, the defendant was   A
conferred some form of contractual entitlement to be paid a year's salary on termination
without taking into account by way of mitigation any earnings made by him during the
year. I also reject the suggestion that that sentence amounted to a 'liquidated damages'
provision.

Even, however, as regards the decision to terminate the contract, it does not seem to
me that the reasons given either individually or collectively amount to a justification for   B
the defendant's action being regarded as being in the interests of the company, although
those reasons may well have been a justification in the defendant's mind for his resigning
and claiming damages for constructive dismissal (for which purpose they were originally
pleaded until the claim for constructive dismissal was abandoned). The defendant
towards the end of his evidence conceded in cross-examination that in his mind there was
really little distinction between resignation and termination by the company. He was
asked why, if he found, because of the matters complained of, that it was intolerable for   C
him to continue as managing director of the company, he did not simply resign. The
defendant's answer is interesting. He said that he saw the two 'going hand-in-hand' and
that he did not 'make a distinction between them'. This answer is, of course, itself entirely
disingenuous. The defendant had been advised by counsel that, if he resigned and claimed
damages for wrongful dismissal, he would be unlikely to obtain much, if any, damages
should he be re-employed shortly thereafter, as he fully expected to be. In cross-   D
examination the defendant was able to distil the reasons for his decision to terminate his
service contract under two main heads as follows:

(1) He felt he was neither wanted nor needed by the shareholders in the position of
     managing director and that, had they needed him, they would have at least given
     him the courtesy of saying that they did not have the information which he had
     been seeking.

     Whilst I can well see that this may have led the defendant to conclude that it was   E
     intolerable for him to continue any longer as managing director, whether or not
     the shareholders wanted or needed him was essentially a matter for them. There
     was still work to be done and someone had to do it. Further in the interests of the
     company there would have to be considered the financial consequences of the
     company terminating at that point the defendant's service contract. In my
     judgment, to suggest this as a reason why it was in the interests of the company to   F
     terminate the defendant's service contract comes ill from a person who went out of
     his way to keep what he was doing secret from the shareholders.

(2) He felt that he had clearly reached what he described as an 'impasse' because he
     felt that as a director of the company he could not follow 'certain instructions'
     which he regarded as improper. These instructions, he subsequently explained,   G
     were to do with the transfer of moneys and assets to Wesumat and making staff
     redundant without complying with the regulations. On further cross-examination
     he conceded that no such instructions had by 5 January been given but that he
     anticipated that they would be given at some stage in the future.

     I have to say that I find this explanation entirely unconvincing. There is nothing in
     the evidence adduced before me to suggest that Mr Phillips or anybody else on   H
     behalf of the shareholders had at any stage instructed or threatened to instruct the
     defendant to do anything which would be improper or illegal or in breach of the
     defendant's duties to the company. But – and somewhat ironically – if this truly
     was something that the defendant had in mind at the time, this would afford a
     reason why it was in the interests of the company that he should stay as managing
     director to resist any improper suggestions of the shareholders rather than go.

A   I conclude, therefore, that, in taking the actions which he did on 5 January the defendant acted in breach of his duties as a director of the company. In my judgment the actions which he took were not taken bona fide in the interests of the company but were taken by the defendant solely in his own interests. On that basis, it seems to me, the plaintiff must, prima facie, be entitled to the repayment of the moneys which were paid to and received by the defendant in breach of his fiduciary duties.

B   The defendant has advanced two reasons which, it is suggested should avoid this consequence in whole or in part, with which I must now deal, namely:

(1)   *Relief under s. 727 of the Companies Act 1985*

This section empowers the court to relieve any officer of a company from his liability for breach of duty or breach of trust if it appears to the court that such officer has acted 'honestly and reasonably, and ... having regard to all the circumstances of the case ... he ought fairly to be excused for the ... breach of duty or breach of trust'. Even assuming in the defendant's favour that, having regard to the findings which I have made, it would be proper to regard the defendant as having acted 'honestly', in my judgment it cannot possibly be said, having regard to those findings, that he can be regarded as having acted 'reasonably'. In those circumstances, it does not seem to me that the power conferred by s. 727 arises. Even if it did, I would not regard this as being a case where, having regard to all the circumstances which I have outlined above, ought to exercise it.

(2)   *Power of the court to order restitution on terms*

It is submitted that the court has in this sort of case power to direct repayment but only on terms that the defendant be permitted to retain out of the money in question such sum as to the court seems reasonable. The existence of such a power is essentially founded upon *Phipps v Boardman* [1967] 2 AC 46, where the court, in directing a person in a fiduciary position (the solicitor for a trust) to account for a profit which should have been earned for the trust, directed that in calculating the profit there should be deducted an allowance for the work and trouble of the solicitor in achieving that profit. That case is simply an illustration of an exercise by the court of its inherent power to award remuneration to a trustee (see *Guinness plc v Saunders* [1990] BCC 205, per Lord Templeman at p. 214, per Lord Goff of Chieveley at p. 219). In the *Guinness* case the question at issue was whether a director was bound to return to his company a fee for work done for the company which, as the court held, had in fact never properly been agreed to be paid by the company. The director argued that there ought to be an allowance from the amount in question equal to a reasonable fee calculated on a quantum meruit basis for the work which he had actually done. The House of Lords left open the question whether there was any jurisdiction of the court in effect by this means to award remuneration to a company director (as opposed to a trustee) but decided that, even assuming that the jurisdiction existed, it should be 'restricted to those cases where it cannot have the effect of encouraging trustees in any way to put themselves in a position where their interests conflict with their duties as trustees' – see per Lord Goff at p. 220. In my judgment, the exercise of such a jurisdiction, if it exists, in the present case would fall precisely within this description. Accordingly, in my judgment, it is not a jurisdiction which ought to exercise, even if it exists (a point which I too do not in these circumstances have to decide). I should add that, in addition, it does not seem to me that there can be regarded as having been performed by the defendant any 'service' to the company in respect of which he ought to be remunerated by the exercise of this jurisdiction, if it exists. All that the defendant did was to leave the employment of the company. Even

assuming that such can be regarded as a 'service', if that was done in circumstances   A
which amounted to constructive dismissal, the defendant would have his common
law and statutory remedies. Indeed, the defendant originally was pursuing in these
proceedings a claim for damages for constructive dismissal but, doubtless for good
reason, has abandoned that claim (although he is still pursuing a claim in the
industrial tribunal for compensation for unfair dismissal).

My findings thus far make it strictly unnecessary to deal with the alternative bases   B
upon which the company puts its case, but for the sake of completeness I will do as briefly
as I can.

Insufficient declaration of nature of interest

I have already referred to the judgment of Lightman J. In the light of that judgment,
by which I am bound, the transaction can only be upheld if the defendant is able to
satisfy me that at the board meeting on 5 January he made a 'full and frank declaration   C
... of the precise nature of the interest he holds' and that 'he has in letter and spirit
complied with [s. 317 and reg. 84 of Table A]'. The judge further held that the making of
the declaration 'should be the occasion for a statutory pause for thought about the
existence of a conflict of interest and of the duty to prefer the interests of the company to
[his] own' and 'must be a distinct happening at the meeting which therefore must be
recorded in the minutes' (although the judge went on to hold that the failure to record   D
the declaration in the minutes does not preclude proof that the declaration was in fact
made and s. 317 complied with). Where, judge held that the declaration must 'be made
out loud and in the hearing of those attending and again should be recorded'.

I am unable to conclude on the evidence before me that any such declaration complying
with the judge's determination was made. The defendant's evidence is that at the board
meeting he explained to the company secretary, Peter Phillips, the only other person there
present, that he had decided to terminate his contract as he considered it 'to be in the best   E
interests of the company so to do'. According to the defendant he went on to explain to
Mr Phillips that he felt that there was a 'potential in passing this resolution for a conflict
to exist' but that he had taken advice and in the light of that advice he considered that
there was 'not a conflict'. He also said that he referred Mr Peter Phillips to those
provisions of the company's memorandum and articles which conferred upon him the
power to act as sole director. This evidence, if taken at face value, appears prima facie to   F
be the antithesis of the declaration which Lightman J determined had to be given because,
far from reminding himself of the conflict of interest and making that reminder the
occasion 'for a statutory pause for thought about the existing of the conflict of interest',
the defendant appears to have persuaded himself that, merely because he had been
advised that as a sole director he was entitled to act, the conflict had disappeared
altogether. Mr Peter Phillips' evidence is that it was he, rather than the defendant, who
raised the potential conflict because he was uncomfortable about signing the minute   G
which the defendant had prepared. In para. 4 of Mr Phillips' witness statement it appears
that it was in an attempt to overcome Mr Phillips' concerns on this score that the
defendant directed Mr Phillips to the relevant paragraph of the articles entitling him to
vote upon a contract in which he was interest, notwithstanding that he was sole director,
and then said that 'whilst there was a potential conflict of interest in him voting to
terminate his contract of employment and paying himself the sum of £100,892.62, the
memorandum and articles of association allowed this and he considered it reasonable   H
and proper for him to do so'. I do not regard this statement – made, as it was, not for the
purpose of reminding the defendant of the conflict and of the need for the 'statutory
pause for thought' about its existence but solely for the purpose of overcoming Mr
Phillips' concerns – as being either in letter or spirit a sufficient compliance with s. 317
and the company's articles. The defendant's evidence is that by the time of the meeting

A   he had already written out and signed the letter of authority to the company's bankers to issue him with the draft. The very fact that such was done shows that what followed was a foregone conclusion and somewhat belies any suggestion, in my judgment, that at any stage during the board meeting was there any occasion for any 'pause for thought' about the existence of the conflict. Accordingly, in my judgment there was no or insufficient declaration by the defendant of the nature of his interest to the board meeting on 5 January to satisfy the requirements of the company's articles and s. 317.

B

It is suggested by the defendant that, since all relevant facts were, ex hypothesi, known to the defendant, any omission on this score should be regarded as purely technical and not such as to invalidate the transaction. In this regard reliance is had upon the decision of Simon Brown J in *Runciman v Walter Runciman plc* [1993] BCC 223, particularly the passage at p. 234, and upon the observations of Dillon LJ in *Lee Panavision Ltd v Lee Lighting Ltd* [1991] BCC 620 at p. 637. I have already stated at the commencement of

C   this judgment that the requirement for a sole director to make a declaration to himself of the nature of his interest of which ex hypothesi he knows everything might at first blush appear to be somewhat bizarre and unnecessary. Nevertheless, Lightman J has held that such a declaration in the case of a sole director is both possible and essential for the purposes of validating what would otherwise be a voidable self-dealing transaction. Admittedly Lightman J himself left over what he referred to as 'the vexed question of

D   law' whether the failure to make the declaration was, in the light of the two cases which I have mentioned, to be regarded as no more than 'a mere technical non-declaration' and hence not fatal to the transaction. Despite that, it seems to me that so to hold would, in effect, negate the whole basis of Lightman J's judgment. If a director wishes to take advantage of the provisions of a company's articles which allow self-dealing without the informed consent of the shareholders, he must, as the judge held, scrupulously comply with those provisions. He further held that in the case of a sole director he could take

E   advantage of such provisions provided that he made a full and frank declaration of the nature of his interest to a meeting consisting of himself. To allow validity to the transaction here where no such declaration is found to have been made on the ground that such was 'a mere technical non-declaration' as all the relevant facts were known to the director would be, in effect, to negate altogether the requirement for such a declaration to be made at all. For, wherever there is a sole director he must know all the facts to which the declaration was to relate.

F

Want of authority to make the payment

The defence originally pleaded that the defendant resigned his directorship forthwith after the board meeting of 5 January. This would have been consistent with the defendant's obligations under his service contract, which required him to resign his directorship forthwith upon his service contract being terminated. Given that logically

G   the letter of authority to the bank should have been written only after the board meeting and, further, that the company discovered (from documents obtained from the bank) that in fact the bank had in the afternoon required the defendant to sign as director a further authority in the bank's own form before issuing the draft, it is not surprising that the company sought and obtained from me leave to amend the statement of claim so as to plead that in any event the defendant, having now ceased to be a director, had no authority from the company to instruct the bank to issue the draft. If that was right, then

H   prima facie the money would be repayable as representing money drawn by the defendant from the company's bank account without authority. It is not pleaded that the board resolutions in themselves created any contract between the company and the defendant entitling the defendant to the payment. Nor, indeed, do the resolutions in themselves confer any authority on the defendant to help himself to the payment The letter of authority to the bank should not properly have been signed by the defendant until the

board resolutions had been made – and those resolutions do not record any ratification   A
by the board of that letter. They merely record the decision of the board that such
payment should be made. But, until implemented, it was perfectly open to the board to
reverse this decision. In fact in this regard the defendant was (although this was not
appreciated) in something of a dilemma. He could not properly as sole director make the
payment to himself or authorise himself to make it until such time as his service contract
had been formally terminated and the amount in question resolved to be paid. But, once
this was done, under the terms of his service contract he was supposed immediately to   B
resign as director and hence would no longer have any authority actually to make the
payment.

The defendant's response was with my leave to reamend the defence so as to plead that
in fact the defendant's resignation as director did not take place until 6 January at the
earliest coinciding with the date of a letter which he wrote to White & Bowker informing
them of his resignation. In my judgment the defendant's resignation as director should   C
be regarded as having taken place immediately after the board meeting of 5 January. The
defendant himself gave no evidence on this point and clearly regarded himself as having
resigned as director on 5 January. This was, after all, his pleaded case until the late
amendment. His action in leaving the company on that date points to the same
conclusion. Furthermore, for him now to contend that his resignation did not take effect
until 6 January would involve him in relying upon his own breach of contract (since he   D
was obliged to resign forthwith) in order to sustain his continuing authority to make the
payment to himself. He is thus to that extent seeking to rely for his own benefit on his
own wrong and this is, in my judgment, something which he is not entitled to do.

I thus conclude that, in addition to the other matters upon which I have ruled, the
payment of the money to himself by bankers' draft on 5 January was made by the
defendant without any authority of the company so to do and provides a further reason
why he is obliged, in my judgment, to repay that money to the company.   E

The counterclaim for damages for wrongful dismissal

Finally, I deal with the defendant's counterclaim based on wrongful dismissal. The
allegation is that, on the assumption that the board resolutions of 5 January are invalid,
as I have held, the defendant was dismissed from his employment by the actions of Mr
Phillips on behalf of the shareholders on 6 January and such dismissal was wrongful,   F
being in breach of the terms of his service contract. On 6 January Mr Phillips knew, of
course, nothing about the events of 5 January and had set out to dismiss the defendant
on the basis of a number of complaints, the principal one being the sending out by the
defendant of his circular to the staff of 23 December. I have set out above my findings in
relation to that circular. It was certainly damaging to Wesumat and certainly arguably in
breach by the defendant of his obligations to the company in that it constituted a distinct
encouragement to the engineering staff to leave the company's employment immediately.   G
Its sending out was thus arguably a grave breach by the defendant of his duties to the
company justifying his summary dismissal. I do not, however, have to decide this point
since I have not the slightest doubt that the defendant's actions on 5 January constituted
a repudiatory breach by the defendant of his obligations under the service contract upon
which the company, by its shareholders, is fully entitled now to rely to justify in law the
action which it took on 6 January – see *Boston Deep Sea Fishing and Ice Co v Ansell*   H
(1888) 39 ChD 339. Indeed, in his closing submissions Mr Roberts for the defendant in
effect so conceded. The defendant's counterclaim for damages must, accordingly, be
dismissed. I should add that the defendant has not himself adduced any evidence as to
what damages he has suffered and such evidence as there is concerning the terms of his
subsequent employment with Brushwash suggest that he has not in fact suffered any
damage.

A   There was, however, argument before me whether, assuming I were to reach the findings of fact which I have done, the company's actions by its shareholders on and after 6 January are to be regarded as a dismissal by the company of the defendant (albeit on this hypothesis for good cause) or are to be regarded as an acceptance by the company of the defendant's repudiation of the contract by his actions on 5 January. Strictly speaking it is not necessary for me to determine this point for the purposes of dismissing the counterclaim, but as, so I am informed, the determination of this point may well be

B   relevant to questions that could arise as to the release of the moneys from the joint bank account, with which I have yet to deal, I must do so. It is submitted by Mr Roberts for the defendant and accepted by Miss Jones for the company, that the defendant's actions on 5 January, although, on the basis of the facts which I have held, clearly repudiatory of the defendant's contractual obligations under his service contract, would not in law operate ipso facto to terminate the defendant's service contract unless and until that

C   repudiation was accepted by the company – and that, until that occurs, the contract still continues. It is further submitted by Mr Roberts that there cannot be any acceptance of a repudiation until the relevant facts are known to the other party. Accordingly, so he submits, the actions of the company by its shareholders on 6 January cannot be regarded as an acceptance of his client's repudiation of the contract on 5 January because at that time they were not aware of what the defendant had done.

D   There is little authority on the point. In fact the only authority which seems to bear upon it is the judgment of Evans J in *State Trading Corp of India v M Golodetz Ltd* [1988] 2 Ll Rep 182. In that case it was held that a buyer of goods was excused from his non-performance of the contract by the seller's previous or simultaneous repudiatory breach of contract of which the buyer was not at the time aware. The judge examined two lines of authorities. First, the line of authorities which established that 'given a repudiatory breach by one party, the innocent party has a right to elect whether to rescind or to affirm

E   the contract' (see, ibid, at p. 188). From those authorities the judge concluded that the innocent party could not exercise his right to terminate the contract without knowledge – but qualified this by saying if by that was meant 'a positive exercise of that right of election'. He then went on to examine the other line of authorities, of which (although the judge does not mention this specific one) the *Boston Deep Sea Fishing* case (above) is one, to the effect that a party is entitled to rely to justify a termination of a contract upon beaches by the other party of which he was not aware when he purported to terminate

F   the contract. His conclusion (ibid at p. 190) was that 'if the buyer who has failed to perform his contract is able to point to justification in the sense which I have mentioned,' [i.e. a prior or simultaneous breach of which he was not aware] 'it follows that the non-performance itself can be taken to stand as his acceptance of the previous or simultaneously repudiatory breach'. Accepting, as I do, the correctness of this authority, it follows, in my judgment, that the company's actions on 6 January 1994, can properly

G   be treated as an acceptance by the company of the defendant's repudiatory breach of his service contract the previous day, even though the company, in the shape of Mr Phillips, knew nothing about it on that date.

It therefore follows that, in my judgment, strictly speaking, the company did not dismiss the defendant. This accords with commonsense. The defendant's actions the previous day amounted on the findings which I have made to a resignation by him which he purported to dress up as a termination of his contract by the company. The company

H   by its actions on 6 January is to be regarded as having accepted that resignation.

Conclusions

My conclusions in summary are, therefore, as follows:

(1)   The defendant acted in breach of his fiduciary duties to the company in passing the board resolutions of 5 January 1994 and procuring the payment to himself of

A

the sum of £100,892.62 from the company's bank account by not acting bona fide in the interests of the company but preferring his own interests to those of the company.

(2)   The defendant failed to make a sufficient declaration of the nature of his interest to the board meeting on 5 January in compliance with reg. 84 of Table A and s. 317 of the *Companies Act* 1985 – and this is not something which can be overlooked.

B

(3)   The defendant ceased or is to be regarded as having ceased to be a director immediately after the board resolutions of 5 January were made and thus did not have the authority of the company to make the said payment.

(4)   I have no power to grant relief to the defendant pursuant to s. 727 of the *Companies Act* 1985 since it does not appear to me that the defendant has acted reasonably. If I had the power, I would not in all the circumstances of this case have seen fit to exercise it.

C

(5)   There is no justification in the circumstances of this case for exercising any power which the court might have to subject the company's prima facie entitlement to repayment in full to any term that would allow the defendant to retain some part of the sum wrongly paid.

(6)   The counterclaim for damages for wrongful dismissal is dismissed because the defendant's contract of employment was terminated by the defendant's own wrongful repudiation of it by the action which he took on 5 January 1994 which is to be regarded as accepted by the company by the actions taken by Mr Don Phillips on behalf of the shareholders the following day.

D

(*Order accordingly*)

———————————

E

F

G

H

A # Secretary of State for Trade and Industry v Bannister.

Court of Appeal (Civil Division).
Glidewell and Morritt L JJ and Sir John May.
Judgment delivered 19 July 1995.

Director disqualification – Jurisdiction to stay disqualification order pending
B   *appeal – Company Directors Disqualification Act 1986, s. 1(1), 6, 17.*

This was an application to the Court of Appeal for a stay of a director disqualification order pending an appeal.

Held, refusing the application:

1. The Court of Appeal did have jurisdiction to stay or suspend a disqualification order pending an appeal. No view was expressed on the question whether a county court judge
C   would have the power which a High Court judge had to stay or suspend his order.

2. Leave to act under s. 17 of the Company Directors Disqualification Act was the relief which the disqualified director should normally pursue. The interests of the disqualified director and the protection of the public could be more suitably considered on an application under that section rather than on an application for a stay pending appeal. Thus the discretion to stay or suspend the disqualification order would only be exercised if the
D   applicant showed that his case was an exceptional one in which the alternative remedy under s. 17 was inadequate. The applicant had not done so.

3. It was relevant on an application for a stay pending an appeal from a disqualification order to consider whether and to what extent the protection of the public might reasonably be forgone pending the appeal.

4. The applicant's prospects of obtaining the discharge of the order on appeal were slim.
E   Certainly the grounds of appeal did not satisfy the court that the public did not need some protection from the applicant's activities as a director of a limited company pending the appeal. Therefore the application was refused on the merits.

The following cases were referred to in the judgment of Morritt LJ:

Auto Electro and Powder Finishers, Re (unreported, 5 April 1995, Chadwick J).
Ipcon Fashions Ltd, Re (1989) 5 BCC 773.
F   *Sevenoaks Stationers (Retail) Ltd, Re* [1990] BCC 765; [1991] Ch 164.

David Stockill and M Bleasdale (instructed by George Green, Warley) for the applicant.

Lance Ashworth (instructed by Wragge & Co, Birmingham) for the Secretary of State.

G ## JUDGMENT

Morritt LJ: On 24 February 1995 His Honour Judge Micklem sitting in Birmingham as a deputy judge of the High Court made an order under s. 6 of the *Company Directors Disqualification Act* 1986 that R W Bannister be disqualified from 'acting as a company director for a period of five years commencing 21 days from today'. Mr Bannister's application to the judge for a stay of execution pending an appeal was refused. On 16
H   March 1995 Mr Bannister served notice of appeal and by a summons dated 29 March 1995 applied to the Court of Appeal for a stay pending the determination of that appeal. The Secretary of State contends that on the true construction of the relevant provisions of the Company Directors Disqualification Act there is no power to grant a stay or suspension of the disqualification order. Thus two points arise. First, does this court have jurisdiction to grant the relief sought? Second, if it does, should it exercise it in the circumstances of this case?

First it is necessary to set out the relevant provisions of the Act. Section 1(1) provides:

A

'(1) In the circumstances specified below in this Act a court may, and under section 6 shall, make against a person a disqualification order, that is to say an order that he shall not, without leave of the court–

(a) be a director of a company, or

(b) be a liquidator or administrator of a company, or

B

(c) be a receiver or manager of a company's property, or

(d) in any way, whether directly or indirectly, be concerned or take part in the promotion, formation or management of a company,

for a specified period beginning with the date of the order.'

Sections 2–5 deal with disqualification in consequence of conviction of an indictable offence, persistent breaches of the companies legislation, fraud in a winding up and on summary conviction. So far as relevant s. 6 provides:

C

'(1) The court shall make a disqualification order against a person in any case where, on an application under this section, it is satisfied–

(a) that he is or has been a director of a company which has at any time become insolvent (whether while he was a director or subsequently), and

(b) that his conduct as a director of that company (either taken alone or taken together with his conduct as a director of any other company or companies) makes him unfit to be concerned in the management of a company).

D

. . .

(4) Under this section the minimum period of disqualification is 2 years, and the maximum period is 15 years.'

Section 7 provides, amongst other things, that an application to disqualify under s. 6 should, unless the court otherwise orders, be made within two years of the insolvency of the company in question. Section 17 deals with the courts having jurisdiction to give leave to act notwithstanding the disqualification and provides:

E

'(1) As regards the court to which application must be made for leave under a disqualification order, the following applies–

(a) where the application is for leave to promote or form a company, it is any court with jurisdiction to wind up companies, and

F

(b) where the application is for leave to be a liquidator, administrator or director of, or otherwise to take part in the management of a company, or to be a receiver or manager of a company's property, it is any court having jurisdiction to wind up that company.'

Section 21 provides that s. 6 and 7 are deemed to be included in Pt. I–VII of the Insolvency Act for the purpose of the rule-making power contained in s. 411 of that Act. That section provides that:

G

'(1) Rules may be made–

(a) in relation to England and Wales, by the Lord Chancellor with the concurrence of the Secretary of State, or

(b) in relation to Scotland, by the Secretary of State,

H

for the purpose of giving effect to Parts I to VII of this Act.'

Under that section the *Insolvent Companies (Disqualification of Unfit Directors) Proceedings Rules* 1987 (SI 1987/2023) were made prescribing the procedure to be followed. So far as relevant those rules provide:

A

'2. *Form of application*

An application to which these Rules apply shall be made–

    (a) in the High Court, by originating summons (Form 10 in Appendix A to the Rules of the Supreme Court, with such adaptation as may be appropriate), and

B

    (b) in a county court, by originating application, such an application being nevertheless referred to in these Rules as a summons;

and the Rules of the Supreme Court 1965 or (as the case may be) the County Court Rules 1981 apply accordingly, except where these Rules make provision to inconsistent effect.

. . .

C

9. *Commencement of disqualification order*

Unless the court otherwise orders, a disqualification order takes effect at the beginning of the 21st day after the day on which the order is made.'

The Secretary of State submits that there is no express provision in either the Act, those rules or the Rules of the Supreme Court conferring any power on the court to stay or suspend the operation of an order for the disqualification of a director and that any

D

implied power is ousted by the express provision of s. 1(1) requiring the period of the disqualification to start on the date of the order. He points out that in the case of a company winding-up petition s. 147 of the Insolvency Act confers an express power to stay all further proceedings in the winding up. By way of contrast he relies on the provisions of the *Licensing Act* 1964, s. 100 and 101; the *Gaming Act* 1968, s. 24 and 25 and the *Road Traffic Offenders Act* 1988, s. 37, 39 and 40. To illustrate this point it is only necessary to refer to s. 37 and 39 of the *Road Traffic Offenders Act* 1988 which

E

provide:

'37. *Effect of order of disqualification*

(1) Where the holder of a licence is disqualified by an order of a court, the licence shall be treated as being revoked with effect from the beginning of the period of disqualification.

F

(2) Where the holder of the licence appeals against the order and the disqualification is suspended under section 39 of this Act, the period of disqualification shall be treated for the purpose of subsection (1) above as beginning on the day on which the disqualification ceases to be suspended.

. . .

39. *Suspension of disqualification pending appeal*

(1) Any court in England and Wales (whether a magistrates' court or another)

G

which makes an order disqualifying a person may, if it thinks fit, suspend the disqualification pending an appeal against the order.'

This shows, so the argument runs, that when Parliament confers power on a court to disqualify a person from a specific date, but wishes it to have power to suspend the disqualification pending appeal it makes express provision for that purpose, including the reimposition of the disqualification for the full period if the appeal fails. By contrast

H

in this case not only is there no express power to suspend the disqualification but the exercise of any implied power would shorten the period for which the lower court had made provision.

The Secretary of State submits further that there is no need for such a power as the court is expressly empowered by s. 1(1) and 17 to grant leave to act as a director, etc. notwithstanding the disqualification order.

This is disputed by Mr Bannister. On his behalf it is submitted that the High Court   A
and the Court of Appeal have inherent jurisdiction to stay proceedings including the stay
or suspension of orders as recognised and preserved by s. 49(3) of the *Supreme Court Act*
1981. It is submitted that it would require clear words to oust that jurisdiction and that
Parliament cannot have intended to do so by the words in s. 1 of the Company Directors
Disqualification Act which are no more than a definition of what a disqualification order
is. It is suggested that the time which inevitably lapses between the events in question and
the order do not necessitate the order being effective forthwith and that the power to   B
grant leave to act is no substitute for a power to stay an order pending an appeal.

As a riposte to the argument based on the inherent jurisdiction of the High Court and
the Court of Appeal, counsel for the Secretary of State pointed out that the county court
has no inherent jurisdiction, so that if the argument for Mr Bannister were right it would
reveal an inexplicable difference between the powers of the two courts before whom the
application for a disqualification order might come. Counsel for the Secretary of State   C
frankly accepted that on his argument r. 9 of the Insolvent Companies (Disqualification
of Unfit Directors) Proceedings Rules was ultra vires as it did not on any view 'give effect
to' s. 6 of the *Company Directors Disqualification Act* 1986 and the disqualification order
as defined by s. 1 of that Act which s. 6 required to be made.

The only case to which we were referred in which these and related questions have
arisen is *Re Auto Electro and Powder Finishers Ltd* in which Chadwick J gave judgment   D
on 5 April 1995. In that case a disqualification order had been made and suspended
pending an application for leave to act as a director of a specified company under s. 17.
That company went into liquidation so that the application was not pursued. Chadwick
J was concerned with an application for a further disqualification in relation to that
company. At the conclusion of his judgment he made a number of comments on the
suspension of the earlier disqualification order. First he doubted whether the court had
had jurisdiction to make it. Second he expressed the view that it was not an order which   E
should have been made since as the court could not alter the date at which the
disqualification order commenced, the effect of the suspension was to shorten the period
of the disqualification. He suggested that an interim order giving leave to act as a director
would have been more appropriate.

It is not disputed that an appeal lies to the Court of Appeal from a disqualification
order made in the High Court or the county court. As with any appeal the Court of   F
Appeal has power to make any order which the court below might have made. Thus the
period of the disqualification may be extended or reduced or discharged altogether. In
those circumstances it would be surprising if the court did not possess the lesser power to
stay or suspend its order pending the appeal.

It is true that the court has power to alleviate the effect of the order pending appeal by
giving leave to act as a director pending appeal as permitted by s. 1 and 17. But although   G
this power may be sufficient in the normal run of cases it is not necessarily adequate for
dealing with the extreme case in which the court below went badly wrong and the very
existence of the disqualification order causes irreparable harm to the person apparently
disqualified. In such hard though rare cases the power conferred by s. 17 would not be
sufficient to achieve justice. Accordingly in my view this question must be approached on
the basis that clear words are needed to exclude the usual and necessary power to stay or
suspend an order pending appeal.   H

In form the words said to have achieved this effect are part of a definition of a
disqualification order for they follow the words 'that is to say'. I do not accept the
submission for the Secretary of State that the definition ends with subpara. (d) for the
period is necessarily part of the definition as the court has no power to disqualify for an
unlimited period. It would be surprising if a definition had the effect of excluding the

A   inherent jurisdiction of the court in the way contended for. In my view it does not. The definition without more cannot exclude the jurisdiction to stay or suspend the order being defined. Thus the words 'beginning with the date of the order' do not preclude the suspension of that order. Accordingly that effect must be derived, if at all, from the use of the words 'and under section 6 shall'. But, again, these words cannot be sufficient to exclude the usual power to stay an order pending appeal for a statutory duty to make the order in prescribed circumstances has never, without more, been considered sufficient to
B   exclude or restrict the powers of the Court of Appeal in respect of the order made.

The existence of the express power to stay all further proceedings in the winding up of a company conferred by s. 147 of the *Insolvency Act* 1986 and the equivalent power to annul a bankruptcy order conferred by s. 282 of the *Insolvency Act* 1986 are directed to staying the insolvency process otherwise than pending appeal and do not in my judgment throw any light on the question.

C   The examples relied on by way of analogy are distinguishable in that, in each case, the activity in question, be it selling alcohol, gaming or driving, was unlawful without the licence or qualification being revoked. Thus it would be insufficient to rely on the inherent power to stay or suspend an order pending an appeal without also providing for the temporary reinstatement of the licence of qualification. In so far as those statutory provisions went further and provided that the period of suspension or disqualification
D   should commence when the appeal was disposed of they do demonstrate the necessarily different treatment provided by Parliament in those cases but that is not a good reason for construing the Company Directors Disqualification Act otherwise than in accordance with the clear words used.

This is not an appeal from a disqualification order made in a county court. I express no view on the question whether the judge of such a court would have the power which the judge of the High Court has to stay or suspend his order; the resolution of that
E   question would require further argument on at least the ambit in this respect of s. 76 of the *County Courts Act* 1984. But even if he did not, that is no reason for denying the power to the High Court judge and still less to the Court of Appeal.

For these reasons I do not share the doubt expressed by Chadwick J in *Re Auto Electro and Powder Finishers* but conclude that the Court of Appeal does have jurisdiction to stay or suspend the disqualification order against which Mr Bannister appeals. The
F   question whether r. 9 of the *Insolvent Companies (Disqualification of Unfit Directors) Proceedings Rules* 1987 is ultra vires does not arise for decision; but that does not mean that it is not a question to which the rule making authorities should direct their attention.

So the next question is whether in the exercise of its discretion this court should grant the stay sought. Before considering the facts of this case I should note two submissions made on behalf of Mr Bannister which raise issues of general principle. The first was that
G   on an application to stay or suspend a disqualification order the court was concerned with the hardship to the director and the merits of the appeal and not with the protection of the public. The second was that the existence of the ability of the disqualified director to apply for leave to act under s. 17 was not material to the consideration of whether the court should stay or suspend the order pending the appeal.

In relation to the first it was pointed out that normally the events on which the court
H   determined to disqualify the director occurred some years before. Section 7 allows two years from the insolvency of the company concerned within which to apply and it normally takes a year or more after the application for the order has been launched for the matter to come before the court. Thus at least three years are likely to have elapsed. This is all true but does not establish the proposition in support of which it is advanced. The whole purpose of the Act is to protect the public from the future activities of those who for the prescribed reasons have shown themselves to be unfit to act as directors of a

company. In my view it must be relevant on an application for a stay pending an appeal   A
from the disqualification order to consider whether and to what extent that protection
may reasonably be forgone pending the appeal.

The second point is allied to the first. Section 17 prescribes a method by which a person
disqualified may nevertheless obtain leave to act as a director. Further as Chadwick J
observed in *Re Auto Electro and Powder Finishers* the grant of such leave would not have
the effect which I assume, for it is not necessary to decide, a stay or suspension would   B
have of shortening the period of the disqualification. Though, as I have already observed,
such a dispensation pending appeal may not do justice in all cases in my view, in
agreement with Chadwick J, it is the relief which the disqualified director should normally
pursue. The usual practice is to require the applicant to give details of the financial
standing and management structure of the company concerned. The leave, if granted,
may be on condition or subject to undertakings and is confined to the company in respect
of which the leave is sought. It seems to me that the interests of the disqualified director   C
and the protection of the public can be more suitably considered on an application for
leave to act under that section rather than on an application for a stay pending appeal.
The flexibility which it permits is shown by the order of Hoffmann J in *Re Ipcon Fashions
Ltd* (1989) 5 BCC 773 at p. 776.

Thus the discretion to stay or suspend the disqualification order would, in practice,
only be exercised in favour of the applicant if he showed that his case was one of those   D
exceptional cases in which the alternative remedy under s. 17 was inadequate. This is not
one of those cases, Mr Bannister has not applied to the court prescribed by s. 17 for leave
to act and has not filed any evidence on this application such as the court deciding
whether such leave should be given would require. Accordingly in my judgment this
application should be refused for that reason alone.

However, as the matter was fully argued and there had not been any previous reported   E
case to the effect that, save in exceptional cases, application should be made under s. 17
I will deal briefly with the other submissions made on Mr Bannister's behalf.

The application for the disqualification order was made by the Secretary of State for
Trade and Industry in relation to the affairs of Sectional Shotblasting (Dudley) Ltd. That
company was incorporated on 6 November 1989 with an authorised capital of £100 of
which only £2 was issued, one to Mr Bannister and one to Mr Taylor. There were three
directors, Mr Bannister, his wife and Mr Taylor. The company was to trade from   F
premises leased to it by Mr Bannister and both Mr Bannister and Mr Taylor were to put
in £25,000 as working capital. Arrangements were made by Mr Bannister for the
company to have overdraft facilities of £40,000 and for the acquisition of a shot blasting
machine.

By August 1990 Mr Bannister was aware that the company was insolvent but he
allowed the company to continue to trade until 26 January 1991. During that period the   G
deficiency regarding creditors increased by a further £34,000. On 6 March 1991 the
company went into creditors' voluntary liquidation with an estimated deficiency
regarding creditors of £125,411.

On 7 March 1993 these proceedings were commenced. The grounds of unfitness alleged
were trading without reasonable prospect of the payment of creditors, failure to give
sufficient attention to the financial affairs of the company and failure to maintain the   H
statutory records.

Judge Micklem found all these matters proved. In his judgment he described Mr
Bannister as:

> 'a bad witness, evasive and unhelpful. I accept his evidence on important issues
> only where supported by some other witness or documentary evidence.'

A   Later he said:

> 'I bear in mind the period of the company's life was a period of recession in the
> construction industry on which the company's business depended. I bear in mind
> also that Mr Bannister has himself lost a substantial sum of money and has been
> required to honour guarantees given on behalf of the company. Mr Bannister is
> not guilty of any lack of commercial probity. But he has been, as it seems to me,
B   > extremely negligent or incompetent. Counsel has said everything that could be said
> in his behalf, but I have come to the clear conclusion that Mr Bannister is unfit to
> be concerned in the management of a company.

After reference to the judgment of Dillon LJ in *Re Sevenoaks Stationers (Retail) Ltd*
[1990] BCC 765 for guidance on the length of the period of disqualification he continued:

C   > 'Mr Bannister had the primary responsibility for controlling the finances of this
> company and made wholly inadequate attempts to do so. He had the empty
> register at his premises. He was the more experienced and could be expected to be
> the more knowledgeable director in company matters, but he simply left the book
> blank.'

Mr Bannister filed two affidavits in support of this application testifying to the serious
D   financial hardship which the disqualification order had occasioned to him. In his affidavit
sworn on 26 May 1995 he stated that since November 1994 he had ceased to be involved
in the affairs of Pressvess Engineering Ltd and R & B Castings. As a result his income
had been reduced and his family was suffering hardship. There is a similar affidavit from
his solicitor. By a further affidavit sworn by Mr Bannister on 27 June 1995 he reiterated
and re-emphasised his financial problems to which he added medical and nervous
E   disorders. His counsel indicated the merits of his appeal by reference to the arguments he
proposes to adduce in due course.

But with regard to those arguments it did not appear to me that the primary facts were
in dispute, rather whether there were any exculpatory features. Thus it is not disputed
that Mr Bannister knew that the company was insolvent in August 1990 but permitted it
to continue to trade until January 1991 when the deficiency increased by a further
F   £34,000. It is sought to justify that conduct by reference to the fact that a person who
helped the company with its books, Mr Lawrence, had told Mr Bannister that one option
open to him was to continue trading in order to trade out of the difficulty. There is no
dispute that the statutory records have not been kept but Mr Bannister says that it was
the responsibility of Mr Lawrence to complete them. In these circumstances whilst Mr
Bannister may succeed in reducing the period of his disqualification to the statutory
G   minimum of two years his prospects of obtaining the discharge of the order altogether
seem slim. Certainly the grounds of appeal do not satisfy me that the public do not need
some protection from Mr Bannister's activities as a director of a limited company
pending the appeal. Moreover the alleged financial hardship is not shown to be in
consequence of the order appealed from as Mr Bannister resigned from the board of the
company in question before the order was made and the order does not impede him in
conducting the affairs of the other but unincorporated trading organisation to which he
H   refers.

For all these reasons in my judgment this application should be rejected on its merits.

Sir John May: I agree that Mr Bannister's application for a stay pending his appeal
should be refused for the reasons set out in the judgment which Morritt LJ has just
delivered.

A

Glidewell LJ: For the reasons set out in the judgment of Morritt LJ, I agree that Mr Bannister's application for a stay pending his appeal should be refused.

Despite the persuasive argument advanced on behalf of the Secretary of State, I also am clearly of the opinion that the High Court and the Court of Appeal have an inherent power to grant a stay of an order disqualifying a person from acting as a company director. Nevertheless I wish to emphasise that this power should only be exercised in exceptional circumstances. In most cases, the provisions of s. 17 of the Act entitling the person subject to a disqualification order to apply for leave to act, pending appeal, as a director of a specified company is sufficient to ensure that no unjust hardship is caused. Moreover, this course has the advantage that the grant of such leave may be subject to conditions, which should ensure leave is only granted if the court is satisfied that the company has proper financial advice and control. If, therefore, the court is minded to exercise discretion in favour of the disqualified director at all, in the great majority of cases an application under s. 17 will be the appropriate course to enable it to do so.

B

C

(*Order accordingly*)

D

E

F

G

H

A
Re Brian Sheridan Cars Ltd.

Chancery Division (Companies Court).
David Neuberger QC (sitting as a deputy judge of the Chancery Division).
Judgment delivered 24 July 1995.

B
*Director disqualification – Whether disqualification order not incorporating all
statutory words invalid – Whether order could be corrected under 'slip rule',
inherent jurisdiction or Insolvency Rules – Whether correction would prejudice
respondent – Company Directors Disqualification Act 1986, s. 1(1); Insolvency
Rules 1986 (SI 1986/1925), r. 7.47, 7.51; Rules of the Supreme Court, O. 20,
r. 11.*

C
*Application for variation with retrospective effect of order giving leave to act as
director – Application to have order extended – Discretion of court to backdate
order – Company Directors Disqualification Act 1986, s. 17.*

These were an application by the official receiver to alter a disqualification order made
against the respondent, and the respondent's application to vary an order giving leave to act
as a director under s. 17 of the Company Directors Disqualification Act 1986.

D
The court made a disqualification order for a term of three years against the respondent
arising out of his directorship of two companies following a hearing in which the respondent
conceded that a disqualification order should be made and the only issue was the appropriate
period of disqualification (a procedure approved in Re Carecraft Construction Co Ltd [1993]
BCC 336).

The official receiver's summons and the order agreed and entered incorporated the
wording of s. 1(1)(a) and (d) of the 1986 Act and not s. 1(1)(b) or (c). Following various
decisions indicating that a disqualification order might only be valid if it incorporated the
E provisions of the whole of s. 1(1), the official receiver applied to have the order amended so
that it complied with the provisions of s. 1(1)(a)–(d). The official receiver contended that the
order could be amended pursuant to RSC, O. 20, r. 11 ('the slip rule'), the inherent
jurisdiction of the court or r. 7.47 of the Insolvency Rules.

After making the disqualification order the court gave the respondent leave under s. 17 to
act as a director of three companies subject to certain conditions for a year on the basis that
F the period could be renewed if appropriate on the respondent's application. The respondent,
having failed to comply with the terms of the order, applied to vary the order with
retrospective effect and to renew the order for a further 12 months on different terms.

Held, allowing the official receiver's application to alter the form of the order, and varying
the terms of the s. 17 order without retrospective effect, and extending the order for a further
year:

G
1. Whether or not the Insolvency Rules applied, there was nothing in r. 7.47 which was
inconsistent with the slip rule. Accordingly, even if the Rules did apply, r. 7.51 thereof
enabled the slip rule to be invoked.

2. The court had jurisdiction to alter the form of the disqualification order pursuant to
the slip rule. There was no question of any prejudice to the respondent if the order was
altered as the official receiver requested. Further, the prejudice to the public if the
H application was refused would be potentially severe.

3. If the slip rule could not be invoked to achieve that result, the court would grant the
official receiver's application under r. 7.47 or the inherent jurisdiction.

4. With very considerable hesitation, the leave granted to the respondent to continue to
act as a director was extended for a further year. The court took into account various
mitigating factors and the fact that, in relation to at least some of the failures to comply,

the respondent was acting on his solicitors' advice. There was no suggestion that any of the
failures had of themselves caused any danger, let alone any damage, to the public and the
two trading companies of which the respondent had been permitted to be a director had
traded successfully. The terms would be broadly similar to the terms imposed by the original
order, with a new condition for the respondent within 21 days to lodge an affidavit with the
court (with a copy to the official receiver) confirming that each and every one of the terms
had been satisfied.

5. Even assuming the court had a virtually unfettered discretion to backdate an order,
there were sufficient aspects of the respondent's failure to comply with the terms of the order
and of other, connected, unsatisfactory conduct on his part in relation to the proceedings to
render it inappropriate to backdate any order varying the s. 17 order.

The following cases were referred to in the judgment on the official receiver's
application:

Carecraft Construction Co Ltd, Re [1993] BCC 336; [1994] 1 WLR 172.
Chessum & Sons v Gordon [1901] 1 QB 694.
Circle Holidays International plc, Re [1994] BCC 226.
Dobson & Anor v Hastings & Ors [1992] Ch 394.
Fritz v Hobson (1880) 14 ChD 542.
Gower Enterprises Ltd, Re (No. 2) [1995] BCC 1081.
Hatton v Harris [1892] AC 547.
Inchcape (Earl), Re [1942] Ch 394.
Isaacs v Robertson [1985] AC 97.
Kuwait Airways Corp v Iraqi Airways Co & Anor (No. 2) [1994] 1 WLR 985.
Navimprex Centrala Navala v George Moundreas & Co SA (1983) 127 SJ 392.
Polly Peck International plc, Re [1993] BCC 890.
Seagull Manufacturing Co Ltd, Re (No. 3) [1995] BCC 1088.
Tak Ming Co Ltd v Yee Sang Metal Supplies Co [1973] 1 WLR 300.
Tasbian Ltd, Re (No. 2) [1990] BCC 322.
Thynne v Thynne [1955] P 272.

The following cases were referred to in the judgment on the respondent's application:

Kuwait Airways Corporation v Iraqi Airways Co & Anor (No. 2) [1994] 1 WLR 985.
Palata Investments Ltd & Ors v Burt & Sinfield Ltd & Ors [1985] 1 WLR 942.
R v Secretary of State for the Home Department, ex parte Mahta [1975] 1 WLR 1084.
Williams (Rex) Leisure plc, Re [1993] BCC 79.

Malcolm Davis-White (instructed by the Treasury Solicitor) for the official receiver.

J McLinden (instructed by Mackrell Turner Garrett) for the respondent.

JUDGMENT ON OFFICIAL RECEIVER'S APPLICATION

David Neuberger QC: This is an application by the official receiver to alter a
disqualification order which I made on 13 June 1994 against the respondent. The
application is made on the ground that the order does not comply with the requirements
of the *Company Directors Disqualification Act* 1986 ('the Act') and that it should be
altered so that it does so comply. I understand that the point is of some general relevance,
because a large number of disqualification orders made pursuant to the Act suffer from
the same defect as the order in the instant case, and as a result, if they are not altered so
as to comply with the Act, they may be liable to be discharged.

The proceedings in the instant case were issued against the respondent by the official
receiver on 1 May 1992. The relief claimed was:

'An order under s. 6 of the [Act] that the respondent shall not, without leave of the
court, be a director of, or in any way, whether directly or indirectly, be concerned

A   or take part of the promotion, formation or management of a company for a period of not less than two years and not exceeding 15 years from the date of such order.

. . .

3. Such further or other order as the court shall deem proper.'

B   When the matter first came before me, the respondent accepted that a disqualification order should be made, and the only issue was the length of that order (in other words, the procedure adopted was that considered and approved by Ferris J in *Re Carecraft Construction Co Ltd* [1993] BCC 336). On 13 June 1994, I decided that the appropriate period of disqualification was three years, and it was left to the parties to agree the precise form of the order. The order was duly agreed and drawn up, and it was duly passed and entered on 1 July 1994. The operative part of the order read as follows:

C   '*It is ordered*

      (1) that pursuant to s. 6 of the [Act] that the respondent . . . shall not without the leave of the court be a director of a company or in any way, whether directly or indirectly, be concerned in or take part in the promotion, formation or management of a company for a period of three years commencing from the date hereof . . .'

D   Having heard further arguments following my judgment on 13 June 1994, I gave leave, subject to certain conditions, to the respondent on 14 June 1994 to continue as a director and to be concerned in and take part in the management of certain specified companies, pursuant to s. 17 of the Act.

Section 1(1) of the Act provides that, where, as in the present case, the court makes an order under s. 6, the order is to be:

E   'an order that he shall not, without leave of the court–

      (a) be a director of a company, or

      (b) be a liquidator or administration of a company, or

      (c) be a receiver or manager of a company's property, or

      (d) in any way, whether directly or indirectly, be concerned or take part in the
F   promotion, formation or management of a company,

for a specified period beginning with the date of the order.'

It will be observed that the order drawn up on 1 July 1994 incorporates s. 1(1)(a) and (d), but does not incorporate s. 1(1)(b) or (c), of the Act. In this, the order reflected the summons issued by the official receiver. This form of summons and this form of order are fairly standard in this sort of proceedings. That is presumably because the official
G   receiver has taken the view that businessmen such as the respondent in this case, with no professional qualifications, will not become liquidators, administrators, or receivers or managers, in any event.

In *Re Gower Enterprises Ltd (No. 2)* [1995] BCC 1081 Mr Robert Reid QC, sitting as a deputy judge, considered an argument that a summons substantially in the form of the summons in the instant case was invalid, because it only sought relief under part of s. 1(1) of the Act. He held, following the obiter observation of Lindsay J in *Re Polly Peck*
H   *International plc* [1993] BCC 890 at p. 897A, that a disqualification order could only be validly made by the court if it incorporated the provisions of the whole s. 1(1) of the Act: in other words, the word 'or' is, in the context of s. 1(1) of the Act, conjunctive.

It is right to add that, having so decided, the deputy judge went on to give leave to the official receiver, the applicant in that case, to amend the summons so as to extend the relief sought to s. 1(1)(b) and (c) of the Act.

The substantive decision of Mr Reid was not challenged on behalf of the official A
receiver before Blackburne J in *Re Seagull Manufacturing Co Ltd (No. 3)* [1995] BCC
1088 and he cast no doubt on its correctness. Similarly, before me, counsel for the official
receiver's submissions proceed on the basis that the decision of Mr Reid QC is correct
and I am content to make the same assumption.

In these circumstances, the order drawn up in this case and entered on 1 July 1994 was
defective. It may very well be that, if the order remains unaltered, an application by the B
respondent to have it set aside will be brought and will succeed.

Accordingly, the official receiver invites me to amend the order drawn up following
my judgment on 13 June 1994 so that it complies with the provisions of s. 1(1)(a) to (d)
inclusive, in accordance with the judgment of Mr Reid QC to which I have referred.

The primary basis upon which I am invited to make such an order is pursuant to
O. 20, r. 11 of the *Rules of the Supreme Court* 1965, as amended ('the slip rule'). This C
provides:

> 'Clerical mistakes in judgments or orders, or errors arising therein from any
> accidental slip or omission, may at any time be corrected by the court on motion
> or summons without an appeal.'

In the alternative, counsel for the official receiver contends that I can and should amend
the order pursuant to the inherent jurisdiction of the court or pursuant to r. 7.47(1) of D
the *Insolvency Rules* 1986.

I propose to consider the matter first on the basis of the slip rule. The first question is
whether the slip rule applies at all. Rule 2 of the *Insolvent Companies (Disqualification of
Unfit Directors) Proceedings Rules* 1987 (SI 1987/2023) provides that, in relation to an
application for disqualification of a company director pursuant to the 1986 Act in the
High Court: E

> 'the Rules of the Supreme Court 1965 . . . apply . . . except where these Rules make
> provision to inconsistent effect.'

If that were the end of the matter, the slip rule would clearly be applicable. However,
there is an argument that the power of the court under r. 7.47(1) of the Insolvency Rules
applies in the present type of proceedings (see *Re Tasbian (No. 2)* [1990] BCC 322)
although that is not by any means clear (see *Dobson & Anor v Hastings & Ors* [1992] Ch F
394 and the discussion in *Re Circle Holidays International plc* [1994] BCC 226). I do not
consider that I need to decide whether or not r. 7.47 of the Insolvency Rules applies. Rule
7.47(1) provides:

> 'Every court having jurisdiction under the [Insolvency] Act to wind up companies
> may review, rescind or vary any order made by it in the exercise of that
> jurisdiction.' G

However, r. 7.51 of the Insolvency Rules provides:

> 'Except so far as inconsistent with the Insolvency Rules, the Rules of the Supreme
> Court and the practice of the High Court apply to insolvency proceedings in the
> High Court . . . with any necessary modifications.'

It appears to me to be clear that, even if the Insolvency Rules apply, there is nothing
in r. 7.47 which is inconsistent with the slip rule. Accordingly even if the Insolvency Rules H
apply, r. 7.51 thereof enables the slip rule to be invoked.

I turn to consider whether the slip rule may be relied on in a case such as the present,
where the form of the order reflected the form of the official receiver's summons, and is
sought to be corrected on the ground that an error of law was made when its terms were
agreed between counsel and passed and entered by the court.

A In *Re Earl of Inchcape* [1942] Ch 394, Morton J had given judgment on a summons in favour of the plaintiff together with costs. At the conclusion of his judgment, he had specifically asked counsel for the plaintiff as to whether anything further arose on the summons, and counsel stated that it did not. The order was then drawn up. Subsequently, the plaintiff's legal advisers appreciated that counsel had failed to ask for an order that the plaintiff have the costs of certain items which, in order to be recovered, had to be the subject of a specific order. Accordingly, the plaintiff made an application to Morton J to alter the order.

B

In his judgment, Morton J referred to the predecessor of the present slip rule (then O. 28, r. 11). At p. 398 he said this:

'The error which it is now sought to set right, if it can be properly described as an error, did not arise from an omission to embody in the order something which I in fact ordered to be done, but it arose from an accidental omission of counsel to ask that a particular thing might be done.'

C

However, relying on the reasoning of Fry J in *Fritz v Hobson* (1880) 14 ChD 542 and on the observations of A L Smith MR in *Chessum & Sons v Gordon* [1901] 1 QB 694, Morton J concluded at p. 399 that he had power to alter an order pursuant to the slip rule in 'cases where the omissions arose by a slip on the part of counsel, on the part of a solicitor and on the part of a party to the action'. He went on to say that the slip rule could be invoked notwithstanding that:

D

'I made the order which I intended to make in regard to the costs for which I was asked to make provision, but there was an accidental omission on the part of counsel, and I did not make the order which I would have made if that accidental omission had not occurred.'

The decision in *Inchcape* appears to have been cited with approval, and indeed applied, by the Court of Appeal in *Navinprex Centrala Navala v George Moundreas & Co SA* (17 March 1983) briefly reported at 127 SJ 392. It was also cited with approval by the Privy Council in *Tak Ming Co Ltd v Yee Sang Metal Supplies Co* [1973] 1 WLR 300 at p. 304E.

E

Clearly, it would be inappropriate to amend an order under the slip rule in such a way as would cause prejudice to the respondent: see the observations of Lord Watson in *Hatton v Harris* [1892] AC 547 at p. 560. However, it seems clear, both on principle and on authority that the mere fact that there is a substantial delay in applying to alter the order does not justify the application to alter being rejected, unless of course the alteration results in prejudice to the respondent: see *Tak Ming* at p. 306F–307B.

F

Of course, in a case such as this, the sort of prejudice which the respondent can invoke to oppose the alteration of the order would be prejudice resulting from the fact that the order has been amended to incorporate s. 1(1)(b) and (c) of the Act some 13 months after the original drawing up of the order, rather than when the order was first drawn up. For instance, the respondent might show that, because the order had not restrained him from acting as a liquidator of a company, he had so acted; even in those circumstances, however, I apprehend that the order could be altered in such a way as to ensure that he would in no way be liable for having so acted.

G

In the present case, however, I am quite satisfied that there can be no question of any prejudice to the respondent if the order were altered as the official receiver requests. Until the present application of the official receiver to alter the order was made, the respondent and his advisers had clearly been proceeding on the assumption that the order was valid. Further, there is no question of the respondent having acted as a liquidator, administrator, receiver, or manager of a company since the order was made. Accordingly, there is no possibility of prejudice to the respondent in the instant case if I were to decide that the order should be amended pursuant to the slip rule in the manner sought by the official receiver.

H

On the other hand, it seems to me that the prejudice if I did not allow the application   A
of the official receiver would be potentially severe. The purpose of the Act, as has been
frequently stated and authoritatively stated, is to protect the public. In the present case,
the court concluded (indeed the respondent conceded) that the policy of the Act, and
therefore the protection of the public, required the making of a disqualification order. If,
as a result of a pure technicality, that protection is liable to be revoked, or even cut down,
I consider that that represents significant prejudice, and, therefore, a strong reason in   B
favour of granting the official receiver's application.

On behalf of the respondent, it is, however, suggested that the slip rule cannot be relied
on to amend the order. First, it is said that the order, in its present form, is a nullity, and
the slip rule cannot be relied on to convert a nullity into a valid order.

I do not accept that argument. First, there is no reason in principle why the slip rule
cannot be relied on to convert an order which is invalid on its face into an order which is   C
valid on its face. Indeed, one would have thought that, if the court has the power to
invoke the slip rule to correct a valid order, it would be a fortiori that the slip rule could
be invoked to make a correction which renders valid an order which is, on its face,
invalid. Secondly, there is nothing in the wording of the slip rule which suggests that it
can only be invoked to correct orders which are valid on their face. It seems to me quite
inappropriate to imply into the slip rule a provision to the effect that it cannot be invoked
in a case such as this. Thirdly, this is in any event not a case where the order of the court   D
is invalid in the sense that it is a nonsense or unenforceable on its face: it is merely a case
of the order not going as far as it should have gone. Thus, if the order in its present form
were broken by the respondent, he would be in breach of an order of the court: see *Isaacs
v Robertson* [1985] AC 97.

Secondly, it is submitted on behalf of the respondent that the error which led to the
order being in its current form was an error of law rather than an oversight. I can see no   E
reason why the slip rule should be confined to oversights, which are not errors of law.
The facts of *Inchcape* provide a good example as to why that should be so. On the
respondent's argument, it would seem that in that case, the slip rule could have been
invoked by the plaintiff if the failure to ask for the specific order for costs had been due
to counsel not having carried out his instructions due to an oversight, but it could not
have been invoked if counsel had failed to ask for the specific costs because, mistaken in
law, he assumed that they would be included in the general order for costs. I do not see   F
how that distinction can be right. Furthermore, given the way in which Morton J
formulated the application of the slip rule to an oversight by the parties, I cannot see any
justification for limiting the very beneficial application of the slip rule as demonstrated
by that case in the way in which the respondent suggests.

Thirdly, the respondent suggests that the slip rule cannot be invoked where the form
of the order has been agreed by counsel and reflected the form of the summons issued by   G
the official receiver. Again, that point does not seem to me to have any force. As the
decision of Mr Reid QC shows, the court would, unless there is good reason, have given
the official receiver leave to amend the summons in the instant case appropriately. There
does not seem to me to be any good reason why, given that the slip rule can be invoked,
the same sort of approach is inappropriate when the order has been drawn up, unless of
course some sort of prejudice is thereby suffered by the respondent. Furthermore, there   H
is no doubt whatever that in this case the court intended to make a disqualification order
under s. 6 of the Act (and, indeed, as I have already mentioned, the respondent accepted
that such an order should be made). There was no dispute or argument as to the terms or
extent of the disqualification order (other than as to its duration). Accordingly, if the
disqualification order stands in its present form, which is defective, and may even amount
to a nullity, it does not reflect the court's manifest intention (or indeed the manifest

A   intention of the parties). If, on the other hand, it is altered as the official receiver seeks, it
     will accord with that intention.

     Finally, it is suggested that the slip rule should be invoked with particular reluctance
     in a case such as this, where the order which is sought to be altered is somewhat draconian
     in its effect. In my judgment, that point is answered by the fact that the respondent is
     already protected by the principle that the slip rule cannot be invoked in such a way as
B   to cause prejudice to the party against whom the order is altered. The fact that the order
     is one whose terms are somewhat severe on the respondent means, at the most, that the
     court would be particularly vigilant, when considering applications to alter the order, to
     ensure that the respondent will not thereby be prejudiced.

     In all these circumstances, I have come to the clear conclusion that I have jurisdiction
     to order that the form of disqualification order entered on 1 July 1994 be amended as the
     official receiver seeks pursuant to the slip rule. Further I have no hesitation in deciding
C   to exercise my discretion to allow the official receiver's application to that effect.

     It is right to add that, if I am wrong in my view that the slip rule can be invoked to
     achieve this result, then I would still have granted the official receiver's application. First,
     on the assumption that r. 7.47 of the Insolvency Rules applies, it seems to me that the
     terms of that rule, which I have quoted above, are wide enough to encompass the sort of
     alteration of the order which the official receiver seeks, and, essentially for the reasons
D   already given in relation to the slip rule, I would have thought it right to make the
     alteration. In addition, albeit with more hesitation, I consider that, even if the slip rule
     and r. 7.47 of the Insolvency Rules cannot be invoked, there would be inherent
     jurisdiction in the court to alter the order: see *Thynne v Thynne* [1955] P 272, especially at
     pp. 307 and 313.

     As I understand the submissions on behalf of the official receiver, if, as is the case, I
E   am prepared to alter the order entered on 1 July 1994 pursuant to the provisions of the
     slip rule, it is not necessary to consider whether that amendment is to be backdated to 1
     July 1994 pursuant to O. 42, r. 3 of the Rules of the Supreme Court, on the basis that an
     amendment of an order pursuant to the slip rule is automatically backdated to the date
     of the original order. I do not understand that proposition to be challenged by counsel
     for the respondent. In any event it seems to me that, where an order is amended pursuant
     to the slip rule, the alteration must, as a matter of logic, be automatically backdated to
F   the date of the original order. However, in case I am wrong on the point, it is right to
     record that I would have been prepared to backdate any amendments to the order
     pursuant to the power to backdate orders under O. 42, r. 3 of the Rules of the Supreme
     Court. Following the reasoning of the Court of Appeal in *Kuwait Airways Corp v Iraqi
     Airways Co & Anor (No. 2)* [1994] 1 WLR 985, it appears to me that the jurisdiction to
     backdate orders is rather less circumscribed than had been thought to be the case, and I
G   would have considered, essentially for the reasons I have already given, that this would
     be an appropriate case to exercise the power to backdate the order, were it necessary so
     to do.

     In these circumstances, I propose to allow the official receiver's application, and would
     invite counsel to agree the appropriate altered form of the order which was entered on 1
     July 1994.

H   (*Order accordingly*)

JUDGMENT ON RESPONDENT'S APPLICATION   A

David Neuberger QC: Introduction

This is an application by the respondent:

(1)   to vary an order dated 4 July 1994 ('the order'), whereby I permitted the respondent to be a director of certain companies notwithstanding the fact that I had just disqualified him from acting as a director pursuant to the provisions of s. 1 and 6 of the *Company Directors Disqualification Act* 1986 ('the Act');   B

(2)   that such variations take effect retrospectively to 4 July 1994 or such other date as I consider appropriate;

(3)   to give the respondent leave to continue to act as a director of certain companies for a further 12 months from 5 July 1995.

On 13 June 1994, I decided to make a disqualification order for a term of three years against the respondent arising out of his directorships of two companies called Brian Sheridan Cars Ltd and Brian Sheridan Cars (Hounslow) Ltd. This followed a hearing in which the respondent conceded that a disqualification order should be made, and the only issue was the appropriate period of disqualification.   C

Immediately after making this order I considered an application by him under s. 17 of the Act for leave to act as a director of three companies, Mercury Group Ltd ('Mercury'), Autoparks UK Ltd ('Autoparks') and J R Reynolds Design Builders Ltd ('Reynolds'). On 14 June 1994, I gave the respondent leave to act as a director of those companies, subject to certain conditions, for a year from 4 July 1994 on the basis that this period could be renewed if appropriate on the respondent's application.   D

The order was duly drawn up and entered on 4 July 1994. It provided that the respondent could act as a director of the three companies:

'For a period of 12 months from 4 July 1994 subject to and so long as the following conditions are complied with: E

(a)   Andrew Donald Gordon Mackenzie (or failing him, a solicitor of the Supreme Court with a current practising certificate) and Alan Willan Ross (or failing him, a fellow of the Institute of Chartered Accountants in England and Wales with a current practising certificate or individual with equivalent professional qualifications) be appointed as executive directors (and in the case of Alan Willan Ross, or failing him such chartered accountant as aforesaid, as finance director) of each of the companies by 4 July 1994 and that they continue as such directors;   F

(b)   Anthony Wasikowski or such other individual as may be agreed to in writing by the applicant be appointed as director of J L Reynolds (Design Builders) Ltd by 1 October 1994 or within such further time as may be agreed in writing between the parties and that such individual continue as such director;   G

(c)   Williams Allen be retained as the companies' accountants to provide and that they provide each of the companies with the services set out in para. 4 of the affidavit of Donald Brame sworn herein on 31 May 1994 as being services that it had been recommended Williams Allen should provide;

(d)   there be made available to Williams Allen on a monthly basis such financial records of the companies as that firm shall require;   H

(e)   that Price Waterhouse be appointed as the auditors of each of the companies by 4 July 1994 and that they continue to hold such offices;

(f)   that copies of the approved judgments and of the orders made herein on 13 and 14 June 1994 in these proceedings be made available on or before 4 July

A   1994 (or within such other period as may be agreed to in writing by the applicant) to General Accident Fire and Life Assurance Corporation, to Andrew Donald Gordon Mackenzie (or such other solicitor as is appointed director in his place pursuant to para. (1) hereof), Alan Willan Ross (or such other chartered accountant who is appointed director in his place pursuant to para. (1) hereof) and Anthony Wasikowski and, on or prior to its appointment as aforesaid, the firm of Price Waterhouse.'

B

The respondent failed to comply with the terms set out in that order, in three of respects. First, Price Waterhouse were not appointed auditors to any of the companies by 4 July 1994 or at all. In fact, Price Waterhouse decided that they were not prepared to act as auditors to any of the companies. Ernst & Young were approached, and they agreed to act as auditors for each of the companies, and have duly been appointed to act.

C   Secondly, neither Mr Wasikowski nor any other person has been appointed a director of Reynolds by 1 October 1994 or at all.

Thirdly, it does not appear that copies of my judgments were duly served upon Price Waterhouse or upon Mr Wasikowski.

During the hearing of this application, counsel for the respondent indicated that he wished to call oral evidence to add to the affidavit evidence which was already before me on his behalf, and also, I apprehend, to answer some of the points raised on behalf of the

D   official receiver. It seemed to me to be inappropriate to accede to this suggestion. In most cases of this sort, as in the present case, the parties will have had ample time to exchange affidavit evidence, and the respondent will be well aware of the points and arguments and queries raised by the official receiver. It would therefore only be in a rare case (such as the late raising of a new point of evidence by the official receiver) that it would be right to permit the respondent to add to his affidavit evidence by oral testimony. Insofar as the

E   respondent wished to have oral evidence before the court so that any dispute of fact which appeared from the affidavits could be tested by cross-examination, or so that the court could be satisfied that the respondent's witnesses were truthful, it seems to me that it would only be in a rare case that this course was justified. In this connection, I draw support from the approach of the court in similar types of applications (e.g. under s. 127 of the *Insolvency Act* 1986), and from the observations of Sir Donald Nicholls V-C in *Re*

F   *Rex Williams Leisure plc* [1993] BCC 79.

The appointment of auditors

The reason that there was express reference in the order of 4 July 1994 to Price Waterhouse being appointed auditors of the companies was that I had been told in clear terms on instructions by counsel for the respondent that Price Waterhouse had indicated

G   that they were prepared to act as auditors. It appears that a local partner of Price Waterhouse had indicated to the respondent that Price Waterhouse would be prepared so to act, and this is confirmed by Mr Ross. However, the evidence before me, which includes correspondence with Price Waterhouse, does not suggest that any sort of commitment was given by that firm. Price Waterhouse made it clear to Mr Ross that they were not prepared to act as auditors to the companies by letter dated 8 August 1994.

H   The respondent, his solicitors, and his co-directors appreciated the importance of having as auditors of the companies a firm of international repute. Accordingly, once Price Waterhouse had declined to act, Mr Ross promptly approached Ernst & Young, who had agreed to act as auditors by the middle of September 1994. Mr Ross says in his affidavit, and I accept, that, in practice, no harm has been caused by Ernst & Young acting as auditors instead of Price Waterhouse, nor by their having been appointed later than the court order required.

Nonetheless, in my judgment, the history relating to the appointment of auditors gives   A
rise to three points of concern. First, the respondent appears to have been rather casual
and over-confident in informing the court that Price Waterhouse were prepared to act as
auditors, and in permitting his legal advisers to approve an order with an unqualified
requirement to that effect. I appreciate that it is easy for the court, particularly with
wisdom of hindsight, to be over-critical of a businessman, who is not professionally
qualified, on this sort of point, but it is relevant to bear in mind that the respondent was
putting forward Price Waterhouse as auditors in circumstances where he knew that his   B
behaviour as a director had been, and would be, under close scrutiny, and when he was
seeking the indulgence of the court under s. 17 of the Act.

Secondly, the respondent did not apply promptly to the court for variation of the
terms of the order, so that the reference to Price Waterhouse could be replaced by Ernst
& Young. He carried on as a director of the companies where the terms upon which he
was permitted to act as director were being breached. Indeed, it was only when the   C
Treasury solicitor pointed out to the respondent's solicitors that by continuing to act as
a director in the circumstances the respondent was in breach of the Act, that the
respondent applied to the court to vary the terms upon which he would be permitted to
continue to act as a director of the companies. Even then it took him nearly two months
to make the appropriate application.

The respondent is, in my judgment, entitled to rely in partial mitigation upon the fact   D
that he was relying upon the advice given by his solicitors. That advice was that Price
Waterhouse's refusal to act as auditors did not, as it were, go to the root of the terms
upon which the respondent was entitled to act as a director, and that the problem could
effectively be cured by Ernst & Young acting as auditors, and that the matter should be
dealt with, as it were, by agreement with the official receiver, rather than by an application
to the court.

In taking this view, I consider that the respondent's solicitor was wrong. As counsel   E
for the official receiver has rightly emphasised, it is the court which decides whether or
not a director is to be disqualified, for how long he is to be disqualified, whether he
should be nonetheless entitled to act as director of certain companies, and if so on what
terms. It involves a misunderstanding of the Act to think that the official receiver has any
decision-making role let alone that he can agree to vary a court order.

The third concern raised by this history relating to the non-compliance with this term   F
is the fact that neither of the two professional directors, namely Mr Ross nor Mr
Mackenzie, seem to have appreciated that one of their co-directors, namely the
respondent, was disqualified from acting as a director of the companies by virtue of not
having complied with the terms upon which he was permitted to act as a director. One of
the reasons I thought it appropriate to require a solicitor and an accountant to be co-
directors of the respondent was because, as professional people, they would help to   G
ensure that the companies were properly run. In my judgment, it scarcely gives grounds
for confidence in their role if they permitted the respondent to continue to act as a
director of those companies in breach of the terms of the order permitting him so to do,
without any expression of concern.

However, it would be wrong to make too much of this fact. Mr Ross and Mr
Mackenzie are entitled to say that, so far as the respondent's disqualification proceedings   H
were concerned, they were being dealt with by the respondent's solicitors. While I do not
consider that that is by any means a complete answer to the point, it seems to me to be a
significant mitigating factor. The primary role of Mr Ross as an accountant and Mr
Mackenzie, as a solicitor, was to ensure that the legal and accountancy proprieties were
complied with. The reason I required their presence as directors of the companies was to
ensure that the public was protected.

Mr Wasikowski

Neither Mr Wasikowski nor any other person was appointed as a director of Reynolds. In practical terms, this is explicable on the basis that Reynolds' function was to carry out construction work, and, in the event, no construction work has been contemplated, let alone carried out, since the order was drawn up. However, the respondent became and remained a director of Reynolds, and nothing was done on behalf of the respondent so far as non-compliance with this term of the order was concerned, until, once again, concern was forcefully expressed by the Treasury Solicitor on behalf of the official receiver after 1 October 1994.

This demonstrates an unacceptable degree of casualness on the part of the respondent. It was not until the very last minute, namely 29 September 1994, that the respondent's solicitors even raised in clear terms with the Treasury Solicitor the fact that neither Mr Wasikowski nor anyone else was to be appointed director of Reynolds. In answer to the suggestion of the respondent's solicitor that the time for the appointment of an expert such as Mr Wasikowski as a director of Reynolds be extended generally, until such time as construction works were contemplated, the Treasury Solicitor made it clear by his letter of 7 October 1994 that this was quite unacceptable. Despite this, it took some three months before the respondent even brought the matter before the court.

Once again, however, it is fair to say that the respondent's attitude seems to have been based upon the advice he received from his solicitors, who appear to have assumed that this aspect was also one which should be sorted out with the official receiver, rather than by bringing the matter back to court promptly. In this connection, it is fair to say that the terms of the order did envisage the identity of the director (if not Mr Wasikowski) and the time within which he was to be appointed being negotiated between the respondent and the official receiver, without reference to the court. However, even on this basis, the respondent left the initiation of any discussions with the official receiver to an unacceptably late stage.

Service of judgment

The failure to serve copies of my judgments on Mr Wasikowski and upon Price Waterhouse is admitted by the respondent, but I have not been given any explanation as to why that happened. So far as Mr Wasikowski is concerned he made it clear fairly soon after 4 July 1994 that he was not prepared to act. Nonetheless, in view of the terms of the order agreed between the parties, he should obviously have been served with copies of the judgment, given that the order specifically required service on him by 4 July 1994.

The position with regard to Price Waterhouse is somewhat harder to understand. Although Price Waterhouse ultimately did not agree to act as auditors, they were clearly asked in correspondence to accept formal appointment as auditors. Although they asked for relevant information, it does not appear that they were ever provided with copies of the judgments.

The failure to serve copies of the judgments on Mr Wasikowski and on Price Waterhouse, without any explanation, is more than regrettable.

General Accident

It is convenient to refer to another point of concern. It will be recalled that a copy of the judgments was also to be served on General Accident Fire and Life Assurance Corporation ('General Accident'). That was because General Accident was to be, in effect, the financier of the schemes which the companies were formed to put into effect.

I was told at the hearing of 14 June 1994, both by the respondent's solicitor on affidavit, and by the respondent's counsel on instructions from the respondent, that General

Accident were aware of the disqualification application brought against the respondent   A
by the official receiver.

The state of the evidence now before me as to General Accident's alleged knowledge
of the proceedings as at June 1994 is thoroughly unsatisfactory. On the respondent's own
evidence, he merely informed the director of a subsidiary of General Accident that he
was involved in litigation with the official receiver: thus, he did not inform General
Accident directly of the fact that he was the subject of disqualification proceedings, and,   B
in so far as he informed anyone connected with General Accident, all he said was that he
was involved in litigation with the official receiver. That is a far cry from what I was told
by counsel, in his presence, or by his solicitor on affidavit on his instructions. It is also
right to say that the director of the General Accident subsidiary whom the respondent
claims that he informed does not recall having been so informed.

The issue relating to General Accident is of concern. It demonstrates, to my mind, a
casualness on the part of the respondent in circumstances where one would have expected   C
him to be at his most punctilious. If he cannot be relied upon to be truthful and accurate
in what he tells his solicitor and his counsel at a time when he is seeking the indulgence
of the court to permit him to continue to act as a director of certain companies when he
has just been disqualified from acting as a director under the 1986 Act, one is bound to
ask oneself whether he can be relied on in any circumstances.

D

More general considerations

On behalf of the respondent, Mr McLinden has urged me not to look only at the
deficiencies of the respondent in complying with the detailed terms of the order entered
on 4 July 1994, but rather to look at the broader aspect which he says is positive. First,
this is not a case where the respondent or his advisers were seeking to hide the facts from
the official receiver, the Treasury Solicitor, or the court. The respondent was relying upon
the advice given by his solicitors, and he cannot be blamed if that advice was wrong;   E
similarly Mr Ross and Mr Mackenzie were entitled to assume that the respondent was
being advised by his solicitor in relation to the disqualification proceedings and the terms
upon which he was permitted to act as a director, and it would be unrealistic to blame
them for any failure on his part. I think that there is some substance in these submissions.
However, it does not seem to me that the respondent can be wholly exonerated in relation
to any of the criticisms, and, in relation to the non-service of the judgment and what I   F
was told in connection with General Accident, there are no mitigating factors.

Mr McLinden further relies upon the fact that Mr Ross and Mr Mackenzie are
unstinting of their praise for the manner in which the respondent has carried out his role
as director of Mercury and Autoparks. They have regularly attended board meetings,
and have been closely involved in the running of those two companies for the past year
or so. Furthermore, in accordance with the terms of the order of 4 July 1994, Mr Ross   G
confirms that he received all relevant documents relating to Autoparks and Mercury,
who had been supplying monthly statements to his firm.

Furthermore, I am told that, if the respondent is unable to continue as a director of
Mercury and Autoparks, the successful business ventures so far developed through those
companies may well grind to a halt, and the companies themselves may well cease trading.
Furthermore, it appears that the two companies employ 11 people or thereabouts, and,
if the order is not extended to enable the respondent to continue to act as a director of   H
Mercury and Autoparks, their jobs may well be in jeopardy.

The report and accounts of Mercury and Autoparks as at 31 March 1995 have been
prepared and exhibited to Mr Ross's affidavit, and the consolidated accounts of the
holding company, Mercury, show a profit for the year of over £800,000. Overall, the two
companies appear to have traded very successfully, and the accounts bear out the

A   comments of Mr Ross and Mr Mackenzie as to the entrepreneurial ability of the respondent. It is fair to say that the respondent appears to have been paid substantial sums as consultancy fees. However, on the basis of the evidence, I accept that he has been working hard and successfully on behalf of the two companies, and that this has been reflected in the success of the companies as revealed by the accounts prepared for the year ending 31 March 1995.

B

The application to renew the s. 17 order

In these circumstances, I turn to consider the relief claimed by the respondent. I think it right to begin by considering the relief claimed in so far as it relates to the future. Should the respondent be permitted to continue to act as a director of all or any of the companies, and if so on what terms? In relation to Reynolds, the respondent resigned on 25 January 1995 and there is no reason for his directorship to be resumed. On his own

C   evidence, Reynolds is not trading, and there are no plans for it to do so. If there is a change of intention so far as Reynolds is concerned, then no doubt the respondent can make further application to the court under s. 17 of the Act, and such an application would be considered on its merits.

I find the issue much more difficult in relation to Mercury and Autoparks. The arguments for and against permitting the respondent to continue to act as a director are, I apprehend, tolerably clear from the above recital of the facts. On the one hand, there is

D   the fact that the respondent has failed to comply with the terms upon which he was granted what amounts to an indulgence, namely leave to act as a director of companies in circumstances where he had been disqualified from so doing under the Act, and where his attitude to those terms and, indeed, in connection with aspects of the court proceedings, gives considerable cause for concern. Furthermore, it can fairly be said that to extend an order entitling a person to act as a director of certain companies, when he

E   has been the subject of a disqualification order under the Act, and where he has failed to comply with the terms previously permitting him to act as a director in circumstances such as those arising here, sends out quite the wrong message. When considering whether, and if so for how long, to make a disqualification order, the court has frequently emphasised that the purpose of the Act is to protect the public, and to make it clear that casualness or worse on the part of directors, who seek to shelter behind the privilege of limited liability, is not acceptable. That is all the more so where, as here, one is considering

F   whether to extend an order made under s. 17 of the Act.

On the other hand, there is no suggestion that any of the failures of the respondent have of themselves caused any danger, let alone any damage, to the public. The two trading companies of which he has been permitted to be a director have traded successfully, and, if one looks at the matter broadly, the safeguards which I sought to

G   impose in my earlier order appear to have been effective.

With very considerable hesitation, I have come to the conclusion that I can extend the leave granted to the respondent to continue to act as a director of Mercury and Autoparks for a further year with effect from 5 July 1995. In reaching this conclusion, I take into account the factors pressed on me by Mr McLinden, and the fact that, in relation to at least some of the complaints raised against the respondent, he was acting on his solicitors' advice. Now that it has been the subject of detailed discussion and

H   analysis, it is plain that that advice was wrong, but I think that it would be unreasonable for me to conclude that, to a person in the position of the respondent, it should have been obvious, or even apparent, that the advice was wrong.

In his closing submissions on behalf of the official receiver, counsel suggested that it might be appropriate for me to extend the leave granted to the respondent to act as a director of the two companies for a further year if I felt satisfied that, in all the

circumstances, the respondent and, indeed, Mr Ross and Mr Mackenzie had 'learnt their
lesson'. I do not think that I can improve upon that way of putting it. It seems to me
that, in view of the various criticisms which can be made of the respondent, he has come
virtually as close to having his application for an extension period of the s. 17 order
refused as he could have done, without actually having it refused. Clearly, as I am
extending that order for a further year, he will be aware that an application could be
made at any time to discharge that leave during the year in question, and that, even if no
such application is made, he will have to make a further application for leave for the
third year to take effect from 4 July 1996. It is, I trust, clear to him that if he fails to
comply with any of the terms of the order permitting his directorship of the two
companies to continue, or if there is any other criticism which can be made of his conduct
as a director, the court will be most unlikely to permit him to continue acting as a director
of the two companies.

So far as the terms are concerned, they will be broadly similar to the terms imposed by
the order of 4 July 1994, save that condition (b) will be removed, condition (e) will involve
the substitution of Price Waterhouse by Ernst & Young, and condition (f) will require a
copy of this judgment to be served upon General Accident, Mr Ross, Mr Mackenzie and
Ernst & Young within 14 days of today. Finally, there will be a new condition, namely
that, within 21 days from today, the respondent must lodge an affidavit with the court
(with a copy to the official receiver) confirming that each and every one of the terms has
been satisfied. I will leave the details of the terms to be drafted by counsel, with liberty to
apply in case of disagreement.

Variation of the order of 4 July 1994

I now turn to consider the respondent's application to vary the s. 17 order entered on
4 July 1994, with retrospective effect to that date. Under O. 42, r. 3 of the *Rules of the
Supreme Court* 1965, it is clear that the court has power to backdate any order.
Furthermore, in light of the decision of the Court of Appeal in *Kuwait Airways
Corporation v Iraqi Airways Co & Anor (No. 2)* [1994] 1 WLR 985, it would appear that
the power of the court to backdate an order may not be as circumscribed as was
previously thought.

The reason why the respondent is anxious that I should not merely amend the s. 17
order, but also backdate it, is that it would thereby validate the respondent's directorship
of the companies, whereas, if I did not backdate any amending order, the respondent
would have been acting as a director of the companies contrary to the provisions of the
1986 Act, because he would not have been complying with the terms on which the court
had given him leave to act as director of the companies.

In support of the proposition that the court should amend the order of 4 July 1994 and
backdate any amendments to that date, I have been referred to a number of cases where
the courts have been prepared to extend time for the making of an application by a party,
whose application is made out of time due to an oversight by his solicitors: see for
instance *Palata Investments Ltd & Ors v Burt & Sinfield Ltd & Ors* [1985] 1 WLR 942, the
cases cited therein, and, in a slightly different jurisdiction, *R v Secretary of State for the
Home Department, ex parte Mahta* [1975] 1 WLR 1084.

I have come to the clear conclusion that if I amend the terms of the order as the
respondent seeks, I should not grant the respondent's application to backdate the
amendments to 4 July 1994. First, although the respondent's failure to comply with some
of the terms of the order of 4 July 1994 may be mitigated (but not exonerated) by
reference to the advice that he obtained from his solicitors, that is not a complete answer
to those failures, and others of his failures cannot be explained by reference to the advice
he obtained from his solicitors. Secondly, I consider that, taken as a whole, the

A   circumstances of this case make it inappropriate to backdate any order amending the s. 17 order to 4 July 1994 to assist the respondent: there are sufficient aspects of his failure to comply with the terms of that order, and of other, connected, unsatisfactory conduct on his part in relation to these proceedings, to render it inappropriate for me to grant him, at any rate in full, the assistance he seeks by backdating the order. Thirdly, having extended by a further year the period during which the respondent can act as a director of Autoparks and Mercury, it seems to me that if I were additionally to amend the order

B   of 4 July 1994 retrospectively to that date, I would be close to indicating that the court did not take the provisions of the Act seriously. If I granted in full the respondent the relief he seeks, the message which might justifiably be said to be sent out is that the court does not really expect directors who were granted the indulgence contemplated by a s. 17 order to take their responsibilities seriously. Nothing would be more regrettable or inappropriate, or, indeed, inconsistent with the clear purpose of the Act.

C   However, there is a stronger case for backdating any amendments to 5 December 1994, when the respondent's present application was made. It seems to me that, had the respondent made his application promptly, as he should have done, the court might well have been prepared to backdate any amendment to 4 July 1994. In fact, he did not make his application until 5 December 1994. The reason for the delay between that date and the hearing of his application was partly due to the need to put in evidence, and partly

D   because of the difficulty of finding a date when all the relevant parties were available for hearing. It can be said with some apparent force that he should not suffer for that component of the delay.

     However, I have come to the conclusion that I should not backdate the amendments to 5 December 1994, or even to some later date. While the delay since the issuing of the respondent's application on 5 December 1994 has been due to the time it has taken to get

E   all the necessary evidence together and the difficulty in finding a hearing date convenient to all parties, one has, as it seems to me, to bear in mind the reason for that. In my judgment, the reason is that the respondent has had to explain, in so far as he could, why he failed to comply with three of the terms of the order, and has also had to explain, so far as he can, why the court was misled as to the information he imparted to General Accident. If, for instance, the only problem faced by the respondent was that Price Waterhouse had declined to be appointed as auditors, and the respondent had, as he

F   should have done, promptly made an application to the court to vary the order, then, in the absence of any other problems, the application would not have involved much evidence, and could have been promptly disposed of. It is really only because there are a number of aspects of the respondent's behaviour which require a detailed explanation (and which have not been explained fully satisfactorily in any case, and in some cases have not been explained at all) that it has been necessary for the parties to prepare

G   evidence for, and to make time available for, a full day's hearing.

     Even assuming, as the respondent suggests, that the effect of the decision of the Court of Appeal in *Kuwait Airways* is to give the court a virtually unfettered discretion to backdate an order where in the circumstances it is just to do so, it does not seem to me that it would be appropriate to backdate any variations I make to the order. I refer once again to the purpose of the Act, as it has been explained on a number of occasions by the

H   court. On the facts of this case, although the respondent has persuaded me to extend to him the indulgence available under s. 17 of the Act for a further year, I consider that it would be wholly inappropriate for me to grant him the further indulgence of backdating any amendments which I am prepared to make to the order of 4 July 1994 to the date of that order, particularly bearing in mind the purpose for which he seeks the backdating, namely to absolve him from the consequences of his own non-compliance with an order of the court which was of itself something of an indulgence to him. However, I am

prepared to backdate to 5 July 1995 the order granting him a further year under s. 17 of   A
the Act in relation to his directorships of Autoparks and Mercury.

Accordingly, I am prepared to make the variations to the order of 4 July 1994 as
sought by the respondent, but I am not prepared to backdate them. Whether, given that
I am prepared to backdate to 5 July 1995 the order permitting him to act as a director
from that date, I am not sure whether there is any benefit to him in granting him the
variations to the order of 4 July 1994, which is now spent.   B

General comments

Finally, counsel for the official receiver suggested that it might be useful if I could
indicate whether there were any general lessons to be learnt from this case. I do so, albeit
with some diffidence. In my judgment, this case serves to highlight the following points:

(1)   A person disqualified from acting as a director pursuant to s. 1 of the Act, who is   C
       then granted leave to act as a director of specified companies pursuant to s. 17
       should be aware that he is being accorded a privilege by the court, and that that
       privilege is liable to be withdrawn if he is casual in any way in relation to his
       conduct as a director or with regard to any aspect of the proceedings.

(2)   Where the s. 17 order permits a person to act as a director on specific terms, it is of
       cardinal importance that those terms are strictly observed: the respondent in this
       case can count himself lucky in having leave under s. 17 extended despite his failure   D
       to observe all the terms imposed upon him, and it must be doubtful whether the
       court would be so indulgent in the future.

(3)   A person who is permitted to continue as a director of a company under s. 17 on
       certain terms, and who fails to observe those terms, should be in no doubt that by
       acting as a director he is contravening the Act: if a person is permitted to act as a
       director only on certain terms, and he does not observe those terms scrupulously,   E
       then he is not acting pursuant to the leave granted to him. He is therefore liable
       under s. 13 (criminal penalties) and s. 15 (personal liability for company's debts)
       of the Act.

(4)   Similar potential personal liability for the companies' debts under s. 15 of the Act
       could be faced by other persons involved with the management of a company,
       where a disqualified person is continuing to act as a director of that company   F
       purportedly pursuant to an order under s. 17, but in fact in breach of the terms of
       that order.

(5)   As my decision in this case shows, even where the court is prepared to extend any
       s. 17 order where the person concerned has been in breach of the terms of a
       previous s. 17 order, he (and, quite possibly, his co-directors and other officers of
       the company) will still be vulnerable in relation to the period when he was   G
       continuing to act as a director in breach of the terms of the s. 17 order.

(6)   If a court makes a s. 17 order on terms which have to be complied with by a certain
       time, it would, at least in general, be a desirable practice for the court to require
       the respondent to lodge an affidavit (with a copy to the official receiver) within a
       specified time confirming that the various terms had been complied with; if such a
       term had been included in the order of 4 July 1994 in the instant case, it would
       have served both to concentrate the mind of the respondent and his advisers on   H
       the necessity to comply strictly with the terms of that order, and would have
       brought to the attention of the official receiver and of the court, in good time, the
       failure of the respondent to comply with those terms.

(7)   It is normally inappropriate for the court to impose as a term of a s. 17 order a
       requirement that the respondent do something to the satisfaction of the official

A   receiver. First, the official receiver's function is to assist the court, but it is for the court, and not for the official receiver, to be satisfied of relevant matters in relation to a s. 17 order, just as much as it is for the court to be satisfied that it is appropriate to make a disqualification order or a s. 17 order. Secondly, it is unfair on the official receiver to expect him to get involved with agreeing matters with the representatives of a director who is the subject of a s. 17 order: it would be adding to his already substantial burdens if that was required of him.

(*Order accordingly*)

Re N P Engineering and Security Products Ltd.

A

Chancery Division.
Harman J.
Judgment delivered 27 July 1995.

Disqualifying unfit directors of insolvent companies – Disqualification application made by official receiver in county court after dissolution of company – Whether proceedings were a nullity – Whether proceedings could and should be transferred to High Court – Whether Secretary of State could and should be added as party – Whether proceedings should be struck out – Whether Secretary of State should have leave to commence disqualification proceedings out of time – County Courts Act 1984, s. 41(1), 42(1); Company Directors Disqualification Act 1986, s. 7(2).

B

These were applications by the respondents to director disqualification proceedings in the county court for the proceedings to be struck out under s. 42(1) of the County Courts Act 1984, and by the official receiver and Secretary of State for those proceedings to be transferred to the High Court and for the Secretary of State to be substituted for the official receiver as plaintiff. Alternatively, the Secretary of State sought leave to commence disqualification proceedings against the respondents out of time.

C

The disqualification proceedings were started by the official receiver in the county court after the company had been dissolved notwithstanding the terms of s. 6(3)(d) and 7(1)(a) of the Company Directors Disqualification Act 1986.

D

Held, striking out the proceedings, and refusing the Secretary of State leave to commence disqualification proceedings out of time:

1. Applications for disqualification of directors brought after the relevant company had been dissolved had to be brought in the High Court by the Secretary of State. These were statutory requirements which had to be satisfied if disqualification proceedings started after dissolution were to be valid. It followed that the proceedings were constituted in breach of the statute under which they were brought. (Re Working Project Ltd [1995] BCC 197 followed.)

E

2. The court had no power under RSC, O. 20, r. 5(3) to amend the parties to the proceedings by substituting or adding the Secretary of State. The identity of the official receiver was quite different from the identity of the Secretary of State and the name chosen in which to sue was not a mere misnomer but the deliberate choice of one officer rather than another. (Re Probe Data Systems Ltd (1989) 5 BCC 384 followed.)

F

3. Considering the respondents' summons after transfer to the High Court on the same basis as would have applied without transfer, the county court deciding the summons under s. 42(1) should have struck out the proceedings.

4. Imposing a period of disqualification would prejudice the respondents because disqualification would last for a total period far longer than would have been appropriate if the proceedings had been properly constituted and brought. There was also delay in making the application for leave. Bearing in mind all the material points and the whole conduct and seriousness of the application to disqualify, leave should not be granted.

G

The following cases were referred to in the judgment:

Al Tawwab, The [1991] 1 Ll Rep 201.
Carecraft Construction Co Ltd, Re [1993] BCC 336; [1994] 1 WLR 172.
Cedac Ltd, Re [1990] BCC 555.
Dubai Bank Ltd v Galadari (unreported, 12 February 1990, Morritt J).
Miller-Mead v Minister of Housing and Local Government & Anor [1963] 2 QB 196.
Probe Data Systems Ltd, Re (1989) 5 BCC 384.
Probe Data Systems Ltd, Re (No. 3) [1991] BCC 428.
Restick v Crickmore [1994] 1 WLR 420.

H

A   *Sevenoaks Stationers (Retail) Ltd, Re* [1990] BCC 765; [1991] Ch 164.
Town Investments Ltd & Ors v Department of the Environment [1978] AC 359.
Working Project Ltd, Re [1995] BCC 197.

Philip Jones (instructed by the Treasury Solicitor) for the official receiver and Secretary of State.

Lord Meston (instructed by Franklins) for Mr and Mrs Pafundo.

B

JUDGMENT

Harman J: I have to determine both an application made to this court and an application made to the Milton Keynes County Court. By an originating summons issued in the Chancery Division on 22 February 1995 the official receiver and the Secretary of State for Trade and Industry as joint applicants (although described in the body of the originating summons as 'plaintiffs') sought orders against Mr and Mrs Pafundo. The relief sought was, first, that Case No. 69CD of 1992 proceeding in the Milton Keynes County Court be transferred to the Companies Court and secondly that the Secretary of State be substituted for the official receiver as plaintiff in that action. Alternatively, and quite separately, relief was sought by the grant of leave by this court to the Secretary of State (sometimes known as the President of the Board of Trade) to issue an originating application in the Companies Court against Mr and Mrs Pafundo seeking their disqualification from acting as directors of a company despite the period of two years from the winding up of the company stipulated by s. 7(2) of the *Company Directors Disqualification Act* 1986 (hereafter 'the Act of 1986') having elapsed.

By what has been called an ordinary summons issued in the Milton Keynes County Court on 4 January 1995, Mr and Mrs Pafundo as respondents in Case No. 69CD of 1992, wherein the official receiver was the applicant, sought an order that those proceedings be struck out pursuant to s. 42(1) of the *County Courts Act* 1984 (hereafter 'the Act of 1984') as substituted by the *Courts and Legal Services Act* 1990. Grounds were carefully set out; first, that N P Engineering and Security Products Ltd (hereafter 'the company') was wound up by order of this court on 12 December 1990 and was dissolved on 8 August 1992; in the same paragraph but secondly, that the originating application No. 69CD of 1992 was issued on 12 October 1992 well after the dissolution of the company; thirdly that the proceedings were wrongly commenced in the Milton Keynes (or any) County Court so that there was no jurisdiction to hear or determine the originating application. The summons added a third paragraph stating that Mr and Mrs Pafundo had not acted as directors of any company since the insolvency of the company in 1990 and it would be oppressive to transfer the county court action to the High Court. Thus before the originating summons was issued the respondents had claimed that the county court proceedings were brought without jurisdiction.

G   I have already transferred, pursuant to the powers in s. 41(1) of the Act of 1984 from the Milton Keynes County Court to this court a summons by the respondents seeking to have Case No. 69CD of 1992 struck out for want of prosecution. I have delivered judgment on that summons holding that the delays which have occurred, regrettably, in the proceedings were not 'inordinate and inexcusable' and that a fair trial was still possible. Accordingly I have refused to strike out Case No. 69CD of 1992 for want of prosecution.

H   I now have to consider Mr and Mrs Pafundo's summons of 4 January 1995 which I have directed shall be transferred to be heard by me. I have so ordered exercising the powers conferred by s. 41(1) of the Act of 1984, it being agreed by counsel, and I so hold, that 'it [is] desirable that . . . part of [the proceedings] . . . should be heard and determined in the High Court'. I have not at present considered the exercise of the power to transfer in respect of the originating application dated 12 October 1992 itself.

Thus the first in time of the applications now before me is Mr and Mrs Pafundo's   **A**
summons and the Secretary of State's originating summons comes second. Part of the
argument before me proceeded on the footing that the originating application in the
county court was a nullity. That argument was based on what might seem the self-evident
proposition that proceedings before a court which had no power to entertain them must
be a nullity. However it is clear from s. 42(1) of the Act of 1984 that proceedings beyond
the jurisdiction of the county court can yet be transferred to the High Court. If the
proceedings beyond jurisdiction were in truth a nullity, that is a thing writ in water and   **B**
of no effect, they could not be transferred since they would be a mere *brutum fulmen*. The
proceedings in the county court are no doubt invalid, in that no effective order can be
made in them, but they are not a nullity.

The exposition of the difference between nullity and invalidity, admittedly in a totally
different field, by Upjohn LJ in *Miller-Mead v Minister of Housing and Local Government
& Anor* [1963] 2 QB 196 at p. 226 after the first break to p. 228 top paragraph, seems to   **C**
me helpful on the general approach of the courts but in this case the statutory creation of
a power to transfer what might otherwise be thought to be a nullity in my judgment
prevents there being any nullity argument based on lack of jurisdiction.

However, that is not the end of Lord Meston's argument in support of this summons.
He called my attention to s. 42(1) of the Act of 1984 as now substituted. That provides
that where a county court is satisfied that (I summarise) proceedings are beyond its   **D**
jurisdiction it shall (a) transfer proceedings to the High Court or (b) if satisfied that the
person bringing the proceedings (here the applicant official receiver) knew or ought to
have known of that requirement order that (the proceedings) be struck out. Lord Meston
argued that on any application to the Milton Keynes County Court to transfer Case No.
69CD of 1992 to the High Court the judge of the county court ought not to have exercised
the power to transfer and should have struck out the originating application. Lord
Meston submitted that I should approach this summons after transfer under s. 41(1) on   **E**
the same basis as would have applied without transfer. In my judgment that is the correct
approach.

The basis of Lord Meston's submission as to the exercise of jurisdiction under s. 42(1)
is said to be fourfold:

(1)   the official receiver ought to know the basis of the jurisdiction of the court; he is   **F**
       an experienced office-holder with special familiarity with the winding up of
       companies and the consequences thereof;

(2)   the proceedings were not only brought in a court which had no jurisdiction but by
       the wrong person; the Secretary of State and the official receiver should, as holders
       of offices under the Crown, surely be familiar with the statutory requirements of
       the Act of 1986 and perhaps a fortiori where the relevant Act is a recent Act
       promoted by the very department of which the Secretary of State is head;   **G**

(3)   the length of time that has passed since the winding up of the company on 12
       December 1990; the lapse of time since 12 August 1992 when the so-called ten-day
       notice was given to the respondents and since 12 October 1992 when the originating
       application was issued; although there has not been inordinate delay and it is
       possible to have a fair trial (as I have held) the delay is still prejudicial to the
       respondents and can be prayed in aid in favour of the exercise of the discretion to   **H**
       opt for para. (b) in s. 42(1);

(4)   the fact that since the ten-day notice was given neither of the respondents has acted
       as a director of a company and if the proceedings are now transferred and heard
       in the High Court, perhaps in December but more likely in January or February
       next year, the minimum period of disqualification, if that were thought suitable,

A   would result in the respondents being unable to act as directors until 1998, six
years after the ten-day notice was given or the originating application began.

All these factors undoubtedly exist. All have some weight. Mr Jones for the official
receiver arguing that the summons of 4 January 1995 should be dismissed and that the
court in considering the originating summons should now exercise its power under
s. 41(1) of the Act of 1984 to transfer the county court originating application, did not
B   challenge the existence of these factors. He argued in effect that there was no difference
between disqualification proceedings brought in the High Court and such proceedings
brought in the county court. He argued that there was no relevant difference between the
Secretary of State, who should have brought the proceedings, and the official receiver.
On that basis he urged that the provisions inserted by Parliament in the Act of 1986 were
of small significance. There was no need for these distinctions, no substantial reality
turned upon them and no policy could be perceived which would be carried out by
C   adherence to the statutory requirements. In his submission the court should ignore the
errors on the ground that they have done the defendants no substantial harm.

All judges nowadays are familiar with purposive constructions of statutes so as to
produce a result which although it does some slight violence to the language of a statute
yet can be seen to carry out the policy behind the statutory provisions. Here Mr Jones,
instructed by the Treasury Solicitor, does not attempt to suggest that a policy can be seen
D   which can be achieved despite infelicities of language to give effect to the purpose
intended by those enacting the statute. His submission was, in essence, that no policy
could be discerned and no purpose was served by the provisions of s. 6(3)(a) in contrast
to s. 6(3)(d) or by the provisions of s. 7(1)(a) in contrast to s. 7(1)(b). He submitted that
the particular holder of the office of official receiver who brought Case No. 69CD of
1992 did so on the direction of the Secretary of State although by his own title. The
decision to bring the disqualification proceedings was the decision of the Secretary of
E   State and not that of the official receiver.

It followed, said Mr Jones, that the court should not be concerned to distinguish
between the Secretary of State, whose decision governed the start and continuance of the
application in the case whether it was brought in the High Court or the county court,
and the official receiver. Both were emanations of the Crown (a perhaps unhappy phase
when one considers the speeches in *Town Investments Ltd & Ors v Department of the
F   Environment* [1978] AC 359, especially Lord Diplock's comments at 380Cff. and per Lord
Morris of Borth-y-Gest at p. 390Cff.) and it mattered not who was the plaintiff, or
applicant if that be the correct title, in proceedings to disqualify a person from acting as
a director. Mr Jones further submitted that since the county courts, in cases properly
within their jurisdiction, had the same powers to disqualify directors and very similar
procedures (save that all solicitors have rights of audience in county courts whereas the
G   Bar and a few specially qualified solicitors have rights of audience in the High Court)
there could be no purpose in the statute providing that disqualification cases brought
after dissolution of a company are not within the powers of a county court. From these
two submissions Mr Jones drew the conclusion that I should ignore the differences,
transfer Case No. 69CD of 1992 from the county court, where no order could ever be
made upon it, to this court, and change the style of the officer of the Crown bringing the
proceedings.

H   I regret that I regard that as a wholly fallacious approach. I accept that a statute ought
to be construed so as to effect the purpose for which it was enacted even if the statutory
words are inept or unsuitable on their face. But where a statute has been enacted
containing provisions which are clear enough but seem to serve no useful purpose, or at
least none is suggested, then in my judgment the only thing to do is to apply the words
and assume that Parliament knew what it was doing when it made the provisions now

desired to be ignored. On that basis I must hold that applications for disqualification of   A
directors brought after the relevant company has been dissolved must be brought in the
High Court and that the only officer who can bring these disqualification proceedings is
the Secretary of State. These are statutory requirements which must be satisfied if
disqualification proceedings started after dissolution are to be valid. It must follow that
Case No. 69CD is constituted in breach of the statute under which it is brought. In this I
follow the decision of Carnwath J in *Re Working Project Ltd* [1995] BCC 197. I take
comfort from the reasoning in that judgment at p. 201C–E where that judge commented   B
that words in s. 6(3) gave no jurisdiction to county courts for cases started after the
winding up was complete which occurred on dissolution.

I notice that in *Re Probe Data Systems Ltd* (1989) 5 BCC 384 Millett J dealing with an
originating summons under the Act of 1986 which had been brought by the official
receiver under his own style against a director of a company which had gone into
voluntary liquidation (unlike on its facts this case, which is one of compulsory   C
liquidation), where the provisions of s. 7(1)(b) Act of 1986 gave the official receiver no
locus standi, struck out the originating summons. Millett J held that RSC, O. 20, r. 5(3)
could not apply to such a case. The judge pointed out that in considering the power to
amend parties 'the crucial question is as to the identity of the person intended to be made
a party' (at p. 387B), applying a decision of the Court of Appeal. He also held that in
that case, 'the official receiver clearly intended to make the application in his own name'
and therefore there was no 'mistake' within O. 20, r. 5(3). The present case is at least as   D
strong on its facts as *Re Probe Data Systems Ltd* (above) and in my judgment I have no
power under O. 20, r. 5(3) to amend the parties to the proceedings by deleting the style
of the official receiver and substituting the style of the Secretary of State, nor can I see
any power to double-up the applicants, or plaintiffs, by simply adding to the official
receiver the Secretary of State who is the only officer who had, both on 12 October 1992
and now, locus standi to bring these proceedings, it now being long past the period of   E
two years from the date of the company's insolvency within which, by s. 7(2) of the Act
of 1986, applications for disqualification must be made.

I was urged by Mr Jones to exercise the powers conferred by O. 15, r. 6 to order the
Secretary of State to be added as a party. These well-known powers were not relied upon
before Millett J in *Re Probe Data Systems Ltd* (above), although O. 20, r. 5(1) begins
with a reference to O. 15, r. 6, and I prefer to follow that judgment. It was argued that
the decision in *The Al Tawwab* [1991] 1 Ll Rep 201, in which O. 20, r. 3 was relied upon   F
and not O. 15, r. 6, had 'overtaken' the decision in *Re Probe Data Systems Ltd* (above).
It appears that Millett J's decision was not cited to the Court of Appeal in the Admiralty
Court. However, Morritt J's decision in *Dubai Bank Ltd v Galadari* (unreported) was
approved (see per Lloyd LJ at p. 205, 2nd column), where Morritt J held that there was
no jurisdiction to join a person as plaintiff to proceedings. The essence of Lloyd LJ's
judgment can be seen at p. 207, 2nd column, the second and third sidelining. He held that   G
the mistake as to the name of the party was 'a mistake as to name not a mistake as to
identity'. Stocker LJ at p. 208, 2nd column, 4th sidelining, is to the same effect and Sir
George Waller agreed. In this case, in my judgment, the identity of the official receiver is
quite different from the identity of the Secretary of State and the name chosen in which
to sue was not a mere misnomer but the deliberate choice of one officer rather than
another. I can see no inconsistency between *Re Probe Data Systems Ltd* (above) and *The*   H
Al Tawwab (above).

Lord Meston, in directing my attention to s. 42(1) of the Act of 1984 as substituted,
and in support of the respondents' summons to strike out, relying on para. (b) of the
subsection, referred me to a decision of the Court of Appeal in *Restick v Crickmore* [1994]
1 WLR 420. That decision turned upon the terms of s. 40(1) of the Act of 1984 as
substituted, and not upon the terms of s. 42(1) but the words of the two subsections are

A   almost identical and in my judgment I should endeavour in this case to apply the principles enunciated by the Court of Appeal. In *Restick v Crickmore* (above) the Court of Appeal held that upon the true construction of s. 40(1) there was a mandatory obligation, by virtue of the word 'shall' in the body of the subsection, upon the court to do one of two things, either order a transfer or strike out the proceedings where a condition was satisfied. But the court had a discretion as to which of the two possible orders it should make. The court held, by the judgment of Stuart-Smith LJ with which

B   the other members of the court agreed, that the policy of the courts was not to strike out proceedings because of 'some mistake of procedure' on the part of the plaintiff – see at p. 427E–F.

However, Stuart-Smith LJ went on to qualify that broad statement. On p. 427F he held that 'the draconian sanction of striking out an otherwise properly constituted action, [for failure] to comply with the rules of court, is not part of the court's function.' In the

C   present case the action No. 69CD of 1992 is not 'properly constituted'. It is brought by a person having no locus standi to seek the relief claimed. The failure to make the application to the correct court is not non-compliance with rules of court but failure to satisfy the specific requirements of the statute pursuant to which the originating application purported to be made. In my judgment the guidance I obtain from *Restick v Crickmore* (above) does not point to one rather than another exercise of discretion in this

D   present case. As it seems to me on the whole of the matters I have set out I ought to hold that under s. 42(1) of the Act of 1984 a county court deciding Mr and Mrs Pafundo's summons should have refused to transfer and should have struck out the originating application.

In those circumstances it would be unjust to Mr and Mrs Pafundo to allow the Secretary of State's application by originating summons for transfer under s. 41(1) of the Act of 1984, to avoid the proper consequences of the decision which should have been

E   made in the county court. Further s. 41(3) of the Act of 1984 itself provides that the power to transfer is to be exercised 'subject to any provision [of] any other enactment'. As I have set out above the originating application is completely outwith the requirements of s. 7 of the Act of 1986. In all the circumstances I refuse to exercise my discretion under s. 41 of the Act of 1984 to transfer the originating application to this court. I hold that the originating application ought to be struck out.

F   I now turn to consider the second part of the originating summons issued by the Secretary of State. By that application leave is sought pursuant to s. 7(2) of the Act of 1986 to apply for a disqualification order notwithstanding that the two-year period since the company became insolvent has long elapsed. The decision in *Re Cedac Ltd* [1990] BCC 555 was naturally cited to me on this point. The judgment of Mummery J at p. 564B to the end bears directly upon matters which will influence the court to exercise

G   its discretion whether or not to permit a disqualification application to be made out of time. I was urged that in the present case, as in *Re Cedac Ltd*, all the evidence bearing on the case has been filed and the new application can be made ready for trial very speedily. I accept that that is so.

However Mummery J then considered whether prejudice would be caused to the director, and held in that case it would not. In the present case the conduct complained

H   of took place in or before 1989. If a new originating summons is issued it is unlikely, even with all proper expedition, to be heard this year. If the summons were heard in the Hilary sittings of 1996 and a disqualification order for the minimum term – two years – was made, Mr and Mrs Pafundo will suffer until 1998. It is usual for the court when making a disqualification order to take account in determining the length of the disqualification of how long has passed since the events, and the director's conduct in the meantime. No court could impose a period of disqualification in this case without causing the

disqualification to last for a total period far longer than would have been appropriate if   A
the proceedings had been properly constituted and brought. Thus Mr and Mrs Pafundo
would be prejudiced in suffering far longer effective disqualification than the court would
have imposed if the wrong steps had not been taken.

Mummery J also referred at p. 565B to the seriousness of the allegations against the
director in that case. In the present case I am told that before the flaw in the county court
proceedings had been noticed negotiations had taken place for resolution of Case No.   B
69CD of 1992 by the *Carecraft* procedure – referring to *Re Carecraft Construction Co
Ltd* [1993] BCC 336 – and the band of disqualification appropriate had been agreed as
band 1. The case is therefore not one of very serious allegations, since it was agreed to
fall into the lowest of the three bands defined by the Court of Appeal in *Re Sevenoaks
Stationers (Retail) Ltd* [1990] BCC 765.

I have also to consider the delay in making this application for leave. As I have held in
my separate judgment on the application to strike out for want of prosecution there were   C
considerable delays on the part of the applicant although not such as to amount to
inordinate or unexcusable delay. The deplorable lack of answer to letters from solicitors
acting for Mr and Mrs Pafundo, indicating to me a lack of frankness on the part of the
applicant, is a factor for me to bear in mind in weighing the balance.

I was also referred to my own decision in *Re Probe Data Systems (No. 3)* [1991] BCC
428 where I refused to overturn the registrar's decision to grant leave under s. 7(2) of the   D
Act of 1986. I do not find any particular help from my own decision. It turned upon the
facts in that case, as all exercises of discretion must do.

I have tried to bear in mind all the material points and the whole conduct and
seriousness of this application to disqualify. In my judgment I should not grant leave to
the Secretary of State in this case.

(Order accordingly)   E

F

G

H

A

Barclays Bank plc & Ors v British & Commonwealth Holdings plc.

Court of Appeal (Civil Division).
Kennedy and Aldous L JJ and Sir Roger Parker.
Judgment delivered 28 July 1995.

B
Maintenance of capital – Purchase of own shares – Redemption of preference shares – Scheme of arrangement – Reduction of capital – Shareholder wishing to sell stake issued with redeemable preference shares – Redemption underwritten by banks – Scheme sanctioned by court and reduction of capital confirmed – Company became insolvent – Banks obliged to purchase worthless shares – Banks claimed as creditors – Whether agreement which substituted claim as creditor for claim as shareholder on insolvency was objectionable – Whether claim 'in respect

C
of' failure to redeem shares – Whether there was 'financial assistance by way of indemnity' – Materiality of court order sanctioning scheme – Companies Act 1985, s. 151–153, 178, 425.

This was an appeal by the defendant in an action, British and Commonwealth Holdings plc ('B & C'), against parts of an order of Harman J made after he answered ten questions posed in a special case (see [1995] BCC 19). The plaintiffs, six banks and a company called

D
Tindalk Ltd, sought to support the judge's conclusion.

Tindalk was the vehicle for the redemption of certain redeemable shares in B & C issued in connection with the disposal by its owner, 'Caledonia', of a substantial stake in B & C. The scheme by which Caledonia was to cease to be a shareholder involved the cancellation of stock units in B & C held by Caledonia partly by purchase by B & C and partly by cancellation in exchange for the issue to Caledonia of new redeemable preference shares in

E
B & C. The new redeemable preference shares would be redeemed in four equal tranches at a price of approximately £81.1m for each tranche at the wish of either the holder or B & C on 31 December in each of the years 1988 to 1991. If B & C failed to redeem the relevant tranche of the shares, Caledonia was to be granted the right to sell those tranches of its redeemable preference shares at the redemption prices to Tindalk, a company formed for the purpose and to be financed by the plaintiff banks in return for B & C's covenant.

F
The scheme involved a reduction of the capital of B & C and in October 1987 the court made an order sanctioning the scheme under s. 425 of the Companies Act 1985 and confirming the reduction of capital.

The first two tranches of shares were redeemed by B & C, but it became insolvent and administrators were appointed in 1990 and the last two tranches were not redeemed. Caledonia exercised its right to require Tindalk to purchase those shares and the banks, having financed Tindalk's purchase of the shares, claimed damages for breach of covenant

G
by B & C in the amount paid to finance the two purchases. The effect was that instead of the sum required to redeem the shares being paid out of shareholders' funds, and therefore ranking behind creditors, the sum claimed by the six banks as damages would rank as a creditor's claim equally with other creditors.

Harman J held that the damages sought in the action were not damages 'in respect of' any failure to redeem any shares within the meaning of s. 178(2) of the Companies Act 1985; and that there was no 'indemnity' associated with any of the transactions and

H
accordingly no 'financial assistance' within the meaning of s. 152(1)(a)(ii) of the 1985 Act was provided by B & C in connection with those transactions. He also held that the agreement was objectionable by reason of the rule in Trevor v Whitworth (1887) 12 App Cas 409 as an obligation by B & C to make a gratuitous payment at a time when it had no distributable profits. However, the order of the court sanctioning the scheme had the effect of rendering the obligation of B & C lawful. In relation to claims in misrepresentation the

judge held that they were capable of being pursued since they related to misrepresentations   A
about the status of the agreement which was validated by the order of the court.

Held, dismissing the appeal:

1. The judge was right to conclude that the damages claimed by the plaintiffs were not in
respect of B & C's failure to redeem the shares and therefore B & C was not excluded from
liability pursuant to s. 178(2) of the 1985 Act.

2. The judge rightly concluded that s. 151 of the 1985 Act did not preclude the plaintiffs'   B
claims. There was no indemnity under s. 152(1)(a)(ii). Indemnity had a recognised legal
meaning. The fact that a party might recover under a contract the same amount by way of
damages as he would have recovered under an indemnity did not convert that contract into
an indemnity. There was no financial assistance under s. 152(1)(a)(iv). The words 'financial
assistance' were of a commercial rather than a conveyancing kind and the form of the
obligation or transaction would not be conclusive. The covenants were bona fide covenants
the performance of which did not involve giving any financial assistance. The fact that   C
breach of the covenants might render B & C liable to damages did not mean that B & C
gave financial assistance thereby.

3. It was not open to B & C to assert that the terms of an agreement which became
binding on B & C and Caledonia pursuant to the order of the court were ultra vires and void
as between them. No more could B & C contend that the covenants were ultra vires and void
when sought to be enforced by a third party to the scheme of arrangement who entered into   D
the agreement which had been sanctioned by the court.

4. It was possible for representations to amount to an act beyond the corporate capacity
of a company, but the principles of law which affected a company's right to buy its own
shares and give away property did not prevent B & C from making the representations relied
on by the relevant plaintiffs nor prevent B & C from being liable for the consequences.

The following cases were referred to in the judgment of Aldous LJ: E

A & C Constructions Pty Ltd, Re [1970] SASR 565.
Ackbar v C F Green & Co Ltd [1975] QB 582.
Bank of New South Wales v The Commonwealth (1948) 76 CLR 1.
Birmingham & District Land Co v London & North Western Rly Co (1886) 34 ChD 261.
Burton v Palmer [1980] 2 NSWLR 878.
Charterhouse Investment Trust Ltd & Ors v Tempest Diesels Ltd (1985) 1 BCC 99,544.
Glendale Land Development Ltd, Re (1982) 1 ACLC 540.   F
Glendale Land Development Ltd, Re (No. 2) (1982) 1 ACLC 562.
Howe & Ors v David Brown Tractors (Retail) Ltd [1991] 4 All ER 30.
Industrial Equity Ltd v Tocpar Pty Ltd [1972] 2 NSWLR 505.
Isles v Daily Mail Newspaper Ltd (1912) 14 CLR 193.
Leslie (R) Ltd v Sheill [1914] 3 KB 607.
Lietzke (Installations) Pty Ltd v EMJ Morgan Pty Ltd & Dean (1973) 5 SASR 88.   G
McGahie v Union of Shop Distributive & Allied Workers 1966 SLT 74.
Nicholl v Eberhardt Co Ltd (1889) 59 LT 860; (1889) 1 Meg 402 (CA).
Pepper v Hart [1992] BTC 591; [1993] AC 593.
Plaut & Anor v Steiner & Ors (1989) 5 BCC 352.
R v Londonderry Justices [1971] NI 91.
Speller & Co v Bristol Steam Navigation Co (1884) 13 QBD 96.
Trevor v Whitworth (1887) 12 App Cas 409.   H
Trustees, Executors and Agency Co Ltd v Reilly [1941] VLR 110.
Walters' Deed of Guarantee, Re [1933] Ch 321.
Yeoman Credit Ltd v Latter [1961] 1 WLR 828.

Robin Potts QC and Christopher Butcher (instructed by Clifford Chance) for the
plaintiffs.

A   William Stubbs QC and Sir Thomas Stockdale (instructed by Wilde Sapte) for the defendants.

JUDGMENT

Aldous LJ: The defendants in this action, British and Commonwealth Holdings plc ('B & C'), appeal against certain parts of the order of Harman J dated 14 November 1994, in which he answered ten questions posed in a special case (see [1995] BCC 19). The

B   plaintiffs, which consist of six banks and a company called Tindalk Ltd, seek to support the judge's conclusion not only upon the grounds stated by him but also upon further grounds contained in their respondents' notice.

These proceedings arise out of the collapse of B & C in 1990. It was incorporated on 1 November 1955, under the name the British and Commonwealth Shipping Co Ltd. It changed its name on 15 February 1982, to the British and Commonwealth Shipping Co

C   plc and then on 13 January 1987 to British and Commonwealth Holdings plc. It was placed in administration on 3 June 1990.

As of August 1987 B & C's capital consisted of £54m divided into 324,036,401 ordinary stock units of 10p each and 215,963,599 shares of 10p each. None of the shares had been issued. However a company called Caledonia Investments Ltd ('Caledonia') together with an associated company were the owners of 101,478,412 of the ordinary stock units which therefore amounted to just less than a third of the issued share capital of B & C.

D   Caledonia was a company owned by the Cayzer family who in 1987 wished to cease being a large shareholder in B & C. Thus it was decided that Caledonia would divest itself of its interest in B & C. The way that that was achieved was concisely set out by the judge (at pp. 21D–22C):

'In order that Caledonia could avoid placing very large numbers of B & C's shares on the Stock Exchange, which might have led to a substantial fall in the share price to the detriment of Caledonia and the dissatisfaction of the board of B & C, an

E   elaborate and ingenious scheme was formulated by some of the best known solicitors practising in the City of London with the advice of well-known specialist counsel. The scheme involved the cancellation of 90m stock units in B & C held by Caledonia partly by purchase by B & C of some stock units for £100m and partly by cancellation of the remaining stock units in exchange for the issue to Caledonia of new redeemable preference shares in B & C. The new redeemable preference

F   shares would be redeemed in four equal tranches at a price of approximately £81.1m for each tranche at the wish of either the holder or B & C on 31 December of each of the years 1988–1991. There were provisions as to dividends which are immaterial for the present purposes.

In order for Caledonia to be sure that it would receive its £81.1m-odd in each of the years 1988–1991 even if B & C failed to redeem the relevant tranche of the

G   shares, Caledonia was to be granted the right to sell those tranches of its redeemable preference shares at the redemption prices to a company called Tindalk Ltd (hereafter "Tindalk") formed for the purpose which would be financed by six banks. Further B & C was to covenant with the six banks that it would conduct its affairs so as to maintain certain asset rates. Any breach of covenant would give rise to a claim in damages by the banks against B & C.

H   The scheme involved a reduction of the capital of B & C and therefore required the sanction of the court. On 12 October 1987 this court made an order sanctioning the scheme and confirming the reduction of capital. On 16 October 1987 B & C purchased 21m-odd stock units from Caledonia for £100m and issued the new redeemable preference shares to Caledonia. Thereafter the first tranche of "A" class redeemable preference shares was redeemed at its proper price on 31 December 1988, and the second tranche of "B" class of such shares was so

redeemed on 31 December 1989. As I have said, in the summer of 1990 B & C was   A
held to be or to be likely to become insolvent and was placed in administration.
The administrators are still running B & C and endeavouring to sort out the
various claims. Naturally B & C did not redeem either the "C" class redeemable
preference shares on 31 December 1990 or the "D" class redeemable preference
shares on 31 December 1991. Further B & C was in breach of its covenants to the
six banks.
                                                                                  B
Caledonia exercised its right to require Tindalk to purchase the third tranche of C
class preference shares which was effected on 27 June 1991, and the fourth tranche
of D class preference shares which was effected on 23 July 1992 – a date after issue
of the writ herein. Tindalk was provided with finance to make its purchases from
Caledonia by loans from the six banks. Those loans are likely to be irrecoverable
from Tindalk since the preference shares held by it are unlikely to be of any value.
                                                                                  C
Thus Caledonia has received the same sum of money as it would have received as
a shareholder if all its preference shares in B & C had been redeemed although two
tranches were not so redeemed. The six banks have financed Tindalk's purchase of
two tranches of preference shares and the six banks claim damages for breach of
covenant by B & C in the amount paid to finance the two purchases. The economic
effect is that instead of the sum required to redeem the class C and class D
preference shares being paid out of the shareholders' funds, and therefore ranking   D
behind creditors, the sum claimed by the six banks as damages (which is the same
amount and has been paid to the former shareholder Caledonia) will rank as a
creditors' claim equally with other creditors. Plainly creditors of B & C will be
much disadvantaged by the result which is said to have been arranged.'

The scheme of arrangement was achieved using three agreements. The loan agreement
dated 8 October 1987, was between five of the banks and Tindalk. Under that agreement   E
the banks made available a loan facility to Tindalk for the sole purpose of enabling
Tindalk to comply with the obligation in the option agreement to purchase the
redeemable preference shares from Caledonia. On the same day the same banks,
Caledonia and B & C signed the 'stand-by agreement'. The purpose of the stand-by
agreement was to provide a facility for use by B & C if it had sufficient distributable
reserves but insufficient cash flow to enable it to make dividend or redemption payments
in relation to the preference shares on the due date. The stand-by agreement contained in   F
cl. 18 a covenant by B & C to the banks to comply with the covenants and undertakings
in an agreement that was proposed called the option agreement and in cl. 19 to indemnify
the banks against any loss or expense which any of them might sustain or incur as a
consequence of default by B & C in the performance of any obligations expressed to be
assumed by it in the stand-by agreement.
                                                                                  G
After the order of the court of 12 October 1987, sanctioning the scheme and the
reduction of capital, B & C, the first five plaintiffs and Caledonia entered into the option
agreement on 16 October 1987. It contained terms the effect of which are set out in the
judge's summary of events which I have quoted. In effect Tindalk granted to Caledonia
the right (a put option) to require Tindalk to purchase all or some of Caledonia's
preference shares at a price equal to that which would have been payable by the company
on redemption. Tindalk also granted to Caledonia the right to require Tindalk to pay to   H
Caledonia an amount equal to the price which would have been payable by the company
on redemption in respect of each preference share then held by Caledonia. The obligation
of Tindalk in relation to the put option would be guaranteed by the banks in proportions
in which they had agreed to participate in the option agreement. It also contained in
cl. 6.01 covenants by B & C of which the following are relevant:

A   '6. *Covenants and undertakings*

6.01 B & C shall:

. . .

(3) Procure that the amounts standing to the credit of the Redemption Reserve shall at all times be equal to the amounts set out below:

From the date hereof up to and including 31 December 1988, £275m

B   From 1 January 1989 until all the preference shares have been redeemed, an amount equal to the amount required to redeem the outstanding preference shares (including the premium on redemption) together with all dividends which would fall due to be paid thereon in respect of any period down to the due date of redemption;

(4) Procure that the profit on ordinary activity before finance charges, taxation C   and extraordinary items in each of B & C's financial years (as shown by the audited consolidated profit and loss account of the Group for the relevant financial year) will be at least 175 per cent of the aggregate of the finance charges of such financial years;

. . .

(8) Make or agree to make any prepayment of any sums payable under the D   CULS (the existing convertible subordinated unsecured loan) . . .

. . .

(10)   (a) Procure that the outstanding principal amount, including any fixed or minimum premium payable on final redemption (for the time being outstanding) of all moneys borrowed (whether secured or not) of B & C and the non-financial subsidiaries (excluding moneys borrowed by B & C from a non-financial subsidiary or by a non-financial subsidiary E   upon B & C or another non-financial subsidiary) shall not exceed an amount equal to four times the adjusted capital and reserves of B & C;

(b) Procure that the outstanding principal amounts (including any fixed or minimum premium payable on final redemption) for the time being outstanding of all moneys borrowed of B & C (whether secured or F   not) shall not exceed an amount equal to twice the adjusted capital and reserves of B & C;

. . .

(12) Supply the company with copies of its published audited consolidated and unconsolidated financial statements, together with an auditors certificate . . .'

G   The sixth defendant was not party to the option agreement, but the statement of claim alleges that on or about 19 July 1989 the third and sixth defendant banks were shown a draft supplemental agreement with a view to them taking over the obligations of one of the other banks which had signed the option agreement. That draft contained representations by B & C that it was not in breach of any of the covenants and undertakings contained in cl. 6.01 of the option agreement. It is said by the third and sixth defendants that they entered into the supplemental agreement of 5 October 1989 H   relying upon those representations. Thus the option agreement was modified in 1989 with the result that the second and sixth defendants took over the obligations of one of the banks which had originally entered into it with certain immaterial modifications.

On 16 July 1991 the six banks and Tindalk issued a writ against B & C claiming damages for breach of contract, a declaration that B & C was liable to indemnify the banks against loss and damage, and, in the case of the third and sixth defendants,

damages for misrepresentation. The claims made by the plaintiffs fell into three   A
categories: first, claims by five of the banks for damages for breach of contract by reason
of B & C's failure to perform the covenants in cl. 6.01 of the option agreement to which
I have referred – in the special case those claims are referred to as the primary creditor
claims; second, claims pursuant to cl. 18 and 19 of the stand-by agreement because it is
alleged that B & C was liable to indemnify the plaintiffs in respect of all losses and
expenses they suffered as a result of the breaches of covenant and for breach of the stand-
by agreement – those claims are referred to in the special case as the further creditor   B
claims; third, claims by the third and sixth defendants for loss caused as a result of the
alleged misrepresentations made by B & C in the draft agreement which ultimately
became the supplemental agreement of 1989 – those claims were referred to as the
misrepresentation claims.

The defence is contained in 43 pages of pleadings which includes two pages of
definitions. I need not refer to all the matters pleaded, but it is sufficient to record that B   C
& C allege inter alia that the claims made cannot succeed having regard to certain
principles of law and because they offend s. 151 and 178 of the *Companies Act* 1985. That
encouraged the parties to agree 'A special case for the opinion of the court'. The matters
upon which the opinion of the court were sought are set out in para. 48, 49 and 50 of that
special case. It is those questions which the judge answered and which are the subject of
this appeal. All the questions were the subject of appeal and I will therefore deal with
each of them in, I believe, a logical order, using the paragraph numbers of the special   D
case.

1. Section 178 of the Companies Act 1985

(A) *Question 48(d)(ii) (primary creditor claims)*

'Whether liability on the part of the company, as claimed in the primary creditor
claims, is precluded by s. 178(2) of the 1985 Act.'   E

Section 178 of the Act is as follows:

'178. *Effect of company's failure to redeem or purchase*

(1) This section has effect where a company has, on or after 15 June 1982,–

     (a) issued shares on terms that they are or are liable to be redeemed, or

     (b) agreed to purchase any of its own shares.   F

(2) The company is not liable in damages in respect of any failure on its part to
redeem or purchase any of the shares.

(3) Subsection (2) is without prejudice to any right of the holder of the shares
other than his right to sue the company for damages in respect of its failure; but
the court shall not grant an order for specific performance of the terms of
redemption or purchase if the company shows that it is unable to meet the costs of   G
redeeming or purchasing the shares in question out of distributable profits.

(4) If the company is wound up and at the commencement of the winding up any
of the shares have not been redeemed or purchased, the terms of redemption or
purchase may be enforced against the company; and when shares are redeemed or
purchased under this subsection, they are treated as cancelled.

(5) However, subsection (4) does not apply if–   H

     (a) the terms provided for the redemption or purchase to take place at a date
later than that of the commencement of the winding up, or

     (b) during the period beginning with the date on which the redemption or
purchase was to have taken place and ending with the commencement of the
winding up the company could not at any time have lawfully made a

A distribution equal in value to the price at which the shares were to have been redeemed or purchased.

(6) There shall be paid in priority to any amount which the company is liable under subsection (4) to pay in respect of any shares–

(a) all other debts and liabilities of the company (other than any due to members in their character as such),

B (b) if other shares carry rights (whether as to capital or as to income) which are preferred to the rights as to capital attaching to the first- mentioned shares, any amount due in satisfaction of those preferred rights;

but, subject to that, any such amount shall be paid in priority to any amounts due to members in satisfaction of their rights (whether as to capital or income) as members.'

C It is common ground that preference shares were issued to Caledonia upon terms that they would be redeemed by B & C and therefore the requirements of subs. (1) of the section are satisfied. The dispute between the parties concerns the words 'damages in respect of any failure on its part' in subs. (2).

On behalf of B & C, Mr Stubbs QC submitted that the words 'in respect of' had the meaning of 'some connection or relation between the two subject-matters to which the words refer'. That being so, he submitted, there could be no doubt that the section

D applied to the primary creditor claims with the result that B & C were not liable to pay damages to the banks. B & C had failed to redeem the preference shares and the damages sought were connected and had a relationship with that claim because the breaches of covenant in cl. 6 of the option agreement and the failure to redeem arose from the same cause. Further the payment to the banks as damages of sums equivalent to those lent to Tindalk which were then paid to Caledonia would be the same as paying the redemption value of the preference shares. The covenants in the option agreement had precisely the

E same effect as a covenant by B & C to the plaintiff banks that B & C would redeem the preference shares as and when required.

On behalf of the plaintiffs, Mr Potts QC submitted that the words 'in respect of' referred to the damages which B & C would (apart from the subsection) be liable to pay for breach of its obligations under the terms of the issue to redeem the shares. He went on to submit that the subsection, read in the context of the Act as a whole, was only

F concerned with remedies of shareholders in respect of a failure to redeem. In essence damages for breach of the contract requiring redemption.

The judge did not accept or reject Mr Potts' argument that the subsection was only concerned with claims by shareholders, but accepted his main submission that the subsection was only concerned with damages for the failure of the obligation to redeem. He therefore decided the question in the negative.

G Both parties cited authority as to the way that courts have construed the words 'in respect of' as used in other statutes. For myself I have only found those authorities of limited help, as words such as those under consideration have to be construed in context and therefore caution is necessary before adopting reasoning used by judges when considering the same words in a different context.

The words in the subsection are in my view clear. To decide whether a company is

H excused liability to pay damages, the court should ask itself whether there has been a failure to redeem and if so, are the claimed damages in respect of that failure, in the sense of being damages recoverable because of the failure to redeem. The loose connection or relationship suggested by B & C is not sufficient. The damages claimed by the plaintiffs in the present case are in respect of breaches of covenants in the option agreement and not in respect of the failure to redeem. That conclusion is I believe consistent with the Act as a whole. Section 159 gives a company the right to issue redeemable shares which

are liable to be redeemed at the option of the company or the shareholder. Section 160   A
provides for the way that such shares may be redeemed. Sections 160–169 are concerned
with the powers and duties of companies to purchase their own shares. Section 178
contemplates a case where the company has either agreed to purchase its shares or to
redeem shares from shareholders and fails to do so. The section then provides the result
namely no damages are recoverable (s. 178(2)) and specific performance cannot be
ordered (s. 178(3)), but the shareholder has the right to enforce redemption (s. 178(4) and
(5)) with deferred priority (s. 178(6)).   B

There is in my view much force in the submission by Mr Potts that the damages
referred to in subs. (2) are damages claimed by a shareholder in respect of the failure by
the company to redeem. However, I do not believe it necessary to come to any concluded
view upon the matter.

The cases cited support the construction of s. 178(2) to which I have arrived. In   C
McGahie v Union of Shop, Distributive and Allied Workers 1966 SLT 74, Lord Fraser
considered a claim by a member of a trade union brought against the union for damages
in respect of the failure by the union timeously to pursue a claim on her behalf against
her employers in respect of injury which she had sustained in their employment. The
accident occurred in 1957 and her action was raised in February 1964. The union pleaded
that the action was time barred by virtue of s. 6(1)(a) of the *Law Reform (Limitation of
Actions) Act* 1954. The relevant parts of that Act were to this effect: D

'6(1) No action of damages where the damages claimed consist of or include
damages or solatium in respect of personal injuries to any person shall be brought
in Scotland against any person unless it is commenced within the appropriate
period.'

Lord Fraser held that the claim was not statute barred since the damages claimed were
not damages 'in respect of personal injuries', but were damages for allowing her right of   E
action against her employers to lapse. His reasons are encapsulated in this passage from
his judgment, at p. 75:

'The matter was put correctly, I think, by senior counsel for the pursuer, thus: The
expression "damages in respect of personal injuries" may be paraphrased as
"compensation for a wrong consisting of personal injuries"; but the pursuer in this
action seeks compensation for a wrong consisting of allowing her right of action
against her employers to lapse without having been exercised. Therefore, said   F
senior counsel, the damages are not in respect of personal injuries. No doubt this
action will necessitate enquiry into the nature and extent of the personal injuries
sustained by the pursuer, but that is, in my opinion, only for the purpose of
evaluating the right that she has lost or (what is the same thing) of quantifying her
loss.'

The reasoning of Lord Fraser is apposite to the present case. The damages the plaintiffs   G
seek are compensation for breach of the covenants in cl. 6 of the option agreement; not
compensation in respect of the failure to redeem. No doubt the action for breach of
covenant will necessitate enquiry as to the cost of the failure to redeem the shares, but
that is only for ascertaining the value of the loss for breach of the covenant.

McGahie was cited to Croom-Johnson J in *Ackbar v C F Green & Co Ltd* [1975] 1 QB
582. The plaintiff in that case had been injured in an accident while travelling as a   H
passenger in his own lorry. He discovered that the defendants, his insurance brokers, had
failed to carry out his instructions to obtain passenger liability insurance for the lorry.
More than three years but less than six years after the date of the accident the plaintiff,
who had been unable to recover his losses from any insurers, issued a writ claiming
damages from the defendants for breach of their contractual duty to obtain the insurance.
The defendants contended inter alia that the damages claimed were statute barred

A   because they did 'consist of or include damages in respect of personal injuries'. At p. 588 the judge said this:

> 'In the end if one asks the question here, "What is this action all about?", one gets the answer that it is about an alleged breach of contract by the defendants, as a result of which the plaintiff lost the chance or right to recover his loss either from the driver or from his own insurers. I do not think that the damages sought in this action consist of or include damages in respect of personal injuries. Those damages, which might have been recovered heretofore, are only the measure of the damages now claimed. Accordingly, I find that the proviso has no application and that the period of limitation is six years in this case.'

What is the plaintiffs' action all about in this case? It is about a breach of contract for failure to comply with the covenants. It may be that the damages will be equivalent to the damages for failure to redeem, but that does not mean that the damages are in respect of the failure to redeem.

C

Mr Stubbs submitted that as *McGahie* and *Ackbar* were decisions upon the wording of the Limitation Act, they could not be determinative of the meaning of the words 'in respect of' in the Companies Act. That submission is right. However, I believe the reasoning of the judges to be persuasive. He also submitted that those cases differed from the present because the causes of action were based on a further wrong, whereas in the present case the action was, in effect, about the failure of B & C to redeem the shares. That submission is wrong. In *McGahie* and *Ackbar* there were accidents and the causes of action relied on were in contract. In the present case there was a failure to redeem and the cause of action was the breaches of the covenants in the option agreement.

Mr Stubbs also referred us to authority which he submitted supported his construction of the words 'in respect of'. In *Trustees Executors & Agency Co Ltd v Reilly* [1941] VLR 110, a mortgagee sought possession for failure to pay the interest due. The defence was that no notice had been given to one of the defendants, a farmer, as was required by the *Farmers Protection Act* 1940. The application for possession came before the Police Magistrate. He held that the application was not a step in an action, process or proceeding whether judicial or extra-judicial, in respect of a debt. Clearly the magistrate was wrong as the Chief Justice of Victoria pointed out. Mann CJ said (at p. 111):

> 'The words "in respect of" are difficult of definition, but they have the widest possible meaning of any expression intended to convey some connection or relation between the two subject matters to which the words refer. This was a proceeding in which the complainant had to prove, firstly, that the defendant was his tenant. He did that by production of the mortgage and reference to the attornment clause therein. He then had to prove that the tenancy thereby created had been duly determined and the magistrate found that the tenancy had been terminated because the defendant had given grounds for such determination by not paying the interest due under the mortgage. That was a breach of covenant which under the express terms of the mortgage authorised the mortgagee in the position of a landlord to bring the tenancy to an end, and but for proof of that breach of covenant, or in other words, of non-payment of a debt due, the whole proceedings must have failed because the complainant would have failed to show that the tenancy had been duly determined by notice to quit. Those facts are sufficient to justify the use of the language of s. 5(1), and to make it a case which could rightly be said to be a proceeding "in respect of" a debt of the defendant. The defendant being a farmer, the case consequently came within s. 5 and, therefore, the proceedings were admittedly not well founded by reason of the absence of notice to the farmer pursuant to that section.'

In that case, an essential, perhaps the essential, ingredient to establish the right to possession was the debt. Thus the application was in respect of a debt although it was

not to recover the debt. That can be contrasted with the present case where the cause of   A
action for breach of the covenants did not depend upon the failure to redeem. The
statement that the words in respect of have 'the widest possible meaning of any expression
intended to convey some connection or relation between two subject matters', when read
in context, are not persuasive as to the meaning of s. 178(2) of the *Companies Act* 1985.

Mr Stubbs also relied on *Howe v David Brown Tractors (Retail) Ltd* [1991] 4 All ER
30. In that case the plaintiff and his father were farmers trading under the name of W &
J Howe. In August 1982 the defendants supplied the firm with a tractor and recotiller.   B
On 23 January 1985, the plaintiff was standing on the recotiller when the guard gave way
and his leg came into contact with the machinery which was in motion. As a result his leg
had to be amputated. The primary limitation period for any claim by the plaintiff in
respect of his injuries expired on 22 January 1988, three years after the accident. The writ
was issued on 8 July 1988, claiming damages in tort for negligence and breach of statutory
duty. The defence pleaded the statute of limitations. Thereafter the plaintiff took out a   C
summons seeking an order under s. 33 of the *Limitation Act* 1980 to disapply s. 11 and to
add the firm as a plaintiff so as to allege breach of contract by the defendants. That
application to amend was opposed. As a requirement of deciding whether the amendment
should be allowed, the Court of Appeal had to decide whether the claim for breach of
contract fell within s. 11 of the Limitation Act. Stuart Smith LJ after citing *Ackbar* and
McGahie said, at p. 36:

>   D
> '... "What is the firm's action all about?" [T]he answer is that it is a claim for
> damages consisting of loss of profit caused by breach of contract or negligence on
> the part of the defendant, resulting from the personal injury to the plaintiff. The
> essential distinction between the present case and *Ackbar's* case is that the same
> facts which give rise to the personal injury and breach of duty to the plaintiff give
> rise to the breach of duty, albeit a different duty, owed to the firm. It is the supply
> of a dangerous machine which constitutes the breach of duty in tort to the plaintiff   E
> and causes his personal injury and pecuniary loss resulting from such injury. It is
> the supply of the dangerous machine which constitutes the breach of contractual
> duty owed to the firm to supply a machine of merchantable quality fit for its
> purpose; this breach of duty only causes financial loss to the firm because of the
> loss resulting from the personal injury to the plaintiff. In my judgment the words
> "in respect of" are wide enough to embrace such a claim and I find nothing
> inconsistent in this result with the reasoning of Croom-Johnson J in *Ackbar's* case.'   F

Mr Stubbs submitted that that case afforded a near perfect analogy with the present
case where the breach of covenant caused the failure to redeem and that failure to redeem
in turn caused pecuniary damage to the covenantee. I cannot accept that submission. In
Howe there were two causes of action relied on, namely breach of contract by the firm
and negligence by the individual plaintiff. The same facts lay at the root of both claims
and the damages arising from the breach of contract were the losses incurred as a direct   G
result of injury. In the present case the plaintiffs' claim is for breach of the covenants and
the damages claimed are those arising as a direct result of those breaches. The action is
not for breach of the agreement to redeem the shares which is a different act to breaches
of the covenant nor is it for the damage arising from the failure to redeem.

It was also submitted that guidance could be obtained from the judgments in *Bank of
New South Wales v The Commonwealth* (1948) 76 CLR 1 and *R v Londonderry Justices*
[1972] NI 91 and that what was said in those cases should be preferred to the reasoning   H
in *Ackbar* and *McGahie*. I think not. I, like the judge, do not find the decisions in those
cases upon constitutional matters to be helpful.

For myself, I have no doubt that the judge was right to conclude that the primary
creditor claims were not for damages in respect of the failure by B & C to redeem the
shares and therefore B & C was not excluded from liability pursuant to s. 178(2) of the

A Act. The words in the subsection are in my view concerned with claims for damages for breach of a company's duty to redeem shares. If there had been doubt upon the matter, it would, pursuant to the principles enunciated in *Pepper v Hart* [1993] AC 593, have been appropriate to look at proceedings in Parliament to see whether there was a clear statement of intention directed to the issue. That being so, we had drawn to our attention certain questions asked in the House of Lords *Hansard* 1980–81, vol. 10, 1001, and the answers given by Lord Mackay of Clashfern. Lord Bruce of Donington quoted the

B amendments which became subs. (2) and (3) to s. 178 and asked for an explanation. Lord Mackay said:

> 'Yes, my Lords. The purpose of subs. (2) is to prevent the remedy of damages for reasons which I explained earlier, because it would mean that this shareholder would have a priority over others in a liquidation. What subs. (3) is saying is that subs. (2), cutting off the right of damages is without prejudice to the other rights
C > to enforce the contract that the shareholder has.

> Lord Wedderburn of Charlton: My Lords, perhaps the noble and learned Lord could add a little more. Are we to understand that the word "damages", which is excluded, does not include compensation for breach of equitable obligations, other types of compensation in restitution or remedies of that kind?

> Lord Mackay of Clashfern: My Lords, the intention is to exclude rights of action
D > for damages for breach of contract, the contract being the contract for the redemption or purchase of the shares. It is that right of action which is excluded.'

Although I am not certain that Lord Mackay had in mind all the considerations that were placed before us, I take comfort from the fact that the conclusion that I have come to as to the construction of s. 178(2) coincides with the intention that was expressed in the passage from *Hansard* that I have quoted.

E (B) *Paragraph 49(ii) (further creditor claims)*
(C) *Paragraph 50(i) (misrepresentation claims)*

These paragraphs raised for consideration the question whether liability for the further creditor claims and the misrepresentation claims was precluded by s. 178(2) of the Act. As the parties accepted that the arguments in relation to these questions were essentially the same as those that I have considered in relation to para. 48(d)(ii) and that the conclusion reached must be the same, I decide that the judge correctly answered both the

F above questions in the negative.

2. Section 151 of the Companies Act 1985

(A) *Paragraph 48(d)(iii) (primary creditor claims)*

> '(3) Whether to the extent that breaches of the covenants by the company would impose a liability in damages upon the company as claimed in the primary creditor
G > claims the entry into and execution of the option agreement by the company was (but for the provisions of s. 153(3)(e) of the 1985 Act) unlawful by reason of s. 151(1) of that Act when read in conjunction with s. 152(1)(a)(ii) of that Act.'

The relevant parts of s. 151 and 152 are:

> '151. *Financial assistance generally prohibited*

> (1) Subject to the following provisions of this Chapter, where a person is acquiring
H > or is proposing to acquire shares in a company, it is not lawful for the company or any of its subsidiaries to give financial assistance directly or indirectly for the purpose of that acquisition before or at the same time as the acquisition takes place.

> (2) Subject to those provisions, where a person has acquired shares in a company and any liability has been incurred (by that or any other person), for the purpose

of that acquisition, it is not lawful for the company or any of its subsidiaries to
give financial assistance directly or indirectly for the purpose of reducing or
discharging the liability so incurred.

(3) If a company acts in contravention of this section, it is liable to a fine, and
every officer of it who is in default is liable to imprisonment or a fine, or both.

152. *Definitions for this Chapter*

(1) In this Chapter–

    (a) "financial assistance" means–

        (i) financial assistance given by way of gift,

       (ii) financial assistance given by way of guarantee, security or indemnity,
other than an indemnity in respect of the indemnifier's own neglect or
default, or by way of release or waiver,

      (iii) financial assistance given by way of a loan or any other agreement
under which any of the obligations of the person giving the assistance
are to be fulfilled at a time when in accordance with the agreement
any obligation of another party to the agreement remains unfulfilled,
or by way of the novation of, or the assignment of rights arising under,
a loan or such other agreement, or

      (iv) any other financial assistance given by a company the net assets of
which are thereby reduced to a material extent or which has no net
assets . . .'

It is the contention of B & C that the entry into the option agreement and in particular
the covenants in cl. 6 constituted 'financial assistance' for the purpose of the original
acquisition by Caledonia of the preference shares issued to it under the scheme and the
respective acquisitions of preference shares by Tindalk on the exercise by Caledonia of
the put option. It was submitted that the financial assistance given was by way of
'indemnity' (s. 152(1)(a)(ii)) or alternatively 'other financial assistance' as referred to in
s. 152(1)(a)(iv).

The plaintiffs submitted that B & C had not provided assistance; let alone financial
assistance; let alone financial assistance for the purpose of the acquisition of shares and
in any case nothing that was agreed between them and B & C constituted an indemnity.

The judge held that there was 'no indemnity concerned with any of the three relevant
transactions and accordingly under the definition no financial assistance was accorded
by B & C in connection with any of those transactions'.

Section 152(1) contains definitions of the words 'financial assistance', but by using the
words 'financial assistance' in each form of definition it is a requirement that the actual
transaction must be of the type mentioned, and must also amount to financial assistance.
Thus under s. 152(1)(a)(ii) there must, for instance, be an indemnity which gives
assistance for the purpose of acquisition of the shares which is of a financial nature.
Against that background I turn first to decide whether the covenants amounted to an
indemnity.

Mr Stubbs submitted that the word 'indemnity' should be given its ordinary dictionary
meaning, namely – a security or protection against contingent hurt, damage or loss or
compensation for loss. That being so B & C, by entering into the option agreement
(containing the covenants), gave an indemnity by providing the banks with security or
protection against contingent hurt or loss or compensation for loss.

I cannot accept that submission as it starts from the dictionary definition of the word
'indemnity' when the word is used in the statute in a legal sense and the submission then
seeks to equate covenants in the agreement, which give a right to damages, with an
indemnity. Section 152 contains reference to a number of legal terms of which 'indemnity'

A   is only one. All have their normal legal meaning. A guarantee is different to an indemnity. Both words have a recognised legal meaning, namely that given by Holroyd Pearce LJ in *Yeoman Credit Ltd v Latter* [1961] 1 WLR 828 at p. 831:

> 'An indemnity is a contract by one party to keep the other harmless against loss, but a contract of guarantee is a contract to answer for the debt, default or miscarriage of another who is to be primary liable to the promisee.'

B   The fact that there may be a contract under which a party may recover the same amount by way of damages as he would have recovered under an indemnity is not sufficient to convert that contract into an indemnity (see *Speller & Co v Bristol Steam Navigation Co* (1884) 13 QBD 96 at p. 101 and *Birmingham and District Land Co v London and North Western Railway Co* (1886) 34 ChD 261 at p. 271).

    Mr Stubbs sought to persuade us that the word 'indemnity' should not be given its normal legal meaning with the aid of certain conclusions of Hoffmann J in *Charterhouse*
C   *Investment Trust Ltd v Tempest Diesels Ltd* (1985) 1 BCC 99,544. At pp. 99,551–99,552 he said:

> 'There are two elements in the commission of an offence under s. 54 [the section that preceded s. 151]. The first is the giving of financial assistance and the second is that it should have been given "for the purpose of or in connection with", in this case, a purchase of shares ...

D   There is no definition of giving financial assistance in the section, although some examples are given. The words have no technical meaning and their frame of reference is in my judgment the language of ordinary commerce. One must examine the commercial realities of the transaction and decide whether it can properly be described as the giving of financial assistance by the company, bearing in mind that the section is a penal one and should not be strained to cover transactions which are not fairly within it.'

E   It was submitted that as the words 'financial assistance' had no technical meaning and their frame of reference was the language of ordinary commerce, the word 'indemnity' should be similarly construed. The fallacy in that submission is clear. The words 'financial assistance' are not words which have any recognised legal significance whereas the word 'indemnity' does. It is used in the section as one of a number of words having a recognised legal meaning.

F   Mr Stubbs also referred us to *Plaut v Steiner* (1989) 5 BCC 352. In that case Morritt J held that two transactions amounted to financial assistance by way of a gift within s. 152(1)(a)(i). The first concerned a sum of £5,778 which did not represent consideration for any asset acquired, but was a compensatory payment designed with others to secure equality of value between two groups. The second related to about £145,000 of a payment of £395,000 which was made to make an option attractive. He held that they were payments for which the particular companies did not receive any consideration and
G   concluded that the obligations to pay involved giving financial assistance by way of a gift. It was submitted that to arrive at the conclusion he did, the judge had to construe the word 'gift' as covering transactions which would not in law amount to a gift in that they were just overpayments. It is not apparent to me that the judge did not attach to the word 'gift' in s. 152(1)(a)(i) its normal legal meaning. Overpayments may or may not be gifts depending upon the circumstances and in that case, I believe, the judge took into account the reality of the transactions rather than their form. In any case the judgment
H   does not throw light upon the true meaning of the word 'indemnity' in subs. (1)(a)(ii). Therefore this authority does not suggest that the conclusion that I have reached was wrong.

    B & C also submitted that the scheme amounted to financial assistance as defined by s. 152(1)(a)(iv). Thus it is necessary to decide whether the scheme constituted financial assistance for the purpose of acquiring the shares.

I have already read the relevant part of Hoffmann J's judgment in *Charterhouse Investment Trust Ltd* in which he pointed out that the term financial assistance shall be given its normal commercial meaning. Thus the section requires that there should be assistance or help for the purpose of acquiring the shares and that that assistance should be financial.

The plaintiffs submitted that B & C had never provided assistance, let alone financial assistance for the purpose of acquiring the shares. They accept that the giving of the covenants in cl. 6 may have induced the plaintiffs to enter into the commitments that they did, but submitted that the covenants did not financially assist anybody to buy shares.

Mr Potts drew to our attention *Industrial Equity Ltd v Tocpar Pty Ltd* [1972] 2 NSWLR 505 in which Helsham J drew a similar distinction between financial assistance and inducement. The facts of that case are complicated but his reasoning is apparent from this passage of his judgment, at p. 514:

> 'The plaintiff argues that Country Producers is required to, or will at some stage in the future, provide money to a company to be formed so as to enable each share in that new company to have an asset backing of 75c per share . . . The requirement of Country Producers to provide this money for this purpose is claimed to be the giving of financial assistance by Country Producers in connection with the purchase by Tocpar of shares in Country Producers to be acquired pursuant to the take-over scheme from present shareholders. But the possibility, probability or enforceable requirement of Country Producers to provide in the future an asset backing for shares in the company to be formed by payment of a premium by it on shares to be acquired by it in that company cannot, in my view, be said to be the giving of financial assistance in connection with the acquisition of shares under the take-over scheme . . . An offer of an advance, if that is what Country Producers offered, to be made to a third party if a purchase, without any help from it, of its shares is concluded, cannot in my view be said to be an agreement or threat to give financial assistance in connection with the purchase of its shares. The offer of Country Producers, if it constituted an offer, or the indication of intention to provide an asset backing for a new company might amount to encouragement by Country Producers for its shareholders to accept the take-over offer, and was certainly intended as an inducement to them to accept Tocpar's offer and to reject that of Jeperion. But to say that it amounts to a promise to give financial assistance in connection with the purchase of the shares when the purchase will have been completed is to attempt to extend s. 67 beyond its limits.'

A similar view was expressed by the Supreme Court of New South Wales in *Burton v Palmer* [1980] 2 NSWLR 878. Mahoney J said at p. 889F:

> 'The fact that a company undertakes obligations, absolute or contingent, in connection with the proposal for the transfer of its shares does not of itself constitute the giving of financial assistance. As I have said, the fact that a company facilitates a proposal for such a transfer will not involve it necessarily in a contravention of s. 67. Thus, a company may answer requests for information relevant to the proposed transfer knowing that it does so in circumstances such that it will be liable for damages if, for lack of care, the information is incorrect: cf. *Mutual Life and Citizens Assurance Co Ltd v Evatt* ([1971] AC 793). But, by answering such requests, the company does not thereby give financial assistance.
>
> There may, of course, be circumstances in which the obligations entered into by a company are entered into for a collateral purpose: in such circumstances it may be that the company will, in the particular case, be giving financial assistance. But, collateral purposes aside, if s. 67 is to be relevant, there must be more than the

A   incurring, in connection with the transfer of shares, of an obligation which may involve the company in the payment of money. The obligation must be such that it is properly to be categorised as financial assistance. An obligation of a different kind, e.g., an obligation to permit inspection of its books and records, will not constitute the giving of financial assistance simply because, if it is broken, the company will be liable to pay damages.

B   I do not mean by this that the relevance of s. 67 is to be determined by a schematic analysis of the obligation undertaken. The words "financial assistance" are words of a commercial rather than a conveyancing kind and the form of the obligation or transaction will not be conclusive. Thus a loan ostensibly given by a third party may, in the context of a 'round robin' of cheques, be seen as financial assistance in connection with the sale of the shares: see *Wallersteiner v Moir* ([1974] 1 WLR 991). And a loan given by a company after the sale has been completed may, in

C   particular circumstances, be such: in the example given in the Greene Report, the Act might be contravened: cf. *Glennon v Commissioner of Taxation* ((1972) 127 CLR 503 at p. 510). Similarly, a warranty given with the intention that the company will be called upon to pay damages and to provide funds in connection with the transfer of its shares will contravene the section. That is not the present case.'

D   That statement of the way to approach s. 67 of the Australian Act is, I believe, applicable to s. 151 of the 1985 Act. No doubt, as pointed out by Mahoney J, there will be cases where the court will look behind the form to see whether there was a collateral purpose and if so conclude that financial assistance was provided; this is not such a case. The purpose of the covenants in the option agreement was to reassure Caledonia. The covenants were bona fide covenants the performance of which did not involve giving of any financial assistance. The fact that breach of the covenants might render B & C liable

E   to damages did not mean that B & C gave financial assistance thereby.

The judge rightly in my view concluded that s. 151 did not preclude the primary creditor claims. The option agreement did not amount to financial assistance for the purpose of acquisition of the shares. He correctly answered question 48(d)(iii) in the negative.

F   (B) *Question 49(iii) (further creditor claims)*

The parties agreed that their submissions as to the effect of s. 151 upon the further creditor claims were essentially the same as those made on the primary creditor claims. Therefore for the reasons already given, I conclude that the judge correctly answered this question in the negative.

(C) *Question 50(iii) (misrepresentation claims)*

G   B & C put forward the same submissions on s. 151 in respect of the misrepresentations claims, but also submitted that by making the alleged misrepresentations with the intention that they would be acted on, they provided the two banks concerned with an indemnity within the meaning of that word. Alternatively, B & C by making the representations with the intention that they would be acted on, entered into a transaction which, even if not taking the form of a contract indemnity, had precisely the same effect.

H   From what I have already said, it is quite clear that those submissions cannot be accepted. I cannot understand how the making of misrepresentations by B & C could amount to the provision by them of an indemnity. The misrepresentations may have amounted to a wrong for which the law provides a remedy in the form of damages which could be equivalent in amount to the sum that would be awarded pursuant to a contract of indemnity; but to suggest that the misrepresentations themselves amount to an indemnity is in my submission totally unsupportable.

3. The effect of the order of the court

(A) *Question 48(d)(iv)*

A

'Whether the order dated 12 October 1987 sanctioning the scheme of arrangement was capable of rendering lawful financial assistance (namely, to the extent that breaches of the covenants by the company would impose a liability in damages upon the company as claimed in the primary creditor claims, the entry into and the execution of the option agreement) which would otherwise whether by reason of s. 152(1)(a)(ii) or by reason of s. 152(1)(a)(iv) have been unlawful.'

B

The order of 12 October 1987, was that 'This court does hereby sanction the scheme of arrangement as set forth in the schedule to the said petition and in the first schedule hereto'. The schedule describes the scheme. Paragraph 1 of the scheme made provision for the capital of the company to be reduced by cancelling and extinguishing the Caledonia stock units and the issue of certain preference shares to Caledonia. Paragraph 2 stated 'The company and Caledonia shall enter into and execute the option agreement'.

C

The order sanctioning the scheme was made under the powers given by s. 425, the relevant parts of which are as follows:

'(1) Where a compromise or arrangement is proposed between a company and its creditors, or any class of them, or between the company and its members, or any class of them, the court may on the application of the company or any creditor or member of it or, in the case of a company being wound up, or an administration order being in force in relation to a company, of the liquidator or administrator, order a meeting of the creditors or class of creditors, or of the members of the company or class of members (as the case may be), to be summoned in such manner as the court directs.

D

(2) If a majority in number representing three-fourths in value of the creditors or class of creditors or members or class of members (as the case may be), present and voting either in person or by proxy at the meeting, agree to any compromise or arrangement, the compromise or arrangement, if sanctioned by the court, is binding on all the creditors or the class of creditors, or on the members or class of members (as the case may be), and also on the company or, in the case of a company in the course of being wound up, on the liquidator and contributories of the company.'

E

F

The judge held that the option agreement had been sanctioned by the order of the court and as it had not been set aside, it could not be impugned by B & C. The result was that B & C could not contend that the covenants in the option agreement were ultra vires so as to prevent the plaintiffs from succeeding on the primary creditor claims.

Not surprisingly the plaintiffs supported both the reasoning and conclusion of the judge. However B & C submitted that the judge had erred in a number of respects which had consequently led him to a wrong conclusion. First, it was submitted that the judge was wrong to hold that the option agreement was part of the scheme that had been approved by the court. All that the order required was that B & C and Caledonia should enter into the agreement and that obligation was wholly spent as soon as the agreement was signed; second that, if the effect of the order was to create rights between B & C and Caledonia, it did not mean that enforceable rights were created between B & C and the plaintiffs; third, s. 425 contained an implied limitation to the effect that if and to the extent that a scheme of arrangement sanctioned by s. 425(2) obliged the company to do something which would infringe some other statutory provision, the scheme did not become binding upon the company. That being so, the scheme did not bind B & C as the order obliged B & C to enter into an agreement that was contrary to the statute. I will consider each of B & C's submissions.

G

H

A   I have already quoted the relevant terms of the order and the scheme which is scheduled to it. The order sanctioned the scheme as set forth in the schedule and the scheme required B & C to enter into and execute the option agreement which was defined in the document scheduled to the order. The actual agreement signed conformed with that definition. It follows that the court approved B & C and Caledonia entering into the option agreement containing as it did the covenants in cl. 6. It seems to me unarguable that the court did not also sanction the option agreement as and when it was signed. The submission that

B   the only effect of the order was that B & C and Caledonia should become parties to the option agreement without also sanctioning the agreement itself with the effect that the parties became bound by its terms is unacceptable and contrary to sense. There could be no purpose in the court approving the act of B & C and Caledonia executing the agreement unless it was to make the terms of the agreement binding, at least between B & C and Caledonia.

C   The second submission of B & C starts from the assumption that the order of the court approved the option agreement with the result that it became binding as between the parties mentioned in the order, namely B & C and Caledonia. Even so it was submitted that the order did not make the agreement binding as between B & C and any other parties as s. 425 only states that if an arrangement is sanctioned by the courts, then it becomes binding upon the company, its creditors and members, one of which was

D   Caledonia. It is correct that s. 425 provides that agreed compromises and arrangements, if sanctioned by the court, are binding between the company, its creditors and members as the case may be; but that does not solve the matter in dispute, namely whether a term of an agreement which is binding between a company and its members is also binding upon another party.

   The plaintiffs submitted that, the effect of the court order was to make the covenants

E   binding as between B & C and Caledonia. Thus B & C cannot contend that the act of entering into the covenants was ultra vires as it was an act authorised by the court. It followed that B & C had corporate capacity to enter into the covenants and cannot contend that it did not have that capacity when the covenants are sought to be enforced by the plaintiffs.

   B & C sought to support its submission that the court order did not prevent it from

F   establishing that the covenants were unenforceable at the suit of the plaintiffs by a number of Australian cases.

   The first case relied on was *Isles v Daily Mail Newspaper Ltd* (1912) 14 CLR 193. In that case the High Court of Australia considered the position of a plaintiff who was a debenture holder. He had sued the newspaper company for a declaration that an agreement between the company and the other debenture holders was not binding upon him. The court held that it had power under an equivalent provision in the Australian

G   Act to s. 425 of the 1985 Act to sanction the arrangement and refused to make the declaration. Isaacs J said at p. 204-205:

     'Is the arrangement one which the court would have jurisdiction to sanction under s. 35? The only arrangements which it has jurisdiction to sanction are those between the debtor and the creditor; putting it shortly, none others are stated to be bound, and therefore there are no others with whom, by force of the statute

H   operating on the curial order, the minority can be brought into compulsory contractual relation.'

   That statement of the law is applicable to s. 425, but it does not throw any light upon the issues in this case. There is no dispute that the court had power to sanction the agreement as between B & C and Caledonia and did not have power to sanction it as between B & C and the plaintiffs and did not do so. However that does not throw light upon whether

the order made had the effect of preventing the company (B & C) from resisting claims   A
from parties to the agreement who were not members or creditors.

The second case relied on was *Re A & C Constructions Pty Ltd* [1970] SASR 565. In
that case the Supreme Court of South Australia concluded that it would not refuse to
sanction a scheme of arrangement because a person, other than a company, a creditor or
a member, was a party to the agreement to be approved. Bray CJ pointed out, as Isaacs
J had done in the *Isles* case, that the sanctioning order only bound the company, its   B
members and creditors. He went on to say at p. 568:

> 'It is, however, in my view, a fallacy to assume that therefore no other person can
> be a party to the scheme. In my view, so long as the scheme can properly be
> described as a compromise or arrangement between a company and its members
> or creditors or any class of them within the meaning of s. 181(l), it is immaterial
> that other persons are parties to it, but its binding force upon such other parties
> will derive from the scheme as a contract, or from some other contract, and not   C
> from the order of the court.'

That statement of the law is accepted to be correct by the plaintiffs and applicable to the
facts of the case before this court. The effect of the order of the court was to sanction an
arrangement which would, but for the court's order, have been ultra vires the company.
The rights of the plaintiffs stem from the option agreement not from the court's order.

Bright J said at p. 573:   D

> 'There are, as it seems to me, two problems which deserve more attention in this
> type of scheme. The first is the position of the scheme manager, who is assuming
> what may turn out to be inconsistent obligations as agent of both the existing
> creditors and the scheme purchaser. He is already the liquidator of the company.
> The second is the distinction which the scheme makes between the existing creditors
> and their assignee. The scheme creditors receive their composition as vendors of   E
> choses in action, viz. of their debts. They have agreed to reduce their debts by one
> cent in the dollar, and that is, no doubt, an agreement between them and the
> company, and therefore an arrangement within s. 181. But the agreement for the
> sale of the choses in action is not an arrangement between the creditors and the
> company, for the company is not interested in that sale nor affected by it. Perhaps
> par. 8 of the scheme is inserted with this in mind although, if this is so, it is not
> aptly expressed.   F

> In other words, I do not think that s. 181 enables a court to bind persons (albeit
> described as creditors) to sell their debts to a third person. They can be bound to
> reduce their debts and also to accept an immediate composition in discharge of
> their debts. In either case the agreement can be described as one made between a
> company and its creditors or any class of them. But an agreement to sell the debts
> to a third person is not such an agreement, and the approval of a scheme   G
> containing, in addition to agreements which fall within s. 181, an agreement which
> does not, does not give any greater force to the last mentioned agreement than it
> derives from its nature as a contract.'

In that passage the judge was concerned with whether an agreement would be binding
upon a person who was not a creditor or member. He did not consider whether an
obligation entered into by the company in an agreement which had been sanctioned   H
could be avoided by the company when sought to be enforced by a party to the agreement
who was not a creditor or member.

Mr Stubbs placed special emphasis upon *Lietzke (Installations) Pty Ltd v EMJ
Morgan Pty Ltd & Dean* (1973) 5 SASR 88. The creditors of the defendant company, in
that case, agreed a scheme of arrangement which was approved by the court. As a result
the defendant, Dean, became the special manager of the company under the scheme of

A   arrangement which provided that in his dealings with third parties he should, so far as reasonably practicable, conduct them in the name of the company and disclosing his authority as special manager. The plaintiff entered into a contract with the defendant company and was not told of the position of Dean. The plaintiff performed the contract but failed to obtain payment. Thereafter the plaintiff sued Dean for negligence. The court by a majority held that Dean was not under a duty of care to the plaintiff and therefore the plaintiff's claim was bound to fail.

B   It was submitted that the facts of that case were directly relevant to the present case in that the scheme provided for a third party to have rights as well as obligations vis-à-vis the company. That is true, but the issue before the court was whether the plaintiff, who was not a party to the scheme, had a cause of action in negligence against Dean who did not carry out his obligations under the scheme. The court said that no action lay because no duty arose. The statements of the judges must be read in context and when so read give no guidance on the issue before this court.

C   Mr Stubbs also drew our attention to *Re Glendale Land Development Ltd* (1982) 1 ACLC 540 and *Re Glendale Land Development Ltd (No. 2)* (1982) 1 ACLC 562. In both those cases the court considered whether approval of a scheme of arrangement could bind a person who was not either the company, a creditor or a member. The answer given was 'no'. That conclusion does not throw light upon whether a company who is a party to an approved agreement can contend that it had no corporate capacity to enter into parts of that agreement when those parts are sought to be enforced by a third party.

D   The only case which I believe throws light upon the way that the issue between the parties is to be answered is that cited by the plaintiffs. *Nicholl v Eberhardt Co* (1889) 59 LT 860 was decided by Kekewich J. His judgment was appealed and the judgments of the Court of Appeal are reported in a number of reports. I have not found any material difference in those reports and will refer to the report in (1889) 1 Meg 402.

E   In 1885 the Eberhardt Co went into voluntary liquidation. By an agreement later that year a contract was made for the sale of the assets of the old company to a new company as paid up to the extent of 15 shillings. The agreement also provided that any shares in the new company that had not been applied for by a time to be determined by the directors of the new company could be sold by it. On 18 November 1988 the scheme was approved by the court. Thereafter it was implemented. The plaintiffs were the executors of Mr Towne who had held 570 fully paid shares in the old company. They had been unable to take up his shares in the new company as probate had not been obtained in time. After probate was obtained, the executors applied for shares in the new company. Their application, being out of time, was refused. That prompted them to start the action against the old company, its liquidators and the new company for a declaration that the approved agreement was ultra vires and void and an injunction to prevent it being carried into effect. Both Kekewich J and the Court of Appeal held that the plaintiffs were not in a position to challenge the scheme owing to the sanction of the court. Kekewich J said at p. 863 of the LT Report:

> 'I express no opinion upon the scheme, but what I do hold is, that the order having been made in the required form is, according to the Act of 1870, binding, not only on the creditors, not only on the liquidators, but on all the members of the company. As long as that order stands I cannot hear the plaintiffs say that they are not bound by the scheme sanctioned by that order, which is substantially the same scheme as that embodied in the agreement for sale and transfer of the assets.'

In the Court of Appeal Lord Esher MR said at p. 408:

> 'An arrangement and agreement was come to between the liquidator of the company and that class of creditors; and three years ago that compromise or arrangement was brought before the court as between the liquidator and that class

of creditors, namely, the bond holders, and that arrangement was based upon, and   A
is really, practically, the arrangement which is now sought to say is ultra vires and
void. But that arrangement was sanctioned by an order of the court. If it were not
for the Joint Stock Companies Arrangement Act of 1870, that arrangement would
not be binding upon people who were not parties to it, and in one sense were not
before the court; but by the very plain terms of the second section of that Act, it is
enacted that while such an arrangement is before the court, as between the
liquidator and that class of creditors, not only can the majority of those creditors   B
bind the minority of those creditors, but the sanction of the court makes that
arrangement binding also on the liquidator and the contributories of the company.
Words more plain I cannot conceive.'

From the *Nicholl* case it is clear that agreements which might be ultra vires and void
become binding when approved by order of the court pursuant to s. 425 of the Act. The
result in that case was that the new company, which was not a party to the scheme, took   C
advantage of what would otherwise have been an invalid agreement and the court held
that its acts could not be challenged. Similarly in the present case, the option agreement
became binding upon B & C and Caledonia, pursuant to the order of the court, and
therefore it is not open to B & C to assert that the terms of the agreement were ultra vires
and void as between them. Further I can see no reason why B & C should be able to
contend that the covenants are ultra vires and void when sought to be enforced by a third
party to the scheme of arrangement who entered into the agreement which had been   D
sanctioned by the court.

Finally I come to the submission that some words should be implied into s. 425. I can
find no basis for implying any words into the section nor is there in my view a need to do
so. Petitions for approval of schemes come before specialist judges who do, with the help
of those who appear before them, protect the interests of creditors and members of the
public.   E

I conclude that the judge was right to answer this question in the affirmative. He was
right to hold at p. 34F:

'The attack upon the validity of the provisions under the rules of company law
that I have endeavoured to express above cannot be made because, by virtue of the
statute and the order made under it on 12 October 1987, the option agreement is
binding on B & C. The administrators who control B & C's affairs were not   F
suggested to be, and in my judgment are not, in any different position. It follows
that the whole attack on the option agreement based on the principle of the
maintenance of capital must fail.'

4. Principles of law (Trevor v Whitworth)

(A) *Question 48(d)(i) (primary creditor claims)*   G

'Whether to the extent that breaches of the covenants by the company would
impose a liability in damages on the company claimed in the primary creditor
claims the option agreement was, so far as the company was concerned, ultra vires
and unenforceable against the company or such a liability on the part of the
company is precluded having regard to the principles applied in *Trevor v Whitworth*
(1887) 12 App Cas 409 and *Re Walters' Deed of Guarantee* [1933] 1 Ch 321 and/or
having regard to the provisions of Ch. IV of Pt. V (reduction of capital) and   H
Pt. VIII (distribution) of the 1985 Act.'

The judge affirmed the rule in *Trevor v Whitworth*. He said (at p. 22F):

'The first set of questions set out in para. 48 concerns the rule of company law
usually called 'the rule in *Trevor v Whitworth*'. In my judgment there are two
fundamental principles of company law which can be seen in the cases cited. The

A   first of those principles goes back to the earliest days of English limited liability
companies. The principle is that a company cannot return capital to its members
save by a reduction of capital sanctioned by the court.'

He went on to review the authorities in which that principle had been enunciated from
the middle of the 19th century until the present day. At p. 29F of his judgment he came
to the second principle which he stated in this way:

B   'The second fundamental principle of company law established by the cases is that
no company may make truly gratuitous dispositions of its assets.'

After reviewing the authorities in which that principle had been applied, he concluded
that an obligation to pay damages by B & C to the banks was not a return of capital, but
was an obligation to make a gratuitous payment by B & C at a time when it had no
distributable profits. That being so, he concluded that the obligation could not be
enforced and was ultra vires. He therefore would have answered this question in the
C   affirmative and in B & C's favour. However, he went on, as required by the question
posed in para. 48(d)(iv) to decide whether the order of the court which sanctioned the
scheme of arrangement had the effect of rendering the obligation of B & C lawful. He
decided that it did and therefore answered the question in the negative. B & C appealed
against that conclusion and the plaintiffs served a respondents' notice in which it was
averred that the principles of law enunciated by the judge did not impinge upon the
D   obligations of B & C under the option or stand-by agreements.

As we came to the conclusion that the judge was right in his view of the effect of the
order sanctioning the scheme of arrangement, we did not feel it necessary to hear
submissions as to whether the particular matters raised in the respondents' notice of the
plaintiffs were correct.

Having regard to the reasons expressed above in relation to question 48(d)(iv), this
E   question was correctly answered by the judge in the negative.

(B) *Question 49(i) (further creditor claims)*

This question is similar to question 48(d)(i) and the judge dealt with it upon the same
basis having held that the covenants in cl. 6 of the option agreement offended one of the
principles of law to which he had referred. He concluded that both covenants were
enforceable having regard to the order sanctioning the scheme. In his further judgment
F   he said ([1995] BCC 19 at p. 39F):

'As it seems to me the whole essence of the stand-by agreement depends upon the
validity of the option agreement. If that is valid the terms of the stand-by
agreement do not, in my own view, require further validation by an express
reference.'

I believe the judge was right. The stand-by agreement simply incorporated, as part of
that agreement, relevant terms of the option agreement, the entering into which was
G   sanctioned by the scheme order. In the circumstance where the entering into the precise
obligations complained of were sanctioned by the court, it would be absurd if it could be
said that the undertaking of those self-same obligations in the stand-by agreement was
illegal as being ultra vires.

(C) *Question 50(ii) (misrepresentation claims)*

The judge after the further hearing concluded that these claims related to
H   misrepresentations about the status of the option agreement and that because the option
agreement was validated by the order of the court, the misrepresentation claims were also
capable of being pursued. Thus he answered this question in the negative.

The plaintiffs did not feel able to support the reasoning of the judge, but submitted
that he came to the right answer. Even though they did not accept that the two principles
of law in question applied to the scheme, they submitted that no principle of law

A

prevented the two banks concerned from seeking damages for misrepresentation. What, asked Mr Potts, was the act which B & C did not have the capacity to do? He answered the question – certainly not the uttering of representations as there was no legal principle to the effect that it was ultra vires for a company to utter representations which may turn out to be false.

On behalf of B & C it was submitted that a company cannot make a representation unless it has the corporate capacity to do so and, in the present case, it did not have the corporate capacity to make the particular representations relied on in the misrepresentation claims. No authority was cited for that proposition, but some reliance was sought to be placed upon *R Leslie Ltd v Sheill* [1914] 3 KB 607. That case is of no relevance as the incapacity of the person who made the misrepresentation was provided for in the *Infants' Relief Act* 1874.

B

There is no fetter upon companies preventing them making representations and if the representations turn out to be false, they will be liable for the consequences. That does not mean that a company can avoid its inability to contract by the substitution of a representation giving apparent rights to the representee. The courts will look not only at the form, but also the reality of the transaction. Thus representations made for a collateral purpose may amount to an act beyond the corporate capacity of a company (see *Burton v Palmer* (1980) 2 NSWLR 878 at p. 889F). That is not this case. The representations were made to induce two of the plaintiffs to take over the obligations of one of the signatories to the option agreement.

C

D

In my view principles of law which affect a company's right to buy its own shares and give away property cannot and did not prevent B & C making the representations relied on by the relevant plaintiffs nor prevent B & C from being liable for the consequences. I therefore conclude that the question posed should be answered in the negative.

For the reasons given, I have come to the conclusion that the judge correctly answered the questions posed in the special case. I would dismiss the appeal.

Sir Roger Parker: I agree.

E

Kennedy LJ: I also agree.

(*Appeal dismissed. Leave to appeal refused*)

F

G

H

A Re Gower Enterprises Ltd (No. 2).

Chancery Division (Companies Court).
Robert Reid QC (sitting as a deputy High Court judge).
Judgment delivered 23 May 1995.

B
> *Director disqualification – Official receiver sought disqualification order in terms of s. 1(1)(a) and (d) of Disqualification Act – Whether disqualification order and application had to contain provisions of s. 1(1)(a)–(d) – Whether official receiver's application needed to be amended – Whether official receiver should have leave to amend notwithstanding expiry of two-year period – Company Directors Disqualification Act 1986, s. 1(1), 6, 7(2).*

C
1. A disqualification order under s. 1 of the Company Directors Disqualification Act 1986 (and an originating summons applying for such an order under s. 6) had to contain all the wording of s. 1(1)(a)–(d); those provisions were cumulative, the 'or' which joined them being conjunctive.

2. The claim for 'further and other relief' in the official receiver's summons was sufficient in the particular circumstances of the case to encompass a disqualification order in terms of s. 1(1)(a)–(d), notwithstanding that certain parts of s. 1(1) were not mentioned in para. 1 of the summons. The order sought was clearly an order under s. 6 and the fact that it was
D **spelled out in a deficient manner was not a fatal defect.**

3. Leave would in any event have been given to amend the official receiver's application which sought an order in terms of subs. (1)(a) and (d), notwithstanding the expiry of the two-year period in s. 7(2).

The following cases were referred to in the judgment:

E
Carecraft Construction Co Ltd, Re [1993] BCC 336; [1994] 1 WLR 172.
Cedac Ltd, Re [1990] BCC 555.
Flatbolt Ltd, Re (unreported, 21 February 1986, Harman J).
Pepper v Hart [1992] BTC 591; [1993] AC 593.
Polly Peck International plc, Re (No. 2) [1993] BCC 890.
Probe Data Systems Ltd, Re (No. 3) [1992] BCC 110.
Rolus Properties Ltd & Anor, Re (1988) 4 BCC 446.

F
Philip Jones (instructed by the Treasury Solicitor) for the official receiver.

Kathryn Lampard (instructed by Wedlake Bell) for the second respondent.

JUDGMENT

Robert Reid QC: The point that I now have to decide can be described as being 'What is a disqualification order?' In para. 1 of the originating summons, which is before me,
G the official receiver has asked in what has now become, I think, practically a standard form for an order under the *Company Directors Disqualification Act* 1986 that:

> 'Each of the respondents, the said Kenneth John Moore and Malcolm Leslie Patrick, shall not without the leave of the court be a director of or in any way whether directly or indirectly be concerned or take part in the promotion, formation or management of a company for a period of not less than two years
H and not exceeding 15 years from the date of such order.'

The application is made under s. 6 of that Act, and that section provides as follows:

> '(1) The court shall make a disqualification order against a person in any case where, on an application under this section, it is satisfied–
>
> (a) that he is or has been a director of a company which has at any time become insolvent (whether while he was a director or subsequently), and

(b) that his conduct as a director of that company (either taken alone or taken　A
together with his conduct as a director of any other company or companies)
makes him unfit to be concerned in the management of a company.'

I need not read the rest of the section. It will be observed that it is mandatory on the
court under s. 6 to make a disqualification order.

The question then is what is such an order. Under s. 1 the Act provides as follows:

'(1) In the circumstances specified below in this Act a court may, and under section　B
6 shall, make against a person a disqualification order, that is to say an order that
he shall not, without leave of the court–

(a) be a director of a company, or

(b) be a liquidator or an administrator of a company, or

(c) be a receiver or a manager of a company's property, or

(d) in any way, whether directly or indirectly, be concerned or take part in the　C
promotion, formation or management of a company,

for a specified period beginning with the date of the order.'

What is said on behalf of the respondent is that a disqualification order is an order
that the person the subject of the order shall not without leave of the court do any of the
four things set out in heads (a)–(d) and that if a summons asks for less than that, it is not
in truth asking for a disqualification order.　　　　　　　　　　　　　　　　　　　　D

I have heard submissions on behalf of the official receiver from Mr Jones and on behalf
of the second respondent from Miss Lampard. It is as well, I think, just to begin by
looking back very briefly at some of the legislative history of the section, because the
section in its present form is in an Act which is said to be an Act to consolidate certain
enactments relating to the disqualification of persons from being directors of companies
and from being otherwise concerned with the company's affairs. That Act contains　　E
material from the *Insolvency Act* 1985, which in its turn contains material from the
Insolvency Act 1976, which had been amended by the *Companies Act* 1981. Back at the
time of the 1976 Act the equivalent section was drafted so as to take in only heads (a)
and (d) of what is now s. 1(1) of the 1986 Act. Heads (b) and (c) were added later. There
is, I think, otherwise no material alteration after the accretions of the 1981 Act between
then and the 1986 Act.

The submissions before me have included a *Pepper v Hart* ([1993] AC 593; [1992] BTC　F
591) submission by virtue of which I was shown a passage in *Hansard* when the House
was considering what was at that stage cl. 63 of the Companies (No. 2) Bill. I shall at this
point read the material passage from *Hansard*, though I should say that in my view the
wording of the section is not ambiguous and, therefore, although I read this for
completeness this is not something which has been a factor in the decision which I make.
The passage is as follows:　　　　　　　　　　　　　　　　　　　　　　　　　　G

'Mr Eyre: The amendments would extend both the grounds for application for
disqualification order and the coverage of such an order to include receivers. I
believe that the committee is indebted to the Law Society for raising this point, and
I am glad to propose amendments that will make cl. 63 more effective.

The Opposition amendments No. 191 and 193, which are included in this debate,
are intended to extend the coverage of the orders so that they would prevent a
disqualified person from acting as a receiver and, consequentially, to enable him to　H
apply for leave to do so. We believe that that is the right approach, as it is quite
inconsistent that people who are considered unfit to run companies as directors
should also be able to run them as receivers.

I am advised that our amendments to the same effect, namely, amendments
No. 201 and 204, are superior in their drafting, in that by referring to 'a receiver

A   or manager of the property of a company' rather than simply 'a receiver or manager', they pick up the phrase that is used in Pt. VI of the *Companies Act* 1948.'

There were two occasions before the 1986 Act came into force when the position under what is now s. 1 of that Act was considered. The first was in an unreported decision of Harman J on 21 February 1986 (*Re Flatbolt Ltd*) where it is clear that the point was not argued before him and he merely mentioned the matter in passing. He said:

B   'The summons seeks an order under what is now s. 300 of the *Companies Act* 1985, that Mr Griffiths shall not, without the leave of the court, be a director of or in any way, directly or indirectly, concerned or take part in the promotion, formation or management of a company. There are two subparagraphs, (b) and (c), to be a liquidator and to be a receiver or manager. The official receiver, by counsel, does not seek to press those two subparagraphs which, indeed, since the coming into force of the Insolvency Act are probably no longer material since Mr Griffiths would not be qualified for those offices.'

C

So there the judge was taking the view, without benefit of argument, that he could, so to speak, pick and choose as to which of the four heads of what is now s. 1(1) were included in the order that he was in due course going to make in that case.

The other case, again a decision of Harman J, was *Re Rolus Properties Ltd & Anor* (1988) 4 BCC 446, the judgment, in fact, having been delivered on 21 March 1986. There he said:

D

E   'I have before me a summons issued on 19 October 1983, for an order under s. 9 of the *Insolvency Act* 1976 that Ira Constantine Whyte shall not be a director of or in any way directly or indirectly be concerned or take part in the promotion, formation or management of a company. There are two further subparagraphs in the summons which are not opened or pressed before me, they being effectively overtaken by the *Insolvency Act* 1985 and the qualifications for liquidations and receiverships thereby imposed.'

So there again without the benefit of argument the judge was making the assumption that he could pick and choose.

That is the limit of authority at the time when the 1986 Act came into force. At the time when the 1986 Act came into force there was some correspondence between Mr Baker, the chief clerk of the Companies Court, and Mr Sibley of the Department of Trade and Industry about the form of disqualification orders. This obviously is not material to the construction of the statute, but it explains, it seems to me, how it has come about that the present practice of making what I might loosely call pick-and-choose orders has become enshrined in the way in which the Companies Court does its business. On 19 May 1987 Mr Baker wrote to Mr Sibley in the third paragraph of his letter:

F

G   'It is my view that the operative part of the order must disqualify the respondent from acting in any of the capacities therein set out even though there is no suggestion that he has any intention of, for instance, being a liquidator or a receiver. My reasoning is that s. 2–6 of the Act empower the court to make "a disqualification order" and that is defined in s. 1(1) of the Act as an order that he shall not, without leave of the court, act in any of the four capacities set out in the section.'

H

He evidently received a response on 22 June, which has not survived, and he then wrote again to Mr Sibley on 29 June 1987. In that letter he wrote in the second paragraph:

'In view of the differing way in which the Treasury Solicitor interprets s. 1(1) of the Act to my own I thought it right to discuss the matter with both Mr Registrar Bradburn, who, as you know, will be hearing the majority of the applications, and with Mr Justice Harman who appeared from the Treasury Solicitor's letter to you

to have taken a view which supported that of the Treasury Solicitor. Both the A
registrar and the judge were initially of my own view of the section but, upon
reflection, felt that it was open to either interpretation. The judge also said that, if
he has a choice, his own preference would be to be able to select any one or more
of the four capacities set out in the section as he did in the *Flatbolt* case to which
the Treasury Solicitor referred in his letter. He agreed, however, that if a case arose
– and here I cited the *Chancery Lane Registrars* case to him – where it was apparent B
that a liquidator had been failing in his duties as liquidator that he might also wish
to disqualify him as a director for his opportunities to misbehave would be
considerably greater as a director than as a liquidator. We all, I think, agree with
the Treasury Solicitor's view that he cannot get an order in terms wider than his
summons so that it might perhaps be worth the Treasury Solicitors considering
going back to the form of summons which the official receiver appears to have
adopted initially, i.e. to ask for disqualification from all four capacities and leave C
it to the court to choose one or more or all of them.'

The upshot of the correspondence was a standard form of order being produced and
from that has flowed the custom of the Treasury Solicitor in cases of this type of asking
in the majority, if not all, cases for disqualification simply in terms of s. 1(1)(a) and
1(1)(d).

Miss Lampard on behalf of the respondent has submitted that the view of Mr Baker D
and the initial view of Harman J and Mr Registrar Bradburn is the correct view. She says
that if one looks at s. 1(1) it refers to the court making a disqualification order rather
than an order or orders, and she points out that throughout the Act there is reference to
an order in the singular. There is no reference, for example, in s. 6 to a disqualification
order or orders. She goes on by saying that the section then defines what a disqualification
order is. It is 'that is to say, an order that he shall not without leave of the court . . .' and E
then it sets out heads (a)–(d). She submits that the words, 'that is to say,' clearly indicate
that all the words that follow, including all of the matters (a)–(d), are comprised within
the definition of a disqualification order.

I have already referred to Mr Baker's letter in which he mentions Harman J's statement
that he would prefer to be able to select any one or more of the four capacities, and Miss
Lampard says with considerable force, in my view, that had it been the intention of F
Parliament to give court that choice there would have been wording such as 'that is to
say, an order that he shall not without leave of the court act in some or all of the
following capacities . . .' or perhaps the section would have referred to an order 'in all or
in any of the following terms.' She further points out that the last line of s. 1(1) reads 'for
a specified period beginning with the date of the order'. There is no provision, she says,
for allowing different periods to be specified for different capacities. So it is not possible,
for example, to disqualify someone from being a director for seven years but being a G
liquidator or administrator for only five years. And she submits that it would be logical
for the court to be at liberty to decide differing periods of disqualification for differing
activities, depending on the degree of unfitness the person might show in relation to each
activity.

She then goes on to point out that s. 6 provides for the mandatory making of a H
disqualification order in a case where the court is satisfied that the person's conduct as a
director of a company either taken alone or taken together with his conduct as a director
of any other company or companies makes him unfit to be concerned in the management
of a company. She says that if it were intended that the order could be made disqualifying
a person from some or all of the activities (a)–(d) in s. 1(1), it is illogical that s. 6 does not
require the court to be satisfied that the director's conduct makes him unfit to undertake

A   each of the various activities in subs. (1)(a)–(d) but only requires the court to be satisfied that he is unfit in respect of one of them – that is, in his conduct as a director.

The next point argued somewhat faintly, and if I may say so rightly, I think, somewhat faintly, was that s. 390(4) of the *Insolvency Act* 1986, which came into force on the same day as the Company Directors Disqualification Act, provides that:

'A person is not qualified to act as an insolvency practitioner at any time if at that
B   time . . .

     (b)   he is subject to a disqualification order made under the Company Directors Disqualification Act 1986 . . .'

She suggests that the fact that s. 390(4) does not refer to a person being disqualified to act as an insolvency practitioner where he is subject to disqualification under s. 1(1)(b) tends to suggest that there is no power under the Company Directors Disqualification
C   Act to pick and choose between the activities in s. 1(1)(a)–(d).

As I said, I think she was right to argue that somewhat faintly. It seems to me equally plausible that Parliament should have taken the view that nobody should be qualified to act as an insolvency practitioner at any time when they had been subject to any disqualification under any part of s. 1, whether the whole or, if the pick-and-choose construction be correct, one or more of those parts. Were that her only point, I would be
D   against her.

However, it is not her only point. It seemed to me that Mr Jones on behalf of the official receiver was in the end driven back simply to saying, 'Ah well, look at the scheme of the Act. There must be intended to be a discretion. And you should construe the word "or" between each of (a), (b), (c), and (d) in s. 1(1) as being "and/or".' In doing that he was seeking to persuade me that the considered obiter dictum of Lindsay J in *Re Polly Peck International plc (No. 2)* reported at [1993] BCC 890 at p. 897A was incorrect.
E   There the judge said in his reserved judgment:

'However, quite apart from the answers that I have already given, it is plain that there is no such direct relationship; s. 6(1)(b) provides that if a director's specified conduct makes him unfit to be concerned in the *management* of a company then it is not only from the management of a company from which he is (without leave) barred but also, because the provisions of s. 1(1)(a)–(d) are cumulative (the "or"
F   which joins them is plainly intended to be conjunctive), from being a liquidator, an administrator, a receiver or manager of a company's property or concerned in the promotion or formation of a company.'

I respectfully agree with Lindsay J that the 'or' is intended to be conjunctive and that the meaning of s. 1(1) of the Act is that a disqualification order is an order that a person without the leave of the court shall not be a director of a company, and shall not be a
G   liquidator or an administrator of a company, and shall not be a receiver or manager of a company's property, and shall not be in any way, whether directly or indirectly, concerned and shall not take part in the promotion, formation or management of a company; and that an order which does not prevent a person from doing all of those things is not a disqualification order within the terms of s. 1(1) of the Act.

It follows that I accept Miss Lampard's submissions and take the view, admittedly with some trepidation, that the practice that has grown up over the past years is incorrect.
H

Leave to amend

The question that now falls to be decided is whether the applicant, the official receiver, needs leave to amend his originating summons and, if so, whether, given the passage of time, he is entitled to that leave. As I indicated earlier in my judgment, the form of relief which he seeks by s. 1 of his originating summons is defective in that it refers to an

application for an order under s. 6 of the 1986 Act that each of the respondents 'shall not   A
without the leave of the court be a director of a company ... or in any way whether
directly or indirectly be concerned or take part in the promotion, formation or
management of a company for a period of not less than two years and not exceeding 15
years from the date of such order' – that is to say, an order in accordance with s. 1(1)(a)
and (d) but not (b) and (c). I have held that an order under s. 6 must be all or nothing –
that is to say, it must be an order disqualifying in relation to each of the four matters set
out in s. 1(1) and cannot be an order simply in relation to some of the matters set out in   B
subs. (1).

It is argued first of all that since the originating summons in para. 3 contains a claim
for such further or other orders the court shall deem proper, the originating summons
itself is presently still in an adequate form, and I could properly on that summons as
unamended make an order for disqualification. It is said that the relief sought is an order
under s. 6 and is 'further or other relief' in so far as it concerns matters under s. 1(1)(b)   C
and (c). Against that it is said that the court could not properly construe the originating
summons in that way and that an application for further or other relief is really a sort of
mopping-up operation to cover little bits and pieces but is not intended to add further
substantive claims.

On balance it seems to me that the claim for 'further and other relief' is sufficient in the
particular circumstances of this case to encompass a full disqualification order,   D
notwithstanding that certain parts of s. 1(1) are not mentioned in para. 1 of the
originating summons. The order sought is clearly an order under s. 6 and the fact that it
is spelled out in a deficient manner does not seem to me to be a fatal defect. I would,
therefore, on that short first ground hold that the originating summons was adequate as
drawn. It would, however, I think, in any event be desirable that it should be amended
so that the whole of the relief sought is specifically spelled out in para. 1, and I will give
leave for that amendment to be made.   E

I should add that even if I had taken a contrary view I would have taken the view that
it was appropriate in the circumstances of this case to grant leave to amend. In my
judgment, even though the two-year period for the commencement of a fresh originating
process for disqualification has now elapsed, no prejudice is caused by the amendment.
This is clearly a case in which, were I to strike these proceedings out, further proceedings
could be launched, because leave to launch those proceedings would be obtained under   F
s. 7(2) of the Act.

The four specific matters referred to in *Re Cedac Ltd* [1990] BCC 555 and referred to
also in the Court of Appeal subsequently in *Re Probe Data Systems (No. 3)* [1992] BCC
110 seem to me to be amply fulfilled. Taking the Court of Appeal case first; first, the
length of delay: here there would be a substantial delay before fresh proceedings were
launched from the date of liquidation, but for all practical purposes there have been   G
proceedings on foot for the whole of that period. Second, the reasons for the delay: the
reason for the delay is a misunderstanding as to what I have held to be the legal position,
a misunderstanding arising quite reasonably, in my view, because it was a point which
had hitherto escaped everybody's notice until the industry of counsel brought it to light
shortly before this case. Thirdly, the strength of the case against the director: this is a
case where it is intended, as I understand it, if the matter is allowed to proceed, that what
might loosely be called the plea bargain under *Re Carecraft Construction Co Ltd* [1993]   H
BCC 336 would be presented to me. So clearly there is a case which the director
acknowledges is overwhelming. Fourthly, the degree of prejudice caused, which in my
view is nil.

Turning then to an alternative way of putting those four heads, as Mummery J dealt
with them in *Cedac*: is there going to be any substantive change in these proceedings?

A　　Answer: no. There will simply be a change in the nature of the relief sought. Secondly, is there prejudice apart from potential loss of the two-year limitation period? As I have already said, none. Thirdly, what is the effect of the refusal of leave? Answer: grave and substantially admitted allegations would then go undetermined by the court and, more to the point, the public would go unprotected. It must be borne in mind that this is primarily a jurisdiction for the protection of the public. It may have quasi-penal consequences, but it is not a penal jurisdiction. Fourthly, is there any unexplained delay

B　　in this case? No, save in so far as nobody has been able to explain how this point escaped the combined wisdom of the Company Bar for ten years.

　　In those circumstances, even if I did not hold on the first point that leave to amend was not strictly needed, I would hold that it was an appropriate case to grant leave to amend, notwithstanding the expiry of the two-year period. I therefore propose to grant leave to amend as prayed.

C
　　　　　　　　　　　　　　(*Order accordingly*)

D

E

F

G

H

Re Seagull Manufacturing Co Ltd (No. 3).

A

Chancery Division.
Blackburne J.
Judgment delivered 6 June 1995.

*Director disqualification – Official receiver sought disqualification order in terms
of s. 1(1)(a) and (d) of Disqualification Act – Whether disqualification order
and application had to contain provisions of s. 1(1)(a)–(d) – Whether official
receiver's application needed to be amended – Company Directors Disqualification
Act 1986, s. 1(1), 6, 7(2).*

B

**The court refused to dismiss an originating summons by the official receiver, seeking a
disqualification order under s. 6 of the Company Directors Disqualification Act 1986, on
the ground that the summons omitted any reference to para. (b) and (c) of s. 1(1) of the Act.
Assuming that a disqualification order could not be limited in scope to some only of the
paragraphs set out in s. 1(1) of the Act, it followed that if the official receiver established
the conditions set out in s. 6(1), the scope of the order would follow as a matter of course.
The fact that the summons unnecessarily and incorrectly described the scope of the order
was of no consequence.**

C

The following case was referred to in the judgment:

Gower Enterprises Ltd, Re (No. 2) [1995] BCC 1081.

D

Paul Girolami (instructed by the Treasury Solicitor) for the official receiver.

Nicholas Asprey (instructed by Silvermans, Barnet) for the respondent.

JUDGMENT

Blackburne J: I have before me an originating summons by the official receiver in
which he seeks a disqualification order under s. 6 of the *Company Directors
Disqualification Act* 1986 against Colin John Slinn. He does so on the basis that Mr Slinn
is or has been a director of a company, Seagull Manufacturing Co Ltd, which has become
insolvent, and that his conduct as a director of that company and of another company
called Scott & Partners Ltd makes him unfit to be concerned in the management of a
company. If the official receiver makes good those matters, s. 6 of the Act obliges the
court to make a disqualification order against Mr Slinn. Section 1 of the Act defines what
is meant by a disqualification order. It provides as follows:

E

F

'(1) In the circumstances specified below in this Act a court may, and under section
6 shall, make against a person a disqualification order, that is to say an order that
he shall not, without leave of the court–

(a) be a director of a company, or

(b) be a liquidator or administrator of a company, or

G

(c) be a receiver or manager of a company's property, or

(d) in any way, whether directly or indirectly, be concerned or take part in the
promotion, formation or management of a company,

for a specified period beginning with the date of the order.'

I need read no further.

H

The originating summons in this matter was issued on 1 April 1992, the company
Seagull Manufacturing Co Ltd having gone into compulsory liquidation on I think 4
April 1990. The other company, Scott & Partners Ltd, was wound up by order of the
court on 8 August 1988. The relief sought on the originating summons so far as material
is as follows:

A

'1. An order under s. 6 of the *Company Directors Disqualification Act* 1986 that the respondent Colin John Slinn shall not, without the leave of the court, be a director of, or in any way whether directly or indirectly be concerned or take part in the promotion, formation or management of a company for a period of not less than two years and not exceeding 15 years from the date of such order.

2. An order that the respondent pay to the applicant his costs of and incidental to this application.

B

3. Such further or other order as the court shall deem proper.'

In claiming that relief, which it will be observed embraces para. (a) and (d) only of s. 1(1), the official receiver was following what I am told has been the long standing practice of limiting the scope of the disqualification order sought to those matters to which the evidence has related upon the basis of which the order was sought. In this case the matters in question are concerned with the respondent's conduct as a director of a company and, I assume, with his management of a company, that is to say matters which are in terms referred to in para. (a) and (d) of s. 1(1).

C

For the respondent, Mr Asprey applies to have the originating summons struck out on the ground that it discloses no cause of action because it seeks an order which, because it is too narrowly stated, the court has no jurisdiction to make. He does so in reliance upon a decision in a case called *Re Gower Enterprises Ltd (No. 2)* ([1995] BCC 1081) in which Mr Robert Reid QC, sitting as a deputy High Court judge in this division, held that the court had no jurisdiction when making a disqualification order to limit the scope of the order to some but not all of the paragraphs set out in s. 1(1) and that the order, if made, must extend to all four paragraphs of the subsection. I have not seen, because none is so far available, a transcript of that decision, but I have seen a note of it approved, as I understand it, by counsel who were involved in it.

D

Mr Girolami, who appears before me on behalf of the official receiver, does not seek to challenge the correctness of that decision as I have endeavoured to summarise it. He submits, however, that the fact that the form of the disqualification order which the originating summons seeks is too narrowly stated is immaterial because if he makes out his case for a disqualification order under s. 6 of the Act the form of the order will simply follow what it is now accepted by the official receiver is its correct scope as described in s. 1(1). Alternatively, if the relief which he is seeking needs to be correctly described on the originating summons he seeks leave to amend para. 1 in order correctly to describe the scope of the order sought.

E

F

It is to be observed that in the *Gower Enterprises* case, the judge considered that, notwithstanding that in that case the form of the order sought was defective having regard to the terms of s. 1(1), nevertheless the matter could be dealt with by the court on the basis of a claim to further or other relief set out elsewhere on the originating summons before him. He also came to the conclusion – and this part of his decision was, I think, obiter – that he would in any event have been minded to give leave to the official receiver to amend the proceedings so as to set out correctly the full scope of the disqualification order which in those proceedings the official receiver was seeking.

G

Mr Asprey submits that the court has no jurisdiction to make an order which is wider in scope than that which is claimed and no jurisdiction to make an order in the narrow form in which it is claimed. Mr Asprey further submits that the court has no power to grant relief in the wider form under the guise of para. 3 of the originating summons which claims 'Such further or other order as the court shall deem proper' – that, he says, being an impermissible use of the limited power in the court under such a paragraph. To that extent, as I understand it, Mr Asprey takes issue with the decision in the *Gower Enterprises* case. He therefore submits that, as it stands, the originating summons discloses no cause of action and should be dismissed.

H

He further submits that I ought not to grant leave to the official receiver to amend para. 1 of the originating summons by including reference to para. (b) and (c) of s. 1(1) because to do so would, he submits, be depriving him of a defence to which he would otherwise be entitled under s. 7(2) of the Act. He submits therefore that the course of action which I should follow is to dismiss the originating summons and leave it to the official receiver, if he is so minded, to make an application to bring fresh disqualification proceedings against Mr Slinn which necessarily would be outside the two year period within which, under s. 7(2) – otherwise than with the court's leave – the proceedings must be brought, and that were such an application to be made for leave to bring fresh proceedings out of time he would seek to adduce evidence of one kind or another to demonstrate why in the circumstances it would not be appropriate for such leave to be granted.

I cannot, for my part, accede to Mr Asprey's submissions. If the official receiver makes out his case under s. 6 of the Act (and that is the nature of the proceedings which are being brought against Mr Slinn as is apparent from the opening words of para. 1 of the originating summons) the court, as I have mentioned, is obliged to make a disqualification order. Section 1 defines what is meant by a disqualification order. Assuming, without going into the matter, that a disqualification order cannot be limited in scope to some only of the paragraph set out in s. 1(1) of the Act, it follows, in my view, that if the official receiver establishes the conditions set out in s. 6(1), the scope of the order will follow as a matter of course, the court having on this assumption no choice in the matter. The fact that the scope of the order sought is too narrowly described in para. 1 of the originating summons seems to me therefore to be of no consequence at all. I should say that in referring to the scope of the order sought by para. 1, I am not of course referring to the period of any disqualification order.

Indeed, it seems to me that para. 1 of the originating summons could simply have claimed, as Mr Girolami submitted to me, an order under s. 6 of the *Company Directors Disqualification Act* 1986, full stop, without condescending to set out, as para. 1 does, what that order should contain. Mr Asprey accepted that if para. 1 had contained, in error, an additional prohibition on the activities of the respondent (additional, that is, to those set out in s. 1(1)) the court could quite properly – within the context of the existing proceedings – ignore the incorrect addition. Equally he accepted that if, in setting out the scope of the prohibition contained in s. 1(1), the official receiver had omitted, for example, 'formation' from para. (d) or 'administrator' from para. (b) the proceedings would not be liable to be struck out. He was unable, however, to suggest what it was that rendered the proceedings defective and liable to be struck out where, as here, two of the paragraph of s. 1(1) have been omitted. These considerations reinforce my view that the fact that para. 1 unnecessarily and incorrectly describes the scope of the order by omitting any reference to para. (b) and (c) of s. 1(1) is a matter of the merest technicality. Mr Asprey's application accordingly fails.

I do not propose to give leave at this stage to make any amendment to para. 1 because it seems to me to be unnecessary. I need not therefore concern myself with the question with which Mr Reid in the *Gower Enterprises* case concerned himself, which is whether, if leave were necessary, it would be appropriate in all the circumstances to grant it.

(*Order accordingly*)

A   # Re AGB Research plc.
     # Redleaf Investments Ltd v Talbot.

Chancery Division (Companies Court).
Vinelott J.
Judgment delivered 22 April 1994.

B   *Administration order – Company voluntary arrangement – Whether landlord had*
     forfeited lease of company in administration – Insolvency Act 1986, s. 11(3).

This was an application by a landlord ('Redleaf') seeking a declaration that a lease of premises to a company ('AGB') subject to an administration order was subsisting.

A voluntary arrangement had been approved unanimously by the creditors of AGB who attended a meeting to approve the arrangement. No provision was made in the arrangement
C   for arrears of rent, or for rent prospectively payable under the lease. The landlord argued that it was entitled to prove for rent due and to become due, and that approval of the arrangement should be revoked or suspended and a further meeting convened at which it could attend and vote in respect of its claim.

The administrators argued that the lease to AGB had been forfeited by the grant of a new lease to another company (which had since become insolvent). The landlord submitted that
D   as the new lease was executed without the consent of the administrators under s. 11(3) of the Insolvency Act 1986, it took effect subject to AGB's lease.

Held, declaring that the lease to AGB was forfeited by the grant of a new lease:

The administrators, when they learned of the lease, could have relied upon the failure to obtain their consent or an order of the court as a ground for claiming that the lease had not been forfeited, but Redleaf, having asserted its right to re-enter by giving possession to a
E   new tenant, could not claim against the administrators that the lease was still in existence.

The following cases were referred to in the judgment:

Exchange Travel Agency Ltd v Triton Property Trust plc & Anor [1991] BCC 341.
Expert Clothing Service & Sales Ltd v Hillgate House Ltd & Anor [1986] Ch 340.
Olympia & York Canary Wharf Ltd, Re [1993] BCC 154.
Segal Securities Ltd v Thoseby [1963] 1 QB 887.

F   David Neuberger QC and Susan Prevezer (instructed by Allen & Overy) for the administrators.

Nicholas Patten QC (instructed by Halliwell Landau) for the landlord.

JUDGMENT

Vinelott J: Redleaf Investments Ltd ('Redleaf') is the registered proprietor of a
G   property known as Audley House, Berkhamstead in Hertfordshire. At the material time the property was subject to a lease dated 9 January 1991, which was made between Redleaf's predecessor in title, Frogmore Developments Ltd, as landlord, AGB Research plc ('AGB') as tenant, and Pergamon Holdings Ltd, which later changed its name to Headington Holdings Ltd, as guarantor. The lease was for a term of 25 years commencing on 25 December 1990 at a rent of £175,000 payable quarterly in advance, with provisions for review on each fifth anniversary of the commencement of the lease.
H   The lease provided for payment of interest if instalments of rent were paid late, and it also contained a usual provision for forfeiture if an instalment of rent was unpaid for a period of 14 days after it became payable whether formally demanded or not. Joint administrators of AGB were appointed on 6 December 1991.

The issue between Redleaf and the administrators is whether the lease was forfeited. It is a curious case of role reversal. The administrators claim that the lease was forfeited on or about November 1992. Redleaf claims that it has never been forfeited. The reason for the reversal of roles is that a voluntary arrangement has been approved unanimously by those of the creditors of AGB, which is heavily insolvent, who attended a meeting on 15 November 1993 to approve the arrangement. No provision is made in the arrangement for arrears of rent, or for rent prospectively payable under the lease.

Redleaf now seek a declaration that the lease is still subsisting, and that it is entitled to prove for rent due and to become due, and that approval of the arrangement should be revoked or suspended and a further meeting convened at which Redleaf can attend and vote in respect of its claim.

The background is shortly as follows. Following the appointment of administrators of AGB, an arrangement was made between them and Redleaf under which rent and insurance premiums were paid monthly and treated as expenses of the administration. The arrangement came to an end in May, and AGB vacated the premises. In June one of the administrators (both are partners in Arthur Andersen) writing to Redleaf's agents, Jones Lang Wootten ('JLW'), asserted that the leasehold interest had no value, and offered to surrender it. He enclosed a draft deed of surrender.

At about that time the administrators gave the keys to JLW. JLW, writing to the administrators on 1 July 1992, said that they understood that the property was vacant, and asked for confirmation that adequate security cover was in force, and for information as to the steps that were being taken to protect the building.

There followed further correspondence as to the work needed to preserve the property and to meet the insurers' requirements. There was some correspondence between Landau Nock & Co, the solicitors acting for Redleaf, and the administrators concerning the administration, whether a proof of debt could be submitted by Redleaf, and whether Redleaf should have been given notice of the creditors' meeting.

On 11 September Berwin Leighton ('BL'), who were acting as solicitors to Redleaf, wrote to the administrators to say their property department would be writing to Arthur Andersen's property department concerning the possibility of surrender at a future date, and made it clear that these discussions would be 'without prejudice to our client's right of forfeiture or other rights under the lease'.

On 21 September BL wrote again, enclosing a draft deed of surrender. They said that they were seeking further information as to the value of the lease, and reserved the right to amend the consideration shown in the draft deed, a nominal £10 to be paid by Redleaf, on receipt of this information.

An instalment of rent, one quarter's rent, payable in advance, became due on 29 September. On 6 October BL wrote to the administrators to say that Redleaf were proposing to grant a new tenancy to another tenant, and added that, 'if for any reason the proposed new lease is not executed, then our clients reserve the right to treat the lease as still subsisting'. They suggested that the administrators might prefer to take a new lease 'which will crystallise the company's liability'.

There was no reply to that letter, and on 14 October, the day after the expiration of 14 days from the September quarter day, JLW wrote to the administrators to say that rent of £102,988.23 was due, and that unless paid 'appropriate action will be taken for recovery'. BL followed this on 19 October 1992 with a renewed request for comments on their draft deed of surrender.

On 9 November 1992 the administrators of Headington Holdings Ltd wrote to BL to say that they understood that Redleaf had arranged a new letting of the premises to Ouvah Highfields Ltd ('Ouvah'), 'which clearly demonstrates that the lease has some value', and suggested that if they wished to proceed with the surrender they should make an offer.

A   BL wrote on 17 November to say that they were taking instructions. In fact a new lease, between Redleaf and Ouvah, had been executed on 10 November. The solicitors who acted for Redleaf in relation to the new lease were Landau Nock, which is no doubt why BL needed to take instructions. The new lease was for a term of 25 years from 10 November 1992, also at a rent of £175,000, with five-yearly upwards only reviews after the expiry of the first ten years. However, Ouvah was entitled to a rent-free period until 10 May 1993, and was paid a reverse premium of £108,000.

B   Ouvah covenanted to carry out work to the property, specified in a schedule, and Redleaf agreed to contribute £175,000 towards the cost of the work, payable as to £50,000 on the grant of the lease and as to the balance by instalments as the work proceeded. The lease contained the usual covenant by Redleaf that from and including possession date, the date of the lease, Ouvah would be permitted peaceably and quietly to own and enjoy the premises without any interruption or disturbance from or by Redleaf or any person claiming under or in trust for Redleaf.

C   On 23 November BL wrote further to say that a lease had been agreed, but on terms which included a payment as a result of a reverse premium, 'which clearly demonstrate that the lease has no value'. They added that they had instructions to commence proceedings for forfeiture, and would be making an application to the Companies Court for leave to issue proceedings.

D   These are the salient events, and the salient correspondence. I should however say something about the subsequent events, and the curious reversal of roles that took place later.

        Landau Nock wrote to the administrators on 6 January to say that the lease had been forfeited by the grant of a lease to Ouvah on 10 November, but that the forfeiture was 'without prejudice to our client's rights and remedies which may then have accrued in respect of any antecedent breach'. They claimed the loss to Redleaf by way of loss of rent, dilapidations and diminution in value was £400,000–£500,000.

E   JLW wrote to the administrators on 14 January, claiming arrears of rent of £105,170.23, the rent previously claimed, with rent for the period from 29 September to 10 November, and further interest. It is significant that no rent was sought for the period after 10 November.

F   The administrators' reply on 6 May was that Redleaf had accepted the surrender by accepting the keys on 26 or 27 July, and that Redleaf's agents had obtained access on a number of occasions following the handing over of the keys, 'indicating acceptance of the surrender'. The significance of an earlier surrender would of course be that Redleaf would have had no claim for the payment of rent due after the end of May.

        The claim was clearly misconceived, and was not pursued before me. The administrators drew attention to the failure to obtain an order authorising the forfeiture of the lease, but added that they confirmed, for the avoidance of doubt, that to the extent AGB's interests had not previously been surrendered, 'our clients accept the forfeiture of the lease and confirm their retrospective consent to it'.

G   By this time Ouvah had proved to be no more successful as a tenant than AGB. An order for its compulsory winding up was made on 28 April 1993. It is that that led to an entire change of front by Redleaf. New solicitors, Halliwell Landau, wrote to the administrators' solicitors, Allen & Overy ('A & O'), on 14 June to say that they did not accept that the administrators were entitled to retrospectively consent to a forfeiture, and that a consent could only operate, if at all, from receipt of the letter of 6 May.

H   Mr Patten's first submission was that as rent was payable in advance the demand for rent made on 14 October operated as a waiver of the right to forfeit the lease for non-payment of rent for the period up to the next quarter day, 25 December 1992. He relied

upon the decision of Sachs J in *Segal Securities Ltd v Thoseby* [1963] 1 QB 887, that a
demand for rent has the same effect as acceptance of rent and that, as in the case of
acceptance of rent, a landlord cannot preclude its operation as a waiver by merely stating
that it is without prejudice to his rights of forfeiture.

It is unnecessary for me to consider whether this decision can have any application
where the breach of covenant relied on is a failure to pay the rent, the demand for which
is relied on as a waiver, and if it does, whether I should follow it. The point was left open
by the Court of Appeal in *Expert Clothing Service & Sales Ltd v Hillgate House Ltd &
Anor* [1986] Ch 340 at p. 359.

The short answer to Mr Patten's submission is that the demand was for rent payable
on 29 September, and could not operate as a waiver of the landlord's right to forfeit for
failure to pay the rent before the expiry of 14 days from that date.

Mr Patten's alternative submission was that Redleaf waived its right to forfeit by
continuing negotiations for the surrender of the lease. The answer to that submission is
that although the possibility of a surrender had been discussed before 14 October, there
were no negotiations between that date and the grant of the new lease. Nothing was said
on behalf of Redleaf which could amount to a representation that the right to forfeit the
lease would not be enforced.

Mr Patten's main submission was founded on s. 11(3) of the *Insolvency Act* 1986,
which provides, so far as material, that while an administration order is in force no steps
may be taken to enforce any security over the property of a company except with the
consent of the administrators or the leave of the court.

It was held by Harman J in *Exchange Travel Agency Ltd v Triton Property Trust plc &
Anor* [1991] BCC 341 that these words are wide enough to comprehend the exercise of a
right of re-entry by a landlord, and in *Re Olympia & York Canary Wharf Ltd* [1993] BCC
154, Millett J expressly agreed with that decision.

Mr Neuberger did not seek to contend to the contrary, although he reserved his right
to do so in a higher court.

Mr Patten erected an ingenious edifice on these foundations. He submitted that as the
lease to Ouvah was executed without the consent of the administrators, it took effect
subject to AGB's lease. Ouvah would have been entitled to have the lease to it set aside if
the administrators had taken steps to recover possession, but until those steps were taken
Ouvah had no more than the right to rent under a lease to AGB accrued since the grant
of the lease to it.

In my judgment the foundation of this submission is unsound. The grant of a lease to
Ouvah was an unequivocal assertion by Redleaf of its right to re-enter. The lease was
clearly intended to take effect in possession. To give it effect as a reversionary lease would
be inconsistent with the obligation imposed on Ouvah to carry out works of repair and
alteration.

The administrators, when they learned of the lease, could have relied upon the failure
to obtain their consent or an order of the court as a ground for claiming that the lease
had not been forfeited, but in my judgment Redleaf, having asserted their right to re-
enter by giving possession to Ouvah, cannot now claim against the administrators that
the lease is still in existence.

In my judgment the contentions advanced on behalf of Redleaf are devoid of merit or
substance. I will declare that the lease to AGB was forfeited by the grant of a lease to
Ouvah. I will hear any further submissions counsel may wish to make as to the
appropriate order to be made in the application by Redleaf as to costs and otherwise.

(*Order accordingly*)

A
R v Chance, ex parte Smith & Ors.

Queen's Bench Division (Divisional Court).
Henry LJ and Kay J.
Judgment delivered 21 December 1994.

B
Judicial review – Chartered accountants' Joint Disciplinary Scheme – Executive counsel refused to stay scheme inquiry pending outcome of civil proceedings – Whether continuance of inquiry would be unjust.

The Divisional Court refused an application for judicial review of a decision by the executive counsel of the chartered accountants' Joint Disciplinary Scheme refusing the applicant accountants' request for a stay of a scheme enquiry and anticipated consequent disciplinary proceedings against the firm and/or individual named partners pending the

C
disposal of various substantial civil actions for damages against the applicants arising out of the same matters. (R v Panel on Takeovers & Mergers, ex parte Fayed & Ors [1992] BCC 524 applied; R v ICAEW, ex parte Brindle & Ors [1994] BCC 297 distinguished.)

The following cases were referred to in the judgment of the court:

A & Ors v B (Governor of the Bank of England intervening) [1991] 1 Bank LR 60.
Associated Provincial Picture Houses Ltd v Wednesbury Corporation [1948] 1 KB 223.

D
Conteh v Onslow-Fane The Times, 26 June 1975, CA.
R v ICAEW, ex parte Brindle & Ors [1993] BCC 736 (DC); [1994] BCC 297 (CA).
R v Panel on Takeovers & Mergers, ex parte Fayed & Ors [1992] BCC 524.
R v Panel on Takeovers & Mergers, ex parte Guinness plc (1988) 4 BCC 714; [1990] 1 QB 146.

Christopher Clarke QC and Andrew Simmonds (instructed by Barlow Lyde & Gilbert) for the applicants.

E
Michael Beloff QC and Tim Kerr (instructed by Bates Wells & Braithwaite) for the respondent.

JUDGMENT OF THE COURT
(Delivered by Henry LJ)

F
This is an application for judicial review in which the applicants are the UK partnership of Coopers & Lybrand, the well-known chartered accountants, and three named individual partners. The respondent is the executive counsel appointed for the purposes of the Joint Disciplinary Scheme ('the scheme') of the Institute of Chartered Accountants in England and Wales ('ICAEW'), which is the applicants' professional body. The application challenges a decision by the respondent refusing the applicants' request for a stay of the scheme enquiry and anticipated consequent disciplinary

G
proceedings against the firm and/or the individual named partners pending the disposal of various substantial civil actions for damages against the applicants arising out of the same matters.

Only the broad outlines of the background facts are necessary for the purposes of this judgment. On 5 November 1991, Robert Maxwell, the chairman of the Mirror Group of Newspapers plc ('MGN') and the effective controller of a web of private family companies, died. Following his death, it became apparent that there had been large-scale

H
misappropriation of assets belonging to the pension funds of various public companies with which he was concerned. Other Maxwell companies were the trustees and/or managers of the assets in question. Coopers & Lybrand were the auditors both of the pension funds and of the companies that were the trustees and managers of the relevant assets of those funds. Their stewardship as auditors has come under scrutiny in three areas.

First, they have played (and may continue to play) an important role in various   A
enquiries and investigations consequent upon the discoveries. They are:

(1)   An enquiry by inspectors appointed by the Department of Trade and Industry
under s. 432(2) and 442 of the *Companies Act* 1985.

(2)   An investigation by the Serious Fraud Office into possible criminal conduct which
resulted in criminal proceedings against a number of individuals connected with
Maxwell group companies. The first criminal trial is due to commence in April   B
1995.

(3)   Enquiries by the Social Security Committee of the House of Commons under the
chairmanship of Mr Frank Field MP.

(4)   An investigation into Coopers & Lybrand's audit procedures and controls by the
Audit Registration Committee ('ARC') and the Joint Monitoring Unit ('JMU') of
the ICAEW. (But given the nature of that investigation, we do not consider it to   C
be of central relevance to the issue we have to decide.)

The applicants have co-operated with those investigations.

Second, the applicants are (or anticipate they may be) defendants in various substantial
civil claims for damages. These are:

(1)   The liquidators of Bishopsgate Investment Management Ltd ('BIM') have   D
indicated a claim and have delivered a very lengthy draft statement of claim
claiming £305m. The claims relate to the losses suffered by the pension schemes'
common investment fund ('CIF') and allege negligence in the 1988 and 1989 audits
of the CIF and the 1988, 1989 and 1990 audits of London and Bishopsgate
International Investment Management Ltd ('LBI'), which managed the assets of
the CIF and FTIT (see below in 3).

(2)   A separate claim is to be made by the trustee of the Mirror Group Pension Scheme.   E
This in part relates to the same subject-matter as the BIM claim but there is an
additional claim for £50m and $47m. A draft of the statement of claim is again
available.

(3)   The liquidators of First Tokyo Index Trust Ltd ('FTIT') have begun proceedings
against Morgan Stanley as custodians of the portfolio of shares which it is alleged
were disposed of improperly. Morgan Stanley have recently joined a number of   F
third parties including Coopers & Lybrand. It is anticipated that the liquidators of
FTIT will in due course bring a claim against Coopers & Lybrand as well. The
claim in this case is for £56m.

(4)   There is a possibility of further claims by the administrators of some of the
Maxwell companies on the private side (as opposed to the public companies).

    This stay is sought pending the trial of those actions. Those actions are the subject of   G
a mediation initiative headed by Sir John Cuckney with the assistance of Sir Peter
Webster. No assumptions as to the success or otherwise of this initiative can be made at
the present time. It should also be noted that the liquidators in the BIM action have
made extensive use of their powers to obtain documents and information from the
applicants under s. 236 of the *Insolvency Act* 1986. Also, where there is overlap between
the various investigations and actions, each feeds on the other, in that information   H
obtained in one is likely to be used in others.

    Thirdly, there are the disciplinary proceedings under the scheme, which it is now sought
to stay.

    The scheme has both a Community and statutory backing. The Community source
relates to the Eighth Directive (84/253 of 10 April 1984), dealing with 'co-ordination

A   measures' relating to the qualification, competence, and standards of auditors within the Community, and the responsibilities of member states for their regulation.

Article 23 provides:

> 'Member States shall prescribe that persons approved for the statutory auditing of the documents referred to in Article 1(1) shall carry out such audits with professional integrity.'

B   Article 26 provides:

> 'Member States shall ensure that approved persons are liable to appropriate sanctions when they do not carry out audits in accordance with Article 23 . . .'

Effect is given to the directive in England and Wales by the *Companies Act* 1989. The framework of domestic law was fully reviewed by Mann LJ in this court in the case of *R v ICAEW, ex parte Brindle* [1993] BCC 736 and we gratefully draw upon his judgment (at pp. 738–739) in order to set the matter out on this occasion:

C

> '*Statutory background*
>
> The "main purposes" of Pt. II of the *Companies Act* 1989 are,
>
> > "to secure that only persons who are properly supervised and appropriately qualified are appointed company auditors, and that audits by persons so appointed are carried out properly and with integrity and with a proper degree of independence." (Section 24(1).)

D

> In order to secure those objectives a person or a firm is eligible for appointment as an auditor only if he is a member of a recognised supervisory body (s. 25(1)). Such a body means a body established in the UK which maintains and enforces rules as to (a) the eligibility of persons to seek positions as company auditors and (b) the conduct of company audit work, which are binding on persons seeking appointment as or acting as company auditors (s. 30(1)). The requirements for recognition as a supervisory body are contained in Pt. 2 of Sch. 11 to the Act. Paragraph 6(1) of the Schedule provides that:

E

> > "The body must have adequate rules and practices designed to ensure that the persons eligible under its rules for appointment as a company auditor are fit and proper persons to be so appointed."

F

> Paragraph 7(1) provides that:
>
> > "The body must have adequate rules and practices designed to ensure–
> >
> > (a) that company audit work is conducted properly and with integrity . . ."

> Paragraph 9 provides:

G

> > "The body must have rules and practices designed to ensure that persons eligible under its rules for appointment as a company auditor continue to maintain an appropriate level of competence in the conduct of company audits."

> Paragraph 10(1) provides that:
>
> > "The body must have adequate arrangements and resources for the effective monitoring and enforcement of compliance with its rules."

H

> Paragraph 12(1) provides that:
>
> > "The body must have effective arrangements for the investigation of complaints–
> >
> > (a) against persons who are eligible under its rules to be appointed company auditor . . ."

The recognition of a supervisory body is a matter for (now) the President of the   A
Board of Trade; and the Institute of Chartered Accountants in England and Wales,
the Institute of Chartered Accountants of Scotland and the Chartered Association
of Certified Certified Accountants all received recognition. They are each bodies
incorporated by Royal Charter . . .'

Additionally it is important to note the statutory basis for the Auditing Guideline
relating to the auditor's responsibility in relation to fraud and other irregularities, to be   B
found in s. 109 and 180(1)(q) of the *Financial Services Act* 1986.

We are concerned here with the revised version of the scheme, which became effective
on 21 January 1993. The scheme is part of the machinery relating to the regulation of
company auditors required to be in place under Pt. II of the *Companies Act* 1989, in
compliance with the UK's obligations under the directive. The scheme 'sets out the
procedures for investigating and regulating [members'] professional and business
conduct, efficiency and competence *in circumstances which give rise to public concern*'   C
(emphasis added). Its objectives are:

'to promote the highest possible standards of professional and business conduct,
efficiency and competence . . . by providing a system for the investigation and
regulation of the activity of Members . . . so as to secure their adherence to all
professional criteria . . .'

The scheme is administered by an executive committee. The first stage in the scheme is   D
when that committee receives a report concerning the conduct, efficiency or competence
of a member and the committee certifies that in its opinion the circumstances of the
matter 'are ones which give rise to public concern'. They will then refer the report to the
executive counsel, who must be legally qualified.

The report that triggered this investigation was a report by the regulator IMRO to the
Securities and Investments Board, under the *Financial Services Act* 1986. And when the   E
committee referred that report to the executive counsel, the second stage of the process
was initiated.

This stage is covered by para. 6(c)–(e) of the scheme. Under para. 11 members and
member firms are under a duty to co-operate fully with the executive counsel in his
enquiries.

So the respondent began his enquiries. On 12 July 1993 he gave notice to Coopers &   F
Lybrand that the firm was under enquiry and forwarded a copy of the report and
certificate of the investigation committee. The respondent called for production of
documents and answers to a number of questions required for his enquiry pursuant to
his powers under the scheme. Approximately 67,000 documents and the answers to the
questions posed were provided on 5 October 1993.

On 11 November 1993, the respondent gave notice that Mr Cowling, the second named   G
applicant, one of the partners in Coopers & Lybrand concerned with the relevant audits,
was the subject of enquiry in his personal capacity as a member of the ICAEW.

On 10 and 11 January 1994, the respondent interviewed Mr Cowling. On 14 January
the respondent notified Coopers & Lybrand that he wished to interview eight further
partners and employees.

On 4 February solicitors acting for Coopers & Lybrand wrote to the respondent and   H
formally requested a stay of the enquiry. The request sought a stay until anticipated
litigation referred to in the letter had been concluded. The letter placed reliance upon the
decision of the Court of Appeal in *R v ICAEW, ex parte Brindle* [1994] BCC 297. It dealt
with the anticipated litigation to which reference has been made. The letter claimed that
the matters which would be litigated in such proceedings were the principal subject-
matter of the respondent's enquiry and that it was inherently unfair that the same issues

A   should be considered by two different tribunals. It was said that the duplication would result in unfairness because it would place an unreasonable strain on the relatively few individuals involved and that the enquiry would generate documents discoverable in the litigation. Reference was made to the other enquiries and the criminal proceedings and the additional burden that these would place on the firm and individual members. The letter pointed to the ARC and JMU investigation and said that the fact that no regulatory action had been proposed indicated that there was no pressing public need for the
B   respondent's enquiry to proceed without delay.

By a letter dated 18 March 1994, the respondent replied notifying two decisions. The first read:

     '*Scope of the investigation*

C   Under para. 5(d)(ix) and 6(e) of the Scheme the Executive Committee, after consultation with the Investigation Committee of the ICAEW, has given authority for the scope of my enquiries to include the work of Coopers & Lybrand concerning:

       (a) the comfort given by Coopers & Lybrand to Samuel Montagu & Co Ltd in April 1991 in relation to the undertakings given by the Maxwell Private Interests on the flotation of Mirror Group Newspapers plc;

D   (b) the arrangements for the ring-fencing of financial and treasury matters within the newly floated company and for the approval of transactions with Maxwell-related entities; and

       (c) the solvency and cash-flow of Robert Maxwell Group plc and its subsidiaries and the meeting of the board of directors on 23 July 1991.'

The second decision notified was the refusal of the request for a stay and it is that
E   decision that is the subject of this application for judicial review.

On 3 May 1994, the respondent notified Messrs Wootten and Walsh, the third and fourth named applicants, that they were the subject of enquiry in their personal capacity.

On 27 May 1994, these proceedings were commenced. When Latham J granted leave, he granted an interim stay by consent. The enquiry has thus been suspended during this period.
F   So these proceedings were stayed before the second stage under the scheme was complete. Had the enquiry been completed, para. 6(f) sets out the most serious of the three courses of action which may follow on as the third stage:

     '(f) If, following his enquiry, the Executive Counsel is of opinion that there are grounds upon which a Joint Disciplinary Tribunal could make an adverse finding concerning the professional or business conduct, efficiency or competence of a
G   Member . . . he shall request the Executive Committee to appoint such a tribunal at the same time delivering to the Executive Committee a formal complaint specifying the manner in which he alleges that the conduct or quality of work of the Member . . . fell below that which was to be expected . . .'

While the respondent had not completed his enquiries under this stage, those enquiries were sufficiently well advanced for him to be able to indicate that the likelihood was that
H   on completion of those enquiries he would request the matter to be referred to the tribunal, and would be making allegations concerning not only the competence but also the integrity of the named partners.

But under this stage of the process, the respondent would be bound to notify the firm and its named partners of the action he proposed, to give them an opportunity of making written representation to him (para. 6(h)). If those representations were unsuccessful,

then the fourth stage of the process would be the appointment of a Joint Disciplinary   A
Tribunal.

Such a tribunal shall consist of three or five persons, with a legally qualified chairman. The procedures before that tribunal are essentially adversarial, with the respondent acting as complainant. There is the right to cross-examine and to call evidence. Legal representation is allowed. The hearing is in private.

If the finding of the tribunal is adverse to the member or the member firm, the tribunal   B
has power to reprimand, severely reprimand and/or fine the member firm or member, and additionally, in the case of the member firm, to withdraw their registration as an auditor and their investment business certificate, and in relation to the member order him to be ineligible for a practising certificate or excluded from membership. Additionally there is a power to order costs.

The final stage of the process is an appeal against any finding and/or order made by   C
the tribunal. This appeal lies to an appeal tribunal appointed by the executive committee. It shall consist of not less than three persons, and shall be chaired by a member or former member of the judiciary or a Queen's Counsel. Here, as in the hearing before the tribunal, the strict rules of evidence shall not apply but the appeal tribunal has discretion to rehear any witness and to receive fresh evidence. It has full powers to affirm, vary or rescind any finding or order. At the conclusion of the process the tribunal's or appeal tribunal's   D
report shall be published as soon as practicable.

Those then are the disciplinary proceedings under the scheme that it is sought to stay until the disposal of the civil actions. The allegations made in those proceedings are hotly contested, particularly in so far as they relate to the integrity of the named individuals. And it is common ground that there is a considerable factual overlap between the matters in issue in the disciplinary proceedings and the allegations made in the civil actions. This will often be the case where both are concerned with the auditors' responsibility as to   E
detecting and dealing with fraud, irregularities, and other errors under the Auditing Guideline set up under s. 109 and 180(1)(q) of the *Financial Services Act* 1986.

The test we have to apply in this case is clear. It was enunciated by Neill LJ in *R v Panel on Takeovers & Mergers, ex parte Fayed* [1992] BCC 524 at p. 531E:

'It is clear that the court has power to intervene to prevent injustice where the continuation of one set of proceedings may prejudice the fairness of the trial of   F
other proceedings ... But it is a power which has to be exercised with great care and only where there is a real risk of serious prejudice which may lead to injustice.'

It is common ground between the parties that this court is required to conduct that balancing exercise of weighing the public interest in the prompt and efficient operation of the scheme against the risk of serious prejudice to the fairness of the trial of other proceedings, which may result in injustice. This court is not therefore concerned with a   G
Wednesbury review of the respondent's decision not to stay proceedings under the scheme. And in that balancing exercise the court will take into account all the evidence before it, including such evidence as relates to matters subsequent to the respondent's decision not to stay the proceedings.

So there is broad agreement between the parties as to the test to be applied by us in this matter, and the dispute has centred on its application. In the debate as to its   H
application, much time has been spent on considering the Court of Appeal decision in the case of *R v ICAEW, ex parte Brindle* [1994] BCC 297. That case bears superficial similarities to the case before us, and there the disciplinary proceedings were stayed. The court there applied Neill LJ's test as laid down in *ex parte Fayed*. That we take to be the true ratio of the decision, though it will also be necessary to consider two potential glosses on that test to be found in Hirst LJ's judgment, namely first that the power to intervene

A   to stay disciplinary proceedings be 'most sparingly exercised, . . . only in exceptional cases' (p. 310D) and second, that 'it is inherently unfair that two tribunals should contemporaneously be considering the same issue (*Conteh v Onslow-Fane*, The Times, 26 June 1975, CAT No. 291)' (p. 311A).

The applicants attach particular importance to *ex parte Brindle* because of its superficial factual similarities to the case which we have to consider. The respondent

B   regards it as a dangerous precedent and a threat to the proper working of the scheme because of the encouragement he believes it to have given to other applications for stays of disciplinary proceedings under investigation by him pending the resolution of civil proceedings (e.g. in the Astra investigation and the Polly Peck investigation). Additionally, three other firms of auditors are awaiting the outcome of the present proceedings before deciding whether to seek stays of the executive counsel's enquiries under the scheme.

C

We have concluded that *ex parte Brindle* was decided on its own facts, and is clearly distinguishable. We deal with that case and our reasons for distinguishing it in a separate schedule attached to this judgment.

As the first step in the balancing exercise which we must carry out, we seek to identify the public interest in the disciplinary proceedings under the scheme, first in general terms,

D   and then in relation to this particular case. As is clear from the legal framework of the scheme as we have examined it, the conduct and regulation of auditors is a matter of both Community and Parliamentary concern. The UK is obliged by treaty (and has responded by statute) to bring the responsibilities and conduct of auditors within the system of overall statutory control of multi-disciplinary regulation imposed under the framework of the *Financial Services Act* 1986 – which marked the beginning of the end of what too often was the 'cosy club' of self-regulation. (One of the problems of self-

E   regulation was that in many disciplines it was seen to have no teeth: one of the perceptions of the 1980s was that from some self-regulatory bodies there was nothing to fear but 'a slap on the wrist'. Hence the need to impose a statutory framework on such regulation.)

As has been made clear by our citation of the workings of the scheme, the executive counsel only comes to be involved when the executive committee are of opinion that 'the circumstances of the matter are ones which give rise to public concern'. In our judgment

F   the evaluation of that public concern is a matter for those who have to weigh it under the provisions of the scheme at each of its stages, and this court should give great weight to the views of those persons or bodies, and should not lightly decide that that person or body has acted or proposes to act unfairly: see *R v Panel on Takeovers & Mergers, ex parte Guinness plc* (1988) 4 BCC 714; [1990] 1 QB 146 per Lloyd LJ at p. 747; 184D–E. And where there is such public concern, there is an obvious need for that concern to be met with all speed consistent with justice. If the disciplinary proceedings designed to

G   address that concern are stayed pending resolution of the civil proceedings, we are doubtful whether that public concern will often be met when it has to await the prior resolution of those civil proceedings. Even where the civil proceedings are focused on the area covered by the regulatory functions, the remedies of fine and disqualification that may be required to meet the public concern are not available in those proceedings. Often the civil actions will settle without pronouncement by the court and a long time after the events that initially caused the concern. By then it may be too late for the disciplinary

H   proceedings to play their allotted role in meeting that concern. When dealing with public concern as to the auditing process, there will usually be a considerable degree of factual overlap between the likely issues in civil proceedings and under the disciplinary scheme. But this should not in our judgment be allowed to blur the different functions and different objectives of the two types of proceeding. Mr Chance, the executive counsel, says in his first affidavit:

'Were an expectation to develop that my investigations would routinely be stayed   A
for lengthy periods when civil actions were initiated or imminent, there would
inevitably be a loss of public confidence in the regulatory and disciplinary
arrangements for chartered and certified accountants in the very cases that matter
most and the UK's obligations under the Eighth Company Law Directive would
not be met.'

He then expresses his view as to the gravity of the complaints that are likely to be laid   B
against the applicants and its individual partners if his investigation is allowed to proceed
and states that in his judgment 'failure to take action to expose or prevent dishonesty,
deception and fraud is a matter which may justify exclusion from the membership of the
Institute'.

The applicants here have attempted to mount a factual challenge to that provisional
evaluation based on the present state of the respondent's enquiries (which are necessarily
incomplete because of the interim stay imposed in these proceedings). If the processes of   C
judicial review are routinely available to mount a challenge at one or more stages of the
disciplinary processes under the scheme, it is difficult to see how the scheme can operate
in practice. Steyn LJ said in *ex parte Fayed* ([1992] BCC 524 at p. 535H):

'But is it possible to challenge in judicial review proceedings the preliminary
decision of the executive that there is a prima facie case to initiate disciplinary
proceedings? The decision of the executive to bring disciplinary charges is not an   D
adjudicative act: it is preliminary in character. Here the analogy of a decision to
prosecute in criminal proceedings is instructive. Such a decision can be most
damaging to a defendant. Nevertheless it is a decision which almost invariably lies
beyond the legitimate domain of judicial review. In *Wiseman v Borneman* [1971]
AC 297 Lord Reid observed (at p. 308E):

"It is, I think, not entirely irrelevant to have in mind that it is very unusual for   E
there to be a judicial determination of the question whether there is a prima
facie case. Every public officer who has to decide whether to prosecute or raise
proceedings ought first to decide whether there is a prima facie case, but no one
supposes that justice requires that he should first seek the comments of the
accused or defendant on the material before him. So there is nothing inherently
unjust in reaching such a decision in the absence of the other party."

... In the developing field of judicial review it is usually unwise to say "never".   F
But it seems to me that, in the absence of evidence of fraud, corruption or mala
fides, judicial review will not be allowed to probe a decision to charge individuals
in criminal proceedings. The law must take a practical view of the limits of judicial
review. It would be unworkable to extend judicial review into this field. If this
reasoning is sound, a similar approach seems applicable to the initiation of
disciplinary proceedings. There is therefore no reason why judicial review should   G
be allowed to issue on the question whether there are prima facie grounds to take
disciplinary proceedings under the code of the Takeover Panel.'

In the light of the authority of *ex parte Guinness plc* (above) and that dictum, as
Parliament has entrusted the initial valuation of the case against the applicants to the
respondent, and has built into the disciplinary scheme adequate procedural protections
for the applicants, we believe that absent quite exceptional circumstances such as those
listed by Steyn LJ (which we do not find to be present in this case) we should not get   H
involved in a detailed consideration of the merits, but accept the respondent's valuation
that there is a strong public interest in the continuance of this enquiry (which could lead
to disciplinary proceedings) not being delayed by order of the court.

This brings us to the first potential gloss on Neill LJ's principle suggested by Hirst LJ
in *ex parte Brindle* (above). There he said (at p. 310D):

A
'I accept Mr Carnwath's submission, which is fully in line with the approach of the Court of Appeal in the *Fayed* case, that the power to intervene should be most sparingly exercised, and that it is only in exceptional cases that the disciplinary process (to which the institute rightly attaches great importance in the public interest) should not be allowed to go ahead unhindered.'

We respectfully agree that the considerations we set out above fully justify that view.
B We agree too with what Hirst LJ went on to say:

'However, it is clear that the adjudication which the court has to make is a balancing exercise, and that, heavily though the scales will initially weigh in the institute's favour, there may be cases where the considerations of serious prejudice to the member are so strong that they will prevail.

When assessing the weight of the considerations on the Institute's side of the scale,
C the intrinsic importance of the disciplinary process is clearly a very significant but not an overriding factor; it will also be necessary to evaluate the degree of public importance to the case under consideration, the seriousness of the allegation of professional incompetence and/or professional misconduct, and the urgency of their resolution in the disciplinary context. Thus, for example, allegations of dishonesty or other professional malpractice which, if proved, would be likely to lead to the striking off of a member must clearly weigh heavily or perhaps even
D overwhelmingly on the institute's side of the scale.'

But in our evaluation of those matters, we should not lightly depart from the views of the person or body entrusted with that evaluation the respondent. We see no reason for not accepting his evaluation of the seriousness of the allegations and the degree of the public importance of the disciplinary proceedings in this case. As Hirst J said in another context in *A & Ors v B (Governor of the Bank of England intervening)* [1991] 1 Bank LR
E 60 at p. 68):

'I cannot stress too strongly the importance which should be attached to the Bank of England having, within the limits laid down by the Act and general law, unfettered and unimpeded scope for the exercise of their most important public duties of regulation in the interests of the public, who are surely entitled to rely on the Bank of England to exercise those powers with integrity.'

F
There is no room here for the suppressed premise identified by Steyn LJ in *ex parte Fayed* (at p. 537G):

'There is no basis for a contention that the applicants will not be given a full and adequate opportunity to challenge the inspectors' report and to present their case. The unexpressed, but implied, contention was that compared to the court proceedings the disciplinary proceedings will only afford a second-class form of
G justice to the applicants. There is no warrant for such an assumption. There is no reason to doubt that the disciplinary proceedings will be conducted efficiently, properly and fairly, and with a full regard to the protections to which the applicants are entitled.'

In *ex parte Brindle* the court had to consider an earlier disciplinary scheme, and the court accepted that justifiable criticisms had been made of the fairness of that scheme. No such criticisms have been made of the present scheme. And there is no warrant for
H thinking that the respondent and those involved in the scheme will not operate it fairly.

Those considerations cause us to have great difficulty with a second gloss on the test in *ex parte Fayed* which it is submitted is binding on us. Hirst LJ, having stated that the overlap of the issues in the disciplinary proceedings and the liquidator's actions in the case before him was so close as to amount to 'virtual total eclipse' went on to say this (at p. 311A):

        A

'This to my mind is a most important consideration, because in my judgment it is inherently unfair that two tribunals should contemporaneously be considering the same issue (*Conteh v Onslow-Fane*, The Times, 26 June 1975, CAT 1975 No. 291) and because it affects the evaluation of [the burden of parallel proceedings on Price Waterhouse and its key personnel involved in the disciplinary inquiry before him].'

        B

In our judgment Hirst LJ was not there laying down any general proposition, because it would contradict the logic of all he had said when accepting the submission that 'the power to intervene should be most sparingly exercised' (at p. 310D). *Conteh v Onslow-Fane* was a case where the issue before both the British Boxing Board of Control's disciplinary proceedings and the civil action was a simple question of breach of contract. The issue – the sanctity or otherwise of boxers' contracts with managers and promoters – had no public law interest or element in it. We would not accept that any presumption against duplication expressed in those proceedings must apply in proceedings where the public law interest in the prompt resolution of the disciplinary proceedings is as strong as we take this interest to be.

        C

We turn then to consider the risk of prejudice to the civil proceedings. It is not suggested that civil proceedings tried (as these would be) by judge alone could be prejudiced by the earlier determination of the disciplinary proceedings. The case is put on the basis that having to defend parallel proceedings, disciplinary and civil, at the same time brings with it a real risk of serious prejudice that may lead to injustice.

        D

First the risk of inconsistent decisions is raised. Where two fact-finding tribunals are considering the same issue, there will always be the risk of inconsistent decisions. That risk can only be avoided by a procedure under which there is one determinative fact-finding exercise. Under our law as it is, disciplinary proceedings are necessary both in order to ensure that regulatory questions arousing public concern are addressed within a reasonable time-scale, and that they are addressed by a body with power to deal with them by way of fine and disqualification. Both the Community and Parliament have seen the need for such proceedings, and they would not be properly efficacious if they had to await the resolution – whether by compromise or otherwise – of civil proceedings, which might happen long after the event. And, given the nature of the disciplinary scheme in this case, there is no warrant for assuming that such proceedings would arrive at an erroneous conclusion.

        E

        F

Next it is objected that having to fight this particular battle on two fronts will cause injustice in that it will prejudice the defence on both fronts. And it is submitted that it is not simply a question of those two fronts – the other enquiries and investigations increase the demands on the three named individuals concerned in the disciplinary proceedings and the consequent strains on them.

        G

Given the nature of the allegations against them, we accept without hesitation the strains that are on them. But these strains must be greatly reduced by the fact that they have the support of their employers (and of their considerable resources) in all of this. Additionally, the disciplinary allegations are specific, they are not general and wide-ranging. The extent of the overlap will mean that the proper preparation for defence on the one front will also serve as the defence on the other front. If difficulties arise as a result of different tribunals requiring different things of the named individuals at the same time, then this can be sorted out by the tribunals responsible for the conflicting demands. But there is nothing on the information before us that would justify us in concluding that the additional burden of the disciplinary enquiry might be the last straw that would prevent a proper defence being made to the civil proceedings.

        H

Next, complaint is made that the disciplinary proceedings would generate their own documents which may be used to the applicants' disadvantage in the civil proceedings.

A   The principal documents identified before us were the transcripts of what the individuals might say in relation to the issues in interviews conducted under the scheme, and in evidence before the tribunal. If there was a real inconsistency between what they then said and what was said in the civil proceedings thereafter, then the reason for that inconsistency would have to be investigated. If there was an explanation for it, the inconsistency would not harm them. If there was no such explanation, the inconsistency would be rightly taken into account. There would be no injustice in that. The only other

B   identified documents were the possibility that additional accountants' reports might be generated – this might be so, but it is difficult to see how it could lead to injustice in the second set of proceedings. Surprise is the enemy of justice, and we see no likely injustice in having to give two different accounts on oath of the same incident.

Next it is alleged that, were the initial disciplinary proceedings to come to the wrong conclusion, an injustice would be done in that a subsequent vindication in the civil

C   proceedings would come too late. This is simply a re-heat of the risk of inconsistent decisions. There would be force in it only if the disciplinary proceedings would, in Steyn LJ's words in *Fayed* at p. 537G, 'only afford a second-class form of justice'. There are no grounds for making such an assumption. This court has no grounds for concluding that the risks of the body entrusted by Parliament with the enforcement of the disciplinary process getting it wrong are such that that process should be stayed pending the

D   resolution of the civil actions.

Next it is said that, whilst the disciplinary procedure is intrinsically important, there are in truth no special considerations of seriousness or urgency which demand the immediate resumption of the enquiry in this case. We disagree. We are satisfied that the respondent is right in concluding that the plunder of the MGN pension funds poses questions of real public concern as to the protection afforded by professional auditors. We agree with the respondent that that question should be addressed promptly, and its

E   resolution should not await and be dependent on the final resolution of civil proceedings, which may be some years off, and which when it happens may occur without any public pronouncement on the rights and wrongs of these matters.

Nor are we impressed by the suggestion that the investigations by the ARC and the JMU of the applicants' current audit procedures and controls are a substitute for a disciplinary hearing. As we have already indicated, that enquiry was into Coopers &

F   Lybrand's auditing systems current at the date of the enquiry and did not relate to the audits with which the disciplinary proceedings would be concerned. Second and more important, the disciplinary proceedings are concerned with individual conduct, and not with systems. ARC/JMU investigations do not in any significant way reduce the need for a disciplinary enquiry.

Nor should such an enquiry await the publication of the DTI inspectors' report. Many

G   considerations can delay such publication (as a quick mental check on the unpublished reports relating to financial scandals dating from the 1980s will confirm). Nor can it be said that 'it would be positively beneficial if the JDS enquiry were postponed until after the trial of the civil litigation' – we are back to the impermissible assumption that disciplinary proceedings would only provide a second-class system of justice.

Lastly the suggestion is made that the continuation of the JDS enquiry might prejudice

H   the criminal trials. The parties and the court in those trials will be alive to any potential risk of prejudice to them. The responsibility for preservation of the integrity of those trials rests with the court in those trials. In the unlikely event of their integrity being threatened by the hearing (in private in the first instance) of the disciplinary proceedings or the publication of the findings thereof, then the criminal court has ample powers to obtain an order restraining publication until after the conclusion of the criminal trials. There are no grounds for this court interfering at this stage on that score.

Therefore we see no grounds for granting any stay of the disciplinary proceedings in   A
this case. Accordingly, in our judgment, this application must be dismissed.

But before we leave this subject, we wish to add this. Mr Beloff QC on behalf of the
respondent, while submitting that no stay could be imposed at this stage, as a fall-back
position was prepared to contemplate the possibility that judicial review might lie at a
later stage on completion of the enquiry when and if the respondent committed the case
to the tribunal. While, as Steyn LJ in *Fayed* pointed out, it is unwise to say 'never' in the   B
developing field of judicial review, we would point out that too ready a grant of leave at
that stage would, if not frustrate, at least reduce the intended efficacy of disciplinary
proceedings in meeting the public concern. Parliament has entrusted such disciplinary
proceedings to a responsible body, the procedures under which that body operates have
built into them proper protection for the applicants, and in those circumstances we would
suggest that it should require strong evidence before the judge granting leave concluded
that there was an arguable case for the court to intervene before the disciplinary   C
procedures were complete.

SCHEDULE

This matter arises out of the collapse of the bank of Credit and Commerce
International. The well-known accountants, Price Waterhouse, co-ordinated the world-
wide auditors of that group, and reviewed the consolidation of its accounts. The world-   D
wide collapse of that banking group was massive in scale, and generated many enquiries
and investigations, and many law suits – and not only in this country. Price Waterhouse
were both centrally involved in the investigation and enquiries, and also were the target
of many of the law suits. They and the six of their partners who were centrally involved
in the BCCI audits were the subject of a disciplinary enquiry under the scheme's
predecessor. They sought a stay of that enquiry until the resolution of the civil actions
against them. The divisional court (Mann LJ and Sedley J) refused the stay. The Court   E
of Appeal (Nolan and Hirst L JJ and Sir Roger Parker) allowed the appeal, and granted
the stay.

We draw the following distinctions between the court's findings in that case and ours
in this.

(1)   There, the open-ended nature and scale of the disciplinary proceedings was such
        that to pursue them contemporaneously with the civil proceedings would prejudice   F
        the defence of those civil proceedings. Here the disciplinary proceedings are
        specific, do not impose such 'daunting . . . unprecedented' burdens, and would not
        jeopardise the proper defence of the civil proceedings.

(2)   There, there was no special consideration of seriousness or urgency in the
        disciplinary proceedings: no seriousness because there was no allegation of
        misconduct, no urgency because the disciplinary proceedings would not be   G
        complete for years and no sooner than the civil actions in any event. Here, serious
        allegations are made, and the disciplinary proceedings clearly could be completed
        before the civil proceedings – viz. the submissions on inconsistent verdicts which
        were predicated on that basis.

(3)   There, the scale of the civil proceedings was such that even 'if only partly successful,
        it might destroy the appellants' business'. Here, there is no evidence that the   H
        litigation poses that threat.

(4)   There, the disciplinary proceedings were under the old (and arguably unfair)
        scheme. No such criticisms are made of the new scheme.

(5)   There, the court attached importance to the ARC/JMU clearance. We do not, for
        the reasons given.

A   (6)   There, it was felt that the mere commencement of the disciplinary proceedings met the public concern. We did not feel that.

    In short, there, the court took the view that on its facts there was little public interest in the pursuit of the disciplinary proceedings, and a real risk of serious prejudice to the civil proceedings were they not stayed, and we on our facts took a diametrically opposite view to theirs on each side of the balance.

B

(Order accordingly)

———————————

C

D

E

F

G

H

Weisgard v Pilkington & Anor.

A

Chancery Division (Liverpool).
Judge Maddocks.
Judgment delivered 14 June 1995.

Liquidation – Preferences – Property development company in financial difficulties granted leases of flats to directors – Whether directors could rebut presumption of desire to prefer – Insolvency Act 1986, s. 239.

B

This was an application by the liquidator of Hotswap Ltd under s. 239 of the Insolvency Act 1986 seeking to reverse the disposition by the company to two directors of six flats.

The company was in liquidation. It had been developing a property consisting of a ground floor restaurant with flats above. The property was charged to secure the loan used to acquire it and the respondent directors had given personal guarantees of the company's overdraft. The company ran into financial difficulties and four months before the company went into liquidation it granted leases of six flats to the respondents for a consideration said to be based on an assessment of their value in their then undeveloped state. No money actually passed from the respondents to the company, the leases being taken in discharge of sums owed to them by the company. Two of the flats were then charged to the bank to secure the company's overdraft. One flat was later sold and the proceeds expended, it was said, as to £10,000 on legal costs and as to £19,500 on converting the remaining flats. The transfers were at a relevant time and the presumption in s. 239(6) on a transfer to a connected person applied.

C

D

Held, ordering the respondents to transfer the leases to the liquidator and to repay the sum of £29,500 (but with liberty to the respondents to apply if so advised for payment by the liquidator out of the proceeds of sale of the flats of any sums they might claim to have expended in the conversion or development or sale of the flats to the extent of any benefit thereby conferred):

E

1. The transfers by way of the two leases taken in satisfaction of the respondents' debts plainly put them in a better position than they would have been in under an insolvent liquidation. That had to be qualified slightly in relation to the two flats immediately charged to the bank but even in relation to those flats the charges afforded some benefit in mitigating their guarantee liabilities.

F

2. The respondents had failed to displace the presumption. Their explanation that the transaction was seen by them as simply a way of restructuring the development of the property so as to relieve the company of responsibility for completing the flats and that in so far as they were preferred that was merely in incident of the scheme, became wholly unconvincing when tested by the facts and by their own conduct and could not be accepted.

The following cases were referred to in the judgment:

G

Beacon Leisure Ltd, Re [1991] BCC 213.
Ledingham-Smith (a bankrupt), ex parte the trustee of the bankrupt v Pannell Kerr Forster (a firm), Re [1993] BCLC 635.
M C Bacon Ltd, Re [1990] BCC 78.

Hugo Groves (instructed by Davies Arnold Cooper) for the petitioner.

The respondents did not appear and were not represented.

H

JUDGMENT

Judge Maddocks: This is an application by the liquidator of the company Hotswap Ltd ('Hotswap') for relief under s. 239 of the *Insolvency Act* 1986. It relates to the disposition by the company to the two respondents, Mr Yeomans and Mr Pilkington, on

A   24 July 1991 of six flats belonging to the company. In the alternative the liquidator seeks relief under s. 238.

The company went into creditors' voluntary liquidation on 26 November 1991.

The facts shortly are that Hotswap was incorporated on 21 July 1989 and traded from 23/24 Union Street, Ryde on the Isle of Wight. The initial directors following formation were Mr Paul Thomas Brommel and Mr Kerry Yeomans, the second respondent, both

B   appointed on 25 September 1989. Mr Dale Pilkington, the first respondent, was appointed on 7 June 1990. Each director held one of the three issued shares of £1.

In February 1990 the company completed the purchase of the premises 23/24 Union Street, a building erected at the turn of the century which then comprised a restaurant called The Galleon Restaurant which had been closed for some time, and a retail unit and two upper floors which had planning consent for conversion into eight one-bedroom

C   flats.

The purchase was financed by a loan from Coopers of Wessex Ltd, which became Ind Coope, of £210,000 secured by a fixed legal charge on the property dated 22 February 1990. The scheme was to convert the ground floor to a new restaurant or cafe bar and the two upper floors to residential accommodation which ultimately was to take the form of six self-contained flats.

D   On 3 May 1990 a valuation was obtained from a firm of surveyors, Messrs Deakins, on the basis of the refurbishment of all parts being completed. On that basis a value of between £500,000 and £550,000 was attributed to the property with the eight flats being marketed at between £35,000 and £40,000 each, that is to say £280,000 to £320,000 in total.

The first stage was completed by 1 August 1990 when the restaurant opened as Brommel's Cafe Bar. Mr Pilkington told me that he initially provided £25,000 for the

E   project, later increased to £40,000 on the understanding that his finance would be secured by a second charge on the property with the benefit of a deed of priority agreed with Coopers. Drafts were certainly prepared by solicitors acting for the company, Davis Blank and Furniss. The terms of the deed of priority as accepted in principle by Coopers were that he be entitled to priority over the Coopers' debt so far as it exceeded £260,000.

That is confirmed by a letter dated 5 July 1990 from Davis Blank and Furniss referring

F   to the drafts prepared and to the mortgage being now required for £40,000.

In early July 1990 Mr Pilkington was on a business trip to Kuwait, he was caught up in the Iraqi invasion of 2 August 1990 and on 6 August 1990 was taken with his family and others to Iraq where he was detained until 10 December 1990. It was an unhappy and distressing experience for which he is certainly entitled to sympathy.

On 10 August 1990 Mr Yeomans suffered a heart attack. This left the business under

G   the control of Mr Brommel until mid-December 1990. When the respondents returned in that month they were dissatisfied with the way in which Mr Brommel had been running the business. Indeed, they considered that he had been guilty of dishonesty and made a report to the local CID.

They removed him from control and ran the business themselves. It was clearly in financial difficulties at this point with debts overdue for payment, but they were prepared to give it their backing. The bank account was originally with Lloyds but had been frozen

H   as a consequence of Mr Pilkington's detention in Iraq so that a new account was opened with the National Westminster Bank in August 1990.

As at the end of December 1990 the account stood at approximately £13,000 overdrawn but Mr Yeomans and Mr Pilkington were able to arrange an increase in the facility on the basis that a charge would be given over two of the flats to be released from the Coopers' charge as referred to in certain of the correspondence.

In the meantime, however, on 21 February 1991 each of the respondents gave a
personal guarantee to the bank for the company's account with a limit of £45,000.
Despite the increase in the overdraft limit to £42,000 and then to £50,000 bills continued
to be unpaid and on 29 May 1991 one creditor, Jewson Ltd, issued a winding-up petition
based on a county court judgment dated 30 November 1990 for £7,045.

By a letter dated 9 July 1991 the bank confirmed its agreement to extend the overdraft
limit to £65,000 for the development of two flats, the overdraft to be repaid out of the
proceeds of sale of these two flats, when the bank would consider releasing the
guarantees. At this point, after consultation with the company accountant, Mr Julian
Behrman, the company entered into the transactions with Mr Yeomans and Mr
Pilkington which are now challenged by the liquidator. There were the following deeds
all drawn up by the solicitors and executed on 24 July 1991:

(1)   A lease of flats 1 and 2 being two flats on the first floor for a term of 999 years, the
       consideration expressed being £20,000.

(2)   A lease of flats 3, 4, 5 and 6 being the remaining flat on the first floor and all the
       second floor flats for 999 years. The consideration was expressed to be £40,000.

(3)   A declaration of trust reciting the leases by which Mr Pilkington and Mr Yeomans
       agreed to divide the proceeds of sale first in payment of £66,899.86 to Mr
       Pilkington and, secondly, as to the balance in equal shares.

This deed was first produced by Mr Pilkington in his affidavit of 10 November 1993 in
which he explained that the £66,899.86 represented the difference between the amount
owing to him by the company, that is £73,149.86, and the amount owing to Mr Yeomans
of £6,125, a total of £79,374.86.

In evidence he said he had provided a list to the company's solicitors but this was not
now forthcoming from them or from him. He said the figures of £20,000 and £40,000
were based on an assessment of the value of the flat units, in their then undeveloped state,
at £10,000 each. No money actually passed from the lessees to the company, the leases
being taken in discharge of the sums owed to them.

In addition to these deeds there were also produced:

(4)   A legal mortgage by Mr Pilkington in favour of National Westminster Bank on
       flat number 1 to secure the company's account up to £70,000.

(5)   A like charge/mortgage over flat number 2 with the same limit.

I should here note that Coopers on the same date, July 1991, were content to release
their charge over the freehold of all six flats. That is to say the first and second floors of
the building.

The flats were then developed and flats 3 and 6 were brought up to completion. It
emerged from the evidence at the hearing that notwithstanding the leases, the costs, or
certainly a large part of the costs, of converting the flats were paid out of the company's
bank account making use of the increased overdraft facility of up to £70,000.

In September 1991 Mr Pilkington and Mr Yeomans accepted that the company was
insolvent and could no longer continue to trade. On the advice of Mr Behrman, the
company accountant, they instructed Mr Weisgard, an insolvency practitioner, to place
the company in creditors' voluntary winding up rather than accede to the petition still
pending, for compulsory winding up, which petition, following an amendment reducing
the debt to £6,077 plus costs, was due to be heard on Monday, 7 October 1991.

On 17 September 1991 Mr Weisgard wrote to the respondents. His letter noted that
the company had no assets so that he must look to them for the costs, he noted also that
the sale of the flats would appear to constitute a preference; he also emphasised the need
to treat all creditors on an equal basis in the period running up to the date of the creditors'

A   meeting. Despite these warnings Mr Yeomans and Mr Pilkington continued with the development of the flats seemingly still using money from the company's bank account.

On 3 October 1991 the major creditor, Eastcheap Ltd, trading as Peter Green Contracts gave notice of their intention to support the petition for their debt of £15,427.20.

B   On 7 October 1991 Mr Yeomans and Mr Pilkington obtained a valuation of the flats for mortgage purposes from a firm, Kingston and Grist. It stated, 'Work of conversion is complete on one unit, proceeding to completion on another', those I should note are flats 3 and 6 respectively, 'and with work at various stages in the further four'. The valuation was put at £60,000 or £50,000 on a forced sale basis. This, however, would appear to have excluded the two flats at or nearing completion, three and six, as these were treated as sold on 99-year leases at a ground rent. As number 3 was sold shortly afterwards for £30,000 that would appear to add about £60,000 to the valuation.

C   On 24 October 1991 a further deed was executed being a deed of variation whereby there were added to the leases rights to use six of the 12 parking spaces. This was no doubt caused by a conveyancing oversight, nevertheless it was an action detracting from the assets of the company for the benefit of the two directors almost on the eve of liquidation.

D   It has since emerged that on 1 November 1991 flat number 3, the fully completed flat, was transferred to Mr Keeley, or agreed to be transferred to Mr Keeley, possibly on a 99-year lease for a consideration of £30,000. No documentary evidence of the transaction has ever been forthcoming from the respondents or their solicitors but at the hearing Mr Yeomans said that the amount received by their solicitors on completion was £29,500 from which the solicitors deducted approximately £10,000 in respect of costs. The remaining £19,500, he said, had been expended in paying the costs of converting the flats, E   but, again, no particulars or documentary evidence were forthcoming.

On 20 November 1991 the solicitors, Davis Blank and Furniss wrote:

> 'The directors were aware that the company did not have sufficient funds to develop the flats but they formed the view that the company was not insolvent and was capable of continuing to trade strictly within the terms of the Insolvency Act. They therefore determined that they themselves would develop the flats using their F   own moneys.
>
> Clearly it was not in the company's best interests for the flats above to remain vacant and in their previous state for any great period of time. They were clearly owed substantial sums by the company for loan moneys advanced by them and they agreed to forego those loans.
>
> Further, they agreed the request of the company's bankers to provide a guarantee G   for the company's bank borrowing without which the bank had threatened to withdraw its support. We enclose copies of those guarantees and we are authorised to tell you that the bank has made a demand upon each of the directors for payment of the sum of £70,000.'

In answer to further questions on 25 November they wrote this:

> '(1) I think that the correct analysis is that it never occurred to the directors that H   the company was anything but solvent and capable of continuing to trade because they were paying their debts as they fell due and had a reliable offer of finance both from the bank and also from the brewery whose support they enjoyed. I have not discussed this issue directly with them but I do not think they ever formally sat down and addressed the question.'

Those letters, I am bound to say, do somewhat misrepresent the position.

(1)   The directors had each already guaranteed the bank account in February 1991.   A

(2)   There is abundant evidence that the company was unable to pay its debts as they fell due.

(3)   The directors continued to use company funds to develop the flats.

(4)   The new guarantee was simply a charge over flats 1 and 2.

On 26 November 1991 the resolution for voluntary winding up was passed. I can here refer to the statement of affairs which shows that the only assets of the company were the property 23/24 Union Street effectively limited by the leases to the ground floor, estimated to realise £290,000 less the sum due to Coopers, now Ind Coope, of £210,000 and furniture etc. estimated to realise £1,900, there is nothing else at all.

Preferential creditors were £8,993 leaving nothing for unsecured creditors. Lloyds Bank was still owed £6,165 and trade creditors were owed £103,112. The overall estimated total deficiency as regards creditors was £266,665.   C

On the evidence there is nothing to suggest that the position was significantly different as at 24 July 1991 save that the assets then included the six flats albeit unconverted and the directors had claims as unsecured creditors which they put at £79,149.

The notes for the information of creditors include the following passage based on statements by the directors:

'All possible efforts were made to make payments against debts incurred to December 1990 as well as paying invoices as we went. However, the debts to December 1990 were far in excess of our anticipation. Initially the very lack of funds prevented any action by the liquidator from issuing these proceedings.'

Mr Weisgard did however seek further explanations.

On 24 March 1992 Mr Pilkington wrote, 'I will write a full and detailed explanation as I understand it and will forward to you within the next few days.' That explanation never arrived.

When, however, the liquidation was about to be closed the liquidator was placed in funds and pursued the claims further. On 4 February 1993 he sent a detailed questionnaire to each of the respondents. Mr Yeomans replied in fairly short terms with only the minimum of detail, Mr Pilkington did not reply at all.

These proceedings were issued on 10 June 1993. Mr Pilkington swore an affidavit on 10 November 1993 which, for the first time, revealed the declaration of trust. Both respondents appeared before me at the hearing and gave evidence. It is fair to note Mr Yeomans now spends most of his time on business abroad.

I turn then to the issues. The first is whether the leases constituted preferences within s. 239. I shall not read the sections in full. The date 24 June 1991 was plainly a relevant time within s. 240 being within the period of six months before voluntary winding up. I   G am satisfied, and, indeed, I do not think it was disputed, that as at 24 July 1991 the company was unable to pay its debts within the meaning of s. 123.

I turn then to s. 239(4)–(6):

'(4) For the purposes of this section and section 241, a company gives a preference to a person if–

(a) that person is one of the company's creditors or a surety or guarantor for   H any of the company's debts or other liabilities, and

(b) the company does anything or suffers anything to be done which (in either case) has the effect of putting that person into a position which, in the event of the company going into insolvent liquidation, will be better than the position he would have been in if that thing had not been done.

A   (5) The court shall not make an order under this section in respect of a preference given to any person unless the company which gave the preference was influenced in deciding to give it by a desire to produce in relation to that person the effect mentioned in subsection (4)(b).

(6) A company which has given a preference to a person connected with the company (otherwise than by reason only of being its employee) at the time the
B   preference was given is presumed, unless the contrary is shown, to have been influenced in deciding to give it by such a desire as is mentioned in subsection (5).'

Here it is clear that the respondents were creditors and on their evidence were creditors owed respectively, £6,125, and £73,149.86 those sums being unsecured. They were also guarantors of the company's bank account for up to £45,000 each. The six flats were plainly assets of value, that value on their evidence being put at £10,000 per unit.

C   The transfers by way of the two leases were taken in satisfaction of their debts. They plainly put the respondents in a better position than they would have been in under an insolvent liquidation. That must be qualified slightly in relation to flats 1 and 2 by the immediate charges to the bank but even in relation to those flats the charges afforded some benefit in mitigating their guarantee liabilities.

The crucial question is that which arises under subs. (5) and (6) which I have read. The
D   respondents here were the two controlling directors of the company which gave the preferences, the presumption under subs. (6) therefore applies and that was accepted.

I was referred by Mr Groves for the liquidator to three authorities all which are particularly helpful on this section, *Re M C Bacon Ltd* [1990] BCC 78, a decision of Millett J, *Re Beacon Leisure Ltd* [1991] BCC 213, a decision of Mr Robert Wright QC sitting as a deputy judge of the High Court and finally *Re Ledingham-Smith* which is a
E   bankruptcy case reported at [1993] BCLC 635, the decision of Morritt J.

I am here content to follow the words of Morritt J in the last case at p. 641 where he said:

> 'In my judgment "desire" and "influenced by" are ordinary English words which are not susceptible of further useful definition. It is a question of applying them to the facts of the case.'

F
So it appears to me. The wording of the Insolvency Act has been carefully drawn to adopt language which can be so applied.

The question then is whether the respondents have displaced the presumption. I am satisfied they have not. In reaching this conclusion I am influenced by the following factors.

G   (1)   The respondents together had full control of the company and were persons who had knowledge of its property and financial position. They also had the advantage of the advice and assistance of accountants and solicitors. They could not be said to have been acting in ignorance or without a proper understanding of what the situation was or what was taking place.

(2)   Mr Pilkington in particular was aware that he was still unsecured, because the
H   proposed legal charge in his favour had never been executed. Indeed, his evidence in para. 7 of his affidavit is that the leases were in substitution for the proposed legal charge. The whole purpose of such a legal charge would, of course, have been to place the chargee in a better position than that of an unsecured creditor.

(3)   The directors were aware of the debts and judgments against the company and particularly of the pending winding-up petition.

(4)   Despite repeated requests from the liquidator they were throughout less than forthcoming with any of the material information and documents which he required.

The case as presented by Mr Pilkington and Mr Yeomans was that the transaction was seen by them as simply a way of restructuring the development of the property so as to relieve the company of responsibility for completing the flats. They had no desire to achieve a preference for themselves and the transaction was not influenced by such a desire. In so far as that happened it was merely in incident of the scheme.

However, when tested by the facts and by their own conduct that explanation becomes wholly unconvincing and I cannot accept it. If the leases fall to be treated as preferences the deed of variation must suffer the same fate. I think on balance it was probably intended to correct an oversight at the time of the leases but in that case it cannot be treated any differently.

On the view I take as to the application of s. 239 I do not propose to deal with the alternative claim under s. 238, but if the leases had not been made in satisfaction of the debts then one of two consequences would have followed, either the liquidator would have had a claim against the respondents for the unpaid consideration of £60,000 or the leases would manifestly have been transactions at an undervalue. However, the case really rests on s. 239.

I come finally to flat number 3 which has been sold possibly by way of under lease for 99 years. The respondents by their solicitors received, on their evidence, the consideration of £29,500. They have not, despite every opportunity, given any account of that money or provided any documentary evidence in relation to it. It seems to me that the right order is that they should repay that sum to the liquidator.

However, I do not exclude the possibility that they may be in the position to establish that money has been expended by them personally on the conversion of the flats or in relation to the sale of flat number 3 which had the effect of enhancing the value of the property to the liquidator for the purpose of the liquidation as compared with the value at the time of the transactions in question.

Mr Groves urged that as they were guilty of misfeasance in granting the leases they are not entitled to any indulgence and, having failed to provide any proper particulars, no further indulgence should be afforded.

Under s. 239(3), however, the court is required to make such order as it thinks fit for restoring the position to what it would have been if the company had not given that preference. It seems to me that despite the submissions of Mr Groves I should at least allow the respondents an opportunity to make a claim if they can show that they have in fact expended money which has had the effect of enhancing the value of these properties.

The course I therefore propose is to give liberty to the respondents to apply if so advised for payment by the liquidator out of the proceeds of sale of the flats of any sums they may claim to have expended in the conversion or development or sale of the flats to the extent of any benefit thereby conferred.

I turn to the orders, and Mr Robinson may be able to assist me with his observations here, but if I go to the originating summons the course I propose is, first, to make a declaration as sought in para. 1 both in relation to the leases and in relation to the deeds of variation which were supplemental thereto.

I will also order that the respondents do transfer the leases to the liquidator. I will order that the respondents do pay to the liquidator the sum of £29,500 to which I have referred. I will give liberty to the respondents to apply in the terms I have already set out and it may be also I should make an order if required for delivery up of vacant possession with the exception of flat 3 and I will give liberty for the applicant or any person affected

A   by this order to apply for any such person to be joined in the proceedings and to apply
for any consequential relief.

Finally, I indicated that the costs will follow the event when both parties were fully
represented, that is when Mr Pilkington was before me on Monday and Mr Weisgard by
counsel, subject to any observations the applicant would have had if the decision had
gone against him. As it is, it seems to me costs must plainly follow the event and I order

B   the respondents to pay the applicant's costs.

(Order accordingly)

C

D

E

F

G

H

1,116

Re John Slack Ltd.

A

Chancery Division.
Scott J.
Judgment delivered 2 July 1990.

*Administration order – Whether administrator could pay pre-administration order
creditors in full – Insolvency Act 1986, s. 8(2), (3), Sch. 1, para. 13.*

B

**An administrator had power, if the assets of the company permitted him to do so, to pay
off the pre-administration order creditors in full. That was one of the steps which he might
take in order to ensure the survival of the company as a going concern. (Accordingly, for
the protection of the administrator, who had brought the matter to court, the court made an
order giving him leave to make the payments to creditors, but he would have been entitled
to have done it of his own motion without coming to court.) (Re St Ives Windings Ltd (1987)
3 BCC 634 distinguished.)**

C

The following case was referred to in the judgment:

St Ives Windings Ltd, Re (1987) 3 BCC 634.

John Higham (instructed by Abson Hall, Stockport) for the administrator.

JUDGMENT

D

Scott J: An administration order was made in respect of John Slack Ltd on 19
September 1988. There were two statutory purposes set out in the order. One was the
survival of the company or of any part of its undertaking as a going concern. The other
was a more advantageous realisation of the company's assets than would be effected on
a winding up. At the time the order was made the company was being pressed by its
creditors and had inadequate cash flow to enable its debts to be paid. So the effect of the
administration order was to give the company relief from creditors' pressure and to give
it time to be brought to a more satisfactory state of viability.

E

The purpose of the administration order has succeeded. The administrator has sold a
part of some land owned by the company for a very favourable price. The proceeds of
this sale has produced enough money to enable all the pre-administration creditors to be
paid in full, to enable provision to be made for payment in full of all the liabilities of the
administration and for the expected remuneration of the administrator. That having been
done, there will still be a substantial surplus of assets still owned by the company which
will enable the company to resume trading under the control of its directors.

F

By the application before me this morning the administrators seek an order giving
them leave to make payment to the creditors of the full amount of the debts owing to
them. As the administrator has observed in the affidavit he has sworn, those creditors
have been very patient and have been waiting for a long time to be paid the money that
is owing to them. The question arises whether it was necessary for this application to be
made, or whether the administrator could not simply have paid the creditors the debts
owing to them out of the funds realised by him in discharge of his duties as administrator.
That would have seemed the convenient course. But the administrator has been inhibited
in taking that course because of the possible implications of a decision of Harman J in
Re St Ives Windings Ltd (1987) 3 BCC 634.

G

The facts of that case were not the same as those of the present case. That was a case
where an administration order had been made for the purpose either of obtaining the
survival of the company as a going concern or of achieving a more advantageous
realisation of its assets than would be effected in a winding up, but it was not a company
which was solvent on a balance sheet footing; its assets did not exceed its liabilities. After
the administrator had done what he could and had realised the company's assets more
advantageously than would have been possible in a winding up, after, therefore, the

H

A   purpose of the administration order had been achieved, the administrator desired to make a distribution to the creditors. He proposed to make a pro rata distribution because there were not sufficient assets to pay creditors in full. Harman J took the view that a pro rata distribution was not something that an administrator had power to do. It could be done either by means of a voluntary arrangement pursuant to the relevant section of the *Insolvency Act* 1986, or, of course, could be done by a liquidator if the company went into liquidation. Accordingly the solution in that case was that an extra purpose, namely,

B   obtaining the approval by creditors to a voluntary arrangement, was added to the purposes for which the administration order was made, and the matter proceeded in that way. The case is only briefly reported, but I have indicated, I think, sufficient of the basis on which the judgment was given.

      Harman J summed up the main point of the case by posing the question, 'whether there is a power under a simple administration for the purposes for which this

C   administration order was made to approve or sanction in any binding way so as to bind dissentients to such a distribution.' The distribution, I repeat, was a pro rata distribution; it was not a payment of the creditors in full. Here, on the other hand, a payment of the creditors in full is proposed. There are not going to be any dissentients. The creditors will receive the full amount of their respective debts.

      Mr Higham has drawn my attention to provisions of the *Insolvency Act* 1986 which

D   justify the conclusion that an administrator does have power to pay pre-administration order creditors in full. In s. 8(2) it is provided:

> 'An administration order is an order directing that, during the period for which the order is in force, the affairs,' – I would stress that noun – 'business and property of the company shall be managed by a person ("the administrator") . . .'

Schedule 1 to the Act, which sets out the powers of the administrator during the period an administration order is in effect, provides under para. 13 that he may make any

E   payment which is necessary or incidental to the performance of his functions. One would suppose that the payment of creditors of the company was incidental to the performance of the administrator's function in bringing about the survival of the company as a going concern.

      I am satisfied that an administrator does have power, if the assets of the company permit him to do so, to pay off the pre-administration order creditors in full. That is one

F   of the steps which he may take, and is likely to have to take, in order to ensure the survival of the company as a going concern. That was not the point that arose in Harman J's case. There the payments proposed to be made were, in effect, payments as on a winding up, a liquidation of the company. Accordingly, for the protection of the administrator, as he has brought the matter to court, I am prepared to make the order sought giving him leave to make the payments to creditors, but, in my opinion, he would have been entitled to have done it of his own motion without coming to court.

G   I will simply say this by way of addition. This case was transferred to London from the Stockport County Court because it raised a point of insolvency practice which it was thought desired the attention of a High Court judge. As to bringing the matter before a High Court judge, I am in full agreement with the opinion of counsel that that was the right course. As to the transfer of the case to London, I am entirely in disagreement with the proposition that that was the right course to take. This case should have been

H   transferred from the Stockport County Court to be heard by a High Court judge in Manchester. I hope in future that will be done.

(Order accordingly)

Re WBSL Realisations 1992 Ltd.   A

Chancery Division.
Knox J.
Judgment delivered 17 July 1995.

> *Administration orders – Distributions to creditors – Administrators appointed to*
> *holding company and subsidiary – More advantageous realisation of assets*   B
> *achieved – Administrators sought to pay off creditors of subsidiary in full –*
> *Prospect of further substantial realisation if holding company not wound up –*
> *Whether administrators could pay holding company's creditors on basis of*
> *notional winding up – Insolvency Act 1986, Sch. 1, para. 13.*

These were applications by the administrators of two companies, 'WBSL' and 'PLC',
asking the court to sanction distributions by the administrators to the companies' creditors.
                                                                                C
The purpose of both administrations was a more advantageous realisation of the assets
than would be effected on a winding up. In the case of WBSL the administrators were able
to pay all the creditors in full. In the case of PLC the administrators wished to pay off those
who would be preferential creditors in a subsequent liquidation and make payments to other
unsecured creditors on a pari passu basis. There was a prospect of a further substantial
realisation in the case of PLC which would cease to be distributable if PLC was wound up.
There were also factors which meant that a voluntary arrangement was not convenient or   D
practicable.

Held, sanctioning payment to the creditors of WBSL and to the preferential creditors of
PLC on the basis of a notional winding up at the date when the administration order was
made, and to the unsecured creditors on a pari passu basis and on terms that they brought
the payments received into account on a subsequent liquidation:

The breadth of the power in Sch. 1, para. 13 to the Insolvency Act 1986 was wide enough   E
to permit a distribution in the special circumstances of the case, which were that, unless that
was done, there would be a significant prejudice to the creditors of PLC, coupled with the
fact that creditors of PLC had approved the proposed application, and supported it through
the creditors' committee, and the fact that there was evidence that there was no significant
or practical risk of creditors emerging thereafter who were not known.

The following cases were referred to in the judgment: F

Mount Banking plc, Re (unreported, 25 January 1993).
St Ives Windings Ltd, Re (1987) 3 BCC 634.
Slack (John) Ltd, Re [1995] BCC 1116.

Susan Prevezer (instructed by Hammond Suddards, Leeds) for the applicant.

JUDGMENT   G

Knox J: There are two applications before me, both by the joint administrators of a
company. One company is WBSL Realisations 1992 Ltd. It is a subsidiary of the other
company, Ward Group plc. As I have said, both are in administration. The
administration orders were made as long ago as 5 June 1992, and the only purpose in the
administration orders was the fourth in the list in the *Insolvency Act* 1986, s. 8(3), the
more advantageous realisation of the company's assets than would be effected on a   H
winding up.

The administrations have been successful, more especially in relation to WBSL
Realisations, in that the evidence now is that there is more than enough to pay all
creditors in full. I am asked to sanction the administrators doing that in the ordinary
application with regard to that company.

A   The situation is less straightforward in Ward Group plc. The application asks for a direction that the applicants have power to and/or be at liberty to agree the claims of all creditors who, if Ward Group plc were to enter into a compulsory liquidation on the discharge of the administration order, would rank as unsecured creditors within the scope of s. 386 and Sch. 6 of the Insolvency Act, that is with preferential debts; secondly, a direction that the applicants may make a payment in respect of such claims on the footing that they are necessary or incidental to the performance of the administrator's functions under para. 13 of Sch. 1 to the Insolvency Act; thirdly, a direction that the applicants have power to and/or be at liberty to agree the claims of all creditors who, if Ward Group plc were to enter into compulsory liquidation on the discharge of the administration order, would rank as unsecured creditors within the meaning of s. 248(a), i.e. the non-preferential unsecured creditors; and a direction that in so far as the applicants hold funds enabling them to do so, payment may be made in respect of such claims on a pari passu basis, such payments being necessary or incidental to the performance of the administrator's functions pursuant to para. 13 of Sch. 1.

The administrators hold substantial sums, as I have already said, in relation to the WBSL Realisation company, enough to pay all the preferential and non-preferential creditors. In PLC, as I will call the other company, they have realised over £4.5m, and it is anticipated that there is to come rather more than another £4m, in particular a payment up from WBSL, the other company which is a subsidiary, of the amount of its prospective surplus after all creditors have been paid.

What is special in this unusual case is that there is a prospect of a realisation of another £1.5m in relation to the pension scheme which PLC has, and which is at present in substantial surplus. There is a complex situation there in that the businesses have been sold to an outside party, and there is a provision, if there is a transfer of the pension scheme to that outside party, that a substantial payment will be made in respect of that surplus. But there were also other possibilities; notably, the one which would be detrimental to the creditors of PLC is that the surplus would, if there was a compulsory winding up of PLC, become distributable within the pension scheme otherwise than to PLC itself, notably to the members.

The members of the pension scheme are not, as I see it, in any way affected by what is proposed to be done. The creditors of PLC would be seriously affected if the live possibility of recovering £1.5m from the pension scheme surplus became impossible of realisation, and that could, as matters now stand, be triggered by an insistence by unsecured creditors of PLC through the administration or an attempt by them to procure the compulsory winding up of the company, notwithstanding the administration order, on the footing that all the assets effectively are now secured or in view and the court ought not to allow the administration to go on indefinitely.

There is therefore something of a dilemma raised by observations that have been made in the past in relation to the ability of administrators to make payments to creditors otherwise than through the vehicle of a voluntary arrangement or a scheme of arrangement. In particular, the voluntary arrangement path is not readily available as a solution to the present problem, partly because there is a confidentiality clause in the sale agreement to the third party that I have mentioned, which would make the explanation of the voluntary arrangements peculiarly difficult for those concerned to get it approved, and partly because it is perfectly clear that PLC is entirely insolvent, and therefore its members have nothing to lose. Their consent cannot be guaranteed, although it would be needed, for a voluntary arrangement to become effective.

So I accept that a voluntary arrangement is not a convenient, or probably practicable, way out of the present impasse.

So far as the authorities on this point are concerned, I have been referred to a decision of Scott J dated 2 July 1990 in a case called *Re John Slack Ltd* [1995] BCC 1116, in which he held that, where there was (as there was in that case) an administration with two purposes, not only the purpose that is the one for this administration but also the survival of the company and the whole of any part of its undertaking as a going concern, and there was a surplus sufficient to pay off all creditors, it was proper and possible for administrators to pay off creditors in that set of circumstances. He pointed out that there was no possibility of any dissentient. He took into account the main contrary indication on the question of whether there is power to do such a thing as is now proposed, a decision of Harman J in *Re St Ives Windings Ltd* (1987) 3 BCC 634, where Harman J expressed a preliminary view that the payment by administrators to creditors was not what the court could sanction. At p. 634 he said:

> 'In my present and, as I say, provisional view, there is no power in the court to sanction an administrator making distributions where he has been appointed for the purposes such as this administrator was, that is under s. 8(3)(a) and (d) of the Act. However, there is a power to appoint an administrator with a view to the approval of a voluntary arrangement, that is s. 8(3)(b).'

He took that way out which was available in those circumstances and which, for reasons which I have sought briefly to explain, is not available to me in this case.

Scott J dealt with that by saying that the distribution that was proposed to Harman J was a pro rata distribution, it was not a payment of the creditors in full, and Scott J said (at p. 1117C):

> 'Here, on the other hand, a payment of the creditors in full is proposed. There are not going to be any dissentients.'

He proceeded to hold that the administrators did have power to pay out pre-administration order creditors in full.

Finally, I am told by counsel, and I am referred to a textbook in which this is supported, that in a case which is unreported, decided by Ferris J, called *Re Mount Banking plc* on 25 January 1993, it was held by Ferris J that, pending administrators' attempts to achieve the purposes for which they were appointed, in that case para. (a) and (d), the administrators did have power to make a payment on account to depositors with the bank, the company in question. There were precautions taken in that the amount was calculated so as not to exceed the amount that they would have received in the event of a liquidation, and the payment was to be made on terms that the depositors undertook to bring into account on a subsequent liquidation the payments they received from the administrators and hold any dividends received by them in any such liquidation on trust for other creditors so far as necessary to ensure that other creditors were not prejudiced by the payment on account. In that particular case it appears that the payment on account was justified on the basis that it was needed to preserve the goodwill of the company's business pending the attempt to achieve the survival of the company and its business.

In my judgment, the breadth of the power in Sch. 1, para. 13 to the Insolvency Act is wide enough to permit a distribution in the special circumstances of this case, which are that, unless this is done, there will be a significant prejudice to the creditors of PLC, coupled with the fact that creditors of PLC have approved the proposed application, and support it through the creditors' committee, and the fact that there is evidence before me which satisfies me that there is no significant or practical risk of creditors emerging hereafter who are not known. That is the conclusion I draw from the fact that this is an administration that has gone on since the middle of 1992, and there has therefore been a very full opportunity to discover who all the creditors are, and the fact that the company

A　　in question, PLC, is not a trading company and has not been a trading company, but has traded through its several subsidiaries.

All those circumstances, including in particular the possibility of obtaining the £1.5m from the pension fund of PLC as its surplus, persuade me that this is a sufficiently special case for me to order what I entirely accept is a very unusual provision for administrators to make the payments out to preferential creditors on the basis that there is a notional

B　　winding up at the date when the administration order was made, and to the unsecured creditors on a pari passu basis and on the same terms as were mentioned in the decision of Ferris J.

I therefore propose to make the order as asked.

(Order accordingly)

C

D

E

F

G

H

Davis v Martin-Sklan.

A

Chancery Division (in bankruptcy).
Blackburne J.
Judgment delivered 28 July 1995.

*Voluntary arrangement – Subsequent bankruptcy order on supervisor's petition –
Whether voluntary arrangement terminated – Effect of termination of voluntary
arrangement – Insolvency Act 1986, s. 264(1)(c), 276(2).*

B

**The making of a bankruptcy order on the petition of the supervisor of a voluntary
arrangement under s. 264(1)(c) of the Insolvency Act 1986, terminated the voluntary
arrangement with the result that £20,000 in the supervisor's hands (subject to any claim by
the person who had provided it for the purposes of the arrangement (if not the debtor))
became part of the debtor's estate and payable to the debtor's trustee in bankruptcy for
distribution to the debtor's creditors (including the creditors previously bound by the
voluntary arrangement) subject to a first charge in favour of the supervisor under s. 276(2)
of the Act in respect of any expenses properly incurred by him as expenses of the
administration of the voluntary arrangement. (Re McKeen (a Debtor) [1995] BCC 412 and
Re Bradley-Hole (a Bankrupt), ex parte Knight [1995] BCC 418 distinguished.)**

C

The following cases were referred to in the judgment:

Bradley-Hole (a Bankrupt), Re, ex parte Knight [1995] BCC 418; [1995] 1 WLR 1097.
McKeen (a Debtor), Re [1995] BCC 412.

D

Edward Bailey (instructed by Edwin Coe) for the trustee.

The supervisor appeared in person.

JUDGMENT

E

Blackburne J: This is an appeal against a decision of Mr Registrar Scott made on 18
May 1995 on an application for directions by the supervisor under a voluntary
arrangement entered into by a debtor with his creditors under Pt. VIII of the *Insolvency
Act* 1986 ('the Act'). It raises a short question concerning the effect on the voluntary
arrangement of a subsequent bankruptcy order against the debtor made on the petition
of the supervisor under s. 264(1)(c) of the Act.

The relevant facts are simply stated. At a meeting on 12 November 1992 the debtor's
creditors approved, by a large majority and with certain modifications, the debtor's
proposals for a voluntary arrangement. Those proposals, as modified were, so far as
material, as follows:

F

(1) That Alex Martin-Sklan, who is the respondent to the appeal, would be the
supervisor.

(2) That from the profits of his dry cleaning and shoe repairing business the debtor
would make moneys available sufficient to enable quarterly payments of £3,500 to
be made to the supervisor on 31 March, 30 June, 30 September, and 31 December
1993 and quarterly payments of £5,000 to be made on 31 March, 30 June, 30
September, and 31 December in each of the six years 1994–1999.

G

(3) That the four quarterly payments to be made in 1993 would be paid from a sum of
£20,000 already deposited with the nominee (and said to have been provided by a
third party).

H

(4) That, subject to retaining sufficient funds to petition for the debtor's bankruptcy
in the event of a payment under (2) above not being received within three months
of the due date of payment, the payments received under (2) above would be
applied, first, in paying the fees and expenses of the supervisor, secondly in paying

A   the claims of preferential creditors, thirdly in paying the claims of ordinary unsecured creditors, and fourthly in the payment of any surplus to the debtor.

(5)   That the supervisor would annually review the debtor's financial position to see whether he could increase the quarterly payments on the basis that if in any year he should earn in excess of £120,000, 80 per cent of the excess would be made available for creditors.

B   (6)   That the debtor would pay to the supervisor 100 per cent of any windfall receipts received during the period of the arrangement.

(7)   That the first distribution to unsecured creditors would be by 12 December 1993 and that subsequent distributions would be made annually thereafter.

(8)   That creditors' claims would not bear interest from the date of implementation of the arrangement.

C   (9)   That the arrangement would last for so long as necessary to enable liabilities to be agreed, funds to be distributed to creditors and all matters to be dealt with that were to arise under the arrangement.

(10)   That when all assets to be made available under the arrangement had been realised and distributed to creditors in accordance with the terms of the arrangement the debtor would be released from any further liability to his creditors in respect of claims provable in the voluntary arrangement.

D

Mr Martin-Sklan, who was both nominee and supervisor and who chaired the meeting of creditors, reported to the court on 13 November 1992 under s. 259 of the Act.

The creditors bound by the arrangement amounted in value to £232,000. In addition there were a number of partially secured creditors who could participate in respect of their unsecured balances. Those balances were estimated as at 5 October 1992 at £336,000-odd. Under the arrangement the total amount to be made available for distribution to creditors, excluding additional contributions should the debtor earn more than £120,000 in any year or receive a windfall, was £134,000. The understanding and expectation of creditors bound by the arrangement was, therefore, that, assuming no windfall receipts and earnings above £120,000 in any year and provided the debtor paid the instalments stipulated by the arrangement, they would accept substantially less than 100 pence in the pound in satisfaction of their claims against the debtor provable in the arrangement.

The debtor made no payments to the supervisor in March and June 1994. Indeed, apart from the sum of £20,000 deposited with Mr Martin-Sklan as nominee and applied under the arrangements described in (3) above, nothing at all was paid to him.

On 7 July 1994 Mr Martin-Sklan, as supervisor, presented a petition under s. 264(1)(c) for a bankruptcy order against the debtor on the ground that he had failed to comply with his obligations under the voluntary arrangement in that he had failed to make the payments due on 31 March and 30 June 1994 and had failed to provide Mr Martin-Sklan with information and accounts to enable him to review the debtor's financial position. On 1 September 1994 a bankruptcy order was made on that petition and on 4 November 1994 Norman Harold Davis, the appellant before me, was appointed trustee of the debtor's estate.

On 15 March 1995 Mr Martin-Sklan, as supervisor, applied to the court for directions under s. 263(4) of the Act. Notice of the application was given to the trustee, Mr Davis. The question before the court related to the manner in which the £20,000 in Mr Martin-Sklan's hands should be dealt with after deduction of his fees and expenses as supervisor. Although the amount of the fees and expenses was not in evidence, the argument proceeded, both before the registrar and before me, on the basis that a substantial proportion of that sum will remain available after payment of those fees and expenses. I should add, because it explains why the manner in which the £20,000 is to be dealt with is important, that the debtor's creditors at the time of the bankruptcy order include many who were not bound by the voluntary arrangement, presumably because their claims have arisen since 12 November 1992.

The question before the registrar was whether, as the trustee contended, the effect of the bankruptcy order was to terminate the voluntary arrangement with the result that the £20,000 in the supervisor's hands thereupon became a part of the debtor's estate and payable therefore to the trustee for distribution to the debtor's creditors (including the creditors previously bound by the voluntary arrangement) subject only to a first charge in favour of the supervisor under s. 276(2) of the Act in respect of any expenses properly incurred by him as expenses of the administration of the voluntary arrangement. The registrar concluded that the bankruptcy order did not have that effect and that, as he had contended, Mr Martin-Sklan continued to hold the £20,000 upon the terms of the voluntary arrangement – i.e. after payment of his expenses, for the benefit of the creditors bound by the arrangement. He came to that conclusion after a consideration of *Re McKeen (a Debtor)* [1995] BCC 412 and *Re Bradley-Hole (a Bankrupt), ex parte Knight* [1995] BCC 418 to which I return later. He summarised his conclusion as follows:

> 'In the light of those decisions my conclusion as to the status or continued existence of the IVA in this case is that it is not brought to an end . . . I can find nothing in the Act to warrant the conclusion that it is brought to an end by the making of a s. 264(1)(c) order, or to differentiate in this respect between a s. 264(1)(c) petition and an ordinary creditor's petition.'

The trustee now appeals against that conclusion.

Mr Bailey for the trustee submitted that a bankruptcy order made on the petition under s. 264(1)(c) of a supervisor of, or a person (other than the debtor) bound by, a voluntary arrangement brings that arrangement to an end and that this is so whatever the position may be where the bankruptcy order is made on the petition of someone falling under one of the other paragraphs of s. 264(1). This result, he submitted, is the inevitable consequence of s. 276(2).

Section 276 provides as follows:

> '(1) The court shall not make a bankruptcy order on a petition under section 264(1)(c) (supervisor of, or person bound by, voluntary arrangement proposed and approved) unless it is satisfied–
>
>   (a) that the debtor has failed to comply with his obligations under the voluntary arrangement, or
>
>   (b) that information which was false or misleading in any material particular or which contained material omissions–
>
>   (i) was contained in any statement of affairs or other documents supplied by the debtor under Part VIII to any person, or
>
>   (ii) was otherwise made available by the debtor to his creditors at or in connection with a meeting summoned under that Part, or
>
>   (c) that the debtor has failed to do all such things as may for the purposes of voluntary arrangement have been reasonably required of him by the supervisor of the arrangement.
>
> (2) Where a bankruptcy order is made on a petition under section 264(1)(c), any expenses properly incurred as expenses of the administration of the voluntary arrangement in question shall be a first charge on the bankrupt's estate.'

© **1995 CCH Editions Limited**
bcp95 bcp   177 Mp   1124   —bcp177   85

A   In my judgment Mr Bailey is correct in this submission. The scheme of the Act is to provide an insolvent person, who can persuade a sufficient majority in value of his creditors to accept his proposal for a voluntary arrangement, with a mode of insolvent administration of his estate alternative to that provided by bankruptcy. The effect of a voluntary arrangement, once approved by the required majority at a meeting of creditors summoned under s. 257, is to prevent any creditor bound by the arrangement from pursuing the debtor personally (whether by bankruptcy petition or otherwise) in respect

B   of debts provable in the arrangement except in accordance with the terms of the arrangement. This, in my view, is the effect of s. 260(2) which provides as follows:

'(2) The approved arrangement–

(a) takes effect as if made by the debtor at the meeting, and

(b) binds every person who in accordance with the rules had notice of, and was
C   entitled to vote at, a meeting (whether or not he was present or represented at it) as if he were a party to the arrangement.'

In other words approval of the arrangement gives rise to a species of statutory contract binding on the debtor and the creditors referred to in para. (b) of that subsection.

Section 276(1) nevertheless empowers the court, in certain defined circumstances, to make a bankruptcy order on the petition of the supervisor of, or any person (other than the debtor) bound by, the arrangement. Broadly stated those circumstances are: false or
D   misleading information supplied by the debtor at or in connection with the meeting of creditors which resolved to approve the arrangement; and failure by the debtor to adhere to his obligations under the arrangement or to do what is reasonably required of him by the supervisor for the purposes of the arrangement. In short they are acts or omissions on the part of the debtor which might be thought to vitiate the creditors' approval of the arrangement at the meeting summoned under s. 257 or which hinder or prevent

E   implementation of the arrangement. By making a bankruptcy order on a petition under s. 264(1)(c) by or (through the supervisor) on behalf of the persons bound by the voluntary arrangement, the court recognises that it is no longer appropriate for the arrangement to remain in being. It therefore releases the creditors hitherto bound by the statutory contract (constituted by the approved voluntary arrangement) from further observance of its terms by substituting bankruptcy in place of the voluntary arrangement as the regime for the administration of the debtor's estate.

F   This view is supported by s. 276(2). The expenses of the administration of the voluntary arrangement are by that provision to be a first charge on the bankrupt's estate. Those expenses would otherwise be provided for in accordance with the terms of the voluntary arrangement. The consequence to a voluntary arrangement of a bankruptcy order made on a petition under s. 264(1)(c) cannot simply be to charge those expenses on the bankrupt's estate and, if there are any, to exonerate the assets subject to the voluntary
G   arrangement from the burden of those expenses thereby increasing the assets available for distribution to the creditors bound by the arrangement. In my view the subsection assumes that, upon the making of a bankruptcy order under s. 264(1)(c), the terms of the voluntary arrangement thereupon cease to apply and the assets, if any, held by the supervisor for distribution in accordance with the voluntary arrangement become part of the bankrupt's estate, to be administered and distributed in accordance with the provisions of Pt. IX of the Act. Provision was needed to enable the expenses of the

H   voluntary arrangement to be discharged: it is the object of the subsection to make that provision. Creditors hitherto bound by the arrangement are released from the arrangement and are left to prove in the debtor's bankruptcy for the balance of their claims.

As is evident from the passage in his judgment which I have quoted, the registrar, in coming to his conclusion, was influenced by the decisions in the two reported cases to which I have referred. It is right therefore that I should examine them to see whether they support the registrar's conclusion. Although in each of them the court held that a voluntary arrangement was not terminated on the making of a subsequent bankruptcy order, in each the circumstances were very different from the present.

In *Re McKeen (a Debtor)* [1995] BCC 412, the voluntary arrangement approved by the creditors provided for the assignment by the debtor to the supervisor of certain assets to be dealt with in accordance with the terms of the arrangement. The debtor later became indebted for rent to his landlord who, after non-payment, obtained a bankruptcy order. The debt and costs having been paid, the debtor applied to the court for annulment of the bankruptcy order under s. 282(1)(b) of the Act. The district judge had refused to annul the bankruptcy order on the ground that the debts owed to the creditors under the voluntary arrangement were bankruptcy debts as defined by s. 382 of the Act and that, as they had not been paid in full or secured to the satisfaction of the court, the requirements of s. 282(1)(b) had not been satisfied with the result that the application failed. In allowing the debtor's appeal and annulling the bankruptcy order Morritt J, after drawing attention to the provisions of s. 264(1)(c) and 276 of the Act, and after stating that there were no circumstances which could bring any of those provisions into operation, held that there was nothing in the terms of the arrangement before him which provided, either expressly or by necessary implication, for its determination in the event of the subsequent bankruptcy of the debtor and that, on the making of the bankruptcy order, the trustee took the property comprised in the voluntary arrangement subject to the right of the creditors under the arrangement to have it applied for their benefit in accordance with the terms of the arrangement. In other words the property comprised in the voluntary arrangement did not form part of the debtor's estate for the purposes of his bankruptcy but continued to be available for the creditors bound by the voluntary arrangement to be applied in their favour in accordance with the arrangement. He went on to observe that the rights conferred on creditors bound by the voluntary arrangement were in satisfaction of their pre-existing debts and that they had no right to receive anything from the debtor personally. He therefore concluded that, as the voluntary arrangement continued notwithstanding the bankruptcy order, the debtor was not subject to any debt or liability on the date of the bankruptcy order in respect of the creditors' claims under the arrangement. This had the result that (there being no other creditors) the requirements of s. 282(1)(b) were satisfied, and he was free to annul the bankruptcy order.

Re Bradley-Hole (a Bankrupt), ex parte Knight [1995] BCC 418 was concerned with a number of issues. So far as material, under the voluntary arrangement in that case the bankrupt (she was a bankrupt under an earlier bankruptcy order at the time of the approval of the voluntary arrangement) made available for the benefit of her creditors under the voluntary arrangement the whole of her assets to which she was entitled at the date of that earlier bankruptcy order and to which she might become entitled up to the date of the approval by her creditors of her proposals for a voluntary arrangement. There was a provision for the net post-tax trading profits of a public house held under a lease to be paid to the supervisor but that provision lapsed when the lease of the public house was not renewed. The claims of creditors bound by the voluntary arrangement were to be discharged from the assets made thus available and, I infer, from no others. Two and a half years later a bankruptcy order was made on the petition of a creditor whose debt had been incurred after the approval of the voluntary arrangement. One of the questions which arose for decision was whether the making of the bankruptcy order brought the voluntary arrangement to an end. Whether it did rested upon the provisions of the Act, there being no suggestion that there was any express or implied provision of the arrangement that it should come to an end on the making of a subsequent bankruptcy order. Holding that the subsequent bankruptcy order did not bring the arrangement to

A   an end. Rimer J stated that he did not find in any of the provisions in the Act to which his attention had been drawn any sufficient warrant for the inference that a bankruptcy order, at any rate one made on a petition presented by someone other than a s. 264(1)(c) petitioner, was intended to have the effect of automatically terminating a prior voluntary arrangement. He specifically left open whether a bankruptcy order made on a petition brought under s. 264(1)(c) automatically terminated a prior voluntary arrangement.

B   I find nothing in either of those decisions which leads me to a different view of the position in the present case. The petitions upon which the bankruptcy orders were made were not brought under the provisions of s. 264(1)(c) and 276; there was nothing to indicate that there had been any breach of the terms of the voluntary arrangements; the terms of the voluntary arrangements did not provide, either expressly or by necessary implication, for the voluntary arrangement to come to an end in the event to the making of the subsequent bankruptcy order; and there was nothing in the legislation to justify

C   the conclusion that, by reason of the making of a subsequent bankruptcy order, the voluntary arrangement had been terminated. It is true that in the *McKeen* case Morritt J observed, at p. 417, that the effect of a bankruptcy order 'under s. 276' (meaning, I think, an order made on a petition brought under s. 264(1)(c)) would be 'to enable the court in the bankruptcy to remedy the default which justified the order in the first place. It would not necessarily require termination of the voluntary arrangement.' I am not at all sure quite what Morritt J had in mind when making those observations but, in any event, his

D   remarks were plainly obiter as, of course, he was not concerned with an order made on such a petition.

I therefore hold to my view that Mr Bailey's submission is correct and that upon the making of the bankruptcy order on 1 September 1994 on the petition of Mr Martin-Sklan, as supervisor, the voluntary arrangement was terminated and the moneys which were in his hands in accordance with the terms of the voluntary arrangement became a

E   part of the debtor's estate available for administration and distribution in his bankruptcy subject only to a first charge in respect of any expenses properly incurred as expenses of the voluntary arrangement.

Mr Bailey also pointed out that a term of the voluntary arrangement was that the supervisor was to retain sufficient funds to petition for the debtor's bankruptcy in the event of one of the £5,000 instalments not being received within three months of its due

F   date for payment, and that a likely, if not inevitable, consequence of a bankruptcy order would be that, either as a result of the vesting of the debtor's property in the trustee or of the making of an income payments order under s. 310 of the Act, the debtor would be unable to make any further payment to the supervisor under the terms of the arrangement. This showed, he submitted, that the voluntary arrangement provided by necessary implication for its termination in the event of a subsequent bankruptcy of the debtor for non-payment of an instalment. I see the force of these points but doubt

G   whether they add much to Mr Bailey's principal submission. A related question which arose in argument was whether the voluntary arrangement would automatically have terminated if a bankruptcy order had been made on the petition of a creditor not bound by the voluntary arrangement. The question does not arise but I incline to the view that if, at the time of the order, there had been no breach of the terms of the voluntary arrangement there is no reason why the making of the order would have had that effect

H   as I do not consider that the terms of the arrangement would by necessary implication have provided for its termination in that event and, consistently with the decisions in the *McKeen* and *Bradley-Hole* cases, I see nothing in the Act to bring about that result. What the position would have been if, at the time of the making of such a bankruptcy order (i.e. one made on the petition of a creditor not bound by the arrangement) there had existed a breach of the terms of the arrangement which would have entitled the supervisor, or a creditor bound by it, to bring a petition under s. 264(1)(c) is rather more

problematical. That question likewise does not arise but I am inclined to think that, in   A
that event, it was implicit in the terms of the arrangement that the arrangement would
have come to an end.

In the course of argument, a question arose concerning the right, if any, of the provider
of the £20,000 to its return if, as I have held, the making of the bankruptcy order brought
the voluntary arrangement to an end. The identity of the provider of that sum is
unknown, although the trustee has issued an application, which is shortly to be heard,   B
designed to require the bank from which the sum emanated to identify its source. In this
connection I should say that the trustee suspects that the provider may have been none
other than the debtor himself. I raised in argument as a possibility that the provider,
assuming he is not the debtor, may wish to claim the return of that sum now that the
voluntary arrangement has ended. As to that I would merely observe that there is nothing
in the evidence to indicate that the sum was received by Mr Martin-Sklan impressed with
any trust other than that the sum should be applied in the voluntary arrangement as it   C
has been. In particular there is nothing to indicate that there was a term binding on Mr
Martin-Sklan that the moneys should become repayable to the provider in the event that
the voluntary arrangement should at any subsequent date be terminated.

In *Re Bradley-Hole* Rimer J stated that the assets held by the supervisor on the terms
of the arrangement in that case were held by him on trust for the creditors who were
parties to the arrangement. Relying, I think, on the reasoning which had led to that   D
conclusion Mr Martin-Sklan, who appeared in person before me, submitted that the
£20,000 in his hands at the time of the bankruptcy order were held by him upon trust,
subject to the payment of his own proper fees and expenses, for the creditors who were
bound by the arrangement even if the consequence of the bankruptcy order for which he
had successfully petitioned was to terminate the arrangement of which he was supervisor.
He submitted, and Mr Bailey did not disagree, that if he had distributed the £20,000, less
his expenses, to creditors under the arrangement prior to the making of the bankruptcy   E
order there could be no question of the trustee subsequently seeking to recover the
amount so distributed. He then submitted that up to the moment of distribution he held
those moneys on trust for those creditors. Why then, he asked, should the creditors' right
under that trust to receive those moneys have ceased merely because the voluntary
arrangement came to an end upon the making of a bankruptcy order? The answer to that
is that the trusts upon which, under the voluntary arrangement, Mr Martin-Sklan as   F
supervisor held the £20,000 ceased on the making of the bankruptcy order on his petition
under s. 264(1)(c). Thereafter, subject to any claim to that sum which the third party
provider of it might be able to establish, he held the sum on different trusts, namely trusts
to give effect to the scheme of administration of the debtor's estate established under
Pt. IX of the Act subject only to the charge for expenses properly incurred conferred by
s. 276(2).

It follows that this appeal succeeds, that the registrar's order must be set aside and that   G
instead I shall direct that, hands at the time of the bankruptcy order became a part of the
debtor's estate for the purposes of his bankruptcy subject only to a first charge in respect
of any expenses properly incurred as expenses of the administration of his voluntary
arrangement.

(*Order accordingly*)

H

A
Practice Direction No. 1 of 1995.
Insolvency Appeals (Individuals)
Chancery Division (Bankruptcy).
28 July 1995.

B
1. As from 1 October 1995 the attached *Practice Direction: Insolvency Appeals (Individuals)* shall come into effect and shall apply to insolvency appeals relating to individuals.

2. As from the above date *Practice Direction (Insolvency and Revenue Appeals in North)* [1991] 1 WLR 103; [1991] 1 All ER 608 shall be revoked in so far as it relates to insolvency only.

C
3. As from the above date *Practice Direction No. 3 of 1992 (Insolvency Appeals: Hearings outside London)* [1992] BCC 998; [1992] 1 WLR 791 shall be revoked in its entirety.

Scott V-C

INSOLVENCY APPEALS (INDIVIDUALS)

D
(1) An appeal from a decision made in a county court by a circuit or district judge or in the High Court by a registrar in bankruptcy lies to a single judge of the High Court: s. 375(2) of the *Insolvency Act* 1986 and r. 7.48(2) of the *Insolvency Rules* 1986.

(2) Such appeals are set down and heard as follows:

(i) An appeal from a decision of a registrar in bankruptcy shall or from any decision made in any county court may be set down and heard in London by a High Court judge of the Chancery Division or by a deputy designated to sit as a judge of the
E Chancery Division under s. 9 of the *Supreme Court Act* 1981.

(ii) An appeal from a decision made in a county court exercising jurisdiction over an area within the Northern and North Eastern Circuits may be set down in Manchester for hearing in Leeds, Liverpool, Manchester or Newcastle upon Tyne by the Vice Chancellor of the County Palatine or by a circuit judge designated under s. 9 of the *Supreme Court Act* 1981 to sit as a judge of the Chancery Division
F at the above venues and at Preston.

(iii) An appeal from a decision made in a county court exercising jurisdiction over an area within the Birmingham, Bristol or Cardiff Chancery District Registries may be set down in the registry appropriate to the area in which the decision was made for hearing in Birmingham, Bristol or Cardiff by the Chancery Supervising Judge or by a circuit judge designated under s. 9 of the *Supreme Court Act* 1981 to sit as
G a judge of the Chancery Division in Birmingham, Bristol or Cardiff.

(3) The procedure and practice of the Supreme Court relating to appeals to the Court of Appeal applies to appeals in insolvency proceedings: r. 7.49(1). Thus RSC, O. 59 applies to insolvency appeals.

(4) In relation to any appeal under s. 375(2) to a single judge of the Chancery Division any reference to the Court of Appeal in the Rules of the Supreme Court is replaced by
H reference to that judge and any reference to the Registrar of Civil Appeals is replaced by a reference to a bankruptcy registrar who deals with insolvency proceedings referred to below as the Registrar of Bankruptcy Appeals: r. 7.49(2).

(5) The single judge sits in open court to hear the appeal and hears applications:

● for injunctions pending the substantive hearing of the appeal;

● by way of appeal from the Registrar of Bankruptcy Appeals;

- for expedition or vacation of the hearing date of an appeal.

A

(6) The Registrar of Bankruptcy Appeals sits in Chambers in London and hears applications for:

- an extension of time for serving a notice of appeal;
- an extension of time for setting down a notice of appeal;
- an extension of time for serving a respondent's notice;

B

- leave to amend a notice of appeal or a respondent's notice;
- security for costs of an appeal;
- leave to adduce further evidence on an appeal.

(7)(i) A form of notice of appeal appropriate to insolvency appeals to a single judge is set out in *Atkins Court Forms*, vol. 7, or may be adapted from the form set out in RSC, O. 59 or may be obtained in London from the fees room, Thomas More Building, The Royal Courts of Justice or from the addresses set out in para. 8(iv) below.

C

(ii) Applications to the Registrar of Bankruptcy Appeals may be made on Bankruptcy Application Form 7.2 which may be obtained from the fees room, Thomas More Building, The Royal Courts of Justice or from the addresses set out in para. 8(iv) below and should be lodged at the address set out in para. 8(iv)(a) below.

(8) The following practice applies to all appeals to the single judge of the High Court whether set down in London, or set down at one of the other venues referred to in para. (2) above.

D

(i)   A notice of appeal must be served not later than 28 days, such time to run:

     (a)   in the case of an appeal from an order made in a county court from the date the order is made (RSC, O. 59, r. 4 and r. 19(3));

E

     (b)   in the case of an appeal from an order made by a registrar in bankruptcy from the date on which the order is sealed (RSC, O. 59, r. 4(1)).

(ii)   Notice of appeal must be served on all parties to the proceedings below who are directly affected by the appeal. This will include the district judge of the appropriate county court (see RSC, O. 59, r. 19(2)) and where a bankruptcy order has been made, the official receiver.

F

     Service of the notice of appeal may be effected by the following methods:

     (a)   by leaving the document at the proper address of the person to be served;

     (b)   by post;

     (c)   through a document exchange;

     (d)   if both appellant and respondent are represented by solicitors by fax together with a hard copy posted to the party concerned on the same day as the fax is sent;

G

     (e)   by substituted service with the leave of the court.

(RSC, note 59/3/13).

(iii)   After service the appellant must set down the notice of appeal within the time limits set out in RSC, O. 59, r. 5 by lodging the documents listed below:

H

     (a)   two copies of the notice of appeal, one of which must be endorsed with a certificate of the date and method of service and stamped with the appropriate fee;

     (b)   a copy of the order under appeal;

     (c)   the estimate of time for the hearing.

A   (iv)   The above documents may be lodged personally or by post at the address of the appropriate venue listed below:

          (a)   If the appeal is to be set down and heard in London the documents must be lodged at Room 206, Thomas More Building, The Royal Courts of Justice, Strand, London WC2A 2LL.

B   (b)   If the appeal is to be set down in Manchester the documents must be lodged at the Chancery Section, Courts of Justice, Crown Square, Manchester M3 3FL.

          (c)   (i)   If the appeal is to be set down in Birmingham, the documents must be lodged at the District Registry of the Chancery Division of the High Court, 33 Bull Street, Birmingham B4 6DS.

C   (ii)   If the appeal is to be set down in Bristol the documents must be lodged at the District Registry of the Chancery Division of the High Court, 3rd Floor, Greyfriars, Lewins Mead, Bristol BS1 2NR;

               (iii)   If the appeal is to be set down in Cardiff the documents must be lodged at the District Registry of the Chancery Division of the High Court, 1st Floor, 2 Park Street, Cardiff CF1 INR.

D   (v)   If the documents are correct and in order the court at which the documents are lodged will fix a hearing date and under subpara. 8(iv)(b) and (c) above will also fix the place of hearing. That court will send letters to all the parties to the appeal informing them of the date and place of hearing and indicating the time estimate given by the appellant. The parties will be invited to notify the court of any alternative or revised time estimate. In the absence of any such notification the estimate of the appellant will be taken as agreed. The court will also send to the appellant a document setting out the court's requirements concerning the form and content of the bundle of documents for the use of the judge. Such bundle of documents must be lodged by the appellant at the address of the appropriate venue as set out in para. 8(iv) above not later than seven days before the date fixed for the hearing. Failure to do so may result in the appeal being dismissed by the judge.

E

    (vi)   Skeleton arguments, accompanied by a written chronology of events relevant to the appeal, should be lodged at the address of the appropriate venue as set out in para. 8(iv) above, at least two clear days before the date fixed for the hearing. Failure to lodge may result in an adverse order by the judge on the hearing of the appeal.

F

    (vii)   A notice of appeal and a respondent's notice may be amended:

          (a)   with the leave of the Registrar of Bankruptcy Appeals or the single judge at any time;

G   (b)   without leave by supplementary notice served:

               (i)   in the case of a notice of appeal, not later than five days after setting down the notice of appeal;

               (ii)   in the case of a respondent's notice, not later than five days after setting down the respondent's notice.

H   After service two copies of the amended notice must be lodged at the address of the appropriate venue as set out in para. 8(iv) above, one copy endorsed with the date on which service was effected and stamped with the appropriate fee.

    (viii)   Where an appellant does not wish to continue with the appeal or where the appeal has been settled, the appeal may be dismissed by consent on paper without a hearing. An order to that effect signed by each party or letters of consent from each party must be lodged not later than 24 hours before the date fixed for the hearing of the appeal at the address of the appropriate venue as set out in para. 8(iv) above.

(9) An appeal from a decision made by the single judge lies with the leave of that judge or of the Court of Appeal to the Court of Appeal (see IR 1986, r. 7.48(2)). Applications for such leave to appeal should be made to the single judge at the conclusion of his judgment on the appeal. If a party fails to apply that party may apply ex parte by notice of application. Such notice together with draft intended grounds of appeal must be lodged at the address of the appropriate venue as set out in para. 8(iv) above within 28 days of the sealing of the order made on the appeal. The application will first be considered ex parte by the judge who heard the appeal who may refuse leave or give such directions as he or she thinks fit for the disposal of the application. Applications made after the 28-day period has expired must be made direct to the Court of Appeal.

A
Re Cancol Ltd.

Chancery Division (Companies Court).
Knox J.
Judgment delivered 4 October 1995.

B
Company voluntary arrangement – Landlord's proxy in respect of arrears of rent counted against proposed arrangement – Landlord did not attend creditors' meeting claiming that liability to future rent was outside arrangement – Whether future rent capable of inclusion in company voluntary arrangement – Whether landlord not entitled to vote because minimum value of claim for future rent not agreed – Whether there was unfair prejudice or material irregularity – Insolvency Act 1986, s. 6; Insolvency Rules 1986 (SI 1986/1925), r. 1.17.

C
This was an application by a landlord for a declaration that future rent under a lease was payable by the tenant to the landlord in full and was not affected by a voluntary arrangement approved in relation to the tenant company. Alternatively, there was a claim for the approval of the voluntary arrangement to be revoked or suspended.

The landlord's proxy was counted against the proposed arrangement in respect of arrears of rent but the landlord did not attend the creditors' meeting, arguing that future rent was incapable of inclusion as a matter of law in a company voluntary arrangement. Alternatively,
D
the landlord argued (on the basis that the landlord was a creditor for the purposes of r. 1.17 and therefore potentially entitled to vote), first, that the requirements of r. 1.17(3) were not satisfied because no minimum value for the claim to future rent had been agreed between the landlord and the chairman of the creditors' meeting; secondly, that there was unfair prejudice within the meaning of s. 6 of the Insolvency Act 1986 in that some future creditors were to be paid in full under the arrangement; thirdly, that there was a material irregularity in that another landlord of premises leased by the company voted for a large amount of
E
future rent.

Held, dismissing the landlord's application:

1. The word 'creditor' in r. 1.17(1) included those entitled to a right to a future payment under an existing valid instrument such as a lease. The argument to the contrary was based on the proposition that the word 'creditor' had a natural or ordinary meaning which was narrow and only included those with presently enforceable claims. Although that was a
F
possible meaning, it was not one which prevailed over other possible meanings notwithstanding the many indications to the contrary from the context and the purpose of the legislation.

2. There was no relevant difference between the legislation relating to individual and company voluntary arrangements and it had been held that future rent was capable of inclusion in an individual voluntary arrangement. (Doorbar v Alltime Securities Ltd [1994]
G
BCC 994 considered.)

3. It was undisputed that both in bankruptcy and winding up, claims to future rent were susceptible of being included as relevant claims. Moreover, the power of a company with the approval of the court to enter into schemes of arrangement under s. 425 of the Companies Act 1985 extended to schemes of arrangement which affected the rights of creditors with debts payable in the future as well as those payable at present. It would be anomalous if company voluntary arrangements, which were intended to be an alternative to liquidation,
H
and s. 425 compromises or arrangements did not have the same potential ambit. (Re Midland Coal, Coke and Iron Co [1895] 1 Ch 267 considered.)

4. Rule 1.17(3) did not require the creditor in question to agree to a minimum value being placed on the claim. If the creditor stayed away he could not say that the chairman had not agreed. Equally, the rule did not say that the chairman had to put a value and tell the creditor before the meeting. (Doorbar v Alltime Securities Ltd [1994] BCC 994 considered.)

5. It was not unfair within the meaning of s. 6 to make a differentiation between members
of the class of creditors with future claims on the basis that some creditors would be paid in
full so long as the asset in question was used to earn the profits envisaged by the voluntary
arrangement while those whose assets were no longer so used were left to a dividend in
respect of their claim under the arrangement. As far as the landlord was concerned, if and
so long as the premises were occupied by the company the rent would be paid in full; once
vacated the landlord would rank for a dividend in the proposals. The landlord had a right of
forfeiture once the rent ceased to be paid in full. The proposals did not deprive him of that,
so he was not without a remedy.

6. The applicant landlord was not accorded the same treatment so far as voting on its
future right to rent was concerned as the other landlord. However it was not an irregularity
not to give the landlord any particular voting rights if and so long as it claimed that future
rent could not be included in the arrangement. It was not necessary to investigate how the
other landlord's claim was valued because if its vote was left out altogether the result on the
figures would have been the same.

The following cases were referred to in the judgment:

Cranley Mansions Ltd, Re [1994] BCC 576; [1994] 1 WLR 1610.
Doorbar v Alltime Securities Ltd [1994] BCC 994.
Midland Coal, Coke and Iron Co, Re [1895] 1 Ch 267.

Stephen Schaw-Miller (instructed by Abbott King & Troen) for the landlord.

Jonathan Nash (instructed by Lovell White Durrant) for the respondents.

JUDGMENT

Knox J: The applicant before the court is a company, which I will call 'the landlords'.
It is the freehold owner of premises ('the premises') at Victoria Wharf, Dragoon Road,
London SE8. The first respondent ('the company') is the original tenant under a lease
which was granted by a predecessor of the landlords. The lease itself is not fully in
evidence but the material particulars regarding it are as follows. It was dated 6 February
1989. It demised, of course, the premises. The commencement of the term was 4 August
1988. The term was one of 20 years. The rent was initially £46,000 per annum
commencing to be paid on the date of the commencement of the term and there were
three rent review dates at five-year intervals on 4 August in the years 1993, 1998 and
2003. The passing rent at the material time was £59,750 p.a. and it is a fairly clear
deduction that that was the result of the rent review on the first of the three rent review
dates. I infer, and no one has suggested the contrary, that the lease contained a forfeiture
clause for non-payment of rent among other things.

The second and third respondents are the joint supervisors of a voluntary arrangement
concerning the company which was approved by a meeting of creditors on 23 June 1995,
and it is with regard to that voluntary arrangement that this application is made. The
application asks for an order declaring that all money falling due on or after the next
day, which is the midsummer quarter day, under the lease is payable to the landlords in
full and not affected by the voluntary arrangement that was approved on 23 June.
Alternatively, there is a claim, if the declaration thus sought is not made, that the
approval of the voluntary arrangement given by that meeting of creditors be revoked or
suspended on such terms as the court should decide were just; and there is the usual claim
for further or other relief and costs.

The declaration sought is based on a pure point of law, namely that a company
voluntary arrangement, as opposed to an individual voluntary arrangement under the
Insolvency Act 1986, cannot as a matter of law, it is said, bind persons entitled to future
or contingently payable debts such as future payments of rent to fall due under an

A   existing lease, but can only bind persons entitled to the benefit of present as opposed to future or contingent liabilities.

The landlords were entitled to accrued rent arrears at the date of the approval of the voluntary arrangement in the sum of £10,430.44. No problems arise with regard to that. That was clearly a debt in respect of which the landlords were entitled to vote, and indeed did vote.

B   Voluntary arrangements under the Insolvency Act only bind persons who have notice of a meeting of creditors and are entitled to vote at it. That in relation to company voluntary arrangements comes from s. 5 of the *Insolvency Act* 1986. Subsection (2) reads:

'The approved voluntary arrangement–

. . .

C   (b) binds every person who in accordance with the rules had notice of, and was entitled to vote at, that meeting (whether or not he was present or represented at the meeting) as if he were a party to the voluntary arrangement.'

One can, perhaps, discern there an intention that one should not be able to avoid the effect of a voluntary arrangement by the rather simple expedient of staying away.

D   No issue on this application arises as to notice of the proposal that led to the voluntary arrangement. The issues arise with regard to entitlement to vote under the rules, as the subsection which I have just read mentions. The relevant rules are to be found in the *Insolvency Rules* 1986, notably r. 1.17(1), which reads:

'(1) Subject as follows, every creditor who was given notice of the creditors' meeting is entitled to vote at the meeting or any adjournment of it.'

E   It will be convenient to read subr. (3) as well:

'(3) A creditor shall not vote in respect of a debt for an unliquidated amount, or any debt whose value is not ascertained, except where the chairman agrees to put upon the debt an estimated minimum value for the purpose of entitlement to vote.'

F   Exactly the same provisions are in the Insolvency Rules, r. 5.17(1) and (3) as regards entitlement to vote on a voluntary arrangement regarding an individual as opposed to a company. 'Creditor' is not given a specific statutory definition in relation to company voluntary arrangements. It is, at least by implication, given an extended definition in company winding up by a definition of debt or liability, which is to be found in the Insolvency Rules, r. 13.12, subr. (3) of which reads:

G   '(3) For the purposes of references in any provision of the [Insolvency] Act or the [Insolvency] Rules about winding up to a debt or liability, it is immaterial whether the debt or liability is present or future, whether it is certain or contingent, or whether its amount is fixed or liquidated, or is capable of being ascertained by fixed rules or as a matter of opinion; and references in any such provision to owing a debt are to be read accordingly.'

H   Winding up is fairly clearly and uncontroversially dealt with in s. 73 of the Insolvency Act. It is not a term which admits of very much doubt. Section 73 states the well-known alternative modes of winding up – either voluntary, dealt with in Ch. II, III, IV and V of Pt. IV of the *Insolvency Act* 1986, or by the court, which is dealt with by Ch. VI.

Equally, there is an extended definition, at any rate of 'debt' and 'liability' to be found in individual bankruptcy and individual voluntary arrangements. That comes from s. 380–385 of the *Insolvency Act* 1986. Section 380 says:

'The next five sections have effect for the interpretation of the provisions of this
Act which are comprised in this Group of Parts; and where a definition is provided
for a particular expression, it applies except so far as the context otherwise
requires.'

–and the second Group of Parts which is 'this Group' deals with personal insolvency.

In those following five sections one finds in s. 383 a definition in subs. (1) of the word
'creditor' in the context of bankruptcy. What the subsection provides is:

' "Creditor"–

   (a) in relation to a bankrupt, means a person to whom any of the bankruptcy
debts is owed . . .

   (b) in relation to an individual to whom a bankruptcy petition relates, means a
person who would be a creditor in the bankruptcy if a bankruptcy order
were made on that petition.'

That is all in the context of either an actual bankruptcy or a prospective one when there
is on the file a bankruptcy petition. That ties in with the definition in s. 382 of 'bankruptcy
debt', which I need not read.

Section 385 deals with miscellaneous definitions, and notably amongst those in
subs. (1) one has:

' "debt" is to be construed in accordance with section 382(3) . . .'

One turns back to that and one finds in that subsection:

'For the purposes of references in this Group of Parts to a debt or liability, it is
immaterial whether the debt or liability is present or future, whether it is certain or
contingent or whether its amount is fixed or liquidated, or is capable of being
ascertained by fixed rules or as a matter of opinion; and references in this Group
of Parts to owing a debt are to be read accordingly.'

That, of course, has very strong echoes of what I read from the company insolvency
legislation and the rules in r. 13.12, which is only applicable in winding up.

It was argued by Mr Miller for the landlords that in relation to company voluntary
arrangements the word 'creditor' has to be given what he called its 'ordinary meaning';
that is, he said, a person entitled to the benefit of a liability presently due, whether or not
quantified by judgment, where there is a liability to pay damages. That does not, of
course, cover rent due in the future under an existing lease because, Mr Miller submitted,
that is a liability which is both future and contingent. I would for my part prefer to call it
'defeasible' by the determination of the lease rather than 'contingent', but nothing much
turns on that distinction and I need not pursue it. The liability in question is an existing
one but payment is only due in the future.

I do not accept that a liability to future rent is incapable of inclusion as a matter of law
in a company voluntary arrangement. My reasons for that conclusion are both general
and specific. As to the general ones, I rejected such an argument in the context of an
individual arrangement in the decision *Doorbar v Alltime Securities Ltd* [1994] BCC 994.
In that case, at p. 1003F, I said:

'Miss Tipples' second submission'– Miss Tipples in that case was appearing for the
landlord – 'was that future rent under a lease was, as a matter of law, incapable of
being included in a voluntary arrangement. This submission was made on the basis
of what His Honour Judge Cooke said in *Burford Midland Properties Ltd v Marley
Extrusions Ltd & Ors* [1994] BCC 604. The issue there was whether the terms of a
voluntary arrangement which had elaborate provisions defining such expressions
as "unascertained liabilities", "ascertained liabilities" and "liabilities" was apt to
include future payments of rent under a lease. Judge Cooke was not concerned

A   with the question of whether it was legally permissible or possible to include such payments within a voluntary arrangement, but rather whether it had in fact been done, although it is to be observed that, had it been a legal impossibility, the questions of construction debated at some considerable length in his judgment could have been omitted. For it to be established that it is not possible to include future payments of rent under a lease, it would in my view have to be shown that the expression in s. 253(1) "a scheme of arrangement of his affairs" was not wide

B   enough to comprehend the liability to make such future payments. That is not a subject addressed by Judge Cooke in the *Burford Midland Properties* case, and I derive no assistance from it on what I have to decide. No other authority was cited in favour of the proposition that it is legally impossible to include liabilities to make future payments of rent under an existing lease in a voluntary arrangement and I do not feel able to accept such a proposition.'

C   Mr Miller distinguished that decision on the ground that it was an individual voluntary arrangement and not a company voluntary arrangement and that for the former the definitions referred to above in the passages I have read from s. 380–385 showed that liabilities, and by the same token the expression 'creditor', were made wide enough where there was an individual voluntary arrangement to include future payments of rent. But because of the absence of such expanded definitions otherwise than in relation to winding up in the company insolvency legislation he submitted that the word 'creditor' had in

D   that context its narrower and, as he called it, natural meaning.

In terms I based my decision in the *Doorbar* case on the width of the words which defined a voluntary arrangement, and here there is no relevant difference between the individual and the company voluntary arrangement legislation. Section 1(1) of the *Insolvency Act* 1986 reads:

E   'The directors of a company ... may make a proposal under this Part to the company and to its creditors for a composition in satisfaction of its debts or a scheme of arrangement of its affairs (from here on referred to, in either case, as a "voluntary arrangement").'

That is exactly paralleled by the expression in s. 253(1):

F   'Application to the court for an interim order may be made where the debtor intends to make a proposal to his creditors for a composition in satisfaction of his debts or a scheme of arrangement of his affairs (from here on referred to, in either case, as a "voluntary arrangement").'

It would indeed be strange if, with that identity in description, different arrangements were intended to be referred to.

Mr Miller sought to meet this consideration by submitting that it was the individual voluntary arrangement that was anomalous in extending so wide, as he accepted it did

G   because he did not challenge the correctness of my decision in *Doorbar* on this particular point. Even if that was correct, it would not in my view be an answer because it is the existence of the anomaly at all that needs explaining and not an identification of which of the two disparate definitions is the anomalous one. If the word 'creditor' in the Insolvency Rules, r. 1.17(1) is wide enough to include the person entitled to receive future rent under an existing lease, there is no anomaly at all because both individual and company voluntary arrangements are capable of including it.

H   Mr Miller also relied on the fact that in bankruptcy and liquidation there is a power of disclaimer of onerous continuing liabilities but that there is no such facility in voluntary arrangements. That is, of course, true so far as it goes but I am unable to see that it can provide a justification for an important difference between the possible ambit of an individual voluntary arrangement on the one hand and a company voluntary arrangement on the other.

Secondly, on the general aspect, I accept Mr Nash's submission that the purpose of   A
voluntary arrangements, both individual and company, is to provide a cheaper and
commercially more beneficial alternative to bankruptcy or winding up. It is undisputed
that both in bankruptcy and winding-up claims, claims to future rent are susceptible of
being included as relevant claims. Moreover, the power of a company with the approval
of a court to enter into schemes of arrangement under s. 425 of the *Companies Act* 1985
in my judgment extends to schemes of arrangements which affect the rights of creditors
with debts payable in the future as well as those payable at present. This was decided in   B
relation to s. 2 of the *Joint Stock Companies Arrangement Act* 1870, in *Re Midland Coal,
Coke and Iron Co* [1895] 1 Ch 267. The headnote reads, so far as material:

> 'The lessee of certain mines assigned his leases to a company which covenanted to
> indemnify him against liability thereunder. The company went into liquidation,
> and a scheme of arrangement under the *Joint Stock Companies Arrangement Act*,
> 1870, was adopted and approved by the Court for forming a new company which   C
> should take over the assets and liabilities of the old company, and should pay or
> satisfy the unsecured creditors of the old company within three months of the
> approval of the scheme by the Court. After the new company was incorporated
> the lessee applied in the liquidation to have a sum provided to meet his contingent
> liability for rents, royalties, and breaches of covenant:-
>
> *Held* (affirming the decision of *Wright* J.), that the *Joint Stock Companies*   D
> *Arrangement Act*, 1870, applied to every person having a pecuniary claim against
> a company, whether actual or contingent, that the lessee was bound by the scheme,
> and that the application failed.'

The lessee was only liable if the company lessee, his assign, failed to pay the rent. So he
was truly only contingently liable. Nevertheless he was held to be bound and Lindley LJ,
giving the judgment of the Court of Appeal, said at p. 277:   E

> 'Whether the Court is bound to give effect to his'– that is Mr Craig, the original
> lessee –'opposition is a different question, and depends on the meaning of the word
> "creditor" in the *Joint Stock Companies Arrangement Act*, 1870. Considering that
> that Act was passed in order to enlarge the powers conferred by sect. 159 of the
> *Companies Act*, 1862, we agree with Mr Justice *Wright* in thinking that the word
> "creditor" is used in the Act of 1870 in the widest sense, and that it includes all
> persons having any pecuniary claims against the company. Any other construction   F
> would render the Act practically useless. If we are right in this interpretation of the
> Act of 1870, Mr. *Craig* is bound by the scheme approved by the Court; and in our
> opinion he is so bound. This is of itself enough for the decision of this appeal.'

They went on to deal with other matters.

Section 2 of the *Joint Stock Companies Arrangement Act* 1870, provided as follows:

> 'Where any compromise or arrangement shall be proposed between a company   G
> which is, at the time of the passing of this Act or afterwards, in the course of being
> wound up, either voluntarily or by or under the supervision of the court, under the
> Companies Acts 1862 and 1867, or either of them, and the creditors of such
> company, or any class of such creditors, it shall be lawful for the court, in addition
> to any other of its powers, on the application in a summary way of any creditor or
> the liquidator, to order that a meeting of such creditors or class of creditors shall
> be summoned in such manner as the court shall direct, and if a majority in number   H
> representing three fourths in value of such creditors or class of creditors present
> either in person or by proxy at such meeting shall agree to any arrangement or
> compromise, such arrangement or compromise shall, if sanctioned by an order of
> the court, be binding on all such creditors or class of creditors, as the case may be,
> and also on the liquidator and contributories of the said company.'

A   That provision is the direct ancestor of s. 425 of the *Companies Act* 1985 but both that latter provision and its immediate predecessor, s. 206 of the *Companies Act* 1948, applied both where the company was in liquidation – in this respect like s. 2 of the 1870 Act – but also where it was not, unlike that enactment.

Section 206(1) of the 1948 Act is in virtually identical terms with the present s. 425(1) of the 1985 Companies Act, and it reads:

B   '(1) Where a compromise or arrangement is proposed between a company and its creditors or any class of them or between the company and its members or any class of them, the court may, on the application in a summary way of the company or of any creditor or member of the company, or, in the case of a company being wound up, of the liquidator, order a meeting of the creditors or class of creditors, or of the members of the company or class of members, as the case may be, to be summoned in such manner as the court directs.'

C
–and then it goes on to provide that if there is a requisite majority that arrangement, if approved by the court, will be binding on all parties.

Buckley on the Companies Acts (14th edn) contains a note on that section which reads as follows, at p. 469:

'*Creditors*

D   Every person who has a pecuniary claim against the company, whether actual or contingent, is a creditor within the Act. Thus a lessee of mines who had assigned the lease to a company taking the company's covenant to indemnify him against rents, royalties and covenants was a person capable of being bound as a 'creditor' under the Act.'

The authority for that, of course, is *Re Midland Coal, Coke and Iron Co* which I have

E   referred to. That treats the *Midland Coal, Coke and Iron* case as still relevant to define the type of creditor capable of being bound. The same can, in my view, be said of s. 425 of the *Companies Act* 1985. So one has the situation that compromises or arrangements approved under s. 425 of the *Companies Act* 1985 are capable of including contingent creditors. Again it would, in my view, be highly anomalous if company voluntary arrangements under the Insolvency Act, which are intended to be an alternative to liquidation, and s. 425 compromises or arrangements did not have the same potential

F   ambit.

Mr Miller referred me to s. 158 of the *Companies Act* 1862, which was in force of course when the *Midland Coal, Coke and Iron Co* case was decided. That reads as follows:

'In the event of any company being wound up under this Act, all debts payable on a contingency, and all claims against the company, present or future, certain or contingent, ascertained or sounding only in damages, shall be admissible to proof

G   against the company, a just estimate being made, so far as is possible, of the value of all such debts or claims as may be subject to any contingency or sound only in damages, or for some other reason do not bear a certain value.'

He submitted that that was the explanation for *Re Midland Coal, Coke and Iron Co* being decided in the way in which it was because it was only concerned with a liquidation winding up situation.

H
There are two difficulties with that argument. The first is that it is not in fact the basis upon which Lindley LJ, giving the judgment of the Court of Appeal, based his reasoning in the passage which I have read. The second difficulty is that, unlike s. 2 of the *Joint Stock Companies Arrangement Act* 1870, the later enactments, such as s. 206 of the 1948 Act and s. 425 of the 1985 Act, are not limited to winding up of companies but apply generally and there is no authority cited or known to me for the proposition that

contingent creditors are excluded from the ambit of those sections. The passage in *Buckley* which I have cited is to the contrary effect and seems to me to be correct.

A

Those are the general reasons, and I now come to the particular reasons for my view that the expression 'creditor' in the Insolvency Rules, r. 1.17(1) is wide enough to include a landlord with a right to future rent.

First, there is r. 1.3(2)(a)(ii). This deals with the requirement that the directors' proposals should have certain contents, and the relevant passage is as follows in relation to that directors' proposal:

B

> '(2) The following matters shall be stated, or otherwise dealt with, in the directors' proposal–
>
> (a) the following matters, so far as within the directors' immediate knowledge–
>
>   . . .
>
>   (ii) the extent (if any) to which the assets are charged in favour of creditors
>   . . .'

C

If Mr Miller is right in his submission regarding the meaning of the word 'creditor' the directors would appear to have to exclude secured creditors on a contingency such as a debt made payable on demand, a very common case, which would be outside the scheme of the voluntary arrangement because 'creditors' on this hypothesis only includes those with a present right to payment, and that does seem very anomalous.

D

Secondly, r. 1.17(3) dealing with company voluntary arrangements (which I have read) would have a different meaning from the identical wording of r. 5.17(3) which deals with individual voluntary arrangements. I need not read them again. If Mr Miller is right r. 1.17(3) only includes creditors with an accrued but unliquidated claim or one where the value of the debt was not ascertained although presently payable, whereas r. 5.17(3) includes in the self-same words contingent creditors and creditors with an established right to the future payment of a fixed sum. It is very difficult to believe that the draftsman intended identical sentences in different parts of the same set of rules to have a different meaning.

E

Thirdly and lastly, Mr Miller's arguments did not deal with the problems posed by s. 425 of the *Companies Act* 1985, which with immaterial alterations, as I have said, re-enacts s. 206 of the 1948 Act. Either the word 'creditors' in s. 425(1) includes creditors who have claims which are not presently enforceable, such as a landlord with a right to future rent, or it does not. If it does, it goes a long way towards destroying Mr Miller's thesis regarding the natural or ordinary meaning of the word creditors because there is no relevant statutory enlargement of the term. If it does not and *Re Midland Coal, Coke and Iron Co* (above), contrary to the views expressed in *Buckley*, is no longer good law in relation to s. 425 of the *Companies Act* 1985, Parliament has radically restricted a power of compromise with creditors in a way which would deprive it of a great deal of its usefulness. The only other possibility that I can see would be that the word 'creditor' would have a variable meaning according to whether or not the company in question was in liquidation with the wider construction applicable to those that were in liquidation and the narrower for those that were not in liquidation. That is also a profoundly unsatisfactory construction, giving a single word different meanings in the same sentence in relation to different situations.

F

G

Mr Miller's argument on this aspect was that *Re Midland Coal, Coke and Iron Co* might have to be reconsidered and he remained, as he said, agnostic regarding the meaning of s. 425. This rather Olympian attitude enabled Mr Miller to remain unimpaled above the horns of a rather difficult dilemma, which is there if one gets down to considering what s. 425 actually means. In my view, s. 425 is a very considerable obstacle in the path of those who, like Mr Miller, seek to argue that the word 'creditor' has a

H

A   single ordinary or natural meaning which is not capable of taking its meaning from the legislative context in which it is found.

For all those reasons, both general and specific, I prefer the construction of the word 'creditor' in r. 1.17(1), which includes those entitled to a right to a future payment under an existing valid instrument such as a lease. The argument to the contrary is based on the proposition that the word 'creditor' has a natural or ordinary meaning which is narrow
B   and only includes those with presently enforceable claims. Although that is a possible meaning, I do not accept that it is one which must prevail over other possible meanings notwithstanding the many indications to the contrary from the context and the purpose of the legislation.

I turn to the other arguments advanced on behalf of the landlords. These are based on the assumption, which I have found to be correct, that the landlords were a creditor for the purposes of r. 1.17(1) and therefore potentially entitled to vote. It is necessary for this
C   aspect of the case to look at the evidence regarding the facts, and this is as follows so far as material.

Notice was given of the decision to hold a meeting of creditors pursuant to s. 3 of the Insolvency Act on Friday, 23 June 1995 at 10.30 am for the purpose of considering and, if thought fit, approving the proposals of the directors for a voluntary arrangement as set out in that Act. The notice was dated 8 June, and it is accepted that it was received by the
D   landlords in due time. A copy of the proposals was, of course, included with the notice and they included the following. Paragraph 1 contained definitions, headed with the phrase:

> 'In this voluntary arrangement proposal the following definitions shall apply unless the context otherwise requires'.

Among the definitions one finds 'creditors', 'secured creditors', 'preferential creditors'
E   and 'unsecured creditors'.

> ' "Fixed Date": the date, if any, of approval of this voluntary arrangement.

> "Unsecured creditors": creditors of the company who would have been entitled to prove in a liquidation had the company gone into creditors' voluntary liquidation on the fixed date, including prospective and contingent creditors, other than–

> > (i)   secured creditors to the extent of their security;

F   > > (ii) preferential creditors . . .'

–and 'preferential creditors' and 'secured creditors' are also defined – the latter as including those companies listed in para. 7.1.1 as having supplied assets to the company on the terms of hire, hire-purchase, lease or similar agreements.

The proposals contained this about the company's then financial position:

G   > '4.4 After adjusting the book values of the company to take effect of'– certain points above –'there is a surplus of liabilities over assets of approximately £330,000. The company is therefore insolvent on a balance sheet basis. The company has exhausted its financing facilities and has for some time been trading under severe cash flow pressure.'

The proposals are contained in para. 5 of the document, and that includes the following:

H   > '5.1 The intention of the directors is to save the business, retain their livelihood and that of their employees and provide the company's creditors with a greater return than they would otherwise receive in a winding up.

> 5.2 In summary, the voluntary arrangement is to provide for the business to trade and make payments to the supervisors from profits/cashflow over the life of the voluntary arrangement for the benefit of the creditors of the company.

. . .

5.5 It is anticipated that the factoring agreement with Royal Bank Invoice Finance Ltd will continue as will all the necessary payments in respect of asset lease agreements which the company wishes to retain. The company will not require any continuing overdraft facility and will trade with a credit account.

. . .

5.15 The company presently trades from Victoria Wharf, Dragoon Road, London SE8'– that, of course, is the premises –'under the terms of a lease which has an unexpired term of approximately 13 years. These premises are too large for the present business and it is therefore proposed that the company will trade from leasehold premises in Clement's Road, London SE16, under the terms of a lease held by CDL . . .'

–that is an associated company. There are then details given of the costs of the lease of the premises, and para. 5.16 also says:

'5.16 . . . The company will bear one-third of the Clement's Road lease which will represent £20,833 per annum for the period to 30 November 1995 and £41,667 per annum thereafter.'

Paragraph 5.17 is of critical importance and reads:

'5.17 The landlord and/or any intermediate lessee of the premises in Dragoon Road'– in fact there was no such intermediate lessee –'will have a claim against the company not only for arrears of rent up to 4 May 1995 but also in damages for the failure of the company to honour the terms of the lease. The company will move into Clement's Road as soon after the fixed date as possible and will continue to pay the rent in respect of the period from the fixed date to vacation. The company shall then offer to surrender the lease in respect of Dragoon Road and the supervisors shall appoint an independent agent to negotiate with the landlord and/or any intermediate lessee the extent of his claim for damages.

5.18 The company also holds a further lease in respect of Maritime Industrial Estate, Woolwich Road, Greenwich which has an unexpired period of approximately 11 years and a cost of £16,000 per annum. It is proposed as part of this arrangement that the company will offer to surrender the lease and the supervisors shall appoint an independent agent to negotiate with the landlord and/or any intermediate lessee the extent of his claim.

5.19 The company further stands as surety to a lease for 20 Boughton Road, Thamesmead which has an unexpired term of 16 months at a cost of £16,221 per annum. It is proposed that upon any disclaimer of this lease by the liquidator of R & P'– that was the lessee, of course –'that the company shall not accept a new lease from the landlord and the supervisors will appoint an independent agent to negotiate with the landlord the extent of the company's guarantee liability.

5.20 For the sake of clarification, any claim under para. 5.17, 5.18 or 5.19 shall whether in relation to any arrears outstanding as at the fixed date or any future rent or any other sums which may become payable be claimable only in the voluntary arrangement and not against the company outside the terms of the voluntary arrangement.'

Then passing over irrelevant passages, para. 5.30 and 5.31 read as follows:

'5.30 Should the company proceed into liquidation we believe that whilst preferential creditors may receive a minimal dividend, no dividend would be payable to the unsecured creditors.

A   5.31 With the exception of any rent payable in respect of Victoria Wharf from the
     fixed date to the date of vacation and subject to the provisions of para. 5.19, any
     creditors whose debts have been incurred by the company in the carrying on of the
     business of the company after the fixed date will be paid from the ongoing trade
     outside the voluntary arrangement.'

B   There was a schedule in the usual way of unsecured creditors and amongst that one
     finds the landlords in at the figure for accrued rent, about which there is no problem,
     £10,430.44, and one finds another creditor called London Industrial plc, which was in
     fact the landlord of the other premises in respect of which there was a lease in favour of
     the company. That is in at £7,015.34.

     Correspondence ensued between the landlords and their solicitors on the one hand and
     the company and its solicitors on the other. The landlords wrote on 14 June, the first of
     more than one letter. The first letter included the following:

C   'Whatever the outcome of the creditors' meeting the company's liabilities under
     this lease will continue, i.e. we will demand that all rental moneys are paid on the
     usual quarter days'– and they are specified –'together with any other moneys due
     under the terms of the lease. If any of these payments are not met C I Holdings
     Ltd [the landlords] immediately will issue a winding-up petition against the
     company.'

D   The same day, but presumably later, the landlords wrote the following:

     'Further to my letter of 14 June, I write to advise that our lawyers and insolvency
     consultants have now had the opportunity to study your notice to creditors and
     have pointed out to us that the debt of £10,430.44 admitted to the landlords is
     incorrect. We are advised that the debt admitted should cover all rental moneys
     including tax under the terms of the lease to August 4th, 2008'

E   – that is the whole of the unexpired term of the lease, of course–

     'We are advised, therefore, that we are entitled to vote at the meeting of creditors
     in respect of the full amount of all rental moneys under the terms of the lease,
     being £10,430.44 in arrears, plus £920,375.07 in future rents, making a total of
     moneys owing to creditors of £1,808,987.80, of which £930,805.51 is owed to the
     landlords.'

F   Again the same day there was a letter demanding the quarter's rent that was due the next
     day, that Midsummer Day, and a threat that if it was not paid there would be a winding-
     up petition issued.

     A proxy was sent simultaneously with that shoal of letters on 14 June and that named
     two directors of the landlords as proxy holders and included as voting instructions the
     following:

G   '1. That the resolution 5.17 be deleted'

     – that is a reference to the proposals, of course–

     '2. That the company should continue to honour its lease on the premises at
     Dragoon Road until such time as the lease can be assigned.'

     The answer came from the insolvency practitioners for the company on 16 June 1995 and
     there is only one paragraph that I need read, on the second page, which reads as follows:

H   'With regard to your second letter, your lawyers and insolvency consultants should
     also have pointed out to you that you have a duty to mitigate any potential loss
     under the terms of the lease. No doubt your advisers will also have advised you
     with regard to the contents of r. 1.17(3). The material point in question in
     determining the value of your claim for voting purposes is the time in which you
     would be expected to re-let the vacant property. I believe in the present market you

would be able to re-let the property within approximately six months of it   A
becoming vacant.'

There then ensued a change of heart on the part of the landlords through their
solicitors, who wrote a letter dated 21 June 1995, in which they said (I am not reading
the whole of the letter but such parts of it as seem to be material):

'The proposal appears to be made in order to assist the tenant of the Clement's
Road property rather than the creditors. It is in any event equivocal. Paragraphs   B
5.17 and 5.20 are inconsistent. The suggestion made by the terms of para. 5.20 is
beyond the scope of the Insolvency Rules.'

It will be recalled that para. 5.20 is the paragraph that said in terms that any claim by,
notably, the landlords for future rent or other sums which might become payable would
be claimable only in the voluntary arrangement and not outside the terms of the
voluntary arrangement. Going on with the letter from the landlord's solicitors, it contains   C
this:

'The wording of para. 5.17 of the voluntary arrangement does not contemplate
any claims accruing to our client for rent falling due on each quarter day after the
meeting and if, as we expect will be the case, our client does not agree to accept
any surrender it will have a claim for a new debt arising on each quarter day which
again will be unaffected by any voluntary arrangements made as future rent is   D
outside the scope of para. 5.17 of the arrangement.'

Then a little later:

'If it is the intention of the proposal for the arrangement either that by para. 5.17
or para. 5.20 to offer our client the opportunity to vote in respect of future claims
you must please make clear how much it is proposed our client is to be entitled to
vote for in relation to those claims. In order that we may advise our client we will   E
require a breakdown of any figure you suggest our client may be entitled to vote
for.'

The last paragraph I need read reads as follows:

'This letter supersedes all previous correspondence you have had from our client
or anyone writing on their behalf about this matter and all previous comments
made by our client in relation to the value of their voting entitlement are   F
unequivocally and irrevocably withdrawn, such that they are nugatory and of no
effect.'

A further proxy was sent in the alternative in favour of the two directors, whom I
mentioned earlier, and the third possibility of a chairman but the voting instructions were
as follows:

'1. Vote against the proposed voluntary arrangement on the basis that it is   G
modified to make clear that only claims to a total value of £10,430.44 by the
landlords are covered by the voluntary arrangement and all and any other claims
by the landlords are not covered by the voluntary arrangement.'

In fact no reply was given to that request for information as to how much the landlords
would be allowed to vote for. The meeting was held, as I have said, on 23 June 1995 and
the proposal, subject to some modifications upon which nothing turns, was approved.   H
The voting particulars are set out in the schedule which is in evidence and they include
London Industrial plc as voting in favour in a sum of £297,275 and the landlords as
voting against in the sum of accrued rent £10,430.44. Whether that was a proper use of
the proxy I need not pause to consider because it is at least arguable that the proxy was
conditional on the landlords' propositions regarding its future claims being accepted, but
nothing turns on that aspect.

A

A report was sent – perhaps not as fast as it should have been – to the landlords and they replied through their solicitors on 18 July 1995:

'We look forward to receipt of a breakdown of the sum of £297,275 for which London Industrial plc was granted voting rights, as requested by our letter to you of 13 July 1995 . . .'

–which indeed it had been.

B

The affidavits deal with this matter, so far as relevant, as follows. The affidavit sworn on behalf of the landlords by one of its directors includes the following:

'It will be seen that the letter of 21 June 1995 requested that if it was the intention of the proposal to offer my company the opportunity to vote in respect of future claims Mr Calcott should make clear how much the voting rights were. No response was received to this letter. I know that Mr Calcott'–

C

he was a representative of the insolvency practitioners dealing with this matter on behalf of the company–

'had it prior to the meeting as I spoke to Mr Brown of Cancol Ltd on 22 June 1995 and he told me consideration was being given as to how to deal with the letter. Neither I nor Bob Irving'– the other director of the landlords –'attended the meeting on 23 June 1995. The chairman voted against the proposal in the sum of £10,430.44 as instructed by the new proxy.'

D

Then passing over a mention of the fact that there had been correspondence, which of course is true:

'One point which should be noted'– it said in relation to that correspondence –'is in relation to London Industrial plc. I know from conversations I had prior to 23 June 1995 with Mr Richard Purcell of that company that it is the landlord of the premises referred to in para. 5.18 of the voluntary arrangement. London Industrial plc was given voting rights of £297,275. Presumably some arrangement was made with that creditor that it could vote for its future rent. It will be seen from p. 34 that in the list of unsecured creditors the amount due to London Industrial was put at £7,015.34, which I take to be the sum accrued due to that company down to 23 June 1995. As I say, the amount voted by the chairman in accordance with the proxy on behalf of the landlords was £10,430.44, the precise sum due to the landlords down to 23 June 1995, and the same sum appears in the schedule of unsecured creditors. It is clear from this and from the correspondence to which I have referred that the landlords did not have any voting rights in relation to rent due to it on or after 24 June, the proposal for the voluntary arrangement. It did not agree to vote in relation to its future rent in the voluntary arrangement and it was not offered any sum by way of voting rights for that future rent.'

E

F

G

He asked for an order declaring that future rent and other moneys are not covered by the voluntary arrangement or 'for such other relief as the court may decide is fit'.

Finally, Mr Fry swore an affidavit on behalf of the company in which he said this with regard to what was said in relation to London Industrial plc:

'5. The claim of the applicant against the company in respect of future rent is covered by the terms of the voluntary arrangement. This is made clear in para. 5.20 of the voluntary arrangement. The claim of the applicant in the voluntary arrangement in respect of, inter alia, the unexpired term of the lease of the premises is set out at para. 5.17 of the voluntary arrangement. The claims against the company of London Industrial plc in respect of the lease of the premises at Maritime Industrial Estate, which the company had previously vacated, are dealt with in the same manner in the voluntary arrangement. London Industrial plc was

H

entitled to vote in the voluntary arrangement not because of "some arrangement" as suggested in para. 9 of the affidavit of Mr Cassidy but because London Industrial plc had received notice of the s. 3 creditors' meeting and the chairman of the meeting was agreeable to putting an estimated minimum value on the claim for voting purposes within r. 1.17(3) of the *Insolvency Rules* 1986. The applicant was entitled to vote at the s. 3 creditors' meeting on precisely the same basis as London Industrial plc. However, for reasons of its own the applicant determined not to exercise that entitlement.'

Finally, in para. 11:

'11. The valuation of the claim in respect of future rent for voting purposes was based upon a professional valuation obtained by the joint nominees of the voluntary arrangement . . .'

–and he exhibits a copy of that valuation:

'The same procedure was used for the claim of London Industrial plc, although in the latter case a greater percentage of the claim was allowed for voting purposes because the valuation indicated that the relevant premises would be very difficult to let.'

The valuation that was exhibited dealt with what I am calling the premises and it contained a statement of opinion by the valuers that they would suggest that the property could be on the market for, say, six to twelve months before a suitable tenant could be found.

'In addition, it is likely that a new tenant would require a rent-free period as an incentive to take possession and this could be for, say, six to nine months.'

There is an issue which in my view is of no significance regarding when the company's solicitors received the letter dated 21 June from the landlords' solicitors. It was received before the meeting but may have been faxed on 21 (the landlords' evidence) or received on 22 (the company's evidence). Nothing turns on this. The rest of the correspondence between the solicitors is not strictly in evidence and I do not propose to read it because all that it shows is that an attempt was made on behalf of the landlords to see the valuation which Mr Fry referred to in his affidavit regarding the claim of London Industrial plc. This was unsuccessful because the advice was said to be oral. There is also in that correspondence a certain amount of debate between solicitors of, sadly, frequent occurrence in which debating points about the behaviour of the opposite side and its advisers are made. It is unnecessary to refer to it and it was very properly omitted from the evidence. On that evidence, Mr Miller makes three points.

First, he submitted that the requirements of r. 1.17(3) were not satisfied in that the chairman of the meeting did not agree to place a minimum value for voting on the landlords' right to future rent and the word used in that subrule 'agrees' involves, he said, a consensual agreement. I dealt with this aspect of the rule in the *Doorbar* case (above). There does, unfortunately, appear to me to be some difference of opinion between the judgment that Ferris J gave in *Re Cranley Mansions Ltd* [1994] BCC 576 and myself as expressed in the *Doorbar* case. I do not propose to repeat the arguments on this subject, which can be found in my decision in *Doorbar*, beyond saying that I remain of the opinion which I expressed in my conclusion at p. 1007B in the *Doorbar* case, when I said:

'I should, of course, normally follow what one of my brethren in this division had previously held but I am not bound to do so, and in the light of the argument addressed to me by Mr Zacaroli'– he was for the individual bankrupt in that case –'which was not, so far as I could see, addressed to Ferris J, I have reached the conclusion that the only agreement that subr. 5.17(3) requires is an expressed willingness by the chairman to put an estimated minimum value on the debt in

A question. If the subrule is thus interpreted it avoids the undesirable result that the relevant creditor can avoid the consequence of being in a minority of 25 per cent or less and be bound by the 75 per cent or more majority by the simple expedient of refusing to agree any minimum value for any purpose, and it gives the appeal procedure a proper field within which to operate.'

B In the case now before the court the landlords did not attend the meeting, having expressed in very forceful terms through their solicitors the view that their claim to future rent was outside the voluntary arrangement. They had been given an indication of how their claim would be likely to be valued without further elaboration. Mr Miller submitted that the rule requires the creditor in question to agree to a minimum value being placed on the claim. I do not accept this. Whilst it is true that the word 'agrees' suggests a bilateral activity, it is to be noted that the rule requires the chairman to agree; it does not say 'agree with the creditor'. If a creditor stays away I do not think it lies in his mouth to C say that the chairman has not agreed. That enables the voluntary arrangement to be frustrated in just the same way as it would be by interpreting the rules requiring agreement on the value to be reached between chairman and creditor. Equally, I reject the submission that was made that the chairman must put a value and tell the creditor before the meeting. The answer to that submission is that the rule does not say so.

D Secondly, it was submitted that there was unfair prejudice. This arises under the provisions of s. 6 of the *Insolvency Act* 1986, which allows challenges of decisions of a chairman at a meeting of creditors on certain terms. Subsection (1) provides:

'(1) Subject to this section, an application to the court may be made, by any of the persons specified below, on one or both of the following grounds, namely–

(a) that a voluntary arrangement approved at the meetings summoned under section 3 unfairly prejudices the interests of a creditor, member or E contributory of the company;

(b) that there has been some material irregularity at or in relation to either of the meetings.'

Subsection (2) defines the persons who may apply and includes a person entitled in accordance with the rules to vote at either of the meetings. Under this head it is said that future creditors were dealt with differently in the proposal. Some creditors with leasing arrangements in favour of the company were to be paid in full, and reference was made F to para. 5.5 of the proposals, which it will be recalled said:

'It is anticipated that the factoring agreement with Royal Bank Invoice Finance Ltd will continue, as will all the necessary payments in respect of asset lease agreements which the company wishes to retain.'

Equally, in para. 5.17 there was different treatment put forward in relation to the G landlords' claim but the same treatment so long as the company actually remained in occupation. I have read the paragraph once and need not repeat it.

The question arises: does it constitute unfair prejudice for those creditors with future rights to be paid in full so long as the asset in question is used to earn the profits envisaged by the voluntary arrangement while those whose assets are no longer so used are left to a dividend in respect of their claim under the arrangement? That is indeed how I construe the proposals, which are not entirely explicit on this subject. I construe them as meaning H this: if and so long as the premises were occupied by the company the rent would be paid in full; once vacated the landlords would rank for a dividend in the proposals, either on the claim for damages for failure to honour the terms of the lease (as the proposals call it) if there was an agreement between the independent agent envisaged by para. 5.17 and the company or, if no such agreement was reached, on the rental payments as they fell due. It is not necessary for me to go into the question whether damages for failure to

honour the terms of the lease is in fact an apt expression. That was not fully argued   A
before me and I express no views on the point.

To return to the question of unfair prejudice, I do not consider that it is unfair within
the meaning of the section to make a differentiation between members of the class of
creditors with future claims on the basis proposed. The landlord has a right of forfeiture
once the rent ceases to be paid in full. The proposals do not deprive him of that, so he is
not without a remedy. Of course, it is a much less attractive remedy in terms of static or   B
falling rents than in terms of rent inflation, but I do not consider that the fact that the
remedy which the landlord has is not very attractive to him means that it should not be
taken into account. Equally, the distinction proposed between the categories of future
creditors does seem to me to be a realistic and commercially sensible one, and on that
basis I reject the argument that there was here unfair prejudice.

Finally, it was submitted to me that there was a material irregularity in the differential
treatment of the claim of London Industrial plc and the landlords' claim to future rent.   C
That turns on the fact that London Industrial plc, or their representative, turned up at
the meeting and persuaded the chairman to increase their figure for voting to a
remarkable extent. This point was not taken in the affidavits, or indeed in Mr Miller's
skeleton argument, and the evidence justifying the increase in the figure for London
Industrial plc's vote is exceedingly thin. It does not explain how it is that the figure
allowed appears to exceed the sum of the number of years in the London Industrial lease,   D
which is unexpired, multiplied by the annual rent payable under that lease. Had I been
persuaded that the inclusion at that increased figure of London Industrial plc's vote could
have had an effect on the outcome I would have stood over this application for further
evidence on how it was valued, but the fact is that even if it is left out altogether the result
on the figures would have been the same, and on that basis I do not think it would be
justifiable to involve the parties in such further expense.

The other side of the coin is that the landlords were not accorded the same treatment   E
so far as voting on their future right to rent is concerned as London Industrial plc. Here,
however, I do not think that the landlords can complain because they stayed away and
took their stand on the proposition that future rent could not be included and that they
retained their right to it in full outside the voluntary arrangement. In those circumstances
it is not, in my judgment, an irregularity not to give them any particular voting rights if
and so long as they claim in effect not to be creditors, save of course for the accrued rent   F
claim, as to which there is no issue.

For those reasons, I dismiss this application.

(Order accordingly)

G

H

A # Doorbar v Alltime Securities Ltd.

Court of Appeal (Civil Division).
Hirst and Peter Gibson L JJ and Forbes J.
Judgment delivered 30 November 1995.

B *Individual voluntary arrangement – Voting rights – Chairman at creditors' meeting allowed landlord to vote for one year's future rent – Whether arrangement capable of including future rent – Whether creditor had to agree with chairman's estimated minimum value of debt – Landlord had rights under lease exercisable against debtor's wife on bankruptcy – Whether inability to invoke clause was unfairly prejudicial – Whether rights under lease were interests of landlord as a creditor – Whether there was a material irregularity in valuing landlord's claim –*
C *Whether approval of arrangement should be revoked – Insolvency Act 1986, s. 258, 260(2), 262(1)(a), (b); Insolvency Rules 1986 (SI 1986/1925), r. 5.17.*

These were appeals from two decisions of Knox J in which he held that a debtor's future liability under a lease was included in an individual voluntary arrangement (see [1994] BCC 994) and that there was no unfair prejudice or material irregularity in approval of the arrangement (see [1995] BCC 728).

D The proposal for a voluntary arrangement of the debtor's affairs purported to cover his liability for future rent under a lease. The landlord voted against the proposal in respect of arrears of rent (and interest). The landlord also sought to vote for the whole of the rent payable for the remaining term of the lease. The chairman offered to value the landlord's claim under that head at a minimum of one year's rent for voting purposes. The landlord did not agree that figure and no vote was cast in respect of that claim. Knox J held that the future rent payments were intended to be within the arrangement, that future rent was capable of being included in a voluntary arrangement, and that r. 5.17(3) of the Insolvency
E Rules 1986 required the chairman's agreement to put a minimum value on a debt and not to agree the minimum value with the creditor. Accordingly the landlord was entitled to vote in respect of the claim for future rent and was bound by the voluntary arrangement in respect of that claim.

The landlord further argued that approval of the voluntary arrangement was unfairly prejudicial to its interests under s. 262(1)(a) of the Insolvency Act 1986, because the lease
F contained a clause which provided that the debtor and his wife would take a new lease on the debtor's bankruptcy. The landlord attached value to its rights against the wife under the clause. If it was bound by the arrangement in respect of future rent it could not petition for bankruptcy and inability to activate the clause constituted unfair prejudice.

The landlord also alleged that the chairman's refusal to value the future rent under the lease for voting purposes as the annual rent multiplied by the number of years left to run
G was a material irregularity under s. 262(1)(b).

Knox J held that the landlord's rights under the clause were not within the ambit of the landlord's interests as a creditor of the debtor under s. 262. In any event any prejudice would not be unfair, because the landlord retained its security against the debtor in the shape of a right of re-entry unaffected by the voluntary arrangement. On the question of material irregularity, the chairman of the meeting was justified in making allowance for the
H probability of re-entry and effectively treating the landlord as not standing to lose the rent for the whole of the rest of the term. The landlord appealed.

Held, dismissing the appeal:

1. The context of the crucial words in r. 5.17(3) was that there was a general prohibition on voting by the creditor with an unliquidated or unascertained claim, to which prohibition there was an exception if the chairman agreed. That agreement was not expressed to be

with the creditor or anyone else. It was not an agreement on the value (that was for the   A
supervisor): the chairman only agreed to put on the debt an estimated minimum value. It
was sufficient if the chairman expressed his willingness to put, and put, an estimated
minimum value on the debt.

2. Any irregularity in the estimate of the minimum value would not be material unless
that value was increased threefold. Only then would the landlord have had 25 per cent or
more of the voting power at the meeting. No attempt was made by the landlord to provide   B
the chairman with any estimate or evidence of the then present value of its claim; it simply
claimed the aggregate of the whole of the future rent. It was also not in dispute that the
right of re-entry remained unaffected by the arrangement. In those circumstances, it was
entirely realistic of the chairman to put a minimum value on the landlord's claim by
estimating what was likely to happen, and making allowance for the possibility of re-entry.
The landlord's approach of treating the minimum value of the future rent liability as equal
to the whole of that liability was wrong in principle.   C

3. The judge was right in his analysis and conclusion that in the light of the characteristics
of the alleged prejudice and more especially of the fact that the right in question was one
exercisable against a person other than the debtor and arose on the determination through
disclaimer by the trustee of the debtor's liability and was therefore a substitute for rather
than a constituent part of the debtor's indebtedness, the landlord's interest was outside the
ambit of s. 262(1)(a) and that therefore there was no prejudice of which it could complain.   D

The following cases were referred to in the judgment of Peter Gibson LJ:

Beverley Group plc v McClue [1995] BCC 751.
Bradley-Hole, Re [1995] BCC 418; [1995] 1 WLR 1097.
Cancol Ltd, Re [1995] BCC 1133.
Cranley Mansions Ltd, Re [1994] BCC 576; [1994] 1 WLR 1610.
Davis v Martin-Sklan [1995] BCC 1122.   E
McKeen, Re [1995] BCC 412.
Naeem (a bankrupt), Re [1990] 1 WLR 48.

Amanda Tipples (instructed by Tinklin Springall, Beckenham) for the landlord.

Antony Zacaroli (instructed by Charles Marlowe, Brighton) for the debtor.

JUDGMENT   F

Peter Gibson LJ: Among the innovations introduced by the *Insolvency Act* 1986 were
provisions in Pt. VIII of the Act enabling an individual debtor to make a proposal to his
creditors for a composition in satisfaction of his debts or a scheme of arrangement of his
affairs (in either case called a voluntary arrangement), and for carrying that voluntary
arrangement into effect. There were corresponding provisions for corporate debtors in
Pt. I of the Act. These appeals raise questions as to the meaning of the statutory   G
provisions and rules relating to individual voluntary arrangements and their effect in the
particular circumstances of this case.

It is convenient to commence by summarising the statutory scheme for individual
voluntary arrangements. The debtor who intends to propose a voluntary arrangement is
required to apply to the court for an interim order under s. 253. His proposal must
provide for some person ('the nominee') to act in relation to the voluntary arrangement   H
as trustee or otherwise for the purpose of supervising its implementation. The matters to
be dealt with in the proposal include his assets and their estimated values, any property,
other than the assets of the debtor himself, which is to be included in the voluntary
arrangement, the nature and amount of his liabilities, the duration of the voluntary
arrangement, and the functions which are to be undertaken by the supervisor of the
voluntary arrangement (r. 5.3 of the *Insolvency Rules* 1986). Both the nominee and the

A   supervisor have to be insolvency practitioners (s. 255(1)(d) and r. 5.3(2)(p)). If the court makes an interim order, no bankruptcy petition may be presented or proceeded with and no other proceedings and no execution or other legal process may be commenced or continued against the debtor without leave (s. 252). The order ceases to have effect after 14 days and before it does the nominee must submit a report to the court, stating whether a creditors' meeting should be summoned to consider the debtor's proposal (s. 255(6) and 256(1)). The debtor is required to submit to the nominee a statement of his affairs

B   (s. 256(2)). If the court is satisfied that there should be a creditors' meeting, the interim order is extended until the meeting (s. 256(5)) and the nominee summons every creditor to the meeting (s. 257). The creditors' meeting decides whether to approve the proposed voluntary arrangement and may do so with modifications to which the debtor consents (s. 258(1) and (2)). But the meeting shall not approve any proposal or modification which affects the right of a secured creditor to enforce his security, except with the creditor's

C   concurrence (s. 258(4)).

The nominee, if able to attend, is the chairman of the meeting (r. 5.15(1)). Voting rights are dealt with in r. 5.17:

'(1) Subject as follows, every creditor who was given notice of the creditors' meeting is entitled to vote at the meeting or any adjournment of it.

D   (2) . . . votes are calculated . . . in Case 2 [relating to a case where the debtor is other than an undischarged bankrupt] according to the amount of the debt as at the date of the meeting.

(3) A creditor shall not vote in respect of a debt for an unliquidated amount or any debt whose value is not ascertained, except where the chairman agrees to put upon the debt an estimated minimum value for the purpose of entitlement to vote.

E   (4) The chairman has power to admit or reject a creditor's claim for the purpose of his entitlement to vote, and the power is exercisable with respect to the whole or any part of the claim.

(5) The chairman's decision on entitlement to vote is subject to appeal to the court by any creditor, or by the debtor.

(6) If the chairman is in doubt whether a claim should be admitted or rejected, he shall mark it as objected to and allow the creditor to vote, subject to his vote being

F   subsequently declared invalid if the objection to the claim is sustained.

(7) If on an appeal the chairman's decision is reversed or varied, or a creditor's vote is declared invalid, the court may order another meeting to be summoned, or make such other order as it thinks just.

The court's power to make an order under this paragraph is exercisable only if it considers that the matter is such as to give rise to unfair prejudice or a material

G   irregularity.

(8) An application to the court by way of appeal under this Rule against the chairman's decision shall not be made after the end of the period of 28 days beginning with the day on which the chairman's report to the court is made under section 259.'

H   By r. 5.18(1) for any resolution to pass approving any proposal or modification there must be a majority in excess of three-quarters in value of the creditors present in person or by proxy and voting on the resolution.

The effect of the approval is stated in s. 260. By subs. (2):

'The approved arrangement—

(a) takes effect as if made by the debtor at the meeting, and

(b) binds every person who in accordance with the rules had notice of, and was   A
entitled to vote at, the meeting (whether or not he was present or represented
at it) as if he were a party to the arrangement.'

Section 262 provides for challenges of the meeting's decision, allowing, amongst others,
a person entitled to vote at the meeting to apply to the court on one or both of the
following grounds (s. 262(1)):

'(a) that a voluntary arrangement approved by a creditors' meeting summoned   B
under section 257 unfairly prejudices the interests of a creditor of the debtor;

(b) that there has been some material irregularity at or in relation to such a
meeting.'

The court if satisfied on either of those grounds may revoke or suspend any approval
given by the meeting and may direct a further meeting to be summoned.

Where a voluntary arrangement takes effect, the supervisor performs the functions   C
allotted to him by that arrangement. If the debtor or any creditor or other person is
dissatisfied with any act, omission or decision of the supervisor, he may apply to the
court under s. 263(3).

By s. 264(1)(c) the supervisor or any person (other than the debtor) who is for the time
being bound by an approved voluntary arrangement may present a bankruptcy petition
against the debtor, but a bankruptcy order will not be made on such petition unless the   D
court is satisfied of a default by the debtor in connection with the voluntary arrangement
(s. 276(1)). In contrast, any creditor who is not bound by the approved arrangement may
present a petition relying on his debt (s. 264(1)(a)).

I turn to the facts. On 3 April 1981 the appellant, Alltime Securities Ltd ('Alltime'), as
the landlord granted a lease of business premises, 343 Eden Park Avenue, Bromley to
Menage Graphic Productions as the tenant for a term of 20 years at £7,500 per annum   E
subject to five-year rent reviews and an additional annual rent for insurance. From 29
September 1990 the annual rent was increased to £13,830. The tenant is in fact the
respondent debtor, Mr Doorbar, by his trade name. There was provision in cl. 4 for
reentry by the landlord in usual form on the failure to pay the rent thereby reserved for
21 days after becoming payable or if the tenant should become bankrupt or enter into
any composition with his creditors. Also named as parties to the lease were Mr Doorbar
and his then wife, who were called in the lease 'the sureties'. By cl. 5:   F

'If the tenant shall go into liquidation and the liquidator shall disclaim this lease
or if the tenant shall be wound up or cease to exist (or if the tenant for the time
being shall be an individual and shall become bankrupt and the trustee in
bankruptcy shall disclaim this lease) and if the landlord shall within three months
after such disclaimer or other event putting an end to the effect of this lease as
aforesaid so far as concerns the tenant by notice in writing require the surety to   G
accept a lease of the premises for a term commensurate with the residue which if
there had been no disclaimer or if this lease had continued to have had effect as
aforesaid would have remained of the term hereby granted at the same rent and
subject to the like covenants and conditions as are reserved by and contained in
this lease (with the exception of this clause) the said new lease and the rights and
liabilities thereunder to take effect as from the date of the said disclaimer or of this
lease ceasing to have effect as aforesaid then and in such case the surety shall pay   H
the costs of and accept such new lease accordingly and will execute and deliver to
the landlord a counterpart thereof.'

Although that clause only refers to 'the surety' in the singular, Mr Zacaroli for Mr
Doorbar does not dispute that if the conditions for the operation of cl. 5 are satisfied,
Alltime may require Mrs Doorbar to take a lease for the remainder of the term. It is to

A be noted that those conditions are more limited than the conditions for forfeiture in cl. 4, in particular in that they do not include the condition if the tenant should enter into any composition with his creditors.

Mr Doorbar fell into arrears with his rent and on 24 April 1993 Alltime served a statutory demand on him, requiring payment of £7,434 arrears. Mr Doorbar did not pay the sum demanded but sought unsuccessfully to set aside the demand. Alltime presented

B a bankruptcy petition based on that demand. The hearing was fixed for 24 August 1993, but Mr Doorbar applied under s. 253 for, and on 24 August 1993 obtained, an interim order on the basis of a proposal for a voluntary arrangement. His statement of affairs, appended to his proposal, showed that his only asset, a leasehold property, had a negative equity while his liabilities were some £35,000 (including a debt to Alltime of £7,434). That total proved to be a gross underestimate. His proposal was based on monthly payments out of his anticipated income. He proposed paying £250 per month for six months, £350

C per month for the next six months and £500 per month for the remainder of the term of the arrangement which he proposed should last for four years. He named Mr Kenneth Bradshaw as the nominee and Mr Michael Matthews as the supervisor. The supervisor's functions were to include agreeing creditors' claims. Dividends were to be paid to creditors where it was possible to pay at least 10p in the £ on proved debts. Paragraph 12 stated:

D 'All future liabilities arising under the guarantee on property owned by Alltime . . . are to be included in the arrangement'.

It is common ground that the liability to Alltime of Mr Doorbar as tenant for future rent under the lease is covered by that paragraph.

A meeting of creditors was summoned by the nominee for 20 September 1993 but adjourned to 4 October 1993. Prior to the adjourned meeting Alltime had indicated to

E the nominee that it objected to the inclusion of para. 12 but had not put any value on its claim based on future rent under the lease. The nominee was chairman of the adjourned meeting.

At the meeting Alltime's managing director, Mr Springall, raised the question of the liability of Mr Doorbar for future rent. Mr Springall in his affidavit of 15 October said:

F '. . . whilst the chairman permitted all future liabilities under the lease to be included in the voluntary arrangement, he would not allow [Alltime], as creditor, the value of this future liability for voting purposes.'

The nominee in his report to the court on the meeting said:

'Mr Bradshaw was asked about cl. 12 of the proposals, and it was confirmed that it was intended that any liabilities arising under the lease of premises should be included in the arrangement. Mr Springall suggested that the whole of the future

G rent should therefore be included, but Mr Bradshaw said that this could not be so because there had to be mitigation for the likelihood of the property being re-let, and it was therefore not possible to quantify a liquidated sum due. The only liquidated sum due at today's date was the figure claimed in Alltime Securities Ltd's proof of debt in the sum of £32,911.61. The most which would be accepted for future liability at this stage would be one year's future rent.'

H In his affidavit of 22 November 1993 the nominee amplified this:

'I invited the applicant to submit a claim for the future rent liabilities in the sum of one year's rent. I would not accept a calculation of all the future rent because there was a duty to mitigate, but I would have been prepared to accept one year's future rent. The applicant did not ask for such a sum to be included in the voting and as such its vote was in the sum of £32,911.61. Even if one year's rent (in the sum of

£13,830) had been admitted for the purposes of voting, the proposal would still   A
have been approved by the requisite majority.'

And a little later in that affidavit he said that he indicated to Mr Springall that he would allow Alltime to vote in relation to the future liabilities restricted to the future rent for the period of one year. But that was not acceptable to Mr Springall, who only voted for Alltime as creditor in respect of arrears of rent and interest thereon in the sum of £32,911.61.   B

Certain modifications of the proposed arrangement were approved, including the extension of the term of the arrangement to five years, and creditors with debts of £226,898 approved the modified arrangement, only Alltime voting against; that is to say creditors with 87.34 per cent of the total debts (on the footing that Alltime was a creditor in only the sum of £32,911.61) were in favour. The effect of the approved arrangement is that if it includes the future rent under the lease and Alltime is bound thereby, it cannot   C
proceed with its bankruptcy petition to obtain a bankruptcy order against Mr Doorbar and so cannot invoke cl. 5 of the lease requiring Mrs Doorbar to take a lease for the remainder of the term.

On 18 October 1993 Alltime applied under s. 262 in the Eastbourne County Court, seeking by its amended summons three orders:

(1)   a declaration that the arrangement does not include future rent under the lease and   D
does not affect Mr Doorbar's liability for the same;

(2)   the revocation of the approval given to the arrangement at the creditors' meeting on 4 October 1993 on the ground that the arrangement unfairly prejudiced the interests of Alltime as a creditor of Mr Doorbar; and

(3)   the revocation or suspension of that approval on the ground that there was a material irregularity at the meeting.   E

On 5 July 1994 District Judge Hollis made the first order sought, saying that he could not see how a future debt, particularly where the amount was unliquidated, could be included in a voluntary arrangement unless there was agreement between the debtor and the creditor. He therefore did not deal with the second and third orders sought. Mr Doorbar appealed to the High Court. Knox J on 3 November 1994 allowed the appeal, holding that the voluntary arrangement did include the future rent under the lease and that Alltime was bound in respect of the same (see [1994] BCC 994). He granted Alltime   F
leave to appeal. Alltime then applied for the rest of its summons to be restored for hearing and on 17 February 1995 Deputy District Judge Gamba ordered that the approval to the arrangement be revoked on the grounds stated in the second and third orders sought. He said that the inability to activate cl. 5 of the lease constituted unfair prejudice to Alltime and that there was a material irregularity in that the chairman did not make a reasonable valuation of the future rent but wrongly concerned himself with the duty to mitigate.   G
Again that decision was the subject of an appeal by Mr Doorbar and this appeal too was allowed by Knox J on 16 June 1995 (see [1995] BCC 728). He held that the interests of Alltime were not prejudiced unfairly or at all. He further held that while there may have been an irregularity in that the chairman was wrong to rely, if he did, on a duty to mitigate, there was no material irregularity involved in the chairman's willingness to put upon Alltime's claim for future rent a minimum value of one year's rent. Again Knox J granted leave to appeal.   H

Alltime now appeals to this court against both decisions of Knox J. It is not suggested by Miss Tipples, appearing for Alltime, that a future rent liability could not be included in a voluntary arrangement nor that that liability does not fall within the words of r. 5.17(3) 'a debt for an unliquidated amount, or any debt whose value is not ascertained'. She makes the following submissions on the facts of this case:

A   (1)   Alltime was not bound by the arrangement in relation to the future rent liability because the chairman did not agree with Alltime to put upon that debt the estimated minimum value of one year's rent;

    (2)   if it was bound, the court should revoke the approval given at the creditors' meeting of the voluntary arrangement on either or both of the following grounds:

        (a)   the chairman's valuation of the future rent liability was a material
B   irregularity;

        (b)   the arrangement unfairly prejudiced Alltime's interests.

I shall consider these submissions in turn.

(1) Is Alltime bound by the arrangement?

C   If Alltime was entitled to vote at the creditors' meeting in respect of the future rent liability owed to it, by virtue of s. 260(2)(b) Alltime would be bound by the arrangement. The question whether Alltime was entitled to vote turns on the true construction of r. 5.17(3) and in particular the word 'agrees'. Does it connote some element of bilateral concurrence between the chairman and the creditor, or an expression of willingness by the chairman?

D   The former was the conclusion of Ferris J in *Re Cranley Mansions Ltd* [1994] BCC 576; [1994] 1 WLR 1610. That was a decision on a company voluntary arrangement. As the corresponding rule, r. 1.17(3) of the *Insolvency Rules* 1986, uses the same wording as r. 5.17(3), it cannot be suggested that the two rules have different meanings. In that case a leaseholder, Mrs Saigol, claimed damages against the landlord company in respect of defects in works undertaken by the company to her property. A company voluntary arrangement was proposed. Mrs Saigol lodged a claim in the sum of £900,000 but the chairman of the creditors' meeting considered that the value of the debt was not
E   ascertained and placed an estimated minimum value of £1 on the debt for the purposes of entitlement to vote. If the minimum value of her debt had been estimated at over £1,700 the proposal would have been defeated. The proposal was approved by the creditors' meeting. Mrs Saigol sought an order revoking or suspending that approval. She succeeded in her submission that there had been a material irregularity in the conduct of the meeting in that the chairman had purported to admit her vote in respect of £1,
F   whereas r. 1.17(3) was inapplicable, as no estimated minimum value was agreed with her to be put on her debt.

    Ferris J said (at pp. 592D; 1628–1629):

> 'Both [counsel for the company] and [counsel for the chairman] pointed out that unless the chairman is entitled to put a value upon the claim of a creditor which is unliquidated or unascertained without regard to the wishes of that creditor, the
G   > utility of the statutory provisions in respect of corporate voluntary arrangements (and, indeed, individual voluntary arrangements and other matters to be decided at meetings governed by rules as to voting equivalent to r. 1.17) would be greatly reduced. If a creditor is not entitled to vote in respect of such a claim without a value being put upon the claim under r. 1.17(3) or its equivalent (which is a matter to be considered in a moment) a disaffected creditor could stultify proposals for a
H   > voluntary arrangement by the simple expedient of failing to concur in a value being put on his claim. The arrangement might then be approved by the requisite majorities of those entitled to vote on it, but it would not be binding on the disaffected creditor. In most, if not all, cases there would be no point in having an arrangement which is not binding upon all creditors.
>
> I see the force of this submission which causes me some anxiety because my decision is likely to affect many other cases. Nevertheless I cannot escape the fact

that the relevant words of r. 1.17(3) are "where the chairman agrees to put upon   A
the debt an estimated minimum value", not "where the chairman puts upon the
debt an estimated minimum value". Moreover I think it would be perverse to say
that the requirement imported by the word "agrees" can be satisfied by an
agreement between the chairman and someone other than the creditor, such as the
company, as was suggested in argument. In my judgment "agrees" requires some
element of bilateral concurrence between the chairman and the creditor in question.
If the creditor puts forward an estimated minimum value without prejudice to a   B
contention that his real claim is much larger and if the chairman accepts this, the
words of the rule would, in my view, clearly be satisfied notwithstanding that there
is nothing in the nature of a contract between the chairman and the creditor. The
same would be the case if the chairman took the initiative in suggesting a value
and the creditor concurred in this suggestion for the purpose of r. 1.17(3), although
not for the purpose of limiting the claim. The matter would be more difficult if   C
the chairman put forward a value for the purpose of r. 1.17(3) and the creditor
rejected this for all purposes but nevertheless insisted upon voting. The outcome
would, in my view, then depend upon an evaluation of precisely what was said and
done.'

In the first of the decisions under appeal before us, Knox J took a different view of the
meaning of r. 5.17(3). He said (at p. 1006H):   D

'Mr Zacaroli invited me not to follow that decision and advanced a different
argument from that which appears to have been advanced before Ferris J, namely
that what the subrule requires is the chairman's agreement to put a minimum value
and not an agreement upon or in relation to the minimum value. He submitted
that an agreement by the chairman to put a value was satisfied on 4 October by
Mr Bradshaw's expression of willingness to put a value of £13,830, one year's rent,   E
upon the debt. The fact that that was not acceptable to Mr Springall does not
detract from the effect of Mr Bradshaw's willingness to put a minimum value. In
support of that construction Mr Zacaroli pointed out that the appeal machinery in
r. 5.17(5), which applies to subr. (3) just as much as to subr. (4), would be rendered
effectively nugatory since it would only be if there was agreement that a minimum
value could be placed upon the debt, and, if there was agreement, it is difficult to
see how there could be an effective appeal. It is apparent that Ferris J himself was   F
caused anxiety by what he took to be the inescapable requirement of bilateral
concurrence between the creditor and the chairman, and I respectfully share that
anxiety. I should, of course, normally follow what one of my brethren in this
division had previously held but I am not bound to do so, and in the light of the
argument addressed to me by Mr Zacaroli, which was not, so far as I could see,
addressed to Ferris J, I have reached the conclusion that the only agreement that   G
subr. 5.17(3) requires is an expressed willingness by the chairman to put an
estimated minimum value on the debt in question. If the subrule is thus interpreted
it avoids the undesirable result that the relevant creditor can avoid the
consequences of being in a minority of 25 per cent or less and be bound by the
75 per cent or more majority by the simple expedient of refusing to agree any
minimum value for any purpose, and it gives the appeal procedure a proper field
within which to operate.'   H

Accordingly he held that on the facts what the chairman did amounted to expressing a
willingness to put a minimum value on Alltime's claim, and that therefore the exception
in r. 5.17(3) applied. In two subsequent cases, *Beverley Group plc v McClue* [1995] BCC
751 at p. 759 and *Re Cancol Ltd* [1995] BCC 1133, he adhered to his view of the word
'agrees' in the context of r. 5.17(3).

A   Miss Tipples submitted that Ferris J's view was to be preferred to that of Knox J. She said that Knox J was construing the subrule as though it read 'except where the chairman puts upon the debt an estimated minimum value', and that gave no meaning to the word 'agrees'. She criticised Knox J's acceptance of the argument that the appeal machinery in r. 5.17(5) would on her construction be rendered nugatory, pointing out that that machinery would still apply to r. 5.17(3) on an appeal by a person other than the creditor in question, for example the debtor. In answer to the point that a creditor with an unliquidated claim could avoid being bound by not agreeing with the chairman she submitted that it was in the commercial interest of the creditor to reach agreement in order to be bound by the arrangement and receive dividends thereunder. Although the creditor who is not bound by the arrangement might later make the debtor bankrupt, that in itself would not necessarily defeat the voluntary arrangement which would continue in operation, the assets subject to the arrangement being held by the supervisor on trust only for the creditors bound by the arrangement (*Re McKeen* [1995] BCC 412 and *Re Bradley-Hole* [1995] BCC 418; [1995] 1 WLR 1097).

     I see the force of these submissions and of the considerations which led Ferris J to the construction which he put on the subrule, but I am not persuaded by them. The context of the crucial words in r. 5.17(3) is that there is a general prohibition on voting by the creditor with an unliquidated or unascertained claim, to which prohibition there is an exception if the chairman agrees. That agreement significantly is not expressed to be with the creditor or anyone else. It is not an agreement on the value (that, in the voluntary arrangement, is for the supervisor who might arrive at a significantly higher value): the chairman only agrees to put on the debt an estimated minimum value. That is an unlikely subject of a bilateral agreement and to my mind it suggests that it is left to the chairman alone to decide 'At the very least the claim is worth £x', rather than to arrive at an agreement with the creditor on that minimum value. Given that the chairman is not a lawyer but an insolvency practitioner at a meeting of creditors, it seems to me unlikely that the draftsman contemplated the necessity of agreement with the creditor on each debt of this character. It is sufficient if the chairman expresses his willingness to put, and puts, an estimated minimum value on the debt.

     Knox J's interpretation seems to me to derive support from consideration of other parts of the legislation. For there to be a voluntary arrangement, there must be a composition in satisfaction of the debtor's debts or a scheme of arrangement of his affairs, and the intention must have been to bind all the creditors so far as possible even if creditors holding up to 25 per cent in value of the debts do not agree. Of course the very wording of r. 5.17(3) contemplates that the chairman may not agree to put an estimated minimum value on some unliquidated and unascertained claims, and so there may be some such creditors (as well as creditors inadvertently omitted) not bound by the arrangement; but it would in my opinion materially diminish the utility of voluntary arrangements if creditors with such claims were free not to be bound by the arrangement by simply choosing not to agree a minimum value which was not to their liking. A creditor not so bound is free to make the debtor bankrupt.

     Mr Zacaroli for the purposes of this appeal did not challenge the correctness of the decisions in *Re McKeen* and *Re Bradley-Hole*, although both are first instance decisions. For completeness he drew to our attention the recent decision of Blackburne J in *Davis v Martin-Sklan* [1995] BCC 1122 in which it was held that the making of a bankruptcy order on a petition presented by a petitioner within s. 264(1)(c) automatically brought the arrangement to an end, and it may be that the decisions in *Re McKeen* and *Re Bradley-Hole* will on a future occasion need reconsideration. But I shall proceed like Mr Zacaroli did, on the footing that if a creditor not bound by the arrangement makes the debtor bankrupt, the arrangement will nevertheless not be terminated and the assets subject to the arrangement will remain subject to a trust from which the creditors not so bound are excluded. As Mr Zacaroli pointed out, it may be in such a creditor's commercial interest to petition for the debtor's bankruptcy, notwithstanding the existence of a voluntary arrangement, particularly in a case like the present where the only assets of the arrangement are to come from the debtor's future income. The trustee in bankruptcy can apply for an income payments order, claiming for the bankrupt's estate the bankrupt's surplus income (s. 310). Such an order in a case like the present would imperil the arrangement, dependent as it is on the debtor's payments out of income to fund it. Any creditor not bound by the arrangement is therefore a threat to its efficacy.

Finally, r. 5.17(5) seems to me to offer further support to Knox J's construction. It is plain that that subrule applies to r. 5.17(3) and on its face, by allowing any creditor the right to appeal against the chairman's decision on entitlement, would give the creditor aggrieved by the chairman's decision on the estimated minimum value of his unliquidated claim the opportunity to appeal. On Miss Tipples' construction, that creditor could hardly appeal what he has agreed.

For these reasons, which are essentially those advanced by Mr Zacaroli in support of the first decision of Knox J, I would hold that Alltime was bound by the arrangement.

(2)(a) Was the chairman's valuation of the future liability a material irregularity?

Miss Tipples submitted that the whole of Mr Doorbar's future rent liability for the remaining seven years of the term of the lease should have been treated rateably for voting purposes. She said that instead, by being allowed to vote only in respect of one year's future rent, Alltime had been placed in the worst possible position: it had no voting power at the meeting and is now bound by the arrangement in respect of all the future rent liability. She complained that the chairman failed to make any real attempt to value Alltime's claim, that the chairman was wrong to make any allowance for what he may have considered to be the possibility of re-entry, and that he therefore failed to put an estimated minimum value on the claim. She points out that had Alltime been allowed to vote in respect of the whole of the future rent liability, the arrangement would not have been approved.

To take the last point first, any irregularity in the estimate of the minimum value would not be material unless that value was increased threefold. Only then would Alltime have had 25 per cent or more of the voting power at the meeting. In considering this question it must be borne in mind that no attempt was made by Alltime to provide the chairman with any estimate or evidence of the then present value of its claim; it simply claimed the aggregate of the whole of the future rent. It is also not in dispute that the right of re-entry remained unaffected by the arrangement (s. 258(4) and see *Re Naeem (a bankrupt)* [1990] 1 WLR 48). It was presently exercisable by Alltime at the time of the meeting by reason of the arrears of rent and would continue thereafter to be exercisable in relation both to the arrears and to the future rent reserved by the lease if it was not paid within 21 days of each payment being due. On the figures there was no possibility of such payments.

In those circumstances, while the chairman should not have taken account of any duty to mitigate nor should he have considered, as he put in his report, 'the most which would be accepted for future liability', it was entirely realistic of him to put a minimum value on Alltime's claim by estimating what was likely to happen, and making allowance for the possibility that Alltime would exercise its power of re-entry. In my judgment Alltime's approach of treating the minimum value of the future rent liability as equal to the whole of that liability was wrong in principle. In agreement therefore with the judge, I do not see any material irregularity in the chairman's estimate of the minimum value which he put on Alltime's debt.

A   **(2)(b) Did the arrangement unfairly prejudice Alltime's interests?**

Miss Tipples submitted that the term 'interests' is one of wide import by reference to the authorities on s. 459 of the *Companies Act* 1985, where the concept of unfair prejudice to a member's interests is found. However it is common ground that the relevant interests in the context of s. 262(1)(a) are the interests of the creditor as a creditor, and for my part I do not derive much assistance from consideration of the authorities on s. 459 with its

B   very different context. Miss Tipples said that Alltime's right arising under cl. 5 of the lease was inextricably linked with its right to receive payment from Mr Doorbar of the future rent liability and as such it was an interest of Alltime as creditor. Clause 5, she said, enabled Alltime, on Mr Doorbar's bankruptcy and the subsequent disclaimer by the trustee of the lease, to require the surety, Mrs Doorbar, to accept a lease and so Alltime had a legitimate expectation to recover from Mrs Doorbar all the future rent.

C   She said that the unfairness in this case arises because by reason of the voluntary arrangement Alltime is unable to proceed with its bankruptcy petition, and it is in a unique position in relation to all the other creditors because it had the means by cl. 5 of suffering no loss in respect of its claim for future rent, and so, by being denied the ability to activate cl. 5, it had been unfairly prejudiced by the terms of the arrangement.

I cannot do better on this point then refer to the analysis of the judge (at p. 734F):

D   'The prejudice which is relied upon has the following features. First, it is a restriction of a right prospectively exercisable against a person other than the debtor. Second, it is the product of the statutory consequences of the approval of the voluntary arrangement, which includes the right to future rent, rather than the result of any particular term of the arrangement. Third, the right which is prejudicially affected is one which arises under the lease and therefore pre-exists the voluntary arrangement and has no connection with the voluntary arrangement

E   save that its value increases if and to the extent that the debtor is insolvent. Fourth, the right which is prejudicially affected is not a right over the debtor's property but a contingent personal right against the third party, the debtor's ex-wife. Five, the right prejudicially affected is one to substitute in place of rights against the debtor corresponding rights against the debtor and another. It is therefore in practice a right to release the debtor and substitute another. The new covenant by the debtor

F   ex hypothesi after his bankruptcy is practically worthless and would involve a merger of the debtor's existing covenant. Finally, there is no question of Alltime's rights of re-entry having been prejudiced by the voluntary arrangement.'

The judge said that in the light of those characteristics and more especially of the fact that the right in question was one exercisable against a person other than the debtor and arose on the determination through disclaimer by the trustee of the debtor's liability and

G   was therefore a substitute for rather than a constituent part of the debtor's indebtedness, the interest of Alltime was outside the ambit of s. 262(1)(a) and that therefore there was no prejudice of which it could complain. I agree with that analysis and that conclusion.

The judge also gave his answer to the question where the balance lies as between the prejudice to Alltime in having its right against the debtor's ex-wife restricted on the one hand and the prejudice to the general body of creditors in being prevented from having

H   the benefits of any voluntary arrangement which includes future payments of rent under the lease on the other. He considered that the prejudice to Alltime would not in the circumstances be unfair, primarily because Alltime had its security against Mr Doorbar in the shape of the right of re-entry unaffected by the voluntary arrangement. That is a conclusion with which I would not think it right for this court to interfere, the judge having taken into account all the relevant circumstances.

For these reasons therefore in my judgment the judge came to unassailable conclusions in his second decision.

I would dismiss this appeal.

Forbes J: I agree.

Hirst LJ: I also agree.

(*Appeal dismissed. Leave to appeal refused*)

CASES CITED

This table lists alphabetically all cases referred to in judgments of the courts reported in British Company Cases in 1995. References are to the first page of the relevant case.

LEGISLATION FINDING LIST

The following Legislation Finding List covers all cases reported in British Company Cases 1995. References to legislative provisions are to section numbers unless otherwise stated. References are to the first page of the relevant case.

TOPICAL INDEX

References are to the first page of the relevant case.